This modern text is designed to prepare you for your future professional career. While theories, ideas, techniques, and data are dynamic, the information contained in this volume will provide you a quick and useful reference as well as a guide for future learning for many years to come. Your familiarity with the contents of this book will make it an important volume in your professional library.

EX LIBRIS

Business Law
Text and Cases

Business Law
Text and Cases

PHILLIP J. SCALETTA, Jr.
Krannert Graduate School
of Management
Purdue University

GEORGE D. CAMERON III
Graduate School
of Business Administration
University of Michigan

1982

BUSINESS PUBLICATIONS, INC.
Plano, Texas   75075

© BUSINESS PUBLICATIONS, INC., 1982

ISBN 0-256-02440-5

Library of Congress Catalog Card No. 81–70516

Printed in the United States of America

1 2 3 4 5 6 7 8 9 0 D 9 8 7 6 5 4 3 2

To our families, colleagues, and friends,
for their support and understanding
during the years this book was in process

Preface

This book is the product of our combined 30-plus years of experience in teaching Business Law. We have taught all levels of students, from freshmen to graduate students to adult education classes, in several different types of colleges and universities. Over the years we have used several of the leading Business Law texts. We have reviewed others at the request of their publishers and have examined several dozen more for possible classroom use. Like many authors, when we didn't find what we wanted, we decided to write our own.

Most Business Law professors are probably looking for the same things in a text that we were: completeness, accuracy, organization, and readability. In terms of completeness, we felt that the text should at least cover the required topics listed for the CPA and CPS exams. Even if a school's normal course sequence does not specifically include all of these topics, a student studying for the exams should be able to find specific coverage of all the topics. This text has them all, with illustrative cases and review problems. The AACSB (American Association of Collegiate Schools of Business) has recently emphasized the importance of having the international dimensions of business operations in the curriculum. We have included a chapter on International Law, with several of the old classic cases showing the constitutional basis of International Law in U.S. courts, and several significant recent cases to show current applications. Completeness in a Business Law text also means a reasonable depth of coverage within individual topics. In our chapter on contractual capacity, for example, we have included a discussion of some of the remaining anomalies in the legal status of married women and Native Americans, with illustrative cases.

Accuracy to us means that the text's statements of legal rules conform to the UCC, the various restatements, the cases, the recognized authorities such as Corbin, Williston, C.J.S., *Am. Jr.* —and common sense. In the Statute of Frauds chapter, for instance, we note that the "party to be charged" on a contract is not *always* the defendant, since the existence of an alleged contract may be raised as a defense or setoff by a defendant against the plaintiff. Since this is a text rather than a research monograph, we have not used footnotes. We have, however, made extensive references to the UCC sections when dealing with Code topics. We also note the existence of major splits of authority, although in many cases we simply indicate that one rule appears to be the majority rule or that it represents the modern trend.

One of the difficulties Business Law teachers have always had to face is the dichotomy between general Contract Law and the UCC's treatment of Sales of Goods. There are clearly two sets of rules that we need to communicate to our students. With increasing peer pressure for inclusion of more environmental material in our courses, we cannot afford the luxury of reteaching the formation and enforceability rules when we cover contracts for the Sale of Goods. Our Contracts chapters, therefore, fully integrate the UCC's special rules for the Sale of Goods in each topic—Offer, Acceptance, Consideration, Statute of Frauds, and so on. Our Sales chapters cover only those matters which are specifically applicable to sales contracts, such as Passing of Risk of Loss and Products Liability. We believe that our teaching units are organized to provide the instructor with maximum flexibility in selecting the topics to cover in a particular course.

A good text must be readable. We are confronting our students with new theoretical concepts and a new technical terminology. Perhaps our greatest challenge as Business Law instructors is to present this technical material in an interesting and yet challenging and accurate manner. Our big job, in other words, is translation—of the treatises, cases, and legislation for our students. We have used technical terms in this text only where we felt they were necessary and have tried to define them as clearly and simply as possible. Throughout we have attempted to use plain English rather than legalese in presenting the legal rules. Of necessity, quotations taken from cases will contain some legal jargon, but the students should have some background from the chapter as a basis for translating it.

We have one final major criterion for a good Business Law text. It must contain cases—real cases—with substantial quotes from the actual opinions of the courts, not just editorial summaries by the authors. All of our end-of-chapter discussion cases are directly quoted from the courts' opinions. Nearly all of our in-chapter case briefs contain substantial quotes from the courts in the "Reasons" section. We strongly believe that the students need and enjoy this direct exposure to the courts' decision-making process. Court cases are the ingredient that make our Business Law courses unique and interesting; we should not lose that extra margin of excitement by giving the students only editorial summaries of the cases.

In selecting cases for inclusion, we of course used a lot of our old favorites; we hope Business Law professors will find many of their favorites here, too. Some classic cases, like *Lefkowitz* and *Mitchill*, demand inclusion. When we didn't find appropriate case examples in our own files or from the various case reporting services, we used the LEXIS system to generate new cases. We think many of these newer cases may also become classics. Nearly all the problems at the ends of chapters are also taken from actual cases; again, many of these were generated through the LEXIS system. We have found similar problems to be very useful teaching tools; most of the problems at the end of the Contracts and UCC chapters have been classroom tested.

No project of this size and scope can be brought to a successful conclusion without significant contributions from a number of people. Our secretarial staffs did yeoman work in typing the chapters and the discussion cases. Our schools have been generous with their support and encouragement. Dr. Al Edwards of the Division of Research, University of Michigan Graduate School of Business Administration, provided support for several research assistants who helped in drafting the problems for many of the earlier chapters. Dr. Jay W. Wiley, Director of Graduate Studies and Research Administration of the Krannert Graduate School of Management of Purdue University, provided support for several research assistants who helped the authors with the Study Guide. Ms. Tamara Savage was of great help in preparing the Instructor's Manual, and Ms. Valerie Franklin and Mrs. Cheryl Royer turned many rough drafts into finished copy.

We also give special thanks and express our sincere appreciation to our wives and families for their encouragement and support.

>   **Phillip J. Scaletta, Jr.**
>   **George D. Cameron III**

Contents

Part I

Introduction to Law
and the Legal System

1 | The Definition, Source, and Function of Law

WHAT IS LAW?

Before commencing a study of the law, a student must first have an understanding of the meaning of the term *law*. What is law? Whom does it affect? Why do we need law? Where does law come from? Why should you study law?

First, how do we define law? Aristotle, the famous philosopher, said, "Law is a form of order." That would seem to be a good definition, for when we think of law, we think of law and order—the orderly protection of society against the wrongdoers who might injure us or our property.

We also may visualize the police officers on their beats protecting us from the disorderly and criminal element of society. But is there more to law than keeping order in society? What about compensation for the damages to a person or propery that are incurred as the result of another person's negligence in an automobile accident? What about the need for enforcement of a contract where one party refuses to perform the required contractual duties? What about protection of the individual from invasion of privacy by the computer? What about environmental and consumer problems? What about legal regulation of business in areas such as safety, equal rights, competition, antitrust, and so forth? This list could go on endlessly to cover nearly every aspect of business as well as almost every aspect of our individual lives.

For centuries philosophers and legal scholars have attempted to compose a comprehensive definition of law, but without success. A very generalized definition of law in *Black's Law Dictionary* reads as follows:

That which is laid down, ordained, or established. A rule or method according to which phenomena or actions co-exist or follow each other. A system of principles and rules of human conduct, being the aggregate of those commandments and principles which are either prescribed or recognized by the governing power in an organized jural society as its will in relation to the conduct of the members of such society, and which it undertakes to maintain and sanction and to use as the criteria of the actions of such members.

As you read this definition you find that law is the aggregate of all those principles and rules of human conduct both present and past which the governing power of a society prescribes and adopts for the conduct of the members of that society. The governing power of our society is exercised by national, state, and local bodies.

The principles and rules include the Constitution of the United States; treaties with other nations approved by the U.S. Congress; the constitutions of the various states; the statutes passed by the Congress of the United States and the various state legislatures; the laws passed by the various county governing bodies, cities, and towns; the decisions of the courts—national, state, and local; and the regulations of the many administrative agencies of government—national, state, and local.

These principles and rules, of and for human conduct of the members of a society, cannot simply be laid down, ordained, or established on a permanent basis. They must change as the will of society changes. Law must meet the needs of the society which it governs. For example, in recent years we have seen drastic changes in the laws concerning the rights of women, the rights of minorities, and the rights of individual members of society—such as the right of privacy.

The ultimate goal of law is justice for all; however, that goal is seldom achieved. We must remember that law is made by human beings to govern human beings, and human beings are not perfect creatures. Thus law and justice are often not synonymous.

In the foregoing definition of law, the governing power not only prescribes the principles and rules of conduct but also undertakes to maintain, sanction, and use these principles and rules to govern the actions of the members of society. Thus we have a second dimension to the law: that of enforcement.

Thus law is not only principles and rules of conduct; it is also the processes for resolving disputes as well as prosecuting wrongs and preventing wrongs before they are committed.

WHOM DOES THE LAW AFFECT?

Law affects every human being from womb to tomb. There are abortion laws that protect the unborn child; there are probate laws that regulate the distribution of a person's assets after death; and, of course, there are a multitude of laws that affect individuals in their various relationships with other individuals and society as they go through life.

Law not only affects natural persons but also creates and regulates legal entities such as corporations, cooperatives, limited partnerships, and other business and nonbusiness entities.

WHY DO WE NEED LAW?

Law is essential for human survival. Let us for the moment contemplate what a society would be like if there were no law. The individuals in such a society would be so busy trying to protect themselves and their property from others that they would have no time for individual development or for the development of the society.

If we look back in history, we find that one of the first priorities of a primitive society was to set up a system of law. This comprised not only a set of rules for the members of the society to live by but also a procedure to enforce those rules and tribunals to try the accused and pronounce punishments. In the primitive society law was needed primarily to keep the peace. Keeping the peace is still a primary need for law.

In the primitive society people were comparatively self-sufficient. They grew or hunted for food, built their own shelters, and made their own clothes. They had little contact with other members of society. As society developed, we find members of society becoming more dependent upon one another. They need to barter or buy food, clothing, shelter, and other necessities from other members of society. Thus a second need for law is a need for standards of conduct in trade and in individual and personal relationships among members of society. For example, we now have the Uniform Commercial Code, which governs the sale of goods and establishes principles and rules governing such contracts between members of society. We have tort law, which defines legal rights and legal duties regarding both personal and business relationships and provides for money damages to reimburse persons for damages that result from interference with their legal rights. We also have a myriad of statutes and court decisions setting forth legal standards of conduct covering nearly every relationship among the various members of society. Examples are domestic relations law, covering relationships between husband and wife; property law, covering the ownership, purchase, and sale of real estate and personal property; and labor law, covering relationships between employer and employees.

A third need for law is to bridge the gap between the present and the future and to develop principles and rules that meet the changing needs of society. New technology brings about new problems which require new rules and regulations for human conduct. Space law is needed to regulate rights and duties in space. With new medical technology we are now able to transplant hearts, kidneys, and other organs from a deceased person to a living person. When is a person legally dead? The computerization of personal records about individuals has also opened up a Pandora's box of new problems. What is your right to privacy? What is your right to know what is in the record about you? As energy becomes scarce, we must look for new sources of energy. Who owns the sun? What right do you have to the rays of the sun for solar energy? Who owns the oil deposits under the sea? New problems and new technology require new rules and regulations and interpretations of rights and duties not previously contemplated. Law must be responsive to the ever-changing needs of society if society is to progress and prosper.

The fourth need for law is stability and predictability. While law must be responsive to the needs of society, it must also be stable and reasonably predictable. This may seem paradoxical. However, if we are to have a workable system of law, members of society must be able to plan, forecast, and predict the future.

A business cannot simply operate day by day; it must plan ahead for several years. The business executive must be knowledgeable about the law that affects his or her business and should be able to rely on that law to predict and plan future business activities. While law must change to meet the needs of society, such change must be predictable and orderly. It has often been said that the wheels of justice move slowly. While this slow movement can be criticized by some, it certainly results in predictability.

In this complex technological society in which we live, our lives, our property, our human rights, and our human dignity are subjects of the law. Without the law we would have no protection, no rights, no duties, no society.

WHERE DOES OUR LAW COME FROM?

It is often said that the source of American law is the English common law. It is true that the early settlers of our country were primarily of English origin, and it naturally followed that their legal traditions influenced the American legal system. Our legal system is, however, independent of the English legal system and not a strict adoption of it.

The Constitution of the United States is the supreme law of this land. All other laws of whatever nature must adhere to the Constitution of the United States, or they will be declared null or void. We will hereafter use the adjective *national* rather than *federal* to refer to the U.S. government and its agencies, since *federal* really describes the entire system of a national government and 50 state governments.

Article I of the Constitution of the United States established the legislative branch of government, the Congress of the United States, and further specifically set out its powers and the limitations on those powers.

Article II of the Constitution of the United States established the office of the president of the United States and the executive branch of government and set out the powers of and limitations on that branch of government.

Article III of the Constitution of the United States created the judicial branch of the national government. Article III provides that the judicial power of the United States shall be vested one supreme court, and in such inferior courts as the Congress may from time to time ordain and establish.

These three articles of the Constitution created the three branches of our national governmental system—the legislative to create law, the executive to administer and enforce the law, and the judicial to interpret the law and to act as guardian of the Constitution.

Article II, Section 2 of the Constitution also gave the president the power to make treaties; however, all treaties must be made with the advice and consent of the Senate of the United States. This source of law is increasingly important in our relationships with foreign nations, as treaties affect not only defense and military matters, but also our business and trade relationships with the other nations of our world. With today's satellite communication and interbank and intercompany computer networks interwoven across the boundaries of the nations of the world, we need new international legal agreements and new principles and rules for the conduct of international business. Treaty power is the source for those needs.

The treaty power of the United States is a source of law not only for international affairs but also for internal affairs. A treaty, once approved by the Senate, has the same force and effect as laws enacted by the U.S. Congress. Thus a treaty concerning U.S. internal affairs is superior to any state law or any state constitution.

The following case illustrates the supremacy of treaties over state law.

People of the State of Michigan v. *Le Blanc*
223 N.W.2d 305 (Michigan, 1974)

FACTS   Albert B. Le Blanc, a full-blooded Chippewa Indian, was convicted for fishing without a license and for fishing with a gill net in violation of Michigan state law. Le Blanc appealed on the basis that in 1836 a federal treaty executed with the Chippewa Indians granted them perpetual fishing rights. No subsequent treaty has changed those rights.

ISSUE   Is the treaty of 1836 granting fishing rights superior to Michigan conservation law?

DECISION   Yes. The treaty of 1836 is superior to Michigan law. The conviction for fishing without a license is reversed. The conviction for fishing with a gill net is remanded to the lower court to determine whether the statute outlawing the use of such nets is necessary to prevent a substantial depletion of fish supply. If the outlawing of such nets is necessary from a conservation standpoint, then that conviction will stand.

REASON   The federal treaty with the Indians guaranteed the Indians the right to fish on the lands ceded to the U.S., and no later treaty changed those rights. The federal treaty is superior to Michigan law. With regard to conservation efforts the court found that although treaty rights granted Indians cannot be qualified or conditioned by state law, the state can, consistent with the mandates of the Constitution, regulate the time and manner in which such rights are exercised, provided the regulation is nondiscriminatory and is necessary for the conservation of fish.

Next we have state legal systems. The 10th Amendment to the Constitution provides that the powers not delegated to the United States by the Constitution or prohibited by it to the states are reserved to the states respectively or to the people. This amendment is often referred to as the states' rights amendment.

This amendment, the last of the 10 amendments to the Constitution which are referred to as the Bill of Rights, in effect allows the states to govern themselves in all areas where the Constitution does not specify national regulation. For example, Article I, Section 8 of the Constitution grants Congress the power to regulate commerce with foreign nations and among the several states, the power to establish post offices; the power to raise and support an army, the power to provide and maintain a navy, the power to coin money, and various other powers which relate to the operation of the national government. The 13 states were originally separate governments. They realized that for self-protection and for economic reasons it would be better to give one national government the power to provide an army and navy, a uniform system of coins and currency, a national postal system, and to regulate interstate problems. Each of the states, however, also wanted to retain the right to have its own state government to govern internal affairs within the state. Thus each state has a constitution which sets up a state, county, and municipal legislative system, an executive system, and a court system.

In addition to the national and state constitutions, the national and state legislatures, and the various county and city legislative bodies, and the national and state courts, we have another source of law. That source is the various regulations and pronouncements of a myriad of administrative agencies, both national and state. On the national level we have agencies such as the National Labor Relations Board (NLRB), the Federal Trade Commission (FTC), the Interstate Commerce Commission (ICC), and the Equal Employment Opportunity Commission (EEOC). On the state level we have agencies such as the Public Utilities Commission (PUC), the Workers' Compensation Board, and various consumer commissions.

These administrative agencies are creatures of the legislatures. An administrative agency is created by an enactment of a national or state legislature specifically delegating certain tasks and functions to the agency. The legislature may later limit the agency's authority or dispose of the agency entirely.

The theory of administrative agencies is that since the members and staff of an agency are dealing with a specific area of law, they become expert in that area and are more capable of legislating in that area than is the legislature at large. An example here would be the Environmental Protection Agency (EPA). The legislature set up the agency with power to establish regulations as to air, water, and land pollution. The directors of the agency deal with problems in the area of pollution on a daily basis.

In addition to making regulations, many administrative agencies have quasi-judicial powers; for example, the National Labor Relations Board hears complaints concerning unfair labor practices and renders decisions which have the force of law. Nearly all actions and rules of an administrative agency are subject to judicial review. These actions and rules may be reviewed by a court of law to determine whether they violate the constitutional rights of the individuals affected, whether they are discriminatory to certain individuals, whether they are arbitrary or capricious, and whether they are consistent with the authority that the legislature has delegated to the agency.

In addition to delegating authority to formal administrative agencies, the state legislatures have delegated rule-making authority to state universities and other state-supported institutions. These institutions can make rules and regulations necessary for their operation. But the rules and actions of these institutions, like those of administrative agencies, are subject to judicial review.

Too often, legislation is drafted in broad and general terms, and the specific rights and duties of the parties involved are not spelled out. When a situation arises where the rights and duties of the parties are not clear, a court upon request may review the case and make an interpretation of the statute and specifically declare the rights and duties of the parties involved.

The following case involves a court interpretation of a statute passed by the Wisconsin state legislature concerning rule-making authority for the operation of the University of Wisconsin.

Student Assn. of University of Wisconsin–Milwaukee
v. Chancellor Baum and the Board of Regents
246 N.W.2d 622 (Wisconsin, 1976)

FACTS   The Wisconsin legislature in 1974 passed a statute stating that the "students of each institution or campus . . . shall be active participants in the immediate governance of and policy development for such institutions. As such, students shall have primary responsibility for the formulation and review of policies concerning student life, services and interests. . . . The students of each institution or campus shall have the right to organize themselves in a manner they determine and to select their representatives to participate in institutional governance." The students have a Student Association, and the constitution of the Student Association authorizes the president of the Student Association to appoint student members to the various university committees. The Student Association president made his appointments, and the chancellor of the university declared them to be illegal and made appointments of his own. The Student Association filed this lawsuit for a declaratory judgment to declare that the Student Association had the exclusive right to appoint student members to these committees. The Dane County Circuit Court granted the defendants' motion for a summary judgment in their favor, and the case was dismissed. The Student Association appealed.

ISSUE   Who has the exclusive right to appoint student members to the university committees—the Student Association or the chancellor?

DECISION   The Student Association has the power to make the appointments of student members to the university committees.

REASONS   Where a statute is ambiguous or unclear in its wording, the court must look to the intent of the legislative body which enacted the statute. The court felt that the intent of the legislature was to give students the statutory right to select their own representatives to participate and represent the student body in the governing of the university.

The court reasoned as follows: "If the right to organize and to select representatives is seen as two distinct rights without an integral relationship to each other, the possible effect could be the negation of one of these rights. For example, if a chancellor retains the right to dictate, students shall be selected by election with two from this organization and one or two from other organizations, or persons with special interests, as was done here, the right to organize becomes meaningless. While students retain their right to organize, the administration can thwart the authority of the organization and deal with other students more to its liking. . . . In addition, if the chancellor retains the power to direct that students shall be elected from some organization or another, does he not also have the power to say a particular committee requires that students be in the upper 10 percent of their academic class. And if this power is present, the students' right to select their representatives could be only an illusion. . . . In order to give effect to the legislative intent of this section, the right to organize and select representatives must be seen as one right, which must be free of administrative interference if it is, in reality, to be a right."

WHY SHOULD YOU STUDY LAW?

In this increasingly legalistic age, every individual should be aware of his or her contract rights, property rights, civil rights, and personal rights. Everyone should know and understand the background of our legal system, the basis for our laws, and the procedure by which the rights of individuals and the rights of society are protected in the courts and administrative bodies of our governments.

In the past, law was viewed by the public as a mysterious set of principles and rules known only to judges and lawyers and in the minds of most laypersons it was something to be feared. The layperson often tends to view the law as independent of the acts of human beings, when, in fact, law is established and enforced by human acts and the purpose of the law is to protect, not persecute, the individual. Fear is the result of ignorance; respect is the result of understanding. Progress is made on the basis of understanding, not on the basis of fear. Hopefully, this course wil give the student an understanding of and respect for the law.

The medical profession has very successfully publicized the danger signals for cancer and heart disease, and it has promoted the teaching of first aid wherever possible. The dental profession has publicized the care and hygiene of the teeth. The law, on the other hand, is still a deep, dark secret for many people. Ordinary laypeople do not know the danger signals of a serious legal problem, and ignorance in this respect may cost them their entire worldly possessions. Shouldn't laypeople learn enough about the law so that they will know when to call the expert, the lawyer, before a legal problem becomes terminal in character?

This text does not propose to make you a legal expert. We only want to educate you as to your basic rights and duties under the law. We want to teach you the legal danger signals, the legal pitfalls to avoid, and respect and tolerance for the law, so that you can become better members of society and so that you can contribute to an orderly and properly functioning legal system. This in turn will promote the ultimate good of society.

CLASSIFICATIONS OF LAW

Substantive and Procedural Law.   To begin with, the study of law must be divided into two basic categories: substantive law and procedural law. Substantive law is the body of constitutions, treaties, statutes, ordinances, judicial decisions, and regulations and decisions of administrative bodies which define the rights and duties of individuals and institutions in their mutual relationships. In a jury trial, for example, after the jurors have heard the evidence, the judge instructs them on the law. The judge is giving them the substantive law of the case. In that same trial, procedural rules of law governed the admission of evidence, the sequence of the lawsuit, and possible appeal. This second body of law is essentially concerned with the rules of the game and not necessarily with the outcome.

Procedural law will be discussed further in Chapter 2 when we review the court system and court procedure.

Criminal, Civil, and Equity Law. Substantive law is divided into three basic classifications: criminal law, civil law, and equity law. Criminal law encompasses national and state statutes and city and town ordinances which make the commission or omission of certain acts punishable by fine or imprisonment. In criminal law the people, that is to say, the city, state, or national government, prosecute the person who disobeyed the criminal law. For example, Harry Horrible mugged a little old lady, took her pocketbook, and ran. The police arrested him; and he was prosecuted for assault and battery and theft, found guilty, and sentenced to jail. The little old lady lost her purse and several dollars, missed several days of work at her job, and she still has unpaid doctor and hospital bills because of her injuries. The criminal law does not give her the right to get her bills paid and to get paid for her pain and suffering and the cost of a new purse. The criminal law only attempts to fine or imprison the wrongdoer. The wrong being punished is a wrong against society.

Next we come to civil law. This is the body of statutory and case law which sets out the rights and duties of the individual to other individuals in society. For example, in the previous situation the criminal law might put Harry Horrible in jail, but who is going to pay the bills and reimburse the little old lady for her loss? Under civil law, more specifically tort law, the little old lady could sue Harry Horrible for money damages. This would be a separate lawsuit, and it would be conducted in a different court than the criminal trial. Civil law also emcompasses the law of contracts, the law of property, and many other areas of the law where the remedy sought is money damages, not punishment by fine or imprisonment.

Next we have equity law, a specialized branch of civil law. In many situations the act is not a crime and a civil lawsuit for money damages is not an adequate remedy. For example, you have made a contract to purchase a famous racehorse and now the seller refuses to go through with the sale. What recourse do you have? You can sue for breach of contract for damages, but what are the damages? Who knows what races the horse may win or perhaps lose? Since the horse is a unique object, no other horse would be exactly the same and thus this case would have to be decided under equity law. You would ask the court to order the seller to specifically perform the contract. Another situation which might be handled under equity law would be one in which the teachers in a certain school district strike illegally. The teachers may or may not be committing a crime. You could sue each teacher individually under civil law for breach of his or her contract and recover damages, but the desired remedy is to get the teachers back to work. Thus you ask a court with equity powers for an injunction to order them back to work. If they refuse to obey the injunction, they can be fined or imprisoned for being in contempt of court.

Other common situations in which cases are brought in equity courts are suits for rescission or reformation of a contract, suits to partition property, suits to quiet title to real estate, and suits for an accounting by one business partner against another. The theme in all of these situations is a request that the court take action, not just award money. Also cases in equity court are normally tried before the judge only, no jury is allowed except in specific cases where the state or national procedural law specifies the use of a jury as a fact finder. An example would be a suit to contest the sanity of a deceased person at the time that person made his or her last will and testament. Courts of equity tend to use equitable maxims such as the following instead of strict rules of law:

1. "Equality is equity."
2. "He who seeks equity must do equity."
3. "He who comes into equity must do so with clean hands."
4. "Equity will not suffer a right to exist without a remedy."
5. "Equity aids the vigilant."
6. "Where there is equal equity, the law must prevail."
7. "Equity regards as done that which ought to be done."

Public Law and Private Law. Law is also often classified as public law and private law. Public law encompasses criminal law, constitutional law, and administrative or governmental law. These areas of law involve societal interests rather than the personal interests of individuals. The major thrust of public law is the regulation of society. Private law, on the other hand, encompasses the areas of law which govern an individual's rights and duties with regard to relationships with other individuals. Private law includes contract law, agency law, tort law, property law, the law of sales, the law governing commercial paper, consumer law, and other areas of law that are concerned with the problems of individuals rather than the problems of society as a whole.

Written and "Unwritten" Law. When we speak of written law we are referring to the national and state constitutions, to treaties, and to national and state statutes, ordinances, administrative regulations, and similar enactments. The "unwritten" law refers to the vast body of case law that has been developed by the various courts in our country over the years. The term *unwritten law* came about because in early English times the decisions of the courts were not written down. In the United States, of course, the decisions of the courts are recorded, and the full text of the decisions of the various appellate and supreme courts is kept in book form in the chronological order of the decision dates. These decisions are also indexed as to subject matter so that lawyers and judges may locate previous decisions on which to base their contentions in the cases they are now handling. This is called referring to precedent.

Referring to precedent is done in order to comply with the rule of *stare decisis*. *Stare decisis* is a Latin term which means "let the decision stand." As we stated earlier, among the needs of law are stability and predictability. The rule of stare decisis provides that if a ruling has already been made on the legal issue in question, then that ruling should be used to determine the outcome of the current dispute. Stability and predictability in the law are certainly necessary; however, legal change is also necessary. Thus, in deciding a legal issue, the court must not only consider the previous rulings but must also consider the present and the future. If the court believes that the previous rulings are no longer appropriate because of societal changes, then the court does not have to follow precedent. This is a weighty responsibility and one not taken lightly by our courts.

Operation of the Doctrine of Precedent. The Anglo-American legal system cannot by fully understood without a working knowledge of how the doctrine of precedent operates. Our legal system assumes that the body of the law is in the cases unless and until the case law rule has been changed by statute or constitutional provision. Even where such changes have been made, precedent operates to explain the meaning of the statutory change as cases involving the change are decided.

The doctrine of precedent operates in three different ways or on three different levels: the effect of the decisions of a higher court on the lower courts within the same system; the effect of prior decisions of the same court on a current case; and the effect of prior decisions in other states or countries on a current case. Where there is a clearly applicable precedent case, a lower court in the same jurisdiction should follow the precedent and apply the rule it lays down—100 percent of the time. In practice, the rule is not quite that simple because trial judges may try to avoid the precedent by one means or another if they disagree with the result it produces in the case at hand. When that happens, the trial court will of course be reversed on appeal unless the higher court wishes to change its mind and reverse or modify its own precedent.

Typically, when judges, lawyers, and commentators refer to the doctrine of precedent they are referring to its second level of operation—the relationship between prior decisions of the same court and the case which is to be decided now. What impact should these prior decisions in similar cases have on the case at hand? Most courts, most of the time, will simply follow their established precedent cases, particularly in the commercial law areas which we are emphasizing in this book. Perhaps the most extreme example of following a precedent is seen in the professional baseball cases. In 1922, in what has been described as "not one of his happier days," Justice Holmes, speaking for a unanimous U.S. Supreme Court in *Federal Baseball Club*, decided that baseball was not commerce. It was not, therefore, subject to regulation by Congress under the Sherman Antitrust Act of 1890. Despite heavy criticism and the advent of radio and television broadcasts, that mistaken ruling was adhered to by the Court in 1953, 1972, and 1981—solely on the basis of the doctrine of precedent. Despite its disagreement with Justice Holmes' conclusion, the Court has repeatedly told us that the matter has been decided and that it is better to perpetuate error consistently than to reevaluate the underlying analysis.

Where a later court disagrees with the results that a precedent will produce in the case under consideration, it may use any one of several devices to avoid the precedent. Occasionally, a court will simply ignore one of its own precedents, although this is hard to do if one of the lawyers has included the precedent case in his or her brief or argument. The most frequently used tactic is called "distinguishing the precedent on the facts," meaning that the court shows how the precedent case really involved facts which were different enough to justify a different result in the case now up for decision. That process was at work in the following case.

Radovich v. National Football League
352 U.S. 445 (U.S. Supreme Court, 1957)

FACTS William Radovich, a professional football player, alleged that the NFL had black-listed him and had prevented him from getting a coaching job in the Pacific Coast League. Radovich had started with the Detroit Lions and had became an all-pro guard there. After four seasons he joined the Navy, from 1942 to 1945. He played the 1945 season for Detroit but then asked for a transfer to a West Coast NFL club because his father was ill and living in California. When the Lions refused, Radovich jumped the NFL and played for the Los Angeles Dons, a member club of the All-America Conference. In 1948 the San Francisco Clippers, a member club of the Pacific Coast League and an affiliate of the NFL, offered Radovich a job as player-coach. The NFL then told the Clippers not to hire him because he had jumped out of the NFL previously. Radovich sued for $35,000 damages, which would be trebled under antitrust law. The lower courts dismissed the case, applying the *Federal Baseball* and *Toolson* (1953) precedents to include all "team sports." Radovich appealed.

ISSUE Should the baseball precedents also apply to other professional team sports?

DECISION No. Judgment reversed and case remanded for trial on the facts.

REASONS The U.S. Supreme Court divided 6 to 3 in this case, with the dissenters being unable to distinguish the two forms of organized sport for antitrust purposes. For the major-ity, Justice Clark said that the only reason for reaffirming the *Federal Baseball* prece-dent in the 1953 *Toolson* case was that the justices felt that more harm would come from overturning it than from reaffirming it. The Court had already distinguished baseball from professional boxing and professional theater exhibitions, which, while just as "local" as baseball, had been subjected to the antitrust laws in two 1955 decisions. Clark stated that the Court was now specifically limiting the rule from the baseball precedents "to the facts there involved, i.e., the buisness of organized pro-fessional baseball.

"If this ruling is unrealistic, inconsistent, or illogical, it is sufficient to answer, aside from the distinctions between the businesses, that were we considering the question of baseball for the first time upon a clean slate we would have no doubts. But *Federal Baseball* held the business of baseball outside the scope of the Act. No other business claiming the coverage of those cases has such an adjudication. We, therefore, conclude that the orderly way to eliminate error or discrimination, if any there be, is by legislature and not by court decision."

In the years since *Radovich*, the Court has continued to uphold the baseball-exemption from antitrust, while at the same time subjecting other professional sports to antitrust regulation. See the *Flood* case at the end of this chapter.

Another mechanism for avoiding an undesirable precedent is to "distinguish the precedent on the law." The precedent is a precedent only for the rule of law which was actually necessary to the decision in the case. The judge writing the opinion of the court may have said a lot of things, but not everything in the opinion is necessarily a binding rule for future cases. These nonbinding, "extra" statements in opinions are called *obiter dicta*, or just *dicta*, meaning that the court is saying things that are not actually necessary to decide the case. Perhaps the most famous example of such *dicta* is Chief Justice John Marshall's opinion in *Marbury* v. *Madison*.

Read

Marbury v. *Madison*
1 Cranch 137, 2 L.Ed. 60 (U.S. Supreme Court, 1803)

FACTS   When the Federalist Party lost both the presidency and the Congress to Jefferson's Democratic-Republicans in the election of 1800, John Adams and his followers decided to try to ensure Federalist control of the judiciary for as long as possible. The Federalist "lame duck" Congress passed the Judiciary Act of 1801 (on February 13), which authorized the appointment of 16 new circuit court judges (so that the U.S. Supreme Court justices would not have to "ride circuit"). Two weeks later, Congress authorized the president to appoint for five-year terms as many justices of the peace for the District of Columbia as he thought necessary. The last few days of Adams' administration were a flurry of activity, and Adams tried to fill the total of 58 new judgeships. He was still signing their commissions on the evening of March 3, with Jefferson scheduled to be inaugurated as president the next day. The commissions of William Marbury and three other newly appointed JPs had been signed by Adams but had not been delivered by the secretary of state—John Marshall. The commissions were discovered the next day by the new secretary of state, James Madison, who was told by Jefferson not to deliver them. Marbury sued Madison under a provision of the Judiciary Act of 1789, which authorized the U.S. Supreme Court to issue writs of mandamus (orders to officials to do their official duties) in original proceedings.

ISSUE   Does the U.S. Supreme Court have jurisdiction to issue writs of mandamus in original proceedings?

DECISION   No. Case dismissed.

REASONS   Chief Justice Marshall (who had also been acting as secretary of state and had caused the whole problem by not delivering the commissions in the first place) obviously didn't want to issue any orders to the executive. Madison and Jefferson probably would have disregarded any order he made anyway. At the same time, he didn't want to miss the opportunity to say that the new president had done something legally wrong, so he wrote a long analysis of the merits of Marbury's case—even though he was going to dismiss it because the Court lacked jurisdiction! Marshall pointed out that the appointment had been properly made, that Marbury was entitled to his commission, and that the writ of mandamus was the proper procedural device to use. He then proceeded to dismiss the case because the Court could not exercise original jurisdiction that was not given in the Constitution and because the section of the Judiciary Act of 1789 that purported to give the court the power of mandamus was unconstitutional. He thus announced a powerful new check on the legislature and the executive, while at the same time avoiding a direct confrontation, since he didn't order anyone to do anything. The sections of the opinion quoted below deal with that new check.

"If an Act of the Legislature, repugnant to the Constitution, is void, does it, notwith-standing its invalidity, bind the courts, and oblige them to give it effect? Or, in other words, though it be not law, does it constitute a rule as operative as if it was a law? This would seem . . . an absurdity too gross to be insisted on . . .

"It is emphatically the province and duty of the judicial department to say what the law is. Those who apply the rule to particular cases, must of necessity expound and interpret that rule. If two laws conflict with each other, the courts must decide on the operation of each.

"So if a law be in opposition to the Constitution; if both the law and the Constitution apply to a particular case, so that the court must either decide that case conformably to the law, disregarding the Constitution; or conformably to the Constitution, disregarding the law, the court must determine which of these conflicting rules governs the case. This is of the very essence of judicial duty.

"If, then, the courts are to regard the Constitution, and the Constitution is superior to any ordinary Act of the Legislature, the Constitution, and not such ordinary Act, must govern the case to which they both apply."

Nothing that Marshall had to say about the merits of Marbury's case or about the appropriateness of using a writ of mandamus against executive officers is really precedent for future cases, since that's not what the Court decided.

The ultimate "avoidance" technique for a bad precedent is to take it head on and reverse it. Reversals do occur, but not too frequently. Courts are more willing to reexamine points of constitutional law, criminal law, and tort law than they are to upset established rules in contract law and commercial law, where parties have structured their relationships on the basis of the existing rules. The *Brown* case at the end of this chapter shows the U.S. Supreme Court reversing its "separate but equal" rule, which had been the law of the land for nearly 60 years.

Finally, the doctrine of precedent operates in a third way. Suppose that the case which has to be decided today is "unprecedented," that is, there are no decided cases in this state which have ever dealt with the problem? There are two possible responses from the court. One approach is to simply dismiss the complaint for failure to state a cause of action; this usually occurs where the plaintiff wants the court to recognize a new right or a new theory of liability. Where the underlying theory of liability has been recognized, but there is simply no case applying it to the given situation, the courts will use precedents in a third way—by borrowing some from other states, or even from other countries (particularly from countries with similar legal systems). The *Cohen* case at the end of this chapter illustrates this borrowing of precedents. The other states' decisions are not binding rules in this state unless and until they are accepted as precedents by courts here in cases decided here.

UNIFORM LAWS

We have 51 different legal systems in the United States. Each state has its own legal system, and of course we have the national system. When this nation

15

was young, transportation was limited, communication was slow, and commerce between states was minimal. Today we can fly persons or merchandise from coast to coast in hours and we can communicate from coast to coast in seconds. Under the 10th Amendment of the U.S. Constitution, each state has the right to govern itself and the business within it so long as its law does not conflict with the national Constitution or national laws. The problem was that the various states had different laws governing property and business. A business had to be aware of and conform to different standards of law in its various transactions as it did business from state to state. Thus there was a need for uniformity of state law, especially in the area of business law. The National Conference of Commissioners on Uniform State Laws was created, and representatives from each of the states, the District of Columbia, and Puerto Rico gathered for the purpose of promoting uniformity in state laws.

The conferees reviewed the various state laws and judicial decisions, and then, in cooperation with the American Law Institute, they drafted model statutes governing various areas of business law. Afterward they attempted to get the legislatures of the various states to adopt these new model laws and to repeal their previous laws, with the ultimate goal of having uniform state business laws throughout the country. The most notable accomplishment of the National Conference of Commissioners on Uniform State Laws is the Uniform Commercial Code, which has been adopted in 49 states. Louisiana is the only state which has not adopted the entire Uniform Commercial Code.

The Uniform Commercial Code covers such areas as sales, commercial paper, checks, drafts, promissory notes, bank deposits and collections, letters of credit, bulk sales of goods, documents of title, investment securities, and secured transactions.

In addition to the Uniform Commercial Code the National Conference of Commissioners has drafted uniform laws for the settling or probating of estates and for partnerships. One of its most recent uniform laws is the Uniform Consumer Credit Code, which will be discussed in Chapter 5.

RESTATEMENTS OF THE LAW

In addition to the uniform codes drafted by the National Conference of Commissioners with the help of the American Law Institute, there has been effort toward uniformity of law throughout the states. The American Law Institute publishes treatises called Restatements of the Law. These treatises cover many business-related areas, such as torts, property, trusts, and conflicts of the laws. The American Law Institute writers have attempted to review the vast volume of case law and to set out in organized, encyclopedia-like form the generally accepted rules of law on specific topics. These Restatements are not like the statutes of a state. They are only for reference, and they are constantly revised and updated. They serve a very useful purpose, as they allow lawyers and judges to quickly see what the generally accepted rule of law is on a specific legal point. Judges often adopt the rules set out in the Restatements of the Law, thus making the Restatements actual law.

When commencing the study of a new subject, one often finds terms and phrases not used in other subject areas. It is helpful to learn such terms and phrases before advancing further into the study of the subject.

Legal Right. What does it mean to have a legal right? Simply stated, a legal right is a relationship between the individual and other members of society. When an individual has a legal right, he or she may be entitled to either action or forbearance by other members of society and the failure of members of society to respect this right will be penalized, in some cases by criminal action and in other cases by civil action. For example, if I have legal rights in real estate, I can legally prevent other persons from trespassing on my premises and I can legally charge sums of money for the use of my premises. What about my so-called moral rights? I may feel I have a moral right to do a certain act, but unless the constitution, a statute, or case law grants that right, it is not enforceable.

Legal Duty. Whenever there is a legal right, there is a corresponding legal duty. For example, if I have legal rights in real estate, you have a legal duty not to trespass upon my real estate. We often speak of ethics, of moral duties; however, a legal duty does not exist unless constitutional, statutory, or case law creates it.

Litigation. A lawsuit serves the purpose of securing a decision concerning a dispute over a legal right of the plaintiff (the party bringing the action) and a legal duty of the defendant (the party being sued).

Res Judicata. This Latin term means "the thing has been decided." Res judicata is a principle of law which says that once you get a final decision in a lawsuit, that is, after all appeals have been made, you cannot go back and start a new lawsuit to see whether you can get a different decision.

The Court. The phrase "the court" refers to the judge in a trial-level court and to the judges as a group in an appellate or reviewing court. For example, the Supreme Court of the United States is a nine-member court, whereas the local county court is simply a one-person court.

Jurisdiction. This term can be defined as the authority, power, or right of a court to act in certain matters. Each court has a defined jurisdiction. Jurisdiction can be over the person, the subject matter, or the value of the case. As you will see in Chapter 2, some courts are limited as to the monetary value of the cases they can hear, some as to the subject matter, and some as to the persons involved.

Property. This appears to be a common term. You say, "I own this property." Acutally property is not a tangible item. It is a legal concept of ownership. It is a "bundle of rights" in a tangible or intangible item.

Let's take real estate. For example, you have property rights in real estate; you have the right to sell it, to lease it, to cut down the trees. Or perhaps you don't have the right to cut down the trees because when you made the purchase, there was a restriction against cutting trees of a certain size without the developer's permission. You have the right to the use of minerals below the surface of the ground and to the use of the air above the ground. All of these are separate rights. You may own the entire bundle of rights, or you may own less than the entire bundle. For example, the mineral rights may have been sold to an oil company before you bought the land.

CASES FOR DISCUSSION

CONGREGATIONAL B'NAI SHOLOM v. MARTIN

173 N.W. 2d 504 (Michigan, 1969)

Adams, Justice

In January of 1959, defendant Morris Martin became chairman of the Synagogue Building Committee. On April 22, 1959, plaintiff contracted Ira J. Miller, a professional fund raiser, to assist in raising funds to build a new synagogue. . . .

On or about June 1, 1959, Morris Martin delivered to plaintiff's campaign office four partially filled in pledge cards. The first three were signed, respectively, by Irving Martin, Jack Martin, and Morris Martin. The fourth was signed by Morris Martin in the name of Bessie Martin Steinberg. The four pledge cards were not filled out as to amount. Morris Martin wrote the words, "Total Donation $25,000.00" on an attached scrap of paper. . . .

Later in the year 1959, disputes arose between Morris Martin, chairman of the Synagogue Building Committee, and other members of the Congregation. On October 29, 1959, and again on November 8, 1959, Morris Martin attempted to withdraw the pledge. . . .

On December 20, 1962, plaintiff, a nonprofit corporation, brought suit against Morris Martin, Irving Martin, Jack Martin, and Bessie Martin Steinberg. . . .

At a pretrial conference on March 10, 1965, the trial judge ordered the parties to file motions

for summary judgment or accelerated judgment. On November 17, 1965, the defendants filed a motion for leave to amend their answer. The proposed amendment would have added an affirmative defense to the effect that

. . . Jewish religious law and the custom and usage of Plaintiff synagogue prohibits the institution of a law suit in a nonreligious court before resort is had to Beth Din, or religious courts. There has been no effort on the part of Plaintiff to seek relief in a Beth Din. Whether or not the cards on which Plaintiff relies would otherwise form a legally binding contract, it was the intent of the parties that the Jewish law should govern the transaction. Since the Jewish law prohibits the institution of this suit, the parties did not intend to enter into a contract which is legally enforceable under Michigan law.

The defendants' motions for leave to amend were supported by the affidavit of a Dr. Rabbi Bernard D. Perlow, a rabbi for 25 years and a scholar. After stating his qualifications as an expert witness, he gave his opinion as follows:

5. That the religious customs, practices and laws binding on all Jews are codified in the work known as the *Shulchan Aruch*; that this code is generally regarded as binding as a matter of religious faith by both Orthodox and Conservative Jews. . . .

6. That in the opinion of this deponent, the *Shulchan Aruch*, as well as the custom and tradition for more than a thousand years, prohibits the bringing of a suit in the civil courts of any state by a synagogue against any of its members or vice versa and is contrary to Jewish law and is prohibited; that any such civil controversy must be first brought before the Jewish religion court known as the Beth Din (a Jewish rabbinical court); that under Jewish law, matters of charity to the

synagogue go to the heart of the Jewish religion; that a charitable contribution to a synagogue is considered a religious matter by and between the synagogue and the member; that for a synagogue to file a suit against one of its members upon an alleged charitable contribution without submitting it to a Beth Din is what is known in Jewish law as a "Chillul Hashem" which is a profanation of God's name and such action is such a grave sin in Jewish law, that it warrants excommunication. . . .

7. That it is expressly stated in Hyman E. Goldin's translation of Rabbi Solomon Ganzfried's *Code of Jewish Law, Kidzur Schulchan Aruch* published in New York City by the Hebrew Publishing Company in 1961, volume 4, page 67, that it is forbidden to bring a suit in the civil courts even if their decision would be in accordance with the law of Israel; that even if the two litigants are willing to try the case before such a court, it is forbidden; that even if they make an oral or a written agreement to that effect, it is of no avail; that whoever takes a case against another Jew involving religious matters, is a Godless person and he has violated and defiled the law of Moses.

On December 10, 1965, the trial judge denied defendants' two motions for leave to amend answer. Motion to reconsider was denied on April 21, 1966. On August 24, 1966, the trial judge issued a supplemental opinion in which he granted a summary judgment in favor of plaintiff against defendant Morris Martin for the sum of $25,000, plus interest at 5 percent from June 30, 1964; Morris Martin was granted the right within 30 days to introduce a third party action for contribution from defendants Jack Martin and Irving Martin. Appeal was taken from the final judgment in favor of plaintiff and against Morris Martin to the Court of Appeals. The Court affirmed the trial judge. . . .

The trial judge erred in denying defendants' motions for leave to amend for the reason that the affidavit of Dr. Rabbi Bernard B. Perlow raised a question of fact as to Jewish custom which may be controlling upon the parties. . . .

Nothing appears in the record before us in this case to warrant the trial judge's denial of the motion. When the rights of the parties are being tested on motions for summary judgment filed, not at the election of the parties themselves but at the behest of the trial judge, a defendant should most certainly be allowed to amend to assert any

defense he may have before the court has ruled. . . .

Reversed and remanded for further proceedings in accordance with this opinion. Costs to appellant.

FLOOD v. KUHN

407 U.S. 258 (U.S. Supreme Court, 1972)

Justice Blackmun

For the third time in 50 years the Court is asked specifically to rule that professional baseball's reserve system is within the reach of the federal antitrust laws. Collateral issues of state law and of federal labor policy are also advanced.

I
The Game

It is a century and a quarter since the New York Nine defeated the Knickerbockers 23 to 1 on Hoboken's Elysian Fields June 19, 1846, with Alexander Jay Cartwright as the instigator and the umpire. The teams were amateur, but the contest marked a significant date in baseball's beginnings. That early game led ultimately to the development of professional baseball and its tightly organized structure.

The Cincinnati Red Stockings came into existence in 1869 upon an outpouring of local pride. With only one Cincinnatian on the payroll, this professional team traveled over 11,000 miles that summer, winning 56 games and tying one. . . .

The ensuing colorful days are well known. The ardent follower and the student of baseball know of General Abner Doubleday; the formation of the National League in 1876; Chicago's supremacy in the first year's competition under the leadership of Al Spalding and with Cap Anson at third base; the formation of the American Association and then of the Union Association in the 1880's. . . .

Then there are the many names, celebrated for one reason or another, that have sparked the diamond and its environs and that have provided tinder for recaptured thrills, for reminiscence and

19

comparisons, and for conversation and anticipation in-season and off-season: Ty Cobb, Babe Ruth, Tris Speaker, Walter Johnson, Henry Chadwick, Eddie Collins, Lou Gehrig, Grover Cleveland Alexander, Rogers Hornsby, Harry Hopper, Goose Goslin. . . .

II
Petitioner

The petitioner, Curtis Charles Flood, born in 1938, began his major league career in 1956 when he signed a contract with the Cincinnati Reds for the salary of $4,000 for the season. He had no attorney or agent to advise him on that occasion. He was traded to the St. Louis Cardinals before the 1958 season. Flood rose to fame as a center fielder with the Cardinals during the years 1958–1969. . . .

But at the age of 31, in October 1969, Flood was traded to the Philadelphia Phillies of the National League in a multi-player transaction. He was not consulted about the trade. He was informed by telephone and received formal notice only after the deal had been consummated. In December he complained to the Commissioner of Baseball and asked that he be made a free agent and be placed at liberty to strike his own bargain with any other major league team. His request was denied.

Flood then instituted this antitrust suit in January 1970 in federal court for the Southern District of New York. . . . In general, the complaint charged violations of the federal antitrust laws and civil rights statutes, violation of state statutes and the common law, and the imposition of a form of peonage and involuntary service contrary to the 13th Amendment. . . . Petitioner sought declaratory and injunctive relief and treble damages. . . .

III
The Present Litigation

Judge Cooper in a detailed opinion, first denied a preliminary injunction, 309 F. Supp. 793 (S.D.N.Y. 1970), observing on the way:

Baseball has been the national pastime for over one hundred years and enjoys a unique place in our Ameri-

can heritage. Major league professional baseball is avidly followed by millions of fans, looked upon with fervor and pride and provides a special source of inspiration and competitive team spirit especially for the young.

Baseball's status in the life of the nation is so pervasive that it would strain credulity to say the Court can take judicial notice that baseball is everybody's business. To put it mildly and with restraint, it would be unfortunate indeed if a fine sport and profession, which brings surcease from daily travail and an escape from the ordinary to most inhabitants of this land, were to suffer in the least because of undue concentration by any one or any group on commercial and profit considerations. The game is on higher ground; it behooves every one to keep it there. . . .

Trial to the court took place in May and June 1970. An extensive record was developed.

He then held that *Federal Baseball Club* v. *National League*, 259 U.S. 200 . . . (1922), and *Toolson* v. *New York Yankees, Inc.* 346 U.S. 356 (1953), were controlling; that it was not necessary to reach the issue whether exemption from the antitrust laws would result because aspects of baseball now are a subject of collective bargaining; that the plaintiff's state-law claims, those based on common law as well as on statute, were to be denied because baseball was not "a matter which admits of diversity of treatment," 316 F. Supp., at 280; that the involuntary servitude claim failed because of the absence of "the essential element of this cause of action, a showing of compulsory service," 316 F. Supp., at 281–282; and that judgment was to be entered for the defendants.

On appeal, the Second Circuit felt "compelled to affirm." 443 F.2d 264, 265 (1971).

IV
The Legal Background

A. *Federal Baseball Club* v. *National League* . . . was a suit for treble damages instituted by a member of the Federal League (Baltimore) against the National and American Leagues and others. . . .

Mr. Justice Holmes, in speaking succinctly for a unanimous Court, said:

The business is giving exhibitions of baseball, which

are purely state affairs. . . . But the fact that in order to give the exhibitions the Leagues must induce free persons to cross state lines and must arrange and pay for their doing so is not enough to change the character of the business. . . . [T]he transport is a mere incident, not the essential thing. That to which it is incident, the exhibition, although made for money would not be called trade or commerce in the commonly accepted use of those words. As it is put by the defendant, personal effort, not related to production, is not a subject of commerce. That which in its consummation is not commerce does not become commerce among the States because the transportation that we have mentioned takes place. . . .

In the years that followed, baseball continued to be subject to intermittent antitrust attack. The courts, however, rejected these challenges on the authority of *Federal Baseball*. In some cases stress was laid, although unsuccessfully, on new factors such as the development of radio and television with their substantial additional revenues to baseball. For the most part, however, the Holmes opinion was generally and necessarily accepted as controlling authority. . . .

C. The Court granted certiorari . . . in the *Toolson*, *Kowalksi*, and *Corbett* cases . . . and affirmed the judgments of the respective courts of appeals in those three cases . . . *Federal Baseball* was cited as holding "that the business of providing public baseball games for profit between clubs of professional baseball players was not within the scope of the federal antitrust laws," and:

Congress has had the ruling under consideration but has not seen fit to bring such business under these laws by legislation having prospective effect. The business has thus been left for thirty years to develop, on the understanding that it was not subject to existing antitrust legislation. The present cases ask us to overrule the prior decision and, with retrospective effect, hold the legislation applicable. We think that if there are evils in this field which now warrant application to it of the antitrust laws it should be by legislation. Without re-examination of the underlying issues, the judgments below are affirmed on the authority of *Federal Baseball Club of Baltimore* v. *National League of Professional Baseball Clubs*, supra, so far as that decision determines that Congress had no intention of including the business of baseball within the scope of the federal antitrust laws. . . .

H. This series of decisions understandably spawned extensive commentary, some of it mildly critical and much of it not; nearly all of it looked to Congress for any remedy that might be deemed essential.

I. Legislative proposals have been numerous and persistent. Since *Toolson* more than 50 bills have been introduced in Congress relative to the applicability or nonapplicability of the antitrust laws to baseball. A few of these passed one house or the other. Those that did would have expanded, not restricted, the reserve system's exemption to other professional league sports.

V

In view of all this, it seems appropriate now to say that:

1. Professional baseball is a business and it is engaged in interstate commerce.

2. With its reserve system enjoying exemption from the federal antitrust laws, baseball is, in a very distinct sense, an exception and an anomaly. *Federal Baseball* and *Toolson* have become an aberration confined to baseball.

3. Even though others might regard this as "unrealistic, inconsistent, or illogical," see *Radovich*, 352 U.S., at 452, 77 S. Ct., at 394, the aberration is an established one, and one that has been recognized not only in *Federal Baseball* and *Toolson*, but in *Shubert*, *International Boxing*, and *Radovich*, as well, a total of five consecutive cases in this Court. It is an aberration that has been with us now for half a century, one heretofore deemed fully entitled to the benefit of stare decisis, and one that has survived the Court's expanding concept of interstate commerce. It rests on a recognition and an acceptance of baseball's unique characteristics and needs.

4. Other professional sports operating interstate—football, boxing, basketball, and presumably, hockey and golf—are not so exempt.

5. The advent of radio and television, with their consequent increased coverage and additional revenues, has not occasioned an overruling of *Federal Baseball* and *Toolson*.

6. The Court has emphasized that since 1922 baseball, with full and continuing congressional awareness, has been allowed to develop and to

expand unhindered by federal legislative action. Remedial legislation has been introduced repeatedly in Congress, but none has ever been enacted. The Court, accordingly, has concluded that Congress as yet has had no intention to subject baseball's reserve system to the reach of the antitrust statutes. This, obviously, has been deemed to be something other than mere congressional silence and passivity. . . .

7. The Court has expressed concern about the confusion and the retroactivity problems that inevitably would result with a judicial overturning of *Federal Baseball*. It has voiced a perference that if any change is made, it come by legislative action that, by its nature, is only prospective in operation.

8. The Court noted in *Radovich*, that the slate with respect to baseball is not clean. Indeed, it has not been clean for half a century.

This emphasis and this concern are still with us. We continue to loath, 50 years after *Federal Baseball* and almost two decades after *Toolson*, to overturn those cases judicially when Congress, by its positive inaction, has allowed those decisions to stand for so long and, far beyond mere inference and implication, has clearly evinced a desire not to disapprove them legislatively.

Accordingly, we adhere once again to *Federal Baseball* and *Toolson* and to their application to professional baseball. We adhere also to *International Boxing* and *Radovich* and to their respective applications to professional boxing and professional football. If there is any inconsistency or illogic in all this, it is an inconsistency and illogic of long standing that is to be remedied by the Congress and not by this Court. If we were to act otherwise, we would be withdrawing from the conclusion as to congressional intent made in *Toolson* and from the concerns as to retrospectivity therein expressed. Under these circumstances, there is merit in consistency even though some might claim that beneath that consistency is a layer of inconsistency. . . .

[W]hat the Court said in *Federal Baseball* in 1922 and what is said in *Toolson* in 1953, we say again here in 1972: the remedy, if any is indicated, is for congressional, and not judicial, action.

The judgment of the Court of Appeals is affirmed. . . .

WINKLE v. KROPP
403 F.2d 661 (U.S. Sixth Circuit, 1968)
Per Curiam

Appellee was convicted in the Circuit Court of Lenawee County, Michigan, in 1958, for carrying concealed weapons and for possession of burglary tools. The Supreme Court of Michigan affirmed the conviction. *People v. Winkle*, 358 Mich. 551, 100 N.W.2d 309 (1960). Thereafter the Supreme Court of Michigan denied, in an unreported order, Winkle's petition for habeas corpus and certiorari. The Supreme Court of the United States granted certiorari and upon the suggestion of the Attorney General of Michigan, remanded the case to the Supreme Court of Michigan for consideration in the light of *Mapp* v. *Ohio*, 367 U.S. 643 . . . (1961). *Winkle* v. *Bannan* 368 U.S. 34 (1961).

Upon receipt of the mandate from the United States Supreme Court, the Supreme Court of Michigan vacated its earlier denial of habeas corpus and ordered the cause to be rebriefed and reargued, and again denied the writ. All seven Judges agreed, although for different reasons, that there was no unlawful search and seizure of appellee's automobile. *In re Winkle*, 372 Mich. 292, 125 N.W.2d 875 (1964). Certiorari was denied by the United States Supreme Court, *Winkle* v. *Bannan*, 379 U.S. 645 . . . (1965), and a rehearing was denied, 380 U.S. 967 . . . (1965).

Appellee then filed a habeas corpus action in the District Court for the Eastern District of Michigan, 279 F. Supp. 532, and the District Court granted the writ, disagreeing with the Supreme Court of Michigan, and holding that Article 2, Section 10 of the Michigan Constitution of 1908 was in violation of the Fourth Amendment to the United States Constitution.

Appellant contends that the case is controlled by *Wolf* v. *People of State of Colorado*, 338 U.S. 25 . . . (1949), which was overruled in *Mapp* v. *Ohio*, 367 U.S. 643 . . . (1961). Appellant further contends that the judgment of conviction in the present case had become final before *Mapp* was decided and that *Mapp* should not have been retrospectively applied by the District Court. He relies on *Linkletter* v. *Walker*, 381 U.S. 618 . . . (1965).

The question whether *Mapp* should be retrospectively applied apparently was not brought up in the District Court as everyone assumed that the rule in *Mapp* was controlling. It is not understandable why counsel for appellant did not present the point. However, irrespective of whether this question of law was raised by counsel for appellant, it is clear from *Linkletter* that it was error to apply *Mapp* retrospectively. The rule in *Wolf* should have been applied.

Since *Wolf* was applicable, the question whether Article 2, Section 10 of the Michigan Constitution of 1908 offends the Fourth Amendment to the Constitution of the United States was not properly before the District Court; nor is it properly before us, and we express no opinion on it.

The judgment of the District Court is vacated, and the cause is remanded for further proceedings in conformity with this opinion.

BROWN ET AL. v. BOARD OF EDUCATION OF TOPEKA

347 U.S. 483 (U.S. Supreme Court, 1954)

Chief Justice Warren

These cases come to us from the States of Kansas, South Carolina, Virginia, and Delaware. They are premised on different facts and different local conditions, but a common legal question justifies their consideration together in this consolidated opinion.

In each of the cases, minors of the Negro race, through their legal representatives, seek the aid of the courts in obtaining admission to the public schools of their community on a nonsegregated basis. In each instance, they have been denied admission to schools attended by white children under laws requiring or permitting segregation according to race. This segregation was alleged to deprive the plaintiffs of the equal protection of the laws under the 14th Amendment. In each of the cases other than the Delaware case, a three-judge federal district court denied relief to the plaintiffs on the so-called "separate but equal" doctrine announced by this Court in *Plessy* v. *Ferguson*, 163 U.S. 537. . . . Under the doctrine, equality of treatment is accorded when the races are provided substantially equal facilities, even though these facilities be separate. In the Delaware case, the Supreme Court of Delaware adhered to the doctrine, but ordered that the plaintiffs be admitted to the white schools because of their superiority to the Negro schools.

The plaintiffs contend that segregated public schools are not "equal," and cannot be made "equal," and that hence they are deprived of the equal protection of the laws. Because of the obvious importance of the question presented, the Court took jurisdiction. Argument was heard in the 1952 Term, and reargument was heard this Term on certain questions propounded by the Court.

Reargument was largely devoted to the circumstances surrounding the adoption of the 14th Amendment in 1868. It covered exhaustively consideration of the Amendment in Congress, ratification by the states, then existing practices in racial segregation, and the views of proponents and opponents of the Amendment. This discussion and our own investigation convince us that, although these sources cast some light, it is not enough to resolve the problem with which we are faced. At best, they are inconclusive. The most avid proponents of the post-War Amendments undoubtedly intended them to remove all legal distinctions among "all persons born or naturalized in the United States." Their opponents, just as certainly, were antagonistic to both the letter and the spirit of the Amendments and wished them to have the limited effect. What others in Congress and the state legislatures had in mind cannot be determined with any degree of certainty.

An additional reason for the inconclusive nature of the Amendment's history, with respect to segregated schools, is the status of public education at that time. In the South, the movement toward free common schools supported by general taxation, had not yet taken hold. Education of white children was largely in the hands of private groups. Education of Negroes was almost nonexistent, and practically all of the race were illiterate. In fact, any education of Negroes was forbidden by law in some states. Today, in contrast, many Negroes have achieved outstanding success in the arts and sciences as well as in the business and professional world. It is true that public school education at the time of the Amendment had advanced further in the North, but the effect of the Amendment on Northern states was generally ignored in the congressional debates. Even in the North, the conditions of public education did not approximate those existing today. The curriculum was usually rudimentary; ungraded schools were common in rural areas; the school term was but three months a year in many states; and compulsory school attendance was virtually unknown. As a consequence, it is not surprising that there should be so little in the history of the 14th Amendment relating to its intended effect on public education. . . .

Here . . . there are findings below that the Negro and white schools involved have been equalized, or are being equalized, with respect to buildings, curricula, qualifications and salaries of teachers, and other "tangible" factors. Our decision, therefore, cannot turn on merely a comparison of these tangible factors in the Negro and white schools involved in each of the cases. We must look instead to the effect of segregation itself on public education.

In approaching this problem, we cannot turn the clock back to 1868 when the Amendment was adopted, or even to 1896 when *Plessy* v. *Ferguson* was written. We must consider public education in the light of its full development and its present place in American life throughout the Nation. Only in this way can it be determined if segregation in public schools deprives these plaintiffs of the equal protection of the laws.

Today, education is perhaps the most important function of state and local governments. Compulsory school attendance laws and the great expenditures for education both demonstrate our

recognition of the importance of education to our democratic society. It is required in the performance of our most basic public responsibilities, even service in the armed forces. It is the very foundation of good citizenship. Today it is a principal instrument in awakening the child to cultural values, in preparing him for later professional training, and in helping him adjust normally to his environment. In these days, it is doubtful that any child may reasonably be expected to succeed in life if he is denied the opportunity of an education. Such an opportunity, where the state has undertaken to provide it, is a right which must be made available to all on equal terms.

We come then to the question presented: Does segregation of children in public schools solely on the basis of race, even though the physical facilities and other "tangible" factors may be equal, deprive the children of the minority group of equal educational opportunities? We believe that it does. . . .

To separate them from others of similar age and qualifications solely because of their race generates a feeling of inferiority as to their status in the community that may affect their hearts and minds in a way unlikely ever to be undone. The effect of this separation on their educational opportunities was well stated by a finding in the Kansas case by a court which nevertheless felt compelled to rule against the Negro plaintiffs:

Segregation of white and colored children in public schools has a detrimental effect upon the colored children. The impact is greater when it has the sanction of the law; for the policy of separating the races is usually interpreted as denoting the inferiority of the negro group. A sense of inferiority affects the motivation of a child to learn. . . .

Whatever may have been the extent of psychological knowledge at the time of *Plessy* v. *Ferguson*, this finding is amply supported by modern authority. Any language in *Plessy* v. *Ferguson* contrary to this finding is rejected.

We conclude that in the field of public education the doctrine of "separate but equal" has no place. Separate educational facilities are inherently unequal. Therefore, we hold that the plaintiffs and others similarly situated for whom the actions have been brought are, by reason of the segregation complained of, deprived of the equal protection of the laws guaranteed by the 14th Amendment. This disposition makes unnecessary any discussion whether such segregation also violates the Due Process Clause of the 14th Amendment.

Because these are class actions, because of the wide applicability of this decision, and because of the great variety of local conditions, the formulation of decrees in these cases presents problems of considerable complexity. . . . In order that we may have the full assistance of the parties in formulating decrees, the cases will be restored to the docket, and the parties are requested to present further argument on Questions 4 and 5 previously propounded by the Court for the reargument this Term. The Attorney General of the United States is again invited to participate. The Attorneys General of the states requiring or permitting segregation in public education will also be permitted to appear as *amici curiae* upon request to do so by September 15, 1954, and submission of briefs by October 1, 1954.

It is so ordered.

COHEN v. BAYSIDE FEDERAL SAVINGS AND LOAN ASSOCIATION
309 N.Y.S.2d 980 (New York, 1970)

Tessler, Justice

The fundamental question presented to this court in an agreed statement of facts submitted by the parties is:

Can an engagement ring, given in contemplation of marriage, be recovered from a "donee," by the estate of the "donor," when the contemplated marriage fails to occur because of the death of the "donor"?

The undisputed facts can be summarized as follows: Richard Alan Rothchild became engaged to be married to Carol Sue Cohen, the plaintiff in this action. Both were over 21 years of age. Richard gave Carol a diamond "engagement" ring which is valued at $1,000. Shortly before the wedding date, Richard was killed in an automobile accident, and his estate has instituted this action to recover the ring. The sole question for determination by this court is: "Who is entitled to the ring?"

Actions for return of engagement rings have had an interesting and confusing history in New York. These actions were permitted at common law prior to 1935. However, in 1935 the Legislature of this State enacted Article 2-A of the Civil Practice Act (the heart balm statute) which was later interpreted by the courts so as to bar actions for the return of engagement rings in most instances. . . . These results were widely criticized. . . . In response to this criticism, in 1965 the Legislature amended section 80-b of the Civil Rights Law to permit recovery of engagement rings where "justice so requires."

In *Lowe* v. *Quinn*, 32 A.D.2d 269, 301 N.Y.S.2d 361, the Appellate Division, First Department, held that the common law rules formulated before 1935 would again be applicable. . . .

However, reference to these common law rules formulated prior to 1935 is of little help in the present instance since this case appears to be one of first impression in this State. In the absence of any controlling authority, this court has sought help by looking to applicable decisional law in other jurisdictions, the general principles underlying engagement ring cases in general and, finally, to what justice requires in this situation.

An examination of the relevant authorities in other states indicates that they are split. One approach is illustrated in the decision in *Urbanus* v. *Burns*, 300 Ill.App. 207, 20 N.E.2d 869. In that case, the court denied the donor recovery of an engagement ring and other jewelry he had given his fiancée, whose death had prevented the marriage. . . .

However, a different approach was taken in a Pennsylvania case (*Ruehling* v. *Hornung*, 98 Pa.Super. 535 at page 540) in which the court stated:

Such a ring is given as a pledge or symbol of the contract to marry. We think that it is always given subject to the implied condition that if the marriage does not take place either because of the death, or a disability recognized by the law on the part of either party, or by breach of the contract by the donee, or its dissolution by mutual consent, the gift shall be returned. It only becomes the absolute property of the recipient if the marriage takes place. Good sense usually secures the return of the ring. The English cases seem to be in harmony on this question. . . .

Nor does an examination of the principles underlying the gift of engagement ring cases in general clearly point the way to a particular result. The results set forth in the decisions in gift of engagement ring cases are usually predictable and understandable. However, the legal principles and rationales relied upon by the courts are often divergent and muddled. For example, it is settled that where a fiancée breaks an engagement without the fault of the donor, she must return the ring. . . . It is also well settled that where the donor breaks the engagement, the ring may be kept by the donee . . . and, generally, where the engagement is broken by mutual consent, the ring also goes back to the donor. . . .

Thus, a confusing body of law has grown up around the engagement ring and, after careful consideration of these principles, this court has decided that Carol should keep the ring because that result is equitable and because "justice so requires" for the following reasons:

While the engagement ring to some people in the "mod" world of today is just another material possession, and while it has not been unknown in some circles for recipients of these rings to flaunt them, to compare their luster, number of carats, etc., with the rings of their friends, for the vast majority the ring still remains a hallowed symbol of the love and devotion that a prospective husband and wife bear for each other. In my judgment, no gift given during a lifetime can approach the meaningfulness and significance of the engagement ring. When Richard gave the ring to Carol, he obviously intended that she have it and

keep it unless she affirmatively did something to prevent the marriage of the parties. While it is improbable that at the time of the gift either gave a thought to the consequences that would arise in the event of the death of one of the parties, I firmly believe that had Richard thought of these consequences he would have intended that in the event of his untimely death Carol should keep the ring as a symbol of his love and affection. There appears to be no reason, in logic or morals, to prevent such a result.

This court frankly acknowledges that implicit in this determination is a recognition that the gift of an engagement ring is a special occasion interwoven with romance and mutual love. It is a meaningful act symbolic of much more than the ordinary and usual business transaction. I am convinced that it is time for a change in our approach to this area. The traditional approach of applying the sound and settled principles of business law and the law of gifts to the giving of an engagement ring has resulted in a myriad of decisional law in this area, which is, to say the least, in much confusion and determinative of little.

I can not believe that the age-old ritual of giving an engagement ring to bind the mutual premarital vows can be or is intended to be treated as an exchange of consideration as practiced in the everyday market place. Can it be seriously urged that the giving of this ring by the decedent "groom" to his loved one and bride-to-be can be treated as the ordinary commercial or business transaction requiring the ultimate in consideration and payment? I think not. To treat this special and usually once in a lifetime occasion as one requiring quid pro quo, is a mistake and unrealistic.

Accordingly the ring shall remain with Carol and judgment shall be entered accordingly.

1. Define *law* in your own words.

2. What are the needs for law in our society?

3. What are equitable maxims?

4. What is the supreme law of our country?

5. What amendment of the U.S. Constitution is referred to as the states' rights amendment?

6. Define stare decisis.

7. Give an example of the use of res judicata.

8. What is the difference between private law and public law?

9. What is the "unwritten" law?

10. What is the difference between substantive law and procedural law?

11. Alumsports, Inc., a manufacturer of baseball bats, sued Batoff Company for alleged patent infringement. Alumsports said that it had the patent on a certain design for aluminum baseball bats and that Batoff was making the same product. Batoff argues that the patent is invalid since baseball is not commerce and Congress lacks the power to regulate it. Thus the congressionally established patent system can not be applied to baseball equipment. What result, and why?

12. Harold owns and operates a traveling dog and poney show. He gives exhibitions in several states. The U.S. secretary of agriculture attempted to impose regulations on Harold as to the care and feeding of his animals, pursuant to authority granted under the Animal Welfare Act. Harold says that his exhibitions are not interstate commerce and that he is therefore not subject to congressional regulation, under the authority of the *Federal Baseball* case. How should the court rule, and why? Would there be a different result if Harold had a permanent location and gave exhibitions only in that one place?

13. The National Hockey League permits a player to become a "free agent" if he plays for one year for his old club without a contract. After that year he is free to negotiate with any other club in the league. If he is signed by another club, however, his former club can claim a player of equal value in compensation. Harry Handsome became a free agent under these rules and signed a very lucrative contract with the Buffalo Bingos. His former team, the Sudbury Suds, was quite angry and demanded the Bingos' ace goaltender, Roger Redder, as compensation. The Suds' claim was upheld by the league commissioner, and Roger was ordered to report to the Suds. Roger refused, alleging that this system amounted to an illegal conspiracy under the U.S. antitrust laws. The league and the commissioner argue that they ought to be exempt from the antitrust laws, just like baseball. How should the court rule on these claims, and why?

14. Hap Hapless, the former owner of a now-bankrupt minor league baseball team, sues the commissioner of major league baseball and all the major league club owners for damages sustained to his franchise when a major league team moved into the same geographic area. Hap alleges that the fans went to see the major league games, rather than coming to see his minor league team play. He says that the loss in revenues which resulted forced him to go out of business. He claims damages for unfair competition under the appropriate sections of the antitrust laws. The commissioner and the owners argue that the case should be dismissed, under the authority of *Federal Baseball*. How should the court rule, and why?

2 | Dispute Resolution and Enforcement of the Law

Legal principles and rules are meaningless without an effective procedure for resolving disputes concerning the law and an effective procedure for enforcement of the law.

In Chapter 1 we referred to laws as being divided into two major classifications, procedural law and substantive law. This chapter deals primarily with procedural law, the law that governs the resolution and enforcement of substantive law.

In the United States we do not have a single system for resolving disputes and enforcing the law; we have several. We have the national judicial system, 50 different state judicial systems, the quasi-judicial systems of the various national and state administrative agencies, and a nonjudicial dispute-resolving system called arbitration.

In this chapter we will look at these systems and review the procedure of a typical lawsuit, the procedure of an administrative agency, and the procedure of arbitration. Our purpose is not to make lawyers of you, but rather to give you some familiarity with the procedures that your lawyer must pursue in a lawsuit, administrative hearing, or arbitration hearing.

STATE COURT SYSTEMS

Each state has a state court system which has been designed to fit its own needs. Thus there is no uniform pattern that applies to all of the states in the United States. There is, however, a general pattern which most of the states follow. It is a four-tier judicial system, as illustrated in the accompanying chart.

In the first tier or lowest level of the typical state judicial system, we find specialty courts of limited jurisdiction. The justice of the peace court is perhaps the oldest of these specialty courts. Normally this court has jurisdiction over civil cases involving small amounts and over nonfelony criminal matters, typically traffic cases where the charged person is willing to plead guilty. There is

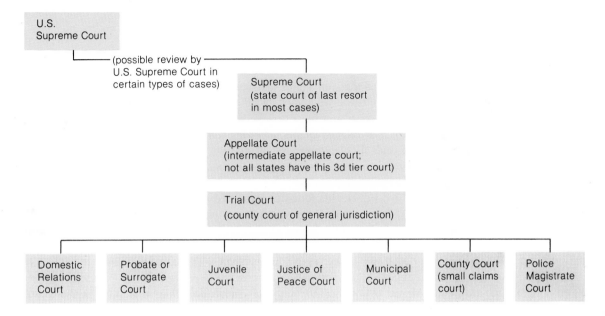

STATE COURT SYSTEM

normally no provision for a jury trial in this court. The judge in most instances serves part time only; he or she is often not a lawyer; and often the court is held in the judge's home or other place of business. Today many states have abolished the justice of the peace court and replaced it with a county court or a small claims court with a full-time judge who must meet certain educational requirements. Typically these courts do not have provision for trial by jury.

In this first tier we also find police magistrate courts and municipal courts. Police magistrate courts are usually created to handle traffic offenses and minor criminal matters. Depending on the particular state, municipal courts may handle minor civil matters and may also handle minor criminal matters. Municipal courts often allow trial by jury, whereas police magistrate courts normally do not. These courts are quick and inexpensive. The great majority of the persons who come before them are not represented by a lawyer. There is, of course, a right to appeal from their decisions. Generally, these courts do not record all testimony and proceedings and the appeal is made to the trial court of general jurisdiction. There the case is tried de novo, which means that a complete new trial is held, rather than just a review of the record. However, in some states where a record of testimony and proceedings is kept, the appeal is direct to an appellate court for review rather than for a retrial.

In this first tier we also find domestic relations courts, which generally handle marital relations problems, child custody problems, and other domestic problems. Probate courts, also known as surrogate courts, generally handle the administration of decedents' estates, the guardianship of minor children and persons declared incompetent to handle their own affairs, and matters involving juveniles. In most states juveniles are persons under 17 years of age. Typically there is no provision for trial by jury in the domestic relations, probate, and juvenile courts. These courts are generally answerable to the trial court of general jurisdiction, but in some states an appeal can be made directly to an appellate court.

In the second tier of this four-tier structure we find the trial courts with general jurisdiction. These courts may be called district courts, superior courts, or common pleas courts; in New York this court is called the Supreme Court. Generally speaking, our states are divided into counties and each county has one or more of these trial courts with general jurisdiction. Counties with large populations have a number of trial courts with general jurisdiction. This court in all states is a court of record, meaning that all testimony and proceedings are recorded and all pleadings are in writing. Usually there is no limit on the monetary amounts involved in cases in these courts. The courts handle criminal, civil, and equity matters.

The third tier in this four-tier structure is an intermediate appellate court. This court hears appeals from judgments entered by the courts below it. The appellate court is a reviewing court, and no new evidence is presented to it. The court will review the transcript of the record, the testimony, and the decision of the lower court. The attorneys for each side will submit written briefs of the law which they contend applies, and the court will in some cases listen to oral arguments of the attorneys for each side. Then this court will make its decision to approve and affirm the lower court's decision, to reverse the lower court's decision and give judgment to the party that appealed, or to reverse the lower court's decision and send the case back for a new trial or other proceedings in accordance with this court's opinion.

In order to appeal a judgment of a lower court, the party making the appeal, called the appellant, must allege error in the trial. For example, perhaps the judge in the trial court allowed the jury to hear inadmissible hearsay evidence, or perhaps he or she gave incorrect instructions on the law to the jury.

In some states the title of the appellate case may be reversed from the title of the case in the lower court. For example, Smith sued Jones in the lower court. Smith won; Jones appeals. Some states now list the case as *Jones* v. *Smith*.

This third tier, the intermediate appellate court, is not found in all states. It is usually needed in states with large populations and a large volume of cases.

Next we come to the fourth tier, which is the state's court of final resort. This court may be called the supreme court, the supreme court of errors and appeals, the supreme judicial court, the supreme court of appeals, or simply the court of appeals, depending on the particular state court system. Like the intermediate appellate court, this court is a reviewing court, and no new trial is held by it. The procedure for review in this court is similar to the procedure for review at the intermediate appellate court level. This court, however, is the party's last resort for appeal in the great majority of the cases which originate in the state court system. There is the opportunity for review of the highest state court's decision by the Supreme Court of the United States in cases where such a decision is against the validity of a U.S. treaty or statute or in favor of the validity of a state statute when it has been charged that the state statute violates the U.S. Constitution. These appeals are allowed as a matter of right. The Supreme Court of the United States may be requested to review cases where a federal question is involved. Here there is no automatic right of appeal. The party requesting the review must submit a petition for a writ of certioriari, a formal request for review. This petition is then circulated among the nine justices of the U.S. Supreme Court, who decide whether a federal question is involved and whether it is important enough to warrant a full hearing before the Supreme Court. Several thousand cases are submitted to the U.S. Supreme Court for review each year; however, only a few hundred cases eventually receive a formal hearing by the Court. If at least four of the nine justices vote in favor of a review, then the writ of certioriari is granted and the case is scheduled for a formal hearing. Transcripts of testimony and the decisions of the lower courts together with briefs of the law prepared by the attorneys for both sides are submitted for review, and the attorneys are given an opportunity to argue their contentions before the Court.

THE NATIONAL COURT SYSTEM

As was noted in Chapter 1, the Constitution of the United States established the Supreme Court and gave Congress the right to establish inferior national courts as it desired. The national court system is also a four-tier system, as shown in the accompanying illustration.

The first, or lower tier, is comprised of specialty courts such as the customs court, the patent office, and the court of customs and patent appeals, and the court of claims. Appeals from these courts can be made directly to the Supreme Court of the United States.

In the second tier we find the United States district courts. Most have national jurisdiction only, but some have both local and national jurisdiction. The United States district courts in the District of Columbia, the Virgin Islands, and Guam not only have to handle the typical matters which a U.S. District Court

THE NATIONAL COURT SYSTEM

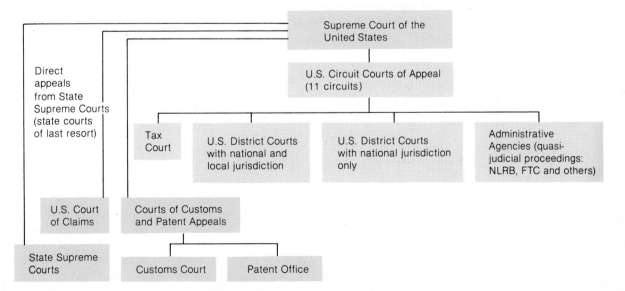

would normally handle, but they also decide normal civil cases since there are no state courts in these areas. United States district courts with national jurisdiction only, are found in all 50 states and Puerto Rico. Also in the second tier are administrative quasi-judicial agencies such as the Tax Court, the Federal Trade Commission, the National Labor Relations Board, and other federal administrative agencies too numerous to list here. The United States district courts are courts of general jurisdiction with regard to national law. They have authority to hear civil, criminal and equity cases and power to enforce their decisions by court orders which can result in fines or imprisonment.

The administrative quasi-judicial agencies are limited in jurisdiction to cases involving their specialty area. They are also limited in their power to enforce their decisions. Generally speaking, if the party being charged by the particular agency does not desire to voluntarily comply with the agency decision, the party charged may appeal the decision to the U.S. court of appeals for review or the agency may request the U.S. court of appeals to approve and enforce their decision by court order.

In the third tier we find the U.S. courts of appeal, also called U.S. circuit courts of appeal. There are 11 circuits throughout the country. Basically these courts are reviewing courts similar to the state appellate courts; no new evidence may be submitted to them. Their hearing is not a trial; it is simply a review. The procedure followed by these courts is similar to the procedure of the state appellate courts.

The fourth tier is the Supreme Court of the United States. This is the court of final resort for appeal for any case. The U.S. Supreme Court is generally a reviewing court; however, the U.S. Constitution, Article III, Section 2, provides that in addition to being a court of appellate or reviewing jurisdiction, the Supreme Court of the United States can also in certain cases be a trial court. In cases affecting ambassadors, other public ministers, and consuls and cases in which a state is a party, the Supreme Court has original jurisdiction and may act as a trial court. Note, however, that the word used is *may* and not *must*. Thus the Supreme Court decides whether or not to hear such cases. The following case illustrates the exercise of this latitude by the Supreme Court.

Ohio v. *Wyandotte Chemicals Corporation*
401 U.S. 493 (U.S. Supreme Court, 1971)

FACTS The state of Ohio petitioned the U.S. Supreme Court for permission to file a lawsuit against a corporation allegedly polluting Lake Erie, directly in the U.S. Supreme Court under the original jurisdiction authority of the Court, which allows it to have an original trial in cases in which a state is a party and in cases affecting ambassadors, public ministers, and consuls. The defendants were not Ohio corporations or Ohio citizens. The purpose of the lawsuit was to prevent further pollution by the defendants.

ISSUE Should the U.S. Supreme Court accept original jurisdiction of this lawsuit?

DECISION   The U.S. Supreme Court declined to exercise its power of original jurisdiction in this case.

REASONS   The U.S. Supreme Court's paramount responsibilities lie in the domain of federal law. While the Court does have the constitutional power to accept original jurisdiction in cases involving a state and a citizen or citizens of another state, it is not required to do so. The primary role of the Court is to perform as an appellate tribunal, not a trial court. Only in a case justified by the strictest necessity will the Court accept original jurisdiction.

Justice Harlan's opinion for the Court emphasized the extreme complexity of interstate and international claims relating to air and water pollution and the tremendous number of such lawsuits that could be filed. He felt that the U.S. Supreme Court could not afford to take a large block of time away from its unique responsibilities as administrator and umpire in the total federal court system, to do a job for which it was ill-equipped anyway.

"[T]he evolution of this Court's responsibilities in the American legal system has brought matters to a point where much would be sacrificed, and little gained, by our exercising original jurisdiction over issues bottomed on local law. This Court's paramount responsibilities to the national system lie almost without exception in the domain of federal law. As the impact on the social structure of federal common, statutory, and constitutional law has expanded, our attention has necessarily been drawn more and more to such matters. We have no claim to special competence in dealing with the numerous conflicts between States and nonresident individuals that raise no serious issues of federal law.

"This Court is, moreover, structured to perform as an appellate tribunal, ill-equipped for the task of factfinding and so forced, in original cases, awkwardly to play the role of fact-finder without actually presiding over the introduction of evidence. . . .

"Finally, in what has been said it is vitally important to stress that we are not called upon by this lawsuit to resolve difficult or important problems of federal law and that nothing in Ohio's complaint distinguishes it from any one of a host of such actions that might, with equal justification, be commenced in this Court. Thus, entertaining this complaint not only would fail to serve those responsibilities we are principally charged with, but could well pave the way for putting this Court into a quandary whereby we must opt either to pick and choose arbitrarily among similarly situated litigants or to devote truly enormous portions of our energies to such matters."

With regard to the appellate or reviewing jurisdiction of the U.S. Supreme Court, we have already noted that there is a provision for appeal directly from a state supreme court, or state court of last resort, to the U.S. Supreme Court in cases where the validity of a U.S. treaty or statute is challenged or where a state statute is alleged to be in violation of the U.S. Constitution. The right to petition for a writ of certiorari exists in cases involving a "federal question" or the relationship between national and state laws. In addition to hearing appeals and considering petitions for writs of certiorari from the state courts, the U.S. Supreme Court reviews cases from the various courts of appeal of the United States. Thus there are three routes to the Supreme Court: appeal, certiorari, and certification. Appeal can be made where a constitutional question is involved. A petition for a writ of certiorari will be granted where the U.S. Supreme Court feels that the issue of law involved is of considerable public concern or where there is a difference of opinion among the various U.S. appellate courts and a decision by the U.S. Supreme Court will bring uniformity to the decisions of the appellate courts. Certification is a procedure whereby the appellate court secures instructions as to a point of law from the Supreme Court without a formal hearing. There are also provisions for appeal or a petition for a writ of certiorari direct to the Supreme Court from the Court of Customs or the Court of Patent Appeals. There are also some situations where an appeal from a U.S. district court can bypass the appellate court level and be heard directly by the Supreme Court. An example would be a situation where a three-judge panel has either granted or denied an injunction and the subject matter is of considerable national concern. Going through the appellate court would only delay the final resolution of an issue which requires prompt action. There is also provision for bypassing the appellate court in cases where the United States or any agency, officer, or employee thereof is a party in a civil lawsuit and in cases where the district court decision finds an act of Congress unconstitutional. In criminal actions where a conviction or indictment is dismissed or set aside based on the invalidity or interpretation of a national statute, there is the possibility of a direct appeal to the U.S. Supreme Court.

JURISDICTION OF NATIONAL AND STATE COURTS

A far greater volume of court cases is handled by the state courts than is handled by the national courts. The national courts have jurisdiction in the areas of criminal law, civil law, and equity law. In the area of criminal law the national courts have jurisdiction only if a national crime was committed. For example, if someone steals a car in Indiana, the theft of the car is a crime in the state of Indiana and would be prosecuted in the Indiana state court system. If the thief drove the car across the state line of Indiana into Ohio, then a national crime was committed, since stolen goods were transported across state lines.

The national courts are also concerned with civil matters involving national law, such as bankruptcy laws, patent and copyright laws, and other such national statutes creating rights and duties.

In the areas of civil law which do not involve national questions and in which money damages are requested—areas such as contract law and tort law—the jurisdiction of the U.S. district court is limited to cases with complete diversity of citizenship. This means that any or all of the parties plaintiff must be citizens of states different from the states of any of the defendants. If any plaintiff is a citizen of the same state as any of the defendants, there is no diversity of citizenship. In addition to the requirement that diversity of citizenship be complete, it is also required that the amount in controversy exceed $10,000.

If a case involves more than one plaintiff, the claim of each plaintiff must meet the minimum requirement of $10,000. The claims of the plaintiffs may not be aggregated to meet a basic minimum amount of $10,000 unless this is specifically allowed by statutory law. There have been many proposals to lower this minimum to allow consumer class actions in cases where individual claims amount to less than $10,000 but where the aggregate claim of the class exceeds $10,000. Cases where money damages are requested and there is either no diversity of citizenship or the amount in controversy is less than $10,000 must be tried in the state court system. Such a case may be filed in the state court at the place of the accident or in the state court where the defendant resides. Both the national court and the state court have jurisdiction in cases where money damages are requested and there is diversity of citizenship and the amount in controversy exceeds $10,000. That is, both courts have the power to hear and try such cases. This is called concurrent jurisdiction. The plaintiff may file his or her case in the state court; however, if there is diversity of citizenship and over $10,000 is involved, the defendant has the right to have the case transferred to the national court.

Next we come to the equity jursidiction of the national courts. The national court has equity jurisdiction in cases which involve a "federal question." An example here would be a request for an injunction in a labor dispute. If the labor dispute involved an employer and a union involved in interstate commerce, then the national court would have jurisdiction and the national court would hear the case and make the required decision.

WHAT LAW APPLIES IN NATIONAL COURTS

National courts use their own procedural rules, the Federal Rules of Civil Procedure (FRCP), for civil cases tried in U.S. district courts. Where a national court is hearing a case involving the U.S. Constitution, an act of Congress, or a treaty, it is clear that national law is being applied. It is not quite so clear what ought to be done when a case is being tried in a U.S. district court because of diversity of citizenship, but the issues are matters of ordinary tort or commercial law. Should U.S. district courts use the applicable state law or develop their own national common law? That was the problem confronting Justice Brandeis in the following landmark case.

Erie Railroad Co. v. *Tompkins*
304 U.S. 64 (U.S. Supreme Court, 1938)

FACTS   Harry J. Tompkins, a Pennsylvania resident, was walking alongside Erie's railroad tracks in Hughestown, Pennsylvania, when he was struck by an open door on a passing freight train. Erie was not a Pennsylvania corporation, and more than $10,000 in damages was alleged, so the case was brought in a U.S. district court. Relying on the precedent of *Swift* v. *Tyson,* the trial judge instructed the jury on his version of the "national common law" rather than on the basis of Pennsylvania law, which would have denied recovery to a trespasser. The jury awarded Tompkins $30,000 damages. Erie appealed.

ISSUE   Is there a national substantive law which should be applied to ordinary civil matters litigated in U.S. district courts because of diversity?

35

Erie Railroad Co. v. Tompkins (continued)

DECISION   No. Judgment reversed and case remanded for a new trial.

REASONS   Justice Brandeis emphasized that the *Swift* rule had resulted in a considerable amount of uncertainty and unfairness and had encouraged "forumshopping" by litigants, since it increased the chances of different courts applying different substantive rules to the same case, depending on where the case was tried.

"The federal courts assumed, in the broad field of 'general law,' the power to declare rules of decision which Congress was confessedly without power to enact as statutes. . . .

"Experience in applying the doctrine of *Swift* v. *Tyson* had revealed its defects, political and social; and the benefits expected to flow from the rule did not accrue. . . . [T]he impossibility of discovering a satisfactory line of demarcation between the province of general law and that of local law developed a new well of uncertainties.

"On the other hand, the mischievous results of the doctrine had become apparent. . . . It made rights enjoyed under the unwritten 'general law' vary according to whether enforcement was sought in the state or in the federal court. . . .

"Except in matters governed by the Federal Constitution or by acts of Congress, the law to be applied in any case is the law of the state. And whether the law of the state shall be declared by its Legislature in a statute or by its highest court in a decision is not a matter of federal concern. There is no federal general common law. Congress has no power to declare substantive rules of common law applicable in a state whether they be local in their nature or 'general,' be they commercial law or a part of the law of torts. And no clause in the Constitution purports to confer such a power upon the federal courts."

THE TRIAL OF A CIVIL LAWSUIT

Before a student can properly study the substantive law, he or she must first have some understanding of the procedural law of how a case is brought to the courts and the procedure of the trial and appeal of a case. For purposes of illustration we will divide the trial of a lawsuit into three stages: the pleading stage, the discovery and pretrial stage, and the trial stage.

The Pleading Stage

The first step in filing a lawsuit is the preparation of a complaint, sometimes called a petition or a declaration. This complaint will state the names of the parties involved. The party bringing the action is called the plaintiff, and the party being sued is called the defendant. The complaint will then go on to state the plaintiff's version of what happened, where it happened, when it happened, how it happened, and why it happened, and it will allege that it happened as the result of the defendant's wrongful acts. Then it will state what the injuries or damages were. Lastly, it will contain a request for an amount of money.

The attorney for the plaintiff will file this complaint with the clerk of the court where the case is being filed. The clerk of the court will issue a summons which will be served on the defendant. The summons gives the defendant notification of the lawsuit and tells the defendant when and where an appearance must be made if the defendant wishes to defend. Usually a copy of the complaint is served along with the summons so that the defendant will know the particulars of the lawsuit. The rules with regard to the service of the summons differ for different types of lawsuits and also differ somewhat from state to state. The most common method of service is service to the defendant in person by a sheriff or another official authorized to serve a summons. Service may also be made by registered or certified mail with a return receipt. In some jurisdictions a summons may be legally served if it is handed to a member of the defendant's household; however, there are restrictions as to the age of the party receiving the summons. For example, handing the summons to the defendant's husband or wife would be proper service, but handing it to the defendant's eight-year-old child would not. There may also be a requirement that another copy of the summons be mailed to the defendant.

In many cases the defendant will be a resident of another state. Traditionally the plaintiff had to travel to the state of the defendant's residence to file suit because the courts did not have jurisdiction over residents of other states. Today states have what are termed *long arm statutes*, which allow service of a summons on persons or corporations residing beyond the state boundaries. For example, in the case of an automobile accident which occurred in Chicago, where the plaintiff is an Illinois resident and the defendant is an Indiana resident, valid service on a case filed in the Illinois courts may be made by sending the summons and a copy of the complaint to the secretary of state of Illinois as the defendant's agent for service and by sending a copy of the summons and complaint directly to the defendant in Indiana. Corporations incorporated in another state may be sued in your state if they are doing business in that state. Someone who owns property in a state may be sued even though he or she is a resident of another state. Generally speaking, a long arm statute allows service to be made on a nonresident of the state if the person or corporation being sued is doing business in the state or has made some contract in the state upon which a lawsuit is being filed, or if the person being sued has committed a tort within the state, or if the person being sued owns property within the state, provided the claim being litigated arises out of a transaction or occurrence within the state.

Roberts v. Jack Richards Aircraft Co.
536 P.2d 353 (Oklahoma, 1975)

FACTS Roberts, as the representative of the deceased's estate and as the guardian ad litem for three surviving minor children, sues Jack Richards Aircraft Co., Eastern Airlines, and Mohawk Airlines. Jack Richards Company was operating the aircraft at the time of the fatal crash. The plane had apparently been previously owned by the defendants Eastern Airlines and Mohawk Airlines, which are alleged to have sold it in defective condition. No specific acts by Eastern or Mohawk in Oklahoma are alleged, but Eastern commercials are seen on TV in Oklahoma, Eastern has a telephone

37

Roberts v. Jack Richards Aircraft Co. (continued)

listing in Oklahoma City, and a travel agency in Oklahoma City sells tickets for both Eastern and Mohawk. The crash of the Jack Richards plane occurred in Colorado. The trial court sustained objections by Eastern and Mohawk to the Oklahoma courts' jurisdiction. Roberts appeals.

ISSUE   Does the long arm statute of Oklahoma provide jurisdiction here?

DECISION   No. Judgment for defendants affirmed.

REASONS   Justice Lavender did not feel that either of these two defendants had done anything in Oklahoma to bring the long arm provisions into play. Nor did he think that there was any connection between the things that they had done and the claim which was being asserted for the accident.

"To assert personam jurisdiction over a foreign corporation. . . , the record should show a voluntarily committed act of the defendant by which that defendant purposefully availed itself for the privilege of conducting activities within the State so as to invoke the benefits and protection of the laws of Oklahoma. . . . National televised commercials viewed within Oklahoma fall far short of 'purposefully availed itself of the privilege of conducting activities within the State.' The possibility of a travel agency selling tickets to flights on Eastern and Mohawk is not a 'comitted act.' The strongest fact set forth in the affidavit is the Eastern listing in the Oklahoma City telephone directory. Eastern argues such listing was not until 1973. Roberts does not dispute this. His affidavit fixes no date for the listing. . . .

"Here the cause of action as to Eastern and Mohawk appears from the record . . . to arise out of their individual acts during their separate sale of the aircraft some time prior to the crash. All of this occurred outside the State of Oklahoma. These are not the same acts of Eastern and Mohawk alleged to confer jurisdiction in personam by 'doing business within the State.' There is no relation between the two sets of acts, (1) as to liability, and (2) as to doing business within the State."

In some types of cases notice of the suit can be made by publication in a local newspaper for a required number of times. An example would be an adoption case in which the whereabouts of one of the natural parents is unknown and thus service cannot be made on that parent either personally or by certified mail. Whenever we refer to state law, it must be remembered that procedures may differ slightly from state to state. Thus, before a lawsuit is filed in a particular state, the exact procedure in that state must be determined.

Once the complaint has been filed with the clerk of the court and the summons has been properly served on the defendant, then the defendant is required to make an appearance in court, either in person or by an attorney, within a stated number of days. Normally the defendant is required to appear within 20 days after receipt of the summons. The summons will inform the defendant of this duty. If the defendant fails to make an appearance either in person or by an attorney within the required number of days after service of the summons, the court will enter a default judgment against the defendant. The defendant's failure to appear is treated as an admission of guilt in the case. Thus

a default judgment will be rendered. Under certain circumstances the defendant may have this default judgment set aside. It will be set aside, for example, if
the defendant can show that the service of the summons was not made in
accordance with the procedural requirements of that type of case, so that the
defendant did not in fact have notice of the lawsuit.

Now let us assume that the defendant has made an appearance in court
during the required time. The plaintiff has filed a complaint against the defendant. It is now the defendant's turn to defend. The first question the defendant
must address is whether the lawsuit was filed within the proper statutory period. This period is set by the state's statute of limitations. For a tort action the
period will normally vary from one year to five years after the date of the
occurrence, depending on the law of the state where the occurrence took place.
In a breach of contract case the period may vary from 5 to 10 years. There are
special provisions if the defendant is a city, a county, a state, or the national
government, as notice of intent to sue may be required within three to six
months after the occurrence, depending on the particular state law.

Next the defendant may challenge the sufficiency of the complaint, attack
the complaint with motions concerning jurisdiction or venue, and file an answer and/or counterclaim. First, let's look at the sufficiency of the complaint. In
order to be legally sufficient, a complaint must state a cause of action. That is,
the complaint filed by the plaintiff must state that the plaintiff had a specific
legal right, that the defendant had a legal duty and breached it, and that the
plaintiff was injured as a proximate result of the breach.

A simple example of this would be a situation involving a two-lane highway
going north and south. The plaintiff was southbound on the two-lane highway,
and the defendant was northbound. The plaintiff had a legal right to travel in
the southbound lane. The defendant had a legal duty not to cross the centerline
and drive in the southbound lane since the plaintiff was northbound. The defendant, who was lighting a cigarette, dropped the cigarette, was reaching
down to get it, and lost control of the car. The car veered across the centerline,
striking the plaintiff's vehicle. In this case the defendant breached a legal duty
and caused damage to the plaintiff as a proximate result of that breach.

Now, let's take a hypothetical case where Henry Hunter climbs over a
barbed wire fence marked "no trespassing" and enters a cornfield belonging to
Freddie Farmer. While roaming in the cornstalks, Henry Hunter comes face-
to-face with Freddie Farmer's prize bull. The bull proceeds to expedite Henry's exit from the cornfield by throwing him over the fence. Henry Hunter
brings a lawsuit against Freddie Farmer for his injuries. In this case Freddie
Farmer's attorney would challenge the sufficiency of the complaint. Did Henry
Hunter have a legal right to be on the premises where he was injured? Did
Freddie Farmer have a legal duty to prevent injury to Henry Hunter? In this
case the defendant's attorney would file a demurrer asking that the case be
dismissed. In many states, and in the national system, the demurrer has been
replaced by a motion to dismiss for failure to state a cause of action. This is a
very important phase of a lawsuit since if the plaintiff files a lawsuit and in fact
there is no legal right on the part of the plantiff and no legal duty on the part of
the defendant, then the case should be dismissed without further expense to
the defendant and without the expenditure of valuable court time.

Let us assume that the complaint did state a valid cause of action, and thus no demurrer or motion to dismiss for failure to state a cause of action would be filed. The defendant may feel that a fair trial could not be held at the place where the complaint was filed. For example, the defendant might be a student at a large university in a relatively small town who was involved in an automobile accident with a well-known local citizen. The student might feel that prejudices against students precluded a fair jury trial in the local area. In that case the attorney for the student would make a motion to change venue. The attorney would request that the trial be changed to a court in an adjoining county. Thus the jury would be selected from persons residing in the adjoining county and there would be less possibility of prejudice against the student or favoritism toward the local citizen. Other challenges to the complaint can be made by motions; however, time and space do not permit a full review of trial procedures.

The next important pleading is the answer. The defendant must now affirm or deny the allegations made by the plaintiff in the complaint. The defendant may very well affirm or admit the facts, such as when the accident happened, where it happened, the parties involved, the type of vehicle involved, and so on. The defendant would, however, deny allegations regarding his or her negligence. Now the defendant has an opportunity to make claim for his or her damages, if any. If the defendant desires to pursue a claim for damages, a counterclaim must be filed. This is also called a cross complaint in some states. In this pleading the defendant will allege that the plaintiff was negligent and will state a claim for damages. The plaintiff must answer the cross complaint or counterclaim. This pleading is called a reply.

Now the parties have their legal swords drawn. Both parties have stated their claims and have asked that they be awarded damages. The court can now determine what issues are in dispute. Allegations in either the complaint or the answer which the other side admits are not issues in dispute. The only issues in dispute are allegations which the other party has denied. In the actual trial, only evidence to prove the issues in dispute will be allowed. Evidence on issues not included in the pleadings will not be allowed unless an amendment is made to the pleadings, and this is normally done only at the discretion of the trial judge.

The Discovery and Pretrial Stage

We come now to the second stage of the trial, called the discovery and pretrial stage. In most major metropolitan areas there is a long backlog of cases. Thus a case filed today may not come up for trial for several years. This presents several problems. First, witnesses tend to forget as time goes by. Second, witnesses die, or they move away and perhaps their whereabouts are unknown, or they move out of the jurisdiction and cannot legally be brought back for trial. Third, if there is to be a possibility of an amicable settlement, then both parties should know all the facts. Thus we have the discovery stage.

There are three general methods of discovery. First, the plaintiff may file interrogatories against the defendant. Interrogatories are a series of questions which are propounded in order to get information about a person, about the incident, and about the damages. The questions must be relevant.

Interrogatories are generally simply a "fishing expedition" and are not admissible as evidence in court.

Interrogatories are normally followed by depositions. A deposition is sworn testimony which is subject to cross-examination. A deposition is admissible as evidence in the trial of the case. Interrogatories may only be served on the parties to the action, whereas depositions may be taken from the parties and also from witnesses, both witnesses to the incident and expert witnesses such as doctors, engineers, and economists. Depositions basically serve two purposes. First, they discover the testimony. A party who has testified under oath will be guilty of perjury if he or she materially changes the testimony later. Second, they preserve the testimony in case the witness dies or moves from the area and cannot be found. Doctors and other experts testifying in a case may not be able to appear at the trial. If so, depositions can be used instead of their personal testimony. In the past, depositions have typically been taken in the presence of a court reporter. The court reporter takes down the testimony and types it up, and if the deposition has to be used at the trial, it is simply read in court. Today many courts throughout the United States are experimenting with videotape depositions. Here the deposition is taken on videotape and thus can be played back in the courtroom like a movie. This technique will speed up trials that would otherwise have to be postponed or delayed because of scheduling problems with expert witnesses such as doctors who are called out on emergencies or for other reasons.

A third discovery procedure is a motion by one party to have the other party produce certain items of evidence for review. For example, the defendant may very well ask the the plaintiff to produce copies of medical reports, medical bills, photographs, and various other evidential material which the plaintiff intends to submit at the trial.

After the discovery has been completed by both sides, the court will schedule a pretrial hearing or a pretrial conference. The purpose of the pretrial hearing is twofold. First, it enables the judge to get the attorneys representing the plaintiff and the defendant together and to determine whether or not there can be an amicable settlement. Here the judge acts more as a mediator than as a judge. If there is a possibility of a settlement, the judge will try to get the parties to negotiate and thus get the case settled and dismissed. If, on the other hand, there appears to be no possibility of a settlement, the judge will try to determine whether there are any items of evidence which can be admitted without objection in order to save time at the actual trial of the case. In some jurisdictions the judge will have the parties exchange lists of the witnesses they are going to have testify. Thus each party has a complete list of the other party's witnesses. The theory is that there should be no surprises and that each party should have an opportunity to know the other party's evidence. If it appears that the case will have to be tried, a trial date will be set.

The Trial Stage

The third stage is the actual trial of the lawsuit. This stage is a series of events which we will review in the order of their occurrence.

1. Selection of a Jury. The first step in the trial of the case is the selection of a jury—if a jury is to hear the case. Traditionally in the United States a jury was composed of 12 persons with one or two alternates selected in cases which were expected to run for a considerable time. In many jurisdictions the number of persons required for a jury has now been reduced from 12 to 6, at least for some cases. Selecting the jury is a very important phase of the trial. In order to have a fair trial, jurors must be unbiased and must be willing to be fair and impartial. Before each term of court a jury list is selected at random from the eligible voters in the county where a state court lawsuit is to be tried or in the court district where a national district court suit is to be tried. Prospective jurors are seated in the jury box of the courtroom, and the attorneys for the plaintiff and the defendant then have the opportunity to question them to determine any bias they might have or to find any reason why they could not serve as fair and impartial jurors. For example, the prospective jurors may be asked whether they are related to any of the parties in the lawsuit or any of the attorneys, or whether they have had business dealings with the parties, or whether they know the parties socially. They may also be asked whether they have read about the particular incident in the newspapers and whether they have already made up their mind concerning the guilt or innocence of the parties. The purpose of the examination, of course, is to determine whether any of the jurors have biases or prejudices that might affect their judgment of the case. This examination is called voir dire. If a prospective juror admits bias or prejudice or if there appears to be a possibility of bias or prejudice due to a relationship, he or she will be challenged for cause. If the court feels that the prospective juror is in fact biased or prejudiced or cannot be a fair and impartial juror, he or she will be dismissed. In addition to the challenges for cause, each side in the lawsuit will be given a certain number of peremptory challenges. No cause need be stated for making a peremptory challenge. The purpose of the peremptory challenge is to give each side an opportunity to dismiss certain jurors who for one reason or another the attorney feels may be prejudiced against his or her client. Peremptory challenges may or may not be used.

2. Preliminary Instructions by the Court.   After the jury has been selected and seated in the jury box, the judge will give the jury preliminary instructions concerning the trial. The judge will outline the issue for trial and explain the burden of proof, the credibility of witnesses, and the manner in which the jurors should weigh the testimony they are about to hear.

3. Opening Statements by the Attorneys.   The plaintiff in the American legal system has the burden of proof. The plaintiff is the complaining party and thus has the first opening statement. In the opening statement the plaintiff's attorney simply tells the jurors what type of case they are to hear and briefly explains the complaint of the plaintiff and what the plaintiff intends to prove. The opening statement is not evidence; it is only a preview of coming attractions. The defendant's attorney then has an opportunity to make an opening statement and to tell the jury what the defendant expects to prove. After the opening statements have been made, the jury, now having a general overview of what the case is all about and what the parties expect to prove, is ready to hear the evidence.

4. Plaintiff's Evidence.   The plaintiff, the party having the burden of proof, will be called upon first to present evidence. The plaintiff's attorney will then call the first witness and will ask this witness questions; this is called direct examination. After this questioning is concluded, the defendant's attorney will be entitled to cross-examine the witness; and after the cross-examination is completed, the plaintiff's attorney will have an opportunity for redirect examination. Exhibits such as photographs, charts, documents, and articles of clothing will be submitted as evidence. This process will continue with witness after witness until all of the plaintiff's witnesses have testified. The plaintiff will then rest his or her case.

5. *Motion for Directed Verdict or Directed Judgment.* We have now reached the second "safety valve" in the litigation. You will recall that after the complaint was filed and the summons was served, the defendant had an opportunity to file a demurrer, or a motion to dismiss for failure to state a cause of action, and to have the case dismissed if in fact there was no legal right or legal duty. Now, after the plaintiff has presented evidence and rested his or her case, the defendant may make a motion for a directed verdict if there is a jury. If the judge feels that there is no issue of fact to be decided by the jury, then the judge will direct a verdict in favor of the defendant. If there is no jury, a motion can be made for a directed judgment in favor of the defendant. Given the frequent tendency of jurors to decide for sympathy rather than the facts, it is certainly preferable to have the case dismissed by the judge rather than have the jury decide it. If there is an issue of fact raised for the jury to decide, then the trial must go on.

6. *Defendant's Evidence.* The defendant's attorney will now call the defense witnesses, and the same process of questioning will occur. The defendant's attorney will ask questions under direct examination; the plaintiff's attorney will cross-examine; and the defendant's attorney will have an opportunity for redirect examination of the witnesses. The defendant may submit exhibits of evidential material for the defense. Then the defendant rests.

7. *Plaintiff's Rebuttal Evidence.* The plaintiff has the right to recall witnesses or to call additional witnesses for the sole purpose of rebutting the defendant's evidence.

8. *Final Instructions by the Judge.* The judge gave preliminary instructions to the jury before the opening statements by the attorneys. Since that time the jury has heard testimony by several witnesses as to the facts surrounding the case and as to the injuries and damages. The jurors now need to know what the substantive law of the case is. To meet that need, the judge will read prepared instructions on the law to the jury. In most jurisdictions the attorneys for each side prepare proposed instructions to be given to the jury and the judge then picks the instructions that he or she feels are appropriate for the case. The judge may also add instructions not submitted by either attorney.

9. *Final Arguments.* Since the plaintiff has the burden of proving his or her case against the defendant, the plaintiff is entitled to present the first closing argument. This is also called a summation. Here the plaintiff's attorney reviews all the testimony and tries to convince the jurors that the plaintiff's evidence is stronger than the defendant's evidence and that the plaintiff should win. In a civil case the jury decides not only who is right and who is wrong but also how much the verdict will be. Thus the plaintiff's attorney also argues the value of the plaintiff's claim. The defendant then argues his or her case. Then the plaintiff is entitled to a rebuttal or closing argument.

10. Jury Deliberations.   After the jurors have heard the instructions on the law, they are taken to the jury room. The first order of business is to select a foreman. Then the jurors' deliberations commence.

11. The Verdict.   When the jurors have agreed upon a verdict, they will return to the courtroom and the foreman will read the verdict. The verdict must be unanimous under the current rules of procedure in most jurisdictions. Since the jury in a civil case decides both questions of fact and the dollar amount of the verdict, there is seldom a "hung jury" in a civil suit.

12. Judgment Notwithstanding the Verdict.   Here we have a third safety valve in the system. The judge has a veto power over the jury in the rare situations where the jury has obviously failed to follow the instructions on the law. At such times the judge can throw the verdict out and enter a judgment contrary to the verdict.

CIVIL APPELLATE PROCEDURE

After the verdict has been rendered and the judgment entered, the losing party has a right to an appeal if he or she complies with the procedural requirements of the state system or the national system. Notice of intent to appeal must be given within a specified time after the judgment is rendered. The procedure before the appellate court has been discussed earlier in this chapter. After all appeal procedures have been exhausted, a final judgment will be rendered, provided the court judgment has been affirmed. Of course, if, there was a reversal, then we are faced with a new trial or other action in accordance with the apellate court's instructions.

In the great majority of cases no appeal is filed and at the end of the time allotted for filing an appeal, the judgment becomes final. Thus we come to the next step in the trial of a civil case—enforcement of the judgment.

ENFORCEMENT OF JUDGMENTS

A judgment rendered against a party is worthless without a procedure to enforce and collect that judgment. In years past persons were put in debtors' prison for failing to pay their bills, but no such procedure exists today. Today, if a person obtains a judgment for money against another person, there are basically three ways to collect that judgment. One way is for the party on whose behalf the judgment was rendered to levy execution on the property of the party against whom the judgment was rendered. The debtor's property not exempt from execution under the particular state or national law may be sold at a public sale, and the proceeds may be applied against the judgment. A second way to collect is to have the wages of the person against whom the judgment was rendered garnished, subject, of course, to the state and national laws concerning garnishment. There are exemptions under the national and state laws which do not allow the owner of a judgment to secure the total wages of the debtor. The specifics of these laws will be discussed in a later chapter. The third way to collect is to secure a lien against property owned by the debtor. For example, a lien may be placed against real estate owned by the debtor. Thus the debtor cannot sell the real estate without first paying the lien.

In some cases the judgment debtor may not have enough property in the state which issued the judgment to satisfy it. If the debtor owns property in other states, it may be necessary to take the judgment from State 1 to those other states and to ask for its enforcement there. When this happens, the "Full Faith and Credit" clause in Article IV of the U.S. Constitution comes into play. The clause requires each state to give "full faith and credit" to the public acts, records, and judicial proceedings of other states. The successful party in State 1 cannot be forced to relitigate the whole case in other states in order to enforce his or her claim; other states can, however, examine the judgment to make sure that the court which issued it had jurisdiction. If the court in State 1 had jurisdiction, the other states have no choice; they must enforce the judgment just as they would one of their own. The ultimate decision as to what are adequate jurisdictional bases is made by the U.S. Supreme Court, since a matter of constitutional interpretation is at issue.

Keck V. Keck
309 N.E.2d 217 (Illinois, 1974)

FACTS   James E. Keck filed a divorce petition in Cook County, Illinois, in December 1967. He charged his wife, Dolores, with mental cruelty and constructive desertion. Dolores answered the complaint and asked for separate maintenance, charging James with desertion. In October 1968, while the Illinois case was still pending, James moved to Nevada. On December 5, 1968, Dolores was served with a summons and complaint from a Nevada divorce action. On December 23, James asked the Illinois court to dismiss their action, but it was scheduled for further hearings on January 14, 1969, and James was enjoined from proceeding further with the Nevada divorce and was ordered to pay temporary alimony and child support. On December 27, 1968, a default decree was entered against Dolores in the Nevada divorce. James then moved back to Chicago, where he denied liability for any further "support" payments because the parties were now divorced. The trial court upheld Dolores' claim that the Nevada decree was invalid, but the appeals court reversed, saying that the Nevada decree must be given full faith and credit.

ISSUE   Did the Nevada courts have jurisdiction to issue the divorce decree?

DECISION   No. Trial court judgment for Dolores affirmed; appeals court reversed.

REASONS   Justice Davis acknowledged that divorce proceedings are a special case, in that a decree is valid if the issuing court has jurisdiction over *one* spouse (the plaintiff), at least as to the termination of the marriage, and that jurisdiction over the defendant spouse is not necessary. The issue was thus narrowed to whether the Nevada courts had jurisdiction over James, and that depended in turn on whether he had established domicile there.

"[W]hile plaintiff's domicile must be *bona fide,* when the decree is challenged in another jurisdiction, there is a presumption favoring the requisite domicile. . . .

"A foreign divorce decree may be collaterally attacked in our courts as to matters going to jurisdiction. . . .

"[T]he evidence presented . . . overcame the presumption of such domicile created by the introduction into evidence of the Nevada divorce decree. It is well established that the question of domicile is largely one of intention and that to establish a new domicile a person must physically go to a new home and live there with the intention of making it his permanent home. . . . Here plaintiff lived in Nevada only two months, he returned immediately upon obtaining his decree, he retained his apartment in Chicago and returned there, he retained his job in Chicago and returned to it, he retained his Chicago bank accounts and his Illinois driver's license. Within one or two days after arriving in Nevada, he contacted a lawyer about getting a divorce. The evidence presented to the trial court clearly supports the conclusion that the plaintiff went to Nevada for the purpose of obtaining a divorce and with the intent of returning to Illinois. The plaintiff did not establish a *bona fide* domicile in Nevada, and the trial court was warranted in concluding that the Nevada decree was invalid and in denying it full faith and credit."

CLASS ACTIONS

Traditionally each plaintiff has pursued his or her claim in a court of law on an individual basis. However, courts have occasionally permitted plaintiffs to represent a large class of claimants where the claims of all the parties are similar and arise out of the same occurrence. The most common situation is a case in which one shareholder brings an action against the corporation for some alleged mismanagement and resulting loss and also represents all other similar stockholders who were similarly damaged. Obviously, it is more expeditious and less costly for the court to hear one case rather than hundreds or thousands of similar cases.

Also, there is the problem of inequality of means. The big corporation can afford litigation costs more than the little plaintiff. However, if a large number of plaintiffs can join as a class, the expense is far less for each of the plaintiffs.

The increased citizen interest in litigation brought about by the environmental and consumer movements has made class actions increasingly popular. Environmentalists and consumer advocates see the class action as a means to pursue their goals. For example, the class action is potentially one of the most effective ways to force polluters to internalize the social costs of their activities. The class action makes it possible for the individuals who are damaged to bargain collectively with polluters. It also makes it feasible to assert claims for damages that would otherwise be too small to warrant the large expense of environmental litigation. This same reasoning is used by consumer advocates. Some manufacturers do not worry about small claims caused by the malfunctioning or the poor quality of their products as the cost of litigation normally exceeds the individual's claim and thus the individual is normally discouraged from pursuing the claim. If, however, all persons injured or damaged by a company in the same way joined in a class action, then the company would have to pay for the damages caused by its negligence and carelessness. This result would produce a higher degree of care on the part of manufacturers.

Under the current Federal Rules of Civil Procedure four prerequisites must be met before a class action may be maintained in national court:

1. The class is so numerous that joinder of all its members is impractical.
2. The class members have common questions of law or fact.
3. The claim or defense of the class representative is typical of that of the absent class members.
4. The representative will fairly and adequately protect the interests of the class.

The rules also provide that one of the following conditions must exist:

1. The prosecution of separate actions might result in inconsistent or varying judgments.
2. The prosecution of separate actions might in practice dispose of the interests of other members or impede their ability to protect those interests.
3. The defendant has acted or refused to act on grounds generally applicable to all members of the class, so that injunctive or declaratory relief for the whole class is appropriate.
4. The court finds that a class action is the best method to adjudicate the controversy.

The requirement that the amount per claim be at least $10,000 prevents the national courts from being flooded with class actions. The individual states also have rules for class actions, many of which are similar to the Federal Rules, with the notable exception that no minimum amount per claim is required. Also, many states have passed specific environmental and consumer laws authorizing class actions under certain circumstances.

QUASI-JUDICIAL PROCEDURE IN ADMINISTRATIVE AGENCIES

The National Labor Relations Board, the Federal Trade Commission, the Environmental Protection Agency, the Occupational Safety and Health Administration, and many other national and state administrative agencies daily hear disputes concerning violations of their rules and regulations. Typically the businessperson will have more contact with administrative agencies than with the court system. The procedure of judicial determination is much less formal, less costly, and more speedy in the administrative agency system than in the court system. The procedure for the determination of disputes in the administrative agency system is termed *quasi judicial* because it does not have the full authority of a court and because the party being tried does not have the right to trial by jury. The decisions of administrative bodies are subject to judicial review by an appellate court.

To give the student an understanding of a typical administrative agency quasi-judicial procedure, we will follow a National Labor Relations Board case from beginning to end.

The Charge

The National Labor Relations Board has been notified that an employer or a union is engaged in one or more unfair labor practices. This means that the employer or the union has violated the specific statutory rules by which both labor unions and management must conduct themselves. The complaining party is then asked to complete a charge, which is simply a form specifying what unfair labor practice has been engaged in and by whom. Once a charge is filed, a field examiner makes an investigation. This is done to determine whether there is sufficient evidence of a violation to proceed to a formal hearing. If the evidence indicates that the case should be pursued, then a formal complaint will be filed. This complaint is similar to the complaint filed in a civil action. If the field examiner does not find evidence sufficient to support further activity in the case, then the charge will be dismissed.

The Formal Complaint

If the evidence found was sufficient to justify pursuing the case, then a formal complaint will be filed and it will be served upon the employer or the labor union which was alleged to be in violation. The party accused of the violation is given an opportunity to reply to the charges. This reply is called an answer.

The Answer

The answer filed in this case is similar to the answer filed in a civil case. The answer will no doubt deny some allegations and admit others. Typically allegations concerning violation of the National Labor Relations Act will be denied and allegations concerning time and place will be admitted.

The Hearing

A hearing is then scheduled, and at the hearing an administrative law judge hears testimony. Witnesses are presented by both parties in a manner similar to that of the trial in a civil lawsuit. At the end of the testimony the parties are allowed to make their summarization statements to the administrative law judge.

Findings of Fact and Conclusions of Law

The administrative law judge will take the case under advisement and will prepare a written decision entitled "Findings of Fact and Conclusions of Law." This decision will summarize the facts and give the administrative law judge's decision concerning the facts and the law. After the administrative law judge has rendered a decision, either of the parties may file a statement of exceptions and request an appeal. This must be done within 20 days after the decision. If exceptions are not filed and an appeal is not requested, the decision of the administrative law judge becomes final. If a request for an appeal is made, then the parties will file a legal brief to support the exceptions which they have enumerated and may request oral argument before the National Labor Relations Board, a five-person board which sits in Washington, D.C.

NLRB Board Review

The Board will review the briefs of the parties, hear oral arguments, and render a decision and order. Again, either party may appeal this decision to the U.S. circuit court of appeals. The NLRB itself has no legal power to enforce its order. If the finding is against the employer or the union and that party refuses to comply with the Board's order, than the Board must ask the U.S. circuit court of appeals for a judgment to enforce its order. Or if the employer or the union feels that the NLRB decision is incorrect or unfair, it may appeal the decision to the circuit court of appeals. The U.S. circuit court of appeals will then review the decision of the National Labor Relations Board to ascertain whether there was substantial evidence to support the findings and whether the Board followed the correct substantive law.

Review by the Supreme Court of the United States

Either party may petition the Supreme Court of the United States for a writ of certiorari to review the decision of the circuit court of appeals. If the writ of certiorari is granted, a review will be had and the parties will have to comply with the final judgment of the Supreme Court. If the Supreme Court refuses to issue a writ of certiorari, then the judgment of the circuit court of appeals is final. A judgment will be rendered, and a court order will be made. The failure of a party to obey a court order can be punishable as either civil or criminal contempt of court.

The procedure of the National Labor Relations Board is typical of the procedure used by most of the administrative agencies that have quasi-judicial authority. In other words, an investigation will be made and an initial hearing will be had before an administrative law judge, with the right of an appeal to a quasi-judicial board and with the right of a later appeal to an appellate court. The legal justification for not giving the right to trial by jury in these cases is that they are not legal trials and that the decision rendered is not a civil judgment for money. They are more like equity injunctions—an order to comply with the law, or an order to pay back wages, or an order to rehire.

ARBITRATION AS A METHOD OF DISPUTE RESOLUTION

When one thinks of arbitration, one normally thinks of labor law and the arbitration of grievances and the arbitration clauses in labor contracts. Arbitration, of course, has been used extensively as a method of settling grievance disputes in labor-management relations. However, arbitration has also been used as a method of determining contract terms.

In the public bargaining sector, public employees are not allowed to strike and thus it is common for agreements between labor and management to be reached by submitting the offers of both parties to one or more arbitrators for a final decision as to the contract terms. This procedure is being more extensively used as unionization spreads among public employees.

Another type of arbitration has also been growing in popularity. This is the commercial arbitration of business disputes that would normally be handled in civil lawsuits, such as disputes involving a breach of contract. If such a case were filed in a civil court, there would be considerable expense for court costs and legal fees for both parties and there would be considerable delay in getting the case to trial. Also, the typical judge does not have expertise in all fields. In commercial arbitration the arbitrator selected often has specific expertise in the area which the dispute involves. For example, the parties have a dispute concerning their obligations under a contract to build a multimillion-dollar building. Time is of the essence. The parties cannot wait six or seven years for this case to come up before a court. If the case is submitted to arbitration, they can get a decision within a very short time and can then go about their businesses.

In arbitration there is no set procedure such as one would find in a formal court of law or even in an administrative agency. There is, however, one prerequisite to arbitration, namely, that both parties agree to submit the dispute to arbitration. This can be done by inserting an arbitration clause in the original document, such as a contract. If there is no such clause, the parties may still agree at a later date to submit a dispute to arbitration. They thus waive their day in court. The parties may also determine the method of arbitration. For example, they may agree to have the case heard by a single arbitrator or by a panel of three arbitrators. If they agree to use three arbitrators, they may decide that each party will select an arbitrator of its choice and that the two arbitrators they select will choose the third arbitrator.

The American Arbitration Association was formed as a national not-for-profit association to encourage the use of arbitration in resolving disputes. It has a panel of recommended arbitrators who will hear commercial arbitration disputes. It also has panels of recommended arbitrators who will hear labor disputes.

The Federal Mediation and Conciliation Service, a governmental agency, also has a panel of recommended arbitrators for labor disputes. Both the American Arbitration Association and the Federal Mediation and Conciliation Service offer to supply the names of recommended arbitrators; the parties select the arbitrator they want and pay the arbitrator directly. Usually the two sides share the arbitrator's fee equally.

The main objections to the use of arbitration for resolving disputes are that there is no direct right of appeal and that there is no direct power or procedure for enforcement of the arbitrator's decision.

When you agree to submit a dispute to arbitraton you also agree to abide by the arbitrator's ruling. The only exceptions would be if you could prove that the arbitrator had a financial or personal interest in the matter which prejudiced the decision, or that fraud or perjury was involved in the testimony, or that the arbitrator mistakenly failed to follow the law on a material issue. Otherwise, the arbitrator's decision is final. If you can prove one of the above exceptions, a court will set aside the arbitrator's decision.

The next problem is enforcement. If the loser refuses to abide by the arbitrator's decision, the winner's only recourse is to go to court to have the arbitrator's decision enforced.

Arbitration is a fast, inexpensive method for resolving commercial disputes. However, its effectiveness depends greatly upon the attitude of the parties. Most businesses today want their legal disputes settled out of court and as cheaply and quickly as possible. Arbitration can be the answer to commercial business disputes.

CASES FOR DISCUSSION

WORLD-WIDE VOLKSWAGEN CORP. v. WOODSON

100 S. Ct. 559 (U.S. Supreme Court, 1980)

Justice White

The facts presented to the District Court showed that World-Wide is incorporated and has its business office in New York. It distributes vehicles, parts, and accessories, under contract with Volkswagen, to retail dealers in New York, New Jersey, and Connecticut. Seaway, one of these retail dealers, is incorporated and has its place of business in New York. Insofar as the record reveals, Seaway and World-Wide are fully independent corporations whose relations with each other and with Volkswagen and Audi are contractual only. Respondents adduced no evidence that either World-Wide or Seaway does any business in Oklahoma, ships or sells any products to or in the State, has an agent to receive process there, or purchases advertisements in any media calculated to reach Oklahoma. In fact, as respondents' counsel conceded at oral argument, Tr. of Oral Arg. 32, there was no showing that any automobile sold by World-Wide or Seaway has ever entered Oklahoma with the single exception of the vehicle involved in the present case.

Despite the apparent paucity of contacts between petitioners and Oklahoma, the District Court rejected their constitutional claim and reaffirmed that ruling in denying petitioners' motion for reconsideration. Petitioners then sought a writ of prohibition in the Supreme Court of Oklahoma to restrain the District Judge, respondent Charles S. Woodson, from exercising *in personam* jurisdiction over them. They renewed their contention that because they had no "minimal contacts" with the State of Oklahoma, the actions of the District Judge were in violation of their rights under the Due Process Clause.

The Supreme Court of Oklahoma denied the writ . . . holding that personal jurisdiction over petitioners was authorized by Oklahoma's "Long-Arm" Statute. . . .

We granted certiorari to consider an important constitutional question with respect to state-court jurisdiction and to resolve a conflict between the Supreme Court of Oklahoma and the highest courts of at least four other States. We reverse.

The Due Process Clause of the 14th Amendment limits the power of a state court to render a valid personal judgment against a nonresident defendant. . . . A judgment rendered in violation of due process is void in the rendering State and is not entitled to full faith and credit elsewhere. . . . Due process requires that the defendant be given adequate notice of the suit . . . and be subject to the personal jurisdiction of the court. . . . In the present case, it is not contended that notice was inadequate; the only question is whether these particular petitioners were subject to the jurisdiction of the Oklahoma courts.

As has long been settled, and as we reaffirm today, a state court may exercise personal jurisdiction over a nonresident defendant only so long as there exist "minimum contacts" between the defendant and the forum State. . . . The concept of minimum contacts, in turn, can be seen to perform two related, but distinguishable, functions. It protects the defendant against the burdens of litigating in a distant or inconvenient forum. And it acts to ensure that the States through their courts, do not reach out beyond the limits imposed on them by their status as coequal sovereigns in a federal system.

The protection against inconvenient litigation is typically described in terms of "reasonableness" or "fairness." We have said that the defendant's contacts with the forum State must be such that maintenance of the suit "does not offend 'traditional notions of fair play and substantial justice.'" . . . The relationship between the defendant and the forum must be such that it is "reasonable . . . to require the corporation to defend the particular suit which is brought there." . . . Implicit in this emphasis on reasonableness is the understanding that the burden on the defendant, while always a primary concern, will in an appropriate case be considered in light of other relevant factors, including the forum State's interest in adjudicating the dispute . . . the plaintiff's interest in obtaining convenient and effective relief . . . the interstate judicial system's interest in obtaining the most efficient resolution of controversies; and the shared interest of the several States in furthering fundamental substantive social policies. . . .

The limits imposed on state jurisdiction by the Due Process Clause, in its role as a guarantor against inconvenient litigation, has been substantially relaxed over the years.

Nevertheless, we have never accepted the proposition that state lines are irrelevant for jurisdictional purposes, nor could we and remain faithful to the principles of interstate federalism embodied in the Constitution. The economic interdependence of the States was foreseen and desired by the Framers. In the Commerce Clause, they provided that the Nation was to be a common market, a "free trade unit" in which the States are debarred from acting as separable economic entities. *H. P. Hood & Sons, Inc.* v. *Du Mond*, 336 U.S. 525, 69 S. Ct. 657, 665, 93 L.Ed. 865 (1949). But the Framers also intended that the States retain many essential attributes of sovereignty including, in particular, the sovereign power to try causes in their courts. The sovereignty of each State, in turn, implied a limita-

tion on the sovereignty of all of its sister States—a limitation express or implicit in both the original scheme of the Constitution and the 14th Amendment.

Hence, even while abandoning the shibboleth that "[t]he authority of every tribunal is necessarily restricted by the territorial limits of the State in which it is established," *Pennoyer* v. *Neff*, supra, 95 U.S., at 720, we emphasized that the reasonableness of asserting jurisdiction over the defendant must be assessed "in the context of our federal system of government," *International Shoe Co.* v. *Washington*, supra, 326 U.S. at 317, 66 S. Ct., at 158, and stressed that the Due Process Clause ensures, not only fairness, but also the "orderly administration of the laws," id., at 319, 66 S. Ct., at 159. As we noted in *Hanson* v. *Denckla*, 357 U.S. 235, 250–251, 78 S. Ct. 1228, 2 L.Ed.2d 1283 (1958):

As technological progress has increased the flow of commerce between the States, the need for jurisdiction over nonresidents has undergone a similar increase. At the same time, progress in communications and transportations has made the defense of a suit in a foreign tribunal less burdensome. In response to these changes, the requirements for personal jurisdiction over nonresidents have evolved from the rigid rule of *Pennoyer* v. *Neff*, 95 U.S. 714, 24 L.Ed. 565, to the flexible standard of *International Shoe Co.* v. *Washington*, 326 U.S. 310, 66 S. Ct. 154, 90 L.Ed. 95. But it is a mistake to assume that this trend heralds the eventual demise of all restrictions on the personal jurisdiction of state courts. [Citation omitted.] Those restrictions are more than a guarantee of immunity from inconvenient or distant litigation. They are a consequence of territorial limitations on the power of the respective States.

Thus, the Due Process Clause "does not contemplate that a state may make binding a judgment *in personam* against an individual or corporate defendant with which the state has no contacts, ties, or relations." . . . Even if the defendant would suffer minimal or no inconvenience from being forced to litigate before the tribunals of another State; even if the forum State has a strong interest in applying its law to the controversy; even if the forum State is the most convenient location for litigation, the Due Process Clause, acting as an instrument of interstate federalism, may sometimes act to divest the State of its power to render a valid judgment. . . .

III

Applying these principles to the case at hand, we find in the record before us a total absence of those affiliating circumstances that are a necessary predicate to any exercise of state-court jurisdiction. Petitioners carry on no activity whatsoever in Oklahoma. They close no sales and perform no services there. They avail themselves of none of the privileges and benefits of Oklahoma law. They solicit no business there either through salespersons or through advertising reasonably calculated to reach the State. Nor does the record show that they regularly sell cars at wholesale or retail to Oklahoma customers or residents or that they indirectly, through others, serve or seek to serve the Oklahoma market. In short, respondents seek to base jurisdiction on one, isolated occurrence and whatever inferences can be drawn therefrom: the fortuitous circumstance that a single Audi automobile, sold in New York to New York residents, happened to suffer an accident while passing through Oklahoma.

It is argued, however, that because an automobile is mobile by its very design and purpose it was "foreseeable" that the Robinsons' Audi would cause injury in Oklahoma. Yet "foreseeability" alone has never been a sufficient benchmark for personal jurisdiction under the Due Process Clause. . . .

This is not to say, of course, that foreseeability is wholly irrelevant. But the foreseeability that is critical to due process analysis is not the mere likelihood that a product will find its way into the forum State. Rather, it is that the defendant's conduct and connection with the forum State are such that he should reasonably anticipate being haled into court there. . . .

When a corporation "purposefully avails itself of the privilege of conducting activities within the forum State," it has clear notice that it is subject to suit there, and can act to alleviate the risk of burdensome litigation by procuring insurance, passing the expected costs on to customers, or, if

the risks are too great, severing its connection with the State. . . .

But there is no such or similar basis for Oklahoma jurisdiction over World-Wide or Seaway in this case. Seaway's sales are made in Massena, N.Y. World-Wide's market, although substantially larger, is limited to dealers in New York, New Jersey, and Connecticut. There is no evidence of record that any automobiles distributed by World-Wide are sold to retail customers outside this tri-State area. It is foreseeable that the purchasers of automobiles sold by World-Wide and Seaway may take them to Oklahoma. But the mere "unilateral activity of those who claim some relationship with a nonresident defendant cannot satisfy the requirement of contact with the forum State." . . .

CALIFORNIA v. ARIZONA

99 S. Ct. 919 (U.S. Supreme Court, 1979)

Justice Stewart

Since the admission of California to the Union in 1850, the southeastern boundary of the State has been the middle of the channel of the Colorado River. Act of September 9, 1850, 9 Stat. 452 (1850). Neither the Gadsden Purchase in 1853 nor the admission of Arizona to statehood in 1912 changed the location of this 229-mile border. The location of the river did change, however, from causes both natural and artificial. These shifts created confusion about the location of the political boundary between California and Arizona. This problem was resolved through an interstate compact, ratified by the Congress in 1966. The Compact fixed the boundary by stations of longitude and latitude, divorced from the continuing shifts of the Colorado River.

California has taken the position, however, that the Compact settled only questions of political jurisdiction, not questions of ownership of real property, since, under the "equal footing doctrine," California holds title to all lands beneath the navigable waters within its boundaries at the time of its admission to the Union. . . . In the early 1970's the California State Lands Commission made a study of a stretch of 11.3 miles along the river to determine what land California owns. Both Arizona and the United States have a direct interest in such a determination. Arizona, of course, has the same rights under the equal footing doctrine as does California. The United States is the principal riparian owner in this region, and determination of the width and location of the old river bed thus will necessarily affect its property interest. California has presented the determinations of its Lands Commission to both Arizona and the United States; neither has acquiesced in the Commissions' conclusions.

California seeks to invoke the Court's original jurisdiction in this suit to quiet title of the lands it claims, and thus resolve its dispute with Arizona and the United States. To sue Arizona, it relies on 28 U.S.C. § 1251(a), which confers on this Court "original and exclusive jurisdiction of . . . all controversies between two or more States." To sue the United States, it relies on 28 U.S.C. § 1251(b) which confers on this Court "original but not exclusive jurisdiction of . . . [a]ll controversies between the United States and a State." Both these heads of original jurisdiction find their source in Art. III, § 2 of the Constitution : "In all Cases . . . in which a State shall be Party, the Supreme Court shall have original Jurisdiction."

It is undisputed that both Arizona and the United States are indispensable parties to this litigation, and it is California's need to sue both Arizona and the United States that creates the problem before us. Specifically, Arizona and the United States contend that the United States has not agreed to be a defendant in a quiet title action in this Court. Yet this is the only federal court in which California can sue Arizona, because Congress has conferred upon it "original and exclusive jurisdiction." [emphasis added] over controversies between States. 28 U.S.C. § 1251(a) (1).

It is settled that the United States must give its consent to be sued even when one of the States invokes this Court's original jurisdiction. . . .

Yet the Court has recognized that an action in equity cannot be maintained without the joinder of indispensable parties. . . . Thus, if the United States has not consented to be sued in an action such as this, California's motion for leave to file a complaint must be denied. . . .

The suit, then, could not be maintained in any court. This Court could not hear the claims against the United States because it has not waived its sovereign immunity, and a district court could not hear the claims against Arizona, because this Court has exclusive jurisdiction over such claims. . . . However, we have concluded that the United States has already waived its sovereign immunity to suit in this case. . . .

In 1972 Congress passed Pub.L. 92–562. The Act made two relevant changes in Title 28 of the United State Code. First, it created a new § 2409a. Subsection (a) of this new section provides:

The United States may be named as a party defendant in a civil action under this section to adjudicate a disputed title to real property in which the United States claims an interest other than a security interest or water rights. . . .

The remainder of the section defines the procedures to be followed in such suits. Second, the Congress amended § 1346 to add a new subsection (f). That subsection provides:

The district courts shall have exclusive original jurisdiction of civil actions under section 2409a to quiet title to an estate or interest in real property in which an interest is claimed by the United States.

It is thus clear that the United States has waived its immunity to suit in actions brought against it to quiet title to land. The question is whether suits brought under that waiver may be heard in this Court.

The Solicitor General argues that they may not, that § 1346(f) operates both to confer original jurisdiction over such a case on the federal district courts and simultaneously to withdraw the original jurisdiction of this Court. If this contention were accepted, a grave constitutional question would immediately arise. The question, quite simply, is whether Congress can deprive this Court of original jurisdiction conferred upon it by the Constitution.

The original jurisdiction of the Supreme Court is conferred not by the Congress but by the Constitution itself. This jurisdiction is self-executing, and needs no legislative implementation. . . . It is clear, of course, that Congress could refuse to waive the Nation's sovereign immunity in all cases or only in some cases but in all courts. Either action would bind this Court even in the exercise of its original jurisdiction. It is similarly clear that the original jurisdiction of this Court is not constitutionally exclusive—that other courts can be awarded concurrent jurisdiction by statute. . . . But once Congress has waived the Nation's sovereign immunity, it's far from clear that it can withdraw the constitutional jurisdiction of this Court over such suits.

The constitutional grant to this Court of original jurisdiction is limited to cases involving the States and the envoys of foreign nations. The Framers seem to have been concerned with matching the dignity of the parties to the status of the court. . . .

See *The Federalist*, No. 81, 507–509 (Lodge ed. 1888) (A. Hamilton). Elimination of this Court's original jurisdiction would require these sovereign parties to go to another court, in derogation of this constitutional purpose. Congress has broad powers over the jurisdiction of the federal courts and over the sovereign immunity of the United States, but it is extremely doubtful that they include the power to limit in this manner the original jurisdiction conferred upon this Court by the Constutition.

Happily, we need not decide this constitutional question, for the statute in question can readily be construed in such a way as to obviate it. In so construing the statute, we no more than follow the long practice of the Court to forego the resolution of constitutional issues except when absolutely necessary. . . .

The legislative history of § 1346(f) is sparse, but the intent of Congress seems reasonably clear. The congressional purpose was simply to confine jurisdiction to the federal courts and to exclude the courts of the States, which otherwise might be presumed to have jurisdiction over quiet title suits against the United States, once its sovereign immunity had been waived. . . . The legislative history shows no intention to divest this Court of jurisdiction over quiet title actions against the United States in cases otherwise within our original jurisdiction. We find, there-fore, that § 1346(f), by vesting "exclusive original jurisdiction" of quiet title actions against the United States in the federal district courts, did not more than assure that such jurisdiction was not conferred upon the courts of any State.

For these reasons we conclude that there is no bar to this original suit in the Supreme Court between California as plaintiff, and Arizona and the United States as defendants. Accordingly, the motion of California for leave to file its complaint is granted, and the defendants are allowed 45 days in which to answer or otherwise respond.

APPLICATION OF HANSEN

(275 N.W.2d 790 (Minnesota, 1978)

Kelly, Justice

This case comes before the court pursuant to petitioner's request for review of a decision by the State Board of Law Examiners (Board) that petitioner would not be allowed to sit for the Minnesota State Bar examination because he had not graduated from an approved law school as required by Rule II(4) of the Supreme Court Rules for Admission to the Bar. We affirm.

Petitioner, originally a Minnesota resident, is a 1977 graduate of Western State University College of Law (Western State), San Diego, California. Although not admitted to the University of Minnesota Law School, petitioner had the opportunity to attend a number of the 166 law schools accredited by the American Bar Association (ABA). After one month at Marquette University Law School, petitioner decided to transfer to Western State Law School. Western State has never applied to the ABA for accreditation. It has been accredited both by the California Committee of Bar Examiners and by the Western Association of Schools and Colleges.

Prior to leaving Marquette, petitioner had a conference with the Dean, who advised him to remain at Marquette, partly because of its ABA-approved status. Nevertheless, petitioner decided to leave Marquette and enroll at Western State.

In the fall of 1976, when petitioner was a senior student at Western State, he applied to the

Board for permission to sit for the July, 1977, bar examination. The Board denied his application because he was not a graduate of an approved law school. According to the Rules for Admission to the Bar, an approved law school is one "that is provisionally or fully approved by the Section of Legal Education for Admissions to the Bar of the American Bar Association."

Thereafter, petitioner requested and was granted a formal hearing before the Board, pursuant to Rule X, Rules for Admission to the Bar. On March 11, 1977, after a full hearing, at which petitioner waived his right to appear, the Board found that he did not satisfy the requirements of Rule II(4) and therefore again denied him permission to sit for the bar examination.

On May 11, 1977, petitioner sought a hearing before this court which was denied on June 7, 1977. His request for a reconsideration of his petition, filed on August 22, 1977, was granted. During this interim period petitioner wrote and passed the California Bar Examination and was admitted to practice in California in January, 1978.

This case presents the following issues for decision:

(1) Whether Rule II(4) of the Supreme Court Rules for Admission to the Bar is constitutional; and,

(2) Whether, granting its constitutionality, the requirement of graduating from an ABA-accredited law school should be waived in this case.

Petitioner and Western State, as amicus curiae, suggest that Minnesota's rule requiring proof of graduation from an ABA-approved law school as a prerequisite to sitting for the bar examination is unconstitutional under both the due process and the equal protection clauses of the 14th Amendment to the United States Constitution. We disagree. As long as the requirements established by state supreme courts to regulate the practice of law are reasonable ones, they comply with applicable constitutional principles.

All United States Supreme Court decisions concerning state regulation of the practice of law recognize that a state has a substantial interest in the qualifications of those it admits to the legal profession. . . . As the Supreme Court noted

recently in *Goldfarb* v. *Virgina State Bar*, 421 U.S. 773 (1975):

. . . [T]he States have a compelling interest in the practice of professions within their boundaries, and . . . as part of their power to protect the public health, safety, and other valid interests they have broad power to establish standards for licensing practitioners. . . . The interest of the States in regulating lawyers is especially great since lawyers are essential to the primary governmental function of administering justice, and have historically been "officers of the courts."

Nevertheless, the Court has also recognized that "[t]he practice of law is not a matter of grace, but of right for one who is qualified by his learning and his moral character." . . . Thus, while "[a] state can require high standards of qualifications, such as good moral character or proficiency in its law, before it admits an applicant to the bar, . . . any qualification must have a rational connection with the applicant's fitness or capacity to practice law." . . .

The test that emerges from these cases is that, despite the strong interest of the applicant in being able to practice law, the state can regulate admission as long as such regulation is reasonably related to its interest in a competent bar. A procedure is reasonable as long as it is not arbitrary and capricious. Only if the complainant is a member of a suspect class or if the procedure at issue violates a fundamental right must the state demonstrate a compelling state interest for its system of regulation to pass constitutional muster. . . .

The procedure being challenged in this case is Minnesota's requirement that an applicant wishing to take the bar examination demonstrate, among other things, that he graduated from a law school which is provisionally or fully accredited by the American Bar Association. . . . Although there have been numerous challenges over the years to educational requirements similar to those of Rule II, both state and federal courts have consistently found such requirements to be constitutional. . . .

In all the decisions upholding a state's educational requirements as a valid prerequisite to admission to the bar, courts have required only that there be a rational reason for the imposition of the requirements. . . .

It is also rational for a state supreme court to conclude that the ABA is best equipped to perform the function of accrediting law schools. . . .

Clearly, it is reasonable for Minnesota to require proof that an applicant's legal education was of a high quality as a general prerequisite to admission to the bar. Similarly, it is neither arbitrary nor capricious for us to measure the quality of legal education with the same standards as those utilized by the ABA. . . .

The only extenuating circumstance that petitioner presents is the inconvenience to him of practicing law away from his family. Yet, because he knew that his transfer to Western State could create this hardship, he cannot be heard to complain to us at this time. . . .

Finally, we reject the contention that we should accept the decision of some other accrediting organization that Western State offers its students a quality education. The Western Association of Schools and Colleges is a general regional accrediting organization. According to the ABA, Western State is the only law school that it has accredited. Thus, we do not believe that its expertise is comparable to that of the ABA which specializes in evaluating legal education. . . .

Nothing forced petitioner to attend a nonaccredited law school. . . . He chose to transfer from an ABA-approved school to a nonaccredited one far away from his home state, knowing that his move would pose problems for him if he later wanted to return to Minnesota to practice law. Thus, equity requires no waiver here. Were we to grant the waiver as requested, we would have to consider similar requests by students from other nonaccredited law schools with chaotic results. . . .

Affirmed.

REVIEW QUESTIONS AND PROBLEMS

1. What is a demurrer? What purpose does it serve?

2. When will a writ of certiorari be granted?

3. What are the advantages of arbitration over a civil lawsuit?

4. What are the differences between depositions and interrogatories?

5. Once you have a judgment against a person, how can you collect it?

6. What is a peremptory challenge?

7. When would you change venue in a case?

8. When will a default judgment be rendered?

9. What is a directed verdict, and when in the course of a trial will it be requested, and under what circumstances will it be granted?

10. How can an administrative agency enforce its quasi-judicial findings?

11. Sometime in March 1977, Herman disclosed an idea for a business machine to his trusted business advisor, Plato. Plato promised that he wouldn't tell anyone else about the idea until Herman had had a chance to patent it. In June 1977, while Herman was still trying to get the money together to process a patent application, he learned that Plato had disclosed the idea to at least one company which might be interested in manufacturing the machine. By October 1977 that company, ABM Machines, was advertising and selling a machine which seemed to be copied from Herman's, and Plato was receiving royalties on the machine from ABM. Herman filed a lawsuit against Plato on August 15, 1979. The state has a two-year statute of limitations for any action "on a contract, obligation, or liability not founded on an instrument in writing." Is Herman's lawsuit barred by this statute? Discuss.

12. Aleoni packages and sells soil and fertilizer products in Oshkosh, Wisconsin. He met Orville, a representative of Mildoo Farms, at a convention in St. Louis, Mis-

souri. Mildoo is located in Byback, Arkansas. Pursuant to an oral contract made at the convention, Aleoni sent a shipment of fertilizer to Mildoo in Arkansas. The shipment was sent by railroad, FOB Oshkosh. Thereafter a dispute arose over the amount of the contract price, which the parties were unable to settle. Aleoni sues in the Wisconsin courts, alleging that that state's long arm statute provides jurisdiction over Mildoo, since it covers persons who transact business or own property in the state. Mildoo moves to dismiss for lack of personal jurisdiction. How should the court rule? Discuss.

13. Frisco Company sued Swayback Corporation, alleging that Swayback had committed several antitrust violations which injured Frisco. Frisco asked the trial court for a discovery order against certain of Swayback's books and records which related to Swayback's marketing practices and market shares. Humble, who was vice president for finance at Swayback, said that the company did not have such records available. When the court ordered production, Humble swore under oath that he was unable to comply. It has now been learned that Swayback did have such records available. What sorts of remedial action might the court take now? Discuss.

14. One of the statutes setting up the U.S. Veterans Administration provides that all records under its jurisdiction shall be "confidential and privileged." Sanchez, who had been treated in a VA hospital in New Mexico for certain service-related injuries, was involved in a car accident. Sanchez sued Knoze, the other driver, alleging that Knoze was at fault and that Sanchez was permanently disabled. Knoze's lawyer thinks that Sanchez may be using the accident to try to recover for his war injuries and asks for a discovery order against Sanchez' VA hospital records. How should the court rule, and why?

Criminal Law and Business | 3

T raditionally the businessperson has been less concerned about criminal law than about contract law, tort law, corporation law, and other mainstream business law subjects. Today, however, criminal law, particularly as it applies to white-collar crimes, is becoming an area of considerable concern for businesspersons. There are a number of business crimes of which the businessperson must be aware. One of the newest types of business crimes is computer theft. Computer theft encompasses embezzlement of funds, theft of computer programs, and theft of confidential business information and records—all through the use and manipulation of computers and other electronic devices.

In addition to having to concern themselves with white-collar or business crimes, the corporate officer and corporate director now find that they are not only subject to civil lawsuits for their actions but that they may also be criminally liable, with resulting jail terms, or large fines.

WHAT IS A CRIME?

A crime can be defined as a public wrong. In order to maintain an orderly society, certain standards of conduct must be set which the members of society must observe. Failure to observe these standards must be enforced by some form of societal pressure such as fines, or imprisonment. A crime may involve either the commission of a specific act or the omission or failure to act under certain circumstances. For the commission or omission of an act to be classified as a crime, the legislature, either national, state, or local, must have passed a statute or ordinance declaring the commission or omission of that act to be a crime.

Many of the acts or omissions which have been statutorily termed crimes may also be torts. A tort is a private wrong for which the wronged person may recover monetary damages. A typical example is the crime of assault and battery in which someone is mugged on the street. Society has decreed by statute that such acts of assault and battery against a person shall be considered crimes and shall be punished appropriately. The person who has been mugged, on the other hand, was the victim of a private wrong and has a legal right to bring a civil action at his or her own expense in order to recover monetary damages for the loss suffered.

CLASSIFICATIONS OF CRIME

Basically crimes may be classified as felonies or misdemeanors. There is also the crime of treason; however, it is not normally associated with business law and therefore will not be discussed here. Traditionally felonies have been serious crimes, such as murder, rape, robbery, burglary, arson, theft, and larceny. A crime is not a felony, however, unless it is designated as such by the particular statute or ordinance making it a crime. Felonies are normally punishable by jail sentences of at least one year, plus possible fines.

Misdemeanors are criminal offenses other than felonies. Typically misdemeanors are punished by small fines and/or jail sentences not exceeding one year. Normally the person who has been convicted of a misdemeanor is confined in a county jail rather than the state penitentiary. The fines imposed for misdemeanors are normally smaller than the fines imposed for felonies. There is, however, no standard that is common to all states, and different states have different crime classifications and different levels of punishment. Each state has the responsibility of creating its own criminal law. State criminal law may not however, conflict with any applicable national law.

BUSINESS CRIMES

Since the object of this textbook is to focus on business-related legal matters, we will only discuss crimes which are relevant to the operation of a business. The following are some typical business crimes.

1. Larceny. Larceny, or theft as it is commonly called, is simply the unlawful taking of another person's personal property with the intent of depriving the owner of his or her property. Shoplifting is an example of larceny with which the businessperson has to be concerned. Larceny is also committed by employees who carry off goods and merchandise.

2. Robbery. Robbery, like larceny, involves the unlawful taking of personal property. However, robbery differs from larceny in that the unlawful taking involves the use of force putting other persons in fear of injury. Thus, robbery is a more serious crime than larceny since it has the potential of physical harm to individuals.

3. Embezzlement. Embezzlement differs from larceny in that the party charged with this crime had lawful possession of the money or property involved. However, the embezzler simply used the property or money for his or her own purposes. A typical case here would be a bank employee who was in charge of certain funds and used some of the funds for personal purposes. Most embezzlers borrow money with the intent of paying it back later. In most jurisdictions the person who takes money with the intent of returning it is still guilty of embezzlement.

4. Arson. Arson is willfully setting fire to and burning someone else's building. In old English common law, arson referred primarily to the burning of someone else's dwelling house.

Under most state statutes, arson now covers the burning of business buildings as well as dwellings. Burning one's own home or building traditionally was not arson. You had a right to tear your own building down, burn it, or destroy it in any other manner as long as you didn't injure the property of others. A problem arises, however, when the building being burned is covered by fire insurance and the intent of burning it is to collect the insurance. The offense in that situation is actually criminal fraud against an insurance company.

5. Defrauding Consumers by Use of the Mails. It is a crime to use the mails to solicit money for fraudulent purposes. This could include schemes to sell phony corporate stocks and bonds, false statements about products which when received are not as advertised, and a myriad of other situations in which people use the mails to convey false information for the purpose of committing fraud. National laws also make it a crime to send pornographic materials through the mails.

6. Defrauding Consumers by Using False Labels, Measures, and Weights. In recent years a number of national and state laws have been passed concerning false weights, measures, and labels. Again, intention is a key factor in this crime. A simple mistake in weight or measurement is not a crime. There must be an intent to defraud or cheat the consumer.

7. Forgery. Forgery is the false or fraudulent making, or the material alteration with the intent to defraud, of any writing which if it were genuine would be of legal effect and create legal liability. When we think of forgery we think of a situation where one person signs another person's name to a check. Forgery also includes the changing of a legal document in such a way as to change the legal liability of the document. One of the most common acts of forgery today relates to the use of credit cards. How often are you asked to furnish your driver's license or other identification when you want to use your gasoline credit card?

8. Computer Crime. This is the newest and perhaps the most important area of criminal law of concern to business managers. Computer-related crimes range from the theft of a computer program worth thousands of dollars to the use of computers to embezzle millions of dollars. As we enter the new cashless society, electronic fund transfer systems are replacing the traditional cash and check method of payment and deposit of funds. Thus most of our funds are stored magnetically and electronically as data in various computer memory banks, and fund transfers are made over communication circuits of various types from those computer memory banks to other computer memory banks. It is comparatively easy for a skilled and knowledgeable computer technician with access to an electronic data processing system to reprogram the computer in such a way as to shift, hide, or manipulate funds. Moreover, detection is difficult, as an erasure or an addition of data in a magnetic file leaves no traceable evidence. In a case involving the New York City Union Dime Savings Bank, a chief teller was accused of embezzling over $1.5 million. The chief teller simply reprogrammed the computer to electronically transfer electronic money from legitimate accounts into his fraudulently created computer accounts, and he could then withdraw actual money from those accounts. He electronically redeposited these electronic funds just before regular quarterly interest payment dates so that everything seemed to balance out.

In addition to the cases involving computerized embezzlement or manipulation of funds, we find an increasing number of cases where valuable computer programs and confidential business information have been stolen. Thousands of dollars are often invested in developing computer programs, or "software," and confidential business information can often be very valuable in the hands of competitors. Back in the days when records were kept in time-locked, steel-walled safes or vaults, it was difficult to steal such information. Today a majority of businesses store their information and records in a computerized system. Also, some businesses cannot afford their own internal computer system and use an outside time-sharing system, which increases the possibility of theft. The fact is that in most systems computerized files can be easily accessed by a number of different persons, and the odds against detection are considerably greater than they were in the traditional theft of records cases, where there was physical evidence of theft.

Thus far, we have probably seen only the tip of the iceberg in the area of computer crime. Businesspersons must be aware of the potential for loss and liability in this area, and take appropriate precautions. As a matter of fact, the Federal Corrupt Practices Act imposes a duty on corporate officers and directors to ensure the adequacy of "internal controls" over business records and expenditures.

9. Criminal Liability of Accountants. This is also a new area of criminal law. Traditionally professionals such as accountants, lawyers, and doctors were found liable for civil damages for malpractice but were not prosecuted criminally for acts of mere negligence. In recent years a number of criminal cases have been brought against accountants, particularly in connection with their failure to discover and report fraud by corporate officers or employees. This problem is discussed further in a later chapter.

10. Commercial Bribery. In recent years the press has exposed many cases of commercial bribery and payoffs to politicians and various cases of illegal campaign contributions. The problem in these cases is that a corporation typically makes the illegal contribution or pays the bribe. You can fine a corporation, but you can't put a corporation in jail. Shouldn't the executive who made the decision to have the corporation disobey the law be criminally liable?

11. Criminal Liability of Corporate Executives. In stockholder actions against managers, corporate directors, and corporate officers, these persons have always been individually accountable in civil court for their acts of negligence in the operation of the business. With regard to criminal charges, typically the corporation is charged with the crime, and since a corporation cannot be jailed, the corporation simply paid the fine and the case was closed. There seemed to be a protective shield between the manager, corporate director, or corporate officer and the criminal prosecutor. The first major instance in which this corporate shield was pierced was the electrical industry price-fixing conspiracy case in 1960. In that case several corporate executives were sent to jail. The corporate shield has been disintegrating ever since.

New regulations and new laws are aiming criminal prosecution, not at the corporate entity, an artificial person, but more realistically at the natural persons whose decision caused the criminal act. Thus corporate executives must weigh their decisions not only on the corporate profit-loss scale but also against the possibility of personal criminal punishment. In the past a corporate executive might have decided to violate the law because the anticipated profit of doing so exceeded the antcipated corporate fines that would have to be paid if the violation were detected. Now the executive may not want to risk violating the law if this means that he or she may face individual criminal prosecution.

YOUR RIGHTS UNDER CRIMINAL LAW

Your rights under criminal law are considerably different from your rights under civil law. Under civil law, if you are sued for breach of contract or for the commission of a tort, the remedy is monetary damages. None of us want to lose money. However, if we are unfortunate enough to have a very large judgment assessed against us and we do not have the funds to satisfy the judgment, we do have the opportunity to file for bankruptcy. A person who is adjudicated a bankrupt is free from all prior debts and in effect is born again as far as his or her financial life is concerned. However, a person who is convicted of a crime may be jailed and/or assessed a fine, and if the crime is a felony, the person may lose some of his or her civil rights. In some states convicted felons lose the right to vote, the right to serve on juries, and the right to hold public office. Also, if the person convicted of a crime is a professional practitioner such as a lawyer, he or she may be disbarred as a result of the conviction. Thus a criminal conviction carries with it more serious consequences than does a simple civil judgment for money. A person convicted of a crime will carry this record for the rest of his or her life. In fact, if capital punishment is allowed, the person may lose his or her life. Thus the guarantees which the law must give to a person charged with a crime are much greater than the guarantees which must be given in a civil trial for monetary damages.

Following are some of the guarantees which are essential in a criminal law trial but need not be provided in a civil law trial.

1. The Right to a Speedy Public Trial by Jury. The Sixth Amendment to the Constitution of the United States guarantees a speedy public trial by jury in criminal cases. In civil cases in large metropolitan areas there may be a delay of several years between the time of filing a lawsuit and the time of trial. A person charged with a crime should have his or her day in court promptly. The trial should be before a jury of his or her peers, and it must be public.

Reid v. *Covert*
354 U.S. 1 (U.S. Supreme Court, 1957)

FACTS   This case and *Kinsella* v. *Krueger* were decided together, since they raised the same constitutional problems. Mrs. Clarice Covert killed her husband, a U.S. Air Force sergeant, at an air base in England, where they were stationed. Mrs. Dorothy Smith killed her husband, a U.S. Army officer, at an Army post in Japan. Each was tried by a military court-martial, in accordance with agreements entered into with the host country which provided for such trials of dependents of service personnel) rather than trial in the courts of the host country. Each woman pleaded insanity as a defense; each was found guilty by the court-martial panel; each was sentenced to life imprisonment. The U.S. district court for the District of Columbia granted Mrs. Covert's motion for habeas corpus, and the government appealed. Mrs. Smith's fa-

Reid v. Covert (continued)

ther filed a similar petition in the U.S. district court in West Virginia, which refused it. While an appeal to the U.S. circuit court was pending, the government also requested certiorari for that case.

ISSUE   Does the criminal trial of a civilian military dependent by a court-martial unconstitutionally deprive her of the right to jury trial?

DECISION   Yes. Both habeaus corpus petitions must be granted.

REASONS   Justice Black's opinion reviewed basic constitutional doctrines and some of the historical origins of the Bill of Rights protections. He also distinguished earlier cases which had limited the application of the Bill of Rights in proceedings outside this country.

"At the beginning we reject the idea that when the United States acts against citizens abroad it can do so free of the Bill of Rights. The United States is entirely a creature of the Constitution. Its power and authority have no other source. It can only act in accordance with all the limitations imposed by the Constitution. When the Government reaches out to punish a citizen who is abroad, the shield which the Bill of Rights and other parts of the Constitution provide to protect his life and liberty should not be stripped away just because he happens to be in another land. This is not a novel concept. To the contrary, it is as old as government. It was recognized long before Paul successfully invoked his right as a Roman citizen to be tried in strict accordance with Roman law. . . .

"This Court and other federal courts have held or asserted that various constitutional limitations apply to the Government when it acts outside the continental United States. While it has been suggested that only those constitutional rights which are 'fundamental' protect Americans abroad, we can find no warrant, in logic or otherwise, for picking and choosing among the remarkable collection of 'Thou shalt nots' which were explicitly fastened on all departments and agencies of the Federal Government by the Constitution and its Amendments. Moreover, in view of our heritage and the history of the adoption of the Constitution and the Bill of Rights, it seems peculiarly anomalous to say that trial before a civilian judge and by an independent jury picked from the common citizenry are not fundamenmtal rights."

2. You are Innocent until Proven Guilty. The jury in a criminal trial must be instructed by the judge that the defendant, the party charged with the crime, is innocent until proven guilty. The jury is instructed that the state or the national government, whoever the charging party may be, must prove the case against the defendant beyond a reasonable doubt. There must also be a unanimous verdict. In a civil case the plaintiff must simply prove his or her case by a preponderance of the evidence. This means that the jury must simply believe the plaintiff's story more than it believes the defendant's story. Also, in a criminal case the jury in most jurisdictions has only one thing to decide, and that is guilt or innocence. The punishment is normally decided by the judge or at a second deliberation of the jury. In civil cases the jury not only decides whether the plaintiff gets a verdict or the defendant gets a verdict, but it also has the option of deciding how much money the plaintiff will be awarded.

3. Self-Incrimination. In a criminal case the person charged with a crime cannot be forced to testify against himself or herself. This, of course, is the guarantee against self-incrimination which is provided by the Fifth Amendment of the U.S. Constitution. In an ordinary civil trial, however, a defendant may be required to testify or be found in civil contempt of court.

Slochower v. Board of Higher Education of New York City
350 U.S. 551 (U.S. Supreme Court, 1956)

FACTS Section 903 of the charter of New York City provided that whenever a city employee used the privilege against self-incrimination to avoid answering questions relating to his official conduct, "his term or tenure of office or employment shall terminate." Slochower, an associate professor at Brooklyn College, was called to testify at a hearing of the U.S. Senate Internal Security Subcommittee, which was investigating subversive influences in the educational system. He had been identified by one Bernard Grebanier as having been a member of the Communist Party in 1941. When called, Professor Slochower said he was not now a member of the Communist Party and that he would answer all questions about his associations since 1941. He declined to answer questions about 1940 and 1941, however, on the ground that the answers might tend to incriminate him. Shortly thereafter, he was fired. The New York courts upheld the discharge, indicating that his "taking the Fifth" was equivalent to a resignation under section 903.

ISSUE Can a state automatically attach such penalties to the assertion of a constitutional privilege?

DECISION No. The dismissal is reversed and the case remanded.

REASONS Justice Clark first noted that Slochower, with 27 years' experience, had tenure under New York's law and was therefore generally dischargeable only for cause and only after proper notice, a hearing, and an appeal. All those "due process" steps were denied under section 903.

"At the outset we must condemn the practice of imputing a sinister meaning to the exercise of a person's constitutional right under the Fifth Amendment. The right of an accused person to refuse to testify, which had been in England merely a rule of evidence, was so important to our forefathers that they raised it to the dignity of a constitutional enactment, and it has been recognized as 'one of the most valuable prerogatives of the citizen.' . . . We have reaffirmed our faith in this principle recently. . . . [W]e scored the assumption that those who claim this privilege are either criminals or perjurers. The privilege against a self-incrimination would be reduced to a hollow mockery if its exercise could be taken as equivalent either to a confession of guilt or a conclusive presumption of perjury. . . . [A] witness may have a reasonable fear of prosecution and yet be innocent of any wrongdoing. The privilege serves to protect the innocent who otherwise might be ensnared by ambiguous circumstances."

Justice Clark said that his decision did not mean that Professor Slochower had a constitutional right to teach at Brooklyn College, only that he must be given a due process hearing.

4. Right to Counsel. The Sixth Amendment to the U.S. Constitution provides that the accused in a criminal trial shall have the right to assistance of counsel for his or her defense. If the accused cannot afford an attorney, an attorney will be appointed for the accused by the court at the expense of the state. In most civil cases no attorney is appointed for a defendant. The defendant must hire an attorney at his or her own expense or act as his or her own counsel. Many metropolitan areas and many university towns now have legal aid societies which furnish free legal counsel to people who cannot afford the services of an attorney.

5. The Accused Is Entitled to a Miranda-type Warning. The famous case of *Miranda* v. *State of Arizona,* 86 S. Ct. 1602 (1966) initiated the so-called Miranda-type warning which now must be given to an accused at the time of arrest. Briefly, the accused must be told that he or she has the right to remain silent, that anything he or she says can be used against him or her in court, that he or she has the right to have an attorney present when he or she is questioned, and that if he or she cannot afford an attorney, an attorney will be appointed for him or her.

6. Double Jeopardy. In criminal trials there is also the Fifth Amendment guarantee against double jeopardy. If a person charged with a crime has been found innocent, even though later evidence may prove that the person was in fact guilty of the crime, the person may not be tried again. The state may not appeal a verdict of not guilty. Once a person has been tried and found innocent, that is the end of the case. In a civil case either party may appeal a decision.

7. Mens rea. In a criminal case a person may not be found guilty of a crime unless the person had a mental intent to commit the crime: We often hear about the defense of temporary insanity in criminal cases. If a person charged with the commission of a crime did not know what he or she was doing, then the person is not guilty of the crime since there was no mental intent to commit it. Some states have a doctrine called irresistible impulse. In those states, if the person had an irresistible impulse to commit the criminal act, then the person is not guilty. The typical case here would be a husband or wife finding his or her mate in bed with another person and striking or shooting them in a rage of temper.

A person who is intoxicated or under the influence of drugs may not be guilty for acts committed while he or she is in that condition. However, in such cases the question arises as to whether the person became intoxicated or fell under the influence of drugs voluntarily or involuntarily, and whether the person was incapable of having a mental intent. If the person became intoxicated or fell under the influence of drugs voluntarily and was still capable of a mental intent, then the majority of courts would find the person guilty. For example, Sam Soak went to a party, voluntarily imbibed too much liquor, and then got into his car to drive home. While swerving down the street, Sam hit a pedestrian in the crosswalk and killed the pedestrian. Sam may very well be found guilty of manslaughter.

If the person who committed a crime was a child under the age of reason, than the child would not legally have sufficient mens rea, or mental intent, to be guilty of the crime. In most states a child under seven years of age is presumed to be incapable of the mental intent to commit a crime. Over the age of seven years the individual child's capability of mental intent becomes an open question. Here again, the laws of the various states will differ and the particular law of the state where the crime was committed must be consulted.

CRIMINAL PROCEDURE

The procedure in a criminal trial differs considerably from the procedure in a civil trial, which we reviewed in Chapter 2. The accompanying illustration shows a typical criminal trial procedure from the investigation of a crime to the point where the person is released from prison.

In a civil case the injured party simply secures legal counsel of his or her own choice and proceeds to file a civil lawsuit at his or her own expense. That party can control the lawsuit; that is, the injured party, the plaintiff, can settle the case out of court, pursue the case through trial, or dismiss the case entirely at any point during the proceedings. In a criminal case the injured party simply reports the commission of a crime to the proper authority and the state or

PROCEDURE IN A CRIMINAL TRIAL

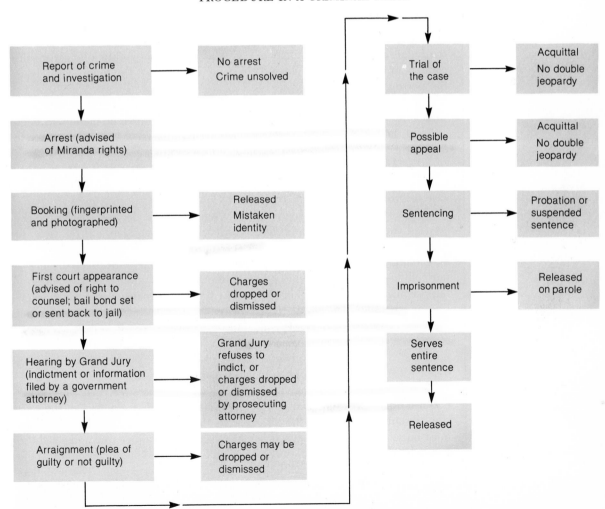

national government then takes over. The injured individual has no further control over the case.

The first step in the procedure of a criminal case is the report of the crime and the investigation. If the investigators are unable to find evidence sufficient to prosecute, then no arrest is made. Many cases will fall into the unsolved category. If the investigation does produce evidence which would support prosecution of the case, then an arrest is made. At the time of the arrest the arresting officer must inform the person being arrested of his or her rights. The officer must tell the accused person that he or she has the right to remain silent, that anything he or she says can be used against him or her in court, and that he or she has the right to the presence of an attorney and to have an attorney appointed before questioning if he or she cannot afford one. After having been arrested, the person will be booked. This process involves photographing and fingerprinting the subject and making up a record containing the subject's name, address, age, weight, height, and other pertinent information. The person now has a "police record."

The accused will then be entitled to an appearance before a judge. The accused is informed that he or she has the right to have counsel present. At this hearing the judge must determine whether the person shall be released on bail or without bail or returned to jail. If the person is to be released on bail, then the judge must set the amount of bail which must be paid or pledged to the court before he or she is released. In many minor cases the judge will release the person without bail.

The next step in the criminal process is to determine whether or not there is sufficient evidence to try the person for the crime of which he or she has been accused. In serious crimes a grand jury will be impaneled to hear evidence to determine whether or not there is sufficient cause to proceed to a regular trial. If the grand jury finds sufficient evidence, it will issue an indictment. In other cases the prosecuting attorney will file an "information" which will allow the case to proceed to a regular trial.

At this stage of the proceeding the prosecutor must decide what crime the accused should be prosecuted for. Probably the prosecution and the defense will engage in the process called plea bargaining. A very typical example of plea bargaining would take place where a person was arrested for drunken driving— normally punishable by a fine, possible imprisonment, and suspension of driving privileges. If the blood alcohol test or the breathanalyzer test was borderline or just slightly over the legal limit, the prosecuting attorney will often agree to reduce the charge to speeding or reckless driving, which are lesser offenses, if the accused will plead guilty. The prosecutor realizes that the case is not too strong and thus a conviction for a lesser offense is better than a possible defense verdict on the drunken driving charge.

The next step is the arraignment hearing. Here the accused party must plead either not guilty or guilty. If the party pleads guilty, then, of course, the next step is sentencing. If, on the other hand, the party pleads not guilty, a trial must be scheduled. The accused person has a right to a jury trial and a right to a speedy trial. After the trial the party is either acquitted and released, or, if the jury found the party guilty, there is the possibility of appeal. The appellate court may affirm the conviction, or it may reverse and order a retrial. If the appellate procedure has been exhausted and the party has not been acquitted or released, then the party is sentenced to a jail term and/or fines. At this point the judge may see fit to put the person on probation or a suspended sentence or to send the person to jail. If the person goes to jail, he or she can be paroled within a stated period of time or serve out the entire sentence, at which time he or she is released to go back into society.

We often hear the comment that the rise in crime rates is the fault of weak judges and a weak criminal law system. It is true that a system can only be as good as the persons who operate it. We must remember, however, that under our system of law, when a person is charged with a crime, he or she is presumed innocent until proven guilty beyond a reasonable doubt. Let us remember, too, that in most of the cases which go to trial, the crucial decision of guilty or not guilty is made, not by the judge, but by a jury of people selected at random from the community.

CASES FOR DISCUSSION

U.S. v. PARK
421 U.S. 658 (U.S. Supreme Court, 1975)

Chief Justice Burger

Acme Markets, Inc., is a national retail food chain with approximately 36,000 employees, 874 retail outlets, 12 general warehouses, and four special warehouses. Its headquarters, including the office of the president, respondent Park, who is chief executive officer of the corporation, are located in Philadelphia, Pennsylvania. In a five-count information filed in the United States District Court for the District of Maryland, the Government charged Acme and respondent with violations of the Federal Food, Drug, and Cosmetic Act. Each count of the information alleged that the defendants had received food that had been shipped in interstate commerce and that, while the food was being held for sale in Acme's Baltimore warehouse following shipment in interstate commerce, they caused it to be held in a building accessible to rodents and to be exposed to contamination by rodents. These acts were alleged to have resulted in the food being adulterated within the meaning of 21 U.S.C. §§ 342(a) (3) and (4). . . .

Acme pleaded guilty to each count of the infor-

mation. Respondent pleaded not guilty. The evidence at trial demonstrated that in April 1970 the Food and Drug Adminstration (FDA) advised respondent by letter of unsanitary conditions in Acme's Philadelphia warehouse. In 1971 FDA found that similar conditions existed in the firm's Baltimore warehouse. An FDA consumer safety officer testified concerning evidence of rodent infestation and other unsanitary conditions discovered during a 12-day inspection of the Baltimore warehouse in November and December 1971. He also related that a second inspection of the warehouse had been conducted in March 1972. On that occasion the inspectors found that there had been improvement in the sanitary conditions, but that, "there was still evidence of rodent activity in the building and in the warehouse and we found some rodent-contaminated lots of food items."

The Government also presented testimony by the Chief of Compliance of FDA's Baltimore office, who informed respondent by letter of the conditions at the Baltimore warehouse after the first inspection. There was testimony by Acme's Baltimore division vice president, who had responded to the letter on behalf of Acme and respondent and who described the steps taken to remedy the unsanitary conditions discovered by both inspections. The Government's final witness, Acme's vice president for legal affairs and assistant secretary, identified respondent as the president and chief executive officer of the company and read a bylaw prescribing the duties of the chief executive officer. He testified that respondent functioned by delegating "normal operating duties," including sanitation, but that he retained "certain things, which are the big, broad, principles of the operation of the company," and had "the responsibility of seeing that they all work together." . . .

At the close of the Government's case-in-chief, respondent moved for a judgment of acquittal on the ground that the "evidence in chief has shown that Mr. Park is not personally concerned in this Food and Drug violation." The trial judge denied the motion. . . .

Respondent was the only defense witness. He testified that, although all of Acme's employees were in a sense under his general direction, the company had an "organizational structure for responsibilities for certain functions" according to which different phases of its operation were "assigned to individuals who, in turn, have staff and departments under them." He identified those individuals responsible for sanitation and related that upon receipt of the January 1972 FDA letter, he had conferred with the vice president for legal affairs, who informed him that the Baltimore division vice president "was investigating the situation immediately and would be taking corrective action and would be preparing a summary of the corrective action to reply to the letter." Respondent stated that he did not "believe there was anything [he] could have done more constructively than what [he] found was being done." . . .

On cross-examination, respondent conceded that providing sanitary conditions for food offered for sale to the public was something that he was "responsible for in the entire operation of the company," and he stated that it was one of many phases of the company that he assigned to "dependable subordinates." Respondent was asked about and, over the objections of his counsel, admitted receiving, the April 1970 letter addressed to him from FDA regarding unsanitary conditions at Acme's Philadelphia warehouse. He acknowledged that, with the exception of the di-

vision vice president, the same individuals had responsibility for sanitation in both Baltimore and Philadelphia. Finally, in response to questions concerning the Philadelphia and Baltimore incidents, respondent admitted that the Baltimore problem indicated the system for handling sanitation "wasn't working perfectly" and that as Acme's chief executive officer he was responsible for "any result which occurs in our company." . . .

At the close of the evidence, respondent's renewed motion for judgment of acquittal was denied. . . . Respondent's counsel objected to the (jury) instructions on the ground that they failed to reflect our decision in *United States* v. *Dotterweich* . . . and to define "'responsible relationship.'" The trial judge overruled the objection. The jury found respondent guilty on all counts of the information, and he was subsequently sentenced to pay a fine of $50 on each count.

The Court of Appeals reversed the conviction and remanded for a new trial. . . .

We granted certiorari because of an apparent conflict among the courts of appeals with respect to the standard of liability of corporate officers under the Federal Food, Drug, and Cosmetic Act as construed in *United States* v. *Dotterweich* . . . and because of the importance of the question to the Government's enforcement program. We reverse.

The question presented by the Government's petition for certiorari in *United States* v. *Dotterweich* . . . and the focus of this Court's opinion, was whether "the manager of a corporation, as well as the corporation itself, may be prosecuted under the Federal Food, Drug, and Cosmetic Act of 1938 for the introduction of misbranded and adulterated articles into interstate commerce. . . . In *Dotterweich*, a jury had disagreed as to the corporation, a jobber purchasing drugs from manufacturers and shipping them in interstate commerce under its own label, but had convicted Dotterweich, the corporation's president and general manager. The Court of Appeals reversed the conviction on the ground that only the drug dealer, whether corporation or individual, was subject to the criminal provision of the Act, and that where the dealer was a corporation, an individual connected therewith might be held personally only if he was operating the corporation "as his 'alter ego.'" . . .

In reversing the judgment of the Court of Appeals and reinstating Dotterweich's conviction, this Court looked to the purposes of the Act and noted that they "touch phases of the lives and health of people which, in the circumstances of modern industrialism, are largely beyond self-protection." . . . It observed that the Act is of "a now familiar type" which "dispenses with the conventional requirement for criminal conduct—awareness of some wrongdoing. In the interest of the larger good it puts the burden of acting at hazard upon a person otherwise innocent but standing in responsible relation to a public danger." . . .

Central to the Court's conclusion that individuals other than proprietors are subject to the criminal provisions of the act was the reality that "the only way in which a corporation can act is through the individuals who act on its behalf." . . .

The Court recognized that, because the Act dispenses with the need to prove "consciousness of wrongdoing," it may result in hardship even as applied to those who share "a responsibility in the business process resulting in" a violation. It regarded as "too treacherous" an attempt to "to define or even to indicate by way of illustration the class of employees which stands in such a responsible relation." The question of responsibility, the Court said, depends "on the evidence produced at the trial and its submission—assuming the evidence warrants it—to the jury under appropriate guidance." The Court added: "In such matters the good sense of prosecutors, the wise guidance of trial judges, and the ultimate judgment of juries must be trusted." . . .

II

The rule that corporate employees who have "a responsible share in the furtherance of the transaction which the statute outlaws" are subject to the criminal provision of the Act was not formulated in a vacuum. . . . [T]he principle had been recognized that a corporate agent, through whose act, default, or omission the corporation committed a crime, was himself guilty individually of that crime. The principle has been applied whether or not the crime required "consciousness of wrongdoing," and it has been applied not only to those corporate agents who themselves committed the criminal act, but also to those who by virtue of their managerial positions or other similar relations to the act could be deemed responsible for its commission. . . .

Thus, *Dotterweich* and the cases which have followed reveal that in providing sanctions which reach and touch the individuals who execute the corporate mission—and this is by no means necessarily confined to a single corporate agent or employee—the Act imposes not only a positive duty to seek out and remedy violations when they occur but also, and primarily, a duty to implement measures that will insure that violations will not occur. The requirements of foresight and vigilance imposed on responsible corporate agents are beyond question demanding, and perhaps onerous, but they are no more stringent than the public has a right to expect from those who voluntarily assume positions of authority in business enterprises whose services and products affect the health and well-being of the public that supports them. . . .

III

Reading the entire charge satisfied us that the jury's attention was adequately focused on the issue of respondent's authority with respect to the conditions that formed the basis of the alleged violations. Viewed as a whole, the charge did not permit the jury to find guilt solely on the basis of respondent's position in the corporation; rather, it fairly advised the jury that to find guilt it must find respondent "had a responsible relation to the situation" and "by virtue of his position . . . had authority and responsibility" to deal with the situation. The situation referred to could only be "food . . . held in unsanitary conditions in a

71

warehouse with the result that it consisted, in part, of filth or . . . may have been contaminated with filth."

MIRANDA v. STATE OF ARIZONA

86 S. Ct. 1602 (U.S. Supreme Court, 1966)

Chief Justice Warren

The cases before us raise questions which go to the roots of our concepts of American criminal jurisprudence: the restraints society must observe consistent with the Federal Constitution in prosecuting individuals for crime. More specifically, we deal with the admissibility of statements obtained from an individual who is subjected to custodial police interrogation and the necessity for procedures which assure that the individual is accorded his privilege under the Fifth Amendment to the Constitution not to be compelled to incriminate himself.

We dealt with certain phases of this problem recently in *Escobedo* v. *State of Illinois.* . . . There, as in the four cases before us, law enforcement officials took the defendant into custody and interrogated him in a police station for the purpose of obtaining a confession. The police did not effectively advise him of his right to remain silent or of his right to consult with his attorney. . . . During this interrogation, the police denied his request to speak to his attorney, and they prevented his retained attorney, who had come to the police station, from consulting with him. At his trial, the State, over his objection, introduced the confession against him. We held that the statements thus made were constitutionally inadmissible.

* * * * *

We start here, as we did in *Escobedo*, with the premise that our holding is not an innovation in our jurisprudence, but is an application of principles long recognized and applied in other settings. We have undertaken a thorough re-examination of the *Escobedo* decision and the principles it announced, and we reaffirm it. That case was but

72

an explication of basic rights that are enshrined in our Constitution—that "No person . . . shall be compelled in any criminal case to be a witness against himself," and that "the accused shall . . . have the Assistance of Counsel"—rights which were put in jeopardy in that case through official overbearing.

* * * * *

Our holding . . . is this: the prosecution may not use statements, whether exculpatory or inculpatory, stemming from custodial interrogation of the defendant unless it demonstrates the use of procedural safeguards effective to secure the privilege against self-incrimination. By custodial interrogation, we mean questioning initiated by law enforcement officers after a person has been taken into custody or otherwise deprived of his freedom of action in any significant way. As for the procedural safeguards to be employed, unless other fully effective means are devised to inform accused persons of their right of silence and to assure a continuous opportunity to exercise it, the following measures are required. Prior to any questioning, the person must be warned that any statement he does make may be used as evidence against him, and that he has a right to the presence of an attorney, either retained or appointed. The defendant may waive effectuation of these rights, provided the waiver is made voluntarily, knowingly and intelligently. If, however, he indicates in any manner and at any stage of the process that he wishes to consult with an attorney before speaking, there can be no questioning. Likewise, if the individual is alone and indicates in any manner that he does not wish to be interrogated, the police may not question him. The mere fact that he may have answered some questions or volunteered some statements on his own does not deprive him of the right to refrain from answering any further inquiries until he has consulted with an attorney and thereafter consents to be questioned.

* * * * *

Today . . there can be no doubt that the Fifth Amendment privilege is available outside of criminal court proceedings and serves to protect persons in all settings in which their freedom of action is curtailed in any significant way from being compelled to incriminate themselves. We have concluded that without proper safeguards the process of in-custody interrogation of persons suspected or accused of crime contains inherently compelling pressures which work to undermine the individual's will to resist and to compel him to speak where he would not otherwise do so freely. In order to combat these pressures and to permit a full opportunity to exercise the privilege against self-incrimination, the accused must be adequately and effectively apprised of his rights and the exercise of those rights must be fully honored.

It is impossible for us to foresee the potential alternatives for protecting the privilege which might be devised by Congress or the States in the exercise of their creative rule-making capacities. Therefore, we cannot say that the Constitution necessarily requires adherence to any particular solution for the inherent compulsions of the interrogation process as it is presently conducted. Our decision in no way creates a constitutional straitjacket which will handicap sound efforts at reform, nor is it intended to have this effect. We encourage Congress and the States to continue their laudable search for increasingly effective ways of protecting the right of the individual while promoting efficient enforcement of our criminal laws. . . .

* * * * *

The Fifth Amendment privilege is so fundamental to our system of constitutional rule and the expedient of giving an adequate warning as to the availability of the privilege so simple, we will not pause to inquire in individual cases whether the defendant was aware of his rights without a warning being given. . . .

The warning of the right to remain silent must be accompanied by the explanation that anything said can and will be used against the individual in court. This warning is needed in order to make him aware not only of the privilege, but also of the consequences of foregoing it. It is only

through an awareness of these consequences that there can be any assurance of real understanding and intelligent exercise of the privilege. Moreover, this warning may serve to make the individual more acutely aware that he is faced with a phase of the adversary system—that he is not in the presence of persons acting solely in his interest.

The circumstances surrounding in-custody interrogation can operate very quickly to overbear the will of one merely made aware of his privilege by his interrogators. Therefore, the right to have counsel present at the interrogation is indispensable to the protection of the Fifth Amendment privilege under the system we delineate today. Our aim is to assure that the individual's right to choose between silence and speech remains unfettered throughout the interrogation process. A once-stated warning, delivered by those who will conduct the interrogation, cannot itself suffice to that end among those who most require knowledge of their rights. A mere warning given by the interrogators is not alone sufficient to accomplish that end.

* * * * *

Accordingly, we hold that an individual held for interrogation must be clearly informed that he has the right to consult with a lawyer and to have the lawyer with him during interrogation under the system for protecting the privilege we delineate today. As with the warnings of the right to remain silent and that anything stated can be used in evidence against him, this warning is an absolute prerequisite to interrogation. No amount of circumstantial evidence that the person may have been aware of this right will suffice to stand in its stead. Only through such a warning is there ascertainable assurance that the accused was aware of his right.

* * * * *

In order fully to apprise a person interrogated of the extent of his rights under this system then, it is necessary to warn him not only that he has the right to consult with an attorney, but also that if he is indigent a lawyer will be appointed to represent him. Without this additional warning, the admonition of the right to consult with counsel would often be understood as meaning only that he can consult with a lawyer if he has one or has the funds to obtain one. The warning of a right to counsel would be hollow if not couched in terms that would convey to the indigent—the person most often subjected to interrogation—the knowledge that he too has a right to have counsel present.

* * * * *

Our decision is not intended to hamper the traditional function of police officers in investigating crime. . . . When an individual is in custody on probable cause, the police may, of course, seek out evidence in the field to be used at trial against him. Such investigation may include inquiry of persons not under restraint. General on-the-scene questioning as to facts surrounding a crime or other general questioning of citizens in the fact-finding process is not affected by our holding.

* * * * *

In dealing with statements obtained through interrogation, we do not purport to find all confessions inadmissible. Confessions remain a proper element in law enforcement. Any statement given freely and voluntarily without any compelling influences is, of course, admissible in evidence. The fundamental import of the privilege while an individual is in custody is not whether he is allowed to talk to the police without the benefit of warnings and counsel, but whether he can be interrogated. There is no requirement that police stop a person who enters a police station and states that he wishes to confess to a crime, or a person who calls the police to offer a confession or any other statment he desires to make. Volunteered statements of any kind are not barred by the Fifth Amendment and their admissibility is not affected by our holding today. . . .

Because of the nature of the problem and because of its recurrent significance in numerous cases, we have to this point discussed the relationship of the Fifth Amendment privilege to po-

lice interrogation without specific concentration on the facts of the cases before us. . . . In each instance, we have concluded that statements were obtained from the defendant under circumstances that did not meet constitutional standards for protection of the privilege.

SHEPPARD v. MAXWELL, WARDEN
86 S. Ct. 1507 (U.S. Supreme Court, 1966)

Sheppard was arrested, tried, and convicted of murdering his wife. The trial was held in the common pleas court of Cuyahoga County, Ohio. Sheppard's conviction was affirmed by the Supreme Court of Ohio. Sheppard filed a petition for habeas corpus in U.S. district court against the prison warden, seeking release from custody. His contention was that he was denied a fair trial because the trial judge failed to protect him from inherently prejudicial publicity which saturated the community and also because the judge allowed extensive newspaper, radio, and television coverage of his trial in the courtroom itself. The district court ruled in favor, of the petition for habeas corpus; the U.S. court of appeals reversed; and the Supreme Court of the United States granted certiorari.

Justice Clark

This federal habeas corpus application involves the question of whether Sheppard was deprived of a fair trial in his state conviction for the second-degree murder of his wife because of the trial judge's failure to protect Sheppard sufficiently from the massive, pervasive, and prejudicial publicity that attended his prosecution. The United States District Court held that he was not afforded a fair trial and granted the writ subject to the State's right to put Sheppard to trial again. . . . The Court of Appeals for the Sixth Circuit reversed by a divided vote. . . . We have concluded that Sheppard did not receive a fair trial consistent with the Due Process Clause of the 14th Amendment and, therefore, reverse the judgment.

Marilyn Sheppard, petitioner's pregnant wife, was bludgeoned to death in the upstairs bedroom of their lakeshore home in Bay Village, Ohio, a suburb of Cleveland.

* * * * *

On July 7, the day of Marilyn Sheppard's funeral, a newspaper story appeared in which Assistant County Attorney Mahon—later the chief prosecutor of Sheppard—sharply criticized the refusal of the Sheppard family to permit his immediate questioning. From there on, headline stories repeatedly stressed Sheppard's lack of cooperation with the police and other officials. . . . The newspapers also played up Sheppard's refusal to take a lie detector test and "the protective ring" thrown up by his family. Front-page newpaper headlines announced on the same day the "Doctor Balks At Lie Test; Retells Story." . . .

* * * * *

On the 20th, the "editorial artillery" opened fire with a front-page charge that somebody is "getting away with murder." The editorial attributed the ineptness of the investigation to "friendships, relationships, hired lawyers, a husband who ought to have been subjected instantly to the same third-degree to which any other person under similar circumstances is subjected. . . ." The following day, July 21, another page-one editorial was headed: "Why No Inquest? Do It Now, Dr. Gerber." The Coroner called an inquest the same day and subpoenaed Sheppard. It was staged the next day in a school gymnasium; the Coroner presided with the County Prosecutor as his advisor and two detectives as bailiffs. In the front of the room was a long table occupied by reporters, television and radio personnel, and broadcasting equipment. The hearing was broadcast with live microphones placed at the Coroner's seat and the witness stand. A swarm of reporters and photographers attended. Sheppard was brought into the room by police who searched him in full view of several hundred spectators. Sheppard's counsel were present during the three-day inquest but were not permitted to participate. When Sheppard's chief counsel attempted to place some documents in the record, he was forcibly ejected from the room by the

Coroner, who received cheers, hugs, and kisses from ladies in the audience.

* * * * *

With this background the case came on for trial two weeks before the November general election at which the . . . trial judge . . was a candidate to succeed himself. Twenty-five days before the case was set, 75 veniremen were called as prospective jurors. All three Cleveland newspapers published the names and addresses of the veniremen. As a consequence, anonymous letters and telephone calls, as well as calls from friends, regarding the impending prosecution were received by all of the prospective jurors. The selection of the jury began on October 18, 1954.

The courtroom in which the trial was held measured 26 by 48 feet. A long temporary table was set up inside the bar, in back of the single counsel table. It ran the width of the courtroom, parallel to the bar railing, with one end less than three feet from the jury box. Approximately 20 representatives of newspapers and wire services were assigned seats at this table by the court. Behind the bar railing there were four rows of benches. These seats were likewise assigned by the court for the entire trial. The first row was occupied by representatives of television and radio stations, and the second and third rows by reporters from out-of-town newspapers and magazines. . . . Representatives of the news media also used all the rooms on the courtroom floor, including the room where cases were ordinarily called and assigned for trial. Private telephone lines and telegraphic equipment were installed in these rooms so that reports from the trial could be speeded to the papers. . . .

* * * * *

The principle that justice cannot survive behind walls of silence has long been reflected in the "Anglo-American distrust for secret trials." . . . A responsible press has always been regarded as the handmaiden of effective judicial administration, especially in the criminal field. Its function in this regard is documented by an impressive record of service over several centuries. The press does not simply publish information about trials but guards against the miscarriage of justice by subjecting the police, prosecutors, and judicial processes to extensive public scrutiny and criticism. This Court has, therefore, been unwilling to place any direct limitations on the freedom traditionally exercised by the news media for "[w]hat transpires in the court room is public property." . . . The unqualified prohibitions laid down by the framers were intended to give to liberty of the press. . . . the broadest scope that could be countenanced in an orderly society." . . . And where there was "no threat or menace to the integrity of the trial," we have consistently required that the press have a free hand, even though we sometimes deplored its sensationalism.

But the Court has also pointed out that "[l]egal trials are not like elections, to be won through the use of the meeting-hall, the radio, and the newspaper." . . . And the Court has insisted that no one be punished for a crime without "a charge fairly made and fairly tried in a public tribunal free of prejudice, passion, excitement, and tyrannical power." . . . Freedom of discussion should be given the widest range compatible with the essential requirement of the fair and orderly administration of justice." . . . But it must not be allowed to divert the trial from the "very purpose of a court system . . . to adjudicate controversies, both criminal and civil, in the calmness and solemnity of the courtroom according to legal procedures." . . . Among these "legal procedures" is the requirement that the jury's verdict be based on evidence received in open court, not from outside sources. Thus, in *Marshall* v. *United States,* . . . we set aside a federal conviction where the jurors were exposed "through news accounts" to information that was not admitted at trial. We held that the prejudice from such material "may indeed be greater" than when it is part of the prosecution's evidence "for it is then not tempered by protective procedures." . . .

* * * * *

While we cannot say that Sheppard was denied due process by the judge's refusal to take precautions against the influence of pretrial publicity alone, the court's later rulings must be con-

sidered against the setting in which the trial was held. In light of this background, we believe that the arrangements made by the judge with the news media caused Sheppard to be deprived of that "judicial serenity and calm to which [he] was entitled." . . . The fact is that bedlam reigned at the courthouse during the trial and newsmen took over practically the entire courtroom, hounding most of the participants in the trial, especially Sheppard. At a temporary table within a few feet of the jury box and counsel table sat some 20 reporters staring at Sheppard and taking notes. The erection of a press table for reporters inside the bar is unprecedented. The bar of the court is reserved for counsel, providing them a safe place in which to keep papers and exhibits, and to confer privately with client and co-counsel. It is designed to protect the witness and the jury from any distractions, intrusions, or influences, and to permit bench discussions of the judge's rulings away from the hearing of the public and the jury. Having assigned almost all of the available seats in the courtroom to the news media, the judge lost his ability to supervise that environment. The movement of the reporters in and out of the courtroom caused frequent confusion and disruption of the trial. And the record reveals constant commotion within the bar. Moreover, the judge gave the throng of newsmen gathered in the corridors of the courthouse absolute free rein. Participants in the trial, including the jury, were forced to run a gantlet of reporters and photographers each time they entered or left the courtroom. The total lack of consideration for the privacy of the jury was demonstrated by the assignment to the broadcasting station of space next to the jury room on the floor above the courtroom, as well as the fact that jurors were allowed to make telephone calls during their five-day deliberation.

There can be no question about the nature of the publicity which surrounded Sheppard's trial. We agree, as did the Court of Appeals, with the findings in Judge Bell's opinion for the Ohio Supreme Court:

Murder and mystery, society, sex and suspense were combined in this case in such a manner as to intrigue and captivate the public fancy to a degree per-haps unparalleled in recent annals. Throughout the preindictment investigation, the subsequent legal skirmishes and the nine-week trial, circulation-conscious editors catered to the insatiable interest to the American public in the bizarre. . . . In this atmosphere of a "Roman Holiday" for the news media, Sam Sheppard stood trial for his life. . . .

Indeed, every court that has considered this case, save the court that tried it, has deplored the manner in which the news media inflamed and prejudiced the public.

Since the state trial judge did not fulfill his duty to protect Sheppard from the inherently prejudicial publicity which saturated the community and to control disruptive influences in the courtroom, we must reverse the denial of the habeas petition. The case is remanded to the District Court with instructions to issue the writ and order that Sheppard be released from custody unless the State puts him to its charges again within a reasonable time.

It is so ordered.

* * * * *

REVIEW QUESTIONS AND PROBLEMS FOR DISCUSSION

1. What is a white-collar crime?
2. How does a crime differ from a tort?
3. How does a felony differ from a misdemeanor?
4. What is a Miranda-type warning? When is it given?
5. When can a child be capable of committing a crime?
6. What types of documents can be the subject of forgery?
7. On what basis have accountants been held criminally liable?
8. What is plea bargaining?
9. What happens at an arraignment hearing?
10. What is the constitutional guarantee against double jeopardy?
11. Acting on a tip from an informant, two police officers went to Boscoe's home while he was at school. They identified themselves and explained that they had a tip that Boscoe had been taking dangerous weapons to school. They asked Boscoe's mother if they could search his room. She let them do so, and they found a zip gun and a switchblade. Possession of either of these items is a crime under state law. If Boscoe is prosecuted, can he ask that the evidence be thrown out because the search was unlawful? Discuss. Would it make any difference how old Boscoe was?
12. Francien was a student at Vermont State University (VSU). She received two tickets on her car windshield on October 6, one for parking in a restricted area and one for failing to register the car with the university, as required by university regulations. The tickets stated that the fines would be doubled if not paid within one week. She also testified that a "wheel lock" was put on her car so that she could not move the vehicle without contacting the university police. The VSU Traffic Appeals Committee upheld the validity of the tickets. Francien now sues in district court, alleging that the VSU procedures for issuing and enforcing tickets violate her rights to due process of law. Does she have a case? Discuss.
13. Smoot was a student at Vixberg High School. The school officials were concerned about what they perceived as the widespread use of marijuana by the students, so they asked the city police for assistance. The city police came to the high school with a dog which had been trained to "sniff out" the scent of marijuana. The dog indicated that there was marijuana in Smoot's locker. When the locker was opened

by the school officials, marijuana was found there. If Smoot is prosecuted, can he claim that the use of the dog constituted an illegal search and seizure of the evidence? Discuss.

14. The Uniform Code of Military Justice provides for trial by court-martial where crimes are charged against civilians who accompany U.S. military personnel overseas, where the foreign nation has agreed to such a procedure. Marice killed her husband, a U.S. Army corporal, at a base in France. She was tried by a military tribunal composed of U.S. service personnel and sentenced to 90 years in prison. Marice claims that she was unconstitutionally deprived of her right to trial by jury. Does she have a valid claim. Discuss.

15. Weeks was driving his pickup truck in Idaho when he was involved in a collision with a car. The driver of the car was killed, and Weeks was seriously injured. Police officers found a pint of whiskey, almost empty, in the glove box of the pickup truck. Weeks was taken to a hospital, where the smell of whiskey was detected on his breath. While he was still unconscious, a blood sample was taken. Laboratory analysis showed that Weeks' blood contained about 0.17 percent alcohol. Weeks was charged with involuntary manslaughter, and the blood sample was used as evidence that he had been driving under the influence of liquor. On appeal, Weeks contends that the seizure of the whiskey bottle and the taking of the blood sample violated his due process rights. How should the court rule? Discuss.

16. Hogg was charged with having robbed three men who were together in a tavern at the time of the robbery. He was acquitted by a jury. The state then charged Hogg with having robbed a fourth man who was also in the group at the tavern. This time, Hogg was found guilty by the jury. On appeal, Hogg says that the second prosecution violated his due process rights. How should the court rule? Discuss.

Tort Law and Business | 4

Today more than ever the business manager must be concerned about the law of torts and business. The general public is becoming more knowledgeable about its legal rights, and incidents that might not have resulted in a lawsuit a few years ago may very well be litigated today.

WHAT IS A TORT?

A tort is a civil wrong committed when one individual, having a legal duty not to invade the legal rights of another individual, breaches that legal duty and invades the legal rights of another individual, causing damage to the person, property, or reputation of that individual. The person whose rights have been invaded and who has suffered damage may then bring action in a civil court to recover monetary damages suffered because of the invasion of his or her rights. These rights and duties may be derived from statutory or common law. When we speak of an individual we mean a legal individual, such as a corporation, as well as a natural individual, the human being.

A tort may also be a crime. For example, a drunken driver runs a red light and hits your car in the intersection. You have a cause of action in tort against the drunken driver for your property damage and personal injury. The drunken driver may also be prosecuted criminally for driving a motor vehicle under the influence of intoxicating beverages. Most nonintentional torts, however, are not crimes.

Also, a tortious civil wrong must be distinguished from a contractual civil wrong, where the rights and duties arise out of a specific contractual agreement. In a tort the rights and duties are imposed by general laws which apply to others under similar circumstances, such as traffic laws and general laws of negligence.

CLASSIFICATION OF TORTS

Torts can be classified into three general categories. First, there are intentional torts. These are wrongs which the wrongdoers intended to commit. Second, there are negligent torts. These are wrongs which the wrongdoers did not mean to commit. They simply failed to act as ordinary prudent reasonable persons would have acted under similar circumstances. For example, in the typical automobile accident, the driver of the automobile does not mean to strike another automobile and damage it or to damage his or her own automobile. He or she was simply not careful and was not acting as a reasonable and prudent person. Third, there are strict liability torts. This classification comprises situations in which the law finds that the person or persons committing the torts are "strictly liable," meaning that there is no need for the plaintiff to prove negligence on the part of the defendant. The defendant is simply liable, as a matter of law, for the harmful results caused.

INTENTIONAL TORTS

An intentional tort is an intentional breach of one's legal duty to another person, which breach of duty invades that person's rights and causes physical or mental damage to that person or damage to that person's reputation or property.

Intentional torts can be subdivided into three categories: torts against the physical person, torts against the reputation of the person, and torts against the property of the person. Following are some of the common torts against the physical person.

Torts against the Physical Person

Assault. An assault is an intentional act by one person which causes another person to be in immediate apprehension for his or her safety. Apprehension does not necessarily mean fear, since fear is a very subjective term. Some persons may be in apprehension for their safety without actually being frightened, whereas other persons may be frightened without justifiable cause. Courts have held that mere words are not sufficient to prove a case of assault, even if the words are provoking or insulting. Also, threats of future injury are not the basis for assault. In order to prove a case of assault, it must be shown that the defendant committed a specific act or acts which put the plaintiff in apprehension for his or her immediate safety, not simply his or her future safety. Although the tort of assault is classified as an intentional tort, it is not necessary to prove that the defendant actually intended to harm the plaintiff. It is sufficient to show that a reasonable person under the circumstances would have been in apprehension for his or her safety.

The following case is an example of an assault with an unloaded gun.

Allen v. *Hannaford*
244 p. 700 (Washington, 1926)

FACTS   The plaintiff was a tenant in the defendant's apartment house, and the plaintiff was in the process of moving her furniture out of the apartment when the defendant appeared on the scene with a pistol. He threatened her and told her not to move anything out as he had a lien on the goods because of the unpaid rents. The gun was unloaded, but the plaintiff didn't know that. The plaintiff sued for assault. The verdict was rendered for the plaintiff, and the defendant appealed.

ISSUE   Since the defendant meant no actual harm and the gun was unloaded, was this actually an assault?

DECISION   Yes. Verdict affirmed.

REASONS   Justice Mair said that it doesn't matter whether the gun was loaded or not loaded. Nor does the intent of the person holding the gun matter. The law simply looks to see whether the person threatened was in apprehension or in fear of harmful or offensive conduct. The court quoted from the opinion in a previous case, *Beach* v. *Hancock*, 27 N.H. 223, saying:

"One of the most important objects to be attained by the enactment of laws and the institutions of civilized society is, each of us shall feel secure against unlawful assaults. Without such security society loses most of its value. Peace and order and domestic happiness, inexpressibly more precious than mere forms of government, cannot be enjoyed without the sense of perfect security. We have a right to live in society without being put in fear of personal harm. But it must be a reasonable fear of which we complain. And it surely is not unreasonable for a person to entertain a fear of personal injury, when a pistol is pointed at him in a threatening manner, when, for aught he knows, it may be loaded, and may occasion his immediate death. The business of the world could not be carried on with comfort, if such things could be done with impunity."

Then the Washington court went on to say:

"Whether there is an assault in a given case depends more upon the apprehensions created in the mind of the person assaulted than upon what may be the secret intentions of the person committing the assault."

Assault can also be a crime. In the foregoing case the crime would be assault with a deadly weapon.

Battery.   Battery is the intentional contact or touching of another person without that person's permission and without legal justification. The contact or touching must cause injury. It is not necessary that there be a specific intent to cause harm. Nor is it necessary that the contact be directly with the person. For example, the tort of battery is committed if one person puts in motion an object which strikes another person, say, by shooting a gun or throwing a knife, or if one person strikes another person with an object in hand.

Not all touching or contact is considered battery. For example, people are often bumped, pushed, and jostled when they walk through the crowded aisles of department stores or walk out of crowded sports stadiums. Here there is physical contact and touching by other persons which may cause discomfort and which may be offensive. From a legal standpoint, however, these are not considered batteries because there is an implied consent to such "touching."

Technical Battery.   When we defined the tort of battery we stated that it was the intentional contact or touching of another person without that person's permission. A technical battery occurs when the person gives consent to physical contact of one sort and then a different kind of contact occurs, or the terms of the consent are exceeded. Damages may be claimed under this theory against a surgeon who performs "extra" surgical procedures while the patient is under anesthesia. In the absence of some sort of emergency, the surgeon's act is tortious and the patient could recover damages. This is a very different kind of liability than that in a malpractice action, in which the claim is that the physician did not perform the agreed treatment or procedure in accordance with reasonable professional standards.

Intentional Infliction of Mental Distress. Courts in the various states are now recognizing the intentional infliction of emotional or mental distress as a tort, without the necessity of showing either physical injury or a threat of physical contact, such as one would find in the torts of assault and battery. The tort of intentional infliction of emotional or mental distress is an entirely separate tort from the torts of assault and battery. This tort may be defined as an act or the use of words by a person with the intent of causing another person to experience anxiety, fright, terror, or some other form of emotional and mental distress.

Historically, the courts have discouraged and denied claims for emotional and mental distress unless the person had also suffered some accompanying physical injury. They thought that allowing claims for mental or emotional distress would encourage fictitious claims. Physical injury can be verified by X ray and visual appearance. Emotional and mental distress is a very subjective claim, and until recently such injuries often could not be objectively verified. However, advances in medical science have given us more accurate methods of measuring and verifying such injuries.

The courts are still concerned about the potential for misuse of this particular tort. Generally, courts have held that in order to have recovery, it must be shown that the mental distress or disturbance is real and not simply an annoyance or hurt feelings or something of that nature. Actual mental injury must be shown. The courts also require that before one can recover for this tort, it must be shown that the conduct of the defendant has been outrageous in character and generally of a type which is intolerable in a civilized community.

False Imprisonment. False imprisonment can be defined as the intentional detention of a person without that person's permission. It is not necessary that there be actual physical detention. However, the courts have required that the detained person be detained by at least a threat of force, either expressed or implied. Also, the detention must be for more than a reasonable time.

The following case illustrates a typical false imprisonment case. The majority of false imprisonment cases arise from the detention of persons accused of shoplifting.

Southwest Drug Stores of Mississippi, Inc. v. Garner
195 So.2d 837 (Mississippi, 1967)

FACTS   Mrs. Garner went into a drug store to buy some soap. She left her father, who was ill, in her car in the parking lot in front of the store. She found the bar of soap she wanted, took it to the cashier, paid for it, and received a sales ticket. The cashier put the soap in a small bag. Mrs. Garner's sister had come to the store with her and had not finished shopping, so Mrs. Garner said that she thought she should go out to the car and check to see if their father was all right and that she would take some of the sister's packages with her to the car. She walked out of the store, but before she got to her car, the manager of the store yelled out at her, telling her to stop and accused her of stealing the bar of soap. She denied it, but he told her she would have to go back into the store with him to prove that she hadn't stolen the soap. There were a number of people in the parking lot who heard the manager's loud and rude accusations. When the manager and Mrs. Garner got back to the store, the cashier verified that Mrs. Garner had paid for the soap. Mrs. Garner was then released. She became ill and distressed as a result of the incident. She required medical treatment for her distress.

The Mississippi law allows a merchant or any employee of the merchant to stop a person and question that person if the merchant or the employee has reasonable grounds to believe that the person is committing or attempting to commit the crime of shoplifting. Mrs. Garner sued Southwest Drug Stores for false imprisonment and slander, and a verdict was rendered in her favor in the lower court. The defendant, Southwest Drug Stores, appealed.

ISSUE   Is Southwest Drug Stores of Mississippi, Inc., liable to the plaintiff for slander and false imprisonment in view of the fact that the law allows a merchant or employee to question a person suspected of shoplifting?

DECISION   Yes. Judgment of the lower court affirmed.

REASON   Justice Inzer found that the law did permit the merchant or his employee to question a person suspected of attempting or committing a crime of shoplifting. In this case the manager of the drugstore overstepped the bounds of privilege when he went out into the parking lot and yelled in a rude and loud manner, accusing the plaintiff of stealing and also coercing her to return to the drugstore. Thus the law would allow the manager to stop a person suspected of shoplifting and to question the person politely and quietly, and in such a situation the manager and the establishment would not be guilty of imprisonment or slander.

"[I]nstead of making inquiry in a reasonable manner, he accused Mrs. Garner of stealing a bar of soap. When he did so he exceeded the qualified privilege. In order for a communication to be privileged the person making it must be careful to go no further than his interest or duties require. . . .

"Whether privilege is available as a defense may depend on the manner in which the communication is made. The protection of a qualified privilege may be lost by the manner of its exercise, although belief in the truth of the charge exists."

False Arrest.   False arrest is similar to false imprisonment in that it is the intentional detention of an individual without that person's permission. In the case of false arrest the detention is imposed under an asserted legal authority. If, in fact, the person making the arrest does not have proper legal authority to do so, then we would have the tort of false arrest. In the case of false arrest, as in the case of false imprisonment, it is not necessary that the person detaining the suspect use force. For example, a person dressed in a police uniform with a badge indicating authority states to you: "You are under arrest. I am taking you to the police station." Most people would go along peacefully rather than resist arrest. If, in fact, there was no reasonable ground, no probable cause, to believe that you had committed a specific crime, then you were wrongfully deprived of your freedom and you would have an action for false arrest and false imprisonment.

Torts against the Reputation of the Person

Next we come to intentional torts which injure the person's reputation. These are often classified as defamation of character.

Libel and Slander.   Libel and slander are both torts involving intentional defamation of character by the tort-feasor. Libel is defamation of character which can be read or seen, and slander is defamation of character which can be heard. In both libel and slander cases it must be proven that a defamatory statement or defamatory material was published. In the case of libel, this means that the defamatory material was published in a book, magazine, or newspaper or in the form of a movie, pictures, a statue, or some other physical form whereby the material came into the hands of a person or persons other than the person about whom the material was published. If you write a personal letter to an individual and make defamatory statements about the individual in that letter, this does not constitute publication, since no one other than the individual to whom you are writing is intended to see the letter. In the case of slander, publication means that the statement was heard by someone other than the person whom the defamatory statement or material was about. Thus the simple test in slander and libel cases is: Did anyone other than the subject of the defamatory statement or material hear, read, or see the statement or material? If no third person heard, read, or saw the statement or material, then there is no slander or libel. If a third person did hear the defamatory statement or read or see the defamatory material, then we have a potential lawsuit for defamation of character.

The next issue is the truth of the defamatory statement or material. Generally speaking, truth is a defense to slander or libel. The exception is a situation where the party publishing the defamatory statement or material is doing so with a malicious intent to injure the other party. This is called a technical tort. An example of this would be the publication of the fact that a person now well established in society committed a crime while a teenager. Let's say that as a teenager the person stole an automobile and took it for a joyride, was arrested and convicted, and paid his or her debt to society. Then, some years later, after the person had established a good reputation in society, someone found out about this skeleton in the closet and published the information with the sole purpose of maligning the person's character. Here, even though the statement is true, it was obviously made for malicious purposes, and thus there would be a right of action for this defamation of character.

There are also cases where defamatory statements may be either absolutely privileged or conditionally privileged. Lawyers and judges may not be sued for slander for the statements made by them during the trial of a lawsuit. Also, if a member of Congress makes a defamatory statement on the floor of Congress, the congressman may not be held liable for the statement. There is also a different standard with regard to slander and libel when the statement is made about a public official or a public figure, rather than a private individual. The following case set the precedent with regard to liability for defamatory statements about public officials.

New York Times Co. v. Sullivan
376 U.S. 254 (U.S. Supreme Court, 1964)

FACTS Sullivan was an elected official in the state of Alabama. The New York Times published an editorial advertisement which stated that Mr. Sullivan and others were engaged in a "wave of terror" against Negroes. The advertisement encouraged readers to contribute funds to help Negroes in a fight for their constitutional rights. Sullivan claimed that the advertisement contained false and defamatory statements about him. The jury gave Sullivan a verdict in the amount of $500,000. The case was appealed to the Supreme Court of Alabama, which affirmed the decision of the lower court. The defendant then petitioned for a writ of certiorari to the Supreme Court of the United States, and the Supreme Court granted certiorari.

ISSUE Does the First Amendment right of freedom of the press protect the New York Times Company from a libel suit where statements are made about a public official?

DECISION Yes. The Supreme Court of the United States reversed the decision of the lower court.

REASONS The plaintiff in this case was a public official. As a public official, he was a person of public interest and concern. The things he said and the things he did were of public interest and concern.

Justice Brennan stated:

"[W]e consider this case against the background of a profound national commitment to the principle that debate on public issues should be uninhibited, robust, and wide-open, and that it may well include vehement, caustic, and sometimes unpleasantly sharp attacks on government and public officials. . . . The present advertisement, as an expression of grievance and protest on one of the major public issues of our time, would seem clearly to qualify for the constitutional protection. The question is whether it forfeits that protection by the falsity of some of its factual statements and by its alleged defamation of respondent.

Authoritative interpretations of the First Amendment guarantees have consistently refused to recognize an exception for any test of truth—whether administered by judges, juries, or administrative officials—and especially one that puts the burden of proving truth on the speaker. . . . The constitutional protection does not turn upon "the truth, popularity, or social utility of the ideas and beliefs which are offered." . . . As Madison said, "Some degree of abuse is inseparable from the proper use of every thing; and in no instance is this more true than in that of the press." . . . [E]rroneous statement is inevitable in free debate, and . . . it must be protected if the freedoms of expression are to have the "breathing space" that they "need . . . to survive." . . .

The constitutional guarantees require, we think, a federal rule that prohibits a public official from recovering damages for a defamatory falsehood relating to his official conduct unless he proves that the statement was made with "actual malice"—that is, with knowledge that it was false or with reckless disregard of whether it was false or not."

Invasion of Privacy. The area of individual privacy has been very highly publicized in recent years, and several state and national statutes have been passed concerning the individual's right to privacy. These new laws are primarily concerned with invasion of privacy by the computer with regard to credit records and bank records which contain sensitive information about individuals.

In 1970 the Congress of the United States passed the Fair Credit Reporting Act. This gave the consumer the right to see the credit file compiled on him or her and to correct or explain any misleading or incorrect information. The law also generally limited access to the individual's credit record to the persons to whom or the companies to which the individual had applied for credit, insurance, or employment.

In 1974 the Congress passed the Privacy Act. This act gave the individual access to records concerning himself or herself, restricted the use of the social security number as a universal identifier, and placed many restrictions on the record keeping of national agencies and the handling of their records. The act also established the Federal Privacy Protection Study Commission to study and make recommendations on data banks and information processing programs which might affect individual privacy both in the public sector and the private sector.

In 1974 the U.S. Congress also passed the Family Educational Rights and Privacy Act, which allowed the student and/or the parents, depending on particular situations, to inspect and review and secure copies of the student's educational record to ensure its accuracy. The act made provision for the correction, deletion, and explanation of incorrect or misleading information. It also provided that the university shall not allow access to confidential information about the student without permission of the student or the parent, depending on the student's age.

In 1974 Congress also created a National Commission on Electronic Fund Transfers which was to look into possible invasions of privacy as well as other aspects of the new cashless society created by electronic fund transfers.

Several states have enacted privacy statutes, and other states have established commissions to study the privacy problems of public sector and private sector record keeping and handling.

In addition to the current concern about invasion of privacy by the computer and various electronic data processing procedures, there has been a concern about many more traditional invasions of the individual's privacy. One of the most common of these invasions of privacy is eavesdropping by wiretapping or other electronic devices. Such eavesdropping is a national crime as well as a tort, and it is prohibited except in the rare cases where it has been authorized by national statutory law. Another invasion of privacy is the use of a person's photograph under objectionable circumstances. Simply turning the television camera and taking pictures of the persons in the bleachers at a baseball game is not an invasion of privacy. However, if someone takes an embarrassing picture of you and uses it without your permission, you may have an action for invasion of privacy.

Similarly, a persons' picture may not be used for commercial purposes without his or her specific consent. For example, a street photographer snaps your picture and a few days later you see the picture in a newspaper advertisement for some product. You do not need to prove any specific monetary damage for such an invasion of your privacy. A jury may award nominal damages or whatever damages it feels are fair and just.

As with libel and slander, we again have a conflict with the constitutional protection of freedom of speech and freedom of the press. Thus, if you are involved in a matter of public interest, your rights of privacy are affected accordingly. For example, if you are involved in an automobile accident, newspaper photographers may be snapping photographs of you at the scene of the accident; or if you are arrested, the TV cameras may be directed toward you. Here you are news; thus your right of privacy must be secondary to the freedom of the press to publish the news. For similar reasons a public figure does not have the same right of privacy as an ordinary citizen.

Torts to the Person's Property

Next we have the torts which injure the person's property.

Trespass to Real Property. The general rule of law with regard to trespass to real property is that the owner of real property has the right not only to exclusive possession of a specific piece of ground and the buildings and the appurtenances on that ground but also to exclusive possession of the airspace above the ground and the area below the ground. The old common-law rule was that the owner of land owned all of the airspace above the land and the area below the land all the way to the middle of the earth. This rule had to be modified when we started to use airspace for airplane travel. Now the landowner still owns the airspace above his or her land, subject, however, to the right of airplanes to fly through that airspace. With regard to the space below the land, the possessor of the land surface also possesses the soil and space below the surface to the extent that he or she can effectively use that soil or space, either now or in the future. When we talk about space below the land we are talking about the ownership of the oil, gas, coal, water, and other valuable minerals and resources which may be present under the surface.

In order to have the tort of trespass to your land, it is not necessary that there be actual damage to your land. In all of the other torts previously mentioned, damage had to be proven before a recovery could be made. In the tort of trespass to land, you can sue the trespasser even though there was no actual damage and the court will award nominal damages, perhaps $1 and costs.

Trespass to Personal Property. This tort allows the owner of personal property to bring an action against a person or persons who interfere with his or her exclusive possession of an item of personal property. Unlike the plaintiff in a case involving trespass to real property, the plaintiff in a case involving trespass to personal property must show and prove monetary damage in order to get a verdict against the trespasser.

Conversion. The tort of conversion is the unlawful taking and use of personal property owned by another person. In other words, it is the conversion of another person's property to your own use. This sounds like theft. However, you will recall that in order to have theft, one has to have a mens rea, or mental intent, to steal. In the tort of conversion, the person converting the property to his or her own use does not have the intent to steal. The person feels that he or she has the right to use the property. A good example of conversion would be a case where the branches of your neighbor's apple tree hang over the lot line so that the apples are over your property. You honestly feel that you have a right to these apples; after all, they are over your property in your airspace. After you pick the apples, your neighbors tells you that the apples belong to him and that you should give them to him. If you fail to give your neighbor the apples, you are guilty of the tort of conversion. The apples and the branches that hung over the lot line are in effect trespassing on your airspace; however, you do not have the right of ownership to them. You may, however, cut off the branches at the lot line and put them on your neighbor's land. You cannot keep them.

Deceit-Fraud. The tort of deceit, also called fraud, involves a situation where one or more parties, fraudulently and with the intent to deceive, misrepresent certain facts, either through oral or written statement or through an artifice or device of some type, and another party relies upon the misrepresentation and is damaged.

Abuse of Civil Process. This tort involves an intentional use of the civil legal process for a purpose which is wrongful and for which the process was not designed. A person may bring a civil action against you simply to harass you and cause you the expense of defending the lawsuit, when in fact the person has no legitimate claim against you. You may sue him or her for your damages as a result of this wrongful use of the civil process.

Malicious Prosecution. The tort of malicious prosecution is similar to the tort of abuse of civil process. However, it involves the criminal process. An example would be a case where the police and the court system take action against you because a person has maliciously and without probable cause sworn out a criminal complaint against you. You can sue that person for malicious prosecution and recover damages.

Interference with Economic Relations. This tort concerns your right to conduct your business free from malicious and intentional interference which might destroy the business. The free enterprise system is based on the competitive marketplace. However, competition must be kept within reasonable bounds. It is certainly permissible for one business to lower its price in an effort to competitively secure a market advantage. However, when a person or a business intentionally uses economic resources to injure another person or business for reasons other than the legal reasons for competition, the tort of interference with economic relations has been committed.

In the following case we see another type of economic interference.

Chemical Corporation of America v. _Anheuser-Busch, Inc._
306 F.2d 433 (U.S. Fifth Circuit, 1962)

FACTS   The manufacturer of Budweiser beer, which used the advertising phrase "Where there's life, there's Bud," sued to enjoin the use of a similar slogan. Chemical was selling a combination floor wax and insecticide under the slogan "Where there's life, there's Bugs." The plaintiff was concerned that people would start associating "Bugs" with "Bud," and thus wouldn't buy its beer. Judge G. Harrold Carswell of the U.S. district court for the Northern District of Florida issued the injunction, and Chemical appealed.

ISSUE   Was Chemical's use of its slogan an interference with plaintiff's economic relations?

DECISION   Yes. Judgment for plaintiff affirmed.

REASONS   Chief Judge Tuttle said for the court of appeals that the court should not let itself be swayed by "its instinctive reaction" that this was a "brazen and cheap effort . . . to capitalize on the good will created by the tremendous expenditure in advertising by the plaintiff." Nevertheless, he felt that a tort had clearly been committed.

"[T]he trial court is amply supported by the decisions of the Florida courts showing great concern for the rights of a person who after establishing a substantial market by an expensive advertising campaign and otherwise enjoying an established business identified with the name, slogan, or other attribute of good will, is then damaged by the use by another of his name or slogan. . . .

"These cases make it clear that in Florida a cause of action may exist where simulation of another's name or slogan causes damage on grounds entirely separate from actual confusion between competitors as to the source of the product. . . .

"Finding, as we do, the liberal trend in the equity courts of the state of Florida, toward the protection of trade names and slogans from unfair attacks by others, we are not reluctant to conclude that what is here morally reprehensible is also legally impermissible."

The tort of interference with economic relations also encompasses interference with contractual relations. If Johnny Rich, a nightclub owner, induces a famous entertainer to breach his or her contract with another nightclub to come

4. Tort Law
and Business

89

and work for him, the employer who had a contract with the entertainer can sue Johnny Rich for interference with his contractual relations.

Nuisance Torts to Person and Property.   Nuisance torts are wrongs that arise from the unreasonable or unlawful use by a person of his or her own property in such a manner as to interfere with the rights of others, with resulting damage.

Nuisance torts may be classified as private or public. An example of a private nuisance situation would be one in which your neighbor is an amateur inventor who produces various offensive odors and smoke that make it unpleasant for you to go outside your house. Another example would be a situation in which your neighbor has a dog that howls all night. The test with regard to a nuisance case is whether the interference with your enjoyment of your property is substantial and unreasonable and whether that interference would be offensive or inconvenient to a reasonable or prudent person. The victim may sue for money damages, an injunction, or both remedies together.

A public nuisance can be defined as the doing of something or the failure to do something as a result of which the safety, health, or morals of the public are injuriously affected. Public nuisances may be criminal as well as civil. Examples of public nuisances are the storing of explosives on a person's premises, allowing persons to smoke marijuana on the premises, and nearly any other use of the premises which could adversely affect the safety, health, or morals of the community. The shooting of fireworks in the streets is also a public nuisance. Many public nuisances may also be private nuisances. A public nuisance is an offense against the state, and as such it is subject to criminal prosecution if it is a specifically criminal act and it may be subject to abatement by governmental order. If the public nuisance also injures private parties, those private parties may have their own actions separate from the government, since private parties are concerned with damages for their own injuries.

NEGLIGENT TORTS

Each person in society is bound to take reasonable care not to injure the person, the reputation, or the property of those persons whom he or she must reasonably consider as likely to be affected by his or her behavior. Any act or omission in breach of that duty which causes damage to others may cause a person to be liable for damages to the person or persons affected by that act or omission. In the negligent tort case the question is not, as it was with the intentional tort, Did the person intend to cause the injury or damage? The question is simply, Did the person act in a negligent manner?

What Constitutes Negligence?

The standard which is used to determine the absence or presence of negligence is a very simple one. The standard is simply, did the person act in a manner similar to that in which a reasonable and prudent person would have acted under the same or similar circumstances? Would the reasonable and prudent person have foreseen the dangers of his or her action, and was the damage or injury proximately caused by the action or the failure to act of the individual being charged with the tort? The question then arises: Who is this reasonable and prudent person? The reasonable and prudent person is an imaginary person, and when deciding a case involving a negligent tort, jurors are instructed not to use themselves as examples of the reasonable and prudent person. The jurors must determine not what they individually would have done in the same or a similar situation but what that imaginary person called the reasonable and prudent person would have done. Obviously, this standard is not very precise and it is certainly subject to great variations. The standard, however, has operated very successfully over the years since it does take into consideration changes in technology and changes in societal mores which the jury will impute to the reasonable and prudent person. Also, it would be impossible to have a specific statutory code that would cover every possible act or omission which could be considered negligent. Thus negligence continues to be decided on a case-by-case basis.

Proximate Cause

A person may commit a negligent act or may negligently fail to act under certain circumstances. However, that person will not be liable to any person who is damaged or injured as a result of such act or omission unless it can be shown that the damage or injury was proximately caused by the negligent act or omission. For a negligent act or omission to be a proximate cause of damage or injury, it must be a cause which in a natural and continuous sequence, unbroken by any intervening cause, produced the injury, and it must be a cause without which the injury would not have occurred. An example would be a motorist who was driving at a high rate of speed, hit a chuckhole, lost control of the vehicle, struck a water hydrant, breaking off the hydrant and causing the street to flood and water to flow into the basement of a house near the hydrant. The driver would be liable not only for the damage to the water hydrant, but also for the damage to the house, as that damage was proximately caused by the driver's negligence.

If, while the street was flooded, a city bus came down the street and stopped and let off an elderly lady who stepped into the water and slipped, fell, and broke her hip, would the driver of the vehicle that struck the water hydrant be responsible for her injuries? Were her injuries proximately caused by his negligence? The answer would be no. The lady was not injured as a result of a natural and continuous chain of events commencing with the motorist's negligent driving. There was an intervening cause—the negligence of the bus driver entering a dangerously flooded area and the negligence of the elderly lady stepping off the bus into the flooded street.

There are situations where the actions or omissions of more than one person are a proximate cause of damage or injury to a person or property. If two cars collide in an intersection and one of the cars strikes a legally parked car, it may be found that the negligence of both of the drivers in the collision proximately caused the damage to the parked car. Thus, it is not necessary that any one act or omission be the sole proximate cause of damage or injury.

Foreseeability

For a defendant to be liable to a plaintiff for a tortious act or omission to act, not only must the act or omission be a proximate cause of the damage or injury, but the ultimate damage or injury must also be foreseeable by the reasonable and prudent person. The following case is an example of an injury which was caused by an unbroken chain of events. However, it was not foreseeable to the reasonable and prudent person that the actions which triggered the chain of events could ultimately cause injury to the plaintiff.

Palsgraf v. *Long Island R.R.*
162 N.E. 99 (New York, 1928)

FACTS The plaintiff was standing on a railroad platform waiting for a train to Rockaway Beach. Another train stopped to let off and board passengers and then started moving. A man carrying a small package under his arm ran to catch the moving train and jumped aboard it. Then he seemed unsteady, as if about to fall. A guard on the train, who was holding the door open, reached out to help him in, and a guard on the platform ran up and pushed him from behind. As this was being done, the package which the man had under his arm became dislodged and fell. The package exploded, and the shock of the explosion knocked over some scales at the other end of the platform. The scales struck the plaintiff, causing injuries to her. The package, which was about 15 inches long and was covered by a newspaper, contained fireworks. The plaintiff sued the railroad for injuries. The jury found for the plaintiff. The defendant appealed.

ISSUE Should the railroad be responsible for the injury to the plaintiff ? Was the injury to the plaintiff foreseeable when the defendant's employees attempted to help the passenger onto the train?

DECISION No. Lower court verdict reversed. Judgment for the defendant railroad.

REASONS Chief Justice Cardozo argued that the outward appearance of the package gave no clue as to what was in the package. The reasonable person would not assume that the package was full of explosives or other dangerous material. Helping the passenger onto the train was not an act that foreseeably could injure a person standing at the other end of the platform. The court felt that the wrongdoer was the man who carried the explosives and not the persons who innocently dislodged a package from the man's arm, without any suspicion that the package could be dangerous. The orbit of danger in the eyes of a reasonable vigilant person is the orbit of duty. In this case no legal duty to the plaintiff was violated.

Justice Cardozo continued: "The range of reasonable apprehension is at times a question for the court, and at times, if varying inferences are possible, a question for the jury. Here, by concession, there was nothing in the situation to suggest to the most cautious mind that the parcel wrapped in newspaper would spread wreckage through the station. If the guard had thrown it down knowingly and willfully, he would not have threatened the plaintiff's safety, so far as appearances could warn him. His conduct would not have involved, even then, an unreasonable probability of invasion of her bodily security. Liability can be no greater where the act is inadvertent.''

OTHER THEORIES OF LIABILITY OR TORT

Res Ipsa Loquitur

The term *res ipsa loquitur* means "the thing speaks for itself." The plaintiff normally has the burden of proving that the defendant failed to act in a reasonable and prudent manner, that the accident was foreseeable, and that the damage or injury was a proximate cause of the defendant's action. Normally the plaintiff has at his or her disposal various types of evidence, such as skid marks and eyewitnesses.

In some cases it is obvious that the accident would not have happened had it not been for negligence on the part of the defendant, but the plaintiff does not have access to information which would verify or prove such negligence. An example would be a situation where a person was a passenger in an airplane and the airplane struck a mountain. The plane was demolished, and all its occupants died. In this case the next of kin of the passengers will bring suit for the wrongful deaths. However, a plaintiff here lacks access to the physical evidence needed to prove this case. We know that airplanes normally do not run into mountains, and that someone's negligence probably caused the accident. The cause may have been a malfunction or a breakdown in the aircraft itself; it may have been a manufacturing defect; or it may have been a failure on the part of the airline to properly service and inspect. It may also have been pilot error or error on the part of air traffic control. In such cases the plaintiff pleads the theory of res ipsa loquitur and the burden is shifted to the defendant to prove that he or she wasn't negligent.

Respondeat Superior

This doctrine provides that the boss will pay. You might also call this the "deep pocket" doctrine. Under the doctrine of respondeat superior a principal may be liable for the tortious acts of his or her agent provided the agent was acting in the scope of his or her employment by the principal. Also, in the case of a simple employer-employee relationship, if the employee is acting in the scope of his or her employment, that is, doing the employer's job, and commits a negligent act, then the employer will be liable under the doctrine of respondeat superior. It is important to note here that the employee is still liable for his or her own actions. In other words, both employee and employer or both agent and principal could be liable in tort. This rule is discussed further in the chapters on agency.

Last Clear Chance Doctrine

Simply stated, this doctrine provides that the liable party is the party who had the last clear chance to avoid damage or injury to the other party. This doctrine imposes a duty upon one party to exercise care in avoiding injury to another party who has negligently placed himself or herself in a situation of danger. For example, suppose that a motorist on a very cold day started up his or her automobile, drove up to an intersection while the motor was still cold, and proceeded to pull out into the intersection. The motor died, causing the car to stall crosswise in the intersection. Cars approaching the stalled vehicle would then have a duty to exercise reasonable care to try to avoid injury to the driver who had negligently placed himself or herself in a position of peril. Thus, if an oncoming motorist could swerve to the right or the left and go around this stalled car, or could stop before hitting it, then he or she would have a duty to do so.

DEFENSES TO NEGLIGENT TORTS

There are three basic defenses to negligent torts. They are (1) contributory negligence, (2) assumption of risk, and (3) act of God.

Traditionally, contributory negligence on the part of the plaintiff has been a complete bar to his or her recovery. Many states have adopted the comparative negligence rule, which means that the negligence of the plaintiff will not necessarily bar him or her from recovery. The negligence of the plaintiff will, however, diminish the plaintiff's damages proportionately. If the plaintiff was found to be 10 percent negligent and the defendant was found to be 90 percent negligent, then the plaintiff would recover only 90 percent of his or her damages, rather than the 100 percent that would have been recovered had no negligence been found against the plaintiff. In a contributory negligence state the plaintiff would have recovered nothing.

A simple example of contributory negligence would be a situation where Mr. Leadfoot was northbound on a through highway at a speed of 75 miles per hour in a 30-mile-per-hour zone. Ms. Badsite was driving without her glasses, which she was required to wear when driving, and, not seeing a stop sign, drove into the intersection, into the side of Mr. Leadfoots' car. Obviously, Ms. Badsite was negligent for driving without prescription glasses and for failing to stop at the stop sign. Also, her negligence was a proximate cause of the accident since it directly contributed to the accident. On the other hand, Mr. Leadfoot was contributorily negligent since he was driving in excess of the speed limit and his speed was a contributing factor to the collision. Thus, in a contributory negligence state neither of them will recover from the other.

The defense of assumption of risk may also be a complete defense to a plaintiff's negligent tort action. When a person is aware of the danger in a situation, yet continues to expose himself or herself to that danger and is then injured, that person cannot complain of the defendant's negligence.

The third defense is the defense of act of God. If lightning strikes a large tree in your yard, causing the tree to fall on and crush your neighbor's car, you would not be liable, as the proximate cause of the damage was a so-called act of God. Similarly, if a tornado swept your tree into your neighbor's house, you would not be liable. If, however, you had a dead tree in your backyard which you intended to cut down because the tree was rotten and dangerous, and one day a strong breeze toppled the tree onto your neighbor's car, then you would not be able to use the defense of act of God, because you were aware of the condition of the tree and also should have been aware of the possibility that a windstorm would cause the tree to fall and do damage to others.

IMMUNITY FROM TORT ACTION

Certain persons, organizations, and governmental bodies have traditionally been immune from tort liability under certain circumstances.

At common law a husband could not sue his wife and a wife could not sue her husband for personal torts. The theory of courts was that such litigation would destroy family unity. Today, of course, if a husband wanted to sue his wife for a tort action, this would only be because insurance proceeds were available. Also, traditionally a child could not sue his or her father or mother. These common-law intrafamily immunities are gradually being eroded as the reason for the immunity is no longer as strong as it used to be, since in most cases the spouse or the child is not actually suing the other spouse or the parent, but in effect is going after insurance proceeds. The spouse or the parent is a defendant in name only.

Charitable organizations traditionally were immune to tort liability. The theory was that to impose tort liability on the funds of the charitable organization would cripple its good work and would discourage donations to the organization. This immunity is also being eroded or completely eliminated in many states. Here again, the original reasons for the immunity are no longer valid. A charitable organization today can buy liability insurance, and the cost of this insurance can be part of its regular budget. Thus the organization needs no more protection than any other business and it should be liable for injury caused to innocent persons. An example would be the charitable hospital. A person negligently injured when a patient in a charitable hospital certainly should have the same rights of recovery in tort against the charitable hospital as he or she would have had if the injury had occurred in a private hospital.

The third traditional immunity is called sovereign immunity; simply stated, this means that the government may not be sued for its torts. The government can be defined as the U.S. government, state governments, municipal or county governments, or any governmental subdivision. The national government enacted the U.S. Tort Claims Act in 1946. This act established certain conditions for lawsuits and claims against the national government. Many states have also passed tort claims acts or other legislative acts, limiting the sovereign immunity of the state, cities, and other governmental units. Some states, however, have established dollar limits on claims which can be recovered from them. The general trend in sovereign immunity is toward its elimination. Here again, the state, city, or other governmental subdivision can purchase liability insurance and thus budget the cost on an annual basis.

STRICT LIABILITY

Strict liabilty is liability without fault. In a strict liability case the defendant will be liable for injuries caused by his or her actions, even though the defendant was not negligent in any way and the defendant did not intentionally injure the plaintiff. This concept of liability without fault is comparatively new in our legal system. The traditional theories of tort involve either the intentional wrongful acts which we referred to under intentional torts or the negligent acts or omissions where the person didn't intend to injure the other party wrongfully, but through his or her carelessness or negligence the other party was injured and thus should have a right to recover. In developing the theory of no fault or liability without fault, the courts and the legislatures are not really looking at right or wrong but at who can best bear the cost of the loss. In other words, if you are going to engage in certain types of activities, then you must realize that persons might be injured by your activities even though you do nothing legally wrong and do not intend to hurt anyone. When you enter into certain activities you must simply be prepared to pay for the consequences of your actions, regardless of any legal fault on your part.

Strict liability has been imposed on owners or possessors of animals. If you keep a wild animal on your premises, you are going to be strictly liable for any damages which that animal does to other persons or to the property of other persons. The owner or possessor of hard-hooved animals, such as cattle, horses, and donkeys, may also be held strictly liable for injuries caused by those animals. The owner or possessor of a dog or a cat would not normally be liable unless he or she knows the animal to be dangerous. The common-law rule was that a dog is entitled to its first bite. This, of course, meant that until the dog has bitten someone it is not known to be dangerous. This would be true with regard to a small dog. However, if a person kept a large Doberman that was constantly growling and baring its teeth at anyone who came near to it, obviously this dog appears to have dangerous propensities and its owner would be strictly liable for any injury or damage caused by it.

Strict liability has also been imposed on persons who are responsible for activities, the production of products, or conditions on their property which are dangerous and which might cause injury to other persons. The theory of attractive nuisance comes under this area of strict liability. For example, if an old refrigerator and an old junk car are sitting on your premises, these are called attractive nuisances, because they simply invite young children to come over and climb around on them. If these children are injured, you are strictly liable for injuries to them, even though you did not intentionally do anything wrong and in fact the children were trespassing on your property. Another example would be a construction contractor blasting out stumps or blasting hard rock in excavating for a building. If the blasting caused structural damage to nearby buildings or homes or if personal property within the buildings or homes were damaged by the concussion of the explosions, then the contractor would be strictly liable.

A third area of strict liability involves products liability. Traditionally we had the theory of caveat emptor, which meant "let the buyer beware." The theory was that the buyer had a duty to inspect the goods which he or she purchased, and unless there was intentional fraud or deceit, the buyer was simply stuck with them. This third area of strict liability will be discussed more fully in Chapter 17.

CASES FOR DISCUSSION

CATANIA v. UNIVERSITY OF NEBRASKA

282 N.W.2d 27 (Nebraska, 1979)

Hastings, Justice

This is an action brought by the plaintiff for personal injuries resulting from the alleged negligence of the defendant, The University of Nebraska, a corporate governmental body, more accurately described as the Board of Regents of the University of Nebraska. Plaintiff was a student at the University and suffered injury and permanent disability when struck in the right eye by a plastic practice golf ball during a physical education class session held on the Lincoln campus. The case was tried before a judge of the District Court for Douglas County, and resulted in a judgment in favor of the plaintiff in the amount of $60,000. The University has appealed, setting forth as errors improper venue, failure of the evidence to support the judgment, and excessive damages.

In her original petition filed on March 21, 1977, plaintiff alleged the facts of the accident as briefly outlined above, after claiming the action was brought pursuant to the Political Subdivisions Tort Claims Act, section 23–2401 et seq., R.R.S.1943, and that she had filed a claim with the secretary of the Board of Regents more than six months prior to the filing of the petition. . . . Thereafter, the plaintiff apparently had second thoughts about having followed the proper procedure, so she filed a claim with the secretary of the State Claims Board under the provisions of the Tort Claims Act, section 81–8, 209 et seq., R.R.S.1943. . . . For its answers to the amended petition the University again denied the claim on its merits, but also objected to the jurisdiction of the court because the action should have been filed in Lancaster County. In the final analysis, plaintiff was attempting to proceed simultaneously under both the Political Subdivisions Tort Claims Act and the Tort Claims Act, so it is necessary to examine each of them in some detail.

The Political Subdivisions Tort Claims Act declares that no political subdivision of the State of Nebraska shall be liable for any torts and no suit may be maintained except to the extent provided by the act. . . . "Jurisdiction, venue, procedure, and rights of appeal . . . shall be determined in the same manner as if the suits involved private individuals. . . ." This would indicate that venue would be governed by the general venue statute as applied to suits against residents, section 25–409, R.R.S.1943, which permits a suit to "be brought in the county where the . . . plaintiff resides and the defendant . . . may be summoned." In this case, the plaintiff was a resident of Douglas County and apparently, there being no objection or showing to the contrary, the University was properly summoned . . . .

On the other hand, the Tort Claims Act, section 81–8, 209 et seq., R.R.S.1943, prohibits suits against the state or any state except as provided in that act. . . . Suits shall be brought in the District Court of the county where the act or omission complained of occurred, s.81–8, 214, R.R.S.1943.

From a reading of the foregoing two acts it becomes readily apparent that it is essential in this case to decide whether the University is a political subdivision or a state agency. . . .

[C]onsidering our own statutes and constitutional provisions as well as our own case law, we believe and hold that the Board of Regents of the University of Nebraska is an agency of the state. Therefore, this claim should have been brought under the provisions of section 81–8, 209 et seq., R.R.S.1943, and the suit filed in the District Court for Lancaster County, Nebraska. . . .

In order to sue the State of Nebraska or one of its agencies under the Tort Claims Act, the requirements of the act must be followed strictly and the petition filed in the District Court for the county in which the alleged wrongful act or omission took place. In the absence of specific legislative authority, neither the state nor one of its agencies may waive those jurisdictional requirements.

It is fundamental that want of jurisdiction of the subject matter of the action is a defect which requires the court to proceed by dismissal of the case or other suitable action. . . . The trial court should have sustained the University's motion to dismiss.

Accordingly, the judgment of the trial court is reversed and the cause remanded with directions to vacate the judgment in favor of the plaintiff and to dismiss the action without prejudice.

MIKKELSON v. RISOVI

141 N.W.2d 150 (North Dakota, 1966)

Englert, District Judge

This appeal involves an action for personal injuries sustained by Richard A. Mikkelson, a minor, brought in said minor's behalf by his mother, as guardian ad litem, and also on her own behalf for medical expenses incurred, against Frank Risovi and Mike Kurtz, a construction partnership. The injuries resulted from a fall while climbing on and jumping from scaffolding erected in connection with the construction of a new home by the defendants. The case was tried to a jury. At the close of plaintiffs' evidence, and again at the close of all of the evidence, the trial court denied motions by the defendants for a directed verdict. The jury returned a verdict in favor of Richard in the amount of $2,000 and in favor of his mother in the sum of $2,335. The defendants moved for judgment in their favor notwithstanding the verdict.

* * * * *

This being a negligence case, the burden of proof is upon the plaintiff's to establish negligence on the part of the defendants against whom they seek to recover. The case is founded upon the theory that the defendants owed a legal duty to the plaintiffs, which they failed without lawful excuse to perform, and that, because of such failure, the plaintiffs suffered injury for which the defendants should respond in damages. There can, of course, be no actionable negligence unless there be a failure to perform a legal duty owing the person injured.

* * * * *

The plaintiff Richard Mikkelson was injured while a trespasser upon a scaffold erected adjacent to a house which the defendants were constructing. The incident occurred in the evening after the defendants and their employees had left the construction site. The action was tried upon what is usually called the attractive-nuisance doctrine. The attractive-nuisance doctrine or, as it is sometimes called, the turntable doctrine, is a subject upon which there has been a great amount of confusion and a wide diversity of opinion. Much conflict exists in the decisions of the courts. . . .

* * * * *

It appears that the so-called attractive-nuisance doctrine or, as it is sometimes called, the turntable doctrine, has not been adopted in this State in any previous decision, nor has it

been rejected. Thus this is one of first impression in this jurisdiction.

What has been said in previous cases in this State, insofar as the attractive-nuisance doctrine has been considered, is in no way contrary to five principles set forth in Section 339, Second Edition, *Restatement of the Law, Torts*, which states as follows:

A possessor of land is subject to liability for physical harm to children trespassing thereon caused by an artificial condition upon the land if

(a)   the place where the condition exists is one upon which the possessor knows or has reason to know that children are likely to trespass, and

(b)   the condition is one of which the possessor knows or has reason to know and which he realizes or should realize will involve an unreasonable risk of death or serious bodily harm to such children, and

(c)   the children because of their youth do not discover the condition or realize the risk involved in intermeddling with it or in coming within the area made dangerous by it, and

(d)   the utility to the possessor of maintaining the condition and the burden of eliminating the danger are slight as compared with the risk to children involved, and

(e)   the possessor fails to exercise reasonable care to eliminate the danger or otherwise to protect the children.

* * * * *

We accept the principle as stated in Section 339, Second Edition, *Restatement of the Law*, as the rule applicable in this case.

* * * * *

These important questions must be decided by this court: Were the defendants negligent in leaving a metal scaffold of the type used in this house-building project unfenced and unguarded? And, further, should they be required, at the end of each day's work, to dismantle such scaffolding in order to avoid being charged with negligence? From a review of the evidence in the case, and as a matter of law, this court is of the opinion that these two questions must be answered in the negative. A scaffold which is not defective is considered to be an essential and necessary part of the construction work and is no more dangerous than uncompleted portions of the house being built. A child could injure himself as well by a fall from or in jumping over a dismantled section of the scaffolding upon the existence of certain conditions. To require the fencing or guarding of every house under construction, or the taking down of scaffolding at the end of each day, would impose an unreasonable expense and hardship upon the builder.

A possessor of land is not under a duty to prevent every possibility of harm but only to exercise due care as to those risks which he should realize are unreasonably great and threaten serious bodily harm in a way unlikely to be appreciated by children whose trespass he could foresee. The duty under the law is to maintain the premises so as not to create an inherently dangerous condition.

We are of the opinion that the evidence does not sustain the verdict in that we must conclude that the condition, as shown by the evidence to exist, was not, as a matter of law, one which the possessor would know or should know would involve an unreasonable risk of death or serious harm to children. Therefore, the proof required in regard to clause (b) of Section 339 of *Restatement of the Law, Torts*, Second Edition, has not been met so as to entitle plaintiffs to recover, damages for injuries sustained in said fall.

The order denying defendants' motion for judgment notwithstanding the verdict is reversed, and the case is remanded to the district court for entry of judgment in favor of the defendants.

GALELLA v. ONASSIS

487 F.2d 986 (U.S. Second Circuit, 1973)

Smith, Circuit Judge

Donald Galella, a free-lance photographer, appeals from a summary judgment dismissing his complaint against three Secret Service agents for false arrest, malicious prosecution and interference with trade . . . ; the dismissal after trial of his identical complaint against Jacqueline Onassis and the grant of injunctive relief to defendant Onassis on her counterclaim and to the

intervenor, the United States, on its intervening complaint and third judgment retaxing transcript costs to plaintiff. . . . In addition to numerous alleged procedural errors, Galella raises the First Amendment as an absolute shield against liability to any sanctions. . . .

Galella is a free-lance photographer specializing in the making and sale of photographs of well-known persons. Defendant Onassis is the widow of the late President John F. Kennedy, mother of the two Kennedy children, John and Caroline, and is the wife of Aristotle Onassis, widely known shipping figure and reputed multimillionaire. John Walsh, James Kalafatis, and John Connelly are U.S. Secret Service agents assigned to the duty of protecting the Kennedy children under 18 U.S.C. § 3056, which provides for protection of the children of deceased presidents up to the age of 16.

Galella fancies himself as a "paparazzo" (literally a kind of annoying insect, perhaps roughly equivalent to the English "gadfly"). Paparazzi make themselves as visible to the public and obnoxious to their photographic subjects as possible to aid in the advertisement and wide sale of their works.

Some examples of Galella's conduct brought out at trial are illustrative. Galella took pictures of John Kennedy riding his bicycle in Central Park across the way from his home. He jumped out into the boy's path, causing the agents concern for John's safety. The agents' reaction and interrogation of Galella led to Galella's arrest and his action against the agents; Galella on other occasions interrupted Caroline at tennis and invaded the children's private schools. At one time he came uncomfortably close in a power boat to Mrs. Onassis swimming. He often jumped and postured around while taking pictures of her party, notably at a theater opening but also on numerous other occasions. He followed a practice of bribing apartment house, restaurant, and nightclub doormen as well as romancing a family servant to keep him advised of the movements of the family.

After detention and arrest following complaint by the Secret Service agents protecting Mrs. Onassis' son and his acquittal in the state court,

Galella filed suit in state court against the agents and Mrs. Onassis. Galella claimed that under orders from Mrs. Onassis, the three agents had falsely arrested and maliciously prosecuted him, and that this incident in addition to several others described in the complaint constituted an unlawful intereference with his trade.

Mrs. Onassis answered, denying any role in the arrest or any part in the claimed interference with his attempts to photograph her, and counterclaimed for damages and injunctive relief, charging that Galella had invaded her privacy, assaulted and battered her, intentionally inflicted emotional distress, and engaged in a campaign of harassment.

The action was removed under 28 U.S.C. § 1442(a) to the United States District Court. On a motion for summary judgment, Galella's claim against the Secret Service agents was dismissed, the court finding that the agents were acting within the scope of their authority and thus were immune from prosecution. At the same time, the government intervened, requesting injunctive relief from the activities of Galella which obstructed the Secret Service's ability to protect Mrs. Onassis' children. Galella's motion to remand the case to state court, just prior to trial, was denied. . . .

After a six-week trial the court dismissed Galella's claim and granted relief to both the defendant and the intervenor. Galella was enjoined from (1) keeping the defendant and her children under surveillance or following any of them; (2) approaching within 100 yards of the home of defendant or her children, or within 100 yards of either child's school or within 75 yards of either child or 50 yards of defendant; (3) using the name, portrait, or picture of defendant or her children for advertising; (4) attempting to communicate with defendant or her children except through her attorney.

We conclude that grant of summary judgment and dismissal of Galella's claim against the Secret Service agents was proper. Federal agents when charged with duties which require the exercise of discretion are immune from liability for actions within the scope of their authority. . . . The protective duties assigned the agents under this statute. . . . require the instant exercise of

judgment which should be protected. The agents saw Galella jump into the path of John Kennedy who was forced to swerve his bike dangerously as he left Central Park and was about to enter Fifth Avenue, whereupon the agents gave chase to the photographer. Galella indicated that he was a press photographer listed with the New York City Police; he and the agents went to the police station to check on the story, where one of the agents made the complaint on which the state court charges were based. Certainly it was reasonable that the agents "check out" an individual who has endangered their charge, and seek prosecution for apparent violation of state law which interferes with them in the discharge of their duties. . . .

Discrediting all of Galella's testimony, the court found the photographer guilty of harassment, intentional infliction of emotional distress, assault and battery, commercial exploitation of defendant's personality, and invasion of privacy. Fully crediting defendant's testimony, the court found no liability on Galella's claim. Evidence offered by the defense showed that Galella had on occasion intentionally physically touched Mrs. Onassis and her daughter, caused fear of physical contact in his frenzied attempts to get their pictures, followed defendant and her children too closely in an automobile, endangered the safety of the children while they were swimming, water skiing, and horseback riding. Galella cannot successfully challenge the court's finding of tortious conduct.

Finding that Galella had "insinuated himself into the very fabric of Mrs. Onassis' life . . ." the court framed its relief in part on the need to prevent further invasion of the defendant's privacy. Whether or not this accords with present New York law, there is no doubt that it is sustainable under New York's prescription of harassment.

Of course legitimate countervailing social needs may warrant some intrusion despite an individual's reasonable expectation of privacy and freedom from harassment. However the interference allowed may be no greater than that necessary to protect the overriding public interest. Mrs. Onassis was properly found to be a public figure and thus subject to news coverage. . . .

Nonetheless, Galella's action went far beyond the reasonable bounds of news gathering. When weighed against the de minimis public importance of the daily activities of the defendant, Galella's constant surveillance, his obtrusive and intruding presence, was unwarranted and unreasonable. If there were any doubt in our minds, Galella's inexcusable conduct toward defendant's minor children would resolve it.

Galella does not seriously dispute the court's finding of tortious conduct. Rather, he sets up the First Amendment as a wall of immunity protecting newsmen from any liability for their conduct while gathering news. There is no such scope to the First Amendment right. Crimes and torts committed in news gathering are not protected. . . .

The injunction, however, is broader than is required to protect the defendant. Relief must be tailored to protect Mrs. Onassis from the "paparazzo" attack which distinguishes Galella's behavior from that of other photographers; it should not unnecessarily infringe on reasonable efforts to "cover" defendant. Therefore, we modify the court's order to prohibit only (1) any approach within twenty-five (25) feet of defendant or any touching of the person of the defendant Jacqueline Onassis; (2) any blocking of her movement in public places and thoroughfares; (3) any act foreseeably or reasonably calculated to place the life and safety of defendant in jeopardy; and (4) any conduct which would reasonably be foreseen to harass, alarm, or frighten the defendant. . . .

Likewise, we affirm the grant of injunctive relief to the government modified to prohibit any action interfering with Secret Service agents' protective duties. Galella thus may be enjoined from (a) entering the children's schools or play areas; (b) engaging in action calculated or reasonably foreseen to place the children's safety or well-being in jeopardy, or which would threaten or create physical injury; (c) taking any action which could reasonably be foreseen to harass, alarm, or frighten the children; and (d) from approaching within thirty (30) feet of the children. . . .

As modified, the relief granted fully allows Galella the opportunity to photograph and report on Mrs. Onassis' public activities. Any prior restraint on news gathering is miniscule and fully supported by the findings.

Affirmed in part, reversed in part, and remanded for modification of the judgment in accordance with this opinion. Costs on appeal to be taxed in favor of appellees.

Timbers, Circuit Judge (concurring in part and dissenting in part)

With one exception, I concur in the judgment of the Court and in the able majority opinion of Judge Smith.

With the utmost deference to and respect for my colleagues, however, I am constrained to dissent from the judgment of the Court and the majority opinion to the extent that they modify the injunctive relief found necessary by the district court to protect Jacqueline Onassis and her children, Caroline B. and John F. Kennedy, Jr., from the continued predatory conduct of the self-proclaimed paparazzo Galella. . . .

In the instant case, after a six week trial at which 25 witnesses testified, hundreds of exhibits were received, and a 4,714 page record was compiled, Judge Cooper filed a careful, comprehensive 40 page opinion, 353 F. Supp. 194, which meticulously sets forth detailed findings of fact and conclusions of law. As for the provisions of the injunction requiring Galella to keep certain distances away from Mrs. Onassis and her children (from the modification of which I dissent), Judge Cooper stated his reasons for these provisions as follows:

For practical reasons, the injunction cannot be couched in terms of prohibitions upon Galella's leaping, blocking, taunting, grunting, hiding, and the like. Nor have abstract concepts—harassing, endangering proved workable. No effective relief seems possible without the fixing of prescribed distances.

We must, moreover, make certain plaintiff keeps sufficiently far enough away to avoid problems as to compliance with the injunction and injurious disobedience. Disputes concerning his compliance may be frequent, thereby necessitating repeated application to the Court. Hence, the restraint must be clear, simple, and effective so that Galella's substantial compliance cannot seriously be disputed unless a violation occurs.

Of major importance in determining the scope of

the relief to be afforded here is the attitude which Galella has demonstrated toward the process of this Court in the past. Galella blatantly violated our restraining orders of October 8 and December 2, 1971. He did so deliberately and in full knowledge of the fact of his violation. His deliberate disobedience to the subpoena and his attempts to obstruct justice with respect to Exhibit G, together with the perjury that infected his testimony, do not warrant mere token relief.

In light of Galella's repeated misbehavior, it is clear that only a strong restraint—an injunction which will clearly protect Mrs. Onassis' rights and leave no room for quibbling about compliance and no room for evasion or circumvention—is appropriate in this case.

* * * * *

As for the actual distance to be prescribed, we must bear in mind that plaintiff never moved to modify the distances heretofore imposed by our restraining order, even after the Court had clearly and explicitly invited him to do so if he could prove it was too harsh. . . .

I have set forth the foregoing explanation by Judge Cooper of his reasons for the critical distance provisions of the injunction because they are weighty findings by the trial judge who had the benefit of seeing the parties before him and who obviously was in a better position than we to judge their demeanor. I feel very strongly that such findings should not be set aside or drastically modified by our Court unless they are clearly erroneous; and I do not understand the majority to suggest that they are.

Distance Galella Is Required to Maintain	As Provided in District Court Injunction	As Modified by Court of Appeals Majority
From home of Mrs. Onassis and her children	100 yards	No restriction
From children's schools	100 yards	Restricted only from entering schools or play areas
From Mrs. Onassis personally	50 yards	25 feet and not to touch her
From children personally	75 yards	30 feet

In addition to modifying the distance restriction of the injunction, the majority also has directed that Galella be prohibited from blocking Mrs. Onassis' movement in public places and thoroughfares, from any act "foreseeably or reasonably calculated" to place Mrs. Onassis' life and safety in jeopardy (and similarly with respect to her children); and from any conduct which would "reasonably be foreseen" to harass, alarm, or frighten Mrs. Onassis (and similarly with respect to her children).

With deference, I believe the majority's modification of the injunction in the respects indicated above to be unwarranted and unworkable. . . .

PROBLEMS FOR DISCUSSION

1. Reynolds was standing outside his store when Trotter came up to him, took hold of his arm, and began talking to him. Pierson, sort of a practical joker, walked by, grabbed Trotter's arm, and jerked on it. Since Trotter was holding onto Reynolds, Reynolds was pulled off balance too. Reynolds fell down, hitting his head on the side of the building. Reynolds sues Pierson. What result, and why?

2. Dr. Snively was supposed to operate on Mrs. Biggs' nose. He did so, but while she was under anesthesia, he also removed her tonsils. There was no particular reason for doing so, except that Dr. Snively says that it's "common practice" to remove the tonsils when a patient is under general anesthesia for another operation. Mrs. Biggs sues for damages. What result, and why?

3. Judge Roibean, after reviewing a petition filed in his court, ordered that Mrs. Mary Meek be hospitalized for an examination of her mental condition. There was apparently some concern that she might be dangerous to herself or to others. Deputy Sheriff Bilbo, with a warrant, found Mrs. Meek in her neighbor's home

and told her: "Mrs. Meek, I'm terribly sorry to have to tell you this, but your husband has been seriously injured in a car accident, and you should come down to the county hospital right now." Mrs. Meek went with Bilbo to the hospital. When they arrived, Mrs. Meek discovered the truth. Bilbo said: "Well, I just had to tell you that to get you down here." Mrs. Meek was then placed in the psychiatric ward for observation. At no time had Bilbo told her that he had a valid warrant for her detention. Mrs. Meek later sued Bilbo, alleging that she had suffered severe emotional distress as the result of his statements about her husband. What result, and why?

4. Police officer Bark, investigating a fire at the Saddle Shoe Store, was told that Trinma had stolen several pairs of shoes during the fire. Bark and two other officers went to Trinma's home that night, got Trinma and his wife out of bed, and told Trinma: "Consider yourself under arrest. You've got to come downtown with us right now." Trinma asked to see their warrant and was told: "That's all right, you have to go with us." Trinma agreed to go with them but asked them to search the house for the missing shoes. Bark and the other two officers searched the house but did not find the shoes. At that point they told Trinma that it would be OK if he came down to the police station in the morning. Trinma did so, but no warrant had been issued for his arrest and no charges were ever filed against him for stealing any shoes. Trinma sues Bark and the other two officers. What result, and why?

5. *Persons* magazine published an article in its "Current Events" section which read: "DIVORCED. By Bobby Brass, heir to the silver fortune—Betty Burpee Tinhorne Brass, his third wife, a former schoolteacher; on grounds of extreme cruelty and adultery; after five years of marriage, one daughter. The 16-month off-and-on trial produced enough testimony of extramarital adventures on both sides, said the judge, 'to make Dr. Freud's hair curl'."

Betty demanded a retraction, saying that part of this article was false and defamatory. *Persons* refused, saying that it was just reporting the news. The statement attributed to the judge was in fact false. Betty sued *Persons*. What result, and why?

6. Northern Air Company owns and operates a small airport near Biddeford, Maine. Reinhard owns a parcel of land which adjoins the airport. Northern's planes, in taking off and landing, fly as low as 100 feet over a wooded area on Reinhard's land. There are no dwellings or other structures in the wooded area. Reinhard sues for damages and for an injunction to prohibit Northern from flying lower than 500 feet above his land. What result, and why?

7. Mrs. Wilma Winsomme, married and the mother of two sons aged 8 and 10 years, has lived in Culpepper County, Tennessee, all her life (35 years). While they were attending the county fair, her sons wanted to go into the "Fun House" but wanted her to come with them. Wilma had never been in a "fun house" before and didn't quite know what to expect, but she went in anyway. As she was coming out the exit door, a blast of air from holes in the floor blew her skirt up, exposing the lower part of her body. At that moment, without her knowledge, a newspaper photographer snapped her picture. Three days later the picture appeared on the front page of the local paper. Wilma sues the newspaper. What result, and why?

8. Robin owned and operated the only barbershop in Chilly, North Dakota. The wealthy president of the town's only bank, Tuck Dollerz, disliked Robin very much. Tuck disliked Robin so much that he always drove 40 miles to the next town to get his haircuts and advised anyone who would listen to do the same. When Robin needed a business loan, Tuck refused to give it to him and Robin had to go to another bank. Finally, Tuck set up another barbershop in Chilly, with cut-rate

prices designed to drive Robin out of business. Are any of Tuck's actions common-law torts? Explain.

9. Millicent Innocent was riding on a train from Buffalo to Albany, New York. Her scheduled stop was the small town of Erewhon, about 20 miles outside Albany. For some reason the train failed to stop at Erewhon. Millicent immediately alerted the conductor, but by the time the train was stopped, it was three quarters of a mile past Erewhon. The conductor refused to back up the train and told Millicent she could either get off and walk back or go on to Albany and take the next train back. Millicent decided to get off. While she was walking by an area known as Hobo Hollow, she was mugged by a hobo and her purse was stolen. Millicent sues the railroad for the $50 that was in her purse and for her other damages. Does she have a basis for recovery? What is the main issue in this case? Explain.

10. Myron had been cutting wood on his farm and was using his donkey and a small donkey cart to haul the wood back to the farmhouse. When it was time for his lunch, Myron unhitched the donkey, fettered the donkey's feet so it wouldn't run away, and left it to graze by the side of the road. While Myron was still inside having lunch, Victor ran over the donkey cart with his car. Myron sues for value of the donkey, but Victor says that Myron was negligent in leaving the donkey in the road. Does Myron have any basis for recovery? Why or why not?

11. Russo and Olive Dribble owned a large male goat, which they kept in a pen. One morning the Dribbles' two sons, aged 10 and 7, missed the school bus. Their parents had already left for work, so the boys were home alone. They let the goat out of his pen to play with him. At this point the goat was still within the Dribbles' fenced-in front yard. When the boys went across the street to visit their friend Mr. Pappe, the goat jumped the fence and followed them. Pappe poked the goat in the side with his cane to try to get the goat off his property. The goat attacked Pappe and seriously injured him. Pappe was taken to the hospital, treated for a month, and then released. He was readmitted about three months later and died about a month after that. Pappe's estate sues the Dribbles. Is there any basis for tort liability here? Discuss.

Part II
Contracts

5 | Formation of the Agreement

Our basic contract formula may be stated as follows: Contract = Agreement + Consideration. That is, in order for promises to have legal consequences as contracts, there must be an agreement between the parties that they will have such consequences and that agreement must involve an exchange of legally sufficient considerations, or values.

This chapter examines the "Agreement" part of the formula, which may be stated as a subformula: Agreement = Offer + Acceptance. In order to know how to discover whether there was a contractual agreement, we will need to know the answers to three main questions: What is an "offer"? How long is an offer open for acceptance? What is an effective acceptance?

WHAT IS AN OFFER?

Preliminary Negotiations Distinguished from Offers. Parties may engage in extended preliminary discussions before they finally arrive at the point where one of them makes a direct business proposition to the other. Buyers typically want to compare prices and payment terms, and may therefore request such information from several prospective sellers. Sellers may have only one or a limited number of items available, but they will contact a number of prospective buyers to see whether any of them is interested. Thus, if the buyer asks, "What will you take for your car?" he or she is only seeking price information and is not making an offer to buy. Likewise, if the would-be seller responds, "$400," he or she is only supplying the requested information and is not making an offer to sell at that price, to this buyer or to anyone else.

The element that distinguishes an offer from such preliminary negotiations, the thing that makes it an offer, is a promise to do business. The promise may be stated expressly, in so many words ("I'll give you $400 for your car"), or it may be implied from the language used and the surrounding facts and circumstances. This promise gives the offeree, the person to whom the offer is made, the power to change the legal relationships between the parties by accepting the offer and forming a contract) Because, typically, price quotations and advertisements do not contain such promises, they are not considered to be offers. However, stores which advertise products for sale to the public are required by state false advertising statutes and by Federal Trade Commission regulations to have "reasonable quantities" of the advertised items available for sale. (They can't, in other words, rely on the general contract law rule that "advertisements are not offers" without being liable for fines under the "false advertising" laws.)

Identity of Offeree. (Since, as a general rule, you have no legal duty to do business with anyone unless and until a contract is made, you can as an offeror specify the person or persons to whom your offer is made. You can make the offer to as many or as few persons as you wish, on whatever basis you wish. Today, however, an offeror's power to pick and choose the persons with whom he or she is willing to do business is subject to some important limitations by both state and national "civil rights" acts.

Not all types of contracts, or all potential offerors, or all possible bases of "discrimination" between offerees, are prohibited by these acts. Each such statute must be read carefully to see exactly what forms of discrimination are covered. Usually it is illegal to discriminate on the basis of race, color, religion, sex, or national origin, for contracts involving employment, real estate purchase or rental, or places of "public accommodation." Employment discrimination is discussed further in Chapter 51.

Law professors and students everywhere should be grateful to Mr. Lefkowitz for having had the tenacity to litigate the following case to his state's supreme court. It is a classic illustration of the application of these first two points about "offers."

Lefkowitz v. *Great Minneapolis Surplus Store*
86 N.W.2d 689 (Minnesota, 1957)

FACTS   On April 6, 1956, the defendant published the following advertisement in a Minneapolis newspaper:

SATURDAY 9 A.M. SHARP
3 BRAND NEW
FUR COATS
Worth to $100.00
First Come
First Served
$1
EACH

Lefkowitz v. *Great Minneapolis Surplus Store (continued)*

On April 13, the defendant published a similar advertisement:

SATURDAY 9 A.M.
2 BRAND NEW PASTEL
MINK 3-SKIN SCARFS
Selling for $89.50
Out they go
Saturday. Each $1.00
1 BLACK LAPIN STOLE
Beautiful,
Worth $139.50 .... $1.00
FIRST COME
FIRST SERVED

On each Saturday the plaintiff was the first to present himself at the appropriate counter in the defendant's store. On the first Saturday he demanded the advertised coat, and on the second Saturday he demanded the advertised stole. On both occasions he indicated his readiness to pay the sales price of $1, and on both occasions the defendant refused to sell the merchandise to the plaintiff, stating at the time of the plaintiff's first visit that by a "house rule" the offer was intended for women only and sales would not be made to men, and at the time of the second visit that the plaintiff knew the defendant's house rules. The defendant appealed the trial court's award of $138.50 damages.

ISSUE   Were the newspaper advertisements offers? If so, was Lefkowitz an intended offeree?

DECISION   Yes. Yes. Judgment affirmed.

REASONS   Justice Murphy first cited Professor Williston: "The test of whether a binding obligation may originate in advertisements addressed to the general public is whether the facts show that some performance was promised in positive terms in return for something requested."

Justice Murphy then stated that "where the offer is clear, definite, and explicit, and leaves nothing open for negotiation, it constitutes an offer, acceptance of which will complete the contract. Whether in any individual instance a newspaper advertisement is an offer rather than an invitation to make an offer depends on the legal intention of the parties and the surrounding circumstances. We are of the view on the facts before us that the offer by the defendant of the sale of the Lapin fur was clear, definite, and explicit, and left nothing open for negotiation. The plaintiff having successfully managed to be the first one to appear at the seller's place of business to be served, as requested by the advertisement, and having offered the stated purchase price of the article, he was entitled to performance on the part of the defendant. We think the trial court was correct."

This case thus tells advertisers who only wish to consider offers from others to be very careful in their choice of words. Don't say "First come, first served" or "First $400 takes it away" or anything else from which a court can imply your promise to do business.

Communication to Offeree.   It's really no more than common sense to say that an offer has no legal effect as an offer until it has been communicated to the intended offeree or offerees. If I mail you a letter containing an offer, but then change my mind and get the letter back from the post office before it's delivered to you, no offer has been made. Even if you somehow learn what happened, there would be nothing for you to "accept." If the letter were on my desk waiting for my signature, and you or one of your agents happened to be in my office and read the letter without my having authorized you to do so, no offer would have been made to you. In other words, it's *my* offer, and it's not effective until I intend that it be effective.

Manner of Acceptance.   Also, since it's my offer, I determine the manner of acceptance; I tell you what you have to do to accept it. The required acceptance can be as ridiculous, as stupid, or as difficult as I choose to make it; if you want to accept, you must do so on whatever terms I specify. Of course, you are not obligated to accept my terms; you can propose your own terms or ignore the offer completely. Your counterproposal, however, does not create a contract; it is a counteroffer which has the effect of rejecting (and thus terminating) my original offer.

Where the offeror requests a return promise, he or she has offered a "bilateral contract" (a promise in return for a promise). Where the offeror requests that the offeree accept by performing some act ("I offer $50 reward for the return of my lost poodle, Fifi"), he or she has offered a "unilateral contract."

The main issue in the following case is whether the plaintiff has in fact done what the defendant requested in return for the offered reward.

James v. *Turilli*

473 S.W.2d 757 (Missouri, 1971)

FACTS On February 27, 1967, Rudy Turilli, owner of the Jesse James Museum at Stanton, Missouri, appeared on Joe Pyne's late-evening TV "talk show." Rudy discussed his theory that Jesse James (the famous train and bank robber) had not really been shot in the back and killed by Robert Ford in 1882 but has lived into the 1950s and had actually stayed with Rudy at his museum. During the course of the discussion, Rudy said he believed his theory so strongly that he "would pay $10,000 to anyone, yourself, Mr. Pyne, Mr. Gruber, the audience, and the network audience, to anyone who could prove me wrong."

Stella James (Jesse's daughter-in-law) and her two daughters claimed the $10,000 on the basis of several affidavits, from persons in and acquainted with the James family, stating facts which tended to prove that Jesse was killed in 1882. Rudy refused to pay, and Stella James and her two daughters brought suit to collect the reward. Rudy appealed the judgment for the plaintiffs.

109

James v. Turilli (continued)

ISSUE   Have the plaintiffs complied with the terms of the offer of the reward?

DECISION   Yes. Judgment for plaintiffs affirmed.

REASONS   "The parties' dispute hinges on the word *prove,* a word of ordinary meaning. For present purposes we accept defendant's own definition of the word: Under ordinary rules of construction 'to prove' is to determine or persuade that a thing does or does not exist.

"We hold the trial court properly denied defendant's motion to dismiss the petition. It pleaded an offer to pay a reward if the plaintiffs proved him wrong about Jesse W. James being alive after 1882. Whether the plaintiffs' affidavits were sufficient to persuade an ordinary man that Jesse W. James was killed in 1882 was an issue to be determined by the trier of fact.

"Defendant contends the offer attributed to him by plaintiffs was incomplete in that Mrs. James quoted him as saying he would pay the reward to anyone who could prove me wrong but they neglected to establish what it was they were to prove [me] wrong about. In determining the sufficiency of plaintiffs' evidence, we must give them the benefit of every reasonable favorable inference which the evidence tends to support. Can it reasonably be inferred that when defendant offered the reward to anyone who could prove him wrong he was referring to Jesse W. James being alive after 1882?

"Considering all this en masse, it supported an inference that when defendant offered the reward to anyone who could prove him wrong he was referring to his contention that Jesse W. James was not killed in 1882 but lived for many years thereafter.

"As pointed out earlier, the offer of a reward is a unilateral contract which becomes complete when accepted by performance of the act called for in the offer. A claimant to a reward needs only to show substantial performance. As with other contracts, literal performance is not required."

(Reasonably) Definite Terms Necessary. The *James* case also illustrates the point that courts do not require that exact agreement be reached on all points for a contract to be enforceable. Obviously, the more specific and complete the terms are, the less chance there is for misunderstanding and possible lawsuit. However, the courts are aware that parties very often intend agreements but do not bother to spell out the terms completely.

At some point, however, the "terms" become so vague and indefinite that a court can only hold that there was no contract made because the parties never really agreed on anything. Confronted with an employee's claim that he had been promised "some share of the profits" of the business, a Wisconsin court had to say that there was no way for it to enforce such a "promise," since it could not know what share the parties might have had in mind.

The UCC (Sections 2–204, 2–305, 2–306) has liberalized this requirement to some extent for sales of goods contracts, by permitting the parties to use "requirements" or "output" as quantity terms and to leave the price term "open" (unspecified). Even here, however, there are limits. There must be a "real" promise, not just an "illusory" one ("I promise to buy as much as I want to buy"). To be enforceable, the promise must be definite enough to restrict the promisor's freedom of action.

Intent to Contract.   In most cases where the parties have exchanged promises, there probably has been a real "meeting of the minds"; that is, each party intended his or her promise in the same way that it was understood by the other. Such a mutual understanding obviously forms the contractual agreement.

There are cases, however, where one of the parties claims that no contract was ever formed because he or she did not "intend" that his or her promise be taken seriously, that it have contractual effect. In such cases a court will not require the other party to prove an actual "meeting of the minds"; it is enough if the trier of fact is convinced that a "reasonable person" would have believed that the promise was seriously intended. What counts, in other words, is not what the promisor "really" intended but the impression that his or her words and actions created in the mind of the other party. If the "joke" was convincing enough to fool a reasonable person, and if the other party was not aware of the joke when he or she accepted the offer, there is a contract.

Another aspect of the "intent to contract" problem arises when one party claims that certain parts of a written contract which he or she signed are not binding because he or she did not read the contract or did not understand it when he or she read it. Absent special facts (e.g., fraud, illiteracy), courts generally will not accept this argument. In general, the rule is that you are bound by what you sign—read or unread, understood or not understood.

General Motors Acceptance Corp. v. Blanco
149 N.W.2d 516 (Nebraska, 1967)

FACTS   Joe Blanco bought a new car which was financed through GMAC. On the reverse side of the written financing contract which he signed were provisions giving GMAC the right to repossess and resell the car if the buyer was in default on his monthly payments. Joe claimed that he was not bound by the provisions on the back of the written contract since he signed only the front side. GMAC filed suit and won in the lower court. Blanco appeals.

ISSUE   Are the provisions on the back of the written contract part of the agreement?

DECISION   Yes. Judgment for GMAC affirmed.

REASONS   The court first rejected Blanco's claim that the contract was fraudulent. "Defendant's argument is bottomed upon the premise that the language of the contract is so unintelligible, vague, ambiguous, so contrary to public policy, and so consciously loaded in favor of the plaintiff, that its execution constituted a fraud on the defendant, and that fraud vitiated or rendered the contract void. A short description of the contract is necessary to an understanding of the defendant's contention. On the front side of the

111

contract, immediately following the title in solid capitals, 'CONDITIONAL SALE CONTRACT,' is the following sentence: 'The undersigned seller hereby sells, and undersigned buyer or buyers, jointly and severally hereby purchase(s), subject to the terms and conditions set forth below *and upon the reverse side hereof,* the following property, delivery and acceptance of which in good order are hereby acknowledged by buyer. . . .' (Italics supplied.)

"On the reverse side of this instrument, under the title 'Provisions,' are 12 numbered sections, some of which have several paragraphs. The type is small but readable. Provision No. 1 is as follows: 'For the purpose of securing payment of the obligation hereunder, seller reserves title, and shall have a security interest, in said property until said obligation is fully paid in cash.'

"The defendant does not deny that he received a copy of the contract after its execution.

"Defendant tries to make much of the fact that he did not read the reverse side of the contract. Generally in the absence of fraud, one who does not choose to read a contract before signing it cannot later relieve himself of its burdens. We realize there may be situations in modern commercial life where the relative position of the parties is such that one of them has unconscionably taken advantage of the necessities of the other and certain provisions of the contract should not be enforced as a matter of public policy. Here the defendant is not attempting to void some specific provision of the contract which for reasons of public policy should not be enforced, but by expanding the thrust of that case, he is attempting to void the contract itself. To adopt defendant's illusory premise would void all sale contracts where the relative bargaining opportunities of the parties are unequal. To so apply it would be to pervert the principle involved and serve to destroy the very freedom of opportunity it is designed to protect. While there may be provisions of the contract to which the argument would be applicable, a question we do not need to decide, it would strain credulity to believe that the defendant did not fully understand that the intent of the agreement signed by him herein was to retain a security interest in the seller until the obligation was paid."

HOW LONG IS AN OFFER OPEN FOR ACCEPTANCE?

Lapse of Time. Even though no specific termination date or length of time during which the offer will remain open is stated, the offer will not be open for acceptance forever. In such cases the offer will terminate at the expiration of a "reasonable time." What is a reasonable time depends on the facts of the particular case, and litigations will result because one party claims to have accepted in time and the other party claims that the acceptance was too late because a reasonable time had already elapsed. Where an offer is made during a person-to-person conversation (face-to-face or over the telephone), and nothing is stated about its being open for some period of time, the presumption is that the offer terminates when the conversation ends.

Where an offer states that it will terminate on a specific date ("This offer will end August 14, 1978"), the day named is the last day on which an acceptance can occur. Unless facts and circumstances indicate otherwise, an acceptance which took legal effect anytime on that date would form a contract. Where an offer sent by letter indicates that it will be open for a period of time ("This offer is good for 30 days"), the time period normally begins to run as of the date of the writing, even though the letter is not received through the mails for several days. But if the offer says that the offeree has a certain period of time within which "to consider" or "to accept" it, the time period does not commence until the letter is delivered.

Revocability of Offers. In most cases, even though the offeror has stated that the offer will remain open for a period of time, he or she has both the power and the right to revoke it if his or her revocation takes legal effect prior to an acceptance. Since these so-called continuing offers are not supported by any value given by the offeree to the offeror, the offeror is not bound by his or her promise to keep the offer open. Usually, therefore, in order to be sure that he or she has the promised 30 days to investigate and consider the offer, an offeree must "buy" the 30 days by forming a preliminary "option contract" with the offeror. Once the offeror has received the agreed consideration in exchange for his or her "30 days" promise, he or she is no longer free to revoke the offer without being liable for breach of the option contract. (Note that there is still no contract on the main offer; the offeree may decide, after thinking about the main offer for the 30 days, that he or she does not wish to do business after all.)

For offers to buy or sell goods, the UCC (2–205) contains a new rule on revocability. If such an offer is made by a "merchant," is in a signed writing, and by its terms gives assurance that it will remain open for some period of time, it is not revocable because of the "lack of consideration" principle explained above. The merchant is bound to keep the "firm offer" open for the time period stated, or for a reasonable time if the offer gives such assurance but does not state a specific cutoff date; but in no case is the merchant bound for more than three months.

The *Burgess* case at the end of Chapter 7 illustrates the general rules on revocation of offers and on option contracts.

Revocation. If an offer is revocable, it may be revoked expressly or impliedly. Implied revocation occurs when the court feels that underlying facts and circumstances have changed to such an extent that the agreement contemplated by the offer can no longer be made. The death or insanity of either the offeror or the offeree, for instance, impliedly revokes any outstanding offers, because one of the intended parties no longer has the capacity to contract. Likewise, the destruction of the intended subject matter of the contract operates to terminate any unaccepted offers for its purchase or sale. In a situation where a seller-offeror sells an item to a third party, the offeror's first offer to buyer 1 is not terminated unless and until buyer 1 learns of the sale. If, in the meantime, buyer 1 has effectively accepted the offer, the seller is bound to two contracts for the same item and will be guilty of breaching one of the contracts unless he or she can get one of the buyers to accept a substitute.

With an express revocation, the offeror's intent is usually clear enough: "I revoke"; "The deal's off"; "My offer is hereby canceled." The main problem in these cases is not whether the offeror meant to revoke but whether the offeror's revocation took legal effect before the offeree's acceptance. If a revocation takes legal effect before the intended acceptance, there is no contract and the would-be "acceptance" is only a counteroffer. If an acceptance takes legal effect first, there is a contract and the revocation is inoperative.

Where the parties are dealing face-to-face or over the telephone, the jury (or judge) must determine, as a matter of fact, which party spoke the "magic words" first. Where the parties are communicating by letter or telegram, there is an additional complexity in the case because of the fact that communications may cross each other in transit—a revocation and an acceptance may be in the mail at the same time. Many such problems are solved by applying two presumptions that courts have worked out as to when communications take legal effect: generally a revocation is not effective until it is *received*, while an acceptance letter takes legal effect as soon as it is *mailed*. In general, a letter is "received" when the post office gets finished handling it, that is, when the letter is delivered at the place a party has designated as the place for receipt of such communications. If you have a mailbox on your front porch and you have left a letter of acceptance of my offer in the mailbox for the mail carrier to pick up, the jury will then have to decide whether the mail carrier dropped my letter of revocation in the mailbox first, and then took out your letter of acceptance, or vice versa. In the first case, there is no contract; in the second case, there is a contract.

There is one other conceptually difficult problem regarding revocations. This problem arises where the offeror has offered a unilateral contract. Suppose an offeree, intending to accept, has started to perform the requested act and then is notified by the offeror that the offer is revoked. There is no acceptance unless and until the offeree completes the performance requested, but shouldn't he or she, in all fairness, be given the chance to finish once he or she has started? Courts disagree here; there are at least three rules. Some states, following the old common law, permit the offer to be withdrawn anytime prior to complete performance of the requested act, on the basis that every offeree should know that this can happen in a unilateral contract situation. Other courts use a rule which says that an offeree's commencement of performance makes the offer irrevocable for a reasonable period of time, so that he or she is given a chance to finish the performance. If the offeree does render complete performance as requested, then the offeror must perform his or her promise. A few states go one step further and say that where an offeree has made substantial preparations to perform, the offeree must be given a chance to do so.

The following case illustrates the older common-law rule as well as the rules for revoking a "public" offer.

Shuey v. *United States*
92 U.S. 73 (U.S. Supreme Court, 1875)

FACTS   Henry B. Ste. Marie sued in the U.S. Court of Claims to recover the sum of $15,000, the balance alleged to be due him of the reward of $25,000 offered in a proclamation by the secretary of war on April 20, 1865, for the apprehension of John H. Surratt, one of Booth's alleged accomplices in the murder of President Lincoln. The proclamation also promised that "liberal rewards will be paid for any information that shall conduce to the arrest of either of the above-named criminals or their accomplices." The proclamation was not limited in terms to any specific period, and it was signed "Edwin M. Stanton, Secretary of War." On November 24, 1865, President Andrew Johnson published an order revoking the reward offered for the arrest of Surratt.

In April 1866, both Surratt and the claimant were Zouaves in the military service of the papal government. During that month the claimant communicated to Mr. King, the American minister at Rome, the fact that he had discovered and identified Surratt, who had confessed to him his participation in the assassination plot against President Lincoln. The claimant subsequently communicated further information to the same effect and kept watch over Surratt at the American minister's request. Thereupon, certain diplomatic correspondence passed between the government of the United States and the papal government regarding the arrest and extradition of Suratt; and on November 6, 1866, the papal government, at the request of the United States, ordered that Surratt, who was then at Veroli, be arrested and brought to Rome.

Surratt was arrested under this order of the papal government, but as he left the prison at Veroli he escaped from the guard who had him in custody and, crossing the frontier of the papal territory, embarked at Naples, and escaped to Alexandria in Egypt. Immediately after Surratt's escape, and both before and after his embarkation at Naples, the American minister at Rome, having been informed of the escape by the Papal government, took measures to rearrest him. This was done in Alexandria, from which he was conveyed by the American government to the United States. Before his departure the American minister, having procured the discharge of the claimant from the papal military service, sent the claimant to Alexandria to identify Surratt.

From the time of the claimant's first interview with the American minister until the final capture of Surratt, both the claimant and the American minister were ignorant of the fact that the reward offered by the secretary of war for Surratt's arrest had been revoked by President Johnson. The discovery and arrest of Surratt were due entirely to the claimant's disclosures to the American minister at Rome; but the arrests at Veroli and Alexandria were not made by the claimant.

The plaintiff appealed a judgment for the U.S. government.

ISSUES   Was the offer of the reward effectively revoked?

DECISION   Yes. Judgment for the U.S. government affirmed.

REASONS   The Court first decided "that at most the claimant was entitled to the 'liberal reward' promised for information conducing to the arrest, and that reward he has received.

"But, if this were not so, the judgment given by the Court of Claims is correct. The offer of a reward for the apprehension of Surratt was revoked on the Twenty-fourth day of November, 1865; and notice of the revocation was published. It is not to be doubted that the offer was revocable at any time before it was accepted, and before any thing had been done in reliance upon it. There was no contract until its terms were compiled with. Like any other offer of a contract, it might, therefore, be withdrawn before rights had accrued under it; and it was withdrawn through the same channel in which it was made. The same notoriety was given to the revocation that was given to the offer; and the findings of fact do not show that any information was given by the claimant, or that he did any thing to entitle him to the reward offered, until five months after the offer had been withdrawn. True, it is found that then, and at all times until the arrest was actually made, he was ignorant of the withdrawal; but that is the immaterial fact. The offer of the reward not having been made to him directly, but by means of a published proclamation, he should have known that it could be revoked in the manner in which it was made.''

Rejection or Counteroffer. A rejection by the offeree indicates that the offeree does not wish to do business at all. A counteroffer indicates that the offeree is willing to contract, but on terms different from those stated in the original offer. Either of these responses by an offeree operates to terminate the original offer; each of them takes legal effect when it is received by the offeror. A counteroffer gives the original offeror the power to form a contract on the basis of the new terms, by accepting the counteroffer. If the offeree inquires about the possibility of alternative terms but does not indicate an unwillingness to accept the terms offered, such an inquiry is not considered a rejection.

WHAT IS AN EFFECTIVE ACCEPTANCE?

When Effective. Like all other person-to-person communications, words of acceptance spoken during a conversation and heard at almost the same instant take legal effect immediately. As we have seen, most litigations arise where the parties have been negotiating by correspondence and their communications have crossed in transit.

As a convenient method of solving some of these problems, the courts have created the "mailbox rule," which states that a letter of acceptance is effective when it is *mailed*. This has the effect of placing the risk of lost, delayed, or misdelivered communications on the offeror. The rule holds that there is a contract at the instant the letter is placed in the mailbox, even though the letter is delivered late or not delivered at all.

The following case provides a practical example of the significance of the mailbox rule.

Morrison v. Thoelke
155 S.2d 889 (Florida, 1963)

FACTS   The plaintiff-appellees, owners of certain realty, sued to quiet title, specifically requesting that the defendant-appellants be enjoined from making any claim under a recorded contract for the sale of the subject realty. The defendant-appellants counterclaimed, seeking specific performance of the same contract and conveyance of the subject property to them. The lower court, after a hearing, entered a summary decree for the plaintiffs.

Among the undisputed facts established by the pleadings were the following: the appellees were the owners of the subject property, located in Orange County; on November 26, 1957, the appellants, as purchasers, executed a contract for the sale and purchase of the subject property and mailed the contract to the appellees, who were in Texas; on November 27, 1957, the appellees executed the contract and mailed it to the appellants' attorney in Florida. It was also undisputed that after mailing the contract, but prior to its receipt in Florida, the appellees called the appellants' attorney and canceled and repudiated the execution and contract. Nonetheless, the appellants, upon receiving the contract, caused it to be recorded.

ISSUE   Was the sellers' revocation by telephone effective?

DECISION   No. Judgment for buyers; decree for sellers reversed.

REASONS   The question is whether a contract is complete and binding when a letter of acceptance is mailed, thus barring repudiation prior to delivery to the offeror, or when the letter of acceptance is received, thus permitting repudiation prior to receipt.

"The rule that a contract is complete upon deposit of the acceptance in the mails . . . had its origin, insofar as the common law is concerned, in *Adams* v. *Lindsell.*

"Examination of the decision in *Adams* v. *Lindsell* reveals three distinct factors deserving consideration. The first and most significant is the court's obvious concern with the necessity of drawing a line, with establishing some point at which a contract is deemed complete, and their equally obvious concern with the thought that if communication of each party's assent were necessary, the negotiations would be interminable. A second factor, again a practical one, was the court's apparent desire to limit but not overrule the decision in *Cooke.* v. *Oxley,* 3 T.R. 653 (1790), that an offer was revocable at any time prior to acceptance. In application to contracts negotiated by mail, this latter rule would permit revocation even after unqualified assent unless the assent was deemed effective upon posting. Finally, having chosen a point at which negotiations would terminate and having effectively circumvented the inequities of *Cooke* v. *Oxley,* the court, apparently constrained to offer some theoretical justification for its decision, designated a mailed offer as 'continuing' and found a meeting of the minds upon the instant of posting assent. Significantly, the factor of the offeree's loss of control of his acceptance is not mentioned.

"A better explanation of the existing rule seems to be that in such cases the mailing of a letter has long been a customary and expected way of accepting the offer. It is ordinary business usage.''

Exceptions to the Mailbox Rule. There are several situations where a response intended as an acceptance is not effective when it is sent but only if and when it is received. Perhaps the most obvious of these is the situation where the letter does not give the offeror's correct address or does not have sufficient postage to be delivered through regular postal procedures. Here the risk of misdelivery should be borne by the offeree and the letter is an effective acceptance only when it is delivered (if it is delivered at all).

Section 39 of the restatement of contracts also indicates that there is no mailbox presumption in effect where the offeree first sends a rejection communication, and then tries to accept. The second communication is only a counteroffer unless it overtakes the earlier rejection and is received by the offeror before the rejection is received.

A third exception is the situation where the offeror has specified in the offer that the offeror must receive the offeree's acceptance communication before the acceptance is effective. The mailbox rule is only a presumption; it applies unless the offeror says otherwise (e.g., "We must have your acceptance in our main office by the close of business next Friday").

Fourth, there may be no mailbox rule where the offeree responds by using a communication means different from the means of communication that the offeror used for the offer. Generally, if the offeror did not specify the use of a particular means of communication, the offeree may use a different, but still reasonable means of communicating an acceptance, and have the acceptance effective when sent (e.g., offer by letter, acceptance-response by telegram). However, if the offeree uses another means of communication which the court feels is "unreasonable" and therefore not "intended" by the offeror, the acceptance is effective only if and when it is delivered (e.g., offer by letter, acceptance-response by carrier pigeon). Finally, if the offeror has specified *the one means* by which the acceptance must be communicated, a response by any other means is not an acceptance but only a counteroffer.

Nature of an Effective Acceptance. There are three main problem-situations regarding the nature of an effective acceptance. First, what happens when an offeree responds by saying that the offeree wants to do business, but adds, deletes, or modifies one or more of the terms of the offer? Second, what happens when a seller-offeree responds to an order for goods by shipping "nonconforming" (different) goods? And third, when, if ever, does silence by an offeree constitute an effective acceptance?

Offeree Changes Terms. At common law, in order to be an effective acceptance, a response-communication must agree exactly with the terms of the offer; courts often say it must be a "miror image" of the offer. This mirror image rule does not mean that the acceptance must literally restate all the terms of the offer, just that it must *agree* with all of them. Given the right set of facts, a response as simple as "OK" could be interpreted as an acceptance. What the rule does mean is that a response which changes one or more terms is most likely a counteroffer rather than an acceptance, so that no contract is formed when the response is sent. (If an employer writes you a letter offering you a job, starting June 1, and you reply, "I accept, but I can't start until June 20," at that point you do *not* have a job. You have simply made a counteroffer.)

As applied by the courts, this rule meant that there was no contract on the buyer's terms in the very frequently occurring situation where the buyer-offeror sends the seller an order for goods and the seller responds with an acknowledgment/invoice form which contains additional or different terms. If the seller ships the goods and the buyer receives and uses them, there is a contract on the seller's terms. The buyer's use is an acceptance of the seller's counteroffer. If the buyer refused to accept the goods on those terms (e.g., "There are no warranties, express or implied"), there is no contract and the seller will have to absorb the shipping charges. Dissatisfaction with these results led to a specific UCC provision, 2–207, to deal with this problem in the sale of goods situation.

UCC 2–207 first says that a response from the seller which indicates that the seller wants to do business is an acceptance, not a counteroffer, even though it contains terms "additional to or different from" those in the offer. The only way for the offeree (seller) to avoid this result is to make the acceptance *expressly* "conditional on assent to the additional or different terms"—in other words, to clearly make it a counteroffer.

Having thus created a contract for the sale of goods, the Code then proceeds to answer this question: On whose terms? The general rule states: "The additional terms are to be construed as proposals for addition to the contract." In other words, they are *not* part of the contract unless they are specifically agreed to by the offeror; otherwise, there is a contract on the terms of the original offer. Where *both* parties are "merchants" (e.g., GM and a parts supplier), the additional terms become part of the contract unless (*a*) the original offer said otherwise, or (*b*) they materially alter the original offer, or (*c*) the offeror objects to their inclusion within a reasonable time after the offeror has notice of them. Where the offeree-merchant has included such terms and the offeror-merchant has said nothing specific about their inclusion, the litigation will focus on whether or not the new terms "materially alter" the original offer.

Seller Ships Nonconforming Goods. Exactly the same sort of problem, with exactly the same results under the common-law rules, is presented by the seller who responds to an order by shipping goods which do not conform to the terms of the order. Buyers were frequently placed in a situation where they either had to accept the nonconforming goods and make whatever use they could of them, paying for any modifications out of their own pocket, or send the nonconforming goods back and sustain "shut-down-the-plant" losses. (Buyer orders blue widgets; seller ships green. If buyer uses green, buyer has accepted seller's counteroffer and there is a contract for *green*.)

The UCC also has a specific provision, 2–206(1)(b), to deal with this sale of goods problem. The new Code rule states that even a shipment of nonconforming goods by the seller, in response to an order, is to be interpreted as an acceptance rather than a counteroffer. (Under the Code, in the example above, there is a contract for *blue* widgets and the seller has breached this contract and is liable for damages unless the seller sends blue widgets to the buyer within the time permitted by the contract.) The buyer is protected; whether the buyer uses the nonconforming goods or rejects them and buys elsewhere, the buyer can still collect whatever damages are sustained.

119

Silence as Acceptance.   Since, normally, an offeree has no duty to respond to an offer, the offeree's failure to respond cannot be given any particular legal significance. The offeree's silence is therefore not effective as an acceptance in most cases. The common law did, however, recognize four exceptions to this general rule.

First, where an offeree has the opportunity to reject offered services, but instead takes the benefit of them, the offeree's silence does imply an acceptance. By permitting the offeror to perform services which a reasonable person should have known were not being offered for nothing, the offeree has impliedly agreed to pay a fair market price for them.

Second, where the offeror has told the offeree that he or she can accept the offer by not saying or doing anything, just by remaining silent, and the offeree *actually* does intend his or her silence to have that effect, it does.

Third, where because of previous dealings (such as standing order with a book or record club) the offeree has indicated to the offeror that nonnotification by the offeree means that the standing order should be continued, the offeree's silence has the effect of continuing the standing order.

Finally, where nonordered merchandise is sent to the offeree and the offeree exercises "dominion" over it (e.g., by reading an unordered book or magazine or by giving it to someone else), this dominion has the effect of an acceptance and an implied promise to pay the offered contract price.

The second and fourth rules have now been substantially changed because nearly all states have "unordered goods" statutes. These laws vary; the strongest ones make such unsolicited goods an absolute, out-and-out gift to the recipient, who has no obligation to return them, to pay for them, or to account for them in anyway.

IS THE CONTRACT SUBJECT TO A SPECIAL "CANCELLATION" RULE?

At the point where the agreement had been formed by offer and acceptance (and assuming an exchange of legally sufficient considerations), the common-law analysis would have said there was a binding contract. This result still follows from the vast majority of contract situations. However, a growing trend in new statutes and regulations has been to create new rules which give the consumer/buyer a "cancellation" privilege for at least a limited period of time, even after the contract has been entered into.

For example, FTC regulations and statutes in several states give the consumer a three-day cancellation option where the contract is entered into in the consumers' home and is for more than a specified minimum amount. Each of these new laws is likely to contain some exceptions; life insurance sales and emergency home repairs may not be covered, for instance.

The national Truth-in-Lending Act gives a similar three-day rescission option where the borrower's residence has been used as security for a loan, except for the first mortgage to finance the original purchase of the house. The National Interstate Land Sales Act gives a buyer 48 hours to revoke a purchase of land where the buyer has not been given the required "property report" on the land. Many of the states have separate laws covering these same general areas.

If the proposed Uniform Consumer Credit Code is widely adopted by the states, it will cover more transactions than any of the above examples; its three-day cancellation privilege applies to any consumer transaction for goods *or* services, with no dollar minimum, where the sale is made in the buyer's home, or where the home is used as collateral (other than in the original purchase of the home).

For consumer transactions, at least, it appears that we will have to ask this fourth question about many agreements in the very near future.

CASES FOR DISCUSSION

LUCY v. ZEHMER

84 S.E.2d 516 (Virginia, 1954)

(W. O. Lucy and J. C. Lucy sued A. H. Zehmer and Ida S. Zehmer, his wife, to have specific performance of a contract by which the Zehmers were alleged to have sold to W. O. Lucy, a tract of land known as the Ferguson Farm for $50,000. J. C. Lucy, the other complainant, was a brother of W. O. Lucy, to whom W. O. Lucy had transferred a half interest in his alleged purchase.)

Buchanan, Justice

The instrument sought to be enforced was written by A. H. Zehmer on December 20, 1952, in these words: "We hereby agree to sell to W. O. Lucy the Ferguson Farm complete for $50,000.00, title satisfactory to buyer," and signed by the defendants, A. H. Zehmer and Ida S. Zehmer.

The answer of A. H. Zehmer admitted that at the time mentioned W. O. Lucy offered him $50,000 cash for the farm, but that Zehmer considered that the offer was made in jest; that so thinking, and both he and Lucy having had several drinks, he wrote out "the memorandum" quoted above and induced his wife to sign it; that he did not deliver the memorandum to Lucy, but that Lucy picked it up, read it, put it in his pocket, attempted to offer Zehmer $5 to bind the bargain, which Zehmer refused to accept, and realizing for the first time that Lucy was serious, Zehmer assured him that he had no intention of selling the farm and that the whole matter was a

joke. Lucy left the premises insisting that he had purchased the farm. . . .

In his testimony Zehmer claimed that he "was high as a Georgia pine," and that the transaction "was just a bunch of two doggoned drunks bluffing to see who could talk the biggest and say the most." That claim is inconsistent with his attempt to testify in great detail as to what was said and what was done. It is contradicted by other evidence as to the condition of both parties, and rendered of no weight by the testimony of his wife that when Lucy left the restaurant she suggested that Zehmer drive him home. The record is convincing that Zehmer was not intoxicated to the extent of being unable to comprehend the nature and consequences of the instrument he executed, and hence that instrument is not to be invalidated on that ground. It was in fact conceded by defendants' counsel in oral argument that under the evidence Zehmer was not too drunk to make a valid contract.

The appearance of the contract; the fact that it was under discussion for 40 minutes or more before it was signed; Lucy's objection to the first draft because it was written in the singular, and he wanted Mrs. Zehmer to sign it also; the rewriting to meet that objection and the signing by Mrs. Zehmer, the discussion of what was to be included in the sale, the provision for the examination of the title, the completeness of the instrument that was executed, the taking possession of it by Lucy with no request or suggestion by either of the defendants that he give it back, are facts which furnish persuasive evidence that the execution of the contract was a serious business transaction rather than a casual, jesting matter as defendants now contend.

121

Not only did Lucy actually believe, but the evidence shows he was warranted in believing, that the contract represented a serious business transaction and a good faith sale and purchase of the farm.

In the field of contracts, as generally elsewhere, "We must look to the outward expression of a person as manifesting his intention rather than to his secret and unexpressed intention. The law imputes to a person an intention corresponding to the reasonable meaning of his words and acts." At no time prior to the execution of the contract had Zehmer indicated to Lucy by word or act that he was not in earnest about selling the farm. They had argued about it and discussed its terms, as Zehmer admitted, for a long time. Lucy testified that if there was any jesting, it was about paying $50,000 that night.

The mental assent of the parties is not requisite for the formation of a contract. If the words or other acts of one of the parties have but one reasonable meaning, his undisclosed intention is immaterial except when an unreasonable meaning which he attaches to his manifestations is known to the other party.

An agreement or mutual assent is of course essential to a valid contract, but the law imputes to a person an intention corresponding to the reasonable meaning of his words and acts. If his words and acts, judged by a reasonable standard, manifest an intention to agree, it is immaterial what may be the real but unexpressed state of his mind.

So a person cannot set up that he was merely jesting when his conduct and words would warrant a reasonable person in believing that he intended a real agreement.

Whether the writing signed by the defendants and now sought to be enforced by the complainants was the result of a serious offer by Lucy and a serious acceptance by the defendants, or was a serious offer by Lucy and an acceptance in secret jest by the defendants, in either event it constituted a binding contract of sale between the parties.

STRETCH v. GENERAL MOTORS CORP.

126 N.E.2d 389 (Illinois, 1955)

Justice McCormick

This is an appeal from an order of the Circuit Court of Cook County sustaining a motion to dismiss the plaintiff's fifth amended complaint. The complaint was filed in an action for damages occasioned by the defendant's alleged wrongful cancellation of a contract.

Plaintiff's theory on appeal is that there was as a matter of law a binding contract between the parties as set out in the amended complaint. The theory of the defendant is that the plaintiff had declared on an alleged contract which, on the face of the complaint, was not sustainable.

In the plaintiff's fifth amended complaint he alleged that the defendant had entered into a written contract with the plaintiff for certain air magnet valves, as evidenced by defendant's purchase order No. 11925.

Among other things, the "purchase order" stated:

Deliveries are to be made both in quantities and at times specified in schedules furnished by Buyer. Buyer will have no liability for payment for material or items delivered to Buyer which are in excess of quantities specified in the delivery schedules. Buyer may from time to time change delivery schedules or direct temporary suspension of scheduled shipments.

Buyer reserves the right to cancel all or any of the undelivered portion of this order if Seller does not make deliveries as specified in the schedules, or if Seller breaches any of the terms hereof, including the warranties of Seller.

There is no question but that under the law a contract properly entered into whereby the buyer agrees to buy all its requirements of a commodity for a certain period, and the seller agrees to sell the same as ordered, is a valid and enforceable contract and is not void for uncertainty and want of mutuality. . . . The contract in the instant case is not such a contract. Purchase order No. 11925 states that it is issued to cover "shipments of this part, to be received by us from September 1, 1948, to August 31, 1949, as released and scheduled on our series 48 'Purchase Order release and Shipping Schedule' No. 478412 attached and all subsequent Purchase Order releases." Construing the letter of April 1, 1948, as an integral part of the contract, the provisions therein contained are merely that it "now becomes necessary to issue our 48 series 'Open End' purchase order for our requirements from September 1, 1948, through August 31, 1949." Reading and construing the two documents together, notwithstanding the detailed provisions contained on the reverse side of the purchase order, the result is an agreement on the part of the seller to sell a certain identified valve at a certain fixed price in such quantities as the buyer may designate, when and if it issues a purchase order for the same. The word "release" as used throughout these documents is treated by both parties as equivalent to "order."

In Corbin on Contracts, Vol. 1, Sec. 157, the author says:

In what purports to be a bilateral contract, one party sometimes promises to supply another, on specified terms with all the goods or services that the other may order from time to time within a stated period. A mere statement by the other party that he assents to this, or "accepts" it, is not a promise to order any goods or to pay anything. There is no consideration of any sort for the seller's promise; and he is not bound by it. This remains true, even though the parties think that a contract has been made and expressly label their agreement a "contract." In cases like this, there may be no good reason for implying any kind of promise by the offeree. Indeed, the proposal and promise of the seller has the form of an invitation for orders; and the mode of making an operative acceptance is to send in an order for a specific amount. By such order, if there has been no previous notice of revocation, a contract is consummated binding both parties. The standing offer is one of those that empowers the offeree to accept more than once and to create a series of separate obligations. The sending in of one order and the filling of it by the seller does not make the offer irrevocable as to additional amounts if the parties have not so agreed.

* * * * *

Here, the buyer proffers purchase order 11925, with its 25 or more clauses, to the seller for acceptance. In the instrument it makes no promise to do anything. On the surface it appears to be an attempt to initiate a valid bilateral contract. The seller accepts, and as by a flash of leg-erdemain the positions of the buyer and the seller shift. The buyer now becomes the promisee and the seller the promisor. The promise of the seller to furnish identified items at a stated price is merely an offer and cannot become a contract until the buyer issues a release or order for a designated number of items. Until this action is taken, the buyer has made no promise to do anything, and either party may withdraw. The promise is illusory, and the chimerical contract vanishes. "An agreement to sell to another such of the seller's goods, wares, and merchandise as the other might from time to time desire to purchase is lacking in mutuality because it does not bind the buyer to purchase any of the goods of the seller, as such matter is left wholly at the option or pleasure of the buyer. . . ."

* * * * *

The agreement in question is an adaptation of what was termed an "open-end contract," which was used extensively by the federal government during the late war. However, it was used only in cases where the commodities dealt with were staples and either in the possession of or easily accessible to the seller. In this case the use of the contract is shifted and extended to cover commodities which must be manufactured before they are available for sale. According to the admitted statements in the complaints, special tools had to be manufactured in order to produce the item herein involved. The seller here, misled by the many and detailed provisions contained in purchase order No 11925 and ordinarily applicable to an enforceable bilateral contract, undoubtedly, as he alleged in his complaint, did go to considerable expense in providing tools and machines, only to find that by the accepted agreement the buyer had promised to do absolutely nothing. A statement of expectation creates no duty. Courts are not clothed with the power to make contracts for parties, nor can they, under the guise of interpretation, supply provisions actually lacking or impose obligations not actually assumed.

* * * * *

The agreement contained in purchase order No. 11925 was artfully prepared. It contains, in print to fine as to be scarcely legible, more than 23 clauses, most of which are applicable to bilateral contracts. It has all the indicia of a binding and enforceable contract, but it was not a binding and enforceable contract because the promise was made in the higher echelons of business, overshadowed by the aura of business ethics. To say the least, the agreement was deceptive. In a more subterranean atmosphere and between persons of lower ethical standards it might, without any strain on the language, be denominated by a less deterged appellation.

Nevertheless, as the law is today, on the pleadings in the instant case, the trial court could do nothing but sustain the motion to dismiss the complaint. The judgment of the Circuit Court is affirmed.

AMERICAN PARTS CO., INC. v. AMERICAN ARBITRATION ASS'N

154 N.W.2d 5 (Michigan, 1967)

Justice Levin

This action was commenced by American Parts Co. [the purchaser] against American Arbitration Association and Deering Milliken, Inc. The purchaser seeks a stay of arbitration proceedings demanded by the seller on July 19, 1966, pursuant to the arbitration provision of alleged contracts on printed forms called "confirmation of order," which were prepared, signed, and mailed by the seller to the purchaser but were never signed by the purchaser.

On May 28, 1965, Gerrish H. Milliken, Jr., and Albert M. Kaufman, officers respectively of the seller and the purchaser, met in New York City to discuss the sale by the seller to the purchaser of a quantity of fabrics to be used in automobile seat covers. The parties agree that some "understanding" was reached, but disagree as to the terms thereof.

Shortly after the meeting, the seller prepared, signed, and mailed to the purchaser confirmation of order No. 8387, which document Mr. Milliken asserts embodies a "firm agreement" for the sale and purchase of fabrics entered into by Mr. Kauf-

man and himself at their May 28, 1965, New York City meeting. In contrast, Mr. Kaufman states that "after some discussion [at the New York City meeting], it was suggested that Deering prepare a written contract along the lines discussed and submit the same to Detroit Body Products [Division of the purchaser] for its *approval* and execution." Mr. Kaufman further asserts that upon returning to Detroit from an extended trip he found 8387 and immediately responded by a letter dated June 25, 1965, addressed to the seller:

After going over this contract, I found everything to be satisfactory with the exception of the Rivoli Pattern. I noted that your figures and your contract call for $1.75 per yard. I cannot recall acknowledging $1.75 on this fabric and my figures show $1.50. This would be the maximum we could go for this particular number.

If this price meets with your approval and the proper change noted on the contract, it could be signed by us and forwarded to your office immediately.

Mr. Milliken replied in a letter dated June 28, 1965, asserting that 8387 correctly reflects a "firm agreement" entered into by the parties in New York City and requested return of a signed copy of 8387. The purchaser did not reply in writing to the seller's letter of June 28, 1965, but Mr. Kaufman asserts that in further discussions with seller's representatives concerning 8387 he and other representatives of the purchaser continually maintained that 8387 did not reflect the understanding reached between Mr. Milliken and himself and had never been executed or accepted in any manner by the purchaser and, therefore, the purchaser was not bound by 8387.

On September 10, 1965, Mr. Milliken wrote Mr. Kaufman referring to "your attempts to have the price" for the Rivoli pattern "changed" from $1.75 to $1.50 per yard. Mr. Milliken's letter continued:

"This contract with you was made by Deering Milliken in good faith after all of the styles, yardages and prices had been worked out with you in detail here in New York and *the agreement, as made, was confirmed in writing to you with contract 8387.*" (Emphasis added.)

The purchaser replied by letter dated September 29, 1965, stating that a contract in writing had never been executed "because there was never a complete meeting of the minds" and that the completed deliveries had been "on the basis of specific transactions, and neither you nor we have been under any legal obligation except on specific purchases."

Nevertheless, from July, 1965, to February, 1966, the seller shipped to the purchaser well over 135,000 yards of fabrics, including quantities of the Rivoli pattern. All such fabrics were accepted and paid for in full by the purchaser, including the invoices covering the Rivoli pattern, which pattern was invoiced to and paid for by the purchaser at the $1.75 price alleged by the seller.

The seller contends that the purchaser may not challenge the effectiveness of 8387 because 8387 is a written confirmation within the meaning of section 2–(201) of the uniform commercial code . . . adopted both in New York and Michigan; the parties being merchants and the purchaser having failed to object to 8387 within 10 days of its receipt. However, it is clear that the only effect of section 2–(201) "is to take away from the party who fails to answer [within the 10-day period mentioned in that section] the defense of the Statute of Frauds; the burden of persuading the trier of the fact that a contract was in fact made orally prior to the written confirmation is unaffected."

The parties also disagree concerning the application of section 2–(207) of the uniform commercial code; and here again the question which emerges is whether 8387 is a written confirmation of a prior oral contract.

We are also satisfied that neither the reference to 8387 by its number in the seller's numerous invoices accompanying the various deliveries of fabrics nor the purchaser's acceptance and payment for large quantities of fabrics, including the Rivoli pattern, may be regarded as acts manifesting the purchaser's assent to an "additional term."

Section 2–(207) seeks to avoid the imposition on businessmen of unagreed terms. Prior to section 2–(207) terms not agreed upon were often imposed upon one party, generally the purchaser, in consequence of that party's performance of an informal agreement following receipt by such party of a document setting forth additional, often boiler plate, terms. The comments of the National Conference of Commissioners on Uniform State Laws and the American Law Institute indicate that material additional terms do not become part of the contract "unless *expressly* agreed to by the other party." . . .

Under section 2–(207), a party, except a merchant in the case of an immaterial term, may ignore additional terms, and proceed with performance of the agreement actually negotiated by the parties without fear that such performance will be interpreted by court or jury as acceptance of the other party's additional terms. The fact that, following an oral agreement, one or both of the parties resort to what some call the battle of forms, does not, under section 2–(207), change the agreement or prevent the formation of the contract, or place one party or another in the position of waiving the benefit of the agreement or becoming bound to unagreed small or large print by proceeding with performance of those terms upon which the parties, in fact, did orally agree.

From a commercial point-of-view our decision has the advantage of holding the purchaser to any oral agreement reached in New York City which was confirmed by 8387. At the same time it prevents the seller from imposing on the purchaser on obligation to arbitrate merely because the purchaser proceeded with performance unless the purchaser has agreed to the arbitration clause or the parties are found to be merchants and the arbitration clause is found to be an immaterial term.

Reversed and remanded for further proceedings not inconsistent with this opinion. Costs awarded to the party who ultimately prevails.

1. Reinhold Miller leased a building from George Bloomberg. The lease contained the following provision: "At any time during the original term of the lease or any extension thereof, lessee shall have the option to purchase the premises for the then prevailing market price." After three years of occupancy Reinhold notified his landlord of his intention to exercise the option. Both parties ordered an appraisal of the property. After receiving the appraisal report of the landlord, Reinhold offered $80,000 for the property. The offer was rejected, and Reinhold sued George Bloomberg for specific performance. What arguments can George Bloomberg marshal, and who will win?

2. In the winter of 1972 Priceless Foods purchased a piece of property on which to build a store. The property lacked access to the street, and Priceless approached its neighbor Dolly's Clothes to gain an easement across Dolly's property to the street. Since Dolly's had been contemplating an expansion of its building which would have consumed most of its parking lot, the two parties signed an agreement in early 1973 whereby they exchanged easements on their properties and Priceless agreed to pave the area covered by the easements.

    Six months later both parties had abandoned their building plans and Priceless had large "For Sale" signs on its land. In the fall of 1977 Priceless asked Dolly's for a release from the easement on its land in anticipation of a sale. Dolly's then demanded that Priceless perform the paving, and when Priceless refused, Dolly's sued Priceless for damages. Can Dolly's collect?

3. On June 20, 1975, John Thompson entered into a real estate purchase agreement with Steve Quinlan to buy 80 acres of Quinlan's property. The agreement was contingent on Thompson's being able to close purchases on several adjacent pieces of land, and it also stated that any crops growing on the land at the time of closing belonged to Quinlan.

    When the closing was deferred because of title difficulties with the adjacent properties, Quinlan planted the land in wheat on September 2. The closing finally occurred on October 22, and the following June Quinlan returned to harvest the wheat. Thompson sought to receive one third of the proceeds from the sale of the wheat as the owner's share. Does he have a right to this share?

4. In the spring of 1971 Jim Horst opened Sounds, a retail audio store. Within a year Sounds was in financial trouble, and after a series of meetings with Samuel Kowalski, president of Alright, Inc., Horst entered into an agreement with Alright in June 1972 whereby Alright would receive title to all the assets and liabilities of Sounds in exchange for $30,000.

    Horst continued to run Sounds under the general direction of Kowalski, who controlled the disbursements of funds via advances from Alright. In April 1973 Kowalski cut off further funds and Horst learned that Kowalski considered their earlier agreement a secured loan.

    Horst had always considered the agreement a sale, and he pointed to a credit application, signed by Kowalski, listing Sounds as a subsidiary of Alright and Kowalski as principal owner. In addition, Kowalski had been introduced on several occasions to Sounds' employees as the new owner and had never objected. Kowalski pointed to the fact that he had listed the advances to Sounds as loans on the books of Alright and had never taken a tax deduction for Sounds' losses. Finally, he claimed that all the essential terms for a sale had never been agreed on. Who owns Sounds?

5. After 15 years of work as an engineer for Federal Motors Corporation, Horace Hanke was "separated" from the company. He sued to receive severance pay from

his former employers, based on a description of a "separation allowance plan" contained in an employment handbook given to him when he started work at Federal Motors. The plan was designed to provide income for separated employees, and Hanke claimed that it constituted a unilateral offer which he had accepted by working.

The first paragraph describing the separation allowance plan stated that the description of the plan in the handbook was not intended to create a contractual relationship but was for information only. A similar general disclaimer, italicized and outlined in red, appeared at the back of the handbook. Can Hanke collect severance pay?

6. Passfast, Inc., is a driving school for truck drivers which operates franchised schools in several states. Jonathan Shift, one of Passfast's franchisees, had his franchise terminated when he allegedly failed to live up to his franchise agreement. The contract stipulated that "he will produce . . . a minimum of 15 enrollments per month or the School can declare this agreement null and void."

   Jonathan brings a suit for breach of contract, claiming that the agreement is ambiguous in that it fails to state whether "15 enrollments per month" is a yearly average, an average up to date, or a minimum for each and every month. What result?

7. The Millers contracted with Homepride, Inc., for the construction of a new residence. They received a rough estimate of the costs, "around $30,000 to $32,000." There was no written agreement regarding either construction details or a fixed price for the house.

   The Millers made monthly payments as the construction progressed. Several extras were added, and by the time the house was finished, the Millers had paid about $40,000. Several months later Homepride, Inc., sent a final bill demanding another $8,000. It claimed that the final agreement between Homepride and the Millers had been for "cost plus 10 percent profit." The Millers deny that the phrase was ever used in their conversations with Homepride's representatives and refuse further payments. Can Homepride collect the $8,000 in court?

8. Purchaser Company conducted oral negotiations with Seller Corporation for the sale of fabric to be used in seat covers. Shortly thereafter, Seller Corporation sent to Purchaser Company a purchase order confirmation. Purchaser Company rejected the price stipulated for one of the fabrics, insisting that the orally agreed price had been lower. Seller Corporation, arguing that the purchase order confirmation was its acceptance of Purchaser's offer, sued Purchaser for breach of contract. Decision?

9. Morris offered his farm for sale to Charles. The written offer gave a description of the land, the price, and the payment terms, but it did not mention a time of possession. The offer was to be good for 30 days. Charles had trouble financing the down payment, and the negotiations continued for some time. Two months after the written offer was made, Morris moved away from his property. However, when after a few more months he heard that Charles had still not occupied the land, he moved back and informed Charles that he considered the offer to be void. Now Charles sues Morris for specific performance. Decision?

10. Theo Sass entered into a franchise agreement with Fat-Sow, a Nebraska corporation selling vitamins and minerals to be used as additives to livestock feed. He received a $1,000 advance from the franchisor, or "$125 per week drawn against commissions earned from sales of products for eight weeks." During the first eight weeks Theo made no sales, but later business picked up and he earned commissions of about $12,000. Fat-Sow Corporation later became dissatisfied with Theo's

work, terminated the franchise, and asked for payment of the $1,000 advance. Theo claimed that he had made no sales and earned no commissions during the specified eight weeks and that consequently he did not have to return the $1,000. Fat-Sow Corporation sues Theo Sass. Who wins?

11. As a special attraction at the 1978 annual Labor Day Golf Tournament, sponsored by the Ritzy Country Club of Smalltown, Frederick Fender, the local Buick dealer, offered a brand-new Buick to "the first entry who shoots a hole in one on the eighth hole." The golf course of the Ritzy Country Club had only 9 holes, but it could be played as an 18-hole course by going around it twice. Each hole thus carried two numbers, and hole 8 was also marked as hole 17. Archibald Green scored his hole in one on hole 8 on the first day of the tournament while playing from the 17th tee in an 18-hole match. When he claimed his prize, Frederick Fender refused to give it to him. Who wins in a suit by Archibald against Frederick?

Consideration | 6

This chapter is concerned with the second part of our contract "formula"—the requirement of "consideration." Once again, we need to know the answers to three main questions: What does the law mean by consideration? What are the basic methods of complying with this requirement? What do the courts accept as legally sufficient consideration?

We will use Uncle Ned and his nephew Johnny to provide some factually simple hypothetical examples of how the consideration rules work.

WHAT IS THE CONSIDERATION REQUIREMENT?

Basic Definitions. In our legal system a promise is generally not enforceable as a contract, even if it is agreed to by the promisee, unless the promise is supported by legally sufficient consideration. Stated another way, a completely one-sided promise of benefits (a promise of "something for nothing") does not generally bind the promisor to performance or make him or her liable in the event of nonperformance. If Uncle Ned promises to give Johnny $5,000 as a Christmas present and then changes his mind, Johnny cannot sue and collect the $5,000, even if the promise was written and signed or was made in front of witnesses. The consideration requirement, most simply stated, means that unless *something* is given in return for the promise, the promise is not legally enforceable.

Source and Recipient of Consideration. The required consideration may be supplied by the promisee himself or herself, or by a third person. Uncle Ned would be contractually obligated if he had promised Johnny the $5,000 in return for a house-painting job and Johnny saw to it that the job was done, whether or not Johnny did the work. When Uncle Ned gets his house painted according to the terms of the agreement, he owes Johnny the $5,000.

The benefits given in return for the promise may be given to the promisor himself or herself, or to a third person. If Uncle Ned promised the $5,000 to Johnny if Johnny would paint H. O. Moaner's house, he is bound to pay the money if Johnny does the job. Even if no one receives anything that most people would think of as a "benefit," there is legally sufficient consideration if the promisee has assumed (a *burden*, by doing something which he or she was not already legally bound to do.) If Uncle Ned promises the $5,000 to Johnny if Johnny stops smoking until age 21, and Johnny does so, Uncle Ned is legally obligated to pay the money. In each of these last two examples, (Uncle Ned has received a *legal* benefit, in the sense that he got the performance he bargained for as the price for his promise, and he has therefore received consideration.)

HOW DOES ONE COMPLY WITH THE CONSIDERATION REQUIREMENT?

There are four ways in which the consideration requirement may be satisfied, so that the promisor is legally bound to perform his or her promise: (1) a bargained-for exchange of values; (2) a change of legal position by the promisee in reliance on the promise; (3) the seal; and (4) a statutory exception to the requirement.

Bargained-for Exchange of Values. The basic meaning of the consideration requirement is that there must be a "bargain" in order for there to be a contract; promises which are gifts, with nothing given in return, are not legally enforceable. The usual method of complying with the consideration requirement, therefore, is to prove the existence of a bargain, to prove that something *was* given or promised in return. Since the law generally does not concern itself with whether the bargain was a good one or a bad one, but only with the question of whether there was in fact a bargain, the promisee should be able to enforce the promise made to him or her by showing that there was an agreement for any sort of exchange of benefits.

Wood v. Lucy, Lady Duff-Gordon
118 N.E. 214 (New York, 1917)

FACTS "The defendant styles herself a 'creator of fashions.' . . . Manufacturers of dresses, millinery, and like articles are glad to pay for a certificate of her approval. The things which she designs, fabrics, parasols, and what not, have a new value in the public mind when issued in her name. She employed the plaintiff to help her turn this vogue into money. He was to have the exclusive right, subject always to her approval, to place her indorsements on the designs of others. He was also to have the exclusive right to place her own designs on sale, or to license others to market them. In return, she was to have one half of 'all profits and revenues' derived from any contracts he might make. The exclusive right was to last at least one year from April 1, 1915, and thereafter from year to year unless terminated by notice of 90 days. The plaintiff says that he kept the contract on his part, and that the defendant broke it. She placed her indorsement on fabrics, dresses, and millinery without his knowledge, and withheld the profits." The plaintiff filed suit for damages. The defendant filed a demurrer to the complaint, and the demurrer was denied. The defendant appealed.

ISSUE Did Wood assume any real performance obligation under the contract?

130

DECISION   Yes. Judgment of trial court, denying defendant's motion for dismissal, is affirmed. Plaintiff is entitled to damages.

REASONS   "An agreement of employment is signed by both parties. . . . The defendant insists, however, that it lacks the elements of a contract. She says that the plaintiff does not bind himself to anything. It is true that he does not promise in so many words that he will use reasonable efforts to place the defendant's indorsements and market her designs. We think, however, that such a promise is fairly to be implied. The law has outgrown its primitive stage of formalism when the precise word was the sovereign talisman and every slip was fatal. It takes a broader view to-day. A promise may be lacking, and yet the whole writing may be 'instinct with an obligation,' imperfectly expressed. . . . If that is so, there is a contract.

"The implication of a promise here finds support in many circumstances. The defendant gave an *exclusive* privilege. She was to have no right for at least a year to place her own indorsements or market her own designs except through the agency of the plaintiff. The acceptance of the exclusive agency was an assumption of its duties. . . . We are not to suppose that one party was to be placed at the mercy of the other. . . . Many other terms of the agreement point the same way. We are told at the outset by way of recital that 'the said Otis F. Wood possesses a business organization adapted to the placing of such indorsements as the said Lucy, Lady Duff-Gordon has approved.' The implication is that the plaintiff's business organization will be used for the purpose for which it is adapted. But the terms of the defendant's compensation are even more significant. Her sole compensation for the grant of an exclusive agency is to be one-half of all the profits resulting from the plaintiff's efforts. Unless he gave his efforts, she could never get anything. Without an implied promise, the transaction cannot have such business 'efficacy as both parties must have intended that at all events it should have.' . . . But the contract does not stop there. The plaintiff goes on to promise that he will account monthly for all moneys received by him, and that he will take out all such patents and copyrights and trade-marks as may in his judgment be necessary to protect the rights and articles affected by the agreement. It is true, of course, . . . that if he was under no duty to try to market designs or to place certificates of indorsement, his promise to account for profits or take out copyrights would be valueless. But in determining the intention of the parties, the promise *has* a value. It helps to enforce the conclusion that the plaintiff *had* some duties. His promise to pay the defendant one-half of the profits and revenues resulting from the exclusive agency and to render accounts monthly, was a promise to use reasonable efforts to being profits and revenues into existence. . . ." Thus there was a valid contract.

In most cases the existence or nonexistence of a bargain can be seen pretty clearly, but there are a few situations where the facts are somewhat ambiguous. One of the most difficult distinctions to draw is that between a condition attached to the promise of a gift (no contract) and a burden undertaken as part of a bargain (contract). Suppose that Uncle Ned says to Johnny, "Come over to the house Saturday night, and I'll fix you a steak dinner." Is Uncle Ned contractually obligated to provide a steak dinner when Johnny arrives as requested? No, he's not—for two reasons. First, Uncle Ned's promise is not intended by him, or reasonably understood by Johnny, as a contractual arrangement. Second,

131

"coming over to the house" is neither intended nor understood as the price of the steak dinner. But what about the case where Uncle Ned tells Johnny, "When you get married, I'll give you $5,000," and Johnny does in fact get married? Whether Johnny's marriage supplies consideration for Uncle Ned's promise depends on the parties' intent, as derived by the court from the surrounding facts and circumstances. If Johnny already had his wedding planned and the date set and Uncle Ned was just making a promise of a cash wedding gift, there is probably no consideration for the promise and thus no contract. But if Uncle Ned is trying to induce Johnny away from life as a "swinging single," the initiative for the marriage comes from *Uncle Ned* rather than Johnny, and Johnny in response to the promise does as his uncle requests and gets married, Uncle Ned is contractually bound to pay the money.

Devecmon v. *Shaw & Devries*
14 A. 464 (Maryland, 1888)

FACTS   John Semmes Devecmon brought suit against the executors of John S. Combs, deceased. After judgment by default a jury was sworn to assess the damages sustained by the plaintiff. The evidence consisted of certain accounts taken from the books of the deceased and testimony that the plaintiff was a nephew of the deceased, lived for several years in his family, and was in his service as clerk for several years. The plaintiff then made an offer to testimony, which is thus stated in the bill of exceptions: "That the plaintiff took a trip to Europe in 1878, and that said trip was taken by said plaintiff, and the money on said trip was spent by the said plaintiff at the instance and request of said Combs, and upon a promise from him that he would reimburse and repay to the plaintiff all money expended by him in said trip; and that the trip was so taken and the money so expended by the said plaintiff, but that the said trip had no connection with the business of said Combs; and that said Combs spoke to the witness of his conduct in being this willing to pay his nephew's expenses as liberal and generous on his part." On objection, the court refused to permit the evidence to be given and the plaintiff excepted. The trial court gave judgment to the defendants, executors of the estate of John Combs, deceased, and the plaintiff appealed.

ISSUE   Did the plaintiff provide consideration, so that the defendant was bound to pay for the trip? Was there a valid contract?

DECISION   Yes. Judgment reversed and new trial ordered.

REASONS   "It might very well be, and probably was the case, that the plaintiff would not have taken a trip to Europe at his own expense. But whether this be so or not, the testimony would have tended to show that the plaintiff incurred expense at the instance and request of the deceased, and upon an express promise by him that he would repay the money spent. It was a burden incurred at the request of the other party, and was certainly a sufficient consideration for a promise to pay. Great injury might be done by inducing persons to make expenditures beyond their means, on express promise of repayment, if the law were otherwise. It is an entirely different case from a promise to make another a present;' or render him a gratuitous service. It is nothing

Change of Position in Reliance. Most courts today accept the rule stated in Section 90 of the *Restatement of the Law of Contracts*: "A promise which the promisor should reasonably expect to induce action or forbearance of a definite and substantial character on the part of the promisee and which does induce such action or forbearance is binding if injustice can be avoided only by enforcement of the promise." In other words, where the promisee, reasonably relying on the promise of benefits, makes a substantial change in his or her legal position, a court will estop (prevent) the promisor from using the "no consideration" argument when he or she is sued on the promise. The courts usually refer to this concept as "promissory estoppel."

If, when Uncle Ned makes his promise of a $5,000 gift, Johnny goes out and buys a new car, which he would not have bought except for his reliance on the promise, Uncle Ned is probably estopped from asserting a no consideration defense when Johnny sues him for the money.

The following case illustrates the application of this doctrine and the difficulty which the court may have in figuring out how much the promisee should recover in such cases.

Hoffman v. Red Owl Stores, Inc.
26 N.W.2d 683 (Wisconsin, 1964)

FACTS   Relying on the representations of Lukowitz, a representative of Red Owl Stores, that the company would set him up in business in a franchised Red Owl grocery store for a capital investment of $18,000, Hoffman and his wife did the following: sold their existing bakery business and building; bought a small grocery store, ran it for several months "to get some experience," and then resold it; took an option on the proposed site for the Red Owl store and made a down payment on the lot; moved the family's home; and rented a house in the town where the new store was to be located. Red Owl kept increasing the capital requirements, and the deal for the new store fell through without the parties ever having agreed to a contract. Hoffman and his wife sued for the damages they sustained as a result of the above transactions. The trial court ordered judgment for the plaintiffs, based on the jury's verdict, but said a new trial would be required to determine the exact amount of the loss suffered by the sale of the small grocery store. Both parties appealed.

ISSUE   Is this a case for the application of the doctrine of "promissory estoppel"?

Hoffman v. Red Owl Stores, Inc. (continued)

DECISION   Yes. Judgment affirmed, including the order for a new trial to determine the damages from the sale of the grocery store.

REASONS   The court first quoted Section 90 of the *Restatement.* Chief Justice Currie then said: "The record here discloses a number of promises and assurances given to Hoffman by Lukowitz in behalf of Red Owl upon which plaintiffs relied and acted upon to their detriment.

*****

"There remains for consideration the question of law raised by defendants that agreement was never reached on essential factors necessary to establish a contract between Hoffman and Red Owl. Among these were the size, cost, design, and layout of the store building; and the terms of the lease with respect to rent, maintenance, renewal,and purchase options. This poses the question of whether the promise necessary to sustain a cause of action for promissory estoppel must embrace all essential details of a proposed transaction between promisor and promisee so as to be the equivalent of an offer that would result in a binding contract between the parties if the promisee were to accept the same.

"However, Sec. 90 of *Restatment, 1 Contracts,* does not impose the requirement that the promise giving rise to the cause of action must be so comprehensive in scope as to meet the requirements of an offer that would ripen into a contract if accepted by the promisee. Rather the conditions imposed are:

(1)   Was the promise one which the promisor should reasonably expect to induce the action of forbearance of a definite and substantial character on the part of the promisee?
(2)   Did the promise induce such action or forbearance?
(3)   Can injustice be avoided only by enforcement of the promise?

"We deem it would be a mistake to regard an action grounded on promissory estoppel as the equivalent of a breach-of-contract action. As Dean Boyer points out, it is desirable that fluidity in the application of the concept be maintained. While the first two of the above-listed three requirements . . . present issues of fact which ordinarily will be resolved by a jury, the third requirement, that the remedy can only be invoked where necessary to avoid injustice, is one that involves a policy decision by the court. Such a policy decision necessarily embraces an element of discretion.

"We conclude that injustice would result here if plaintiffs were not granted some relief because of the failure of defendants to keep their promises which induced plaintiffs to act to their detriment."

The Seal.   As an alternative method of holding persons to promises made and accepted, the common law said that if the promise was made in writing and the writing was signed and "sealed," there was a conclusive presumption that consideration had been given in return. The promisor, in other words, was not able to make the no consideration argument against his signed and sealed written promise. The use of the word *seal* or the initials "L. S." before or after the promisor's signature was sufficient.

Only a few states follow this rule today. In about half of the states a seal on the signed writing supplies a *rebuttable* presumption of consideration, meaning that the promisor still has a chance to prove that no consideration was given for the promise. Similarly, in many states the presence of a corporate seal on a document creates a rebuttable presumption that the document was executed by someone who had authority to act for the corporation. In about half of the states the presence of a seal on a signed, written document creates no presumption at all as to consideration: the promisee must prove consideration by one of the other methods. This last, "no-effect-at-all" rule is adopted by the UCC (2–203) for the sale of goods, so that many states now have two rules on the seal—one for goods and one for other contracts. The problem of the seal is further complicated by the fact that many states allow a longer "statute of limitations" period in which to bring suit where the contract is "sealed."

Statutory Exceptions to the Consideration Requirement. A respectable body of legal opinion holds that the consideration requirement has caused more problems than it has prevented, and that a person should be bound to perform whatever he or she promised to perform, at least where the promise was made in a signed writing, whether or not the person gets anything in return. These same ideas may have been the rationale for the common-law rule on the seal; they find their modern expression in various statutes which provide that certain promises are enforceable even though no consideration was given in return. One such provision is the "firm offer" rule discussed in Chapter 5: if a merchant's signed, written offer to buy or sell goods, says that the offer will remain open for acceptance, it is not revocable by the merchant even though the merchant has received no consideration for the promise to keep the offer open. Similarly, the Model Business Corporation Act, Section 17, provides that an offer to subscribe to shares of stock is not revocable for a period of six months unless otherwise agreed.

The UCC contains two other "no-consideration- required" sections that have very broad potential application (and are thus very important). UCC 1–107 permits a party to a contract to waive any claim the party may have for an alleged breach of the contract by means of a signed writing. No special form is required, and no consideration need be received by the person giving up the contract claim. Since this section is in Article 1 of the Code, it applies to all of the types of contracts covered in any other section of the Code.
UCC 2–209(1) applies only to contracts for the sale of goods, but it is also a very significant exception to the consideration requirement. It provides that any agreement modifying a preexisting contract for the sale of goods needs no consideration to be binding. Suppose you contract to buy a new car but decide after you've driven it for two days that you'd like rear-seat stereo speakers for the radio. You call up the dealer and talk to your salesman, and the salesman promises to install the speakers for no additional charge if you bring the car in next Monday. If the jury believes your testimony that such a modification of the original car contract was agreed to, the dealer is now contractually bound to install the speakers. Without 2–209(1), the dealer would *not* be bound, since the dealer received no new consideration for the speakers. (*Remember* that this new rule applies *only* to goods contracts. If you want to modify contracts for land, services, etc., there must be consideration moving both ways.)

In addition to these Code provisions, special statutory provisions applying the no-consideration-required rule to other types of contracts have been adopted by some states. The following statute, adopted by Michigan in 1941, is an example: "Agreements to Modify or Discharge Contracts, Sec. 1. An agreement hereafter made to change or modify, or to discharge in whole or in part, any contract, obligation, or lease, or any mortgage or other security interest in personal or real property, shall not be invalid because of the absence of consideration: Provided, that the agreement changing, modifying, or discharging such contract, obligation, lease, mortgage or security interest shall not be valid or binding unless it shall be in writing and signed by the party against whom it is sought to enforce the change, modification, or discharge."

Although the working of this Michigan statute makes it potentially applicable to *any* contract, it was apparently little known and less used, because the *Belt* case, following, is the first reported appellate court decision which cited it in deciding a case.

Belt v. *Wolpin Co.*
197 N.W.2d 129 (Michigan, 1972)

FACTS Belt sued for breach of a contract to lease certain trucking equipment. Wolpin Company said that its liability under the contract was discharged when Belt indorsed and cashed payment checks which contained a notation that the payee by indorsing or cashing the check acknowledged payment in full of the underlying debt.

ISSUE Does the cashing of the check with such a notation discharge the debt in full, under M.C.L.A. 566.1?

DECISION Yes. Summary judgment for defendants affirmed.

REASONS "The record shows that several checks which defendants mailed to plaintiff in response to the latter's rental invoices bore certain conditions at the time of mailing, but that additional modifying clauses appeared on these checks when they were returned by defendants' bank after payment. The language on the final check, dated June 26, 1961, is typical and reads as follows:

" 'In full and final settlement, payment and discharge of any and all claims of every nature and description and whether accrued or contingent to date hereof including any claims under contract terminated May 15, 1961.'

"After this check had been indorsed and cashed by plaintiff, and was returned by defendants' bank, it contained the additional words "but, it is understood that this payment applies only to truck rental charges." An affidavit filed by plaintiff stated that he did not recall seeing the notations on the checks, and that he had no information or knowledge as to the origin of the additional modifying clause. The trial judge concluded that defendants had satisfactorily established the fact that they had entered settlement provisions upon the checks, and that plaintiff had not succeeded in raising a factual issue on this point. The trial judge then decided that plaintiff's indorsement and cashing of these checks, bearing the condition therein stated, effectively released defendants from all liability for breach of contract, either under the doctrine of accord and satisfaction, or alternatively, under the theory that the indorsed checks constituted a signed writing discharging defendants' obligations pursuant to M.C.L.A. 566.1, M.S.A, 26.978(1).

"Our examination of the evidence confirms the correctness of the trial court's decision. The provision appearing on the check of June 26, 1961, clearly discharged any claim plaintiff might have had for breach of a written leasing agreement. We hold that this check, when indorsed and cashed by plaintiff, constituted a signed writing which effectively discharged defendants' obligations, pursuant to the above cited statute. . . . It is, of course, well known that the subsequent addition by second parties of purported modifying clauses could not alter the legal effect of the settlement provision originally placed upon the checks by defendants. . . . Having concluded that there was a legally sufficient discharge of defendants' obligations, we need not decide whether accord and satisfaction occurred in the instant case."

WHAT DO THE COURTS ACCEPT AS LEGALLY SUFFICIENT CONSIDERATION?

Legal Sufficiency versus Adequacy. As noted previously, the courts do not generally concern themselves with whether the parties have made a "good deal" or a "bad deal"; they will enforce stupid and unreasonable contracts as well as wise and reasonable ones. To be legally sufficient, a consideration need not be "adequate," in the sense of being a reasonable estimate of a jury's idea of fair market value. Unless there are unusual circumstances, such as fraud, duress, or undue influence, it is enough that something of value was received in return as the price of the promise, even though that "something" does not seem very desirable to the judge or jury. Freedom of contract means that you have the power to make your own bargains and that you are generally bound by the bargains you make once you have agreed to them.

Courts continue to state these general rules, and yet they seem more and more willing to "remake" contracts so as to arrive at "fair" results. For one thing, the *gross* inadequacy of the consideration received by one party is *some* evidence to support that party's claim to have been defrauded or subjected to duress or undue influence. Also, where a court finds such gross inadequacy it will generally refuse to exercise its equity powers to order specific performance of the unfair contract, since "He who seeks equity must do equity." A court may even refuse to award money damages in such a case, by using the newly popular concept of "unconscionability" (basically meaning that the contract is so terribly unfair that it should not be enforced as written). For the purpose of calculating amounts due under the U.S. estate and gift taxes, the Internal Revenue Code requires examination of alleged "contracts" to make sure that each party has received "an adequate (and full) consideration in money and money's worth." (If Uncle Ned promises Johnny $50,000 for painting a picket fence, there may technically be a contract, but the IRS will view the transaction as a gift by Uncle Ned of the difference between $50,000 and the fair market value of the painting job.)

The following paragraphs discuss some of the other "returns" which the court do *not* generally accept as supplying a legally sufficient consideration.

Nominal Consideration. *Nominal* means "in name only" or "very small." "Nominal consideration" usually refers to the recital of $1 as consideration. There is nothing inherently wrong with $1 or any other very small amount as consideration for a return promise, if that amount is *in fact* intended and agreed to as the price of the bargain. Most courts, however, do not accept the mere recital of a fictitious dollar bill as legally sufficient consideration. (See the discussion of this point in the *Burgess* case, at the end of Chapter 7.)

Good Consideration. As it appears in most legal forms ("and other good and valuable consideration"), *good* seems to be used as a synonym for *valuable* (and thus legally sufficient) consideration. However, that is not the meaning given to the term by most authoritative legal texts; they generally define *good consideration* in terms of a promise to be a "good relative," and thus *not* legally sufficient. "Nice family feelings" do not provide a legally sufficient consideration. When Johnny promises to be a "good nephew" (kind, loyal, loving, etc., etc.) in return for Uncle Ned's promise of $5,000, there is no consideration for Uncle Ned's promise, and Uncle Ned is not contractually bound to pay the money.

Past Consideration. A promise of benefits is not changed from a gift into a contract by the fact that the promisee has given something to the promisor in a previous, separate transaction. Such so-called past consideration is no consideration for the new promise of benefits. It is this rule which requires that a modification of a preexisting contract must be supported by a new exchange of considerations in order to be enforceable, except for UCC 2–209(1). Likewise, this rule generally prevents a "good Samaritan" from enforcing a promise to repay the good Samaritan for benefits previously conferred on the promisor as a gift. Since no contract was entered into or intended at the time the benefits were originally provided, those benefits—a completed gift—constitute past consideration.

Moral Consideration. Generally, the courts treat the existence of a moral obligation in the same way that they treat past consideration. The fact that a person is morally obligated to provide certain benefits does not supply consideration for his or her promise to provide them. By most standards the person who received aid and comfort from the good Samaritan would be morally obligated to repay the good Samaritan when able to do so, but the courts do not regard this moral obligation as a legally sufficient consideration.

There are three situations where the courts *will* generally enforce a promise on the basis of some idea of moral obligation. Two of them are closely related—new promises to pay a debt barred by a discharge in bankruptcy or by the running of the statute of limitations. In each of these cases the debtor has received the values the debtor contracted for but has not paid for them; in each case the debtor has a technical defense which would prevent a successful lawsuit to collect the debt. Nevertheless, when the debtor makes a new promise to pay the debt in either of these cases, most courts will hold the debtor to the new promise, even though the debtor has received no *new* consideration, on the theory that "a person ought to pay his or her debts." In most states one or both of these new promises must be made in a signed writing to be enforceable.

The third situation relates to promises made to charitable organizations. These are almost uniformly enforceable, though the courts do not always agree on why they are. Some courts imply mutual promises between and among the donors not to revoke their pledges to the charity. Where the charity has "moved in reliance on the promises" (for example, by hiring an architect to design a new building, or by taking an option on land), the doctrine of promissory estoppel can be applied. Even without applying either of these ideas, some courts apparently enforce promises to charitable organizations on the basis of some underlying "moral obligation" to support good works.

Preexisting Duty. \A promise to do or the actual doing of something which one is already bound to do anyway does not supply consideration for a return promise.\Thus, when a landowner promises an extra bonus to a builder if the builder will get a job done on time, in accordance with the terms of the original contract, the builder cannot collect this promised bonus even if the builder does get the job done on time⸨The builder was already legally obligated to do so and has promised nothing new in return for the bonus. Similarly, police officers usually cannot collect rewards offered for the capture of criminals when they make the arrest in their own jurisdiction, in the line of their official duties. The following case presents the application of this rule in a slightly different factual context.

Reif v. *Paige*
13 N.W. 473 (Wisconsin, 1882)

FACTS   During the afternoon of December 3, 1880, a hotel in the city of Oshkosh, known as the Beckwith House, was destroyed by fire. The defendant and his wife lived in this hotel, occupying rooms on the fourth story. When the fire broke out, Mrs. Paige was in those rooms and perished in the flames. The members of the Oshkosh fire department placed a ladder at the window near where Mrs. Paige was supposed to be, and at least two firemen attemped to enter the window and rescue her but were driven back by the smoke and flames. The ladder was then removed, but it was subsequently replaced at the same window. About this time, after the fire had been raging about 30 minutes or more, the defendant, who had been absent, reached the scene of the fire and, as alleged in the complaint, promised to pay a reward of $5,000 to any person who would rescue his wife from the burning building, dead or alive. The plaintiff claimed that he had earned the reward and brought this action to recover it. The plaintiff's complaint was dismissed by the trial court.

ISSUE   Was the fireman under a preexisting duty to perform the acts requested here?

DECISION   No. Judgment for plaintiff. Trial court reversed.

REASONS   "The offer of a reward by the defendant for rescuing the body of his wife, and the rescue of her remains by the plaintiff, with knowledge of such offer, and with a view to obtaining the reward offered, constituted a contract between the parties, which was fully and completely executed by the plaintiff. The offer, which the proofs tend to show the defendant made, was, in substance, 'I will give $5,000 to any person who will bring the body of my wife out of that building, dead or alive.' There were no restrictions or limitations to the offer, and no additional requirement upon the claimant of the offered bounty. Hence, when the plaintiff, with a view of obtaining the offered reward, rescued the body of Mrs. Paige, he had done all that the offer required him to do, and if he has any cause of action it was then complete.

"There was considerable discussion by counsel as to what are the duties of firemen. We know of no guide for ascertaining those duties other than the charter of the municipality in which they are employed, and the ordinances or by-laws enacted pursuant thereto. The ordinances of the city of Oshkosh in respect to its fire department were read in evidence, and reference made to the city charter in that behalf. We do not care to comment upon these, for we are clear that there is nothing in them which made it the duty of the plaintiff to enter the fourth story of the burning building and rescue the body of Mrs. Paige from the flames, at the imminent hazard of losing his own life. That he incurred such hazard there can be no doubt from the testimony. . . .

"It follows, from the views above expressed, that inasmuch as the plaintiff could not rescue the body of Mrs. Paige from the burning building without imminent peril of losing his own life, and inasmuch as it was not his duty as a paid officer and member of the fire department to do so, he is in a position to claim the reward alleged to have been offered by the defendant for such rescue."

One of the most common applications of the preexisting duty rule is in cases where a debtor offers to pay part of the debt if the creditor will accept the part payment as full satisfaction of the debt. Obviously, in most cases the creditor is willing to agree to anything in order to get some cash, especially if the debt is past due and the debtor is in questionable financial condition. Does such an agreement prevent the creditor from later suing to collect the unpaid balance of the original debt? At common law the general rule was clear: no, the creditor is not prevented from collecting the balance, because the debtor's part payment was nothing more (in fact less) than the debtor was already legally obligated to pay.

Only under special circumstances would the part payment legally discharge the debt in full. If the part payment was made and accepted by the creditor as payment in full before the debt was in fact due, the creditor would be bound by the acceptance of this "early payment." The creditor in this case did receive new consideration for the agreement to surrender the balance of the debt because the creditor had no right to receive any payment on the date that the payment was actually made. There is likewise consideration for the discharge of the entire debt if the part payment is accompanied by "some new item," received and accepted by the creditor, which the creditor was not previously legally entitled to receive. There is consideration (at least technically), and the debt is (probably) discharged, when a creditor agrees to accept a ball-point pen and $600 in cash in full satisfaction of a $1,000 debt. Finally, where there is an honest, good faith dispute over the amount that is actually owed and the creditor agrees to take a lesser sum in full payment, the creditor is bound and the debt is discharged.

The following case shows that the courts are likely to be quite liberal in their definition of such a "new item."

Jaffray v. *Davis*
124 N.Y. 164 (1891)

FACTS   The facts found by the trial court in this case were agreed upon. They were simple and presented a familiar question of law. The facts were that on December 8, 1886, the defendants owed the plaintiffs for goods sold between that date and the previous May at an agreed price, the sum of $7,714.37; that on December 27, 1886, the defendants delivered to the plaintiffs three promissory notes amounting in the aggregate to $3,462.24 secured by a *chattel mortgage on* the stock, fixtures, and other property of the defendants, located in East Saginaw, Michigan; and that these notes and the chattel mortgage were received by plaintiffs under an agreement to accept them in full satisfaction and discharge of the indebtedness.

ISSUE   Did the creditor receive new consideration for his promise to discharge the debt in full?

DECISION   Yes. Judgment for the debtor (Jaffray). Trial court reversed.

REASONS   The court first stated the general rule: "One of the elements embraced in the question presented upon this appeal is whether the payment of a sum less than the amount of a liquidated debt under an agreement to accept the same in satisfaction of such debt forms a bar to the recovery of the balance of the debt. This single question was presented to the English court in 1602, when it was resolved (if not decided) in *Pinnel's* case, 'that payment of a lesser sum on the day in satisfaction of a greater, cannot be any satisfaction for the whole,' and that this is so, although it was agreed that such payment should satisfy the whole. This simple question has since arisen in the English courts and in the courts of this country in almost numberless instances, and has received the same solution, notwithstanding the courts, while so ruling, have rarely failed, upon any recurrence of the question, to criticize and condemn its reasonableness, justice, fairness, or honesty. No respectable authority that I have been able to find has, after such unanimous disapproval by all the courts, held otherwise."

The Court then described the exceptions to the rule. "Lord Blackburn said in his opinion in *Foakes* v. *Beer* . . . , while maintaining the doctrine 'that a lesser sum cannot be satisfaction of a greater sum, but the gift of a horse, hawk or robe, etc., in satisfaction is good,' quite regardless of the amount of the debt. And it was further said by him in the same opinion 'that payment and acceptance of a parcel before the day of payment of a larger sum would be a good satisfaction in regard to the circumstance of time, and so if I am bound in 20 pounds to pay you 10 pounds at Westminster, and you request me to pay you 5 pounds at the day at York, and you will accept it in full satisfaction for the whole 10 pounds, it is a good satisfaction. . . . [A] negotiable security may operate, if so given and taken in satisfaction of a debt of a greater amount; the circumstance of negotiability making it in fact a different thing and more advantageous than the original debt which was not negotiable.' "

The court then decided that this was an "exception" case. "Under the cases

141

above cited, and upon principle, this new agreement was supported by a sufficient consideration to make it a valid agreement, and this agreement was by the parties substituted in place of the former. The consideration of the new agreement was that the plaintiffs, in place of an open book account for goods sold, got the defendants' promissory notes, probably negotiable in form, signed by the defendants, thus saving the plaintiffs perhaps trouble or expense of proving their account, and for security upon all the defendants' personal property for the payment of the sum specified in the notes, where before they had no security."

There have been suggestions by some legal writers that under UCC 1–107, 2–209(1), and 3–408, the cashing of a part-payment check discharges the debt in full if the check so indicates, even without the existence of a dispute. Most of the cases decided since the adoption of the Code, however, continue to apply the common-law rules discussed above, without reference to any of these Code sections. It is thus not clear how a court would apply these sections if they were properly briefed and argued. It certainly appears that creditors would be much safer in sending such checks back and suing for the entire balance due. At the very least, a creditor should be aware that by cashing such a check he or she *may* be giving up the right to sue for the balance of the debt.

CASES FOR DISCUSSION

MELICK v. NAUMAN VANDERVOORT, INC.

220 N.W.2d 748 (Michigan, 1974)

McGregor, Judge

After a trial on the merits, judgment was entered against the defendant by the trial court on plaintiffs' action for damages resulting from the incorrect valuation of plaintiffs' stock which had been redeemed by defendant corporation. Damages were assessed by the trial court in the amount of $7,720 for plaintiff Melick and $3,860 for plaintiff Phillips.

An agreement was entered into between plaintiffs and the defendant whereby the defendant corporation would redeem its stock, owned by the plaintiffs, for its book value per share, as determined by acceptable accounting principles. The parties agreed that the redemption value of the stock would be determined as of July 31, 1970. On August 28, 1970, defendant notified the plaintiffs by letters that the book value of their stock, as of July 31, 1970, was 95 cents per share. Included in these letters to the plaintiffs were checks drawn on defendant's account to the order of the plaintiffs for the full amount due and owing on the redemption of their stock, computed at the value of 95 cents per share. On the reverse side of each check, defendant had inscribed the words, "Final Payment" and attached to each check was defendant's voucher which stated "Final Payment re purchase Capital Stock." In the accompanying letters, defendant stated that the checks were submitted "in full and final settlement of our agreement."

Neither plaintiff was satisfied with defendant's valuation of their stock and both protested to the defendant. Defendant refused to change its valuation of plaintiffs' stock and plaintiffs commenced this action on October 8, 1970.

However, prior to commencing this action,

plaintiffs endorsed their checks to the order of their attorneys, on September 18, 1970, and the checks were presented by the attorneys at defendant's bank and were certified. The checks were not presented for payment at the defendant's bank until January 6, 1971, after the circuit court's order of December 21, 1970, which allowed the transfer of the funds to an interest-bearing account. Plaintiffs testified that the purpose of having the checks certified was to provide security in the event that the defendant later was unable to pay the amounts of the checks.

During trial, the principal issue between the parties concerned the correct valuation of plaintiffs' stock and the methods used by defendant to arrive at that valuation. The trial court resolved this dispute in favor of plaintiffs, by finding that defendant had wrongfully deducted several items from the corporation assets when it computed the redemption value of plaintiffs' stock. The redemption value of the stock was recomputed, and the trial court entered its award of damages on the basis of the difference between the two valuations. The trial court specifically found that the parties did not intend an accord and satisfaction by the action of the plaintiffs in holding the checks and the certification of the same by their attorneys. The court based this finding on the fact that there had been no agreement between the plaintiffs and the defendant on an accord and satisfaction.

* * * * *

Plaintiffs contend that there was no accord and satisfaction because there was no consideration, since the defendant sent checks to the plaintiffs in an amount only equal to what the defendant determined was due to them, citing *Puett* v. *Walker*, 332 Mich, 117, 50 N.W.2d 740 (1952), and hold that defendant was merely doing what it was legally bound to do under the agreement between these parties and that such payment, therefore, could not constitute consideration. Plaintiffs' reliance on *Puett* is misplaced because, there, the claim was not unliquidated.

Puett, supra, is further distinguishable on its facts, because there, "the tender of the check was not a conditional one nor in final settlement of the

rights of the parties." . . . The Court, in *Puett*, did not consider the effect of M.C.L.A. 566,1; M.S.A. 26.978(1), which provides that an agreement to change any contract or obligation is not invalid because of the absence of consideration, provided the modification is in writing and signed by the party against whom enforcement is sought.

This statute has been construed to apply to a creditor's cashing of a check from a debtor which had a condition above the space for the creditor's endorsement providing that the payment was in full discharge of any and all obligations. *Belt* v. *Wolpin Co.*, 39 Mich. App. 40, 43–44, 197 N.W.3d 129 (1972). Thus, where an accord and satisfaction is in writing and signed by the party against whom enforcement is sought as in the instant case with the checks at issue, no consideration is necessary, albeit where the accord and satisfaction is oral, additional consideration is required. *Green* v. *Millman Bros., Inc.*, 7 Mich. App. 450, 151 N.W.2d 860 (1967).

Plaintiffs further contend that no accord and satisfaction was accomplished in the instant case, because there was never a meeting of minds between the parties to such effect; that the plaintiffs continually and constantly protested as insufficient the amounts of the checks tendered to them.

The fundamental error of the trial court in this matter was to confuse a meeting of the minds in fact with a meeting of the minds in law. . . .

It has been held consistently that, where there is a dispute of an amount due, acceptance of a check received and designated as payment in full constitutes settlement and satisfaction of the debt. The additional condition that there be an agreement in fact as to settlement of the debt has never before been attached to the conditional-check-compromise situation. . . .

Since defendant's checks to the plaintiffs were tendered as full and final payment of the disputed debt, the retention of the checks by the plaintiffs, who were fully informed of the condition, constituted a meeting of minds of the parties by implication, because there could be no severance of the condition from their acceptance. . . .

Albeit plaintiffs may not have understood the legal significance of their retention of defendant's checks as effecting an accord and satisfaction, such mistake is not sufficient to set aside the settlement. . . . This is in accordance with the long-established policy that settlements of disputes are favored by the law. . . .

In these circumstances, the trial court's finding that because plaintiffs did not understand the legal significance of their holding defendant's checks, there was no accord and satisfaction, is reversible error. There was no misunderstanding or uncertainty in the instant case as to which claims of plaintiffs the checks were intended to satisfy. . . .

Judgment of the circuit court for plaintiffs is reversed. Costs to defendant.

McGOWAN v. BEACH

86 S.E.2d 763 (North Carolina, 1955)

This civil action was brought to recover from the estate of Wade H. McGowan (who died on April 6, 1951, survived by his widow, the plaintiff, but no lineal descendants) the sum of $15,000, together with interest on that sum, from January 2, 1945, until paid.

It was alleged in the complaint and admitted in the answer that the plaintiff and the defendant were citizens and residents of Caldwell County, North Carolina; that the defendant was the duly qualified and acting administrator of the estate of Wade H. McGowan, having qualified as such on April 23, 1952, before the clerk of the Superior Court of Caldwell County; that on November 25, 1953, the plaintiff filed with the defendant, as administrator, her verified claim against the estate of Wade H. McGowan in the amount set forth above; and that the administrator denied the claim on February 4, 1954.

The plaintiff alleged in her complaint that on or about January 2, 1945, Wade H. McGowan borrowed from her the sum of $15,000, and as evidence of his indebtedness executed under seal his memorandum in words and figures as follows: "January 2, 1945. I owe my wife Lois McGowan $15,000. Wade H. McGowan (Seal)." She also alleged that on the memorandum as credit for interest payments: the following items were entered "Interest paid $100.00 Jan. 6, 1947.

Interest paid $50.00 Jan. 5, 1948." The plaintiff introduced this instrument in evidence as her Exhibit No. 36.

The defendant denied, upon information and belief, that Wade H. McGowan, on January 2, 1945, or at any other time, had borrowed the sum of $15,000 from the plaintiff and further denied that Wade H. McGowan had executed any such instrument as that alleged by the plaintiff. These issues were submitted to the jury and answered as follows:

1. Did W. H. McGowan sign the instrument described as Plaintiff's Exhibit No. 36, as alleged in the Complaint? Answer: Yes.
2. If so, did W. H. McGowan deliver the same to the plaintiff? Answer: Yes.
3. If so, was the said instrument based upon a valuable consideration? Answer: Yes.

Judgment was entered on the verdict, and the defendant appealed, assigning error.

Denny, Justice.

The defendant interposed no objection to the issues submitted to the jury but excepts and assigns as error the refusal of the court below to submit the following issue: "Did the plaintiff loan the deceased, Wade H. McGowan, the sum of $15,000, as alleged by the plaintiff?"

It should be kept in mind that the alleged transaction, which resulted in the execution of the instrument upon which the plaintiff brings this action, was a personal transaction between the plaintiff and her deceased husband. Therefore, it was not permissable under the provisions of G.S. #8.51 for the plaintiff to have testified that she loaned her deceased husband the alleged sum of $15,000, or that she saw him sign the instrument and that he delivered it to her. . . . Any right to recover on the instrument must flow from its legal effect as written, coupled with the fact that the plaintiff had it in her possession and introduced it in evidence at the trial. . . .

The instrument in this action purports to be under seal and wholly in the handwriting of the executant thereof, and the plaintiff offered evidence to the effect that the entire instrument was

144

in the handwriting of W. H. McGowan. More-over, the defendant does not attack the suffi-ciency of the evidence to support the answer of the jury to the first issue, except by motion to nonsuit. However, in his belief, the only argu-ment in support of this motion is to the effect that the plaintiff offered no proof that the word "seal" was written after the name of the maker at the time he executed the instrument and, if so, that he adopted it as his seal. There is no contention on the part of the defendant that if the maker of the instrument wrote the word "seal" after his name at the time he executed the instrument and adopted it as his seal, the defendant would be entitled to a nonsuit. We think that where an in-strument is wholly in the handwriting of the maker, it would be strange indeed for him to go to the trouble of writing the word "seal" after his name unless it was his intention to adopt it as his seal, and such intention will be presumed. In fact, our Court has held that a seal appearing upon an instrument, opposite the name of the maker, in the place where the seal belongs, will in the absence of proof that the maker intended otherwise, be valid as a seal. ". . . [I]n any event, the maker would have the burden of over-coming the presumption arising from the pres-ence of a seal." Furthermore, the defendant ad-mits in his belief that in the trial below, "no questions were asked about the seal, and no evi-dence offered tending to show its presence or adoption."

From an examination of the evidence, it is quite clear that the battle below was waged over the question as to whether the instrument intro-duced by the plaintiff was executed by W. H. McGowan, deceased. Moreover, counsel for de-fendant in the oral argument before this Court admitted that the questions now urged with re-spect to the seal were not raised in the trial below. . . . Therefore, since the question as to whether the seal was placed on the instrument by the maker and adopted by him, was not raised in the trial below, except by a general denial of the genuineness of the instrument, and no issue having been tendered with respect thereto, the motion for judgment as of nonsuit will be denied. Consequently, the plaintiff's right to recover

must turn soley upon the legal effect of the in-strument as written, including the seal, since the jury found that W. H. McGowan executed it as alleged in the complaint.

It is said in 12 Am. Jur., Contracts under Seal, section 74 page 567: "At common law a promise under seal, but without any consideration, is binding because no consideration is required in such a case or, as is sometimes said, because the seal imports, or gives rise to a presumption of, consideration. It has been said that the solemnity of a sealed instrument imports consideration or, to speak more accurately, estops a covenantor from denying a consideration except for fraud." . . .

Hoke, Jr. (late Chief Justice), in speaking for the Court in the last cited case, said: "It is the accepted principle of the common law that instru-ments under seal require no consideration to sup-port them. Whether this should rest on the posi-tion that a seal conclusively imports a consid-eration, or that the solemnity of the act imports such reflection and care that a consideration is regarded as unnecessary, such instruments are held to be binding agreements enforceable in all actions before the common-law courts."

Whether we construe the instrument under consideration to be a nonnegotiable note, a due bill, or merely an acknowledgment by W. H. McGowan of a debt to his wife in the sum of $15,000, the fact that it was executed under seal, which in the absence of proof to the contrary, imports a consideration, the instrument is suffi-cient as an acknowledgment of such debt.

* * * * *

No error. Judgment of lower court affirmed.

PITTS v. McGRAW-EDISON COMPANY
329 F.2d 412 (U.S. Sixth Circuit, 1964)
Shackelford Miller, Jr., Circuit Judge

Plaintiff, L. U. Pitts, brought this action in the District Court to recover damages in the amount of $15,000 for an alleged breach of a retirement contract by the defendant. . . . Plaintiff appeals from a judgment dismissing the action.

The facts, which are mostly undisputed, are as follows. Plaintiff was a manufacturer's representative in Memphis, Tennessee, for a period of many years prior to July 1, 1955. For approximately 25 years preceding that date, he sold the products of the defendant's predecessor and the defendant, McGraw-Edison Company, on a commission basis in an assigned territory comprising several southern states. In his capacity as a manufacturer's representative he was an independent business man, hiring and firing his own employees, paying his own expenses and overhead, and managing his business as he saw fit. He had no written contract with the defendant, and the defendant had no obligation to him except to compensate him on a commission basis for sales made in the assigned territory. The relationship between the parties was independent and was not that of employer and employee. It was terminable at will, without notice by either party at any time. The plaintiff was free to handle any other products he desired, including those of competitors of the defendant, and he did so until early in 1954, when on his own volition and without any requirement by the defendant, he discontinued his representation of other manufacturers.

At no time during the relationship of the parties did the plaintiff make contributions to a pension fund or a retirement fund of any kind.

In April 1955, when the plaintiff was approximately 67 years of age, he accompanied O. Dee Harrison, the sales manager for the defendant, to Little Rock, Arkansas, for a meeting with one Paul Thurman, who had formerly worked for the plaintiff but at the time was working the State of Arkansas as a factory representative for the defendant and others. At that meeting Mr. Harrison, told the plaintiff that the defendant was making arrangements for the plaintiff to retire at a time shortly thereafter and for Thurman to take over the plaintiff's territory, with the plaintiff receiving an overwrite commission of 1 percent from the defendant on all sales made in the territory. Thereafter the plaintiff received a letter dated July 1, 1955, from O. Dee Harrison reading in part as follows:

Dear Lou:

Whether you know it or not, you are on retirement effective July 1st. But to make the matter of retirement a little less distasteful, we are going ahead as you and I talked last time we were together by paying each month 1 percent of the . . . sales from the Mississippi and Tennessee states. You will get your check each month just as you have been in the habit of getting our check on commissions. Let us hope that there is enough to help keep a few pork chops on the table and a few biscuits in the oven.

We are going to keep you on the list for bulletins, Lou, so that you will know what is going on. I know that you will help Paul in every way that you can, and I know that your help will be greatly appreciated by Paul.

A letter dated July 20 also said:

We will keep you on the mailing list and any time you can throw a little weight our way we will appreciate any effort you make, Lou. And any time you have any questions, don't be afraid to ask us about them.

The plaintiff received a check from the defendant each month regularly from July 1955 through June 1960 covering the 1 percent commission on sales in the specified territory.

Under date of July 23, 1960, the plaintiff was advised by letter from the Division Controller of the defendant reading in part as follows:

Dear Mr. Pitts:

I am enclosing our check #50064752 for $238.51 which, according to our records, completes the five year series of payments to be paid after your retirement from the Company.

This action followed. Following a trial to the Court without a jury, the District Judge held that the plaintiff was not entitled to recover any amount whatever and dismissed his complaint.

Plaintiff contends that the negotiations between the Company and him leading to his retirement were in substance an offer on the part of the Company that if he would retire as a manufacturer's representative on July 1, 1955, and turn over to his successor representative all of his customer account records containing valuable information on active and inactive accounts, which had been built up over a period of 20 years or more, the Company would pay him monthly thereafter a 1 percent overwrite commission on sales by the defendant in the territory which was at that time alotted to him; that after considering the offer, he accepted it and thereafter carried it out by retiring as a manufacturer's representative and turning over to his successor the stipulated records; and that the defendant breached the contract by refusing to make the payments after July 1, 1960.

In considering these contentions, it must be kept in mind that the plaintiff was an independent business man, not an employee of the defendant. His relationship with the defendant could be terminated by either party at any time without notice and without liability therefor. The plaintiff in his testimony concedes this, and it was so found as a fact by the District Judge. Unless the plaintiff is able to establish a valid contract obligating the defendant to pay the "retirement" benefits claimed, he has no cause of action.

Assuming, without so holding, that there was a promise by the defendant to pay the plaintiff the retirement benefits claimed, we are faced with the question of what consideration passed from the plaintiff to the defendant to make this promise enforceable.

Plaintiff vigorously argues that although he did not *promise* to do anything or to refrain from doing anything, as plainly appears from the two letters, and so conceded by him, consideration nevertheless exists because of the action taken by him at the request of the defendant, namely, his retirement as a manufacturer's representative, including other manufacturers as well as the defendant, and his turning over to the defendant his personal records pertaining to customers and sales over a period of years in the past. There would be merit in this contention if it was supported by the facts.

* * * * *

However, these factual contentions of the plaintiff were disputed by the evidence of the defendant. The District Judge made findings of fact that the plaintiff was not required by the terms of the letters, or by any other statements on the part of the defendant, or its agents, to do anything whatsoever; that upon his retirement of July 1, 1955, the plaintiff was free to handle the products of any other manufacturer or competitor if he so desired, to seek other employment, or to do as he pleased; that nothing in the arrangement circumscribed the plaintiff's actions or rights in any manner; and that the plaintiff was not obligated to perform any duties on behalf of the defendant. These findings are fully supported by the evidence. In fact, they were substantially conceded by the plaintiff in the cross-examination of him as a witness, in which he apparently contended that he did certain things for the defendant after his retirement although he was not required to do so.

On the basis of these facts, the District Judge ruled that the payments to the plaintiff over the period of July 1, 1955, to July 1, 1960, were without consideration, were the result of voluntary action on the part of the defendant, and were mere gratuities terminable by the defendant at will.

The court also rejected Pitts' claim under promissory estoppel since "the plaintiff in no way altered his position for the worse by reason of defendant's letters of July 1 and July 20, 1955. The District Judge found as a fact that the plaintiff gave up nothing to which he was legally entitled and was restricted in no way in his activities thereafter. Plaintiff gave up nothing in accepting retirement that he would not have lost if he had refused to accept it."

COLLINS v. COLLINS
88 N.Y.S.2d 136 (New York, 1949)

Carlin, Justice

This motion to dismiss the amended complaint for insufficiency on its face, which was heretofore granted by default, has been, by consents, restored to the calendar and is now considered on the merits.

This is an action, as shown in the complaint, by a mother, allegedly aged and destitute, against her son. It is set forth in the complaint that the defendant, the son, agreed to pay to the plaintiff, the mother, the sum of $50 per month for her support and that the agreement was based upon "good and valuable consideration." The defendant demanded a bill of particulars, and plaintiff served one, in which the consideration for such agreement is stated to be "love and affection." This application to dismiss the amended complaint, under Rule 112, Rules of Civil Practice, is predicated upon the complaint as limited by the bill of particulars.

"Love and affection" is not a sufficient consideration to support an executory contract. The case would be different if an executed deed, assignment, or mortgage were involved; if in fact the transaction were accomplished.

The plaintiff relies upon *Calhoun* v. *Calhoun*, 49 App. Div. 520, 63 N.Y.S. 601, but that action was founded upon a mortgage which had been executed and delivered. It is true that it was stated in the opinion that love and affection or the moral obligation to support, constituted a suffi-cient consideration. But such statement was unnecessary to the decision, which could have rested either upon the fact that the mortgage in suit had been delivered and the transaction was therefore executed; or upon the fact that the defendant had undertaken to support the plaintiff, his mother, partly at least, because she conveyed a farm to him. The view expressed in that opinion that love and affection alone, or a moral obligation to support, is a sufficient consideration is not, wherever an executory agreement is involved, in accord with the rule in this state.

It appears in the pleadings that the plaintiff is not a resident of New York, but of Pennsylvania. Any rights which she might have had, if she had been a resident, under Section 101, Social Welfare Law, are therefore not germane to a consideration of this case.

As plaintiff does not, upon any suggested theory, have a good cause of action against the defendant, the complaint should be dismissed without leave to plead over.

PROBLEMS FOR DISCUSSION

1. On October 19, 1975, Ellis Valente and Jarle Ottesen engaged in a barroom brawl in which Ottesen was seriously injured and consequently sued Valente for assault and battery. About six weeks after the fight Valente (70 years old) transferred all of his assets except for a small amount of cash to his wife and children for estate-planning purposes and in consideration of love and affection.

   In April, 1976 Ottesen instituted an action to set aside the transfer of assets, claiming that the transfer had had the effect of defrauding him. Who wins the case?

2. In December 1970 Clyde sustained serious injuries while riding as a passenger in a car. The car was insured by Travelers' Insurance, and the insurance company arranged for the necessary surgery and paid all hospital bills. A representative of Travelers' Insurance also assured Clyde that he need not bother to institute any other claims proceedings because Travelers' would settle equitably with him once his condition had stabilized and his situation could be assessed properly. Three years later, after the statute of limitations regarding actions for injuries had run out, the insurance company had still not made a settlement and actually refused to do so. What rights does Clyde have?

3. In June Richard Axminster listed his house with Speedy Real Estate Company in an exclusive selling agreement. The contract specified a 6 percent commission if the house were sold during the three month's listing period or within three months thereafter either by Speedy or by the owner. No buyer was procured by Speedy, and in October Richard sold the house to a buyer with whom he had negotiated directly. Speedy still wants to collect the commission, which Richard refuses to pay since Speedy never showed the property to anyone, never made an offer, and did not even know the final buyer. Can Speedy collect?

4. The township of Floodsville contracted with Canale Construction Company for an extension of a water main. When the town fathers received the final bill, which was much higher than expected, they refused to pay more than the originally estimated price. Lengthy oral negotiations with Canale ensued, the exact outcome of which remains in dispute. However, the court has in hand a canceled check made out by the town of Floodsville to Canale Construction Company. The check bears the restriction "Final Payment," and it was promptly endorsed and cashed by Canale. The check was for the originally estimated price. Canale is now suing the township for the difference between the estimated price and the final bill. Will Canale win?

5. In 1968 Nebraska Power and Light Company signed a contract for the purchase of a power line easement across the land of Jack and Jill Grubb. The Grubbs claim that there had also been an oral agreement between the parties and that Nebraska Power and Light had promised that "if any other landowners get more money, then you will get more money." When the Grubbs heard that Nebraska Power and Light had purchased a similar easement in the county for a higher price, they instituted a suit for an additional payment. Will Grubbs win?

6. John Frontier, acting on behalf of several farmers in Corn County, agreed over the phone to sell 90,000 bushels of No. 2 grade yellow corn to Farmland Co-op. The agreed price was $1.39 per bushel, and the corn was to be delivered during June, July, and August. Later John Frontier found out that he could get a better price by selling to another co-op and called off the deal. Farmland Co-op, which had already entered into several resale agreements for the corn, then sued John Frontier for damages for breach of contract. Can Farmland Co-op collect damages?

7. Blitz Electric Company, of doubtful credit rating, was performing electrical work in an apartment complex under construction. It asked Construction Science, Inc., for assistance in getting needed materials from Supplier Corporation. In a telephone conversation between Construction Science, Inc., and Supplier Corporation, Supplier agreed to sell to Blitz if Construction Science made certain guarantees. A letter from Supplier followed, repeating the terms of the conversation and asking Construction Science to return a copy of the letter with its acknowledgment. The disputed paragraph ran: "We will expect your firm to guarantee payment of all our invoices for material furnished . . . and it is understood that joint payable checks will be made out to Supplier and Blitz." Construction Science returned the copy, stamped "Acknowledged and accepted."

    When several claims arose under the construction project, Construction Science argued that it had merely assured Supplier Corporation of payment by joint check but had not itself guaranteed payment. What decision?

8. Mr. and Mrs. Homeowner contracted with Mortar Construction Company to have some improvements made on their home. Throughout the work they made various cash payments. Upon completion, Mortar Construction Company demanded an additional $2,000 in payment. The Homeowners claimed that several cash payments had not been credited to their account and that they therefore owed only $500. They mailed a check for $500 to Mortar Construction Company, on the back of which they typed: "Settlement in full for all labor and material to date." Mortar Construction Company scratched out the typing, replaced it with the handwritten addition "Restriction of payment in full refused," and cashed the check. Then it proceeded to sue the Homeowners for the remaining $1,500. What decision?

9. Horatio began working for Steel Chain Company in 1921, as an order clerk. He subsequently became traffic manager, sales representative, president, and finally, chairman of the board of directors. In 1960, while he was chairman, the six other directors prepared a proposed agreement for his retirement. Horatio knew nothing

about it until the agreement was presented to him at a board meeting. The agreement provided that the company would pay Horatio $20,000 for the current fiscal year and $15,000 a year for the rest of his life and that Horatio, in turn would be available for consultation and would not compete with the company in its domestic or overseas markets. Horatio signed the agreement. In 1963 the company stopped making the promised annual payments to Horatio and asked him to accept smaller payments. He refused and sued for breach of contract. Who wins?

The Statute of Frauds and the Parol Evidence Rule   **7**

Although the parties have entered into an agreement and their agreement is supported by an exchange of legally sufficient considerations, (there are many situations where a court will refuse to enforce some or all of the promises exchanged unless the alleged promises can be proved by something more than oral testimony.) The statute of frauds requires that certain types of contractual promises be contained in a signed writing in order to be enforceable in court. The parol evidence rule prevents a party from contradicting the terms of a complete written contract, once signed, by the use of outside, or parol, evidence.

THE STATUTE OF FRAUDS: ORIGINS, DEVELOPMENT, AND BASIC PURPOSE

One year after the United States celebrated its bicentennial, the statute of frauds celebrated its "tricentennial." The English Parliament passed the original statute in 1677 to deal with what was perceived to be a serious legal problem: the possibility that a court would force a party to perform a contract which had never really been made, solely on the basis of perjured oral testimony. The solution to this problem seemed simple enough: require that a contract be proved by something more than oral testimony before you enforce it. Thus the statute of frauds ("An Act for Prevention of Frauds and Perjuries") was adopted.

Parliament did not go all the way and require that *all* contracts be evidenced by a signed writing in order to be enforceable in court. Rather, it confined this new requirement to what seemed to be "important" contracts and to other situations where intentional perjury or mistaken testimony seemed likely. As a result, the following types of contracts had to be in writing in order to be enforceable in court: the sale of any interest in real estate; the sale of goods worth 10 pounds or more; any contract which by its terms could not possibly be completed within one year from the date it was made; any promise to pay the debt of another party; any promise by the executor or administrator of a decedent's estate to pay the estate's debts out of his or her own funds; any promise made "in consideration of marriage." This list formed the basis for similar statutes in nearly all of our states.

To see how the statute of frauds works today, we need to know the answers to three questions: What contracts are now subject to the statute of frauds? How does one comply with the statute of frauds requirement? What results follow if the statute of frauds applies and has not been satisfied?

WHAT CONTRACTS ARE SUBJECT TO THE STATUTE OF FRAUDS?

Pre-UCC Holdovers. Three provisions of the 1677 statute that have general commercial significance have, on the whole, survived in their original form: the transfer of any interest in real estate, any promise to pay the debt of another, any contract which by its terms cannot be performed within one year. Prior to the UCC, many states had also adopted a statute of frauds provision which required all "assignments," or transfers, of contract rights to be made in writing. (Assignments are discussed more fully in Chapter 11.)

Real Estate Transfers. "Any interest" in land means just that: every case where a party is voluntarily creating such an interest in another or divesting himself or herself of such an interest. Most courts agree that leases, mortgages, easements, and options on real estate are all subject to this requirement, although options might be excluded in some states. Also, most states do have a statutory exception for short-term leases; if the term of an oral lease is not more than one year, the lease is enforceable. Although a real estate broker does not have an "interest" in the real estate under this section of the statute of frauds, in most states a real estate broker is required by a separate statutory provision to have his or her commission arrangement in writing in order to enforce it.

There are some definitional problems where the contract relates to things which are growing on, attached to, or contained in the land. Generally, these questions will be answered by reference to UCC 2–107. If the contract requires the seller to "sever" minerals or the like, or a structure or its materials, the contract is a sale of goods within Article 2. If the buyer is to do the severing, until the buyer does so, the contract would be assumed to deal with an "interest" in the land. Where the subject matter of the contract is timber, growing crops, "or other things attached to realty and capable of severance without material harm thereto," but not covered under the first rule, the contract is a sale of goods, regardless of who does the severing. The significance of the distinction can be seen later, in the discussion of what is a sufficient compliance with the statute of frauds provision which applies to the contract.

Promises to Pay the Debt of Another. Parliament probably included this provision because both the principal debtor and the creditor have an incentive to commit perjury in this case. Here, too, there are definitional questions to be resolved. This section does not apply to direct, "original" promises to confer benefits on a third party—only to "secondary" or supplemental promises. This section of the statute of frauds does not apply where the promisor's main motive in making the promise is to benefit *himself* or *herself* rather than just to "back-stop" the principal debtor's credit. Finally, the section does not apply where the secondary promise is made to the principal debtor rather than to the creditor.

Peterson v. Rowe
314 P.2d 892 (New Mexico, 1957)

FACTS   Between the approximate dates of July 26, 1955, and September 11, 1955, the plaintiff provided hospital care, laboratory facilities, and medication to the patient William H. Rowe at the special instance and request of Rowe's sons, M. H. Rowe and William W. Rowe. When Dr. Peterson sued the sons, the trial court gave him $2,739.25, the account balance.

ISSUE   Are the sons' promises subject to the statute of frauds and therefore unenforceable because they were made orally?

DECISION   No. Judgment for Dr. Peterson affirmed.

REASONS   The court reviewed the nature of the promises which the sons had made. "A review of the evidence convinces us that appellants are original promisors and not guarantors. . . .

"The evidence discloses at least four conversations between the parties concerning payment for services to be furnished the patient. Appellants were at the hospital the day after William H. Rowe was admitted, and while there, discussed with appellee the matter of making financial arrangements. Appellee explained to appellants that the patient was very ill and would require extensive treatment. Appellants informed appellee that their father had no financial means; nevertheless, appellant M. H. Rowe stated that appellants themselves would pay for such service. His exact statement was: 'You go right ahead and give him whatever is necessary to save his life and I will pay for it.' Subsequently, on July 29, appellants, accompanied by their wives, came to the hospital, and again appellant M. H. Rowe stated to appellee: 'Well, we want you to do everything you can to save his life, and we don't want you to spare any expense, because whatever he needs, doctor, you go ahead and get it and I will pay you.' On July 31, the date of the operation, appellants were at the hospital, and again the question of payment of expenses was renewed. At that time, M. H. Rowe voluntarily authorized the services of special nurses, stating: '[B]ecause whatever he needs, I want him to have it and I will pay you for it.' To which appellant William W. Rowe assented as follows: 'That is correct, anything that—any expense. Do not spare any expense on my father, and I will pay you for it.' The testimony of both Dr. Kinne and Dr. Andrews lends strong support to appellee. This evidence is substantial. Further, some three weeks later, the business manager of the hospital phoned appellants and advised them that the expenses were continuing to mount, and asked them to come in and discuss the matter. They did, but stated that they were just then short of cash. Appellant M. H. Rowe said: 'We will pay you $200 now, and then we will pay you $200 every month.' He stated further: 'My father has some property back in Missouri, and we will put it on the market for sale, and when we sell the property, why, we will pay the entire balance off in full.' Appellant William W.

Rowe spoke up, saying, '[T]hat is correct.' They then paid $200, and $45 later when threatened with litigation.

"Of course, in the absence of an expressed contract, appellants would have been under no legal obligation to pay for the services rendered to their father. But it was at appellants' request, and for their benefit, that the services were furnished; hence, the promise to pay was an original undertaking and is without the statute."

Contracts Impossible to Perform within One Year. The probable reason for inclusion of the "year clause" was the likelihood that the parties and witnesses would tend to forget the provisions of the contract, or would remember them differently, where the performances extended over a relatively long period of time. Thus, if on the day a contract is made, the parties can see that there is absolutely no way to perform it within one year from that date, the contract must be evidenced by a signed writing. As applied by the courts, the test is not how long the performances were likely to take or, with hindsight, how long they actually took. The test is whether there was any conceivable way that the contract *could* have been fully performed, according to its terms, within a year from the date it was made. If it *could* have been performed within a year, the oral contract is perfectly valid and perfectly enforceable in court (assuming that the jury believes the oral testimony).

Thus an oral contract for lifetime employment, where performance is to start within one year of the date the contract is made, is enforceable, since the employee could conceivably die within the first year. But where the employee is hired for more than one year, or where he or she is not to start performing until some future date and then is to work for at least a year, the oral contract is not enforceable, as Mr. Sinclair learned to his sorrow in the following case.

Sinclair v. *Sullivan Chevrolet Co.*
311 Ill. App. 2d 507 (Illinois, 1964)

FACTS   "The plaintiff alleged that on May 30, 1960, he entered into an oral contract with the defendant whereby he was to be employed as sales manager for a one-year period starting June 6, 1960. According to further allegations, plaintiff was to receive a salary of $1,200 per month plus a bonus to be later agreed upon but with a guaranteed minimum annual remuneration of $20,000. In addition, the employer was to pay plaintiff's moving expenses, provide him with a company automobile, and reduce the agreement to writing on June 6, 1960. It is further alleged that said representations were falsely made by the defendant without intention of performance, but this being unknown to the plaintiff, he quit his job in St. Louis, moved his family to Champaign, and assumed his duties pursuant to the agreement. However, defendant did not abide by said agreement, as a result of which plaintiff terminated his employment on March 18, 1961. He claimed damages of $12,527."

ISSUE   Does the "year clause" of the statute of frauds make this oral contract unenforceable?

DECISION   Yes. Judgment for defendant employer affirmed.

REASONS   "It is agreed that either on May 30 or May 31 plaintiff was employed for a one-year period starting June 6, 1960. This was a contract which could not on the date made have been performed within a year, and it was therefore of the class generally made unenforceable by the Statute of Frauds. However, in certain instances where fraud or material misrepresentation has occurred, the guilty party may be estopped to assert this particular defense.

"When the instant contract was entered into, there appears to have been no concealment or misrepresentation of fact but mere oral promises concerning future performances which the law did not regard as binding. We hold that the present suit was barred by statute as a matter of law and that the trial court was correct in granting summary judgment for the defendant."

UCC Statute of Frauds Provisions. The Code contains several specific statute of frauds provisions. Contracts for the sale of goods worth $500 or more, investment securities, or intangible personal property worth $5,000 or more and contracts creating a security interest or establishing a letter of credit must be evidenced by some sort of writing. In addition, "negotiable instruments" under Article 3 and "documents" under Article 7, by definition, involve signed writings with particular characteristics.

Sales of Goods for $500 or More. As defined in Section 2–105(1), *goods* means tangible, movable personal property, but it can also refer to things which are currently attached to land. (See the discussion earlier in this chapter.) There can be a contract for the sale of goods which do not exist yet, with the seller promising to produce them or get them from a third party prior to the delivery date specified in the contract.

There are some cases where it is hard to decide whether the contract is a contract for the sale of goods or a contract for services. The distinction is very important here since there is no statute of frauds which is generally applicable to services contracts. If a services contract (such as a promise to construct a building on land already owned by the customer) can be performed within one year, it can be oral and still be enforceable, no matter how much money it involves. If a contract is for goods worth $500 or more, 2–201 applies. A contract to buy a $600 color TV is pretty clearly a contract for the sale of goods even if the seller also promises to deliver and "set up" the TV as part of the contract. Likewise, if you buy all the parts for a TV set in a "kit," and then hire a TV technician to put the set together for you, your contract with the technician is clearly a services contract. Many contracts are more ambiguous, however, such as your contract for the purchase of a custom-made suit from a tailor, or your contract with an artist to have your portrait painted, or your contract to have your car fixed or your house aluminum-sided, all of which involve both labor and materials. (Most probably, a court would decide that the suit and portrait contracts are primarily for goods and that the car repair and aluminum siding contracts are primarily for services.)

Sales of Investment Securities. Most simply put, "investment securities" are stocks and bonds. Stock warrants and other such special devices, which are commonly traded in securities markets, would also be covered here. No dollar minimum is specified, so that every contract for the sale of securities must be in writing to be enforceable. However, nearly all the cases in point have held that this statute of frauds section (8–319) does not apply to your "agency" contract with your broker, so you can sue your broker for failing to follow your oral instructions.

Sales of Intangible Personal Property for $5,000 or More. After eliminating goods, investment securities, and security agreements, Section 1–206 covers "personal property." Included here are the sales of such things as copyrights, patents, royalties, trademarks, and trade names, and tort claims for damages. If the contract price of such items is $5,000 or more, there must be a signed writing.

Security Agreements. Where a creditor ("secured party") wishes to use a piece of personal property as collateral for the payment of some obligation, the creditor must have a written security agreement which creates or provides for such a "security interest" and the writing must be signed by the debtor. Without such a writing the creditor has no rights against the specific collateral when the debtor goes into default unless the creditor actually has possession of the collateral.

Letters of Credit. Letters of credit are widely used in international trade, where the credit standing of a buyer may not be known to the seller. Before leaving his or her country, the buyer arranges to have his or her bank honor drafts (orders for money) up to a certain amount. With such a written agreement from a recognized bank in the buyer's own country, the buyer can have ready access to funds from banks in a foreign country. Obviously, any such letter of credit, and any modification thereof, must be contained in a signed writing.

Modifications. Because of the general common-law requirement that a document must contain all the material terms in order to comply with the statute of frauds, subsequently agreed-to modifications of such a document must also be evidenced by a signed writing to be enforceable. Such changes can be written on the original document and initialed, or a new document covering the modifications can be prepared and signed by the parties. In a real estate transaction, for example, any later agreement to modify the signed writing by changing the total contract price, the monthly payments, the acreage involved, the interest rate, or even such things as the date of possession almost certainly has to be written to be enforced in court.

For sales of goods, however, the rules are quite different because of the wording of the applicable Code provisions. Because the signed writing here does *not* have to contain all the terms agreed on, or even all the material terms, oral modifications of a previous written contract for goods should be enforceable in nearly every case. The one thing which Section 2–201(1) does not permit is an oral modification which increases the quantity term stated in the signed writing. (For example, the parties enter into a written contract for 1,000 bushels of wheat at $3 per bushel. They can later orally agree to raise or lower the price, to change the delivery date, or to lower the quantity to 700 bushels. What they cannot do without a new writing is to increase the quantity to 1,200 bushels. The quantity term in the original writing can't be increased orally, and 200 more bushels means $600 worth of goods, so this "modification" has to be evidenced by a new writing.) Where there was originally an enforceable oral contract for under $500 and the agreed modification brings the price to over $500, the contract as modified must be evidenced by a writing, or else the modification cannot be enforced and the original terms stand. (For example, the parties orally agree to a contract for 150 bushels of wheat at $3 per bushel. Later they agree to raise the price per bushel to $3.50, for a total price of $525. This modification must be in writing to be enforced.)

Remember from the last chapter that such modifications need no new exchange of considerations in a sale of goods case; they can be completely one-sided and still be binding under Section 2–209(1). For other types of contracts, however, remember that there has to be new consideration moving both ways for such modifications to be enforceable, even if the modifications are in writing.

Consideration Substitutes. Chapter 6 contained several examples of statutory provisions which made certain kinds of promises enforceable even without consideration. Typically, such promises will have to be contained in a signed writing to be enforceable. UCC 2–209(1) does not require modifications of a preexisting sale of goods contract to be in writing, nor, in some states, do the statutes which cover new promises to pay debts barred by the statute of limitations or by a bankruptcy discharge. (As always, of course, it's good idea to have the promise in writing even though no statute requires it, simply because a signed written promise is easier to prove in court.)

HOW DOES ONE COMPLY WITH THE STATUTE OF FRAUDS?

General Common-Law Rule. The method of compliance intended by the original 1677 statute was a signed writing. As interpreted by the courts, this requirement came to mean that the writing had to contain "all the material terms" and that a writing which did not clearly spell out all the important provisions of the contract was not sufficient to comply with the statute. In general, this "all-material-terms" rule continues to be used for those statute of frauds provisions described above as common-law "holdovers."

The all-material-terms rule can be seen operating most clearly in real estate transactions, where most courts have used the "4-P's" interpretation. To comply with the statute for real estate, the signed writing has to at least contain the Parties, the Property, the Price, and the Payment terms. If the terms are simple, a very short memorandum could conceivably contain all these elements. In the *Lucy* case in Chapter 5, Zehmer signed a writing which identified Lucy as the buyer and the property as the Ferguson Farm, which named the price ($50,000), and which specified the payment terms ("cash"). All of the necessary terms were included. More typically, however, payment for real estate is to be made over an extended period of time, interest must be calculated on the unpaid balance and paid periodically, and other special provisions are agreed to. In such cases the parties run a very real risk that a court may later find their document to be insufficient to comply with the statute. The following case illustrates this danger.

Klipfel v. *Brandenburger*
156 N.W.2d 774 (North Dakota, 1968)

FACTS The defendant put certain personal and real property up for sale at public auction, to be sold by a licensed auctioneer. The sale was held on October 15, 1964. At the auction the plaintiff was the successful bidder on 640 acres of the defendant's land.

After the sale the auctioneer prepared a memorandum which read: "Terms not over 20 percent down Bal 5 yr. 5% Int Henry agreed to pay 50¢ per acre for land sold Oct 15—64 Henry Brandenburger. Auction Land sold to Wilbur Erlinbush 240 acres at 44.00 per acre Alvin Klipfel 640 acres at 39.00 per acre. Earl Thorpe"

Thorpe, the auctioneer, testified that he had prepared the above memorandum, not for the purpose of complying with the law but for the purpose of showing the commission that was due him.

The trial court found for the plaintiff and ordered the defendant to specifically perform. The defendant appealed.

ISSUE Was the memorandum signed by the auctioneer sufficient to comply with the real estate statute of frauds?

DECISION No. Judgment reversed and plaintiff's complaint dismissed.

REASONS "The statute of frauds, as it pertains to sales of real estate, applies to sales of privately owned land sold at public auction. And where such sale is at public auction, the statute vests in the auctioneer the authority to make the required memorandum on behalf of both the buyer and the seller, in the form required by statute.

"In the case before us, the auctioneer did make a memorandum. We must determine if that memorandum complies with the requirements of the statute of frauds. It is conceded that the writing relied upon contains many of the necessary provisions of the agreement. It states the selling price per acre. The down-payment is stated as being 'not over 20 percent down,' which, although vague, can be held to mean 20 percent. Interest is to be at 5 percent of the balance due. Whether such interest is payable annually, or at the end of the five years, is not stated. The memorandum provides that such balance is to be paid in five years. But is such balance to be paid in annual installments, or is it to be paid at the end of the five years? The memorandum does not provide at what time or in what manner such balance is to be paid.

"The memorandum relied upon also fails to specifically describe the land which was being sold, other than to provide: 'Alvin Klipfel 640 acres at 39.00 per acre.' Testimony produced at the trial discloses that the defendant was the owner of 880 acres of land, 240 acres of which were sold to Wilbur Erlinbush. But what particular tract went to Erlinbush and what tract was to go to the plaintiff cannot be determined from the memorandum of the auctioneer or from any other writing in evidence without resort to parol. Thus we believe the writing is insufficient to properly describe the real estate which is the subject of this contract.

> "The terms of the agreement in this case cannot be determined except by parol evidence. To be sufficient under the statute of frauds, the memorandum must be complete in itself and leave nothing to rest in parol. It must be definite and certain as to the property to be sold, the consideration to be paid, and the manner and time of performance."

Sale of Goods Compliance: Five Alternatives. The UCC, Section 2–201, provides five alternative methods of compliance: a signed writing, a writing in confirmation, special manufacture, admission in court, and part performance.

Unlike the general common-law rule, the signed writing for the sale of goods need not contain all the material terms: "a writing is not insufficient because it omits or incorrectly states a term agreed upon." The writing must indicate that a contract for sale has been made; it must be signed by the party against whom enforcement is sought or by that party's authorized agent; and it must contain the quantity term ("the contract is not enforceable under this paragraph beyond the quantity of goods stated"). Price, packaging, and delivery terms can all be omitted and then filled in by supplementary evidence. A very simple notation on the check given for the down payment would be sufficient (for example, "Down payment on one 1969 Buick"). The buyer's signature on the check binds the buyer to the contract; the seller is also bound when the seller indorses the check so that the check can be cashed or deposited to the seller's account.

Where both parties are merchants and there is no writing which evidences a contract because agreement has been reached over the telephone or in personal conversation, the Code provides a method of compliance called "a writing in confirmation." This is a brand-new Code concept, unknown in prior law. It is a "bootstrap" method: our contract becomes enforceable by me against you on the basis of a writing signed by *me*, not by you. If within a reasonable time after the oral contract has been made, one merchant sends the other a written confirmation of the contract and the confirmation is a sufficient writing against the sender-merchant, it also becomes a sufficient writing against the receiver-merchant unless the receiver-merchant sends back notice of objection to its contents within 10 days after receiving it. This new rule is saying two things to merchants: first, to be on the safe side, always send written confirmation of the contract (preferably by registered mail) before you expend time and money in reliance on an oral agreement; and second, *read your mail!*

To protect the seller of goods against a potentially unfair result, this section provides a separate alternative for specially manufactured goods. Where the buyer has a change of mind and tries to cancel an oral order for custom-made goods, the seller can enforce the oral contract if the seller can convince the jury that the goods the seller is making are "for the buyer," that the seller has substantially started to produce the goods or has made commitments to get them from someone else, and that the goods cannot be readily resold in the ordinary course of the seller's business. This case thus presents several fact questions; basically, the jury has to be convinced that the seller will be stuck

159

with the proverbial "white elephant" if the oral contract, actually made, is not enforced.

The oral contract is also enforceable against a party who admits its existence in pleadings; testimony, or otherwise *in court*. As with the "writing" alternatives, the contract is not enforceable under this provision beyond the quantity of goods admitted.

Finally, the "part performance" alternative has been substantially changed by the Code. Previously, either party could use the other's receipt and acceptance of a partial performance as evidence of a much larger contract. For example, a seller could show that the seller had delivered and the buyer had accepted 50 bushels of wheat and then allege that this was merely the first installment on an oral contract for 1,000 bushels of wheat; if the jury believed the seller, the seller could get the contract enforced on that basis. The drafters of the Code felt that this result circumvented the policy of the statute of frauds, so they provided that partial performance by one party makes the contract enforceable against the other party only to the same, pro rata extent. Thus in the above example the seller can only collect the contract price for the 50 bushels of wheat delivered and accepted; the rest of the oral contract remains unenforceable. However, if the goods are an indivisible unit, such as a car or a Boeing 707, the buyer's payment of part of the contract price, received and accepted by the seller, does have the effect of making the entire contract enforceable.

Compliance Alternatives under Other Code Sections.   For investment securities, the Code permits the use of these same basic alternatives, with the exception of "special manufacture." To be sufficient, a writing under this section (8–319) must also contain the price term. The writing in confirmation procedure can be used between any buyer and seller; it is not limited to situations where both parties are, or are represented by, brokers or other securities "experts." Since these securities would normally exist in divisible units, partial performance here should nearly always result in only partial enforceability.

For security agreements, there must be a writing by which the debtor grants the secured party a security interest in the described collateral, and only if the *debtor* signs the writing will the secured party have the right to repossess and resell the collateral if the debtor goes into default. Such a writing is not required only in cases where the secured party keeps possession of the collateral ("pledge" or "pawn" transactions). Secured transactions are discussed in more detail in Chapters 20 and 21.

For sales of miscellaneous intangibles at a contract price of $5,000 or more, no alternative to the writing is provided. The signed writing must indicate that a contract has been made, must describe the subject matter of the contract, and must contain a price term.

WHAT RESULTS FOLLOW IF THE STATUTE OF FRAUDS APPLIES AND IT HAS NOT BEEN SATISFIED

Unenforceable in Court.   In the vast majority of cases where the statute of frauds applies and has not been complied with, the contract is unenforceable in court. This does not mean that the contract is illegal in any way or that the parties have violated any criminal law. Nor does it mean that if the parties perform the contract in full, one of the parties can later move to rescind the performances on the basis that the contract should have been evidenced by a writing and never was. "Unenforceable" as applied here simply means that there will be no court remedy for the enforcement of such a contract, that the court will not assist either party with its sanctions for nonperformance of the contract unless the contract can be proved by the required writing.

This result is not changed by the fact that one party has relied in good faith (but stupidly) on the existence of the unenforceable oral contract. Courts do not generally feel that they are permitted to work out a result forbidden by the statute of frauds just because a particular plaintiff presents an appealing set of facts. The following case illustrates this point, with the court refusing to override the legislative policy expressed in the statute even though it doesn't particularly like the results produced.

Davis v. Crown Central Petroleum Corp.
483 F.2d 1014 (U.S. Fourth Circuit, 1973)

FACTS   The plaintiffs, both citizens of North Carolina, were small independent oil dealers with their main operations in North Carolina. The defendant was a refiner, dependent almost entirely on producers for its supply of crude oil. It had for some years been selling its product to the plaintiffs. In anticipation of the oil shortage, which all parties in the industry apparently foresaw, discussions as to future supplies were held among the parties. It was contended by the plaintiffs that the defendant agreed to supply them with certain fixed quantities of gasoline. As the energy crisis deepened, the defendant's suppliers drastically reduced its supply of crude oil. The defendant accordingly proceeded to allocate on a lower percentage its deliveries to its contract customers and to notify customers such as the plaintiffs, whom it denominated noncontract customers, that it would make no further sales to them. These actions followed the notification. Preliminary injunctive relief was sought in both cases by the plaintiffs and was granted in both instances by the district court having jurisdiction over the actions. In each case the defendant appealed from these grants of injunctive relief.

ISSUE   Can these contracts be enforced despite the statute of frauds?

DECISION   No. Judgment for defendant in both cases.

REASONS   "We find it necessary to consider only the contention based on the Statute of Frauds. The Findings of Fact in each case made it clear that any agreement between the plaintiffs and the defendant was within the North Carolina Statute of Frauds. . . . On the basis of the present Findings of Fact in each case, the statute would be a complete bar to a ruling that there was a valid contract or agreement between the plaintiffs . . . and the defendant. . . . It is true, as the plaintiffs have argued, that in exceptional cases, courts of equity will find an estoppel against the enforcement of the statute, but such an estoppel can arise in North Carolina only 'upon grounds of fraud' on the part of him who relies on the statute. The District Court in neither case made a finding of 'fraud' on the part of the defendant, and, absent such finding, there can be no estoppel. Nor, on the facts in the record before us, would it appear that any such finding would have been in order. . . .

> A mere failure or refusal to perform an oral contract, within the statute, is not such fraud, within the meaning of this rule, as will take the case out of the operation of the statute, and this is ordinarily true even though the other party has changed his position to his injury.

"After all, as the District Court in one of the cases observed, the plight of the defendant was not substantially different from that of the plaintiffs. It was experiencing hardships which forced it to take action it obviously did not relish.

"The claim of the plaintiffs is appealing, and our sympathies are with them. As the District Courts indicated, it is equitable in periods of scarcity of basic materials for the Government to inaugurate a program of mandatory allocations of the materials. This, however, is a power to be exercised by the legislative branch of Government. The power of the Court extends only to the enforcement of valid contracts and does not comprehend the power to make mandatory allocations of scarce products on the basis of any consideration of the public interest."

"Part Performance" Exceptions. The UCC's exceptions where part performance of an oral contract for goods or securities has taken place, have already been discussed as "alternatives." In addition, courts have worked out limited exceptions to the unenforceability result for contracts involving real estate or the one-year clause.

Where one party has in good faith conferred benefits on the other under an oral contract which is unenforceable because of the one-year clause, a court will generally permit recovery in quasi contract of the fair market value of the benefits so as to prevent "unjust enrichment." An employee who worked for three months under a two-year oral contract would thus be able to recover the fair market value of any services for which he or she had not been paid already. This exception would not, however, permit the recovery of moving expenses, bonuses, or other special compensation promised as part of the unenforceable oral agreement. The entire contract is enforceable, according to the *Restatement of Contracts*, only where one party has *fully* performed his or her obligations; that party can then enforce the other party's full return performance.

For real estate contracts, the courts have developed a doctrine called "equitable estoppel," which prevents a party from relying on the statute of frauds under certain limited circumstances and thus has the effect of making an oral contract enforceable. The courts have permitted either party to enforce an oral contract where the buyer has taken possession of real estate with the seller's permission and has made substantial permanent physical improvements or (perhaps) where the buyer has taken possession and has made a part payment on the contract price. This doctrine is generally not applicable in cases where there has been only a part payment of the price or only a taking of possession by the buyer, or only "reliance" expenditures such as preparation of documents by the seller or moving expenses by the buyer. The following case shows that, legally speaking, ignorance is sometimes better than expertise.

Burke v. *Fine*
51 N.W.2d 818 (Minnesota, 1952)

FACTS   This suit was commenced in August 1945 for the specific performance of an alleged oral contract to convey a vacant lot to the plaintiff.

The plaintiff claimed that the contract was taken out of the statute of frauds by virtue of his having taken possession of the lot under the contract and his having made certain valuable improvements. No payment was ever made, but at the commencement of this action the plaintiff paid into court $1,477.98, representing the alleged contract price.

The property involved lay directly to the rear of the plaintiff's home. It was covered with underbrush and debris and was described as more or less like a jungle. The only trees on the lot were crooked box elders. According to the plaintiff's testimony, rats came out of the dump on lot 6 and in April 1943 he tried to burn them out.

In the spring of 1943, the plaintiff and Duell, who had had some association with him for years and often visited at his home, spent weekends and holidays working in the plaintiff's yard. On April 3, 1943, while they were working on lot 6, Jacob Fine appeared, and the plaintiff claimed that the alleged contract was formed at that time. Subsequent to this meeting, the plaintiff hired a bulldozer to rough-grade lot 6, had it leveled, planted a lawn and hedge along its north and west sides, and planted some trees, bushes, and plants on it.

ISSUE   Is this a proper case for application of the doctrine of "equitable estoppel," so that the statute of frauds cannot be used against the alleged buyer.

DECISION   No. Trial court reversed; judgment for defendants ("sellers").

REASONS   "The doctrine of part performance as it has been developed by the courts is essentially a compromise between the policy of the statute of frauds and the need presented by some cases for at least some flexibility in applying it. Application of the doctrine in some cases has been explained by the extreme hardship which would result if the statute were applied; while in others the court has felt that the policy behind the statute was adequately protected if acts of performance unequivocally referable to the contract were shown. Thus, where plaintiff shows that his acts of part performance in reliance upon the contract have so altered his position that he will incur unjust and irreparable injury in the event that defendant is permitted to rely on the statute of frauds, equity requires that the contract be specifically enforced. Or where the relationship of the parties, as shown by their acts rather than by the alleged contract, cannot reasonably be explained except by reference to some contract between them, the oral contract is taken out of the statute of frauds and may be specifically enforced. It is our opinion that plaintiff here has failed to show part performance sufficient to satisfy either or these theories.

"It is reasonable to believe that he was interested in the improvement of lot 6 because of its location immediately adjacent to the rear of his home. The improvements relied on have provided plaintiff with a spacious and attractive backyard, which he and his family have used since 1943. . . . Nor does the record disclose

Burke v. *Fine (continued)*

any acts of defendants which point unequivocally to a contract relationship between the parties. Defendants did not vacate the premises or perform any other act to give possession to plaintiff.

"Under the record in the instant case, it cannot be said that defendants' failure to object to the making of the improvements unequivocally refers to a contract.

"Aside from the unequivocal reference theory, plaintiff does not present equities sufficient to take the contract out of the statute of frauds. He shows no affirmative act of defendants which induced him to make the improvements. . . . Rather than being induced by defendants to make the improvements, it appears that plaintiff proceeded on his own initiative, fully aware of the possible consequences.

"Plaintiff argues that, being a lawyer, he knew that an oral contract was taken out of the statute of frauds by part performance, so that in effect he was induced to make the improvements. This argument misconceives the nature of the part-performance doctrine. It definitely is not an alternative method for the deliberate creation of a binding contract to convey land. A party aware that his claim is unenforceable should take steps to comply with the statute rather than make improvements and later complain that the application of the statute will work a fraud on him. To rule otherwise would be to invite the unfortunate situations which these cases of part performance always represent. By this we do not mean to say that an attorney, such as plaintiff, may never have a case where part performance will take an oral contract out of the statute of frauds; but where, as here, there is nothing about the actions of the parties which unequivocally refers to a contract between them, the claim by an attorney that the statute of frauds is being used to work a fraud against him will be carefully scrutinized.

"Since the facts and circumstances of this case fail to bring it under either of the theories upon which the doctrine of part performance is based, the statute of frauds must be given effect."

It is never advisable to rely on the slim chance that a court will salvage your situation by applying one of the exceptions to the statute of frauds. The only safe course is to *Get it in writing* (and make sure the other party signs the writing)!

THE PAROL EVIDENCE RULE

Nature and Operation of the Rule. Just as the operation of the statute of frauds can be summarized in the sentence "Get it in writing," so can the significance of the parol evidence rule be summarized by slightly modifying the sentence to read: *"Get it **all** in writing!"*

Although the application of the parol evidence rule may seem to produce harsh or unfair results in particular situations (such as the *Mitchill* case, reported below), the equities are not all on one side. There are sound, practical reasons for the rule's existence. It is, ultimately, another example of the courts' efforts to find and enforce the intent of the parties. The contracting parties may have engaged in extended negotiations before reaching their agreement. They may have exchanged numerous oral and written proposals and counterproposals, some accepted by the other side, some rejected. Then, at the end of this lengthy process, they signed a document which either expressly or impliedly stated that it was intended by them as the full, final, and complete written expression of their agreement.

At this point, the parol evidence rule comes into operation. Once a party has signed such a document, the rule prevents that party from unilaterally changing or modifying its terms by using parol, or outside, evidence. The document means what it says: "blue" means blue, not green; "10 tons" means 10 tons, not 100 tons or 10 pounds. If a term or a provision on a particular subject is not contained in the document, the presumption is that it was left out on purpose, because the parties did not intend that it be included. In short, the rule operates against the "add-on-a-term" person, who is trying to say, "Yes, that's the contract I signed. Yes, that's the deal I made. But—there's something else that we agreed on that's not in the document." In general, the "add-on" person will (and should) lose this argument; parol evidence will not be admitted to change the terms of the written document.

Mrs. Mitchill provides the classic example of the operation of the parol evidence rule.

Mitchill v. Lath
247 N.Y. 377 (1928)

FACTS | "In the fall of 1923 the Laths owned a farm. This they wished to sell. Across the road, on land belonging to Lieutenant-Governor Lunn, they had an ice house which they might remove. Mrs. Mitchill looked over the land with a view to its purchase. She found the ice house objectionable. Thereupon 'the defendants orally promised and agreed, for and in consideration of the purchase of their farm by the plaintiff, to remove the said ice house in the spring of 1924.' Relying upon this promise, she made a written contract to buy the property for $8,400, for cash and a mortgage and containing various provisions usual in such papers. Later receiving a deed, she entered into possession and has spent considerable sums in improving the property for use as a summer residence. The defendants have not fulfilled their promise as to the ice house and do not intend to do so."

ISSUE | Should the buyer be permitted to prove the alleged "extra" promise made by the sellers to tear down their icehouse?

DECISION | No. Trial court decree for plaintiff reversed.

REASONS | "This requires a discussion of the parol evidence rule—a rule of law which defines the limits of the contract to be construed. . . . It is, at times, troublesome to draw the line. . . . It is claimed that the defendants are called upon to do more than is required by their written contract in connection with the sale as to which it deals.
"Under our decisions, before such an oral agreement as the present is received to vary the written contract, at least three conditions must exist, (1) the agreement must in form be a collateral one; (2) it must not contradict express or implied provisions of the written contract; (3) it must be one that parties would not ordinarily be expected to embody in the writing; or put in another way, an inspection of the written contract, read in the light of surrounding circumstances, must not indicate that the

writing appears 'to contain the engagements of the parties, and to define the object and measure the extent of such engagement.' Or again, it must not be so clearly connected with the principal transaction as to be part and parcel of it.

"[An] inspection of this contract shows a full and complete agreement, setting forth in detail the obligations of each party. On reading it one would conclude that the reciprocal obligations of the parties were fully detailed. Nor would his opinion alter if he knew the surrounding circumstances. The presence of the ice house, even the knowledge that Mrs. Mitchill thought it objectionable, would not lead to the belief that a separate agreement existed with regard to it. Were such an agreement made, it would seem most natural that the inquirer should find it in the contract. Collateral in form it is found to be, but it is closely related to the subject dealt with in the written agreement—so closely that we hold it may not be proved."

If you're feeling too sorry for Mrs. Mitchill, note that the court itself makes the point that if she can impose additional obligations on the sellers by adding on a term, they could do likewise to her. In other words, the parol evidence rule operates to protect *both* parties, by guaranteeing the integrity of the document they both signed and intended as "the contract." Consider also the point that once we open the door and let Mrs. Mitchill add on the "ice house" term this year, who's to say that she won't be back next year and allege that the Laths also promised to blacktop her driveway, or paint the barn, or aluminum-side the house, or landscape the yard, etc., etc., etc.? The rule is really not saying anything more "unfair" than that a person is, generally, bound by what he or she has signed. If the document isn't "right," if it doesn't contain all the terms you have agreed on, *Don't sign it!*

Situations Not Covered by the Rule. Since the purpose of the parol evidence rule is to make final a document which the parties intended to be final, the rule has no application in contract situations where no such full, final, and complete document has ever been signed. If the seller has simply given the buyer a sales receipt, or if the parties have merely exchanged letters, no such complete document exists, so all evidence is admissible to show what the parties intended to include as part of the contract. For sales of goods, a "final" writing may be "explained or supplemented," but not "contradicted," by "consistent additional terms," "unless the court finds the writing to have been intended also as a complete and exclusive statement of the terms of the agreement" (UCC, 2–202[b]). What this means in plain English is that a court *may* be a little more reluctant to apply the parol evidence rule in a sale of goods case where the contract does not contain a specific "This is it" statement.

Again remembering the basic purpose of the parol evidence rule, it obviously has no application in situations where the alleged modification of the terms in the document occurred *after* the document was signed. The document is presumed final as of the time it was signed. The parties may decide to modify it later, and the parol evidence rule does not prevent either of them from trying to convince a jury that such modifications were in fact agreed to. (There may, however, be both consideration and statute of frauds problems as to such subsequent modifications, as noted previously.)

Third, and even more obviously, the rule has no application where there are *two* contracts, one evidenced by a complete writing, the other oral. The fact that one contract is written does not prevent a party from trying to prove that there was a second, oral contract. If you buy a used car from your next-door neighbor for $900, and he or she also agrees to let you park the car in his or her garage for the next six months for $10 a month, the fact that you have signed a complete written contract for the sale of the car will not prevent you from trying to prove the existence of the separate oral contract to rent the garage space. (But note that if the "garage" promise was not a *separate* rental contract, but just part of the deal for the car, and that promise was not included in the written car contract, you'd be right where Mrs. Mitchill was.

Exceptions to the Operation of the Parol Evidence Rule. Like many of the other rules of evidence, the parol evidence rule is subject to some important exceptions. That is, the trier of fact can consider parol evidence in some situations, at least for some purposes, even though a complete written document exists and even though the evidentiary facts occurred before the document was signed.

Stated most simply, parol evidence is admissible where it is being offered to help the court interpret the terms of the written contract or to show the existence of a defense against the written contract, not to *change* the terms of the written contract. The line is not always easy to draw, although in some cases the correct result seems fairly obvious.

The easiest cases to decide are those where the writing makes no sense by itself, due to ambiguities, contradictory provisions, or coded "nonsense" terms. In these cases a court must use extrinsic evidence to discover what the parties "really meant." Where both parties are engaged in a particular trade or business and certain words have acquired a customary meaning in that business, courts generally permit either party to prove that special meaning even though the words have a "plain English" meaning too. Thus an Oregon court permitted a seller to prove that "50 percent protein" really meant *49.50 percent* protein in the dog food business, and the seller could therefore collect the full contract price per ton for all shipments of dog food scraps with a protein content of at least 49.50 percent. For sales of goods, the UCC now permits the parties to explain or supplement a "final" writing by course of dealing, usage of trade, or course of performance.

Most courts will also allow a party to show that the written contract was intended to be subject to an orally agreed-upon condition precedent, that they intended no deal at all unless and until some special condition was satisfied. Similarly, if the writing states as a fact something that is just not so, a party can usually prove the truth. For instance, if your contract to buy a new TV set not only describes the set and states the price and the payment terms, but also goes on to say that the set "has been delivered," when in fact it has not been delivered, you can prove that you didn't get the TV set as promised. (But the parol evidence rule will generally prevent you from changing "one TV" into *two* TVs, or "$600" into $450, or "TV" into stereo.)

Courts are quite liberal in allowing proof of the existence of a defense against liability on the written contract. In most cases this is not really a "contradiction" of the writing because the writing does not usually contain such provisions as "This contract is legal" or "There was no duress." The contract may, however, contain a representation that the party signing it is of full legal age, and there are some courts which prevent a minor from asserting his or her lack of capacity if the minor has stated otherwise in writing. (The next chapter has a more complete discussion of this point.)

The following case shows that a court is likely to be *very* sympathetic where fraud is alleged, even though the contract langauge is clear and emphatic on the point of dispute. Indeed, one wonders what else the company could have said in its written contract to avoid the result in this case.

Central Construction Company v. Osbahr
180 N.W.2d 139 (Nebraska, 1970)

FACTS "This was an action to foreclose a mechanics lien. It was based on a contract involving the installation of plastic siding and aluminum windows and doors on defendants' residence. The district court found that the written contract was procured by the plaintiff by fraud and misrepresentation, ordered that the written contract be reformed to conform to the oral agreement of the parties, and dismissed plaintiff's petition.

"Two representatives of the plaintiff called on defendants at their home. After several hours, the salesmen departed with a printed form contract which had been signed by the defendants. One paragraph of the printed agreement provided: 'There are no representations, guarantees or warranties except such as may herein be incorporated, if any, nor any agreement collateral hereto, nor is this contract dependent upon or subject to any conditions not herein stated. Any subsequent agreement in reference hereto shall be binding only if in writing and if signed by all parties. Owner(s) understand and agree that Contractor does not make, and no agent of Contractor is authorized to make, any agreement with Owner(s) either concerning any payments, credits or commissions to be received by Owner(s) for referrals of prospective customers. Owner(s) further understand and agree that, in the event Owner(s) make any such agreements with any person whomsoever, Contractor has no responsibility whatsoever for the performance of such agreements. Contractor does hereby expressly disaffirm any such agreements purportedly made on its behalf.'

". . . Defendants testified that plaintiff's salesmen represented to them the defendants' residence would be used by the plaintiff as a 'model home,' and that certain payments resulting from the sale of plaintiff's products arising out of such use of defendants' home would be credited to and discharge defendants' obligations under the contract. The entire installation would, in effect, be at no cost to defendants.

"There was also evidence that plaintiff's representatives told the defendants there was no need to read the contract. Whenever they attempted to read it, or inquire about or objected to portions of the contract they read, the representatives would explain to them that it did not apply to them because theirs was to be a model home and the printed form was the form for standard contracts."

ISSUE Can the defendants introduce parol evidence to show that the written contract was procured by fraud?

CASES FOR DISCUSSION

BOARD OF CONTROL OF EASTERN MICH. UNIV. v. BURGESS

206 N.W.2d 256 (Michigan, 1973)

R. B. Burns, Judge

On February 15, 1966, defendant [Renee M. Burgess] signed a document which purported to grant to plaintiff a 60-day option to purchase defendant's home. That document, which was drafted by plaintiff's agent, acknowledged receipt by defendant of "One and no/100 ($1.00) Dollar and other valuable consideration." Plaintiff concedes that neither the one dollar nor any other consideration was ever paid or even tendered to defendant. On April 14, 1966, plaintiff delivered to defendant written notice of its intention to exercise the option. On the closing date defendant rejected plaintiff's tender of the purchase price. Thereupon, plaintiff commenced this action for specific performance.

At trial defendant claimed that the purported option was void for want of consideration, that any underlying offer by defendant had been re-

voked prior to acceptance by plaintiff, and that the agreed purchase price was the product of fraud and mutual mistake. The trial judge concluded that no fraud was involved, and that any mutual mistake was not material. He also held that defendant's acknowledgment of receipt of consideration bars any subsequent contention to the contrary. Accordingly, the trial judge entered judgment for plaintiff.

Defendant appeals. She claims that acknowledgment of receipt of consideration does not bar the defense of failure of consideration. She further claims that the trial judge's findings of fact as to the absence of fraud and material mistake are in error, and that the record supports a finding that defendant was the victim of plaintiff's coercion.

Options for the purchase of land, if based on valid consideration, are contracts which may be specifically enforced. . . . Conversely, that which purports to be an option, but which is not based on valid consideration, is not a contract and will not be enforced. . . . One dollar is valid consideration for an option to purchase land, provided the dollar is paid or at least tendered. . . . In the instant case defendant received no consideration for the purported option of February 15, 1966.

A written acknowledgment of receipt of consideration merely creates a rebuttable presumption that consideration has, in fact, passed. Neither the parol evidence rule nor the doctrine of estoppel bars the presentation of evidence to contradict any such acknowledgment. . . .

It is our opinion that the document signed by defendant on February 15, 1966, is not an enforceable option, and that defendant is not barred from so asserting.

* * * * *

That which purports to be an option for the purchase of land, but which is not based on valid consideration, is a simple offer to sell the same land. . . . An option is a contract collateral to an offer to sell whereby the offer is made irrevocable for a specified period. . . . Ordinarily, an offer is revocable at the will of the offeror. Accordingly, a failure of consideration affects only the collateral contract to keep the offer open, not the underlying offer.

A simple offer may be revoked for any reason or for no reason by the offeror at any time prior to its acceptance by the offeree. . . . Thus, the question in this case becomes, "Did defendant effectively revoke her offer to sell before plaintiff accepted that offer?"

We disagree with plaintiff that to be effective the revocation of a written offer to sell land must itself be in writing. The Statute of Frauds applies only to contracts and conveyances of interests in land. . . . An offer is not a contract. . . . An offer to sell land creates no interest in that land. . . . Therefore, the Statute of Frauds does not require that the revocation of an offer to sell land be in writing. . . . Contract law does not require written revocation of a written offer. . . . A revocation of an offer is effective if merely communicated to the offeree. . . .

Defendant testified that within hours of signing the purported option she telephoned plaintiff's agent and informed him that she would not abide by the option unless the purchase price was increased. Defendant also testified that when plaintiff's agent delivered to her on April 14,

1966, plaintiff's notice of its intention to exercise the purported option, she told him that "the option was off."

Plaintiff's agent testified that defendant did not communicate to him any dissatisfaction until sometime in July, 1966.

If defendant is telling the truth, she effectively revoked her offer several weeks before plaintiff accepted that offer, and no contract of sale was created. If plaintiff's agent is telling the truth, defendant's offer was still open when plaintiff accepted that offer, and an enforceable contract was created. The trial judge thought it unnecessary to resolve this particular dispute. In light of our holding the dispute must be resolved.

An appellate court cannot assess the credibility of witnesses. We have neither seen nor heard them testify. . . . Accordingly, we remand this case to the trial court for additional findings of fact based on the record already before the court.

* * * * *

SIERENS v. CLAUSEN
328 N.E.2d 559 (Illinois, 1975)

Goldenhersh, Justice

Plaintiffs, Kenneth Sierens and James Thompson, a partnership, d/b/a Mineral Elevator Company, appealed from the judgment of the circuit court of Bureau County entered in favor of defendant, Edwin Clausen, upon allowance of his "motion to strike complaint." The appellate court affirmed (21 Ill. App. 3d 540, 315 N.E.2d 897), and we allowed plaintiffs' petition for leave to appeal.

In their amended complaint plaintiffs alleged that they had entered into two oral agreements with defendant whereby defendant agreed to sell and plaintiffs agreed to buy 3,500 bushels of soybeans, for future delivery; that plaintiffs furnished defendant with a written confirmation of the agreement; "that all of the foregoing was done in accordance with the practices, customs and usages of the grain business and the commodities market and that defendant is a grower and seller of farm commodities and such has been at

170

all times pertinent to this lawsuit well familiar with said practices, customs and usages"; that subsequently defendant, in writing, "repudiated" the contracts; that by reason of defendant's failure to deliver the soybeans plaintiffs suffered substantial damages.

In the motion to strike the amended complaint, defendant asserts that each contract was for the sale of goods for more than $500 and "that there was no writing signed by the defendant; all in violation of section 2–201 of the Commercial Code (I.R.S., ch. 26, par. 2–201)"; that "par. 2–201(2) concerning confirmations is applicable only between merchants; that the complaint does not allege that defendant is a merchant; and that he is, in fact, not a merchant within the meaning of the above-mentioned statute."

* * * * *

The circuit court found that at the time the oral contracts were made defendant was a farmer and not a "merchant within the meaning of Section 2–201(2) of the Uniform Commercial Code" and that the contracts were not enforceable. It struck the amended complaint and dismissed the action. The appellate court, finding that "the defendant, as described in the complaint before us, was a casual seller" (see UCC Comment Sec. 2–104, comments 1 and 2), held that defendant was not a merchant and affirmed the judgment.

The defense presented by defendant's motion to strike is based on the Statute of Frauds, and the procedure is governed by section 48 of the Civil Practice Act (Ill. Rev. Stat. 1971, ch. 110, par. 48), which provides in pertinent part:

"(1) Defendant may, within the time for pleading, file a motion for dismissal of the action or for other appropriate relief upon any of the following grounds. If the grounds do not appear on the face of the pleading attacked, the motion shall be supported by affidavit:

* * * * *

"(g) That the claim or demand asserted is unenforceable under the provisions of the Statute of Frauds."

There were no affidavits filed by the parties,

but the circuit court had before it defendant's answers to interrogatories submitted by plaintiffs. Our rules provide that "Answers to interrogatories may be used in evidence to the same extent as a discovery deposition" (Rule 213[f], Ill. Rev. Stat. 1973, ch. 110A, # 213[f]), and that discovery depositions may be used "for any purpose for which an affidavit may be used" (Rule 212[a][4]). The facts stated in defendant's answers to the interrogatories were therefore before the circuit court for its consideration when it ruled on defendant's motion. The answers show that defendant had been engaged in farming for 34 years, that at that time he had under cultivation approximately 180 acres of corn and 150 acres of soybeans, and that for a period of at lest five years he had sold his crops to grain elevators both in "cash sales" and "future contracts."

The briefs of the parties, and our own research, indicate that the question whether a farmer may under the circumstances here shown be a "merchant" under the Uniform Commercial Code, has been decided on three prior occasions. In *Campbell* v. *Yokel*, 20 Ill. App. 3d 702, 313 N.E.2d 628, the appellate court held that farmers who marketed their crops on a regular basis are merchants within the contemplation of section 2–201 of the Uniform Commercial Code. In *Cook Grains, Inc.* v. *Fallis* (1965), 239 Ark. 962, 395 S.W.2d 555, the court held that a merchant under Section 2-104(1) of the Uniform Commercial Code is one who trades in goods or commodities on a professional basis and a farmer who "sells the commodities he has raised" is not a merchant. In *Ohio Grain Co.* v. *Swisshelm* (1973), 40 Ohio App. 2d 203, 318 N.E.2d 428, 69 Ohio Op. 2d 192, the court held that the defendant, an experienced farmer who had previously sold soybeans and kept abreast of the market, was a "merchant" when selling his current crop of soybeans.

The practice of grain and soybean growers in selling their products in the manner described in plaintiffs' amended complaint is well known and widely followed. We know of no reason why under the circumstances shown here the defendant, admittedly a farmer, cannot at the time of the sale be a "merchant." On this record we hold that he was a merchant and that Section 2–201 of the

Uniform Commercial Code applied to those transactions.

In his motion to strike the complain defendant has attacked the sufficiency of the written confirmations of the agreements sent by plaintiffs. We have examined the documents and hold them to be sufficient under the provisions of Section 2–201 of the Uniform Commercial Code.

Although for purposes of the motion all facts well pleaded are taken as true, defendant's letter "repudiating" the agreements, which appears in the record as an exhibit attached to plaintiffs' amended complaint, purports to raise the question whether the parties entered into the oral contracts. Although we have determined as a matter of law defendant's status and the sufficiency of the confirmations, the remaining question is one for the trier of fact.

For the reasons stated, the judgments of the appellate and circuit courts are reversed and the cause is remanded to the circuit court of Bureau County for further proceedings.

Reversed and remanded.

LEWIS v. HUGHES

346 A.2d 231 (Maryland, 1975)

Digges, Judge

Whether the writing requirement of the Statute of Frauds contained in Title 2 of the Uniform Commercial Code, 2–201, prevents the enforcement of an oral contract for the sale of a mobile home is the question we must settle in this case. Judge Robert E. Clapp, Jr., sitting without a jury in the Circuit Court for Montgomery County, resolved this issue by deciding that under #2–201(1) the contract between Bettie Lewis, the plaintiff-appellant, and Dr. Herbert H. Hughes, the defendant-appellee, was not enforceable because the writing evidencing the contract, though signed by an agent of the appellee, was inadequately subscribed inasmuch as the agent did not have authority to execute such a memorandum on behalf of the doctor. Without determining whether the circuit court was correct in holding that this agreement cannot pass muster under the signature requirement of

#2–201(1), we conclude that it can be enforced under #2–201(3)(b) since Dr. Hughes admitted in his testimony at trial the case for an assessment of damages.

The chronicle of this case begins in the spring of 1973 when the appellant agreed to sell her 1967 Hillcrest mobile home to Phillip and Joyce Walters subject to the condition that Midway Mobile Home Park, located in Laurel, Maryland, permit the purchasers to rent the space on which the house trailer was then situated. Mrs. Lewis immediately sought the consent of the trailer park's managers, who informed her that no decision would be made until a formal application was filed; however, the managers added that these prospective occupants were unlikely to be accepted since Mrs. Walters' brother already lived in the mobile home park and park rules prohibited relatives of current residents from becoming tenants. Piqued by this rule, the appellant protested to Dr. Hughes, the owner of the trailer park, who indicated that he had no knowledge that such a rule existed but would look into the matter; Mrs. Lewis then complained to James L. Baer, Esq., an attorney appellant knew to have represented the doctor in the past, who in turn relayed her message to the appellee. On May 2 or 3 the doctor informed Mr. Baer that he had revoked the rule prohibiting relatives as tenants and asked him to so notify the appellant. This, unfortunately, did not end the dispute, as on May 4 or 5 Dr. Hughes advised the attorney that the trailer park superintendents were upset at being overruled by him and that, in order to mollify both his managers and the appellant, he would consider purchasing the mobile home himself. At the doctor's request Mr. Baer, on May 7, apprised Mrs. Lewis of the appellee's plight and of his resulting interest in acquiring the trailer; later that same day the appellant replied to the attorney that she was willing to sell the house trailer to Dr. Hughes for $5,000. On May 7 Mr. Baer reported appellant's offer to Dr. Hughes, who, without comment as to terms of payment, assented to the $5,000 purchase price. The attorney then signed and mailed to Dr. Hughes a letter, dated May 8, 1973, in confirmation of that conversation. Mrs. Lewis was notified on May 9 by

Mr. Baer of the doctor's acceptance of her offer. However, the appellee on May 21 informed Mrs. Lewis that he would not pay the full $5,000 at the time of settlement, offering instead $3,500 cash, or alternatively, $5,000 over a period of time, which prompted the appellant to sell the mobile home elsewhere and to institute this suit for fraud and breach of contract.

The circuit court, relying on those facts, held that there was an oral contract between the appellant and Dr. Hughes for the sale of the house trailer, a conclusion which appellee does not challenge on this appeal. Nonetheless, the court decided that the contract was unenforceable under #2–201(1) of the UCC. . . .

The appellant asserts that Dr. Hughes repeatedly acknowledged the existence of the contract in his testimony and that therefore, regardless of its enforceability under #2–201(1), the agreement is enforceable under #2–201(3)(b).

The next step in deciding whether the statute bars enforcement of the contract is to determine just what, if anything, Dr. Hughes did admit concerning the agreement during the course of his testimony at trial. An examination of the record discloses that the doctor testified as follows:

Q. This . . . conversation [with Mr. Baer], did you regard that as a meeting of the minds that you were to buy a trailer from Mrs. Lewis for $5,000 then or in the immediate future?

A. No, sir, I did not.

Q. What was your understanding of your relationship with Mrs. Lewis at that time?

A. My understanding was we were in a negotiation state really of reaching an agreement as to the purchase of the trailer, and I did not really agree to the terms how to purchase the trailer. But the price I had agreed with Mr. Baer on.

Q. Now I take it, sir, that you were not willing at any time to pay $5,000 cash?

A. That is correct.

* * * * *

Q. Did you tell [Mr. Baer], as he says, 'O.K. I will buy it at that price,' or not?

A. Yes.

Q. Now the essence of your version, if I understand it correctly, is that your statement was misinter-

preted. You did not intend to mean that you would pay $5,000 cash. You intended that you would pay $5,000 on terms of some down and some over a period of time, is that right?

A. That was not even discussed.

Q. I understand that. But am I correct that when you said, 'O.K. I will buy it at that price,' that in your mind, at that time, you meant that you would buy it for $2,500 down, whatever it is, plus the rest over a period of time, although you did not say so?

A. That is right.

* * * * *

Q. You have already agreed to $5,000 as the price?

A. Yes.

Q. In your mind there exists a reservation as to method of payment that you have not communicated to anyone, is that right?

A. That is right.

In sum, it is apparent from this, as well as from other portions of the appellee's testimony not here quoted, that at the trial the doctor admitted he told Mr. Baer, without mention of any terms of payment, that he would purchase the mobile home for $5,000. Of course, it is legally irrelevant, in the face of Dr. Hughes' objective manifestation of unconditional assent to the offer, that the doctor thought the contract was still being negotiated and had a subjective desire to impose certain conditions on the manner of payment. . . . Consequently, when on May 9, the lawyer, in accordance with his agency authority, informed appellant of Dr. Hughes' assent, there was an acceptance of the offer and a contract, as a matter of law, came into existence.

However, before reaching the principal issue posed by this case, we must, it seems, decide whether an admission that a contract was made is a valid admission for purposes of #2–201(3)(b) if made involuntarily, since it has several times been said that there is a conflict of authority on the question. . . . It is true that some cases decided prior to the adoption of the UCC by any state indicate that involuntary admissions as to the making of a contract will not satisfy the common law Statute of Frauds. . . . and that some commentators have apparently associated those decisions with #2–201(3)(b). . . . Nevertheless, the cases reaching this issue under the UCC are uniform in concluding that involuntary admissions are sufficient for purposes of #2–201(3)(b). . . . We therefore hold that involuntary admissions can be used to satisfy the Statute of Frauds under #2–201(3)(b).

We come then to the basic issue in this case, which is whether the Statute of Frauds is satisfied pursuant to #2–201(3)(b) when the party denying the existence of the contract and relying on the statute takes the stand and, without admitting explicitly that a contract was made, testifies to facts which as a matter of law establish that a contract was formed. While we have found no case specifically deciding this question, numerous cases dealing with #2–201(3)(b) seem to say that in such a situation the requirements of the statute have been fulfilled. . . .

Since it is implicit in the trial judge's findings of fact that he concluded that there was a breach of the contract by the appellee, we will remand the proceedings of the circuit court for entry of judgment in favor of the appellant and for assessment of such damages as that court determines to be proper.

SHPILBERG v. MERRILL LYNCH, PIERCE, ETC.

535 S.W.2d 227 (Kentucky, 1976)

Per Curiam

George Y. Shpilberg appeals from a judgment holding him liable to the brokerage firm of Merrill Lynch, Pierce, Fenner & Smith, in the sum of $22,300, as damages for breach of an alleged contract under which Shpilberg agreed to purchase $1 million face amount of TVA bonds at the price of $1,005 per $1,000 bond. The circuit court made a summary determination that Shpilberg had breached the contract, and then conducted a trial on the issue of damages.

Shpilberg's primary contention on this appeal is that the summary determination that he had breached the contract was error because there was a genuine issue of fact as to whether there was a contract in existence. He maintains that

Merrill Lynch had the burden of proving that there was a contract, or at the least he was entitled to offer proof that there was no contract.

The problem grows out of the fact that the alleged contract on which Merrill Lynch sued was evidenced only by a broker's confirmation slip which was mailed to Shpilberg and to which he made no written objection within 10 days of its receipt by him. The circuit court held that under KRS 355.8–319 (a section of the Uniform Commercial Code) the confirmation slip, not objected to in writing within 10 days, established the existence of a contract, which could not be contradicted by mere testimony that the parties never had reached a firm oral agreement. Shpilberg maintains that the statute merely lifted the bar of the Statute of Frauds, and that Merrill Lynch was not relieved of the burden of proving that there was an oral contract in the terms stated in the confirmation slip, or in any event Shpilberg was entitled to offer proof that there was no oral contract.

Admittedly, Merrill Lynch mailed to Shpilberg a confirmation slip, signed by Merrill Lynch, describing the securities sold, stating the quantity, and stating the price per $1,000 bond and the gross price, and he did not within 10 days of receipt of the slip send written objections. He did, however, on the day the slip was placed in the mail and before he received it, have a telephone conversation with Merrill Lynch concerning the bond transaction. On the motion for summary judgment the showing was that his testimony would be that he told Merrill Lynch that he did not desire to make an agreement to buy the bonds, the parties not then having advanced beyond the negotiating stage, while the evidence for Merrill Lynch would be that he said he wanted to get out of his agreement to buy the bonds, which definitely had been made. Our question is whether the circuit court correctly interpreted the statute to mean that the confirmation slip, unobjected to, established the existence of the contract, not subject to contradiction by mere testimony that there was no contract.

We think the clear meaning to be derived from the words of the statute is that the party who has received the writing and not objected to it is in the same legal position, as concerns enforceability, as the party who signed the writing. We cannot find in the statute any basis for holding that where the party against whom enforcement is sought is the party to whom the writing was sent, and to which he did not object, he has any greater rights than the party who signed and sent the writing.

Calamari, in *The Law of Contracts*, in effect agrees with our interpretation of the statute because in a footnote to Section 313, Chapter 16 of his work, on page 487, in reference to the comparable provision of Section 2–201 of the Commercial Code (relating to sales of goods), he says that the nonobjecting receiver of the writing is in the equivalent position of having *signed* the writing. The official comment under Section 2–201 says the same thing.

We are aware that the official comment under Section 2–201 of the Commercial Code goes on to say that the only effect of the failure to give written notice of objection is to deprive the party who received the writing of the defense of the Statute of Frauds, and that the burden of persuading the trier of fact that a contract was in fact made orally prior to the sending of the written confirmation is unaffected. We are aware also of the decision of some courts interpreting Section 2–201 as the comment would indicate. However, the comment obviously does not mean that the *writing*, which under the statute is required to be sufficient to "indicate that a contract has been made," is not acceptable *evidence* of the fact that a contract was made. In *Tripp* v. *Pay 'N Pak Stores, Inc.* (1974), Or., 518 P.2d 1298, the court specifically held that the writing was evidence sufficient to sustain the findings of the trial court that there was a contract. The holding in *Harry Rubin & Sons*, supra, was to the same effect. And, of course, the whole purpose of the writing required by a Statute of Frauds is to provide *evidence* of a contract. . . .

Since it appears that the writing is acceptable evidence of the existence of a contract, the question then is *how conclusive* evidence is it? We think the answer must be that if the writing contains all of the essential elements of a contract, rather than being merely a skeleton memorandum, it should be treated as conclusive evidence of the existence of the contract, subject to attack only on the grounds on which a written contract may be attacked. Surely where, as here, the writing recites that on a stated day the broker sold a stated quantity of clearly described securities at a stated price per unit with a stated settlement date, and the broker has signed the writing, he, if sued, would not be heard to say that there was no contract, unless he offered to explain away the writing. And the statute puts the nonobjecting receiver of the writing in the same legal position as the signer.

In accord is the law under the traditional Statute of Frauds. In 37 C.J.S. Frauds, Statute of #281, p. 809, the general rule is stated to be that a memorandum sufficient under the statute may not be *contradicted* by parol evidence, though it may be attacked on the grounds of fraud or mistake. This means, we think, that if the writing clearly shows the existence of a contract, it is conclusive evidence of that fact to the extent that it cannot be contradicted simply by parol evidence that there was no agreement.

In the instant case the confirmation slip set forth all of the elements of a complete contract. Shpilberg did not claim by way of defense that his failure to send written objections (which put him in the equivalent position of having signed the writing) was due to fraud, mistake, or other excusing cause. He simply stated that the parties never got beyond the negotiating stage to the point of reaching a firm agreement for the sale of bonds. In these circumstances we think the confirmation slip was entitled to be treated as conclusive evidence of the contract, warranting summary judgment for Merrill Lynch.

The judgment is affirmed.

1. George Marley claimed that on September 1, 1976, he entered into a written agreement with Quark Labs, Inc., to work for Quark from December 1, 1976, to December 1, 1977, for 5 percent of the gross sales in that period. Marley was fired April 1, 1977, after which he sued Quark for breach of contract to recover 5 percent of the gross sales for the year mentioned above.

    Quark denied the existence of any written agreement, and no evidence of one can be found. Quark offered to pay Marley 5 percent of gross sales from December 1, 1976, to April 1, 1977. Can Marley collect for the remainder of the year?

2. In the fall of 1959 Ralph Schultz became ill and unable to operate his 1,200-acre farm. At that time he promised his only son, Lance, that if Lance and his wife, Rosie, would come and operate the farm, he would leave it to them upon his death. Shortly thereafter, Lance gave up his engineer's job with the state and began running the farm.

    In 1962 Ralph's wife died, and three years later Ralph married Esther England. Esther owned an 80-acre farm herself and did not need support but was interested in marriage for companionship. Two days before the marriage Ralph and Esther signed an agreement stating that upon death the land each owned prior to marriage would go to their respective children. In 1972 Ralph died and Esther received personal property and cash worth $65,000 from his estate. She then sued to receive a portion of Ralph's land as his surviving spouse, claiming that she had not understood the agreement signed prior to their marriage. Is she entitled to some of the land?

3. On June 29, Irma Embea, eager to get started in a business of her own, entered into a written agreement for the purchase of Sweet Corner Candy Shop from retiring John Olds. She paid earnest money of $1,000, with the remaining $15,000 due on July 26, the agreed closing date. When Irma could not obtain financing by July 26, she telephoned John Olds, who extended the deadline until August 31. Irma was not able to meet this deadline either and asked for a new extension over the phone. She claims that it was granted to her. John Olds, however, denies having granted a second extension. He subsequently sold the candy store to a third party. Now Irma Embea sues John Olds for specific performance of the sales contract. What decision?

4. Lewis and Martha Fields, a couple in their 80s, listed their farm with a realtor for $150,000. The realtor received an offer for $110,000 from Buyup Land Company and forwarded the contract to the Fields. Martha, the more robust of the two, signed both names on the contract. Later the realtor sent Mrs. Bails, a local notary, to the Fields farm to have the two signatures notarized. Mrs. Bails supposedly did not specifically ask who had actually signed the contract, but she did advise the Fields that she was there to notarize their signatures on the contract for the sale of their farm. Neither of the two objected. They looked at the contract and handed it back to her, and she notarized the signatures. Lewis now claims that the contract is invalid since he never signed it and since he was not advised of the purpose of the notary's visit. Buyup Land Company sues the Fields for specific performance. Who wins?

5. Jon Bear, who operates a brokerage business, brings this action against his customer Albert Loss. Albert placed two trading orders by phone to one of John Bear's employees, one Jeremiah Daef. Albert claims that he instructed Daef to buy 50,000 bushels of July soybeans at $5.80. Daef claims that he was given a sell order. In addition, a few more disputed transactions took place in the course of several days, resulting a loss to Albert. John Bear requested that Albert send him a

check for $21,000 so that Albert could hold his position in the market. The check bounced. Closing out the account caused Albert to lose another $13,000, for which he also sent a bad check. John Bear now demands payment from Albert Loss, and Albert refuses, claiming that his losses were the result of Jeremiah Daef's failure to follow his instructions. Who wins?

6. The city of Sunset, Arizona, entered into a written contract with Masterbuilder Construction Company for the erection of a nursing home. The building was to cost $384,386, and the contract contained detailed specifications on how it was to be constructed. Among other things the contract specified solid-core or hollow-core birch doors throughout the interior. Later Masterbuilder sent shop drawings to the city architect which showed cheaper particle board doors, and the architect's office returned the drawings stamped "approved." After all 46 doors had been installed, the fire marshal inspected the building and notified the city that the doors presented a fire hazard and needed to be replaced. This was done, and now Masterbuilder, pointing to the usual contract provision for "changes in work by written order," claims that the city of Sunset is responsible for the extra cost. The city fathers balk, and the case is taken to court. Who wins?

7. Joe Taken, a real estate broker, was engaged by Mr. and Mrs. Tight to find a buyer for their property. For his efforts he was to receive a 5 percent commission. A buyer was found, and a sales contract was executed between the buyer and the seller which contained the provision for a 5 percent commission to be paid upon the first installment payment by the buyer to the seller. Eventually a dispute between the buyer and the seller arose. It dragged on for several years and was settled by a court order for specific performance. Throughout the proceedings the buyer kept up his payments. The Tights refuse to pay the commission, claiming that an oral promise to pay a real estate commission is unenforceable and that the sales contract containing the commission stipulation does not bind them since it was not signed by the realtor. Are they correct?

8. Eugene Feudal brings this action against Mr. and Mrs. Trustee. The two parties had entered into an oral rental agreement which continued for several years. In September the Trustees suddenly stopped payment. When they had not paid any rent by December, Eugene brought an action against them. The Trustees countered by claiming that they were the owners of the disputed premises, which Eugene Feudal had sold to them in an oral contract two years ago. They said that they had stopped payment when their obligation under the oral contract had been fulfilled. Mrs. Trustee testified that she had heard her husband and Feudal discussing the possibility of a sale. Mr. Trustee told his attorney that Feudal would contact him to draw up a contract. Was there an enforceable contract?

9. Theissen's, Inc., agreed to build a new store and to lease it to the Red Owl supermarket. The lease specified that the lessee would pay each year a percentage of the increase in the tax assessment over the taxes of a prescribed base year. The language of the lease was ambiguous as to the base year. Theissen's claimed it to be the year before the store was built, when taxes were assessed on the vacant lot, while Red Owl asserted that the base year was the first year in which the store building was in existence. How should the judge handle this ambiguity?

10. In 1954 Robert Hifly was hired as a copilot by Ford Motor Company. He was also a brigadier general in the National Guard, a job he resigned when he became chief pilot for Ford in 1970. Robert claimed that he handed in his resignation at Ford's urging and upon Ford's assurance that his salary at Ford would more than make up for the difference. However, no employment contract was ever drawn up. In 1972 Robert Hifly was fired and could not find a comparable job. As a result, his income

dropped by over 25 percent and he sued Ford for breach of contract. What could the defense assert?

11. Alex Dominic executed a purchase agreement for a piece of land owned by Mr. George Obrest. The price was $26,000, and closing was to take place between June 1 and June 30, 1973. The sale was not made contingent upon the buyer obtaining financing. In June Alex asked for a postponement of the closing date, a request which was granted orally. Alex made improvements on the land worth $3,000, but the sale was never perfected. By December 1974, the assessed value of the land had increased, and Obrest negotiated with Dominic for a higher price. No agreement was reached, and the land was ultimately sold to another buyer. Dominic now claims breach of contract and seeks specific performance, while Obrest claims that the purchase agreement was void when Dominic could not meet the first closing date. Decision?

12. On July 3, 1977, Archie Hieb agreed over the telephone to sell 10,000 bushels of wheat for $2.65 a bushel to Jamestown Terminal Elevator, Inc. He was to deliver the wheat within a couple of weeks. Jamestown immediately sold the contracted grain to a third party. Archie failed to deliver the wheat, and in order to fulfill its own contract obligation to the third party, Jamestown Terminal had to buy wheat at $6.75 per bushel. Who would win in a lawsuit by Jamestown against Archie for $41,500, the price difference for 10,000 bushels of wheat?

Defenses—Lack of Capacity | 8

Even though what appears to be a complete contract has been entered into, and the agreement is enforceable under the statute of frauds, there may still be defenses against liability on the contract. Depending on the defense proved, the contract may be voidable at the option of one or both parties, or some parts of it or the whole contract may be unenforceable, or the entire agreement may be void.

We consider, first, defenses based on a party's lack of capacity to contract. Capacity questions may be raised with regard to minors, insane persons, intoxicated persons, persons under the influence of drugs, aliens, American Indians, convicts, married women, and private and governmental corporations. Determinations of these questions are usually made according to the law of the place where the contract is entered into, except where real estate is involved; for realty, the law of the state where the realty is located determines capacity questions.

MINORS, OR "LEGAL INFANTS"

It is sometimes said that "minors can't make contracts." That is patently not so; minors can and do make millions of dollars' worth of contracts every day. What is distinctive about the minor's contract is that it is voidable at his or her option; the minor can later elect not to be bound by it. But make no mistake; the other party, unless that party too lacks full contractual capacity, *is* bound to the agreement with the minor. The common-law judges were concerned with the possibility that the "infant" might be taken advantage of, and so gave the minor the virtually absolute right of disaffirmance. Although minors today may be more sophisticated at an earlier age, this rule continues to be applied by the courts.

We need, then, to examine the scope of the minor's power to disaffirm his or her contracts and to see when a minor may be liable under five different "theories of liability."

Scope of the Minor's Power to Disaffirm. The common law set the age of legal majority at 21; until quite recently that was also the age used for full contractual capacity in nearly all states. The adoption of the Voting Rights Amendment, setting the voting age at 18, has led most states to similarly lower their age of majority to 18 (except perhaps for the age at which one can lawfully buy alcoholic beverages). Different ages, however, may still exist in some states for such matters as criminal responsibility, marriage without parental consent, and making a valid will. However, we are concerned here only with the legal capacity to make fully binding contracts. Whatever age is established in a state, it refers strictly to chronological age. How old the minor "looks," or how "experienced" he or she is, is completely irrelevant to the minor's power to disaffirm his or her contracts. Likewise irrelevant is the fact that the minor is living away from his or her parents and is totally free of their control (i.e., is "emancipated").

In general, the minor has the power to disaffirm any contract he or she makes while still a minor. In some states certain contracts are made binding against the minor by special statutes (bank accounts and life insurance contracts are typical examples); but these are special, and very limited, exceptions.

In most states a minor can disaffirm a contract anytime while he or she is still a minor and for a reasonable time after arriving at the age of majority. For contracts involving real estate, most states say that a minor cannot disaffirm until the minor reaches the age of majority, and then he or she has a reasonable time in which to make the election to affirm or disaffirm. What is a reasonable time within which to disaffirm is a question to be determined by the facts of each case, with the courts paying particular attention to whether the minor was aware of the right to disaffirm.

Any words or actions which indicate the minor's intent not to be bound by the contract are sufficient notice of disaffirmance. Asking for the money back or offering to return items he or she bought while a minor would be clear indications of an intent to disaffirm. Where the contract is completely "executory" (unperformed by either side), even the minor's silence may amount to a disaffirmance. The minor's failure to confirm the unperformed contract after age 18 indicates an unwillingness to be bound by it, but the receipt and retention of benefits or the making of a payment on the contract by the former minor would probably be a ratification of the contract. Silence has the opposite implication where the minor has received the performance of the other party and has given his or her own performance in return, while still a minor, and then the minor turns 18 but says nothing about wanting to disaffirm. In this case silence beyond the reasonable time for disaffirmance equals ratification.

All states agree that ratification by the minor can occur only after the minor has arrived at the age of majority; otherwise, any "ratification" can be disaffirmed since it too occurred while the person was a minor. In addition to the "silence" case described above, ratification can be made by express statements ("I'll keep the car") or it may be implied from the retention of benefits or from payments made after the minor has reached the age of 18.

Logan County Bank v. Taylor
295 N.E.2d 743 (Illinois, 1973)

FACTS   While a minor, James Taylor, the defendant, executed a note. He used the proceeds of the note for the purchase of an automobile. He made two payments and was then drafted. He left the car with a friend "when I went into the service, and it set there until I contacted the bank to pick it up." He was 20 when all this occurred. The bank did pick it up and sold it for salvage—$30. The note, when executed in December 1964, was for $377.40. Subsequently, in 1969, the bank called the defendant in and demanded payment. The defendant advised the bank that he was a minor at the time the loan was executed, but he was told that this fact was of no consequence, and he thereupon agreed to make payments of $10 or $15 a month—which he never did. In February 1972 the bank "confessed judgment" against him. The defendant sought to have the judgment set aside, arguing that he had disaffirmed the note. The lower court, however, confirmed the judgment, and he appealed.

ISSUE   Did James Taylor effectively disaffirm his contract (the note)?

DECISION   Yes. Judgment reversed.

REASONS   "We are not presented with the question more often present than not, as to whether the disaffirmance, if such was the case, was timely, that is, made within a reasonable time after reaching majority. Here, the disaffirmance, if there was one, was prior to majority and therefore about as timely as it could be. A minor can in most instances disaffirm a contract during his minority. But the question remains, was the act of calling the bank and telling them to 'pick it up' a renunciation or disaffirmance. For the defendant here to avoid the note, the renunciation must be unequivocal. . . .

"The bank argues that defendant's direction to pick the car up was not an act of disaffirmance and points to the fact that defendant did not demand the return of two payments previously made. It argues further that disaffirmance can only come after majority—thus, whatever the implications of picking up the car might be, it has no bearing in our context.

"We think otherwise. As we have seen, a minor can disaffirm his contract during minority, and the question here is whether he did so in having the car picked up by the bank. Disaffirmance or renunciation is a question of intent, and it seems to us that when he told the bank to pick up the car, it was his intent to disaffirm the note. There are no circumstances present that militate against such conclusion by implication, such as making another payment, or expressly, by advising the bank at the time that he still intended to pay off the note. In our opinion, his contacting the bank and telling them to pick up the car was an unequivocal renunciation and disaffirmance.

"The bank points to the subsequent conversations with it in 1959 and characterizes such as 'reaffirmance.' But you can't reaffirm that which has been disaffirmed. In our opinion, there was *nothing* to reaffirm—defendant's disaffirmance in legal effect obliterated the note. Reaffirmance cannot be premised on an effort to reverse that which has been legally avoided. Accordingly, we hold that defendant disaffirmed the contract during his minority."

Effect of Minor's Disaffirmance on the Contract. Once a minor has effectively exercised the power to disaffirm a contract, the minor can no longer be held liable for any promises made therein; the minor's contract was voidable, and the minor has elected to avoid it. Thus, where a minor purchased an automobile and promised to make installment payments for the balance of the contract price, if the minor disaffirms, then the minor is no longer liable for the balance still due. Likewise, when a minor disaffirms such a voidable contract, the minor has the legal right to receive back all benefits already transferred by the minor to the other party; in the car purchase case, the minor is entitled to the return of all monies the minor has already paid to the seller of the car. If the minor gave the seller a trade-in car as part of the down payment, the minor is entitled to the return of that too, or of its fair market value if the seller no longer has it. Where the benefits given by the minor have been retransferred to third parties, the minor can generally sue such third parties and demand the return of such property. Thus a minor who sells real estate while a minor would be able to reclaim it even as against a good faith third party who bought the real estate from the minor's buyer. As exceptions to the general third-party rule, the Code protects good-faith-purchaser third parties against such claims by minors in two situations: where the minor's goods have been resold by his or her buyer to a good faith purchaser or where a promissory note or other "negotiable instrument" executed by a minor has gotten into the hands of a "holder in due course" (basically, just another name for a good faith purchaser).

Liabilty in Quasi Contract for Necessaries. In order to prevent "unjust enrichment" and to provide a remedy for persons who have transferred benefits but have no enforceable contract claim for their price, the common-law courts developed the concept of "quasi contract." While acknowledging that there is no enforceable contract claim, this theory permits a plaintiff to collect the reasonable market value of benefits that the plaintiff has conferred, "as if" a contract existed.

A minor is liable in quasi contract for the reasonable market value of "necessaries" actually furnished to the minor pursuant to the minor's now-disaffirmed contract. The other party has the burden of proving that whatever was furnished was actually a necessary to the *particular* minor whom the party dealt with; proof that general categories of necessaries, such as food, clothing, shelter, or medical services, were furnished to the minor is not sufficient to establish the seller's right to recovery. It must also be shown that the minor in question had no source of supply of these items and that the items were furnished to the minor in reasonable amounts. An apartment would not be a necessary, for example, if the minor could live with his or her parents; and even if *an* apartment were a necessary for the particular minor, a 10-room penthouse would probably not be. Although courts today are somewhat more liberal in defining necessaries, sellers of such obvious "luxury" items as stereos, TVs, and vacation trips probably have no case under this theory. Even where an item is found to be a necessary, the proper measure of recovery is only its fair market value (a fact question), not its contract price, and that *only* for the benefits already conferred on and used by the minor. In the case of the apartment found to be a necessary, the landlord can collect only what a jury determines to be the fair market value and only for the period of time that the minor stayed in the apartment.

Minor's Duty to Make Restitution.   Under the general rule, as applied in most states, a minor who wishes to disaffirm a contract has the duty to return to the other party whatever contract benefits are still in the minor's possession at the time of disaffirmance. In most states the minor has no duty to reimburse the other party for that portion of the consideration which the minor has lost, wasted, or disposed of during infancy. In the classic example, the minor buys a new Cadillac, drives it until he or she is almost 18, then "totals" it in an accident. In most states the minor's only duty of restitution is to return the wreck; the minor is not liable for the use value of the car while the minor had it or for the extensive "depreciation" in the value of the car. (Similarly, if the minor had resold the car and spent the proceeds, the minor would have nothing at all to restore but could still disaffirm the original purchase contract and get back whatever payment the minor had made to the original seller) (In short, car dealers are repeatedly warned: "Don't sell to minors!")(The same result—no restitution at all by the minor—occurs when the minor has received intangible benefits such as a vacation trip or services.

Bowling v. *Sperry*
184 N.E.2d 901 (Indiana, 1962)

FACTS   Larry Bowling was a minor, 16 years of age. On June 29, 1957, he purchased from appellee a 1947 Plymouth automobile for the sum of $140 in cash. He paid $50 down on that day, and he returned on July 1, 1957, to pay the balance of $90 and take possession of the car. The appellee delivered to him a certificate of title and a written receipt. This receipt stated that as of June 29, 1957, Max Sperry Ford Sales sold to Larry Bowling a 1947 Plymouth for the amount of $140, cash, paid in full.

Larry drove the car several times during the following week and discovered that the main bearing was burned out. He had the car brought back to the appellee's place of business, where he was informed that it would cost him from $45 to $95 to make repairs. He declined to pay this amount and left the car on the appellee's lot. Subsequently he mailed a letter to the appellee to the effect that he disaffirmed the contract of purchase and demanded the return of his money. Upon the appellee's refusal to pay back the $140, this lawsuit followed.

ISSUES   Was the car a necessary? Can Larry effectively disaffirm the contract on these facts?

DECISION   No. Yes. Judgment reversed.

REASONS   "In so far as the agreement and sale is concerned, there was sufficient evidence to show that it was made between appellee and Larry, and no one else. It is of no consequence that his aunt and grandmother accompanied him at the time of purchase; and the fact that his aunt made payment of the $90 balance due could have no effect upon Larry's right to take advantage of his minority in an action to recover such payment. Appellee was fully aware of Larry's age when the sale was negotiated. The written receipt was in Larry's name alone. This contract was squarely between an adult and a minor and falls within the rule pronounced above. Larry had every right to disaffirm it and set it aside.

"The evidence revealed that at the time of this transaction, Larry was living with his grandmother in Cromwell, Indiana, where he had lived for the past 15 years; that his mother was dead and his father resided in Fort Wayne; that he was a student at Cromwell High School, but was on vacation; that he had a summer job working at a restaurant in the town of Syracuse, Indiana, which was eight or nine miles away from his home; that his usual means of transportation back and forth was with the cook; that on occasion he could 'bum' rides with other people. . . .

"We are well aware of the overwhelming increase in the use and number of automobiles in this country since World War II. What once was a great luxury for only the wealthy has become a matter of common necessity for the ordinary work-ingman, farmer, and businessman. The automobile is as important to the modern household as food, clothing, and shelter. The problem here is whether the car in question was so needed by Larry, in view of his situation in life, his social status, and his financial position, that he could not be maintained properly or suitably without it. The burden of showing this was upon appellee. From the evidence presented, we do not think appellee met this burden. While every high school boy today wants a car of his own, and many of them own automobiles which under given circumstances may be considered as necessaries, we do not consider the car in this case so vital to Larry's existence that it could be classified as a necessary."

Estoppel to Assert Minority. As applied in most states, the above rules are hard enough on the adult seller, but even harsher results occur in those cases where the minor misrepresented his or her age and thus induced the other party to contract on the assumption that an adult was being dealt with.

"Estoppel," remember, is the legal rule that prevents a party from denying the legal effectiveness of what he or she stated earlier, after another party has changed his or her position in reliance on the earlier statement. Shouldn't that rule be applied where the other party has made a contract in reliance on the minor's statement that the minor was of legal age to contract? Shouldn't the minor, in other words, be estopped from asserting his or her minority in such a case? Some courts do apply estoppel against the minor here, but the majority do not. A special California statute provides a procedure for court approval of employment contracts for minor athletes and artists; the minor-employee is bound to the contract once the court approves it.

Tort Liability for Misrepresentation of Age. Minors are, as a general rule, liable for their own torts; intentional misrepresentation is a tort—fraud. Should not the other party, having been damaged by reasonable reliance on the minor's misrepresentation of age, be able to sue the minor on a tort theory of liability even though the contract has been disaffirmed? Once again, the courts are split on this point. A slight majority still follows the older view that the minor cannot be sued in tort, where to do so would amount to holding the minor liable on his or her contract. The policy protecting the minor against improvident contracts is more important to most courts than the policy of hold-ing the minor liable for his or her torts.

It probably should also be noted at this point that a minor's parents are not generally liable for the minor's torts or the minor's contracts, although they are legally obligated to support the minor with the necessities of life.

PERSONS WHO ARE INSANE, INTOXICATED, OR DRUGGED

Contracts made by persons who lack contractual capacity because their abil-ity to make decisions has been impaired by mental disease or defect, or by alcohol or drugs, are treated in much the same way as contracts made by mi-nors. As a general rule, where a person's mental faculties are so impaired that the person does not understand the nature and consequences of the transac-tion, the resulting contract is voidable at that person's option when the person recovers, or at the option of his or her subsequently appointed guardian. If any such person has previously been taken before a (probate) court, adjudged in-competent to manage his or her own affairs, and had a guardian appointed, then later contracts made by that person are not just voidable but totally void. The person need take no action to disaffirm the contracts; they simply will not be recognized by the courts.

Such persons are generally liable in quasi contract for the fair market value of necessaries furnished to them during their period of disability (assuming that these needs are not already being met by a guardian), under basically the same rules as those that apply to minors. Much more strictly than with the minor(the courts require the mentally disabled person to make full restitution in money or the equivalent if he or she wishes to disaffirm contracts entered into in good faith by the other party.)

ALIENS

Aliens in the United States are not generally subject to any contractual disa-bilities unless they are in the country illegally or their country is at war with ours. In either case they will usually not be able to use our courts to enforce contracts. Aside from these two exceptional cases, there have been efforts by some of the states (and even the national government) to reserve to citizens certain rights and privileges—real estate ownership, practice of such profes-sions as law and medicine, government employment.

Aliens do not have to be given the "privileges and immunities of citizenship" under the 14th Amendment, since they are obviously not citizens. But they are "persons," and thus they are protected by the due process of law clauses of the 5th and 14th amendments and by the equal protection clause of the 14th Amendment. The courts' problem, when such "citizens-only" laws are chal-lenged, is to try to decide which rights and privileges fall into which category. Voting in political elections and holding political office are obviously rights which do not have to be extended to aliens. The present tendency of the courts is to invalidate all other restrictions on aliens. (See the "government employ-ment" cases noted in Chapter 51.)

Takahashi v. Fish and Game Commission
334 U.S. 410 (1948)

FACTS Takahashi, born in Japan, came to this country and became a resident of California in 1907. U.S. laws then in force, based on distinctions of "color and race," permitted Japanese and certain other nonwhite racial groups to enter and reside in the country but made them ineligible for U.S. citizenship. In 1943, during the period of war and Japanese evacuation, an amendment to the California Fish and Game Code was adopted prohibiting issuance of a license to any "alien Japanese." In 1945 the state code was again amended by striking the 1943 provision for fear that it might be declared unconstitutional because directed only "against alien Japanese." The new amendment banned the issuance of licenses to any "person ineligible to citizenship," which classification included Japanese. Because of this state provision barring the issuance of commercial fishing licenses to persons ineligible for citizenship under federal law, Takahashi, who met all other state requirements, was denied a license by the California Fish and Game Commission upon his return to California in 1945.

ISSUE Can a lawfully resident alien be denied a commercial fishing license by the state?

DECISION No. Judgment reversed.

REASONS "[F]or purposes of our decision we may assume that the code provision was passed to conserve fish in the California coastal waters, or to protect California citizens engaged in commercial fishing from competition by Japanese aliens, or for both reasons.

"It does not follow, as California seems to argue, that because the United States regulates immigration and naturalization in part on the basis of race and color classifications, a state can adopt one or more of the same classifications to prevent lawfully admitted aliens within its borders from earning a living in the same way other state inhabitants earn their living. The Federal Government has broad constitutional powers in determining what aliens shall be admitted to the United States, the period they may remain, regulation of their conduct before naturalization. Under the Constitution the states are granted no such powers; they can neither add to nor take from the conditions lawfully imposed by Congress upon admission, naturalization, and residence of aliens in the United States or the several states. . . . Moreover, Congress, in the enactment of a comprehensive legislative plan for the nation-wide control and regulation of immigration and naturalization has broadly provided:

> All persons within the jurisdiction of the United States shall have the same right in every State and Territory to make and enforce contracts, to sue, be parties, give evidence, and to the full and equal benefit of all laws and proceedings for the security of persons and property as is enjoyed by white citizens, and shall be subject to like punishment, pains, penalties, taxes, licenses, and exactions of every kind, and to no other.

"The protection of this section has been held to extend to aliens as well as to citizens. Consequently the section and the 14th Amendment on which it rests in part protect 'all persons' against state legislation bearing unequally upon them either because of alienage or color. The 14th Amendment and the laws adopted under its authority thus embody a general policy that all persons lawfully in this country shall

abide 'in any state' on an equality of legal privileges with all citizens under nondiscriminatory laws.''

(The Court also rejected California's claim that its "ownership" of the fish within
the three-mile limit gave it special regulatory powers.)

AMERICAN INDIANS

It sounds very strange to stay it, some 200 years after the birth of the United
States, but it is nonetheless true: The original inhabitants of this country, the
American Indians, may still be subject to different legal rules because of their
"national origin." This special legal status is not necessarily all bad; it may
involve special privileges and immunities as well as disabilities. As noted in
Chapter 1, Albert B. Le Blanc, a full-blooded Chippewa Indian, did not have to
get a commercial fishing license from the Michigan Department of Natural
Resources since an 1836 treaty with the U.S. government reserved such fishing
rights to the Chippewa nation. Likewise, a Navajo woman, Rosalind Mc-
Clanahan, could not be required to pay Arizona state income tax on income she
earned on the Navajo reservation. Inheritance of property, particularly for Indians living on reservations, may still be governed by tribal law rather than the
general inheritance law of the particular state. Reservation businesses and the
Bureau of Indian Affairs may engage in preferential hiring of Indians without
violating the 1964 Civil Rights Act.

While the foregoing examples would probably be thought of as advantages
enjoyed by Indians because of their special status, members of particular Indian tribes may still be subject to some residual contractual disabilities under
old U.S. treaties and statutes. The following case illustration involves the statutes relating to the Osage Indians.

Osage County Motor Co. v. United States
33 F.2d 21 (U.S. Tenth Circuit, 1929)

FACTS   On February 4, 1926, the day following his becoming of age, Roosevelt Pappin, an
Osage Indian of 9/64 Indian blood and fully enrolled as such, executed five promissory notes aggregating $5,649.70, payable to the Osage County Motor Company,
defendant below, appellant here, and secured them by mortgages on his unrestricted
allotted lands. No statutory certificate of competency had ever been issued to
Pappin, and these contracts for debt, evidenced by the notes, were never approved
by the secretary of the interior.

The government brought this suit on behalf of Pappin to have the notes and
mortgages canceled and set aside, alleging that they were void under that part of
Section 6 of the Act of Congress, February 27, 1925, which states:

No contract for debt hereafter made with a member of the Osage Tribe of Indians
not having a certificate of competency, shall have any validity, unless approved
by the Secretary of the Interior.

Judgment was entered for the government, holding the notes null and void and decreeing the cancellation of the mortgages. The defendant appealed.

ISSUES   Does the statute apply to a person "of less than one-half degree Indian blood, whose allotted lands are alienable"? If it does apply, is the statute constitutional?

DECISION   Yes. Yes. Judgment affirmed.

REASONS   "The Act of February 27, 1925, when compared with the previous acts, discloses no revolutionary change in the Indian policy of the federal government. All the statutes that we are discussing are by their very terms amendatory of their predecessors, starting with the Act of June 28, 1906, and, though they may differ in detail, they all disclose the intent of Congress to exercise its unquestioned plenary power over the Indians. They all contain references to certificates of competency, and make restrictions and classifications depending on that, as well as other factors. . . . [W]hether the Act of 1921 repealed as to members of the Osage Tribe of less than one-half blood that part of the act authorizing the issuance of certificates of competency we do not have to decide, for, admitting that the necessity thereof no longer exists as to this class, it does not follow that it was the intent of Congress to make such Indians competent for all purposes, or to free them entirely from government control as to their persons or property.

"The contract in question could, under the statute, have been presented to the Secretary of the Interior for his approval, irrespective of whether Pappin held a certificate of competency or not.

"Second, appellant contends that section 6 of the 1925 act is unconstitutional under the Fifth Amendment to the Federal Constitution, as interfering with the right to contract; the Indian, Pappin, being a citizen of the United States. We cannot take this proposition seriously. The right to contract about one's affairs is a part of the liberty of the individual protected by the Fifth Amendment, but, as said in *Adkins* v. *Children's Hospital:* 'There is, of course, no such thing as absolute freedom of contract. It is subject to a great variety of restraints.'"

CONVICTS

Upon conviction for certain crimes, a person may be sentenced to confinement in a U.S. or state prison. Such a sentence does not, however, mean that the person loses his or her general capacity to contract and to own property. Likewise, even in prison the person is still protected by the U.S. and state constitutions. Even in prison the person has the capacity to appoint agents and attorneys and through them to make contracts and manage his or her property and affairs; such contracts made on the prisoner's behalf are, generally, fully enforceable by and against the prisoner.

Conviction of crimes involving force or fraud may, however, carry certain other disabilities. A person who has been released after having served the required sentence may be prevented from holding political (or labor union) office for some period of time. The person may also be prevented from practicing some of the licensed professions, such as law or medicine (e.g., Spiro Agnew was disbarred as a lawyer after pleading "no contest" to tax evasion charges).

MARRIED WOMEN

At common law, husband and wife are regarded legally as "one person." As applied in contract and tort situations, this doctrine of "coverture" meant that the wife lacked the capacity to manage even her separately owned property or separate income and that no tort liability could exist between the spouses; the contracts which a married woman attempted to make were totally void. The wife could, however, obligate her *husband* in quasi contract for necessaries furnished to her for herself, their children, or their home.

In nearly all states these rules have been changed by statute or constitution, so that a married woman enjoys the same legal rights and powers as her husband. She can own, manage, and dispose of her own property and has joint control of the jointly owned property. She, not he, is legally entitled to receive her earnings from her job. State courts have also been permitting the spouses to sue each other in tort, at least in some cases. Also, under modern interpretations, a wife would be similarly obligated in quasi contract for necessaries furnished to her husband where she had income or property and he did not.

Minor residues of the common-law rules remain in a few states, where a married woman may not be able to convey real estate, to mortgage jointly owned property, or act as a guarantor of someone else's debt without the husband's consent. Until 1963, Texas continued to apply the basic rules of coverture, so that a married woman lacked the capacity to contract unless she went through a special court procedure which removed her disability. Now only Michigan continues to apply the coverture rules, and it does so despite Article 10, Section 1 of its 1963 constitution, which says: "The disabilities of coverture as to property are abolished."

The following Michigan case shows the court's reluctance to abandon the "protections" given to married women by this doctrine.

City Finance Company v. *Kloostra*
209 N.W.2d 498 (Michigan, 1973)

FACTS   Pat Kloostra and her husband, Harold, cosigned a promissory note for $472.24 and used the money to buy a used car. At that time Pat had no separately owned property or separate income. A little over a year later, Pat and Harold were divorced and Harold "departed for parts unknown" with the car. The balance still due on the loan was $400.12. The trial judge held that the 1963 constitution superseded the married women's statutes and entered summary judgment for the plaintiff. The circuit court affirmed, and the court of appeals originally denied leave to appeal, but the state supreme court reversed and remanded to the court of appeals for consideration on the merits of the appeal.

ISSUE   Has the Michigan law on coverture been completely abolished by the 1963 constitution?

DECISION   No. Judgment for defendant as to her separately owned property.

REASONS   "Const. 1963, art. 10, § 1 provides:

> *The disabilities of coverture as to property are abolished.* The real and personal estate of every woman acquired before marriage and all real and personal property to which she may afterwards become entitled shall be and remain the estate and property of such woman, and shall not be liable for the debts, obligations or engagements of her husband, and may be dealt with and disposed of by her as if she were unmarried. Dower may be relinquished or conveyed as provided by law. (Emphasis added.)

"Plaintiff claims that the limited liability sought by defendant and obviously authorized by 1917 P.A. 158 is one of those 'disabilities of coverture as to property' abolished by our 1963 constitution. Defendant responds that the framers of the new constitution had no intention of altering the married women's property act; that the limited liability she seeks is not a disability but a protection; and that, if a disability of coverture is involved, it is not a disability 'as to property.'

"Although the married women's property act has gone far toward making a wife equal of her husband, at least in the eyes of the law, it does not abolish all the common-law distinctions between husband and wife. One of the remaining distinctions is at issue herein: If a married man co-signs a promissory note with his wife, he is jointly and severally liable thereon. That means that any judgment entered on the note may be satisfied out of any property held jointly with his wife and also out of any property held by him separately, even though consideration for the note inured solely to the joint estate. On the other hand, if a married woman co-signs a promissory note with her husband, she is jointly liable thereon. That means that judgment entered on the note may be satisfied only out of property held jointly with her husband. The wife's separate estate is not liable, unless consideration for the note passed directly to her separate estate."

The Equal Rights Amendment to the U.S. Constitution, when and if ratified, will almost certainly overturn any state laws which provide for different legal results based solely on sex.

CORPORATIONS

Private Corporations. Since corporations are "artificial" persons, existing only in the eyes of the law, they can have and exercise only those powers which the law gives them. In this sense, they have limited legal capacity; they can make contracts only in those areas of activity in which they have been authorized to be engaged. Modern corporation statutes are generally very liberal in granting corporate powers, and even if a corporation makes a contract which is outside its charter powers, most courts today do not permit either of the parties to the contract to raise that fact as a defense when sued on the contract. These matters are discussed more fully in Chapter 43.

Public (Municipal) Corporations. Like both profit and nonprofit private corporations, public corporations are creatures of limited legal authority, possessing only those powers given to them by constitutional or statutory provisions. The courts will normally not permit any enforcement of contracts made by a public corporation in excess of its powers, on the theory that to do so would injure the public through the illegal expenditure of public funds. Contracting procedures for public bodies are usually subject to very specific regulations, which must be complied with if one hopes to have an enforceable contract with them.

In summary, limitations on contractual capacity exist with respect to a very large number of persons. Before entering into any important contract, it is a good idea to check the laws of the particular state so as to make sure that one is dealing with a competent party.

CASES FOR DISCUSSION

KIEFER v. FRED HOWE MOTORS, INC.
158 N.W.2d 288 (Wisconsin, 1968)

On August 9, 1965, the plaintiff, Steven Kiefer, entered into a contract with the defendant, Fred Howe Motors, Inc. (the dealer), for the purchase of a 1960 Willys station wagon. Kiefer paid the contract price of $412 and took possession of the car. At the time of the sale Kiefer was 20 years old, married, and the father of one child.

Kiefer had difficulty with the car, which he claimed was caused by a cracked block. Kiefer contacted the dealer and asked it to take the car back. Several other attempts to secure some adjustment with the dealer failed, and Kiefer contacted Paul C. Konnor, an attorney. Konnor wrote a letter to the dealer, advising it that Kiefer was under 21 at the time of the sale. The letter declared the contract void, tendered return of the automobile, and demanded repayment of the purchase price. There was no response, so this action was commenced to recover the $412 purchase price. After a trial to the court, a judgment for the plaintiff was entered and the defendant appealed.)

Wilkie, Justice

Three issues are presented on this appeal. They are:

1. Should an emancipated minor over the age of 18 be legally responsible for his contracts?
2. Was the contract effectively disaffirmed?
3. Is the plaintiff liable in tort for misrepresentation?

Legal Responsibility of Emancipated Minor

The law governing agreements made during infancy reaches back over many centuries. The general rule is that ". . . the contract of a minor, other than for necessaries, is either void or voidable at his option." The only other exceptions to the rule permitting disaffirmance are statutory or involve contracts which deal with duties imposed by law such as a contract of marriage or an agreement to support an illegitimate child. The general rule is not affected by the minor's status as emancipated or unemancipated.

Appellant does not advance any argument that would put this case within one of the exceptions to the general rule, but rather urges that this court, as a matter of public policy, adopt a rule that an emancipated minor over 18 years of age be made legally responsible for his contracts.

The underpinnings of the general rule allowing the minor to disaffirm his contracts were undoubtedly the protection of the minor. It was

191

thought that the minor was immature in both mind and experience and that, therefore, he should be protected from his own bad judgments as well as from adults who would take advantage of him. The doctrine of the voidability of minors' contracts often seems commendable and just. If the beans that the young naive Jack purchased from the crafty old man in the fairy tale "Jack and the Bean Stalk" had been worthless rather than magical, it would have been only fair to allow Jack to disaffirm the bargain and reclaim his cow. However, in today's modern and sophisticated society the "infancy doctrine" seems to lose some of its gloss.

* * * * *

No one really questions that a line as to age must be drawn somewhere below which a legally defined minor must be able to disaffirm his contracts for nonnecessities. The law over the centuries has considered this age to be 21. Legislatures in other states have lowered the age. We suggest that the appellant might better seek the change it proposes in the legislative halls rather than this court.

Undoubtedly, the infancy doctrine is an obstacle when a major purchase is involved. However, we believe that the reasons for allowing that obstacle to remain viable at this point outweigh those for casting it aside. Minors require some protection from the pitfalls of the market place. Reasonable minds will always differ on the extent of the protection that should be afforded. For this court to adopt a rule that the appellant suggests and remove the contractual disabilities from a minor simply because he becomes emancipated, which in most cases would be the result of marriage, would be to suggest that the married minor is somehow vested with more wisdom and maturity than his single counterpart. However, logic would not seem to dictate this result, especially when today a youthful marriage is oftentimes indicative of a lack of wisdom and maturity.

Disaffirmance

Williston, while discussing how a minor may disaffirm a contract, states:

"Any act which clearly shows an intent to disaffirm a contract or sale is sufficient for the purpose. Thus a notice by the infant of his purpose to disaffirm . . . a tender or even an offer to return the consideration or its proceeds to the vendor, . . . is sufficient."

The testimony of Steven Kiefer and the letter from his attorney to the dealer clearly establish that there was an effective disaffirmance of the contract.

Misrepresentation

Appellant's last argument is that the respondent should be held liable in tort for damages because he misrepresented his age. Appellant would use these damages as a setoff against the contract price sought to be reclaimed by respondent.

The 19th-century view was that a minor's lying about his age was inconsequential because a fraudulent representation of capacity was not the equivalent of actual capacity. This rule has been altered by time. There appear to be two possible methods that now can be employed to bind the defrauding minor: He may be estopped from denying his alleged majority, in which case the contract will be enforced or contract damages will be allowed; or he may be allowed to disaffirm his contract but be liable in tort for damages. Wisconsin follows the latter approach. . . .

Having established that there is a remedy against the defrauding minor, the question becomes whether the requisites for a tort action in misrepresentation are present in this case.

The trial produced conflicting testimony regarding whether Steven Kiefer had been asked his age or had replied that he was "21." Steven and his wife, Jacqueline, said "No," and Frank McHalsky, appellant's salesman, said "Yes." Confronted with this conflict, the question of credibility was for the trial court to decide, which it did by holding that Steven did not orally represent that he was "21." This finding is not contrary to the great weight and clear preponderance of the evidence and must be affirmed.

Even accepting the trial court's conclusion that Steven Kiefer had not orally represented his age to be over 21, the appellant argues that there was still a misrepresentation. The "motor vehicle purchase contract" signed by Steven Kiefer contained the following language just above the purchaser's signature:

"I represent that I am 21 years of age or over and recognize that the dealer sells the above vehicle upon this representation."

Whether the inclusion of this sentence constitutes a misrepresentation depends on whether elements of the tort have been satisfied. They were not.

No evidence was adduced to show that the plaintiff had an intent to defraud the dealer. To the contrary, it is at least arguable that the majority of minors are, as the plaintiff here might well have been, unaware of the legal consequences of their acts.

. . . We fail to see how the dealer could be justified in the mere reliance on the fact that the plaintiff signed a contract containing a sentence that said he was 21 or over. The trial court observed that the plaintiff was sufficiently immature looking to arouse suspicion. The appellant never took any affirmative steps to determine whether the plaintiff was in fact over 21. It never asked to see a draft card, identification card, or the most logical indicium of age under the circumstances, a driver's license. Therefore, because there was no intent to deceive, and no justifiable reliance, the appellant's action for misrepresentation must fail.

Judgment affirmed.

ROBERTSON v. KING

280 S.W.2d 402 (Arkansas, 1955)

Robinson, Justice

The principal issue here is whether appellant, a minor, may rescind a contract to purchase a pick-up truck. On the 20th day of March, 1954, L. D. Robertson, a minor, entered into a conditional sales agreement whereby he purchased from Turner King and J. W. Julian, doing business as the Julian Pontiac Company, a pick-up truck for the agreed price of $1,743.85. On the day of the purchase, Robertson was 17 years of age, and did not have his 18th birthday until April 8th. Robertson traded in a passenger car for which he was given a credit of $723.85 on the purchase price, leaving a balance of $1,020 paya-

ble in 23 monthly installments of $52.66 plus one payment of $52.83. He paid the April installment of $52.66.

It appears that Robertson had considerable trouble with the wiring on the truck. He returned it to the automobile dealers for repairs, but the defective condition was not remedied. On May 2nd, the truck caught fire and was practically destroyed. He notified the automobile concern, and they stated that they would send the insurance man to see him. It appears that the insurance representative, upon finding out that Robertson was only 17 years of age, refused to deal with him.

On June 7th, appellees filed suit to replevy the damaged truck from Robertson. By his father and next friend, Robertson filed a cross-complaint in which he alleged that he is a minor and asked that the contract of purchase be rescinded and sought to recover that part of the purchase price he had paid, which he alleges is the amount of $723.85, allowed by the dealers on the car traded in, plus the one monthly payment of $52.66, totalling $776.51. A jury was waived, and the cause was submitted to the court. There was a judgment for King and Julian on the complaint and the cross-complaint. On appeal, Robertson contends that he was 17 years of age at the time of the alleged purchase and that he has a right under the law to rescind the contract and to recover the portion of the purchase price he has paid.

Appellees contend that the judgment should be sustained because Robertson did not return the damaged truck to the automobile dealers. However, the judgment of the court states: "The court further finds the proof to be that the plaintiff has possession of the said GMC pick-up truck." Hence, there is no merit to this contention. Appellees also contend that Act 337 of 1953 applies in that a minor cannot rescind a contract of purchase without reimbursing the seller for any loss that he may have sustained by reason of such recission. This statute deals with situations where a minor is 18 years of age at the time of making a purchase. The statute is not applicable here because according to the undisputed evidence Robertson was only 17 years of age at the time of entering into the purchase agreement.

Appellees further contend that the minor is

bound by the contract because the automobile was a necessary. The record does not contain any substantial evidence to support this contention. The only evidence on this issue is that the boy quit school in 1951 and has been earning his own living since that time, and that he has been working for a construction company and traveling around the country to different jobs with his father in his father's truck. The boy lives at home with his parents, and there is no showing whatever that he needed the truck in connection with any work he was doing. One of the witnesses for the appellees testified that the boy stated he wanted to use the truck in a farming operation. The record contains no evidence that he was engaged in farming at any time. . . . In a suit by a minor to rescind a contract the burden is on the defendant to show that the article was a necessary. . . .

It is our conclusion that the evidence does not sustain a finding that the truck was a necessary to Robertson. . . . The law is settled in this State that a minor may rescind a contract to purchase where the property involved is not a necessary. . . .

The automobile dealers have disposed of the car they received in the trade, and cannot restore it to the minor. In a situation of this kind, the weight of authority is that the actual value of the property given as part of the purchase price by the minor is the correct measure of damages. Neither side is bound by the agreement reached as to the value of the car at the time the trade was made. This is true because the contract has been rescinded and there is no contract fixing the value. It is said in 43 C.J.S., Infants, #47, p. 117: "While it is generally held that, where property traded in by the infant as part of the price is beyond reach of the seller, the infant is entitled to the reasonable value of the property at the time of the purchase, rather than the value fixed in the purchase agreement, it has also been held that he is entitled to receive the value fixed in the agreement."

* * * * *

In the case at bar, although the minor was allowed over $700 on his car in trade, there is evidence to the effect that it was actually worth about $350. Although there is conflict among the authorities as pointed out above, we believe the better rule holds that the value of an article given in trade by a minor as a part of the purchase price is the reasonable market value of the article at the time of the purchase, and that neither party is bound by the value fixed in the purchase agreement.

Young Robertson is a minor; the truck was not a necessary; and Act 337 of 1953 is not applicable. Hence, the court erred in finding for the automobile dealers, and the cause is therefore reversed and remanded for a new trial.

Holt, Justice, dissents.

BROWN v. WOOD
291 N.W. 255 (Michigan, 1940)

North, J.

These four cases, consolidated and tried as one, were brought to recover damages resulting from an automobile collision. The plaintiffs Susanne Brown and Wallace Blodgett are minors who were riding in defendant's automobile at the time of the accident. These minors suffered personal injuries, and suit in behalf of each was brought by a guardian. Erwin Brown is the father of Susanne Brown, and Murray Blodgett is the father of Wallace Blodgett. Each of these parents brought suit for loss of services and earnings of the minor child and for money expended for necessary hospital, nurses' and physicians' care. The defendants Archie Wood and Harold Elliott were the drivers of the two automobiles involved in this collision accident. In the circuit court judgment in each case was entered in favor of defendant Elliott and no appeal has been taken. It is stipulated that negligence on the part of the defendant Archie Wood was the proximate cause of the accident. On trial without a jury the circuit judge in each case rendered a judgment against this defendant. He has appealed.

Like the two personally injured plaintiffs, defendant Archie Wood was a minor. He lived some 8 or 10 miles from Bay City where he was attend-

194

ing high school in October, 1937. Each school day he drove an automobile which he owned to Bay City and was accompanied to and from Bay City by the two minor plaintiffs and other high school students. In the declaration in each of these cases it is alleged that the injured minor was a passenger for hire at the time the collision occurred. All of the parties to the alleged passenger-for-hire contracts were minors. By an agreement between themselves each of these minor plaintiffs was paying defendant Wood 15 cents a day or 75 cents per week for riding with him to and from the Bay City Central High School.

The controlling question is whether under the circumstances of this case the defendant Archie Wood, being a minor and the accident having occurred while the minor plaintiffs were passengers in his automobile being carried for a consideration, can be held liable in this tort action.

It is elementary that an infant's contract, with certain exceptions not here involved, is voidable. And as a general rule an infant is liable for his torts provided he possessed the capacity, mental or physical or both, requisite to the commission of the tort with which he is charged. . . . But it is also a general rule that if the tort with which an infant is charged is so connected with his contract that commission of the tort constitutes a breach of the contract, or if the tort is predicated on a transaction with the infant based upon contract, so that holding the infant liable in tort would in effect enforce a liability arising out of his contract, then, since the infant cannot be held *ex contractu*, he cannot be held liable for his tort. The injured party is not permitted to enforce against the infant indirectly by an action in tort a liability which he could not enforce directly against the infant by an action based upon contract. In the instant case a contract to which all parties were minors is disclosed. Were it not for the fact that the contract was voidable because of defendant's minority, there would have been imposed upon him the obligation to carry the minor plaintiffs safely. This, by his negligence which resulted in the automobile collision, the defendant failed to do. Neither by their pleadings nor the testimony have plaintiffs attempted to establish a right of recovery under the Michigan guest passenger

act. . . . Nor could there be recovery under the guest act because, so far as disclosed by the record, the defendant was guilty of ordinary negligence only. The sole ground upon which plaintiffs assert a right of recovery is the relation or "status" which existed between the minor plaintiffs and the minor defendant. . . .

* * * * *

From our review of this record we are unable to conceive how the tort aspect of these actions can be separated from the contractual relation which these minor plaintiffs entered into with the minor defendant.

* * * * *

"Torts based on or connected with contracts. — The law is solicitous in holding the infant liable for his torts, not to impair the immunity given him against liability on his contracts. The tort must be a '*tort simpliciter*,' and not one the essence of which is a breach of contract, and in a case of doubt the tendency has been to favor the infant, and to hold it more important to preserve his immunity from contract liability than to enforce his liability for torts. It has been said that the only satisfactory test is, can the infant be held liable without directly or indirectly enforcing his promise." . . .

* * * * *

While this court has not heretofore had occasion to pass upon a case wherein the factual aspect duplicated that of the instant case, nonetheless in its former decisions reference has been made to the phase of the law just above noted and its soundness has, at least by implication, been approved. . . .

* * * * *

In both counts of their declaration these plaintiffs have alleged that the minor plaintiff "was a passenger for hire in the said motor vehicle owned and operated by the said Archie Wood." Not only because of its being so alleged in the respective declarations but also under the stipulated facts in this case, it must be held that these minor plaintiffs at the time of the accident were passengers for hire, notwithstanding the agreement for such transportation was voidable on the part of the minor plaintiffs because of their minority.

For the reasons hereinbefore indicated, the judgments entered in the circuit court are reversed, without new trials. Appellant will have costs of this appeal.

PROBLEMS FOR DISCUSSION

1. In December 1974 George Jenks borrowed $50,000 from the Inland Michigan Bank. The loan was guaranteed by his wife, Irene. In 1975 Jenks defaulted on the loan and the bank instituted suit to recover its money, charging at the same time that it had been defrauded by George, who had falsely claimed ownership of property in Inland in fact owned by his wife. Who is liable for the loan, and whose property can be seized in satisfaction of it?

2. Cecil, age 15, was hired by Temp-Help, Inc., a firm which provided temporary employees as they were needed by other companies or individuals. On his application for employment, Cecil had listed his age as 18. Temp-Help sent Cecil out to work for Young Industries, where he was put to work on a power press. While running the press, Cecil had a serious accident which resulted in the amputation of part of his right hand. The state's Workers' Compensation Act provides that it is the exclusive remedy for any person in the service of another under a "contract for hire." Cecil wants to sue Temp-Help and Young in a tort action. Is he bound by the Workers' Compensation Act?

3. Cora, age 17, applied for insurance for her new motorcycle. As required by state statute, Neutral Insurance Company offered her a policy which gave her the option of having uninsured motorist coverage. Under the statute the insured had to be given this choice but did not have to purchase the uninsured motorist coverage. Cora accepted the rest of the policy but declined the uninsured motorist coverage.

   This policy was in force when Cora had a collision with an automobile while riding her motorcycle. The driver of the car was uninsured, and his negligence caused the accident. Cora now wishes to disaffirm her earlier rejection of the uninsured motorist coverage and to collect her damages from her insurance company, Neutral. What result, and why?

4. Freda, age 17, misrepresented her age (as 19) on a student loan application. Bigger Bank loaned her $1,000. When Freda defaulted on her loan payments, Bigger set off the $300 balance she had in her checking account against the amount she still owed them. Freda sues to force the bank to turn over the $300. Bigger Bank counterclaims for the remaining balance still due on the loan, after deducting the $300. What result, and why?

5. Filbert, nearly 21 years old but still a minor in his state, went to work in a beauty parlor. Brunehilde, the owner of the beauty parlor, had him sign an employment contract in which he promised not to work for a competing firm within a 10-mile radius of her shop for two years after he left her employ. About six months later, Filbert quit Brunehilde's shop and opened his own about three doors down the street. Brunehilde sues for an injunction and damages. What result, and why?

6. Zachariah, in his will, created a "power of appointment" as to certain of his assets in favor of his nephew Zeb; that is, he gave Zeb the right to decide who the next owner of these assets would be. When Zachariah died and the will was probated, Zeb was still a minor. The executor of Zachariah's estate claims that the power of

appointment is thus ineffective and that these assets must be distributed as part of the residue of the estate. Zeb wants to exercise this power of appointment. What result, and why?

7. Yolanda, using money that she had saved from her newspaper route, bought an expensive stereo set when she was 15 years old. She paid cash for the set. After using it for about $2^1/_2$ years, Yolanda decided that she would rather have a sports car instead, so she asked the seller (Big Bennie) if she could have her money back. She offered to give the set back to Bennie. Bennie refused to take the set and give her her money back unless she agreed to compensate him for the depreciation on the set. Yolanda sues to recover the contract price of the stereo and set. What result, and why?

8. Standing Bull, a Navajo Indian residing on a reservation, went to a bank in Gallup, New Mexico, and borrowed $5,000. When he defaulted on the loan, the bank sued in the New Mexico state courts. Standing Bull claims that the state courts have no jurisdiction over him, since he is a reservation Indian. What result, and why?

9. Pierre, an alien who had not been lawfully admitted to the United States, rented a furnished apartment from Herman. Pierre was seriously injured when the gas stove in the apartment blew up. Pierre sued Herman, and also the manufacturer of the stove, for the damages caused by the defective goods. The defendants asked the court to dismiss the suit, since Pierre was not a lawful U.S. resident. What result, and why?

10. Goodie, the minor son of a rich architect, was an undergraduate at Stale University. Trash sold him about $2,000 worth of expensive clothing items. Goodie later refused to pay, and Trash sued for the contract price, alleging that these items were necessaries. Goodie's father, Lord Toshues, testified that Goodie was already being supplied with sufficient clothes for school. What result, and why?

8. Defenses—Lack of Capacity

9 | Defenses—Lack of Real Consent

A second group of defenses center on the idea that one of the parties did not really consent to the terms of the contract which the other wishes to enforce. While courts generally continue to require both parties to live up to the bargain they made, the problem in many of these cases is to discover exactly what they really did agree to. Included here are cases involving fraud, innocent misrepresentation, duress, undue influence, and mistake.

FRAUD

Many types of fraud may be crimes, so that criminal charges can be filed against the wrongdoer. False advertising and other deceptive practices may also result in administrative proceedings before the Federal Trade Commission and/or similar state bodies. We are concerned here, however, with the civil aspects of fraud, with its impact on the contract which resulted from the fraud.

Civil fraud is of two kinds: fraud in the inducement and fraud in the execution. Fraud in the execution describes a situation where one party is deceived as to the very nature of the transaction. The party does not know he or she is making a contract at all, or at least that he or she is making the one which the plaintiff now seeks to enforce. Elvis Presley, fighting his way toward the exit from a concert hall, in the midst of a screaming mass of fans, was signing autograph books as fast as he could. One clever person shoved a folded piece of paper at him, and Elvis signed, not knowing that the unseen part of the paper contained a contract to buy a new set of *Encyclopedia Junkana*. On these facts, there is fraud in the execution and the purported "contract" is totally void. Elvis was deceived as to the very nature of the "transaction" he was entering into, without having had a reasonable opportunity to discover the truth.

The far more common kind of civil fraud is fraud in the inducement, where the defrauded party does know that he or she is entering into a contract and does intend to enter the contract but has been deceived as to some aspect of the contract. Usually this type of fraud involves misrepresentation of what the defrauded party is to receive (e.g., a used car is falsely represented as being in "A-1 mechanical condition").

198

Although different courts may use slightly different formulations, the typical fraud case requires proof of five elements: (1) misrepresentation of a material fact, (2) made with knowledge, (3) made with intent to deceive, (4) reasonably relied on by the other party, and (5) with damage resulting to the other party. Because fraud is so easily alleged by anyone having second thoughts about a contract, courts typically require proof of fraud by "independent" evidence which is "clear and convincing."

Misrepresentation of Material Fact. A statement must contain a factual assertion in order to provide the basis for a fraud case. Statements of opinion are therefore not generally treated as statements of fact, so long as the statements do in fact represent the speaker's honestly held opinion. Sellers are also given some latitude in "puffing" their wares, so that such statements as "It's the best car for the money" or "It looks great on you" are not normally intended or understood as factual descriptions. Thus a statement by an individual selling his or her used car that he or she "thinks it's in good shape mechanically" would not be fraudulent unless the buyer could show that the seller knew that there were mechanical defects in the car when he or she made the statements. A car dealer making the same kind of statement, however, would be making a misrepresentation of fact, since "expert opinions" are generally treated as statements of fact.

Predictions of future events over which the speaker has no control are generally not regarded as statements of fact. Where the speaker is making promises as to the speaker's own future behavior, however, there is a misrepresentation of fact if it can be proved that the speaker had no such intention when he or she made the statements. If a buyer promises to use a piece of land for residential purposes only, there is fraud where the seller can show that the buyer had already signed construction and lease contracts for a gasoline station at the time the buyer made the "residential use" statement.

Although a party to an "arm's-length" transaction between equals generally has no affirmative duty to disclose facts which he or she knows, there are several situations where nondisclosure or silence can be interpreted as a fraudulent misrepresentation. The most obvious case requiring affirmative disclosure is one where the party knowing the actual facts has created a mistaken belief in the mind of the other person through actions (concealment) or prior communications (which were true when spoken but have become false). A second obvious case requiring full disclosure occurs where the transaction is not arm's-length but rather involves a fiduciary relationship, such as lawyer-client or guardian-ward. A lawyer who buys a piece of real estate from his or her client and has a resale deal with Disney World already lined up, would have a duty to tell the client about the resale deal, whereas a buyer in an ordinary transaction would not. A third group of cases is more difficult to define. Most courts today are increasingly willing to impose fraud remedies for nondisclosure where one party (usually the buyer) has had no reasonable opportunity to discover the truth and where the undisclosed fact is so significant that the contract might not have been made at all if the fact had been known. Examples are the house with a serious termite infestation and the used car with dangerously defective brakes. The following case is another example of this last rule in operation.

Janinda v. *Lanning*

390 P.2d 826 (Idaho, 1964)

FACTS   In December 1961 Harold M. Janinda was transferred by his employer from Denver, Colorado, to Mountain Home, Idaho. He considered settling in Mountain Home, and in looking for housing for his family and for income-producing property, he consulted a local real estate agency. A Mr. Swearingen of that agency showed the respondent several parcels of real estate, including Mrs. Lanning's rental and residence property consisting of duplex apartments, six trailer spaces, and a three-bedroom house. This property was located a short distance outside the city limits of Mountain Home, within the county, and obtained its water supply from two shallow wells on the property.

On January 24, 1962, Mrs. Lanning received information indicating that one of the wells was contaminated, but she did not disclose this fact to Mr. Swearingen while he asked about the water supply. About two weeks later, Janinda bought the property. Janinda now sues to rescind the contract.

ISSUE   Was Mrs. Lanning's nondisclosure a fraudulent misrepresentation?

DECISION   Yes. Judgment for plaintiff affirmed.

REASONS   The court felt that there were several aspects of the case that required Mrs. Lanning to make disclosure of the poisoned water, despite the fact that the parties were dealing at arm's length. "Particularly, the duty of disclosure is required to be observed 'in cases involving latent dangerous physical conditions of land' *Prosser on Torts,* § 87 at 535 (2nd ed. 1955). Appellant regarded her property as income producing property and was fully aware, as was her agent, that respondents intended buying it for the same purpose; and admitted on cross examination that if 'I had gone on owning the place and I had had contamination, . . . I probably would have put in a chlorine system.' Respondents relied upon appellant's representations and were under no duty to make an independent investigation of their own.

"The rule decisive of the issue is stated in *Restatement of Contracts,* sec. 472, Comment b (1932):

> . . . if a fact known by one party and not the other is so vital that if the mistake were mutual the contract would be voidable, and the party knowing the fact also knows that the other does not know it, non-disclosure is not privileged and is fraudulent."

Knowledge of Falsity. There is no fraud unless it can be shown that the speaker made a misrepresentation with knowledge that it was false. However, there are three ways to prove this "knowledge" element. The most obvious way is to show that the speaker actually knew when he or she made the statement that it was a lie. The speaker knew the car was not in "A-1 mechanical shape" because the garage mechanic had said the day before that he or she had better get rid of the car or be prepared to spend a lot of money, because it needed a lot of work. Even if the speaker didn't actually know from personal inspection or from the mechanic that the car was in bad shape, there was "knowledge" if the speaker had "reason to know" that he or she was not telling the truth about the car's condition. Presumably, every reasonable car driver knows that a car in A-1 mechanical shape does not burn a quart of oil every 100 miles or require repeated pumping of the brake pedal to get the car to stop. If the speaker knew of these operating characteristics, then the speaker certainly had reason to know that the car was not in A-1 shape. Finally, "knowledge" can be proved by proving *lack* of knowledge. Assume that a car dealership has just taken a used car as a trade-in; no complete mechanical inspection of the car has been made yet. Nevertheless, when a buyer comes to the used-car lot and inquires about the car, the buyer is told that it is in "A-1 shape" and buys it on that basis. If the car has serious defects, fraud has been committed in this case. The salesperson who made the "A-1" statement *knew* that he or she didn't know anything at all about the car's real mechanical condition; thus the salesperson was lying about the extent of information he or she had on the car, and the salesperson *knew* he or she was lying.

Intent to Deceive.   In most cases knowledge of the lie and intent to deceive go so closely hand in hand that some courts do not even consider them separately. But what about the person who says, "Yes, I knew I was lying. But I didn't intend that the other party should be hurt by it. I thought things would come out all right in the end." For want of a better label, we might refer to this as the "Nixon defense": "Yes,' I lied, and I knew I was lying, but I did it for your own good." The few cases that have considered this argument have rejected it, the requirement is not proof of intent to *injure* or do harm, only of intent to *deceive*. Deception for any motive, good or bad, is fraud (assuming that the other four elements are also proved).

Reasonable Reliance.   Even though the liar is the nastiest person imaginable, the liar has not committed fraud unless the other party can show that he or she reasonably relied on the misrepresentation. It is not enough to show that the person was in fact deceived; the person complaining must also convince the trier of fact that he or she was reasonable in relying on the misstatement. There is clearly no fraud if the other party knows the truth but goes ahead and makes the contract anyway. On the other hand, reliance is reasonable where an independent verification of the representation would require considerable time, money, and effort. Where the truth is readily ascertainable, it is probably not reasonable to rely on the misstatement. If the used-car salesman tells you the car has only 25,000 miles and the odometer in the car shows the mileage is 48,000, most juries would probably decide that a reasonable person would have checked the odometer before relying on the salesperson's statement. Each case ultimately rests on its own facts.

Capitol Dodge, Inc. v. Haley
288 N.E.2d 766 (Indiana, 1972)

FACTS The record discloses that Thomas Haley, together with his parents, Loren M. Haley and Edna Haley, executed a retail installment contract on April 10, 1970, for the purchase by the son of an automobile from Capitol Dodge.

Thomas Haley testified that he had told Allen, the salesman, before the contract was signed that he had to make sure that he could have "full coverage" and "that [he] wouldn't have anything to do with the car unless it had full coverage insurance." According to Loren Haley, Allen assured him that he had nothing to worry about and that Thomas would be fully covered. Mr. Haley then signed the contract. He indicated, however, that he had not read the contract prior to signing it.

No liability coverage was afforded by the contract. The face of the contract, otherwise printed in blue ink, contained a provision in red letters near the point at which the Haleys signed as follows:

> The Insurance Contracted for in Connection with This Retail Installment Sale Does Not Provide for Liability Insurance for Bodily Injury and Property Damage.

Nothing of record, however, indicates that Haley's attention was specifically called to the exclusionary language.

The line immediately above the space provided in the contract for the purchaser's signature read as follows:

> NOTICE TO THE BUYER: Do not sign this contract before you read it or if it contains any blank spaces. You are entitled to an exact copy of the contract you sign.

Thomas Haley also stated that he eventually demanded that both Capitol Dodge and Chrysler Credit that the contract be rescinded, that his down payment of $395 be returned to him within 14 days, and that the sum of $495.70 representing a trade-in by Haley be returned to him within the same period. Upon refusal of his demand and having discontinued payments, he returned the car to Capitol Dodge. Chrysler Credit, in turn, repossessed the car and sued Haley for the deficiency. A jury returned a verdict in favor of Haley for $874.90 as compensatory damages and $2,000 punitive damages. Chrysler in its suit received a verdict against Haley and his parents for $1,226.44, representing the deficiency balance upon the auto. Judgments were entered upon the verdicts.

ISSUES Did the evidence support Haley's fraud case? Is this a proper case for punitive damages?

DECISION Yes. Yes. Judgment affirmed.

REASONS The court first decided that punitive damages were particularly appropriate in cases of "consumer fraud."

"There can be no dispute that the installment contract in question did not provide for liability insurance coverage. The 'full coverage' representation by Capitol's salesman, Mr. Allen, was therefore patently false.

"The statements heretofore alluded to as made by Capitol's salesman could have reasonably been found by the jury to have been made recklessly and without regard to their truth or falsity. Such unconcern for the truth may serve as an imputation of scienter.

> "Capitol's most plausible argument concerns the matter of reliance by Haley upon the representations made by Allen, and we are inclined to agree that it perhaps harbors a measure of naiveté to conclude, without reservation or hesitance, that a literate adult who insists upon the inclusion of a particular subject in a purchase contract would bind himself to that contract without availing himself of the opportunity to read the document in order to satisfy himself that the desired subject was within the contract terms. Nevertheless, the question whether Thomas Haley reasonably relied upon Allen's assurances, which were in conflict with the limited insurance coverage specifically recited in the contract, was for the jury's determination. We are not at liberty to substitute our assessment of the evidence. It is but to repeat a truism that the question of reliance is one of fact to be determined by the jury, and that upon appeal from a jury verdict this court will not weigh the evidence. . . .
>
> "With respect, therefore, to the appeal by Capitol Dodge against the verdict and judgment awarded Thomas Haley, we affirm. . . .
>
> "The judgment below in favor of Chrysler Credit Corporation against the Haleys is also affirmed."

Damage to the Defrauded Party. As a final essential part of his or her case, the defrauded party must prove that he or she has sustained damage as a result of the misrepresentation. If a seller of land fraudulently represents that there is gold on it, and there is no gold but there is oil, so that the land is actually worth more than it would have been, the buyer probably does not have a case of fraud. (The buyer probably will not want to rescind anyway.) Even in the gold/oil case, however, the buyer has wound up with a contract different from the one the buyer intended to have, so in that sense the buyer may have suffered an "injury" which would permit the buyer to rescind if the buyer wanted to. Generally, to justify rescission of the entire contract, the misrepresented fact must relate to an essential part of the bargain. If the defrauded party wishes to keep the contract in force and collect "make-it-right" or difference-in-value damages, the party must prove the amount of the dollar loss which the party has sustained because of the fraud. Since fraud is an intentional tort, punitive damages (over and above the actual loss) may also be collected in many of these cases.

INNOCENT MISREPRESENTATION

Even though the speaker honestly and reasonably believed that he or she was telling the truth and had no intent to mislead anyone, if the speaker in fact misrepresented the truth, the other party is just as badly off as he or she would have been if there had been fraud. (The net effect is the same, whether the misrepresentation was made fraudulently or "innocently.") For this reason, where the fact innocently misstated has been proved to be a very important part of the contract, most courts will permit rescission by the other party. In most states, if the misrepresented fact is not material enough to justify rescission, the contract stands as is; no damages remedy is given. In a few states damages can be recovered even for an innocent misrepresentation, as an alternative remedy to rescission. (Since there has been no intentional tort, punitive damages are not recoverable for innocent misrepresentation.)

203

UNDUE INFLUENCE

(As noted above, where any sort of fiduciary relationship exists (lawyer-client, guardian-ward, doctor-patient), there is a distinct possibility that one of the parties to the transaction has misused the trust and confidence which the other has given, in order to benefit at the other's expense. The party may be relying on the advice of the trusted lawyer, doctor, or guardian as the basis for entering into a contract) Where such an underlying relationship exists between the contracting parties, the courts will examine their bargain very carefully to make sure that it represents the true intent of the "subordinate" party and that all the facts had been disclosed to that party. Even without an underlying fiduciary relationship, it is possible to prove that a contract was entered into because of undue influence rather than by free choice, although this case is not nearly as easy to prove.

DURESS

Closely related to the idea of undue influence is that of duress. |Duress means something more than just pressure or "hard selling." The most obvious cases involve violence or threats of violence against the contracting party.) Threats to commence a criminal prosecution unless money is paid or promised also constitute duress, but simply threatening to bring a civil suit for money allegedly owed is not duress. The following case illustrates these principles.

Great American Indemnity Co. v. Berryessa
122 Utah 243 (1952)

FACTS The Great American Indemnity Company brought this suit against Frank Berryessa and W. S. Berryessa, the obligors on a joint promissory note. Frank Berryessa was not served with a summons and did not participate in the trial. W. S. Berryessa pleaded as defenses duress and lack of consideration and also counterclaimed for the return of $1,500 paid by him and the cancellation of a personal check given by him and not cashed at the time of the suit. This appeal was from a jury verdict and the judgment thereon in favor of W. S. Berryessa.

Frank Berryessa, a son of W. S. Berryessa, misappropriated some funds of his employer, the Eccles Hotel Company, which operated the Ben Lomond Hotel in Ogden, Utah. When the father first learned of this, it was thought that the sum involved was approximately $2,000 and he agreed to repay this amount if the bonding company would not be notified and no publicity would be given to the matter. He gave the hotel his promissory note for $2,186 to cover the shortage. Before this note became due, it was discovered that the shortage would probably be over $6,000 and therefore the manager of the hotel called W. S. Berryessa in for a conference. W. S. Berryessa knew that he couldn't pay this larger sum, and it was decided that the bonding company, the Great American Indemnity Company, should be advised of the shortages. After the bonding company was notified, its agent had several conferences with the Berryessas and the hotel management in which it was ascertained that the total shortage amounted to $6,865.28 and Frank Berryessa signed a statement that he had misappropriated that amount. At a further meeting of the Berryessas with the agent, W. S. Berryessa indicated that he did not think his son Frank would be able to make the payments of $250 quarterly suggested and that he was sure he personally would not be able to do so and therefore did not want to sign the note. W. S. Berryessa then testified, though this was denied by the agent, that the agent thereupon swore, pounded his fists on his desk, and told him, "You can't come here and tell me what you will do," and then told them that if W. S. Berryessa would pay $2,000 in cash and sign a note with Frank Berryessa for $4,865.20, payable at the rate of $50 a month, Frank would not be prosecuted, but that if W. S. Berryessa did not sign, Frank would have to be prosecuted. Thereupon, W. S. Berryessa agreed to do this. A couple of days later, he signed the note sued upon herein, and about a month later, having secured a loan by mortgaging his home, he gave the agent a cashier's check in the amount of $500 as payment for the $2,000 cash agreed upon.

ISSUE   Were either of the father's promises based on duress?

DECISION   Yes, as to the $4,865.20 note. Judgment affirmed.

REASONS   "It is well settled that a note given to suppress a criminal prosecution is against public policy and is not enforceable between the parties. . . .

"In this case respondent relied on two separate defenses, duress and illegal consideration, either one of which is sufficient to nullify this note. So if the jury found that the note was the result of duress or that respondent signed the note because appellant promised to refrain from criminal prosecution of his son, either one would be sufficient to invalidate the note and would constitute a defense thereto.

"The uncashed check and the payment of $1,500 cash present a different problem. Respondent had given the hotel a note for slightly over $2,000 to pay for son's defalcations. At the time this note was given, there can be no question that no coercion was exercised against respondent and that his act was voluntary and at his own suggestion. There is nothing in the record to indicate that this note was given under duress or a promise to suppress prosecution."

MISTAKE

The contracting parties can be "mistaken" about so many things that it is impossible to catalog all of the conceivable factual combinations. ("Mistakes" may occur in the formation of the agreement, in writing up the deal, or in performance.) Rather than a comprehensive list, what follows is merely a discussion of some of the most frequent kinds of mistakes: mutual mistake in basic assumptions, material unilateral mistake, mistake in integration, and mistake in performance.)

Mutual Mistake in Basic Assumptions. Where both parties enter into a contract assuming the existence of some particular fact or condition which later turns out not to have been so, there is no contract at all if the fact is "basic" (material) to the contract. Efrem Zimbalist, Sr., the famous concert violinist, bought two violins which both he and the seller assumed were a genuine Stradivarius and a genuine Guarnerius. In fact, both violins were merely good copies. When he discovered the truth, Zimbalist was entitled to get his money back; neither party intended a contract for *fake* violins.

Many "mutual mistake" cases arise from a latent ambiguity in the terms of the contract; that is, a word or phrase really describes more than one thing, and each party understands it to mean something different. In the classic example, a buyer and a seller contracted in England for "certain goods, to wit, 125 bales Surat cotton to arrive ex ship Peerless from Bombay." Unknown to either the buyer or the seller, there were *two* ships called *Peerless*, and both were in Bombay and both had some Surat cotton on board. To make the story complete, incredible though it may seem, they were both bound for London, one to arrive in October, and one in December. The buyer knew only about the "October" *Peerless*; the seller knew only about the "December" *Peerless*. When the buyer's cotton was not delivered in October and the buyer sued for breach of contract the English court correctly held that no damages were recoverable since no contract had ever really been made. The parties were talking about two different things and had never really agreed. The following case is a modern example of the *Peerless* principle in action.

Oswald v. Allen
417 F.2d 43 (U.S. Second Circuit, 1969)

FACTS Dr. Oswald, a coin collector from Switzerland, was interested in Mrs. Allen's collection of Swiss coins. In April 1964 Dr. Oswald was in the United States and arranged to see Mrs. Allen's coins. The parties drove to the Newburgh Savings Bank of Newburgh, New York, where two of Mrs. Allen's collections, referred to as the Swiss Coin Collection and the Rarity Coin Collection, were located in separate vault boxes. After examining and taking notes on the coins in the Swiss Coin Collection, Dr. Oswald was shown several valuable Swiss coins from the Rarity Coin Collection. He also took notes on these coins, and he later testified that he did not know that they were in a separate "collection." The evidence showed that each collection had a different key number and was housed in labeled cigar boxes.

On the return to New York City, Dr. Oswald sat in the front seat of the car while Mrs. Allen sat in the back with Dr. Oswald's brother, Mr. Victor Oswald, and Mr. Cantarella of the Chase Manhattan Bank's Money Museum, who had helped arrange the meeting and had served as Dr. Oswald's agent. Dr. Oswald could speak practically no English and so depended on his brother to conduct the transaction. After some negotiation a price of $50,000 was agreed upon. Apparently the parties never realized that the references to "Swiss coins" and the "Swiss Coin Collection" were ambiguous. The trial judge found that Dr. Oswald thought the offer he had authorized his brother to make was for all of the Swiss coins, while Mrs. Allen thought she was selling only the Swiss Coin Collection and not the Swiss coins in the Rarity Coin Collection.

ISSUE Did the parties reach an agreement? Was there a signed writing adequate to satisfy the statute of frauds?

DECISION No. No. Judgment for defendant affirmed.

There is no "mistake," and thus there is a binding contract, where both parties are aware of their lack of knowledge as to a particular fact of condition, and take their mutual ignorance into account in setting the terms of the contract. In a Wisconsin case the finder of a pretty stone in a field took the stone to a friend and asked the friend what he thought it was worth. The friend said he didn't know either but that he'd pay the finder $1 for it. After the sale the stone was identified as an uncut diamond, worth $700. There was no "mistake" in this case, in the legal sense, since both parties were aware when they contracted that they did not know the true identity or worth of the stone.

Because much of modern commerce is based on differing estimates of the value of land, goods, and securities, most courts also adhere to a rule which says that mistake relief will not be given where the only error is as to the *value* of an item rather than a mistake as to its *identity*. The mistake in the Zimbalist case, for example, was not as to the value of fake violins but as to whether the violins were genuine or fake. This difference is probably easy enough to see in most cases, but some cases are a little harder to decide.

Material Unilateral Mistake.   Generally, the fact that one party to the contract has made a mistake of some sort affords no basis for relief, so long as the other party was unaware of the mistake and was acting in good faith. Most courts do, however, say that there is no contract where the mistake was so "gross" that the other party should have been aware of it. This situation arises most frequently where bids are being solicited for a certain job. Several bid-offers are submitted, and one is way out of line. Courts usually will not permit the offeree to "snap up" what the offeree has good reason to know must be a mistaken bid, thus binding the honestly mistaken bidder to an unfair contract. Just how gross the mistake has to be to trigger this rule is a question of fact.

Mistake in Integration.   Both the courts and the *Restatement* continue to state as the general rule that one is bound by what he or she signs. Yet, almost in the same breath, courts everywhere also continue to grant relief ("reformation") for what is commonly termed "mistake in integration." In such a case one party alleges that a written document is incorrect, that it does not accurately state the terms actually agreed on. If there is evidence to support this claim, a court with equity powers can "reform" the document to make it agree with the actual intent of the parties, and then enforce the document as corrected.

Mistake in Performance. Perhaps the most difficult cases of all in which to work out a mutually fair result are those involving a "mistake in performance." (Someone performs for the wrong person, or at the wrong time, or in the wrong place, or when he or she was not really contractually obligated to perform at all.) Where the performance involves money or a tangible object which can be easily returned, the solution is simple; the person who has received the money or other item by mistake must return it. Where construction or demolition takes place at the wrong site, however, the problem is not so easily resolved. What does one do for the owner of the apartment house which the wrecking crew tore down "by mistake"? Even if the owner is given the full fair market value of the old building, plus lost rentals, until a new one is built, he or she has still been the unwilling participant in a forced sale of the old building, with all sorts of possible adverse tax consequences. How about the landowner who gets a new house put up on his or her lot "by mistake"? Should that person have to pay for the new house, and if so, how much? Or should he or she be able to force the removal of the house and the restoration of the pristine ecology? For these, as for many other "mistake" questions, there are no easy or universal answers.

CASES FOR DISCUSSION

KENNEDY v. FLO-TRONICS, INC.

143 N.W.2d 827 (Minnesota, 1966)

Otis, Justice

This is an appeal from a judgment against defendants for $15,000 arising out of alleged misrepresentations made to plaintiff concerning the future value of corporate stock.

The contract out of which this litigation arose was entered February 23, 1961. By its terms plaintiff transferred to defendant Flo-Tronics, Inc., all of the assets in a business he was conducting under the name of Kenco Plastics, in return for which plaintiff received 4,000 shares of stock in Flo-Tronics, having a market value of $8.50 per share. Under the contract, plaintiff was obliged to retire the debts he then owed. To that end the stock he received was pledged with a bank as collateral for a loan in the sum of $17,500.

In addition he executed a second mortgage on his home for $5,000. Plaintiff claims he was induced to enter the contract by the assurances of one of defendants' officers, Earl Nelson, that the value of Flo-Tronics stock would rise from $8.50 per share to $25 a share by January 1, 1962. The stock did increase in market value to $17 per share by April 18, 1961. However, plaintiff was advised that under S.E.C. regulations he was not permitted to sell it until he had retained it for six months. By March 1962, the market value had fallen to approximately $3 a share. At that time the bank sold the stock for the sum of $10,367.65. In addition the second mortgage on plaintiff's home was foreclosed.

The court charged the jury that in order to recover, plaintiff had the burden of proving (1) that defendants made a false representation of a material fact; (2) that Nelson stood in a relation of trust and confidence to plaintiff which justified his relying on Nelson's opinion regarding the future value of Flo-Tronics stock; and (3) that plaintiff had reasonable cause to believe that Nelson would act only in plaintiff's best interests. In a well-considered memorandum accompanying his order denying a new trial, the court made the following observations:

". . . It seems to me that there is a sound basis for distinguishing between a promise to do an act in the future and an opinion. With respect to the latter, I view the decisions as showing a disposition on the part of the courts to treat as representations of existing facts those opinions which are expressed as unqualified affirmations by a person in a position to have knowledge of the facts necessary to make such affirmation. . . . Thus, in the present case where the jury has found a confidential relationship to have existed as between plaintiff and Nelson, and the latter, by reason of his dealings and position with defendants, might reasonably be expected to know the facts upon which he based his unqualified affirmation of value, no reason is perceived in law or in reason for not according to such affirmation the legal status of a misrepresentation of fact. As such, the misrepresentation was actionable irrespective of the defendants' knowledge of its falsity."

Since it is the general rule that, in the absence of an intent to deceive, an innocent misrepresentation of future value does not give rise to an action for fraud unless there is such a disparity in the positions of the parties that the law infers an overreaching, the disposition of the instant case hinges on the relationship of the parties and the sequence of events which gave rise to the litigation.

Plaintiff Kennedy and Earl Nelson met in 1954 at Camp McCoy. Nelson, then 45, was a colonel, and Kennedy, then 33, a private, acting as Nelson's radio operator. Kennedy had attended a junior college in Iowa, as well as Oklahoma A. and M., and had earned 187 credits towards graduation. He studied mathematics, science, physics, and aerodynamics, and subsequently attended a radio school in Kansas City. In addition, he took extension courses at the University of Minnesota. He was successively a radio operator for Northwest Airlines, in the United States Air Force, and, having received the highest marks in a competitive examination, postmaster for five years at the Ah-Gwah-Ching Sanitarium. He operated various sport shops, and in 1954 commenced a plastics business in the basement of his home at Walker, Minnesota.

Nelson's educational background included 160 college credits and a correspondence course in accounting. He was president of defendant Wilcox Products Company, also dealing in plastics. As a result of Kennedy's acquaintance with Nelson in the Army, Kennedy got in touch with Nelson and began doing business with him in the fall of 1954. Their relationship continued on a friendly basis for the next six years, during which time they contracted with one another in business and occasionally visited one another's home. In the summer of 1960, Nelson proposed that Kennedy merge his business with Flo-Tronics, which meanwhile had purchased the Wilcox stock from Nelson and others. Nelson had become a vice president of Flo-Tronics, although not on its board, and held approximately 23,000 shares of its stock. He remained president of Wilcox and later became the comptroller and treasurer of Thermotech Industries, a wholly owned subsidiary of Flo-Tronics to which Wilcox was sold. At that time Kennedy was not interested in a merger and declined to consider the proposition when it was broached again by Nelson that fall. However, in December 1960, Kennedy's business had expanded to a point where he had moved it out of his home and it had 13 employees. While his volume had risen to about $35,000 a year, he found he was operating without sufficient capital because of a great many accounts receivable. He was therefore receptive to Nelson's proposal to merge and began negotiations in December 1960 which culminated in the contract of February 23, 1961, under which he transferred assets valued at approximately $28,000 for stock worth approximately $34,000.

Kennedy rejected Nelson's overtures on at least two occasions and only acquiesced in the so-called merger when he found himself overextended and without sufficient capital. There was a striking similarity between the educational and intellectual capacity of the two men. Although Nelson undoubtedly had broader experience,

Kennedy had himself shown an unusual aptitude in the business world. Nevertheless, Kennedy insists that when Nelson expressed the opinion Flo-Tronics stock would triple in value within a year, Nelson's position in the companies of which he was an officer gave rise to an inference he was speaking from the vantage of one having information not generally available to the public. We do not agree. The fact is that Kennedy received stock which was equivalent in value to the assets he transferred. Nelson did not represent that he had any undisclosed information. He did not suggest, for example, that Flo-Tronics was about to enter a particularly favorable contract for the sale of its products, or that it had discovered a valuable process which would give it an advantage in the competitive market, or that it was about to accomplish a profitable merger with some other concern. Nelson did quite truthfully observe that he had a profit in the stock, although there is a dispute as to whether or not it was merely a paper profit. The rise in market value he anticipated was in fact very shortly realized, if not to the full extent that he predicted.

Here . . . the record does not support the finding implicit in the verdict that Kennedy was "simple and unwary" or relied blindly on Nelson's judgment. Clearly, in the instant case the prediction of a spectacular increase in value in such a brief period of time was not a representation of fact which was "susceptible of knowledge" within the meaning of the *Hollerman* case.

In the light of Kennedy's background, experience, and intelligence, we hold he was not justified in assuming that Nelson was omniscient or infallible in a matter as patently fraught with uncertainty as the state of the securities market at a given date in the future.

Reversed.

M. F. KEMPER CONSTRUCTION CO. v. CITY OF LOS ANGELES

235 P.2d 7 (California, 1951)

Gibson, Chief Justice

The M. F. Kemper Construction Company brought this action against the City of Los Angeles to cancel a bid it had submitted on public construction work and to obtain discharge of its bid bond. The city cross-complained for forfeiture of the bond and for damages. The trial court cancelled the bid, discharged the bond, and allowed appellant city nothing on its cross-complaint. The sole issue is whether the company is entitled to relief on the ground of unilateral mistake.

On July 28, 1948, the city Board of Public Works published a notice inviting bids for the construction of the general piping system for the Hyperion sewer project. Pursuant to the city charter, the notice provided that each bid must be accompanied by a certified check or surety bond for an amount not less than 10 percent of the sum of the bid "as a guarantee that the bidder will enter into the proposed contract if it is awarded to him," and that the bond or check and the proceeds thereof "will become the property of the city of Los Angeles, if the bidder fails or refuses to execute the required contract. . . ." The notice inviting bids reserved to the board the right to reject any and all bids, and both it and the official bid form stated that bidders "will not be released on account of errors."

Respondent company learned of the invitation for bids on August 17 and immediately began to prepare its proposal. Over a thousand different items were involved in the estimates. The actual computations were performed by three men, each of whom calculated the costs of different parts of the work, and in order to complete their estimates, they all worked until 2:00 o'clock on the morning of the day the bids were to be opened. Their final effort required the addition and transposition of the figures arrived at by each man for his portion of the work from his "work sheet" to a "final accumulation sheet" from which the total amount of the bid was taken. One item estimated on a work sheet in the amount of $301,769 was inadvertently omitted from the final accumulation sheet and was overlooked in computing the total amount of the bid. The error was caused by the fact that the men were exhausted after working long hours under pressure. When the bids were opened on August 25, it was found that respondent company's bid was $780,305 and the bids of the other three contractors were $1,049,592, $1,183,000, and $1,278,895.

The company discovered its error several

hours after the bids were opened and immediately notified a member of the board of its mistake in omitting one item while preparing the final accumulation of figures for its bid. On August 27 the company explained its mistake to the board and withdrew its bid. A few days later, at the board's invitation, it submitted evidence which showed the unintentional omission of the $301,769 item. The board, however, passed a resolution accepting the erroneous bid of $780,305, and the company refused to enter into a written contract at that figure. On October 15, 1948, without readvertising, the board awarded the contract to the next lowest bidder. The city then demanded forfeiture of the Kemper Company's bond, and the company commenced the present action to cancel its bid and obtain discharge of the bond.

The trial court found that the bid had been submitted as the result of an excusable and honest mistake of a material and fundamental character, that the company had not been negligent in preparing the proposal, that it had acted promptly to notify the board of the mistake and to rescind the bid, and that the board had accepted the bid with knowledge of the error. The court further found and concluded that it would be unconscionable to require the company to perform for the amount of the bid, that no intervening rights had accrued, and that the city had suffered no damage or prejudice.

Once opened and declared, the company's bid was in the nature of an irrevocable option, a contract right of which the city could not be deprived without its consent unless the requirements for rescission were satisifed. . . . The company seeks to enforce rescission of its bid on the ground of mistake. . . . The city contends that a party is entitled to relief on that ground only where the mistake is mutual, and it points to the fact that the mistake in the bid submitted was wholly unilateral. . . . However, the city had actual notice of the error in the estimates before it attempted to accept the bid, and knowledge by one party that the other is acting under mistake is treated as equivalent to mutual mistake for purposes of rescission. . . . Relief from mistaken bids is consistently allowed where one party knows or has reason to know of the other's error

and the requirements for rescission are fulfilled. . . .

Omission of the $301,769 item from the company's bid was, of course, a material mistake. The city claims that the company is barred from relief because it was negligent in preparing the estimates, but even if we assume that the error was due to some carelessness, it does not follow that the company is without remedy. . . . The type of error here involved is one which will sometimes occur in the conduct of reasonable and cautious businessmen, and, under all the circumstances, we cannot say as a matter of law that it constituted a neglect of legal duty such as would bar the right to equitable relief.

The evidence clearly supports the conclusion that it would be unconscionable to hold the company to its bid at the mistaken figure. The city had knowledge before the bid was accepted that the company had made a clerical error which resulted in the omission of an item amounting to nearly one-third of the amount intended to be bid, and, under all the circumstances, it appears that it would be unjust and unfair to permit the city to take advantage of the company's mistake. There is no reason for denying relief on the ground that the city cannot be restored to status quo. It had ample time in which to award the contract without readvertising, the contract was actually awarded to the next lowest bidder, and the city will not be heard to complain that it cannot be placed in status quo because it will not have the benefit of an inequitable bargain. . . . Finally, the company gave notice promptly upon discovering the facts entitling it to rescind, and no offer of restoration was necessary because it had received nothing of value which it could restore. . . . We are satisfied that all the requirements for rescission have been met.

There is no merit in the city's contention that, even assuming the company is entitled to cancellation of the bid and is not liable for breach of contract, the bid bond should nevertheless be enforced because the company failed to enter into a written contract. It is argued that forfeiture of the bond is provided for by charter and that equity cannot relieve from a statutory forfeiture. We do not agree however that the city charter should be construed as requiring forfeiture of bid bonds in situations where the bidder has a legal excuse for refusing to enter into a formal written contract. Under such circumstances the contingency which would give rise to a forfeiture has not occurred. . . . In line with the general policy of construing against forfeiture wherever possible, decisions from other jurisdictions permitting rescission of bids uniformly excuse the contractors from similar provisions relating to forfeiture of bid bonds or deposits. . . .

The judgment is affirmed.

SHERWOOD v. WALKER

33 N.W. 919 (Michigan, 1887)

Morse, J.

Replevin for a cow. Suit commenced in justice's court. Judgment for plaintiff. Appealed to circuit court of Wayne county. The defendants bring error, and set out 25 assignments of the same.

The main controversy depends upon the construction of a contract for the sale of the cow.

The plaintiff claims that the title passed, and bases his action upon such claim.

The defendants contend that the contract was executory, and by its terms no title to the animal was acquired by plaintiff.

The defendants reside at Detroit, but are in business at Walkerville, Ontario, and have a farm at Greenfield, in Wayne county, upon which were some blooded cattle supposed to be barren as breeders. The Walkers are importers and breeders of polled Angus cattle.

The plaintiff is a banker living at Plymouth, in Wayne county. He called upon the defendants at Walkerville for the purchase of some of their stock, but found none there that suited him. Meeting one of the defendants afterwards, he was informed that they had a few head upon this Greenfield farm. He was asked to go out and look at them, with the statement at the time that they were probably barren, and would not breed.

May 5, 1886, plaintiff went out to Greenfield and saw the cattle. A few days thereafter, he called upon one of the defendants with the view of purchasing a cow, known as "Rose 2d of

212

Aberlone." After considerable talk, it was agreed that defendants would telephone Sherwood at his home in Plymouth in reference to the price. The second morning after this talk he was called up by telephone, and the terms of the sale were finally agreed upon. He was to pay $5\frac{1}{2}$ cents per pound, live weight, 50 pounds shrinkage. He was asked how he intended to take the cow home, and replied that he might ship her from King's cattle-yard. He requested defendants to confirm the sale in writing, which they did by sending him the following letter:

T. C. Sherwood,
President, etc.,—

Dear Sir:

We confirm sale to you of the cow Rose 2d of Aberlone, lot 56 of our catalogue, at $5\frac{1}{2}$ cents per pound, less 50 pounds shrink. We inclose herewith order in Mr. Graham for the cow. You might leave check with him, or mail to us here, as you prefer.

Yours truly,

Hiram Walker & Sons

The order upon Graham inclosed in the letter read as follows:

Walkerville, May 15, 1886.

George Graham:

You will please deliver at King's cattle-yard to Mr. T. C. Sherwood, Plymouth, the cow Rose 2d of Aberlone, lot 56 of our catalogue. Send halter with cow, and have her weighed.

Yours truly,

Hiram Walker & Sons

On the 21st of the same month the plaintiff went to defendants' farm at Greenfield, and presented the order and letter to Graham, who informed him that the defendants had instructed him not to deliver the cow. Walker refused to take the money or deliver the cow. The plaintiff then instituted this suit.

* * * * *

The defendants . . . introduced evidence tending to show that at the time of the alleged sale it was believed by both the plaintiff and themselves that the cow was barren and would not breed; that she [had] cost $850 and if not barren would be worth from $750 to $1,000; that after the date of the letter, and the order to Graham, the defendants were informed by said Graham that in his judgment the cow was with calf, and therefore they instructed him not to deliver her to plaintiff, and on the 20th of May, 1886, telegraphed to the plaintiff what Graham thought about the cow being with calf, and that consequently they could not sell her. The cow had a calf in the month of October following.

* * * * *

It appears from the record that both parties supposed this cow was barren and would not breed, and she was sold by the pound for an insignificant sum as compared with her real value if a breeder. She was evidently sold and purchased on the relation of her value for beef, unless the plaintiff had learned of her true condition, and concealed knowledge from the defendants. Before the plaintiff secured possession of the animal, the defendants learned that she was with calf, and therefore of great value, and undertook to rescind the sale by refusing to deliver her. The question arises whether they had a right to do so.

The circuit judge ruled that this fact did not avoid the sale, and it made no difference whether she was barren or not. I am of the opinion that the court erred in this holding. I know that this is a close question, and the dividing line between the adjudicated cases is not easily discerned. But it must be considered as well settled that a party who has given an apparent consent to a contract of sale may refuse to execute it, or he may avoid it after it has been completed, if the asset was founded, or the contract made, upon the mistake of a material fact—such as the subject-matter of the sale, the price, or some collateral fact materially inducing the agreement; and this can be done when the mistake is mutual.

* * * * *

If there is a difference or misapprehension as to the substance of the thing bargained for, if the thing actually delivered or received is different in substance from the thing bargained for and intended to be sold, then there is no contract; but if it be only a difference in some quality or accident, even though the mistake may have been the actuating motive to the purchaser or seller, or both of them, yet the contract remains binding.

* * * * *

It seems to me, however, in the case made by this record, that the mistake or misapprehension of the parties went to the whole substance of the agreement. If the cow was a breeder, she was worth at least $750; if barren, she was worth not over $80. The parties would not have made the contract of sale except upon the understanding and belief that she was incapable of breeding, and of no use as a cow. It is true she is now the identical animal that they thought her to be when the contract was made; there is no mistake as to the identity of the creature. Yet the mistake was not of the mere quality of the animal, but went to the very nature of the thing.

The court should have instructed the jury that if they found that the cow was sold, or contracted to be sold, upon the understanding of both parties that she was barren, and useless for the purpose of breeding, and that in fact she was not barren, but capable of breeding, then the defendants had a right to rescind, and to refuse to deliver, and the verdict should be in their favor.

The judgment of the court below must be reversed, and a new trial granted, with costs of this Court to defendants.

* * * * *

Sherwood, J. (*dissenting*)

I do not concur in the opinion given by my brethren in this case. I think the judgments before the justice and at the circuit were right.

* * * * *

There is no question but that the defendants sold the cow representing her of the breed and quality they believed the cow to be, and that the purchaser so understood it. And the buyer purchased her believing her to be of the breed represented by the sellers, and possessing all the qualities stated, and even more. He believed she

213

would breed. There is no pretense that the plaintiff bought the cow for beef, and there is nothing in the record indicating that he would have bought her at all only that he thought she might be made to breed. Under the foregoing facts—and these are all that are contained in the record material to the contract—it is held that because it turned out that the plaintiff was more correct in his judgment as to one quality of the cow than the defendants, and a quality, too, which could not by any possibility be positively known at the time by either party to exist, the contract may be annulled by the defendants at their pleasure. I know of no law, and have not been referred to any, which will justify any such holding, and I think the circuit judge was right in his construction of the contract between the parties.

* * * * *

The judgment should be affirmed.

WOODWORTH v. PRUDENTIAL INSURANCE CO.

258 App. Div. 103 (New York, 1939)

Dore, Justice

The complaint, the sufficiency of which has been sustained at Special Term, seeks to rescind a nonrefunding annuity policy issued by defendant to Chauncey C. Woodworth on May 1, 1936, on the theory of a unilateral material mistake of fact, viz., that Woodworth, the annuitant, at the time the policy was issued, was wholly unaware that he was then suffering from serious constitutional diseases which would cause his death in less than two years, and had he known of such condition would not have made the contract.

The action is brought by plaintiffs as executors of Woodworth, deceased. The complaint alleges that on May 1, 1936, Woodworth (herein-after referred to as "the annuitant") paid defendant $100,000 cash in advance in consideration of defendant issuing an annuity policy providing for quarterly payments to him of $1,571 for the remainder of his life; that he was then 52 years of age and had a life expectancy of 19 and $^{49}/_{100}$ths years; that at the time he made the contract he was unaware of the fact that then and for some time previous thereto he had been suffering from diseases of such serious nature that it was a physical impossibility for him to live more than two years; that had he known of this he would not have paid the $100,000; that he died July 15, 1937, from such diseases, before which date he had received only four quarterly payments totaling $6,284; that defendant retains the balance of $93,716 and is, therefore, unjustly enriched. The complaint demands rescission and return of the balance retained by defendant.

The Special Term held if plaintiffs could prove that a disease, unknown but pre-existing on May 1, 1936, the time of making the contract, caused the annuitant's death on July 15, 1937, plaintiffs should recover; that defendant would merely be deprived of the benefit of the annuitant's mistake, a benefit to which it was never entitled; and that no injury would result to any one. . . .

We think the ruling was in error and that the complaint does not state facts sufficient to constitute a cause of action. There is no claim of mental incapacity, fraud, overreaching, undue influence, duress, misrepresentation, the existence of any fiduciary relationship, or that defendant had any knowledge of the alleged diseases. By the express terms of the annuity contract, as pleaded, the annuitant was to receive quarterly payments only so long as he lived, without any payment upon or after death. The complaint alleges that under the terms of the contract the quarterly payments were to be made while the annuitant lived, "but without credit or promise to pay anything whatever to anyone whomsoever on any quarter day succeeding the death of said Chauncey C. Woodworth or to give any credit to his estate, regardless of how few quarter-annual payments should be made prior to the death of the said Chauncey C. Woodworth and subsequent to the execution and delivery to him of the annuity policy or contract hereinbefore referred to." That was the agreement to which both parties assented. On the facts pleaded, it is binding on both parties. It may not be rescinded by plaintiffs because, as the event showed, there were few quarterly payments made before death, and it could not be rescinded by defendant on analogous facts if the event were otherwise and there were many quarterly payments made, even beyond the expectancy period of the class in which annuitant was when the contract was made.

When it is said that the annuitant had a life expectancy at the age of 52 of about 19 years, that means the annuitant was in a class which at his age, based upon the calculation of actuarial tables covering a large number of lives, had an average expectancy of 19 years. Of that class, as indicated by the actuarial tables themselves, a certain number would die within one year, that is, at the age of 53, and another estimated number in each succeeding year. In *Hartley* v. *Eagle Ins. Co.* (222 N.Y. 178, 186) the court said that "tables of mortality are at best only slight evidence of the expectancy of life of any particular person," and that "such tables show only the average length of life among the classes whose lives are taken into consideration in preparing the tables."

The Combined Annuity Tables are prescribed by subdivision 5 of section 84 of the Insurance Law as a minimum standard for the valuation of annuities issued after January 1, 1931. Whatever table or valuation standard is used to calculate the price of an annuity, it is contemplated that the annuitant is a member of a class whose average expectancy under the annuity table is a specified number of years, but that some of the class will die within the first year thereafter and others within succeeding years before reaching the average normal expectancy. It was unsound, therefore, to assume that in entering into an annuity contract the parties did not contemplate the very possibility that here happened, namely, that the annuitant might die before his average life expectancy and receive a small fraction in return for the purchase price paid. The parties also contemplate that the individual annuitant might live to and even far beyond the average expectancy, in which case, under the terms of the policy herein, the insurance company is bound to continue quarterly annuity payments during the annuitant's life no matter how far prolonged.

The insurance company need not require that the annuitant take a physical examination before making the contract. If for his own protection he desired such examination, on the facts pleaded the company did nothing whatever to prevent it.

The result is not an unjust enrichment of defendant. That assumption is based on the erroneous notion that defendant has a profit for itself of the balance of the $100,000 not paid the annuitant during his lifetime. But the entire purchase price of the contract and the balance remaining unpaid become part of a required reserve fund for the benefit of all annuitants in the class. Annuity contracts issued by responsible companies are necessarily issued on a basis that will establish a reserve computed in accordance with a proper minimum valuation standard and sufficient to meet all contracts as they accrue. Annuitants who die early receive less than the amount paid; those who survive beyond the expectancy period receive more than they paid. Annuity contracts could not be written nor could proper reserves be with certainty assured if upon proof after death of unknown illness when the contracts were written a recovery of the premium could be had.

The orders appealed from should be reversed, with $20 costs and disbursements, and the motion to dismiss the complaint granted.

PROBLEMS FOR DISCUSSION

1. Theresa Pate slipped on the ice of the Strike and Spare lanes in February 1975, sustaining minor injuries. The following July she signed a release for any future claim for injuries in return for consideration of $150. Both parties at the time believed that case law in the state would have made litigation on the case "fruitless." In October 1975 the prior case law was overruled, allowing litigation in such cases, though not retroactively. In November 1975 Theresa sued Strike and Spare for her injuries, stating that the release was invalid because of a mutual mistake of law. Does she have a right to sue?

2. The diocese of Detroit contracted with School Equipment Distributors, Inc., for the purchase of certain equipment. School Equipment received a quotation from one of its suppliers, Scientific Manufacturing Company for $32,000, including freight and installation, and School Equipment mailed a purchase order. A few days later Scientific Manufacturing Company requested that the contract between the diocese and School Equipment be assigned to it, a measure necessitated by School Equipment's poor credit rating. Scientific Manufacturing Company would bill the diocese directly and send School Equipment the difference between the retail price and its dealer price. The letter also explained that a mistake had been made and the quoted price of $32,000 did not include freight and installation, which would cost an additional $3,000. The equipment was delivered, and Scientific Manufacturing Company received payment and sent a portion to School Equipment as promised. However, a mistake was made and Scientific's check was $2,500 more than it should have been. School Equipment refuses to return the money and claims that it should receive an additional $500, based on the original quotation by Scientific. What decision?

3. Joe Cleen purchased a Laundromat operation from Shirley Bubbles. The agreement mentioned that all equipment was in good condition. It also stated that in 1972 the business had grossed $26,000, with $16,000 in taxable income, and that the business had been growing steadily. The buyer was given the right to examine the books for the years 1970, 1971, and 1972. It is uncertain whether Joe actually looked at the books before the purchase. Soon after he took over the business, the equipment started to break down, business was less than expected, and upon examination he found that the 1972 gross receipts had been $25,761, with taxable income of $8,774. He claims that he has been defrauded by Shirley Bubbles and wants to rescind the contract. Will the court allow rescission in this case?

4. In 1940 Philip Reich purchased a large tract of land. In a later survey he divided the property by a 434-foot-long line and built a shopping center on the southern portion, while the northern portion was used for a restaurant. The land in between was used for parking for both establishments. Sometime later the restaurant was reorganized as a corporation, with the Reichs and Mr. and Mrs. Thauros being the only shareholders. Upon Philip Reich's death a dispute arose between Mrs. Reich and the Thauroses, and Mrs. Reich sold out her interest in the restaurant. She made it clear that restaurant patrons could not park in the shopping center parking lot any longer but would have to stay north of the boundary line.

   Mr. and Mrs. Thauros bring an action arguing that the 434-foot boundary must be a mistake since it leaves the restaurant with virtually no parking space and Philip Reich would never have wanted such a nonsensical division. Mrs. Reich counters with a claim for an injunction to restrain trespassing. Who will win?

5. Billy Joe Smith contracted to purchase a certain piece of land from Jeremiah Bluegrass. The land consisted of the Bluegrass homesite, 1.65 acres, and an 80-acre tract of land containing the famous tourist attraction Wildcat Cave. After Billy Joe had paid for the 81.65 acres, he discovered that the homesite was on U.S. Forest Service land, that the cave had been flooded during the previous year, that the gross income was $6,000 rather than $9,000, and that the number of billboards advertising the cave was considerably less than represented. What can Billy Joe do?

6. Mrs. Wealthy, who had inherited several houses from her husband, decided to sell one of her houses, which had been converted into apartments. It lay next to the house that she and her son occupied and was separated from her house only by her driveway and that of the other house. Mr. Wilkinson bought the property through a real estate office. The realtor had been given a description of the property over the

216

phone which was the same as the one in effect before the Wealthys' present residence had been built. The deed drawn up according to that description gave possession of both driveways to the apartment house owner. Several weeks later Mr. Wilkinson informed Mrs. Wealthy that he claimed his property included the driveway next to her house. Mrs. Wealthy filed an action to rescind the contract, claiming that a mistake must have been made since the deed did not allow her access to her garage without trespassing. Decision?

7. Hi-Way Motor Company entered into an agreement with International Harvester to become an IH franchised dealer. Orally, International Harvester assured Hi-Way Motor Company that it would not franchise any other dealers, but the written contract which was drawn up later did not mention any such promise. Three years later another franchise was granted to an area dealer. Hi-Way Motor Company unilaterally terminated its franchised agreement and sought damages, claiming fraud. What decision?

8. Cora owned a farm which she had never seen. Ringer came to her home and said that he wanted to buy the pasture portion of the farm. Ringer told Cora that the pasture was poor land and worth only $400 and that the only reason he wanted to buy it was because it adjoined a piece of land that he owned and that was being used for access to the pasture. Ringer said that he just wanted to end the annoyance of having the access over his land. Cora told Ringer to see her lawyer, Fumble. Ringer told Fumble the same story. As a result, Cora sold the entire farm to Ringer for $4,000. She later learned that there was a valuable, undeveloped granite quarry on the farm. She now sues for rescission of the contract and deed. What decision?

10 | Defenses—Illegality and "Public Policy"

Ⅰn the vast majority of cases, both the formation of the contract and the performances which it requires are lawful. Where a bargain transaction is illegal, either in its formation or in the performances required, the court attempts to do exactly the opposite of what it normally does; instead of enforcing the intent of the parties, the court tries to frustrate it. Since the bargain is illegal in some respect, the court will try to prevent the illegality from occurring if it can and will try to discourage similar illegal bargains from being made in the future. Although the specific results vary from case to case, this policy underlies all "illegality" cases.

This chapter discusses the results which the courts work out in some of the most frequent illegality cases as well as several examples of courts refusing to enforce contract provisions which are not specifically illegal but just against public policy.

ILLEGAL BARGAINS

Commission of Crime or Tort. The clearest case for the application of these illegality rules occurs where the would-be contract calls for a performance specifically defined as criminal under applicable state statutory law or involves the commission of an intentional tort against some third party. In popular jargon, the arrangement between the local Big Boss and Murder, Inc., which calls for the removal of the crosstown competition is called a contract. Clearly, the courts should not (and will not) have any part in the enforcement of such a contract, regardless of the stage of performance or nonperformance in which it is brought to the attention of the court. Whether the "hit-man" has taken the money and has refused to perform or has done the job in an unworkmanlike way, or the Big Boss has refused to pay for the services rendered, the court should refuse to recognize any rights or duties flowing from such a contract and simply leave these equally guilty parties where it finds them, with no relief to either. Conspiracy to commit murder is itself a crime, so very few such contracts are brought to the attention of a court. The following case, however, shows that occasionally such contracts do get litigated. (Note the methods used by the old common-law court in the precedent case to discourage the making of such illegal bargains.)

Central Trust & Safe Deposit Co. v. Respass
112 Ky. 606 (1902)

FACTS Jerome B. Respass and Solomon L. Sharp appeared to have formed a copartnership, extending over several years, in the business of managing a racing stable, and in connection with that business they were engaged in bookmaking, or making wagers upon racehorses. They had no regular time for making settlements with each other, but at various times, when requested, the cashier made out statements of the bookmaking business of the firm. Sharp died suddenly, before any such settlement was made. The money in the bankroll was on deposit to Sharp's credit. Respass brought suit against Sharp's executors for a settlement of the partnership accounts.

ISSUE Should the gains and losses from gambling be considered in settling the partnership accounts?

DECISION No. Judgment reversed.

REASONS "Another item to which exception is taken consists of $700; being the amount of two bets made, lost and paid by Respass. . . . In view of the statutory law of Kentucky, we are unable to see how any legal consideration can exist from a promise to reimburse to a partner any portion of any sum lost upon a bet on a horse race. . . . It is a contract for an illegal venture. The whole contract is illegal. No right of action can arise out of that contract. . . . Such a contract cannot be enforced in this State.

"A closer question is presented by the claim for a division of the 'bank roll.' This $4,724 was, as found by the chancellor, earned by the firm composed of Respass and Sharp in carrying on an illegal business—that of 'bookmaking'—in the State of Illinois.

"It does not seem to be seriously contended that the business of 'bookmaking,' whether carried on in Chicago or in this Commonwealth, was legal, for by the common law of this country all wagers are illegal. One of the most interesting cases upon this subject is that of Everet V. Williams—the celebrated Highwaymen's Case—an account of which is given in 9 *Law Quart. Rev.*, 197. That was a bill for an accounting of a partnership in the business of highwaymen, though the true nature of the partnership was veiled in ambiguous language. The bill set up the partnership between defendant and plaintiff, who was 'skilled in dealing in several sorts of commodities'; that they 'proceeded jointly in the said dealings with good success on Hounslow Heath, where they dealt with a gentleman for a gold watch'; that defendant had informed plaintiff that Finchley 'was a good and convenient place to deal in,' such commodities being 'very plenty' there, and if they were to deal there 'it would be almost all gain to them'; that they accordingly 'dealt with several gentlemen for divers watches, rings, swords, canes, hats, cloaks, horses, bridles, saddles, and other things, to the value of £2000 and upwards'; that a gentleman of Blackheath had several articles which defendant thought 'might be had for a little or no money, in case they could prevail on the said gentleman to part with the said things'; and that, 'after some small discourse with the said gentleman,' the said things were dealt for 'at a very cheap rate.' The dealings were alleged to have amounted to £2000 and upwards. This case, while interesting, from the views it gives of the audacity of the parties and their solicitors, sheds little light upon the legal questions involved, for the bill was condemned for scandal and impertinence; the solicitors were taken into custody, and 'fyned' £50 each for 'reflecting upon the honor and dignity of this court'; the counsel whose name was signed to the bill required to pay the costs; and both the litigants were subsequently hanged, at Tyburn and Maidstone, respectively; while one of the solicitors was transported.

"We conclude in this country, in the case of a partnership in a business confessedly illegal, whatever may be the doctrine where there has been a new contract in relation to, or a new investment of, the profits of such illegal business, and whatever may be the doctrine as to the rights or liabilities of a third person who assumes obligations with respect to such profits, or by law becomes responsible therefor, the decided weight of authority is that a court of equity will not entertain a bill for an accounting."

Gambling, Lotteries, and Games of Chance. Although nearly all forms of gambling are illegal in nearly all states, and although the parties to an illegal bet are clearly *in pari delicto* (i.e., they are equally guilty of violating the law, so that there should be no reason to prefer one over the other), different legal rules are applied to the bet case. Since the illegal purpose of a bet is to pay money to the winner based on the outcome of a game, race, fight, or whatever, the courts attempt to frustrate that purpose by permitting the loser of the bet to "repent" and repudiate the bet (*and* get his or her money back) at any time before the money is actually paid to the winner. If you "see the light" only after your team has lost, you can still (legally) repudiate your bet and keep your money (or get it back from the stakeholder), as long as you indicate your intent to do so before the money is actually paid over to the winner.) The same rule applies when you try unsuccessfully to fill an inside straight in poker: you can take your money back from the pot (though you may lose a lot of friends, and hands, in doing so).

Most state gambling statutes are broad enough to cover lotteries, license-plate bingo, and similar games of chance; some states also have separate statutes to cover these other forms of gambling. States are also attempting to prohibit newer forms of risk taking, such as so-called chainletter and pyramid forms of selling. All of these statutes are subject to judicial interpretation as to just what they prohibit and just what the courts should refuse to enforce, as the *Radikopf* (discussion) case shows.

Licensing Statutes. A 1969 study the U.S. Labor Department estimated that over 500 different occupations required a license of some sort from at least one governmental body, including such jobs as beekeeper, rainmaker, tattoo artist, and fund raiser. The "illegality" problem here occurs when an unlicensed person performs services for which a license is required. Should the client-customer be required to pay for the services received from the unlicensed practitioner?

Courts usually try to answer this question by first categorizing the licensing statute in question as either "regulatory" or "revenue raising." Of course, many statutes will include both legislative purposes, but what the court is trying to decide is whether the basic reason for the license is to protect persons from unqualified or unscrupulous practitioners or just to raise some money for the government. If the licensing statute contains educational and experiential requirements and specifies that a standardized test must be passed in order to get a license, it is pretty clearly regulatory in character. The fewer such standards it contains, the more it looks like just a revenue raiser.)

If a statute is regulatory in nature, the results of not being properly licensed under it are serious. In addition to being liable for whatever punishments are provided for practicing without the required license and for any malpractice against the client, the practitioner will usually be denied any recovery for the services performed even if he or she later gets licensed. (Contrariwise, if the statute is only designed to bring in money, the worst that will happen to the unlicensed practitioner is that he or she may have to get licensed before being able to sue to recover for services already performed. /

Tom Welch Accounting Service v. Walby
138 N.W.2d 139 (Wisconsin, 1965)

FACTS Tom Welch, d/b/a Tom Welch Accounting Service, sued to recover $1,429.75 for bookkeeping services performed and bookkeeping materials furnished for the defendant, Roger Walby, at his request between July 5, 1960, and September 26, 1961. Welch was not licensed under a statute which required that public accountants and CPAs be licensed.

Judgment was entered April 7, 1965, in behalf of the plaintiff against the defendant for $1,029.75 together with costs. The defendant appealed.

ISSUE Did the plaintiff violate the licensing statute for public accountants?

DECISION No. Judgment for plaintiff affirmed.

REASONS "The principal contention advanced by defendant on this appeal is that plaintiff, although not licensed as a public accountant or CPA, held himself out to defendant as being such, and, therefore, is precluded from recovering for the services rendered for which recovery is sought in the instant action.

"Apparently defendant interprets [the precedent case] as meaning that a non-registered accountant such as plaintiff is prohibited by the statute from holding himself out as an accountant, and can only practice his occupation under the title of bookkeeper or offering bookkeeping services. We think this is too narrow a construction of the statute.

"'When this court stated . . . that the work of a nonregistered accountant 'cannot be put before the public as work of a public accountant or certified public

221

accountant' it put its finger upon the public aspect of the practice of accountancy which the statute prohibits. The statute does not concern itself with the methods used by a nonregistered accountant to gain employment from members of the public so long as these means do not deceive the public into believing he is a public acccount or CPA. Ch. 135, Stats., has now been in effect for 30 years, and we believe that the distinction between a nonregistered accountant and a public accountant is generally recognized. One has only to turn to the yellow pages of a telephone directory to see the distinction maintained.

"We conclude that plaintiff did not violate sec. 135.11(5) and (6), Stats., when he did business under the name of 'Tom Welch Accounting Service' or listed himself under that name in the Shawano telephone directory under the occupational heading of 'Accountants.' No claim is here made that the services he actually performed for defendant violated any of the prohibitions of ch. 135. Therefore, because plaintiff did not violate the statute, there is no illegality in his contract of employment by defendant which would bar him from recovering the reasonable value of the services rendered.''

Usury. Usury is very easy to define: it is the charging of an illegally high rate of interest. This simple definition is not always so easy to apply to particular cases. The court must decide two subsidiary questions: What is interest, and what is an illegally high rate? State courts do not agree on the answers to these questions.

Interest is generally defined as the charge for a loan of money or for the forbearance of a debt. Since the impact on the buyer-debtor is the same in either case, and since the seller-lender ought not to be able to evade the maximum rate by merely calling interest something else, most courts today would probably hold that a "time-price differential" charged in a credit sale is in fact interest, but there are cases reaching the opposite result. Monthly service charges on revolving charge accounts have been held to be interest by nearly every court to consider the problem since 1970. Some states have specific statutes regulating these special kinds of credit arrangements and permitting the creditor to charge a higher rate of interest than that permitted by the state's general usury law. Nearly all courts agree that bona fide charges for separate services, such as credit reports on the debtor, appraisals of collateral, and filing fees, are valid and are not to be calculated as part of the interest charge.

How high is too high? The general usury law in most states specifies a maximum annual interest rate of from 7 to 10 percent. In most states corporations are not protected by usury laws, and this same idea has been extended in several states to any loan to a business, incorporated or not. Small loan companies are typically governed by their own statute, which permits them to charge a much higher interest rate (usually 24 to 36 percent). Credit unions and other special lenders may also have their own special statutory rate. One of the main objectives of the Uniform Consumer Credit Code is to simplify this hodgepodge of existing laws.

The states disagree not only on the definition of interest and the rate permitted but also on what the remedy should be when a lender tries to charge a usurious rate. At least four types of results have been worked out: (1) forfeiture of only the excessive amount of interest; (2) forfeiture of all interest; (3) forfeiture of double or triple the amount of interest charged; and (4) forfeiture of the entire debt, both principal and interest.

Sunday Laws. About half of the states have some sort of statute prohibiting the doing of business, or at least some types of business, on Sunday. Some of the more recently enacted statutes give the target merchants the option of closing either Sunday or Saturday. These statutes are an obvious outgrowth of the old colonial blue laws, under which it was made illegal to do almost anything on Sunday but go to church. Although these laws clearly interfere with the "free exercise of religion," and clearly "establish" the Christian Sunday (in most cases) as *the* official day of rest, the U.S. Supreme Court upheld their constitutionality in 1961.

Merchants who wish to remain open on Sunday have fared better by challenging these laws in state courts, under the state's own constitution, either on the "religion" ground or on the ground that the legislation arbitrarily discriminates between products and businesses.

Arlan's Department Stores, Inc. v. *Kelley*
130 N.W.2d 892 (Michigan, 1964)

FACTS   These actions were filed to seek a declaratory judgment and to enjoin enforcement of P.A. 1962, No. 128. The plaintiffs, operators of retail stores, sought to have the act declared unconstitutional and invalid. The circuit court, on motions for summary judgment heard considerable testimony, dismissed the complaints, and entered judgments for the defendant's. The plaintiffs appealed.

The act purported to be "to promote the health, recreation and welfare of the state." It forbade the sale by certain merchants on any successive Saturday and Sunday of various articles and merchandise. The act made any violation of it a misdemeanor, subject to a fine of not more than $100 for the first offense and not more than $500 for the second and subsequent offenses. A court might suspend or revoke the license to do business of any person so convicted. The operation of any business contrary to the act was declared to be a public nuisance, subject to injunction proceedings. Any transaction in violation of the act was voidable at the option of the purchaser within one year upon tender of the property sold. Since the act was a penal statute, it had to be strictly construed.

ISSUE   Is the Sunday law a valid exercise of the state's police power?

DECISION   No. Judgment reversed.

REASONS   While all eight justices agreed that the act was unconstitutional, three different opinions were written as to *why* it was unconstitutional. Three judges thought it improperly delegated state legislative power to the counties. Three more agreed with that conclusion and also held that the act was unconstitutional because it "neither enhanced nor promoted" the general welfare.

The most interesting opinion was written by Justice O'Hara, who was joined by Justice Dethmers:

"Act. No. 128 of the Public Acts of 1962 is unconstitutional for so many reasons it offers the member of a multi-judge appellate court an attractive variety of bases upon which so to hold.

"I am content to rest my concurrence herein on the ground that it imposes criminal liability in language so vague and contradictory as to render its enforcement ludicrously impossible and farcical. For example, the sale of clothing is prohibited except 'rainwear.' Is Bulldog Drummond's traditional trench coat exempt or included? He wears it, rain or shine, as I do mine. Optical goods are included, sun glasses excluded. If the lenses are tinted, do prescription glasses become sun glasses? Mattresses are prohibited unless the mattress is primarily intended for outdoor camping; then it is exempted. Does the clerk obtain an affidavit attesting it for outdoor camping use only? Pet supplies are barred, except food. If the owner demands ground sirloin for pampered Phydo, does the harried merchant sell it? Grooming supplies are not prohibited except power-operated devices. If the beep-beep blade user is shaved by another, does his razor become a power-operated shaver? When does plumbing equipment which is barred become 'emergency plumbing' equipment which is permitted? Must the purchaser wait until the emergency has become socially menacing, or may he anticipate the emergency and, if so, by how long? Most intriguing is the test to be applied to athletic equipment necessary to participate in recreational activities. If the item is to be used 'on the premises where it is sold' or 'within 1 mile, measured directly,' the sale has the Act's blessing. If not, the sale subjects the seller to fines of up to $500. Does the clerk make a daily tour of the area of '1 mile, measured directly' to see if there are baseball diamonds, golf courses, miniature and otherwise, ski tows, swimming pools, et cetera *ad infinitum?* Even with this intelligence, who follows the purchaser to see that he doesn't utilize his new golf clubs at a course more distant than a mile?

"If the high and lofty motive of one-day closing per week is to be attained under its proclaimed banner of 'protecting all persons from physical and moral debasement which comes from uninterrupted labor,' the statute enacted to accomplish it, when it makes violation criminally punishable, must be definite and certain enough so that violation thereof becomes ascertainable in some manner other than by extra-sensory perception, moon gazing, or resort to a crystal ball.

"I too hold the Act to be unconstitutional."

Where there is a valid Sunday law in force, some rather surprising results may occur, as illustrated by an old New Hampshire case where two cows were sold on a Sunday with the price to be paid later. When the buyer didn't pay and the seller repossessed the cows, the seller was held liable for trespass since an absolute ownership of the cows had passed to the buyer. But when the seller sued for the contract price, the court permitted the buyer to use the illegality defense since the contract had been made on a Sunday. The court's main reason for this result was that the parties were equally guilty and should therefore have been left where they were when performance of the illegal bargain ceased—the buyer with the cows, the seller without the money. In many states today, a court would construct an "implied promise" to pay the contract price if the buyer retained the property and would say that this promise was legal because it was "made" on a weekday.

Common-Law Restraint of Trade. While contracts which produce unreasonable restraints of trade were illegal under the common law, as they are under many modern state and national statutes, the courts have long recognized that certain types of "restraints" serve a legitimate business function. In two situations in particular, the courts have recognized and enforced reasonable "restraints of trade." When a business is sold, the courts permit the buyer to protect the goodwill which the buyer has purchased by requiring the seller not to engage in a competing business within a reasonable geographic area for a reasonable period of time. If this restraint were not permitted, the seller could immediately regain most or all of his or her old customers by going back into business right across the street. Similarly, former employees, partners, or other business associates can be "restrained" from going to work for a competing firm, within reasonable area and time limits, if this is necessary to protect a former employer's goodwill, customer lists, or trade secrets.

Where the area of time limitations are unreasonable, and therefore illegal, the courts do not agree on what should happen. Some courts throw out the restraint entirely, thus giving the other party a better bargain than the party made for himself or herself. Other courts use a "blue pencil" and rewrite the limitations so as to make them reasonable. The problem with this approach is that it encourages the buyer or employer to write in unreasonable limitations since if these are challenged in court, they will only be made reasonable anyway.

The following case is a recent illustration of the common use made of such restraints in professional partnerships.

Middlesex Neurological Associates, Inc. v. *Cohen*
324 N.E.2d 911 (Massachusetts, 1975)

FACTS   This was a bill in equity to enforce a restrictive covenant by enjoining the defendant, a physician specializing in neurology, from practicing his specialty in Malden and surrounding communities and in various named hospitals. Both parties appealed from a final decree, entered on a master's report, enjoining the defendant from such practice substantially in the words of the covenant.

The master's subsidiary findings, which were no longer challenged, established that the plaintiff's assignor, a neurosurgeon named Fusillo, engaged in discussions with the defendant in the summer and fall of 1971 which led to an oral understanding that the defendant would associate with Fusillo in the practice of neurology in Malden and vicinity, where Fusillo had been in practice since 1963. The association began on November 6, 1971. About a week later Fusillo asked the defendant to sign an "employment agreement," which stated that it represented the entire agreement

225

of the parties and contained the restrictive covenant. The defendant expressed reluctance to sign it but did so after consulting with an attorney. The plaintiff corporation, of which Fusillo was president and sole stockholder, was chartered on December 3, 1971, and Fusillo assigned the employment agreement to it on December 7.

ISSUE   Is the covenant enforceable as a reasonable restraint?

DECISION   Yes. Judgment for plaintiff.

REASONS   The court first rejected the defendant's arguments that he received no consideration for his promise not to compete and that the plaintiff had not lived up to its part of the contract.

"The defendant further contends that the restrictive covenant is unreasonably broad in its territorial coverage. The defendant's argument is addressed to the inclusion in the restriction of the entire 'Malden, Melrose, Wakefield, Everett, Winchester, Stoneham community,' which, according to the defendant's brief, exceeds 250,000 in population. In view of the master's finding that Fusillo actively practices throughout the area, the covenant's territorial scope is not broader than the plaintiff's legitimate interests require. 'The master's findings, supported by the evidence reported on one of the defendant's objections, established that several neurologists and neurosurgeons other than Fusillo and the defendant practice (although not exclusively) in the area, and that no patients have suffered due to the unavailability of a neurologist.'

"The duration of the striction (two years) was reasonable. The good will sought to be protected by the restrictive covenant was of long-term significance, relating not only to Fusillo's patients during the period of employment but also to the medical community from which a neurologist must derive patients by referral.

"The defendant [also] argues that enforcement of the restrictive covenant is not necessary for the economic protection of the plaintiff.

"We concur in the judge's conclusion. The subsidiary findings do not establish that the plaintiff has not suffered some loss in gross volume of business. The defendant's assumption that the defendant was the source of half of the volume of business during the six months of association lacks a priori validity and is not buttressed by findings concerning Fusillo's volume of business in the six months preceding the association. But even if the subsidiary findings did establish that the plaintiff has suffered no loss in volume of business, that without more would not establish that the plaintiff has not suffered a loss of the good will which it is the lawful purpose of the covenant to protect. On the contrary, the master's findings that the defendant has been treating former patients of the plaintiff and has accepted referrals from doctors who formerly made referrals to the plaintiff suggest loss of good will in fact."

Improper Interference with Governmental Processes. In the wake of Watergate, with the absolutely unprecedented loss through resignation of both a president and a vice president of the United States and with the disclosures of illegal political contributions by some of our largest national corporations, many people have been made much more aware of the possibilities for the corruption of governmental processes. Coercion or bribery of public officials is clearly illegal, and any "contract" involving such "services" would be void. Lobbying, on the other hand, is perfectly lawful and an essential part of the democratic process, and lobbying contracts which do not involve any improper means are valid and enforceable in court.

While in most states mere failure to report a crime (misprision) is no longer itself criminal, crimes are committed when a person actively aids in concealing a crime or agrees not to file criminal charges in return for a consideration. Perjury and jury tampering are both crimes. While at one time "maintenance" (stirring up litigation) was a crime, this rule has been modified as a result of the activities of such organizations as the NAACP Legal Defense Fund and Nader's Raiders. The old common-law judges were so jealous of their prerogatives that they even held arbitration agreements to be illegal "obstructions of justice," but this view has been almost completely repudiated.

The Watergate scandal has left this entire area of the law somewhat unsettled, as new legislation has been adopted to limit private political contributions and new attempts are under way to repeal the Hatch Act so as to permit political activities by employees of the U.S. government.

BARGAINS AGAINST PUBLIC POLICY AND UNCONSCIONABLE CONTRACTS

Courts have become increasingly willing to refuse enforcement of contract provisions which are not specifically illegal but which they just plain don't like. Traditionally the emphasis of the common law has been on freedom of contract, or letting the parties make any sort of contractual arrangement they want so long as it is not illegal. More and more, however, recognizing that contracts in modern society do not always represent real bargaining between equals, courts have been rewriting contracts by refusing to enforce provisions which they regard as unduly harsh, oppressive, or unjust. As the following case shows, courts have been discovering that they have always had a common-law power to refuse enforcement of such "unconscionable" provisions, even without Section 2–302 of the UCC.

Williams v. *Walker-Thomas Furniture Company*
350 F.2d 445 (District of Columbia Circuit, 1965)

FACTS   Walker-Thomas Furniture Company operated a retail furniture store in the District of Columbia. During the period from 1957 to 1962 Ora Lee Williams purchased a number of household items from Walker-Thomas, for which payment was to be made in installments. The terms of each purchase were contained in a printed form contract which set forth the value of the purchased item and purported to lease the item to the appellant for a stipulated monthly rent payment. The contract then provided, in substance, that title would remain in Walker-Thomas until the total of all the monthly payments equaled the stated value of the item, at which time the appellant could take title. In the event of a default in the payment of any monthly installment, Walker-Thomas could repossess the item.

Williams v. Walker-Thomas Furniture Company *(continued)*

The contract further provided that "the amount of each periodical installment payment to be made by [purchaser] to the Company under this present lease shall be inclusive of and not in addition to the amount of each installment payment to be made by [purchaser] under such prior leases, bills or accounts; *and all payments now and hereafter made by [purchaser] shall be credited pro rata on all outstanding leases, bills and accounts* due the Company by [purchaser at the time each such payment is made." (Emphasis added.)

On April 17, 1962, appellant Williams bought a stereo set whose stated value was $514.95. She defaulted shortly thereafter, and the appellee sought to replevy all the items Williams had purchased since December 1957. The court of general sessions granted judgment for the appellee. The District of Columbia Court of Appeals affirmed.

ISSUE   Is the pro rata payment clause valid?

DECISION   No. Judgment reversed.

REASONS   Chief Judge Wright did not think that "unconscionability" applied only under U.C.C. 2–302.

Appellants' principal contention, rejected by both the trial and the appellate courts below, is that these contracts, or at least some of them, are unconscionable and, hence, not enforceable. . . .

"We do not agree that the court lacked the power to refuse enforcement to contracts found to be unconscionable. In other jurisdictions, it has been held as a matter of common law that unconscionable contracts are not enforceable. While no decision of this court so holding has been found, the notion that an unconscionable bargain should not be given full enforcement is by no means novel. . . .

"In determining reasonableness or fairness, the primary concern must be with the terms of the contract considered in light of the circumstances existing when the contract was made. The test is not simple, nor can it be mechanically applied. The terms are to be considered "in the light of the general commercial background and the commercial needs of the particular trade or case." Corbin suggests the test as being whether the terms are "so extreme as to appear unconscionable according to the mores and business practices of the time and place." We think this formulation correctly states the test to be applied in those cases where no meaningful choice was exercised upon entering the contract.

"Because the trial court and the appellate court did not feel that enforcement could be refused, no findings were made on the possible unconscionability of the contracts in these cases. Since the record is not sufficient for our deciding the issue as a matter of law, the cases must be remanded to the trial court for further proceedings."

Among other kinds of provisions challengeable as "against public policy" are those attempting to insulate landlords, employers, and bailees from liability for their own negligence and those which purport to waive or give up specific statutory protections. Anyone who has ever rented a house or an apartment knows that landlords' lawyers are particularly adept at coming up with objectionable lease provisions: no pets, no motorcycles, no waterbeds, no alcohol; tenant waives right to trial by jury; landlord may inspect the premises at any hour of the day or night, with or without notice to the tenant; etc., etc. While the landlord surely has a legitimate concern with what happens on the premises, some of the preceding seem to constitute an unwarranted intrusion into the tenant's affairs; this balance has not yet been fully and finally defined. The *Lamont* (discussion) case is one early attempt by the Ohio courts to deal with a landlord's "no children" policy.

These are not closed categories. As society's values change, provisions which are readily accepted and enforced today may become "against public policy" and thus unenforceable. In any case where the results called for by the terms of the contract seem unduly harsh, this argument should be presented to the court. What can you lose?

CASES FOR DISCUSSION

HARPER v. STATE

394 So.2d 311 (Mississippi, 1981)

Broom, Justice

Check forgery is the offense for which the defendant, Lindsey Harper, was convicted in the Circuit Court of the First Judicial District of Hinds County. Sentenced to 15 years' imprisonment with 5 years suspended, he appeals contending that (1) the indictment charged no crime, (2) his motion for continuance was erroneously overruled, and (3) the evidence was insufficient to support the verdict of guilty. We affirm.

Briefly stated, the facts are as follows. On October 22, 1979, the defendant presented to First National Bank in Jackson, Mississippi, a check dated the preceding day, October 21, 1979, which was a Sunday. Payee of the check was the defendant. He testified the check was given him by some woman for painting, but he failed to name or identify her. The check was drawn upon the joint checking account of R. M. Thompson (for whom the defendant previously did some work) and Mrs. Jan Johnston and had on it what

appeared to be the signature of Ms. Jan Johnston (not "Mrs.") as maker. Mrs. Johnston, Thompson's daughter, denied signing the check. The defendant endorsed the check, but First National Bank refused payment. That same date, October 22, 1979, the defendant was arrested and charged, and the November 1979 grand jury indicted him for uttering and publishing as true the check knowing it to be forged. Trial was on January 29, 1980, and the jury found him guilty as charged.

The thrust of his first argument is that the check bearing a notation "for painting" was a written contract—void because made on Sunday. He contends that being void on its face, the check is not the subject of forgery. . . . Therefore, according to him the trial court erred in overruling his motion to quash the indictment based upon Mississippi Code Annotated § 97–23–63 and § 97–23–67 (1972). In substance, these "Blue Law" statutes prohibit certain work and business activities on Sundays. Although these statutes prohibit certain activities on Sundays, they exempt certain other activities and business transactions and, as pointed out by the defendant, "painting" is not one of the exempted activities. In support of his argument that contracts entered into on Sunday are void, the defendant cited several Mississippi cases. He now argues that the lower court erroneously overruled his motion because the check, being a contract dated on Sunday issued in payment "for painting," was void on its face and could not be the subject of forgery or basis for a valid indictment.

Our view is that the position of the defendant, if followed by this Court, would allow forgers and the like to observe the calendar, date their forged instruments on a Sunday, and thus be immunized from prosecution. It is true that according to our case law, in order for an instrument to be a basis of forgery, it must possess some legal efficacy. The rationale is that otherwise the instrument would not contain the potential to defraud and injure another. We have held, therefore, that if the instrument in question could not create a liability, it could not be the basis for a forgery. . . .

Thus presented here is the question: Could the check in question create a liability and have worked a fraud? The answer to this question has to be affirmative. When someone presents a check to a bank for cashing, the bank's main inquiry is whether it has on deposit sufficient funds in the check maker's account to cover the check. Banks in this regard take reasonable precautions in accord with Mississippi code Annotated § 75–3–505 (1972) to insure that the presentor of the check is authorized to do so. First National's alert teller took these precautions and did not cash the check because it was a forgery, not because it was dated on Sunday. Under Mississippi Code Annotated § 75–3–417 (1972), one who obtains payment through presentation of commercial paper, such as a check, warrants to the good faith payor that the presentor has good title to the instrument. Good title presumes a valid instrument based on a legal transaction, and accordingly banks may safely cash checks regardless of whether dated on a Sunday. Notwithstanding the defendant's argument, this Sunday-dated check was cashable and therefore possessed sufficient legal efficacy to create a liability.

We have held that even though a contract is signed and finalized on a Sunday, evidence that it had been negotiated and agreed upon on a secular day will validate the contract. . . . Similarly, a contract executed by one party on a Sunday without the knowledge of the other party is valid and enforceable as to the innocent party. . . . As against the innocent party, to permit the wrongdoer to avoid the contract on these facts and take advantage of his own wrong would be unconscionable. Likewise to exonerate the defendant on his theory that this check is void, which check he obviously desired that the bank honor, would amount to telling "Sunday forgers" that they may with impunity reap the benefits of forgery while defrauding others. Our decision here gives reasonable interpretation to our "Blue Laws" statutes and those relating to the utterance of forged checks. We are unwilling to construe our "Blue Laws" so as to hold that all checks dated on Sunday are void and thereby immunize badcheck artists who date checks on Sunday and pass them on Monday. As previously held by us, we will not impute an unjust or unwise purpose to the legislators who enact statutes for the public good as they intended in enacting the "Blue Laws" and laws on forgery. . . . Our "Blue Laws" making certain otherwise legal activities unlawful if performed on Sunday cannot be reasonably construed to have the ludicrous result of making the crime of forgery lawful if perpetrated on Sunday.

MILLER v. RADIKOPF

228 N.W.2d 386 (Michigan, 1975)

Levin, Justice

The question is whether a contract to share the proceeds of an Irish Sweepstakes ticket is judicially enforceable.

Miller claims that he and Radikopf jointly sold sweepstakes tickets. For each 20 sold, they received 2 tickets as compensation. Although each would put his name on one of the tickets, Miller claims they agreed that the tickets were jointly owned and all winnings would be divided equally.

A ticket bearing Radikopf's name won and yielded in excess of $487,000. After Radikopf refused to surrender any of the proceeds, Miller commenced this action.

The trial court, stating that the alleged agreement was "spawned in violation of statute," granted Radikopf a summary judgment.

The Court of Appeals, referring to #372 of the Penal Code which prohibits the "set[ting] up or promot[ion of a] lottery," affirmed:

It is true that receiving a lottery award voluntarily paid, is not prohibited. . . . The general policy of this state against the holding of lotteries, M.C.L.A. 750.372 et seq.; M.S.A. 28.604 et seq., would be seriously compromised, however, if lottery winners were allowed to successfully bring suit for their prizes. Although the Court will not interfere where a lottery prize is voluntarily given the winner, public policy demands that courts not give support to the maintenance of lotteries in this state by allowing prize winners judicial process to collect their winnings. . . .

This is not, however, an action to collect prize winnings from a lottery promoter.

The narrow question to be decided is whether a contractual claim to a share of money legally paid by the Irish Sweepstakes and legally possessed by the defendant may be enforced.

We would hold that the public policy of this state does not preclude Miller from attempting to enforce his claim and, accordingly, would reverse and remand for trial.

It is a crime to "set up or promote" a lottery in this state. It is similarly a crime for a person to "sell," "offer for sale," or "have in his possession with intent to sell or offer for sale" lottery tickets.

However, it does not appear that Irish law prohibits the payment of money to holders of winning sweepstakes tickets. Nor does any statute or rule of law of this state prohibit the holder of a winning ticket from receiving and retaining proceeds paid voluntarily by a lottery without legal action.

There being no statute barring enforcement of the claim asserted in this case, the question whether its enforcement would be in accord with public policy is for judicial decision.

There were several contracts preceding the contract sued upon. Miller and Radikopf agreed to sell sweepstakes tickets and to accept as consideration "free" tickets. Each ticket so received by them was a separate contract binding the lottery promoters to pay the holder of a winning ticket.

As neither Miller nor Radikopf is presently attempting to enforce the antecedent contracts, their possible illegality and attendant public policy ramifications need not concern us. Whatever their legality, those contractual obligations were fulfilled. A different question would be presented if Miller or Radikopf sought by legal action to collect either their compensation for selling tickets or lottery winnings directly from the promoters of the sweepstakes.

Miller in this action seeks to enforce the agreement he claims was made by him and Radikopf "that should either of the tickets win any prize, the prize would be split equally between the two of them." The consideration exchanged by each was a promise to the other to pay one-half of any proceeds won on tickets held in his name. Since receipt and retention of sweepstakes winnings voluntarily paid by the Irish promoter violates no Irish or Michigan statute or rule of law, a promise to share amounts so received constitutes legal consideration. A contract based on the exchange of legal consideration is a legal contract, and its enforcement does not violate public policy.

Agreements to share possible proceeds from Irish Sweepstakes tickets are not an "essential part" of the sale and distribution of those tickets. The continued success of the Irish Sweepstakes in this state is in no way dependant on the enforceability of agreements to share winnings. Miller's and Radikopf's collateral agreement to divide their prospective winnings was not an essential part of their sale and distribution of those tickets. Nor was their agreement dependant on illegal conduct in the acquisition of the lottery tickets; they might have acquired the tickets in a manner free of any suggestion of illegality and then entered into an agreement to share proceeds.

However this case is decided, the courts of this state will continue to refuse to entertain action seeking an accounting of proceeds obtained from illegal enterprises such as the illegal sale of narcotics and bank robberies. Additionally, enforcement or an accounting will be denied, without regard to whether the proceeds sought to be divided have been legally obtained, if the consideration offered is illegal.

The judicial nonenforcement of agreements deemed against public policy is considered a deterrent for those who might otherwise become involved in such transactions. While nonenforcement of Miller's claim might tend to discourage people from agreeing to split their legal winnings, nonenforcement would not tend to discourage people from buying or selling Irish Sweepstakes tickets. Both Miller and Radikopf have been compensated for selling the tickets, and Radikopf has received the winnings as the holder of a particular ticket. No interest of the state would be furthered by nonenforcement of Miller's claim that he is the owner of one-half of those legal winnings.

It is consonant with the public policy of this state to encourage performance of legal contracts and to foster the just resolution of disputes. Nonenforcement of the agreement claimed by Miller would not tend to discourage the sale of Irish Sweepstakes tickets. It could reward, without any corresponding benefit, promissory default. We conclude that public policy would not be offended by enforcement of the claimed agreement.

LAMONT BDG. CO. v. COURT
70 N.E.2d 447 (Ohio, 1946)

On February 19, 1945, the plaintiff rented to the defendant, on a month-to-month basis, an apartment in a building in the city of Cleveland. At the time, the defendant was advised that the month's rent receipt given the defendant was the notation "Specific rental rule—No pets—adults only."

The defendant and his wife moved into the apartment. The wife was then pregnant, which fact was not known to the plaintiff. In the course of a few months a child was born to the defendant's wife and came to live in the apartment with its parents.

Thereafter, the plaintiff gave written notice to the defendant that he must arrange for the occupancy of the apartment by adults only or vacate. The defendant did not comply with the notice, and an action in forcible entry and detainer was brought in the municipal court of the city of Cleveland. Trial before the court and a jury resulted in a verdict for the defendant, upon which judgment was entered.

The plaintiff thereupon took its appeal to the court of appeals on questions of law. That court affirmed the judgment below on the ground that the plaintiff's rule against permitting children to occupy its premise was against public policy and void.

In its material aspects, the evidence was undisputed. The Office of Price Administration of the national government made no appearance in the proceedings. The plaintiff gave as the reasons for its rule against allowing children to occupy its premises that the partition walls inside the building were thin and that the premises lacked facilities for and were unadapted to the proper accommodation of children.)

Zimmerman, Judge

As succinctly stated in 12 American Jurisprudence 641, Section 149:

"It is the inherent and inalienable right of every man freely to deal or refuse to deal with his fellow man. Competent persons ordinarily have the utmost liberty of contracting, and their agreements voluntarily and fairly made will be held valid and enforced in the courts. Parties may incorporate in their agreements any provisions that are not illegal or violative of public policy."

Ordinarily, the owner of real property may surround its occupation and use by others with such reasonable restrictions as he may deem fit and proper. Here, plaintiff was in the control of the apartment building. Defendant rented an apartment and moved into it with knowledge of the condition that its occupancy was to be solely by adults. In bringing a child to dwell in the apartment against plaintiff's stipulation to the contrary, the defendant breached a material part of the agreement.

We know of no constitutional provision, statutory enactment, or decision by this court denying plaintiff the privilege of imposing a condition of the kind involved here. Nor can we conceive that such a condition may be classed as injurious to the public or in contravention of any established interest of society. Although we are aware that a temporary housing shortage exists in this state, the argument that plaintiff's rule against permitting children to live in its property would encourage race suicide is hardly tenable.

At best, "public policy" is an uncertain and indefinite term. When judges come to apply the doctrine, they must take care not to infringe on the rights of parties to make contracts which are not clearly opposed to some principle or policy of the law. Notwithstanding we may be sympathetic toward the defendant and his problem of securing living accommodations for himself and his family, we cannot allow that sympathy to prevail over plaintiff's legal rights.

Plaintiff did not say to the defendant, "You cannot have children"; it said, merely, "If you do have children, they may not occupy my premises."

In summation, plaintiff and the defendant agreed on the terms and conditions under which defendant would become plaintiff's tenant. Defendant became a tenant upon the conditions prescribed and exercised his privilege of having a child. When defendant brought such child to live in plaintiff's property, he plainly violated an important feature of the rental agreement, which gave plaintiff the option of reclaiming the apartment by an action in forcible entry and detainer.

Consequently, the judgment of the Court of Appeals is reversed and final judgment is entered for the plaintiff.

Judgment reversed.

PROBLEMS FOR DISCUSSION

1. R. E. Fuse operates a garbage collection service in the towns of Cleen and Teidy. In June 1974 he made an oral agreement with Wesley Trashy to hire him as a garbage truck driver. In November R.E. Fuse handed Wesley a written document which stated that, upon severance of employment, Trashy would not engage in garbage collection within 15 miles of Cleen and Teidy for a period of 5 years. Trashy, who knew that his signature on the document was a precondition for continued employment, signed the agreement. In September 1975 Wesley Trashy quit his job and immediately went into the garbage collection business for himself. R.E. Fuse now brings an action against Trashy for breach of contract. What decision? Why?

2. Mr. and Mrs. Molly are the sole shareholders of Crossroads, Inc., which owns a restaurant with an adjacent parking lot and several acres nearby. In July 1969 the corporation sold the restaurant business to Ulcers, Inc., and in a separate agreement leased the restaurant building and the parking lot to the same corporation for 20 years. The original lease stated that during the term of the lease neither Crossroads, Inc., nor the Mollys "shall have an interest in a restaurant business within a radius of 10 miles. . . . or lease or sell any facility or land to any other restaurant." Closing of the lease was delayed for several months. The final lease agreement between the two corporations, which incidentally was not signed by Mr. and Mrs. Molly individually, read: "or lease or sell any facility to any other restaurant."

   A few years later the Mollys negotiated the sale of the nearby land to Developers Realty. Developers was an association of two parties, one of which was an agent for a national motel-restaurant chain. Now Ulcers, Inc., sues the Mollys for breach of contract and seeks an injunction to prevent sale. Who wins? Why?

3. Perry and Gerry Gray of Galesburg, father and son, were arrested by Sergeant Tough for disorderly conduct. In the course of the arrest, Sergeant Tough inflicted unnecessary damages to the Grays' property and the Grays threatened him and the city of Galesburg with a suit. At the trial the Grays were asked to sign a release of the city and the police officer from any claims in return for a dismissal of their charge of disorderly conduct. Discuss the legality of this contract.

4. Worgess Agency, a successful insurance broker, bought out Elmer Lane, Inc., another insurance agency in the town of Norisk, Michigan, and hired Elmer Lane as its solicitor. The sales agreement contained a clause forbidding the seller to engage in the insurance business for five years from the date of sale in the city and within a radius of 50 miles.

   After seven years Elmer Lane left Worgess Agency and became an agent for Auto-Owners Insurance Company, one of the companies which Worgess represented. With the help of the Auto-Owners files, Elmer was able to contact the customers he had served at Worgess and establish himself again as a successful agent. At that time he was still receiving payments from Worgess on the sale of the agency.

   Who would win if Worgess sued Elmer for breach of contract? Under what theory can Worgess sue Auto-Owners?

5. One afternoon, Collamer and Day were talking in Collamer's office when a large, expensive luxury car drove by the front window. Day asked: "Whose car is that?" Collamer replied: "It's Dr. Denison's." Day said: "No, I'm sure it's not; I know Dr. Denison's car. I'll bet my watch against yours that it's not Denison's." Collamer agreed, and each party took off his watch and laid it on Collamer's desk. They then telephoned Dr. Denison's office and learned that the car was not Dr. Denison's. At that point Day picked up his watch and left the office. Collamer sues for possession of the watch. What result, and why?

6. On the evening of December 31, Joel Jones held a party and dance at his home. Rice and several other uninvited persons attempted to crash the party, and there was a small riot. The police were called, and criminal charges were filed against Rice and his friends. Later Jones and the other guests who were injured in the riot agreed that if Rice would pay $1,800 to them, including $500 for their actual injuries, they would drop all criminal charges. Rice promised to pay the $1,800, and Jones and his friends caused all criminal charges to be dropped. Rice has now refused to pay the $1,800, and Jones sues to collect. What result, and why?

7. After some lengthy negotiations, Hammermill Paper Company agreed to appoint Nashua River Supply Company as its exclusive sales agent for the state of Massachusetts. A comprehensive written contract was drafted and executed. One provision of the contract read as follows: "no action at law or in equity shall be instituted or maintained by Nashua in any court of any State of the United States, or in any United States Districe Court, or elsewhere, against Hammermill, other than in the state courts of Pennsylvania." Disputes arose over the terms of the agency agreement, and Nashua sued in Massachusetts. Hammermill asks the Massachusetts court to dismiss the case, based on the above-quoted contract clause. What result, and why?

8. Henry Van Riper promised May Wood, his executive secretary, that he would pay her $5,000 if she refrained from marrying until after his death and stayed in his employ, "attending to and caring for the wants of said Henry Van Riper until his death." Henry executed a promissory note to this effect, payable 30 days after his death. May fulfilled her part of the bargain; Henry died; and May now sues to collect on the note. Henry's executor claims that the agreement is against public policy. What result, and why?

Assignment and Third-Party Beneficiary Contracts | 11

The problems discussed in this chapter are quite different from any we have considered so far. Here our basic question is whether persons other than the parties who actually negotiated and agreed to the contract should be given the right to demand performance under it. The answer given by the early common law was simple: No! Today, however, courts do recognize the rights of these "strangers"—both assignees and third-party beneficiaries—at least in some situations and subject to many complicated and technical limitations.

THIRD-PARTY BENEFICIARY CONTRACTS

Basic Concepts and Definitions. A third-party beneficiary contract is one in which at least one of the performances called for is intended for the direct benefit of a person or persons other than the parties who actually made the contract. A donee beneficiary is one who is receiving this benefit as a gift, without any duty on anyone's part to provide him with the benefit. In most cases persons named as the beneficiaries in life insurance policies are donees. A creditor beneficiary is one to whom the benefit is actually owed, as a result of a prior legal relationship. If creditors have sold or financed purchases of such items as cars, appliances, or real estate to buyers who resell the as-yet-unpaid-for items to purchasers who agree to take over the payments, the creditors are third-party creditor beneficiaries of the take-over-the-payments contracts.

The Uniform Commercial Code does not deal with third-party beneficiaries in any comprehensive way. It does, however, contain one very important third-party provision 2–318, which provides that whatever warranties are made by a seller of goods are also by law extended to members of the buyer's family and household and to guests in the buyer's home. The section further provides that its effect cannot be limited by any contrary agreement between the seller and the buyer.

Incidental Beneficiaries. Many courts are still quite reluctant to permit "non-participant" third parties to enforce contracts which they had no part in making and will therefore demand clear proof of an intent to benefit a third party. Incidental beneficiaries are persons who derive some indirect benefit from a contract but cannot show such an intent on the part of the contracting parties; such persons have no right to sue to enforce the contract.

It is not necessary that the third party be specifically named or indentified at the time the contract is made. A shopkeeper-tenant was held to have enforceable rights against a contractor who had promised the owner-landlord that the remodeling job would be done "in such a way as to cause a minimum of disturbance to the daytime operations in the building." The following case does show, however, that courts look very carefully for the contracting parties' intent.

Winnebago Homes, Inc. v. Sheldon
139 N.W.2d 606 (Wisconsin, 1966)

FACTS "A contract for the construction of a home for the price of $15,900 was entered into between the plaintiff and Richard and Kathleen Sheldon on April 22, 1961. The plaintiff brought the Sheldons to Advance Mortgage Corporation to obtain a mortgage loan for $15,200 to finance the home construction. Such loan was to be 'insured' by the Federal Housing Administration (FHA).

"The plaintiff received a letter from Advance Mortgage on June 26, 1961, informing the plaintiff that the FHA had issued its firm commitment regarding the mortgage loan in question. John Vishnevsky, plaintiff's president, testified that he understood the term 'firm commitment' to mean that the FHA would insure the loan without the necessity of performing any further conditions. He stated that he relied on this letter to begin the construction of the home and that no work had been commenced prior to the receipt of the letter. . . .

"The note and mortgage were executed on FHA forms and recorded by Advance Mortgage, and the money was allocated to the Sheldon construction project. The Sheldons moved into the substantially completed home in January, 1962.

"At the Sheldons' direction Advance Mortgage paid to the plaintiff the sum of $8,289.75 representing compensation for work completed on the home as of December 18, 1961. The plaintiff continued construction and requested progress draws but was informed by Advance Mortgage that the latter's new policy was to make a final payment only upon completion of the building.

"Mr. Vishnevsky testified that in the spring of 1962 he was informed by Advance Mortgage that full payment would not be made until final clearance from FHA was obtained. He stated that this conversation led him to understand that the balance of the moneys loaned would be available once the FHA clearance was obtained.

"The FHA certificate of final inspection was obtained on August 1, 1962, whereupon the plaintiff made demand upon Advance Mortgage for final payment. Advance Mortgage refused on the grounds that the Sheldons were eight months behind in their mortgage payments.

"A meeting was held on October 27, 1962, between the Sheldons, Advance Mortgage, and the plaintiff for the purpose of closing the transaction. Mr. Robert Koch, the attorney for Advance Mortgage, was authorized to disburse the balance of the loan proceeds upon compliance with all the FHA requirements by both the Sheldons and the plaintiff.

"At the closing conference, it was determined that the Sheldons would have to provide $1,400 in addition to the loan proceeds in order to pay the plaintiff the full amount due on the construction contract. The Sheldons refused to pay any amount of money, claiming that the building was improperly constructed. They asked for setoffs, and they specifically refused to authorize any further payments to the plaintiff." The Sheldons subsequently went through bankruptcy and were not involved in this appeal.

ISSUE   Is the builder a third-party beneficiary of the loan contract?

DECISION   No. Judgment for defendant. The court rejected all three of Winnebago's arguments—third-party beneficiary, promissory estoppel, and garnishment.

REASONS   "There was no promise, either express or implied, that Advance Mortgage was to pay the amount of the loan to Winnebago Homes even if the Sheldons were in default or even if FHA insurance was never issued. The lender's commitment to supply the money to the Sheldons was circumscribed with numerous conditions. In order to entitle a stranger to a contract to recover thereon, the contract must indicate an intention to secure some benefit to such third party.

"Our examination of the relevant instruments pursuades us that there was no contract wherein Advance Mortgage agreed to do anything for the benefit of Winnebago Homes. While the latter may have indirectly benefited from the agreement, such benefit was only incidental to the agreement between the mortgagor and the mortgagee. However, even if an express promise to pay Winnebago Homes could be spelled out of these instruments, we see no reason why it would not be subject to the same conditions that existed between the principals to the agreement. Thus, if Advance Mortgage did not have to pay the moneys to the Sheldons because FHA insurance was not obtained, this condition would preclude any responsibility by Advance Mortgage to Winnebago Homes. In *Watkins* v. *Watkins* . . . this court stated:

> It has been repeatedly held by this court, however, that when a right has been created by contract, the third party claiming the benefit of the contract takes the right subject to all the terms and conditions of the contract creating the right."

Mutual Rescission of the Contract.   Generally, the parties to a contract can agree to call off the deal anytime they want to. The problem is complicated by the presence of a third-party beneficiary: Must the original contracting parties also get his or her consent to the rescission?

In answering this question, the *Restatement* distinguishes between the donee beneficiary and the creditor beneficiary. In the case of the donee beneficiary, the gift is considered to be complete and therefore nonrescindable when the contract is made. Thus the parties to a life insurance contract, for example, cannot rescind the gift by agreeing to a change of beneficiaries unless the right to change beneficiaries has been reserved. On the other hand, where a creditor beneficiary is involved, the contract can be rescinded at any time before he or she learns of it or acts in reliance on it unless the rescission amounts to a fraud on the creditor.

237

ASSIGNMENT OF CONTRACT RIGHTS

Basic Concepts and Definitions. *Assignment* simply means transfer; the "owner" of the right to receive benefits under a contract is simply transferring this right to someone else. The transfer may itself be part of a second contract (as it usually is), or it may be made as a gift. No special language is required for an effective assignment; any manifestation of an intent to make such a transfer is sufficient. Some states require all assignments to be in writing to be enforceable; others do not. For the kinds of assignments it covers (9–102[1][b], 9–104[f], 9–106), Article 9 of the UCC requires assignments to be in writing.

Assignability of a Right. As noted above, the common law emphasized freedom of contract; no one should be required to deal with another unless he or she had in fact agreed to do so. Contract prohibitions against assignment were given full force and effect. An obligor (the person who had a duty to perform) could in effect veto an assignment by refusing to perform for the new obligee. Although the validity of transfers of contract rights is now generally recognized and such assignments provide the mechanism for financing a large part of modern business, there are still many technical legal rules on this subject. The *Talco* (discussion) case illustrates both the modern general rule and some of these complexities.

One of the first distinctions which must be drawn is the difference between assigning a right and delegating a duty. Duties can never be assigned, only delegated, the difference being that someone who delegates his or her own duty of performance to another remains personally responsible for its proper and timely performance. In our example above, if the repurchaser of the stereo in the take-over-the-payments deal does not make the payments as promised, the original buyer remains personally liable and can be sued by the original seller. Where a right has been validly assigned, however, the assignee completely displaces the original owner of the right, to whom performance was due. However, the original debtor is free of liability for a delegated duty only if the original obligee (creditor) agrees to the substitution of the new obligor (debtor) in place of the original one and agrees to discharge the original one. Without the obligee's consent, the performance of a duty cannot even be delegated to another person if the duty involves an individualized service or if there is a particular reason for dealing with one certain person.

As to whether rights are assignable or not, contracts must be grouped into three categories. First, there are contracts whose rights are not assignable unless the obligor specifically agrees to the assignment. This category includes contracts involving some personal element such as the personal service of the obligor or the personal credit or requirements of the obligee, and contracts where the performance of the duty would be materially changed if the assignment were recognized. The UCC adopts this same basic approach for sales of goods in Section 2–210(2).

Probably the vast majority of contracts fall into the second category, in which the rights are assignable unless there is a specific contract prohibition against assignment. In most cases, in other words, contract rights for such things as land, securities, or goods would be presumed to be transferable to others unless the parties had specifically agreed otherwise. Section 2–210(3) of the UCC says that in order to prohibit assignment of the right to receive goods, a contract clause must very clearly specify that result; a general prohibition of "the contract" is only effective to prohibit a delegation of duties. The validity of a "no assignment" clause is at issue in the following case.

National Lumber Company v. Goodman
123 N.W.2d 147 (Michigan, 1963)

FACTS   "On January 18, 1956, defendant Goodman contracted to sell, by land contract, 101 lots in Venetian Village subdivision, Macomb county, Michigan, to Elliott-Jared Investment Company. Elliott-Jared was one of a group of companies owned and controlled by Elliott Schubiner. The contract contained the following provision:

> No assignment or conveyance by the purchaser shall create any liability whatsoever against the seller until a duplicate thereof, duly witnessed and acknowledged, together with the residence address of such assignee, shall be delivered to and accepted by the seller, and receipt thereof indorsed thereon.

"In September 1958, three of the building corporations controlled by Schubiner executed notes and mortgages on five lots to plaintiff Rocform Corporation to secure indebtedness owed Rocform for materials supplied for the construction of houses in the subdivision.

"In March 1960, two of his building corporations executed notes and mortgages to plaintiff National Lumber Company covering three other lots.

"At no time prior to the expiration date of the land contract were duplicates of these mortgages or assignments presented to the vendor in accordance with the applicable provision of the contract. . . .

"By December 1, 1960, one month before the expiration of the contract, there existed on the eight lots in question houses in various stages of construction. In order to protect their interest plaintiffs entered into negotiations with defendant Goodman. Plaintiffs offered to pay Goodman whatever moneys were due and owing under the release provisions of the contract with respect to the eight lots upon which they held mortgages. Goodman refused to deal with the corporations, but did offer to extend the contract for 1 year or 1½ years upon payment of accrued interest and back taxes on the entire contract if plaintiffs could reach some agreement with Elliott Schubiner. Plaintiffs were unable to do this. Mr. Schubiner, on behalf of Elliott-Jared, refused to become a party to any agreement unless he was paid. The amount demanded varied throughout the negotiations from $7,000 to $15,000. No agreement was reached. Plaintiffs did not make a formal tender of the amount necessary to release the eight lots. However, the trial court found as a fact plaintiffs made their offer to pay and the offer was refused by Goodman.

"After January 1, 1961, when the entire contract balance became due, defendant Goodman instituted foreclosure action in the form of summary proceedings. On May 8, 1961, Goodman obtained judgment in the total sum of $102,383.25. Elliott-Jared Investment Company and the affiliated building corporations were subsequently adjudicated as bankrupts. This suit was instituted August 13, 1961, some weeks before the expiration of the redemption period, in an attempt to stop the foreclosure proceedings and to have National and Rocform substituted as the buyers of the eight lots in question."

National Lumber Company v. Goodman (continued)

ISSUE   Are plaintiff corporations entitled to enforce their assignments?

DECISION   No. Judgment dismissing complaints is affirmed.

REASONS   (Opinion by Justice Kavanagh.) "A similar provision to the one present in this land contract restricting alienation has been held by this Court not to be invalid because of being in restraint of alienation, since it does not bar assignment of the contract but merely is an agreement between the contracting parties as to the method in which an assignment or conveyance must be made to affect the rights of the vendor. . . .

"It is not disputed that at the time the negotiations took place between plaintiffs and defendant Goodman, the vendee, Elliott-Jared Investment Company, had the right to a release of any or all of the remaining lots upon payment of the same amounts offered by plaintiffs. Defendant Goodman testified he had a legal obligation to convey upon payment by Elliott-Jared Investment Company of such sums.

"Plaintiffs contend that as mortgages of a vendee's interest under a land contract, they have the right to step in the shoes of their mortgagor and exercise the right to obtain a release of the eight lots in order to protect their interest. Accepting, *arguendo*, this basic contention, plaintiffs face a second hurdle, namely, whether their offer of payment is a sufficient basis for granting equitable relief, even though they breached the contract provisions requiring presentation and indorsement of the conveyance. Authority exists for such a rule where the assignee of the vendee has acquired the full interest of the vendee and tenders full payment of the contract price.

"The record in the instant case discloses there were several extensions and modifications of the contract, which were obviously concessions to the vendee to enable it to perform. This, together with the provisions relating to presentation and indorsement of an assignment or conveyance, indicates the contract was of a personal nature.

"The law recognizes the right of a person to choose those with whom he would contract. It would appear for reasons best known to himself, perhaps because of the promotional ability of Elliott Schubiner, that defendant Goodman was willing to grant personal extensions and release lots to him, fully confident that he would be able to perform the remainder of the contract.

"'We conclude that this personal element, which in no way affected the assignability of the contract, prevented any equities arising that would interfere with the vendor's right to insist upon strict compliance with the contract terms."

The third group of contracts results from the Code's effort to make sure that businesses will be able to use their accounts as financing collateral without having to get each account debtor's consent. Section 9–318(4) says that even if the contract specifically prohibits assignment of the right to receive payment for goods sold or leased or services performed, the creditor can go ahead and assign the account anyway, without the debtor's consent; the contract provision will not be enforced. (When you buy your new TV on time, even getting a specific clause written into your contract will not enable you to avoid dealing with a finance company if the dealer wants to assign your contract.)

As a rule, present assignments of future rights are fully effective; that is, one can effectively transfer ownership now of the right, under an existing contract, to receive a performance at some future date. However, any purported assignment of rights under a contract which does not exist yet, but is merely anticipated, is totally void. An unemployed person has not made an effective assignment when he signs a contract with an employment agency by which he purports to assign one third of his first month's wages to the agency when it gets him a new job. In addition, most states have specific regulatory statutes covering wage assignments and limiting the percentage share that can be assigned.

Warranties of Assignor to Assignee. Where a contract right has been transferred for value, the *Restatement* says that the assignor makes three warranties to his assignee: (1) that he will do nothing to defeat or impair the value of the assignment; (2) that the right, as assigned, actually exists and is subject to no limitations of defenses except those stated or apparent; and (3) that any token, writing, etc., given or shown to the assignee as evidence of the right is genuine and what it purports to be. In addition, the seller/assignor of the right can be sued for breach of warranty and/or fraud for any express misstatements he made (for example, that he had made a credit check on the buyer/obligor or that the buyer/obligor had a steady job). Note that there is no implied guarantee that the buyer/obligor will in fact perform. In most cases where accounts receivable are being assigned on a regular basis (a GM dealer to GMAC, for example), the assignment agreement itself will specify the conditions under which the assignee can force the assignor to refund money paid for accounts that prove to be uncollectible.

Delegation of Duty to Assignee. Courts are not agreed as to whether, in taking the assignment, an assignee is also impliedly agreeing to perform any remaining duties owed by his assignor to the other original party. Most of the older cases say that no such promise is implied; many of the newer ones have adopted a contrary rule. In any event, all of the surrounding facts and circumstances, and especially the language of the assignment itself, will be examined to see whether such a promise should be implied. The simplest solution to this problem is to specify the result desired in the assignment itself.

For the sale of goods, the Code adopts the view of the newer cases, so that an acceptance by the assignee of a general assignment is also his promise to perform all of his assignor's remaining duties, unless the language of the assignment or the circumstances indicate otherwise.

The significance of such a promise by the assignee is that nonperformance of the reciprocal duty gives (or may give) the other party an excuse for withholding his required performance or even a basis for bringing his own lawsuit against the assignee for breach of contract.

Notice to Obligor. All courts agree that, as between the assignor and the assignee, the assignment is effective when it is made, even though notice of the assignment has not been communicated to the obligor. However, notice (or its absence) does have some important legal consequences. Payment or other performance that the obligor gives to the assignor before receiving notice that the obligation has been assigned and that the performance should now be made to the assignee, completely discharges that part of the original contract obligation. The assignee cannot sue the obligor and force a repeat performance but instead would have to sue his assignor. Similarly, the obligor can assert defenses or counterclaims against the assignee even on totally unrelated transactions between the obligor and the assignor if such claims arose before the obligor received notice of the assignment. For example: Dull buys a used car and a new car from Sharpie. Dull pays cash for the used car and finances the new car. Sharpie assigns the financing contract on the new car to the Bigger Bank. Until Dull gets notice of this assignment he can use as a defense against paying the balance due not only any defects in the new car but also any defects in the used car. Once Dull gets notice of the assignment of his new-car contract to Bigger he can use only defects in the new car as his reason for nonpayment; after notice has been received, any problems with the used car will have to be taken up separately with Sharpie.

Notice is also significant in working out the problems which arise when the assignor has made more than one assignment of the same right. Although this should not occur and the assignor is clearly liable for breach of his implied warranties to both assignees, the situation does arise and rules have been developed to deal with it. To a retailer or a construction firm caught in a temporary cash flow squeeze, a "temporary" double assignment of the accounts receivable looks like a painless solution, with no one ever being the wiser; too often, however, the optimism is not justified and the double financing is discovered in a bankruptcy proceeding. The problem, then, is that there is only one sum of money to be paid and there are two assignee-claimants. Which one should be paid first?

The states do not agree on the answer to this question. In the states which follow the "English" rule (probably still the minority), the assignee who first gives notice to the obligor is entitled to priority of payment. In the states which follow the "American" rule, the first assignment in point of time is given priority, but subject to several exceptions where notice has not been given. Even in an American-rule state, therefore, it is important to give notice to the obligor immediately, so that he does not perform for some subsequent assignee.

Boulevard National Bank of Miami v. *Air Metals Industries, Inc.*
176 So.2d 94 (Florida, 1965)

FACTS "Tompkins-Beckwith was the contractor on a construction project which had entered into a subcontract with a division of Air Metal Industries, Inc. Air Metal procured American Fire and Casualty Company to be surety on certain bonds in connection with contracts it was performing for Tompkins-Beckwith and others. As security for such bonds, Air Metal executed, on January 3, 1962, a 'contractor's General Agreement of Indemnity' which contains an assignment to American Fire of 'all monthly, final or other estimates and retained percentages; pertaining to or arising out of or in connection with any contracts performed or being performed or to be performed, such assignment to be in full force and effect as of the date hereof, in the event of default in the performance of any contract as to which the surety has issued, or shall issue, any [surety bonds or undertakings].'

"On November 26, 1962, the petitioner bank lent money to Air Metal and to secure the loans Air Metal purported to assign to the bank certain accounts receivable it had with Tompkins-Beckwith which arose out of subcontracts being done for that contractor.

"In June, 1963, Air Metal defaulted on various contracts bonded by American Fire. On July 1, 1963, American Fire served formal notice on Tompkins-Beckwith of Air Metal's assignment. Tompkins-Beckwith acknowledged the assignment and agreed to pay. On August 12, 1963, the petitioner bank notified Tompkins-Beckwith of its assignment and claim thereunder. The claim was not recognized, and on September 26, 1963, this action was filed in the trial court. On October 9, 1963, Tomplins-Beckwith paid all remaining funds which had accrued to Air Metal to American Fire." The bank's claim that it should have received the money was rejected by the lower courts.

ISSUE   Which assignee is entitled to priority?

DECISION   American Fire, which gave notice first. Judgment affirmed.

REASONS   "The 'Question' which was passed upon by the certifying court is whether the law of Florida requires recognition of the so-called English rule or American rule of priority between assignees of successive assignments of an account receivable or other similar chose in action. Stated in its simplest form, the American rule would give priority to the assignee first in point of time of assignment, while the English rule would give preference to the assignment of which the debtor was first given notice. Both rules presuppose the absence of any estoppel or other special equities in favor of or against either assignee. The English rule giving priority to the assignee first giving notice to the debtor is specifically qualified as applying 'unless he takes a later assignment with notice of a previous one or without a valuable consideration.' The American rule giving the first assignee in point of time the preference is applicable only when the equities are equal between the contending assignees, and if a subsequent assignee has a stronger equity than an earlier one, he would prevail.

"In the case here there are no special equities and no rights, such as subrogation, which would arise outside of the assignments. Also we regard that any conditions precedent to the assignments, which the parties have expressly or impliedly stipulated, have occurred. In this posture, we are thus free to adjudicate which of these two rules, described as being 'clearly defined and irreconcilable,' is in harmony with out jurisprudence.

"The American rule for which petitioner contends is based upon the reasoning that an account or other chose in action may be assigned at will by the owner; that the notice to the debtor is not essential to complete the assignment; and that when such assignment is made, the property rights become vested in the assignee so that the assignor no longer has any interest in the account or chose which he may subsequently assign to another.

"It is undoubted that the creditor of an account receivable or other similar chose in action arising out of contract may assign it to another so that the assignee may sue on it in his own name and make recovery. Formal requisites of such an assignment are not prescribed by statute, and it may be accomplished by parol, by instrument in writing, or other mode, such as delivery of evidences of the debt, as may demonstrate an intent to transfer and an acceptance of it. . . .

"It seems to be generally agreed that notice to a debtor of an assignment is necessary to impose on the debtor the duty of payment to the assignee, and that if before receiving such notice he pays the debt to the assignor, or to a subsequent assignee, he will be discharged from the debt. . . . It would seem to follow that the mere private dealing between the creditor and his assignee unaccompanied by any manifestations discernable to others having or considering the acquiring of an interest in the account would not meet the requirement of delivery and acceptance of possession which is essential to the consummation of the assignment. Proper notice to the debtor of the assignment is a manifestation of such delivery. It fixes the accountability of the debtor to the assignee instead of the assignor and enables all involved to deal more safely. . . .

"We thus find that the so-called English rule which the trial and appellant court approved and applied is harmonious with our jurisprudence, whereas the so-called American rule is not."

The Code will be of some help in dealing with this problem, since Article 9 covers most assignments for value as "secured transactions" and generally requires the public filing of a notice that such financing arrangements are in force in order for them to be effective against third parties. Where such a filing is required by Article 9 and has not yet occurred, a subsequent assignee of the accounts who gave value for them, had no knowledge of the first assignment, and filed its own public notice would be entitled to priority. It is therefore important for the first assignee to file the required public notice as well as to notify the obligor.

Availability of Defenses against Assignee. As it began to recognize the validity of assignments, the common law developed a rule which said that the assignee took the assigned contract right subject to all claims and defenses which the obligor could assert against the assignor. The assignee stepped into the assignor's legal shoes, and the shoes didn't get any bigger just because someone else was wearing them. While the assignee could at least cut off the obligor's claims on unrelated transactions by getting notice to him or her, there was no way that the assignee could stand in any better enforcement position than his or her assignor with respect to the assigned contract itself.

Obviously, a promise to pay money or render some other performance is rendered much more uncertain, and therefore much less valuable, if it is subject to all sorts of unknown contingencies. To deal with this problem, the merchant community developed the "negotiable instrument," which is basically just a written promise to pay money stated in a particular way. The law merchant said that if a promise to pay money was in negotiable form and was properly transferred to a good faith purchaser, then the debtor would not be able to assert most voidable-type defenses against the transferee. This was a "negotiation," not just an assignment. Where the buyer-debtor had signed a negotiable promissory note for his or her 100 bushels of wheat which the seller had never delivered, the buyer would have to pay the amount of the note to the bank or finance company to which the note had been sold and then bring his or her own lawsuit for breach of contract against the seller. Article 9 of the code permitted the parties to work out this same basic result without using a negotiable instrument, by simply placing a provision to that effect (a waiver-of-defenses clause) in the contract itself.

These two "exceptions"—the negotiable instrument and the waiver-of-defenses clause—came into such widespread and common use that they all but swallowed up the general rule. The result was that many, many buyers had to pay for a "dead horse"—the undelivered wheat, the fraudulently represented car, the unperformed services. As a result of the consumer movement of the 1960s and 1970s, first some of the states and then the FTC adopted rules which invalidated both of these devices in consumer contracts. As the law stands today, these devices are available only where the debtor is a business or other "nonconsumer." One important "loophole" does remain, however: where the consumer goes to the financing agency and makes his or her own loan, and *then* gives the cash to the seller, the dead horse result still occurs. Legislation is being considered to close this loophole.

The following case illustrates the old dead horse result, since it occurred before the FTC rule took effect and before the state had any consumer protection law of its own.

Jennings v. Universal C.I.T. Credit Corporation
442 S.W.2d 565 (Kentucky, 1969)

FACTS   "O. G. Jennings purchased an automobile from Scott-McGaw Motor Company under a conditional sales contract which was assigned to Universal C.I.T. Credit Corporation. Jennings apparently defaulted in making his payments, and Universal repossessed and sold the automobile. However, when the automobile was sold it did not bring a sufficient amount to pay the balance due under the contract.

"Universal filed this action against appellant to collect the deficiency, alleging that $1,119.26 was due under the contract. Jennings admitted that he executed the contract with Scott-McGaw Motor Company and that the contract was assigned to Universal, but he denied that he had defaulted in making his payments and that there was $1,119.26, or any sum, due Universal. Jennings, by counterclaim, alleged that, although the contract he entered into with Scott-McGaw Motor Company provided delivery of a new automobile, it delivered to him a used automobile. Jennings sought to recover damages in the sum of $500.

"Universal's motion to dismiss the counterclaim was sustained on the ground that the counterclaim failed to state a claim against them. Universals's motion for summary judgment was also sustained." Jennings appealed.

ISSUE   Can Jennings assert his fraud defense against C.I.T.?

DECISION   No. Judgment reversed and remanded on the second issue.

REASONS   The court first upheld the validity of the waiver-of-defenses clause in the contract, which stated:

> If Seller assigns this contract, Seller shall not be assignee's agent for transmission of payments or for any purpose; Customer will settle, directly with Seller, all claims, defenses, set-offs and counterclaims there may be against Seller, and not set up any thereof against assignee. Upon full payment of Customer's obligation, assignee may deliver all original papers, including any certificate of title, to Seller as Customer's agent.

The court referred to UCC 9–206(1): "This provision was apparently inserted into the subject contract pursuant to KRS 355.9–206(1). . . .

"The validity of this statutory provision authorizing the inclusion of waiver of defense clause in commercial contracts has been upheld. In the instant case the waiver of defense clause constitutes a complete defense to appellant's claim because appellee took the assignment for value, in good faith, and without notice of a claim or defense to the debt. In these circumstances appellee was entitled to recover against appellant the amount owing under the assigned contract, independently of any claim to damages appellant may have against Scott-McGaw Motor Company for its alleged breach of its contract."

The court stated, however, that while Jennings could not assert his fraud defense, he was entitled to a hearing to determine whether he did default and, if so, how much he still owed Universal.

CASES FOR DISCUSSION

MOCH CO. v. RENSSELAER WATER CO.

159 N.E. 896 (New York, 1928)

Cardozo, Chief Justice

The defendant, a water works company under the law of this State, made a contract with the city of Rensselaer for the supply of water during a term of years. Water was to be furnished to the city for sewer flushing and street sprinkling; for service to schools and public buildings; and for service at fire hydrants, the latter service at the rate of $42.50 a year for each hydrant. Water was to be furnished to private takers within the city at their homes and factories and other industries at reasonable rates, not exceeding a stated schedule. While this contract was in force, a building caught fire. The flames, spreading to the plaintiff's warehouse near by, destroyed it and its contents. [The firemen were there and could have put out the fire, but there was no water at the hydrant.] By reason of the failure of the defendant to "fulfill the provisions of the contract between it and the city of Rensselaer," the plaintiff is said to have suffered damage, for which judgment is demanded. A motion, in the nature of a demurrer, to dismiss the complaint, was denied at Special Term. The Appellate Division reversed by a divided court.

(1) We think the action is not maintainable as one for breach of contract.

No legal duty rests upon a city to supply its inhabitants with protection against fire. That being so, a member of the public may not maintain an action under *Lawrence* v. *Fox* against one contracting with the city to furnish water at the hydrants, unless an intention appears that the promisor is to be answerable to individual members of the public as well as to the city for any loss ensuing from the failure to fulfill the promise. No such intention is discernible here. On the contrary, the contract is significantly divided into two branches: one a promise to the city for the benefit of the city in its corporate capacity, in which branch is included the service at the hydrants; and the other promise to the city for the benefit of private takers, in which branch is included the service at their homes and factories. In a broad sense it is true that every city contract, not improvident or wasteful, is for the benefit of the public. More than this, however, must be shown to give a right of action to a member of the public not formally a party. The benefit, as it is sometimes said, must be one that is not merely incidental and secondary. It must be primary and immediate in such a sense and to such a degree as to bespeak the assumption of a duty to make reparation directly to the individual members of the public if the benefit is lost. The field of obligation would be expanded beyond reasonable limits if less than this were to be demanded as a condition of liability. A promisor undertakes to supply fuel for heating a public building. He is not liable for breach of contract to a visitor who finds the building without fuel, and thus contracts a cold. The list of illustrations can be indefinitely extended. The carrier of the mails under contract with the government is not answerable to the merchant who has lost the benefit of a bargain through negligent delay. The householder is without a remedy against manufacturers of hose and engines, though prompt performance of their contracts would have stayed the ravages of fire. "The law does not spread its protection so far."

So with the case at hand. By the vast preponderance of authority, a contract between a city and a water company to furnish water at the city hydrants has in view a benefit to the public that is incidental rather than immediate, an assumption of duty to the city and not to its inhabitants. Such is the ruling of the Supreme Court of the United States. Such has been the ruling in this State though the question is still open in this court. Such with few exceptions has been the ruling in other jurisdictions. The diligence of counsel has brought together decisions to that effect from 26 States. Only a few States have held otherwise. An intention to assume an obligation of indefinite extension to every member of the public is seen to be the more improbable when we recall the crushing burden that the obligation would impose. The consequences invited would bear no reasonable proportion to those attached by law to defaults not greatly different. If the plaintiff is to prevail, one who negligently omits to supply sufficient pressure to extinguish a fire started by another, assumes an obligation to pay the ensuing damage, though the whole city is laid low. A promisor will not be deemed to have had in mind the assumption of a risk so overwhelming for any trivial reward.

The cases that have applied the rule of *Lawrence* v. *Fox* to contracts made by a city for the benefit of the public are not at war with this conclusion. Through them all there runs a unifying principle, the presence of an intention to compensate the individual members of the public in the event of a default.

(2) We think the action is not maintainable as one for a common-law tort.

"It is ancient learning that one who assumes to act, even though gratuitously, may thereby become subject to the duty of acting carefully, if he acts at all." The plaintiff would bring its case within the orbit of that principle. The hand once set to a task may not always be withdrawn with impunity though liability would fail if it had never been applied at all. A time-honored formula often phrases the distinction as one between misfeasance and nonfeasance. Incomplete the formula is, and so at times misleading. Given a relation involving in its existence a duty of care irrespective of a contract, a tort may result as well from acts of omission as of commission in the fulfillment of the duty thus recognized by law. What we need to know is not so much the conduct to be avoided when the relation and its attendant duty are established as existing. What we need to know is the conduct that engenders the relation. It is here that the formula, however incomplete, has its value and significance. If conduct has gone forward to such a stage that inaction would commonly result, not negatively merely in withholding a benefit, but positively or actively in working an injury, there exists a relation out of which

247

arises a duty to go forward. The query always is whether the punitive wrongdoer has advanced to such a point as to have launched a force or instrument of harm, or has stopped where inaction is at most a refusal to become an instrument for good.

The plaintiff would have us hold that the defendant, when once it entered upon the performance of its contract with the city, was brought into such a relation with every one who might potentially be benefited through the supply of water at the hydrants as to give to negligent performance, without reasonable notice of a refusal to continue, the quality of a tort. We are satisfied that liability would be unduly and indeed indefinitely extended by this enlargement of the zone of duty.

What we are dealing with at this time is a mere negligent omission, unaccompanied by malice or other aggravating elements. The failure in such circumstances to furnish an adequate supply of water is at most the denial of a benefit. It is not the commission of a wrong.

BAYS v. U.S. CAMERA PUBLISHING CORP.

171 N.W.2d 232 (Michigan, 1969)

Pratt, Judge

Beginning in the June, 1958, issue of its magazine, the defendant-publisher announced a photographic contest with various prizes to be awarded winners. The announcement contained "Official Contest Rules" which were set off in bold black lines from the other portions of the article listing and describing various prizes.

Pertinent to the issues here is the first paragraph of the contest rules which reads as follows:

1. Anyone is eligible to enter this contest with the exception of employees of U.S. Camera Publishing Corp. and their families. Entries will be accepted from anywhere in the world, although U.S. Camera Publishing Corp. will not assume any responsibility for postage or customs duties due on entries received. The sponsor will exercise all possible care for entries but cannot accept responsibility for loss or damage. Entries will be returned if sufficient first class return postage is enclosed. Model releases and original negatives must be available on request.

248

Plaintiff, a resident of Windsor, Ontario, Canada, entered the contest, submitting a photograph and in December, 1958, was advised by letter that he had been awarded the second prize, a fully equipped and installed 18' × 36' swimming pool. The letter also contained the following language:

(These pools cannot be assigned or transferred to someone other than yourself without the express consent of the International Swimming Pool Corporation.) As soon as arrangements for the delivery and installation of your swimming pool have been completed, we will contact you.

Faced with the restrictions against assignment or transfer, the plaintiff, who owned no home of his own, attempted the subterfuge involving the transfer of deeds with a homeowning friend who would eventually obtain the pool and pay the plaintiff $3,500. However, the pool supplier had no distributor in the area of plaintiff's residence and during the ensuing delay, plaintiff's arrangements with his friend became impractical. In the late summer, a representative of the pool supplier contacted the plaintiff but it was mutually agreed that installation in the fall of 1959 would be imprudent and that the pool would be installed in the spring of 1960. Before the spring of 1960, the pool supplier became insolvent and could not deliver the pool. The defendant publisher then refused delivery.

From a judgment by the trial court in favor of the plaintiff in the amount of $5,437.50, the defendant-publisher appeals, and contends that the assignment or transfer restriction contained in its letter did not constitute a breach of contract by the defendant, that the agreement between the pool supplier and plaintiff to delay installation until the spring of 1960 excused defendant from performance, that plaintiff failed to sustain his burden as to the value of the pool, and that plaintiff's damages should be limited to the $3,500 amount of the abortive agreement with plaintiff's friend.

Defendant contends that the restriction against assignment or transfer of the pool was not a new provision or condition of the contract but on the contrary was a more explicit recitation of an implicit condition contained in the original contest announcement. Defendant bases this argument on that portion of the announcement which describes the swimming pool prize and includes the following:

How would you like to have one of these wonderful pools completely installed in your backyard? . . . A magnificent recreational swimming pool for any homeowner.

Thus, defendant asserts, since the pool was to be installed "in your own backyard," it could obviously not be assigned or transferred and the subsequent restriction merely reiterated this condition in more definite terms. We cannot accept such a circuitous argument. The language of the "Official Contest Rules" is simple, clear, and unequivocal, i.e., "Anyone is eligible . . . anywhere in the world. . . ." The official rules are set apart from the prize descriptions, and the latter cannot in our view be considered as conditions of the offering. As is stated in 17 Am.Jur. 2d, Contracts Section 263, p. 668, the "plain meaning expressed in the contract cannot be varied or added to by such extrinsic matters."

The defendant had no legal right after the plaintiff accepted the defendant's offer to enter the contest to impose a restriction on assignment and transfer not set forth in the contest rules. Accordingly, the plaintiff was justified in ignoring the restriction which the defendant attempted to impose.

Defendant also contends that the agreement of plaintiff with the pool supplier, and the ensuing delay, excuses defendant from any obligation under the contest contract.

Such is not the case here. The initial delay was caused by the lack of a distributor of the pool supplier in the area, and the plaintiff, according to the record, urged installation from the time he was notified in December, 1958, to August, 1959. The delay agreed upon in August, 1959, by the pool supplier and plaintiff was prompted as much by weather hazards, both as to construction and as to use, as by any other reason. No different contract was entered into with the supplier.

With respect to the award of damages, we find no error in the reliance of the trial court on the competency of plaintiff's expert as to the value of the awarded pool. Further, plaintiff was entitled to recover damages in an amount equal to the fair market value of the installed and equipped pool, and his fruitless agreement with his friend does not allow a variation of that rule under the circumstances of this case.

The record discloses that the plaintiff agreed to allow his friend to have the pool for only $3,500, but this fact alone would not justify our finding as a matter of law that $3,500 was the true market value of the pool.

The price agreed upon by the plaintiff and his friend, in light of their personal relationship, may have been a bargain price. If defendant wanted to show that the market value of the pool was less than the replacement value, the defendant should have offered testimony or proof establishing that fact. Since it failed to do so, it cannot object that the trial judge adopted the only record evidence as to the value of the pool.

The decision of the trial court is affirmed with costs to appellee.

TALCO CAPITAL CORP. v. STATE UNDERGROUND PARKING COMMISSION

324 N.E.2d 762 (Ohio, 1974)

Holmes, Judge

This matter involves the appeal of a judgment of the Court of Common Pleas of Franklin County, which found in favor of the plaintiff Talco Capital Corporation (Talco), the assignee of a creditor's claim against the State Underground Parking Commission and the Seaboard Surety Company, the latter having previously issued a surety policy to the Commission.

The facts in brief are that a certain company by the name of Kenny Brown and Associates, Inc. (Kenny Brown), had a contract with defendant State Underground Parking Commission for the erection within the parking garage of an automatic vehicle counting and control system. Kenny Brown entered into a contract with the National Automation Company (NAC), by which

NAC was to supply an automatic vehicle counting and control system and was also to supply overall supervision of the installation of the equipment. It appears from the record that a good portion of the equipment was delivered and installed by the time of the opening of the parking garage on November 16, 1964, but that the system was not complete on such date. It would appear that NAC was last on the job at or about June 11, 1965.

The facts further show that, on November 30, 1964, NAC assigned its accounts receivable from Kenny Brown to the Long Island Trust Company of New York, such assignment being in connection with certain loans made to NAC by the Long Island Trust Company. The Long Island Trust Company made a further assignment of these accounts receivable to the present plaintiff Talco by assignment dated November 1, 1965.

Difference developed between NAC and Kenny Brown as to what was due NAC under the contract. On September 22, 1965, NAC filed with the Parking Commission an "Affidavit for Mechanic's Lien" intended to be pursuant to R.C. 1311.26. In such affidavit NAC alleged that there was the sum of $38,540 due it from Kenny Brown under the "base contract" between them, which base contract was alleged to have been completed by November 1964. The affidavit also alleged that NAC was due the sum of $19,128.98 for "extra labor" performed from November 11, 1964, to June 11, 1965.

Within 10 days of the filing of the affidavit, Kenny Brown filed with the Commission its notice of intention to dispute the lien and claim of NAC. On or about August 5, 1966, Seaboard Surety Company and Kenny Brown gave a bond to the Commission, and Kenny Brown was paid the funds remaining due under Kenny Brown's electrical contract with the Commission.

Thereafter, NAC brought an action against Kenny Brown in the Court of Common Pleas of Franklin County, seeking to recover the sum of $57,668.98; it alleged that $38,540 was due under its contract and that $19,128.98 was due for extra work performed up to June 11, 1965. No claim was made in that action with respect to the validity or propriety of the alleged mechanic's lien of NAC. In that case the trial court found that Kenny Brown was not obligated to pay for any

"extra services" claimed by NAC, but that NAC was entitled to receive $20,572.71 under its contract, with interest at 6 percent from August 5, 1966. That judgment became final and was not appealed and, according to the original stipulation filed herein, such judgment was not satisfied. Kenny Brown, it appears, sometime thereafter discontinued its operations and is no longer in business. On January 12, 1967, Talco purchased all of the rights, title, and interest of the trustee in bankruptcy of NAC in the accounts receivable of the bankrupt company.

Subsequently, Talco brought this action against Seaboard and the Commission for the purpose of establishing the validity of the mechanic's lien acquired by NAC. The trial court, in this action, found there to be due from the defendants to the plaintiff the sum of $20,572.71 with interest, and there to be a valid lien filed by NAC. It is from that lower court's judgment that this appeal has been taken.

The assignments of error, as set forth in the defendants' brief, are as follows:

The trial court erred in finding that National Automation Corporation (NAC), predecessor in interest to Talco Capital Corporation (Talco), had a right to file an attested account (lien) in the name of NAC subsequent to an assignment by NAC to Long Island Trust Company of all of the right, title, and interest of NAC to any and all sums due to NAC from Kenny Brown and Associates, Inc. (KBA).

The first question to be resolved is, What rights of assignment does such lien claimant have? The question of rights of assignment on the part of the lien claimant arises both as to the chose in action, the account receivable, as well as to the mechanic's lien which secures such account receivable.

As to the assignability generally of a chose in action, we find at 5 Ohio Jurisprudence 2d 156, Assignments, Section 6, the following:

The early common-law rule that a chose in action was not assignable, at least not so as to vest the assignee with the legal title and enable him to maintain an action at law in his own name, has been so materially modified by judicial decision and by statute that assignability of choses in action is now the rule, and nonassignability the exception.

Assignments of a chose in action, such as accounts receivable, may take a variety of forms, according to the needs, circumstances, and requirements of the particular parties assignor and assignee. In a given instance, the one party owning the account receivable may assign his account as security for the repayment of loans entered into, or to be entered into. In another instance, the account receivable may be absolutely sold and assigned to the lender in payment of the debt. Additionally, such account receivable may be sold to a third-party factor, often such sale to be at a discount in allowance for the uncollectibility of such account.

The assignability of a lien on a public works fund is a much more difficult and complex question. This question seemingly is an open one in Ohio and has as yet not been judicially answered; at least no reported decisions are to be found. In some jurisdictions this question has been answered by way of statute. Some statutes grant the right to the lien claimant to assign the lien only after properly perfecting such. Other statutes extend the right of assignment to the lien claimant, either before or after perfecting such lien.

We agree with the statement found within 36 Ohio Jurisprudence 2d 655, Mechanics' Liens, Section 183, that: "Although there is a conflict on this question, the great weight of authority, as well as the better reasoning, is in favor of permitting such an assignment."

It has been held in Ohio, in construing assignments of mechanics' liens, both before and after the passage of R.C. 1311.22, that the right to the lien is not assignable until it has been established in the manner provided by law. It is our view that such principle of law in like manner should be applied to mechanics' liens asserted upon public improvements.

Having determined that a mechanic's lien, or attested account, where properly perfected, may be assigned, we come next to the question of whether NAC, the lien claimant, had a right to obtain a lien even though the debt, by way of the account receivable from the subcontractor, had been assigned to the Long Island Trust Company.

We believe that the plaintiff has stated the preferable law to be applied to this particular issue of the case. Such law is to be found in 53

American Jurisprudence 2d 822, Mechanics' Liens, Section 286, as follows:

In those jurisdictions where a lienable claim may be assigned, if one entitled to a mechanic's lien makes an absolute assignment of the sum due him, and not merely as security, a lien statement filed by him on his own account after such assignment, although within the statutory time, is void, and will not, therefore, inure to the benefit of his assignee. It also has been held that by assignment of all rights to the money to come due under a contract the contractor waived his right to a lien, since such right is incidental to the right to exact compensation. But if the sum due is assigned as collateral security for the payment of a debt, the assignor still has sufficient interest to entitle him to file a lien statement afterward within the statutory time, which will secure his equitable rights in the claim assigned and also to inure to the benefit of his assignee.

We hereby adopt such principle of law as being within the intent and purpose of the lien laws, to provide a more meaningful and tangible benefit to lien claimants; i.e., the marketability of that which represents the fruits of their labors. Merely stating the law to be applied to this case, unfortunately, does not resolve all of the problems presented here, in that the evidence before the trial court by way of the stipulations and the exhibits does not entirely clarify the issue as to whether NAC, the lien claimant, had merely assigned its accounts receivable from Kenny Brown by way of security for its loans as negotiated, or whether such assignment was absolute and in that sense a sale of such accounts in satisfaction of the notes due.

The pertinent exhibit in this regard is exhibit A where, at page 1, we find the following:

Whereas, on the 30th day of November, 1964, in consideration of mutual promises and loans then and thereafter made by Long Island Trust Company to National Automation Corporation, said National Automation Corporation did assign certain accounts receivable to said Long Island Trust Company by an agreement of said date; and. . . .

This wording is not determinative of the exact nature of the transaction between the parties. Conceivably, such could have been an absolute assignment, or the assignment could have been only by way of security for the loan. We feel that such a determination must be made by the trial court prior to applying the appropriate law as pronounced in this decision.

Therefore, the judgment of the Court of Common Pleas of Franklin County is reversed, and is hereby remanded for the limited purpose of a finding, as to whether the assignment of the accounts receivable due NAC from Kenny Brown were absolutely sold and assigned without recourse, or whether such assignment was merely for the purpose of securing certain obligations.

If the finding is the former, judgment should be entered for the defendant Seaboard; if the finding be the latter, judgment should be entered for the plaintiff Talco Corporation.

Judgment reversed and cause remanded.

PROBLEMS FOR DISCUSSION

1. Ethel Widow sued Pipeline Oil Corporation and its franchised service station operator on the New York State Thruway, Carl Pump, for failure to provide road services to her husband. Their car developed a flat tire, and a passing state trooper ordered Carl Pump to come to the aid of the stranded motorists. Carl neglected to do so, and after waiting for over two hours, Ethel's husband, a stout accountant, tried to change the tire himself. The work exhausted him, so that he collapsed. He died shortly thereafter of a heart attack. What result, and why?

2. Izzy graduated from Free School District. Although he received failing grades in several subjects and lacked basic reading and writing skills, he was given a diploma anyway. Izzy later hired tutors so that he could attain these basic language skills and be more employable. He now sues for $5 million, alleging that he was the third-party beneficiary of a provision of the state constitution which requires the state legislature to maintain and support "a system of free common schools, wherein all the children of this state may be educated." What result, and why?

3. American Bridge, assignee from Coburn of "all the moneys due or which may hereafter become due" to Coburn under two building contracts which Coburn had with the city of Boston, sues to collect the alleged contract balances. After notification of the assignment had been received by Boston, Coburn defaulted on his performance obligations. Boston wishes to deduct the damages caused by Coburn's default from the amounts due under the contracts. What result, and why?

4. Pitzoo Snak Shops agreed to have Kookie Cola vending machines installed in each of its 23 Pitzoo locations. Kookie Cola was later bought out by Burpsi Cola, and this contract with Pitzoo was assigned to Burpsi. Pitzoo objected to doing business with Burpsi and attempted to terminate the contract. Burpsi sued Pitzoo for breach. What result, and why?

5. Clifford and his wife, Patricia, owned two businesses in Flagstaff, Arizona, Cliff's Clothing and Cliff's Shoes. They sold Cliff's Clothing to Pawnee Clothing, Inc. As part of the contract, Pawnee agreed "not to compete with the Seller in the sale of shoes and other footwear and footwear accessories in Flagstaff, Arizona, for a period of five years from this date." The contract also stated: "This contract shall be binding upon the heirs, executors, and administrators of the parties hereto." About five months later Cliff and Patricia sold their other business, Cliff's Shoes, to Hamblet. Shortly thereafter, Pawnee started selling shoes at Cliff's Clothing's old store. Cliff and Patricia then executed an assignment of all their rights under their contract with Pawnee to Hamblet. Hamblet sues for an injunction to prevent Pawnee from selling shoes at the clothing store location. What result, and why?

6. While he was walking by the Nickeldimes' house, on the public sidewalk, Frodo was attacked by the Nickeldimes' dog. Frodo died as a result of the injuries he sus-

tained. His widow, Elizabeth, sued the Nickeldimes, alleging that they had been negligent in the care and treatment of their dog. At the time of the incident, the Nickeldimes did not have a homeowner's liability insurance policy in force because their mortgage company, Esanel, had failed to purchase such insurance with the funds that the Nickeldimes had paid into their escrow account at Esanel for that purpose. Elizabeth, learning these facts, now amends her complaint and sues Esanel as a third-party beneficiary of the escrow agreement between Esanel and the Nickeldimes. Esanel moves to dismiss this amendment to Elizabeth's complaint. How should the court rule, and why?

7. Goodtread Tire Company licensed Adolph and Hermann as its exclusive agents for the state of New York, except for New York City, for a period of one year. (Goodtread could license other distributors only in New York City.) This agreement was renewable for another year by Adolph and Hermann if they gave notice of their intent to renew at least 30 days prior to the expiration date of the original contract. By the terms of the agreement, Goodtread sent its tires to Adolph and Hermann on consignment (ownership of the tires remained in Goodtread until they were sold to customers), and Adolph and Hermann had to account to Goodtread each month for all sales made.

About three months before the contract was due to expire, Adolph assigned his interest in the contract to Hermann. Hermann then properly notified Goodtread of his intent to renew the contract for another year, but Goodtread refused to do so. Hermann sues for breach of contract. What result, and why?

8. Mickey and Minnie bought a $50,000 house for $10,000 down, with a mortgage for $40,000 at a 9 percent interest rate. About four years later, Mickey and Minnie wanted to move to another home. They found a buyer for their first home (Ned Needy) who was willing to cash out their equity in the house and assume the mortgage (i.e., take an assignment of rights and accept a delegation of the duty to pay off the mortgage according to its terms). But when they checked with the holder of their mortgage, the Octopus Bank, Mickey and Minnie were told that their mortgage was not assignable because it contained a "due on sale" clause. According to that clause, if and when Mickey and Minnie ever sold their house, the entire remaining balance on the mortgage would then become due and payable. Octopus says it would be willing to consider a loan application from Ned for a new loan, at the current interest rate of 16 percent. Ned does not want to pay 16 percent or the cost of processing a new mortgage. Does the bank have to accept Ned as the assignee of the original mortgage despite the due on sale clause? Discuss.

12 | Excuses for Nonperformance

While the vast majority of contracts are performed according to their terms, many are not. Not all nonperformances will produce liability for breach of contract, however; in some of these cases the nonperforming party will have a legal excuse for his or her failure. These legal excuses, or discharges of liability, can be placed in five general groupings: (1) conditions, (2) breach by the other party, (3) discharge by new agreement, (4) discharge by "merger," and (5) discharge by "operation of law." We now proceed to consider each of these groups.

CONDITIONS

Basic Concepts and Definitions. A "condition" is an act, event, or set of facts to which the parties have attached some special legal significance. The parties have included it in their contract, either expressly or impliedly, with the intent that its occurrence or nonoccurrence will operate to modify, suspend, or completely discharge a performance duty under the contract.

In terms of how they operate, conditions are classified as precedent, concurrent, and subsequent. A condition precedent operates to prevent a contract duty from arising until it occurs. If a tailor promises that you will be personally satisfied with your new custom-made suit, and you're not satisifed, you don't have to take the suit and pay for it—no "personal satisfaction" (the condition precedent), no duty to take the suit. Concurrent conditions, which are usually implied by law, operate so that each party's duty to perform is conditioned on the other party's being ready, willing, and able to render the required return performance. The most typical example of concurrent conditions in action is the "cash sale" transaction, as seen in the following case.

Vidal v. Transcontinental & Western Air
120 F.2d 67 (U.S. Third Circuit, 1941)

FACTS "This action for breach of contract was tried by the court below without a jury. This appeal by the plaintiffs is from the action of the trial court in dismissing their complaint. By the terms of the contract, which bears date of Apirl 14, 1937, the defendant agreed to sell and the plaintiff agreed to buy four used airplanes of a specified type belonging to the seller. The price was stipulated, and payment was to be made by certified check upon delivery of the airplanes to the buyer at the Municipal Airport, Kansas City, Missouri. The date for delivery was stated to be June 1, 1937. As to the date of delivery, however, the seller's obligation to deliver on June 1 was qualified by saying 'unless on that date we have not received a sufficient number of Douglas DC-3 or SDT airplanes to enable us to withdraw from service the airplanes to be purchased by you, in which event such airplanes shall be delivered to you and you agree to make payment within five (5) days after notice from us to you that such airplanes are ready for delivery to you.' The buyers were privileged, by a following clause, to withdraw from the agreement if the seller was unable to deliver on or before July 1, 1937.

"Twelve days later one of the buyers telegraphed to Mr. Frye, president of the defendant corporation (the seller), asking 'Can you let us know approximate dates delivery. . . ?' Mr. Frye replied the same day: 'Can deliver first ship June 1st and others by July 10th subject no further delays by Douglas.' Plaintiffs did not answer this telegram. The trial court found as a fact that on June 1 the defendant was ready, able, and willing to deliver one of the planes described in the contract to the plaintiffs at Municipal Airport in Kansas City, Missouri, and that after June 1 and prior to July 10 the defendant was ready, able, and willing to deliver all of the four airplanes at the place specified. It was also found as a fact that the plaintiffs did not on June 1 or any other date either tender payment on any or all of the machines nor request delivery. Plaintiffs' action for damages was begun in the United States District Court for the District of Delaware on October 8, 1938."

ISSUE Was the defendant (seller) in default because of its failure to deliver the planes?

DECISION No. Judgment affirmed.

REASONS (Opinion by Justice Goodrich.) "What are the respective rights and duties of the parties in a contract of this kind? . . . Payment and delivery are concurrent conditions since both parties are bound to render performance at the same time. *Restatement, Contracts,* § 251. In such a case, as Williston points out, neither party can maintain an action against the other without first making an offer of performance himself. Otherwise, if each stayed at home ready and willing to perform, each would have a right of action against the other. . . . '[T]o maintain an action at law the plaintiff must not only be ready and willing but he must have manifested this before bringing his action, by some offer of performance to the defendant. . . . It is one of the consequences of concurrent conditions that a situation may arise where no right of action ever arises against either party. . . . so long as both parties remain inactive, neither is liable.' . . . This statement by the learned author not only has the force of his authority and that of many decisions from many states, but is also sound common sense. It is not an unfair requirement that a party complaining of another's conduct should be required to show that the other has fallen short in the performance of a legal obligation. . . .

"The conclusion is, therefore, that the defendant is not in default. Neither side having demanded performance by the other, neither side is in a position to complain or to assert any claim in an action of law against the other. This view of the case makes it unnecessary to examine the testimony which asserts that the buyers either abandoned or repudiated the contract prior to the time of the performance."

Conditions subsequent operate to discharge or excuse an existing duty of performance. An automobile liability insurance policy, for example, may provide that the insurance company's duty to defend liability claims under the policy is excused where the insured admits his or her liability for the accident. Or a property insurance policy may specify that coverage lapses where a structure is unoccupied for more than a certain period of time. Whether a condition exists or has occurred is generally a question of fact, to be proved like any other.

Conditions of Approval or Satisfaction. Especially in large construction contracts, the parties may specify that a third party's approval is required before the final payment has to be made. In construction, this third party is typically the architect who drew the plans and specifications for the job. Until the builder can convince the architect that the job has been done in conformity to the plans, the landowner/customer does not have to make the final payment on the contract price. Where the architect is withholding his or her approval in bad faith, or as part of a fraudulent scheme against the builder, most courts would probably hold this condition to have been satisfied and require the landowner/customer to pay the balance due.

There are also contracts in which "personal satisfaction" of the buyer/customer is guaranteed, with the parties' intent being that if he or she is not satisfied, he or she is not bound to pay the contract price. In trying to determine whether such a condition has been met, so that the seller can collect the contract price, the courts use two different tests: an individualized, or "subjective," test and a "reasonable person," or "objective," test. The first says that if the particular buyer is not satisfied, the buyer is not bound to pay; the second says that if the buyer, as a reasonable person, *should* be satisfied, then he must pay. Where the contract is for an item involving personal taste, such as a custom-tailored suit, a portrait, or a statue, "personal satisfaction" probably means just that: no deal unless the individual buyer indicates that he or she is satisfied. Where the contract involves an item of everyday mechanical utility, such as a furnace, "personal satisfaction" is probably a jury question under the reasonable person test: either the furnace is working properly, or it is not; if it is, the buyer ought to be satisfied with it. Besides the nature of the item, the other main factor considered by the courts in determining which test to use is what happens to the item if the satisfaction condition is not met. The suit, portrait, or sculpture stays with the seller; there is no "unjust enrichment" of the buyer, though the seller may be stuck with an unmarketable item. With something like an aluminum siding job, however, the situation is quite different, since it is somewhat uneconomic to un-aluminum-side a house; the courts would almost certainly apply the reasonable person test to the job.

Timely Performance as a Condition Precedent. What happens when one party is late in performing or offering to perform his contract obligations? Any provable damages resulting from the delay in performance should be collectable without question. But the real question is whether the other party can refuse to accept the offered late performance and use the failure to perform on time as a basis for rescinding the whole contract. Courts generally consider this problem in terms of whether "time is of the essence," meaning that the parties have either expressly or impliedly made timely performance a condition precedent.

While there are apparently a few early cases stating that time is presumed to be of the essence in a sale of goods, this does not seem to be the general rule, and it is clearly not the rule for real estate or construction contracts. Where the parties have not clearly specified in the contract that time is of the essence, the court must determine, as a question of fact, whether such a condition precedent should be implied.

Arrowhead Growers Sales Co. v. Central Sands Produce, Inc.
180 N.W.2d 567 (Wisconsin, 1970)

FACTS   "Plaintiff-appellant, Arrowhead Growers Sales Company, Inc., is a Wisconsin corporation engaged in the business of selling potatoes for producers. Defendant-respondent, Central Sands Produce, Inc., is a Wisconsin corporation engaged in the business of storing, grading, and packaging potatoes for the producers who are its stockholders. Defendant's potatoes were sold exclusively by the plaintiff under an oral contract in 1963, and pursuant to a written agreement in 1964. The parties entered another three-year contract, effective July 1, 1965, whereby the plaintiff agreed to market all potatoes stored and processed by the defendant, receiving a commission in the amount of $0.20 per cwt. Plaintiff agreed to sell the defendant's potatoes with dispatch. The contract further provided that the dealings of the parties were to conform to the provisions of the Perishable Agricultural Commodities Act (PACA).

"In the early part of 1966 the defendant attempted to terminate the contract by mutual agreement, but the plaintiff was unwilling to do so. On March 3, 1966, the defendant notified the plaintiff by letter that it considered the contract terminated.

"In August, 1966, this action was commenced on the complaint of the plaintiff seeking specific performance of the contract, damages for sales in violation of the contract, and an injunction restraining sales by the defendant in violation of the contract. The defendant filed an answer and counterclaim alleging five causes of action. The demurrer of the plaintiff to the second, third, fourth, and fifth causes of action was sustained. Trial was to the court.

"The court found the plaintiff had materially breached the contract by failing to

Arrowhead Growers Sales Co. v. Central Sands Produce, Inc. (continued)

market the defendant's potatoes expeditiously and in the manner contemplated by the contract, and in failing to furnish the individual growers itemized information on the sales. Judgment was entered dismissing plaintiff's complaint and awarding the defendant damages on the first cause of action set forth in its counterclaim.

"The plaintiff has appealed from that part of the trial court's judgment dismissing the plaintiff's cause of action."

ISSUES (1) Did the plaintiff breach the contract in failing to market the defendant's potatoes with dispatch, and, if so, was the breach material? (2) Did the plaintiff breach the contract in failing to furnish defendant's growers with itemized information as to sales, and, if so, was the breach material?

DECISION Yes. No. Judgment affirmed.

REASONS (Opinion by Justice Hansen.) "We have reviewed the rather extensive record, and as might be presumed, there is a conflict in the testimony presented by the respective parties as to whether the plaintiff marketed the defendant's product with dispatch, as provided in the contract. The growers brought their product to the shed of the defendant. The defendant had the responsibility for moving sufficient potatoes from the bins to meet the orders from the plaintiff, together with a sufficient allowance for potatoes which would not pass the required grade. The potatoes making up the orders were promptly shipped and the remaining potatoes, which resulted from any overestimate of the amount required to fill the order and those potatoes which did not meet the grade but were salable, became part of the floor inventory. Potatoes comprising the floor inventory could be sold directly from the floor or used to fill orders on sales effected by the plaintiff. . . .

"Plaintiff contends that its adequate performance under the contract was shown by testimony that the plaintiff was doing the best he could. Our attention is directed to *Ekstrom v. State* (1969), 45 Wis.2d 218, 172 N.W.2d 660, for the proposition that breach is not shown by mere error in judgment. However, the court in that case was discussing the conditions under which a 'satisfaction' clause may be dispensed with. The plaintiff's obligation under the contract in this case was not to use his best judgment in marketing or to market to the best of his ability, but to market 'with dispatch.' The trial court, in its decision, stated that the nature of the product and the nature of the contract 'casts a strong burden on the Plaintiff to see that the Defendant's potatoes were marketed expeditiously.' . . .

"The trial court found that the plaintiff did not furnish to the individual growers prompt, itemized information as to the sales of potatoes, as provided in the contract; that such failure constituted a breach of contract and was material.

"We agree that failure to supply the itemized information to the growers as to sales constituted a breach of the contract; however, we do not consider it a material breach in this case. . . .

"Having acquiesced in the reporting methods used by the plaintiff for three years prior to the termination of the contract, the defendant cannot now assert the plaintiff's failure to comply with the PACA regulations is a material breach of the contract. Therefore, the breach of failure to report information on sales, as required by the contract, does not constitute a material breach under the facts of this case."

Doctrine of Substantial Performance. Courts are reluctant to excuse a party's contractual obligations completely just because the other party has committed a relatively minor breach. Just as there are many cases where the simple, one-shot performances called for are given exactly in accordance with the contract terms, there are also cases, such as construction contracts, where the required performances are more complex and extend over a considerable period of time. In construction contracts it is a rare situation indeed when the job is completed *exactly* in accordance with the agreed plans and specifications. Should minor deviations by the builder permit the buyer to rescind the whole contract?

The courts have answered this question in the negative, by applying the doctrine of "substantial performance." What this doctrine says is that if the builder has acted in good faith and has done the job in *substantial* compliance with the contract, the builder can enforce the contract and collect his or her contract price. Any damages which result from any noncompliance, no matter how trivial, can be collected by the buyer or deducted from the amount of the contractor's recovery. Perfection is not required. The buyer of a new house would not be able to rescind the contract just because the kitchen was painted green instead of blue, but he or she could force the builder to repaint, or he or she could deduct the price of the paint job from the contract price if the builder refused.

The doctrine of substantial performance will not be applied where the builder has intentionally substituted inferior materials or used other production shortcuts in a fraudulent attempt to make extra money. Nor will it be applied where the builder has only partially, rather than substantially, performed. In such cases the buyer can rescind the whole contract. If the partially built structure has been placed on land already owned by the buyer, he is probably liable in quasi contract for the fair market value of the labor and materials, but even in this case he or she can probably deduct any provable damages he or she has sustained.

BREACH BY OTHER PARTY

In General. When the plaintiff brings his or her action for breach of contract, a possible response by the defendant is the argument "You breached first." That is, the defendant argues that his or her own nonperformance was not a breach, because the plaintiff's prior nonperformance justified the defendant's refusal to perform. Although in some cases the courts have treated the reciprocal performances as "independent," they generally accept this argument as a sufficient excuse where the prior breach by the plaintiff was a material one. It would, generally, be unfair to require the defendant to perform or hold the defendant liable for not performing if he or she has not received what the plaintiff promised him or her in return. However, it would be equally unfair for the defendant to repudiate the whole contract and completely refuse to perform if the plaintiff has committed only a minor, relatively insignificant breach.

Breach of Installment Contract. It is even more difficult to work out a fair result where the contract calls for a series of performances by one or both parties, rather than just a single exchange. What should the measure of recovery be when a party partially performs and then fails to deliver one or more of the installments still due?

The courts usually try to solve this problem by first determining whether the contract is divisible or indivisible. If the contract is held to be divisible into a series of pro rata exchanges, the court will usually permit the breaching party to recover the agreed reciprocal performance, less any damages his or her breach has caused to the other party. An employee who quits after having worked for three months under a one-year contract would usually be able to collect the agreed contract salary for the three months worked, less any damages which the employer sustains as a result of the breach. If the contract is held to be indivisible, or "entire," a party guilty of a material breach should collect only the fair market value of any benefits retained by the other party, less damages caused by the breach. The following case shows that each case must be decided on its own facts and that the divisible/indivisible analysis may be used by the breaching party too.

New Era Homes Corporation v. *Forster et al.*
86 N.E.2d 757 (New York, 1959)

FACTS   "Plaintiff entered into a written agreement with defendants, to make extensive alterations to defendants' home, the reference therein to price and payment being as follows:

All above material, and labor to erect and install same to be supplied for $3,075.00 to be paid as follows:

$ 150.00   on signing of contract,
$1,000.00   upon delivery of materials and starting of work,
$1,500.00   on completion of rough carpentry and rough plumbing,
$ 425.00   upon job being completed.

"The work was commenced and partly finished, and the first two stipulated payments were made. Then, when the 'rough work' was done, plaintiff asked for the third installment of $1,500 but defendants would not pay it, so plaintiff stopped work and brought suit for the whole of the balance, that is, for the two payments of $1,500 and $425. On the trial plaintiff stipulated to reduce its demand to $1,500, its theory being that, since all the necessary 'rough carpentry and rough plumbing' had been done, the time had arrived for it to collect $1,500. It offered no other proof as to its damages. Defendants conceded their default but argued at the trial, and argue here, that plaintiff was entitled not to the $1,500 third payment, but to such amount as it could establish by way of actual loss sustained from defendants' breach. In other words, defendants say the correct measure of damage was the value of the work actually done, less payments made, plus lost profits. The jury, however, by its verdict gave plaintiff its $1,500. The Appellate Division, Second Department, affirmed the judgment, and we granted defendants leave to appeal to this court."

ISSUE   Does the provision for periodic payments make the contract divisible?

DECISION   No. Judgment reversed.

REASONS   (Opinion by Justice Desmond.) "The whole question is as to the meaning of so much of the agreement as we have quoted above. Did that language make it an entire contract, with one consideration for the doing of the whole work, and payments on account at fixed points in the progress of the job, or was the bargain a severable or divisible one in the sense that, of the total consideration, $1,150 was to be the full and fixed payment for 'delivery of materials and starting of work,' $1,500 the full and fixed payment for work done up to and including 'completion of rough carpentry and rough plumbing,' and $425 for the rest. We hold that the total price of $3,075 was the single consideration for the whole of the work, and that the separately listed payments were not allocated absolutely to certain parts of the undertaking, but were scheduled part payments, mutually convenient to the builder and the owner. That conclusion, we think, is a necessary one from the very words of the writing, since the arrangement there stated was not that separate items of work be done for separate amounts of money, but that the whole alteration project, including material and labor, as 'to be supplied for $3,075.00.' There is nothing in the record to suggest that the parties had intended to group, in this contract, several separate engagements, each with its own separate consideration. They did not say, for instance, that the price for all the work up to the completion of rough carpentry and plumbing was to be $1,500. They did agree that at that point $1,500 would be due, but as a part payment on the whole price. To illustrate: it is hardly conceivable that the amount of $150, payable 'on signing of contract,' was a reward to plaintiff for the act of affixing its corporate name and seal.

"We would, in short, be writing a new contract for these people if we broke this single promise up into separate deals; and the new contract so written by us might be, for all we know, most unjust to one or the other party.

"We find no controlling New York case, but the trend of authority in this State, and elsewhere, is that such agreements express an intent that payment be conditioned and dependent upon completion of all the agreed work. We think that is the reasonable rule—after all, a householder who remodels his home is, usually, committing himself to one plan and one result, not a series of unrelated projects. The parties to a construction or alteration contract may, of course, make it divisible and stipulate the value of each divisible part. But there is no sign that these people so intended. It follows that plaintiff, on defendants' default, could collect either in quantum meruit for what had been finished, or in contract for the value of what plaintiff had lost—that is, the contract price, less payments made and less the cost of completion."

Anticipatory Repudiation.   An anticipatory repudiation occurs when one party, by words or conduct, indicates that he or she will not be willing or able to perform his or her contract duties when the time for performance arrives. In other words, he or she announces in advance that he or she is not going to perform as scheduled. In nearly all cases the courts treat such an unequivocal repudiation of the contract as a present breach, giving the injured party the right to make other arrangements immediately and sue for any damages caused or to wait and see what happens and then sue for any damages caused, if in fact performance does not occur. The courts do not apply this rule to promises to pay money at a future date; a present statement of intention not to pay a future debt normally does not accelerate the due date of the debt unless there is a special provision to that effect. The courts also normally permit a party to retract his or her repudiation if he or she does so before the other party has made any substantial change in his or her legal position because of the repudiation.

Adequate Assurance. For the sale of goods, the UCC's rules for dealing with breach and repudiation problems are substantially the same as the common-law principles discussed above. (See UCC 2–106(3) and (4), 2–610, 2–611, and 2–712.) The Code does, however, give the injured party one very important new protection: the right to demand "adequate assurance" (2–609).

Even though a breach by one of the parties to a goods contract is not material enough in itself to justify rescission of the whole contract (e.g., a two- or three-day delay in delivery of one month's shipment of goods on an installment contract), such a break may create a doubt in the mind of the other party as to whether he or she will be able and willing to continue to perform. The same is true where one party has repudiated and then retracted: Does he or she mean it or not? When will he or she change his or her mind again?

In any case where one party has reasonable grounds for feeling "insecure," he or she may make a written demand that the other party furnish him or her with "adequate assurance of due performance." So long as he or she is being commercially reasonable, he or she can withhold any performance of his or her own "for which he or she has not already received the agreed return" until he or she gets a reasonable assurance that the other party will perform. Where a proper demand for assurance has been made, the other party's failure to respond within a reasonable time (not over 30 days) is treated as a repudiation of the contract. At that point, the party who made the demand can go ahead and make other arrangements, without him- or herself being guilty of a breach, and sue for any damages he or she sustains because of the other party's repudiation.

DISCHARGE BY NEW AGREEMENT

The parties themselves created their reciprocal rights and duties by making the agreement. It's their contract, and unless the rights of third parties are involved in some way, the parties can call off their agreement anytime they both wish to do so, or they can substitute a new arrangement for the old one. There are many technical terms to describe the different types of new agreements, but they all come down to the same basic argument: "My nonperformance under the original contract was excused because we made a new deal." We now consider the main types of "new deals."

Mutual Rescission. As a rule, the parties can call off their existing contract anytime they wish, as long as they both agree to do so. This case is called a "mutual rescission," to distinguish it from the case where the *remedy* of rescission is given to one party because of a material breach by the other. If the parties have mutually agreed to a rescission, neither can later claim that the other's nonperformance of the contract was a breach.

Where partial performance has already occurred, the mutual rescission agreement should provide for part payment or restitution. If there is no such provision in the rescission agreement, any retained benefits would almost certainly have to be paid for at fair market value.

Novation. Although the derivation and commonsense meaning of the term *novation* would seem to apply to any new agreement which the parties intend to substitute for their existing contract, the courts generally apply the term only to those new arrangements which involve a substitution of parties. That is, a new debtor is substituted for the original debtor, with the consent of the creditor, or the obligation is assigned to a new creditor for whom the debtor agrees to perform.

If, in the take-over-the-payments example used in the last chapter, the mortgage/creditor agrees to accept the resale buyer as the sole obligor and to discharge the original mortgage/debtor, there has been a novation. Whether the new agreement is called a "novation" or simply a "new contract," it must itself be a valid contract in order to have the effect of discharging the original one.

Accord and Satisfaction. This term is usually applied to a situation where the obligee/creditor has agreed to accept a substituted performance, in place of the one originally agreed to. For example, Dan Debtor owes Car Creditor $1,000. Dan does not have the cash, but he does own a used car, which he offers to convey to Carl in lieu of the $1,000. Carl, of course, does not have to take the car; he can sue Dan for the $1,000 if it is not paid when due. If Carl does agree to take the car, there is an "accord." At that point, the $1,000 debt is not yet discharged; if Carl does not get the car, he can sue Dan either for $1,000 or for breach of the accord. When Dan delivers the car as agreed, however, the $1,000 debt has been discharged by an *accord and satisfaction.*"

Unfortunately, from the standpoint of clarity, courts also use the term *accord and satisfaction* to refer to situations involving part payment of a debt, especially where the debt is in dispute. (See our earlier discussion of this problem in Chapter 6.) The creditor's cashing of the "in full" check is his agreement to the "accord and satisfaction" and his acceptance of the substituted performance thereunder.

Waiver or Estoppel. A waiver is the intentional surrender of a known right or benefit; a person simply chooses not to demand that something which is due him or her be given. Your apartment lease, for example, specifies that the rent must be paid in advance on the 1st of each month, but the landlord tells you that payment can be made by the 10th; this is a waiver of his right to insist on payment by the 1st. Ordinarily, this kind of waiver "before breach" can be retracted by proper notice to the other party, unless consideration was given for the waiver or unless the other party has made a substantial change of position in reliance on the waiver. Contrariwise, courts usually hold that a waiver of the right to sue for a breach which has already occurred does not require any new consideration to be binding. (See UCC 1–107, previously referred to in Chapter 6.) A waiver may also be inferred from a party's conduct.

Release. A release also involves the giving up of some right, but it is based on a written contract. Releases are commonly used in situations where there is a contingent or disputed liability, as in auto accident cases or in employment termination agreements. The law generally favors compromises and settlements of disputes, particularly in light of the tremendous backlog of civil litigation that is clogging the courts. Traditionally, therefore, courts have been reluctant to permit a party to avoid the effect of a release he or she has previously given unless there is very strong evidence of fraud, undue influence, mistake, and so on. While courts today are more and more willing to stretch a point in favor of the "little guy," the *Stetzel* (discussion) case shows that they will still look for some evidence to support the claimed defense against the effect of a release.

Account Stated. The "account stated" is based on the same fundamental principle as accord and satisfaction: the law favors settlements. Where, after a series of transactions between them, the parties have agreed on a final statement of the net amount due, there is an account stated. No further reliance can be placed on the earlier transactions; the amount which is now due and owing is that agreed to in the account stated. An account stated can arise when the creditor sends a summary statement of the account and the debtor retains the statement without objection beyond a reasonable time. In other words, the agreement to the account stated can be implied as well as expressed.

DISCHARGE BY "MERGER"

In general. As used here, the doctrine of "merger" means that the prior obligation has been superseded by a "better" one, better in the sense of being easier to prove, to transfer, or to collect. Merger may be effected by a new agreement between the parties or by judgment. The three most common examples of such better legal obligations (other than a judgment) are the sealed contract, the negotiable instrument, and the secured debt. Since many states have abolished by statute the common-law effect of the seal on the presumption of consideration, there would be no merger effect in those states, if a sealed contract were given in satisfaction of an unsealed one. In a state where the seal makes the contract easier to prove in court, or (perhaps) even if the seal only has the effect of keeping the debt alive for a longer time, the acceptance of a sealed contract by the creditor in place of the unsealed one should have the merger effect.

A negotiable instrument is clearly a much better form of legal obligation than an ordinary "open-book account." For example, you owe your dentist, Dr. Peter Pullit, $300 for services rendered. If he sues to collect, he will have to produce office records, witnesses, and so forth, to prove that he in fact gave you this consideration and that you agreed to pay for it at his prices. Such a collection suit would involve substantial disruption of his regular office routine and a loss of time and money, even though he would ultimately win. If he accepts your offer of a 90-day negotiable promissory note for $250 as satisfaction of the account, he could in fact be net dollars ahead even if he is forced to sue on the note, since the note carries a presumption of consideration which *you* would have to overcome with evidence. Because of this fact, the note is much more readily transferable than the account. If your dentist doesn't want to wait the 90 days and collect the interest, he will have a much easier time selling your note to a bank than he would have in assigning your account.

Finally, if the debt is made more certain of collection because the debtor gives the creditor a mortgage or other security interest against a specific piece of the debtor's property, that is clearly a better deal for the creditor. If your dentist agrees to take your new contract promise to pay $250, secured by your used car as collateral, in satisfaction of the $300 open-book amount, there has been a merger and the old account debt is discharged.

Judgment. The doctrine of res judicata says that once "the thing has been adjudicated," it cannot be relitigated. Whatever rights and duties may have been alleged as the result of the prior legal relationship, they have been superseded by the court's final judgment; the prior obligations have been merged into the judgment.

The following case illustrates the doctrine of res judicata and also shows the important distinction between a "joint" debt (where all debtors must be sued at the same time if they are to be held liable) and a "joint and several" obligation (where the creditor may get a judgment against one or more the debtors and still retain the right to sue the others). The same result would follow if the creditor released one joint debtor; he has released the entire debt against all the joint debtors.

B-OK, Inc. v. *Storey*
473 P.2d 426 (Washington, 1970)

FACTS   "For several years prior to April 30, 1962, defendants were partners in the petroleum products business at Cle Elum, doing business as Storey Distributing Company. On April 30, 1962, the defendants dissolved their partnership. At the time of dissolution of the partnership, defendants' account with plaintiff had a balance of $3,515.80.

"On December 27, 1963, plaintiff obtained a judgment against defendant Earl Storey, in Cause No. 15849 . . . for $3,735.47. Defendant William E. Storey was not a named defendant in Cause No. 15849. The judgment in Cause No. 15849 was based upon the identical account involved in this action.

"Plaintiff and defendants had a debtor-creditor relationship regarding this account which was based upon the sale of petroleum products by plaintiff to defendants. Defendants incurred this debt while they were partners. Defendants' liability toward plaintiff in no way involved a breach of trust or a tortious situation.

"The dissolution of the partnership by the defendants on April 30, 1962, in no way involved any fraudulent transactions between them affecting their creditors. It was a bona fide dissolution and division of assets, without any evidence of fraud on their creditors.

265

"There was no prayer for relief against defendant Earl Storey and his wife in the Amended Complaint herein.

"After April 30, 1962, defendant Earl Storey continued doing business selling petroleum products in Cle Elum, at the same location as before, without any visible alteration of the premises, under the assumed name of Storey Distributing Company, for approximately three years.

"Plaintiff concedes that he is charged with notice of the partnership dissolution and that Earl M. Storey was continuing to do business as the Storey Distributing Company, as the 'only person conducting or intending to conduct said business or having interest therein.'"

ISSUE   Is William Storey still liable on this partnership obligation?

DECISION   No. Judgment affirmed.

REASONS   (Opinion by Chief Justice Evans.) "The conclusion by the trial court that defendant William E. Storey should be dismissed is based on the Uniform Partnership Act and *Warren* v. *Rickles,* 129 Wash. 443, 225 p. 422 (1924), holding that:

> It is a very generally accepted rule of law that, where an obligation is joint and not joint and several, a judgment rendered on such obligation against one or more, but less than the whole number of obligors, is a bar to any action on the same claim against the obligors not parties to the judgment, because the claim is merged in the judgment and is extinguished thereby.

"We hold the trial court correctly concluded that after dissolution the liability of the retiring partner William Storey to plaintiff remained a joint liability, and that plaintiff's claim against him was merged in the prior judgment taken against the continuing partner, Earl Storey. The trial court, therefore, did not err in dismissing William Storey."

DISCHARGE BY "OPERATION OF LAW"

Statute of Limitations. At least in most states, debts do not last forever. At some point, it becomes rather unfair for an alleged creditor to revive ancient history and begin a litigation over a matter which should have been long forgotten (and probably has been by nearly everyone else). Again, the law encourages the parties to settle their disputes and requires them to commence any necessary litigation before memories fade completely. At some point, if no action has been taken to enforce an alleged obligation, it is good public policy to declare that the debtor has a defense if he or she does not wish to pay the ancient debt. This "statute of limitations" defense is a technical one, and it is not particularly favored by the courts, but where it does apply it is a complete defense against a lawsuit based on the old debt. In most states the limitations period for tort actions is considerably shorter than the one for contracts.

Bankruptcy: Composition with Creditors. A discharge in a bankruptcy proceeding also operates as a technical defense in favor of the debtor, as to all debts and claims provable under bankruptcy rules. This same result occurs whether the debtor has filed his or her own, "voluntary" petition with the bankruptcy court or has been forced into an "involuntary" bankruptcy by one or more of his or her creditors (see Chapter 51). Like the statute of limitations, a bankruptcy discharge is a technical defense which can be waived by the debtor when he or she makes a new promise after bankruptcy to pay the old debt.

To avoid the administrative costs and (some of) the legal expenses incident to a bankruptcy proceeding, a person's creditors may as a group voluntarily agree to accept less than full payment in full satisfaction of their debts. A creditor cannot be forced to make such an agreement, but he or she may wish to do so in order to get a higher percentage of his or her claim paid than he or she would if the debtor were forced through bankruptcy. Such a "composition with creditors" operates like an accord and satisfaction.

Subsequent Illegality.   Where the performances called for by the contract were legal when made but were subsequently made illegal by statute or administrative regulation, the now-illegal contract duties are discharged by "operation by law." This is clearly the only fair result: neither party normally assumes this kind of risk, and neither ought to be forced to perform if by doing so, he or she is breaking the law. The adoption of the 18th Amendment and the Volstead Act, which made it illegal to manufacture, transport, or sell alcoholic beverages, provided one illustration of this rule in operation. More current examples might involve changes in the legal rules pertaining to foreign investments, currency exchange, ownership of gold by U.S. citizens, sale of "strategic" materials to Communist-bloc countries, and the like.

Impossibility.   Where a contract specifies performance by one certain party or where the performance requires the existence of a particular thing, the death or disability of the party or the destruction of the thing will normally operate to discharge the performance obligation through "objective impossibility." That is, because the contract is so specific, no one at all can render the required performance. A promise to deliver "all of my tomato crop" is discharged if the tomato crop is destroyed without any fault on the part of the grower. A promise to deliver "1,000 tons of tomatoes" is probably not discharged when the grower's own crop fails, because he or she could buy other tomatoes on the market and deliver them; where no specific thing is identified, there is only "subjective impossibility," which does not operate to discharge contract obligations.

Christy v. *Pilkinton*
273 S.W.2d 533 (1954)

FACTS   "The parties executed a valid written contract by which the Christys agreed to buy an apartment house from Mr. Pilkinton for $30,000. The vendor's title is admittedly good. When the time came for performance, the purchasers, although not insolvent, were unable to raise enough money to carry out their contract. Mrs. Pilkinton, after having tendered a deed to the property, brought this suit. At the trial the defendants' evidence tended to show that, as a result of a decline in Christy's used car business, they do not possess and cannot borrow the unpaid balance of $29,900."

ISSUE   Does defendants' financial inability to perform constitute "impossibility"?

DECISION   No. Judgment affirmed.

REASONS   (Opinion by Justice Smith.) "Proof of this kind does not establish the type of impossibility that constitutes a defense. There is a familiar distinction between objective impossibility, which amounts to saying, 'The thing cannot be done,' and subjective impossibility—'I cannot do it.' The latter, which is well illustrated by a promisor's financial inability to pay, does not discharge a contractual duty and is therefore not a bar to a decree for specific performance.

"Much of the appellants' brief is devoted to a discussion of the difficulty that the chancellor may have in enforcing his decree; but that problem is not now before us. By the decree the defendants were allowed a period of 20 days in which to perform their obligation. If their default continues, it will, of course, be for the chancellor to say whether further relief should be granted, as by a foreclosure of the vendor's lien or by other process available to a court of equity. At present it is enough to observe that foreseeable obstacles to the enforcement of a judgment are not a sufficient reason for denying the relief to which the plaintiff is entitled."

Commercial Impracticability and Frustation. Closely related to the idea of impossibility are the ideas of "impracticability" and "frustration." A performance may not actually be impossible to render, but it may be financially impracticable to do it, in the sense that it is stupid or nonsensical to require the performance. If a trucking company has a contract to transport a racehorse to Churchill Downs for the Kentucky Derby, and the horse dies, it would clearly be commercially impracticable to require the owner to pay the trucking company for transporting the dead horse to Churchill Downs, although that performance is not impossible. The UCC contains specific provisions, in Section 2–615, for dealing with this problem in sale of goods cases.

"Frustration" is also closely related to "impossibility." Again, the performance specified in the contract is not technically impossible, but the entire *purpose* or reason for making the contract no longer exists because of the happening of some unforeseeable event. The classic case of frustration involved the renting of rooms in London for exorbitant prices so as to be able to see the coronation parade of King Edward VII. On the day designated in the "leases," there was no parade because the king had caught a cold and postponed it. Although there was nothing impossible about performance by either the landlord or the tenant, at least one English court agreed that the contract duty should be discharged.

The following case is a more recent example of these infrequently litigated points.

Wood v. Bartolino
146 P.2d 883 (New Mexico, 1944)

FACTS "The appellant leased a building to appellees 'for use solely as a filling station and not for a restaurant or lunch counter purposes,' at a rental of $100 per month for a term of five years commencing June 1, 1939. It was operated by sub-lessees until February 1, 1941, and thereafter until July 1, 1942, by appellees, when the latter ceased its operation and offered to restore possession of the premises upon the alleged ground that the lease contract had been terminated because of 'commercial frustration' resulting from government rules, regulations, and orders freezing automobiles, tires, and tubes and rationing the sale of gasoline, so that it was 'impossible and impracticable to use or operate the leased premises as a filling station' at any time after the first of December, 1942; and that such 'impossibility and impracticability' still continued and would continue throughout the term of lease. . . .

"The filling station in question is located near the center of the business district of Raton, New Mexico, on the main highway passing through that city. Appellees' customers were mainly tourists and commercial travellers who used this highway. Ordinarily tourist travel is heavy, beginning in May and continuing through the summer and autumn. The Federal rules and regulations which limited and restricted the sales of tires, tubes, and automobiles became effective about the first of 1942 and have since continued in effect. These regulations so seriously reduced the operation of motor vehicles that the travel of tourists and commercial travellers practically and abruptly ceased."

ISSUE Was the contract discharged by commercial frustration?

DECISION No. Judgment reversed.

REASONS (Opinion by Justice Brice.) "The parties, at the time the lease contract was entered into, did not contemplate, and could not reasonably have contemplated, that such laws, rules, and regulations would be enacted, promulgated, or enforced, or that they would materially and substantially change the conditions of the business operated in the leased premises.

"Appellees' evidence shows that the total income for the 11 months during which the filling station was operated by them in 1941 was $1,568.93, and that during the same time the expense of operation was $2,096.69, leaving a deficit of $527.76, or an average deficit of $47.98 per month. . . .

"It would appear from the facts just stated that it was not impossible to operate the filling station prior or subsequent to the effective dates of the laws, orders, and regulations of the Federal Government to which reference has been made; but that from the beginning of its operation by appellees, it was impracticable in the sense that it could only be operated at a loss, and that the effect of the enforcement of the Federal rules, laws, and regulations only made bad matters worse by increasing the deficit of a worthless business.

"[I]t is the rule that in the absence of an eviction, actual or constructive, or a complete destruction of the leasehold, a tenant is bound to discharge his covenant to pay rent, unless he is relieved therefrom by the happening of some event which by the covenants of the lease terminates it.

"This rule is based upon the common-law principle that a leasehold is an interest in real property and that the lessee is obligated to pay the purchase price (rent) unless relieved by its terms or by eviction, actual or constructive, or by a complete destruction of the leasehold.

"There are no Federal regulations prohibiting the sale of gasoline, oil, tires, tubes, and other merchandise ordinarily sold at filling stations, though the enforcement of such regulations has drastically reduced appellees' income, which before was less than operating expenses; nor has any Federal law, rule, or regulation deprived appellees of the use of the premises as a filling station. It follows that the trial court erred in denying recovery of rent by appellant.

"It is just, and no doubt to the best interest of landlords, for them to voluntarily shoulder a portion of the burden, and that it is being done generally, we are advised. But the appellant may enforce the covenant to pay her rent. In such cases relief lies only in the conscience of the landlord, to which in this case, it appears, fruitless appeals for relief have been made."

CASES FOR DISCUSSION

BABB'S, INC. v. BABB
169 N.W.2d 211 (Iowa, 1969)

Stuart, Justice

Plaintiff purchased a business property from defendants on contract. After plaintiff had operated it for several months, defendants took possession without court authority under claim of right by virtue of statutory forfeiture proceedings under chapter 656, Code of Iowa. Plaintiff brought this action in forcible entry to recover possession, claiming defendants waived the right to proceed with the forfeiture by accepting payment of some of the delinquencies. The trial court ordered the petition dismissed, ruled the contract had been forfeited, and confirmed possession and title in defendants. We reverse.

On October 1, 1966, plaintiff contracted to purchase Babb's, a cocktail lounge, café, and apartment complex in Coralville, from defendants for $103,309.39 with $10,000 down and $1,000 per month commencing November 1, 1966. Plaintiff entered into possession in October and made payments on time for November and

December 1966 and January and February 1967. The monthly payments for March and April were not made, and defendants had notice of forfeiture served on plaintiff April 26, 1967. On May 29, 1967, plaintiff paid defendants $3,000 representing the March, April, and May payments. Mr. Dean Coglan, president of plaintiff corporation, was advised future payments were to be made when due.

Failing to receive timely payment of the installment due June 1, 1967, defendants caused plaintiff to be served with notice of forfeiture on June 9. This notice alleged default on the $1,000 payment due June 1 and the first half of the 1966 real estate taxes amounting to $872.63 due March 1, 1967, which became delinquent June 1, 1967. On June 15 and July 1, plaintiff paid and defendants accepted the $1,000 payments for June and July 1967. The taxes were not paid.

By June plaintiff had accumulated $20–25,000 in accounts payable. Between June and September it attempted to sell the property, but was unable to find a purchaser who would pay enough down to make the additional cash payment to defendants required by the contract in the event of a sale. Defendants knew of the negotiations and refused to take less cash than called for in the contract.

Defendants, who were renting one of the apartments, paid plaintiff the monthly rental for July, August, and September after the notice of forfeiture was served June 9.

On August 15, 1967, the notice of forfeiture was recorded as required by chapter 656, Code of Iowa. On September 1, 1967, plaintiff was served with a three day notice to quit. On September 5, defendants took possession without filing a lawsuit, changed the locks on the building, and kept plaintiff out of possession.

Plaintiff instituted this action. At the time of trial plaintiff had not made or tendered any further payments on the contract and had not paid any real or personal taxes.

I. Plaintiff concedes defendants complied with the provisions of chapter 656. It contends defendants waived their rights to declare a forfeiture under the notice served June 9, 1967. The specific question for our determination is whether defendants, by accepting two $1,000 payments, after the notice of forfeiture was served, waived their rights to declare a forfeiture for failure to pay delinquent real estate taxes also listed as a default in the notice of forfeiture.

Forfeitures are not favored in either law or equity, and they are enforced only when it is shown the equities clearly required forfeiture.

Waiver is the voluntary and intentional relinquishment of a known right. It is largely a matter of intent which may be ascertained from a person's conduct.

We believe the record here shows defendants did not intend to stand upon the notice of forfeiture and waived their rights to proceed thereunder.

Defendants' conduct was inconsistent with any intention to treat the contract as retained partial payments under the contract. They made rental payments to the contract purchaser. They did not object to plaintiff's negotiations for a sale of the premises.

There is authority in other states for the proposition that the acceptance of partial payment of the delinquencies after notice of forfeiture has been served amounts to a waiver of any right to claim forfeiture under such notice.

"A forfeiture is waived where the vendor, after serving the vendee a notice of forfeiture, accepts some payment on the contract."

We have not passed directly on the point, but have, by dictum, clearly indicated our acceptance of the rule set out above.

Both parties cite *Janes* v. *Towne*, 201 Iowa 690, 207 N.W. 790, and *Moore* v. *Elliott*, 213 Iowa 374, 239 N.W.32. Each points to language therein which is favorable to it. However, the cases do not reach the precise issue before us here. In *Janes*, purchaser sought to defend against a forfeiture because vendor had accepted late and partial payments of interest in the past. The notice of forfeiture was for the balance of an interest payment which was not paid within the 30 days. Vendor did not accept a partial payment after the notice of forfeiture was served.

Moore v. *Elliott* involved a tender of a partial payment which vendors refused, and the refusal was claimed as a waiver.

We have already pointed out that *Janes* v. *Towne*, supra, does not reach our issue. *Jewell* v. *Logsdon*, supra, and *Collins* v. *Nagel*, supra, do not involve forfeitures, but foreclosures of real estate mortgages. They hold acceptance of partial payment did not waive the right to foreclose. The vendor's rights under forfeiture and foreclosure are quite different. One can accept partial payments of real estate mortgage obligation quite consistently with foreclosure. Such payments merely reduce the balance due the mortgage. "The mortgagee cannot be penalized for the mere receipt of that to which he is, in equity and good conscience, entitled."

It is not consistent or equitable for a party to declare a contract forfeited and continue to accept partial payments thereunder. The vendor takes the property back and keeps the payments made. Any payments received and retained after the declaration of forfeiture would be windfall to which the vendor is not in equity entitled.

Now, the plaintiff could not be allowed to accept partial payment, and say at the same time that, the payment being partial, the contract is void, and the partial payment thus made is forfeited. The very act of accepting partial payment was a waiver of strict performance as to the balance of that payment. No other theory would consist with good faith. The acceptance, to be sure, was not a waiver of the payment of the

271

balance, and the plaintiff, unless there was an agreement to the contrary, might probably demand it at any time. But, after accepting partial payment, we think that the plaintiff should have demanded the balance before he could properly claim that Lint was in default.

In so far as *Cassiday* v. *Adamson* is contrary to our holding here, it is overruled.

We do not mean to indicate that there might not be some instances in which the entire record would show an intent to pursue the forfeiture even though a partial payment had been accepted. But when, as here, partial payment has been accepted and retained beyond a reasonable time after purchasers failed to pay the full delinquency within the 30 day period; where vendors knew purchaser was attempting to negotiate a sale and apparently approved of this procedure; and where vendors continued to pay rent to purchaser after notice of forfeiture, we believe it is clear they recognized the existence of the contract and intended to waive the right to forfeit it. There was no indication of any different intent until the notice and return of service were filed August 15.

II. Although defendants had started legal proceedings to obtain possession, they, claiming waste, entered into possession by stealth and barred plaintiff from possession. We need not decide the effect of this action in this particular instance, but believe it advisable to state there is considerable merit in plaintiff's contention that defendants acted unlawfully in doing so.

The plaintiffs were in peaceable possession of the premises in controversy. They had never been ejected by legal proceedings nor otherwise. The marshal had destroyed the fence so far as it was in what was claimed to be streets and alleys, but he did not attempt to interfere with the possession of the plaintiffs as to the remainder of the premises. If the defendant had owned them with the right to immediate possession when he destroyed the fence, his acts would, nevertheless, have been wrongful. The law has provided a remedy in such cases, and will not permit the owner to enter into possession by stealth or force.

III. Defendants argue a party seeking relief from a forfeiture must tender full performance of

his defaulted obligations. This general rule has no application where the rights to forfeit have been waived. Defendants treat the waiver argument, which we have held determinative, in a rather offhand manner. It may be because they, as we, have not found authority to the contrary.

We hold defendants acted without proper authority of law in taking possession of these premises September 5, 1967, under the notice of forfeiture and plaintiffs should not have been ousted from possession thereunder.

We understand Babb's has been operated since that time. We do not know by whom or under what sort of an arrangement. We realize this decision necessarily leaves many questions unanswered and many equities between these parties undetermined. These matters cannot properly be considered in a forcible entry which is intended to be a summary remedy to place the proper party in possession.

For the reasons stated this case is reversed and remanded for judgment entry in accordance herewith.

All Justices concur.

TRANSATLANTIC FINANCING CORP. v. UNITED STATES
363 F.2d 312 (District of Columbia Circuit, 1966)

J. Skelly Wright, Circuit Judge

This appeal involves a voyage charter between Transatlantic Financing Corporation, operator of the SS *Christos*, and the United States covering carriage of a full cargo of wheat from a United States Gulf port to a safe port in Iran. The District Court dismissed a libel filed by Transatlantic against the United States for costs attributable to the ship's diversion from the normal sea route caused by the closing of the Suez Canal. We affirm.

On July 26, 1956, the Government of Egypt nationalized the Suez Canal Company and took over operation of the Canal. On October 2, 1956, during the international crisis which resulted from the seizure, the voyage charter in suit was executed between representatives of Transatlantic and the United States. The charter indicated the termini of the voyage but not the route. On October 27, 1956, the SS *Christos* sailed from Galveston for Bandar Shapur, Iran, on a course which would have taken her through Gibralter and the Suez Canal. On October 29, 1956, Israel invaded Egypt. On October 31, 1956, Great Britain and France invaded the Suez Canal Zone. The Government of Egypt obstructed the Suez Canal with sunken vessels and closed it to traffic.

On or about November 7, 1956, Beckmann, representing Transatlantic, contacted Potosky, an employee of the United States Department of Agriculture, who appellant concedes was unauthorized to bind the Government, requesting instructions concerning disposition of the cargo and seeking an agreement for payment of additional compensation for a voyage around the Cape of Good Hope. Potosky advised Beckmann that Transatlantic was expected to perform the charter according to its terms, that he did not believe Transatlantic was entitled to additional compensation for a voyage around the Cape, but that Transatlantic was free to file such a claim. Following this discussion, the *Christos* changed course for the Cape of Good Hope and eventually arrived in Bandar Shapur on December 30, 1956.

Transatlantic's claim is based on the following train of argument. The charter was a contract for a voyage from a Gulf port to Iran. Admiralty principles and practices, especially stemming from the doctrine of deviation, require us to imply into the contract the term that the voyage was to be performed by the "usual and customary" route. The usual and customary route from Texas to Iran was, at the time of contract, via Suez, so the contract was for a voyage from Texas to Iran via Suez. When Suez was closed, this contract became impossible to perform. Consequently, appellant's argument continues, when Transatlantic delivered the cargo by going around the Cape of Good Hope, in compliance with the Government's demand under claim of right, it conferred a benefit upon the United States for which it should be paid in quantum meruit.

The doctrine of impossibility of performance has gradually been freed from the earlier fictional and unrealistic strictures of such tests as the "implied term" and the parties' "contemplation."

It is now recognized that "'A thing is impossible in legal contemplation when it is not practicable; and a thing is impracticable when it can only be done at an excessive and unreasonable cost.'" The doctrine ultimately represents the ever-shifting line, drawn by courts hopefully responsive to commercial practices and mores, at which the community's interest in having contracts enforced according to their terms is outweighed by the commercial senselessness of requiring performance. When the issue is raised, the court is asked to construct a condition of performance based on the changed circumstances, a process which involves at least three reasonably definable steps. First, a contingency—something unexpected—must have occurred. Second, the risk of the unexpected occurrence must not have been allocated either by agreement or by custom. Finally, occurrence of the contingency must have rendered performance commercially impracticable. Unless the court finds these three requirements satisfied, the plea of impossibility must fail.

The first requirement was met here. It seems reasonable, where no route is mentioned in a contract, to assume the parties expected performance by the usual and customary route at the time of contract. Since the usual and customary route from Texas to Iran at the time of contract was through Suez, closure of the Canal made impossible the expected method of performance, but this unexpected development raises rather than resolves the impossibility issue, which turns additionally on whether the risk of the contingency's occurrence had been allocated and, if not, whether performance by alternative routes was rendered impracticable.

Proof that the risk of a contingency's occurrence has been allocated may be expressed in or implied from the agreement. Such proof may also be found in the surrounding circumstances, including custom and usage of the trade. The contract in this case does not expressly condition performance upon availability of the Suez route. Nor does it specify "via Suez" or, on the other hand, "via Suez or Cape of Good Hope." Nor are there provisions in the contract from which we may properly imply that the continued availability of

Suez was a condition of performance. Nor is there anything in customer or trade usage, or in the surrounding circumstances generally, which would support our constructing a condition of performance. The numerous cases requiring performance around the Cape when Suez was closed, indicate that the Cape route is generally regarded as an alternative means of performance. So the implied expectation that the route would be via Suez is hardly adequate proof of an allocation of the promises of the risk of closure. In some cases, even an express expectation may not amount to a condition of performance. The doctrine of deviation supports our assumption that parties normally expect performance by the usual and customary route, but it adds nothing beyond this that is probative of an allocation of the risk.

If anything, the circumstances surrounding this contract indicate that the risk of the Canal's closure may be deemed to have been allocated to Transatlantic. We know or may safely assume that the parties were aware, as were most commercial men with interests affected by the Suez situation, that the Canal might become a dangerous area. No doubt the tension affected freight rates, and it is arguable that the risk of closure became part of the dickered terms.

We do not deem the risk of closure so allocated, however. Foreseeability or even recognition of a risk does not necessarily prove its allocation. Parties to a contract are not always able to provide for all the possibilities of which they are aware, sometimes because they cannot agree, often simply because they are too busy. Moreover, that some abnormal risk was contemplated is probative but does not necessarily establish an allocation of the risk of the contingency which actually occurs. In this case, for example, nationalization by Egypt of the Canal Corporation and formation of the Suez Users Group did not necessarily indicate that the Canal would be blocked even if a confrontation resulted. The surrounding circumstances do indicate, however, a willingness by Transatlantic to assume abnormal risks, and this fact should legitimately cause us to judge the impracticability of performance by an alternative route in stricter terms than we would were the contingency unforeseen.

274

We turn then to the question whether occurrence of the contingency rendered performance commercially impracticable under the circumstances of this case. The goods shipped were not subject to harm from the longer, less temperate Southern route. The vessel and crew were fit to proceed around the Cape. Transatlantic was no less able than the United States to purchase insurance to cover the contingency's occurrence. If anything, it is more reasonable to expect owner-operator of vessels to insure against the hazards of war. They are in the best position to calculate the cost of performance by alternative routes (and therefore to estimate the amount of insurance required), and are undoubtedly sensitive to international troubles which uniquely affect the demand for and cost of their services. The only factor operating here in appellant's favor is the added expense, allegedly $43,972.00 above and beyond the contract price of $305,842.92, of extending a 10,000 mile voyage by approximately 3,000 miles. While it may be an overstatement to say that increased cost and difficulty of performance never constitute impracticability, to justify relief there must be more of a variation between expected costs and the cost of performing by an available alternative than is present in this case, where the promisor can legitimately be presumed to have accepted some degree of abnormal risk, and where impracticability is urged on the basis of added expense alone.

We conclude, therefore, as have most other courts considering related issues arising out of the Suez closure, that performance of this contract was not rendered legally impossible. Even if we agreed with appellant, its theory of relief seems untenable. When performance of a contract is deemed impossible, it is a nullity. In the case of the charter party involving carriage of goods, the carrier may return to an appropriate port and unload its cargo, subject of course to required steps to minimize damages. If the performance rendered has value, recovery in quantum meruit for the entire performance is proper. But here Transatlantic has collected its contract price, and now seeks quantum meruit relief for the additional expense of the trip around the Cape. If the contract is a nullity, Transatlantic's theory of relief should have been quantum meruit for the entire trip, rather than only for the extra expense. Transatlantic attempts to take its profit on the contract, and then force the Government to absorb the cost of the additional voyage. When impracticability without fault occurs, the law seeks an equitable solution, and quantum meruit is one of its potent devices to achieve this end. There is no interest in casting the entire burden of commercial disaster on one party in order to preserve the other's profit. Apparently the contract price in this case was advantageous enough to deter appellant from taking a stance on damages consistent with its theory of liability. In any event, there is no basis for relief.

Affirmed.

STETZEL v. DICKENSON
174 N.W.2d 438 (Iowa, 1970)

LeGrand, Justice

This case arises out of an intersection accident which occurred in Iowa City on September 27, 1965, as a result of which plaintiff sustained certain personal injuries. On December 2, 1965, she executed a release and was paid $400 by defendant's insurance carrier.

Being dissatisfied with her settlement, plaintiff subsequently brought this action against defendant, seeking damages for her injuries. Defendant relied on the release as a complete defense. Plaintiff then alleged the settlement was the result of mutual mistake and was not voluntarily entered into because of the "extreme mental pressure" exerted upon her and the "high-pressure tactics" practiced by the insurance carrier. These issues were submitted to the jury over defendant's timely motion for directed verdict. The jury found for plaintiff the amount of $3,000. Defendant filed a motion for judgment notwithstanding the verdict under rule 243, Rules of Civil Procedure, which was also overruled.

Certain rules have evolved which are determinative of this appeal:

1. A release is a contract, and its validity is governed by the rules related to contract;

2. A release may be set aside for mutual mistake of a material past or present fact, and the one who seeks that relief has the burden of proof;

3. There is a definite trend toward granting relief liberally where the injured party has released a claim under the false impression he was fully informed as to the nature and extent of his injuries;

4. In determining if there was mutual mistake, we consider whether the settlement amount was based on an item-by-item computation or was a lump-sum payment for the damages sustained; whether the question of liability was compromised as part of the settlement; and whether the amount paid was so inadequate as to indicate the matter of settling future or unknown damages was not within the contemplation of the parties;

5. It is the manifest intent of the parties, not the particular language used, which controls; and

6. An agreement to compromise unknown injuries and future damages is valid and enforceable if the parties intended that result at the time the settlement agreement was made.

We might add that each case depends on its own peculiar facts and circumstances and, to repeat once more a familiar cliché, that the rules above set out are easy to state but difficult to apply. . . .

We recognized this recently when we said in *Thomas v. Sheehan,* supra, 260 Iowa at page 624, 149 N.W.2d at page 845:

We are not unaware of the dilemma in which claims adjusters find themselves in trying to settle as against unknown injuries and future developments. . . . But we are not convinced that the alleviation of a harsh rule [which would hold releases to be final regardless of mistake] is necessarily bad. The development of the law permitting correction of mistakes has been in the interest of justice. The doctrine that courts favor compromises still has meaning, but when it appears that a mistake has been made it is proper to take a look at the factual situation as it existed when the words were written.

It seems unnecessary to point out that not every mistake will vitiate a settlement. It must be mutual, and it must be material; and it must be concerned with a present or past fact. . . .

Plaintiff's injury occurred when the accident impact threw her sideways, causing her head to strike the window. Almost immediately she experienced a headache. She went to the Student Health Center—she was then a student at the University of Iowa—where she was kept overnight. She was attended by a Dr. Dewey, who released her to return home the following day. Her headaches continued. She stated it was "a headache like you would expect to have if you got hit on the head." For some weeks she "didn't feel good," by which she said she meant she had headaches. The doctor gave her "pain pills," and when necessary she would take a pill and lie down. She said as long as she was "lying down, it was sort of gone." She testified that the headaches interfered with her ability to study, that her concentration was affected, and that her classes suffered.

During this time she asserts she was being importuned by the insurance company adjuster to sign a release and settle her claim. She declares she was reluctant to talk with him, but he was so persistent she was unable to avoid him. Finally, on December 2, 1965, she signed a release for $400. As far as the evidence shows, she then had incurred no medical or other expense of any kind. She was not employed and had no loss of income, although there is some suggestion she would have sought employment except for the accident.

Shortly, if not immediately, after the settlement her symptoms began to change. The type of pain was different although it will still confined to headaches. They merely became more severe. At the end of December, or the first of January, she noticed something different with reference to the use of her hands. She seemed to have difficulty picking things up at times. This was not present before she signed the release. She also noticed that after the accident her eyes would tire more easily, particularly her right one. Sometimes, too, she seemed to be forgetful, a condition which did not exist prior to the accident. She testified she was still having headaches at the time of the trial, although they had become infrequent.

We are convinced plaintiff's case fits the pattern of *Wieland* v. *Cedar Rapids & Iowa City Railway Co.*, where we said:

Here there was a settlement for a lump sum having no relation to any computation based on estimated loss of time and expense. The parties clearly intended to cover future developments, whatever they might be. . . .

Plaintiff testifies that if she had known she would "experience and suffer the conditions" that have arisen, she would not have made the settlement. But that does not help her. Practically every settlement for personal injury involves the element of chance as to future consequences and developments. There are usually unknown and unknowable conditions (congenital or otherwise) that may affect the ultimate recovery or failure of recovery. Mutual ignorance of their existence cannot constitute "mutual mistake." No two persons have the same power of recuperation, and the settlement is an agreement by which both take the chance that the amount paid eventually prove to have been too great or too small.

Perhaps we have spent too much time on this matter since we find there is another, and greater obstacle, to plaintiff's cause. We have already mentioned a claimant may foreclose future damages, even those arising from injuries then unknown, if that is the intention at the time the settlement is made. Here we cannot escape the conclusion that the parties did intend that result. On cross-examination plaintiff testified as follows:

As far as I know I told the representative of the insurance company about the difficulties I was having when I visited with him. The accident happened in September, and it was in December that I signed a release and accepted a draft for $400. *I understood what the paper was and that they were paying me for damages as a result of the accident. I understood the paper that I signed, but I didn't want to sign it. It was my understanding that I was releasing them from all further claims when I signed the release. It was explained to me that this would be conclusion and settlement and end to it. I knew what the agreement was that I was signing, and I read and understood it.* . . . (Emphasis supplied.)

Under the principles we have previously referred to, we find this was meant by the parties to be a final and complete settlement of plaintiff's claim, that it was so understood by plaintiff, and that no evidence upon which it could be set aside was produced by her.

We must also consider plaintiff's allegations that the release was obtained by "extreme mental pressure" and "high-pressure" tactics of the insurance adjuster. The parties considered this as a pleading that the release was the result of undue influence. The case was tried and submitted on that theory. We so consider it here.

Undue influence is defined as any "improper or wrongful constraint, machination, or urgency of persuasion whereby the will of a person is overpowered and he is induced to do or forbear an act which he would not do or would do if left to act freely." *Black's Law Dictionary*, rev. 4th ed.

In 17 Am.Jr.2d, Contracts, section 154, page 505, we find this, "Generally, in order to invalidate a contract, undue influence must operate to deprive a party of his free agency or will." A similar statement is found in 13 Am.Jur.2d, Cancellation of Instruments, section 29, page 522. . . .

We find no evidence here to support a finding that plaintiff executed the release as the result of undue influence. The fact that the adjuster was boorish and intruded upon plaintiff's privacy is not significant unless it resulted in depriving her of her independence of action and substituted his will for hers at the time the release was signed.

There is a total absence of evidence that it did. In fact the record proves conclusively to the contrary.

Plaintiff places great importance on her testimony that she did not want to sign. This is by no means the same as saying undue influence was exercised upon her. Plaintiff was a well-educated, highly intelligent young lady. Her scholastic record was outstanding. Before signing the release, she sought independent advice from her landlady, in whom she apparently had considerable confidence, and from an Iowa City lawyer—not counsel now representing her—whose help she now denounces. Whether his advice was good or bad is not the question we here consider. The fact that she sought and received independent advice is a proper matter to consider on the question of undue influence.

In addition to all this is the testimony heretofore set out in which plaintiff concedes she knew the purpose of the instrument, read it, understood it, and realized its consequences before signing. We hold all these circumstances refute undue influence as a matter of law.

We conclude defendant was entitled to a directed verdict, and the judgment for plaintiff is therefore reversed. We enter judgment for defendant as permitted under rule 349, Rules of Civil Procedure.

PROBLEMS FOR DISCUSSION

1. Sylvia Miklas was hired by the Naples, North Dakota, school board in February 1968 to teach home economics during the school year starting in September 1969. On September 1, 1969, not enough students had enrolled in the home economics courses to qualify the school to receive federal aid for them. As a result, Ms. Miklas was fired and she sued the school board for breach of contract. Her contract stated that the home economics program was to be carried out in keeping with the policies of the school board. The board claims that the power to hire teachers carries with it implicitly the power to fire them. Who wins?

2. Melissa Bowen was hired by the Copake school board to teach kindergarten and physical education at the Copake elementary school. When it was discovered that she lacked the valid certificates to teach these subjects, as required by her contract, she was assigned to be a study hall supervisor at the Stinson Educational Center, 25 miles from Copake but still in the school district. Melissa then sued the school board for breach of contract. The board said that her lack of certification constituted a failure to perform conditions precedent. Who wins?

3. In 1975 Edwin Shaw, a tenured professor in the School of Pharmacy of Carlisle University was fired because a cutback in federal funds to the pharmacy school greatly increased the pharmacy school's already existing deficit. Shaw's contract stated that he could be fired in the event of financial exigency on the part of the institution. Financial exigency was defined to include bona fide discontinuance of a program or department of instruction or reduction in size thereof. The university as a whole was not in financial trouble, and Shaw claimed that he could not be fired unless that were true. Can he get his job back?

4. In May 1974 Frank Spier contracted away his patent rights on the Superscope to the Olney Corporation in return for adequate consideration, including 50 percent of the shares in a planned corporation for marketing the device. The following year the Superscope Corporation was formed and the patent rights to the Superscope were assigned to it by the Olney Corporation. Spier agreed that the earlier agreement was canceled and received the right to buy one third of the shares of Superscope Corporation. The assignment of the patent rights to Superscope Corporation was declared void for lack of consideration. Spier now claims he owns the rights because no novation has canceled the original agreement. Who owns the patent rights?

5. In September 1973 Century Savings & Loan agreed to lend Molloy Construction $2 million to finance the construction of a building. When Molloy was delayed in obtaining a building permit, Century Savings withheld scheduled progress payments, and by the time the agreement expired in July 1975, Century Savings had lent Molloy only $1 million. In September 1975 the two parties entered into a new loan agreement, at a substantially higher interest rate. The agreement stated that its acceptance would constitute revocation and cancellation of the prior agreement. Now Molloy is suing Century Savings for failure to lend all the money promised in their original agreement. Molloy contends that cancellation of the original contract does not cancel its right to sue for breach of that contract. Who wins?

6. Benjamin Enterprise engaged Don Dough, a mortgage broker, to secure for him a loan which he needed to finance his newest real estate deal, Seedy Acres. The written contract stipulated a 2 percent fee if Don could secure a loan in accordance with Ben's terms or on different but still acceptable terms. A loan with different but still acceptable terms was found, and Ben accepted it. However, the commencement of construction on Seedy Acres was delayed and the loan agreement was never consummated. By the time Ben had straightened out his affairs the loan commitment period had expired and he had to secure a new loan. Don Dough, pointing to the letter of the contract, still wants his money. Benjamin Enterprises refuses to pay, claiming that the only reasonable interpretation of the contract was, of course, that the fee be contingent upon the actual consummation of the loan.

7. On December 27, 1974, Homer Haas sold Michael Mullin 50 milk cows, telling Mullin the cows were "clean," even though they had not been tested for brucellosis (a highly contagious cattle disease) as required by state law. In April 1975 Haas learned that the cows he sold Mullin might be contaminated with brucellosis and paid to have all of them tested. Two cows were identified as suspect and sold for slaughter; the rest of the herd received a clean bill of health. In June Haas approached Mullin and asked him what it would take to make things right. Mullin said that he had paid for 50 cows and he wanted fifty cows, and they agreed on $600. Later in the year more of the cows contracted brucellosis and the entire herd had to be sold for slaughter. Mullin sued Haas for the loss from the diseased cattle. Haas said the $600 he had already paid discharged any claim. Can Mullin collect from Haas for additional damages?

8. The G & M Construction Corporation entered into a contract to perform earth-moving and grading work for a golf course being built by the Heather Woods Corporation. The contract stipulated that all fairways would be covered with at least six inches of topsoil upon completion of the work. In general, the work was completed successfully, but Heather Woods withheld the final $3,000 payment from the total contract price of $19,000 when the topsoil depth was found to be inadequate in several places. It cost Heather Woods $2,000 to correct the situation when G & M didn't do so. G & M sued to receive its final $3,000 payment. Heather Woods countersued, asking $10,000 damages and claiming that the contract had been breached by G & M's failure to perform according to the specifications. Who wins, and how much?

9. In August 1970 Gordon listed his farm to be sold with a real estate broker. An employee of the broker found a buyer shortly thereafter, and on September 18 Gordon accepted an offer of $160,425 for the property. Pfab (the buyer) made a $5,000 advance payment, to be held by the broker until the installment contract was executed, which was to be on or before March 1, 1971.

    Soon after his offer was accepted, Pfab began to inquire about the productivity of the land and began to have doubts about whether the farm was as good as he had been led to believe. In October 1970 Pfab stopped payment on the $5,000 check. Pfab discussed the situation with the broker. Then, still unsatisfied as to his complaints, Pfab went directly to Gordon and asked for an agreement which would allow Pfab to forgo principal payments under the installment contract in any year in which corn production fell below a certain level. Gordon agreed. Pfab then issued another check for the advance payment.

    On February 22, 1971, Pfab sent Gordon a letter refusing to complete the contract and asking for the return of the $5,000. Upon receiving the letter, Gordon rented the farm to a new tenant for the coming crop year and sued Pfab for damages. Who wins? Why?

10. David and Marietta Kruger owned a 3,000-acre farm which they listed with Bowman Real Estate Company. Mr. and Mrs. Soreide indicated their interest in the land and signed a purchase agreement for $300,000. Being unsure about their ability to finance the purchase, the Soreides had the following clause inserted: "This sale is subject to buyer receiving Federal Land Bank financing." The financing fell through since Mr. Soreide did not agree to some of the bank's mortgage terms. The Krugers had to relist the property with Bowman which could find no buyer for them. Later the Krugers sold the property themselves, to a buyer who paid them $250,000. Now the Krugers are suing the Soreides and the realtor for $50,000, and the realtor has counterclaimed with a suit for his commission. Who wins? Why?

11. Vincent Erikson, an insurance agent, entered into an Agency Incentive Agreement with United Life Insurance Company. Under the agreement he was to be compensated for the policies he wrote, based on monthly accounting statements of the insurance company. In case of a disagreement he was to inform United in writing. A year later the agreement was terminated and United sent accounting statements to which Vincent made no objections in writing. However, he claims that he complained repeatedly over the phone. After three years Vincent's complaints had still not been answered by United and he proceeded to file a suit asking for an accounting. Decision?

13 | Remedies for Breach

Court Costs and Attorney Fees. A rational decision to litigate a claim must be based on economic, psychological and legal factors. In many cases a party can be a "legal winner"—that is, get a judgment in his or her favor—and still be an "economic loser," in the sense of not being compensated for all of his or her economic losses, to say nothing of the psychological strains endured during the litigation process. The potential litigant faces the distinct possibility of not recovering all out-of-pocket expenses for court costs and attorney fees. In addition, his or her "downtime" during litigation is not compensable; that is, he or she may collect lost revenue resulting from a breach of contract but will not collect "lost revenue" resulting from having to be in court. Also, any "mental stress" resulting from the pressures of the litigation process is not compensable.

Court costs (filing fees, jury fees, witness fees, transcripts, etc.) are usually assessed against the losing party. Where a "public question" is involved, however, the court may decide to let the taxpayers, rather than one of the parties, bear the costs of the litigation. The trial judge generally has great discretion in determining which items of costs were really necessary to the litigation and should therefore be paid by the loser.

Almost alone among the legal systems of the civilized world, the common-law system did not permit victorious litigants to recover their lawyers' charges as part of court costs. In large part, this rule resulted because each lawyer-client contract was the result of a private agreement, with no official fee schedule limiting the amount that could be charged. Since there was no general court control over legal fees, it was felt that the court could not properly charge them against the losing party. Lawyers' fees are still not generally included as court costs. To assess them against the losing party, there must be a specific provision to that effect in the contract of the parties or in a statute covering the kind of claim being litigated.

All of the above factors should be very carefully considered by anyone contemplating litigation. Even if you win legally, you may still lose financially.

Election of Remedies. The strict application of logical principles does not always produce "justice" in particular cases, and the early common law always tried to be logical. Where a plaintiff had two alternative remedies for an alleged breach of contract, for example, common-law rules of pleading required him or her to choose between them if they were "inconsistent." The two most clearly inconsistent remedies are specific performance and rescission and restitution. In the first, the plaintiff is insisting that the contract be performed as agreed; in the second, he or she wants to call off the whole deal and put everything back where it was.

The plaintiff's main difficulty under these early rules was that the choice had to be made the complaint was filed, that is, at a time when the plaintiff did not yet know whether he or she would be able to prove his or her case for restitution. A court might find that the plaintiff had waited too long to rescind, for example, and deny him or her the restitution remedy. But if the plaintiff then tried to sue for damages in a second case, the early civil procedure rules would say that he or she couldn't do that either because a binding "election of remedies" had been made when the first lawsuit was filed. As a result, in some cases the plaintiff received no remedy at all, just because he or she (or the lawyer) had guessed wrong initially.

Some of the injustice inherent in these rules has been removed by the adoption of civil procedure rules which permit the plaintiff to file a complaint asking for such inconsistent remedies in the alternative ("I want *either* rescission and restitution *or* damages"). Such alternative pleading is possible in a majority of states and in the U.S. district courts. Even with this liberalization, however, the plaintiff must still make an election of remedies at some point in the litigation. He or she must still decide whether he or she wants to keep the house with the leaky basement and get damages for the wet furniture and for fixing the leak or whether he or she wants the money back and a rescission of the house deal. If he or she gets the latter, he or she does *not* also get damages for the wet furniture; he or she bears those damages him- or herself if the contract is rescinded. Because of the potential harshness of election rules, it becomes important to know which remedies are inconsistent and thus require an election. The following case speaks to that point.

Billy Williams Builders & Development Inc. v. *Hillerich*
446 S.W.2d 280 (Kentucky, 1969)

FACTS   Hillerich sued Williams Builders for specific performance of a contract for sale of a house (which Williams was to build) and lot, for damages resulting from defective construction, and for damages resulting from delay in completion. An equity court ordered the specific performance and then transferred the case to the law docket, where a jury awarded Hillerich $3,318 in damages for the defective construction and $910.38 for the delay. Williams appealed.

ISSUE   Is the plaintiff asking for inconsistent remedies?

DECISION   No. Judgment affirmed.

Billy Williams Builders & Development Inc. v. Hillerich (continued)

REASONS   Justice Hill first summarized the defendant's argument: "Williams argues that by complying with the judgment for specific performance and by accepting the deed to the property, Hillerich elected to have one of two inconsistent remedies; and by so doing, he cannot back up to the 'forks of the road' and take a road different from the one on which he 'first embarked.' " The court said that specific performance could be combined with damages for delay in performance but that "damages for deficiency of quantity or quality present a more complex question on which there is some conflict among the authorities."

The court quoted the *Restatement of Contracts,* Section 365:

> The fact that a part of the promised performance cannot be rendered . . . does not prevent the specific enforcement of the remainder, if in all other respects the requisites for specific enforcement of that remainder exist. Compensation for the partial breach that still remains may be awarded in the same proceeding, either as damages, restitution, or an abatement in price.

A similar rule was cited from Thompson on Real Property.

Justice Hill then stated for the court: "We need to keep in mind that in the contract in question vendor (appellant) agreed to sell lot 102 and to construct a house according to 'submitted plans and specification' Not only did appellant agree to convey the lot and residence to be built, but he undertook to build the house according to the 'plans and specifications.'

"This court decided in *Preece* v. *Wolford* . . . that vendee may have 'specific performance as to such title as the vendor can furnish, and may also have a just abatement from the purchase money for the deficiency of title or quantity or *quality* of the estate.' (Our emphasis.) We can see no reason for a distinction between a deficiency in quantity (short acreage or lack of title) and deficiency in quality (defective construction).

"We conclude that appellee's remedies were not inconsistent so as to require an election of remedies and that the chancellor did not err in granting specific performance and directing that damages be ascertained by the common law division of the court."

The best possible rule for the plaintiff is found in the UCC rules for the sale of goods, which do not require the plaintiff to make any election at all. Buyers who prove their case for rescission can get their money back and can also collect all provable damages which they have sustained while the goods were in their possession. The following case illustrates a buyer's recovery under both of these "inconsistent" theories.

Riley v. *Ford Motor Company*
442 F.2d 670 (U.S. Third Circuit, 1971)

FACTS   "A jury awarded the purchaser of a 1969 Lincoln Mark III automobile $30,000 in damages against Ford Motor Company for breach of warranty and negligent repair of certain defects. Appellant Ford insists that the district court erred in withdrawing from the jury the question whether the dealer acted as its agent, and argues that the damages were excessive as a matter of law.

"Appellee purchase his new automobile from a Florida dealer at a cost of $8,476.00, and Ford issued a self-styled 'New Vehicle Warranty.' Shortly thereafter he took the car to Robinson Brothers, an Alabama Ford dealer, for repair of a window and removal of a noise in the rear end. According to Riley these defects were not corrected. At trial he testified that in the weeks following the requested repairs, and before the car was returned to Robinson Brothers for further repairs, these additional malfunctions developed: air conditioning did not work, speed control did not function, power seats became inoperative, the radio aerial functioned spasmodically, the rear seat did not fit, headlight panels were not synchronized, the cigarette lighter was missing, windshield wipers were defective, engine knocked upon acceleration, the transmission did not function properly, gear shift lever would not function, and the left door would not close properly.

"Dissatisfied with the car's condition, appellee wrote to Ford setting forth in detail his complaints, and requesting Ford 'to direct me to a dealer employing trained service personnel, or furnish me with someone capable of overseeing service personnel available in order to insure that the defects in my automobile are properly corrected in an expert and dependable manner.' Ford dispatched a Technical Service Representative who road tested the automobile, agreed that it was not functioning properly, and offered to take it to Robinson Brothers where he would personally supervise its repair. The owner believed he had a better idea. Refusing to again leave his car with Robinson's, he brought this action against Ford seeking recovery on two theories: breach of warranty and negligent repair."

ISSUES   Was the dealer acting as Ford's agent? Was the jury's award of damages supported by the evidence?

DECISION   The jury must be free to decide this issue on the facts. No, the damage award was clearly incorrect. Judgment reversed and case remanded for a new trial.

REASONS   Judge Aldisert's opinion first noted that the trial court had committed reversible error by telling the jury that the dealer was "acting for Ford Motor Company" rather than letting the jury decide this as a question of fact. He then discussed the award of damages.

"We turn now to the argument that the award of damages was excessive as a matter of law. Ford offers two theories in support of this contention: (1) any recovery should have been limited, under the warranty . . . to 'the cost of repairing or replacing any part or parts of the plaintiff's automobile that were defective,' and, under the negligence count, to 'certain other compensatory damages'; (2) assuming that the district court's charge permitting greater recovery was correct, there was no evidence to justify the jury's verdict of $30,000.

"Title 7A Code of Alabama § 2–316(2) permits a seller to 'exclude or modify' the common law warranties of merchantability and fitness,' and provides in subsection

(4) that '[r]emedies for breach of warranty can be limited in accordance with the provisions of this article.' Section 2–719 deals specifically with contractual modification or limitation of remedies. It states in subsection (1)(a) that an agreement may limit 'the buyer's remedies . . . to repair and replacement of non-conforming parts.' It further provides, however, in subsection (2) that '[w]here circumstances cause an exclusive or limited remedy to fail of its essential purpose, remedy may be had as provided in this title.'

"The question whether the remedy provided in Ford's warranty did 'fail to its essential purpose' was presented to the jury in somewhat different terms. The district court charged that it was for the jury to decide whether 'the defendant, Ford Motor Company, has breached its warranty and [whether] they were given a reasonable opportunity to repair it, and they didn't.' That the jury refused to give effect to the limitation of remedy contained in the warranty is manifest in light of the size of the verdict it returned. Under the facts of this case, we are unable to conclude that the jury was unjustified in its implicit finding that the warranty operated to deprive the purchaser 'of the substantial value of the bargain.'

"At the same time, however, we cannot validate the jury's award of $30,000. The district court correctly instructed as to the measure of damages:

> Now, I charge you that if you find that the defendant Ford Motor Company, has breached its warranty and that they were given a reasonable opportunity to repair it, and they didn't, then the proper measure of damages for breach of warranty is this: the difference in the value of the automobile as it was represented and warranted to be and the value it really was at the time of its delivery.
>
> The measure of damages may also include any incidental damage, as you may think is proper, such as any expenses, reasonably incurred, in acquiring any substitute means of transportation during such reasonable time as it would take to repair the defects in the automobile.

"This instruction was consistent with the directive of 7A Code of Alabama § 2–714. . . . Under this standard, the jury's award here was clearly excessive.

"The purchase price of the automobile was $8,476. In response to questions propounded by the trial court, plaintiff declared that the car 'hasn't been worth anything to me.' Even accepting this testimony as sufficient to establish that the automobile was worthless at the time of delivery, 'the difference in the value of the automobile as it was represented and warranted to be and the value it was at the time of delivery' could not have exceeded the price of $8,476. Adding to this the reasonably incurred cost of a substitute means of transportation, which, at the most, amounted to $430.43, plaintiff's total recovery would have been limited to $8,906.43.

"We agree that that $30,000 jury verdict was not supported by the evidence. The court erred in entering judgment upon it."

DAMAGES

Underlying Factors. In determining the amount of damages that a plaintiff can collect for a breach of contract, the court will subject the claimed damages to four tests: causation, certainty, foreseeability, and mitigation. To be collectible, compensatory damages must meet each of these tests.

First, the plaintiff must prove that the alleged damages were caused by the breach and not by something else. Lost profits which result when a supplier fails to deliver may be recoverable, but if the plaintiff's lower sales are due to a general economic downturn, the breaching seller should not be liable because his or her breach did not cause the "injury."

Second, the plaintiff must be able to prove the amount of his or her damages with *reasonable* certainty. Damages for lost profits and for mental stress are difficult to collect, in part, for this reason; courts are reluctant to permit jury speculation and sympathy to substitute for solid evidence of amount of injury. However, as the following case shows, a plaintiff can collect "mental stress" damages even for a simple breach of contract if the right sort of case is proved.

Lamm v. *Shingleton*
55 S.E.2d 810 (North Carolina, 1949)

FACTS The plaintiff's first husband, Larry Waddell, died August 3, 1946. She employed the defendant undertakers to conduct the funeral and purchased a casket and vault from them. The vault had two sections: a base on which the casket rested and a metal cover which fitted over the casket and locked to the base. The defendants represented and warranted that the vault was watertight and would protect the body from water for years.

On the Wednesday before Thanksgiving Day, the plaintiff discovered that during a very rainy spell of weather the vault had risen above the level of the ground, the top of one end being about six inches above the ground level. She reported the condition to the defendants and to the cemetery authorities. The defendants (or the cemetery authorities) undertook to reinter the body.

On the following Saturday, employees of the defendant and of the cemetery authorities met at the grave for the purpose of placing the vault in an adjoining grave. The plaintiff was present. When the vault, including the base, was raised, it was discovered that water and mud had entered it and that the casket was wet.

The plaintiff testified that "seeing the vault out of the ground that first time" caused her considerable shock and made her extremely nervous, as a result of which she became a nervous wreck. She also testified that after the men at the grave had discussed getting the mud out of the vault, defendant Shingleton had said he was not going to get it out and "To hell with the whole damned business—it's no concern of mine" and that this had made her so nervous she could hardly stand up.

The trial judge ruled that there was no cause of action for breach of warranty and then asked the jury to determine whether the plaintiff had been damaged by the "unlawful, willful negligence and carelessness" of the defendant. The jury said no and awarded no damages. The plaintiff appealed.

ISSUE Must the plaintiff prove that a willful tort was committed in order to recover damages for mental anguish?

DECISION No. Judgment reversed and this case is remanded for a new trial.

REASONS "This is essentially an action for damages for breach of contract. Plaintiff alleges a contract to furnish a casket and watertight vault and conduct the funeral and inter the body, the breach thereof by failure to lock the vault, and damages resulting from the

285

breach. The further allegation that the defendants' failure to lock the vault . . . was due to their negligence and carelessness does not convert it into an action in tort. . . .

"[C]ontracts are usually commercial in nature and relate to property or to services to be rendered in connection with business or professional operations. Pecuniary interest is dominant. Therefore, as a general rule, damages for mental anguish suffered by reason of the breach thereof are not recoverable. Some type of mental anguish, anxiety, or distress is apt to result from the breach of any contract which causes pecuniary loss. Yet damages therefore are deemed to be too remote to have been in the contemplation of the parties at the time the contract was entered into to be considered as an element of compensatory damages.

"The rule is not absolute. Indeed, the trend of modern decisions tends to leave it in a state of flux. . . . [T]o some extent the courts have modified the common law rule.

"In this process of modification a definite exception to the doctrine has developed. Where the contract is personal in nature and the contractual duty or obligation is so coupled with matters of mental concern or solicitude, or with the sensibilities of the party to whom the duty is owed, that a breach of that duty will necessarily or reasonably result in mental anguish or suffering, and it should be known to the parties from the nature of the contrct that such suffering will result from its breach, compensatory damages therefore may be recovered. . . .

"The tenderest feelings of the human heart center around the remains of the dead. When the defendants contracted with plaintiff to inter the body of her deceased husband in a workmanlike manner they did so with the knowledge that she was the widow and would naturally and probably suffer mental anguish if they failed to fulfill their contractual obligation in the manner here charged. The contract was predominantly personal in nature, and no substantial pecuniary loss would follow its breach. Her mental concern, her sensibilities, and her solicitude were the prime considerations in the contract, and the contract itself was such as to put the defendants on notice that a failure on their part to inter the body properly would probably produce mental suffering on her part. It cannot be said, therefore, that such damages were not within the contemplation of the parties at the time the contract was made."

A third significant limitation on the amount of damages awarded is that the damages sustained must have been reasonably foreseeable at the time the contract was made. That is, a party is not held legally responsible for damages which result from a breach of contract unless the party ought to have known that damages of that sort would occur if he or she didn't perform. Damages for lost profits which result from a "shut down the plant" situation are especially difficult to collect because of the application of this foreseeability principle. Obviously, your safeguard here is to make sure that your suppliers and contractors are fully informed as to your requirements and of the consequences of their failure to perform.

Finally, it is only common sense to require the injured party to take reasonable steps to "mitigate," or hold down, his or her losses. Even though one party has breached, it wouldn't be fair to that party to allow the other party to simply sit back and watch the damages mount up, without making any effort to get an alternative performance from someone else. The law, therefore, generally requires the injured party to make reasonable efforts to mitigate his or her damages.

Because a lease of real estate is a conveyance of an interest in the land as well as a contract, courts at one time did not apply the mitigation rule to landlords; landlords could simply sue for the agreed rental price whether the tenant was using the premises or not. The following case illustrates a growing trend toward removing this exception, thereby forcing the landlord to mitigate by rerenting the premises before he or she can collect damages against a tenant who has moved out prior to the expiration of the lease.

Wright v. *Baumann*
398 P.2d 119 (Oregon, 1965)

FACTS "Plaintiffs seek to recover for a breach of agreement under which plaintiffs agreed to erect an office building and defendant, a dentist, agreed to enter into a lease of one of the offices after the building was constructed. Both parties waived a jury trial. Defendant appeals from a judgment for plaintiffs.

"Defendant's principal assignments of error are directed at the trial court's rejection of evidence tending to show that plaintiffs had the opportunity to mitigate damages but refused to do so. Plaintiffs' objections to defendant's questions relating to mitigation were sustained by the trial court, apparently on the ground that the instrument signed by the parties was a lease rather than a contract and that, being a lease, the lessor had no obligation to mitigate damages. . . .

"[P]laintiffs notified defendant on August 27, 1956, that the building would be ready for occupancy on September 24, 1956. On September 6, 1956, defendant notified plaintiffs that he did not desire to enter into a lease of any part of the building. It was further shown that defendant informed two doctors that the space allotted to him was available and that during September, 1956, the two doctors had offered to lease the space allotted to defendant on the terms and conditions specified in the 'Agreement' in question but that plaintiffs refused to lease the office space to them, giving no reasons for the refusal to do so."

ISSUE Is the landlord required to mitigate his or her damages when the tenant breaches?

DECISION Yes. Judgment reversed and case remanded.

REASONS Justice O'Connell's opinion emphasized the policy concerns involved. "A majority of the courts, including Oregon, hold that a lessor is not required to mitigate damages when the lessee abandons the leasehold. In a few states it is incumbent upon the lessor to use reasonable means to mitigate damages. If the transaction is a contract to make a lease rather than an executed lease, it is universally recognized that the landowner has an obligation to mitigate damages upon a breach of the contract by the promisor.

"The majority view, absolving the lessor from any obligation to mitigate, is based on the theory that the lessee becomes the owner of the premises for a term and therefore the lessor need not concern himself with the lessee's abandonment of his

287

own property. That view might have some validity in those cases where there is simply a lease of the land alone with no covenants except the covenant to pay rent. But a modern business lease is predominantly an exchange of promises and only incidentally a sale of a part of the lessor's interest in the land. . . . These covenants in a modern business lease, particularly where only a part of the space in a building is leased, relate for the most part to the use of the space. The lessor's duties do not end with the execution of the lease. . . .

"The covenants in the instrument in the present case relate to the continuing obligations of the respective parties. The transaction is essentially a contract. There is no reason why the principle of mitigation of damages should not be applied to it. '. . . [I]t is important that the rules for awarding damages should be such as to discourage even persons against whom wrongs have been committed from passively suffering economic loss which could be averted by reasonable efforts. . . .' McCormick, *Damages*, p. 127 (1935).

"Lessors as well as contract promisors should be made to serve this salutary policy. To borrow again from McCormick, 'the realities of feudal tenure have vanished and a new system based upon a theory of contractual obligations has in general taken its place.' He reminds us that in disregarding the contractual nature of modern leases we have 'neglected the caution of Mr. Justice Holmes, "that continuity with the past is only a necessity and not a duty."' Writing in 1925, McCormick predicted that eventually 'the logic, inescapable according to the standards of a "jurisprudence of conceptions" which permits the landlord to stand idly by the vacant, abandoned premises and treat them as the property of the tenant and recover full rent, will yield to the more realistic notions of social advantage which in other fields of the law have forbidden a recovery for damages which the plaintiff by reasonable efforts could have avoided.' We believe that it is time for McCormick's prediction to become a reality."

Compensatory Damages. The basic purpose of the damages remedy is to compensate the injured party for the loss sustained by the other party's breach, that is, to put the injured party, so far as possible, in the place he or she would have been if the contract had been properly and fully performed. The measure of compensatory damages is the difference between the performance promised and the performance given; thus general compensatory damages are sometimes called "difference-money" damages. For example, if a used car is represented to be in "A-1 shape," and it is not, compensatory damages would give the buyer the amount of money necessary to put the car into "A-1 shape."

"Special" compensatory damages are awarded for losses which are further down in the chain of causation, losses over and above the difference-money losses which are caused by the breach. For example, if the buyer of the above used car had to take a cab to work twice because the car wouldn't start, special compensatory damages should be given to cover the cab fare.

Nominal Damages and Punitive Damages. Where there has been a breach of contract but the injured party is unable to show that he or she has sustained any actual losses as a result, he or she will be awarded "nominal" damages (almost always $1) and his or her court costs if he or she sues and proves his or her case. Obviously, most such cases will not be litigated. But nominal damages play an important part in a case which contains the right combination of facts for "punitive" damages to be awarded. Once the injured party proves his or her case for breach of contract, an award of punitive damages can be added on, to punish the defendant who has been guilty of repeated, willful violations of the rights of others (again, even though no actual damages can be proved to have resulted). Cases involving fraudulent or other intentionally tortious conduct are particularly appropriate for punitive damage awards.

Liquidated Damages. The general policy of the law to favor settlements of claims after they arise also operates to validate "remedy" provisions agreed to in advance, as part of the original contract. The parties are generally free to specify in advance what steps can be taken if their contract is breached by one of them. However, since many contracts are entered into between parties with unequal bargaining power, and since in many cases form contracts drafted by one party are used, the courts examine such "liquidated damages" provisions very carefully, to make sure that they are basically fair and that a substantial forfeiture of rights does not result from a relatively minor breach. Where a valid liquidated damages provision exists, the amount specified can be collected for a breach without any proof of actual damages.

OTHER REMEDIES

In addition to the damages remedy, several other remedies may be available to the injured plaintiff, depending on the facts of his or her case. Most of these alternative remedies were first developed by the courts of equity, to deal with situations where the "remedy at law" (i.e., damages) was felt to be inadequate to solve the plaintiff's problem. The main alternative remedies for breach of contract are discussed below; certain special remedies for breach of sale of goods contracts and secured financing contracts are discussed in the chapters dealing with those topics.

Specific Performance. Where the parties have contracted for the purchase and sale of a "unique" item, the buyer, particularly, may want the court to specifically enforce the contract, because it will usually be very hard for him or her to prove damages in the absence of an established market and because even if he or she got damages, he or she would still not be able to get the thing bargained for. In the eyes of the law every piece of land is unique, so the specific performance remedy is available to either party to a real estate contract. Such items as goods and securities are legally unique if no alternative source of supply is reasonably available. Fifty shares of stock in a small, closely held corporation might very well be unique; 50 shares of U.S. Steel would not be. A 1973 Ford is probably not unique; 1904 Stanley Steamer almost certainly is.

As a general rule, specific performance is not available as a remedy for breach of personal services contracts, for two main reasons. First, courts have been reluctant (at least traditionally) to get involved in extensive supervision of contract performances on a day-to-day basis. And second, an order forcing one person to work for another smacks of "involuntary servitude," which is prohibited by the U.S. Constitution. Because performances under construction contracts can normally be judged against an agreed set of plans and specifications, specific performance is available in such cases.

Injunction. Injunction is another remedy that has been developed in equity; a court orders someone to do something or to stop doing something. In breach of contract situations, a *negative* injunction may be granted to prevent a breaching party from performing for others while he is still under a contractual duty to perform for the plaintiff. For the reasons stated above, the plaintiff does not get a positive decree ordering the defendant to perform for him or her; the plaintiff only gets a negative order directing the defendant not to perform for others. In the following case, Professor Felch (or his lawyer) failed to appreciate this difference.

Felch v. Findlay College
200 N.E.2d 353 (Ohio, 1963)

FACTS

"This is an appeal on questions of law and fact from a judgment of the Common Pleas Court for the defendant, Findlay College, a private nonprofit corporation.
"Plaintiff, William E. Felch, alleges, among other things, that he was employed by the defendant as a member of its faculty on a continuing basis and that contrary to and without compliance with the provisions for dismissal contained in administrative memoranda purporting to require certain hearings, the board of trustees of defendant on August 22, 1961, approved the action of its president on July 20, 1961, dismissing the plaintiff effective August 11, 1961. Plaintiff prays that 'defendant be enjoined from carrying into effect the dismissal of this plaintiff as a member of the faculty . . . and that the defendant may be ordered to continue plaintiff as such member of the faculty of Findlay College, Findlay, Ohio, and that defendant be ordered to pay to this plaintiff the salary therefore agreed upon.' "

ISSUE

Is an injunction a proper remedy in this case?

DECISION

No. Judgment affirmed.

REASONS

Judge Guernsey first stated that Felch "in essence and in legal effect" was really asking for specific performance. He then cited three authorities to support the court's denial of that remedy.
"In *Masetta* v. *National Bronze & Aluminum Foundry Co.,* 159 Ohio St. 306, 112 N.E.2d 15, the Supreme Court held that '[a] court of equity will not, by means of mandatory injunction, decree specific performance of a labor contract existing between an employer and its employees so as to require the employer to continue any such employee in its service or to rehire such employee if discharged,' and in Judge Middleton's opinion, unanimously concurred in, it was stated, at page 311, 112 N.E.2d at page 18:

It has long been settled law that a court of equity will not decree specific performance of a contract for personal services. This court has recognized this principle of
law whenever occasion arose.

"In 81 C.J.S. Specific Performance § 82, p. 591, the rule is stated as follows:

In general, specific performance does not lie to enforce a provision in a contract
for the performance of personal services requiring special knowledge, ability,
experience, or the exercise of judgment, skill, taste, discretion, labor, tact, energy,
or integrity, particularly where the performance of such services would be continuous over a long period of time. This rule is based on the fact that mischief likely
to result from an enforced continuance of the relationship incident to the service
after it has become personally obnoxious to one of the parties is so great that the
interests of society require that the remedy be denied, and on the fact that the
enforcement of a decree requiring the performance of such a contract would
impose too great a burden on the courts. . . .

On the other hand, where services have unique and peculiar value, specific
performance has been awarded under some circumstances.

"Assuming plaintiff's claim of continuing contract status, the services to be performed would 'be continuous over a long period of time' and although his services
might once have had a unique and peculiar value, they no longer have any value as
far as the defendant is concerned. Moreover, the rule of uniqueness is applicable to
an action to require specific performance of a contract by an employee who refuses
to perform personal services and not applicable to an action to require specific
performance by the employer.

"The same rule is reiterated in 2 *Restatement of the Law of Contracts,* 703, Section
379, and it is stated therein in comment:

c. Among the many varieties of personal service contracts to which the rule of the
Section applies are those requiring performance as . . . a teacher. . . .
d. The refusal of affirmative specific enforcement in these cases is based . . . in
part upon the undesirability of compelling the continuance of personal association after disputes have arisen and confidence and loyalty are gone.

"For these reasons it is the opinion and judgment of this court that the remedy of
specific performance, either in itself or by means of the injunctive process, is not
available to the plaintiff to enforce the provisions of the employment contract which
he claims to exist between himself and defendant private college."

Rescission and Restitution. A court will not lightly undo the parties' whole
agreement and order the restoration of benefits already given. The rescission
and restitution remedy is provided only if there has been fraud, material
breach, or similar failure; only if the injured party asks for this remedy with
reasonable promptness; and only if the rights of third parties or other equitable
factors have not intervened. The objective of "R & R" is to terminate the contract and to put the parties back where they were before it was made; the more
difficult and complex it is to achieve this objective, the less likely it is that
R & R will be used as a remedy.

Quasi Contract. Because the old common-law courts only heard cases which fell into certain categories, lawyers became somewhat creative in constructing fact combinations to fit those categories. *Quasi contract* means in essence "almost like a real contract, but not quite"; it describes a situation where a party has received and retained benefits but has made no actual promise to pay for them. It is in fact a remedy which the courts developed to prevent such a party from being "unjustly enriched." The circumstances are such that it wouldn't be fair for him or her to keep the benefits without paying anything for them. This principle is the justification for requiring a minor to pay the fair market value for necessaries which he or she has received, even though the minor has exercised the option of disaffirming the contract which he or she made to pay for them. Quasi contract also applies to all sorts of other situations, such as benefits conferred on the wrong person by mistake or partial performance given to one party to a breach of contract.

Since a court will not (and should not) give unrequested remedies, one of the lawyer's main jobs is to figure out the remedy or the combination of remedies which will best solve the client's problem. If you do go to litigation, make sure you fully understand what your options are and what you chances are of receiving each possible remedy.

CASES FOR DISCUSSION

ALBERS v. KOCH

173 N.W.2d 293 (Nebraska, 1969)

Smith, Justice

Donald F. Albers and wife sued for $4,500, which they had paid down on the purchase price of farmland. They contended that sellers, Raymond Koch and wife, had breached contractual provisions for possession. Kochs cross-petitioned for specific performance and for $160, which they had paid for fall plowing. After trial the district court rendered judgment against Kochs for $2,841 as partial restitution. The cross-petition was dismissed. Kochs have appealed. Alberses have cross-appealed.

Alberses had paid Kochs the $4,500 upon making the agreement in May 1968, promising to pay $4,500 on December 1, $14,000 on March 1, 1969, and the balance of the $87,000 purchase price in 20 annual installments. Actual possession was to be delivered on March 1, 1969. Time was to be of the essence. The agreement also provided: ". . . in case . . . defects in the title . . . cannot be cured . . . , [the $4,500 down payment] is to be refunded, and in the event of the refusal or failure of the Buyer to consummate the purchase, to be retained by the Seller as liquidated damages. . . . Buyers shall have the privilege . . . to fix fences, remove trees and to fall plow after the 1968 crop is harvested. The Buyers shall not disturb the Tenants growing crops or fall grazing privileges."

Grazing on part of the tract, 240 acres which included 47 acres of trees and roads, were cattle of Raymond Koch's brother Herman, a subtenant. Another brother, Donald, was in possession of the tract under a year-to-year tenancy from March 1. Raymond had orally notified brother Donald in April 1968 that Raymond was listing the tract for sale with possession on March 1, 1969.

On September 4, 1968, Raymond, a California resident, in a letter with copy to Alberses, who lived 17 miles from the tract, informed Donald Koch of the sale: "I agreed . . . that he can fall plow after the 1968 crop is harvested. I don't know how many acres you had into small grain or soil bank, but I understood that Mr. Albers would like to fall plow close to 60 acres. . . . I also said

292

that Mr. Albers can fix fence or remove trees if it doesn't disturb your fall grazing."

Donald Albers visited Raymond's brother after September 4, 1968, about entering on the land that fall. The gate was padlocked, and "No trespassing" signs were posted. Donald Koch left the entry decision to Herman, whose language was unequivocal: Albers had no right there; should he trespass, Herman would shoot him.

The situation brought Raymond to Nebraska, where Alberses on October 21, 1968, notified him that the tenant's refusal constituted a breach of the contract. Restitution was demanded. On October 23 an order in a suit by Raymond restrained his brothers from interference with performance of the purchase agreement. On the same day Donald Koch signed this consent: ". . . Raymond Koch, his agents or assignees will have immediate right to fall plow the 40 acres from which the crop has been harvested or which has been summer fallowed. . . . the undersigned also agrees to permit . . . [them] to remove trees, to repair fences, as long as they do not disturb his crops or grazing privileges on the balance of the land . . . not fall plowed. The . . . lease terminates February 28, 1969."

Shortly after October 23, 1968, Donald Miller, Raymond's agent, engaged Valgene Stratman, a custom farmer, to plow 40 acres of the tract. Raymond's attorney promptly notified Alberses in a letter enclosing copies of the restraining order and Donald Koch's consent. The plowing was completed that month, and the $160 charge was paid by Donald Koch. There is testimony of Miller to authority from Alberses in August to engage Stratman. Testimony of Donald Albers to a meeting with a Stratman that month is that "we didn't ask him to . . . plow for sure." Testimony of Donald Albers' father to an August meeting with Miller is: "**Q** . . . did either you or your son agree to pay the cost of fall plowing? **A** No. . . . **Q** Did your son agree to have Valgene Stratman plow the ground? **A** Well, he said if anybody would plow it, he thought Valgene would be the best."

Until the trial Alberses did not complain that the number of acres plowed was only 40. After October 23, 1968, no one denied them entry. On November 29, 1968, they again demanded restitution for refusal of entry and for sellers' "failure to . . . obtain or be assured of obtaining possession . . . on March 1, 1969." Holding over as tenant after February 28, 1969, had been the subject of three separate conversations between Donald Koch and Donald Albers. The latter had requested a written statement of intention to hold over. Donald Koch refused. He and Herman were still occupying the land at the time of trial in April 1969.

The remedy of restitution for breach of contract is available to a plaintiff only in case defendant's breach is total. A slight breach does not terminate the duty of the injured person unless nonperformance of an express condition requires that result. *Restatement, Contracts*, s. 347, Comment e, p. 587.

Specific performance may properly be decreed in spite of a minor breach by plaintiff, the breach involving no substantial failure of the exchange for the performance to be compelled. *Restatment, Contracts*, s. 375(2), p. 691.

The fact that a contract provides for payment of liquidated damages for breach of promise is not a bar to specific enforcement of the promise. Where a contract provides for such payment as a true alternative performance, the promisor's election to pay this price will prevent specific enforcement of the alternative against him. *Restatement, Contracts*, s. 378, p. 700. To the extent of conflict *Boehmer* v. *Wellensiek*, 107 Neb. 478, 186 N.W. 326 (1922), is disapproved.

We find neither total breach of contract by defendants Koch nor nonperformance of a condition that terminated Alberses' duty of performance. Existence of the tenancy to March 1, 1969, under the circumstances afforded Alberses no excuse for refusing to proceed with the contract. See 6 Williston on Contracts (3d ed., 1962), ss. 878 and 879, pp. 357 and 366. Liquidated damages were not to be a true alternative performance. Alberses did not contract to pay the $160 charge for fall plowing. They were not entitled to restitution. Defendants Koch were entitled to a decree of specific performance.

That part of the judgment dismissing the crossclaim for fall plowing is affirmed. The other parts are reversed and the cause remanded for proceedings consistent with this opinion. Costs on opinion are taxed to Alberses.

Affirmed in part, and in part reversed and remanded.

AMERICAN FINANCIAL LEASING & SERV. CO. v. MILLER

322 N.E.2d 149 (Ohio, 1974)

Holmes, Judge

This matter involves the appeal of that portion of a judgment of the Court of Common Pleas of Franklin County which awarded the plaintiff American Financial Leasing and Services Company the amount of $2,119.79, which the plaintiff argued and the trial court agreed was "stipulated damages" included in a lease contract by and between the parties hereto.

The defendants appeal, assigning one error to the effect that such amount was erroneously awarded, in that such amount constituted a "penalty" rather than a lawful "stipulated damage."

The facts of this case are basically that the defendants wished to engage in the business of gasoline sales in combination with a car wash operation in Columbus, Ohio. In order to finance the car wash equipment, the defendants, in 1967, entered into a financing arrangement with the plaintiff company, such arrangement being in the form of an equipment lease.

The lease, as drawn by the plaintiff company, provided for the leasing of the equipment to the defendants for an initial period of five years, with the right to renew for three one-year periods, at the end of which time the plaintiff company would "abandon the equipment to the defendants."

The defendants made all of the payments due under the lease from the date of entering into such in 1967 until May of 1971, at which time defendants lost their real estate lease and were evicted. Plaintiff repossessed the equipment and thereafter sold such to another operator, and then brought an action in the Common Pleas Court of Franklin County to recover pursuant to the terms of the lease.

The items of damage, and the method of calculation therof, were set forth in plaintiff's Exhibit C. Such items included 11 unpaid rental payments as of October 16, 1971, interest charges, certain miscellaneous charges, and a charge of $2,119.79 which was listed as "10 percent of cost per lease." It is this item which the defendants now contend is not proper.

Such amount is sought by the plaintiff lessor on the specific basis of paragraph 21(c) of the lease herein. For the purpose of availing the reader the opportunity of seeing paragraph 21(c) in relationship to its surrounding lease provisions, we set it forth in its entirety:

21. Default. If lessee fails to pay any rent or other amount herein provided within ten (10) days after the same is due and payable, or if lessee fails to perform any other provision hereof within ten (10) days after lessor shall have demanded in writing performance thereof, or if any proceeding in bankruptcy, receivership or insolvency shall be commenced by or against lessee or its property, or if lessee makes any assignment for the benefit of its creditors, lessor shall have the right, but shall not be obligated, to exercise any one or more of the following remedies: (a) to sue for and recover all rents and other amounts then due or thereafter accruing under this lease; (b) to take possession of any or all of the equipment, wherever it may be located, without demand or notice, without any court order or other process of law, and without incurring any liability to lessee for any damages occasioned by such taking of possession; (c) to sell any or all of the equipment at public or private sale for cash or on credit and to recover from lessee all costs of taking possession, storing, repairing and selling the equipment, an amount equal to ten percent (10%) of the actual cost to lessor of the equipment sold, and the unpaid balance of the total rent for the initial term of this lease attributable to the equipment sold, less the net proceeds of such sale; (d) to terminate this lease as to any or all items of equipment; (e) in the event lessor elects to terminate this lease as to any or all items of equipment, to recover from lessee as to each item subject to said termination the worth at the time of such termination, of the excees, if any, of the amount of rent reserved herein for said item for the balance of the term hereof over the then reasonable rental value of said items for

294

the same period of time; (f) to pursue any other remedy now or hereafter existing at law or in equity.

Notwithstanding any such action that lessor may take, including taking possession of any or all of the equipment, lessee shall remain liable for the full performance of all its obligations hereunder, provided, however, that if lessor in writing terminates this lease, as to any item of equipment, lessee shall not be liable for rent in respect of such item accruing after the date of such termination.

In addition to the foregoing, lessee shall pay lessor all costs and expenses, including reasonable attorneys' fees, incurred by lessor in exercising any of its rights or remedies hereunder.

In the event that one or more of the lesses in the within lease is a lessee under any other lease from the lessor herein, default in the terms of this lease shall be and constitute a default under any other lease then in force and similarly a default in any one or more of such other leases shall constitute a default under this lease.

It is quite generally accepted that a clause in a contract providing for liquidated damages in the event of a default is valid and enforceable.

The text of the Ohio Jurisprudence article calls one's attention to the difference between a liquidated damage provision and a penalty provision that might be found in a contract. More particularly, the article points out the differences of the courts' view as between the two.

Ohio Jurisprudence 2d (Revised) 154, Damages, Section 133, reads as follows:

While provisions for liquidated damages in a contract are valid and enforceable, courts avoid the enforcement of a provision for liquidated damages when it is actually in the nature of a penalty. As distinguished from liquidated damages, a "penalty" is a sum inserted in a contract, not as the measure of compensation for its breach, but rather as a punishment for default, or by way of security for actual damages which may be sustained by reason of nonperformance, and it involves the idea of punishment. Stipulations for liquidated damages are often treated as penalties because of the inequities that would result from the strict enforcement of the stipulations, and there is a marked tendency on the part of the courts to construe stipulations for liquidated damages as penalties. . . .

Every contract, and the specific wording thereof, must be viewed in its entirety in determining the intent of the parties and in arriving at conclusions with regard to the validity of a provision seeking a certain sum of money in the event of a breach of contract.

The aforestated textual article sets forth the proposition, which we accept as being valid, that most Ohio cases hold that there must be three elements appearing in order that the provision may be construed as one for liquidated damages, rather than a penalty. It is stated therein, at page 155, that ". . . it must, according to most cases, appear that the sum stipulated bears a reasonable proportion to the loss actually sustained; that the actual damages occasioned by the breach are uncertain or difficult to ascertain; and most important of all, that a construction of the contract as a whole evinces a conscious intention of the parties deliberately to consider and adjust the damages that might flow from the breach. . . ."

It is our belief that the main element to be considered in arriving at the determination of the validity of such a provision is whether it expressed the intention of the parties that any such stipulated amount represents the reasonable damages for the breach of the general provisions of the contract, which damage, because of the nature of the transaction, would be difficult to ascertain.

If the provision is not on its face unconscionable, the element of fraud is not present, and the amount can reasonably be related to the loss that may have been experienced by a party due to the breach, the reviewing court should uphold the provisions of the contract.

However, where, upon a review of the terms of the specific agreement, all of the elements in the rule do not fall into place, a contrary conclusion must be reached. Such is the case before this court.

In the first instance, the actual damages that would be sustained by the lessor, in the event of a breach by the lessees, would not be difficult to ascertain or prove. There would be little or no uncertainty in determining actual damages. Such damages would be the unpaid portion of the lease and, if the property had been repossessed, the costs of repossession and sale, and any deficiency remaining after such sale.

Secondly, we must look to the reasonableness of the 10 percent to be exacted from the lessees pursuant to the "Default" paragraph of the contract.

It should be noted that in the "Default" paragraph, upon the occurrence of one of the events constituting a default, the lessor had a wide range of options available to him. . . .

It being inconceivable that the print used in the production of the instrument could have been any smaller, it appears that the only way in which additional default provisions favorable to the drafter could be included would be by way of adding further pages to the contract.

In any event, going specifically to the reasonableness of the stipulation exacting 10 percent of the contract price in the event of default, we hold that such amount, in light of the other provisions covering the recoupment of the lessor's actual damage in the event of a breach, neither bears a reasonable relationship to such damage, nor is in a reasonable proportion thereto.

Such amount is patently in excess of the actual damage which could be suffered by the lessor, and therefore must be considered as a "penalty" rather than a stipulated "liquidated damage."

Further, a reading of the contract in its totality, and most particularly the paragraph entitled "Default," shows that there are ample provisions which reasonably consider and adjust any damages which might flow from a breach. On the other hand, we are not convinced that it was the intent and understanding of the parties hereto that the enforcement of the clause questioned would reasonably adjust the actual damages that might flow from any breach.

As previously stated, the courts are generally reluctant to step in reform contracts of individuals, in that our business world demands, and should be afforded, a free right of contract. Yet the underlying philosophy pertains that our courts abhor penalties, and such legal philosophy must be applied to the instant contract.

Therefore, the single assignment of error is sustained, and the judgment of the Court of

Common Pleas of Franklin County is hereby reversed and a final judgment is entered accordingly.

MARSHALL v. MARVIN H. ANDERSON CONSTRUCTION CO.

167 N.W.2d 724 (Minnesota, 1969)

Nelson, Justice

Appeal from an order of the District Court of Hennepin County denying defendant's motion for judgment notwithstanding the verdict or for a new trial.

This case consists of a claim of either breach of warranty or negligence in the construction of a new home. The facts appear to be that on May 30, 1961, plaintiffs, William and Patricia Marshall, contracted to purchase a home from defendant, Marvin H. Anderson Construction Company, for $15,400, the house to be completed during the last week of August 1961. The purchase price was paid. In addition to giving plaintiffs a written warranty as to workmanship and material, defendant explicitly orally warranted the home's workmanship and materials to be "of the highest" order. However, from the time plaintiffs moved into the new home down to the time of trial, their basement was continually wet or flooded during and for weeks after steady or prolonged rains and during and after the spring thaw.

When plaintiffs complained, defendant first assured them that the situation was temporary and would correct itself. Afterwards defendant took certain half-measures, such as applying putty to the walls, and, finally, four years later and against plaintiffs' wishes, put in an inadequate drain field and sump-pump device which even defendant admitted did not work or solve the problem. It appears that numerous persons saw the flooded condition of the basement many times over the years and there was testimony that even during dry periods the basement was never free from mildew or mold.

Plaintiffs claim that they have been deprived of the use of their basement for seven years; that they have been deprived for a good part of each year of storage, living, entertaining, and playing space, as well as surroundings properly fitting into the performance of their household tasks; and that for all practical purposes they bought a house without a basement. They allege that they lost personal property, such as furniture, luggage, clothing, and appliances, of the value of $450 to $500 due to repeated floodings and the mustiness and mildew which followed in their wake. Witnesses verified these losses and also the claim that the room used by plaintiffs' little girl was never heated properly by defendant's heating installation.

Plaintiffs also claim the ventilation of the roof was faulty, causing moisture and condensation inside the house which stained the walls and peeled the paper on the entire north wall each year during their occupancy.

Rudy Ocel, a highly qualified, experienced contractor and former building inspector who was unacquainted with the parties, made a careful inspection of the home and found it, with respect to the foregoing problems (except the heating problem, which he did not inspect), to have been built negligently, improperly, and below the standard of workmanship in the community. He set out in detail the many respects in which the drain field was inadequate in its function and the ventilation in the home was insufficient. Mr. Ocel testified as to what would be needed at a minimum to correct the problems, apart from the heating, and said the cost of such corrections would be at least $3,000.

In addition to providing evidence as to personal property loss, Mrs. Marshall testified that the house was worth $5,400 less than the price they had paid. Mr. Marshall concurred in this estimate. Their estimates did not include any valuation of the loss of use of portions of the home.

The record indicates that plaintiffs phoned and wrote letters from time to time, protesting personally to Marvin H. Anderson, defendant's president, about their numerous problems during the period they had lived in the home. Anderson promised to take care of the matters but failed to do so. It appears that defendant only urged plaintiffs to be patient, saying that problems were to be expected and would in time subside.

Defendant suggests that the case presents the following legal issues: (1) Even though the defects are as plaintiffs claimed, is the evidence sufficient to support recovery on the basis of either breach of warranty or negligence? (2) Where defects in construction of a home and resultant damages were alleged, did the trial court err in refusing to permit the jury to view the premises? (3) Where damages are claimed for breach of warranty or negligence in construction of the home and the jury is permitted to award damages for the difference in the value of the product contracted for and the value of the product as delivered, may the jury, in addition, be permitted to award consequential damages for (a) damage to property and (b) partial loss of use of the property, and, if so, for what period of time? (4) Did plaintiffs make any attempt to mitigate damages, and did the jury consider mitigation? (5) Were the damages awarded by the jury in the instant case excessive?

[3] A view of premises in a case such as the instant one is generally conceded to be discretionary with the trial court. Upon the state of the record herein, it must be held that there was no abuse of that discretion in the trial court's refusal to order a view.

3. In the *Droher* case this court reviewed at length the rule of damages applicable to facts somewhat similar to those in the instant case, stating:

. . . [W]here there is a substantial good-faith effort to perform the contract but there are defects of such a nature that the contract has not been performed according to its terms, which defects can be remedied without the destruction of a substantial part of the building, the owner is entitled to recover the cost of making the work conform to the contract but, where it appears that the cost of remedying the defects is grossly disproportionate to the benefits to be derived therefrom, the owner is entitled to recover the difference between the value of the property as it would have been if the contract had been performed according to its terms and the value in its condition as constructed.

We think, in view of the extensive damage and the costs to which plaintiffs would have been exposed as a result of any effort to properly correct the defects in this house, it was proper for the trial court to apply the difference-in-value theory in assessing damages.

This court in the *Droher* case also said:

The applicable rule is to be found in *Restatement, Constracts*, § 346, as follows:

> (a) For defective or unfinished construction he can get judgment for either
>
> (i) the reasonable cost of construction and completion in accordance with the contract, if this is possible and does not involve unreasonable economic waste; or
>
> (ii) the difference between the value that the product contracted for would have had and the value of the performance that has been received by the plaintiff, if construction and completion in accordance with the contract would involve unreasonable economic waste.

Defendant argues that the court erred in permitting the jury to consider plaintiffs' personal property loss due to defendant's faulty construction. We think the record clearly established this damage and that the loss in the value of the property was from $450 to $500. It is clear from the holding in the *Droher* case that in any such case the full proper measure of damages includes the actual cost of labor and materials, increased overhead, damage caused by the delay, and any other matters found from the preponderance of the evidence to have naturally flowed from the breach of contract.

This court in the *Droher* case did not consider loss of use. However, *Restatement, Contracts*, § 346(1)(b), specifically provides:

For any delay in completion fairly chargeable to the builder, the plaintiff can get judgment for the value of the use of the product, if it was being constructed for use. . . .

Incidentally, the jury might or might not have included in the instant case the element of loss of use in arriving at its verdict of $4,900. It undoubtedly allowed plaintiffs $500 for loss of personal property. The remaining $4,400 of the verdict was less than the $5,400 general damages for defects in the construction testified to by plaintiffs.

4. We think the trial court properly charged the jury on damages. . . .

Defendant's claim that plaintiffs made no attempt to mitigate damages and that the jury did not properly consider mitigation ignores relevant facts and the court's instructions. The record shows that plaintiffs bought and used at least three trailer loads of black dirt and applied it to their yard themselves to try to remedy the water problems and that they had put in extra dirt on another occasion, which defendant admitted. Plaintiffs also contend that Mr. Marshall regraded the house and banked it as well as he was able and actually put in 1,300 rolls of sod by himself. The Marshalls also did some landscaping and planting around the house, repainted the interior north wall of the house each year for seven years to try to cope with the stains and moisture marks caused by the inadequately ventilated and constructed roof, and called in plumbers at their expense to remedy other building defects. They also bought and used an auxiliary heating device to try to remedy the lack of heat in their daughter's bedroom. It was for the jury under the charge and the evidence submitted to consider mitigation of damages and to apply its judgment on that issue.

5. Defendant contends that the amount of the damages allowed by the jury was excessive. Upon reviewing the evidence in the light most favorable to plaintiffs' verdict, we hold the amount of the damages awarded to be within the limits permitted by the evidence.

The trial court's order denying defendant's motion for judgment notwithstanding the verdict or for a new trial is affirmed.

1. Sylvia Beedlebaum, a tenured teacher, was fired by her local school board because they disagreed with her teaching philosophy, even though her students were equal in achievement and abilities to the students of other teachers. She brought suit for reinstatement, which the court ordered. At that point, she had been out of her job for a year. Is she entitled to her salary for that time?

2. Earl and Daniel Cutter are copartners in a hay contracting business. As such, they signed an agreement with Christopher Clover which provided that they were to stack "all of the hay located on Cloverdale Ranch . . . which will yield approximately 5,000 tons of hay." The price was to be $6.50 per ton. The work proceeded very slowly, and by the time the stacking was customarily completed, at the beginning of September, much less than 5,000 tons had been stacked. The haystacks were also smaller than was usual in the business and were loosely packed, with "doughnuts" in the middle, where water could seep in and ruin the hay. During their work the Cutters had been paid some $6,000. Christopher, however, estimates that they packed at the most 642 tons of hay, entitling them to only $4,173. He wants back the difference, and the Cutters feel that they are entitled to an amount equal to what they would have earned had they stacked 5,000 tons of hay. Who wins?

3. Gerald and Ophelia Plumb executed a purchase contract in which they offered to buy Mrs. Wilma Day's house for $50,000. The offer was accepted, and the defendants made a $100 deposit. Closing was to take place within a month. Before the closing date the Plumbs informed Mrs. Day's realtor that they did not want to go through with the deal. At that time, Mrs. Day had been dead for three weeks, a fact unknown to the Plumbs. Her estate administrator advised the Plumbs that he would sue them for any difference in the selling price if the house had to be sold for less to another buyer. A year later the house was sold for $40,000. The administrator then sued the Plumbs for $10,000. What would be your decision?

4. Larry lost the use of his airplane for 75 days because of damage caused by the negligence of an employee of Airserv, Inc. He sued Airserv, proved his case, and was awarded $900 damages by the trial court. The trial court measured damages based on Larry's actual out-of-pocket costs, including the cost of several plane rentals. On appeal, Larry contends that he should receive damages based on his loss of the use of his plane for the entire 75 days, or $3,500, even though he didn't actually rent the plane each day. What is the proper measure of Larry's damages?

5. Gloria claims that in 1965 she entered into an oral agreement with Norma to "take care of" Norma until Norma's death, in return for which Norma would bequeath her farm to Gloria. Neither Gloria's neighbors nor her son was aware of this agreement. Gloria was indefinite as to the terms and the conditions of performance required of her by the agreement. From 1965 to 1975 Gloria did many favors for Norma, but so did other neighbors and friends. In 1975 Norma died without indicating in her will that Gloria was to receive the farm. Gloria sues for specific performance or, in the alternative, compensation for services rendered. What result, and why?

6. The Garnet Construction Company entered into a contract with the Nevada Highway Department to pave a section of highway for $530,000. The contract stated that if Garnet failed to complete the job within the allotted time, the state would withhold $210 for each day that the work remained uncompleted. Garnet was 67 days late in completing the job, and the state withheld $14,070 from the final payment. Garnet sued to recover this amount. The state admits that any damage, loss, or expense caused by the delay was unknown. What result, and why?

7. On September 1, 1974, Munch entered into a contract with Wilson, sole stock-holder of Wilson Motors, Inc., to purchase 49 percent of Wilson Motors' stock. The contract also provided that Munch would become comanager of Wilson Motors at a salary of $2,000 per month plus quarterly bonuses. Munch paid $6,000 down on the stock and agreed to pay off the $49,000 balance at a rate of $7,000 plus interest on each succeeding September 1. During the summer of 1975, car sales were off and the dealership was having cash flow problems. At that point, Wilson told Munch that neither of them would draw a salary until the cash balance improved. In October, with three months' salary unpaid, Munch sued to rescind the contract and collect his unpaid salary. Wilson counterclaimed, alleging that Munch had breached by failing to make the $7,000 payment on the stock purchase which had been due September 1. Who wins, and why?

8. Barrett was interested in buying a resort property which consisted of 100 acres and 14 cabins and abutted Lake Ontario. This property was completely surrounded by 1,200 acres owned by Dr. McCraw, who spent the summer months and Christmas on his property. McCraw loaned Barrett $5,000 as a down payment for the resort property, in return for a mortgage on other property that Barrett owned and a written promise by Barrett that for 25 years he would make no improvements on the resort property closer to McCraw's property than the improvements already in existence. The next year, 1970, Barrett repaid the loan. From 1971 to 1974 he spent another $20,000 to improve the existing cabins, but resort income fell off and Barrett had trouble making his mortgage payments. At that point, in violation of his agreement with McCraw, Barrett started construction of a trailer park and campsite. McCraw sues for an injunction to stop further construction. What result, and why?

9. On the advice of her insurance agent, Mellors, May Cosper signed a listing agreement on her farm with a realtor, Orr. Both Orr and Mellors then urged May to sign a sales contract on the farm, even though the offer which had been received from the prospective buyer, Stanley Zeller, differed from the listing agreement in several material terms. Several hours later, after she had thought it over, May notified Orr and Zeller that she was not going to go through with the deal. Zeller, through Orr and Mellors, made several other offers to buy the farm, but May refused them all. Zeller sues for specific performance of the first sales contract. May says that Orr and Mellors were not acting in her best interests and that she had been misled into thinking that she had to sign the sales contract because she had signed the listing. Should specific performance be granted here?

Part III
Agency

14 | Agency—Creation and Termination

Agency is a very ancient and very important legal concept. Agency law and contract law describe the two most basic legal relationships. On this foundation many of the other, more specialized legal relationships are erected. The modern law of agency can be traced to the Roman law concerning the owner and slave; the law merchant, a private system of rules and courts which traders and merchants established to govern themselves during the Middle Ages; and the English common law. Because individuals and businesses everywhere must on many occasions conduct their affairs through others, every legal system must somehow deal with the concept of agency. Every contract entered into by corporations and partnerships and many of the contracts made by individuals and unincorporated associations involve the principles of agency law.

Although the law of agency obviously has very great "commercial" significance, it is not covered in the Uniform Commercial Code. One reason for this omission may be that when the Uniform Commercial Code was formulated, the basic rules of agency law were already pretty well agreed on by the states and were already summarized in the *Restatement of the Law of Agency, Second*. The *Restatement* does not have the force of law, but it is considered to be an authoritative source and it is followed most of the time by most courts

Before we look at the various ways in which the agency relationship can be created (and terminated), it is necessary to distinguish and explain another relationship which involves the use of others to conduct one's affairs—the "independent contractor" relationship.

INDEPENDENT CONTRACTORS

Independent Contractors Distinguished from Agents/Employees. As a general rule, a person who employs an "independent contractor" to perform services for him or her is liable neither for torts committed by the independent contractor in performing the job nor for subcontracts made by the independent contractor in order to get the job done. Independent contractors are, of course, liable for their own torts (and for the torts of their agents and employees) and for their own contracts. Litigation frequently arises, however, when the independent contractor has gone out of business, or lacks the financial resources to cover a substantial claim, or is simply out of the jurisdiction and not available (or not conveniently available) for suit. The key issue in these cases is whether the relationship in question was really an independent contractor–employer relationship (resulting in nonliability) or was a principal-agent or employer-employee relationship (resulting in the principal/employer's being held liable in tort and/or contract).

The primary test used by the courts to distinguish these legal relationships is the degree of control which the employer/principal exercises over the "person in the middle" (the independent contractor or the agent/employee). The general idea is that with independent contractors the employer contracts only for results and leaves the details of the job to the independent contractors, although given the right set of facts, these too could be agents/employees. Put in simplest terms, a person using an independent contractor controls *what* gets done, but the independent contractor decides *how* it gets done. With an agent/employee, the principal/employer not only determines *what* gets done but also has the power to determine *how* it gets done. If you hire an employee to help you put aluminum siding on your house, you can tell him or her what size hammer to use, what size nails to use, where to place the nails, and so on. If you hire Mr. Shatturglas, "the aluminum siding king," to do the job for you, you contract only for a good, skillful job, and Shatturglas determines the nail placement and all the other details of how the job gets done.

The nature of the relationship which the parties have actually created is essentially a fact question, for determination by the court. The label that the parties have attached to that relationship is not conclusive, nor is the "intent" of the parties, nor is what the parties "thought" they were creating. The facts speak for themselves in each case, since the parties may easily be mistaken as to what the law is or they may be attempting to avoid legal responsibilities by using the independent contractor label as a smokescreen. Among the factors which a court may consider significant are "whether the one employed is engaged in a distinct business, whether in the locality the work is usually done under supervision or by a specialist without supervision, skill required, furnishing of tools and equipment, time limit of employment, method of payment, whether [the] work is a part of [the] regular business of [the] employer, whether [the] parties believe they are creating one or the other relationship, and whether the principal is or is not in business." The *Newman* (discussion) case illustrates the application of these tests.

Independent Contractors under Statutes Regulating Employer-Employee Relationships. The nonliability aspects of the independent contractor relationship as compared to the agent/employee relationship tend to make businesses and individuals prefer to conduct their affairs through independent contractors whenever possible. However, the tort and contract areas are not the only areas where the law deals differently with independent contractors and their employers. In general, employers of independent contractors escape regulation under statutes designed to "protect" employees. Employers of independent contractors do not have to withhold state or national income tax, do not have to withhold or pay social security taxes, do not have to pay unemployment compensation taxes, do not have to provide workers' compensation coverage for the independent contractors, and are not subject to minimum wage or employment discrimination statutes. Moreover, independent contractors have no rights to organization and collective bargaining under the National Labor Relations Act. Statutes often contain their own definition, for their purposes, of who is an "employee" and who is an "independent contractor." Typically the board or agency charged with the enforcement of such a statute may make its own administrative determination as to who is subject to the statute's provisions, and often employers have to challenge the board or agency in court if they wish to claim an exemption for independent contractors employed by them.

The following case involves the protection of the Norris-LaGuardia Act, which the U.S. Congress passed to protect unions and employees from injunctions by employers in labor disputes from which violence or other illegal action was absent. In this case the court had to determine whether the relationship between the parties was the type of relationship that was meant to be covered by the law.

Columbia River Packers Assn. v. Hinton
315 U.S. 143 (U.S. Supreme Court, 1942)

FACTS The Columbia River Packers Association was in the business of processing and canning fish. The defendants were the Pacific Coast Fishermans Union, its officers and members, and two individuals.

The union was affiliated with the CIO. The union was primarily a fishermen's association, composed of fishermen who either owned their own fishing boats or leased fishing boats and simply went out and caught fish which they sold to the canneries. The union acted as a collective bargaining agent in the sale of the fish caught by its members. The union constitution and bylaws provided that union members would sell their fish in accordance with the union agreements with the canneries. The union also tried to get agreements from the canneries that they would not buy fish from nonmembers of the union.

The union made demands on the Columbia River Packers Association that it would buy fish only from union members and that it would refuse to buy fish from nonmembers. The Columbia River Packers Association would not accept such an agreement, and the union then induced its members not to sell fish to it. This boycott prevented the Columbia River Packers Association from obtaining the fish it needed to carry on its business.

The Columbia River Packers Association filed a petition for an injunction in the U.S. district court, alleging that the defendants were attempting to monopolize the fish industry in Oregon, Washington, and Alaska in violation of the Sherman Anti-Trust Act. The Norris-LaGuardia Act prohibited a U.S. district court from issuing an injunction in a case which involved a labor dispute, except under certain specified circumstances—circumstances which were not present in this case. The district court issued an injunction instructing the defendants to cease and desist the actions which damaged the plaintiff. The case was appealed to the U.S. circuit court of appeals, which reversed the district court decision on the basis that a labor dispute was involved and the district court was without jurisdiction to issue the injunction. A petition for Certiorari was granted by the Supreme Court of the United States.

ISSUE
The legal issue in this case was whether or not the boycott complained of arose out of a labor dispute as defined by the Norris-LaGuardia Act. If there was a labor dispute, then no injunction could be issued by the district court. If, on the other hand, the circumstances did not fall within the statutory definition of a labor dispute, then an injunction could be issued. The key issue was whether the relationship between the plaintiff, Columbia River Packers Association, and the union members was an employer-employee relationship or an independent contractor relationship.

DECISION
No labor dispute existed. The union members were independent contractors, not employees. The injunction would be granted.

REASONS
This case did not involve employer and employees, and it did not involve wages, hours and conditions of employment. The fishermen were independent contractors, not employees. The Columbia River Packers Association was not an employer; it was simply a buyer that wished to buy fish from independent contractor fishermen. The union was not a union of employees but a union of independent businesspersons whose sole objective was to secure higher prices for the sale of their goods, namely the fish they caught.

Franchisees as Independent Contractors. A business which sells a widely advertised product or service through local franchised "dealers" (e.g., McDonald's, Kentucky Fried Chicken, and General Motors) must avoid overstepping the boundaries that separate the independent contractor relationship from the principal-agent relationship. The business wants to minimize its legal liability and regulatory exposures by using independent contractors to sell its products or services. At the same time, however, it wants to ensure that certain quality standards are met by each franchisee-dealer. The dilemma is that the greater the degree of "quality control" it exercises, the more likely it is that the franchisee will be held to be an agent-employee rather than an independent contractor, for both liability and regulatory purposes.

The following case is an example of a situation where the franchisor wanted to make the franchise relationship an employer–independent contractor relationship but the court found that in fact there was a principal-agent relationship.

Van Pelt v. *Paull*
150 N.W. 2d 185 (Michigan, 1967)

FACTS
The plaintiff contracted with the Arthur Murray School of Dancing at the Traverse City, Michigan, Arthur Murray Studio, which was operated and owned by defendant Paull. The plaintiff paid $3,687.50 for 315 hours of instruction, and after only 107 hours of instruction Paull closed his doors and filed bankruptcy. The plaintiff started this lawsuit to recover the money she had paid for 208 hours of lessons which she never received. She first sued Paull. She then joined Arthur Murray Studios of Michigan, Inc., Doris Eaton Travis, Inc., and Doris Eaton Travis individually, alleging that

Paull was their agent and thus they were liable for his contracts. Travis and her corporation had leased the premises on which the dance studio had operated and had subleased the premises to Mr. Paull. Arthur Murray Studios of Michigan, Inc., had contracted with Paull and had sold him the franchise to run the Arthur Murray Studio. The district court granted a judgment for the plaintiff against all of the defendants except Paull. He was never served with a summons due to his bankruptcy proceedings. The defendants appealed.

ISSUE Was there an agency relationship between Paull and the other defendants, or was Paull an independent contractor?

DECISION The district court judgment for the plaintiff is affirmed. Paull was an agent.

REASONS The franchise contract between Paull and Arthur Murray Studios of Michigan, Inc., provided that Paull was to pay a percentage of his gross receipts to Arthur Murray Studios of Michigan, Inc. He had to have his books available for the corporation's inspection; he had to conduct his business on premises either owned or controlled by the corporation; he had to honor unused lessons sold by other franchises of Arthur Murray around the country; and he could not borrow money without the consent of the corporation. Also the contracts which customers signed simply stated "Arthur Murray School of Dancing" and did not specifically limit liability to Paull. The court felt that these facts sufficiently established an agency relationship rather than an independent contractor relationship. The court felt the law regarding the issue in this case was best summarized in 3 Am. Jur. 2d, Agency, paragraph 21, p. 43: "The question whether an agency has been created is ordinarily a question of fact which may be established the same as any other fact, either by direct or by circumstantial evidence; and whether an agency has in fact been created is to be determined by the relations of the parties as they exist under their agreements or acts, with the question being ultimately one of intention. The question is to be determined by the fact that one represents and is acting for another, and not by the consideration that it will be inconvenient or unjust if he is not held to be the agent of such other; and if relations exist which will constitute an agency, it will be an agency whether the parties understood the exact nature of the relation or not. Moreover, the manner in which the parties designate the relationship is not controlling and if an act done by one person in behalf of another is in its essential nature one of agency, the one is the agent of such other notwithstanding he is not so called."

Exceptions to the Nonliability Rule for Contracts and Torts of Independent Contractors. There are at least three well-recognized exceptions to the nonliability aspects of employing independent contractors.

First, as to contracts by the independent contractor, nearly all states have mechanic's lien statutes, which provide that persons who supply labor or materials for improvements on real estate can file claims against the real estate if they are not paid. These laws generally do not make the owners of the real estate personally liable for the debts which their independent contractors owes to laborers or materialmen, but the results are about the same as if they were, since they must pay off the claims to clear the title to the real estate. Of course, the landowner who is forced to pay off such third-party claims can recover from the independent contractor if the independent contractor is still solvent and available for suit.

The two other exceptions where liability is imposed on the employer for torts by his or her independent contractor involve "extra-hazardous activities" and "nondelegable duties." Extra-hazardous activities where there is a foreseeable risk of harm to others may result in the employer's being held liable for an independent contractor's torts in a situation where the employer knew that the independent contractor was inexperienced, lacked proper or safe equipment for the job, or was engaging in unnecessarily dangerous practices. Also, if the work is being done on the employer's land, the employer must exercise reasonable care to prevent injury to invited persons who might enter upon the land to persons and property adjacent to the land. Briefly, employers who hire independent contractors to do extra-hazardous work cannot simply close their eyes to what is being done and expect to be free from liability just because the work is being done by an independent contractor rather than an employee.

Nondelegable duties may be imposed by statute or derived from the common law; they generally exist in favor of the public at large. The *Nash* (discussion) case illustrates a store's nondelegable duty to its customers.

CREATION OF THE AGENCY RELATIONSHIP

In General. The agency relationship is created by the mutual consent of the parties thereto, the principal and the agent, but whether it exists or not depends on the legal significance of what the parties actually said and did rather than what they "really intended." In other words, a court may find that agency exists even though the parties did not really intend that result. As a general rule, agency may be created by oral or written words or by conduct. There is no generally applicable statute of frauds section for agency agreements, although many states require written authority if the agent is to execute real estate documents for his or her principal. Depending on the state, other particular types of agency agreements may also have to be in writing. A signed, written statement of agency authority is usually called a "power of attorney," making the agent an "attorney in fact" for his or her principal as to the matters contained in the document.

Although agency is usually based on a contract, with the agent being compensated for his or her services, the relationship can also exist without any contract at all. For example, your roommate agrees to take your coat to the cleaner for you, as he or she is going to the cleaner anyway. Your roommate is acting as your agent when he or she makes the contract with the cleaner to have the coat cleaned, even though he or she is just doing it as a favor, with no compensation at all. If the cleaner ruins your coat, you could sue it for breach of contract because an agency was created and your agent made an offer on your behalf and the cleaner accepted the coat for cleaning. You would not, however, be able to sue your roommate for breach of contract if he or she decided not to take your coat to the cleaner after all, since there was no agency contract.

Since the agent is to contract on behalf of the principal, the principal is the party who must have contractual capacity. Principals who are minors have the same rights of disaffirmance as they would have if they had made a contract in person, including the right to disaffirm whatever contract they may have made with their agents. The fact that agents are minors, or lack contractual capacity for some other reason, would not generally have any impact on the contracts which they made on behalf of their principals. However, agents who are minors can disaffirm any employment contract which they made with their principals.

The burden of proving that an agency relationship exists is on the person alleging it, typically the third party who dealt with the alleged agent. The third party has no case against the alleged principal unless he or she can show that the principal gave the agent the authority to do the acts in question. In order to hold the principal liable for the agent's actions, the third party must show that the agent had express authority, implied authority, apparent authority, or authority by ratification.

Express Authority. Express authority is authority which has been given specifically, in so many words. Orally or in writing, the principal has told the agent what he or she wants the agent to do: "Sell my GM stock"; or "Take my car to the garage, and have them fix the brakes"; or "Go over to the lumberyard, and buy us 10 more two-by-fours." In these simple examples it's pretty clear what is intended, but there are many situations where the principal's meaning is not so easy to determine. Where the words used are more general, or where the agent is to conduct a series of complicated transactions, or where the agent is left "in charge" for a period of time, a court may be called on to see whether the principal's instructions did or did not include the acts in question.

The *Restatement of Contracts* is of some help here, at least as to what is involved in "managing" a business. Section 73 lists these things: buying supplies and equipment, making repairs, hiring and firing employees, selling goods held for sale, paying and receiving payment of debts, and doing those things which are incidental, usual, necessary, or ordinary in such a business. In the following case the New York courts tried to define *manage* in another context.

Keyes v. Metropolitan Trust Co.
115 N.E. 455 (New York, 1910)

FACTS This was a lawsuit to collect a promissory note for $20,000 payable to a person now deceased. The plaintiff was the executor of the estate. The note was signed in the name of Alexander McDonald by Edmund K. Stallo, his attorney in fact. Stallo was acting under powers of attorney executed by McDonald in 1903 and 1907 which gave him certain powers to act in McDonald's behalf. McDonald was now deceased, and it was his estate that was being sued. The defense of McDonald's estate was that the powers of attorney did not authorize Stallo to sign the promissory note in question. Substantially the same wording was employed in the powers of the attorney granted in 1903 and 1907. Stallo was authorized to "collect all debts due or to become due to me; to collect and receive all dividends on stock of incorporated companies owned or held by me; to collect and receive all rents due or accruing to me . . . and to give valid receipts and acquittances for all money received by him for me and in my behalf; to make, sign, execute and deliver for me and in my name, all bills of exchange, promissory notes and other evidences of indebtedness; to sell, transfer and assign all personal property of whatever description which I own or to which I have any right or title; to vote as my proxy at all stockholders meetings of companies and corporations in which I now own or may hereafter own stock or shares and to give valid proxies to said substitutes hereunder on my behalf as my said attorney in fact may select; to guarantee the payment of promissory notes, obligations and debts of companies to which I may be or become stockholder, especially . . . and generally in the sale and management of my personal property and in other matters above mentioned to do and to perform everything which I could do and perform if personally present." The trial court held that these powers of attorney conferred power upon Stallo to make the note in question and directed judgment for the plaintiff. The defendant then appealed from the trial court to the appellate division, the intermediate court in the New York court system. That court reversed the trial court and ordered a new trial. It felt that the powers of attorney did not confer authority upon Stallo to sign the promissory note in question. The plaintiff then appealed the decision of the appellate division to the court of appeals of New York.

ISSUE   Did the powers of attorney executed by McDonald to Stallo in 1903 and 1907 grant Stallo the authority to purchase property and execute a promissory note in payment of the purchase price, or was Stallo limited by the words *other evidences of indebtedness* to indebtedness existing at the time the powers of attorney were executed?

DECISION   The court found that the authority conferred by the powers of attorney conferred the power to execute promissory notes for new indebtedness as well as indebtedness existing prior to the execution of the powers of attorney. The decision of the appellate division was reversed, and the judgment of the trial court was reinstated.

REASONS   Justice McLaughlin stated: "The purpose of a written power of attorney is not to define the authority of the agent to the third parties with whom the agent deals." In reversing the trial court, the found that the powers of attorney did not expressly give Stallo the authority to buy, as they specifically said that Stallo had authority to sell, transfer, and assign all personal property, but they did not give him specific authority to buy. Thus the trial court felt that Stallo's authority to sign promissory notes was limited to present indebtedness at the time the promissory notes were executed and did not extend to the execution of a promissory note for a new purchase. The court of appeals felt that this view placed too narrow a construction upon the powers of attorney and pointed out that the powers of attorney also gave Stallo authority "generally in the sale and management of my personal property and in other matters above mentioned to do and perform everything which I could do and perform if personally present." The appellate court found that to manage money meant to employ it or invest it, not necessarily just to sell things. It looked at the general intention of the powers of attorney and did not simply try to pick out words which would narrowly construe their meaning. It concluded that if McDonald had wanted to restrict Stallo's authority, he could have specifically done so in the instruments. But he did not choose to do so.

Most of the difficulty in the above case centers on the fact that the courts are very reluctant to imply the power to issue negotiable instruments, since such a power, quite literally, gives the agent a blank check with the principal's name on it. As a general rule, third parties should not take such instruments signed by an alleged agent unless these parties have so dealt with the agent in the past or unless they have a clear express statement of authority from the principal.

Implied Authority. Not every detail needs to be stated expressly for actual authority to exist. Once an agent has been given the express authority to do a particular job, the implication is that the principal also intended the agent to have the authority to do whatever was necessary and appropriate to get the main job done. By implication, the agent has the authority to take care of all incidental details. Also, when an emergency threatens the success of the enterprise, the agent on the spot, in charge of the principal's affairs, is assumed to have the authority to meet and deal with the emergency. And finally, implied authority may exist on the basis of a course of prior transactions between the principal and the agent or on the basis of custom in their trade or business.

Any implied authority which might otherwise exist would be negated by express instructions to the contrary, but third parties might still be able to rely on the "appearance" of authority unless they were aware of the specific instructions.

The following case illustrates the principle of implied authority.

Magenau v. Aetna Freight Lines
257 F.2d 445 (U.S. Third Circuit, 1958)

FACTS   Schroyer, a truck driver for Aetna Freight Lines, Inc., was driving a truck for Aetna to Midland, Pennsylvania, when the accident involved in this lawsuit occurred. A few days before the accident he had experienced brake problems with the truck, and the company mechanics at Buffalo had endeavored to adjust the brakes before he took off on this trip. He stopped at Jones Tavern at Waterford, Pennsylvania, and told the bartender he was still having trouble with his brakes. Ormsbee was in the tavern. Schroyer offered Ormsbee $25 to accompany him on the remainder of the trip to Midland, as he was afraid he was going to have mechanical trouble and he wanted someone else along. The two men got into the truck, and this was the last time they were seen alive. State police found the tractor-trailer off the highway over an embankment and both men dead. The administrator of the estate of Norman Ormsbee, Jr., sued Aetna Freight Lines for Ormsbee's wrongful death. The case was tried in the U.S. District Court for the Western District of Pennsylvania, and the jury entered a verdict in favor of the deceased. The defendant, Aetna Freight Lines, appealed the judgment of the lower court.

ISSUE   Did Schroyer have authority to hire a helper, Ormsbee, to accompany him on the trip?

DECISION   Yes. Schroyer had authority to hire Ormsbee, and Ormsbee then became an employee of Aetna Freight Lines. The verdict of the jury was replaced with an award for workers compensation benefits. Since Ormsbee was found to be an employee, he was only entitled to workers' compensation benefits.

REASONS   The rule of law governing this situation is stated in the *Restatement of Agency* as follows: "unless otherwise ageed, an agent is authorized to appoint another agent for the principal if . . . an unforeseen contingency arises making it impracticable to communicate with the principal and making such appointment reasonably necessary for the protection of the interests of the principal entrusted to the agent." After hearing the evidence, the jury found that an unforeseen contingency had arisen which made it reasonably necessary that the driver, Schroyer, engage Ormsbee to accompany him for the remainder of the trip for the protection of the defendant's interests.

In addition to these general ideas on implied authority, many rules as to whether particular powers have been given to the agent are generally agreed on, through long-established usage and custom and by expression in the *Restatement of Agency*. For instance, once an agency relationship has been established, notice to the agent is effectively notice to the principal, as to those facts related to the conduct of the agency. Likewise, admissions by the agent, as to matters within the scope of his or her authority, bind the principal. And although there are some earlier cases to the contrary, most courts today would probably hold the principal liable for representations made by the agent about the subject matter of the agency.

Third parties dealing with agents should be particularly careful about making payments to them, since the courts are reluctant to imply the power to receive payment unless there is a clear industry custom or a history of prior dealing between the parties. Store clerks who sell merchandise usually have the power to receive payments; traveling salespersons who merely solicit orders for goods or services usually do not. Where an agent does have authority to receive payments, he or she can only accept money, checks (usually), or credit cards (in accordance with the principal's policies). The agent cannot take other forms of property or services in payment unless expressly authorized to do so.

Apparent Authority.   Even though the principal did not actually give the alleged agent the express or implied authority to do the acts in question, the principal may be held liable nonetheless if he or she has created the "appearance" of authority. That is, if the principal has created a situation where it appears to a reasonable third party that the agent was authorized to do what he or she did, the principal is estopped to deny that an agency relationship existed once the third party has changed his or her legal position in reliance on the apperances.

Apparent authority may arise where secret instructions or limitations of authority are communicated to the agent but not to third parties. Or it may arise where actual authority was terminated (as where the agent was fired) but third parties were not notified of the termination. The following case shows that apparent authority may also arise from some other business relationship between the "principal" and the "agent" and even in a situation where there is no business relationship between them at all.

Duluth Herald & News Tribune v. Plymouth Optical Company
176 N.W.2d 552 (Minnesota, 1970)

FACTS   This was an action to recover the balance due on an advertising contract. In 1964 Paul McJames and Dr. Warren Reyburn (an optometrist) organized Paul's Opticians, Inc., a Minnesota corporation. Paul's entered into a franchise agreement with Plymouth Optical Company whereby the latter authorized the former to use the Plymouth Optical Company trade name in connection with the operation of Paul's Duluth store.

McJames as the president and general manager of "Plymouth Optical Company" entered into a contract with the plaintiff which provided that the plaintiff would print advertisements in its papers at specified rates for "Plymouth Optical Company," located in Duluth. This contract was executed on November 22, 1964. It was renewed by McJames and William R. Srnec, the store manager, in the name of "Plymouth Optical Company" on November 1, 1965, and renewed again by Srnec as store manager in the name of "Plymouth Optical Company" on November 1, 1966.

Under the 1966 renewal the plaintiff provided advertising services in the sum of $2,470.10 which Paul's failed to pay. The plaintiff sued the defendant on the theory of the apparent authority of Paul's representatives to bind the defendant.

Not only did Paul's Duluth store use the name "Plymouth Optical Company" in executing the contract with the plaintiff, but it also paid the plaintiff with checks imprinted with the name "Plymouth Optical Company." Its advertisements in the plaintiff's papers were in the name of "Plymouth Optical Company"; it had that name on its office sign and door; and it was listed in the telephone and city directories as "Plymouth Optical Company." Paul's Duluth store, in fact, was merely a franchise holder of the defendant with no actual or implied authority to bind the defendant.

The case was tried to the court without a jury. The trial judge entered judgment for the plaintiff, and the defendant appealed.

ISSUE   Was the plaintiff entitled to rely on the apparent authority of Paul McJames and William R. Srnec to bind Plymouth Optical Company in contract?

DECISION   Yes. Judgment of the trial court is affirmed.

REASONS   The court stated: "It is well settled that, in so far as third parties are concerned, the relationship of principal and agent may be evidenced by acts on the part of the alleged principal or appearances of authority he permits another to have which lead to the belief that an agency has been created."

The court also quoted the *Restatement of Agency, Second*, Section 8, comments (a) and (b) as follows:

(a)   Apparent authority results from a manifestation by a person that another is his agent, the manifestation being made to a third person and not, as where authority is created, to the agent.

(b)   The manifestation of the principal may be made directly to a third person, or may be made to the community, by signs, by advertising, by authorizing the agent to state that he is authorized, or by continuously employing the agent.

> The court then concluded:

> that the conduct of defendant franchiser in authorizing and permitting the franchisee in this case to use the name "Plymouth Optical Company" for three years under the circumstances disclosed, created an apparent authority in the franchisee to bind defendant franchiser, and accordingly defendant is liable as principal for the advertising services furnished it by plaintiff.

Ratification. Finally the principal may be held liable for his or her agent's actions on the basis of ratification. Where the agent acted without authority but the principal wishes to accept the results of the agent's action anyway, the principal can do so if he or she wants to. In most states the principal must act to ratify before the third party discovers the agent's lack of authority and decides to repudiate the contract. If the principal does so, the third party ends up with exactly the contract he thought he was making and should have no basis for complaint.

Ratification may be express ("I agree to be bound on this contract"), or it may be implied from the principal's retention of the benefits of the unauthorized transaction or from other conduct of the principal which indicates an intent to be bound to the contract. Obviously, the principal must have knowledge of the transaction when he or she speaks or acts to ratify; the principal generally will not be held to have ratified something he or she did not know about. Equally obvious, the principal has to ratify the entire transaction; the principal can't just accept the benefits and refuse to assume the reciprocal obligations. Generally, when the principal does ratify an unauthorized contract, the courts say that the principal has also agreed to accept responsibility for whatever conduct of the agent produced the contract, including false warranties and fraud.

Ratification, like any of the other cases against the alleged principal, must be proved by evidence; agency is not necessarily assumed just because some other relationship exists.

UNDISCLOSED PRINCIPAL

A principal is "undisclosed" when the third party is unaware of the principal's existence or identity; that is, the third party either doesn't know that an agent is being dealt with or knows that an agent is being dealt with but doesn't know whom the agent represents. In most cases it probably makes no difference to the third party who is being dealt with, as long as the third party gets the return performance contracted for. An undisclosed principal is given substantially the same rights to enforce the contract as are given to a disclosed principal.

Because in certain circumstances it would be unfair to force the third party to do business with an undisclosed principal, the courts have worked out some limitations. These limitations are much the same as the limitations covering the assignment of contract rights. For instance, a third party cannot be forced to perform personal services for an undisclosed principal, or to loan an

313

undisclosed principal money, or to sell to an undisclosed principal on credit. In such cases the third party's rights might be prejudiced by being forced to do business with someone other than the party believed to have been contracted with—the agent. A court may also refuse to force the third party to perform for an undisclosed principal where both the principal and the agent were aware that the third party would have refused to make the contract if the principal's identity had been disclosed.

Said v. Butt
King's Bench Div., Eng., 1919 (1920), 3 K.B. 497

FACTS The plaintiff was a Russian gentleman of independent means. The defendant was the managing director of the Palace Theatre, Ltd. ("the company"), the proprietor of the Palace Theatre, London, England.

In July 1919 an opera was produced at the Palace Theatre by the company under a financial agreement with the plaintiff. During the run of the opera, differences arose between the plaintiff and the defendant and the plaintiff made charges against the defendant and other officials of the theater with regard to the sale of tickets for the performances of the opera. These charges were untrue, though the plaintiff believed them to be true, and they were deeply resented by the defendant and other officials of the theater. The opera was canceled on October 18, and December 23 was set as the date of the first performance of a new play at the Palace Theatre.

The plaintiff desired to be present at the December 23 performance. He twice applied to the company in his own name for a ticket, but his applications were refused. The plaintiff, knowing that any application in his own name would be rejected, asked a friend of his, Pollock, to buy a ticket for him. Pollock bought a ticket for a seat at the December 23 performance without disclosing that the ticket had been bought for the plaintiff. Had this been known, the ticket would not have been given to him. The plaintiff paid Pollock for the ticket, and on the evening of December 23 he went to the theater in order to occupy the seat for which Pollock had bought the ticket. The defendant happened to see the plaintiff in the vestibule of the theater, and he immediately gave orders to the attendants that if the plaintiff had a ticket, he was not to be allowed to occupy his seat and his money was to be returned to him. As a result, the plaintiff was refused admission to the performance and he left the theater. The money paid for the ticket was offered to him, but he declined to take it.

The plaintiff sued the manager for damages, alleging that the manager had wrongfully and maliciously caused the company to break a contract made by it with the plaintiff through his agent.

ISSUE Was there a valid contract between the plaintiff and the company?

DECISION No. There was not a valid contract. Thus there was no breach when the plaintiff was refused seating at the performance.

REASONS The defendant's counsel argued that no valid contract existed between the Palace Theatre, Ltd., and the plaintiff. He contended that the Palace Theatre had never knowingly contracted with the plaintiff for the sale of a ticket for his own use and that upon discovering that the plaintiff was in fact the purchaser of a ticket it would be entitled to put an end to any apparent contract on the ground that where personal considerations enter into a contract, error as to the person with whom the contract is made annuls the contract.

It was also pointed out that a theater stands on a wholly different footing from a public inn or from a public service such as a railway. A public inn, for example, is under a common-law duty to supply to all who come, provided that accommodation exists and provided that the guest is of proper character and behavior. But a theater may sell or refuse to sell tickets at its own option. The public cannot compel a theater to grant admission.

The court found in favor of the defendant, stating, "In my opinion the defendant can rightly say, upon the special circumstances of this case, that no contract existed on December 23, 1919, upon which the plaintiff could have sued the Palace Theatre. The personal element was here strikingly present. The plaintiff knew that the Palace Theatre would not contract with him for the sale of a seat for December 23. They had expressly refused to do so. He was well aware of their reasons. I hold that by the mere device of utilizing the name and services of Mr. Pollock, the plaintiff could not constitute himself a contractor with the Palace Theatre against their knowledge, and contrary to their express refusal. He is disabled from asserting that he was the undisclosed principal of Mr. Pollock."

In order to make sure that the third party's rights are fully protected, the third party is given the choice of holding *either* the agent *or* the undisclosed principal liable for the promised return performance, once the third party discovers the principal's identity. This election may be made either expressly or impliedly, after the principal becomes known. The undisclosed principal is not liable to the third party under such an election where the third party has already received full performance under the contract, where the principal has already settled accounts with the agent on the basis of conduct by the third party, or where the principal's name does not appear on a negotiable instrument (because of the special liability rules for negotiable instruments).

PRINCIPAL'S LIABILITY FOR AGENT'S TORTS

When a person chooses to conduct his or her affairs through agents or employees, the doctrine of respondent superior holds the person liable for any wrongs they commit in trying to accomplish that person's business. The agent or employee is, of course, always liable for his or her own torts; the only question is whether the torts were committed within the "scope of employment" or the "scope of authority," so that the principal/employer is also liable. This is a form of vicarious liability—that is, liability for the wrongful acts of another, not for one's own conduct.

The main question to be decided in such cases is one of fact: Was the tort committed by the agent or employee within the scope of employment? If the answer is yes, both the principal/employer and the agent/employee are liable for the tort; if the answer is no, the agent/employee is liable but the principal/employer is not. As seen in the *Nash* (discussion) case, an agent/employee may have been within the "scope of employment" even where he or she violated direct instructions, so long as the trier of fact feels that he was attempting to accomplish the job that was assigned to him. On the other hand, if the agent is off "on a frolic of his or her own" (i.e., doing his or her own thing), the principal is not liable for the agent's actions. The "frolic" rule, however, may be subject to special motor vehicle statutory liabilities.

Two other important variables in deciding the scope of authority question are the character and the location of the tort. If the tort was intentionally committed, rather than just negligence, the agent/employee may have been motivated by his or her own reasons rather than the employer's needs; if the intentional tort was so motivated, the employer ought not to be held liable. The place where the tort occurred may be important in proving its connection with the principal/employer's business. As the *Sandman* (discussion) case shows, however, acts on the "premises" may not be within the scope of employment. Likewise, acts by agents or employees off the premises may still be within the scope of employment.

TERMINATION OF THE AGENCY RELATIONSHIP

In general, in discussing the termination of the agency relationship, we must first distinguish between the principal's *power* to terminate and the principal's *right* to do so. As a general rule, the principal has the power to terminate the agency at any time by revocation, provided the principal gives proper notice of termination to the agent and to third parties. Whether the principal also has the right to do so depends on the principal's arrangement with the agent. If there is a contract between them, the principal's wrongful termination may make the principal liable to the agent for breach, even though the agent's power to make contracts with third parties has been effectively terminated. The same distinction applies to the agent; the agent can effectively terminate the relationship at any time by simply refusing to continue as agent but may be liable to the principal for breach of contract.

The agency relationship may also be terminated, without liability for breach, by mutual agreement between the principal and the agent, by fulfillment of the purpose of the agency, or by expiration of an agreed duration. An agency may also be terminated without liability by the same sort of "impossibility" excuses as apply to contracts generally: the death, insanity, or bankruptcy of either party; the subsequent illegality of the agency's purpose; the destruction of the subject matter of the agency; a substantial change in business conditions; or war.

Notice of Termination. As a general rule, where termination has occurred by the act of either the principal or the agent, or by their mutual agreement, notice of the termination must be given to third parties. Otherwise, the agent may continue to have apparent authority to do the things he or she has been doing. Any third party who has actually dealt with the agent as an agent in the past must be given actual notice, either orally or in writing. A newspaper ad or similar "constructive notice" is sufficient for all other third parties, whether or not they ever read the ad or have it called to their attention. Generally, where the termination of an agency occurs by "operation of law," no notice at all need be given to third parties, except that an insane principal is bound on contracts made by third parties in good faith before he or she is judicially declared incompetent or before the third parties receive other notice of his or her incapacity.

Agency Coupled with an Interest. As an exception to the general rule which gives the principal the power to revoke an agency at any time, the principal cannot revoke an agency in which the agent has a personal interest in the subject matter—an "agency coupled with an interest." This phrase describes the cases where the agent is more than just a hired hand, where there is some other underlying relationship between the parties—most typically, a debtor-creditor relationship. The agency power has been given to the agent as the creditor of the principal, to try to make sure that the agent gets paid. In such cases, the principal cannot revoke the agent's power and the agent's power is not terminated by the subsequent incapacity of either party.

Following the precedent established by Chief Justice Marshall in the *Hunt* case, which follows, most courts have said that the agent's power is terminated by the principal's death unless the principal has also transferred some sort of ownership interest in the subject matter to the agent. In other words, if the principal had merely authorized the agent to sell a specific piece of property in order to pay the principal's debt to the agent, the principal's death would terminate the power to sell; if the principal had given the agent a mortgage on the property (an "interest") plus the power to sell, the principal's death would not terminate that power.

Hunt v. *Rousmanier's Administrators*
21 U.S. 174 (U.S. Supreme Court, 1823)

FACTS   In January 1820 Lewis Rousmanier asked Hunt for a loan of $1,450. As security for repayment, Rousmanier offered to give Hunt a bill of sale or a mortgage of his interest in the Ship *Nereus,* which was then at sea. Hunt made the loan, and Rousmanier executed two promissory notes for the amount, but on the advice of counsel Rousmanier gave Hunt a power of attorney to sell the *Nereus* rather than a mortgage. The power recited that it was given as security for repayment of the notes and was to become void when they were repaid. On March 21, Hunt made a second loan of $700 to Rousmanier and received a similar power of attorney to sell the schooner *Industry.*

Rousmanier died insolvent in May 1820, having paid only $200 on these loans. When Hunt tried to sell the two ships, the administrators of Rousmanier's estate refused to approve the sale. Hunt brought a bill in equity in the U.S. circuit court (then the trial court) in Rhode Island to compel the administrators to join in the deeds. The defendants' demurrer was sustained, and Hunt appealed.

ISSUES   (1) Was this a power coupled with an interest? (2) Was the power revoked by

Rousmanier's death? (3) Does a court of equity have the power to give relief for a mistake of law?

DECISION (1) No. (2) Yes. (3) Yes. Judgment reversed and cause remanded.

REASONS Chief Justice Marshall first analyzed what the parties had actually done, legally (as opposed to what they thought they had done). In looking at the power of attorney, he found that it "contains no words of conveyance or of assignment, but is a simple power to sell and convey." He then stated the general rule of agency law: "As the power of one man to act for another depends on the will and license of that other, the power ceases when the will, or this permission, is withdrawn." ("Dead men sell no ships," in other words.)

Marshall distinguished three types of powers: (1) the ordinary power of attorney would be revocable by the principal at any time and would be revoked automatically by his or her death; (2) a power given as security would not be revocable by the principal at will but would still be automatically revoked by the principal's death; (3) a power given as security *and* "coupled with an interest" in the subject matter of the power (the thing to which the power pertained) was not revocable at the principal's will or by the principal's death. Although these parties wanted the third type of power, and because of their lawyer's mistaken advice, thought that they had it, this did not change the fact that they really had the second type. Marshall said: "It is, then, deemed perfectly clear that the power given in this case is a naked power, not coupled with an interest, which, though irrevocable by Rousmanier himself, expired on his death."

After some further explanation in the opinion, however, Marshall did rule that a court of equity had the power to provide relief from a mistake of law as well as a mistake of fact. Since there were also other creditors of the insolvent estate, the case was remanded to a lower court so that it could work out an equitable result.

Since the intent of the parties is basically the same in both cases, some modern decisions do not follow this distinction and hold that either a power given as security or a power "coupled with an interest" would survive the principal's death.

Such powers to sell collateral in the event of default would be terminated by the principal's bankruptcy, unless a proper filing of the security agreement or a financing statement has been made or other steps have been taken in accordance with bankruptcy law to establish priority over other creditors.

CASES FOR DISCUSSION

MARBURY MANAGEMENT, INC. v. KOHN

629 F.2nd 705 (U.S. Second Circuit, 1980)

Dooling, District Judge

Marbury Management, Inc. ("Marbury"), and Harry Bader sued Alfred Kohn and Wood, Walker & Co., the brokerage house that employed Kohn, for losses incurred on securities purchased through Wood, Walker allegedly on the faith of Kohn's representations that he was a "lawfully licensed registered representative," authorized to transact buy and sell orders on behalf of Wood, Walker. After a nonjury trial before the Honorable Lee P. Gagliardi, District Judge, the court found that Kohn was employed by Wood, Walker as a trainee and that his repeated statements that he was a stockbroker and his use of a business card stating that he was a "portfolio management specialist" were undeniably false; the court found further that Kohn made the statements with intent to deceive, manipulate, or defraud in making them and that his misstatements were material. The court found that Kohn's misrepresentations about his employment status caused Marbury and Bader to purchase securities from Kohn between summer 1967 and April 1969. The district court also found that the predictive statements Kohn made about various securities were not fraudulently made, and that there was no evidence that they were made without a firm basis. . . .

Judge Gagliardi dismissed the plaintiffs' claims against Wood, Walker on the ground of plaintiffs' failure to prove that Wood, Walker participated in the fraudulent manipulation or intended to deceive plaintiffs; treating plaintiffs as basing their claims against Wood, Walker solely on the theory that the firm aided and abetted Kohn's fraud, the court found that the evidence supported neither a finding of conscious wrongful participation by the firm nor a legally equivalent recklessness but at best a finding of negligence in supervision. . . .

The court did not consider Wood, Walker's possible liability under the respondeat superior theory, or as a "controlling person" under Section 20(a) of the Securities Act of 1934, 15 U.S.C. § 78(a). It is concluded on this branch of the case, that the court's disposition of the "aider and abettor" issues was correct, but that it was error, on the record before the court, not to consider and determine whether Wood, Walker was liable as a controlling person or as Kohn's employer. . . .

While plaintiffs have not denominated their argument in this court and in the district court a respondeat superior argument and the complaint did not contain the traditional allegation that Kohn made the representations relief upon in the course of his employment with Wood, Walker, the evidence upon which plaintiffs rely in this court, as in the district court, and the allegations of fact made in the complaint are alike completely descriptive of the transactions and of the roles of the actors in them, and they are the evidence and allegations relevant to a determination of the respondeat superior issue, and inevitably, of the Section 20(a) issue. Plaintiffs' counsel argued the respondeat superior issue orally at the trial, and the bare failure to reiterate it in the closing brief in the district court cannot be considered an abandonment of the point.

The way in which the case was tried, and the shift in the emphasis of argument on the motion to dismiss arising from the introduction of *Ernst & Ernst* into the discussion, may explain Judge Gagliardi's taking the position that he had to consider only the aider and abettor analysis, but the record evidence tending to support the plaintiffs' claim on the other two grounds was before the court, and, on the whole of that evidence, the three theories of liability—aider and abettor, controlling person, and respondeat superior—equally presented themselves for resolution. There was evidence of Kohn's hiring, his compensation, his authority to accept orders over the telephone at the firm's Bronx office, the execution by Wood, Walker of the orders Kohn obtained from plaintiffs, the fact that Wood, Walker received the brokerage commission on all the transactions, the extent to which and the circumstances in which Kohn was authorized to recommend securities to the firm's customers, the uncertain provenance of Kohn's Wood, Walker business card, and the relation of the Bronx office of Wood, Walker to its main office. . . .

It was then error not to pass on the resondeat superior and Section 20(a) issues which lurked in the record, unless resort to respondeat superior is precluded by Section 20(a) and the district court's rejection of the claim that Wood, Walker aided and abetted Kohn's violations implies a finding that Wood, Walker has a "good faith" defense under Section 20(a). . . .

While the precise standard of supervision required of broker-dealers to make good the good faith defense of Section 20(a) is uncertain, where, as in the present case, the erring salesman completes the transactions through the employing brokerage house and the brokerage house receives a commission on the transactions, the burden of proving good faith is shifted to the brokerage house . . . and requires it to show at least that it has not been negligent in supervision . . . and that it has maintained and enforced a reasonable and proper system of supervision and internal control over sales personnel. . . . That Wood, Walker has successfully met the charge that it aided and abetted Kohn does not establish that it has borne the burden of proving "good faith" under the last clause of Section 20(a). . . .

Different considerations control the application of respondeat superior principles. Here the concern is simply with scope or course of employment and whether the acts of the employee Kohn can fairly be considered to be within the scope of his employment. . . . The evidence of record in the present case presents substantial issues of credibility and interpretation, but it indicates, if taken at face value, that Kohn at all times acted as an employee of Wood, Walker, and accounted to Wood, Walker for the transactions. The evidence contains no indication that he profited by any of the transactions other than by reason of his compensation from Wood, Walker as one of its employees. Whatever the specific limitations on his authority as between him and his employer, the evidence, again, indicates, although with some uncertainty, that it was his function as a trainee to be an intermediary in the making of transactions in securities, but that there were certain limitations on the manner in which he was to carry on his activities. Kohn's deviant conduct, while it may have induced the purchase of securities that would not otherwise have been purchased, did not appear, on the record made at the trial, to mark a deviation from Kohn's services to his employer. Arguably, what he did was done in Wood, Walker's service, though it was done badly and contrary to the practices of the industry and the standing instructions of the firm. The record on the respondeat superior issue more than sufficed to require the trier of the fact to dispose of the issue on the merits.

The judgment against defendant Kohn is affirmed and the judgment in favor of Wood, Walker & Co. is reversed, and a new trial of the claims of Marbury Management and Harry Bader against Wood, Walker & Co. is granted.

NASH v. SEARS, ROEBUCK & CO.

163 N.W.2d 471 (Michigan, 1968)

Lesinski, Chief Judge

The plaintiff brought action against Sears, Heidt's, and Arthur Keolian for false arrest, false imprisonment, and assault and battery committed by Keolian who was an employee of Heidt's, with whom Sears had contracted to furnish guard service at its store located at 8000 Gratiot at Van Dyke in Detroit. An amendment to plaintiff's complaint added a further count of negligence against the two corporate defendants based on the employment of Keolian as guard.

The incident which gave rise to plaintiff's cause of action took place on September 4, 1962, when Keolian, in guard uniform, apprehended the plaintiff, a departing Sears customer, on the sidewalk adjacent to the store. He noticed she had loose merchandise and demanded to see receipts. Plaintiff was able to produce only one. Keolian tried to get her back to the store; however, she refused to go and struck Keolian with her umbrella and started to walk away. Keolian then shoved her to the ground, straddled her body, and pinned her arms above her head. They remained in this position until a crowd gathered and the police arrived. A subsequent examination of plaintiff's possessions by the police revealed that the shoplifting charge was without foundation.

According to Keolian's testimony, he was summoned to the lingerie department in response to a bell call in the store. A saleslady told him that a woman had taken some merchandise, stuffed it into a shopping bag, and left the store. Keolian stated that when he was unable to find the suspected party on the basis of the sparse description of her attire given to him initially, he returned to get his informant, and that the saleslady accompanied him to the door and pointed the plaintiff out to him.

The plaintiff alleged and proved physical injuries and expenses, as well as accompanying humiliation, pain, and suffering resulting therefrom, none of which are at issue here.

The testimony showed that Sears and Heidt's, through their agents, had entered into an oral contract in 1957 whereby Heidt's was to furnish guards on a part-time basis to the Sears store at Gratiot and Van Dyke. Sears paid Heidt's for this service at the rate of $2 per hour per guard supplied. Heidt's paid the guards. . . .

Sears does not contend that there was not, as a matter of law, an assault and battery and false arrest, but argues that it was not liable therefor.

Sears' argument is that Heidt's was an independent contractor, for whose torts Sears, as employer, should not be held liable. . . .

Sears' principal argument on this issue, however, is that the exception to the employer's nonliability is found where the work delegated is intrinsically or inherently dangerous. Although this exception is well settled in Michigan law, it is not the exclusive exception, as Sears would imply. . . .

In the absence of Michigan case law on the question of whether or not this fact situation presents a nondelegable duty, we consider the authority cited from out-of-state and find it valid.

The responsibility owed the public by storekeepers to keep invitees safe from attacks such as was suffered by the plaintiff here cannot be delegated by an invitor so as to free the invitor from liability when its contractor, through its agent, commits a wrongful act. . . .

This is not the case of a contractor doing his work negligently. Where negligence is the sole basis of the liability, the doctrine of respondeat superior has been held inapplicable to independent contracts. Negligence does not enter into the tort of false arrest. . . . Immunity from vicarious liability would permit any storekeeper to subject his customers to the hazards of an irresponsible detective agency without peril to himself. . . . The opportunities for gross injustice afforded by such a doctrine are too manifest to permit its incorporation into the jurisprudence of our state, without compelling reason.

Thus the first issue raised by Sears must be determined in the plaintiff's favor.

Next we discuss the issue raised by defendant Heidt's relative to the court's determination that the intentional torts were proved as matter of law. Heidt's alleges that there was conflicting evidence as to the false arrest, and that therefore a jury question was presented. It notes that under the shoplifting statute, any larceny is a felony. On this point, Heidt's is correct. Heidt's then states that a private citizen may arrest without a warrant where the person arrested has in fact committed a felony even though it was not committed in his presence. Again, Heidt's is correct. However, Heidt's employs these rules of law to reach a conclusion which is fallacious. Heidt's says that since there was unobjected-to hearsay evidence to the effect that the saleslady said some merchandise was taken, this evidence of a felony should have gone to the jury, because if believed by the jury, there would have been no false arrest. Heidt's misinterprets the admission of the evidence here discussed. The evidence was not admitted as hearsay—to prove the truth of the matter asserted—but rather to prove the fact of an assertion—that the saleslady said something relevant to the cause at issue. There was not testimony that a theft had been committed—no evidence therefore of a felony, and the trial court correctly found that there was a false arrest—an arrest without legal authority. There was, according to the undisputed evidence, an assault and battery. The trial court committed no error in so finding and charging. Heidt's assignment of error as to this issue is without merit. . . .

Heidt's responsibility, if any, to Sears could only be founded on contract. The issue, consequently, was whether the kind of guard contracted for was provided. The instruction requested by Sears based on tort and the matter of proximate cause has no bearing on the breach or nonbreach of the contract. . . .

Affirmed. Costs to appellee.

SANDMAN v. HAGAN

154 N.W.2d 113 (Iowa, 1967)

Larson, Justice

[O]n November 7, 1963, the plaintiff Jerry Sandman, employed by the Sioux City Sewer Department, was directed to inspect a job . . . and arrived on the job between 8 and 9 A.M. His duty that particular morning was to inspect the installation, the hookup, and the backfill of the connection to the city water system being done by Beane Plumbing and Heating Co., hereafter referred to as the employer. The defendant Montagne and two other employees of Beane Plumbing and Heating Co., Lloyd Brunssen and Martin Wilde, were doing the actual work. A hole had been dug in the street approximately three to four feet wide, five feet long, and six feet deep. The installation and hookup had been completed, and the backfill operation involving the refilling of the hole was awaiting the arrival of Sandman. In this operation a small quantity of dirt is first dumped into the excavation and then this dirt must be firmly tamped beneath the water pipe and main. This process is repeated until there is sufficient dirt under the pipe and main so that there is no gap between the dirt and the main. If a gap is present, in time this could cause the water main to come apart and undermine and wash out the pavement. Inspector Sandman was there to see that the dirt was properly compacted under the main by the installing workmen. At the time of this incident defendant Montagne was on the street helping scoop dirt into the hole with a hand shovel. Brunssen was in the hole spreading the dirt and tamping it under the pipes, and Wilde was on the street near the hole attending his front-end loader tractor. An air compressor nearby that powered a pneumatic tamper was running during this time, which made it difficult to hear conversations in the area.

Sandman testified he was observing the backfill operation from above when he noticed that dirt had not been properly compacted under the main, and he brought this to the attention of Brunssen. Not being satisfied with the results of his directions, he jumped down in the hole to show Brunssen that there was a void under the main.

Brunssen testified that Sandman had said nothing to him about improper backfilling, but rather jumped into the hole with him and began shoving dirt into a gap under the main. Both testified that no altercation or abusive language

322

occurred until Sandman had demonstrated to Brunssen that there was indeed a gap between the main and the ground. At this point Sandman testified that Brunssen called him an s.o.b. and other derogatory names, told him to get out of the hole, and said he had no business down there. . . .

Immediately following this name-calling, a fight took place between Sandman and Brunssen. Sandman testified that to the best of his recollection he struck Brunssen only once and that the fight lasted about two minutes. Brunssen testified that he did not strike Sandman, but doubled up to protect himself, and that Sandman struck him several times on the face and body, and that the fight lasted about 15 to 30 seconds.

Montagne testified that he did not hear the conversation between Sandman and Brunssen prior to the fight because the noisy air compressor was running at the time, that the first thing he knew Sandman was pounding on Brunssen and he yelled at Sandman to stop but that he did not stop, and that he (Montagne) became scared that Brunssen might be hurt. Montagne then struck Sandman on the back of the head with a shovel. . . .

It further appears there was a dispute between Sandman and Montagne over another backfill job two weeks before, in the presence of the employer's foreman. At that time Sandman said Montagne picked up a shovel and gave it a toss and it careened off the tires of a machine some distance away. The alarmed foreman asked what was the matter, retrieved the shovel, and proceeded to do the work of tamping himself. Montagne got out of the hole entirely. . . .

The difficulty encountered by various courts in cases of willful torts committed by servants has resulted in irreconcilable decisions, and unless carefully scrutinized, the authorities seem to be in hopeless confusion. . . .

It is safe to say that "within the scope of employment" requires that the conduct complained of must be of the same general nature as that authorized or incidental to the conduct authorized. . . . [T]o determine whether an agent's act is within the scope of employment so as to make the master liable therefor, the question is whether the agent's conduct is so unlike that authorized that it is "substantially different." . . .

Generally speaking, an employer is responsible to third persons for his servant's tortious acts if committed while the servant is engaged in furthering the employer's business or interests within the scope of employment. . . .

We are satisfied here that the employee Montagne's assault on Inspector Sandman was a substantial deviation from his duties, that his act was substantially different in nature from that authorized by the employer, and that at the time thereof he was acting outside the scope of his employment. . . .

Having found no basis for reversal, the judgment of the trial court must be affirmed.

NEWMAN v. SEARS, ROEBUCK & CO.

43 N.W.2d 411 (North Dakota, 1950)

Grimson, Judge

The defendant, Alfred S. Dale, was the owner of an apartment house in the City of Bismarck, North Dakota. In August 1947, he ordered from Sears, Roebuck & Company, three folding beds. Sears, Roebuck & Company contracted their supply of said beds from the manufacturer, Superior Sleeprite Corporation of Chicago. When the Dale order was received, Sears, Roebuck & Company directed the shipment of three beds to be made by the Superior Sleeprite Corporation direct to the defendant, Dale, at Bismarck. When they were received, defendant Dale had one Christ Nelson install one of these beds in one of his furnished apartments. A Mrs. Holum was then the occupant of the apartment and immediately made use of the bed. Later defendant, Dale, and his wife occupied the apartment and used the bed. Then about the 27th day of December 1947, the plaintiff and his wife rented the premises, including the bed. About 10 o'clock on the evening of February 28, 1948, after plaintiff had gone to bed, the bed collapsed and plaintiff was seriously injured. For the damages so sustained, plaintiff brings this action. . . .

A jury was waived and the case tried to the court. After hearing the evidence and the argument of counsel, the court found for the defendants and dismissed the action. This appeal was taken and a trial de novo demanded.

The evidence shows that this folding bed is made of iron; that the feet under the head of the bed are welded to an angle iron frame which has seven holes through which lag screws attach it to the floor; that there were furnished with the bed for the purpose seven lag screws, of a size and design specified to have a sufficient holding power when screwed into a wooden floor to hold the bed in place. These lag screws were $1^1/_2$ inches long, $5/_{16}$ inch in diameter. Connecting the angle iron and the frame of the bed were six coil springs about $3/_4$ of an inch in diameter and $11^1/_2$ inches long. The coil was of 12 gauge steel wire, a little heavier than the wire used for tenpenny nails. As the bed is lifted up or down, these springs act as a counterbalance making it easier to raise or lower the bed.

The District Court found that there was no fault in the design or manufacture of the folding bed and that there was nothing inherently dangerous in its construction or operation; that sufficient lag screws were furnished by the manufacturer for the proper installation of the bed; that the defendant, Sears, Roebuck & Company, had nothing to do with the installation and was in nowise liable for the collapse of the bed or injuries of the plaintiff. That finding is in accord with the evidence.

The evidence further shows that there was a double floor $1^1/_2$ inches thick in the Dale apartment where this bed was installed. The top floor was of $13/_{16}$ inch oak, comparatively new. While Nelson testified that he did not remember the kind of screws he used in attaching the bed to the floor, the evidence warrants the conclusion that he did not use the lag screws furnished, but, instead, used ordinary wood screws $1^1/_2$ inches long but only $5/_{32}$ inch in diameter. Not only the size but also the threads of the screws show that the lag screws designated to hold the bed in place had at least four times the holding power of the wood screws used.

As the bed is lowered, the coil springs

stretched and pull up on the angle iron with considerable force. When the angle iron becomes loosened from the floor, the pull of these springs causes the bed to roll forward, fall to the floor, and the head to collapse over the bed. The evidence shows that that is what happened.

Assuming that the use by Nelson of those wood screws for fastening the bed was negligence and was the proximate cause of the bed becoming loose and collapsing to the injury of the plantiff, the question arises whether the defendant, Dale, is liable therefor. That raises the question whether Nelson was an independent contractor or a servant of Dale. . . .

"One of the most important tests to be applied in determining whether a person who is doing work for another is an employee or an independent contractor is whether the person for whom the work is done has the right to control, not merely the result, but the manner in which the work is done, as well as the method used." . . .

In determining whether a workman is an independent contractor or employee, all the circumstances of the case and the attitude and intent of the parties must be considered. . . .

The evidence shows that Nelson was a carpenter of many years' experience; that his brother and his two sons worked together; that there was a general agreement between Dale and Nelson that Nelson should make repairs on Dale's apartments whenever called by Dale or his tenants; that the only instruction given by Dale to Nelson was to make the repairs called for according to his best judgment; that instructions were given by Dale to his tenants to call Nelson if carpenter repairs were needed. Nelson drew no salary. Instead such repairs were paid by Dale on a bill rendered at the completion of each job. Dale exercised no supervision over any particular job. Nelson had the right to hire help or to have others do the job for him in case he was otherwise employed. The particular job here involved was an installation of a folding bed, making it a processed, usable article. Nelson was, by the owner, Dale, given the right to possession of the premises as far as necessary for the installation, which provision was acquiesced in by Mrs. Holum, the tenant at the time. Some alterations in a partition were necessary. It required the special skill of a carpenter. That work was not a part of Dale's regular business but was in line with Nelson's regular work. No directions were given as to when or how the job should be done. Neither Dale nor his wife was present when it was done. They accepted the finished product of the work. From that evidence it is clear that Dale had no control and reserved no right of control over how Nelson performed the work of installation nor the methods he used. . . .

Considering that finding an all the circumstances shown in evidence, Nelson must be held to have been an independent contractor in installing the bed. . . .

The only agreement between the plaintiff and Dale for the renting of this apartment shown in the evidence is that a sister of plaintiff's wife plaintiff could rent that apartment, which request was granted. There were no inducements or representations made by Dale or his wife to the plaintiff or his agent to secure him as a tenant. No warranties of any kind as to the apartment or its furnishings were made to the plaintiff. Dale had no knowledge of the latent defect in the installation of the folding bed. No deceit or fraud on his part appears in the evidence. The plaintiff had not called upon Dale for any repairs, nor given any notice of any defects. Under these circumstances Dale can not be held for damages resulting from a latent defect in the folding bed here involved. "Generally, a landlord is not liable for injuries to tenant resulting from latent defect in premises, in absence of proof of knowledge and concealment on his part." . . .

The judgment of the District Court is affirmed.

PROBLEMS FOR DISCUSSION

1. Cloris James opened a Servu Revolving Charge Account at the local Servu Store. She signed the application "Mrs. Ralph James." Cloris made over $600 worth of credit purchases on the account before Servu terminated her charging privileges because of nonpayment. Cloris has no separate job and no available personal assets. Servu sued her husband, Ralph, for the balance due on the account. There is no indication that Ralph ever used the charge account or that he ever made any of the payments credited on it. What result, and why?

2. Orville went to the home of Reverend Flowers and asked to borrow Flowers' car so that he could go pick up his paycheck. Flowers agreed to let him take the car but told him to be back by 11:30 that morning, since Flowers had to use the car himself. When Orville didn't come back on time, Flowers called his home, his employer, and several hospitals. Finally, Flowers called the city police and explained that his car was missing. The police told him to come down and file a stolen car report if the car wasn't back by the next day. About 2 A.M. Orville called Flowers and told him that he had had an accident with the car. At that point, Flowers had not yet filed any stolen car report with the police. The state's motor vehicle code makes the owner liable for accidents while a vehicle is being driven with the owner's permission. Minnie, the driver of the other car involved in the accident, suffered serious personal injuries. She sues Flowers. What result, and why?

3. Major went into the Finepoint Inn and ordered a dinner "special" for $7.95. He specified that he had to have olive oil and vinegar dressing on his salad. When the bill came, it included an extra charge of 55 cents for the salad dressing. Major refused to pay the extra charge. Rudy Manners, the headwaiter, was then summoned. The argument continued, and Rudy followed Major out of the inn and next door to the motel where Major was staying. Although they were separate businesses, the inn and the motel had worked out an arrangement whereby the food bills of motel guests could be placed on their motel bill, so that the guest would only have to pay once for room and meals. Rudy gave the motel clerk the food bill and told him to put it on "this person's bill." Major then asked Rudy to "step outside," made a sweeping motion at him, and called him a bad name. Rudy picked up an ashtray and hit Major over the head with it. Major sues Finepoint Inn. What result, and why?

4. Lucious, the sales manager, left his home one evening, supposedly to meet a client of his construction firm employer at a local restaurant. Lucious told his wife and the maid where he was going. When the maid asked when she could get her paycheck for the week, Lucious told her that he'd be back in a little while and write out her paycheck then. Less than an hour later, Lucious was shot and killed by an unknown person. When his wife filed for death benefits under workers' compensation, her claim was opposed by the employer. There was no record at Lucious' office of any such business appointment, nor did anyone at the construction firm know anything about it. (Workers' compensation, of course, covers only on-the-job injuries to employees.) Should Lucious' widow collect death benefits? Why or why not? Would it make any difference if he had been killed at the restaurant where he said he was going to be? Why?

5. Dewey owned an ice-cream parlor. He bought his ice cream from Dairy Products, Inc. The ice cream was delivered twice a week, as ordered by Dewey, by a Dairy truck driver who had instructions to collect the price when he left the ice cream. One hot July day, Dewey refused to accept a delivery of ice cream, saying it was "soft." Bonzo, the truck driver, said Dewey could do as he wished with the ice cream but that the price had to be paid. Dewey refused to pay, so Bonzo moved

toward the cash register. Dewey was quicker and locked the cash register before Bonzo could take out any money. Bonzo then picked up the cash register and started to walk out with it. Dewey grabbed him, and they started to fight. Bonzo yelled for Herman, his assistant, who had been waiting on the truck, and the two of them beat Dewey severely. Dewey sues Dairy for damages. What result, and why?

6. The state's workers' compensation statute provides that the benefits payable thereunder are the exclusive remedy for on-the-job injuries sustained by employees. Needing a summer job, Geraldine signed up with Partimees, Inc., a firm that provided part-time and temporary help to individuals and businesses. Partimees paid Geraldine $2 per hour and charged its clients $4 per hour for all the hours she worked for them. Geraldine had the right to choose from whatever jobs were available each day, and she didn't have to take any job she didn't like. After having been sent out to three different companies for various periods of time, she was told one morning that there was a job at Humdrum Tool Company. While she was operating a machine at Humdrum she was seriously injured. Geraldine has collected from Partimees, under its workers' compensation coverage. Since these benefits are so limited, Geraldine also wants to collect tort damages from Humdrum. Can she do so? Discuss.

7. Patricia Hartless was vice president and stockholder of Realistic, Inc., a real estate firm. Buddy Buryme was originally employed by Realistic as a salesman. After he had been with the firm about two years, Patricia (who had also hired Buddy) told him that he was promoted to sales manager of one of the company's offices, and that he would receive 10 percent of the net monthly profits of that office as a semiannual bonus. When he left the company about six months later Buddy was not paid any bonus for the time he had worked there. Realistic said that Patricia was not authorized to promise such bonuses, that the company directors had discussed the problem and decided not to give Buddy a bonus, and that while Patricia might be personally liable to Buddy, the company was not. Buddy sues Realistic. What result, and why?

8. The state of Indiana seeks an injunction to prohibit Medina, Inc., from continuing to operate there without being properly licensed as a foreign corporation and from using certain fraudulent sales practices. Medina, incorporated in Delaware, denies that it is operating in Indiana and says that the persons representing it there are independent contractors. It is a book and magazine discounter. Subscriptions are taken by door-to-door solicitors, who work in crews of 5 to 20 persons, under the direction of a "contractor." Each contractor hires his or her own solicitors, negotiates commissions with them, tells them where and when to solicit, and pays their expenses. At the end of the day, each contractor prepares a daily report form, which is submitted to Medina along with the day's orders. Contractors are paid a percentage of the sales made. Should this injunction issue? Do the Indiana courts even have jurisdiction over Medina? Discuss.

Agency—Other Legal Relationships | 15

DUTIES AND LIABILITIES OF PRINCIPAL TO AGENT

Principal's Duty to Compensate Agent.   Many of the cases in which an agent is suing his or her principal involve the principal's duty to compensate the agent. It is assumed that the principal owes the agent whatever salary or commission was agreed on for doing the acts required, and it is also assumed that the principal should reimburse the agent for any expenses which the agent reasonably and necessarily incurred in carrying out the principal's instructions. If the agent is to pay his or her own expenses, this should be stated in the contract. In the absence of any specific agreement, it is also assumed that the agent should be reimbursed for any personal loss or damage which he or she has sustained as a result of following the principal's instructions.

There are special "compensation" rules for real estate brokers. Usually the broker does not actually have the power to sell the listed property but only to conduct negotiations with prospective buyers. The broker, therefore, has normally earned the commission when he or she "brings in a deal," that is, when the broker produces a buyer who is ready, willing, and able to meet the purchase terms specified by the seller in the listing agreement. The following case shows the significance of these special rules for brokers.

Hecht v. Meller
244 N.E.2d 77 (New York, 1968)

FACTS   Helen Hecht, the plaintiff, a real estate broker, entered into a written contract with Herbert and Joyce Meller, the defendants, by which she became the exclusive selling agent for the sale of their residence. Through the plaintiff's efforts suitable buyers were introduced to the Mellers, and on May 30, 1963, a contract for the sale of the property was signed which acknowledged that Hecht had brought the parties together, established a sale price of $60,000, and set August 1 as the closing date.

On July 20, without fault of either party, the dwelling house on the property was substantially destroyed by fire. The buyers elected to rescind the contract, as provided for by New York State statutory law. The Mellers returned the buyers' down payment. The present action was commenced by the real estate broker when the sellers refused to pay the $3,600 commission allegedly earned by the broker in bringing the contracting parties together. The lower court found for the plaintiff. The defendants appealed to the appellate division, which reversed the lower court. The plaintiff then appealed that decision to the court of appeals of New York.

ISSUE   Is a real estate broker entitled to commissions on the sale of real property if the purchaser asserts a statutory privilege to rescind the contract of sale because the property has been substantially destroyed by fire after the contract was executed but before the buyer took title or possession?

DECISION   Yes. The broker is entitled to her commission. The court of appeals reversed the appellate division and reinstated the judgment for the plaintiff.

REASONS   The court stated "that a real estate broker's right to commissions attaches when he procures a buyer who meets the requirements established by the seller. . . . At the juncture that the broker produces an acceptable buyer he has fully performed his part of the agreement with the vendor and his right to commission becomes enforceable. The broker's ultimate right to compensation has never been held to be dependent upon the performance of the realty contract or the receipt by the seller of the selling price unless the brokerage agreement with the vendor specifically so conditioned payment. . . . As stated in *Gilder* v. *Davis* . . . : 'If from a defect in the title of the vendor, or a refusal to consummate the contract on the part of the purchaser for any reason in no way attributable to the broker, the sale falls through, nevertheless the broker is entitled to his commissions, for the simple reason that he has performed his contract.'"

Principal's Liability for Breach of Agency Contract. If the principal wrongfully prevents the agent from carrying out their contract and thus earning the agreed compensation, the principal like any other employer, is liable to the agent for breach. Some of these cases involve an unjustified discharge of the agent; others result from the principal's improper interference with the agent's conduct of the agency, such as failing to provide the agent with new price and product information or attempting to impose arbitrary and discriminatory paperwork requirements. If the agent is not meeting his or her duties under the contract, the principal may be justified in firing the agent. Generally, if the agency has not been set up for a specific period of time (i.e., it is "at will"), the agent may be fired at any time, with or without reason, and the agent will have no case for breach of contract. While the following case involves a nonagent employee, it does show that there may be some "outer limits" on the right to discharge an employee even where the term of employment is "at will."

FACTS   The plaintiff was hired in September 1968 at $1.84 per hour to work in the defendant's factory and was allegedly told that if she worked well, she would get a better job with better pay. The term of the contract was at will. The plaintiff claimed that she was harassed by her foreman because she refused to go out with him and that his hostility, condoned if not shared by the defendant's personnel manager, ultimately resulted in her being fired. Trial by jury resulted in a verdict for the plaintiff in the amount of $2,500. The defendant appealed.

ISSUE   In an employment contract where the term of employment is at will, can the employee recover damages from the employer for breach of contract if the employee is discharged without reason?

DECISION   Yes. The employee can collect damages in certain cases. The court affirmed the right of the plaintiff to collect damages but remanded the case to the trial court on the issue of damages.

REASONS   The court stated: "In all employment contracts, whether at will or for a definite term, the employer's interest in running his business as he sees fit must be balanced against the interest of the employee in maintaining his employment and the public's interest in maintaining a proper balance between the two. . . . We hold that a termination by the employer of a contract of employment at will which is motivated by bad faith or malice or based on retaliation is not in the best interest of the economic system or the public good and constitutes a breach of the employment contract. . . . Such a rule affords the employee a certain stability of employment and does not interfere with the employer's normal exercise of his right to discharge, which is necessary to permit him to operate his business efficiently and profitably." With regard to the amount of damages recoverable, the court stated that the verdict included elements of damage not properly recoverable. The plaintiff lost 20 weeks' employment at an average pay of $70.81 per week. This would account for $1,416.20 of the verdict, leaving $1,083.80 attributable to mental suffering. Damages for mental suffering are not generally recoverable in a contract action. Thus the plaintiff would only get $1,416.20 instead of $2,500.

DUTIES AND LIABILITIES OF AGENT TO PRINCIPAL

In General. The agency relationship is based on the trust and confidence which the principal has placed in the agent, by giving the agent the power to manage the principal's affairs. The agent is thus a fiduciary, owing to the principal a duty of honesty and fair dealing in their relationship. The following specific aspects of this fiduciary duty may be easier to remember if you recall the boy scout's pledge: "Trustworthy, Loyal, Helpful, Friendly, Courteous, Kind, Obedient, Cheerful, Thrifty, Brave, Clean, and Reverent." Nearly all of these desirable characteristics of a successful scout also apply to the agent.

Loyalty and Good Faith. Loyalty to the principal's interests and good faith in dealing with them are the most basic parts of the agent's fiduciary duty. Under the rule that a person "cannot faithfully serve two masters," an agent is prohibited from representing two persons with opposing interests, such as the two parties to a business transaction, unless both of them know of the dual agency and agree to it. A principal who does not know of the dual agency can rescind the resulting transaction when he or she learns the truth. Likewise, the agent can neither buy from nor sell to himself or herself nor derive any other secret benefit for himself or herself from conducting the principal's affairs. The receipt of secret bribes, payoffs, or presents by the agent from third parties will justify dismissal of the agent and may also involve civil or criminal penalties against the agent. The following case involved a dual agency where the agent acted for both parties in a real estate transaction without disclosing the fact of his dual agency to either party.

Taborsky v. *Mathews*
121 So.2d 61 (Florida, 1960)

FACTS   This is an action by the sellers of real estate to foreclose on a purchase-money mortgage signed by the purchasers when they purchased certain real estate from the sellers. The facts disclosed that the real estate agent who acted for the defendants was also the agent for the plaintiffs in this transaction. The agent received a commission from both parties, and the defendants had no knowledge of the dual agency. The defendants counterclaimed to recover the portion of the purchase price which they paid and asked that the entire transaction be avoided and canceled. The plaintiffs won in the lower court. The defendants appealed.

ISSUE   In an action to foreclose a money mortgage upon certain real property where a real estate broker, without disclosing the dual nature of his agency to the purchasers, acted as agent for both parties in negotiating the sale of the property, have the purchasers the right, upon discovering the dual agency, to avoid the sale and purchase-money mortgage?

DECISION   Yes. Lower court reversed.

REASONS   The court stated: "In our jurisprudence it is well established that an agent for one party to a transaction cannot act for the other party without the consent of both principals. Where an agent assumes to act in such a dual capacity without such assent, the transaction is voidable as a matter of public policy. Perhaps the best statement of the law applicable to the inquiry at bar is that found in *Evans* v. *Brown,* 1912, 33 Okla. 323, 125, p. 469, 470: No principle is better settled than that a man cannot be the agent of both the seller and the buyer in the same transaction, without the intelligent consent of both. Loyalty to his trust is the most important duty which the agent owes to his principal. Reliance upon his integrity, fidelity, and ability is the main consideration in the selection of agents; and so careful is the law in guarding this fiduciary relation that it will not allow an agent to act for himself and his principal, nor to act for two principals on opposite sides in the same transaction. In such cases the amount of consideration, the absence of undue advantage, and other like features are wholly immaterial. Nothing will defeat the principal's right of remedy, except his own confirmation, after full knowledge of all the facts. Actual injury is not the principle upon which the law holds such transactions voidable. The chief object of the principle is not to compel restitution where actual fraud has been committed, or unjust advantage gained, but it is to prevent the agent from putting himself in a position in which to be honest must be a strain on him, and to elevate him to a position where he cannot be tempted to betray his principal.'''

A related problem, and one which arises with some frequency in a technological society, is the conflict between employer and employee over who owns patents developed by the employee and other "secret" information used by the employee on the job (for example, customer lists). Courts generally hold that the fiduciary duty does not end simply because employment is terminated, and thus the employee (or agent) does not have the right to use formulas, processes, customer lists, or other trade secrets in competition with his or her former employer. As to patented devices and processes which the employee developed on the job, the employee may become the owner by having them patented in his or her own name, but the employer has a "shop right" to make use of them in the employer's business without paying royalties. Specific language in the employment contract will probably head off most of these problems.

BBF Group Inc. v. Kontrols, Inc.
326 N.E.2d 18 (Massachusetts, 1975)

FACTS   Laczko was an employee of BBF Group and had a valid contract with BBF Group requiring him to turn over to it the title to and all supporting documents concerning any improvements on certain plastic molding devices which he developed while working for it. Laczko developed certain improvements while in the plaintiff's employ, and during that time he also organized the defendant company, Kontrols, Inc. He then quit BBF Group and marketed the improvements through this new company. The plaintiff, BBF Group, sued Laczko and Kontrols, Inc., for misappropriating trade secrets. The lower court found for the plaintiff, and the defendants appealed.

ISSUE   Are the defendants liable for the misappropriation of trade secrets when the information and material involved were the developments of the defendant Laczko?

DECISION   Yes. Lower court decision affirmed.

REASONS   The contract which Laczko signed with BBF Group was sufficient to allow BBF Group to successfully win an action against its former employee and his corporation for misappropriation of trade secrets. These trade secrets were defined as the improvements which the former employee had made on certain plastic molding devices while he worked for BBF Group, Inc.

Care and Skill of His or Her Calling.   Once a person accepts appointment as an agent, he or she has the duty to use that degree of care and skill possessed by a reasonably competent practitioner in that line of business. A salesperson, for example, would be required to have and to exercise the knowledge, training, and diligence of "average" salespersons in the field involved. The existence of this duty means that an agent can be held liable for misfeasance (not doing lawful acts in a proper manner), malfeasance (doing a wrongful act), or nonfeasance (not being diligent in performing his or her job).

Personal Performance.   A person is chosen as an agent of a principal, and placed in position of trust and confidence, on the basis of his or her unique personal characteristics. It therefore follows logically that the agent owes a duty to use those personal qualities in performing the assigned job and that the agent should not be able to delegate to others the exercise of his or her discretionary powers as an agent. Absent any specific agreement, delegation by the agent is permitted only where the nature of the business requires it, or where a known and established custom permits it, or where the delegation involves purely ministerial or mechanical acts (such as answering the telephone or typing correspondence). Except in these situations, the principal will not be liable to third parties for the acts of such "subagents" and their appointment by the original agent would be a breach of his or her duty to the principal.

Obedience to Instructions and Good Conduct.   Like the boy scout, a good agent is obedient. The agent must obey the principal's instructions, even if he or she considers them stupid or unreasonable; this control over methods, remember, is the main distinction between the agent/employee and the independent contractor. In general, the agent's only excuses for not obeying instructions are that they require him or her to do something illegal or that it has become impossible to comply with them. The law is not too clear on the degree to which agents must subject themselves to personal danger in order to comply with the principal's instructions, although the *Restatement of Agency* does indicate that agents can disregard such instructions in order to "protect the agents' own superior interests." It is clear that the agent will have to follow instructions which are merely "unreasonable," unless the relationship involves an agency coupled with an interest and the unreasonable instructions would interefere with the agent's rights in the subject matter of the agency.

As far as third parties are concerned, the agent is the principal. This holds true particularly for agents who represent business concerns. The image and reputation of a business are in large part determined by the way its agents and employees conduct themselves toward third parties. The agent, and to some extent even the employee, therefore owes a duty of "good conduct." This requirement clearly covers on-the-job conduct, so that things like dress codes can be enforced if they are reasonably and uniformly applied (see the cases in Chapter 51). The *Restatement of Agency* also indicates that this duty extends to off-the-job conduct which might affect the principal's business, such as the conduct of the bank teller who becomes known in the community as a "patron of the races." The exact degree to which agents can be legally required to surrender their personality in order to keep their jobs remains an open question.

Use of Principal's Property.   The agent is liable for any misuse of property which the principal has entrusted to the agent or which comes into the agent's possession as part of his or her activities as agent. As part of this duty, the agent is not to commingle money or other property of the principal with his or her money or other property and the agent is required to provide the principal with correct and reasonably detailed statements of account.

The agent also has a duty to communicate to the principal any information that he or she possesses which might materially affect the agency.

Principal's Ratification of Agent's Unauthorized Act.   As a general rule, where the principal has a clear choice and ratifies with full knowledge that the agent's actions were unauthorized, the agent is excused of any further liability to the principal. The *Restatement* says that the agent will remain liable for breach of duty either where the principal "is obliged to affirm the act in order to protect his own interest" or where the principal is induced to ratify by the agent's fraud or duress.

LIABILITY OF AGENT TO THIRD PARTY

Agent Acts beyond Authority.   In most states, when the agent in a disclosed agency transaction acts beyond the scope of his or her authority, so that the third party has no contract with the principal, the third party has no contract with the agent either. In these states the third party's remedy against the agent is a tort claim for fraud (if the agent knowingly misrepresented his or her authority) or a case for breach by the agent of his or her "implied warranty of authority." As a rule, it is assumed that the agent makes such a warranty to the third party. There is no such warranty, however, if the third party knew that the agent was unauthorized, or if the agent in good faith disclosed to the third party all the facts regarding the extent of his or her authority, or if the contract contains a disclaimer of the agent's liability. In a minority of states the agent could also be sued directly on the contract which the agent was not authorized to make for the principal.

Principal Nonexistent or Incompetent.   The two most common examples of the "nonexistent" principal are the corporation which has not yet been formed and the unincorporated association (which is usually not recognized as a separate legal person). In these cases the agent is personally liable on the contracts he or she makes with the third party, even if the third party knows of the "non-existence," unless the contracts specifically exempt the agent from personal liability.

Where the principal totally lacks contractual capacity at the time the contract is made (e.g., a person who has been judicially declared insane), most courts will probably arrive at the same result as would be reached if the principal were "nonexistent." Also, the agent would clearly be liable if the agent fraudulently misrepresented or concealed the principal's lack of capacity. Where the principal has merely exercised an option to disaffirm the contract, however, the results are not so clear-cut, but even in such cases many courts would hold the agent liable.

Agent Pledges Personal Credit. An agent who has pledged his or her personal credit on the contract, as surety for the principal, is also clearly liable to the third party. This occurs very frequently where the agent is acting on behalf of a small, brand-new corporation that has not yet established its own credit standing; in such cases the third party will often demand that the agent-promoter-shareholder cosign the contract. If the agent does so, the agent is liable according to the terms of the contract.

Because this situation is so common, the agent may also be held personally liable where the contract language or the signatures on the contract indicate his or her liability. If it appears that the agent was a party (or the other party) to the contract, the agent may be prevented by the parol evidence rule from proving otherwise. If the principal's name does not appear on a negotiable instrument, and the agent's does, the agent is liable on it and the principal is not. To avoid these unintended results, the agent should always sign "Peter Principal, by John Able, agent"—thus clearly indicating that he or she is signing in a representative capacity.

The following case involves a small corporation and the question of the liability of the party singing the contract.

Henderson v. Phillips
195 A.2d 400 (District of Columbia, 1963)

FACTS Henderson was a plumbing contractor. Phillips telephoned Henderson to request an estimate on the cost of doing some plumbing work on a particular house, identifying himself as the president of the firm that was constructing the house. After inspecting the house, Henderson prepared two written contracts addressed to "Design for Modern Living" and mailed them to the corporation. Each was accepted under the signature of "James O. Phillips" and remailed to Henderson in an envelope bearing in the upper left-hand corner the name "Designed for Living, Inc., 2814 Pennsylvania Avenue, N.W., Washington 7, D.C.," within the outline of a picture of a house. Thereafter, payment on account was made by checks mailed in a similar envelope. Printed on the first check in the upper left-hand corner was "Metropolitan Designed for Living, Inc.," showing the Pennsylvania Avenue address. It was signed by two persons, one of whom was Phillips, under the printed name of the corporation, with no indication as to the capacity of either signor. A second check, similarly drawn, was not paid upon presentment. Henderson then sued both the corporation and Phillips.

The lower court found the corporation liable but found that Phillips was not individually liable for the balance due on the contracts. The plaintiff appealed.

ISSUE The sole question upon appeal was whether the appellee, Phillips, president of Metropolitan Designed for Living, Inc., was personally liable under two contracts for plumbing services rendered by the appellant.

DECISION Phillips is not personally liable.

REASONS The court felt that the facts revealed that Henderson knew he was dealing with a corporation of which Phillips was an agent. The court stated: "The prior dealing between appellant and Phillips was sufficient to impute notice of the agency relationship of Phillips. The checks in payment for the work performed by Henderson were definitely revealing as to the corporate identity of the builder. The present contracts were again negotiated through Phillips who identified himself as president of the corporation. It is true that he 'accepted' the written contracts without indicating his agency capacity, but he did the same when co-signing the corporation check in payment for both jobs by Henderson. Henderson recognized that he was dealing with a corporate entity when he addressed his contracts to 'Design for Modern Living.' It is also significant that Henderson never testified that he thought he was dealing only with Phillips and intended to rely upon him for payment and not upon the corporate builder. Neither contract contained any words expressly binding Phillips personally or indicating any intent by him to be responsible for payment in the event the corporation defaulted. The identity of the principal being known and the agency of Phillips being established at the time of the transaction, upon default of the disclosed principal, personal liability could not be imposed upon its agent."

Undisclosed Principal. As indicated in the last chapter, where the existence or identity of the principal is not disclosed at the time the contract is made, the third party has the option of holding the agent personally liable on the contract. The only way to avoid this liability is to disclose the principal.

Agent Commits Tort against Third Party. As also stated in the last chapter, an agent is personally liable for the torts which the agent commits against third parties. Where the agent's tort was within the scope of his authority, the third party can sue *both* the agent and the principal and they are both liable, although the third party cannot collect damages twice.

As a rule, the agent is not liable to third parties for breach of a duty which is owed only to the principal, at least if the breach involves only nonfeasance or misfeasance.

Sawyer v. *Tildahl*
148 N.W.2d 131 (Minnesota, 1967)

FACTS   The owner-sellers listed their property with the defendant broker. The plaintiffs contacted the broker, who showed the property to them. It had come to the attention of the plaintiffs that some of the homes in the area had a water problem in the basement. The plaintiffs were told, "You will never have a water problem with this basement. You couldn't possibly have a water problem in this home because you are south of Highway 10 and your land is very close to Rice Creek and this land all drains to Rice Creek."

The plaintiffs relied on the representations of the broker, completed a contract for purchase, and finally bought the house about April 17, 1962. On taking possession, they discovered that the basement floor was covered with from 1 to 1½ inches of water. Various explanations were offered as to where the water came from. The flooding was attributed to unseasonable rains, the possibility that the house had penetrated the water table, the appearance of an "underground spring," and a possible faulty pipe connection with the city water main. In any event the record established that before the sellers moved they had made an attempt to correct the seepage problem by plugging certain cracks and installing a sump pump to siphon off the water. The siphoning was continued by the plaintiffs after they took possession and until the problem either corrected itself or disappeared. The record also indicates that about two years prior to the sale a neighbor observed a pump siphoning water from the excavation that was now the basement. It also appeared that a babysitter who was present in the home some months before the sale, while the property was occupied by the Tildahls, observed that there was water on the basement floor and that the walls of the basement were damp.

The purchase price of the house, including certain equipment, was $17,000. There was testimony from a qualified real estate appraiser that the existence of the water problem reduced the value of the property by $3,000 to $3,400. At the time this witness inspected the property, which was several months after the purchase, he observed water on the basement floor.

The plaintiffs sued the broker for damages for misrepresentation. The verdict was for the plaintiffs, for $3,000 and $100 punitive damages. The defendant appealed.

ISSUE   Where a real estate broker-agent makes a false representation of past or existing material fact which is susceptible of knowledge, without actually knowing its truth or falsity but with the intent to induce the hearer to act in reliance on the representation, or where the representation is made under circumstances justifying the hearer in so acting and the hearer does so to his pecuniary damage, is the broker-agent liable for fraud?

DECISION   Yes. The lower court verdict was affirmed as to the compensatory damages of $3,000, but the court did not allow the punitive damages of $100.

REASONS   The court in holding for the plaintiff stated: "It should be conceded that a water problem in the basement of a home is of 'material' consideration to a prospective buyer and in this case was of such importance that plaintiffs would not have considered purchasing the home if they had not been assured by the broker that they would have no seepage problem. While it may be true that the broker did not actually know that there had been water seepage in the home, that fact was nevertheless susceptible of knowledge. It would seem that that information should be available to an experienced real estate broker who 'knew his merchandise.'"

LIABILITY OF THIRD PARTY TO AGENT

Agent Suing on His or Her Own Behalf. There are only a few situations where the agent will sue the third party on his or her own behalf. If the agent was also made a party to the original contract, or if the agent owns the contract rights by assignment from the principal, the agent can sue the third party. The agent can also sue a third party for wrongful interference in the contract relationship between the agent and his or her principal or for any other tort which the third party commits against the agent. Finally, where the agent has delivered money or goods to the third party under circumstances where the third party would be unjustly enriched at the agent's expense (e.g., the agent by mistake pays the third party more than the principal owes the third party), the agent can sue in his or her own name to prevent such unjust enrichment.

Agent Suing for His or Her Principal.   Generally, an agent cannot sue in his or her own name to enforce a contract that the agent made on behalf of his or her principal; the principal has to sue the third party. If specifically authorized to so, an agent may be able to bring suit as an agent for collection; also, an assignment may be made to such an agent for the purpose of collection only. An agent can also sue on the principal's behalf to recover goods which the agent delivered to the third party by mistake, or for interference by the third party with the agent's possession of the principal's goods.

Thus, while the main agency case is the third party's suit against the principal, based on an alleged contract or on the agent's tort, any of the three parties to this relationship may have a case against either of the other two.

CASES FOR DISCUSSION

J. D. MARSHALL INTERNATIONAL, INC., v. FRADKIN

409 N.E.2d 4 (Illinois, 1980)

McNamara, Justice

Plaintiff, J. D. Marshall International, Inc., brought this action for injunctive relief against defendants Leslie Fradkin, Richard Ellis, Aldon International, Inc., and Thomas McShane, seeking to enforce post-employment restrictive covenants and prevent tortious interference with its business relationships. Plaintiff appeals the trial court's allowance of defendants' motions to dismiss the complaint. . . .

Plaintiff, an Illinois corporation, is engaged in the business of buying products manufactured by various domestic companies and then selling and exporting these products to foreign customers. The business operates primarily under agreements giving plaintiff the exclusive right to export the products of certain domestic suppliers.

Fradkin, Ellis, and McShane were employees of plaintiff. Fradkin was employed by plaintiff from March 1, 1976 through December 31, 1978.

Fradkin was director of the construction equipment division, and his duties included procuring construction equipment from domestic producers and exporting such products to foreign customers. Fradkin's written employment agreement with plaintiff provided, in relevant part:

In consideration of the fact that you are employing me as an executive of your company, in a position of confidence, I agree that in the event that my employment is terminated, for any reason whatsoever, I will not for a period of two years, either accept employment or accept to represent, or seek employment with, or seek to represent in any capacity whatsoever, as an office worker, manager, consultant, salesman, sales representative or sales agent—any manufacturer, fabricator, exporter or importer whom you are representing or with whom you have commercial relations at the time of termination of my employment or that you had represented or with whom you had commercial relations during the period of my employment with you.

Ellis was employed on May 2, 1977 through December 31, 1978, as director of plaintiff's power generator set division, and was responsible for buying power generator sets from domestic suppliers for export to foreign customers. McShane, another executive, was hired on August 27, 1977, and was in plaintiff's employ when this action was instituted. Ellis and McShane both executed employment agreements containing the following provisions:

In consideration of your employing me as an executive or your company in a position of trust and confidence, I agree that in the event my employment is terminated for any reason whatsoever, I will not for a period of two years following the termination of my employment: (a) directly or indirectly (i) seek or accept employment with any manufacturer, fabricator or supplier with whom I have directly or indirectly contacted during my employment with you; or (ii) represent in any capacity whatsoever as an employee, owner, consultant, salesman, sales representative or agent any manufacturer, fabricator or supplier with whom I have directly or indirectly contacted during my employment with you; and (b) communicate, furnish or divulge the identity of any entity with which you have conducted business or any information concerning your business, which information was communicated to me by virtue of my employment with you.

In addition to the post-employment restrictive covenants, each of the three employees agreed that during his period of employment with plaintiff, he would not, without plaintiff's consent, engage in any remunerative or commercial activities other than his work for plaintiff.

On May 22, 1979, plaintiff filed its four-count complaint for injunctive relief against defendants. Count I alleged that, while employed by plaintiff, Fradkin, Ellis, and McShane entered into a conspiracy to appropriate plaintiff's business to their own benefit by diverting orders from plaintiff's foreign customers and by causing other companies to fill these orders through purchases from plaintiff's domestic suppliers. Plaintiff charged that in furtherance of this conspiracy, defendants incorporated Aldon for the purpose of receiving and filling orders thus diverted. Plaintiff also alleged that McShane, while employed by plaintiff, procured orders from one of plaintiff's exclusive distributors and diverted the orders to Aldon. Plaintiff accused Ellis and Aldon of having paid or promised to pay McShane a portion of Aldon's profits as compensation for securing these orders. . . .

Enforceability of a restrictive covenant is conditioned upon its reasonableness in terms of its effect upon parties to the contract and the pub-

lic. . . . Whether a restrictive covenant is reasonable and enforceable is a question of law. . . .

In the present case, the restrictive provisions set out in the pleadings are "activity" covenants designed not to prohibit competition, but to protect plaintiff's relations with its suppliers, and as such, do not require a geographic limitation. Therefore the covenants are not void as a matter of law. Under the covenants, defendants are required to refrain from seeking or accepting employment with or representing plaintiff's suppliers. They are not precluded from participating in the export industry as competitors or from soliciting other domestic suppliers. The covenants evidence an intent to protect plaintiff's contracts and business relations with its suppliers, and to avoid the loss of suppliers to defendants. As these suppliers are located nationwide, delineating a geographic area would serve no purpose. . . . By these covenants, plaintiff sought merely to prevent defendants from dealing with certain designated suppliers, not to impose a world-wide restriction upon defendants' activities in the export industry. . . .

Defendants argue that the complaint does not allege the existence of a legitimate business interest which would justify enforcement of the post-employment restrictive covenants. The protection of an established clientele from takeover by a former employee is recognized as a legitimate interest of the employer. . . .

For the reasons stated, the order of the circuit court of Cook county dismissing plaintiff's complaint is reversed, and the cause is remanded for further proceedings consistent with the holdings of this opinion.

STUEMPGES v. PARKE, DAVIS & COMPANY

297 N.W.2d 252 (Minnesota, 1980)

Sheran, Chief Justice

This is an appeal by Parke, Davis & Company challenging a jury verdict that plaintiff-respondent Neil Stuempges had been defamed by Parke Davis employees and its award of $17,250 for actual pecuniary loss, $10,500 in compensatory damages, and $10,000 in punitive damages. We affirm. . . .

Parke Davis, a pharmaceutical manufacturer, employed Neil Stuempges as one of its Minneapolis sales representatives for 16 years from 1958 until February 25, 1974, when it asked him to resign or be fired. During the first 15 years of his employment, Stuempges had never been disparaged for his lack of ability as a salesperson and had even received commendations over the years for his outstanding behavior. In the period from 1969 through 1973, for example, Stuempges won awards for his sales performance in promoting specific drugs. One of the awards he received in 1973 was presented by the president of the company and involved as a prize a free trip to the Bahamas. He was also often asked to train new salespersons in how to call on physicians and retailers.

In July, 1973, Robert Jones became the new district manager of the Minneapolis area in which Stuempges' sales territory was located. From the beginning, they clashed in their approaches to a number of issues. Jones felt that Stuempges incorrectly "sold on the basis of friendship" rather than using planned presentations, which Stuempges rejected as "canned." Stuempges refused to conduct a drug survey instituted by Jones because he believed that reviewing prescription records on file with pharmacies was an unethical invasion of patients' privacy. There was also friction between them regarding the change in Stuempges' sales territory and Stuempges' refusal to set what Jones considered to be sufficiently high goals for his sales performance.

On February 25, 1974, at Jones' request, Stuempges met with him and Donald Burgett, Jones' immediate supervisor. At this meeting Stuempges was asked to resign and was promised a good recommendation if he did so. If he refused to resign, however, Jones told him that he would be "blackballed" in industry. Shortly thereafter, Stuempges submitted his resignation.

On March 5, 1974, Stuempges sought assistance in finding another job through Sales Consultants, Inc., an employment agency specializing in sales personnel. He was interviewed by Robert Hammer, at which time he listed Parke Davis as his most recent employer and Jones as

his most recent supervisor and gave permission for Sales Consultants to check his references at Parke Davis. At this meeting Hammer told him that he "was a terrific piece of flesh to sell, had a terrific sales record, and there would be no problems whatsoever in placing [him] in a similar position."

Shortly after Stuempges left, Hammer called Jones for a reference. Jones told Hammer that Stuempges was a poor salesperson and was not industrious and that he was fired because he sold on friendship, would not get products out, was hard to motivate, and could not sell. He concluded their conversation by telling Hammer that Stuempges did not belong in sales. As a result of what Hammer characterized to Stuempges as the worst recommendation he had ever received, he told Stuempges that he would not try to place him.

When Jones' superiors at Parke Davis heard about his conversation with Hammer, they attempted to rectify the situation. A few weeks after the fateful conversation Hammer received a call from Robert Luchsinger, the Parke Davis regional manager, who told him to discard Jones' reference check and promised that, if further references were needed for Stuempges, Luchsinger would provide excellent ones. Another former supervisor of Stuempges also called Hammer and volunteered a good reference. Nevertheless, Hammer continued to refuse to find potential employment for Stuempges.

In July, 1974, Stuempges took a franchise dealership for American LaFrance fire equipment. He was paid on straight commission and did not begin to derive "net income" from his job until July, 1975. . . .

The following issues are presented by this appeal:

1. Were appellant's statements nondefamatory because they were true?
2. Were the statements qualifiedly privileged and thus not actionable?
3. Did the trial court correctly instruct the jury on the definition of malice?
4. Were the damage awards proper?

1. The elements of a common law defamation action are well settled. In order for a statement to be considered defamatory it must be communi-

cated to someone other than the plaintiff, it must be false, and it must tend to harm the plaintiff's reputation and to lower him in the estimation of the community. . . . Slanders affecting the plaintiff in his business, trade, profession, office or calling are slanders per se and thus actionable without any proof of actual damages. . . . Truth, however, is a complete defense, and true statements, however disparaging, are not actionable.

Although Jones' words to Hammer clearly related to Stuempges' reputation in his profession, Parke Davis contends that they were not slanderous because substantially true. . . . There are indications in the record that Jones himself acknowledged the falsity or at least distortion of his statements to Hammer. The injury accepted Stuempges' version and found the statements made by Jones to Hammer to be false. . . .

2. Parke Davis also argues that Jones' statements to Hammer are not defamatory because they were conditionally privileged. Thus, even if the statements were slanders per se, by pleading and proving the existence of a conditional privilege, it has rebutted the presumption of common law malice. . . .

We agree with Parke Davis that an employer called upon to give information about a former employee should be protected so that he can give an accurate assessment of the employee's qualifications. It is certainly in the public interest that this kind of information be readily available to prospective employers, and we are concerned that, unless a significant privilege is recognized by the courts, employers will decline to evaluate honestly their former employees' work records. We believe, however, that the falsity of the statements made by Jones to Hammer, after he had on February 25 indicated that he had a favorable impression of Stuempges' capabilities as a salesperson and would give a good recommendation to prospective employers, takes this case out of the realm of privilege. Thus, Parke Davis cannot be relieved of responsibility on the basis of this theory.

The underpinning of Stuempges' defamation action is that Jones was motivated by malice to give him a bad recommendation. . . .

One of the underpinnings of Stuempges' case

was that Jones was motivated by malice toward him and that the statements to Hammer were an attempt to blackball him in the profession. He introduced evidence that a personality conflict existed between him and Jones, that Jones was hostile toward him because he refused to conduct the prescription survey, and that Jones told him during the February 25 meeting that he would be blackballed in the industry unless he resigned. Although Parke Davis introduced contrary evidence, the jury was not compelled to accept its interpretation. Since the evidence supports a jury finding that Jones acted with malice in making the statement to Hammer, it was reasonable for the jury to have determined that the conditional privilege of fair comment concerning the character of a past employee had been abused.

4. Finally, Parke Davis attacks the jury's award of damages to Stuempges. . . .

Since media self-censorship is not involved in this case and since "[t]he imposition of liability for private defamation does not abridge the freedom of public speech or any other freedom protected by the First Amendment," . . . we are free to permit juries to award punitive damages to punish defendants for this type of unsanctioned behavior.

Affirmed.

LONG v. ARTHUR RUBLOFF & CO.

327 N.E.2d 346 (Illinois, 1975)

Stamos, Justice

Plaintiff, Arthur Long, brought this action against defendant, Arthur Rubloff & Company (hereinafter Rubloff), for breach of an oral agreement of employment and for the "wrongful appropriation" of plaintiff's property. After a bench trial, judgment was entered in favor of plaintiff for $20,000. From that judgment, defendant appeals. . . .

In a one-count amended complaint, plaintiff alleged, inter alia, that in 1967 he was employed by defendant on a month-to-month basis as a real estate broker, salesman, and solicitor; that defendant agreed to pay plaintiff the sum of $1,000 per month, plus a commission of 10 percent on all business brought in by plaintiff for the listing and sale of real estate; and that on February 20, 1968, defendant terminated plaintiff's employment without notice, breached the employment agreement, and "wrongfully appropriated" plaintiff's personal files and listings. As a result of the above, plaintiff sought damages, inter alia, for three days' salary ($150), for failure to give 30 days' notice of termination ($1,000), for two weeks' vacation pay ($500), for the commission due for the listing of property owned by Libby, McNeill & Libby ($9,750), and for damages sustained due to defendant's taking of plaintiff's personal files and listings ($5,000).

Arthur Long testified that he was a licensed real estate broker in the State of Illinois for the past 16 years, specializing in leasing. In March of 1967, he was approached by Thomas Curley, manager of the Office Leasing Department at Rubloff, in regard to a possible employment relationship. Mr. Curley stated that he had recently assumed charge of the Office Leasing Department and needed assistance from someone with experience in the field. The witness told Mr. Curley that he was in possession of a file reflecting a list of buildings with relevant leasing information. Mr. Curley was interested, and subsequently Mr. Curley and several other men from Rubloff examined the file.

The witness described the file as being approximately six inches thick and containing leasing information on 40 to 50 buildings. Each building in the file contained the names of tenants, their lease-expiration dates, the name of the contact, the number of square feet occupied, the amount paid per square foot, whether the tenant contemplated expanding, and similarly pertinent information. Plaintiff stated that he had been compiling the list since 1960 and placed the value of the listings at $25,000.

After exhibiting the file to Mr. Curley, the two discussed the terms of employment. Plaintiff told Mr. Curley that he would require $1,000 per month plus 10 percent of the commission received on leases or sales generated through plaintiff's efforts. On direct examination, plaintiff stated that Mr. Curley made no reply to his request; on redirect examination, he stated that

Mr. Curley specifically told the witness that he would receive a $1,000 a month salary and 10 percent of all commissions or listing fees which were generated by him. The terms of the contract of employment were never reduced to writing. . . .

We initially dismiss the contention that plaintiff was not entitled to two weeks' vacation pay. . . .

We find merit, however, in defendant's assertion that the evidence does not support the alleged damages of $1,000 for failure to give 30 days' notice of termination and of $150 representing salary for the three days subsequent to plaintiff's discharge. . . . There appears to be no dispute that although Long was hired at a monthly salary and paid twice a month, no definite term of employment was specified. Under these circumstances, plaintiff is not entitled to compensation for a period beyond the actual date of discharge. In this state the rule has long been established that a hiring at a monthly or annual salary, if no duration is specified in the contract, is presumed to be at will and either party may terminate the hiring at his pleasure without liability. . . .

The terms upon which plaintiff was employed were crucial to plaintiff's case. Yet, even if undisputed, we do not regard plaintiff's testimoney as very clear and satisfactory in proving the terms of the contract. Had his evidence on this point been direct and internally consistent, the mere fact that it was sharply controverted, both directly and circumstantially, would not justify a reversal of the trial court's finding. But when, as here, plaintiff's testimony is weak, inconsistent, and contradicted by a substantial body of evidence, the presumptive finding of the trial court cannot be sustained. This court is always reluctant to disturb the findings of the trial judge who saw the witnesses and heard them testify, but under the posture of the present case, we can only hold that any finding that plaintiff was entitled to commissions, either as to leases or as to the Libby sale, under the contract of employment was contrary to the manifest weight of the evidence.

We turn next to the contention that plaintiff is not entitled to damages for defendant's taking of lists and files from Long's office. . . . There was no testimony that the terms of employment included the sale to Rubloff of Long's personal lists and files; and in the absence of an agreement to the contrary, we are unaware of any rule which would deprive an employee of his personal property merely because its use during the employment relationship accrued to the benefit of the employer. Taken as a whole, the evidence was merely conflicting and we cannot say that its resolution in favor of plaintiff was against the manifest weight of the evidence.

The remaining question is whether the award of damages is sustained by the pleadings and the evidence. Generally, the measure of damages for conversion is the market value of the property at the time of conversion. . . .

[O]ther than plaintiff's opinion, there was absolutely no testimony from which the trier of fact could determine the value of the leasing data to plaintiff. . . . However, plaintiff's opinion, unsupported by the requisite foundation, was insufficient to establish damages. . . .

Accordingly, the judgment is reversed and remanded for further proceedings not inconsistent with the views herein expressed.

GOLDFINGER v. DOHERTY

276 N.Y.S. 289 (New York, 1934)

Shientag, Justice

The plaintiff sued the defendant Doherty, disaffirming certain purchases of stock, made in her behalf by her duly authorized agent, alleging that she was an infant at the time of the transactions, and that she now elected to rescind and offered to return the stock, together with the stock and cash dividends received thereon. The defendant Doherty thereupon obtained an order permitting him to serve a supplemental summons and complaint on the agent Samuel Goldfinger. . . . The supplemental pleading alleged, in substance, that the agent purchased the stock from Doherty on behalf of the alleged infant "without disclosing the infancy of his principal." It further alleged that, if plaintiff should recover against Doherty, then the defendant Goldfinger, plaintiff's agent, will be liable to defendant

Doherty for damages sustained through the rescission of the contracts by plaintiff, "on the ground that defendant Samuel Goldfinger has breached his implied warranty that he was authorized to enter into binding contracts for the plaintiff."

The supplemental pleading was dismissed below for insufficiency, no opinion being rendered. From that determination, the defendant Doherty has appealed to this court.

The fair inference to be drawn from the pleading is that at the time of the transactions in suit the infant was at least 16 years old; that she has disaffirmed, not the authority of the agent to act in her behalf, but the transactions entered into by her duly authorized agent. The relationship between the infant and the agent is not disclosed by the pleading, nor is there any allegation that, at the time of the transaction, the agent knew, or had reasonable cause to know, of his principal's infancy, or that the other contracting party, Doherty, was in ignorance thereof.

A contract made by an infant is not void. He has the capacity to enter into an agreement which will bind the other contracting party. An infant's contract is said to be voidable. Another way of putting it is that the law, for the protection of the infant, gives him the privilege, under certain conditions, of disaffirming his contract. This privilege is not without its limitations. . . .

An infant's appointment of an agent is not void; it is merely voidable, like any other contract he makes. . . .

There is, therefore, no basis for the contention of the appellant that disaffirmance by the infant of a contract entered into on his behalf by his agent renders the transaction void ab initio, so that the agent is deemed to have acted without any authority. The infant, without questioning the authority of his agent, may disaffirm the contract entered into on his behalf, in the same manner as if he had made the contract directly. The infant may disaffirm the contract of agency; he may disaffirm the contract entered into by his agent. Either contract is voidable; neither is void.

The general rule is that, if, in making a contract in the name of his principal, the agent acts without authority or beyond it, he becomes liable. As the agent assumes to represent the principal he cannot be heard to say that he had no authority, or that there was, in fact, no principal to be bound; he impliedly warrants that there is a principal, and that he is authorized to act for him. . . .

"An agent does not warrant that his principal has full contractual capacity, any more than he warrants that his principal is solvent. Thus an agent for one not of legal age is not necessarily liable if the infant avoids the obligation of the contract made on his acount." Comment (a) on section 332, *Restatement of the Law of Agency*. . . .

Assuming that the agent knows or has reason to know of his principal's lack of full capacity, and of the other party's ignorance thereof, what, if any, is the agent's liability?

Clear authority on this point is lacking. Ordinarily, the duty to speak has been limited to a situation where there is either a pre-existing fiduciary relationship, or one expressly created by a repose of confidence, or where the contract itself calls for disclosure.

In a case as here presented, however, the duty imposed, if any, must rest on a broader basis. Concealment involves a suppression of truth, and, when accompanied by a statement in itself true, they together may create such a misleading impression as to cause the statement made to be in effect false and actionable. . . .

The basis of the liability of an agent, in a situation such as we are here considering, is that he has produced 'a false impression upon the mind of the other party; and, if this result is accomplished, it is unimportant whether the means of accomplishing it are words or acts of the defendant, or his concealment or suppression of material facts not equally within the knowledge or reach of the plaintiff." . . . We believe that the correct rule is that set forth in the *Restatement of the Law of Agency* as follows: "§ 332. Agent of partially incompetent principal. An agent making a contract for a disclosed principal whose contracts are voidable because of lack of full capacity to contract, or for a principal who, although having capacity to contract generally, is incompetent to enter into the particular transaction, is not thereby liable to the other party. He does not become liable by reason of the failure of the principal to perform, unless he contracts or represents that the principal has capacity or unless he has reason to know of the principal's lack of capacity and of the other party's ignorance thereof." . . .

Drawing the most favorable inferences from the pleading under consideration, we find that it fails to set forth enough facts to constitute a cause of action. We feel, however, that the defendant Doherty should have an opportunity to amend, if he be so advised, so as to conform his pleading to the requirements herein set forth.

PROBLEMS FOR DISCUSSION

1. Repke began working as a custodian for the Fragile School District in 1965. In 1975, after a union was organized among school employees, the school board and the union reached agreement on wages, vacations, retirement, and certain other terms of employment. Repke was fired in August 1976. He relies in his complaint on a written document titled "Working Agreement for Male Custodians." The document is not signed by anyone, and it mentions no individual employees by name; it purports to cover the period from June 1, 1975, to May 31, 1976. it says nothing about the duration of employment of any specific employee. Repke sues for $119,115.68 damages, alleging wrongful discharge. What result, and why?

2. While working at the jobsite, Lupo, an employee of Dubletalk Brothers Construction, fell through an unguarded opening in a platform and was seriously injured. Mr. and Mrs. Lupo sued the general contractor on the project, Zinger Builders, for workers' compensation benefits. (Dubletalk was the subcontractor for the electrical work.) The workers' compensation statute says that it is the employee's exclusive

remedy, except that the injured employee may sue a fellow employee whose conduct has contributed to the injury. Zinger brought a third-party claim against Dubletalk's supervisor, Gireis, for negligent failure to properly supervise Lupo and the safety conditions at the jobsite. Is Gireis liable to Zinger under this theory? Discuss.

3. Remle and his brother Philo organized and operated a business of selling farm products to farmers in the area of Andof, Montana. The business was quite successful, and the brothers were approached by a representative of Ace Company, which was interested in buying them out. The brothers agreed to sell, and as part of the deal Ace agreed to employ Remle as its plant manager at a nearby plant. Remle was fired about two years later. He sues for wrongful discharge, alleging that the Ace representative had told him he could manage the plant as long as he wished to do so and that he was maintaining the plant's production at a satisfactory level. How should this lawsuit be resolved? Discuss.

4. Marner owned a machine shop in which he designed and manufactured tools and processes which his customers needed to make specific products. Blaux and Rakow were his employees. Goodwrench, Inc., asked Marner to develop machines for sharpening certain steel blades and for punching holes in a certain plastic part. Marner designed and produced the necessary machines, assisted by Blaux and Rakow. Blaux and Rakow quit about three years later and opened their own machine shop. Marner later learned that they were underbidding him for work at Goodwrench, using a process similar to his. Expert witnesses state that Marner's blade-sharpening machine includes many principles generally known in the industry. The hole-punching machine had originally been sold by Marner to Goodwrench. Marner now sues Blaux and Rakow for damages and an injunction. What result, and why?

5. Sonya, a real estate broker for the Warden Company, was retained as a broker by H. O. Moaner, to try to find a buyer for Moaner's property. Barabbas said he would be interested in buying the property, so Sonya had him sign an offer to purchase it. Barabbas gave Sonya the signed purchase offer and made a down payment of $2,000. The purchase offer stated that it was irrevocable for 10 days, "in consideration of the Broker's effort to obtain approval from the Seller of this offer." Three days later, Barabbas called Sonya and said he wanted to cancel his offer. She said he could not do so, and got Moaner's acceptance the next day. Was the offer to purchase irrevocable? Discuss.

6. Relee inherited his father's farm. He was inexperienced in real estate matters but was able to operate the farm successfully. Shortly thereafter, he learned that a larger farm in the county was for sale and he contacted Freeman, the broker with whom it was listed. Relee told Freeman that he wanted to sell his present farm and buy the larger one but that he didn't have the cash to do it. Freeman told him that he could borrow $20,000 on a 90-day note at the local bank and use his present farm as collateral. Freeman assured Relee that he could sell Relee's present farm for him for over $60,000 with "no trouble" and that Relee could then use that money to pay off the loan at the bank. Relee borrowed the money and bought the new farm (on which Freeman of course earned his broker's commission). Freeman did not sell the old farm for Relee, and the bank foreclosed on its mortgage against the farm. Freeman bought the old farm at the foreclosure sale for $30,000. Relee sues Freeman and asks for all appropriate relief. Discuss and decide.

7. Mavis, the purchasing agent for Wirthles Corporation, was told that the company needed 30 new cars for its sales representatives. Mavis bought the cars from a dealer who promised to give her a new car for half of the list price if she bought Wirthles'

cars from him. Mavis then resold that car for the full list price, $8,000. What rights does Wirthles have when it discovers what Mavis has done? Discuss.

8. Lynseed, a sales representative for ABM Computers, calls at the home office of Deuce Hardware to try to sell it a computer system for its business. The president of Deuce, Spiro Ragsnow, asked several questions about what guarantees and services came with the computer system and told Lynseed that he would not buy without assurances from ABM on these matters. At that point, to close the sale, Lynseed showed Spiro a letter, purporting to be written by the president of ABM, which stated that Lynseed had "full authority" to deal with ABM's customers. In fact, Lynseed had written and signed the letter himself, for use in case any potential customers questioned his authority. If Deuce sues to enforce statements made by Lynseed about the computer system sold to it, does it have any rights against either ABM or Lynseed? Discuss.

Part IV
Sales of Goods

16 | Sales: Title, Risk of Loss, and Other Interests

BASIC CONCEPTS AND DEFINITIONS

UCC Coverage. Since a "sale of goods" is one specific type of contract, the general principles of contract law apply to such sales, but most of the rules relating specifically to sales of goods have been codified, supplemented, and sometimes changed by the Uniform Commercial Code. Article 2, the longest article in the Uniform Commercial Code, specifically covers sales of goods, but other portions of the UCC may also apply. If the goods are to be stored or transported as part of the transaction, Article 7 may apply. The general principles and definitions stated in Article 1 apply to all Code transactions.

Many of the special sales rules have already been discussed in the contracts chapters covering offer and acceptance, consideration, the statute of frauds, and assignments. This chapter and the next three chapters will focus on other major areas of difference between the law of sales and general contract law.

Definitions. The basic purpose of a contract for the sale of goods is to pass the various ownership interests recognized by the Code from the seller to the buyer, for a consideration called the price. The transaction is not a gift of the goods, because the seller is receiving a price for them; it is not a bailment of the goods, because the buyer will become the owner of them. Whether a particular contract is a sale of goods or a services contract depends on which element—goods or services—predominates.

As defined in 2–105(1), *goods* means tangible, movable personal property. Investment securities (stocks and bonds) and other "things in action" (intangibles) are excluded from the definition of goods; specifically included are such things as growing crops, the unborn young of animals, and specially manufactured goods. Goods which are not both existing and identified when the contract is made are called "future goods," and a contract involving such goods is a "contract to sell." "Fungible goods" are goods whose units are indistinguishable from one another, such as grain in a grain elevator, fuel oil in a tank car, or coal in a pile.

The "price" is whatever value is received by the seller for the goods; it may be money, other goods, services, or land—or a promise by the buyer to deliver any of these things.

A "merchant" (2–104[1]) is defined as a person who (a) deals in goods of the kind being sold; or (b) by his or her occupation holds himself or herself out as having special knowledge about the goods or practices involved in the sale; or (c) is represented by someone who is held out as having such special knowledge. The question of whether or not a farmer is a merchant for Code purposes has not been answered uniformly by the courts. The following case shows one importance of the "merchant" definition.

Cook Grains, Inc. v. Fallis
395 S.W.2d 555 (Arkansas, 1965)

FACTS Fallis, a farmer, made an oral agreement with Cook Grains, Inc., a grain dealer, to sell and deliver 5,000 bushels of soy beans to it. Following the oral discussion between Fallis and Horton, the agent of Cook Grains, Inc., Horton prepared and mailed to Fallis, for his signature, a written contract for the sale of 5,000 bushels of soy beans. The contract had already been signed by Cook Grains, Inc. Fallis never signed the contract, and later he refused to deliver the beans. Cook Grains, Inc., then filed this action for breach of contract.

Fallis used the statute of frauds as a defense, saying that there was no written contract. Cook Grains Inc., alleged that Fallis was a merchant, and thus, since a written confirmation of the agreement had been sent to him, he had 10 days to object after receiving the confirmation, and if he didn't object, which he did not, then he was liable under the terms of the contract. The lower court found in favor of Fallis, and Cook Grains, Inc., appealed.

ISSUE The issue in this case is whether the appellee, Fallis, is a "merchant" within the meaning of the statute. The Ark. Stat. Ann. 85–2–104 (1961 Addendum) provides: "'Merchant' means a person who deals in goods of the kind or otherwise by his occupation holds himself out as having knowledge or skill peculiar to the practices or goods involved in the transaction or to whom such knowledge or skill may be attributed by his employment of an agent or broker or other intermediary who by his occupation holds himself out as having such knowledge or skill. . . .

DECISION The farmer in this case was found not to be a merchant. Lower court decision affirmed.

REASON The court stated: "The evidence in this case is that appellee is a farmer and nothing else. He farms about 550 acres, and there is no showing that he has any other occupation. In Vol. 16, Words and Phrases, beginning at page 401 there are many cases cited giving the definition of a farmer, such as: 'A "farmer" is one devoted to the tillage of the soil, such as an agriculturalist.' . . .

"If the General Assembly had intended that in the circumstances of this case a farmer should be considered a merchant and therefore liable on an alleged contract

---

to sell his commodities, which he did not sign, no doubt clear and explicit language would have been used in the statute to that effect. There is nothing whatever in the statute indicating that the word 'merchant' should apply to a farmer when he is acting in the capacity of a farmer, and he comes within that category when he is merely trying to sell the commodities he has raised. . . .

"Notes 1 and 2 under Ark. Stat. Ann. 85–2–104 (1961 Addendum), (Uniform Commercial Code) defining merchant indicate that this provision of the statute is meant to apply to professional traders. In Note 1 it is stated: 'This section lays the foundation of this policy defining those who are to be regarded as professionals or merchants.' . . . It is said in Note 2: 'The term "merchant" as defined here roots in the "law merchant" concept of a professional in business.'"

Significance of the "Goods" Definition. What difference does it make whether a contract is for the sale of goods, or for the sale of services, or for the sale of land? The *Cook Grains* case, above, illustrates one difference: different statute of frauds requirements apply to goods. As we discussed in Chapter 7, for real estate, no oral contract except a short-term lease is enforceable, and a writing sufficient to make a real estate contract enforceable must contain all of the material terms. For services, any oral contract is fully enforceable (if proved) unless the term of the contract is definitely for over one year. For goods priced at under $500, an oral contract is enforceable; for goods priced at $500 or more, one of the five alternatives listed in UCC 2–201 must be complied with.

A second important difference was discussed in Chapter 6: For sales of goods, modifications agreed to after the contract was originally formed are binding without a new exchange of considerations, and in many cases this holds true even if the modifications are oral. For services, unless new values are exchanged, such modifications would not be binding, but the modifications can usually be oral. For land, subsequent modifications would require a new exchange of considerations and would almost certainly have to be in writing.

A third important difference between sales of goods, services, and land has to do with "quality guarantees": What sort of performance standards does the law require of the seller? There are some very important distinctions between goods, on the one hand, and services or land, on the other. For land, although some states now follow a different rule (at least for the seller of a new home), the general rule is that the buyer takes the land as he or she finds it; unless the buyer can prove that the seller committed fraud or made a specific guarantee as part of the contract, the buyer has no case for alleged defects in the real estate. For services, unless a specific guarantee of results has been made, the buyer-customer has to prove malpractice in order to recover; that is, the buyer-customer has to show that the seller's performance fell below the standard of a reasonably competent practitioner. For sales of goods, however, a merchant-

350

seller is held to an automatic quality warranty that the goods are merchantable, even though the merchant-seller has said nothing specific about their quality and even though the merchant-seller is not guilty of any negligence in handling or delivering the goods. Betty Epstein's case, as well as a number of cases involving blood tranfusions by hospitals, involves the question of what is a sale of goods.

Epstein v. Giannattasio et al.
197 A.2d 342 (Connecticut), 1963)

FACTS Mrs. Epstein went to a beauty parlor owned and operated by Marie Giannattasio for a beauty treatment. Giannattasio used a product called "Zotos 30 day color" manufactured by defendant Sales Affiliates, Inc., and a prebleach manufactured by defendant Clairol, Inc. The plaintiff claimed that as a result of the treatment she suffered acute dermatitis, disfigurement resulting from loss of hair, and other injuries and damages. The complaint set forth two causes of action against each defendant, the first in negligence and the second in breach of warranty. Each of the defendants demurred to the latter: Giannattasio and Sales Affiliates, Inc., on the single ground that the transaction did not amount to a contract for the sale of goods; Clairol, Inc., on that ground and also on the ground that any warranties which might have been given by it did not extend to the plaintiff. The lower court sustained the demurrers in favor of the defendants. The plaintiff appealed.

ISSUE Can the plaintiff recover from the beautician and the other defendants on a breach of implied warranty?

DECISION No. Demurrers sustained in favor of defendants as to the cause of action concerning breach of warranty. Case remanded to the lower court to be tried on the cause of action in negligence.

REASON The court stated: "The issue reduced itself to the simple one of whether or not the use of the product involved in the course of the beauty treatment amounts to a sale or a contract for sale of goods under the pertinent sections of the code. . . . As the complaint alleges, the plaintiff asked Giannattasio for a beauty treatment, and not for the purchase of goods. From such language, it could not be inferred that it was the intention of either party that the transaction be a transaction in goods within the meaning of the code. . . . There is another line of cases which involves blood transfusions received by patients in the course of medical care and treatment in hospitals. These concern the claim that injuries caused by such transfusions ground a recovery under the Sales Act. This claim has been universally rejected. Such a contract is clearly one for services, and just as clearly, it is not divisible. . . . It has long been recognized, that, when service predominates, and transfer of personal property is but an incidental feature of the transaction, the transaction is not deemed a sale within the Sales Act."

The court also referred to cases involving the service of food in a restaurant and quoted the following from *Lynch* v. *Hotel Bond Co.*, 117 Conn. 128, 167A99 (1933): "The only thing 'sold' is the personal service rendered in the preparation and presentation of the food, the various essentials to its comfortable consumption or other facilities provided, and the privilege of consuming so much of the meal ordered as the guest may desire. Service is the predominant feature of the transaction. If there is a transfer of title to the food actually consumed, it is merely incidental and does not constitute a sale of goods within the contemplation of the Sales Act . . . , and there is therefore no implied warranty of its quality under the law of sales."

PASSING OF OWNERSHIP INTERESTS IN THE GOODS

In general, one special (and somewhat complicated) problem in the law of sales is that of determining when the various ownership interests recognized by the Code pass from the seller to the buyer. The UCC recognizes six different ownership interests in the goods—"special property," "insurable interest," "title," "risk of loss," "right to possession," and "security interest." These six interests represent packages of rights and duties with respect to the goods. They can all exist at the same time, as to the same goods, and they may be parceled out among the seller, the buyer, and different third parties in any number of combinations.

Under the Code, most of the cases between the buyer and the seller will be "risk of loss" cases. Where third parties are involved in the litigation, the solution will nearly always depend on the location of one of the other five interests.

Presumptions.   Article 2 contains a rather extensive set of statutory presumptions as to when each of the various interests in the goods passes to the buyer; the most important sections are 2–401, 2–501, and 2–509. In general, these presumptions may be overcome by the parties' specific agreement; that is, the parties are free to make any specific agreement they with as to when a particular ownership interest will pass to the buyer, but if they say nothing, the Code presumptions apply. In most cases the contract probably will not say anything specific about when these ownership interests pass.

One inflexible rule is stated in the Code (2–105[2]): "Goods must be both existing and identified before any interest in them can pass." In other words, even if they both agree to do so, the buyer and the seller cannot pass any interest to anyone unless the goods are both existing and identified. Once the goods come into existence and are identified as the goods for the given contract, the buyer and the seller are free to parcel out the six ownership interests in any way they choose. Although the following case arose under the old Uniform Sales Act (now repealed by the Code), and the court used the word *appropriation* instead of the word *identification*, the case provides an excellent illustration of the Code's one inflexible rule in action.

Lamborn v. *Seggerman Brothers, Inc.*
240 N.Y. 118 (1925)

FACTS   Lamborn as the buyer and the Seggermans as the sellers entered into a written contract for the sale of "1200/50 lb. boxes Calif. Evap. apples—Extra Choice Quality—1919 crop." The contract was made on July 30; shipment was to occur in September or October 1919. (The Seggermans had, in turn, made arrangements to buy 1,200 boxes of dried apples from a supplier, Rosenberg Brothers.) Lamborn was to pay 22½ cents per pound "F.O.B. Pacific Coast Rail Shipping Point. . . . Payment to be made against draft with documents attached." The Rosenbergs loaded a Southern Pacific railroad car with 1,770 boxes of dried apples and received an "order" bill of lading which provided for shipment to New York. Once they knew the apples were on the way, the Seggermans billed Lamborn for 1,200 boxes and gave Lamborn an order addressed to their delivery clerk at their place of business. Seeing these documents, Lamborn paid the contract price as agreed—$13,377. The apples never arrived in New York; they were seized en route by agents of the U.S. government, for reasons not disclosed by the court. Lamborn sued for a refund but lost in the lower court.

ISSUE   Has the risk of loss on the 1,200 boxes of apples passed to Lamborn?

DECISION   No. Judgment reversed (Lamborn gets the contract price back.)

REASONS   Since this was a pre-Code case, the New York court of appeals talked about the passing of title as implying the passing of risk of loss, and used the word *appropriation* rather than the word *identification* in referring to specific goods; the underlying principles are the same.

Judge Lehman pointed out that neither the Rosenbergs nor the Seggermans had ever set aside 1,200 specific boxes for Lamborn. "[I]n the present case there has been no . . . . appropriation by the defendant of any ascertained goods to the plaintiffs' contract. . . . A delivery by a seller to a carrier, even for the purpose of transmission to the buyer, of a quantity greater than the amount called for by the contract does not constitute an appropriation of goods to the buyer's contract . . . sufficient to pass property in any of the goods." Further, said Judge Lehman, the sellers had exceeded the "shipment" authority given to them by Lamborn and had not really complied with the contract. "The plaintiffs never agreed to purchase an undivided share in a mass; they never authorized shipment of 1,200 boxes of apples as part of a mass or even as part of a pool car, for their contract refers to a specific carload and to 1,200 boxes of apples to be ascertained and appropriated before shipment and no title to any apples has ever passed to the plaintiffs."

This was a unanimous opinion by all seven judges, including Benjamin Cardozo and Roscoe Pound.

Identification. Identification is the act of specifying exactly which goods are to be delivered by the seller to the buyer in order to satisfy the terms of a particular contract. Identification may be made by either the seller or the buyer, in any manner they agree to have it made. As an important change from prior law, the goods do not necessarily have to be in "deliverable condition" per the terms of the contract, in order for identification to occur. If the parties so agree,

353

individual shares of a mass of fungible goods can be "identified," and thus sold, even though these shares have not yet been parceled out. For example, the parties could agree to buy and sell one half of the fuel oil in Penn-Central railroad car #35790; that would be a sufficient identification.

In the absence of any specific agreement, Section 2–501 says that identification is presumed to occur; (a) when the contract is made, if it is for goods already existing and identified in the parties' negotiations (a particular used car, for example); (b) for future goods generally, when the goods are "shipped, marked, or otherwise designated" by the seller (when the seller tags one new car in his or her inventory with the buyer's order number, for example); or (c) for agricultural products such as crops and the young of animals when the crops are planted and the as-yet-unborn young are conceived.

Once identification has occurred, ownership interests can then be passed to the buyer as the parties wish; "special property" and "insurable interest" are presumed to pass to the buyer as soon as identification occurs.

Special Property. The special property interest which the UCC gives to the buyer once particular goods have been identified to the contract, is a brand-new concept; nothing like it existed under pre-Code law. The purpose of this new Code interest is to provide some protection for the buyer, both as to the seller and as to third parties, as soon as the buyer's goods have been identified, even though the buyer is not yet technically "the owner" of the goods (i.e., legal title has not yet passed to the buyer).

In addition to an "insurable interest," the buyer's special property interest gives the buyer a package of three rights against his or her goods: (a) The buyer has the right to inspect the goods at a reasonable time and place. (b) The buyer has the right to recover damages that the buyer sustains if a third party wrongfully interferes with the buyer's possession of the identified goods. (c) The buyer has a right to sue for possession of the identified goods where the seller refuses to deliver them and the buyer can't get substitute goods or where the seller goes insolvent within 10 days after receiving the first installment on the contract price.

Insurable Interest. As soon as the goods are identified, the Code gives the buyer an "insurable interest," meaning that the buyer can then get a valid insurance policy protecting the buyer against financial losses relating to his or her goods. The extent to which a preexisting "blanket" insurance policy on all property "owned" by the buyer would apply to such identified goods has not yet been determined in most states, but this question can be resolved by a carefully drafted policy provision.

More than one person may have an insurable interest in the same goods at the same time. This does not mean that several persons will recover for the same damages but that several persons may suffer different financial losses when the goods are lost or damaged. Each such person has an insurable interest to the extent of his or her potential loss. The seller, for example, retains an insurable interest so long as he or she holds title to the goods or a security interest against the goods. Where the goods are shipped or stored, the carrier or the warehouse has an insurable interest in the goods while they are in its possession. Any party with an insurable interest in the goods can sue a third party who has caused him or her financial loss by injuring the goods.

Title. The concept of "title" generally refers to legal ownership, with all its attendant rights and liabilities. For the purpose of Article 2, however, title is given a much more restricted meaning, since most of the litigations between the buyer and the seller, and even some litigations involving third parties, are solved by using other ownership interests and the location of the legal title is irrelevant. Title is still an important concept because even under the Code many cases involving third parties will depend on whether the buyer or the seller had title to the goods at some particular point in time. Such cases might involve liability for required taxes, registration, or insurance on the goods, or liability resulting from use of the goods, or adverse claims against the goods by the creditors of the buyer or the seller.

The main presumptions as to when title passes are contained in Section 2–401; this section states a general rule and four specific applications. These presumptions are all based on common sense; if the parties want a special result, they will have to so expressly agree. The general rule is that title passes to the buyer "at the time and place at which the seller completes his or her performance with respect to the physical delivery of the goods." This rule applies even though, for financing reasons, using the goods as collateral for the unpaid balance of the purchase price, the seller has reserved a "security interest" in the goods, or even though a "document of title" (bill of lading or warehouse receipt) is to be delivered to the buyer at a different time or place.

The four specific rules cover the two common arrangements where the goods are to be moved as part of the contract for sale and the two common situations not involving any further movement of the goods by the seller. If the contract merely authorizes the seller to make the arrangment for shipping the goods to the buyer, but it does not require the seller to deliver the goods at their destination, title is presumed to pass at the time and place of shipment. In the other "movement" case, where the seller is required to make delivery of the goods at their destination, a tender means that the seller must get the goods to the place where they are to be delivered to the buyer and give the buyer any notice reasonably necessary to enable the buyer to receive delivery.

In the two "nonmovement" cases, the goods are already at the location where the buyer is to take delivery. In one case, they are in the possession of a third party (usually a warehouse); in the other, they are in the seller's possession. If the seller is not required to move the goods but is required to deliver to the buyer a "document of title" (warehouse receipt or bill of lading) covering them, title is presumed to pass when the required document is delivered. (In this case the seller is only required to give the buyer the document; the buyer can then go over to the warehouse whenever he or she wants to and get the goods.) Where the seller is not required to move the goods or to deliver any documents, and the specific goods to which the contract applies have already been identified, title is presumed to pass "at the time and place of contracting," i.e., at the instant the contract is made. And the Code assumes that the place of delivery is the seller's place of business. In the typical used-car purchase, for example, "title" to the used car passes to the buyer at the instant he or she says,

"I'll take it," since the seller has possession and is not required to move the car to any other location to make delivery. (In most states this presumption would hold even though the state's motor vehicle registration requirements had not yet been complied with.)

The following case illustrates one important consequence of the passing of title.

Waggoner v. Wilson
507 P.2d 482 (Colorado, 1973)

FACTS   The plaintiff, Ms. Waggoner, was injured when she was struck by a 1961 Ford Thunderbird driven by Mrs. Wilson. She sued Mrs. Wilson and recovered a judgment for $39,727.80. She was now attempting to collect that judgment from State Farm, Mrs. Wilson's insurance company. The trial court ruled that her policy did not cover the 1961 Ford, since it was not a "non-owned automobile" as defined in the policy. The plaintiff appealed that ruling.

Mr. and Mrs. Wilson were in the process of selling the 1961 Ford to Charles Beucker. Beucker had orally agreed to buy the car and had made payments to the Wilsons, but neither the license plates nor the registration certificate had been transferred to him. Beucker had the car, but the Wilsons had kept the registration certificate until he paid the balance due. Mrs. Wilson had borrowed the car from Beucker, to use it temporarily.

The State Farm policy covered Mrs. Wilson if she were driving a "non-owned automobile," defined as one not "(1) owned by, (2) registered in the name of, or (3) furnished or available for the frequent or regular use of the named insured." The appeal was based on these definitions.

ISSUE   Is the car a "non-owned automobile" as defined in the policy?

DECISION   Yes. Judgment reversed. (Ms. Waggoner collects from State Farm.)

REASONS   Judge Smith first decided that Beucker "owned" the car, since there was an enforceable contract for sale and he had been given possession. And even though the motor vehicle statute expressly stated that no purchaser would acquire "any right, title or interest" in a vehicle until he obtained a certificate of title, Judge Smith stated: "[N]on-delivery of the certificate of title does not prevent change of ownership as between the parties to the transaction."

When he came to the question of "registration," however, Judge Smith interpreted the statute *very* literally. The statute provided that when an owner of a registered vehicle "transfers or assigns his title or interest thereto, the registration of such vehicle shall expire." Therefore, said the judge, because the Wilsons had sold their car, their registration on it had "expired," so that it was not "registered" even though Beucker had not yet gotten it reregistered in his name. (This seems questionable.)

Finally, the court ruled that Beucker had general control of the car, so that it was not available for regular use by the Wilsons. Mrs. Wilson had got specific permission from him to use it.

Thus the 1961 Ford was indeed a "non-owned automobile," and Mrs. Wilson's use of it was covered under her State Farm policy, and Ms. Waggoner collected her judgment from State Farm.

Where title has already passed to the buyer under the above presumptions, it is passed back to the seller either by the buyer's rejection of the goods, whether the rejection is justified or not, or by the buyer's revocation of his or her previous acceptance, but only if such revocation is justified. In other words, if the buyer refuses delivery and sends the goods back, the goods again "belong to" the seller on the way back; but if the buyer has accepted the goods and *then* tries to revoke that acceptance by sending the goods back, title is not revested in the seller unless the buyer can show a justification for his or her action.

Risk of Loss. Article 2 treats "risk of loss" as a separate and distinct ownership interest. Stated most simply, risk of loss means responsibility for the goods: As between the buyer and the seller, who gets stuck for the value of the goods when they are destroyed or damaged by an "act of God" or by a third party. Who has to try to recover from the third party or from an insurance company?

Once the goods are identified, the parties can allocate the risk of loss on the goods in any way they wish or divide it between themselves. Merely giving the buyer a right to inspect the goods at a particular time and place does not postpone the passing of risk of loss, unless that result is also specified. If the parties have not made any specific agreement as to when risk of loss passes, Article 2 again provides a set of commonsense presumptions.

In the two "movement" cases, the presumptions for risk of loss are basically the same as those for the passing of title. If the seller is authorized to ship out but is not required to deliver, risk passes when the goods are delivered to the carrier, even though the seller has reserved the right to possession (COD shipment) or a security interest against the goods. If the seller is required to deliver, risk of loss stays with him or her until the goods arrive at their destination and are duly tendered to the buyer.

Where the goods are in the possession of a bailee (a warehouse or a carrier) and are to be delivered to the buyer without further movement to another place, risk of loss passes when any one of three things happens: (*a*) when the buyer receives a negotiable document of title on the goods; or (*b*) when the buyer receives a nonnegotiable document of title on the goods *and* has had a reasonable amount of time to present the bailee with it and to pick up the goods; or (*c*) when the bailee acknowledges the buyer's right to possession of the goods.

Where the goods are in the seller's possession and the buyer is to come over and pick them up, there are two different rules as to when risk passes, depending on whether the seller is a merchant or not. If the seller is not a merchant, risk passes when he or she tenders delivery to the buyer; but if the seller is a merchant, risk does not pass to the buyer until he or she actually receives the goods. This special "risk" rule where the seller is a merchant represents an important change from prior law; it is illustrated by the following case.

Caudle v. Sherrard Motor Company
525 S.W.2d 238 (Texas, 1975)

FACTS   John Caudle bought a house trailer from the plaintiff, Sherrard. He gave Sherrard a check for $2,685 for the down payment and signed a promissory note for $4,005 for the balance. While Sherrard was preparing the house trailer for delivery, Caudle got a call from his business office in Dallas, telling him that he had to be there at once. Caudle told Sherrard that he'd have to come back to Denison and pick up the trailer later. The sale occurred on February 10; the trailer was stolen from Sherrard's place of business sometime between February 12 and 14, before Caudle had a chance to pick it up. Caudle thereupon stopped payment on his check, and Sherrard sued for the full contract price. The jury found the Caudle had breached but that Sherrard had sustained no damages, but the trial judge entered a judgment notwithstanding the verdict for Sherrard for $6,285.70. Caudle appealed.

ISSUE   Had the risk of loss on the house trailer passed to the buyer when the theft occurred?

DESICISION   No. Judgment reversed. (Caudle does not have to pay for it.)

REASONS   The court first disposed of Sherrard's two arguments as to when the risk of loss passed. Sharrard argued that since it was "acting as" a bailee and since the goods were to be delivered without being physically moved further, risk of loss had passed under UCC 2–509(b). the court said that this section referred to goods in the possession of a commercial bailee who had issued a document of title (a bill of lading or a warehouse receipt) on them; the section was not intended to cover the situation where the seller was a "bailee' because title had already passed to the buyer.

A more difficult question was presented by Sherrard's argument that the contract itself provided for the passing of risk to the buyer, under 2–509(d). The contract stated: "No transfer, renewal, extension or assignment of this agreement or any interest hereunder, and no loss, damage or destruction of said motor vehicle shall release buyer from his obligation hereunder." The court said that this language was not sufficiently clear to pass the risk to the buyer before delivery of possession but rather that it was intended to cover what happened *after* the buyer had taken delivery and was primarily for the benefit of the bank or finance company to which Sherrard assigned the contract. "To hold otherwise would be to set a trap for the unwary. If parties intend to shift the burden of the risk of loss from the seller to the buyer before delivery of the goods, then such must be done in clear and unequivocal language."

The court concluded that the applicable provision was 2–509(c), which stated that where the seller was a merchant, risk of loss did not pass to the buyer until he or she received the goods. Since it was undisputed that Caudle had never received possession of the goods, the merchant seller (Sherrard) still had the risk of loss when the theft occurred. Since Caudle didn't get his trailer, he was entitled to stop payment on his check and was not liable for the contract price.

Where the seller's tender of delivery or the seller's delivery "fails to conform to the contract" so as to give the buyer the right to reject the goods, the risk of loss stays with the seller until he or she "cures" the problem or until the buyer agrees to accept the goods anyway. Where the buyer rightfully revokes his or her prior acceptance, he or she can force the seller to bear any loss not covered by the buyer's insurance. Where the buyer breaches after conforming goods have been identified to the contract but before risk has passed to the buyer, the seller may force the buyer to bear any loss not covered by the seller's insurance. In these breach cases, the basic risk of loss rule is: "The bad guy loses."

Right to Possession of the Goods. The Code also recognizes that a party may have title and risk of loss and yet not have an immediate "right to the goods." One obvious case where this result occurs is the COD contract: When the seller ships the goods as agreed, the buyer has title, risk of loss, and a special property interest and an insurable interest in the goods, but he or she does not yet have the right to possession because the COD term requires him or her to pay in order to get delivery. Another common separation of the right to possession from title and risk occurs when goods are shipped or stored by a carrier or a warehouse. Article 7 of the Code gives such persons a possessory "lien" for their services, meaning that they can hold (and if necessary sell) the goods until their charges are paid. Either the buyer or the seller may have title and risk of loss, but neither of them has the right to possession of the goods until the carrier or warehouse gets paid.

Security Interest. Finally, where the goods are being used as collateral to secure payment of the balance due on the contract price, the financing agency (the seller or a bank or other lender) has a "security interest" in them. Stated most simply, this security interest means that if the debtor defaults, the creditor (the "secured party") has the right to get possession of the goods, to resell them, and to apply the proceeds to pay off the balance due on the debt. Section 2–401(1) says that any attempt by the seller to withhold "title" on goods which he or she has shipped or delivered to the Buyer "is limited in effect to a reservation of a security interest." What the seller has to do to make sure he or she has a valid security interest. The other details of such secured transactions are covered in Article 9 of the UCC; Chapters 20 and 21 will discuss secured transactions at greater length.

Special Sale Arrangements. The Code also provides specific rules to cover several frequently used special sale arrangements: sale on approval, sale or return, consignment, and sale by auction. Where the buyer has the option of returning goods even though they conform to the contract, the transaction is presumed to be a sale on approval if the buyer bought primarily for his or her own use and a sale or return if he or she bought the goods primarily for resale to others.

In a sale on approval, the buyer has possession of someone else's goods as a bailee, to use them according to the terms of the trial contract; the seller still "owns" the goods (i.e., he or she has both title and risk of loss). Title and risk do not pass to the buyer until the buyer accepts the goods, either expressly or by doing something which indicates that he or she considers them to be his or hers, or until the agreed trial period expires with the buyer still in possession and not having notified the seller that he or she wants to return them.

In a sale or return, title and risk pass to the buyer under the normal presumptions, but he or she has the option of returning the goods in accordance with the terms of the contract. Any such "return" is at the buyer's risk and expense, unless otherwise agreed.

In a consigment arrangment, the "buyer" (a retail store, for example) is not really a buyer at all, but rather a bailee-agent who has possession of someone else's goods and the power to sell the goods to third parties. As between this "consignee" (the retail store) and the "consignor" (a manufacturer, for example), the consignor retains title and risk on the goods until they are sold to third parties. Out of fairness to the creditors of the consignee, however, the Code says that they can treat the transaction like a sale or return, unless the consignee's creditors know generally that the consignee engages in such transactions or unless the consignor publicly files a financing statement under Article 9's provisions or posts a sign on the consignee's premises in accordance with an applicable state statute.

Section 2–328 contains some special "offer and acceptance" rules for sales by auction. When the auctioneer, Colonel Fasthammer, receives offers in the form of bids, his acceptance occurs when he raps his hammer (and hollers "Sold!") or in any other customary manner. Until the hammer falls, any bid can be withdrawn, but such a withdrawal does not revive any previous bid. Whether the goods have to be sold to the highest bidder depends on whether the sale is "with reserve" or "without reserve." Unless specific notice is given otherwise, it is assumed that the auction is with reserve, meaning that the auctioneer "may withdraw the goods at any time until he announces completion of the sale." Since the goods are already identified and (usually) no further delivery by the seller is required, title and risk would be presumed to pass to the buyer when the auctioneer's acceptance occurs.

Common Shipping Terms. Since in the "movement" cases the location of title and risk will probably depend on whether the seller has met his or her contract duties, it is important to know what certain commonly used shipping terms require the seller to do. In addition to the COD (collect on delivery) term discussed above, the abbreviations FOB (free on board), FAS (free alongside), and CIF (cost, insurance, and freight) are commonly used.

The FOB term is used in combination with a named city, for example, FOB Chicago. The seller's obligation is to get the goods into the possession of a carrier and to get them to the specified place. Whether this is a shipment contract or a delivery contract depends on whether "Chicago" is the seller's city or the buyer's city. If the FOB contract also specifies a vessel, car, or other vehicle, the seller must also "at his own expense and risk load the goods on board"; in other words, the seller is responsible for getting the goods into the buyer's designated carrier. The FAS term is used in connection with a particular vessel, for example, FAS SS *Mariner*. The seller must deliver the goods alongside that vessel in accordance with the port's custom, or on a dock specified by the buyer; the seller must also get a receipt for the goods and tender it to the buyer so that the buyer can get a bill of lading from the vessel's operator.

The CIF contract provides the buyer with the convenience of making one lump-sum payment to the seller, after the seller has made all the arrangements for shipping the goods. The seller is obligated to pay the carrier's freight charges (or to get credit from the carrier) and to obtain the customary insurance policy on the goods while they are in transit. (A C&F contract omits the insurance requirement.) The seller then forwards to the buyer all the required paperwork: the freight receipt, the bill of lading, the insurance policy, his or her own invoice for the package price, and a negotiable draft for the total invoice price. Normally these papers will be sent to a bank in the buyer's city where the buyer has made credit arrangements; the bank has instructions to give the buyer the negotiable bill of lading (without which the buyer can't get the goods) only after the buyer signs the negotiable draft, thus indicating that he or she will pay the draft when it becomes due. The bank then buys the draft from the seller and sends the seller the cash. Everyone's happy: the buyer has his or her goods and whatever credit period is specified in the draft in which to pay for them; the seller has his or her cash, with no risk of nonpayment; and the buyer's bank earns the interest rate provided for in the draft. This very common transaction shows how Articles 2, 3, 4, and 7 come together to cover the various aspects of a single commercial transaction. The following case provides a specific example of a C&F contract's effect on the risk of loss.

Val Decker Packing Co. v. *Armour & Co.*
184 N.E.2d 548 (Ohio, 1962).

FACTS   About 5 P.M. on December 26, 1956, Irwin Busse telephoned Decker's place of business in Piqua, Ohio, and bought a truckload of dressed hogs for Armour, at a price of $8,885.51. The hogs were to be shipped CAF to Western Pork Packers, Inc., in Worchester, Massachusetts. The truck left Piqua at 12:25 P.M. on December 27. Sometime before 3 P.M. on December 28, the truck driver called Armour's manager in Worchester and reported mechanical trouble with the truck. The manager said that delivery by 6 A.M. on December 29 would be acceptable, but the truck did not arrive until December 31, at which time Armour refused the shipment. Decker resold the shipment for $7,203.99 and sued for damages. Armour's written confirmation indicated its "desire to unload these hogs not later than 3:00 P.M. Friday 12/28 and as much sooner as possible." The trial court held for Decker.

ISSUES   When does risk of loss (delay) pass to the buyer in a CAF contract? Had Decker complied with the terms of the contract?

DECISION   On delivery to the carrier. Yes. Judgment of Decker affirmed.

REASONS   The court indicated that the normal presumption in a C&F (or CAF) contract was that title and risk passed to the buyer when the goods were delivered to the carrier. It was, in other words, treated as a "shipment" rather than a "delivery" contract. Nothing appeared in this transaction to change the normal commercial presumption.
    As to whether Decker had fulfilled its part of the contract, there was no indication or requirement of a specific date on which *shipment* was to be made; rather, there was a desired delivery date. The truck carrying the hogs left Piqua at 12:25 P.M. on December 27. The normal driving time was 24 hours, so the shipment should have arrived in Worcester some 2½ hours before the desired time. The confirmation did indicate that Armour's manager should be called if there was any delay, and this was done by the truck driver when the mechanical problem arose.

361

MULTIPLASTICS, INC. v. ARCH INDUSTRIES, INC.

348 A.2d 618 (Connecticut, 1974)

Bogdanski, Associate Justice

The plaintiff, Multiplastics, Inc., brought this action to recover damages from the defendant, Arch Industries, Inc., for the breach of a contract to purchase 40,000 pounds of plastic pellets. From a judgment rendered for the plaintiff, the defendant has appealed to this court.

The facts may be summarized as follows: The plaintiff, a manufacturer of plastic resin pellets, agreed with the defendant on June 30, 1971, to manufacture and deliver 40,000 pounds of brown polystyrene plastic pellets for 19 cents a pound. The pellets were specially made for the defendant, who agreed to accept delivery at the rate of 1,000 pounds per day after completion of production. The defendant's confirming order contained the notation "make and hold for release. Confirmation." The plaintiff produced the order of pellets within two weeks and requested release orders from the defendant. The defendant refused to issue the release orders, citing labor difficulties and its vacation schedule. On August 18, 1971, the plaintiff sent the defendant the following letter: "Against P.O. 0946, we produced 40,000 lbs. of brown high impact styrene, and you have issued no releases. You indicated to us that you would be using 1,000 lbs. per day. We have warehoused these products for more than 40 days, as we agreed to do. However, we cannot warehouse these products indefinitely, and request that you send us shipping instructions. We have done everything we agreed to do." After August 18, 1971, the plaintiff made numerous telephone calls to the defendant to seek payment and delivery instructions. In response, beginning August 20, 1971, the defendant agreed to issue release orders but in fact never did.

On September 22, 1971, the plaintiff's plant, containing the pellets manufactured for the defendant, was destroyed by fire. The plaintiff's fire

insurance did not cover the loss of the pellets. The plaintiff brought this action against the defendant to recover the contract price.

The trial court concluded that the plaintiff made a valid tender of delivery by its letter of August 18, 1971, and by its subsequent requests for delivery instructions; that the defendant repudiated and breached the contract by refusing to accept delivery on August 20, 1971; that the period from August 20, 1971, to September 22, 1971, was not a commercially unreasonable time for the plaintiff to treat the risk of loss as resting on the defendant under General Statutes § 42a–2–510(3); and that the plaintiff was entitled to recover the contract price plus interest. . . .

The defendant contends that § 42a–510 is not applicable because its failure to issue delivery instructions did not constitute either a repudiation or a breach of the agreement. The defendant also argues that even if § 42a–2–510 were applicable, the period from August 20, 1971, to September 22, 1971, was not a commercially reasonable period of time within which to treat the risk of loss as resting on the buyer. The defendant does not claim that the destroyed pellets were not "conforming goods already identified to the contract for sale," as required by General Statutes § 42a–2–510(3), nor does it protest the computation of damages. . . .

The trial court's conclusion that the defendant was in breach is supported by its finding that the defendant agreed to accept delivery of the pellets at the rate of 1,000 pounds per day after completion of production. The defendant argues that since the confirming order instructed the defendant to "make and hold for release," the contract did not specify an exact delivery date. This argument fails, however, because nothing in the finding suggests that the notation in the confirming order was part of the agreement between the parties. Since, as the trial court found, the plaintiff made a proper tender of delivery, beginning with its letter of August 18, 1971, the plaintiff was entitled to acceptance of the goods and to payment according to the contract. . . .

The present case does not involve repudiation of an executory promise, however, since the defendant breached the contract by failing to accept the goods when acceptance became due.

The defendant next claims that the plaintiff acquiesced in the defendant's refusal to accept delivery by continuing to urge compliance with the contract and by failing to pursue any of the remedies provided aggrieved sellers by General Statutes § 42a–2–703. In essence, the defendant's argument rests on the doctrines of waiver and estoppel, which are available defenses under the Uniform Commercial Code. . . .

The remaining question is whether, under General Statues § 42a–2–510(3), the period of time from August 20, 1971, the date of the breach, to September 22, 1971, the date of the fire, was a "commercially reasonable" period within which to treat the risk of loss as resting on the buyer. The trial court concluded that it was "not, on the facts in this case, a commercially unreasonable time," which we take to mean that it was a commercially reasonably period. The time limitation in § 42a–2–510(3) is designed to enable the seller to obtain the additional requisite insurance coverage. . . .

As already stated, the trial court found that the defendant repeatedly agreed to transmit delivery instructions and that the pellets were specially made to fill the defendant's order. Under those circumstances, it was reasonable for the plaintiff to believe that the goods would soon be taken off its hands and so to forego procuring the needed insurance. . . .

LUMBER SALES, INC., v. JULIOUS BROWN, d/b/a JULIOUS BROWN LUMBER COMPANY

469 S.W.2d 888 (Tennessee, 1971)

Puryear, Judge

Plaintiff sued the defendant for $5,163.23 alleged to be due and owing to plaintiff for a carload of lumber sold by plaintiff to defendant. . . .

The plaintiff contends and defendant admits that on or about the 6th day of November, 1968, the defendant agreed to purchase from plaintiff five carloads of lumber, which the plaintiff agreed to sell and deliver to defendant at a certain railroad siding near Radnor Yards in Nashville, Tennessee, which siding was known and designated by the railroad carrier as No. 609–A.

Plaintiff contends that all five carloads of lumber were delivered to defendant at said railroad siding in Nashville, Tennessee, and the defendant admits that four carloads thereof were received by him, but he denies that the fifth carload of lumber, which was to consist of two-by-four pine studs, was ever delivered to him or received by him. . . .

The plaintiff's contention that this fifth carload of lumber was duly delivered to defendant and the defendant's denial that same was delivered to or received by him is the substance of the controversy between the parties.

The case was tried upon oral testimony and documentary evidence before Honorable Sam L. Felts, Jr., Circuit Judge, without the intervention of a jury, on January 21, 1970, as a result of which trial the Circuit Judge found the issue in favor of plaintiff and against defendant and rendered a judgment in favor of plaintiff in the sum of $5,163.20 and costs, from which judgment the defendant has prayed and perfected an appeal and filed a single assignment of error as follows:

The trial court erred in rendering a judgment for plaintiff, as plaintiff failed to deliver the lumber in question to defendant as required by the sales provisions of the Uniform Commerical Code. In the absence of delivery, as therein spelled out, the seller must bear the risk of loss.

The railroad siding at which the lumber was to be delivered, according to agreement of the parties, is located about one-half mile from the defendant's place of business and is known as a "team track," which designation means that it is available for use by several parties, which in this case included the defendant. Track location 609–A on this siding is a point where a loading platform is located.

The uncontroverted evidence shows that during the early morning hours of November 27, 1968, the Louisville and Nashville Railroad Company, to which we will hereinafter refer as the carrier, placed a boxcar loaded with lumber consigned to the defendant on this siding at track location 609–A.

This boxcar was designated as NW 54938, and it was inspected by an employee of the carrier between 8:00 A.M. and 8:30 A.M. on November 27, 1968, at which time it was found loaded with cargo and so designated upon the carrier's records.

At 11:07 A.M. on November 27, 1968, the carrier notified one of defendant's employees that the carload of lumber had been delivered at track location 609–A.

At approximately 4:00 P.M. on that same day an employee of the carrier again inspected this boxcar at track location 609–A, found one of the seals on it to be broken, and resealed it at that time. The evidence does not show whether the car was still loaded with cargo at that time or not.

The following day, November 28th, was Thanksgiving Day, and the record does not disclose that the carrier inspected the boxcar on that date. But on November 29, 1968, between 8:00 A.M. and 8:30 A.M. an employee of the carrier inspected the car and found it empty.

From evidence in the record before us it is impossible to reach any logical conclusion as to what happened to this carload of lumber without indulging in speculation and conjecture, but the defendant earnestly insists that he did not unload it and there is no evidence to the contrary. . . .

The trial Court held that the risk of loss in this case did, in fact, pass to the defendant buyer. . . .

There is competent evidence in the record which shows that on November 27, 1968, at 11:07 A.M. the carrier notified the defendant's employee, Mr. Caldwell, at defendant's business office, that the carload of lumber had been delivered at track location 609–A. Mr. Caldwell did not testify, so this evidence is uncontroverted.

There is no evidence in the record to the effect that the defendant declined to accept delivery at that time or asked for a postponement of such delivery until a later time.

The defendant testified that it would normally require about four or five hours for him and his employees to unload a carload of lumber and that on November 27, 1968, he and his employees were so busily engaged in other necessary work that he could not unload the lumber on that day and since the following day was Thanksgiving, he could not unload it until November 29th, at which time, of course, the carrier found the car to be empty.

The defendant also testified, on cross-examination, as follows:

Q. Mr. Brown, did you, in fact see NW 54938?

A. I did see that car somewhere on some track.

Q. And that was at Radnor Yards?

A. I said I seen the car on some track because I have a crossmark where I have seen the car. When I see a car I put a crossmark. When I unload a car I mark him out.

Q. All right, Mr. Brown, let me ask you this: Is this your records right here?

A. Yes.

[Tendering documents.]

Q. All right, sir, so you have—now, these are your business records?

A. Yes, sir, I keep that in my car, I go by the railroad and check for my cars. I knew several cars were coming in at that time.

Q. Yes, sir, and you keep this memo in your car?

A. In my car, so when I go to breakfast I go by and check; when I go to lunch I go by and check. At night I check. I carry the bookkeeper home. I have a night-time bookkeeper, and when I carry the bookkeeper home I go by and check.

Q. All right, sir, you put down in your book NW 54938 and you put a check by it, is that correct, sir?

A. That is correct.

Q. All right.

A. That shows I have seen the car.

Q. You have physically seen the car?

A. Yes.

Q. Now, does that mean, also, that you have opened the door on the car to check its contents?

A. No, sir, it does not.

Q. Then when you have unloaded it you scratch it off, is that correct, sir?

A. That is right, sir." (B. of E., pp. 90, 01)

One Kenneth E. Crye, freight agent of the carrier, Louisville and Nashville Railroad Company, testified that on Thanksgiving Day, November

28th, he saw what he believed to be a railroad car being unloaded at track location 609–A, but he could not identify the car or the persons whom he believed to be unloading it. He qualified this testimony by saying that he was not positive that the car was being unloaded, but there was some lumber and some kind of activity on the platform, none of which appeared to be unusual. . . .

Counsel for defendant argues that the lumber in question was not duly "so tendered as to enable the buyer to take delivery" as required by T.C.A. § 47–2–509.

However, this argument seems to be based upon the premise that it was not convenient for the defendant to unload the lumber on November 27th, the day on which it was delivered at track location 609–A and defendant was duly notified of such delivery.

This was an ordinary business day, and the time of 11:07 A.M. was a reasonable business hour. If it was not convenient with the defendant to unload the lumber within a few hours after being duly notified of delivery, then he should have protected himself against risk of loss by directing someone to guard the cargo against loss by theft and other hazards.

To hold that the seller or the carrier should, under the circumstances existing in a case of this kind, continue to protect the goods until such time as the buyer may find it convenient to unload them would impose an undue burden upon the seller or the carrier and unnecessarily obstruct the channels of commerce.

The language of sub-section(1)(b) of T.C.A. § 47–2–509 does not impose such a burden upon the seller, in the absence of some material breach of the contract for delivery, and we think a reasonable construction of such language only requires the seller to place the goods at the buyer's disposal so that he has access to them and may remove them from the carrier's conveyance without lawful obstruction, with the proviso, however, that due notice of such delivery be given to the buyer. . . .

For the foregoing reasons herein set forth, the assignment of error is respectfully overruled and the judgment of the trial Court is affirmed.

MEINHARD-COMMERCIAL CORPORATION v. HARGO WOOLEN MILLS ET AL.

300 A.2d 321 (Delaware, 1972)

Grimes, Justice

The issue presented by this case is the correctness of the master's rulings as to who has ownership or title in the disputed goods. Hargo Woolen Mills, Inc., and its wholly owned subsidiary, Wallisford Mills, Inc., were respectively the seller and the manufacturer of woolen cloth. Meinhard-Commercial Corporation, the factor for and principal secured creditor of Hargo, instituted equity receivership proceedings against Hargo and Wallisford. On December 15, 1967, the Cheshire County Superior Court appointed a receiver who took possession of Hargo's and Wallisford's assets.

Shabry Trading Co. was in the business of trading waste material and for over 10 years prior to the receivership had sold card waste, used in the production of cloth, to Hargo.

On or about May 17, 1966, Shabry shipped and invoiced to Hargo 24 bales of card waste. Hargo did not wish to purchase the material at that time, and so on May 25, 1966, Shabry and Hargo made an oral agreement whereby Hargo was to store the goods on its premises but was not to pay for or be charged for the goods until Hargo notified Shabry that it was using them in its mill operation. Hargo returned the invoice for the goods to Shabry. Shabry marked the invoice "pro-forma" and returned it to Hargo. This invoice fixed the price at which these bales could be purchased by Hargo. In September of 1966 Hargo notified Shabry that it could use eight bales. Shabry invoiced them as of the original invoice date of May 17, 1966; Hargo had this revised to September since the parties had agreed Hargo was to be billed only at the time it used the goods. Hargo then used the goods, and Shabry received part payment for the eight bales (the balance being lost to Shabry as a general creditor in the receivership).

The remaining 16 bales were never used by or billed to Hargo except upon the "pro-forma" invoice of May 17. The receiver took possession of the bales on or about December 15, 1967.

Shabry on February 21, 1968, demanded possession of the 16 bales from the receiver, claiming that Hargo never owned the bales since title was retained by Shabry until use of the bales by Hargo. The receiver sold the 16 bales, and pursuant to the final decree by the Superior Court in the receivership proceedings (Dunfey, J.) on March 27, 1969, a sum of $7,500 covering the value of the bales was delivered by the receiver to a joint account of Shabry's and Meinhard's counsel, subject to further proceedings of the Superior Court to determine Shabry's claim. This final decree also found Meinhard the holder of a first lien against all of Hargo's inventory and proceeds thereof and as such the residuary beneficiary of all of Hargo's funds, credits, and deposits after payment of certain specific items, none of which are in issue here except for the purported claim of Shabry. The court obliged Meinhard to defend the claim of Shabry on behalf of Hargo's receiver. There was no evidence that Meinhard relied on the card waste as belonging to Hargo in extending its credit.

Meinhard and Shabry subsequently appeared before a master to settle the issue of whether Shabry had retained title to the 16 bales of card waste prior to Hargo's receivership or whether title had passed on to Hargo prior to receivership. The Master, N. Michael Plaut, found as a matter of law under RSA 382–A:1–201(37) and 2–401(1) that when Shabry delivered the bales to Hargo, title passed to Hargo and a security interest was concurrently created for Shabry. Shabry, never having perfected his security interest in the goods prior to appointment of the receiver, was left in the status of an unsecured creditor of Hargo.

The master found as a matter of fact that Hargo and Shabry believed and intended that title to the 16 bales would not pass until Hargo notified Shabry of their use. Hargo was under no obligation to buy, and Shabry was free to sell the goods to other buyers. Hargo never took the 16 bales into its inventory, and the bales were separately stored and distinctly marked as not being included in Hargo's general raw materials inventory.

The master's report was approved by the Superior Court (Loughlin, J.) subject to Shabry's exception, and the case was transferred to us reserving all questions of law raised by the parties' exceptions of record.

Whether this transaction was a sale or some other type of transaction is a question of the intent of the parties, which is a question for the trier of fact to determine. . . .

Given these findings, it is clear that the parties' agreement concerning the delivered card waste created no contract for sale by the passage of title for a price. The parties showed no intent to pass title. . . .

The mere fact that goods are delivered to the premises of a prospective buyer does not in and of itself create a sale, where neither party considered it a sale. . . .

The parties did agree as to the placement of the goods on Hargo's premises, and Shabry did make an offer on the pro-forma invoice of a price if Hargo wished to buy. The parties' course of dealings in card waste helps us interpret the meaning of this agreement. . . .

Hargo was nothing more than a bailee with an option to buy if the goods were not sold to others. . . .

We therefore hold that, since there was no sale, title to these goods cannot be determined by RSA 382–A:2–401 and, since no other provisions of the code apply, the rights of the parties are determined by the law of contracts. . . .

The master found the parties' stated intentions to be that title to these 16 bales never passed to Hargo. We therefore hold that title remained in Shabry and that the receiver wrongfully withheld return of the 16 bales to Shabry.

Exceptions of Shabry Trading Co. sustained; remanded.

PROBLEMS FOR DISCUSSION

1. H & R Railroad Materials, Inc., made a contract with Rusty Industries, Inc., for the sale of old relay rails salvaged from a discontinued railroad. The parties agreed on a down payment of $20,000, with the balance due before removal of the rails from the seller's premises. The $20,000 having been paid, H & R sent its driver, James Husky, to fetch the iron. While removing the 17th load, Husky was informed by Joe Tougharm, an employee of Rusty, Inc., that the $20,000 had been used up and that a balance of $750 would have to be paid before Husky could leave town. Husky, who denied having received those instructions, stayed for one night before he set out for his trip home, with the 17th load. On the freeway he was stopped by a road patrol, which had been alerted by Tougharm, and arrested for larceny. Who had title to the iron when Husky was arrested for "stealing" it?

2. Hermann Ehrlich, owner of a disputed piece of property, had planted alfalfa on land which was occupied by his tenant Will Mills. Later, Ehrlich's title was disputed by Mrs. Terry, the district court decided in her favor, and Will Mills had to leave the land. At harvestime, Mrs. Terry hired Joe Cut and Jack Dry to cut and bale the alfalfa, promising them half of the hay for their labor. At about that time, the district court's decision was overturned by the state supreme court and Hermann Ehrlich had possession of the land restored to him until the issue could be settled by the Department of the Interior. Shortly after this decision, Will Mills returned to the land, saw the neatly stacked bales of hay, and hauled them happily to his barn. Now the two hay balers are suing Will for conversion of the hay. Who will win? Why?

3. The *People's Voice*, a newspaper of dubious credit rating, wanted to buy a printing press from Safeplay Company. The conditional sales agreement stated that the buyer would be responsible for all loss or damage to the goods and that loss or damage to the goods through any casualty would not release the buyer from its obligation to pay for the goods. The seller also required that the buyer carry an insurance policy on the goods. The *People's Voice* took out insurance on all of its assets, without, however, specifically naming Safeplay as the recipient. Safeplay itself carried insurance on all the merchandise that it sold on conditional terms. Shortly thereafter, a fire destroyed many assets of the *People's Voice'* including the press. Safeplay received the unpaid balance from its own insurance company. Nevertheless, it is suing the buyer for the unpaid balance on the press. Who wins? Why?

4. Dave Craig and Roger Holler ordered from Implement Company a 1962 International chassis and cab for use in their business. Implement did not have the necessary vehicle in stock, but it found one at a dealership in a neighboring city and notified the buyers. Holler drove to the city and took physical delivery of the truck. When Holler asked for some sort of ownership document or certificate, the dealership said that it did not have such documentation on hand. Holler drove the vehicle back anyway. Craig and Holler were in the process of installing a hoist and a dump bed on the truck, when a fire destroyed the vehicle completely. Implement sued for the contract price, but the defendants argued that title (and risk) had not yet passed. Discuss and decide.

5. EXIM Corporation bought 4,000 pounds of yarn from Knitwear Corporation at $1.35 per pound, to be loaded into a container at the seller's premises for reshipment to South America. EXIM had a trucking company deliver an empty semitruck container to the seller's premises. Knitwear loaded the container with the yarn and notified EXIM that the container was ready to be picked up. Before EXIM's driver appeared, a thief drove up with another semicab, signed for the goods, hooked up the container, and drove off. Seller sues for the contract price. Discuss and decide.

6. Harmless, Inc., had assembly plants, which used brilligs, in several different cities. Harmless sent orders for brilligs to be manufactured to its specifications to Stainless Metals, Inc., located in Norwalk, Connecticut. Stainless accepted the orders FOB Norwalk, but Harmless had supplied Stainless with "ship to" addresses, indicating the different plants to which the brilligs were to be sent, both inside and outside Connecticut. The brilligs were damaged in transit, and Harmless refused to pay the full contract price. Stainless sues. Discuss and decide.

7. Aeroflop Airlines sold a used twin-engine Cessna to Richtofen on June 12, with delivery and payment of the contract price to occur on July 1. On June 20, without fault on the part of either the buyer or the seller, the plane was destroyed by a fire of unknown origin. Aeroflop had an insurance policy in force on all its planes, but its claim on the plane in question was denied by the insurance company, Massive Insurance. Aeroflop sues Massive. Discuss and decide.

8. Freda Construction Company, working on a large electrical project, ordered three reels of burial cable from Cableus, Inc. By mistake, Cableus shipped one reel of burial cable and two reels of aerial cable, although all three cartons were labeled "burial cable." Freda's foreman rejected the two reels of aerial cable but left them at the construction site because of their size and weight. Cableus was notified of the rejection but did not come out to pick up the two reels. Freda was unable to reship the two reels because of a trucker's strike. About four months later, the two reels of aerial cable were stolen from the construction site. Cableus sues for the contract price for the two cables. Discuss and decide.

9. Mercury, Inc., delivered a shipment of stereo equipment and stereotapes to I. M. Greeze, for resale in his gasoline service station. The contract provided: "Terms 30–60–90. This equipment will be picked up if not sold in 90 days." Greeze's service station was robbed, and the merchandise in question was stolen. Mercury sues Greeze for the contract price. Discuss and decide.

Warranties and Products Liability | 17

Stop and think for a minute. How many times each day do you entrust your health and safety, and even your life, to a manufactured product? Your new electric blanket that you left on all night, the can of frozen orange juice that you opened for breakfast this morning (and the electric can opener that you used to open it), the car or bus that you used to get to school (and all the other motor vehicles that were on the highway at the same time)—a malfunction in any one of these or in thousands of other products that we encounter every day could produce sickness, injury, or even death. No product can be made absolutely safe, under any and all circumstances. Malfunctions do occur, with resulting personal injury, property damage, and financial loss. The law's function in this area is to provide the rules by which the burden of such lossess will be allocated.

Earlier legal doctrine tended to "leave the loss where it was incurred," that is, to force the injured parties to pay for their own injuries, or to buy their own insurance to cover such losses. The modern legal trend, which has accelerated sharply during the last two decades, is to pass these losses back up the chain of distribution, to sellers and manufacturers, as one of the costs of doing business. The net result of the modern product liability rules is that all of us as consumers will pay higher prices for products and that some of the smaller manufacturers in "high-risk" industries such as chemicals and machinery may be forced out of business because they cannot absorb these additional overhead costs. The courts' willingness to apply these modern theories of liability and to disallow traditional defenses has produced a crisis of major proportions and worldwide impact.

Plaintiffs, Defendants, and Theories of Liability. In addition to the buyer of "defective" goods, other possible plaintiffs include members of the buyer's family and household and guests in the buyer's home; the buyer's employees and customers; and "bystanders" who have had no previous relationship with the buyer. In addition to the seller, possible defendants include the manufacturer or assembler of the product, the designer, the supplier of the defective component part, and any intermediate distributors. The availability of the manufacturer as a defendant becomes crucial in those cases where the seller is unable to pay the judgment, or where the injured buyer cannot remember where he bought the brand name product that caused the injury, or where the injury results from long-continued use of the brand name product (e.g., lung cancer from smoking).

Modern courts have a wide selection of theories of liability which can be used to impose damages back up the chain of distribution: fraud, innocent misrepresentation, negligence, breach of express or implied warranty, and strict liability. Although these different theories of liabilty require different forms of proof and are subject to different defenses and different statutes of limitations, the courts are not always careful to distinguish which theory is being applied to produce liability in a particular case.

Fraud and Innocent Misrepresentation. The most obvious case for "product liability" is the seller (or manufacturer) who has fraudulently misrepresented his product. He or she should clearly be held liable for all the losses which are caused by the misrepresentation, and probably for punitive damages as well. However, as previously noted in Part II, Contracts, fraud is easy to allege but difficult to prove, and it probably applies to only a tiny fraction of product liability cases.

As noted in Chapter 9, most courts permit rescission (but not recovery of damages) where a buyer has been damaged because of reasonable reliance on the seller's honestly made, but mistaken, statement of fact. The most recent version of the *Restatement of the Law of Torts, Second*, includes a revised Section 402B, which would substantially modify this general rule for sales of goods. Under Section 402B, a seller of goods is liable for "physical harm to a consumer" which results from reliance on the seller's material misrepresentation, even though "not made fraudulently or negligently" and even though "the consumer has not bought the chattel from or entered into any contractual relation with the seller." Essentially, what this section does is to restate the law of express warranty, without the requirement of "privity" (relationship) of contract.

Negligence. Like fraud, negligence is easy to allege but sometimes very difficult to prove. The fact that one part fails and causes injury is not much evidence of negligent manufacture, if tens of thousands of identical parts have been and are functioning properly. Indeed, in most cases such statistics would present a pretty convincing case that the manufacturer was doing an excellent job of product design, manufacture, and inspection. Where negligence can be proved against either the manufacturer or the seller or both, the injured party should be able to collect all the damages which result. Courts today generally recognize that the manufacturer's liability for negligence extends not only to the buyer of the product but also to other persons "whom he should expect to be endangered by its probable use" (if the product is not properly made). In a few situations, such as the case of the dead mouse in the bottle of cola, the courts may apply the doctrine of *res ipsa loquitur* ("the thing speaks for itself"), meaning that such things do not occur without negligent or purposeful conduct.

The following case is a classic application of negligence as a theory of product liability.

MacPherson v. Buick Motor Co.
111 N.E. 1050 (New York, 1916)

FACTS   MacPherson bought a Buick from a retail dealer. He was injured while driving the car when the wooden spokes on one of the wheels crumbled into fragments. The defective wheel had been supplied to Buick Motor Company by a parts manufacturer. There was evidence tending to show that a reasonable inspection by Buick would have disclosed the defective wheel but that Buick failed to make such an inspection. The trial court held for the plaintiff.

ISSUE   Does a manufacturer owe a duty of care to the ultimate purchaser (consumer) who has bought the item from an independent distributor?

DECISION   Yes. Judgment affirmed.

REASONS   Justice Cardozo first discussed many of the precedents in the field of products liability. The basic New York case imposing such liability on the manufacturer-producer involved a mislabeled poison, where there was a clearly foreseeable risk of injury to persons other than the initial buyer-distributor. Other cases imposed liability for a collapsing scaffold and an exploding coffee urn. Justice Cardozo then concluded that the rule should be applied to any product which was dangerous if negligently made, not just to products which were inherently dangerous (such as poisons and explosives).

"From this survey of the decisions, there thus emerges a definition of the duty of a manufacturer which enables us to measure this defendant's liability. Beyond all question, the nature of an automobile gives warning of probable danger if its construction is defective. This automobile was designed to go 50 miles an hour. Unless its wheels were sound and strong, injury was almost certain. It was as much a thing of danger as a defective engine for a railroad. The defendant knew the danger. It also knew that the car would be used by persons other than the buyer. . . . The dealer was indeed the one person of whom it might be said with some approach to certainty that by him the car would not be used. Yet the defendant would have us say that he was the one person whom it was under a legal duty to protect. The law does not lead us to so inconsequent a conclusion. Precedents drawn from the days of travel by stagecoach do not fit the conditions of travel today. The principle that the danger must be imminent does not change, but the things subject to the principle change. They are whatever the needs of life in a developing civilization require them to be."

Breach of Warranty. *Warranty* is simply another word for guarantee. Depending on the facts and circumstances, the seller may make several different types of warranties on the goods he or she is selling—warranties relating to his or her title to the goods or to the characteristics, qualities, or capabilities of the goods. In a simpler economy, where most sellers produced what they sold, where such manufactured goods as there were could be readily inspected and understood by the buyers, and where there was a rough equality in the bargaining power of the parties, *caveat emptor* ("let the buyer beware") may have been a workable rule for the law of sales. As products became more intricate and the distribution system became more impersonal, courts and legislatures saw the necessity of changing this early rule to provide more protection to buyers and users. It is one thing to say that Walter Woodcutter ought to be able to tell a bad ax from a good one when he deals with the village blacksmith; it is quite another to apply the same standard to a weekend hobbyist when he or she buys a gasoline-driven chain saw from the local hardware store. The law of warranty has changed, and is still changing, to meet changes in the economy.

Although the UCC does not make any revolutionary changes in the law of warranties, it does contain several provisions which extend warranty liability, or which make such liability more difficult to disclaim. The Code sections cover three types of warranties: express, implied, and title warranties.

Although the title warranties are not specifically labeled "implied," they are such, in the sense that they are automatically written into the transaction by the law unless the parties agree otherwise or the circumstances clearly indicate otherwise. The seller guarantees that he or she has a good title to the goods, that he or she has the right to sell them, and that there are no liens or encumbrances against them. In addition, where the seller is a merchant who regularly deals in such goods, he or she also warrants that the sale will not subject the buyer to suit by any third party claiming infringement on a patent, copyright, trademark, and so forth.

Express Warranties.   Under the Code, express warranties are created in one of three ways: an affirmation of fact or a promise, which relates to the goods and becomes part of the basis of the bargain; a description of the goods; or a sample or model of the goods. In each of these three cases, the assumption is that the seller and the buyer have specifically included the guarantee as an integral part of their sales contract. An express warranty is thus virtually impossible to disclaim by form language in a written sales contract. It is not necessary to prove that the seller used the word *warranty* or *guarantee*, or that he or she had the specific intent to make a warranty. If the statement is a factual one and it is made in the context of negotiations on the sales contract, it is assumed to be a warranty unless the facts clearly indicate otherwise. In the case of a description, sample, or model, there is an express warranty that the goods will conform to the description, sample, or model. Even statements made in advertisements, if factual, may be held to be express warranties.

Alafoss, h.f. v. *Premium Corporation of America*
448 F. Supp. 95 (1978)

FACTS   Alafoss, h.f., a corporation organized under the laws of Iceland, was engaged in the export and sale of garments and other products made from the fur and wool of Icelandic sheep. During 1972 a PCA designer worked with Alafoss in developing a full-collared wraparound coat for resale by PCA in its mail marketing business to American Express Card holders. The body of the coat was to be all-white wool, with a detachable white fur collar made from the fur of Icelandic sheep. Alafoss supplied samples of the coat to PCA; these samples had full, solid white collars of a silky texture. In 1973 PCA ordered 8,225 coats at a price of $88.11 each, delivered in Chicago. PCA offered the coats to American Express Card holders for $199.90. After filling a number of orders, PCA discovered that a large number of the collars had a significant yellow discoloration and that about 1,400 coats had loosely sewn pockets. Alafoss agreed to have 4,350 collars treated at a cost of $5.55 per collar and to have the pockets resewn for $2 each. A large number of the coats already sold were returned. PCA resold the coats on hand to Alden's, a Chicago discounter. Alafoss sues for the original contract price, and PCA counterclaims for damages.

ISSUE   Did the seller breach the sample warranty?

DECISION   Yes. Judgment for PCA for damages sustained.

REASONS   Judge MacLaughlin found that the coats delivered did not match the samples, so that the damages sustained were the difference between the goods delivered and the goods as warranted. A fair resale price was $25 per coat, or $63.11 × 3,736 coats, or $238,758.96 in damages. PCA still owed $132,470 on the purchase price; the difference was $106,288.96. Alafoss also owed PCA for the $26,986.90 spent in repairing the coats.

". . . [T]he samples of the wrap coats were made a part of the basis of the bargain and created an express warranty that the whole of the goods would conform to the sample or model. . . .

"Alafoss breaches the express warranty created by the sample and the express and implied warranty of fitness for a particular purpose by its delivery of at least 3,736 wrap coats which did not conform to the sample and which were not fit for PCA's resale in its direct mail business. Proper notice was given by PCA to Alafoss of the breach of these warranties."

Implied Warranty of Merchantability. (Where the seller is a merchant with respect to the type of goods involved in the contract, he or she makes an implied warranty that the goods are "merchantable.") This is a minimum quality guarantee, defined in UCC 2–314, which is imposed on the seller unless the buyer and the seller clearly agree otherwise. (Among other requirements, to be merchantable goods must at least be "fit for the ordinary purposes for which such goods are used"; be "adequately contained, packaged, and labeled as the agreement may require"; and "conform to the promises or affirmations of fact made on the container or label if any."

   Prior to the adoption of the Code some courts drew a distinction between food purchased in "carryout" restaurants, to be consumed off the premises, and food purchase in "service" restaurants, where the diners ate on the premises. The latter case was held to be a services contract, not a sale of goods, and thus there was no implied warranty that food or drink purchased for consumption on the premises was "merchantable." The Code specifically repudiates this distinction, so that your hamburger must be merchantable whether you eat it on or off the restaurant premises. The fact questions involved in such situations are illustrated by the following case.

Hochberg v. *O'Donnell's Restaurant, Inc.*
272 A.2d 846 (District of Columbia, 1971)

FACTS   Philip Hochberg ordered a vodka martini in O'Donnell's Restaurant. He took the olive out of the drink with his fingers, saw a hole in the end of the olive, placed the olive in his mouth, and bit down. He uttered an exclamation, and told his fellow diners that he had broken a tooth on an olive pit. The manager was called to the table and was shown the olive pit and a piece of the tooth.

   Hochberg sued O'Donnell's for his damages alleging negligence and breach of the implied warranty of merchantability. O'Donnell's in turn sued its olive supplier, which also sued the food company from which it had purchased the olives. The trial court first granted a directed verdict on the negligence count and then did the same with the warranty claim, since Hochberg had failed to prove that the food served was "unwholesome or contained foreign matter." Judgments were also entered in favor of the olive supplier and the food company. Hochberg appealed.

ISSUE   Was the olive in the martini "merchantable"?

DECISION   This is a fact question for the jury. Reversed and remanded for a new trial.

REASONS   Judge Gallagher first noted that there was a split of authority as to the proper test of merchantability for food. He cited cases from California, Illinois, Louisiana, and North Carolina as holding that there was no breach of warranty where the object in the food which caused injury was "natural" to the food served. In Wisconsin, Maryland, Pennsylvania, and Rhode Island, the test was "what should reasonably be expected by the consumer to be in the food served to him." Judge Gallagher thought that the second test was fairer and more realistic. "In our view it is unrealistic to deny recovery *as a matter of law* if, for example, a person is injured from a chicken bone while eating a sliced chicken sandwich in a restaurant, simply because the bone is natural to chicken. The exposure to injury is not much different than if a sliver of glass were there. 'Naturalness of the substance to any ingredients in the food served is important only in determining whether the consumer may reasonably expect to find such substance in the particular type of dish or style of food served.' . . . Because a substance is natural to a product in one stage of preparation does not mean necessarily that it will be reasonably anticipated by the consumer in the final product served."

   The evidence in this case presented a jury question as to whether Hochberg acted reasonably. A new trial was necessary.

Implied Warranty of Fitness. The Code has also made an important extension in the seller's liability under the implied warranty of fitness. Where this warranty applies, the seller is not only guaranteeing that the goods are of fair average quality and that they will do what most buyers expect them to do but also that they are suitable for the *particular* needs of the given buyer. The fitness warranty does not arise unless the buyer makes known to the seller his or her special needs and the fact that he or she is relying on the seller to select or furnish suitable goods to meet those special needs. Prior to the Code, this fitness warranty could not apply where the goods were sold under a brand name or a trade name; under UCC 2–315, a brand name on the goods is only one fact to be considered in determining whether the buyer relied on the seller to furnish suitable goods.

Exclusion or Modification of Warranties. The Code generally makes it more difficult for the seller to disclaim warranties once they are made. For all practical purposes, it is impossible for the seller to disclaim an express warranty unless the entire transaction is renegotiated or unless the parties agree on a final written contract which does not include the express warranty and which indicates that it is intended as a complete statement of all the terms of the contract. With such a clause in the final contract, any prior express warranty would be excluded by the operation of the parol evidence section of Article 2 (2–202). Otherwise, where an express warranty has been made it overrides any attempted disclaimer of warranty to the extent that the two provisions are inconsistent.

Theoretically, at least, the implied warranties of merchantability and fitness can be disclaimed if the appropriate Code sections are complied with. As a practical matter, however, courts have been reluctant to enforce such disclaimers unless there is evidence that the buyer understood and intended that result (for example, where a used item is bought "as is" or where the buyer is also a business, such as TWA buying jumbo jets from Boeing). In order to stand *any* chance of being enforceable, the disclaimer of warranties must comply with the Code's requirements. Merchantability may be disclaimed either orally or in writing, but the word *merchantability* must be used; moreover, if the disclaimer is part of a written contract, it must be stated "conspicuously" in the writing. The fitness warranty cannot be excluded except by a writing, and the disclaimer must be a conspicuous part of the writing. UCC 1–201(10) defines *conspicuous* as being "so written that a reasonable person against whom it is to operate ought to have noticed it," for instance, in a contrasting type style or color.

Even where all the Code's requirements as to the language and form of the disclaimer have been met, a court may still refuse to enforce the disclaimer, on the grounds that it is an attempt to avoid the seller's basic obligations of "good faith, diligence, reasonableness and care" (1–102[3]), or that it is "unconscionable" (2–302), or that it is against "public policy." The following case is perhaps the most significant single case on product liability since it started the modern trend by repudiating the "privity" requirement and by refusing to enforce the auto manufacturer's form disclaimer.

Henningsen v. *Bloomfield Motors, Inc.*
161 A.2d 69 (New Jersey, 1960)

FACTS   Clause Henningsen bought his wife a new Plymouth as a Mother's Day present. Ten days later, while driving the car, she heard a loud noise from under the hood; she said it "felt as if something had cracked." The steering wheel spun in her hands, and the car veered sharply to the right and crashed into a brick wall. The Henningsens sued Bloomfield (the dealer) and Chrysler (the manufacturer). The sales contract stated that the manufacturer's only warranty on the car was a promise to replace defective parts at the factory and that the warranty was given in lieu of all other warranties, express or implied. The trial court held for the plaintiffs, and the defendants appealed.

ISSUE   Should the disclaimer of warranties be given full effect?

DECISION   No. Judgment affirmed.

REASONS   The disclaimer appeared in fine print on the back of the contract form. Clause did not read it at the time of purchase. A statement on the front of the form that the buyer had read the entire contract appeared in even finer print; it too was unread by Clause. Justice Francis' opinion then reviewed the law of warranty and indicated that Chrysler's normally implied warranty of merchantability would run directly to the purchasers. He also held that the "large scale advertising programs" of Chrysler and others, to the extent that they contained factual representations, "constitute an express warranty running directly to a buyer who purchases in reliance thereon." He then noted that the form disclaimer was "a sad commentary upon the automobile manufacturers' marketing practices." Even though he recognized the fundamental principle of freedom of contract, he felt that this provision should not be enforced.

"[W]arranties originated in the law to safeguard the buyer and not to limit the liability of the seller or manufacturer. It seems obvious in this instance that the motive was to avoid the warranty obligations which are normally incidental to such sales. The language gave little and withdrew much. In return for the delusive remedy of replacement of defective parts at the factory, the buyer is said to have accepted the exclusion of the maker's liability for personal injuries arising from the breach of the warranty. An instinctively felt sense of justice cries out against such a sharp bargain. . . .

"The warranty before us is a standardized form designed for mass use. It is imposed upon the automobile consumer. He takes it or leaves it, and he must take it to buy an automobile. No bargaining is engaged in with respect to it. In fact, the dealer through whom it comes to the buyer is without authority to alter it; his function is ministerial—simply to deliver it. . . .

"The gross inequality for bargaining position occupied by the consumer in the automobile industry is thus apparent. There is no competition among the car makers in the area of express warranty. . . .

"In the area of sale of goods, the legislative will has imposed an implied warranty of merchantability as a general incident of sale of an automobile by description. The warranty does not depend upon the affirmative intention of the parties. It is a child of the law; it annexes itself to the contract because of the very nature of the transaction. . . . The disclaimer of the implied warranty and exclusion of all obligations except those specifically assumed by the express warranty signify a studied effort to frustrate that protection."

There are two other important limitations on warranty disclaimers. A seller
who has made warranties to his or her buyer cannot "exclude or limit" the
operation of Section 2–318, which extends the warranties automatically to "any
natural person who is in the family or household of his or her buyer or who is
a guest in his or her home." Also, although Section 2–316 permits the parties to
agree to limit the remedies for breach of warranty, in accordance with Sections
2–718 and 2–719, Section 2–719 states that any limitation "of consequential
damages for injury to the person in the case of consumer goods is prima facie
unconscionable" (and therefore not enforceable).

The Code also provides that warranties, whether express or implied, are to
be construed as consistent with each other and cumulative (i.e., *all* the warranties which apply on the facts are made) unless such a construction is unreasonable.

Strict Liability in Tort.   As the new case law was developing during the 1960s,
courts gradually came to realize that the liability they were enforcing for product failure could no longer be properly described in terms of contract warranties. When manufacturers are held liable to retail buyers with whom they have
no contract, when both manufacturers and sellers are held liable to persons
other than the buyer, when both manufacturers and sellers are held liable
despite clear and conspicuous written disclaimers of implied quality warranties,
and when liability is imposed even before a sale is made (as in a "self-serve"
store), it is no longer quite accurate to describe this liability as "breach of
warranty." Most courts now recognize that this is a socially imposed, *tort*
liability rather than a self-imposed, *contract* liability; in many cases liability is
being enforced despite contrary provisions in the parties' contract or even
where there is no contract at all between them.

Moreover, since proof of negligence is not required and proof of the plaintiff's contributory negligence is not fatal in his or her case, this is a new theory
of tort liability, usually described as "strict liability in tort," or liability without
fault. Historically, strict tort liability was imposed only on the keepers of dangerous wild animals and on persons who engaged in "extra-hazardous activities." What the courts have done, in effect, is to extend this theory of liability to
manufacturers, sellers, and renters of products, so that the supplier of a defective product will be liable for the damage it causes, irrespective of any contract.

Of course, the plaintiff must still prove his or her case, but this is a much
easier case to prove, and a much more difficult case to defend, than either
negligence or breach of warranty. The fact that only this one product failed out
of 5 million produced and used may prevent recovery for negligent manufacture, but it will not prevent recovery based on strict liability. The plaintiff need
only prove that the product was made by the defendant, that it was "defective,"
that the defect caused his or her injury, and that he or she has sustained damages in a certain amount. The defendant can try to show that the product was
not defective, but instead failed as the result of normal wear and tear, or improper maintenance, or misuse by the plaintiff. But the courts have in some
cases indicated that the manufacturer should reasonably foresee the possibility
of misuse or improper maintenance, and thus design "idiot-proof" products. In
one recent case the manufacturer of a bench saw, made for the U.S. Navy in

1942 and originally equipped with the required safety guard (and apparently used without incident for nearly *30 years!*), was required to pay $50,000 to a worker who was injured while using the saw in 1971 and whose employer had bought the saw from a dealer who had removed the safety guard. It is this kind of Alice-in-Wonderland decision that is causing the "product liability crisis." Once they adopt the theory of strict liability, the courts generally have been reluctant to recognize any defenses which would prevent the injured plaintiff from recovering for his or her injuries.

The following case shows a court in the process of developing this new tort liability.

Suvada v. *White Motor Company*
201 N.E.2d 313 (Illinois, 1964)

FACTS On February 11, 1957, Suvada bought a used, reconditioned tractor-trailer unit from White Motor Company for use in the plaintiffs' milk delivery business. The vehicle was equipped with a brake system manufactured by Bendix. On June 24, 1960, the brakes failed and the truck collided with a bus operated by the Chicago Transit Authority. Several people were injured, and the plaintiffs were sued by those third parties. The plaintiffs brought this suit to recover for damages to their tractor-trailer and for the costs involved in the defense and settlement of the lawsuits which were brought against them. The trial court dismissed all of the counts which asked for such reimbursement.

ISSUE Is a manufacturer-seller liable to persons beyond its buyer for injuries resulting from product defects?

DECISION Yes. Judgment reversed; case remanded for trial.

REASONS Justice Burke first reviewed the then-developing case law, which was imposing liability for "inherently dangerous" products, and the reasons for this extension: "Today's manufacturer, selling to distributors or wholesalers, is still interested in the subsequent sales of the product. His advertising is not aimed at his distributors. The historical relative equality of seller and buyer no longer exists. A product that is inherently dangerous or defectively made constitutes an exception to the requirement of privity in an action between the user of the product and its manufacturer. . . .

"The exception to the privity requirement is not superseded nor is it modified by the provisions of the Uniform Commercial Code."

Justice Burke then indicated that the tractor-trailer unit with the defective brakes was clearly "inherently dangerous." He then answered the defendants' argument that damages should not include the amounts expended in defending the lawsuits by the third parties injured in the collision with the bus: "Plaintiffs are not volunteers. They are the owners of the tractor-trailer unit that collided with the bus, and as the owners of this unit or an employer of the driver of the unit, they were subject to being sued. The owner of the unit was under a duty to operate the motor vehicle with adequate brakes in Illinois, and failure to do so subjects the operator to liability. The failure of the brakes made plaintiffs answerable to third parties. Under the allegations of the complaint plaintiffs are not volunteers and have a right to prosecute their counts for indemnifications from the defendants."

Magnuson-Moss Warranty Act. One would have imagined that if there was any field of law under the sun where additional "protective" legislation was not needed, it was the law of product liability. Indeed, if a problem in this field required legislative attention, it was exactly the opposite problem: how to *limit* skyrocketing product liability costs before all but the very largest manufacturers were driven out of business. Congress, however, did not see it that way. Either unaware of or unimpressed by the product liability "revolution" which had occurred during the preceding 15 years, Congress in 1975 passed the Magnuson-Moss Warranty Act, thereby adding one more large straw to the already weakened camel's back.

Like most "remedial" legislation, the act has high-minded objectives which it is impossible to oppose: to provide consumers with clearer and truer warranties and to give dissatisfied consumers a remedy for defective products. The act says that the manufacturer must designate whether the written warranty is a "full" or "limited" one, but the act's definitions of these terms have been criticized as being incomplete and ambiguous. The net result in the marketplace so far has been that very few manufacturers have tried to claim that they are giving full warranties on their products, and some have stopped giving written warranties altogether. Faced with the act's uncertainties, only the very hardiest (or foolhardiest) manufacturers will run the risk of extended jousting with the FTC staff. Whether this act represents a net gain for consumers remains to be seen.

CASES FOR DISCUSSION

TROPPI v. SCARF

187 N.W.2d 511 (Michigan, 1971)

Levin, Presiding Judge

In this case we consider the civil liability of a pharmacist who negligently supplied the wrong drug to a married woman who had ordered an oral contraceptive and, as a consequence, became pregnant and delivered a normal, healthy child.

I

A summary judgment was entered dismissing the complaint of the plaintiffs, John and Dorothy Troppi, on the ground that it does not state a claim upon which relief can be granted. In our appraisal of the correctness of the trial judge's ruling we accept as true plaintiffs' factual allegations.

In August 1964, plaintiffs were the parents of seven children, ranging in age from 6 to 16 years of age. John Troppi was 43 years old, his wife 37.

While pregnant with an eighth child, Mrs. Troppi suffered a miscarriage. She and her husband consulted with their physician and decided to limit the size of their family. The physician prescribed an oral contraceptive, Norinyl, as the most desirable means of insuring that Mrs. Troppi would bear no more children. He telephoned the prescription to defendant, Frank H. Scarf, a licensed pharmacist. Instead of filling the prescription, Scarf negligently supplied Mrs. Troppi with a drug called Nardil, a mild tranquilizer.

Believing that the pills she had purchased were contraceptives, Mrs. Troppi took them on a daily basis. In December 1964, Mrs. Troppi became pregnant. She delivered a well-born son on August 12, 1965.

Plaintiffs' complaint alleges four separate items of damage: (1) Mrs. Troppi's lost wages; (2) medical and hospital expenses; (3) the pain and anxiety of pregnancy and childbirth; and (4) the economic costs of rearing the eight child.

In dismissing the complaint, the judge declared that whatever damage plaintiffs suffered was more than offset by the benefit to them of having a healthy child.

II

Contraception, conjugal relations, and childbirth are highly charged subjects. It is all the more important, then, to emphasize that resolution of the case before us requires no intrusion into the domain of moral philosophy. At issue here is simply the extent to which defendant is civilly liable for the consequences of his negligence. In reversing and remanding for trial, we go no further than to apply settled common-law principles.

We begin by noting that the fundamental conditions of tort liability are present here. The defendant's conduct constituted a clear breach of duty. A pharmacist is held to a very high standard of care in filling prescriptions. When he negligently supplies a drug other than the drug requested, he is liable for resulting harm to the purchaser. . . .

We assume, for the purpose of appraising the correctness of the ruling dismissing the complaint, that the defendant's negligence was a cause in fact of Mrs. Troppi's pregnancy. The possibility that she might become pregnant was certainly a foreseeable consequence of the defendant's failure to fill a prescription for birth control pills; we therefore could not say that it was not a proximate cause of the birth of the child.

Setting aside, for the moment, the subtleties of the damage question, it is at least clear that the plaintiffs have expended significant sums of money as a direct and proximate result of the defendant's negligence. The medical and hospital expenses of Mrs. Troppi's confinement and her loss of wages arose from the defendant's failure to fill the prescription properly. Pain and suffering, like that accompanying childbirth, have long been recognized as compensable injuries.

This review of the elements of tort liability points up the extraordinary nature of the trial court's holding that the plaintiffs were entitled to no recovery as a matter of law. We have here a negligent, wrongful act by the defendant, which act directly and proximately caused injury to the plaintiffs. . . .

III

The trial judge based his decision upon what he perceived to be the law "announced by a majority of the courts in this country." But, as yet, no appellate court has passed upon the liability of a pharmacist for negligently dispensing oral contraceptives. Several cases have, indeed, dealt with the liability of physicians for failure to exercise due care in the therapeutic or elective sterilization of patients. Because the elements of damage in these cases correspond to some of the damages prayed for here, the decisions deserve scrutiny. . . .

IV

Our review has been conducted to determine whether the defendant in this case should be exempted from the consequences of his negligence. We conclude that there is no valid reason why the trier of fact should not be free to assess damages as it would in any other negligence case. . . .

. . . It has been suggested that parents who seek to recover for the birth of an unwanted child are under a duty to mitigate damages by placing the child for adoption. If the child is "unwanted," why should they object to placing him for adoption, thereby reducing the financial burden on defendant for his maintenance? . . .

While the reasonableness of a plaintiff's efforts to mitigate is ordinarily to be decided by the trier of fact, we are persuaded to rule, as a matter of law, that no mother, wed or unwed, can reasonably be required to abort (even if legal) or place her child for adoption. The plaintiffs are entitled to have the jurors instructed that if they find that negligence of the defendant was a cause in fact of the plaintiffs' injury, they may not, in computing the amount, if any, of the plaintiffs' damages, take into consideration the fact that the plaintiffs might have aborted the child or placed the child for adoption. . . .

Michigan law is clear that there need only be a basis for reasonable ascertainment of the amount of the damages. Where the fact of liability is proven, difficulty in determining damages will not bar recovery. . . .

The assessment of damages in this case is properly within the competence of the trier of fact. The element of uncertainty in the net recovery does not render the damages unduly speculative. Reversed and remanded for trial.

WEBSTER v. BLUE SHIP TEA ROOM, INC.

198 N.E. 2d 309 (Massachusetts, 1964)

Reardon, Justice

This is a case which by its nature evokes earnest study not only of the law but also of the culinary traditions of the Commonwealth which bear so heavily upon its outcome. It is action to recover damages for personal injuries sustained by reason of a breach of implied warranty of food served by the defendant in its restaurant. . . .

The jury could have found the following facts: On Saturday, April 25, 1959, about 1 P.M., the plaintiff, accompanied by her sister and her aunt, entered the Blue Ship Tea Room operated by the defendant. The group was seated at a table and supplied with menus.

This restaurant, which the plaintiff characterized as "quaint," was located in Boston "on the third floor of an old building on T Wharf, which overlooks the ocean."

The plaintiff, who had been born and brought up in New England (a fact of some consequence), ordered clam chowder and crabmeat salad. Within a few minutes she received tidings to the effect that "there was no more clam chowder." Presently, there was set before her a "a small bowl of fish chowder." She had previously enjoyed a breakfast about 9 A.M. which had given her no difficulty. "The fish chowder contained haddock, potatoes, milk, water, and seasoning. The chowder was milky in color and not clear. The haddock and potatoes were in chunks" (also a fact of consequence). "She agitated it a little with the spoon and observed that it was a fairly full bowl. . . . It was hot when she got it, but she did not sip it with her spoon because it was

hot . . . but stirred it in an up and under motion. She denied that she did this because she was looking for something, but it was rather because she wanted an even distribution of fish and potatoes." "She started to eat it, alternating between the chowder and crackers which were on the table with . . . [some] rolls. She ate about three or four spoonfuls, then stopped. She looked at the spoonfuls as she was eating. She saw equal parts of liquid, potato, and fish as she spooned it into her mouth. She did not see anything unusual about it. After three or four spoonfuls she was aware that something had lodged in her throat because she couldn't swallow and couldn't clear her throat by gulping and she could feel it." This misadventure led to two esophagoscopies at the Massachusetts General Hospital, in the second of which, on April 27, 1959, a fish bone was found and removed. The sequence of events produced injury to the plaintiff which was not insubstantial.

We must decide whether a fish bone lurking in a fish chowder, about the ingredients of which there is no other complaint, constitutes a breach of implied warranty under applicable provisions of the Uniform Commercial Code. . . . As the judge put it in his charge, "Was the fish chowder fit to be eaten and wholesome? . . . [N]obody is claiming that the fish itself wasn't wholesome. . . . But the bone of contention here—I don't mean that for a pun—but was this fish bone a foreign substance that made the fish chowder unwholesome or not fit to be eaten?"

The plaintiff has vigorously reminded us of the high standards imposed by this court where the sale of food is involved . . . and has made reference to cases involving stones in beans . . . and to certain other cases, here and elsewhere, serving to bolster her contention of breach of warranty.

The defendant asserts that here was a native New Englander eating fish chowder in a "quaint" Boston dining place where she had been before; that "[f]ish chowder, as it is served and enjoyed by New Englanders, is a hearty dish, originally designed to satisfy the appetites of our seamen and fishermen"; that "[t]his court knows well that we are not talking of some insipid broth as is customarily served to convalescents." We are asked to rule in such fashion that no chef is forced "to reduce the pieces of fish in the chowder to miniscule size in an effort to ascertain if they contained any pieces of bone. In so ruling," we are told (in the defendant's brief), "the court will not only uphold its reputation for legal knowledge and acumen, but will, as loyal sons of Massachusetts, save our world-renowned fish chowder from degenerating into an insipid broth containing the mere essence of its former stature as a culinary masterpiece." Notwithstanding these passionate entreaties we are bound to examine with detachment the nature of fish chowder and what might happen to it under varying interpretations of the Uniform Commercial Code.

Chowder is an ancient dish preexisting even "the appetites of our seamen and fishermen." It was perhaps the common ancestor of the "more refined cream soups, purees, and bisques." [Berolzheimer, *The American Woman's Cook Book* (Publisher's Guild Inc., New York, 1941), p. 176.] The word *chowder* comes from the French *chaudière*, meaning a "cauldron" or "pot." "In the fishing villages of Brittany . . . 'faire la chaudière' means to supply a cauldron in which is cooked a mess of fish and biscuit with some savoury condiments, a hodge-podge contributed by the fishermen themselves, each of whom in return receives his share of the prepared dish. The Breton fishermen probably carried the custom to Newfoundland, long famous for its chowder, whence it has spread to Nova Scotia, New Brunswick, and New England." [*A New English Dictionary* (Macmillan, 1893), p. 386.] Our literature over the years abounds in references not only to the delights of chowder but also to its manufacture. A namesake of the plaintiff, Daniel Webster, had a recipe of fish chowder which has survived into a number of modern cookbooks*

and in which the removal of fish bones is not mentioned at all. One old time recipe recited in the *New English Dictionary* study defines chowder as "A dish made of fresh fish (esp. cod) or clams, stewed with slices of pork or bacon, onions, and biscuit. 'Cider and champagne are sometimes added.'" A chowder variant, cod "Muddle," was made in Plymouth in the 1890s by taking "a three or four pound codfish, head added. Season with salt and pepper and boil in just enough water to keep from burning. When cooked, add milk and piece of butter." [Atwood, *Receipts for Cooking Fish* (Avery & Doten, Plymouth, 1896), p. 8.] The recitation of these ancient formulae suffices to indicate that in construction of chowders in these parts in other years, worries about fish bones played no role whatsoever. This broad outlook on chowders has persisted in more modern cookbooks. The all-embracing Fannie Farmer states, in a portion of her recipe, fish chowder is made with a "fish skinned, but head and tail left on. Cut off head and tail and remove fish from backbone. Cut fish in 2-inch pieces and set aside. Put head, tail and backbone broken in pieces, in stewpan; add 2 cups cold water and bring slowly to boiling point. . . ." The liquor thus produced from the bones is added to the balance of the chowder. [Farmer, *The Boston Cooking School Cook Book* (Little, Brown, 1937), p. 166.]

Thus, we consider a dish which for many long years, if well made, has been made generally as outlined above. It is not too much to say that a person sitting down in New England to consume a good New England fish chowder embarks on a gustatory adventure which may entail the removal of some fish bones from his bowl as he proceeds. We are not inclined to tamper with age-old recipes by an amendment reflecting the plaintiff's view of the effect of the Uniform Commercial

---

* "Take a cod of ten pounds, well cleaned, leaving on the skin. Cut into pieces one and a half pounds thick, preserving the head whole. Take one and a half pounds of clear, fat salt pork, cut in thin slices. Do the same with twelve potatoes. Take the largest pot you have. Fry out the pork first, then take out the pieces of pork, leaving in the drippings. Add to that three parts of water, a layer of fish, so as to cover the bottom of the pot; next a layer of potatoes, then two tablespoons of salt, 1 teaspoon of pepper, then the pork, another layer of fish, and the remainder of the potatoes. Fill the pot with the

water to cover the ingredients. Put over a good fire. Let the chowder boil twenty-five minutes. When this is done, have a quart of boiling milk ready, and ten hard crackers split and dipped in cold water. Add milk and crackers. Let the whole boil five minutes. The chowder is then ready to be first-rate if you have followed the directions. An onion may be added if you like the flavor." "This chowder," he adds, "is suitable for a large fishing party." [Wolcott, *The Yankee Cook Book* (Coward-McCann, New York, 1939), p. 9.]

Code upon them. We are aware of the heavy body of case law involving foreign substances in food, but we sense a strong distinction between them and those relative to unwholesomeness of the food itself, e.g., tainted mackerel, and a fish bone in a fish chowder. Certain Massachusetts cooks might cavil at the ingredients contained in the chowder in this case in that it lacked the heartening lift of salt pork. In any event, we consider that the joys of life in New England include the ready availability of fresh fish chowder.

GREENO v. CLARK EQUIPMENT COMPANY

237 F. Supp. 427 (Indiana, 1965)

Eschbach, District Judge

This products liability action was commenced by the filing of an original complaint in three counts, federal jurisdiction being based on diverse citizenship. Plaintiff's original three counts were grounded in breach of implied warranty, negligence, and breach of express warranty, respectively. Thereafter, with leave of Court, plaintiff amended his original complaint by the addition of Counts Four and Five. Bared of the usual formalities, plaintiff's additional counts are grounded upon theories of strict liability and wilful and wanton misconduct, respectively. Defendant has filed timely motions to dismiss Counts Four and Five from plaintiff's complaint on the grounds that each fails to state a claim upon which relief can be granted. Addressing first the defendant's motion to dismiss Count Four, the precise question involved has never been presented to Indiana courts, and state guidelines are not easily ascertainable in this rapidly developing field of the law, commonly designated "Products Liability."

Plaintiff, in Count Four, contends essentially that the defendant designed, manufactured, and sold a fork lift truck which was defective. The specific defects allegedly existing are not relevant to the question now before the Court. In Count Four it is alleged that Materials Handling Equipment Corporation, an Indiana corporation not a part in this litigation, leased to Dana Corpora-

tion, plaintiff's employer, a certain fork lift truck, designed, manufactured, and sold by defendant Clark Equipment Company. There is no allegation as to how Materials Handling Equipment Corporation acquired the truck nor any alleged relationship between it and Clark Equipment Company. The fork lift truck in question is alleged to have been sold by defendant in a "defective condition," and that while using it in the normal course of his employment, plaintiff received serious permanent injuries as a proximate result of an industrial accident caused by one or another of the alleged defects. Unlike Count One, based on implied warranty, Count Four contains no allegation of privity of contract or of any other relationship between Clark Equipment Company and Materials Handling Equipment Corporation or between Clark and plaintiff, except that Clark manufactured and plaintiff used the equipment. In his brief, plaintiff contends that Count Four as alleged is sufficient in law to support recovery upon the theory of "Strict Liability" in the field of products liability and as recognized by the *Restatement (Second), Torts* § 402A (approved May 1964). Unquestionably, the allegation of Count Four of plaintiff's complaint meet the standards imposed by the *Restatement* supra. The remaining and more difficult question is whether "Strict Liability," so-called, as understood by this court and explained infra, is properly the law of Indiana. This court now concludes that it is.

While strict liability in certain forms is not a stranger to the law of Indiana, notably in workmen's compensation and as ultra-hazardous activity, . . . it is of recent vintage in the area of products liability. This opinion will consider the theory of strict liability only in context of products liability. When so confined, its least ambiguous definition appears in *Restatement (Second), Torts* § 402A.

Without attempting an exhaustive explanation, it may fairly be said that the liability which this section would impose is hardly more than what exists under implied warranty when stripped of the contract doctrines of privity, disclaimer, requirements of notice of defect, and limitation through inconsistencies with express warranties. . . . The conditions of liability which may not be self-evident in the above text are a "defective condition" at the time the product leaves the seller's control and which causes harm to a user or consumer. A "defective condition" is a condition not contemplated by the consumer/user and which is "unreasonably dangerous" to him or his property, that is, more dangerous than would be contemplated by the ordinary consumer/user with the ordinary knowledge of the community as to its characteristics and uses. . . . Recovery in strict liability is not conditioned on privity of contract, or reliance or notice to the seller of a defect, and the seller cannot disclaim or by contract alter a duty which the law would impose upon him. Nor can inconsistent express warranties dilute the seller's duty to refrain from injecting into the stream of commerce goods in a "defective condition." . . . Neither would contributory negligence constitute a defense, although use different from or more strenuous than that contemplated to be safe by ordinary users/consumers, that is, "misuse," would refute either a defective condition or causation. "Misuse" would include much conduct otherwise labeled contributory negligence and would constitute a defense. Incurring a known and appreciated risk is likewise a defense.

While at one time the relevant law of Indiana generally required privity of contract in product liability cases based on negligence of the manufacturer or seller . . . privity was not required where the product was "imminently dangerous." . . . The concept of "imminently dangerous" was an amorphous one, and even included the undrained pipes of a discontinued heating system which caused extensive water damage to the property of an adjoining tenant when ice burst the pipes. . . .

These Indiana cases represent a trend toward permitting a product user to recover from a remote manufacturer for injuries inflicted by the product's defective condition. . . .

It is generally recognized that implied warranty is more properly a matter of public policy beyond the power of the seller to alter unilaterally with disclaimers and inconsistent express warranties. . . . Where there is implied in law a certain duty to persons not in contract privity, it

seems preposterous that the seller should escape that duty by inserting into a noncontractual relationship a contractual disclaimer of which the remote injured person would be unaware. Even as between parties to a contract, where the law would imply in a sale the reasonable fitness of the product for ordinary purposes, it seems unconscionable that the seller should by disclaimers avoid the duty of selling merchantable products or shift the risk of defect, unless the total circumstances of the transaction indicate the buyer's awareness of defects or acceptance of risk. This warranty imposed by law, irrespective of privity and based on public policy, is more aptly called "strict liability." . . .

Accordingly, defendant's motion to dismiss Count Four is hereby denied.

GLADYS FLIPPO v. MODE O'DAY FROCK SHOPS OF HOLLYWOOD ET AL.

449 S.W.2d (Arkansas, 1970)

Carleton Harris, Chief Justice

This litigation is occasioned by a spider bite. Gladys Flippo, appellant herein, went into a ladies clothing store in Batesville, operated by Rosie Goforth, and known as Mode O'Day Frock Shops of Hollywood. Mrs. Flippo tried on two pairs of pants, or slacks, which were shown to her by Mr. Goforth. The first pair proved to be too small, and according to appellant's evidence, when Mrs. Flippo put on the second pair, she suddenly felt a burning sensation on her thigh; she immediately removed the pants, shook them, and a spider fell to the floor which was then stepped upon. An examination of her thigh revealed a reddened area, which progressively grew worse. Mrs. Flippo was subsequently hospitalized for approximately 30 days. According to her physician, the injury was caused by the bite of a brown recluse spider. Suit for damages was instituted against Mode O'Day Frock Shops and Rosie Goforth, the complaint asserting three grounds for recovery, first that a pair of slacks in a defective condition (by reason of the presence of a poisonous spider) and unreasonably dangerous was sold to appellant; second, that both appellees were guilty of several acts of negligence; and third, that there was an implied warranty that the slacks were fit for the purpose for which they were purchased, though actually not fit, because of the poisonous spider concealed therein. On trial, the court refused requested instructions offered by appellant on theories of implied warranty and strict tort liability, and instructed the jury only on the issue of appellees' alleged negligence as the proximate cause of the injury. The jury returned a verdict for both appellees, and judgment was entered accordingly. From the judgment so entered, appellant brings this appeal, not, however, appealing from the finding of no negligence; instead, the appeal is based entirely upon the court's refusal to submit the case upon implied warranty and strict tort liability theories. . . .

We cannot agree that the law of implied warranty of merchantability is applicable to a case of this nature. The pair of pants itself was fit for the ordinary purposes for which stretch pants are used; there was nothing wrong from a manufacturing standpoint. In fact, the evidence reflects that Mrs. Flippo bought these particular pants after being bitten, and she has worn and laundered them since the accident. There is absolutely no evidence that the goods were defective in any manner. It is, of course, readily apparent that the spider was not a part of the product, and there is no evidence that either the manufacturer or retailer had any control of the spider, or caused it to be in the pants. . . .

Irrespective of whether the spider attached itself to the garment in Kansas City, or in Batesville, it was not a part of the garment. The three cases cited by appellant as authority for the common law implied warranty of merchantability, all deal with a defective product, which is not the situation in the present litigation. Perhaps our position can best be made clear by simply stating that the spider was not a part of the manufactured article, and the injury to Mrs. Flippo was caused by the spider—and not the product. We find no cause of action under either the statute or the common law.

Nor can we agree that the trial court erred in refusing to instruct the jury upon the principles of strict tort liability. . . .

It is at once obvious that the product sold in the instant case was a pair of slacks, and the slacks were not in a defective condition; nor were they unreasonably dangerous; in fact, they were not dangerous at all; still further, the slacks did not cause any physical harm to Mrs. Flippo.

Were we inclined to a more liberal view of the theory of strict tort liability, it would not be applied in this case, for we have no hesitancy in stating that the facts in the instant litigation do not support the submission of the case on the theory. This case was properly submitted upon the issue of negligence, and it would have been improper for the court to have given the instructions sought by appellant.

Affirmed.

PROBLEMS FOR DISCUSSION

1. Excelsior Steel Company sold $9,000 worth of steel to Hardedge Steel Company, which in turn sold the steel to one of its customers. The order did not specify a particular grade of steel. When the customer used the steel, it cracked during a rather ordinary welding process. The steel was returned to Hardedge for a refund, and now Hardedge refuses to pay the remaining balance on its bill from Excelsior, claiming that the steel did not have the commercially usual carbon content of 1010 to 1020. Is Hardedge right in refusing to pay Excelsior? Why?

2. Plaintiff, Hardhat Concrete Company, entered into a contract for the manufacture and sale of concrete slabs to be used in the construction of apartments by defendant, Tilt Construction Company. The price was set at $31,000, $15,000 of which was paid by Tilt. Tilt refuses to pay the remaining $16,000, however, claiming that

the slabs were defective and could only be used after a $2,000 repair job had been done by it. Does Tilt owe the remaining $16,000? Discuss.

3. Carl Craft, owner of a small printshop, was considering the purchasing of a new printing press. He observed one possible model in action at the Reliable, Inc., distributorship and read advertising material on another model, made by Neverfail Corporation. The advertising copy stated what sizes and weights of paper could be printed and at what operating speeds, and it made further claims regarding the inking system and its control.

Reliable's president visited Carl Craft's establishment and recommended the Neverfail model to him. Carl ordered the recommended model, which was delivered to him directly from the factory. It never worked properly, and the angry Carl promptly reported the defects to the manufacturer. He also contacted the dealer who sent an experienced repairer. The press still could not be made to operate properly.

Since Carl had not yet paid any installments on the press to the distributor, the distributor asked him to sign a security agreement which contained in bold capital letters a disclaimer of express warranties and the implied warranty of merchantability. However, the president of the Reliable, Inc., distributorship assured Carl that he would "make that press print and stand behind that 100 percent." So Carl signed the agreement and made several installment payments.

When the press still did not work, Carl purchased a new machine in order to minimize his losses. He had incurred considerable expenses in overtime to his employees, wasted his own time, and lost business. Carl sued for damages. What was the result? Why?

4. Joseph Versatile conducted a profitable hide, fur, and junk business. To branch out, he bought batteries from Louie Loaded, a distributor for the Waterless Battery Company, in order to sell them to retail customers. Each battery carried a warranty promising free replacement of any faulty battery unless it showed signs of abuse.

Joseph received 150 batteries, all of which were allegedly defective and had to be replaced. When he applied for refund, Louis wanted to see the defective batteries in order to make sure that the defect was not due to abuse. Joseph, however, could produce only 30 batteries. He claimed that the other 120 had been junked for $1 each. Joseph sues for a refund. What is the result? Why?

5. August H., a paraplegic, was a passenger in a brand-new sports car. The owner, Judy K., had purchased the vehicle from the authorized dealer several days earlier and was showing her new car to her friends. In an S curve she lost control and the car veered off the road and overturned. Both passengers were injured. August was hospitalized for months, required skin grafts, and had to have a leg amputated. The accident occurred around midnight. The roads were clear, and Judy was driving between 40 and 45 mph.

Just before the accident Judy had noticed that the steering wheel turned hard, with a clicking sound. This had also been noticed by a friend to whom Judy had loaned the car. Shortly after the accident, Judy received a letter from the manufacturer in which she was advised to have the retaining bolts for the steering gear checked. After the accident a mechanic of the dealer came out and tightened some bolts on the steering gear. The car had not yet been examined at that time.

Whom and under what theory may August H. sue? What would be your decision in those suits?

6. John P. was employed by Apex Die Casting Company as a hydraulic press operator. In order to operate the press, two palm buttons, located at the side of the machine far away from the cutting mechanism, had to be pushed. Then a ram would come down, cut the metal, and return to its original position until the buttons were pressed again. After the ram had returned to its original position, the operator would remove the centerpiece of the casting by hand. The control mechanism for this press was located in a box sealed by the manufacturer. The press was rather new, and the box had never been opened.

   After one cutting operation, while John P. was removing the centerpiece, the ram came down without the buttons having been pressed, and cut off his arm. Right after this accident the ram came down by itself for a second time.

   What recourse is open to John P.?

7. Grassland Implement Company, a manufacturer of farm tools, contracted with Acme Tool & Die Company for the manufacture and sale of a machine which was to produce teeth for hayrakes. The machine was delivered and set up at Grassland's place of business in April 1972. However, neither the quality of the rake teeth produced nor the rate of hourly production was as Grassland had expected. The plaintiff made several complaints to Acme Tool & Die, but by November 1973 the machine's performance was still not up to Grassland's standards. Therefore, it brought an action against Acme Tool & Die for breach of warranty. How should the lawyer for Acme Tool & Die argue the case?

8. Mrs. Jones, a welfare mother, brought an action against the manufacturer of charcoal briquettes which she had used in a brazier to heat her bedroom after the gas heat had been cut off. The bag containing the briquettes carried a warning in bold letters: "**CAUTION—FOR INDOOR USE—COOK ONLY IN PROPERLY VENTILATED AREAS.**"

   Mrs. Jones had used the briquettes as a heating fuel for some time when she and her daughters started to feel ill. She called the hospital for an appointment. However, the next morning she found her 11-year-old daughter dead and her 4-year-old daughter severely ill. It was subsequently determined that the death and illness had been caused by the carbon monoxide fumes given off by the briquettes.

   How might the two parties argue, and what would your decision be?

9. Peter G., an experienced auto mechanic, was injured when a ratchet wrench he was using on a repair job slipped and struck him in the face. On his next service call to the auto repair shop, the sales representative for the manufacturer of the wrench was informed of the accident. Upon examination, he found that a gear tooth had been sheared, a defect which might have caused the accident. However, an examiner for the wrench manufacturer also found that grease and debris had built up in the gear housing which should have been removed periodically in order to avoid any slippage in the gear-engaging mechanism. Peter G. now sues the tool company for negligently designing the tool. What arguments could the defense bring up, and how would you decide the case?

10. In 1969 Mary J. was injured while working at a power punch press. Her employer, a die casting company, had bought the press in 1955 through a dealer. The manufacturer no longer existed, but the dealer did. At the time of the injury the press was equipped with dies owned by Chrysler Corporation. Chrysler was not the manufacturer, however, but had purchased them from Mary's employer. Mary J. now sues Chrysler on the theory of negligence and implied warranty. How would you decide this case?

11. Linda Ambers bought a Christmas tree. She paid $2 extra for a tree which, according to John Woodsy, the seller, had been treated with a chemical that would retard the dropping of the needles and act as a fireproofing agent. The tree was used in her father's house, where it caught on fire and damaged the house. Luckily, no one was injured. The fire insurance company paid for the damages to the house, and it is now suing John Woodsy for breach of warranty. To whom does Woodsy's liability extend?

Special Performance and Breach Rules | 18

A rticle 2 of the Uniform Commercial Code covers in some detail the respective performance requirements of the buyer and the seller, and the remedies which are available to each in the event of breach by the other. Many of these points, however, have already been discussed in Part II, Contracts. This chapter thus includes only those major "performance and breach" rules which have not yet been mentioned.

PERFORMANCE REQUIREMENTS OF SELLER AND BUYER

Basic Requirements.   Article 2 generally permits the parties to structure their contract for the sale of goods as they wish and to specify what will or will not be required of each. This general "freedom of contract" is, however, subject to a few qualifying provisions. Any clause of the contract, or the entire contract, is subject to modification if the court finds it to be "unconscionable" under Section 2–302. One of the generally applicable provisions of Article 1 (1–102[3]) also states that a party cannot disclaim his or her basic obligations of "good faith, diligence, reasonableness and care" or effectively agree to "manifestly unreasonable" standards by which the performance of such obligations is to be judged. A court may also rely on its general notions of "public policy" to refuse enforcement of a particularly unfair contract term. Within these very broad limits, the buyer and the seller can pretty much "do their own thing."

The most succinct statement of the parties' obligations is Section 2–301: "The obligation of the seller is to transfer and deliver and that of the buyer is to accept and pay in accordance with the contract." Each party thus has the right to expect the other to perform these minimum obligations in accordance with their specific agreement. When these justifiable expectations are impaired— because one party has delegated his or her performance to another person, or because he or she has repudiated the contract and then tried to reinstate it, or for any other reason—the party having reasonable grounds for "insecurity" may demand in writing that the other party provide him or her with "adequate assurance of due performance of his or her own for which he or she has not already received the reciprocal performance, and if he or she receives no such assurance within a reasonable time not over 30 days, he or she can treat the other party's silence as a repudiation of the whole contract. The basic performance duties of the parties to a contract may also be discharged or suspended by a party's "anticipatory repudiation" (2–610) or by "impracticability" (2–615), as discussed in Chapter 12.

Mishara Construction Co., Inc., v. Transit-Mixed Concrete Corp.
310 N.E.2d 363 (Massachusetts, 1974)

FACTS Mishara was the general contractor on a housing project for the elderly, Rose Manor, which was being built for the Pittsfield Housing Authority. Mishara contracted with Transit to supply all the ready mixed concrete for the project at $13.25 per cubic yard, with deliveries to be made at the times and in the amounts ordered by Mishara. The contract was signed on September 21, 1966, and it was performed satisfactorily until April 1967. In April there was a labor dispute at the jobsite. Work resumed on June 15, but a picket line was maintained until the job was completed in 1969. Transit made only a "very few" deliveries during this period, despite repeated requests by Mishara. After notifying Transit, Mishara met the balance of its concrete requirements elsewhere. It then sued Transit for difference-money damages and for the costs involved in finding the second source. The trial court jury held for Transit.

ISSUE Was the seller's duty discharged by impracticability due to the strike and picket line at the buyer's jobsite?

DECISION Yes, as properly submitted to the jury and determined by it.

REASONS Justice Reardon's opinion concentrated on Mishara's claim that the trial court judge had made errors in failing to instruct the jury that Transit had clearly breached the contract by failing to deliver despite the picket line. Reardon reviewed the difference between *impossibility* and the UCC's term, *impracticability*. He felt that there had been no "radical change" in the basic idea: What was involved was a drastic increase in the difficulty and expense of the contemplated performance, unanticipated by the parties.

"It is, of course, the very essence of contract that it is directed at the elimination of some risks for each party in exchange for others. Each receives the certainty of price, quantity, and time, and assumes the risk of changing market prices, superior opportunity, or added costs. It is implicit in the doctrine of impossibility (and in the companion rule of 'frustration of purpose') that certain risks are so unusual and have such severe consequences that they must have been beyond the scope of the assignment of risks inherent in the contract. . . . To require performance in that case would be to grant the promisee an advantage for which he could not be said to have bargained in making the contract. . . . The question is, given the commercial circumstances in which the parties dealt: Was the contingency which developed one which the parties could reasonably be thought to have foreseen as a real possibility which could affect performance? . . . If it were, performance will be required. If it could not be so considered, performance is excused."

Justice Reardon then rejected Mishara's claim that a labor dispute could never provide such an excuse; it might or it might not. "Much must depend on the facts known to the parties at the time of contracting with respect to the history of and prospects for labor difficulties during the period of performance of the contract, as well as the likely severity of the effect of such disputes on the ability to perform." The determination was thus properly given to the jury in this case.

Delivery and Payment. Unless otherwise agreed, the Code assumes that the seller's duty to deliver the goods and the buyer's duty to pay the price are each conditioned on the other party's tender of the reciprocal performance (2–507; 2–511[1]); this is the doctrine of "concurrent conditions," as also discussed in Chapter 12. The requirements for the seller's tender of delivery of the goods are spelled out in 2–503 (and the parties' contract); generally, tender "requires that the seller put and hold conforming goods at the buyer's disposition and give the buyer any notification reasonably necessary to enable him to take delivery." It is generally assumed that the place for delivery is the seller's place of business, unless there is a specific agreement or trade practice that it should be otherwise (2–308).

The buyer's tender of payment can be made "by any means or in any manner current in the ordinary course of business," including check or credit card. If the seller wants cash, he or she must demand cash and he or she must give the buyer "any extension of time reasonably necessary to procure it" (2–511[2]). If the buyer does pay by check, the payment is conditional, the condition being that the check will be honored by the buyer's bank when it is duly presented (2–511[3]).

Inspection. Unless otherwise agreed, where goods are tendered or delivered or have been identified, the buyer has the right to inspect them before he or she accepts or pays for them (2–513[1]). This inspection must be at a reasonable time and place and in a reasonable manner, and the assumption is that the buyer bears the expenses of such inspection, though he or she can recover against the seller if the goods do not conform to the contract (2–513[2]). Where there is a specific agreement on the place or manner of inspection, the place or manner is presumed to be exclusive, unless compliance becomes impossible. The impossibility of performing the inspection as agreed may or may not discharge the whole contract, depending on how the court views the parties' intent (2–513[4]). As a rule, where the contract requires a COD delivery or payment as soon as shipping documents are presented to the buyer, he or she must pay for the goods prior to inspection (2–513[3]).

When a claim or dispute arises as to whether the goods conform to the contract, either party has the right to inspect, test, and sample goods in the possession of the other party by giving that party reasonable notification, so that the facts can be ascertained and evidence preserved (2–515[a]). Further, the parties may by agreement provide for such an inspection by a third party (who acts as a sort of arbitrator) and may agree that his or her findings shall be binding upon them in any subsequent litigation (2–515[b]).

Buyer's Acceptance of Goods. Under the Code, acceptance of the goods by the buyer occurs when, having had a reasonable opportunity to inspect them, he or she indicates that they do conform to the contract or that he or she will take them in spite of some nonconformity, or when he or she simply fails to effectively reject them (2–606[1][a] and [b]). Any act by the buyer which is inconsistent with the seller's ownership of the goods is likewise an acceptance, but if the act is wrongful as against the seller, it is an acceptance only if it is ratified by the seller (2–606[1][c]). "Acceptance of a part of any commercial unit is acceptance of that entire unit" (2–606[2]).

Once the buyer has accepted the goods, he or she must pay for them at the contract rate (2–607[1]). Further, the burden is now on the buyer to prove any alleged breach with respect to the accepted goods (2–607[4]). The buyer must also prove that he or she notified the seller of the breach within a reasonable time after he or she discovered it or should have discovered it (2–607[3][a]). If the buyer has accepted the goods, it follows logically that he or she can no longer "reject" them. Nor can he or she revoke his or her acceptance where he or she knew of the nonconformity at the time he or she accepted unless he or she did so with the reasonable assumption that the nonconformity would be cured (2–607[2]). Except for the foregoing provisions, acceptance does not prevent the buyer from pursuing any other remedy provided for nonconformity of the goods.

The buyer may revoke or withdraw his or her acceptance of any lot or commercial unit which is subsequently discovered to have a substantial nonconformity if he or she could not reasonably have discovered the defect before acceptance or if he or she was induced to accept the goods by the seller's assurances (2–608[1][b]). The buyer can also revoke an acceptance based on the seller's assurance that a known defect would be cured if the seller has not seasonably cured the defect (2–608[1][a]). The buyer must revoke his or her acceptance within a reasonable time after he or she discovers or should have discovered the defect "and before any substantial change in condition of the goods which is not caused by their own defects" (2–608[2]). Once the buyer has notified the seller of such a proper revocation, he or she has the same rights against the goods as if he or she had rejected them initially.

Lang v. Fleet
165 A.2d 258 (Pennsylvania, 1960)

FACTS   On April 30, 1957, Fleet purchased from Lang an ice-cream freezer and a refrigeration compressor unit, paying only $200 down, though agreeing to pay $860 down and the balance in 18 payments of $78.72 (total sales price of $2,160). Fleet made no further payments. On July 30, 1959, Lang brought suit for replevin, because of Fleet's failure to pay.

Before this, Fleet had disconnected the compressor from the freezer and connected it to an air conditioner. Yet he now alleged that the equipment was defective and was wholly unusable for the purpose intended, and he demanded the return of the down payment, the cost of maintaining the equipment while it was in his possession, and court costs. The trial court decided for Lang.

ISSUE Could Fleet still revoke his acceptance of the goods?

DECISION No. Judgment affirmed.

REASONS The court said that Fleet had waited too long and done too much to the freezer to rescind his acceptance of it.

"In the instant case the defendants exercised dominion over the compressor unit by using it to operate an air conditioner. This is completely inconsistent with the seller's ownership. The seller in this case by entering judgment for the unpaid balance ratified the sale as represented by the installment sales contract. The seller never accepted or agreed to a rescission by the defendants. Therefore, under the cited provisions of the Commercial Code the buyer is deemed to have accepted the goods and is precluded from unilaterally asserting a rescission of the sales contract.

"A recission based on breach of warranty must be made within a reasonable time and cannot be made if the buyer exercises an act of dominion over the goods or permits the goods to be altered or changed while in his exclusive possession.

"We are convinced that there is no valid defense to the plaintiff's claim and, hence, we discharged the defendants' rule to open the judgment."

Buyer's Rejection of Goods. A buyer wishing to reject goods because of their nonconformity must do so within a reasonable time after delivery or tender and must also "seasonally" notify the seller that he or she has done so (2–602[1]). Once the buyer has rejected the goods, any exercise of ownership over them by the buyer is wrongful as against the seller. Further, unless the buyer is entitled to retain possession under 2–711(3), he or she is required to take reasonable care of the seller's rejected goods until the seller has had a reasonable chance to remove them (2–602[2]). Where the buyer is a merchant and the seller does not have an agent or a place of business nearby, the buyer must follow the seller's reasonable instructions with respect to the disposition of the rejected goods or must make reasonable efforts to sell the goods for the seller if the seller does not send such instructions and the goods are perishable or otherwise subject to a rapid decline in value (2–603).

Davis v. *Colonial Mobile Homes*
220 S.E.2d 802 (North Carolina, 1975)

FACTS The plaintiff, Ralph W. Davis, bought a mobile home for $5,359 cash. He alleged a number of serious defects in the unit as a result of negligent delivery (it was hauled a considerable distance on a flat tire) and improper installation on the lot. He had to wait three weeks to inspect the interior because no keys were delivered with the unit. When he did so he found that the doors on the cabinets, the refrigerator, and the

Davis v. Colonial Mobile Homes (continued)

trailer itself would not close properly. There was a large gap on the outside of the trailer, between the paneling and the frame; sections of both the exterior metal and the frame were twisted and bent. After each rain, water would drain from the walls into the trailer for up to three hours, causing the electrical connections to short-circuit. Davis had his attorney demand a replacement or a refund about one month after delivery (about July 3), and he moved out of the trailer in September. After the first trial, Davis was awarded only $900 in damages, but the appellate court ordered a new trial to determine whether Davis had rejected or revoked his acceptance. The second trial court decided that he had rejected, but it awarded Davis only the return of the purchase price. Both parties appealed this second decision.

ISSUE   Did the buyer make an effective rejection? If so, was he entitled to the damages he sustained as well as the return of his purchase price?

DECISION   Yes. Yes. Judgment affirmed as to rejection; remanded for findings on buyer's damages.

REASONS   Judge Morris began with the rule that the buyer is entitled to a reasonable time period in which to inspect goods and to reject them if he finds that they do not conform. The fact that the goods were already paid for did not change this rule. The evidence here clearly showed that Davis was justifiably dissatisfied with the trailer and that the seller was well aware of his complaints, since it made several attempts to fix up the trailer.

"We think the evidence in this case supports a conclusion that plaintiff revoked his acceptance. The fact that plaintiff stayed in the unit after allegedly revoking or rejecting the unit does not alone necessarily vitiate any of the buyer's rights. . . .

"However, any error committed by the District Court in finding a rejection instead of a revocation of acceptance must be deemed harmless in view of our determination that the evidence warrants a finding of revocation. In either case the plaintiff's relief is the same."

Judge Morris said that Davis should get his contract price back, plus all incidental and consequential damages. Finally, Judge Morris rejected the sellers' argument that it should have been permitted further time to fix the trailer and make a retender of it. "By their own testimony, defendants were not able to and did not make a conforming delivery within a 'reasonable time' or within the 'contract time.' Under these circumstances, the plaintiff buyer has no further obligations to purchase or accept any mobile home from defendants, whether the original unit repaired or a replacement."

REMEDIES OF THE SELLER

In General. The basic policy of Article 2 is that the injured party should have available whatever combination of remedies best solves his or her problem. The technical doctrine of election of remedies is officially rejected; the remedies listed for the seller in 2–703 are "essentially cumulative in nature" (Comment 1). "Whether the pursuit of one remedy bars another depends entirely on the facts of the individual case" (Comment 1). Further, the drafters of the Code intended that its remedies of breach "be liberally administered" (Comment 4). The intent of the Code is to put the injured party in the position he or she would have been had the breach not occurred.

Against the Goods.   Where the seller discovers that the buyer is insolvent, he or she may withhold delivery of the goods, unless the buyer is prepared to pay cash, including payment for all goods already delivered under the same contract (2–702[1]). Where the goods are already in transit, the seller can order the bailee to stop delivery if the bailee has not acknowledged the buyer's right to possession and if the buyer has not received a negotiable document of title covering the goods (2–705).

Where the goods have already been delivered on credit to an insolvent buyer, the seller has a very limited right to reclaim them. He or she must demand their return within 10 days after the buyer received them, unless the buyer made a written statement that he or she was solvent within three months prior to the delivery; then the 10-day limitation does not apply. In any case, however, the seller's right of repossession is subject to the rights of buyers in the ordinary course of business or other good faith purchasers and to the rights of lien creditors. Where the seller decides on repossession, this remedy excludes all others (2–702[3]).

In Re Bel Air Carpets, Inc.
452 F.2d 1210 (U.S. Ninth Circuit, 1971)

FACTS   Bel Air, now bankrupt, applied for a line of credit at Mand Carpet Mills in late June or early July 1969. Bel Air submitted a financial statement dated June 30, 1968. Morteza T. Meskin, Bel Air's president, told Mand's credit manager not to worry about the statement's being a year old, that a new one was being prepared, and that it would show Bel Air to be in substantially the same financial condition. The new statement was never given to Mand, but Mand extended credit to Bel Air anyway, after checking with Dun & Bradstreet and with a factor who had sold to Bel Air on credit. Mand's credit manager approved the extension of credit to Bel Air on July 9, 1969, and within five weeks Bel Air had bought $10,365.52 worth of goods on credit. Mand delivered the last shipment, worth $539.08, on August 13. The next day Bel Air declared that it was insolvent, and on September 10 it filed an involuntary bankruptcy petition. Meanwhile, another carpet mill had sued Bel Air in California and had attached almost all of its carpet inventories. Mand filed a third-party claim in that case, and it recovered goods worth $3,871.92, taking delivery on September 19.

ISSUE   Is the unpaid seller permitted to recover these goods under UCC 2–702, even against the buyer's trustee in bankruptcy?

DECISION   Yes. The referee's decision is affirmed.

REASONS   Judge Choy first decided that the key date for establishing Mand's rights was August 19, when it filed its third-party claim in the California lawsuit. That was the date of the "transfer" to Mand, and it was prior to the date of bankruptcy. Normally a seller must make its demand for the return of goods within 10 days after delivery to the buyer. Mand was relying on the exception to that rule which existed where the buyer had made a written misrepresentation of solvency within three months prior to the delivery. The Code section itself said only that the misrepresentation must have been *made* within the prior three months, but the official comment to that section said that the written misrepresentation must have been *dated* within the prior three months. Judge Choy disregarded the official comment.

"The protection afforded the seller would be severely limited by allowing the loophole the Trustee would have us create. Reliance upon a financial statement such as that delivered to Mand takes place on the date the statement is delivered, not on the date in the past on which it was purportedly prepared. . . .

"There would be little doubt that, had the Bankrupt sent Mand the 1968 financial statement with a current cover letter incorporated the enclosed statement, S.2–702(2) would be fully operative. There is no reason for a different result in this case. . . . Whatever the reason behind the arbitrary time requirement, it was not designed to achieve such an anomalous result as the Trustee espouses, which is patently contrary to common sense and to the intent of the Code. Mand was entitled to rescind its contract with the Bankrupt and to retain the entire sum it recovered."

If the buyer breaches before the seller has finished manufacturing the goods, the seller (as long as he or she is exercising "reasonable commercial judgment") has the options of completing the goods and identifying them to the contract, or of selling the unfinished goods for scrap or salvage, or of pursuing any other reasonable alternative (2–704[2]).

For Damages. The general measure of the seller's damages is "difference money," that is, the difference between the contract price and the (lower) market price at the time and place of tender (2–708[1]). Obviously, if another buyer pays more for the goods and the seller had only one item for sale, he or she should not collect any difference-money damages. The seller can also recover any "incidental" damages which he or she sustained because of the buyer's breach, such as additional storage charges on the goods or the cost of an advertisement needed to resell the goods (2–710). Where the buyer's breach means that the seller "loses" that sale, in the sense that he or she has many of the same items for sale (as would be true for a car dealer) and could have sold another one to buyer 2, the seller should collect the profit he or she would have made on that other sale as damages from buyer 1 (2–708[2]).

Chicago Roller Skate Mfg. Co. v. Sokol Mfg. Co.
177 N.W.2d 25 (Nebraska, 1970)

FACTS   Sokol bought a quantity of truck and wheel assemblies from Chicago, for use by Sokol in manufacturing skateboards. Demand for the skateboards fell off, and Sokol returned some of the assemblies to Chicago, without Chicago's consent. Sokol still owed $12,860 on the contract price, and the assemblies could not be resold "as is" since they were not suitable for other uses. After seven months Chicago offered a credit of 70 cents per unit returned, but Sokol still did not respond. Chicago then disassembled, cleaned, and rebuilt the units for use on roller skates, at an expense of $3,540.76. Chicago's lost profits on the canceled sale to Sokol were $2,572. Chicago credited 70 cents per unit against its total damages and sued for the balance, $4,285. Chicago won in the trial court, and Sokol appealed.

ISSUE   Was the seller entitled to recover for both types of damages?

DECISION   Yes. Judgment for Chicago affirmed.

REASONS   Justice Newton first reviewed the UCC's general policies in Sections 1–103, 1–106, 1–203, and 2–718(4). He then said that Chicago could have elected to sue for the entire contract price under 2–709, since the goods were not resalable. Instead, Chicago very kindly attempted to mitigate the losses that Sokol would sustain by converting the goods to another use. "In so doing, plaintiff was evidencing good faith and conforming to the general rule requiring one damaged by another's breach of contract to reduce or mitigate damages."

Justice Newton said that the buyer was not entitled to a credit of the full original contract price of the goods returned, since they had become worthless. Sokol was credited for the reasonable value of the goods, as contemplated by 2–718(4). The correct measure of the damages was found in 2–718(4).

"This section provides that the measure of damages is the profit which the seller would have made from full performance by the buyer, together with any incidental damages resulting from the breach and costs reasonably incurred. Defendant overlooks the provision for allowance of incidental damages and costs incurred. The loss of profits, together with the additional costs or damage sustained by plaintiff, amount to $6,112.76, a sum considerably in excess of that sought and recovered by plaintiff."

For the Contract Price. The seller can sue and collect the full contract price from the buyer only in certain limited situations. He or she can, of course, sue for the full price on any goods which the buyer has accepted. He or she can also get the contract price for conforming goods which have been lost or damaged within a commercially reasonable time after the risk of loss passed to the buyer. Finally, he or she can collect the contract price from the buyer for goods which have been identified to the contract and which cannot be resold at a reasonable price (2–709).

REMEDIES OF THE BUYER

Against the Goods. The buyer's right to specific performance of the contract by the seller has been expanded by the Code. In addition to cases involving "unique" goods such as works of art, this remedy is also available "in other proper circumstances," such as "output and requirements contracts involving a particular or peculiarly available source or market" (2–716[1]). As to any goods which have been identified to the contract, the buyer can sue for possession if he or she is unable to buy similar goods elsewhere or if the goods were shipped under reservation of a security interest and the buyer has made or tendered the required performance (2–716[3]).

In the "extreme hardship" case, where the seller has become insolvent within 10 days after receiving the first installment on the contract price, the buyer has the right to obtain possession of "his [or her]" goods by tendering any unpaid part of the contract price. This is part of the buyer's "special property" in the goods once they have been identified to the contract. If the buyer has made the identification, he or she has this right to possession only if the goods conform to the contract (2–502).

If the buyer is in possession or control of goods which he or she has rightfully rejected because of their nonconformity, he or she has a security interest in them for any payments already made on the price and for all reasonable expenses incurred in inspecting and handling them. The buyer can sell such goods and apply the proceeds to satisfy his or her claim (2–711[3]).

To Cancel. Where the seller has been guilty of a material breach, the buyer has the right to cancel the contract and to recover any payments he or she has already made on the price and any damages he or she has sustained (2–711[1]). On an installment contract the breach is material and justifies cancellation of the whole contract if it "substantially impairs the value of the whole contract" (2–612[3]).

For Damages. If the seller has failed to deliver or the buyer has rightfully rejected or justifiably revoked his or her acceptance, the buyer may obtain substitute goods from another source and sue the seller for difference-money damages. The buyer may also recover any "incidental and consequential damages" (2–715), which are defined as any expenses incurred in inspecting or handling the goods or obtaining substitute goods and any other reasonable expenses incident to the delay ("incidental"), any loss resulting from the buyer's requirements for the goods of which the seller had reason to know and which could not be avoided, and any injury to person or property resulting from breach of warranty (2–712).

As to goods which the buyer has accepted but which are nonconforming, he or she may recover damages for any "loss resulting in the ordinary course of events" from the seller's breach (2–714[1]). For a breach of warranty the buyer may recover damages for the difference between the value of the goods accepted and what the value of the goods would have been if the warranty had been met, "unless special circumstances show proximate damages of a different amount" (2–714[2]).

Limitation of Damages. Liability for consequential damages may be limited by the parties' agreement unless the limitation is "unconscionable." Such a limitation for personal injuries from consumer goods is prima facie unconscionable, but a limitation for commercial losses is not (2–719).

Wilson Trading Corporation v. David Ferguson, Ltd.
244 N.E.2d 685 (New York, 1968)

FACTS   Wilson sold Ferguson a specified quantity of yarn. After the yarn had been delivered, cut, and knit into sweaters, the finished product was washed, and it was then discovered that the color of the yarn had "shaded," rendering the sweaters "unmarketable." The seller sued for the contract price after the defendant had refused payment. The sales contract provided, in pertinent part:

2. No claims relating to excessive moisture content, short weight, count variations, twist, quality, or shade shall be allowed if made after weaving, knitting, or processing, or more than 10 days after receipt of shipment. . . .

4. This instrument constitutes the entire agreement between the parties. . . . It is expressly agreed that no representations or warranties, express or implied, have been or are made by the seller except as stated herein. . . . being limited to the delivery of good merchantable yarn of the description stated herein.

Relying on these contract clauses, the trial court granted summary judgment for the seller. The appellate division affirmed. The plaintiff and the defendant buyer appealed.

ISSUE   Is the time limitation clause effective, so as to prevent the buyer from asserting its defense of unmerchantability?

DECISION   No.

REASONS   Judge Jasen's opinion emphasized the unfairness of this time clause on the facts presented. "The plaintiff does not seriously dispute the fact that its yarn was unmerchantable, but instead, like Special Term, relies upon the failure of defendant to give notice of the breach of warranty within the time limits prescribed by paragraph 2 of the contract. . . . Parties to a contract are given broad latitude within which to fashion their own remedies for breach of contract (Uniform Commercial Code, § 2–316), subd. [4]; §§ 2–718—2–719). Nevertheless, it is clear from the official comments to section 2–719 of the Uniform Commercial Code that it is the very essence of a sales contract that at least minimum adequate remedies be available for its breach. . . .

"It is unnecessary to decide the issue of whether the time limitation is unconscionable on this appeal for section 2–719 (subd. [2]) of the Uniform Commercial Code provides that the general remedy provisions of the code apply when 'circumstances cause an exclusive or limited remedy to fail of its essential purpose.' As explained by the official comments to this section: 'where an apparently fair and reasonable clause because of circumstances fails in its purpose or operates to deprive either party of the substantial value of the bargain, it must give way to the general remedy provisions of this Article.' (Uniform Commercial Code § 2–719, official comment 1.) Here, paragraph 2 of the contract bars all claims for shade and other specified defects made after knitting and processing. Its effect is to eliminate any remedy for shade defects not reasonably discoverable within the time limitation period. It is true that parties may set by agreement any time not manifestly unreasonable whenever the code 'requires any action to be taken within a reasonable time' (Uniform Commercial Code, § 1–104, subd. [1]), but here the time provision eliminates all remedy for defects not discoverable before knitting and processing and section 2–719, (subd. [2]) of the Uniform Commercial Code therefore applies.

"Defendant's affidavits allege that sweaters manufactured from the yarn were rendered unmarketable because of latent shading defects not reasonably discoverable before knitting and processing of the yarn into sweaters. If these factual allegations are established at trial, the limited remedy established by paragraph 2 has failed its 'essential purpose' and the buyer is, in effect, without remedy. The time limitation clause of the contract, therefore, insofar as it applies to defects not reasonably discoverable within the time limits established by the contract, must give way to the general code rule that a buyer has a reasonable time to notify the seller of breach of contract after he discovers or should have discovered the defect. . . .

"Here, the contract expressly creates an unlimited express warranty of merchantability while in a separate clause it purports to indirectly modify the warranty without expressly mentioning the word merchantability. Under these circumstances, the language creating the unlimited express warranty must prevail over the time limitation insofar as the latter modifies the warranty. It follows that the express warranty of merchantability includes latent shading defects, and defendant may claim for such defects not reasonably discoverable within the time limits established by the contract if plaintiff was notified of these defects within a reasonable time after they were or should have been discovered."

CASES FOR DISCUSSION

WILSON v. SCAMPOLI

228 A.2d 848 (District of Columbia, 1967)

Myers, Associate Judge

This is an appeal from an order of the trial court granting rescission of a sales contract for a color television set and directing the return of the purchase price plus interest and costs.

Appellee purchased the set in question on November 4, 1965, paying the total purchase price in cash. The transaction was evidenced by a sales ticket showing the price paid and guaranteeing 90 days' free service and replacement of any defective tube and parts for a period of one year. Two days after the purchase the set was delivered and uncrated, the antennas adjusted and the set plugged into an electrical outlet to "cook out." When the set was turned on, however, it did not function properly, the picture having a reddish tinge. Appellant's delivery man advised the buy-

er's daughter, Mrs. Kolley, that it was not his duty to tune in or adjust the color but that a service representative would shortly call at her house for that purpose. After the departure of the delivery man, Mrs. Kolley unplugged the set and did not use it.*

On November 8, 1965, a service representative arrived, and after spending an hour in an effort to eliminate the red cast from the picture advised Mrs. Kolley that he would have to remove the chassis from the cabinet and take it to the shop as he could not determine the cause of the difficulty from his examination at the house. He also made a written memorandum of his service call, noting that the television "Needs Shop Work (Red Screen)." Mrs. Kolley refused to allow the chassis to be removed, asserting she did not want a "repaired" set but another "brand new" set. Later she demanded the return of the pur-

---

*Appellee, who made his home with Mrs. Kolley, had been hospitalized shortly before delivery of the set. The remaining negotiations were carried on by Mrs. Kolley, acting on behalf of her father.

chase price, although retaining the set. Appellant refused to refund the purchase price, but renewed his offer to adjust, repair, or, if the set could not be made to function properly, to replace it. Ultimately, appellee instituted this suit against appellant seeking a refund of the purchase price. . . .

Appellant does not contest the jurisdiction of the trial court to order rescission in a proper case, but contends the trial judge erred in holding that rescission here was appropriate. He argues that he was always willing to comply with the terms of the sale either by correcting the malfunction by minor repairs or, in the event the set could not be made thereby properly operative, by replacement; that as he was denied the opportunity to try to correct the difficulty, he did not breach the contract of sale or any warranty thereunder, expressed or implied. . . .

A retail dealer would certainly expect and have reasonable grounds to believe that merchandise like color television sets, new and delivered as crated at the factory, would be acceptable as delivered and that, if defective in some way, he would have the right to substitute a conforming tender. The question then resolves itself to whether the dealer may conform his tender by adjustment or minor repair or whether he must conform by substituting brand new merchandise. The problem seems to be one of first impression in other jurisdictions adopting the Uniform Commercial Code as well as in the District of Columbia.

Although the Official Code Comments do not reach this precise issue, there are cases and comments under other provisions of the Code which indicate that under certain circumstances repairs and adjustments are contemplated as remedies under implied warranties. . . .

While these cases provide no mandate to require the buyer to accept patchwork goods or substantially repaired articles in lieu of flawless merchandise, they do indicate that minor repairs or reasonable adjustments are frequently the means by which an imperfect tender may be cured. . . .

Removal of a television chassis for a short period of time in order to determine the cause of color malfunction and ascertain the extent of adjustment or correction needed to effect full operational efficiency presents no great inconvenience to the buyer. In the instant case, appellant's expert witness testified that this was not infrequently necessary with new televisions. Should the set be defective in workmanship or parts, the loss would be upon the manufacturer who warranted it free from mechanical defect. Here the adamant refusal of Mrs. Kolley, acting on behalf of appellee, to allow inspection essential to the determination of the cause of the excessive red tinge to the picture defeated any effort by the seller to provide timely repair or even replacement of the set if the difficulty could not be corrected. The cause of the defect might have been minor and easily adjusted, or it may have been substantial and required replacement by another new set—but the seller was never given an adequate opportunity to make a determination.

We do not hold that appellant has no liability to appellee, but as he was denied access and a reasonable opportunity to repair, appellee has not shown a breach of warranty entitling him either to a brand new set or to rescission. We therefore reverse the judgment of the trial court granting rescission and directing the return of the purchase price of the set.

WOLPERT v. FOSTER

254 N.W.2d 348 (Minnesota, 1977)

Kelly, Justice

Defendants appeal from a judgment of the Hennepin County District Court entitling plaintiff to recover damages arising from a contractual relationship with defendants. We affirm in part and reverse in part.

Plaintiff, Herschel Wolpert, was the sole proprietor of Sales Enterprises for the years in question, 1967 to 1970. The principal business of Sales Enterprises was the sale of fishing equipment to distributors and retail outlets. Defendant Charles R. Foster was the owner of defendant Strike Master, Inc., a concern whose principal business was the manufacture and sale of terminal fishing tackle and ice fishing equipment to wholesalers and major chain stores. Defendant in 1967 was having financial difficulties, and the parties worked out a two-part arrangement to aid him. The arrangement was intended to be temporary only, but no suitable permanent financing was discovered. The first part was a lending agreement, wherein defendant would assign his accounts receivable to plaintiff in exchange for a cash loan equalling an agreed percentage of the amount of the invoice. The second method of providing financial assistance is the focus of this appeal.

Defendant was having difficulty obtaining credit from suppliers. Plaintiff offered to use his cash or credit to purchase merchandise defendant desired; defendant, in turn, agreed to purchase those goods from plaintiff. The contract price was to be plaintiff's cost, plus a markup of 10 percent for domestic and 20 percent for foreign merchandise, unless otherwise agreed. Payment originally was intended to be in cash or merchandise, but plaintiff gradually permitted defendant to make an increasing number of purchases from him on unsecured credit, on a so-called "open account." Plaintiff charged no interest on this account, because the markup charged defendant for the merchandise was in part to cover the cost of money and because the parties did not anticipate that large amounts of credit would be involved.

In 1969, however, the amount of cedit extended to defendant on the open account had grown to $55,000. Plaintiff was also concerned because he discovered defendant had diverted some $32,000 in receipts from him in connection with the first part of the arrangement. Thus, in the fall of 1969, plaintiff advised defendant that if the parties were to continue to do business, plaintiff would charge defendant interest at the rate of 1 percent per month on the unpaid open account balance, commencing in January 1970. No agreement was reached, but defendant continued to deal with plaintiff through July 1970, when defendant arranged alternative financing.

On July 24, 1970, defendant terminated the arrangement. Plaintiff held inventory he had purchased for defendant at a cost of $19,055.08. He offered to sell it en masse to defendant at cost plus markup, but refused to permit defendant to purchase only the most desirable items. When the parties could not agree as to disposition of the inventory, plaintiff undertook to minimize his damages by selling or using it. Some of the inventory plaintiff used as components for his own products; some of it he sold in the regular course of his business or at cost or on a distress sale basis. The inventory consisted of thousands of items, disposed of in a multitude of transactions. By the time of trial, he had reduced the inventory to items that he could not dispose of and that had a cost to him of $4,703.43, and had a contract price to defendant of $5,515.56. As of July 31, 1970, the open account had a principal balance of $2,817.50. By the time of trial, surplus monies received from the assigned account receivables reduced the balance to $12,886.59.

Plaintiff commenced the instant action in May 1971 to recover the principal and interest on the open account and the contract price for the remaining inventory. Sitting without a jury, the trial court found in plaintiff's favor. Defendant appeals from the judgment and challenges the award of interest and of the contract price for the remaining goods.

1. Plaintiff brought this action for the price of the remaining inventory under Minn. St. 336.2–709. . . . Plaintiff holds the remaining goods for delivery to defendant upon payment of the contract price. Defendant concedes the goods have been identified to the contract and does not challenge the reasonableness of plaintiff's efforts to resell the remaining inventory. Instead, defendant contends that plaintiff has failed to adequately credit under § 336.2–709(2) the part of the inventory that plaintiff was able to resell, because those resales did not comport with Minn. St. 336.2–706. It should be noted that plaintiff is not seeking damages with respect to that part of the inventory which has been resold. The trial court found that plaintiff "neither made nor lost any substantial amount of money" on the resales. Our perception of the evidence similarly reveals that the net proceeds from the resales were less than the contract price for those goods.

We find that § 336.2–709 does not incorporate the resale requirements of § 336.2–706. The Uniform Commercial Code makes it clear that a seller's remedies are cumulative. . . . A resale of goods conforming to the requirement of § 336.2–706 entitles a seller to damages measured by the resale price. . . . A resale failing to conform to these requirements may relegate the seller to measurement of his damages based on the market price at the time and place of tender. . . . An action for the price arises in this situation only when reasonable resale efforts do not dispose of the goods. It is a remedy distinct from an action for damages under § 336.2–706 or § 336.2–708, and thus we would hesitate to incorporate the requirements of § 336.2–706 with respect to the goods that have been sold as a prerequisite for maintaining an action under § 336.2–709 for the price of the remaining goods. Minn.St. § 336.2–709 confirms our conclusion. It mandates crediting resale proceeds only of goods still held for the buyer at the time of suit and not of goods amenable to sale by reasonable efforts and for which no action for the price would lie. Minn.St. 336.2–709(2): ". . . The net proceeds of any *such* resale. . . ." (Italics supplied.) Because the trial court found that the plaintiff handled the resold goods in a commercially reasonable manner and because plaintiff's net proceeds from the resale were less than the contract price for the items, no factor appears in the instant case to alter our conclusion.

In sum, plaintiff resold some of the goods identified to the contract but decided not to seek damages with respect to those goods. Instead, he sought to recover the contract price for the goods he could not resell. He has satisfied the requirements of § 336.2–709 and is entitled to the contract price, even though he failed to comply with the requirements § 336.2–706 imposes on an action to recover damages measured by the resale price. Thus, the trial court's judgment in this respect is affirmed, and defendant is entitled to the goods in plaintiff's possession upon payment of the contract price. . . .

[The] trial court erred in awarding plaintiff interest calculated at a 12 percent rate. Plaintiff is entitled to only 6 percent interest on the unpaid balance of the open account from January 1970. But for this modification, and the modification of the judgment to entitle defendant to the remain-

ing goods upon payment of the contract price, the judgment of the trial court is affirmed.

McMILLAN v. MEUSER MATERIAL & EQUIP. CO.

541 S.W.2d 911 (Arkansas, 1976)

Holt, Justice

The trial court, sitting as a jury, found appellant McMillan breached a contract to buy a bulldozer from appellee Meuser and assessed $2,700 as appellee's damages (\$2,595 actual and \$105 incidental). From that judgment comes this appeal.

On December 13, 1973, the parties entered into their agreement. The purchase price, including a bellhousing, was \$9,825, f.o.b. Springdale. Meuser arranged transportation of the bulldozer to Greeley, Colorado, the residence of appellant. On December 24, 1973, McMillan stopped payment on his check, asserting that since the agreed delivery date was December 21, the delivery was past due. Appellee's version is that the delivery date was January 1, 1974. After unsuccessful negotiations between the parties or about two months after the appellant purchaser stopped payment on his check, appellee brought this action. On March 5, 1975, or about 14 months following the alleged breach of the purchase contract, appellee sold the bulldozer for \$7,230 at a private sale. During this 14 month interval, the equipment remained unsheltered, although regularly serviced, on an Arkansas farm, which was its situs when the sale contract was made.

We first consider appellant's assertion that the resale by appellee did not constitute the good faith and commercial reasonableness which is required. . . . Appellee responds that this defense was not properly raised at trial. We must disagree with appellee. Appellee alleged in its complaint that it had made reasonable efforts to resell the bulldozer. The length of time between the alleged breach and the resale were joined in issue by appellee's direct testimony. . . .

We turn now to appellant's contention that the resale by appellee Meuser was not in accordance with the requirements of § 85-2–706. . . .

In order to recover the damages prescribed in subsection (1), subsection (2) requires that every aspect of the resale including the method, manner, time, place, and terms must be commercially reasonable. The purpose of the resale provisions is discussed in Anderson, Uniform Commercial Code 2d § 2–706:19, at p. 385, where it is stated:

. . . the object of the resale is simply to determine exactly the seller's damages. The damages are the difference between the contract price and the market price at the time and place when performance should have been made by the buyer. The object of the resale in such a case is to determine what the market price in fact was. Unless the resale is made at about the time when performance was due it will of slight probative value, especially if the goods are of a kind which fluctuate rapidly in value, to show what the market price actually was at the only time which is legally important.

In Comment 5 following § 85–2–706, the writers make it clear that "what is such a reasonable time depends upon the nature of the goods, the conditions of the market and the other circumstances of the case."

Here, even though we accord a liberal interpretation to the U.C.C. § 85–1–106, which mandates that remedies be so administered, we are of the view that the resale of the bulldozer, in excess of 14 months after the alleged breach, will be of "slight probative value" as an indication of the market price at the time of the breach. Appellee Meuser is in the construction business and "deal[s] in bulldozers." Meuser himself testified that he was "aware of the state of the economy in the bulldozer market" and since the time of the alleged breach in December, 1973, the market for bulldozers had declined due to recession in the construction industry and high fuel prices. As indicated, he testified he made no effort to resell the goods for in excess of a year. . . .

Neither can we agree with appellant's contention that the measure of damages provided by § 85–2–706 on resale of goods after breach by the buyer is not applicable here because of asserted noncompliance by appellee with the notice requirements. . . . Appellee's complaint alleged it had made reasonable efforts to resell the goods. In answer to appellant's interrogatories, before the resale, appellee fully described his efforts to resell the bulldozer. Certainly, it must be said that the appellant received notice of appellee's intention to resell the equipment.

Appellant also claims error in the trial court's finding that cancellation of the contract was unjustified. Apellant asserts his cancellation of the contract was valid under Ark. Stat. Ann. § 85–2–504(Add. 1961). Appellant's argument turns upon a disputed issue of fact as to the actual date of delivery. The appellee produced evidence that the delivery date was January 1, 1974. This was disputed by the appellant whose evidence was to the effect that the delivery date was December 21, 1973. On appeal we are not concerned with determining where the preponderance of the evidence lies, but only whether there was any substantial evidence to support the verdict which, if supported by any substantial evidence, must be affirmed on appeal. . . . In the case at bar, it was for the trial court, sitting as a jury, to resolve the conflicting versions as to the delivery date. There is ample substantial evidence to support the court's finding.

The court's award of $105 for incidental expenses incurred by appellee in servicing the bulldozer during the 14 months from appellant's breach of the contract until appellee sold the equipment is supported by substantial evidence. In fact, appellee's testimony as to the necessity and the beneficial results of the servicing and maintenance of the equipment appears undisputed. As to the resale of the bulldozer, the appellee, admittedly, is in the construction business, sells bulldozers, and was aware of the declining market. As previously indicated, as a matter of law, the long delay in the resale of the bulldozer by the appellee is commercially unreasonable. Consequently, the judgment is affirmed upon the condition that the award of $2,595 for actual damages is offered as a remittitur within the next 17 days. Otherwise, the judgment is reversed and remanded. Affirmed upon condition of remittitur.

PROBLEMS FOR DISCUSSION

1. On November 30, Mr. and Mrs. Farmer purchased three used combines from Harvest, Inc. Their price was $2,200, of which they paid $200 as a down payment, with the remainder due when they picked up the machines at Harvest, Inc.'s place of business. When the Farmers had not picked up the combines by February 20, Harvest returned the down payment to them and sold the three combines to another customer. Harvest's check was not cashed, and the Farmers instituted a suit against Harvest for breach of contract. They also claimed damages amounting to $8,000, since they could have sold the three combines to an interested party for that amount. What is the result? Why?

2. Mildred Mifflin, owner of the Gaiety Shoppe, customarily ordered her inventory from the Baggy Clothing Company, whose salesman, Herb Neet, visited her four times a year. On one occasion she missed Herb's visit. Herb testified that he had telephoned her and that they had agreed "to order the usual." Mildred denied this, adding that at that time she had made numerous complaints to Baggy Clothing Company for keeping her overstocked on some items and short on others, regardless of her actual order. Therefore, she refused to pay a bill for $1,500, part of which covered the disputed telephone order and the rest of which covered overstocked items. Baggy Clothing Company sues Mildred Mifflin for the disputed $1,500. What is the decision? Why?

3. Ralph Red verbally agreed to sell Arthur Adobe a pile of bricks located at Ralph's property for a unit price. Later he made Arthur another offer for building materials located at a second site which Ralph could purchase for $1,000. Arthur removed some materials from both sites and sent Ralph a check for $150, the unit price for the materials he had taken. Ralph refused to take the check, claiming that Arthur must pay for the whole lot, even though he had only removed parts of it so far. Arthur, on the other hand, claimed that he had never agreed to anything but a sale per unit. Who is right? Why?

4. Earthy, a potato grower, made a contract with Fastdeal, a potato broker, in which he promised to sell Fastdeal 25 cwt of potatoes. Soon difficulties arose between the two; Earthy accused Fastdeal of being slow in his payments, and Fastdeal accused Earthy of withholding his shipments. When Fastdeal's payments were still slow several months later, Earthy told Fastdeal in a letter that he considered the contract breached. A few days later, however, the two parties got together, talked things over, and decided to go ahead with the contract. The precise agreement is under dispute, with Earthy claiming that Fastdeal promised to pay from now on within 15 days of each shipment and Fastdeal claiming that he only promised to pay "promptly."

   On at least one occasion thereafter, Fastdeal did not pay within 15 days but Earthy continued to ship his potatoes. A few weeks after that, at a time when Fastdeal had become current in his payments but still owed money on earlier shipments, Earthy notified Fastdeal by letter that he would not deliver any more potatoes. Now the parties are suing each other for breach of contract. Who wins? Why?

5. On September 25, 1972, Robert Durum signed an agreement with Farmers' Co-op for the sale of 27,500 bushels of wheat at $1.93 per bushel. The wheat was to be delivered on or before May 30, 1973, with a possible extension of the delivery time at the buyer's option. Durum claims that he tried to reach Farmers' Co-op a number of times in January, February, and March to arrange for an earlier delivery of his wheat, since he feared that a May delivery might interfere with spring planting. His messages were never returned, and he was put off time and again. Finally, on May

15, he informed the co-op over the phone that the deal was off. He wrote it a letter to this effect, which Farmers' Co-op supposedly never received. In July 1973 Farmers' Co-op called Durum about the wheat and he delivered 21,500 bushels. By that time the price of wheat had climbed to $6.47 and Durum refused to deliver the remaining 6,000 bushels at $1.93. Now Farmers' Co-op sues him for the sum of ($6.47 − $1.93) × 6,000 and Durum countersues it for ($6.47 − $1.93) × 21,500, claiming that his July deliveries had not been made under the old contract, which had been voided on May 15, but were for the July market price. Who wins? Why?

6. Fritz bought a used combine from Novak, a John Deere implement dealer. He made a down payment and promised subsequent installments. The conditional sales contract was assigned to John Deere Company, as was customary under financing agreements. When the combine failed to perform properly despite attempts to fix it, Fritz wanted to return the machine to Novak. He refused to accept it, and Fritz stopped making his payments. Subsequently, the machine was repossessed by John Deere and the manufacturer brought a suit against Fritz on the open account. Fritz filed a counterclaim to rescind the contract. Who wins? Why?

7. Plastic Molding Company contracted with Power-Screw, Inc., for the manufacture of a special stud driver which was to cost $12,000. Delivery of the machine was promised within 12 weeks from receipt of the order and certain samples. The order was received on January 11, and in the acknowledgment Power-Screw stated March 31 as the likely delivery date. The samples were not delivered until February 10. In mid-March, Plastic Molding informed Power-Screw that the studs which were to be used with the new machine had been changed. It was determined that the stud driver required some redesign, at a price of $600. However, the buyer still insisted on the original delivery date. There is no evidence as to whether Power-Screw accepted that date. When the machine was not completed by the beginning of April, Plastic Molding told the manufacturer to stop working on it. The bill for the unfinished machine was refused by the buyer, and Power-Screw then sued Plastic Molding for breach of contract. Who wins? Why?

8. Sweet Tooth Sugar Company supplied 800 bags of sugar to Red Cheek Apple Orchards, which used the sugar in processing frozen diced apples under contract for J. Fussy Company. An inspector for Red Cheek noticed the presence of a contaminant, and Red Cheek returned 68 bags of sugar to Sweet Tooth. They were promptly replaced. Red Cheek used the other 732 bags, even though its inspectors had noticed the presence of some contaminants in them as well.

   When delivering the frozen apples to its customer some months later, Red Cheek was told that they did not measure up to J. Fussy Company's exacting quality standards. Red Cheek had to take them back and later sold them at a great loss. Red Cheek then refused to pay for the defective 732 bags of sugar, and Sweet Tooth sued Red Cheek. Red Cheek brought a countersuit for breach of warranty. What is the decision? Why?

9. On May 29, Gin Mills, Inc., and Boffo entered into a written contract for the sale of 50,000 bushels of no. 2 yellow corn at $2.20 per bushel. Gin Mills specified in the written contract that delivery should be made during October, November, or December of that year, at its option. When Gin Mills requested delivery, Boffo refused on the ground that he had not been able to produce 50,000 bushels that year. Boffo offered to deliver 40,000 bushels if Gin Mills would take that amount in full satisfaction of the contract. Gin Mills refused to accept the partial delivery, covered at $3.02 per bushel, and sued for damages. What is the decision? Why?

Special "Entrusting" and Bulk Sales Rules

Two special situations involving claims by third parties against the goods have arisen frequently enough to require special legal rules. The "title" sections of Article 2 provide the rules for settling disputes which occur because of "defects" in the seller's title to the goods. "Bulk sales" problems are dealt with in Article 6.

SALE BY SELLER WITH VOID OR VOIDABLE TITLE

Defects in Seller's Title.   There are any number of situations where a person has possession of goods which he or she doesn't own or as to which his title is voidable because someone else has the power to rescind a previous sale transaction. What happens when such goods are sold by the person in possession to a good faith purchaser? Which of the two innocent parties should the law protect—the original owner or the good faith purchaser? Since only one of these parties can win the litigation for ownership of the goods, the other party will sustain a loss unless he or she can find and collect against the "middleman." If you lend one of your books to a friend, and he or she sells it along with some of his or her own books, either intentionally or by mistake, you can clearly sue your friend for the value of the book; the more basic question, however, is whether you can get the book back from the buyer, if you can find him.

The Code's basic approach to this sort of problem is to distinguish between a seller who has a "void" title (i.e., no title at all) and a seller whose title to the goods is voidable because of some irregularity in the transaction in which he or she became the owner of the goods. Except for the very special case discussed below, the general rule is that a person with no title passes no title to his or her buyer. Where your watch is lost, stolen, or lent and then sold by the finder, thief, or bailee, you get the watch back from the buyer if you can prove what happened, even if the buyer was acting in good faith. On the other hand, where there was in fact a sales transaction between the original owner and the seller and the original owner intended at that time to make the seller the owner of the goods, a good faith purchaser from the seller keeps the goods, even though the original sale is voidable because of minority, fraud, duress, nonpayment, etc., etc.

Appearance of Authority to Sell. However, where the original owner created a situation in which it appeared to reasonable third parties that his bailee was really the owner of the goods or that his bailee had the power to sell the goods for the owner, a good faith purchaser from the bailee would keep the goods. The main problem in such a case, both before and after the adoption of the Code, has been to determine what actions by the original owner are sufficient to create this "appearance of authority" to sell. The following pre-Code case illustrates this problem.

Zendman v. Harry Winston, Inc.
111 N.E.2d 871 (New York, 1953)

FACTS   On November 28, 1947, Jane Zendman bought a diamond ring for $12,500 at an auction held at the gallery of Brand, Inc., on the boardwalk at Atlantic City, New Jersey.

   The ring had been entrusted to Brand by the defendant, Harry Winston, a diamond merchant located in New York City, under memorandums stating that the goods were for the jeweler's examination only and that title was not to pass until he had made his selection and had notified the defendant of his agreement to pay the stated price. Records disclosed that in the past other goods had been sent and later sold with payment accepted. A judgment in Zendman's favor in the trial court was reversed by the appellate division, and she appealed to the court of appeals.

ISSUE   Did Brand, Inc., have "apparent authority" to sell the diamond ring?

DECISION   Yes. Judgment reversed (for plaintiff).

REASONS   The court first noted that the applicable law in New Jersey (the place of sale) was identical with that of New York, since both had adopted Section 23 of the Uniform Sales Act. Justice Fuld then discussed the policies underlying this "estoppel" rule.

   "Generally, we seek a proper balance between the competing interests of an owner who has entrusted his property to another for purposes other than sale, and of an innocent purchaser who has in good faith bought that property from the latter without notice of the seller's lack of title or authority to sell. In resolving this conflict, the courts have evolved certain principles 'akin to estoppel,' . . . based on the maxim that 'As between two innocent victims of the fraud, the one who made possible the fraud on the other should suffer.' . . .

   "The courts have generally acknowledged that 'The rightful owner may be estopped by his own acts from asserting his title. If he has invested another with the usual evidence of title, or an apparent authority to dispose of it, he will not be allowed to make claim against an innocent purchaser dealing on the faith of such apparent ownership.' . . .

"The trial court was fully justified in holding that defendant was precluded from denying Brand's authority to sell. For more than a month, defendant acquiesced in Brand's public display of the ring unsegregated from other wares properly up for sale. Defendant's officer, Raticoff, knew of the ring's display, and yet no effort was made to inform the public that it was exhibited only to solicit offers and not for immediate sale. Moreover, as noted above, the evidence revealed a regular course of dealing between Brand and Winston regarding jewelry received 'on memorandum,' under which Winston appears to have accepted either Brand's check or money or customers' checks for sales made by Brand, without insisting on compliance with the limitations of the memoranda. Winston was thus responsible for the appearance of a general, unrestricted authority in Brand to sell items received on such memoranda. And, relying on Brand's apparent authority to sell the diamond, plaintiff bid at the auction sale and bought the ring.

"Nor can there be any question that such reliance on plaintiff's part was reasonable, if not, indeed, inevitable. In the eyes of the public, auction galleries exist solely to sell merchandise, and the public thus regards the entrusting of goods to an auction house as tantamount to the entrusting of the power to sell such goods. In the words of Lord Ellenborough, uttered more than a century ago, 'if one send goods to an auction-room, can it be supposed that he sent them thither merely for safe custody?'

"An owner must be fully aware of the potentialities for fraud created when, for purposes of sale, he entrusts merchandise to a retail dealer, regularly engaged in selling such goods, and the dangers are many times multiplied if that dealer happens to be an auctioneer. It ill behooves the owner to complain if he is not permitted to rely upon his private and secret agreement, when he himself has failed to require strict adherence to its terms and has thus become responsible for the dealer's apparent authority to sell."

Entrusting to a Merchant. The Code lists only one situation in which such an "appearance of authority" is conclusively created—an "entrusting" of possession of goods to a merchant who deals in goods of that kind. Entrusting is defined in 2–403(3) as including any delivery of possession or any acquiescence in retention of possession. Where such an entrusting occurs, the merchant has the *power* (not the right) to transfer all rights of the *entruster* to a buyer in the ordinary course of business (BIOC). If you left your watch for repair at a jewelry store that sold watches, or if you bought a new watch at the store but left it there on a layaway plan until you could pay for it, you have given the watch merchant the power to transfer all your rights in the watch to a good faith purchaser (BIOC). The buyer keeps "your" watch; you have to sue the merchant for wrongfully selling your property. Notice, however, that if a thief stole your watch and left it for repair, you could still recover it from a BIOC, since the merchant only had the power to pass whatever title the thief had (none). This section thus goes further than the law ever has in protecting good faith purchasers.

409

Couch v. Cockroft
490 S.W.2d 713 (Tennessee, 1972)

FACTS   Couch, a dealer in new and used cars, sold a new 1967 Cadillac to Sartain, also a dealer in used cars. The related papers of sale were held by Couch and were to be sent to Sartain after Sartain's check cleared. After Couch had delivered the car, but before the check had cleared, Sartain sold the car to Cockroft, a BFP (bona fide purchaser). The check bounced. Couch filed for replevin, regained the Cadillac, and then resold it.

The chancery court held that the seller had no right to replevy the car and that Cockroft was entitled to the value of the automobile from the seller for wrongful replevy. Couch appealed.

ISSUE   Was Cockroft a BIOC (buyer in the ordinary course of business) even though he had not yet received a motor vehicle registration certificate?

DECISION   Yes. Judgment affirmed.

REASONS   After reviewing the facts surrounding the sale and Section 2–403, Judge Matherne got to the main issue:

"The plaintiff insists the defendant Cockroft is not a buyer in the ordinary course of business because he accepted the automobile without the instruments of title as required by the Motor Vehicle Title and Registration law. . . . We do not find a reported Tennessee case on the issue. This Court has, however, repeatedly held a failure to comply with the title and registration laws does not render the sale of an automobile void. . . .

"We therefore conclude the failure of the purchaser to obtain from the seller a certificate of title, or other instrument showing compliance with the Motor Vehicle Title and Registration laws, does not in and of itself deny the purchaser the status of a buyer in ordinary course of business. . . .

"The plaintiff further insists the defendant Cockroft did not act in 'good faith' wherein he had experience as an automobile dealer, but he accepted a new Cadillac automobile from a nonfranchised dealer without receiving the manufacturer's certificate of origin to that vehicle. The evidence reveals Cockroft had about 10 years' experience as a dealer in used and new automobiles. This experience ended, however, about 15 years prior to the trial date of this lawsuit, and prior to the adoption of the Uniform Commercial Code by the General Assembly of the State of Tennessee. The good faith of Cockroft is further challenged on the ground he knew the Cadillac was purchased by Sartain by telephone to fill Cockroft's specific order and therefore Cockroft in good faith would be required to demand complete title papers with the delivery to him of the automobile.

"Under the facts we hold the purchase by Cockroft was not a transaction 'between merchants' as contemplated by T.C.A. § 47–2–104(3), so as to charge Cockroft with 'knowledge of skill of merchants.' Under the facts we hold the defendant Cockroft under no greater burden of exhibiting good faith than applicable to a member of the general public.

"The legislative intent by the enactment of T.C.A. § 47–2–403(2) and (3) was to protect the purchaser of goods entrusted to another who is engaged in the business of selling goods of that kind. We hold the fact Sartain obtained the Cadillac from some source unknown to the defendant Cockroft in order to meet the demand of the defendant for a certain type vehicle did not put the defendant on notice to demand proof the vehicle was clear of liens. Under the facts of this case, all elements of the 'entrustment statutes' were met. The Cadillac in the possession of Sartain was subject to sale the same as any other vehicle on Sartain's lot."

BULK SALES

The Problem Defined. Bulk sales also involve third parties who may have claims against the seller's goods and who wish to assert those claims even though the goods are now in the hands of a good faith purchaser. This problem, however, arises in a different context. The seller here is a merchant "whose principal business is the sale of merchandise from stock, including those who manufacture what they sell" (6–102[3]); this definition excludes farmers, contractors, and service enterprises. The seller does own the goods involved—his inventory—but instead of selling it in the normal course of his business, he is making a "bulk transfer," that is, a single transfer involving a "major part" of his inventory. The problem arises because some sellers want to play "take the money and run"; that is, they sell all their inventory to an innocent buyer, pocket the cash, and leave town without paying off their business creditors. The purpose of prior bulk sales laws and of Article 6 of the Code is to try to protect both the seller's creditors and the buyer by specifying a required procedure for bulk transfers, with the main burden of compliance placed on the bulk seller.

The court in the following case was trying to decide what is the "ordinary course of business."

Sternberg v. *Rubenstein*
305 N.Y. 235 (1953)

FACTS   Three weeks before Christmas 1948, Fink opened a family shoe store in Buffalo, New York. In May he still had $19,000 worth of winter-style shoes. He sold 1,300 pairs for $3,549 to Rubenstein to clear his shelves of off-season shoes as well as to obtain cash to pay his debts and thus obtain credit for the purchase of new summer stock. Fink continued in business for six months after the sale, until the filing of a petition in bankruptcy in November 1949. The plaintiff, the trustee in bankruptcy, acting on behalf of the creditors, sued to hold the defendant, Jack Rubenstein, accountable under the Bulk Sales Act. The trial court held for Rubenstein, but the appellate division reversed. Rubenstein appealed.

ISSUE   Is a retailer's bulk disposition of off-season merchandise "in the ordinary course of business"?

DECISION   Yes. Judgment reversed (for Rubenstein).

REASONS   After reviewing the facts, the majority opinion emphasized the policy and spirit of the Bulk Sales Act.

"In our view, both the design and scope of this section make clear that the words, 'otherwise than in the ordinary course of trade and in the regular prosecution of . . . business,' were meant to exempt the sale of 'off-season' shoes—merchandise rendered 'obsolete' by the passage of time. . . .

"The record here shows that in the business of shoe retailing the sale of 'off-season' wares is no rare and irregular occurrence, but rather an established operating pattern, no attempt to defraud creditors, but rather an inevitable incident to the conduct of business. Shoe styles may vary sharply from season to season and year to year, with the result that last year's 'rage' may clog this season's shelves. As seasons change, a merchant seeks to clear his store, and as rapidly as possible, of shoes still unsold. Larger stores may resort to much publicized 'clearance sales' or operate their own 'special outlet' stores. But the smaller, independent retailer, lacking the means for extensive advertising or a separate store, must, of necessity, rely on dealers specializing in unseasonable obsolete shoes. Thus, as the record reveals, Rubenstein alone regularly dealt with as many as 'several hundred' retailers in 'smaller towns . . . throughout northern and western New York.'

"Such recurring sales, vital as these may be to the operation of the smaller independent retailer, must be regarded, in the words of the statute, as sales made 'in the ordinary course of trade and in the regular prosecution of said business.' Indeed, to subject such transactions to the requirements prescribed by section 44 would tell creditors little more than they already know. They are forewarned, by industry and trade custom, that 'off-season' sales are regular occurrences and, entirely apart from the Bulk Sales Act, they may anticipate usual sales of obsolete leftovers and scrutinize such transactions beforehand. And, if fraud or covert advantage is later unearthed, a creditor may set it aside as a fraudulent conveyance under state law or as a preference or fraudulent conveyance under federal statute.

"In point of fact, to hold that these frequently repeated transactions are controlled by section 44 might, contrary to the aim of the statute, render the creditor's lot more hazardous. Even if a dealer could be found to purchase 'off-season' stock on the terms prescribed by the statute, the prices realized would almost certainly be lower. Small retailers might, therefore, be forced to rely upon markdown sales or below-cost clearances—which, as one expert testified at the trial, 'would' make it 'difficult . . . to sell the same customers other shoes at the list price.' . . . The result, it is easy to see, might well be to curtail the retailer's business and thus endanger prompt payment to his creditors."

Basic Requirements. In most cases the required procedure should be easy enough to follow. The buyer and seller prepare a schedule of the goods to be transferred. The seller furnishes the buyer with a list of the seller's creditors and their addresses; this list must be sworn to by the seller, and the buyer is not liable for any inaccuracies unless he or she actually knows that a creditor's name has been omitted. The buyer is then responsible for notifying each listed creditor, either in person or by registered or certified mail, that the bulk transfer is to occur. This notice must be given at least 10 days before the buyer takes possession of the goods or makes a payment on the price. The notice must also contain the names and business addresses of the seller and the buyer and, if provision has been made for paying off the creditors, the address to which they should send their bills for payment. If no arrangement has been made for paying off the creditors, a "long form" notice must be used, which includes the estimated total of the seller's debts, the description and location of the goods to be transferred, the address where the creditor list and property schedule may be inspected, and the consideration received by the seller for the goods. The buyer is responsible for preserving the schedule and list for six months, for inspection, or he or she can simply file this information with the specified public official.

If these steps have been followed, the buyer owns the goods free and clear of any claims of the seller's unsecured creditors, except in those few states which have adopted optional Section 6–106, which makes the buyer personally responsible for seeing to it that the purchase price is applied to pay off the seller's creditors. If the required steps have not been followed, the seller's creditors can have the bulk goods seized and sold to satisfy their claims if they bring suit within six months after the transfer occurred or, if the transfer was "concealed," within six months after they discover what happened. In any case, a good faith purchaser from the bulk transferee owns the goods free and clear of claims of the original seller's creditors.

The following case illustrates the application of these provisions.

Adrian Tabin Corp. v. Climax Boutique
338 N.Y.S.2d 59 (1972)

FACTS   L.D.J. Dresses, Inc., operated a dress shop in Jamaica, Queens. It was indebted to Tabin, a garment supplier, at the time it sold the business in bulk to Warman, who in turn sold the business to Climax Boutique (of which Warman was a principal).

Prior to the purchase, Warman received an affidavit from the president of L.D.J. stating that the seller was not indebted to anyone and had no creditors. Warman even had a lien search made, which found no outstanding liens. Tabin was not notified of the sale and sued to have it declared void. Tabin won in the trial term.

ISSUE   Does a bulk transferee who receives an affidavit from the bulk seller stating "no creditors" have a duty to try to verify it?

DECISION   No. Judgment reversed (Climax Boutique wins.)

REASONS   Justice Shapiro's opinion emphasized the changes in the UCC's bulk sales section.

"Prior to the adoption of the Uniform Commercial Code in 1962, bulk sales were governed by the provisions of former section 44 of the Personal Property Law. That section was, in many respects, similar to the bulk transfer provisions contained in article 6 of the Uniform Commercial Code. Many of the cases which interpreted section 44 (including those relied upon by the Special Term in this case) held that, in addition to taking the required list of creditors from the seller, the purchasers were under a duty to make careful inquiry as to the possible existence of other creditors. . . .

"In our opinion, such cases are no longer applicable. Subdivision (3) of section 6–104 of the Uniform Commercial Code (which has no counterpart in former section

---

413

44 of the Personal Property Law) provides that 'responsibility for the completeness and accuracy of the list of creditors rests on the transferor, and the transfer is not rendered ineffective by errors or omissions therein unless the transferee is shown to have had knowledge.' Section 1–201 of the Uniform Commercial Code, the general definitions section of that code, provides, in subdivision (25), that 'a person "knows" or has "knowledge" of fact when he has actual knowledge of it.' It is therefore apparent that a bulk sale may not be set aside as to creditors not listed by the seller in the affidavit requested by the purchaser, of whom the purchaser had no actual knowledge. As the purchasers concededly had no actual knowledge of the plaintiff, the possibility of whose existence as a creditor was denied by the seller in an affidavit (the purchasers having no reason to disbelieve the truthfulness of the affidavit), the bulk sale may not be set aside as to the plaintiff.

"We note, in passing, that even were the purchasers under a duty to make careful inquiry, they complied with that responsibility in this case by making a lien search and by making inquiry of the seller's attorney, who represented that all creditors had been paid and that he had seen the checks sent out to them in payment of the seller's obligations."

In those states which have adopted optional Section 6–106, the bulk buyer needs to be much more careful, as may be seen in the following case.

Darby v. *Ewing's Home Furnishings*
278 F. Supp. 917 (Oklahoma, 1967)

FACTS   Darby was the trustee in bankruptcy for Trend House Furniture, Inc. Ewing's, a partnership, bought virtually all of the inventories of Trend House, including damaged merchandise, discontinued styles, and odds and ends, for about 70 to 75 percent of the wholesale invoice cost. Darby sued for the alleged fair market value of the goods, $13,052.50. Ewing's filed a motion to dismiss and a motion for summary judgment, since it claimed it bought the goods for a fair consideration, in good faith, and in an arm's-length transaction.

ISSUE   Can a bona fide purchaser (BFP), buying in a bulk transfer, be held personally liable for the value of the goods if the purchase price is not used to pay off the transferor's creditors?

DECISION   Yes, if UCC 6–106 is in force in the state.

REASONS   Judge Eubanks first indicated that Oklahoma law prior to the UCC would probably have protected a BFP under these circumstances. But he felt that the law had been changed by 6–106. He relied primarily on a textbook by law professors Willier and Hart, which stated: "Section 6–106 makes the transferee *personally liable* to holders of debts owed by the transferor if there is a failure to comply with this provision." (Judge Eubanks' emphasis.)

He then said: "From the foregoing it is abundantly clear that a 'Bulk Sales' transferee who fails to comply . . . renders himself personally liable to creditors of the transferor for the value of the property purchased or for the amount he paid therefor. . . .

"Since defendant makes no contention of compliance . . . but only contends that he paid a fair consideration for the goods at an 'arms-length' transaction, the motion for summary judgment and motion to dismiss are without merit and accordingly are overruled."

Notice that Judge Eubanks said that the transferee could be held liable *either* for the amount he paid for the property *or* for its fair market value.

Exceptions. Certain extraordinary transfers are not subject to the requirements of Article 6. Transfers pursuant to judicial processes or to satisfy certain preexisting obligations and transfers of property which is exempt from creditors' claims can be made without complying with Article 6. (see 6–103). Article 6 also contains two exemptions which were not found in most of the old bulk sales statutes.

These two new exemptions will permit the sale of a business, including its inventories, without the necessity of compliance, where the buyer has an established, solvent business and agrees to assume the seller's debts, or where the buyer is a new enterprise organized to take over and continue the seller's business and the seller receives nothing from the bulk transfer except an interest in the new enterprise which is subordinate to the claims of its creditors. In both cases an unspecified "public notice" must be given, but otherwise these exceptions should provide considerable flexibility in reorganizing an existing business.

CASES FOR DISCUSSION

JEFFERSON v. JONES

408 A.2d 1036 (Maryland, 1979)

Digges, Judge

In the present case, we are called upon to decide an issue arising under the Maryland Uniform Commercial Code that this Court has not before had occasion to consider—whether a purchaser of goods must prove that a third party has a superior or paramount title to those goods in order to substantiate a claim that a seller's warranty of title as established by section 2–312 of the Commercial Law Article, Md. Code (1975), has been breached?

The genesis of this dispute was the sale of a Honda motorcycle by appellee Lawrence V. Jones to appellant Thomas N. Jefferson in July, 1975. At the time of sale, although the appellant received immediate possession of the cycle, the seller retained the title certificate as security for the unpaid portion of the agreed purchase price. Upon the receipt of the balance due, Jones executed an assignment of the certificate to Jefferson, which was then reissued in the new owner's name by the Maryland Motor Vehicle Administration. Approximately two years later, while Jefferson was having the motorcycle repaired at a garage in the District of Columbia, he was asked by the D.C. police, for reasons not apparent in the record, to prove his entitlement to the vehicle. In an effort to establish his ownership,

Jefferson produced his title certificate, but when the identification number listed on it (CB450E1009012) did not correspond to the one embossed on the frame of the vehicle (CB4501010009), the police became suspicious and seized the motorcycle. Following the denial of his demand that possession of the motorcycle be relinquished to him, Jefferson instituted an action in the Superior Court of the District of Columbia against the police in replevin and for conversion. Before trial, the matter was settled and the motorcycle was returned to Jefferson. He then asked Jones to indemnify him for the legal expenses which he had incurred in retrieving the vehicle, and when Jones refused, the appellant filed the present breach of warranty action.

In deciding in favor of the appellee, the District Court (Fisher, J.) made the following factual and legal rulings:

[T]itle to the motorcycle in question is in the plaintiff, . . . it has been in the plaintiff since the day the title was delivered to him and . . . recorded by an Officer of the State Government by the issuance of a registration card and a certificate of title. . . . [T]he history of the title . . . shows that there has been no change, [and that] nobody in authority has made a claim against that title. . . . *There has been no superior or paramount title shown, hence, I feel I have no alternative under the circumstances [but] to grant a judgment in favor of the defendant.* . . . (Emphasis added.)

Jefferson appealed this ruling to the Circuit Court for Prince George's County (Woods, J.), which, with one minor exception, affirmed Judge Fisher's findings of fact and his interpretation of the relevant law. We granted certiorari, and now explain why we disagree with the two earlier court interpretations of section 2–312 in this action as requiring the buyer to prove superior or paramount title in a third party before a breach of the warranty of title is established.

Section 2–312 of the Maryland Uniform Commercial Code sets forth the warranty of title, relevant here, that is inherent in every sale of goods in this State. . . . Of primary concern in this case is the requirement imposed upon the seller by subsection (1)(a) that a good title be rightfully

transferred. In analyzing its meaning, we mention that the term "good title" is not one of art with a fixed significance in the law of property . . . nor is it in any way defined by the provisions of the Commercial Law Article. Consequently, as is so often the case with legislative enactments, we must resort to the principles of statutory construction if we are to understand the obligation which section 2–312 establishes. . . .

Unlike most state statutory enactments, the U.C.C. is accompanied by a useful aid for determining the purpose of its provisions—the official comments of the Code's draftsmen. While these comments are not controlling authority and may not be used to vary the plain language of the statute, . . . they are an excellent place to begin a search for the legislature's intent when it adopted the Code. . . . A perusal of the applicable comments here reveals that the purpose of section 2–312 is to provide for a "buyer's basic needs in respect to a title. . . ." Md. Code (1975), Commercial Law Art., § 2–312, comment 1. A seller accomplishes this objective whenever he transfers to his purchaser "a good, clean title . . . in a rightful manner so that [the buyer] will not be exposed to a lawsuit in order to protect it."

Our holding here, that proof of a superior title is not necessary, does not mean, however, that all claims, no matter how unfounded, which may be made against the buyer's title should result in a breach of the warranty. "Good title" is "usually taken to mean that the title which the seller gives to the buyer is 'free from reasonable doubt, that is, not only a valid title in fact, but [also] one that can again be sold to a reasonable purchaser or mortgaged to a person of reasonable prudence.'" . . . As such, "there is some point at which [a] third party's claim against the goods becomes so attenuated that we should not regard it as an interference against which the seller has warranted." . . . All that a purchaser should expect from a seller of property is that he be protected from colorable claims against his title and not from all claims. Spurious title claims can be made by anyone at any time.

Whether a given claim relating to title is sufficient to establish a breach of the warranty under section 2–312 is a mixed question of law and fact. . . . When analyzing the legal questions presented, a court, in our opinion, may profitably draw upon the principles which this Court has developed over the years for deciding whether title to real property is marketable. . . . The criteria which have developed essentially require a determination of whether the claim is of such a substantial nature that it may reasonably subject the buyer to serious litigation. . . .

When we examine the facts of the case now before us, in light of the legal standard just mentioned, we conclude that, as a matter of law, there exists a warranty of title that has been breached here. An undisputed aspect of possessing good title is that a purchaser be "enable[d] . . . to hold the [property] in peace and, if he wishes to sell it, to be reasonably certain that no flaw will appear to disturb its market value." . . . Whenever the title to personal property is evidenced by a document which is an aid to proving ownership, as is true in the case of motor vehicles, see Md. Code (1977), Transportation Art., § 13–101.1, any substantial defect in that document necessarily creates a reasonable doubt as to that ownership. A certificate of title, which, with limited exceptions, all owners of motor vehicles must have in this State, id. §§ 13–101.1, –102, is prima facie evidence of ownership. . . . To be valid, such a certificate must include, among other things, the vehicle's identification number, . . . and while the owner of the vehicle may prove his title by means other than the certificate, . . . any seller of a motor vehicle who executes, as required by section 13–112(a) of the Transportation Article, an assignment of the vehicle's certificate of title that contains identifying information that is different from that on the vehicle itself, knows or should know that problems concerning the buyer's ownership would arise. Without a valid title certificate, the owner of a vehicle cannot register, drive, or sell it, . . . and if problems do arise, as in this case, the seller is responsible for any damages caused.

McKESSON ROBBINS v. BRUNO'S, INC.

368 So.2d 1 (Alabama, 1979)

Maddox, Justice

Sav-On Drugs operated a drugstore in Clanton, Alabama. It owed First Alabama Bank of Birmingham a substantial debt for a loan of money which was personally guaranteed by its president, Donald R. Dennis. Dennis has obligations to First Alabama other than this guaranty. Except for the personal guarantee, these debts were not secured.

At the request of First Alabama Bank, Sav-On Drugs sold all, or a major portion of its inventory to Bruno's Inc. d/b/a Big B Discount Store for $82,500.00. The proceeds from this sale were by endorsement, paid to the First Alabama Bank in the form received. These proceeds were applied by the bank to the debts due the bank by Sav-On Drugs and to the debts due the bank by Donald R. Dennis.

Prior to the sale of the inventory, Sav-On Drugs did not give Bruno's a list of the names and addresses of its creditors.

Prior to the sale, Bruno's did not cause a notice of the sale to be sent to the creditors of Sav-On Drugs.

At the time of the transfer, McKesson Robbins was a creditor of Sav-On Drugs, having an obligation of $11,260.44 due by account for the sale and purchase of inventory.

The trial judge granted a motion to dismiss by the defendants. The record does not show that the trial judge considered matters outside the motion in dismissing the cause. . . . Plaintiff appealed.

Where there is a bulk transfer of inventory, does the creditor of the transferor have any action against the transferee where the transferee has failed to comply with the provisions of Article 6 of the UCC of Alabama on Bulk Transfers . . . ?

Plaintiff's main argument is that the trial judge considered only the allegations of the complaint, as amended, and the motions to dismiss, and did not consider anything outside the pleadings, and

417

that its complaint, as amended, alleges facts that give rise to the conclusion that the appellees, along with those defendants who were not dismissed as defendants, participated in a scheme, artifice, or device to hinder or delay the appellant in the collection of its debt by a secret conversion of Sav-On Drugs' assets into proceeds that were placed beyond the reach of the ordinary processes of law.

Appellees claim that the complaint was due to be dismissed because it failed to allege fraud, much less with particularity, and that there was a failure to state a claim for relief for damages for violation of the Commercial Code's Bulk Sale requirement.

We reverse and remand.

Rule 8 provides that all pleadings shall be construed as to do substantial justice. We conclude that plaintiff McKesson Robbins' allegations are "more than bare bones pleadings. The meat thereon more than satisfies Rule 8." . . .

On Rehearing

Maddox, Justice

On application of rehearing, First Alabama Bank contends that the *original opinion claims* the bank violated the Bulk Sales Act. The opinion does nothing of the kind. The holding of the original opinion is quite simple.

A complaint which alleges, in substance, that a party or parties "participated in a scheme, artifice, or device to hinder or delay [a creditor] in the collection of a debt," is more than "bare bones pleading." The trial judge was faced with a motion to dismiss which alleges (1) that the complaint fails to state a claim and (2) that the complaint does not allege fraud with particularity. He considered *nothing outside the pleading;* therefore, he should not have dismissed the complaint.

The original opinion deals with a question of law relative to *pleading,* not *liability.* We expressed no opinion on whether the plaintiff could or could not succeed on its complaint, or at what stage the action might be *correctly* terminated, only that the plaintiff, under our new rules of procedure, should not have been thrown out of court by a mere motion to dismiss its complaint.

The original opinion is extended, and the application for rehearing is denied.

JOHNSON v. VINCENT BRASS & ALUMINUM COMPANY

244 Ga. 412 (Georgia, 1979)

Marshall, Justice

G. R. Johnson entered into an employment contract with Mid States Screw & Bolt Company in 1974. Johnson's term of employment extended through December 31, 1976. In the employment contract, Mid States agreed that if Johnson was terminated during the term of the contract for other than specific causes, he would be paid his compensation on a monthly basis for the remaining term of the contract. . . .

On November 21, 1975, Johnson was terminated by Mid States for a reason other than cause. In April of 1976, Johnson filed suit against Mid States in the Civil Court of Richmond County, seeking to recover his monthly compensation from the date of his termination through the month of April 1976.

In March of 1977, Vincent Brass & Aluminum Company contracted to purchase the assets of Mid States. The contract provided that Mid States would remain liable to Johnson in the civil action Johnson was then prosecuting against Mid States in Richmond County. Johnson was not included on the list of creditors which Mid States furnished to Vincent Brass, as required by Code Ann. § 109A–6—104(1)(a). . . . Therefore, Johnson did not receive formal notice, as provided in Code Ann. § 109A–6—107, of the transfer of Mid States' assets to Vincent Brass. However, Johnson was negotiating for possible employment with Vincent Brass at the time of the sale, and Vincent Brass alleged at trial that Johnson had actual knowledge of the impending sale weeks in advance.

On May 16, 1977, Johnson obtained a judgment against Mid States for his unpaid monthly compensation through April of 1976. He then filed another suit against Mid States in the Richmond County Superior Court, seeking to recover the balance due him for compensation from May of 1976 through December of 1976. Johnson's motion for summary judgment in this action was granted. Johnson subsequently filed the present garnishment action against Vincent Brass. Johnson's motion for summary judgment was granted by the trial court. On appeal, the Court of Appeals reversed. We granted certiorari. . . .

Code Ann. §§ 109A–6—105 and 109A–6—107 required that "all the persons shown on the list of creditors furnished by the transferor" and "all other persons who are known to the transferee to hold or assert claims against the transferor (Code Ann. § 109A–6—107[3]) be given rather extensive notice that a bulk transfer is about to be made. The transfer is not rendered ineffective by the omission of creditor(s) from the list of creditors "unless the transferee is shown to have had knowledge." . . . The few cases which have considered the question have held that "knowledge" under UCC § 6–104(3) requires "actual knowledge" under UCC § 1–201(25). . . .

It affirmatively appears from the record that Johnson was a person actually known to Vincent Brass to be asserting a claim against Mid States. Therefore, under Code Ann. § 109–6—107(3), Vincent Brass was required to give Johnson the rather detailed notice of the transfer specified in Code Ann. § 109A–6—107(1), (2). It is undisputed that this was not done. Therefore, the trial court was correct in granting Johnson's motion for summary judgment. Accordingly, the judgment of the Court of Appeals is reversed.

PROBLEMS FOR DISCUSSION

1. Edward Flibinite operated Queen's Furniture Store. He borrowed $20,000 from Arrow Bank to buy additional inventory. Arrow filed a financing statement against Edward's inventory, but by mistake filed it with the local register of deeds rather than with the secretary of state. This mistaken filing meant that Arrow was merely a general unsecured creditor for the amount of the loan. Shortly before declaring bankruptcy, Flibinite sold his entire remaining inventory to Federal Liquidators for $13,000. Flibinite told Federal that there were "no liens of any kind against the inventory" but did not furnish Federal with a written statement to that effect. As a result, Federal did not notify anyone of the bulk sale. Arrow claims against the inventory sold to Federal. What result, and why?

2. Hernando owned a 1977 Lincoln which was insured against theft by Casualty Insurance. It was stolen, and Casualty paid Hernando $8,000 under the terms of the policy. Hernando assigned his vehicle registration certificate (the "title") to Casualty. Meanwhile, the thief had forged a registration certificate and sold the stolen car in another state, where a new registration certificate was issued. Bingo Bank loaned the purchase money to the buyer and had its security interest in the car noted on the new registration certificate. With the help of the FBI, Casualty tracked down the car, repossessed it, and resold it for $5,000. Bingo Bank sues Casualty for the $5,000. What result, and why?

3. Jaybird Corporation, a mass marketing organization, transferred almost all of its assets, including its merchandise inventories, to Marketers, Inc. Prior to the transfer, Deliverance, Inc., had performed delivery services for Jaybird, totalling more than $57,000, and had not been paid. Jaybird is insolvent, and Deliverance wants to assert its claim against Marketers. Marketers argues that it should not be held liable, since its contract with Jaybird indicates that a fair consideration was to be paid for the merchandise. No notice of the transfer was given to Deliverance or any of Jaybird's other creditors. What result, and why?

419

4. Friedrich was interested in trading in his used car for a newer model. He went to Karl, a used-car dealer, to discuss the possibility of a trade-in. Karl said he could allow only $1,500 on the trade-in. Friedrich said he thought the car was worth at least $2,000. Karl told Friedrich to leave the car and said that he would show it to customers and see if anyone would pay $2,000 for it. Karl sold the car for $1,800 but never turned the money over to Friedrich or got Friedrich's specific approval for the sale at that price. Karl is now bankrupt. Friedrich sues to recover his car from .the buyer, Nikolai. What result, and why?

5. Road Machinery Company was a dealer in heavy equipment. It leased a set of truck scales to Ore Company for a period of 24 months, at $600 per month. At the end of the lease, Ore had an option to buy the scales if it wished to do so. Ore never made any lease payments, but instead resold the truck scales to Clyde for $9,000. Prior to buying the scales, Clyde checked the public records and found no financing statements or any other indication that anyone had a claim against them. Road sues Clyde for the return of the scales. What result, and why?

6. JCM Trucking assigned all its assets, including its trucks, accounts receivable, and operating licenses and permits, to Ceso, Inc. Suppliers Company had furnished about $4,500 worth of parts and service to JCM before it went out of business and had not been paid. JCM is bankrupt. No notice of the assignment of assets was given to any of JCM's creditors. Suppliers sues Ceso for the $4,500. What result, and why?

7. Frank Foxx operated a car dealership. Foxx agreed to sell Holmes the business, including its new and used-car and parts and equipment inventories, for $350,000. Foxx was required to furnish a list of all his business creditors. Notices were sent out to these creditors, stating that a bulk sale was to be made and that the deal would be closed on April 1, 1979, and 1202 North Main, Ham Harbor, Michigan. Simon, a creditor of Foxx who had received such a notice, showed up at that address on April 1, but no one there had any information concerning the Foxx-Holmes sale. As it turned out, Foxx and Holmes actually closed the sale several days later, in another city, and Holmes had actually taken possession of the business about a month earlier. Simon seeks to assert his claim against Holmes. What result, and why?

8. Beante Company, holder of an unpaid mortgage against certain real estate of the Outland Printing Company, sued Outland's officers and directors for alleged losses caused to Beante by their negligence mismanagement of Outland. Specifically, Beante's complaint alleged that these officers and directors "did cause or allow Outland to be transferred to Braggart in violation of the Bulk Sales Law." No notices had even been sent out by Braggart or Outland to Outland's creditors. The defendants move for dismissal of the complaint. How should the court rule, and why?

Part V
Secured Transactions

20 | Definition; Creation ("Attachment")

Perhaps no single area is so crucial to the functioning of a modern economy, or so little understood by the "average" participant in the economic game, as the area of secured financing. It is hard to imagine a modern business enterprise functioning effectively on a "cash on the barrelhead" basis; credit is the oil that keeps the economic wheels turning. It is true that some holdouts among the ranks of consumers still insist that they always "pay cash for everything," but for most individuals this is just as much a credit economy as it is for business firms. The great majority of us will have occasion, not just once, but many times, to buy things on credit and to borrow money. Credit buying, borrowing, and financing is the name of modern economic game, and that's what "secured transactions" are all about.

This chapter and the next are intended to convey to you the basic concepts and problems involved, and to give you some idea of what you need to do to protect your rights, either as an individual or as a businessperson.

The following are hypothetical examples which illustrate the range of transactions covered by Article 9 of the Uniform Commercial Code:

1. Carole Consumer wants to buy a new car on credit. Whether she arranges her own financing at her bank or credit union or signs a time payment contract which her car dealer sells to a bank or finance company, this is a "secured transaction" if the new car is used as collateral to secure payment of the balance of the purchase price.
2. Dan Debtor needs to borrow $1,500. His bank (or credit union, or finance company) will not make the loan on Dan's signature alone, but requires collateral. Dan owns an expensive stereo set and a refrigerator-freezer, which are both paid for and which his bank accepts as sufficient collateral. This is a "secured transaction."
3. Big Bennie's Appliance Store orders a shipment of new TVs on credit. This is a "secured transaction" if the credit seller (manufacturer or wholesaler) wants to use the TVs as collateral for the unpaid contract price. Alternatively, Bennie could borrow the contract price from a bank or finance company and use the TVs as collateral for the loan. Either way, since the

creditor (the "secured party") wants to use the TVs as collateral, this is a "secured transaction."

4. Mr. Shatturglas (the home improvement king) needs to borrow $50,000 for added working capital. His bank (or finance company) will not lend him the money without collateral. His only available asset is his accounts receivable—the amounts due him for work performed. Whether Shatturglas merely pledges his accounts to the bank or sells the accounts outright for cash, this is a "secured transaction."

5. Freddy Farmer leases a new tractor from an equipment rental company for two years at $300 per month. At the end of the two-year lease term, Freddy has the option of buying the tractor for an additional $300. This is a "secured transaction."

SECURITY AND PRE-CODE LAW

Creditor's Need for Security

Creditors as a group are notoriously unwanted, unloved, misunderstood, and *insecure*. A creditor is someone who has permitted the other party with whom he or she has dealt to receive his or her goods, services, or other value without its having been fully paid for by return value. This other party (the debtor) has been permitted to enjoy the benefits of the transaction but has not yet returned the full value which he or she promised to the creditor. The unsecured creditor thus has only the debtor's word that he or she will fulfill his or her promise, subject to all the human and economic infirmities which may come "twixt the cup and the lip."

In many personal business situations the debtor's word may be good enough. The debtor's financial standing may be such that there is little risk of nonpayment. In many other situations the creditor has good reason to feel insecure, particularly since in the event of bankruptcy he or she will stand in a group at the end of a long line of preferred claims.

Types of Security, or Collateral

The creditor seeking the warm feeling of "security" may use any one of the three basic types of "collateral" to try to ensure the payment of the debt. He or she may require a second person to back up the debtor by also agreeing to pay the debt (a "surety") or by agreeing to pay the debt if the debtor does not (a "guarantor"). The parties may agree that the creditor will have certain rights against the piece of real estate if the debtor defaults. Finally, the parties may agree that the creditor will have certain rights against an item or items of personal property as collateral if the debtor defaults on his or her obligation. It is with this third situation that we are concerned here.

Personal Property as Collateral in Pre-Code Law

Pre-Code law confronted our creditor with a bewildering array of personal property security devices—some based on ancient common-law ideas, some statutory. Typically, different filing systems were required for the different devices and there were other conflicting provisions. Also, certain devices could be used only for certain kinds of transactions and were unavailable for other kinds of transactions.

The effects of legal technicalities under such a hodgepodge nonsystem is illustrated by the case of *Hughbanks* v. *Gourley*. A farmer bought a tractor, giving a down payment and promising the balance in installments. A finance company paid the seller in full and was to receive the farmer's monthly payments. The arrangement was described as a conditional sale and filed accordingly. When a different judgment creditor of the farmer seized the tractor, the court held that the finance company did not have a valid prior claim because the transaction was "really" a chattel mortgage, not a conditional sale, and the filing was therefore ineffective to perfect the interest as a chattel mortgage interest.

SECURED TRANSACTIONS, ARTICLE 9, UNIFORM COMMERCIAL CODE

Purpose, Policy, and General Characteristics

The basic objectives of Article 9 in the field of personal property secured financing are uniformity, unity, and simplicity. Lawyers and nonlawyers struggling with the new Code concepts and terminology may wonder whether the third objective has really been advanced very far, but it is clear that the first two have. The Code is now in force, with only relatively minor variations, in all U.S. jurisdictions except Louisiana, thus ending the pre-Code jungle of drastically conflicting state laws and the attendant conflict-of-laws problems. And even though it was necessary to make distinctions in Article 9 and to deal with different security situations and problems in different ways, such differences were placed within the context of an overall scheme of security law and their nature and effects were carefully calculated.

Being practical persons concerned with real problems, the drafters of Article 9 were also concerned with the marketplace effects of their efforts. They make this evident in the official "Uniform Code Comment" to Section 9–101:

The aim of this Article is to provide a simple and unified structure within which the immense variety of present-day secured financing transaction can go forward with less cost and with greater certainty.

. . . Despite the statutory simplification a greater degree of flexibility in the financing transaction is allowed than is possible under existing law.

Thus the Code is also intended to be responsive to the needs of the marketplace for swift, sure, and cheap methods of secured financing. Needless complexities and formalities are breeders of uncertainty and litigation, which inevitably increase costs, to the detriment of both businesses and consumers. Stated most succinctly, Article 9 is trying to provide a system that works better for all concerned.

It should be noted at the outset, particularly for the nonlawyer, that Article 9, while "comprehensive" in intent and organization, does not embrace all the law dealing with interests in personal property. It is, after all, part of the Code;

all the "General Provisions" of Article 1 apply to a particular transaction, and other parts of the Code may also be involved. For example, if the secured transaction involves a credit sale of goods, the warranty sections and other parts of Article 2 may be relevant. The most important single piece of non-Code law applicable to financing transactions is the U.S. Bankruptcy Act (U.S. Code, Title 11); one of the main contenders that a secured creditor is trying to defeat is the trustee in bankruptcy, who is seeking the debtor's assets for pro rata distribution to all of the debtor's creditors. Problems as to priority of claims between the secured creditor and persons such as a garage operator who is given a statutory lien also require reference to sources outside the Code. A secured transaction involving a motor vehicle will probably require reference to the state's motor vehicle code. And so on. Moreover, in some areas the coverage of the Code will depend on prior state law (e.g., the definition of a "fixture") and in other areas the Code's applicability is unclear (e.g., mobile homes).

Finally, some kinds of transactions are specifically excluded from Article 9's coverage (see below). In sum, while Article 9 goes further than the law ever has in providing "unity" in personal property security law, it is still necessary to be aware of other applicable Code and non-Code law outside Article 9.

Like the Code generally, Article 9 is characterized by a considerable degree of "freedom of contract." Some sections contain rules which are explicitly made subject to a different agreement by the parties, usually with the words *unless otherwise agreed* (see, e.g., 9–207[2]). A few sections specifically state that they cannot be varied by the parties (see, e.g., 9–501[3]). But the bulk of the Article 9 sections contain no specific statement as to whether the parties may, by agreement, change or modify the rules the sections contain. In light of the Code's general commonsense approach and its downgrading of legal technicalities, it would seem that the parties would be given considerable latitude to "do their thing" in their own agreement, unless otherwise specified, subject only to the requirements of good faith, reasonableness, diligence, and care (the "Four Horsemen" of 1–102[3]) and to the idea of unconscionability expressed in 2–302.

Seen in outline form, the organizational scheme of Article 9 is almost deceptively simple; in terms of actual content, only Article 2 on sales of goods is longer. Article 9 consists of five parts:

1. Short Title, Applicability and Definitions.
2. Validity of Security Agreement and Rights of Parties Thereto.
3. Rights of Third Parties; Perfected and Unperfected Security Interests; Rules of Priority.
4. Filing.
5. Default.

This pattern of Article 9 is thus based on a practical, step-by-step, problem-solving approach in dealing with a secured transaction. The first question we must answer is whether Article 9 applies to the transaction; the answer will be based on the 9–100 sections in Part 1 and on the general definitions contained in 1–201. Our next problem is to create a security interest in the collateral which will be effective as between the immediate parties to the transaction;

here we use the 9–200 sections. Our next job is to perfect the security interest so as to try to maximize our rights against third parties; here we need to consult the 9–300s and 9–400s. Where there are conflicting claims against the collateral, we need to determine the relative priorities of these claims; for this we will use the 9–300s. And finally, in the event of a default by the debtor, we need to know what we can or must do to enforce our security interest against the collateral; these procedures are outlined in the 9–500 sections. We now proceed to consider each of these matters in greater detail.

Applicability and Definitions

Transactions Covered; Transactions Excluded. The coverage intended by the drafters of Article 9 is very broad indeed. Coverage is extended by 9–102(1):

(a) to any transaction (regardless of its form) which is intended to create a security interest in personal property or fixtures including goods, documents, instruments, general intangibles, chattel paper, accounts or contract rights; and also

(b) to any sale of accounts, contract rights or chattel paper.

In 9–102(2) the drafters reiterate their intent to cover all security interests created by contract," including pledge, assignment, chattel mortgage, chattel trust, factor's lien, equipment trust, conditional sale, trust receipt, other lien or title retention contract and lease or consignment intended as security." The comment states that this listing of the old pre-Code security devices is illustrative only; any contractual arrangement, new or old, which is intended to create a security interest in personal property is included.

Since in many cases Article 9's applicability is made dependent on the intent of the parties to the transaction, litigation frequently arises as to what the parties did intend. A third-party claimant will usually raise the question that the parties' arrangement is not effective as against him because it was really "intended" as a secured transaction and it was not properly filed as such. The "lease" and "consignment" cases are particularly troublesome. The problem arose so often that a special new section on consignment was added by the 1972 amendments. In general, this section requires the consignor to give the same kind of notice to other inventory financers as if he were selling on credit rather than consigning.

In 1–201(37) the code also provides some guidance for the courts as to when "leases" are intended as security devices:

Whether a lease is intended as security is to be determined by the facts of each case; however, (a) the inclusion of an option to purchase does not of itself make the lease one intended for security, and (b) an agreement that upon compliance with the terms of the lease the lessee shall become or has the option to become the owner of the property for no additional consideration or for a nominal consideration does make the lease one intended for security.

The court had occasion to apply this definition in *Wheatland*, where the "lease" had not been filed as a secured transaction and where a third-party claimant was involved. The court said that the lease provision which required the lessee to make a minimum additional payment of about 25 percent of the total lease price of the goods in order to become the owner did not indicate a "nominal" consideration. Therefore, the lease was really just a lease, not one intended as security, and it did not have to be filed in order to be effective against third parties, so the lessor won. (*In re Wheatland Electric Products Co.*, 237 F. Supp. 820 [Pennsylvania, 1964].) The *James Talcott* case is another example of this continuing definitional problem.

Having made such brave claims for the comprehensiveness of Article 9's coverage, we must now consider the lengthy list of specific exclusions (*a* through *k*) which the Code enumerates in 9–104. Generally, these exclusions refer to liens and transactions which are outside the scope of normal financing arrangements. For example, landlords' liens, wage assignments, and transfers of insurance claims, tort claims, and bank deposits are among the exclusions. Also excluded are security interests that are subject to a supervening national statute, such as the Ship Mortgage Act of 1920. The general theme underlying these exclusions is to omit Code coverage for transactions which are not normally used in commercial situations, particularly transactions which are already adequately covered under existing law. Financing based on railway equipment trusts, formerly exempted from Article 9 coverage, are covered in the 1972 amendments.

Conflict-of-Law Rules. Section 9–103 lays down some basic rules for dealing with multistate transactions in three situations which caused problems under prior law. The validity and perfection of security interests against accounts and contract rights is to be determined according to the law of the state where the debtor keeps his office records concerning them (9–103[1]). Similarly, the law of the State where the debtor has his principal place of business governs security interests in mobile equipment and general intangibles (9–103[2]). Where personal property of other kinds already subject to a security interest is brought into a Code state, then its validity is to be determined by the law of the state where the property was located when the security interest attached. If such an interest was already perfected when the property was brought into the state, it remains perfected in the new state for four months, within which time it may also be perfected in that state (9–103[3]). Where a certificate of title is issued on property under a state statute which requires notation on such a certificate in order to perfect a security interest, then perfection is governed by the law of the state which issued the certificate (9–103[4]).

Although the adoption of the Code in all jurisdictions except Louisiana has had the effect of substantially minimizing the areas of interstate conflict, these 9–103 rules retain considerable significance. One still needs to know where to file in order to perfect a security interest, whether to have a notation made on a certificate of title, and what to do to protect the interest where the debtor will be using the collateral in more than one state. Moreover, some significant changes have been made by the 1972 amendments, which have not yet been adopted by all states.

Definitions. To avoid as many ambiguities and differences in interpretation as possible, the drafters of the Code provided a set of definitions, some found in 1–201 and generally applicable throughout the Code and some contained in each article. For secured transactions the drafters felt it desirable to use new terminology which would not be encumbered and encrusted with residues from pre-Code law. The *secured party* (lender, credit seller) and the *debtor* enter into a contract (the *security agreement*) which provides that the secured party shall have a *security interest* in the described *collateral*. This is a *secured transaction* (see 9–105).

Collateral is classified generally into 10 categories. The definitions used are basically functional definitions, based on the nature of the item and/or the use to which it is being put by the debtor at the time the security interest attaches to it. The significance of these categories stems from the different treatment given the different types of collateral. Such differences are observable:

1. In the available methods of perfecting the security interest.
2. In the place of filing and the necessity therefor.
3. In the priority of claims against the collateral.
4. In determining the rights of buyers from the debtor.
5. In the respective rights and remedies of the parties on default.

Section 9–109 recognizes four classes of "goods":

(1) "consumer goods" if they are used or bought for use primarily for personal, family or household purposes;
(2) "equipment" if they are used or bought for use primarily in business (including farming or a profession) or by a debtor who is a non-profit organization or a governmental subdivision or agency or if the goods are not included in the definitions of inventory, farm products or consumer goods;
(3) "farm products" if they are crops or livestock or supplies used or produced in farming operations or if they are products of crops or livestock in their unmanufactured states . . . , and if they are in the possession of a debtor engaged in . . . farming operations . . . ;
(4) "inventory" if they are held by a person who holds them for sale or lease or to be furnished under contracts of service or if he has so furnished them, or if they are raw materials, work in process or materials used or consumed in a business. . . .

The comment to this section makes clear that these categories are mutually exclusive. While the same goods can fall into different categories at different times, "the same property cannot at the same time and as to the same person be both equipment and inventory, for example." "Equipment" is the residuary category; if the goods do not fit one of the other definitions, they are equipment. (What about a Modigliani painting in the hands of a museum?)

The significance of these differences is illustrated by *In re Midas Stamp & Coin Co.*, 264 F. Supp. 193 (Missouri, 1967). The bank which had lent money to Midas was holding a large batch of the coins which Midas kept for sale to its customers. If these coins are defined as "inventory," then the lending bank had a security interest in them which was effectively perfected against Midas' trustee in bankruptcy by the bank's possession of them. If these coins were defined as money (presumably a "general intangible"), then the only effective method of perfecting the bank's security interest would have been by filing (which the bank hadn't done). The court determined that inasmuch as the coins were goods held by the debtor for sale to others they were inventory, and thus the bank won.

The *Nicolosi* case is another illustration of the differences in legal results that flow from these differences in the categorization of the collateral.

In Re Nicolosi
4 UCC Rptr. 111 (U.S. District Court, Southern District Ohio, 1966)

FACTS   Nicolosi bought a diamond engagement ring for his fiancée for $1,237.35 from Rike-Kumler Company. He executed a purchase-money security agreement for the unpaid contract price, with the ring as collateral. Rike-Kumler did not file a financing statement. Nicolosi gave the ring to his fiancée prior to his bankruptcy. After he was declared bankrupt, she called off the engagement and gave the ring to the trustee. The trustee wanted to sell the ring for the benefit of all of Nicolosi's creditors; Rike-Kumler claimed priority as a secured party.

ISSUE   Was Rike-Kumler's security interest automatically perfected against the ring so as to give priority against the trustee in bankruptcy?

DECISION   Yes. Rike-Kumler takes priority.

REASONS   The court first considered whether the ring was indeed "consumer goods." Apparently the question was raised because Nicolosi did not buy the ring to wear himself. It was purchased, however, for his own "purposes," that is, as a gift to his fiancée. The court also noted that "by a process of exclusion," a diamond engagement ring (as to the debtor Nicolosi) could not be defined as "equipment," "farm products," or "inventory." The court then felt it necessary to consider whether the trustee had succeeded to the fiancée's special status as another consumer who had "bought" the goods in good faith.

"Another problem is implicit, although not covered by the briefs.

"By the foregoing summary analysis, it is apparent that the diamond ring, when the interest of the bankrupt attached, was consumer goods since it could have been no other class of goods. Unless the fiancée had a special status under the code provision protecting a bona fide buyer, without knowledge, for value, of consumer goods, the failure to file a financing statement is not crucial. No evidence has been adduced on the scienter question.

"Is a promise, as valid contractual consideration, included under the term 'value'? In other words, was the ring given to his betrothed in consideration of marriage (promise for promise)? If so, and 'value' has been given, the transferee is a 'buyer' under traditional concepts. . . .

"The Uniform Commercial Code definition of 'value' . . . very definitely covers a promise for a promise. The definition reads that 'a person gives value for rights if he acquires them . . . (4) generally, in return for any consideration sufficient to support a simple contract.'

"It would seem unrealistic, nevertheless, to apply contract law concepts historically developed into the law of marriage relations in the context of new concepts developed for uniform commercial practices. They are not, in reality, the same juristic manifold. The purpose of uniformity of the code should not be defeated by the obsessions of the code drafters to be all inclusive for secured creditors.

"Even if the trustee, in behalf of the unsecured creditors, would feel inclined to insert love, romance, and morals into commercial law, he is appearing in the wrong era, and possibly in the wrong court."

Section 9–106 defines three kinds of intangible property which may serve as collateral: *account, contract right,* and *general intangible.*

"Account" means any right to payment for goods sold or leased or for services rendered which is not evidenced by an instrument or chattel paper. "Contract right" means any right to payment under a contract not yet earned by performance and not evidenced by an instrument or chattel paper. "General intangibles" means any personal property (including things in action) other than goods, accounts, contract rights, chattel paper, documents and instruments.

The distinction between an account and a contract right has been eliminated by the 1972 amendments.

The last three general types of collateral under Article 9 are also "intangible," but they relate to rights which are embodied in pieces of paper which are physically transferred from party to party as the rights they represent are sold, pledged, or mortgaged. In other words, these pieces of paper are used as a convenient way of handling any transfer of these intangible rights. These three categories are "documents," "instruments," and "chattel paper." "Document" means a document of title, defined in 1–201(15) as including bills of lading, warehouse receipts, and the like, covering goods in the possession of a bailee and giving the possessor of the document the right to dispose of it and of the goods it represents. "Instrument" means a negotiable instrument as defined in 3–104 (notes, drafts, checks, and certificates of deposit), or an investment security as defined in 8–102 (stocks and bonds), or any other similar writing (9–105[1][g]). The "chattel paper" definition is new (9–105[1][b]).

"Chattel paper" means a writing or writings which evidence both a monetary obligation and a security interest in or lease of specific goods.

Chattel paper is thus the retail installment contract you sign when you buy your new car; you promise to pay the balance of the contract price in easy monthly installments, and the seller (or his or her financing agency) reserves a security interest in the goods in the event that you default. This piece of paper has value to the car dealer; he or she can sell it to a financing agency, or use it as collateral for his or her own loan.

Article 9 also singles out certain specific types of collateral for special treatment under some of the provisions to be discussed below. Motor vehicles, fixtures, and the proceeds derived from the sale of collateral are examples of collateral to which such special treatment is applied.

Sufficiency of Description of Collateral. Both the immediate parties to the secured transaction and third parties need to know the identity of the collateral which it covers. Thus both the security agreement itself (9–203[1][b]) and any financing statement which is to be publicly filed (9–402[1]) require a description of the collateral. Once again, the drafters of Article 9 clearly express their intent that this requirement should not become encumbered with extreme technicalities and legalisms. Section 9–110 says:

For the purpose of this Article any description of personal property or real estate is sufficient whether or not it is specific if it reasonably identifies what is described.

The courts seem, in general, to be accepting this "reasonableness" approach. In the *Drane* case the court accepted the validity of a description of consumer goods collateral which read: "1–2 piece living room suite, wine; 1–5 piece chrome dinette set, yellow; 1–3 piece panel bedroom suite, lime oak, mattress and springs." The court felt that such a description was sufficiently precise and definite where the debtor was a consumer and where it was very unlikely that there would be any ambiguity about which pieces of furniture in the debtor's house were being described. (*In re Drane*, 202 F. Supp. 221 [Kentucky, 1962].) One of the issues present in the *Fort Pitt Packaging* case was whether a description of the collateral as (in part) "all present and future accounts receivable submitted" was legally sufficient. The court ruled that it was: the description did "reasonably identify" the thing described. Note also the discussion of this issue in the *National Cash Register* and *James Talcott* cases in Chapter 21.

The *Waychus* case, involving "farm products," provides another illustration of the "reasonableness" approach of the Code.

First State Bank of Nora Springs v. Waychus
183 N.W.2d 728 (Iowa, 1971)

FACTS From time to time during 1968 Waychus had borrowed money from the bank and had executed promissory notes and security agreements. A financing statement had been filed on October 17, 1968, with the recorder of Cerro Gordo County. The financing statement identified the collateral as "All Farm Machinery, All Brood Sows & the increase, All Crops, feed and roughage." The financing statement also contained a real estate description of land located in Floyd County, whereas Waychus in fact resided in Cerro Gordo County.

Johnson, who had no actual knowledge of the bank's interest, bought hogs from Waychus. The trial court held that Johnson was subject to the bank's perfected security interest. Johnson appealed.

ISSUE Was the financing statement with the erroneous real estate description "seriously misleading" so as to make the filing invalid?

DECISION No. Judgment for the bank affirmed.

REASONS Justice Rees rejected Johnson's attempt to use a pre-Code case as a precedent. He held that the old chattel mortgage acts were quite different since they required a filing of the chattel mortgage itself rather than a simple notice. He did not think the mistaken real estate description was very serious.

"It is apparent there is no present requirement under the law that the location of livestock be set out in the financing statement. Certainly the erroneous description would be insufficient to impart constructive notice as to a claimed security interest in crops, but the erroneous description or for that matter the lack of a description entirely would not impair the efficacy of the financing statement insofar as it imparts constructive notice as to a security interest in hogs or other livestock. . . .

"[T]he test of the sufficiency of a description of property is that the description does the job assigned to it—that it makes possible the identification of the thing described. Certainly the financing statement was sufficient to direct inquiry and therefore to impart constructive notice."

As for Johnson's claim that the financing statement was "fatally misleading," Justice Rees noted that Johnson never checked the records and never saw the financing statement, so he could hardly claim that it had misled *him* in any way. In any case, it clearly stated *"All* Brood Sows & the increase," which should have put any hog buyer on notice of the bank's possible claim.

(**Note:** Even though Johnson was probably a buyer in the ordinary course of Waychus' business, he was not protected by the special BIOC rule of UCC 9–307[1] because "farm products" are specifically excluded from that section. This is another example of the different rules for different categories of collateral.)

Validity of Security Agreement and Rights of Parties Thereto

General Validity. As noted previously, both the Code generally and Article 9 specifically provide for a great deal of freedom of contract between the immediate parties to a transaction. This deference to the intent of the parties is observable in both the text and the comment to Section 9–201. The section says, in part:

Except as otherwise provided by this Act a security agreement is effective according to its terms between the parties, against purchasers of the collateral and against creditors.

The section then goes on to point out that Article 9 is not intended to modify in any way any existing *regulatory* legislation in the state pertaining to financial transactions. The comment reads in part as follows:

. . . In general the security agreement is effective between the parties; it is likewise effective against third parties. Exceptions to this general rule arise where there is a specific provision in any Article of this Act.

The Code's general commonsense approach and its repudiation of needless legalisms is evidenced by Section 9–202:

Each provision of this Article with regard to rights, obligations and remedies applies whether title to collateral is in the secured party or in the debtor.

This section is intended to make it clear that for the purposes of Article 9 formalistic distinctions based on whether the secured party has "title" to the collateral or "only" a lien on the collateral are no longer applicable. The parties are still free to structure their approach either way, but for the purposes of rights and remedies under Article 9 it makes no difference which form they choose to use. The location of "title" to the collateral may still be important for other reasons, however; tax, regulatory, and other non-Code liability problems may be solved by reference to the location of title.

Enforceability; Formal Requisites. Article 9 does include a "statute of frauds" requirement, 9–203(1), which states a general rule requiring a security interest to be in writing in order to be enforceable either against the *debtor* or against third parties. As an alternative to the writing (the "security agreement"), the secured party may keep possession of the collateral. There are also two limited exceptions to this requirement—the security interest of a "collecting bank" (4–208) and a security interest arising under Article 2 on sales of goods (9–113).

What, then, constitutes a sufficient writing to make the security interest enforceable under Article 9? On its face, Section 9–203(1) is deceptively simple. It provides that the interest is not enforceable unless

20. Definition; Creation ("Attachment")

(b) the debtor has signed a security agreement which contains a description of the collateral and in addition, when the security interest covers crops or oil, gas or minerals to be extracted or timber to be cut, a description of the land concerned. In describing collateral, the word "proceeds" is sufficient without further description to cover proceeds of any character.

The "deception" arises because the term *security agreement* is itself defined in Section 9–105(1)(h) as "an agreement which creates or provides for a security interest." In other words, the writing signed by the debtor must not only *describe* the collateral; it must also *create* or *provide for* a security interest in favor of the secured party. Thus a security agreement which was signed by both parties and contained their addresses and an adequate description of the collateral could be filed as a financing statement. However, since a financing statement would not normally provide for the *creation* of the security interest and would not normally embody any "agreement," it could not do double duty as the "security agreement." The terms are distinct and not interchangeable, and confusion (and loss of security) can occur unless the prospective secured party is adequately informed on this point.

As an example of the results which can occur when the creditor does not understand this distinction, consider the *American Card* case.

American Card Company v. H.M.H. Co.
196 A.2d 150 (Rhode Island, 1963)

FACTS On February 21, 1962, American Card Company executed a promissory note for $12,373.33, payable to Oscar A. Hillman & Sons. On March 14, both parties signed a financing statement which designated certain "tools and dies" as collateral and they filed the financing statement with the secretary of state, as required by UCC 9–402. On July 2, an equity receivership was begun against American Card and the receivers disallowed Hillman's claim for priority against the tools and dies. The lower court agreed with the receivers' decision, and Hillman appealed.

ISSUE Did Hillman have an enforceable security interest against the tools and dies?

DECISION No. Judgment for the receivers affirmed.

REASONS Even though the debtor might admit to the existence of an oral security agreement, Section 9–203 required a written security agreement if the collateral was in the debtor's possession. Where the creditor seeking priority as a secured party was challenged by other creditors, he had to prove that the Code's requirements were met.

433

Hillman was unable to do that here since neither the promissory note nor the financing statement met the Code's definition of "security agreement."

Chief Justice Condon noted that "while it is possible for a financing statement and a security agreement to be one and the same document as argued by claimants, it is not possible for a financing statement which does not contain the debtor's grant of security interest to serve as a security agreement." He also cited a law review article which stated: "The financing statement does not of itself create a security interest." In summarizing, he said:

"The financing statement which the claimants filed clearly fails to qualify also as a security agreement because nowhere in the form is there any evidence of an agreement by the debtor to grant claimants a security interest. As for the testimony of the claimants' agent upon which they also rely to prove the intention of the debtor to make such a grant, our answer is that his testimony is without probative force to supply the absence of a required security agreement in writing. Therefore the trial justice did not err in holding as she did that the financing statement and the evidence before her did not prove the existence of a security agreement within the contemplation of the language of the statute."

Attachment of the Security Interest. The words *attach* and *attachment* as used in Article 9 merely refer to the coming into existence of the security interest with respect to the collateral involved. The point in time at which the security interest "attaches" to the collateral is significant for several reasons. It is at this point in time that the collateral is classified under the definitions discussed above. Many priority rules among conflicting claims to the collateral will hinge on "attachment." And so on.

Section 9–204(1) contains the rules for making this determination:

A security interest cannot attach until there is agreement (subsection [3] of Section 1–201) that it attach and value is given and the debtor has rights in the collateral. It attaches as soon as all of the events in the preceding sentence have taken place unless explicit agreement postpones the time of attaching.

To rephrase the rules: The parties may provide that attachment occurs at any time *after* these three events have occurred; even by agreement, they cannot provide for attachment *prior* to their occurrence.

Some explanations are provided as to when the debtor has "rights" in the collateral (9–204[2]):

For the purposes of this section the debtor has no rights

(a) in crops until they are planted or otherwise become growing crops, in the young of livestock until they are conceived;

(b) in fish until caught, in oil, gas or minerals until they are extracted, in timber until it is cut;

(c) in a contract right until the contract has been made;

(d) in an account until it comes into existence.

Aside from these explanations, the general rules of contract and sales law presumably apply to determine when the debtor has "rights" in the collateral.

Subject to limited exceptions for crops and consumer goods, the Code expressly permits the parties to provide in their agreement "that collateral, whenever acquired, shall secure all obligations covered by the security agreement" (9–204[3]). For all subsequent creditors, the word is: "Look out for the person with this 'security blanket.'"

This section also permits the security agreement to cover "future advances" of value by the secured party, whether he or she is obligated to make them or has the discretion to make them (9–204[5]).

Use of Collateral by Debtor; Statement of Account. Section 9–205 and its explanatory comment decisively repudiate the rule derived from *Benedict* v. *Ratner*, 268 U.S. 353 (U.S. Supreme Court, 1925). The U.S. Supreme Court held here that under the law of New York a security interest was invalid where the debtor was given complete dominion over a shifting stock of inventory or accounts receivable and was not required by the agreement to provide the would-be secured party with an adequate accounting of his or her proceeds. The imposition of this legal rule forced such lenders "to observe a number of needless and costly formalities" and forced "financing arrangements in this field toward a self-liquidating basis" (9–205, Comment 1). Article 9 expressly validates such financing arrangements and lets the parties determine to what extent the debtor should "police" the inventory or accounts. In general, third-party creditors in such situations should be adequately protected by the requirement that a financing statement on the shifting stock of collateral be publicly filed. Where there has been no such filing and the validity of the security interest depends on possession of the collateral by the secured party, the common-law rules on "pledge" still apply (9–205, Comment 6).

For the protection of both the debtor and any third parties involved, Section 9–208 provides that the debtor can require the secured party to verify periodic "progress reports" on the total amount the debtor believes to be due and on the collateral which he believes to be subject to the security agreement. The secured party must comply with such a request within two weeks after he receives it, by sending a written correction or approval, and he may become liable to the debtor and to third parties if he fails to comply without "reasonable excuse." The debtor can request one such statement without charge every six months; the secured party may charge a fee of up to $10 for each additional statement.

Collateral in Possession of Secured Party. In general, Section 9–207 continues the case law rules which had been developed under the common law of pledge. Where the collateral is being held by the secured party, he or she has the obligation of using reasonable care in its custody and preservation—and of keeping collateral other than fungible goods identifiable. However, the risk of loss of damage to the collateral remains on the debtor to the extent of any deficiency in effective insurance coverage.

The secured party has the right to recover his reasonable expenses from the debtor, to hold any increase or profits (except money) received from the collateral as additional security for the debt, and to repledge the collateral so long as he or she does not impair the debtor's right to redeem. The secured party also has the right to use or operate the collateral in order to preserve it or its value, or pursuant to a court order, or in accordance with the provisions of the security agreement itself (9–207[4]).

If any loss occurs because the secured party fails to meet his or her obligations under 9–207(1) or (2), he or she is liable therefor, but he or she does not lose his or her security interest in the collateral (9–207[3]).

CASES FOR DISCUSSION

MOTTAZ v. KEIDEL

613 F.2d 172 (U.S. Seventh Circuit, 1980)

Cudahy, Circuit Judge

This is an appeal by a putative secured creditor from an order of the district court affirming the decision of a bankruptcy judge requiring appellant First National Bank of Wood River to turn over to the trustee in bankruptcy $3,500, representing the value of a mobile home. The issue presented is the priority in bankruptcy between the holder of the security interest in the mobile home and the trustee.

On May 17, 1977, the bankrupt, Esther Keidel, borrowed $3,500 from the First National Bank of Wood River to finance the purchase of a mobile home. Keidel signed a security agreement with the Bank and executed a promissory note. She received from the Bank a check for $3,500 payable jointly to her, to Kenneth and Rose Mitchell (the sellers), and to Olin Employees' Credit Union (the prior lienholder). When the check was issued by the Bank it was taken to the business office of the Credit Union, where the money changed hands and various notations were made on the old certificate of title. The bankrupt was advised immediately to apply for a new certificate of title.

The mobile home was purchased by the bankrupt from the Mitchells by assignment of the old certificate of title. The old certificate showed by notation of the assignment, the release of its lien by the Credit Union, and the existence of a security agreement in favor of the First National Bank of Wood River. The bankrupt attempted to apply for a new certificate of title but failed in (and finally desisted from) her efforts.

The petition in bankruptcy was filed on November 7, 1977. About one month later, the Bank delivered an application for a new certificate of title to the Secretary of State of Illinois. A new certificate was issued on December 15, 1977. Subsequently, the trustee filed a complaint for turnover, which was sustained by the bankruptcy judge. The district court approved the bankruptcy judge's order. We affirm.

Under Illinois law, security interests in personal property are, in general, governed by the Uniform Commercial Code as adopted in Illinois. . . . With respect to the means of perfection of security interest in motor vehicles (including mobile homes), however, the Illinois Vehicle Code exclusively controls. . . . Thus, the Illinois Vehicle Code provides that:

A security interest is perfected by delivery to the Secretary of State of the existing certificate of title, if any, an application for a certificate of title containing the name and address of the lienholder and the date of his security agreement and the required fee. It is perfected as of the time of its creation if the delivery is completed within 21 days thereafter, otherwise as of the time of the delivery. Ill. Rev. Stat. ch. 95 ½, § 3–202(b).

In the instant case the old certificate of title and an application for a new certificate were not delivered to the Secretary of State until shortly before December 15, 1977. But the security interest of the First National Bank of Wood River was created on May 17, 1977, when the security agreement and the promissory note were signed. . . . Therefore, since the security interest was not perfected within 21 days of its creation, it was not perfected until the application was delivered to the Secretary of State—well after the date of bankruptcy (November 7, 1977). . . . On November 7, 1977, therefore, the security interest of the Bank was unperfected.

But the trustee in the bankruptcy came into the position of a lien creditor of the bankrupt (whether or not such a creditor actually existed) as of the date of bankruptcy—that is, on November 7, 1977. Bankruptcy Act § 70(c); 11 U.S.C. § 110(c). The Illinois Vehicle Code, as of the date of bankruptcy, spells out the respective rights of holders of unperfected security interests and the trustee in bankruptcy (standing in the shoes of a lienholder) as follows:

. . . a security interest in a vehicle of a type for which a certificate of title is required is not valid against subsequent transferees or lienholders of the vehicle unless perfected as provided in this Act.

Hence, as of the date of the bankruptcy, the rights of the Bank, as the holder of an unperfected security interest, were subordinate to those of the trustee in bankruptcy, who stood in the position of a lien creditor or lienholder. . . . This result illustrates the general rule that a lien creditor or lienholder (in whose shoes the trustee stands) prevails over the holder of an unperfected security interest but is defeated by the holder of a perfected security interest. Under the Uniform Commercial Code, the rule, which is intended to reward diligence in perfection, applies even when the competing creditor has knowledge of the unperfected security interest. . . .

In the instant case, the First National Bank of Wood River failed to perfect its security interest by carrying out its statutory duty of "immediately [, after execution and delivery by the bankrupt, causing] the certificate, application and the required fee to be mailed or delivered to the Secretary of State. . . ." In fact, such delivery to the Secretary of State did not take place until after bankruptcy. Hence, the interest of the Bank cannot be sustained against that of the trustee.

The Bank asserts that the certificate of title was never in its hands, but was surrendered to the bankrupt by the Credit Union. The Bank also claims that the bankrupt was fully instructed to secure the title. But none of these circumstances are of help to the Bank since the bankrupt was under a statutory duty to "cause the certificate, application and the required fee to be delivered to the lienholder [bank]," and the Bank could

have enforced this requirement by making its performance a condition of advancing funds. . . .

The Bank also argues that a portion of Section 67(c)(1) of the Bankruptcy Act, pertaining to the invalidity of statutory liens against the trustee in bankruptcy, somehow vindicates its position. . . . The statute in question provides, inter alia, that a statutory lien which is not enforceable at the date of bankruptcy against a bona fide purchaser from the debtor on that date is invalid against the trustee. The Bank suggests, based on the cited provision, that a lien which is good against a bona fide purchaser is good against the trustee. . . . The argument continues that the lien of the Bank in the instant case was valid against a bona fide purchaser because notice of the security interest was provided by the notation on the old certificate of title. The Bank cites *Commerce Bank, N.A.* v. *Chambers*, 519 F.2d 356 (10th Circuit, 1975) for the proposition that under Kansas law, notation of a lien on a bill of sale is adequate to place a potential buyer or creditor (in whose shoes the trustee stands) on notice.

We reject these arguments. In the first place, the subsections of the Bankruptcy Act upon which the Bank relies are addressed to "statutory" liens. But the term "statutory lien" is defined to mean "a lien arising solely by force of statute upon specified circumstances or conditions, but shall not include any lien provided by or dependent upon an agreement to give security, whether or not such lien is also provided by or is also dependent upon statute and whether or not the agreement or lien is made fully effective by statute." . . . The security interest of the Bank here is not a "statutory lien," as defined in the Bankruptcy Act; it is a consensual lien created by agreement between the bankrupt and the Bank. Hence, Section 67(c)(1) of the Bankruptcy Act, cited by the Bank, is not here relevant.

In the second place, the interpretation of the law of Kansas made by the Tenth Circuit, upon which the Bank relies, is quite different than the law of Illinois which governs the instant case. "The statutory scheme in Kansas clearly contemplates that it is the responsibility of the purchaser of a new vehicle to obtain [a] certificate of title, and the cases have so held." . . . In Illinois the statutory scheme reposes sold responsibility in the Bank to deliver the application to secure the certificate. . . .

The Bank contends that the result here produces a windfall for the bankrupt's estate at the expense of the secured creditor, which furnished the purchase price of the mobile home. This may indeed be the result in this case, but the Bank has only itself to blame for failure to perform its statutory duty prescribing application for a new title. The Illinois law applicable to secured transactions in personal property, including motor vehicles, places strong emphasis on the need for diligence in perfection of the security interest in accordance with the statutory methods. . . . The strong policy favoring diligence in perfection (and the consequent gain in certainty and regularity) outweighs the possibility here of "unjust enrichment" or a "windfall."

Affirmed.

FIRST NATIONAL BANK OF BRUSH v. BOSTRON

564 P.2d 964 (Colorado, 1977)

Sternberg, Judge

The issues presented by this appeal are whether, under the Uniform Commercial Code, a perfected security interest in feed survives after consumption of the feed by cattle in which the secured party has no interest, and if so, whether the secured party is entitled to any of the proceeds from the sale of these cattle. We answer these questions in the negative and therefore affirm the judgment of the trial court.

One Eldon Weiss owned a ranch on which he raised cattle and feed crops. As a separate and distinct part of this operation Weiss entered into a joint venture with the defendant, Reinhold Bostron, under which Bostron was to supply the money and Weiss the labor necessary to raise Holstein heifers. The heifers were purchased by Bostron and Weiss with money borrowed from the plaintiff, First National Bank of Brush, which retained a perfected purchase money security interest in the animals. The Bostron-Weiss joint

venture cattle were segregated from other cattle on the Weiss ranch. Feed for all the cattle, however, was commingled and fed to the animals Weiss owned individually and to those owned by the Bostron-Weiss joint venture. Intervenor, Colorado High Plains Agricultural Credit Corporation, held a perfected security interest given by Weiss, individually, in, among other things, "all feed now owned or hereafter acquired, all crops now growing or to be grown, proceeds and products of collateral."

The cattle raised by the joint venture were eventually sold at a loss, and consequently, even after paying most of the proceeds from the sale to First National Bank of Brush, there was a deficiency owing that bank. None of the proceeds from the sale of the Bostron-Weiss cattle were paid to the intervenor.

Plaintiff bank sued Weiss and Bostron to recover the remaining balance of the loan, and Colorado High Plains intervened, claiming an interest in any recovery which the bank might obtain against Bostron. Weiss was adjudicated a bankrupt, and proceedings against him in this action were stayed. Since the intervenor's security interest attached only to the feed owned by Weiss, its right of recovery, if any, from Bostron must be premised on the benefit which Bostron individually received from the joint venture as a result of the Weiss feed being fed to the joint venture cattle. . . .

[C]attle are neither a "product" nor a "mass" as these terms are used in the statute. The reference in subsection (a) to "manufactured, processed, assembled, or commingled" precludes any other interpretation. The feed which the cattle ate did not undergo any of these transformations, that is, it was not manufactured, processed, assembled, or commingled with the cattle. Cattle consume food as motor vehicles do gasoline. Once eaten, the feed not only loses its identity, but in essence it ceases to exist and thus does not become part of the mass in the sense that the code uses the phrase. Section 4–9–315, C.R.S.1973 (Comment 3), makes this evident:

This section applies not only to cases where flour, sugar and eggs are commingled into cake mix or cake, but also to cases where components are assembled into a machine.

438

Feed as consumed by cattle is distinguishable from this notion of accession which the code's drafters visualized.

Moreover, since the financing statement did not specifically cover the product "into which the goods have been manufactured, processed or assembled," the language of § 4–9–315(1)(b), C.R.S.1973, does not support intervenor's claim.

Relying on § 4–9–306, C.R.S.1973, intervenor next contends that the cattle are proceeds of the feed as that term is defined in that portion of the code. . . .

The contention also is unavailing for several reasons. First, the trial court found that the intervenor lost its interest in the proceeds because it authorized the disposition of its collateral, i.e., the feed, by Weiss to the Bostron-Weiss joint venture. . . . This finding is supported by evidence in the record and therefore is dispositive. However, we also conclude that even if the intervenor had not authorized the use of the feed subject to its security interest by the joint venture, nevertheless intervenor's interest still would not have survived its consumption by the cattle.

Weiss received nothing when he disposed of the collateral by feeding it to the joint venture cattle. As noted in our discussion of § 4–9–315, C.R.S.1973, the collateral was consumed, and there are not traceable proceeds to which the security interest may be said to have attached. To interpret § 4–9–306 C.R.S.1973, as intervenor urges would extend the security interest of one in the position of the intervenor to the parts of the butchered animal, into the supermarket, and ultimately into the hands of the consumers. We cannot attribute such legislative intent to the General Assembly when it adopted this section of the UCC.

Intervenor's final contention is that by § 4–9–307(1), C.R.S.1973, it had an interest in the cattle which ate the feed. . . .

Assuming, without deciding, that the joint venture was a buyer in the ordinary course of business from Weiss, a cursory reading of this portion of the code would suggest, as intervenor asserts, that its security interest continues into the cattle. However, the joint venture did not sell the feed; rather, it sold the cattle to which it was fed. As previously noted, in our analysis of § 4–9–315, C.R.S.1973, the collateral in which the security interest was initially taken is, after having been fed to the cattle, nonexistent, and thus buyers of the cattle cannot reasonably be equated with buyers of the feed in which there exists a security interest.

DRAPER v. MINNEAPOLIS-MOLINE, INC.

241 N.E.2d 342 (Illinois, 1968)

Culbertson, Justice

On December 30, 1966, plaintiff entered into a written contract with Larry Meiners, a farm equipment dealer who handled defendant's products, for the purchase of a new Minneapolis-Moline tractor and new six bottom plow for use on plaintiff's farm. By the terms of the contract various extras, including a cab and radio, were to be installed on the tractor by the dealer; plaintiff was to trade in an old tractor and an old plow; and delivery was to be "by" April 1, 1967. The net purchase price of $5,300.00 was to be paid on delivery. Subsequently, on a date not entirely clear from the record, the old and the new plows were exchanged but nothing was paid on the contract.

At the time the contract was entered into, the dealer did not have the required tractor in stock, but received one from defendant on or about January 26, 1967. This machine was delivered under a trust receipt and a trust receipt financing agreement, both of which gave Meiners the right to sell the tractor at retail in the ordinary course of business, and provided that to the extent permitted by law, the security interest would attach to the proceeds of sale. In this regard, it is undisputed that defendant retained and perfected a valid security interest. By one of the provisions of the trust receipt, it was provided that the machine could be repossessed if the dealer defaulted in the terms of payment.

Shortly after the dealer received the machine, plaintiff came to the store and was shown the tractor and was told that it was his. At the trial plaintiff recalled that the last three digits of the serial number on the tractor shown to him were "804," and this coincided with the number shown on the purchase agreement between the dealer and defendant. The dealer had not as yet received the cab called for by the contract, and this appears to have delayed delivery of the tractor to the plaintiff. On one occasion, apparently in February, 1967, the dealer offered to let plaintiff take the tractor without the cab but plaintiff refused the offer.

During the last week of February, 1967, the completion of a routine audit disclosed the dealer to be greatly in arrears for substantial sums of money owed to defendant. When it became apparent that he was not financially able to correct or alleviate the situation, defendant repossessed all of its products on the store premises for which it had not been paid, including the tractor plaintiff had been told would be delivered to him under his contract. At the time plaintiff had neither turned in his old tractor nor had he paid anything to the dealer. Plaintiff then negotiated directly with defendant to complete the deal, but the negotiations fell through because defendant, as a manufacturer, was in no position to accept a trade-in or to provide and install the contract extras. It is undisputed that plaintiff thereafter did his spring plowing with his old tractor, and that he incurred expenses of $396.70 he would not have had if the new tractor had been available to him. This action against defendant for damages soon followed.

The authority for plaintiff's action is found in Section 2–722 of Article 2 of the Uniform Commercial Code (hereinafter referred to as the Code), which, in substance, gives to one having a special property interest in goods a right of action against a third party who "so deals with goods which have been identified to a contract for sale as to cause actionable injury to a party to that contract." . . . The quoted language, we believe, intends that a third party would be liable for conversion, physical damage to the goods, or interference with the rights of a buyer in the goods. Section 2–103(1)(a) of Article 2 states that in such Article: "'Buyer' means a person who buys or contracts to buy goods." . . .

While defendant makes a mild argument that the tractor did not conform to the contract because the extras had not been installed when it was pointed out by the dealer, we think it manifest from the evidence that there was a complete and sufficient identification of the tractor to the contract within the purview of Section 2–501(1). It is apparent, too, that defendant's conduct made it impossible for the dealer to deliver the tractor to plaintiff, and that defendant so dealt with the goods as to interfere with plaintiff's special property interest. And, without more, it could be said that plaintiff has standing to maintain an action for damages as authorized by Section 2–722. However, there next arises the question of whether plaintiff obtained his special property interest, and its attendant rights, free and clear of defendant's security interest. . . .

Here the sale of the tractor to plaintiff was not unauthorized. Rather, both the trust receipt and the trust receipt financing agreement gave the dealer (seller) the express authority to sell the tractor at retail in the ordinary course of business, and provided that the security interest would attach to the proceeds of sale. The very intent of the commercial papers involved was that the tractor could be sold to a buyer (see: Section 2–103[1][a]), free and clear of the security interest of the seller's creditor. Accordingly, we hold the plaintiff obtained his special property interest in the tractor free and clear of defendant's security interest, and that such security interest is no bar to the action for damages given to plaintiff by Section 2–722.

The remaining issue for determination relates to damages which, as previously noted, were awarded to plaintiff in the amount of $2,396.70, of which $396.70 is undisputed and represents expenses incurred by plaintiff because he was denied the use of the new tractor for his 1967 spring plowing. The remaining $2,000, which is disputed, was awarded by the trial court as "cover" under Section 2–712 of the Code . . . and was based on plaintiff's testimony that the contract price was $2,000 less than that quoted to him by another Minneapolis-Moline dealer (his brother-in-law) for the same kind of tractor.

We are in accord with the contention of defendant that the trial court erred in awarding $2,000 as "cover." While we think the competency of the proof by which the $2,000 figure was established is suspect . . . it is enough to say that Section 2–712 is inapplicable under the facts of this case. That section, in unambiguous terms, has application only where a buyer actually buys goods in substitution for the goods he expected to receive from the seller, and provides as the measure of damages the difference between the cost of cover and the contract price. The plaintiff here did not purchase another tractor as cover, thus the award $2,000 was a windfall to which he was not entitled.

For reasons stated, the judgment of the circuit court of Whiteside County is affirmed in part and reversed in part, and the cause is remanded to the court with directions to enter judgment for the plaintiff in the amount of $396.70.

PROBLEMS FOR DISCUSSION

1. Ned Ninepins, owner of Lucky Lane bowling alley, bought six automatic pinsetters from Leisure Equipment, Inc. He entered into a retail installment contract with the seller which specified that upon default the total contract price would become due. After several payments Ned defaulted, and six months later Leisure Equipment, Inc., brought a foreclosure action against him. Under a warrant of seizure the local sheriff entered the building and rendered the pinsetters inoperative but left them in their place. Ned counterclaimed for damages, arguing that personal property had been converted and that the sheriff's failure to remove the seized equipment made it impossible for Ned to use the building in any other way. Was the seizure legal?

2. Joann Paragon bought a new Pontiac from Barney's Pontiac dealership. She borrowed $3,000 from Friendly Credit Union and signed a promissory note in favor of it. When making out the draft to Barney and Joann, Friendly noted on the back that Barney should notify the secretary of state of the lien when completing the title application. Barney failed to do so, and Joann subsequently received a title certificate with no reference to the lien. She defaulted on her payments and sold the car to Bonnie Fide, keeping the proceeds. How should Friendly proceed with regard to Joann, Barney, and Bonnie? Who wins? Why?

3. Andrew purchased a new Toronado from Mars Oldsmobile on an installment contract and executed a negotiable promissory note for $3,000. The note, which contained a confession of judgment clause, was negotiated to Smallsville Bank. Andrew made a few payments to the bank, but eventually he fell behind in his payments. The bank sent him a notice of repossession by registered mail, but Andrew had moved and the letter was returned to the bank as undeliverable. The bank then repossessed the car, sold it for $300, and sued Andrew for the difference. Was the bank's action legal? Why?

4. In April 1963 Jack Coyle, a car dealer, bought a new station wagon, which he financed through a loan from Oscoda State Bank. The loan was secured by a properly registered chattel mortgage, but no certificate of title was issued. Donald MacAllister bought the car from Coyle and obtained a certificate of title from the secretary of state. It contained no reference to the mortgage lien. Coyle defaulted on his payments, and the bank seized the car from Donald, claiming that he had constructive notice of the chattel mortgage. How can Donald get his car back?

5. Donley Bindery bought a paper cutter from Harris Corporation under an installment sales contract. The seller was to retain title and the right to possession if the purchaser defaulted. Donley was unable to meet its payments, and Harris wants to regain possession of the paper cutter. Can it do so? Why?

6. James Carver, a cattle rancher in Syracuse, Kansas, received a loan from Easyterm Finance Corporation (EFC) to purchase 161 head of cattle for which he executed a

perfected security agreement. The agreement required Carver to obtain written permission before selling any of the secured cattle. Carver made several sales, properly endorsed the checks he received for his cows to EFC for application on his indebtedness, but never bothered to obtain the written consent required in the loan agreement. EFC, in turn, never reprimanded him for his failure to do so. Eventually Carver sold all 161 head of cattle and closed another deal with Jonathan and Jeremiah Augustin, who agreed to purchase another 165 head of cattle. Carver went to EFC for additional financing of this purchase, bought the cows, and delivered them to the Augustin brothers. Four were rejected, but Carver received a sight draft of over $30,000 for the others. Carver endorsed the draft as usual and sent it to the EFC for application toward his debt. The check was returned for insufficient funds. In the meantime, the Augustin brothers had resold the cattle to Jack Lannan. EFC, learning of the resale to Lannan, immediately filed a financing statement covering the 161 cows and tried to repossess the herd. Whose loss is it?

7. Robert Broke borrowed $14,000 from Farmland Bank for which he gave the bank a security interest in "all farm equipment now owned or hereafter acquired and all livestock now owned or hereafter acquired and the young of such livestock." A financing statement was filed on August 23, 1965. Several other loans were made, and on April 10, 1967, another financing statement was filed. Beginning in August 1966, Robert had purchased cattle from Joe Ranch, 43 head in all. The transactions were secured by properly filed conditional sales notes and later by a chattel mortgage on a grinder-mixer, which was also filed with the county. Eventually Robert was unable to meet his commitments, and now Joe Ranch and the Farmland Bank both claim an interest in the 28 head of cattle still in Roberts' possession and the grinder-mixer. Who has priority?

8. P and K Pontiac Dealership, Inc., sold a GM automobile to its own president, Walter Keil, on a conditional sales contract which called for payment in 36 monthly installments. The lien was noted on the certificate of title; however, the certificate was never transferred to Walter personally but remained with the dealership. A year later, the same car, which was exhibited in the dealership showroom, was sold to Jerry Lemon. He never received a certificate of title, and he was unaware of the lien until he received a friendly admonishment from GM Acceptance Corporation. Now GM is suing him and Walter Keil for repossession of the car. Decision?

Perfection, Priorities, and Remedies

Methods of Perfection

For the purpose of Article 9, the term *perfection* is used to describe a process—the steps which a secured party must take to make his or her security interest effective against third parties, particularly the debtor's general creditors or their representative in an insolvency proceeding. The very idea of "security" is to have an available source of funds from which the secured debt can be paid in the event of default by the debtor; that objective is defeated if the asset in question or its proceeds are distributed pro rata to all creditors.

To be more specific and more technically correct, perfection of the security interest in the collateral is necessary in order to best "a person who becomes a lien creditor without knowledge of the security interest and before it is perfected" (9–301[1][b]). *Lien creditor* is defined to include a creditor with a levy or attachment against the property involved, or an assignee for the benefit of creditors, or a receiver in equity, or a trustee in bankruptcy (9–301[3]). The secured party needs to perfect in order to prevent these people from making priority claims against "his" item of collateral. A secured party who has provided the purchase-money credit or loan (which enabled the debtor to purchase the collateral) does have a 10-day grace period within which to perfect his or her security interest and still beat out these lien creditors (9–301[2]), but as a rule the secured party must perfect *before* the lien creditor becomes such, or lose priority. Subsections 9–301(1)(c) & (d) extend similar protection to certain unknowing transferees of goods, instruments, documents, chattel paper, accounts, contract rights, and general intangibles; they too will beat the unperfected security interest of the would-be secured party to the extent that they give value without knowledge of his or her interest.

Perfection will also assist the secured party in beating out some other kinds of third-party claimants, at least in some situations. But since it is possible to have more than one perfected security interest in the same collateral, and since even a perfected security interest is subordinate to certain types of third-party claims in certain situations, it must be remembered that a secured party with a perfected security interest is not always "the first to be paid." Priorities of payment under Article 9 are discussed below

There are three general methods of perfection—filing, possession of the collateral, and automatic perfection—plus some variations (such as different places to file for different types of collateral). Filing is effective for every type of collateral except "instruments." Filing is the only method of perfecting against accounts, contract rights, and general intangibles since there is nothing in these situations which can really be effectively "possessed." Possession of the item of collateral by the secured party is an effective method of perfection for all types of goods and for the "paper intangibles"—documents, instruments, and chattel paper. Since these pieces of paper are commonly dealt with in the commercial world as embodying the rights which they represent, and since they are capable of being physically possessed, the drafters of Article 9 provided that a security interest in such pieces of paper could be perfected by the secured party's retention of them. Indeed, for instruments, except for a limited 21-day perfection against the debtor's other creditors, possession is the only acceptable method of perfection.

For *purchase-money* security interests in most consumer goods and (under the 1962 Code) in most farm equipment with a purchase price of not over $2,500, Article 9 provides a third alternative. The "purchase-money person" (the seller or the financing agency that provided the cash or credit which the debtor used to buy the collateral) is given the benefit of an "automatic" perfection as soon as his or her security interest "attaches" to the collateral. (This automatic perfection alternative is not available where the consumer goods or farm equipment is defined as "fixtures" or is a motor vehicle required to be licensed.) Even without filing and with the debtor in possession of the consumer goods or farm equipment, the purchase-money person will still be protected against nearly all other possible claimants—lien creditors, other general creditors, the trustee in bankruptcy, another dealer to whom the collateral was sold or traded in, a donee to whom the collateral was given, or a buyer who had knowledge of the security interest. Aside from the common priority problems, only one sort of claimant—a bona fide purchaser (BFP)—takes the collateral free and clear of the *unfiled* purchase-money security interest (9–307[2]). The BFP must buy without knowledge of the unfiled security interest, for value, and for his or her own personal, family or household purposes (consumer goods) or his or her own farming operations (farm equipment). Given this extensive protection of the unfiled security interest, the retailer or financer of these types of collateral can then decide whether protection against BFPs is worth the filing fee and the clerical expense involved in filing a financing statement. If the dealer does file, he or she will prevail even against a BFP, so buyers of consumer goods or farm equipment from other individuals do have to check these filing records in order to make sure that the item they're buying is indeed "free and clear." Note again that this third perfection alternative applies only to the purchase-money person; all other secured parties must file or possess to perfect. The 1972 amendments eliminate this third alternative as to farm equipment; it will remain only for most types of consumer goods.

Perfection as against Proceeds

Section 9–306 provides an extensive and careful coverage for security interests in "proceeds," meaning "whatever is received when collateral or proceeds is sold, exchanged, collected or otherwise disposed of" (9–306[1]). "Money, checks and the like are 'cash proceeds.' All other proceeds are 'non-cash proceeds'" (9–306[1]). The general intent of this section is to give the secured party with a security interest in collateral, a similar security in anything which the debtor received from third parties in exchange for that collateral.

As a general rule, unless he or she authorized his or her debtor to make the sale or exchange of the collateral, a secured party can elect to pursue the collateral in the hands of a third party as well as the proceeds in the hands of his debtor. A dealer who filed against a TV set which was bought on credit could, for example, repossess the TV from a third party to whom the set was sold if the debtor was in default under the original security agreement. The secured party will not get the debt paid twice, but he or she will have two sources to look to for payment (9–306, Comment 3). This general rule is subject to several exceptions, including the buyer in the ordinary course of business (BIOC) who buys goods (usually from a dealer's inventory). This BIOC takes the goods free and clear of a security interest created by his or her seller, even though that interest is perfected and even though he or she knows about it (9–307[1]). For other exceptions, see Sections 9–301, 9–308, and 9–309.

What does the secured party need to do to perfect his or her security interest against "proceeds"? If he or she has already filed a financing statement which indicates the security interest applies to proceeds as well as the original collateral, he or she need do nothing more; he or she has a continuously perfected security interest against the proceeds. Where his or her original financing statement does not so indicate, or where he or she has perfected against the original collateral by another method, that perfection still applies to proceeds, continuously and automatically, for a 10-day grace period. Within that period, the secured party needs to file or to take possession of the proceeds in order to perfect (9–306[3]).

In the event of insolvency proceedings, then, the secured party with a perfected security interest against proceeds will be able to assert his or her rights in any of the debtor's assets which he or she can "identify" as being derived from his or her original collateral and in "all cash and bank accounts of the debtor," even if "his" cash proceeds cannot be identified because they have been commingled with other funds (9–306[4]).

Subsection (5) of 9–306 contains a detailed set of priority rules to cover situations where "a sale of goods results in an account or chattel paper which is transferred by the seller to a secured party, and . . . the goods are returned to or are repossessed by the seller or the secured party."

Perfection against Fixtures

Many complex problems may arise where goods are attached to real estate and both the goods and the real estate are subject to the claims of financing agencies or good faith purchasers. The Code was not intended to regulate real property law, but in this area Article 9 does impact on real property doctrines. In general, fixtures are defined by the general law of the state where the realty is located. The Code does exclude structural materials from the "fixtures" definition.

Under the 1962 version of the Code, the secured party whose interest *attached* to the goods before they became affixed to the realty took priority over all earlier interests in the realty and only had to file a financing statement to take priority over subsequent real estate interests as well. Where his or her interest did not attach until after affixation of the goods to the realty, he or she lost as to earlier realty interests (unless they agreed to take a subordinate position) but could file and win against later realty claimants.

The 1972 revision of Section 9–313 has substantially changed the rules, in favor of the realty claimants. First, a construction mortgagee (who makes advances of funds to finance the building of structures on the land) is given a special priority over all fixture financers even as to such items as dishwashers and refrigerators. As to other existing interests in the real estate (such as a land contract seller or the holder of the purchase mortgage), the fixture financer must make a *"fixture filing"* either before or within 10 days after the goods become attached to the real estate. This is a special rule for purchase-money security interests in the fixtures. Otherwise, there is a first-to-file rule for fixtures. For example, the seller of a new furnace on credit could obtain priority over the holder of an existing mortgage by making the proper fixture filing. But if the existing mortgage had already been properly recorded, a non-purchase-money creditor who wished to use existing fixtures as collateral could not take priority over the mortgagee unless the latter agreed. Financers of "readily-removable factory or office machines or readily-removable replacements of domestic appliances which are consumer goods" are given priority over conflicting real estate interests if their security interest is perfected before the goods become fixtures. Most stoves, refrigerators, washers, and dryers would seem to be "readily-removable"; most furnaces would not. A catchall provision indicates that a conflicting real estate interest takes priority against any security interest which is not properly perfected.

To avoid the problem which arose in states where the fixture financer did not have to file on the real estate records but merely in the *office* where real estate claims were filed, the 1972 amendments specify that a fixture filing must be made in the real estate records. It must include a legal description of the real estate to which the fixture is being attached and also the name of the real estate owner if that person is not the debtor who is using the fixture as collateral. Thus, the fixture claim should appear in any title search of the real estate records.

Karp Bros., Inc. v. West Ward Savings & Loan Assn.
271 A.2d 493 (Pennsylvania, 1970)

FACTS   On April 29, 1964, Mr. and Mrs. McCown, owners of the Ranch Court Motel in State College, Pennsylvania, borrowed $240,000 from West Ward. As security for this loan, they executed a mortgage on the motel; the mortgage was duly recorded. On January 8, 1965, the McCowns made a credit purchase of 50 items of restaurant equipment from Karp, a wholesaler. These items were to be used in an addition to the motel. On February 10, Karp filed a financing statement with the proper county and state officers. On March 8, Karp and the McCowns executed a "bailment lease" covering the equipment; this contract was assigned to the Hollidaysburg Trust Company. After the McCowns had made 10 payments under this security agreement, a new bailment lease for the balance due was executed on January 11, 1966. This new contract was also assigned to Hollidaysburg.

West Ward foreclosed on November 25, 1966, and bought the motel itself at the sheriff's sale on January 31, 1967. It refused to let Karp remove the equipment, and Karp sued for replevin. West Ward appealed from a money judgment in favor of Karp. (Prior to trial, Hollidaysburg had reassigned to Karp.)

ISSUE   Did the holder of the prior real estate mortgage take priority over the secured party (Karp)?

DECISION   No. Judgment for Karp affirmed.

REASONS   Justice Eagen first discussed briefly whether the equipment had become part of the real estate. There were no findings on this point by the trial court, but Eagen stated that in this case that didn't matter.

The 1962 version of Article 9 was in effect at the time, and 9–313(2) said: "A security interest which attaches to goods before they become fixtures takes priority as to the goods over the claims of all persons who have an interest in the real estate except as stated in subsection (4)." The only exception in (4) which had any relevance to these facts was a "subsequent purchaser for value" of the real estate. But (4) also made clear that this exception did not include a real estate mortgagee buying the land at its own foreclosure sale, as West Ward did here.

The court decided that these bailment leases were clearly intended as security agreements, so the main question for decision was whether Karp's security interest attached to the goods before they became fixtures (if indeed they ever did).

"When the first, 'Bailment Lease' was executed on March 8, 1965, there was a manifest agreement that the security interest attach, and value given, in that credit was thereby extended to the bailment lessees. . . . Moreover, the lessee-debtors had rights in the collateral in that the lease gave them a right to possession of the goods. All this occurred before the goods could possibly have become affixed to the realty, since there was testimony found to be true by the court below that none of the goods referred to in the lease were delivered prior to the execution of the first bailment agreement."

The court also decided that the second bailment lease, after affixation of the goods, was merely a refinancing of the original debt and thus did not affect the priority which had already been established.

Priorities

For a creditor, priority of payment is that the "security" game is all about. Obviously, if the debtor had enough funds to go around, there would be no problem of who got paid first and no need for this sort of litigation. Litigation to establish priority occurs because someone who has extended credit to an insolvent debtor is going to get "stuck" for some or all of his or her claim against the debtor. Other types of claimants, such as good faith purchasers of collateral from the debtor, will also be interested in determining whether they hold the property in question free and clear or subject to the claims of a creditor or creditors. Different potential claimants and different types of financing transactions combine to produce a great range of specific fact situations. Part of what appears to be a terrible complexity in Article 9's priority rules stems directly from the need to provide a number of different rules to deal with a number of quite different fact variations. We thus need to consider both the "general rules" and about 15 special situations covered by a special priority rule.

For the first general rule on priority, we return to 9–201:

> Except as otherwise provided by this Act a security agreement is effective according to its terms between the parties, against purchasers of the collateral and against creditors.

In other words, the security agreement itself controls priority unless a Code provision covers the situation and provides otherwise. One of the leading authorities on the Code, Roy Steinheimer, describes this 9–201 "except" provision as "the biggest 'except' clause in the history of Western Civilization," and he's probably not far wrong. What he's getting at is that nearly all typical authority priority situations are in fact covered by a Code rule, so that the security agreement itself is operative only within a limited range insofar as priority rules are concerned. The significance of the legally effective "residue" remaining in 9–201 can be seen in *U.S.* v. *Lebanon Woolen Mills*, 241 F. Supp. 393 (1964), where an *unfiled* conditional sales contract was given priority over a U.S. tax lien which purported to attach to all the debtor's property before the seller filed.

One of the special priority rules (9–316) does provide that secured parties may agree among themselves as to their relatives priority positions. Such an arrangement, of course, would be effective only as between the parties who agreed to it.

A second look at 9–301 indicates that even a secured party with an unfiled, unperfected security interest receives some protection in terms of priority. If the interest has attached to the collateral, he or she does have rights in the collateral as against his or her debtor, and *generally* his or her interest will take priority as against buyers of the collateral or lien creditors who have *knowledge* of his or her security interest when they become such.

Section 9–312 is the basic priorities section. It provides the general rules for determining priorities between conflicting security interests in the same collateral (9–312[5]); it spells out special purchase-money rules for inventory and noninventory collateral (9–312[3] and [4]); it provides a special priority rule where "crops" are used as collateral (9–312[2]); and it cross-references 12 other sections containing special priority rules (9–312[1]).

The general priority rules from 9–312(5) are simple and logical. As between the competing security interests, priority is determined:

1. In order of filing if both security interests have been perfected by filing, regardless of which security interest attached first and whether it attached before or after filing.
2. In order of perfection unless both security interests have been perfected by

filing, again regardless of which security interest attached first and of whether any filed security interest attached before or after it was filed.

3. In order of attachment of the security interests to the collateral so long as neither security interest has been perfected.

For purposes of applying these three priority rules, the method by which the security interest is first perfected is the one that counts (9–312[6]).

Special purchase-money rules for inventory and noninventory collateral are set out in 9–312(3) and (4). A purchase-money security interest in inventory collateral has priority over a conflicting security interest in the same collateral if (a) the purchase-money security interest is perfected when the debtor gets possession of the collateral; *and* (b) notification of the purchase-money security interest is received by any other "known" or "filed" secured party before the debtor gets possession of the collateral; *and* (c) the notification states that the purchase-money person has or intends to acquire a purchase-money security interest in the debtor's inventory, "describing such inventory by item of type" (9–312[3]). Because there is much less of a commingling problem with non-inventory collateral, the purchase-money person's requirements for priority in such collateral are much simpler. He or she just has to have his or her interest perfected when the debtor takes possession of the noninventory collateral, or within 10 days thereafter (3–312[4]).

Purchase-money priorities are illustrated by the *National Cash Register* case.

National Cash Register Co. v. Firestone Co.
191 N.E.2d 471 (Massachusetts, 1963)

FACTS On June 15, 1960, NCR sold a new cash register to Edmund Carroll, who was doing business as the "Kozy Kitchen" in Canton, Massachusetts. This sale was designated as a conditional sale. The cash register was delivered sometime between November 19 and November 25. On November 25, the parties canceled the June 15 contract and replaced it with one providing easier payment terms. NCR filed financing statements with the town clerk of Canton on December 20 and with the secretary of state on December 21.

Meanwhile, Carroll had borrowed $1,911 from Firestone on November 18 and had executed a security agreement covering "the following goods, chattels, and automobiles, namely: The business located at and numbered 574 Washington Street, Canton Mass. together with all its good-will, fixtures, equipment, and merchandise. The fixtures specifically consist of the following: *All contents of luncheonette including equipment such as: booths and tables; stand and counter; tables; chairs; booths; steam tables; salad unit; potato peeler; U.S. slicer; range; case; fryer; compressor; bobtail; milk dispenser; Silex; 100 class air conditioner; signs; pastry case; mixer; dishes; silverware; tables; hot fudge; Haven Ex.; 2 door station wagon 1957 Ford A57R107215,* together with all property and articles now, and which may hereafter be, used or mixed with, added or attached to, and/or substituted for, any of the foregoing described property." Firestone filed financing statements on November 18 and 25 which identified the collateral with the italicized words from the security agreement description.

21. Perfection, Priorities, and Remedies

National Cash Register Co. v. Firestone Co. (continued)

When Carroll went into default on both contracts, Firestone repossessed and sold the contents of the luncheonette, including the cash register. NCR sued for the tort of conversion of "its" cash register. The lower courts held for NCR.

ISSUE   Was the cash register covered by Firestone's financing statement, without a specific mention of after-acquired property or of a cash register?

DECISION   Yes. Judgment reversed; Firestone takes priority.

REASONS   Chief Justice Wilkins first dismissed NCR's argument that Carroll did not intend to give Firestone security interest in the cash register: "The debtor's intent must be judged by the language of the security agreement. Even if Firestone had enough security without the cash register (which is not apparent from the facts), Firestone is entitled to whatever priority it received by compliance with the Code.

"The description in the security agreement is clearly broad enough to reach the cash register. It said 'All contents'; 'equipment such as': and 'used . . . with.' The cash register is covered by all of these phrases. Likewise, the financing statements cover the cash register by their use of the first two phrases—'All contents': 'equipment such as.'"

NCR also tried to argue that the financing statement was defective because it spelled "Kozy' with a C ("Cozy") rather than with a *K*. The court felt that this error was not seriously misleading because the filing was done under Carroll's name and because the address of the business was correctly stated.

The court held that the words *All contents . . . including equipment* "were enough to put the plaintiff on notice to ascertain what those contents were. This is not a harsh result as to the plaintiff, to which, as we have indicated, S. 9–312(4) made available a simple and sure procedure for completely protecting its purchase money security interest."

Some of the other sections listed by 9–312(1) as containing special priority rules have already been referred to above: 9–301, dealing with unperfected security interest and lien creditors; 9–306, covering proceeds and repossessions; 9–307, on good faith purchasers of goods (more on this in the next section of this chapter); 9–313, on fixtures; 9–316, on contractual subordination. For the sake of brevity, the remaining special priority rules are presented in summary fashion:

Section 4–208 gives a bank which has given credit against an item being handled for collection a high-priority security interest against the item itself and any accompanying documents, even without a separate security agreement and without filing.

Section 9–304 provides a set of special rules for dealing with instruments, documents, and goods covered by documents, including a provision for limited and temporary (21 days) perfection without filing and without possession.

Section 9–308 provides a special rule protecting BFPs of chattel paper or nonnegotiable instruments where the conflicting security interest is perfected under 9–304's rules on permissive filing or temporary perfection.

Section 9–309 preserves the superior rights of good faith buyers of negotiable pieces of paper—instruments, documents, and investment securities; filing under Article 9 is not notice of the security interest to these parties.

Section 9–310 grants priority to any lien created by statute or case law in favor of a person who furnishes services or materials with respect to goods subject to a security interest.

Section 9–314 adopts a set of detailed rules for dealing with the common problem of "accessions" where goods become installed in or affixed to other goods (e.g., the new motor in the old car); these rules are similar to the 1962 fixture rules.

Section 9–315 attempts to cover the situation where goods are commingled or processed so that they lose their distinct identity; the general idea is that the security interest continues against the mass or product; where there is more than one such security interest, they have equal priority and share pro rata in the product.

Protection for Certain Good Faith Purchasers

Section 9–307 contains two special rules designed for the protection of good faith purchasers of goods. These rules were referred to in the preceding section of this chapter; and the *Nicolosi* case illustrates their application in one fact situation.

Subsection (1) of 9–307 protects the "buyer in the ordinary course of business," who is defined by 1–201(9) as follows:

"Buyer in ordinary course of business" means a person who in good faith and without knowledge that the sale to him is in violation of the ownership rights or security interest of a third party in the goods buys in ordinary course from a person in the business of selling goods of that kind.

Stated more simply, the BIOC is a buyer from a dealer's inventory. The BIOC "takes free of a security interest created by this seller even though the security interest is perfected and even though the buyer knows of its existence."

The limitations inherent in 9–307(1) have been brought out by several car dealer cases. In *National Shawmut Bank of Boston* v. *Jones*, 236 A.2d 484 (1967), the Supreme Court of New Hampshire held that Jones was not protected under either 9–307(1) or (2) because a security interest had not been created by *his* seller and because the bank's security interest had been filed. Jones had bought the car in good faith from a dealer to whom it had been resold by the original buyer. When the original buyer went into default on his installment payments, the bank sued to foreclose on its security interest and won.

Moreover, where the BIOC not only knows of the existence of a security interest but also knows that the sale to him is in violation of it, he takes subject to the security interest. This point was explained in *O. M. Scott Credit Corporation* v. *Apex, Inc.*, 198 A.2d 673 (1964). The Rhode Island court found as a matter of fact that Apex, a wholesaler, was told by an employee of the seller (Massachusetts Hardware) that the seller was not authorized to sell to wholesalers, but only to retail customers. Presumably, that warning should have put Apex on notice that somebody else had something to say about the seller's handling of the goods in question (300 bags of fertilizer).

Section 9–307(1) also specifically excludes from its protection "a person buying farm products from a person engaged in farming operations." Thus buyer Johnson did not get BIOC protection in the *Waychus* case.

Equally significant is the limitation which 9–307(2) places on the operation of the automatic perfection alternative for consumer goods and for farm equipment with a purchase price of not over $2,500. Where the secured party is relying on automatic perfection (i.e., where there has been no filing and the debtor is in possession of the goods), a BFP takes free of the security interest if he buys without knowledge and for his own personal, family, or household purposes or his own farming operations. The unfiled (and unsatisfied) security interest in the TV set is thus ineffective against another BFP consumer to whom the TV is resold by the debtor-buyer.

Debtor's Defenses against Assignee

The great bulk of time-sale contracts are not held by the seller until maturity, but are transferred or "assigned" to a bank or other financing agency. The early common law absolutely prohibited such assignments since it was felt that their result was to force the debtor to do business with a stranger with whom he or she had never contacted. Only within the last hundred years has their validity been accepted, and "traces of the absolute common law prohibition have survived almost to our own day" (9–318, Comment 4).

One of the most significant common-law rules developed to protect account debtors in the assignment situation is the one which makes the assignee subject to all defenses which the debtor has against the assignor (seller). The assignee steps into the assignor's shoes; they don't get any larger just because someone else is wearing them; if they pinch a little bit, too bad. For its own protection, the financial community has been able to get statutes passed in some states which modify this general rule. Michigan, for example, passed a statute in 1966 giving the debtor 15 days after he or she received notice that his or her account had been assigned to notify the assignee of any defenses which he or she had against the assignor-seller; otherwise, the defense cannot be used against the assignee. In a similar statute Arizona gives the debtor 90 days. The seller could also insulate the financing agency from most of the debtor's usual defenses (nondelivery, defective merchandise, fraud in the inducement) by having the debtor sign a negotiable instrument and then negotiating it to the financing agency as a "holder in due course."

The drafters of Article 9 continued the general rule on debtors' defenses against the assignee in substantially unchanged form, in 9–318(1):

Unless an account debtor has made an enforceable agreement not to assert defenses or claims arising out of a sale as provided in Section 9–206 the rights of an assignee are subject to:

(a) all the terms of the contract between the account debtor and assignor and any defense or claim arising therefrom; and

(b) any other defense or claim of the account debtor against the assignor which accrues before the account debtor receives notification of the assignment.

As was true under the common law, therefore, the account debtor cannot only assert any defense he has under the assigned contract against the assignee but can also use any defense or claim he or she has against the assignor on totally unrelated matters, up to the time when he or she receives notice that his or her account has been assigned. For example, Biff Baker buys two cars, one new and one used, from Able's Auto Sales. Biff pays cash for the used car and finances the new car over 36 months. Able's Auto assigns the financing contract to the E-Z Money Company. If anything goes wrong with *either* car, Biff can use that defect (breach of warranty) as a defense when he is sued by E-Z Money, up to the point when Biff is notified of the assignment. After that, Biff can only assert claims he has under the new-car contract against E-Z and has to go back to Able's Auto for any claims he had on the used car.

The references in 9–318(1) to Section 9–206 are important because 9–206 specifically validates a contractual agreement by the debtor-buyer "that he will not assert against an assignee any claim or defense which he may have against the seller." For an assignee to claim the protection afforded by this section, he must take his assignment "for value, in good faith and without notice of a claim or defense." Moreover, this section does not prevent the debtor from asserting defenses which he could assert against the holder in due course of a negotiable instrument (e.g., minority, illegality, fraud in the execution). And finally, and perhaps most significantly, 9–206 states that it is subject to "any statute or decision which establishes a different rule for buyers of consumer goods." If a state wishes to modify the seeming harshness of this section so as to protect consumers, this is easily done, either legislatively or judicially. Massachusetts took the lead by passing the bill which abolished the "holder in due course" concept for consumer sales; most states have now adopted such legislation. Under its rule-making powers, the FTC held extensive hearings and then adopted an "unfair method of competition" rule at the national level. It now seems only a question of time until the "holder in due course" doctrine will be almost completely removed from the consumer-sales field. In that event, 9–206 waiver clauses will be valid only for nonconsumer buyers (who, presumably, are better able to take care of themselves from a legal and contractual standpoint).

Section 9–206 makes it clear that any "disclaimer, limitation or modification of the seller's warranties" must be made in accordance with Article 2 and not under this section. Pennsylvania's original version of this subsection was applied in *L & N Sales Company* v. *Stuski*, 146 A.2d 154 (1958), where the court held that an implied warranty of fitness was preserved against the seller's argument that a conditional sales contract, executed after the original sales agreement, operated to modify the agreement by disclaiming all warranties except an expressly written warranty of merchantability.

The operation of 9–206(1) is illustrated by the *Molina* case.

Star Credit Corporation v. Molina
298 N.Y.S.2d 570 (1969)

FACTS On July 25, 1966, Mr. and Mrs. Cecilio Molina bought a freezer from Peoples Foods, Inc., for $1,222.15. On July 30, Mr. Molina bought $445.82 worth of frozen and packaged foods on a "food plan" from Peoples Food Packaging Corporation. Both of these retail installment contracts were immediately assigned to Star Credit. The freezer and one third of the food products were delivered. The Molinas paid $169.75 on the first contract and $111.47 on the second. Peoples Food Packaging went out of business without delivering the rest of the food, and the Molinas stopped making payments.

ISSUE Is Star Credit a bona fide purchaser assignee of the contracts and therefore not subject to the Molinas' defenses?

DECISION No. The defenses may be proved.

REASONS At the time, both 9–206(1) and New York's Personal Property Law permitted waiver of defenses clauses in retail installment contracts. The main fact question here was whether Star had acquired the contracts in "good faith," and Justice Younger decided that Star had not.

He began with the UCC definition, "honesty in fact in the conduct or transaction concerned," and with the official comment, which said that the phrase "means at least what is here stated." He emphasized that this was a consumer, not a business, signing a contract which waived defenses. "Although the Molinas are literate, they are hardly sophisticated enough to understand the 'cut-off' provision of the contracts they signed. There was no parity of bargaining power between the Molinas and their sellers. If the Molinas are indeed 'cut-off' from asserting their claims and defenses, they will be required without further remedy to pay for foods they will never receive."

In reviewing the facts, Justice Younger noted that each contract had a printed assignment form on its reverse side; that each contract was in fact assigned to Star within 24 hours of being signed by the Molinas; that each contract contained provisions dealing with assignees' rights; that Star took each contract at a 20 percent discount; that Star used the same account numbers as the sellers; and that each contract was signed by the seller "subject to approval of Buyer's credit." Younger felt that "[n]o credit investigation could possibly have been made by the seller between the time of execution and the time of assignment." Yet Star wrote a letter saying it had decided to accept the contracts "in view of your excellent credit rating and fine character references." Younger felt that Peoples' main intent was to get contracts that it could assign, not to sell freezers and food, and that Star was well aware of what was going on.

The Molinas introduced no evidence of fraud or unconscionability, as they had claimed, but they did show a material breach of the contract by Peoples. Justice Younger treated the freezer and food contracts as one, since both the salesman and the documents referred to a "food plan." One third of the food would be worth $148.61; the Molinas had paid a total of $281.22. The balance of $132.61 Justice Younger allocated to Star as payment for the use of the freezer (for about three years). Star got the freezer back.

Place and Manner of Filing

One place where the "uniformity" desired by the drafters of the Code has broken down is in the requirements for a valid "filing" so as to give notice to third parties of the existence of a security interest against the collateral. Solid policy arguments can be made both for central filing (there's only one place to check, particularly for a mobile debtor) and for local filing (it's much more convenient). The Code originally contained a simple filing scheme: for fixtures, file with the register of deeds in the county where the real estate is located; for motor vehicles required to be licensed, file by making a notation on the vehicle registration certificate; for all else, file with the secretary of state. Alternatives provided in the Code, combined with the effects of having each state legislature "do its own thing," have produced some major variations in these filing requirements. Each state's filing requirements must be checked to ensure the validity of a filing there.

To take one example, the original Michigan version of the Code required that fixtures be filed as indicated above but that motor vehicles other than inventory required a filing with the register of deeds (plus, presumably, a notation on the vehicle registration certificate) and that for all other collateral, *dual* filing with the secretary of state and the local register of deeds was necessary. (Apparently the Lansing lawmakers were impressed with the policy arguments on both sides, so they required both filings.) This original version was amended almost immediately so as to eliminate the expense and complexities of a generally required dual filing. As amended, only local filing is required for fixtures, noninventory motor vehicles (plus registration certification notation), consumer goods, farm equipment, farm products, and resulting intangibles. Where the collateral is crops of the debtor-farmer, filing is also required in the county where the crops are located (if different). For all other types of collateral, only central filing with the secretary of state is now required. Each state may have its own similar variations of these filing requirements.

Where the secured party makes a good faith attempt to file but files in an improper place or in only one of two required places, the filing is nonetheless effective as to anyone who has knowledge of the contents of the financing statement and also of any types of collateral as to which the filing is correct (9–410[2]). An effective filing is not invalidated by a change in the debtor's residence or his or her place of business or in the location of the collateral, but some states have adopted alternative language which requires a new filing in the new county, even within the same state (9–403[3]) and Alternate 3). "Filing" is defined as meaning *either* "[p]resentation for filing of a financing statement and tender of the filing fee" *or* "acceptance of the statement by the filing officer." (The alternative language is included just in case the local filing officer gets funny and refuses to accept your financing statement because "it's not in proper form," etc.)

The effects of an improper filing under a multiple-filing requirement, and the application of 9–401(2), can be seen in *Matter of Babcock Box Co.*, 200 F. Supp. 80 (1961). Financing statements covering two conditional sales of machinery to the debtor Babcock were filed with the Massachusetts secretary of state and the county register of deeds, but not with the city clerk of Attleboro, where the debtor had its only business location in the state. The filing was thus ineffective against the trustee in bankruptcy unless 9–402 applied. The trustee knew the contents of the financing statements, but there was no evidence to indicate that *all* of the creditors he represented had such knowledge and his personal knowledge could be imputed to them (9–301[3]). The secured party, Verson Allsteel Press Company, lost its priority against the machinery.

Financing Statement

What must a "financing statement" contain in order to be effective? Since the only purpose of the financing statement is to serve as a "red flag" to third parties who may wish to deal with the collateral, the requirements are held to a minimum. A valid financing statement must contain the signature and address of both the debtor and the secured party and "a statement indicating the types, or describing the items, of collateral." In addition, where crops or fixtures are involved, there must also be a description of the real estate involved. (Remember that any description is sufficient which "reasonably identifies" the collateral.) No legal mumbo jumbo is required—no witnesses, no affidavits, no notarization. The 1972 amendments eliminate the need for the secured party's signature.

Moreover, substantial compliance is sufficient under 9–402(5):

A financing statement substantially complying with the requirements of this section is effective even though it contains minor errors which are not seriously misleading.

A financing statement that inadvertently described the debtor (Excel Stores, Inc.) as "Excel Department Stores" was held to be in substantial compliance under 9–402(5) so as to protect the secured party (National Cash Register) against the claims of the debtor's trustee in bankruptcy (*In re Excel Stores, Inc.*, 341 F.2d 961 [1965]). Misspelling of the debtor's name, however, has been held to be an error which is seriously misleading, making the filing ineffective (*John Deere Co., v. Pahl*, 300 N.Y.S.2d 701 [1969]): "Ranalli" filed as "Ranelli Construction, Inc." (This decision seems a bit dubious even in a state as large as New York. How many Ranalli or Ranelli construction companies are there where the third party would be required to make inquiry if the filing had been held to be effective?)

As previously noted, *security agreement* and *financing statement* are not used synonymously in Article 9; they are distinct terms, with distinct functions. It would be possible for a security agreement which contained the names and addresses of both parties to be filed as a valid financing statement. The disadvantage of this procedure is that it puts all the "gory details" of the transaction on the public record. But the greater potential danger to the secured party arises when he attempts to have his financing statement do double duty as the security agreement. Since the typical financing statement form will not embody any agreement, or provide for the creation of a security interest in the collateral, the secured party may very well wind up with an interest which is not even enforceable against the debtor. (Refer again to the *American Card* case.)

When properly filed, the original financing statement is effective for the period it specifies, up to five years. It lapses at the end of the five-year period or 60 days after the expiration date where a shorter period is specified. "Upon such lapse the security interest becomes unperfected" (9–403[1]).

If an extension of time is desired, a "continuation statement" may be filed by the secured party anytime within the six-month period prior to the specified expiration date or within the 60-day grace period referred to in the preceding paragraph. The requirements for this continuation statement are absolutely minimal: "Any such continuation statement must be signed by the secured party, identify the original statement by file number and state that the original statement is still effective" (9–403[3]). As long as he complies with the provisions each time, a secured party may thus renew his filing any number of times and thus preserve his perfection against the collateral.

This section also imposes the duties of filing, dating, numbering, and indexing on the filing officer. The statements are to be held "for public inspection" (9–403[4]). Unless he is prohibited by another "public records" statute from doing so, the filing officer "may remove a lapsed statement from the files and destroy it" (9–403[3]). Further duties are imposed by 9–407.

When the secured debt has been paid and the secured party has no obligation to make further advances of money or credit to the debtor, the secured party must on written demand by the debtor send the debtor a "termination statement," saying that "he no longer claims a security interest under the financing statement, which shall be identified by file number" (9–404[1]). A termination statement signed by someone other than the secured party of record must be accompanied by a statement of assignment from the secured party of record (9–404[1]). Where the secured party fails to send the statement within 10 days after a proper demand by the debtor, the debtor can recover a penalty of $100 in addition to any loss he or she can show he or she sustained because of the secured party's refusal (9–404[1]).

When the termination statement is presented to the filing officer, he must note it in the index. He must then remove the financing statement, any continuation statement, and any statement of assignment or release. He marks these statements "terminated" and sends them to the secured party (9–404[2]).

Section 9–405 and 9–406 contain provisions for handling an "Assignment of Security Interest" and a "Release of Collateral," respectively.

DEFAULT AND REMEDIES

Most of our discussion of secured transactions to this point has concerned the problems confronted by the secured party when third-party claimants contest his or her right to "priority" against the collateral. Most of Article 9 is directed toward those problems, but Part 5, Default, does step into the transaction between the immediate parties, to regulate the rights and remedies as between them in the event that the debtor defaults.

Section 9–501(1) makes clear the intent of the UCC drafters that the secured party should be entitled to pursue all available remedies until the debt to him or her is satisfied. He or she has the rights and remedies provided by Part 5 and 9–207, those provided in the security agreement itself (subject to the limitations in 9–501[3]), and "any available judicial procedure" for debt enforcement under applicable state law. "The rights and remedies referred to in this subsection are cumulative" (9–501[1]).

Similarly, the debtor has the rights and remedies provided in Part 5, in Section 9–207, and in the security agreement. The policy of the Code and of Article 9 is to provide substantial freedom of contract between the immediate parties to the particular transaction. That policy is continued, to a degree, as regards default procedures, but 9–501(3) imposes a set of "minimum procedural requirements" on default, for the protection of the debtor. This section is important enough to merit an extensive quotation:

To the extent that they give rights to the debtor and impose duties on the secured party, the rules stated in the subsections referred to below may not be waived or varied except as provided with respect to compulsory disposition of collateral (subsection [1] of Section 9–505) and with respect to redemption of collateral [Section 9–506] but the parties may by agreement determine the standards by which the fulfillment of these rights and duties is to be measured if such standards are not manifestly unreasonable.

Included in this list are 9–502(2) and 9–504(2), which require the secured party to account for surplus proceeds of collateral; 9–504(3) and 9–505(1), which cover the disposition of collateral; 9–505(2), which deals with the secured party's acceptance of the collateral in satisfaction of the debt; 9–506, which deals with the debtor's right to redeem the collateral; and 9–507(1), which imposes liability on the secured party for failure to follow these prescribed procedures. (In addition to these prescribed minima, the parties' freedom to agree to "whatever they want" may also be limited by 1–102[3] and 2–302, as noted above.)

The objective in these default sections, then, is to balance the rights and remedies of both parties and to ensure that the debtor is protected by requiring that certain steps be taken when default occurs. *Default*, however, is not specifically defined; its definition is left to the agreement itself and to generally applicable legal principles.

Collection

On default, or whenever so agreed, the secured party has the right to notify an account debtor or the obligor on an instrument to start making payments to him or her and the right to take control of any proceeds to which he or she is entitled under Section 9–306. This rule applies even though the assignor (i.e., the "debtor" under the security agreement) was previously making the collections himself or herself and then remitting them to the secured party (9–502[1]).

Where the agreement provides that the secured party is entitled to charge back against the debtor any "uncollected" collateral and the secured party elects to do his or her own collecting, he or she "must proceed in a commercially reasonable manner." He or she is entitled to the reasonable expenses he or she incurs in the collection process. Provision is also made for both "deficiency" and "surplus" situations (9–502[2]):

If the security agreement secures an indebtedness, the secured party must account to the debtor for any surplus, and unless otherwise agreed, the debtor is liable for any deficiency. But, if the underlying transaction was a sale of accounts, contract rights, or chattel paper, the debtor is entitled to any surplus or is liable for any deficiency only if the security agreement so provides.

Repossession

The creditor's classic remedy on default has been to "repo" the collateral. This remedy is continued for the secured party, pretty much as it existed under prior law, by 9–503:

Unless otherwise agreed, a secured party has on default the right to take possession of the collateral. In taking possession a secured party may proceed without judicial process if this can be done without breach of the peace or may proceed by action.

Traditionally the main question in these cases has been the definition of what constitutes a "breach of the peace" by the creditor when he or she repossesses without court order. Parked on the street or in a public parking lot, the debtor's car seems to be fair game for the repo person. Even if it's in the debtor's driveway or parked on private property, the repo person can probably still seize it and drive or tow it away. The line of demarcation seems to be the point at which the repo person opens a door or gate, either by force or fraud, or threatens the debtor in any way. (See, e.g., *Dominick* v. *Rea*, 226 Mich. 594 [1924]. These lines of decision under prior law will presumably continue under 9–503.

The 1972 U.S. Supreme Court decision in the landmark *Fuentes* case seemed to throw into doubt the whole idea of repossession without a hearing. In effect, it seemed to amend the second sentence of 9–503 so as to require the secured party to proceed by "action" if he or she wished to repossess the collateral. Nearly all subsequent decisions have continued to recognize the legal validity of self-help repossession on default.

On the other hand, repossession by court process, after default by the debtor, and when done in good faith by the creditor in an attempt to realize on the security that he or she has been given by agreement, should not subject the creditor to liability. A clearly erroneous trial court judgment which awarded the debtor (Edith Gustafson) $20,500 actual damages and $15,000 punitive damages on an "abuse of process" theory was reversed by the Kentucky court of appeals in *Fort Knox Bank* v. *Gustafson*, 385 S.W.2d 196 (1964). There was no indication that the bank had acted otherwise than in good faith in activating its acceleration clause and foreclosing on the collateral (a mobile diner); the only basis for the so-called abuse of process was a technical defect in the replevin bond filed by the bank when it repossessed. The case was remanded for further evidence as to whether the bank disposed of the diner in a "commercially reasonable manner."

Section 9–503 also provides two new repo alternatives:

> If the security agreement so provides the secured party may require the debtor to assemble the collateral and make it available to the secured party at a place to be designated by the secured party which is reasonably convenient to both parties.

And:

> Without removal a secured party may render equipment unusable, and may dispose of collateral on the debtor's premises under Section 9–504.

These two provisions give the secured party additional options under his or her general right to repossession.

Disposition

After default by the debtor, the secured party has the right to dispose of the collateral and to apply the proceeds—first, to pay his or her reasonable selling expenses; second, to satisfy his or her security interest; and third, to pay any subordinate security interest as to which he or she receives a written demand for payment prior to distribution of the proceeds (9–504[1]). Where there is an underlying debt, "the secured party must account to the debtor for any surplus, and, unless otherwise agreed, the debtor is liable for any deficiency" (9–504[2]). Contrariwise, if the transaction was a sale of accounts, contract rights, or chattel paper, "the debtor is entitled to any surplus or is liable for any deficiency only if the security agreement so provides" (9–504[2]).

As regards the disposition itself, 9–504 allows maximum flexibility as to details. The disposition may be made by public or private sale, in one or more contracts, as a unit or in parcels, at any time and place, and on any terms. The secured party may buy the collateral at any public sale, or at a private sale if the collateral is of a type sold in a recognized market or subject to widely distributed standard price quotations. This considerable flexibility is, however, subject to a basic good faith limitation: "every aspect of the disposition including the method, manner, time, place and terms must be commercially reasonable." Also, except where the collateral is perishable, or threatens to decline speedily in value, or is customarily sold on a recognized market, the secured party must give the debtor reasonable notification of the intended sale. Except for consumer goods, notification must also be sent to any other secured party who has filed against the collateral or whose interest is known to the secured party (9–504[3]). The debtor can thus challenge the legal effects of the sale either under the "commercially reasonable" requirement or on the basis that he did not get "reasonable notification." The issue is most often raised when the debtor is sued for a deficiency judgment, where the secured party says that the sale did not bring enough to pay off the debt.

The Tennessee Supreme Court had occasion to define the "reasonable notification" requirement in *Mallicott* v. *Volunteer Finance & Loan Corporation*, 415 S.W.2d 347 (1966). The Mallicotts were in default on their installment payments on a car. Volunteer's manager testified that he had sent a registered letter notice of the sale but that it had come back; he initially claimed that there had been notice by poster-advertisement but then admitted that he could not remember when or where that had occurred. Volunteer made no *further* effort to contract the debtor, despite the fact that it knew where Mr. Mallicott worked, where his parents lived, and that he lived in Knoxville, where the secured party had its place of business and where the sale had been made. The court held that Volunteer had not met its obligations under this section and that the Mallicotts were entitled to a penalty award under 9–507(1), to be offset against the balance they owed on the car.

The effect of improper sales procedure on the secured party's rights is also at issue in the *Nuss* case.

Grant County Tractor Co. v. Nuss
496 P.2d 966 (Washington, 1972)

FACTS   On August 15, 1968, Mr. and Mrs. Vernon Nuss bought a Model 1850 Oliver diesel tractor, a Howard rotovator, and a Brillion packer from the plaintiff. They executed a written purchase-money security agreement. They used the equipment in their farming operations and made the required installment payments for about one year. On July 1, 1969, they decided to trade in the 1850 model tractor on a 1950 T model, and executed a new security agreement. The first annual payment of $3,867.10 under the new agreement was due on September 1, 1969. The Nusses defaulted on this payment. On January 8, 1970, on their own initiative, they returned the new tractor, the rotovator, and the packer to the plaintiff's sales yard. On January 13, their attorney told the plaintiff that they were rescinding the contract.

The plaintiff's employees decided that the rotovator and the packer were not worth repairing but had only salvage value. The plaintiff did resell the new tractor in April 1970 but failed to give notice of the sale to the Nusses. The trial court found that the Nusses still owed the plaintiff $3,507 but refused to enter a deficiency judgment for that amount because of the lack of notice. It also refused to award damages to the Nusses on their claim that the equipment was defective. Both parties appealed.

ISSUE   Does the secured party's failure to give the required notice prevent it from receiving a deficiency judgment for the balance due?

DECISION   No. Judgment reversed; Grant County collects $3,507.

REASONS   Judge Green first reviewed UCC 9–504(2) and (3), which made the debtor liable for any deficiency unless otherwise agreed. Disposition was not limited to a "sale" of the collateral, but notice to the debtor was required. In this case, only the tractor had been resold without notice and there was no evidence that the lack of notice had caused any loss to the Nusses. Had such a loss been proved, under UCC 9–507(1) they could have recovered that loss or offset it against the amount they still owed. The court felt that 9–507(1) gave the debtor adequate protection and that it was not necessary to also prevent the secured party from collecting an amount that was admittedly still due on the contract. Further, in this case the $3,507 was the balance due for the rotovator and packer, after allowing credits of $300 and $50 for their salvage values. Moreover, the Nusses had voluntarily returned the collateral and given notice of their intent to rescind the contract. "It has been held that such con-

461

duct constitutes a waiver of the debtor's right to reasonable notice of an impending sale or estops the debtor from claiming a violation of the statute."

Judge Green noted that there was a wide-open split of authority on this point, with New York, New Mexico, Georgia, and Pennsylvania cases holding for the debtor and Arkansas, Alaska, New Jersey, and Tennessee cases permitting the entry of a deficiency judgment. Because of the debtor's right to offset any loss under 9–507(1), Judge Green said, "[W]e are of the opinion the writers of the Uniform Commercial Code did not intend that the creditor's failure to give notice would result in a forfeiture of the creditor's right to a deficiency."

Section 9–504(4) deals with the rights acquired by the purchaser of the collateral at the disposition sale. The disposition gives the purchaser all rights of the debtor, and it discharges the security interest under which the sale was made and any subordinate interest or lien. Even though the secured party does not follow proper sale procedures, the purchaser is protected at a public sale if he or she has no knowledge of the defects in the sale and does not buy in collusion and in any other case if he or she acts in good faith.

Compulsory Disposition

A secured party who has repossessed the collateral *must* dispose of it in accordance with Section 9–504 where the consumer-debtor has paid 60 percent of the cash price or of the loan and has not signed *after default* a statement renouncing or modifying his or her rights under Part 5. If the secured party fails to comply with this section within 90 days after he or she takes possession, the debtor may either sue for conversion of the collateral or recover damages and a penalty as specified under 9–501(7) (9–505[1]).

Except for the above consumer goods situation, a secured party who is in possession of the collateral may propose *after default* that he or she will retain it in satisfaction of the debt. The secured party must send written notice of his or her "proposal" to the debtor and, except for consumer goods, to any other secured party who has filed or who is known to the secured party with possession. The debtor or any secured party entitled to notification has 30 days from receipt of the notification to object in writing to the proposal; any other secured party claiming an interest in the collateral has 30 days from the time that secured party 1 obtained possession of the collateral. If anyone does object, secured party 1 cannot retain the collateral as he or she proposed but must dispose of it under 9–504; if there is no objection, he or she can keep the collateral in satisfaction of the obligation (9–505[2]).

Redemption by Debtor

At any time before the secured party has disposed or contracted to dispose of the collateral under 9–504 or has discharged the obligation by retention of the collateral under 9–505(2), the debtor or any other secured party has the right to redeem the collateral. In order to redeem, there must be a tender to the secured party of (*a*) all obligations secured by the collateral; (*b*) "the expenses reasonably incurred by the secured party in retaking, holding and preparing the collateral for disposition, in arranging for the sale;" and (*c*) "to the extent provided in the agreement and not prohibited by law, his reasonable attorneys' fees and legal expenses."

The debtor or any other secured party may agree *in writing, after default,* to waive this right to redeem (9–506).

Secured Party Liability for Failure to Comply

Section 9–507 does two things. It defines more precisely the requirement that the secured party proceed after default in a "commercially reasonable" manner (9–507[2]); and it provides remedies for the debtor where the secured party does not proceed in accordance with the provisions of Part 5.

Section 9–507(2) establishes several principles regarding "commercial reasonableness":

> "The fact that a better price could have been obtained by a sale at a different time or in a different method from that selected by the secured party is not of itself sufficient to establish that the sale was not made in a commercially reasonably manner."

> "If the secured party either sells the collateral in the usual manner in any recognized market therefore or if he sells at the price current in such market at the time of his sale or if he has otherwise sold in conformity with reasonable commercial practices among dealers in the type of property sold he has sold in a commercially reasonably manner."

> "The principles stated in the two preceding sentences with respect to sales also apply as may be appropriate to other types of disposition."

> "A disposition which has been approved in any judicial proceeding or by any bona fide creditors' committee or representative of creditors shall conclusively be deemed to be commercially reasonable, but this sentence does not indicate that any such approval must be obtained in any case nor does it indicate that any disposition not so approved is not commercially reasonable."

Section 9–507(1) establishes the debtor's right to recover for a secured party's violation of the default provisions of Part 5. Where such violation has occurred:

a. " . . . [D]isposition may be ordered or restrained on appropriate terms and conditions."

b. "If the disposition has occurred the debtor or any person entitled to notification or whose security interest has been made known to the secured party prior to disposition has a right to recover from the secured party any loss caused by a failure to comply with the provisions of this Part."

c. "If the collateral is consumer goods, the debtor has a right to recover in any event an amount not less than the credit service charge plus ten percent of the principal amount of the debt or the time price differential plus ten percent of the cash price."

These Code sections thus provide significant protections for both consumer and nonconsumer debtors even after they have gone into default on their obligations under a security agreement.

CASES FOR DISCUSSION

MESSENGER v. SANDY MOTORS, INC.

205 A.2d 402 (New Jersey, 1972)

Herbert, Justice

* * * * *

On July 10, 1970 plaintiff bought a used automobile from defendant Sandy Motors, Inc. The price was $1,674.75. The cash paid was $674.75, and plaintiff agreed to pay the balance, plus interest and insurance charges, in 24 equal monthly installments of $52.01 each. The details of the transaction were set out in a written agreement signed by plaintiff, by defendant Sandy Motors, and by plaintiff's wife as coobligor. A printed form furnished by defendant Peoples Trust Company of New Jersey was used, and immediately following the transaction between plaintiff and Sandy Motors, Inc., the latter assigned all of its rights to the Trust Company.

The agreement of July 10, 1970 provided that:

Seller retains a purchase money Security Interest in the Vehicle and all accessions until Buyer fully performs hereunder.

On the reverse side of the one-sheet document a number of contract terms are to be found, including the following.

In the event of default by Buyer hereunder, (1) the entire unpaid balance of the Total Payments shall, at the option of Holder, become immediately due and payable, and (2) Buyer, upon demand, shall deliver the vehicle to Holder, or Holder may, with or without previous notice or demand for performance, enter any premises wherein the vehicle may be and take possession of the same, together with anything in the vehicle.

Though easily readable, this quotation as well as the entire reverse side of the agreement is in

fine print. On the other side, where the signatures appear, there is a reference in relatively large capital letters to the terms printed on the back of the document.

When plaintiff's payment for October, 1971 fell due it was not made on time. Prior to October 1971 plaintiff had been more than 10 days late with 12 payments out of a total of 14, and for two short intervals he had been in arrears for two payments at once. This history of the account bears upon the reasons of defendant bank for the action it took when the October 1971 payment was not received, and it shows considerable tolerance in the treatment of defaults.

By November 9, 1971 the bank had not received plaintiff's payment for October and had no word from him about that payment. It decided to demand possession of the car, was unable to reach plaintiff by telephone, and sent by ordinary mail to plaintiff at his residence a written demand which he says was not received by him. Having received no payment from plaintiff and having heard nothing from him by way of explanation of his delay, the bank instructed an agency to repossess the car. On November 17, 1971 the car was taken from a parking area behind the building in which plaintiff had his apartment. Repossession took place without judicial process and without any breach of the peace. In fact, the car was taken away from the parking place without any physical confrontation with anyone. Plaintiff first learned about what happened from the Linden police, who had been notified immediately by the agent who acted for the bank.

On November 17, 1971, the date of repossession, the bank received through the mail from plaintiff the payment for October. At the time of repossession the bank's collection department was not yet aware that payment had arrived. The payment due on November 13, 1971 was not made at the same time and was delinquent by four days when the repossession took place.

Having taken possession of the car, defendant Trust Company proposed to sell it (N.J.S.A. 12A:9–504) and so notified plaintiff. He then brought this action. Among other things, he sought an interlocutory injunction against the sale. An order to show cause containing a preliminary restraint was issued. That was followed by a negotiated arrangement between the parties by which plaintiff got the car back and the account was reinstated. In relation to the negotiations an order was entered on December 3, 1971, consented to by the attorneys and by plaintiff personally, which provided in part that claims for nominal damages on certain counts of the complaint would survive. Plaintiff now urges that section 503 of the Uniform Commercial Code, by authorizing a secured creditor to take possession of security without a judicial proceeding, is in conflict with the Due Process Clause of the Federal Constitution. He also argues violation of the Fourth Amendment and of Article I, paragraphs 1 and 7 of New Jersey's Constitution. He says that his car was, therefore, taken unlawfully by the bank's agents on November 17, 1971 and that he is entitled to damages—though only nominal—for the unlawful taking. Plaintiff initially named the State as a defendant, but later a consent judgment of dismissal was entered on application of the Attorney General.

It is quite common for secured creditors, after default, to repossess automobiles by the peaceful use of self-help. Rarely, however, have the questions presented here been litigated. Yet it now seems apparent that those questions are before long going to be placed before the United States Supreme Court. The federal court for the Southern District of California, in cases involving peaceful repossession of automobiles following default under installment purchase contracts, has held sections 9503 and 9504 of the California Commercial Code unconstitutional under the Due Process Clause of the 14th Amendment of the United States Constitution. *Adams* v. *Egley*— *Posadas* v. *Star and Crescent Fed. Credit Union* (two cases), 338 F. Supp. 614 (S.D. Cal. 1972). The federal court for the Northern District of

California on similar facts has reached the opposite result. . . .

Section 9503 in California is identical with N.J.S.A. 12A:9–503. Section 9504 is identical with N.J.S.A. 12A:9–504, which provides for disposition of the collateral after it has been repossessed.

Two main questions are presented: (*a*) Is there a sufficient element of state action involved to make the 14th Amendment to the Federal Constitution applicable to all? And (*b*) If the 14th Amendment does apply, has plaintiff been denied due process? . . .

Section 9–503 of the Code limits a creditor's use of self-help to peaceful situations, but does it create or substantially contribute to the creation of the right of self-help? I think not. It appears to me that section 503 in its first sentence says that the secured party has the right to take possession on default even though the agreement is silent on the subject, but says in effect that where the parties have agreed about possession after default, their agreement is to control. The agreement here is the creative thing, and the first three words of section 503 ("Unless otherwise agreed") merely make it clear that the statute does not bar the parties from making contracts as they see fit about possession after default.

Although it can be argued to the contrary that the enactment of section 9–503 either created the right to repossession under which defendant Trust Company acted, or so influenced the draftsman of the contract form signed by plaintiff that the repossession provisions would not have been inserted if section 9–503 had never been put on the statute books, my conclusion is that the existence of the section did not make the taking of the automobile on November 17, 1971 an action under color of state law, within the meaning of the 14th Amendment of the Federal Constitution. It might be difficult to sustain this conclusion if self-help never had been legally recognized prior to the adoption of the Uniform Commercial Code. However, self-help has been known to the common law for centuries. . . .

If I am mistaken in concluding that the 14th Amendment does not apply to this case, then plaintiff's contention that he was denied due process is to be considered. The record here contains much information about the business of financing automobile purchases as that business is carried on by a number of representative lenders. . . . There is a substantial degree of uniformity. Once a loan has been made or contract acquired, the necessary data about it is made part of a computer system. The computer is then relied upon to get out bills in advance of due dates and get out a late notice a few days after a failure to pay on time. If the debtor does not respond to a computerized notice that his account is delinquent, then the usual practice is to try to reach him by telephone. Much effort is made to keep accounts alive by adjusting the payment schedule and otherwise. Repossession is treated as a last resort, and when the decision is made to repossess, it is usual practice to mail to the debtor notice of intent to repossess before a professional agency is directed to try to pick up the car. . . .

The witnesses before me were firm in their opinions that changes in recaption procedure to meet the requirements of *Adams*, supra, would impose substantial costs of doing business. It was testified that under present practices the bank or finance company sustains losses in a large percentage of repossession cases. This indicates a limited possibility of passing along to a particular defaulting car buyer the direct costs of repossessing his automobile by a legal proceeding, and further indicates that much of the burden of doing business in the new way ultimately would be borne by all who buy cars on credit. Witnesses also expressed the view that the only practical way to minimize the costs of conforming with the *Adams* case would be to select credit risks with greater care, thus keeping down the number of replevin cases. Professor Johnson also points out other elements of cost which would bear on the situation: the cost to the public of substantial volume of additional court cases, a longer time to get possession of a car after a contract goes into default, great car depreciation, and so on.

Among thousands of recaptions a year one can imagine there are some in which car buyers get harsh treatment, but there is nothing before me to prove unfair tactics are in any degree usual. . . .

Thousands of cars are repossessed each year. It is difficult to believe the buying public is not well informed of the likelihood of repossession by the bank or finance company if installments are not paid. Plaintiff does not say that he lacked knowledge of such likelihood or that he was unaware of the express terms of his contract; the argument for him is that with or without knowledge of the consequences of default, he and those similarly situated are entitled by the Constitution to a hearing on notice before recaption. I think that argument must be rejected. A car buyer, having a wealth of experience all around him to draw upon and make him aware of the possibility of repossession, is not in a situation where he can properly claim that recaption of his car is a violation of his right to due process because, and only because, no prior hearing or notice to him took place.

My conclusion is that if the 14th Amendment has any application at all to this case, there has been no violation of the Due Process Clause. . . .

Judgment will be entered for defendants against plaintiff.

JAMES TALCOTT, INC. v. FRANKLIN NATIONAL BANK OF MINNEAPOLIS
194 N.W.2d 775 (Minnesota, 1972)

Ronald E. Hackey, Justice

This is an appeal taken from a summary judgment in favor of defendant, Franklin National Bank of Minneapolis. The action was commenced for the recovery of possession of several motor vehicles, or their value, in which plaintiff, James Talcott, Inc., claimed a superior security interest.

The case was heard on stipulated facts. On February 20, 1968, Noyes Paving Company, hereinafter referred to as "debtor," entered into a conditional sales contract with Northern Contracting Company, as seller, covering the purchase, on an installment basis, of two dump trucks and other construction equipment. On that same day, the seller assigned, without recourse, the conditional sales contract to plaintiff, together with all sums payable thereunder and all right, title, and interest in and to the equipment covered by the contract. On February 21, 1968, a financing statement was filed with the secretary of state naming Noyes Paving Company as debtor, Northern Contracting Company as secured party, and James Talcott, Inc., as assignee of the secured party. The financing statement covered the following items of property: "Construction Equipment, Motor Vehicles."

On May 1, debtor entered into an equipment lease with defendant bank covering one dump truck; and on May 31, a similar lease agreement was entered into between the same parties covering two additional dump trucks and other equipment. Each lease provided that debtor, if not in default, could purchase the leased goods at the end of the lease term for the sum of $1. Defendant did not at that time file a financing statement regarding the equipment described in the two lease agreements.

During the latter part of the year 1968, debtor experienced difficulty in making payments on the conditional sales contract. On *January 30, 1969,* debtor and plaintiff entered into an agreement extending the time for payment. In consideration of the extension granted, debtor gave plaintiff a *security interest "in all goods (as defined in Article 9 of the Uniform Commercial Code) whether now owned or hereafter acquired."* An attached schedule merely repeated in substantially identical form the list of goods attached to the original conditional sales agreement. The new agreement went on to provide that the security interest was granted to secure the payment of all loans, advances, debts, liabilities, obligations, covenants, and duties owing by debtor to plaintiff, including, without limitation, any debt, liability, or obligation owing from debtor to others which plaintiff may have obtained by assignment or otherwise. No additional financing statement was filed in connection with the extension agreement of January 30. At that time, plaintiff did not know of the existence of the motor vehicles and other equipment listed in defendant's two equipment leases and did not rely upon their existence in entering into the extension agreement.

Following the date of the extension agreement, debtor ran into more financial difficulty

and defaulted in payments with respect to both the conditional sales contract and the equipment leases. On May 21, 1970, copies of the leases were filed by defendant bank as financing statements with the secretary of state. Sometime during May 1970, defendant repossessed the equipment in question and this action ensued. The precise date on which defendant made the repossession is not clear from the record. The parties agreed that it took place during the month of May 1970. All of the equipment was located with the exception of one item. By agreement between plaintiff and defendant, the equipment was sold, and the proceeds were placed in a special account pending the outcome of this case.

The issues on appeal are: (1) Whether an equipment lease which gives the lessee the right to acquire title to the equipment for $1 upon compliance with the lease terms is a "security agreement" within the meaning of Article 9 of the Uniform Commercial Code (Minn. St. 336.9–101, et seq.); (2) whether debtor had sufficient ownership of the leased equipment so that it became secured property under the extension agreement with plaintiff; (3) whether the description of the secured property, as it appeared in the extension agreement, was sufficient to meet the requirements of Art. 9 of the Uniform Commercial Code; (4) whether the financing statement filed at the time the first security agreement was assigned to plaintiff was sufficient to perfect a security interest in the property covered by the extension agreement; and (5) which security interest was entitled to priority. . . .

1. Were the leases security agreements?

This question is extremely significant because plaintiff's right to recovery is dependent upon a finding that the lease agreements between defendant and debtor were, in effect, security agreements. Plaintiff claims that, because the procedures set out in the code were not followed in a timely manner by defendant, the latter has lost its priority rights to the collateral. It is the clear policy of Art. 9 of the code to look to the substance, rather than to the form, of an agreement to determine whether or not it is a security

467

agreement. This policy is expressed in the code itself in § 336.9–102(1). . . .

The language of the code specifically determines whether or not a lease creates a security interest in the collateral. Section 336.1–201(37). . . . The words of that section are unequivocal. An option given to the lessee to purchase the leased property for a nominal consideration does make the lease one intended for security. Hence, the options to buy the equipment in the instant case for thé combined sum of $2, nominal an amount when compared to the total rental of $73,303.32, created security interests. The leases in question were precisely the type that Art. 9 was intended to cover, i.e., transactions in goods which were in substance, although not in form, security agreements. . . .

Defendant bank did not file a financing statement with the secretary of state at the time of the making of the leases. Accordingly, the security interests of the bank in the equipment which it financed were unperfected at that time. Presumably, defendant was laboring under a misapprehension concerning the nature of the equipment leases. Had it filed a financing statement with 10 days after the leases were signed, under § 336.9–312(4) it would have perfected its security interest in the equipment which it had financed, which, in turn, would have afforded protection against execution creditors, trustees in bankruptcy, and secured parties whose financing statements were filed later. In addition, if the statement had been filed within the prescribed 10-day period, defendant, having a perfected purchase money security interest in the equipment, would have had priority under § 336.9–312(4) over conflicting security interests perfected earlier, including any conflicting security interest plaintiff might have had as a result of its filing the financing statement on February 21, 1968.

2. Did the debtor "own" the leased property so that it was included as secured property under plaintiff's security agreement?

This question is a part of the critical issue in the case inasmuch as the second security agreement between plaintiff and debtor (the extension agreement of January 30, 1969) gave plaintiff a security interest in "all goods . . . whether now owned or hereafter acquired" by debtor. The issue turns on whether or not debtor can be deemed to have owned the leased property at the time it entered into the extension agreement. Minn. St. 336.9–202 provides:

Each provision of this article with regard to rights, obligations and remedies applies whether title to collateral is in the secured party or in the debtor.

Thus the draftsmen of the code intended that its provisions should not be circumvented by manipulation of the locus of title. For this reason, consignment sales, conditional sales, and other arrangements or devices whereby title is retained in the seller for a period following possession by the debtor are all treated under Art. 9 as though the title had been transferred to the debtor and the creditor-seller had retained only a security interest in the goods. For the purpose of analyzing rights of ownership under Art. 9, we hold, based upon the stipulated facts of this case, that defendant had only a security interest in the equipment despite a purported reservation of title and that debtor "owned" the equipment at the time that the extension agreement was executed.

3. Was the description of the secured property, as it appeared in the extension agreement, sufficient to meet the requirements of Art. 9; that is, did the description reasonably identify what was being described?

Upon examination of the code, it is readily apparent that its provisions give scant guidance in the resolution of this problem.* Where this issue has arisen, a number of courts have sustained security agreements containing descriptions almost as general as the one in question in the instant case.

Minn. St. 336–203(1)(b) sets out one of the elements required to make a security agreement

---

*In contrast to the requirements of a financing statement, for which the code expressly states that the description may be by item or by type, there is no guiding reference relative to the description required in a security agreement.

enforceable against a debtor. It states that it must contain "a description of the collateral." . . .

The principal function of a description of the collateral in a security agreement is to enable the parties themselves or their successors in interest to identify it, particularly if the secured party has to repossess the collateral or reclaim it in a legal proceeding. If the debtor himself is willing to give a creditor a security interest in everything he owns, the code does not prevent it, whether his action is prudent or not. Upon default, the creditor takes everything to which the debtor previously agreed; hence, identification is no problem.

The description of the collateral in the extension agreement did what it was meant to do—namely, it included all of the goods then owned, or to be owned in the future, by the debtor. The term "goods" was defined to be those goods as comprehended within the meaning of Art. 9 of the code. The definition selected is embodied in the statute, a definition that is used and applied frequently. The parties sought to create a security interest in substantially all of the debtor's property. That is what was stated, and that is what was meant. The parties did not particularize any further, and the statute does not require it. . . .

A security agreement should not be held unenforceable unless it is so ambiguous that its meaning cannot reasonably be construed from the language of the agreement itself. Such a test appears to have been intended by the draftsmen of the code and should be applied in this case. We fail to find an impelling reason why we should not approve the description used in this case, and we hold that it suffices within the terms of the statute. We further hold specifically that the description used in the extension agreement between debtor and plaintiff includes the equipment financed by defendant bank.

4. Was the financing statement, filed at the time the first security agreement was assigned to plaintiff, sufficient to reflect a security interest in the property covered by the extension agreement?

Defendant argues that plaintiff did not perfect its security interest in the equipment covered by the second security agreement (the extension agreement of January 30, 1969) because of the failure to file an amendment to the financing statement. The trial court also followed this line of reasoning in arriving at its decision that plaintiff had not perfected its security interest.

Section 336.402(1) provides that "[a] financing statement may be filed before a security agreement is made or a security interest otherwise attaches." This is what happened in the instant case. The financing statement filed February 21, 1968, met all requirements of the code since it described by type ("Construction Equipment, Motor Vehicles") not only the property covered by the original sales agreement which was assigned to plaintiff but also the property, which likewise consisted of motor vehicles and construction equipment, financed by defendant. The code does not require a reference in the financing statement to after-acquired property. . . .

When §§ 336.9–402(1) and 336.9–204(3) are read together, it is clear they sanction the essential elements of the transaction in the instant case. The financing statement was filed February 21, 1968, and described the type of goods covered as "Construction Equipment, Motor Vehicles." It was sufficient to give notice of the security agreement entered into on February 20, 1968, and was also sufficient to give notice of the second security agreement of January 30, 1969. As pointed out herein, § 336.9–402(1) specifically permits the filing of a financing statement in advance of the making of the security agreement itself.

The whole purpose of notice filing would be nullified if a financing statement had to be filed whenever a new transaction took place between a secured party and a debtor. Once a financing statement is on file describing property by type, the entire world is warned, not only that the secured party may already have a security interest in the property of that type (as did plaintiff in the property originally financed), but that it may later acquire a perfected security interest in property of the same type acquired by the debtor in the future. When the debtor does acquire more property of the type referred to in the financing statement already on file, and when a security interest attaches to that property, the perfection is instantaneous and automatic. § 336.9–303(1). . . .

5. Priority.

As has been pointed out, the record is not clear as to what date defendant repossessed the equipment. The exact date the conflict arose would be helpful in determining which portion of § 336.9–312 should be applied in determining priorities.

From an examination of the record, it is clear that § 336.9–312(4) is inapplicable inasmuch as defendant's security was not perfected within the allotted time thereunder—that is, no financing statement had been filed at the time that the debtor received the equipment or within 10 days thereafter. Had a financing statement covering the equipment leases been filed at the time the transaction between debtor and defendant took place or within 10 days thereafter, defendant would have had priority under this section of the code. Unfortunate as it may be for defendant, this did not take place; hence, § 336.9–312(4) does not govern despite the bank's later filing.

Turning our attention to § 336.9–312(5), we must determine whether paragraph (a) or paragraph (b) governs. Again, the date that the dispute arose is not clear. The parties have agreed that it arose sometime during the month of May 1970. Hence, whether the filing of the financing statement (equipment leases) by defendant was prior to or subsequent to the repossession date is not established. It then follows that § 336.9–312(5)(a) may or may not be applicable.

With certain exceptions not applicable in the case at bar, a security interest is perfected when a financing statement is filed. Therefore, a reading of paragraph (a) leads us to the conclusion that, if a dispute arises over priority of perfected security interests (both having been perfected by filing before the dispute arose), then the order of filing of the financing statement governs. We are aware of the date that the defendant filed its financing statement (May 21, 1970), but, again, the record is not clear as to the date that the dispute arose (i.e., the date of repossession). Defendant might have filed first and then repossessed, or it might have repossessed first, and, upon being confronted with a dispute over priorities, decided to file forthwith. As we have said, if defendant filed first and then repossessed, § 336.9–312(5)(a) governs.

Conversely, if the dispute arose first and thereafter the bank filed, then paragraph (a) of § 336.9–312(5) is inapplicable, and we direct our attention to paragraph (b), which gives the following alternative method of determining priorities under this subsection:

In the order of perfection unless both are perfected by filing, regardless of which security interest attached first under section 336.9–204(1) and, in the case of a filed security interest, whether it attached before or after filing."

Defendant's security interest did attach first, but (assuming it was filed after repossession) it was not perfected. Plaintiff's security interest attached later—actually after its filing had occurred. But neither of these factors is material in the application of the first-to-perfect rule. Accordingly, when the conflict arose (still assuming it was before defendant had filed), plaintiff was entitled to priority. Once plaintiff's priority had been acquired, no subsequent filing by defendant (more than 10 days after debtor received possession) could alter the situation. Moreover, even if § 336.9–312(5)(a) should apply, plaintiff would still have priority under the first-to-file rule as its filing preceded defendant's by many months.

In passing, it could be said that plaintiff is to receive an unearned windfall, being the beneficiary of a security interest in property of which it wasn't even aware. Unquestionably, defendant bank, through misunderstanding of the applicable provisions of the code, will suffer a substantial loss. By its own failure to conform to and comply with very simple and obvious provisions of the code, it has found itself entangled in other provisions which are admittedly more complex but which are absolutely essential to the whole concept of notice filing. The fundamental purpose of Art. 9 of the code is to make the process of perfecting a security interest easy, simple, and certain. It was intended to be a complete reversal of prior chattel security law and to rid the unaware of the traps of requirement of specific types of acknowledgements, technical affidavits of consideration, selection of specific property forms, and other pitfalls that were not uncommon. The code very simply and briefly provides for a notice-filing procedure with a minimum of information required to be publicized in a filed financing statement. All that is required is a minimal description, and it may be by type of kind. The statement need not necessarily contain detail as to collateral, nor any statement of quantity, size, description or specifications, or serial numbers. No preciseness is required with respect to whether the collateral exists at the time of filing or is to be acquired thereafter, and no statement of charges, payment schedule, or maturity date need be included in the statement. The first to file shall prevail. Although there are a few exceptions, they are very clearly and definitely stated. To affirm here would amount to a limitation upon the efficacy of the first-to-file rule, which is basic and essential to the certainty that Art. 9 seeks to achieve. Moreover, to hold that plaintiff was required to file an additional financing statement to cover the extension agreement of January 30, 1969, would have a disastrous effect upon financing transactions.

The summary judgment for defendant is reversed, and the matter is remanded with directions to enter judgment for plaintiff. . . .

PROBLEMS FOR DISCUSSION

1. Tom Teemster's truck broke down while en route to Menomanee Falls. He had it towed to Harry Fixall's Truck Repair, but Harry hesitated to start with the repairs since Tom still owed him money on previous repair jobs. The truck in question was mortgaged to Easycome Credit Company as security for an installment note totaling $21,000. Tom notified Easycome of the needed repairs without asking for financing. Nevertheless, a few days later Easycome's finance manager, Joe Cents, came to the garage to inspect the truck. No estimate was given, and Cents did not mention that his company would pay for the repairs. Harry, however, went ahead and repaired the truck for $3,000. Shortly thereafter, Tom Teemster declared bankruptcy. Easycome, listed as one of his creditors, received the truck from the referee in bankruptcy. Harry was not listed as one of Tom's creditors. What arguments might he use to get his $3,000? Who will prevail?

2. Becky Miller, MBA, decided to open a Texaco station. She purchased equipment from Leek Oil Equipment Company, for which she delivered to the seller a promissory note for $3,000. Under the conditional sales agreement she was to pay monthly installments and title to the equipment would remain with the seller until the entire purchase price was paid. After making three payments, she defaulted. Leek repossessed the equipment, estimated to be worth $2,000, credited the promissory note for this amount, and sued Becky for another $1,000. Becky protests, claiming that the repossession wipes out the entire debt. Decision?

3. Timothy Gillespie bought a new Plymouth on a retail installment contract, which the dealer assigned to Chrysler Credit Company. Six months later, after Timothy had driven it to Texas, the car broke down and needed extensive repair on its transmission. Timothy was informed that the car warranty did not extend to the transmission. So he left the car in Harry's garage in Texas and went back home to Chicago by Dachshound Bus. While reading his accumulated mail, he found a letter from Chrysler Credit Company informing him that he had defaulted on his last four payments. Thereupon Timothy moved to a new apartment and got an unlisted telephone number. What is likely to happen in the next act?

4. In 1966 Pedro Agricola, a farmer, bought a pickup for which he executed a promissory note to Flatland Bank. The note was secured by a properly executed and

perfected security agreement. Pedro also had other loans outstanding with Flatland Bank which were secured by mortgages on other equipment and on his 16 pigs. Two years later Pedro borrowed money from his neighbor Lilly White and gave her a promissory note, but soon afterward he defaulted on both notes. Lilly took possession of the truck, claiming that the bank should satisfy its claim by taking possession of Pedro's other assets, namely the 10-year-old equipment and the 16 2-year-old pigs. Who has prior claim on the truck?

5. Robert and Christine Liggett purchased $23,000 worth of equipment from J. F. England & Sons. The conditional sales agreement stipulated monthly payments, reserved title with the seller until full payment, and gave the seller the right to repossess the goods "without notice . . . or legal process" and to sell them "at any time thereafter with or without notice," with the proceeds applied to the debt and any excess due to the purchaser. Does this agreement meet the statutory requirements for repossession?

6. Larry Leche, an independent milk distributor, had a contract with the Chicago Board of Education for milk delivery within the Chicago school system. Being in need of financing, Larry granted his supplier, Dairy Pride Company, an interest in his contract rights and accounts receivable. The agreement was duly executed and perfected, and the school board was instructed to make direct payments to Dairy Pride Company.

A few months later, in November, when Larry still owed Dairy Pride over $50,000, he severed his connection with Dairy Pride and began to purchase his milk from Alpine Milk Company. The new supplier obtained from Larry an assignment of all contract rights under the milk contract with the Chicago Board of Education as of November 15, but Alpine did not obtain a properly executed and perfected security agreement or release of the prior assignment. The school board, which always paid for its milk one month late, sent its November payment to Dairy Pride even though the milk for November had been supplied by Alpine. Now Larry Leche and Alpine sue Dairy Pride and the school board for the November payment. Decision?

7. Joe Munns purchased a used pickup truck from Lou Leventhal, a dealer. As down payment he paid $100 in cash and left his $150 Buick. For the remaining $350 he executed a conditional sales agreement which gave Lou a lien on the car until full payment. The next day Joe, having discovered that Lou had not reinspected the truck as required by law, took it to a garage and found that it could not pass inspection. Joe drove the truck back to Lou, and only after a lengthy conversation, which included a phone call to the police, could Joe persuade Lou to rescind the deal. However, when Lou wanted to take back the Buick, the title certificate, and the truck, Joe kept the truck until further notice. Lou asked him repeatedly to apply for a duplicate title, which Joe did not want to do. Instead he kept making his payments on the truck. Lou repeatedly threatened to take back the truck if Joe would not cooperate, and one morning the truck was gone. It was found by police in Harold's Body Shop, where Lou had taken it for repairs. Discuss the lawfulness of the repossession.

8. John Shepler purchased a $26,000 tractor-truck from the McCormick Company. He paid $5,000 down and executed a retail installment contract for the remainder. The agreement provided for payments at the beginning of each month, with the right to repossession without notice in case of default. The title was to remain with the seller until full payment. McCormick sold the contract to Payday Credit Corporation.

From the start, John had trouble meeting his obligations. Since he could not afford the insurance on the truck, he leased it to Tim Trucker, who drove it down to Florida. John waited until May 28 to make his May payment, at which time he also paid for the month of June. On the same day, the truck was repossessed by one of Payday Credit Corporation's agents in Florida. John Shepler sued for conversion of property. What issues must be decided, and who wins?

9. Richard Fancy built Sunshine Haven, an apartment complex located in Arctic, Minnesota. The apartments were to face into an enclosed courtyard which contained a heated pool surrounded by tropical plants. The heating and plumbing system of the apartment complex was designed in such a way that the apartments would be unheatable in winter without the enclosed heated courtyard.

   In July 1963 Richard Fancy entered into a conditional sales agreement with Structural Plastics, Inc., for the sale of various roofing materials to be used on the courtyard roof. The contract stated that "the roofs shall remain chattels and personal property at all times . . . and shall not become part of the realty." Structural Plastics, Inc., received partial payment for its work from the general contractor.

   In December 1963, when the roof was already completed, a mortgage was executed with Frestland Life Insurance Company to finance the apartment complex. At that time, Structural Plastics, Inc., delivered a mechanic's lien waiver for the unpaid balance on the conditional sales agreement.

   In April 1964 Structural Plastics filed a mechanic's lien on the premises for the value of an additional layer of plastic sheeting which had been installed on the roof. Later it filed a mechanic's lien foreclosure action. Which claim has priority, the insurance company's or Structural Plastics'?

10. Kelly Goodheart, registered owner of a highway tractor, leased his tractor to Morse Crash. However, the rental agreement was in actuality a conditional sales or title-retaining contract, under which Morse agreed to pay $300 for 15 weeks and then was to receive title. Morse also was to pay all repair bills and to provide insurance coverage. The vehicle was damaged in an accident and later repaired by Frank Hammer's Collision Service for $600. Morse decided to move for destinations unknown, leaving Kelly and Frank to fight over the tractor. How would you decide these conflicting claims?

Part VI
Commercial Paper

22 | Types of Instruments; Requirements of Negotiability

Negotiable instruments were developed by Western European merchants several centuries ago to meet the needs of trade and commerce. Carrying large sums of money was (and still is) a risky operation, with highwaymen and bandits then making the roads unsafe. Goods and services could conceivably be purchased on the buyer's credit, but that arrangement also entailed substantial risks of nonpayment in the days before Dun & Bradstreet and credit bureaus. What the merchant wanted was something that would be as acceptable as money in most commercial transactions but could be carried from place to place with greater safety than money. Through custom and usuage, merchants and their special commercial courts came to agree that instruments written in the proper form would have the characteristics they desired (1) these instruments would be freely transferable from person to person (under the old English common law, at least, a transferee of contract rights could not sue the debtor directly); (2) they would be presumed to have been issued for value, and the debtor would have the burden of proving otherwise; and (3) the debtor would not be able to assert certain defenses (generally, "voidable" defenses) when a good faith purchaser ("holder in due course") sued to enforce an instrument and collect the money. Negotiable instruments law, as part of the law merchant, was assimilated into English common law during the 17th and 18th centuries. An English statute codifying these practices was passed in 1882, and the Uniform NIL was proposed in 1896 and subsequently adopted by nearly all states in the U.S. The NIL has now been superseded by the UCC's Article 3, Commerical Paper. Article 4, Bank Deposits and Collections, brings together the rules regarding bank processing of such instruments. More recently, several states and the FTC have adopted new rules eliminating the "no defenses" result where the instrument was executed by a consumer-debtor.

In discussing negotiable instruments problems, we need to focus on five questions: (1) Is this writing a negotiable instrument? (2) If it is, is the defendant liable on it? (3) Has the instrument been properly negotiated to the plaintiff, so that he or she is the holder of the instrument and the proper party to enforce it? (4) If the defendant has a defense against liability, does the plaintiff qualify as a holder in due course (HDC)? (5) Which defenses are available against HDCs, and which are not? As with sales and secured transactions, our primary source for answering these questions will be the UCC. Cases in this area will focus on the Code's provisions dealing with one or more of the above questions.

Types of Commercial Paper. The Code defines four types of commercial paper under Article 3: the draft or bill of exchange, the check, the note, and the certificate of deposit. A draft is an *order* from a "drawer" directed to a "drawee" to pay money to a payee. If the drawee is a bank, and if the draft is payable on demand, it is a check. A note is a *promise* by a "maker" to pay money to a payee. A certificate of deposit is "an acknowledgement by a bank of receipt of money with an engagement to repay it" (3–104[2]). This section also says that the same four terms may be used to refer to instruments which do not meet the requirements of negotiability, depending on the context of the particular Code provision (3–104[3]). "An 'order' is a direction to pay and must be more than an authorization or request" (3–102[1][b]). If you have a checking account, look at your checks—they don't even say "Please pay"; some smart lawyer might try to argue that such courteous language is only a request and not an order. "A 'promise' is an undertaking to pay and must be more than an acknowledgement of an obligation" (3–102[1][c]), which is why an IOU does not qualify as a negotiable instrument even though it is in writing and signed. Unlike the NIL, where some ambiguity existed, Article 3 of the Code specifically excludes "investment securities" (stocks and bonds) from its coverage, along with money and "documents of title." Article 8 covers investment securities, and documents of title are covered in Article 7. Both securities and documents may be issued in "negotiable" form, as discussed in later chapters, but they are not used as money substitutes in the same way as "negotiable instruments" (commercial paper).

Requirements of Negotiability. Negotiability is strictly a matter of form. If an instrument is written so that it complies with the requirements of UCC 3–104(1), it is negotiable; if not, it is not negotiable, though it may be enforceable as an ordinary written contract. Negotiability, in other words, does not depend on the parties' intent, or their agreement, or their understanding, but on their compliance with the Code's requirements. The drafters of the Code have expressed this policy very clearly in several of their official comments: "The negotiability of an instrument is always to be determined by what appears on the face of the instrument alone" (3–119, Comment 5); "either the language of the section or a clear equivalent must be found, and . . . in doubtful cases the decision should be against negotiability" (3–104, Comment 5). The courts are thus directed not to produce the very special negotiability results unless the debtor has signed a writing which clearly conforms to Article 3's requirements.

What are these requirements? They are listed in Section 3–104(1): the writing must "(*a*) be signed by the maker or drawer; and (*b*) contain an unconditional promise or order to pay a sum certain in money and no other promise, order, obligation or power given by the maker or drawer except as authorized by this Article; and (*c*) be payable on demand or at a definite time; and (*d*) be payable to order or to bearer." Each of these requirements is further defined and explained in other Code sections. One of the defendant-debtor's main arguments against liability will be that the instrument he or she signed is not negotiable and that the plaintiff-creditor is therefore subject to any defense which can be proved.

Signed by Maker or Drawer. *Signed* is defined in the general definitions section of Article 1 (1–201[39]) to include "any symbol executed or adopted by a party with present intention to authenticate a writing." Thus a signature need not be written out fully in script; it can be printed, typed, stamped, initialed, or reproduced mechanically by a checkwriter. Because of the special characteristics of negotiable instruments, Section 3–401(1) states a very important rule for them: "No person is liable on an instrument unless his signature appears thereon." A person may be liable on some other basis to the plaintiff, but he or she is not liable *on an instrument* unless his or her signature is on the instrument, though it does not necessarily have to appear at the bottom. It may be made by trade name, assumed name, mark (X), or even thumbprint (3–401, Comment 2). It may be made by a properly authorized agent, though the agent may be held personally liable to subsequent holders of the instrument if he or she does not clearly indicate that the signing is being done only on behalf of his or her principal (3–403). Where someone who is not authorized to do so signs another's name, the signature operates as that of "the unauthorized signer in favor of any person who in good faith pays the instrument or takes it for value" (3–404).

Griffin v. Ellinger
530 S.W.2d 329 (Texas, 1975)

FACTS   Ellinger had furnished labor and materials to Greenway Building Company, of which Griffin was president. Griffin signed three drafts, totaling $3,950, in payment for the work done. The drafts were drawn against Greenway's account at the Northeast Bank of Houston, which refused payment because of insufficient funds. Griffin's signatures did not show that he was signing in a representative capacity only. Ellinger was not told who owned the building project, or who would pay him, or who would be responsible for the payments. Ellinger had received other payments from Greenway officers and had never looked to them personally for payment. The trial court found for Ellinger.

ISSUE   Is an authorized agent who signs his name without indicating his status as agent personally liable on the instrument to the payee?

DECISION   Yes. Judgment for Ellinger affirmed.

REASONS   Justice Shannon cited Section 3–403. He noted that the drafts did contain the printed name of Greenway but that Griffin's signatures did not show his agency status. Under these circumstances Griffin was liable unless he could use the statutory exception "except as otherwise established between the immediate parties." This phrase means that the signer may introduce parol evidence to rebut the presumption of personal obligation. The Texas Supreme Court had previously ruled that this could include evidence showing "an understanding between the parties, or prior dealings between the parties, or a disclosure by the signer at the time of the execution of the instrument." Griffin did not conceal his principal, but Justice Shannon said that he also had to show that he had signed properly. Justice Shannon also discounted the prior transactions with other Greenway officers, since those transactions had not been with Griffin but with other persons.

"Appellant states, correctly, that the record shows he did not make any personal representations that he would personally guarantee the drafts. Appellant then argues that before he could be personally obligated on the drafts appellee would have to prove that appellant guaranteed them. Appellant's argument ignores the plain language of S.3.403, which makes the signer personally obligated if the instrument he signs does not show that he signed in a representative capacity."

Unconditional Promise or Order. Section 3–105 lists a number of rules for determining when a promise or an order is or is not "unconditional"; most of these rules are designed to meet particular problems which have come up in prior cases. Instruments frequently refer to the transaction out of which they arose, or to the consideration received or to be received for them, or to the fact that payment is secured by mortgage or otherwise. Within limits, the Code permits such references; the promise or order is still "unconditional," and the instrument is still negotiable. But when a promise or order states "That it is subject to or governed by any other agreement," it is conditional and thus not negotiable. (The instrument may still be enforced like any ordinary written contract, however; *not negotiable* just means that the plaintiff is subject to any defense which the defendant can prove.)

Holly Hill Acres, Ltd. v. *Charter Bank of Gainesville*
314 So.2d 209 (Florida, 1975)

FACTS   Charter sued to foreclose on a note and mortgage given by Holly Hill. The note contained the following provision: "The terms of said mortgage are by this reference made a part thereof." Rogers and Blythe had sold to Holly Hill, received the note and mortgage, and then assigned both to Charter. Holly Hill alleged that Rogers and Blythe had committed fraud in the sale. The trial court entered summary judgment against Holly Hill, since it ruled that Charter was a holder in due course of a negotiable instrument.

ISSUE   Was the note negotiable, so that Charter could be an HDC?

DECISION   No. Summary judgment for Charter reversed; case remanded for trial.

REASONS   Judge Scheb went right to the main issue: "The note, having incorporated the terms of the purchase money mortgage, was not negotiable." Therefore, the bank could not be an HDC and was not entitled to summary judgment.

"The note, incorporating by reference the terms of the mortgage, did not contain the unconditional promise to pay required by . . . 3–104(1)(b). . . .

"Mere reference to a note being secured by mortgage is a common commercial practice, and such reference in itself does not impede the negotiability of the note. There is, however, a significant difference in a note stating that it is 'secured by a mortgage' from one which provides, 'the terms of said mortgage are by this reference made a part hereof.' In the former instance the note merely refers to a separate agreement which does not impede its negotiability, while in the latter instance the note is rendered nonnegotiable. . . .

"As a general rule the assignee of a mortgage securing a nonnegotiable note, even though a bona fide purchaser for value, takes subject to all defenses available as against the mortgagee."

Similar rules are stated with regard to the source of funds to pay the instrument. Generally, an instrument which "is to be paid only out of a particular fund" is conditional (and therefore not negotiable), because that one source may or may not be sufficient to pay the obligation. The instrument can, however, indicate that it is to be charged against or reimbursed from a particular account, for bookkeeping purposes, so long as it is issued in general terms. As an exception to the "particular fund" doctrine, the Code permits negotiable instruments to be issued against the "entire assets" of a partnership, unincorporated association, trust, or estate. As a further exception, governmental agencies can issue negotiable instruments with payment limited to a particular fund or source (3–105).

Sum Certain. The Code also provides some detailed rules for determining when the amount to be paid is a "sum certain" (3–106). Most typical provisions regarding interest, installment payments, and discounts or penalties for early payment require only a little mathematics to determine the "sum" due and are thus permissable. The interest rates and other percentages must be specified, however, so that the calculations can be made from the information appearing on the face of the instrument. Many instruments, particularly promissory notes, will include a provision requiring the payment of collection costs and attorney fees if the debtor defaults and litigation is necessary; the Code validates such provisions. Aside from the fact that "attorneys" drafted the Code, the rationale for this provision is that the basic sum due at maturity is "certain" and that these additional costs arise only because of the debtor's default.

In Money. *Money* is defined in the general definitions section of the Code (1–201[24]) as "a medium of exchange authorized or adopted by a domestic or foreign government as a part of its currency." The official comment to this section says that the "official governmental currency" test is broader than just saying "legal tender"; thus an instrument is payable in "money" even though it is payable in the United States in foreign currency. Unless it specifies otherwise, such an instrument may be paid in dollars equivalent to the stated amount of foreign currency on the due date (3–107).

No Other Promise or Order Except as Article 3 Authorizes. Negotiable instruments used to be described as "couriers without luggage." The obligations which they imposed were to be stated clearly and simply; thus any language providing for performances in addition to the payment of money was to be regarded with suspicion. Comment 3 to Section 3–104 refers us to Section 3–112 for a list of provisions which are permitted to be included in (or omitted from) an instrument without destroying its negotiability. Provisions relating to collateral given to secure payment of the instrument may be included. A draft may contain a statement that "the payee by indorsing or cashing it acknowledges full satisfaction of an obligation of the drawer." Section 3–112 permits the inclusion of terms which waive the benefit of any law intended to protect debtors and by which the debtor authorizes the creditor to go into court on his or her behalf and "confess judgment" (admit that the debtor owes the money). Many states would probably not permit their consumer protection laws to be overridden in this way, and only a few states recognize the confession of judgment procedure; 3–112 merely permits such provisions where they are otherwise lawful. An instrument need not state the consideration received for it, nor need it include any indication of where it was drawn or where it is to be paid.

Universal C.I.T. Credit Corp. v. Ingel
196 N.E.2d 847 (Massachusetts, 1964)

FACTS   Albert and Dora Ingel had an aluminum siding job done on their home by Allied Aluminum Associates, Inc. In payment, they executed a promissory note for $1,890. The note, together with a certificate indicating that the job had been completed, was transferred for value to the plaintiff. After making several monthly payments, the Ingels alleged that the job had not been done properly and that Allied was guilty of breach of warranties, breach of contract, and/or fraud. CIT sued for the balance due, claiming that it was a holder in due course, and recovered $1,630.12 in the trial court. The Ingels appealed, alleging that the note was nonnegotiable and that the holder (CIT) was subject to any defense which the Ingels could prove.

ISSUE   Was the note negotiable?

DECISION   Yes. Judgment for CIT affirmed.

REASONS   Justice Spiegel first reviewed the facts, including the language of the note itself. He found nothing to indicate that the note and the completion certificate were "part of the same instrument" even though they may have been given to CIT at the same time. Any statements in the certificate were not "other promises" which would render the note nonnegotiable.

"We are equally satisfied that the insurance clause in the note does not affect negotiability under S.3–104(1)(b) since it is clear that the 'no other promise' provision refers only to promises by the maker.

"The provision in the note for 'interest after maturity at the highest lawful' rate does not render the note nonnegotiable for failure to state a sum certain as required by S.3–104(1)(b). We are of the opinion that after maturity the interest rate is that indicated in G.L. c. 107, S.3, since in this case there is no agreement in writing for any other rate after default. This being the case, we do not treat this note differently from one payable 'with interest.' The latter note would clearly be negotiable under G.L. c. 106, S.3–118(d)."

Spiegel rejected the claim that the note had been materially altered where the date of the first payment had been changed from June to July by writing "ly" over "ne." The Ingels had made the first payment, and the amount due was not at issue anyway.

Spiegel also ruled that CIT was a holder in due course, even though it had worked with Allied on various aspects of the financing arrangement and even though it knew of complaints from some of Allied's previous customers.

Payable on Demand or at a Definite Time. For an instrument to be negotiable, not only must its amount be certain, but the holder must also be able to determine when he can get the money if he wants it. Where the instrument is payable "on demand," the money is due whenever the holder asks for it. Demand instruments include "those payable at sight or on presentation" (essentially the same thing as saying "on demand") and those "in which no time for payment is stated." Checks, for example, usually do not include any statement as to when they are to be paid, so they are assumed to be demand instruments (3–108).

The rules for determining whether an instrument is payable at a definite time are a little more complicated. The clearest cases are those where the instrument is payable "on or before a stated date or at a fixed period after a stated date." Also fairly easy to decide are those where the instruments are payable "at a fixed period after sight." The "acceleration clause" and the "extension clause," two provisions frequently inserted in instruments, may cause some difficulties with respect to the "definite time" requirement. An acceleration clause advances the due date; an extension clause delays it. The Code says that *any* type of acceleration clause may be inserted without destroying negotiability, whether the acceleration occurs only when the debtor defaults in paying principal or interest or anytime the holder feels insecure about getting his or her money. The rationale for this rule is that such an instrument is at least as certain as to due date as a demand instrument, which has always been recognized as being negotiable. A holder who wishes to accelerate because he or she feels insecure, however, can do so "only if he in good faith believes that the prospect of payment or performance is impaired" (1–208). Such a holder's good faith is presumed; the party against whom he or she is accelerating must prove otherwise.

Barton v. *Scott Hudgens Realty & Mortgage, Inc.*
222 S.E.2d 126 (Georgia, 1975)

FACTS   Barton signed a promissory note for $3,000 which would become due and payable "upon evidence of an acceptable permanent loan of $290,000 for Barton-Ludwig Cains Hill Place Office Building, Atlanta, Georgia, from one of SHRAM's investors and upon acceptance of the commitment by the undersigned." Barton admitted that SHRAM did get such a loan commitment and that Barton did execute the commitment. Barton claimed, however, that since the loan had not in fact been made, he didn't owe the $3,000 loan fee. The trial court entered judgment for SHRAM on the pleadings. Barton appealed.

ISSUE   Was the note negotiable?

DECISION   No, but the summary judgment for Barton is affirmed anyway since on the admitted facts he had no defense which would justify nonpayment.

REASONS   UCC 3–307(2) recognizes the validity of summary judgment where the execution of a negotiable note is admitted and where no affirmative defense is raised. Judge Deen said that that rule wouldn't work in this case, however, because this note wasn't negotiable.

"This 'promissory note' by its terms was made payable 'upon evidence of an acceptable permanent loan . . . and upon acceptance of the [loan] commitment'; however under Code Ann. Ch. 109A–3–104(1)(c) a negotiable instrument must 'be payable on demand or at a definite time.' The 'note' here was not payable on demand under the language of S. 109A–3–108, and under S. 109A–3–109(2) '[a]n instrument which by its terms is otherwise payable only upon an act or event uncertain as to time of occurrence is not payable at a definite time even though the act or event has occurred.'"

Judge Deen found that the $3,000 had clearly been earned by SHRAM when the loan commitment was accepted by Barton, and so a summary judgment for SHRAM was the correct result even though the note was not negotiable.

As the person to whom the money is owed, the holder can grant any extension of the time for payment he or she wishes, as far as the maker or drawer is concerned. The main reason for inserting an express provision for such extension is to preserve the liability of indorsers and parties who have cosigned the instrument for the "accommodation" of the maker or drawer. Where the maker or acceptor/drawee is given the option of extending the time of payment or where an extension is to occur automatically upon the happening of a specified event, the extension must be to "a further definite time," for example, six months or one year. "Unless otherwise specified consent to extension authorizes a single extension for not longer than the original period" (3–118[f]). The holder cannot, however, refuse a proper tender of payment and continue to earn interest on the instrument where the maker, acceptor, or other party tenders full payment on the due date (3–118[f]). Section 3–109(2) states one further rule, intended to cover the "death notes" sometimes issued by the beneficiaries of estates ("90 days after Uncle Ned's death"): "An instrument which by its terms is otherwise payable only upon an act or event uncertain as to time of occurrence is not payable at a definite time even though the act or event has occurred." The drafters of the Code made a conscious policy choice that such instruments should not be negotiable and that all the maker's defenses should be preserved as against subsequent holders of such notes (3–109, Comment 1).

Payable to Order or to Bearer. These are "the magic words of negotiability," used to indicate clearly that an instrument is intended to pass freely from hand to hand, to circulate in commerce as a money substitute. Sections 3–110 (order) and 3–111 (bearer) specify the words and phrases which can be used to achieve these results. Bearer instruments include those which are made payable to bearer, to the order of bearer, to a specified person or bearer, to cash, to the order or cash, or to "any other indication which does not purport to designate a specific payee." As examples of the last phrase, Comment 2 lists "Pay bills payable" and "Pay to the order of one keg of nails."

Broadway Management Corp. v. *Briggs*
332 N.E.2d 131 (Illinois, 1975)

FACTS   Conan Briggs signed a promissory note for $3,498.45. The note permitted the holder to accelerate the due date if it felt insecure and authorized a "confession of judgment" if the note were not paid when due. After the phrase "promise to pay to the order of," the note read: "Three Thousand Four Hundred Ninety Eight and 45/100 - - - - - - - -Dollars." No payee's name had been filled in, just the amount. The trial court entered a "judgment by confession" and issued a garnishment order against a third party who was holding stock certificates owned by Briggs. Briggs appealed.

ISSUE   Is this note payable to order or to bearer?

DECISION   To order; judgment and garnishment order vacated.

REASONS   Justice Craven said that "confession of judgment" clauses, although legal in Illinois, must be strictly construed. If such a drastic remedy is given to a particular person, only that person can exercise the power. Therefore, if the note is order paper, and if the identity of the payee who is to exercise the "confession of judgment" cannot be determined, then the power cannot be used. Broadway's action would be permitted only if the note were bearer paper and the "confession" power had therefore been given to any holder of the instrument. Justice Craven looked at UCC 3–111.

   "The official comments to the section note that an instrument payable 'to the order of _____' is not bearer paper but an incomplete order instrument unenforceable until completed in accordance with authority. . . .

> "The instrument here is not bearer paper. We cannot say that it does not purport to designate a specific payee.' Rather, we believe the wording of the instrument is clear in its implication that the payee's name is to be inserted between the promise and the amount, so that the literal absence of blanks is legally insignificant.
>
> "Since the holder could not be determined from the face of the instrument, the trial court was in error in allowing plaintiff . . . to exercise the warrant of attorney granted by this instrument to its holder."

Order instruments are those payable to "the order or assigns of any person therein specified with reasonable certainty, or to him or his order, or when it is conspicuously designated on its face as 'exchange' or the like and names a payee." The section then goes on to list the various possible types of order-payees: (1) the maker or drawer; (2) the drawee; (3) a payee who is not a maker, drawer, or drawee; (4) two or more payees together or in the alternative; (5) an estate, trust, or fund; (6) an office or an officer by his title as such; and (7) a partnership or an unincorporated association. If you fill in your own (drawer's) name on your check to get some cash at the bank, that check would fall in to the first category of order paper. An example of the second type would be a check made out to your own drawee bank as an installment loan payment. Checks to the landlord or a grocery store would be in the third group. An income tax refund check payable to a husband and wife would fall into the fourth category. A check for a donation to a scholarship fund would be an example of the fifth category. When you make out your check for a parking ticket in favor of "City Treasurer, Ham Harbor, Mythigan," that's the sixth category; the check is payable to the city, but the incumbent officeholder may indorse and deposit it as if he or she were the holder. A check made out to a partnership or an unincorporated association (such as a fraternity or a sorority), the seventh category, "may be indorsed or transferred by any person thereto authorized" (3–110[1][g]). Finally, a requirement in an instrument which is not otherwise payable to order that it is payable when "properly indorsed" does not make the instrument negotiable (3–110[2]).

CASES FOR DISCUSSION

SMITH v. GENTILOTTI

371 Mass. 839 (1977)

Braucher, J.

The plaintiffs, mother and son, sued the father's executrix on an instrument in the form of a check payable to the order of the son for $20,000, executed by the father in 1969, and delivered to the mother, postdated November 4, 1984. The check was indorsed by the father as follows: "For Edward Joseph Smith Gentilotti My Son If I should pass away The amount of $20,000.00 dollars Shall be taken from My Estate at death. S. Gentilotti 11–25–69".

We summarize the judge's findings, based on stipulations of the parties and the testimony of the mother. The father's will is dated August 1, 1962. The son was born in Michigan on November 4, 1964. From August 1, 1964, to September 15, 1972, the father paid the mother more than $14,000 by 49 checks and paid her additional sums in cash; she also received stock later sold for $1,500. From time to time the father asked the mother whether she still had the check in suit, expressed approval that she still had it, and requested her to keep it. Both mother and father expected it to be enforceable. She did not transfer or negotiate the check, and did not bring any paternity proceedings against the father. He died May 31, 1973. Demand for payment has been duly made and refused.

The case is governed by the Uniform Commercial Code, G. L. c. 106. Under § 3–104, the instrument in question is on its face a check drawn on a bank in Milford, Massachusetts, payable on demand, and a negotiable instrument. Its negotiability is not affected by the fact that it was postdated 15 years; the time when it is payable is determined by the stated date. § 3–114 (1), (2). The indorsement modifies the check by providing for acceleration of the time of payment and for direct payment by the drawer's estate. . . . The acceleration provision is authorized by § 3–109 (1) (c). As for direct payment, the drawee bank was not authorized to pay the check more than 10 days after the drawer's death, if it knew of the fact of death. § 4–405. Hence presentment to that bank was entirely excused as a futile gesture. § 3–511 (2). . . . Thus, the provision for direct payment merely restates the result prescribed by law. §§ 3–413 (2), 3–507 (1) (b). We need not consider the plaintiff's argument that the indorsement is a draft drawn on the drawer, effective as a note under § 3–118 (a).

The principal contentions of the defendant are, first, that the instrument sued on is not a negotiable instrument, and, second, that it is unenforceable for want of consideration or reliance. We hold that the instrument was a negotiable instrument. The plaintiffs, unless they have the rights of a holder in due course, took the instrument subject to the defense of want of consideration. §§ 3–306 (c), 3–408. But the signatures were admitted, and in such cases "production of the instrument entitles a holder to recover on it unless the defendant establishes a defense." § 3–307 (2). . . . The judge here did not find that the defense of want of consideration had been established, and neither his findings nor the stipulation and evidence compel such a finding.* . . .

The defendant suggests that the instrument was given in lieu of an inheritance. She does not argue that, if otherwise valid, it fails because it is testamentary in character. Such an argument could not prevail, since a valid contract may properly serve as a substitute for a will. . . .

Judgment is to be entered for the plaintiffs. So ordered.

VAN HORN v. VAN DE WOL, INC.

497 P.2d 252 (Washington, 1972)

James, Judge

Defendant Van De Wol, Inc. operates a golf course. Plaintiff Van Horn, while a stockholder in defendant corporation, made several loans to defendant, totaling $37,000, and received unsecured demand notes in return. Subsequently, before selling his stock to an investor produced by the corporation, plaintiff entered into an agreement providing, among other things, that he would not accelerate payment of the notes so long as the terms of the agreement were complied with, but that if he should at any time deem himself insecure he would have the right to demand payment of the notes.

Approximately one year after liquidating his stock and entering into the agreement, plaintiff, asserting that he deemed himself insecure, demanded payment of the notes. This suit followed when defendant failed to discharge the notes.

The trial judge found that plaintiff, in good faith, deemed himself insecure and granted judgment for the balances due upon the notes. This appeal is from the denial of defendant's motion for a new trial.

Defendant contends that the trial judge erred in holding that plaintiff "in good faith," deemed himself insecure, because plaintiff erroneously believed defendant had been denied a bank loan, when in fact defendant had not been denied a loan.

The trial judge found as a fact that plaintiff knew defendant corporation lost money during the prior business year; that defendant corporation was faced with increasing competition from a newly established public golf course; that the new stockholder refused to hold him harmless on corporate notes which he had signed as a guarantor; and that the corporation refused to refrain from mortgaging the corporate realty until after plaintiff had been paid.

The Uniform Commercial Code, RCW, 62A.1–208 provides that the term, "'when he deems himself insecure'" shall be construed "to mean that he shall have power to do so only if he in good faith believes that the prospect of payment or performance is impaired." RCW 62A.1–201(19) provides that "'[g]ood faith' means honesty in fact in the conduct or transaction concerned."

The "honesty in fact" standard which the trier of fact must apply has been described as follows:

Section 1–201(19) defines "good faith" as "honesty in fact" and thus follows a number of the uniform commercial acts in making negligence irrelevant to good faith. The adoption of this "subjective" test, sometimes known as the rule of "the pure heart and the empty head," dates back more than a hundred years in the law of negotiable instruments, to the abandonment of the "objective" standard announced in *Gill* v. *Cubitt*. . . .

Plaintiff, as an unsecured creditor, had to consider the overall financial stability of defendant to determine the likelihood of payment. Anything which adversely affected the corporation adversely affected plaintiff's prospect of payment.

Even if plaintiff was negligent in not checking to determine whether defendant had in fact been denied a loan, negligence is irrelevant to good faith. The standard is what plaintiff actually knew, or believed he knew, not what he could or should have known. Because plaintiff believed defendant had been denied a loan, and acted in accordance with that belief, he acted in good faith.

Plaintiff's "good faith" is a question of fact. Our review of the record discloses that the trial judge's finding that plaintiff acted in good faith is supported by substantial evidence. The matter of the loan was but one consideration, and even if it were resolved in defendant's favor, that would not eliminate the other substantial bases for plaintiff's insecurity. We may not substitute our judgment for that of the trial judge. . . .

FERRI v. SYLVIA
214 A.2d 470 (Rhode Island, 1965)

Joslin, Justice

This action of assumpsit based upon a promissory note was tried before a justice of the superior court sitting without a jury and resulted in a decision for the plaintiff of $2,600. The defendants prosecute their exceptions to evidentiary rulings and to the decision.

The note, which is dated May 25, 1963, obligates defendants to pay to plaintiff or her order $3,000 "within ten (10) years after date." The trial justice determined that the maturity of the note was uncertain, admitted testimony of the parties as to both their intentions and prior agreements, and premised upon such extrinsic evidence found that plaintiff "could have the balance that may be due at any time she needed it and that she could call for and demand the full payment of any balance that may be due or owing her at the time of her demand.

The question is whether the note is payable at a fixed or determinable future time. If the phrase "within ten (10) years after date" lacks explicitness or is ambiguous, then clearly parol evidence was admissable for the purpose of ascertaining the intention of the parties. . . . Moreover, if it was apparent from an inspection of the note that it did not include the entire agreement of the parties, then it was permissible to accept extrinsic evidence of their prior agreements relative to its due date in supplementation and explanation of the writing; provided, however, that the collateral terms were consistent therewith and such as would normally have been excluded by the parties from the note. . . . While the trial justice in admitting and accepting the extrinsic evidence apparently relied on these principles, neither is applicable because the payment provisions of the note are not uncertain nor are they incomplete.

At the law merchant it was generally settled that a promissory note or a bill of exchange payable "on or before" a specified date fixed with certainty the time of payment. . . . The same rule has been fixed by statute first under the negotiable instruments of law, G.L. 1956, § 6–18–10, subd. 2, and now pursuant to the uniform commercial code. . . .

The courts in the cases we cite were primarily concerned with whether a provision for payment "on or before" a specified date impaired the negotiability of an instrument. Collaterally, of course, they necessarily considered whether such an instrument was payable at a fixed or determinable future time, for unless it was, an essential prerequisite to negotiability was lacking.

They said that the legal rights of the holder of an "on or before" instrument were clearly fixed and entitled him to payment upon an event that was certain to come, even though the maker might be privileged to pay sooner if he so elected. They held, therefore, that the due date of such an instrument was fixed with certainty and that its negotiability was unaffected by the privilege given the maker to accelerate payment. . . .

On principle no valid distinction can be drawn between an instrument payable "on or before" a fixed date and one which calls for payment "within" a stipulated period. . . .

We follow the lead of the Maine court and equate the word "within" with the phrase "on or before." So construed, it fixes both the beginning and the end of the period, and insofar as it means the former it is applicable to the right of a maker to prepay, and insofar as it means the latter it is referable to the date the instrument matures. We hold that the payment provision of a negotiable instrument payable "within" a stated period is certain as well as complete on its face and that such an instrument does not mature until the time fixed arrives.

For the foregoing reasons it is clear that the parties unequivocally agreed that the plaintiff could not demand payment of the note until the expiration of the 10-year period. . . .

The defendants' exception to the trial justice's decision is sustained. . . .

ECKLEY v. STEINBRECHER

482 P.2d 392 (Colorado, 1971)

Coyte, Judge

The original complaint was initiated by the plaintiffs, Steinbrecher and Dworak, to recover on a check given by defendant Eckley to a couple named Ferguson, and endorsed by them to the plaintiffs. The check was dishonored by the bank because of insufficient funds.

The factual background of this case disclosed that in 1962 the Fergusons contacted Dworak Realty Co. in order to purchase a farm from the plaintiff Steinbrecher. As a down payment on the contract the Fergusons sought a loan from defendant Eckley in the amount of $2,000. On July 25, 1962, Eckley executed and delivered his check postdated July 29, 1962, payable to the Fergusons. On the face of the check was written "Loan on farm." The Fergusons then endorsed the check and delivered it to the plaintiffs. The check was dishonored by the bank due to insufficient funds in Eckley's account, and the transaction for the sale of the property was never completed.

In July of 1967, this suit was brought to recover on the check. Both the Fergusons and Eckley were named as defendants. A default judgment was entered into against the Fergusons, and they are not parties to this appeal. Trial was held to the court, which found that the check being sued on was a negotiable instrument and that plaintiffs were holders in due course, and entered judgment against Eckley for $2,000.

Eckley appeals, claiming the trial court misapplied the facts in this case when it held the check to be a negotiable instrument and the plaintiffs to be holders in due course. Since the transaction occurred in 1962, we must refer to C.R.S. 1963, 95–1–1, et. seq., for disposition of this case rather than Art. 3 of the subsequently enacted Uniform Commercial Code.

Defendant's first argument is that the check was defective on its face and nonnegotiable since it was postdated and bore the notation "Loan on farm." In order for the check to be nonnegotiable, it would have to have a patent defect, which would mean that the check does not meet the requirements for negotiability set forth in C.R.S. 1963, 95–1–1. . . .

Since there is no denial of the fact that the check was signed by the defendant, or that it was for a sum certain, or that it was payable at a definite future time to a definite drawee, the defect assigned by the defendant must go to the requirement that it be an unconditional promise to pay. C.R.S. 1963, 95–1–3(1) (c), states that a promise is not qualified or made conditional merely because it recites: ". . . the transaction which gives rise to the instrument." The notation on the check does not affect the negotiability of the check as this section of the statute is applicable to the notation "Loan on farm."

The mere fact that the check was postdated does not render it void, but merely defers negotiability to a subsequent time. . . . Nor does it qualify or make the promise conditional. C.R.S. 1963, 95–1–12, specifically provides that postdated instruments are not made invalid unless done for some illegal purpose. Since the defendant does not claim, nor prove, that the postdating was done for such an illegal purpose, the check remains valid.

The next argument raised is that the plaintiffs are not holders in due course because no value was given in return for the check, as is required by C.R.S. 1963, 91–1–52(1) (d). The value spoken of in this section is consideration given by the plaintiffs for the check, not consideration given to Eckley by the Fergusons in return for execution of this check in their favor.

The evidence supports the finding that plaintiffs did give value in the form of a promise to convey the farm in return for the check as earnest money, and therefore plaintiffs' claim of being holders in due course cannot be defeated by this assertion.

We must conclude, therefore, that the check was negotiable within the meaning of the statute and that the plaintiffs did become holders in due course, entitling them to enforce the provisions of the check. . . .

PROBLEMS FOR DISCUSSION

Assume that in each of the following examples the plaintiff is a bona fide purchaser (BFP) of the instrument, who would qualify as a holder in due course if the instrument were negotiable. The only defense against liability on the instrument is the personal defense of fraud in the inducement, so that the business debtor (drawer or maker) will have to pay if the instrument is negotiable. In each case, only the quoted provision is in question.

1. "Borrower hereby authorizes Bank to pay the total hereon upon presentation hereof."   *BFP v. Drawer*

    DR ⟶ Payee ⟶ BFP (HDC) ⟶ DE (dishonors)

2. "The sum of up to $5,000."   *BFP v. Drawer*

    DR ⟶ Payee ⟶ BFP (HDC) ⟶ DE (dishonors)

3. "This instrument given for one color TV."   *BFP v. Maker*

    M ⟶ Payee ⟶ BFP (HDC)

4. "This instrument payable if one color TV is delivered.   *BFP v. Maker*

    M ⟶ Payee ⟶ BFP (HDC)

5. "This instrument is payable when one color TV is delivered."   *BFP v. Maker*

    M ⟶ Payee ⟶ BFP (HDC)

6. "This instrument is given in payment for one color TV, which the Buyer promises to keep insured against loss."   *BFP v. Maker*

    M ⟶ Payee ⟶ BFP (HDC)

7. "This instrument is payable 90 days after Richard M. Nixon resigns the presidency."

    M ⟶ Payee ⟶ BFP (HDC)

    BFP v. *Maker*

8. "This instrument is payable as per a contract this same date for one color TV."

    M ⟶ Payee ⟶ BFP (HDC)

    BFP v. *Maker*

9. "This instrument is payable subject to a contract of this same date for one color TV."

    M ⟶ Payee ⟶ BFP (HDC)

    BFP v. *Maker*

10. "Maker also promises to pay all applicable personal property taxes."

    M ⟶ Payee ⟶ BFP (HDC)

    BFP v. *Maker*

Liabilities of Parties | 23

Having determined that an instrument is negotiable, the next problem is to determine whether the defendant is liable on it and what the nature of his or her liability is. Negotiable instruments are a combination of property and contract concepts, so that liability may be based either on the contract which a person has made with respect to the instrument or on the fact that he or she transferred a piece of property. In addition, persons intentionally or negligently dealing with such instruments so as to cause loss to others may be held liable on a tort theory. We now proceed to examine each of these types of liability.

Primary Contract Liability. Someone who has made a direct, unqualified promise to pay an instrument when it is due, has assumed primary contract liability on the instrument. Only two parties make such a primary promise—the maker of a promissory note and the acceptor of a draft or check. Where the draft has not been presented to the drawee (or drawee bank) and accepted (certified) by him or her, *no one* has primary contract liability on the draft or check. The draft or check is an *order* to the drawee to pay, and the drawer's normal assumption is that the order will be honored by the drawee. If the payee or some later holder of the draft has some doubts about whether it will be honored, or if the payee refuses to send merchandise or perform services without receiving a certified check, then the instrument can be presented to the drawee to find out whether he or she will agree to pay it when it is presented for payment. A drawee who agrees to the order and directly promises to pay the money when due, writes "accepted" or "certified" on the instrument, signs his or her name, and gives the instrument back to the holder. Once the drawee does this, he or she has become an acceptor with primary contract liability; until the drawee does this, no one has primary contract liability on the draft or check, and the drawee or drawee bank is not liable on the instrument at all—to anyone.

Secondary Contract Liability. A party with secondary contract liability does not expect to pay the instrument; if everything goes right, someone else will pay. His or her signature on the instrument implies a kind of backstop promise: I'll pay if necessary—*if* you make a proper, timely presentment of the instrument to the person who is supposed to pay, *and if* he or she dishonors the instrument, *and if* you give me proper notice of the dishonor, *then* bring it to me and I'll give you your money. This kind of "if—then" promise is quite different from that of the party who simply says, "I'll pay." Drawers of drafts and checks and indorsers of all types of negotiable instruments make this secondary contract promise. Furthermore, the drawer or indorser may *disclaim* even this secondary promise by drawing or indorsing "without recourse" (3–413[2] and 3–414[1]). If the instrument is a draft which appears to be drawn or payable outside the United States, there is a further requirement: The holder must also send the drawer and indorsers a "protest," which is an official notarized statement of the fact of dishonor (3–501[3] and 3–509[1]).

Implicit in the conditional promise of the drawer or indorser is the idea that if the above conditions are not met, his or her liability is excused. For a drawer, this is true only to a limited extent. An unexcused failure to make a proper presentment or to send a notice of dishonor excuses the drawer only where he or she "is deprived of funds maintained with the drawee or payor bank to cover the instrument" because the drawee or payor bank becomes insolvent during the delay." When such bank insolvency occurs, the drawer can become free of any further liability for such instruments by making a written assignment to the holder of his or her rights against the insolvent bank. As a practical matter, this means that few drawers will be excused by a holder's failure to present or to give notice of dishonor. Where a protest is required, failure of the holder to furnish it to the drawer will discharge the drawer (3–502[2]). As to indorsers, any unexcused delay in complying with the requirements for presentment, notice, or protest is a complete discharge (3–502[1][a] and [2]). Compliance with these requirements thus becomes very important to the holder, to make sure that the secondary contract liability of drawers and indorsers is preserved, so that they are available if the instrument is dishonored. The details of these requirements are spelled out in various provisions of Article 3.

Presentment, Notice of Dishonor, Protest. As to the time when presentment must be made, if the instrument is payable on a specific date, presentment is also due then (3–503[1][c]). If it is payable "after sight," it must "either be presented for acceptance or negotiated within a reasonable time after date or issue whichever is later" (3–503[1][b]). In order to enforce the instrument against a secondary party, presentment of any other instrument "is due within a reasonable time after such party becomes liable thereon" (3–503[1][e]). For an uncertified domestic check, a "reasonable time" is *presumed* to be 30 days after date or issue, whichever is later, for the drawer to be held liable; for an indorser, 7 days after his or her indorsement (3–503[2][b] and [b]). If presentment is due on a day which is not a full business day for either party, it is postponed to the next day which is a full business day for both (3–503[3]). Presentment must be made at a reasonable hour; if it is made at a bank, during its banking day (3–503[4]).

Hane v. Exten
259 A.2d 290 (Maryland, 1969)

FACTS John B. Hane was the assignee-holder of a note issued by Theta Electronics Laboratories, Inc., in the amount of $15,377.07, plus 6 percent interest. The note, dated August 10, 1964, provided that the first monthly payment of $320.47 would be due on January 10, 1965. The note contained an acceleration clause. Gerald M. Exten, Emil L. O'Neil, James W. Hane, and their wives all indorsed the note. The original payees, George B. and Marguerite F. Thompson, assigned the note without recourse to Hane on November 26, 1965. Some $2,222.13 had been paid on the note up to that point. Exten had originally been the corporate president of Theta but had been removed in April or May 1965. Although no more than six payments were made (through June 1965), Hane took no action until June 7, 1967, when he filed a confession of judgment against all of the indorsers except the Thompsons. The Extens demanded and received a trial on the merits, after which the judge found them not liable.

ISSUE Have the conditions to the Extens' liability as indorsers been met?

DECISION No. Judgment for the Extens affirmed.

REASONS Judge Slingley first reviewed the UCC provisions and noted: "S.3–502(1)(a) makes it clear that unless presentment or notice of dishonor is waived or excused, unreasonable delay will discharge an indorser." The record indicated that Hane waited about 18 months before making any sort of demand for payment. Judge Singley further noted that the UCC rules indicated that what was a reasonable time was primarily a fact question. The trial court was certainly justified in finding that a delay of 18 months in making presentment for payment was unreasonable.

As to the giving of notice of Theta's dishonor, Hane's brother testified that demand for payment had been made on April 15, 1967, and that he was uncertain as to exactly when he notified Exten, but he said that it was "within a week." For nonbank parties, the UCC specifies that notice of dishonor must be given before midnight of the third business day following the dishonor. Exten denied receiving any notice at all prior to the default judgment on June 7.

Hane next tried to argue that the late presentment and notice were excused "because Exten himself had dishonored the note or had no reason to expect that it would be paid. . . . The court below rejected this contention on the ground that there was no evidence that Exten dishonored the note in his individual capacity.

"There is an even more persuasive reason which negates the contention that Exten had reason to expect that the note would not be paid. . . . While the manner in which $2,222.13 had been paid was unexplained, it would appear that at least six monthly payments of $320.47 had been met, with the result that payments were current for the period when Exten was president. . . . In the face of this Hane offered no proof that Exten, in his capacity as president of Theta, knew or should have known that the note would not be paid. An indorser's knowledge of the maker's insolvency, standing alone, will not excuse the giving of notice of dishonor. . . .

"Hane makes much of the fact that he is a holder in due course. We doubt that he was, since there is some evidence that he took the note with notice that it was overdue. . . . Whether Hane was or was not a holder in the course has no relevance to the issue here presented. In either case timely presentment and notice of dishonor were required to hold the Extens."

Presentment is the holder's demand for acceptance or payment of the instrument (3–504[1]). It may be made by mail, through a clearinghouse, or in person at the place specified (3–504[2]). The party to whom presentment is made may require the presenter to show the instrument, to identify himself or herself, to note a receipt for partial or full payment on the instrument, and to surrender the instrument if it is paid in full (3–505[1]).

Dishonor of the instrument occurs when it is properly presented and acceptance or payment is refused (3–507[1][a]). The party to whom presentment is made has only a limited period within which to decide whether or not he or she is going to pay or accept. The party has until the close of the next business day to decide whether to accept, but the holder may give him or her one extra business day, at the holder's option (3–506[1]). If payment is requested, it can be deferred "pending reasonable examination to determine whether it is properly payable," but only until the close of business on the day of presentment. There are only two exceptions to this "pay-same-day" rule: first, where the party to pay agrees to an earlier time for payment; second, where "documentary drafts" (4–104[1][f]) are being presented under a "letter of credit" (5–103[1][a]), in which case the bank to which such drafts are presented may defer honor until "the third banking day following receipt of the documents" (5–112[1][a]). Where an instrument has not been properly indorsed, returning it to the holder so that he or she can get the required indorsement is not a dishonor (3–507[3]), but a bank may certify the instrument if it wants to, before returning it for the proper indorsement (3–411[3]). Since a check is a demand instrument which is normally intended to have only limited circulation and then to be paid, the drawee bank "has no obligation to certify a check" (3–411[3]). The bank's refusal to pay the check would, of course, be a dishonor. The holder is entitled to have the instrument accepted as presented and can treat any variation or qualification in the acceptance as a dishonor (3–412[1]). If the holder does agree to take the acceptance with the changed terms, he or she discharges the drawer and indorser and has only the obligation of the drawee/acceptor according to the changed terms. The holder who is placed in this situation thus has to decide in which way he or she is more likely to get his or her money.

Where a proper presentment has been made and the instrument has been dishonored, something has obviously gone wrong; the original expectations of the parties have somehow been frustrated. Where such dishonor occurs, the drawer of a draft or check and indorsers of any sort of instrument are entitled to receive prompt notice, so that they can take steps to protect their rights. Notice is usually given by the holder, but 3–508(1) says that it may be given by "any other party who can be compelled to pay the instrument," such as a prior indorser. "Any reasonable manner" of notification is sufficient; even oral notice is permitted, if it can be proved. The Code also specifically recognizes the validity of the common banking procedure of simply returning the item with a stamp or attached ticket indicating the dishonor, or just sending back a debit notice to the party who gave the instrument to the bank (3–508[3]). Banks must give such required notice before their "midnight deadline," which means that a bank must send the word back up the line to others by midnight of the next banking day after the day of dishonor or the day of its own receipt from some other party of notice of dishonor (3–508[2]). Nonbank parties are given until midnight of the *third* business day following dishonor or their receipt of notice (3–508[2]). Since a "written notice is given when sent although it is not received" (3–508[4]), it is important to be able to prove exactly when letters were posted or telegrams given to the telegraph company. Once properly given, "notice operates for the benefit of all parties who have rights on the instrument against the party notified (3–508[8]). If a holder sent notice to prior indorsers Archie and Bernice, for example, Bernice's rights against Archie would be preserved even though *she* didn't send Archie any notice.

Samples v. Trust Company of Georgia
163 S.E.2d 325 (Georgia, 1968)

FACTS On January 30, 1967, Ed Samples received a check for $170.75 in payment for auto repair work. The check was signed by Carolyn D. Jordan and drawn against the Trust Company of Georgia. Samples indorsed the check and presented it to the Citizens and Southern National Bank, which paid him the money on February 1. On February 2, Citizens sent the check to Trust Company, which paid it on the same day. Trust Company then mistakenly debited the check to the account of one its employees, Carolyn Jordan, and sent the check out with her bank statement. On February 16, Carolyn told Trust Company that the check was not hers. Trust Company then recredited her account, took the check back, and sent the check to Citizens. Citizens returned the check to Trust Company and refused to return Trust Company's money. Trust Company sued and recovered in the trial court.

ISSUE Is the payor bank (Trust Company) entitled to the return of its funds?

DECISION No. Judgment reversed. (Citizens wins.)

REASONS Judge Bell referred to the requirement of UCC 3–501(2) that a bank must give notice of dishonor by its midnight deadline—"midnight on its next banking day following the banking day on which it receives the relevant item"—and to UCC 4–104(h), which discharges any indorser if the bank fails any such necessary notice. In this case, he said:
"The plaintiff bank's failure to give notice of the dishonor within the prescribed time was not due to 'circumstances beyond the control of the bank' and was not excused by any provision of the Code, but was due to the bank's error in mistaking the signature of a check for the signature of one of its customers with a similar name. A bank is bound to know the signatures of its depositors."
Further, Judge Bell said that UCC 4–302 required the same result, since it also held the payor bank liable if it did not send notice of dishonor until after its midnight deadline, unless the payor bank had a valid defense to such a breach of a presentment warranty. Trust Company had no such defense.

Parties with secondary contract liability may still be held on an instrument where there is an excuse for a delay in meeting these requirements or for a failure to meet them at all. If a holder does not know that an instrument has been accelerated by a prior holder, for example, his or her delay in making presentment would be excused. Similarly, where a delay is due to "circumstances beyond his control," a party has an excuse for late presentment, notice, or protest, so long as he or she "exercises reasonable diligence after the cause of the delay ceases to operate" (3–511[1]). Any of these requirements is "entirely excused" where (a) the party to be charged has waived it, or (b) he or she has no reason to expect the instrument to be paid or accepted (e.g., where the drawer of a check issues a stop pay order to his or her drawee bank, or (c) the requirement cannot be met "by reasonable diligence" (3–511[2]). Presentment is also excused by the death or subsequent insolvency of the maker, acceptor, or drawee "of any instrument except a documentary draft," or where "acceptance or payment is refused but not for want of proper presentment" (3–511[3]). In line with general commercial understanding, a waiver of protest is also a waiver of presentment and notice, even though protest is not required (3–511[3]). If the waiver language is part of the body of the instrument, it is binding on all secondary parties; if it is written above the signature of an indorser, it binds only him or her (3–511[6]).

Liability of Accommodation Parties and Guarantors. In many cases the person desiring to obtain a loan or credit may not have sufficient income or assets to make the creditor feel reasonably secure about receiving repayment when it is due. One form of additional security which can be used is to have another person, someone who does have a good credit rating, also promise to pay the debt. These "backstop" promises on negotiable instruments can take several forms.

An "accommodation party" is someone who has signed an instrument in some capacity (maker, indorser, acceptor) for the purpose of lending his or her credit standing to another party to the instrument. Common sense and the Code (3–415[2]) dictate that the accommodation party be liable in whatever capacity he or she signs to third parties who take the instrument for value. If Jones can't get a bank loan in his own name and his friend Smith agrees to cosign the note with him as a joint maker, Smith (the accommodation party) is liable to third parties as a maker. Had Smith indorsed the note after Jones signed as a sole maker, Smith would be liable to third parties as an indorser (and entitled to presentment, notice, and protest). Generally, these results occur even if the third party knows that Smith signed only to accommodate Jones. As between Smith and Jones, however, Smith has the right to demand reimbursement from Jones if Smith has to pay a third party, regardless of the order or the capacity in which they signed the instrument. The debt is really Jones' debt, and Jones should repay Smith.

Kerr v. DeKalb County Bank
217 S.E.2d 434 (Georgia, 1975)

FACTS   Kerr, Mott, and Thurston signed a promissory note, all three signing in the lower right-hand corner. The note was dated December 29, 1972, and stated that it was for 180 days, due on June 18, 1973. The bank admitted that Thurston's credit was insufficient to support a loan in any amount. Kerr and Mott argued that they were only accommodation parties, but the bank president testified that they said "they had a percentage interest in this production." After default, demand for payment was sent to each of these three persons by letters dated January 15, 1974. Suit was filed, and summary judgment was issued against all three. Kerr and Mott appealed.

ISSUE   Are Mott and Kerr primarily liable, as makers?

DECISION   Yes. Judgment for the bank affirmed.

REASONS   Judge Deen first cited the UCC rule from 3–415(2): "When the instrument has been taken for value before it is due the accommodation party is liable in the capacity in which he has signed even though the taker knows of the accommodation." In this case, not only had Kerr and Mott signed the note as makers, but the certified check for the proceeds was made out to them jointly with Thurston. The official comment to Section 3–415 indicated that recourse against the principal debtor was not a prerequisite to suit against the accommodation maker.

    The seven-month delay after maturity in making a demand for payment was also irrelevant here. "A demand for payment is not necessary in order to charge the maker of a promissory note; and hence . . . is not a prerequisite to the institution and maintenance of a suit on the note against the maker."

Words of guaranty may also be added to a signature. *Payment guaranteed* means that the holder of the instrument can present it directly to the person so signing if it is not paid when due. *Collection guaranteed* means that before the signer-guarantor is obligated to pay, the holder must first get a judgment against the maker or acceptor and show that the judgment is uncollectible. Where an indorser so guarantees payment or collection, he or she waives presentment, notice, and protest (3–416[5]).

Warranty Liability. Because the parties are dealing with the instrument as a piece of property, the Code provides that certain implied warranties are made when the instrument is transferred for value or presented for payment or acceptance. Just as implied warranties are imposed against the seller of goods under Article 2, so, too, five implied warranties are imposed on the person who transfers an instrument and receives consideration. If the transfer is by indorsement, these five warranties run to all subsequent good faith holders of the instrument; if the transfer is by delivery alone, they run only to the immediate transferee.

    The transferor for value warrants (*a*) that he or she has good title or is authorized to act for a person who has and that the transfer is otherwise rightful; (*b*)

497

that all signatures are genuine or authorized; (*c*) that the instrument has not been materially altered; (*d*) that no prior party who is liable on the instrument has a defense which is good as against the transferor; and (*e*) that he or she has no knowledge of any insolvency proceeding instituted with respect to the maker, acceptor, or drawer of an unaccepted instrument (3–417[2]). Comment 1 to this section states that these warranties may be disclaimed by agreement between the immediate parties but that an indorser cannot escape such warranty liability to subsequent holders unless his or her disclaimer is part of his or her indorsement. Where the indorsement contains only the words *without recourse*, the indorser-transferor still makes five warranties, but warranty (*d*) changes to a warranty that he or she has no *knowledge* that any defense of a prior party is good as against him or her (3–417[3]). A selling agent or broker who does not disclose his or her status makes all the warranties provided in this section; if such a seller does disclose that he or she is acting only as a representative, the seller warrants only his or her good faith and authority (3–417[4]).

Primarily in an effort to make sure that the proper party gets the money, Article 3 also imposes three warranties when the instrument is presented for payment or acceptance. These three warranties are imposed not only on the person who obtains the payment or acceptance but also on any prior transferor. The warranties are (*a*) that the person who presents the instrument has a good title to it or is authorized to act for someone who does; (*b*) that he or she has no knowledge of any unauthorized signature of a maker or drawer, except that a holder in due course does not warrant the maker's *own* signature to the maker, or the drawer's *own* signature to the drawer, or the drawer's signature to the acceptor if the holder took the instrument after acceptance or if the holder obtained the acceptance without knowledge of the unauthorized drawer's signature; and (*c*) that the instrument has not been materially altered, except that a holder in due course does not make this warranty either to those persons who should know the original terms of the instrument—the maker, the drawer, and the acceptor (3–417[1]). The exceptions under (*b*) and (*c*) are made to ensure fairness and are based on the old English case of *Price* v. *Neal*, 3 Burr. 1354 (1762). The idea is that at some point payment should be "final"; the Code draws this line at the point where payment is made to a holder in due course, acting in good faith. If the maker, drawer, or acceptor isn't sharp enough to catch the fact that the instrument has been altered or that his or her signature has been forged (or in the case of the acceptor-drawee, that his or her drawer's signature has been forged), it's simply not fair to let him or her recover the money paid to a holder in due course who was acting in good faith. Probably the most typical situation where the money has to be paid back and the instrument has to be kicked back up the chain of title is the case where a required indorsement is missing, so that the person making the presentment did not really have a "good title." These indorsement cases are considered in the next chapter.

Tort Liability. There are also special sections in Article 3 which impose liability for the torts of negligence and conversion. Section 3–406 says: "Any person who by his negligence substantially contributes to a material alteration of the instrument or to the making of an unauthorized signature is precluded from asserting the alteration or lack of authority against a holder in due course or against a drawee or other payor who pays the instrument in good faith and in accordance with the reasonable commercial standards of the drawee's or payor's business." If you fill out a check with a blank space after "Six" and before "dollars," and you also leave a blank when you write $6   .00" and if someone alters that check to read "Six Hundred" and the check is paid by your bank, you would be prevented from arguing the alteration as a basis for having the bank put $594 bank in your account. However, if the words *six* and *hundred* were written in ink of a different color, or if the handwritings were obviously dissimilar, your counterargument would be that the bank had not paid the check in good faith or had not exercised reasonable care in doing so. Another fairly typical case of this sort would involve the negligence of a business which printed its checks on a checkwriter. If the business had not taken reasonable precautions to prevent unauthorized persons from using the checkwriter, it would be precluded from asserting their lack of authority where the drawee bank had paid the checks in good faith. The net result of this section is that the negligent party is stuck with the loss, unless he or she can find and recover from the person who inserted the alteration or the unauthorized signature.

As with other types of personal property, a person who deals with an instrument in a manner inconsistent with the rights of the true owner is guilty of the tort of conversion. Section 3–419 says that an instrument is converted where (*a*) a drawee to whom it was presented for acceptance refuses to return it, or (*b*) a person to whom it was delivered for payment refuses to either pay or return it, or (*c*) it is paid on a forged (required) indorsement. If any of these things occurs, the amount of tort damages which the owner can collect against the wrongdoer will usually be the face amount of the instrument (3–419[2]). Banks which are merely acting as agents for their customers in trying to collect for deposited items are not liable as converters under this section, so long as they have exercised reasonable commercial standards in dealing with such an item and so long as they turn over any of the proceeds remaining in their possession to the true owner (3–419[3]); the customer is the converter, not the bank.

Gast v. American Casualty Co. of Reading, Pa.
2240 A.2d 682 (New Jersey, 1968)

FACTS   The Reverend Stuart F. Gast and his wife, Elizabeth, contracted to sell a house to Mark and Gertrude Hanna. Pursuant to the contract, the Hannas bought a fire insurance policy on the property, with the proceeds payable to the Gasts in the event of loss or damage. After a fire damaged the building, an amount of $3,435.92 was agreed on as the settlement. American issued a draft in that amount, drawn on itself, payable through Berks County Trust Company, and naming the insurance adjuster, the Gasts, and the Hannas as payees. The adjuster indorsed the draft, but when the Gasts' attorney sent the note to the Hannas for their signature, they forged the Gasts' indorsements, cashed the draft, and absconded with the money. The Gasts sued the drawee for conversion. The jury found for the drawee, and the Gasts appealed.

ISSUE   Was the drawee liable for conversion of the draft?

499

DECISION   Yes. Judgment reversed, and judgment entered for the Gasts.

REASONS   Judge Carton first set out the UCC 3–419 absolute liability rule when an instrument is paid on a forged indorsement. He said that the trial judge had made a material error by instructing the jury that the Gasts were required to prove that the drawee was negligent.

        The drawee tried to show that the Gasts' own negligence had "substantially contributed" to the making of the forged indorsement and that the Gasts were therefore barred from recovery under UC 3–406. Judge Carton thought that there was no jury question on this point. "We fail to see how any of plaintiffs' conduct constituted negligence which substantially contributed to the forgery and payment on the forged indorsement. The action of plaintiffs' attorney in forwarding the draft to the Hannas' attorney was entirely proper. . . . Neither plaintiffs nor their attorney was required to anticipate that, as a result of this mailing in escrow, the Hannas might appropriate the draft or that plaintiffs' signatures would be forged. . . .

        "Accordingly, the defense that plaintiff had substantially contributed to the making of the unauthorized signatures was not supported by the evidence and this issue should not have been submitted to the jury."

CASES FOR DISCUSSION

WILLIAMS v. MONTANA NATIONAL BANK OF BOZEMAN

534 P.2d 1247 (Montana, 1975)

James T. Harrison, Chief Justice

This is an appeal from a judgment for plaintiff entered in the district court, Gallatin County, following a jury verdict in the sum of $6,840, and denial of a motion for new trial.

Mrs. Rosa J. Williams, wife of plaintiff D. M. Williams, testified that on July 19, 1973, she was at their rural home when she saw a man coming up the walk. There was another man in a car who did not get out. The man told Mrs. Williams that he heard they had been having some bad electrical storms and that he was with a lightning rod company; that he heard she had been having a little trouble with the lightning rod and wanted to talk to him. He advised her that she needed a new clamp on the lightning rod, and she authorized him to put it on.

Mrs. Williams further testified the man talked fast and moved fast, moved his feet a little, and kept edging off as she talked to him, which she considered unusual. The man advised her the clamp would be $1.26 and that he had to have a check so he could mail it in to the company. She secured her check book and a pen. The man said he would fill in the check for her, and she gave him the check book. He filled it in by writing $1.26 in figures and in longhand, putting a date on it. He advised her that he would stamp the check with the company stamp. She looked the check over, and it looked alright to her, although it was not as she would have written it. The check was written so that the figures were so far to the right hand side that there was ample space to write the additional figures 684 to the left without any appearance of change. The words were written on the lower line so close to the word "Dollars" that there was ample space to write "Six thousand eight hundred forty" ahead of it without any appearance of alteration.

On cross-examination, Mrs. Williams testified the individual did not introduce himself, did not give her a business card or anything to identify him; she did not check the work before paying; she gave the man her entire check book; and he filled out the check while it was in the check book.

The teller who cashed the check at defendant Montana National Bank, where plaintiff had an account, and with its predecessor since about 1918 or 1919, testified that she went to the journal and checked the funds to see if there was enough money in the account. She also checked the person's signature to see if the signature on the check and on the signature card at the bank were the same; they were, so she cashed the check. Other witnesses testified as to the usual and reasonable commercial standards existing in the defendant bank and other banks in Bozeman. . . .

At the conclusion of plaintiff's case, defendant moved for a directed verdict and dismissal of the case, which was denied. . . .

As to the plaintiff's negligence, his wife and agent knew how to write a check and sign the check in question contrary to the manner in which she usually made out a check, according to her own testimony. She knew there was plenty of space for insertion of larger amounts ahead of the figures and words of amount in the check and was also negligent in not requiring that the payee's name be inserted in the check and in making delivery of the check under the circumstances. . . .

Under these definitions of negligence the jury could find that plaintiff was negligent since he knew that his wife had in the past signed checks prepared by others and thereby authorized her to do so, since he had done nothing to stop her from this procedure. His wife should have foreseen that there was a likelihood of raising the check when she left it the way it had been written, permitting the placing of the figures and the words so far to the right so as to permit what occurred. . . .

The jury under the fact situation here could then determine there would have been no loss "but for" the negligence of Mrs. Williams, wife-agent of plaintiff, as hereinbefore related. . . .

Here plaintiff charged defendant was negligent in cashing the check in that the bank breached its general obligation to handle plaintiff's account by acting contrary to reasonable commercial standards. Surely then the bank should be allowed to have the jury instructed as to what reasonable commercial standards are, as set forth in the Uniform Commercial Code.

The judgment is reversed and the cause remanded for new trial.

PORT CITY STATE BANK v. AMERICAN NATIONAL BANK, LAWTON, OKLAHOMA

486 F.2d 196 (U.S. 10th Circuit, 1973)

Hill, Circuit Judge

This appeal is from a judgment entered against appellant Port City State Bank in its suit to collect upon two checks forwarded to appellee and not returned as insufficient before the appropriate midnight deadline. Following a trial without jury, the United States District Court for the Western District of Oklahoma ruled that the failure to notify of dishonor prior to the deadline was excused in this case by Regulation J of the Federal Reserve Regulations, 12 C.F.R. 210.14, and 12A O.S.A. 4–108(2).

This court has jurisdiction by virtue of the diversity of citizenship of the parties and the allegation in the complaint of liability greatly exceeding the jurisdictional amount.

The record discloses that appellant was the holder of two checks drawn upon the J. H. McClung Coin Shop account with American National. Both items were forwarded through collecting channels for payment. The first check arrived at American National on Friday, November 28, 1969. That check contained two conflicting amounts: in figures $72,000.00 and in words seventy-two dollars and no/100 dollars. It was processed manually and stamped insufficient funds on Saturday, November 29; however, it was not returned immediately but was placed in Monday's business to determine if any deposits were forthcoming on Monday which would balance the account. Notice of dishonor was given to the last endorser of the check, the Federal Reserve Bank at Oklahoma City, on Wednesday, December 3, and the check was returned to the Federal Reserve Bank at Oklahoma City, on Wednesday, December 3, and the check was returned to the Federal Reserve on December 4.

The second check, in the amount of $120,377.20, arrived at American National on Tuesday, December 2, 1969. The first notice of its dishonor was by telephone to the Federal Reserve on Friday, December 5; it was returned to the Federal Reserve the same day.

It was stipulated by the parties that the "midnight deadline" for these items as established by Regulation J, 12 C.F.R. 210.12, and 12A O.S.A. 4–104(1)(h) was midnight December 1 for the first check and midnight December 3 for the second check. Additionally, it was stipulated that neither check was dishonored before the applicable deadline.

These facts establish a prima facie case for the application of 12 C.F.R. 210.12 and 12A O.S.A. 4–302(a), both concerning the necessity of fulfilling the midnight deadline, and thus it became the obligation of appellee at the trial to prove an excuse from these provisions under 12 C.F.R. 210.14 and 12A O.S.A. 4–108(2). The latter regulations in essence prevent the operation of the midnight deadline in cases when the delay by the payor bank is caused by the interruption of communication facilities, suspension of payments by another bank, war, emergency condition, or other circumstances beyond the control of the bank, provided it exercises such diligence as the circumstances require.

In furtherance of its contention, American National presented evidence that prior to December 1, 1969, it had performed its bookkeeping functions by machine posting, a so-called manual system. During 1969, however, a decision was made to implement a computer bookkeeping operation, and a rental agreement was entered into with a large computer company. That lease provided that all repairs and maintenance were the obligation of the computer firm, and American National was not authorized to undertake any such tasks. After the installation of the computer, American National paralleled its

manual system with computer operations for approximately two weeks. Finally the decision was made to change over to computer processing beginning on December 1. A last manual posting was made on Saturday, November 29, and the manual bookkeeping equipment was removed from the bank during that weekend.

At approximately 10:00 A.M. on December 1, the first day for use of computer operations, the American National computer developed a "memory error" which rendered it unusable. Though the computer manufacturer indicated repairs would not take "too long," they lasted until late Monday night and the testing procedure extended into the early hours of Tuesday, December 2.

In reliance upon the belief that the computer would be required without prolonged delay, American National took no extraordinary steps to process Monday's business during the business day. However, when it became apparent that evening that the computer was not going to be ready immediately, American National decided to utilize an identical computer in a bank which was a trip of some 2½ hours away, in accord with a backup agreement they had made with the other banking institution. Thus at about 11:30 P.M. personnel from American National and the computer company began processing Monday's business on the backup computer and continued processing through the night. This work had proceeded to the point of capturing the items on discs when, because the backup computer was required by its owner and because they were informed their own computer was operational, the American National personnel returned to their bank to complete the work on their own machine. After returning to American National, the work was processed to the point of completing the printing of the trial balances when another memory error developed which again rendered the computer unusable. No further use could be made of the appellee's computer until a new memory module was installed on Thursday, December 4.

Because of the second failure, American National was forced to utilize the backup computer both Wednesday and Thursday during times it was not required by its owner. Monday's business was completed and work was begun on Tuesday's items the evening of Tuesday, December 2. Tuesday's items were not completed until either Wednesday, the third, or Thursday, the fourth. When the second check arrived in Tuesday's business, it was held to determine if a later deposit had balanced the account. Through the use of the backup computer and then its own computer during the next weekend, American National was fully "caught up" by Monday, December 8.

Based upon this evidence, the trial court held that the computer malfunction suffered by American National was the cause of its failure to meet its required midnight deadline of the checks, and that such malfunction constituted both an emergency condition and a circumstance beyond the control of the bank as outlined in 12 C.F.R. 210.14 and 12A O.S.A. 4–108(2). The court further held that the reaction to the situation by American National fulfilled the requirements of diligence imposed by those regulations, and therefore the court entered judgment for American National on both checks. . . .

As to the first check, it is true that it was processed and stamped insufficient on Saturday; however, it was held for Monday's business to allow any deposits made on Monday to balance the account before notice was required. This procedure is reasonable, and only the subsequent computer breakdown prevented timely notice upon the check. In the case of the second check, appellant contends that problems involved in balancing the "proof batches" caused the delay, not the unavailability of the computer. Such a contention ignores the problems encountered by the bank on Tuesday as a result of the delay in processing Monday's business. Tuesday's work was delayed first by the necessity of driving 2½ hours each day before work could commence, and second by the necessity that Monday's business be completed first. Without doubt, both of these delays resulted from the computer problems at American National.

Further, appellant contends that a computer failure, as a matter of law, is not an event which can impose the application of 12A O.S.A. 4–108(2). In our opinion, such a determination is a mixed question of fact and law; however, neither treatment justifies the reversal of the trial court's determination in this case. Factually, it was in no way erroneous to conclude that the malfunction created an emergency condition in the bank and was also a condition beyond the control of the bank. . . .

Port City next alleges that the trial court erred in its determination that American National exercised "such diligence" as the circumstances required. Basically, appellant asserts three alternative procedures that American National could have employed, and asserts that if any of these alternatives would have resulted in meeting the deadline, then appellee did not exercise diligence under the circumstances. As the trial court correctly concluded, the statute does not require perfection on the part of the appellee, and American National's performance should not be judged on the basis of 20–20 hindsight.

It must first be noted that appellee quickly notified the computer firm of the breakdown, and that company began an immediate repair effort. Further, there was evidence to indicate that such computer breakdowns are generally repaired very quickly. Thus it would appear that appellee was justified in its initial delay in adopting emergency procedures based on its belief such measures would prove unnecessary. Additionally, we must agree with the trial court that appellee's duty under these circumstances was much broader than one requiring merely that it meet its midnight deadline. It was further obligated to keep the bank open and to serve its customers. To abandon the orderly day-by-day process of bookkeeping to adopt radical emergency measures would have likely prolonged the delay in returning the bank to normal operations.

As to appellant's assertion that appellee should be returned to manual posting, it was shown that the equipment for this procedure was no longer in the bank. Further, no clear evidence was presented to indicate such a procedure would have allowed appellee to fulfill its deadlines if the procedure had been implemented. Any decision to return to manual posting would have to have been made very soon after the discovery of the initial failure. At that time, because of their own experience with computers and the industry history, and also because the manufacturer did not foresee the serious nature of the repairs, American National was justified in believing its computer would be back in service soon. Their delay in commencing emergency operations was reasonable, and these facts prevented a return to manual posting in time to fulfill the deadlines.

As to the possiblity of utilizing another backup computer at the regional headquarters of the computer leasing firm, we must agree with the trial court that there was no evidence that this alternative would have proved any more success-ful than the method actually employed by appellee.

In regard to the last alternative, "sight posting," the evidence is conflicting but sufficient to indicate it is not clear this alternative was so obviously superior as to be mandated under these circumstances. There were differing estimates as to the time required, and it was indicated such a procedure would upset and delay the eventual computer bookkeeping required to return the bank to current status. And as in the consideration of the previous alternatives, it was not clearly demonstrated that this procedure would have allowed American National to meet its deadlines even if it had been adopted. . . .

PROBLEMS FOR DISCUSSION

In each of the following examples, the instrument is negotiable and the plaintiff is a bona fide purchaser who would qualify as a holder in due course (HDC) if the instrument has been properly negotiated to him or her. The issue in these cases is whether a particular defendant—M (Maker), X, DR (Drawer), DE (Drawee), P (Payee), DE Bank (Drawee Bank) or Dep. Bank (Depositary Bank)—is liable to the plaintiff on the facts given in the example.

Fact situations	*What result?*
1. $M \xrightarrow[\text{(fraud)}]{\text{due }7/1}$ Payee $\rightarrow$ X $\rightarrow$ HDC (HDC presents 12/1; M dishonors)	HDC v. M HDC v. X
2. DR $\xrightarrow[\text{(fraud)}]{\text{due }7/1}$ Payee $\rightarrow$ X $\rightarrow$ HDC (HDC presents 12/1; DE dishonors)	HDC v. DR HDC v. X HDC v. DE
3. DR $\xrightarrow[\text{(fraud)}]{\text{due }7/1}$ Payee $\rightarrow$ X $\rightarrow$ HDC (HDC presents 7/1; DE dishonors; no notice to X)	HDC v. DR HDC v. X HDC v. DE
4. Same, except that X did receive notice of dishonor but had indorsed "without recourse"	HDC v. X
5. DR $\rightarrow$ Order of Payee $\rightarrow$ X (finds and forges Payee's indorsement) $\rightarrow$ HDC DE (Payee presents; DE accepts liability)	HDC v. DR HDC v. P HDC v. DE
6. Same, except that Payee indorses and then loses instrument	HDC v. DR HDC v. P HDC v. DE

	Fact situations	*What result?*

7. DR → Payee or Bearer → X (finds and forges Payee's indorsement) → HDC

DE (Payee presents; DE accepts liability)

HDC v. DR   HDC v. P
HDC v. DE

8. Same, except that Payee indorses and then loses instrument

HDC v. DR   HDC v. P
HDC v. DE

9. Same, except that Payee indorses "without recourse" and then loses instrument

HDC v. P

10. DR → Payee → Thief → HDC → Depositary Bank → DE Bank (DE Bank pays and charges DR's account)

P v. DR (P v. HDC)
DR v. DE Bank
DE v. Dep. Bk.
Dep. Bk. v. HDC

24 | Negotiation and Holders in Due Course

W e now have an instrument which is negotiable and on which one or more parties are liable. In order to get the special "negotiability" results, however, our plaintiff who is seeking to enforce the instrument must meet an additional set of requirements. Unless he or she has taken the instrument through a special form of transfer called "negotiation" and under circumstances which qualify him or her as a "holder in due course," our plaintiff holds the instrument subject to all the defenses and claims which would be available against the assignee of a simple written contract.

NEGOTIATION

Today, as indicated in Chapter 11, most contracts can be assigned. Only a negotiable instrument, however, can be "negotiated." Negotiation is a transfer "in such form that the transferee becomes a holder" (3–202[1]). There must be physical delivery of the instrument, and if the instrument is payable to order, it must be indorsed (3–202[1]). A holder is a person who is in possession of an instrument "drawn, issued or indorsed to him or her or to his or her order or to bearer or in blank" (1–201[20]). Where you make your check payable to "cash," or where you indorse your paycheck on the back by simply signing your name, any person who subsequently gains possession of the instrument is a holder, even without any further indorsements. (Not every holder is a holder in due course, however; that status depends on the circumstances under which the holder acquired the instrument.)

Where an instrument is drawn to someone's order (your rent check to your landlord, for example) or is indorsed to someone's order (you indorsed a dividend check to your bank as payment on a loan), negotiation cannot occur unless there is a proper indorsement by the person to whose order the instrument is now payable. In other words, the finder of an unindorsed order instrument would not be a holder nor would any subsequent transferee from the finder.

506

The missing required indorsement breaks the "chain of title" to the instrument, so that no later person, even though in possession of the instrument itself, is a "holder." To qualify as a holder in due course so as to own an instrument free of most claims and defenses, a person must first be a holder. The proper indorsement of an order instrument is therefore crucial to the HDC status of later possessors. If you simply sign your name on the back of your paycheck and then lose it on the way to the bank, the finder would not be an HDC (since he or she gave no value for it), but the finder would be a *holder* and the store where he or she used it to buy merchandise could qualify as an HDC. The net result is that you lose the value represented by your paycheck just as if you had cashed it and then lost the cash. To change this example: If you lost your paycheck before you indorsed it, the finder would not be a holder and neither would the store, even if the finder forged your indorsement on the back of the check. The net result is that you get your money back and the store gets stuck. For this reason, many stores and banks are reluctant to cash checks where the person asking for the money is not the original payee.

INDORSEMENT

General Rules. An indorsement is made by signing your name on the instrument, normally on the back. An indorser could sign on the front of the instrument, but this would entail the risk of being held liable as a comaker of the note or as a codrawer of the draft if that's what the signature seemed to be. Section 3–402 is some help: "Unless the instrument clearly indicates that a signature is made in some other capacity it is an indorsement." The Code also contains a presumption (3–414[2]) as to the sequence in which indorsers are liable: "in the order in which they indorse, which is presumed to be the order in which their signatures appear on the instrument." Where an instrument has been transferred so many times that there is no room on it for further indorsements, these may be made on a "permanently" attached piece of paper, called an "allonge" (3–202[2]).

An indorsement is effective for negotiation only when it conveys the entire amount due on the instrument. Any attempt to indorse over only part of what's due is not a negotiation but operates as only a partial assignment. (Therefore, no transferee under such a partial indorsement could be an HDC.) Additional words of assignment, condition, waiver, or limitation of liability "do not affect its character as an indorsement" (3–202[3] and [4]). Where the name of the person to whose order the instrument is payable is misspelled or otherwise incorrect, he or she may indorse with the incorrect name or the correct name or both. Anyone giving value for the instrument can require the double indorsement (3–203). Unless the instrument is already payable to the bearer, any transferee for value can demand that the transferor indorse (3–201[3]).

Where an instrument is payable to two or more persons jointly ("pay to the order of Jones and Green"), all of them must indorse in order to negotiate the instrument. Where an instrument is payable to two or more persons in the alternative ("pay to the order of Jones or Green"), the single indorsement of any of them is sufficient to negotiate it (3–116).

Clinger v. *Clinger*

503 P.2d 363 (Colorado, 1972)

FACTS   Ross Clinger and George Laumeyer owned Rockwell Concrete Products, Inc. Dennis Clinger (Ross' twin brother) owned Republic Concrete Construction Company. Republic owed Rockwell $3,952.71; Rockwell owed Republic $3,848.30. Dennis and his wife issued a check on the Republic account at the Continental National Bank for $3,952.71, payable to Dennis Clinger and Rockwell Concrete Products. The brothers had the check certified and then went to the Southwest State Bank, where Ross indorsed as agent for Rockwell and deposited the check. Dennis did not indorse the check. Southwest then issued a cashier's check to Ross for $3,848.30, payable to Republic, which Ross gave to Dennis. When the $3,952.71 check was presented to Continental, it refused payment. This check came back to Ross, who added Dennis' signature and presented the check a second time. Payment was again refused, and Continental finally released the amount it had been holding out of the Republic account. Ross, George, and Rockwell sued Dennis, Republic, and Continental. The trial court held Dennis and Republic liable but dismissed the case against Continental. The plaintiffs appealed the dismissal order as to the Continental Bank.

ISSUE   Did the defendant bank wrongfully refuse to pay the certified check?

DECISION   No. Judgment for the Continental Bank affirmed.

REASONS   Judge Coyte first reviewed the facts and then cited UCC 3–409 and 3–411. The bank, on acceptance/certification, had an obligation "to pay the check upon presentment when properly endorsed." "The statutory effect of the bank's certification was to create the bank's direct liability on the instrument when properly endorsed and presented for payment. The fact that the bank released the funds from the drawer's account created no new liability on the part of the bank. Even after release of the funds, if the certified check were presented in a properly endorsed form, the bank would have been liable on it.

    "Continental National Bank's obligation was on the instrument and was to make payment upon proper presentment. Since the check was made payable to the order of Dennis Clinger and Rockwell Concrete Products, the signatures of both payees were required for negotiation. . . . Refusal of the bank to pay the check was not a breach of its obligation on the instrument."

Imposters and Defrauders. Article 3 contains some very special rules to cover situations where instruments are issued to imposters, crooked employees and agents, and other defrauders. In the imposter case, someone who is not Henry Forge comes into your office, says "I am Henry Forge," convinces you that he is, and persuades you to enter into a transaction which results in your making out a check payable to the order of "Henry Forge." He tricked you. The Code (3–405[1][a]) says that *anyone* can effectively indorse this instrument by signing "Henry Forge." The fake Henry Forge can do so. If he loses it or it's stolen from him, the thief or finder can indorse "Henry Forge" and effectively negotiate the instrument. This doesn't mean that some or all of these persons can't be prosecuted criminally; it just means that subsequent transferees can be holders and can therefore qualify as HDCs if they meet all of the other requirements. The same rule applies where a corporations' bookkeeper or payroll clerk "pads the payroll" with extra fake names and then indorses and cashes these extra checks. The crook's indorsements in the names of the named payees are effective; the drawee bank honoring these checks when presented has paid the right party; and the corporation is stuck unless it can get the money back from the crook. Most simply, the Code's rule for these cases is: "The sucker always pays!" The Code also provides for similar results where the negotiation of an instrument is subject to rescission because of minority or other incapacity, illegality, breach of duty, or fraud, duress, or mistake. Such a negotiation is at least temporarily effective, and these "defects'" in the transaction cannot be used so as to recover the instrument from a later HDC (3–207). A minor's negotiation of an instrument, for example, would make all later transferees "holders," so that one of them could qualify as an HDC. If there were a subsequent HDC in the chain of title, the minor could not get the instrument back; if there were no subsequent HDC, the minor could exercise his or her rescission rights to recover the instrument from the current holder. In either case, the minor could use minority as a defense against having to actually pay the instrument (3–305[2][a]).

TYPES OF INDORSEMENT

There are at least three features to every indorsement: the method it requires for making further negotiations, or at least the next one; the nature of the liability it imposes on the indorser; and the kind of restrictions, if any, which it attempts to place on further transfers. These three features may be combined in various ways.

Blank Indorsements and Special Indorsements. The last indorsement controls the status of the instrument as order paper or bearer paper, regardless of the form in which it was originally issued. A blank indorsement consists merely of the indorser's signature: "John Smith." If the last or the only indorsement is a blank indorsement, the instrument is now bearer paper and may be negotiated from now on by delivery, without further indorsement. A special indorsement names the next transferee: "Pay to Judy Jones. John Smith." Regardless of how it was originally made payable, this instrument is now order paper and Judy must now indorse in order to negotiate the instrument further. (Note that the words of negotiability—*order* or *bearer*—do not have to be used in an indorsement; the preceding example is payable to the order of Judy Jones.)

509

Klomann v. Sol K. Graff & Sons
317 N.E.2d 608 (Illinois, 1974)

FACTS Graff & Sons, a real estate brokerage partnership, represented Fred Klomann in his trading of certain real estate for the Countryside Shopping Plaza. The firm owed Klomann $13,000 as a result, and Robert Graff (a partner) gave him three notes, one for $5,000 and two for $4,000 each. Klomann hired Graff & Sons to manage the shopping center and orally promised that the commissions which the firm earned for that work could be offset against the amount that Graff owed him. Robert Graff estimated that his salary of $300 a month (total $14,700) more than offset the firm's debt to Klomann. Klomann specially indorsed the notes to his daughter, Candace Klomann. She examined them and then handed them back to her father so that he could collect them for her. Klomann later scratched out Candace's name, inserted his wife Georgia's name, and delivered the notes to Georgia. Georgia sued to collect. The trial court ruled that the money earned by Robert as manager of the shopping center could not be offset against the money that Graff & Sons owed Klomann, and it entered a summary judgment for Georgia.

ISSUE Can Georgia Klomann enforce the notes?

DECISION No. Judgment reversed and cause remanded.

REASONS After reviewing the facts, Justice Dieringer discussed the plaintiff's reliance on UCC 3–306(d): "The claim of any third person to the instrument is not otherwise available as a defense to any party liable thereon unless the third person himself defends the action for such party." Dieringer thought that the case was controlled by UCC 3–204 and 3–201, regarding the propriety of the indorsement as vesting ownership in the transferee.

"Fred Klomann specially indorsed the promissory notes to his daughter, Candace, in August, 1967. The notes, therefore, could only be further negotiated by Candace. Examination of the record further reveals Candace, the special indorsee, has never negotiated the notes. . . . When Fred Klomann assigned the notes in question to his daughter he no longer had any interest in them. His attempted assignment to Georgia approximately three years later conveyed only that interest which he had in the notes, which was nothing. Plaintiff, therefore, has no interest in the notes sued on in the instant case. We do not believe, as the plaintiff contends, that the Uniform Commercial Code intends . . . to not allow the maker of the note to look into the situation and see where title really lies."

Qualified and Unqualified Indorsements. As indicated in Chapter 23, an indorser may disclaim his or her secondary contract liability by using the words *without recourse* or similar language. This is called a qualified indorsement. If such language is not used, the indorsement is unqualified, meaning that the indorser is assuming the normal secondary contract liability—to pay the instrument on dishonor.

Restrictive Indorsements. Indorsers sometimes attempt, in various ways, to restrict or limit the further negotiation of an instrument. Under the Code's rules, some such restrictions are fully effective, some are partially effective, and some are without legal effect. Section 3–206(1) states that no indorser can effectively prohibit the further negotiation of a negotiable instrument. If John Smith indorsed "Pay only Judy Jones" or "Pay Judy Jones and no one else," the "only" language is completely ineffective. Judy can indorse and renegotiate the instrument just as if John had indorsed "Pay to the order of Judy Jones." Furthermore, Comment 2 to Section 3–206 says that such an "only" indorsement "does not of itself give notice to subsequent parties of any defense or claim of the indorser"; there's not necessarily an indication that there's something wrong back up the line, so as to prevent later holders from qualifying as HDCs.

The promise or order contained in the body of the instrument itself cannot be conditional without destroying its negotiability. This is not true, however, of indorsements. Conditions can be included in indorsements without affecting an instrument's negotiability. What's more, the Code makes such conditions fully effective as against all subsequent holders of the instrument other than banks handling it for collection purposes (3–206[3]). For example, Biff Bosox buys a new TV from Big Bennie's Appliance Store. As payment, Biff indorses his payroll check: "Pay to Big Bennie if he delivers one new Zenith TV to my home. Biff Bosox." Bennie is not supposed to get the money unless he delivers the TV as promised, and the Code says that all later holders of the instrument are responsible for checking and seeing that he has done so before they take the instrument. If Bennie has not delivered the TV but gets the money from someone anyway, that later holder of the instrument is not an HDC (3–206[3]). Similarly, all subsequent holders other than intermediary banks are fully bound by such language in the indorsement as "For deposit only" or "For collection." It is very hard to imagine a situation where a nonbank person taking an instrument after such an indorsement could ever qualify as an HDC; such language clearly indicates that the instrument is intended to circulate only through the bank collection process.

Where the restrictive indorsement indicates that the proceeds are to be paid to one person for the benefit of another ("Pay to Ollie Orkin for the benefit of Shirley Trample"), only the first taker after the indorsement is bound by it. In order to be a holder for value so as to (perhaps) qualify as an HDC, the immediate transferee must pay any value given "consistently with the indorsement." Unless later holders of the instrument actually know that the trustee or other fiduciary has misapplied these funds, they are not affected in any way by the "benefit" type of restrictive indorsement.

HOLDER IN DUE COURSE

Generally. The essence of the whole concept of negotiability is the elimination or nonassertability of most common defenses when the instrument gets into the hands of a good faith purchaser. The technical term for such a BFP in the negotiable instruments context is *holder in due course*. The requirements for becoming an HDC are set out in Section 3–302, and then they are more specifically defined in other sections. Whether a particular person has met this set of requirements presents a complex combination of legal and factual issues which have been subject to considerable litigation. Since, as previously noted, consumer debtors are now permitted to assert any defense they may have, against anyone, HDC status has become virtually meaningless in consumer transactions. For businesses, however, these issues are still vital where merchandise has been fraudulently misrepresented or has not been delivered at all. Whether a business debtor will be able to assert such defenses or will be forced to pay for the proverbial "dead horse," will depend on a later holder's status as an HDC.

A holder in due course first has to be a holder (as discussed above) and then must meet an additional set of qualifications. He or she must have taken the instrument "for value, and in good faith, and without notice that it is overdue or has been dishonored or of any defense against or claim to it on the part of any person." Section 3–302 also contains several specific rules: a payee can qualify as an HDC; a purchaser of a limited interest in an instrument can be an HDC only to that extent; and a person cannot become an HDC by buying an instrument at a judicial sale or as part of a bulk transaction not in the ordinary course of business or by acquiring it through legal process or in taking over an estate (3–302[2], [3], and [4]).

Value. *Value,* as used here, is a much more limited concept than "consideration." A holder for value must have performed the agreed consideration for the note. If Axle Greez promises to buy a certain promissory note from Henna Rinz for $600, there is a contract, but Axle is not a holder for value until he actually pays Henna the $600. If he is notified of an existing defense before he pays, he can't become an HDC. A person who acquires security interests or other liens against instruments, other than by judicial process, is a holder for value. So is a person who "takes the instrument in payment of or as security for an antecedent claim against any person whether or not the claim is due" (3–303[b]). Similarly, someone who makes an "irrevocable commitment to a third person" (a binding agreement for an extension of credit, for example) is thereby a holder for value. Finally, value is given by giving another negotiable instrument. In the above example, if Axle had given Henna his check for $600 in payment for the promissory note he bought from her, Axle would be a holder for value of the note (3–303[c]).

Korzenik v. *Supreme Radio, Inc.*
197 N.E.2d 702 (Massachusetts, 1964)

FACTS   On October 31, 1961, Armand Korzenik's law firm had received $15,000 in trade acceptances from its client, Southern New England Distributing Corporation, "as a retainer for services to be performed." Korzenik had been retained by Southern on October 25 in connection with certain antitrust litigation. He did some work for Southern from October 25 to October 31, but there was no evidence as to its value. He also paid cocounsel in the antitrust case some money, but there was no indication of the specific amount. Korzenik sued to collect on two of the trade acceptances, due November 1 and December 1, 1961, in a total amount of $1,900. Southern had defrauded Supreme, although Korzenik didn't know that when he took the trade acceptances. The lower courts found for Supreme.

ISSUE   Had Korzenik given "value" for the trade acceptances, so that he qualified as an HDC?

DECISION   No. Judgment for Supreme affirmed.

REASONS   According to Justice Whttemore, the key was UCC 3–303(a): "A holder takes the instrument for value (a) to the extent that the agreed consideration has been performed." The agreement with Korzenik clearly related to future legal services, and the burden was on him to prove the extent to which those services had already been performed when he learned of the fraud defense.

"The Uniform Laws Comment to S.3–303 points out that in this article 'value is divorced from consideration' and that except as provided in paragraph (c) '[a]n executory promise to give value is not . . . value. . . . The underlying reason of policy is that when the purchaser learns of a defense . . . he is not required to enforce the instrument, but is free to rescind the transaction for breach of the transferor's warranty.' . . .

"The only other possible issue under S.3–303 is whether, because of or in connection with taking the assignments, Korzenik made 'an irrevocable commitment to a third person.' There is no evidence of such a commitment. The finding as to a payment to cocounsel shows only that some of the proceeds of other assigned items have been expended by Korzenik."

Good Faith. Article 3 contains no special definition of *good faith* other than that in the general definitions section (1–201[19]). It is a subjective test, to be applied by the trier of fact: "honesty in fact in the conduct or transaction concerned." Such facts as the relationship between the parties, the size of any discount from the fact amount of the instrument, the proximity of the transfer to the instrument's due date, the appearance of the instrument, and the time and place of the transfer would be relevant in deciding whether a particular holder had bought in "good faith."

No Notice of Claim or Defense. Article 3 (3–304) does contain several specific rules for determining when a purchaser has "notice" that an instrument is overdue, has been dishonored, or is subject to a claim or defense. The basic rule is nothing more than common sense: A purchaser has notice of a claim or defense where "the instrument is so incomplete, bears such visible evidence of forgery or alteration, or is otherwise so irregular as to call into question its validity, terms or ownership or to create an ambiguity as to the party to pay." A purchaser also has notice if he or she is made aware "that the obligation of any party is voidable in whole or in part, or that all parties have been discharged." Where a fiduciary has negotiated an instrument for his or her own benefit, the purchaser must have had knowledge of that fact when he or she took the instrument. Remember the difference between "knowledge" and "notice"; *knowl-*

edge means actual, "inside-the-head" information, whereas *notice* includes both acts from which a reasonable person should infer other information and the receipt of notices containing information, whether those notices are actually read or not. Knowledge is therefore only one form of "notice." This section does say that the filing or recording of a document does not of itself constitute notice so as to prevent a person from being an HDC, and it also says that for notice to be effective, it must be received "at such time and in such manner as to give a reasonable opportunity to act on it."

Briand v. Wild
268 A.2d 896 (New Hampshire, 1970)

FACTS Norman and Lois Wild were negotiating for the purchase of certain land from Romeo and Jean Briand. On March 31, 1965, Mrs. Wild sent Briand a letter which read: "[C]onfirming our telephone conversation of yesterday, I am enclosing herewith my check in the amount of $400.00 (dated May 1st as suggested by you) to cover . . . Lot #33." The letter also asked for an option on the lot next door, and it said that "Norman will return from Hawaii sometime between the 15th and 20th of April, and at that time he will contact you to arrange for the balance of payment on Lot #33." Prior to May 1, the Wilds decided not to buy the lot and stopped payment on the $400 check. The trial court held for the plaintiffs.

ISSUE Were the plaintiffs HDCs?

DECISION No. Judgment reversed; defendants are not liable on the check.

REASONS The UCC specifically permits the payee to be a holder in due course if he or she meets all the requirements. The Code also states that the negotiability of a check is not affected by the fact that it is postdated. But Justice Kenison saw another problem here. ". . . [A] purchaser of a postdated instrument who knows at the time of his purchase of an asserted defense or of facts or circumstances which may create a defense, is precluded from being a holder in due course. . . .

"The plaintiff Romeo Briand, the payee of the check, had notice that the check was postdated and that the sale might not be completed when defendant Norman Wild returned if the terms of payment could not be worked out. The plaintiff as payee does not qualify as a holder in due course, for he is charged with notice of the claim of the defendants to the $400 if the sale were not completed. . . . Plaintiff took the check subject to 'all defenses' the defendants have 'available in an action on a simple contract' and 'the defenses of want or failure of consideration, [and] nonperformance of any condition precedent.'"

Section 3–304 also specifies certain things which do not necessarily give the purchaser notice of a claim or defense and thus prevent him or her from qualifying as an HDC. These things include the fact that the instrument is antedated or postdated; that the instrument was originally incomplete and has been completed (unless there is also notice that the completion was improper); that one or more persons have signed the instrument as accommodation parties; that any person negotiating the instrument is or was a fiduciary; that the instrument was issued or negotiated in return for an executory promise or was accompanied by a separate agreement; that there has been a default in interest payments on the instrument or in payment on any other instrument, except where the defaulted instrument was part of a series with this one (a series of corporate notes, for example).

No Notice That Instrument Is Overdue. Section 3–304(3) provides a few rules for determining when a purchaser has notice that an instrument is "overdue." Where the instrument is a demand instrument, rather than one with a specific due date, the purchaser has notice that it's overdue if he or she is taking it after a demand for payment has already been made by a prior holder or after more than a reasonable time from the date it was issued. The section contains a presumption that 30 days is such a reasonable time for an uncertified check payable in the United States, but it does not contain similar guidelines for drafts or notes. (Presumably, the reasonable time for these other instruments would be longer than that for an uncertified check.) The purchaser also has such notice when he or she is aware that a prior acceleration of the due date has been made. Finally, there is notice that an instrument is overdue when the purchaser has reason to know that part of the principal is overdue (a missed installment payment, for example) or that "there is an uncured default in payment of another instrument of the same series." There is no stated rule for the most obvious case: the stated due date is July 1, and you buy the instrument on July 2; you can clearly see that the instrument is overdue when you buy it, and you are not an HDC.

SHELTER RULE

Under the Code, a transferee of a negotiable instrument (including one who is not even a holder) in most instances receives whatever rights to it his or her transferor had. A holder who is not an HDC (a donee, for example) would nevertheless have whatever enforcement rights his or her transferor had. Because of this general rule, any holder of an instrument after an HDC succeeds to all the rights of the HDC, even though the later holder or holders, don't personally meet all the requirments for being an HDC. The donee of the instrument can't personally qualify as an HDC, because he or she gave no value for it. But if the donor or some prior party was an HDC, the donee would have all the rights to the instrument that the HDC did. In simplest terms, once there is an HDC in an instrument's chain of title, all later holders of the instrument receive the "shelter" of that person's HDC status even though they can't meet the HDC tests.

Canyonville Bible Academy v. Lobemaster
247 N.E.2d 623 (Illinois, 1969)

FACTS   Louis and Bernice Lobemaster signed a promissory note for $12,694.22 in favor of Lobmaster Trailer Sales, Inc., owned and operated by Samuel D. Lobmaster. Prior to the due date of the first installment, Samuel indorsed and discounted the note to the Jefferson Bank in the corporations' name. He had previously guaranteed payment to the bank on all such trailer contracts discounted to it, and he had procured a life insurance policy for $200,000 to be paid to the bank in the event of this death in order to satisfy the bank's claims, with the balance, if any, to be paid to Canyonville. Prudential Insurance paid the $200,000 to the bank; the bank charged the $9,674.30 still due on the note against this $200,000 fund; and then the bank assigned the note to Canyonville. Canyonville sued to enforce the note, but the trial court held for the defendants.

ISSUE   Must the holder prove that it gave value to enforce the note?

DECISION   No. Judgment for the plaintiff (Canyonville).

REASONS   Justiced Trapp first disposed of the argument that Samuel Lobmaster's estate rather than Canyonville should be suing. He then decided that Canyonville was protected under the "shelter rule," UCC 3–201. He cited the comment to 3–201: "This subsection eliminates the requirement of value for the purposes of transferring the rights of the holder. It is in accord with Illinois case law indicating that a valid transfer may be made by way of gift. . . . The transfer of rights is not limited to transfers for value. An instrument may be transferred as a gift, and the donee acquires whatever rights the donor had." He felt that those rules clearly applied here.

   "Since the Bank was a holder in due course and plaintiff was not a prior holder, the plaintiff by transfer from the Bank acquired the rights of a holder in due course irrespective of the question of value. Also we think that since the guaranty by Samuel Lobmaster was general and involved many notes which the Bank was required to handle and questions could arise as to whether certain liabilities really existed or could be paid out of the insurance proceeds, a consideration in the nature of a detriment to plaintiff was involved in agreeing to the satisfaction of the guaranty from the insurance fund."

There are two exceptions to this shelter rule. A person who is a party to some fraud or illegality affecting an instrument cannot improve his or her legal position by transferring the instrument to an HDC and then reacquiring it. Nor can a person who has notice of a claim or defense to an instrument, then transfers the instrument to an HDC, and later reacquires the instrument.

NEW AMSTERDAM CASUALTY CO. v. FIRST PENNSYLVANIA B. & T. CO.

451 F. 2d 892 (U.S. Third Circuit, 1971).

Adams, Circuit Judge

The question here is whether an employee supplied to his employer the names of payees within the meaning of Section 3–405(1)(c) . . . intending the payees to have no interest in the proceeds of the checks. If Emanuel Wexler, an employee of E. W. Smith Co. (Smith), did so, his forged indorsements on the checks are effective as between Smith and The First Pennsylvania Banking and Trust Co. (Bank), which charged Smith's checking account with the sum of the checks.

Preliminarily, several points must be dealt with in the interest of clarity. The plaintiff in the action before us is Smith's insurer. After forged indorsements by its employee, Wexler, were discovered by Smith, New Amsterdam Casualty Co., pursuant to the employee dishonesty provisions of its fidelity bond, paid Smith's losses. All of Wexler's peculations relate to his employment at Smith, and since Smith has assigned its rights to New Amsterdam, New Amsterdam will be referred to as Smith for the purposes of this opinion. . . .

The case came on for a jury trial September 16, 1970. At the close of the evidence, both the Bank and Smith moved for directed verdicts under Rule 50, Fed.R.Civ.P. The District Court granted the Bank's motion, denied Smith's motion, and entered judgment in the Bank's favor. . . .

Wexler, from 1959 until he was discharged on January 14, 1965, was employed by Smith as a registered representative. During a period lasting almost two years, Wexler improperly obtained some 47 checks made out to customers of Smith with a total value of $88,213.82, forged the customers' endorsements on the reverse side of the checks, cashed the checks at check-cashing agencies and other banks, and then converted the proceeds to his own use. . . .

Wexler turned this course of business into a money-making venture. Aware of the quantity and type of stock which his customer kept on account at Smith, Wexler would, without authorization from a customer, fill out a sell order with appropriate and verifiable information. The following day, Wexler would stop by the desk where confirmations were typed out, and tell the secretary that since he, Wexler, was going to see the customer he would take the confirmation slip and give it to the customer personally. Wexler would not transmit the slip, and the customer, of course, never received the confirmation. Then, on the fourth trading day following the sale, when he knew the check would be prepared pursuant to the course of events which he had intiated, Wexler would approach Smith's cashier with the same story he had given the person preparing confirmations, adding, however, that the customer had authorized Wexler's receipt of the check. After receiving the check, Wexler would forge on the reverse side of it the indorsement of the payee and either deposit the check in one of Wexler's accounts at banks other than First Pennsylvania, or cash the checks with one of the third-party defendant check-cashing agencies. In no case did the checks go directly from Wexler to the First Pennsylvania. . . .

Clearly, the protection afforded the drawee bank under 3–405(1)(c) is much broader than that afforded by Section 9(3). Whereas Section 9(3) held the bank harmless only when the fraud involved was that of the actual drawer or maker of the check, Section 3–405(1)(d) extends that protection when the fraud is committed in the drawer's establishment, whether by the maker himself or by some subordinate employee who furnishes the name of the payee. The word "supplied" in (1)(c) must, therefore, cover cases running from the padded payroll to the one in which an employee starts the wheels of normal business procedure in motion to produce a check for a nonauthorized transaction.

For the purpose of giving meaning to the word

"supplied" in Section 3–405(1)(c), we can find no viable place to draw the line within the business enterprise of the drawer. . . . When Wexler, by submitting the fraudulent sell order to the trading room at Smith, initiated normal business practice to produce a check payable to a named payee, and Wexler intended the payee to have no interest in the proceeds of the check, he "supplied" Smith with the name of the payee, thereby making his forged indorsement effective as between Smith and the drawee Bank.

Thus, the Bank properly charged Smith's account for the checks in question, and, therefore, the granting of the Bank's motion for a directed verdict was correct. Accordingly, the judgment of the District Court will be affirmed.

BOWLING GREEN , INC. v. STATE STREET BANK AND TRUST CO.

425 F.2d 81 (U.S. First Circuit, 1970)

Coffin, Circuit Judge

On September 26, 1966, plaintiff Bowling Green, Inc., the operator of a bowling alley, negotiated a United States government check for $15,306 to Bowl-Mor, Inc., a manufacturer of bowling alley equipment. The check, which plaintiff had acquired through a Small Business Administration loan, represented the first installment on a conditional sales contract for the purchase of candlepin setting machines. On the following day, September 27, a representative of Bowl-Mor deposited the check in defendant State Street Bank and Trust Co. The Bank immediately credited $5,024.85 of the check against an overdraft in Bowl-Mor's account. Later that day, when the Bank learned that Bowl-Mor had filed a petition for reorganization under Chapter X of the Bankruptcy Act, it transferred $233.61 of Bowl-Mor's funds to another account and applied the remaining $10,047.54 against debts which Bowl-Mor owed the Bank. Shortly thereafter, Bowl-Mor's petition for reorganization was dismissed and the firm was adjudicated a bankrupt. Plaintiff has never received the pinsetting ma-

chines for which it contracted. Its part payment remains in the hands of defendant Bank. . . .

Plaintiff's appeal challenges the conclusion of the district court in three respects. First, plaintiff maintains that the Bank has not met its burden of establishing that it was a "holder" of the item within the meaning of Mass. Gen. Laws Ann. c. 106 § 1–201(20), and thus cannot be a "holder in due course" within the meaning of § 4–209 and § 3–302. Second, plaintiff argues that the Bank's close working relation with Bowl-Mor prevented it from becoming a holder in good faith. Finally, plaintiff denies that defendant gave value within the meaning of § 4–209 for the $10,047.54 which it set off against Bowl-Mor's loan account.

Plaintiff's first objection arises from a technical failure of proof. The district court found that plaintiff had endorsed the item in question to Bowl-Mor, but there was no evidence that Bowl-Mor supplied its own endorsement before depositing the item in the Bank. Thus we cannot tell whether the Bank is a holder within the meaning of § 1–201(20), which defines holder as one who takes an instrument indorsed to him, or to bearer, or in blank. But, argues plaintiff, once it is shown that a defense to an instrument exists, the Bank has the burden of showing that it is in all respects a holder in due course. This failure of proof, in plaintiff's eyes, is fatal to the Bank's case. . . .

The issue, however, is not whether the Bank bears the burden of proof, but whether it must establish that it took the item in question by endorsement in order to meet its burden. We think not. The evidence in this case indicates that the Bank's transferor, Bowl-Mor, was a holder. Under Mass. Gen. Laws Ann. c. 106, § 3–201(a), transfer of an instrument vests in the transferee all the rights of the transferor. As the official comment to § 3–201 indicates, one who is not a holder must first establish the transaction by which he acquired the instrument before enforcing it, but the Bank has met this burden here.

We doubt, moreover, whether the concept of "holder" as defined in § 1–201(20) applies with full force to Article 4. Article 4 establishes a comprehensive scheme for simplifying and expediting

518

bank collections. Its provisions govern the more general rules of Article 3 wherever inconsistent. . . . As part of this expediting process, Article 4 recognizes the common bank practice of accepting unendorsed checks for deposit. . . . § 4–201(1) provides that the lack of an endorsement shall not affect the bank's status as agent for collection, and § 4–205(1) authorizes the collecting bank to supply the missing endorsements as a matter of course. In practice, banks comply with § 4–205 by stamping the item "deposited to the account of the named payee" or some similar formula. . . . We doubt whether the bank's status should turn on proof of whether a clerk employed the appropriate stamp, and we hesitate to penalize a bank which accepted unendorsed checks for deposit in reliance on the Code, at least when, as here, the customer himself clearly satisfies the definition of "holder." Section 4–209 does provide that a bank must comply "with the requirements of section 3–302 on what constitutes a holder in due course," but we think this language refers to the enumerated requirements of good faith and lack of notice rather than to the status of holder, a status which § 3–302 assumes rather than requires. We therefore hold that a bank which takes an item for collection from a customer who was himself a holder need not establish that it took the item by negotiation in order to satisfy § 4–209.

Plaintiff's second objection arises from the intimate relationship between Bowl-Mor and the Bank, a relationship which plaintiff maintains precludes a finding of good faith. The record shows that the Bank was one of Bowl-Mor's three major creditors, and that it regularly provided short-term financing for Bowl-Mor against the security of Bowl-Mor's inventory and unperformed contracts. The loan officer in charge of Bowl-Mor's account, Francis Haydock, was also a director of Bowl-Mor until August 1966. Haydock knew of Bowl-Mor's poor financial health and of its inability to satisfy all its creditors during 1966. In the five months before the transaction in question, the Bank charged $1 million of Bowl-Mor's debt to the Bank's reserve for bad debts. However, the record also shows that the Bank continued to make loans to Bowl-Mor until September 12.

The Bank was also aware of the underlying transaction between Bowl-Mor and the plaintiff which led to the deposit on September 26. During the week prior to this transaction, Bowl-Mor had overdrawn its checking account with the Bank to meet a payroll. In order to persuade the Bank to honor the overdraft, officials of Bowl-Mor contacted Haydock and informed him that a check for $15,000 would be deposited as soon as plaintiff could obtain the funds from the Small Business Administration. The district court found, however, that the Bank was not aware that the directors of Bowl-Mor had authorized a Chapter X petition or that Bowl-Mor officials planned to file the petition on September 27.

On the basis of this record, the district court found that the Bank acted in good faith and without notice of any defense to the instrument. . . . Since the application of these definitions turns so heavily on the facts of an individual case, rulings of a district court under §§ 3–302(1)(b) and 3–302(1)(c) should never be reversed unless clearly erroneous. In this case, the evidence indicated that Bowl-Mor had persevered in spite of long-term financial ill health, and that the event which precipitated its demise was the withdrawal of financial support by another major creditor, Otis Elevator Co., on the morning of September 27, after the deposit of plaintiff's check. Thus, at the time of deposit, the Bank might reasonably have expected Bowl-Mor to continue its shambling pace rather than cease business immediately. The findings of the district court are not, therefore, clearly erroneous. . . .

This brings us to plaintiff's final argument, that the Bank gave value only to the extent of the $5,024.85 overdraft, and thus cannot be a holder in due course with respect to the remaining $10,047.54 which the Bank credited against Bowl-Mor's loan account. Our consideration of this argument is confined by the narrow scope of the district court's findings. The Bank may well have given value under § 4–208(1)(a) when it credited the balance of Bowl-Mor's checking account against its outstanding indebtedness. . . .

But by that time the Bank knew of Bowl-Mor's petition for reorganization, additional information which the district court did not consider in finding that the Bank acted in good faith and without notice at the time it received the item. We must therefore decide whether the Bank gave value for the additional $10,047.54 at the time the item was deposited.

Resolution of this issue depends on the proper interpretation of § 4–209, which provides that a collecting bank has given value to the extent that it has acquired a "security interest" in an item. In plaintiff's view, a collecting bank can satisfy § 4–209 only by extending credit against an item in compliance with § 4–208(1). The district court, on the other hand, adopted the view that a security interest is a security interest, however acquired. The court then found that defendant and Bowl-Mor had entered a security agreement which gave defendant a floating lien on Bowl-Mor's chattel paper. Since the item in question was part of the proceeds of a Bowl-Mor contract, the court concluded that defendant had given value for the full $15,306 at the time it received the deposit.

With this conclusion we agree. Section 1–201(37) defines "security interest" as an interest in personal property which secures payment or performance of an obligation. There is no indication in § 4–209 that the term is used in a more narrow or specialized sense. Moreover, as the official comment to § 4–209 observes, this provision is in accord with prior law and with § 3–303, both of which provide that a holder gives value when he accepts an instrument as security for an antecedent debt. . . .

Finally, we note that if one of the Bank's prior loans to Bowl-Mor had been made in the expectation that this particular instrument would be deposited, the terms of § 4–208(1)(c) would have been literally satisfied. We do not think the case is significantly different when the Bank advances credit on the strength of a continuing flow of items of this kind. We therefore conclude that the Bank gave value for the full $15,306 at the time it accepted the deposit.

We see no discrepancy between this result and

520

the realities of commercial life. Each party, of course, chose to do business with an eventually irresponsible third party. The Bank, though perhaps unwise in prolonging its hopes for a prospering customer, nevertheless protected itself through security arrangements as far as possible without hobbling each deposit and withdrawal. Plaintiff, on the other hand, not only placed its initial faith in Bowl-Mor, but later became aware that Bowl-Mor was having difficulties in meeting its payroll. It seems not too unjust that this vestige of caveat emptor survives.

SALSMAN v. NATIONAL COMMUNITY BANK OF RUTHERFORD

246 A.2d 162 (New Jersey, 1968)

Botter, Justice

In May 1965 plaintiff Elizabeth A. Odgers (now Elizabeth A. Salsman) retained an attorney, Harold Breslow, to handle matters arising out of the death of her husband, Arthur J. Odgers. Breslow was recommended to Mrs. Odgers by her personal physician, Dr. S. It is stipulated that Breslow enjoyed a good reputation in the community at that time. Arthur J. Odgers had been an officer and stockholder in a company in which he had a one-third interest. He participated in the company's profit-sharing plan and had designated his wife as sole beneficiary. In payment of benefits under the plan, Mrs. Odgers received a cashier's check of the First National City Bank made out to her order in the amount of $159,770.02. The check is dated August 13, 1965. Breslow then informed Mrs. Odgers that the check was not hers but belonged to the estate, and that the proceeds must be held in a separate account for payment of taxes and other purposes. Mrs. Odgers was told by Breslow that the check "must be put in the estate account of Arthur Odgers." Breslow testified that at no time did he indicate or inform Mrs. Odgers that the money was to go or would go into his attorney's trust account.

Breslow wrote on the back of the cashier's check, "Pay to the order of Estate of Arthur J.

Odgers." He requested Mrs. Odgers to endorse the check in this fashion, and she did so. Under this special endorsement, when he was no longer in the presence of Mrs. Odgers, Breslow wrote, "Estate of Arthur J. Odgers—for deposit. Harold Breslow, Trustee." Under this purported endorsement Breslow's secretary then wrote, "For deposit Harold Breslow Trustee." Mrs. Odgers had no knowledge of the subsequent endorsements. The check was then sent by mail to defendant National Community Bank of Rutherford for collection, and the proceeds were collected and deposited in Breslow's general trustee account. Defendant bank did not inquire into the authority of Breslow to endorse the checks for the estate. There was no estate account in defendant's bank, although Mrs. Odgers had qualified as administratrix of the estate on July 9, 1965.

From August 1965 until March 1966 Mrs. Odgers inquired of Breslow on many occasions as to the status of the profit-sharing funds. She was anxious to have the funds invested so that she could use the income for current expenses. Breslow put her off with a variety of delaying tactics and misrepresentations. Ultimately he told her the funds were invested in Treasury notes. As time passed, Mrs. Odgers became more suspicious and began to investigate the disposition of the funds. In March 1966 she called defendant bank to get information concerning the alleged Treasury notes. The bank advised her that there was no record of an account for the estate of Arthur J. Odgers. Mrs. Odgers then contacted another attorney, and he assisted her in further investigation. She obtained a copy of the original check from the First National Bank in New York City. She took the check to several lawyers for their advice. An appointment was then made with Breslow for March 30. On that date, at his office, Breslow confessed to Mrs. Odgers and her present husband, Salsman, that he had appropriated the funds for his own use, but that he had some money left in his account. They immediately took Breslow to defendant bank where he paid over to Mrs. Odgers funds which were still in his account. Later that day Mrs. Odgers and

Salsman went to Salsman's attorney, who called defendant concerning the matter. . . . Mrs. Odgers was also advised to file a criminal complaint against Breslow, and she did so promptly. Breslow has since pleaded guilty to the charge of embezzlement and misappropriation of funds and is presently serving a prison sentence. He also resigned from the New Jersey Bar. In April 1966 Mrs. Odgers started an action against Breslow and on June 3, 1966 obtained a judgment in her favor. Some monies were recovered by execution on that judgment. The balance not yet recovered is $117,437.43. . . .

In the absence of defenses such as negligence, estoppel, or ratification, the payee of a check is entitled to recover against a bank making collection from the drawee based upon a forged or unauthorized endorsement of a check. . . . This has been the established law throughout the country and continues to be the rule in states which have adopted the Uniform Commercial Code. . . .

The check in question was endorsed by the payee, Mrs. Odgers, to the order of the Estate of Arthur J. Odgers. There was no valid endorsement thereafter by the estate of Arthur J. Odgers. . . . The check was not endorsed by the administratrix of the estate, the only person who had authority in law to endorse the check. Breslow was not a trustee of the estate, and the purported endorsement for the estate by "Harold Breslow, Trustee" was unauthorized and ineffective. Breslow testified that he never told plaintiff that he would act as her agent. His purported endorsement was not authorized as the agent for the administratrix nor as a representative of the estate. . . .

The check in question could not be negotiated without an authorized endorsement of the special endorsee, the estate of Arthur J. Odgers. . . . There is no evidence in this case which shows a ratification by Mrs. Odgers of the conduct of Breslow; there has been nothing shown to preclude her from denying the endorsements in question, and there is no evidence of any negligence on her part which contributed to the misapplication of the funds. . . .

Receiving the funds without a proper endorsement and crediting the funds to one not entitled thereto constitutes a conversion of the funds. . . .

N.J.S. 12A:3–419(3), N.J.S.A. clearly implies the liability of a depositary or collecting bank in conversion when it deals with an instrument or its proceeds on behalf of one who is not the true owner, where the bank does not act in accordance with "reasonable commercial standards."

PROBLEMS FOR DISCUSSION

In each of the following examples, the question is whether the person who is the last transferee can collect the instrument against any of the other parties mentioned. In problems 1–8, the last transferee may or may not be a holder. In problems 9–14, he or she may or may not be a holder in due course.

Fact situations	What result?
1. M → (cash) Payee → Thief (forges) → BFP	*BFP* v. *M* *P* v. *BFP*
2. M → Order of Payee → Thief (forges) → BFP	*BFP* v. *M* *P* v. *BFP*
3. M → Order of Payee (indorses) → Thief → BFP	*BFP* v. *M* *BFP* v. *P* *P* v. *BFP*
4. DR → Order of Payee → Thief (forges) → BFP ↓ stop order DE Bank refuses to pay. ←	*BFP* v. *DR* *BFP* v. *P* *BFP* v. *DE Bank* *P* v. *BFP*
5. Same, except that there is no stop order, so DE Bank pays when instrument is presented	*P* v. *DE Bank* *DR* v. *DE Bank* *DE Bank* v. *BFP*
6. DR → Order of cash → Thief (forges) → BFP ↓ stop order DE Bank refuses to pay. ←	*BFP* v. *DR* *BFP* v. *P* *BFP* v. *DE Bank* *P* v. *BFP*
7. DR → Order of Payee (indorses) → Thief → BFP ↓ stop order DE Bank refuses to pay. ←	*BFP* v. *DR* *BFP* v. *P* *BFP* v. *DE Bank* *P* v. *BFP*
8. Same, except that DE Bank pays	*P* v. *DE Bank* and *DR* v. *DE Bank* *DE Bank* v. *BFP*
9. M $\xrightarrow[\text{(fraud)}]{}$ Payee $\xrightarrow[\text{(gift)}]{}$ Uncle Ned	*Uncle Ned* v. *M* *Uncle Ned* v. *P*
10. M $\xrightarrow[\text{(fraud)}]{\text{due 7/1}}$ Payee $\xrightarrow[\text{(on 7/5)}]{}$ H	*H* v. *M* *H* v. *Payee*
11. DR $\xrightarrow[\text{(fraud)}]{}$ Payee → H DE Bank ← DE Bank dishonors and stamps.	*H* v. *DR* *H* v. *Payee* *H* v. *DE Bank*

Fact situations	*What result?*

12. DR $\xrightarrow[\text{(fraud)}]{}$ Payee (for deposit only) →   *H* v. *DR*   *H* v. *Finder*

      Finder → H

13. M $\xrightarrow[\text{(fraud)}]{\text{due 7/1}}$ Payee $\xrightarrow[\text{(on 6/1)}]{}$ HDC $\xrightarrow[\text{(on 7/6)}]{}$ X   *X* v. *M*

14. M $\xrightarrow[\text{(fraud)}]{\text{due 7/1}}$ Payee $\xrightarrow[\text{(on 6/1)}]{}$ HDC $\xrightarrow[\text{(on 7/6)}]{}$ P   *P* v. *M*

25 | Defenses and Discharge

The main purpose of the merchant community in developing negotiable instruments and the main significance of negotiability today is the nonassertability of most common defenses against liability when an instrument gets into the hands of an HDC. HDC status does not, however, eliminate *all* defenses. Some defenses can still be asserted against an HDC and, if proved, will defeat or reduce his or her recovery on an instrument. Those defenses which cannot be asserted against an HDC or an HHDC (a holder through a holder in due course) are called "personal" or "limited" defenses. Personal defenses can still be asserted against anyone who is not an HDC or a holder through an HDC. Those defenses which can be used against anyone, including an HDC or an HHDC, are called "real" or "universal" defenses. The most obvious example of these defenses is forgery; certainly a person whose name has been forged on an instrument should not be required to pay it, even to an HDC. The basic distinction is between "void"-type defenses (= real) and "voidable"-type defenses (= personal), except for minority, which is recognized as a real defense. If a defense is one which "makes the obligation a nullity," it is a real defense. If there is no contract, there is no contract even if the instrument is in the hands of an HDC. On the other hand, if a defense merely relates to some problem between two of the parties on an instrument, it is a personal defense and it cannot be asserted against an HDC.

REAL DEFENSES

Article 3's main list of real defenses is found in Section 3–305. In addition, 3–404 (unauthorized signatures) and 3–407 (alteration) describe real defenses.

Unauthorized Signature or Forgery. When someone signs your name to an instrument without your permission, you're not liable, even to an HDC. The result is the same whether your name is simply forged or whether it is signed with an indication of agency authority which doesn't exist. The section says that this unauthorized signature is "wholly inoperative" against you unless you ratify it or are estopped by your conduct from denying its validity. It is, however, effective to impose full liability on the instrument against the forger, in favor of someone who pays or takes the instrument in good faith.

Material Alteration. Where the contract of any party to an instrument has been changed "in any respect" by an alteration, Section 3–407 says that the alteration is material. If this material alteration is also fraudulent, the party whose contract is changed is discharged from further liability on the instrument unless he or she assents to the change or is estopped from asserting it. As the one exception to this rule, an HDC can still enforce the instrument "according to its original tenor," that is, the terms prior to the alteration. A nonmaterial or nonfraudulent alteration does not discharge any party.

As an example of these rules, if you signed a blank check and lost it, and the finder filled in $600 as the amount, an HDC could force you to pay the $600. If you signed a check and filled it in for $6.00, and someone found or stole the check and altered it to read $600, an HDC could force you to pay only the original $6.00. However, if you filled in the amount spaces with blanks after the number 6 and the word *Six*, so that the thief or finder could very easily add "00" and "Hundred," you would be estopped from asserting the alteration and would have to pay the full $600.

Thomas v. Osborn
536 P.2d 8 (Washington, 1975)

FACTS   William Thomas sued to collect on a note executed by James and Bernice Osborn for $2,000. The note was apparently given in settlement of a dispute over the value of a redwood table which had been delivered by Thomas to the Osborns and over claims for certain other work performed. The note was dated October 30, 1969, and was due one year later, subject to an acceleration clause which provided that if a certain described piece of real estate was sold before the due date, the note would become immediately payable. To make sure that any third-party buyer of the land knew about his claim against the Osborns, Thomas had the note recorded in the real estate records. In order to do so, he had a notary public write on an acknowledgment of James Osborn's signature and notarize it. Since the note was recorded, it was also so stamped by a clerk in the recorder's office. The trial court held for the plaintiff, and the Osborns appealed.

ISSUE   Did the acknowledgment, notarization, and recording stamp operate as material alterations, so as to discharge the Osborns from liability?

DECISION   No. Judgment affirmed.

REASONS   Judge Callow quickly disposed of the Osborns' claim that the table wasn't worth $2,000 and that there was no consideration for the note. It had been given in settlement of this dispute, he said. He then examined their argument that the recording of the note had added the relationship of mortgagor-mortgagee to that of maker-payee and thus constituted a material alteration.

"Ostensibly, the terms of the note include the legal description of the real property for the purpose of inserting an acceleration provision into the note. This is the apparent reason for the presence of the property description since the terms provide for payment in full on sale of the property rather than granting a security interest

525

which might be looked to for recourse in the event of a default in payment. We cannot read into the instrument an unmanifested intent of the parties. The note was not ambiguous when it was signed by the makers, and it does not purport either a purpose to convey or to encumber the property. . . . The note does not contain the expression of an intent to impose a lien upon the property. . . .

"We conclude that neither the recording of the instrument nor the addition of the addendum to the instrument changed the relationship of the parties, materially affected the form of the document, the time of payment, or the sum payable. The alteration did not attempt to acquire for the payee any funds to which he was not entitled.

"We also find that the evidence does not indicate that the plaintiff acted fraudulently. . . .

"The actions of the parties here are best characterized by the term 'misguided.' The trial court did not find a dishonest, fraudulent intent in the payee, and the chaotic dealings of the parties reveal that their understanding of the legal ramifications of their actions was limited. While the plaintiff attempted to overreach his position as payee by his effort to achieve security for payment of the debt, his ineffective attempt was not such a fraudulent intent to achieve something to which he was not entitled as would justify excusing the liability of the makers and granting them a windfall."

Minority. Although minority or infancy generally results in a voidable obligation rather than a void one, Section 3–305 makes it a real defense to liability on a negotiable instrument. Infancy is a defense to the same extent that it would be against liability on a simple contract. In other words, infancy can be asserted against an HDC. On the other hand, since this section distinguishes between "defenses" and "claims" and states that an HDC owns the instrument free of *all* adverse ownership claims, the minor cannot get back the instrument that he or she signed. Remember that the indorsement sections make the minor's indorsement fully effective to transfer ownership of the instrument, so that there can be later HDCs in the chain of title.

Other Incapacity. As to other types of contractual incapacity, 3–305 makes these a real defense only if they void the contract (render "the obligation of the party a nullity"). This rule thus refers us to the applicable state law on insanity, aliens, married women, and so on, as discussed in Chapter 8. Ultra vires acts by corporations or governmental agencies which resulted in the issuance of negotiable instruments would probably also fall into this category.

Void-Type Duress. Duress may be either a real or a personal defense, depending on whether it results in a void or a voidable obligation. "Gun-to-the-head" duress "renders the obligation of the party a nullity" and can thus be asserted against an HDC. The "threat-of-criminal-prosecution" type of duress would make a contract only voidable, not void, and thus it cannot be asserted against an HDC.

Void-Type Illegality. Where some part of a transaction violates a criminal statute, the state's statutory and case law may make the contract involved either void or voidable. Section 3–305 again refers us to these state law distinctions to see whether the particular illegality is a real or only a personal defense. The following case illustrates how the courts will try to make this determination.

Commercial Bank & Trust Co. v. *Middle Georgia Livestock Sales*
182 S.E.2d 533 (Georgia, 1971)

FACTS   Middle Georgia bought some stolen cattle at an auction sale and paid for them with a check. When it learned that the cattle were stolen, it ordered its bank to stop payment on the check. Meanwhile, the plaintiff bank had cashed the check for the seller. When payment was refused by the drawee bank, the plaintiff bank sued the drawer, Middle Georgia. Middle Georgia appealed from the trial court's decision against it.

ISSUE   Did the fact that the consideration given for the check was stolen make the drawer's obligation a nullity?

DECISION   Yes. Judgment reversed.

REASONS   The court first indicated that the case must be decided by local state law, and it cited UCC 3–305(2)(6).
"The case then turns on the question of whether the sale of the stolen [cattle] . . . , presuming the seller possessed guilty knowledge of the fact but the buyer did not, represents an 'illegal consideration' so as to render it absolutely void. 'A contract to do an immoral or illegal thing is void.' Code S.20–501. A sale of stolen goods, although to a bona fide purchaser for value, cannot transfer any lawful interest in the property and does not divest the title of the true owner.
"Knowingly disposing of stolen property is . . . a type of theft and a statutory offense. Being prohibited by statute, it is an illegal transaction within the meaning of Code Ann. 109A–3–305(2)(b). . . . This accords with the decisions of our courts. In *Smith* v. *Wood*, 36 S.E. 649, it was held: 'A note given for something . . . which the law absolutely prohibits and makes penal is based upon an illegal consideration, and is consequently void in the hands of any holder thereof. The thing for which the note is given is outlawed, and the note standing upon such a foundation is outlawed also.' . . .
"It follows that the note is unenforceable even in the hands of a holder in due course, and the trial court erred in granting summary judgment for the plaintiff."

Fraud in the Execution. The most obvious example of fraud in the execution occurs when the nature of the instrument itself is misrepresented. You are told you're merely signing a receipt for delivery of merchandise, or an authorization form for repairs on your car, but the document is folded, or covered, or switched, so that you can't see it's really a negotiable instrument. The section also extends this defense to the case where you *do* know you're signing a negotiable instrument but you don't have a reasonable opportunity to obtain knowledge of its "essential terms." In either of these cases, you must show that your ignorance of the character and terms of the instrument was "excusable ignorance"—in other words, that you acted reasonably under the circumstances. This is a fact question, depending on such things as the signer's age, education, business experience, and literacy; the nature of the representations made to the signer and his or her reasons for relying on them; the availability of independent information; and the need to act quickly. If your ignorance was "excusable," you have a real defense, good even as against an HDC; otherwise, you don't.

Discharge in Bankruptcy.   Section 3–305 also spells out a result that should be obvious anyway: The debtor's discharge in bankruptcy or other insolvency proceedings can be asserted against anyone, even the HDC of a negotiable instrument signed by the debtor.

Notice of Other Discharge.   A holder can't qualify as an HDC if he or she takes the instrument with notice that *all* parties have been discharged. But it's possible to become an HDC with notice that one or more parties have been discharged, as long as there's no notice that *all* have been. The holder then qualifies as an HDC as to the remaining parties, but he can't collect against the ones he knew had been discharged when he took the instrument. Discharge of an indorser by canceling his or her signature would be a typical example of this rule. The HDC couldn't collect against that indorser, but he or she would still be an HDC as to all the remaining parties.

PERSONAL DEFENSES

Since Section 3–305 says that an HDC can enforce an instrument free of "all defenses except," any other defense against liability on the instrument is only a personal defense. Section 3–306 lists some of these personal defenses.

Ordinary Contract Defenses.   Any defense which a party has which could be asserted if he or she were sued on a simple contract can be asserted against anyone who does not have the rights of an HDC. This general rule would include such things as undue influence, breach of contract by the plaintiff (including any counterclaim by the defendant), and setoffs which the defendant might have from unrelated transactions.

Consideration Defenses.   Section 3–306 mentions "want or failure of consideration" specifically because there is an initial presumption that the negotiable instrument was issued for legally sufficient consideration. If it was not, or if the promised consideration was not properly delivered, the burden of proving the defense is on the defendant. These consideration defenses are only personal ones, and thus they can't be used against an HDC.

Voidable Defenses.   Tying back into Section 3–305, any defense based on lack of capacity, duress, or illegality which does not "render the obligation of the party a nullity" (void) is only a personal defense. Remember that minority is a real defense even though the minor's contracts are voidable rather than void.

Fraud in the Inducement.   In contrast to fraud in the execution, fraud in the inducement, which is the typical fraud case, provides only a personal defense.

Here the party does know that he or she is entering into a contract but is deceived as to the consideration to be received or the other terms and conditions of the contract. The following case shows that fraud in the inducement also exists where a party could *reasonably* have discovered the nature of the contract he or she signed, but simply didn't bother to read it. The contract was misrepresented, but on the facts there's only a personal defense, and so the HDC collects. Since the Burchetts and the Beevers are consumers, the result in this case would have been reversed under the new FTC regulations.

Burchett v. Allied Concord Financial Corporation
396 P.2d 186 (New Mexico, 1964)

FACTS   John and Connie Burchett and Harold and Marie Beevers bought an aluminum siding job on their homes from a man named Kelly, who represented Consolidated Products of Roswell. In each case, Kelly promised that the buyers would receive a $100 credit off the price of their job for each other customer who signed up after seeing these "demonstration homes." Kelly said that the Burchetts and the Beevers would in effect be getting their own jobs for nothing. While these buyers were reading the contract forms given to them by Kelly, he was busy filling out other forms. In each case, these buyers signed the filled-in forms without reading them, although they had never seen Kelly before. The signed filled-in forms were notes, and mortgages against the homes as security for the notes. Although the work was done, these buyers were not completely satisfied with the jobs, and there was nothing in the signed contracts about $100 credits. Consolidated negotiated the notes and assigned the mortgages to Allied Concord, an HDC. The trial court held the notes void, and Allied Concord appealed.

ISSUE   Does the fraud involved here make the notes totally void?

DECISION   No. Judgment reversed.

REASONS   Judge Carmody's opinion started with UCC 3–305(2)(c) and its key phrase, "reasonable opportunity to obtain knowledge." He then cited Official Comment 7 to this section, which discusses "excusable ignorance" and the facts which may be considered in deciding whether there was reasonable care exercised by the party signing the instrument. He decided that in this case the reliance on Kelly's representations was not reasonable.
    "We recognize that the reasonable opportunity to obtain knowledge may be excused if the maker places reasonable reliance on the representations. The difficulty in the instant case is that the reliance upon the representations of a complete stranger (Kelly) was not reasonable, and all of the parties were of sufficient age, intelligence, education, and business experience to know better. In this connection, it is noted that the contracts clearly stated, on the same page which bore the signatures of the various appellees, the following: No one is authorized on behalf of this company to represent this job to be 'A SAMPLE HOME OR A FREE JOB.'
    "Although we have sympathy with the appellees, we cannot allow it to influence our decision. They were certainly victimized, but because of their failure to exercise ordinary care for their own protection, an innocent party cannot be made to suffer."

Delivery Defenses.   Numerous cases have arisen involving some irregularity in the delivery or completion of an instrument. Where an instrument has been signed or indorsed so that it is in bearer form, the fact that it has been negotiated by a thief or finder will not prevent a later party from being an HDC and collecting on the instrument. The fact that you just signed your check as drawer, intending to fill in the payee's name and the amount later, and that the check was completed by the thief or finder, won't change this result; the HDC still collects. An HDC would also collect where you signed a check and delivered it to your intended payee with instructions to fill in the amount you owed, but your payee filled it in for a larger, unauthorized amount. Finally, an HDC is also protected where a check has been properly filled in and delivered, but delivered subject to some oral condition which is not expressed in the instrument. If the condition is not fulfilled, a defense exists which could be asserted only against someone not having the rights of an HDC.

Agency Defenses.   Where someone signing on behalf of a corporation, a partnership, or an individual has general authority to sign negotiable instruments, the fact that a particular instrument was improperly signed is only a personal defense.

FTC REGULATION

Since the courts decided in the early 1970s that the FTC could issue rules with industry-wide application, the FTC has been much more vigorous in the "consumer protection" field. One of the most important and widely discussed FTC rules relates to the HDC status of holders of consumer installment sales contracts. While the rule does not say so in so many words, the net effect is that in most cases there are no longer any real defenses against consumers who have signed negotiable instruments. Likewise, no waiver-of-defenses clause in an installment contract for the purchase of goods or services is effective against the consumer-buyer. Holders and assignees are thus remitted to their position under the old common law: The assignee "steps into the shoes of the assignor" and is subject to all available defenses which can be proved by the debtor. While the exact dimensions of this FTC rule are still subject to litigation, revolving charge accounts (such as a Sears charge account) signed before August 1, 1977, and credit card accounts have been exempted from its operation.

ESTOPPEL

It has been, and still is, true that a person with a claim or defense may be estopped by his or her conduct from asserting it. This is as true of real defenses as of personal defenses. If you typically signed your checks with a rubber stamp, and you lost the stamp and didn't bother to alert your bank; you probably ought to get stuck when your bank continues to honor the checks that someone else has prepared in your name with your lost signature stamp. Estoppel clearly applies where you have made out your check or note in such a way as to permit alteration very easily (large, inviting gaps after words and numbers, for example). A more interesting question for litigation is whether persons as gullible as the Burchetts and the Beevers ought to be permitted to assert the new FTC rule to avoid liability on the notes they signed, under circumstances similar to the fact pattern in that case.

DISCHARGE

In addition to the defenses discussed above and the conditions precedent to indorsers' liability discussed in Chapter 23, parties may be discharged from liability on an instrument in several other ways.

Payment. The most obvious and most frequent method of discharge is payment of the instrument to the holder. Perhaps the most important rule for most of us is found in Section 3–802(1)(b): "Unless otherwise agreed, where an instrument is taken for an underlying obligation . . . discharge of the underlying obligor on the instrument also discharges him on the obligation." In other words, when your check is paid by your bank, you are not only discharged of liability on the check but also of liability on the underlying debt for which it was given as payment. The one danger point here is that this discharge is not effective against a later HDC of the instrument if he or she does not have notice of it. If you pay your promissory note, but you don't get it back from the holder, and there's no indication on it that it has been paid or that it's overdue, a later HDC could make you pay it again.

Tender of Payment. Where payment is offered to a holder at or after the due date of the instrument and the holder refuses payment for some reason, the party offering full payment is discharged only to the extent of any additional interest, court costs, or attorney fees later incurred. This rule also applies where the maker or acceptor of a nondemand instrument is ready and able to make payment on the due date at the place or places specified in the instrument, and payment is not demanded by the holder (3–604[3]). The holder's refusal of tender "wholly discharges" any party who has a right of recourse against the party making the tender.

Simple Contract Discharge. As between themselves, any two parties can agree that the liability of one to the other is discharged by any mechanism which is sufficient to discharge liability on a simple contract. All the forms of new agreements discussed in Chapter 12 also apply here: novation, rescission, release, waiver, accord, and satisfaction. Once again, no HDC is bound by these new arrangements unless he or she is aware of them.

Cancellation or Renunciation. As a special negotiable instruments rule, Section 3–605 provides that any holder may discharge any party from further liability on an instrument by destruction or mutilation of the instrument, by canceling the party's signature, by surrendering the instrument to the party, or by a separate writing signed and delivered to the party. All of these but the last would seem to be sufficient to put third parties on notice of the discharge.

Reacquisition Rules. Because of the very special nature of indorsers' liability, Section 3–208 provides some specific rules for the discharge of intermediate parties where someone reacquires an instrument. As against the reacquirer, such parties are discharged. If Arnie, Bernice, and Carole have signed an instrument as indorsers and Arnie reacquires it, he can't sue Bernice or Carole. Arnie could, however, renegotiate the instrument to Donald, who could sue Bernice or Carole if he qualified as an HDC. On the other hand, if Arnie crossed out the signatures of Bernice and Carole, Donald would be on notice that they had been discharged and so he could not sue them either.

Suretyship Rules. As is true under the law of suretyship generally (see Chapter 28), a holder of an obligation who impairs someone's rights of recourse or repayment from another person discharges the party whose rights are impaired. In the above example, if Donald had crossed out Bernice's signature, he would have discharged her from liability on the instrument, thus impairing Carole's rights against Bernice, and so Carole would have also been discharged. A holder can avoid such an "automatic discharge" by expressly reserving his or her rights against the other party (Carole), but when he (Donald) does so, that has the effect of preserving the right of secondary recourse (by Carole against Bernice). Donald can say: "I won't sue Bernice, but I reserve my right to sue Carole." This also preserves Carole's right to sue Bernice if Carole has to pay Donald.

Likewise, where some piece of property is being used as collateral for an obligation, and through the negligence or intentional conduct of the holder its value is lessened or lost, secondary parties are discharged to that extent (3–606[1][b]).

CASES FOR DISCUSSION

STEWART v. THORNTON

568 P.2d 414 (Arizona, 1977)

Struckmeyer, Justice

On May 23, 1971, Thornton signed an agreement to purchase a lot, received a deed thereto, and in return executed a promissory note and mortgage on the lot in the amount of fifty-three hundred sixty-eight and 44/100 dollars ($5,368.44), payable to the order of Cochise College Park, Inc. (College Park). Two days later, on May 25, 1971, Thornton rescinded the transaction. Her down payment was returned by College Park, but, on the same day, College Park assigned her note and mortgage to Stewart for a consideration of thirty-five hundred fifty dollars ($3,550). . . .

As an affirmative defense to appellant's suit for collection of the note, Thornton set up that she had not received a property report as required by

the Interstate Land Sales Full Disclosure Act, 15 U.S.C.A. § 1701 et seq., and that her rescission of the transaction made the purchase agreement, the promissory note, and the realty mortgage void by operation of law, § 1703(b) of the Act.

The trial court, sitting without a jury, held that Stewart was not a holder in due course and that the note was subject to any defenses which Thornton could assert against College Park. Her position on appeal is that Stewart was not a holder in due course because he was charged with constructive notice of § 1703(b), supra, and that he had actual knowledge of the facts which should have alerted him to possible defenses defeating his claimed status as a holder in due course. . . .

It is sometimes said that a purchaser of a note is under no duty to ascertain from the maker the actual status of the contract arrangement. . . . This is because were there such a duty, it would impose unnecessary and perhaps crippling restrictions on the free alienation of commercial paper. . . .

But notice under the UCC requires some inquiry if the purchaser has actual knowledge of facts which would apprise him of possible irregularities. . . . The protection afforded a holder in due course cannot be used to shield one who simply refuses to investigate when the facts known to him suggest an irregularity concerning the commercial paper he purchases.

By the express terms of § 1703(b), the sales agreement for the purchase of the lot must provide that a "purchaser may revoke such . . . agreement within forty-eight hours, where he has received the property report less than forty-eight hours before he signed the contract or agreement. . . ." Stewart was, of course, charged with notice of the statute. He was also charged with knowing that a purchaser who received the property report, has inspected the lot in advance of signing the sales agreement and acknowledged by his signature on the agreement that he has made such inspection, and has read and understood such report, may stipulate in the agreement of purchase that the right to revoke for 48 hours shall not apply.

The promissory note signed by appellee, dated May 23, 1971, provided that it was delivered in payment for certain real property in College Park. Neither the note nor mortgage indicate that the purchaser received a property report and inspected the lot to be purchased in advance of their execution; neither do they show when or that a property report was received by the purchaser. Nor does the written sales agreement signed by Thornton as part of the transaction on May 23, 1971, show that she ever inspected the lot or received a property report pursuant to § 1703(b).

In the instant case the note was not purchased for full value. It was discounted one-third. That fact alone is sufficient to alert a prospective purchaser to a possible defense. Moreover, it was sold in the 48-hour period during which the purchaser of the property could have voided the purchase agreement. By examining the written sales agreement in possession of the seller of the note, Stewart could have ascertained that Mrs. Thornton had not inspected the lot or received a property report pursuant to § 1703(b). We think

under these circumstances bad faith could have reasonably been inferred by the trial judge, and he could have concluded that Stewart was not a holder in due course within the meaning and intent of the UCC. To hold otherwise would open to rampant abuse the fraud which Congress' Act, § 1703(b), seeks to prohibit.

Judgment of the trial court is affirmed.

Cameron, Chief Justice, and Hays, Holohan, and Gordon, Justices, concur.

FIRST NATIONAL BANK OF LIBERTY v. LATIMER

486 S.W.2d 262 (Missouri, 1972)

Houser, Commissioner

First National Bank of Liberty, Missouri (hereinafter "the bank"), filed suit on a promissory note in the original amount of $22,500, date January 10, 1964, due in 30 days, payable to the bank, signed as follows:

> National School of Aeronautics
> by Jean Price Latimer, Pres.
> _____, V. Pres.
> Jean Price Latimer
> J. E. Latimer.

The prayer for the balance due on the note, including interest, was for $24,227.62. Jean P. Latimer went bankrupt. During pendency of the suit the bank received a sum through the bankruptcy court, which reduced the amount claimed to $22,105, plus interest. Neither National School of Aeronautics nor Jean Price Latimer was named as a party defendant. The sole named defendant was J. E. Latimer. . . .

By deposition, certified to by the notary (signature having been waived), J. E. Latimer stated as facts the following: Latimer and Jean Price were married January 1, 1961; divorced the first part of 1965. On January 1, 1964 Jean P. Latimer was president of the school and owner of all of the stock of the corporation. J. E. Latimer was vice-president, office manager, and personnel manager in charge of expense accounts, at a salary of $2,000 per month. J. E. Latimer at no time owned any stock of the school corporation. Some of his salary checks were not honored, and the school "wasn't in the best condition." He and Latimer Motors, Ltd. were buying notes signed by students at the school in payment of tuition and endorsed by the school. The $2,658.33 check of Latimer Motors, Ltd. to the bank (credited on the original $25,000 note) was in fact payment for paper bought by Latimer Motors, Ltd. from the school. When Latimer signed the original note for $25,000 he and his motor company owned school paper, endorsed by the school with recourse, in the sum of "quite a few thousand dollars." J. E. Latimer had nothing to do with making the deal for the original $25,000 loan, or the renewal note in suit. All these dealings were between his wife and the officers at the bank. J. E. Latimer had not previously discussed a loan with the president of the bank, Mr. James, or any other officer of the bank, and he was not asked for a financial statement. All arrangements for the loan had been made before J. E. Latimer was called in and asked to sign the note. Latimer's wife, after indicating to him that she was borrowing $25,000 from the bank and that she had made a "deal" with Mr. James as to how the money was to be repaid, asked him to accompany her to the bank. It was then that Mr. James asked J. E. Latimer to sign the note "with her," and told Latimer that he need not worry about the note; "it's all set up." She's going to sell the building and pay this back, and I just need your signature on here because we don't have any mortgage or anything." Latimer did not sign the note in suit "with the knowledge that [he] was going to pay it"; the bank, through its president, "knew that [he] wasn't signing it to pay it back." The loan was to the school. J. E. Latimer "didn't get any of it." When the note sued on matured, J. E. Latimer refused to sign a renewal note or grant an extension of time. At the time the note was extended in February or March of 1964, the bank could have collected on the note because the school then had "plenty of assets over there that they could have come in and gotten" and Jean P. Latimer had at least $20,000–$25,000 in personal assets that were "clear." . . .

In this state of the record each party filed a motion for summary judgment. . . .

The court overruled the bank's motion for summary judgment, sustained Latimer's motion for summary judgment, and rendered judgment for Latimer. In due course the bank appealed. . . .

The following facts were admitted by the bank: The note in suit was given as a renewal for the balance due on the original note. The bank extended the time of payment of the renewal note 11 times, dealing with Jean P. Latimer in reaching these agreements, and making no agreements with any other person. The extension agreements were supported by legal consideration.

On the basis of these facts we are obliged to rule as follows: J. E. Latimer was an accommodation maker of the original note. . . . He signed the note as a maker without receiving value therefor and for the purpose of lending his name to the bank, which was the accommodated party. He was also surety for the principal obligor, the school corporation. "[O]ne may be both an accommodation maker and a surety on the same note." . . . The foregoing relationships continued upon the execution of the renewal note in suit.

The bank, as payee, was not a holder in due course as between itself and J. E. Latimer, and therefore under § 401.058 the note was subject to the same defenses as if it were nonnegotiable. The bank, as the party accommodated by J. E. Latimer, acquired no rights against the latter, there being no consideration between them, particularly in view of the mutual understanding between the bank and J. E. Latimer that he need not worry about the note; that the bank would look elsewhere for payment. . . .

Furthermore, J. E. Latimer, on suretyship principles apart from N.I.L., as surety for the principal obligor, was discharged from liability on this note because the bank entered into binding agreements with the principal obligor extending the time of payment of the note for definite periods of time, without the knowledge or consent of J. E. Latimer. . . .

The bank's position is that consideration is to be found, and that J. E. Latimer is deprived of his status as a surety, because of his admissions that he was an officer, creditor, and husband of the president of the principal obligor. No authority is cited for this proposition. In some cases consideration is found when a person interested in a partnership, corporation, or business enterprise as a partner or stockholder gives his individual note for money loaned or advanced to the partnership, corporation, or business . . . but J. E. Latimer was not interested in the school corporation as a stockholder. He had no demonstrated financial interest in the business as an owner. . . . J. E. Latimer's interest in the payment of salary checks for his services as employee is too remote to constitute the basis for a finding of consideration, at least in the absence of proof that the $25,000 was borrowed to keep the school open, was placed to the credit of the school and used to pay salaries, none of which has been shown. . . . There is no consideration arising out of the marital relationship where a husband signs the note of a corporation of which the wife is president, where the corporation and not the husband receives the proceeds of the note. . . .

Judgment affirmed.

NATIONWIDE ACCEPTANCE CORPORATION v. HENNE

194 So.2d 434 (Louisiana, 1967)

Samuel, Judge

This suit on a promissory note was instituted by the holder against the makers thereof. The petition prays for judgment in the amount of $773.19, the alleged balance due on the principal amount of $843.48. The defendants answered admitting execution of the note in the principal amount of $100, admitted payments of $79.20, and averred material alterations of the note, that the principal amount had been changed from $100 to $843.48 and the number of monthly installments had been changed from 4 to 36. There was judgment in the trial court in favor of the defendants, dismissing plaintiff's suit. Plaintiff has appealed therefrom. . . .

* * * * *

Two representatives of Rich Plan of New Orleans, Inc. visited defendants in the latter's home and sold them a home food plan for the price of $100. They wanted the defendants to sign a note

in blank, but the latter refused. One of the representatives then filled in the space reserved in the note for the principal amount with the figure 100 and the space reserved for the number of installments with the figure 4, both figures being written in ink. The defendants then signed the note, and they have never made, authorized, or assented to any alteration thereof. Several days later defendants received a payment book from plaintiff, which had acquired the note from Rich Plan of New Orleans, Inc., showing the amount due on the note to be $843.48, payable in 36 monthly installments of $23.43 each. Defendants almost immediately protested to Rich Plan of New Orleans, Inc. and to plaintiff that there was an error in the amount, but to no avail. They also consulted with their district attorney and on advice of counsel made three of the payments. They refused to make further payments, and this action followed. The note now contains the figures $843.48 as the principal amount and 36 as the number of installments. The original figures 100 and 4, which were written in ink, have been erased and the present figures typed over the erasures.

The trial court found as a fact that the alterations were "obvious to the naked eye." Our examination of the instrument reveals that the erasures around and under the typewritten figures 843.48 and 36, although somewhat cleverly done, are easily seen. In addition, there appears under the first figure a small ink line, in all probability a part of the figure 1 as it originally appeared in 100, and another small ink mark under the figure 36. We hold that the alterations are apparent to the naked eye on the face of the note by the use of ordinary care in inspecting the instrument.

Even if the plaintiff is a holder in due course as it contends, under the second paragraph of N.I.L. § 124 . . . it could enforce payment only in accordance with the note's original tenor, i.e., it could recover only the original principal amount of $100, subject to a credit for the three payments made. However, under the facts and circumstances here present and under the pertinent portion of N.I.L. § 52 . . . plaintiff is not a holder in due course. The portion of § 52 referred to reads: "A holder in due course is a holder who has taken the instrument under the following conditions: (1) That it is complete and regular upon its face. . . ." Here plaintiff acquired an instrument which was not complete and regular upon its face because of alterations apparent to the naked eye by the use of ordinary care in inspecting that instrument. . . .

N.I.L. § 124 . . . is determinative of the instant case and prevents any recovery by the plaintiff on the note in suit. That paragraph reads:

Where a negotiable instrument is materially altered without the assent of all parties liable thereon, it is avoided, except as against a party who has himself made, authorized, or assented to the alteration, and subsequent indorsers.

The judgment appealed from is affirmed.

PROBLEMS FOR DISCUSSION

1. Sharpe exhibited a personal promissory note for $500 to his friend Gulliver and asked Gulliver to indorse it for him as an accommodation indorser, Gulliver agreed to do so and went to get a pen. While Gulliver was out of the room, Sharpe switched notes, substituting one for $25,000. Since the note was upside down on the table, ready for his indorsement, Gulliver simply signed it without turning it over and rereading it. Sharpe then negotiated the note to the Slate City Bank, an HDC. Sharpe defaulted, and the bank sued Gulliver. What result, and why?

2. Mona operated a small grocery store that was open 24 hours a day. Clem managed the store for her from 10 P.M. to 6 A.M.; usually he was the only employee in the store during that period of time. Mona had been unable to balance her cash totals and merchandise inventories for several weeks, and she finally decided that Clem was stealing cash and/or merchandise. She told Clem that he was fired and that unless he signed a promissory note for the total amount missing, $1,500, she would file criminal charges against him. Reluctantly, Clem signed the note. Mona transferred the note to Bigger Bank, an HDC. When Bigger sued Clem to collect, he claimed that he had not stolen anything, that he had been forced to sign the note, and that he had received no consideration for it. Are Clem's arguments effective against the bank? Why or why not?

3. Herman wrote a note for $9,000 to pay certain gambling debts which he had incurred. The payee on the note, Sharpie, transferred the note to his bank, Enbede, for value and prior to its maturity date. When Enbede Bank sued Herman to collect the $9,000, he claimed that the note was void because it was issued in payment of gambling debts. Is this a valid argument? Why or why not? Would the result change if gambling were legal in this state?

4. Marjorie purchased a lot in Sawtooth Acres, New Mexico, from Donald, who was an authorized representative of Sawtooth. Marjorie paid only $100 down and signed a promissory note for $5,300 for the balance; the note was payable in 48 monthly installments. This sale to Marjorie occurred in Nevada, and it was subject to the U.S. Interstate Land Sales Full Disclosure Act. The act provides that such land sales are voidable at the purchaser's option if the seller has not given the buyer a required report on the property at least 48 hours prior to the execution of the contract. Marjorie never received the required property report, nor had she personally inspected the property. She exercised her option of avoiding the contract within the first 48 hours. Meanwhile, Donald and Sawtooth Acres had sold her note to Reno Bank. When Marjorie refused to make payments on the note, Reno Bank sued her to collect. What result, and why?

5. Kolokos borrowed $30,000 to buy certain equipment for his business. He signed a note at the Bozey Bank for that amount, plus interest at the rate of 11.75 percent.

The state usury statute provided for a maximum rate of 10 percent, and it further provided that a debtor may collect "double the amount of interest which the note carries" if usury were proved. The total interest "added on" to this note was $6,000. Bozey Bank says that it did not intend to extract a usurious rate of interest, that it acted in good faith throughout and was thus an HDC, and that in any event Kolokos should only collect the difference between the rate charged and the maximum legal rate. How should this problem be resolved? Discuss.

6. Sand and Gravel Company borrowed $60,000 from Humble, giving her a note for that amount plus interest. The note was executed for Sand by its president (Laurel) and its secretary (Hardy). Laurel and Hardy also signed the note individually, to the left of the corporation's signature. The note provided: "All signers of this note are principals." Sand also executed a security agreement on its inventory in favor of Humble, but she did not properly file a financing statement so as to perfect her security interest in the inventory as collateral for the note. Sand got into financial trouble and sold its inventory to another company. At that time, the value of the inventory would have been sufficient to pay off the balance due on the note. Laurel and Hardy say that they are discharged from liability on the note because of the "unjustifiable impairment of collateral" under UCC 3–606. Humble sues them for the balance due on the note. What result, and why?

7. Lucinda was given an undated check for $185 for her net weekly earnings by her employer, Society Shoppes. Lucinda had the check in a jacket pocket when she went into a coffee shop. She set her jacket down on the seat next to hers. She left for a few minutes to make a telephone call, and the jacket was missing when she got back. Romeo took the jacket, found the check, first tore up the check, then decided he would try to cash it and taped it back together. Romeo cashed the check at Safeshop Market, telling the store's manager that his children had torn up the check by mistake. Romeo had forged Lucinda's indorsement and was arrested and charged with "uttering and publishing a forged negotiable instrument." Romeo's lawyer says that the charge should be dismissed, since the materially altered and destroyed check was no longer a negotiable instrument. Is this a valid argument? Why or why not?

8. Sopel executed a promissory note in favor of Inenbe Bank for $8,000. He defaulted on the note, and Inenbe filed suit to collect the principal amount, interest, court costs, and attorney's fees (total due $10,000), as provided in the note. Sopel admitted that the note was in default but said that he had talked to one of the bank's officers about it and that the officer had told him that he could renew the note for the total amount due if he would give the bank a mortgage on certain real estate which he owned. Sopel says that he has offered to deliver such a mortgage but that the bank now wants to enforce the original note. Should the bank be able to sue on the original note? Why or why not?

26 | Bank Deposits and Collections

Commercial banking in the United States is a huge industry. *U.S. News* reported in mid-1979 that the nation's 14,700 commercial banks held nearly $1.3 *trillion* in assets and that reported earnings for 1978 revealed an increase of 57.1 percent over earnings reported in 1974. Banks are responsible for funding many business purchases of land, buildings, and equipment and also provide many other services to business. The banking industry has been subjected to a considerable amount of governmental regulation, and more is probably on the way, in part as a reaction to the Bert Lance scandal. This chapter will not attempt to cover all of the various banking regulations but will focus instead on Article 4 of the UCC, Bank Deposits and Collections. Article 4 sets out the basic legal rules for the relationship between a bank and its customers and for the processing of negotiable (and nonnegotiable) instruments.

CHECKS: THE COLLECTION PROCESS

Clearinghouses and Federal Reserve Banks. The next time you get back a canceled check that you've sent to an out-of-state creditor (a book club or a record club, for example), take a look at its reverse side. All of those funny multicolored stamps indicate that your humble little check has passed through several banks, and goodness knows how many computers, on its way back to you.

If both the payee and the drawer do business at the same bank, the collection process is quite simple: out of one account and into the other. If both are in the same city but customers of different banks, a local clearinghouse association of banks probably handles the collection of the check. At the end of each business day, if a bank has presented more (total dollar) items for payment than have been presented against it, it gets a check for the difference from the clearinghouse. If the reverse is true, it writes a check for the total dollar difference to the clearinghouse.

Many "correspondent" bank arrangements also exist for collecting checks and other items, particularly between large metropolitan banks and smaller banks in the same geographic region. The small local bank receiving a check for collection would forward it to its large correspondent bank, which would in turn present it directly to the payor bank or would forward it through one of the

13 federal reserve banks if the payor bank were located in a different federal reserve district. Your check to your out-of-state creditor might pass through his or her local bank, a large nearby metropolitan bank, a federal reserve bank in that district, a federal reserve bank in your district, a large metropolitan bank close to your bank, and finally get presented at your bank for payment (by which time you had better have the money in your account). In 1979 *Forbes* magazine estimated that about $54 million worth of checks were "floating" through this national collection process on any given day. It's therefore obvious that banks (and their customers) need to have a set of legal rules to ensure that this process goes smoothly.

Banks under Article 4.   In order to better spell out the rights and duties of banks in the collection process, Article 4 defines different categories of banks according to their function in the various stages of that process. A "depositary bank" is "the first bank to which an item is transferred for collection even though it is also the payor bank." (The depositor, usually the payee/creditor of the drawer, although he or she could be a later holder of the instrument, takes the item to his or her bank and either cashes it or deposits it.) The "payor bank" is the bank "by which an item is payable as drawn or accepted." (In the simplest case, where both the drawer and the "depositor" have accounts at the same bank, no other banks will be involved.) An "intermediary bank" is any bank "to which an item is transferred in course of collection except the depositary or payor bank." (In the example in the preceeding paragraph, the correspondent banks and the federal reserve banks would be "intermediary banks.") Where the depositary bank is not also the payor bank, it and all intermediary banks are also called "collecting banks." (They're "collecting," or trying to collect, your paycheck for you.) The last bank in the collection process, the one that actually presents the item to the payor/drawee for payment, is called the "presenting bank." (A payor bank "presenting" the item to itself is excluded from this definition.) Finally, when the instrument is honored and the banks actually get the money (or a credit), all the banks passing the money back up the line to the depositary bank are called "remitting banks." (This definition includes the payor bank, since it is the source of the funds and is "remitting" them to pay the instrument.) The accompanying simplified diagram shows how these definitions fit together.

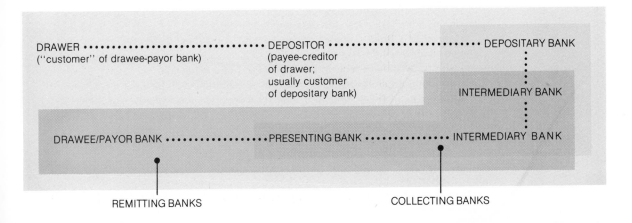

| **DEPOSITOR AND DEPOSITARY BANK**

Agency Relationship. In the normal transaction, the depositor remains the owner of the check or other item which is being processed for collection by his or her bank. This rule protects the depositary and intermediary banks by leaving all the risks of ownership of the item with the depositor; all the banks in the collection process are protected so long as they exercise reasonable care in processing the item. This basic rule applies unless there is a clear agreement otherwise, regardless of the form of the indorsement or of the fact that the depositor is permitted to make withdrawals against these funds (4–201 and 4–202).

Phillips Home Furnishings, Inc. v. *Continental Bank*

331 A.2d 840 (Pennsylvania, 1974)

FACTS
Max Shectman, owner of Phillips, made out a bank deposit for $5,669 in receipts from the business, stopped to pick up his wife at her place of employment, drove to an office of the defendant, and made his deposit by placing it in the bank's "Night Depositary Safe." Five days later, when he asked why he had received no confirmation of this deposit, the bank said that it had no record of the deposit. The agreement signed by Shectman put the risk of all such losses on the depositor, unless and until the items actually came into the bank's possession the next morning, when the safe was opened by an authorized bank employee. Relying on the agreement, the trial court granted summary judgment for the bank. Shectman appealed.

ISSUE
Is the provision in the deposit agreement effective, so as to limit the bank's liability in this way?

DECISION
No. Judgment reversed, and case remanded for trial.

REASONS
While the courts in most other states appeared to uphold the validity of such agreements between banks and customers, Judge Jacobs felt that general bailment law principles should be applied here. In Pennsylvania, he said, the rule was that a "bailee cannot stipulate against liability for his own negligence." By leaving his personal property with the bank for deposit, Shectman had entered into what was essentially a bailment relationship. Since banks were so heavily regulated, and had to be licensed in order to operate, Judge Jacobs felt that they were analogous to common carriers—they owed a duty of care to the public, which could not be totally disclaimed by a simple contract clause. He also pointed to UCC 4–103, which prevented a bank from disclaiming its liability for lack of good faith or failure to exercise ordinary care in connection with bank deposits and collections.

"We find the public need for professional and competent banking services too great and the legitimate and justifiable reliance upon the integrity and safety of financial institutions too strong to permit a bank to contract away its liability for its failure to provide service and protections its customers justifiably expect, that is, for its failure to exercise due care and good faith. The Bank, while acting as a bailee, was also acting in its capacity as a bank. . . . Although the parties could delay the initiations of the normal depositor-creditor relationship, they could not erase the relationship of bank-customer."

Withdrawals of Deposited Funds. A cash deposit can be withdrawn "as a matter of right" at the opening of the next banking day following its receipt by the bank unless the bank has the right to offset the deposited funds against amounts owed it by the depositor/customer. Where the deposit is in the form of a check or other instrument, however, the credit to the customer's account is only "provisional"; that is, the credit is subject to revocation if the instrument is not honored when it is presented to the drawee bank. The depositor/customer thus does not have the right to withdraw these funds until his depositary bank has received a "final settlement" for the item (4–212 and 4–213). Where the depositary bank is also the payor bank and the item is paid from the drawer's account, the depositor/customer has the right to withdraw the funds at the opening of the second banking day following receipt of the item.

CUSTOMER/DEPOSITOR/HOLDER (AND COLLECTING BANKS AS AGENTS) AND PAYOR BANK

As between the holder of an instrument who is trying to collect on it and the payor/drawee bank that is supposedly going to pay it when it's presented, the most important rule is found in Article 3: "A check or other draft does not of itself operate as an assignment of any funds in the hands of the drawee available for its payment, and the drawee is not liable on the instrument until he accepts it" (3–409[1]). Even if the money is in the drawer's checking account, in other words, the drawee bank owes no direct duty to the holder to pay the instrument. The drawee bank may be liable to its customer, the drawer, for a wrongful dishonor of the instrument, as discussed below, but that does not mean that the holder/depositor has any direct claim against the payor bank.

Obviously, a drawee bank which has certified a check or accepted a draft is primarily liable on it to the holder thereof and can be sued if it doesn't pay the check or draft when it is properly presented.

CUSTOMER/DEPOSITOR/HOLDER AND DRAWEE

If a deposited item is not paid, for whatever reason, the holder who deposited the item for collection may proceed against the drawer on the basis of secondary contract liability, subject to the rules discussed in Chapter 23. In addition, the depositor/holder may have a case against one or more of the collecting banks, where their negligent mishandling of the instrument was the reason for its dishonor. However, a collecting bank is not liable solely on the basis of some *prior* bank's mishandling of the instrument; its own negligence must be established.

DRAWER/CUSTOMER AND DRAWEE/PAYOR BANK

Article 4 also provides some detailed rules for handling the problems that may occur between a drawer and his or her drawee bank.

Charging Items against Customer's Account. The drawee bank has a general contractual duty to its drawer/customer to pay items when, presented, assuming that there are sufficient funds in his or her account. As a general rule, when the drawee bank does pay such items in good faith, it can charge the items against the customer's account. Even if an item causes an overdraft to a customer's account, the drawee/payor bank may honor the item anyway, and it has a claim against its customer for the amount of the overdraft.

This general rule is, however, subject to some important exceptions. The key phrase in Section 4–401 is "otherwise properly payable from that account." If the drawer's signature has been forged, the instrument is *not* "properly payable" from the drawer's account and the bank will have to put the money back even if it paid in good faith. The same result occurs where the required signature of an indorser is forged; the money must be returned to the drawer's account because the bank has not paid the right party. If the instrument has been materially altered, the bank which has paid it can charge the drawer's account only "according to the original tenor of his altered item." The drawer's own negligence may prevent him or her from asserting any of these irregularities against the drawee bank unless the bank was also negligent in paying the item; that is, the bank did not pay in good faith and according to reasonable commercial standards (3–406 and 4–406).

Cairo Cooperative Exchange v. First National Bank of Cunningham
620 P.2d 805 (Kansas, 1980)

FACTS K. C. Jones, the manager of Cairo's branch in Cunningham, was authorized to draw checks against Cairo's account. From September 30, 1969, to March 6, 1976, Jones drew 101 checks for various amounts to various customers of Cairo. Jones forged the customers' signatures on 10 of these checks and cashed the checks. As to these checks, Cairo made no claim for reimbursement from the bank. As to the other 91 checks, after forging the customers' indorsements, Jones used the co-op's own restrictive indorsement stamp, which read: "Pay to the order of First National Bank, Cunningham, Kansas. For Deposit Only, Cairo Co-op Equity Exchange, Farmer's Co-op." Jones got a total of $46,564.46 in cash at the bank for these checks. The trial court granted summary judgment for the bank, and Cairo appealed.

ISSUE Is the bank guilty of conversion and/or failure to act in good faith and with reasonable care, in paying cash for checks which have been restrictively indorsed?

DECISION Yes. Judgment reversed as to the 91 checks.

REASONS Justice Herd first reviewed the facts and the UCC provisions dealing with the effect of restrictive indorsements. He then stated that a "course of conduct" could not vary the duties imposed by a restrictive indorsement and to monitor and investigate a series of irregular transactions." Further, he said that Jones could not modify the bank's obligations.

"We find no evidence to support modification. Jones and the bank entered into a contract commonly called a signature card. Nothing in that contract can be construed as an agreement to vary the application of K.S.A. 84–3–206(3). The only evidence of an agreement to vary is Jones' course of conduct. As we have previously indicated, good practice dictates that an agreement to vary a restrictive indorsement be in writing and noted on the instrument by a person with proper authority."

Wrongful Dishonor. Whether mistakenly ("computer error") or intentionally, the drawee bank may dishonor an instrument which it should have paid. When this happens, the drawer is at least temporarily embarrassed since his or her good credit is impugned when the check bounces. When this happens by an honest mistake, Article 4 protects the drawee bank by providing that the drawer can recover only damages which were "proximately caused" and "actually proved"; there will be no punitive damages, in other words, for a simple mistake by the drawee bank. Further, the dishonor of a check is not per se defamation of a drawer's reputation, so that actual damages must be proved there too. Finally, damages resulting from the arrest and prosecution of the drawer under an "insufficient funds" criminal statute may be recovered from the drawee bank if they are proved to have been proximately caused by the dishonor.

Stop Payment Orders. A check is an order by the customer/drawer to the drawee/payor bank to pay money to the order of the named payee. At least until the check is certified by the drawee bank, the drawer has the right to stop payment, in other words, to countermand the original order. An oral stop-pay order is valid for only 14 calendar days unless it is reconfirmed in writing within that period. A written stop-pay order is valid for six months unless it is similarly reconfirmed. In either case, the stop-pay order must be received by the drawee/payor bank "at such time and in such manner as to afford the bank a reasonable opportunity to act on it prior to any action by the bank with respect to the item" (4–403). If the drawee/payor bank pays the item anyway, it can still charge its customer's account unless the customer can show that he or she suffered a loss as a result. (That would be the case, for example, where the customer had a defense which was valid against the holder, so that the holder really shouldn't have gotten the money. The bank would have to put that money back in its customer's account.) Obviously, once a check has been certified, the customer loses the right to stop payment.

Granite Equipment Leasing Corp. v. *Hempstead Bank*
326 N.Y.S.2d 881 (New York, 1971)

FACTS   On October 10, 1968, Granite drew a check against its account at Hempstead, made payable to Overseas Equipment Company. Five days later, when Overseas notified Granite that it had not received the check, Granite issued a written stop-pay order on the check and directed Hempstead to simply wire the funds directly to Overseas. Hempstead did so. Granite never renewed its stop-pay order. On November 10, 1969, the original check was presented for payment. Without any notice or inquiry to Granite, Hempstead simply paid the stale check and charged Granite's account.

ISSUE   Does a bank have a duty to make inquiry of the drawer before paying a stale check as to which there had been a valid stop-pay order?

DECISION   No. Judgment for defendant bank.

REASONS   Justice Harnett pointed out that the official comment to UCC 4–403 specifically

543

rejected the rule in the New York pre-Code precedents which held banks liable under similar circumstances. The section obligated the drawer to renew the stop-pay order after six months if he wished it to continue; if he did not renew, the bank might pay the item.

"Neither may Granite predicate a claim of liability upon the Bank's payment of a stale check. The legal principles applicable to this circumstance are codified in UCC S.4–404. . . . Here too, the *Goldberg* case reasoning is discarded in the official commentary. There is no obligation under the statute of the Bank to search its records to discover old lapsed stop payment orders. The Bank does not have to pay a stale check, but it may pay one in 'good faith.' . . . In the absence of any facts which could justify a finding of dishonesty, bad faith, recklessness, or lack of ordinary care, in the face of circumstances actually known, or which should have been known, the Bank is not liable to Granite for its payment of the check drawn to Overseas. . . .

"One statute invalidates stop payment orders not renewed within six months. Another statute allows payment in good faith of stale checks. Granite cannot combine the two statutes to reach a synergistic result not contemplated by either separately.

"Granite's complete remedy lies in its pending Florida action against Overseas to recover the extra payment."

Stale Checks. Where an uncertified check has been circulating for more than six months, the drawee/payor bank is under no obligation to its checking account customer to pay the check. The bank may dishonor the check without any liability for damage even if there is enough money in the account to cover it. If the bank does pay the stale check, in good faith, it may charge the item against its customer's account. It's completely up to the bank, as long as the bank acts in good faith (4–404).

Customer's Death or Incompetence. The Code's rules generally protect a bank from liability in the case where the customer dies or becomes legally incompetent. "Neither death nor incompetence of a customer revokes [a bank's] authority to accept, pay, collect or account until the bank knows of the fact of death or of an adjudication of incompetence and has reasonable opportunity to act on it" (4–405). Moreover, even after a bank learns of its customer's death, it may pay or certify previously issued checks for a period of 10 days, unless ordered not to by someone claiming an interest in the account. A customer's bankruptcy probably does not terminate the bank's authority to process items until the bank has knowledge or notice of it.

Customer's Duty to Inspect Statements. When a bank makes available an itemized statement and the canceled items, its customer has a duty to exercise reasonable care and promptness in inspecting the charges and reporting any improper ones to the bank. The customer's failure to do so may prevent him or her from forcing the bank to put money back in the account where an item has been altered or paid over a forged signature or indorsement (4–406[2]). However, if the bank failed to exercise ordinary care in paying an item (for example, if it paid an item which was obviously altered), the customer could still force the bank to put the money back in his or her account. Finally, whether the customer, the bank, or both were guilty of negligence, this section protects the bank by imposing a one-year statute of limitations period for claims of alteration or forgery of the drawer's signature and a three-year period for claims of forged indorsements. In other words, if you don't notify the bank of the irregularities within those time periods, you can't make it put the money back in your account even if your signature on the check was forged. The lesson is clear: Read your bank statement and verify your checks right away.

Silvia v. Industrial National Bank of Rhode Island
403 A.2d 1075 (Rhode Island, 1979)

FACTS   John Mahoney had prepared Antone Silvia's tax returns for over 25 years. Mahoney would make out the return and a check for any tax due to the IRS and would then take the documents to Silvia for his signature. In 1967, "apparently in need of some extra cash," Mahoney added $7,000 of nonexistent business profits to Silvia's return, thereby increasing Silvia's tax liability from about $2,000 to $4,625. Mahoney made out one of Silvia's checks to "Internal Revenue Services" and had Silvia sign the check and the return. Mahoney then added "by John J. Mahoney" in the space for the payee's name, indorsed the check "Internal Revenue Services by John J. Mahoney," and exchanged Silvia's check for several cashier's checks at Industrial National Bank. Mahoney used these cashier's checks to pay his personal creditors. Silvia did not notice the alterations made by his accountant when he received the canceled check with his bank statement in February 1968. Silvia first became aware of the problem in April 1969, when the IRS notified him that he had not paid his taxes for 1967. By that time, Mahoney had died. Silvia sued Industrial to force it to recredit his account. The trial court held for the bank; Silvia appealed.

ISSUE   Which UCC statute of limitations controls, the one-year period for alterations on the face of the item or the three-year period for unauthorized indorsements?

DECISION   The one-year statute controls. Judgment for the bank affirmed.

REASONS   After reviewing the facts, Justice Kelleher focused on UCC 4–406 and the policy underlying it. The reason for the two different time periods, he explained, was that the customer was not necessarily familiar with all the indorsers' signatures, so he or she needed a longer time in which to discover unauthorized indorsements.
　　"Here, the alteration and unauthorized endorsement were identical, that is, 'Internal Revenue Services by John J. Mahoney.' Once the alteration was made, Mahoney could negotiate the check solely through the use of an unauthorized endorsement. Accordingly, discovery of the alteration would have been tantamount to discovery of the unauthorized endorsement. The presence of an altered payee on a canceled check should have automatically alerted Silvia to the existence of the unauthorized endorsement. Since the drafters of S.6A–4–406(4) considered one year more than sufficient time to discover a material alteration, we cannot allow Silvia to

545

circumvent that policy when, as here, the unauthorized endorsement arises out of and is part of the scheme which caused the alteration. . . .

"Had he looked at the face of the check, he would have known that the instrument also contained an unauthorized endorsement. To allow Silvia to recover on this endorsement after the one-year period had elapsed would defeat the policies underlying prompt discovery and notice of material alterations. Such a suit is in actuality a suit upon the alteration itself."

Bank's Right to Subrogation. The drawee/payor bank is further protected by being subrogated to the rights of other parties where it has made a payment despite a stop order or under other circumstances where the drawer or maker has "a basis for objection." Where such an "improper" payment has occurred, the bank steps into the shoes of (1) an HDC, as against the drawer or maker; (2) the payee or any other holder, as against the drawer or maker, either on the paid item itself or on the underlying transaction; and (3) the drawer or maker, as against the payee or any other holder on the underlying transaction. In other words, if the bank has paid someone when it should not have done so, it shouldn't get stuck for the money but should have recourse against another party. The only problem may be finding that other party.

ELECTRONIC FUNDS TRANSFER

Just as the use of checks and credit cards has made us to a very large extent a "cashless" society, there have been predictions for several years that the use of computer-controlled electronic funds transfer (EFT) systems will make us a "checkless" society. With billions of checks being processed each year, the practical need for such a system is very clear. Properly implemented, it could speed payments, reduce errors, and lower costs. However, EFT presents its own set of problems, with which the law is just beginning to deal.

Some phases of EFT are already in widespread use; probably the most common is the "24-hour money machine," located at bank branches, where a customer can use a magnetic card to receive cash, make deposits, pay bills, and transfer funds between accounts. Another frequently used EFT system makes direct deposits of paychecks to employees' bank accounts. More recently, banks have begun to offer their customers the option of paying bills with a telephone call to the bank's computer system; this method saves the customer's time and money. Not yet widely adopted is the most revolutionary EFT system: immediate payment from the customer's checking account through point-of-sale computer terminals located in stores.

It's not hard to imagine some of the problems involved in implementing each of these EFT systems. There is inevitably some customer resistance from those who fear that they will lose control of their money. Some workers like to see their actual paycheck, if only for a few minutes on the way to the bank. (Anyone who has ever been paid by an employer in cash can probably appreciate the different feeling you get from being able to actually see what you've earned in your own hands.) The money machines are a great convenience, but they also involve security risks late at night and the possibility of lost cards and unauthorized withdrawals. The major difficulty involved with the point-of-sale payment, aside from the loss of the float period which would exist if the bills were totaled once a month and mailed out, is the problem of how to preserve consumer defenses where defective merchandise or services are delivered.

New legal rules to deal with these and other problems have been proposed, both as amendments to the UCC and as separate legislation. New laws have such provisions as: (1) the bank must send each customer a written agreement which includes his or her rights as a user of the EFT card; (2) the bank must provide a monthly statement of all EFT transactions to the customer; (3) the customer must be given a receipt for each EFT transaction; (4) the bank is liable for unauthorized use of the EFT card in the machine unless the customer has been negligent; (5) the bank may not send out unsolicited EFT cards unless the recipients are already its customers; and (6) the bank may not release a customer's financial records without his or her permission or a court order. These statutes may provide civil and criminal penalties for violation by the bank.

The entire area of electronic funds transfer will continue to challenge the ingenuity of judges, lawyers, and legislators.

CASES FOR DISCUSSION

BLAKE v. WOODFORD BANK & TRUST CO.

555 S.W.2d 589 (Kentucky, 1977)

Park, Justice

On December 6, 1973, Blake deposited a check in the amount of $16,449.84 to his account at the Morristown Bank, of Morristown, Ohio. This check was payable to Blake's order and was drawn on the K & K Farm Account at the Woodford Bank and Trust Company. The check was dated December 3, 1973.

On December, 19, 1973, Blake deposited a second check in the amount of $11,200 to his account in the Morristown Bank. The second check was also drawn on the K & K Farm Account at the Woodford Bank and Trust Company and made payable to Blake's order. The second check was dated December 17, 1973.

When Blake deposited the second check on

December 19, he was informed by the Morristown Bank that the first check had been dishonored and returned because of insufficient funds. Blake instructed the Morristown Bank to re-present the first check along with the second check. Blake was a cattle trader, and the two checks represented the purchase price for cattle sold by Blake to James Knight who maintained the K & K Farm Account. Blake testified that he had been doing business with Knight for several years. On other occasions, checks had been returned for insufficient funds but had been paid when re-presented.

The two checks were forwarded for collections through the Cincinnati Branch of the Federal Reserve Bank of Cleveland. From the Federal Reserve Bank, the two checks were delivered to the Woodford Bank and Trust Company by means of the Purolator Courier Corp. The checks arrived at the Woodford Bank and Trust Company on Monday, December 24, 1973, shortly before the opening of the bank for business. The next day, Christmas, was not a banking day. The two checks were returned by the Woodford Bank and

Trust Company to the Cincinnati Branch of the Federal Reserve Bank by means of Purolator on Thursday, December 27, 1973.

The two checks were received by the bank on Monday, December 24. The next banking day was Wednesday, December 26. Thus, the bank's "midnight deadline" was midnight on Wednesday, December 26. KRS 355.4—104(1)(h). As the bank retained the two checks beyond its midnight deadline, Blake asserts that the bank is "accountable" for the amount of two checks under KRS 355.4—302(1)(a). . . .

The basic facts found by the circuit court can be summarized as follows: (a) the bank had no intention of holding the checks beyond the midnight deadline in order to accommodate its customer; (b) there was an increased volume of checks to be handled by reason of the Christmas holiday; (c) two posting machines were broken down for a period of time on December 26; (d) one regular bookkeeper was absent because of illness. Standing alone, the bank's intention not to favor its customer by retaining an item beyond the midnight deadline would not justify the application of § 4–108(2). The application of the exemption statute necessarily will turn upon the findings relating to heavy volume, machine breakdown, and absence of a bookkeeper.

The bank's president testified that 4,200 to 4,600 checks were processed on a normal day. Because the bank was closed for Christmas on Tuesday, the bank was required to process 6,995 checks on December 26. The bank had four posting machines. On the morning of December 26, two of the machines were temporarily inoperable. One of the machines required 2½ hours to repair. The second machine was repaired in 1½ hours. As the bank had four bookkeepers, the machine breakdown required the bookkeepers to take turns using the posting machines for a time in the morning. One of the four bookkeepers who regularly operated the posting machines was absent because of illness on December 26. This bookkeeper was replaced by the head bookkeeper, who had experience on the posting machines, although he was not as proficient as a regular posting machine operator.

Because of the cumulative effect of the heavy volume, machine breakdown, and absence of a regular bookkeeper, the bank claims it was unable to process the two checks in time to deliver them to the courier from Purolator for return to the Federal Reserve Bank on December 26. As the bank's president testified:

Because we couldn't get them ready for the Purolator carrier to pick them up by 4:00, and we tried to get all our work down there to him by 4:00, for him to pick up, and these two checks were still being processed in our bookkeeping department, and it was impossible for those to get into returns for that day.

The validity of this claim must be considered in light of the testimony of the bank's bookkeeper who processed the two checks.

Betty Stratton was the regular bookkeeper who posted all of the accounts from "D" through "K," and she processed the two checks in question on December 26. While two posting machines were being repaired, Mrs. Stratton shared her posting machine with Garnetta Bunch, another regular bookkeeper and posting machine operator. Since the substitute bookkeeper was not processing the two checks in question and was not sharing a posting machine with Mrs. Stratton, it is difficult to see how the absence of one of the regular bookkeepers could have delayed the posting of the two checks in question.

Mrs. Stratton testified that she did not complete the posting of all of the checks in the "H" through "K" accounts until after 4:00. Had it not been for the extra volume of checks to be handled and the breakdown in the posting machines, she should have completed the process of posting by 12:30 P.M. In accordance with her operating instructions, Mrs. Stratton took the two checks to Susan Williams, the bank employee with the duty of handling any checks which were to be returned because of insufficient funds. Because of the lateness of the hour, Ms. Williams and all responsible officers of the bank had left for the day. Mrs. Stratton left the two checks on Ms. Williams' desk. Mrs. Stratton testified on cross-examination:

X50: And Ms. Williams was not there?

A.: No.

X51: Did you make any effort, Mrs. Stratton, to find anybody to give the check to?

A.: No.

X52: Were you aware that if that check was not returned timely that the bank might be subject to some liability?

A.: No, sir.

The two checks were returned to the Cincinnati branch of the Federal Reserve Bank by the regular Purolator courier on Thursday afternoon, December 27.

The increased volume of items to be processed the day after Christmas was clearly foreseeable. The breakdown of the posting machines was not an unusual occurrence, although it was unusual to have two machines broken down at the same time. In any event, it should have been foreseeable to the responsible officers of the bank that the bookkeepers would be delayed in completing posting of the checks on December 26. Nevertheless, the undisputed evidence establishes that no arrangements of any kind were made for return of "bad" items which might be discovered by the bookkeepers after the departure of the Purolator courier. The two checks in question were in fact determined by Mrs. Stratton to be "bad" on December 26. The checks were not returned because the regular employee responsible for handling "bad" checks had left for the day, and Mrs. Stratton had no instructions to cover the situation.

Even though the bank missed returning the two checks by the Purolator courier, it was still possible for the bank to have returned the checks by its midnight deadline. Under UCC § 4–301(4)(b) an item is returned when it is "sent" to the bank's transferor, in this case the Federal Reserve Bank. Under UCC § 1–201(38) an item is "sent" when it is deposited in the mail. . . . Thus, the bank could have returned the two checks before the midnight deadline by the simple procedure of depositing the two checks in the mail, properly addressed to the Cincinnati branch of the Federal Reserve Bank.

This court concludes that circumstances beyond the control of the bank did not prevent it from returning the two checks in question before its midnight deadline on December 26. The circumstances causing delay in the bookkeeping department were foreseeable. On December 26, the bank actually discovered that the checks were "bad," but the responsible employees and officers had left the bank without leaving any instructions to the bookkeepers. The circuit court erred in holding that the bank was excused under § 4–108 from meeting its midnight deadline. The facts found by the circuit court do not support its conclusion that the circumstances in the case were beyond the control of the bank. . . .

HARDEX-STEUBENVILLE CORPORATION v. WESTERN PENNSYLVANIA NATIONAL BANK

446 Pa. 446 (Pennsylvania, 1971)

Pomeroy, Justice

We are concerned on this appeal with the right of a depositor in a bank to recoup from the bank the sums paid from his bank account on forged checks, and the defenses available to the bank against its customer's claim. Appellant here sued appellee bank to recover amounts so charged against its account. After a jury trial a verdict was returned in favor of the appellee bank. Appellant's motion for a new trial was denied, and judgment was entered on the verdict. . . .

In 1962 Hardex-Steubenville Corporation, Inc., appellant (herein "the Customer"), opened a checking account with appellee (herein "the Bank"), executing signature cards which, inter alia, authorized Myron Swartz, the President of the Customer, to sign checks on its behalf. In 1963 the Customer employed one Frank Iskra as an office manager and accountant. Early in 1964, Mr. Iskra began forging Mr. Swartz' signature to checks purportedly made by the Customer, payable to Mr. Iskra's order. Mr. Iskra continued this practice until it was detected in January, 1967. In the three-year period before discovery Mr. Iskra forged and the Bank paid checks in amounts totaling $97,000. Recovery is sought in the present suit only for these checks forged between January, 1966 and January, 1967, in amounts aggregating $63,105.28.

As is revealed by Mr. Iskra's deposition which

was read into the record at trial, he was in an ideal position to carry off this fraud. As office manager, he received the Bank's monthly statements of his employer's accounts, together with the month's cancelled checks. From the latter, he removed the forged checks and altered the Customer's books so as to make the missing funds appear to be attributable to inventory pilferage. The Customer notified the Bank promptly upon discovery of Mr. Iskra's defalcations, but the Bank refused to credit the Customer's account with the amounts it had paid out on the forged checks.

At trial the Customer introduced testimony tending to show that the Bank had been negligent in honoring the forged checks. The Bank introduced testimony to the contrary and showing that during the period involved it had sent to the Customer regular monthly statements of its accounts, together with the Customer's cancelled checks for each month.

The agreement between the Bank and the Customer under which the checking accounts here involved were established contained the normal provision that the Bank will accept sums deposited with it by the Customer and will pay out all or any part of these sums to a payee named in a check drawn by the Customer and bearing a signature authorized by the Customer. Except to the extent that the relationships of the parties are embodied in an agreement, they are governed in Pennsylvania by the Uniform Commercial Code. . . . [T]he fundamental rule of the Code with respect to an unauthorized signature on an instrument is that it "is wholly inoperative as that of the person whose name is signed unless he ratifies it or is precluded from denying it. . . ." Thus under the Code a bank breaches its agreement with a customer when it pays the holder of a forged check. It is this breach which constitutes the customer's cause of action against a bank to recover the sums paid out on checks bearing forged signatures.

The defense in the case at bar was not that the instruments were genuine but that the Customer had failed in its duty to discover and promptly notify the Bank of the forgeries. This duty and the effect of a customer's failure to discharge it are set

forth in subsections (1) and (2), respectively, of Section 4–406. . . .

As indicated above, there was evidence that the Customer failed to exercise reasonable care to examine his statement and cancelled checks and to notify the Bank of unauthorized signatures discovered in the course of that examination. The trial court correctly instructed the jury with respect thereto in the light of subsections 4–406(1) and (2) and in charging that such a failure, if found by the jury to have occurred, may preclude the customer from recovering.

Where the learned trial court fell into what we consider to have been prejudicial error, however, was in failing to instruct the jury properly concerning the next Code provision, viz., subsection 4–406(3), 12A P.S. subsection 4–406(3), which provides: "The preclusion under subsection (2) does not apply if the customer establishes lack of ordinary care on the part of the bank in paying the item." While the court did mention this section to the jury, it went on to state: "But if you find that the customer himself did not exercise reasonable care and he was careless and did not fulfill the necessary requirements and duties as described here in the language established in the code, and if you find also that the bank itself did not exercise reasonable care in carrying out its duties, you have two parties here at fault, and neither exercising ordinary care nor exercising reasonable care, and therefore the status quo should be preserved and no recovery should be had by the Plaintiff."

Under the court's instruction, if the jury found both that the Bank had failed to use ordinary care in paying the checks and that the Customer had failed to exercise reasonable care in discovering the forgeries, the jury would have had to return a verdict for the Bank. This was not an accurate statement, for under subsection 4–406(3) of the Code, if the Customer's evidence had convinced the jury that the Bank exhibited a lack of ordinary care in paying the checks forged by Mr. Iskra, then the failure of the Customer to exercise reasonable care in examining the statements and checks and notifying the Bank of the forgeries would not preclude the Customer from asserting the unauthorized signatures on the checks and the Bank's breach of its agreement with the customer.

Finally, the Bank argues that the Customer's recovery here is barred by the rule of subsection 4–406(4) of the Code the regardless of the care or lack of care of either the bank or the customer, "a customer who does not within one year from the time the statement and items are made available to the customer (subsection [1]) discover and report his unauthorized signature. . . . is precluded from asserting against the bank such unauthorized signature." . . . While we agree that this subsection precludes the Customer from recovering from the Bank for any forged check the latter paid and returned to the Customer more than one year prior to the Customer's discovery of the forgery, we do not read the subsection as precluding the Customer here from recovering for checks which had been paid and returned to it within the one year period preceding the date on which the forgeries were first reported to the Bank. The Customer apparently read this Code provision as do we, since it did not seek recovery with respect to any forged checks paid and returned to it more than one year before it discovered the forgeries. The return to the Customer of each month's statement together with the cancelled checks covered thereby started anew the one year period within which the Customer was required to detect the forgeries on the checks returned with that statement or be forever barred from asserting his cause of action against the Bank.

Because we hold that a crucial portion of the trial court's charge, to which prompt and specific exception was taken, was erroneous, the judgment must be reversed and the case remanded for a new trial.

KIRBY v. FIRST AND MERCHANTS NATIONAL BANK

168 S.E.2d 273 (Virginia, 1969)

Gordon, Justice

On December 30, 1966, defendant Margaret Kirby handed (a $2,500 check drawn against plaintiff by Neuse Engineering) to a teller at a branch of plaintiff First & Merchants National Bank. . . .

The back of the check bore the signatures of the payees, Mr. and Mrs. Kirby.

Mrs. Kirby, who also had an account with the Bank, gave the teller a deposit ticket (for $2,300 "currency"). . . .

The teller handed $200 in cash to Mrs. Kirby, and the Bank credited her account with $2,300 on the next business day, January 3, 1967. The teller or another Bank employee made the notation "Cash for Dep." under Mr. and Mrs. Kirby's signature on the back of the Neuse check.

On January 4 the Bank discovered that the Neuse check was drawn against insufficient funds. Instead of giving written notice, a Bank officer called Mr. and Mrs. Kirby on January 5 to advise that the Bank had dishonored the check and to request reimbursement. Mr. and Mrs. Kirby said they would come to the Bank to cover the check, but they did not. On January 10 the Bank charged Mrs. Kirby's account with $2,500, creating an overdraft of $543.47.

On January 18 the Bank instituted this action to recover $543.47 from Mr. and Mrs. Kirby. At the trial a Bank officer, the only witness in the case, testified:

Q.: Did you cash the check (the Neuse check for $2,500) before you credited (the deposit of $2,300 to Mrs. Kirby's account)?

A.: Yes, sir.

Q.: So the bank, in effect, cashed the check for $2,500 and then gave defendant a credit of $2,300 to their [sic] account and gave them [sic] $200 in cash?

A.: Correct.

* * * * *

Q.: So you cashed the check for $2,500?

A.: Yes, sir.

The trial court, sitting without a jury, entered judgment for the plaintiff First & Merchants, and the defendants Mr. and Mrs. Kirby appeal. The question is whether the Bank had the right to charge Mrs. Kirby's account with $2,500 on January 10 and to recover from Mr. and Mrs. Kirby the overdraft created by the charge ($543.47).

U.C.C. § 4–213 provides:

(1) An item is finally paid by a payor bank when the bank has done any of the following, whichever happens first:

(*a*) paid the item in cash.

So if First & Merchants paid the Neuse check in cash on December 30, it then made final payment and could not sue Mr. and Mrs. Kirby on the check except for breach of warranty.

When Mrs. Kirby presented the $2,500 Neuse check to the Bank on December 30, the Bank paid her $200 in cash and accepted a deposit of $2,300. The Bank officer said that the Bank cashed the check for $2,500, which could mean only that Mrs. Kirby deposited $2,300 in cash.

And the documentary evidence shows that cash was deposited. The deposit of cash is evidenced by the word "currency" before $2,300.00" on the deposit ticket and by the words "Cash for Dep." on the back of the check. The Bank's ledger, which shows a credit of $2,300 to Mrs. Kirby's account rather than a credit of $2,500 and a debit of $200, is consistent with a cashing of the Neuse check and a depositing of part of the proceeds. We must conclude that First & Merchants paid the Neuse check in cash on December 30 and, therefore, had no right thereafter to charge Mrs. Kirby's account with the amount of the check.

The trial court apparently decided that Mr. and Mrs. Kirby were liable to the Bank because they had indorsed the Neuse check. But under U.C.C. § 3–414(1) an indorser contracts to pay an instrument only if the instrument is dishonored. And, as we have pointed out, the Bank did not dishonor the Neuse check, but paid the check in cash when Mrs. Kirby presented it. . . .

Nevertheless, First & Merchants contends that under the terms of its deposit contract with Mrs. Kirby, the settlement was provisional and therefore subject to revocation whether or not the Neuse check was paid in cash on December 30. It contends that in this regard the deposit contract changes the rule set forth in the Uniform Commercial Code. But in providing that "all items are credited subject to final payment," the contract recognized the settlement for an item is provisional only until the item is finally paid. Since the deposit contract does not change the applicable rule as set forth in the Uniform Commercial Code, we do not decide whether a bank can provide by deposit contract that payment of a check in cash is provisional.

Even if the Bank's settlement for the Neuse check had been provisional, the Bank had the right to change that item back to Mrs. Kirby's account only if it complied with U.C.C. §§ 4–212(3) and 4–301. . . .

The Bank concedes that it neither sent written notice of dishonor nor returned the Neuse check before the "midnight deadline." So the Bank had no right to charge the item back to Mrs. Kirby's account.

For the reasons set forth, the trial court erred in entering judgment for First & Merchants against Mr. and Mrs. Kirby.

Reversed and final judgment.

BANK OF LOUISVILLE ROYAL v. SIMS
435 S.W.2d 57 (Kentucky, 1968)

Clay, Commissioner

Appellee recovered $631.50 for the wrongful dishonor of two small checks. This sum included the following items of damage: $1.50 for a telephone call; $130 for two weeks' lost wages; and $500 for "illness, harassment, embarrassment and inconvenience." The trial court, trying the case without a jury, found that the dishonor was due to a mistake and it was not malicious. . . .

[UCC 4–403] does not define "consequential" damages, but it is clear they must be proximately caused by the wrongful dishonor. It appears this statute codifies the common law measure of the damages as it heretofore existed in Kentucky. . . . As in other cases of breach of contract, "proximately caused" damages, whether direct or consequential, would be those which could be reasonably foreseeable by the parties as the natural and probable result of the breach. . . .

The plaintiff deposited for her account with appellant a check for $756, drawn on an out-of-town bank. In order to permit such a check to clear, it was apparently customary for the bank to delay crediting the account for a period of three days. By mistake one of appellant's clerks posted a 10-day hold on this check, and during that period two of plaintiff's checks were dishonored and returned with the notation "Drawn against Uncollected Funds." Apparently she had some difficulty getting the matter straightened out.

The plaintiff had respiratory trouble and, because of it and a case of "nerves," her doctor advised her to take a two-week leave of absence from her place of employment, which she did. She testified she was embarrassed, humiliated, and mortified, but her principal complaint seems to be of the difficulty and delay in getting the bank to correct its mistake.

In *American Nat. Bank* v. *Morey*, 113 Ky. 857, 69 S.W. 759, 58 L.R.A. 956, it was held that if there was no basis for punitive damages for the dishonor of a check, recovery cannot be had for humiliation or mortification. It was also held that plaintiff's "nervous chill" was not the natural result of the dishonor or such a thing as could be reasonably anticipated. In *Berea Bank and Trust Co.* v. *Mokwa*, 194 Ky. 556, 239 S.W. 1044, it

was recognized that loss of time could be a proper item of damages provided it was the direct and proximate result of the bank's refusal to honor a check.

On the authority of *Morey*, the plaintiff was not entitled to recover for her hurt feelings or for her "nerves." It follows, therefore, that she was likewise not entitled to recover for her two weeks' lost time from work even if her mental state actually contributed to this loss. From the proximate cause standpoint, these nebulous items of damage bore no reasonable relationship to the dishonor of her two checks and consequently they could not be classified as "actual damages proved." (Had the action of the bank been willful or malicious, justifying a punitive award, damages of this kind might have been recoverable as naturally flowing from this type of tortious misconduct, but we do not have that question here.)

The charge for the telephone call was a proper item of damages.

The judgment is reversed, with directions to enter judgment for the plaintiff in the sum of $1.50.

PROBLEMS FOR DISCUSSION

1. Raskell sent two undated drafts to Lonnie, one for $21,000 and one for $27,000. Raskell's account balance at Rosie Bank, the drawee on both drafts, showed sufficient deposits to cover the drafts, but some of these deposits were checks and other were drafts for which Rosie had not yet collected the money. Without these uncollected items, Raskell's account did not have sufficient funds to cover his drafts to Lonnie. When Lonnie presented the drafts, Rosie Bank dishonored them. Lonnie sues Raskell and Rosie Bank on the drafts, and Raskell cross-claims against Rosie Bank for wrongful dishonor of his drafts. What result, and why?

2. Fayette Zappa was the bookkeeper for Ace Corporation. Every month she prepared Ace's payroll, including the payroll checks, which she presented to Ace's president, LaSalad, for his signature. Between August 1972 and June 1974, Fayette drew 55 such checks, of which 33 actually went to Ace's employees and 22 were fraudulent. Fayette would present the fraudulent checks to Royalty Bank, where Ace had its payroll account, and would get the bank to issue new checks to other persons, usually one of her friends or a relative. The 22 fraudulent checks totaled $130,000. Ace sues Royalty Bank for the return of this amount; Royalty says Ace is estopped from making such a claim. What result, and why?

3. Zepka drew a check for $4,800 on his account at Socie Bank, payable to SAB Company, and gave the check to Mishmash, one of SAB's sales agents. Mishmash forged SAB's indorsement, signed his own name, and exchanged the check for a cashier's

check for the same amount at Socie Bank. The cashier's check was also made out to SAB, so Mishmash again forged SAB's signature and then deposited the check in an account titled "Doors, Inc.," which he had at Capie Bank. Capie Bank sent the check to Commie Bank for collection. Commie Bank collected on the check from Socie Bank. More than a year later, Zepka told Socie Bank that the indorsement on his original check had been forged and Socie put the money back in his account. Socie now sues Capie and Commie. What result, and why?

4. Musso gave a check for $6,000 to Eveson Company on the evening of May 3. She learned from her bookkeeper the next morning that a check to Eveson had already been sent for the $6,000 billing, so she went directly to Uncertain Bank, the drawee, and gave it a written stop-pay order on the second check. Musso gave Uncertain Bank the stop-pay order at 9:30 A.M. on May 4. At 11:10 A.M. on May 4, Eveson presented the second check (on which the stop-pay order had been issued) and got it certified. At that point, Uncertain deducted $6,000 from Musso's account. Since there was no stop-pay order on the first check (the one mailed out by the bookkeeper), it was also paid by Uncertain when it was presented by Eveson. Musso sues Uncertain for certifying the check after a stop-pay order had been given to it; Uncertain says it's not liable unless it can be proved negligent in some way. What result, and why?

5. Millard had a checking account at City Bank. Seer Heating Company also had its checking account at City. On April 9, Seer gave Millard a check for $2,000 drawn on Seer's account at City, payable to Millard. That same day, Millard took the check to City, filled out a deposit slip to his account, and gave the check to the teller. She stamped the check in red ink: April 9, 1980. Pay to any bank—P.E.G., City Bank, Sun City, Arizona." As of the close of business on April 9, Seer's account did not have sufficient funds to cover the check, so City charged the $2,000 back against Millard's account, and on April 10 it notified him of what had happened. Millard sues City Bank; he claims that it accepted the check and could not later dishonor it. (In banking practice, P.E.G. means "prior endorsements guaranteed.") What result, and why?

6. Contractors, Inc., employed Rena in its accounting department. Rena's duties included verification of all bills and invoices, preparation of payment checks therefor, submission of the bills and checks to company officers for signatures, and mailing out of the checks. During 1977 and 1978, Rena submitted 10 fake invoices from firms with which Contractors did a lot of business. Rena then forged the indorsements of those payee firms. She used fake stamps similar to those used by the companies themselves; she apparently had the fake stamps made up in order to have the indorsements seem normal. These indorsement stamps contained the usual restrictive language used by companies for indorsing incoming payment checks: "For Deposit Only," followed the company's name.

Enwhy Bank cashed 11 such checks, totaling $450,000, for Rena or one of her coconspirators. Enwhy either paid the amount in cash or deposited it to a savings account in the crook's name. The checks were then sent to Checking Bank, where Contractors had its account and where they were paid. Contractors sues Enwhy Bank for $450,000. Does it have any theory of liability under which it can recover the money? Discuss.

7. Cleveland had been a member and officer of Ardmoor Church for over 20 years, finally being elected its financial secretary. As such, he received all of the church's bank statements and handled most of its financial affairs, although two signatures were required for any withdrawal, his own and that of Herbie Thompson. During 1973 and 1974, Cleveland made out 53 checks to himself as payee, forging Herbie's

countersignature on each check. Many of these checks were indorsed by Southern Racers, Inc., after Cleveland's indorsement. Southern Racers operated a racetrack where betting occurred. Memory Bank, the drawee, paid all of these checks without objection. Ardmoor Church sues Memory Bank for $4,488.50, the total amount of these 53 checks. What result, and why?

8. Merry Lyncher, a stockbroker, gave a check for $260,000 to Swindler, one of her customers, on Thursday, June 11. Later that same day, Swindler deposited the check to his account at the Wessie Bank. On the next morning, the check was presented through the city's clearinghouse to the drawee bank, Navy Bank. On Friday evening, Navy began processing the check. It was stamped "PAID," charged against Merry's account, and run through Navy's computer system. Navy's computer prepared a "large item" report for all items over $500; this check appeared on that report. On Monday, June 15, Navy's accountant looked over the large item report, and since there were no deficiencies, this check was photographed, canceled, and filed in Merry's account for return to her as a canceled check. About 4 P.M. on Monday, Navy discovered that a check issued by Swindler to Merry for $275,000 had to be dishonored due to insufficient funds. Navy immediately notified Merry, who told Navy to stop payment on her check to Swindler. At that point, Navy took the canceled check out of Merry's file, reversed all computer entries, stamped the check "Payment stopped. Canceled in error," and sent the check back to Wessie Bank. Wessie says that Navy owes it the $260,000 since the check had been paid and it was too late to reverse the process. What result, and why?

Part VII
Insurance and Suretyship

27 Insurance: Nature, Types; Special Legal Problems

An insurance policy is a contract in which the risk of financial loss resulting from certain specified occurrences is shifted from the insured to the insurance company. The company agrees to bear these risks and to reimburse the insured (or some other person) in return for the payment of the agreed premiums. In addition to being a method of "risk bearing," insurance is also a method of "risk sharing," since the insurance company collects a relatively small amount from each insured and reimburses only those insureds who suffer actual losses. Each insured pays a little so that none of the insured loses a lot. Basically the same principle was used by the pioneer families who distributed their family possessions in several wagons in a wagon train so that if one wagon were destroyed, a family wouldn't lose everything it owned.

HISTORY AND REGULATION

Arrangements similar to today's insurance have been known since the earliest historical times. Babylonian traders apparently used an insurance-like financing arrangement for assuming the risks of the caravan trade, a practice that was legally recognized in the Code of Hammurabi. The Phoenicians, the Greeks, and the Romans followed this precedent for seaborne trade. The Romans also appear to have worked out a sort of life insurance for the payment of burial expenses and survivor benefits. Marine insurance was widely used by the trading nations of medieval Europe; the oldest known marine insurance contract, from Genoa, is dated 1347. The first life insurance policy in the modern sense was issued in England in 1583. The oldest continuously existing insurance organization, the famous Lloyd's of London, was organized about 100 years later, in 1689, in Edward Lloyd's London coffeehouse. According to most sources, the term *underwriter* stems from the procedure used by syndicates such as Lloyd's, in which each member of the syndicate would sign his name and the amount of liability he wished to assume for particular ships.

Insurance law in the United States was originally subject to considerable English influence. Both life insurance and fire insurance existed in the colonies and continued to develop during the early years of nationhood. From a legal standpoint, the most important early precedent dealing with insurance was established in 1869, when the U.S. Supreme Court decided in *Paul* v. *Virginia* that insurance was not interstate commerce and therefore not subject to regulation by Congress. Based on this decision, the various states constructed rather elaborate regulatory schemes of their own. While the details and the enforcement procedures vary considerably, the state insurance regulations typically include qualifications which foreign insurance corporations must meet in order to write insurance in the state, limitations on investments by insurance companies so as to provide protection against company insolvency, and the licensing and control of insurance agents and brokers.

The states' comprehensive regulatory schemes were cast into question when, in *U.S.* v. *Southeastern Underwriters*, the U.S. Supreme Court reversed 75 years of precedents and held that insurance *was* commerce. Congress responded by passing the McCarran-Ferguson Act, which delegated the regulatory power of Congress to the states. The insurance industry was given broad exemption from the U.S. antitrust acts, which were to apply to insurance only "to the extent that such business is not regulated by state law." Since then, the Supreme Court has been experiencing continuing difficulties in defining the scope of this exemption. More recently, several proposals have been made in Congress to repeal or substantially amend the McCarran-Ferguson Act.

ORGANIZATIONAL FORMS OF INSURANCE COMPANIES

The two major types of insurance companies are stock companies and mutual companies. Stock companies are organized as profit-making corporations, with the policyholders as the companies' customers. Some individuals may be both stockholders and customers as is true with any publicly traded corporation, such as GM or Ford, but there is no necessary connection between the two groups. Except for life insurance, stock companies have historically dominated the insurance industry in this country. Mutual companies, at least theoretically, are a sort of "cooperative," in which each policyholder pays an initial "membership fee" to join the organization. If a mutual company is operated at a profit, this surplus is distributed to the owner-customers as rebates on the premiums charged. For most day-to-day purposes, there is little difference in how these two kinds of companies operate.

Relatively small amounts of life insurance and health insurance are written by fraternal organizations for their members. Governmental agencies may also issue life insurance and other insurance-like "guarantees." The U.S. government provides life insurance for members of the military. Social security provides certain kinds of insurance benefits. U.S. agencies also insure bank deposits and guarantee the payment of residential mortgages. State governmental agencies may be involved in a variety of other insurance programs.

TYPES OF INSURANCE

Most types of insurance are well known. These can be grouped into five basic categories: life insurance, health and accident insurance, property insurance, marine insurance, and liability insurance.

There are many specific varieties of life insurance, containing different combinations of the "protection" element and the "savings" element and many different special clauses. Term life insurance commits the insurance company for only a limited period (five years, for example); if the insured wishes to renew coverage beyond that period, he or she must usually submit a new application, including evidence of good health. If a new term policy is issued, the premium is normally higher than that for the first five-year period since the insured is now five years older. Term insurance usually does not provide for "cash surrender value" or other savings features. Ordinary life insurance provides coverage, and level premium payments, throughout the insured's life. Ordinary life accumulates a cash surrender value.

Greater emphasis on the savings feature of insurance is found in limited-payment life policies and endowment policies. In a limited-payment life policy, the premiums are paid only for a specified number of years, such as 10 or 20. At the end of that time, the policy is fully paid up and coverage continues for the life of the insured. This sort of policy is particularly appropriate for use during high earning years, in contrast to term insurance, which is useful for persons who want maximum protection at minimum cost. An endowment policy also has a limited-pay feature, but the insured is to receive the face amount at a given age. If the insured dies before that date, the proceeds are payable to a named beneficiary. An annuity contract obligates the company to make regular periodic payments to the insured once he or she reaches a certain age. (See the *Woodworth* case in Chapter 9.)

Health insurance provides for the direct payment or reimbursement of expenses incurred by the insured as a result of illness, such as hospital costs, doctors' fees, X-ray examinations, and medicines. It may also provide for periodic payments to make up for lost wages. Such "income maintenance" protection is especially important where the insured is the sole or principal wage earner in the family unit. Accident insurance provides similar coverage for costs arising from accidental injuries. It usually contains a provision for a lump-sum payment in the event of accidental death, with percentage of that amount payable for permanent disabilities such as the loss of an eye or an arm.

Property insurance of various kinds reimburses the insured for losses sustained from damage to or destruction of property. Fire insurance usually sets a maximum amount for which the company is liable, but the insured can collect only the actual cash value of the insured property at the time of the loss. Loss of a TV set which cost $500 new but had depreciated in value to $200 would permit the insured to recover only $200. A "valued" fire insurance policy, on the other hand, specifies the amount which will be paid in the event of loss by fire. An "extended coverage" indorsement to the policy would protect against loss due to other causes, such as windstorm, hail, aircraft, riot, vehicles, explosion, or smoke ("WHARVES" coverage). For an auto, collision coverage is appropriate if the vehicle has any value at all. Where property is used in a business so that its loss or nonfunctioning might prevent the business from continuing, "business interruption" coverage is also important.

Both ocean marine and inland marine insurance are basically concerned with transportation losses, but there are some differences. The loss and liability rules for ocean marine rely heavily on concepts drawn from the law of the sea and international law generally. Because of the requirements for international uniformity, ocean marine is subject to much less regulation by the states. While inland marine basically covers losses due to transportation mishaps occurring within the United States, it may also cover protection against the loss of such things as tunnels, bridges, and pipelines. Inland marine companies also write "personal property floater" coverage for items which are used in different places at different times, such as a set of golf clubs or this book, or for property which is composed of different specific units at different times, such as the inventory of a shoe store.

Liability insurance, sometimes classified as "casualty" insurance, is also very important for both business firms and individuals. Owners and occupiers of real estate need protection against the claims of persons who are injured while on the premises. Owners and operators of motor vehicles need similar protection. Professionals need insurance to cover malpractice liability claims. Businesses need workers' compensation coverage for on-the-job injuries to employees. Manufacturers and sellers of products need product liability insurance (although today some firms may not be able to afford the premiums). The list could be extended considerably.

Finally, title insurance protection can be obtained in many locations. For a one-time premium, the title insurance company promises to litigate, if necessary, to maintain the validity of the title to particular real estate and to reimburse the purchaser and/or mortgage lender if another person proves to have a superior title to the real estate.

INSURANCE AS A CONTRACT

As noted earlier, an insurance policy is a contract, though subject to extensive regulation and to some special rules. All of the problems that can arise in the formation, execution, and enforcement of contracts generally can also arise with respect to the purchase of insurance. In general, contract law principles apply to insurance contracts unless these are superseded by special statutory rules or specific "insurance" precedents.

Offer and acceptance problems occur when it becomes necessary to determine the exact time at which insurance became effective because a loss occurred before the insured actually received the policy. In the absence of a specific agreement, the courts generally agree that a life insurance policy takes effect when it is mailed to the insured or even to the company's agent for delivery to the insured. Many insurance applications, however, also require that the insured be in good health as of the effective date of the policy and that the first premium be paid before the policy comes into force. For property and liability insurance, an authorized agent may be able to commit the company even without a written policy. In many cases the agent can at least issue a written "binder" which provides temporary insurance coverage until the company accepts or rejects the proposed policy. Once again, specific language as to what was intended should control.

Turner v. Worth Insurance Company
464 P.2d 990 (Arizona, 1970)

FACTS   Worth brought a declaratory judgment action to have the court decide whether it was liable for a car accident under an alleged insurance contract entered into by Liken, its agent. The trial court decided that there was no valid contact, and Turner, the driver of the other car (who would have been able to file a claim against Worth if it were liable), appealed.

Wilson went to the Liken Insurance Agency on August 17, 1964, to buy the car insurance he needed in order to operate his car at the airbase where he worked. He filled out an application, paid Liken $30.80, and received a receipt. Wilson said that he thought he was covered at this point, but Liken said that her intention was that coverage be subject to company approval. On August 25, Liken informed Wilson by letter that a higher premium would be required and asked him "to let us know if the policy should be issued." On September 18, not having heard from Wilson, Liken wrote him that his application had been rejected. Meanwhile, on August 23, Wilson had had the accident in question.

ISSUE   Had Liken bound the Worth Insurance Company on at least a temporary basis?

DECISION   No. Judgment for Worth affirmed.

REASONS   Although an Arizona statute did provide that temporary contracts for insurance might be made orally or in writing, the court decided that neither Liken nor Worth had done anything to accept Wilson's application. Wilson's belief that he was covered immediately was not reasonable, said the court, in light of the sentence which appeared right below his signature, in boldface type: "No coverage is in effect until a binder in writing on a policy is issued by a policy-writing office of International Service Group."

Judge Hathaway continued: "While Mr. Wilson received a written receipt from Mrs. Liken, this appears to be for the $30.80 advance payment made by Wilson in applying for the insurance and not an insurance contract itself. And even though an application for insurance is accompanied by payment of premium, a contract of insurance is not consummated until the acceptance by the company."

The court further stated that there was no contract here since there was no "mutual assent," because each party had a different understanding of what had been agreed to.

By statute, many states permit minors to buy life insurance on their own lives and to designate certain persons as beneficiaries (usually spouse, parent[s], sibling[s]). In the absence of such a statute, a minor can usually disaffirm his or her purchase of insurance and recover all premiums paid since insurance is not viewed as a necessary.

As to the assignability of rights under insurance contracts, there are different rules, depending on the type of insurance. Since the identity of the user of property is a material element in determining the nature of the risk involved, property insurance normally is not assignable without the consent of the insurer before a loss occurs. Once claims under a property insurance policy arise, they are assignable, like any chose in action. The right to receive the proceeds from a fire or extended coverage policy may be assigned to a creditor with a lien against the insured property; the nature of the risk does not change since the insured-owner is still using the property. Unless expressly prohibited by the terms of the policy, life insurance is normally assignable by the insured without the consent of the company. The policy may be assigned as a gift, or it may be assigned only temporarily as collateral for a loan. In either case, conflicting claims may arise between the assignee and the designated beneficiary. If the right to change beneficiaries has been expressly reserved in the policy, most courts hold that the assignee prevails. To avoid this problem, the named insured need only make himself or herself the beneficiary and then assign the policy.

PARTS OF THE POLICY

The states regulate to a considerable degree the contents of insurance policies, including the basic coverages which may be written, the special provisions or "riders" which may be included, and to some extent even the actual wording. Recently, several states have tried to require by statute that insurance policies be written in "plain English." (If you don't think this is a real problem, try to read a policy sometime.) Most insurance contracts contain five major parts, though these are not always clearly separated or always in the same order: the definitions, the declarations, the insuring agreements, the exclusions, and the conditions.

In any lengthy and detailed contract, it's a good idea to have a list of agreed definitions of terms. This is particularly true where technical terms are used, or where an everyday term has a technical meaning, or where one of the parties is a consumer or other nonexpert. The results of not carefully defining terms can be seen in the following case.

Youse v. *Employers Fire Insurance Co.*
238 P.2d 472 (Kansas 1941)

FACTS   Employers had issued a standard form policy to Mr. and Mrs. Youse, covering their household goods and personal property "against all direct loss or damage by fire." Mrs. Youse was carrying one of her rings, wrapped in a handkerchief, in her purse. When she got home she put the handkerchief and some Kleenex tissues on the dresser in her bedroom. Her maid threw both the handkerchief and the Kleenex tissues into a wastebasket. Later, another member of the household staff emptied the wastebasket into the trash burner at the rear of the house and then burned the contents of the trash burner. About a week later, the missing ring was discovered in the ashes; it had been damaged to the tune of $900. Youse sued when Employers refused to pay for the damage.

ISSUE   Was the damage to the ring covered under the fire insurance policy?

DECISION   No. Judgment for Employers.

REASONS The court said that, even without specific definitions in the policy itself, most cases distinguished between "friendly" fires and "hostile" fires.

"A friendly fire is defined as being a fire lighted and contained in a usual place for fire, such as a furnace, stove, incinerator, and the like, and used for the purposes of heating, cooking, manufacturing, or other common and usual everyday purposes.

"A hostile fire is defined as being a fire unexpected, unintended, not anticipated, in a place not intended for it to be and where fire is not ordinarily maintained, or as one which has escaped in the usual and ordinary sense of the word. A fire originally friendly, by escaping, becomes hostile, and ordinarily recovery may be had for loss or damage resulting thereby. . . .

"In our opinion there can be no question but that the fire which damaged or destroyed the sapphire ring was what in law is known as a 'friendly' fire. It was intentionally lighted, was for the usual and ordinary purpose of burning trash, and was at all times confined to the place where it was intended, and did not escape."

Declarations are factual statements in the policy concerning such things as the name, age, residence, and occupation of the insured. Some such statements would obviously be material to the risk undertaken by the insurance company; others would not. The courts traditionally distinguished between "representation," and "warranties," holding that a false representation of fact not contained in the policy was a basis for rescinding the policy only if the misrepresented fact was material to the insured risk, whereas a false warranty (contained in the policy itself) was always a basis for rescission. Today, either by statute or newer decisions, most courts would probably require the insurance company to show that a false "warranty" by the insured was also material before permitting the company to deny liability under the policy. An error in stating the vehicle number or the color of an insured car would probably not permit the insurance company to rescind the policy.

The essence of the insurance policy is the insuring agreements. These are the company's statements of the risks which it is agreeing to assume. The insuring agreements obviously need to be read very carefully, in conjunction with the exclusions, which are specific statements of the risks which the insurance company is *not* assuming. These two parts of the policy must be read together to see exactly what occurrences are covered. Equally important are the policy's specifically stated conditions relating to such matters as what the insured must do to reinstate a lapsed policy, what notice and proof of loss are required, and what circumstances may cause termination of coverage. The next case shows how some of these provisions fit together.

Stark v. Grange Mutual Insurance Company of Custer County
277 N.W.2d 679 (Nebraska 1979)

FACTS   Virgil Stark, doing business as Stark Electric, bought a fire insurance policy covering his building and its contents from Grange. The policy was written for five years, from December 5, 1973, to December 5, 1978, with annual premiums due on December 5. Stark did not pay the premium due on December 5, 1974, until December 18, 1974. Stark had not paid the premium due on December 5, 1975, when his building and its contents were destroyed by fire on December 13, 1975. Stark claimed that his late payment on December 18, 1974, gave him insurance for one year from that date, so that the fire loss was covered. The trial court denied recovery. The key policy provision read in part as follows: "This policy shall stand suspended if any default shall be made in the payment of any assessment on or before the date specified. . . . The company shall in no event be liable for any loss or damage occurring during such period of suspension. This policy may be reinstated and placed in full force according to its terms to cover losses thereafter occurring and insured against under this policy, upon payment to and acceptance by the Company of such delinquent premium or assessment."

ISSUE   Did acceptance of the late premium payment reinstate the policy for one year from the date of payment?

DECISION   No. Judgment for defendant insurer affirmed.

REASONS   The court had no doubt what the provision in question meant.
"This provision is not ambiguous, nor its meaning uncertain; its meaning is clear, and since it is not illegal or opposed to public policy, it will be enforced as it is made. . . .
"This provision provides that the policy shall stand suspended if any default in the premium payment occurs on a certain date and the company shall not be liable for any loss occurring to the insured during the period of suspension. This provision is valid and enforceable. . . . It is clear from these terms that the coverage of the policy extended from the 5th day of December of each year to the 5th day of December of the following year, and that the policy coverage would terminate and expire on December 5, 1978. Any other interpretation of this provision would stretch the policy period beyond December 5, 1978, and in effect make a new contract for the parties. The plaintiff was aware of his provision when he paid the premium on December 18, 1974. He was under no obligation to reinstate the policy. If he had desired coverage for a full year from December 18, 1974, he could have bought a new policy or made a new contract with the defendant. He chose instead to reinstate the policy according to its terms, and thus when he paid the premium on December 18, 1974, he acquired coverage from December 5, 1974, to December 5, 1975, and when he did not pay the premium due on December 5, 1975, the policy stood suspended. Accordingly, he had no coverage on December 13, 1975, the date of the fire, and the decision of the trial court was correct and is affirmed."

SPECIAL PROBLEMS AND POLICY PROVISIONS

Insurable Interest. To prevent people from using insurance as another form of gambling and to discourage intentional destruction of the insured property or person, the law requires that the insured have an "insurable interest" in the subject matter of the policy in order for the policy to be valid and enforceable. If such an insurable interest does not exist according to the applicable rules for the particular type of insurance, the policy is void and no recovery will be permitted.

Anyone who will suffer direct financial injury from the loss or destruction of an item of property has an insurable interest in it. The holder of the legal title to the property obviously has such an interest in its continued existence. But so has a tenant in a building, even though the lease gives the tenant only a temporary right to possession. So has a creditor with a mortgage or other security interest against the property. A partner has an insurable interest in the property of the partnership even though the partnership is the legal owner of its specific assets; by extension, a few cases have applied the same rule to the stockholders with respect to the property of a closely held corporation. The insurable interest must exist at the time the loss occurs; unless so provided by statute, it need not exist when the policy is issued. For example, a creditor who anticipates making a loan might buy insurance coverage on the building which is to be used as collateral. If the loan is made and a mortgage executed, the creditor would be able to recover under the policy. If the loan is not made, the would-be creditor has no insurable interest in the building and cannot recover if the building is destroyed. Likewise, if the loan is repaid by the debtor, the creditor no longer has an insurable interest in the building and cannot recover for any damage which occurs after he or she has been repaid.

Universal C.I.T. Credit Corp. v. *Foundation Reserve Insurance Co.*

450 P.2d 194 (New Mexico, 1969)

FACTS   Norman Bowman bought a car for use by his 17-year-old cousin, Jimmy Don Bowman, during the school year 1965–66. Jimmy Don was living with Norman and needed transportation to school and to work. Norman bought, registered, and financed the vehicle in his own name. Knowing that Jimmy Don did not own the car, Foundation's agent nevertheless issued an insurance policy on the car to Jimmy Don. A specific policy provision stated that facts known to its agent would not estop the company from asserting lack of an insurable interest.

When the school year ended, Jimmy Don returned to Washington to live with his father, leaving the car with Norman. In July Norman let a prospective buyer drive the car to try it out. The car was totaled in a one-car accident, and the (unpaid) finance company sued to collect under the policy which Jimmy Don had purchased. The trial court held for Foundation.

ISSUE   Did Jimmy Don have an insurable interest in the car?

DECISION   No. Judgment for defendant affirmed.

REASONS CIT tried to argue that Jimmy Don did have an insurable interest in the car "by virtue of the fact that he might incur liability because of his operation or use of it." It could also be argued that Jimmy Don would have sustained a direct loss if the car had been destroyed while he was using it. However, the court decided that neither of those arguments could be applied on the facts of this case.

"When the insured voluntarily abandoned the use of the vehicle, his insurable interest, if any, ceased to exist. An insurable interest must exist at the time of loss. . . . There was no contractual obligation between Jimmy Don with [sic] anyone. He could not have suffered loss by its destruction. He had no interest in the vehicle, and he lost nothing."

Every person has an insurable interest in his or her own life and can contract for insurance and designate anyone he or she wishes as beneficiary. In such a case the beneficiary need have no insurable interest in the life of the insured. Questions arise when one person buys life insurance on the life of another person. For such a policy to be valid, the buyer/beneficiary must have an insurable interest in the life of the person insured. In contrast to property insurance, this interest must exist when the policy is purchased but need not exist when the loss (death) occurs. Just which persons have such interests in the lives of other persons is not absolutely clear since the courts generally test each case on its own facts. It is generally assumed that spouses and partners have an insurable interest in each other's lives; and by analogy, a corporation probably has an insurable interest in the lives of its key employees. A creditor usually has an insurable interest in the life of his or her debtor, at least to the extent of the debt. Based on specific sets of facts, parents and children and brothers and sisters may or may not have an insurable interest in each other's lives; the courts will usually demand something more than just the blood relationship to validate the policy.

Incontestability Clause. By statute in many states and by common practice in others, life insurance policies typically contain a clause specifying that the insurance company cannot raise certain defenses to avoid liability after a policy has been in force for a stated period of time (usually two years). Not all of the company's defenses are removed by such a clause, however. Lack of an insurable interest, certain types of criminal fraud, no required proof of death, and the statute of limitations (and perhaps some other defenses) could still be asserted by the company.

Waiver and Estoppel. As is true with contracts generally, rights under an insurance contract may be waived or a party may be estopped by his or her conduct from asserting them. An insurance company, acting through its authorized agents, can waive its rights under the contract, such as its right to cancel a life insurance policy where the insured has been hospitalized prior to delivery of the policy. An insurance company may also be estopped by the conduct of its agents from asserting a defense on which it could otherwise have relied. It

567

would be virtually impossible to prevent the company from asserting the lack of an insurable interest by either of these legal doctrines.

Nonforfeiture Provision.   Since the insured's financial situation may change drastically for any number of reasons and he or she may become unable to pay premiums when due, many life insurance policies contain a nonforfeiture provision and/or a waiver-of-premiums clause. If the required premiums are not paid within the permitted grace period, the policy may provide that the insured can choose one of several options: a paid-up-for-life policy in a smaller amount, a term insurance policy for the original face amount for whatever term the accumulated values will cover, or return to the insured of the cash surrender value of the policy. Such a provision will also contain a presumption as to which choice is made if the insured does not specifically indicate a choice. Where sickness or other disability prevents the insured from paying the premiums, there may be a waiver-of-premiums clause which states that the policy remains in full force and effect for the duration of the disability. Obviously, such a clause is very important in a single-income family. It can usually be obtained for a slightly higher premium.

Double Indemnity Clause.   Life insurance policies frequently contain a provision requiring the company to pay twice the face amount of the policy in the event of "accidental" death. These clauses have produced much litigation as to what is an accidental death. An insured killed while playing Russian roulette? Probably not. An insured who dies of sunstroke after staying out in the sun too long? Possibly not. An insured who dies from serum hepatitis contracted as a result of a blood transfusion necessitated by a car wreck? Perhaps accidental, necessitating the double payment. The cases are not uniform.

Iron-Safe Clause.   To protect the insurance company against false claims of loss by fire or burglary, particularly where the property insured is a changing inventory of business goods, the policy may require that the insured firm keep adequate inventory records and lock them in a fireproof safe when the firm is not open for business. These records will then have to be produced to substantiate any loss claimed under the policy.

Coinsurance Clause.   Unless prohibited by statute, property insurance policies typically require that coverage be purchased for some specified percentage of the total value if the insured wishes to collect the full amount of any loss. If a building had a value of $100,000 and the policy contained an 80 percent coinsurance clause, the insured would have to buy at least $80,000 worth of coverage in order to collect his or her full loss from the company. If the insured bought only $60,000 worth of insurance on the building, he or she could collect only three fourths of any losses ($60,000/$80,000 × Amount of loss). With or without coinsurance clauses, the insured's recovery could not exceed the face amount of the policy.

TITUS v. WEST AMERICAN INSURANCE COMPANY

143 N.J. Super. 195 (New Jersey, 1976)

Beetel, J.C.C.

Temporarily assigned. This is an action for breach of an automobile insurance contract which raises the novel question of the insurer's liability for the theft of a used automobile in "customized" or "restored" condition.

Plaintiff filed suit seeking judgment in the amount of $2,000, together with interest and costs of suit, alleging that this amount represents the "actual cost value" (ACV) of plaintiff's automobile at the time it was stolen. Alternatively, plaintiff sought the appointment of a disinterested and competent umpire under Section 10, Part 3, of the insurance contract, which provides:

If the insured and the company fail to agree as to the amount of loss, either may, within 60 days after proof of loss is filed, demand an appraisal of the loss. In such event the insured and the company shall each select a competent appraiser, and the appraisers shall select a competent and disinterested umpire. The appraisers shall state separately the actual cash value and the amount of loss and failing to agree shall submit their differences to the umpire. An award in writing of any two shall determine the amount of loss. The insured and the company shall each pay his chosen appraiser and shall bear equally the other expenses of appraisal and umpire.

The matter was pretried on June 5, 1975, and this court directed both sides to produce their appraisers in court on June 13, 1975, at which time the two appraisers would select the umpire. When defendant failed to produce its appraiser on the day set, the court ordered that Anthony Berezny of Sunset Tire Service, Inc., Route 12, Baptistown, New Jersey, be appointed the umpire for the purposes of making an award and determining the actual cash value of the automobile in question.

After some delay and a further order of this court, Berezny and the appraisers met and agreed that the market value of plaintiff's particular car at the time of the theft was $2,000. However, they also agreed that the value of a vehicle of the same model and year in excellent condition, equipped with standard options, would be worth no more than $1,000. Neither of them knew which value was applicable under the law.

Thereafter, plaintiff's motion for summary judgment was denied and the matter proceeded to trial before the court on April 29, 1976. Defendant withdrew its jury demand and admitted liability. The case was then heard before the court without a jury, limited to the issue of damages.

Plaintiff is a young man who operates his own auto body repair shop and who has been an auto body mechanic all his working life. On March 16, 1972 he purchased a used 1966 Mustang convertible for a purchase price of $472.50 (including $22.50 in sales tax). About three weeks later he contacted his insurance broker, Robert Herdman, and requested that this vehicle be added to his current insurance policy underwritten by defendant. At this time he wanted only coverage for liability.

Plaintiff purchased this car with the idea of "customizing" it. He enjoys working with automobiles and wanted to make his 1966 Mustang something special. To this end he did extensive work on the automobile. During the first seven months he owned the car he repainted it, added new tires, installed a new canvas top, and added several other small items to the automobile. Evidence was submitted by plaintiff showing that during these seven months he spent approximately $350 on parts alone, exclusive of his own labor.

In September 1972 he contacted his insurance broker again and requested that "comprehensive" (theft and property damage) coverage be added to his policy. The broker, Herdman, testified that when this coverage was added plaintiff never mentioned to him that the car was in the process of being extensively remodeled or customized. Herdman admitted that he knew from casual observation that plaintiff's car had been repainted and that new tires had been added, but he stated that this alone gave him no cause to suspect that the car was being customized or that these changes represented any increase in the insurable risk. The broker duly purchased this additional coverage at a cost of $9.18 a year.

Thereafter, plaintiff continued to improve and customize his vehicle. In March 1973 he rebuilt the engine at a cost of $156.10 (including labor). In May 1973 he purchased a second set of tires and a set of "mag wheels" at a total cost of $293.52 (including wheel locks). He also spent nearly $450 on other parts and equipment. During this time his automobile insurance policy was automatically renewed semi-annually. At no time did plaintiff inform the company or his broker of the extensive modification he made on the automobile.

On February 23, 1974 plaintiff's automobile was stolen. To this date it has not been returned. Shortly thereafter, plaintiff filed a claim with defendant insurance company giving a description of the car and indicating that the odometer read 89,000 miles at the time of the theft. Lengthy negotiations ensued which resulted in the instant suit and the failure of the appraisers and the umpire to agree upon the standard upon which value should be determined.

At trial each side adduced expert testimony regarding the question of value and the method of evaluating auto insurance losses. Like the court-appointed umpire and defendant's appraiser, these experts were in substantial agreement regarding the market value of plaintiff's customized 1966 Mustang convertible. Among aficionados of such vehicles, plaintiff's car would have sold for $2,000 on the date of the theft. Plaintiff introduced pictures of his late beloved vehicle into evidence, and from viewing these photos this court finds that there is no question that the car was in excellent, indeed "cream puff," condition. Thus, this court finds as a fact that the market value of plaintiff's car, with the special equipment he added, was $2,000 on February 23, 1974.

The experts could not agree on the value of a 1966 Mustang convertible with full standard options in excellent condition. Defendant's expert, an appraiser with many years of experience, testi-

fied that the "book value" of such a car was $375. "Book value," he explained, refers to two publications used throughout the auto and insurance industries to evaluate used automobiles, the *Red Book* published by National Market Reports, Inc., and the *N.A.D.A. Official Used Car Guide* published by the National Automobile Dealer's Association. He testified, further, that the maximum value of such a vehicle would be double the "book" price, or $750. Plaintiff's experts testified that such a vehicle would have sold for about $1,000. They rejected the book value method of evaluation as the only guide toward the determination of actual cash value. Berezny, the umpire, agreed with plaintiff's experts and thus iterated his previous findings made during arbitrations.

If this court were to make independent findings of fact on this issue, it might place the value of a fully equipped, "cream puff" 1966 Mustang convertible at something closer to the double book value standard espoused by defendant's expert. However, for the reasons which follow, this court finds that $1,000 was the actual cash value of such a vehicle on the date of the theft under the terms of the insurance contract in question.

In determining the meaning of actual cash value generally, there appears to be a split of authority. . . . Some courts adopt a market value test; others look to a formula reflecting reproduction or replacement cost; others have adopted the so-called "broad evidence rule" under which any evidence is received which logically tends to establish actual cash value; and some courts have held that actual cash value is an independent test to be applied without reference to other criteria. . . .

Unrestrained by controlling precedent, this court is in the position to adopt what appears to be the better rule for determining the actual cash value of an automobile, and that is, its market value. . . . As these authorities point out, there is a readily determinable market value for used automobiles, and this value adequately compensates the insured and adequately reflects his reasonable expectations. The broad evidence rule, while helpful in indemnifying owners of property which might be unique or which, when sold on the market, would not bring a reasonable return (e.g., used furniture or clothing), is too uncertain a standard to be applied to the day-to-day business of adjusting automobile insurance claims.

This conclusion is buttressed by the testimony of witnesses in this action. They all assumed that when you talk of value, you are talking about market value. They disagreed over whether the industry guidebooks were the only evidence of market value, but they agreed that market value governs.

Thus, this court holds that actual cash value means market value. This leads again to a familiar principle of law. Market value is "measured by the price which, in all probability, would voluntarily be agreed upon in fair negotiations between an owner willing (but not forced) to sell and a buyer willing (but not forced) to buy." . . .

The final question to be resolved is what automobile is to be evaluated. Plaintiff argues strenuously that it is his car, as he had equipped it, which should be the subject matter of the evaluation. Defendant argues with equal intensity that the subject matter of the evaluation is an automobile of the same model, year, and condition, equipped with standard options. Surprisingly, research had disclosed no case directly on point, nor do the commentators provide significant enlightenment.

Defendant insurer presented uncontradicted expert testimony by an experienced insurance underwriter regarding long-established industry custom and usage. He stated that comprehensive coverage is geared to insure the ordinarily equipped automobile and that this was widely known and employed by all insurers. He further opined that the insurance buying public is aware of this custom, and that the extremely modest premiums payable for such coverage should, at a minimum, put the insured on notice that what was being insured was an ordinary risk. . . .

Based on this testimony defendant argues that the subject matter of this policy was a "1966 Mustang with standard options," not a "customized 1966 Mustang with a rebuilt high-powered engine, mag wheels, racing tires, and front sloping chassis, and special paint." To point to the logical absurdity of plaintiff's position, counsel for de-

fendant advanced a "horrible hypothetical"—a solid gold 1966 Mustang with mink seat-covers studded with precious gems. Surely, he urges, such a vehicle could not be insured at full value for the paltry sum of $9.18 a year.

Defendant's logically extreme example is compelling. It would be patently unreasonable for the owner of such a vehicle to expect full coverage in case of loss. Plaintiff's vehicle is not, however, positioned at this extreme. Surely an owner who maintains his car in excellent condition by regular servicing and the replacement of worn parts can reasonably expect to be covered for the full value of his automobile. In fact, by providing for arbitration in its policy, the insurer recognized that individual automobiles of the same model year do vary in value, and thus makes allowance for these legitimate expectations. This plaintiff, however, did something more than merely maintain his car in excellent condition. He added equipment which did more than make the vehicle safe and convenient, and more than was necessary to make it a running car. . . . It is undisputed that the special improvements placed on the vehicle more than doubled its value. Thus, plaintiff could not reasonably expect to receive full value for the addition of nonessential and nonstandard equipment. . . .

Here, plaintiff represented that his car was a "1966 Mustang convertible" when in fact it was (or became) a "customized 1966 Mustang convertible." Such a misstatement was certainly "material to the risk," since it both increased the potential liability of the insurer and the likelihood that the vehicle might be purloined. Had not defendant graciously admitted liability, it may well have been able to advance the argument that the policy should have been avoided on this ground.

There also exists another reason why plaintiff's claim for an additional $1,000 must be denied. . . .

In the instant case most of the modifications to the vehicle were made after plaintiff met with his broker and purchased the comprehensive coverage. These subsequent modifications (the rebuilt engine, the racing tires, and the mag wheels) were primarily responsible for the doubling of the car's market value.

For the reasons stated above, this court finds in favor of plaintiff in the amount of $1,000 plus taxed costs and interest. Because of the novel questions of law involved and defendant's lack of bad faith, taxed costs shall not include an award of counsel fees.

SFI, INC. v. UNITED STATES FIRE INS. CO.

453 F. Supp. 502 (Louisiana, 1978)

E. Gordon West, District Judge

Sometime between midnight, Saturday, October 18, 1975, and 7 A.M., Monday morning, October 20, 1975, the office trailer and main workshop of SFI, Inc., an industrial pump repair company located in Zachary, Louisiana, was burglarized. Tools and equipment valued between $19,257.63 and $21,078.65 were stolen. At the time of this burglary a multi-peril insurance policy issued by the defendant, United States Fire Insurance Company, was in effect covering theft and other losses. After the burglary, the president of SFI, Inc., Chester Efferson, notified the defendant of the burglary. The defendant investigated, but did not deny or affirm coverage for several months, the exact time lapse being unclear in the record. Eventually the defendant did deny coverage on the grounds that the plaintiff failed to comply with protective safeguards clause of the policy. The plaintiff then brought suit against the defendant insurance company to compel payment under the policy. The case, removed from the 19th Judicial District Court for the Parish of East Baton Rouge, State of Louisiana on the basis of diversity jurisdiction, . . . was tried without a jury.

The sole defense of the insurance company is that the plaintiff allegedly failed to comply with certain clauses of the policy. The pertinent clauses provide that:

It is a condition of this insurance that the insured shall maintain so far as within his control such protective safeguards as are set forth by endorsement hereto.

Failure to maintain such protective safeguards shall suspend this insurance, only as respects the location or situation affected, for the time of such discontinuance.

572

The protective safeguards clause states:

In consideration of the premium at which this policy is written, based on the protection of the premises by the protective safeguards system described below (local alarm, with telephone dialer service) [sic], it is a condition of this policy that, the insured shall exercise due diligence in maintaining in complete working order all equipment and services pertaining to the system and the insured shall give immediate notice of any impairment in or suspension of such equipment or service (within the knowledge of the insured) to this company.

It should be noted at the outset that this defense applies only to the coverage of tools and equipment located in the main workshop as this protective safeguards clause did not at the time of the theft apply to the office trailer.

A preponderance of the evidence in this case indicates that the burglar alarm system, while apparently in working condition, was not turned on at the time of the burglary. It is for this reason that the defendant asserts that the plaintiff failed to comply with the protective safeguards clause by failing to "exercise due diligence in maintaining the system." Irrespective of the fact that the system was not turned on, the plaintiff asserts three theories of recovery: (1) "due diligence" to maintain the system does not require the system to be "on" but merely in good working order; (2) delay in notifying the plaintiff of the denial of coverage until after the receipt of a subsequent premium payment estops the defendant from asserting the denial of coverage; and (3) the one failure to activate the system does not qualify as a failure of "due diligence in maintaining" the system in working order.

After the initial policy was issued in May of 1973, the defendant requested but did not require that the plaintiff install a burglar alarm system. The plaintiff complied with this request by installing a burglar alarm system which sounded an alarm on the premises and dialed the preselected telephone numbers of two employees of SFI, Inc., the Zachary Police Department, and the East Baton Rouge Sheriff's Department. After the defendant was notified that the system was installed, it issued the protective safeguards clause and required the clause to be incorporated into the policy without any reduction in premium. This occurred on April 28, 1975, and was in effect with respect to the workshop at the time of the burglary.

Between midnight, Saturday, October 18, 1975, and 7:00 A.M., Monday morning, October 20, 1975, someone cut the hurricane fence surrounding SFI, Inc., and broke into the office trailer and main workshop. Using one of the plaintiff's pickup trucks, the burglars removed between $19,257.63 and $21,078.65 worth of tools and equipment. This difference in amounts results from a failure of the parties to agree as to whether or not a roll of monel wire having a value of $1,821.02 was taken in the theft. Otherwise the parties have agreed by stipulation to the amount of damages. At no time did the alarm system sound an alarm or dial any of its pre-selected numbers. The two employees, as well as representatives from the East Baton Rouge Sheriff's Department and the Zachary Volunteer Fire Department (who handle weekend calls for the Zachary Police Department) testified that no calls were received by them. Chester Efferson stated that he did not think the alarm system was activated at the time of the burglary, and Glen Brown, a former employee of SFI, Inc., told Officer Dunaway of the Zachary Police Department that the system had not been turned on.

The burglar alarm system is not complicated but does require knowledgeable implementation. All personnel have to be out of the building and all doors and windows must be closed and locked before activating a series of key-switches on the office trailer and the workshop. Four keys exist which may activate the system. Chester Efferson, Wayne Cavin, and Billy Lively each had one. The other one is left in a drawer of the workshop during the day and is removed and used by the last shift foreman of the day, either Glen Brown or Ed Shaneyfelt, when he leaves. Each of these men had been individually instructed in the mechanics of closing down the business and activating the system, and each knew when it was his responsibility to activate the system. There existed a clear-cut procedure whereby the last supervisory employee left on the premises was in charge of activating the system after all employees had left.

Although there is dispute as to who the night shift foreman was the night of Saturday, October 18, 1975, there is no dispute as to what supervisory employee was to close up—the night shift foreman. There was no confusion resulting from overlapping responsibilities or the simultaneous presence of two supervisory employees.

In summary, the facts are rather simple and undisputed. When the shop closed down Saturday night, the night shift foreman failed to activate the system—a job he had been trained to do and one which he knew he was supposed to do. When the burglars broke into the workshop, no alarm went off, no one was called, and consequently, no one discovered the burglary until Monday morning when SFI, Inc., opened for business.

The plaintiff's first contention, that the protective safeguards clause only required the system to be in working order but not "on," is an attempt to have the clause interpreted narrowly—much too narrowly for this Court to accept. To interpret "due diligence in maintaining the system in working order" in this fashion would be to utterly disregard the reason for insertion of such a clause. Clearly the whole point of requiring any alarm system was to frustrate burglars and lessen the chance or amount of loss, and the resulting liability of the insurance company. Such a construction would render the clause meaningless. Furthermore there exists no evidence that any officer of SFI, Inc., interpreted the clause in such a manner, or that they were in any way misled as to the requirements of the clause. Louisiana law mandates that a clause be interpreted as the parties intended and without ridiculous results. Louisiana Civil Code article 1945 states in pertinent part:

Legal agreements having the effects of law upon the parties, none but the parties can abrogate or modify them. Upon this principle are established the following rules:

* * * * *

Third—That the intent is to be determined by the words of the contract, when these are clear and explicit and lead to no absurd consequences. . . .

This principle is backed by legend case law. . . .

573

According to the evidence the defendant did not notify the insured of its decision to deny coverage until after the plaintiff renewed its policy by submitting another premium payment to the insurer. In fact, the defendant did not notify the plaintiff of its denial of coverage until the plaintiff had complained of the nonpayment and sought relief from the Louisiana State Insurance Commission. The plaintiff asserts that this subsequent acceptance of a premium payment estops the defendant from asserting the failure of a breach of a condition as a defense. Plaintiff cites to the Court numerous cases stating general principles of estoppel, but little which aids in resolving the problem at hand. . . . [I]n the present case no evidence was produced which proved or even suggested that any agent of the defendant, at the time of the acceptance of the premium, knew that the plaintiff had been determined to be in violation of any such condition. Without any such proof the claim of estoppel under this theory must fall. Furthermore an essential element of the theory of estoppel in Louisiana is detrimental reliance. . . . No harm was proved to have resulted from the defendant's delay in notifying the plaintiff of its denial of coverage. . . .

The final question before us is whether the one negligent act of the shift foreman in not properly activating the system qualifies as a failure to "exercise due diligence in maintaining in complete working order all equipment and services pertaining to the system. . . ." "Due diligence in law means everything reasonable and not everything possible." . . . "Due diligence is that which is expected of persons of ordinary prudence under similar circumstances. . . ." Above all, however, the Court must analyze and consider the surrounding facts and circumstances to determine whether due diligence has been exercised. . . .

Each supervising employee testified that he knew when to activate the system—when he had been supervising and was the last one to leave. The procedure was not adequate. It was the night shift foreman's failure to follow that established procedure that was inadquate.

In summary it appears that the insured, SFI, Inc., did all that could be reasonably expected to assure that the system was operational; an approved burglar alarm system was installed, each responsible employee was trained in the operation of the system, and it was made clear to the employee in charge at the end of the day that he was to activate the system. . . .

With regard to damages, it is the plaintiff's burden to prove those damages which he has sustained. . . . In this case, the plaintiff has done so with respect to all except the monel wire. There is simply a failure on the part of the plaintiff to develop any connexity between the loss of the monel wire and the burglary. . . .

The plaintiff also seeks a penalty and attorney's fees under La.R.S.22:658 for the defendant's alleged failure and refusal, arbitrarily, capriciously, and without probable cause, to pay the claim. Such penalties and attorney's fees should not be awarded where a reasonable defense had been presented in good faith. . . . The issue of the applicability of the defense was not so clearcut that its assertion could be called unreasonable. This Court denies the plaintiff's request for a penalty and attorney's fees.

For these reasons, the Court concludes that the evidence in this case preponderates in favor of a holding that, as a matter of fact and law, the plaintiff did use due diligence in complying with all of the terms and conditions of the insurance policy in question and that the plaintiff is entitled to recover from the defendant the sum of $19,257.63, together with interest at the legal rate from the date this suit was filed until paid, and for all costs, properly assessable, of this suit. Judgment will be entered accordingly.

CITIZENS INSURANCE CO. OF AMERICA v. TUTTLE

294 N.W.2d 224 (Michigan, 1980)

Beasley, Judge

This is another case of first impression under Michigan no-fault insurance law and, in particular, M.C.L. § 500.3135; M.S.A. § 24.13135. The question posed is the interpretation to be given to the phrase "tort liability arising from the ownership, maintenance or use within this state of a motor vehicle . . . is abolished," in the light of the peculiar fact situation presented in the instant case.

Plaintiff Edgar Schaedig was driving a tractor and trailer owned by Zaiger Beverage Company on U.S. Highway 2 in Schoolcraft County when he collided with defendant's cow, which was running at large on the highway. The truck-trailer unit jackknifed, ran into a ditch, and suffered extensive damage.

Citizens Insurance Company of America, the insurer of the truck, paid for the damage to the truck and became subrogated to that claim of the Zaiger Beverage Company. Citizens filed suit to recover the amount paid, and both Schaedig and Zaiger were allowed to join the suit to recover lost wages and additional costs respectively. Plaintiffs' claims were based on defendant's allowing the cow to run at large on the highway in violation of M.C.L. § 433.11 et seq.; M.S.A. § 18.789(1) et seq. and, also, that he was negligent in not fencing in and restraining the cow.

Defendant brought a motion for summary judgment pursuant to GCR 1963, 117.2(1), alleging the plaintiffs' cause of action was barred by the no-fault act, M.C.L. § 500.3135; M.S.A. § 24.13135. The trial judge granted the motion and awarded summary judgment to defendant. Plaintiffs appeal as of right.

M.C.L. § 500.3135; M.S.A. § 24.13135 provides:

Sec. 3135 (1) A person remains subject to tort liability for noneconomic loss caused by his ownership, maintenance or use of a motor vehicle only if the injured person has suffered death, serious impairment of body function or permanent serious disfigurement.

(2) Notwithstanding any other provision of law, tort liability arising from the ownership, maintenance or use within this state of a motor vehicle with respect to which the security required by subsections (3) and (4) of section 3101 was in effect is abolished except as to:

(a) Intentionally caused harm to person or property. Even though a person knows that harm to person or property is substantially certain to be caused by his act or omission, he does not cause or suffer such harm intentionally if he acts or refrains from acting for the purpose of averting injury to any person, including himself, or for the purpose of averting damage to tangible property.

(b) Damages for noneconomic loss as provided and limited in subsection (1).

(c) Damages for allowable expenses, work loss and survivor's loss as defined in sections 3107 and 3110 in excess of the daily, monthly and three year limitations contained in those sections. The party liable for damages is entitled to an exemption reducing his liability by the amount of taxes that would have been payable on account of income the injured person would have received if he had not been injured. (Footnotes omitted.)

On appeal, plaintiffs argue that if defendant's tort did not arise from his use of a motor vehicle, defendant's liability is not abolished by virtue of § 3135. Defendant counters, arguing that any time a motor vehicle is involved in an accident, tort liability is abolished by this section, and the vehicle owner must look to his own insurance company for coverage.

Thus, the issue is to what extent the Legislature intended to abolish tort liability under M.C.L. § 500.3135; M.S.A. § 24.13135. If we determine that the Legislature intended that, aside from the enumerated exceptions, tort liability is to be precluded whenever an automobile is involved in any way, even if the cause of the accident could in no way be attributed to the vehicle, we must affirm the ruling of the trial court. We determine that the Legislature did so intend and affirm.

In *Shavers* v. *Attorney General*, the Michigan Supreme Court upheld the constitutionality of the no-fault insurance act with respect to the abolition of tort liability for property damage, enumerating four legislative goals which would be served by the no-fault plan:

First, with the shift from liability to collision insurance resulting from the abolition of tort liability, there would be a new emphasis on the value and repairability of the insured's own motor vehicle; rates would be calculated on the basis of repair costs for the vehicle, rather than, as in liability insurance, on the potential damage to a vehicle of unknown value.

Second, an additional anticipated effect of relating premium costs to the insured's car was that this system would create incentives for safer cars.

Third, the abolition of tort liability eliminates the

necessity for accident investigations, because a determination of fault is irrelevant to the payment of compensation. The elimination of such investigation, it was hoped, would result in the decreased administrative costs and resultant savings on insurance premiums.

Finally, by shifting from a liability to a no-fault system which emphasizes the risk to the insured, not the exposure to some unknown third party, the Legislature anticipated that group insurance would become feasible. Group insurance has been shown to be far less expensive to administer and more likely to result in lower costs. Furthermore, this potential for group insurance may draw large life and group insurance underwriters into the automobile insurance field, resulting in beneficial competition. (Footnotes omitted.)

Since a legitimate state interest was involved, the statute's constitutionality was upheld against a due process attack. The court also rejected a claim that the statute unconstitutionality denied equal protection, using the following language which is instructive in analyzing the problem posed in the instant case:

The different treatment of moving vehicles and tangible property and properly parked vehicles is related to the second conceptual difficulty relating to the use of fault in a no-fault act. Common sense would indicate, and actuarial studies have shown, that in accidents involving motor vehicles and tangible property, the motor vehicle is usually at fault. Consequently, the act makes the motorist strictly liable for the damage he does to tangible property and requires him to purchase insurance for such damage.[58]

[58]It is possible that a motorist's insurer will be liable to the owners of stray animals, trains or other nonstationary tangible property which may occasion the damage. The equal protection clause does not, in this context, require that statutory classification be drawn with great precision. *New Orleans* v. *Dukes*, 427 U.S. 297, 303–304, 96 S. Ct. 2513, 2516–2517, 49 L.Ed.2d 511 (1976).

The system, however, functions without regard to fault. That is, there is no determination in each accident of who was at fault. Thus, the appellation "no-fault" is a misnomer only if one concentrates on the initial legislative allocation of responsibility. However, if one looks at the operational effect of the act, it remains a system of insurance without fault.

In the quoted dictum, the *Shavers* court appears to have rejected the "fault investigation"

requirement even in the case where a stray animal may occasion the damage. Thus, the insurer of the driver of an automobile who does damage to property would be strictly liable for the damage regardless of who was at fault.

Plaintiffs also argue that the language of § 3135 seems to indicate otherwise. M.C.L. § 500.3135(1); M.S.A. § 24.13135(1) speaks of "tort liability . . . caused by his ownership, maintenance or use of a motor vehicle." M.C.L. § 500.3135(2); M.S.A. § 24.13135(2) states "tort liability arising from the ownership, maintenance or use." This language indicates that the tort liability must arise from the ownership of the vehicle. What the language does not state is whether it must be from a vehicle driven by plaintiff, by defendant, or by either. We find that to fulfill the objectives of the Legislature, the statute must be construed to apply to a vehicle "owned, maintained or used" by either plaintiff or defendant. Where ambiguities exist in a statute, or if a statute is susceptible of two or more meanings, courts may construe the statute in a reasonable fashion, considering its purpose and objectives.

Under the circumstances of the case at bar, the fact that the cow was a stray on the highway and, therefore allegedly caused the accident, does not absolve the motorist's insurance company from liability to pay for the damage to the vehicle. Otherwise, an investigation to determine fault would be required, in contravention of the Legislature's purpose in enacting the no-fault statute.

Under M.C.L. § 500.3101; M.S.A. § 24.13101, and under M.C.L. § 500.3121; M.S.A. § 24.13121, plaintiffs, as owners of a motor vehicle and trailer, were required to furnish insurance to protect against damage to personal property. If the owner or operator of a vehicle desires to protect against the loss or damage to his vehicle, he must provide for his own insurance. Regardless of who is at fault, one looks to one's own insurance carrier to pay for the damage to property. The effect of § 3135(2) is to do away with tort liability unless a claimant fits within one of the enumerated exceptions to the statute. Since none of the exceptions are applicable in the instant case, the only claims made related to property damage by plaintiff driver. . . .

No-fault was enacted in order to provide a method of prompt compensation for persons and property involved in automobile accidents. If the Legislature had intended to limit § 3135(2) to the defendant's use of a motor vehicle, it could have achieved this purpose by abolishing "tort liability arising from the defendant's ownership." Or, the statute could have abolished "tort liability caused by the ownership of a motor vehicle." The use of the broad term "arising from" indicates that the Legislature did not intend to limit § 3135(2) to accidents caused by a defendant's use of a motor vehicle.

The trial judge's conclusion that § 3135(2) applies to actions arising out of a plaintiff's use of a motor vehicle is correct. Plaintiffs' claims are barred by the no-fault act.

Affirmed.

PROBLEMS FOR DISCUSSION

1. Ronald was insured under a Standard Fire Insurance Policy issued by Farmers Insurance Company. In 1973 he constructed a hog barn on his farm. The hog barn was heated by a furnace which was located just outside the barn and which blew hot air into the barn. The furnace was regulated by a thermostat which would shut off the furnace and fan at a preset temperature.

    On January 1, 1976, Ronald discovered that 15 of the 16 sows then in the hog barn were dead. Later investigation revealed that the hogs had died from a lack of oxygen, caused by extremely high temperature. The thermostat on the furnace had been set at 75 degrees but had shorted out, so that the furnace stayed on until the temperature reached 120 degrees and the safety control shut off the furnace. The fire inside the furnace burned normally at all times, and no damage was done to the furnace or the barn. Farmers thus refused to compensate Ronald for his dead hogs under the fire insurance policy. Ronald sues. What result, and why?

2. On February 16, a car driven by Deborah collided with a parked car, causing damages of $1,800 to the parked car. The car driven by Deborah was owned by Shirley, whose minor son Jeffrey was a passenger at the time of the accident. Shirley's car was insured by Casualty Company. Although the car was titled and insured in Shirley's name only, she had bought it for Jeffrey's use. She kept the keys to the car, however, and Jeffrey was required to ask her for them each time he wished to use the car. Shirley had expressly forbidden him from allowing anyone else to use the car, including Deborah. On the evening in question, Shirley had given Jeffrey the car. He had then picked up Deborah, and they had driven around for about three hours. When Jeffrey hurt his hand (in an unrelated accident), Deborah took over the driving, and she had been driving for about two hours when the accident occurred. The insurer of the parked car, having paid the owner the $1,800 damage, sues Shirley and Casualty to recover for the loss. What result, and why?

3. Juliet sues to recover the "double indemnity" death benefits for "accidental injury or death" under a life insurance policy issued to her late husband, Romeo, by the Friendly Life Insurance Company. Romeo, a chronic alcoholic, died as the result of an all-night drinking bout. Friendly claims that it is not liable under the accidental death clause. What result, and why?

4. Casualty Company issued to Ace Corporation a property damage insurance policy, which included cargo insurance. On August 22, 1969, Ace shipped five large transformers by common carrier truck. The truck turned over on August 24, and the transformers were damaged. This damage was covered under Ace's policy. Ace learned of the accident shortly after it happened and filed a claim against the common carrier. On June 3, 1970, Ace sent a letter to Casualty's agent advising it of the accident but not supplying any details. Casualty did not respond to this letter. On

April 6, 1971, Ace again wrote to Casualty, this time specifying the amount of the loss and indicating that the carrier's insurance company had rejected the claim. Ace suggested that Casualty sue the carrier's insurance company before the statute of limitations expired. Ace provided no further details and sent no proof of the loss. On May 6, 1971, Casualty wrote to Ace and disclaimed liability since Ace had failed to comply with the policy provisions requiring prompt notice of loss and proof of loss. Ace sues Casualty. What result, and why?

5. In early February 1975, Dean purchased a tavern known as the Sand Bar. On February 26, he bought from Fire Insurance Company an insurance policy which included $60,000 coverage on the building and $20,000 coverage for personal property in the building. Dean claimed that his purchase price for the tavern was $50,000 and that the purchase contract required him to buy adequate insurance coverage until the full purchase price was paid. About one month later, the building and its contents were totally destroyed by fire. Dean made several demands for the policy amounts, but payment was refused. Fire said that Dean had misrepresented the value of the property to be insured when he filled out his application and that the true value of the building was only $15,000. Fire wants to cancel the policy for fraud. What result, and why?

6. Underwriters appeals from a trial court judgment against it for $7,500 in actual damages and $35,000 in punitive damages because of its "willful, wanton, and malicious refusal" to pay insurance proceeds. The plaintiff, Olson, operated a trucking company and had insured his trucks with Underwriters since 1969. In 1975 Olson was told that Underwriters was leaving the state and that he would have to get his insurance from another company. Olson contacted his insurance agent, Rookie, who handled other insurance for Olson. Rookie discovered that Underwriters was merely moving its home office to another state and that it would continue to operate in his state. Olson told Rookie to send in an application to renew the coverage on his trucks, which were then insured for $5,000 each. When Olson saw the new policy he told Rookie that he wanted the amount of the coverage per truck raised to $10,000. Rookie so informed Underwriters, but it never changed the policy amounts.

On December 24, 1975, two of Olson's trucks were damaged in a fire, each sustaining damage of more than $12,000. Underwriters offered to pay $5,000 per truck if Olson would sign a complete release for any further claims against it. Olson refused since he claimed $10,000 coverage on each truck. Olson sold the two damaged trucks for salvage and bought two others. Underwriters did not even pay the undisputed amount until July 1976. Should the trial court's damages award be sustained? Discuss.

7. Yorick was killed in a severe two-car accident while driving a car owned by Hamlet. The proximate cause of the accident was the negligence of the other car's driver, who was uninsured. Hamlet owned two vehicles, both of which were covered by one insurance policy, but with the premiums separately calculated. The policy on both cars had a death benefit coverage of $20,000 per person where the accident involved an uninsured motorist. Mrs. Yorick, suing for herself and for her deceased husband's estate, claims that she is entitled to recover the death benefits under both parts of Hamlet's policy. She wants to "stack" the two uninsured motorist clauses so that she recovers $40,000. How should the court rule, and why?

8. Neutral Insurance sues to rescind a policy of health and accident insurance which it issued to Oliver, covering Oliver and his wife. Neutral claims that Oliver misrepresented his wife's health in the application. Neutral raised the problem with Oliver

and indicated to him that it wished to rescind the policy. At one point, Neutral sent Oliver a check "in full settlement and termination of policy." Oliver received and cashed the check. (Oliver is a lawyer.) What result, and why?

9. James Hane purchased a farm from Paul Fish in December 1969 under a contract for deed (a land contract). Pursuant to the contract, Hane bought fire insurance on the farmhouse and buildings. On April 17, 1972, due to financial problems (and a pending cancellation of the land contract for nonpayment), Hane assigned his vendee's interest in the contract to Braget. Braget made up all of the missed payments to Fish. At the same time, an informal understanding was apparently reached which would allow Hane to help manage the farm and would give him the chance to buy back the farm at a later date. On April 26, 1972, the farmhouse was destroyed by fire. The insurer refused payment under the policy issued to Hane, and Hane sues to collect. What result, and why?

28 | Suretyship: Types; Special Legal Rules

Nature of the Relationship. Suretyship is a special form of contractual agreement by which one party promises to make good for the default of another. It occurs in two common situations. Where a lender or seller does not feel that the debtor's personal financial situation warrants the extension of credit, the lender or seller may require a cosigner, that is, another person who also agrees to become liable for payment of the debt. This sort of arrangement may be used as the only additional security which the creditor requires, or it may be used in combination with personal property or real estate as specific collateral securing the debt. The person who actually receives the money or credit is spoken of as the "principal debtor"; the cosigner is the surety.

The other frequently occurring suretyship transaction involves "bonding." Here a company issuing a surety bond promises to pay a certain sum of money if the "debtor" defaults on his or her performance obligations. For example, with the performance bonds required of building contractors, the bonding company promises to pay the landowner/customer in the event of nonperformance or improper performance by the builder. Because courts have disagreed as to whether such a bond also covers the claims of unpaid laborers or material suppliers, the builder may also be required to furnish, a bond which specifically provides for the payment of these claims. Many public officials, particularly those who have custody of public funds, are required to file bonds guaranteeing that the bonding company will replace any missing monies. Bonds are also required in many types of judicial proceedings in order to protect the other party and to guarantee performance of court-imposed obligations, for example, a bail bond to ensure a party's appearance for trial. Although perhaps not technically surety bonds, fidelity bonds are frequently required by employers for employees in "sensitive" jobs; specified defaults by such an employee give the employer the right to recover the amount of the bond from the bonding company.

FACTS   National Surety issued a fidelity bond to State Bank of Prairie City. The bond covered "any loss through any dishonest, fraudulent, or criminal act of any of the employees" of the bank. The bank's president, Harry Soults, was very liberal in making loans, including several that were beyond the bank's $25,000 limit. When bank examiners criticized this practice, Soults apparently stopped, and the last examination before bankruptcy showed a "marked improvement." Soults had continued to make these unauthorized loans, however, and had merely been covering his tracks by juggling the books and making illegal transfers from escrow accounts. The FDIC took over the insolvent bank and sued as its receiver. The trial court found that the amount of loss caused by Soults was $914,935.66, and it held National Surety liable for that amount. National Surety appealed.

ISSUES   Was Soults' misconduct covered by the fidelity bond? Should the bank's failure to give National Surety notice of Soults' misconduct prevent recovery on the bond?

DECISION   Yes. No. Judgment affirmed.

REASONS   Justice LeGrand first dismissed National Surety's claim that it had been improperly a jury trial, since it had not made a proper demand in state court for one. After reviewing the facts, he turned to the terms of the bond.

"The terms 'dishonest' and 'fraudulent' as used in fidelity bonds have a broad meaning. They include acts which show a 'want of integrity' or 'breach of trust.' . . . They also include acts in disregard of an employer's interest, which are likely to subject the employer to loss. . . . The fact that one knowingly makes unauthorized loans in excess of authority has been called 'such breach of trust as will constitute fraud or dishonesty within the meaning of the law.'"

He then discussed the defendant's claim that it had been exposed to greater liability then it should have been because the bank failed to notify it when Soults' acts were first discovered. He felt that the facts did not support this argument. "Although the directors had knowledge that excess loans had been made, they were nevertheless justified in believing these loans had been repaid and that the making of such loans would not be repeated. It was only after the bank had been closed that the extent of the fraudulent and dishonest practices became apparent."

Finally, Justice LeGrand said that Soults had not been in "sole control" of the bank, so as to charge it with knowledge of everything he did.

Most courts continue to draw a distinction between "suretyship," strictly defined, and "guaranty." A surety makes the same promise to the creditor as does the principal debtor; the surety says, "I will pay." When the debt falls due, the creditor can sue the surety without first demanding payment from the principal debtor. A guarantor makes a different sort of promise; he or she says, "If the principal debtor doesn't pay, then I'll pay." The creditor is required to demand the money from the principal debtor and to notify the guarantor of the principal debtor's default before the guarantor becomes liable to "pick up the check." The guarantor's promise is similar to the conditional contract liability of the indorser of a negotiable instrument. A "guarantor of collectibility" makes an even more limited promise; the creditor must normally get a judgment against the principal debtor and have the judgment returned unsatisfied before the guarantor of collectibility becomes liable. Many of the following legal rules, however, are applied by the courts to both suretyship and guaranty.

Contract Aspects of Suretyship. Since suretyship is a contract, there must be offer and acceptance, supported by consideration, in order to form the contract. Whether the creditor-offeree is required to give notice of acceptance to the surety-offeror depends on the facts and circumstances of the particular situation. In many cases the creditor's acceptance of the surety's offer will be obvious. Where there has been a continuing guaranty of payment, intended to cover a number of possible transactions, many courts will require notice of a creditor's acceptance, so that the guarantor knows the extent of the obligations which the creditor has undertaken.

American Chain Co. v. *Arrow Grip Mfg. Co.*
235 N.Y.S. 228 (New York, 1929)

FACTS   Prior to 1923, Arrow purchased chains from American. Arrow usually had to sign a draft as acceptor for the purchase price of each shipment, the draft being attached to the bill of lading. To secure better credit terms for Arrow, a contract of guaranty was executed between American, Arrow, and certain of Arrow's directors and stockholders as guarantors. Tait and Burns were named in, and executed, the guaranty contract. Underwood, Emerson, and Gelshenen were not named in the body of the contract, but they signed it as guarantors. These three persons died in 1923 and 1924, but there was no indication that American knew this when it furnished goods to Arrow in 1927 and 1928. The guaranty contract provided that death would not terminate liability unless and until notice to that effect was given to American. No such notice was ever given, and American sued for $34,556.74 worth of goods furnished to Arrow in 1927 and 1928. Summary judgment for the plaintiff was granted as to Arrow, Tait, and Burns.

ISSUE   Was this continuing guaranty revoked by death, without notice to American?

DECISION   Yes. Judgment for the estates of Underwood, Emerson, and Gelshenen.

REASONS   Justice Heffernan quickly disposed of the claim that the decedents were not liable as guarantors because they were not named as such in the body of the contract. This fact, he felt, was "of no importance." They had signed the contract and had clearly intended to be bound by it. The more difficult question was whether death revoked the continuing guaranty, without notice to American. Justice Heffernan found no New York precedent on this point, and the language of this contract was not substantially identical to that used in the cases from other states.
"It is well settled that after the intention of the parties or the scope of the guarantor's undertaking has been determined by the ordinary rules of construction, either from the instrument itself in which it is clearly expressed or from the instrument and the surrounding circumstances, the rule of *strictissimi juris* applies, that is,

that the guarantor is entitled to have his undertaking as thus determined strictly construed, and that it cannot be extended by construction or implication beyond the precise terms of his contract; and in this respect a guarantor is said to be, like a surety a favorite of the law. . . .

"In case of a continuing guaranty, each advance made by the guarantor constitutes a fresh consideration and, when made, an irrevocable promise on the part of the living guarantor. Guaranties have, therefore, been divided into two classes. The first is where the entire consideration passes wholly at one time; the other where it passes at different times and is separable or divisible. The former are not revocable by the guarantor and are not affected by his death. The latter, on the contrary, may be revoked as to subsequent transactions by the guarantor upon notice to that effect and are determined by his death. The guaranty in the case at bar is in the latter class. . . .

"The continuance of an offer is in the nature of its constant repetition, which necessarily requires someone capable of making a repetition. . . . A dead guarantor can make no promise, nor can it be held that the creditor made the advance at the request of a dead man. . . . [T]he offer of the guarantors could have been withdrawn by them at any time as to future sales. Therefore, it logically follows that . . . their death operated as a withdrawal and no liability can be asserted against their estates on sales made after their decease."

In the simplest sort of transaction, both the principal debtor and the surety sign the loan agreement at the same time. The bank's payment of the loan funds to the principal debtor is consideration for both promises of payment. Since a contract of guaranty is typically a "reassurance" of payment sometime after the primary debt was made, new consideration is required in order to bind the guarantor to his or her promise. This new consideration may be an extension of the time for payment, smaller monthly installments, forbearance from suit, or any other agreed modification by the creditor, but *some* new consideration has to be present in order to hold the guarantor liable.

The precise form in which the "backstop" promise is made may also determine whether the statute of frauds applies. Clearly the guarantor's "if-then" promise is covered, and it is therefore required to be evidenced by a signed writing. Courts may not always draw the technical distinction between suretyship and guaranty, however, and they may require a writing for suretyship contracts as well. Special state statutes may also produce the same result. As always, it's a good idea to "get it in writing."

Special Rights of the Surety. Because the surety has been placed in a rather special position by promising to pay someone else's debt, the law gives the surety a set of special rights in order to produce fair ultimate results wherever possible.

"Exoneration" is the right of the surety to demand that the principal debtor pay the debt when it falls due and before the creditor collects it from the surety. The surety can also get a similar equity order against cosureties, forcing each to pay his or her proportinate share of the debt where the debtor is insolvent or otherwise in default.

583

After the surety has paid some or all of the debt, he or she is entitled to "reimbursement" or "indemnification" from the debtor; this was really the debtor's obligation, and it's only fair that the debtor repay the surety. If there were two or more cosureties, any of them that paid more than his or her fair share is entitled to "contribution" from the cosureties, so that each surety bears the agreed proportionate part of the loss. To assist the surety in obtaining reimbursement from the principal debtor, the surety who has paid off the creditor acquires, through a process called "subrogation," the same legal status that the creditor had. The surety automatically acquires whatever rights the creditor had in property which served as collateral for the debt, and he or she can take whatever enforcement steps the creditor could have taken against the collateral.

Defenses of the Surety. The law provides the surety with some special defenses because of the surety's unique situation. In addition, the surety can use some, but not all, of the defenses that can be used by the principal debtor as well as any defenses which may be personal to the surety.

Because of the surety's special legal situation, to prevent unfair results, the courts generally hold that any of the following acts by the creditor will discharge the surety's liability.

Release of the Principal Debtor. Unless the surety consents to such a release, or unless the creditor specifically reserves his or her rights against the surety, or unless an arrangement is made to indemnify the surety (for example, turning over to the surety sufficient collateral to cover the debt), a release of the principal debtor also releases the surety. Where the creditor releases the principal debtor but reserves the right to sue the surety, the surety's rights against the principal debtor must be preserved too, so that the principal debtor ultimately pays.

Release of Collateral. The courts have generally said that a release of rights against property held as collateral security for the debt will also release the surety *if* he or she can show that his or her rights are prejudiced in some material way by such release. Some courts have reached similar results where the value of the items held as collateral has been substantially diminished by negligence of the creditor.

Material Alteration of Terms. Again, out of fairness to the surety, who has agreed to assume the debt of another under certain terms and conditions, any material change in those terms, if not agreed to by the surety, should discharge his or her liability. Materiality here is a fact question, but changes in the amount of the debt, the maturity date, or the place of payment would almost certainly be held to be material. Most modern cases require that a surety who has been paid for acting as such must show that the change in terms prejudices his or her rights.

Wexler v. McLucas
121 Cal. Rptr. 453 (California, 1975)

FACTS
Floyd McLucas and his wife wanted to buy some furniture but were told by the store that the sale could not be made to them on credit. (Floyd was 22 years old; his wife 18.) Floyd was told that he needed a cosigner. He brought his friend James McWilliams to the store, and McWilliams also signed the contract. The store was still not satisfied, so Floyd brought his mother, Catherine McLucas, and she cosigned too. At that point, the sale was made. The store assigned the contract to the plaintiff, Wexler, who sued Catherine when Floyd and his wife defaulted on their payments. The trial court held for Wexler, and Catherine McLucas appealed. After the complaint was served on Catherine, Floyd had gone to Wexler's office and Wexler had agreed to let him pay off the account at $10 per week, thereby lengthening the term of the contract.

ISSUES
Was Catherine a principal or a surety? If a surety, did the change in the payment terms exonerate her from further liability?

DECSION
A surety. Yes. Judgment reversed.

REASONS
After reviewing the facts and the testimony of the parties, Judge Marshall examined the word cosign. He said that its meaning had not been previously adjudicated and that it had not acquired a clear common meaning. In other words, Catherine could have "cosigned" *either* as a principal *or* as a surety. The terms of the contract were not conclusive as to how she had signed. Further, a state statute provided that a person who appeared to be a principal might show that he or she was in fact a surety except as against persons who had relied on the appearances. There was no evidence to put the store or Wexler within the exception; in fact, the contract named only Floyd and his wife, Roseanna, as purchasers in its first paragraph. Oral testimony was therefore admissible.

"The uncontradicted testimony indicates that the defendant intended to be a surety and not a principal or purchaser (even though she may have been asked to sign as a co-signer). Her testimony, corroborated by her son, was that she neither bought nor possessed the furniture and that she only agreed to pay for it if her son failed to do so. Such agreement is that of a surety: one who promises to answer for the default of another. . . . The defendant is a classic example of a nonprofessional surety: a mother who seeks to help her 22-year-old son and her 18-year-old daughter-in-law to acquire furniture. Suretyship law throws up many defenses around such a person.

"Among such defense is exoneration of liability where the principal obligation is altered in any respect or where the remedies of the creditor are impaired or suspended in any way."

Judge Marshall held that Wexler's agreement to change the payment terms automatically discharged Catherine, as did Wexler's failure to ask in his complaint for repossession of the furniture.

Rejection of Tender of Payment. Where the creditor refuses a valid tender of payment by either the principal debtor or the surety, the surety is discharged. If the debtor is willing to pay the amount as agreed and the tender is refused by the creditor, it certainly wouldn't be fair for the creditor to then be able to sue the surety. If the surety's tender of payment is refused, it wouldn't be fair to extend his or her liability any further, since he or she could have sued the principal debtor immediately if the creditor had taken the money.

Like any other party who is liable on a contract, the surety has available any defense which applies to his or her individual situation, such as lack of agreement, lack of consideration, lack of contractual capacity, and fraud. The courts have generally held, however, that when sued by the creditor, the surety cannot use fraud by the principal debtor against the surety as a defense unless the creditor is also somehow responsible for the fraud.

Because of the special suretyship arrangement, the surety can also assert many of the defenses of the principal debtor, especially those relating to the formation or performance of the agreement. Where a defense such as fraud or duress against the principal debtor makes the contract voidable at his or her option, the surety can use the same defense if the principal debtor elects to avoid the contract. If the principal debtor elects to affirm the contract, the surety remains bound. Where the whole contract is void because of illegality, that defense would of course also be available to the surety. Where the principal debtor's defense is his or her lack of capacity, the surety would still be bound. Indeed, such lack of capacity would in many cases be the very reason for having the cosigner. However, where a minor has disaffirmed the contract and returned the consideration received to the creditor, the surety is discharged, at least to the extent of the value of the consideration when returned. Bankruptcy of the principal debtor does not discharge the surety.

McKee v. Harwood Automotive Co.
183 N.E. 646 (Indiana, 1932)

FACTS   Clyde McKee, a minor under 21, bought a 1924 Ford sedan from the defendant on July 15, 1925. He paid $11.40 down and promised to pay the $570 balance at the rate of $11.40 per week. The contract provided that the seller would retain title to the car until it was paid for, could repossess it on default, and could retain all payments made prior to default as compensation for the use of the car. Clement and Laura McKee signed the accompanying promissory note as sureties.

Clyde had paid $197 when he disaffirmed the contract and returned the car on February 26, 1926. Harwood refused to return his $197 and told him that it was holding the car for him at a storage fee of 50 cents a day. Clyde sued for his money, and Harwood cross-claimed against Clement and Laura for the entire contract price plus $90 attorney fees. The trial court held for Clyde but against Clement and Laura. Clement and Laura appealed.

ISSUE   Does the discharge of the principal debtor also discharge the sureties?

DECISION   No. Judgment affirmed.

The court first stated that none of the exceptions to a minor's nonliability had been proved, so that Clyde was not liable once he disaffirmed. The court then discussed the liability of the sureties.

"The general rule is that a surety is discharged when the liability of his principal is extinguished. This rule is subject to an exception in the case of a surety for a minor or other person incapable of contracting, and the extinction of the contract and discharge of the principal by operation of law because of the principal's legal incapacity does not release the surety. . . . In such a case the surety is bound, unless the minor in disaffirming the contract restores to the creditor everything received by him under the contract."

Although Clyde had given back the car, he had had the use of it for free for some seven months, during which time it had depreciated. Harwood was thus not given back "everything" it had given to Clyde, and Clyde's sureties were properly held liable. However, the court did say that the sureties would own the car when they had paid the judgment to Harwood.

CASES FOR DISCUSSION

UNITED STATES v. SOUTHERN CYCLE ACCESS, INC.

567 F.2d 296 (U.S. Fifth Circuit, 1978)

Per Curiam

The United States brought this action against the debtor and five individuals who were signatories to a Small Business Administration Standard Form Guaranty Agreement. The undisputed facts are as follows:

On February 28, 1972, Southern Cycle Accessories, Inc., executed and delivered to Bossier Bank and Trust Company a promissory note in the amount of $21,000 and a chattel mortgage as security on the note. On the same day a guaranty agreement was signed by Estell R. Raforth, Carl and Margaret Ann Le Croy, Eugene J. Evans, Billie Jo Evans, Jimmy Ray Raforth, and Grace Gill, the appellant. The Small Business Administration (SBA) became owner and holder of the note by endorsement and assignment.

The maker defaulted on the note. On September 8, 1975, the United States, on behalf of the SBA, filed this action against the maker and five of the guarantors to recover the remaining balance on the note and for foreclosure of the chattel mortgage. Default judgment was entered against the maker of the note, but the judgment could not be enforced. An agreement between the plaintiff and the Le Croys was reached and the suit against the Le Croys was dismissed with prejudice, only insofar as it pertained to the Le Croys. The suit was dismissed against the Evans, as the district court lacked jurisdiction over them.

Grace Gill, the appellant, filed an answer and a third party complaint against the Le Croys, who had been dismissed from the suit. She also filed a motion for summary judgment on the grounds that plaintiff failed to reserve its rights against the other defendants when the Le Croys were dismissed from the suit. This motion was denied. The plaintiff also filed a motion for summary judgment which was granted. Appellant appeals from this order granting summary judgment.

On the appeal appellant raises four basic issues:

1. In the absence of a reservation of rights she had been released from her debt due to the settlement between the plaintiff and the Le Croys;

2. If there was an effective reservation of rights, her liability should be reduced by the pro rata share of the parties released;

3. Lack of jurisdiction over the parties jeopardizes her right to contribution; and

4. She is only liable as a guarantor with the other cosigners.

After reviewing the pleadings which were before the district court we find no error in granting summary judgment to the plaintiff.

Appellant first contends that the judgment of dismissal as to the guarantors released all the other cosigners of the guaranty because there was no reservation of rights against the other defendants. . . . The SBA guaranty signed by appellant was unconditional and was a collateral agreement to pay the debt of the primary obligor. Appellant expressly agreed that the releases of other collateral would not affect her liability. Consequently, the release of the Le Croys by settlement did not release appellant. Although the release as to the Le Croys contained a specific reservation of rights, it did not have to contain such a provision. Accordingly, the court's order did not have to contain such a provision.

Appellant next contends that her liability should be reduced by the pro rata share of the parties released instead of a credit for the release of the Le Croys. The standard form guarantee agreement of the SBA in totally unconditional language indicating this is as follows:

. . . the Undersigned hereby unconditionally guarantees to Lender its successors and assigns, the due and punctual payment when due . . . with respect to the note of the Debtor. . . . The term "collateral" as used herein shall mean any . . . guaranties. . . .

The term "Undersigned" as used in this agreement shall mean the signer or signers of this agreement, and such signers, if more than one, shall be jointly and severally liable hereunder. The Undersigned further agrees that all liability hereunder shall continue notwithstanding the incapacity, lack of authority, death, or disability of any one or more of the Undersigned, and that any failure by Lender or its assigns to file or enforce a claim against the estate of any of the Undersigned shall not operate to release any other of the Undersigned from liability hereunder. . . .

Such language clearly implies a waiver of the right to contribution. . . . These terms reflect that each signer was obligated to pay the whole debt and release of part of the indebtedness does

588

not lessen the individual several liability of the appellant for the whole. . . .

Appellant's next contention, that lack of jurisdiction over the parties not residing in Louisiana jeopardized her right to contribution, is without merit. Appellant, citing Louisiana law, argues that the plaintiff by not suing in Texas, where four guarantors reside, has failed to preserve the rights and security interests of appellant. Under the following terms of the guaranty agreement, the guarantors agreed to waive any right they might have had to require the plaintiff to bring suit against the other guarantors.

. . . The Undersigned hereby grants to Lender full power, in its uncontrolled discretion and without notice to the Undersigned, but subject to the provisions of any agreement between the Debtor or any other party and Lender at the time in force, to deal in any manner with the Liabilities and collateral, including but without limiting the generality of the foregoing, the following powers:

* * * * *

(d) To consent to the substitution, exchange, or release of all or any part of the collateral, whether or not the collateral, if any, received by Lender upon any such substitution, exchange, or release shall be of the same or of a different character or value than the collateral surrendered by Lender:

* * * * *

The obligations of the Undersigned hereunder shall not be released, discharged, or in any way affected, nor shall the Undersigned have any rights or recourse against Lender, by reason of any action Lender may take or omit to take under the foregoing powers. . . .

The risk of appellant was not increased by plaintiff's action because her obligations are absolute and unconditional. . . .

Appellant next contends that she is liable only as a guarantor with the other six cosigners and not primarily liable with the principal debtor. Again, she relies on Louisiana law to support her position. In situations such as this, federal law and not state law applies. . . . Under the guaranty agreement appellant agreed to be jointly and severally liable. The agreement was totally unconditional. Appellant agreed to pay the debt in case of default. This obligation can be enforced separately from the primary obligation and without the necessity of proceeding against the primary debtor. . . .

Affirmed.

REGENTS OF THE UNIVERSITY OF CALIFORNIA v. HARTFORD ACCIDENT AND INDEMNITY COMPANY

581 P.2d 197 (California, 1978)

Tobriner, Justice

In April and May of 1960 plaintiff contracted with an architect to design a married students apartment project. On December 8, 1960, plaintiff entered into a construction contract with the general contractor, and on December 19, defendant surety executed a bond guaranteeing the performance of the general contractor. The work of improvement was substantially completed by September 2, 1962.

In January of 1972, about 9½ years after completion, plaintiff first discovered that portions of the project's balconies and the structural members supporting them were beginning to deteriorate because of dry rot. Whether any deficiency in the design of construction of the balconies was apparent to reasonable inspection prior to January of 1972 is disputed factual issue; for the purpose of testing the correctness of the summary judgment we must assume the defect was not reasonably discoverable.

In 1971 the Legislature enacted Code of Civil Procedure section 337.15, effective March 4, 1972. . . . [S]ection 337.15 imposed a 10-year period of limitation, running from the date of substantial completion, on any suit for latent defects against an architect or general contractor. That 10-year period as to plaintiff's apartment project expired September 2, 1971. Plaintiff, however, did not file suit against the architect, general contractor, and surety until July 15, 1974.

Plaintiff's complaint asserted a cause of action against the general contractor based upon negligence, implied warranty, and breach of contract; each of these grounds was also assigned as a basis for recovery from the surety under the performance bond. The court granted defendants' motion for summary judgment based on section 337.15. Plaintiff appeals from the portion of the judgment in favor of defendant surety.

Plaintiff contends, and defendant surety does not dispute, that in the absence of section 337.15 the statute of limitations would not begin to run against plaintiff's action until the plaintiff discovered or would in the exercise of reasonable diligence discover the defect in the buildings. If plaintiff's action against the contractor rests on a breach of a prospective warranty or work or materials furnished under that contract, the appropriate period of limitation is four years (Code Civ. Proc., § 377, subd. 1). . . . Since plaintiff filed suit within 2½ years of the alleged date of discovery of the defect, neither section 337 nor section 338 would bar plaintiff's suit against the contractor. Plaintiff's action against defendant surety, based on the written surety bond, is also governed by the four-year period of section 337, subdivision 1. . . . [I]n accord with the "general rule . . . that the liability of a surety accrues at the same time as that of the principal," . . . plaintiff's suit would also be timely against the surety. . . .

Defendant surety claims that section 337.15 provides it with a defense to the instant action. Defendant advances three contentions to support this claim: (1) that although section 337.15 does not expressly mention sureties, the statute should be interpreted to extend its protection to such defendants; (2) that under California statutes on suretyship the running of the statute of limitations on the principal obligation automatically exonerates the surety; and (3) that under the terms of the surety bond all defenses of the principal inhere to the benefit of the surety. . . .

The language of section 337.15 states explicitly the persons who may assert that statute as a defense: persons who develop, design, survey, plan, supervise, test or observe the construction of an improvement to real property. A construction surety does not come within the statutory description. . . .

In brief, section 337.15 merely describes actions against contractors and other parties as prin-

589

cipal obligors, without any reference to the duties or liabilities of a surety. Prior California decisions have clearly established that statutes of limitation so worded do not govern suits against a surety. . . .

Section 337.15, thus, was enacted against a background of established precedent that a statute of limitations which describes only an action against the principal does not bar suits against the surety. Under these circumstances—and in the absence of any contrary legislative intent—we view the Legislature's failure to mention sureties as among those parties entitled to the protection of section 337.15 as indicating that the section does not govern actions against construction sureties. As with suits against all sureties whose obligation is founded upon a written instrument, actions against construction sureties remain governed by the limitation of section 337, subdivision 1.

The question whether a creditor's failure to sue the principal within the period of the statute of limitations exonerates the surety is a question of statutory interpretation. Unfortunately the statutes governing suretyship do not explicitly resolve that problem. . . .

In terms of the statutory language, the question of whether the running of the period of limitation on the principal obligation exonerates the surety depends on whether that event constitutes a "mere personal disability" of the principal under section 2810 or "mere delay" on the creditor's part under section 2823 (in which case it does not exonerate the surety) or whether it constitutes an "omission of the creditor" under section 2825 (in which case it exonerates the surety). Questions such as these have vexed the California courts for well over 100 years.

The primary remedy that the surety can actually invoke against the principal is a suit based on the implied obligation of reimbursement. Because an action for reimbursement is a new cause of action, arising only when the surety pays the creditor, it is unaffected by the running of the period of limitation on the original debt. Consequently a rule of exoneration is not necessary to avoid impairment of the surety's right to reimbursement.

In summary, the purpose of a surety's agreement is to protect the creditor against the danger that he will be unable to collect from the debtor for any failure in the performance of the contract. In the majority of states, and in California since 1934, the possibility that the statute of limitations will bar a claim against the debtor has been recognized as one of those risks against which a surety bond will protect. Professional sureties such as the present defendant are cognizant of that rule . . . and able to adjust their changes accordingly.

We thus perceive no reason to overthrow well established authority or to repudiate a rule which has served as a protection to the creditor, as an incentive for the purchase of surety bonds, and as a basis for the calculation of rates. Whatever merits defendant surety's defense may suggest as an original theoretical proposition, we deal here with an established ruling, announced by one case over 40 years ago and by another almost 20 years ago. Many transactions have since been founded upon these decisions. We do not lightly disregard stare decisis, and surely not here when we can find no compelling reason, in policy or theory, which would justify such uprooting of precedent. We therefore conclude that under California law the running of the statute of limitations on the principal obligation does not exonerate the surety. . . .

To construe the bond literally, as defendant surety advocates, would place upon its language an interpretation which in all likelihood defeats the intent of the parties. If liability of principal and surety are at all times coextensive, as defendant claims, then all personal defenses of the principal would inure to the surety's benefit. In particular, the bankruptcy of the principal would exonerate the surety, thus leaving the owner without remedy. A literal interpretation of the quoted language thus would render the protection of the surety bond illusory. . . .

We therefore conclude that the summary judgment in favor of defendant surety cannot be sustained on the ground that the language of the bond compels exoneration of the surety. . . .

The judgment is reversed.

J. R. WATKINS CO. v. LANKFORD

256 S.W.2d 788 (Missouri, 1953)

Hyde, Judge

This is an action on an account for merchandise sold to John Baker (one of the defendants sued herein) under the terms of a dealer's contract, payment of which was guaranteed by the other defendants as his sureties. The jury's verdict was against Baker for $640.34 without interest and in favor of the other defendants. On plaintiff's appeal, the Springfield Court of Appeals reversed and remanded with directions to enter judgment against all defendants for $640.34 with interest thereon at 6 percent from May 28, 1940. . . .

Defendants' evidence was that their signatures as sureties were obtained by fraud by Baker and Paul Corbin, who was with him when Sanders signed, saying the paper was only a recommendation. In the case of Sanders (who is the only defendant not contesting plaintiff's right to judgment) Baker and Corbin drove out to his home and found him in the driveway. Baker got out first and asked Sanders to sign (saying it was a recommendation) while Corbin remained in the car. (Baker said he had never read the document but took Corbin's word for what was in it.) Sanders said, after he had talked with Baker, "he [Corbin] got out and said that he wanted me to sign this recommendation for Mr. Baker to sell Watkins' products, and I said that I didn't have my glasses and couldn't read without them, and I said that I didn't want to sign anything that would hurt me in any way, and he said there was nothing there that would hurt me and that it was just a recommendation for Mr. Baker." Sanders then signed without going into the house for his glasses. Baker's contract and the suretyship agreement were both printed on one long (legal size) sheet of paper. Defendants' evidence showed that Sanders could not read without his glasses, but had 20–20 vision with them.

Plaintiff's evidence was that it wrote letters dated March 28, 1939, to each of the sureties on Baker's contract (date March 25, 1939, and terminating April 1, 1940) which were sent by registered mail with directions "Deliver to addressee only. Personal receipt required." The letter to Sanders said: "We are pleased to inform you that we have received and accepted the Agreements of Mr. John Baker dated March 25, 1939, which you signed as surety, together with Louis Wilkerson and J. L. Lankford." Plaintiff had a registered mail receipt, dated April 6, 1939, signed "T. J. Sanders." However, Sanders denied receiving the letter and said he did not think the signature on the receipt was his signature. We must, of course, consider that the jury found against plaintiff on the fact issues.

The first question is whether the fact that the suretyship agreement was fraudulently misrepresented to Sanders by the principal Baker, and also by Corbin, as only a recommendation, is any defense to plaintiff's action on the agreement. Of course, as authorities hereinafter referred to hold, that would be a defense if either Baker or Corbin were agents to plaintiff to make the contract. However, as hereinafter shown, defendants had no substantial evidence of such agency. . . .

The rule is thus stated in *Restatement of Security*, Sec. 119: "Where the surety by fraud or duress of the principal has been induced to become bound to the creditor, the fraud or duress is not a defense against the creditor, if, without knowledge of the fraud, he has extended credit to the principal on the security of the surety's promise or, relying on the promise, has changed his position in respect of the principal." The following illustration is given: "P induced S to sign an instrument guaranteeing an extension of credit by C to P. S had an opportunity to read the instrument but did not do so and relied upon P's representation that it was a letter of recommendation. P exhibited the instrument to C, who extended the credit without knowledge of P's fraud. S is liable to C." That illustration fits this case completely. Sanders could have gone into his house, got his glasses, and read the agreement before he signed it, or he could have had it read to him. There is no evidence that plaintiff had any knowledge of the alleged misrepresentations. Thus there are no facts in evidence to show that the general rule should not apply in this case. . . .

The contract between plaintiff and Baker is in the record and clearly does not create the relation

591

of principal and agent but provides only for sale of merchandise to him at wholesale prices for a period of one year. It appears that Corbin had the same kind of contract with plaintiff. (Each contract was limited to specified territory.) As to the status of Corbin with plaintiff, both Baker and Sanders said all they knew about it was what Corbin told them. The Court of Appeals correctly held. . . . "neither the fact nor scope of agency can be established by the mere out of court declarations of the alleged agent." . . .

Our conclusion is that this evidence is insufficient to establish the relation of principal and agent between plaintiff and Corbin, with authority to make any representations concerning the subject matter of the contract, at the time Sanders signed as surety. At most, it only shows that plaintiff paid him for a completed result; that is, sending in a signed contract on plaintiff's printed form for its acceptance. Thus his status would be in the nature of an independent contractor. This could give him no authority to negotiate a contract, accept it for plaintiff, vary its terms, or make representations about its contents or effect. . . .

Baker admitted at the trial that he owed plaintiff the amount of $640.34. However, as heretofore noted, the verdict was for that amount without interest. . . . Plaintiff filed no motion asking any relief at all against Baker or for any different judgment against him; and neither of its motions specifically mentioned the matter of judgment for interest against any party. Thus the judgment for $640.34 without interest has become final as to Baker, and his liability is finally fixed by it. . . .

"Since the obligation of a surety is accessory to that of a principal debtor, it follows as a corollary that the liability of the surety is ordinarily measured by the liability of the principal, and cannot exceed it. So, generally, the surety is not liable if the principal is not." . . . Thus it is clear that plaintiff is not entitled to a judgment against the sureties for interest from May 28, 1940, as ordered by the Court of Appeals.

The judgment for the sureties is reversed and the cause remanded with directions to enter judgment against them for $640.34 with interest at 6 percent from the date of the judgment against their principal, namely, April 18, 1951.

PROBLEMS FOR DISCUSSION

1. Denver and Gary were both officers of Sunny Mobile Homes, Inc. Both of them had indorsed several of the company's notes for loans to it. They had also signed a guaranty agreement for the loans, which stated: "Liability hereunder is not affected or impaired by any surrender, compromise, settlement, release, renewal, extension, authorization, substitution, exchange, modification, or other disposition of any of said indebtedness and obligations." At one point, all of the company's outstanding loans were consolidated into one renewal note. Gary signed the renewal note, but Denver did not. Denver now claims that his liability as guarantor was discharged by a novation between the bank (the lender), the company (Sunny), and Gary, since the renewal note did not include his signature. What result, and why?

2. James was branch manager for a large construction firm, Charles Company. Over an 11-month period, James stole some 200 checks made out by customers to the company, indorsed them "Charles Company by James," and cashed them at Modern Market. Modern Market then indorsed the checks and deposited them to its account at the Birdie Bank. When Charles Company discovered the thefts, it collected the total loss (over $175,000) from Bonding Company, which had issued a fidelity bond on James. Charles assigned all its rights against James, Modern, and Birdie Bank to Bonding. Bonding sues Birdie Bank, which claims that it is not liable to Bonding based on the assignment. What result, and why?

3. Piggy Bank sued Hot Dog Shops, Inc., on a promissory note for $35,000. Piggy also sued Clem, Hot Dog's president, on a guaranty contract which he had signed per-

sonally at the same time he had executed the note for the corporation. No dollar amount appeared on the guaranty contract. In one blank space on the guaranty form, someone filled in "Hot Dog Shops, Inc.," before the word *Dollars*. The other space provided on the form for writing in an amount was simply left blank. The trial court gave summary judgment for Piggy against both defendants. Clem appeals. How should the appeals court rule, and why?

4. Statutes in the state of Georgia require drivers of motor vehicles to provide proof of financial responsibility in order to be licensed to drive. This requirement may be met either by buying normal liability insurance or by posting a financial responsibility bond. Veeman and Brubeck were involved in a car accident in which Brubeck was killed. At the time of the accident, Veeman had a family car insurance policy with $30,000 liability coverage, issued by Conklin Insurance, and had also posted a financial responsibility bond for $20,000, issued by Regressive Insurance. The Conklin policy provided that it would pay only a pro rata part of any claim if the insured had "other insurance" in force when the loss occurred. The Regressive bond provided that if the principal (Veeman) had insurance in force, the amount of the bond would be "excess protection over and above the amount of such insurance." Brubeck's estate sues Veeman and both insurance companies. Conklin says that it is liable for only three fifths of any judgment, up to a maximum of $30,000; Regressive says that it is not liable at all unless the estate gets a judgment for more than $30,000. Who's right, and why?

5. Underhand was the sole shareholder in Homeright, Inc., a mobile home dealer. Homeright's inventory of mobile homes was financed through a floor-planning arrangement with Esanel bank. Esanel provided the funds to buy the units from the manufacturers and was to be repaid from the proceeds as the units were sold by Homeright. Underhand had signed this floor-planning contract as a guarantor. Underhand had hired Dwayne to manage the business and only stopped by about once a month to see how things were going. Over a period of nine months, Dwayne sold about $70,000 worth of trailers which he did not report to the bank or to Underhand. Esanel sues Underhand on his guaranty. Underhand claims that Esanel was negligent in failing to adequately inspect the mobile home inventory to make sure that its collateral was in place and that this negligence discharges his liability as guarantor. What result, and why?

6. Pennsey Corporation entered into a contract with Demac Construction for the erection of a building which Pennsey intended to lease to Major Motors. As required by the contract, Demac bought a performance bond from Bayside Casualty. The bond stated that the construction contract "is by reference made a part hereof." The contract contained an arbitration clause. Problems and delays occurred when the city objected to the height of the building, and Pennsey and Demac asked for arbitration. Bayside was not notified of the arbitration hearing and did not participate. The arbitrator ruled that Demac was in default on the construction contract. Pennsey sues Bayside to collect on the performance bond and says that the arbitrator's decision is at least prima facie evidence of the validity of its claim against Demac. Bayside argues that it never agreed to arbitrate and that it can't be bound at all by a proceeding in which it didn't participate. Who's right, and why?

7. Enbee Bank bought a fidelity bond from Fidip Company, covering losses of up to $1 million resulting from the dishonest acts of its employees. Enbee's executive vice president, Cansen, embezzled $906,000. Enbee Bank sues Fidip to collect on the bond, Fidip makes two arguments: (1) the bond terminated because the bank had had notice of prior dishonest acts by Cansen and did not fire him; and (2) if Fidip is liable to the Bank, it has a right of subrogation against the bank's officers and directors for negligently failing to supervise Cansen. Are these arguments valid? Discuss.

8. Ducky Stores contracted with Ceevee Company for the construction of a building. Ceevee provided a performance bond purchased from Yewes Bonding, which named Ducky Stores as the Obligee and stated that Yewes would "repay to said Obligee all sums of money which the said Obligee may pay to other persons on account of work and labor done or materials furnished on or for said contract." Ceevee subcontracted the installation of the electrical system to Louie Lighting. Louie did the electrical work as agreed, at a price of $8,200, but it was not paid. Ceevee became bankrupt. Louie sues Yewes on the performance bond. Yewes says that it is not liable to Louie but only to the named Obligee, Ducky Stores. What result, and why?

Part VIII
Property Relationships

29 | Introduction to Property Law

HUMAN RIGHTS, PROPERTY RIGHTS AND PERSONAL RIGHTS

You'll often hear it stated, particularly by proponents of various regulatory and wealth redistribution schemes, that "human rights are more important than property rights." By any meaningful set of definitions, that statement is illogical and ridiculous. The *things* which are the subject matter of property rights—cars, books, TVs, parcels of real estate—have no "rights" at all, in and of themselves. Property *rights* are held by persons, including human beings and corporate persons and various other kinds of legal entities. Among the most important rights of human beings are property rights—the right to acquire, possess, use, enjoy, and dispose of the things which are the subject matter of those rights. Your TV set has no "rights"; *you* do: The right to acquire it, to watch it when you want to, to turn it off when you want to study, and to sell it or give it away (when it's paid for). At least equally important is your property right in the results of your labor—the money and other rewards you earn through your physical and mental efforts. Those things are yours because you worked for them, and your "property rights" protect your freedom to save or spend, as you see fit, when you wish, where you wish. Property rights are very important to all of us as individual human beings. They are what enables us to enjoy music, art, poetry, literature, and all sorts of leisure and productive activity. In short, they are a large part of what separates us from the beasts of the jungle and makes life worth living.

WHAT IS PROPERTY?

Property may be defined as the bundle of rights concerning a specific parcel of land or any other thing of value, tangible or intangible, visible or invisible. Some of the rights included in this bundle of rights are the right to possess, to use, to sell, to lease, to dispose of, or to destroy the land or thing in a legal way and the right to exclude others from trespassing or interfering with the land or thing. Since property may be described as the bundle of rights concerning land or a thing, we often find that we do not have absolute or unconditional property since someone else may have certain rights in the land or thing. For example, although the owner of a parcel of land may say, "That is my property," the parcel of land may be leased to a tenant and thus the tenant has property rights in the land—the right to use it and the right to use the proceeds from it according to the terms of the lease contract. Also, a public utility company may have an easement across the parcel of land, allowing it to come in and repair or replace underground or overhead power lines. An easement is simply a right to enter upon the land of another for a specific purpose. If the land is situated in an area where there are mineral, oil, or gas deposits, the rights to the mineral, oil, or gas deposits may be owned by a person or persons other than the landowner. Moreover, if the purchaser of the land took out a purchase-money mortgage, that is, if he or she borrowed money to buy the land, the mortgagee has certain rights in the land as security for payment of the mortgage. Thus it is not uncommon for several persons to have property in the same land.

We normally tend to think of property in terms of tangible and visible objects or things, such as cars, furniture, houses, and land. However, there is also property in intangible things, such as patents granted by the U.S. Patent Office or copyrights granted by the U.S. Copyright Office. Here the property is simply the right to prevent others from using your invention or copying your book, your song, or other copyrighted material and to secure damages from those persons who do so without your permission.

The following case is an example of a copyright infringement action whose primary purpose was not to win money damages but to stop "music pirates" from illegally copying records and to seize the equipment and machinery that were being used to copy the records. This case also reviews the compulsory license provision of the copyright act. The patent law does not have any such provision. If a patent owner does not give others permission to use the patent, they may not do so.

Duchess Music Corp. v. *Stern et al.*
458 F.2d 1305 (1972)

FACTS This was a copyright infringement action. Duchess Music Corporation, the plaintiff, owned the copyrights to musical compositions by Elvis Presley, Johnny Cash, and other well-known performers. The defendants were alleged to be music pirates who made cassette tapes of phonograph records issued by Duchess Music Corporation from copyrighted compositions. The plaintiff found the location of these music pirates and secured a temporary restraining order and a writ of seizure from a U.S. district court. A U.S. marshall seized and impounded equipment and machinery used to copy tapes. Also seized were 25,000 completed tape copies of records and many blank tapes. The defendants objected to the seizure at a hearing in U.S. district court, and the court ordered the return of all tape recording machinery and equipment, blank tapes, and unmarked packaging materials. The court also held that the defendants could again copy the copyrighted material under the compulsory license provision of the Copyright Act. The plaintiff appealed to the circuit court of appeals.

ISSUE   Does the owner of a copyright have the right to seize and impound illegal copies and the machinery and equipment used to manufacture such copies? Does the compulsory license provision of the Copyright Act allow an alleged infringer to make tape recordings of phonograph records produced by the copyright owner?

DECISION   The appellate court reversed the decision of the district court. The appellate court held that it was proper to seize illegal copies of records and any equipment or machinery which was used to make them. The court also held that the compulsory license provision of the Copyright Act did not allow the defendants to copy the plaintiff's records; it simply allowed a party to record the copyright owner's songs if the party hired musicians, artists, and technicians and if it paid royalty to the copyright owner.

REASONS   The court stated: ''The Copyright Act of 1909 provides for injunctive and monetary relief for infringement, and also for impoundment and destruction of infringing articles.'' The court further stated: ''In dealing with copyright infringers, Congress did not halt at injunctive and monetary relief. It prescribed impoundment and destruction.'' The court went on to explain that Congress intended to allow not only the seizure and impoundment of the infringing copies but of all the equipment used to make them even though some of that equipment could be used for other purposes.

   With regard to the compulsory license provision, the court quoted Seciton 1(e) of the Copyright Act: ''And as a condition of extending the copyright control of such mechanical reproductions, that whenever the owner of a musical copyright has used or permitted or . . . knowingly acquiesced in the use of the copyrighted work, any other person may make similar use of the copyrighted work, upon payment to the copyright proprietor of a royalty of 2 cents on each such part manufactured, to be paid by the manufacturer thereof. . . .''

   The question which the court had to resolve was the interpretation of the phrase *similar use.* The court stated that the copying of the plaintiff's records onto tapes was not ''similar use.'' The court explained that the defendants could record the plaintiff's copyrighted songs if they hired musicians, artists, and technicians, and then paid a royalty for use of the songs. Here the defendants were simply stealing the genius and talent of others. The court found that the defendants had no legal right to copy the plaintiff's records.

CLASSIFICATIONS OF PROPERTY

1. Real Property.   When we speak of real property we are referring to land and to any buildings or permanent fixtures which have been erected on or affixed to land. Crops, trees, or any other objects that are growing on land are generally considered real property until they are severed from the land.

2. Personal Property.   This term is used to designate anything of value which is subject to ownership and is not classified as real property. Personal property can be divided into two classifications, tangible and intangible. Tangible personal property includes animals, furniture, books, clothes, many kinds of personal items, and merchandise in stores. Intangible personal property includes a person's rights in patents, copyrights, corporate shares of stock, insurance policies, and many similar legal documents.

3. Public Property.   This term is used to designate the land and things which are owned by the national government, a state government, a city, or some other political subdivision and are therefore considered to be owned by the public, the people in general. This classification includes parks, public buildings, the national archives, and so on.

4. Private Property.   In contrast to public property, this is property belonging to an individual or a corporation or other private legal entity. The property of Notre Dame University is private property, whereas the property of Michigan State University is public property.

TYPES OF OWNERSHIP

1. Ownership in Severalty.   This is ownership in the name of one person, with no one else having any legal interest in the real or personal property involved.

2. Tenancy in Common.   Here there are two or more co-owners of real property or personal property. Under this type of co-ownership, the co-owners or cotenants have equal rights to possess and use the property. A co-owner's interest in a tenancy in common may be transferred by a last will and testament, may be sold, and is subject to levy of execution by a creditor who has secured a judgment against the owner.

Tenants in common need not be equal owners. For example, grandfather had a will which said that all of his property would be divided equally among his children and that any deceased child's share should go to that child's children. When grandfather died, only one of his children survived him, the other two having predeceased him. However, one of the deceased children had five children and the other had four. Thus one third of grandfather's real and personal property went to his surviving child and the third which was willed to each of his other children was co-owned by their children. Thus all of the heirs are tenants in common, yet not all of the tenants in common have equal shares.

In this example, the heirs could continue as tenants in common and any rents or profits from the property would have to be divided according to the proportionate share of each person, or the entire property or parts of the property could be sold and the money received from the sale would be divided according to each person's proportionate share. Often the parties prefer not to have the property sold and they ask the probate court to divide up the property in accordance with their various shares. With a divisible property such as farmland, the court would divide up the acreage according to the interests of the parties. In addition to arising from inherited property, tenancy in common arises when title to real or personal property is transferred to two or more persons and it is not declared to be joint tenancy or tenancy by the entirety.

3. Joint Tenancy. Joint tenancy is a form of co-ownership where certain land or personal property is owned by two or more persons. These persons enjoy equal rights to share in the use and profits of the property involved, but if any one of the joint tenants dies, the entire property passes to the surviving joint tenants. If Charlie Jones, Sam Smith, and Harvey Brown owned an acre of land as joint tenants with right of survivorship and Charlie Jones died, then Charlie's interest would simply pass automatically to Sam Smith and Harvey Brown. Charlie Jones' heirs would receive nothing. Then, if Sam Smith died, Harvey Brown would own the property in severalty. The interest of a joint tenant cannot be willed to the joint tenant's heirs because the deceased's interest terminates at death.

Joint tenancy is not necessarily a "till death do us part" ownership. A joint tenant may sell and convey his or her share in the joint tenancy, and if this is done, the joint tenancy is severed and the tenants or co-owners become tenants in common. Also, a joint tenant's interest is subject to the rights of his or her creditors, and these creditors may secure judgment and levy execution against the joint tenant's interest and have that interest sold and the joint tenancy severed.

Historically, joint tenancy was only applicable to real estate. Today, however, one can have a joint tenancy in almost any type of personal property—bank accounts, stock shares, automobiles, and so on.

Many states have passed specific joint tenancy statutes which modify the common-law concept, and thus the applicable state law must be referred to in any case involving a joint tenancy relationship.

In the following case the parties attempted to create a joint tenancy relationship and the legality of the deed was questioned in court.

Cleaver v. *Long*
126 N.E.2d 479 (Ohio, 1955)

FACTS This was an action to determine the validity and legal effect of a quitclaim deed. The deed was signed by Marion E. Cleaver and Florence Cleaver, husband and wife, as grantors conveying to themselves as joint tenants with the right of survivorship, and not as tenants in common. At the time the deed was signed, Mr. Cleaver owned the real estate and his wife, Florence, had a right of dower which would have given her a one-third interest in the real estate if she survived her husband. The intent of the deed was to change the title from tenancy in common to joint tenancy with the right of survivorship.

ISSUE Can a husband legally convey his real estate directly to himself and his wife and create a joint tenancy relationship?

DECISION Yes. The deed was held to be effective as an instrument creating the relationship of joint tenancy with the right of survivorship, and not as tenants in common, and upon the death of either Mr. or Mrs. Cleaver, the real estate would become the absolute property in fee simple of the survivor.

4. Tenancy by the Entirety. Tenancy by the entirety is essentially a joint tenancy with the right of survivorship; however, it is limited to a husband-and-wife relationship. The prime characteristc which distinguishes tenancy by the entirety from joint tenancy is that tenancy by the entirety cannot be changed except by joint action of the husband and wife during their lifetimes, whereas a joint tenancy with the right of survivorship is terminated when any one of the tenants conveys his or her interest or when a levy of execution is made by a creditor against a joint tenant's interest. If a husband and wife take title to a home as tenants by the entireties and the husband has a judgment rendered against him for damages that result from an automobile accident, the person who was awarded the damages cannot have the judgment executed against the home. If, however, both the husband and wife are jointly liable on a debt, then the creditor may secure a judgment and execute it against the home.

Like joint tenancy, tenancy by the entirety was historically confined to real estate ownership and did not extend to ownership of personal property. However, some states have extended the concept to personal property. About 20 states recognize tenancy by the entirety, but here again the state laws are not uniform and the individual state law must be referred to in each case.

A problem that often arises in tenancies by the entirety involves the fact that these can only apply where there is a husband-and-wife relationship. What happens when the parties seek a divorce or a legal separation? The following case involves this problem.

D'Ercole v. *D'Ercole*
407 F. Supp. 1377 (1976)

FACTS   Mary E. D'Ercole, the estranged wife of Alghier D'Ercole, brought suit in the U.S. district court in Massachusetts seeking declaratory and injunctive relief. She claimed that the common-law concept of tenancy by the entirety deprived her of due process and equal protection of the law in that it gave her husband the right of possession and control of their home during his lifetime.

The plaintiff and the defendant bought a house in 1962 and then separated in

1971. Proceedings for legal separation and for divorce were pending in the Middlesex County Probate Court. The defendant husband was seeking a divorce. The plaintiff wife was seeking a separation and vehemently opposed a divorce on factual and religious grounds. The husband had refused to share their marital home with the plaintiff by allowing her sole occupancy for part of the year, by selling the house and dividing the proceeds, by paying the plaintiff her share of the equity of the house, or by renting the premises and dividing the proceeds. In support of his position, the husband pointed out that the property in question was held under a tenancy by the entirety which gave both him and his wife an indefeasible right of survivorship but gave him the exclusive right to possession and control during his lifetime. He stated that he would grant the plaintiff one half of the equity in the house if she would grant him an uncontested divorce.

ISSUE Does the separation of husband and wife end tenancy by the entirety? Does the common-law concept of tenancy by the entirety deprive the plaintiff of the due process and equal protection of the law guaranteed by the Constitution and the Bill of Rights?

DECISION No, the separation of married persons does not end tenancy by the entirety even if that separation is ratified by a formal court decree. Divorce does terminate tenancy by the entirety and it allows the parties to divide the property or the proceeds. No, the common-law concept of tenancy by the entirety does not deprive the plaintiff of her constitutional rights to due process and equal protection of the law.

REASON The court stated: "When two or more persons wish to hold property together in Massachusetts they may select one of three common law forms of ownership: the tenancy in common, joint tenancy, or tenancy by the entirety." The court went on to explain: "The tenancy by the entirety is designed particularly for married couples and may be employed only by them. Until 1973 unless there was clear language to the contrary a conveyance to a married couple was presumed to create a tenancy by the entirety. This form of property ownership differs from the joint tenancy in two respects. First, each tenant has an indefeasible right of survivorship in the entire tenancy, which cannot be defeated by any act taken individually by either spouse during his or her lifetime. There can be no partition. Second, the spouses do not have an equal right to control and possession of the property. The husband during his lifetime has paramount rights in the property. In the event of divorce the tenancy by the entirety becomes a tenancy in common unless the divorce decree reflects that a joint tenancy is intended."

In answer to the charge that the law was illegal because it discriminated on grounds of sex, the court stated: "[I]t is true that the only Massachusetts tenancy tailored exclusively for married persons appears to be balanced in favor of males. There is no equivalent female-biased tenancy, nor is there a "neutral" married persons' tenancy providing for indefeasible survivorship but not vesting paramount lifetime rights in the male. Married couples may, it is true, elect a joint tenancy, a tenancy in common, or a sole tenancy. . . . A wife who wants the security of indefeasible survivorship can achieve it only by means of a male-dominated tenancy."

Thus the court in the above case simply felt that since there was a choice among the three forms of property ownership and since there did not appear to be any evidence of fraud, coercion, or wrongdoing, the husband and wife must now live with the choice that they had made. It should also be noted here that with the increased concern of legislatures concerning the problems of sex discrimination in the various areas of the law, we may see legislative changes concerning the effect of the tenancy by the entirety relationship as between husband and wife.

5. Community Property. Only eight states currently use the community property system. The main feature of the community property system is that property acquired after marriage by either the husband or the wife automatically becomes the joint property of the husband and wife. Under the common law, if a husband earned $50,000 per year, he was legally obligated to provide the necessities for his wife's support with that amount; however, his wife had no rights in any money over and above that amount which was required to provide the necessities for her support. Also, under the common law, if a wife were employed outside of the home, her income was also her husband's. Under the community property theory, the income and the property acquired by both parties are simply put into the pot, so to speak, and the parties share and share alike. Possible exceptions to the joint ownership of property acquired after marriage would be property acquired by gift or inheritance or property received in exchange for property owned by one of the parties prior to the marriage.

The community property system is a statutory type of ownership which, if it is adopted by a specific state, will cover all of the persons in the relationship of husband and wife who are subject to that statute. Unlike the previous types of ownership discussed in this chapter, it is not a voluntary type of ownership. Also, the various states which have adopted this form of ownership have not followed any uniform pattern. Answers to such questions as whether a spouse's share in the community property will descend to his or her heirs or will automatically go to the surviving spouse, or whether the spouse's share is subject to levy of execution of creditors, or how the property is to be divided in case of divorce must be determined by looking at the specific statute of the state involved. The eight states that have community property laws at present are Arizona, California, Idaho, Louisiana, New Mexico, Nevada, Texas, and Washington.

6. Condominium Ownership. Today we are seeing a rapid growth in condominium ownership. Condominium ownership is a combination of ownership in severalty and tenancy in common. Condominiums are multiple-unit buildings or developments of several buildings where an owner owns his or her own apartment or building and the land and common areas used by all tenants are owned by them as tenants in common. For example, each condominium owner in a 100-unit development may own a one-hundredth share of the total land and of such common areas as walks and hallways. The owners of the various individual apartments or buildings pay a management fee to a condominium corporation to manage the complex and keep the common areas repaired, cleaned, and so on.

Nearly all of the states have enacted some type of condominium law to regulate condominium ownership and construction. These laws vary from state to state, and a person should be familiar with the particular state condominium law before making any decisions regarding condominium ownership or construction.

7. Time-Sharing Ownership. This is a new property concept which has been developed in recent years, particularly with regard to resort properties.

The theory of time-sharing ownership is very simple. In the past, you purchased a condominium in Florida, hoping to rent it out for most of the year and to reserve it for yourself for two months in the winter. The problem was that the capital investment was quite sizable. Now you can simply buy the right to use a condominium unit or an apartment in a resort area for a specific period of time, perhaps 2 weeks a year; the other 50 weeks are sold to other individuals. You have simply purchased two weeks of use per year for your life or forever, as the case may be. You can trade your two weeks to one of the other time-share owners if you want to use the apartment at a different time, or you can sell or lease your right to use the apartment. The obvious benefit of time-sharing ownership is that you have to pay only a fraction of the total value of the unit and yet you do own an exclusive right to use the unit for a specific time every year.

As with condominium ownership, there may be specific state laws regulating this type of ownership, so before any decision is made regarding such purchases, the laws of the state where the real estate is located should be reviewed.

RIGHTS OF GOVERNMENTS VERSUS RIGHTS OF INDIVIDUAL PROPERTY OWNERS

Property rights are not absolute; they are subject to government regulations and intervention. The national, state, and local governments have the right to take your property by eminent domain. This is the right of the government to assert, either temporarily or permanently, dominion over property, real or personal, for a public purpose, such as the right to take your land for a highway or a school. You will, of course, be paid a fair and reasonable price for the property, but you have no choice if it is determined that eminent domain is in the best interest of the public. Also, in time of war or insurrection, authorities may take over your land and your buildings or other personal objects.

The local area planning and zoning board may regulate the use of your land. For example, some areas are zoned for single-family dwellings only; other areas are zoned for multiple-family dwellings; and still other areas are zoned for industry. Criminal laws may restrict the ownership by individuals of guns or other deadly weapons or explosives. In addition, the government may tax your real and personal property, and if you fail to pay the tax, the property may be sold at a tax sale.

Thus, in the chapters that follow, remember that when we refer to a person's property we are referring to a bundle of rights, not all of which are necessarily possessed by the same person. Remember also that all property rights are subject to governmental seizure, regulation, and taxation, in accordance with due process of law under national and state constitutions.

29. Introduction to Property Law

CASES FOR DISCUSSION

HISQUIERDO v. HISQUIERDO

99 S. Ct. 802 (U.S. Supreme Court, 1979)

Blackmun, Justice

Petitioner Jess H. Hisquierdo in 1975 sued to dissolve his marriage with respondent Angela Hisquierdo. The Supreme Court of California, in applying the State's community property rules, awarded respondent an interest in petitioner's expectation of ultimately receiving benefits under the Railroad Retirement Act of 1974. . . . The issue here is whether the Act prohibits this allocation and division of benefits.

The Railroad Retirement Act, first passed in 1934, 48 Stat. 1283, provides a system of retirement and disability benefits for persons who pursue careers in the railroad industry. Its sponsors felt that the Act would encourage older workers to retire by providing them with the means "to enjoy the closing days of their lives with peace of mind and physical comfort," and so would "assure more rapid advancement in the service" and also more jobs for younger workers. Both employees and carriers pay a federal tax which funds a Railroad Retirement Account. The Railroad Retirement Board, provided for by the Act, . . . disburses benefits from the account to each eligible "individual." . . .

In its modern form, the Act resembles both a private pension program and a social welfare plan. It provides two tiers of benefits. The upper tier, like a private pension, is tied to earnings and career service. An employee, to be eligible for benefits, must work in the industry 10 years. Absent disability, no benefit is paid, however, until the employee either reaches age 62 or is at least 60 years old and has completed 30 years of service. . . . Like a social welfare or insurance scheme, the taxes paid by and on behalf of an employee do not necessarily correlate with the benefits to which the employee may be entitled. . . .

The lower, and larger, tier of benefits corresponds exactly to those an employee would expect to receive were he covered by the Social Security Act. . . . The Act provides special benefits for the children or parent of a worker who dies. . . . It also makes detailed provision for a worker's spouse; the spouse qualifies for an individual benefit if the spouse lives with the employee, and receives regular contributions from the employee for support, or is entitled to support from the employee pursuant to a court order. The benefits terminate, however, when the spouse and the employee are absolutely divorced. . . .

Like Social Security, and unlike most private pension plans, railroad retirement benefits are not contractual. Congress may alter, and even eliminate, them at any time. This vulnerability to congressional edict contrasts strongly with the protection Congress has afforded recipients from creditors, taxgatherers, and all those who would "anticipate" the receipt of benefits:

Notwithstanding any other law of the United States, or of any State, territory, or the District of Columbia, no annuity or supplemental annuity shall be assignable or be subject to any tax or to garnishment, attachment, or other legal process under any circumstances whatsoever, nor shall the payment thereof be anticipated. . . .

In 1975, Congress made an exception to § 213m and similar provisions in all other federal benefit plans. Concerned about recipients who were evading support obligations and thereby throwing children and divorced spouses on the public dole, Congress amended the Social Security Act by adding a new provision, § 459, to the effect that, notwithstanding any contrary law, federal benefits may be reached to satisfy a legal obligation for child support or alimony. . . . In 1977, shortly before the issuance of the Supreme Court of California's opinion in this case, Congress added to the Social Security Act a definitional statute, § 462(c), which relates to § 459 and limits "alimony" to its traditional common-law meaning of spousal support. That statute states specifically that "alimony"

does not include any payment or transfer of property or its value by an individual to his spouse or former spouse in compliance with any community property settlement, equitable distribution of property, or other division of property between spouses or former spouses. . . .

On the theory that petitioner acquired an expectation of receiving Railroad Retirement Act benefits due in part to his labors while married, respondent (but not petitioner) in California divorce proceeding listed that expectation as an item of community property subject to division upon dissolution of the marriage. . . .

Respondent calculated that she was entitled to half the benefits attributable to his labor during the 14 years of their marriage, or, by her estimate, 19.6 percent of the total benefits to be received. The couple had no children.

Respondent in 1975 was 53. She had worked for the preceding eight years in a factory. She had been gainfully employed for 35 years and had an expectation that upon her retirement she would be entitled to benefits under the Social Security Act. Neither petitioner nor respondent claimed that her expectation of receiving those benefits was community property. . . .

Insofar as marriage is within temporal control, the States lay on the guiding hand. . . . On rare occasions when state family law has come into conflict with a federal statute, this Court has limited review under the Supremacy Clause to a determination whether Congress has "positively required by direct enactment that state law be pre-empted." . . . State family and family-property law must do "major damage" to "clear and substantial" federal interests before the Supremacy Clause will demand that state law be overridden. . . .

Here, California must defer to the federal statutory scheme for allocating Railroad Retirement Act benefits insofar as the terms of federal law require. The critical terms here include a specified beneficiary protected by a flat prohibition against attachment and anticipation. . . .

Congress has made a choice, and § 213m protects it. It is for Congress to decide how these finite funds are to be allocated. The statutory balance is delicate. Congress has fixed an amount thought appropriate to support an employee's old age and to encourage the employee to retire. Any automatic diminution of that amount frustrates the congressional objective. By reducing benefits received, it discourages the divorced employee from retiring. And it provides the employee with an incentive to keep working, because the former spouse has no community property claim to salary earned after the marital community is dissolved. Section 213m shields the distribution of benefits from state decisions that would actually reverse the flow of incentives Congress originally intended.

ABBEY, PUBLIC ADMINISTRATOR v. LORD

336 P.2d 226 (California, 1959)

Griffin, Justice

In July, 1950, defendant-appellant Joseph R. Lord married Regina Dion. He had a separate estate of approximately $12,000, and she had one valued at approximately $20,000. In December, 1953, they separated under a property settlement agreement. They agreed to divide and apportion their properties in accordance with the contributions each had made to the common fund at the time of their marriage. Under the agreement defendant received about $12,338.87 and Mrs. Lord $20,958.83. An interlocutory decree of divorce was obtained by Mrs. Lord. They later agreed to return to live together as husband and wife, and according to Mr. Lord, in consideration of his returning to live with her, they agreed to pool their assets and that each would have a one-half interest therein. Later, some domestic or financial difficulty arose between them. On February 20,

1956, Joseph Lord killed his wife Regina. He was charged with murder, and he entered a plea of guilty of manslaughter. The court determined the same to be voluntary. Probation was granted upon the condition, among other things, that defendant serve one year in the county jail. Thereafter, plaintiff, the public administrator, was appointed to administer her estate and brought an action against Joseph Lord to quiet title, to establish a constructive trust in the property, and to obtain declaratory relief.

After they resumed marital relationship and at the time of her death the parties owned, as tenants in common: (a) a fully paid investment certificate No. 10,029, in the sum of $10,000; (b) investment certificate No. 11,020 in the sum of $3,370.95; (c) investment certificate No. 9522 in the sum of $10,299.63; (d) a bank account in the sum of $2,323.77, claimed by Mr. Lord to be in joint tenancy with his wife; and (e) 500 shares of telephone stock value at $5,000, likewise held in joint tenancy, all totaling $30,994.35.

The trial court found after taking considerable evidence, that all of the property was owned by them as tenants in common except the 500 shares of telephone stock, which was held in joint tenancy; that when defendant husband killed his wife, he destroyed the joint tenancy and thereby converted the stock into a tenancy in common; that it would be unconscionable for defendant to recover out of the common estate more than he ever owned of it or contributed to it; that he only contributed separate property worth 37 per cent of its total value and Regina contributed separate property worth 63 per cent thereof at the time of their marriage and each regained the same proportionate amounts by virtue of the executed property settlement agreement; and that Regina Lord never made any gift or transfer of ownership of any of her separate property to defendant and at the time of her death she was still the owner of 63 per cent of the common estate held with defendant. Judgment was entered that plaintiff's title to 63 per cent of the common fund in cash value, equivalent to $19,526.44, be quieted, together with 63 per cent of the gross income accumulated since her death.

It is the defendant's position that he was entitled to a one-half interest in items (a), (b), and (c), and was entitled to the full amount of items (d) and (e) because of the joint tenancy holding, he being the survivor. . . .

Some question arises as to the nature of the holding in reference to item (d), the bank account. Plaintiff produced a banker who testified he opened the account for these parties on October 26, 1954, and prepared the signature card and ledger sheet; that Mrs. Lord did all of the talking about it even though Mr. Lord stood by and listened; that Mrs. Lord said she wanted to put the money in the bank so Mr. Lord could not get it without her knowing it or without her signature; that she referred to it as "my money"; that the bank used the same card for joint and common accounts; that the Lord transaction was unusual and that he explained to her that if he opened an account requiring both signatures neither could draw money without the signature of the other; and she said that was the way she wanted it. The ledger sheet used the word "and" between the two signatures and used no words indicating a joint tenancy account. It was marked "Both signatures required." The signature card reads in part as follows: "(1) That this account is to be carried by such bank as a commercial account . . . (2) That all funds now to the credit of or which may hereafter be placed to the credit of account are and shall be the property of the undersigned as joint tenants to be withdrawn as follows: . . . Both signatures required." In this connection the banker testified that he asked Mrs. Lord if she wanted the account in joint tenancy; that he told her in that case what would happen to the money in the event of the death of one party and said it was unusual to open a joint tenancy account requiring both signatures; that she said she did not know what joint tenancy meant but she wanted it arranged so that both would have to sign for withdrawals.

Defendant Lord testified in reference to another bank account in Los Gatos opened by them both in names that he "didn't know anything about joint tenancy or joint accounts or anything like that": that "it was both names" and knew he did not have the privilege of withdrawing money from it without both signatures; that she could not do so either; and that the account in the Santa Ana bank was opened under the same arrangement.

It is concluded that the telephone stock (*e*) was held in joint tenancy. Appellant contends that the taking of title in the name of the spouses as joint tenants is tantamount to a binding agreement between them that the same shall not thereafter be held as common property but instead as joint tenancy with all the characteristics of such an estate. . . .

While this is the general rule it has long been held that the character of property thus held may be changed by executed oral agreement between the parties. . . . It has likewise been held that to create a joint tenancy interest it is necessary to comply with section 683 of the Civil Code. At common law, estates in joint tenancy were favored over tenancies in common, and it was necessary to add restrictive words to limit the grantees' estate to that of tenancy in common. This rule has been abrogated by statute in this state. The intention to create a joint tenancy must now appear expressly in the instrument. Without such a declaration there is no compliance with the statute and no joint tenancy results. . . .

In view of the evidence and circumstances related, the trial court was not bound to accept the testimony of Mr. Lord that his wife Regina said she was making a gift of a portion of her separate property to Lord, or that they thereafter agreed to hold their property "fifty–fifty." . . . [T]he court held that the uncorroborated testimony as to an oral declaration of a deceased person is the weakest form of evidence and is open to suspicion; but where admissible, it may be weighed by the trier of facts the same as other evidence and may be disregarded where shown to be unconvincing or insubstantial, or because of the witness' interest in the outcome of the case and close relationship. . . . It may be further observed that even Lord's testimony, set forth in his deposition, indicates that he was at least in doubt as to the intended nature of the joint tenancy bank account.

Although it might well appear that a joint tenancy account was never intended, we conclude, under the reasoning hereinafter expressed in respect to the claimed destruction of the joint tenancy holding pertaining to item (*e*), the telephone stock, it will be unnecessary to determine this issue.

Appellant urges in substance this proposition, that the logic of the strict common-law rule must be applied to any apparent joint tenancy title; that therefore defendant is the sole owner of any property so held at the instant he killed the other joint tenant, and argues against weight and trend of authority. It seems to us that he is opposed by modern views. The decisive fact in the case at bar is the voluntary, unlawful, and felonious killing of one joint tenant by the other as distinguished from an unintentional killing. It appears that defendant stabbed his wife with a butcher knife in the abdomen and throat, causing her immediate death in an argument over the deceased wife's refusal to join with him in signing a check drawn on the joint tenancy account here involved. The controlling facts cannot possibly be disregarded in a just determination of this case. Conversely, there would seem to be no justification whatsoever for disposing of this case as though Regina Lord had died of natural causes, for no amount of lucubration can dissolve the crucial distinction in circumstances. . . .

In the instant case the trial court concluded that the joint tenancy in the stock was destroyed and terminated by the act of killing the decedent. The court converted the joint tenancy into a tenancy in common. As readily the court could have found the joint tenancy was preserved and that the defendant was a constructive trustee, and that half or all of the property passed thereby to plaintiff. The court however adopted a practical solution fairest to the plaintiff and to the defendant. This court does not believe that it should countenance the addition of homicide as the approved method of terminating a joint tenancy without affecting the results found by the trial court.

It will be remembered that defendant's contention was that his wife, after making the property settlement agreement, later told him if he would return to her she would make a gift of some of her property to him so they would hold their property "fifty-fifty" and that she later did make such a gift and division. Of course the decedent herself was unable to personally rebut that testimony. Over objections of defendant, plaintiff produced witnesses who testified that in December 1955, after the placing of the stock in joint tenancy Mrs. Lord told them she was worried because she had dividend checks coming from them and she had an idea that the defendant had taken them. The witness testified that when the Lords sold their home she wanted to keep her money separate from his, but defendant would not agree, and about four months before she was killed Mrs. Lord told her they had agreed to a divorce, but Mr. Lord wanted half of the property and she wanted all of her property, which was more than half. The argument is that this conversation was hearsay and selfserving, not being in the presence of defendant, and that the hidden intention of one party, not disclosed by the other, was not admissible. . . .

It is the general rule that evidence of intention or mental state of a person at a particular time, when material to an issue under trial, is admissible. . . . The trial court was entitled to draw from this evidence an inference that there never was an oral agreement to divide the property 50–50, as claimed by the defendant, and Mrs. Lord never intended to make a gift of it to him.

No prejudicial error appears in the reception of evidence, and no miscarriage of justice has resulted. We conclude that the trial court applied the sound equitable principles that a man should not profit from his own crime and that no common-law fiction ought to impair the judgment.

PROBLEMS FOR DISCUSSION

1. Annie and Dennie Cracker had been married for six years when they filed a joint petition for divorce. Annie had been employed full time throughout the marriage and had also done most of the couple's housework and cooking. Dennie had worked only part time and had gone to school full time for four out of the six years. He had finished a BS in Engineering and had then received an MBA. The trial court found that the only marital "asset" of any value that the parties had accumulated during the marriage was Dennie's MBA degree. It placed a value of $82,000 on his future extra earnings due to the degree, and it awarded Annie $33,000 of this amount, which Dennie was to pay off at the rate of $100 per month. Dennie appeals from this award, saying his MBA isn't really "property." How should the appeals court rule? Explain.

2. Blaine and Nadyne Waring, husband and wife, owned their home as joint tenants. Blaine's employer told him he was being transferred to the company's office in Utah, so Blaine made arrangements to sell the house. Minnie Maus called Nadyne and asked if the house was for sale. Nadyne said she wasn't sure they wanted to sell, but when Minnie and her husband, Mickey, looked at the house, they offered to buy it for 89,500. Blaine accepted, and he and Mickey went to a lawyer's office where they signed a purchase contract for the house. Mickey gave Blaine a down payment check for $1,000, made out to Blaine and Nadyne. Blaine and Nadyne indorsed and cashed the check. Two weeks later, they found out that Blaine's transfer had been called off and they called Mickey and Minnie and told them the deal for the house was off. The state's homestead statute prohibits the transfer of a family home without the signatures of both spouses. Nadyne never signed the purchase agreement, but Mickey and Minnie say that her signature on the check should be enough. What should the court do with this litigation? Discuss.

3. The University Nook is incorporated as a nonprofit corporation to operate the student bookstore at the University of Tecnosis, a state university. Its board of directors is composed of five students, two faculty members, and one member appointed by the university president. Incorporation of the Nook was originally authorized by

the university's board of governors, and on termination, any assets remaining will revert to the board. The Nook's directors make no reports to the board of governors, and the board does not exercise any other control. The city of Normal, where the Nook is located, sought to impose the city's personal property tax on the Nook's book inventories and other personal property. The Nook claims that it is exempt from local taxation because it is a state agency. Are these assets taxable? Why or why not?

4. Merwin and Marcedes Grisel, husband and wife, owned several pieces of real estate as tenants by the entirety. Merwin moved to Nevada, got a Nevada divorce, and remarried. The Nevada divorce decree made no property division between the spouses, and Marcedes did not participate in the divorce proceedings. Merwin died; his will left all his property, wherever situated, to his second wife, Flora. Marcedes claimed that she owned the tenancy by the entirety property, since the Nevada decree could not (and did not) affect title to property in another state without personal service of process on the defendant spouse. Flora claims that she owns Merwin's half of this real estate, since the divorce made Merwin and Marcedes tenants in common. Which wife prevails, and why?

5. Ulrich and Amanda Alconey were married in 1963. At that time, each had only a small amount of personal assets and savings. When Ulrich petitioned for divorce in 1979, the parties had accumulated considerable asset values and Ulrich was the owner of a very profitable financial consulting firm. When the trial court entered a divorce decree, Ulrich claimed that the court had made two errors in dividing the property: it had excluded the value of jewelry owned by Amanda which she had received as gifts from Ulrich, and it had included $30,000 in fees which Ulrich expected to receive for work to be performed for clients. Ulrich appeals this portion of the decree. How should the appeals court rule here? Discuss.

6. Ben Roberto was the sole record owner of a certain piece of real estate. When this real estate was sold in 1974, the land contract was signed by both Ben and his wife, Inez, as "Sellers." The down payment check for $55,000 was made out to and indorsed by both Ben and Inez. About $100,000 was still due and payable on the contract when Ben died in 1977. Inez claims she owns these funds as the surviving joint owner. Hopeful Hospital, the beneficiary under Ben's will, says that the balance due under this contract is an asset of Ben's estate. Who is right, and why?

7. When their father, Bert Balakowski, died, Billie, Millie, Freida, Sophie, and Karl received the large family farm through his will, as tenants in common. Billie was living in Arizona at the time. The other four children, who were living on or near the farm, decided to sell it. They called Billie, and she agreed to sell too. Karl found a buyer, Casimir Hirpich, and told Casimir that he had authority to speak for all the co-owners. A contract for the sale of the farm was drawn up and signed by Millie, Freida, Sophie, and Karl. When a copy of the contract was mailed to Billie for her signature, she tore it up. Casimir went into possession of the farm and made all the payments called for by the sales contract. Billie now sues to recover possession of the farm. Does she have a case? Explain.

8. Helga Scarface and her husband, Lauren, owned real estate as tenants by the entirety. In 1979 Helga listed the land for sale with Fine Time Realtors. She represented that she was authorized to act for Lauren as well. After some negotiations Helga signed a contract to sell the land to ABM Industries, Inc. She also signed for Lauren, and she showed ABM and Fine Time a power of attorney executed by Lauren. The sale was conditioned on ABM's being able to get the land rezoned for commercial use. After considerable expense ABM did get the land rezoned, but Helga refused to execute a deed and close the deal. When ABM sued for specific

performance, Helga proved that Lauren had been suffering from brain damage when he executed the power of attorney and that he had later been adjudged mentally incompetent. Since the power of attorney was invalid, she says, Lauren never signed the contract and the contract was therefore invalid. Later Lauren died. How should the court resolve this problem? Discuss.

30 | Personal Property

Personal property rights are the bundles of rights in anything of value, either tangible or intangible, that is subject to ownership and is not considered to be real property. These rights include the right to possess, to use, to sell, to lend, and even to destroy these things, subject of course to any restrictions or regulation by state and national laws.

CLASSIFICATION OF PERSONAL PROPERTY

Personal property can be divided into two major classifications: (1) Tangible and movable things which are not attached or annexed to land or a building. In this classification are such things as furniture, clothing, books, and automobiles. These tangible, movable things are called chattels. (2) Property interests in intangibles, such as a promissory note, a stock certificate, an insurance policy, a patent, a copyright, a claim for wages, a right against another party arising out of a contract, or perhaps a right against another party which results from injuries or property damages received in an automobile accident. These intangible property rights are called choses in action.

WHEN DOES PERSONAL PROPERTY BECOME
REAL PROPERTY?

When purchasing a home, the buyer may ask, "Do these drapes go with the house?" "Does this chandelier stay with the house?" "Does the carpet in the family room go with the house?" The crucial legal question here is whether these items which were once personal property have now become fixtures to the real property and are thus a part of the real property and inseparable from it.

Here again, the specific law of the state in which the property is located will determine whether a particular item is still movable personal property or whether it has become a fixture and part of the real property.

Generally speaking, the court will use three guidelines to determine whether an item remains personal property or whether it has become a part of the real property. (1) Has the item become permanently affixed to the land or

612

the building? If an item has been attached to the land or the building in such a manner that it cannot be removed without damaging the building or the land or the item itself, then the item is considered to be part of the real property. If in the family room of a house, the floor is concrete slab and the carpet is glued to the floor, the carpet is typically considered to be part of the real estate and no longer personal property, since removing the carpet would leave a bare unusable floor and would no doubt destroy the carpet. Drapes or curtains can normally be removed from curtain rods or other types of hangers without damaging either the curtains or the fixtures upon which they are hanging. However, the curtain rods themselves are considered permanent fixtures because they are permanently attached to the wall and cannot be removed without leaving holes in it. (2) What was the intent of the owner of the personal property when the personal property was affixed to the real property? Here we may go beyond the actual physical method of affixing the property and look to what the owner's intent was when the property was affixed. (3) How is the property being carried on the books of the business? Is it still considered personal property, or is it considered to be part of the real estate? If a person rents a store building and installs a freezer, counters, showcases, and other equipment necessary to run the store, will these items be considered personal property, or will they be part of the real estate? The freezer may be anchored to the floor with bolts to prevent vibration, and the counters may be anchored to the floor so that they will not be moved around by persons leaning against them. Usually, if a person affixes personal property to the land or building of another, the owner of the land or building becomes the owner of the affixed items. But in a situation such as the above, most courts would probably say that the tenant remains the owner of the items even though it becomes necessary to unbolt them from the floor or to disconnect electric wires or water pipes before the items can be removed from the building. It is normally not the intent of the tenant to make a gift of such items to the landlord.

Intent is really the most important test. However, in many cases there is no evidence of intent other than the actual method of affixing the items to the real estate. The following case shows a court faced with this problem.

Strain v. *Green*
172 P.2d 216 (Washington, 1946)

FACTS   Mr. and Mrs. Jacob Green agreed to sell their house to Mr. and Mrs. Strain. A warranty deed was executed and delivered to the purchasers, and the purchasers paid the purchase price. Then the sellers moved out, and they took the hot-water tank and an enclosed electric heater from the basement. They also took the venetian blinds, certain lighting fixtures and three mirrors which had been firmly attached to the walls. The buyers then requested that these items be returned, and when the sellers refused, the buyers filed this suit.

The trial court held that the automatic hot-water tank was a fixture and must be returned. The venetian blinds were also held to be fixtures and ordered returned. Money damages were awarded with respect to the reinstallation of these items. The

613

trial court, however, then held that the lighting fixtures and mirrors were personal property, which the defendants had a right to remove, and it was from that holding that this appeal was taken.

ISSUE   Are items such as lighting fixtures and mirrors firmly attached to the walls fixtures or personal property?

DECISION   The chandelier and other lighting fixtures are fixtures which were annexed to the real estate and cannot be taken. The mirrors that were physically attached to the walls by bolts or screws are fixtures and may not be removed.

REASONS   All of the items that were taken except one mirror had been attached to the walls or floors. The defendants stated that their reason for taking these items was that they had never intended these items to become a part of the real estate. The court in its opinion addressed that contention as follows: "We do not wish it to be understood that we in any way question the veracity of the respondents, but we are here considering, an alleged rule that may be involved in future cases, and treating the matter wholly impersonally, if a witness testifies that, when he put a chandelier in a house, he intended to take it out if he should ever sell the house, in what possible way can his evidence be disputed? And, passing that, by what ex post facto system of mind reading could a purchaser determine the vendor's state of mind when he installed the chandelier? There is no evidence whatever in the instant case that the respondents told the appellants that they had ever had such an intention until after the appellants had bought, and paid for, the house. If it be held in this case that the secret intention of the defendants is determinative of the question whether or not the articles involved are fixtures, that holding will encourage and invite persons less honest than the respondents to attempt to remove from premises sold every at-all-movable article that can be disconnected without breakage.

"It has never been the law of this jurisdiction, nor, we think, of any other, that the secret intention of the owner who affixed the disputed article, of itself determines whether or not it was a fixture or a personal chattel."

Courts are generally more liberal in permitting removal where items have been attached for the tenant's specific business or agricultural use or to add to the comfort and convenience of a residence. In all of these situations, however, it is advisable to have a clause in the lease specifying what items are to be removable by the tenant and are not to be considered part of the realty even though there is evidence of permanent attachment.

The following case involves personal property described as trade fixtures and discusses the rights of the parties concerning these fixtures.

Central Chrysler Plymouth, Inc. v. Holt
266 N.W.2d 177 (Minnesota, 1978)

FACTS   Central Chrysler Plymouth, Inc. was an automobile dealership which rented a build-ing from Holt. Central had hoists installed in the building for its use in repairing cars. Later Central moved its dealership and agreed to sell the hoists to the new tenant, another automobile dealership. The landlord claimed that Central had no right to sell the hoists as they had become a part of the real estate once they were installed. Central sued Holt and won a judgment. Holt appealed from that judgment.

ISSUE   Are hoists installed by the tenant and firmly attached to the realty to be considered trade fixtures which are removable by the tenant or are subject to sale by the tenant to others?

DECISION   Yes. The hoists were found to be trade fixtures and did not become the property of the landlord.

REASON   The court acknowledged the landlord's contention that items permanently attached to the real estate by a tenant may be considered a part of the realty and thus the property of the owner-landlord. Obviously, the hoists were permanently affixed. However, they could be removed without causing structural damage.

   The court found that these items were trade fixtures which the tenant used in his business and not improvements to the real estate. There was no intent on the tenant's part that these hoists would become the property of the landlord. The court noted that if the tenant had put in new windows or replaced doors or other parts of the structure, those items would have been improvements and would not have been removable when the tenant vacated.

WHEN DOES REAL PROPERTY BECOME PERSONAL PROPERTY?

When a fixture is severed from the real estate, it becomes personal property. A built-in stove and oven in your kitchen is considered part of the real estate and goes with the house. However, if you decide to replace it with a new one and you take it out, once the old stove and oven has been physically severed from the real estate it returns to the status of personal property. Growing timber or growing crops are part of the real estate; however, once they are severed from the real estate they become personal property. Coal in the ground is part of the real estate; however, when it is mined and severed from the ground it becomes personal property.

ACQUISITION OF TITLE TO PERSONAL PROPERTY

Title to personal property may be acquired in many different ways. Acquisition may be the result of voluntary action on the part of the former owner and the new owner, or it may occur simply by the operation of the law. Following are some of the common methods of acquisition of title to personal property.

1. Purchase of Personal Property. When you go to the grocery store and buy groceries for the week you have acquired personal property by purchase. No certificate of title is attached to each item in your grocery sack; mere possession is evidence of title to such items. If you purchase an automobile, or a motorcycle, or a motor home, however, the seller will give you a certificate of title which you then must register with the specific state authorities so that the title can be registered in your name on the state records. If you purchase the equipment and trade fixtures of a business, you will normally require that a bill of sale specifically describe each item or object which is part of the purchase. This bill of sale does not need to be recorded with the state or county; however, it will be your evidence of title.

2. Title to Personal Property by a Gift. Title to personal property may be transferred from one person to other persons by gift. A gift is a voluntary action on the part of the giver, with no expectation of consideration from the person receiving the gift. The transfer of personal property by gift can be divided into three basic classifications. An inter vivos gift is a gift made by a living person to another living person. A gift causa mortis is a gift which is given in contemplation of the giver's death. A testamentary gift is a gift which is given in a person's will. The three types of gifts differ mainly with regard to revocability. Once an inter vivos gift has been delivered, it is generally irrevocable. Since a gift causa mortis is made in contemplation of death, if the giver recovers, then the giver can have the property back. The causa mortis gift may be revoked by the giver before he or she dies. It may also be revoked if the person to whom the gift is made dies before the giver dies. A testamentary gift may be revoked by revoking or amending the will.

The question often arises as to when an inter vivos gift becomes effective. There are two tests which must be met. First, it must be shown that the giver intended to divest himself or herself of certain rights in the property. It is not necessary that all rights be given in order for a gift to be valid. For example, an owner of corporate stock may give the dividends of the stock to another person but retain ownership of the actual shares of stock. Intent may be evidenced by a writing, by actions of the giver, or by other documents such as the signature card of a joint bank account. The second test of a gift is delivery. Delivery is simply the transfer of possession or control from one person to another. Delivery does not have to be made to the recipient of the gift; it can be made to a third person as agent or trustee for the recipient. A bank will often be the trustee for the recipient if the recipient is a minor or if the recipient is an elderly person who is incapable of handling the property. The key with regard to delivery is that the giver surrenders all rights to possession and control of the property which is the subject of the gift. In some instances you cannot pick the gift up and hand it to the recipient. With an automobile, for example, delivery would consist of handing over the keys. This would be called symbolic delivery. If the gift involves intangible property, then delivery would consist of turning over some document which transfers title to the intangible property to the donee, such as an assignment of a patent or a copyright or a properly indorsed stock certificate.

The following case involved a gift and symbolic delivery of the contents of a safe-deposit box by delivery of the keys to the safe-deposit box.

In Re Estate of Evans
356 A.2d 778 (Pennsylvania, 1976)

FACTS   Arthur Evans, now deceased, had rented a safe-deposit box and had stored valuables in the box. His niece Mrs. Kellows had worked for the family since she was 16, and she continued to care for Evans until he died. Before Evans went into the hospital, just prior to his death, he gave the keys to the box to Kellows and witnesses testified that she had kept them beneath her mattress. Reverend Cummings visited Evans shortly before he died, and Evans told Cummings that he was giving $10,000 to the church and that he had given the rest of his possessions and the keys to the safe-deposit box to Kellows. The executor considered the contents of the safe-deposit box, valued at approximately $80,000, to be assets of the estate and not the specific property of Kellows. Kellows filed objections, stating that there had been a gift and that she owned the contents of the box. She had the keys; however, her name was not on the rental agreement and the bank had no notice that she had any interest in the box.

Ordinarily, The trial court held that the decedent's delivery of the keys to the safe-deposit box to the claimant did not constitute sufficient delivery where the box remained registered in the decedent's name and the claimant could not have gained access to it even with the keys. Kellows appealed from that decision.

ISSUE   Did the decedent's delivery of the keys to the safe-deposit box before his death constitute a gift of the contents of the safe-deposit box?

DECISION   No. The delivery of the keys was not sufficient delivery to support the plaintiff's contention that an inter vivos gift of the contents of the box had been made.

REASONS   The court admitted that there was evidence that the decedent intended to give his estate to Mrs. Kellows. However, the court also noted that there had been ample opportunity for the decedent to remove the contents of the box and give them to Kellows or to take her to the bank and transfer the rental of the box to her. The decedent did in fact visit the bank and get out the safe-deposit box less than one month before he died. His delivery of the keys was intended to ensure the safekeeping of the keys and not to signify delivery of the contents of the safe-deposit box, as was indicated by the fact that Kellows could not get into the safe-deposit box without the decedent's specific authorization. Thus delivery of the keys to a safe-deposit box is not symbolic delivery of the contents of the safe-deposit box.

Two uniform laws apply to gifts of personal property: the Uniform Gifts to Minors Act and the Uniform Anatomical Gift Act.

The Uniform Gifts to Minors Act.   In the past many parents who wanted to give money to their children would set up a savings account in a bank in the name of the minor child. The account would show one of the parents as parent and guardian, and normally the money could be taken out of the account only by the parent. The question arose as to whether or not there was an actual gift, since the parent still retained control over the property. Was there really delivery? The Uniform Gifts to Minors Act (UGMA) was drafted to set up a procedure for making legal gifts to minors. This act has been adopted in nearly all of the states. It provides a method for making gifts of money and of registered and unregistered securities to minors. If the gift is money, the money may simply be deposited in a bank in the name of the giver or some other adult, or of some corporate trustee such as a bank, with the statement that the party in whose name the account is registered is a custodian for the minor under the UGMA. If the gift is a registered security, then the giver registers the security as custodian for the minor under the UGMA. If the security is unregistered, it has to be delivered to another adult or to a bank or some other financial institution as trustee, together with a statement of the gift and an acknowledgment accepting the role of custodian of the security for and on behalf of the minor. The custodian has very broad powers as to the use and disposition of the property. The property can be exchanged or sold without the permission of the minor who is the beneficiary of the gift. Of course, the custodian is not permitted to use any of the property or any of the proceeds for his or her benefit.

The Uniform Anatomical Gift Act.   Traditionally we didn't think of the human body or parts of the human body as things of monetary value, and thus we were not concerned about property rights in our body or various parts of our body. Now that medical technology has developed processes for transplanting parts of one body to another body, it has become necessary to treat the human body and the parts thereof as property and to establish some procedure for making gifts of the human body or its parts. Under the Uniform Anatomical Gift Act (UAGA) any person 18 years of age or older may make a gift of his or her entire body or any part of his or her body. However, the gift does not take effect until the death of the giver. Such gifts are of course revocable at any time. They are usually included in the giver's last will and testament.

During a person's lifetime he or she may sell or give blood to a blood bank or may give a kidney, an eye, or some other organ whose loss does not automatically cause death. Such gifts are not covered by the UAGA since they are not given at death.

3. Title by Inheritance.   As indicated previously, you may become the owner of personal property as a result of a specific bequest in a deceased person's will. You may also become the owner of personal property through the process of intestate succession, which means that you are an heir under state statute and that you will receive a designated share of the decedent's personal property if there is no valid will which disposes of it.

4. Title by Accession.   Accession simply means an addition to what you already have. You are the owner of a cow, and that cow bears a calf. Since you were the owner of the cow, you now also own the new animal. You acquired ownership of that animal by accession. Another example of accession would be a situation where the lawn mower which your neighbor borrowed for the weekend broke down and he had to have it repaired. When your neighbor returned the lawn mower to you, you became the owner of the repairs by accession. Problems in this type of acquisition of personal property arise where the accession is made without the property owner's consent where the accession is of considerable value, and where the original item has been changed or altered so that identification is difficult. A trespasser cuts down small trees on my land, makes rustic lawn chairs from the trees, and sets up a stand along the highway to sell the lawn chairs. Who owns the chairs which were previously my timber? There is no simple answer to this question as the courts in the various jurisdictions have not agreed on one solution, especially if the original material was taken as the result of an innocent mistake. If, on the other hand, the taking was intentional and wrongful, the original owner will no doubt be awarded the chairs.

5. Title by Possession and Control. Title to personal property may be acquired in some instances by simply taking possession of an item and exercising rights of ownership and control over that item. Some common situations where title by possession could be legally exercised are as follows.

Title to Wildlife. Title to fish, birds, or wild animals may in some instances be acquired simply by taking possession and control of the fish, birds, or animals. Title by possession can only occur, however, where the fish, birds, or animals are not owned by another party or where such taking and control would not violate national, state, or local laws for the conservation and protection of wildlife. If you trespass upon a farmer's land and catch fish in the farmer's private pond, the fish belong to the farmer, not to you. If you go hunting during a period of time when it is not legal to hunt a certain species of animal, then you will not be allowed to keep the slain animal and you may have to pay a fine for your wrongful action.

Abandoned Personal Property. An item of personal property has been abandoned if the owner has intentionally and voluntarily relinquished control and possession of the item and has not transferred the title to the item in any matter to another person. The intent of the owner is simply to have nothing more to do with the item. If you go down to the city dump and find an old bicycle which has been cast there to rust and deteriorate, and you pick it up and take it home, you will have acquired title to abandoned property. In that case it seems obvious that the circumstances surrounding the object reveal an intent to abandon it. If, on the other hand, while walking home one day, you see a bicycle lying along the side of the road and you proceed to pick it up, climb on it, and ride it home, you may find yourself talking to a policeman and answering a charge of theft. It may well be the owner of the bicycle simply left it there, intending to come back for it at a later time. Thus the question of whether or not an article has been abandoned will be a question, of the fact of intent of each case.

Lost or Mislaid Property. Lost property is property which the owner accidentally dropped or property which was accidentally separated from the owner. The owner has no knowledge of the location of the lost property. Mislaid property is property which was voluntarily and intentionally placed somewhere by the owner and then forgotten. Lost or mislaid personal property, unlike abandoned personal property, is still the property of the owner who lost or mislaid it. However, it is generally held that the finder of lost property has a right to possession and contract until the item is claimed by the true owner if the item is found in a publicly accessible place, such as a street, a parking lot, or a store. On the other hand, if you find a billfold in an office or an apartment, the courts will generally say that the landowner or occupier has the right to possession of the billfold. Mislaid property generally stays with the owner/occupier of the place where it was discovered.

619

Dolitsky v. *Dollar Savings Bank*
118 N.Y.S.2d 65 (New York, 1952)

FACTS   The plaintiff went into the bank safe-deposit vault area to look into her safe-deposit box, and she took her safe-deposit box to a booth provided by the bank for the use of its customers. The plaintiff found a $100 bill in a folder advertising bank life insurance; the folder was in a rack attached to the wall above the booth. The plaintiff gave the bill to the vault attendant, and he turned it over to his superior. A year passed, and no one ever claimed the $100 bill. The plaintiff then brought action in small claims court to have the bill returned to her as the finder. The court refused to grant the plaintiff's request and dismissed the case.

ISSUE   Is the finder of the mislaid property entitled to the possession of the property if the owner never claims it?

DECISION   No. The discoverer of mislaid property has the duty to leave it with the proprietor of the premises, and the proprietor has the duty to hold it for the owner.

REASONS   The first question to be decided was whether the $100 bill was to be considered lost property or mislaid property. Lost property is property which the owner has casually and involuntarily parted with, so that the mind had no knowledge of the parting. Mislaid property is property which the owner has voluntarily and intentionally placed and then forgotten. The court found that the $100 bill was mislaid property, not lost property. In coming to this conclusion, the court stated: "Property in someone's possession cannot be found in the sense of common law lost property. If the article is in the custody of the owner of the place when it is discovered, it is not lost in the legal sense; instead it is mislaid. Thus if a chattel is discovered anywhere in a private place where only a limited class of people have a right to be and they are customers of the owner of the premises who has the duty of preserving the property of his customers, it is in the possession of the owner of the premises."
    In this case the bank simply had the duty to redeliver the $100 bill to the owner. There was no time limit, and the bank could not hand over the bill to the finder or anyone other than the owner.

The identity of the lost or mislaid item is also a factor in determining who has the better right to possession. A lost billfold will normally have the owner's identification in it, whereas a wrist watch that fell off the owner's wrist when the band broke would not be so identifiable. Courts may also consider the status of the finder. Trespassers usually have to turn over any property they find; so do employees whose job includes such a duty.

Kalyvakis v. The T.S.S. Olympia
181 F. Supp. 32 (New York, 1960)

FACTS   The plaintiff was employed as an assistant steward aboard the T.S.S. *Olympia,* a passenger vessel owned by the defendant. He was a Greek national. The defendant was a Greek corporation with an office and place of business within the jurisdiction of the court. The *Olympia* was documented under the laws of Liberia and flew the Liberian flag.

On June 6, 1956, while the *Olympia* was moored at a pier in New York City and receiving passengers for an imminent sailing, the plaintiff found $3,010 in U.S. currency on the floor of a public men's room on the upper deck. The room was accessible to passengers and their guests, visitors, and the ship's personnel. The bills, which were scattered on the floor of the men's room, were found shortly before visitors and guests were required to disembark and return to the pier. After the vessel had sailed, the plaintiff deposited the money with the chief steward to be held for the true owner, should he make any claim to it. Although more than three years had elapsed, no claim had been made for the funds. The plaintiff then asked that the money be returned to him.

ISSUE   Did the steward who found the currency have a claim to it since the true owner had not claimed the currency and more than three years had passed since the lost currency was found?

DECISION   Yes. The steward has a right to the money. The employer has no right to retain the money.

REASONS   In deciding this issue, the court stated: "Research by Court and counsel has failed to bring to light any controlling case under the general maritime law of the United States. In the absence of an applicable rule the Court may look to state law. The most appropriate state law is that of New York, where the vessel was moored when the money was found. Under New York law the money in question would be considered lost or abandoned. And since it was found in a public place, the finder would be entitled to it against all but the owner. This is so regardless of the fact that the money was found during the course of his employment. The New York view is in accord with the weight of American authority which tends to reject any master-servant exception to the law of finders." The court awarded the lost money in the amount of $3,010 to the plaintiff.

Many states have "finders' statutes" which enable the finder to become the new owner of lost or mislaid property by advertising or posting notices. If the owner does not return and claim the property within the statutory period (e.g., one year), the finder can become the new owner. Some of these statutes require the finder to pay the state part of the value of the item in order to become the new owner.

Bishop v. *Ellsworth*
234 N.E.2d 49 (Illinois, 1968)

FACTS
The plaintiff filed a complaint alleging that on July 21, 1965, the defendants, Mark and Jeff Ellsworth and David Gibson, three small boys, entered his salvage yard without his permission and that while there they found a bottle partially embedded in the loose earth on top of a landfill, wherein they discovered the sum of $12,590 in U.S. currency. The boys delivered the money to the chief of police, who deposited it with the defendant Canton State Bank. The defendants caused preliminary notices to be given as required by Ill. Rev. Stat., Chap. 50, Subsections 27 and 28 (1965). The plaintiff asked that the court appoint a guardian ad litem for the minor defendants and adjudicate the rights of the parties with respect to the currency. To this complaint an attorney, on behalf of the next friends and natural guardians of the minor defendants, filed a motion to dismiss on the ground that no cause of action was stated. The trial court, after hearing arguments, sustained this motion. The plaintiff appealed.

ISSUE
Can trespassers claim ownership of lost property that they find on land on which they are trespassing?

DECISION
No. Trespassers have no claim to possession or ownership of property found while trespassing.

REASONS
"The defendants rely on the provision of Ill. Rev. Stat., Chap. 50, Subsection 27 and 28. The relevant portions read as follows: '27. Lost goods. . . . If any person or persons find any lost goods, money, bank notes, or other choses in action, of any description whatever, such person or persons shall inform the owner thereof, if known, and shall make restitution of the same, without any compensation whatever, except the same shall be voluntarily given on the part of the owner. If the owner be unknown, and if such property found is of the value of $15 or upwards, the finder . . . shall within 5 days after such finding . . . appear before some judge or magistrate . . . and make affidavit of the description thereof, the time and place when and where the same was found, that no alteration has been made in the appearance thereof since the findings of the same, that the owner thereof is unknown to him, and that he has not secreted, withheld, or disposed of any part thereof. The judge or magistrate shall enter the value of the property found as near as he can ascertain in his estray book, together with the affidavit of the finder, and shall also, within 10 days after the proceedings have been entered on his estray book, transmit to the county clerk a certified copy thereof, to be by him recorded in his estray book and to file the same in his office. . . .' '28. Advertisement. . . . If the value thereof exceeds the sum of $15, the county clerk, within 20 days after receiving the certified copy of the judge or magistrate's estray record, shall cause an advertisement to be set up on the court house door, and in 3 other of the most public places in the county, and also a notice thereof to be published for 3 weeks successively in some public newspaper printed in this state, and if the owner of such goods, money, bank notes, or other choses in action does not appear and claim the same and pay the finder's charges and expenses within one year after the advertisement thereof as aforesaid, the ownership of such property shall vest in the finder.'"

The defendant minors stated that they had complied with the statute and that they should be entitled to the money. The court gave the following reasons for finding that the statute did not apply to this case:

"We think it apparent that the statute to which defendants make reference provides a means of vesting title to lost property in the finder where the prescribed search for the owner proves fruitless. This statute does not purport to provide for the disposition of property deemed mislaid or abandoned, nor does it purport to describe or determine the right to possession against any other party other than the true owner. The plain meaning of this statute does not support plaintiff's position that common law is wholly abrogated thereby. The provisions of the statute are designed to provide a procedure whereby the discoverer of 'lost' property may be vested with the ownership of said property even as against the true owner thereof, a right which theretofore did not exist at common law. In the absence of any language in the statute from which the contrary can be inferred, it must be assumed that the term 'lost' was used in its generally accepted legal sense and no extension of the term was intended. Thus the right to possession of discovered property still depends upon the relative rights of the discoverer and the owner of the locus in quo and the distinction which exists between property which is abandoned, mislaid, lost, or is treasure trove. The statute assumes that the discoverer is in the rightful possession of lost property, and proceedings under such statute are not a bar where the issue is a claim to the contrary.

"There is a presumption that the owner or occupant of land or premises has custody of property found on it or actually imbedded in the land. . . . The ownership or possession of the locus in quo is related to the right to possession of property discovered thereon or imbedded therein in two respects. First, if the premises on which the property is discovered are private, it is deemed that the property discovered thereon is and always has been in the constructive possession of the owner of said premises and in a legal sense the property can be neither mislaid or lost. . . . Second, the question of whether the property is mislaid or lost in a legal sense depends upon the intent of the true owner. The ownership or possession of the premises is an important factor in determining such intent. If the property be determined to be mislaid, the owner of the premises is entitled to the possession thereof against the discoverer. It would also appear that if the discoverer is a trespasser, such trespasser can have no claim to possession of such property even if it might otherwise be considered lost."

6. Confusion. Title to personal property may be acquired when the property of different owners is so intermingled that the property of the individual owners cannot be identified or separated and returned to the specific owners. Confusion is most common when dealing with such fungible goods as corn, wheat, milk, and oil.

If three persons owning 1,000 bushels of wheat of the same grade and quality agree to intermingle their property for purposes of storage, there would be no problem since the intermingling was voluntary, and each party will simply have a one-third ownership in the total volume of wheat. The problem involving title to personal property arises where one person intentionally and wrongfully intermingles his or her goods with those of another person so that the goods of each owner can no longer be separated or distinguished. The majority of the courts, in a case where the commingling was deliberate and wrongful and without the permission of the other party, will simply grant the innocent party title to the entire volume of goods and will punish the wrongdoer by depriving that person of any further right or title to the property. If the intermingling of the goods is not an intentional and wrongful act and instead is simply an accident where grains or such liquids as milk or oil become commingled, then if the goods are of the same kind and quality, courts will usually hold that each owner now owns a proportionate share of the total mixed goods.

7. Title by Creation. Property is created when a new invention is made, when a new song or book is written, or when a new painting is created. These creations are the result of intellectual production. Title by creation differs from title by accession since in title by accession you already own the basic property such as a cow, and then when the cow gives birth to a calf, you automatically own the calf. You didn't create the calf; the calf was simply an accession to property you already owned. Here you are intellectually creating a new idea to which the law grants property rights. The U.S. Congress has enacted the patent law, which gives inventors certain property rights in the inventions which they create, and the Copyright Act, which gives writers, composers, and producers of other copyrightable material certain property rights in their creations.

CASES FOR DISCUSSION

MORRISON v. UNITED STATES

492 F.2d 1219 (U.S. Court of Claims, 1974)

Durfee, Senior Judge

Opinion

Per Curiam

This case comes before the court having been submitted on plaintiff's exceptions to the recommended decision, filed April 26, 1973, by Trial Judge Kenneth R. Harkins pursuant to Rule 134(h). The court has considered the case on the briefs of the parties with oral argument of counsel. Since the court agrees with the recommended decision of the trial judge, as hereinafter set forth, it hereby affirms and adopts the same as the basis for its judgment in this case. Therefore, it is concluded that plaintiff is not entitled to recover and the petition is dismissed.

Opinion of Trial Judge

Harkins, Trial Judge

On July 31, 1968, plaintiff was a Sergeant E–5 in command of a squad of the 3d Platoon, B Com-

pany, 1st Battalion, 50th Infantry, on a search-and-destroy patrol in the Central Highlands of South Vietnam. During the course of this patrol, plaintiff's squad searched a cave and discovered, among other items, $150,000 in United States currency and 550,000 South Vietnamese piasters. The $150,000 in United States currency and the South Vietnamese piasters were turned over to plaintiff's platoon leader and, through channels, delivered to the custody of defendant. Plaintiff contends that he is a "finder" of "treasure trove" and that defendant's refusal to deliver the money to him constitutes a taking of private property for public use without just compensation in violation of the Fifth Amendment of the Constitution of the United States.

Plaintiff is not a "finder" of the $150,000. When plaintiff discovered the money and took it into possession, he did so as an agent of the United States; the $150,000 was "captured" public property taken from the enemy or "abandoned" property within the meaning of Article 103 of the Uniform Code of Military Justice. Accordingly, plaintiff's petition must be dismissed.

* * * * *

On July 31, 1968, plaintiff was subject to Article 103 of the Uniform Code of Military Justice. This article deals with captured or abandoned property, and is derived from the constitutional power of Congress to "make Rules concerning Captures on Land and Water." Article 103 requires military personnel on duty in a combat zone, on penalty of court martial to (a) secure all public property that is taken from the enemy and (b) turn over to the proper authority all captured or abandoned property in their possession, custody, or control. In addition, Article 103 prohibits military personnel from buying, selling, trading, or dealing in captured or abandoned property in his own account or from engaging in looting or pillaging. Article 103 reflects the policy that a soldier may not make a profit out of the disorders of war. The article recognizes the difficulties involved in policing an army when abandoned property situations and looting situations are involved.

* * * * *

A directive of the United States Military Assistance Command implements the provisions of Article 103 for captured or seized currencies taken in field operations in Vietnam. This directive applies to all United States forces conducting operations within the Republic of Vietnam and was in force at the time plaintiff's squad located and searched the cave on July 31, 1968. MACV Dir. 37–20 applies to any currency, either public currency or private currency, including United States dollars, Military Payment Certificates (MPC), and GVN or NVN piasters, that United States forces personnel may capture or seize in the possession of a detainee or as part of a cache.

All public currency so taken is stated to be the "property of the United States Government." Public currency is defined as all currency which is the "property of the enemy force, state, government, or political subdivision thereof."

Private currency is property that can be identified by the individual who can establish ownership. Private currency is any currency seized or captured by United States forces personnel and "identifiable as the personal property of an individual."

The source of, or the true owner of the money located in the cave is unknown. The record does not establish the identity of the parties that de-

posited the money in the ammunition cans or placed the cans in the cave. No individual has identified or established a claim to the money as personal property. In the circumstances of this case, the $150,000 must be treated as public property unless or until the true owner identifies it and establishes a superior personal property right. Until proven otherwise, the currency found in the cave should be considered to be public currency and, as such, the property of the United States Government.

When in the cave, and when he saw and took possession of the money, plaintiff was in a combat situation in an area not under effective control of either the South Vietnam forces or the United States forces. If the currency was property of the enemy, it was taken in combat and is captured public property. As a general rule, all property located in enemy territory, regardless of its ownership, in time of war is regarded as enemy property subject to the laws of war.

Hypothetically, the currency located in the cave could be considered to be private currency placed in the cave by unknown South Vietnamese or other civilian parties, or even by South Vietnamese or American military personnel. In such event, the $150,000 private currency would be contraband under local law and would be abandoned property as that term is used in Article 103. In Article 103, the word "abandoned" covers not only property abandoned by the enemy, but also by civilian populations "in flight from the perils of the combat zone." The term "abandoned" in Article 103 is broader than the common law concept of "abandoned" property in that it includes property that was left behind or cast aside in situations where the right to possession was not voluntarily surrendered. In the circumstances of this case, the nature of the war in Vietnam would have caused any private owner of the money to abandon it to escape the "perils of the combat zone." No South Vietnamese or American, civilian or military, who had cached profits from black market operations would assert title to the money in the cave in the circumstances, particularly when its discovery occurred on a search-and-destroy patrol by heavily armed combat troops. In such event, the $150,000 would be private property cast aside and abandoned with no intent of asserting ownership or possessory rights.

Plaintiff's claim is disposed of by the nature of plaintiff's mission at the time the discovery was made. Seizure of the currency was plaintiff's military responsibility, and possession of the currency was taken as an agent of the United States. Plaintiff can assert no right to possession. This case is not concerned with, and no decision is made as to, what the result would be if plaintiff were not on a combat mission and acting well within the scope of his assigned official duties. Nor is this case concerned with a "finding" made by a member of an army of occupation or by military personnel in pursuit of wholly personal activities that lay outside the scope of assigned official responsibilities.

Conclusion of Law

Upon the findings of fact and the foregoing opinion, which are adopted by the court and made a part of the judgment herein, the court concludes as a matter of law that plaintiff is not entitled to recover, and the petition is dismissed.

BANK OF AMERICA NAT. T. & S. ASS'N v. COUNTY OF LOS ANGELES

36 Cal. Rptr. 413 (California, 1964)

Burke, Justice

Plaintiff seeks a refund of taxes paid under protest to defendants, the County of Los Angeles and certain cities for which it collects taxes. The taxes in question were levied on several electronic computer systems installed in various buildings owned by plaintiff. The trial court held the systems to be fixtures and taxable as improvements to real property. Plaintiff appeals from such judgment.

The sole issue before the trial court was the taxability of such property as fixtures. If such equipment constitutes personal property, defendants admittedly have no power to tax it. . . .

Plaintiff contends that an article is not a fixture unless permanently attached to the land or to improvements on the land, . . . that permanence is a matter of manifested intention, citing *M. P. Moller, Inc.* v. *Wilson*, 8 Cal. 2d 31, 37, 63 P.2d 818, 821, which states: "This court has recognized the test of intention to make the article a permanent addition to the realty as manifested by the physical facts, and has accepted the character of the annexation and the use for which the article is designed as subsidiary elements employed for the purpose of testing the intention of permanency."

The physical facts, plaintiff asserts, demonstrate the intention to have the equipment retain its character as personal property, because (a) the function performed is the same as that formerly performed by bookkeepers using manually operated, electrically driven mechanical equipment; (b) the dimension, weight, and physical characteristics of the equipment lend to the conclusion that it is personal property (the equipment weighed less than the manually operated counterparts and occupied less area; sorter-readers, for example, are equipped with rollaway casters, and sorters can be divided into three sections which are readily movable); (c) the method of connection between the components manifests a temporary condition (some plug connections were used); (d) the assessed equipment in one building occupied only 5 per cent of the building; the floor design was to obtain flexibility to permit movement of the equipment; the temperature and humidity controls were established with minimums and maximums to satisfy the needs of the employees, not the equipment (the defendants' own witness was in doubt at first as to the proper classification for the equipment; the buildings were designed as accounting centers, and this does not render the computer installations improvements to the real property); (e) the bank moved many components in the past and intended to do so in the future; (f) the usual life of the equipment ranges from 6 to 10 years, and that of the building approximately 50 years; (g) double taxation would result in this case since national banks pay an excess franchise tax in lieu of personal property taxes from which they are exempt, as heretofore indicated. . . .

Here, the trial court viewed the installations

and upon conclusion of the trial decided for defendants. The court made the following findings of fact, in part:

IV

All of said systems included several major components as described in plaintiff's Exhibit 12 which were interconnected by a mass of thousands of signal wires and cables housed underneath the floor on which they were installed. Some of the individual major components can be separately operated for special purposes, but the major component parts are principally operated as an accounting unit. Each and every part of each system is essential to the performance of the overall accounting functions for which the systems are designed.

V

The component parts of each system were effectively held in place by their substantial weight, by the mass of interconnecting wiring passing beneath the floor on which said components were installed, and by other devices.

VI

The two data bossers and related equipment which were the subject of the 1960 tax assessment in the third cause of action in Case No. 758,864 and the subject of the 1961 tax assessment in the eighth cause of action in Case No. 784,689 are effectively held in place by their substantial weight and are further affixed by rigid metal compressed air pipes which join them with an air compressor installed in the same building. They produce credit cards used in plaintiff's business. Because they are now functionally obsolete, plaintiff plans to move one data bosser from Los Angeles to San Francisco for modification, and to replace it with a modified data bosser which was in San Francisco at the time of trial, such modification costing approximately Twenty-Seven Thousand Dollars ($27,000.00).

VII

The physical facts indicate that, except for emergencies, plaintiff intends and intended all of these electronic computer systems and the two data bossers and their related equipment to remain in place until necessary to remove them for repair or improvement or because of economic or functional obsolescence.

Our review of the proceedings indicates that there was substantial evidence to sustain the findings of the trial judge and that the findings support the judgment. We concur in the contention of defendants that the equipment in question was properly taxable as fixtures because:

(1) The buildings themselves (six out of the seven) were special purpose buildings, designed as accounting centers requiring the computer systems . . . ; (2) the components of each system were interconnected by hundreds of signal and power cables; the floors of the buildings were raised to accommodate the cables, each of which contained from 2 to 50 wires; (3) air conditioning and humidity controls were installed for optimum operating efficiency of the computers as the magnetic tapes which were utilized were sensitive to heat and humidity changes; (4) the buildings had fewer windows than the usual commercial building and were located with ready access to freeways or main arteries and a constant electrical power source; (5) less expensive sites were used avoiding prime military target areas; (6) each building was designed with room for expansion; (7) the raised floor was particularly a deviation in construction, at great cost, solely for the computer systems and was not installed throughout the entire building; (8) the great expense incident to moving heavy equipment makes for permanence of location . . . ; (9) the size and weight (11 tons to each system) likewise militate against moving, regardless of the method of attachment to the building . . . (the court quoted from Corpus Juris to the effect that "Retention in place by gravity, without any fastening, has been not infrequently held to be insufficient, but the later cases usually regard this as sufficient provided the intention to make the article part of the realty plainly appears and the article or structure is so heavy that it is as effectively kept in place by gravity as if it were fastened"); (10) the difficulty attending removal is indicative of intended permanency; substantial expense was entailed in relocation of any of the components, requiring much labor and highly skilled electronic technicians; (11) actual physical connection was present in the instant case, hundreds of cables containing thousands of wires passed beneath the floors and connected the component units; (12) in the case of the data bosser machines, used to print plastic credit cards, connections to air compressors were

627

made to rigid iron pipes in another room; (13) the case of *Southern California Telephone Co.* v. *State Board* . . . enunciates a unit-for-use rule which is applicable here: "The fact that articles affixed are necessary or convenient to the use of a building for the purpose for which it is designed is generally treated as tending to indicate they are realty"; (14) function is not determined as a test of annexation . . . ; (15) the administrative interpretation by the assessor may be considered by the court and given such weight as it sees fit . . . ; (16) the law presumes the assessment to be correct, and the burden of proof otherwise is upon plaintiff; (17) permanence is to be distinguished from perpetuity; (18) the issue of taxability is a question of fact determinable by the trial court upon the evidence regarding annexation showing intention with which the computers were annexed as manifested by reasonable outward appearances. . . .

The trial court personally viewed the premises involved and inspected the installations. Such view is evidence though not reflected in the record. . . . Such visual observation may have been the deciding factor in the court's testing of the intention of permanency as manifested by the physical facts. But without such evidence the record otherwise disclosed adequate evidence to support the factual determination of the trial court.

No errors of law appear in the record. The court's conclusion that the computer systems were fixtures is supported by substantial evidence, and absent error, is conclusive upon this court.

SNEDEKER v. WARING

12 N.Y. 170 (New York, 1854)

Parker, Justice

The facts in this case are undisputed, and it is a question of law whether the statue and sundial were real or personal property. The plaintiffs claim they are personal property, having purchased them as such. . . . The defendant claims they are real property, having bought the farm on which they were erected at a foreclosure sale under a mortgage, executed . . . before the erection of the statue and sundial. . . . The claim of the defendent under the mortgage sale is not impaired by the fact that the property in controversy was put on the place after the execution of the mortgage. . . . Permanent erections and other improvements, made by the mortgagor on the land mortgaged, become a part of the realty and are covered by the mortgage.

Governed, then, by the rule prevailing between grantor and grantee, if the statue and dial were fixtures, actual or constructive, they passed to the defendant as part of the realty.

No case has been found in either the English or American courts, deciding in what cases statuary placed in a house or in grounds shall be deemed real and in what cases personal property. This question must therefore be determined upon principle. All will agree that statuary exposed for sale in a workshop, or wherever it may be before it shall be permanently placed, is personal property; nor will it be controverted that where statuary is placed upon a building, or so connected with it as to be considered part of it, it will be deemed real property and pass with a deed of the land. But the doubt in this case arises from the peculiar position and character of this statue, it being placed in a courtyard before the house, on a base erected on an artificial mound for the purpose of supporting it. The statue was not fastened to the base by either clamps or cement, but it rested as firmly on it by its own weight, which was three or four tons, as if otherwise affixed to it. The base was of masonary, the seams being pointed with cement, though the stones were not laid in either cement or mortar; and the mound was an artificial and permanent erection, raised some two or three feet above the surrounding land, with a substantial stone foundation.

If the statue had been actually affixed to the base by cement or clamps or in any other manner, it would be conceded to be a fixture and belong to the realty. But as it was, it could have been removed without fracture to the base on which it rested. But is that circumstance controlling? A building of wood, weighing even less than the statue, but resting on a substantial foundation of masonry, would have belonged to the realty. A thing may be as firmly affixed to the land by gravitation as by clamps or cement. Its character may depend much upon the object of its erection. Its destination, the intention of the person making the erection, often exercise a controlling influence, and its connection with the land is looked at principally for the purpose of ascertaining whether that intent was that the thing in question should retain its original chattel character, or whether it was designed to make it a permanent accession to the lands.

By the civil law, columns, figures, and statues, used to spout water at fountains, were regarded as immovable, or real; . . . though it was inferred that statues resting on a base of masonry were not immovable, because they were there, not as part of the construction, but as ornaments. . . .

By the French law, statues placed in a niche made expressly to receive them, though they could be removed without fracture or deterioration, are immovable, or part of the realty. . . . But the statues standing on pedestals in houses, courtyards, and gardens retain their character of "movable" or personal. . . . This has reference to statues only which do not stand on a substantial and permanent base or separate pedestal made expressly for them. For when a statue is placed on a pedestal or base of masonry constructed expressly for it, it is governed by the same rule as when placed on a niche made expressly to receive it, and is immovable. . . . The statue in such case is regarded as making part of the same thing with the permanent base upon which it rests. . . .

[T]he law will presume the proprietor intended them as immovable, when they cannot be taken away without fracture or deterioration, or leaving a gap or vacancy. A statue is regarded as integral with the permanent base on which it rests and which was erected expressly for it, when the removal of the statue will offend the eye by presenting before it a distasteful gap . . . , a foundation and base no longer appropriate or useful. . . . Things immovable by destination are said to be those objects movable in their nature, which, without being actually held to the ground,

are destined to remain there perpetually attached for use, improvement, or ornament. . . .

I think the French law, as applicable to statuary, is in accordance with reason and justice. It effectuates the intention of the proprietor. No evidence could be received more satisfactory of the intent of the proprietor to make a statue a part of his realty than the fact of his having prepared a niche or erected a permanent base of masonry expressly to receive it; and to remove a statue from its place, under such circumstances, would produce as great an injury and do as much violence to the hold, by leaving an unseemly and uncovered base, as it would have done if torn rudely from a fastening by which it had been connected with the land. The mound and base in this case, though designed in connection with the statue as an ornament to the grounds, would, when deprived of the statue, become a most objectionable deformity.

There are circumstances in this case, not necessary under the French law, to indicate the intention to make the statue a permanent erection, but greatly strengthening the presumption of such intent. The base was made of red sandstone, the same material as the statue, giving to both the statue and base the appearance of being but a single block, and both were also of the same materials as the house. The statue was thus peculiarly fitted as an ornament for the grounds in front of that particular house. It was also of colossal size and was not adapted to any other destination than a permanent ornament to the realty. The design and location of the statue were in every respect appropriate, in good taste, and in harmony with the surrounding objects and circumstances.

I lay entirely out of view in this case the fact that Thom testified that he intended to sell the statue when an opportunity should offer. His secret intention in that respect can have no legitimate bearing on the question. He clearly intended to make use of the statue to ornament his grounds, when he erected for it a permanent mound and base; and a purchaser had a right to infer and to be governed by the manifest and unmistakable evidences of intention. . . .

There is no good reason for calling the statue personal because it was erected for ornament only, if it was clearly designed to be permanent. If Thom had erected a bower or summerhouse of wicker work, and had placed it on a permanent foundation in an appropriate place in front of his house, no one would doubt it belonged to the realty; and I think this statue as clearly belongs to the realty as a statue would, placed on the house, or as one of the two statues placed on the gate post at the entrance to the grounds.

* * * * *

The sundial stands on a somewhat different footing. It was made for use as well as for ornament, and could not be useful except when firmly placed in the open air and in the light of the sun. Though it does not appear that the stone on which it was placed was made expressly for it, it was appropriately located on a solid and durable foundation. There is good reason to believe it was designed to be a permanent fixture, because the material of which it was made was the same as that of the house and the statue, and because it was in every respect adapted to the place.

Johnson, J. (dissenting)

. . . [T]he statue and sundial were originally personal property. To lose that character they must have been annexed or attached in some sufficient manner to the freehold. If they have never been so annexed or attached, then they retain their chattel character, and were subject to sale on execution as personal property. The question then is, whether their resting by their own mere weight upon substructures prepared for their support, but to which they were not in any manner fastened or attached, is in the sense of the law an annexation or affixing to the freehold. . . .

The general rule requires physical annexation to the freehold. To this rule there are some exceptions under the head of constructive annexation, as the deeds of an estate, the chest containing them, deer in a park, fish in a pond, doves in a dovecote; so also the keys of doors, locks, windows, and articles of the like nature, which form as much a part of the structure of a house as the walls, although not annexed to it at all, or not in such a manner as to be incapable of removal without injury to the house. These are incidents to the house, and from the nature of their use can be no[t] otherwise annexed to it without the entire subversion of the purpose for which they are intended. But this class of exceptions does not, in the reason of the rule, nor according to the decided cases, extend to articles merely of ornament not physically annexed to the soil.

I have been unable to find any case at common law, or any statement in any text-book, upon the precise case of a statue; though it seems that the question must, in England, frequently have arisen in practice, and if it forms an exception to the general rule, it is not a little singular that no mention is anywhere made of the fact.

It seems clear that a statue of ordinary size, standing upon a movable pedestal in a house, would not pass by a conveyance of the house, any more than a porcelain vase or any other ornamental article of furniture. Nor do I think if the same statue were set out of doors it would thereby lose its character of personality. The mere difference in weight between such a statue and that in question does not seem to me a sufficient ground on which to establish a different rule. It stands for ornament alone, and is not fastened to the freehold, and its character must depend upon the general rule.

PROBLEMS FOR DISCUSSION

1. Early Eyesore Products, Inc., manufactures and sells an assembly kit for a steel farm silo for the storage of fodder. The kit includes 100 steel sheets, about 7,300 bolts, and a sealant. Early's dealers assemble the kits for farmers on a concrete slab that weighs about 65 tons. The silo is about 22 feet in diameter and 72 feet high. It weighs about 32 tons and costs over $20,000. Kansas levies a state sales tax which includes sales of building materials to builders for the erection of buildings or struc-

tures or for the alteration or improvement of real property. Early claims that its silos, after installation, remain personal property and that they are therefore not covered by this sales tax. The Kansas tax collector says that Early owes $160,000 for silo sales made in Kansas. Who's right, and why?

2. Tina Bracht rented a Mavis rental car. When she opened the glove compartment to see whether any city maps were there, she discovered $800 in currency. When Tina returned the rental car she told the attendant what had happened and gave him the $800 to return to the true owner if he or she could be identified. Mavis checked with persons who had previously rented the car, but none of them could satisfactorily identify the money as belonging to him or her. Tina now claims that the money should be turned over to her as the finder. Is she right? Explain.

3. Germaine Gerwin contracted to sell her ranch to Honcho Ranches, Inc. On March 15, the date on which the deal was to be closed, possession transferred, and the money paid, Gerwin was unable to deliver possession. Her tenant, Ronald Relson, refused to turn over possession because he had planted 150 acres of winter wheat the previous fall and it would not be ready to harvest until the middle of the summer. Ronald also claimed two thirds of the wheat crop under the terms of the lease. Honcho claims that it bought the wheat with the ranch. Gerwin's deed to Honcho did not exempt the wheat crop and warranted that she had good and clear title. Gerwin's lease to Ronald expired on March 10, however, she had permitted previous tenants to harvest their winter wheat crops, as was the customary practice in the area. Honcho sues Gerwin and Ronald for possession of the wheat crop or for damages. How should the court resolve this dispute? Explain.

4. Lem Webcar leased a commercial building from Alph Centauri. Alph had been using the building for storage and so had never installed heating equipment. Lem knew this when he leased the building. Lem installed an oil burner and a boiler in the basement so that he could heat the building, since he intended to use it as his workshop. Alph sold the building to Betty Bluster. When Lem's lease expired, Lem and Betty were unable to agree on terms for a renewal, so Lem prepared to move out—with the heating equipment. Upon learning that Lem planned to remove the oil burner and boiler, Betty sued for an injunction. Should the injunction be granted? Why or why not?

5. While Harvey Heist was on duty with the U.S. Army in World War II, he and two companions entered an apartment which had formerly been occupied by Benito Mussolini, the Italian dictator, who had fled to northern Italy. Harvey picked up several items of personal property, including two hats, four medals, and several pictures. He brought these items with him when he returned to the United States in 1945. In 1969 Harvey's collection was stolen from him by an employee, Frank Faithless, who sold it to a dealer in war souvenirs. The dealer sold it to another collector, Gus Gudgy, who was unaware at the time that the collection had been stolen. Harvey discovered that Gus had the collection and sued to get it back. Gus says that he bought the collection in good faith and that Harvey stole it in the first place anyway. Who has the better right to possession, and why?

6. Horace Humble bought a 60-acre farm from Oskar Bismark. When Horace looked at the farm, prior to buying it, he observed an irrigation well, complete with a pump and motor. The pump was in the well, and the motor was bolted to a concrete pad next to the well. Irrigation pipe and a sprinkler system were unassembled and had been stacked behind the barn. Horace mentioned at the time that he would "have no use for" the pipe and the sprinkler system. The contract was a printed form. The printed part said that the sale included "all fixtures and equipment permanently attached to said premises." The space on the form for filling in personal property

which was included in the sale was left blank. This typewritten sentence was added to the form: "The irrigation equipment is not included in this sale." Adolph Avid paid Oskar $5,000 for the pump, motor, pipe, and sprinker system and had them all removed before Horace took possession of the farm. Horace sues Oskar and Adolph for the value of the pump and motor, which he says he thought were included with the farm. Oskar says they were not. Who's right, and why?

7. While riding on the subway, Lindy Larson noticed a package on the seat across the aisle. She went over and picked it up. It was wrapped in plain paper and tied with string. When Lindy got to her stop, as she was about to get off with the package, she was stopped by the conductor. "I saw what happened," he said. "Where are you going with that package?" Lindy explained that she was going to take it with her and advertise for the owner, but the conductor wasn't satisfied. When Lindy refused to give him the package, he called a policeman and had Lindy arrested and charged with petty larceny. When the package was opened, it was found to contain two loaves of bread. Lindy sues the conductor and the city (which owns and operates the subway) for false arrest. How should the courts dispose of these various charges?

8. Television station WSDS had county real property taxes assessed against its television tower, antenna, and other transmission equipment; the value of these items was nearly $700,000. WSDS claimed that they were personal property and should not be taxed as real estate. The tower was over 1,800 feet high and consisted of steel components bolted to each other. The tower was then bolted to a concrete foundation. Three ground wires were welded to each of the tower's three legs and run into the ground, where they were attached to steel rods. The tower was supported by 27 guy lines running from it to nine concrete anchors; three lines were attached to each anchor by U-bolts. The entire assembly could be removed without altering the tower, the foundation, or the anchors. If disassembled, the tower could be shipped by truck in 30-foot sections and reassembled as one tower or as three smaller ones. WSDS sues to have these items removed from the real estate tax rolls; the tax assessor says they are part of the land. Who's right, and why?

Bailments | 31

Have you ever loaned your car to a friend? Have you ever taken your stereo set back to the dealer for repairs? Have you ever checked your coat and hat at a restaurant? These are all bailments. A bailment exists when the possessor of personal property gives up its possession and control to another person with the agreement that there is no transfer of title to the object and that the transfer of possession is temporary. The person who had possession of the personal property and is giving up possession is a bailor, and the person who is receiving the personal property is a bailee.

Essential Elements of Bailment

1. The first essential element of a bailment is an agreement between the parties. This can be expressed either orally or in writing, or it may be implied from the facts and circumstances of the situation. The agreement of bailment would normally cover consideration, if any, to the bailor for the use of the bailed property; what the property is going to be used for or how it is going to be used; when, where, and how the bailed item is to be returned to the bailor, delivered to someone else, or disposed of in some other manner; and the rights and duties of the parties.

In a simple situation such as leaving your coat with the attendant in the cloakroom of a restaurant, you normally receive a wood, plastic, or metal token with a number on it. This is your receipt for the coat you entrusted to the cloakroom attendant, and normally when you hand this token back to the attendant you would get your coat. Here there is an implied agreement of bailment when you hand the attendant the coat, as the attendant knows that you are not transferring title to him or her and that your intent is to have the coat returned to you when you leave the premises. The attendant is also aware that there is a duty on his or her part to take care not to damage the coat.

If you rent a car from a car rental agency, you will sign a rental agreement which is in effect an agreement of bailment. The agreement will specify the consideration that you will pay for the use of the car, the restrictions on its use, when and where the car is to be returned, and specific details as to the rights and duties of the parties in case of damage to the car or damage to a third party.

2. In order to have a bailment, the bailor must have physical possession of the object to be bailed. The bailor need not be the owner of the property. In fact, the bailor may be a bailee. For example, as the bailee of the car you rented from Hertz, you may entrust it to a parking attendant and thus become its bailor.

Theobald v. *Satterthwaite*
190 P.2d 714 (Washington, 1948)

FACTS   On December 24, 1946, Mae Theobald came to the Crystal Palace Barber and Beauty Shop, owned by Guy and Helen Satterthwaite, for a permanent wave. There were three rooms at Crystal: the front room was the waiting room; the middle room was the beauty shop; and the back room was the barbershop. Persons on the street could see into the waiting room through the front window, but persons in the waiting room could not see into the beauty shop, or vice versa. Mae was wearing her new fur coat. When Helen called her to come into the beauty shop, Mae hung her coat on a hook in the waiting room. On a prior visit, Mae had asked Helen whether it was safe to leave her coat there and Helen had told her that it was safe, that nothing had been stolen in 20 years. This time Mae's coat was stolen. The trial court gave Mae $300, the value of the coat, on the basis that there had been a bailment and that the waiting room was not a safe place since there was no bell or other warning device on the front door and since the waiting room was visible from the street. Guy and Helen appealed.

ISSUE   Was there a bailment of the customer's coat?

DECISION   No. Judgment reversed.

REASONS   After reviewing the facts, Chief Justice Mallery first noted that on this occasion the proprietors of the shop had had no knowledge of the presence of Mae's coat and that therefore there could not be a bailment. But the main reason for the decision was that there had been no transfer of possession of the coat.

"[T]here is another and better ground upon which the appellants must prevail. That is that there was no change of possession or delivery in this case. . . .

"While we are not inclined to view the element of delivery in any technical sense, still we think there can be no delivery unless there is a change of possession of an article from one person to another. Where property is stolen, the loss will lie where it falls unless the owner can prove that it was due to the negligent act of another who had a duty of care with regard to it. The duty of care falls upon the bailee because he possesses the article and has the power of custody or control over it. This situation will not arise unless the owner parts with control over the article as a result of the bailee coming into possession of it. One who takes off a garment and deposits it in his own presence, as one would do in a restaurant, retains the power of surveillance and control in himself and the burden of care is not transferred with regard to such an article because the operators of the restaurant have not knowingly received the exclusive possession and dominion over it. In the instant case the respondent may not have had an adequate opportunity for surveillance; nevertheless she had not transferred control of it to the appellants by a delivery and they were unaware that a valuable fur coat had been left in the reception room. . . .

"It follows that, in the absence of a bailment, the appellants owed the respondent no duty of care and were not negligent in failing to guard it effectively."

3. There must be delivery of the object to be bailed from the bailor to the bailee, and the bailee must accept delivery of the object. Since size, weight, and location prevent some items of personal property from being physically handed over to another person, we may have constructive delivery, such as handing a person the keys to a rental car in the parking lot and telling the person to go ahead and take it. Where the bailed property contains other items, there is no bailment as to those items unless the bailee knows or has reason to know of their existence.

Allen v. Houserman
250 A.2d 389 (Delaware, 1969)

FACTS   Frank Houserman left his car in Allen's Parking Lot. The keys, including the trunk key were left in the car. The car was taken from the lot by unknown persons but was later recovered. Missing from the trunk, however, were Frank's golf clubs, valued at $373.53. Frank had not told the attendant that the clubs were in the trunk. Frank sued for the value of the clubs.

ISSUE   Since there was a bailment of the car, was there also a bailment of the golf clubs in the trunk?

DECISION   No. Summary judgment entered for defendant Allen.

REASONS   In a very brief opinion Judge Quillen held that there could be no bailment of the clubs unless Allen knew of them or should have known of them.

"[T]he duty of the bailee parking lot depends upon notice, actual or constructive, of the presence of golf clubs. . . . It is clear under the stipulated facts that there was no actual or express notice given by plaintiff to the defendant.

"The case thus turns on constructive notice. It has been held that constructive notice may be established by the presence in a car of personal property in plain view which was or should have been seen by the employees of the parking lot. . . . This is especially true when the property is such that its presence would normally be anticipated. . . . But such authority does not help the plaintiff where the property is locked out of sight in the trunk. And, notwithstanding the growing band of golf devotees, it can hardly be reasonably said that a downtown parking lot should impliedly anticipate the presence of golf clubs in the trunk of each patron's car.

"Since there is no genuine issue of fact and no evidence of actual notice and no facts which could constitute constructive notice, the defendant is entitled to judgment as a matter of law."

---

4. The bailee must have a duty to return the personal property to the bailor or to deliver the property to a third person or to dispose the property in accordance with the wishes of the bailor. Let's say that you rent a U-Haul truck to move your household goods from Los Angeles to New York. As the bailee, you will have a duty to return the specific property, namely the truck, to the bailor or to any person the bailor may designate. In this case, let's say that the bailor does not have an office in New York but that the bailor directs you to deliver the truck to a specific location where an employee of the bailor will pick it up and drive it back. Thus the important factor here is that the object is still the bailor's

property and that the bailee has the duty to give up possession of the object at the time and place that the bailor designates.

Custody Situations Where a Bailment Will Not Normally Exist

In the typical university parking lot you either pay by the month and get a sticker for your windshield or you go through a gate and get a claim check which requires payment when you leave the lot. Typically, you park your own car and keep the keys, and therefore no bailment exists. You have not entrusted your car to the owner or the attendant of the parking lot. You were simply renting space on which to park your car. If, however, you take your car to a parking garage and as you enter the garage, the attendant gives you a claim check, takes your car and parks it, and retains the keys, then there is a delivery to the bailee and acceptance by the bailee. In the case involving the university parking lot there was no delivery to the bailee or acceptance by the bailee. You simply drove your car in and parked it.

Another example of custody without bailment would be a situation where, upon entering the university bookstore, you are asked to check the books you are carrying so that there will be no confusion as to what you purchased when you leave the store. If an attendant accepts delivery of the books and gives you a claim check, there would be a bailment. However, if you simply leave your books in the shelves and boxes which the bookstore has provided for that purpose, then there is no bailment and generally there is no liability on the part of the store if your books are stolen or damaged. With no delivery and no acceptance as bailee by the bookstore, it would be liable only for loss or damage due to its specific negligent or intentional conduct.

Central Parking System v. Miller
586 S.W.2d 262 (Kentucky, 1979)

FACTS   Stephen Miller regularly parked his car in Central's six-story self-park structure and walked to work at a nearby office building in Louisville. As the customer drove up, the ticket machine issued a time-stamped parking ticket. The customer picked a parking space and took the keys to the car with him. The customer paid at a cashier's booth near the garage exit. The structure was patrolled three times daily by garage personnel. On three occasions Miller had expensive wire wheels stolen from his car. He recovered $854.97 in the lower courts.

ISSUE   Was Central liable *as a bailee?*

DECISION   No. Judgment reversed.

REASONS   Justice Stephenson said that the lower courts' reliance on a 1925 precedent was incorrect, given the facts of the present case and the nature of modern-day parking operations.

"The standards that were applicable to a liveryman should not be applicable to a parking garage where hundreds of cars are parked daily. While it may have been that these standards were applicable to a parking garage in 1925, it is not practical to them to garages of today. There are more automobiles in existence today, more and larger parking facilities, and easier access to these facilities as a result of automatic ticket machines and other technological advances. No longer is entry into a lot or garage and the parking of a car dependent upon the presence of the owner or an attendant or an express agreement between the garage and car owner. For these reasons we hold that . . . the facts in the case at bar do not create a bailment.

"Therefore, Central Parking is not liable to Miller in the absence of negligence. . . . The effect of this holding is that the owner of the car must offer proof of specific acts of negligence by the operator or his employees if he is to recover for loss or damage. . . . The trial court made no finding that Central Parking was negligent, holding only that there was a bailment created and Miller had met his burden of proof. However, as a result of our holding Miller must prove specific acts of negligence on the part of Central Parking in order to recover for his stolen wheels. In the absence of such evidence, Central Parking is not liable."

Justice Sternberg dissented, since he apparently didn't understand the difference between saying that Central had to exercise reasonable care and would be liable if Miller could *prove* it had not done so and saying that Central was a bailee and was thereby *presumed* negligent unless it could explain the loss. His solution was to make Central a bailee even though on the facts here it clearly was not one.

Rights and Duties of the Bailee

Since a bailment is based on an expressed or implied agreement between two parties, each party has rights and duties with regard to the use, care, and eventual return of the object of the bailment.

1. Rights of the Bailee. The bailee has the right to possess, use, and control the object during the period of the bailment, subject to any legal restrictions and to the restrictions in any expressed or implied contractual agreement. Let's say that you take your car to the garage to have the motor tuned up. The garage will no doubt write out a work order showing the work to be done on the car and will give you a copy of the work order. You park the car in the garage's parking lot, and you hand the keys to an employee of the garage. Impliedly, you have given the garage owner or his employees permission to drive the car from the parking lot into the garage where repairs will be made and to test-drive the car after the repairs have been made. Thus the bailee has the right to possess, use, and exercise control over your car for the purposes of the bailment, namely, to tune up the motor and test-drive the car. The bailee in this instance does not have the right to drive the car home and use it for pleasure over the weekend before returning it to you on Monday.

Barrett v. Freed
35 A.2d 180 (District of Columbia, 1944)

FACTS   Mr. and Mrs. Freed stored certain household furniture and personal effects with Alva Barrett, D.B.A. Barrett's Transfer Company. The warehouse receipt was issued in the name of Mrs. Freed (Bettye). Mr. Freed bought a fire insurance policy which covered the goods while they were in storage. The warehouse receipt expressly disclaimed liability for loss by fire and instructed the bailee to make sure the goods were covered by insurance. The warehouse receipt indicated that the goods would be stored in a warehouse at "rear 618 Eye Street, N.W., Washington, D.C." Mr. Freed's insurance policy gave the same location and indicated that the goods were only insured while they were stored there. Some of the goods were later relocated at 612 H Street. No notice was given to the Freeds that their goods had been moved. The fire occurred at 612 H Street. The trial court directed verdict for the insurance company, since the goods had been moved, and against Mr. Freed, since he was not named in the warehouse receipt. Mrs. Freed was awarded $450 by the jury. Barrett appealed.

ISSUE   Did the bailee's movement of the goods without the bailor's consent make the bailee liable for the loss by fire despite the contract provision?

DECISION   Yes. Judgments affirmed.

REASONS   Judge Hood was clear that English and American precedents made the bailee liable under such circumstances.

"One storing goods has a right to know where the goods shall be stored. Especially this is true where the warehouseman does not assume responsibility for loss by fire. The location and type of building affect the risk which the owner assumes. . . . The contract of bailment called for storage at a particular place, and the bailee breached his contract by removing the goods to another place. It is well established that if a bailee without authority deviates from the contract as to place of storage and a loss occurs, which would not have occurred had the property been kept at the agreed place, the bailee is liable for such loss, even though he is not negligent. . . .

"If a bailee elects to deal with the property entrusted to him in a way not authorized by the bailor, he takes upon himself the risks of so doing, except where the risk is independent of his acts and inherent in the property itself.' . . .

"The rule laid down above has been generally accepted by American authorities, and we hold that when Barrett, without authority from or notice to the owner of the goods, removed them from the place of storage specified in the warehouse receipt, he breached his contract of bailment and assumed the risk of the destruction of the property. . . .

"The removal of the goods from the designated place of storage was a willful act on the part of Barrett. Indeed, removal of the goods without notice to the owner, thereby causing him to lose the protection of his insurance, was gross negligence on the part of the warehouseman. . . .

"All appellant's trouble arises from his failure to carry out his contract."

2. Duty of Care for the Bailed Property. The standard of care owed by a bailee to the bailed property differs with the type of bailment involved. Basically there are three types of bailment. First, there is a type of bailment where both parties benefit from the bailment. Before leaving school, you rent a rug shampooer from a rental agency so that you can clean up your apartment and get your security deposit back. You are paying for the use of the rug shampooer, and thus the bailor is receiving benefit, and in exchange for your payment you are receiving the right to possess, use, and control the rug shampooer for a specified time. Second, there is a type of bailment where the bailor is the only person who benefits from the arrangement. An example of such a bailment would be the situation where you found out that you neighbor was going to the store where you bought your stereo set, which has to be taken back for adjustment, and you asked your neighbor whether he would take the set to the store for you and save you the trip. Your neighbor agreed, and you delivered the set to him for the purpose of taking it to the store for repairs. Obviously, your neighbor was doing you a favor and there was no benefit to him. Finally, there is a type of bailment where the bailee is the only person who benefits. Your roommate borrows your car for the evening. No payment is to be made. The bailment is simply for the benefit of the bailee.

With regard to the difference in the duty of care owed by the bailee in these three different types of bailments, the courts have found that in a bailment where there is benefit to both parties, the bailee owes a duty of ordinary care. This means reasonable care to protect the object of the bailment from foreseeable damage, or the care that a reasonable and prudent person would take of his or her own goods under similar circumstances. In a bailment which benefits only the bailor, such as the case where your neighbor takes your stereo set to the store, the bailee does not owe the same degree of care as does the bailee in a mutual benefit bailment. Here the bailee owes only a slight degree of care. Thus, if your neighbor put your stereo set on the back seat and then struck a chuckhole on the way to the store, so that the set slid off the seat and was damaged, your neighbor would not be liable to you for the damage. In a bailment where the bailee receives the sole benefit, the bailee owes a high degree of care. If your neighbor wanted to borrow your stereo set for use at a party, the bailment would be solely for the benefit of the bailee, your neighbor. In that situation your neighbor-bailee would owe a high degree of care for the safety and condition of your stereo set. The differences in the bailee's duties of care in the three different types of bailments make good sense. However, problems arise when the courts try to apply these duties of care to actual situations. What is slight care, ordinary care, and a high degree of care will depend on the type of object bailed, the circumstances surrounding the bailment, and whether the bailment was gratuitous or for consideration. If you loaned a friend a brand-new car with less than 1,000 miles on it, you would expect the friend to be more careful about where he or she parked the car, what roads he or she drove on, and so on, than if you loaned a friend a beat-up 1965 Chevy, especially if the Chevy already had some dents in it and the paint was faded. Thus each case will have to be decided in light of all the factors mentioned above.

In view of the uncertainty as to just what the common-law liability of the bailee may be, in certain circumstances it is advisable to specify the bailee's liability in the bailment contract. This is especially true for a professional bailee such as a garage, a warehouse, or a repair shop. A parking garage will normally have a clause in the bailment contract stating that the garage will not be responsible for theft of or damage to the automobile while the automobile is in its custody. Typically, this clause is printed on a parking ticket which you receive as you enter the parking lot. Also typically, the terms are in very small print. This clause may be effective in relieving the bailee of liability for damage to your car if the clause is called to your attention when you leave the car, except in cases where the bailee or its agents or employees negligently or willfully damage the bailed property. Thus, if the parking attendant backed your car into a post, the bailee would be liable for the damages even though a clause in the bailment contract disclaimed all liability. If, on the other hand, the brakes of another parked car failed and that car ran into your parked car, no negligence would be attributed to the bailee or its employees or agents, and thus the clause would relieve the bailee of liability.

Some courts have held such disclaimers to be against public policy and thus not effective to limit the "professional" bailee's liability.

Julius Garfinkel & Co. v. *Firemen's Insurance Co. of Washington, D.C.*
288 A.2d 662 (District of Columbia, 1972)

FACTS   Mrs. Earl Ryan left three fur pieces with Garfinkel's for storage. Six months later, two of the three furs were apparently redelivered to someone else. The storage contract which Mrs. Ryan signed contained a limitation of liability, to a maximum of the value stated in the contract for each item. Mrs. Ryan said that she asked the clerk for advice in filling in the value and was told that if the items were already covered by insurance, she could avoid higher storage charges by stating a nominal value for them. The missing furs had been stated as having a value of $100 and $200, respectively. The driver for the delivery company which had been hired by Garfinkel's to deliver the goods to Mrs. Ryan said that he had not required the return of a delivery receipt for the goods because they were under the valuation for which a receipt was required. Mrs. Ryan collected $3,622.50 from her insurance company, which then sued Garfinkel's. Garfinkel's appealed from a trial court judgment against it for the full value.

ISSUE   Is the limitation of liability effective?

DECISION   Yes. Judgment reversed and case remanded for entry of a $300 judgment.

REASONS   After an extensive review of the facts. Justice Reilly summarized the legal rules on bailees' limitations of liability.

"It is well settled in this jurisdiction that a bailee for hire can limit his liability by contract, and such limitation will be honored by the courts, unless the bailee has been guilty of gross negligence or willful misconduct. . . .

"Such a limitation can be shown by evidence of notice to the bailor at the time he places his property in the hands of the bailee. . . . It should be noted, however, that attempts to limit liability by contract have been deemed ineffective in situations where the only notice consists of fine print on a parking lot claims check not presented to the bailor until after the bailee has taken possession . . . or on a laundry slip placed on bundles of finished work returned to customers. . . .

"In our opinion, there is no testimony in this case which could support a finding that Mrs. Ryan was not effectively put on notice that the valuation she herself placed on her furs at storage established a ceiling on a potential liability of Garfinkel's. Her own account of her colloquy with appellant's clerk reveals that she understood that because the furs were already fully insured by reason of her Firemen's policy, it was not to her economic advantage to pay a higher premium for equivalent Garfinkel coverage. . . .

"Nor can the judgment of the trial court be sustained by the text of the limitation of liability clauses. In our view, the court erred in placing so narrow a construction upon the previously quoted language in the storage receipt. A fair reading of the entire document indicates the Garfinkel's was not merely concerned with protecting itself against claims arising out of fire and theft, but also against loss or damage of any sort."

Justice Reilly also said that a mere failure of the deliveryman to get a receipt for the returned item did not amount to gross negligence, so as to avoid the terms of the contract.

The other extreme with regard to a contract clause concerns the bailee's assumption of full liability for the bailed object. If you take your diamond ring to the jeweler for cleaning, the jeweler may well issue a bailment contract which is in effect an insurance policy for the safety of your ring. Thus, if the jewelry store is broken into and your ring is stolen, the jeweler or its insurance company will reimburse you for the value of the ring. Rental contracts for cars, trailers, and equipment typically contain similar clauses, which purport to make the bailee liable for any loss to the property.

Statutory Liability of the Bailee

In certain types of bailments, the bailee has a statutory duty rather than a simple common-law duty of care. Common carriers and innkeepers, discussed in the next chapter, are by law held to a higher degree of care with regard to bailed property. Special statutes may also exist in particular states for parking lots, repair shops, dry cleaners, and other specific categories of bailees. Such statutes typically give the bailee a lien for services performed and the power to sell the property, if necessary, to enforce the lien.

Bailor's Liability for Defects

The traditional bailment litigation is that of a bailor suing a bailee for loss of or damage to the bailed property. Even though the amounts involved in many of these cases are relatively small, the results are important to the parties.

Increasingly, in our modern, complex urban society, people are renting all kinds of items from professional rental companies. Hundreds of thousands of cars are rented each year. Many businesses have discovered that it is more economical to rent trucks when they need them than to own and maintain their own fleets. College students rent furniture, TVs, and refrigerators. Do-it-youselfers rent all types of tools and equipment. Businesses rent computers, software, and other office equipment. As a result of these developments, legal rules have had to be formulated to deal with cases in which the rented property is defective in some way and causes injury to the bailee or to third persons.

Where the bailor simply loans an item to a friend, the bailor's only duty is to inform the friend-bailee of any known hazards or defects in the item. The bailor has no obligation to inspect the item or to discover existing defects. If the bailee has been informed of all known defects, the bailor has no further liability.

In the mutual benefit bailment, the bailor's obligation is much more extensive. Most courts which have looked at this problem in recent years have applied to the "professional" bailor the same three theories of product liability which are applied to the seller of goods. In such cases a bailor may be held liable for negligence, because of a failure to exercise reasonable care in maintaining, servicing, and inspecting equipment which is being rented for immediate use. The bailor may also be held liable for breach of warranty—either express warranty or the implied warranties of merchantability and fitness. The most recent development has been the extension to professional bailors of strict liability in tort for defects in their rented items.

Cintrone v. Hertz Truck Leasing & Rental Service
212 A.2d 769 (New Jersey, 1965)

FACTS Francisco Cintrone was injured when the brakes failed on a 1959 Ford truck which his employer, Contract Packers, had leased from Hertz. Cintrone had driven the truck for three days during the previous week. Cintrone said that he had complained to Hertz each day about the brakes, but Hertz had no record of the three alleged complaint slips. When the accident occurred, Cintrone was a passenger in the truck; the driver was Robert Sottilare. Sottilare said that prior to the accident he had had no difficulty with the brakes: "they wasn't perfect"; "they were a little low, but they held." Both men were injured when the top of the truck hit a low bridge; the brakes had failed completely. The trial judge refused to charge the jury on Cintrone's breach of warranty claim, and the jury found for Hertz on the negligence claim, apparently feeling that neither party had been guilty of any negligence. Cintrone appealed.

ISSUE Did the trial judge err in refusing to charge the jury on a breach of warranty theory?

DECISION Yes. Judgment reversed and case remanded for a new trial.

REASON Justice Francis reviewed the facts extensively and then delivered a long opinion which summarized the law of bailors' warranties. He noted that *Henningsen* had made it clear that a car puchaser would have a case against a seller under these same circumstances and that the UCC comments indicated that implied warranties were not restricted to *sales* of goods.

"There is no good reason for restricting such warranties to sales. Warranties of fitness are regarded by law as an incident of a transaction because one party to the relationship is in a better position than the other to know and control the condition of the chattel transferred and to distribute the losses which may occur because of a dangerous condition the chattel possesses. These factors make it likely that the party acquiring possession of the article will assume it is in a safe condition for use and therefore refrain from taking precautionary measures himself. . . .

"We may take judicial notice of the growth of the business of renting motor vehicles, trucks, and pleasure cars.

"The nature of the U-drive-it enterprise is such that a heavy burden of responsibility for the safety of lessees and for members of the public must be imposed upon it. . . . [T]he offering to the public of trucks and pleasure vehicles for hire necessarily carries with it a representation that they are fit for operation. This representation is of major significance because both new and used cars and trucks are rented. In fact, . . . the rental rates are the same whether a new or used vehicle is supplied. In other words, the lessor in effect says to the customer that the representation of fitness for use is the same whether the vehicle supplied is new or old. . . . The nature of the business is such that the customer is expected to, and in fact must, rely ordinarily on the express or implied representation of fitness for immediate use. . . . [I]f a traveler comes into an airport and needs a car for a short period and rents one from a U-drive-it agency, when he is 'put in the driver's seat' his reliance on the fitness of the car assigned to him for the rental period whether new or used usually is absolute. In such circumstances the relationship between the parties fairly calls for an implied warranty of fitness for use, at least equal to that assumed by a new car manufacturer. The content of such warranty must be that the car will not fail mechanically during the rental period."

Justice Francis also noted that a finding of "no negligence" by the jury would not necessarily prevent liability based on breach of warranty.

CASES FOR DISCUSSION

LISSIE v. SOUTHERN NEW ENGLAND TELEPHONE CO.

359 A.2d 187 (Connecticut, 1976)

Sponzo, Judge

The plaintiffs were employed by the defendant in its commercial department located on the second floor of a two-story structure maintained by it in the North Meadows area of Hartford. The plaintiffs were not permitted to leave their coats by their desks or in their working area. Because there were no facilities available for the plaintiffs' coats on the second floor, they were assigned one of two areas on the first floor. On November 29, 1972, the plaintiffs left their coats in one of the areas on the first floor. They were unable to see their coats in the coatroom from their working area on the second floor. The location of the coatroom in question was primarily for the convenience of the defendant. On said date, after working from 8 A.M. to 8 P.M., the plaintiffs discovered that their coats were missing from the area on the first floor where they had been left after the plaintiffs returned from lunch at 2 P.M.

No charge was made by the defendant to the plaintiffs for hanging their coats, nor did the defendant have an attendant or custodian on duty at the coatroom to receive the coats. The plaintiffs knew that the area in which they hung their coats was unguarded. On the day in question members of the general public had access to the coatroom and the building until 5 P.M. without being required to show identification. After 5 P.M., ingress to the building could only be obtained by ringing a bell and showing identification. The coatroom in question did not have security supervision from 2 P.M. to 5 P.M. on November 29, 1972, nor was there evidence that a security guard was in fact on the premises between 5 P.M. and 10 P.M. The one security guard at the location each day between 5 P.M. and 10 P.M. was responsible for 35,000 square feet, four acres of property and 175 parking spaces. The security measures taken were for the benefit of the defendant and not for the protection of the employees' personal belongings. Prior to moving into the North Meadows area in 1969, the defendant discussed various security measures to be taken, including the security of employees' coats, but no such measures were taken because it was decided they would be counterproductive. The defendant refused to reimburse the plaintiffs for the loss of their coats. . . .

The principal issues raised by the defendant are whether the court erred in concluding that a bailment was created, in finding that the defendant presented no evidence of the actual circumstances of the loss, and in not considering the question of the degree of care exercised by the defendant.

Whether an arrangement between employer and employee for storing personal property during working hours, such as the one revealed by the facts in this case, gives rise to a bailment is an issue of first impression before this court. The essential element of bailment is the express or implied assumption of control over the property by the bailee. Applying that principle to the instant case it is apparent that the defendant required the plaintiffs to leave their coats in the first-floor coatrooms and prohibited them from bringing their coats into their working area on the second floor. The defendant had knowledge that during working hours the plaintiffs' coats, together with the coats of other employees, would be left in those areas specifically designated by it. By requiring its employees to comply with that procedure, the defendant implicitly assumed exclusive, albeit temporary, custody and control over their personal property during working hours. The trial court correctly concluded that

the plaintiffs surrendered custody and control of their coats to the defendant during working hours, thereby creating a bailment. . . .

We are in agreement with the trial court that the bailment in the instant case was one for mutual benefit. The standard of care required of a bailee in a mutual benefit bailment is due care. . . . When a bailor establishes that his property has not been returned, however, a presumption arises that the loss of the bailed property was due to the bailee's negligence, notwithstanding the standard of care to which the bailee is held. . . . In order to rebut the presumption, the bailee must prove "the actual circumstances involved in the loss of the property." . . . "The isolated fact of destruction by fire or of loss by theft rebuts nothing. The bailee must prove something more if he is to overcome the presumption. He must prove the actual circumstances connected with the origin of the fire or the theft, and these include the precautions taken to prevent the loss." . . . "The proof must go so far as to establish what, if any, human conduct materially contributed to that immediate cause." . . .

Whether the bailee has proved the actual circumstances of the loss and rebutted the presumption of negligence is a question for the trier of fact. . . . Although there was testimony by the plaintiffs that their coats were "stolen" and testimony on behalf of the defendant regarding security measures taken for the protection of its premises, we cannot say that the trial court erred in finding that the defendant failed to rebut the presumption of negligence. No evidence was presented as to the conduct that materially contributed to the loss and the evidence of security measures instituted by the defendant does not establish conclusively that it fulfilled the duty of using reasonable care to prevent the plaintiffs' loss. The trial court correctly concluded that the defendant failed to rebut the presumption of negligence on its part as bailee.

KLOTZ v. EL MOROCCO INTERNATIONAL, LTD.

288 N.Y.S.2d 684 (New York, 1967)

Arnold L. Fein, Judge

On Saturday, October 29, 1966, at about 1:00 A.M., plaintiff drove his specially equipped 1965 Cadillac up to El Morocco, the corporate defendant's night club. Other cars were parked at the curb, so plaintiff double-parked his car. A man wearing a French Foreign Legion type uniform, in front of the premises, helped plaintiff and his guests out of the car. Plaintiff testified the uniformed man said he would park the car and that plaintiff should "leave the keys in the ignition." Plaintiff left the car with the motor running and the keys in the ignition and entered El Morocco with his guests, after telling the uniformed man to be careful not to "nick" the car while parking it.

They remained in the club until about 3:00 A.M. When they emerged, the uniformed man handed plaintiff the car keys and said, "The car is gone. It's not here." Plaintiff went back into the club and complained to the maitre de, at whose suggestion and in whose presence plaintiff phoned the police, who had not been previously advised of the car's disappearance. Plaintiff then went outside and walked around the block looking for his car.

On cross-examination plaintiff testified he had been at defendant's club on many prior occasions. In the courtroom, he identified the man with whom he had left the car. Plaintiff did not receive a claim check, nor did he pay any fee. He did not tell the man where to park the car. Plaintiff testified without objection he "assumed it would be parked in front of El Morocco." When plaintiff came out of the establishment, the uniformed man stated he had parked plaintiff's car on Second Avenue, between 54th and 55th Streets, around the corner from El Morocco, and that it was gone. After plaintiff notified the police, and before their arrival, he again talked to the uniformed man. Plaintiff then walked around the block with a man he described as the uniformed man's assistant, looking for the car without suc-

cess. Later that night, plaintiff and a police detective toured the area looking for the car, which was never found. . . .

Defendant's witness, Vincent DiGiovanni, the person identified by plaintiff as the uniformed man in front of El Morocco, testified that he was the doorman at El Morocco. He greeted patrons of El Morocco, assisted them out of cabs and cars, called cabs and cars for patrons, and parked cars when asked to by patrons. He wore a uniform which he supplied. He worked several nights a week, always at the door, outside the club. He had no assistants, and no one took his place on nights he was not there. No one else parked cars at El Morocco, although sometimes patrons' chauffeurs helped him. He parked about 30 to 35 cars on the night of the incident. He normally parked approximately 60 to 70 cars during a six-day week. Most of the cars were "classy" cars. He knew there was a public parking lot on the same block and a public garage in the area. However, he customarily parked the cars of El Morocco's patrons on 54th Street, west of Second Avenue, in the same block as the club, and also east of Second Avenue, toward First Avenue, and on the west side of Second Avenue, between 54th and 55th Streets. He also parked cars for the patrons of other restaurants in the area.

He confirmed plaintiff's testimony as to what had occurred on plaintiff's arrival at the club except that he testified plaintiff asked him to park the car. After assisting plaintiff and his guests into the club, DiGiovanni drove the car around the corner and parked it on the west side of Second Avenue, between 54th and 55th Streets, at a point which could not be observed from in front of the club. He locked the car, returned to El Morocco, and put the keys on an unattended key rack inside the club, with other patrons' car keys. Sometime before 3:00 A.M., when he went around the corner for another patron's car, he observed plaintiff's car was gone. He thought plaintiff might have taken the car himself. DiGiovanni had been around the corner several times between 1:30 and 3:00 A.M. for other patrons' cars. He had not observed plaintiff's car was missing prior to 2:45 A.M. at the earliest. He returned to El Morocco and saw that plaintiff's keys were still on the rack. He took them off the rack and started looking for the car. When he could not locate it, he went back to El Morocco. Plaintiff was just emerging. He told plaintiff what had happened and gave him the keys. The man who helped plaintiff look for the car was a chauffeur whom DiGiovanni had asked to help because plaintiff was angry and doubted DiGiovanni's word as to what happened and where he parked the car.

DiGiovanni claims he was not questioned by the police until two days later. . . .

Plaintiff established a prima facie case by proving delivery to defendant's agent and failure to redeliver upon demand. The burden of going forward shifted to defendant bailee. . . . It was necessary for defendant to go forward with evidence "to show the circumstances of the loss in order to rebut the presumption of negligence" arising from the failure to return or redeliver. . . .

DiGiovanni's testimony added little except that it more firmly established the fact of his agency, finally conceded by defendant's stipulation at the close of the case. The question is whether his conduct rose to the dignity of that degree of care requisite in a bailment for mutual benefit, the care and diligence which prudent men exercise in the conduct of their own affairs. . . . Although one might have assumed that a night club such as El Morocco would provide garage or parking lot facilities, there was no evidence in this case on which to base such conclusion. Moreover, plaintiff's voluntary testimony that he presumed the car would be parked in front of El Morocco negates any such determination. It amounted to a concession he expected his car would be parked in the street. "A person who parks his car in the street of course takes the risk of leaving it unattended." . . . However, parking a car in front of El Morocco does not mean parking it just anywhere. It implies at least parking it where it could be kept under some degree of observation. Although there was no evidence such instruction was given to or agreed to by DiGiovanni, it is appropriate to find this degree of care warranted under the circumstances.

The burden of proof on the whole case was on the plaintiff to show the loss was occasioned by the negligence of the defendant. . . . It is common knowledge that the streets of New York City have become one vast parking lot, day and night, sometimes to the profit of the city. The court must judicially notice that a host of people park their own cars overnight, unattended, in the city streets. However, this does not necessarily measure the standard of care. The test is not the care one actually uses for his own property, although this is entitled to consideration. . . . The fact that DiGiovanni left the keys on an unattended rack in the night club for two hours evidenced negligence, although there was no proof the keys had been removed by anyone except DiGiovanni. . . .

DiGiovanni testified he parked the car on Second Avenue at a point where it could not be observed from his station in front of the night club. He conceded it was a "classy" car, but he did not inspect its location or make any patrol during the two-hour period involved. He parked other "classy" cars equally far from his sight. As long ago as 1912, it was held that a bailee who parked a horse and wagon for a similar period and did not keep it under observation was chargeable with negligence. . . . Although the horse and buggy days are gone and a locked car is not a horse and wagon, the applicable degree of care under the circumstances has not lessened. The point of that case is that the bailee is required to use that degree of care requisite under the circumstances. As there stated, "It seems to me that the defendants exercised absolutely no care to safeguard the plaintiff's property." . . . It is easier to steal a horse and wagon than a locked car. However, the theft of a locked car, not under some measure of observation, is unfortunately no great feat. There was a failure to keep the car within view or some measure of observation for two hours. Whether parking in that location for that period violates the traffic regulations does not appear. The circumstances of the parties and the nature of the subject of the bailment are pertinent factors. . . . Defendant was negligent in that it failed to exercise that degree of care required of a reasonably prudent operator of a night club such as El Morocco for motor vehicles of the type owned by plaintiff.

After trial, judgment for the plaintiff in the stipulated sum of $2,000 against the defendant El Morocco International Ltd. only. DiGiovanni not served.

FARNUM v. CONNECTICUT BANK AND TRUST CO.

168 A.2d 168 (Connecticut, 1960)

Colter, Justice

The plaintiff, a retired professor 76 years of age, sues to recover securities or their value, which he claims to have placed in a safe deposit box.

He rented the box from the defendant at its Willimantic branch. . . . He purchased negotiable bonds valued at approximately $8,400, represented by five certificates, on October 18, 1957, from Wood, Struthers and Company of New York. . . . He opened the envelope at that time, examined the certificate, and then placed the unsealed envelope containing them in an unlocked deep filing drawer in a desk at his home in Hampton, Connecticut. He left Hampton October 20, Sunday, in company with his wife, to visit their daughter in New York, placing the bonds in a small zipper brief case which he packed in a larger suitcase for travel by automobile. They returned to Willimantic on October 25, Friday, after visiting with their daughter and her family, arriving in front of the bank about noontime. He parked at a meter, purportedly took the zipper case out of the suitcase, proceeded to remove the manila envelope, then its contents, and inserted them in a smaller envelope, about $9\frac{1}{2}$ inches by $4\frac{1}{8}$ inches, which he placed in the inside pocket of his suit coat. He went into the bank and after going through the necessary procedures received his box, took it into a small room, removed the securities from the small envelope which he took from his coat pocket, and supposedly placed them in the box. He closed and latched the box and returned it to the attendant, who placed it in the vault within the plaintiff's line of vision. The plaintiff had not examined the bonds from the

time he left on October 20 through the time he allegedly put them in the box on October 25. He made a visit to the box on December 31 to put in another security. On January 24, 1958, the plaintiff, at the request of his son-in-law, who was about to make out the plaintiff's income tax return, opened the box at the bank to list the securities he owned. He then discovered that the bonds he thought he had left in the vault on October 25, 1957, were not in the box.

The court visited the bank, viewed the premises, and heard testimony there. The vault and boxes were made and installed by the Moseley Company. To enter the vault the customer signs a card, the attendant opens a grill door by key, then a guard key is inserted in the box lock, and the customer's key, given to the attendant, is inserted. The lock is opened, and the box is taken out and given to the customer, who takes it to a booth. When he returns with the box, the grill door is opened by the key again and the keys inserted, the box locked, and the customer's key returned. There are only two customer keys, which are kept by the customer, and if they are lost, the box must be drilled open. In such a case the lock is changed and the customer given a new box and new keys. The customer's key cannot be returned to him unless the box space is locked.

What happened to the bonds is a mystery. Duplicates were issued for all the bonds except the $5,000 Federal Land Banks $4\frac{1}{2}$ percent. In a letter to Wood, Struthers and Company dated January 27, 1958, the plaintiff states in part:

Dear Sirs:

* * * * *

On Friday, October 25, I took them to the bank and supposedly placed them in the box with other securities. My wife recalls telling me to tuck them safely in an inside pocket when I left the car to enter the bank. I signed for the box and to the best of my knowledge put these securities in it and saw that the box was returned to its space in the vault.

Upon checking up on the contents of the box on Friday, January 24, 1958, I discovered that four of these securities were missing. I am completely mystified over the situation. I certainly had the securities and took my box out in which to file them. The securities made a sizable package. In leaving the small room in which I had them with the box, it would seem that I could hardly have failed to notice them had I closed the box without placing them inside, and left them on the table. And yet this is the only conclusion I can come to.

At all events the securities are gone, either lost in some manner or stolen.

I have notified the bank. I have searched and re-searched my home. My wife and I have carefully reviewed our movements. She remembers, confidently, my placing them from brief case into my inner coat pocket and going directly to the bank.

I left the bank with a distinct sense of relief that they were safely cared for. As a rule I try to be extremely careful, especially about matters of this kind, but I am forced to acknowledge that I must have made a careless move somewhere. I was completely dumfounded to discover them gone.

I fear the securities have been stolen, but I am hoping that in some way recovery in part or in whole may be made, that the situation isn't entirely hopeless.

The first notice of claim against the bank was made in a letter dated July 23, 1959, prepared by a New York lawyer.

In a case such as this, where the bank leases a safe deposit box, the relationship of bailor and bailee exists as to securities or valuables placed in such box, even though the bank has no knowledge as to the property deposited. . . . It is a bailment for hire and mutual benefit. This is true even though access to the contents can be had only by use of a key retained by the lessee, and the relationship is distinguished from that of landlord and tenant. In general the rights, duties, and liabilities of the parties seem to be that the bank "holds out to the public the implied agreement that property placed in its custody will be protected so far as reasonable human foresight will permit, from the ordinary dangers to which valuables . . . are exposed." . . . There appeared no special contract between the parties herein limiting any rights, duties, or liabilities.

Generally, a bailee owes the duty to return or account for the property deposited. . . . On demand, the bank must produce the contents, and if it cannot do so it must account for its failure by showing some reason to excuse such failure. It has been held that a loss through theft excuses the bank from its obligation to redeliver, in the

event it has exercised ordinary care to prevent the theft. . . .

Under the above authorities, it has been held that the bank must exercise reasonable care in keeping such property, in the selection of its employees and in the supervision of their conduct and is liable only when the loss results from a failure to exercise ordinary care, since the bank is not an insurer except by special contract or statute. . . . They likewise hold that a prima facie case is made out when the contract, delivery of property, and failure to return the contents on demand are shown, but it does not shift the burden of proof, since "although the duty to go forward and rebut the prima facie case is on the defendant, the risk of nonpersuasion on the whole issue is on the bailor as plaintiff." . . .

Proof of nonproduction makes out a prima facie case; the bailee must then prove the actual circumstances; and thereafter the burden on the whole case is upon the bailor. . . . The bank showed upon all the circumstances it used proper care. . . . The plaintiff is uncertain as to the happenings; a fortiori, the court is uncertain. In argument, counsel suggested that the attendant might have palmed the plaintiff's key and made a wax impression of it. This is pure conjecture from the circumstances as related to the court. There were too many safeguards thrown up by the bank, and the young lady attendants seemed far from having the legerdemain of a Houdini to accomplish such a feat in view of a customer or others.

The issues are found, and judgment may enter, for the defendant.

LUCAS v. AUTO CITY PARKING
62 A.2d 557 (District of Columbia, 1948)

Cayton, Chief Justice

Mr. and Mrs. Lucas were medical students at George Washington University, which is just across an alley from defendant's parking lot. . . . Mr. Lucas testified that just before 4:00 P.M. on October 28, 1947, he drove his wife's automobile into the alley adjoining the parking lot; that he had many times driven into this parking lot and was well known to the attendant; that in accordance with his usual custom, he drove into the alley and he and his wife got out of the car as they saw the parking lot attendant coming toward the car; that he left the keys in the car; that the attendant gave him no ticket because he was in a hurry, and, as was frequently the case, the two plaintiffs ran on into the school leaving the car for the attendant to park; that he left on the floor of the back seat a black medical leather bag containing medical instruments belonging to himself, and a fountain pen belonging to his wife; that when the door on the left side is opened, the rear seat floor is exposed so that it is readily visible to anyone getting into the car and that the black bag was readily visible; that he was accustomed to leaving articles of clothing, books, and his bag of medical instruments in the car when he drove into the lot, and that no one ever told him not to; that before this occurrence he had never seen any sign stating that the lot was not responsible nor had he seen any printed matter to that effect on the ticket; that he had many times received a ticket and usually did receive one, except when he was in an unusual hurry, as on the occasion in question; that he drove his car into this parking lot four or five times a week, and had done so for 18 months, during his attendance at the medical school; that he returned about 5:00 P.M. for his car, and it could not be found; that the attendant then gave him a parking ticket which was offered in evidence; that plaintiff noticed the time stamped on the bottom of the ticket that day and had noticed the time stamped on the bottom of the ticket on a few previous occasions; and that the car was afterwards found in a slightly damaged condition.

* * * * *

An attendant employed by defendant testified on that day in question Mr. Lucas brought the car into the alley and disappeared and when he got to the car no one was there; that he did not see a black bag on the floor of the car and did not know it was there; that he took the car and parked it in the northwest corner of the lot facing the alley; that on the right hand side of the car there were iron posts which would prevent the car being taken out at the north end, but that it could

be driven onto the alley and then north out to Eye Street without passing the cashier's booth; that he remembers moving the car at least once, at 4:00 P.M., to get another car out but that he put it back in the same place; that the car was taken without his permission and he did not know by whom; that he gave Mr. Lucas a ticket and reported the matter to the company. He testified that the cashier's window at the front of H Street side of the lot is so constructed that the cashier can see over the whole lot. He also testified as to a sign on the cashier's booth stating in part "Not responsible for articles left in car."

More specific testimony as to this sign was given by defendant's manager who said that since March or April it had been on the north or front side of the cashier's booth where customers pay their fees; that it is 2½ by 3 or 3½ feet; that the top portion is in letters three inches high and reads "Cars left after closing hours will be locked and the keys will be available the next weekday morning at 8:00 A.M."; that the lower portion is in letters about two inches high and reads "Not responsible for articles left in car"; that all the lettering is in black on a white background. The manager also testified that he designed the form of customer's parking ticket which had been in use at the lot since March or April 1947 (during the 18 months the plaintiffs had been parking their car there). The particular ticket which plaintiffs received on the day of the theft was in evidence, and contains these words in the largest type on the ticket "COMPANY NOT RESPONSIBLE FOR ARTICLES LEFT IN CAR." Also in bold type is a provision reading "No Employee Has Authority to Change Above Conditions."

In contending that they were entitled to be compensated for the loss of their personal property left in the car, plaintiffs contended (1) that the trial judge should have held that defendant was a bailee of such articles, and (2) that even if not a bailee, defendant's negligence in failing to prevent the theft of the automobile was the proximate cause of the loss of the articles therein.

The trial judge in a written memorandum held that there was no agreement, express or implied, as to the safekeeping of the medical bag, and we think the finding was fully warranted by the evidence. There was no proof that the medical bag was in any way entrusted to the care and custody of defendant. The evidence was simply that plaintiff's car was driven into the alley next to defendant's lot and left there. . . . [T]he attendant swore that he never saw it. The burden was on the plaintiff to prove that the articles lost had been entrusted to and accepted by an employee of defendant, and without proof of such acceptance there could be no bailor-bailee relationship. We rule that the trial court was justified under the evidence in holding as it did that there was no agreement between the parties for the safekeeping of articles.

Plaintiffs argue that a custom had grown up under which they and others had repeatedly left personal belongings in cars parked on the lot and that liability should be predicated on such custom. However, if such custom existed, reliance on it was entirely unilateral, for there was no evidence that defendant or its agents agreed to the custom or even knew of it. A custom, to be binding, "must be certainly shown to be the general usage of the trade. . . . It must be definite, uniform, and well known, and should be established by clear and satisfactory evidence." Thus the only bailment proven was that of the automobile itself, together with its usual ordinary equipment. But a medical bag containing medical instruments cannot be considered the usual, ordinary equipment of an automobile, for which a garage or parking lot would normally be expected to answer in case of loss.

Plaintiffs also advance the argument that there was at least a gratuitous bailment of these articles and that defendant as a gratuitous bailee was guilty of gross negligence in allowing the car to be stolen, and is liable on that theory. But as we have said, the evidence showed no bailment at all except of the automobile itself; hence this argument must fail.

The trial court based its decision in part on the limitation of liability printed on the claim check and rule that plaintiffs knew or should have known thereof. This court has held that unless a customer knows of the terms of a limitation of liability on a ticket or claim check the limitation is not binding upon him but that when the customer does have knowledge of such terms he is bound thereby. In the circumstances of this case the question as to whether plaintiffs knew of the limitation was one of fact and the judge's finding thereon must stand, for there was sufficient evidence to support it.

Next we consider plaintiffs' contention that even if there was no bailment defendant is liable because its negligence in permitting the automobile to be stolen was the proximate cause of the loss of the bag. There is, of course, no question of defendant's liability for theft of the automobile and the ensuing damage thereto. And such liability was recognized and established by the judgment below. But there was no proof whatever, and no fact from which any sound inference could be drawn, as to when or by whom or under what circumstances the bag was stolen from the car. Perhaps it was stolen by the same thief who took the car, and perhaps not. Perhaps it was stolen from the car before the car was taken from the lot or after the thief abandoned the car. We can easily get lost in a tangle of speculation on the subject. But neither we nor the trial court can predicate a valid finding on such speculations.

It must be remembered that as to this feature of the case plaintiffs are not in as preferred a position as on the claim of bailment, with the attendant presumptions operating in their favor. On this theory of the case they are making a specific charge: that the proximate cause of the loss of the bag was defendant's negligence in failing to prevent the theft of the automobile. There was no evidence of support to that charge.

It follows from what we have said that the judgment must be and is Affirmed.

1. Gaspane Restaurant required its waitresses to wear uniforms while on the job. It provided a room, with a clothes rack and lockers, where the waitresses could change into their uniforms and leave their purses and other personal property. The room was unattended, although waitresses came in and out at various times, either on breaks or when their shift was over. The room was at the rear of the restaurant, which had a city alley running directly behind it. The rear window had been locked, but it had been jimmied open with a crowbar. Sally Simple's new coat and purse were stolen. The coat was worth about $300, and the purse $45. Salley had just cashed her paycheck at the bank, and she had nearly $400 in the purse. Gaspane has refused to reimburse her. Is Gaspane liable for the loss of any of this property? Discuss.

2. Bennie Berb parked his car on a parking lot owned by Brovas Parking, Inc. He drove up, took a claim check from the automatic machine, parked his car, and took the keys. His car was about 100 feet from the attendant's office, which had windows on all sides. The lot was well lighted. Later that evening an unidentified customer told the attendant that something was happening to one of the cars on the lot. The attendant went over to Bennie's car and saw a man looking under the hood. The man told the attendant that something was wrong with the car, which was his brother's, and that he was trying to fix it. The attendant made no further inquiry or observation, nor did he call the police, as he had been told to do if he saw a car being tampered with by unknown persons. When Bennie got back, the transmission was missing from his car. When Bennie sued, Brovas denied liability on the basis that no bailment had been established. What result here, and why?

3. Ralph Ruff and his wife, Renata, went to the Classy Clothes Store to pick out a new suit for Ralph. They found a style they both liked, and Ralph told the salesman that he wanted to try on a particular suit. The salesman told Ralph that he had better leave his wallet and pocket watch in a drawer under the counter rather than in the changing room, saying: "It will be safe here, I think." Renata and the salesman went over to a mirror where Ralph was seeing how he liked the fit of the new suit. Ralph decided to buy it, and Renata and the salesman waited at the mirror for Ralph to come out of the changing room. When Ralph came out he had the salesman write up the sale and then said: "Now I need my watch and wallet." Neither item was in the drawer. Classy denied that there was a bailment and also said that Ralph was as much at fault for his loss as the store. Can Ralph recover here? Why or why not?

4. Floyd Babbyng sued his employer, Rapid Repairs, Inc., for the loss of his toolbox and its contents, worth a total of $850. Floyd was required to furnish his own tools on the job, and because of the size and weight of the toolbox it was not practical to take it back and forth each day. Employees' tools were thus stored in the repair shop, at first in a locked crib, later just in the work area. The shop was located on a major highway, in a large one-story building. The premises were lighted both inside and outside at night. On two sides of the building were four electrically activated overhead doors, each weighing about 900 pounds and about 12 feet wide by 16 feet high. Rapid said that each door was equipped with a factory-installed locking mechanism, but Floyd said that the locks didn't always work and that Rapid had installed steel locking pins in the tracks on which the doors ran up and down. Floyd also said that it was possible to operate the doors manually. The thief had cut a hole in a glass pane in one of the doors, through which he could reach the locking pin and the electric switch but not the locking mechanism. When Floyd sued, Rapid said that it had met its standard of care. Had it? Discuss.

5. Homey Hotel was located near a large resort area. In addition to its apartment hotel, it owned a large attached public garage with eight parking levels. Homey reserved 100 spaces in its garage for the cars of its tenants. It rented 50 spaces for other cars on a regular basis to local commercial establishments. Another 100 spaces were rented to local residents and vacationers for boat storage. Les Lepeck rented a space in the garage to store his boat. Homey told all its boat storage customers that they could get access to the garage only by calling the office from the outside and requesting that the building engineer come down and open the garage doors. Boat storage customers were not given keys to the garage, and Les said that he thought the procedure was the same for all parking customers, including those who were just parking cars. Unknown to Les, however, all of the customers parking cars had keys to open the garage doors. Les's boat is now missing, and he wants to hold Homey liable for the loss. Can he do so? Explain.

6. Vera Valla was a patient of Dr. Horace Poldleo. One morning, when she came to his office for her weekly appointment, she was wearing her new fur coat, worth $1,800. She took off her coat and hung it in the small clothes closet located in the waiting room. Dr. Poldleo and his partner each had a private consulting office attached to the waiting room, but there was no receptionist or other staff person regularly in the waiting room. When Vera came out after her appointment, her new coat was gone. Dr. Poldleo denies liability. Can Vera recover for her coat? Why or why not?

7. Olga Orson, staying in town for a business conference, parked her car at the Saf-T Parking Garage on Thursday morning. Saf-T was a "valet" parking garage, where the customer drove up, turned over possession of the car to an attendant, and was given a claim check. When Olga returned for her car late Friday afternoon and presented her claim check, the car could not be located. When Olga described her car and its out-of-state license plates, one of the attendants said he remembered giving that car to someone else who had also presented a claim check for it. When the other claim check was examined closely, it proved to be a forgery. The number on the duplicate check matched the number on Olga's. Is Saf-T liable for the missing car? Discuss.

8. Dawkins Construction Company sustained about $40,000 in extra costs and other economic losses when a large section of scaffolding collapsed at one of its construction sites. Dawkins had leased the scaffolding from Mayhew Company, an equipment rental firm. The scaffolding had been manufactured by Staco Corporation. Mayhew had solicited Dawkins' business by sending it one of Staco's brochures, which stated that its product would carry up to 20,000 pounds per panel, or twice the load of conventional steel scaffolding. The supporting scaffolding collapsed as Dawkins was pouring the concrete roof on a building. After making a number of tests, an engineering expert testified that the collapse had been due to an imperfection in the center of the connectors which were used to hold the scaffolding together. Under what theories of liability, if any, can Dawkins collect its losses from Mayhew? Explain.

Carriers, Warehouses, and Innkeepers | 32

In Chapter 31 we addressed bailments in general. In this chapter we will discuss the special problems and the law governing bailments where the bailee is a common carrier, for example, a truckline; a public warehouse (an establishment where the public may contract to store furniture or other goods); or an innkeeper (a motel or hotel). There are also special problems and specific law concerning the documents of title which are issued by the common carrier and the public warehouse but are not required in the ordinary bailment relationship referred to in Chapter 31.

Definition of a Common Carrier

A common carrier is an organization such as a railroad, a truckline, an airline, a bus company, a moving company, or any other type of business that holds itself out to the public as a transporter of goods. Private carriers also transport goods from one place to another; however, they do so on an individual basis only for persons who contract with them for their services. They are not bound by law to serve any or all people who request their services.

A common carrier must be licensed by the Interstate Commerce Commission if it transports goods over state lines and also has to be licensed by the individual commerce commissions of the various states where it is allowed to transport goods. The license granted to a common carrier designates the routes and territory over which the common carrier is allowed to travel and do business. The common carrier may also be restricted to the transportation of a certain type of goods. For example, the large household moving companies move only household goods and do not have to accept commercial goods for transportation.

Another difference between the common carrier and the private carrier is that the rates of the common carrier are uniform and are regulated by the Interstate Commerce Commission and the various state commerce commissions. That is, if you contact two common carriers in the same city to move your goods to a destination 500 miles away, both will have to quote the identical rates per pound for the move. The private carrier, on the other hand, may charge whatever the traffic will bear. Airlines, railroads, and bus lines are common carriers that carry passengers as well as goods. In the past, their rates were strictly regulated; however there is now a move toward the deregulation of rates, which will allow rate competition among the various carriers. To be classified as a common carrier, an organization must furnish transportation of goods or persons to those members of the public who request its services and must charge the rates set by the various regulatory commissions which regulate its operations. It must be licensed, and it must comply with the limitations as to territory and the type of services which it is allowed to perform under the licenses which it is granted as a common carrier.

Duties of a Common Carrier as a Bailee

In Chapter 31 we discussed the duty of care for bailed property and found that in a situation where both parties benefit from the bailment, the bailee owes a duty of ordinary care. This was explained to mean reasonable care for the protection of the object of the bailment from foreseeable damage. The contract of bailment between an owner of goods and a common carrier which is contracting to transport and deliver the goods is a mutual benefit bailment, since both parties benefit. The common carrier is receiving a fee for its services, and the bailor is getting the goods transported and delivered to a new destination. The basic difference between the duty of care required of the bailee in the ordinary bailment and that required in the common carrier bailment is that by law the common carrier bailee is an absolute insurer of the goods being transported from the time that it receives the goods until the time that it delivers them to their final destination. This is a very high duty of care, and there have been many instances where goods have been lost or damaged in transportation or delivery despite the fact that the common carrier used reasonable care.

It might be said that the common carrier is strictly liable for damage to the bailor's goods while they are in its possession. At first glance, this rule may seem very harsh, as there are situations where loss or damage to goods is caused by elements beyond the control or foreseeability of the common carrier. For this reason, five exceptions to the strict liability or absolute insurer rule have been carved out to reduce the common carrier's liability in certain circumstances. These exceptions are damage to goods or the loss of goods which is caused (1) by an act of God (for example, a tornado destroys the shipment); (2) by action of an alien enemy (this would include damage in an invasion by enemy forces); (3) by an order of public authority (for example, if goods in shipment were in close proximity to a nuclear power plant radiation leak, the public authorities might condemn the shipment and have it disposed of); (4) by the inherent nature of the goods, which renders them easily subject to damage or spoilage (for example, if goods are perishable, the bailor who is contracting to have them transported must notify the bailee of the problem and the bailee may not want to accept the goods unless it has proper facilities for refrigeration and some guarantee of speedy transportation and delivery); and (5) by the bailor's negligence in packaging or crating (this one is the most used exception). To illustrate the last exception, if you are moving your household furnishings, and you pack the dishes yourself, and you do not properly wrap them individually, and you do not use enough packing material around them to ensure their safety against the normal and expected bouncing around, then when you find the dishes broken at their final destination, you may not have a claim unless you can show that the box in which the dishes were packed was mishandled. For this reason, many bailors will have the bailee pack their breakable goods. Thus, if improper packing was done, the bailee is still liable, since the bailment started at the point of packing. Apart from situations involving one of the five exceptions described above, the duty of a common carrier with regard to the care of the goods in its possession for transportation and delivery is one of strict liability.

Southern Pacific Co. v. *Loden*
508 P.2d 347 (Arizona, 1973)

FACTS   Lou Loden was a produce broker whose business was located in Nogales, Arizona; he inspected and bought produce for various customers throughout the United States. On January 24, 1969, about 1:30 P.M., he gave the defendant two refrigerated vans, each containing 725 crates of cucumbers, for delivery to two of his customers in Los Angeles. The train with the cucumbers left Nogales at 4:15 A.M. on January 25, and it should have arrived in Los Angeles that same evening, but it did not arrive until 6:40 A.M. on January 29. The train was stopped at Yuma from 8:55 P.M., January 25, until 5:30 P.M., January 28, because heavy rains in the area had washed out both railroad bridges at Thermal, California, and had weakened several others. It had been raining for about a week before January 25, when the defendant first sent out its local bridge inspector to check the line. No weather records for earlier years were placed in evidence. The trial awarded Loden his damages from spoilage, $10,047.68.

ISSUE   Had the carrier proved its "act of God" defense?

DECISION   No. Judgment affirmed.

REASONS   Judge Howard described the high standard of care required of the common carrier and indicated that Southern Pacific had not done a very good job of proving its defense in this case.

"Common carriers impliedly agree to carry safely, and at common law they are held to a very strict accountability for the loss or damage of goods received by them. . . . In this state a common carrier's liability for damage to goods in transit is based on the substantive rule of law that the carrier is an insurer for the safe transportation of goods entrusted to its care, unless the loss is caused by an act of God, the public enemy, negligence of the shipper, or the inherent nature of the goods themselves. . . .

"Furthermore, common carriers undertaking to carry perishable goods are held to a higher degree of care than when engaged in the shipment of other articles not inherently perishable, and a failure to comply with this duty which results in a loss or injury to the shipper renders the carrier liable for the loss sustained, unless a proper defense is alleged and proved. . . .

"In addition, common carriers undertaking to transport property must, in the absence of an express contract providing for the time of delivery, carry and deliver within a reasonable time. . . .

"The law recognizes various fact situations as an excuse for delay which constitutes a good defense. . . . The delay, however, must have been due to an occurrence such as could not have been anticipated in the exercise by the carrier of reasonable prudence, diligence and care. . . .

"[E]very strong wind, snowstorm, or rainstorm cannot be termed an act of God merely because it is of unusual or more than average intensity. . . . Ordinary, expectable, and gradual weather conditions are not regarded as acts of God even though they may have produced a disaster, because man had the opportunity to control their effects. . . .

"Appellant did not offer any evidence of the condition of the bridge at Thermal on or before January 25, 1969. . . . [T]here was no evidence shown of a causal connection between the rainfall and the destruction of the bridge. . . .

"The rainfall in the instant case was not shown to be totally unforeseeable or of greater intensity than other rainfalls in the region so as to justify being called an 'act of God' and, therefore, the judgment of the trial court is affirmed."

One problem that seems to come up constantly is that of the liability of the initial bailee versus the liability of the various connecting carriers or subbailees. If you were shipping goods from New York City to Los Angeles, you would make a bailment contract with a shipper-bailee in New York City and that shipper would accept the goods for transportation and final delivery. However, as indicated above, common carriers are limited in the routes and territory over which they can operate, and therefore the New York common carrier might transfer the goods to several connecting common carriers before the goods are finally delivered in Los Angeles. Assume that the goods were in good condition when the bailor delivered them to the bailee carrier but were severely damaged when they were finally delivered in Los Angeles. Who damaged them— the original bailee, one of the connecting carriers, or the delivering carrier? Obviously, in many cases it is impossible to know which of the carriers caused the damage. Since there is strict liability for damage to the goods, the bailor may collect the full amount of the loss. The bailor may make the claim against either the initial bailee or the delivering bailee, and that bailee may then in turn seek restitution from the other carriers involved. Thus the loss may be shared by all of the parties that handled the goods.

What is the duty of the common carrier when the objects of transportation are persons rather than goods? Common carriers which transport human beings, such as railroads, airlines, and buses, are not held to be absolute insurers of the safety of their passengers; however, their duty of care for their passengers' safety is still very high. The injured passenger must prove that the common carrier was guilty of at least some negligence. The courts, while not making the common carrier strictly liable, do hold the common carrier to a very high degree of care for the safety of its passengers.

Vogel v. *State*
124 N.Y.S.2d 563 (New York, 1953)

FACTS   On March 4, 1950, Vogel (an attorney) went with some friends to ski at Belleayre Mountain Ski Center, which was owned and operated by the state of New York. The chair lift was about 3,000 feet in length, rose 784 feet, and consisted of a series of chairs suspended about 75 feet apart from a continuous cable. During skiing hours the cable usually moved continuously, with the skiers getting on and off while the chairs were in motion. Vogel had never used a chair lift, though she was classed as an intermediate skier. She watched the operation of the chair lift for about 40 minutes. She asked her friends about it and was told that it was "simple." When she got on the lift, the attendant shouted that her ski poles were in the wrong hand, so she shifted her poles. When she arrived at the intermediate station, where she wanted to get off, she discovered that she had lodged her poles in the chair. While she was attempting to disengage them, the chair bumped her from the rear. She panicked and threw herself to the right, falling and breaking her leg. She sued for damages.

ISSUE   Did the state, operating the chair lift as a common carrier of passengers, meet its standard of care?

DECISION   Yes. Vogel's claim is dismissed.

REASONS   In a very thorough opinion, Judge Young reviewed the operation of the chair lift, the state's status and obligations as a common carrier, the way in which the accident had occurred, and the possibilities of preventing it. Vogel's main argument was that the state had been negligent in not having properly assisted her in alighting from the lift and, specifically, in not having had a second attendant, on the right side of the chair, to help her off.

"The time has arrived when such transportation devices should be scrutinized by the Courts, and the concern which the operators show must be defined. . . .

"The duty owed by a common carrier of passengers is to use the utmost foresight as to possible dangers and the utmost prudence in guarding against them. . . . This includes making provision for the passenger to safely alight. . . . 'The degree of care to be exercised is commensurate with the danger to be avoided.' . . .

"It is a manifest impossibility for the operator of a ski resort to oversee and classify for his own protection the ability of every skier who may come to ski on his slope. Consequently, he must rely on each skier being a competent judge of his own abilities. . . .

"Likewise, the skier should bring to the riding of the chair lift the same degree of facility with skis that he employs in going down the hill. Barring any hidden defects or latent dangers, the skier who judges himself capable of skiing down a mountain from an intermediate station or the summit, must also judge himself capable of riding on a lift up to that station and alighting from a chair moving 500 feet a minute. If his talents fail him, through overconfidence or through no one else's fault, he alone must suffer consequences.

"In the instant case, the speed at which the lift was moving was obvious to the claimant. It was also obvious to her that she would have to alight from the chair while it was moving, and this with a pair of steel-edged boards strapped to her feet and carrying a pair of poles in her hand. The question which presented itself to her was simply whether or not she had the ability to do it. She gauged the situation for herself, assessed her own ability, was reassured by her friends, and made her own decision. . . .

"About the only thing not done was to stop each chair to let the skier alight. We do not feel that the State was called upon to do this as it could rely on the skier's ability to execute this simple maneuver, proof of the pudding lying in the fact that this was the first such accident in 30,000 rides.

"The proximate cause of the accident was the claimant's own negligence in permitting her poles to become entangled in the chair."

Rights of a Common Carrier To Limit Its Liability To Bailors

In the absence of any specific state or national law or regulation, a common carrier has the right to limit its liability to its own negligence rather than the strict liability or absolute safety standard by a provision in its contract with the shipper-bailor, provided, however, that the shipper-bailor is given a reduced rate in exchange for accepting the carrier's limited liability. In other words, if the shipper-bailor and the carrier-bailee agree to a limited liability contract, the courts will generally enforce the contract unless fraud, duress, or unconscionability was involved in the transaction. If the shipper-bailor so requests, however, the carrier-bailee must accept the shipment from the shipper-bailor with full liability, charging the full rate.

The common carrier may also make an agreement with the shipper regarding the value of the goods being shipped. Generally, the courts will accept this figure for loss purposes unless the amount appears to be unreasonable. Specific regulations of the Interstate Commerce Commission have further limited the liability of certain common carriers which transport goods in interstate commerce. These regulations do not affect the legal liability of the carrier for loss or damage. The liability is still strict liability with the exceptions previously noted. However, a limit is placed on the amount that the carrier must pay for loss of or damage to the goods. If you are moving your household goods from Chicago to New Orleans, the carrier is responsible for damage to or loss of individual items up to a maximum of 60 cents per pound. If a table lamp worth $100 were broken in shipment, the carrier would only have to pay 60 cents per pound for the amount the lamp weighed. Thus, if the lamp weighed 20 pounds, the carrier would only have to pay $12. If a refrigerator that weighed 300 pounds were lost, the carrier's payment would be $180. Thus, while the insurer is absolutely responsible for the safety of the goods being transported, there may be a limitation on their value based on their weight. If the shipper-bailor desires protection up to the full value of the goods, then the shipper-bailor may buy value insurance from the carrier or the carrier's insurance company. Specific regulations also limit the liability of common carriers which handle commercial freight rather than household goods. The value per pound is usually less for commercial freight. It should also be noted that the Interstate Commerce Commission regulations will change from time to time. Shipper-bailors should make themselves aware of the pertinent regulations concerning the transportation of their goods by common carriers.

As previously indicated, the Interstate Commerce Commission issues regulations governing the transportation of goods and persons in interstate commerce within the boundaries of the United States. However many common carriers carry passengers and goods by air and sea outside the territorial limits of the United States. Thus, there is a need for limitations on the liability of common carriers involved in international commerce and travel. The Warsaw Convention is a treaty which limits the liability of airlines carrying passengers in international travel. The Carriage of Goods by Sea Act similarly limits the liability of carriers operating in international waters. Thus, even though the common carrier is an absolute insurer of the safety of the goods it carries, limits have been set on the amounts which it must pay.

Limitations of Liability for Baggage Carried by Common Carrier

Common carriers which carry passengers, such as airlines, railroads, and bus lines, are required to have certain facilities for carrying the passengers' baggage. Regulations stipulate the number of bags that each passenger can transport and the maximum weight of each bag or the maximum weight of each passenger's total baggage. Limits have also been set to the common carrier's liability for loss of or damage to the baggage. The common carrier is not an absolute insurer of the passenger's baggage but is responsible only for its negligence in handling that baggage. Such negligence is defined as a lack of reasonable care in handling the baggage.

Shirazi v. Greyhound Corporation
401 P.2d 559 (Montana, 1965)

FACTS   Ebrahim Shirazi, an Iranian citizen, came to the United States in 1961 to attend school. He first attended school in Michigan, where he learned to speak about 400 English words. He then enrolled at Montana State College in Bozeman. In the summer of 1962, he took a trip to California, from which he returned to Bozeman by bus. At the bus depot in Redding, California, he checked a suitcase and two boxes of books as his luggage and was given a receipt. The books arrived in Bozeman but not the suitcase. In accordance with ICC regulations, Greyhound had filed a tariff limiting its liability for lost luggage to $25 unless excess value were declared and a higher fee paid. Notices to that effect were posted at the luggage counter where Shirazi checked his luggage and were printed on the back of the receipt that was given to him. Shirazi received a $680 judgment from the trial court. Greyhound appealed.

ISSUE   Was the limitation of liability effective?

DECISION   Yes. Judgment reversed.

659

REASONS   Justice Castles emphasized the fact that this case was controlled by U.S. law and that all applicable ICC procedures had been complied with by Greyhound.

"First, we must determine whether the plaintiff was given sufficient notice of the limitation. The rule that the shipper be given notice of the limitation of liability requires that he be given a fair and reasonable opportunity to discover the limitation. . . . It does not require actual knowledge of the limitation on the part of the passenger. . . .

" '[W]here a regulation limiting liability is so filed it is binding on the carrier and on the passenger, even though the passenger has no knowledge thereof. . . . [T]he effect of such filing is to permit the carrier by such a regulation to obtain commensurate compensation for the responsibility assumed.' . . .

"[I]n the case before us, Mr. Shirazi knew that the baggage receipt presented to him by the defendant's agent was concerned with the transaction of checking and shipping his luggage. It was incumbent upon Mr. Shirazi, who knew of his own inability to read the English language, to acquaint himself with the contents of the ticket. It was not incumbent upon the defendant to discover the plaintiff's inability and then inform him of the limitation contained in the matter printed on the baggage receipt and on the notice posted at the baggage counter. . . .

"The finding of the court below that it was unreasonable for the defendant to limit its liability to $25 is also error. If liability were limited to $25 without provision for obtaining greater coverage, the determination of the lower court may have been valid. However, plaintiff was given adequate notice of the opportunity to declare a higher value, pay a higher fare, and obtain greater coverage. It seems only fair that the transportation company be allowed to require that the compensation paid bear a reasonable relation to the risk and responsibility assumed. . . .

"The final argument of the plaintiff is that since defendant violated its tariff by accepting for transportation plaintiff's pasteboard boxes of books, it waived its limitation of liability and was responsible for the entire loss. . . . [W]here baggage accepted for carriage in conformity with the tariff filed by the carrier is lost, an otherwise valid limitation of liability is not waived by the acceptance for carriage of other baggage in violation of the carrier's tariff and this is not lost.

"The judgment of the district court awarding the plaintiff $680 plus costs is reduced to $25 plus costs."

The Bill of Lading—Document of Title

With the exception of automobiles, boats, airplanes, and other personal property which has to be specifically licensed to be used, the owner of personal property normally does not have a specific ownership document for such property. This is the origin of the expression "Possession is nine points of the law." In other words, it is assumed that the possessor owns the objects in his or her possession unless such ownership is challenged by another person. Thus, for most of the goods which are shipped, such as household goods or commercial goods, there are no specific title registration certificates. The shipper-bailor simply delivers the goods to the common carriers with instructions to transport and deliver them, or the common carrier comes to the residence or business of the shipper and picks up the goods with instructions as to their transportation and delivery.

At the point where the shipper-bailor turns over possession to the common carrier–bailee, a document showing ownership of the particular goods is necessary. This document is called a bill of lading if the transportation is by land or sea, and it is called an air bill if the transportation is by air. The bill of lading or air bill serves as both a receipt for the goods and as a contract which states the terms of the agreement to transport and deliver the goods. Title to the goods may be transferred from the shipper to another person or organization by transferring the bill of lading or air bill.

A bill of lading or an air bill can be negotiable or nonnegotiable. If the bill is to be negotiable, then it will state that the goods are to be delivered to the bearer of the bill or to the order of a specific person or organization. If the bill simply consigns the goods to a specific person or organization at the point of delivery, then it is nonnegotiable and it is called a straight bill of lading or a straight air bill.

The bill of lading or air bill must describe the goods. Typically, the weight of the goods will be stated and the number of items and the content of the shipment will be described in such a manner that the person receiving the goods will be able to identify them as those which were entrusted to the carrier for shipment.

Article 7 of the Uniform Commercial Code, Warehouse Receipts, Bills of Lading and Other Documents of Title, contains specific provisions governing the issuance and use of bills of lading. Normally the bill of lading is issued to the shipper-bailor. The shipper-bailor can then mail the bill of lading to the person or organization that is to receive the goods at their final destination. However, Uniform Commercial Code Section 7–305(1) allows the shipper to request that the common carrier issue the bill of lading directly to the person or organization receiving the goods at the final destination or at any other place which the shipper-bailor may request. Obviously, there are situations where it would be unwise to mail the bill of lading to the receiver of the goods and where it would be best to have the bill of lading issued by the carrier directly to the person or organization receiving the goods prior to or at the time of delivery.

If the bill of lading is negotiable, then the carrier may not deliver the goods without getting the bill of lading properly indorsed by the person or organization receiving them. If the goods are shipped under a nonnegotiable bill of lading, the carrier can simply deliver them to the person or organization named as consignee in the bill and the bill of lading need not be indorsed by the receiving party. The carrier must verify that the receiving party is in fact the party to whom the shipment was supposed to be delivered. If the carrier delivers the goods to the wrong person, the carrier will be responsible to the shipper-bailor.

Definition of a Warehouse

A public warehouse holds itself out to the public as a business engaged in the storing for members of the public for a fee. A private warehouse is a storage business which is not open to the public but only leases storage space to one person or company or to a select number of persons or companies.

Duties of a Warehouse as a Bailee

A warehouse is liable for damage to or loss of the goods being stored by the bailor only if the warehouse fails to exercise reasonable care in their storage and handling. Thus the warehouse is generally not held to the same standard of care as that required of the common carrier. What constitutes reasonable care has to be resolved in each case. The care required to store goods which are subject to damage or to deterioration by freezing would certainly be different from the care required to store lawn furniture for the winter. Fragile goods require more care than nonfragile goods. It would not be reasonable to stack heavy cartons on top of fragile antique tables. Certain types of goods require protection from freezing, whereas others are unaffected by temperature. Thus the standard of care depends on the type and the condition of the goods being stored, and the warehouse must provide facilities suitable for the goods being stored.

Rights of a Warehouse as a Bailee

The public warehouse is entitled to a lien for the amount of the storage charges on the goods stored by the bailor. If the stored goods are not picked up by the bailor at the designated time, the warehouse may, after giving proper legal notice to the owner of the goods or to any other persons having an interest in the goods, sell the goods to pay off the lien. It should be noted that most states have specific laws relating to the operation of warehouses and setting out the rights and duties of warehouses with regard to the claiming of liens for storage fees and with regard to the sale of stored goods to satisfy their bills.

Rights of a Warehouse to Limit Its Liability to Bailors

Like common carriers, warehouses may arrive at an agreement with the bailor on the values of the items being stored, and the courts will generally accept these figures assessing losses unless the amounts appear to be unreasonable.

Warehouses may also limit their liability as to the amount which they will pay if stored goods are lost or damaged. Such a limit on liability is a contractual agreement between the bailor and the warehouse. The warehouse gives the bailor a reduced rate, and the bailor agrees to a maximum amount for which the warehouse will be liable if the stored item is lost or damaged. For example, when you want to store the antique dresser you inherited from your grandmother, the warehouse may state in its receipt that its limit of liability for this item is $250. If, as the bailor, you exercise your right to reject the warehouse's limited liability figure, the warehouse may then charge you a higher rate to compensate it for the higher risk it assumes. The warehouse's liability limit must be stated for each item or each unit of weight and not simply as a standard dollar amount per customer.

Kimberly-Clark Corp. v. *Lake Erie Warehouse*
375 N.Y.S.2d 918 (New York, 1975)

FACTS   The plaintiff had stored paper at Lake Erie's warehouse. The paper was damaged by water, allegedly as a result of Lake Erie's negligence. Lake Erie said that it was not liable because the warehouse receipt issued to the plaintiff contained a provision which exempted Lake Erie from any liability for goods covered by the bailor's insurance. The plaintiff did have insurance coverage on the paper. At the end of the trial the trial court granted the defendant's motion to dismiss the plaintiff's case. The plaintiff appealed.

ISSUE   Did Lake Erie's disclaimer effectively exempt it from liability?

DECISION   No. Judgment reversed and case remanded for a new trial.

REASONS   Justice Del Vecchio said that the UCC clearly stated the circumstances under which and the extent to which a warehouse could limit its liability. Any other attempted limitations were ineffective.

"[A] warehouseman's liability is fixed by section 7–204(1) of the Uniform Commercial Code. . . .

"Subdivision (2) of the same statutory section provides the extent to and manner in which the liability imposed by the proceeding subdivisions may be modified. . . .

"Section 7–202 of the Code, relating to terms in a warehouse receipt, provides in part:

(3) A warehouseman may insert in his receipt any other terms which are not contrary to the provisions of this Act and *do not impair* his obligation of delivery (Section 7–403) or *his duty of care* (Section 7–204). *Any contrary provisions shall be ineffective.* (Emphasis supplied.) . . .

"The Uniform Commercial Code does not authorize exculpatory provisions like those contained in sections 7(c) and 20 of the defendant's Rate Schedule Agreement, under which the warehouseman is totally exempt from liability in a particular situation—i.e., when the bailor has secured insurance against the peril resulting in the damage of the goods stored."

Warehouse Receipts—Another Document of Title

Every warehouse which stores goods for the public must issue a warehouse receipt to the bailor when the bailor leaves the goods for storage. There is no specific statutory form that must be used. However, the receipt must contain certain essential terms, such as the location of the warehouse, the date the receipt is issued, the consecutive number of the receipt, and a statement as to whether the goods will be delivered either to the bearer of the receipt or to the order of a specified person, thus making the receipt negotiable, or whether the goods are to be delivered only to a specified person, thus making the receipt nonnegotiable. The rates to be charged must also be stated, and the goods must be described so that they can later be identified. The receipt must be signed by the warehouse or its agent, and if any advances have been made or any liabilities incurred, a statement of explanation must be made on the receipt. Section 7–202 of the Uniform Commercial Code governs the contents of the warehouse receipt.

Definition of an Innkeeper

An innkeeper, more commonly known today as a hotelkeeper, is any person or organization that operates a hotel, motel, or other business which offers sleeping and living accommodations to transient persons. The owner of an apartment complex is not an innkeeper, since he or she is not in the business of offering sleeping and living accommodations to transient persons.

Liability of the Innkeeper for Loss of or Damage to Goods of Its Guests

Traditionally the innkeeper was an insurer of the safety of the goods of its guests. The innkeeper's liability was subject to the same general exceptions that we found when we reviewed the liability of the common carrier for the bailor's goods. Thus the innkeeper was not liable for damage to the guest's goods caused by an act of God, a public enemy, the nature of the goods, some act of a public authority, or negligence or fault of the guest. (The bailor in this instance is the guest.) Most states have passed laws to limit the common-law liabilities of the innkeeper. Many statutes allow the innkeeper to limit its liability by posting a notice of the limitations. Frequently a notice will be placed on the door of a hotel room or a card will be left in the room which states that the hotel will not be responsible for the theft of money, jewelry, or similar valuables and which advises you to deposit these valuables with the innkeeper to be put in its safe until you are ready to leave.

Federal Insurance Co. v. Waldorf-Astoria Hotel
303 N.Y.S.2d 297 (New York, 1969)

FACTS Cesar Caceras, a guest at the Waldorf, discovered that his gold cuff links had been stolen from his room sometime between the evening of May 18 and the morning of May 19. Each cuff link was decorated with a nine-millimeter pearl; the cuff links were worth $175. The hotel denied liability under the innkeeper statute, saying that the cuff links were "jewels," "ornaments," or "precious stones" which should have been placed in the hotel safe.

ISSUE Were the cuff links "safe" property?

DECISION No. Defendant's motion for summary judgment denied; plaintiff's motion for summary judgment granted.

REASONS Judge Schwartz indicated that the only question was one of statutory interpretation. She reviewed several precedents for help in determining the meaning of the words in question. Items which had been held not to be "safe" property included a gold watch, a purse, a rosary, silver table forks, a silver soup ladle, a gold pen and pencil case, a traveling bag, a knife, and a diamond-studded watch.

"Section 200 of the General Business Law, being in derogation of the common law relative to the liability of innkeepers, is strictly construed. . . . The exemption is limited to the particular species of property named and, being strictly construed, cannot be extended in its application by doubtful construction so as to include property not fairly within its terms. . . .

"By analogy, the cuff-links in suit, even though fashioned of gold and ornamented with a pearl in each, cannot be considered as jewels or ornaments, as these terms are used and understood in common parlance. . . . Cuff-links are not used as jewels or ornaments but to close the cuffs, otherwise buttonless, of shirts. They are articles of utilitarian and ordinary wear in daily use, on all occasions, with business clothes as well as clothes designed for leisure, in the daytime as well as the evening. They are carried principally for use and convenience and not for ornament. Cuff-links, as with watches and other articles of ordinary wear, may be made of precious metals and even made more elaborate with precious stones, but these do not change their essential description as articles of ordinary wear."

Other states besides New York have enacted laws which limit the maximum amount for which an innkeeper can be held liable. Such a law might say that the innkeeper cannot be held liable for any amount in excess of $500 for loss or damage to the goods of a single guest. Some states have simply reduced the high standard of care that the common law required of innkeepers to a standard of ordinary care, basically the same care that any bailee must use with regard to bailed property. In no case, however, can an innkeeper be held liable for more than the actual value of the guest's goods. Moreover, the innkeeper is not liable for any consequential damages that may result from damage to or loss of the guest's property. For example, a manufacturer's representative rents a hotel room for one day, and he has two large suitcases full of samples which he uses to demonstrate his products to prospective customers. The suitcases are stolen from the room, and the representative loses an untold amount of sales because he cannot demonstrate the samples to his prospective customers. The innkeeper could be responsible for the value of the samples and the suitcase, provided that this does not exceed the statutory limit in that particular state and that the state law requires the innkeeper to be an insurer of the safety of the goods of the guest-bailor and does not hold the innkeeper simply to the standard of ordinary care. The hotel would not, however, be liable for the lost sales.

Rights of the Innkeeper

The innkeeper is given a lien on all goods brought onto the premises by the guest, for the charges for the accommodations. In most states the innkeeper can hold those goods until it is paid and can ultimately sell those goods to enforce the lien.

J. ARON AND COMPANY, INC. v. SERVICE TRANSPORTATION COMPANY

486 F. Supp. 1070 (Maryland, 1980)

Blair, District Judge

Early in the morning of June 29, 1977, Service Transportation's truck terminal warehouse burned to the ground. This is a diversity action brought by J. Aron and Company, Inc., the owner of a large shipment of coffee which was destroyed or seriously damaged in the fire. The plaintiff alleges that the defendant breached its duty as warehouseman/bailee. The defendant has counterclaimed for storage charges accruing after the fire. Additionally, the defendant has impleaded Fireman's Fund, its insurance carrier. The case was tried to the court. . . .

In June 1977, Service Transportation received 1,000 bags of the plaintiff's coffee, in good condition and invoiced at $442,378.15. The coffee was held at the defendant's Baltimore terminal pending release by the Food and Drug Administration. By letter of June 23, 1977, Service Transportation notified J. Aron and Company, Inc., that it was holding coffee "at the risk of the owner" and "as warehouseman only" and that storage charges would be assessed. . . . The defendant stored the coffee in four trailers backed up against the doors of its terminal. The coffee was severely damaged by a fire of unknown origin which occurred on June 29, 1977.

Thus the plaintiff proved the three elements necessary and sufficient to establish a prima facie case for recovery: delivery of its goods to the defendant, bailment for hire, and the defendant's failure to return the property in the condition in which it was received. . . .

The burden then shifted to the defendant to come forward and present evidence of nonliability, evidence either excusing its failure to return the bailed goods or evidence tending to show that it exercised due care in safeguarding the plaintiff's property. The Maryland version of the Uniform Commercial Code, Md.Ann.code, Comm.L. Article § 7–403(1)(b) is not to the contrary. The code places the ultimate burden of proof upon the owner of the bailed goods, but this burden does not even arise until the warehouseman or bailee establishes some evidence which would legally excuse nondelivery. Once the bailee articulates a legally sufficient excuse, a question for the trier of fact is presented, and the bailor must proceed affirmatively to demonstrate negligence.

In recognition of its burden, Service Transportation adduced the following evidence: that the fire was of unknown and possibly suspicious origin . . . ; that there was no history of fires in the neighborhood and that its building had never burned . . . ; that there was greater danger of theft than of fire, and that as precaution against theft, Service had backed the coffee-laden trailers close against the terminal doors . . . and equipped the terminal with a very sensitive ADT burglar alarm system . . . ; that the building was locked on the night of the fire; that Service generally provided overnight transfer service, with the result that goods were only very rarely stored on the dock overnight; and that the premises were attended from approximately 4:00 A.M. until 1:00 A.M. every day. . . .

If this were a jury trial, the court would have to determine at this point whether the defendant bailee had articulated sufficient evidence of excuse or due care to warrant sending the case to the jury. The court is of the opinion that the defendant probably did not make a sufficient showing of nonliability. . . . Nevertheless, since the court sat as the trier of fact, the court has assumed that the bailee's showing was sufficient, and required the plaintiff to prove affirmatively the bailee's negligence.

To this end, J. Aron proved the following facts: the Service Transportation terminal building was neither fireproof nor fire resistant. . . . It had masonry walls, a pitched, wood-trussed roof constructed of tarpaper and asphalt shingles, and seven wooden garage-type doors running down either side of the storage area, against which trailers were backed. . . . The building was described by one expert as "combustible," and is classified under the Baltimore City Building Code as "ordinary." . . . There was no fire alarm, smoke detection, or fire abatement system on the premises. . . . There was no round-the-clock guard service: in fact, the premises were routinely left unattended between 1:00 and 4:00 A.M. . . . The fire originated in the office area and within 30 to 40 minutes spread the entire length of the warehouse, engaging the roof and spreading to the trailers containing the plaintiff's coffee.

Finally, the plaintiff proved that, in violation of the Baltimore City Fire Code, there were stored on the premises on the night of the fire five 55-gallon drums of a "Class II" flammable liquid called Kure-n-Seal and five 55-gallon drums of a "Class I" flammable liquid printer's ink. The flash point of the two liquids is 108° and 25° Fahrenheit respectively. . . . The drums were stored near the middle of the dock, approximately opposite the doors at which the trailers containing J. Aron's coffee were parked. The Class II liquid had been stored on the Service Transportation premises for several weeks prior to June 29.

In the absence of the "highly hazardous room" required by the City code, acceptable alternatives where flammable liquid must be stored include sprinkler systems, buried vaults, water deluge systems, remote storage areas 40 feet or more away from occupied structures and dry chemicals. . . . Service Transportation had none of these. The minimum safety precaution which might pass muster where flammable liquids are occasionally handled for short periods of time would be to store the liquids in an empty locked trailer, away from the warehouse proper. . . . Again, Service did not store the drums away from its combustible building or away from the combustible and highly valuable cargo of coffee. Service did not even take the very slightest precaution available, that is, to store the flammables at the far end of the terminal against a masonry wall and away from the office and the coffee. . . . There was evidence that other companies in the area, when forced to store flammable liquids for a short time, store them either in a remote trailer or at the extreme end of the terminal building. . . .

Under Maryland law, it is well-settled that mere violation of a statute does not constitute negligence per se unless the violation was the proximate cause of the injury. . . . This court finds as a fact that the 550 gallons of flammable liquids stored on the dock on June 29, 1977, contributed to the spread of the fire to the trailers and to the coffee contained in them.

The defendant sought to rebut the plaintiff's case by showing that it was common practice in the local trucking industry to store small quantities of flammable liquids temporarily. Neither witness who testified concerning the practice in the industry, however, stated that his firm handled flammable liquids in the manner Service Transportation did. . . . This court concludes from all the evidence presented that Service Transportation failed to demonstrate ordinary care and diligence under the circumstances and thus failed to rebut J. Aron's affirmative showing of negligence. Accordingly, judgment will be entered for the plaintiff. . . .

There remains only the assessment of the plaintiff's damages. The parties agree that the price per pound of green Nicaraguan coffee was $2.67 on the date of the fire. Based upon an estimated net weight per bag of coffee at 152.076 lbs. (Plaintiff's Exhibit 3), the court finds the plaintiff's damages to be as follows:

Total value of coffee on 6/29/77
(1,000 bags nt. wt. ea. 152.076 at
$2.67/lb.) $406,042.92
Salvage expenses:
S. A. Wald & Co., Inc. 19,071.01
Belt's Wharf Whse., Inc. 849.34
Peter F. Luard & Co., Inc. Surveyors . . . 1,797.50
Freight (Baltimore to S. A. Wald &
Co., Inc. in New Jersey). 1,159.09
FDA charges: supervision of disposal
of unsalvageable coffee 122.75
$429,042.61
Less: Salvage proceeds to plaintiff. . . . . . $ 40,426.75
Storage charges, the subject of
defendant's counterclaim 8,909.25
$ 49,336.00
Total damages $379,706.61

DAVID CRYSTAL INC. v. EHRLICH-NEWMARK TRUCKING CO.

314 N.Y.S.2d 559 (New York, 1970)

Kassal, Justice

Plaintiff's applicaton for leave to reargue is granted. Upon such reargument and reconsideration of the original and additional papers presented, the decision of this Court is recalled and the following is substituted in place thereof.

Defendant, as a common carrier for hire in interstate commerce, concededly received and failed to deliver a property shipment received from plaintiff. The defense, in essence, is that the loss resulted from a hijacking on the streets of New York City of the defendant's truck, containing this shipment. Defendant contends that the loss resulted by reason of the act of a "public enemy" and that it is therefore not responsible for such loss.

The general rule is that a common carrier is an insurer against the loss of property received by it for transportation. The only exceptions are losses arising from an act of God or from acts of the public enemy. . . .

However, the Court decides to the contrary. In its general usage, the phrase "public enemy" connotes the existence of an actual state of war and refers to the government of a foreign nation at war with the carrier's government. It has also been expanded to include pirates on the high seas (who are considered enemies of all civilized nations) and in some instances, rebels in insurrection against their own government.

Thieves, rioters, and robbers, although at war with social order, are not to be classed as "public enemies" in a legal sense but are merely depredators for whose acts the carrier remains liable. . . .

The Court is of the opinion that despite the enormous increase in crimes generally and hijacking specifically, domestic criminals, whether or not they have achieved the status of having been singled out by the F.B.I. so that they become numbered public enemies, do not fall within the scope of "public enemies" for purpose of being an exception to the insurer liability of a common carrier for its shipments. . . .

Accordingly, the motion for summary judgment is granted to the extent of directing an assessment of damages. The amount thereof shall be entered as a judgment in favor of plaintiff against defendant.

UNION MARINE & GENERAL INS. CO. v. AMERICAN EXPORT LINES, INC.

247 F. Supp. 123 (New Jersey, 1966)

Cooper, District Judge

This is a claim for cargo lost on July 21, 1959, consisting of five barrels of sheep casings shipped aboard respondent's vessel, the S.S. *Excalibur*, from Beirut, Lebanon, to Hoboken, New Jersey. . . .

Filed July 15, 1960, the complaint seeks recovery against both the carrier, American Export Lines, Inc. (hereinafter known as "Export"), and McRoberts Protective Agency, Inc. (hereinafter "McRoberts"), a firm engaged by Export to protect cargo.

The evidence shows that all the barrels of casings involved here, valued at some $14,000, actually were last seen on July 21, 1959, while being discharged from the ship's crib at Pier B in Hoboken. When last observed, this cargo was in a hoist preliminary to discharge to the pier. Although due demand was made, the casings were never delivered to the intended consignee. . . .

Union Marine predicates its claim against Export on breach of the bill of lading which incorporated the provisions of the Carriage of Goods by Sea Act ("COGSA"), 46 U.S.C. Secs. 1300–1315. Prior to the commencement of trial, Export settled Union Marine's claim against it for the sum of $2,000. Seeking indemnity in the amount of its settlement, Export, in turn, cross-claims against defendant, McRoberts.

Union Marine's direct claim against McRoberts for the balance of the $14,000 loss is sought to be buttressed on several theories: (1) warranty, (2) tort, and (3) bailment. First, the complaint . . .

alleges, in substance, that the agreement between McRoberts and Export inured to the benefit of the consignee and "defendant negligently failed to perform its duty owing to the plaintiff to adequately observe the discharge of plaintiff's cargo. . . ." In its trial memorandum . . . Union Marine argues that McRoberts breached its warranty of workmanlike service, implied in such agreement, and that Union Marine was a third party beneficiary thereof. Alternatively, Union Marine argues that the consignee can take advantage of such a warranty even if it is not a third party beneficiary, since the warranty is not limited to the zone of direct contractual relations.

Second, in its post-trial memorandum . . . , Union Marine cites the principle, not grounded in contract, that an agent such as McRoberts is directly liable to plaintiff for the negligent performance of responsibilities which it undertook. Third, Union Marine contended by notice dated May 2, 1966, that it would prove at trial that McRoberts, as plaintiff's cargo bailee, failed in its burden of accounting for nondelivery. . . .

After a careful study of the total evidence adduced and the theories upon which plaintiff relies, we find plaintiff has failed to meet its requisite burden of proof.

THE FACTS

The Export-McRoberts Agreement

The substance of the 1958 oral agreement between Export and McRoberts is not in dispute. It provided, in essence, that the latter was to watch all cargo on the carrier's ships and piers, and be responsible for the safekeeping of "special" cargo.

As more fully set forth in Exhibit 2, . . . the agreement provided:

Export designated the items of "special cargo," preparing from time to time a list of such cargo which was delivered to McRoberts. When "special cargo" was discharged or received on the pier, McRoberts arranged with Export employees for its prompt transfer to a "safe room" or "crib" where it was held under McRoberts custody. McRoberts kept appropriate records of such cargo. Its men noted transfer to whom, by whom, and when such cargo was delivered out to an authorized person.

These general responsibilities encompassed in the oral agreement seem to represent no more than the normal customs and practices, as proved at trial, incident to McRoberts' daily work.

Security Procedures during Unloading

Special cargo is often discharged from the ship along with general cargo as it is in mixed storage in the hatches. Special cargo is usually carried in the locked compartments of a hatch called "security lockers" or "cribs," and a McRoberts guard on the ship in addition to the ship's mate (who holds the key) and crew of stevedores, is present on the outturn. McRoberts guards, stationed both on the ship and the pier, do not physically handle either special or general cargo.

From its initial landing on the stringpiece, cargo is taken by the stevedores via hi-lo equipment to various "sorting piles" on the pier. Here, Export's sorter designates where on the pier general cargo is to be placed pending delivery to the consignee's trucker.

If there is special cargo expected, Export's delivery clerk prepares a list indicating the specific cargo and gives one copy each to the sorter and accompanying McRoberts guard. In the words of McRoberts' supervisor, Buckridge, "we post a man at the sorting pile with the sheet to see that those [special cargo] are put on a special pallet and sent to the crib. In other words, . . . if the sorter misses something, the guard will pick it up and send it to the crib." . . .

The Cargo Loss

Turning our attention to the day in question, July 21, 1959, the five barrels of casings were last seen as they were lifted over the vessel, after being taken from the crib in hatch no. 2. . . . Although there was no direct evidence that the barrels landed on the pier, it may be so inferred under the circumstances.

According to Buckridge's uncontroverted testimony, there was no guard stationed at the stringpiece, because George Hinte, the

McRoberts guard at the sorting pile, "was so close to the stringpiece he had it in view all the time." . . .

Furthermore, while there was no liaison between Cusimano, the McRoberts guard at hatch no. 2, and other McRoberts guards on the pier, this procedure is compelled neither by the agreement nor by custom and usage. . . .

There being no credible evidence otherwise, we find, contrary to what should have taken place, that the casings were not on the list of special cargo compiled by Export's clerk and given to McRoberts personnel on the pier. . . .

THE LAW

Breach of Warranty

With regard to the alleged breach of warranty, we find general maritime law applicable. The general rule is that maritime contract is one having reference to maritime transactions, and thus we look to the subject matter of the contract. . . .

Such contracts of work and labor contain an implied warranty that the work will be done in a skilled and workmanlike manner. . . .

Union Marine contends, in substance, that McRoberts breached its warranty of workmanlike service in failing to have "kept the barrels under constant surveilance until they were safely stored in the pier . . . 'safe room,' as they agreed to do." Trial Memorandum, p. 35. In this connection Union Marine argues that Cusimano, McRoberts' no. 2 hatch guard, should have notified the pier in some manner that the barrels were about to be discharged.

Assuming Union Marine has standing to sue for breach thereof, we find that under the terms of the contract McRoberts did not agree and was not expressly required to maintain constant surveillance of each individual piece of special cargo, and failure to do so is not a breach of the implied warranty of workmanlike service. It is not an insurer. Further, its guards on the pier did not have actual notice of the casings. Moreover, they were not put on notice by virtue of the list.

The law compels McRoberts to exercise its best efforts in maximizing the security of the cargo. Whether it had notice or not, breach of warranty under these circumstances is predicated on the normal tort standard of negligence. . . .

We find the record barren of any proof of specific negligent acts or omissions attributed to McRoberts and connected with the disappearance of the shipment. "There is no rule requiring the testimony of eyewitnesses, or requiring a defendant voluntarily to testify because the plaintiff cannot otherwise ascertain the facts, or requiring defendant to prove affirmatively that he was not negligent." . . . The attendant circumstances are not such that we could reasonably draw an inference of negligence or causation from the mere loss of the cargo.

McRoberts was not negligent in failing to establish a liaison between the ship and the pier. The necessity therefore would seem obviated by the special cargo list. We are not told how the liaison should be accomplished or why it would be more efficacious than present security means so as to warrant change. . . .

The Tort Claim

Union Marine claims McRoberts as agent for the carrier is liable to plaintiff for its own negligence. . . . While it is a generally recognized principle that an agent is liable to third persons for his own misfeasance, the controlling standard of care is no different than that which we applied to the warranty claim. Accordingly, since there is no proof of negligence, we find the tort claim, founded upon the same factual allegations, without merit.

Bailment

Union Marine seeks to place the burden of explaining the loss on McRoberts. It is asserted that "custody of the barrels in the hands of McRoberts, began with the presence of its guard, Mr. Cusimano, in the hold. . . . Once having assumed custody of the barrels, the burden is on McRoberts to explain their disappearance. . . ."

Certainly, the burden of producing evidence to avoid an unfavorable inference would be cast on McRoberts were it deemed a bailee. . . . The rule finds its justification in the degree of control normally exercised by the bailee on the theory that nothing could have happened to the property if due care were used. "This is but a particular application of the doctrine of res ipsa loquitur. . . ."

There is no claim here, nor could there be with justification, that the casings were received by McRoberts at the "safe room" or "crib" on the pier. We are thus left with the question whether Cusimano, Hinte, or other McRoberts guards (not in the safe room) constituted bailees. We find no proof of any delivery and knowledgeable acceptance which would be the basis for a bailment relationship. Requisite possession and control is thus absent from the facts adduced. . . .

* * * * *

Based upon a quantitative and qualitative review of the entire record and the reasonable and natural inferences to be drawn therefrom, Union Marine has failed to prove its claim against McRoberts by a preponderance of the credible evidence. Export has similarly failed to prove its cross-claim.

The complaint and cross-claim are dismissed. Judgment shall be entered for defendant.

MORSE v. PIEDMONT HOTEL COMPANY

139 S.E.2d 133 (Georgia, 1964)

Hall, Justice

This petition alleged in essence that the plaintiff, a jewelry salesman, was a guest of the defendant Hotel and entrusted to the Hotel's bell boy a sample case containing valuable jewelry to take and place on a bus of the defendant Cab Company for transportation from the Hotel to the Atlanta airport. The bell boy placed the jewelry case in the baggage compartment of the airport bus, and the plaintiff boarded the bus. When the bus reached the airport, the sample case had been stolen as a result of alleged negligent acts and omissions of the defendants' agents in failing to protect it. The sample case and contents were the property of the plaintiff's employer. The plaintiff's employer was compensated for its loss

by an insurer, but the insurer cancelled its policy and no other insurance company would thereafter insure the plaintiff as a jewelry salesman. This caused the plaintiff to be fired from his employment and to be unable to obtain other employment and to suffer great mental pain and shock, shattering of his nervous system, a heart attack, and confinement to his home for two months. The petition alleged that as a result of the defendants' negligence and the larceny of the sample case the plaintiff had been deprived wrongfully of carrying on the business of selling of diamonds and jewelry in which he had been engaged for 40 years, and was damaged in the loss of earning capacity, at the rate of $20,000 per year, in the amount of $100,000 and because of pain and suffering in the amount of $25,000.

The plaintiff relies on the decision in *G. C. G. Jewelry Manufacturing Corp.* v. *Atlanta Baggage & Cab Co.*, 109 Ga. App. 469, 136 S.E. 419, another case which arose out of the loss of the jewelry sample case which allegedly caused the damages the plaintiff sues for in the present case. There the plaintiff's employer sued the defendant Cab Company as a bailee for the loss of the sample case, and this court held the petition set forth a cause of action. That was an action for property damages caused by the bailee's negligence, for which a bailee is clearly liable. . . . The decision does not support the present action, against allegedly negligent bailees, which seeks damages for the plaintiff's inability, resulting from the theft of the jewelry sample case, to obtain insurance covering him as a jewelry salesman and the consequent loss of his employment and earning capacity in this occupation and physical and mental pain and suffering.

In this petition the only duty allegedly owed to the plaintiff and breached by the defendant is the duty to protect the property the plaintiff entrusted to the defendants. The only damages that the plaintiff claims to have resulted to him from this alleged breach of duty are consequent to the loss of an insurance company which had to compensate the plaintiff's employer for its loss of the stolen jewelry case. For such indirect damages the law does not allow recovery. . . .

Generally a person is not liable for the unintentional invasion of the interest of another in his contractual or employment relationships with third persons. The rights or interests of the plaintiff which he alleges have been damaged—the interest in retaining insurance protection and the interest in his employment—he had by virtue of relations with others than the defendants in this case. The petition does not show that the plaintiff had property rights in his relationships with the insurance company or his employer, but such interests of the plaintiff as were damaged inhered in these relationships. The law does not place upon these defendants the duty to protect these interests of the plaintiff against unintentional invasion. . . .

The trial court did not err in disallowing the amendment to the petition and in sustaining the defendants' general demurrers.

PROBLEMS FOR DISCUSSION

1. Bosy Construction Company is engaged in road building and other heavy construction projects. It hired Jonsby Truck Line, Inc., to transport a large Caterpillar tractor from one of its jobsites to another. The tractor was damaged when the truck carrying it slipped off the dirt road at the jobsite, causing the tractor to break the tie-down chains holding it and to roll upside down. In its complaint Bosy alleged (1) that Jonsby's driver had negligently loaded the tractor and/or (2) that he had negligently operated the truck. In its answer Jonsby denied that it had been negligent in any way and said that the accident was due to Bosy's negligence in constructing and/or maintaining the road on its jobsite. At the trial Bosy offered no proof of the specific negligence charged other than the general presumption in a bailment case. Jonsby moved to dismiss. How should the court rule, and why?

2. A steel fabricating company, Twistem, Inc., needed to expand its facilities. It found a steel mill of United Metals, Inc., which was not being used and leased some space from the steel company. United Metals, Inc., had left a considerable amount of equipment in the mill. Some of this equipment could be used by Twistem, so Twistem entered into a second contract with United to rent that equipment. One of Twistem's employees lost a hand and most of an arm in a shearing machine which Twistem rented from United. The employee sues United for breach of bailor's warranties and for strict liability in tort. Does he have a case?

3. Sunny Electronics shipped a piggyback truckload of stereo components to New York on the Reading Railroad. In the piggyback shipping arrangement, a semitruck drives the load to the railroad's loading area, the van part of the truck is unhitched, and the van is then loaded onto a railroad flatcar for shipment to destination. At destination the van is off-loaded, rehitched to another truck, and driven away. Sunny's van of stereo components was badly damaged when it was dropped by the crane which was lifting it off the flatcar in New York. Reading sold what was left of the components for salvage and sent Sunny a letter to that effect, but Sunny filed no claim for over a year. When Sunny's claim finally was filed, Reading denied liability, relying on a clause in the bill of lading which stated that claims for loss had to be filed within nine months. Reading's letter to Sunny had been sent within the nine-month period. Does Sunny still have a valid claim? Why or why not?

4. Sirhan Shiftee, a sales agent for the Junky Jewelry Company, rented a room at the Palamo Motel. Sirhan was showing Junky's new line of items to prospective customers and was carrying a sample case with $90,000 worth of samples in it. The sample case was stolen from the motel room while he was asleep. Ranover Insurance Company reimbursed Junky for the loss to the extent of its policy coverage— $50,000. Junky sues Palamo for the balance of the loss ($40,000), the Ranover sues

Palamo for the $50,000 it paid Junky. This state's version of the innkeeper's iron safe statute says that an innkeeper is not obligated to take more than $500 in value from any one guest, for storage in the hotel's iron safe. It also says that for property other than jewelry and the like, the maximum recoverable is $250. What result in this case, and why?

5. M-T Potatoes, Inc., sued Yolanda Yassu for $7,500 allegedly due under a contract for storage of 14,000 hundredweight (cwt) of potatoes on M-Ts premises. Yolanda counterclaimed for damages to her potatoes caused by M-T's negligence in storing them; she said that the potatoes had been made unmarketable for potato chips and that her damages were $21,000. M-T was to store the potatoes and to maintain all controls for temperature and humidity. M-T charged 50 cents per cwt for storing the potatoes, 30 cents per cwt for the climate control arrangement, and 15 cents per cwt if the customer wanted it to load the potatoes onto trucks for shipment. Yolanda periodically inspected her potatoes, and she found water dripping on the inside of the bins, doors inside and outside the storage area improperly left open during the winter, and insulation missing in places. M-T says that it is not liable on Yolanda's counterclaim because (1) it is not a bailee but only a landlord and (2) there should be no presumption of a bailee's negligence where the goods are perishable. Are these valid arguments? Explain.

6. Mindy Morko, age 12, and her mother were visiting Mindy's grandparents, who were staying at the Landless Motel. At around 2:30 P.M., Mindy left the swimming pool area at the back of the motel and went to look at the rock garden and statue on the premises of the adjoining restaurant, the Landless Inn. Although both businesses had the same name, the inn was operated by a separate company and was not open for business at the time. Mindy spent several minutes looking at the inn's rock garden and statue. As she was skipping back to the motel, she was struck by a car driven by Hap Hapless in the driveway that separated the inn from the motel. Because of the shrubbery and other decorations, Mindy and Hap could not see each other. There was no warning sign to either pedestrians or drivers. Mindy sues the motel and the inn. Both deny liability on the grounds that she was not a guest, that she was trespassing on the inn's property, and that she was guilty of contributory negligence. Can Mindy recover for her injuries? Discuss.

7. Medstrong Company shipped 15,500 pounds of freight on the Seeanen Railroad. The shipping order named Krown Kartage Kompany as the consignee for the shipment but provided that 14,000 pounds should be left at the Little M Warehouse in St. Louis, that all freight charges should be billed to Little M, and that only the balance of the shipment should be taken to Krown's warehouse in Bismarck, North Dakota. When Seeanen tried to collect from Little M, it discovered that Little M was bankrupt. Seeanen now sues Krown for the freight charges on the entire shipment, since it was named as consignee. Seeanen relies on an ICC regulation which provides that if a consignee is acting only as an agent and has no beneficial interest in the goods being sent to it, it must notify the carrier in writing of that fact in order to avoid liability for the freight charges. Krown sent no such writing. On these facts, should Krown be held liable for the total freight bill? Explain.

8. Grouse Brothers Moving Company contracted to move Jocko Janisary's household goods to his new home in Missoula. Since it was a relatively short trip and the weather forecast was favorable, Grouse elected to use an open-top truck. The furniture and other goods were properly loaded, and a heavy tarpaulin was tied over the top of the load. As the truck approached the city of Fernwood, the driver and his helper noticed that weeds were being burned along the south side of the road and that dense smoke was blowing across the road. They debated about whether to go

through or not, but since the road itself was visible, they decided to go ahead. After they had driven another two miles, a car passed them, blowing its horn, with the driver of the car shouting that their load was on fire. By this time Jocko's goods were a total loss. Grouse denies liability since (1) Jocko had seen the nature of the truck, so the loss was due to an act of the shipper; (2) the city had done the burning, so this was an act of the state; and (3) the wind was an act of God. Can Jocko collect here? Why or why not?

Real Property— 33
Acquisition and Transfer of Ownership; Financing of Real Estate Transactions

The law concerning the rights and duties of the owners of real property differs considerably from the law concerning the rights and duties of the owners of personal property. Some objects of personal property can be picked up and taken from state to state or even from country to country. With regard to such objects we often hear the expression "Possession is nine tenths of the law." Exception for motor vehicles, most objects of personal property do not have registered titles to them.

When we deal with real property, we are dealing with land and with the permanent fixtures and buildings attached to it. The land cannot be picked up and taken across state lines; it is part of the earth's surface. The fixtures and buildings on the land may depreciate, burn down, or be destroyed otherwise; however, the land itself remains the same, century after century. Also, the land cannot be possessed physically as an item of personal property is possessed.

NATURE OF REAL PROPERTY

Real property is a term that describes the bundle of rights to a specific parcel of land. It includes not only the buildings and permanent fixtures attached to the surface of the land and the trees, crops, and any other vegetation growing on the surface of the land but also rights to the ground below the surface of the land and rights to the air and sky above the land. Thus the owner of a parcel of land has rights to the airspace above that parcel, to water on it, to things growing on or attached to its surface, and to the minerals, underground waters, and whatever else may be found below its surface.

Technically, the owner of a tract of land, and therefore of the airspace above it, could prevent anyone from trespassing into his or her airspace. This presented a problem since landowners could not be allowed to restrict the large volume of interstate or even intrastate air travel. Thus the American Law Institute formulated a rule to govern trespasses into the airspace above a land-owner's parcel of land. Such an overflight is privileged if it is made at a reasonable height and if it is in accordance with all applicable government regulations. Many states have passed specific statutory provisions clarifying the use of airspace which are similar in content to the common-law rules set out in the *Restatement of Torts.*

Burnham v. *Beverly Airways, Inc.*
42 N.E.2d 575 (Massachusetts, 1942)

FACTS
The plaintiffs owned a 174-acre country estate in Wenham, on which were located a "commodious" house, a garage, a water tower, and other buildings occupied by a caretaker. Beverly operated an airport on an adjoining 40-acre tract. It also stored and repaired planes, gave flying lessons, sold gasoline and other supplies, and carried passengers for hire. Military planes occasionally made use of the airport. Activities there had gradually increased. The plaintiffs asked for an injunction and damages. The trial court enjoined Beverly from flying its planes over the house and the immediately adjacent grounds at a height of less than 500 feet except when this was necessary for a safe emergency landing, and it granted damages of $1. Beverly appealed.

ISSUE
Is the plaintiff entitled to injunctive relief which protects 500 feet of airspace above the house?

DECISION
Yes. Judgment affirmed.

REASONS
Justice Qua stated that since the overflights had not been frequent enough or annoying enough to "affect the health, habits, or material comfort of a normal person," they could not be classified as a nuisance. He did feel, however, that they could be called a continuing trespass under the doctrine announced in the 1930 *Smith* precedent. He noted that the decisions in other jurisdictions since *Smith* had not been uniform but that the 500-foot rule had been adopted legislatively. He refused to discard *Smith's* trespass approach for a nuisance theory, which would be less favorable to the landowner.

"We see no occasion to disturb the fundamental basis of the decision in the *Smith* case. That case was not a slavish application of the ancient maxim *cujus est solumejus et usque ad coelum.* The just demands of modern progress were recognized, and room was left for their reasonable satisfaction, while at the same time protection was given to the landowner against that which he might naturally and justly regard as unwarranted intrusion. Ordinarily there would seem to be no sufficient reason for making flights lower than the limits fixed by the commission. The statute in expressly providing for the right of navigation above fixed limits by implication negatives the existence of any such general right below those limits in instances where the limits are applicable. . . .

"The facts in the case before us fail to justify flights below the level of 500 feet over the plaintiffs' house and the immediately surrounding grounds. No public necessity is involved. . . . Flying over the house or the surrounding grounds at a level below 500 feet is certain to produce noise to which the plaintiffs have a right to object, even if, in view of all the factors, it does not amount to a nuisance. . . . This case is distinguishable from the *Smith* case, where the court refused an injunction against trespasses over unused brush and woodland. . . . Here the injunction was rightly granted, and damages in the sum of $1 were rightly assessed against the defendant, Beverly Airways, Inc."

The most obvious area of real property is the surface of the land. In Chapter 30 we discussed the question of when fixtures become real property and how certain things which are part of real property, such as growing crops, may be severed from the real property and become personal property. Thus the rules are fairly clear concerning most of the land surface and the buildings, fixtures, trees, and growing objects, which are generally affixed and stay affixed to it until they are severed by people or by an act of God such as a tornado. The water that is present on the land surface is in constant motion, and it changes course and swells and shrinks in height and width with the seasons and the years.

Water rights are a concern of those who own land which abuts a lake, river, or other body of water. These rights are called riparian rights. Generally speaking, the owner of the land next to a stream, river, or lake may take or use the water as needed for natural and domestic purposes on the land adjoining the water. For example, the water could be taken for use in irrigation or for washing or drinking purposes. A riparian owner would not, however, have the right to divert the entire stream for his or her purposes and thus deprive landowners downstream of its use. Riparian rights also concern the property boundary lines of land next to a river, stream, or lake. Does your ownership extend to the edge of the river, 10 feet out into the river, or just where? The river or stream will run at different levels depending on the time of year. The general rule is that the property line will be at the point of normal flow of the river or stream. However, the law concerning riparian rights varies from state to state, because different areas of the country have different problems with regard to water. In areas where water is scarce and irrigation is a necessity, then of course rules with regard to the use of water from running streams will be stricter. Also different problems are involved if the property abuts a creek rather than a navigable river. In addition, many national and state statutes govern what a riparian landowner can or cannot do which might affect water quality.

With regard to what lies under the land's surface, the law covering minerals such as coal or metals is quite clear. If you own the land, you own everything below the surface unless the mineral rights were previously sold to someone else. Such sales of mineral rights are very common in Texas, Oklahoma, and other oil-producing states. If there is oil or water under your land and your neighbor's land, how much do you own? How much does your neighbor own? If you pump out the pool under your land, will you be taking your neighbor's oil or water? Since liquids seek their own level, you cannot just separate and take your part of the oil or water, beneath a large area of land. Thus the courts are constantly having to settle such problems. The *Restatement of the Law of Torts,* Section 833, adopts the reasonable use test.

Acker v. Guinn
464 S.W.2d 348 (Texas, 1971)

FACTS   J. P. Acker, Jr., brought this declaratory judgment action against M. M. Guinn to determine whether certain mineral rights passed under a deed executed in 1941. The deed conveyed "an undivided ½ interest in and to all of the oil, gas and other minerals in and under, and that may be produced from" a tract of 86½ acres in Cherokee County. Acker who held through the grantee, claimed that the deed included an interest in the iron ore on the land; Guinn, who held under the grantor, said that the deed did not include the iron ore. Over the years the main use made of iron ore from Cherokee County had been as a foundation base for road construction; iron ore was also used in the manufacture of cement. Because of its high silica content, this iron ore had to be mixed with other ores to make pig iron. The ore deposits were solid beds, varying in thickness from a few inches to three or four feet. There were outcrops of the ore deposits at some places, and the deposits ranged in depth to as much as 50 feet below the surface. The ore had to be strip-mined, which would destroy or substantially impair the use of the surface for farming, ranching, or timber production. The trial court granted Acker's motion for summary judgment; the court of civil appeals reversed.

ISSUE   Did the grant of "other minerals" include the iron ore?

DECISION   No. Judgment of appeals court affirmed.

REASONS   Justice Walker began with a discussion of the *ejusdem generis* rule of interpretation—that general words following specifics mean things of the same kind or nature as the particulars enumerated. Here this would mean the same kinds of minerals as those enumerated. The deed used was a form deed with the standard oil and gas clause; it stated that the oil and gas was already under lease to another but that if the lease were canceled, the grantee would own one half of the rights to oil, gas, and other minerals. Justice Walker then discussed the precedents and said that the correct test should be to find the "general intent" of the parties.

"A grant or reservation of minerals by the fee owner effects a horizontal severance and the creation of two separate and distinct estates: an estate in the surface and an estate in the minerals. . . . The parties to a mineral lease or deed usually think of the mineral estate as including valuable substances that are removed from the ground by means of wells or mine shafts. This estate is dominant, of course, and its owner is entitled to make reasonable use of the surface for the production of his minerals. It is not ordinarily contemplated, however, that the utility of the surface for agricultural or grazing purposes will be destroyed or substantially impaired. Unless the contrary intention is affirmatively and fairly expressed, therefore, a grant or reservation of 'minerals' or 'mineral rights' should not be construed to include a substance that must be removed by methods that will, in effect, consume or deplete the surface estate. . . .

"That is the rule to be applied in determining whether an interest in the iron ore was conveyed by the deed in this case. In terms of its location with respect to the surface, methods by which it must be mined, and the effect of production upon the surface, the ore is quite similar to gravel and limestone. Aside from the general reference to 'other minerals,' moreover, there is nothing in the deed even remotely suggesting an intention to vest in the grantee the right to destroy the surface. It is our

678

> opinion that in these circumstances the ore, like gravel and limestone, should be considered as belonging to the surface estate and not as part of the minerals. We accordingly hold that as a matter of law no interest in the ore passed by the deed."

LAND DESCRIPTION AND TITLE REGISTRATION

Personal property is capable of a simple description—for example, "a red 1980 Dodge Mirada two-door sedan." People can readily recognize the personal property in question by that description. On the other hand, if a person says that he or she owns 300 acres of land, we must have some method of description by which the boundaries of the land may be determined. Moreover, the method of description must be similar to the method used to describe the adjoining parcels of land. For these reasons some type of uniform system for describing and identifying land became necessary.

Basically there are two methods of land description—the metes and bounds description and the rectangular survey description. The metes and bounds description is the traditional method. It involves picking a starting point and marking it with a permanent stake or post so that it can always be referred to and then simply measuring distances and angles until you return to the starting point. This system was used for land description in the original 13 states of the United States. In 1875 the U.S. government adopted a rectangular survey system which is now used in the majority of the states. This system divides the land into rectangular squares called sections. These sections are divided into quarter sections and can be further subdivided as needed. A section is a square mile. Where the rectangular survey system has been adopted, there will be maps or plats of the entire surface area of the land in a county, divided into one-mile squares. Such plots are filed in the county courthouse. If the land involved lies within the limits of a city or town, it will be divided further into various subdivisions, which in turn are subdivided into lots.

Unlike personal property, for which physical possession is a strong indicator of ownership, ownership of land is proved by registration of title to it. A system of land registration has been developed. If you purchase land, you will be given a deed transferring ownership from the previous owner to you. This deed has to be filed or registered with the proper authority in the county where the land is located. The title will then be public record, and anyone may check the county records to find out who owns that particular tract of land. Land registration is also needed for taxation purposes. Real estate is a prime source of tax revenue for municipal, county, and state governments, and an ad valorem tax is imposed upon the registered title holder of a tract of land.

VARIOUS TYPES OF RIGHTS TO OWNERSHIP IN REAL PROPERTY

The bundle of rights to most objects of personal property is owned by one person. Seldom would a person have only a life interest in a book or a chair or an automobile. This, of course, is because personal property typically does not have perpetual life, as most items of personal property will fall apart, rot, or be destroyed in some other manner over a period of time. Land, however, as previously noted, will always be there. Thus there is a need to have a different set of ownership rights for real property than for personal property.

Following are the various rights which persons may possess in real property.

1. Fee Simple Estate. Fee simple title is the best title that an owner can have. This means that the owner has all of the so-called bundle of rights and that the owner has these rights forever. The owner of the fee simple estate can sell all of his or her rights in the land or any part thereof. If the owner dies, his or her heirs will inherit the fee simple estate and the title can go on and on through generations.

2. Life Estate. A life estate is an interest in land which is limited to the life of the person or persons to whom the life estate was granted. The owner of the life estate may not sell the land or cause permanent injury to it. The owner of the life estate simply has the right to use the land and the right to profit from it during his or her lifetime. An owner of a life estate may be viewed as a tenant who has free rent until he or she dies. Then the land will either revert to the owner who gave the life estate or, if the owner is now dead, it will go to the owner's heirs or to whomever the owner has designated in his or her will.

Medlin v. *Medlin*

203 S.W.2d 635 (Texas, 1947)

FACTS   T. W. Medlin died in 1939, survived by his wife Minnie and nine children. Five of the children—W. A. Medlin, Thomas, Marie, Julia, and Alice—sued Minnie and the other four children (Richard, John Keyes, Marie, and Geraldine) for a declaratory judgment interpreting T. W.'s will. The will gave Minnie all of T. W.'s property "to have the use and benefit of the same during her natural life, and at her death, all of such property in her hands shall completely vest in my children, share and share alike." In another paragraph the will gave Minnie "the full and complete management, use and enjoyment of all of my property during her said lifetime, including all rents and revenues to be derived therefrom." The plaintiffs argued that Minnie received only a limited life estate, for her use and benefit, rather than a general life estate and that, similarly, the rents and revenues earned during her lifetime were not hers absolutely but were only to be used for her reasonable support. The trial court rejected both of these arguments. The plaintiffs appealed.

ISSUE   Did the will create a general life estate in Minnie?

DECISION   Yes. Judgment affirmed.

REASONS   Justice Stokes first reviewed the terms of the will and the parties' conflicting interpretations of it. He then tried to ascertain T. W.'s intent when the will was executed.
"We find nothing in the will which indicates a purpose on the part of the testator to limit in respect to her welfare and support the life estate bequeathed to his surviv-

ing wife. The adjectives 'reasonable' and 'comfortable' are not used in the will and to ingraft their implications of limitation upon the bequest to her would be to change completely a material portion of the will and the benefits which obviously the testator intended to confer upon her. It bequeaths to her, during her lifetime, all of the testator's property with the remainder to the children, share and share alike, and then goes further and confers upon the wife the power and authority to sell, transfer, mortgage, and convey part or all of the property during her lifetime. . . .

"The use of the phrases 'use and enjoyment' and 'use and benefit' in other portions of the will was not a limitation of the estate bequeathed. If it had any effect, it made more positive the absolute life estate bequeathed to her. The use and benefit of the property bequeathed constitute the essential features of a life estate and, in fact, themselves constitute such an estate. No particular form of words is necessary for the creation of a life estate. Where a will bequeaths the use of rents or revenues or use and benefit during a life in being, its effect is to bequeath a life estate whether the technical term is use or not. . . .

"From the entire will here involved, it is obvious that the main plan and purpose of the testator was to provide for the comfort, maintenance, and support of his wife. In order to make it certain that this purpose was carried out, the provision was inserted a number of times that her judgment should control, and he enjoined his children in most solemn and appealing terms to aid her and recognize the fact that he had utmost confidence in her judgment. He provided in terms that her judgment was to be exercised in any matter pertaining to the handling and managment of his estate and our interpretation of the will is that the surviving wife, Minnie Medlin, took a life estate in the property, together with the power and authority to manage, control, mortgage, sell, and convey the property or any part of it for such purposes and under such conditions as she might see fit and proper in order to pay the debts, provide for her own comfort and support, and to keep and preserve the estate."

3. Leasehold Estate. The owner of a leasehold estate has the right to occupy and use the described real estate. A leasehold estate may be for a specified period such as a year or 10 years, or it may be a tenancy at will, which means that either the tenant or the owner-landlord may terminate the leasehold at any time without reason, simply by giving a required notice. If you rent an apartment during the school year and you sign a lease, you will have acquired a leasehold interest in land.

4. Easements. Easements may also be described as rights-of-way over land. If you buy a lot in a subdivision on which you intend to build a home, no doubt there will be an easement across the back of the lot for the use of public utilities. The easement will allow the water company, the electric company, and the gas company to come upon that specific area of land and erect poles, dig trenches for water lines, bury cable lines, and so forth. You still own the land covered by an easement, but the easement allows another person or persons to come upon that portion of the land for certain purposes. An easement is an interest in land which is usually evidenced by a written document called a deed of easement, and this deed must be registered with the appropriate county official in the county where the land is located. There is an exception to this

681

general rule, which is called easement by prescription or easement by adverse possession. Here there is no written easement and in fact there is no agreement that there should be an easement. This is simply a situation where the owner of the land has allowed another person or persons to use a certain portion of the land continuously for a number of years and the owner is now estopped from denying the rights of that person or persons to continue to use the land. This is also referred to as "squatter's rights." Thus, even though no formal easement was granted, the courts will enforce the right of the "squatter" provided that he or she has occupied the land continuously for a long period of time. Most states have a specific statutory time before easement by prescription or easement by adverse possession will be effective.

Downie v. City of Renton
9 P.2d 372 (Washington, 1932)

FACTS In 1908 the city of Renton built a 500,000-gallon concrete reservoir. About once a year, from 1908 to 1929, the city had to drain and clean the reservoir to prevent the buildup of contamination. The wastewater pipe ran from the base of the reservoir out some 600 feet, where the wastewater was discharged into a small gully. The wastewater then ran down another 450 feet into a small stream, which crossed Downie's land. Downie bought his two acres in 1921; it was then "unused, unimproved, unoccupied, unfenced, and covered with underbrush and second growth trees." In 1928 Downie dammed up the stream and created a one-third acre pond, which he stocked with 25,000 fish. The city's cleaning of the reservoir in September 1929 resulted in the discharge of wastewater, debris, and mud into Downie's pond. The trial court dismissed Downie's suit for an injunction, holding that the city had acquired an easement by prescription. Downie appealed.

ISSUE Had the city acquired an easement by prescription?

DECISION No. Judgment reversed and case remanded for a perpetual injunction.

REASONS Justice Beeler started with the proposition that prescriptive rights were not favored by the law since they involved a forfeiture of the rights of someone else. All of the required elements must therefore be clearly proved.

"To acquire an easement by prescription the owner must know of and acquiesce in the adverse user, or the use must be so open, notorious, visible, and uninterrupted that knowledge and acquiescence will be presumed. . . .

"The inquiry then is whether the asserted adverse user by the city was of a sufficiently open, notorious, and hostile character so as to charge the appellant's predecessor in interest with presumptive knowledge or constructive notice of the isolated acts of user. The word 'notorious' is defined by Webster as 'generally known and talked about by the public; usually believed to be true; manifest to the world; evident.' . . .

"Where . . . there has been no actual notice, it is necessary to show that the possession of his disseisor was so open, notorious, and visible, as to warrant the inference that the owner must, or should, have known it; otherwise a mere trespass might be evidence of ouster.' . . .

"[T]he property from 1908 to 1921 was unfenced, unused, and unimproved, a wild stretch of acreage almost as nature left it. Neither the appellant's vendor nor the appellant himself when he became the purchaser could have discovered by passing over the land any indication of adverse user, and the acts of user relied upon by the respondent were of such a nature as to negative the very idea of presumptive notice. . . . Nor was there anything about the manner in which the reservoir was claimed [sic] or drained that would in any wise bring knowledge to his attention. This took but from 2 to 2½ hours and occurred, according to the most reliable testimony in the record, only once a year between 1908 and 1929. . . .

"In addition to having open, notorious, and hostile possession, it is also essential that such possession, in order to ripen into a prescriptive right, be shown to have been continuous and uninterrupted for the full statutory period. . . .

"The acts of user relied upon by respondent consist at most of desultory acts of trespass, of short duration, and occurring at widely separated intervals. . . . The separate acts of draining the reservoir were wholly lacking in continuity and were not sufficiently open and notorious so as to charge the appellant's grantor or the appellant himself with presumptive notice of such occasional use."

5. Profits. In the law of real property, a "profit" is the right to remove part of someone else's land, for example, timber, crops, or minerals. Most modern cases treat profits under the same general rules as are applied to easements. Like easements, a profit may be appurtenant (attached to the ownership of other land) or "in gross" (owned by someone other than the landowner, without regard to whether that someone owns other real estate). An example of the first type would be a neighbor who has the right to cut as much wood as he needs for his fireplace. A profit in gross would exist where the landowner has simply sold or given someone the right to remove firewood from the land. As is seen in the following case, legal problems can arise when the owner of a profit tries to convey it to someone else.

Stanton v. *Herbert & Sons*
211 S.W. 353 (Tennessee, 1918)

FACTS   This was a suit for damages and for an injunction to prevent the defendants from removing sand and gravel from Hill's Island in the Cumberland River. Hill's Island, located about 20 miles above Nashville, was formerly owned by Mary Nolan and William Jordan. On June 12, 1911, they conveyed it to the plaintiffs, Elizabeth Stanton and Rush Hawes. The warranty deed contained an exception which reserved the right to remove sand for 10 years. The grantors then assigned their right to remove sand to three of the largest contractors in Nashville, who were removing "tremendous" quantities of sand for their construction projects.

ISSUE   Did the assignment of the right to the three defendants violate the implied terms of the deed?

DECISION   Yes. Judgment reversed and case remanded for further proceedings.

REASONS   Justice Green first reviewed the facts and then defined the nature of the controversy. The key was whether there had been a reservation of all mineral rights or only of a personal right to a "profit."

"We think the right to remove sand reserved to the grantors under this deed was not exclusive. There is nothing in the language used in the deed to indicate that such right was intended to be exclusive. The right was described as 'an easement, right, or privilege.' The indefinite article 'an' was used, not 'the.' . . . There is nothing to show an intention to deprive Stanton and Hawes of the right to remove sand themselves. Under the authorities, the presumption is against an exclusive grant or reservation of this nature. . . .

"'A profit à *prendre* is a right to take something off another person's land; such a right does not prevent the owner from taking the same sort of thing from off his own land; the first right may limit, but does not exclude the second. An exclusive right to all the profit of a particular kind can no doubt be granted; but such a right cannot be inferred from the language when it is not clear and explicit.' . . .

"[A] mere grant of the right or privilege of removing minerals from the land of another does not in itself create an exclusive right or privilege in the grantees. Such cases are to be distinguished from those in which there is a grant of all the minerals in certain property or a grant of an exclusive right to remove the minerals. . . .

"The effect of the distinction is this: If all the minerals are conveyed, or an exclusive right thereto, an interest in the land passes. This is a corporeal interest, which may be assigned, divided, or dealt with as any other interest in land. If, under the grant, there passes only a right to remove minerals in common with the grantor, an incorporeal hereditament results. . . .

"It is not . . . a revocable license, and it is not an easement that is personal in the grantee. It is a profit à *prendre,* and under the weight of authority a profit à *prendre* is both inheritable and assignable. . . .

"While a profit à *prendre* is assignable, it is not divisible. . . .

"[I]t is manifest that the grantors by the reservation contained in their deed only obtained a right in common with their grantees to remove sand from this island. Such a right was a mere incorporeal hereditament, and could not be divided as here undertaken. The attempted division has destroyed the reservation. The assignees of the grantors, therefore, were not entitled to this sand."

6. Licenses. A license is permission to enter upon the land of another person. It is not an easement since it is not truly an interest in land but simply temporary permission to go upon another person's land for a specific purpose. I have an apple orchard, and I agree to sell you all of the apples in the orchard for a specific price. Part of the agreement is that you will have to go into the orchard and pick the apples. You would have a license to go onto the land and pick the apples and to take them away to market. You do not have a permanent easement to traverse that area at a later time or for any other reason.

7. Dower Rights. Under the common law a widow had dower rights in her husband's real property. This meant that she had a life estate in one third of all the real property which the husband had owned during his lifetime, provided she had not signed away her dower rights in a transfer of any of that real property to another person. The purpose of the dower interest was to ensure that the widow would have some means to support herself if her husband died. Typically in those days a woman was not a wage earner outside the home.

The widow's dower interest is still recognized in many states. However, some states have limited it to only that real estate which the husband owned at the time of his decease, thus preventing the widow from claiming an interest in real estate which the husband had transferred to others during his lifetime.

8. Curtesy Rights. Under the common law the husband, upon the decease of his wife, was entitled to a life estate in all of the real property his wife owned which was subject to inheritance. One requirement had to be met before the husband was granted curtesy rights: a child which could have inherited the real property had to have been born alive. Most states have replaced the common-law right of curtesy with specific statutory provisions concerning a husband's right in his wife's estate.

9. Liens against the Real Property. A lien is a claim which some person or persons may have against an owner of real property for the payment of some debt, obligation, or duty. A lien may be either voluntary or involuntary. An example of a voluntary lien would be the lien of a mortgage which is created when the owner of real estate borrows money and pledges the real estate security for repayment of the loan. The lending institution, the mortgagee, then files the mortgage agreement with the county recorder in the county where the land is located and thus has a lien against the property. The owner of the real property cannot sell the real estate and give clear title until the mortgage lien is satisfied by full payment or unless the mortgagee agrees to let a new buyer assume the present mortgage lien, which means that the new buyer will have to pay off the mortgage.

Examples of involuntary liens are such liens as a tax lien, and a judgment lien, and a mechanic's lien. If the owner of real estate fails to pay the property taxes, then the property taxes become a lien against the real estate. As with a mortgage, the real estate may not be sold with a clear title unless the lien is paid off. A judgment lien would involve a situation where the owner of real estate has been sued, the court has rendered a judgment against the owner, and the owner has not paid off the judgment; thus the unpaid judgment and interest become an involuntary lien against the real estate. A mechanic's lien is a lien of a person or persons who furnish building materials and/or labor for the improvement of the owner's real estate, such as contractors, carpenters, plumbers, and electricians. If such persons are not paid, the law gives them the right to file a lien against the real estate. Here again, the real estate cannot be sold with a clear title unless the mechanic's lien is paid off. The mechanic's lien is a statutory lien, and the statutory language will differ from state to state. In some states, if a mechanic's lien is not satisfied within a specified period of time, the person holding the mechanic's lien may sue the owner, get a judgment, and have the real estate sold at a sheriff's auction to satisfy the lien. Since the mechanic's lien statutes do differ from state to state, it is advisable to find out what the law is in your state. Otherwise, you might find your home sold for a very minor debt.

ACQUISITION OF OWNERSHIP TO REAL PROPERTY

Real property may be acquired in various ways. First, it may be acquired by legislative grant from the national government or by a patent. A patent is a document similar to a deed which the government issues to convey a portion of the public lands to one or more persons. In the early days of our country, the national Homestead Act allowed settlers to establish their homestead on public land, and after the passage of a specified period of time and compliance with the requirements of the act, the homesteader would be granted a patent to this land. Second, real property may be acquired by purchase. This, of course, is the most common method of acquisition. Third, it may be acquired by inheritance. You may inherit land from your parents or from grandparents or other persons who die and name you in their will, or if you are the legal heir, you would inherit by intestate succession. This will be covered further in Chapter 36. A fourth method of acquiring land is by gift. An owner of land may decide to give a certain parcel of land to his or her children, to some other person or persons, or to some charity during his or her lifetime. A gift is not valid unless there is a proper deed which evidences a transfer of title from the donor, or giver, to the donee, or beneficiary, the person receiving the gift. A fifth method of acquiring real estate is by accretion. Accretion simply means that the owner of land has acquired more land because of a change in the course of a river or stream which runs alongside the property. For example, over a period of years sand and soil have been deposited on your side of a stream, thus increasing the actual land that you can use. A stream may also recede, giving more land between the previous bank and the present level of the stream. In these situations you would acquire land by accretion. A sixth way of acquiring land is by adverse possession, as mentioned earlier in this chapter. After you use or occupy land for a statutory period of time, the original owner loses his or her right to object to your possession of the land. A seventh method of acquiring land applies to governmental entities such as school districts, cities, states, and the national government. This method of acquisition is called eminent domain and is often also referred to as condemnation. It is the right of government to take private property for the use of the public. The owner of the private property must be paid a fair amount for the land taken. An eighth method of acquiring land, which also applies only to governmental entities, is acquisition through dedication. A real estate developer of a new subdivision dedicates the streets to the city. The streets then become public property. Dedication is a gift by the landowner to a governmental entity, and it is an effective acquisition only if the governmental entity accepts the gift. For example, a person may want to dedicate certain land to a city for use as a park that will be named after the donor. The city may or may not accept the gift with that condition. If the gift is accepted, then appropriate documents are executed and the land becomes public property that is owned and maintained by the city.

PROCESS OF TRANSFER OF OWNERSHIP

The transfer of land from the present owner or owners to the acquiring owner or owners must be evidenced by a written document which can be recorded in the records of the county where the land is located.

The transfer document used in an acquisition by purchase or by gift is a deed. This is a written document which is signed by the owner of the real property and which conveys or transfers the owner's rights, title, and interest in specifically described real estate to the person or persons who are acquiring the ownership. The present owner or owners are called the grantors and the person or persons acquiring ownership are called the grantees. The grantors must sign the deed in the presence of a notary public who will verify that they signed it. The deed may be in the form of a warranty deed or a quitclaim deed. A warranty deed contains language whereby the grantor expressly guarantees that the ownership being transferred is free from the claims of others. That is, the grantor guarantees to the grantee that the grantor is transferring a clear and merchantable title. A quitclaim deed states that the grantor is transferring all of his or her rights, title, and interest in the real property to the grantee, but the grantor makes no guarantee that the grantee will have a clear title free from the claims of others.

The grantor or grantors in a warranty deed may reserve some rights or may make the warranty subject to certain rights of others. For example, the grantors in a warranty deed may reserve subsurface mineral rights. Then, if oil is ever found under the land, it belongs to the grantor. If there is a mortgage on the land, the grantor-seller may deed the title subject to the rights of the mortgagee, normally a bank or other lending institution. Thus the new purchaser gets title subject to the lien of the mortgage. If there are private restrictions on the real estate, the deed will transfer title subject to those restrictions. Since taxes are a lien, the deed will also specify that the transfer of title is subject to unpaid taxes if any remain unpaid at the time of the transfer of title.

Thus it is important to remember the bundle of rights concept, as it is possible to deed only part of the bundle of rights. The warranty deed will, however, transfer all rights except those specifically reserved by the grantor or those to which the transfer is made subject, such as the mortgage.

Brown v. Lober
379 N.E.2d 1354 (Illinois, 1978)

FACTS   In 1957 James and Dolly Brown, husband and wife, purchased 80 acres of land in Montgomery County from William and Faith Bost, joint tenants. The Bosts gave the Browns a statutory warranty deed which included the covenants of seisin (ownership), right to convey, quiet enjoyment, and against incumbrances. The deed was absolute on its face, and it purported to convey an estate in fee simple. In fact, a prior owner in the chain of title had conveyed a two-thirds interest in the mineral rights in 1947. This prior conveyance was apparently not discovered in title searches which the Bosts had done in 1958 and 1968, when they used the land as collateral for loans.

687

Faith Bost died in 1974; William had died earlier. Maureen Lober was appointed as executor of Faith's estate. On May 8, 1974, the Browns granted a coal option to the Consolidated Coal Company for $6,000. On May 4, 1976, the Browns learned that they owned only one third of the coal rights. They accepted $2,000 from the coal company and then sued Faith's estate for damages of $4,000. The trial court dismissed the lawsuit, holding that only the first two warranties in the Bosts' deed had been breached, that this had occurred in 1957, when the deed was delivered, and that the claim was thus barred by the 10-year statute of limitations. The Browns appealed.

ISSUE   Did the Bosts only breach the convenants of seisin and the right to convey?

DECISION   No. Judgment reversed and case remanded.

REASONS   Justice Wineland agreed with the trial court that the first two covenants were either met or breached when the deed took effect and that a cause of action for their breach would accrue at that time. He felt, however, that the Bosts had also breached the covenant of quiet enjoyment, and perhaps the covenant against incumbrances.

"In the instant case it is agreed by the parties that the plaintiffs had no knowledge of the previous grant of the sub-surface minerals until 1976. But if they did have, it would have been of no moment because they could not have brought suit for breach of [the] covenant of quiet enjoyment until they were actually or constructively evicted. It was at this time that the plaintiffs were advised by the coal company of the outstanding incumbrance in the underlying minerals. It was at this time that plaintiffs yielded as they had a right to do, to the paramount title to the two-thirds interest in the coal. The coal purchaser refused to pay them for the coal rights warranted to them by the Bosts. It would seem to be at this time that the covenant of quiet and peaceable possession was disturbed for the first time since 1957 and that this suit was brought. The Statute of Limitations could not be operative until plaintiffs' rights were disturbed in the possession of their title by the sale of the underlying coal. . . .

"It would appear here that the defect in title would constitute an incumbrance as it would seem to be a claim, lien, charge, or liability attached to and binding real property. . . .

"A covenant against incumbrances does not depend for its existence upon the extent or amount of diminution of value, but extends to cases where, by reason of the burden, claim, or right, the owner does not acquire complete dominion over the land conveyed by his conveyance or deed. . . . A burden may be only inchoate, yet if it is a right which may be enforced against the property and against the will of [*sic*] the consent of the owners, it is within the category of an incumbrance."

FINANCING OF REAL ESTATE TRANSACTIONS

The great majority of real estate transactions involve some type of financing arrangement, since few people have the cash required in exchange for the title to real property. Financing can be handled through either a land contract or a real estate mortgage.

LAND CONTRACTS

A land contract is an agreement between a buyer and a seller regarding the purchase of a parcel of land. The contract is a conditional sale of the land subject to payment of the purchase price by the buyer. Typically the buyer will make a down payment and will agree to make periodic payments of interest and principal for a specified period of time, either until the entire balance of the principal is paid or until the principal balance is paid down to a level where the buyer can secure a real estate mortgage from a lending institution. Typically the down payment required for a land contract transaction is less than that required in a transaction involving a real estate mortgage.

The buyer in a land contract transaction does not acquire a fee simple title to the land until the entire contract purchase price has been paid. The seller retains the fee simple title, and if the buyer breaches the terms of the contract, either by not making the scheduled payments or by breaching other terms of the contract, the seller may give the buyer notice of the breach, reenter the premises, and evict the buyer from possession, and in some instances the buyer's down payment and other payments may be forfeited. In some states, however, the same procedure is followed in the foreclosure of a land contract sale as would be followed in the foreclosure of a mortgage.

Upon execution of a land contract, the buyer is entitled to possession and control of the land and the improvements thereon. The buyer is the equitable owner of the rights to possess and control the land subject to the legal rights of the fee simple title holder who is selling the land. The buyer may not use the land in any way he or she wants to, and the buyer has the duty to keep the premises insured against fire and other risks of loss. The buyer may not add to or tear down the improvements without the specific permission of the seller. The buyer has the right to use, control, and enjoy the land and improvements, but he or she may not materially change the land or improvements.

In a real estate purchase involving a mortgage, the buyer receives fee simple title to the real estate and then executes a mortgage to secure the payment of the loan which the bank or lending institution has made to enable him or her to purchase the real estate. The seller is then paid off and deeds over all of his or her property rights in the real estate. In the land contract transaction the seller still holds property rights and thus a certain amount of control until the last payment has been made on the contract.

REAL ESTATE MORTGAGES

A real estate mortgage is simply a document wherein the owner of real estate pledges it as security for the payment of a debt or some other obligation. The owner of the property, who is called the mortgagor, does not transfer title to the land in this document; the mortgagee, normally a bank or other lending institution, obtains a nonpossessory interest in the real estate. If the debt or obligation is not satisfied within the required time period or in accordance with the required conditions for repayment as set out in the mortgage document, the mortgagee may commence legal proceedings to foreclose on the mortgage and to have the property sold at a sheriff's sale. The proceeds will then be applied to the balance owed on the mortgage. The owner-mortgagor will receive any proceeds which remain after the payment of the mortgage balance plus reasonable attorney's fees and court costs.

TYPES OF REAL ESTATE MORTGAGES

Purchase-Money Mortgage. A purchase-money mortgage is a mortgage which is executed to obtain money to purchase the land which is to be pledged in the mortgage. Typically an individual or individuals contemplating the purchase of a home will go to a bank first and get a commitment from the bank to lend them money for the purchase of a certain piece of property. Then, relying on that commitment the individual or individuals will negotiate the purchase of the real estate. After all preliminary legal matters have been taken care of, the seller will convey the title to the buyer, the buyer will sign a purchase-money mortgage with the bank, and the bank in turn will pay the amount of the loan to the seller or to the seller's mortgagee if there is a mortgage on the property at the time it is sold.

Non-Purchase-Money Mortgage. This mortgage is executed on real property, not for the purpose of purchasing real property. For example, your parents own their home, debt-free, and they need money to send their children to college. Thus they borrow money from a bank and pledge their home in the form of a mortgage for the repayment of this money to the bank.

Construction Mortgage. This mortgage is used when the mortgagor-owner owns a parcel of land and wants to build a building or buildings on the land. The bank or lending institution will review the owner's building plans and building estimates, and if it approves these, it will make a commitment to lend a certain sum to the mortgagor. Typically the agreement is not to pay the entire amount out in a lump sum, as would be done with a purchase-money mortgage, but to pay out portions of the loan as necessary to pay the costs of construction. When construction has been completed, the loan funds will be paid out in full to the mortgagor or his or her assigns, and then the procedure for payment and/or foreclosure is the same as that of any other mortgage.

REAL PROPERTY WHICH IS SUBJECT TO MORTGAGE

A mortgage may be executed which covers any interest in real property that the mortgagor has, even after-acquired real estate. This, of course, would be an exceptional situation, as mortgages normally cover specifically described real estate.

Once a mortgage covering a specific described parcel of land has been executed, the mortgage lien will cover any and all improvements which are at present on the real estate, such as a house, and it will automatically cover any additional improvements which are made on the real estate during the term of the mortgage. For example, you build an additional room onto your home. The new improvement as well as the basic structure previously on the land is subject to the mortgage lien.

Under the Uniform Commercial Code, Article 9, a fixture which has become permanently attached to the real estate will be subject to the mortgage lien unless there is a prior security interest. If there is a valid security interest, then the mortgage lien will be secondary to that interest.

The corn growing in the field is subject to the mortgage lien covering that land. However, the farmer-mortgagor may go ahead and pick the corn, and once the corn has been picked, it is considered severed from the real estate and then becomes the sole property of the farmer-mortgagor. If, however, the farmer-mortgagor was in default on his mortgage, that is, had failed to pay the payments or to live up to the conditions of the mortgage, and if proper notice was given to him, then the crops would be subject to the lien on the mortgage.

CONTENTS OF THE TYPICAL MORTGAGE DOCUMENT

The typical mortgage document will contain the names of the parties, that is, the mortgagor or mortgagors and the mortgagee, the bank or other person lending the money; a description of the particular parcel of land; a statement of the dollar amount of the debt which is secured by the mortgage and, if construction is anticipated and more money will be needed for construction, of the future advances which are to be made; and, of course, the rate of interest and the terms for repayment. The mortgage payments can be made monthly, which is typical in a purchase-money mortgage for a home, or they can be made annually, semiannually, or in any other manner which is agreed to by the parties.

Typically the mortgagor covenants or promises to pay the debt secured by the mortgage and to make payments in accordance with the terms of a separate promissory note signed by the mortgagor. Failure to do so will result in a default by the mortgagor and in the mortgagee's right to foreclosure. The mortgagor also promises to pay all taxes and special assessments which are levied against the property, to keep the improvements on the property insured for at least the amount of the mortgage, keep the property in a good state of repair, and to keep the property free from all other liens.

The mortgagee, on the other hand, simply agrees to release the lien on the real estate upon the payment of the debt plus interest.

There are also provisions which refer to late payments and extra charges for such payments.

FILING AND RECORDING REQUIREMENTS OF A MORTGAGE

A mortgage need not be filed or recorded in any public office for its lien to be valid between the mortgagor and the mortgagee. However, if a mortgage is not filed and recorded in the office of the recorder of the county where the real estate is located, then the mortgagee's lien will not be superior to any subsequent liens which may be placed against the real estate. For example, an individual borrows money, executes a promissory note, and signs a mortgage on his or her real estate, but the mortgagee doesn't file and record the mortgage. Then the property owner, the mortgagor, has some improvements made to the real estate but does not pay for them, so a mechanic's lien is filed against the real estate. Or perhaps the owner of the real estate was involved in an automobile accident and suit was filed and a judgment rendered against him or her. If the mortgage was not filed and recorded properly, it would not have priority over the mechanic's lien or the judgment. Thus, immediately after a mortgage is executed, it is very important to file and record the mortgage with the recorder of the county where the real estate is located.

DEFAULTS IN PAYMENT OF THE MORTGAGE

The mortgagor may be in default on the mortgage by failing to pay the mortgage payments, the real estate taxes, or the payments for insurance against fire and extended coverage as they become due, or by doing any act which would endanger the security interest of the mortgagee.

If the mortgagor fails to make the mortgage payments when they become due or defaults in any of the other ways just stated, then the mortgagee may file a suit of foreclosure against the mortgagor. At that time, the entire balance of the mortgage is due and payable, and if the court awards the mortgagee a judgment of foreclosure, the property will be sold at a sheriff's sale. The proceeds of the sale of the real estate will be applied first to the unpaid balance of the mortgage plus interest and to the legal fees and court costs of the foreclosure suit, and the balance will then be paid to the mortgagee. If the sale does not bring enough money to pay off the mortgage debt, the mortgagor will remain liable for any deficiency.

The above procedure appears to be very one-sided in favor of the mortgagee, the lending institution. However, most lending institutions do not normally proceed with a foreclosure suit except in situations where there has been a continued pattern of default by the mortgagor. Moreover, many states have enacted statutes which allow the mortgagor to get a delay of foreclosure in certain hardship cases. Another statutory procedure that favors the mortgagor is called the right of redemption. This is the mortgagor's statutory right to repurchase the real estate within a specified time after the foreclosure. In other words, the mortgagor who can get the money together can have his or her property back for the amount for which it was sold plus the expenses incurred in the foreclosure and sale.

In the case where the real property was sold by the sheriff, the sheriff is authorized by law to execute to the purchaser a sheriff's deed which is free and clear of the mortgage lien.

NATIONAL LAWS AFFECTING THE TRANSFER OF TITLE TO REAL ESTATE

The U.S. Real Estate Settlement Procedures Act, which was passed in 1974, requires the disclosure of all the costs of a real estate transaction to the buyer prior to the consummation of such a transaction. The costs which must be disclosed are the loan origination fees, loan discount points, appraisal fees, attorney's fees, inspection fees, charges for title search or title insurance, and land survey fees. The purpose of this law is primarily to let the buyer know just what he or she is paying for. The law also prohibits certain practices which are not in the best interests of the buyer. The lending institution is not allowed to give a kickback to any person for referring the borrower to them, to charge or accept fees except for services actually performed, or to require that the borrower purchase title insurance from a particular title company. The borrower may purchase title insurance from any title insurance company that he or she desires. The parties may also select their own attorneys and cannot be forced to use an attorney which the lending institution selects.

WARRANTIES OF TITLE IN THE SALE OF REAL ESTATE

The person transferring title, known as the grantor, is presumed to have made certain warranties of title even though those warranties were not expressly stated in the deed. The grantor warrants that he or she owns the real estate which is being conveyed subject to the restriction, unpaid taxes, mortgage, easements, or any other liens against it. The grantor also warrants that he or she has the right to convey the property and is not restricted with regard to his or her right to make the conveyance. In the case of the transfer of title by a corporation, the officers signing the deed warrant that they have authority to act for the corporation. It is good practice for the purchaser to have the corporate officers furnish him or her with a resolution whereby the corporation's board of directors had authorized those officers to sign a transfer of title for the corporation. The grantor also guarantees that the land is not encumbered by any right or interest other than the liens or easements which are stated in the deed. Thus the grantor is guaranteeing that the purchaser will have the right to enjoy the use of the property without interference by the grantors or others at a later date.

Even though the grantor guarantees that the buyer is being given a clear title and will have the right to undisturbed enjoyment of the premises, free from liens and encumbrances other than those shown in the deed, the buyer should request further assurances since, after all, should there be problems at a later date, the grantor who made those guarantees may have spent the money that the buyer paid for the real estate, may have moved out of the area, may have died, may have filed bankruptcy, or may simply be judgment-proof. Thus, prior to consummating the purchase of real estate, the buyer should require from the seller either an abstract of title showing good and merchantable title certified to the date of the closing of the transaction or a policy of title insurance to the real estate.

An abstract of title is a history of the title to a property. Usually beginning with the original transfer from the U.S. government to the homesteader, it then contains brief copies of every deed, every mortgage, every document which affects the transfer of the title from that date to the present. It also contains copies of any liens or encumbrances which have been filed against the real estate. The abstract of title, however, only covers those documents which have been recorded in the county recorder's office in the county where the real estate is situated. It does not cover any unrecorded documents which may have been agreed upon by parties involved in the chain of title.

The abstractor, the person preparing the abstract, does not certify that the title is clear from liens and encumbrances and is merchantable. The abstract must be taken to an attorney who will examine the chain of title and then give an opinion stating whether or not the title is merchantable and what liens and encumbrances may be against it. A policy of title insurance is an insurance policy which states that if any person or persons later challenge the title, the insurance company will pay the cost of any judgment against you and will pay the legal fees and court costs required to defend you in any action brought by the person or persons claiming title against you. Before the title insurance company issues a title insurance policy, it first searches the title and verifies that the title is clear from liens and encumbrances and is merchantable, and if it feels that the title is clear and merchantable, it will issue a policy of title insurance.

The warranties made by the seller-grantor, the issuance of a title insurance policy, and the preparation and examination of an abstract of title do not protect the buyer against any defects in the improvements on the real estate, such as the house, the garage, or the other buildings on it. The courts tend to use the doctrine of caveat emptor with regard to the condition of the improvements on the real estate. Caveat emptor means "Let the buyer beware." The buyer had an opportunity to examine the real estate, and if the buyer did not request any express warranties or agreement as to the buildings, then the buyer gets what he or she sees. The exception, of course, is where there was fraud or misrepresentation by the seller in the sale of the real estate. If the seller lied to the buyer about some material fact and this concerned a condition that the buyer could not have checked with the use of ordinary inspection methods, then the courts will simply void the transaction and the buyer may be able to secure money damages in addition to having the transfer voided.

An exception is also made to the general rule of caveat emptor with regard to the buildings on the real estate being transferred in the case where a new home has been constructed on the real estate. Many states have specific laws which make the builder responsible for defects in the new home for a specific period of time, usually one year. Since this is a matter of state law, the buyer of real estate should either secure an express warranty from the seller or check the statutory law in the given state.

With regard to certain latent defects which have not been discovered until the statutory period had expired, some states have held the builder responsible for a longer period of time. While the common law placed the burden squarely upon the buyer, using the doctrine of caveat emptor, the current trend in this area of law has been to hold the builder responsible for defects in the construction of a home, especially where the defects are such that the buyer could not readily find them by a reasonable inspection of the home at the time of purchase.

STATE EX REL. BROWN v. NEWPORT CONCRETE CO.

336 N.E.2d 453 (Ohio, 1975)

Holmes, Justice

This matter involves the appeal of a summary judgment granted by the Court of Common Pleas of Hamilton County, which court, after a review of the pleadings, affidavits, and answers to interrogatories, entered a judgment compelling the defendant, Newport Concrete Company, to remove a certain concrete structure from the bed of the Little Miami River that the trial court had found to interfere with the public's free use of such stream for navigation purposes.

The original Complaint was filed by the Attorney General of Ohio on behalf of the state and its citizens. It alleged that the state is the owner in trust of the Little Miami River, "a navigable stream and watercourse used by the citizens of Ohio and the United States."

The Complaint stated, and the facts show, that the defendant owned land on the bank of the Little Miami River, as well as land on an island in the middle of the river adjacent to the main bank of the river. The defendant constructed a concrete causeway or ford, runnng from the south bank of the river to the island. This causeway was constructed in order that the defendant's trucks might move from the south bank to the island, and haul sand and gravel that had been extracted from the island to the defendant's processing plant on the south bank of the river.

The facts show that the causeway was constructed by placing three prestressed concrete tubes, 5 feet square and 30 feet long, with 48-inch round openings, in the bed of such stream, permitting the water to flow through. On top of such tubes was placed a concrete slab as a roadway for the defendant's trucks. The water, depending upon its volume or height, would either flow over the causeway or through the tubes.

Evidence adduced by way of an affidavit on behalf of the state pursuant to a motion for summary judgment showed that such causeway was an obstacle to the free passage of boats or canoes along that portion of the Little Miami River. More particularly, the affidavit of Mr. Ross E. Terrell stated that he was the owner of a canoe livery, which was operating upstream from the causeway, and that he was experiencing economic detriment in that his customers could not canoe downstream from the livery without being impeded by the defendant's causeway. Consequently, Mr. Terrell stated, there is only the more difficult upstream canoeing.

There was also evidence, by way of an affidavit, that the defendant's causeway had occasioned a tragic mishap when two young men, who were wading in the water nearby, were drawn into the tube, as a result of the rapidity of the current and flow of the water occasioned by the placement of such tubes, and one of the young men was drowned. The trial court, in sustaining the motion of the state of Ohio for summary judgment, and in granting the injunction sought by the state, found the Little Miami River to be a "navigable stream" and applied the theory that the streams and bodies of water, as other natural resources within the state, are held in trust by the state of Ohio for all its citizens.

The trial court ordered the defendant to remove its causeway from the river. Further, the court permanently enjoined the defendant from "obstructing, impeding, or interfering with navigation, fishing, recreational activities, or other uses of the waters of the state of Ohio, specifically, the Little Miami River. . . ." Interestingly, the court also ordered the defendant to pay into the general revenue fund of the state of Ohio compensatory damages in the sum of one cent.

The basic issue involved in this case is whether or not the Little Miami River in the general area under consideration is in fact a "navigable river" under the interpretation of such term in Ohio law. Such determination of whether a given body of water is navigable is important from the standpoint of deciding whether there are certain inherent rights that the public has in the free and uminterrupted use of such waters. . . .

Therefore, the questions to be resolved are (1)

what is the legal definition of "navigable" water? and (2) did the facts presented to the trial court logically and lawfully permit it to find that the Little Miami River at this location was navigable? The nature of the elements, requisites, and factors involved in determining these questions has been well stated in 56 American Jurisprudence 645, Waters, Section 179, as follows:

Navigability, in the sense of actual usability for navigation or navigability in fact, as a legal concept embracing both public and private interests, is not susceptible of definition or determination by a precise formula which fits every type of stream or body of water under all circumstances and at all times. A general definition or test which has frequently been approved is that rivers or other bodies of water are navigable when they are used, or are susceptible of being used, in their ordinary condition, as highways for commerce, over which trade and travel are or may be conducted in the customary modes of trade and travel on water.

The aforestated quotation expresses the historical view of whether or not a stream or body of water may be characterized as "navigable." In this regard, we find that in pertinent cases in the United States Supreme Court the emphasis in the past has been upon a determination whether the water is navigable for some purpose useful to trade or commerce. . . .

Exemplary of the adherence to such criteria for the legal determination of whether a body of water is "navigable" is the statement to be found within the early Ohio case of *Hickok* v. *Hine* (1872), 23 Ohio St. 523, 527, as follows:

A river is regarded as navigable which is capable of floating to market the products of the country through which it passes, or upon which commerce may be conducted; and, from the fact of its being so navigable, it becomes in law a public river or highway. The character of a river, as such highway, is not so much determined by the frequency of its use for that purpose as it is by its capacity of being used by the public for purposes of transportation and commerce. . . .

Further, the cases seem to have generally held that a stream or body of water may be legally determined to be navigable even though there may be found at various locations thereon certain natural barriers or obstructions, such as rapids, sand-

bars, or falls. Such natural restrictions have been found not to preclude the finding that a stream is legally navigable in at least certain stretches thereof. . . .

The state legislative bodies in a number of states have seen fit to enact laws defining the term "navigable waters" for general application within those states. However, the Ohio General Assembly has not provided a general definition to be applied to bodies of water for purposes of determining whether such have "navigable" characteristics. There is, however, a definition of "navigable waters" to be found at R.C. 1547.01(J) which is made specifically applicable to the chapter dealing with laws pertaining to watercraft. The definition reads as follows:

(J) "Navigable waters," for the purposes of Chapter 1547 of the Revised Code, means waters which come under the jurisdiction of the department of the army of the United States and any waterways within or adjacent to this state, except inland lakes having neither a navigable inlet or outlet.

This definition, as it would relate to the control of watercraft using the waters of this state, is at least indicative that the General Assembly viewed the need for control over watercraft on the larger bodies of water under the jurisdiction of the Army Corps of Engineers, bodies which might historically have been viewed as capable of commercial use, as well as the need for control of watercraft using "any waterways within or adjacent to this state (except inland lakes having neither inlet or outlet)."

As in other areas of legal interpretation of words and phrases, especially where it involves the changing public uses, activity, and involvement in such areas of concern, the definition of "navigable waters" and "navigability" has not been a static one. Pertinent is the language to be found in the early case of *Pollock* v. *Cleveland Ship Building Co.* (1897), 56 Ohio St. 665 at page 668, 47 N.E. 582 at page 583, as follows:

Clearly the term "easement of navigation," should not be construed in any narrow, scientific sense, but, having in mind the reservation of the easement by the state is for the benefit of the public in its use of the highway, it should receive a construction in harmony with the nature of the uses of the water by the public, and the objects of a public nature to be accomplished by such uses.

There is to be found a further development of such philosophy, that legal construction should be in harmony with the nature of the uses of the water by the public, in *Coleman* v. *Schaeffer* (1955), 163 Ohio St. 202, 126 N.E.2d 444, which case specifically expanded the test of navigability to include a stream's availability for boating and recreation, as well as the use of the stream for pecuniary profit. The transition was yet further developed in the case of *Mentor Harbor Yachting Club* v. *Mentor Lagoons, Inc.*, supra, 170 Ohio St. at 200, 163 N.E.2d at 378, where the Supreme Court stated:

. . . [T]his increased recreational use of our waters has been accompanied by a corresponding lessening of their use for commerce. We are in accord with the modern view that navigation for pleasure and recreation is as important in the eyes of the law as navigation for a commercial purpose.

We hold that the modern utilization of our waters by our citizens requires that our courts, in their judicial interpretation of the navigability of such waters, consider their recreational use as well as the more traditional criteria of commercial use. In the instant case, the facts as presented to the trial court show that such stream is in fact used for recreational purposes. . . .

The evidence before the trial court upon the question of a summary judgment would reasonably permit the finding that the stream in the area of the defendant's property could be concluded to be navigable. . . .

Based upon all of the foregoing, the judgment of the Common Pleas Court of Hamilton County, Ohio, is hereby affirmed.

TAVARES v. HORSTMAN

542 P.2d 1275 (Wyoming, 1975)

Raper, Justice

The defendant, a land developer and builder, sold the plaintiffs a tract of land; the defendant built a home for plaintiffs on the property under an oral agreement with no express warranty. A warranty deed with only the usual covenants of title was delivered. Within a little over a year, the septic tank system backed sewage to a depth of about three inches into the plaintiffs' basement before it was discovered. A plumber was called; after pumping out the tanks a couple of times, he advised that something would have to be done about the system. Defendant was called and informed of this nasty predicament. He dug down to the discharge pipe, perforated the line, and let the raw sewage flow into an open trench. Nothing further was done. Plaintiffs called him to do something further, but he said he could not work on it because he had to go on a vacation. The stinking situation was so deplorable that plaintiffs called in an experienced septic tank contractor. The system had to be rebuilt because of its inadequacy. The soil in the area of the drainage field was of tight gumbo, so a particular design and manner of installation was necessary. The contractor who rebuilt the system testified that the problems with the one he replaced were several. The defendant had installed foundation drainage pipe all around the house and connected it to discharge into the septic tank system, causing an overload of the sewage disposal scheme. There was not enough capacity for the size home it was to serve. The excess water caused the drainage field to waterlog, backed effluent into the tanks, killed the bacterial actions supposed to be taking place there, and, in turn, blocked the flow of sewage from the house. Having no place else to go, the noxious wastes covered the basement floor. Plaintiffs expended $2,083 to correct the condition.

Defendant had obtained no permit for construction of the system. He testified that he had but could not find it. The issuing agency could find no record of its issuance. Such permits are issued by the Casper-Natrona County Health Department. . . . The trial judge was justified in concluding that defendant skipped this important step, which finding is an element of the court's general finding. . . .

The court made only a general finding in favor of plaintiffs and against defendant. Judgment for plaintiffs in the sum of $2,083 was entered. . . .

We have accordingly given no credence to defendant's claim of sole or contributory negligence of the plaintiffs in the erection of a barn over part of the drain field. Furthermore, the plaintiffs cannot be charged with negligence for a condition to which they were not alerted by a proper warning even if some act on their part may have contributed to the failure of the septic tank system. . . .

From the cases which we shall cite in this opinion, it appears that the rule of the past and still existing in a few jurisdictions is that no implied warranties of quality in the sale of realty existed in the common law. The doctrine of caveat emptor reigned supreme. Cracks, however, began to appear in that tenet with respect to the sale of new housing. Favorite references used in the cases and work of scholars come from the thoughts of Cardozo, *The Nature of the Judicial Process* (1921). . . .

In Wyoming, this court has had no occasion to sustain the concept of caveat emptor in a real estate transaction. . . . We therefore have the advantage over many other courts in not having to set aside a principle of long standing in our jurisprudence.

Since World War II homes have been built in tremendous numbers. There have come into being developer-builders operating on a large scale. Many firms and persons, large and small operators, hold themselves out as skilled in home construction and are in the business of building and selling to individual owners. Developers contract with builders to construct for resale. Building construction by modern methods is complex and intertwined with governmental codes and regulations. The ordinary home buyer is not in a position, by skill or training, to discover defects lurking in the plumbing, the electrical wiring, the structure itself, all of which is usually covered up and not open for inspection.

A home buyer should be able to place reliance on the builder or developer who sells him a new house. The improved real estate the average family buys gives it thoughtful pause not only because of the base price but the interest involved over a long period of time. This is usually the largest single purchase a family makes for a lifetime. Some may be able to pay cash, but we cannot single out that buyer in the formulation of a rule.

It ought to be an implicit understanding of the

698

parties that when an agreed price is paid that the home is reasonably fit for the purpose for which it is to be used—that it is reasonably fit for habitation. Illusory value is a poor substitute for quality. There is no need for the buyer to be subjected to the harassment caused by defects, and he deserves the focus of the law and its concern. The significant purchase of a new home leads logically to the buyer's expectation that he be judicially protected. Any other result would be intolerable and unjust. . . .

We now reach defendant's claim that it is not necessary that the work be done perfectly and any implied warranty that may have existed has expired. Some question exists as to what should be the period of implied warranty. We appreciate that different parts of construction may have a different expected life, such as a foundation compared to a roof. We have no problem in the present case because the septic tank system failed before a minimum life expectancy had been reached; its breakdown is traced to the negligent design and is considered a major component of a residence not served by a county or municipal sewer system. . . .

In summary then, we hold that under the circumstances of this case, the rule of caveat emptor no longer protects the builder-vendor because it is unrealistic in the light of the change that has emerged in the morals of the marketplace. That doctrine was based upon an arm's-length transaction between seller and buyer and contemplated comparable skill and experience, which does not now exist; they are not in an equal bargaining position, and the buyer is forced to rely on the skill and knowledge of the builder.

We further hold along with a vast majority of courts that where a vendor builds new houses for the purpose of sale, the sale carries with it an implied warranty that it is constructed in a reasonably workmanlike manner and is fit for habitation. For the moment, we confine this holding to the sale of new housing. It is perceived the boundaries of implied warranties will be circumscribed by experience in future cases. In the many cases studied, we see lines being drawn but a definitive determination will necessarily depend upon the circumstances of each particular case. We do not include used housing in our holding but visualize that circumstances may require consideration of some sales as included. We do not exclude the possibility that industrial property and vacant land in a proper setting may be embraced, but make no ruling in that regard.

We finally hold that a buyer may proceed not only upon the basis of implied warranty but upon the basis of negligent design and construction. There obviously can be and probably is in some cases an indistinguishable overlap, but an implied warranty would embrace a wider range of causes and be less restrictive in proof.

There was no error.

SOUTHWEST WEATHER RESEARCH, INC. v. DUNCAN

319 S.W.2d 940 (Texas, 1959)

Per Curiam

This is an appeal from a judgment of the 83rd District Court, Jeff Davis County, Texas, said judgment being in the form of an injunction commanding the appellants "to refrain from seeding the clouds by artificial nucleation or otherwise and from in any other manner or way interfering with the clouds and the natural condition of the air, sky, atmosphere and air space of plaintiffs' lands and in the area of plaintiffs' lands to in any manner, degree or way affect, control or modify the weather condition on or about said lands, pending final hearing and determination of this cause; and from further flying over the above-described lands of plaintiffs and discharging any chemicals or other matter or material into the clouds over said lands." Appellees are ranchmen residing in Jeff Davis County, and appellants are owners and operators of certain airplanes and equipment generally used in what they call a "weather modification program," and those who contracted and arranged for their services.

It is not disputed that appellants did operate their airplanes at various times over portions of lands belonging to the appellees, for the purpose of and while engaged in what is commonly called "cloud seeding." Appellants do not deny having done this, and testified through the president of the company that the operation would continue unless restrained. He stated, "We seeded the clouds to attempt to suppress the hail." The controversy is really over appellants' right to seed clouds or otherwise modify weather conditions over appellees' property; the manner of so doing; and the effects resulting therefrom. Appellants stoutly maintained that they can treat clouds in such manner as will prevent the clouds from precipitating hail, and that such operation does not and cannot decrease either the present or ultimate rainfall from any cloud or clouds so treated. Appellants were hired on a hail suppression program by a large number of farmers in and around Fort Stockton and other areas generally east, or easterly, of Jeff Davis County. It was developed that the farmers' land was frequently ravaged by damaging hail storms, which appellants claim originated in and over the Davis Mountains in the Jeff Davis County area.

The appellees' testimony, on the other hand, which was elicited from some 11 witnesses, was to the effect that this program of cloud seeding destroyed potential rain clouds over their property.

The trial court, in granting the temporary injunction, found as a matter of fact that appellants were engaging in day to day flying airplanes over appellees' lands and into the clouds over appellees' lands, and expelling a foreign substance into the clouds above appellees' lands in such a manner that there was a change in the contents of the clouds, causing them to be dissipated and scattered, with the results that the clouds over plaintiffs' lands were prevented from following their natural and usual course of developing rain upon and over and near plaintiffs' lands, thereby resulting in retarded rainfall upon plaintiffs' properties. The court further held that such was injurious to appellees and was in interference of their property rights, and would cause irreparable damage if not restrained.

So summing up the fact situation or evidence that was before the trial court, we find that the three appellees and other witnesses testified that they had visually observed the destruction of potential rain clouds over their own property by the equipment of the appellants. They testified that they had seen this happen more than once. The experts differed sharply in the probable effects of a hail suppression program accomplished by the cloud seeding methods used here. The trial court apparently, as reflected by his findings included in the judgment, believed the testimony of the lay witnesses and that part of the expert testimony in harmony with his judgment. This he had a right to do as the trier of facts.

We have carefully considered the voluminous record and exhibits that were admitted in evidence, and have concluded that the trial court had ample evidence on which to base his findings and with which to justify the issuance of the injunction.

Now we must turn to the objections of the appellants, who protest the issuance of the injunction on the grounds, generally, that appellants had every right to do what they were doing in order to protect their crops from hail, and that the facts or credible evidence did not justify the issuance of the injunction. Appellants maintain that appellees have no right to prevent them from flying over appellees' lands; that no one owns the clouds unless it be the State; and that the trial court was without legal right to restrain appellants from pursuing a lawful occupation; also, that the injunction is too broad in its terms.

First of all, it must be noted that here we do not have any governmental agency, State or Federal, and find no legislative regulation. This is exclusively a dispute between private interests. It has been said there is no precedent and no legal justification for the trial court's action. It has long been understood that equity was created for the man who had a right without a remedy, and as later modified, without an adequate remedy. Appellees urge here that the owner of land also owns in connection therewith certain so-called natural rights, and cite us the following quotation from *Spann* v. *City of Dallas*, 111 Tex. 350, 235 S.W. 513, 514, in which Chief Justice Nelson Phillips states:

Property in a thing consists not merely in its ownership and possession but in unrestricted right of use, enjoyment and disposal. Anything which destroys any of these elements of property, to that extent destroys the property itself. The substantial value of property lies in its use. If the right of use be denied, the value of the property is annihilated and ownership is rendered a barren right. . . .

. . . The very essence of American constitutions is that the material rights of no man shall be subject to the mere will of another. *Yick Wo* v. *Hopkins*, 118 U.S. 356, 6 S. Ct. 1064, 30 L. Ed. 220.

In Volume 34, *Marquette Law Review*, at Page 275, this is said:

Considering the property right of every man to the use and enjoyment of his land, and considering the profound effect which natural rainfall has upon the realization of this right, it would appear that the benefits of natural rainfall should come within the scope of judicial protection, and a duty should be imposed on adjoining landowners not to interfere therewith.

In the *Stanford Law Review*, November 1948, Volume 1, in an article entitled "Who Owns the Clouds?" the following statements occur:

The landowner does have rights in the water in clouds, however. The basis for these rights is the common law doctrine of natural rights. Literally, the term "natural rights" is well chosen; these rights protect the landowner's use of his land in its natural condition. . . .

All forms of natural precipitation should be elements of the natural condition of the land. Precipitation, like air, oxygen, sunlight, and the soil itself, is an essential to many reasonable uses of the land. The plant and animal life on the land are both ultimately dependent upon rainfall. To the extent that rain is important to the use of land, the landowner should be entitled to the natural rainfall.

In *California Law Review*, December 1957, Volume 45, No. 5, in an article, "Weather Modification," are found the following statements:

What are the rights of the landowner or public body to natural rainfall? It has been suggested that the right to receive rainfall is one of those "natural rights" which are inherent in the full use of land from the fact of its natural contact with moisture in the air. . . .

Any use of such air or space by others which is injurious to his land, or which constitutes an actual interference with his possession or his beneficial use thereof, would be a trespass for which he would have remedy. *Hinman* v. *Pacific Air Transport*, 9 Cir., 84 F.2d 755, 758.

* * * * *

We believe that under our system of government the landowner is entitled to such precipitation as Nature deigns to bestow. We believe that the landowner is entitled, therefore and thereby, to such rainfall as may come from clouds over his own property that Nature, in her caprice, may provide. It follows, therefore, that this enjoyment of or entitlement to the benefits of Nature should be protected by the courts if interfered with improperly and unlawfully. It must be noted that defendants' planes were based at Fort Stockton, in Pecos County, and had to fly many miles to seed clouds over defendants' lands in Jeff Davis County. We do not mean to say or imply at this time or under the conditions present in this particular case that the landowner had a right to prevent or control weather modification over land not his own. We do not pass upon that point here, and we do not intend any implication to that effect.

There is ample evidence here to sustain the fact findings of the trial court that clouds were destroyed over property of appellees by operations of the appellants. The trial court chose to believe the evidence to that effect, and we hold there was ample evidence to support him in so holding and finding. We further hold that the trial court was justified in restraining appellants from modifying or attempting to modify any clouds or weather over or in the air space over lands of the appellees.

However, we do find that the temporary injunction granted by the trial court was too broad in its terms, in that it purports to restrain appellants from any activity with reference to land in the area of "plaintiffs' lands." The trial court's injunction is, therefore, modified so as to restrain appellants from the activities therein described only as they apply to the lands of appellees.

FONTAINEBLEAU HOTEL CORP. v. FORTY FIVE TWENTY-FIVE, INC.

114 So.2d 357 (Florida, 1959)

Per Curiam

This is an interlocutory appeal from an order temporarily enjoining the appellants from continuing with the construction of a 14-story addition to the Fontainebleau Hotel, owned and operated by the appellants. Appellee, plaintiff below, owns the Eden Roc Hotel, which was constructed in 1955, about a year after the Fontainebleau, and adjoins the Fontainebleau on the north. Both are luxury hotels, facing the Atlantic Ocean. The proposed addition to the Fontainebleau is being constructed 20 feet from its north property line, 130 feet from the mean high water mark of the Atlantic Ocean, and 76 feet 8 inches from the ocean bulkhead line. The 14-story tower will extend 160 feet above grade in height and is 416 feet long from east to west. During the winter months, from around two o'clock in the afternoon for the remainder of the day, the shadow of the addition will extend over the cabana, swimming pool, and sunbathing areas of the Eden Roc, which are located in the southern portion of its property.

In this action, plaintiff-appellee sought to enjoin the defendants-appellants from proceeding with the construction of the addition to the Fontainebleau (it appears to have been roughly eight stories high at the time the suit was filed), alleging that the construction would interfere with the light and air on the beach in front of the Eden Roc and cast a shadow of such size as to render the beach wholly unfitted for the use and enjoyment of its guests, to the irreparable injury of the plaintiff; further, that the construction of such addition on the north side of defendants' property rather than the south side, was actuated by malice and ill will on the part of the defendants' president toward the plaintiff's president; and that the construction was in violation of a building ordinance requiring a 100-foot setback from the ocean. It was also alleged that the construction would interfere with the easements of light and air enjoyed by the plaintiff and its predecessors in title for more than 20 years and "impliedly granted by virtue of the acts of the plaintiff's predecessors in title, as well as under the common law and the express recognition of such rights by virtue of Chapter 9837, Laws of Florida 1923. . . ." Some attempt was also made to allege an easement by implication in favor of the plaintiff's property, as the dominant, and against the defendants' property as the servient, tenement.

701

The defendants' answer denied the material allegations of the complaint, pleaded laches and estoppel by judgment.

The chancellor heard considerable testimony on the issue made by the complaint and the answer and, as noted, entered a temporary injunction restraining the defendants from continuing with the construction of the addition. His reason for so doing was stated by him, in a memorandum opinion, as follows:

In granting the temporary injunction in this case, the Court wishes to make several things very clear. The ruling is not based on any alleged presumptive title, nor is it based on any deed restrictions nor recorded plats in the title of the plaintiff nor the defendants nor of any plat of record. It is not based on any zoning ordinance nor on any provision of the building code of the City of Miami Beach nor on the decision of any court, nisi prius or appellate. It is based solely on the proposition that no one has a right to use his property to injury of another. In this case it is clear from the evidence that the proposed use by the Fontainebleau will materially damage the Eden Roc. There is evidence indicating that the construction of the proposed annex by the Fontainebleau is malicious or deliberate for the purpose of injuring the Eden Roc, but it is scarcely sufficient, standing alone, to afford a basis for equitable relief.

This is indeed a novel application of the maxim *sic utere tuo ut alienum non laedas*. This maxim does not mean that one must never use his own property in such a way as to do any injury to his neighbor. . . . It means only that one must use his property so as not to injure the lawful rights of another. . . . [U]nder this maxim, it was stated that "it is well settled that a property owner may put his own property to any reasonable and lawful use, so long as he does not thereby deprive the adjoining landowner of any right of enjoyment of his property which is recognized and protected by law, and so long as his use is not such a one as the law will pronounce a nuisance."

No American decision has been cited, and independent research has revealed none, in which it has been held that—in the absence of some contractual or statutory obligation—a landowner has a legal right to the free flow of light and air across the adjoining land of his neighbor. Even at common law, the landowner had no legal right, in the absence of an easement or uninterrupted use and enjoyment for a period of 20 years, to unobstructed light and air from the adjoining land. . . . And the English doctrine of "ancient lights" has been unanimously repudiated in this country. . . .

There being then no legal right to the free flow of light and air from the adjoining land, it is universally held that where a structure serves a useful and beneficial purpose, it does not give rise to a cause of action, either for damages or for an injunction under the maxim *sic utere tuo ut alienum non laedas*, even though it causes injury to another by cutting off the light and air and interfering with the view that would otherwise be available over adjoining land in its natural state, regardless of the fact that the structure may have been erected partly for spite. . . .

We see no reason for departing from this universal rule. If, as contended on behalf of plaintiff, public policy demands a landowner in the Miami Beach area refrain from constructing buildings on his premises that will cast a shadow on the adjoining premises, an amendment of its comprehensive planning and zoning ordinance, applicable to the public as a whole, is the means by which such purpose should be achieved. (No opinion is expressed here as to the validity of such an ordinance, if one should be enacted pursuant to the requirements of law. Cf. *City of Miami Beach* v. *State ex rel. Fontainebleau Hotel Corp.*, Fla. App. 1959, 108 So.2d 614, 619; certiorari denied, Fla. 1959, 111 So.2d 437.) But to change the universal rule—and the custom followed in that state since its inception—that adjoining landowners have an equal right under the law to build to the line of their respective tracts and to such a height as is desired by them (in the absence, of course, of building restrictions or regulations) amounts, in our opinion, to judicial legislation. . . .

* * * * *

The record affirmatively shows that no statutory basis for the right sought to be enforced by plaintiff exists. The so-called Shadow Ordinance enacted by the City of Miami Beach at plaintiff's behest was held invalid in *City of Miami Beach* v.

State ex rel. Fontainebleau Hotel Corp., supra. It also affirmatively appears that there is no possible basis for holding that plaintiff has an easement for light and air, either express or implied, across defendants' property, nor any prescriptive right thereto—even if it be assumed, arguendo, that the common-law right of prescription as to "ancient lights" is in effect in this state. And from what we have said heretofore in this opinion, it is perhaps superfluous to add that we have no desire to dissent from the unanimous holding in this country repudiating the English doctrine of ancient lights.

* * * * *

While the chancellor did not decide the question of whether the setback ordinance had been violated, it is our view that, even if there was such a violation, the plaintiff would have no cause of action against the defendants based on such violation. The application of simple mathematics to the sun studies filed in evidence by plaintiff in support of its claim demonstrates conclusively that to move the existing structure back some 23 feet from the ocean would make no appreciable difference in the problem which is the subject of this controversy. . . . The construction of the 14-story addition is proceeding under a permit issued by the city pursuant to the mandate of this court in *City of Miami Beach* v. *State ex rel. Fontainebleau Hotel Corp.*, supra, which permit authorizes completion of the 14-story addition according to a plan showing a 76-foot setback from the ocean bulkhead line. Moreover, the plaintiff's objection to the distance of the structure from the ocean appears to have been made for the first time in the instant suit, which was filed almost a year after the beginning of the construction of the addition, at a time when it was roughly eight stories in height, representing the expenditure by defendants of several million dollars. In these circumstances, it is our view that the plaintiff has stated no cause of action for equitable relief based on the violation of the ordinance—assuming, arguendo, that there has been a violation.

Since it affirmatively appears that the plaintiff has not established a cause of action against the defendants by reason of the structure here in question, the order granting a temporary injunction should be and it is hereby reversed with the directions to dismiss the complaint.

PROBLEMS FOR DISCUSSION

1. Bowie James bought a large apartment complex in the city of Cleveland from Melissa Montalvo. Melissa gave Bowie a warranty deed to the land, which was subject only to the zoning ordinances of the city. Bowie later learned that the city had condemned (taken by eminent domain) a sewer easement 150 feet under the surface. A sewer line was constructed at that level. Bowie claims that the existence of the sewer easement is a breach of Melissa's covenant against encumbrances, and he asks for rescission of the land sale or damages. How should the court decide this lawsuit? Explain.

2. Greg Kasu claims ownership of 36 acres of land by adverse possession, as against the record owner, Olive Smiley. This parcel lay across the river from Olive's other land, and she used it only occasionally in the winter. Greg erected no fences around the parcel since it was bounded by the river and his other land. Greg regularly farmed 22 of the 36 acres, and Olive concedes that he owns that much by adverse possession. The other 14 acres were wooded and along the river. Greg had begun clearing trees in that area in 1955 and had cleared it off slowly over a number of years, with most of the clearing occurring after 1958. In the meantime, Greg had grazed cattle on some of the uncleared land. Greg brought a quiet title action in 1976, claiming that the 20-year period for adverse possession had run and that he owned all 36 acres. Olive says that the 20 years could not start until he had completely cleared the land, since he hadn't fenced it off. Who's right, and why?

3. Karil Clancy brought a declaratory judgment action to clarify a deed which had been given by a prior owner of her land to the Nifty Northland Railroad. The deed had conveyed a strip of land to the railroad "for said railroad and for railroad purposes only, to have and to hold the same to said company, their successor and assigns, forever." Nifty has now abandoned this railroad line, and Karil claims that the land has automatically to reverted to her, since the railroad had only an easement. Nifty says it was granted a fee simple estate to the strip of land. How should the court rule here, and why?

4. Olaf Reelin owned a 100-acre tract of land which Vic Grab wanted to purchase. Olaf told Vic he wasn't interested in selling the land just yet, but he did give Vic a lease on the land with an option to purchase at the end of the five-year lease period. The lease was to run from January 1, 1971, to January 1, 1976, with the annual rental of $1,000 payable in advance on each January 1. Vic was required to give six months' advance notice if he intended to exercise the option to buy. Vic died in July 1973. His widow or his estate made the rental payments for 1974 and 1975, which were accepted. On June 15, 1975, the administrator of his estate notified Olaf that the estate was exercising Vic's option to buy the land. Olaf refused to convey, and the estate brings an action for specific performance. What result, and why?

5. Finster and Maymie Fauman moved into their new house in 1952 and immediately constructed a gravel driveway in front of the house. The driveway was partially within a highway right-of-way which crossed the corner of the property across the street, owned by Reuben and Lesah Rumrow. The Faumans used their driveway without objection until 1971, when the city dug up the portion of the driveway within the highway right-of-way in order to lay sewer pipe. In return for the sewer easement, the city agreed to pave the portion of the driveway within the highway right-of-way. At that point, the Rumrows sued for an injunction. The Faumans claim an easement by prescription. Should an injunction be issued? Why or why not?

6. Jerry Lagaro filed a mechanic's lien against Viennese Village, Inc., for work done on its restaurant building. Jerry had submitted a bill for $6,000 on June 26 for work done to date, but the bank which held the mortgage on the restaurant had required him to sign a mechanic's lien waiver before it released any money to pay his bill. Jerry did so. The waiver form stated: "The undersigned hereby waive any and all claims or right of lien which the undersigned now have or may have hereafter for labor rendered or material supplied." Jerry was paid this first $6,000. He then performed another $5,800 worth of work on the restaurant, and when he was not paid, he filed a mechanic's lien against the property. Viennese brings an action to declare this second mechanic's lien invalid because of Jerry's earlier waiver. Does Jerry have a valid lien here? Discuss.

7. Fred Champain had a trench dug near the boundary line of his property in order to put up a retaining wall. The trench was about seven feet long, four feet wide, and seven feet deep. Because the excavation was on his property, Fred did not cover it or light it. Milo Stalker was visiting Bibi Ransom, who lived next door to Fred. About 11 P.M., Bibi's dog began to growl and Milo thought he heard a strange noise, so he ran out of Bibi's house and around the side next to Fred's. At this point, he fell into Fred's ditch and was seriously injured. Milo sues Fred. Does he have a case? Why or why not?

8. In 1925 the Buffalo Land Company conveyed certain real estate to Gertie Gravell. The deed to Gertie contained the following reservation: "Reserving and excepting from the same, coal and mineral rights in such lands as are now known or shall hereafter be ascertained to contain coal or iron and also the use of such surface ground as may be necessary for mining operations." Gertie's successors in interest

claim that they own the mineral rights because this reservation is contradictory and because no coal or iron was known or mined for 50 years after the deed was given to Gertie. Alternatively, they argue that only coal and iron rights were reserved if the reservation is valid. Buffalo says it kept all the mineral rights. How should the court interpret this deed provision? Explain.

9. Johann Karz and Zelda Karz had two children, Ned and Eileen. Zelda died in 1915, and Johann married Wanda. Wanda cared for the children as if they were her own. Johann and Wanda bought a farm in 1917 as tenants by the entirety. Johann died in 1952, making Wanda the sole owner. Wanda married Harvey Terkiel in 1954. Wanda had her attorney draft a will which she executed in 1967 and which left two thirds of her property to the children and one third to Harvey. In 1970 Wanda went back to her attorney and had him draft a deed which she executed, conveying the farm to herself and Harvey as tenants by the entirety. Wanda died in 1971, and Harvey became sole owner of the farm. Ned and Eileen sue to have the deed set aside as having been executed under undue influence. They argue that Wanda was 72 when she executed the deed and that she had been hospitalized several times in the prior two years; that, as her husband, Harvey had a fiduciary relationship with her; that he had the opportunity to influence her decision; and that he personally benefited from the deed, for which he paid nothing. Harvey's lawyer argues that Wanda was a strong-willed woman, that she consulted her own lawyer, and that even when Harvey was with her, she always did all the talking. Should the court set aside this deed? Discuss.

34 | Real Property—Landlord and Tenant

The problems, rights, and duties involved in the landlord-tenant relationship are very relevant to the students who will be reading this textbook as nearly all of them will be involved in such a relationship. For a student who lives in a dormitory, there is a landlord-tenant relationship in which the university is the landlord and the student is the tenant. For a student who lives in an apartment, the landlord is the owner of the premises in which the apartment is located. In this chapter we will try to answer some of the questions that are often posed concerning the landlord-tenant relationship.

TYPES OF TENANCIES

Tenancies at Will. Tenancy is simply the right of the tenant, or the lessee as he or she is often called, to occupy the premises. The simplest form of tenancy is called tenancy at will. This occurs when the landlord allows the tenant to occupy the premises and there is no agreement as to a specific time period. Thus either the landlord or the tenant may terminate the tenancy whenever he or she wants to. Also, a tenancy at will is automatically terminated by the death of either party. Most states do require that the terminating party give the other party advance notice of the termination. The length of this notice varies from state to state, but its usual length is 30 days. This, of course, assumes that the rent has been paid. If the tenant fails to pay the rent, then the landlord can simply give the tenant notice that the lease has been terminated for that reason. In this situation a different notice requirement would be imposed.

No reason need be given in order to terminate the tenancy at will. The landlord may terminate the tenancy at will simply because he or she doesn't want the tenant living there any longer. The tenant, on the other hand, may terminate it simply because he or she wants to move out.

The tenancy at will can be oral or in writing. You recall that in Chapter 7 we discussed the statute of frauds and learned that any agreement concerning an interest in land must be in writing in order to be enforced in the courts. That was a general rule, and there are statutory exceptions from state to state.

Tenancies for a Specified Period.   The great majority of residential tenancies are for a period of one year. In a college community, however, the period of tenancy may be governed by the school year. For example, the landlord may lease an apartment from August to May to one student and then lease the apartment for a two-month period during the summer to a student going to summer school. Typically a commercial lease will be for a longer period of time than one year for reasons of expediency. A tenancy for a specified period is automatically terminated by the expiration of its term, and there is no requirement that either party give any notice. Both parties are aware of the term, and when the term ends, the tenancy ends.

Normally tenancies for a specified period will be in writing because it is in the best interest of both parties to have written evidence of their agreement and of the term of the tenancy. In this type of tenancy neither the landlord nor the tenant may terminate the tenancy until the expiration of its term unless the tenant fails to pay the rent when due, in which case the landlord may terminate the tenancy, or unless one of the parties fails to live up to the requirements of the agreement, in which case the other party may terminate the tenancy based on that breach of the agreement. For example, if the landlord turns off the heat in below-zero weather, the tenant would certainly have a right to terminate the lease and to move out of the premises since it would be unsafe for the tenant to continue living there.

Tenancies by Sufferance.   This type of tenancy occurs after the tenancy for a specified period expires. For example, a student had a 10-month lease which expired on May 31. The student had a duty to move out on May 31 but for one reason or another needed to stay in the area for an additional time and continued to occupy the premises. He or she was then a tenant by sufferance. The landlord may treat the tenant by sufferance as a trespasser and have him or her evicted, or the landlord may work out some type of rental arrangement with such a tenant for the period of time that the tenant needs to stay. A person remains a tenant by sufferance until the landlord decides to evict him or her or to agree to a new term of tenancy.

NATURE OF A LEASE

The lease is a contract, and thus it must comply with the requirements for the formation and enforcement of a contract. There must be offer, acceptance, consideration, capacity to contract, and lawful purpose. The lease contract may be oral or written. If it is oral and for a term exceeding one year, it will not be legally enforceable in most states. There are, however, a few states which allow the enforcement of oral lease contracts for a period of up to three years.

Many tenants have the misconception that an oral lease is better for them. Actually a written lease provides better protection for both parties. With an oral lease, there is always the question of who said what and whom the court will believe. In a written lease, the rights and duties of both parties are stated and the landlord cannot raise the rent, evict the tenant, or make any new rules during the term of the lease. In a college town where living space is limited, these protections can be very important. But a written lease also prevents the tenant from moving out merely because he or she feels like it. If the landlord fails to comply with the terms of the lease, the tenant can move out legally, or force the landlord to comply with the terms, or sue for damages.

The lease agreement must give the tenant-lessee the right to occupy, use, and enjoy the apartment or the parcel of land and the improvements thereon as defined in the agreement. Since the intent is not to permanently convey any rights to the lessee, the agreement must state when the landlord is allowed to retake possession. It must also state the consideration—how much rent the tenant is required to pay. The lease should specify what security deposit must be paid and when rental payments are due and to whom they are paid. There will also be lease terms which govern the tenant's use, enjoyment, and possession of the premises and preserve the landlord's right of inspection. In addition, many other terms may be inserted in a lease agreement. Many landlords do not want animals on the premises and therefore have a clause in the lease which prohibits the tenant from having an animal pet. Another common clause restricts the subletting of the premises. Normally the tenant may sublet the premises to another person, provided the landlord agrees to the sublease. Landlords also frequently include clauses which purport to limit their liability for accidents on the premises. The following case illustrates the effect of such an exculpatory clause.

State Farm Fire & Casualty Co. v. *Home Insurance Co.*
276 N.W. 2d 349 (Wisconsin, 1979)

FACTS   In October 1974 Charlotte Kirsch and her son moved into a ground floor apartment in a building in Burlington owned by Manuel Mendez. Mendez employed Lawrence Middleton as caretaker for the building. Kirsch lived there for one month before she was required to sign a one-year lease. The lease contained a clause disclaiming the landlord's liability for any damage done by plumbing, gas, steam, water, or other pipes. Kirsch did not read this clause at the time, nor was it explained to her. Her apartment had a "sleeve" for an air conditioning unit, but there was no air conditioning unit. Instead, a piece of cardboard covered the opening where the unit would have been. Lex Hickman and Dennis Cramer moved into the apartment above Kirsch's in November. Their air conditioner was also missing, and during the winter they filed about 50 complaints with Middleton about the cardboard blowing off the hole and letting in cold air. Middleton did nothing about the problem. On February 2, 1975, Kirsch received a call at work telling her to come back to her apartment. A copper tube in the baseboard radiation system had broken, and her apartment was flooded with water. The cold air coming in upstairs had apparently frozen the pipe, and it broke. Kirsch was paid $1,646.24 by her insurance company, State Farm. State Farm got $155 in salvage of her items, and sued Mendez' insurance company, Home, for $1,491.24. State Farm won a jury verdict, but the trial court entered a judgment N.O.V. for Home. State Farm appealed.

ISSUE   Does the disclaimer clause in the lease protect the landlord from liabilty?

DECISION   No. Judgment reversed; case remanded for entry of judgment on jury's award.

708

REASONS   Judge Bode first considered whether the exculpatory clause was valid at all. He restated the factors to be used: "the circumstances under which the lease was negotiated, including the type of lease involved—whether a standard form or an individualized contract—the type of housing which the lease covers, the relative positions of the parties at the time the lease was entered into, and the scope of the exculpatory language." He also said that the general rule was to favor freedom of contract and to invalidate exculpatory clauses only where such freedom was "nothing more than an illusion." He did not think that that was the case here.

"Kirsch was free to sign the lease or to move elsewhere. There is no evidence that alternative apartments were not available or that she could not afford a different unit. She was not placed in a position of either signing or having no place to go. Moreover, there is no indication that the lease requirement came as a surprise to her. . . . If a prospective tenant is illiterate, unable to read English, or for some other reason unable to comprehend the written terms of a lease, there may be an obligation on the part of a landlord to explain them. However, that is not the case here. . . . To hold an unambiguous portion of a contract invalid simply because it was not read would be ludicrous. Failure to read a contract before signing it will generally not affect its validity. A court will not protect a person who fails to take reasonable steps for his own protection. . . .

"The general rule is that an exculpatory clause exempting a landlord from liability resulting from a condition of the premises does not apply where the damage sustained is caused by the active or affirmative negligence of the landlord. . . .

"Middleton's actions did not amount to mere inadvertent acts or omissions. . . . Hickman and Cramer had repeatedly brought the lack of insulation in the air conditioning sleeve to Middleton's attention. His intentional failure to take action to correct the defect under the circumstances was an affirmative act constituting active negligence. Having concluded that Middleton's negligence was active, the exculpatory clause may not be used to exempt Mendez from liability."

Landlord's Rights and Obligations

Once a lease agreement has been made, either orally or in writing, the landlord has a duty to give the tenant possession of the premises specified in the lease agreement. The landlord also has the duty not to interfere with the right of the tenant to use, possess, and enjoy the premises for the term of the agreement, provided that the tenant does not breach any of the conditions or convenants that he or she is to perform and that the tenant pays the rent as scheduled in the lease agreement. The landlord also has the right to inspect the premises at reasonable times, with the tenant's permission, to see that the premises are not being mistreated or damaged.

Under the common law the landlord did not have to worry about the condition of the premises when he or she rented them to a tenant. The tenant was subject to the rule of caveat emptor and simply took the premises as they were or refused to rent them. If the premises were filthy or infested with rats and other vermin and the tenant knowingly agreed to take them, then the tenant assumed the risk and the landlord would not be responsible for injuries and damages that the tenant might suffer as a result of living in the premises. The rule of caveat emptor has generally been replaced by the rule of caveat vendor—

that is, "Let the seller (in this case the landlord) beware." The landlord-tenant relationship has become the target of many consumer groups, and as a result many states, cities, and counties have enacted housing codes which set minimum standards with regard to the rental of premises for residential occupancy. Most cities and counties now have housing inspectors who will respond to the complaints of tenants and whose job is to see that rental units are in fact safe and habitable and free from such dangers as bare electrical wires which would cause a fire and the infestation of rodents and other vermin which could cause unhealthy and unsanitary conditions.

Green v. Superior Court of City and County of San Francisco
517 P.2d 1168 (California, 1974)

FACTS Roger Green was sued by his landlord, Jack Sumski, for possession of the leased apartment and $300 in back rent. Roger defended on the ground that the landlord had breached the implied warranty of habitability. The small claims court awarded possession and $225. Roger appealed to the superior court, where a new trial was held. Roger introduced a Department of Public Works inspection report which listed 80 housing code violations in the apartment, including a collapsed bathroom ceiling, vermin and cockroaches, no heat in four rooms, plumbing blockages, exposed and faulty wiring, and an illegally installed and dangerous stove. The superior court entered the same judgment for the landlord, holding that the tenant's only remedy for such violations was a separate action under the city housing code. Roger then asked the court of appeal for a writ of mandamus, which was denied. Finally, he appealed to the state Supreme Court, which stayed the execution of the superior court's judgment pending the outcome of the appeal.

ISSUE Can a landlord's breach of the implied warranty of habitability be used as a defense by a tenant who is sued for back rent?

DECISION Yes. Judgment reversed, and case remanded for further proceedings.

REASONS Justice Tobriner said that the old common-law rule of caveat emptor had been rejected in a growing number of modern decisions by the highest courts of other states. He noted that the new rule of caveat vendor had also been recognized in a prior case by the California court of appeal and held that the time had come for California to adopt the new rule.

"[A]s the recent line of out-of-state cases comprehensively demonstrate, the factual and legal premises underlying the original common law rule in this area have long ceased to exist; continued adherence to the time-worn doctrine conflicts with the expectations and demands of the contemporary landlord-tenant relationship and with modern legal principles in analogous fields. To remain viable, the common law must reflect the realities of present-day society; an implied warranty of habitability in residential leases must therefore be recognized. . . .

"[T]he 'repair and deduct' provisions of Civil Code section 1941 et seq. do not preclude this development in the common law, for such enactments were never intended to be the exclusive remedy for tenants but have always been viewed as complementary to existing common law rights.

"Finally, we have concluded that a landlord's breach of this warranty of habitability may be raised as a defense in an unlawful detainer action. Past California cases have established that a defendant in an unlawful detainer action may raise any affirmative defense which, if established, will preserve the tenant's possession of the premises. As we shall explain, a landlord's breach of a warranty of habitability directly relates to whether any rent is 'due and owing' by the tenant; hence, such breach may be determinative of whether the landlord or tenant is entitled to possession of the premises upon nonpayment of rent. Accordingly, the tenant may properly raise the issue of warranty of habitability in an unlawful detainer action. . . .

"The transformation which the residential lease has undergone since the Middle Ages . . . has completely eroded the underpinnings of the 'independent covenant' rule. Today the habitability of the dwelling unit has become the very essence of the residental lease; the landlord can as materially frustrate the purpose of such a lease by permitting the premises to become uninhabitable as by withdrawing the use of a portion of the premises."

In many recent cases, landlords have been found civilly liable for injury to tenants because the landlords failed to provide sufficient security and because the landlords' employees were responsible for theft or injury to tenants.

Whether the landlord is liable in such cases depends heavily on the circumstances. If the apartment complex advertises that it provides security for its tenants, then it has assumed that duty; if, however, no security has been promised or provided, then the tenant will be faced with caveat emptor. As to theft, the landlord will normally have a clause in the lease stating that the landlord is not responsible for theft. With regard to attacks by employees, the landlord will allege that the persons who perpetrated them were not acting as agents or employees and that the employer is not responsible for criminal acts of employees. We must, however, keep in mind that the pendulum of the law is constantly swinging in favor of the consumer-tenant and against the seller-landlord. Thus the wise landlord will insure adequately against such situations, as this area of landlord's rights and obligations is still a questionable one.

Braitman v. Overlook Terrace Corp.
346 A.2d 76 (New Jersey, 1975)

FACTS   Overlook Terrace is a 600-unit, middle-income, high-rise apartment complex located at 5701 Boulevard East, West New York, New Jersey. Nathan and Olga Braitman leased their apartment on January 30, 1971, with the lease term to start on March 1. They did not actually take possession until March 16, and Nathan noticed at that time that the dead-bolt lock on the door was not working properly. He notified the management office several hours later and was told that things would be "taken care of." When nothing was done, Nathan repeated his complaint on two other occasions, but the lock was still not fixed. Nathan also complained at least twice to the building superintendent, and Olga complained to the management several times. On March

24, the Braitmans' apartment was robbed of $6,100 worth of personal property, mostly jewelry. The investigating police officer said that he had slipped the slip lock on the door with "a piece of celluloid" and that the dead-bolt lock was not working. The evidence also showed that Nathan had tried to get his own locksmith to install a new lock but that the locksmith had been told by a security guard that "you're not allowed to install locks." The trial court awarded $6,100, and the appellate division affirmed. Overlook appealed.

ISSUE   Was the landlord's negligence the proximate cause of the tenant's loss?

DECISION   Yes. Judgment affirmed.

REASONS   Justice Pashman began his analysis by restating the general common-law rules that one private person had no duty to protect another from the criminal acts of third persons and that a landlord had no duty to protect a tenant from such criminal acts. He noted, however, "that there has been a recent judicial trend toward expanding the scope of duty on the part of landlords with respect to tenant security." According to these newer precedents, the underlying rationale for the old rules was missing in the context of modern-day urban apartment living, particularly where the landlord retained control of the common portions of the building, including entrances, and provided general building security. The *Restatement of Torts, Second,* also recognized that liability might result where negligent conduct exposed another person to unreasonable risk of harm by the criminal acts of third parties. Here there was negligence and the results were foreseeable.

"In light of the foregoing, it is clear that whether we base our conclusion on the decisions of other states which have identified a duty on the part of landlords to take reasonable measures to safeguard tenants from foreseeable criminal conduct . . . or upon a logical extension of the principles of our own case law dealing with the relationship between the foreseeability and criminal conduct . . . , the result is the same. A residental tenant can recover damages from his landlord upon proof that that latter unreasonably enhanced the risk of loss due to theft by failing to supply adequate locks to safeguard the tenant's premises after suitable notice of the defect."

Justice Pashman also noted that the failure to provide a working dead-bolt lock was a violation of a regulation adopted by the commissioner of community affairs pursuant to the state's Hotel and Multiple Dwelling Law.

While all seven judges agreed on the affirmance of the lower court's decision, Justices Pashman and Sullivan and Chief Justice Hughes went on to state that the Supreme Court might soon have to extend the landlord's liability for security measures. Justices Clifford and Schreiber concurred in the result but filed a separate opinion stating that they did so based on traditional negligence theory and that they saw no need to go further in order to decide this case.

Tenant's Rights and Obligations

The most important right that a tenant has is what the law terms "quiet enjoyment of the premises." This means that, with a few exceptions, the tenant has the right to use the house or apartment which he or she is renting in generally the same manner as if the tenant owned the premises. To be more specific, if you are a tenant, you may invite anyone you wish to visit you, and you may carry on any activities which are not forbidden by the lease or by law. The key here is reasonable use of the premises. For example, you rent a house with a large yard and the house is a considerable distance from other houses. In that case, you can play your stereo as loud as you want to and have loud parties, as long as you don't destroy or damage the rented property. On the other hand, if you live in an apartment building, your right to play the stereo loud and to have loud parties would be limited because as the tenant in an apartment house, you not only have the right to quiet enjoyment of the premises but you also have an obligation not to unreasonably disturb the other tenants, who also have the right to quiet enjoyment of the premises. The tenant should always read the fine print in the lease agreement, as the agreement may prohibit many activities which are not expressly forbidden by law, and such provisions are contractual and will generally be enforced by courts.

As stated in the preceding section on the landlord's rights and obligations, the landlord has a right to inspect the rented premises to see that they are being kept in good condition and that no damage to them has occurred. However, during the period of the lease the landlord does not have the right to enter the house or apartment whenever he or she pleases and without the tenant's permission. The landlord who is going to inspect the premises must do so at reasonable times when his or her entry will not interfere with the quiet enjoyment of the premises by the tenant. A landlord could be civilly liable in a trespass action for forcing his or her way into the rented premises or for entering the rented premises periodically when the tenant is not at home simply to snoop.

Another common problem experienced by tenants is that of liability for repairs. What repairs are the landlord's duty, and what repairs are the duty of the tenant? The landlord's obligation to make repairs inside the rented house or apartment will vary from state to state and from locality to locality and may also be dictated by the terms of the lease. As a general rule, however, the landlord is required to make major repairs except when the damage which requires repairs is caused by the tenant's negligence. If the tenant is having a wild party and something is thrown through a window, the tenant will be obligated to replace the window. If a windstorm blows off part of the roofing and water drips through the ceiling causing the plaster to fall, the landlord will be responsible for making the necessary repairs. A general rule of thumb in these cases would be that the tenant has a duty to make minor repairs to keep the premises in as good a condition as they were when he or she rented them, excluding, of course, normal wear and tear. Most landlords require a security deposit for use in making such minor repairs when the tenant vacates the premises. If the tenant's furniture marked up the walls, then the tenant would be obligated to have the walls repainted in order to cover the damage. If the furnace broke down, that is a major repair which would be the landlord's obligation.

Borders v. *Roseberry*

532 P.2d 1366 (Kansas, 1975)

FACTS   Rienecker leased a single-family house from Agnes Roseberry in 1970. Agnes had just had some remodeling done on the house, including the installation of a new roof. The roofers had removed the gutters from the front of the house but had not reinstalled them. Without gutters, water ran off the front side of the roof onto the front steps. On January 9, 1971, ice had accumulated on the steps and Rienecker worked that afternoon to clean them off. Gary Borders arrived at about 4 P.M. in response to a dinner invitation. When Gary left that evening, about 9 P.M., he slipped and fell on the icy steps, and sustained personal injuries. Gary sued Agnes. He appealed from a trial court ruling that Agnes owed no duty to a social guest of the tenant in a single-family house where the injury was the result of a known hazard.

ISSUE   Is the landlord liable for a known defective condition which existed when the tenant took possession of the premises?

DECISION   No. Judgment affirmed.

REASONS   After stating the facts, Justice Prager began by reiterating the common-law rule of nonliability of the landlord for defective conditions existing at the time the lease is executed and possession is transferred. He then reviewed each of the recognized exceptions; (1) unknown dangerous conditions; (2) conditions dangerous to persons outside the premises; (3) land leased for purpose of admitting the public; (4) lessor retains control of parts which lessee is permitted to use; (5) lessor contracts to repair; and (6) lessor makes repairs negligently. Only exception 6 had any possible connection with this case.

"As to exception 6, although it is obvious that the repairs to the roof were not completed by installation of the guttering and although the landlord expressed his [*sic*] intention to replace the guttering, we do not believe that the factual circumstances bring the plaintiff within the application of exception 6 where the lessor has been negligent in making repairs. As pointed out above, that exception comes into play only when the lessee lacks knowledge that the purported repairs have not been made or have been negligently made. Here it is undisputed that the tenant had full knowledge of the icy condition on the steps created by the absence of guttering. It seems to us that the landlord could reasonably assume that the tenant would inform his guest about the icy condition on the front steps. We have concluded that the factual circumstances do not establish liability on the landlord on the basis of negligent repairs made by him."

As indicated previously, many states, cities, and counties have passed housing codes which are for the most part tenant oriented since they usually require the landlord to maintain the premises in a manner that complies with the codes. Typically the housing authorities do not police the rented premises but rely upon complaints from tenants. If a tenant complains that the premises are not being maintained according to the housing code, the landlord can be forced to make the necessary repairs and perhaps fined for the violation, depending on the particular law.

714   Tenants' rights as to heat, water, and electricity will depend primarily upon

the lease agreement. If the landlord is to provide the heat and he or she turns the thermostats down to a point at which the heat is inadequate for living purposes, then the tenant may terminate the lease and leave, or heat the premises at his or her expense and deduct the cost from the rent, or report the landlord to the local housing authority.

Another question that often arises is: Who bears the responsibility for the loss of the tenant's furniture, clothing, and personal effects if the rented apartment or house burns down? The lease agreement will often expressly state that the tenant assumes the responsibility for carrying fire insurance on his or her contents. If there is no such agreement in the lease, then the courts will usually hold that the landlord is responsible for damages to the tenant's contents if the fire or other damage was caused as a result of the landlord's negligence. The wise thing for the tenant to do is to carry renter's insurance on his or her contents, as the law and the obligation of the landlord will vary from jurisdiction to jurisdiction and with the factual situation. Also, it is often difficult to determine who, if anyone, was negligent in a major fire or catastrophe.

Another common question concerns the extent to which a tenant can make changes or additions, such as putting pictures on walls, installing shelves, or changing curtain rods. Again, the lease often specifies that the tenant may not paint the premises, hang pictures, or make any alterations to the premises without the landlord's permission. If there is no such provision in the lease, then a reasonable approach applies. If the tenant hangs pictures on the wall, he or she will be obligated to patch any holes and to paint any areas that have been marred, so that the premises are restored to their original condition when the lease comes to an end. If the tenant makes any major additions, such as bookshelves, a room divider, or other fixtures, the landlord automatically becomes the owner of those fixtures when the tenant leaves, unless the fixtures can be removed without causing any damage to the rented property.

When Can the Tenant Break the Lease? When Can the Landlord Evict the Tenant?

If the lease is for a fixed period of time, it is rather difficult for the tenant to break the lease. It is to be noted that a landlord and a tenant can always end the lease by a mutual agreement, regardless of the term of the lease. Thus, if the tenant and the landlord agree that the tenant may move out before the lease expires, then the lease may be terminated by mutual consent. It is a good idea to put this in writing to prevent the landlord from coming back later and trying to enforce the lease.

The tenant may also terminate the lease without the landlord's agreement if the landlord has interfered with the tenant's quiet enjoyment or if the landlord has in some way failed to meet his or her obligations and such failure has caused the premises to be uninhabitable or not up to the required health standards. The landlord can evict a tenant for nonpayment of rent. The landlord can evict a tenant if the tenant stays in possession of the premises after the term of the lease has expired. The landlord can evict a tenant if the tenant violates the rules and regulations of the lease. For example, if your lease states that no pets are allowed and you keep a pet, the landlord can evict you unless you get rid of the pet.

Thorpe v. Housing Authority of the City of Durham
393 U.S. 268 (1969)

FACTS On November 11, 1964, Joyce Thorpe and her children began a month-to-month tenancy at McDougald Terrace, a federally assisted low-rent housing project owned by the City Housing Authority. The lease provided for automatic one-month renewals, provided that her family income and composition did not change and that she did not violate the terms of the lease. The lease further provided that either party could terminate the tenancy by giving notice at least 15 days before the end of a monthly term. On August 10, 1965, Joyce was elected president of a tenants' organization called the Parents' Club. The very next day the City Housing Authority notified her that her lease would be canceled as of August 31. No reasons were given. She refused to leave, so the authority brought eviction proceedings. The justice court ordered eviction; so did the superior court after a trial de novo. The eviction order was affirmed by the state Supreme Court. Joyce asked for certiorari. Meanwhile, HUD sent out a new circular, so the U.S. Supreme Court remanded the case for reconsideration. The state Supreme Court refused to apply the new HUD procedures retroactively, so the case came back up to the U.S. Supreme Court.

ISSUE Should the new HUD rule, which requires a specification of the reasons for an eviction, be applied to this case?

DECISION Yes. Judgment reversed and case remanded.

REASONS After reviewing the facts, Chief Justice Warren considered the nature of the HUD rule. It had been validly adopted, in accordance with HUD's general rule-making power. It was mandatory, not optional, as could be clearly seen by contrasting the new circular with the one it replaced. It did not "impair" the contract between HUD and the City Housing Authority or the contract between the authority and Thorpe. "HUD has merely provided for a particular type of notification that must precede eviction; and '[i]n modes of proceeding and forms to enforce the contract the legislature has the control, and may enlarge, limit, or alter them, provided it does not deny a remedy or so embarrass it with conditions or restrictions as seriously to impair the value of the right.' " He said further, "We . . . cannot hold that the circular's requirements bear no reasonable relationship to the purposes for which HUD's rule-making power was authorized." Finally, the chief justice met the argument that the new regulation should not be applied to an existing dispute.

"The general rule . . . is that an appellate court must apply the law in effect at the time it renders its decision. Since the law we are concerned with in this case is embodied in a federal administration regulation, the applicability of this general rule is necessarily governed by federal law. Chief Justice Marshall explained the rule over 150 years ago. . . . This same reasoning has been applied where the change was constitutional, statutory, or judicial. Surely it applies with equal force where the change is made by an administrative agency acting pursuant to legislative authorization. Exceptions have been made to prevent manifest injustice, but this is not such a case.

"To the contrary, the general rule is particularly applicable here."

RAGIN v. SCHWARTZ

393 F. Supp. 152 (Pennsylvania, 1975)

Snyder, District Judge

This is an action for declaratory judgment and injunctive relief challenging the constitutionality of those portions of Article III of the Pennsylvania Landlord and Tenant Act of 1951 (The Act) which authorize a landlord's seizure and sale of a tenant's property for unpaid rent without prior notice or opportunity to present a defense. We find those portions of Article III violate Due Process requirements and will grant the requested relief.

On July 30, 1973, Darlene Ragin entered into a written lease agreement for an apartment with Allegheny Commons East Associates, through its agent, Regional Sales, Inc., for a term of 12 months, at a monthly rental of $171.50, payable in advance. On April 20, 1974, after default in the payment due April 1, 1974, Mrs. Ragin found posted on her front door a "Notice of Distraint" which stated as follows:

NOTICE OF DISTRAINT

To Darlene Ragin   You are hereby notified that by authority and on behalf of your Landlord, Regional Sales, Inc., I have this day distrained the several goods and chattels specified in the inventory hereto annexed, the same being ALL THE GOODS AND CHATTELS LOCATED AT Ally Common apt. 112F in Pittsburgh County of Ally and State of Pennsylvania, for arrearages of rent due 1st day of April and unpaid for the amount of $171.50 Dollars; and if you do not pay the same, together with the costs of this proceeding, or replevy said goods and chattels according to the law, within five days hereafter, I shall cause the said goods and chattels to be appraised, and proceed to sell the same, according to the Act of Assembly in such case made and provided.

Given under my hand, this 20th day of April, 1974

RENT PER MONTH: 171.50 /s/ Allan Schwartz
OTHER CHARGES: Constable
    2569 PARK HILL DRIVE—PGH., PA.
    15221—731-5701

Attached to the Notice was an inventory list of property distrained which included various items of furniture from the kitchen, living room, and bedroom.

On April 24, 1974, Judge Hubert I. Teitelbaum of this Court issued a Temporary Restraining Order enjoining Constable Schwartz from selling Mrs. Ragin's property. At the Hearing for Preliminary Injunction on April 26, 1974, the Temporary Restraining Order was dissolved on the assurance of Constable Schwartz that he would not sell the property in question, and at that time a request was made for the convening of a Three Judge Court pursuant to Title 28, Section 2281. The Plaintiff promptly moved for an Order that the Action be maintained as a Rule 23(b) (2), F.R.Civ.P., Class Action, with the Class to be "all residents of Allegheny County, Pennsylvania, who rent their residences and who, therefore, are subject to a levy and/or sale authorized by Article III, Section 302 et seq. of the Pennsylvania Landlord and Tenant Act of 1951, 68 P.S. Sec. 250.302, et seq." On July 30, 1974, the Class was certified. Counsel for the Plaintiffs then moved for Summary Judgment. Argument was held thereon by the Three Judge Court on September 16, 1974, at which time counsel for the Commonwealth of Pennsylvania orally moved for a Cross-Motion for Summary Judgment. Shortly thereafter, a member of the Class, Dorthy R. Ashcraft, moved for a Temporary Restraining Order against Constable Schwartz to restrain the threatened sale of her property and the levying upon, distraining, or selling of the property of any and all members of the Class. This Order was granted.

* * * * *

The power to distrain is delineated by Sec. 250.302. . . .

The tenant is given five days within which he may bring an action of replevin for the goods (Sec. 250.306), and also may bring an action to compel the landlord to set-off any account which the tenant may have against such landlord. In this latter action, the Court may determine the amount of rent in arrears and the amount of the set-off, if any, and enter judgment in favor of the

717

proper party (Sec. 250.307), with the option in the landlord if he prevails to execute on such judgment or proceed with the distress.

In the context of this case, the question is whether the seizure of property without a chance to be heard violates this procedural due process. While there is available to the tenant the Trespass Action, the Replevin Action, and the Action for Defalcation just as in *Sniadach*, supra, the tenant here is deprived of the unfettered use of property during the interim between the Distraint and the outcome of any of these actions. In many instances these actions themselves involve court costs and collection fees which make the entire process a taking of one's property where there is the need of the less affluent for the protection provided by the Constitution. . . .

The Plaintiffs have shown that the Constable in this case acted pursuant to the Act, as the Distraint Notice itself indicates, and, without prior notice, entered the Plaintiff's premises and made a physical levy on the property as set forth in the Inventory. This indeed is an adequate basis for finding the provisions of Article III of the Act to be violative of the 14th Amendment. . . .

There is sufficient State involvement in the levy and the sale because a State official performed the sale. . . . Here, the public official has power to act only because he is an official, and thus performs "under color of law" as required by 42 U.S.C. Sec. 1983. . . .

The United States Supreme Court since *Sniadach* . . . has rendered a series of decisions striking prejudgment remedies which fail to provide prior notice and an opportunity for a hearing to determine the validity of the creditor's claim. . . .

We believe, in light of *Fuentes* v. *Shevin*, . . . where the Court held that . . . "an individual be given an opportunity for a hearing before he is deprived of any significant property interest" . . . , making exceptions only when ". . . the seizure has been directly necessary to secure an important governmental or general public interest" . . . , it is sufficient here to emphasize that the landlord-tenant situation involves self interested private parties and not important governmental concerns. . . .

We thus hold that in the instant case and in accord with the great weight of authority, that the Act here involved is violative of Due Process requirements and the Plaintiffs' suit, founded on Section 1983, is solidly supported by the law.

TOM'S POINT APARTMENTS v. GOUDZWARD

339 N.Y.S.2d 281 (New York, 1972)

Diamond, Judge

This is a holdover proceeding in which the landlord-petitioner seeks possession of the demised premises. The tenant's defense is retaliatory eviction.

The basic facts are not in dispute. The parties entered into a lease on August 17, 1966, for a two-year period commencing September 1, 1966. The lease was renewed twice, each time for a two-year period. The last renewal expired August 31, 1972.

In October, 1971, the tenant invited a group of fellow tenants to meet in her apartment to consider the possibility of forming a tenants' organization to deal with the landlord with respect to several grievances.

In April, 1972, and again in June, 1972, the tenant was advised that her lease would not be further renewed. Despite notice tenant failed to vacate the premises. On the 5th day of October, 1972, this proceeding was begun.

At the trial, the tenant raised the affirmative defense of "retaliatory eviction." She claimed that the landlord's refusal to renew her lease was solely in retaliation for her actions with her fellow tenants in opposing the landlord. The landlord contends that the tenant has failed to sustain the burden of proof required and, further, that the defense of retaliatory eviction does not apply in this case.

Tenant seeks to dismiss the action and have the Court order the landlord to renew the lease on terms equal to those offered other tenants.

The Court has before it the question whether a landlord has the right to pick his tenants and refuse to renew the tenancy of a person he finds undesirable for any reason, or whether the right is affected by the defense of retaliatory eviction.

The defense of retaliatory eviction in New York State is a comparatively new one. Retaliatory eviction has been defined in many ways. . . .

The defense of retaliatory eviction in a holdover proceeding was not available at common law, nor do we in New York have any statutes specifically prohibiting retaliatory eviction. A few states have recently enacted such statutes. . . .

The cases in New York are not in complete agreement on the interpretation of retaliatory eviction. Some New York cases have recognized it as a proper defense in holdover proceedings. . . . The Federal courts have also recognized the defense. . . .

There is no dispute between the parties that absent the defense of retaliatory eviction the Court must grant the landlord's petition of eviction. Testimony at the trial indicates that the tenant did hold a meeting of the tenants in her apartment and that she had testified at a hearing concerning the dismissal of the landlord's custodian. There was some testimony that the tenant had concerned herself with such matters as lack of services, rent increases, and inequities in rent. The tenant testified that she complained to the Attorney General's Office regarding the failure of the landlord to pay interest on rent security deposits and that she appeared at a "hearing" of the superintendent who was fired by the landlord. The landlord during the trial neither admitted nor denied the testimony of the tenant regarding these activities. . . .

The Court rejects tenant's argument that if the Court finds a retaliatory eviction it should grant the remedy of ordering a new lease. There seems to be no authority, public policy, or any other justification for disturbing the well settled law in New York that there is no way, legal or equitable, to compel a renewal of a lease.

In reviewing the New York, Federal, and out of state cases discussed above, the Court finds that the basis for accepting the defense of retaliatory eviction is as follows:

A tenant has the constitutional right . . . to discuss the conditions of the building he is living in with his co-tenants; to encourage them to use legal means to remedy improper conditions; hold meetings; form tenants' associations; and inform public officials of their complaints. These rights would for all practical purposes be meaningless if the threat of eviction would coerce the most justifiable complaints into a submissive silence.

Failure to recognize the defense of retaliatory eviction might result in the continuation of undesirable housing conditions contrary to the strong public policy of creating and/or maintaining proper housing in New York State. Our Court should not by the granting of an eviction of a complaining tenant encourage the landlord to evade his responsibility to abide by the law.

The Court is in accord with the reasoning behind the acceptance of the defense of retaliatory eviction in an action by a landlord to recover possession. Once having accepted that concept, the Court is faced with the problem as to what elements are necessary to create a valid retaliatory eviction defense. In reviewing the cases, we find no definite guidelines to follow.

It seems to this Court that *all* of the following should be presented for the tenant to prevail:

1. The tenant must have exercised a constitutional right in the action he undertook.
2. The grievance complained of by the tenant must be bona fide, reasonable, serious in nature, and have a foundation in fact. However, the grievance need not have been adjudicated by the agency reviewing the complaint.
3. The tenant did not create the condition upon which the complaint is based.
4. The grievance complained of must be present at the time the landlord commences his proceeding.
5. The overriding reason the landlord is seeking the eviction is to retaliate against the tenant for exercising his constitutional rights.

Applying facts in the present case to the above criteria, the Court finds that at the time the landlord commenced this action and, at the present time, none of the original grievances existed. The tenant testified that the tenants' association never came into being; that the tenants had collected the interest due them; that the problem with the superintendant had been resolved. Moreover, the tenant failed to show any current complaint against the landlord.

In *Edwards* v. *Habib* . . . , the Court cautioned that even if a tenant can prove a retaliatory defense, he would not be entitled to remain in possession in perpetuity. "If this illegal purpose is dissipated, the landlord can, in the absence of legislation or a binding contract, evict his tenants or raise their rents for economic or other legitimate reasons, or even for no reason at all."

The Court finds that the tenant has failed to prove the elements necessary to sustain the alleged retaliatory eviction defense. Accordingly, the decision of the Court is as follows:

Final Judgment in favor of the landlord against the tenant. Execution of the warrant stayed to February 28, 1973.

McCUTCHEON v. UNITED HOMES CORPORATION

469 P.2d 997 (Washington, 1970)

Petrie, Judge

Two tenants living in an apartment complex instituted independent actions to recover damages for injuries allegedly caused by the landlord's negligent maintenance of common passageways. Tenant McCutcheon alleged injuries from a fall down an unlighted interior stairway. Tenant Fuller alleged injuries when he fell down an exterior wooden stairway. Both tenants had previously signed a lease which contained the following exculpatory clause:

That neither the Lessor, nor his Agent, shall be liable for any injury to Lessee, his family, guests or employees or any other person entering the premises or the building of which the demised premises are a part.

The landlord, in each lawsuit, set up as an affirmative defense the exculpatory provision of the lease and moved for summary judgment. The trial court granted the motion and dismissed the complaints. Both tenants appeal from the summary judgment, and their appeals have been consolidated.

The scope of the exculpatory clause is not questioned because the tenants concede that if the clause is valid, it is an effective bar to their lawsuit. The sole issue presented upon this appeal is the validity of exculpatory clauses appearing within residential lease agreements. Tenants

contend that such clauses are void as against the public policy of the state of Washington.

The prevailing rule in regard to the validity of exculpatory agreements is succinctly stated in *Restatement of Contracts* S.574 (1932). . . .

It is clear that Washington follows the *Restatement* rule. . . .

The stated exceptions contained in S.575 of the *Restatement* prohibit contractual exculpation from the consequences of (1) willful breach of duty; (2) simple breach of duty arising out of the employment relationship; and (3) breach of duty by a person charged with a duty of public service.

Most courts, which have been called upon to determine the question, have upheld the validity of exculpatory clauses appearing within residential or apartment lease agreements. . . . The relatively few courts which have declared such agreements invalid have done so on the strength of specific legislation, such as public housing codes, which place affirmative public duties upon landlords. . . . In addition, three states, Maryland, Massachusetts, and New York, have enacted specific legislation declaring such agreements to be void. New Hampshire prohibits any waiver of the common law duty of ordinary care. . . .

Tenants in the instant case have made no contention that the exculpatory clause contravenes any Washington statute, nor has our attention been called to any such enactment. . . .

In light of this state's policy of validating exculpatory agreements in general, . . . and in the absence of any legislative expression to the contrary, we can discern no public policy which is violated by the exculpatory clause in question. We view this as an area for distinct concern because of the potentiality for unwarranted abuse, but nevertheless deem this a subject peculiarly appropriate for legislative, rather than judicial action.

The judgment is affirmed. . . .

Armstrong, Chief Judge (concurring)

I concur in the majority opinion because it expresses the rule in the state of Washington as well as the overwhelming authority in our nation.

In my judgment the legislature should consider abolishing exculpatory clauses in leases in at least ghetto and multiple family housing. I recognize there is a disparity in bargaining power in many contracts, but when that disparity is accompanied by the tendency of exculpatory clauses in leases to increase the incidence of uncompensated injury and to discourage incentive for safety precautions which potential liability creates, there is a sound basis for declaring such exculpatory clauses to be contrary to public policy.

PROBLEMS FOR DISCUSSION

1. Matilda Mango, age 83, lived alone in an apartment which she rented from Durban Rentals, Inc. Several of the other tenants in the building had seen mice on numerous occasions and had heard noises in the walls. Exterminators serviced the building about once a month, but without much effect. The building had incinerators for the disposal of waste and garbage. Matilda was so startled when a mouse jumped out of her oven that she fell and broke her hip, requiring surgery. Prior to this accident she had been in good health. Matilda sues Durban for her medical injuries and emotional distress. What result, and why?

2. Rinky Dinky Stores, Inc., decided to develop a 20-acre corner tract as a shopping center, with about 2.5 acres of that to be used for one of its large stores and parking facilities. When Pickollo Drugs learned of this project, it inquired about putting one of its drugstores in the shopping center. As a result of further negotiations, Pickollo leased a room in Rinky Dinky's store building in the shopping center. Pickollo agreed not to sell groceries in competition with Rinky Dinky, and the lease in turn gave Pickollo "the right to the exclusive operation of a retail drugstore upon the location hereinabove described." The description referred to was that of a room leased in a building in Kribbs, Idaho, "as shown on the attached plot plan marked Exhibit B." Alan Kublai later bought control of Rinky Dinky, and now he wants to lease space in one of the other buildings in the shopping center to another drugstore. Kublai says that Rinky Dinky is only prevented from leasing to another drugstore in its building; Pickollo says that the provision covers the whole shopping center. Who's right, and why?

3. Norman and Tammi Overmyer purchased on a land contract Horace Huffy's chiropractic practice, his office supplies and equipment, and the apartment building in which the practice was located. After about one year the Overmyers defaulted on several monthly payments on the land contract. The parties got together again and agreed to rescind the land contract and to forgive all past indebtednesses. The Overmyers then agreed to lease the office and facilities for six months, beginning June 1, with the rent to be $800 per month "payable in advance." The June 1 rent was received on time. The July 1 rent was received in the mail on July 5. When Huffy did not receive the July 1 rent on time, he wrote the following letter on July 2: "if this is not paid immediately and next month's rent received before the 1st, I shall consider it a violation of our agreement and withdraw my equipment from the office and request that you be moved immediately." The August 1 rent was not received on time, so Huffy and his agents went to the office and removed the equipment. The Overmyers were out of town on August 1. When they got back and learned what happened, they immediately tendered the August rent (on August 2), but Huffy refused to take the check. The Overmyers sued for actual and punitive damages for wrongful eviction. Do they have a case? Discuss.

4. Alva Sproker owned and operated Sproker's Bar for several years. As part of the business, he had been granted a state liquor license. Alva sold the business to Cecil and Cindy Estover but retained ownership of the building in which it was located. The Estovers leased the building from Alva. One provision of the lease stated that

721

on termination of the lease the lessee would surrender all licenses to serve liquor to the lessor. The Estovers were duly licensed by the state to serve liquor. About halfway through their one-year lease, they bought the building next door to Sproker's. They then applied to the local city council for permission to move the location of their licensed liquor establishment into the other building. The city council granted permission. Sproker learned what was going on and sued for an injunction and damages. The Estovers argue that the lease provision is invalid since state liquor law controls the issuance and transfer of liquor licenses. Who's right, and why?

5. Lillie Molen and Cyril Molen rented an apartment from Greg Davoriva on June 1, 1973. They never had a written lease on the apartment but simply paid the rent on a month-to-month basis. On January 28, 1975, at about 9:30 A.M., Cyril left the apartment to buy groceries. He went out the front door, which opened onto a staircase leading to the ground level. The staircase was for the sole use of the Molens' apartment. A handrail extended the full length of the staircase on the right side; on the left side there was a railing from the ground level up to the side of the building. The edge of the building roof extended partially over the stairs, but there were no gutters. Water had dripped off the roof and frozen on the stairs. Cyril descended the stairs without slipping, got his groceries, and returned. Because he lacked two fingers on his right hand he carried the groceries in his right arm and held the left handrail as he ascended the stairs. When he reached the second or third step from the top he let go of the handrail to open the door. He then slipped and broke his hip. Cyril sues for damages. What result, and why?

6. Areta Rankin leased an apartment from Hermann House, Inc., under a written lease which contained a clause exempting the landlord from any liability resulting from lack of repairs, accident, or act of the tenant or any other occupant of the building or any other person. Areta picked this building in large part because of its security system. Areta returned one night to find that $4,500 worth of jewelry was missing from her apartment. There was no evidence of the thief's identity or means of access, although the entry door between the parking lot and the elevator was sometimes left open. Without further proof, Areta said that the theft must have been due to the failure of the security system and to the landlord's negligent failure to maintain it properly. Hermann House relies on the lease clause, which it says requires a summary judgment in its favor. Who's right, and why?

7. Jess Eneker went to Krazy Kenny's Kar Wash to wash his pickup truck. Kenny's was a self-service car wash. The entrance door was closed, so Jess got out of his truck and pushed the up button to open the door. The door went up about three feet and stopped. Jess then pushed the down button, and the door went down. When he pushed the up botton again, the door went all the way up and he drove in. When Jess was ready to leave he pushed the inside up button, and the door came up about three feet. Jess noticed a loop in the door cable and bent over to look at it. The cable snapped, striking him in the left eye and causing substantial loss of vision. Kenny's leased the car wash from Proteus Petro, Inc., under a written lease which provided that the lessor would keep the premises in good repair and that the lessee would indemnify the lessor for any damages claims arising from injury to anyone on the premises. Kenny testified that he and his wife inspected the car wash every morning and that he repaired anything that needed repair and sent the bills to Proteus. Jess has sued both Kenny and Proteus. Does he have a case against either? Discuss.

8. On August 15, 1971, Harvey Hustle signed a lease for a retail gasoline station with Nobil Oil Company. The lease was for three years, and it provided for the payment of a monthly rental of two cents per gallon of gasoline sold or $300, whichever was

greater. No new written lease was executed after August 15, 1974, but Harvey was permitted to stay on for the same monthly rental. Nobil decided to withdraw its brand name marketing from the area in which the gasoline station was located, and it sold all of its local assets, including Harvey's station, to Sunshine Oil Company, which had been organized by Nobil's local distribution manager. This sale was closed on February 1, 1975. On June 15, 1975, Sunshine notified Harvey that his lease was terminated effective July 31, 1975. When Harvey refused to vacate, Sunshine brought an eviction proceeding. Harvey says that he is protected from arbitrary termination as a dealer under a statute which requires good cause for any franchisee-dealer's termination on any contract entered into after May 1, 1975. He claims that each month's lease is a new contract. Is Harvey correct? Explain.

34. Real Property—
Landlord and Tenant

35 | Real Property—Zoning, Environmental Regulation, and Eminent Domain

This chapter deals with the many problems involved in the use of real estate by its owner. The initial reaction from most people is: "It's my land, and I ought to be able to use it as I see fit." If we look back in time to the era of our grandfathers or perhaps our great-grandfathers, we would find that the owner of real estate could use his or her land in any way that he or she saw fit, provided it was not used so as to cause a nuisance as defined by the law. Such a nuisance would do harm to the neighboring property owners or would interfere with their peaceable use and enjoyment of their real estate. There were no restrictions on house sizes, on the erection of fences or any outbuildings, on the number of families housed on a property, or on the use of a home to operate a beauty shop, a barbershop, a small appliance repair shop, or some similar type of business. In those days, we did not have the density problem or the traffic problem that we have today in most cities. Plenty of land was available, and far fewer people were making a demand for its use. Cities simply grew and grew, and in most cases there was no master plan. Thus we ended up with industrial plants and apartment complexes in single-family residental areas and with commercial buildings scattered here and there.

Florio v. *State*
119 So.2d 305 (Florida, 1960)

FACTS A. L. Epperson and other riparian owners around Egypt Lake complained to the state that the operation of Stew's Ski School on the lake constituted a nuisance under state law. The statutes referred to nuisances which tended "to annoy the community" or which were "manifestly injurious to the public health and safety." Egypt Lake was approximately 75 acres in area. The Florios operated a 29-acre public beach along the lake and leased a portion of this land to Stew McDonald, who ran a ski school on the lake. Another defendant, the Tampa Ski Bees, was an unincorporated association whose members water-skied on the lake and presented a 45-minute ski show every Sunday afternoon. The plaintiff owners also water-skied on the lake, but they objected to the noise, annoyance, and interference caused by the defendants, to erosion of the beaches, and to the defendants' domination of the lake by their use of high-powered speedboats and their negligent and reckless skiing. The trial court issued an injunction against the operation of the ski school and against the Ski Bees' use of the lake. The defendants appealed.

ISSUE   Was the injunction justified by the defendants' conduct?

DECISION   Partially. Judgment affirmed in part, reversed in part, and remanded.

REASONS   Judge Kanner thought that the injunction issued by the trial court was overbroad and discriminated unfairly against the defendants. He remanded the case for modification of the injunction.

"The testimony clearly, convincingly, and satisfactorily established that the activities and conduct of the defendants resulted in physical dangers and hazards to the resident home owners and renters, their children and visitors, in the use of the lake; that there was usurpation, deprivation, and unreasonable interference with the use of the lake for fishing, swimming, skiing, and boating; that there were damages to the shores through erosion; that there were also debris, mud, and grass washed and thrown on the beaches; and that such conduct created and caused a continued annoyance and discomfort to the community around the lake. This is not a complaint between neighbor and neighbor but one created through wrongful conduct of the defendants that has seriously affected the entire lake community. . . . Unquestionably the evidence sustains the findings of fact of the chancellor. . . .

"[T]he injunction against the Tampa Ski Bees . . . since it was not founded upon service on the members individually, is without basis. This defect, however, does not weaken the injunction as it applies to the other defendants. . . .

"The final point argued by defendants relates to the question whether the injunctive decree constituted an arbitrary and unjust discrimination against them and deprived them of equal protection.

"The rights of riparian proprietors to the use of waters in the nonnavigable lake are equal, and each riparian owner has the right to use the water in the lake for lawful purposes, so long as his use is not detrimental to the rights of the other riparian owners. . . . One riparian owner is not entitled to use the lake to the exclusion of other riparian owners. . . .

"The parties recognize that water skiing is not a nuisance per se. Normally it is a legitimate and wholesome pursuit. The chancellor found it to be a nuisance here because of the extent to which it was pursued under the circumstances delineated and determined. However, the court's order was so broad as to prohibit all water skiing activities by the defendant McDonald . . . and to prohibit the leasing of property by defendants Florio to the other defendants for water skiing purposes, consequently amounting in effect to wrongful discrimination against the defendants. . . .

"[I]t . . . should be modified so as to provide reasonable use by all parties of their rights under appropriate regulations."

With the increased population density in our cities, environmental problems such as industrial air pollution, industrial water pollution, solid waste pollution, traffic congestion, and noise pollution have become problems to be solved. In order to solve such problems, we have had to resort to governmental regulation of the use of various land areas. Today most cities develop industrial parks and encourage industry to build and operate within these areas. Most cities have developed zoning ordinances which restrict the use of the land in various areas. For example, single-family dwellings will be allowed in some areas, two-family dwellings will be allowed in other areas, and multifamily dwellings such as large apartment houses will be allowed in still other areas. In addition, commercial businesses will be excluded from certain areas. At first glance, this may seem unfair to the owner of real estate since under these ordinances the owner may not use the real estate as he or she sees fit but is limited to the uses prescribed by the law. It is true that zoning ordinances do take away certain rights of the individual owner. However, when one looks at the overall picture, it is clear that some type of land use regulation is in the best interest of all the residents of the various city areas, as such regulation guarantees a more peaceful enjoyment of the owners' premises for the purposes which are allowed in an area and also preserves the property values for the owners in that area. For example, if you live in an area of single-family dwellings, you certainly would object to having a developer put an apartment complex next to your home, since this would increase the traffic in front of your residence, would increase the parking problem in the area, and in general would reduce the value of your real estate.

Another problem regarding land use is that of eminent domain. With our increased population we need more schools, more parks, and more public buildings and public services. If a new school is needed to serve a housing area, then the school has to be built in the area or in close proximity to it. If no vacant land is available, then the governmental body responsible for building the school will have to use the process of eminent domain, power which allows governmental bodies to take private property for public use.

History of Zoning Laws

The first zoning law in the United States was a zoning ordinance adopted in 1916 by New York City. This ordinance regulated both the location and the use of buildings in the city.

The basic constitutionality of zoning laws was upheld as a valid exercise of the local government's police power in the landmark case of *Euclid* v. *Ambler Realty Co.*, which was decided by the U.S. Supreme Court in 1926. Zoning and land use restrictions of other kinds may still be held unconstitutional, however, if they unreasonably interfere with a property owner's rights or if they violate some other constitutional restriction.

City of Burbank v. Lockheed Air Terminal, Inc.
411 U.S. 624 (1973)

FACTS

The City Council of Burbank passed an ordinance making it illegal for jet aircraft to take off from the Hollywood-Burbank Airport between the hours of 11 P.M. and 7 A.M. The only regularly scheduled flight affected by the ordinance was an intrastate flight of Pacific Southwest Airlines which originated in Oakland and departed from the Hollywood-Burbank Airport for San Diego every Sunday night at 11:30 P.M. The plaintiff, Lockheed, brought suit for an injunction against enforcement of the ordinance, alleging that it was invalid under the Commerce Clause and the Supremacy Clause of the U.S. Constitution. The U.S. district court granted the injunction, and the U.S. court of appeals affirmed. The city of Burbank appealed.

ISSUE

Has the field of airport operations been preempted by national regulation?

DECISION

Yes. Judgment affirmed.

REASONS

Justice Douglas felt that there had been an implied preemption due to the necessity for a national system of air traffic control and to the comprehensiveness of national statutes and regulations dealing with the subject. Not only was the FAA involved; Congress had also legislated with respect to aircraft noise, and provided for EPA involvement.

"There is, to be sure, no express provision of preemption in the 1972 Act. That, however, is not decisive. . . . It is the pervasive nature of the scheme of federal regulation of aircraft noise that leads us to conclude that there is preemption. . . . 'Federal control is intensive and exclusive. Planes do not wander about in the sky like vagrant clouds. They move only by federal permission, subject to federal inspection, in the hands of federally certified personnel and under an intricate system of federal commands. The moment a ship taxis onto a runway it is caught up in an elaborate and detailed system of controls.' . . .

"The Senate Report stated: 'States and local governments are preempted from establishing or enforcing noise emission standards for aircraft unless such standards are identical to standards prescribed under this bill.' . . .

"The Secretary [of Transportation] requested leave to submit a written opinion, and in a letter dated June 22, 1968, he stated: 'The courts have held that the Federal Government presently preempts the field of noise regulation insofar as it involves controlling the flight of aircraft. . . . H.R. 3400 would merely expand the Federal Government's role in a field already preempted. It would not change this preemption. State and local governments will remain unable to use their police powers to control aircraft noise by regulating the flight of aircraft.' . . .

"When the blended provisions of the present Act were before the House, Congressman Staggers, Chairman of the House Committee on Interstate and Foreign Commerce, in urging the House to accept the amended version, said: 'I cannot say what the industry's intention may be, but I can say to the gentleman what my intention is in trying to get this bill passed. We have evidence that across America some cities and States are trying to pass noise regulations. Certainly we do not want that to happen. It would harass industry and progress in America. That is the reason why I want to get this bill passed during this session.' . . .

"When the President signed the bill he stated that 'many of the most significant sources of noise move in interstate commece and can be effectively regulated only at the national level.' . . .

"If we were to uphold the Burbank ordinance and a significant number of municipalities followed suit, it is obvious that fractionalized control of the timing of takeoffs and landings would severely limit the flexibility of FAA in controlling air traffic flow."

The need for zoning regulation was initially a problem of the cities, and through enabling legislation the various states granted their cities the power to pass zoning ordinances. Then the population grew, and new developments both residential and commercial, sprang up outside the city limits and therefore outside the legal jurisdiction of the city. Thus a need arose for county zoning regulation to prevent the misuse and haphazard development of land. The states again responded, and a majority of the states passed enabling legislation giving counties the power to pass zoning laws. Another approach to the problem was for a state to create planning regions which were not limited to the boundaries of any city or county but could cover parts of some counties and all of others. Each planning region would then be delegated the authority to make zoning regulations for the entire region. A third approach was for a state to grant extraterritorial zoning powers to a city, giving it the power to regulate and control subdivisions contiguous to the city but not actually within its limits. This approach has been adopted by only a few states as it presents the possibility of constitutional problems since the persons being regulated in the extraterritorial areas are unrepresented in the city legislative body which does the regulating.

Today nearly every city and urban area is controlled by some form of zoning law. In addition, in most cities a master plan has been adopted for the purpose of guiding and coordinating the future development of the city. Zoning is only one phase of this master plan. Zoning laws do not regulate the installation of utilities or the location of schools and parks or other public recreational facilities. Nor do these laws regulate the outward appearance of buildings or the materials used in building construction. In the past, these matters have been covered by separte city ordinances. However, with the adoption of a master plan for city planning, many cities have combined all of the old separate ordinances into a comprehensive land development control ordinance.

Zoning Defined

Zoning can be defined as the division of a city, a township, or a county or other governmental unit into specific districts for the purpose of regulating the type of building structure that may be built in each district, the placement of the buildings upon the land, and the permitted use or uses of the buildings and the land. For example, certain districts will be zoned R–1, which means that only single-family residential buildings would be allowed in them. Two-family buildings would be allowed in an R–2 district. Multifamily buildings such as apartment houses would be allowed in an R–3 district. A G–B district would allow general businesses such as office buidings, stores, shopping centers, motels, and hotels. An L–I would allow light industry such as assembly-type factories and warehouses. An H–I would allow heavy industry such as manufacturing plants with the potential for noise and air pollution. Typically these industrial districts are located as far away from residential areas as possible.

The use of the identifying terms R–1, R–2, R–3, G–B, L–I, and H–I is not universal. Some areas classify their zoning districts alphabetically, referring, for example, to A or B districts, or use other methods to identify their various zoning districts.

Within each zoning district there may be further regulations regarding the architecture, the location, and the occupancy of buildings. Examples of such regulations are regulation of the height of buildings and regulations specifying a minimum distance from the front, side, and rear property lines within which no building may be constructed. This type of regulation helps control the density of buildings and protects the property owner from encroachment upon his or her airspace and access to sunlight. For example, a neighbor would not be allowed to construct a 16-foot fence that blocks your view or blocks sunlight from your windows, or to build an addition that brings his or her house right up to the property line and thus reduces the space between the houses.

Most cities or counties now have specific building construction codes. These codes are primarily for safety and health purposes. They regulate construction methods and the use of construction materials and typically set a minimum standard for the area. Building codes will differ in different parts of the country because different standards are dictated by regional differences in such respects as temperature, the density of buildings, the possibility of earthquakes, and freezing and thawing problems.

In addition to physical regulations regarding the structure and placement of buildings, many zoning districts may have regulations concerning businesses which may be undesirable to property owners. For example, certain districts may not allow bars or the selling of intoxicating beverages or may exclude funeral homes or cemeteries.

One of the problems which has plagued city planners is that zoning must be prospective rather than retroactive in effect. Thus, if a zoning ordinance zones a certain area exclusively for single-family residential dwellings, the little corner grocery store or the lady who has her beauty shop in her home cannot be forced to cease doing business. Thus most zoning laws have a "grandfather clause" which allows a business that was in the area before the passage of the zoning ordinance to operate until it is sold or disposed of in some other manner.

Another exception to zoning regulations is the "variance." Often there are situations where the strict adherence to a zoning regulation would cause undue hardship to a property owner. In such situations the regulatory agency can grant a variance to allow the land to be used in a manner not in strict conformance with the zoning regulation. Variances are, however, not automatic but are granted only in exceptional situations.

Private Restrictive Covenants as a Method of Land Use Regulation

Zoning laws are usually general in character and often do not cover certain specific areas of concern with regard to land use. For example, zoning laws do not forbid the parking of large boats or campers in a driveway, yet such action may be unsightly and disturbing to the adjoining residents. Thus a land developer may desire to place certain restrictions in the land deeds to protect the value of the real estate in a new residential subdivision. Therefore, when the land is being developed and sold, the contract of sale and deed will contain certain restrictions, such as the requirement to submit house plans not only to the public agency for a building permit but *also* to a committee in the subdivision for its approval. Other restrictions might ban outside clothes lines, the construction of outbuildings, the construction of fences without prior approval, and the parking of boats and campers on driveways. Should a homeowner violate these restrictions, he or she may be taken to court. The court may enjoin further violations and cause the party to tear down the building or fence, move the camper or trailer, or perhaps pay damages to neighbors if damages to them were incurred. Failure to comply with the court order could result in fines and/or imprisonment for civil contempt of court.

Thus we have public zoning and private restrictive zoning. Before purchasing any parcel of real estate, the purchaser should be aware not only of public zoning restrictions but of any private restrictions which may affect his or her future use of this land.

Schaefers v. Apel
328 So.2d 274 (Alabama, 1976)

FACTS In 1961 Mary Schaefers divided her real estate and conveyed it to her four children—William, Jr., Elfreda, Julienne, and Rosemary Schaefers Sandlin. The deed to Rosemary reserved a life estate in the described real estate, which was the family home, to Mary. It then provided: "It is further mutually agreed by and between the grantor and the grantee that as a part of the consideration set out above, the grantee agrees to provide a permanent home for my daughter, Elfreda Schaefers, should she desire or request one and for my son, William Schaefers, Jr., should he desire or request one. However, it is further mutually agreed between the parties that the grantee herein is required only to furnish a permanent home for either Elfreda Schaefers, or William Schaefers, Jr., upon their request; however, this request and requirement will not and shall not apply to either of their dependents or spouse. Failure to perform the above will be considered a material breach of the consideration set out herein." The deed then granted Rosemary a fee simple estate. Mary died. Rosemary conveyed the land to Edward and Arthur Apel in 1974. Elfreda was living with Rosemary in another house and had given her a quitclaim deed to the family home. William, Jr., brought suit to set aside Rosemary's deed to the Apels because he claimed it violated his mother's deed to Rosemary. The trial court held that the quoted provision was void as an illegal restraint on alienation (transfer) of the property. William Jr. appeals.

ISSUE Is the deed provision a condition subsequent to the estate granted?

730

DECISION   No. Dismissal of complaint affirmed; decree modified.

REASONS   Justice Jones and the state Supreme Court took a very different view of the nature of the quoted provision in Mary's deed. It was valid, they said, and was not inconsistent with the grant of a fee simple estate to Rosemary. It was only a personal covenant between Mary and Rosemary, however, and not a covenant which would "run with the land" so as to prevent Rosemary from effectively conveying the land to someone else. Since it didn't prevent conveyance, it couldn't be an illegal restraint on alienation.

"[W]e find that Mary Schaefers did intend to solicit Rosemary's promise to provide a permanent home for William and Elfreda in consideration for the conveyance, and that the provision manifests that intention; therefore, it is not void. This finding brings us to the problems of determining the nature and operation of the provision.

"To set aside the Sandlin-Apel conveyance, the plaintiff must prove that the restrictive provision is a condition subsequent. If the provision is a condition subsequent, it creates a right of entry in Mrs. Schaefers' estate which may be exercised by William for a condition broken. The right of entry is not subject to the rule against perpetuities in Alabama; therefore, it creates a cloud on title which will endure indefinitely. . . .

"Thus, Alabama courts do not favor construing restrictive provisions in deeds of conveyance as conditions subsequent. And in cases where the intention of the grantor is not clear, this Court prefers to construe a restriction as a covenant—not to be confused with a covenant running with the land—rather than a condition subsequent. . . .

"The restrictive portion . . . makes no reference to the property conveyed as the permanent home which Rosemary is required to furnish, nor does it contain a divestiture or re-entry clause. . . . Such a drastic remedy as the divestiture of a fee simple estate must be expressed more precisely than this. [T]he restrictive language in the deed to Rosemary is a covenant in the nature of a personal obligation, not a covenant running with the land. . . .

"The covenant is merely a personal obligation from Rosemary to William to provide him a permanent home in some location if he requests one. Since William has made no request, Rosemary has not breached the covenant. The provision remains valid within this context."

Legality of Zoning Laws and Land Use Regulations

Each state has inherent rights to exercise police power to regulate private property for the public interest, convenience, and necessity. The states have delegated this regulatory power to the local governments, such as counties and cities. Under this delegated regulatory power, most cities and counties have enacted zoning regulations to regulate the use of land within their boundaries, housing codes to regulate the use and occupancy of residential property, and building codes to ensure the safe construction of buildings—for example, to see that a minimum standard is met in the electrical wiring, the plumbing, and the general construction of the building, including the concrete work and the roofing materials. The structural design must be adequate if a building is to withstand the stress and strain of the expected weather conditions. Thus a construction code for housing to be built in Minnesota might be more stringent with regard to roof construction than would a construction code for housing to be built in southern Arizona, simply because in Minnesota a roof would be expected to withstand the weight of extreme amounts of snow, whereas in Arizona that problem would not exist.

In addition to zoning regulations, housing codes, and building codes, most cities and counties now have subdivision controls and regulations, since housing density is becoming more and more of a problem. When a group of new homes are to be built in an area, there must be a preliminary investigation to determine whether any health or other environmental hazard will be caused by this new group of dwellings. Today many subdivisions are being created in areas where there are no public sewage systems or public water systems. In such areas it is important to make sure that the soil will allow proper drainage and filtering of the wastes from the various septic tanks of the new dwellings. It must also be determined that the water supply will not be contaminated by the septic systems. Another problem that must be considered is the drainage of storm water. For example, if a subdivision with 300 or 400 homes is built in a rural area which has had natural drainage across farmlands for years and no apparent drainage problems, each new home that is built changes the drainage situation, by replacing land that ordinarily absorbs water with a concrete slab or basement and concrete or asphalt roadways. These changes reduce the absorptive capacity of the land. However, the storm water has to go somewhere, and since less of it is absorbed by the land, it will run across the land, where it may well cause damage to buildings, the erosion of topsoil, and other problems.

Environment

The use of one's land as he or she wished was a cherished right in our country for many years. One day, only a few decades ago, people began looking around and seeing that our streams, rivers, and lakes had become polluted to such an extent that we couldn't enjoy the waters and that the air had become hazy, smelly, and acrid, often burning our eyes. The landscape was cluttered with old car bodies, beer cans, junk, and solid waste of every description. Citizen groups began calling for governmental regulation of the environment, to protect it against air pollution, water pollution, and solid waste pollution.

On the national level, Congress passed the National Environmental Policy Act and created the Environmental Protection Agency to act as the watchdog against continued pollution of our air, water, and land. Congress also passed legislation to control specific areas of pollution, such as the Clean Air Act, the Water Pollution Control Act, the Noise Control Act, and the Solid Waste Disposal Act.

Tennessee Valley Authority v. Hill
98 S. Ct. 2279 (U.S. Supreme Court, 1978)

FACTS   In 1967 the Tennessee Valley Authority (TVA) began construction on the Tellico Dam and Reservoir Project, a combined flood control, electric power, and recreation project. A dam was commenced on the Little Tennessee River; when completed, it would create a deep reservoir covering 16,500 acres. Local residents and environmental groups objected to the dam, and it was temporarily enjoined because an environmental impact statement (EIS) had not been filed, as required by the Environmental Protection Act. This injunction was lifted when the required EIS was filed in 1972, but the EIS did not mention the fish in the river.

In 1973 Congress passed the Endangered Species Act, which required all national agencies to see that they did not jeopardize the continued existence of such endangered species or destroy or modify their habitats. Just before the first injunction was lifted, a previously unknown species of perch, the snail darter, was discovered in the Little Tennessee River by a University of Tennessee ichthyologist. (There are about 130 known species of darters, including 85 to 90 in Tennessee.) The secretary of the interior declared the snail darter an endangered species and the Little Tennessee a "critical habitat." This case was then filed, in February 1976, asking for a new injunction against the dam, which was then 80 percent complete. In May 1976 the U.S. district court refused the injunction. Congress continued to appropriate money for Tellico, and the dam was 90 percent complete when an injunction was finally ordered by the U.S. court of appeals, on January 31, 1977. TVA appealed.

ISSUE   Do the provisions of the Endangered Species Act apply to existing and almost completed projects?

DECISION   Yes. Judgment of court of appeals affirmed.

REASONS   After reviewing the facts at some length, Chief Justice Burger began his analysis with the admitted fact that the completion and operation of the dam would destroy the snail darter's habitat on the Little Tennessee River. He also noted that the secretary of the interior had exclusive authority to determine when a species was endangered.

"It may seem curious to some that the survival of a relatively small number of three-inch fish among all the countless millions of species extant would require the permanent halting of a virtually completed dam for which Congress has expended more than $100 million. The paradox is not minimized by the fact that Congress continued to appropriate large sums of public money for the project, even after congressional appropriations committees were apprised of its apparent impact upon the survival of the snail darter. We conclude, however, that the explicit provisions of the Endangered Species Act require precisely that result.

"One would be hard-pressed to find a statutory provision whose terms were any plainer than those in S.7 of the Endangered Species Act. Its very words affirmatively command all federal agencies 'to *insure* that actions *authorized, funded,* or *carried out* by them do not *jeopardize* the continued existence of an endangered species or *result* in the destruction or modification of [the] habitat of such species. . . .' This language admits of no exception. . . .

"Concededly, this view of the Act will produce results requiring the sacrifice of the anticipated benefits of the project and of many millions of dollars of public funds. But examination of the language, history, and structure of the legislation under review here indicates beyond doubt that Congress intended endangered species to be afforded the highest of priorities. . . .

"Our individual appraisal of the wisdom or unwisdom of a particular course consciously selected by the Congress is to be put aside in the process of interpreting a statute. Once the meaning of an enactment is discerned and its constitutionality determined, the judicial process comes to an end."

Many states, counties, and cities have enacted environmental laws, and in some instances these laws have set even more stringent pollution standards than the national pollution laws. Many states have also created their own environmental protection agencies to control and regulate pollution within their boundaries. A recent development in the control of solid waste pollution has been the passage of so-called bottle bills by several states. These laws require stores to take deposits from the customer on beverage containers and to return the deposit when the cans or bottles are returned empty. These same laws have also banned the use of pull-top cans for beverages. The following case represents an unsuccessful challenge of a "bottle bill" by American Can Company and other industry members.

American Can Co. v. *Oregon Liquor Control Commission*
517 P.2d 691 (Oregon, 1974)

FACTS   In 1971 the Oregon legislature passed a bottle bill, to take effect on October 1, 1972. The bill prohibited the sale of pull-top beverage cans in the state and required deposits on all cans and bottles of beer and carbonated soft drinks. The plaintiffs in this suit included can and bottle manufacturers, bottlers of beer and soft drinks, and the Oregon Soft Drink Association. The plaintiffs alleged that the statute was invalid under the Due Process and Equal Protection clauses of the 14th Amendment and under the Commerce Clause. They said that it also violated similar provisions in the state constitution. All of their witnesses emphasized the inconvenience and extra expense involved in complying with the law. The trial court held that the statute was valid.

ISSUE   Does the statute violate the U.S. Constitution, specifically the Commerce Clause, the Due Process Clause, or the Equal Protection Clause?

DECISION   No. Judgment affirmed.

REASONS   Judge Tanzer devoted most of his lengthy opinion to an analysis of the Commerce Clause, feeling that this clause was the plaintiffs' strongest argument. He noted that the beverage industry had reorganized to take advantage of the economies permitted by one-way containers.

"The purpose of the Commerce Clause . . . was to assure to the commercial enterprises in every state substantial equality of access to a free national market. It was not meant to usurp the police power of the states which was reserved under the 10th Amendment. Therefore, although most exercises of the police power affect interstate commerce to some degree, not every such exercise is invalid under the Commerce Clause. . . .

"The cases consistently hold that the Commerce Clause bars state police action only where:

"(1) federal action has preempted regulation of the activity;

"(2) the state action impedes the free physical flow of commerce from one state to another; or

"(3) protectionist state action, even though under the guise of the police power, discriminates against interstate commerce.

"In this case there is no claim of federal preemption, so we are concerned only with the latter two concepts, interstate transportation and economic protectionism. No party cited and we were unable to find any case striking down state action under the Commerce Clause which did not come within one of these two categories. . . .

"The blight of the landscape, the appropriation of lands for solid waste disposal, and the injury to children's feet caused by pull tops discarded in the sands of our ocean shores are concerns not divisible by the same units of measurement as is economic loss to elements of the beverage industry, and we are unable to weigh them, one against the other. . . .

"The bottle bill is unquestionably a legitimate legislative exercise of the police power."

Judge Tanzer then proceeded to make short work of the plaintiffs' other constitutional arguments: there was no "taking" of anyone's property, just some added costs of doing business, and all members of the industry were treated alike.

Further environmental problems have been caused by the expansion of our cities into what was previously the domain of the farmer. No cattle feedlot or hog feedlot is pleasing to the nostrils, and we must accept the fact that such farming operations are not desirable next door to a residential area. What happens when the city expands to the point where the rights of the parties conflict? The following case illustrates this problem, and the court was forced to make a difficult decision.

Spur Industries, Inc. v. *Del E. Webb Development Co.*
494 P.2d 700 (Arizona, 1972)

FACTS   The small retirement community of Youngtown was founded in 1954, just off the Phoenix-Wickenburg Highway (Grand Avenue), about 14 or 15 miles west of the urban area of Phoenix. Farming operations had been conducted in the area since 1911, and Spur's predecessors had started a feedlot about 2½ miles south of Youngtown in 1956. By 1959 there were 25 cattle feeding or dairy operations in the area. In 1959 Del Webb began planning the development of a large retirement com-

Spur Industries, Inc. v. Del E. Webb Development Co. (continued)

munity, Sun City, and purchased some 20,000 acres of land south of Grand Avenue and directly east of Youngtown. One year later, 450 to 500 homes were completed or under construction. The units just south of Grand Avenue sold well, but sales resistance increased as the location of the homes got closer and closer to the feedlots. By 1962 Spur had expanded its operation from 35 to 114 acres. By 1963 Del Webb's housing manager said that it was impossible to sell any home in the southwestern portion of Del Webb's land. By 1967 the properties were within 500 feet of each other at one point, and Spur was feeding between 20,000 and 30,000 head of cattle on its lots, producing over a million pounds of wet manure per day. Del Webb sued to enjoin Spur as a public nuisance, due to the flies and odor. The trial court entered an injunction, and Spur appealed.

ISSUE   Is the feedlot a public nuisance which should be enjoined?

DECISION   Yes. Judgment affirmed but remanded for a damages award to Spur.

REASONS   Vice Chief Justice Cameron thought that the feedlot clearly met the definition of a public nuisance and that it should be enjoined from continuing to operate. But he also thought that there needed to be a balancing of the equities.

"The difference between a private nuisance and a public nuisance is generally one of degree. A private nuisance is one affecting a single individual or a definite small number of persons in the enjoyment of private rights not common to the public, while a public nuisance is one affecting the rights enjoyed by citizens as a part of the public. To constitute a public nuisance, the nuisance must affect a considerable number of people or an entire community or neighborhood. . . .

"Where the injury is slight, the remedy for minor inconvenience lies in an action for damages rather than in one for an injunction. . . .

"By . . . statute, before an otherwise lawful (and necessary) business may be declared a public nuisance, there must be a 'populous' area in which people are injured. . . .

"It is clear that as to the citizens of Sun City, the operation of Spur's feedlot was both a public and a private nuisance. . . .

"A suit to enjoin a nuisance sounds in equity and the courts have long recognized a special responsibility to the public when acting as a court of equity. . . .

"In addition to protecting the public interest, however, courts of equity are concerned with protecting the operator of a lawful, albeit obnoxious, business from the result of a knowing and willful encroachment by others near his business. . . .

"It does not equitably or legally follow . . . that Webb, being entitled to the injunction, is then free of any liability to Spur if Webb has in fact been the cause of the damage Spur has sustained. It does not seem harsh to require a developer, who has taken advantage of the lesser land values in a rural area as well as the availability of large tracts of land on which to build and develop a new town or city in the area, to indemnify those who are forced to leave as a result."

The previous case illustrates the need for community planning and proper zoning to prevent such situations from occurring.

Thus we no longer have the cherished right to use our land, water, and airspace in any way we choose; there are too many of us, and we live too close together for that. You can't burn trash in an outside incinerator anymore in most large cities. The burning of leaves may also be banned. You can't install a septic system for your home unless it is approved by a local agency. You can't use your backyard to store your collection of junk cars.

Today, before you can construct a building on your land, or add to an existing one, or conduct any business, or manufacture any product, you must first check all applicable pollution regulations—national, state, and local. You must also secure a building permit before you can begin construction.

Eminent Domain

The Fifth Amendment, which is a part of the Bill of Rights of the U.S. Constitution, provides that the national government shall not take private property without the payment of just compensation. The 14th Amendment extended this provision to the various states. The states also have similar provisions in their constitutions, allowing them to exercise the power of eminent domain.

Most simply stated, the power of eminent domain is the power of government to take real estate from a private owner for the use of the public. This very basic governmental power is necessary for the government to function properly and efficiently. For example, if the government is building a highway across the state, the highway must be laid out in as straight a line as possible, considering the topography of the land. It would not be in the best interest of the public if the highway had to jog around various pieces of property whose owners had decided not to sell to the government. The power of eminent domain is also used to acquire land for new school buildings, public parks, public housing projects, public buildings, and other public projects. The government simply must have the right to take over private property if this is in the best interest of the public. The owner of such property does, however, have a right to just compensation. The two key problems are, first, that the land may be taken only for a public purpose and, second, that the owner must receive just compensation. What is a public purpose is often a question which must be resolved in the courts. What is just compensation is also not an easy question to resolve in many cases, and thus a lawsuit may be filed and a jury called upon to decide what just compensation would be for a certain parcel of land.

SOUTHERN BURLINGTON COUNTY N.A.A.C.P. v. TOWNSHIP OF MOUNT LAUREL

336 A.2d 713 (New Jersey, 1975).

Hall, Judge

This case attacks the system of land use regulation by defendant Township of Mount Laurel on the ground that low and moderate income families are thereby unlawfully excluded from the municipality. The trial court so found . . . , and declared the township zoning ordinance invalid. . . .

The implications of the issue presented are indeed broad and far-reaching, extending much beyond these particular plaintiffs and the boundaries of this particular municipality.

There is not the slightest doubt that New Jersey has been, and continues to be, faced with a desperate need for housing, especially of decent living accommodations economically suitable for low and moderate income families. The situation was characterized as a "crisis" and fully explored and documented by Governor Cahill in two special messages to the Legislature. . . .

Plaintiffs represent the minority group poor (black and Hispanic) seeking such quarters. But they are not the only category of persons barred from so many municipalities by reason of restrictive land use regulations. We have reference to young and elderly couples, single persons, and large, growing families not in the poverty class, but who still cannot afford the only kinds of housing realistically permitted in most places—relatively high-priced, single-family detached dwellings on sizeable lots and, in some municipalities, expensive apartments. . . .

As already intimated, the issue here is not confined to Mount Laurel. The same question arises with respect to any number of other municipalities of sizeable land area outside the central cities and older built-up suburbs of our North and South Jersey metropolitan areas . . . which,

like Mount Laurel, have substantially shed rural characteristics and have undergone great population increase since World War II, or are now in the process of doing so, but still are not completely developed and remain in the path of inevitable future residential, commerical, and industrial demand and growth. . . .

Mount Laurel is a flat, sprawling township, 22 square miles, or about 14,000 acres, in area, on the west central edge of Burlington County. . . .

The growth of the township has been spurred by the construction or improvement of main highways through or near it. . . .

The location and nature of development has been, as usual, controlled by the local zoning enactments. The general ordinance presently in force, which was declared invalid by the trial court, was adopted in 1964. . . .

Under the present ordinance, 29.2 percent of all the land in the township, or 4,121 acres, is zoned for industry. This amounts to 2,800 more acres than were so zoned by the 1954 ordinance. . . . Only industry meeting specified performance standards is permitted. The effect is to limit the use substantially to light manufacturing, research, distribution of goods, offices, and the like. . . . At the time of trial, no more than 100 acres . . . were actually occupied by industrial users. . . .

The amount of land zoned for retail business use under the general ordinance is relatively small—169 acres, or 1.2 percent of the total. . . .

The balance of the land area, almost 10,000 acres, has been developed until recently in the conventional form of major subdivisions. The general ordinance provides for four residential zones, designated R–1, R–1D, R–2, and R–3. All permit only single-family, detached dwellings, one house per lot—the usual form of grid development. Attached town houses, apartments (except on farms for agricultural workers), and mobile homes are not allowed anywhere in the township under the general ordinance. . . .

The general ordinance requirements, while not as restrictive as those in many similar municipalities, nonetheless realistically allow only homes within the financial reach of persons of at least middle income. . . .

A variation from conventional development has recently occurred in some parts of Mount Laurel, as in a number of other similar municipalities, by use of the land use regulation device known as "planned unit development" (PUD). . . . The idea may be basically thought of as the creation of "new towns" in virgin territory. . . .

The projects . . . are very substantial and involve at least 10,000 sale and rental housing units of various types to be erected over a period of years. . . . While multi-family housing in the form of rental garden, medium rise, and high rise apartments and attached town houses is for the first time provided for, as well as single-family detached dwellings for sale, it is not designed to accommodate and is beyond the financial reach of low and moderate income families, especially those with young children. The aim is quite the contrary; as with the single-family homes in the older conventional subdivisions, only persons of medium and upper income are sought as residents. . . .

Still another restrictive land use regulation was adopted by the township . . . in September 1972, creating a new zone, R–4, Planned Adult Retirement Community (PARC). . . . The highly restrictive nature of the zone is found in the requirement that all permanent residents must be at least 52 years of age (except a spouse, immediate family member other than a child, live-in domestic, companion, or nurse). Children are limited to a maximum of one, over age 18, residing with a parent, and there may be no more than three permanent residents in any one dwelling unit.

All this affirmative action for the benefit of certain segments of the population is in sharp contrast to the lack of action, and indeed hostility, with respect to affording any opportunity for decent housing for the township's own poor living in substandard accommodations, found largely in the section known as Springville (R–3 zone). . . . The continuous official reaction has been rather a negative policy of waiting for dilapidated premises to be vacated and then forbidding further occupancy. . . .

The legal question before us . . . is whether a developing municipality like Mount Laurel may validly, by a system of land use regulation, make it physically and economically impossible to provide low and moderate income housing in the municipality for the various categories of persons who need and want it and thereby, as Mount Laurel has, exclude such people from living within its confines because of the limited extent of their income and resources. Necessarily implicated are the broader questions of the right of such municipalities to limit the kinds of available housing and of any obligation to make possible a variety and choice of types of living accommodations.

We conclude that every such municipality must, by its land use regulations, presumptively make realistically possible an appropriate variety and choice of housing. More specifically, presumptively it cannot foreclose the opportunity of the classes of people mentioned for low and moderate income housing and in its regulations must affirmatively afford that opportunity, at least to the extent of the municipality's fair share of the present and prospective regional need therefor. These obligations must be met unless the particular municipality can sustain the heavy burden of demonstrating peculiar circumstances which dictate that it should not be required to do so.

We reach this conclusion under state law and so do not find it necessary to consider the federal constitutional grounds urged by plaintiffs. . . .

It is elementary theory that all police power enactments, no matter at what level of government, must conform to the basic state constitutional requirements of substantive due process and equal protection of the laws. . . . It is required that, affirmatively, a zoning regulation, like any police power enactment, must promote public health, safety, morals, or the general welfare. Conversely, a zoning enactment which is contrary to the general welfare is invalid. . . .

The demarcation between the valid and the invalid in the field of land use regulation is difficult to determine, not always clear, and subject to change. . . .

[I]t is fundamental and not to be forgotten that the zoning power is a police power of the state and the local authority is acting only as a delegate of that power and is restricted in the same manner as the state. So, when regulation does have a substantial external impact, the welfare of the state's citizens beyond the borders of the particular municipality cannot be disregarded and must be recognized and served. . . .

It is plain beyond dispute that proper provision for adequate housing of all categories of people is certainly an absolute essential in promotion of the general welfare required in all local land use regulation. Further the universal and constant need for such housing is so important and of such broad public interest that the general welfare which developing municipalities like Mount Laurel must consider extends beyond their boundaries and cannot be parochially confined to the claimed good of the particular municipality. . . .

By way of summary, what we have said comes down to this. As a developing municipality, Mount Laurel must, by its land use regulations, make realistically possible the opportunity for an appropriate variety and choice of housing for all categories of people who may desire to live there, of course including those of low and moderate income. . . .

The municipality should first have full opportunity to itself act without judicial supervision. We trust it will do so in the spirit we have suggested, both by appropriate zoning ordinance amendments and whatever additional action encouraging the fulfillment of its fair share of the regional need for low and moderate income housing may be indicated as necessary and advisable. . . . Should Mount Laurel not perform as we expect, further judicial action may be sought by supplemental pleading in this cause.

UNITED STATES v. 564.54 ACRES OF LAND

506 E.2d 796 (U.S. Third Circuit, 1974)

Gibbons, Circuit Judge

This interlocutory appeal which the district court certified involves a controlling question of law as to which there is a substantial ground for a difference of opinion. . . . The order appealed from arose in an action by the United States for the condemnation of three recreational camps in the proposed Tocks Island recreational area which were owned and operated on a not-for-profit basis by or on behalf of the Southeastern Pennsylvania Synod of the Lutheran Church in America. The land and improvements, according to the owner, have a special character designed specifically for camping purposes.

The order under review was entered during pre-trial proceedings on the government's request for a ruling that the cost of "substitute facilities" is not a proper measure of compensation for the taking of defendant's property, and that evidence at the trial should be restricted to fair market value as of the date of taking, or if that measure is unavailable, to depreciated replacement cost of the properties on the same date. The district court held that the cost of substitute facilities measure of compensation was available only to a governmental condemnee. However, recognizing that if its ruling was in error a fruitless trial might result, the trial court certified the case for an interlocutory appeal on that issue. We reverse.

Appellant Southeastern Pennsylvania Synod of the Lutheran Church in America owned and operated three summer camps located on three separate tracts totaling 305.81 acres along the Delaware River in Monroe County, Pennsylvania. On June 15, 1970 the United States acquired the three camps by filing a notice of taking, and has offered compensation totaling $485,400. The condemnees have offered to prove that the camps have been operated on a nondenominational basis for many years at continuous losses, which losses have been underwritten by the Synod; that there is no ready market for such not-for-profit facilities; that by virtue of grandfather clauses in the Pennsylvania legislation governing recreational camps the Synod could have continued operating the camps with their present somewhat primitive facilities; that because of the same legislation as well as recently enacted federal environmental legislation the development of new camps would require far more elaborate facilities, especially for housing and sewage treatment; and that the cost of development of the new site will total in excess of $5.8 million. At this stage of the case there has been no ruling as to whether all of the items of cost included in appellant's $5.8 million estimate would actually be needed for the development of substitute facilities, but it is undisputed that $485,000 would fall far short of providing for them.

Whether the Lutheran Synod operates camping facilities at a loss because it believes camping builds character, or because it feels a charitable obligation to afford recreational opportunities to persons who would not otherwise be able to afford them, it seems clear that the reason for operating the camps is related to the Synod's religious mission. Thus the question presented is the extent to which owners of single purpose facilities, operated not-for-profit for a religious or charitable purpose (and having no ready market), are entitled to be indemnified when the federal government condemns the facilities. . . .

The basic principle underlying the constitutional requirement of "just compensation" is one of indemnity. The condemnee "is entitled to be put in as good a position pecuniarily as if his property had not been taken. He must be made whole but he is entitled to no more." . . .

There are facilities which are unique, for which there is no ready market, and which are operated for motives other than profit. With respect to such facilities, neither a fair market value nor a capitalized earnings approach as the measure of the government's constitutional duty to indemnify will produce a fair result.

With respect to some unique facilities it may be possible to afford just compensation by calculating depreciated replacement cost to arrive at an approximation of otherwise unavailable proof of market value. For others, however, such a measure will not be fair. . . . Fair indemnification in such circumstances requires compensation sufficient to provide a substitution for the unique facilities so that the functions carried out by or on behalf of members of the community may be continued. Depreciated replacement cost often will not permit continuation of such functions. To meet the requirement of fair indemnification for the taking of community facilities the courts have developed the "substitute facilities" measure of compensation. . . .

Even in those comparatively rare instances where there is a market value for the community facility taken (for example a possible sale of a public building for private use) the government's duty to indemnify is to provide the cost of a more expensive public substitute facility. . . . The community entity is entitled to be made whole, and making it whole means more than forcing it to abandon its nonprofit community use and accept what it could obtain in the marketplace from a profit motivated purchaser. Simply stated, this method insures that sufficient damages will be awarded to finance a replacement for the condemned facility. Nothing less would afford just compensation. And since the owner of a facility devoted to a nonprofit, public use has a proprietary as well as a community interest in it, if the fair market value exceeds the cost of the substitute facility, such an owner should be entitled to the higher of the two measures of compensation.

The government urges that no operator of a public nonprofit facility other than a governmental entity under a legal obligation to replace a condemned facility should be entitled to indemnification to the extent of the substitute facilities measure of just compensation. . . . But such a holding would produce the anomalous result that the federal government's Fifth Amendment duty of fair compensation, which would seem to be equally applicable throughout the country, would vary according to the vagaries of local law. . . .

The government also urges that the substitute facilities measure of just compensation is totally inapplicable to any condemnee other than a governmental entity. This position was accepted by the district court. No Supreme Court or court of appeals decision has ever considered that issue.

For several reasons we think the government's position with respect to private owners of nonprofit community facilities is untenable. In the first place we are dealing with the measure of the duty of indemnification imposed by the "taking clause" in the Fifth Amendment. . . . In view of the express reference to private property and the absence of any reference to public property, it is inconceivable that the framers of the amendment intended to impose a greater obligation of indemnification on the national government toward the states and their subdivisions than to-

741

ward private owners. . . . It seems to us an impermissible suggestion that the Fifth Amendment puts the government in the position of making such choices on the basis that it would be required to pay less by way of fair compensation to the private owners of such community facilities. . . .

We conclude that the substitution of facilities measure of fair compensation is available to private owners of nonprofit community facilities as well as to public owners of such facilities, in appropriate cases. In the preliminary stage in which the case is before us, we have no occasion to decide whether this is an appropriate case.

The order appealed from will be reversed.

LIDKE v. MARTIN
500 p.2d 1184 (Colorado, 1972)
Enoch, Judge

This action was brought by certain residents of Hillcrest Heights Subdivision in Jefferson County to enjoin defendants from erecting two apartment buildings on the back portion of a platted lot owned by defendants and located in the same subdivision. The trial court entered judgment for plaintiffs on the grounds that the proposed apartment buildings would violate the subdivision's protective covenants and that defendants' use of a portion of two adjacent lots for access to the apartment would render those lots in violation of the zoning ordinance. We affirm this judgment.

I

The trial court based its conclusion that defendants' proposed apartment buildings would violate the subdivision's protective covenants upon the following clause of the covenants:

A. All lots in this subdivision shall be Residential One (R–1) only. No structure shall be erected, altered, placed, or permitted to remain on any lot other than one detached single-family dwelling not to exceed two and one-half stories in height, a private garage for not more than three cars, and other outbuildings incidental to residential use only.

Defendants concede that, if otherwise valid, this clause standing alone would prohibit the con-

struction of the proposed apartment buildings. They contend, however, that since another clause in the restrictive covenants incorporates an existing zoning classification that allows apartment buildings, the apartment buildings would not violate the protective covenants. The clause relied on by defendants provides as follows:

L. None of the foregoing shall be construed as conflicting with any terms or regulations of the present or future Jefferson County zoning ordinance which shall form a part of this instrument and shall govern their use of all land herein described.

We do not agree with defendants that this clause allows a resident to make any use of his property permitted under applicable zoning regulations. Read as a whole, the protective covenants envision and provide for a single-family residential subdivision. To interpret Clause L in the manner argued for by defendants would render these other covenants meaningless and allow their circumvention. Actually, Clause L provides a rule of construction for the covenants, the effect of which is to incorporate those portions of the applicable zoning ordinances which provide more restrictive standards than the covenants or which prescribe regulations not covered by the covenants. This result is consistent with section 31 of the applicable zoning ordinance which provides:

. . . It is not intended by this Resolution to interfere with or abrogate or annul any easements, covenants or agreements between parties, provided, however, that wherever this Resolution imposes a greater restriction upon the use of buildings or land or upon the location or height of buildings or structures or required larger open spaces about buildings than are imposed or required by other laws, resolutions or by easements, covenants or agreements between parties, the provisions of this Resolution shall govern.

In this case, the new zone permitted the construction of apartment buildings. However, the covenants are controlling because they require a more restrictive use of the land than is permitted under the applicable zoning requirements.

II

Defendants' proposed plans for the apartment buildings included access by means of a 25-foot

742

easement across two adjacent residential lots in the same subdivision. The access road in question would involve the use of 10 feet of the side yard of one lot and 15 feet of the side yard of the other lot. Plaintiffs contend that the easement area reduces the area of the residential lots and renders said lots nonconforming under the applicable zoning restrictions. Defendants argue that the easement area should be included in the area of the two lots because it is a "private driveway." We find no merit in this contention and agree with the trial court that the area occupied by the easement cannot be considered a part of the two adjacent lots for the purpose of determining compliance with zoning area requirements. . . .

Under the circumstances of this case, the fact that the easement was to remain "private" does not change this result. The effect of a roadway upon the area of a lot is not dependent upon its technical ownership, but upon its use. Where a private easement, as in the present case, is to be used by a large number of persons as the only access to two apartment buildings, it is the functional equivalent of a public street, and should be given the same effect in determining area requirements.

PROBLEMS FOR DISCUSSION

1. Bobby and Tessie Swinghammer owned a lot in the Scenic Vista Recreation Area. They bought the lot for camping on weekends and planned to leave their travel trailer on the lot during the week as well as on weekends. All property in the area was subject to a restrictive covenant which permitted the lot owner to use the lot for camping for a maximum of five years after purchase before building a permanent structure, so long as the owner did not leave camping equipment on the lot when it was not in use. After the Swinghammers had left their travel trailer on the lot for several weeks, even when they weren't there to use it, and had indicated that they intended to continue to do so, the SVRA Property Owners' Association brought suit for an injunction to enforce the restrictive covenant. The Swinghammers argue that (1) their trailer is not "camping equipment" under the meaning of the covenant; (2) their trailer is "in use," even though only on weekends; and (3) the agent who sold them their lot said that they could use it in this way. Are any of these arguments valid? Explain.

2. Cliffen College was a private college with an enrollment of about 1,000 students. Its campus was located on the north shore of Louisa Lake and extended north to the city of Hopeville. On both the east and west sides of the campus were one-family residential areas. The Village of Louisa Lake was incorporated in 1971, and it adopted a zoning ordinance soon afterward. Cliffen had been given building permits during the 1970s to remodel some of its buildings. In 1980 Cliffen was given $3 million to build a fine arts center. Cliffen's request for a special-use permit to construct another building in an area zoned residential was rejected by the city council after a neighborhood group protested, even though the planning commission had unanimously recommended that the permit be granted. Shortly thereafter, Bethlehem College, another small private college, located in another residential area of Louisa Lake, had its application to expand its fine arts center approved. The zoning was changed for Bethlehem, from residential to "limited business," and Bethlehem's application was then approved. Cliffen now brings suit, challenging the denial of its special-use permit. Does it have any basis for a claim here? Discuss.

3. Aireout Productions, Inc., wanted to hold a rock concert at the Knokdowne Racetrack. Aireout's president, Janice Jodpurr, met with the chairman of the county planning and zoning commission, Howdy Harper, and one of the commission members, Ben Barnstorme, who had been the principal author of the County's zoning ordinance. Janice says that Howdy and Ben told her that they didn't think she would need a permit in order to hold the rock concert and that in reliance on their advice

she expended some $90,000 in promoting and preparing for the concert. The county then advised her that a permit would be required and got an injunction against holding the concert without one. Janice then sued Howdy, Ben, and the county in a tort action for negligent misrepresentation. Does she have a case? Why or why not?

4. Denny Destry bought a town house in Armadillo Acres, a large condominium development. All housing units in the development were subject to a series of restrictive covenants, including one which required the express written approval of a majority of the homeowners prior to any alteration, so as to maintain "general appearance, exterior color or colors, harmony of external design, location in relation to topography and surroundings and other relevant architectural factors, quality of construction, size, and suitability for clustered residential purposes." Denny had previously installed an exterior front door and a beveled glass window without approval and without objection, but when he started to install a skylight, other owners objected. Other owners had installed a front door knocker, front doors of a different color, and a patio, without any owners' vote. Several of Denny's neighbors sued for an injunction to enforce the restrictive covenant. What result, and why?

5. Rolling Acres, Inc., purchased a 400-acre tract of land in Montana. Although the land was accessible with four-wheel-drive vehicles over two rugged trails, the easiest access was over a certain dirt road. This road ran over U.S. Forest Service land, then over property belonging to the Tinder Timber Company, and then across 10 acres belonging to Bessie Bristle, before it got to the 400 acres. Prior to Rolling Acres' purchase of the land, some members of the general public had used the road for access to remote hunting and fishing areas. There was a state statute which provided that mere use of a route of travel across private or public land, by the public, should not establish the route as a public highway. Rolling Acres applied to the county to have the road paved, but the county refused to do so. Rolling Acres sold several homesites on the 400 acres, and the new owners were driving up and down the road all day. The road passed within 25 feet of Bessie's house, and she wanted the traffic stopped. To make it impassable, she dug a ditch through the road and placed large rocks and boulders on it. Rolling Acres wants to pave the road for its home buyers, and sues for an unjunction against Bessie. How should the court rule here? Explain.

6. Zane Fonder, president of the Nonukes Alliance, filed a lawsuit challenging certain actions of the U.S. Nuclear Regulatory Commission. The NRC had held general public hearings on the problem of nuclear waste disposal, after which it had adopted an administrative rule which approved the practice of storing such wastes on-site at nuclear power plants, with appropriate safeguards. It subsequently issued operating permits to two nuclear power plants which proposed to use on-site storage of wastes. Now, however, it was again considering the problem of how best to handle nuclear wastes. Zane says that the two operating permits were improperly issued because (1) a generic, rule-making hearing on this subject was inappropriate and (2) no licenses should have been issued until the new rules were adopted. How should the court respond to this lawsuit? Discuss.

7. Sandy Snidely, doing business as the Misfit Cleaners, had his business property condemned by the State Highway Commission, to make way for a new road. Sandy says he was told that he would be given a relocation payment but would not be compensated for any equipment left in the building. Relying on this advice, he removed his dry cleaning equipment. Because of the age and nature of the equipment, and because of changes in the city's laws and building codes, Sandy says that he was prohibited from relocating his business in the city and that the equipment

now has only scrap value. Sandy did accept a relocation payment, but now he says that he is also entitled to the difference in value of the equipment resulting from the condemnation of his business location. The state says that he can't have both. Who's right, and why?

8. Lucy Lovelace lost her lease on the building where she operated a beauty shop. She decided to operate the business in her home and made certain additions and modifications to her home in order to do so. Her neighbors objected, and they filed suit for an injunction to prohibit the operation of the beauty shop. The tract of land on which Lucy's house and the other houses in the neighborhood were located was originally conveyed subject to a restrictive covenant that it be used "solely and wholly for residential purposes." All of the deeds in the area, however, also stated that the land was being conveyed "subject to all governmental regulations, including zoning ordinances, affecting said premises." The town's zoning ordinance permitted "customary home occupations" in residential areas. Lucy says that the reference to zoning ordinances in the deeds means that she can do whatever is permitted by the town's zoning ordinance. Is she correct? Why or why not?

Part IX
Trusts and
Decedents' Estates

36 | Administration of Decedents' Estates and Intestate Succession

In the preceding chapters we were concerned with personal and real property relationships during the lifetime of the owners of real and personal property. In this chapter we are concerned with the law and the procedures governing the disposition of both real property and personal property when the owner of that property dies. There is no national law which governs the descent and distribution of the property of a deceased person, although the U.S. estate tax has a great impact on estate planning. The laws that govern the descent and distribution of the property of deceased persons are state laws, and they vary from state to state.

Since our population is very mobile today and people often own property in several states, there is a need for uniformity in the descent and distribution laws of the various states. The National Conference of Commissioners on Uniform State Laws has drafted a Uniform Probate Code which it is hoped will be adopted by all the states. The first draft of the code was approved and submitted to the various state legislatures in 1969, and the code was amended in 1975. Thus far, only a few states have adopted the Uniform Probate Code.

There are two procedures for the distribution of property, both real and personal, which are common to all the states. First, there is distribution by last will and testament. This procedure is called testate distribution. If a person makes a will, his or her property after the payment of all valid debts will be distributed according to the wishes of the deceased as set out in the will, unless the will is found to be legally invalid. If the deceased person did not make a will, then the real and personal property of the deceased person will be distributed to his or her legal heirs in accordance with specific statutory laws of descent and distribution. This procedure is called intestate distribution. Real property will be distributed in accordance with the statutes of the state where it is located; personal property will be distributed in accordance with the statutes of the state where the decedent resided. Thus, if a person with a legal residence in Minnesota and real estate in Wisconsin and Illinois dies in Florida, several different state laws would be involved in the distribution of his or her estate. If the person died without leaving a will and he or she had no legal heirs, then the property would be acquired by the state, through a process called escheat.

The last will and testament is simply a written statement of a person's desires as to the distribution of his or her real and personal property when he or she dies. The person who makes a will is called a testator if a man and a testatrix if a women.

TYPES OF WILLS

The Formal Will.   The formal will is a written document specifically stating the desires of the testator or testatrix as to the disposition of his or her real and personal property. The will is signed by the testator or testatrix in the presence of witnesses who also sign the document. The testator or testatrix has indicated to the witnesses that he or she knows that the document is his or her last will and testament. Formal wills are recognized as legal in all jurisdictions. However, some states have particular requirements as to the formalities, such as the number of witnesses.

Nuncupative Wills.   A nuncupative will is an oral will. It might also be called a dying will since it is an oral will made in a person's dying hours or minutes. Nuncupative wills are valid only for the distribution of personal property, and usually only the personal property which the dying person has in his or her immediate possession. The problems in this type of will are to prove that the statements concerning the disposition of property were actually made and that the person who made them was of sound mind. In addition, there must be witnesses other than the persons benefiting from the will. Not all states recognize nuncupative wills. Some states extend the privilege of making nuncupative wills to wartime military personnel in a battle zone. Here again, the law would like to abide by the wishes of the dying person. However, problems of proof, fraud, undue influence, and perjury arise in these situations. Again, only personal property can be distributed by this type of will. Real property will be distributed to the heirs in accordance with the intestate succession laws of the state where the real estate is located.

Holographic Wills.   A holographic will is a will written out and signed by the testator or testatrix. There are no witnesses to the signature. Not all states recognize holographic wills as being legal wills. The problem with regard to a holographic will is that the person who made it is now deceased and cannot verify that the handwriting and the signature was his or hers. Thus a court is faced with the possibility of forgery.

Hammer v. Atchison
536 P. 2d 151 (Wyoming, 1975)

FACTS   On December 9, 1966, Joe Snoddy and Leona Georgen entered into a prenuptial agreement; they were married less than a week later. On November 22, 1968, Joe executed a new will. He died on December 19, 1970, and his will was admitted to probate. The prenuptial agreement provided that Joe would make out a new will, or amend his old one, so as to leave one fourth of his net estate to Leona and that she would pay all state inheritance taxes on her one fourth. The agreement also provided that it did not prevent either party from accepting any bequest made in the other party's will. Joe's will left Leona $100,000 as well as $200 per month until the $100,000 was paid. The trial court gave Leona $101,400 under the terms of the will and one fourth of the net estate (another $170,000). The executors appealed these rulings, claiming that the $101,400 should be considered part of her one fourth.

ISSUE   Were the specific bequests in the will intended as partial satisfaction of the prenuptial agreement?

DECISION   No. Judgments affirmed.

REASONS   Justice Raper noted the existence of a general rule that a devise or legacy was not considered to be given in satisfaction of a debt unless the intent was clear. In the absence of a statute to the contrary, the intention of the testator must govern.

"An antenuptial agreement has long been favored in Wyoming as a family settlement of their affairs. . . . It ought to be carried into effect as expressed in its four corners. Our purpose in this case, then, is to construe the agreement in relation to the will and keep them harmonious with each other. . . .

"The language of the bequest of $100,000 denotes gift which testator says 'I give . . . to my wife . . . ,' We must give meaning to this provision. It is not idle language.

"If the testator here wanted the $100,000 and the $200 per month applied to the one-quarter ($1/4$) of his estate, it would have been simple to so express that desire in his will. When the contract was entered into before execution of the will and testator nevertheless provides for his spouse in that will, he could not have intended that the will be affected by the contract and the survivor deprived of the right to take under the will. There is no way to identify the legacies in the will with a satisfaction or partial satisfaction of the obligation created by the agreement. We note that both documents were apparently drawn by the same skilled and experienced draftsman so we cannot opine that decedent failed to advise him of the existence of the contract when putting together the will.

"This is further borne out by the prenuptial agreement; the bride-to-be was to pay inheritance taxes from the one-quarter ($1/4$) share agreed to be paid. The will provided that taxes be paid from the residue of the estate. There is no way to tie the legacies to the contractual terms. . . .

"Appellee is entitled to recover both the amount of indebtedness incurred as a result of the agreement and the legacies."

CAPACITY TO MAKE A WILL

As a rule, a minor cannot make a valid will. In order to execute a valid will, a person generally must have reached the age of majority, which is now 18 in most states. Some states do, however, permit persons under the age of majority to make valid wills, at least for their personal property.

The testator must be of "sound and disposing mind" at the time the will is executed. This requirement means that the person knows what he or she is doing—in this case, what property is owned and what disposition is being made of it. Many testators may have certain eccentricities, such as the wealthy elderly lady who leaves a small fortune to her cats. If, in fact, she knows what she is doing and wants to do it, the law will respect her wishes. The question as to whether the testator was indeed of sound and disposing mind may be the subject of a will contest. The heirs may well contest the will, alleging that the lady was not of sound and disposing mind when she made it. However, the presumption of validity will be in favor of the testatrix, and in order to invalidate the will the heirs will have the burden of showing incompetency on her part.

WHAT PROPERTY CAN BE DISPOSED OF BY WILL

All real estate in which the testator or testatrix has a fee simple title and all personal property owned by the testator or testatrix may be disposed of by will. Real property in which the testator or testatrix has an interest as a tenant by the entirety or as a joint tenant with right of survivorship cannot be distributed by will because in such cases, when one tenant dies, the other tenant automatically inherits the property. Also, a life estate cannot be devised by will because such a legal interest dissolves upon the death of its possessor, and thus there is nothing to give away. In addition, depending upon the state law, dower statutes, widows' allowances, and exemption statutes may limit the right of the husband with regard to the disposition of property.

MODIFICATION OF WILL BY CODICIL

A will typically reflects the testator's or testatrix's desires, marital status, and family status at the time that the will is executed, and as the years pass, children grow up, financial situations change, and perhaps the spouse dies, the will may become obsolete and need modification. A will need not be completely rewritten every time a change in it is desired. It may be modified by adding a codicil. This is a separate written document which must be executed in accordance with the applicable state law. The codicil can add to or alter the will.

Gasque v. *Sitterding*
156 S.E. 2d 576 (Virginia, 1967)

FACTS   Fritz Sitterding died in 1928, leaving an estate of $2,728,316.89 and three surviving children: Agnes, Fred, Jr., and William. His will named his two sons and Virginia Trust Company as executors and trustees. It established a trust fund of $300,000 which was to last until 21 years after the death of his last child. The income from the trust fund was to be divided quarterly among the children. The disputed provision read: "In the event of the death of any one of my children leaving issue, the share of the income going to such child shall be paid to his or her issue." Agnes died in 1958, unmarried and without issue. Fred, Jr., died in 1961, survived by three children: Fred III, Mary, and (another) Agnes, married to Michael Maiorano. Mary died in 1964, unmarried and without issue, but leaving a will which bequeathed her entire interest in the trust to her niece Cecelia Maiorano. Mary's executor, Gasque, asked that her

751

one sixth of the trust income be paid to him for the benefit of Cecelia. The trustees refused and brought this action for interpretation of the will. The trial court held that no interest vested until 21 years after the death of the last of Fritz' children. Gasque appealed.

ISSUE   Did the right to a share of the trust income vest in Fritz' grandchildren on the death of their father, Fred, Jr.?

DECISION   Yes. Judgment reversed; final decree for Gasque.

REASONS   Justice Spratley noted that there was a rule of interpretation which said that where ambiguity existed, the courts should favor an interpretation which resulted in early vesting of ownership interests. He felt, however, that it was not necessary to invoke that rule here since the provisions of the will were sufficiently clear.

"The parties agree that the primary duty of the court is to ascertain the intention of a testator from the whole of his will, and the words used by him. They also agree that Fritz Sitterding was an intelligent and successful businessman, and say that 'It is obvious that the will was drawn by a skilled draftsman.'

"The primary significance of words should ordinarily attach and does attach, unless it is manifest from the will itself that other definitions are intended. Weight and meaning must be given to every word used if they are to make any sense at all. None are to be deleted and none added, for men make their own wills, nor should we search out obscure or recondite possibilities in simple words.' . . .

"The will of Fritz Sitterding designated a class of persons entitled to receive immediately the income of the trust. This class consisted of the testator's children . . . The will also provided that the right of each of said children to receive income should terminate at his or her death.

"Upon the death of Fred B. Jr., the will provided for the establishment of a new class to receive his share of the income—that is, 'his issue.' Thus, upon Fred B. Jr.'s death, the right to a share of the income from the trust estate vested in right and possession in Fred's daughter, Mary Elizabeth, . . . with her brother, Fred B. III, and her sister, Agnes, without any restriction, condition, or limitation whatever.

"The will . . . provides expressly that the right of each of the testator's *children* to receive income shall cease upon the *child's* death. Furthermore, the will contains a gift-over upon the death of a *child*. . . .

"The will does not direct that the right of a *grandchild* to receive income shall terminate at the *grandchild's* death; nor does it contain any gift-over of a share of income that vested in a *grandchild* in his or her lifetime. . . .

"We, therefore, hold that Mary Elizabeth Sitterding's vested right to receive income from the trust did not terminate at her death; but was a property right, which she could and did bequeath under her will."

REVOCATION OF A WILL

A will is revocable by the testator or testatrix at any time prior to death. The most common reason for revocation is that the testator or testatrix desires to make a new will and the changes are so extensive that it is desirable to revoke and remake the will rather than simply make the changes by codicil. The new will generally contains a clause stating that the testator or testatrix hereby revokes any and all prior wills. Also, a testator or testatrix may simply decide to tear up, burn, or otherwise destroy his or her will and not make another will. The party may simply want to let his or her property go through intestate succession rather than by specific bequest.

Some state statutes have provisions which would revoke a will by operation of law under certain circumstances. A common situation of this kind would be one like the following. A man made a will giving his property to his wife and his two sons, both of whom were named in the will. After the execution of the will, the man and his wife were divorced, he married again, his new wife gave birth to a daughter, and the man then died. In this situation these questions would arise: Does the daughter who was born after the making of the will have any rights in her father's estate? What are the rights of the surviving spouse in her husband's estate? Presuming that no alimony was owed to the divorced wife and that she had no legal right to inherit her ex-husband's property, what rights does she have? Does the will really reflect the testator's intent with regard to the distribution of his property? Obviously, the will does not reflect the testator's current family relationships. Thus, depending upon the state, part or all of the will may be revoked as a result of the changes in family relationships.

INTESTATE SUCCESSION

A person is considered intestate when he or she dies without leaving a will. Succession means the inheriting or succeeding to the ownership of the deceased person's property. Each state has specific statutes regulating the descent and distribution of the real and personal property of the deceased person where the deceased person did not leave a will or where the deceased person's will has been found to be invalid.

As a general rule, the intestate statutes order distribution of the entire estate to the wife or husband if living and to any children if living, or to children of the children who have predeceased the decedent. The shares are determined by the specific state statute. If the decedent had four children and his or her spouse had died previously, then the estate would be divided equally among the four children. If one child had died but was survived by two children, then those children would inherit their parent's share. This descent could go even further. If a grandchild had children and the grandchild was deceased, then the grandchild's share would go to his or her children.

It is interesting to note that these intestate statues are based on blood relationships. In the same example, if one of the four children, a son, had died and was survived by a wife and two children, the wife would get nothing since she was not a blood relative. Only the son's children would inherit. The only exception to this restriction would be legally adopted children. Although not blood relatives, such children would be put in that category because of the legal adoption.

Now, let's take the case where the decedent has no surviving spouse and no surviving children, grandchildren, or great-grandchildren. Then the intestate law looks to the next preferred level of descendants. The first in preference are the deceased's mother and father. If neither the mother nor the father of the decedent is living, then the estate is divided equally among his or her brothers and sisters, and if any of the decedent's brothers or sisters are deceased, then their share will go to their children or to the children of their children should the children be deceased.

In the case of an only child whose parents are both deceased and who had no children of his or her own, the intestate law will generally state that the estate will be divided among so-called collateral relatives. These are people who are not direct descendants of the decedent but are related in some way to the decedent through a common ancestor. This category would include grandparents, aunts, uncles, and cousins. Only in rare cases is this third level of descent and distribution used.

The fourth step in descent and distribution is taken if there are no direct descendants of the deceased person and no collateral relatives. Then the property is distributed to the state where it is located. This is called escheat to the state.

It can readily be seen that if a person wishes to have any effect on the distribution of his or her property, then he or she should make a will. In the absence of a will, no part of a deceased person's estate can be given, for example, to a charity, to a friend, to the old alma mater, or to any other institution or person other than those persons designated by the particular state law which has jurisdiction over the person and property of the intestate deceased.

With our high-speed motor vehicle and air travel, and with the other dangers which we face today, it is not uncommon for a husband and wife to die in the same accident. In such a situation, if the wife survived the husband for any period of time, however brief, then her estate would inherit from him. However, if she died first, then, of course, her estate would not inherit from the husband. The Commissioners on Uniform Laws, to whom we have referred previously, have formulated a Uniform Simultaneous Death Act, which has been adopted by many states. This act provides that where two people such as a husband and wife die in a situation such as an airplane crash or an automobile crash and it is impossible to determine which of them died first, then each of their estates would be handled and the property in that estate would be distributed as if each of the deceased persons had survived the other deceased person.

The obvious problem which this solved here is that if the husband owned a considerable amount of property and died first, the wife would inherit from him and her estate would have to pay tax on the inheritance, and then if she died a few hours later, her estate would be distributed again and tax would be levied again. Thus there would be the possibility of double taxation on both the state and the national level. With the Uniform Simultaneous Death Act, the property of each deceased spouse passes directly to other heirs of that spouse, disregarding the estate of the other deceased spouse. Thus the property of each spouse is distributed only once and there is no immediate second taxation of the assets.

If a will is prepared, then the testator can provide for the possibility of simultaneous death in the will itself. For example, it is common to provide that property is willed to a spouse if the spouse survives the decedent by 30 days. In the event of simultaneous death or any other occurrence which prevents that from happening, the property does not pass to the spouse but directly to children or other beneficiaries.

PROBATING THE ESTATE

Whether the deceased left a will or not, there still has to be a legal procedure and administration to distribute the deceased's assets, both real and personal, both tangible and intangible, and to pay the deceased's inheritance taxes and any income taxes that the deceased owed when he or she died, to pay off the deceased's creditors, and to pay any final doctor and hospital bills. Thus one can see that a lot of details have to be handled when a person dies. Of course, if the deceased's property was of minimal value, the statutes in many states would waive the necessity of formally probating his or her estate.

The Probate Court.   In Chapter 2 the reader was given a diagram of the typical state court system and an explanation of the various courts. It was noted there that the probate court, also known as the surrogate court, generally handles the administration of decedent's estates and the guardianship of minor children and persons declared incompetent to handle their own affairs. In the smaller areas, the county court judge will act as both a probate judge and a trial court judge. In the larger jurisdictions a special judge will handle only probate matters. The specific procedures with regard to the probating or administering of estates differ slightly from state to state.

The Process of Probating the Deceased's Estate.   When a person dies, the first step is for the immediate family to search through the deceased's papers and find out whether the deceased left a will and whether the deceased had insurance policies, savings accounts, a safe-deposit box, certificates of deposit, stocks and bonds, and so on. If the deceased had a safe-deposit box, the bank will not let an heir simply go to the bank and look into it. Before anyone is allowed to take anything out of the safe-deposit box, the county assessor's office or the local assessor, depending on the jurisdiction, will have to be informed of the person's death, and then a representative from the assessor's office will accompany one of the heirs to the bank and the bank will allow the parties to view the contents of the safe-deposit box. A listing and an appraisal of the contents will be made by the tax assessor, and the contents may not be distributed to any relatives or heirs until an estate has been opened if the estate falls within the dollar amount which requires a formal probate proceeding in the given jurisdiction.

If the deceased left a will, then the will should contain the name of the person or the financial institution that the deceased desired to act as the executor or executrix of the estate. (Executor is the term used if the party is a male or a financial institution such as a bank; *executrix* is the term used if the party is a female.) The executor (executrix) of the estate is the party that gathers together all the assets, makes the required reports to the taxing authorities, makes the required reports to the court, and administers the estate in accordance with the desires of the deceased.

If the deceased left no will, then one of the heirs must petition the probate court to open an estate and appoint an administrator or administrix to administer the assets and pay the debts of the deceased. Typically the court will appoint the surviving spouse, if that spouse is capable, or an adult child of the deceased, provided that person lives within the jurisdiction of the court to act as the administrator or administratrix. In order to be an administrator or administratrix, a person must live within the jurisdiction of the court.

Once an estate has been opened, either by a petition to open it presented to the probate court by the person or financial institution named as the executor or executrix in a will or, if there was no will, by the surviving spouse, a child, or some other heir at law, and the executor (executrix) or administrator (administratrix) has been appointed by the court, then the process of administering the estate begins.

The first step in the administration process is for the executor or administrator to publish legal notice advising creditors to present their claims against the estate of the deceased. The notice must be published in a newspaper of general circulation in the county where the estate is opened. The length of time that the notice must be published will depend upon the individual state laws. The notice will advise creditors that they have a limited time in which to present their claims. Generally, this will not exceed six months. Different states set different time limits for presentations against an estate.

The next step is to take care of the deceased's widow during the period of administration, which could be up to six months or a year. Although the widow may be entitled to inherit all of her husband's money and property, she does not have the right to spend the money or to make any transfer of the property until settlement of the estate is approved by the court. Most states provide for the payment of a widow's allowance by the administrator or executor during the period of administration. The widow's allowance would have priority over other claims.

The third step is for the executor or administrator to make an inventory of all the assets which the deceased owned prior to his death. This, of course, would include all cash on hand, all bank accounts, and all stocks and bonds. If real estate is involved, then a professional appraiser would be called in to appraise it, and if personal property is involved, an appraiser should be called in to appraise it. The executor or administrator is required to file a report to the court setting out a complete inventory of the real and personal property and its total value. This report is then used to determine whether national or state taxes will be due on the estate.

The next step is for the administrator or executor to begin paying the debts of the deceased. First, the expenses of the deceased's last illness and of his or her funeral and burial expenses must be paid. Next an income tax return must be completed for the period of the calendar year or fiscal year, depending on the tax year used by the deceased, up to the date of death. Then the administrator or executor must file tax return forms with the state inheritance tax division and pay the appropriate tax. The state inheritance taxes are the liability of the individual or institution that was willed a gift by the deceased or the statutory share of an intestate estate where there was no will. The amount of tax due depends not only on the amount of the gift or statutory share but on the relationship to the deceased of the person receiving it. No tax will be due unless the amount received exceeds the exemption amount, but the exemption amount will be larger for a spouse than for children. Generally, the exemption becomes smaller as the relationship to the deceased becomes more distant.

If the deceased person left a will, it is possible to have all of the inheritance taxes paid out of the general funds of the estate which are not specifically given to persons or institutions. The will may simply state that its beneficiaries will not have to pay the inheritance taxes from their shares and that these taxes will be paid out of the general funds of the estate. This is especially helpful if the deceased gave his or her residential property to a son or daughter. If the son or daughter had to pay the inheritance taxes, he or she might have to sell the real estate in order to get the money to do so.

Haerry v. Hoffschneider
276 N.W. 2d 196 (Nebraska, 1979)

FACTS   Elise Hoffschneider, a widow, had two children, Melba Marie Holm and Alfred Hoffschneider. In 1965 she gave Alfred a farm consisting of one quarter section of land. On November 29, 1966, accompanied by Alfred, she consulted her lawyer and had him prepare three documents: (1) a deed conveying another quarter-section farm to Alfred but reserving a life estate for herself; (2) a will which left another quarter-section farm to Melba if she survived Elise; otherwise, this farm and the balance of Elise's estate would go to Alfred; and (3) an agreement which recited the execution of the deed and the will and said that in consideration thereof Alfred agreed to pay sufficient sums to cover the debts of Elise's estate, if necessary, so that the real estate left to Melba could pass to her. Elise signed all three documents, and Alfred signed the agreement. Elise died in 1975, leaving personal property assets of $2,270.28, debts and taxes due of $31,596.11, and the land devised to Melba. Haerry, as her executor, demanded payment from Alfred and then sued. Alfred appealed the trial court's award.

ISSUE   Is the agreement legally binding against Alfred?

DECISION   Yes. Judgment affirmed.

REASONS   Judge Kuns thought that neither of Alfred's arguments were valid. Alfred had claimed that since the agreement was testamentary, it was invalid because it had not properly executed under the will statute, and that in any case it had been revoked by Elise's will.
    "It should be noted that the agreement simply recites the execution of the deed and the will and contains no independent provisions disposing of any property or rights belonging to Elise Hoffschneider. . . . The time of death is simply a time of performance. . . . A will is a unilateral disposition of property binding only from the death of the maker; a contract is an agreement drawing its binding force from the meeting of the minds of the parties. . . . Since the agreement is bilateral and not testamentary, execution in accordance with section 30-204, R.R.S. 1943, was not required. . . .
    "Although the deed, the will, and the agreement were all executed upon the same date and may be read together for the purpose of ascertaining intention, it should be

757

noted that the will refers to the previous conveyance by the deed and the agreement refers to the previous execution of the will. Appellant's argument . . . must fail because the agreement, although contemplated, was not in existence at the time of the execution of the will and for the further reason that such a revocation would be completely inconsistent with the general estate plan of Elise Hoffschneider as manifested in the three documents. A revocation of the agreement would bring about the complete reverse of the stated intention of Elise Hoffschneider that the devise to Melba should be subject only to the mortgage to the Federal Land Bank. . . . The testatrix was entitled to plan so that the land she had owned would stay in the family without being subject to possible sale by the executor to meet estate debts. The trial court construed the deed, the will, and the agreement correctly and properly imposed liability upon the appellant."

With regard to U.S. estate taxes, the Tax Reform Act of 1976 set up a unified tax credit system to replace the separate schedules for estate tax and gift tax. The unified tax credit is roughly equivalent to a lifetime exemption of $175,625. If a deceased's estate does not exceed that amount, no U.S. estate tax is due. Further, a surviving spouse is entitled to a marital deduction of one half of the value of assets received due to the decedent's death, up to a maximum of $250,000. Thus, if a husband leaves an estate of $500,000 to his wife, she can deduct $250,000 (the marital deduction maximum), plus another $175,625, and would pay a U.S. estate tax on only $74,375. The Economic Recovery Tax Act of 1981 will raise the exemption each year, to a maximum of $600,000 by 1987. This act provides that *all* property left to a surviving spouse is free of U.S. estate taxes. Furthermore, an individual may now give up to $10,000 per year, per person, with no gift tax liability; if a spouse joins in making the gift, the tax-free amount is $20,000 per year per person. Thus, under the new tax law only a small number of decedents' estates will be liable for U.S. estate taxes.

The next step in the administration of the estate is to sell real estate and personal property which is not specifically given to any particular person or institution. The cash is used to pay the creditors of the estate, provided they prove the validity of their claims to the satisfaction of the court. The administrator or executor must then submit a final report to the court, showing all the assets which have been accumulated, including interest earned on bank accounts, life insurance proceeds collected, cash received from the sale of assets, and other monies, as well as all debts which have been paid. A hearing is scheduled, to allow anyone with an interest in the estate to object to any part of the report. After the hearing the court will decide whether to approve or disapprove the final report of the administrator or executor.

Once the final report has been approved, the executor or administrator will distribute the assets in accordance with either the provisions of the will or the statutory law in the given jurisdiction. The executor's services will be paid for with a fee which is approved by the court or in accordance with a statutory fee schedule. After distribution of the assets and payment of the appropriate fee, the executor or administrator will again go back to the court for a final order to close the estate. At that time, the administrator or executor will also ask the court to release any bonds that the executor or administrator had to file with it during the administration of the estate.

CASES FOR DISCUSSION

HORTON v. KEATING

535 P. 2d 796 (Nevada, 1975)

Per Curiam

By Last Will dated November 6, 1970, Myles Keating bequeathed his estate to his friend and business partner, Larry Horten, and also appointed Horton executor. Keating was not then married. On September 23, 1972, Keating married Myrtle McAvin, to whom he remained married until his death. Provision was not made for Myrtle by marriage contract, by the aforementioned Last Will, nor was she mentioned therein to show an intention not to make provision for her. The decedent left no issue, father, mother, brother or sister surviving. The record does not establish whether his estate was his separate property, or his interest in community property.

If he attempted to bequeath his separate estate, and the dispositive provision of his will was nullified by his subsequent marriage to Myrtle, then NRS 134.050 (4) provides that such separate property shall go to the surviving wife, since, in truth, he died intestate. On the other hand, if he attempted to bequeath his interest in community property, and the bequest was nullified by reason of his later marriage, such interest would go to Myrtle as his surviving spouse.

Following a contest of the dispositive provision of the will by Myrtle, the surviving spouse, the district court ruled that the decedent's estate was to go to Myrtle as though the decedent had died intestate, since, in the circumstances related, the Last Will was revoked by his subsequent marriage to her. That ruling was correct. The will was revoked as to Myrtle, and whatever interest she would have taken had her husband died intestate goes to her as the surviving spouse unaffected by the provisions of the will.

Affirmed.

DEVECMON v. SHAW AND DEVRIES

70 Md. 219 (Maryland, 1889)

Alvey, Chief Judge

This case in its present stage has been submitted on briefs of counsel, for the purpose of obtaining a judicial construction of the last will and testament of the late John S. Combs, deceased, with respect to certain questions supposed to be of doubtful solution.

The testator was the owner of a considerable estate, both real and personal, and he left surviving him a daughter, Althea Louisa Combs, his only child and heir-at-law, who is still a minor, and his widow, Wilhelmina J. Combs, who is still living.

By the will, after giving some pecuniary legacies to certain persons named, and devising a house and lot as a law office, and its contents, in the City of Cumberland, to his nephew, the testator makes provision for his wife, by devising and bequeathing to her absolutely, certain portion of his estate, both real and personal. This provision made for the widow she has renounced, and elected to take such portion of the estate as the law allows her to take.

The testator, after thus providing for his widow, proceeds to dispose of the great bulk of his estate in favor of his daughter. He devises to her certain described parcels of real estate, generally, without words of limitation; and then, in the same clause of the will, he gives her certain moneys, bonds, and stocks, by general words of gift, without limitation or restriction. But at the end of the paragraph of his will, containing these devises and bequests, the testator adds this provision: "But in case my said daughter should die without leaving any child or children AT THE TIME OF HER DEATH, or if leaving such child or children, such child OR ALL SUCH CHILDREN should die before arriving at the age of twenty-one years, then all the real estate and personal estate devised to my said daughter shall go to my sister, Althea M. Devecmon, and her children and grandchildren then living, in equal proportions; such grandchildren to stand in the place of their deceased parents." . . .

McSherry, Justice

The record now before us brings up for review a decree of the Circuit Court for Allegany County, construing the will of the late John S. Combs. The opinion filed by Chief Judge Alvey in the Court below is full, clear, and satisfactory, and nothing we might say could add to its conclusiveness. We accordingly adopt that opinion as our own. It is, however, necessary to notice a question raised in the argument in this Court. It was suggested that the part of the decree which determines that the daughter of the testator took a fee in the realty devised, and an absolute interest in the personalty bequeathed to her, defeasible upon the happening of the contingencies mentioned in the will, ought to be reversed because prematurely passed, inasmuch as no one of those contingencies has yet come to pass. . . .

By the will of Mr. Combs there were trustees appointed to collect the rents and income from the real and personal estate given to his daughter. These trustees are charged with certain duties in regard to the investment and disbursement of the trust funds; and desiring to have the guidance and direction of the Court in the discharge of those duties, they filed the bill now before us. Every person interested, in any way under the will, in the estate was made a party; and the question chiefly discussed was whether Althea Louisa Combs, the daughter, took only a life estate or a defeasible fee under the will. It is true the Court might have declined to consider that question, but the appellants having themselves sought a construction of this part of the will, in the Court below; and having on this appeal elaborately argued that the conclusion reached by the Circuit Court is erroneous; they are scarcely in a position to ask this Court to reverse that portion of the decree, if it be otherwise correct, merely because it was prematurely passed. They had the undoubted right to insist in the Circuit Court, that the proper time for deciding what estate the daughter took had not arrived; but they relied upon no such defense. On the contrary, they submitted all their rights to the Court, and, by their own contention, invited a construction of that clause of the will. They have done the same thing in this Court; but they insist here, that if this Court should agree with the Circuit Court's construction, they are entitled to a reversal, upon the ground that the very question which they sought a decision upon ought not to have been decided at all. They have taken in both Courts whatever change they supposed there was to secure a construction favorable to themselves. They did this with full knowledge that the contingencies, upon the happening of which they would, under the will, be entitled to the property, had not occurred; but as the decision was adverse to them on the merits, they ask us, if we concur in the Circuit Court's interpretation of the will, to reverse the decree, because they were wrong in consenting that the Court should, in anticipation of those contingencies, pass upon those merits, and the Court was wrong in acceding to their request. No court can sanction any such practice as that.

For the reasons set forth in the opinion of Judge Alvey, we shall affirm the decree with costs.

PROBLEMS FOR DISCUSSION

1. Merwin Branish and Minnie Adalla lived together as man and wife for some 33 years. They were never married, though Minnie performed all the tasks of a farm-wife—cooking, cleaning, gardening, shopping, etc. Nearly all of Merwin's property was held in partnership with his brothers; none was put in Minnie's name. The couple had no joint bank account; Merwin paid all the household expenses or gave Minnie cash to pay them. Minnie had a separate account in her own name in which she deposited money earned by selling chickens and eggs. She had her own post office box, kept her medical records in her own name, and filed for social security in her own name. When she admitted Merwin to the hospital, she signed herself as "friend." Merwin filed his income and property tax returns as a single person. The state statute providing for common-law marriage said that it could exist where there had been "a mutual assumption of marital rights, duties or obligations." Merwin died intestate, and Minnie files a claim as his common-law wife. What result, and why?

2. In 1975 Allen Larch executed a will which distributed his estate to his son, Rolf Larch, and several other person. Although Allen's potential estate was in excess of $250,000, Rolf was given only a $10,000 bequest. In 1976 Allen executed a second will, apparently believing that he had been unfair to Rolf in the first one. About two months later, Allen received information which indicated that Rolf's behavior had again deteriorated; Allen then tore up and burned the second will. Allen died there-after, and his first will was admitted to probate. Rolf challenges the status of the first will, claiming that it had been revoked under a statute which provided: "A prior will is not revoked by a subsequent will unless the latter contains an express revocation, or provisions wholly inconsistent with the terms of the former will; but in other cases the prior will remains effectual so far as consistent with the provisions of the subsequent will." There are no other copies of the second will. The other legatees and devisees under the first will say that it is still in effect and that Rolf is only entitled to $10,000. Who is right, and why?

3. Biff Botts died intestate at age 41, survived by two older brothers, Frank and Hank, and three older sisters, Lange, Olive, and Marti. Biff had lived with his father until the father died in 1960. He had then moved in with Lange and her family, where he paid $15 per week for room and board. He had dropped out of school in the eighth grade and had been working for about 10 years as a truck driver. His financial affairs had been handled by his father; after 1960 Frank took over. Frank helped Biff open two savings accounts in their joint names, assisted Biff in buying a car, and had Biff's income tax returns filled out. Frank deposited all of Biff's wages in the ac-counts and made withdrawals from them as requested by Biff. Biff was very self-conscious and shy of strangers, probably because of his weight (350 pounds). He spent most of his time at home or in a local bar. Frank has now filed for a summary estate disposition since the two savings accounts name him as a joint tenant. Hank and the three sisters object, claiming an interest as Biff's heirs. How should the court handle this estate? Explain.

4. Sybil Oxxey executed a will which left "all my stocks, bonds, and/or securities" to her daughter, Cleo Oxxey. She then left the "rest, residue, and remainder" of her estate to her nephew, Greg Blankston. The total value of the estate was just under $100,000, $60,000 of which was represented by several certificates of deposit. Cleo and Greg each claim the CDs. Who gets them, and why?

5. Rudy Mavrodafne and his wife, Geniah, acquired three parcels of property between 1956 and 1970, taking title to each as joint tenants. In 1975 Rudy discovered that he had terminal cancer and only a few months to live. Rudy and Geniah then conveyed

three parcels to themselves as tenants in common. Rudy died about four months later. Geniah included one half the value of the parcels when she filed a state inheritance tax return and a U.S. estate tax return. Both tax collectors claim that the full value of the parcels should be included, because a transfer in contemplation of death was made. Both statutes provide as follows: "Every transfer of property composing a material part of the transferor's estate, made within 2 years prior to the death of the transferor, and without adequate and full consideration in money or money's worth, shall be deemed made in contemplation of death within the meaning of this subchapter, unless shown to the contrary." Geniah says no "transfer" occurred. Who's right, and why?

6. Nemano Porale died intestate, survived by his daughter, Bertha Rivosha, and two sons, Broderic and Yorick. For about five years prior to his death, Nemano had lived with Bertha and her family. She provided him with food, clothing, and care. She testified that he had told her he had some bonds which he wanted her to have and that his sons had no use for him and he had no use for them. Bertha's husband, Buster, generally corroborated her story. No transfer of the bonds was ever made; they were worth about $15,000. Bertha filed a claim against her father's estate for the value of services provided to him, in the amount of $11,367. Broderic and Yorick claim that her services were gratuitous. How should the court rule, and why?

7. Milo Noonan died in 1956, survived by his wife, Erma, and two children, Bernie and Kitty. Milo's will left his farm of some 350 acres to Erma for life, and then to his children for life, with the remainder in fee simple to the heirs of their bodies, per stirpes. Erma is now 68, and she has not remarried. Bernie is 35; Kitty is 39. Both Bernie and Kitty are unmarried and childless at present. Because of a severe physical disability, Kitty is unlikely to ever bear children. The farm is located on rough, hilly land, with poor soil. It has not been very profitable. Erma, Bernie, and Kitty have petitioned the court for permission to sell it. The applicable statute provides: "On the petition of the life tenant, with the consent of the holder of the reversion, the court may order the sale of the property in such estate." The trial court refused to permit a sale, since it held that Erma, Bernie, and Kitty were only the successive life tenants and that the statute therefore did not apply. Should the appellate court affirm this judgment? Discuss.

8. Aldough Cellah and his wife, Violet, entered into a contract to buy certain real estate by land contract from Samson Crooker. They made the down payment of 29 percent as required, went into possession on June 1, 1971, and made the required annual payments of principal and interest each year until 1978, when their check was returned uncashed. Samson died on January 20, 1973. The final date for filing creditors' claims against his estate was set as June 20, 1973, and a decree barring further claims was entered on June 21, 1973. In November 1973 Samson's widow, Hortense, elected to take her statutory widow's share against the terms of the will. Aldough and Violet received no notice of this election or of any prospective breach of contract until the spring of 1976, when they were told that Hortense had filed an action against another land contract purchaser who had bought from Samson. Hortense had never signed the land contracts, disclaiming her dower rights or her rights as a co-owner. Aldough and Violet now want to file a contingent claim for breach of the land contract against Samson's estate, if Hortense files a claim against them. Samson's executor says that no further claims can be filed since more than two years has elapsed since Samson's death. Should the court permit the filing of this claim? Why or why not?

Trusts and | 37
Estate Planning

In the previous chapter we discussed the administration of the deceased person's estate, both where the deceased had executed a last will and testament prior to his or her death and where the deceased died intestate. In this chapter we want to discuss the concept and the process of estate planning and the use of trusts in the estate plan and during the lifetime of the testator.

What Is Estate Planning?

The word *estate* means the interest which an individual has in real property or in personal property, either tangible or intangible. Estate planning is the process of planning for the future distribution of a person's property, both prior to and after that person's death. Estate planning is not just making a last will and testament, putting it in a safe-deposit box, and leaving it there until the testator dies. An estate plan should be made by an individual early in life and should be changed periodically as the goals of the plan change. For example, once the children are grown and educated, a new plan with new goals needs to be formulated. Also, as a person's accumulation of assets increases, changes need to be considered. Thus estate planning should not be a one-shot proposition but should be a continuing plan throughout the adult life of the testator.

The Goals of Estate Planning

The primary goal of any estate plan is to ensure that the testator's property will be distributed to his or her heirs, or to whomever else the testator desires that it be distributed, in the shares and the manner desired by the testator and in accordance with the national and state laws which would apply to the plan.

A second goal of an estate plan is to provide for the care and support of minor children and for the care and support of the surviving spouse for the remainder of his or her life. Especially where the testator's estate is quite large, there is the fear that if a child were to receive the inheritance, the child might soon squander it. Thus wills often set up a trust whereby a trustee manages the child's inheritance and pays out only specific amounts until the child reaches a certain age or accomplishes a specified act, such as completing college or getting married. If the spouse inherits a large sum, there is always the danger that the spouse might remarry and that the new wife or husband would benefit from the inheritance to the detriment of the children who were to later inherit from the spouse. One method of handling this problem is to create a trust in the last will and testament whereby the property is deeded to a trustee and the trustee is instructed to pay the surviving spouse the income from the property being managed by the trust, with the understanding that in case of need the capital funds could be used for the care and support of the spouse and that upon the spouse's death the remainder of the assets in the trust would be distributed to the children. Thus the spouse would be cared for and supported during his or her lifetime and yet the assets of the estate would not be squandered. Another method is to give the surviving spouse a life estate in the real property, which means that the surviving spouse could live on or rent out the real property but could not sell it.

A third goal of an estate plan is to minimize the impact of death taxes and estate settlement costs. The individual planning his or her estate should be aware of the national and state death taxes which may be assessed upon the estate at the time of his or her death. Taxes must be paid prior to the distribution of assets to the heirs. The tax liability can be reduced by distributing property as gifts during the testator's lifetime, thus reducing the value of the assets owned at death. The new tax law allows the testator to make annual tax-free gifts to donees of up to $10,000 per year per donee, (up to $20,000 per year if the spouse joins in making the gift). Thus, over a period of years, a considerable amount of cash or other assets may be distributed to children, grandchildren, charities, and other beneficiaries without any taxes having to be paid.

A fourth goal of an estate plan is to prevent the forced sale of assets from the estate in order to pay death taxes and estate settlement costs. This goal is particularly important when the major asset in the estate is a family business or farm, or residential or commerical real estate. Too often in such cases, the liquid assets (cash, stocks, and the like) are insufficient to meet the necessary costs and taxes. When that happens, major assets or portions of them must be sold, quite often at less than their market value, since the sale must be made quickly and for cash. A good estate plan would provide for life insurance in a sum sufficient to meet all of the immediate cash needs of the estate and the survivors, and thus obviate the need for any forced sale of major assets.

Nature of a Trust

A trust is any arrangement whereby the owner of property transfers its ownership to a natural or corporate person, called the trustee, that is instructed to hold the property for the benefit of a person or persons who are designated as beneficiaries. A trust can be created for any purpose that is legal and not against public policy. The owner of the property interest that is being transferred must instruct the trustee as to how that interest is to be administered for the beneficiaries. For example, an owner of an interest in property may transfer that interest to the trustee for a beneficiary's benefit and may instruct the trustee to distribute only the earnings on the property and not to distribute the principal, or corpus, of the trust until a later date. It is important that the trustee have specific instructions as to how the property is to be administered for the beneficiaries.

Types of Trusts

Trusts are divided into two basic categories. A living trust, also called an inter vivos trust, is a trust which takes effect and is administered during the lifetime of the transferor of the property. A testamentary trust is created prior to the death of the person who sets it up but does not take effect until that person's death.

As a remedy for the fraudulent acquisition of property, a court of equity may impose a "constructive" trust in favor of the real or intended owner.

Marco v. Marco
242 N.W.2d 867 (Nebraska, 1976)

FACTS Lawrence and Mary Marco had two sons, Jerry and Jim, who were 3½ and 1½ when Mary died. Lawrence married Dorothy in 1946, when both boys were still very young. Lawrence and Dorothy had 12 other children, 11 of whom were still living at the time of trial. Jerry began to work at his father's service station at age 12, and Jim did the same shortly thereafter. In 1959 the father began A–1 Auto Parts, with Jim running the office and Jerry salvaging the parts. Each boy received a small weekly salary at age 21. Each later built a house on land owned by A–1; neither paid rent or property taxes. In 1969 Jim began A–1 Auto Sales on land owned by Lawrence and Dorothy as joint tenants. When Lawrence died in 1973, it was discovered that he had conveyed all of A–1's real estate to himself and Dorothy as joint tenants and that his will left his entire estate to her. Jerry and Jim claimed that she got the deeds fraudulently, that their "houses" really belonged to them, and that the court should impose a constructive trust on the property. The trial court dismissed their claims and enjoined them from interfering with Dorothy's operation of A–1 Auto Parts. They appealed.

ISSUE Should the court impose a constructive trust on the real estate?

DECISION No. Judgment affirmed.

REASONS Justice Clinton suggested that the sons might be entitled to some other form of relief, but he did not think that they had proved their case for the relief sought here.

"'Constructive trusts arise from actual or constructive fraud or imposition, committed by one party on another. Thus if one person procures the legal title to property from another by fraud or misrepresentation, or by an abuse of some influential or confidential relation which he holds toward the owner of the legal title, obtains such title from him upon more advantageous terms than he could otherwise have obtained it, the law constructs a trust in favor of the party upon whom the fraud or imposition has been practiced. If a party obtains the legal title to property by virtue of a confidential relation, under such circumstances that he ought not, according to the rules of equity and good conscience . . . , hold and enjoy the benefits, out of such circumstances or relations, a court of equity will raise a trust by construction and fasten it upon the conscience of the offending party and convert him into a trustee of the legal title.' . . .

"The record is completely devoid of any evidence, direct or by inference, to show that Dorothy was named as a grantee in the deeds through some abuse of a confidential relationship. When the deed of 1967 was made, Dorothy and Lawrence had been married for more than 20 years. They then had a large family. At least one child was born after that time. When the deed of 1971 was made, they had been married about 26 years. It was at that time that their youngest child was born. Eighteen thousand dollars was paid for the last-mentioned acquisition and the evidence is completely devoid of anything which would support an inference that any of this money was Jerry's. There is no evidence in the record whatever as to the circumstances surrounding the acquisition of the property acquired from Dorothy's parents and on which 'Jim's house' is located.

"The evidence therefore does not establish prima facie that Dorothy obtained title by virtue of a confidential relationship, under such circumstances that she ought not, according to the rules of equity and good conscience as administered in chancery, hold and enjoy the benefits of title to the property in question. Under the circumstances shown, equity need not raise a trust by construction upon the legal title to the real estate in question."

How Are Trusts Created?

A trust is not a contract, since no consideration is required from the beneficiaries. It is in effect a gift from the giver, also called the settlor, to the beneficiary through a middle person, namely the trustee. In order to create an express trust, there must be a written document, which is normally called a trust agreement or a deed of trust. While it is not necessary for any specific language to be used, there are certain requirements which must be met. If the trust involves an interest in land, then the statute of frauds requires that the details of the transfer of that interest be set out in writing.

There is also a limit to how long a trust may exist before the interest vests in beneficiaries. The rule to be complied with here is called "the rule against perpetuities." This rule prohibits a person from creating a trust which remains in existence forever. A general statement of the rule is that an interest in property, if conveyed for the benefit of a beneficiary, must be turned over or vested in the beneficiary no more than 21 years plus the period of gestation of a new life after the expiration of the life or lives of some person or persons who were in being when the trust was created. There are exceptions to this rule if the purpose of the trust is charitable. Most states have a statutory maximum time during which a trust may remain operative. Here the specific state laws would govern.

Revocability and Modification of Trusts

An inter vivos trust may be declared either revocable or irrevocable. If a person sets up an irrevocable trust for the benefit of beneficiaries, then that person, the settlor, may not revoke or change the trust at a later date. Such a trust may be modified, with the consent of all the beneficiaries, provided such modification would not frustrate its original intent. However, this would only be possible in exceptional circumstances, as the courts will not allow a change in a trust if this would change the trust's original intended purpose. If the settlor sets up a revocable trust, this means that he or she transfers title to certain property to a trustee for the benefit of specific beneficiaries, but may at any time change his or her mind and take back the corpus of the trust from the trustee.

Many wealthy persons deed property over to a trustee so that the trustee can manage the property for them. Thus these persons are both settlor and beneficiary. A professional manages their property for them, thus relieving them of the responsibilities of management, and gives them the income less a managerial service charge. If such a trust is revocable, the settlor can change his or her mind and terminate the trust at any time.

Testamentary trusts do not become effective until the death of the settlor, and they are not revocable after the settlor's death. But anytime before the settlor's death, he or she may revoke such a trust simply by changing the last will and testament which contains or refers to it.

The Trustee—Rights and Obligations

A trustee can be an individual or an institution such as a bank, a trust company, or a similar financial institution. The trustee is governed by given state's laws concerning the handling of trust funds. These laws very from state to state. A trustee generally has the right to make decisions concerning the investment of the trust corpus in accordance with the settlor's directions, provided those directions are not contrary to the law of the particular jurisdiction. For example, a trustee must generally invest trust funds more conservatively than he or she would invest his or her own funds. A trustee may not commingle the property of a trust with property that the trustee owns individually or with property that the trustee is administering as the trustee of another trust. Generally speaking the trustee owes a duty of loyalty to the beneficiaries; that is, the trustee's job is to conserve the corpus for the beneficiaries' benefit and yet to secure the best income and growth possible. The trustee will be required to use the skill, judgment, and care reasonably expected of a person in that capacity. Banks, trust companies, and other corporate trustees will of course be required to use a high degree of skill, care, and judgment in the management of trusts since that is their profession. An individual who is acting as a trustee would not be required to use the same high degree of skill, care, and judgment but would be required to use reasonable care and judgment in the handling of the trust funds. Most trusts involving large sums of money or property will be administered by corporate trustees who have professional investment knowledge and expertise.

Schug v. Michael
245 N.W.2d 587 (Minnesota, 1976)

FACTS   James Michael, an attorney, was an original incorporator, the chairman of the board, and the owner of 50,000 shares (50 percent) of Mustang Investment Corporation. Kenneth Schug was a shareholder. Michael assigned the beneficial interest in 30,000 of his shares to various persons, including Schug. Schug purchased 7,000 of these shares for $0.50 per share through a "Trust Agreement" drafted by Michael. Schug as beneficiary was to receive the income for Michael's lifetime and then to receive the stock absolutely. Charles Quigley joined Mustang's board in 1969 and almost immediately had policy differences with Michael. Quigley made repeated offers to buy out Michael, but Michael never informed Schug of these offers. On November 2, 1970, Michael bought 6,000 shares back from Schug and then sold them and 24,000 more to Quigley for $3.50 per share. Morris, a lawyer representing Michael, then asked Schug to transfer the Trust Agreement to him, so that he could get the stock released by the commissioner of securities. Schug indorsed the agreement in blank and gave it to Morris. Morris later died, and the agreement could not be located. Michael said that he owned the other 1,000 shares as well. Schug also died. Schug's estate sued for damages of $15,000 on the repurchase of 6,000 shares and of $14,500 on the other 1,000 shares. The trial court gave damages.

ISSUE   Did the defendant breach his fiduciary duties as trustee so as to incur liability for damages?

DECISION   Yes. Judgment affirmed but remanded for clarification.

REASONS   Justice Kelly made short work of Michael's arguments. It was clear to him that there had been a breach of fiduciary duty.

"While use of the words 'trust agreement,' 'trustee,' and 'beneficiary' in the instrument executed by the parties is not dispositive of the question of a trust relationship . . . , it is persuasive evidence that defendant, an attorney who drafted the instrument himself, intended a trust relationship. . . .

"Defendant undertook to sell Schug a portion of his own insider stock and to retain control of that stock under the trust agreement. Defendant conceded that this was in direct violation of his escrow agreement that he not sell the stock, and even argued before the trial court that this was criminal violation of Minnesota securities law which voided the trust agreement. Nevertheless, after having illegally sold a beneficial interest to Schug and other parties, defendant continued to seek for himself the best of all possible worlds. He apparently represented to others, including Quigley, that he owned a full 50,000 shares, and he even stated falsely in an affidavit in his own shareholder's action that he owned 50,000 shares. He then proceeded to engage in further trafficking of the escrowed shares by buying them back from Schug and other beneficiaires of similar trusts to aid in his control dispute with Quigley. The result was a substantial profit for him and a somewhat lesser return for his ill-used beneficiaries.

"Defendant's course of conduct reveals violations of several important duties to his beneficiary. First, he breached his duty of loyalty by purchasing (and trafficking in) trust property. . . . [H]e failed to disclose his offers from and disputes with Quigley, which were obviously material facts to Schug. . . .

> "Second, defendant also breached duties to take and keep control of trust property, to preserve trust property, and to keep trust property separate from his own."
>
> Justice Kelly also held that Michael had converted the other 1,000 shares and was liable for the highest value those shares reached within a reasonable time after Schug had knowledge of the conversion.

The Use of Trusts in Estate Planning

A primary use of trusts is to conserve estates. If the testator, the person making the will, has minor children, the testator may want to set up a testamentary trust in the will. This trust will become effective at the testator's death. At that time, certain specified property will be transferred to a person or organization named as the trustee. The trustee will then hold and manage the trust and will normally distribute its earnings to the beneficiaries. In some instances, if the amount involved is not sufficient to care for the beneficiaries' needs, the trustee is allowed to invade the trust principal and to pay out portions of that principal as necessary until the beneficiaries reach a specific age, at which time the trust will be dissolved and the remainder of the principal will be divided among the beneficiaries. A testator can also set up a testamentary trust for the benefit of his or her spouse. This is often done where the spouse is too ill or too old to care for himself or herself. In effect, the testamentary trust allows the testator to control the distribution of his or her estate long after death since the testator's instructions to the trustee will dictate the handling and the distribution of the estate throughout the duration of the trust.

A second use of trusts is to save inheritance taxes. Generation-skipping trusts serve this purpose. For example, if grandfather died and left his estate to grandmother, she would pay inheritance taxes. Then, when grandmother died, her sons and daughters would inherit and would pay another round of inheritance taxes. When they died, the grandchildren would inherit and would pay taxes again. Thus generation-skipping trust, whereby grandfather gives his property in trust for the grandchildren, would skip two levels of taxation. Grandfather pays a gift tax when he gives the property, and the grandchildren thus gain more net property than they would if the property went through the normal inheritance process and much of the principal were reduced by taxation. Generation skipping trusts are, however, subject to Internal Revenue Service regulations, and recent regulations have limited the amount that can skip taxation.

A third use of trusts is to reduce estate settlement costs at death. Estate settlement costs are based on the value of the testator's estate at the time of death and on the legal procedures necessary to probate the estate. If a large portion of the estate has already been deeded to trusts, then the estate of the testator is relatively small and the probate process is much simpler and thus much cheaper.

CHILDREN OF THE CHIPPEWA, OTTAWA AND POTAWATOMY TRIBES v. THE UNIVERSITY OF MICHIGAN

305 N.W.2d 522 (Michigan, 1981)

Per Curiam

On September 29, 1817, the Treaty of Fort Meigs . . . was executed. The Chippewa, Ottawa, and Potawatomy Tribes were signatories of the first part, and the government of the United States of America was the signatory of the second part. The treaty was drafted entirely by the representative of the United States. The Defendant at bar was not a party to the Treaty.

Notwithstanding this latter fact, the Plaintiffs, who are descendants of the members of the signatory Indian Tribes, brought an action in equity before the Circuit Court of Washtenaw County seeking to have a trust declared in their favor against Defendant based on the provisions of this Treaty.

The original complaint was filed August 5, 1971. It was claimed that Article 16 of the Treaty created a trust whereby certain land, belonging to the Indians, was conveyed to defendant for purposes of ensuring that the Indians and their descendants would receive an education in the European fashion. In support of this contention, the complaint cited certain alleged historical events, including the vesting of title of the conveyed parcels of land in the Defendant; the then-University president Lewis Cass's appointment of two trustees to locate and survey these lands; the patenting of these lands to Defendant by the government of the United States in 1824; and the release by one Church of St. Anne of its interest of the lands in favor of Defendant.

The inclusion of St. Anne's Church in the Complaint was occasioned by the Plaintiff's assertion that the Treaty compelled the church to provide for the primary and secondary education of the Indians. The Complaint then contends that the Treaty imposed a concomitant duty upon Defendant to ensure the Indians' college education. It is then claimed that the aforementioned conveyance by the church to the Defendant merged the foregoing duties wholly into Defendant's realm of responsibility.

The Complaint then charged that a breach of these duties had occurred and was continuing to occur. To remedy the alleged breach, Plaintiffs proposed a broad spectrum of equitable remedies.

An accounting of the proceeds realized from sale of the subject parcels was sought. Plaintiffs proposed that upon completion of this accounting, a trust fund composed of proceeds from these sales should be established. Another trust fund, to be composed of monies accounted for from the sale of lands conveyed to Defendant from St. Anne's Church, was also sought.

In addition to the foregoing, Plaintiffs asked for an accounting of all the investments in both trusts, or, in the alternative, payment of a 15 percent interest fee thereon to be compounded annually from 1826 forward.

The Complaint then went on to ask for an accounting of all lands received from the Indians which had not yet been sold together with an accounting of the accrued rent thereon to be computed annually with a compound rate of 15 percent interest to be added thereto.

It was finally requested that the Circuit Court should replace Defendant as the trustee of these funds with a person of its own choosing and that the proceeds from the first trust fund should be directed toward providing Plaintiffs with monies to continue their education at any collegiate institution of their choosing. The funds from the second trust were to be applied toward the primary and secondary education of the Plaintiffs.

On March 28, 1977, Plaintiffs filed an amended complaint and presented a two-pronged attack, again under the theory of equitable trust. After noting the 1974 decision of the trial court to treat the matter as a class action, Plaintiffs proceeded to proffer a claim that the Treaty had created an express trust, with the plaintiffs being the beneficiaries of that trust. The amended Complaint went on to assert that Defendant had sold the lands conveyed to it under the Treaty without either dedicating the monies realized from the sales to the Plaintiffs' educational needs or in any other way accounting to the Plaintiffs for these proceeds. The amended Complaint then sought a trial under the theories of express and/or constructive trust and otherwise repeated the earlier claims.

The Treaty provision that is the primary focus of the present dispute, Article 16, reads:

Some of the Ottawa, Chippewa, and Potawatomy Tribes, being attached to the Catholic religion, and believing they may wish some of their children hereafter educated, do grant to the rector of the Catholic church of St. Anne of Detroit, for the use of the said church, and to the corporation of the college at Detroit, for the use of the said college, to be retained or sold, as the said rector and corporation may judge expedient, each, one half of three sections of land, to contain six hundred and forty acres, on the river Raisin, at a place called Macon; and three sections of land not yet located, which tracts were reserved, for the use of the said Indians, by the treaty of Detroit, in one thousand eight hundred and seven; and the superintendent of Indian affairs, in the territory of Michigan, is authorized, on the part of the said Indians, to select the said tracts of land.

Trial commenced on August 21, 1978. During the trial numerous Exhibits were received along with much expert testimony from all sides. On February 28, 1979, the trial judge issued a meticulously researched and well drafted written opinion, throughly discussing the historical and procedural facets of this novel action and carefully setting forth the law which he believed controlling of this case. The opinion denied relief on all counts.

We have painstakingly reviewed the findings of fact in that opinion and agree with the trial judge in respect to those findings. The task of leaping back over 160 years in time is most difficult, and the trial judge is to be commended for his efforts in that regard. . . .

[I]n setting forth the findings of fact, we choose to incorporate the entire opinion of the trial court

as part of this opinion to accomplish that end. . . .

Following the issuance of the opinion of February 28, 1979, the present appeal was brought as of right. Five issues are raised by Plaintiffs.

It is first asserted that the trial judge erred in finding that the Indians could not have owned fee simple title to any lands conveyed from the year 1790 forward. In so ruling, the trial court found *Oneida Indian Nation* v. *County of Oneida*, 414 U.S. 661 . . . (1974), to be dispositive. We agree. The thrust of *Oneida* is that the 1790 Nonintercourse Act created a right of occupancy rather than a title in fee simple in the Indians as to lands held by them. The trial court held that the Federal Government possesses power to convey the fee as to lands occupied by Indian Tribes and all questions with respect to rights of occupancy and conditions of extinguishment of Indian title are solely for the Federal Government. The trial court went on to say:

This court will concede that in 1817 the Indians could have imposed an express trust on the lands possessed by them and granted to the Church and College by the 1817 Treaty, but this was simply not done at that time.

Given this recognition by the trial court, it is difficult to understand the Plaintiffs' argument on the issue. The trial court's ultimate decision obviates further discussion in any event.

Plaintiffs assert that the trial court erred in relying upon the theories set forth in the first complaint as a point of reference for its opinion. While it is true that the opinion of February 28, 1979, assumes the claims of the earlier Complaint in reference to grants of land, the error is not fatal. A fair reading of the opinion discloses that both theories of recovery in the second Complaint were extensively discussed and refuted. The trial judge clearly comprehended the basis of the relief sought in the second Complaint and carefully interwove those theories with the evidence adduced before ruling against them. . . .

A third issue raised by Plaintiffs is whether the trial court was justified in holding that Article 16 of the Treaty of Fort Meigs constituted a gift of lands to Father Richard and to Defendant. We believe that it did. . . .

The operative language in Article 16 provides that some of the Plaintiffs' forefathers: "*do grant to the . . . church . . . for the use of the said church, and to the . . . college . . . for the use of the said college, to be retained or sold, as the said rector and corporation may judge expedient,* each. . . ." (Emphasis added.)

Clearly, the grant itself is a completed one and not conditional in nature. Nor do its terms encompass more than one transaction. The land is donated jointly to the church and to the corporation. The later divisions of the parcels was a consequence of Father Richard's discretion, a discretion Article 16 allowed him to exercise.

The evidence points to an almost reverential attitude toward Father Richard on the Indians' part. This attitude was commingled with an attitude of filial affection. The evidence also points to a clear donative intent on the Indians' part as regards Father Richard and encompasses a similar attitude toward the educational institution which the Indians very properly regarded as an extension of Father Richard's personality and influence.

We disagree with Plaintiffs' continued assertions that the Treaty, and particularly Article 16, were the sole product of Lewis Cass's efforts. The evidence does not support such a contention in any way. Rather, the Treaty was the cumulative result of extended negotiation involving many leaders on both sides.

Both the expert testimony and the language of the Treaty itself reflect the likelihood of a present donative intent on the part of the Indians at the time of the Treaty's execution. . . .

The next claim of error challenges the trial court's decision that Article 16 created no express trust in the Indians' favor.

It is a general principle of trust law that a trust is created only if the settlor manifests an intention to create a trust, and it is essential that there be an explicit declaration of trust accompanied by a transfer of property to one for the benefit of another. . . .

Further, an express trust in real property must be

in writing, under the hand of the party to be charged. . . .

We find that the Plaintiffs' substantive arguments in support of the theory of an express trust are based on speculation and irrelevancy. . . .

The last claim on appeal concerns the issue of a constructive trust. The trial court rejected this theory for several reasons: (1) the University was not a party to the negotiations and committed no misconduct in the treaty negotiations; (2) the Indians were represented by competent interpreters and a trusted Indian agent; (3) the United States evidenced no unjust conduct at the negotiations, its main intent being to secure a cession of a significant area in Ohio; (4) the Article 16 land was of minimal value when conveyed and when the University tried to sell it; and (5) the two cases cited by Plaintiffs are distinguishable. We agree.

In a pristinely humane world, it might be honorable and fair to compel Defendant to offer comprehensive scholarships in gratitude for the 1817 conveyance. Certainly, the cost of higher education is subject to the rigors of inflation as are all other things and the Plaintiffs, like everyone else, could benefit by the financial assistance they seek. However, constructive trusts are not used to requite obligations imposed by conscience alone. Rather, they are imposed solely where a balancing of equities discloses that it would be unfair to act otherwise. Where, as here, the language of the Treaty and the historical evidence reflect a gift inter vivos and nothing more, the imposition of a constructive trust is neither equitably nor legally desirable.

Based on the foregoing, it is readily apparent that the judgment of the trial court should be and the same is hereby affirmed. No costs, questions of novel impression and public significance being involved.

STAPLETON v. DeVRIES

535 p.2d 1267 (Montana, 1975)

Daly, Justice

Defendants Beverly A. DeVries, individually and as executrix of the estate of Amanda DeVries, deceased; Emma R. Storer; Herman DeVries, Jr.; Loretta M. Kilwein; Gladys J. Weimer; and Marcella K. Buckholz bring this appeal from a judgment of the district court, Carbon County, awarding plaintiffs Louise Stapleton; Dorothy Pihlaja; Ethel Cestnik; and Ruth Johnson, the children of Herman DeVries, deceased, from a prior marriage, each an equal one-tenth share of the estate of Amanda DeVries.

Herman DeVries was married twice. As issue of the first marriage were born the plaintiffs. As issue of the marriage between Herman and Amanda were born the defendants. Herman died June 14, 1951. In his will, he stated:

I give, devise and bequeath to my beloved wife, Amanda DeVries, all the balance, residue and remainder of my property of whatever nature, kind or character which I may own at the time of my death to have and to hold as her sole and separate property. I do this with the knowledge that she will be fair and equitable to all of my children, the issue of myself and my former wife as well as the issue of herself and myself.

On July 15, 1953, in its decree, the district court distributed Herman's estate to his widow Amanda "as her sole and separate property, in accordance with the Last Will and Testament of [Herman DeVries]."

Amanda died on November 8, 1971, leaving a will which was admitted to probate. It left all her property to her children, making no mention of plaintiffs. They contested Amanda's will. Their petition to contest the will was dismissed on the ground that they were not "interested persons" under the statute.

Plaintiffs then filed a complaint alleging, in the alternative, that Herman created a trust for their benefit, or Amanda had contracted to leave a portion of her property to them. On the basis of depositions taken of the four contestants and their proposed witnesses, and on the basis of the estate files of Herman and Amanda, the district court granted summary judgment finding a trust created by Herman for the benefit of his children by previous marriage, the plaintiffs. . . .

Defendants argue there was no constructive trust created by Herman DeVries' will in favor of plaintiffs. Plaintiffs argue that such a trust was

created and that the second article of Herman's will, when read in light of section 91–201, R. C. M. 1947, which provides that a will is to be construed according to the intent of the testator, creates a constructive trust in favor of plaintiffs as to their share of the estate. . . .

This Court in construing the second article finds that there was no trust created for the benefit of the plaintiffs. The will is clear on its face. It gives to Amanda DeVries outright all the property owned by Herman DeVries at the time of his death. The remaining language "with the knowledge that she will be fair and equitable to all of my children, the issue of myself and my former wife, as well as the issue of herself and myself" is merely precatory language, and does not create a trust for the benefit of plaintiffs. . . .

There is no evidence in the record to support the contention that Herman DeVries intended to create a trust in favor of plaintiffs. The language of the will is not sufficient. Therefore, this Court finds no trust created in their favor.

Plaintiffs next contend there was an agreement between Amanda and Herman that Amanda would leave her estate in equal shares to all of the children of Herman DeVries. Plaintiffs reason: that when Herman used the phrase "with the knowledge" that he had to obtain this knowledge from his wife; that when Amanda, an executrix of Herman's estate, signed the final account and petition for distribution of Herman's estate which stated "that in pursuance of and according to the terms and provisions of the Last Will and Testament of Herman DeVries" that she knew part of the terms was that the property would go to her with the knowledge that she would be fair and equitable to all of his children, and that she had some knowledge of an agreement which this Court can imply was a promise to equally distribute the property upon her death.

This Court does not agree with this position of plaintiffs. Nowhere can we find any such knowledge or implication, either from the depositions or from the will itself. Amanda's signing of the final account and petition for distribution merely acknowledged that she was doing so under the authority of and in conformity with the last will and testament of Herman DeVries, and no other implication nor knowledge can be alleged to exist because of the signing. . . .

The judgment of the district court is reversed and remanded with the instruction that a new judgment be entered in conformity with this opinion.

LUX v. LUX

288 A.2d 701 (Rhode Island, 1972)

Kelleher, Justice

The artless efforts of a draftsman have precipitated this suit which seeks the construction of and instructions relating to the will of Philomena Lux who died a resident of Cumberland on August 15, 1968. We hasten to add that the will was drawn by someone other than counsel of record. . . .

Philomena Lux executed her will on May 9, 1966. She left her residuary estate to her husband, Anthony John Lux, and nominated him as executor. Anthony predeceased his wife. His death triggered the following pertinent provisions of Philomena's will:

Fourth: In the event that my said husband, Anthony John Lux, shall predecease me, then I make the following disposition of my estate:

1. . . . .

2. All the rest, residue and remainder of my estate, real and personal of whatsoever kind and nature, and wherever situated, of which I shall die seized and possessed, or over which I may have power of appointment, or to which I may be in any manner entitled at my death, I give, devise and bequeath to my grandchildren, share and share alike.

3. Any real estate included in said residue shall be maintained for the benefit of said grandchildren and shall not be sold until the youngest of said grandchildren has reached twenty-one years of age.

4. Should it become necessary to sell any of said real estate to pay my debts, costs of administration, or to make distribution of my estate or for any other lawful reason, then, in that event, it is my express desire that said real estate be sold to a member of my family.

Philomena was survived by one son, Anthony John Lux, Jr., and five grandchildren whose ages range from two to eight. All the grandchildren were children of Anthony. The youngest grandchild was born after the execution of the will but before Philomena's death. The son is named in the will as the alternate executor. He informed the trial court that he and his wife plan to have more children. At the time of the hearing, Anthony was 30. The Superior Court appointed a guardian ad litem to represent the interests of the grandchildren. It also designated an attorney to represent the rights of individuals who may have an interest under the will but who are at this time unknown, unascertained, or not in being. . . .

At the time of her death, the testatrix owned real estate valued at approximately $35,000 and tangible and intangible personal property, including bank accounts, that totaled some $7,400. The real estate, which consists of two large tenement houses, is located in Cumberland. The sole dispute is as to the nature of the devise of the real estate. Did Philomena make an absolute gift of it to the grandchildren, or did she place it in trust for their benefit? The guardian takes the view that the grandchildren hold the real estate in fee simple. All the other parties take a contrary position.

Admittedly, the language before us is unclear. Accordingly, it is the duty of this court to ascertain the testator's intent as it is expressed in the will, having in mind the circumstances surrounding its formulation, and to effectuate that intent so long as it is not contrary to law. . . .

From the record before us, we believe that Philomena intended that her real estate be held in trust for the benefit of her grandchildren. In reaching this conclusion, we must emphasize that there is no fixed formula as to when a testamentary disposition should be classified as an outright gift or a trust. The result reached depends on the circumstances of each particular case.

We are not unmindful of the formal requirements necessary for the creation of a testamentary trust. It is an elementary proposition of law that a trust is created when legal title to property is held by one person for the benefit of another. It is generally accepted that such a relationship cannot be created by will unless the beneficiaries of the trust are identifiable. . . . However, no particular words are required to create a testamentary trust. The absence of such words as

774

"trust" or "trustee" is immaterial where the requisite intent of the testator can be found. . . .

When the residuary clause in the instant case is viewed in its entirety, it is clear that Philomena did not give her grandchildren a fee simple title to the realty. It appears that she, realizing the nature of this bequest and the age of the beneficiaries, intended that someone would hold and manage the property until they were of sufficient age to do so themselves. The property is income-producing, and apparently she felt that the ultimate interest of her grandchildren would be protected if the realty were left intact until the designated time for distribution. The use of the terms "shall be maintained" and "shall not be sold" is a strong indication of Philomena's intent that the property was to be retained and managed by some person for some considerable time in the future for the benefit of her son's children. This is a duty usually associated with a trustee. We therefore hold that Philomena's will does create a trust on her real estate. . . .

Before determining the individuals who may benefit from Philomena's benevolence, it should be noted that the residuary devise to the grandchildren is a class gift which in no way violates the rule against perpetuities. The rule, in seeking to insure the free administration of property, requires that interest must vest within a life or lives in being at the time of the creation of the future interest plus 21 years thereafter, including an allowance for the period of gestation in those instances where there is a posthumous birth. The person whose life serves as the measuring rod need not be mentioned in the will, nor need he take any interest in the property. He need not be connected in any way with the property or the persons designated to take it. . . . The life in being is Philomena's son. No grandchild will be born to the testatrix once her son dies, with a possible exception of an allowance being made for the gestation period. . . .

Despite our invocation of the rule requiring the class to remain open until the corpus is distributed, we still must determine what Philomena intended when she said that the corpus has to be preserved until the "youngest grandchild" becomes 21.

There are four possible distribution dates depending on the meaning of "youngest." Distribution might be made when the youngest member of the class in being when the will was executed attains 21; or when the youngest in being when the will takes effect becomes 21; or when the youngest of all living class members in being at any one time attains 21 even though it is physically possible for others to be born; or when the youngest whenever it is born attains 21. This last alternative poses a question. Should we delay distribution here and keep the class open until the possibility that Philomena's son can become a father becomes extinct? We think not.

We are conscious of the presumption in the law that a man or a woman is capable of having children so long as life lasts. A construction suit, however, has for its ultimate goal the ascertainment of the average testator's probable intent if he was aware of the problems that lead to this type of litigation. . . .

We hold, therefore, that distribution of the trust corpus shall be made at any time when the youngest of the then living grandchildren has attained the age of 21. When this milestone is reached, there is no longer any necessity to maintain the trust to await the possible conception of additional members of the class.

Although Philomena declared that the real estate was not to be sold until the youngest grandchild became 21, her later statements about the necessity of its sale amounted to her awareness that future circumstances might require the liquidation of her real estate sometime prior to the time her youngest grandchild becomes 21. The Superior Court was informed and documentary evidence was introduced which showed such a precipitous drop in the rental income as would warrant a trustee to seek a better investment. . . .

The impending sale brings into focus the testatrix's "express *desire* that said real estate be sold to a member of my family" (emphasis added). The words "express desire" are purely precatory. We have said that precatory language will be construed as words of command only if it is clear that the testator intended to impose on the individual concerned a legal obligation to make the desired disposition. . . . We think it clear that since Philomena's primary goal was to benefit her grandchildren, we see nothing in the record that would justify a conclusion that she intended that the potential purchasers of her real estate be limited to the members of her family.

PROBLEMS FOR DISCUSSION

1. Hermoine Rance had six grandchildren—Irwin, Merwin, Jennie, Jasper, Torwald, and Rosco. Just before taking an airplane trip, she purchased $50,000 worth of life insurance from a machine at the airport. She filled out the policy, naming Irwin and Merwin as beneficiaries but telling her daughter, who was with her, "There's not enough room for all the kids' names, but if anything happens to me, make sure this gets divided among all of them." She then gave her daughter the insurance policy. Hermoine died when her flight crashed, and the insurance company wants to know who should be paid the $50,000. Irwin and Merwin claim it's theirs, since that's what the policy says. The other children claim Hermoine made Irwin and Merwin trustees for the benefit of all the children. Who's right, and why?

2. Floyd Montfort conveyed certain real estate to Alicia Able, as trustee for the Anytown chapter of the Mission Church, for 10 years. At the end of 10 years, the land would be conveyed outright to the Anytown chapter if it were still in existence, provided that if the national Mission Church built a building on the land within the 10-year period, the land would be conveyed to it. If the Anytown chapter ceased to exist and the national Mission Church had not built on the land, Mabel Montfort would receive the land at the end of 10 years. In 1955, when the 10 years were up, no conveyance was made to anyone. All the members of the Anytown chapter had been suspended for failure to pay required tithes, and the chapter had no listed assets. There were no records of any meetings after that date, but the Anytown chapter was never officially dissolved. The land was rented out, and Alicia put the rents in a bank account titled "A. Able, trustee for Anytown Chapter, Mission Church." In 1975 Alicia turned the land and the rents over to the National Mission Church, which sold the land to Herman Stinglee. Mabel learned what happened, and she now demands the land and accounting for the rents. Does she have a case? Why or why not?

3. Yancey Yoman and his wife, Gertrude, entered into a written contract which provided that the survivor would devise and bequeath one half of their property to the heirs at law of the other. Gertrude died in 1971. The couple had been married for 26 years; they had no children, but Gertrude had two sisters and a brother who survived her. Yancey married Krystal in 1973. At various times during their marriage, Yancey conveyed property to himself and Krystal as joint tenants. Yancey died in 1980. Gertrude's heirs have asked the court to impose a constructive trust on the jointly owned property, which Krystal now owns and for which she paid nothing. Krystal claims that she is in effect a bona fide purchaser of these assets, since when Yancey proposed, he had given her a list of them and said: "I am asking you to marry me. This is what I have to offer. If it is not enough, I will understand." Should the original written contract with Gertrude be enforced against Krystal? Why or why not?

4. Leon Lucullus opened a bank account at the Zoomer National Bank, naming himself as "Trustee" for the benefit of his daughter Lucille. When Leon died several years later, the account contained over $20,000. Lucille claims that she now owns the money in the account. The administrator of Leon's estate says that the attempted trust was invalid, since Leon kept control of the account himself, and that it was

really an attempt by Leon to make a will without complying with the necessary formalities. Who's right, and why?

5. Dulcea Donizetti, as the guardian of her minor son Sancho, was paid $70,000 in settlement of a tort claim which the son had against a third party. She used the money to buy a large tract of land, on which she established a trailer park. All of her other six children helped out in running the trailer park, some more than others. Chico, the only child who did not marry, stayed at the trailer park and managed it full time. Dulcea was characterized as having "Old World ways," "at the very least an autocrat, and at worst a conspiratorial, manipulating dictator." She assured Sancho that he owned the property, and he never checked. At one time, she told Chico that he would own 80 percent of the business. Her will left three fourths of the business to Chico and one fourth to her favorite daughter, Sanctity. Sancho and the other children challenge the will. Do they have a valid claim? Explain.

6. Hilda Sergan left the residue of her estate, some $250,000, in trust in two equal shares to the Crimson Cross Charity Home and "to Vishray University, located at Denizen, Virginia, for its medical school." At the time of Hilda's death, Vishray had a medical college, as a department of the university. Two years later, however, in order to qualify for state support, the medical college severed its formal ties with the university and incorporated separately. Joint medical programs were still conducted, and the College was still located in the same building on the university campus, which was now leased to it. The Crimson Cross Charity Home now contends that since the university no longer has a medical school, it should receive the total trust income under a clause in Hilda's will which provided that this be done if either or the named legatees were "unable to accept the legacy." How should the court construe this trust provision? Discuss.

7. The Bonanza Oil Trust holds several thousand acres of Texas oil lands, which are leased to oil companies under long-term leases. After paying expenses, the trustees distribute the royalties earned to some 1,800 holders of trust certificates. Harvey Hustle, grandson of Ben Bonanza, holds the reversionary interest in the land. The trust was originally created to last for the life of the last of 10 named persons, plus 20 years. All 10 of these persons are deceased, and the 20 years are almost up. On termination, the trustees are instructed to turn over all cash on hand to the certificate holders and any remaining assets to Harvey. The certificate holders now seek to compel the trustees to pump out and sell all of the oil prior to termination of the trust or to convert all trust assets to cash so that a fair distribution can occur on termination. Harvey says that the trustees can only arrange for "orderly" drilling and pumping and that they must maintain the existing assets. Who's right, and why?

8. Rembrandt Dauber's will created a testamentary trust, naming his nephews Ruben Dauber and Van Gogh Dauber as trustees for his controlling block of stock in Aroostok Airlines, Inc. In addition to Ruben and Van, beneficiaries of the trust included Rembrandt's wife, Zelda, and his son, Parsifal. Ruben and Van were the president and secretary of Aroostok. Aroostok's board voted to give them a large cash bonus, which they used to purchase share of Aroostok. As a result of these purchases, the trust lost control of Aroostok. Zelda and Parsifal bring suit, alleging breach of fiduciary duties. What result, and why?

Part X
Business Associations

38 | Organization Forms

There are various forms of business organizations, ranging from one-person proprietorships to such corporate giants as General Motors, AT&T, and U.S. Steel. In this chapter we will look at various forms of business organizations and discuss the pros and cons of each form.

Basic Considerations When Selecting a Form of Business Organization

When you are making plans to set up a new business, there are several factors which you should consider before you decide on a specific form of business organization. These factors are:

1. *Creation of the business organization.* What procedure must you follow in order to create a specific form of business organization? In some cases a statutory procedure must be followed; in other cases a very simple procedure not requiring any governmental review or action may be followed. Also, cost is a factor.

2. *Duration.* Should this business be perpetual, or should it have a specific lifetime in years, or should it dissolve when any of the parties involved dies?

3. *Limitation of liability.* Are you concerned about limiting your liability to third persons? If so, different forms of business organizations have different legal ramifications with regard to your legal liability to others.

4. *Transferability of interest in the organization.* Are you concerned about the ease of transferring or selling interests in the business organization, or are you content to have limited transferability?

5. *Management and control.* How is the organization to be managed? Is it to be managed by a board of directors, or is it to be managed equally by all of the interested parties?

6. *Taxation.* What are the tax benefits of the various forms of business organization?

7. *Litigation by or against the Organization.* Is the organization a legal entity that can sue in its own name, or must any of its suits be brought in the names of the individuals who own the organization? Also, if suit is brought against the

organization, are its individual owners to be joined both as individuals and as members of the organization?

These factors should be weighed when you review any form of business organization whose use you are considering.

We will now try to review briefly the various forms of business organizations. The most commonly used business organizations are the individual proprietorship, the general partnership, the limited partnerships, and the corporation. This chapter will simply define these organizations. Partnerships and corporations will be more specifically treated in later chapters.

The Sole Proprietorship

The sole or individual proprietorship is perhaps the oldest and the simplest form of business organization. Some typical examples of the sole proprietorship are the small-town barbershop, the local hardware store, the shoe repair shop, and other small businesses where the owner is also the active operator of the business. The creation of a sole proprietorship is a relatively simple matter. If you want to start a sole proprietorship, you simply commence doing business. You do not have to get permission from the national, state, or local authorities, and you do not have to pay any fees for the right to commence business. If you are a barber, you would, of course, have to get a barber's license to practice your trade. This would be true whether you were the owner of the business or a barber working for someone, since that is simply a requirement of the trade. If you sell a product and your state has a sales tax, you will have to secure a state sales tax account. If you hire others to work for you, you will have to file appropriate forms with the Internal Revenue Service and the state revenue service. These are inescapable requirements, regardless of the form of the organization.

With regard to duration, a sole proprietorship lives and dies with the owner. If the owner dies, then the business ceases to exist.

The owner of a sole proprietorship is liable for his or her acts of negligence and for the acts of negligence of the employees, if any. He or she is also individually liable for the contracts of the business and for other business liabilities. The liabilities extend not only to the assets of the business but also to the owner's personal assets. Thus the owner is personally liable for all of the debts, losses, and valid claims against the business. This is a very important concern, especially where the business has a high potential for liability losses. Many sole proprietors have transferred their personal assets, such as their house, savings, and personal car to their spouse or some other relative, hoping thereby to prevent persons who claim against the business from getting such assets. A problem here is that the owner must prove that the transfer was not a fraudulent transfer but a valid transfer. Moreover, if the owner and the spouse get divorced, the owner has no claim to the property which was transferred over to the spouse. Thus, transferring property to another in order to avoid claims from the business can be a dangerous procedure.

The management and control of a sole proprietorship are very simple. The owner controls. The owner has the right to decide what products will be manufactured, when, where, how, and at what cost. Although the name of the organization may be Ajax Company, if you were to sue Ajax Company, you would have to sue the sole proprietor, namely, John Doe doing business as Ajax Company and John Doe individually. Also, if Ajax Company wanted to sue someone to collect a debt, John Doe doing business as Ajax Company would have to sue since Ajax Company itself is not a legal entity with power to sue and be sued.

The Partnership

When we speak of a partnership we normally think of a general partnership, which is the most common form of partnership. There is, however, a second form of partnership, called a limited partnership, which will be defined and discussed in the following section.

A general partnership may be defined as an association of two or more persons to carry on a business for profit as co-owners. This is the definition of a partnership as stated in the Uniform Partnership Act. A partnership requires no special statutory filings or governmental approval. It is simply created by an agreement between the parties. This agreement can be oral, or it can be a very specific signed written document. Many of the large accounting firms as well as law firms are partnerships. No specific cost is associated with the creation of a partnership other than the cost of drawing up an agreement if an agreement is desired.

With regard to duration, the partnership, like the sole proprietorship, has a life span no longer than the life of any one of the partners or such time as one of the partners decides to sell his or her share.

With regard to liability for the firm's debts, in the partnership, as in the sole proprietorship, there is unlimited liability. Each partner may be individually liable for any debt of the business or any liability caused by the negligence of any partner or any employee of the partnership. Each partner is the agent of all the other partners.

Transferability of interest is also a problem for the partnership since the interest of each partner is not transferable without the consent of all the other partners. Management and control pose yet another problem, because each partner is entitled to an equal voice in the management and control of the partnership, regardless of his or her share of ownership.

With regard to litigation by and against the partnership, we again have nearly the same situation as exists in the sole proprietorship, namely, that individual partners will be named and must join in any lawsuit.

With regard to U.S. income taxation, the partnership pays no tax as a business organization. All of the profits must be distributed to the partners in accordance with the partnership agreement, and the partners in turn add that income to their personal income. Thus there is no double taxation of the profits.

The Limited Partnership

A limited partnership is more like a corporation than a general partnership because its existence is authorized by statute and it can only be formed by following a statutory procedure and by filing the required documents with the state where the application is being made. In a limited partnership the liability of one or more of the partners, but not all of them, is limited to the investment contributed by those partners when the limited partnership is created. A limited partnership may be formed by two or more persons, at least one of whom is a general partner and at least one of whom is a limited partner. Many states required limited partnerships to add the word *limited* to the company name, just as the abbreviation "Inc." for *incorporated* is added to the name of a corporation.

The Corporation

The sole proprietorship and the partnership are not, in effect, legal entities. The corporation, on the other hand, is, a legal entity; it is a legal person created by the state. It is created by the filing of articles of incorporation by one or more incorporators in accordance with the statutory provisions of the state in which incorporation is sought. Before the business of a corporation may commence, a fee must be paid to the secretary of state of that state, the state must approve the articles of incorporation, and, in some states, the incorporator or incorporators must pledge that a minimum amount of capital will be deposited in the corporation's name. Thus the corporation requires not only filing costs but also the legal costs of drawing up the documents needed to conform to the specific statutory rules regarding incorporation and perhaps also a minimum paid-in capital.

With regard to duration, the corporation may be perpetual, that is, it will live on beyond the death of any of its shareholders.

The corporation provides limited liability for its shareholders. A shareholder is not liable for more than the amount of the shares he or she has purchased, unless, of course, there is some specific agreement to the contrary.

Management and control of the corporation are vested in a board of directors. Shareholders may elect a specific number of directors who have the authority to operate and manage the corporation. Shareholders elect directors for specified terms and have the right to oust them, to demand an accounting from them, or perhaps to bring an action against them for negligent mishandling of the corporate funds.

A corporation may sue or be sued in the corporate name. Even where a single individual owns all of a corporation's stock, that shareholder need not be a party to an action by or against the corporation.

For many years the corporation was not a popular choice of business organization for smaller companies because it had to pay a tax on its net profits and then, when the corporation distributed its profits to its shareholders, the shareholders had to declare their stock dividends in their own income tax reports and to pay tax on the dividends. Thus there was the burden of double taxation, and even though the corporate structure offered limited liability, ease of transferability of interest, and other advantages not offered by the sole proprietorship or the partnership, it was still not feasible for some persons to incorporate. The Internal Revenue Service, however, has remedied this problem by adding a corporate classification called the subchapter S corporation. If your corporation is a small business and it qualifies under the requirements for the subchapter S corporation, the corporation pays no tax whatsoever. However, all of the profits must be distributed annually to the shareholders and the shareholders must declare the profits on their individual tax forms in much the same way as they would if the organization were a partnership. In other words, the subchapter S corporation has all the benefits of a standard corporation, but from a tax standpoint it is treated like a partnership. The subchapter S corporation is created in the same way as any other corporation. Its only difference from other corporations is that it must declare itself to be a subchapter S corporation when it makes a filing for tax purposes.

The Joint Stock Company

The joint stock company is a form of business organization in which the management of the business is placed in the hands of trustees or directors. Shares represented by certificates are then issued to the members of the company, who are, in effect, joint owners of the enterprise. These certificate holders then proceed to elect the board of directors or the board of trustees. Like the shares of a corporation, the shares or certificates are transferable, and their transfer does not cause dissolution, as it would in a partnership. Also, the death of a shareholder does not dissolve the organization, as would be the case for a partnership. The joint stock company exists for the period of time stated in the bylaws. In realty, the joint stock company is a partnership; however, it has many of the advantages of the corporation. Its principle disadvantage is that there is still unlimited personal liability, as in a partnership. Depending on the state statute, the joint stock company may or may not be considered a legal entity for purposes of litigation.

One may wonder why the law recognizes a business organization such as the joint stock company. The joint stock company is a compromise between the partnership and the corporation. It has the partnership's tax advantages since it pays no separate corporation tax, and it has the corporation's advantages of transferability and duration, but it also has the partnership's disadvantage of unlimited liability. At one time, the joint stock company was a popular form of business organization. However, with the advent of the subchapter S corporation, it no longer has great appeal.

The Business Trust

The business trust, or the Massachusetts trust, as it is often called, is a business organization where title to certain property is deeded over to a trustee or a board of trustees who manage and operate the business for the benefit of those parties who contributed property in the form of money or other assets to the trust. The people who contributed money or other assets to the trust are called beneficiaries. They no longer have any legal title to the trust corpus; however, they do have an equitable or beneficial interest in the trust. They are given trust certificates as evidence of their interest in the trust. As beneficiaries of the trust, the certificate holders will receive the profits from the operation and investment of the trust properties. However, the key factor is that the certificate holders do not have any right to control the enterprise. If, in fact, they do have a right to control the actions of the trustees, the courts will normally hold that the trust is a partnership and not a trust.

The main purpose of the business trust is to ensure limited liability to the beneficiaries and yet avoid some of the statutory regulations and reporting procedures of a corporation.

This form of business organization, like the joint stock company, is not used extensively today.

The Cooperative Association

One often hears of farm co-ops or student co-ops. A cooperative association is a union of individuals formed for the purpose of operating an enterprise which is intended to make profits or merely to provide benefits for its members. If it is a profit-making business, the legal rules governing it will be very similar to those that govern a partnership or a joint venture.

If a cooperative is nonprofit and unincorporated, the legal rules governing it are quite different, particularly those relating to the personal liability of the associates. Personal liability for the contract and tort debts of the organization is not automatically assumed on the basis of membership in a nonprofit cooperative. The liability of individual members must be based on proof of an agency relationship; that is, the member whom it is sought to hold personally liable must be shown to have authorized the liability-producing act.

CASES FOR DISCUSSION

LYONS v. AMERICAN LEGION POST NO. 650 REALTY CO.

175 N.E.2d 733 (Ohio, 1961)

Zimmerman, Judge

In the absence of an enabling statute, a voluntary association cannot be sued by its association name. It has no legal existence, and the persons composing it must be joined individually. . . .

[E]ffective on September 30, 1955, the General Assembly enacted legislation which is now Sections 1745.01 through 1745.04, Revised Code. Section 1745.01 provides:

Any unincorporated association may contract or sue in behalf of those who are members and, in its own behalf, be sued as an entity under the name by which it is commonly known and called. . . .

Is it the purpose and intent of the statutes quoted and referred to above to limit actions solely against unincorporated associations as entities in the names they commonly use, as determined by the two lower courts herein, or may the individual members of such associations still be sued as under the former practice? We think the new statutes are no more than cumulative and do not abrogate the right to sue the members of the associations if the suitor chooses to proceed in that way. It is to be noted that Section 1745.01, Revised Code, uses the permissive word, "may," and that, under Section 1745.02, Revised Code, when a suitor does take advantage of the enabling statutes by suing an unincorporated association by the name it uses, the collection of any judgment obtained against such association must be satisfied out of its property alone and the property of its members is immune from seizure. Surely, had the General Assembly intended to

785

eliminate actions against the individuals composing an unincorporated association, it would have so expressed itself. . . .

However, a recognized difference exists between an unincorporated association organized for the transaction of business and one organized for fraternal or social purposes. . . .

In the case of a voluntary association formed for the purpose of engaging in business and making profits, its members are liable, as partners, to third persons upon contracts which are within its scope and are entered into with actual or apparent authority, and a joint judgment against them is justified. . . . But when, as here, the purpose of the association is not business or profit, the liability, if any, of its members is not in its nature that of partners but that arising out of the relation of principal and agent, and only those members who authorize or subsequently ratify an obligation are liable on account of it.

The same principle is recognized in relation to torts. . . .

In the instant case the petition alleges that the defendants, American Legion Post No. 650 Realty Co., Inc., and the individual members of American Legion Post No. 650 "jointly and severally, conducted or caused to be conducted within said building a social affair known as a fish fry for which they charged each person attending the sum of one dollar ($1.00)," and that "defendants, and each of them, were negligent in failing to provide a safe heating system in the building; in equipping and maintaining the building with a defective heating system; in failing to adequately inspect said heating system; in failing to provide proper ventilation in the building; and in failing to warn invitees in the building, including decedent, of the presence of carbon monoxide fumes therein."

Such petition probably states causes of action good as against demurrer so that defendants should plead to conserve their interests, but on the trial of the action to establish liability on the part of individual defendants evidence would have to be produced linking them as active participants in the affair resulting in plaintiff's decedent's alleged injuries, and, furthermore, that they knew or in the exercise of ordinary care

786

should have known of the defective condition of the instrumentality claimed to have caused the injury. And, of course, the other elements necessary to support recovery would have to be proved.

The judgment of the Court of Appeals is reversed, and the cause is remanded to the trial court for further proceedings.

DARLING v. BUDDY

1 S.W.2d 163 (Missouri, 1927)

Lindsay, C.

This is a suit in equity, based upon the provisions of an agreement designated as a "syndicate agreement," to which plaintiffs and defendants and some other persons were parties. The purpose is to have an accounting, and to require contribution by defendants to plaintiffs on account of payment by plaintiffs of two judgments obtained against plaintiffs for an indebtedness contracted by the syndicate managers. . . .

The plaintiffs in their petition alleged that by the agreement the parties "united in a joint adventure," and pleaded the terms of the agreement; alleged that the syndicate managers were empowered to borrow money for the operation of the railroad mentioned, and for such purpose did borrow $20,000 from the Hershey State Bank of Muscatine, Iowa, for which two notes of $10,000 each were given to the said bank. It alleges the nonpayment of the notes, the insolvency of the syndicate, the bringing of the suits in Iowa, in each of which some of the plaintiffs were made defendants, the obtaining of judgments by the bank, and the payment of those judgments by the plaintiffs.

The petition alleges that all of the subscribers to the syndicate agreement, by reason thereof, "became and were partners and cosureties for the Muscatine North & South Syndicate, and became jointly and severally liable for the pecuniary obligations of the syndicate."

The real controversy, the one emphasized by counsel, is whether the agreement created a common-law trust. The agreement does not contain the word "trust" or "trustees," but the fact that these specific words are not used does not of itself determine the question whether the agreement created a trust and is a declaration of trust. The intention of the parties is to be ascertained from the whole of the contract, from the actual relations it created, and not from the fact that the parties use the words "syndicate" or "syndicate managers" and do not in express words denominate the instrument a trust agreement and that the parties occupying the actual relation of trustees are called syndicate managers. "No special form of words is necessary to create an express trust. In a word, then, an express trust is one which defines and limits the uses and purposes to which certain property shall be devoted and defines the duties of the trustee as to its control, management and disposition." . . .

Under the terms of this agreement the title to the entire capital stock of the railway company was in the five persons designated as "syndicate managers," and to them was paid and in them was also vested title to the moneys paid by the several subscribers. Under this agreement, after such payment, the syndicate managers, holding title to all of the property, were authorized to use it according to their own judgment and discretion for the general purpose outlined in the agreement, and the subscribers had no control either of the property or over the syndicate managers. The syndicate managers were to select their own successors. The subscribers had no power to fill any vacancy, or to remove any manager, or to direct or control the syndicate managers in any way. There was no association provided for between the subscribers, nor provision for any meeting of them to be held for any purpose, nor any power to amend the terms of the agreement. They had no voice in determining how long the syndicate should continue. The syndicate managers alone had the power to terminate the contract at any time prior to August 12, 1911, and they alone had the power to continue it as long thereafter as they deemed necessary. The effect of this agreement was that the syndicate managers by title and complete control were the masters of the property, and the subscribers had nothing other than an interest or right, measured by the amount of these several advancements, to share in the profits, if any, or in the property remaining, if any, upon the closing of the enterprise by the managers. . . .

When all the provisions of the agreement are considered, it must be held that the agreement does not create either a partnership or the relation of principal and agent. When it is seen, as here, that the title, possession, and the management of the property is given to the syndicate managers to hold and to manage free from the control of the subscribers who have a beneficial interest therein, the persons so having the title, possession, and control, become the masters by whatever name they be designated. A trustee is a principal and not an agent in his management and control of the property committed to him. . . .

That the agreement created a common-law trust and that the subscribers or members were not liable for the payment of a debt created by the managers is sustained by the greater weight of authority. . . . By these authorities also it is ruled that the true test to determine whether the syndicate or organization formed by the agreement was a trust or a partnership is one of control by the managers or trustees, and not merely of investment by the subscribers. . . .

In the instant case the managers were subscribers, but we can see no reason under the circumstances here existing why each did not occupy the dual relation as beneficiary to the extent of his individual subscription and trustee as to all others. The beneficial interest of a manager to share in the profits as a subscriber to the fund was not commensurate with his interest as a trustee. . . . "Shareholders, as such, are not incapacitated from being trustee for themselves and others; they may be appointed as trustees without affecting the validity of the trust." Dunn, *Business Trusts*, p. 167.

In this action the defendants are not bound by the judgment of the Iowa court against the plaintiffs. . . .

Under the conclusions heretofore stated, the judgment is affirmed.

PEOPLE EX REL. NATIONAL EXPRESS CO. v. COLEMAN

31 N.E. 96 (New York, 1892)

Finch, J.

The relator was taxed upon its capital, on the ground that it had become a corporation within the meaning of the provision of the Revised Statutes which enacts that "all moneyed or stock corporations deriving an income or profit from their capital, or otherwise, shall be liable to taxation on their capital in the manner hereinafter prescribed." . . . The company was formed as a joint-stock company or association, in 1853, by a written agreement of eight individuals with each other, the whole force and effect of which, in constituting and creating the organization, rested upon the common-law rights of the individuals, and their power to contract with each other. The relation they assumed was wholly the product of their mutual agreement, and dependent in no respect upon the grant or authority of the state. It was entered into under no statutory license or permission, neither accepting nor designed to accept any franchise from the sovereign, but founded wholly upon the individual rights of the associates to join their capital and enterprise in a relation similar to that of a partnership. A few years earlier the legislature had explicitly recognized the existence and validity of such organizations, founded upon contract, and evolved from the common-law rights of the citizens. Laws 1849, c. 258. That act provided that any joint-stock company or association which consisted of seven or more members might sue or be sued in the name of its president or treasurer, and with the same force and effect, so far as the joint property and rights were concerned, as if the suit should be prosecuted in the names of the associates; but the act explicitly disclaimed any purpose of converting the joint-stock associations recognized as existing into corporations by a section prohibiting any such construction. Section 5. In 1851 the act was amended in its form and application, but in no respect material to the present inquiry. There is no doubt, therefore, that, when the company was formed and went into operation, the law recognized a distinction and substantial difference between joint-stock companies and corporations, and never confused one with the other; and that the existing statute which taxed the capital of corporations had no reference to or operation upon joint-stock companies or associations. But two things have since occurred. The legislature, while steadily preserving the distinction of names, has, with equal persistence, confused the things, by obliterating substantial and characteristic marks of difference; until it is now claimed that the joint-stock associations have grown into and become corporations by force of the continued bestowal upon them of corporate attributes. It is said, and very probably correctly said, that the legislature may create a corporation without explicitly declaring it to be such, by the bestowal of a corporate franchise or corporate attributes, and the cases of banking associations are referred to as instances of actual occurrence. . . . It is added that such result may happen even without the legislative intent, and because the gift of corporate powers and attributes is tantamount to a corporate creation. It is then asserted that a series of statutes, beginning with the act of 1849, has ended in the gift to joint-stock associations of every essential attribute possessed by and characteristic of corporations, . . . Laws 1853; that the lines of distinction between the two, however far apart in the beginning, have steadily converged, until they have melted into each other and become identical; that every distinguishing mark and characteristic has been obliterated; and no reason remains why joint-stock associations should not be, in all respects, treated and regarded as corporations. Some of this contention is true. . . . And yet the truth remains that all along the line of legislation the distinctive names have been retained as indicative and representative of a difference in the organizations themselves. As recently as the acts of 1880 and 1881, which formed the subject of consideration in the *Wemple* Case, the legislature, dealing with the subject of taxation, and desiring to tax business and franchises, imposed the liability upon "every corporation, joint-stock company, or association whatever, now or hereafter incorporated or organized under any law of this state." It is significant that the words "or organized" were inserted by amendment, and evidently for the understood reason that joint-stock companies could not properly be said to be "incorporated," but might be correctly described as "organized" under the laws of the state. This present distinction in the language of the statutes I should not be inclined to disregard or treat as of no practical consequence, when seeking to arrive at the true intent and proper construction of the statute, even if I were unable to discover any practical or substantial difference between the two classes of organizations upon which it could rest or out of which it grew; for the distinction so sedulously and persistently observed would strongly indicate the legislative intent, and so the correct construction.

But I think there was an original and inherent difference between the corporate and joint-stock companies, known to our law, which legislation has somewhat obscured, but has not destroyed, and that the difference is the one pointed out by the learned counsel for the respondent, and which impresses me as logical, and well supported by authority. It is that the creation of the corporation merges in the artificial body and drowns in it the individual rights and liabilities of the members, while the organization of a joint-stock company leaves the individual rights and liabilities unimpaired and in full force. . . . These last and quite recent enactments show that the legislative intent is still to preserve and not destroy the original difference between the two classes of organizations; to maintain in full force the common-law liability of associates, and not to substitute for it that of corporators; and, preserving in continued operation that normal and distinctive difference, to evince a plain purpose not to merge the two organizations into one, or destroy the boundaries which separate them. . . . The two are alike, but not the same. More or less they crowd upon and overlap each other, but without losing their identity; and so, while we cannot say that the joint-stock company is a corporation, we can say . . . that a joint-stock company is a partnership, with some of the powers of a corporation. Beyond that we do not think it is our duty to go. The order should be affirmed, with costs.

PROBLEMS FOR DISCUSSION

In each of the following situations, indicate what the two most likely organizational forms would be for the proposed business. What would be the two most important factors in making the final decision as to how to organize each proposed business?

1. Sam Suem, Polly Practical, and Percival Prim are three recent law school graduates who want to start their own law firm. Sam can get a loan from his uncle for $5,000 to help the start-up costs, and Polly and Percival think that they could each raise about $3,000.

2. Wilf Wizard has been repairing small electrical appliances as a kind of hobby. He now wants to open an electrical repair shop, since there don't seem to be any in the town. He already has a considerable amount of equipment. For some initial working capital, he could borrow $7,000 against his life insurance. Wilf is not very adept at math, or at bookkeeping.

3. Speed Summers wants to organize a professional auto racing team. He has $10,000 in savings and life insurance and could raise another $30,000 with a second mortgage on his house. He needs a minimum of $250,000 initial working capital; $500,000 would be much better. Speed would drive the racing car himself but would need to have a pit crew to service the car during races. His friend Roosevelt, who is an excellent mechanic, has expressed some interest in getting involved in this venture, possibly as chief mechanic.

4. Freda Fritter and Gus Gastronome are interested in starting a restaurant which would also feature a catering service. The restaurant itself would concentrate on the lengthy-lunch customers and would be open on only a limited basis for dinners. The catering aspect of the business would be heavily promoted. Freda and Gus both have extensive restaurant experience, but they need to raise $50,000 more than they have to invest in the business.

5. Biff Bosox wants to open a shoe store. He has been in the business for nearly 20 years, and now he wants to be his own boss. He can invest $20,000 personally but needs at least another $40,000–$50,000 to start up the store.

6. Hans Wunderkind, who has worked as an automotive designer and production vice president, thinks that the world is ready for the ultimate sports car. Hans wants to organize a new car manufacturing company. He'll need at least $50 million to get going. Hans is well respected in the industry and is a smooth talker, so he may be able to borrow some of the capital he needs.

7. Henrietta Hausfrau is interested in starting a used book exchange, where customers could buy, sell, or trade used books. Because of her other commitments, she would only be able to work part time in the store herself, but she could do all of the accounting work at home. She already has a considerable number of old books, and several of her friends have told her that they would be willing to put their books in her store on consignment. Henrietta thinks she could get started for $5,000, perhaps less.

8. Annie Anxious wants to organize a preschool for children from three to five years old. She plans to use her own home, at least initially, for the business. Annie has a large older home and a large fenced yard. She has raised four children of her own, and she loves kids. She thinks she can get a state license and local zoning approval. Other than some new games, books, and toys, the capital requirements appear to be minimal.

Partnerships—Nature, Creation, and Termination **39**

HISTORICAL BACKGROUND

The partnership is perhaps the oldest and most common form of business organization involving more than one person. We have evidence that the partnership form of organization dates as far back as the Middle Ages and perhaps even before that. Traditionally the partnership was a nonstatutory form of business organization, whose creation was comparatively simple, inexpensive, and informal.

The body of law governing the partnership business organization was developed on a case-by-case basis throughout the court system over the years. Whenever law is developed by the case method, there are bound to be variations in decisions by judges, a lack of uniformity from state to state, and a lack of real clarity as to what the law is on a particular point. Thus the National Conference of Commissioners on Uniform State Laws, which was referred to in an earlier chapter, drafted the Uniform Partnership Act (UPA) in 1914. The purpose of this act was to clarify and codify the maze of court decisions on partnership law into a workable statutory form. The great majority of the states have adopted the Uniform Partnership Act. Thus references will be made to the Uniform Partnership Act throughout the chapters on partnership law.

DEFINITION OF A PARTNERSHIP

Part II, Section 4 of the UPA defines a partnership as follows: "a partnership is an association of two or more persons to carry on as co-owners a business for profit." This definition contains several requirements which must be met before there can be a partnership. First, the partnership must be an association of two or more persons. The word *association* implies that an agreement has been made. Thus we are talking about contract law with regard to whether or not a legal agreement exists. Second, the association must consist of two or more persons. A person can be a natural person or a legal entity such as a corpora-

791

tion. Third, persons must carry on a business as co-owners. Thus a partnership is not simply two or more people working together; it must be two or more people, each of whom has some rights of ownership in the business. It is not required that all of these people have equal rights of ownership; however, each must be a co-owner. Finally, the business must be for profit. This rules out the many organizations which have been established for religious, charitable, educational, and other not-for-profit purposes.

Hartford Accident and Indemnity Company v. *Huddleston*
514 S.W.2d 676 (Kentucky, 1974)

FACTS Lavada Huddleston, administratrix of the estate of Carl Edward Huddleston, sued to collect under the uninsured motorist coverage on a policy which the defendant, Hartford, had issued to City Motor Sales. City was a garage business formed by Clifford Huddleston and Orville Prewitt. Carl was Clifford's son. The uninsured motorist section of the policy read in part: "II. PERSONS INSURED. Each of the following is an insured under this insurance to the extent set forth below: (a) the named insured and any designated insured and, while residents of the same household, the spouse and relatives of either. . . ." Carl was killed as the result of the negligence of an uninsured motorist while riding in a vehicle which was unrelated to the firm's business. Hartford appealed from a judgment for the estate.

ISSUE Was the child of a partner covered under the firm's auto policy?

DECISION Yes. Judgment affirmed.

REASONS Justice Reed first reviewed the facts and the policy language. He then got to the key question of whether Carl was "an insured" under the policy.

"Hartford's policy declarations page lists 'City Motor Sales,' a partnership, as the 'named insured,' the 'designated insured.' Although not expressed directly, the basic premise of Hartford's contention concerning the identity of the insured raises a problem as old as the law of partnerships. There has always been considerable dispute as to whether a partnership is a legal entity or merely an aggregate of persons acting together. Vague expressions in our earlier cases are not helpful. . . . Kentucky adopted the Uniform Partnership Act in 1954. . . . The adoption of the Act did not resolve the question as to the true nature of a partnership.

"We are persuaded the better view is that although the Uniform Partnership Act regards the partnership as a legal entity for many purposes, these purposes are, nevertheless, limited and the 'entity' concept does not possess such attributes of public policy that it must be invoked to achieve an unjust result. . . . The insurance contract with which we are here concerned plainly contracts for the 'aggregate' concept to be applied.

"A legal entity has no 'spouse' nor 'relatives' nor 'household.' A legal entity could not sustain 'bodily injury.' The uninsured-motorist insurance contract plainly embraced the partners and their spouses and relatives living in the same household. The insurer framed the language of the contractual undertaking. The trial judge correctly imposed liability upon Hartford under its contract and the undisputed facts."

It is interesting to note that for tax purposes the Internal Revenue Code, Section 761(a) defines a partnership as "a syndicate, group, pool, joint venture, or other unincorporated organization through . . . which any business . . . is carried on, and which is not . . . a corporation or a trust or estate." The IRS is not concerned about the rights and duties between partners or between partners and third persons; it is only trying to classify business organizations for taxing purposes.

A joint venture is similar to a partnership in that it also involves two or more persons who are engaged in some business activity. Joint ventures differ from partnerships mainly in purpose and duration. A partnership is created to carry on a business for profit for an indefinite period of time and is dissolved by the death or resignation of one of the partners. A joint venture, on the other hand, is created to conduct a specific business activity over a specific period of time. An example of a joint venture would be a situation where two persons purchased an apartment house as an investment for resale and hired a manager to run it until it was sold. The purpose of this venture is specific, and the duration is limited. No general agency is created between the parties; they are simply joint investors.

A syndicate, like a partnership, involves two or more persons who are involved in some business activity. However, a syndicate differs from a partnership in that, like a joint venture, it is formed for a specific business activity and a specific duration. The parties involved in a syndicate can be classified as investors rather than as persons carrying on a business as co-owners. A syndicate was defined in the case of *Hambleton* v. *Rhind*, 84 Md. 456, as "[A]n association of individuals, formed for the purpose of conducting and carrying out some particular business transaction, ordinarily of a financial character in which the members are mutually interested."

The terms *group* and *pool* as used in Section 761(a) are really just Internal Revenue Code language which is used to describe a group of people who are participating in a business activity or a situation where people pool their money to conduct a business for profit.

Rehnberg v. *Minnesota Homes, Inc.*
52 N.W.2d 454 (Minnesota, 1952)

FACTS   Arthur Rehnberg filed an action for an accounting and for breach of an alleged joint venture contract. He also caused a notice of a pending litigation to be filed with the register of deeds, against real property owned by the defendant corporation. The trial court ordered the cancellation of the notice of litigation, and Rehnberg appealed. Rehnberg's complaint alleged that he first conceived of the idea of developing a particular tract of land and building homes on it, that he interested Gilbert C. Hamm and others in the project, that pursuant to his efforts the defendant corporation was formed, and that it entered into contract with Hamm and him. The contract called for the corporation to take title to the land, for Hamm to build the houses for a building fee of $500 each plus 25 percent of the net profit to the corporation from the sale of the houses, and for Rehnberg to sell the houses for a fee of $150 per house plus 25 percent of the corporations' net profit. Rehnberg had received nothing for the sale of the first 26 homes he sold, and Hamm and the corporation were now building 46 more, which they had listed with another sales agent.

ISSUE   Has the plaintiff sufficiently alleged the existence of a joint venture?

DECISION   No. Judgment affirmed (dismissing the litigation).

REASONS   Justice Matson first dealt with the technical point of whether the plaintiff could file a notice against the corporation's real estate. He decided that this would be permissible if a joint venture existed since the plaintiff would be alleging a kind of equitable line against the land, in his favor. Thus the real question was whether a joint venture existed.

"Generally speaking, a joint adventure is created—assuming that a corporation has not been organized and the circumstances do not establish a technical partnership—where two or more persons combine their money, property, time, or skill in a particular business enterprise and agree to share jointly, or in proportion to their respective contributions, in the resulting profits and usually in the losses. In a qualified sense, a joint adventure is a limited partnership, *not limited in a statutory sense as to liability but as to scope and duration.* . . .

"No definite rule has been formulated for identifying the joint adventure relationship in all cases. Each case depends on its own peculiar facts. It is recognized, however, that an enterprise does not constitute a joint adventure unless each of the following four elements are present, namely: (a) *Contribution* . . . , (b) *Joint proprietorship and control* . . . , (c) *Sharing of profits but not necessarily of losses* . . . , (d) *Contract.* . . .

"The first element of *contribution* is here present. . . . The essential element of *joint proprietorship and control* is, however, lacking. There is no showing that plaintiff had any control over the manner in which the enterprise was carried on or that he even had any voice in the management of the corporation. In fact, the contract by its express terms identifies plaintiff's status as simply that of an employee.

"Likewise, the third element of *sharing in the profits* in a manner *consistent with a status of a joint adventure* is absent. It is true, plaintiff was to share in the profits, *but only for the specific purpose of compensating him as an employee.* . . . Furthermore, the indispensable element of a *contract* for the formation of a joint adventure is also absent.

"We have a contract, but it is one that expressly creates an employment relation and thereby negatives any intent to create a joint adventure."

WHO CAN BE A PARTNER?

Part I, Section 2 of the Uniform Partnership Act states that the word *persons* includes individuals, partners, corporations, and other associations. This means that not only individuals but also corporations, partnerships, and other associations may be partners in a partnership. Since the individual states may have specific rules and regulations regarding participation in partnerships by corporations, other partnerships, and other associations, whether these can be partners depends on state laws.

Any natural person having the capacity to contract can become a partner. In Part II, Contracts, we dealt with the question of what persons are competent to contract. Insane persons may not become partners. Minors do not have full contractual capacity; however, they may become partners in a partnership. But, as with simple contracts, minors have the right to disaffirm their partnership contracts at any time before they reach majority and for a reasonable time thereafter. By such disaffirmance, a minor may avoid certain liability to partnership creditors. Also, a minor who disaffirms the partnership agreement is generally entitled to get back his or her capital investment and also to get his or her share of the profits up to that time, provided that such a distribution will not adversely affect the interest of existing partnership creditors.

Generally speaking, the law of contracts concerning the minor's right to enter into a contract and to disaffirm a contract applies to partnerships in the same way as it applies to any other contract. (As previously stated, the partnership agreement is, in effect, a contract.)

CLASSIFICATION OF PARTNERSHIP

Partnerships may be classified as general partnerships or limited partnerships. The general partnership is the more common form. It is a partnership in which all of the partners have unlimited liability for partnership debts. A limited partnership is a partnership in which one or more of the partners are general partners with unlimited liability. However, one or more of the other partners are limited partners, and their liabilities for partnership debts are limited to the extent of their investment in the partnership. Like persons who buy stock in a corporation, they cannot be liable for more than their investment in the business.

Partnerships may be further classified as trading or nontrading partnerships. A trading partnership is engaged in the business of buying or selling goods or real estate for a profit. A nontrading partnership is a business which provides services, such as a law partnership or an accounting partnership.

The law of limited partnerships will be dealt with in detail in Chapter 41.

CLASSIFICATION OF PARTNERS

The partners in a limited partnership may be classified as general partners or as limited partners. The general partners are the managing partners; they make the decisions, and they are personally liable for partnership debts above and beyond the assets of the partnership. The limited partners do not have any decision-making powers; they are simply investors.

None of the partners in a general partnership are granted limited liability. However, the partners in such a partnership may assume several different roles and consequently may be classified separately. Following are some of the most common classifications:

1. *General partner*—this partner is known to be a partner by the public,

one who actively engages in the business and shares in the profits and the losses.

2. *Silent partner*—this partner has invested money in the business and shares in the profits and the losses, but he or she has no vote in the partnership decisions and is not actively involved in the partnership business.

3. *Secret partner*—this partner may take an active part in the management of the business that prefers that his or her membership in the partnership not be known to the public and may be viewed by the public as an employee, not a partner.

4. *Incoming partner*—this is a person who is accepted into an existing partnership.

5. *Retiring partner*—this is a person who leaves an existing partnership.

6. *Surviving partner*—this is a person who survives after his or her partner dies.

7. *Continuing partner*—this is a person who continues running the business after the partnership has been dissolved.

8. *Dormant partner*—this is a person whom the public knows to be a partner but who does not actively participate in the operation of the business.

9. *Ostensible partner*—this is a person who may or may not be a legal partner according to the partnership agreement but who holds himself or herself out to the public as a partner or who lets the partnership publicly indicate that he or she is a partner. To the public this person looks like a partner, as he or she actively participates in the business and gives the public the impression that he or she is a partner.

Even though the partners in a general partnership fall into a number of classifications, it must be remembered that all of these partners may still be personally liable for the debts of the partnership. The only way partners can escape personal liability for amounts above and beyond the partnership assets is by entering into a limited partnership agreement and by complying with the statutory requirements of the limited partnership law in their jurisdiction.

METHODS OF CREATING A GENERAL PARTNERSHIP

The "association" requirement in Section 6 of the UPA means that for a partnership to exist there must be some sort of agreement among the persons involved in it. As is true under general contract law, however, this agreement may be express—either oral or written—or implied. Most courts would refuse to enforce, at least as between the partners themselves, an oral partnership agreement which was to last longer than one year. The statute of frauds might also be applicable where the partnership agreement called for the transfer of land, goods over $500, or miscellaneous intangibles over $5,000.

Although the parties' intent is certainly important in creating a partnership, it is not conclusive. If the parties wanted to create a partnership but left out one of the required elements, they did not form a partnership. Likewise, if the parties did not intend to create a partnership but in fact voluntarily entered into a relationship which contained all of the elements of a partnership, they become partners. No state action is required to form a partnership, though most states do require some sort of registration of the firm, at least where a fictitious name is being used by it. Failure to register under such a statute does not preclude a firm's existence, though it may prevent the firm from suing.

Section 16 of the UPA provides that person who are not actual partners as to each other may be held liable to third parties as if they were partners where they have held themselves out as partners or where they have consented to having another hold them out as partners and where the third party has relied on such representations in making a decision to extend credit to the firm. Where the representation of partnership has been made publicly, no specific proof of reliance is required; reliance is assumed. Section 16 calls this sort of situation a "partnership by estoppel."

Rizzo v. Rizzo
120 N.E.2d 546 (Illinois, 1954)

FACTS Rocco Rizzo, Sr., owned and operated a wastepaper business in Chicago, under the firm name of Rocco Rizzo & Co. Each of his four sons came to work in the business: Michael, in 1910, as general manager; Joseph, in 1913, as receiving clerk; and Rocco, Jr., in 1916, and John in 1920, as truck drivers. None of the sons received wages, but they were given room and board and all of the profits from the business were divided equally. When Michael joined the business, the name was changed to Rocco Rizzo Son & Co., and later it was changed to Rocco Rizzo Sons & Co. Rocco, Sr., retired from the business in 1915 and deeded the business property to Michael in 1929. Rocco, Jr., died in 1931, survived by his widow (the plaintiff) and two minor sons. The plaintiff claimed that at one point she had been promised that the firm would be turned over to her two sons but that later she had been told that she and her sons would get nothing. The plaintiff brought suit against Michael, Joseph, and John, alleging that Rocco, Jr., had been a partner and that an accounting was due. The defendants appealed from a decree ordering an accounting.

ISSUE Did the facts sufficiently indicate the existence of a partnership?

DECISION Yes. Judgment affirmed.

REASONS Justice Bristow first reviewed all the facts and the conflicting testimony at some length. He stated the rule that the findings of a master, when approved by the chancellor, should "not be distributed unless manifestly against the weight of the evidence." These findings agreed with the evidence.

"[A]s between the parties, the existence of a partnership relation is a question of intention to be gathered from all the facts and circumstances. . . . Written articles of agreement are not necessary, for a partnership may exist under a verbal agreement, and circumstances may be sufficient to establish such an agreement. . . . Such factors as the mode in which the parties have dealt with each other; the mode in which each has, with the knowledge of the others, dealt with other people, . . . and the use of a firm name, . . . have been deemed material in determining the existence of a partnership. The essential test, however, is the sharing of profits, . . . but it is not necessary that there be a sharing of the losses in order to constitute a partnership. . . .

"The fact that Michael, as the oldest son, had more authority in the management

797

than the other brothers does not of itself preclude the existence of a partnership, particularly in view of the custom in such closely-knit immigrant families. In fact, Michael stated that the business was turned over to him because he was the oldest son. Furthermore, it is an accepted partnership practice that one partner may be charged with greater managerial responsibilities.

"The fact that the brothers admitted that they all worked in the business, sharing equally in the profits and going without pay if there were none, tends to comply with the essential requirement for a partnership. . . .

"Furthermore, the fact that the firm name, originally Rocco Rizzo & Co., had been changed to Rocco Rizzo Son & Co. when Michael entered the business, and was again changed to Rocco Rizzo Sons & Co., and was so listed in the telephone book and on the truck during the lifetime of Rocco, Jr., is further evidence of the existence of a partnership between the brothers as of 1931. . . .

"Under a partnership, a fiduciary relation is created whereby the partner assuming control of the business is obliged to manage it in the interest of all the partners. . . .

"In the instant case, Michael Rizzo was under a duty as a partner, and as the oldest brother on whom the other children relied, not to take advantage of his fiduciary position."

WHAT SHOULD A PARTNERSHIP AGREEMENT CONTAIN?

A partnership agreement, also called articles of partnership or articles of copartnership, should contain the basic provisions required to form a contract, as a partnership agreement is in fact a contract. In addition to these basic provisions, there will always be certain provisions which relate to the type of business and to special problems connected with the management of that particular business. For example, a considerable number of the provisions in the articles of partnership of a large law firm would not be found in the articles of partnership of a family manufacturing firm. Following are some of the basic provisions which any partnership agreement should contain.

1. The name the business will be using in its dealings with the public. This is called the firm name. The law does not require a partnership to adopt a firm name. However, if a name is adopted in the articles of partnership, then the matter is settled and there will be no dickering later about what the name should be. In many states, if the name of the partnership is different from the name of any of the partners, then the partnership name must be registered with state and/or county officials so that creditors will be able to identify the owners of the firm in case of debts or claims for which owners would be liable. For example, if the name of the partnership were Buildum and Sons, no registration would be necessary; however, if the name were Structures Unlimited, then a name registration would normally be required.

2. The names and addresses of all the partners.

3. The nature and purposes of the business, the location of its principal

offices of the business, and any other location where partnership business will be conducted.

4. The data on which the partnership relationship will commence and how long it will exist. Is it to exist for a specific period of time, or will it exist until it is dissolved by death or voluntary dissolution?

5. The contributions to be made by each partner. Are some partners contributing money, whereas other partners are contributing real estate, personal property, goods and merchandise, expertise, labor, etc.? Also, when are the contributions due and payable?

6. The rights of the partners with regard to management. Will there be senior partners and junior partners, or will all partners have equal voices in management?

7. The duties of the various partners with regard to the operations of the business.

8. Provisions for salaries or drawing account for each partner.

9. A provision concerning the sharing of profits and losses.

10. A provision indicating who will keep the accounts of the partnership. What bookkeeping and accounting methods are to be used, and where are the books to be kept?

11. The requirement for taking in new partners. This provision would be especially important in a law firm or an accounting firm.

12. Any special restrictions, rights, or duties with regard to any particular partner or any group of partners.

13. The general agreement concerning the interest of a retiring partner.

14. A provision setting out the procedures for the purchase of a deceased or retiring partner's share of the partnership.

15. A provision for the arbitration and disposition of grievances which may arise between the partners.

16. A provision concerning the procedure for dissolution of the business and for the final distribution of its assets to the partners.

DISSOLUTION, WINDING UP, AND TERMINATION

A partnership is based on a contract, which may be superseded by the parties' later actions. The firm may be dissolved by agreement of the partners, by acts of the partners, by a decree of court, or by operation of law. In the case of a partnership with a specific time span, it is dissolved at the end of the stipulated period of time. The partnership contract does, however, differ from many other contracts in that it concerns not only the contractual relationship between the parties to the contract but also the contractual relationship between the partnership and its various creditors. Thus, even though the partners may decide to dissolve their contractual relationship between themselves, the partnership is not really terminated until all of its debts are paid and all of its assets are distributed. This procedure is commonly called "winding up." Once the winding-up process has been completed, the partnership is considered terminated. Thus we have a three-step process: dissolution, winding up, and termination.

Dissolution is defined by Section 29 of the Uniform Partnership Act as "the change in the relation of the partners caused by any partner ceasing to be associated in the carrying on as distinguished from the winding up of the business." This change in relation can be voluntary or involuntary. An example of voluntary dissolution would be one in which the partners simply decide to end their relationship and go their separate ways. An example of involuntary dissolution would be one which occurred because a partner died or became mentally or physically incapacitated.

The key legal point to remember is that dissolution in itself does not terminate the partnership entity. Dissolution only triggers the next step, namely the winding-up process. During the winding-up process, the partnership agreement is still legally in force. However, the authority of each partner to act as an agent of the partnership has been legally terminated, except as necessary to wind up partnership affairs.

THE PROCESS OF DISSOLUTION

As has been noted, a partnership may be dissolved by agreement or certain acts of the partners, by court decree, by operation of law, or by lapse of time. If the partnership agreement has a specific time span, at the end of which the partnership is to be dissolved, the partnership is automatically dissolved as of the end of that time span.

1. Dissolution by Agreement of the Partners

The partners may decide to dissolve their partnership for various reasons. This decision must be unanimous unless the partnership agreement specifies otherwise. For example, the agreement could specify that only a majority vote of the partners is needed to dissolve the partnership. Remember, a partnership is a voluntary association, so it can be dissolved by voluntary agreement.

2. Dissolution by Acts of the Partners

a. **Withdrawal by a Partner.** If a partner withdraws from the business, that action causes a dissolution of the partnership. This does not necessarily mean that the business will have to be terminated. If the partnership agreement has been drawn with this problem in mind, it will contain provisions that give the remaining partners the right to buy the withdrawing partner's interest so that they can continue the business.

Although a partner has the power to withdraw from the partnership for any reason that he or she may choose, the withdrawing partner may still be liable to the remaining partners for breach of contract. After all, the partnership agreement is a contract, and if its breach causes damage to the other contracting parties, then the violating party should be liable for such damages. Here again, a well-drawn partnership agreement should anticipate and provide a solution for such problems.

Campbell v. Miller
161 S.E.2d 546 (North Carolina, 1968)

FACTS Taylor Campbell sued his former partner A. C. Miller, and Miller's wife Ruth, for damages for breach of a partnership agreement. The Millers filed a counterclaim, alleging that Campbell had breached the agreement and that they had sustained damages. Campbell, who had had experience as both a butcher and a carpenter, was to supervise the construction of a building on land owned by the Millers, for which he would receive only $75 per week during construction. When the building was finished, Campbell and Miller were to operate a meat-processing plant there and to divide the profits equally. The parties apparently intended to write up their agreement after the plant was built. After about 14 weeks, with some 4 weeks of construction yet to go, Campbell said that he had to wait for a telephone call from a sick relative in another state and that he could not assist in the construction work until later that evening. Campbell claimed that Miller had told him to pick up his tools and leave the job; Miller claimed that Campbell had decided to leave on his own. Miller finished the job with hired help and had operated the business at a loss since it opened. The jury awarded Campbell $9,333.24. Miller appealed.

ISSUE Did the defendant breach the partnership agreement?

DECISION No. Judgment reversed.

REASONS Justice Lake held that neither party had breached the agreement and that both the complaint and the counterclaim should be dismissed. A partnership had clearly been formed prior to the completion of the building, even though the agreement had not yet been written up. The important point was that the partnership formed was a partnership at will.

"There is nothing whatever in the record to indicate any agreement between the parties that their partnership was to continue for a specified term. On the contrary, the plaintiff testified that their understanding was that the site of the building would be leased to the partnership by the defendants for as long as we wanted it.' A partnership is a partnership at will unless some agreement to the contrary can be proved. . . .

"The significance of the partnership being one at will, i.e. without any definite term or undertaking to be accomplished, is that the termination by the election of a partner is not a breach of contract. Having the legal right to terminate, it would seem that there is no liability for its exercise, whatever the motive, and whatever may be the injurious consequences to copartners, who have neglected to protect themselves by an agreement to continue for a definite term. '. . . In view of this rule . . . that a partner may exercise his right to dissolve a partnership at will for any reason which he deems sufficient, or even arbitrarily, he is not liable for damages which have resulted to his copartners by reason of such action.' "

"Since the plaintiff had drawn a total of $1,500 for the 14 weeks he worked, he had already received more than the agreed compensation. Justice Lake did not think that the one conversation was very clear evidence of an intent to dissolve on Miller's part, but he held that even if it was such, Miller had not breached the partnership at will.

b. Expulsion of a Partner. Section 31(d) of the Uniform Partnership Act states that a partnership is dissolved "by the expulsion of any partner from the business bona fide in accordance with such a power conferred by the agreement between the partners." Thus, if the agreement provides for the expulsion of a member under certain circumstances and the remaining partners exercise that power for good and valid cause, then the partnership is dissolved.

c. Death of a Partner. The Uniform Partnership Act, Section 31(4), states that the death of any partner will cause dissolution.

Girard Bank v. *Haley*
332 A.2d 443 (Pennsylvania, 1975)

FACTS   Anna Reid began this action against Haley and her two other partners, alleging that she had dissolved the firm and asking for a distribution of assets. Reid died after the lawsuit was commenced, and her executors were substituted as plaintiffs. Reid had written a letter to her partners, which stated in part: "I hereby notify you that I am terminating the partnership. . . ." Meetings were held, but the partners were unable to agree on a plan for liquidation or on the respective rights of the partners. At that point, Reid started this lawsuit. The partnership agreement gave the surviving partners the right to purchase the interest of a deceased partner, but it contained no such provision in the event that a partner dropped out voluntarily. The chancellor held that Reid's letter did not dissolve the firm but that her death did. He also held that the other partners could exercise their buy-out option by paying her estate $29,165.48 plus Reid's 70 percent of the income for 1971. Reid's executors appealed.

ISSUE   Did the decedent's letter terminate the partnership?

DECISION   Yes. Judgment reversed and case remanded.

REASONS   Justice Pomeroy felt that the chancellor had been somewhat confused as to what the applicable law was. He said that the chancellor appeared to be overly impressed with the fact that Reid had been a "strong-willed person" who dominated the firm and with the fact that she and her representatives had not "justified" her termination.

   "In supposing that justification was necessary, the learned court below fell into error. Dissolution of a partnership is caused, under s.31 of the Act, . . . 'by the express will of any partner.' The expression of that will need not be supported by any justification. If no 'definite term or particular undertaking [is] specified in the partnership agreement,' such an at-will dissolution does not violate the agreement between the partners; indeed, an expression of a will to dissolve is effective as a dissolution even if in contravention of the agreement. . . .

   "There is no doubt in our minds that Mrs. Reid's letter . . . effectively dissolved the partnership between her and her three partners. It was definite and unequivocal. . . . The effective termination date is therefore February 10, 1971, and Mrs. Reid's subsequent death after this litigation was in progress is an irrelevant factor in determining the rights of the parties. . . .

   "In light of our conclusion that an inter-vivos dissolution took place, the provisions of the Act rather than the post-mortem provisions of the agreement, will govern the winding-up of the partnership affairs and the distribution of its assets."

d. **Bankruptcy of a Partner.** The Uniform Partnership Act, Section 31(5), states that the bankruptcy of any partner will cause dissolution.

e. **Addition of a Partner.** The addition of a partner dissolves the partnership.

f. **Assignment of a Partner's Interest for the Benefit of Creditors.** Under the common law the voluntary or involuntary sale or assignment of a partner's interest would dissolve the partnership. Section 27 of the Uniform Partnership Act specifically provides that neither a voluntary nor an involuntary sale for the benefit of creditors automatically dissolves the partnership. The creditors will simply receive the profits which the partner would have received. If, however, a dissolution did occur, then the assignees would get the capital interest of the partner. A few states still follow the old common-law rule of automatic dissolution.

As a general rule of law, a partnership is dissolved whenever its membership changes. When informed of this rule of law, the layperson asks, "If this is true, then how do large law firm and accounting firm partnerships handle the problem, as they are constantly bringing in partners, retiring partners, etc.?" The answer is that the partnership agreement of such firms specifies the procedure to be followed in case of expulsion, voluntary withdrawal, the addition, death, or retirement of a partner, or any other change in membership. In effect, the old partnership is technically dissolved and reorganized in accordance with the provisions of the agreement each time such a situation occurs.

3. Dissolution by Operation of Law

The Uniform Partnership Act, Section 31(3), states, "Dissolution is caused: By any event which makes it unlawful for the business of the partnership to be carried on or for the members to carry it on in the partnership." This simply means that if by either legislative enactment or a court decision the business that the partnership was carrying on is no longer legal, then the partnership is dissolved by operation of the law. To refer back to Part II, Contracts, the partnership agreement is then an illegal bargain and therefore void. As an illustration, let's say that a partnership is operating a casino in Atlantic City and the gaming commission takes away its license or the gambling law is repealed, making gambling illegal. The partnership will then be dissolved by operation of law.

4. Dissolution by Court Decree

Often circumstances arise that require a court determination as to whether a partnership should be dissolved. For example, if an affliction has caused a partner to be of unsound mind and incapable of handling the partnership's affairs, then a remaining partner may petition the court to order the dissolution of the partnership. A court determination might also be desirable if one of the partners has become a drunkard or a drug addict and no longer assumes his or her share of the work and responsibility but refuses to dissolve the partnership voluntarily. Or if fewer than the number of partners required for voluntary dissolution under the agreement will agree to dissolution, then the partners requesting dissolution may request that the court review the situation.

5. Dissolution by Expiration

A partnership may be created for a specified period of time—1 year, 5 years, 10 years, etc. When that period expires, the contract of partnership is dissolved.

RIGHTS AND LIABILITIES OF THE PARTNERS AFTER DISSOLUTION

Dissolution does not change either the existing liability of the partnership or the existing liabilities of the individual partners. Dissolution may be likened to the death of an individual. The person dies, and then an administrator is appointed to settle the affairs of the deceased's estate. The administration of the deceased's estate is a process similar to the winding-up process previously referred to.

The rights of the partners may be likened to the rights of the heirs of a deceased person's estate. The partners have a right to an accounting to see that their interests are being handled properly, and after all the debts have been paid, whatever is left is distributed to them.

RIGHTS OF CREDITORS AFTER DISSOLUTION

All partnership creditors and all other persons who have any current relationship with the partnership should be notified of the dissolution immediately. If these persons are not notified and if they continue to deal with the business after dissolution, the partnership and the individual partners may be liable as if the transactions had occurred prior to dissolution. Thus, once the decision has been made to dissolve the partnership, or once an act of dissolution has occurred, or once a court decree of dissolution has been entered, the first step is to notify in writing everyone who could possibly be concerned with the dissolution and termination of the business.

Ellingson v. Walsh, O'Connor & Barneson
104 P.2d 507 (California, 1940)

FACTS   Ellingson was the receiver of the landlord; the suit was to enforce a lease executed by a partnership. Barneson, one of the partners, disputed his personal liability on the lease because it was executed by the firm before he became a member. After Barneson became a general partner in the firm, it subleased the premises in question for a time, collected rent from the sublessee, and paid its own rent to the landlord. The firm owed $2,374.13 for the period from March 1, 1932, to January 25, 1933. The trial court judgment imposed full liability on Barneson along with the other general partners.

ISSUE   Is an incoming partner personally liable for rentals which become due after he joins the firm, where the lease was executed before he joined it.

DECISION   Yes. Judgment affirmed.

REASONS   Chief Justice Gibson said that Barneson's argument based on Section 17 of the UPA did not apply to a lease obligation.

"This contention would be sound if the only obligation of the partnership in this transaction was one which arose prior to appellant's admission to the firm. . . . But appellant's contention overlooks the fact that tenant of real property is not liable for rent solely by reason of the contract of lease. Tenancies in property need not necessarily be created by valid leases. . . . Where there is a lease, the liability of the tenant arising by operation of law is not superseded by the contractual obligation. Both liabilities exist simultaneously. . . .

"This second partnership did not expressly assume the obligations of the lease, but it occupied the premises. Whether it was liable contractually on the lease is immaterial; it became liable for rent as a tenant. Strangers coming in with consent and occupying the premises would be liable; tenants would be liable even if there were no lease at all; and this second partnership and all its members were liable regardless of any lack of assumption of the obligations of the lease. . . .

"Under the general law the obligation of a tenant arising from occupation of the premises is a continuing one; that is, it arises and binds him continually throughout the period of his occupation. This obligation on the part of appellant first arose when the new partnership, of which he was a member, occupied the premises as a tenant. It follows that his obligations as a tenant arose after his admission to the partnership."

THE PROCESS OF WINDING UP

Winding up, the second step in the process of ending a partnership is the process of liquidating the partnership assets, that is, selling the real and personal property which the partnership owned, collecting any outstanding accounts, and paying any outstanding debts, and closing out any loose ends of the business—canceling orders not yet delivered, canceling any lease or rental agreements, terminating any relationships that the partnership may have had with persons who were not partners, and so on. After all the outstanding accounts have been collected, all the assets have been turned into cash, and all the outstanding bills and claims against the partnership have been paid and settled, then any cash remaining has to be divided among the partners. First, if any of the partners have loaned money to the partnership, those loans are repaid with whatever interest was agreed on. Next, the partners will be given back their initial investment. Finally, if there is still some cash left, it will be divided among the partners as profits and the distribution will be in the same proportions as the distribution of profits in the past and in accordance with the proportions set out in the partnership agreement.

The preceding discussion of the dissolution of assets assumes that the assets of the partnership exceed its outstanding debts. This, of course, is not always the situation of a dissolved partnership which is in the process of winding up. If the assets of the partnership are insufficient to pay its debts, then the personal assets of the various partners may be called upon to pay them. It must be noted, however, that the personal creditors of an individual partner with personal debts may have priority over creditors who are attempting to collect partnership debts from that partner.

WHO HANDLES THE WINDING UP?

The Uniform Partnership Act, Section 35(1)(a), allows a partner to do "any act appropriate for winding up partnership affairs or completing transactions unfinished at dissolution." Thus the winding up can be done by any of the partners, or by a partner whom the other partners designate as the winding-up partner, or by an outsider who is appointed as a receiver for the purpose of winding up the partnership and making the final distribution of its assets.

CONTINUING BUSINESS AFTER DISSOLUTION

As we indicated previously, the dissolution of a partnership does not automatically mean the termination of its business. Among the common situations which cause dissolution are the death or withdrawal of a partner. In such cases the remaining partners do not necessarily want to terminate the business. Thus the winding-up process in such situations will simply be an internal process of buying out the interest of the deceased or withdrawing partner and of making appropriate bookkeeping changes for the reorganization and continued operation of the business. Creditors and persons dealing with the firm may not even know that any changes were made when a partnership has been legally dissolved by death of one of the partners. However, if a partner withdraws from the firm, then it is wise to so notify all creditors and all persons and firms that deal with the partnership.

Remember, in a general partnership each partner is an agent of the partnership. While dissolution terminates that relationship as between the partners, people who have been doing business with the partnership will not know that the person who has withdrawn is no longer a partner. Until such third parties are notified otherwise, the partnership may be liable for certain acts and dealings of the former partner. Thus, even though the business is to continue after dissolution, it is still necessary to give proper notification of the dissolution to all creditors and all persons who might be dealing with the continuing business.

CASES FOR DISCUSSION

STUART v. OVERLAND MEDICAL CENTER

510 S.W.2d 494 (Missouri, 1974)

Weier, Judge

Defendants, physicians practicing at the Overland Medical Center, appeal from a judgment

entered in favor of plaintiff, a physician specializing in dermatology who formerly had practiced at the Center. The judgment ordered the plaintiff recover against defendants the sum of $37,096.74 together with the costs of the action. . . .

Defendants urge four points of error on appeal. The first point challenges the court's conclusion that the relationship between plaintiff and defendants was one of partnership. The three remaining points attack the court's valuation of plaintiff's partnership interest and plaintiff's accounts receivable. We affirm.

Plaintiff, Dr. Wallace Stuart, began practicing dermatology at the Overland Medical Center in 1963. Not long after he had begun practice, plaintiff was approached by one of the defendants, Dr. Mitchell Yanow, the medical administrator, about the possibility of his purchasing the department of dermatology at the Center. The formulas used to determine the consideration for which Dr. Stuart could purchase a 4 percent interest consisted of 10 percent of his gross receipts for a five year period at the beginning of his practice at the Center plus 8 percent of his outstanding accounts receivable at the end of that five year period, none of which were to be over one year old. Plaintiff accepted the offer and began making payments under this formula, and after five years of practice, the total amount was computed to be $17,182.30. Of this sum, $11,297.04 was paid by Dr. Stuart, leaving an unpaid balance of $5,885.26 at the time of the trial.

After working at the Center for a period of eight years (1963 to 1971), Dr. Stuart decided to terminate his association with the Center. He communicated this intention to Dr. Yanow through a letter written by his attorney which was dated May 19, 1971. Dr. Stuart's severance was to be effective on July 31, 1971. Prior to July 31, 1971, Dr. Stuart sent notices to the patients he had been treating at the Center informing them that he was leaving the Center and opening an office elsewhere. Defendants also sent notices to patients informing them that another dermatologist would be available to treat them at the Center beginning August 1, 1971.

By this testimony Dr. Stuart established that the formula used to establish the purchase price had also been agreed to be used to establish the value of his interest to be paid if he withdrew from the partnership. And so when Dr. Stuart left the Center, the amount due him under the formula for five years prior to July 31, 1971, was $30,350 and $28,200 for his outstanding accounts receivable, or a total amount of $58,550. Dr. Stuart admitted that when he left the Center he took some equipment with him which was worth $500. In addition, he had been paid $15,068 on his accounts receivable at the time of the trial. . . .

[D]efendants argue that the evidence showed a relationship between plaintiff and defendants as one of expense-sharing rather than one of partnership, especially since the evidence failed to show that any doctor shared the profits of any other doctor. . . .

A partnership is defined judicially as "a contract of two or more competent persons to place their money, effects, labor and skills, or some or all of them, in lawful commerce or business and to divide the profits and bear the loss in certain proportions." . . . The primary consideration in determining the existence of a partnership is whether the parties intended to carry on as co-owners a business for profit. . . .

Before plaintiff left the Overland Medical Center, he had paid $11,297.04 toward purchasing a 4 percent interest in the Center. The 1970 financial statement of the Center lists plaintiff's equity in the Center at 4 percent. Dr. Mitchell Yanow, one of the founders and for some time medical administrator of the Center, testified plaintiff engaged to purchase a 4 percent interest in the Center and described it as a partnership. Thus, along with the other doctors who had an equity in the Center, plaintiff was a co-owner.

The amount of money each doctor received for practicing his profession at the Center was based upon the billing for services performed by each doctor and collected by and in the name of the Center less a percent of the expenses. . . . Each doctor shared to some extent in the income or profit of the other doctors although the sharing was not the result of proportionally dividing the total amount of money collected by all the doctors without considering the amount of money each doctor collected individually. Rather, the profit sharing was accomplished by the Center's method of allocating the expenses to be deducted from each doctor's collections. It was in this manner that the doctors in the Center actually shared profits. Because the expenses each doctor had to pay bore no relationship to the actual expenses of each doctor, some doctors were receiving profits that otherwise might have been distributed to the doctor or doctors whose actual expenses were slight when compared to the actual expenses of other doctors.

Thus the evidence proved that plaintiff was

practicing his profession with the other doctors in the Center as a co-owner of the Center's facilities for a profit. While co-ownership and the sharing of profits by those engaged in business are not factors which conclusively establish the parties' relationship as that of partnership, they are prima facie evidence of partnership. . . . As such, the presumption of partnership prevails unless evidence sufficient to rebut the presumption is brought forward. In this case, defendants presented no evidence which would lead to the conclusion that the relationship between plaintiff and them was anything other than a partnership. Indeed, defendants' evidence actually aids the conclusion that the relationship was a partnership. By 1970 plaintiff was listed in a financial statement of the Overland Medical Center for the years 1969 through 1971, one of defendants' exhibits, as a partner with an equity interest in the Center of 4 percent. Another defendants' exhibit entitled a "Partnership Agreement" was entered into on January 1, 1954, by the three physicians who started the Overland Medical Center. While plaintiff never signed this agreement, the agreement was evidence that the physicians who founded the Center intended to and actually did practice medicine as partners in a partnership from its inception.

Under these facts and circumstances, combined with the defendant's failure to prove that no partnership relation was intended, the trial court did not err in concluding that the professional arrangement between plaintiff and defendants was a partnership.

CHAIKEN v. EMPLOYMENT SECURITY COMMISSION

274 A.2d 707 (Delaware, 1971)

Storey, Judge

Pursuant to 19 Del.C. § 3359, the Employment Security Commission, hereinafter referred to as the Commission, levied an involuntary assessment against Richard K. Chaiken, complainant, hereinafter referred to as Chaiken, for not filing his unemployment security assessment report. Pursuant to the same statutory section, a hearing was held and a determination made by the Commission that Chaiken was the employer of two barbers in his barber shop and that he should be assessed as an employer for his share of unemployment compensation contributions. Chaiken appealed the Commission's decision. . . .

Both in the administrative hearing and in his appeal brief Chaiken argues that he had entered into partnership agreements with each of his barbers and, therefore, was and is not subject to unemployment compensation assessment. . . .

Chaiken contends that he and his "partners":

(1) properly registered the partnership name and names of partners in the Prothonotary's office, in accordance with 6 Del. C. § 3101,
(2) properly filed federal partnership information returns and paid federal taxes quarterly on an estimated basis, and
(3) duly executed partnership agreements.

Of the three factors, the last is most important. Agreements of "partnership" were executed between Chaiken and Mr. Strazella, a barber in the shop, and between Chaiken and Mr. Spitzer, similarly situated. The agreements were nearly identical. The first paragraph declared the creation of a partnership and the location of business. The second provided that Chaiken would provide barber chair, supplies, and licenses, while the other partner would provide tools of the trade. The paragraph also declared that upon dissolution of the partnership, ownership of items would revert to the party providing them. The third paragraph declared that the income of the partnership would be divided 30 percent for Chaiken, 70 percent for Strazella; 20 percent for Chaiken and 80 percent for Spitzer. The fourth paragraph declared that all partnership policy would be decided by Chaiken, whose decision was final. The fifth paragraph forbade assignment of the agreement without permission of Chaiken. The sixth paragraph required Chaiken to hold and distribute all receipts. The final paragraph stated hours of work for Strazella and Spitzer and holidays.

The mere existence of an agreement labelled "partnership" agreement and the characterization of signatories as "partners" do not conclusively prove the existence of a partnership. Rather, the intention of the parties, as explained by the wording of the agreement, is paramount. . . .

As co-owners of a business, partners have an equal right in the decision-making process. . . . But this right may be abrogated by agreement of the parties without destroying the partnership concept, provided other partnership elements are present. . . .

Thus, while paragraph four reserves for Chaiken all right to determine partnership policy, it is not standing alone, fatal to the partnership concept. Co-owners should also contribute valuable consideration for the creation of the business. Under paragraph two, however, Chaiken provides the barber chair (and implicitly the barber shop itself), mirror, licenses, and linen, while the other partners merely provide their tools and labor—nothing more than any barber-employee would furnish. Standing alone, however, mere contribution of work and skill can be valuable consideration for a partnership agreement. . . .

Partnership interests may be assignable, although it is not a violation of partnership law to prohibit assignment in a partnership agreement. 6 Del.C. § 1527. Therefore, paragraph five on assignment of partnership interests does not violate the partnership concept. On the other hand, distribution of partnership assets to the partners upon dissolution is only allowed after all partnership liabilities are satisfied. . . . But paragraph two of the agreement, in stating the ground rules for dissolution, makes no declaration that the partnership assets will be utilized to pay partnership expenses before reversion to their original owners. This deficiency militates against a finding in favor of partnership intent since it is assumed Chaiken would have inserted such provision had he thought his lesser partners would accept such liability. Partners do accept such liability, employees do not.

Most importantly, co-owners carry on "a business for profit." The phrase has been interpreted to mean that partners share in the profits and the losses of the business. The intent to divide the profits is an indispensable requisite of partnership. . . . Paragraph three of the agreement

declares that each partner shall share in the income of the business. There is no sharing of the profits, and as the agreement is drafted, there are no profits. Merely sharing the gross returns does not establish a partnership. . . . Nor is the sharing of profits prima facie evidence of a partnership where the profits received are in payment of wages. . . .

The failure to share profits, therefore, is fatal to the partnership concept here.

Evaluating Chaiken's agreement in the light of the elements implicity in a partnership, no partnership intent can be found. The absence of the important right of decision making or the important duty to share liabilities upon dissolution individually may not be fatal to a partnership. But when both are absent, coupled with the absence of profit sharing, they become strong factors in discrediting the partnership argument. . . .

In addition, the total circumstances of the case taken together indicate the employer-employee relationship between Chaiken and his barbers. The agreement set forth the hours of work and days off—unusual subjects for partnership agreements. The barbers brought into the relationship only the equipment required of all barber shop operators. And each barber had his own individual "partnership" with Chaiken. Furthermore, Chaiken conducted all transactions with suppliers, and purchased licenses, insurance, and the lease for the business property in his own name. Finally, the name "Richard's Barber Shop" continued to be used after the execution of the so-called partnership agreements.

It is the conclusion of the Court that Chaiken did not carry the burden of proving the existence of partnerships with Spitzer and Strazella. . . .

FLETCHER v. PULLEN & CO.
70 Md. 205 (Maryland, 1889)

Miller, J.

The plaintiffs who are nurserymen in Milford, Delaware, sued Bramble and Fletcher as partners in the same business at Cambridge in this State, for fruit trees sold and delivered to them in the autumn of 1886. Bramble died before the trial, and Fletcher defended upon the ground that he was not a partner. The exceptions relate mainly to the admissibility of evidence upon the question, not whether Fletcher had held himself out, or had permitted himself to be held out, as a partner, so as to become responsible to third parties.

The law on this subject, well established by authority, may be stated thus: The ground of liability of a person as partner who is not so in fact, is that he has held himself out to the world as such, or has permitted others to do so, and by reason thereof is estopped from denying that he is one as against those who have, in good faith, dealt with the firm or with him as a member of it. But it must appear that the person dealing with the firm believed, and had a reasonable right to believe, that the party he seeks to hold as a partner was a member of the firm and that the credit was, to some extent, induced by this belief. It must also appear that the holding out was by the party sought to be charged, or by his authority or with his knowledge or assent. This where it is not the direct act of the party may be inferred from circumstances, such as from advertisements, shop-bills, signs, or cards, and from various other acts from which it is reasonable to infer that the holding out was with his authority, knowledge, or assent. And whether a defendant has so held himself out, or permitted it to be done, is in every case a question of fact, and not of law. . . . These general rules apply to the present case.

The evidence shows that there was, in or near Cambridge, a fruit farm and nursery on about 15 acres of Fletcher's land which Bramble had occupied and managed from the year 1881 to 1887. The plaintiffs then proved that in October and November 1886, they received several letters, postal-cards, telegrams, and circulars from Cambridge, signed "Fletcher & Bramble," representing them to be partners, and the envelopes in which the letters were enclosed were stamped with the same firm name. These letters contained orders for fruit trees, and the first of them gave a reference to a Mr. Van Horst, formerly of Milford, but then residing in Cambridge. The plaintiffs not knowing the firm, nor by whom the letters were written, wrote to Van Horst and others in-

quiring as to its credit and standing, and in reply received information to the effect that Fletcher was entirely responsible, but that Bramble was worth nothing. Upon this information, and receiving no intimation that Fletcher was not a partner, they filled the orders and delivered the trees, relying upon his credit. . . .

The plaintiffs then proved that an advertisement signed "Fletcher & Bramble," calling attention to *their* nursery, offering *their trees* for sale, and soliciting from public continuance of confidence and orders, was published in two weekly newspapers of Cambridge where Fletcher lived for *three months during the year 1884.* In one of these papers there was also a *local notice* of the advertisement. These were also prepared, inserted, and paid for by Bramble without Fletcher's knowledge, but it was proved that during the time of their publication *he was a subscriber* to both papers, and they were *regularly sent to him.* There is also clear proof that he *actually knew* of them while they were being published and never inserted in either of the papers any denial of the partnership. From all this it was competent for a jury to infer that he was held out to the public by Bramble as a partner, with his knowledge and assent, and we are of opinion the plaintiffs were entitled to prove this though they never saw the advertisements and were not influenced by them in trusting the firm. They had already proved they had so trusted it in good faith, and upon good grounds, and we think they had the right to resort to these antecedent advertisements and to this proof for the purpose of showing that Fletcher had been so held out to the public with his knowledge and assent. It was evidence to go to the jury upon that subject, and if uncontradicted would have made him a partner, at least as to all third parties who had trusted the firm in good faith upon that supposition. Having knowledge of these advertisements, it was his duty to deny the partnership if he wished to escape liability. But what was he to do and how much? We do not say he was under a legal obligation to publish a repudiation of the partnership in the same newspapers or in any other, though this would seem to be a very obvious and the most efficient mode of proclaiming such denial, and the fact that

810

he failed to do so was a circumstance to go to the jury. But we take it that the rule upon this subject stated by a very eminent jurist is reasonable and just: "If one is held out as a partner and *he knows it*, he is chargeable as one unless he does all that a reasonable and honest man should do under similar circumstances, to assert and *manifest* his refusal, and thereby prevent innocent parties from being misled." . . .

The errors in rejecting the items of evidence referred to, require us to reverse the judgment and award a new trial. But in view of the fact that the Court below, acting as a jury, found for the plaintiffs notwithstanding they had granted the defendant's fifth prayer, in which all his own testimony in denial of the partnership was expressly submitted to the consideraton of the Judges, we think each party should be required to pay his own costs, both in this Court and in the Court below.

PHILLIPS v. PHILLIPS

49 Ill. 437 (Illinois, 1863)

Caton, Chief Justice

Over 20 years ago John Phillips emigrated from Scotland and settled in Chicago with his family, consisting of a wife and four sons and two daughters. He was then very poor. He was a wood-turner by trade, and commenced that business in a very small way with a foot-lathe. He was frugal, industrious, and honest, and prospered as but few men, even in this country, prosper. He labored hard with his own hands, and as his sons grew up they joined their work to his, all except John S. who, at a proper age, was put as an apprentice to learn the chair-maker's trade, but his health proving delicate, his father made an arrangement with his master by which his time was released when he had but partially learned his trade, then John S. returned home and took a more or less active part in the business of his father. His health was, however, for many years, very delicate, and he was enabled to do but little physical labor. He, however, mostly took charge of the office and books, for which the testimony shows he was very well qualified, and where he rendered efficient service. In the meantime, the business had grown from the smallest beginning, with a single foot-lathe, to a large manufactory, with extensive machinery propelled by steam; and chair-making, which was introduced at an early day, had become the principal or largest branch of the business. Thus this business was begun and continued and prospered, until 1860, when the complainant left his father and the business, and filed this bill for an account as among partners.

The business had always been conducted as it was begun, in the name of John Phillips, the father, although in a few instances bills were made out to John Phillips & Sons by persons with but a superficial acquaintance with them, which were paid without eliciting remark or particular attention. The books were all kept in the name of John Phillips, with the exception of a few entries made by a book-keeper in the name of John Phillips & Sons. Indeed, there is, and can be, no question that if there was a co-partnership embracing the father and sons, the firm name adopted was John Phillips.

The complainant, to show a co-partnership, proves that the sons all devoted their time and attention to the business after they attained their majority, without regular salaries as laborers or servants; that funds which they drew from the concern for their support were charged to each one separately, while neither ever received a credit for labor or services; that the father, upon one or two occasions, stated to third persons that his sons were interested in the business, and he also relied upon the appearances to the outside public, and the interest which all took in the success of the business.

For the defense, it is claimed, that following the habits and customs of their forefathers in Scotland, the sons continued to serve the father in the same relation and with the same fidelity after attaining their majority as before, under the distinct and often declared understanding that all should belong to the father during his life, and at his death the business and property should be left by him to his children, as he should think proper. . . .

If such was the understanding and purpose of

811

the parties, then there was no partnership. Originally, undoubtedly, the entire concern belonged to the father; and it so continued, unless by the agreement of the father the sons were admitted into the concern as partners; for, as before intimated, we know of no means by which the sons could become partners with the father, and thus acquire a title to his property, without his knowledge or consent. Did the father ever consent that his sons, or either of them, should be admitted as partners with him? Did he ever agree that they should be part owners of this property? On repeated occasions the subject of co-partnership with his sons was presented to him, both in the presence of the complainant and his brothers, and he ever repudiated the suggestion in the most emphatic terms. The very suggestion, even, seemed to excite his indignation. Upon one occasion he expressed himself in this characteristic phrase: "Na, na! I will ha' nae sons for partners as long as I live. Damn them! They would put me out of the door." On none of these occasions do we find the complainant, or any of his brothers, claiming the existence of a co-partnership, but, on the contrary, they silently acquiesced in the assertions of the father.

But, to our minds, the controlling features of the evidence in this case consist in the testimony of the complainant himself, and his brothers. The testimony of Alexander A. C. Phillips, Kedzie and Peterson [streets], shows that the complainant was repeatedly examined as witness in cases between John Phillips and other parties, growing out of the business of the concern, and in all of these cases he swore that he was not a partner and had no interest in the concern. He then gave the same account of the relations between the father and sons which his brothers now give. . . .

[T]he question here is, what was the actual fact, and not what observers supposed was the fact from appearances. It is the internal truth we are seeking, and these external appearances are only important as they may enable us to arrive at this truth; and when we so find the truth by indubitable proof in a different direction than that indicated by these external appearances, then these must go for naught. Here we have the positive testimony of every living man who has the absolute knowledge of the facts, including the complainant himself, all testifying most unqualifiedly that there was no partnership. And all these witnesses stand unimpeached, either directly or indirectly. . . .

The decree is reversed and the bill dismissed.

PROBLEMS FOR DISCUSSION

1. Ralph Backworth had been employed by the L. M. Tweet Company, a grain and feed business. Lance Fordson had been the manager at Tweet prior to his death. Ralph started his own grain and feed business. Shortly thereafter, a local newspaper carried a story indicating that Ralph and Lance's widow (Minnie) had formed a partnership for the operation of a grain and feed business. Minnie did not see this news item herself, but she was told about it. She called Ralph and asked him about it. He denied putting the item in the paper but said that he would take care of it. He issued a circular to the trade in general which indicated that his business was a sole proprietorship. Meanwhile, Tom Taddis had sold a carload of grain to Ralph on credit. When Ralph failed to pay, Tom sued Ralph and Minnie as partners. Is Minnie liable here? Why or why not?

2. Brothers Stan and Artie Safer went into business together in 1934, each providing equal capital to start an auto dealership. In 1945 they began buying real estate. No written partnership agreement was ever drawn up. The real estate deeds all listed Stan and Artie as co-owners. In 1948 the auto dealership was separated from the real estate business and incorporated. There was a separate checking account for "Stan Safer and Artie Safer, Real Estate Trust Account, Partnership." On some of the real estate the partners executed leases which indicated that they were partners. They

filed partnership tax returns for the real estate business. Stan died in 1978, and his widow, Rosalynn, in addition to challenging his will, filed a lawsuit claiming that the pieces of real estate had been owned by Stan and Artie as tenants in common and that Stan's estate was entitled to his half. Is she correct? Why or why not?

3. Dawson, Donald, David, and Dunston Stedd, together with their father, I. N. Stedd, were partners in two restaurant businesses, one in Arizona and one in New Mexico. A partnership agreement had been drawn up and signed for the Arizona business, but none existed for the New Mexico business. The Arizona agreement provided that a withdrawing partner would receive only the value of his or her capital account. Dolly Stedd had withdrawn from the New Mexico business firm in 1966 and had received only the value of her capital account. Dawson had withdrawn from the New Mexico firm in 1972 but had later changed his mind and been readmitted without having to pay additional consideration, since no new balance sheet had been prepared showing his withdrawal. The readmission-without-additional-consideration provision was also part of the Arizona written partnership agreement. In 1977 Dawson decided to drop out of both firms. He now says that he is entitled to a determination of the true value of his interest in the New Mexico firm and that he is not bound by the provisions of the Arizona written agreement. Is he correct? Why or why not?

4. Yoland Yutka operated a dry cleaning business in a building she owned. In her will she left the land and building to her three children—Nicholas, Marianna, and Hilda—in equal shares, and the business to Nicholas and Marianna in equal shares. Almost from the beginning, disputes arose as to the operation of the dry cleaning business. Nicholas and Marianna each accused the other of unfair dealing and misappropriation of money. Nicholas sued for a dissolution. Three appraisers agreed that the land and building were worth $51,000 and that the business was worth $48,000. The court appointed a referee to determine what should be done with the business. Nicholas offered to buy out Marianna for $66,000. She made no offer, nor did she appear at the hearing before the referee. The referee entered an order that Marianna sell to Nicholas for $66,000, with $18,000 down and the balance to be paid over 10 years with 12 percent interest. Marianna now appeals from the referee's order, claiming that she should be permitted to submit a bid on the business and that she is owed additional money. How should the court rule? Discuss.

5. Downer, Suam, and Hacker had organized a law partnership, with a written agreement. Their agreement provided that a withdrawing partner was entitled to his or her share of the collected assets of the firm on the date of termination but was not entitled to any share for uncollected accounts receivable or for services performed which had not yet been billed to clients. Another paragraph of the agreement dealt with termination of the firm, which required a two-thirds vote of the partners, in which case all unbilled and uncollected accounts had to be distributed to the partners in accordance with their shares. The paragraph dealing with the duration of the firm said that it was to last from fiscal year to fiscal year, "subject to the right of any partner to terminate pursuant to said agreement." Hacker says that he is terminating the firm, and he wants his share of all the assets. Downer and Suam say that he can only withdraw and that he has no claim for unbilled and uncollected services. Who's right, and why?

6. Helbert, Leland, Cedric, Wilton, and Maxwell formed a rock band known as the Artistics. They gave concerts for about two years, and they made at least one very successful recording. Disputes arose over working arrangements, and the group broke up. Helbert, Leland, and Cedric claim that Wilton and Maxwell dropped out, and they want a permanent injunction against the use of the name Artistics by

Wilton and Maxwell. There was no written partnership agreement, and apparently no oral agreement, as to what would happen to the group's name if a partner withdrew or was expelled. What should happen to the firm name here? (Which partners, if any, have the right to use it?) Discuss.

7. Lemke had managed a hardware store for Crumley for several years, when Lemke got an offer from one of Crumley's competitors for employment at an increased salary and with a profit-sharing plan. Lemke told Crumley that the offer was so good that he was probably going to accept it. Crumley then offered Lemke a partnership in the new store he was opening. Lemke accepted Crumley's offer, and the parties signed an agreement to form a partnership upon the purchase of the new store. Lemke turned down the competitor's offer. After the new store had been open about six months, Crumley sold it without consulting Lemke and terminated Lemke's employment as manager. Lemke sues for damages. What result, and why?

8. Warlock hired Bronson as an auctioneer for a sale of Warlock's surplus and used equipment, materials, and supplies. Bronson was to get 8 percent of the sales price. Bronson, in turn, hired the Biltrite Bank to provide clerking and cashiering services at the sale, for which Bronson would pay it 2 percent of the sales price. Bronson disclosed, through ads and at the sale, that Warlock was the owner of the merchandise being auctioned. Bobber bought several used fuel drums at the auction. About two years later, Merwin and Shirley (both minors) were playing with a cigarette lighter near the drums, when one of them exploded. Merwin and Shirley sue Warlock, Bronson, and the Biltrite Bank as joint venturers. How should the court rule here? Explain.

Partnerships—Operation, Powers, Duties, and Liabilities | 40

In the previous chapter we discussed the creation, dissolution, and termination of the partnership. In this chapter we are concerned with the law which governs the day-to-day operation of the partnership. We are concerned with the legal relationships between partners, that is, the rights and duties between partners, and also with the relationship of partners to third persons. Third persons, of course, include the public and persons doing business with the partnership.

PARTNER'S RIGHTS AND DUTIES WITH REGARD TO OTHER PARTNERS

Right to Participate in Management Decisions. In a general partnership, unless there is a specific agreement to the contrary, each partner should have the right to participate in the partnership's management activities and management decisions. Each partner should also have an equal vote with the other partners in the management and decision making of the partnership. Here a partnership differs from a corporation, since in a corporation a stockholder will have votes for directors in proportion to his or her ownership of stock, whereas in a partnership every partner has an equal voice and vote regardless of the amount of money or services the partner has contributed to the business.

National Biscuit Company, Inc. v. Stroud
106 S.E.2d 692 (North Carolina, 1959)

FACTS   C. N. Stroud and Earl Freeman were equal partners in a grocery store business known as Stroud's Food Center. During 1953, 1954, and 1955 the plaintiff regularly sold bread to the store. Several months prior to February 1956, Stroud told one of the plaintiff's agents that he did not want any more of its bread in the store and that he

---

National Biscuit Company, Inc. v. Stroud (continued)

would not be personally responsible for any more bread purchases from it. From February 6 through February 25, 1956, the plaintiff sold $171.04 worth of bread to the store through this agent. The partnership was dissolved, and Stroud took over the business and paid off all of its existing debts ($12,014.45) except for "his" half of the bread bill, $85.52. The plaintiff recovered a judgment for $171.04, and Stroud appealed.

ISSUE   Can one partner's act within the normal scope of the business bind the firm where there is an equal division of opinion and where the third party has been so notified?

DECISION   Yes. Judgment affirmed.

REASONS   Judge Parker noted that the textbooks disagreed on this point. The problem was not handled in the UPA either, so each state's courts had to make up their own mind as to which was the better rule. (In the few cases that had been decided, the state courts were split too.) Judge Parker began with the idea that this contract was within the ordinary scope of the firm's business and that Freeman was an equal partner, with no limitations in the partnership agreement on his ability to represent the firm. He then cited UPA, Section 18(e), "All partners have equal rights in the management and conduct of the partnership business," and Section 18(h), "Any difference arising as to ordinary matters connected with the partnership business may be decided by a majority of the partners." Freeman thus had equal rights to manage the business.

"Stroud, his co-partner, could not restrict the power and authority of Freeman to buy bread for the partnership as a going concern, for such a purchase was an 'ordinary matter connected with the partnership business,' for the purpose of its business and within its scope, because in the very nature of things Stroud was not, and could not be, a majority of the partners. Therefore, Freeman's purchases of bread from plaintiff for Stroud's Food Center as a going concern bound the partnership and his co-partner Stroud. . . .

"It would seem a fair inference from the agreed statement of facts that the partnership got the benefit of the bread sold and delivered by plaintiff to Stroud's Food Center, at Freeman's request, from 6 February 1956 to 25 February 1956. . . . But whether it did or not, Freeman's acts, as stated above, bound the partnership and Stroud."

With regard to day-to-day business decisions, it is not uncommon for partners to delegate certain decision-making authority to a managing partner. This partner will act as a general manager of the business. In a large law firm or a large accounting firm, for example, it is not possible for the partners to get together daily to make decisions on business matters. Typically the partners will meet on a regular basis to make policy decisions and general management decisions other than the day-to-day decisions which are delegated to the managing partner. Usually a simple majority vote is needed on such matters. For certain types of decisions, however, unanimous action of the partners is required. These include decisions involving an amendment of the original articles of partnership, the addition of a new partner, major changes in the business activities of the partnership, any changes in the division of profits. Again, we must emphasize that a partnership is a contractual arrangement and that the partners may, if they so desire, provide in the partnership agreement that certain changes shall require only a majority vote, a two-thirds vote, a unaminous vote, and so on. Again we emphasize the necessity for having the partnership agreement cover and anticipate these kinds of matters.

Right to Share Profits and Duty to Share Losses. Generally speaking, each partner has a right to share in the profits of the partnership and is liable for its losses. The problem to be resolved is how much each partner's share is. If there is no agreement with regard to the sharing of profits, then the partners would share them equally. However, it is best to have an agreement specifying a formula for sharing profits. This formula can be based on the various partners' contributions of capital and/or services. If there is no such agreement, then the partners will share losses in the same ratio as they share profits. However, if there is a formula for sharing losses, then that formula will be followed as between the partners.

Rights to Salary or Other Compensation. A partner is not, as a matter of right, entitled to a salary or to other compensation for the services he or she renders to the partnership. Absent an agreement which provides for salaries to the various partners, it is assumed that the partners have agreed to share the profits. Obviously, salaries would reduce the total profits. Thus, if salaries or other forms of compensation are contemplated, then a special agreement should be made with regard to these items. It is not uncommon for partners to be paid regular salaries, with profits then being distributed at the end of the calendar or fiscal year.

Right to Inspect Partnership Books of Account. Each partner has the right to inspect the partnership books and to make copies of those books for his or her own records. The partnership books must be kept at the principal office of the partnership unless the partnership agreement specifies otherwise.

Rights in Partnership Property. Section 8 of the Uniform Partnership Act indicates that all property which is contributed when the partnership is formed and all property which the partnership later acquires by purchase or otherwise is considered partnership property and not the property of any individual partner.

Section 25 of the Uniform Partnership Act provides that all the partners in a partnership are co-owners with regard to specific partnership property. Subject to the provisions of the Uniform Partnership Act and also subject to any agreement among the various partners, each partner has an equal right to use partnership property for partnership purposes. A partner, however, has no right to use such property for any other purpose without the consent of the other partners or to assign his or her right in any partnership property to another person unless all the other partners join in an assignment of that property to that person. A partner's interest or property rights in property owned by the partnership is not subject to attachment or execution by an individual creditor of the partner. Partnership property would, of course, be subject to attachment or execution for a debt or a claim against the partnership.

When a partner dies, that partner's interest or property rights in partnership property automatically transfer to the surviving partner or partners. At this point, it becomes important to distinguish between ownership of specific partnership property and simply having an interest in the partnership. Even though the deceased partner's property rights in specific partnership property cease upon his or her death, that partner's heirs will inherit his or her interest in the total assets of the partnership.

Cyrus v. Cyrus
64 N.W.2d 538 (Minnesota, 1954)

FACTS   Edna Cyrus, as the administratrix of the estate of her deceased husband, Cecil Cyrus, sued her brother-in-law, Curtis Cyrus, to establish the existence of a partnership between the brothers from 1936 until her husband's death in 1944. Cecil and Edna were living in North Dakota when Curtis wrote them letters urging them to come to Minnesota and enter into a "partnership" operating a tourist camp on Lake of the Woods. Cecil and Edna moved to Minnesota and began operation of the camp. Curtis owned a 60-acre tract of land and later purchased another 40 acres. Cecil and his father built the first cabin, and Cecil, Edna, and their three children did nearly all the work connected with running the camp. Curtis visited the camp each fall, and the profits were then divided 50–50. Curtis sent Cecil a copy of his will, explaining that he was protecting Cecil in that way until he could deed half of the property to him. After Cecil's death, Curtis told Edna that he would deed half of the property to her, saying, "It's as much yours as mine." However, Curtis or his agents had operated the resort since 1945 without sharing the profits. The trial court found that there had been a partnership and ordered Curtis to pay Edna $5,000 (half of the property's net value in 1944) plus interest since the date of Cecil's death. Curtis appealed.

ISSUE   Does the evidence sustain the trial court's finding that a partnership existed?

DECISION   Yes. Judgment affirmed.

REASONS   Justice Matson indicated that the existence of a partnership was a question of fact and that each case had to be decided "according to its own peculiar facts." Here there were several indications that a partnership existed, even though both tracts of land used in the resort business had always been registered in Curtis' name. The original letters Curtis wrote to Cecil and Edna indicated an intent to form a partnership. Curtis' letter and the copy of his will which he sent to Cecil also spoke in terms of co-ownership of the business. Curtis had told Edna after Cecil died that the business was as much hers as his.

"The evidence as a whole in other respects reasonably tends to indicate an intent of the parties to combine their property, labor, and skill as co-owners of a business for joint profit. There is credible evidence that the resort equipment and improvements were paid for out of the resort earnings. Significantly there was a splitting of the profits each fall. . . . In addition Cecil was never paid a fixed wage or sal-

Right to Return of Capital Contributions. Section 18 of the Uniform Partnership Act provides that absent any agreement to the contrary among the partners, each partner shall be legally entitled to repayment of his or her capital contribution to the partnership. The repayment of capital contributions is considered to be a liability of the partnership. Unless otherwise agreed, a partner is not entitled to interest on his or her capital contribution to the partnership. If, however, a partner contributes more than his or her required share, then the amount in excess of the required contribution will be treated as a loan and interest will be paid on it.

Right to Repayment of Expenses. Each partner has a right to be indemnified for payments which he or she makes and personal liabilities which he or she reasonably incurs in the ordinary and proper conduct of the partnership business or in order to preserve the partnership business or its property.

Right to Decide Who Will Be a Partner. No new partners may be admitted to a partnership without the consent of all the present partners unless there is an agreed procedure to the contrary in the partnership agreement.

Duties of One Partner to the Other Partner. Each partner is an agent of the partnership and thus, in effect, an agent of every other partner in the partnership. As an agent, the partner has a fiduciary relationship with the partnership and with the other partners. This relationship carries with it a number of duties. Among these duties are the following:

1. A partner must be loyal to the partnership and to his or her partners. A partner may not conduct business which will conflict with the partnership unless he or she has the other partners' permission to do so.
2. A partner has a duty to account to the other partners.
3. A partner must use reasonable care in conducting partnership business.
4. If the activities in which a partner engages or the information which a partner has acquired may affect the partnership, the partner has a duty to keep the other partners advised of them.
5. A partner has a legal duty to abide by the terms of the partnership agreement.

819

Belcher v. *Whittemore*
134 Mass. 330 (Massachusetts, 1883)

FACTS John Whittemore, Benjamin Belcher, and another person were partners in a business which manufactured and sold agricultural implements. Using the firm's premises and materials and taking time that he was supposed to be devoting to the firm's business, Whittemore developed certain improvements for agricultural implements, which he then patented in his own name. His partners were aware of all his activities and made no objection. Whittemore was willing to let the firm use these patented inventions on its products, but he said that he owned the patent rights individually. Belcher and the other partner sued to have the patents declared partnership property.

ISSUE Can one partner become the individual owner of patents which he develops by using partnership property and time?

DECISION Yes. Plaintiff's suit dismissed.

REASONS Judge Allen's decision was based primarily on his extremely limited view of the scope of the partnership's business. Specifically, he said: "The inventing and patenting of new and improved machines was no part of the business of manufacturing and selling them, and did not come within the scope of the partnership business." It seems very unlikely that courts today would take such a restricted view of the R&D function of a manufacturing business. Because Whittemore's activities were outside the scope of the firm's business and because his partners knew about these activities but made no objection to them, Judge Allen interpreted their failure to object as their consent to what would otherwise have been a breach of the partnership agreement by Whittemore.

"If he violated his agreement, or used the property of the firm without the consent of his copartners, he was liable therefor. But it does not appear that he did anything to the detriment of the firm, or without the consent of his copartners. The improvements he devised, whether patented or not, were a benefit to the firm by increasing its business, and no objection was made by any member of it, either to the making use by Whittemore of the facilities furnished by the business for making experiments and improvements, or to the procuring of letters patent by him for inventions so made. We know of no principle or decision which, upon the facts in the case, could give to the copartnership any right in the patents."

THE RELATIONSHIP OF PARTNERS TO THIRD PERSONS

Unless there is a contrary agreement, every partner in a general partnership is an agent of the partnership for the purpose of conducting the partnership's business. It is not uncommon for articles of partnership to limit or restrict the agency power of the various partners. This is an agreement between the partners, and such internal limitations or restrictions among the partners themselves would not relieve the partnership of liability to a third person who dealt with a partner who exceeded them unless that third person knew that the partner was limited in his or her authority. Since, generally speaking, each partner is an agent of the partnership, the basic law of agency is applicable to the relationship between partners and third persons.

Phillips v. *Cook*
210 A.2d 743 (Maryland, 1965)

FACTS Daniel Phillips and Isadore Harris were equal partners in a business known as Dan's Used Cars. Neither of them owned a personal car. They had agreed that Harris would use the firm's cars for transportation to and from home. He could demonstrate and sell such cars, and they had "for sale" signs placed in them at various times. He could also use such cars to visit other dealerships and buy cars for the firm's inventory and to stop at the Department of Motor Vehicles so that necessary paperwork could be done for the firm's business. On January 7, 1960, while driving one of the firm's cars, Harris hit a car driven by Smith, which in turn hit a car driven by Dolores Cook. Harris was on his way home at the time. About a week later, the partnership was terminated. Dolores and her husband, Marshall, sued the partnership and received a judgment. Phillips appealed.

ISSUE Did the accident occur within the scope of the firm's business?

DECISION Yes. Judgment affirmed.

REASONS Judge Marbury thought that the trial court had properly instructed the jury and that there was substantial evidence to support the jury's verdict.

"The test of the liability of the partnership and of its members for the torts of any one partner is whether the wrongful act was done within what may reasonably be found to be the scope of the business of the partnership and for its benefit. The extent of the authority of a partner is determined essentially by the same principles as those which measure the scope of an agent's authority. . . .

"In the past, we have held both in workmen's compensation cases and others that where an employer authorizes or furnishes the employee transportation to and from his work as an incident to his employment, or as a benefit to the employer, the employee is considered in the course of his employment when so traveling."

Judge Marbury then pointed out that the very car which Harris was driving was for sale and that Harris often returned to the dealership or called on customers at night. He also pointed to the specific agreement which permitted each partner to use the firm's cars. In addition, Maryland motor vehicle statutes provided a rebuttable presumption that a vehicle titled in the partnership name and being driven by a partner was being used for partnership business. Phillips had not overcome that presumption.

Phillips also tried to argue that he should not be held personally liable, at least not until after the firm's assets had been exhausted. Judge Marbury said, however, that the UPA made each partner jointly and *severally* liable for torts committed by partners, agents, or employees within the scope of the firm's business. The Cooks could collect their judgment directly against Phillips, though he would then have the right to demand contribution from Harris and/or the firm.

It is a general rule of agency that third persons who deal with an agent have the duty to ascertain the nature and the extent of the alleged agent's authority. Third persons cannot simply rely on a person's statement that he or she is an agent and has certain authority. In the case of a partnership, if a third person verifies that a person is a partner, then the third person has a right to believe that the partner-agent has the normal authority of a partner unless he or she is told otherwise. In other words, if a partnership is going to restrict or limit a partner's authority, then the partnership is responsible for notifying all persons who might be dealing with the partner-agent that the partner-agent does not have the full authority that would ordinarily be expected of a person in that capacity.

The partnership is also a principal and the individual partner an agent with regard to any information that the individual partner may secure which relates to the partnership's business affairs. If a partner acquires certain information, then the partnership as the principal is automatically charged with the same information. It is also a general rule of agency that statements and representations made by an agent will bind the principal even though the statements may be untrue, provided the statements were made in the course of the agent's business for the principal and provided the statements were within the normally expected authority of such an agent.

Limitations on a Partner's Authority by Law. Since each partner is an agent of the partnership, it would seem that as long as a partner's acts or transactions are within the scope of the partnership business, then the partnership would be liable for contracts made by a partner on behalf of the partnership. However, there are a number of legal limitations on the authority of individual partners to act for the partnership. The first such limitation concerns a partner's right to act as an agent with regard to the purchase and conveyance of real estate. Section 10 of the Uniform Partnerhip Act deals with the right to convey real property owned by the partnership. Where the partnership holds title to real property in the partnership name, any partner may convey the title to that property by a deed executed in the partnership name by that partner as agent. However, if the other partners have not authorized the partner to make such a conveyance, then the partnership can recover the property from the person to whom it was conveyed. An exception would be made to this right of the partnership to recover the property where the person to whom the conveyance was made transferred the title to an innocent third person who had no knowledge of the situation. Then the innocent third person would prevail over the partnership, provided there was no fraud in the transaction. Another exception would be made where certain acts or past practices of the partnership had created the apparent authority of the particular agent to convey the real estate. The only safe way to purchase real estate from a partnership is to secure both a deed signed by one of the partners and a resolution signed by all of the partners which authorizes the sale of the real estate and also authorizes a specific partner to sign on behalf of the partnership.

Section 9 of the Uniform Partnership Act sets out these further restrictions:

Section 9(3) states "Unless authorized by the other partners or unless they have abandoned the business, one or more but less than all the partners have no authority to: (a) assign the partnership property in trust for creditors or on the assignee's promise to pay the debts of the partnership, (b) dispose of the good-will of the business, (c) do any other act which would make it impossible to carry on the ordinary business of a partnership, (d) confess a judgment, (e) submit a partnership claim or liability to arbitration or reference."

Section 9(4) the UPA further confirms that no act of a partner in a contravention of a restriction on that partner's authority shall bind the partnership to persons having knowledge of the restriction.

Thus, as indicated previously, if there are so-called internal restrictions on the power and authority of a partnership's various agents and if those restrictions have been revealed to third persons, then even though a partner exceeds his or her authority, such third persons have no recourse against the partnership for the partner's unauthorized acts.

Authority to Hire and Fire Employees. Going back to the basic authority of the partner, as set out in Section 9 of the Uniform Partnership Act, every partner is an agent of the partnership for the purpose of its business. Every act of a partner, including the execution in the partnership name of any instrument apparently necessary for carrying on the business of the partnership in the usual way, binds the partnership unless the partner has no authority to act for the partnership in that particular matter and the person with whom he is dealing knows that he has no authority. The articles of partnership could very well state that certain partners are charged with the duty of hiring and firing personnel and that the other partners have no direct authority to do so but have the right to be consulted on matters concerning the employment and tenure of personnel. For example, in a 50-partner law or accounting firm, you could not have each and every partner hiring and firing as he or she saw fit. In a two- or three-member partnership, on the other hand, each of the partners may be involved in the hiring and firing of personnel. Absent an agreement to the contrary between partners, each partner would have the authority to hire persons whose services were reasonably necessary to carry on the partnership business and the further authority to bind the partnership for a reasonable salary for such persons. Each partner would also have the right to dismiss any employee whose services he or she felt were not reasonably necessary to carry on the partnership business. One can immediately see the problems that could arise if such authority were exercised in a firm with a large number of partners. This is why some internal agreement between the partners should specify which partner or partners have the authority to hire and fire personnel and should restrict the other partners accordingly.

Borrowing Money and Mortgaging the Partnership Property. Going back to the general authority clause to which we referred briefly, any partner has the authority to borrow money and execute a mortgage on behalf of the partnership, provided this is done for the purpose of carrying on the partnership business in the usual way. The Uniform Partnership Act does not differentiate between the authority of an agent in a trading partnership and that of an agent in a nontrading partnership. However, in interpreting a partner's authority, courts in many jurisdictions have generally found that partners in a trading partnership which is engaged in buying and selling goods and property have greater implied and apparent authority to buy and sell property, to borrow in the partnership name, and to indorse or execute negotiable instruments in the partnership name if this is reasonably necessary to carry on the partnership business. In partnerships which are considered to be engaged in a nontrading business, such as law firms or accounting firms, courts generally do not feel that individual partners should have the implied and apparent authority to borrow money or to execute or indorse negotiable instruments in the partnership name. Generally speaking, courts have held that the partners in nontrading partnerships do not have the authority to bind the partnership in such situations unless it was customary to do so in given partnership or unless there was an actual necessity to do so. Thus trading partnerships are governed by standards different from the standards that govern partners in nontrading partnerships insofar as their authority with relation to third parties is concerned.

Alabama Cabinet Works v. Benson Hardware Co.
125 So. 214 (Alabama, 1929)

FACTS J. T. Brewer and G. E. Padgett were partners in the Alabama Cabinet Works, which was engaged in home improvement and construction. Padgett bought certain building materials and supplies for the firm from Benson Hardware and signed a promissory note in the firm name for the contract price. Padgett's authority was limited by the partnership agreement, but Benson didn't know of the limitation when he dealt with Padgett. Brewer questioned Padgett's authority to sign the note and argued that at least he should not be held personally liable for the note. Judgment was entered against the firm, Brewer, and Padgett. The firm and Brewer appealed.

ISSUE Was one partner authorized to execute the note for the firm?

DECISION Yes. Judgment affirmed.

REASONS Judge Thomas first decided that the trial court had made no error in charging the jury or in admitting evidence of what happened.

"Padgett, being a full partner in the business of construction, had the authority to sign the partnership name to the note for material and supplies used in that business. . . . That the materials or supplies were sold and credit was given the partnership was not denied. . . .

"The entire management of that business was intrusted to and conducted by Padgett. Those dealing with the partnership and Padgett as such manager were authorized to assume the full authority of the latter in the line and scope of that business. . . .

"'It is a legal consequence of all mercantile partnerships, that each partner is the general agent of the firm, in all transactions within the scope of its business. Within the range of its ordinary business, his acts and engagements are as binding on the firm, as if all the members had united in them. . . . Each partner has an implied authority to make or indorse promissory notes in the name of, and binding on the firm, if they are made or indorsed for the benefit of the partnership, in the course of the partnership business.'"

When the Partnership Goes to Court.   Under the common law a partnership was not a legal entity and therefore a partnership could not sue or be sued in the partnership name. If a third person wanted to sue a partnership, the complaint had to name all of the partners as individual defendants and each partner had to be individually served with a summons. This could be accomplished without too much effort when simple father-son partnerships or three- or four-member partnerships were being dealt with. However, if it had to be done with a modern accounting firm having more than a hundred partners, not all of whom lived in the same jurisdiction, the chore could prove very frustrating. Thus many states have enacted statutes which allow a partnership to be sued as an entity by simply naming the partnership by its firm name. These statutes also allow a partnership to bring action as a legal entity against third persons. Most statutes, however, require that the partners be named as defendants and be served personally with process if this is at all possible. Most statutes also permit the petitioner to secure a judgment against the partnership if the petitioner served at least one of the partners even though several other partners were not served. In a case where the partnership entity was sued and at least one of the partners was named and served process, the judgment can be collected from the partnership assets and any judgment amount not collectible from the partnership assets cannot be collected from the individual partners unless the individual partners were sued, made a party to the lawsuit, and properly served with a summons.

Ragan v. *Smith*
174 S.E. 622 (Georgia, 1934)

FACTS   The plaintiff, Ragan, sought an injunction to restrain the issuance of garnishment orders to persons who were indebted to him, as part of the process of collecting on a judgment entered against his former partnership. One of his partners had died, and the firm had been dissolved. Ragan claimed here that he "as an individual has never had his day in court, was never served with any process or other notice of the pendency of the suit whereupon the execution is based, nor did he waive service, nor did he appear or defend said suit in his own behalf." Smith, the judgment creditor, filed a demurrer to this injunction suit. The demurrer was sustained by the trial court, and Ragan appealed.

ISSUE   Did the judgment against the firm bind the individual partner?

DECISION   Yes. Judgment dismissing the injunction suit affirmed.

REASONS   The Georgia Supreme Court issued a per curiam opinion which briefly summarized the law.
"A judgment recovered in a suit against the partnership binds the partnership assets and the individual assets of the partners served. . . . The judgment need not be rendered expressly against the individual members who are served, in order to bind individual assets. . . .
"Construing the petition and the exhibit most strongly against the plaintiff, as must

be done on demurrer, it is not averred that he was not served as a member, and it is therefore presumed, either that he was served in that capacity, or that service on the partnership was perfected by service upon him. . . .

"The dissolution of a partnership by the death of a member does not absolve the partners from liability from 'transactions that are past.'"

Getting a judgment against a partnership is the first step. The next step is to collect it. Section 40(h) of the Uniform Partnership Act states: "When partnership property and the individual properties of the partners are in possession of a court for distribution, partnership creditors shall have priority on partnership property and separate creditors on individual property, saving the rights of lien or secured creditors as heretofore." In other words, lienholders and secured creditors come first; the partner's individual creditors for his or her individual bills come next; and then the balance can be taken for partnership debts. The new bankruptcy code which became law in October 1980 changes the law of distribution with regard to the assets of partners. It provides that in a case concerning a partnership, if the assets of the partnership are insufficient to satisfy the claims allowed, then each general partner in the partnership will be liable to the trustee in bankruptcy for the full amount of the deficiency. Thus, in the case of a bankrupt partnership the trustee in bankruptcy may now seek to recover the entire deficiency from any one of the general partners who has not already filed bankruptcy for himself or herself.

CASES FOR DISCUSSION

STARR v. INTERNATIONAL REALTY, LTD.

533 P.2d 165 (Oregon, 1975)

Tongue, Justice

This is a suit by the partners in a real estate venture to require the realtor and promoter of the venture, who was also a partner, to account to the partnership for the commission received by him as the realtor without consent of the remaining partners and to hold in trust for the partnership the vendor's interest in the real estate purchased, which he also acquired without their consent. Defendants appeal from an adverse decree, and plaintiffs cross-appeal from other portions of that degree.

The case involves a group of prominent Port-

land doctors and others in high income tax "brackets" and in need of "tax shelters." They were pursuaded by one Stanley G. Harris, a Portland "expert" in real property investments, that by investing $285,000 and joining with him in a partnership for the purchase of an apartment house then under construction, the entire down payment of $265,000 could be treated for federal income tax purposes as "prepaid interest," thereby saving large amounts otherwise payable in income taxes.

It would serve no useful purpose to summarize the entire transaction for the purchase of this property for the sum of $1,010,000 in all of its details, as "put together" by Harris. . . . Harris did not reveal to his partners that the property could have been purchased for $907,500 "net" to the seller (including $207,500 to the seller to "cash [him] out of transaction" and the assumption of a $700,000 mortgage), and that a commission of $100,000, together with an escrow fee of $2,500, was to be paid to International Realty Ltd., of which Harris was president, or that Harris had made an agreement with the seller of the property under which International or Harris would acquire the vendor's interest in the contract under which the property was being purchased by the partnership.

1. Defendants' failure to disclose the receipt of the broker's commission.

The question to be decided in this case . . . is whether the $100,000 commission paid to International, of which Harris was the president, was a "secret" commission. . . .

It appears from the testimony that most of the plaintiffs knew or should have known that Harris and International were in the real estate business and that a realtor's commission in some amount would normally be paid to some realtor on the transaction. Apparently, because their interest in the income tax advantage of the transaction was so dominant and overriding, the doctors did not inquire whether such a commission would be paid to Harris or to International, or in what amount, and Harris did not tell them. It is contended by the doctors, however, that in this case they are entitled to the benefit of the equivalent of a rule more familiar to them in the practice of medicine—that of "informed consent."

When, as in this case, a real estate broker undertakes to join as a member of a partnership or joint venture in the purchase of real property on which he holds a listing, he is also subject to the fiduciary duties of undivided loyalty and complete disclosure owed by one partner to another. Indeed, one of the fundamental duties of any partner who deals on his own account in matters within the scope of his fiduciary relationship is the affirmative duty to make a full disclosure to his partners not only of the fact he is dealing on his own account, but all the facts which are material to the transaction. . . .

It follows that the "consent of the other partners" required by ORS 68,340(1) before any partner may retain "any benefit" from "any transaction connected with the formation [or] conduct" of a partnership must necessarily be an "informed consent" with knowledge of the facts necessary to the giving of an intelligent consent.

In this case, Harris did not inform plaintiffs or disclose to them the fact that this property could have been purchased for $907,500 "net" to the seller or that upon its purchase for $1,010,000 Harris or International (of which Harris was the president) would be paid a commission in the amount of $100,000. In the absence of such a disclosure there could be no effective "consent" by plaintiffs to the payment or retention by Harris of any such "benefit" from that transaction. . . .

For these reasons, we must reject defendants' contention that the broker's commission paid to International was "neither secret nor concealed." For the same reasons, the trial court did not err in requiring defendants to account to the partnership for that commission.

2. Defendants' failure to disclose the agreement to receive an assignment of the vendor's interest in the sales contract.

The acquisition by International (and subsequently by Harris and his wife) of the vendor's interest in the property being purchased under contract by the partnership of which Harris was a member was a "benefit" that was "connected with the formation [and] conduct" of the partnership and was subject to ORS 68,340(1), so as to require "consent" by the other parties and so as also to be subject to the duty of full disclosure to the same extent as the receipt of the commission on the sale, as previously discussed. . . .

It follows that the trial court did not err in holding that Harris holds the vendor's interest in this contract in trust for the benefit of the partnership.

CLEMENT v. CLEMENT

260 A.2d 728 (Pennsylvania, 1970)

Roberts, Justice

Charles and L. W. Clement are brothers whose 40-year partnership has ended in acrimonious litigation. The essence of the conflict lies in Charles' contention that L. W. has over the years wrongfully taken for himself more than his share of the partnership's profits. Charles discovered these misdeeds during negotiations with L. W. over the sale of Charles' interest in the partnership in 1964. He then filed an action in equity, asking for dissolution of the partnership, appointment of a receiver, and an accounting. Dissolution was ordered and a receiver appointed. After lengthy hearings on the issue of the accounting the chancellor decided that L. W., who was the brighter of the two and who kept the partnership books, had diverted partnership funds. The chancellor awarded Charles a one-half interest in several pieces of property owned by L. W. and in several insurance policies on L. W.'s life on the ground that these had been purchased with partnership assets.

The court en banc heard the case and reversed the chancellor's decree in several material respects. The reversal was grounded on two propositions; that Charles' recovery could only be premised on a showing of fraud and that this burden was not met, and that the doctrine of laches foreclosed Charles' right to complain about the bulk of the alleged misdeeds.

We disagree with the court en banc's statement of the applicable law and therefore reverse. Our theory is simple. There is a fiduciary relationship between partners. Where such a relationship exists, actual fraud need not be shown. There was ample evidence of self-dealing and diversion of partnership assets on the part of L. W.—more than enough to sustain the chancellor's conclusion that several substantial investments made by L. W. over the years were bankrolled with funds improperly withdrawn from the partnership. Further, we are of the opinion that the docrine of laches is inapplicable because Charles' delay in asserting his rights was as much a product of L. W.'s concealment and misbehavior as of any negligence on his part. In all this we are strongly motivated by the fact that the chancellor saw and heard the various witnesses for exhausting periods of time and was in a much better position than we could ever hope to be to taste the flavor of the testimony. . . .

One should not have to deal with his partner as though he were the opposite party in an arm's-length transaction. One should be allowed to

828

trust his partner, to expect that he is pursuing a common goal and not working at cross-purposes. This concept of the partnership entity was expressed most ably by Mr. Justice, then Judge, Cardozo. . . .

Joint adventurers, like copartners, owe to one another, while the enterprise continues, the duty of the finest loyalty. Many forms of conduct permissible in a workaday world for those acting at arm's length, are forbidden to those bound by fiduciary ties. A trustee is held to something stricter than the morals of the marketplace. Not honesty alone, but the punctilio of an honor the most sensitive, is then the standard of behavior. As to this there has developed a tradition that is unbending and inveterate. . . . Only thus has the level of conduct for fiduciaries been kept at a level higher than that trodden by the crowd. It will not consciously be lowered by any judgment of this court. . . .

It would be unduly harsh to require that one must prove actual fraud before he can recover for a partner's derelictions. Where one partner has so dealt with the partnership as to raise the probability of wrongdoing, it ought to be his responsibility to negate that inference. It has been held that "where a partner fails to keep a record of partnership transactions, and is unable to account for them, every presumption will be made against him." . . . Likewise, where a partner commingles partnership funds with his own and generally deals loosely with partnership assets he ought to have to shoulder the task of demonstrating the probity of his conduct.

In the instant case L. W. dealt loosely with partnership funds. At various times he made substantial investments in his own name. He was totally unable to explain where he got the funds to make these investments. The court en banc held that Charles had no claim on the fruits of these investments because he could not trace the money that was invested therein dollar for dollar from the partnership. Charles should not have had this burden. He did show that his brother diverted substantial sums from the partnership funds under his control. The inference that these funds provided L. W. with the wherewithal to make investments was a perfectly reasonable one for the chancellor to make, and his decision should have been allowed to stand.

The doctrine of laches has no role to play in the decision of this case. It is true that the transactions complained of cover a period of many years. However, we do not think that it can be said that Charles negligently slept on his rights to the detriment of his brother. L. W. actively concealed much of his wrongdoing. He cannot now rely upon the doctrine of laches—that defense was not intended to reward the successful wrongdoer.

The decree is vacated and the case remanded for further proceedings consistent with this opinion. . . .

Eagen, Justice (dissenting)

In 1923 L. W. Clement and his younger brother, Charles, formed a partnership for the purpose of engaging in the plumbing business under the name of Clement Brothers. They agreed to share the profits of the business equally after payment of the debts. L. W. was the more alert and aggressive of the two. He attended special training schools to upgrade his plumbing skills, and became a master plumber. He alone conducted the business here involved, and had complete control of its finances. He frequently worked nights, Sundays, and holidays. Charles, on the other hand, refused to be "bothered" with the administration of the business or its finances. He insisted also on limiting his work to a regular eight-hour shift and confining his contribution to the business to the performance of various plumbing jobs assigned to him.

Over the years, L. W. accumulated assets which eventually became quite valuable. For instance, in 1945 he purchased two lots of land for $5,500, and subsequently constructed a commercial building thereon. This construction was financed in most part by money secured through placing a mortgage on the property. In 1951 he purchased another piece of real estate for $3,500, and in 1927, 1936, 1938, 1945, 1947, 1955, and 1965 purchased policies of life insurance on his own life. There are presently existing substantial loans against some of these policies.

In 1964 Charles for the first time accused his brother, L. W., of misusing partnership funds to gain the assets he had accumulated. Charles did not have any evidence to substantiate the accusation, but surmised something must be wrong since L. W. had so much while he had so little.

At trial, not a scintilla of evidence was introduced to establish that L. W. diverted any partnership funds to purchase any of his personal assets. In view of this, a majority of the court en banc below ruled that Charles failed to establish that he had any interest or property rights therein. With this I agree. The majority of this Court now rule, in effect, that, because of the fiduciary relationship existing, it is L. W.'s burden to prove that he did not misuse partnership funds. This I cannot accept on the existing record.

Finally, it is clear from the record that as to the real estate involved, Charles had full knowledge for many years of its acquisition by L. W. before making any complaint. While it is true that the mere passage of time is insufficient to warrant the enforcement of the doctrine of laches, there is more in this case than the mere passage of time.

I dissent and would affirm the decree of the court below.

WAAGEN v. GERDE

219 P.2d 595 (Washington, 1950)

Donworth, Justice

Appellant Karl Gerde (who will be referred to as the appellant) and respondent were born in Norway and are first cousins. Each came to the United States in 1923. Respondent took up his residence in San Francisco. He has followed the sea since boyhood and now has a master's license. At various times during the period involved in this case his health had been poor and he required medical care. Of this situation appellant was well aware and in the discussion of their plans told respondent that his state of health would make no difference in their contemplated business relationship.

At the time the parties first discussed the purchase of a fishing vessel, appellant resided in Portland, Oregon. In August, 1941, he and his family moved to Seattle. He was an experienced fisherman, and during the summer he was employed as net foreman by a salmon cannery in Alaska.

The general plan which the parties discussed in 1939, and again early in 1940, was to either build or buy a fishing vessel and fish along the Pacific coast for tuna, halibut, and salmon. The possibility of shark fishing was also mentioned. It was contemplated that respondent would be in charge of the fishing operations during the summer (when appellant usually worked in Alaska) and appellant would be in charge in the winter.

Appellant located the *Princess* in March 1940, and arranged to purchase her for $8,750 and to install a new engine for $700. . . .

Appellant was in Alaska during each summer except 1942 and 1945 and obtained the services of another fisherman to take charge of the boat. Appellant and respondent did not see each other from March 1941, to September 1945. . . .

In November 1941, appellant conceived the idea of fishing for soupfin shark with gill nets. He bought some secondhand salmon nets and experimented with them. He caught some shark, but the nets soon became torn and useless. . . .

[S]hark nets are of two kinds: bottom nets (which are placed vertically in the ocean with the weighted lower edge resting on the bottom and left there for two or three days), and drift nets (which are also placed vertically in the ocean with the upper edge supported by floats about 70 feet below the surface, the nets drifting while still connected with the fishing boat). The assembly and use of bottom nets are described in detail in the *Pacific Fisherman* (January, 1943, p. 18), and the same information regarding drift nets is contained in the March, 1943, issue (p. 21) of the same publication. These articles are illustrated with photographs of the *Princess* and her sets of shark nets.

The total cost of these nets and of keeping them in repair during the period from January 1942 to March 1946 was $20,872.54. During the period appellant, without the knowledge of respondent, took one-half of the boat's one-third share of the "catch" as rental for the use of these nets. The gross amount received by him was $37,705.42. His theory appears to be that since respondent did not expressly authorize the purchase of the nets, they belonged exclusively to appellant and he was entitled to half of the boat's share as rental for their use. When the *Princess* was sold, appellant disposed of the nets for $7,000, which he retained, in addition to the rental ($37,705.42). The profit resulting from the use and sale of these nets was $23,832.88, which was retained by appellant. Half of this sum is claimed by respondent in this suit. . . .

[A]ppellant's letters of December 1, 1941, and January 9, 1942, . . . are strongly indicative of his intention that the shark nets were to be partnership activity. In the last mentioned letter he said regarding the nets:

I wrote you and told you what my plans were when I came to Seattle and wanted to hear what you thought, but since I did not get any reply, I had to do something. I ordered new nets and have gotten them now so I am busy getting them ready. How this will work now after the war is on is hard to say, it probably will be difficult to drift. There are many who have made out fine with nets, especially in California. It will cost quite a lot.

Appellant must have considered at the time he wrote this letter that respondent would be charged for his half of the cost of the nets in the same manner as all other equipment had been charged and paid for. Otherwise, it would have been no concern of respondent whether they would "cost quite a lot." At that time the nets had been ordered but not paid for. If appellant desired to obtain respondent's authority to purchase the nets for the partnership, he should have plainly told respondent that unless respondent advised him that he (respondent) desired the partnership to pay for the nets, he (appellant) would undertake the venture personally. Instead of doing so, he wrote this letter which is susceptible of only one interpretation, to wit, that the nets were to be charged to and paid for by the partnership in the same manner as all other fishing gear had been acquired for the boat.

That appellant regarded the purchase of the nets as a partnership transaction is borne out by the way appellant paid for the nets. . . .

830

Mr. Fry . . . testified that payments on the net account were made by withholding certain amounts from the proceeds of sale of fish caught by the *Princess*. Appellant had no funds of his own when he first ordered the nets and had no means of paying for them until fishing became lucrative in the latter part of 1942 and 1943. If the net venture had been a failure, appellant could not have paid for the nets.

From the evidence above referred to, and other testimony and exhibits in the record, we are convinced that the findings of the trial court, that the parties were partners in connection with the purchase and use of the shark nets, are fully sustained and that appellant's second assignment of error is not well taken. . . .

Appellant's final assignment of error is that the trial court erred in refusing to allow appellant any credit for work done by him in constructing the shark nets.

The evidence shows that appellant with some help from his two sons designed and built the shark nets. Respondent did not in any way assist him in this job. According to appellant, the value of this work was $2,500 and he claims that, even though a partnership should be found to exist, he should be compensated for this work.

The general rule is clear that one partner is not entitled to extra compensation from the partnership, in the absence of an express or implied agreement therefor. Each case must depend largely upon its own facts, and thus other cases are generally of little or no assistance in deciding the case at hand. . . .

While appellant's ingenuity and industry were largely responsible for the success of the *Princess* in shark fishing, we cannot find anything in the record from which an agreement to pay him special compensation could be implied. Appellant did inform respondent that he was busy getting the nets ready and it would "be lots of work to fix" them, but never at any time, did he inform respondent what the work actually entailed or that he expected any compensation for it. Since respondent had so little knowledge of the conduct of the net operations, there could not be any implied agreement for compensation. The trial court found no factual basis for such an allowance, and we can find none in the record.

PROBLEMS FOR DISCUSSION

1. Harvey and Haviland formed a partnership for the purpose of brewing and selling beer and ale. Without Haviland's knowledge or consent, Harvey, in the firm's name, negotiated the takeover of a lease on a brewery. This lease still had seven years to run. Harvey, for the firm, promised to take over the lease and to pay the remaining rentals. The firm operated the brewery for about seven months and then dissolved. The firm sold the equipment and the lease to Dougherty, who also went bankrupt. When the landlord sued for unpaid rentals, Haviland denied that he was liable in any way. What result, and why?

2. Porks and Lozer agreed on a plan for the purchase and resale of a particular tract of land. Lozer was to buy the land, pay off the back taxes, and take title in his own name. Porks was to look for buyers for the property. Lozer bought the land for $45,000 and paid off the back taxes of $3,500. Lozer also paid off a $12,000 "claim" against the land, which was presented to him. Lozer acted in good faith in paying this claim, but if he had checked with Porks, Porks would have told him that the claim was invalid and not to pay it. Lozer then resold the land for $156,000. Porks challenges the $12,000 payment as a proper charge against the partnership profits. What is the proper allocation of profits here? Explain.

3. Winken, Blinken, and Nod were partners in a restaurant business. Winken and Blinken decided that the restaurant needed to be remodeled, and they proposed to borrow $8,000 from Bigger Bank to pay the building contractor, Shatturglas. Nod

did not think that the restaurant needed remodeling, so he notified Bigger and Shatturglas that he would not be personally responsible for any obligations resulting from the remodeling job. If Bigger and/or Shatturglas don't get paid by the firm, does either of them have a claim against Nod personally? Why or why not?

4. Rader and Horning were partners in a real estate and insurance firm. While the firm was still in existence, Horning purchased a tract of land with his own funds, had it platted and improved (streets, sewers, etc.), and listed it with the firm as brokers, to be sold at a 15 percent commission. The land was resold at a substantial profit; the real estate brokerage firm was dissolved; and Rader claims that he is entitled to half of the profit on the sale (representing his half of the firm). Does Rader have a valid claim, through the firm, for half of the profit on the resale of the land? Discuss.

5. Rease and Kole were partners in a theatrical business; they operated a playhouse in Chalk, Michigan. Each week the firm tried to hire a different "name" star to take part in a performance. Most of these were performances of plays, but occasionally musicals or variety shows were presented. After several attempts, Rease was finally successful in signing the TV and recording star, Fern Jillson, to appear at the theater. Fern, however, required that a $10,000 guarantee be posted in advance. Without checking with Kole, Rease borrowed the money from the Last National Bank and posted the guarantee. This was the first promissory note which the firm had ever issued, but the bank did not check with Kole either. If the firm defaults on the note, does the bank have a case against the firm and against Kole personally? Explain.

6. Sam Simple and Dolly Dimple operated a CPA firm as partners. While on his way to call on a client, Sam had an accident with his car. Sam's negligent driving was the cause of the accident, and the driver of the other car involved, Millicent Innocent, recovered a $50,000 judgment against him. Sam and his insurance company paid Millicent's judgment, but they now want Dolly to contribute her fair share (one half, or $25,000), since Sam was on the firm's business at the time the accident occurred. Does Dolly have to contribute one half? Why or why not?

7. Instant Insurance Company issued a liability policy covering a delivery truck operated by Artistics, a partnership consisting of Chip and Dale. Chip and Dale were also partners with Pluto in Real Estate Associates, another partnership. Chip was using the Artistics delivery truck to call on a customer of Real Estate Associates when an accident occurred which was solely Chip's fault. Chip, Dale, and Pluto each paid one third of the $150,000 claim filed by the driver of the other car. Chip and Dale now sue Instant to recover the $100,000 they paid. Does Instant have to pay this claim? Discuss.

8. Paas and Oldman were partners in a grocery store business which operated in a building leased from Uriah, on a 10-year lease. One month, while he was in Uriah's office paying the rent, Paas learned that Uriah was interested in selling the building. Without telling Oldman, Paas bought the building in his own name and then resold it at a $20,000 profit. When Oldman finds out what happened, what are his rights? Explain.

9. Bennie and Beatrice Styles, husband and wife, operate their farm as a partnership. Bennie had a serious accident with his camper-van while he was on a vacation fishing trip. Huffy, the driver of the other car, got a $40,000 judgment against Bennie, which judgment has not been paid. In an attempt to collect the judgment, Huffy had the court issue a writ of execution against all of Bennie's personal property. The sheriff came out to the farm with the writ and seized and sold 50 cows. Beatrice sues the sheriff and his bonding company for conversion of partnership assets. Should Beatrice win this lawsuit? Why or why not?

Limited Partnerships | 41

A limited partnership differs from a general partnership in two major respects. First, a limited partnership allows certain partners to have limited liability for the debts and other liabilities of the partnership. Second, a general partnership may be formed by an express oral or written agreement or by an implied agreement, whereas a limited partnership agreement must be in writing and must conform to the statutory requirements for the formation of such a partnership.

The National Conference of Commissioners on Uniform State Laws has found that limited partnership laws varied from state to state. There was a need for uniformity. In 1916 the commissioners drafted the Uniform Limited Partnership Act. This act was adopted by every state except Louisiana, which has its own limited partnership law. In 1976 the commissioners revised the Uniform Limited Partnership Act. A few states have already adopted the revised act, and it appears that the revised act will be adopted by the other states. In the meantime, however, when the Uniform Limited Partnership Act is discussed, it will be important to note what state is involved and whether the new act or the old act is the effective statutory law in that state. Limited partnerships have become a very popular form of business organization for persons who wish to invest but want limited liability, and who also wish to have their profits treated as partnership profits and not as corporate profits subject to the corporate income tax. There is no income tax on the profits of a limited partnership. The partners divide the profits in accordance with the partnership agreement. The partnership files with the Internal Revenue Service a partnership return which is merely an information return. The individual partner's profit is then shown on his or her income tax return, and the individual pays tax on that profit along with the tax on his or her other income. The limited partnership form of business organization is found mostly in so-called tax shelter ventures, such as land development organizations, oil exploration ventures, and cattle feeding ventures.

Definition of a Limited Partnership

Section 1 of the Uniform Limited Partnership Act defines a limited partnership as a "partnership formed by two or more persons . . . having as members one or more general partners and one or more limited partners." Thus each limited partnership must have at least one general partner with unlimited liability for the business of the partnership and at least one partner with limited liability. The limited partner, like a stockholder in a corporation, cannot be liable for more than his or her investment. However, unlike the corporation stockholder, who has a voice in the control of the business through votes for directors based on the number of stock shares that he or she owns, the limited partner has no voice in the control of the business. In fact, if the limited partner does take a part in the management or control of the business, he or she may be held personally liable for the firm's debts. Thus, if a limited partner wants to retain complete limited liability, he or she should not become involved in any way in the operation of the business.

Holzman v. De Escamilla
195 P.2d 833 (California, 1948)

FACTS Ricardo de Escamilla was raising beans on a farm near Escondido when he organized Hacienda Farms, a limited partnership, with James Russell and H. W. Andrews. Russell and Andrews were the limited partners; Ricardo was the general partner. Hacienda Farms operated only from February to December 1943, when it went bankrupt. Holzman, Hacienda's trustee in bankruptcy, sought to hold Russell and Andrews personally liable for its debts, on the basis that they actively participated in the management of the farm. They appealed from a judgment imposing such liability.

ISSUE Was the participation of these limited partners in management sufficient to impose liability as general partners on them?

DECISION Yes. Judgment affirmed.

REASONS Justice Marks, reviewing the facts, found that Russell and Andrews had participated substantially in the operation of Hacienda Farms. When asked whether he had had conversations with them prior to deciding to plant tomatoes, Ricardo said: "We always conferred and agreed as to what crops we would put in." He also said: "There . . . was never any crop that was planted or contemplated in planting that wasn't thoroughly discussed and agreed upon by the three of us; particularly Andrews and myself." In fact, Andrews and Russell overruled de Escamilla on the planting of peppers, watermelons, and eggplant. They also asked him to resign as manager of Hacienda and replaced him with Harry Miller. Russell and Andrews also seemed to have control of Hacienda's finances.

"The manner of withdrawing money from the bank accounts is particularly illuminating. The two men had absolute power to withdraw all the partnership funds in the banks without the knowledge or consent of the general partner. Either Russell or Andrews could take control of the business from de Escamilla by refusing to sign checks for bills contracted by him and thus limit his activities in the management of the business. They were active in dictating the crops to be planted, some of them against the wish of de Escamilla. This clearly shows they took part in the control of the business of the partnership and thus became liable as general partners."

Creation of the Limited Partnership

A limited partnership certificate must be prepared. This certificate must state the name of the limited partnership—for example, Wildcat Oil Exploration Associates, Ltd. If the revised Uniform Limited Partnership Act of 1976 has been adopted by the state where the limited partnership is being formed, then the name of the limited partnership would have to be Wildcat Oil Exploration Associates, Limited Partnership. In other words, the letters *Ltd.* are no longer allowed since many consumers do not know what *Ltd.* means. If the words *Limited Partnership* are written out in full, the public should be aware of the limited liability of some partners. Next, the certificate must state the purpose of the limited partnership. In this case the purpose would be to conduct oil explorations in the state of Texas. The principal place of business of the limited partnership, the names and addresses of each general and limited partner, the duration of the partnership, and the amount of the contribution that is to be received from each partner must also be stated. Other requirements include a statement as to whether additional partners can be admitted to the partnership and whether the limited partners may sell and assign their interests to other persons. The limited partnership certificate must be filed and recorded in a designated office such as the office of the county recorder or the county clerk in the county where the principal office is located. This gives persons who deal with the limited partnership public notice as to the items of information that are provided on the certificate of limited partnership. In most states it is also necessary to file the limited partnership certificate with a state authority such as the secretary of state's office.

Once the limited partnership certificate has been filed and recorded, the limited partnership may proceed to do business. If the statutory requirements were properly adhered to, the limited partners should be free from liability beyond their investment. However, the partners may desire to draft more detailed articles of partnership in order to provide for matters not considered in the limited partnership certificate.

General Partners' Rights and Duties

The general partner or partners have essentially the same rights and duties as any partner in a general partnership insofar as the partnership's day-to-day business operations are concerned. There is, however, one difference. Such partners cannot, on their own, take in other general partners or other limited partners unless this right has been granted to them in the limited partnership certificate.

Limited Partners—Their Rights and Duties

Basically the limited partner has no specific duties. He or she is simply an investor. However, Section 10 of the Uniform Limited Partnership Act gives the limited partner such rights as the right to inspect and copy the partnership books, the right to demand and be furnished full information on all matters affecting the partnership, and the right to have a formal accounting of the partnership's affairs when circumstances would make such action just and reasonable. Thus the limited partner may not have a voice as such in the management of the limited partnership, but he or she need not stand by and watch as fraudulent or wasteful acts are being committed by the general partner or partners. In addition, a limited partner may petition a court of proper jurisdiction to have a dissolution and winding up of the limited partnership. If that occurs, the limited partner is entitled to receive a share of the profits or compensation as income, and he or she may also be entitled to have his or her contribution returned in accordance with the limited partnership certificate, subject of course to any exceptions under local law.

Allen v. Steinberg
223 A.2d 240 (Maryland, 1966)

FACTS Steinberg and his two general partners owned 84 acres of land in Baltimore County, which land they had encumbered with $365,000 worth of mortgages. To get operating capital, they solicited investments from persons who would become limited partners. The plaintiff's husband was one of those solicited. He said that he and his wife would not be interested in any construction project but that they would be interested in a land deal. Mrs. Allen sent a check for $10,000, after being assured that they were investing in land and that the building operation on that land would be separate. The partnership agreement which Mrs. Allen signed had been redrafted by her husband so that the definition of the firm's business was "the ownership and promotion for development of a tract of land" rather than "the ownership and development of a tract of land." Through various manipulations, the general partners had the firm assume $275,000 worth of utility installation costs and also mortgaged part of the tract for $140,000, all without the knowledge or consent of the limited partners. The firm's assets were lost, and Mrs. Allen sued the general partners for an accounting and for damages resulting from their mismanagement. She appealed from the trial court's dismissal of her suit.

ISSUE Did the general partners act in contravention of the agreement, and/or possess the firm's property for other than the firm's purposes?

DECISION Yes, if plaintiff's allegations are believed. Judgment reversed.

REASONS Chief Judge Hammond felt that the case had to be tried, since Mrs. Allen had made out a prima facie case for recovery, and that Steinberg and the other defendants should be required to rebut her allegations with other evidence if they had any.

"[T]he claims of appellant . . . might be paraphrased to be that she was a sheltered ewe, who, despite the guidance of a learned and experienced shepherd (her husband), was led by the general partners not to the slaughter but to the shearing area where she was fleeced of her investment and anticipated profits. . . .

"If the partnership agreement is looked to alone as the integration of the agreement of the parties, it would appear that the partnership purpose was to hold land and procure and facilitate its development by others. The phrase 'ownership and promotion for development of a tract of land' would seem to negate the conclusion that direct development of or direct participation in development by the partnership was intended. The wording of the partnership agreement might leave open exactly how far and to what extent 'promotion' might go, but it could hardly extend to subordinating ground rents to mortgages or making unsecured loans or mortgaging partnership land without receiving the proceeds of the mortgage. Any doubt as to the meaning intended by the phrase 'promotion for development' was removed, at least in the present posture of the case, by the extrinsic evidence which the chancellor received over objection by the appellee."

Dissolution, Winding Up, and Termination of a Limited Partnership

In Chapter 39 it was noted that the death of a partner in a general partnership, the bankruptcy of a partner in a general partnership, and the withdrawal of a partner from a general partnership were causes for dissolution of the partnership. These rules do not apply to a limited partnership. Since limited partners are simply limited liability investors, they have no voice in management and it is not necessary for the partnership to secure more assets or cash from them, so that there is no specific loss to the limited partnership if a limited partner dies or becomes bankrupt. For the same reasons the substitution of a new limited partner for an old limited partner or the addition of a limited partner will not cause dissolution of a limited partnership. Only if all the limited partners have either died or withdrawn and no substitutions have been made would the death or withdrawal of limited partners necessitate the dissolution of a limited partnership. A limited partnership must have a minimum of one limited partner. Without the limited partner there is no limited partnership.

The death or withdrawal of a general partner from a limited partnership will cause the limited partnership to be dissolved unless there is a provision in the certificate to substitute another person for the deceased or withdrawing general partner.

Thus a limited partnership will normally not be dissolved until the general partners or their replacements decide to dissolve the partnership or until a specific term expires, if the limited partnership was created for a specified term.

Although the limited partnership need not be dissolved upon the death or withdrawal of a general partner if provisions were made for that partner's replacement, the limited partnership still has to file and record an amended limited partnership certificate to inform the public of the change. If a limited partner dies or withdraws and is not replaced, no amendments need be filed and recorded. However, if another person is substituted or added as a limited partner, then the certificate must be amended. Also, if a limited partnership decides to go into a different business or to make any other major changes in the business which concern matters covered in its certificate, it must file and record an amended certificate that gives the public full notice of these changes. Section 24 of the Uniform Limited Partnership Act specifies the various changes in the business which require that an amended certificate be filed.

Changes under the Revised Uniform Limited Partnership Act of 1976

Thus far, the revised ULPA has been adopted by only a few states.

A major reason for the revision of the Uniform Limited Partnership Act was to clarify the question of control. The 1916 ULPA states that a limited partner may not participate in the control of the limited partnership. A limited partner who does participate in the control of the business will be treated in the same way as a general partner and thus will lose his or her limited liability. The problem is simply what is control. Can a limited partner make suggestions to the general partner? Can a limited partner have a vote? Conflicting court decisions have been reached in the various states as to what a limited partner may or may not do insofar as participation in the control of the business is concerned. Some states have even amended their limited partnership statute to grant limited partners a right to vote on certain types of major business decisions.

Because of the concern over the growing nonuniformity of the Uniform Limited Partnership laws, the revised ULPA was drafted. This act specifically allows the limited partner to do certain acts with the understanding that these acts do not constitute participation in the control of the business. The following acts are permitted by the revised ULPA:

1. Being a contractor for, or an agent of, the partnership.
2. Consulting with and advising a partner with respect to the business.
3. Acting as a surety for the partnership.
4. Approving or disapproving of an amendment to the partnership agreement.
5. Voting on such matters as dissolution, winding up, the transfer of all or substantially all of the assets, the incurrence of debt other than in the ordinary course of business, a change in the nature of the business, and the removal of a general partner.

In addition to allowing the limited partner to do the above acts, the revised ULPA also provides that if a limited partner does actively participate in the control of the partnership by doing acts other than those mentioned above, the limited partner will only be liable to those persons who did business with the partnership and who had knowledge of the limited partner's participation in its control. The revised ULPA also makes some general changes in the filing requirements for limited partnerships. It requires that the certificate of limited partnership be filed in the office of the secretary of state in the state where the limited partnership is doing business, and it also requires that the limited partnership designate a resident in the state where it is doing business as the registered agent for the service of process for lawsuits which may be filed against it. These requirements are similar to the filing requirements for corporations.

The original ULPA restricted the limited partner's capital contribution to cash or other property. Under the revised ULPA the limited partner may contribute his or her services as a capital contribution as well as or in place of cash or other property. This is a very important change, since it means that the consulting expertise or other specialized talents of limited partners can now be contributed as a capital contribution to a limited partnership.

Another change in the revised ULPA was previously referred to. That change requires that the full words *limited partnership* be used in the firm name rather than the observation "Ltd.," which is allowed under the original ULPA version.

It must be remembered that at present there is considerable nonuniformity in the limited partnership laws of the various states. Hopefully, the revised ULPA will be adopted by all of the states and there will again be uniformity in this area.

CASES FOR DISCUSSION

STATE v. SIERS

248 N.W.2d 1 (Nebraska, 1976)

Spencer, Justice

Defendant, George J. Siers, appeals from a judgment entered upon a verdict of the jury finding him guilty of embezzlement. . . .

The information under which Siers was charged and tried alleges, so far as material herein, that between the dates of August 3, 1974, and April 7, 1975, inclusive, "George J. Siers . . . , being then and there the agent of Pathfinder II, Ltd., a limited partnership, . . . did then and there by virtue of such position . . . as agent of the said Pathfinder II, Ltd., a limited partnership, receive and take into his possession certain money . . . all of which money was and is the property of . . . his principal, and did then and there fraudulently and unlawfully convert to his own use and embezzle said money, without the consent of the said Pathfinder II, Ltd., a limited partnership, his principal. . . .

The salient facts of this case, so far as material to this appeal, are that Siers and Enlowe A. Hevner, both having had experience as commodity brokers, in 1973 formed a general partnership, Pathfinder II, to trade in commodities and commodity futures. The bookkeeping and accounting was done primarily by Siers, although Hevner also had complete authority and access to the books. Both Siers and Hevner traded through the Pathfinder II account. Sometime later, they conceived the idea of operating limited partnerships in connection with their business for the purpose of trading in commodities, the apparent advantages being the limited liability of limited partners and greater flexibility in operation. With that in mind, in February 1974, Siers set up a small limited partnership with five investors, under the name of Prospector II. All the trading for that and another limited partnership was done through an account opened in the name of one of its investors, Rick Murphy, who was Siers' brother-in-law. Although probably illegal according to the evidence adduced at the trial, Siers did trade through Rick Murphy's account and explained the advantages of so doing on the basis of a reduction in paper work, and in margin requirements. . . .

Plans for the formation of Pathfinder II, Ltd., grew out of discussions between Hevner and Mr. Donald M. Vervaecke. Both Hevner and Vervaecke testified that Hevner was to be the trading agent and that the general partner of the limited partnership had not been determined. Hevner never considered himself a limited partner. Both Hevner and Vervaecke testified that it was their understanding and agreement that before Pathfinder II, Ltd., was to come into existence and commence trading operations, it was necessary to obtain 10 limited partners, each of whom would invest $2,500. . . .

The evidence indicates that Vervaecke sold seven $2,500 shares in Pathfinder II, Ltd., to prospective investors, and turned the money, totalling $17,500, over to Siers. . . .

The State suggests and argues that the following occurred with regard to the $17,500 invested by the Vervaecke group. As previously stated, the money was paid to Siers in early August 1974, by check or checks payable to Pathfinder II, not Pathfinder II, Ltd. The funds were placed in the Pathfinder II bank account, but, according to Hevner, later disappeared. It was the State's theory that Siers, by means of checks whose numbers were out of sequence with the current business transactions, removed the limited partners' money from the Pathfinder II bank account and placed it in the Rick Murphy trading account. . . .

Under both statutory and case law in Nebraska, a partnership has long been considered as an entity separate and apart from the individual partners. . . . The Uniform Partnership Act adopted in Nebraska clearly mandates the entity theory of partnership. . . .

Additionally, section 28–538, R.R.S. 1943, in defining the class of property subject to embezzlement, includes property ". . . which is partly the property of any other persons . . . and partly the property of such officer, attorney at law, agent. . . ." We hold that in Nebraska, both by statutory interpretation and by our adoption of the legal entity theory of partnerships, a partner may be prosecuted for the embezzlement of partnership property. . . .

The fourth and fifth assignments of error concern the question of the existence of Pathfinder II, Ltd., a limited partnership, the alleged victim of the embezzlement. We agree with the State that defendant presented a defense which was based upon the accepted existence of Pathfinder II, Ltd., and sought to prove that he was the general and the trading partner of the limited partnership and in such position could not embezzle the funds of Pathfinder II, Ltd.

The State correctly identified the victim of the embezzlement as Pathfinder II, Ltd. It presented substantial evidence that there had in fact been a partnership formed which the defendant himself titled as Pathfinder II, Ltd., and that the defendant for his own personal use and benefit embez-

zled the funds of that partnership. It might well be argued that the promoters of Pathfinder II, Ltd., did not strictly comply with the provisions of section 67–202, R.R.S. 1943, which specify certain requirements for the formation of a limited partnership. However, subsection (2) of said section provides: "A limited partnership is formed if there has been substantial compliance in good faith with the requirements of subsection (1) of this section."

Siers testified he was to be the trading agent for the limited partnership. There is no question the money collected, totalling $17,500, was turned over to him, and he admits transferring it to the Rick Murphy account. The State's evidence is that Siers was to hold the money in an escrow account until the limited partnership was formed. This Siers denies.

The trial court determined there was substantial compliance in good faith sufficient to create the formation of a limited partnership. That determination, however, is not necessary herein. If there was no limited partnership, there was a partnership agreement and the money was paid under its terms. Any variance in the name would be immaterial because defendant could not have been misled or confused as to the money he was accused of embezzling. . . .

Nationally, some of the more recent cases, with which we agree, hold that proof of the existence of a legal entity capable of owning property is not required in an embezzlement prosecution. . . .

The investors in Pathfinder II, Ltd., entrusted their funds to the defendant during the formative stages of the partnership on the assumption that he was organizing a limited partnership. He testified he had completed its organization by securing the additional partners. It would be a travesty of justice to permit the defendant to go free because he did not complete the existence of the limited partnership. He admitted receiving the money. He admitted using it to cover losses in the Rick Murphy account. The material issue was not the existence of Pathfinder II, Ltd., but whether or not the defendant, George J. Siers, as an agent of Pathfinder II, Ltd., received funds and whether or not he did then convert or embezzle the funds in violation of the law of embezzlement under the charge which is brought in the information. . . .

Brodkey, Justice (dissenting)

The majority opinion states that it "would be a travesty of justice to permit the defendant to go free because he did not complete the existence of the limited partnership." It is also a travesty of justice for a court in its zeal to make bad law simply because it is faced with a hard case. Apparently the law now is that a person can be charged and convicted of embezzling from a partnership which may or may not exist, without a jury determination that the partnership does exist. Such a result defies logic, common sense, and prior law, and I must respectfully dissent. . . .

VIDRICKSEN v. GROVER

363 F.2d 372 (U.S. Ninth Circuit, 1966)

Chambers, Circuit Judge

Dr. Vidricksen intended, when he turned over to Thom $25,000 in July 1952, to become a limited partner with Thom, the general partner, in a Chevrolet car agency business at Dunsmuir, California. Thus, the shoemaker strayed from his last.

Articles of partnership were drawn up, but no effort was made to comply with the California statutory requirement of recording a certificate of limited partnership.

Bankruptcy overtook Thom in September 1961. And the issue here is whether Dr. Vidricksen is a general partner for the purposes of bankruptcy. The referee held he was. On review, the district court sustained the referee. Here on appeal, we affirm.

Apparently the agency developed financial difficulties in March 1961, and the doctor consulted successively two different lawyers. From them, although they could not represent him because of conflict of interest, he did learn he had a problem, to wit, whether in his venture he had attained a real limited partnership and therefore limited liability under California law. The Uniform Limited Partnership Act has been adopted in California with some modification.

On the issue before us, no significant facts occurred until August 1961, when, through another set of attorneys, he filed a complaint against Thom which seemed to seek an accounting. . . .

On September 19, 1961 (eight days after the bankruptcy proceedings started), Dr. Vidricksen filed in the bankruptcy proceedings a renunciation under Section 15511 of the Corporations Code of California. That section reads as follows:

A person who has contributed to the capital of a business conducted by a person or partnership erroneously believing that he has become a limited partner in a limited partnership, is not, by reason of his exercise of the rights of a limited partner, a general partner with the person or in the partnership carrying on the business, or bound by the obligations of such person or partnership; provided, that on ascertaining the mistake he promptly renounces his interest in the profits of the business, or other compensation by way of income.

Was such renunciation timely? We think not.

Appellant would count the time on "promptly" in "promptly renounces" only from August 7, 1961, to September 19, 1961, or a period of 43 days. We disagree. In our view "promptly" began to run when he learned in March 1961 that something was wrong with the organizational setup.

No California case is of help to use in construing the code section, so we must use our best judgment as to what California courts would hold. We do not think Dr. Vidricksen needed a bonded opinion to start the time running. Knowledge that he was probably in trouble was enough. Thus, we conclude that six months from the time he had noticed something was wrong until the actual renunciation is not a prompt renunciation. Even in August when he sued, the doctor was not renouncing, but was apparently accepting the fate of a general partner. It is possible that that action on his part could be held an abandonment of the limited partnership and acceptance of general partnership status. But we do not find it necessary to so hold. Certainly, though, the act went in the wrong direction. And we do not reach the question of his status had he renounced on August 7, 1961, when he instead affirmed general partnership. We simply hold the attempted renunciation was not timely. Thus, the doctor must be held to the pains of a general partner.

The procedure by which Dr. Vidricksen was "backed into" bankruptcy seems a little odd. But the issue was one which federal bankruptcy jurisdiction would cover on subject matter. The doctor had due notice of the proceedings and made no objection to the form of the proceedings. He fully contested the issue. Thus, we think he was bound by the outcome. In fact, even now, he does not contest the form in which the issue was raised and tried. He just objects to the result.

Affirmed.

PROBLEMS FOR DISCUSSION

1. Under the state's Rental Homes Act the owner of a building which contained more than five rental units had to give the tenants the chance to buy the building before it was sold to an outsider if the tenants had previously indicated an interest in buying it and provided that they had "an organization with the legal capacity to hold real estate." Fred Odrog owned the Aperture Apartments, a building complex with 38 housing units. When his tenants found out that he was thinking of selling, they told him they wanted to buy the building. Most of his tenants came to a meeting at which T.W.IN.A.N.E. (Tenants Wildly Incensed About Nearly Everything), Limited, was organized. Bylaws for Twinane specified that each tenant-member would contribute $500 and that all members would have limited liability. Odrog refused to negotiate with Twinane, which then brought an action seeking injunctive relief. What result, and why?

2. Ollie Stanley Company, a brokerage firm with offices in over 30 states, was organized as a limited partnership in the state of New York. One of its offices was located in the state of Illusiana, and a dispute arose there over Ollie Stanley's liability on a certain note. Illusiana had a "common name" statute which provided: "Whenever any business is transacted in this State by an unincorporated association of persons using a common name (ordinary partnerships excepted), suits may be brought against the individuals composing such association by such common name, and judgment recovered therein may be executed by seizure and sale of the personal and real property of such association, and also that of the said persons in the same manner with respect to them as if they had been made parties defendant by their individual names." Marina Lilliman, the plaintiff, had a summons and complaint served on the branch manager at Ollie Stanley's Illusiana office. The complaint also named Ollie Stanley's 86 general partners as individual defendants. These general partners challenge the court's jurisdiction. How should the court rule?

3. Alvin Kafritz, the limited partner in Kafritz Company, sued the general partners, his brothers Archer Kafritz and Adam Kafritz, for reformation of the partnership agreement or dissolution of the firm. The three brothers had been the sole stockholders in Wetland Manor, Inc., a corporation which had owned and operated certain apartment buildings. They organized Kafritz Company as a limited partnership and turned all their Wetland stock over to it as its capital. The partnership agreement provided: "Promptly after the Partnership becomes the owner of the stock of the Corporation, the General Partners shall cause the Corporation to be liquidated, so that the Partnership shall hold the net assets of the Corporation as the capital of the Partnership." Alvin says that his intent was that there should be an immediate distribution of the cash assets of the corporation when it was dissolved, since that was what had happened when the brothers dissolved their other real estate corporation. Archer and Adam refused to make such a cash distribution here. Should the court order the distribution? Discuss.

4. Wilma Banks, a 62-year-old widow, went to the Marble Motor Inn to attend a "free" meeting. At the meeting Verna Shill and Lucinda Sluggs made a presentation which involved mind reading and psychic fortune-telling. After reading Wilma's mind and telling her fortune, Verna and Lucinda asked her to become a limited partner in Papsh Films, Ltd., which was producing religious films for schools and was building a large amusement park. Wilma was an accountant, and Verna and Lucinda promised her that she could do all of the film's bookwork at a generous salary. The three ladies filled out personal financial statements, borrowed $25,000 from the Octopus Bank, and cosigned a promissory note for the amount of the loan. Verna and Lucinda never filed any limited partnership articles with the State but simply took the $25,000 and skipped. Octopus sues Wilma. What result, and why?

5. Ron Wrutsky and Vicki Grinaldi, real estate brokers, decided to form a limited partnership, in which they would be the general partners, to develop a certain tract of land. They signed a purchase agreement for the land on behalf of Lucid Limited Partnership (which had not yet been organized). They then organized Lucid, which was to have 25 limited partners, with each to pay in an initial $10,000 and $15,000 more in the future. As part of the partnership agreement, the limited partners said that they did "hereby ratify and confirm any prior action by the General Partners." Only 7 of the 25 limited partnerships were actually sold. Floyd, Boyd, and Mason agreed to become limited partners. After they signed the partnership agreement, it was modified by Ron and Vicki because the financing arrangements for the land purchase had to be changed. When Floyd learned of the changes he demanded a refund of his initial $10,000 and a cancellation of his subscription; Ron and Vicki gave him back his $10,000. Boyd and Mason didn't learn of the changes until the firm was forced into bankruptcy. Litehead, the trustee in bankruptcy, says that Floyd, Boyd, and Mason each owe $25,000. Is he correct?

6. Funny Fund, a limited partnership, sued Dosee Door, Inc., for breach by Dosee of an agreement to repurchase its stock from Funny, which had bought the stock previously. Several months later, the state legislature amended its statutes so as to allow limited partnerships to sue and be sued in the firm name. Shortly after the amendment took effect, and still within the statute of limitations period, Funny filed a second lawsuit on the same claim, in its firm name. Dosee moves to dismiss the second lawsuit. How should the court rule, and why?

7. As a further complication on the Funny-Dosee dispute, it now appears that the original lawsuit was filed on behalf of Funny by only one of its three general partners—Elmer. Funny's other two general partners, Herman and Ethel, were officers, directors, and stockholders in Dosee Door. Should the first lawsuit be dismissed too? Why or why not?

8. Blank Construction, Inc., entered into a contract with GOW, Limited (a limited partnership), to erect a building. Most of the stock in Blank was owned by the same two persons, Huey and Louie, who were the two general partners in GOW. Blank in turn subcontracted the plumbing, heating, and air conditioning work to Reliant Plumbing and Heating, Inc. The air conditioning did not work properly, and so Blank withheld money from the final contract payment until Reliant fixed or replaced the defective units. Reliant sued for money due, and Blank counterclaimed for damages. Meanwhile, GOW paid Blank in full for the construction job, without making any claim against Blank for damages. At the end of the trial, Reliant moved to dismiss the counterclaim because Blank had failed to prove that it had sustained any damages. Blank then asked the court for leave to amend so as to bring in GOW as the real injured party and to reopen the trial. How should the court rule here? Explain.

42 | Corporations—Nature, Formation, and Powers

A corporation is called a legal person or a legal entity. It may also be called a child of the state, since its birth, existence, and termination are regulated by statutory law. Upon the completion of certain requirements a state will grant a charter of incorporation which is in effect a birth certificate for the corporation. The corporation must abide by the specific statutory law during its existence, and if the corporation is to be terminated, then the termination must comply with the statutory law. Each state has specific statutes governing the creation, regulation, and termination of corporations and also regulating corporations created in other states but doing local business in that state.

CLASSIFICATIONS OF CORPORATIONS

The Private Corporation for Profit.   This is the most common type of corporation. Such a corporation is created for the purpose of conducting private, non-governmental business.

The Public Corporation.   This is a corporation which is created for governmental purposes.

The Not-for-Profit Corporation.   This is a corporation which is created for a civic, charitable, or educational purpose. For example, a fraternity or sorority, if incorporated, would be incorporated as a not-for-profit corporation since its purposes would be social and civic rather than the conduct of a profit-making business. Special tax considerations are given to not-for-profit corporations.

The Domestic Corporation.   This is a corporation which is doing business in the state where it was originally incorporated.

The Foreign Corporation.   This is a corporation which is incorporated in one state and is doing business in another state. Foreign corporations must file certain documents and pay certain fees before doing local business in states other than the state in which they were incorporated.

The Professional Corporation.   Many states now have specific incorporation laws which allow the incorporation of certain professionals; for example, a medical corporation. Such a corporation can be one doctor or many doctors.

Dentists, veterinarians, architects, accountants, and lawyers may also incorporate their businesses under professional corporation statutes. Typically there are different requirements for incorporation and different provisions for regulation under the professional corporation statutes.

FORMATION OF THE CORPORATION

Incorporators.   Incorporators are the persons who actually apply to the state for the incorporation of a business. The incorporators sign a document, usually called articles of incorporation, and file it with the secretary of state of the state where they are requesting incorporation. Some states require the incorporators to be citizens of the incorporation state; others do not. The Model Business Corporation Act, which has been followed by many states, now allows a single incorporator to apply. Thus an individual may incorporate himself or herself and may be the sole shareholder.

Procedure for Incorporation.   While each state has its own individual incorporation statute, the requirements for incorporation are similar in all the states. Generally speaking, the incorporator or incorporators execute and sign articles of incorporation and file this document with the appropriate state official, usually the secretary of state. A filing fee is required, which, of course, varies from state to state. The corporation division of the secretary of state's office will review the articles, and if they comply with the applicable statute, the secretary of state's office will issue a certificate of incorporation which officially gives birth to the corporation. Many states require that a minimum amount of capital be paid into the corporation before it can legally commence business. Some states require that the articles of incorporation be filed in the recorder's office of a county where the corporation holds real estate.

1. Name.   The corporation, like a new baby, must be given a legal name. The incorporators are free to choose nearly any name, so long as it is not same as or similar to the name of another corporation doing business in the state. Thus, before approving a name for the corporation, the state must run a check of all the corporations on file to find out whether this name is the same as or similar to the names of other corporations. Also, the name of the corporation must include the word *Incorporated* or the abbreviation "Inc.," so that people will know that when they deal with this organization they are dealing with a limited liability organization.

2. The Purpose for Which the Corporation Is Formed.   The purpose for which the corporation is formed can be stated in general terms. In most states it is not necessary to state the specific business which the corporation intends to participate in. For example, the purpose may be stated as follows: to transact any and all lawful business for which a corporation may be incorporated under the specific state corporation act.

3. The Address of the Corporation's Principal Office and the Name of Its Registered Agent.   The principal office, of course, will be the mailing address for all corporate correspondence, and the resident agent is the person who can officially accept service of lawsuits against the corporation.

4. The Duration of the Corporation.   A corporation has perpetual existence unless its articles of incorporation provide otherwise.

5. *Issuance of Shares of Stock.* The incorporator or incorporators must here state the total number of shares of stock which the corporation requests authority to issue, the number of shares of stock which are to have a par value, and the number of shares which are to have no par value. If there are to be different classes of stock, different series of stock, and different rights and preferences with regard to different classes of stock, then this information must also be provided. Some states require the names and addresses of the original subscribers to the capital stock and the amount of their subscriptions.

6. *Directors and Officers and Qualifications of Directors.* Many states require the articles of incorporation to include the names of the members of the first board of directors, and often the names of the officers of the corporation are also required.

7. *Provisions for Regulation of Business and Conduct of Affairs of the Corporation.* Many states require specific statements as to the conduct and scheduling of annual and special meetings of shareholders and directors and as to other provisions concerning the conduct of the business.

8. *Requirements Prior to Doing Business.* Many states have specific requirements which must be complied with prior to the commencement of business by the corporation. The most common requirement is the payment of a minimum amount of money, typically $1,000, by subscribers to the corporation before the corporation commences.

THE CHARTER AS A CONTRACT

When the articles are approved or the corporate charter is issued by the state of incorporation, a "contract" is formed between the state and the corporation. This was the main point decided in the *Dartmouth College* case. As a contract, the corporate charter is protected by Article I, Section 10 of the U.S. Constitution, which prohibits a state from passing any law "impairing the obligation of contracts." In the days when each corporate charter was the result of a special statute, this decision barred much state regulation of corporations. Today, however, general corporation laws contain provisions which reserve to the state the power to amend or repeal the statute. The state's power to change the corporate rules thus becomes part of every contract formed with every corporation pursuant to the statute. Courts have also limited the effect of the *Dartmouth College* case by permitting states to exercise their general police power to regulate corporations, as they do other persons.

The corporate charter also acts as a contract between the corporation and its stockholders, in the sense that it states the nature of the corporation's business. The bylaws adopted by the corporation also become part of this contract. To avoid unnecessary litigation, clear procedures for amending the corporate charter/articles and the corporate bylaws should be spelled out, and the power to amend should be specifically stated.

OTHER OBLIGATIONS TO THE STATE
OF INCORPORATION

The obligations of the corporation to its home state do not end with the issuance of the charter. Typically annual reports to the state are required and the corporation must pay an annual fee for the privilege of exercising its corporate powers. Corporation statutes usually provide for suspension or termination of the corporation's privileges for noncompliance with these annual requirements, at least where the default continues for an extended period of time.

THE CORPORATION AS PERSON AND CITIZEN

The corporation is, by definition, a legal person. As such, it enjoys the same constitutional protections as human persons. Under the Fifth Amendment, its life, liberty and property cannot be taken, without due process of law, by the national government or any of its agencies. Under the 14th Amendment, the same due process protection exists against the state governments. Likewise, states cannot deny corporate persons the equal protection of the law. (*Equal* here does not mean identical. It only means that distinctions must have a rational basis; arbitrary, invidious discrimination against corporations is prohibited.)

Corporations are not considered citizens for the purpose of 14th Amendment "privileges and immunities of citizenship." Most obviously, this means that corporations cannot vote in political elections, hold political office, or serve on juries. More important, as discussed in Chapter 46, corporations do not have a citizen's right to conduct business in states other than the domicile state. Corporations wishing to do local business in a second state must secure that state's permission to do so; human persons, as citizens, are exempt from this requirement.

In order to determine whether diversity of citizenship exists (so that an ordinary civil case may be brought into U.S. district court), a corporation *is* considered to be a "citizen" of its state of incorporation. Courts have also recognized that a corporation may acquire a kind of "double citizenship" in the state where it has its principal place of business. If any of the opposing parties in a litigation were a citizen of either of those two states, there would not be complete diversity of citizenship, and the case could not be brought into the U.S. courts, no matter how large an amount was involved.

DEFECTIVE FORMATION

Mistakes are sometimes made during the incorporation process. Forms are filled out incorrectly, or some procedural step is omitted. The effect of such errors on the corporation's existence varies, depending on the seriousness of the mistake and on the intent of the human beings who were representing the corporation.

De Jure Corporation.   Perfection is not required in order to attain full de jure corporate status. As long as any errors are minor, immaterial ones, the corporation's existence cannot be challenged by anyone, including the state of incorporation. Substantial compliance with all mandatory state requirements, in good faith, is all that is required. A mistake as to the last digit in the zip code on the corporation's mailing address would almost certainly be of this nature. If the corporation's name, street number, city, county, and state were correct, its mail would be delivered despite the (slightly) incorrect zip code.

De Facto Corporation. Even though the mandatory requirements of the corporation law have not been substantially complied with, so that the corporation has not attained de jure status, the corporation's de facto ("in fact") existence may nevertheless be recognized. Only very limited challenges against a de facto corporation are permitted. Subscribers cannot be forced to take and pay for stock in a de facto corporation; they are entitled to full de jure status. The state of incorporation, in a direct proceeding (usually called a quo warranto—"by whose authority"), can force the suspension of a de facto corporation's business until the error is corrected. In order to attain de facto status, the promoters/incorporators must have made a good faith attempt to comply with a statute under which the corporation could be organized; they must be in at least "colorable" compliance with the statutory requirements (no mandatory step has been omitted); and the corporation must actually have used its powers. The stockholders of a de facto corporation have limited liability, and the de facto corporation can conduct its business free of third-party challenges.

Corporation by Estoppel. Courts sometimes apply the principle of estoppel against persons who have received benefits from a purported, but really nonexistent, corporation. The recipient of goods and services should have to pay for them, whether or not the provider was validly organized as a corporation. Similarly, insiders who were responsible for the defective organization but then dealt with it to their advantage, should be prevented from asserting its defects.

Bukacek v. Pell City Farms, Inc.
237 So.2d 851 (Alabama, 1970)

FACTS   In 1965 ill health forced James Bukacek to sell his dairy business. His personal problems resulted in a divorce from his wife, Virginia. His financial affairs were also in bad shape. The sheriff was advertising his 300-acre farm for sale, to pay three judgments; he owed the state $15,000 for back taxes; and his mortgage payment was overdue. Bukacek was also unable to exercise the option which Virginia had given him on the 180 acres she owned. At this point, Bukacek went to see Burttram "about saving 'my farm.' " Together with Kelly and Wyatt, they agreed to organize Pell City Farms, Inc. Bukacek conveyed his 300 acres to Pell City, which also exercised the option on Virginia's 180 acres. Pell City (or its promoters) paid off all the back claims and personally assumed the old mortgage and executed a new one. When the deeds from James and Virginia were executed, Pell City's articles had not been filed with the local judge of probate, as required by Alabama law. James filed an action to quiet title to the land in himself, since Pell City was not incorporated and therefore could not take title. The trial court held for Pell City, and James appealed.

ISSUE   Can Bukacek avoid his deed by showing that Pell City was not properly incorporated?

DECISION   No. Judgment affirmed.

REASONS   After reviewing the facts, Justice Maddox first considered whether the failure to file the articles as required by statute meant that there was no corporation. He felt that most states would decide that there was no corporation, either de jure or de facto, until the required filing had occurred. But that did not end the inquiry in this case.

"[T]he incidents of corporate existence may exist as between the parties by virtue of an estoppel. Thus, besides corporations de jure and de facto, there can be a recognition of a third class known as 'Corporations by estoppel.' Corporations by estoppel are not based upon the same principles as corporations de facto. The doctrine de facto corporations has nothing to do with the principle of estoppel. In fact, a corporation de facto cannot be created by estoppel, the only effect of an estoppel being to prevent the raising of the question of the existence of a corporation.

"Bukacek was one of the incorporators; he dealt with the corporation as a corporation both before and after the Articles of Incorporation were filed. Under such facts, Bukacek is estopped to deny the existence of the corporation at the time he voluntarily executed a deed transferring property to the corporation even though the Articles of Incorporation had not been filed at that time.

"Our ruling is limited. It is based on equitable ground which preclude the complainant here from denying corporate existence. . . . We hold, therefore, that Bukacek is estopped to deny the existence of Pell City Farms, Inc., even though it may have neither de facto nor de jure at the time he executed the deed making the corporation, *by its corporate name,* the grantee."

Insiders (promoters, incorporators, officers, directors, and stockholders) who, like Bukacek, know the truth, may be estopped to deny the corporation's existence where *they* have fouled up the incorporation process and have then dealt with their nonexistent corporation as if it had been lawfully performed. Third parties who deal with the nonexistent corporation should not be estopped to deny its existence *unless* they knew the truth at the time.

No Corporation; Partnership Liability. Where the promoters acted in bad faith, or omitted a mandatory procedural step, or for any other reason failed to achieve at least de facto status for the corporation, the result is partnership liability for all the business associates. In such situations stockholders could be held fully liable personally for all the debts of the business. Persons trying to assert claims against the corporation would normally not be estopped from proving that it was not really a corporation and that all associates in the enterprise were personally liable for torts and contracts.

SEPARATE CORPORATE ENTITY/PIERCING THE CORPORATE VEIL

Once a corporation has been successfully organized, it is recognized as a separate and distinct legal person or entity. It owns its own property, makes its own contracts, and pays its own taxes. So long as a corporation's separate identity is preserved by the persons who operate the corporation, that identity should be respected and upheld by the courts and other agencies of government. The fact that all of a corporation's stock is held by only a few persons is not, in itself, a basis for disregarding the separate corporate entity. A court should take this drastic step only where the corporation is being used to produce illegal or fraudulent results or where its human operators are themselves disregarding its existence.

D. I. Felsenthal Co. v. Northern Assurance Co.
120 N.E. 268 (Illinois, 1918)

FACTS   David and Harry Felsenthal and their father, Isaac, owned all 150 shares of the capital stock of Felsenthal Company. When the company was unable to pay a bank loan of $20,000, David went to see an old family friend, Morris L. Fox. Fox paid off the bank loan and received 75 shares of stock, plus assignments of the other 75 shares. About two months prior to the fire which destroyed the premises, Morris and David went to Moe Rosenberg's saloon, had dinner, and discussed the burning out of the business. Moe directed them to Ben Fink, who was in the business of firing properties. They hired Ben, who burned the company's premises with 75 gallons of gasoline. Because of his loans to the company, Morris Fox would ultimately receive all of the insurance proceeds. The trial court and the appeals court found for the insurance company, and Felsenthal Company appealed.

ISSUE   Should the court "pierce the corporate veil" here?

DECISION   Yes. Judgment affirmed.

REASONS   After reviewing the facts which led up to the fire, Chief Justice Duncan decided that the jury could have reasonably believed the testimony of Rosenberg and Fink and disbelieved that of Fox and David Felsenthal. He then proceeded to discuss the applicable law.

"It is true . . . that the general rule of law is that the willful burning of property by a stockholder in a corporation is not a defense against the collection of the insurance by the corporation, and that the corporation cannot be prevented from collecting the insurance because its agents willfully set fire to the property without the participation or authority of the corporation or of all the stockholders of the corporation. When, however, the beneficial owner of practically all of the stock in a corporation, and who has the absolute management and control of its affairs and its property and is its president and a director, sets fire to the property of a corporation or causes it to be done, there is no sound reason to support the contention of appellant that the corporation should be allowed to recover on a policy for the destruction of the corporate property by fire so occasioned. Every principle of insurance law and sound reasoning would seem to be against such contention. . . .

"While the money collected from appellee on this insurance policy would not be paid directly to Fox, still, ultimately, the amount collected would all go, . . . in the settlement of the affairs of the corporation, to Fox. . . . We cannot allow the corporation in this case to be used as a cloak to protect Fox and to aid him in his designs to defraud the insurance company and at the same time to profit by his own wrong or fraud."

Some regulatory and taxation statutes permit enforcement agencies to impose liability on other persons for acts by a corporation. Although this is not quite the same as piercing the corporate veil, in effect the separate corporate entity is disregarded.

Since a corporation is a creature of the law, it possesses only those powers given to it by the law. It can do only those things which it has been authorized to do. Authorization for particular acts of a corporation must be found either in its state's corporation statute or in its own charter. Powers which result from the corporation's existence as a legal person, such as the power to sue and be sued in its corporate name and the power to hold and convey property, are called "inherent" powers. These powers and others specifically stated in the corporation statute are also referred to as "statutory" powers. All corporations formed in the state have them.

"Express" powers are the powers specifically granted to a particular corporation by its charter. Many states permit such powers to be stated very broadly—for example, "to conduct any lawful business which may be conducted by corporations in this state." Corporations also have "implied" powers, that is, the powers which are necessary and appropriate to help carry out their express powers. Where a corporation has not used a very broad statement of its express powers, litigation may occur over whether a particular corporate activity is or is not within its implied powers.

Acts which do not fall within one of the above categories are said to be ultra vires, "outside" the corporation's powers. Courts have not agreed as to what should happen when a corporation engages in such unauthorized activity. The modern tendency is to severely limit such challenges to corporate acts. If a contract has been fully performed by both parties, neither party can raise the ultra vires claim so as to force rescission. If a contract is completely executory, neither party can sue for enforcement. Where only one party has performed, the courts disagree on what should happen; most courts permit the party that has performed to enforce the contract. In any case, the state should be able to enjoin the performance of unauthorized acts; a shareholder should be able to sue for an injunction and damages; and the corporation itself should be able to collect damages against the directors and officers who were responsible for the violation of the charter.

A. P. Smith Mfg. Co. v. Barlow
13 N.J. 145 (New Jersey, 1953)

FACTS   Smith Company made a contribution of $1,500 to Princeton University. Over the years, Smith had contributed to the local community chest, to Upsala College in East Orange and to Newark University. Smith manufactured valves, fire hydrants, and special equipment for the water and gas industries. Barlow and other stockholders challenged the legality of the Princeton gift, since such gifts were neither expressly authorized nor (the stockholders claimed) impliedly authorized. Smith Co. filed a declaratory judgment action in the Chancery Division, which upheld the gift. The stockholders appealed.

ISSUE   Was this gift to a nonprofit educational institution within the corporation's implied powers?

A. P. Smith Mfg. Co. v. Barlow (continued)

DECISION Yes. Judgment affirmed.

REASONS Judge Jacobs noted that Smith's president thought that such contributions benefited the corporation by maintaining a favorable public climate for their business and by ensuring the "free flow of properly trained personnel for administrative and other corporate employment." The chairman of Standard Oil and the former chairman of U.S. Steel expressed similar feelings. Judge Jacobs then reviewed the history of corporate giving.

"In his discussion of the early history of business corporations Professor Williston refers to a 1702 publication where the author stated flatly that 'The general intent and end of all civil incorporations is for better government.' And he points out that the early corporate charters, particularly their recitals, furnish additional support for the notion that the corporate object was the public one of managing and ordering the trade as well as the private one of profit for the members. . . . However, with later economic and social developments and the free availability of the corporate device for all trades, the end of private profit became generally accepted as the controlling one in all businesses other than those classed broadly as public utilities. . . . As a concomitant the common-law rule developed that those who managed the corporation could not disburse any corporate funds for philanthropic or other worthy public cause unless the expenditure would benefit the corporation. . . . Control of economic wealth has passed largely from individual entrepreneurs to dominating corporations, and calls upon the corporations for reasonable philanthropic donations have come to be made with increased public support. In many instances such contributions have been sustained by the courts within the common-law doctrine upon liberal findings that the donations tended reasonably to promote the corporate objectives. . . .

"[C]ourts, while adhering to the terms of the common-law rule, have applied it very broadly to enable worthy corporate donations with indirect benefits to the corporations. . . .

"More and more [corporations] have come to recognize that their salvation rests upon a sound economic and social environment, which in turn rests in no insignificant part upon free and vigorous nongovernmental institutions of learning."

New Jersey had a state statute which encouraged such corporate gifts, but the Barlow group of stockholders said that that law could not be applied to Smith, which had been incorporated before it was passed. Judge Jacobs also rejected this argument, saying that the state had reserved the power to amend its corporation laws and that Smith and other corporations were subject to reasonable further regulation anyway.

PROMOTERS

Definition. The classic definition of a promoter is found in the *Old Dominion* case: "those who undertake to form a corporation and to procure for it the rights, instrumentalities, and capital by which it is to carry out the purposes set forth in its charter and to establish it as fully able to do business." The promoters are the "idea people"; they conceive the idea of incorporation, and then they attempt to implement it. The incorporators, the persons who sign the documents specifically requesting the state of incorporation to recognize the corporation's existence, may or may not be promoters. Persons whose only function in the incorporation process is a professional one, such as lawyers, accountants, or engineers, are not necessarily promoters. The promoters are the driving force behind the corporation.

Liability Inter Se. As between themselves, promoters are in a sense partners, or at least joint venturers. Once agreement has been reached as to what will be done and how it will be done, they owe each other a fiduciary duty. This fiduciary duty does not arise, however, unless and until some agreement has been reached. A person who discloses a "good idea" to another person before any agreement has been reached therefore runs the risk that the other person will appropriate the idea without compensation.

Liability to the Corporation and/or Shareholders. Promoters also occupy a fiduciary relationship to their corporation and its subscribers/shareholders. Promoters should, of course, recover all reasonable expenses which they have incurred during the incorporation process. They are not, however, entitled to retain *secret* profits which they have made during the incorporation process, for example, by reselling assets to the corporation for more than they paid for them. Full disclosure of such proposed profits must be made. The question is: To whom? By the majority rule, disclosure to only the original promoters/subscribers is not sufficient, at least where there is a plan to sell more shares to the public. Full disclosure must be made to an independent (nonpromoters) board of directors, or to all subscribers, or to all shareholders, unless the promoters making the profits have themselves subscribed to all the shares to be issued.

The Corporation's Liability to Promoters' Contracts. Since the corporation does not yet legally exist, the promoters cannot be its agents when they make preincorporation contracts. The promoters are thus personally liable on all preincorporation contracts (with suppliers, landlords, employees, and so on) unless and until the new corporation comes into existence and "adopts" these contracts as its own. If and when that happens, the promoters' personal liability ends, unless they have agreed to be sureties on the corporation's obligations. This liability is subject to any specific agreement by the contracting parties.

CASES FOR DISCUSSION

FIRST NAT. BANK OF BOSTON v. BELLOTTI

435 U.S. 765 (1978)

Powell, Justice

In sustaining a state criminal statute that forbids certain expenditures by banks and business corporations for the purpose of influencing the vote on referendum proposals, the Massachusetts Supreme Judicial Court held that the First Amendment rights of a corporation are limited to issues that materially affect its business, property, or assets. The court rejected appellants' claim that the statute abridges freedom of speech in violation of the 1st and 14th Amendments. The issue presented in this Court. . . . We now reverse.

The statute at issue, Mass. Gen. Laws Ann., ch. 55, § 8 (West Supp. 1977), prohibits appellants, two national banking associations and three business corporations, from making contributions or expenditures "for the purpose of . . . influencing or affecting the vote on any question submitted to the voters, other than one materially affecting any of the property, business or assets of the corporation." The statute further specifies that "[n]o question submitted to the voters solely concerning the taxation of the income, property or transactions of individuals shall be deemed materially to affect the property, business or assets of the corporation." A corporation that violates § 8 may receive a maximum fine of $50,000; a corporate officer, director, or agent who violates the section may receive a maximum fine of $10,000 or imprisonment for up to one year, or both.

Appellants wanted to spend money to publicize their views on a proposed constitutional amendment that was to be submitted to the voters as a ballot question at a general election on November 2, 1976. The amendment would have permitted the legislature to impose a graduated tax on the income of individuals. After appellee, the Attorney General of Massachusetts, informed appellants that he intended to enforce § 8 against them, they brought this action seeking to have the statute declared unconstitutional. . . .

III

The court below framed the principal question in this case as whether and to what extent corporations have First Amendment rights. We believe that the court posed the wrong question. The Constitution often protects interests broader than those of the party seeking their vindication. The First Amendment, in particular, serves significant societal interests. The proper question therefore is not whether corporations "have" First Amendment rights and, if so, whether they are coextensive with those of natural person. Instead, the question must be whether § 8 abridges expression that the First Amendment was meant to protect. We hold that it does.

The speech proposed by appellants is at the heart of the First Amendment's protection.

"The freedom of speech and of the press guaranteed by the Constitution embraces at the least the liberty to discuss publicly and truthfully all matters of public concern without previous restraint or fear of subsequent punishment. . . . Freedom of discussion, if it would fulfill its historic function in this nation, must embrace all issues about which information is needed or appropriate to enable the members of society to cope with the exigencies of their period." . . . The referendum issue that appellants wish to address falls squarely within this description. In appellants' view, the enactment of a graduated personal income tax, as proposed to be authorized by constitutional amendment, would have a seriously adverse effect on the economy of the State. The importance of the referendum issue to the people and government of Massachusetts is not disputed. Its merits, however, are the subject of sharp disagreement.

As the Court said in *Mills* v. *Alabama*, "there is practically universal agreement that a major purpose of [the First] Amendment was to protect the free discussion of governmental affairs." If the speakers here were not corporations, no one would suggest that the State could silence their proposed speech. It is the type of speech indispensable to decision making in a democracy, and this is no less true because the speech comes from a corporation rather than an individual. The inherent worth of the speech in terms of its capacity for informing the public does not depend upon the identity of its source, whether corporation, association, union, or individual. . . .

Freedom of speech and the other freedoms encompassed by the First Amendment always have been viewed as fundamental components of the liberty safeguarded by the Due Process Clause. . . .

The press cases emphasize the special and constitutionally recognized role of that institution in informing and educating the public, offering criticism, and providing a forum for discussion and debate. . . . But the press does not have a monopoly on either the First Amendment or the ability to enlighten.

Nor do our recent commercial speech cases lend support to appellee's business interest theory. They illustrate that the First Amendment goes beyond protection of the press and the self-expression of individuals to prohibit government from limiting the stock of information from which members of the public may draw. A commercial advertisement is constitutionally protected not so much because it pertains to the seller's business as because it furthers the societal interest in the "free flow of commercial information." . . .

C

We thus find no support in the 1st or 14th Amendment, or in the decisions of this Court, for the proposition that speech that otherwise would be within the protection of the 1st Amendment loses that protection simply because its source is a corporation that cannot prove, to the satisfaction of a court, a material effect on its business or property. The "materially affecting" requirement is not an identification of the boundaries of corporate speech etched by the Constitution itself. Rather, it amounts to an impermissible legislative prohibition of speech based on the identity of the interests that spokesmen may represent in public debate over controversial issues and a requirement that the speaker have a sufficiently great interest in the subject to justify communication.

Section 8 permits a corporation to communicate to the public its views on certain referendum subjects—those materially affecting its business—but not others. It also singles out one kind of ballot question—individual taxation—as a subject about which corporations may never make their ideas public. The legislature had drawn the line between permissible and impermissible speech according to whether there is a sufficient nexus, as defined by the legislature, between the issue presented to the voters and the business interests of the speaker.

In the realm of protected speech, the legislature is constitutionally disqualified from dictating the subjects about which persons may speak and the speakers who may address a public is-

sue. . . . If a legislature may direct business corporations to "stick to business," it also may limit other corporations—religious, charitable, or civic—to their respective "business" when addressing the public. Such power in government to channel the expression of views is unacceptable under the First Amendment.

WISCONSIN BIG BOY CORPORATION v. C.I.R.
452 F.2d (U.S. Seventh Circuit, 1971)
Fairchild, Circuit Judge

These appeals involve the allocation under 26 U.S.C. § 482, of all the income of subsidiaries to the parent corporation.

Collectively the business of taxpayers is to operate restaurants in Wisconsin under the Big Boy franchise and trademark. During the years in question there were 10 restaurants. A separate corporation operated each. Wisconsin Big Boy Corporation (WBB) had obtained the franchise from an unrelated California corporation which had developed a particular pattern of restaurant operation. WBB holds all the stock of the 10 restaurant corporations, has granted them subfranchises, and supervises them and performs bookkeeping and other services for them for a fee. The restaurants follow the same pattern of operation. Bon Host Service Corporation sells food to the restaurant corporations at cost plus 2.4 percent of the buyer's gross sales. Marc's Big Boy-Specialty Products, Inc., buys potatoes and resells them to the restaurant corporations. These two corporations do no other business. WBB owns all the stock of Bon Host and Specialty Products.

Ben Marcus owns 45 percent of the stock of WBB and his wife 30 percent. Gene Kilburg owns 25 percent. Mr. Marcus and Mrs. Kilburg are the principal officers of all the corporations and perform the chief management functions of all of them. There are three district managers who perform services as needed by the restaurant corporations.

The Commissioner assessed deficiencies for fiscal years ending in 1963, 1964, and 1965. He gave notice that he had determined that the corporate entities were to be disregarded for income tax purposes and all income and deductions attributed to WBB under 26 U.S.C. § 61. Alternatively he determined that all income and deductions were allocable to WBB under § 482 in order to prevent the evasion of taxes and clearly to reflect income.

The Tax Court upheld the Commissioner's allocation under § 482, upheld the resulting deficiencies of WBB, and found certain overpayments on behalf of the subsidiaries. . . .

A tax advantage resulted from division of the business among a number of corporations because each enjoyed a $25,000 surtax exemption. . . .

It is clear from the description set forth in the Tax Court opinion that the business carried on by the group of taxpayers is indeed highly integrated with all policy making choices and management functions beyond the very limited scope of the individual restaurant managers being performed by Marcus and Kilburg. So much so that it seems very doubtful that unrelated entities, dealing at arm's length, would arrive at a comparable division of functions. Because of the interdependence and overlapping among the segments of the business which have been assigned to the respective corporations, it would be very difficult, merely by adjusting the fee structure, to construct a situation which would conform to the arm's length standard. A hypothetical reconstruction would be fanciful and unreal. . . .

The issue on the instant appeal boils down to the incidence of the burden of proof. Taxpayers would argue that since it is evident that each restaurant operation generated some part of the net income and they have assigned at least the immediate operation of each to a separate corporation they have demonstrated that a total allocation is unreasonable, arbitrary, and capricious, and since the Commissioner failed to prove in the Tax Court that any less extreme allocation was supportable, taxpayers ought to have prevailed. . . .

In the light of the particular facts of this case, we conclude that the Tax Court fairly placed the burden on taxpayers. . . .

In the instant case, taxpayers carried on a business under arrangements where the segments of the business are so interwoven that reconstruction to comply with the arm's length standard is probably not realistic nor feasible, they made no effort to justify the terms of intercorporate transactions with respect to the arm's length test, or to establish the feasibility of reconstructing the transactions so as to comply, and the findings of the trier of the facts were adverse to the taxpayers, and not clearly erroneous.

Accordingly, the decisions of the Tax Court are affirmed.

BRAMWELL v. AIRPORT BLUE PRINT COMPANY

315 P. 2d 360 (California, 1957)

Griffin, Acting Presiding Justice

In this action for an injunction and damages plaintiff and respondent claims that defendants and appellants, after the sale of a business known as Economy Blue Print & Supply Co. in San Diego, violated an agreement not to engage in the same or similar business in San Diego County for 10 years. Previous to April 24, 1950, defendant John F. Mawson owned and operated the business under that name, making blue prints, Diazo prints, photostat work, and selling the necessary material for that purpose. On that date he entered into an agreement for the sale of this business, located at 1127 Fourth Avenue, to plaintiff for $45,000. In paragraph 12 thereof it provides that defendant Mawson agrees not to engage in a similar business in San Diego County for 10 years. He further agreed that if plaintiff should install a lithograph or offset printing plant that Mawson would not engage in such business but might solicit such business to be done in his plant which he had in Los Angeles. Thereafter, plaintiff took over the business and for certain purposes, in addition to the Economy Blue Print & Supply Co. formed corporations known as San Diego Blue Print Company, San Diego Engineers' Supply Company, and San Diego Reproduction Products Company. The business operation of the Economy Blue Print & Supply Co. was segregated, and certain branches of that work were assigned to these respective corporations, all doing business at the same location and under the same management. Plaintiff and his wife were the sole stockholders in said corporations. . . .

It is defendants' claim in this respect that the evidence is not sufficient to show that defendant Airport Blue Print Company was the alter ego of defendant Mawson, the argument being that Mawson only owned 40 percent of the stock in Airport Blue Print Company; that he held no office therein and did not actively solicit accounts for that corporation in San Diego; and that accordingly there was no sufficient showing of unity of interest and ownership therein by him. An examination of the evidence indicates that the trial court's findings in this respect are supported. It appears that Mawson and defendant Grosart were friends and business partners of long standing. They discussed the question of their operating in San Diego County as a partnership after the agreement not to engage in a similar business in San Diego County was signed by Mawson. They also considered whether there was a possibility of their being enjoined under the agreement, and they concluded that they could legally operate as a corporation rather than as individuals. The Airport Blue Print Company was then established. The directors were Mawson, Grosart, and their attorney. Grosart and Mawson each owned 50 per cent of the stock. Blueprinting equipment of Economy was delivered to Airport Blue Print Company, purportedly under a contract of sale, and its vehicles were loaned to Airport Blue Print Company. Several unpaid demand notes were found to be executed in favor of the Airport company by Mawson ($15,464.65) and Grosart ($4,000). It affirmatively appears that the Airport company had been financed almost entirely by Mawson personally, or through loans made by Economy, and that Mawson obtained financial control over the Airport corporation. Thereafter, the manager of Economy came from Los Angeles and solicited an aircraft firm in San Diego, a customer of plaintiff for its business. Two cards were presented, one "Economy Blue Print & Supply Co., Los Angeles" and the other "Airport Blue Print Company." Other similar solicitations were shown. So-called San Diego branch offices were then opened in San Diego by Airport. Defendant Economy Lithograph Co. was another of the Economy companies solely owned by Mawson and his wife. The evidence is sufficient to show that Airport Blue Print Company, a corporation, was formed for the purpose of enabling Mawson to circumvent his convenant with the plaintiff, and that Mawson dominates and controls the said corporations. Under the circumstances the order of the court granting the injunction was authorized. . . .

Judgment affirmed.

PROBLEMS FOR DISCUSSION

1. Sambo's, Inc., a Delaware corporation, owned and operated a chain of 300 family restaurants, which were located in 38 states. It was properly registered and licensed to do business as a foreign corporation in the state of Mythigan. Although Sambo's building plans were approved by the City Building Commission, the City Council of Ham Harbor, Mythigan, would not permit Sambo's to use its name on any sign or billboard within the city. The city had a sign ordinance which regulated the position, size, and content of commercial signs. The City Council said that "Sambo's" could not be used because it implied disrepute or ridicule of blacks. Sambo's sues for injunctive relief. What result, and why?

2. Sharpe and Keene prepared proposed articles of incorporation for Soakem, Inc. The articles were properly and completely filled out, but when they were presented to the State Corporation Bureau for filing, the director of the bureau, Punche, refused to file them and to certify the corporation's existence. The purpose clause in the articles stated that Soakem was organized "to provide loans to noncorporate borrowers at rates of interest in excess of 7 percent per annum, but less than 24 percent per

annum, secured by second mortgages on single-family residential property." Punche said that these rates of interest were usurious under the state's statute and that the proposed corporation's purpose was therefore illegal. Sharpe and Keene bring a mandamus action to force Punche to accept Soakem's articles since these articles are complete and correct. What result, and why?

3. Ferd was employed as a truck driver by Ace Delivery Company, Inc. Leon Crim was the president and principal stockholder of Ace. Ferd quit his job and sued for back wages and bonuses which he claimed were due. Ferd's suit named as defendant "Leon Crim d/b/a Ace Delivery Company, Inc." Crim was served with process as an individual, not as Ace's president. Ace was never served with process. Throughout the trial, Crim denied that he personally was Ferd's employer, but Ferd insisted that he considered Crim and Ace to be "one and the same." The trial court entered judgment against Ace for $2,050 but entered no judgment against Crim. Crim appeals. What should the appeals court do to resolve this case? Explain.

4. Ronald Burberry sued for specific performance of a contract to purchase a large apartment complex. The real estate was owned by Garth, Inc. Garth, Inc., had issued 10 shares of preferred stock, all held by the FHA, which had guaranteed payment of the original purchase price, and 500 shares of common stock. The common was owned by Saul Garth (250 shares); Flora Garth, his wife (240 shares); and Madison Lark, the company's vice president (10 shares). Saul had been president prior to his death, but the office had been left vacant since then. Saul's will left all of his property to Flora. Because of its original mortgage guarantee, the FHA's approval was required prior to any major financial action by Garth, Inc.

   Without getting the FHA's approval, Flora listed the property for sale with the Babble Real Estate Agency. The listing agreement stated that Garth, Inc., was the owner of the property. When Hack Babble drafted the purchase contract he listed Flora Garth as the owner. Flora said that she thought she had the authority to bind the corporation when she signed the purchase contract (even though she really did not have such authority). Ronald Burberry wants the court to pierce the corporate veil. Should it do so? Discuss.

5. Athos, Porthos, and Aramis subscribed for shares of common stock in Lille, Inc., a corporation which was being organized to develop, manufacture, and distribute high-technology medical products. Constance and Harry, the promoters, never filed the articles of incorporation. They nevertheless leased a factory building, bought the necessary equipment, hired several employees, and commenced business. After six months the business was bankrupt. The landlord, the equipment seller, the employees, and several other creditors have unpaid claims. Who may be held liable in this situation? Discuss.

6. Karl and Sophie Ranowski bought a new home which had been constructed by Bill Derr Construction, Inc. The house had been built only a little over 100 feet from the edge of Frisky Lake, and it settled into the soft ground underneath, causing cracking in the basement floor, the foundation walls, the brickwork, and the plaster in the upstairs rooms. In addition to suing the corporation, the Ranowskis joined as defendants Bill Straitedge and Hannibal Derr, who each owned 50 percent of the company's stock. Bill and Hannibal had operated their business as a partnership prior to incorporation, and both were still actively involved in the business. Bill had actually signed the contract with the Ranowskis and had been in general charge of the building of their house. The building contract was signed on one of the old partnership forms, which did not use the word *Incorporated* or "Inc." Can Bill and Hannibal be held personally liable here? Why or why not?

7. Ralph owned some valuable oil properties in Mexico, but he lacked the working

capital necessary to develop them. He called on Green and explained the situation. Green loaned Ralph $20,000 and cosigned a note so that Ralph was able to borrow another $20,000 from the Bigger Bank. Ralph and Green were unable to raise further funds. Green then went to Bart Lurch, president of Lurch Investment Company, and proposed a plan for organizing a corporation to develop Ralph's oil properties. As part of the plan, Lurch agreed that he would personally cosign the corporation's note for $500,000 and that the profits made would be shared equally among himself, Ralph, and Green. The Inland Oil Company was organized, but Lurch refused to cosign its $500,000 note. No bank would advance the $500,000 without Lurch's signature. Lurch said he would go through with the deal if Green would take 5 percent of the profits, rather than one third. Green refused this offer. Lurch then wrote a letter to Green saying that since their deal had fallen through, he was now proceeding to negotiate directly with Ralph. What are Green's rights, if any, under these circumstances? Discuss.

8. The Border Group, a partnership consisting of Rickie, Sherlene, and Teddie acquired certain salvage rights at three abandoned military bases. (The U.S. government had given them the right to remove and to use or resell whatever machinery, equipment, or buildings were left on the bases.) The partners formed a new corporation, Border, Inc., to do the salvage work. Will Clawhamer was hired by Border, Inc., to do certain excavating work at the three bases. Will did all of the agreed excavating work at the first site but was not paid. Border, Inc., had apparently abandoned the project and was insolvent. Will sues Rickie, Sherlene, and Teddie as individuals. Are they personally liable? Explain.

43 | Corporations—Stock; Shareholders' Rights

When a corporation is created, it is granted the power to issue a stated number of shares. The number of shares allowed is stated in the articles of incorporation which are filed in the state of incorporation. As shares of stock are issued by a corporation they are exchanged for cash, property, or services. The owners of the shares of stock issued by a corporation are in effect the owners of the corporation. Each shareholder is entitled to a proportionate share of the profits of the corporations, which, when distributed, are termed dividends, and each shareholder is also entitled to a proportionate amount of the total assets of a corporation if the corporation is dissolved. While the shareholders are in a sense the owners of the corporation, what they own is a proportionate share of the corporation's total value and they do not have any interest or ownership in the specific property owned by the corporation. In other words, a shareholder cannot simply go in and grab an item of property owned by the corporation and say, "I'll trade this for my shares."

In small corporations there is normally only one type of stock. Typically all of the shares in a small corporation have the same value and all of the shareholders have the same rights. This is not true in large corporations. In such corporations it is not uncommon to have several classes and series of stock. Some stock may have a par value, and other stock may have no par value. Some stock may have voting rights, and other stock may not have voting rights. Some stock may be preferred, and other stock may be common.

KINDS OF STOCK

Corporations are normally authorized to issue two or more classes of capital stock or capital shares. Following are some of the most common classes of stock.

1. Common Stock. This is the basic class of stock issued by corporations. Typically a shareholder has one vote for each share of stock and the shareholder is entitled to receive a pro rata share of the corporation's profits in the form of

dividends. The common stockholder is given no guarantees, no special preference. If the business succeeds, the common stockholders receive dividends and
their share value will increase. If the business fails, the common stockholders
get no return on their investment and they may lose the investment itself, as
they share in the balance of the assets after creditors and preferred stockholders
have been paid off.

2. Preferred Stock. As the term indicates, this class of stockholders gets special preference. Typically the preferred stockholder receives a specific, guaranteed dividend before any dividends are paid to the persons owning the corporation's common stock and in case of dissolution of the corporation the preferred
stockholders get their money back before any money is returned to the common stockholders.

The preferred stockholder is not a creditor of the corporation, and normally
the dividend on preferred stock does not have to be paid if the board of directors has no funds with which to pay a dividend.

3. Cumulative Preferred Stock. In some lean years the corporation may not
have enough profits to declare a dividend for either the preferred stockholders
or the common stockholder. This question then arises: Does the preferred
stockholder lose out on the unpaid dividend for such years? Unless the articles
of incorporation so state, the unpaid dividends on preferred stock would not
accumulate. Thus it is important that preferred stock be declared either noncumulative or cumulative. If the preferred stock is noncumulative, then, of
course, if no dividends are declared by the board of directors during a given
year, the preferred stockholders simply lose out for that year. If the stock is
cumulative, then the next year they will get the past year's dividends plus the
new year's dividends before any money is distributed to the common stockholders.

4. Participating Preferred Stock. The preferred stockholder has the advantage of receiving dividends prior to the distribution of dividends to the common
stockholder. Typically, however, the preferred stockholder is entitled to receive only a specific, guaranteed dividend, for example, 6 percent. If the corporation had a good year, the amount left to divide among the common stockholders might well exceed the percentage awarded to the preferred stockholders.
However, if the preferred stockholder has participating preferred stock, then
the preferred stockholder would share in the amount divided after the common
stockholders received a dividend equal to the dividend which was paid to the
preferred stockholders. Thus, if the preferred stockholders get 6 percent on
their stock, then the common stockholders would get 6 percent on their stock
and if there were extra money left over, it would be shared equally between the
two classes of stock.

In addition to the cumulative or noncumulative and participating or nonparticipating provisions of preferred stock, it is not uncommon to find redeemable or convertible provisions. Such provisions say, in effect, that at the election
of the corporation preferred shares may be converted into another class of
shares or may be redeemable by the corporation.

5. Par Value and No Par Value Stock. A corporation may issue stock with or without a par value. The certificates for par value stock state an amount which must be paid per share for the stock. The amount per share of no par value stock is simply determined by the board of directors.

The issuance of par value stock often creates misunderstanding. For example, if a new corporation issues 1,000 shares at a par value of $100 each, and you buy 10 shares at $100 each, you will be given stock certificates which show a face value of $1,000. The corporation, however, proceeds to buy equipment and inventory, to pay the expenses of incorporation and other expenses of doing business, and thus it no longer has a net worth of $10,000 or 1,000 times $100 per share of par value stock. As a result, even though your certificate of stock shows a par value of $100 per share, you could not necessarily sell the stock for $100 per share as the stock is only worth $1/10,000$ of the net worth or book value of the corporation.

SUBSCRIBERS

One of the promoters' most important preincorporation functions is to make arrangements for acquiring the capital necessary to commence the firm's business. Persons making preincorporation offers to buy shares of the firm's stock are called subscribers. Since these offers are made to the corporation, they cannot be accepted until after incorporation. Unfortunately, in many cases proposed corporations fail before they ever commence business or after a very short period of operation. If there are unpaid creditors of the now insolvent corporation, it thus becomes very important to know exactly when subscribers become liable for their shares, and the extent of that liability.

Revocable Offer. The general rule is that a stock subscription, like any offer, is revocable prior to acceptance. This rule creates problems for the promoters, since they can't count on having any set amount of capital until the corporation is formed and accepts the subscription offers. Some courts have found particular subscriptions to be irrevocable on the basis that the promoters' efforts provided consideration for an implied promise by the subscriber not to revoke. Some cases find mutual promise between the several subscribers not to revoke. Section 17 of the MBCA, which has been adopted in several states, makes the subscription offer irrevocable for six months without consideration. Of course, where fraud was committed against the subscriber, the offer can be revoked despite Section 17 or the presence of consideration.

Implied Conditions Precedent. In order for a subscriber to be held liable on a subscription contract, the courts have generally agreed that three conditions must be met. First, the corporation must be fully organized de jure. Second, it must be substantially like the one proposed to the subscriber. And finally, the shares subscribed for must be legally issuable by the corporation (in other words, must not be shares representing an oversubscription).

Express Conditions Precedent/Subscriptions on Special Terms. Some potential subscribers may not be interested in investing in the proposed corporation unless certain return promises are made. These special promises could relate to the corporation's method of operation, the location of its place of business, or other matters. What happens when the corporation is organized, accepts the subscriptions, but goes into bankruptcy before it builds its main plant in Keokuk, as it promised one subscriber? Is that subscriber liable anyway, or was the "plant in Keokuk" an express condition precedent which has not been fulfilled? As between risk-taking investors and unpaid corporate creditors, the equities are all with the creditors. Courts will try as hard as possible to label these special deals as "subscriptions on special terms," so as to hold the subscriber liable for the full price of the shares contracted for. After paying in full, the subscriber then has a claim for damages, if any can be proved, for the corporation's breach of its promise to build the plant. If the parties' intent and the "no contract if no plant" results are spelled out clearly enough in the subscription, the subscriber may avoid liability.

Subscription versus Contract to Purchase Shares. Particularly in cases where the stock is being paid for in installments, it may also be important to distinguish between a subscription and a contract to purchase shares. A subscriber becomes liable for the full price of the shares when the subscription offer is effectively accepted by the corporation. A purchaser does not become a shareholder (and thus become liable for the price of the shares) until a certificate is delivered or tendered. Where corporations have gone into bankruptcy before issuance of the certificates, many courts have held that the purchasers were excused from further liability because they would never receive their certificates. Subscribers in such a case would be bound to pay any balance due on their shares.

Once again, in figuring out which is which, it's a question of the parties' intent and of some legal presumptions and rules. Prior to incorporation, the transaction can only be a subscription, not a purchase. After incorporation, the agreement to buy original, unissued shares may be either. Generally, a purchase is an individual agreement, whereas a subscription may involve several purchasers. If there is any ambiguity at all, most courts will try to impose full liability by classifying the transaction as a subscription.

Minimum Liability Equals Full Par Value. In some instances subscribers may not be willing to pay the full par value per share and the promoters may agree to sell shares at a discount. This is a dangerous practice at best, since all states agree, on one theory or another, that every subscriber must pay at least the full par value for each share taken. One early case held that the corporation's capital was a sort of "trust fund" for the benefit of its creditors. A few states analyze the discount to subscribers as a "fraud" on the firm's creditors. The most sensible analysis simply says that payment of at least full par is the price which the state demands for the privilege of doing business in the corporate form with limited personal liability.

Under any of these theories, creditors can force payment of the difference between the discounted contract price and the full par value. Creditors who knew about the discount when they extended credit, however, might have some difficulty in recovering in a fraud theory state. Stockholders who have paid full par for their shares might also sue to force the discounter to pay up. In some cases the corporation itself or the state of incorporation may bring the suit.

In addition to the original subscriber who bought at a discount (whether or not still a stockholder), possible defendants include knowing transferees of the discounted shares, the directors who approved the sale, and the promoters.

Bing Crosby Minute Maid Corporation v. Eaton
297 P.2d 5 (California, 1956)

FACTS Wallazz Eaton owned and operated a frozen foods business. He organized a corporation and transferred the business to it in return for 4,500 shares of $10 par stock. The corporations commissioner required that 1,022 shares of the stock be placed in escrow and not transferred without his written consent; 1,022 shares were put in escrow in Eaton's name, and the other 3,478 shares were issued directly to him. The plaintiff had a judgment against the corporation for $21,246.42, of which some $15,000 was still unpaid. The corporation was insolvent. The trial court found that the value of the transferred business was $34,780.83 and gave the plaintiff a judgment against Eaton for $10,219.17. Because it had failed to make a finding that the plaintiff relied on some misrepresentation in connection with the watered stock, the trial court granted Eaton a new trial. The plaintiff appealed the order granting a new trial.

ISSUE Must a corporate creditor prove reliance on a misrepresentation in order to recover against the holder of watered stock?

DECISION Yes. Order for new trial affirmed.

REASONS After reciting the facts, Justice Shenk started with the proposition that stockholders were not personally liable for the debts of their corporation unless they had not paid what they promised for their stock or unless they held watered stock. The first exception didn't apply here because there was no proof that Eaton had in fact promised to pay full par for his shares. Justice Shenk did not think that the escrow arrangement made any difference, since Eaton could vote those shares and receive dividends on them. For statutory purposes, Eaton owned them. The real issue was what the plaintiff had to prove to recover.

"In his answer the defendant alleged that in extending credit to the corporation the plaintiff did not rely on the par value of the shares issued, but only on independent investigation and reports as to the corporation's current cash position, its physical assets, and its business experience. . . . Plaintiff's . . . admissions would be sufficient to support a finding that the plaintiff did not rely on any misrepresentation arising out of the issuance of watered stock. The court made no finding on the issue of reliance. If the misrepresentation theory prevails in California, that issue was material and the defendant was entitled to a finding thereon. . . .

"It is therefore necessary to determine which theory prevails in this state. The plaintiff concedes that before the enactment of section 1110 of the Corporations Code . . . in 1931, the misrepresentation theory was the only one available to creditors seeking to recover from holders of watered stock. . . . However, he contends that the enactment of that section reflected a legislative intent to impose on the

> holders of watered stock a statutory obligation to creditors to make good the 'water.' . . . The statute does not expressly impose an obligation to creditors. Most jurisdictions having similar statutes have applied the misrepresentation theory obviously on the ground that creditors are sufficiently protected against stock watering schemes under that theory. . . . In view of the cases in this state prior to 1931 adopting the misrepresentation theory, it is reasonable to assume that the Legislature would have used clear language expressing an intent to broaden the basis of liability of holders of watered stock had it entertained such an intention. In this state the liability of a holder of watered stock may only be based on the misrepresentation theory."

Payment in Property or Services. Another potential area of liability arises when shares are paid for with noncash items. Property or services, to be valid payment for shares, must be usable by the corporation in operating its business. Generally, promises to perform services or to deliver property in the future do not constitute proper payment for shares, and subscribers who receive shares in exchange for such promises could be sued for the full par value of the shares they receive.

Complications arise not only from questions as to whether the corporation was authorized to receive the noncash items but also as to the valuation of those items. States use two very different rules in determining whether at least full par has been paid. The Model Act and most of the newer corporation statutes have adopted the good faith rule: the valuation of the board of directors is conclusive. Whatever the board says the property or services were worth binds the corporation and all its creditors, unless the board was acting fraudulently or was grossly negligent. About half of the states still follow the older true value rule, which holds that any such noncash item had a "true" market value when it was transferred to the firm in payment for shares, that such value presents a question of fact, and that a jury can thus determine the true value of the noncash item. The result of this rule is that jurors are second-guessing the parties, sometimes after a lapse of several years, on the basis of less than perfect information.

No-Par Shares. As noted above, no-par stock does not have any specific dollar figure indicated on the share certificate. Thus most "valuation" problems are avoided when no-par stock is exchanged for a noncash item. The Model Act and most statutes permit no-par shares to be issued for such consideration as is agreed to by the directors (or the existing stockholders). The no-par's price is thus permitted to fluctuate with market conditions, and the no-par stockholders would not be held liable for any "discount." No-par shares cannot, however, be issued as a gift. Moreover, there is case law which indicates that after the initial issue, if the price paid for no-par is not "fair" to the existing stockholders, they can bring suit to enjoin the dilution of their interest in the firm's net assets.

Treasury Shares. The Model Act covers the resale of treasury shares (which were issued but then reacquired by the corporation) with a similar rule: treasury stock may be resold for any consideration fixed by the board of directors. Once again, there should be no "valuation" problem or "discount" liability as long as the directors were acting in good faith.

Shares Issued by Going Concern.   What if the corporation needs additional capital after it has been in operation for some period of time? If it still has original, unissued par stock, can it sell that stock to investors at the market price, or is it still bound to receive at least par value per share? Only in a few states do the corporation statutes recognize this problem and specifically permit the directors, in this case, to sell par stock at the going market price.

Repurchase of Shares.   Having required the payment of at least par value per share by subscribers/investors, courts do not want these risk-takers to be able to escape easily if the firm gets into financial difficulties. Creditors should be paid in full before stockholders recover any part of their investment. Thus, a contract for the repurchase of shares is valid only if the corporation has earned surplus when the contract is made, and for such a contract to be enforceable in court by the shareholder, the corporation must also have earned surplus when payment is to be made to the shareholder. At both points in time, the earned surplus shown on the books must be sufficient to cover the repurchase.

ISSUANCE AND TRANSFER OF SHARES

Registration.   Many securities issues must be registered with either the Securities and Exchange Commission or a similar state agency or with both. This is a very complex area of the law. Chapter 47 discusses the nature of these registration requirements and the potential liabilities involved.

Mechanics of Transfer.   Article 8 of the UCC contains many of the rules covering the transfer of corporate securities (both stocks and bonds). Many customary practices are also involved—stockbrokers' rules for dealing with each other and their customers, regulations adopted by the stock exchanges, and administrative rulings from the SEC. Large corporations usually appoint a bank or trust company to act as their "transfer agent," that is, to record transfer of their securities and to issue new certificates in the new owners' names. Securities, particularly bonds, may also be issued in bearer form, in which case ownership transfers are not registered with the corporation. Bearer bonds are often called coupon bonds, since interest coupons attached to such bonds must be clipped and sent in by the bondholder in order to receive the interest due on the bonds.

Lost or Stolen Securities.   Where the missing securities were in bearer form or had been properly indorsed by the former registered owner, a good faith purchaser from the thief or finder owns the securities. If registered securities are involved, the bona fide purchaser (BFP) is entitled to be registered on the corporation's books as the new owner.

Where the securities were in registered form but the thief or finder forged the indorsement/assignment of the owner, the BFP does not own the certifi-

cates and must return them. If the BFP sends in an old certificate to the transfer agent, however, and the old certificate is canceled and a new one issued to
the BFP, the BFP does own the new certificate. In this last situation the former
owner has a claim against the corporation and its transfer agent for not catching
the forgery. Because of the potential liabilities resulting from such a "double
issuance" of a new certificate, corporations will uniformly require that persons
who claim that their certificates have been lost or stolen post bonds protecting
the corporation against the "reappearance" of the missing securities.

Restrictions.   Corporate securities are generally freely transferable by the
owner. In special situations, however, the persons operating the firm may wish
to place limitations on the retransfer of its stock. In a small closely held corporation, for example, the stockholders might want to give the corporation itself, or
the other stockholders, a right of first refusal before any stock is resold to
outsiders. Similarly, there might be a requirement that shares issued to key
employees, be resold to the firm rather than to outsiders when the employment
ends. For such restrictions to be effective against buyers who don't know about
them, they must be noted conspicuously on the certificate.

SHAREHOLDER RIGHTS

Vested Rights.   As noted earlier, the charter of the corporation is a contract.
This means that the shareholders' rights which the charter establishes cannot
be changed without their consent. Where the power to amend the articles and
the bylaws has been reserved, however, and the amendment procedure is followed, changes can be made in the respective rights and liabilities of the stockholders.

Preemptive Rights.   One right recognized in many older cases is the right to
maintain one's proportionate investment in the corporation. The original stock
issue gave each stockholder a certain percentage of the votes and of any dividends declared. To protect this relationship among the stockholders, courts
required that existing stockholders be given a right of first refusal for a proportionate part of any new issue. That is, the new stock had to be offered to existing
stockholders first, before it could be sold to others. Courts did not agree as to
whether this "preemptive right" also applied to originally authorized but
unissued stock.
   Insistence on such preemptive rights makes it very difficult for a firm to
authorize a new stock issue for executive bonuses, acquisition of assets, mergers with other firms, or other possible business needs. The modern tendency is
to limit or eliminate such preemptive rights unless they are specifically provided for in the articles or by agreement among the stockholders.

Voting Rights.   Except perhaps in Illinois, corporations are permitted to issue
both voting and nonvoting stock. Typically common stock has the right to vote,
while preferred stock does not. Preferred stock may be given voting rights
under special circumstances, such as when dividends have been skipped for
several successive years. Unlike partnerships, where each partner is presumed

to have one vote regardless of the amount he or she has invested, in corporations each share is entitled to one vote.

In order to facilitate minority representation on the board of directors, some corporations provide for cumulative voting. (In some states, in fact, cumulative voting for directors is required by law.) Under this voting system, all directors' vacancies that are to be filled in a given year are voted for at the same time, with each share having as many votes as there are directors to be elected. The idea is that by massing their votes for only one (or a few) candidates, minority stockholders may be able to get at least some representation on the board. A seat on the board enables the minority to obtain information and to present alternative proposals and views. To find out how many shares they need to assemble to be assured of electing their candidates, minority stockholders can use the following formula:

$$X = \frac{a \text{ times } c \text{ plus } 1}{b \text{ plus } 1}$$

where X equals the number of shares needed, a equals the number of shares voting in the election, b equals the number of directors to be elected, and c equals the number of directors the minority want to elect.

In order to assemble the number of shares needed to obtain board representation or to gain or maintain control, shareholder groups can use one of three devices: the proxy, the voting control agreement, or the voting trust. A proxy is merely a revocable agency authority to vote shares. Changing conditions or new information could lead stockholders to withdraw their proxies or to give later proxies to the opposing side. Proxies thus do not provide a very stable coalition.

Some or all of the stockholders, particularly in closely held corporations, may enter into voting control agreements. Such agreements usually provide for reciprocal voting for the board of directors; A, B, and C agree to vote for each other, so that each retains a seat on the board. Such agreements are permitted in most states, at least for a limited period of time. They are not, however, binding on the corporation or on unknowing transferees of stock. A stockholder wishing to break up such an agreement could simply transfer his or her shares to a BFP, who would then be free to vote them as he or she pleased.

The voting trust is the most durable arrangement for accumulating the votes necessary to maintain control of a corporation. Stockholders, the corporation itself, and transferees are all bound by the voting trust, since shares of stock are actually turned over to the voting trustees, who are registered as the owners of the shares on the corporation's books. In return for their shares, the (former) stockholders receive voting trust certificates, which give them all the rights of stockholders *except* the right to vote. Many voting trusts are set up by demand of the firm's creditors, as a condition to the extension of further credit. The creditors want to assure continuity of management, and a voting trust is a good way to do so.

Dividend Rights.   Many persons who invest in corporate stock are mainly motivated by the expectation of dividends. The firm's directors generally determine the timing and amount of dividends, subject to the requirements of the particular state. Most states require that there be earned surplus before dividends may be lawfully declared and paid, but a few states permit the payment of dividends from current earnings even though prior years' losses have not been made up. Once declared, cash dividends become debts of the corporation. If a dividend has been illegally declared, the directors who voted in favor are jointly and severally liable for the entire amount of the dividend. All of the states agree that shareholders who know that a dividend was illegal can be forced to return it, but there is disagreement as to whether innocent stockholders can also be forced to return an illegal dividend.

As to preferred stock, the presumptions are that the shares are cumulative but nonparticipating, unless otherwise agreed.

Stock dividends are not debts of the corporation, and they may be rescinded by the board before new shares are issued.

Dodge v. *Ford Motor Co.*
170 N.W. 668 (Michigan, 1919)

FACTS   Minority stockholders sued to force the directors to declare an additional special dividend. Horace and John Dodge, the plaintiffs, were two of the original stockholders in Ford Motor Company, along with Horace Rackham, James Couzens, and Henry Ford himself. On the capitalization of $2 million, Ford Motor had been paying a quarterly dividend equal to 60 percent per year; it had also paid out a total of $41 million in special dividends. Ford Motor still had a capital surplus of nearly $112 million, however, and sales and profits were up. Henry now proposed a massive capital expansion to produce iron and steel (the Rouge plant) as well as a lowering of the price of the Model T from $440 to $360. At one point, Henry was quoted as saying: "My ambition is to employ still more men, to spread the benefits of this industrial system to the greatest possible number, to help them build up their lives and their homes. To do this, we are putting the greatest share of our profits back in the business." Ford Motor appealed from the trial court's decision ordering payment of a special dividend and enjoining the building of the Rouge plant.

ISSUE   Did the directors abuse their discretion in refusing to grant a dividend?

DECISION   Yes. Judgment affirmed as to dividends, reversed as to injunction.

REASONS   Chief Justice Ostrander first disposed of the claims that Ford Motor's activities had in some way violated its corporate charter. No statutory limits were intended on the size to which corporations might grow, and the Rouge smelter plant seemed closely enough connected with the company's main business so as not to be ultra vires. Likewise, there had been no violation of the antitrust laws. The court also cited several authorities which stated the general rule for the declaration of dividends: "The discretion of the directors will not be interfered with by the courts, unless there has been bad faith, willful neglect, or abuse of discretion." Despite this strong general rule, the court here felt that there had been an abuse of the directors' discretion, due to Ford's personal feelings.

"He had made up his mind in the summer of 1916 that no dividends other than the regular dividends should be paid, 'for the present.' . . .

"The record, and especially the testimony of Mr. Ford, convinces that he has to some extent the attitude towards shareholders of one who has dispensed and distributed to them large gains and that they should be content to take what he chooses to give. His testimony creates the impression, also, that he thinks the Ford Motor Company has made too much money, has had too large profits, and that, although large profits might still be earned, a sharing of them with the public, by reducing the price of the output of the company, ought to be undertaken. We have no doubt that certain sentiments, philanthropic and altruistic, creditable to Mr. Ford, had large influence in determining the policy to be pursued by the Ford Motor Company—the policy which has been herein referred to. . . .

"We are not, however, persuaded that we should interfere with the proposed expansion of the business of the Ford Motor Company. . . . The judges are not business experts. . . . The experience of the Ford Motor Company is evidence of capable management of its affairs."

Management Rights.   In small closely held corporations, where the stockholders are also the directors, officers, and managers, the stockholders may participate in the daily operations of the business. With large corporations like IBM or GM, however, stockholders will usually have only one annual meeting to attend. Special meetings other than the regular annual meeting may be called, but only after proper notice has been sent to all of the stockholders so that they all have a chance to attend. The Model Act specifies that a quorum at a stockholders' meeting is a majority of the voting shares (represented in person or by proxy), unless the articles of the particular firm specify a lower percentage, down to a minimum of one third of the voting shares. Some of the newer statutes permit the stockholders to transact business if any shares are represented, as long as proper notice has been sent. Once a quorum has been established, stockholders cannot prevent the transaction of business by leaving the meeting and then having someone make another quorum call.

The main item of business to be transacted at the stockholders' meeting is the election of directors. As noted above, the cumulative voting system may be used. In most cases the slate of candidates proposed by management is elected without much, if any, opposition. Where a firm has had bad financial results, dissident stockholders may propose their own slate of directors and try to take control of the firm. Each side will solicit support from the rest of the stockholders through personal letters, ads in *The Wall Street Journal*, and other methods. The SEC has extensive regulations on the solicitation and use of proxies in such control battles.

The stockholders generally have no say in making ordinary business decisions for "their" company. By custom and statute, the responsibility for day-to-day management is vested in the board of directors, which in turn delegates much of this authority to the officers. The directors and officers are usually called on to report to the stockholders at the annual meeting, and the stockholders can question them at that time about the decisions made during the year. The stockholders will also usually vote on the selection of the corporation's outside auditors. The independent CPA firm auditing the corporation's books provides another source of information to the stockholders and another method of checking on the directors' and officers' conduct of the firm's business. If changes in a corporations' bylaws are proposed, those will also have to be voted on by the stockholders. Extraordinary business decisions, such as amending the articles to change the nature of the firm's business, or voluntary dissolution of the corporation, or merger or consolidation with another company, must also be presented for stockholder vote. While the Model Act now requires only a majority vote on such extraordinary decisions, many states still require a two-thirds or even a three-fourths favorable vote. (See Chapter 45.)

Medical Committee for Human Rights v. *S.E.C.*
432 F.2d 659 (U.S. District of Columbia Circuit, 1970)

FACTS   On March 11, 1968, Dr. Quentin Young, the national chairman of the Medical Committee, wrote to the secretary of the Dow Chemical Company, stating that the committee had received a few shares of Dow's stock as a gift and asking permission to introduce an amendment to the company's charter at the annual meeting. The amendment would have prohibited Dow from making napalm. The committee was late in making its request, and Dow refused to waive the time limit set by the corporate bylaws. On January 6, 1969, the committee made a timely demand for inclusion of the proposed amendment in Dow's proxy statement for that year's shareholders' meeting. Dow refused to do so, relying on the SEC's proxy rules which said that proposals could be omitted if they were "primarily for the purpose of promoting general economic, political, racial, religious, social or similar causes" or if they requested that "the management take action with respect to a matter relating to the conduct of the ordinary business operations" of the corporation. On February 18, the chief counsel of the SEC's Division of Corporate Finance sent a letter to both parties which said that the division would "not recommend any action . . . if this proposal is omitted from the management's proxy material." On April 2, the SEC approved this "no action" recommendation. The Medical Committee appealed.

ISSUE   Was the SEC's action reviewable by the court? Should the proposal have been included in the proxy statement?

DECISION   Yes. Probably, but a remand to the SEC is necessary. Case remanded.

REASONS   Much of Judge Tamm's opinion dealt with the question of whether such a "no action" decision by the SEC was reviewable by a court of appeals. He decided that the very strong presumption in favor of judicial review of administrative action had not been overcome in this case and that this was in effect a "final order" and thus ready for review. The SEC's proxy procedures were also sufficiently adversary and formal in nature to permit court review of the results. Tamm also felt that the SEC had not done an adequate job of explaining its decision.
    "[T]he Commission has not deigned to address itself to any possible grounds for

871

allowing management to exclude this proposal from its proxy statement. We confess to a similar puzzlement as to how the Commission reached the result which it did, and thus we are forced to remand the controversy for a more illuminating consideration and decision. . . . In aid of this consideration on remand, we feel constrained to explain our difficulties with the position taken by the company and endorsed by the Commission.

"It is obvious to the point of banality to restate the proposition that Congress intended by its enactment of section 14 of the Securities Exchange Act of 1934 to give true vitality to the concept of corporate democracy. The depth of this commitment is reflected in the strong language employed in the legislative history: . . . 'Fair corporate suffrage is an important right that should attach to every equity security bought on a public exchange. Managements of properties owned by the investing public should not be permitted to perpetuate themselves by the misuse of corporate proxies.' . . .

"These two exceptions are, on their face, consistent with the legislative purpose underlying section 14; for it seems fair to infer that Congress desired to make proxy solicitations a vehicle for *corporate* democracy rather than an all-purpose forum for malcontented shareholders to vent their spleen about irrelevant matters, and also realized that management cannot exercise its specialized talents effectively if corporate investors assert the power to dictate the minutiae of daily business decision. However, it is also apparent that the two exceptions . . . can be construed so as to permit the exclusion of practically any shareholder proposal. . . .

"Close examination of the company's arguments only increases doubt as to the reasoning processes which led the Commission to this result."

Generally, the majority stockholders have the right to determine corporate policy as they see fit, through the directors they elect and through the officers whom those directors appoint. The majority control group, however, must act within the limits set by the charter and must act in good faith as far as the rights of the minority stockholders are concerned. Several cases have held that the majority control group occupies a fiduciary position with respect to the minority and that its acts can be challenged where it is abusing its control powers.

Right of Access to Information. Stockholders have the right to receive information regarding the operation of "their" corporation. This right, however, is not unlimited. All of the states agree that financial information such as the firm's annual balance sheet and its profit and loss statement should be available to the stockholders. There is some disagreement as to when an individual stockholder should have access to other information, particularly the firm's general books and business records. With unlimited rights of access, minority stockholders might be able to disrupt normal business operations. Competitors could simply buy one share of a firm's stock and then demand access to all of its trade secrets, formulas, and customer lists. "Junk mailers" of various sorts could buy one share and ask for lists of stockholders. For these reasons, courts have generally required that a stockholder must have a "proper purpose" in

asking for access to corporate books and records. Some states require ownership of a certain percentage of a class of stock, and some also require that the
stock have been owned for some minimum period of time (such as six months)
prior to the demand for information. Where the demand is proper and the
officers refuse to provide the information, the Model Act makes them liable for
10 percent of the value of the stock owned, in addition to any other appropriate
remedy to which the stockholder may be entitled.

State ex rel. Pillsbury v. Honeywell, Inc.
191 N.W.2d 408 (Minnesota, 1971)

FACTS   On July 3, 1969, Pillsbury attended a meeting of a group involved in a so-called
Honeywell Project. He had long opposed the Vietnam War, but it was at this meeting
that he first learned of Honeywell's involvment as a manufacturer of antipersonnel
fragmentation bombs. "Upset" and "shocked" by this information, he determined to
stop Honeywell's munitions production. On July 14, he told his fiscal agent to buy
100 shares of Honeywell. The agent, not knowing that Pillsbury wanted the shares in
his own name, put them in the name of Quad & Co., a family holding company, as
he always did. Upon learning that the 100 shares had not been registered in his
name, Pillsbury bought one share in his own name. Meanwhile, he learned that his
grandmother's trust, of which he was a beneficiary, owned 242 Honeywell shares.
He then made a written demand that Honeywell give him its original shareholder
ledger, its current shareholder ledger, and "all corporate records dealing with weapons and munitions manufacture." Honeywell refused, and Pillsbury filed a petition
for mandamus. He appealed from the trial court's denial of his petition.

ISSUE   Does plaintiff have a right to the corporate records he requested?

DECISION   No. Judgment affirmed.

REASONS   Justice Kelly said that the law of the state of incorporation, Delaware, had to be
applied to this internal dispute. However, he said that this really made no difference
here, since the law of Minnesota (and of most states) agreed with the law of Delaware
on this point. A few states held that a desire to communicate with other shareholders
was per se a proper purpose for inspection of corporate books and records.
    "We believe that a better rule would allow inspection only if the shareholder has
a proper purpose for such communication. . . .
    "The act of inspecting a corporation's shareholder ledger and business records
must be viewed in its proper perspective. In terms of the corporate norm, inspection
is merely the act of the concerned owner checking on what is in part his property. In
the context of the large firm, inspection can be more akin to a weapon in corporate
warfare. The effectiveness of the weapon is considerable. . . .
    "Petitioner's standing as a shareholder is quite tenuous. He owns only one share
in his own name, bought for the purposes of this suit. He had previously ordered his
agent to buy 100 shares, but there is no showing of investment intent. . . . [P]eti-
tioner made no attempt to determine whether Honeywell was a good investment or
whether more profitable shares would have to be sold to finance the Honeywell
purchase. Furthermore, petitioner's agent had the power to sell the Honeywell shares
without his consent. Petitioner also had a contingent beneficial interest in 242

shares. . . . Indicative of petitioner's concern regarding his equitable holdings is the fact that he was unaware of them until he had decided to bring this suit.

"Petitioner had utterly no interest in the affairs of Honeywell before he learned of Honeywell's production of fragmentation bombs. Immediately after obtaining this knowledge, he purchased stock in Honeywell for the sole purpose of asserting ownership privileges in an effort to force Honeywell to cease such production. . . . But for his opposition to Honeywell's policy, petitioner probably would not have bought Honeywell stock, would not be interested in Honeywell's profits, and would not desire to communicate with Honeywell's shareholders. His avowed purpose in buying Honeywell stock was to place himself in a position to try to impress his opinions favoring a reordering of priorities upon Honeywell management and its other shareholders. Such a motivation can hardly be deemed a proper purpose germane to his economic interest as a shareholder. . . .

"His sole motivation was to change Honeywell's course of business because that course was incompatible with his political views. If unsuccessful, petitioner indicated that he would sell the Honeywell stock."

CASES FOR DISCUSSION

WILKES v. SPRINGSIDE NURSING HOME, INC.

353 N.E.2d, 657 (Massachusetts, 1976)

Hennessey, Chief Justice

On August 5, 1971, the plaintiff (Wilkes) filed a bill in equity for declaratory judgment in the Probate Court for Berkshire County, naming as defendants T. Edward Quinn (Quinn), Leon L. Riche (Riche), the First Agricultural National Bank of Berkshire County, and Frank Sutherland MacShane as executors under the will of Lawrence R. Connor (Connor), and the Springside Nursing Home, Inc. (Springside or the corporation). Wilkes alleged that he, Quinn, Riche, and Dr. Hubert A. Pipkin (Pipkin) entered into a partnership agreement in 1951, prior to the incorporation of Springside, which agreement was breached in 1967 when Wilkes's salary was terminated and he was voted out as an officer and director of the corporation. Wilkes sought, among other forms of relief, damages in the amount of

the salary he would have received had he continued as a director and officer of Springside subsequent to March, 1967.

A judge of the Probate Court referred the suit to a master, who, after a lengthy hearing, issued his final report in late 1973. Wilkes's objections to the master's report were overruled after a hearing, and the master's report was confirmed in late 1974. A judgment was entered dismissing Wilkes's action on the merits. We granted direct appellate review. . . . [W]e reverse so much of the judgment as dismisses Wilkes's complaint and order the entry of a judgment substantially granting the relief sought by Wilkes. . . .

Each of the four men invested $1,000 and subscribed to 10 shares of $100 par value stock in Springside. At the time of incorporation it was understood by all of the parties that each would be a director of Springside and each would participate actively in the management and decision making involved in operating the corporation. It was, further, the understanding and intention of all the parties that, corporate resources permitting, each would receive money from the corporation in equal amounts as long as each assumed an active and ongoing responsibility for carrying a portion of the burdens necessary to operate the business.

In *Donahue*, we held that "stockholders in the close corporation owe one another substantially the same fiduciary duty in the operation of the enterprise that partners owe to one another." . . .

In the *Donahue* case we recognized that one peculiar aspect of close corporations was the opportunity afforded to majority stockholders to oppress, disadvantage, or "freeze out" minority stockholders. . . .

"Freeze outs," however, may be accomplished by the use of other devices. One such device which has proved to be particularly effective in accomplishing the purpose of the majority is to deprive minority stockholders of corporate offices and of employment with the corporation. . . . This "freeze-out" technique has been successful because courts fairly consistently have been disinclined to interfere in those facets of internal corporate operations, such as the selection and retention or dismissal of officers, directors, and employees, which essentially involve management decisions subject to the principle of majority control. . . . As one authoritative source has said, "[M]any courts apparently feel that there is a legitimate sphere in which the controlling [directors or] shareholders can act in their own interest even if the minority suffers." . . .

The denial of employment to the minority at the hands of the majority is especially pernicious in some instances. A guaranty of employment with the corporation may have been one of the "basic reasons[s] why a minority owner has invested capital in the firm." . . . The minority stockholder typically depends on his salary as the principal return on his investment, since the "earnings of a close corporation . . . are distributed in major part in salaries, bonuses, and retirement benefits." . . . Other noneconomic interests of the minority stockholder are likewise injuriously affected by barring him from corporate office. . . . Such action severely restricts his participation in the management of the enterprise, and he is relegated to enjoying those benefits incident to this status as a stockholder. . . .

In sum, by terminating a minority stockholder's employment or by severing him from a position as an officer or director, the majority effectively frustrate the minority stockholder's purposes in entering on the corporate venture and also deny him an equal return on his investment.

Therefore, when minority stockholders in a close corporation bring suit against the majority alleging a breach of the strict good faith duty owed to them by the majority, we must carefully analyze the action taken by the controlling stockholders in the individual case. It must be asked whether the controlling group can demonstrate a legitimate business purpose for its action. . . . In asking this question, we acknowledge the fact that the controlling group in a close corporation must have some room to maneuver in establishing the business policy of the corporation. It must have a large measure of discretion, for example, in declaring or withholding dividends, deciding whether to merge or consolidate, establishing the salaries of corporate officers, dismissing directors with or without cause, and hiring and firing corporate employees.

When an asserted business purpose for their action is advanced by the majority, however, we think it is open to minority stockholders to demonstrate that the same legitimate objective could have been achieved through an alternative course of action less harmful to the minority's interest. . . . If called on to settle a dispute, our courts must weigh the legitimate business purpose, if any, against the practicability of a less harmful alternative.

Applying this approach to the instant case, it is apparent that the majority stockholders in Springside have not shown a legitimate business purpose for severing Wilkes from the payroll of the corporation or for refusing to reelect him as a salaried officer and director. . . . There was no showing of misconduct on Wilkes's part as a director, officer, or employee of the corporation which would lead us to approve the majority action as a legitimate response to the disruptive nature of an undesirable individual bent on injuring or destroying the corporation. On the contrary, it appears that Wilkes had always accomplished his assigned share of the duties

875

competently, and that he had never indicated an unwillingness to continue do to so.

It is an inescapable conclusion from all the evidence that the action of the majority stockholders here was a designed "freeze out" for which no legitimate business purpose has been suggested. Furthermore, we may infer that a design to pressure Wilkes into selling his shares to the corporation at a price below their value well may have been at the heart of the majority's plan.

B & H WAREHOUSE, INC. v. ATLAS VAN LINES, INC.

490 F.2d 818 (U.S. Fifth Circuit, 1974).

Lewis R. Morgan, Circuit Judge

This case involves plaintiff-shareholder's claim that the defendant corporation converted plaintiff's shares by restricting plaintiff's right to sell or transfer them. The restriction provides that before alienating the shares, plaintiff must offer them to the corporation at book value, which, plaintiff alleges, is significantly less than the true market value of the shares. Plaintiff seeks damages of $60,000, which is alleged to be the difference between the price which plaintiff could receive in the open market absent the restriction, and the book value of the shares. In the alternative, plaintiff seeks a declaratory judgment that the restriction is invalid as applied to it. At trial, the district court sustained the position of the defendant, holding that an amendment to the corporate charter enacted after plaintiff acquired its shares restricted its right to alienate the stock, and did not constitute a conversion. We reverse.

I

Defendant-appellee Atlas Van Lines, Inc. (Atlas), is a Delaware corporation engaged in the interstate transportation of household goods throughout the continental United States. It was incorporated May 19, 1948. Included in its charter was the following paragraph:

FOURTEENTH. The corporation reserves the right to amend, alter, change or repeal any provision contained in this certificate of incorporation, in the manner now or hereafter prescribed by statute, and all rights conferred upon stockholders herein are granted subject to this restriction.

Plaintiff-appellant B & H Warehouse, Inc. (B & H), a Texas corporation, acquired 30 shares of Class A common stock in Atlas in 1949. At that time, there were no restrictions on the sale of the stock. . . .

In 1966, the Atlas charter was amended to provide that the Class A common stock could not be sold until the shares had first been offered in writing to the corporation at a price equal to the book value of the shares, plus $100.00 per share for good will.

In 1967, the Delaware corporation law was amended by the addition of Section 202(b), which limits the power of corporations to restrict alienability of their stock.

In 1970, Atlas again amended its charter. It now provides that before selling shares of Class A common stock, a shareholder must offer the shares to the corporation for the book value of $333.33 per share. B & H voted against this amendment to the charter. It is conceded that both the 1966 and the 1970 amendments were properly adopted according to the Atlas charter and the existing Delaware law. . . .

We cannot, however, uphold the district court's determination that B & H is bound by the 1966 charter amendment. Although courts in many cases have upheld restrictions similar to the one contained in the 1966 amendment, each of those cases has important distinguishing features.

It should be noted first that the validity of any restriction is to be determined according to the law of the state of incorporation—in this case, Delaware. . . . In spite of both parties' valiant attempts to find a case in point in Delaware law, we are left without any solid precedent for our decision. . . .

After a careful consideration of all of the factors in this area of the law, we conclude that the courts of Delaware would rule that the restriction is invalid. Although the restriction would have been valid had it been in effect when B & H obtained its stock, to add it afterwards contravenes two important policy considerations prevalent in the law of Delaware. The first is the rule that restraints on alienation are disfavored generally. . . . We interpret this rule of law to mean that whenever there is ambiguity or uncertainty, the restraint ought not to be enforced. The second is that restrictions on alienation are to be allowed only so long as they reasonably relate to a valid corporate purpose. There is a valid purpose involved in this case. That is, Atlas is organized as a cooperative association of transport companies, and the restriction was obviously intended to retain control of Atlas among its associated moving companies. Nevertheless, we find that the restraint being challenged is too restrictive to be sustained by reference to this purpose. The interest of Atlas in restricting ownership to associated movers could have been accomplished, at least with respect to those obtaining stock before the amendment took effect, by providing that the corporation would have its right of first refusal based on the market price of the shares. Such a mechanism would have been much more closely related to the valid corporate purpose. But in forcing shareholders to offer their shares to the corporation at book value, Atlas has imposed a restriction significantly broader than necessary to effectuate its purpose. When this occurs, it cannot be said that the general grant of the power to amend contained in the 14th paragraph of the articles of incorporation suffices to validate the amendment. B & H can be held to have assented only to amendments reasonably related to a valid corporate purpose, not to any and all amendments which a majority of shareholders agree upon, regardless of their content. We are unwilling to hold that B & H consented to being bound by the contested restrictions because of the very vague language of the 14th paragraph.

MOLINA v. LARGOSA

465 P.2d 293 (Hawaii, 1970)

Wong, Circuit Judge

Plaintiff bought stock in a newly formed corporation which failed. He sued the promoter of the corporation seeking to recover his investment. The trial held that the promoter of the corporation was not personally liable. We affirm.

On April 15, 1963, plaintiff Henry Molina attended a meeting to discuss the formation of a corporation, Direct Selling Corporation of Hawaii. The corporation was to engage in selling stereo equipment under the trade name Specialties Unlimited. The promoter of the corporation, defendant Rudy Largosa, was already selling stereo equipment under the trade name which he had registered on January 9, 1963.

At the meeting, Molina signed a "subscription form" for the purchase of $2,000 worth of stock (40 shares at $50 per share) in the proposed corporation. The subscription form states, *inter alia*, that "said corporation will engage in the business of wholesale and retail merchandising." The form, however, does not set forth the capital of the proposed corporation or the extent of Molina's proportionate interest therein.

On May 3, 1963, Molina paid Largosa $2,000, which Largosa deposited in a bank account under the name Specialties Unlimited.

On June 25, 1963, the officers of the corporation (including Largosa as president) filed the corporation's Articles of Association, and an affidavit as required by R.L.H. § 172–13 (HRS § 416–15). The affidavit lists Henry Molina as having subscribed 40 shares and paid $2,000, and a total subscription price for all subscribers of $11,750. Thereafter the corporation failed.

Plaintiff contends that because the subscription form did not set out the total capital of the proposed corporation and his proportionate interest in it, there was no valid subscription contract. As a general proposition, in the absence of any statutory requirement (and the Hawaii statute is silent in this respect), no particular form is required if the intent of the parties can be collected from the writing. As one court put it . . . . : "The real question is, Was such paper intended and accepted as a subscription?"

In this case the trial court reached an affirmative answer to that question, which conclusion is supported by the record. Although the subscription form did not state the total capital and Molina's interest, these were ascertainable by merely adding up the investments of all subscribers. This information is also obtainable from the affidavit filed with the corporation's Articles, which listed all subscribers and their respective amounts invested. The interest of any subscriber would then be the amount of his investment divided by the total investment in the corporation.

Upon filing of the said Articles and affidavit, the corporation came into existence. . . . In this jurisdiction, however, the mere fact of incorporation does not amount to an acceptance by the corporation of a subscriber's offer. There must be an expressed or implied acceptance of that offer. . . . After payment of the subscription price by Molina, not only was his name listed as a stockholder in the affidavit filed with the corporation's Articles, but Molina himself on different occasions made inquiries concerning his stock certificate, and from time to time requested Largosa to sell his shares of stock. The acceptance by the corporation of Molina's offer and Molina's acknowledgment of such acceptance are, therefore, clearly supported by the record.

Molina may not now rescind his contract. . . . Molina, who has paid the full amount provided in his stock subscription agreement, has no right to get his money back. . . . It should be noted, in passing, that even if he were entitled to rescission, his action should be against the corporation and not the promoter. . . .

In the case of a subscription contract . . . the objective is a valid incorporation pursuant to the terms of the contract. Once that is accomplished, the contract has been performed. There is no need for a discharge by novation of the promoter from liability as the promoter is liable only if there is failure of such incorporation.

Largosa promised to form a corporation, and he performed this promise. Plaintiff Molina got just what he paid for: stock in a corporation. There was no failure of consideration in the contract; only a failure of a corporation in which Molina had purchased stock. Clearly, if the corporation had succeeded, Molina would have been entitled to his share of the stock appreciation and any dividends declared.

Molina complains that shareholders' meetings were not held, and that his certificate of 40 shares

878

was never delivered. A certificate is not necessary to make him a stockholder. . . . His remedy for this complaint was to compel such meetings and delivery. These are not adequate grounds to support his claim that there was no contract with the corporation.

SPEED ET AL. v. TRANSAMERICA CORP.

99 F. Supp. 808 (Delaware, 1951)

Leahy, Chief Judge

Plaintiffs have sued defendant, Transamerica Corporation, for having purchased from them Class A and Class B stock of the Axton-Fisher Tobacco Company at $40 and $12 per share, respectively, pursuant to a written offer dated November 12, 1942, which Transamerica made to all minority stockholders. The complaint alleges at the time of the sale the true value of the Class A stock was more than $200 per share and such value of the Class B stock was in excess of $100 per share. Plaintiffs allege Transamerica deceived them into selling their shares in the manner hereinafter stated. Plaintiffs seek judgment in an amount equal to the difference between the sales price and the alleged true value. The action purports to be a class action on behalf of all Class A and Class B stockholders who accepted the offer.

The complaint alleges in accepting Transamerica's offer, plaintiffs determined the value of their shares in reliance upon the Axton-Fisher annual report for 1941 and its accompanying letter, which Transamerica had caused to be mailed to the Axton-Fisher stockholders. The 1941 report showed the average cost of Axton-Fisher tobacco inventory to be $7,516,970, and the accompanying letter showed a decline in sales and net income since 1938; whereas, the complaint alleges, at the time when plaintiffs sold their stock the Axton-Fisher tobacco inventory had a real value in excess of $17 million and its earnings were improving.

The complaint further alleges that prior to the time when Transamerica made its offer, it had determined to purchase as many Class A and Class B shares as possible and thereafter to convert its Class A stock into Class B stock, to redeem the remaining Class A stock, and as a final step, to merge or dissolve Axton-Fisher, to the end it might capture for itself the increased but undisclosed value of the Axton-Fisher inventory, all of which Transamerica did. Under these circumstances, the complaint alleges, Transamerica was under a fiduciary duty as a majority stockholder to inform the minority stockholders the real value of the Axton-Fisher inventory was in excess of $17,000,000; that its earnings were improving; and that Transamerica had determined upon a plan which had as its ultimate objective the merger or dissolution of Axton-Fisher; and that if Transamerica had made known these facts to plaintiffs, they would not have sold their stock.

The complaint contains four counts. The first count alleges a common law action of fraud and deceit. The last three counts allege violations of the three sub-paragraphs of Rule X–10B–5 of the Securities and Exchange Commission. . . .

This case turns . . . on the single question as to whether it is a proper inference from all the testimony that Transamerica intended prior to November 12, 1942, to merge, dissolve, or liquidate Axton-Fisher. I now turn to a statement of the facts.

The Facts

Transamerica is a large and powerful investment company which was dominated by the late A. P. Giannini, whose business acumen was said to be legendary. Axton-Fisher was a small tobacco company, the controlling shares of which were purchased by Transamerica for $1 million. . . .

The single inquiry, then, is, did Transamerica plan to capture the Axton-Fisher inventory by merging, dissolving, or liquidating Axton-Fisher at the time it sent its letter of November 12, 1942. There is little direct evidence to support plaintiffs' charge of such plan. The only direct evidence is, indeed, to the contrary, e.g., the testimony of Giannini that there was no such plan contemplated prior to November 12, 1942. Plaintiffs, however, ask me to find Transamerica had such a plan, purely as a matter of inference, and

based primarily on the testimony of Robbins. . . .

From the testimony as a whole, it is palpable so far as decisions were concerned, Transamerica as well as Axton-Fisher were dominated by Giannini. When an important matter arose affecting Axton-Fisher and Transamerica, both Robbins and Cullman did not go to either board of directors but discussed the matter personally and privately with Giannini, *at Giannini's home.* Plaintiffs succeeded in proving . . . that Giannini planned to liquidate Axton-Fisher to capture the inventory profits before November 12, 1942; and this leaves me with the only realistic inference that can be drawn—that Transamerica had a similar intent. . . .

I shall now consider more specifically the letter of November 12, 1942. It will be observed no information relative to the operations of Axton-Fisher was given the minority stockholders. The letter did provide: "Any inquiries regarding the offer may be addressed to us." Concededly, at the time the letter was mailed, the operating position of Axton-Fisher had vastly improved. This fact was well known to the directors of the company and consequently to Transamerica. But, if Transamerica did not at that time intend to liquidate, etc., Axton-Fisher and capture the inventory profit, I think it would specifically have advised the stockholders as fully as possible. It would not have sought to make the stockholders "dig" the information for themselves by making additional inquiries. A radical improvement in the operating position of the company was obviously a matter which every stockholder would be interested in. Transamerica knew this, and consequently the intentional imposition of this burden on the individual stockholder helps to persuade me that Transamerica planned to liquidate, etc., Axton-Fisher at the time it mailed the letter. . . .

Indeed, the price offered was so generous as to indicate there was, in fact, a preexisting intent to liquidate, etc., and that Transamerica wanted to get the stock and rid itself of other stockholders at a price which would be a bargain, when Transamerica decided the time was ripe to capture the inventory appreciation. I think this circumstance is of paramount importance because it is an indication that in this respect, at least, Transamerica overplayed its hand. . . .

Since I find the existence of such a plan to be a fact, it follows defendant must respond in damages.

PROBLEMS FOR DISCUSSION

1. Danny Donaho owned 25 percent of the stock in Loyalty Electric Corporation and was its vice president, but he was not on the board of directors. The other 75 percent of the stock was owned by Larry Hoddy, who was president and chairman of the board. In 1974 Larry put his sons, Kenny and Lennie, who worked for Loyalty, on the board and gave them each 25 shares. The board then voted to buy Larry's remaining 25 shares for $1,000 a share. At a special stockholders' meeting, Danny learned of the repurchase for the first time and voted against a resolution approving it. Danny then offered his 25 shares to Loyalty for $1,000 a share. Loyalty refused to buy Danny's shares. Danny died, and his widow, Ufemia, brings a lawsuit challenging the validity of this repurchase of Larry's shares. What result, and why?

2. Morning Riser, Inc., delivered milk and other dairy and food products to customers' homes. Its founder and president, Eddie Ezee, decided to sell out and retire. Freda Falange, who had been the general manager, contracted to buy the assets and the customer lists. Freda and three of Morning Riser's former truck drivers then formed Milky Way, Inc., with each contributing $2,500 for 25 shares of stock. All four were directors. At a directors' meeting, Freda proposed to sell Milky Way the assets which she had bought from Morning Riser. Her offer was accepted, and she was given another 125 shares in return for these assets. Freda then gave 25 of her shares to her daughter, Fostoria. Wimpy, one of the former truck drivers and now a director/shareholder, says that he was not aware that Milky Way's purchase of assets in return for 125 shares would dilute his ownership interest and that Freda misled him into thinking he would still be a one-fourth owner of the business. Wimpy also challenges Freda's transfer of stock to Fostoria, since the corporation received no consideration for this transfer. Are these claims valid? Discuss.

3. Uriah Grant sues the Peppy Pickle Company, challenging the validity of an amendment to Peppy's articles of incorporation. Grant owned 3,000 shares of $1 par preferred 8 percent cumulative stock in Peppy. Dividends had not been declared (or paid) on Peppy's preferred stock for 10 years. Peppy's articles had expressly reserved the power to amend. Pursuant to the amendment procedure, a majority of Peppy's stockholders voted to cancel the old preferred shares and to issue one new preferred share of 10 percent cumulative preferred for each two old shares. The amendment also canceled the accumulated but undeclared dividends for the 10 years. Grant says that it would be unconstitutional to interpret this amendment so as to deprive him of accrued property rights. What result, and why?

4. Norbert Nostrum, owner of 48 percent of the shares of Snazzy Stores, Inc., sues Kelly Kampin and Lucy Loosely, who each own 26 percent of Snazzy's shares. Kelly is Snazzy's president, and Norbert says that she received "grossly excessive salary and bonuses for 1980." Norbert also challenges payments made to Lucy for "unspecified consulting services and miscellaneous jobs." Norbert's complaint also includes an allegation that Snazzy, a subchapter S corporation, retained earnings far in excess of its reasonable capital needs and arbitrarily refused to declare and pay dividends, even though the individual stockholders were paying taxes on the earnings due to the subchapter S status. Kelly and Lucy move to dismiss the complaint, saying that these separate claims can't be joined together since they allege wrongs to different persons. How should the court rule? Explain.

5. Leo Mello developed an improved lawn mower and received a patent for it. He then organized Mello Mowers, Inc. Leo and his wife, Leona, owned 53 percent of the company's stock; Jock Stanley owned 47 percent. Leo, Leona, and Jock decided to sell the company, and Leo began negotiations with Massive, Inc. Massive agreed to buy all the shares of Mello. Leo and Leona received $20,000 cash and 200 shares of Massive for their shares of Mello. Massive agreed to pay $30,000 cash for Jock's shares. However, Massive discovered that Mello owed a supplier over $10,000, and it claimed that Leo had told it that Mello's total debts were "less than $1,000." Massive also learned that the mower patent was in Leo's name, not that of Mello Mowers. When Massive refused to take and pay for his shares, Jock sued for specific performance. How should the court sort out this mess? Explain.

6. Byron Deznez and his brother Aaron owned all the stock in Deznez Drugs, Inc. Wiley Wonker had worked for them for many years, finally becoming the manager of the retail drugstore the company operated. Wiley got a very good offer from a competitor. He told Byron that he'd probably have to quit Deznez and accept the offer. Byron then promised to increase his salary, provide a bonus plan, and make him the owner of 10 percent of the company's stock if only he'd stay on as manager. Wiley stayed; he received the salary and bonus but not the 10 percent of Deznez' stock. Wiley sues Byron for the stock. Byron says that Wiley's contract is with the company, not with him personally, and so the suit should be dismissed. What result, and why?

7. Nick Nack owned and operated Mr. Nick's Parlor, Inc., a barbershop and beauty shop. Laraine Lerg was one of his most successful hair stylists; many customers asked for Laraine specifically. Laraine had been thinking about opening her own shop for some time, when a real estate broker, Ronald Devine, told her that he had a beauty shop for sale in a good location. Laraine consulted Nick, who said he had previously considered buying that particular shop. Together they retained an attorney, Melba Muffin, to prepare a purchase agreement for the shop. Laraine, Nick, and Melba met with the sellers and their attorney; there was a discussion, but no written agreement was signed. The sellers said they would have to know by the 10th of the month, since they had received another purchase offer for the shop. On the 10th, Nick and Laraine met in Ronald's office to discuss the deal. Laraine and Ronald say that Nick told them he was "too old to start over again" and that he didn't want to buy the new shop. Ronald told Melba, who told the seller's attorney, that "the deal is off." Negotiations with the second buyer fell through, and the seller's attorney called back to see whether Nick and Laraine would reconsider. At this point, Laraine made her own individual offer for the shop and it was accepted. When Nick was told what had happened, he sued Laraine, Melba, and Ronald for breach of fiduciary duties. Does he have a case? Explain.

8. Hiller and Zorpe, together, owned 35 percent of the stock in Ragtime, Inc., and had been two of its seven directors. Since 1960, when it was organized, Ragtime had paid its officers and managers small regular salaries but had had a generous bonus arrangement based on net earnings. Both Hiller and Zorpe were originally officers, but they resigned in 1965 for personal and health reasons. During the Vietnam War, Ragtime's earnings skyrocketed since it supplied metal products to the military. In 1967 the remaining directors adopted a resolution giving the officers indefinite terms of employment and similarly extending the bonus plan. Hiller and Zorpe now bring an action demanding access to the corporate books and records (which had been denied by Ragtime) in order to determine whether improper payments were made. Ragtime says that since these two are no longer officers and directors, they should be satisfied with the company's annual reports. Who is right, and why?

44 | Corporations— Management Duties

DIRECTORS

Authority and Qualifications. The directors are given management control of the normal business operations of the corporation. They are more than just agents for the shareholders, since a large part of their authority and duties flows from the state's corporation statute. Shareholders may try to influence or replace the directors, but shareholders as such have no right to participate in corporate management. So long as the directors are acting in good faith and within the statute, articles, and bylaws, they have exclusive control of the corporation's ordinary business decisions.

Older statutes required three or more directors. Recognizing the reality of the "one-person" corporation, modern corporation codes require only one director. Some states still require directors to be shareholders and/or residents of the state of incorporation. Again, the modern tendency, as seen in Section 35 of the Model Act, is to require neither unless the articles or bylaws of the particular corporation so specify. In other words, let each corporation decide for itself what qualifications its directors must have.

Selection and Removal. As noted in the last chapter, selection of the board of directors is the shareholders' most important management function. While some states require cumulative voting, most statutes permit it but do not require it. Most states also permit corporations to provide for staggered terms for directors, similar to those of U.S. senators. Electing only part of the board each year provides continuity of management and also prevents an outside group from taking over the board all at once, in one election.

The rule in most states is that directors may be removed by the shareholders at any time, with or without cause. Directors, in other words, serve at the pleasure of the shareholders. In this sense, they are like agents. In a few states, such as New York, directors can be removed only if good cause is shown. In any corporation where cumulative voting is in force, a director could not be removed unless he or she failed to get enough votes to win a seat under the cumulative voting system.

Nearly all statutes provide for the replacement of directors by the remaining board members, where vacancies occur, at least until the next shareholders' meeting at which directors are elected. These procedural steps must be followed exactly.

Grossman v. *Liberty Leasing Co., Inc.*
295 A.2d 749 (Delaware, 1972)

FACTS   Liberty was a Delaware corporation, although its main operations were in Chicago. The plaintiffs and their families owned about 20 percent of Liberty's stock. Grossman was its president and treasurer; Gross was its executive vice president and secretary. They were directors, along with Sachnoff and Myers. Liberty's bylaws called for five directors and permitted the directors to amend the bylaws and fill vacancies on the board. The four were unable to agree on a candidate for the single vacancy, but they agreed to amend the bylaws to increase the number of directors to seven and to elect Malkin, Haas, and Roland to fill the three vacancies. The next day Grossman and Gross said that they wanted to rescind the board actions, but Sachnoff (an attorney) told them that this could not be done. At a later board meeting, Grossman and Gross were dismissed as officers and Malkin, Roland, and Haas were elected to the main offices. Grossman and Gross brought suit to declare that both the election of the three new directors and all subsequent board actions were invalid. The new directors moved to dismiss since they had not been personally served in Delaware.

ISSUES   Can the Delaware court determine the validity of directors' elections? Were the three new directors validly elected?

DECISION   Yes. Yes. Defendants' motion to dismiss denied; plaintiffs' motion for injunction denied.

REASONS   Chancellor Duffy first decided that he did have jurisdiction over the defendants since Delaware law governed the validity of directors' elections in Delaware corporations. Personal service of process in Delaware was not required.

    "We are here concerned not with a personal judgment against the individual defendants but only with their respective rights to hold office in a Delaware corporation over which this Court clearly has jurisdiction. That is the contest. In short, defendants' positions, not their pocketbooks, are in jeopardy in this suit."

    Chancellor Duffy then proceeded to the merits of the plaintiffs' claim for injunctive relief.

    "[P]laintiffs argue, a 'vacancy' within the contemplation of S.223 requires a previous incumbency. . . .

    "Plaintiffs say that there was not [a vacancy] because the stockholders had deliberately left the position unfilled at two successive annual meetings called to elect directors. . . .

    "It seems to me that under the circumstances of this case there was indeed a prior incumbency within the requirements of *Johnston*. Nothing in that case requires an 'incumbency' since the last annual meeting of stockholders. . . . The key requirement is not when the office was last filled, but how it was created in the first place. . . .

    "But to discuss the current question in terms of *Johnston* is to apply a test no longer valid. . . . [I]t is quite apparent that there have been significant changes in both S.223 and the purpose it serves. . . .

"[W]hat was once regarded as the prerogative solely of stockholders is now permissible action under S.223. . . . [T]he significant amendment was made in 1949, some three months after *Johnston,* when directors in office were authorized to fill 'newly created directorships resulting from any increase in the authorized number of directors.'" . . .

"Under S.223 directors in office now may fill vacancies in their membership if stockholders do not do so and if other requirements of the statute are met."

Meetings of the Board. The general rule is that the directors must meet as a board in order to take official action for the corporation. Proxy voting is not permitted. Most states today permit the directors to meet outside the state of incorporation; this allows the board to select the most convenient location. Some modern statutes are even more flexible; they permit the directors to have a "meeting" by means of a conference telephone call. Some statutes also permit the directors to take official action by means of a signed document: if they all read and sign the same document, why require them to waste transportation facilities to come together in a meeting room?

Section 42 of the Model Act and the laws in some states permit the directors to designate some board members as an executive committee and to delegate some decision-making authority to the smaller committee. Other similar committees may also be created. The modern tendency is toward flexible management.

If a director wishes to dissent from a decision of the board, the normal rule is that the dissent must be officially entered in the minutes of the board. Otherwise, concurrence with the majority decision is presumed. This rule is significant where a later lawsuit challenges board actions.

Powers and Duties. As noted previously, some extraordinary business decisions are left to the shareholders, but the directors have exclusive control of the ordinary business of the firm. In making these ordinary business decisions, the directors are given the widest possible discretion as long as they are acting in good faith. The individual directors are selected for their business skill and judgment, and courts do not feel that they should second-guess the directors when the directors exercise that judgment. There is, therefore, a very strong presumption in favor of the directors' decisions unless some abuse is shown.

The directors are fiduciaries, and as such, they owe their corporation and its stockholders responsibility and loyalty. Responsibility means that the directors must be more than just personally honest; they must "direct." They must be diligent and careful in managing the firm's business. They are responsible for knowing what's going on, and they may be held personally liable if they don't know but should.

Graham v. Allis-Chalmers Manufacturing Co.
188 A.2d 125 (Delaware, 1963)

FACTS
Graham filed a stockholders' derivative suit against ACM's 14 directors and 4 of its employees. The suit alleged that ACM had sustained damages as a result of antitrust law violations by the four employees, to which criminal charges they and the corporation had pleaded guilty. Three of the four were still ACM employees; the fourth was under contract to it as a consultant. Graham's case against the directors was based on their knowledge, or reason to know, of these illegal activities, or at least on their failure to take proper steps to learn of and prevent such illegal conduct. ACM had over 31,000 employees, in 24 plants and 145 sales offices, and 5,000 dealers. Its operations were divided into two groups; the Industries Group was in turn divided into five divisions. One of these, the Power Equipment Division, was the source of the antitrust violations. The Power Equipment Division had 10 departments, each controlled by a manager. The board had delegated authority to the lowest management level capable of fulfilling given responsibility. The board met once each month to review the general business policy of the company. The antitrust violations commenced in 1956, but the board's first actual notice was a news story in 1959 of a pending investigation of bids by the TVA. In 1937 ACM had entered into two FTC consent decrees relating to earlier price-fixing. The plaintiff appealed from the vice chancellor's ruling for the defendants.

ISSUE
Were the directors guilty of a failure to adequately supervise?

DECISION
No. Judgment affirmed.

REASONS
Justice Wolcott said that only three of the directors knew anything about the 1937 FTC consent decrees and that they had satisfied themselves with an investigation that ACM had done nothing wrong then but had consented so as to avoid extended litigation. "Under the circumstances," he said, "they were notice of nothing."

"The duties of the Allis-Chalmers Directors were fixed by the nature of the enterprise, which employed in excess of 30,000 persons and extended over a large geographical area. By force of necessity, the company's Directors could not know personally all of the company's employees. The very magnitude of the enterprise required them to confine their control to the broad policy decisions. That they did this is clear from the record. At the meetings of the Board in which all Directors participated, these questions were considered and decided on the basis of summaries, reports, and corporate records. These they were entitled to rely on, not only, we think, under general principles of the common law, but by reason of 8 Del. D. S.141(f) as well, which in terms fully protects a director who relies on such in the performance of his duties.

"In the last analysis, the question of whether a corporate director has become liable for losses to the corporation through neglect of duty is determined by the circumstances. If he has recklessly reposed confidence in an obviously untrustworthy employee, has refused or neglected cavalierly to perform his duty as a director, or has ignored either willfully or thorugh inattention obvious danger signs of employee wrongdoing, the law will cast the burden of liability upon him. This is not the case at bar, however, for as soon as it became evident that there were grounds for suspicion, the Board acted promptly to end it and prevent its recurrence. . . .

"[W]e know of no rule of law which requires a corporate director to assume, with no justification whatsoever, that all corporate employees are incipient law violators who, but for a tight checkrein, will give free vent to their unlawful propensities."

A fiduciary must also be loyal. This means at least that the director cannot use his or her position for personal gain at the expense of the corporation. Most states today permit the directors to set their own compensation, but courts would be willing to review such arrangements to make sure there was no abuse of discretion. In any case where the director is dealing with the corporation and receiving a personal benefit, the transaction would be subject to very close judicial review.

OFFICERS

Authority. To a more limited extent, the firm's officers may also get some of their authority from the state's corporation statute. For the most part, the officers derive their authority from the corporation's articles and bylaws and from specific board resolutions. The states do not agree on the amount of power which is given to the corporation's president merely by his or her appointment as such. In some states, the president is presumed to be a kind of "general manager," with automatic authority to make all contracts which are within the scope of the firm's normal business. In other states, the corporation president is only a "figurehead," unless specific powers have been given to the officeholder by articles, bylaws, or resolution. Third parties need to check carefully on whether the individual with whom they are negotiating has authority to bind the corporation. In no state would the president have the authority to execute unusual or extraordinary contracts without specific resolutions.

Goldenberg v. *Bartell Broadcasting Corporation*
262 N.Y.S.2d 274 (New York, 1965)

FACTS   In March 1961 Bernard Goldenberg was hired as assistant to the president of Bartell Broadcasting, Gerald A. Bartell. He was given a three-year contract at a salary of $1,933 per month plus expenses, a private office, and a promise of 12,000 shares of stock to be delivered in three installments in January 1962, 1963, and 1964. In May 1961 his salary was increased to $2,400 per month. He received no salary after November 1961, and no stock at all was delivered. Bartell Broadcasting was merged into McFadden-Bartel Corporation in May 1962. The defendants repudiated Goldenberg's employment contract in July 1962. He sued, and the defendants (BBC and MBC) moved to dismiss the complaint.

ISSUE   Does the complaint state a cause of action? (Did president Bartell have authority to execute this contract for the corporation?)

DECISION   No. (No.) Motion to dismiss the complaint granted.

REASONS   Justice Waltemade first disposed of the plaintiff's claim against the successor corporation, McFadden-Bartell. He said there was no evidence that MBC had ever assumed the obligation of this employment contract, which had been in dispute since the November prior to the merger. The provision in the contract which said it would bind successors of BBC was ineffective.

"Parties to a contract, by the terms of their own agreement, cannot validly cast the obligation of the terms of such contract upon a third party who is not a signatory to the contract. This elementary proposition of law requires no citation of authorities."

He then turned to the question of whether the contract was even valid as against Bartell Broadcasting.

"A corporation can only act through its directors, officers, and employees. They are the conduit by and through which the corporation is given being and from which its power to act and reason springs. Therefore in every action in which a person sues a corporation on a contract executed on behalf of the corporation by one of its officers, one of the issues to be determined is whether the officer had the express, implied, or apparent authority to execute the contract in question. . . .

"There has been no proof offered in this case indicating that Gerald A. Bartell, as president of Bartell Broadcasting Corporation, had express authority to enter into the agreement, dated March 16, 1961. . . .

"*Implied authority* is a species of actual authority, which gives an officer the power to do the necessary acts within the scope of his usual duties. Generally, the president of a corporation has the implied authority to hire and fire corporate employees and to fix their compensation. However, the president of a corporation does *not* have the implied power to execute 'unusual or extraordinary' contracts of employment. . . .

"While the payment of the monthly compensation would not make the contract . . . 'unusual or extraordinary,' the Court is of the opinion that the inclusion in the contract of the provision requiring the delivery to plaintiff of 12,000 shares of 'free registered stock,' does bring the agreement within the category of being an '*unusual and extraordinary*' contract. . . .

"With the varied and broad business experience acquired by the plaintiff in his wide business associations as evidenced by his career résumé furnished to the defendants, . . . it can be truly said that he not only was presumed to have knowledge of the statutory provisions of the law pertaining to corporations, but that he apparently also had actual knowledge of such laws."

Selection, Compensation, and Removal. Corporate officers are selected by the board of directors unless the articles provide otherwise. Officers are usually appointed for one-year, renewable terms, but they continue to serve at the will of the board. In other words, the general rule is that the board can remove an officer at any time, with or without cause. If an officer is removed without good cause, his or her employment contract with the firm would probably require compensation for the remainder of the appointment period, but he or she would no longer be permitted to function as a corporate officer. Most modern corporation statutes do not require more than one officer, though there may be requirements that more than one person sign certain documents for the corporation (deeds to land, for example).

Stott v. *Stott Realty Co.*
224 N.W. 623 (Michigan, 1929)

FACTS   Arthur Stott first brought a lawsuit challenging the power of Stott Realty to mortgage certain of its properties. After a decision in that case in favor of the company, its board of directors passed a resolution ordering its president and secretary to execute the mortgage and the accompanying papers. The president did so, but the secretary, Julia Stott Orloff, refused to sign. At a subsequent board meeting attended by all the directors, including Orloff, the directors voted to remove her as corporate secretary. She thereupon left the meeting. Another member of the board, Thomas Danahey, was then elected secretary. Arthur Stott then commenced this lawsuit, which challenged the validity of Orloff's removal and Danahey's election. Stott appealed from a decision for the company.

ISSUE   Could the board lawfully remove and replace the corporate secretary?

DECISION   Yes. Judgment affirmed.

REASONS   Justice Fellows reviewed the facts and then disposed of the case in a brief statement of the applicable rules.

"Cases will be found holding that the board of directors may remove fellow directors, but the weight of authority is against the proposition. Mrs. Orloff was continued as director. The office of secretary is a ministerial office, may be filled by one not a director, and its occupant, unless a director, has nothing to say about the management of the company. The selection is made by the board of directors. . . . This distinction between a director and a secretary should be kept in mind. The director, being selected by the stockholders, may only be removed by them, while the secretary, being selected by the directors, may be removed by them. . . . 'Below the grade of director and such other officers as are elected by the corporation at large, the general rule is that the officers of private corporations hold their offices during the will of the directors, and are hence removable by the directors without assigning any cause for the removal, except so far as their power may be restrained by contract with the particular officer, just as any other employer may discharge his employee. Speaking generally, it may be said that the power to appoint carries with it the power to remove.' . . .

"The board had power, under the bylaws of the company, to fill vacancies. Mr. Danahey was a member of the board of directors. We need not consider whether he could validly vote for himself, as there was a quorum present without him, and a majority of that quorum voted for his election. With his vote he received a majority of the full board; without it he received the vote of a majority of the quorum which was present after Mrs. Orloff had left the meeting. The rule is recognized by this court and elsewhere that a quorum may act, and a majority vote of such quorum binds the corporation."

Officers' compensation is determined by the board of directors, and their decision will generally not be second-guessed by a court. A director who is also an officer should not be present when the directors set the salary for his or her office. As with any other decision where the board's business judgment is involved, there are limits to the discretion that is given to the board with regard to officers' compensation.

Smith v. *Dunlap*

111 So.2d 1 (Alabama, 1959)

FACTS   Harry Smith, a minority stockholder in Alabama Dry Docks and Shipbuilding Company, Inc., brought a stockholder's derivative suit to recover for the corporation allegedly excessive salaries and bonuses paid to four of its director-officers. Smith tried to get the other directors and stockholders to take action on this matter, but they refused to do so. He then brought this derivative suit on behalf of the corporation. He appealed from the trial court's dismissal of the suit on demurrer.

ISSUE   Did the complaint state a valid cause of action against the directors and officers?

DECISION   Yes. Judgment reversed and case remanded for trial on the merits.

REASONS   Justice Simpson was very clear that allegedly excessive officers' compensation could be challenged in a stockholder's derivative suit.

"[W]here the amount of a bonus payment to officers of a corporation has no reasonable relation to the value of service for which it is given, it is in reality a gift and the majority stockholders have no power to give away corporate property against the protest of a minority stockholder.

"A long line of Alabama cases recognizes the general rule that where officers of a corporation appropriate assets of the corporation to their own use, equity will intervene on behalf of a minority stockholder who is unable to obtain relief within the corporation. . . .

"The question of whether the compensation is so excessive that it bears no reasonable relation to the value of services rendered is a question of fact to be resolved on final hearing. . . . 'To come within the rule of reason the compensation must be in proportion to the executive's ability, services and time devoted to the company, difficulties involved, responsibilities assumed, success achieved, amounts under jurisdiction, corporate earnings, profits and prosperity, increase in volume or quality of business or both, and all other relevant facts and circumstances; nor should it be unfair to stockholders in unduly diminishing dividends properly payable. . . .

"The amount of compensation to be paid to an officer of a corporation is, in the first instance, within the business discretion of the corporation's board of directors, and with this discretion the courts are loath to interfere; generally the decision of the directors as to the amount of such compensation is final; where it appears, however, that the directors have not acted in good faith or that the compensation fixed by them is so excessive that it bears no reasonable relation to the services for which it is given, courts of equity have the power to inquire whether and to what extent payment to the officers constitutes misuse and waste of corporate assets; . . . but courts are reluctant and will proceed with great caution in exercising the power to 'prune' the payments since it is not intended that a court should be called upon to make a yearly audit and adjust salaries; nor is such an inquiry merely to substitute the court's discretion for the discretion of the directors if that has been honestly and fairly exercised."

Liabilities of Directors and Officers. Most of the specific sources of directors' and officers' liability have already been discussed, in this and previous chapters. Directors are liable for the issuance of watered stock and for the declaration of illegal dividends. They may be held liable for refusing a stockholder's justified demand for corporate information or for breaching their fiduciary duty by self-dealing or by stealing a corporate opportunity. Directors and officers may also incur liability under state regulatory statutes for failure to file required reports and income statements. Under the national securities laws (see Chapter 47), such corporate insiders as directors and officers may be held liable for making personal profits at the expense of the corporation or its shareholders. And directors and officers may be held liable to their firm and its shareholders for failing to take reasonable care in the operation of its business.

In recent years, directors and officers have also been subjected to an increasing criminal liability exposure. Criminal prosecutions against the directors and officers responsible for antitrust and other regulatory violations have been becoming more common, as have prison terms for persons convicted of willful violations. (See the *Park* case in Chapter 3.)

Foreign Corrupt Practices Act.   After SEC investigations disclosed that over 300 U.S. firms had made various kinds of payments and gifts to foreign officials to get contracts or favorable regulations, Congress passed the FCPA in 1977. The FCPA amends the 1934 Securities Exchange Act in three main areas: a U.S. firm, whether or not subject to the 1934 Act's registration and disclosure requirements, is prohibited from bribing foreign officials to misuse their official position to benefit the firm; a firm subject to the 1934 Act must maintain books and records which, in reasonable detail, accurately and fairly reflect the firm's transactions, and must also maintain a system of internal accounting controls which reasonably ensures that transactions are properly executed and recorded and that corporate assets are protected; new criminal penalties of up to $1 million for the firm and of up to $10,000 and five years' imprisonment for the individuals involved may be imposed for willful violations. This is a very important new area of potential liability for both corporate and noncorporate managers, but its exact dimensions will not be known until there have been more court interpretations of the FCPA.

CASES FOR DISCUSSION

RARE EARTH, INC. v. HOORELBEKE

401 F. Supp. 26 (New York, 1975)

Cannella, District Judge

Rare Earth, Inc., is not, as one might surmise, an organization dedicated to environmental activism or the preservation of our natural resources. Rather, it is the corporate entity formed by a group of rock and roll musicians who publicly perform as "Rare Earth." From this group "comes the dissonant chord" of an intracorporate battle for control resulting from a schism among the band members in July, 1974.

Predicating jurisdiction on the Lanham Act, the two resultant corporate factions ask the Court to decide which individuals may continue to publicly perform as "Rare Earth." For the reasons expressed in this opinion, we conclude that shareholders Bridges and Guzman possess a controlling interest in Rare Earth, Inc. However, because of the failure of these persons to conform to the dictates of Michigan law, we find that the plaintiff, Rare Earth, Inc., may not obtain the affirmative relief sought in this proceeding. Accordingly, both the complaint and the counterclaims-third-party complaint will be dismissed. . . .

"Rare Earth" is a rock and roll performing group which has recorded several record albums and which enjoys national prominence in rock music circles. The group was organized in the late 1960s and originally consisted of five performers. A sixth member, Edward Guzman, later joined the band.

As the Rare Earth group gained national exposure and the revenues it derived from concerts and recordings increased, the "Rare Earth" name became a valuable asset. As a result, counsel, Henry Baskin, suggested that a corporation be formed. In July 1970 the plaintiff, Rare Earth, Inc., was incorporated under Michigan law. Fifty thousand shares of capital stock were authorized in the articles of incorporation, and 1,200 shares were subscribed to by the band members. As to 1,000 of these shares, it is conceded that the five original band members each received 200 shares. As to the remaining 200 shares, the parties vigorously dispute whether Edward Guzman ever became their lawful owner.

As time passed, three of the original members departed from the Rare Earth group and three new performers were engaged to replace them. It is not disputed that two of the departing members severed all ties with the group and transferred their stock back to the corporation. However, the litigants disagree dramatically concerning the present status in the corporation of the third, Kenneth Folcik.

In a nutshell, both factions concede that Bridges and Hoorelbeke each owns 200 shares of Rare Earth, Inc. In dispute between them is whether Guzman and Folcik are presently shareholders. The Bridges-Guzman faction asserts that Guzman owns 200 shares of Rare Earth, Inc., and that Folcik does not; thus they claim control of 400 to 600 outstanding shares of the corporation. Hoorelbeke, on the other hand, claims that Folcik remains a shareholder and that he, Hoorelbeke, is the voting trustee for the Folcik shares. This claim, when coupled with Hoorelbeke's assertion that Guzman is not a stockholder, allegedly placed working corporate control in his grasp. We discuss the merits of the two contested positions infra (Point IV), and note for present purposes only that each challenged claim of stock ownership turns upon a construction of Michigan law (either the Michigan Business Corporation Act or Article 8 of the Michigan Uniform Commercial Code).

The plaintiff's complaint must be dismissed, albeit without prejudice. . . . [T]he defendants assert that "Neither a majority of the directors nor of the shareholders of Rare Earth, Inc., voting as a duly constituted meeting, authorized counsel to be retained or to initiate suit." . . . Although not for the precise reasons advanced, we find this position well founded in law and fact. . . .

Prior to the dissension which emerged in July 1974 between the members of the Rare Earth group, it is undisputed that Peter Hoorelbeke served as a director and president, as well as a 200 share owner of Rare Earth, Inc. However, in mid-July the Bridges faction became aware (through the musical "grapevine") of Hoorelbeke's purported resignation as a band member and as an officer and director of the corporation. . . .

There is no evidence at bar of a written resignation transmitted by Hoorelbeke to the corporation and thus, as of the July 12th meeting, he remained a director, officer, and shareholder of Rare Earth, Inc. This being so, the failure to notify Hoorelbeke of the meeting and his absence therefrom renders all actions taken by those present invalid and without effect.

With regard to directors' meetings, Michigan law requires that a "special meeting shall be held upon notice as prescribed in the bylaws" (Mich. Comp. Laws Ann. § 450.1521[2] and that a "director is entitled to a notice which will give him ample time to attend the meeting." . . . The statutory requirement that the meeting be convened "upon notice" clearly was not met in the present case, as Hoorelbeke received no notice whatsoever. Thus, it is a settled matter of Michigan law that "where a written notice of the meeting of the board of directors is not given although required by either a statute or the corporate bylaws, any action taken by the meeting at which all the directors are not present is void." . . . The import of the foregoing discussion is plain: the failure to notify Director Hoorelbeke of the July 12th meeting and his absence therefrom renders all actions taken thereat invalid, including such action as was required to commence this suit either directly or through the appointment of Bridges as President. . . .

If the July 12th meeting is deemed a shareholders' meeting, the actions taken thereat similarly must fail for noncompliance with the notice requirements contained in Mich. Comp. Laws Ann. § 450.1404(1) or with the consent provisions contained in § 450.1407. . . .

The improper commencement of the main action on behalf of Rare Earth, Inc., and its dismissal by this Court does not conclude the matter. . . . Although the counterclaim is properly perceived as one which is compulsory under Fed.R.Civ.P. 13(a), it is nonetheless properly before the Court at this time because it is predicated upon federal jurisdiction independent of the complaint. . . .

We find that the receipt of Folcik's certificate by Baskin and, later, by Rosefielde (a corporate functionary who knew not Folcik) satisifed that aspect of delivery specified by § 440.8313(1)(a) and constitutes an acquisition of actual possession of the stock by an appropriate person on behalf of Rare Earth, Inc. The simultaneous issuance of a $5,000 corporate check to Folcik as (at least) partial payment for the stock, the notation which appears in the corporate check book that such check was "for closing" as well as the failure of the corporation to subsequently list Folcik as a shareholder on Rare Earth, Inc., tax returns both individually and collectively evidence that the corporation considered itself to be in receipt of the shares and the owner thereof. . . .

Two separate events in the corporate life of Rare Earth, Inc., cause us to conclude that Guzman has fully paid for his shares and is, therefore, a stockholder. The $5,000 check which Guzman tendered to the Corporation in April 1971 is well perceived as full payment of that portion of his indebtedness to Rare Earth, Inc., which arose on incorporation: $200 for his stock and $4,800 as a loan; as contrasted with his antecedent obligation to the Rare Earth group. . . . If, however, it is assumed arguendo that the April 1971 check served as payment for his earlier obligation, then the subsequent events of September 1971 (the corporation's payment of $7,530 to Bridges,

Hoorelbeke, and Persh) served to discharge the remainder of Guzman's indebtedness to the corporation, including that which was attributable to the subscription contract. . . .

This being so, we conclude that of the 600 shares of Rare Earth, Inc., stock which are presently outstanding, the Bridges-Guzman faction controls 400 shares and represents a two-thirds majority of all shareholders. Thus, it is possessed of working corporate control, which, if necessity, permits it to determine who may use the "Rare Earth" name and mark in connection with musical performances, recordings, and the like. . . .

In the year which has elapsed since the ill-conceived directors' meeting of Rare Earth, Inc., at Los Angeles, the young musicians who once formed "Rare Earth" have expanded substantial time, effort, and funds toward the resolution of the controversy which exists between them. Now, we are at the end of the road, at least insofar as the present litigation is concerned. This is not to suggest that we are entirely convinced that this opinion will stand to quell the raging battle. . . .

The present, somewhat discursive endeavor is well concluded with the following words of the modern poet and popular singer Bob Dylan:

. . . goodbye's too good a word, gal
So I'll just say a fare thee well
I ain't sayin' you treated me unkind
You could have done better but I don't mind
You just kinda wasted my precious time
But don't think twice, it's all right.

SHLENSKY v. WRIGLEY

237 N.E.2d 776 (Illinois, 1968)

Sullivan, Justice

Plaintiff is a minority stockholder of defendant corporation, Chicago National League Ball Club (Inc.), a Delaware corporation with its principal place of business in Chicago, Illinois. Defendant corporation owns and operates the major league professional baseball team known as the Chicago Cubs. The corporation also engages in the operation of Wrigley Field, the Cubs' home park, the concessionaire sales during Cubs' home games, television and radio broadcasts of Cubs' home games, the leasing of the field for football games and other events and receives its share, as visiting team, of admission moneys from games played in other National League stadia. The individual defendants are directors of the Cubs and have served for varying periods of years. Defendant Philip K. Wrigley is also president of the corporation and owner of approximately 80 percent of the stock therein.

Plaintiff alleges that since night baseball was first played in 1935 19 of the 20 major league teams have scheduled night games. In 1966, out of a total of 1,620 games in the major leagues, 932 were played at night. Plaintiff alleges that every member of the major leagues, other than the Cubs, scheduled substantially all of its home games in 1966 at night, exclusive of opening days, Saturdays, Sundays, holidays, and days prohibited by league rules. Allegedly this has been done for the specific purpose of maximizing attendance and thereby maximizing revenue and income.

The Cubs, in the years 1961–65, sustained operating losses from its direct baseball operations. Plaintiff attributes those losses to inadequate attendance at Cubs' home games. He concludes that if the directors continue to refuse to install lights at Wrigley Field and schedule night baseball games, the Cubs will continue to sustain comparable losses and its financial condition will continue to deteriorate. . . .

Plaintiff further alleges that defendant Wrigley has refused to install lights, not because of interest in the welfare of the corporation but because of his personal opinions "that baseball is a 'day-time sport' and that the installation of lights and night baseball games will have a deteriorating effect upon the surrounding neighborhood." . . .

The question on appeal is whether plaintiff's amended complaint states a cause of action. It is plaintiff's position that fraud, illegality, and conflict of interest are not the only bases for a stockholder's derivative action against the directors. Contrariwise, defendants argue that the courts will not step in and interfere with honest business judgment of the directors unless there is a showing of fraud, illegality, or conflict of interest.

The cases in this area are numerous, and each differs from the others on a factual basis. However, the courts have pronounced certain ground rules which appear in all cases and which are then applied to the given factual situation. The court in *Wheeler* v. *Pullman Iron and Steel Company* . . . said:

It is, however, fundamental in the law of corporations, that the majority of its stockholders shall control the policy of the corporation, and regulate and govern the lawful exercise of its franchise and business. . . . Every one purchasing or subscribing for stock in a corporation impliedly agrees that he will be bound by the acts and proceedings done or sanctioned by a majority of the shareholders, or by the agents of the corporation duly chosen by such majority, within the scope of the powers conferred by the charter, and courts of equity will not undertake to control the policy or business methods of a corporation, although it may be seen that a wiser policy might be adopted and the business more successful if other methods were pursued. The majority of shares of its stock, or the agents by the holders thereof lawfully chosen, must be permitted to control the business of the corporation in their discretion, when not in violation of its charter or some public law, or corruptly and fraudulently subversive of the rights and interests of the corporation or of a shareholder. . . .

Plaintiff in the instant case argues that the directors are acting for reasons unrelated to the financial interest and welfare of the Cubs. However, we are not satisfied that the motives assigned to Philip K. Wrigley, and through him to the other directors, are contrary to the best interests of the corporation and the stockholders. By these thoughts we do not mean to say that we have decided that the decision of the directors was a correct one. That is beyond our jurisdiction and ability. We are merely saying that the decision is one properly before directors, and motives alleged in the amended complaint showed no fraud, illegality, or conflict of interest in their making of that decision.

While all the courts do not insist that one or more of the three elements must be present for a stockholder's derivative action to lie, nevertheless we feel that unless the conduct of the defendants at least borders on one of the elements, the courts should not interfere. . . .

We feel that plaintiff's amended complaint was also defective in failing to allege damage to the corporation. . . .

There is no allegation that the night games played by the other 19 teams enhanced their financial position or that the profits, if any, of those teams were directly related to the number of night games scheduled. . . .

Finally, we do not agree with plaintiff's contention that failure to follow the example of the other major clubs in scheduling night games constituted negligence. Plaintiff made no allegation that these teams' night schedules were profitable or that the purpose for which night baseball had been undertaken was fulfilled. Furthermore, it cannot be said that directors, even those of corporations that are losing money, must follow the lead of the other corporations in the field. Directors are elected for their business capabilities and judgment, and the courts cannot require them to forego their judgment because of the decisions of directors of other companies. Courts may not decide these questions in the absence of a clear showing of dereliction of duty on the part of the specific directors, and mere failure to "follow the crowd" is not such a dereliction.

For the foregoing reasons the order of dismissal entered by the trial court is affirmed.

GUTH v. LOFT, INC.

5 A.2d 503 (Delaware, 1939)

Layton, Chief Justice

Corporate officers and directors are not permitted to use their position of trust and confidence to further their private interests. While technically not trustees, they stand in a fiduciary relation to the corporation and its stockholders. A public policy, existing through the years, and derived from a profound knowledge of human characteristics and motives, has established a rule that demands of a corporate officer or director, peremptorily and inexorably, the most scrupulous observance of his duty, not only affirmatively to protect the interests of the corporation committed to his charge, but also to refrain from doing anything that would work injury to the corporation, or to deprive it of profit or advantage which his skill and ability might properly bring to it, or to enable it to make in the reasonable and lawful exercise of its powers. The rule that requires an undivided and unselfish loyalty to the corporation demands that there shall be no conflict between duty and self-interest. The occasions for the determination of honesty, good faith, and loyal conduct are many and varied, and no hard-and-fast rule can be formulated. The standard of loyalty is measured by no fixed scale. . . .

Guth was not merely a director and president of Loft. He was its master. It is admitted that Guth manifested some of the qualities of a dictator. The directors were selected by him. Some of them held salaried positions in the company. All of them held their positions at his favor. Whether they were supine merely, or for sufficient reasons entirely subservient to Guth, it is not profitable to inquire. It is sufficient to say that they either willfully or negligently allowed Guth absolute freedom of action in the management of Loft's activities, and theirs is an unenviable position whether testifying for or against the appellants.

Prior to May 1931 Guth became convinced that Loft was being unfairly discriminated against by the Coca-Cola Company, of whose syrup it was a large purchaser, in that Loft had been refused a jobber's discount on the syrup, although others, whose purchases were of far less importance, had been given such discount. He determined to replace Coca-Cola as a beverage at the Loft stores with some other cola drink, if that could be accomplished. So, on May 19, 1931, he suggested an inquiry with respect to the desirability of discontinuing the use of Coca-Cola, and replacing it with Pepsi-Cola at a greatly reduced price. Pepsi-Cola was the syrup produced by National Pepsi-Cola Company. As a beverage it had been on the market for over 25 years, and while it was not known to consumers in the area of the Loft stores, its formula and trademark were well established. Guth's purpose was to deliver Loft from the thraldom of the Coca-Cola Company, which practically dominated the field of cola beverages, and, at the same time, to gain for Loft a greater margin of profit on its sale of cola beverages. Certainly, the choice of an acceptable substitute for Coca-Cola was not a wide one, and doubtless, his experience in the field of bottle beverages convinced him that it was necessary for him to obtain a cola syrup whose formula and trademark were secure from attack. Although the difficulties and dangers were great, he concluded to make the change. Almost simultaneously, National Pepsi-Cola Company, in which Megargel was predominant and whom Guth knew, went into bankruptcy; and Guth was informed that the long established Pepsi-Cola formula and trademark could be had at a small price. Guth, of course, was Loft; and Loft's determination to replace Coca-Cola with some other cola beverage in its many stores was practically coincidental with the opportunity to acquire the. Pepsi-Cola formula and trademark. This was the condition of affairs when Megargel approached Guth. Guth contended that his negotiation with Megargel in 1931 was but a continuation of a negotiation begun in 1928, when he had no connection with Loft; but the chancellor found to the contrary, and his finding is accepted.

It is urged by the appellants that Megargel offered the Pepsi-Cola opportunity to Guth personally, and not to him as president of Loft. The chancellor said that there was no way of knowing the fact, as Megargel was dead, and the benefit of this testimony could not be had; but that it was not important, for the matter of consequence was how Guth received the proposition.

It was incumbent upon Guth to show that his every act in dealing with the opportunity presented was in the exercise of the utmost good faith to Loft; and the burden was cast upon him satisfactorily to prove tht the offer was made to him individually. Reasonable inferences, drawn from acknowledged facts and circumstances, are powerful factors in arriving at the truth of a disputed matter, and such inferences are not to be ignored in considering the acts and conduct of Megargel. He had been for years engaged in the manufacture and sale of a cola syrup in competition with Coca-Cola. He knew of the difficulties of competition with such a powerful opponent in general, and in particular in securing of a necessary foothold in a new territory where Coca-Cola was supreme. He could not hope to establish the popularity and use of his syrup by the usual advertising means, for he, himself, had no money or resources, and it is entirely unbelievable that he expected Guth to have command of the vast amount of money necessary to popularize Pepsi-Cola by the ordinary methods. He knew of the difficulty, not to say impossibility, of inducing proprietors of soft drink establishments to use a cola drink utterly unknown to their patrons. It would seem clear, from any reasonable point of view, that Megargel sought to interest someone who controlled an existing opportunity to popularize his product by an actual presentation of it to the consuming public. Such person was Guth, the president of Loft. It is entirely reasonable to infer that Megargel approached Guth as president of Loft, operating, as it did, many soft drink fountains in a most necessary and desirable territory where Pepsi-Cola was little known, he well knowing that if the drink could be established in New York and circumjacent territory, its success would be assured. Every reasonable inference points to this conclusion. What was finally agreed upon between Megargel and Guth, and what outward appearance their agreement assumed, is of small importance. It was a matter of indifference to Megargel whether his co-adventurer was Guth personally, or Loft, so long as his terms were met and his object attained. . . .

The real issue is whether the opportunity to secure a very substantial stock interest in a corporation to be formed for the purpose of exploiting a cola beverage on a wholesale scale was so closely associated with the existing business activities of Loft, and so essential thereto, as to bring the transaction within that class of cases where the acquisition of the property would throw the corporate officer purchasing it into competition with his company. This is a factual question to be decided by reasonable inferences from objective facts.

It is asserted that, no matter how diversified the scope of Loft's activities, its primary business was the manufacturing and selling of candy in its own chain of retail stores, and that it never had the idea of turning a subsidiary product into a highly advertised, nation-wide specialty. . . .

Next it is contended that the Pepsi-Cola opportunity was not in the line of Loft's activities, which essentially were of a retail nature. . . .

The manufacture of syrup was the core of the Pepsi-Cola opportunity. The manufacture of syrups was one of Loft's not unimportant activities. It had the necessary resources, facilities, equipment, technical and practical knowledge, and experience. The tie was close between the business of Loft and the Pepsi-Cola enterprise. . . .

Conceding that the essential of an opportunity is reasonably within the scope of a corporation's activities, latitude should be allowed for development and expansion. To deny this would be to deny the history of industrial development. . . .

As a general proposition it may be said that a corporate officer or director is entirely free to engage in an independent, competitive business, so long as he violates no legal or moral duty with respect to the fiduciary relation that exists between the corporation and himself. . . .

In the instant case Guth was Loft, and Guth was Pepsi. He absolutely controlled Loft. His authority over Pepsi was supreme. As Pepsi, he created and controlled the supply of Pepsi-Cola syrup, and he determined the price and the terms. What he offered as Pepsi, he had the power, as Loft, to accept. Upon any consideration of human characteristics and motives, he created a conflict between self-interest and duty. He made himself judge in his own cause. This was the inevitable result of the dual personality which Guth assumed, and his position was one which, upon the least austere view of corporate duty, he had no right to assume. . . .

The fiduciary relation demands something more than the morals of the market place. . . . Guth's abstractions of Loft's money and materials are complacently referred to as borrowings. Whether his acts are to be deemed properly cognizable in a civil court at all, we need not inquire, but certain it is that borrowing is not descriptive of them. A borrower presumes a lender acting freely. Guth took without limit or stint from a helpless corporation, in violation of a statute enacted for the protection of corporations against such abuses, and without the knowledge or authority of the corporation's Board of Directors. Cunning and craft supplanted sincerity. Frank-

ness gave way to concealment. He did not offer the Pepsi-Cola opportunity to Loft, but captured it for himself. He invested little or no money of his own in the venture, but commandeered for his own benefit and advantage the money, resources, and facilities of his corporation and the services of its officials. He thrust upon Loft the hazard, while he reaped the benefit. His time was paid for by Loft. . . . In such manner he acquired for himself and Grace 91 percent of the capital stock of Pepsi, now worth many millions. A genius in his line he may be, but the law makes no distinction between the wrongdoing genius and the one less endowed.

Upon a consideration of all the facts and circumstances as disclosed, we are convinced that the opportunity to acquire the Pepsi-Cola trademark and formula, goodwill and business belonged to the complainant, and that Guth, as its president, had no right to appropriate the opportunity to himself.

BATES v. DRESSER

251 U.S. 524 (1920)

Justice Holmes

This is a bill in equity brought by the receiver of a national bank to charge its former president and directors with the loss of a great part of its assets through the thefts of an employee of the bank while they were in power. The case was sent to a master who found for the defendants; but the District Court entered a decree against all of them. . . . The Circuit Court of Appeals reversed this decree, dismissed the bill as against all except the administrator of Edwin Dresser, the president, cut down the amount with which he was charged[1] and refused to add interest from the date of the decree of the District Court. . . . Dresser's administrator and the receiver both appeal, the latter contending that the decree of the District Court should be affirmed with interest and costs.

The bank was a little bank at Cambridge with the capital of $100,000 and average deposits of

---

[1] To $264,088.02.

somewhere about $300,000. It had a cashier, a bookkeeper, a teller, and a messenger. Before and during the time of the losses Dresser was its president and executive officer, a large stockholder, with an inactive deposit of from $35,000 to $50,000. From July 1903 to the end, Frank L. Earl was cashier. Coleman, who made the trouble, entered the service of the bank as messenger in September 1903. In January 1904, he was promoted to be bookkeeper, being then not quite 18 but having studied bookkeeping. In the previous August an auditor employed on the retirement of a cashier had reported that the daily balance book was very much behind, that it was impossible to prove the deposits, and that a competent bookkeeper should be employed upon the work immediately. Coleman kept the deposit ledger, and this was the work that fell into his hands. There was no cage in the bank, and in 1904 and 1905 there were some small shortages in the accounts of three successive tellers that were not accounted for, and the last of them, Cutting, was asked by Dresser to resign on that ground. Before doing so, he told Dresser that someone had taken the money and that if he might be allowed to stay he would set a trap and catch the man, but Dresser did not care to do that and thought that there was nothing wrong. From Cutting's resignation on October 7, 1905, Coleman acted as paying and receiving teller, in addition to his other duty, until November 1907. During this time there were no shortages disclosed in the teller's accounts. In May 1906, Coleman took $2,000 cash from the vaults of the bank, but restored it the next morning. In November of the same year he began the thefts that come into question here. Perhaps in the beginning he took the money directly. But as he ceased to have charge in the cash in November 1907, he invented another way. Having a small account at the bank, he would draw checks for the amount he wanted, exchange checks with a Boston broker, get cash for the broker's check, and when his own check came to the bank through the clearing house, would abstract it from the envelope, enter the others on his book, and conceal the difference by a charge to some other account or a false addition in the column of drafts or deposits in the depositors'

ledger. He handed to the cashier only the slip from the clearing house that showed the totals. The cashier paid whatever appeared to be due, and thus Coleman's checks were honored. So far as Coleman thought it necessary, in view of the absolute trust in him on the part of all concerned, he took care that his balances should agree with those in the cashier's book.

By May 1, 1907, Coleman had abstracted $17,000, concealing the fact by false additions in the column of total checks, and false balances in the deposit ledger. Then for the moment a safer concealment was effected by charging the whole to Dresser's account. Coleman adopted this method when a bank examiner was expected. Of course when the fraud was disguised by overcharging a depositor it could not be discovered except by calling in the passbooks, or taking all the deposit slips and comparing them with the depositors' ledger in detail. by November 1907, the amount taken by Coleman was $30,100, and the charge on Dresser's account was $20,000. In 1908 the sum was raised from $33,000 to $49,671. In 1909 Coleman's activity began to increase. In January he took $6,829.26; in March, $10,833.73; in June, his previous stealings amounting to $83,390.94, he took $5,152.06; in July, $18,050; in August, $6,250; in September, $17,350; in October, $47,277.08; in November, $51,847; in December, $46,956.44; in January, 1910, $27,395.53; in February, $6,473.97; making a total of $310,143.02, when the bank closed on February 21, 1910. As a result of this the amount of the monthly deposits seemed to decline noticeably and the directors considered the matter in September, but concluded that the falling off was due in part to the springing up of rivals, whose deposits were increasing, but was parallel to a similar decrease in New York. An examination by a bank examiner in December 1909 disclosed nothing wrong to him.

In this connection it should be mentioned that in the previous semiannual examinations by national bank examiners nothing was discovered pointing to malfeasance. The cashier was honest, and everybody believed that they could rely upon him, although in fact he relied too much upon Coleman, who also was unsuspected by all. If

Earl had opened the envelopes from the clearing house, and had seen the checks, or had examined the deposit ledger with any care, he would have found out what was going on. The scrutiny of any-one accustomed to such details would have discovered the false additions and other indicia of fraud that were on the face of the book. But it may be doubted whether anything less than a continuous pursuit of the figures through pages would have done so except by a lucky chance.

The question of the liability of the directors in this case is the question whether they neglected their duty by accepting the cashier's statement of liabilities and failing to inspect the depositors' ledger. The statements of assets always were correct. . . . Of course liabilities as well as assets must be known to know the condition and, as this case shows, peculations may be concealed as well by a false understatement of liabilities as by a false show of assets. But the former is not the direction in which fraud would have been looked for, especially on the part of one who at the time of his principal abstractions was not in contact with the funds. A debtor hardly expects to have his liability understated. Some animals must have given at least one exhibition of dangerous propensities before the owner can be held. This fraud was a novelty in the way of swindling a bank so far as the knowledge of any experience had reached Cambridge before 1910. We are not prepared to reverse the finding of the master and the Circuit Court of Appeals that the directors should not be held answerable for taking the cashier's statement of liabilities to be as correct as the statement of assets always was. If he had not been negligent without their knowledge, it would have been. Their confidence seemed warranted by the semiannual examinations by the Government examiner, and they were encouraged in their belief that all was well by the president, whose responsibility, as executive officer; interest, as large stockholder and depositor; and knowledge, from long daily presence in the bank, were greater than theirs. They were not bound by virtue of the office gratutiously assumed by them to call in the passbooks and compare them with the ledger,

and until the event showed the possibility, they hardly could have seen that their failure to look at the ledger opened a way to fraud. . . .

The position of the president is different. Practically he was the master of the situation. He was daily at the bank for hours, he had the deposit ledger in his hands at times and might have had it at any time. He had had hints and warnings in addition to those that we have mentioned, warnings that should not be magnified unduly, but still that taken with the auditor's report of 1903, the unexplained shortages, the suggestion of the teller, Cutting, in 1905, and the final seeming rapid decline in deposits, would have induced scrutiny but for an invincible repose upon the status quo. In 1908 one Fillmore learned that a package containing $150 left with the bank for safekeeping was not to be found, told Dresser of the loss, wrote to him that he could but conclude that the package had been destroyed or removed by someone connected with the bank, and in later conversation said that it was evident that there was a thief in the bank. He added that he would advise the president to look after Coleman, that he believed he was living at a pretty fast pace, and that he had pretty good authority for thinking that he was supporting a woman. In the same year or the year before, Coleman, whose pay was never more than 12 dollars a week, set up an automobile, as was known to Dresser and commented on unfavorably, to him. There was also some evidence of notice to Dresser that Coleman was dealing in copper stocks. In 1909 came the great and inadequately explained seeming shrinkage in the deposits. No doubt plausible explanations of his conduct came from Coleman and the notice as to speculations may have been slight, but taking the whole story of the relations of the parties, we are not ready to say that the two courts below erred in finding that Dresser had been put upon his guard. However little the warnings may have pointed to the specific facts, had they been accepted they would have led to an examination of the depositors' ledger, a discovery of past and a prevention of future thefts.

PROBLEMS FOR DISCUSSION

1. The bylaws of Ozone Onion Farms, Inc., specify a maximum of 11 directors; there is no indication of any minimum number. Handel, Bach, Mozart, and eight other persons were serving on the board of directors when a special stockholders' meeting was called. Mozart owned 1,400 of the 2,700 shares of stock outstanding. The vote was 1,400 to 1,300 to remove all 11 directors. Mozart, his wife, and Lemming were then elected as directors. The state's statute provided that a corporation must have at least three directors and that the term of a director could not be shortened by amending the bylaws to decrease the number of directors. Handel and Bach file suit, challenging the removal and election. What result, and why?

2. Holly Hustle was area sales manager for Automatic Business Machines, Inc. When she applied for a personal loan of $9,000 at the Strangle Bank she was told that she did not have sufficient personal collateral for the loan but that the bank would make the loan if she could find a proper cosigner. Holly contacted her supervisor, corporate vice president Adam Awesum, and Adam agreed to cosign the loan for her. When the loan fell due, Holly defaulted, and the bank then forced Adam to pay. Adam now brings a lawsuit for reimbursement against Holly. Should he collect? Explain.

3. Willie Wolland was the principal owner and chief executive officer of two companies, Rustic Rooms, Inc., and Handsome Homes, Inc. Slim Shanks worked as the Augusta, Maine, manager for both companies from the fall of 1974 to November 1, 1977. He was paid a salary of $500 per week during this period. Slim also received bonuses at the end of Rustic's fiscal year (September 1)—$2,200 for fiscal 1974, $4,000 for fiscal 1975, and $6,000 for fiscal 1976. The $4,000 was paid half each by the two companies; the $6,000 was paid by Handsome; the first $2,200 bonus was paid by Rustic. Slim says he is due a comparable bonus for fiscal 1977, and sues Willie to collect. Willie moves to dismiss the complaint. How should the court rule? Discuss.

4. Boscoe and Gert Crofty organized Midlife Managers, Inc., as a holding company, to purchase the Oak Tree Bank. Midlife owned nearly all the stock in Oak Tree. Boscoe, Gert, and one Zeb Zlink owned nearly all the stock in Midlife, and served as its three directors. The three of them met whenever they thought it was necessary to conduct business, and did so without formal notices or minutes. The bank began to get into serious financial difficulty shortly after its purchase by Midlife; the suggested ratio of capital to assets and the percentage of delinquent loans varied considerably from the guidelines set by the state banking commissioner. The directors decided to raise some new funds for the bank by selling $250,000 worth of debentures. Herman, Layne, and Maimie each bought $20,000 of these bonds. The directors then used this money to cover some of the bank's bad loans and other losses. Oak Tree Bank is now bankrupt, and Herman, Layne, and Maimie sue to recover their investment from Boscoe, Gert, and Zeb. Boscoe, Gert, and Zeb say that they are not personally liable, since they were never officially elected as directors and they shouldn't be held liable as stockholders for the bank's debts. Who's right, and why?

5. Tarnish Rentals, Inc., sues to collect $38,000 in unpaid rent from Yankem Associates, Inc., a professional dental corporation. Yancy Yankem was the sole stockholder, a director, and the president of Tarnish. He had originally formed Yankem, Inc., to operate his dental office, and had been its sole stockholder, a director, and the president. The lease had been executed between Tarnish and Yankem, Inc., while Yancy served on both boards. Sometime later, Yankem, Inc., had been merged into Yankem Associates, Inc., when Tess Trueblud came into the office as

another dentist. Yancy and Tess each owned 50 percent of Yankem Associates, Inc. The former tenant had paid $420 per month for the building. Tarnish did about $25,000 worth of remodeling and then leased the building to Yankem, Inc., for $880 per month, for five years. Yankem Associates took over this lease but now claims that it is unfair. How should the court try to resolve this dispute?

6. Nanna Nelish, representing her husband Ned's estate, sues the Govel Company, Inc., in which he had been a 45 percent stockholder, and Greg Govel, who also owned 45 percent of the company. Ned and Greg had originally each owned half of the stock but had been forced to sell some additional shares to outsiders to raise more capital. Ned had been president and general manager, and Greg had been corporate counsel. When Ned died, Greg became president. When Greg learned that the 10 percent minority shares were for sale, he bought them himself. Nanna sues to have these shares declared assets of the company or, in the alternative, to be allowed to buy half of them so as to maintain an equal voice in the company. Does she have a valid claim? Discuss.

7. Pearl Tilton sustained a broken arm while working for O-K Hardware, Inc. Pearl was awarded $73 per week, for four months, by a hearing examiner for the state's Workers' Compensation Commission. It was then discovered that O-K had not taken out workers' compensation insurance as required by state statute. The statute provided that where such a failure occurred, the employer lost all exemptions of property from court process (execution and sale). The statute also provided that where a corporation failed to procure such insurance, its officers and directors were personally liable for any uncollected portion of a judgment against the corporation. O-K has gone through bankruptcy proceedings and has received a discharge in bankruptcy from the U.S. district court. Pearl did not file her claim in O-K's bankruptcy proceeding. Nevertheless, she now wants to hold O-K's directors and officers personally liable for the full amount of her award. Can she do so? Explain.

8. Amessa Timber, Inc., was organized by Harlow Hacker in 1953 as an Oregon corporation. Hacker was its president, a director, and the owner of most of its stock until 1978. Barbie Blossom loaned money to Amessa over the course of several years. In 1978 Amessa owed her $76,000; the debt was unsecured. Amessa had executed a first mortgage on all its timberland to the Openend Bank. When Blossom inquired about her status as a creditor, Hacker assured her that the company's assets were more than enough to pay off all claims, that she would be paid first if anything happened, and that all of his interest in the company was subordinate to her loans. Hacker then sold his stock to Gabby Goethe, who was Amessa's treasurer. Goethe was to pay Hacker $220,000 in cash according to a specific schedule. Goethe also agreed to execute in Hacker's favor a second mortgage on all of Amessa's timberland. Blossom sues Amessa, Hacker, and Goethe to collect her $76,000. Are any or all of these persons liable to her? Why or why not?

Corporations—Merger, Dissolution, and Reorganization   **45**

Substantial changes in economic circumstances or regulatory policies may indicate the need for a firm to expand, or to terminate its business. The Model Act and most state statutes contain fairly detailed procedures to cover each of these special situations.

Methods of Expansion.   In addition to growing gradually by selling more of its product or service year by year, a corporation may wish to expand rapidly by entering into various sorts of combinations with other firms. It may wish to buy or lease all the assets of a second firm. It may wish to merge or consolidate with one or more other firms. Or it may wish to simply buy a controlling stock interest in other firms.

In general, the legality of any of the above sorts of combinations would be tested under the national antitrust laws if the firm is engaged in interstate commerce or if its activities have a substantial impact on interstate commerce. Even if a combination met all of the state procedural requirements, the Federal Trade Commission or the U.S. attorney general could still prevent the combination if it would have substantial anticompetitive effects. Antitrust law is discussed more thoroughly in Chapter 48.

Purchase or Lease of Assets.   Where one corporation buys or leases all the existing assets of another, there is no change in the corporate identity of either; they both continue to exist as before. The seller or lessor firm has simply decided to liquidate its operations in one line of business and to reinvest in funds and efforts elsewhere. A TV manufacturer, for example, feels that the present and future competition is too tough, so it sells its TV manufacturing assets and starts making business machines. The stockholders of the seller or lessor firm must approve this extraordinary transaction by majority vote, after recommendation and proper notice of the special meeting from the board of directors. Once shareholder authorization has been given, however, the board may cancel the sale or lease, if conditions change, without further shareholder action. Assuming that all actions have been taken in good faith, the creditors of the seller or lessor firm would have no basis for objecting to the transaction. Since the buyer or lessee is paying fair value for the assets, it should own them free and clear of the seller/lessor's creditors.

Merger and Consolidation.   Two or more firms may decide to combine by means of a merger or a consolidation. In a merger, one of the original firms survives and the others end. In a consolidation, all of the original firms end; a new corporation is formed, and the original ones all become parts of it. In either case, all assets and all liabilities are turned over to the surviving firm. In each case, the Model Act requires approval by the board and by a majority of each class of stock entitled to vote as a class. Since all liabilities are being assumed by the survivor firm, consent of the creditors of the original firms would generally not be required.

Purchase of Controlling Stock Interest.   Where the directors of X Corporation decide to have X buy a controlling stock interest in Y Corporation, both firms continue to exist as before. X Corporation offers to buy shares from Y's stockholders. This is a "tender offer," and it is subject to extensive regulation by the SEC and the states. See the further discussion in Chapter 47, and reread the *Speed* case in Chapter 43.

Rights of Dissenting Shareholders.   The Model Act requires approval by majority stockholder vote in the case of sale or lease of all the firm's assets, merger, or consolidation. In the tender offer, each stockholder makes an individual decision as to whether to sell at the price offered. Generally, consent of the firm's creditors is not required. But what about the minority shareholders who object to this drastic change in their firm's operations?

Section 81 of the Model Act tries to protect the minority by providing a mandatory buy-out procedure. Prior to attendance at the special stockholders' meeting, the dissenter must file written notice of objection to the proposed action. At the meeting, of course, the dissenter would vote against the proposal. If the proposal is passed by the necessary majority vote, the dissenter may then file a written demand with the firm for payment of the fair value of his or her shares as of the day prior to the vote, "excluding any appreciation or depreciation in anticipation of such corporate action." This demand for payment must be made within 10 days after the vote. The theory of this procedure is that the individual should not be forced to maintain his or her investment in a substantially different firm.

Nationwide Ins. Co. v. New York, C. & St. L. R. Co.
211 N.E.2d 854 (Ohio, 1965)

FACTS   On December 21, 1964, the plaintiff filed an action against the defendant, based on a tort claim which arose on December 22, 1962. A summons was served on "the regular freight agent of said railroad company at its Fremont, Ohio, address." On January 21, 1965, the defendant moved to set aside the service of process and to dismiss the claim, since it had been merged into the Norfolk and Western Railway Company, effective October 16, 1964. The relevant section of the Ohio Revised Code (the defendant had been an Ohio corporation) provided: "[A]ny claim existing or action or proceeding pending by or against any of the constituent corporations may be prosecuted to judgment, with right of appeal as in other cases, as if such merger or consolidation had not taken place, or the surviving or new corporation may be substituted in its place." The defendant's motion was granted, and a judgment was entered in its favor. The plaintiff appealed.

ISSUE Can a preexisting tort claim be prosecuted against one constituent corporation after the effective date of a merger?

DECISION Yes. Judgment reversed and case remanded to the trial court.

REASONS Judge Brown first briefly reviewed the facts and cited the statute. The plain meaning of the statute, he felt, covered this case specifically even though he could find no Ohio precedents. He rejected the defendant's argument that a case could not be *commenced* against one of the constituent corporations after the merger had occurred.

"That legal actions were intended by the Legislature, in prescribed circumstances, to be commenced against constituent corporations after the effective date of the merger of a constituent corporation is evidenced by the statutory provisions for service of process on constituent and resulting corporations. Such service of process is not limited to actions commenced before the merger date. . . . The foregoing conclusion is in harmony with the legislative intent, expressed in the General Corporation Law, to save pending rights against consolidating and merging corporations, and such rights cannot be nullified by the sale of the assets of a merged corporation to another corporation. . . .

"Despite a consolidation or merger, creditors may still maintain a legal action against the constituent corporation when the statutes continue the existence of the constituent corporation for the purpose of preserving the rights of creditors, or for the purpose of suit against it by creditors or others in whose favor a liability against it exists. . . . Section 1701.81(A)(6), Revised Code, extends this rule to include 'any claim existing,' and, therefore, applies to a claim ex *contractu* or ex *delicto*."

Dissolution. Assuming that it retained the power to amend, the legislature of the state of incorporation would presumably have the power to terminate the existence of that states' corporations. The state's attorney general or corporation commissioner could ask a court to decree dissolution where a corporation was in continuing default on its duties to file reports and to pay taxes and fees. In those rare cases where the articles did not provide for perpetual existence, the end of the specified time period or the occurrence of the specified event would cause a dissolution of the firm. The shareholders may act voluntarily to terminate their corporation, either by unanimous action or by majority vote, after a recommendation from the board of directors. Normally courts will not interfere with the shareholders' decision.

Anderson v. Cleveland-Cliffs Iron Co.
87 N.E.2d 384 (Ohio, 1948)

FACTS
The plaintiffs, preferred stockholders in CCI, brought suit to enjoin a proposed consolidation. CCI had outstanding 487,238 shares of preferred and 408,296 shares of common. All of the common was owned by Cliffs Corporation; the preferred was owned by various persons. CCI and Cliffs were managed by the same officers, but there was only one person who sat on both boards of directors. A proposal to consolidate the old CCI and Cliffs into a new CCI was approved by a two-thirds majority, as required by state law, at a special stockholders' meeting. Under this proposal, each preferred shareholder in the old CCI would get one share of preferred and one share of common in the new CCI for each share of preferred in the old CCI. Each common share of Cliffs would be exchanged for $2^1/_4$ common shares in the new CCI. The plaintiffs argued that the consolidation was improper because there was no business necessity for it.

ISSUE
May a consolidation lawfully take place even though there is no business or financial necessity for it?

DECISION
Yes. Judgment for defendants.

REASONS
In his opinion, Common Pleas Judge McNamee reviewed several precedent cases which the plaintiffs had cited and which involved attempts to evade or violate the law by use of the consolidation or merger technique. He did not think that any of those situations was present in this case, and thus he saw no reason why the corporations couldn't consolidate if they wanted to do so.

"Here, there is no merger of a parent company with its wholly inactive subsidiary. . . . Nor is this a case where the corporation had recourse to the consolidation statute for the sole purpose of accomplishing an unauthorized result. . . . This case presents no question involving the destruction of vested rights by the retrospective application of statutes or corporate action. Nor does the consolidation impair contractual obligations. There was express legislative authority for the action taken. It is well settled that a shareholder's contract includes the pertinent and appropriate statutory provisions in effect at the time the corporation is created. Section 67 was a part of the preferred shareholders' contracts. By accepting their stock certificates the shareholders of both companies agreed that their corporations might consolidate and determine 'the manner and basis of converting the shares of each of the constituent corporations into shares of the consolidated corporation.' . . .

"It is true, as plaintiffs claim, that the defendant corporation had adequate working capital and that there was no real need for the addition of the liquid assets of Cliffs Corporation. Plaintiffs' position in this regard is confirmed by the statements made by officers of Cliffs at the time dissolution of that company was proposed. But the right of corporations to consolidate is not conditioned upon business exigencies or economic necessity. Courts possess no veto power over purely business judgments of corporate officers or stockholders. Whether the addition of over $20 million of cash and steel stocks was necessary or desirable is a matter peculiarly within the province of the affected interests to determine."

Modern corporation law treats a dissolved corporation in much the same way as a dissolved partnership is treated. That is, the corporation continues to operate for the limited purpose of winding up its affairs—collecting money owed to it, selling off its assets, and paying off its creditors. After the creditors have been paid in full, the preferred shareholders have the first claim on any assets remaining and then, finally, the common stockholders are paid.

Reorganization. Financial reorganizations under the Bankruptcy Act are covered in Chapter 51. An attempt may be made to save the firm by adjusting its debts, or the firm may be dissolved and its assets used to pay off as many claims as possible, according to bankruptcy priorities.

CASES FOR DISCUSSION

JOHNSON v. HELICOPTER & AIRPLANE SERVICES CORPORATION ET AL.

404 F. Supp. 726 (Maryland, 1979)

Joseph H. Young, District Judge

The issue presently, and finally, before this Court is a determination under Fed. R. Civ. P. 17(b) of RAC Corporation's capacity to be sued in this products liability suit. . . .

Facts

RAC was originally incorporated in Delaware in 1931 under the name Siversky Aircraft Corporation. In 1939 the name of the corporation was changed to Republic Aviation Corporation. Throughout its existence, the corporation's principal place of business was in Farmingdale, New York; it procured a license to do business in that state during the 1930's.

In 1965 the corporation sold all of its operating assets to another defendant in the instant action, Fairchild-Hiller Corporation. The corporation then changed its name to RAC Corporation and proceeded to wind up its affairs. On October 1, 1965, RAC's board of directors passed a resolution authorizing the filing of a certificate of dissolution for the company with Delaware's Secretary of State. That certificate was filed on November 19, 1968, and the Secretary issued a formal certificate of dissolution.

RAC has continued to prosecute certain tax claims with the United States and the State of New York in an effort to wind up its affairs prior to liquidation. The continued existence of the corporation is authorized under provisions of the Delaware corporation law which give a dissolved corporation a limited three-year existence to dispose of its affairs. . . .

The corporation has not, however, surrendered its license to do business in New York, asserting that retention of the license is necessary in order to protect its right to pursue tax claims in that state. Those proceedings have not concluded, and RAC is still carrying on significant activities and transactions. It regularly holds meetings of its board of directors, files state and federal tax returns, takes out insurance (including insurance relevant to this case), and issues shareholder reports. RAC has also continued to invest its corporate assets; since 1973, it has invested a substantial percentage of its multi-million dollar assets in short-term commercial paper.

At a hearing on June 1, 1973, this Court granted RAC's motion to dismiss under Fed. R. Civ. P. 12(b) (6) for lack of capacity. That decision was appealed to the Fourth Circuit, which held that the motion should have been treated as one for summary judgment under Fed. R. Civ. P. 56, and remanded to this Court to provide the parties a reasonable time for discovery. . . .

The plaintiff conducted discovery relevant to the jurisdictional and capacity motions, and RAC then renewed its motion to dismiss, asserting that discovery had not uncovered any information requiring a different result than that which the Court reached on June 1, 1973. This is correct. . . .

RAC is bringing to a close its business, and its activities are consistent with that end. While the corporation is still holding assets, it naturally retains a board of directors, holds meetings, issues reports, and invests its assets. To do otherwise might be a breach of the fiduciary duty owed by the directors of the corporation to manage the corporation's affairs. Nevertheless, three years have passed since dissolution, and although RAC is still conducting certain proceedings brought during the winding-up period, it has lost the capacity to sue and be sued in new actions, including the one instituted by the plaintiff here. . . .

Although there certainly may be consequences of RAC's failure to forfeit its license to do business in New York, that failure does not give RAC capacity to be sued in a federal court.

KIRBY ROYALTIES, INC. v. TEXACO, INC.
458 P.2d 101 (Wyoming, 1969)

McIntyre, Justice

Texaco, Inc., brought an action to quiet title to the minerals in 80 acres of land in Carbon County, Wyoming. Kirby Royalties, Inc., was named as a defendant. The State of Wyoming, through its Board of Land Commissioners, has intervened. The district court found for Texaco and held it was the owner of the oil, gas, and other minerals in the subject lands and entitled to the possession thereof as against Kirby and the State of Wyoming. . . .

The common source of title which all parties recognize is the Carbon Oil Company. It received a quitclaim deed for the minerals involved, in 1929, from E. N. Munson. Carbon Oil Company was incorporated in 1925 in the State of Nebraska. Its authorized capital stock was $10,000 divided into 100 shares with a par value of $100 each. . . .

Parties have stipulated that Carbon Oil Company was dissolved by the Secretary of State of the State of Nebraska for nonpayment of taxes on

March 23, 1933. The persons comprising the last board of directors of the corporation, according to the last annual report, were E. N. Munson, C. C. Johnson, and B. F. Roth. All of these directors are deceased, and the last survivor was B. F. Roth, who died January 13, 1946.

Undisputed evidence shows that a diligent search has been made for stock in Carbon Oil Company; for the owners or holders of such stock; for former officers or directors of the corporation; for heirs or successors to any of the former officers or directors; and for creditors, if any. All that could be found was Eliza I. (Isabelle) Roth, widow and sole heir and beneficiary of B. F. Roth. She had possession of Certificate No. 4 dated January 28, 1929 for 10 shares of stock in Carbon Oil Company. The certificate had been issued to B. F. Roth. No other stock or stockholders have been found despite a diligent search for such.

On the basis of the evidence adduced and stipulated to, a total of 100 shares ($10,000 in value) of stock in Carbon Oil Company was issued and became outstanding; Roth owned 10 shares or one tenth of the total outstanding stock; and title to such stock passed to his widow, Eliza I. (Isabelle) Roth. There are no known owners as far as nine-tenths of the stock is concerned.

In 1961 Thomas F. Stroock, acting for Texaco, Inc., took two quitclaim deeds from Mrs. Roth, individually and as trustee for creditors and stockholders of Carbon Oil Company, covering all minerals in the lands we are concerned with. He then conveyed over to Texaco. The consideration paid by Stroock to Mrs. Roth was $7.50 per acre.

On the theory that Mrs. Roth had become successor trustee for creditors and stockhodlers of Carbon Oil Company, after the death of her husband, or that she succeeded to the legal title—subject to a trust for all creditors and stockholders—Texaco claims to be the owner of the property we are dealing with.

In 1966 Mrs. Roth, as the widow and sole heir of B. F. Roth, executed an assignment and a bill of sale by which she purported to sell, transfer, and convey to Kirby Royalties, Inc., all of her rights, title, and interest in and to the 10 shares of stock Roth had owned in Carbon Oil Company.

In 1964 the State of Wyoming issued, without warranty, an oil and gas lease on the 80 acres here involved to Kirby Royalties, Inc. The state's claim of ownership is based on the theory that the minerals in the land had escheated to the State of Wyoming because they did not belong to any person or persons. Kirby therefore claims an interest, as lessee of the state, in and to the oil and gas contained in the land. In addition, it claims under whatever rights it may have obtained, if any, on account of its assignment and bill of sale from Mrs. Roth pertaining to Stock Certificate No. 4. . . .

As far as general statutory trustee for Carbon Oil Company is concerned, Texaco is obliged to look to Nebraska law. Such law, at the time pertinent, specified a successor trustee could be appointed by the district court of the proper county. But none was asked for and none was appointed. As far as a receiver or trustee for the assets in Wyoming is concerned, we have already indicated none was asked for and none was appointed. It follows, then, that Mrs. Roth was not a statutory or appointed trustee under Nebraska law; and she had no status as a trustee or receiver in Wyoming for assets in this state. . . .

It is the general rule that at dissolution of a corporation the equitable title to the distributive shares vests in the respective shareholders; and the unclaimed distributive shares are not available for distribution to the known shareholders. . . .

[A]ssets of a dissolved corporation must be held in trust until such time as they are claimed by the owners or escheated by the state under an appropriate escheat act. . . . [T]he proprietary interest of each stockholder is, at dissolution, transformed into an equitable right to a pro rata distributive share of the assets of the corporation. . . .

[W]here a corporation has been dissolved and there has been no distribution of corporate assets, title to realty becomes vested in the shareholders as tenants in common. . . .

Appellee-Texaco contends corporate property is not subject to escheat because § 9–687 applies only to property which does not belong to any "person"; and because a corporation cannot have "legal heirs" as required in § 9–687.

We are unimpressed with this contention. Not only is the word "person" as used in this statute broad enough to apply to property which does not belong to any corporation, but we have already said the proprietary interest of each stockholder is, at dissolution, transformed into an equitable right to a pro rata distributive share of the assets of the corporation. Thus, the property being escheated is property of the shareholders. . . .

In view of our holding that the proprietary interest of each stockholder is, at dissolution, transformed into an equitable right to a pro rata distributive share of the assets of the corporation, we see no reason why the deed from Mrs. Roth individually to Stroock did not convey to him all of the right, title, and interest of grantor in and to the minerals herein involved. That interest is now owned by Texaco. We have previously indicated this Texaco interest would be one-tenth of the minerals in the land in question.

The remaining interest, being unclaimed by the rightful owners, escheats to the State of Wyoming, subject to the holding provisions set forth in § 9–688(d). The fact that a partial interest only escheats to the state presents no problem. . . .

Accordingly, the judgment of the district court must be modified to quiet the title of plaintiff to an undivided one-tenth interest in such minerals, with judgment for the defendants, Kirby and the State of Wyoming, with respect to the remaining nine-tenths interest.

Remanded for such modification.

1. The Ersatz Edison Company seeks to acquire, through an eminent domain proceeding, a 125-foot-wide easement for an overhead power line across the land of Roswell and Rowena Mouton. Ersatz properly applied for and received from the State Public Service Commission a certificate of public convenience and necessity for the construction of the power line. When the Moutons refused to grant the easement, Ersatz began an eminent domain action in the appropriate state court. The Moutons now argue that Ersatz lacks the power of eminent domain because it was formed by a consolidation of three other companies which was never approved by the state legislature and because the only one of the three companies that had the power of eminent domain has ceased to exist. What result here, and why?

2. Windy Blabhart, one of four director-stockholders in Needy Health Services, Inc., asks for an injunction and damages against his father, Howie Blabhart, and his brothers Charlie and Tommie Blabhart, the other three director-stockholders. Windy's business commitments in other states made it difficult for him to attend board meetings, so he resigned from the board. Windy, however, refused to sell his stock. The other stockholders then devised a plan to merge the old corporation into a new one, Needy Nursing Center, Inc. Under the plan, Windy would be given a new corporate bond in place of his stock in the old company and would not be a stockholder in the new company. The merger was approved by votes of the directors and the stockholders, pursuant to state statute. Windy says, however, that there was no valid business reason for the merger, which he alleges was designed solely to remove him as a stockholder. How should the court rule in this case? Explain.

3. Mavis, Ratucci, and Hessian each owned one third of the stock in MHR Realty, Inc. MHR was organized to take title to certain real estate from Savim Associates, Inc., in which Mavis owned 54 percent of the stock and Ratucci and Hessian owned 23 percent each. Savim then built a building on the land and rented space in it from MHR. Mavis was president, Ratucci vice president, and Hessian treasurer in both firms. These three were the only directors of MHR. Mavis decided that Savim needed to raise more capital, but Ratucci and Hessian were unable to buy more stock, so Mavis terminated their employment at Savim in order to cut overhead costs. At a duly called directors' meeting of MHR, Ratucci and Hessian then voted to fire Mavis as MHR's president and passed a resolution ordering him to turn over all of MHR's books and records to them, as majority directors. Mavis now brings suit asking the court to dissolve MHR, alleging that since it was never intended to be an operating company it no longer serves any useful purpose and that giving control to the majority directors would enable them to use MHR to wreck Savim Associates. How should the court rule?

4. Family, Inc., a nonprofit Delaware corporation, sues Tidown Title Insurance Company to recover legal and other expenses which Family incurred in removing a defect in the title to certain of its real estate. Tidown had originally issued the title insurance policy in question to Family Foundation, Inc., a different corporation. The pertinent part of the policy defined the named insured as: "the insured named in Schedule A and those who succeed to the interest of such insured by operation of law, as distinguished from purchase." Family Foundation had received the land from Mr. and Mrs. Gotbucks, but since Family Foundation had failed to qualify under the tax laws, the Gotbucks were unable to take a deduction for a charitable gift. The land was then conveyed back to the Gotbucks; Family, Inc., was organized; and the land was then conveyed to it. Family, Inc., adopted a name similar to that of Family Foundation, Inc., as well as the purposes and the charter of Family Foundation, Inc. How should the court decide this lawsuit? Explain.

5. Herbie Hassle, as guardian, brings a lawsuit on behalf of his son Marvin against Musty Mechanisms, Inc., the manufacturer of an automatic baseball-throwing machine. One of these machines was sold to the Loon Lake School, which Marvin attended. The machine had been left on the playground with no one supervising it, and Marvin had sustained severe injuries from a blow on the head by the "throwing arm" of the machine. Musty had filed for dissolution in its home state, which had a statutory provision similar to Section 105 of the MBCA, providing for a two-year period for filing claims against a dissolved corporation. This lawsuit was not filed until after a Certificate of Dissolution had been issued to Musty by the secretary of state, but it was filed within two years thereafter. The accident itself did not occur until after the Certificate of Dissolution had been issued. Musty therefore moved to dismiss the complaint, saying that it could not be sued for injuries which occurred after it had been officially dissolved. How should the court rule on this motion to dismiss? Discuss.

6. The Fullup Foundation, Inc., was a nonprofit charitable corporation which had been organized pursuant to the will of Frank C. Fullup and which had operated an orphanage for over 20 years. The trustees of the foundation decided that it was no longer practical to continue operation of the orphanage and began proceedings to liquidate the foundation. The trustees proposed to distribute any remaining assets of the foundation to the State Children's Home and the United Churches Children's Fund. The heirs of Frank Fullup say that they should receive any assets remaining after the foundation is terminated. The Family Saving Institute, another nonprofit corporation, asks to intervene in the liquidation proceedings and to participate in the distribution of assets. How should the assets here be distributed? Explain.

7. The Montana statute regulating credit unions specified that no organization could operate in the state using the words *credit union* in its name or title except those which were organized pursuant to the statute or which were federally organized credit unions. Butterfly Credit Union, organized in Montana, wanted to merge into Giant Credit Union, which was organzied under Idaho law. After the proposed merger, Giant would operate Butterfly's former offices in Montana. Peggy Stiles, the Montana superintendent of banking, refused to approve the proposed merger. Giant and Butterfly bring a mandamus action against Peggy. Should the court order Peggy to approve the proposed merger? Why or why not?

8. Aweful Awnings, Inc., issued a promissory note for $40,000 to Twommers Corporation, to pay for merchandise sold by Twommers to Aweful. Before the note came due, Aweful was placed in liquidation. Twommers wanted to borrow some money at the bank with this note as collateral. Since there was some doubt about whether Aweful would be able to pay off the note, Twommers' president called Ron Pettyman, who owned 60 percent of the stock in Aweful, and asked Ron to indorse the note. Ron did so. Aweful was liquidated and was unable to pay the note. Twommers took the note back from the bank when it paid off its loan, and now it sues to enforce the note against Pettyman. Pettyman says he should not be held personally liable on the note, at least not to Twommers. What result, and why?

46 | Foreign Corporations

What Is a Foreign Corporation? When we see the term *foreign corporation* we normally think of a corporation from some country other than the United States. Actually any corporation for profit, organized and created in one state and doing intrastate business in another state, is a foreign corporation. For example, a corporation organized and created in Illinois is a foreign corporation when it is transacting intrastate business in Wisconsin or Iowa. Corporations organzied in foreign countries and doing business in a state of the United States would technically be classified as "alien" corporations but are also usually regulated as foreign corporations. Simply stated, any corporation not organized in the specific state in which it is doing local buiness or requesting to do local business is a foreign corporation insofar as that state's law is concerned. A corporation organized and doing business in the state in which it is organzied is termed a *domestic corporation*. Thus a corporation can be both a domestic corporation and a foreign corporation, depending upon where it is doing business.

Degrees of "Doing Business." A foreign corporation may be subject to the jurisdiction of a state other than the state of incorporation for litigation, for taxation, or for regulation, on the basis of having done business in the second state. The degree of "doing business" necessary to sustain jurisdiction is not the same, however, in the three cases. One transaction may be sufficient to provide jurisdiction for litigation relating to that transaction. For taxation, the event or relationship being taxed must have occurred within the taxing state. For a corporation to be subject to a second state's regulatory system for foreign corporations, it must conduct some more substantial amount of local business in that state.

Jurisdiction for Litigation. If a foreign corporation has been granted a certificate of authority and it does business within a state, then the foreign corporation must designate a person or another corporation as a resident agent for service of process. Thus there is no problem in securing service of process against a foreign corporation that is admitted and qualified to do business in the state.

A problem arises when a foreign corporation is doing business within a state but has not secured a certificate of authority and does not have an office nor any employees or agents within the state boundaries. In Chapter 2 we indicated that most states now have long arm civil procedure statutes. These statutes allow service of process upon foreign corporations even though they have not registered and have not appointed an agent to receive service of process within the state. Some statutes provide for service of process to the litigation state's secretary of state (who will then forward the notice to the defendant foreign corporation). Other statutes require the plaintiff to send copies of the summons and complaint directly to the out-of-state corporate defendant, by registered or certified mail. In any event, for the long arm process to be constitutionally valid, the defendant foreign corporation must have had some "minimum contact" with persons or property in the plaintiff's state. Exactly how minimal these contacts can be is not yet completely clear. (See the *Volkswagen* case in Chapter 2.)

Harlo Products Corp. v. J. I. Case Company
360 So.2d 1328 (Florida, 1978)

FACTS   Norfolk sued J. I. Case Company to recover for injuries he received when the arm of a forklift owned by Case fell on him. Case filed a third-party claim against Harlo Products, alleging that the accident had been caused by a defective component manufactured by Harlo. Harlo was a Michigan corporation with its principal place of business in Grandville, Michigan. It was not licensed to do business in Florida. Its affidavit stated that it "maintained no offices, agents, employees, bank accounts, books, records, telephone listings or other business activities in Florida." Its components were used on Case forklifts, several of which were in Florida. Harlo appealed from the trial court's refusal to grant its motion to dismiss.

ISSUE   Does Harlo have sufficient "minimum contacts" in Florida to sustain the Florida courts' jurisdiction for a lawsuit against it there?

DECISION   No. Judgment reversed.

REASONS   Judge Mills briefly reviewed the facts and then applied the principles which had been developed by the U.S. Supreme Court and the Florida precedents.
             "Before a state court can acquire personal jurisdiction over a foreign corporation, the foreign corporaton must have certain minimum contacts with the forum state so that the maintenance of the suit does not offend traditional notions of fair play and substantial justice. . . . It is necessary that there be some act by which the foreign corporation purposely avails itself of the privilege of conducting activities within the forum state, thus invoking the benefits and protection of its laws. . . .
             "In *Jack Pickard Dodge, Inc.* . . . , we held that Section 48.193(1)(f)2 was unconstitutional as applied to a North Carolina automobile dealer, who serviced a car owned by Avis who later sold it at auction in Florida to a Florida resident who was injured in Florida. . . .
             "The facts in this case, although not the same, are sufficiently similar to warrant the same result. The only allegation connecting Harlo with Florida is that it manufac-

tured a component of forklifts which are used throughout Florida. The statements in Harlo's affidavit . . . are unrefuted by Case. There are no allegations showing that Harlo purposely availed itself of the privilege of carrying on business activities in Florida or that it had minimum contacts with Florida. We hold that Section 48.193(1)(f)2 is unconstitutional as applied to the facts of this case."

Jurisdiction for Taxation. In order to tax a foreign corporation, the taxing state must show that the corporation has entered into the relationship, within the state, which the tax is designed to reach. Further, if challenged on constitutional grounds, the taxing state must show that the tax does not unfairly discriminate against interstate commerce. Where multistate relationships are involved, some rational apportionment formula must be used to allocate appropriate taxable shares to each state.

With real estate which a foreign corporation owns in the taxing state, the relationship, or "nexus," is clear. The foreign corporation, like any other landowner, will have to pay the assessed real estate taxes. Where personal property of a foreign corporation is being taxed, conflicts may arise if the property is being used in more than one state. For example, trucking companies, airlines, and railroads all have equipment which simply cannot stay in one place all year long. How much of their equipment can be taxed by each of the states where the equipment lands or travels? The following case illustrates the problem.

Braniff Airways v. *Nebraska State Board of Eq. & A.*
347 U.S. 590 (1954)

FACTS   This petition for a declaratory judgment was originally filed by Mid-Continent Airlines, which was later merged into Braniff. The plaintiff claimed that the state tax statute, as applied to its airplane fleet, was unconstitutional. The plaintiff did not challenge the fairness of the apportionment formula, which used an average of three ratios—arrivals and departures, revenue tons of freight, and originating revenue—in each case between the state of Nebraska and the entire airline system. For 1950 these figures were 9 percent, $11\frac{1}{2}$ percent, and 9 percent; and the state tax commissioner assessed a tax of $4,280.44, based on an assessed valuation of $118,901 allocable to Nebraska. The plaintiff made 14 regular stops per day at Omaha and 4 at Lincoln. These were short stops for loading and unloading, and sometimes refueling. The plaintiff owned no repair or storage facilities in Nebraska. The state Supreme Court dismissed the petition, and Braniff appealed.

ISSUE   Can the state constitutionally tax an apportioned part of the plaintiff's airline fleet?

DECISION   Yes. Judgment affirmed.

REASONS   After stating the facts, Justice Reed reviewed the relationship between national regulation of airline operations and the states' sovereignty, and the constitutional limitations on the states' power to tax interstate commerce.

"The provision pertinent to sovereignty over the navigable air space in the Air Commerce Act of 1926 was an assertion of exclusive national sovereignty. . . . The Act, however, did not expressly exclude the sovereign powers of the states. . . .

"Nor has appellant demonstrated that the Commerce Clause otherwise bars this tax as a burden on interstate commerce. We have frequently reiterated that the Commerce Clause does not immunize interstate instrumentalities from all state taxation, but that such commerce may be required to pay a nondiscriminatory share of the tax burden. And appellant does not allege that this Nebraska statute discriminates against it nor, as noted above, does it challenge the reasonableness of the apportionment prescribed by the statute. . . .

"[T]he bare question whether an instrumentality of commerce has tax situs in a state for the purpose of subjection to a property tax is one of due process. . . .

"The limitation imposed by the Due Process Clause upon state power to impose taxes upon such instrumentalities was succinctly stated in the *Ott* case: 'So far as due process is concerned, the only question is whether the tax in practical operation has relation to opportunities, benefits, or protection conferred or afforded by the taxing State.' . . .

"Thus the situs issue devolves into the question of whether 18 stops per day by appellant's aircraft is sufficient contact with Nebraska to sustain that state's power to levy an apportioned ad valorem tax on such aircraft. We think such regular contact is sufficient to establish Nebraska's power to tax even though the same aircraft do not land every day and even though none of the aircraft is continuously within the state."

Even after this decision, no uniform or standardized formula for taxing personal property was used in all states. The threat of multiple taxation continues to be a problem for corporations using property in more than one state.

Many difficulties also exist in the area of income taxation. Each state of course wants to tax as much of the foreign corporation's income as possible. In a landmark case the U.S. Supreme Court upheld the state of Minnesota in its taxation of income of which the Northwestern States Portland Cement Company derived from sales in interstate commerce rather than intrastate business. After the decision in that case Congress enacted the interstate income law, which provides that a tax cannot be imposed on net income of a person or a corporation engaged in interstate business where the only activity of the person or the corporation is to solicit orders for the sale of tangible personal property, the orders are sent outside the state for approval or rejection, and approved orders are shipped or delivered from a point outside the state. The law also exempts income which a foreign corporation derives from selling or soliciting sales through independent contractors, even though the independent contractor may have an office within the state. There will continue to be many litigations in this area, since the revenue needs of the taxing state must be balanced against the discriminatory effect of the tax on interstate commerce and since the tax statute must provide a rational apportionment formula for multistate income.

913

Federated Department Stores, Inc. v. Gerosa
213 N.E.2d 677 (New York, 1965)

FACTS Federated was a Delaware corporation with its princpal office in Cincinnati, Ohio. It owned and operated 42 retail and specialty stores in 11 states, including 3 in New York—Abraham & Straus in Brooklyn and Bloomingdale's in Manhattan and Queens. Some deliveries from the New York stores were made to customers in New Jersey and Connecticut. New York City imposed an excise tax on the privilege of doing business there and authorized its comptroller to develop a formula to allocate that portion of a company's interstate business which was attributable to the city for tax purposes. An earlier formula which provided for a one-third minimum to be taxed by the city had been held invalid by the court. The comptroller then devised a new formula, without the minimum, which weighed "the total property and total wages within and without the city deemed to have produced the interstate business; the amount of wholly taxable business (that done in intrastate transactions); the amount of wholly untaxed business (that done outside the State); and the allocable business (that done in interstate commerce emanating from the city." This new formula made from 45 to 48 percent of Federated's allocable interstate business taxable by the city in the years 1953 to 1959. Federated appealed from the lower courts' determination that it owed the taxes as assessed.

ISSUE Does the formula make a reasonable allocation?

DECISION Yes. Judgment affirmed.

REASONS Justice Bergan, writing for the majority, felt that the basic problem with the plaintiff's case was that the plaintiff had not demonstrated any *actual* unfair results, as the formula had been applied to its operations.

"Even interstate business 'must pay its way.' . . . The ultimate test of local taxability is whether the tax attaches or not to activities 'carried on within the state.' . . .

"Any formula purporting to be general in application must use some artificial assumptions. Business enterprises differ greatly. . . . The formula, however, must serve different kinds of enterprises. What the formula must offer is not perfection but a 'rough approximation' of a just allocation. . . .

"Although the petitioner owns many department stores in other States, the contribution which these operations make to the sale of the three New York City stores of merchandise delivered to New Jersey and Connecticut is, so far as the record demonstrates, nil; and while the policy-making and accounting, and other related control procedures pursued in the main office at Cincinnati, undoubtedly play some part in the interstate activity of the New York City stores, the part played is not shown to have large significance in a fair allocation of the basic activity which produced the sales. . . .

"The business of retail sales is a thing closely related to the place where a store is. . . .

"Petitioner's main argument for invalidity of this formula suggests that the tax tends to increase as a taxpayer's out-of-State and hence wholly nontaxable receipts increase when the relative amounts of property and wages are constant. If one carries through calculations required by the formula, keeping the property and wages at the same level, this can be seen to be borne out. . . .

914

> "[T]he city contends that the actual application of the formula 'is overgenerous to a taxpayer in petitioner's circumstances.'
>
> "Whether it is overgenerous or not, its application is not demonstrated to be unfair or to represent an unreasonable thrust on the interstate activities of petitioner. . . .
>
> "If such cases actually occur, the Comptroller has the power, and it would be his duty, to make adjustments which would keep the formula within a reasonable attribution to the local business activity in the city."

Jurisdiction for Regulation. Since a foreign corporation is not a "citizen" under the 14th Amendment, it has no right to transact intrastate business in states other than the state of its creation. However, all of the states have provisions in their corporation laws which allow foreign corporations to do intrastate business upon compliance with certain filing and licensing requirements. Moreover, a foreign corporation may transact interstate business across a state's borders without being required to file and comply with the state's requirements for foreign corporations. Interstate commerce, that is, commerce among the states, is regulated by the national government under the authority of the Interstate Commerce Clause of the U.S. Constitution (Article I, Section 8). The individual states may not interfere with, burden, or discriminate against interstate commerce by their laws or regulations. The question which then arises is: What is interstate commerce, and what is intrastate commerce. The Model Business Corporation Act sets out some general guidelines as to the activities of foreign corporations which will not be regarded as doing business in a state and will not require filing as a foreign corporation. These activities include selling goods through an independent contractor in another state; soliciting or procuring by mail orders which will be accepted in a home state rather than in the state where they are solicited; conducting isolated transactions; maintaining a bank account; maintaining an office or agency for the transfer, exchange, and registration of the corporation's securities; holding meetings of directors or shareholders; maintaining or defending a lawsuit; or taking out loans or mortgages. The common element in all of these examples is that the foreign corporation is not intending to conduct a long-term business in the state; does not have employees, agents, or property within the state; and thus is dealing in interstate commerce only. Section 106 of the Model Act specifically states that the list it sets out is not exclusive. There is no clear rule of thumb as to what is and what is not interstate commerce. Thus each case is going to have to review separately the amount of business conducted, the type of business conducted, the time span, and so on.

Rochester Capital Leasing Corp. v. Schilling
448 S.W.2d 64 (Tennessee, 1969)

FACTS The plaintiff, a New York corporation with its principal place of business in Rochester, New York, was in the business of leasing machines and equipment. Schilling had leased 25 postage stamp vending machines at $55.35 a month for five years. The machines were delivered, but Schilling claimed that he had been defrauded by the salesman of a Florida company which had initially arranged the lease contract. Schilling refused to pay, and Rochester sued. Rochester was not registered to do business as a foreign corporation in Tennessee. It had no agents or employees there, and all dealings with it in this case had been by mail. The lease contract had been approved by Rochester at its New York office and had provided that all payments should be made there. The trial court dismissed the suit because Rochester was not registered to do business; the court of appeals affirmed; and Rochester then appealed to the Supreme Court.

ISSUE Was Rochester "doing business" in Tennessee so as to require registration?

DECISION No. Judgment reversed and case remanded for a new trial.

REASONS Justice McCanless compared the facts of this case with those of two precedents. In one, where all negotiations were by mail and where the loan contract was made in New York and was to be paid there, a New York corporation which made a loan to a Tennessee resident and used Tennessee land as collateral had been held to be exempt from the registration requirement. In the other, where United Artists rented a local studio in Tennessee, hired an operator there, showed films there to theater owners and the board of censors, and then made contracts with exhibitors, United Artists had been held to be doing local business and had been required to register. Clearly, Justice McCanless felt, Rochester was more like the loan company than like United Artists.

"In this case the plaintiff had no agents in the State, and its only activity that was related to this State was to enter into a contract in the State of New York for the leasing of personal property located in Tennessee in consideration of monthly rent to be paid it at its office in the State of New York. . . .

"Rochester . . . was a mere property owner and investor; it invested in a lease contract providing for the payment to it periodically of a fixed amount of money. Its investment was comparable to the holder of a promissory note of a Tennessee citizen payable to a nonresident payee.

"We conclude that the plaintiff's acts did not constitute doing business in Tennessee within the meaning of Section 48–902, Tennessee Code Annotated, and that it was error for the court to dismiss its suit on that ground."

Procedure for Admission and Regulation of Foreign Corporations. Sections 106 to 111 of the Model Business Corporation Act set out procedures for the admission of foreign corporations and regulations concerning the doing of local business in a particular state. These provisions have been adopted generally by most of the states. However, it must be remembered that this was a "model" act and that not all states adopted it verbatim. Many states have made specific changes to take care of specific problems.

Generally speaking, a foreign corporation doing local business within a state must apply for a certificate of authority. Such an application will normally require the name of the corporation, when and where it was incorporated, the names and addresses of the directors and corporate officers, a breakdown of the number and types of shares issued, and authorization the corporation has regarding the further issuance of stock. The corporation will also be required to estimate the value of the property, both real and personal, that it intends to own within the state and the gross amount of the business that it will transact within the state in the coming year. In addition, it will have to designate some person within the state to be the registered agent upon whom service of process for lawsuits can be made and it will have to maintain a registered office within the state. A license fee must accompany the application. This license fee will differ from state to state. A franchise tax may be assessed annually, based on the corporation's property within the state and the business it conducts there. The foreign corporation must file an annual report similar to the annual reports filed by domestic corporations.

Penalties for Doing Business without Authority to Do So. The Model Business Corporation Act states that a foreign corporation which transacts business within a state without first obtaining a certificate of authority will not be permitted to bring any lawsuit in a court of that state until it has obtained a certificate of authority. The compliance with the requirements for the certificate of authority can be retroactive, thus allowing the corporation to sue on transactions that were consummated prior to the granting of the certificate of authority. The Model Act goes on to state that the failure of a foreign corporation to obtain a certificate of authority to transact business in a state will not impair the validity of any contracts or acts of the corporation and will not prevent the corporation from defending any action brought against it in a court in the state. Thus a corporation does not have the right to bring action as a plaintiff in the courts in a state where it is not authorized to do business; however, it does have the right to defend itself. Next the Model Act states that the foreign corporation will be liable for all fees and franchise taxes which it would have paid had it duly applied for a certificate of authority and received it. Also, many states have statutory penalties for doing business without first obtaining permission. These penalties may be fines imposed upon the corporation or its individual officers, directors, or resident agents. Another penalty imposed by some states is to make the officers, the directors, and any agents involved in contracts personally liable on the contracts, in effect taking away the corporate shield against liability. Again, it must be noted that not all states have adopted the Model Act in its entirety, and thus there are still differences in the treatment of foreign corporations which fail to comply with the requirements of a particular state. Before doing business in a state, a foreign corporation should check out the state's law carefully.

CASES FOR DISCUSSION

MOBIL OIL CORPORATION v. COMMISSIONER OF TAXES OF VERMONT

100 S. Ct. 1223 (1980)

Blackmun, Justice

In this case we are called upon to consider constitutional limits on a nondomiciliary State's taxation of income received by a domestic corporation in the form of dividends from subsidiaries and affiliates doing business abroad. The State of Vermont imposed a tax, calculated by means of an apportionment formula, upon appellant's so-called foreign source dividend income for the taxable years 1970, 1971, and 1972. The Supreme Court of Vermont sustained that tax. . . .

Appellant Mobil Oil Corporation is a corporation organized under the laws of the State of New York. It has its principal place of business and its "commercial domicile" in New York City. It is authorized to do business in Vermont.

Mobil engages in an integrated petroleum business, ranging from exploration for petroleum reserves to production, refining, transportation, and distribution and sale of petroleum and petroleum products. It also engages in related chemical and mining enterprises. It does business in over 40 of our States and in the District of Columbia as well as in a number of foreign countries.

Much of appellant's business abroad is conducted through wholly and partly owned subsidiaries and affiliates. Many of these are corporations organized under the laws of foreign nations; a number, however, are domestically incorporated in States other than Vermont. None of appellant's subsidiaries or affiliates conducts business in Vermont, and appellant's shareholdings in those corporations are controlled and managed elsewhere, presumably from the headquarters in New York City.

In Vermont, appellant's business activities are confined to wholesale and retail marketing of petroleum and related products. Mobil has no oil or

gas production or refineries within the State. Although appellant's business activity in Vermont is by no means insignificant, it forms but a small part of the corporation's worldwide enterprise. . . .

Vermont imposes an annual net income tax on every corporation doing business within the State. Under its scheme, net income is defined as the taxable income of the taxpayer "under the laws of the United States." . . . If a taxpayer corporation does business both within and without Vermont, the State taxes only that portion of the net income attributable to it under a three-factor apportionment formula. In order to determine that portion, net income is multiplied by a fraction representing the arithmetic average of the ratios of sales, payroll, and property values within Vermont to those of the corporation as a whole. . . .

It long has been established that the income of a business operating in interstate commerce is not immune from fairly apportioned state taxation. . . . For a State to tax income generated in interstate commerce, the Due Process Clause of the 14th Amendment imposes two requirements: a "minimal connection" between the interstate activities and the taxing State, and a rational relationship between the income attributed to the State and the intrastate values of the enterprise. . . . The requisite "nexus" is supplied if the corporation avails itself of the "substantial privilege of carrying on business" within the State; and "[t]he fact that a tax is contingent upon events brought to pass without a state does not destroy the nexus between such a tax and transactions within a state for which the tax is an exaction."

We do not understand appellant to contest these general principles. . . . What appellant does seek to establish, in the due process phase of its argument, is that its *dividend* income must be excepted from the general principle of apportionability because it lacks a satisfactory nexus with appellant's business activities in Vermont. To carve that out as an exception, appellant must demonstrate something about the nature of this income that distinguishes it from operating income, a proper portion of which the State concededly may tax. From appellant's argument we discern two potential differentiating factors: the "foreign source" of the income, and the fact that it is received in the form of dividends from subsidiaries and affiliates.

The argument that the source of the income precludes its taxability runs contrary to precedent. In the past, apportionability often has been challenged by the contention that income earned in one State may not be taxed in another if the source of the income may be ascertained by separate geographical accounting. The Court has rejected that contention so long as the intrastate and extra-state activities formed part of a single unitary business. . . .

The Court has applied the same rationale to businesses operating both here and abroad. . . .

[T]he linchpin of apportionability in the field of state income taxation is the unitary business principle. In accord with this principle, what appellant must show, in order to establish that its dividend income is not subject to an apportioned tax in Vermont, is that the income was earned in the course of activities unrelated to the sale of petroleum products in that State. . . . [A]ppellant has made no effort to demonstrate that the foreign operations of its subsidiaries and affiliates are distinct in any business or economic sense from its petroleum sales activities in Vermont. Indeed, all indications in the record are to the contrary, since it appears that these foreign activities are part of appellant's integrated petroleum enterprise. In the absence of any proof of discrete business enterprise, Vermont was entitled to conclude that the dividend income's foreign source did not destroy the requisite nexus with in-state activities. . . .

Nor do we find particularly persuasive Mobil's attempt to identify a separate business in its holding company function. So long as dividends from subsidiaries and affiliates reflect profits derived from a functionally integrated enterprise, those dividends are income to the parent earned in a unitary business. One must look principally at the underlying activity, not at the form of investment, to determine the propriety of apportionability. . . .

In addition to its due process challenge, appellant contends that Vermont's tax imposes a burden on interstate and foreign commerce by subjecting appellant's dividend income to a substantial risk of multiple taxation. . . .

Mobil no doubt enjoys privileges and protections conferred by New York law with respect to ownership of its stock holdings, and its activities in that State no doubt supply some nexus for jurisdiction to tax. . . . But there is no reason in theory why that power should be exclusive when the dividends reflect income from a unitary business, part of which is conducted in other States. . . . Since Vermont seeks to tax income, not ownership, we hold that its interest in taxing a proportionate share of appellant's dividend income is not overridden by any interest of the State of commercial domicile. . . .

In sum, appellant has failed to demonstrate any sound basis, under either the Due Process Clause or the Commerce Clause, for establishing a constitutional preference for allocation of its foreign source dividend income to the State of commercial domicile. Because the issue has not been presented, we need not, and do not, decide what the constituent elements of a fair apportionment formula applicable to such income would be. We do hold, however, that Vermont is not precluded from taxing its proportionate share.

The judgment of the Supreme Court of Vermont is affirmed.

SOUTHERN MACHINE COMPANY v. MOHASCO INDUSTRIES, INC.

401 F.2d 374 (U.S. Sixth Circuit, 1968)

Celebrezze, Circuit Judge

This declaratory judgment action arose out of a licensing agreement between Southern Machine Company, Inc., and Mohasco Industries, Inc. . . . Southern Machine brought the action in the United States District Court for the Eastern District of Tennessee pursuant to 28 U.S.C. § 2201 joining as parties defendant Mohasco and Louisa Carpet Mills, Inc. . . . Upon the motion of Mohasco, the District Court quashed service of process and dismissed the action as to it for lack of in personam jurisdiction. Since jurisdiction over Mohasco is indispensable for the full declaratory relief sought, Southern Machine has appealed the granting of Mohasco's motion. We reverse.

Service of process was made on Mohasco outside the State of Tennessee through the Secretary of State of Tennessee. . . . The questions raised by this appeal relate solely to the power of a Tennessee court to bind Mohasco by judgment in personam. . . .

In 1965 the Tennessee legislature enacted a "long arm" statute, which, among other provisions, purports to give Tennessee courts jurisdiction over nonresidents who engage in the transaction of any business in Tennessee as to "any action or claim for relief" arising out of that business transaction. . . .

The Tennessee Long Arm Statute is a "single act" statute by which the State only purports to assume jurisdiction over causes of action arising out of the defendant's activities in the State. . . . We think it is clear that for causes of action arising out of a nonresident defendant's business activities in the State, the Tennessee legislature intended to extend the jurisdiction of Tennessee courts over a nonresident to the full extent permitted by the 14th Amendment. . . .

Having found that the Tennessee courts are authorized to reach as far as the Constitution will permit, our sole problem is determining the limits that the 14th Amendment places upon a state's extraterritorial exercise of in personam jurisdiction. In approaching that problem, a pedantic quibbling with the wording of the statute is inappropriate. The language is general and was intended to cover any business activity that had a substantial enough contact with the state to satisfy constitutional requirements.

With the issue thus narrowed, we turn to the facts of the instant case. In May, 1962, Mohasco and Southern Machine entered into a license agreement by which Southern Machine was authorized to manufacture and sell various tufting machine attachments on which Mohasco held the patent or licensing rights. The agreement contains the usual patent licensing provisions, disavowing any representation by Mohasco as to the validity and enforceability of the patents and pro-

hibiting Southern Machine from attacking the validity of the patents, and also contains some provisions peculiar to Mohasco's licensing plan. . . .

The nature and quality of a person's contact with a state that will serve as the basis for the exercise of in personam jurisdiction over the person by the state is not a subject of easy description. . . . Presence of the defendant in the forum state at the time process is served is no longer required. . . . Today, it can no longer be doubted, if it ever was, that the doing of an act or the causing of a consequence in the forum state by the defendant can satisfy the requirements of the "minimum contacts" test.

Three criteria emerge for determining the present outer limits of in personam jurisdiction based on a single act. First, the defendant must purposefully avail himself of the privilege of acting in the forum state or causing a consequence in the forum state. Second, the cause of action must arise from the defendant's activities there. Finally, the acts of the defendant or consequences caused by the defendant must have a substantial enough connection with the forum state to make the exercise of jurisdiction over the defendant reasonable.

Applying these criteria to the instant case, we first approach the sine qua non for in personam jurisdiction: Has Mohasco purposefully availed itself of the privilege of transacting business in Tennessee? In considering this question, we can first dispose of those matters that are immaterial. For example, Mohasco has denied that any of its agents have been physically present in Tennessee concerning any matter related to the licensing agreement. Physical presence of an agent is not necessary, however, for the transaction of business in a state. . . . Similarly, the contention that Southern Machine solicited the license agreement from Mohasco is immaterial. . . . Likewise, the technicalities of the execution of the contract and the contractual provisions that the contract was made in New York cannot change the business realities of the transaction. . . .

Mohasco dealt directly with a Tennessee corporation whose only manufacturing plant was located in Chattanooga. The subject of the transaction was a licensing agreement that called for the manufacture of tufting machines at that plant and that contemplated the marketing of the tufting machines in Tennessee as well as other states. Machines manufactured under the agreement have in fact been sold or leased in Tennessee to E'Con Carpet Mills, Inc., and Mohasco has presumably obtained royalties from that buyer or lessee. The license agreement's direct impact on the commerce of Tennessee can hardly be denied, and it can also hardly be denied that the parties contemplated such an impact at the time the license agreement was executed.

So it is clear that Mohasco has purposely availed itself of the privilege of transacting business in Tennessee; therefore, we can proceed to the second inquiry: Does the cause of action rise from the business transacted in the State? . . .

Since it is clear that this cause of action arises from the licensing agreement, we must confront the final question: Does the licensing agreement have a substantial enough connection with Tennessee to make it reasonable to compel Mohasco to come to Tennessee to defend this suit? We think it does. . . .

[W]hen the contract is with a resident of Tennessee, the State's interest in resolving a suit based on the contract and brought by that resident cannot be doubted. . . . Besides this contract is not a one-shot affair. Mohasco has retained substantial control over the manufacture and marketing of the attachments, and it is of no legal significance whether Mohasco has in fact exercised those powers. . . . The agreement contemplates a long continuing relationship between Mohasco and Southern Machine. Mohasco apparently thought that it could profit from such an arrangement, and it has in fact received a return from the agreement. . . . Tennessee has a continuing interest in this continuing relationship, and apparently Mohasco has a continuing interest in profiting from the Tennessee market. It cannot complain if along with the profits from the Tennessee market it must also accept the process from the Tennessee courts. . .

The judgment of the District Court is re-versed, and the case is remanded for further proceedings consistent with this opinion.

TERRAL v. BURKE CONSTRUCTION CO.
257 U.S. 529 (1922)

Taft, Chief Justice

This is an appeal from the District Court under section 238 of the Judicial Code (Comp. St. § 1215) in a case in which the law of a state is claimed to be in contravention of the Constitution of the United States.

The Burke Construction Company, a corporation organized under the laws of the state of Missouri, filed its bill against Terral, Secretary of State of Arkansas, averring that it had been licensed to do business in the state of Arkansas under an act of the Arkansas Legislature approved May 13, 1907 (Laws 1907, p. 744); that it was organized for the purpose of doing construction work, and carrying on interstate commerce, and was actually so engaged in Arkansas; that the right to do business in the state was a valuable privilege, and the revocation of the license would greatly injure it; that it had brought an original suit in the federal court of Arkansas and had removed a suit brought against it to the same federal court; that the Secretary of State was about to revoke the license because of such suit and such removal, acting under the requirement of section 1 of the act of the Legislature of Arkansas of May 13, 1907, reading as follows:

If any company shall, without the consent of the other party to any suit or proceeding brought by or against it in any court of this state, remove said suit or proceeding to any federal court, or shall institute any suit or proceeding against any citizen of this state in any federal court, it shall be the duty of the Secretary of State to forthwith revoke all authority to such company and its agents to do business in this state, and to publish such revocation in some newspaper of general circulation published in this state; and if such corporation shall thereafter continue to do business in this state, it shall be subject to the penalty of this act for each day it shall continue to do business in this state after such revocation.

The penalty fixed is not less than $1,000 a day. The Construction Company avers that this act is in contravention of section 2, article 3, i.e., the judiciary article of the federal Constitution, and of section 1 of the 14th Amendment.

The defendant filed an answer in which there were many denials. One was that the complainant was engaged in interstate commerce. The answer did not deny, however, that the complainant was a foreign corporation, that it had been duly granted a license to do business in the state of Arkansas, that its right to do business in the state thus licensed was a valuable right, that the complainant had brought suit in the federal District Court and removed another case to that court, that such suit and removal were violations of the license granted by the state of Arkansas, or that the defendant intended to cancel the plaintiff's license. . . .

The sole question presented on the record is whether a state law is unconstitutional which revokes a license to a foreign corporation to do business within the state because, while doing only a domestic business in the state, it resorts to the federal court sitting in the state.

The cases in this court in which the conflict between the power of a state to exclude a foreign corporation from doing business within its borders, and the federal constitutional right of such foreign corporation to resort to the federal courts has been considered, cannot be reconciled. . . .

The principle established by the more recent decisions of this court is that a state may not, in imposing conditions upon the privilege of a foreign corporation's doing business in the state, exact from it a waiver of the exercise of its constitutional right to resort to the federal courts, or thereafter withdraw the privilege of doing business because of its exercise of such right, whether waived in advance or not. The principle does not depend for its application on the character of the business the corporation does, whether state or interstate, although that has been suggested as a distinction in some cases. It rests on the ground that the federal Constitution confers upon citizens of one state the right to resort to federal courts in another, that state action, whether legislative or executive, necessarily calculated to curtail the free exercise of the right thus secured is void because the sovereign power of a state in excluding foreign corporations, as in the exercise of all others of its sovereign powers, is subject to the limitations of the supreme fundamental law. . . . The appellant in proposing to comply with the statute in question and revoke the license was about to violate the constitutional right of the appellee. In enjoining him the District Court was right, and its decree is

Affirmed.

PROBLEMS FOR DISCUSSION

1. Volksgeist Motor Corporation, a manufacturer of cars and trucks, challenges the validity of a tax imposed by Texas on the privilege of doing business within that state. The tax was measured by the gross wholesale sales of all motor vehicles, parts, and accessories delivered in the state. These products were all manufactured in other states and countries, but VMC did maintain a branch office in the state. The VMC manager at the branch office called on each of its dealers in the state at least once a month and helped train and motivate dealer personnel. VMC claims that the tax is discriminatory and burdensome to interstate commerce and that it is in effect a tax on the privilege of engaging in interstate commerce and thus unconstitutional. What result, and why?

2. Voyager Travel, Inc., a Vermont corporation, made a contract with Open Arms Hotel, Inc., a Nevada corporation, which specified that Open Arms would provide accommodations for a tour group of 20 of Voyager's clients. Voyager advertised a tour package called Voyager Vegas Vacation, which included rooms in the Open Arms Hotel in Las Vegas. The tour group was turned away when it arrived, because

Open Arms had overbooked. The members of the tour group sustained considerable inconvenience and loss of time and money in finding other rooms. They returned to Vermont, and now they want to sue Open Arms there, based on a provision in the Vermont civil procedure code which permits suit against a foreign corporation that makes a contract with a resident of Vermont to be performed in whole or in part by either party in Vermont. The 20 plaintiffs sue as third party-beneficiaries of the contract between Voyager and Open Arms. Is there jurisdiction in Vermont? Explain.

3. Car Carriers, Inc., was a California corporation which operated in several western states. New cars, manufactured principally in California, were shipped by railroad to major cities, where they were loaded onto Car Carriers' trucks for delivery to individual dealers. This system of delivery was used for Colorado car dealers, with Denver as the rail destination city. Colorado levied its state sales tax on Car Carriers' gross revenues earned from deliveries to Colorado dealers; the tax would be about $40,000 per year. Car Carriers says that this tax is unconstitutional since it is being levied on the privilege of doing interstate business and since Car Carriers' business is not local at all but part of the stream of interstate commerce. Should this tax be upheld? Discuss.

4. Flimsy Materials, Inc., an Idaho corporation which was not licensed to do business in Arizona, filed a lawsuit against Shatturglas Builders, Inc., an Arizona corporation, for materials sold and delivered. Shatturglas moved to dismiss the case on the basis of an Arizona statute which provided that no foreign corporation could maintain an action in an Arizona court arising out of the transaction of business in Arizona until it had secured a certificate of authority to transact business in Arizona. Flimsy filed its lawsuit in June. When Shatturglas filed its motion to dismiss in September, Flimsy had still not secured its certificate of authority from Arizona. How should the court rule? Explain.

5. Duane Hapless bought a "professional" electric razor as a graduation present for his son Harvey. Duane bought the razor from his barber in Little Rock, Arkansas. Harvey took the razor with him when he went to college at Ardmore, Oklahoma. This particular brand of electric razor was manufactured in Italy by Cantare, Inc., an Italian corporation, and distributed in the United States by a New York corporation, Zapper Products, Inc. Harvey received a severe electric shock when the razor fell apart. Can he sue some or all of these persons in Oklahoma? In Arkansas? Explain.

6. A regulatory statute in West Virginia prohibited a producer or refiner of petroleum products from operating any retail gasoline service station in the state. There were over 2,500 such service stations in the state, selling 16 different brands of gasoline. Prior to the adoption of this statute, about 4.5 percent of the stations were company-owned and -operated. Guff Oil Company challenged the constitutionality of this statue. Guff had 12 large company-owned and -operated stations in the state. Guff also owned 150 stations which it leased to individuals who operated them. In most of these stations the gasoline was sold to the dealer outright, and the dealer then resold it to individual retail customers. In a few of its 150 leased stations, however, Guff used a consignment arrangement, in which it retained title to the gasoline until it was sold by the operator of the station. Do any of Guff's arrangements violate the West Virginia statute? Is the statute valid under the Commerce Clause and the Due Process Clause? Discuss.

7. Richiekid Tire Company challenged the constitutionality of a personal property tax levied on its inventory by the state of South Carolina, under the clause of the U.S. Constitution which provides: "No state shall, without the consent of Congress, lay any Imposts or Duties on Imports or Exports, except what may be absolutely neces-

sary for executing its inspection laws." Richiekid had its regional tire warehouse in South Carolina, from which it filled orders from its franchised dealers in eight nearby states. The tires were manufactured in West Germany, loaded in bulk into sea-trucks, driven to the docks where the cab was unhooked, and then loaded onto the ship. The procedure was reversed when the ship docked at Charleston. The tires were sorted for the first time at the warehouse in South Carolina, and then they were stacked and stored, pending dealers' orders. Does Richiekid have to pay this tax? Why or why not?

8. Because of its high unemployment rate and because the oil and gas industry was one of the main sources of employment in the state, Oklahoma passed a statute which required that all oil and gas leases, easements, and right-of-way permits for pipelines contain a provision stating that qualified Oklahoma residents would be hired in preference to nonresidents for any related jobs thereon. Drillin Fools, Inc., a Texas corporation, wanted to develop some oil leases in Oklahoma with its own crews from Texas. Drillin Fools brought a lawsuit challenging the constitutionality of this statute under the Commerce Clause and the Equal Protection Clause. Is the statute valid? Explain.

Part XI
Government Regulation

47 | Securities Law and Accountants' Legal Responsibility

The securities industry is one of the most heavily regulated areas of business activity. Subject to certain exemptions, both the original issue of securities and subsequent trading are subject to detailed and complicated regulations at both the national and state levels. These regulations impose duties and liabilities not only on buyers and sellers of securities but also on the corporate issuer, its officers and directors, and its attorneys, accountants, and other experts. Noncompliance may result in serious civil and criminal penalties as well as the loss of millions of dollars of value.

STATE REGULATION OF SECURITIES

With the great surge of economic development during the late 1800s and early 1900s and the greatly increased use of the corporate form of business organization, many abuses occurred. Promoters of dubious background and resources sold investments to a gullible public in all sort of "speculative schemes which have no more basis than as many feet of blue sky," as one judge put it. To deal with these abuses, the states passed the so-called blue-sky laws, regulating transactions in securities. Standing alone, the state laws were not very effective. Some states had no such law; others did not enforce their statute very effectively. The simplest method for the fraudulent promoter was to operate across state lines from a "friendly" state, beyond the reach of state officials who were trying to enforce their statute. Moreover, the early state laws had many exemptions and were thus relatively easy to evade. Finally, since enforcement depended primarily on the victims' willingness to pursue a lawsuit, the promoters who did get "caught" could escape simply by reaching a financial settlement with the plaintiffs in the lawsuit.

Since the national securities laws specifically permit concurrent regulation by the several states, blue-sky statutes are on the books in nearly all states. The effectiveness with which these statutes are enforced still varies from state to state. The Uniform Securities Act has been adopted by about half the states. It attempts to combine all three types of state regulation: (1) antifraud provisions, which prohibit fraud in the sale of securities and provide for injunctions and criminal penalties; (2) full-disclosure provisions, similar to those in the national act, which require the disclosure of all material information to prospective purchasers of the security; and (3) broker-licensing provisions, which require registration and licensing for persons marketing securities. Most of the states which have not adopted the Uniform Securities Act have at least adopted a full-disclosure statute. Even with the Uniform Act in force, an individual state would have difficulty in preventing securities frauds without the cooperation of other states.

NATIONAL REGULATION OF SECURITIES

The fantastic boom times of the 1920s turned into the depression of the 1930s. Many an investment bubble was punctured by the great stock market crash of 1929. The 1929 crash exposed to the public for the first time the widespread price manipulations and credit abuses which had characterized the stock market of the 1920s. The first New Deal Congress passed the two main pieces of national securities legislation—the Securities Act of 1933 and the Securities Exchange Act of 1934. Other legislation followed, such as the Public Utility Holding Company Act of 1935, the Trust Indenture Act of 1939, the Investment Company Act of 1940, and the Investment Advisors Act of 1940. More recently, Congress passed the Securities Investor Protection Act of 1970 (designed to protect investors against the insolvency of their stockbroker) and the 1975 Amendments to the 1933 Act, which extend the antifraud provisions of the act to dealers in municipal securities.

The SEC. The 1933 Act entrusted enforcement to the Federal Trade Commission, but Congress decided by the next year that this specialized area needed a specialized regulatory body. The 1934 Act thus created the Securities and Exchange Commission and gave it the responsibility for enforcing both acts. Over the years the SEC has accumulated jurisdiction under the various other securities laws that have been passed, and it also exercises important functions in corporate reorganizations in bankruptcy proceedings.

The SEC is headed by five commissioners, appointed for staggered five-year terms by the president with the advice and consent of the Senate. No more than three commissioners may be members of the same political party, but the president does have the power to name the Commission's chairperson. The SEC's headquarters is in Washington, but it has regional offices throughout the country, particularly in the large cities where corporate financing operations are concentrated. The commissioners are assisted by a large organizational staff of lawyers, accountants, economists, securities analysts, and other experts.

GOING PUBLIC: THE 1933 SECURITIES ACT

Basic Purposes. The 1933 Act was aimed solely at the first offering of a securities issue, not at later trading on the stock exchanges or over-the-counter. Its primary objective was "truth in securities": to provide the potential investor with all the information needed to make a rational decision regarding the purchase of the security. Patterned in large part after the English Companies Act of 1900, the 1933 Act did not provide for governmental "approval" of securities, in the sense of deciding whether they were good or bad investments. Its main objective was to require full disclosure by the offering company, so that the potential investor could make an informed decision. Only secondarily did the 1933 Act prohibit fraud and deceit in securities transactions generally.

Even this somewhat limited approach was a big change from the common-law rules. You will recall from Chapter 9 that mere nondisclosure was not usually regarded as a fraudulent misrepresentation unless some special facts were present in the case. The 1933 Act imposed on the offering corporation a positive legal duty to speak out and tell the truth, and the whole truth, about the offered security.

Definition of "Security." The costs involved in complying with the full-disclosure requirement can be very high. With lawyers, accountants, experts, printers, and others all having to be paid professional fees, a quarter of a million dollars doesn't go very far. Since these costs have to be deducted from profits, promoters are always looking for "moneymaking" schemes that don't have to comply with the requirements of the 1933 Act.

Only "securities" are covered by the 1933 Act, but the courts have given that term a very broad definition. So does the Act:

The term "security" means any note, stock, treasury stock, bond, debenture, evidence of indebtedness, certificate of interest or participation in any profit-sharing agreement, collateral-trust certificate, preorganization certificate or subscription, transferable share, investment contract, voting-trust certificate, certificate of deposit for a security, fractional undivided interest in oil, gas, or other mineral rights, or, in general, any interest or instrument commonly known as a "security," or any certificate of interest or participation in, temporary or interim certificate for, receipt for, guarantee of, or warrant or right to subscribe to or purchase, any of the foregoing. . . .

With that definition, it's hard to imagine any investment that's not a "security," but promoters keep trying, as the following case shows.

Securities and Exchange Commission v. *Koscot Interplanetary, Inc.*
497 F.2d 473 (U.S. Fifth Circuit, 1974)

FACTS   The SEC asked for an injunction to stop the sale of unregistered "securities" and to prohibit fraudulent practices in connection with their sale. The U.S. district court denied the injunction, and the SEC appealed.

Koscot was one of the subsidiaries of Glen W. Turner Enterprises; it was organized as a multilevel network of distributors for a line of cosmetics. Distributors received cash bonuses ranging up to $3,000 for each new person who was brought into the plan and advanced up the distribution chain. Prospective distributors were introduced to the plan at "Opportunity Meetings," which were to be run exactly according to a company-prepared script. Distributors were told to dress and live as if they had a very large income, so as to impress the prospects. At the Opportunity Meetings, films were shown, speeches were made, and high-pressure sales tactics were used to try to get the prospects to "make a decision."

The highest level distributorship cost $5,000. It entitled the holder to buy cosmetics for resale or personal use at a 65 percent discount. It also gave the holder the right to recruit prospects and to receive cash bonuses when the new recruits moved to higher levels as well as override commissions on all the sales they made.

ISSUE   Were these franchised distributorships "securities"?

DECISION   Yes. Judgment reversed and case remanded (for injunction).

REASONS   The distributorships did not meet the statutory definition of being "commonly known as a security," so the court of appeals had to look for other authority. Its problem was that the leading U.S. Supreme Court precedent, the *Howey* case, which had been relied on by the district court, said that a security was "a contract, transaction or scheme whereby a person invests his money in a common enterprise and is led to expect profits solely from the efforts of the promoter or a third party." In other words, the investor is not running his or her own business but is simply putting up the money for others to use. In the Koscot scheme, there was clearly an investment of money. But since each investor owned a separate distributorship, and since the investors each earned more or less money as *they* sold the products and recruited new distributors, the *Howey* definition didn't seem to fit too well.

The court of appeals, however, worked its way around the *Howey* case: The critical factor is not the similitude or coincidence of investor input, but rather the uniformity of impact of the promoter's efforts.

". . . [T]he fact that an investor's return is independent of that of other investors in the scheme is not decisive. Rather, the requisite commonality is evidenced by the fact that the fortunes of all investors are inextricably tied to the efficacy of the Koscot meetings and guidelines on recruiting prospects and consummating a sale.

"[T]he critical issue in this case is whether a literal or functional approach to the 'solely from the efforts of others' test should be adopted, i.e., whether the exertion of some effort by an investor is inimical to the holding that an investment scheme falls within the definition.

The court then said that the proper test was one adopted by the Ninth Circuit in an earlier case against Glen Turner Enterprises: "whether the efforts made by those other than the investor are the undeniably significant ones, those essential managerial efforts which affect the success or failure of the enterprise." Since the presentations at the Opportunity Meetings were run from a company script, the court said that "the role of investors at these meetings can be characterized as little more than a perfunctory one"; that the closing of a sale to a new investor "is essentially a ministerial not managerial one"; that following the script was merely a "nominal" function; and that "the critical determinant of the success of the Koscot Enterprise lies with the luring effect of the opportunity meetings." In sum, said the court, "the Koscot scheme does not qualify as a conventional franchising arrangement"; it is a security and must be registered under the 1933 Act.

As a result of this and many other cases filed by state attorneys general, Koscot and similar organizations were virtually run out of business. But new "multilevel" schemes have continued to sprout. Many states now have statutes regulating franchise investments which prohibit or strictly limit the use of such multilevel plans. Because of the ingenuity of promoters, the definition of a security has to be flexible.

Exemptions. Not every offering of securities is subject to the 1933 Act. Some *types* of securities and some *transactions* in securities are exempted. These exemptions only eliminate the need to register the security through SEC procedures; the antifraud (and other) provisions still apply. Short-term commercial paper, ordinarily bought by banks rather than being issued to the general public, is exempt from SEC registration. Securities issued by governmental agencies and nonprofit organizations such as churches and schools are exempt. Transactions which involve only a private offering or which are exclusively intrastate in nature are exempt; in both of these cases the process of qualifying the securities for the exemption requires expert advice. Most individual sales of securities are exempt; the 1933 Act is aimed at the issuer, underwriter, and broker making the initial offering. The SEC is authorized by statute to provide a simplified registration procedure for issues which do not involve more than a minimal amount, currently set at $1,500,000.

Securities and Exchange Commission v. *Ralston Purina Co.*
346 U.S. 119 (1953)

FACTS   Ralston Purina had encouraged its employees to own the company's stock at least since 1911. Between 1947 and 1951 it sold nearly $2 million worth of stock to "key employees" without registering the offering. *Key employees* was defined to include employees who were eligible for promotion, who influenced others, who were sympathetic to management, and who were likely to be promoted. The stock offering was not made to all 7,000 employees. Among those buying stock were persons in the following job categories: artist, bakeshop foreman, chow loading foreman, clerical assistant, copywriter, electrician, stock clerk, mill office clerk, order credit trainee, production trainee, stenographer, and veterinarian. In four of the five years involved here, between 200 and 500 employees had bought stock in the company. The SEC's request for an injunction was dismissed by the U.S. district court, and the court of appeals affirmed.

ISSUE   Were the company's sales of its own stock to its employees a "public offering"?

DECISION   Yes. Judgment reversed.

REASONS   After reviewing the facts, Justice Clark first noted that an offering did not have to be made to the whole world in order to be "public" within the meaning of the 1933 Act. Even the company apparently conceded that an offering to all of its employees would have been a public offering. As Justice Clark saw it, the exemptions in Section 4(1) should be limited to situations where the act's protection wasn't really necessary.

Registration Statement and Prospectus. The corporation issuing nonexempt securities must file multiple copies of a registration statement with the SEC, prior to offering the securities for sale to investors. The registration statement is the basic document for making "full disclosure." It must include information on such things as the company's business, organizational structure, and financial structure and condition; how the proceeds of the new issue are to be used; agreements for the distribution of the new issue; and extraordinary business contracts. The registration statement must be signed by the issuing company, its principal officers, at least a majority of the board of directors, and any expert named as having prepared or certified part of the statement. Certified financial statements for the current year and the last two years must also be filed.

The registration statement becomes effective 20 days after filing unless the SEC advances the effective date or requires further data, in which case the 20 days starts again when the supplement is filed. Technically, the SEC doesn't have the power to "disapprove" a security because it's a bad investment, but by delaying and by requiring many negative disclosure statements, the SEC can certainly try to discourage the issuer. Where there are any delays in the final effective date, all materials in the registration statement must be reviewed to make sure they are still completely accurate.

The prospectus contains most of the information noted above, but not necessarily all of the exhibits or all of the details on how the securities are to be distributed. The prospectus is the document given directly to offeree-buyers. Like the registration statement, it must be accurate *and* complete; literally true information which is misleading in the context in which it is stated, is a violation.

Antifraud Provisions.   In addition to its disclosure requirements, the 1933 Act also contains a very broad prohibition in Section 17 against securities fraud. This section covers "any device, scheme, or artifice to defraud" and "any transaction, practice, or course of business which operates or would operate as a fraud or deceit upon the purchaser." It includes both false statements and material omissions which make otherwise true statements misleading. Securities which are exempt from registration are *not* exempt from these antifraud provisions.

BEING PUBLIC: THE 1934 SECURITIES EXCHANGE ACT

Basic Purposes.   While the 1933 Act dealt primarily with the initial offering of a securities issue, the 1934 Act attempted to deal with the abuses and manipulations which occurred once the stock got into the market. The original basis for regulation was that the security was traded on one of the national stock exchanges (clearly "interstate commerce"), but more recent amendments require registration where the corporation has total assets of $1 million or more and a class of equity securities held by 500 or more persons. (Bonds are not *equity* securities; bondholders are creditors, so a company could have a class of bonds held by more than 500 persons and not have to register under the 1934 Act.) Once these minimum standards apply, all sorts of burdensom (and costly) regulations apply to the corporation and its stockholders. For this reason, there has been a considerable movement in recent years to "go private," that is, to buy back enough shares to reduce the number of stockholders below 500 and "deregister" the stock.

If the 1934 Act applies, the stock must be registered with the SEC, and if the stock is traded on an exchange, it must be registered with the exchange as well. These registration requirements are similar to those under the 1933 Act. In addition, certified annual reports must be filed each year, disclosing such matters as management changes, important legal proceedings, significant asset changes, and other material business events.

Ownership and Proxy Regulations.   The SEC has adopted extensive regulations to try to prevent injury to the corporation or its shareholders by a few dominant "insiders" or by an outside group trying to take control. Within 10 days after becoming the "beneficial owner" of more than 5 percent of a registered equity security, the owner must file a disclosure statement with the SEC and send copies to the issuing corporation and to any stock exchange on which the shares are traded. The owner must disclose who he or she is, why he or she bought the shares, how many shares are owned, and where the funds came from to buy them. Updated reports must be filed 10 days after the end of any month in which the owner has changed the amount of his or her holdings.

Such beneficial owners must turn over to the corporation any "short-swing" profits (purchase and sale of their company's shares within a six-month period) where the owner holds more than 10 percent of the stock. A stockholder with only 9 percent ownership could keep the profits. The corporation's directors and officers are also covered by this rule (Section 16 of the 1934 Act). If the buying and selling transactions extend beyond six months, all of these persons (directors, officers, 10 percent owners) could keep their profits. The basic reason for this short-swing rule is that insiders should not be allowed to take financial advantage of inside corporate information until there is a fair chance for it to be circulated to all investors.

Reliance Electric Co. v. Emerson Electric Co.
404 U.S. 418 (1972)

FACTS   Emerson bought 13.2 percent of the shares of Dodge Manufacturing Company in an attempt to take over Dodge. These shares were bought in June 1967 at a price of $63 per share. Shortly thereafter, Dodge merged with Reliance. Emerson decided to sell its shares in Dodge, since a takeover was no longer possible. On August 28, Emerson sold 37,000 Dodge shares at $68 per share; this sale meant that it then held 9.96 percent of the Dodge shares outstanding. Emerson then sold its remaining shares on September 11, at $69. Reliance, as Dodge's successor, demanded all the profits made by Emerson on both sales. Emerson said that it had not been a 10 percent shareholder when it bought the stock in the first place and that it was liable at most for the profit it made on the first sale. Emerson filed this lawsuit for a declaratory judgment as to its liabilty under Section 16(b) of the 1934 Act. The U.S. district court said that Emerson was liable for all profits, but the U.S. court of appeals said that Emerson only had to give up the profit on the first sale. Reliance asked for certiorari.

ISSUE   Where a stockholder owning more than 10 percent of the shares in a corporation disposes of its holdings in more than one transaction, must it give up all of its profits if it becomes the holder of less than 10 percent after one of these sales?

DECISION   No. Judgment of the court of appeals affirmed.

REASONS   Emerson did not ask the U.S. Supreme Court to review the district court's decision on its first argument—that it was not liable at all under Section 16(b) because it had not owned any stock when it purchased the 13.2 percent. The court of appeals had also agreed that 16(b) applied if the initial purchase of stock made the stockholder the owner of over 10 percent.

In handling the issue that it had to decide, Justice Stewart, writing for the Supreme Court, looked at the reason why 16(b) had been added to the 1934 Act. It had been included as a kind of "strict liability" provision; all profits made within the six-month period were to be turned over to the corporation, regardless of the stockholder's good or bad motives. Justice Stewart noted, however, that Congress did not prohibit *all* transactions by investors with inside information. Investors who weren't "insiders" as defined here could keep all of their profits; so could investors who held their shares longer than six months. The question was whether the two-stage sale of the shares was also a legitimate method of avoiding 16(b) liability.

"Under the approach urged by Reliance, and adopted by the District Court, the apparent immunity of profits derived from Emerson's second sale is lost where the two sales, though independent in every other respect, are 'interrelated parts of a single plan.' . . . But a 'plan' to sell that is conceived within six months of purchase clearly would not fall within S.16(b) if the sale were made after the six months had

933

Whether they are the existing management insiders or a group of outsiders seeking to gain control, persons soliciting proxies from stockholders must file an extensive disclosure statement with the SEC. This information must also be available to the stockholders being solicited. Since the 1968 Amendments to the 1934 Act, similar disclosures must be made in connection with a cash offer to the stockholders to buy all or part of a class of shares. The SEC's proxy rules also attempt to promote "shareholder democracy" by requiring management to include most shareholder proposals in the company's proxy statement and to provide shareholder lists or send out supporting material for the sponsors of such proposals.

Antifraud Provisions. While all of the foregoing rules are important and have probably contributed to better corporate management, the most sweeping and revolutionary section of the 1934 Act is 10(b), the antifraud section. Together with the SEC's Rule 10b–5, as interpreted by the courts, this section potentially covers nearly any aspect of the securities markets one can imagine. It applies not only to the actual buyers and sellers of securities but to all other involved parties as well. It applies not only to the actual purchase and sale of securities but to *any* transaction *in connection with* their purchase and sale. It includes transactions in any securities, whether or not they are required to be listed and whether or not they are traded on an exchange. It covers much more than just common-law fraud, including such things as failure to comply with other securities law requirements, arbitrary withholding of dividends, breaches of fiduciary duty, and disclosure of too much or too little information. (See the *Texas Gulf Sulphur* case at the end of this chapter and the *Speed* case in Chapter 43.) The following landmark case defines accountants' "fraud" liability.

Ernst & Ernst v. Hochfelder
425 U.S. 185 (1976)

FACTS Leston B. Nay, president and owner of 92 percent of the stock of First Securities Company of Chicago, was involved in a fraudulent securities scheme in which Hochfelder and the other plaintiffs had invested. From 1942 to 1966 Hochfelder invested in so-called escrow accounts which supposedly carried a very high interest rate. In fact, no such accounts were listed on the books of First Securities or in the disclosure filings which First Securities sent to the SEC and the Midwest Stock Exchange. Nay was using the money for his own purposes as soon as he got it. To try to hide what he was doing, Nay had a strict rule that any incoming mail addressed to him was not to be opened by anyone else, whether or not he was there at the time. The plaintiffs argued that Ernst & Ernst had failed to use proper auditing procedures on First Securities' accounts and that if they had, they would have discovered Nay's strange rule and thus the fraud. (The fraud was not discovered until 1968, when Nay committed suicide.) The U.S. district court said that there was no case against Ernst & Ernst for *fraud* under Rule 10b–5. The Seventh Circuit Court of Appeals reversed.

ISSUE Does the complaint state a cause of action for fraud under 10b–5?

DECISION No. Judgment reversed (for Ernst & Ernst); case dismissed.

REASONS Justice Powell didn't find a specific statement in the legislative history of the 1934 Act as to whether the act was intended to cover negligent behavior as well as intentional behavior, but he did find some language that helped. One spokesman for the drafters of the act had said: "10(b) says, 'Thou shalt not devise any other cunning devices.' . . . Of course subsection (c) is a catch-all clause to prevent manipulative devices. I do not think there is any objection to that kind of clause. The Commission should have the authority to deal with new manipulative devices."

Justice Powell thought this explanation of the section was significant. "The section was described rightly as a 'catch-all' clause to enable the Commission 'to deal with new manipulative (or cunning) devices.' It is difficult to believe that any lawyer, legislative draftsman, or legislator would use these words if the intent was to create liability for merely negligent acts or omissions. Neither the legislative history nor the briefs supporting Hochfelder identify any usage or authority for construing 'manipulative (or cunning) devices' to include negligence.

"We also consider it significant that each of the express civil remedies in the 1933 Act allowing recovery for negligent conduct is subject to significant procedural restrictions not applicable under 10(b). . . . These restrictions, significantly, were imposed by amendments to the 1933 Act adopted as part of the 1934 Act." In other words, if Congress had meant to include negligent conduct under Section 10(b), it would have treated that section consistently with the other securities law sections covering negligence.

Finally, Justice Powell said that liability under SEC Rule 10(b)–5 could not exceed the power which the Congress had given the SEC in Section 10(b) of the 1934 Act.

Remedies, Liabilities, and Penalties. The SEC uses a variety of court and administrative remedies to enforce the securities laws. It may seek an injunction to halt the sale of unregistered securities. It may ask a court to order the return of illegally received profits. Administratively, it may try to prevent employment of known violators by securities firms. The SEC enters into many voluntary settlements ("consent decrees") with firms and individuals accused of violations. The accused does not admit guilt but agrees to refrain from certain specified practices, or to do certain things, in the future. Sometimes a penalty is accepted as part of the consent decree; sometimes not. Since the courts are usually quite lenient with securities law violators, the SEC feels that these consent decrees are justified in many cases.

Individual investors who have been damaged financially as a result of violations of the securities laws may bring their own lawsuits against those responsible. The problem of suing for individual relief is the same here as in any other case—legal fees. It will undoubtedly cost several thousand dollars to get a securities case instituted, and perhaps as much as $50,000 to see it through all the possible appeals and rehearings. Class action lawsuits are still possible, although the U.S. Supreme Court ruled in 1974 that each member of a "class" of potential plaintiffs has to be notified personally of the lawsuit, so that he or she can decide whether to join in as a plaintiff. Where such a class action is brought, with thousands of plaintiffs, including large institutional investors, damages can add up to millions of dollars very quickly.

Both the 1933 Act and the 1934 Act provide for criminal penalties—up to five years in prison and fines of up to $10,000 for most violations. Failure to file any report under the 1934 Act makes the issuing corporation liable for a fine of $100 per day until the required filing occurs. (A corporation can't be imprisoned, of course, but it can certainly be fined and enjoined.) Criminal cases are brought for the SEC by the U.S. Justice Department, so these two agencies must work together to prepare and present an effective criminal case. The following is one of the rare criminal cases that have been brought against accountants.

United States v. Natelli
527 F.2d 311 (Second Circuit Court of Appeals, 1975)

FACTS   Anthony Natelli and Joseph Scansaroli were prosecuted under Section 32(a) of the 1934 Act for willfully and knowingly making false and misleading statements in a corporation's proxy statement. Both were convicted in U.S. district court, and both appealed.

National Student Marketing Corporation (NSMC) was one of the hottest stocks in the boom market of the 1960s. Formed in 1966, NSMC charged fees to client businesses for marketing their products and services directly to students in an "attractive package" of merchandise. NSMC stock went public in 1968 at $6 a share; five months later it was selling at $80 a share.

Peat, Marwick, Mitchell (PMM) became NSMC's auditors in August 1968. Natelli was the engagement partner for the PMM account and the manager of PMM's office in Washington, D.C. Scansaroli was the audit supervisor for the PMM account.

NSMC counted as earned income all of the fees agreed upon by its various clients even though it would not earn these fees for several years. In making his year-end audit, Natelli decided to use as income only a completion percentage of these amounts. Many of the fee arrangements were only oral commitments. Natelli told Scansaroli to verify these accounts by calling the customers, but he did not tell Scansaroli to get written confirmations. Using NSMC's estimates of completion of its services on the accounts, a year-end adjustment for "unbilled accounts receivable" of $1,700,000 turned a loss into a profit twice that of the previous year. Natelli told NSMC that PMM would count only written commitments for future audits. About $1 million of the oral commitments had been written off by May 1969, most of them invalid because of kickbacks paid to a former NSMC executive. NSMC's 1968 income thereby went down more than $200,000, but Scansaroli and Natelli covered this by "reversing" a deferred tax credit for about the same amount. The financial statements filed with a proxy statement proposing a merger with six other firms did not show any adjustments in NSMC's profit figures for 1968. A $1.2 million commitment from Pontiac (GM) was backdated so as to be included in the period through May 31, 1969. When Natelli raised this question with NSMC, he was told that there was a commitment from Eastern Airlines for a similar amount which could be included, so he let it pass. The financial statements did not show that NSMC had written off $1 million of its 1968 sales and more than $2 million of the unbilled sales for 1968 and 1969. NSMC should have showed no profit for 1969.

ISSUE Do these improper accounting practices constitute criminal fraud?

DECISION Yes, as to Natelli (affirmed); no, as to Scansaroli (reversed).

REASONS "It is hard to probe the intent of a defendant," said Judge Gurfein. "Circumstantial evidence, particularly with proof of motive, where available, is often sufficient to convince a reasonable man of criminal intent beyond a reasonable doubt. When we deal with a defendant who is a professional accountant, it is even harder, at times, to distinguish between simple errors of judgment and errors made with sufficient criminal intent to support a conviction, especially when there is no financial gain to the accountant other than his legitimate fee."

Judge Gurfein said that Natelli's original act of adding in the unbilled sales was contrary to sound accounting practice, thus exposing him to "severe criticism and possible liability." He therefore had a motive for concealing the later write-offs that had to be made. "The accountant owes a duty to the public not to assert a privilege of silence until the next audited annual statement comes around in due time. Since companies were being acquired by Marketing for its shares in this period, Natelli had to know that the 1968 audited statement was being used continuously."

Natelli tried to argue that he didn't have to notify investors of any corrections because the earnings statements were labeled "unaudited." The court said that this might be true in an ordinary case, where the accountant did not actually know of the errors, but that here Natelli *knew* that the statements were materially false and that investors were relying on them.

As to Scansaroli, the court accepted his "following orders" defense. Whether to add in the Eastern Airlines contract was a matter for Natelli's discretion, and Scansaroli just did as he was told in recording it.

Defenses to Civil Liability. There are several possible defenses which may be used to avoid liability under the securities laws. First, the 1933 Act has a relatively short statute of limitations: Suit must be brought within one year from the discovery of the violation or from the date when it would have been discovered using reasonable diligence; in no case, however, can suit be brought more than three years after the sale. With many analysts constantly studying the markets, most large frauds would probably be discovered within that time, but in the *Hochfelder* case Nay defrauded people for some 25 years and was "discovered" only when he committed suicide.

It's at least theoretically possible for the courts to hold that a particular misstatement or omission was not material, but that is unlikely if investors have in fact sustained damage. The definition of *materiality* used in *Escott, Texas Gulf Sulphur* and similar cases is quite liberal: "any fact which *might* reasonably affect the value of the security."

While plaintiffs in securities cases don't have to prove that they specifically relied on a misstatement (as they would in a common-law fraud case), they can't recover if the defendant can prove that they knew when they entered into the securities transaction that the statement was false.

Probably the most important defense, and the one most open to interpretation, is the "due diligence" defense. This defense may be proved by any person other than the issuing corporation. As to parts of a registration statement not based on an expert's authority, the defendant is not liable if he or she can show that he or she "had, after reasonable investigation, reasonable ground to believe and did believe, at the time such part of the registration statement became effective, that the statements therein were true" (and not misleading). The standard of reasonableness specified is "that required of a prudent person in the management of his or her own property." As to the "expertised" sections of the registration statement (those certified by CPAs, engineers, or appraisers, for example), the defendant is not liable if he or she "had no reasonable ground to believe, and did not believe," that the statements were untrue or misleading. In other words, the statements made by experts can be relied on unless the defendant knew or reasonably should have known that the statements were false or misleading. However, lawyers are not necessarily "experts" on everything, under this definition. The court in the *Escott* case rejected the defendants' claim that they could rely on everything in the registration statement because it had been prepared by lawyers. Under this definition, lawyers would only be experts as to specifically legal questions, for example, the nature of the company's contingent liabilities.

SUMMARY

Compliance with the securities laws is burdensome in time, effort, and money. There are no easy shortcuts. But full and accurate compliance is clearly in the company's best interests. For all responsible individuals, the company's compliance should be checked and rechecked so as to avoid the possibility of ruinous damage suits by angry investors.

ESCOTT v. BARCHRIS CONSTRUCTION CORP.

283 F.Supp. 643 (New York, 1968)

McLean, District Judge

This is an action by purchasers of 5½ per cent convertible subordinated 15 year debentures of BarChris Construction Corporation (BarChris). Plaintiffs purport to sue on their own behalf and "on behalf of all other present and former holders" of the debentures. When the action was begun on October 25, 1962, there were nine plaintiffs. Others were subsequently permitted to intervene. At the time of the trial, there were over 60.

The action is brought under Section 11 of the Securities Act of 1933 (15 U.S.C. § 77k). Plaintiffs allege that the registration statement with respect to these debentures filed with the Securities and Exchange Commission, which became effective on May 16, 1961, contained material false statements and material omissions.

Defendants fall into three categories: (1) the persons who signed the registration statement; (2) the underwriters, consisting of eight investment banking firms, led by Drexel & Co. (Drexel); and (3) BarChris's auditors, Peat, Marwick, Mitchell & Co. . . .

The signers, in addition to BarChris itself, were the nine directors of BarChris, plus its controller, defendant Trilling, who was not a director. Of the nine directors, five were officers of BarChris, i.e., defendants Vitolo, president; Russo, executive vice president; Pugliese, vice president; Kircher, treasurer; and Birnbaum, secretary. Of the remaining four, defendant Grant was a member of the firm of Perkins, Daniels, McCormack & Collins, BarChris's attorneys. He became a director in October 1960. Defendant Coleman, a partner in Drexel, became a director on April 17, 1961, as did the other two, Auslander and Rose, who were not otherwise connected with BarChris. . . .

On the main issue of liability, the questions to be decided are (1) did the registration statement contain false statements of fact, or did it omit to state facts which should have been stated in order to prevent it from being misleading; (2) if so, were the facts which were falsely stated or omitted "material" within the meaning of the Act; (3) if so, have defendants established their affirmative defenses? . . .

BarChris was an outgrowth of a business started as a partnership by Vitolo and Pugliese in 1946. The business was incorporated in New York in 1955 under the name of B & C Bowling Alley Builders, Inc. Its name was subsequently changed to BarChris Construction Corporation. . . .

BarChris's sales increased dramatically from 1956 to 1960. According to the prospectus, net sales, in round figures, in 1956 were some $800,000, in 1957 $1,300,000, in 1958 $1,700,000. In 1959 they increased to over $3,300,000, and by 1960 they had leaped to over $9,165,000.

For some years the business had exceeded the managerial capacity of its founders. Vitolo and Pugliese are each men of limited education. Vitolo did not get beyond high school. Pugliese ended his schooling in seventh grade. Pugliese devoted his time to supervising the actual construction work. Vitolo was concerned primarily with obtaining new business. Neither was equipped to handle financial matters.

Rather early in their career they enlisted the aid of Russo, who was trained as an accountant. He first joined them in the days of the partnership, left for a time, and returned as an officer and director of B & C Bowling Alley Builders, Inc., in 1958. He eventually became executive vice president of BarChris. In that capacity he handled many of the transactions which figure in this case.

In 1959 BarChris hired Kircher, a certified public accountant who had been employed by Peat, Marwick. He started as controller and became treasurer in 1960. In October of that year, another ex-Peat, Marwick employee, Trilling, succeeded Kircher as controller. At approximately the same time Birnbaum, a young attorney, was hired as house counsel. He became secretary on April 17, 1961. . . .

Materiality

It is a prerequisite to liability under Section 11 of the Act that the fact which is falsely stated in a registration statement, or the fact that is omitted when it should have been stated to avoid misleading, be "material." . . .

The average prudent investor is not concerned with minor inaccuracies or with errors as to matters which are of no interest to him. The facts which tend to deter him from purchasing a security are facts which have an important bearing upon the nature or condition of the issuing corporation or its business.

Judged by this test, there is no doubt that many of the misstatements and omissions in this prospectus were material. This is true of all of them which relate to the state of affairs in 1961, i.e., the overstatement of sales and gross profit for the first quarter, the understatement of contingent liabilities as of April 30, the overstatement of orders on hand and the failure to disclose the true facts with respect to officers' loans, customers' delinquencies, application of proceeds, and the prospective operation of several alleys.

The misstatments and omissions pertaining to BarChris's status as of December 31, 1960, however, present a much closer question. The 1960 earnings figures, the 1960 balance sheet, and the contingent liabilities as of December 31, 1960 were not nearly as erroneous as plaintiffs have claimed. But they were wrong to some extent, as we have seen. . . .

Would it have made any difference if a prospective purchaser of these debentures had been advised of these facts? There must be some point at which errors in disclosing a company's balance sheet position become material, even to a growth-oriented investor. On all the evidence I find that these balance sheet errors were material within the meaning of Section 11.

Since there was an abundance of material misstatements pertaining to 1961 affairs, whether or not the errors in the 1960 figures were material does not affect the outcome of this case except to the extent that it bears upon liability of Peat, Marwick. That subject will be discussed herein after.

Every defendant, except BarChris itself, to whom, as the issuer, these defenses are not available, and except Peat, Marwick, whose position rests on a different statutory provision, has pleaded these affirmative defenses. Each claims that (1) as to the part of the registration statement purporting to be made on the authority of an expert (which, for convenience, I shall refer to as the "expertised portion"), he had no reasonable ground to believe and did not believe that there were any untrue statements or material omissions, and (2) as to the other parts of the registration statement, he made a reasonable investigation, as a result of which he had reasonable ground to believe and did believe that the registration statement was true and that no material fact was omitted. As to each defendant, the question is whether he has sustained the burden of proving these defenses. Surprising enough, there is little or no judicial authority on this question. No decisions directly in point under Section 11 have been found.

Before considering the evidence, a preliminary matter should be disposed of. The defendants do not agree among themselves as to who the "experts" were or as to the parts of the registration statement which were expertised. . . .

To say that the entire registration statement is expertised because some lawyer prepared it would be an unreasonable construction of the statute. Neither the lawyer for the company nor the lawyer for the underwriters is an expert within the meaning of Section 11. The only expert, in the statutory sense, was Peat, Marwick, and the only parts of the registration statement which purported to be made upon the authority of an expert were the portions which purported to be made on Peat, Marwick's authority. . . .

The Underwriters and Coleman

The underwriters other than Drexel made no investigation of the accuracy of the prospectus. One of them, Peter Morgan, had underwritten the 1959 stock issue and had been a director of

BarChris. He thus had some general familiarity with its affairs, but he knew no more than the other underwriters about the debenture prospectus. They all relied upon Drexel as the "lead" underwriter.

Drexel did make an investigation. The work was in charge of Coleman, a partner of the firm, assisted by Casperson, an associate. Drexel's attorneys acted as attorneys for the entire group of underwriters. Ballard did the work, assisted by Stanton. . . .

After Coleman was elected a director on April 17, 1961, he made no further independent investigation of the accuracy of the prospectus. He assumed that Ballard was taking care of this on his behalf as well as on behalf of the underwriters.

In April 1961 Ballard instructed Stanton to examine BarChris's minutes for the past five years and also to look at "the major contracts of the company." Stanton went to BarChris's office for that purpose on April 24. He asked Birnbaum for the minute books. He read the minutes of the board of directors and discovered interleaved in them a few minutes of executive committee meetings in 1960. He asked Kircher if there were any others. Kircher said that there had been other executive committee meetings but that the minutes had not been written up. . . .

As to the "major contracts," all that Stanton could remember seeing was an insurance policy. Birnbaum told him that there was no file of major contracts. Stanton did not examine the agreements with Talcott. He did not examine the contracts with customers. He did not look to see what contracts comprised the backlog figure. Stanton examined no accounting records of BarChris. His visit, which lasted one day, was devoted primarily to reading the directors' minutes. . . .

The other underwriters, who did nothing and relied solely on Drexel and on the lawyers, are also bound by it. It follows that although Drexel and the other underwriters believed that those portions of the prospectus were true, they had no reasonable ground for that belief, within the meaning of the statute. Hence, they have not established their due diligence defense, except as to the 1960 audited figures.

The same conclusions must apply to Coleman. Although he participated quite actively in the earlier stages of the preparation of the prospectus, and contributed questions and warnings of his own, in addition to the questions of counsel, the fact is that he stopped his participation toward the end of March 1961. He made no investigation after he became a director. When it came to verification, he relied upon his counsel to do it for him. Since counsel failed to do it, Coleman is bound by that failure. Consequently, in his case also, he has not established his due diligence defense except as to the audited 1960 figures. . . .

The 1960 Audit

Peat, Marwick's work was in general charge of a member of the firm, Cummings, and more immediately in charge of Peat, Marwick's manager, Logan. Most of the actual work was performed by a senior accountant, Berardi, who had junior assistants, one of whom was Kennedy.

Berardi was than about 30 years old. He was not yet a C.P.A. He had had no previous experience with the bowling industry. This was his first job as a senior accountant. He could hardly have been given a more difficult assignment.

After obtaining a little background information on BarChris by talking to Logan and reviewing Peat, Marwick's work papers on its 1959 audit, Berardi examined the results of test checks of BarChris's accounting procedures which one of the junior accountants had made, and he prepared an "internal control questionnaire" and an "audit program." Thereafter, for a few days subsequent to December 30, 1960, he inspected BarChris's inventories and examined certain alley construction. Finally, on January 13, 1961, he began his auditing work which he carried on substantially continuously until it was completed on February 24, 1961. Toward the close of the work, Logan reviewed it and made various comments and suggestions to Berardi. . . .

The S–1 Review

The purpose of reviewing events subsequent to the date of a certified balance sheet (referred to as an S–1 review when made with reference to a registration statement) is to ascertain whether any material change has occurred in the company's financial position which should be disclosed in order to prevent the balance sheet figures from being misleading. The scope of such a review, under generally accepted auditing standards, is limited. It does not amount to a complete audit.

Peat, Marwick prepared a written program for such a review. I find that this program conformed to generally accepted auditing standards. . . .

Berardi made the S–1 review in May 1961. He devoted a little over two days to it, a total of $20\frac{1}{2}$ hours. He did not discover any of the errors or omissions pertaining to the state of affairs in 1961 which I have previously discussed at length, all of which were material. The question is whether, despite his failure to find out anything, his investigation was reasonable within the meaning of the statute.

What Berardi did was to look at a consolidating trial balance as of March 31, 1961 which had been prepared by BarChris, compare it with the audited December 31, 1960 figures, discuss with Trilling certain unfavorable developments which the comparison disclosed, and read certain minutes. He did not examine any "important financial records" other than the trial balance. As to minutes, he read only what minutes Birnbaum gave him, which consisted only of the board of directors' minutes of BarChris. He did not read such minutes as there were of the executive committee. He did not know that there was an executive committee, hence he did not discover that Kircher had notes of executive committee minutes which had not been written up. He did not read the minutes of any subsidiary.

In substance, what Berardi did is similar to what Grant and Ballard did. He asked questions, he got answers which he considered satisfactory, and he did nothing to verify them. . . .

There had been a material change for the worse in BarChris's financial position. That change was sufficiently serious so that the failure to disclose it made the 1960 figures misleading. Berardi did not discover it. As far as results were concerned, his S–1 review was useless.

Accountants should not be held to a standard higher than that recognized in their profession. I

942

do not do so here. Berardi's review did not come up to that standard. He did not take some of the steps which Peat, Marwick's written program prescribed. He did not spend an adequate amount of time on a task of this magnitude. Most important of all, he was too easily satisfied with glib answers to his inquiries.

This is not to say that he should have made a complete audit. But there were enough danger signals in the materials which he did examine to require some further investigation on his part. Generally accepted accounting standards required such further investigation under these circumstances. It is not always sufficient merely to ask questions.

Here again, the burden of proof is on Peat, Marwick. I find that that burden has not been satisfied. I conclude that Peat, Marwick has not established its due diligence defense.

SECURITIES AND EXCHANGE COM'N v. TEXAS GULF SULPHUR CO.

401 F.2d 833 (U.S. Second Circuit, 1968)

Waterman, Circuit Judge

This action was commenced in the United States District Court for the Southern District of New York by the Securities and Exchange Commission (the SEC) pursuant to Sec. 21(e) of the Securities Exchange Act of 1934 (the Act), 15 U.S.C. § 78u(e), against Texas Gulf Sulphur Company (TGS) and several of its officers, directors, and employees, to enjoin certain conduct by TGS and the individual defendants said to violate Section 10(B) of the Act, 15 U.S.C. Section 78j(b), and Rule 10b–5 (17 CFR 240.10b–5) (the Rule), promulgated thereunder, and to compel the rescission by the individual defendants of securities transactions assertedly conducted contrary to law. The complaint alleged (1) that defendants Fogarty, Mollison, Darke, Murray, Huntington, O'Neill, Clayton, Crawford, and Coates had either personally or through agents purchased TGS stock or calls thereon from November 12, 1963 through April 16, 1964 on the basis of material inside information concerning the results of TGS drilling in Timmins, Ontario, while such information remained undisclosed to the investing public generally or to the particular sellers; (2) that defendants Darke and Coates had divulged such information to others for use in purchasing TGS stock or calls or recommended its purchase while the information was undisclosed to the public or to the sellers; (3) that defendants Stephens, Fogarty, Mollison, Holyk, and Kline had accepted options to purchase TGS stock on February 20, 1964 without disclosing the material information as to the drilling progress to either the Stock Option Committee or the TGS Board of Directors; and (4) that TGS issued a deceptive press release on April 12, 1964. The case was tried at length before Judge Bonsal of the Southern District of New York, sitting without a jury. Defendants Clayton and Crawford appeal from that part of the decision below which held that they had violated Sec. 10(b) and Rule 10b–5, and the SEC appeals from the remainder of the decision which dismissed the complaint against defendants TGS, Fogarty, Mollison, Holyk, Darke, Stephens, Kline, Murray, and Coates. . . .

This action derives from the exploratory activities of TGS begun in 1957 on the Canadian Shield in eastern Canada. In March of 1959, aerial geophysical surveys were conducted over more than 15,000 square miles of this area by a group led by defendant Mollison, a mining engineer and a Vice President of TGS. The group included defendant Holyk, TGS's chief geologist, defendant Clayton, an electrical engineer and geophysicist, and defendant Darke, a geologist. These operations resulted in the detection of numerous anomalies, i.e., extraordinary variations in the conductivity of rocks, one of which was on the Kidd 55 segment of land located near Timmins, Ontario.

On October 29 and 30, 1963, Clayton conducted a ground geophysical survey on the northeast portion of the Kidd 55 segment which confirmed the presence of an anomaly and indicated the necessity of diamond core drilling for further evaluation. Drilling of the initial hole, K–55–1, at the strongest part of the anomaly was commenced on November 8 and terminated on November 12 at a depth of 655 feet. Visual estimates by Holyk of the core of K–55–1 indicated an average copper content of 1.15 percent and an average zinc content of 8.64 percent over a length of 599 feet. This visual estimate convinced TGS that it was desirable to acquire the remainder of the Kidd 55 segment, and in order to facilitate this acquisition TGS President Stephens instructed the exploration group to keep the results of K–55–1 confidential and undisclosed even as to other officers, directors, and employees of TGS. The hole was concealed, and a barren core was intentionally drilled off the anomaly. Meanwhile, the core of K–55–1 had been shipped to Utah for chemical assay which, when received in early December, revealed an average mineral content of 1.18 percent copper, 8.26 percent zinc, and 3.94 percent ounces of silver per ton over a length of 602 feet. These results were so remarkable that neither Clayton, an experienced geophysicist, nor four other TGS expert witnesses, had never seen or heard of a comparable initial exploratory drill hole in a base metal deposit. . . .

During this period, from November 12, 1963, when K–55–1 was completed, to March 31, 1964, when drilling was resumed, certain of the individual defendants . . . , and persons . . . said to have received "tips" from them, purchased TGS stock or calls thereon. Prior to these transactions these persons had owned 1,135 shares of TGS stock and possessed no calls; thereafter they owned a total of 8,235 shares and possessed 12,300 calls. . . .

Meanwhile, rumors that a major ore strike was in the making had been circulating throughout Canada. On the morning of Saturday, April 11, Stephens at his home in Greenwich, Conn. read in the *New York Herald Tribune* and in the *New York Times* unauthorized reports of the TGS drilling which seemed to infer a rich strike from the fact that the drill cores had been flown to the United States for chemical assay. Stephens immediately contacted Fogarty at his home in Rye, N.Y., who in turn telephoned and later that day visited Mollison at Mollison's home in Greenwich to obtain a current report and evaluation of the drilling progress. The following morning, Sunday, Fogarty again telephoned Mollison, inquiring whether Mollison had any further information and told him to return to Timmins with Holyk,

943

the TGS Chief Geologist, as soon as possible "to move things along." With the aid of one Carroll, a public relations consultant, Fogarty drafted a press release designed to quell the rumors, which release, after having been channeled through Stephens and Huntington, a TGS attorney, was issued at 3:00 p.m. on Sunday, April 12, and which appeared in the morning newspapers of general circulation on Monday, April 13. It read in pertinent part as follows:

NEW YORK, April 12–The following statement was made today by Dr. Charles F. Fogarty, executive vice president of Texas Gulf Sulphur Company, in regard to the company's drilling operations near Timmins, Ontario, Canada. Dr. Fogarty said:

"During the past few days, the exploration activities of Texas Gulf Sulphur in the area of Timmins, Ontario, have been widely reported in the press, coupled with rumors of a substantial copper discovery there. These reports exaggerate the scale of operations, and mention plans and statistics of size and grade of ore that are without factual basis and have evidently originated by speculation of people not connected with TGS.

"The facts are as follows. TGS has been exploring in the Timmins area for six years as part of its overall search in Canada and elsewhere for various minerals— lead, copper, zinc, etc. During the course of this work, in Timmins as well as in Eastern Canada, TGS had conducted explorations entirely on its own, without participation by others. Numerous prospects have been investigated by geophysical means and a large number of selected ones have been core-drilled. These cores are sent to the United States for assay and detailed examination as a matter of routine and on advice of expert Canadian legal counsel. No inferences as to grade can be drawn from this procedure.

"Most of the areas drilled in Eastern Canada have revealed either barren pyrite or graphite without value; a few have resulted in discoveries of small or marginal sulphide ore bodies.

"Recent drilling on one property near Timmins had led to preliminary indications that more drilling would be required for proper evaluation of this prospect. The drilling done to date has not been conclusive, but the statements made by many outside quarters are unreliable and include information and figures that are not available to TGS.

"The work done to date has not been sufficient to reach definite conclusions and any statement as to size and grade of ore would be premature and possibly misleading. When we have progressed to the point where reasonable and logical conclusions can be made, TGS will issue a definite statement to its stockholders and to the public in order to clarify the Timmins project."

The release purported to give the Timmins drilling results as of the release date, April 12. From Mollison, Fogarty had been told of the developments through 7:00 P.M. on April 10, and of remarkable discoveries made up to that time, detailed supra, which discoveries, according to the calculations of the experts who testified for the SEC at the hearing, demonstrated that TGS had already discovered 6.2 to 8.3 million tons of proven ore having gross assay values from $26 to $29 per ton. TGS experts, on the other hand, denied at the hearing that proven or probable ore could have been calculated on April 11 or 12 because there was then no assurance of continuity in the mineralized zone. . . .

During the period of drilling in Timmins, the market price of TGS stock fluctuated but steadily gained overall. On Friday, November 8, when the drilling began, the stock closed at $17^3/8$; on Friday, November 15, after K–55–1 had been completed, it closed at 18. After a slight decline to $16^3/8$ by Friday, November 22, the price rose to $20^7/8$ by December 13, when the chemical assay results of K–55–1 were received, and closed at a high of $24^1/8$ on February 21, the day after the stock options had been issued. It had reached a price of 26 by March 31, after the land acquisition program had been completed and drilling had been resumed, and continued to ascend to $30^1/8$ by the close of trading on April 10, at which time the drilling progress up to then was evaluated for the April 12th press release. On April 13, the day on which the April 12 release was disseminated, TGS opened at $30^1/8$, rose immediately to a high of 32, and gradually tapered off to close at $30^7/8$. It closed at $30^1/4$ the next day; and at $29^3/8$ on April 15. On April 16, the day of the official announcement of the Timmins discovery, the price climbed to a high of 37 and closed at $36^3/8$. By May 15, TGS stock was selling at $58^1/4$. . . .

An insider is not, of course, always foreclosed from investing in his own company merely because he may be more familiar with company operations than are outside investors. An insider's duty to disclose information or his duty to abstain from dealing in his company's securities arises only in "those situations which are essentially extraordinary in nature and which are reasonably certain to have a substantial effect on the market price of the security if [the extraordinary situation is] disclosed." . . .

Nor is an insider obligated to confer upon outside investors the benefit of his superior financial or other expert analysis by disclosing his educated guesses or predictions. . . . The only regulatory objective is that access to material information be enjoyed equally, but this objective requires nothing more than the disclosure of basic facts so that outsiders may draw upon their own evaluative expertise in reaching their own investment decisions with knowledge equal to that of the insiders. . . .

In each case, then, whether facts are material within Rule 10b–5 when the facts relate to a particular event and are undisclosed by those persons who are knowledgeable thereof will depend at any given time upon a balancing of both the indicated probability that the event will occur and the anticipated magnitude of the event in light of the totality of the company activity. Here, notwithstanding the trial court's conclusion that the results of the first drill core, K–55–1, were "too 'remote' . . . to have had any significant impact on the market, i.e., to be deemed material, . . . knowledge of the possibility, which surely was more than marginal, of the existence of a mine of the vast magnitude indicated by the remarkably rich drill core located rather close to the surface (suggesting mineability by the less expensive open-pit method) within the confines of a large anomaly (suggesting an extensive region of mineralization) might well have affected the price of TGS stock and would certainly have been an important fact to a reasonable, if speculative, investor in deciding whether he should buy, sell, or hold. After all, this first drill core was "unusually good and . . . excited the interest and speculation of those who knew about it." . . .

Our survey of the facts found below conclusively establishes that knowledge of the results of the discovery hole, K–55–1, would have been important to a reasonable investor and might have affected the price of the stock. On April 16, *The Northern Miner,* a trade publication in wide circulation among mining stock specialists, called K–55–1, the discovery hole, "one of the most impressive drill holes completed in modern times." Roche, a Canadian broker whose firm specialized in mining securities, characterized the importance to investors of the results of K–55–1. He stated that the completion of "the first drill hole" with "a 600 foot drill core is very, very significant. . . . Anything over 200 feet is just beyond your wildest imagination." . . .

Finally, a major factor in determining whether the K–55–1 discovery was a material fact is the importance attached to the drilling results by those who knew about it. . . . The timing by those who knew of it of their stock purchases and their purchases of short-term calls—purchases in some cases by individuals who had never before purchased calls or even TGS stock—virtually compels the inference that the insiders were influenced by the drilling results. . . .

Our decision to expand the limited protection afforded outside investors by the trial court's narrow definition of materiality is not at all shaken by fears that the elimination of insider trading benefits will deplete the ranks of capable corporate managers by taking away an incentive to accept such employment. Such benefits, in essence, are forms of secret corporate compensation . . . derived at the expense of the uninformed investing public and not at the expense of the corporation which receives the sole benefit from insider incentives. . . .

The core of Rule 10b–5 is the implementation of the congressional purpose that all investors should have equal access to the rewards of participation in securities transactions. It was the intent of Congress that all members of the investing public should be subject to identical market risks—which market risks include, of course, the risk that one's evaluative capacity or one's capital available to put at risk may exceed another's capacity or capital. The insiders here were not trading on an equal footing with the outside investors. They alone were in a position to evaluate the probability and magnitude of what seemed from the outset to be a major ore strike; they alone could invest safely, secure in the expectation that the price of TGS stock would rise substantially in the event such a major strike should materialize, but would decline little, if at all, in the event of failure, for the public, ignorant at the outset of the favorable probabilities, would likewise be unaware of the unproductive exploration, and the additional exploration costs would not significantly affect TGS market prices. Such inequities based upon unequal access to knowledge should not be shrugged off as inevitable in our way of life, or, in view of the congressional concern in the area, remain uncorrected.

We hold, therefore, that all transactions in TGS stock or calls by individuals apprised of the drilling results of K–55–1 were made in violation of Rule 10b–5. Inasmuch as the visual evaluation of that drill core (a generally reliable estimate though less accurate than a chemical assay) constituted material information, those advised of the results of the visual evaluation as well as those informed of the chemical assay traded in violation of law. . . .

Whether the case before us is treated solely as an SEC enforcement proceeding or as a private action, proof of a specific intent to defraud is unnecessary. In an enforcement proceeding for equitable or prophylactic relief, the common law standard of deceptive conduct has been modified in the interest of broader protection for the investing public so that negligent insider conduct has become unlawful. . . .

At 3:00 P.M. on April 12, 1964, evidently believing it desirable to comment upon the rumors concerning the Timmins project, TGS issued the press release quoted in pertinent part, supra. The SEC argued below and maintains on this appeal that this release painted a misleading and deceptive picture of the drilling progress at the time of its issuance, and hence violated Rule 10b–5(2). . . .

We hold only that, in an action for injunctive relief, the district court has the discretionary power under Rule 10b–5 and Section 10(b) to issue an injunction, if the misleading statement resulted from a lack of due diligence on the part of TGS. The trial court did not find it necessary to decide whether TGS exercised such diligence

and has not yet attempted to resolve this issue. While the trial court concluded that TGS had exercised "reasonable business judgment under the circumstances," . . . it applied an incorrect legal standard in appraising whether TGS should have issued its April 12 release on the basis of the facts known to its draftsmen at the time of its preparation . . . and in assuming that disclosure of the full underlying facts of the Timmins situation was not a viable alternative to the vague generalities which were asserted. . . .

It is not altogether certain from the present record that the draftsmen could, as the SEC suggests, have readily obtained current reports of the drilling progress over the weekend of April 10–12, but they certainly should have obtained them if at all possible for them to do so. However, even if it were not possible to evaluate and transmit current data in time to prepare the release on April 12, it would seem that TGS could have delayed the preparation a bit until an accurate report of a rapidly changing situation was possible. . . . At the very least, if TGS felt compelled to respond to the spreading rumors of a spectacular discovery, it would have been more accurate to have stated that the situation was in flux and that the release was prepared as of April 10 information rather than purporting to report the progress "to date." Moreover, it would have obviously been better to have specifically described the known drilling progress as of April 10 by stating the basic facts. Such an explicit disclosure would have permitted the investing public to evaluate the "prospect" of a mine at Timmins without having to read between the lines to understand that preliminary indications were favorable—in itself an understatement.

The choice of an ambiguous general statement rather than a summary of the specific facts cannot reasonably be justified by any claimed urgency. The avoidance of liability for misrepresentation in the event that the Timmins project failed, a highly unlikely event as of April 12 or April 13, did not forbid the accurate and truthful divulgence of detailed results which need not, of course, have been accompanied by conclusory assertions of success. Nor is it any justification that such an explicit disclosure of the truth might

946

have "encouraged the rumor mill which they were seeking to allay."

We conclude, then, that, having established that the release was issued in a manner reasonably calculated to affect the market price of TGS and to influence the investing public, we must remand to the district court to decide whether the release was misleading to the reasonable investor and if found to be misleading, whether the court in its discretion should issue the injunction the SEC seeks.

CHIARELLA v. UNITED STATES

100 S. Ct. 1108 (1980)

Justice Powell

The question in this case is whether a person who learns from the confidential documents of one corporation that it is planning an attempt to secure control of a second corporation violates § 10(b) of the Securities Exchange Act of 1934 if he fails to disclose the impending takeover before trading in the target company's securities.

I

Petitioner is a printer by trade. In 1975 and 1976, he worked as a "markup man" in the New York composing room of Pandick Press, a financial printer. Among documents that petitioner handled were five announcements of corporate takeover bids. When these documents were delivered to the printer, the identities of the acquiring and target corporations were concealed by blank spaces or false names. The true names were sent to the printer on the night of the final printing.

The petitioner, however, was able to deduce the names of the target companies before the final printing from other information contained in the documents. Without disclosing his knowledge, petitioner purchased stock in the target companies and sold shares immediately after the takeover attempts were made public. By this method, petitioner realized a gain of slightly more than $30,000 in the course of 14 months. Subsequently, the Securities and Exchange Commis-

sion (Commission or SEC) began an investigation of his trading activities. In May 1977, petitioner entered into a consent decree with the Commission in which he agreed to return his profits to the sellers of the shares. On the same day, he was discharged by Pandick Press.

In January 1978, petitioner was indicted on 17 counts of violating § 10(b) of the Securities Exchange Act of 1934 (1934 Act) and SEC Rule 10b–5. After petitioner unsuccessfully moved to dismiss the indictment he was brought to trial and convicted on all counts.

The Court of Appeals for the Second Circuit affirmed petitioner's conviction. . . . We granted certiorari, . . . and we now reverse.

The case concerns the legal effect of the petitioner's silence. The District Court's charge permitted the jury to convict the petitioner if it found that he willfully failed to inform sellers of target company securities that he knew of a forthcoming takeover bid that would make their shares more valuable. In order to decide whether silence in such circumstances violates § 10(b), it is necessary to review the language and legislative history of the statute as well as its interpretation by the Commission and the federal courts.

Although the starting point of our inquiry is the language of the statute, § 10(b) does not state whether silence may constitute a manipulative or deceptive device. Section 10(b) was designed as a catchall clause to prevent fraudulent practices. . . . But neither the legislative history nor the statute itself affords specific guidance for the resolution of this case. When Rule 10b–5 was promulgated in 1942, the SEC did not discuss the possibility that failure to provide information might run afoul of § 10(b). . . .

That the relationship between a corporate insider and the stockholders of his corporation gives rise to the disclosure obligation is not a novel twist of the law. At common law, misrepresentation made for the purpose of inducing reliance upon the false statement is fraudulent. But one who fails to disclose material information prior to the consummation of a transaction commits fraud only when he is under a duty to do so. And the duty to disclose arises when one party has information "that the other [party] is entitled

947

to know because of a fiduciary or similar relation of trust and confidence between them."

The Federal courts have found violations of § 10(b) where corporate insiders used undisclosed information for their own benefit. . . . The cases also have emphasized, in accordance with the common-law rule, that "[t]he party charged with failing to disclose market information must be under a duty to disclose it." . . . Accordingly, a purchaser of stock who has no duty to a prospective seller because he is neither an insider nor a fiduciary has been held to have no obligation to reveal material facts. . . . [N]ot every instance of financial unfairness constitutes fraudulent activity under § 10(b). . . . Second, the element required to make silence fraudulent—a duty to disclose—is absent in this case. No duty could arise from petitioner's relationship with the sellers of the target company's securities, for petitioner had no prior dealings with them. He was not their agent, he was not a fiduciary, he was not a person in whom the sellers had placed their trust and confidence. He was, in fact, a complete stranger who dealt with the sellers only through impersonal market transactions.

We cannot affirm petitioner's conviction without recognizing a general duty between all participants in market transactions to forgo actions based on material, nonpublic information. Formulation of such a broad duty, which departs radically from the established doctrine that duty arises from a specific relationship between two parties, . . . should not be undertaken absent some explicit evidence of congressional intent.

PROBLEMS FOR DISCUSSION

1. Vincent, an incorporator of Bronco, Inc., owned 50,000 shares of its initial capital stock. As a condition of a public Bronco stock offering, the state securities commissioner required that all of the insiders' stock (including Vincent's) be placed in escrow. The insiders' stock was escrowed with the Bigger Bank. Shortly thereafter, Vincent sold 2,000 shares of Bronco stock to Katye for $2 per share. Katye was a registered securities dealer who knew that shares escrowed in this way could not be transferred legally. Three years later, when Katye demanded delivery of these shares after the securities commissioner released the escrow, Vincent refused to deliver them. Katye sues for either specific performance or damages for conversion of "her" shares. What result, and why?

2. Danny's Delight, Inc., a real estate development firm, made stock subscription offers to 14 persons, including Ferd, who was also acting as the company's legal adviser. The state's securities law exempted subscriptions from its registration requirements if the number of subscribers did not exceed 10. It also contained a provision exempting offers to sell securities (including subscription offers) which were directed to not more than 15 persons. Danny's never registered its stock. Danny's sues Ferd for the contract price of the shares to which he subscribed. Ferd denies liability. What result, and why?

3. Yankem, a dentist, owned a Piper Cub airplane which he wished to trade in for a larger, two-engine model. Yankem went to Planely Yours, Inc., a Piper dealer, and bought the plane he wanted. Planely allowed $10,000 for the Cub as a trade-in, and Yankem paid the $35,000 balance in cash. Planely gave Yankem a bill of sale which warranted good title, although Planely had floor-planned the plane through Credit Corporation and did not pay off Credit or even report the sale of the plane to it. About six months later, Yankem agreed in writing to sell the plane back to Rooney, who was the president of Planely, for 20 percent of Planely's stock. Planely's financing irregularities had still not been corrected, and Credit Corporation instituted foreclosure proceedings. Rooney sent the stock to Yankem, but Yankem refused to

deliver the plane. Rooney sues for the plane; Yankem alleges violations of the 1933 Act. What result, and why?

4. Dolly Dempsey was convicted of selling unregistered securities in violation of her state's version of the Uniform Securities Act. That act exempted sales of "any negotiable promissory note or commercial paper which arises out of a current transaction and which evidences an obligation to pay cash within 12 months of the date of issuance." Dolly was selling shares in an open-end "trust account" and issuing certificates which indicated that the principal amount invested would be repaid in six months and that four percent interest would be paid monthly. On appeal, Dolly claims that her certificates were exempt from the registration requirement. How should the appeals court rule in this case? Explain.

5. Hoppe sold live silver foxes to about 100 persons at $970 a pair for "full silver" foxes and at $700 a pair for "three-quarter silver" foxes. Each buyer also entered into a "ranching agreement" with Hoppe, in which he agreed to care for the foxes at his ranch, to sell the offspring or their pelts, and to send all of the proceeds to each pair's owner. Hoppe promised to replace foxes lost through escape, theft, or death, and he guaranteed a minimum of three pups per pair in the first year following the purchase. Hoppe's ranching fee was $50 per pair per year. The SEC sues for injunction, alleging that Hoppe is violating the securities laws. What result, and why?

6. Piano Company was a closely held South Carolina corporation. It had only four shareholders—Huey, Louis, Dewey, and Donald. From the time it was incorporated in 1956, it had been unprofitable. In 1964 Donald, who was the only shareholder actively involved in Piano's management, learned that certain market changes would make Piano very profitable. Donald persuaded the other three shareholders to sell their shares to him, without disclosing his new information. All of these representations and statements were made in person by Donald; he sent no letters, and he did not use the telephone. Do the other three shareholders have a case against Donald under Section 10(b) of the 1934 Act? Discuss.

7. Rake bought a large amount of Apco Corporation stock through a broker who used the facilities of the New York Stock Exchange, where Apco was listed. At the time of Rake's purchase, Apco's financial statements contained several serious misrepresentations, specifically, its assets and profits were grossly overstated. When these misrepresentations were disclosed, the price of Apco stock declined sharply and Rake and other investors lost money. Rake brings a class action against Apco's auditors, Beat, Airwick, & Richsell, for failure to use proper accounting techniques in preparing Apco's financial statements, for failure to detect Apco's fraud, and for issuing false financial statements. BA&R says that it should not be held liable, since it engaged in no securities transactions and it made no profit on the information which was misrepresented. Should the auditors (BA&R) be held liable? Discuss.

8. The collective bargaining contract which the Central Teamsters Union entered into with the trucking firms in its region contained a pension plan clause. All employees were required to participate in the plan, but they were not required to pay anything to the plan. The trucking firms made all contributions to the plan. An employee was required to have 20 years of continuous service in order to qualify for a pension under the plan. Herman Heep, who had been a teamster for about 25 years, was denied a pension when he retired because he had been laid off for about seven months some 10 years before and thus did not have 20 years of *continuous* service. (ERISA, which specifically regulates pension plans, had not yet taken effect when Herman retired.) Herman sues the CTU, claiming that it had sold him a security and that it had made material misstatements and omissions in violation of the 1933

and 1934 acts. The CTU denies liability under the securities acts. What result, and why?

9. Merry Lyncher, a stockbroker, developed what she thought was a surefire scheme for making money in the market. After study, she picked stocks which she thought were sure to go down in price and placed "sell" orders with other brokers. She told them that she owned these shares; otherwise, they would have required a margin deposit or refused the orders altogether. Her plan was to buy the stocks when the price went down so that she'd have them by the time she was required to deliver them. Unfortunately, the stocks she selected rose sharply in price and she defaulted on her sales contracts. The other brokers were forced to buy in at the higher market prices to cover sales to their customers, and they now sue Merry for securities fraud. Merry contends that she is not liable, since Section 17(a)(1) of the 1933 Act only protects *investors*, not brokers. Has Merry violated the securities acts? Discuss.

Antitrust | 48

Basic Policy and Interpretation.   It's hard to say whether Senator John Sherman of Ohio would be pleased with the growth of his nearly century-old offspring. The Sherman Act was passed in 1890 as the first attempt by the national government to deal with the perceived abuses of market power by the giant industrial corporations which had grown up after the Civil War. In the broadest possible language, it stated: "Every contract, combination in the form of trust or otherwise, or conspiracy, in restraint of trade or commerce among the several States, or with foreign nations, is hereby declared to be illegal." Section 2 of the act defined another broad category of offenses: "Every person who shall monopolize, or attempt to monopolize, or combine or conspire with any other person or persons, to monopolize any part of the trade or commerce among the several States, or with foreign nations, shall be deemed guilty of a misdemeanor." The act was clearly aimed at the giant concentrations of economic power which existed in many industries—the "trusts." Firms which should have been competing against each other were working together and were in many cases tied together organizationally through voting trusts (see Chapter 43). Quite clearly, the act was intended to reach such anticompetitive schemes as price-fixing, bid-rigging, and market-splitting.

The continuing dilemma of antitrust interpretation is whether the act was intended to go beyond those obvious, specific practices so as to prohibit "bigness" as such. If one company competes aggressively, builds a better product at lower cost, and succeeds in getting nearly all the potential customers to deal with it, has it violated the antitrust laws? Stated most simply, is market success illegal? This is where opinions diverge.

There are two opposing schools of thought on the basic meaning and purpose of the Sherman Act and the other antitrust laws; for want of better terminology, the "legal" school and the "economic" school. The dispute is not quite as simple as the terms suggest, since some economists support the "legal" view and many lawyers and judges take the "economic" view. The legal approach starts with the premise that size alone is not made illegal by the Sherman Act; there is specific support for this approach in the 1890 debates in Congress. To be guilty of an antitrust violation, a company must be shown to have actually abused its position of market power. What counts are the methods used and the intent of those using them. Free and fair competition means that there will be winners *and losers* in the marketplace; the winners should not be penalized if they've won "fair and square." This view of antitrust emphasizes protecting the *process* of competition rather than trying to ensure the survival of specific *competitors*. If customers want to deal with GM and IBM, should the government step in to "preserve" other carmakers and computer manufacturers? Supporters of the legal approach would answer no.

The economic approach starts from the premise that large concentrations of economic power are bad per se, that our democratic society is endangered by such power blocs, and that Congress intended the antitrust laws as a vehicle for preserving an economic structure which embraces a number of smaller independent economic units. In this view, economic efficiencies may at times have to be sacrificed in order to preserve this sort of market structure. The Robinson-Patman act of 1936 (sometimes referred to as the "anti-chain-store act") clearly points in this direction. What counts in this approach is the market structure; large size and market dominance are inherently bad. There is an antitrust violation if a company has the *potential* power to abuse, whether or not it has actually been guilty of any specific abuse. This view of antitrust is clearly most concerned with protecting *competitors*, even with insulating them from the rigors of effective competition.

Unfortunately for students, teachers, lawyers, and most of all for business firms, the antitrust laws have been interpreted *both* ways by various courts with various combinations of judges. Depending in large part on the basic policy view taken by a majority of the justices on the U.S. Supreme Court, a given course of business conduct may or may not be deemed to violate the antitrust laws. If some of the case opinions in this chapter seem to conflict, that's because they probably do conflict.

Penalties for Violation.   These basic questions of interpretation are of more than academic interest to the business community because of the broad reach of the antitrust statutes and the serious penalties which may be imposed for violations. The three basic enforcement mechanisms are criminal prosecution, civil suit by the U.S. government (the Justice Department or the Federal Trade Commission), and civil suit by private parties. Criminal cases are usually instituted by the Justice Department only for conduct which is deemed to be illegal per se (without any test of "reasonableness"), such as price-fixing. If convicted, a corporation now faces a fine of up to $1 million. For individuals, criminal penalties include a fine of up to $100,000 and/or a maximum of three years in jail. Historically, jail sentences were rarely imposed, but there is some evidence that the courts' attitude has been changing. Executives served more time in jail for price-fixing in 1978 than in the entire preceding 87 years of the Sherman Act's existence. The Justice Department was also able to establish in the electrical industry price-fixing cases in the 1960s that it does not have to accept a nolo contendere ("no contest") plea to the criminal charges. This last point is important because a plea of guilty can be used by a civil plaintiff to help prove his case for damages; a nolo plea does not admit guilt.

Because of the much higher standard of proof required in a criminal case (beyond any reasonable doubt) and the general reluctance of juries to subject someone to the chance of prison for nonviolent, business-related conduct, the Justice Department and the FTC prefer to file civil actions in many cases. Anticompetitive conduct may be enjoined; divestiture may be ordered where an illegal merger has taken place; and other civil remedies may be involved. In 1974, for instance, the FTC agreed to a settlement of its complaint against Xerox, by the terms of which Xerox was required to make its entire portfolio of about 2,000 patents available to any other firm that wanted to enter the copier market. Much of the fear of antitrust lawsuits stems from the fact that private parties can recover treble damages plus reasonable attorney fees. This measure of damages is a very real incentive to litigate, and thus a significant deterrent to antitrust violations.

Monopoly Power in One Company. In the first big case under the Sherman Act, the Sugar Trust, which controlled about 98 percent of the U.S. production, escaped liability when the Supreme Court held that manufacturing was not "commerce" and was therefore not covered by the act. This interpretation was soon overruled, and in the famous *Standard Oil* case of 1911 a majority of five justices voted to apply a "rule of reason" in antitrust cases. The Standard Oil majority correctly concluded that a literal reading of the act ("every contract") would produce absurd results since every business contract "restrains" trade in the sense of denying a particular business opportunity to others. (If you contract to buy Smith's used car, Smith has "foreclosed" others from selling you a used car, unless you need more than one. Likewise, you have "foreclosed" Smith's opportunity to sell his used car to other buyers.) Clearly, the act must have been aimed at something other than these normal business contracts with their normal business consequences. While the majority adopted a reasonableness test, they did not really apply it to the facts of the *Standard Oil* case, and ordered the combination split up without much investigation of actual economic performance.

In the landmark *Alcoa* case, in 1945, Circuit Judge Hand stated that monopoly power was illegal per se, regardless of how it had been attained and regardless of whether it had been abused. The case had been started in 1937 in U.S. district court, where Judge Caffey heard 155 witnesses, viewed 1,803 exhibits, and produced a trial record of 58,000 pages. After four years the court decided that Alcoa was not guilty on any of the 140 criminal counts. Hand and the Second Circuit Court of Appeals reversed Judge Caffey on *one* count and took that as the opportunity to radically reinterpret the Sherman Act. The appeals court found a monopoly by a very restrictive definition of the relevant market, which excluded aluminum made from reprocessed scrap and aluminum produced abroad. While the *Alcoa* decision was not reviewed by the Supreme Court, the principal stated there was generally accepted in the Supreme Court's 1946 decision in the *American Tobacco* case. The following case shows how a court's determination of the dimensions of the "relevant market" may be decisive in deciding whether there is a "monopoly."

953

U.S. v. E. I. du Pont de Nemours & Co.
351 U.S. 377 (1956)

FACTS The United States filed a civil suit under Section 4 of the Sherman Act, alleging that Du Pont had monopolized, attempted to monopolize, and conspired to monopolize interstate trade in cellophane, in violation of Section 2 of the Sherman Act. The government asked for an injunction against Du Pont and its officers and for divestiture of some operations. Du Pont produced almost 75 percent of the cellophane sold in the United States, but cellophane constituted less than 20 percent of all sales of "flexible packaging materials." The U.S. district court for Delaware held that the relevant market was all flexible packaging materials and that Du Pont had not, therefore, violated Section 2. The government appealed directly to the U.S. Supreme Court.

ISSUE Does the defendant have monopoly power over a relevant part of trade or commerce?

DECISION No. Judgment affirmed.

REASONS The Supreme Court split 4 to 3, with Justices Clark and Harlan not participating and Justice Frankfurter concurring to provide the four-justice majority. Speaking for the majority, Justice Reed saw the issue as essentially a marketing question: To what extent was there cross-elasticity of demand between and among the various types of flexible packaging materials? Justice Reed said that a decision that Du Pont had no monopoly power would make it unnecessary to decide whether Du Pont could use the "patent monopoly" or "business expertise" defenses. His opinion contained an extensive historical review of the scientific and economic aspects of the development of cellophane, beginning with its discovery in the early 1900s by the Swiss chemist Jacques Brandenberger. He found that the tremendous increase in sales and profits derived from cellophane were the result of "the expansion of the commodity-packaging habits of business" and a "trend in marketing" rather than "elimination of other producers from the relevant market." He also reviewed the policy of the Sherman Act, which was basically directed against practices that threatened competition and controlled prices. He found that Du Pont had done, and could do, neither.

"[A] party has monopoly power if it has, over 'any part of the trade or commerce among the several states,' a power of controlling prices or unreasonably restricting competition. . . .

"Senator Hoar, in discussing S.2, pointed out that monopoly involved something more than extraordinary commercial success, 'that it involved something like the use of means which made it impossible for other persons to engage in fair competition.' . . .

"Monopoly power is the power to control prices or exclude competition. . . . Du Pont has no power to prevent competition from other wrapping materials. . . .

"[W]here there are market alternatives that buyers may readily use for their purposes, illegal monopoly does not exist merely because the product said to be monopolized differs from others. If it were not so, only physically identical products would be a part of the market. . . . New wrappings appear, generally similar to cellophane; is each a monopoly? What is called for is an appraisal of the 'cross-elasticity' of demand in the trade. . . . [C]ommodities reasonably interchangeable by consumers for the same purposes make up that 'part of trade or commerce,' monopolization of which may be illegal."

In the 1960s and 1970s, the government filed monopolization charges against such industrial giants as IBM and AT&T, and threatened several times to try to break up GM. In the early 1970s, the late Senator Philip Hart of Michigan sponsored an "Industrial Reorganization Act" which would have created a new government agency with the power to restructure industries where an "oligopoly" (four or fewer firms with over 50 percent of the market) existed. In the late 1970s, as the energy crisis worsened, several states passed laws prohibiting oil companies (the large refiners) from also owning retail gas stations. Also, at this writing the FTC's case against the four large cereal makers, charging a "shared monopoly" in violation of the Sherman Act, is nearing a final disposition; such a theory would open many firms to prosecution.

Concerted Activities among Competitors. When competing companies get together to fix prices, limit output, or divide markets, the antitrust violation is clear. These practices are so inherently anticompetitive that they are classified as per se violations; that is, there is generally no "rule of reason" defense available. In the 1927 *Trenton Potteries* case, the U.S. Supreme Court held that the defendants' good motives and the reasonableness of the prices they set were both irrelevant; the power to fix reasonable prices was also the power to fix unreasonable prices at some future time. In 1940, in the *Socony-Vacuum Oil* case, the Court said that the government did not have to prove that the defendants had been successful in raising prices, only that they had conspired with the intent to do so. In a 1933 decision that stands virtually alone, the Supreme Court did rule in favor of coal producers who had entered into a "reasonable" price and output agreement; in the midst of a terrible depression, reasonable cooperation in the industry was permitted.

One of the most troublesome "conspiracy" areas involves the cooperative activities of trade associations, especially the collection and reporting of price information. The government's problem in these cases is to prevent the trade association from being used as a price-fixing mechanism while permitting legitimate cooperative activities. In cases dealing with manufacturers of sugar, lumber, and linseed oil, the Supreme Court has indicated that "reporting" of specific prices charged to specific customers is probably evidence of an agreement to charge everyone the same prices. In a case involving cement manufacturers, the Court permitted such reporting, where there was a history of some firms delivering extra, "free" cement, billing the customer, and splitting the extra profits with the contractor. The following case is a more recent example of this continuing problem.

U.S. v. Container Corporation of America
393 U.S. 333 (1969)

FACTS The government brought a civil antitrust action, alleging a price-fixing agreement in violation of Section 1 of the Sherman Act. The defendants were 18 of the 51 producers of corrugated paper containers in the southeastern United States. These 18 accounted for 90 percent of that market, and the top 6 controlled 60 percent. Each of the 18 agreed to supply the others with its latest price quote or with the price it had charged for its latest shipment to particular customers. There was no explicit agree-

955

ment to charge customers the same prices, but in most instances a competitor who received the price information would quote substantially the same price. In some cases competitors undercut prices to get a particular order, and the overall price levels had fallen. During the eight-year period covered by the complaint, the number of sellers had increased from 30 to 51; market entry was very easy since only $50,000 to $75,000 capital was needed to get started. Total demand was increasing. On these facts, the U.S. district court dismissed the complaint. The government then appealed directly to the Supreme Court.

ISSUE   Was there a price-fixing conspiracy, a per se violation?

DECISION   Yes. Judgment reversed (and case remanded for trial).

REASONS   Justice Douglas delivered the opinion of the Court, with Justice Fortas concurring and Justices Marshall, Harlan, and Stewart dissenting. Douglas felt that the agreement was tight enough, and had enough impact on prices, to be condemned under the Sherman Act as a per se violation.

"There was of course freedom to withdraw from the agreement. But the fact remains that when a defendant requested and received price information, it was affirming its willingness to furnish such information in return.

"There was to be sure an infrequency and irregularity of price exchanges between defendants. . . . Yet the essence of the agreement was to furnish price information whenever requested. . . .

"While containers vary as to dimensions, weight, color, and so on, they are substantially identical, no matter who produces them, when made to particular specifications. The prices paid depend on price alternatives. . . .

"The exchange of price information seemed to have the effect of keeping prices within a fairly narrow ambit. . . .

"The result of this reciprocal exchange of prices was to stabilize prices, though at a downward level. Knowledge of a competitor's price usually meant matching that price. The continuation of some price competition is not fatal to the Government's case. The limitation or reduction of price competition brings the case within the ban, for . . . interference with the setting of price by free market forces is unlawful *per se*. Price information exchanged in some markets may have no effect on a truly competitive price. But the corrugated container industry is dominated by relatively few sellers. The product is fungible and the competition for sales is price. The demand is inelastic, as buyers place orders only for immediate, short-run needs. The exchange of price data tends toward price uniformity. . . . Stabilizing prices as well as raising them is within the ban of S.1 of the Sherman Act. . . . The inferences are irresistible that the exchange of price information has had an anticompetitive effect in the industry, chilling the vigor of price competition. . . .

"Price is too critical, too sensitive a control to allow it to be used even in an informal manner to restrain competition."

Another difficult problem relates to the proof necessary to substantiate the conspiracy charge. Price uniformity, in and of itself, does not necessarily indicate the existence of a conspiracy, especially where similar increases can be shown to have stemmed from uniformly increased costs of production and delivery. On the other hand, specific instances of joint price increases and *reductions*, when new firms entered the market, were held to show a conspiracy based on "conscious parallelism" in the 1946 *American Tobacco* case. This doctrine was limited by the 1954 *Theatre Enterprises* decision, which stated that parallel business behavior was not itself illegal nor was it conclusive proof of an illegal conspiracy. In most such cases the existence of a conspiracy is for the jury to decide.

Resale Price Maintenance and Refusals to Deal.   For many years the manufacturers of some products have attempted in various ways to maintain control over the prices at which retailers sell the products, usually by establishing a minimum retail price. The U.S. Supreme Court decided in 1911 in the *Dr. Miles* case that such contracts between a drug manufacturer and distributors were illegal under the Sherman Act. In 1919, however, the Court held in the *Colgate* case that a manufacturer could establish unilaterally the retail prices for its products and could announce in advance that it would refuse to deal with anyone who sold the product for less than the announced price. And in the 1926 *General Electric* case, the Court said that a consignor-manufacturer (which still had title to the products) was free to set any retail price it wanted to, since the retailer was simply acting as the manufacturer's agent and was bound to follow its instructions in selling the product.

Believing that a manufacturer had a legitimate interest in maintaining the "quality image" of its product and in protecting its established dealer network from discounters' price wars, most states passed so-called fair trade laws by 1940. Congress passed the Miller-Tydings Amendment to the Sherman Act in 1937 in order to exempt such state laws from antitrust, but the U.S. Supreme Court ruled in 1951 that the amendment applied only where the retailer had *voluntarily* agreed to the resale prices. Congress then passed the McGuire Amendment to the FTC Act in 1952, so that "nonsigner" plans (if one retailer in a state agreed to the minimum prices, all retailers in that state were bound to adhere to them) were also exempt from antitrust. Even with this legislative support, manufacturers found it very difficult to "police" their minimum prices and they could not prevent an interstate shipment of goods at a lower price from a non–fair trade state. Moreover, at least 10 state courts had declared the nonsigner plant to be a violation of their state constitution by 1957. In 1975 Congress brought the fair trade movement to an end by repealing the 1937 and 1952 amendments; nearly any fair trade arrangement would now be an antitrust violation.

What about refusals to deal, as possible antitrust violations? Except for certain businesses which are bound to deal with all members of the public on an equal basis, such as innkeepers and common carriers, it is generally assumed that a business is free to decide with whom it will deal and on what terms. This principle was applied to antitrust in the *Colgate* case. In the 1960 *Parke, Davis* case, however, the Court said that where the manufacturer "entwined" its wholesalers and retailers in a policing arrangement it had created an illegal conspiracy under the Sherman Act. The following case shows another sort of "entwining."

U.S. v. General Motors Corporation
384 U.S. 127 (1966)

FACTS   The United States brought a civil action to enjoin GM and three associations of Los Angeles–area Chevrolet dealers from conspiring to restrain trade in violation of Section 1 of the Sherman Act. Chevrolet cars and trucks, as well as most other makes, were normally sold through franchised dealerships. The dealer was not restricted as to customer types or location. If a Los Angeles dealer could sell cars to San Francisco customers, he would be free to do so. Dealers were, however, prohibited by their franchise agreement with GM from moving to or establishing a new location without GM's written permission. In the late 1950s, so-called discounters appeared in the Los Angeles area. Through arrangements with a few car dealers, the discounters advertised new cars at bargain prices, usually $250 over the dealer's invoice cost. The retail customer came to the discounter, looked over literature on the cars available (and sometimes inspected a floor model), and signed the contract. The dealer then furnished the car and gave the discounter $50 for making the sale. In some cases the discounter merely referred the customer to the dealer, where the contract was finalized. By 1960 some 2,000 of 100,000 new Chevrolets in the area were sold in this way. Nonparticipating dealers, who were losing sales but being required to provide warranty work on the cars, complained to Chevrolet. After a large letter-writing campaign to GM's offices, conferences with the offending dealers by the Chevrolet regional manager ended the discounting. GM later policed the area to make sure that dealers had stopped discounting, and in several instances dealers bought back discounted cars which had been sold to GM's investigators. The district court entered judgment for the defendants.

ISSUE   Does GM's enforcement of the "location clause" constitute a conspiracy under the antitrust statutes?

DECISION   Yes. Judgment reversed.

REASONS   Justice Fortas said that the Court did not have to decide whether the "location clause" would be an unreasonable restraint of trade if GM had decided to enforce it *unilaterally*. On the facts, however, GM had not acted alone.

"We have here a classic conspiracy in restraint of trade: joint, collaborative action by dealers, the appellee associations, and General Motors to eliminate a class of competitors by terminating business dealings between them and a minority of Chevrolet dealers and to deprive franchised dealers of their freedom to deal through discounters if they so choose. Against this fact of unlawful combination, the 'location clause' is of no avail. Whatever General Motors might or might not lawfully have done to enforce individual Dealer Selling Agreements by action within the borders of those arrangements and the relationship which each defines, is beside the point. . . .

"It is of no consequence, for purposes of determining whether there has been a combination or conspiracy under S.1 of the Sherman Act, that each party acted in its own lawful interest. . . . [I]t has long been settled that explicit agreement is not a necessary part of a Sherman Act conspiracy. . . .

"There can be no doubt that the effect of the combination . . . here was to restrain trade and commerce. . . . Elimination, by joint collaborative action, of discounters from access to the market is a *per se* violation of the Act. . . .

"We note, moreover, that inherent in the success of the combination in this case was a substantial restraint upon price competition—a goal unlawful *per se* when sought to be effected by combination or conspiracy."

Tying Contracts and Exclusive Dealing Agreements. A tying contract is an arrangement whereby the customer is required to buy a product or service it may not want in order to buy the product it does want; in the retail trade, this is sometimes referred to as "full-line forcing." Tying contracts, said the Supreme Court in the 1958 *Northern Pacific Railway* case, are presumed to be illegal "because of their pernicious effect on competition and lack of any redeeming virtue." Unless some very special facts are present, tying contracts are hard to justify. The following case has been bouncing up and down in the courts for two decades.

Fortner Enterprises, Inc. v. *United States Steel Corp.*
394 U.S. 495 (1969)

FACTS   Fortner, a housing developer, brought a civil antitrust suit seeking treble damages for alleged antitrust violations. Fortner claimed that in order to borrow $2 million from U.S. Steel's wholly owned finance subsidiary, U.S. Steel Homes Credit Corporation, it had been required to agree to erect U.S. Steel's prefabricated houses on the land it was buying with the money. Fortner further alleged that U.S. Steel's prices for the houses were unreasonably high and that the houses supplied were defective. The U.S. district court in Kentucky agreed that there was a tying contract, but it entered summary judgment for U.S. Steel because Homes Credit did not have any substantial market power over credit generally and because only an insubstantial amount of commerce was affected. The U.S. court of appeals affirmed without opinion, and Fortner appealed.

ISSUE   Were there sufficient allegations of illegality to require trial on the merits?

DECISION   Yes. Judgment reversed and case remanded for trial.

REASONS   Justice Black gave the opinion for the five-justice majority, with Justices White, Fortas, Harlan, and Stewart dissenting. Black pointed out that the two requirements from the precedent cases—substantial market power over the tying product and substantial commerce involved—had been applied to justify summary judgment *against* defendants under the per se rule. A tying contract without those two requirements might still be judged illegal on its own facts.

"The complaint and affidavits filed here leave no room for doubt that the volume of commerce allegedly foreclosed was substantial. It may be true, as respondents claim, that petitioner's annual purchases of houses from U.S. Steel under the tying arrangement never exceeded $190,000 . . . , but we cannot agree with respondents that a sum of almost $200,000 is paltry or 'insubstantial.' . . . Congress has encouraged private antitrust litigation not merely to compensate those who have been directly injured but also to vindicate the important public interest in free competition. . . . For purposes of determining whether the amount of commerce foreclosed is too insubstantial to warrant prohibition of the practice, therefore, the relevant figure is the total volume of sales tied by the sales policy under challenge, not the portion of this total accounted for by the particular plaintiff who brings suit. . . . In the present case, the annual sales allegedly foreclosed by respondents' tying arrangements throughout the country totaled almost $4 million in 1960, more than $2 million in 1961, and almost $2 million in 1962. These amounts could scarcely be regarded as insubstantial. . . .

"The standard of 'sufficient economic power' does not, as the District Court held, require that the defendant have a monopoly or even a dominant position throughout the market for the tying product. Our tie-in cases have made unmistakably clear that the economic power over the tying product can be sufficient even though the power falls far short of dominance and even though the power exists only with respect to some of the buyers in the market. . . . 'Even absent a showing of market dominance, the crucial economic power may be inferred from the tying product's desirability to consumers or from uniqueness in its attributes.'"

Exclusive dealing arrangements should be analyzed quite differently from tying contracts, since in many situations both the seller and the buyer benefit from such commitments. The buyer has an assured supply and protection against price fluctuations; the seller has an assured market and can plan production more realistically. Such agreements therefore must be tested on a case-by-case basis, under the rule of reason. The motives of the parties are important, and so is the impact of the particular agreement on the relevant market. The following case is probably the leading example of illegal exclusive dealing arrangements.

Standard Oil Co. of California v. *United States*
337 U.S. 293 (1949)

FACTS   California Standard and its wholly owned subsidiary, Standard Stations, Inc., entered into exclusive supplier contracts with some 16 percent of the retail gasoline stations in seven western states. Cal/Standard was the largest gasoline retailer in the area, with over 20 percent of the sales. The next 6 largest competitors had over 40 percent of the sales; over 70 small companies shared the remaining sales. The nearly 6,000 independent dealers (16 percent of the area's retailers) who had signed such exclusive contracts bought over $57 million worth of gasoline and over $8 million worth of other products from Cal/Standard in 1947. The government sought a declaratory judgment that these contracts were illegal under Section 3 of the Clayton Act, which prohibited making a sale conditional on the buyer's agreement not to deal in the goods of a competitor where the effect of such a contract "may be to substantially lessen competition or tend to create a monopoly in any line of commerce." The U.S. district court in California held the contracts illegal and granted an injunction prohibiting the defendants from making or enforcing them. The defendants appealed.

ISSUE   Do these contracts have the prohibited effect on commerce?

DECISION   Yes. Judgment affirmed.

REASONS   Speaking for the Court, Justice Frankfurter reviewed the statistical evidence in the case and the legal tests used by the district court. As he saw it, what the Court had to decide was whether the section was violated simply because a large number of dealers, selling a large amount of products, were involved or whether the government should also be required to prove that competitive activity had diminished or probably would diminish. The precedent case "regarded domination of the market as sufficient in itself to support the inference that competition had been or probably would be lessened." In the *United Shoe Machinery* case, for example, the Court said: "That such restrictive and tying agreements must necessarily lessen competition and tend to monopoly is, we believe, . . . apparent." Frankfurter acknowledged that exclusive dealing contracts might have real economic advantages for both the seller and the buyer, but he still thought that inferences could be used to find the necessary adverse effects on commerce.

"When it is remembered that all the other major suppliers have also been using requirements contracts, and when it is noted that the relative share of business which fell to each has remained about the same during the period of their use, it would not be farfetched to infer that their effect has been to enable the established suppliers individually to maintain their own standing and at the same time collectively, even though not collusively, to prevent a late arrival from wresting away more than an insignficant portion of the market. . . .

"We conclude, therefore, that the qualifying clause of S.3 is satisfied by proof that competition has been foreclosed in a substantial share of the line of commerce affected. It cannot be gainsaid that observance by a dealer of his requirements contract with Standard does effectively foreclose whatever opportunity there might be for competing suppliers to attract his patronage, and it is clear that the affected proportion of retail sales of petroleum products is substantial. In view of the widespread adoption of such contracts by Standard's competitors and the availability of alternative ways of obtaining an assured market, evidence that competitive activity has not actually declined is inconclusive. Standard's use of the contracts creates just such a potential clog on competition as it was the purpose of S.3 to remove wherever, were it to become actual, it would impede a substantial amount of competitive activity."

Mergers and Interlocking Directors. Sections 7 and 8 of the Clayton Act of 1914 were largely ineffective during their first 40 years on the statute books, due to restrictive Supreme Court interpretations and a lack of enforcement vigor. Section 7, in its original version, established a kind of per se rule which prohibited any acquisition by a company of a controlling stock interest in a competitor. In several cases in the 1920s and 1930s, the Supreme Court held that an acquisition of a competitor's *assets* was not prohibited. The following case, filed in 1949, resulted in a drastic reinterpretation of the original Section 7, but it really set no precedent because Congress had in the meantime passed the 1950 Celler-Kefauver Amendment, which substantially reworked Section 7.

U.S. v. E. I. du Pont de Nemours & Co.
353 U.S. 586 (1957)

FACTS   In 1917–19, as part of the reorganization and recapitalization of General Motors, Du Pont acquired 23 percent of GM's stock. In 1946 and 1947 Du Pont supplied about two thirds of GM's requirements for auto paints and finishes. In 1946 GM bought over half of its fabric requirements from Du Pont; for 1947 the figure was 38.5 percent. Since GM was then selling about half the cars in the United States, it was buying about half of the auto industry's requirements for such products. (Both courts used *auto* finishes and fabrics as the relevant markets, rather than *industrial* finishes and fabrics.) The government sued to challenge this stock ownership in a customer, under Section 7 of the Clayton Act as it had existed prior to the 1950 Amendment. After hearing 52 witnesses, seeing over 2,000 exhibits, and producing an 8,283-page transcript for a trial that lasted nearly seven months, the U.S. district court in Illinois held that the government had not proved its case. The government appealed.

ISSUES   Did the unamended Section 7 apply to stock ownership in a customer firm? Did this stock ownership have the prohibited anticompetitive effects?

DECISION   Yes. Yes. Judgment reversed and case remanded.

REASONS   Justice Brennan did not think that the passage of 30 years should prevent the government from bringing the suit so long as the potential adverse effects on competition existed at the time the action was brought. He felt that the old Section 7 clearly covered the acquisition of stock in a customer firm.

"The first paragraph of S.7, written in the disjunctive, plainly is framed to reach not only the corporate acquisition of stock in a competing corporation, where the effect may be substantially to lessen competition between them, but also the corporate acquisition of stock of any corporation, competitor or not, where the effect may be either (1) to restrain commerce in any section or community, or (2) tend to create a monopoly of any line of commerce. . . .

"We hold that any acquisition by one corporation of all or any part of the stock of another corporation, competitor or not, is within the reach of the section whenever the reasonable likelihood appears that the acquisition will result in a restraint of commerce or in the creation of a monopoly of any line of commerce. . . .

"The record shows that automotive finishes and fabrics have sufficient peculiar characteristics and uses to constitute them products sufficiently distinct from all other finishes and fabrics to make them a 'line of commerce' within the meaning of the Clayton Act. . . .

"The market affected must be substantial. . . . Moreover, in order to establish a violation of S.7 the Government must prove a likelihood that competition may be 'foreclosed in a substantial share of . . . [that market].' Both requirements are satisfied in this case. . . .

"The inference is overwhelming that du Pont's commanding position was promoted by its stock interest and was not gained solely on competitive merit. We agree with the trial court that considerations of price, quality, and service were not overlooked by either du Pont or General Motors. Pride in its products and its high financial stake in General Motors' success would naturally lead du Pont to try to supply the best. But the wisdom of this business judgment cannot obscure the fact, plainly revealed by this record, du Pont purposely employed its stock to pry open the General Motors market to entrench itself as the primary supplier of General Motors' requirements for automotive finishes and fabrics."

The amended Section 7 covered one corporation's acquisition of the stock or the assets of another "where in any line of commerce in any section of the country, the effect of such acquisition may be substantially to lessen competition, or to tend to create a monopoly." This new version clearly established an "incipiency" test; the acquisition was illegal if there was a reasonable probability that it would have future anticompetitive effects. Using the revised Section 7, the government was able to stop the proposed merger of Bethlehem Steel and Youngstown Sheet & Tube in 1958 (but Youngstown was subsequently merged into Lykes and Lykes into LTV). The first case to come to the Supreme Court under the new Section 7 was the Brown Shoe acquisition of Kinney Shoes, a merger which had both vertical and horizontal aspects, since both companies were manufacturers and retailers. Using a very restrictive definition of the market which excluded shoe retailers such as Sears, Montgomery Ward, and J. C. Penney and ignoring the fact that Kinney stores bought *more* shoes from independent manufacturers after the merger than it had before, the Supreme Court found the merger illegal. The following case shows the Court attempting to deal with the conglomerate merger boom of the late 1960s.

Federal Trade Commission v. *Procter & Gamble Company*
386 U.S. 568 (1967)

FACTS   In 1957, after deciding against starting up its own bleach product, P&G bought all the assets of Clorox Chemical Company, the leading bleach manufacturer and the only bleach manufacturer which sold its product in all areas of the country. Most firms in the bleach industry had only one plant and sold only in the region where that plant was situated, since shipping costs were high and profit margins were small. Clorox accounted for nearly half of the industry's sales. Purex, its nearest competitor, had

15.7 percent and was available in less than half of the markets nationally. The top six firms had over 80 percent of the industry's sales; 200 small firms shared the rest. The products were chemically identical, so advertising and promotion were crucial. Clorox's market share had been steadily increasing during the five years prior to the merger. P&G had over $1 billion in sales and a half-billion dollars in assets. P&G and its two largest competitors, Colgate-Palmolive and Lever Brothers, accounted for over 80 percent of all packaged detergent sales. In 1957 P&G was the nation's largest advertiser, spending over $80 million on advertising and another $47 million on sales promotion. The FTC ordered P&G to divest itself of Clorox, but the U.S. court of appeals reversed. The FTC asked for certiorari.

ISSUE   Will this merger probably lessen competition?

DECISION   Yes. Judgment of the court of appeals reversed; FTC order affirmed.

REASONS   Justice Douglas thought that the FTC could reasonably use a "market-structure" analysis. (Justice Harlan wrote an extensive concurring opinion.)

"All mergers are within the reach of S.7, and all must be tested by the same standard, whether they are classified as horizontal, vertical, conglomerate, or other. . . . [T]he Commission aptly called this acquisition a 'product-extension merger.' . . .

"The anticompetitive effects with which this product-extension merger is fraught can easily be seen: (1) the substitution of the powerful acquiring firm for the smaller, but already dominant, firm may substantially reduce the competitive structure of the industry by raising entry barriers and by dissuading the smaller firms from aggressively competing; (2) the acquisition eliminates the potential competition of the acquiring firm. . . .

"There is every reason to assume that the smaller firms would become more cautious in competing due to their fear of retaliation by Procter. It is probable that Procter would become the price leader and that oligopoly would become more rigid.

"The acquisition may also have the tendency of raising the barriers to new entry. The major competitive weapon in the successful marketing of bleach is advertising. . . . Procter would be able to use its volume discounts to advantage in advertising Clorox. Thus, a new entrant would be much more reluctant to face the giant Procter than it would have been to face the smaller Clorox. . . .

"It is clear that the existence of Procter at the edge of the industry exerted considerable influence on the market. First, the market behavior of the liquid bleach industry was influenced by each firm's predictions of the market behavior of its competitors, actual and potential. Second, the barriers to entry by a firm of Procter's size and with its advantages were not significant. . . . Third, the number of potential entrants was not so large that the elimination of one would be insignificant. Few firms would have the temerity to challenge a firm as solidly entrenched as Clorox. Fourth, Procter was found by the Commission to be the most likely entrant. These findings of the Commission were amply supported by the evidence."

To resolve some of the uncertainty as to which mergers would be challenged, the Justice Department in 1968 issued its merger "guidelines." These guidelines really did little more than summarize then-existing case law: Horizontal mergers between competitors in a highly concentrated market would be challenged where each firm had as little as 4 percent of the market; vertical mergers would be challenged where the supplier had 10 percent of the sales and the purchaser firm bought at least 6 percent of the goods involved; conglomerate mergers would be brought to court where the acquiring firm was a "potential entrant" into the market through internal expansion, or where the merger created a danger of reciprocal buying, or where the acquiring firm's resources were so extensive as to give the acquired firm an unfair advantage over its smaller competitors.

Interlocking Directorates. As previously noted, there were very few proceedings against "interlocking" directors for the first 40 years after the Clayton Act was passed. Cases against W. T. Grant and Sears, Roebuck were decided in 1953, and Section 8 of the Clayton Act was revived. A district court forced the common director of Sears and B. F. Goodrich to resign from the Sears board, and five years later the same district court held that its decree would be violated if the same person served on the Goodrich board and as a director of Sears' Savings and Profit Sharing Pension Fund. There was renewed emphasis on enforcement of this section in the 1970s, and a common director of Chrysler and General Electric was forced to resign from the GE board because both companies made air conditioners. Potentially, there is a considerable area of antitrust violation under this section.

CASES FOR DISCUSSION   I

GOLDFARB v. VIRGINIA STATE BAR
421 U.S. 773 (1975)

Chief Justice Burger

We granted certiorari to decide whether a minimum-fee schedule for lawyers published by the Fairfax County Bar Association and enforced by the Virginia State Bar violates § 1 of the Sherman Act. . . . The Court of Appeals held that, although the fee schedule and enforcement mechanism substantially restrained competition among lawyers, publication of the schedule by the County Bar was outside the scope of the Act because the practice of law is not "trade or commerce," and enforcement of the schedule by the State Bar was exempt from the Sherman Act as state action. . . .

In 1971 petitioners, husband and wife, contracted to buy a home in Fairfax County, Va. The financing agency required them to secure title insurance; this required a title examination, and only a member of the Virginia State Bar could legally perform that service. Petitioners therefore contacted a lawyer who quoted them the precise fee suggested in a minimum-fee schedule published by respondent Fairfax County Bar Association: the lawyer told them that it was his policy to keep his charges in line with the minimum-fee schedule, which provided for a fee of 1 percent of the value of the property involved. Petitioners then tried to find a lawyer who would examine the title for less than the fee fixed by the schedule. They sent letters to 36 other Fairfax County lawyers requesting their fees. Nineteen replied, and none indicated that he would charge less than the rate fixed by the schedule; several stated that they knew of no attorney who would do so.

The fee schedule the lawyers referred to is a list of recommended minimum prices for common legal services. Respondent Fairfax County Bar Association published the fee schedule although, as a purely voluntary association of attorneys, the County Bar has no formal power to enforce it. Enforcement has been provided by respondent Virginia State Bar, which is the administrative agency through which the Virginia Supreme Court regulates the practice of law in that State; membership in the State Bar is required in order to practice in Virginia. Although the State Bar has never taken formal disciplinary action to compel adherence to any fee schedule, it has published reports condoning fee schedules, and has issued two ethical opinions indicating that fee schedules cannot be ignored. The most recent opinion states that "evidence that an attorney habitually charges less than the suggested minimum fee schedule adopted by his local bar Association, raises a presumption that such lawyer is guilty of misconduct. . . ."

Because petitioners could not find a lawyer willing to charge a fee lower than the schedule dictated, they had their title examined by the lawyer they had first contacted. They then brought this class action against the State Bar and County Bar alleging that the operation of the minimum-fee schedule, as applied to fees for legal services relating to residential real estate transactions, constitutes price fixing in violation of §1 of the Sherman Act. Petitioners sought both injunctive relief and damages.

After a trial soley on the issue of liabilty the District Court held that the minimum-fee schedule violated the Sherman Act. . . .

II

Our inquiry can be divided into four steps: did respondents engage in price fixing? If so, are their activities in interstate commerce or do they affect interstate commerce? If so, are the activities exempt from the Sherman Act, because they involve a "learned Profession"? If not, are the activities "state action" within the meaning of

Parker v. *Brown* . . . and therefore exempt from the Sherman Act?

A

The County Bar argues that because the fee schedule is merely advisory, the schedule and its enforcement mechanism do not constitute price fixing. Its purpose, the argument continues, is only to provide legitimate information to aid member lawyers in complying with Virginia profession regulations. Moreover, the County Bar contends that in practice the schedule has not had the effect of producing fixed fees. The facts found by the trier belie these contentions, and nothing in the record suggests these findings lack support.

A purely advisory fee schedule issued to provide guidelines, or an exchange of price information without a showing of an actual restraint on trade, would present us with a different question. . . . The record here, however, reveals a situation quite different from what would occur under a purely advisory fee schedule. Here a fixed, rigid price floor arose from respondents' activities: every lawyer who responded to petitioners' inquiries adhered to the fee schedule, and no lawyer asked for additional information in order to set an individualized fee. . . .

Moreover, in terms of restraining competition and harming consumers like petitioners the price-fixing activities found here are unusually damaging. A title examination is indispensable in the process of financing a real estate purchase, and since only an attorney licensed to practice in Virginia may legally examine a title, . . . consumers could not turn to alternative sources for the necessary service. All attorneys, of course, were practicing under the constraint of the fee schedule. . . . The County Bar makes much of the fact that it is a voluntary organization; however, the ethical opinions issued by the State Bar provide that any lawyer, whether or not a member of his county bar association, may be disciplined for "*habitually* charg[ing] less than the suggested minimum fee schedule adopted by his local bar Association. . . . "These factors coalesced to create a pricing system that consumers could not realistically escape. On this record respondents' activities constitute a classic illustration of price fixing.

B

The County Bar argues, as the Court of Appeals held, that any effect on interstate commerce caused by the fee schedule's restraint on legal services was incidental and remote. In its view the legal services, which are performed wholly interstate, are essentially local in nature and therefore a restraint with respect to them can never substantially affect interstate commerce. . . . The necessary connection between the interstate transactions and the restraint of trade provided by the minimum-fee schedule is present because, in a practical sense, title examinations are necessary in real estate transactions to assure a lien on a valid title of the borrower. In financing realty purchases lenders require, "as a condition of making the loan, that the title to the property involved by examined. . . ." Thus a title examination is an integral part of an interstate transactions. . . .

Given the substantial volume of commerce involved and the inseparability of this particular legal service from the interstate aspects of real estate transactions, we conclude that interstate commerce has been sufficiently affected. . . .

The fact that there is no showing that home buyers were discouraged by the challenged activities does not mean that interstate commerce was not affected. Otherwise, the magnitude of the effect would control, and our cases have shown that, once an effect is shown, no specific magnitude need be proved. . . .

C

The County Bar argues that Congress never intended to include the learned professions within the terms "trade or commerce" in § 1 of the Sherman Act, and therefore the sale of professional services is exempt from the Act. No explicit exemption or legislative history is provided to support this contention; rather, the existence of state regulation seems to be its primary basis. Also, the County Bar maintains that competition is inconsistent with the practice of a profession because enhancing profit is not the goal of professional activites; the goal is to provide services necessary to the community. That, indeed, is the classic basis traditionally advanced to distinguish professions from trades, businesses, and other occupations, but it loses some of its force when used to support the fee control activities involved here.

In arguing that learned professions are not "trade or commerce" the County Bar seeks a total exclusion from antitrust regulation. Whether state regulation is active or dormant, real or theoretical, lawyers would be able to adopt anticompetitive practices with immunity. We cannot find support for the proposition that Congress intended any such sweeping exclusion. The nature of an occupation, standing alone, does not provide sanctuary from the Sherman Act, . . . nor is the public-service aspect of professional practice controlling in determining whether § 1 includes professions. . . . Congress intended to strike as broadly as it could in § 1 of the Sherman Act, and to read into it so wide an exemption as that urged on us would be at odds with that purpose. . . .

Whatever else it may be, the examination of a land title is a service; the exchange of such a service for money is "commerce" in the most common usage of that word. It is no disparagement of the practice of law as a profession to acknowledge that it has this business aspect. . . .

In the modern world it cannot be denied that the activities of lawyers play an important part in commercial intercourse, and that anticompetitive activities by lawyers may exert a restraint on commerce.

Through its legislature Virginia has authorized its highest court to regulate the practice of law. That court has adopted ethical codes which deal in part with fees, and far from exercising state power to authorize binding price fixing, explicitly directed lawyers not "to be controlled" by fee schedules. The State Bar, a state agency by law, argues that in issuing fee schedule reports and ethical opinions dealing with fee schedules, it was merely implementing the fee provisions of the ethical codes. The County Bar, although it is a voluntary association and not a state agency,

967

claims that the ethical codes and the activities of the State Bar "prompted" it to issue fee schedules, and thus its actions, too, are state action for Sherman Act purposes. . . .

Here we need not inquire further into the state-action question because it cannot fairly be said that the State of Virginia through its Supreme Court Rules required the anticompetitive activities of either respondent. . . .

The fact that the State Bar is a state agency for some limited purposes does not create an antitrust shield that allows it to foster anticompetitive practices for the benefit of its members. . . . The State Bar, by providing that deviation from County Bar minimum fees may lead to disciplinary action, has voluntarily joined in what is essentially a private anticompetitive activity, and in that posture cannot claim it is beyond the reach of the Sherman Act. . . . Its activities resulted in a rigid price floor from which petitioners, as consumers, could not escape if they wished to borrow money to buy a home.

III

We recognize that the States have a compelling interest in the practice of professions within their boundaries, and that as part of their power to protect the public health, safety, and other valid interests they have broad power to establish standards for licensing practitioners and regulating the practice of professions. We also recognize that in some instances the State may decide that "forms of competition usual in the business world may be demoralizing to the ethical standards of a profession." . . . The interest of the States in regulating lawyers is especially great since lawyers are essential to the primary governmental function of administering justice, and have historically been "officers of the courts." . . . In holding that certain anticompetitive conduct by lawyers is within the reach of the Sherman Act, we intend no diminution of the authority of the State to regulate its professions.

The judgment of the Court of Appeals is reversed, and the case is remanded to that court with orders to remand to the District Court for further proceedings consistent with this opinion.

SIMPSON v. UNION OIL COMPANY OF CALIFORNIA
377 U.S. 13 (1964)

Justice Douglas

This is a suit for damages under § 4 of the Clayton Act . . . for violation of §§ 1 and 2 of the Sherman Act. . . . The complaint grows out of a so-called retail dealer "consignment" agreement which, it is alleged, Union Oil requires lessees of its retail outlets to sign, of which Simpson was one. The "consignment" agreement is for one year and thereafter, until cancelled, is terminable by either party at the end of any year and, by its terms, ceases upon any termination of the lease. The lease is also for one year; and it is alleged that it is used to police the retail prices charged by the consignees, renewals not being made if the conditions prescribed by the company are not met. The company, pursuant to the "consignment" agreement, sets the prices at which the retailer sells the gasoline. While "title" to the consigned gasoline "shall remain in Consignor until sold by Consignee," and while the company pays all property taxes on all gasoline in possession of Simpson, he must carry personal liability and property damage insurance by reason of the "consigned" gasoline and is responsible for all losses of the "consigned" gasoline in his possession, save for specified acts of God. Simpson is compensated by a minimum commission and pays all the costs of operation in the familiar manner.

The retail price fixed by the company for the gasoline during the period in question was 29.9 cents per gallon; and Simpson, despite the company's demand that he adhere to the authorized price, sold it at 27.9 cents, allegedly to meet a competitive price. Solely because Simpson sold gasoline below the fixed price, Union Oil refused to renew the lease; termination of the "consignment" agreement ensued; and this suit was filed. Terms of the lease and "consignment" agreement are not in dispute nor the method of their application in this case. The interstate character of Union Oil's business is conceded, as is the extensive use by it of the lease-consignment agreement in eight western States.

After two pretrial hearings, the company moved for a summary judgment. Simpson moved for a partial summary judgment. . . .

The District Court granted the company's motion and denied Simpson's, holding as to the latter that he had not established a violation of the Sherman Act and, even assuming such a violation, that he had not suffered any actionable damage. The Court of Appeals affirmed. . . .

We disagree with the Court of Appeals that there is not actionable wrong or damage if a Sherman Act violation is assumed. . . .

There is actionable wrong whenever the restraint of trade or monopolistic practice has an impact on the market; and it matters not that the complainant may be only one merchant. . . .

Consignments perform an important function in trade and commerce, and their integrity has been recognized by many courts, including this one. . . . Yet consignments, though useful in allocating risks between the parties and determining their rights inter se, do not necessarily control the rights of others, whether they be creditors or sovereigns.

One who sends a rug or a painting or other work of art to a merchant or a gallery for sale at a minimum price can, of course, hold the consignee to the bargain. A retail merchant may, indeed, have inventory on consignment, the terms of which bind the parties inter se. . . . The interests of the Government . . . frequently override agreements that private parties make. Here we have an antitrust policy expressed in Acts of Congress. Accordingly, a consignment, no matter how lawful it might be as a matter of private contract law, must give way before the federal antitrust policy. Thus a consignment is not allowed to be used as a cloak to avoid § 3 of the Clayton Act. . . .

Dealers, like Simpson, are independent businessmen; and they have all or most of the indicia of entrepreneurs, except for the price fixing. The risk of loss of the gasoline is on them, apart from acts of God. Their return is affected by the rise and fall in the market price, their commissions declining as retail prices drop. Practically the only power they have to be wholly independent businessmen whose service depends on their own initiative and enterprise, is taken from them by the provision that they must sell their gasoline at prices fixed by Union Oil. By reason of the lease and "consignment" agreement dealers are coercively laced into an arrangement under which their supplier is able to impose noncompetitive prices on thousands of persons whose prices otherwise might be competitive. The evil of this resale maintenance program . . . is its inexorable potentiality for and even certainty in destroying competition in retail sales of gasoline by these nominal "consignees" who are in reality small struggling competitors seeking retail gas customers.

As we have said, an owner of an article may send it to a dealer who may in turn undertake to sell it only at a price determined by the owner. There is nothing illegal about that arrangement. When, however, a "consignment" device is used to cover a vast gasoline distribution system, fixing prices through many retail outlets, the antitrust laws prevent calling the "consignment" an agency, for then the end result of *United States* v. *Socony Vacuum Oil Co.* . . . would be avoided merely by clever manipulation of words, not by differences in substance. The present, coercive "consignment" device, if successful against challenge under the antitrust laws, furnishes a wooden formula for administering prices on a vast scale.

Reliance is placed on *United States* v. *General Electric Co.,* . . . where a consignment arrangement was utilized to market patented articles. Union Oil correctly argues that the consignment in that case somewhat parallels the one in the instant case. The Court in the *General Electric* case did not restrict its ruling to patented articles; it, indeed, said that the use of the consignment device was available to the owners of articles "patented or otherwise." . . . But whatever may be said of the *General Electric* case on its special facts, involving patents, it is not apposite to the special facts here. . . .

To allow Union Oil to achieve price fixing in this vast distribution system through this "consignment" device would be to make legality for antitrust purposes turn on clever draftsmanship.

We refuse to let a matter so vital to a competitive system rest on such easy manipulation.

We intimate no views on any other issue; we hold only that resale price maintenance through the present, coercive type of "consignment" agreement is illegal under the antitrust laws, and that petitioner suffered actionable wrong or damage.

UNITED STATES v. VON'S GROCERY COMPANY

384 U.S. 270 (1966)

Justice Black

On March 25, 1960, the United States brought this action charging that the acquisition by Von's Grocery Company of its direct competitor Shopping Bag Food Stores, both large retail grocery companies in Los Angeles, California, violated § 7 of the Clayton Act. . . . On March 28, 1960, three days later, the District Court refused to grant the Government's motion for a temporary restraining order and immediately Von's took over all of Shopping Bag's capital stock and assets including 36 grocery stores in the Los Angeles area. After hearing evidence on both sides, the District Court made findings of fact and concluded as a matter of law that there was "not a reasonable probability" that the merger would tend "substantially to lessen competition" or "create a monopoly" in violation of § 7. For this reason the District Court entered judgment for the defendants. . . . The Government appealed directly to this Court as authorized by § 2 of the Expediting Act. The sole question here is whether the District Court properly concluded on the facts before it that the Government had failed to prove a violation of § 7.

The record shows the following facts relevant to our decision. The market involved here is the retail grocery market in the Los Angeles area. In 1958 Von's retail sales ranked third in the area and Shopping Bag's ranked sixth. In 1960 their sales together were 7.5 percent of the total $2½ billion of retail groceries sold in the Los Angeles market each year. For many years before the merger both companies had enjoyed great suc-

cess as rapidly growing companies. From 1948 to 1958 the number of Von's stores in the Los Angeles area practically doubled from 14 to 27, while at the same time the number of Shopping Bag's stores jumped from 14 to 34. During the same decade, Von's sales increased fourfold and its share of the market almost doubled while Shopping Bag's sales multiplied seven times and its share of the market tripled. The merger of these two highly successful, expanding, and aggressive competitors created the second largest grocery chain in Los Angeles with sales of almost $172,488,000 annually. In addition the findings of the District Court show that the number of owners operating single stores in the Los Angeles retail grocery market decreased from 5,365 in 1950 to 3,818 in 1961. By 1963, three years after the merger, the number of single-store owners had dropped still further to 3,590. During roughly the same period, from 1953 to 1962, the number of chains with two or more grocery stores increased from 96 to 150. While the grocery business was being concentrated into the hands of fewer and fewer owners, the small companies were continually being absorbed by the larger firms through mergers. According to an exhibit prepared by one of the Government's expert witnesses, in the period from 1949 to 1958, 9 of the top 20 chains acquired 126 stores from their smaller competitors. . . . These facts alone are enough to cause us to conclude contrary to the District Court that the Von's Shopping Bag merger did violate § 7. Accordingly, we reverse.

From this country's beginning there has been an abiding and widespread fear of the evils which flow from monopoly—that is, the concentration of economic power in the hands of a few. On the basis of this fear, Congress in 1890, when many of the Nation's industries were already concentrated into what it deemed too few hands, passed the Sherman Act in an attempt to prevent further concentration and to preserve competition among a large number of sellers. . . .

Like the Sherman Act in 1980 and the Clayton Act in 1914, the basic purpose of the 1950 Celler-Kefauver Act was to prevent economic concentration in the American economy by keeping a large number of small competitors in business. In stating the purposes of their bill, both of its sponsors, Representative Celler and Senator Kefauver, emphasized their fear, widely shared by other members of Congress, that this concentration was rapidly driving the small businessman out of the market. The period from 1940 to 1947, which was at the center of attention throughout the hearings and debates on the Celler-Kefauver bill, had been characterized by a series of mergers between large corporations and their smaller competitors resulting in the steady erosion of the small independent business in our economy. . . . To arrest this "rising tide" toward concentration into too few hands and to halt the gradual demise of the small businessman, Congress decided to clamp down with vigor on mergers. It both revitalized § 7 of the Clayton Act by "plugging its loophole" and broadened its scope so as not only to prohibit mergers between competitors, the effect of which "may be substantially to lessen competition or to tend to create a monopoly," but to prohibit all mergers having that effect. By using these terms in § 7 which look not merely to the actual present effect of a merger but instead to its effect upon future competition, Congress sought to preserve competition among many small businesses by arresting a trend toward concentration in its incipiency before that trend developed to the point that a market was left in the grip of a few big companies. Thus, where concentration is gaining momentum in a market, we must be alert to carry out Congress' intent to protect competition against ever-increasing concentration through mergers.

The facts of this case present exactly the threatening trend toward concentration which Congress wanted to halt. The number of small grocery companies in the Los Angeles retail grocery market had been declining rapidly before the merger and continued to decline rapidly afterwards. This rapid decline in the number of grocery store owners moved hand in hand with a large number of significant absorptions of the small companies by the larger ones. In the midst of this steadfast trend toward concentration, Von's and Shopping Bag, two of the most successful and largest companies in the area, jointly owning 66 grocery stores, merged to become the sec-

ond largest chain in Los Angeles. This merger cannot be defended on the ground that one of the companies was about to fail or that the two had to merge to save themselves from destruction by some larger and more powerful competitor. What we have on the contrary is simply the case of two already powerful companies merging in a way which makes them even more powerful than they were before. If ever such a merger would not violate § 7, certainly it does when it takes place in a market characterized by a long and continuous trend toward fewer and fewer owner-competitors which is exactly the sort of trend which Congress, with power to do so, declared must be arrested. . . .

Justice Stewart, with whom Justice Harlan joins (dissenting)

The Court makes no effect to appraise the competitive effects of this acquisition in terms of the contemporary economy of the retail food industry in the Los Angeles area. Instead, through a simple exercise in sums, it finds that the number of individual competitors in the market has decreased over the years, and, apparently on the theory that the degree of competition is invariably proportional to the number of competitors, it holds that this historic reduction in the number of competing units is enough under § 7 to invalidate a merger within the market, with no need to examine the economic concentration of the market, the level of competition in the market, or the potential adverse effect of the merger on that competition. This startling per se rule is contrary not only to our previous decisions, but contrary to the language of § 7, contrary to the legislative history of the 1950 amendment, and contrary to economic reality.

Under § 7, as amended, a merger can be invalidated if, and only if, "the effect of such acquisition may be substantially to lessen competition, or to tend to create a monopoly." No question is raised here as to the tendency of the present merger to create a monopoly. Our sole concern is with the question whether the effect of the merger may be substantially to lessen competition. . . .

The legislative history leaves no doubt that the applicable standard for measuring the substantiality of the effect of a merger on competition was that of a "reasonable probability" of lessening competition. The standard was thus more stringent than that of a "mere possibility" on the one hand and more lenient than that of a "certainty" on the other. I cannot agree that the retail grocery business in Los Angeles is in an incipient or any other stage of a trend toward a lessening of competition, or that the effective level of concentration in the industry has increased. Moreover, there in no indication that the present merger, or the trend in this industry as a whole, augurs any danger whatsoever for the small businessman. The Court has substituted bare conjecture for the statutory standard of a reasonable probability that competition may be lessened.

The Court rests its conclusion on the "crucial point" that, in the 11-year period between 1950 and 1961, the number of single-store grocery firms in Los Angeles decreased 29 percent from 5,365 to 3,818. Such a decline should, of course, be no more than a fact calling for further investigation of the competitive trend in the industry. For the Court, however, that decline is made the end, not the beginning, of the analysis. In the counting-of-heads game played today by the Court, the reduction in the number of single-store operators becomes a yardstick for automatic disposition of cases under § 7.

I believe that even the most superficial analysis of the record makes plain the fallacy of the Court's syllogism that competition is necessarily reduced when the bare number of competitors has declined. In any meaningful sense, the structure of the Los Angeles grocery market remains unthreatened by concentration. Local competition is vigorous to a fault, not only among chain stores themselves but also between chain stores and single-store operators. The continuing population explosion of the Los Angeles area, which has outrun the expansion plans of even the largest chains, offers a surfeit of business opportunity for stores of all sizes. Affiliated with cooperatives that give the smallest store the buying strength of its largest competitor, new stores have taken full advantage of the remarkable ease of entry into the

market. And, most important of all, the record simply cries out that the numerical decline in the number of single-store owners is the result of transcending social and technological changes that positively preclude the inference that competition has suffered because of the attrition of competitors.

Section 7 was never intended by Congress for use by the Court as a charter to roll back the supermarket revolution. Yet the Court's opinion is hardly more than a requiem for the so-called "Mom and Pop" grocery stores—the bakery and butcher shops, the vegetable and fish markets—that are now economically and technologically obsolete in many parts of the country. No action by this Court can resurrect the old single-line Los Angeles food stores than have been run over by the automobile or obliterated by the freeway. The transformation of American society since the Second World War has not completely shelved these speciality stores, but it has relegated them to a much less central role in our food economy. Today's dominant enterprise in food retailing is the supermarket. Accessible to the housewife's automobile from a wide radius, it houses under a single roof the entire food requirements of the family. Only through the sort of reactionary philosophy that this Court long ago rejected in the Due Process Clause area can the Court read into the legislative history of § 7 its attempt to make the automobile stand still, to mold the food economy of today into the market pattern of another era. . . .

Between 1948 and 1958, the market share of Safeway, the leading grocery chain in Los Angeles, declined from 14 percent to 8 percent. The combined market shares of the top two chains declined from 21 percent to 14 percent over the same period; for the period 1952–1958, the combined shares of the three, four, and five largest firms also declined. It is true that between 1948 and 1958, the combined shares of the top 20 firms in the market increased from 44 percent to 57 percent. The crucial fact here, however, is that 7 of these top 20 firms in 1958 were not even in existence as chains in 1948. Because of the substantial turnover in the membership of the top 20 firms, the increase in market share of the top 20 as a group is hardly a reliable indicator of any tendency toward market concentration. . . .

The emotional impact of a merger between the third and sixth largest competitors in a given market, however fragmented, is understandable, but that impact cannot substitute for the analysis of the effect of the merger on competition that Congress required by the 1950 amendment. Nothing in the present record indicates that there is more than an ephemeral possibility that the effect of this merger may be substantially to lessen competition. Section 7 clearly takes "reasonable probability" as its standard. That standard has not been met here, and I would therefore affirm the judgment of the District Court.

FORD MOTOR COMPANY v. UNITED STATES

505 U.S. 562 (1972)

Justice Douglas

This is a direct appeal under § 2 of the Expediting Act . . . from a judgment of the District Court . . . holding that Ford Motor Co. (Ford) violated § 7 of the Celler-Kefauver Antimerger Act by acquiring certain assets from Electric Autolite Co. (Autolite). The assets included the Autolite trade name, Autolite's only spark plug plant in this country (located at New Fostoria, Ohio), a battery plant, and extensive rights to its nationwide distribution organization for spark plugs and batteries. The present appeal is limited to that portion of the judgment relating to spark plugs and ordering Ford to divest the Autolite name and the spark plug plant. The ancillary injunctive provisions are also here for review.

Ford, the second-leading producer of automobiles, General Motors, and Chrysler together account for 90 percent of the automobile production in this country. Though Ford makes a substantial portion of its parts, prior to its acquisition of the assets of Autolite it did not make spark plugs or batteries but purchased those parts from independent companies.

The original equipment of new cars, insofar as spark plugs are concerned, is conveniently referred to as the OE tie. The replacement market is referred to as the aftermarket. The independents, including Autolite, furnished the auto manufacturers with OE plugs at cost or less, about six cents a plug, and they continued to sell at that price even when their costs increased threefold. The independents sought to recover their losses on OE sales by profitable sales in the aftermarket where the requirement of each vehicle during its lifetime is about five replacement plug sets. By custom and practice among mechanics, the aftermarket plug is usually the same brand as the OE plug.

Ford was anxious to participate in this aftermarket and, after various efforts not relevant to the present case, concluded that its effective participation in the aftermarket required "an established distribution system with a recognized brand name, a full line of high volume service parts, engineering experience in replacement designs, low volume production facilities and experience, and the opportunity to capitalize on an established car population."

Ford concluded it could develop such a division of its own but decided that course would take from five to eight years and be more costly than an acquisition. To make a long story short, it acquired certain assets of Autolite in 1961.

General Motors had previously entered the spark plug manufacturing field, making the AC brand. The two other major domestic producers were independents—Autolite and Champion. When Ford acquired Autolite, whose share of the domestic spark plug market was about 15 percent, only one major independent was left and that was Champion, whose share of the domestic market declined from just under 50 percent in 1960 to just under 40 percent in 1964 and to about 33 percent in 1966. At the time of the acquisition, General Motors' market share was about 30 percent. There were other small manufacturers of spark plugs, but they had no important share of the market.

The District Court held that the acquisition of Autolite violated § 7 of the Celler-Kefauver Antimerger Act because its effect "may be substantially to lessen competition." It gave two reasons for its decision.

First, prior to 1961 when Ford acquired

973

Autolite it had a "pervasive impact on the aftermarket," . . . in that it was a moderating influence on Champion and on other companies derivatively. It explained that reason as follows:

An interested firm on the outside has a twofold significance. It may someday go in and set the stage for noticeable deconcentration. While it merely stays near the edge, it is a deterrent to current competitors. . . . This was Ford uniquely, as both a prime candidate to manufacture and the major customer of the dominant member of the oligopoly. Given the chance that Autolite would have been doomed to oblivion by defendant's grass-roots entry, which also would have destroyed Ford's soothing influence over replacement prices, Ford may well have been more useful as a potential than it would have been as a real producer, regardless how it began fabrication. Had Ford taken the internal-expansion route, there would have been no illegality; not, however, because the result necessarily would have been commendable, but simply because that course has not been proscribed. . . .

In short, Ford's entry into the spark plug market by means of the acquisition of the factory in Fostoria and the trade name "Autolite" had the effect of raising the barriers to entry into that market as well as removing one of the existing restraints upon the actions of those in the business of manufacturing spark plugs.

It will also be noted that the number of competitors in the spark plug manufacturing industry closely parallels the number of competitors in the automobile manufacturing industry and the barriers to entry into the auto industry was virtually insurmountable at present and will remain so for the foreseeable future. Ford's acquisition of the Autolite assets, particularly when viewed in the context of the original equipment (OE) tie and of GM's ownership of AC, has the result of transmitting the rigidity of the oligopolistic structure of the automobile industry to the spark plug industry, thus reducing the chances of future deconcentration of the spark plug market by forces at work within that market. . . .

It is argued, however, that the acquisition had some beneficial effect in making Autolite a more vigorous and effective competitor against Champion and General Motors than Autolite had been as an independent. But what we said in *United States* v. *Philadelphia National Bank* . . . disposes of that argument. A merger is not saved from illegality under § 7, we said,

because, on some ultimate reckoning of social or economic debits and credits, it may be deemed beneficial. A value choice of such magnitude is beyond the oridinary limits of judicial competence, and in any event has been made for us already, by Congress when it enacted the amended § 7. Congress determined to preserve our traditionally competitive economy. It therefore proscribed anticompetitive mergers, the benign and the malignant alike, fully aware, we must assume, that some price might have to be paid. . . .

Ford argues that the acquisition left the marketplace with a greater number of competitors. To be sure, after Autolite sold its New Fostoria plant to Ford, it constructed another in Decatur, Alabama, which by 1964 had 1.6 percent of the domestic business. Prior to the acquisition, however, there were only two major independent producers and only two significant purchasers of original equipment spark plugs. The acquisition thus aggravated an already oligopolistic market. . . . Moreover, Ford made the acquisition in order to obtain a foothold in the aftermarket. Once established, it would have every incentive to perpetuate the OE tie and thus maintain the virtually insurmountable barriers to entry to the aftermarket.

II

The main controversy here has been over the nature and degree of the relief to be afforded.

During the year following the District Court's finding of a § 7 violation, the parties were unable to agree upon appropriate relief. The District Court then held nine days of hearings on the remedy and, after full consideration, concluded that divestiture and other relief were necessary.

The OE, it held, was in many respects the key to the solution since the propensity of the mechanic in a service station or independent garage is to select as a replacement the spark plug brand that the manufacturer installed in the car. The oligopolistic structure of the spark plug manufacturing industry encourages the continuance of that system. Neither GM nor Autolite sells private-label plugs. It is obviously in the self-interest of OE plug manufacturers to discourage private-brand sales and to encourage the OE tie. There are findings that the private brand sector of the spark plug market will grow substantially in the next decade because mass merchandisers are entering this market in force. They not only sell all brands over the counter but also have service bays where many carry only spark plugs of their own proprietary brand. It is anticipated that by 1980 the total private brand portion of the spark plug market may then represent 17 percent of the total aftermarket. . . .

Accordingly the decree

(1) enjoined Ford for 10 years from manufacturing spark plugs,
(2) ordered Ford for five years to purchase one-half of its total annual requirement of spark plugs from the divested plant under the "Autolite" name,
(3) prohibited Ford for the same period from using its own trade names on plugs,
(4) protected New Fostoria, the town where the Autolite plant is located, by requiring Ford to continue for 10 years its policy of selling spark plugs to its dealers at prices no less than its prevailing minimum suggested jobbers' selling price,
(5) protected employees of the New Fostoria Plant by ordering Ford to condition its divestiture sale on the purchaser's assuming the existing wage and pension obligations and to offer employment to any employee displaced by a transfer of nonplug operations from the divested plant.

The divested plant is given an incentive to provide Ford with terms which will not only satisfy the 50 percent requirement provided for five years by the decree but which even after that period may keep at least some of Ford's ongoing purchases. The divested plant is awarded at least a foothold in the lucrative aftermarket and is provided an incentive to compete aggressively for that market.

PROBLEMS FOR DISCUSSION

1. Bowlerover, Inc., one of the two largest manufacturers of bowling alley equipment, sold its equipment nationwide to many bowling alleys. Some of its customers ran into financial problems, so Bowlerover foreclosed on its equipment mortgages and took over the operation of these unsuccessful customers. Aztec Alleys, Inc., ran a large bowling center in competition with one of the alleys taken over by Bowlerover. Aztec says that the takeover was illegal and that it would have made additional profits if Bowlerover had not taken over the alley. Aztec sues Bowlerover for treble damages. Discuss and decide.

2. Downwind Gas Company acquired all the stock of Pumpy Pipeline Company. The U.S. Justice Department immediately filed suit for divestiture, alleging that the acquisition violated Section 7 of the Clayton Act. Less than a month later, while the lawsuit was still pending, Downwind applied to the Federal Power Commission for authority to acquire Pumpy's assets, in accordance with Section 7 of the Natural Gas Act. Downwind also moved to dismiss the antitrust suit or to stay it until the FPC could act; the U.S. district court denied both motions. The Justice Department wrote four letters to the FPC, asking that it stay its proceedings pending the outcome of the antitrust lawsuit. The FPC held hearings and approved the merger. The court of appeals upheld the FPC. The state of Illusiana, which was permitted to intervene in the FPC hearings, asks the U.S. Supreme Court for certiorari. How should this appeal be decided, and why?

3. Possum Creek Power Company generated electricity and sold it at retail to nearly 500 towns in three states. About 50 other towns in this area had municipally owned power systems. Each of its customer towns granted PCP a 10-to-20-year franchise to distribute electricity there. Sometimes, when these franchises came up for renewal,

proposals were made to convert to a municipally owned system. PCP refused to sell power at wholesale to municipal systems or to permit its transmission lines to be used for power from other generators. Several municipal systems were taken over by PCP. Most of the municipal systems did not have access to any transmission lines other than those of PCP. The U.S. government brought suit, alleging a violation of Section 2 of the Sherman Act (monopolization). Discuss and decide.

4. Fritter's Appliance Company had a retail store in Anytown, Ohio. Two blocks away was an Ace Department Store, which also sold appliances. Ace was a large statewide chain of 50 stores. Fritter had only one location. Ace and the other large chain stores in the area contacted most of the national appliance manufacturers and asked them not to supply merchandise to Fritter, whose discount prices were hurting sales from the chain stores. As a result, Fritter was unable to buy many brand name appliances. Fritter sues Ace and several manufacturers, alleging violations of Sections 1 and 2 of the Sherman Act and asking for treble damages and an injunction. What result, and why?

5. Winners, the nation's largest independent bicycle manufacturer, distributed its product through 20 wholesalers, who in turn supplied the bicycles to some 5,000 dealers nationwide. Dealers might handle competing makes, so long as they gave Winners equal promotion and advertising. A dealer might buy only from the wholesaler authorized to sell in his or her area and might not resell bicycles to unauthorized retailers. Whether they actually bought the bicycles from Winners or acted as agents or consignees for Winners, wholesalers might supply retailers only in their authorized sales area. The United States brings a civil antitrust action alleging violation of Section 1 of the Sherman Act. What result, and why?

6. Blat Publishing Company published the *Daily Clarion* in Halfburg, Mississippi. The paper was sold through independent wholesaler-distributors, who resold to retail customers. Each of the 150 wholesalers had an exclusive home delivery territory. Blat set the maximum retail price at which the papers could be resold. Homer, one of the wholesalers, began charging his customers more than the maximum resale price. Blat told Homer to stop, but he refused to do so. Blat then hired Promotions, Inc., to solicit Homer's retail customers for direct delivery of the paper. About 400 of Homer's 1,300 customers quit Homer for Blat's lower price. Blat then turned these 400 customers over to Myrtle, another wholesaler, who delivered to them. Finally, Blat refused to deal with Homer altogether. Homer sues for treble damages. Does he have a case? Discuss and decide.

7. The state of Floridated and several of its cities and counties sue for treble damages under the Sherman Act. The plaintiffs had all had construction work done for them, by various contractors, using bricks manufactured by the Clammy Clay Company. The plaintiffs allege that Clammy and other brickmakers entered into a price-fixing conspiracy in violation of the Sherman Act, that the price of bricks was set artificially high, that these high prices were passed along to them by the various contractors, and that they were therefore damaged. Clammy asks the trial court to dismiss the complaint, saying that even if it did enter into a price-fixing conspiracy, the plaintiffs were not the proper party to bring the suit. Clammy says, in other words, that an indirect purchaser of goods may not sue for treble damages under the Sherman Act. What result, and why?

8. Siphon Salt Company was the largest producer of salt for industrial and commercial uses. It also manufactured and sold various machines for the utilization of salt in production processes. One such machine, the Mixator, dissolved rock salt into a brine for industrial use. Another, the Saltomatic, injected salt tablets into canned food products during the canning process. Siphon held patents on both machines. It

leased about 800 Mixators and about 100 Saltomatics. In each lease was a clause which required the lessee to purchase all salt used in the machine from Siphon. The United States brings a civil suit for an injunction to prevent the use of such restrictive clauses in the leases, alleging violations of Section 1 of the Sherman Act and Section 3 of the Clayton Act. What result, and why?

9. Electric Company produced and sold electricity to customers in a 1,800-square-mile service area which included several large cities. Because of uncertain oil supplies and opposition to nuclear generators, Electric decided to convert to coal as its power-generating fuel. It signed a contract with the Ashville Coal Company under which Ashville would supply all of Electric's coal requirements at all Electric power-generating locations for the next 20 years—not less than 200,000 tons of coal per generating unit per year. Electric then spent over $10 million to convert its facilities to coal. Just before the first scheduled delivery of coal, Ashville notified Electric that the contract was illegal under Section 3 of the Clayton Act and that it would not deliver any coal. Electric Company sues to enforce the contract; Ashville defends by citing Section 3. Who's right, and why?

49 | Unfair Trade Practices, the FTC, and Consumer Protection

Unfair Trade Practices under the Common Law

Even at common law, there were some limits on the methods that one firm could use to attract customers from its competitors. Where a contract already existed, a third party that induced either of the contracting parties to breach was guilty of a tort. Tort law also recognized a wrong called "product disparagement," a sort of commercial libel; it is only in recent years, with FTC approval, that comparative ads have begun to name the "other product." Both competitor and customer may suffer injury if one firm "passes off" its product for that of a competitor. The *Stiffel* case discusses that problem.

Sears, Roebuck & Co. v. Stiffel Company
376 U.S. 225 (1964)

FACTS   Stiffel secured design and mechanical patents on a pole lamp. Shortly thereafter, Sears began to market a substantially identical lamp. The retail price of the Sears lamp was about the same as the wholesale price of the Stiffel lamp. Stiffel sued in U.S. district court, alleging (1) that the Sears copy infringed Stiffel's patents and (2) that the Sears copy caused confusion in the trade and thereby constituted unfair competition under state (Illinois) law. The district court declared the Stiffel patents invalid due to lack of invention but it upheld the unfair competition charge and awarded an injunction and damages. The court of appeals affirmed, and Sears asked the U.S. Supreme Court for a writ of certiorari.

ISSUE   Can a state's law of unfair competition impose liability for copying a product which is not protected under national patent or copyright laws?

DECISION   No. Judgment reversed.

REASONS   Justice Black reviewed the facts briefly and then discussed the policy and the historical background of the national patent laws.

"[T]he patent system is one in which uniform federal standards are carefully used to promote invention while at the same time preserving free competition. . . . Just as a State cannot encroach upon the federal patent laws directly, it cannot, under some other law, such as that forbidding unfair competition, give protection of a kind that clashes with the objectives of the federal patent laws. . . .

"To allow a State by use of its law of unfair competition to prevent the copying of an article which represents too slight an advance to be patented would be to permit the State to block off from the public something which federal law has said belongs to the public. The result would be that while federal law grants only 14 or 17 years' protection to genuine inventions, . . . States could allow perpetual protection to articles too lacking in novelty to merit any patent at all under federal constitutional standards. This would be too great an encroachment on the federal patent system to be tolerated. . . .

"Doubtless a State may, in appropriate circumstances, require that goods, whether patented or unpatented, be labelled or that other precautionary steps be taken to prevent customers from being misled as to the source, just as it may protect businesses in the use of their trademarks, labels, or distinctive dress in the packaging of goods so as to prevent others, by imitating such markings, from misleading purchasers as to the source of the goods. But because of the federal patent laws a State may not, when the article is unpatented and uncopyrighted, prohibit the copying of the article itself or award the damages for such copying."

Price Discrimination.   One of the most difficult antitrust problems occurs when a seller charges different prices to two or more buyers for the same type of goods. The original Section 2 of the Clayton Act of 1914 did contain a provision aimed at the seller which cut its price in locations where it faced competition and maintained its higher price everywhere else. The early cases, however, interpreted this section to prohibit only discrimination between *competing* buyers, and thus there were few prosecutions under it. By the mid-1930s, grocery store chains had become very powerful buyers and were demanding and getting quantity discounts. As the Supreme Court noted in the *Morton Salt* case, volume discounts of the large chains enabled them to sell Morton salt at retail for less than the price of which independent wholesalers could sell it to their retail-store customers. Under intense pressure from small independent retailers and wholesalers, Congress passed the Robinson-Patman Act to amend the Clayton Act. As noted previously, the Robinson-Patman Act is not fully consistent with the idea of free and open competition; it was designed to prevent large buyers from gaining an undue market price advantage, and thus it has the indirect effect of stifling some price competition at the retail level. The amendment also made it illegal "to sell . . . goods at unreasonably low prices for the purpose of destroying competition or eliminating a competitor." The courts and commentators have usually referred to this last practice as "predatory" price-cutting.

Utah Pie Company v. Continental Baking Co.
386 U.S. 685 (1967)

FACTS

Utah Pie was a small Utah corporation which made and sold fresh and frozen dessert pies. It started selling frozen pies in 1957, and it built a plant in 1958. It marketed frozen pies under its own name, and it also made pies for grocery stores to sell under their labels. The frozen pie market grew rapidly; Utah's share for 1958 was 66.5 percent, but for the next three years its shares were 34.3 percent, 45.5 percent, and 45.3 percent. Continental and two other large national firms—Pet and Carnation—engaged in local price-cutting on their frozen pies at various times during the four-year period involved in this suit. Utah's pies were usually the lowest in price because Utah's factory was locally situated. Utah's wholesale prices dropped from $4.15 per dozen to $2.75 per dozen some 44 months later, when it filed this suit. The jury found for the defendants on the conspiracy charge, but it found for Utah on the price discrimination charge. Judgment was entered for damages and attorney fees, but the court of appeals reversed, holding that the evidence would not permit a jury finding of probable injury to competition under Section 2(a) of the Robinson-Patman Act. Utah requested certiorari.

ISSUE

Was there sufficient evidence to sustain a jury verdict of injury to competition as the result of the defendants' price-cutting?

DECISION

Yes. Judgment of the court of appeals reversed and case remanded.

REASONS

Justice White reviewed the market situation extensively. He said that the jury could reasonably have decided that Pet's lower prices to get Safeway's business were not cost-justified and were made with "predatory intent" to injure Utah Pie. Whether Utah would have got this particular contract otherwise wasn't really the issue, since Pet's price-cutting prevented fair competition by all of the other companies in the market.

Continental sold its pies in Utah for substantially less than it did in other markets. "The Salt Lake City price was less than its direct cost plus an allocation for overhead." After Continental made its drastic price cuts, its "market share increased from 1.8 percent in 1960 to 8.3 percent in 1961." Clearly, someone was being injured by this price-cutting.

"Section 2(a) does not forbid price competition which will probably injure or lessen competition by eliminating competitors, discouraging entry into the market, or enhancing the market shares of the dominant sellers. But Congress has established some ground rules for the game. Sellers may not sell like goods to different purchasers at different prices if the result may be to injure competition in either the sellers' or the buyers' market unless such discriminations are justified as permitted by the Act. This case concerns the sellers' market. . . .

"We believe that the Act reaches price discrimination that erodes competition as much as it does price discrimination that is intended to have immediate destructive impact. In this case, the evidence shows a drastically declining price structure which the jury could rationally attribute to continued or sporadic price discrimination. The jury was entited to conclude that 'the effect of such discrimination,' by each of these respondents, 'may be substantially to lessen competition . . . or to injure, destroy, or prevent competition with any person who either grants or knowingly receives the benefit of such discrimination. . . .' The statutory test is one that necessarily looks forward on the basis of proven conduct in the past. Proper application of that standard here requires reversal of the judgment of the Court of Appeals."

The "Meeting Competition" Defense. Recognizing that in many cases a seller firm must cut its price to meet a lower price quoted by a competitor, Congress specifically provided for such a defense. A seller relying on this defense must be acting in good faith; knowledge that the competitor's lower price is itself illegal would probably prevent a finding of good faith. The following case is the leading example of this defense in action.

Standard Oil Co. v. Federal Trade Commission
340 U.S. 231 (1951)

FACTS   The FTC, after a hearing, ordered Standard to cease and desist from its practice of selling its Red Crown gasoline to four comparatively large "jobber" customers at tank-car prices which were $1\frac{1}{2}$ cents per gallon less than the tank-wagon prices which it charged retail service stations in the Detroit area. The four jobbers were free to resell at retail or wholesale. Each one, at some time, had resold some gasoline at retail; one now did so exclusively. Two of the jobbers had cut prices at the retail level or to their wholesalers. Standard claimed that it had had to reduce jobber prices to keep these customers, since other refiners had offered similar price cuts. The court of appeals ordered enforcement of the order after modifying it slightly. Standard requested certiorari.

ISSUE   Did Standard prove its "meeting competition" defense under 2(b)?

DECISION   Yes. Judgment reversed and case remanded.

REASONS   Justice Burton first determined that the sales made by Standard had been in interstate commerce, so that the national antitrust laws did apply. He noted that there had been no specific finding as to whether the lower prices to the jobbers were cost-justified, but he said that his analysis of the meeting-competition defense proceeded on the assumption that there had not been a cost justification. The FTC had decided that the meeting-competition defense would not apply where there was proof of actual injury to competition as a result of the price discrimination. After an extensive review of precedents and the legislative history of the Robinson-Patman Act, Justice Burton concluded that Congress had not intended to change prior law to the extent indicated by the FTC's decision.

"There is nothing to show a congressional purpose, in such a situation, to compel the seller to choose only between ruinously cutting its prices to all its customers to match the price offered to one, or refusing to meet the competition and then ruinously raising its prices to its remaining customers to cover increased unit costs. There is, on the other hand, plain language and established practice which permits a seller, through S.2(b), to retain a customer by realistically meeting in good faith the price offered to the customer, without necessarily changing the seller's price to its other customers.

"In a case where a seller sustains the burden of proof placed upon it to establish its defense under S.2(b), we find no reason to destroy that defense indirectly, merely because it also appears that the beneficiaries of the seller's price reductions may derive a competitive advantage from them or may, in a natural course of events, reduce their own resale prices to their customers. It must have been obvious to Congress that any price reduction to any dealer may always affect competition at that dealer's level as well as at the dealer's resale level, whether or not the reduction to the dealer is discriminatory. Likewise, it must have been obvious to Congress that any price reductions initiated by a seller's competitor would, if not met by the seller, affect competition at the beneficiary's level or among the beneficiary's customers just as much as if those reductions had been met by the seller. The proviso in S.2(b), as interpreted by the Commission, would not be available when there was or might be an injury to competition at a resale level. So interpreted, the proviso would have such little, if any, applicability as to be practically meaningless. We may, therefore, conclude that Congress meant to permit the natural consequences to follow the seller's action in meeting in good faith a lawful and equally low price of its competitor.''

The "Cost Justification" Defense. In an important proviso to Section 2(a), Congress indicated that it did not wish to outlaw price differentials which could be justified by cost savings. If genuine cost savings could be realized on larger orders, a seller ought to be able to pass them along to the buyer. While the theory of this defense is specifically stated in Section 2(a), actual *proof* of the defense has been next to impossible in practice. The next case illustrates some of these difficulties of proof.

United States v. The Borden Company
370 U.S. 460 (1962)

FACTS   The government sued for an injunction under Section 2(a) of the Clayton Act to prevent price discrimination by Borden Company and Bowman Dairy. Borden and Bowman used a pricing system which granted independent stores discounts based on the average number of units purchased per day but which granted a higher flat discount to chain stores. Borden, for instance, gave independents discounts of up to 4 percent, but Jewel and A&P got 8½ percent and a few larger independents got an extra 1½ percent. Both defendants introduced "voluminous cost studies" to justify their different prices. Borden's study analyzed costs for two classes of customers: Jewel and A&P, with a combined 254 stores, and 1,322 independent stores. The district court accepted the cost justification as evidence that the grouping was not wholly arbitrary. The United States brought a direct appeal.

ISSUE   Did the defendants sufficiently prove a cost justification?

DECISION   No. Judgment reversed and case remanded.

REASONS   Justice Clark felt that the defendants had not done an adequate job of meeting their burden of proof that there were in fact cost justifications for the different prices. He argued that the cost studies did not sufficiently refine the groups of customers for which costs were being compared.

"[T]he practice of grouping customers for pricing purposes has long had the approval of the Federal Trade Commission. We ourselves have noted the 'elusiveness of cost data' in a Robinson-Patman Act proceeding. . . . [T]o completely renounce class pricing as justified by class accounting would be to eliminate in practical effect the cost justification proviso as to sellers having a large number of purchasers, thereby preventing such sellers from passing on economies to their customers. It seems hardly necessary to say that such a result is at war with Congress' language and purpose.

"But this is not to say that price differentials can be justified on the basis of arbitrary classifications or even classifications which are representative of a numerical majority of the individual members. At some point practical considerations shade into a circumvention of the proviso. A balance is struck by the use of classes for cost justification which are composed of members of such selfsameness as to make the averaging of the cost of dealing with the group a valid and reasonable indicium of the cost of dealing with any specific group member. High on the list of 'musts' in the use of the average cost of customer groupings under the proviso of S. 2(a) is a close resemblance of the individual members of the group on the essential point or points which determine the costs considered.

"In this regard we do not find the classifications submitted by the appellees to have been shown to be of sufficient homogeneity. Certainly, the cost factors considered were not necessarily encompassed within the manner in which a customer is owned. Turning first to Borden's justification, we note that it not only failed to show that the economies relied upon were isolated within the favored class but affirmatively revealed that members of the classes utilized were substantially unlike in the cost savings aspects considered. . . . [S]uch a grouping for cost justification purposes, composed as it is of some independents having volumes comparable to, and in some cases larger than, that of the chain stores, created artificial disparities between the larger independents and the chain stores. It is like averaging one horse and one rabbit. . . .

"Nor is the vice in the Borden class justification solely in the paper volumes relied upon, for it attributed to many independents cost factors which were not true indicia of the cost of dealing with those particular customers."

The FTC and Unfair Trade Practices

Section 5 of the Federal Trade Commission Act of 1914 prohibited unfair methods of competition and unfair or deceptive acts or practices. The enforcement emphasis during the early years after 1914 was on deceptive advertising, but this emphasis gradually shifted to unfair methods of competition. The basic problem here is one of definition: Just what are *unfair* methods of competition? Such methods clearly include violations of the Sherman Act and the Clayton Act (including Robinson-Patman) and incipient Sherman Act violations. The Supreme Court has also held that methods which violate the "basic policy" of the Sherman and Clayton Acts, even though not specifically listed in the acts, can be reached under Section 5. Practices which injure customers can be prosecuted without necessarily showing that any competitor has been injured. All types of behavior which might be classified as "bad business morals" can also be reached under Section 5, including such things as tampering with a competitor's goods, deceptive packaging, and delivering unordered goods. In 1972 the Supreme Court decided that the FTC had general rule-making power; that is, the FTC did not have to proceed on a case-by-case basis but could promulgate rules of behavior, just like the NLRB, the SEC, and other agencies. Since then, the FTC has been quite aggressive in adopting rules for competitive conduct. Most recently, there have been attempts in Congress to curb the FTC's growing power over commercial practices.

Federal Trade Commission v. Mary Carter Paint Co.
382 U.S. 46 (1965)

FACTS The FTC issued a cease and desist order which directed Mary Carter to stop advertising its paint-selling policy as "buy one, get one free." The FTC said that Mary Carter had never sold *single* cans of paint but had always sold *two* cans for the advertised price, so that the price of a single can was not really the advertised $6.98. Thus Mary Carter had misrepresented the true nature of the transaction by calling one can "free." Mary Carter was not permitted to prove that the quality of its paint was in fact as good as or superior to other paints selling for $6.98 per can. The U.S. Fifth Circuit Court of Appeals set aside the order, and the FTC appealed.

ISSUE Is there sufficient evidence to sustain the FTC's order?

DECISION Yes. Judgment reversed and case remanded to FTC for clarification of its order.

REASONS In a brief opinion, Justice Brennan decided that the FTC had acted within the range of its administrative discretion and that it should be upheld.

"Although there is some ambiguity in the Commission's opinion, we cannot say that its holding constituted a departure from Commission policy regarding the use of the commercially exploitable word 'free.' Initial efforts to define the term in decisions were followed by 'Guides Against Deceptive Pricing.' These informed businessmen that they might advertise an article as 'free,' even though purchase of another article was required, so long as the terms of the offer were clearly stated, the price of the article required to be purchased was not increased, and its quality and quantity were not diminished. With specific reference to two-for-the-price-of-one offers, the Guides required that either the sales price for the two be 'the advertiser's usual and customary retail price for the single article in the recent, regular course of his business,' or where the advertiser has not previously sold the article, the price for two be the 'usual and customary' price for one in the relevant trade areas. These, of course, were guides, not fixed rules as such, and were designed to inform businessmen of the factors which would guide Commission decision. Although Mary Carter seems to have attempted to tailor its offer to come within their terms, the Commission found that it failed; the offer complied in appearance only. . . .

"[I]t is arguable that any deception was limited to a representation that Mary Carter has a usual and customary price for single cans of paint, when it has no such price. However, it is not for courts to say whether this violates the Act. '[T]he Commission is often in a better position than are courts to determine when a practice is "deceptive" within the meaning of the Act.' . . . There was substantial evidence in the record to support the Commission's finding; its determination that the practice here was deceptive was neither arbitrary nor clearly wrong. The Court of Appeals should have sustained it."

Justice Harlan dissented since he felt that Mary Carter had complied with the "Guides" by clearly spelling out the terms of its two-for-one offer.

Other FTC Jurisdiction. The FTC was also given the responsibility for enforcing a series of labeling acts passed in the 1940s and 1950s: the Wool Products Act (1941), the Fur Products Act (1952), the Textile Fibre Act (1958), and the Flammable Fabrics Act (1954). The enforcement mechanisms include both cease and desist orders and criminal penalties. The FTC also enforces the 1975 Magnuson-Moss Warranty Act, discussed in Chapter 17.

As part of the "consumerism" movement of the 1960s and 1970s, the FTC was given increased enforcement jurisdiction under several new statutes. The Truth in Lending Act, which requires disclosure of the true annual percentage rate of interest and other information to the consumer or farmer borrower, places primary enforcement in the Federal Reserve Board. The Fair Credit Reporting Act creates new debtor rights against credit bureaus, as does the Fair Credit Billing Act in disputes with creditors. Congress also limited debt collection practices with the Fair Debt Collection Practices Act. Many of these new statutes provide the possibility of private damage suits as well as administrative agency action. The FTC was given joint jurisdiction with the Department of Health and Welfare to enforce the new Fair Packaging Act, which requires label disclosures and limits sellers' claims.

Probably because Congress felt that more specific engineering and technical expertise was needed to deal with the problem, the FTC was not given enforcement responsibility under the 1972 Consumer Product Safety Act. A new Consumer Product Safety Commission (CPSC) and a new Advisory Council were created by the act. The CPSC collects and distributes data on product safety and product-related injuries. Injured consumers can bring suits in the U.S. courts if the alleged damages are $10,000 or more, and the further distribution of the "unsafe" product may be enjoined. The manufacturer may also be fined $2,000 for each violation, but the total fine for a single product cannot exceed $500,000.

While the following case deals with an FRB regulation rather than one from the FTC, it does illustrate the scope of the new "consumer protection" statutes.

Mourning v. *Family Publications Service, Inc.*
411 U.S. 356 (1973)

FACTS   Leila Mourning, a 73-year-old widow living in Florida, signed a contract for five-year subscriptions to four magazines, for a total price of $122.45. The contract, solicited by a door-to-door salesman, called for $3.95 down and the same amount each month for 30 months. Leila made only the down payment and then defaulted. The company declared the entire balance due under the contract's acceleration clause and threatened to sue. Leila then brought this suit in U.S. district court, alleging that the company had violated the disclosure requirements of the Truth in Lending Act and the Federal Reserve Board's Regulation Z. Regulation Z required disclosure in credit transactions which called for payment in more than four installments. For violation, the consumer might recover twice the finance charge but not less than $100 nor more than $1,000, plus litigation costs, including attorney fees. The district court granted summary judgment for Leila, but the court of appeals reversed on the ground that the FRB had exceeded its statutory authority. Leila asked for certiorari.

Mourning v. *Family Publications Service, Inc. (continued)*

ISSUE   Does the four-installment rule exceed the authority given to the FRB by the Truth in Lending Act?

DECISION   No. Judgment of the court of appeals reversed.

REASONS   Chief Justice Burger carefully reviewed the legislative history leading up to the passage of the Truth in Lending Act in 1968. The use of credit by consumers had mushroomed, and there were abuses by some lenders.

"The hearings held by Congress reflect the difficulty of the task it sought to accomplish. Whatever legislation was passed had to deal not only with the myriad forms in which credit transactions then occurred, but also with those which would be devised in the future. To accomplish its desired objective, Congress determined to lay the structure of the Act broadly and to entrust its construction to an agency with the necessary experience and resources to monitor its operation. Section 105 delegated to the Federal Reserve Board broad authority to promulgate regulations necessary to render the Act effective. . . .

"One means of circumventing the objectives of the Truth in Lending Act . . . was that of 'burying' the cost of credit in the price of goods sold. Thus in many credit transactions in which creditors claimed that no finance charge had been imposed, the creditor merely assumed the cost of extending credit as an expense of doing business, to be recouped as part of the price charged in the transaction. . . .

"'The Board felt that it was imperative to include transactions involving more than four instalments under the Regulation since without this provision the practice of burying the finance charge in the cash price, a practice which already exists in many cases, would have been encouraged by Truth in Lending. Obviously this would have been directly contrary to Congressional intent.' . . .

"Given that some remedial measure was authorized, the question remaining is whether the measure chosen is reasonably related to its objectives. We see no reason to doubt the Board's conclusion that the rule will deter creditors from engaging in the conduct which the Board sought to eliminate. The burdens imposed on creditors are not severe, when measured against the evils which are avoided. . . .

"The Truth in Lending Act reflects a transition in congressional policy from a philosophy of 'Let the buyer beware' to one of 'Let the seller disclose.' . . . Congress has determined that such purchasers are in need of protection; the Four Installment Rule serves to insure that the protective disclosure mechanism chosen by Congress will not be circumvented.

"That the approach taken may reflect what respondent views as an undue paternalistic concern for the consumer is beside the point. . . . It is not a function of the courts to speculate as to whether the statute is unwise or whether the evils sought to be remedied could better have been regulated in some other manner."

986

GREAT ATLANTIC & PACIFIC TEA CO., INC. v. THE FTC

99 S. Ct. 925 (1979)

Justice Stewart

The question presented in this case is whether the petitioner, the Great Atlantic and Pacific Tea Company (A&P), violated § 2(f) of the Robinson-Patman Act, as amended, 15 U.S.C. § 13(f), by knowingly inducing or receiving illegal price discrimination from the Borden Company (Borden).

The alleged violation was reflected in a 1965 agreement between A&P and Borden under which Borden undertook to supply "private label" milk to more than 200 A&P stores in a Chicago area that included portions of Illinois and Indiana. This agreement resulted from an effort by A&P to achieve cost savings by switching from the sale of "brand label" milk (milk sold under the brand name of the supplying dairy) to the sale of "private label" milk (milk sold under the A&P label).

To implement this plan, A&P asked Borden, its longtime supplier, to submit an offer to supply under private label certain of A&P's milk and other dairy product requirements. After prolonged negotiations, Borden offered to grant A&P a discount for switching to private label milk provided A&P would accept limited delivery service. Borden claimed that this offer would save A&P $410,000 a year compared to what it had been paying for its dairy products. A&P, however, was not satisfied with this offer and solicited offers from other dairies. A competitor of Borden, Bowman Dairy, then submitted an offer which was lower than Borden's.

At this point, A&P's Chicago buyer contacted Borden's chain store sales manager and stated, "I have a bid in my pocket. You [Borden] people are so far out of line it is not even funny. You are not even in the ball park." When the Borden representative asked for more details, he was told nothing except that a $50,000 improvement in Borden's bid "would not be a drop in the bucket."

Borden was thus faced with the problem of deciding whether to rebid. A&P at the time was one of Borden's largest customers in the Chicago area. Moreover, Borden had just invested more than $5 million in a new dairy facility in Illinois. The loss of the A&P account would result in underutilization of this new plant. Under these circumstances, Borden decided to submit a new bid which doubled the estimated annual savings to A&P, from $410,000 to $820,000. In presenting its offer, Borden emphasized to A&P that it needed to keep A&P's business and was making the new offer in order to meet Bowman's bid. A&P then accepted Borden's bid after concluding that it was substantially better than Bowman's.

Based on these facts, the Federal Trade Commission filed a three-count complaint against A&P. Count I charged that A&P had violated § 5 of the Federal Trade Commission Act by misleading Borden in the course of negotiations for the private label contract, in that A&P had failed to inform Borden that its second offer was better than the Bowman bid. Count II, involving the same conduct, charged that A&P had violated § 2(f) of the Robinson-Patman Act by knowingly inducing or receiving price discriminations from Borden. Count III charged that Borden and A&P had violated § 5 of the Federal Trade Commission Act by combining to stabilize and maintain the retail and wholesale prices of milk and other dairy products.

An Administrative Law Judge found, after extended discovery and a hearing that lasted over 110 days, that A&P had acted unfairly and deceptively in accepting the second offer from Borden and had therefore violated § 5 of the Federal Trade Commission Act as charged in Count I. The Administrative Law Judge similarly found that this same conduct had violated § 2(f) of the Robinson-Patman Act. Finally, he dismissed Count III on the ground that the Commission had not satisfied its burden of proof.

On review, the Commission reversed the Administrative Law Judge's finding as to Count I. Pointing out that the question at issue was what amount of disclosure is required of the buyer during contract negotiations, the Commission held that the imposition of a duty of affirmative disclosure would be "contrary to normal business practice and, we think, contrary to the public interest." Despite this ruling, however, the Commission held as to Count II that the identical conduct on the part of A&P had violated § 2(f) of the Robinson-Patman Act, finding that Borden had discriminated in price between A&P and its competitors, that the discrimination had been injurious to competition, and that A&P had known or should have known that it was the beneficiary of unlawful price discrimination. The Commission rejected A&P's defenses that the Borden bid had been made to meet competition and was cost justified.

A&P filed a petition for review of the Commission's order in the Court of Appeals for the Second Circuit. The court held that substantial evidence supported the findings of the Commission, and that as a matter of law A&P could not successfully assert a meeting competition defense because it, unlike Borden, had known that Borden's offer was better than Bowman's. Finally, the court held that the Commission had correctly determined that A&P had no cost justification defense. . . .

The Robinson-Patman Act was passed in response to the problem perceived in the increased market power and coercive practices of chain stores and other big buyers that threatened the existence of small independent retailers. Notwithstanding this concern with buyers, however, the emphasis of the Act is in § 2(a), which prohibits price discrimination by sellers. While the phrase "this section" refers to the entire § 2 of the Act, only subsections (a) and (b) dealing with seller liability involve discriminations in price. Under the plain meaning of § 2(f), therefore, a buyer cannot be liable if a prima facie case could not be established against a seller or if the seller has an affirmative defense. In either situation, there is no price discrimination "prohibited by this section." The legislative history of § 2(f) fully confirms the conclusion that buyer liability under § 2(f) is dependent on seller liabilty under § 2(a). . . .

Congress did not provide in § 2(f) that a buyer can be liable even if the seller has a valid defense. The clear language of § 2(f) states that a buyer can

be liable only if he receives a price discrimination "prohibited by this section." If a seller has a valid meeting competition defense, there is simply no prohibited price discrimination. . . .

In a competitive market, uncertainty among sellers will cause them to compete for business by offering buyers lower prices. Because of the evils of collusive action, the Court has held that the exchange of price information by competitors violates the Sherman Act. . . . Under the view advanced by the respondent, however, a buyer, to avoid liability, must either refuse a seller's bid or at least inform him that his bid has beaten competition. Such a duty of affirmative disclosure would almost inevitably frustrate competitive bidding and, by reducing uncertainty, lead to price matching and anticompetitive cooperation among sellers. . . .

The test for determining when a seller has a valid meeting competition defense is whether a seller can "show the existence of facts which would lead a reasonable and prudent person to believe that the granting of a lower price would in fact meet the equally low price of a competitor." . . . Since good faith, rather than absolute certainty, is the touchstone of the meeting competition defense, a seller can assert the defense even if it has unknowingly made a bid that in fact not only met but beat his competition. . . .

Borden was unable to ascertain the details of the Bowman bid. It requested more information about the bid from the petitioner, but this request was refused. It could not then attempt to verify the existence and terms of the competing offer from Bowman without risking Sherman Act liability. . . . Faced with a substantial loss of business and unable to find out the precise details of the competing bid, Borden made another offer, stating that it was doing so in order to meet competition. Under these circumstances, the conclusion is virtually inescapable that in making that offer Borden acted in a reasonable and good-faith effort to meet its competition, and therefore was entitled to a meeting competition defense.

Since Borden had a meeting competition defense and thus could not be liable under § 2(b) the petitioner who did no more than accept that offer cannot be liable under § 2(f).

FEDERAL TRADE COMMISSION v. BORDEN COMPANY

383 U.S. 637 (1966)

Justice White

The Borden Company, respondent here, produces and sells evaporated milk under the Borden name, a nationally advertised brand. At the same time Borden packs and markets evaporated milk under various private brands owned by its customers. This milk is physically and chemically identical with the milk it distributes under its own brand but is sold at both the wholesale and retail level at prices regularly below those obtained for the Borden brand milk. The Federal Trade Commission found the milk sold under the Borden and the private labels to be of like grade and quality as required for the applicability of § 2(a) of the Robinson-Patman Act, held the price differential to be discriminatory within the meaning of the section, ascertained the requisite adverse effect on commerce, rejected Borden's claim of cost justification, and consequently issued a cease-and-desist order. The Court of Appeals set aside the Commission's order on the sole ground that as a matter of law, the customer label milk was not of the same grade and quality as the milk sold under the Borden brand. . . . We now reverse the decision of the Court of Appeals and remand the case to the court for the determination of the remaining issues raised by respondent Borden in that court. . . .

The position of Borden and of the Court of Appeals is that the determination of like grade and quality, which is a threshold finding essential to the applicability of § 2(a), may not be based solely on the physical properties of the products without regard to the brand names they bear and the relative public acceptance these brands enjoy—"consideration should be given to all commercially significant distinctions which affect market value, whether they be physical or promotional." . . . Here, because the milk bearing the Borden brand regularly sold at a higher price than did the milk with a buyer's label, the court considered the products to be "commercially" different and hence of different "grade" for the purposes of § 2(a) even though they were physically identical and of equal quality. Although a mere difference in brand would not in itself demonstrate a difference in grade, decided consumer preference for one brand over another, reflected in the willingness to pay a higher price for the well-known brand, was, in the view of the Court of Appeals, sufficient to differentiate chemically identical products and to place the price differential beyond the reach of § 2(a).

We reject this construction of § 2(a), as did both the examiner and the Commission in this case. The Commission's view is that labels do not differentiate products for the purpose of determining grade or quality, even though the one label may have more customer appeal and command a higher price in the marketplace from a substantial segment of the public. That this is the Commission's long-standing interpretation of the present Act, as well as of § 2 of the Clayton Act before its amendment by the Robinson-Patman Act, may be gathered from the Commission's decisions dating back to 1936. . . .

Obviously there is nothing in the language of the statute indicating that grade, as distinguished from quality, is not to be determined by the characteristics of the product itself, but by consumer preferences, brand acceptability, or what customers think of it and are willing to pay for it. Moreover, what legislative history there is concerning this question supports the Commission's construction of the statute rather than that of the Court of Appeals. . . .

The Commission's construction of the statute also appears to us to further the purpose and policy of the Robinson-Patman Act. . . . We doubt that Congress intended to foreclose these inquiries in situations where a single seller markets the identical product under several different brands, whether his own, his customers', or both. Such transactions are too laden with potential discrimination and adverse competitive effect to be excluded from the reach of § 2(a) by permitting difference in grade to be established by the label alone or by the label and its consumer appeal.

If two products, physically identical but differently branded, are to be deemed of different grade because the seller regularly and successfully markets some quantity of both at different prices, the seller could, as far as § 2(a) is concerned, make either product available to some customers and deny it to others, however discriminatory this might be and however damaging to competition. Those who offered only one of the two products would be barred from competing for those customers who want or might buy the other. The retailer who was permitted to buy and sell only the more expensive brand would have no chance to sell to those who always buy the cheaper product or to convince others, by experience or otherwise, of the fact which he and all other dealers already know—that the cheaper product is actually identical with that carrying the more expensive label. . . .

Our holding neither ignores the economic realities of the marketplace nor denies that some labels will command a higher price than others, at least from some portion of the public. But it does mean that "the economic factors inherent in brand names and national advertising should not be considered in the jurisdictional inquiry under the statutory 'like grade and quality test.'" . . .

Justice Stewart, with whom Justice Harlan joins (dissenting)

I cannot agree that mere physical or chemical identity between premium and private label brands is, without more, a sufficient basis for a finding of "like grade and quality" within the meaning of § 2(a) of the Robinson-Patman Act. The conclusion that a product that travels at a premium in the marketplace is of "like grade and quality" with products of inferior commercial value is not required by the language of the Robinson-Patman Act, by its logic, or by its legislative history.

It is undisputed that the physical attributes and chemical constituents of Borden's premium and private label brands of evaporated milk are identical. It is also undisputed that the premium and private label brands are not competitive at the same price, and that if the private label milk is to be sold at all, it must be sold at prices substantially below the price commanded by Borden's premium brand. This simple market

fact no more than reflects the obvious economic reality that consumer preferences can and do create significant commercial distinctions between otherwise similar products. By pursuing product comparison only so far as the result of laboratory analysis, the Court ignores a most relevant aspect of the inquiry into the question of "like grade and quality" under § 2(a): Whether the products are different in the eyes of the consumer.

There is nothing intrinsic to the concepts of grade and quality that requires exclusion of the commercial attributes of a product from their definition. The product purchased by a consumer includes not only the chemical components that any competent laboratory can itemize, but also a host of commercial intangibles that distinguish the product in the marketplace. The premium paid for Borden brand milk reflects the consumer's awareness, promoted through advertising, that these commercial attributes are part and parcel of the premium product he is purchasing. The record also indicates that retail purchasers who bought the premium brand did so with the specific expectation of acquiring a product of premium quality. Contrary to the Court's suggestion, . . . this consumer expectation cannot accurately be characterized as a misapprehension. Borden took extensive precautions to insure that a flawed product did not reach the consumer. None of these precautions was taken for the private brand milk packed by Borden. An important ingredient of the premium brand inheres in the consumer's belief, measured by past satisfaction and the market reputation established by Borden for its products, that tomorrow's can will contain the same premium product as that purchased today. To say, as the Court does, that these and other intangibles, which comprise an important part of the commercial value of a product, are not sufficient to confer on Borden's premium brand a "grade" or "quality" different from that of private label brands is to ignore the obvious market acceptance of that difference.

ATLANTIC REFINING COMPANY v. FEDERAL TRADE COMMISSION

381 U.S. 357 (1965)

Justice Clark

The Federal Trade Commission has found that an agreement between the Atlantic Refining Company (Atlantic) and the Goodyear Tire & Rubber Company (Goodyear), under which the former "sponsors" the sale of the tires, batteries, and accessory TBA products of the latter to its wholesale outlets and its retail service station dealers, is an unfair method of competition in violation of the Federal Trade Commission Act. . . .

The Goodyear-Atlantic agreement required Atlantic to assist Goodyear "to the fullest practicable extent in perfecting sales, credit, and merchandising arrangements" with all of Atlantic's outlets. This included announcement to its dealers of its sponsorship of Goodyear products followed by a field representative's call to "suggest . . . the maintenance of adequate stocks of merchandise" and "maintenance of proper identification and advertising" of such merchandise. Atlantic was to instruct its salesmen to urge dealers to "vigorously" represent Goodyear, and to "cooperate with and assist" Goodyear in its "efforts to promote and increase the sale" by Atlantic dealers of Goodyear products. And it was to "maintain adequate dealer training programs in the sale of tires, batteries, and accessories." In addition, the companies organized joint sales organization meetings at which plans were made for perfecting the sales plan. One project was a "double teaming" solicitation of Atlantic outlets by representatives of both companies to convert them to Goodyear products. They were to call on the dealers together, take stock orders, furnish initial price lists, and project future quotas of purchases of Goodyear products. Goodyear also required that each Atlantic dealer be assigned to a supply point maintained by it, such as a warehouse, Goodyear store, independent dealer, or designated Atlantic distributor or retail dealer. Atlantic would not receive any commission on purchases made outside of an assigned supply point. Its commission of 10 percent on sales to Atlantic dealers and 7.5 percent on sales to its wholesalers was paid on the basis of a master sheet prepared by Goodyear and furnished Atlantic each month. This list was broken down so as to show the individual purchases of each dealer (except those whose supply points for Goodyear products were Atlantic wholesalers). Under this reporting technique, the Commission found, "Atlantic may determine the exact amount of sponsored TBA purchased by each Atlantic outlet." . . . Goodyear also furnished, this time at the specific request of Atlantic, a list of the latter's recalcitrant dealers who refused to be identified with the "Goodyear Program." These lists Atlantic forwarded to its district offices for "appropriate action." On one occasion a list of 46 such dealers was furnished Atlantic officials by Goodyear. The Commission found that "the entire group . . . was thereafter signed to Goodyear contracts and Goodyear advertising signs were installed at their stations." . . .

The effectiveness of the program is evidenced by the results. Within seven months after the agreement Goodyear had signed up 96 percent and 98 percent, respectively, of Atlantic's dealers in two of the three areas assigned to it. In 1952 the sale of Goodyear products to Atlantic dealers was $4,175,890—40 percent higher than Atlantic's sales during the last year of its purchase-resale plan with Lee tires and Exide batteries. By 1955 these sales of Goodyear products amounted to $5,700,121. Total sales of Goodyear and Firestone products from June 1950 to June 1956 were over $52,000,000. This enormous increase, the findings indicate, was the result of the effective policing of the plan. The reports of sales by Goodyear to Atlantic enabled it to know exactly the amount of Goodyear products the great majority of its dealers were buying.

The Commission stressed the evidence showing that "Atlantic dealers have been orally advised by sales officials of the oil company that their continued status as Atlantic dealers and lessees will be in jeopardy if they do not purchase sufficient quantities of sponsored" tires, batteries, and accessories. . . . Indeed, some dealers lost their leases after being reported for not complying with the Goodyear sales program. But we need not detail this feature of the case since Atlantic had conceded the point by not perfecting an appeal thereon. . . .

Certainly there is "warrant in the record" for the findings of the Commission here. Substantial evidence supports the conclusion that notwithstanding Atlantic's contention that it and its dealers are mutually dependent upon each other, they simply do not bargain as equals. Among the sources of leverage in Atlantic's hands are its lease and equipment loan contracts with their cancellation and short-term provisions. . . . It must also be remembered that Atlantic controlled the supply of gasoline and oil to its wholesalers and dealers. This was an additional source of economic leverage, . . . as was its extensive control of all advertising on the premises of its dealers.

Furthermore, there was abundant evidence that Atlantic, in some instances with the aid of Goodyear, not only exerted the persuasion that is a natural incident of its economic power, but coupled with it direct and overt threats of reprisal such as are now enjoined by paragraphs 5 and 6 of the order. Indeed, the Commission could properly have concluded that it was for this bundle of persuasion that Goodyear paid Atlantic its commission. We will not repeat the manner in which this sponsorship was carried out. It is sufficient to note that the most impressive evidence of its effectiveness was its undeniable success within a short time of its inception.

The short of it is that Atlantic with Goodyear's encouragement and assistance, has marshaled its full economic power in a continuing campaign to force its dealers and wholesalers to buy Goodyear products. The anticompetitive effects of this program are clear on the record and render unnecessary extensive economic analysis of market percentages or business justifications in determining whether this was a method of competition which Congress had declared unfair and therefore unlawful.

PROBLEMS FOR DISCUSSION

1. Hannibal Solo, doing businss as the Solo Drug Store, sues the Zappo Electric Company for unfair competition. Zappo, a privately owned public utility, was regulated by the State Utility Commission, which approved all rates charged by public utilities and their marketing and billing practices. Since 1890, to encourage use of electricity, Zappo had distributed free light bulbs to its customers. The customer simply brought in the used bulbs and received new ones in exchange. The cost of this program was of course built into the rates which Zappo charged for electricity. Solo claims that the free bulb program unfairly competes with the sale of light bulbs in his drugstore. What result, and why?

2. Stylish Shoe Company, one of the largest manufacturers, sold its shoes through some 600 independent retail stores. It offered these independent dealers the chance to participate in a "Promotion Program," under which they would receive special assistance in store layout, displays, and merchandising help, and a group insurance plan. In return, the dealer had to promise to concentrate his or her business on Stylish Shoes and not to carry any lines of shoes which directly competed with those made by Stylish. Nearly all of the dealers who had been selling Stylish Shoes elected to participate in this program; nonparticipating dealers did not receive the special benefits. The Sorfut Shoe Company brings a lawsuit alleging that the Promotion Program is an unfair method of competition. Does Sorfut have a valid claim for relief? Discuss.

3. Muffy Zelman borrowed $3,000 from the Avid Loan Company. While most of the loan was still unpaid, Muffy received a discharge in bankruptcy. Muffy later went to Avid for a loan of $1,500 and was told that Avid would not make the new loan unless she reaffirmed the earlier debt and promised to pay the balance which had

been discharged in bankruptcy. Muffy did so. Muffy now brings suit against Avid under the state's consumer protection act, claiming that Avid's "reaffirmation" requirement violates the act. Avid claims exemption from the act, since the act contains a section stating that it does not apply to "actions or transactions otherwise permitted, regulated, or prohibited under laws administered by the Director of Insurance, the Public Service Commission, the Federal Power Commission, or any other regulatory body or officer acting under statutory authority of this state or the United States." Avid says that it is regulated by the commissioner of banking, under the state's small loan company statute, and that it is therefore exempt from the consumer protection act. Muffy claims that the interpretation would frustrate the purposes of the consumer protection statute. Who's right, and why?

4. First Alabama National Bank had been in the banking business in Alabama for over 60 years. It first registered its trade name, First Alabama, with the Alabama secretary of state in 1965. At that time it also registered the name First Alabama with the U.S. Patent Office, as a service mark to be used in connection with general banking services. In 1971 Wiley Wichie registered with the secretary of state as First Alabama Home Co. and began building and selling homes. The bank first became aware of Wiley's activities when he opened a checking account there under the name First Alabama Home Co. Bank personnel had also seen a number of Wiley's ads which talked about homes by "First Alabama." The bank now sues for an injunction, alleging trade name infringement and unfair competition. Should the court grant an injunction here? Explain.

5. Roskoe Dairy Products Company began to use the trademark Dairy Maid on some of its products in 1955. It originally marketed nearly all of its products in Augusta, Maine, but had since expanded its marketing to several other cities. In 1963 it began selling dairy products in Biddeford under several names, including Dairy Maid. In 1975 Giant Dairies, Inc. (a nationwide company), began selling its products in Biddeford under the name Dairy Maid, which it used and advertised nationally as one of its brand names. Giant claims that Roskoe "abandoned" the trade name in Biddeford since for several months none of Roskoe's Dairy Maid products were for sale in Biddeford, that Roskoe's Dairy Maid products were carried by only four retail outlets in Biddeford, and that these sales were less than 10 percent of Roskoe's business. Roskoe sues for an injunction to prevent Giant from marketing its products in Biddeford under the name Dairy Maid. What result, and why?

6. Antonio Balistrade, a building contractor, signed a contract with Virgil and Vera Veber to do certain work on their home. The Vebers gave Balistrade a check for $100 as a down payment. The next day, Vera called Balistrade and told him that she and her husband wanted to cancel the deal because they had decided that the price was too high and that they had thought that the job included window and door trim. Balistrade, over the telephone, offered to do all the window and door trim for an additional $250. Vera agreed to that offer. No other written documents were signed. Virgil later signed a criminal complaint against Balistrade, in which three violations of the Home Improvement Act were alleged: failure to specify beginning and ending dates for the job; changing the terms of a written contract without putting the changes in writing; and providing for liquidated damage in excess of the permitted amount. These three requirements were found in regulations adopted by the Department of Commerce, which was the enforcement body named in the Home Improvement Act. The act provided that anyone who "intentionally refuses, neglects or fails to obey any regulation adopted under this Act shall, for each offense, be fined not less than $25 nor more than $1,000, or imprisoned for not more than one year, or both." Balistrade says he can't be charged under the act, since he did not *intentionally* do anything. The district attorney says

that "intentionally" only modifies "refuses" and that Balistrade neglected or failed to obey the regulations. Who is right, and why?

7. For several years Bennie Richards had been president of Crafty Chemicals, Inc. Policy differences arose between Bennie and Crafty's chairman, Herbie Render, who was also the majority stockholder. Bennie left Crafty, taking with him its formula books, cost books, and customer lists. Bennie then went to work for Catchall Chemicals, Inc., which was newly organized as a wholly owned subsidiary of Nollo Corporation. Bennie then wrote a letter to all of Crafty's customers in which he announced his new job, solicited their business, and told them that they could still order from their old catalogs since Catchall's "product numbers are the reverse of the IBM numbers in catalogs past." Catchall's new product catalog used identical format, product prices, and product numbers, and similar product names and descriptions, to those in the crafty catalog. Crafty sues for an injunction and damages. What result, and why?

8. Sally Sweetly, doing business as Magazine Messengers, used telephone solicitation to contact prospective customers for magazine subscriptions. After explaining the selection available, prices, and payment terms, Sally and her agents took orders for subscriptions to specified magazines. The state where she operated had a home solicitation statute which provided for a three-day cancellation privilege where there was a "personal solicitation of the sale at a residence of the buyer, and the buyer's agreement or offer to purchase is there given to the seller or a person acting for him." The local district attorney brings a lawsuit against Sally, asking the court to prohibit her operation unless she complies with the home solicitation statute, which requires written contracts containing the three-day cancellation privilege. Sally says that her operation is not subject to the act. How should the court rule? Explain.

9. Sticky Stamp Company, Inc., provided trading stamps which are given to customers as "bonuses" by grocery stores and other retailers. Customers might save these stamps by pasting them in small books and then redeem them for merchandise at Sticky's "gift centers." Each of Sticky's collection books for the stamps contained a printed notice that the stamps might not be sold to others. Sticky enforced this provision by bringing injunction suits against "trading centers" where customers tried to exchange their partially filled books of one brand of trading stamp for stamps from another company and where customers could buy additional stamps to fill uncompleted books. Sticky had been very successful in closing down these stamp trading centers. The FTC, after an investigation, charges Sticky with unfair methods of competition under Section 5 of the FTC Act. Should this charge be sustained by the Commission and the courts? Discuss.

10. To demonstrate the superior soaking and shaving qualities of its Swift Shave shaving cream, Trendy Products prepared a television commercial using a Plexiglas prop to which sand had been applied. The message read: "Apply, Soak, and Off in a stroke! We even shaved sandpaper with Swift Shave!" Trendy says that the Plexiglas and sand mock-up is necessary because regular sandpaper would appear on TV to be nothing more than plain colored paper. Trendy also can show that actual sandpaper can be shaved with Swift Shave, although some extended soaking is required. The FTC claims that this commercial is false advertising. Trendy says that the commercial is substantially true, and that everyone uses mock-ups on TV because the TV viewing screen does not always accurately convey what takes place in the studio. Should the FTC be able to get this commercial taken off the air? Discuss.

Legal Regulation of the Employment Relationship 50

The significance of "labor law" to modern U.S. business can hardly be overemphasized. Through national and state regulation, developments in this field can reach every firm which employs labor. The scope of potential liability for violations is enormous: back pay awards may reach several million dollars; whole groups of dismissed or retired workers may have to be rehired (with back pay and fringes); abandoned operations and plants may have to be reinstituted (with back pay and fringes for discharged workers). A little managerial "preventive medicine" is clearly desirable in this area, including the possible use of independent contractors rather than employees for some jobs (see Chapter 14).

SOURCES OF LABOR LAW

Where does the law of employer-employee relationships come from? Originally, the employment contract was treated by the common law in much the same way as other types of contracts; it required offer and acceptance, consideration, and the other elements of a valid contract. It was a two-party contract, with each party having the freedom to accept or reject the bargain offered by the other and with the parties being pretty much free to agree on any terms they chose. Specific legal rules also developed to cover this "master-servant" relationship, such as the employer's liability for torts committed by his or her servant within the scope of the employment and the employer's responsibility for furnishing a reasonably safe place in which to work. Much of the common law has now been displaced in this area, as both national and state governments have moved in aggressively to redefine this relationship.

Several broad, comprehensive national statutes exist in each of the two major divisions of labor law—"labor relations" and "labor standards." There is also considerable state regulation of both areas, and the 14th Amendment to the U.S. Constitution may be invoked if the state itself, or one of its agencies or instrumentalities, is directly involved in the relationship as the employer.

In the area of labor relations, the basic piece of national legislation is the National Labor Relations Act of 1935, as amended. The NLRA (also known as the Wagner Act) laid the cornerstone of national labor policy: belief in the process of collective bargaining between the employer and a representative freely chosen by his or her employees. The original act set out a series of forbidden employer "unfair labor practices," so that employers would not interfere with the selection of the bargaining representative and would be required to bargain. The governmental interference here was limited to providing the employees with a freely chosen bargaining representative; it was then up to the union to work out the terms and conditions of employment by bargaining with the employer.

Concern over excessive union power and abuses, coupled with a wave of strikes after World War II, led to the adoption of a series of comprehensive amendments in 1947—the Taft-Hartley Act (or Labor Management Relations Act). Taft-Hartley set out a series of forbidden *union* unfair labor practices and attempted to ensure certain basic employer and employee rights—such as the employer's right to tell his or her side of the story to the employees and the employee's right to *refrain* from participating in union activity if he or she so chose. These amendments also permitted the several states to prohibit agreements between employer and union which required union membership as a condition of employment (state "right-to-work" laws).

Further disenchantment with union operations and evidence of widespread corruption in the internal management of unions, provided by nationally televised hearings of the McClellan subcommittee, resulted in 1959 in a second substantial revision of the NLRA. The Labor-Management Reporting and Disclosure Act (LMRDA), or Landrum-Griffin Act, again attempted to protect employers, individual employees, and the public from certain union abuses, particularly the abuse of exerting indirect pressure on a recalcitrant employer by involving third parties in the bargaining dispute. The LMRDA also placed certain requirements on the internal management of unions and union funds and provided machinery for dealing with so-called national emergency strikes.

As a result of these two sets of amendments, a good deal of the spirit of the original Wagner Act ("Let the union do it") has been dissipated. The rather considerable limitations contained in Taft-Hartley and Landrum-Griffin are not fully consistent with the free collective bargaining envisaged by the Wagner Act, and the law of labor relations thus becomes susceptible of radically different interpretations at several important points.

Labor standards legislation provides direct regulation of the terms and conditions of employment; in that sense, it limits the freedom of the employer and the union, as well as the individual employee, to set their own terms of association with each other. The Wagner Act represented a basic commitment of national labor policy to the collective bargaining process, but the commitment has never been complete or without qualification. The mandatory "social security" system is itself an important piece of labor standards legislation, since it provides a required arrangement for retirement, disability, and dependent benefits. Social security can be supplemented, but not displaced, through collective bargaining.

The main piece of national "wages and hours" legislation is the Fair Labor Standards Act (FLSA) of 1938, as amended. Once again, it sets boundaries to the parties' "freedom of contract" by specifying certain minimum wages and required overtime which must be paid (even if there are persons ready and willing to work for less). Also included in this general category are several national statutes requiring the payment of "prevailing minimum wages" in a particular industry, as determined by the secretary of labor. The two such acts with broadest scope are the Walsh-Healy Act, for manufacturers and dealers supplying the national government with supplies valued at $10,000 or more, and the Davis-Bacon Act, covering building contracts with the national government for more than $2,000. Similar provisions have been inserted in national grant-in-aid legislation for the construction of airports, highways, housing for defense personnel, and urban renewal projects.

There are several important "antidiscrimination" statutes. The Equal Pay Act of 1963, an amendment to the FLSA, forbids employer and/or union conduct which results in pay differentials based on sex ("equal pay for equal work"). Any pay differentials between male and female employees must be justified on some basis other than sex (e.g., seniority or job differentials), or else the employer (and possibly the union) will be subjected to an FLSA proceeding.

Whereas the 1963 Act pertains only to sex discrimination in the payment of wages, Title VII of the 1964 Civil Rights Act is much more comprehensive. It prohibits discrimination by employers, employment agencies, and labor organizations as to hiring, compensation, or any other term, condition, or privilege of employment, on the basis of race, color, religion, sex, or national origin. It also established a new enforcement agency, the Equal Employment Opportunity Commission (EEOC). The 1964 Act does allow such discrimination on the basis of religion, sex, or national origin where "reasonably necessary to the normal operation of that particular business or enterprise" as a "bona fide occupational qualification" (BFOQ). There is no such BFOQ proviso for discrimination based on race or color. Amendments in 1972 extended this antidiscrimination coverage to most state and local government employees.

In 1967 Congress added "age" to the prohibited bases of employment discrimination by enacting the Age Discrimination in Employment Act of 1967 (ADEA). This act prohibits such discrimination against "older" workers (i.e., those between 40 and 70 years of age). Amendments in 1974 extended the act's protection to most governmental employees. The ADEA is enforced through FLSA procedures. Age discrimination is also subject to a BFOQ proviso.

What is potentially the most far-reaching (and therefore the most costly) piece of "labor standards" legislation ever enacted became law in 1970: the Occupational Safety and Health Act. This act is designed to "assure as far as possible every working man and woman in the nation safe and healthful working conditions," by giving the secretary of labor very broad powers to adopt "standards" which will in effect be mandatory health and safety practices. To ensure compliance, the employer's premises are subject to unannounced inspection by "the man from OSHA," either on employee complaint or by random selection. Injunctive relief and criminal penalties are provided for violations.

In 1974 Congress passed another important piece of labor legislation—the Employment Retirement Income Security Act. ERISA establishes a new government agency, financed by contributions from employers with pension plans, to guarantee payment of earned pension benefits. It does not require any employer to establish a pension plan, but when he or she does, the plan must meet certain standards for the funding and management of assets and for the vesting of benefits. ERISA is thus a significant new protection for the more than 30 million workers who are covered by its provisions.

Labor legislation in a particular state may include all of the above types plus some additions. Many states now have statutes regulating collective bargaining by public employees, some of which provide for compulsory arbitration of bargaining disputes which the parties are unable to resolve themselves. The states have also enacted workers' compensation laws, which provide a statutory scheme for compensating employees for virtually all job-related injuries. (A similar national statute, the Federal Employees' Compensation Act, covers U.S. government employees.) Finally, workers who have lost their jobs are provided with at least some temporary help through state systems of unemployment compensation.

LABOR RELATIONS LAW—MAJOR PROBLEM AREAS

Selection of a Bargaining Agent. Assuming that a group of employees have indicated a desire for union representation and that they are subject to NLRA jurisdiction, the first step in the procedure for selecting a bargaining agent is to define the extent of the bargaining unit. In some cases, where there is only one business location and where there is a substantial identity of interests among all concerned employees, this is an easy job. Multiple jobsites create some definitional problems. What if one plant votes "no union" but a majority for all plants operated by the company votes in favor of a union? Do we decide plant by plant or company-wide? The Board has generally favored the company-wide approach. How about employees with substantially different skills, interests, and professional identification? Are they all to be lumped together as an amorphous mass ("one big union"), or are they somehow to be split up (so that some smaller craft unions or even "no union" might have a better chance of winning the separate elections)? Are plumbers working in an auto plant entitled to have their votes counted separately, to see whether they might want the plumbers' union to represent them, or do they just take the plant-wide UAW and like it? Who's included in "faculty" when union-style collective bargaining comes to the campus? Classroom teachers?—certainly. How about teaching fellows? Researchers? Librarians? School nurses (if any)? Dorm counselors? Military personnel teaching ROTC classes? Heads of academic departments who also teach one or more classes? Conflicting equities can make it difficult to arrive at a "fair" resolution of these questions. The Board's general approach has been "one big union," meaning that a group of employees wishing to be excluded from the employer-wide unit must have some strong evidence of their "uniqueness."

American Association of University Professors v. *Board of Regents of the University of Nebraska*
279 N.W.2d 621 (Nebraska, 1979)

FACTS   The Regents appealed an order of the state's Court of Industrial Relations which established a collective bargaining unit at the University of Nebraska at Omaha. The Regents contended that (1) the CIR had no jurisdiction over them; (2) the bargaining unit was inappropriate because it included only employees of U/N at Omaha; (3) the bargaining unit was inappropriate because it should not have included department chairmen, librarians, counselors, assistant instructors, or academic personnel holding special appointments. The U/N–O College Business Administration Faculty Association also appealed from the dismissal of its petition for intervention, which had asked for the establishment of a separate bargaining unit. Intercollegiate athletic coaches and trainers were excluded from the bargaining unit.

ISSUES   Does the CIR have jurisdiction over the University? If so, was the CIR's determination of the bargaining unit correct?

DECISION   Yes. Yes. Judgment affirmed.

REASONS   The largest section of Justice Boslaugh's opinion dealt with the third point raised by the Regents. He quickly disposed of the first two points by noting that the Supreme Court had earlier approved the CIR's similar determination of a separate bargaining unit for the faculty at U/N–Lincoln.

"The remaining assignments of error relate to the composition of the unit. The Regents contend that department chairmen should be excluded from the bargaining unit because they are supervisory personnel and a part of management. . . . [W]here the powers of the chairmen are effectively diffused among the department faculty pursuant to the principal of collegiality, chairmen should be included within the faculty bargaining unit.

"The evidence here is that the department chairmen at UNO are faculty members who serve as chairmen at the pleasure of the dean of the college. . . . In performing their duties, the chairmen consult with the other members of the faculty and, generally, there is little or no disagreement between the chairmen and the faculty of the department concerning recommendations and other decisions which the chairmen make. The evidence sustains the finding of the CIR that chairmen of the department should be included within the faculty bargaining unit.

"Although the library at UNO is not a college, it is considered to be an academic unit in some respects. The librarians do not perform instructional duties, but their work is related to the teaching and research functions performed by the faculty. To that extent there is a community of interest between the faculty and the librarians. . . . We think the record sustains the finding by the CIR that librarians should be included in the faculty bargaining unit. . . .

"During their period of service the personnel holding special appointments function in the same manner as regular members of the faculty. . . .

"Although assistant instructors are considered to have an interim position, they teach and do research in much the same manner as other members of the faculty. While there is a relatively high turnover rate among assistant instructors, the evidence indicates the assistant instructors are a necessary part of the instructional staff.

"There is little in the record concerning the exact nature of the duties performed by the counselors. There is nothing to indicate they are management or supervisory personnel. The title suggests that the counselors work with the students in academic matters, and might be presumed to have some community of interest with the faculty."

The court also dismissed the business faculty's petition since the 20 persons it listed were less than 10 percent of the members of the bargaining unit. The court did indicate that the issue could be raised in a new proceeding, but it noted a "strong policy against undue fragmentation of bargaining units in the public sector."

In addition to determining the appropriate bargaining unit, the Board's preelection hearing also decides which employees are entitled to vote and which unions will appear on the ballot. The original union petitioning for the election is required to present evidence of 30 percent support, typically by means of signature cards from the requisite number of employees. Any other union wishing to appear on the ballot need only show substantial interest, and the "no union" choice will appear automatically. The election is by secret ballot. The winner need only receive a majority of the votes actually cast. If there is no majority, a runoff election is held between the two choices receiving the highest vote totals. While a secret ballot election is clearly the preferred method and the one normally used, the Board does have the power to grant bargaining rights to a union presenting signature cards from a majority, where the cards clearly indicate such an intent, where there has been no union misrepresentation of the purpose of the cards to the individual employees, and where the possibility of holding a fair election is lessened by the employer's serious unfair labor practices.

Section 7 of the NLRA gives employees "the right to self-organization, to form, join or assist labor organizations." Section 8(a)(1) then makes it an unfair labor practice for an employer to "interfere with, restrain or coerce employees in the exercises of the rights guaranteed in Section 7." Labor history contains many cases where unscrupulous employers used puppet unions to forestall genuine representation and to exploit their workers still further. The Board is vigorous and vigilant, therefore, in protecting these important organizing rights, so that the employer's conduct during an organizing campaign must now be circumspect if he or she wishes to avoid an unfair labor practice charge. Taft-Hartley guarantees the employer's (and others') right of "free speech," so long as the employer in presenting his or her views does not make any threat of reprisal or promise any benefit, but the Board has ruled that such conduct may be a basis for invalidating a no-union vote, thus requiring a new election.

Union Security and Membership. Once selected as the official bargaining agent, the union is then legally required to bargain for all employees in the unit, union and nonunion alike, as well as to process the grievances of all employees on an equal basis. Violation of this duty of equal and fair representation could lead to decertification of the union by the NLRB or to charges before the EEOC.

Because it is legally required to represent all, the union makes the superficially logical argument that all employees in the unit should be required to become union members in order to keep their jobs. This is the so-called free rider argument: No nonunion employee should get a free ride on union-won benefits at the expense of his dues-paying fellow employees. The first answer to this argument is that the union not only agreed to accept this status; it aggressively sought it. And second, it should be possible to work up some fair compensation to the union for benefits actually conferred by it on nonunion employees, without forcing them to join and financially support an organization with which they may disagree violently—philosophically, politically, and economically.

From a union's standpoint, the best union-security arrangement is the "closed shop," where only union members are hired and where employees must remain union members to keep their jobs. The closed shop has been outlawed for nearly all industries, but the legally permitted "union shop" is almost as good. Under a union shop, the employee has an initial period of time after hiring, typically 30 days, to decide whether he or she wants to join the union in order to keep the job. An employee who decides not to join is fired at the end of the trial period. In addition to the union shop, the union will probably also negotiate a contract provision for automatic payroll deduction of union dues.

Section 14(b) of Taft-Hartley gave the states the authority to ban compulsory unionism if they wished to do so; there are 20 states with such right-to-work laws. Since Section 14(b) speaks of required "membership" in a union, some of these states permit the "agency shop," under which an employee is not required to join the union but instead pays it a fee which supposedly represents the value of the union's services to him or her as a member of the bargaining unit. Other states in this group hold that the agency shop is illegal too, and in those states the original "open shop" prevails. With an open shop, each individual employee is legally free to decide whether he or she will become, or remain, a union member, and the union leaders are thus responsible to the membership on a continuing basis. Labor's annual drive in Congress to repeal 14(b) has thus far been unsuccessful.

Scope of the Duty to Bargain. Section 8(a)(5) makes it an unfair labor practice for the employer to refuse to bargain collectively with the representative of his or her employees; Section 8(b)(3) contains a similar requirement for the chosen union representative. But the parties are *required* to bargain only as to items which are classified as "mandatory" subjects of collective bargaining. As to those items, not only is it a violation of the NLRA to refuse to bargain, but it is also legally permissible to insist on one's bargaining position as the price of an agreement. That is, where a mandatory subject is involved, either party can use all of the weapons at its command—strike, lockout, picketing, and so on—to enforce the bargaining demand.

What are these mandatory subjects? Generally, they comprise items designated as "wages, hours, and other terms and conditions of employment." Very few bargaining demands would not fall into this category. Pension, profit-sharing, and stock-purchase plans; bonuses and merit raises; seniority and retirement rules; prices for meals and housing furnished by the company; and union security arrangements—all have been ruled mandatory subjects.

"Permissive" subjects of collective bargaining are those which the parties are free to discuss if they *both* wish to, but which neither can insist on as the price of an agreement. Such insistence and/or the use of bargaining weapons would be a violation of the Section 8 duty to bargain and would subject the wrongdoer to unfair labor practice charges. Nearly all demands held to be merely permissive have related to the mechanics of the bargaining process itself, such as the size of the bargaining teams, or the requirement of a secret employee vote on the employer's last offer prior to a strike, or a secret ballot vote on ratification of the new contract. Product selection, distribution, and pricing have likewise thus far been held to be "management prerogatives" and thus not mandatory subjects for collective bargaining. But the contracting out of work which was formerly performed by members of the bargaining unit *is* a mandatory subject, and the NLRB has ordered the resumption of maintenance operations which were so terminated by the company without prior bargaining.

There are a few provisions, such as closed shop and "hot cargo" agreements, which may not be lawfully included in the collective contract even if both parties so desire.

Ford Motor Company v. National Labor Relations Board
99 S. Ct. 1842 (1979)

FACTS   Ford provided in-plant cafeteria and vending machine food services. ARA Services, Inc., an independent caterer, managed these services, but Ford had the right to approve the quality, quantity, and prices for the food served. Ford notified the UAW that food prices in its stamping plant at Chicago Heights, Illinois, would be increased by unspecified amounts. UAW Local 588, representing the 3,600 hourly workers at the plant, asked for bargaining on the prices and services and for information relevant to Ford's involvement in the food services operation. Ford refused, and the UAW filed unfair labor practice charges with the NLRB, alleging a refusal to bargain over a mandatory subject. The Board sustained the charges and ordered Ford to bargain. The U.S. Seventh Circuit Court of Appeals upheld the Board, although it and three other circuit courts had previously refused to do so. Ford asked for certiorari.

ISSUE   Were the in-plant food prices and services a mandatory subject of collective bargaining?

DECISION   Yes. Judgment affirmed.

REASONS   Justice White first noted that the Board had consistently held to this position, even though the courts of appeal had been refusing to enforce its orders. He felt that the Board's judgment should be given "considerable deference."

"Of course, the judgment of the Board is subject to judicial review; but if its construction of the statute is reasonably defensible, it should not be rejected merely because the courts might prefer another view of the statute. . . .

"Construing and applying the duty to bargain and the language of S.8(d), 'other terms and conditions of employment,' are tasks lying at the heart of the Board's function. . . .

> "It is not suggested by petitioner that an employee should work a full eight-hour shift without stopping to eat. It reasonably follows that the availability of food during working hours and the conditions under which it is to be consumed are matters of deep concern to workers, and one need not strain to consider them to be among those 'conditions' of employment that should be subject to the mutual duty to bargain. . . . The terms and conditions under which food is available on the job are plainly germane to the 'working environment.' . . . Furthermore, the company is not in the business of selling food to its employees, and the establishment of in-plant food prices is not among those 'managerial decisions, which lie at the heart of entrepreneurial control.' . . . The Board is in no sense attempting to permit the Union to usurp managerial decision making; nor is it seeking to regulate an area from which Congress intended to exclude it.
>
> "Including within S.8(d) the prices of in-plant supplied food and beverages would also serve the ends of the National Labor Relations Act. . . . National labor policy contemplates that areas of common dispute between employers and employees be funneled into collective bargaining. The assumption is that this is preferable to allowing recurring disputes to fester outside the negotiation process until strikes or other forms of economic warfare occur.
>
> "The trend of industrial practice supports this conclusion. In response to increasing employee concern over this issue, many contracts now are being negotiated that contain provisions concerning in-plant food services."

The duty imposed by the NLRA means that the parties must bargain in "good faith." This at least includes meeting with each other, listening to the other side's proposals, and discussing them. In the case of the employer, the duty to bargain also means providing the union with such relevant information as is within its possession and reasonably available. The NLRA does not require any party to agree to a proposal from the other side, or even to make any concession. Despite these clearly stated rules, however, both the NLRB and the U.S. Second Circuit Court of Appeals held that General Electric committed the unfair labor practice of refusing to bargain by making its "last, best offer" at the start of negotiations and indicating to the employees that that was the best it could do.

Union Tactics and Unfair Labor Practices. The union's main weapons in support of its bargaining demands are the strike, picketing, and the boycott. There are some significant legal limitations (as well as economic ones) on the use of each. In general, both the objectives sought and the tactics used must be lawful.

Both Taft-Hartley and Landrum-Griffin tried to restrict union conduct which had the effect of dragging neutral employers, and their employees, into the primary dispute. The main relevant section of the amended NLRA is Section 8(b)(4). Strikes, refusals to handle or work on certain ("hot") goods, or any other union conduct which threatens, coerces, or restrains any person is illegal if its objective is to (a) force any employer or self-employed person to enter a labor organization or to enter into a "hot cargo" agreement, illegal under 8(e); (b) force any person to cease doing business with any other person; (c) force any employer to bargain with one union where another union has already been certified; or (*d*) force an employer to assign particular work to one group of employees rather than another. Section 8(b)(7) further limits the permissible objectives of picketing. Picketing is unlawful where it is done to force an employer to recognize a union or to force his or her employees to accept it as their agent if (*a*) another union has already been recognized and there is no legal question as to its status; (*b*) a valid election has been held within the past 12 months; or (*c*) such picketing has been conducted for a reasonable time (not to exceed 30 days) and the union has not filed a petition for an election.

In addition to the above legal restrictions on the purposes for which union collective-action weapons may be used, any such concerted activities must themselves be conducted in a lawful manner. In general, this means that the union's tactics must be "peaceful." Violence or threats of violence directed against the employer, his or her premises, employees who choose to go to work, or customers or others who wish to continue to do business with the "target" employer would clearly be illegal. Access to and egress from the target premises must not be impeded. The laws of libel and slander presumably still apply to picket signs and other information media. And so on.

Illegality of the union's objectives or tactics not only subjects it to unfair labor practice charges; there may also be other consequences. The union itself may be liable for the damages caused and/or subject to an injunction to prohibit the unlawful conduct. Civil rights violations could conceivably be involved in the union's conduct. Employees engaging in an "unprotected" strike are subject to lawful dismissal by the employer, with no right to reinstatement when the strike ends. The 1947 and 1959 amendments, coupled with a more critical public attitude toward unions, now make it reasonably clear that union hooliganism will be punished. However, the public still shows a high tolerance level for illegal, but peaceful, union conduct, such as illegal boycotts and illegal public employee strikes. These issues remain unresolved.

Sears, Roebuck & Co. v. San Diego County District Council of Carpenters
436 U.S. 180 (1978)

FACTS   Sears filed a trespass action in state court against the Carpenters Union, which was picketing on Sears' property. The union had learned that certain carpentry work in Sears' store in Chula Vista, California, was being done by persons who had not been sent out from the union's hiring hall, and it had asked the store manager to comply with the hiring hall procedure. Nothing was done, so the union put up picket lines at the store. The pickets were on Sears' property, either on walkways next to the store or in the parking lot. Sears' security manager asked the pickets to leave, and when they refused to do so, a trespass suit was filed. The state trial court granted an injunction, but the state Supreme Court reversed. The U.S. Supreme Court granted certiorari.

ISSUE   Are state trespass actions in labor disputes preempted by the NLRA?

DECISION   No. Judgment of state Supreme Court reversed and case remanded.

REASONS   Justice Stevens reviewed the facts in this case and the history of state court actions in labor disputes since the adoption of the Wagner Act in 1935. He noted that the legality of this picketing under the NLRA was not clear—it might or might not be lawful, depending primarily on the union's motives. It might be illegal under Section 8(b)(4)(D) as an attempt to force assignment of work to members of a particular union or under Section 8(b)(7)(C) as recognition picketing. On the other hand, it might be protected conduct under Section 7 if the union's sole objective was to secure compliance with area standards.

"[T]he history of the labor pre-emption doctrine in this Court does not support an approach which sweeps away state-court jurisdiction over conduct traditionally subject to state regulation without careful consideration of the relative impact of such a jurisdictional bar on the various interests affected. . . .

"In each case, the pertinent inquiry is whether the two potentially conflicting statutes were 'brought to bear on precisely the same conduct.' . . .

"[T]he Court has allowed a State to enforce certain laws of general applicability even though aspects of the challenged conduct were arguably prohibited by S.8 of the NLRA. Thus, for example, the Court has upheld state-court jurisdiction over conduct that touches 'interests so deeply rooted in local feeling and responsibility that, in the absence of compelling congressional direction, we could not infer that Congress had deprived the States of the power to act.' . . .

"The critical inquiry, therefore, is not whether the State is enforcing a law relating specifically to labor relations or one of general application but whether the controversy presented to the state court is identical to . . . or different from . . . that which could have been, but was not presented to the Labor Board. For it is only in the former situation that a state court's exercise of jurisdiction involves a risk of interference with the unfair labor practice jurisdiction of the Board. . . .

"In the present case, the controversy which Sears might have presented to the Labor Board is not the same as the controversy presented to the state court. . . . Accordingly, permitting the state court to adjudicate Sears' trespass claim would create no realistic risk of interference with the Labor Board's primary jurisdiction to enforce the statutory prohibition against unfair labor practices."

Employer Tactics and Unfair Labor Practices. The employer's arsenal of weapons includes some that are roughly comparable to those used by the union, as well as some for which the union has no real equivalent. The counterpart of the union's denial of services through a strike is the employer's denial of access to the workplace (and therefore wages) by means of a "lockout." In lieu of picketing, the employer advises employees, customers, and other members of the public of his or her side of the dispute by advertising, typically in a local newspaper. There is no real employer counterpart to the boycott. In addition to the above "corresponding" weapons, the employer also possesses the ultimate sanctions of plant relocation and termination of the business, though the use of either is severely limited by the Board and the courts. Management may also do some forward planning to cushion the effects of a strike, by stockpiling inventories, readjusting contract schedules, or transferring work from one plant to another. The employer may also attempt to restrict the scope of the union's collective action by means of a court injunction.

A lockout designed to prevent unionization or to discourage union membership would be an unfair labor practice, but an employer may use the lockout to protect his own legitimate economic interests. Where there is a bargaining impasse, the employer may lock out in support of his or her bargaining position. Or, if the union calls or threatens to call a strike, the employer can lock out in retaliation. He or she can also lock out to prevent "economic hardship" to his or her business.

An employer has an absolute right to go out of business at any time, for any reason, even if the employer's sole reason for doing so is his or her anti-union bias. Where an employer closes only part of an operation, however, the employer's motives must be economic ones and not a desire to "chill unionism" at his or her other locations. In general, the legality of a plant relocation ("runaway shop") would be tested in the same manner as that of a partial closing.

Textile Workers Union of America v. Darlington Manufacturing Company
380 U.S. 263 (1965)

FACTS Darlington operated only one textile mill, in South Carolina. A majority of its stock, along with the stock of 16 other manufacturers of textiles, was owned by Deering Milliken Corporation, which was in turn dominated by Roger Milliken and other members of the Milliken family. Roger was president of all but one of the companies and was director of labor relations for all of them. In March 1956 the TWU began an organizing drive at Darlington. It won a narrow victory in an NLRB election on September 6, 1956. On September 12, the directors voted to sell the mill and liquidate Darlington; the stockholders did the same on October 17. The plant closed in November, and the equipment was sold at auction in December. The Darlington Manufacturing Company had been dissolved. The TWU filed charges under 8(a)(1) and (3) and (8)(a)(5). The NLRB, finding that Darlington was part of an employer group characterized by common ownership and common control, ordered back pay until similar jobs were found, preferential hiring at other D–M plants for the discharged Darlington workers, and moving expenses for any of them who wanted to move to another D–M plant. The court of appeals refused to enforce the order.

ISSUE Can a termination of part of an employer's business constitute an unfair labor practice?

DECISION Yes. Judgment reversed and case remanded to the NLRB.

REASONS Justice Harlan very carefully distinguished the charges which had been alleged. Under Section 8(a)(1)—interfering with employees' organizing rights guaranteed under Section 7—employer business decisions with some indirect adverse impact on employee rights would be violations only when the interference outweighed any possible business justification; 8(a)(1) really covered acts which were illegal even without any discriminatory motive. The Board was correct, then, in treating this plant closing case primarily under 8(a)(3)—employer discrimination designed to discourage union membership. As to 8(a)(5), the Board found that the failure to bargain about the plant closing was an unfair labor practice *because* the closing was itself a violation of 8(a)(3).

"We hold that so far as the Labor Relations Act is concerned, an employer has the absolute right to terminate his entire business for any reason he pleases. . . .

> "We consider first the argument . . . that an employer may not go completely out of business without running afoul of the Labor Relations Act if such action is prompted by a desire to avoid unionization. . . . A proposition that a single businessman cannot choose to go out of business if he wants to would represent such a startling innovation that it should not be entertained without the clearest manifestation of legislative intent or unequivocal judicial precedent so construing the Labor Relations Act. We find neither. . . .
>
> "One of the purposes of the Labor Relations Act is to prohibit the discriminatory use of economic weapons in an effort to obtain future benefits. . . . [A] complete liquidation of a business yields no such future benefit for the employer, if the termination is bona fide. It may be motivated more by spite against the union than by business reasons, but it is not the type of discrimination which is prohibited by the Act. The personal satisfaction that such an employer may derive from standing on his beliefs and the mere possibility that other employers will follow his example are surely too remote to be considered dangers at which the labor statutes were aimed. . . .
>
> "On the other hand, a discriminatory partial closing may have repercussions on what remains of the business, affording employer leverage for discouraging the free exercise of S.7 rights among the remaining employees."

Throughout most of the early history of unionism, the courts were on the employer's side. The standard operating procedure when confronted with union collective action was to ask for a court injunction to restrict or terminate the union activities. Employers got an unexpected bonanza when the courts applied the Sherman Anti-Trust Act to union activities, thus further restricting employee collective action.

Congress attempted to limit the use of the courts in labor disputes by including Sections 6 and 20 in the Clayton Act of 1914. Unfortunately, from the union viewpoint, Section 20 said that an injunction could be issued if "necessary to prevent irreparable injury to property, or to a property right," and the courts were very liberal in construing this qualifying phrase. It took the Norris-LaGuardia Act of 1932 to substantially eliminate the labor injunction from the U.S. district courts. (Many states copied this act.) It is still theoretically possible for an employer to get an injunction in a labor dispute, but the strict jurisdictional requirements make this very unlikely. The one exceptional case where the employer will be granted an injunction is where there is a strike in violation of a no-strike clause in an existing collective agreement. (An employer can also get a specific performance order to enforce an arbitration clause in an existing contract.) In addition, the Board and the attorney general are not bound by Norris-LaGuardia and can get injunctions issued.

Conflict Resolution.   As indicated previously, the government's basic approach to management-union disputes is merely to see to it that the parties meet their obligation to bargain with each other in good faith and then to let the economic chips fall where they may. In 1947, however, Congress opted for additional governmental participation in the bargaining process, with the creation of the Federal Mediation and Conciliation Service (FMCS), an independent administrative agency.

The primary responsibility of bargaining out, and living with, their agreement is still left up to the parties. But the services of the FMCS are available at the request of either party, or on its own initiative where the labor dispute involves the public safety and interest or where it threatens to have a substantial adverse impact on interstate commerce. If the parties want to submit their dispute to binding arbitration, the FMCS will also make available to them a list of qualified labor arbitrators from which to select.

Arbitration provides a more civilized method of settling disputes than strikes, lockouts, and the like. It is usually less formal, less complicated, and therefore less time-consuming and less expensive than a court trial. Nearly all arbitration is voluntarily agreed to by the parties, but some states have compulsory arbitration laws for public employees, particularly fire fighters and police officers, and the Taft-Hartley Act contains special procedures for compulsory government action in "national emergency strikes." Today the courts recognize and enforce awards made by third-party arbitrators on matters submitted to them by the parties, and as indicated previously, arbitration clauses in existing contracts are specifically enforceable, despite the Norris-LaGuardia Act.

Internal Union Management; Reporting and Disclosure Requirements. The Landrum-Griffin amendments to the NLRA ushered in a new era in union organization and administration. The Landrum-Griffin Act was passed following the sensational disclosures of the McClellan subcommittee on the extent of corruption and gangster control in the labor movement. The findings received widespread publicity because many of the hearings were televised and because of the popularity of *The Enemy Within*, a book written by subcommittee counsel Robert Kennedy. The result was the passage of the Landrum-Griffin Act, which set out a "bill of rights" for labor union members and imposed substantial reporting and disclosure requirements on unions.

The "bill of rights" is an attempt to provide guarantees of minimum participatory access to the union's decision-making process and to protect the individual member's status within the union. Subject to the union's "reasonable rules," all members are to have equal rights to attend and vote at meetings, to nominate candidates, to vote in elections, and to exercise their freedoms of speech and assembly. Dues increases must be voted by secret ballot at a special membership meeting or by referendum. Except where he fails to pay dues, an individual union member cannot be disciplined by his union unless he is served with written, specific charges and is given a reasonable time to prepare his defense and a full and fair hearing. If his grievance against the union or its officers or agents is not resolved by internal procedures within four months, the member can take his case to court; he can also bring a civil suit in U.S. district court to enforce any of his rights under the act. He can demand a copy of any collective contract which affects him, and the secretary of labor is directed to bring suit on his behalf if he fails to get it.

The union itself is required to file two major types of reports with the secretary of labor—procedural and financial. Each union must adopt a constitution and bylaws, and both must be filed. Existing provisions covering such things as membership qualifications, initiation fees, selection and removal of officers, contract ratification, and strike authorization must also be filed if such matters are not covered in the constitution and bylaws. Yearly financial reports must be filed, and these must cover such matters as assets and liabilities; receipts and their sources; salaries, loans, and other payments to officers and employees; and loans to any business. Full, periodic reports must also be filed when the national union places a local under "trusteeship." To try to prevent conflicts of interest, union officers and employees must file personal financial reports covering transactions with companies which the union has organized or is trying to organize.

The Landrum-Griffin Act thus contains important new legal protections for the individual union member and for the public.

LABOR STANDARDS LEGISLATION

"Fair Labor Standards."   Where it applies, the Fair Labor Standards Act places a floor under wage rates; it does *not* place a ceiling on hours of work, either per day or per week. It is almost inconceivable today, but the first national minimum wage so provided was *25 cents* per hour, with the objective of reaching *40 cents* an hour after the act had been in force for seven years. The 1974 Amendments extended coverage to most employees of public agencies and institutions and to "in-home" domestics workers and babysitters, but the U.S. Supreme Court ruled that Congress could not impose such limits on state and local governments.

Subject again to some exceptions, the FLSA also requires the employer to pay overtime at a rate of time and a half for all hours worked in excess of 40 in the employee's normal workweek. There is no provision for daily overtime; the "workweek" is any seven consecutive days. Overtime must be calculated for each successive seven-day period; the employer gets no "credit' if an employee works fewer than 40 hours in a given week. An hourly wage must be calculated for each employee, but the employer can exclude such things as gifts, discretionary bonuses, and employer payments to certain qualified savings and profit-sharing plans.

The employer is required to keep records of such wage and hour data for up to three years. For violations of the minimum wage and overtime provisions, the injured employee can bring suit personally or request in writing that the secretary of labor do so on his or her behalf. The secretary can also ask the U.S. district court for an injunction to prevent further violations and/or for the removal of goods so produced from interstate commerce.

There are also extensive regulations promulgated by the secretary which pertain to the use of child labor, that is, the use of minors under age 18. Generally, the employment of children under age 14 is prohibited; between 14 and 16, some jobs are permitted, subject to strict limits on work hours; between 16 and 18, employment is prohibited only in those industries which the secretary had found to be "hazardous," such as coal and other mining, slaughterhouses and meat-packing plants, building demolition, and roofing and excavation work. Criminal penalties—up to six months in jail, a fine of up to $10,000, or both—and/or injunctions are possible enforcement measures. Goods produced through the use of illegal child labor are subject to removal from the stream of commerce, but innocent purchasers of the goods, for value, are protected against confiscation if they receive a written certificate of compliance stating that the goods were produced in accordance with FLSA standards.

Antidiscrimination Legislation. Since the Due Process and Equal Protection clauses of the 14th Amendment pertain only to actions by a state or its agencies or instrumentalities, legislation is needed to reach private acts of arbitrary discrimination in the employment field. Once again, the vehicle chosen by Congress is the Commerce Clause.

The Equal Pay Act of 1963 prohibits pay differentials based solely on sex. As indicated previously, it is an amendment to FLSA and applies only to those employees who are covered by the minimum wage provisions of FLSA. Union conduct which causes or attempts to cause such employer discrimination is likewise prohibited.

To show a violation, the government must prove that the jobs in question "require equal skill, equal effort, and equal responsibility and are performed under similar working conditions" (and that males and females are paid different wages for performing them). Then, if the employer wishes to raise one of the exceptions permitted by the Equal Pay Act as a defense (seniority, merit, quality of production, any factor other than sex), he or she has the burden of proving that the differential is based on the exception. "Equal" does not mean identical, and minor, insignificant job differences will not justify such wage discrimination.

Where a violation is shown to exist, the employer is prohibited from reducing anyone's wages to eliminate the differential; someone's wages must be *raised*. Aside from this provision, all the standard FLSA enforcement procedures apply to the Equal Pay provisions, including criminal penalties.

Title VII of the 1964 Civil Rights Act contains much broader antidiscrimination provisions. It applies to any employer who is engaged in an industry affecting commerce and who employs 15 or more employees. It also prohibits discrimination by labor unions and employment agencies.

An employer may not use race, color, religion, sex, or national origin in making employment decisions: hiring, firing, promoting, transferring, compensating, or determining any of the terms, conditions, or privileges of employment. There are, however, several statutory exceptions. Discriminatory *hiring* on the basis of religion, sex, or national origin is permitted where such limitations can be justified as a "bona fide occupational qualification reasonably necessary to the normal operation of that particular business or enterprise." One obvious example would be separate casting for male and female parts in a theater company. A French restaurant might wish to employ only "French" table attendants (or at least French-speaking ones). Religious schools are also specifically exempted; they may prefer members of their own religion in deciding whom to hire. Once the hiring decision has been made, however, there must be substantially equal treatment of the "outsider"-employee. If the French restaurant hired a German, for example, it could not pay the German a lower (or higher) wage on the basis that he or she was German rather than French. Also subject to a specific exemption are businesses located on or near an Indian reservation; such businesses are permitted to have employment practices which gave "preferential treatment" to Indians. Similarly, the U.S. Bureau of Indian Affairs can use preferential hiring for Indians.

By omission, Title VII indicates that there can be no such thing as a bona fide occupational qualification based on race or color. The two cases which always come to mind in this regard are the Harlem Globetrotters basketball team and specifically written "black" or "white" roles in movies, plays, and TV shows. Congress apparently didn't consider such problems, or didn't think they were worth bothering about. In any event, that is the way the act now reads, so that a talented white basketball player who was refused employment by the Globetrotters would seem to have a good case.

Section 703(j) of the act specifically disclaims any requirement that preferential treatment be given to any individual or group so as to "make up" any "statistical imbalance" between an employer's work force and the community as a whole, with regard to the representation of particular groups. There is, in other words, no requirement of "affirmative action" in Title VII. Just because an employer has a disproportionately low number of employees from a particular group does not mean that he or she must prefer applicants from that group for employment or promotion. Indeed, an employer who did so could face a charge under the act from the "majority-group" member who was more qualified and who did not get the job or the promotion solely because of *his* group identity. There were several lower court decisions to this effect, prior to the *Weber* case.

Griggs v. *Duke Power Company*
401 U.S. 424 (1971)

FACTS Willie Griggs bought a class action on behalf of 13 of the 14 black employees at Duke's Dan River Steam Station, located at Draper, North Carolina. Duke's 95 employees there were organized into five departments: Labor, Coal Handling, Operations, Maintenance, and Laboratory and Test. Blacks were employed only in Labor, where the highest paying jobs paid less than the lowest paying jobs in the other four departments, where only whites were employed. Since 1955 Duke had required a high school education for initial hire in any department except Labor and for transfer from Coal Handling to the three inside departments. After Congress passed the 1964 Civil Rights Act, Duke also made a high school education a requirement for transfer from Labor to any other department. Duke also added another requirement for initial placement in any department other than Labor—satisfactory scores on two professionally prepared aptitude tests. Any current employee was permitted to transfer out of Labor or Coal Handling by "passing" the two tests. The lower courts held that there was no violation of Title VII where past discrimination had ceased and where the tests were adopted without any discriminatory intent. Griggs appealed.

ISSUE Was the use of the aptitude tests a violation of Title VII?

DECISION Yes. Judgment reversed.

REASONS Chief Justice Burger first noted that blacks had sustained the burden of an inferior education, due to segregated schools, and that the company had in fact closed the better jobs to them in the past, on a systematic basis.

"Congress did not intend by Title VII, however, to guarantee a job to every person regardless of qualifications. . . . [T]he Act does not command that any person be

---

1011

hired simply because he was formerly the subject of discrimination, or because he is a member of a minority group. Discriminatory preference for any group, minority or majority, is precisely and only what Congress has proscribed. What is required by Congress is the removal of artificial, arbitrary, and unnecessary barriers to employment when the barriers operate invidiously to discriminate on the basis of racial or other impermissible classification. . . .

"The Act proscribes not only overt discrimination but also practices that are fair in form, but discriminatory in operation. The touchstone is business necessity. If an employment practice which operates to exclude Negroes cannot be shown to be related to job performance, the practice is prohibited.

"On the record before us, neither the high school completion requirement nor the general intelligence test is shown to bear a demonstrable relationship to successful performance of the jobs for which it was used. Both were adopted . . . without meaningful study of their relationship to job-performance ability. Rather, a vice president of the Company testified, the requirements were instituted on the Company's judgment that they generally would improve the overall quality of the work force. . . .

"The facts of this case demonstrate the inadequacy of broad and general testing devices as well as the infirmity of using diplomas or degrees as fixed measures of capability. History is filled with examples of men and women who rendered highly effective performance without the conventional badges of accomplishment in terms of certificates, diplomas, or degrees. Diplomas and tests are useful servants, but Congress has mandated the commonsense proposition that they are not to become masters of reality. . . .

"What Congress has commanded is that any tests used must measure the person for the job and not the person in the abstract."

The Age Discrimination in Employment Act of 1967 is limited in its application to acts of discrimination against "older workers," that is, those between 40 and 70; adverse discrimination against workers outside that range, on the basis of age, is not forbidden by the act. Age discrimination against covered workers by employment agencies and labor unions is likewise prohibited. Amendments in 1974 extended ADEA coverage to nearly 14 million national, state, and local government employees.

As with religion, sex, and national origin under Title VII, there is a "bona fide occupational qualification" exception to the ADEA. In addition, the employer may differentiate on the basis of "reasonable factors other than age" (RFOTA). For example, a 40-year-old professional football player who was no longer able to run, block, and tackle with the necessary vigor could presumably be fired on the basis of RFOTA even though age as such was not a BFOQ for a position on the team. The employer may also observe the terms of any bona fide seniority system or employee benefit plan, but he cannot use the benefit plan as an excuse for refusing to hire the older employee. Of course, an employer can still discharge or discipline an employee for good cause. Any company with a mandatory retirement age under 70 is vulnerable under the ADEA. Once again, this new act requires a reexamination of some once standard employment practices.

50. Legal Regulation of the Employment Relationship

Tuohy v. *Ford Motor Company*
490 F. Supp. 258 (U.S. District Court, Michigan, 1980)

FACTS   Jerome Tuohy was a pilot of company airplanes for Ford from 1954 until 1978. When he reached his 60th birthday in December 1978, he was forced to retire due to Ford's rule that no one over age 60 could be employed as a pilot. Tuohy sued, claiming that this was illegal age discrimination under both U.S. and Michigan law. Ford moved for summary judgment, on the basis that its company rule was substantially the same as that of the FAA for commercial airlines and that the FAA rule conclusively established a BFOQ for pilots. The plaintiff wanted to present all of his medical evidence to a jury and to let the jury decide whether the rule was reasonably necessary.

ISSUE   Does the FAA rule conclusively establish age as a BFOQ for pilots?

DECISION   Yes. Ford's motion for summary judgment granted, on both counts.

REASONS   Judge Joiner first reviewed the two leading U.S. circuit court cases dealing with age discrimination—*Hodgson* and *Tamiami*. Both involved bus drivers. Neither case, he felt, provided legal rules which fully covered the present case. Under these cases the employer had to show first, that the job qualification was reasonably necessary to the essence of his or her business, and second, that the use of sex or age as a qualification was necessary because the employer could not deal with applicants as individuals. The parties here disagreed as to whether doctors could in fact predict which individuals would suffer a sudden incapacitating illness.

"If the only thing at stake in this situation were the plaintiff's job, this court would be more than willing to permit the finder of fact to look at the medical evidence and to decide which side's is more convincing. However, this court is compelled to consider more than the plaintiff. If the court were to prohibit the defendant from terminating the plaintiff, and if it then turned out that the defendant's experts had been right, many people might lose their lives. . . .

"[T]he court believes that the second level of the test must be refined. It must be made flexible enough to take into account things such as the public interest which is involved wherever the safety of third persons is potentially threatened. . . .

"Because of the conflicting evidence on the point in question and because of the catastrophic results that could flow from a decision in favor of the plaintiff if that decision turned out to have been incorrect, this court is compelled to find that the Age Discrimination in Employment Act did not mean to force employers to be any more than 'reasonable' in their decisions in this area.

"One must remember that the case before this court presents a situation where the safety factor . . . is enormous; many lives are at stake. . . . This distinction gives as much protection to employees as can be given without unfairly jeopardizing innocent third parties. . . .

"Every court which has dealt with the issue of safety as it comes up in employment discrimination cases has noted that an employer must be given more leeway in cases where a safety factor is present. . . .

"[W]here the BFOQ involves the important safety interests of third persons, a jury should not be permitted to speculate on the sufficiency of the medical evidence as to the reasonable necessity of the defendant's employment rule. Separate juries might reach different conclusions. Third persons, not being parties, might not have their interests protected. . . .

"The defendant uses its fleet of planes and its personnel in much the same way as do the commercial air lines. . . . Persons who ride in these planes are entitled to the same protection as are those on the commercial air lines."

National Government and Government Contractor Employees. Equal employment opportunity in the national government service is guaranteed by a series of executive orders. No. 11246, issued September 24, 1965, prohibits discrimination on the basis of race, creed, color, or national origin. "Sex" as a prohibited basis was added by No. 11375, issued October 13, 1967.

Other sections of these two executive orders provide similar protection for the employees of government contractors. The U.S. government enforces these provisions by simply refusing to deal with contractors who do not guarantee nondiscriminatory treatment in their employment practices. Indeed, the government requires the filing of written "affirmative action" plans for achieving equal employment opportunity.

SUMMARY

Extensive national and state legislation, with its attendant administrative rulings, has substantially altered the nature of the employer-employee relationship. Any employment policy which discriminates, or potentially discriminates, on one of the forbidden bases is subject to challenge. For many industries, the minimum wage and overtime provisions of the FLSA provide significant limitations on the freedom of the parties to agree on their own terms of employment. The rights of employees to organize and bargain collectively are now protected by the NLRB, and employers must recognize and bargain with a lawfully chosen union. In sum, employers must recognize that there is a substantial "public interest" in their employment practices and must take appropriate internal action to make sure that their employment program is in compliance with *all* applicable labor regulations.

CASES FOR DISCUSSION

UNITED STEELWORKERS OF AMERICA v. WEBER

99 S. Ct. 2721 (1979)

Justice Brennan

Challenged here is the legality of an affirmative action plan—collectively bargained by an employer and a union—that reserves for black employees 50 percent of the openings in an in-plant craft training program until the percentage of black craft workers in the plant is commensurate with the percentage of blacks in the local labor force. The question for decision is whether Congress, in Title VII of the Civil Rights Act of 1964 as amended, 42 U.S.C. § 2000e, left employers and unions in the private sector free to take such race-conscious steps to eliminate manifest racial imbalances in traditionally segregated job categories. We hold that Title VII does not prohibit such race-conscious affirmative action plans.

In 1974 petitioner United Steelworkers of America (USWA) and petitioner Kaiser Aluminum & Chemical Corporation (Kaiser) entered into a master collective-bargaining agreement covering terms and conditions of employment at 15 Kaiser plants. The agreement contained, inter alia, an affirmative action plan designed to eliminate conspicuous racial imbalances in Kaiser's then almost exclusively white craft work forces. Black craft hiring goals were set for each Kaiser plant equal to the percentage of blacks in the respective local labor forces. To enable plants to meet these goals, on-the-job training programs were established to teach unskilled production workers—black and white—the skills necessary to become craft workers. The plan reserved for black employees 50 percent of the openings in these newly created in-plant training programs.

This case arose from the operation of the plan at Kaiser's plant in Gramercy, La. Until 1974 Kaiser hired as craft workers for that plant only persons who had had prior craft experience. Because blacks had long been excluded from craft unions, few were able to present such credentials. As a consequence, prior to 1974 only 1.83 percent (5 out of 273) of the skilled craft workers at the Gramercy plant were black, even though the work force in the Gramercy area was approximately 39 percent black.)

Pursuant to the national agreement Kaiser altered its craft hiring practice in the Gramercy plant. Rather than hiring already trained outsiders, Kaiser established a training program to train its production workers to fill craft openings. Selection of craft trainees was made on the basis of seniority, with the proviso that at least 50 percent of the new trainees were to be black until the percentage of black skilled craft workers in the Gramercy plant approximated the percentage of blacks in the local labor force. . . .

During 1974, the first year of the operation of the Kaiser-USWA affirmative action plan, 13 craft trainees were selected from Gramercy's production work force. Of these, seven were black and six white. The most junior black selected into the program had less seniority than several white production workers whose bids for admission were rejected. Thereafter one of those white production workers, respondent Brain Weber, instituted this class action in the United States District Court for the Eastern District of Louisiana.

The complaint alleged that the filling of craft trainee positions at the Gramercy plant pursuant to the affirmative action program had resulted in junior black employees receiving training in preference to more senior white employees, thus discriminating against respondent and other similarly situated white employees in violation of §§ 703(a) and (d) of Title VII. . . .

We emphasize at the outset the narrowness of our inquiry. . . . The only question before us is the narrow statutory issue of whether Title VII forbids private employers and unions from voluntarily agreeing upon bona fide affirmative action plans that accord racial preferences in the manner and for the purpose provided in the Kaiser-USWA plan. . . .

The prohibition against racial discrimination in §§ 703(a) and (d) of Title VII must . . . be read against the background of the legislative history of Title VII and the historical context from which the Act arose. Examination of those sources makes clear that an interpretation of the sections that forbade all race-conscious affirmative action would "bring about an end completely at variance with the purpose of the statute" and must be rejected. . . .

Congress' primary concern in enacting the prohibition against racial discrimination of Title VII of the Civil Rights Act of 1964 was with "the plight of the Negro in our economy." . . .

Congress feared that the goals of the Civil Rights Act—the integration of blacks into the mainstream of American society—could not be achieved unless this trend were reversed. . . .

It plainly appears from the House Report accompanying the Civil Rights Act that Congress did not intend wholly to prohibit private and voluntary affirmative action efforts as one method of solving this problem. . . .

Given this legislative history, we cannot agree with respondent that Congress intended to prohibit the private sector from taking effective steps to accomplish the goal that Congress designed Title VII to achieve. . . .

Our conclusion is further reinforced by examination of the language and legislative history of § 703(j) of Title VII. . . .

The purposes of the plan mirror those of the statute. Both were designed to break down old patterns of racial segregation and hierarchy. Both were structured to "open employment opportunities for Negroes in occupations which have been traditionally closed to them." . . .

Moreover, the plan is a temporary measure; it is not intended to maintain racial balance, but simply to eliminate a manifest racial imbalance. Preferential selection of craft trainees at the Gramercy plant will end as soon as the percentage of black skilled craft workers in the Gramercy plant approximates the percentage of blacks in the local labor force. . . .

We conclude, therefore, that the adoption of the Kaiser-USWA plan for the Gramercy plant falls within the area of discretion left by Title VII to the private sector voluntarily to adopt affirmative action plans designed to eliminate conspicuous racial imbalance in traditionally segregated job categories. Accordingly, the judgment of the Court of Appeals for the Fifth Circuit is reversed.

MARSHALL v. BARLOW'S, INC.

98 S. Ct. 1916 (1978)

Justice White

Section 8(a) of the Occupational Safety and Health Act of 1970 (OSHA or Act) empowers agents of the Secretary of Labor (Secretary) to search the work area of any employment facility within the Act's jurisdiction. The purpose of the search is to inspect for safety hazards and violations of OSHA regulations. No search warrant or other process is expressly required under the Act.

On the morning of September 11, 1975, an OSHA inspector entered the customer service area of Barlow's Inc., an electrical and plumbing installation business located in Pocatello, Idaho. The president and general manager, Ferrol G. "Bill" Barlow, was on hand; and the OSHA inspector, after showing his credentials, informed Mr. Barlow that he wished to conduct a search of the working areas of the business. Mr. Barlow inquired whether any complaint had been received about his company. The inspector answered no, but that Barlow's Inc., had simply turned up in the agency's selection process. The inspector again asked to enter the nonpublic area of the business; Mr. Barlow's response was to inquire whether the inspector had a search warrant. The inspector had none. Thereupon, Mr. Barlow refused the inspector admission to the employee area of his business. He said he was relying on his rights as guaranteed by the Fourth Amendment of the United States Constitution.

Three months later, the Secretary petitioned the United States District Court for the District of Idaho to issue an order compelling Mr. Barlow to admit the inspector. The requested order was issued on December 30, 1975, and was presented to Mr. Barlow on January 5, 1976. Mr. Barlow again refused admission, and he sought his own injunctive relief against the warrantless searches assertedly permitted by OSHA. A three-judge court was convened. On December 30, 1976, it ruled in Mr. Barlow's favor. . . . [T]he court held that the Fourth Amendment required a warrant for the type of search involved here and that the statutory authorization for warrantless inspections was unconstitutional. An injunction against searches or inspections pursuant to § 8(a) was entered. The Secretary appealed, challenging the judgment, and we noted probable jurisdiction. . . .

The Secretary urges that warrantless inspections to enforce OSHA are reasonable within the meaning of the Fourth Amendment. Among other things, he relies on § 8(a) of the Act, 29 U.S.C. § 657(a), which authorizes inspection of business premises without a warrant and which the Secretary urges represents a congressional construction of the Fourth Amendment that the courts should not reject. Regrettably, we are unable to agree.

The Warrant Clause of the Fourth Amendment protects commercial buildings as well as private homes. To hold otherwise would belie the origin of that Amendment and the American colonial experience. . . . The general warrant was a recurring point of contention in the Colonies immediately preceding the Revolution. The particular offensiveness it engendered was acutely felt by the merchants and businessmen whose premises and products were inspected for compliance with the several parliamentary revenue measures that most irritated the colonists. "[T]he Fourth Amendment's commands grew in large measure out of the colonists' experience with the writs of assistance . . . [that] granted sweeping power to customs officials and other agents of the King to search at large for smuggled goods." . . .

The Court has already held that warrantless searches are generally unreasonable, and that this rule applied to commercial premises as well as homes. . . .

If the government intrudes on a person's property, the privacy interest suffers whether the government's motivation is to investigate violations of criminal laws or breaches of other statutory or regulatory standards. . . .

The Secretary urges that an exception from the search warrant requirement has been recognized for "pervasively regulated business[es]" . . . and for "closely regulated" industries "long subject to close supervision and inspection." . . .

These cases are indeed exceptions, but they represent responses to relatively unique circumstances. . . .

The clear import of our cases is that the closely regulated industry of the type involved in *Colonnade* and *Biswell* is the exception. The Secretary would make it the rule. Invoking the Walsh-Healy Act of 1936, . . . the Secretary attempts to support a conclusion that all businesses involved in interstate commerce have long been subjected to close supervision of employee safety and health conditions. But the degree of federal involvement in employee working circumstances has never

been of the order of specificity and pervasiveness that OSHA mandates. . . .

The critical fact in this case is that entry over Mr. Barlow's objection is being sought by a government agent. Employees are not being prohibited from reporting OSHA violations. What they observe in their daily functions is undoubtedly beyond the employer's reasonable expectation of privacy. The government inspector, however, is not an employee. Without a warrant he stands in no better position than a member of the public.

The Secretary submits that warrantless inspections are essential to the proper enforcement of OSHA because they afford the opportunity to inspect without prior notice and hence to preserve the advantages of surprise. . . .

We are unconvinced, however, that requiring warrants to inspect will impose serious burdens on the inspection system or the courts, will prevent inspections necessary to enforce the statute, or will make them less effective. . . .

We hold that Barlow's was entitled to a declaratory judgment that the Act is unconstitutional insofar as it purports to authorize inspections without warrant or its equivalent and to an injunction enjoining the Act's enforcement to that extent. The judgment of the District Court is therefore affirmed.

NATIONAL LEAGUE OF CITIES v. USERY

95. S. Ct. 2465 (1976)

Justice Rehnquist

Nearly 4 years ago Congress enacted the Fair Labor Standards Act, and required employers covered by the Act to pay their employees a minimum hourly wage and to pay them at one and one-half times their regular rate of pay for hours worked in excess of 40 during a work week. By this act covered employers were required to keep certain records to aid in the enforcement of the Act, and to comply with specified child labor standards. This court unanimously upheld the Act as a valid exercise of congressional authority under the commerce power in *United States* v. *Darby*. . . .

Whatever their motive and purpose, regulations of commerce which do not infringe some constitutional prohibition are within the plenary power conferred on Congress by the Commerce Clause. . . .

The original Fair Labor Standards Act passed in 1938 specifically excluded the States and their political subdivisions from its coverage. In 1974, however, Congress enacted the most recent of a series of broadening amendments to the Act. By these amendments Congress has extended the minimum wage and maximum hour provisions to almost all public employees employed by the States and their various political subdivisions. Appellants in these cases include individual cities and States, the National League of Cities, and the National Governors' Conference; they brought an action in the District Court for the District of Columbia which challenged the validity of the 1974 amendments. . . .

Challenging these 1974 amendments in the District Court, appellants sought both declaratory and injunctive relief against the amendments' application to them, and a three-judge court was accordingly convened pursuant to 28 U.S.C. § 2282. That court, after hearing argument on the law from the parties, granted appellee Secretary of Labor's motion to dismiss the complaint for failure to state a claim upon which relief might be granted.

It is established beyond peradventure that the Commerce Clause of Art. 1 of the Constitution is a grant of plenary authority to Congress. . . .

When considering the validity of asserted applications of this power to wholly private activity, the Court has made it clear that

[e]ven activity that is purely intrastate in character may be regulated by Congress, where the activity, combined with like conduct by others similarly situated, affects commerce among the States or with foreign nations. . . .

Congressional power over areas of private endeavor, even when its exercise may preempt express state law determinations contrary to the result which had commended itself to the collective wisdom of Congress, has been held to be limited only by the requirement that "the means chosen by [Congress] must be reasonably adapted to the end permitted by the Constitution." . . .

This Court has never doubted that there are limits upon the power of Congress to override state sovereignty, even when exercising its otherwise plenary powers to tax or to regulate commerce which are conferred by Art. 1 of the Constitution. . . . In *Fry*, . . . the Court recognized that an express declaration of this limitation is found in the 10th Amendment:

While the 10th Amendment has been characterized as a "truism," stating merely that "all is retained which has not been surrendered," . . . it is not without significance. The Amendment expressly declares the constitutional policy that Congress may not exercise power in a fashion that impairs the States' integrity or their ability to function effectively in a federal system.

The expressions in these more recent cases trace back to earlier decisions of this Court recognizing the essential role of the States in our federal system of government. . . .

Both the States and the United States existed before the Constitution. The people, through the instrument, established a more perfect union by substituting a national government, acting, with ample power, directly upon the citizens, instead of the Confederate government which acted with powers, greatly restricted, only upon the States. But in many Articles of the Constitution the necessary existence of the States, and, within their proper spheres, the independent authority of the States, is distinctly recognized. . . .

One undoubted attribute of state sovereignty is the States' power to determine the wages which shall be paid to those whom they employ in order to carry out their governmental functions, what hours those persons will work, and what compensation will be provided where these employees may be called upon to work overtime. The question we must resolve in this case, then, is whether these determinations are "functions essential to separate and independent existence," . . . that Congress may not abrogate the States' otherwise plenary authority to make them.

In their complaint appellants advanced estimates of substantial costs which will be imposed upon them by the 1974 amendments. . . .

Judged solely in terms of increased costs in dollars, these allegations show a significant impact on the functioning of the governmental bodies involved. . . .

Quite apart from the substantial costs imposed upon the States and their political subdivisions, the Act displaces state policies regarding the manner in which they will structure delivery of those governmental services which their citizens require. The Act, speaking directly to the States qua States, requires that they shall pay all but an extremely limited minority of their employees the minimum wage rates currently chosen by Congress. It may well be that as a matter of economic policy it would be desirable that States, just as private employers, comply with these minimum wage requirements. But it cannot be gainsaid that the federal requirement directly supplants the considered policy choices of the States' elected officials and administrators as to how they wish to structure pay scales in state employment. . . .

This congressionally imposed displacement of state decisions may substantially restructure traditional ways in which the local governments have arranged their affairs. . . .

Our examination of the effect of the 1974 amendments, as sought to be extended to the States and their political subdivisions, satisfies us that both the minimum wage and the maximum hour provisions will impermissibly interfere with the integral governmental functions of these bodies. . . . This exercise of congressional authority does not comport with the federal system of government embodied in the Constitution. We hold that insofar as the challenged amendments operate to directly displace the States' freedom to structure integral operations in areas of traditional governmental functions, they are not within the authority granted Congress by Art. 1, § 8, cl. 3. . . .

NATIONAL WOODWORK MANUFACTURERS ASSOCIATION v. N.L.R.B.

386 U.S. 612 (1967)

Justice Brennan

Under the Landrum-Griffin Act amendments enacted in 1959, 73 Stat. 542 § 8(b) (4) (A) of the National Labor Relations Act, 61 Stat. 141, became § 8(b) (4) (B) and § 8(e) was added. The questions here are whether, in the circumstances of these cases, the Metropolitan District Council of Philadelphia and Vicinity of the United Brotherhood of Carpenters and Joiners of America, AFL–CIO . . . committed the unfair labor practices prohibited by §§ 8(e) and 8(b) (4) (B).

Frouge Corporation, a Bridgeport, Connecticut, concern, was the general contractor on a housing project in Philadelphia. Frouge had a collective bargaining agreement with the Carpenters' International Union under which Frouge agreed to be bound by the rules and regulations agreed upon by local unions with contractors in areas in which Frouge had jobs. Frouge was therefore subject to the provisions of a collective bargaining agreement between the Union and an organization of Philadelphia contractors, the General Building Contractors Association, Inc. A sentence in a provision of that agreement entitled Rule 17 provides that ". . . No member of this District Council will handle . . . any doors . . . which have been fitted prior to being furnished on the job. . . ." Fourge's Philadelphia project called for 3,600 doors. Customarily, before the doors could be hung on such projects, "blank" or "blind" doors would be mortised for the knob, routed for the hinges, and beveled to make them fit between jambs. These are tasks traditionally performed in the Philadelphia area by the carpenters employed on the jobsite. However, precut and prefitted doors ready to hang may be purchased from door manufacturers. Although Frouge's contract and job specifications did not call for premachined doors, and "blank" or "blind" could have been ordered, Frouge contracted for the purchase of premachined doors from a Pennsylvania door manufacturer which is a member of the National Woodwork Manufacturers Association. . . . The Union ordered its carpenter members not to hang the doors when they arrived at the jobsite. Frouge thereupon withdrew the prefabricated doors and substituted "blank" doors which were fitted and cut by its carpenters on the jobsite.

The National Woodwork Manufacturers Association and another filed charges with the National Labor Relations Board against the Union, alleging that by including the "will not handle" sentence of Rule 17 in the collective bargaining agreement, the Union committed the unfair labor practice under § 8(e) of entering into an "agreement . . . whereby [the] employer . . . agrees to cease or refrain from handling . . . any of the products of any other employer . . ." and alleging further that in enforcing the sentence against Frouge, the Union committed the unfair labor practice under § 8(b) (4) (B) of "forcing or requiring any person to cease using . . . the products of any other . . . manufacturer. . . ." The National Labor Relations Board dismissed the charges. . . .

Even on the doubtful premise that the words of § 8(e) unambiguously embrace the sentence of Rule 17, this does not end inquiry into Congress' purpose in enacting the section. it is a "familiar rule, that a thing may be within the letter of statute and yet not within the statute, because not within its spirit nor within the intention of its makers." . . . That principle has particular application in the construction of labor legislation which is "to a marked degree, the result of conflict and compromise between strong contending forces and deeply held views on the role of organized labor in the free economic life of the Nation and the appropriate balance to be struck between the uncontrolled power of management and labor to further their respective interests." . . .

Strongly held opposing views have invariably marked controversy over labor's use of the boycott to further its aims by involving an employer in disputes not his own. But congressional action to deal with such conduct has stopped short of proscribing identical activity having the object of pressuring the employer for agreements regulating relations between him and his own employees. That Congress meant §§ 8(e) and 8(b) (4) (B) to prohibit only "secondary" objectives clearly appears from an examination of the history of congressional action on the subject; we may, by such an examination, "reconstitute the gamut of values current at the time when the words were uttered." . . .

Labor abuses of the broad immunity granted by the Norris-LaGuardia Act resulted in the Taft-Hartley Act prohibitions against secondary activities enacted in § 8(b) (4) (A), which, as amended in 1959, is now § 8(b) (4) (B). . . . Senator Taft and others frequently sounded this note that § (b) (4) (A) was designed to eliminate the "secondary boycott," and its proponents uniformly cited examples of union conduct which evidenced labor efforts to draw in neutral employers through pressure calculated to induce them to cease doing business with the primary employer. . . .

Congress in rewriting § 8(b) (4) (A) as § 8(b) (4) (B) took pains to confirm the limited application of the section to such "secondary" conduct. The word "concerted" in former § 8(b) (4) was deleted to reach secondary conduct directed to only one individual. . . . But to make clear that the deletion was not to be read as supporting a construction of the statute as prohibiting the incidental effects of traditional primary activity, Congress added the proviso that nothing in the amended section "shall be construed to make unlawful, where not otherwise unlawful, any primary strike or primary picketing." Many statements and examples proffered in the 1959 debates confirm this congressional acceptance of the distinction between primary and secondary activity.

The Landrum-Griffin Act amendments in 1959 were adopted only to close various loopholes in the application of § 8(b) (4) (A) which had been exposed in Board and court decisions. . . . Section 8(e) simply closed still another loophole. . . .

This loophole-closing measure likewise did not expand the type of conduct which § 8(b) (4) (A) condemned. Although the language of § 8(e) is sweeping, it closely tracks that of § 8(b) (4) (A), and just as the latter and its successor § 8(b) (4) (B) did not reach employees' activity to pressure their employer to preserve for themselves work traditionally done by them, § 8(e) does not prohibit agreements made and maintained for that purpose. . . .

[T]he construction industry proviso, which permits "hot cargo" agreements only for jobsite work, would have the curious and unsupported result of allowing the construction worker to make agreements preserving his traditional tasks against jobsite prefabrication and subcontracting, but not against nonjobsite prefabrication and subcontracting. On the other hand, if the heart of § 8(e) is construed to be directed only to secondary activities, the construction proviso becomes, as it was intended to be, a measure designed to allow agreements pertaining to certain secondary activities on the construction site because of the close community of interests there, but to ban secondary-objective agreements concerning non-jobsite work, in which respect the construction industry is no different from any other. The provisos are therefore substantial probative support that primary work preservation agreements were not to be within the ban of § 8(e). . . .

That the "will not handle" provision was not an unfair labor practice in these cases is clear. The finding of the Trial Examiner, adopted by the Board, was that the objective of the sentence was preservation of work traditionally performed by the jobsite carpenters. This finding is supported by substantial evidence, and therefore the Union's making of the "will not handle" agreement was not a violation of § 8(e).

Similarly, the Union's maintenance of the provision was not a violation of § 8(b) (4) (B). The Union refused to hang prefabricated doors whether or not they bore a union label, and even refused to install prefabricated doors manufactured off the jobsite by members of the Union. This and other substantial evidence supported the finding that the conduct of the Union on the Frouge jobsite related solely to preservation of the traditional tasks of the jobsite carpenters.

PROBLEMS FOR DISCUSSION

1. Louisa Genata applied for a job at the Rustic Manufacturing Company's plant in Amarillo, Texas. Louisa was an alien, and the company said its policy was to hire only U.S. citizens. Louisa filed a lawsuit, claiming that Rustic's refusal to hire her because she was a Mexican national was illegal discrimination on the basis of "national origin." Does she have a case? Explain.

2. The state commissioner of labor filed charges under the state's Occupational Safety and Health Act against the Greater Atlantic Railroad, claiming that conditions in its repair shops and yards violated the act. Greater Atlantic moved to dismiss the complaint, on the basis that the U.S. Railroad Safety Act gave the Department of Transportation complete power to regulate railroad safety. In fact, the U.S. Transportation Department had not exercised this authority. Does the state have jurisdiction here? Why or why not?

3. Ayub Khomeni was a Muslim. He wore a full beard, which he said was required by his religious beliefs. He applied for a job with the Buster Bus Lines, which had a company policy requiring all employees to be clean-shaven. Ayub refused to shave in order to the get the job, and now he sues on the basis that the company's policy, as applied to him, amounted to religious discrimination. Does he have a case? Discuss.

4. Frostee Fizzee Company, a soft-drink bottler, signed a contract with its production and maintenance workers; included in the contract was a no-strike clause. Frostee was unable to reach agreement with its drivers, however, and the drivers went on strike in June. The P&M workers then refused to cross the drivers' picket line to go to work. The company warned the president of the P&M local union that his members' refusal to cross the picket line was an illegal strike under his contract with the company. "I don't care," said the local's president. "It's summertime, and that's the best time to strike a soft-drink company." When the company sued the local union for lost profits and added costs, the union claimed that it wasn't liable since it had not authorized its members' refusal to cross the drivers' picket line. Is the union liable for damages under these circumstances? Why or why not?

1021

5. Elijah Gottfried applied for a job as a cabdriver for Crakup Cab Company. Due to a congenital birth defect, he had no right hand and his right forearm extended only to about three inches below the elbow. He owned and often wore and used a prosthetic device. He held a valid state driver's license, although it limited him to operating motor vehicles equipped with automatic transmission, self-canceling turn signals, and a wheel spinner. All of Crakup's cabs had automatic transmission and self-canceling turn signals, and Elijah was willing to supply his own wheel spinner, which was simply a small knob that attached easily to the steering wheel and enabled the driver to turn the wheel with one hand. While driving on his own, Elijah had been involved in two minor accidents, neither of which was his fault. Crakup said that it had a company policy against hiring one-handed cab drivers and that this was a valid BFOQ. Elijah says that the company illegally discriminated against him because of his handicap. Who's right, and why?

6. Nora Knoluk participated in a swine flu immunization program conducted at the plant of her employer, Evertru Electric Company. The program was part of a government-sponsored effort to head off a swine flu epidemic, and Evertru had volunteered to let the local health service use its company clinic to administer the vaccine to its employees. Although employees were encouraged to participate in the free program, participation was completely voluntary. Nora died from a reaction to the vaccine. Nora's estate sues for the death benefits payable under the state's workers' compensation statute. Are Evertru and its insurance company liable here? Explain.

7. Jonah Jinx had been arrested 15 times by the police, on various charges, but had never been convicted of anything. Jonah applied for a job at Fussy Foods, Inc. One of the questions on the job application asked whether the applicant had ever been arrested. Jonah answered that he had been. On the basis of that answer, Fussy's Personnel Department automatically rejected his application. Jonah brought a suit for illegal discrimination. At the trial, Jonah's lawyer offered proof that this particular question had a statistically disproportionate impact on blacks. Has Jonah proved a case of racial discrimination? Why or why not?

8. Lucinda Mellis worked as a housekeeper for Father Uhlen at the Miracle Mission. Her duties included cleaning, washing, ironing, and cooking. Lucinda was allergic to the pollen on evergreen trees. When she came to work on December 18 she saw that a Christmas tree had been placed in the mission. She told Father Uhlen that she could not work at the mission while the tree was there but that she would check back on January 1 or 2 to see whether the tree had been taken away. On December 20, Father Uhlen wrote her a letter terminating her employment. It stated: "We cannot tolerate anyone walking off the job, especially at this time." Lucinda got another job sometime later, but she filed for unemployment compensation benefits for the time she was off work. The State Department of Labor denied her claim on the ground that she had left her employment voluntarily. Lucinda appeals to the appropriate state court. How should the court rule here? Discuss.

9. Larry, Moe, and Curly worked as truck drivers for the Mishandle Motor Company, a common carrier of goods. One night, all three were caught stealing 10 car batteries from the company's warehouse. None of them had had any prior record of such activity. Larry, who was black, received a reprimand and an entry on his personnel record. Moe and Curly, who were white, were fired. Moe and Curly sue Mishandle, alleging racial discrimination. Do they have a case? Explain.

10. During contract negotiations, the Cinder City Teachers' Union submitted a bargaining proposal relating to the nature of postgraduate education courses necessary

to advance a teacher on the salary schedule. The school board refused to discuss this item, claiming that it raised a question of job qualifications, a management prerogative, and was therefore a subject of permissive but not mandatory collective bargaining. The union filed charges with the State Labor Relations Board, alleging a refusal to bargain in good faith. How should the board rule? Discuss.

11. The Brewers United Union engaged in a lawful economic strike against the Belcher Beer Company and set up picket lines around all its plants. Horatio Hornswogle, a Belcher employee who was a member of the BUU, said he thought the strike was "stupid" and crossed the picket line. For this, he was fined by the BUU, for "conduct unbecoming a union member." BUU sues in court to collect the fine. Horatio files charges with the NLRB, alleging that the union's fine is a violation of Section 8(b)(1)(A), since it was union conduct which restrained or coerced him in the exercise of his right to refrain from concerted activities. The BUU claims that its fine is authorized by the proviso to that section which says "this paragraph shall not impair the right of a labor organization to prescribe its own rules with respect to the acquisition or retention of membership therein." Who's right, and why?

12. Clarkson Company provided a short-term disability plan for its employees. The plan excluded self-inflicted injuries, injuries related to military service, and pregnancy. One of Clarkson's employees, Lucy Lamere, informed her supervisor that she was pregnant and would have to leave her job for a time. Although she applied for benefits under the disability plan, Clarkson refused to pay. She then filed charges of sex discrimination with the EEOC. How should the Commission rule in this case? Discuss.

51 | Bankruptcy

Definition, Goals, Authority, History. Bankruptcy is the process of settling the debts of persons or firms that are no longer able to meet their obligations. Under court supervision, the debtor's assets (or most of them) are collected and sold, and the proceeds are distributed to creditors. Creditors with equal priority status should receive the same proportion of their claims against the debtor. If the correct procedures have been followed, at the end of the process the debtor's obligations (or most of them) are discharged even though they have not been paid in full. The debtor gets a "fresh start."

Congress is empowered to establish uniform bankruptcy laws by the U.S. Constitution, Article I, Section 8. The first national bankruptcy law was passed in 1800. The Bankruptcy Act of 1898 was in force for 80 years, though it was substantially revised by the Chandler Act of 1938. To deal with the administrative problems which had arisen under the Bankruptcy Act and to better implement changes in consumer credit laws and in the UCC, Congress enacted the Bankruptcy Code of 1978, which became generally effective October 1, 1979.

Administration. The 1978 code provides for a new system of bankruptcy courts as of April 1, 1984. Each U.S. judicial district will then have a bankruptcy court as an adjunct to the U.S. district court, with one or more bankruptcy judges, appointed for 14-year terms. The new bankruptcy court will have jurisdiction to decide all controversies affecting the debtor or the debtor's estate, although it can defer to another court if it thinks a particular case can be handled better there. Appeals will go to the U.S. district court or to a panel of three bankruptcy judges unless all parties agree to take an appeal directly to the U.S. court of appeals.

Until 1984 the present "divided jurisdiction" system will be continued in most districts. The U.S. district court supervises the administration of bankruptcy proceedings and resolves controversies between claimants and the representative of the debtor's estate. Most of the details, however, are left to appointed "referees" (now called "bankruptcy judges"). In 18 districts a five-year trial program is in operation, using U.S. trustees to supervise most of the routine bankruptcy matters.

Types of Proceedings. Chapter 7 of the 1978 code provides for "straight bankruptcy," or liquidation. The trustee gathers and sells the debtor's property and pays the creditors; the debtor receives a discharge from all listed debts. Generally, straight bankruptcy proceedings may be voluntary or involuntary; that is, either the debtor or the creditors may institute such proceedings. Involuntary straight bankruptcy proceedings may not be commenced against a farmer or a nonprofit corporation.

Chapter 9 provides for adjustment of the debts of municipal corporations, where this is authorized by applicable state law.

Chapter 11 gives corporations in financial difficulty a chance to "recognize" their financial affairs by staying in business and making periodic payments to their creditors. Chapter 11 proceedings may be voluntary or involuntary. Railroads are limited to Chapter 11 procedures.

Chapter 13 permits similar debt readjustments and payoffs for individuals with regular income. Chapter 13 proceedings can only be voluntary on the part of the debtor.

Insurance companies, banks, savings and loans, and similar financial institutions are governed by their own regulatory agencies and are not subject to the Bankruptcy Act.

Procedure. The debtor commences voluntary proceedings under Chapters 7, 9, 11, and 13 by filing a petition, under the appropriate chapter, with the bankruptcy court. Spouses may file a joint petition, to reduce administrative costs; the bankruptcy court has the power to allocate joint and separate property and debts.

Where the debtor has 12 or more creditors, an involuntary petition under Chapters 7 or 11 must be joined in by 3 of them, who must have unsecured claims totaling at least $5,000. In determining this number, employees and insiders of the debtor are not counted. Where there are fewer than 12 creditors, any one of them with an unsecured claim of $5,000 can file an involuntary petition. In addition, in an involuntary case the petitioning creditor or creditors must show either that the debtor is not paying his or her debts as they fall due or that the debtor has made a general assignment of assets for the benefit of creditors within 120 days prior to the filing of the petition.

In Re Okamoto
491 F.2d 496 (U.S. Ninth Circuit, 1974)

FACTS   On November 28, 1969, one of Ben Okamoto's creditors, Hornblower & Weeks–Hemphill, Noyes, filed a petition that he be adjudged an involuntary bankrupt. Hornblower tried to proceed as the sole petitioning creditor, pursuant to Section 59(b). Okamoto's answer alleged that he was indebted to 21 creditors. The referee found that Okamoto had 19 unsecured creditors, and therefore the referee dismissed the petition, since there were not fewer than 12 creditors as required under 59(b). The U.S. district court affirmed. Hornblower appealed, alleging that eight of the debts should not be counted, since they were for less than $65 each.

ISSUE   Can *de minimis* claims be ignored when counting creditors under 59(b)?

DECISION   No. Judgment affirmed.

REASONS   Judge Ely said that he had not been persuaded by a few early district court decisions supporting Hornblower's position.

"The Congress has explicitly prescribed the procedure that must be followed when less than three creditors join in the petition. In such circumstances the Act provides that the alleged bankrupts *must* have less than 12 creditors and expressly excludes certain types of creditors from the required computation. Since Congress made no distinction between large and small claims, we cannot arrogate to ourselves the power to do so and thereby engraft an additional exception to the Act. Hornblower's argument properly should be addressed to Congress. Our conclusion is reinforced by the fact that Congress has clearly and expressly excluded small claims when it had intended to do so. . . .

"Rejecting Hornblower's first contention, we reach its assertion that the small creditors should be discounted because Okamoto entered into a scheme to circumvent the provisions of the Act. The short answer to this contention is that the Referee concluded that no such scheme or device had existed. We cannot, in the light of the evidence, hold that this finding was clearly erroneous.

"Hornblower also attacks the inclusion of certain creditors as not being creditors of Okamoto. It asserts that two of the debts were incurred by others through the use of credit cards issued in Okamoto's name. The Referee found that the cards were used with Okamoto's consent and that the obligations were owed by him. . . .

"Finally, Hornblower contends that Okamoto Enterprises, a partnership, is indebted to six of the creditors and that these claimants should not be included for section 59 purposes. Even if we assume, *arguendo,* that these creditors were improperly included, the number of creditors still exceeded 11.

"Since Okamoto was indebted to more than 11 creditors and only one claimant filed the petition under section 59(b), the petition was properly dismissed."

In a voluntary case the court's "order for relief" is automatic; this operates to stay collection proceedings against the debtor in state courts. In an involuntary petition the court must determine whether relief should be ordered. Where the creditors' allegations are not proved, the debtor may be awarded court costs and damages for the lost use of property turned over to a trustee as well as actual and punitive damages if the filing was made in bad faith. Once an order for relief has been entered, the debtor is required to prepare schedules of creditors, assets, and liabilities. Where the debtor is claiming personal exemptions, a schedule of those exemptions must also be filed with the court. Based on the list of creditors, the court sends out a notification of the first creditors' meeting.

The court may appoint an interim trustee to hold and manage the debtor's property until a trustee is elected by the creditors. If the creditors fail to elect a trustee, the interim trustee continues to administer the debtor's estate. The trustee's job is to collect all the debtor's property, to separate out exempt property, to determine whether creditors' claims are secured or unsecured, and finally to pay off claims according to their legal priority status.

Debtor's Available Property. The 1898 act permitted each state to specify what items of property the debtor could exempt from the bankruptcy proceeding; these exemptions vary considerably from state to state. The Michigan exemptions, for example, include all family pictures, wearing apparel, "provisions and fuel" for comfortable subsistence for the family for six months, up to $1,000 of household goods and appliances, burial plots, up to $1,000 in the tools of the debtor's trade, disability insurance benefits for sickness or injury, the cash surrender value of life insurance, benefits to be paid under workers compensation, up to $3,500 for a "homestead" exemption (the debtor's equity in the family home), and to each householder "10 sheep, 2 cows, 5 swine, 100 hens, 5 roosters and sufficient hay and grain growing or otherwise to keep such animals and poultry for six months." The foregoing list seems fairly generous if one remembers that the debtor is getting a discharge from most debts and a fresh start.

The 1978 code gives the debtor the option of choosing the exemptions of his or her state or the exemptions provided in the 1978 code. For most debtors in most states, the national exemptions will be a better choice. The exemptions of the 1978 code include a residence exemption of up to $7,500; up to $1,200 for one motor vehicle; up to $200 per item, with no limit on total value, for household goods, wearing apparel, appliances, books, animals, crops, or musical instruments; up to $500 in jewelry owned by the debtor or a dependent; up to $400 for any property plus any unused amount from the $7,500 residence exemption; up to $750 for the tools of the debtor's or a dependent's trade; any unmatured life insurance policy; up to $4,000 in loan value for a life insurance policy; professionally prescribed health aids for the debtor and dependents; and "future earnings" such as social security and veterans' benefits, unemployment compensation, disability payments, and pension plan payments. The debtor is also given the power to avoid judicial liens and nonpossessory, non-purchase-money security interests which impair his or her exemptions for most listed items of tangible personal property (but not liens against the motor vehicle).

The trustee may recover any items of property which the debtor fraudulently transferred to others within one year prior to the filing of the bankruptcy petition. A transfer is fraudulent if the debtor actually intended to hide the asset from his creditors' claims or if the debtor received less than fair consideration for the asset and was insolvent at the time (or became so as a result of the transfer). The trustee may also recover preferential payments made by the debtor 90 or fewer days prior to the petition. A payment is preferential if it is made for a prior unsecured debt, if it gives a creditor more than that creditor would have received in a bankruptcy proceeding, and if the debtor was insolvent at the time the payment was made. The debtor is presumed to have been insolvent during the 90-day period, and the creditor's good faith is irrelevant. The 1978 code does not, however, treat a payment as preferential if it was made in the ordinary course of business within 45 days after the debt was incurred. (This rule suggests that businesses should have a 45-day limit on receivables.)

Creditors' Claims and Priorities. A claim under the 1978 code includes nearly any sort of right to payment, whether or not it is reduced to judgment, liquidated or unliquidated, fixed or contingent, matured or unmatured, disputed or undisputed, legal or equitable, secured or unsecured. It includes the right to equitable remedies where the breach also gives a right to payment. A creditor who has such a claim files a document called a "proof of claim." A secured creditor need not do so unless the claim exceeds the value of the security and the creditor wishes to try to collect the balance in the bankruptcy proceeding. The creditor's "proof" is accepted as prima facie evidence of the existence and the amount of the debt, and such claims will be allowed and paid (to the extent that funds are available) unless objection is made to them by another creditor, the trustee, or the debtor. Under current practice, proofs of claim must be filed within six months after the first date set for the first meeting of creditors; this time limit will probably be retained under the new bankruptcy rules.

Not all claims are paid at the same time or to the same extent. Secured creditors, that is, creditors who have taken the proper steps to establish their rights against specific pieces of collateral, will be paid first from the proceeds of that collateral. If the value of their collateral is sufficient, secured creditors may be paid in full; if not, they are unsecured creditors for the remainder of their claims.

In addition to the claims of secured creditors, there are other claims which are given priority under the Bankruptcy Code. Administrative expenses, including the payment of accountants, appraisers, attorneys, and trustees, are paid first; so are creditors' expenses in discovering and recovering property which the debtor has transferred or concealed. The 1978 code changes priorities by giving second-payment status to unsecured claims for goods, services, or credit which arose in the normal course of the debtor's business between the filing of an involuntary petition and the court's order for relief or appointment of a trustee. Similarly, third priority is given to wage claims of up to $2,000 each which were earned by the debtor's employees in the 90 days preceding the filing of the petition or the cessation of business, and fourth priority is given to claims for contributions to employee benefit plans which were earned within the prior 180 days. Another change of the 1978 code gives consumers a fifth-priority claim of up to $900 per claimant for the return of money deposited with the debtor for purchased or leased goods which were not delivered or for services which were not performed. Claims for unpaid taxes owed to various governmental units have been lowered to sixth-priority status. Only after all of the above priority claims have been paid in turn will the general, unsecured creditors receive any money. In most bankruptcy cases this means that the general creditors will receive little or nothing. (And remember that the debtor is allowed to keep all "exempt" property.)

The 1978 Bankruptcy Code makes one other significant priority change. The creditors of a bankrupt partnership are now entitled to share equally with the unsecured creditors of individual partners against the partners' personal assets. Under the old rule in the Uniform Partnership Act, the firm's unpaid creditors had no claim against personal assets until all the personal creditors had been paid in full. The Bankruptcy Code also contains special rules for community property, and it gives the court general power to change priorities on equitable grounds after a hearing.

Discharge, Objections, and Grounds for Refusal. Most of the individual debtors who file under Chapter 7 will receive a discharge from most of their previous debts at the conclusion of the bankruptcy proceedings. This is the whole idea of the "fresh start." Generally, an individual can be so discharged only once within any six-year period. However, where an individual has worked out a voluntary repayment plan under Chapter 13, has paid off at least 70 percent of the claims filed under it, and has made his or her best efforts in good faith, a discharge may be granted more frequently than once in six years.

Any single creditor or the trustee acting for all of them may file an objection to a discharge. The court must then determine whether there is some reason for denying the discharge. The Bankruptcy Act lists several grounds for denial, including the debtor's destruction or concealment of property with the intent of delaying or defrauding creditors; destroying, concealing, falsifying, or failing to keep books and records; committing a "bankruptcy crime" such as giving a false oath or participating in bribery to obtain some special advantage; failing to explain losses or deficiencies in existing assets; and failing to obey court orders or to answer questions (but *not* including refusals properly based on the constitutional privilege against self-incrimination). Also, even where a debtor is entitled to a discharge he or she may in writing waive the right to one.

Where a discharge has been properly granted, the 1978 code extends the protection given the debtor from the unpaid creditors' further collection efforts for discharged debts. The discharge, of course, voids all existing and future judgments based on such debts. The 1898 act also prohibited creditors from employing "any process" to collect discharged debts; the 1978 code forbids any *act* by creditors to recover such debts. The significance of the 1978 addition can be seen in the following case.

Ryan v. Ohio Edison Co.
611 F.2d 1170 (U.S. Sixth Circuit, 1979)

FACTS   Plaintiffs Ryan and Cox instituted a class action against Ohio Edison and three credit bureau collection agencies. The plaintiffs were customers of Ohio Edison who had filed petitions in bankruptcy which listed it as a creditor. The plaintiffs said that even after they notified Ohio Edison of the "stay" order issued by the bankruptcy court, they had been threatened with the termination of utility service if the debts were not paid or had actually had their service terminiated. They claimed that this action violated Section 14(f)(2), which enjoined "all creditors whose debts are discharged from thereafter instituting or continuing any action or employing any process to collect such debts as personal liabilities of the bankrupt," and that if Ohio Edison were permitted to use such tactics, it would frustrate the purposes of the Bankruptcy Act by gaining an unfair advantage over other creditors and by hindering the debtor's fresh start. They asked for damages and an injunction. The U.S. district court granted the defendants' motion to dimiss, holding that Ohio Edison, as a former creditor, was only prevented from using judicial action to collect.

ISSUE   Did the old Bankruptcy Act prohibit such actions by the creditor?

DECISION   No. Judgment affirmed.

REASONS   Judge Kennedy reviewed both the applicable precedents and the dictionary meanings of the word *process*. Although the dictionary definitions arguably included the
defendants' actions here, she felt that the precedents and the legislative history of the
section supported the defendants' position—that only court process was prohibited
by Section 14(f)(2).

"Section 14(f) was added to the Bankruptcy Act in 1970. . . . The discharge-
ability bills . . . were designed to correct a specific problem which Congress felt
could not wait until the proposed Commission completed its studies and made recommendations. The problem that Congress sought to remedy immediately was that
although the bankruptcy court could determine that a debtor's dischargeable debts
were discharged, it could not determine which debts were so discharged. The state
courts would determine if a particular debt was discharged when the creditor sued in
state court and the debtor affirmatively alleged the debt was one that had been
discharged. Problems arose because of this bifurcated system. . . .

"No discussion appears why the word 'process' was used. At one point during the
hearings, however, Mr. Wiggens mentioned that he received complaints that creditors sued in state court, received judgments, and then obtained garnishments, which
could cost debtors their jobs. . . .

"The word 'process' when used elsewhere in the Bankruptcy Act clearly means
judicial process. . . .

"The legislative history of the 1970 Amendments indicates that the only problem
Congress sought to solve was preventing lawsuits in state courts. No other problems
were addressed except as problems for study by the proposed Bankruptcy Commission. . . . Congress was obviously giving immediate relief to a limited problem
as a stopgap measure until the Commission could study the bankruptcy area as a
whole. No evidence indicates that Congress intended to reach informal measures
like defendants' alleged conduct here before study by the Commission. . . . Further
support for the more narrow reading of the word 'process' can be found in the
language of the new Code. . . . If 'process' included informal activities already, the
inclusion of 'any act' would have been unnecessary."

Debts Not Discharged.   Some debts survive the bankruptcy discharge; that is,
the debtor's liability still exists, and the creditor may use appropriate enforcement procedures. Such nondischargeable debts include taxes incurred for
three years prior to the bankruptcy; alimony and child support payments; sums
owed by a fiduciary because of fraud, misappropriation, or embezzlement; liability based on fraudulent representations or false pretenses; and liability for
intentional torts ("willful and malicious injury"). As to debts in the last three
groups, the creditor involved must specifically request a determination by the
court that the debt is not dischargeable; if there is no such request, such debts
would be discharged. Because of the increasing frequency with which bankruptcies were being filed by recent college graduates, the 1978 code added
another category of nondischargeable debts: educational loans, unless the first
due date was more than five years before the filing of the bankruptcy petition or
unless the continuing liability would impose an "undue hardship" on the debtor
or the debtor's dependents.

In Re Button
8 B.R. 692 (U.S. Bankruptcy Court, W.D. New York, 1981)

FACTS   Ralph Button pleaded guilty to petty larceny. He was placed on probation for three years and ordered to make restitution of $7,597.26 to the victim, Sheridan Oil Company, at a rate of $25 per week. He had paid $425 when he filed his petition in bankruptcy, listing Sheridan, the Seneca County Probation Department, and the Interlaken Village justice, Aubrey Smith, as his creditors. Sheridan made no objection to the discharge, which was granted on September 12, 1980. In October 1980 Button was charged with a violation of probation since he was no longer making the required payments. Judge Smith ordered a hearing on the probation violation. Button applied to the bankruptcy court for an injunction against enforcement of the restitution order.

ISSUE   Is restitution which is made a condition of probation dischargeable in bankruptcy?

DECISION   No. Injunction denied.

REASONS   Bankruptcy Judge Hayes distinguished between the debt owed to the victim for the $7,172.26 balance still due and the sentence of probation imposed by the state criminal court. While the former could be, and was, discharged in bankruptcy, obligations under the state's criminal law were not affected.

"Section 362(b)(1) states that the filing of a bankruptcy petition does not operate as a stay against the continuation of a criminal action or proceeding against the debtor. The legislative history which corresponds to this section, found in House Report No. 95–595, states that '[t]he bankruptcy laws are not a haven for criminal offenders, but are designed to give relief from financial over-extension' and that 'criminal actions and proceedings may proceed in spite of bankruptcy.' . . . Additionally, *Collier* states that the S.362(b)(1) exception 'is consistent with the strong federal policy against federal interference with state court criminal prosecution.' . . .

"[I]t does not appear that restitution could be considered a debt nor that a victim could be considered a creditor. With restitution, the victim has no right to payment. It is the criminal court which sets the restitution amount, and if it is not paid, the victim cannot proceed against the debtor to enforce payment, but instead the probation officer must report the event of nonpayment to the court which in turn determines if a violation of probation has occurred.

"In view of the foregoing, it seems clear that the debt owed by the debtor to the creditor, Sheridan Oil Company, has been discharged because they did not file an objection to discharge under S.523 of the Bankruptcy Code. However, the criminal sentence of restitution as a condition of probation is an entirely different matter. This is part of the punishment for the crime to which the debtor pleaded guilty. The Court cannot see in any section of the Bankruptcy Code an intention by the Federal Government to relieve debtors of criminal responsibilities. Therefore, since the criminal proceeding was a matter entirely within the jurisdiction of the courts of the State of New York, this Court does not believe that it has jurisdiction to interfere with the sentence of the State Court."

Reaffirmation of Debts. The 1978 code changes the rules on debtors' new promises to pay scheduled bankruptcy debts by adding several extra requirements in order for such promises to be enforceable. First, the new promises must be enforceable under the applicable state (nonbankruptcy) law; you'll recall from Chapter 6 that many states require such new promises to be made in writing. The 1978 code requires such new promises to have been made before the bankruptcy discharge becomes effective, and the code further states that such a promise may be rescinded by the debtor for 30 days after it becomes enforceable. In addition, where the debtor is an individual, the court must hold a hearing and advise the debtor of the legal effects of such a promise and that the promise is not required as a condition of the discharge. Where the new promise relates to a consumer debt that is not secured by real property, the court must in addition approve the promise as being in the debtor's "best interest" and not imposing an "undue hardship" or as being part of a good faith agreement for the redemption of some of the debtor's property or for the settlement of a dispute as to whether the debt was or was not dischargeable.

Individual Repayment Plans. An individual in financial difficulty may file a voluntary petition for "adjustment" of debts under Chapter 13 of the 1978 code and thus prevent nearly all further actions by creditors to collect their claims. This Chapter 13 procedure is available to persons who have less than $100,000 in unsecured debts, less than $350,000 in secured debts, and a "regular income." Proprietors of businesses, social security recipients, and wage earners can file under Chapter 13. Within 10 days of filing the petition, the debtor must file with the court a plan which provides for payments of future income to a trustee, for full payment to creditors with priority, for equal treatment of all claims in the same class, and for retention of liens by secured creditors. Such plans usually ask for an extension of time within which to pay the debts; the plan maximum is three years unless the court grants an extension of up to five years for good cause. The debtor may also ask for a "composition" of debts in which the creditors may receive less than 100 percent of their claims.

A bankruptcy judge presides at the hearing for confirmation of the proposed plan. Unsecured creditors do not get to vote on confirming the plan, but the plan must give them at least what they would have received if the debtor had gone through a Chapter 7 bankruptcy/liquidation. Priority claimants must be paid in full, to the extent that money is available, unless these creditors agree to lesser payments. Secured creditors do get to vote on whether to accept the plan, but if a secured creditor disapproves, the court may confirm it anyway if the debtor gives the dissenting creditor the property which secures the claim or if the dissenting creditor retains a lien and the subject property is worth at least as much as the allowed amount of the secured claim. A secured claim against the debtor's principal residence cannot be modified by the plan; other secured claims may be. The payment arrangements of the plan itself may be modified after confirmation, subject to the above limitations, after proper notice and a hearing.

After completing the payments required by the plan, the debtor is discharged from all debts except long-term unsecured debts not covered by the plan and debts for child support, maintenance, and alimony. In cases of "hardship," where modification of the plan is not practicable and where the amounts already paid are equal to Chapter 7 liquidation values, the debtor may receive a hardship discharge if the failure to complete the plan is not his or her fault. Such a hardship discharge does not affect any nondischargeable debts under Chapter 7, or long-term debts not dealt with by the plan, whether secured or unsecured; or debts incurred without the trustee's permission after confirmation of the plan. If the plan was a composition, the debtor cannot receive a second discharge for six years unless the amounts paid were his or her best effort, made in good faith, and at least 70 percent of the required payments were made.

The following case arose under the similar "wage earner" plan provisions of the 1898 act.

Thompson v. Ford Motor Credit Company
475 F.2d 1217 (U.S. Fifth Circuit, 1973)

FACTS On December 8, 1971, Thomas Thompson filed a petition under Chapter 13 to pay his debts through a wage earner plan. He owed Ford a balance on a 1970 Mustang; Ford had a secured claim against the car. The proposed plan, which provided for payments to Ford of $22.90 per week, the same rate as that of the original sales contract, was confirmed over Ford's objections. Ford was enjoined from foreclosing the car. On July 6, 1972, Ford filed a petition to reclaim the car, alleging that Thompson had failed to make the specified payments. The referee denied Ford's petition and its oral motion to dismiss the plan. The U.S. district court reversed the referee's decision and ordered reclamation. Thompson appealed.

ISSUE Did the debtor's failure to make payments justify reclamation by the secured creditor of its security (the car)?

DECISION No. District court judgment reversed; case remanded to referee.

REASONS Judge Wisdom emphasized that "general equitable considerations" should control in such cases. He did not feel that these were "appropriate circumstances" for permitting the objecting creditor to take away its piece of collateral.

"Equitable considerations strongly suggest that foreclosure would be improper in this case. Thompson fell behind in payments not because of any lack of good faith on his part, but because of circumstances beyond his control. His default appears to have been due to an injury which prevented him from working and to his being temporarily put on a part-time schedule by his employer. During the period of his incapacity Thompson regularly submitted his disability check to the trustee. At present Thompson is still employed, and earns enough to cover payments under the plan.

"Foreclosure would seriously threaten Thompson's ability to make payments under the Chapter XIII plan. Loss of the car would endanger his employment. His job requires him to be at work at 6:00 A.M., and the car is his only means for getting to work at that hour. . . . Thompson's other creditors have a substantial stake in the success of the Chapter XIII plan. Though Ford is Thompson's largest single creditor, his total debts to his other secured and unsecured creditors exceed his debt to Ford.

While foreclosure would make Ford whole, it would effectively destroy any hope that Thompson might be able to repay these other creditors. . . .

"Thompson's default has not been so substantial as to impair Ford's security. . . . At the time of the hearing . . . Ford had received $174.04. This sum roughly covered the depreciation on the car, approximately $200 since confirmation of the plan. . . . When the referee considered this case Ford's economic position was fundamentally no worse than when the plan was confirmed.

"Ford is not required by the plan to surrender any essential rights under its contract. The plan contemplates payment at the contract rate. At worst Thompson's default will work some delay in the time required for full payment. In light of all the circumstances in this case, including Thompson's good faith, the interests of the other creditors, and the fact that Ford's security has not been seriously impaired, we do not view this potential delay as substantial enough to require immediate foreclosure."

Judge Wisdom did say, however, that the referee should amend the payment schedule to make sure that Thompson paid up the overdue payments.

Reorganization of Business Debtor. In many cases businesses get into financial difficulty because of dislocations in the production/distribution/collection process over which they have little, if any, control. Embargoes, wars, strikes, materials shortages, defaults by major customers, and other economic occurrences may have serious impact on a business that does not have substantial financial reserves. If a basically sound firm has a temporary cash flow problem, it probably makes sense to try to save the firm rather than push it into a Chapter 7 liquidation. Most reorganizations under Chapter 11 are designed to salvage the debtor businesses, although the creditors sometimes require management changes and the business may be run temporarily by a trustee.

Chapter 11 cases, like Chapter 7 liquidations, may be voluntary or involuntary; most of the same rules apply to both types of proceedings. Under Chapter 11, however, the court must appoint a creditors' committee, usually composed of the seven largest unsecured creditors. This committee examines the affairs of the business to decide whether to continue the business, or to ask the court for a liquidation, or to ask that a trustee be appointed to operate the business in place of the existing management. For the first 120 days after filing, only the debtor can propose a plan for reorganization, but the debtor would normally develop such a plan in consultation with the creditors. A debtor who files a plan within that time has a further 60 days to get the creditors to approve it. The court can reduce or extend these time periods for good cause. After the first 120 days, any party in interest (a creditor or the trustee) can propose a plan.

The proposed plan must classify claims and ownership interests and must spell out which will and which will not be impaired; it must provide equal treatment for all claims or interests in the same class unless the persons with that class of claims or interests agree otherwise; and it must provide adequate means for implementing the plan's payment arrangements. Further, where the debtor business is a corporation, the plan must require that stockholders' voting rights be protected, that no nonvoting stock be issued, and that directors and officers be selected so as to protect the interests of creditors and stockholders. Generally, the plan may modify the rights of creditors and owners, but these persons have the right to vote on whether or not to accept the plan. Normally the bankruptcy court will not confirm a reorganization plan unless it has received the required majority vote of each class of creditors or owners whose rights were modified ("impaired"). Two thirds in dollar amount of each class of such owners must vote in favor of the plan. Each class of such creditors must approve by a majority in number and by two thirds in the dollar amount of allowed claims. The plan may be confirmed without the consent of owners or creditors whose rights were not impaired.

It is possible for the court to confirm a plan which has not received the consent of an impaired class if the persons in that class are treated in a "fair and equitable" manner—for instance, if all members of the class will receive the full current value of their claims or if all members of the class will receive an equal proportion of their claims and classes whose claims and interests have lower priorities will receive nothing. In any case, dissenters are protected by the rule that they must receive from the plan at least what they would have received through a Chapter 7 liquidation.

CASES FOR DISCUSSION

IN RE ARLAN'S DEPARTMENT STORES, INC.

373 F. Supp. 520 (New York, 1974)

Robert L. Carter, District Judge

The Securities and Exchange Commission ("SEC"), by order to show cause, moved, pursuant to Section 328 of the Bankruptcy Act, 11 U.S.C. § 728, for leave to intervene in the pending Chapter XI proceedings of Arlan's Department Stores (the "debtor") and to dismiss the Chapter XI petitions filed by the debtor and the proceedings under Chapter XI and to require proceedings in compliance with Chapter X. . . .

The issue to be resolved is whether the debtor's attempted corporate rehabilitation under the Bankruptcy Act may be conducted under Chapter XI of the Act . . . or whether dismissal of the Chapter XI proceedings and transfer to proceedings under Chapter X . . . are required.

Background Facts

Arlan's Department Stores and its wholly owned subsidiaries make up a retail store chain spread over several states, selling wearing apparel as well as hardlines of various sorts. It is a large public company. Arlan's had three major classes of unsecured creditors whose rights would be affected by whatever arrangement is ordered. As of the filing of the original petition there existed approximately 15,000 trade creditors having claims totalling approximately $35 million. Lending institutions are creditors of the debtor in the sum of approximately $21 million, $6 million of which is on a par with trade creditors, the balance having been subordinated to the trade pursuant to certain loan agreements. The debtor has issued to the public 6 percent convertible subordinated debentures in the sum of $15 million. Those debentures are subordinated to the lending institution debt by virtue of the provisions of the trust indenture. In addition, as a result of the debtor's breach of lease obligations to landlords in connec-

1035

tion with stores it formerly operated, there may be an additional $15 million liability.

Arlan's has outstanding the following issues of securities: (1) the 6 percent convertible subordinated debentures held by approximately 725 widely dispersed public investors, (2) 3,702 shares of preferred stock held by six banks and insurance companies, and (3) 2,775,414 shares of common stock held by approximately 6,000 persons.

For several years Arlan's appeared to be reasonably profitable and expanded rapidly. Its expansion was financed by bank creditors, public investors, and retained earnings. It paid virtually no dividends. However, during fiscal 1970, the year in which the debentures were issued, Arlan's profits declined markedly, and in fiscal 1971 it began suffering substantial losses which have continued unabated. For the three months ended April 29, 1973, Arlan's reported unabated net losses aggregating close to $8 million. The debtor surmises that it is the heavy debt load of the company which led to economic decline and a modification of that load, streamlining its operations, and an infusion of new funds would rehabilitate it.

As a result of the substantial losses incurred during the fiscal year ended January 30, 1971, Arlan's determined to halt further expansion and to dispose of certain stores. At that time, Arlan's operated 119 stores, including 16 "Play World" stores. During the year ended January 1972, Arlan's opened 2 new stores and closed, leased, or sold 41 stores. During the year ended January 1973, Arlan's disposed of 7 additional stores, so that as of the date of the filing of the original petition for an arrangement, May 14, 1973, it operated 73 stores. Since then it has eliminated approximately another 38 stores.

The Proposed Arrangement

A proposed Chapter XI arrangement was promulgated by the various creditor representative groups, among which were representatives of the debenture holders. . . .

Despite the initial predilection for a proceed-

ing under Chapter XI, I must now conclude that Chapter X is the appropriate context for the rehabilitation of this debtor. While retaining concern for doing what is best for the company and the public, I must adhere to and rely upon the thought-out principles set forth by the Supreme Court and our Circuit, which require that in a situation such as the immediate one, the interests of the public will be studied, ascertained, and best served under Chapter X.

The Supreme Court has made it clear that neither this court, nor any other district court, has unbridled discretion in deciding between a proceeding under Chapter X or XI. . . . My discretion is limited to a factual determination of whether the debtor needs a pervasive reorganization rather than a simple composition of unsecured debts. . . . Once that question is decided, then the guidelines established by the Supreme Court on the proper chapter to proceed under must be followed. . . .

It is not the character of the debtor, but rather the degree and nature of the required reorganization that is determinative. Where the rights of public investor creditors are to be adjusted in more than a minor way, then the safeguards and procedures of Chapter X are required. . . .

This is in contrast to the provisions of Chapter XI, which are limited to adjustment of unsecured debt, leave the arrangement and company basically in the hands of the debtor, and do not provide for an independent study by or supervision of a trustee. This procedure is recognized as being primarily concerned with the short-term interests of trade creditors. . . .

Applying these guidelines, it is clear that Chapter X is the necessary context in which to rehabilitate Arlan's. Its debentures are held by approximately 725 widely dispersed public investors who are not closely involved in the operations of the company. The rights of the public debenture holders are being radically adjusted, insofar as publicly held debt is being converted into equity. The capital structure of the company is being subjected to a major reorganization. . . .

I am concerned by the serious possibility that

the debtor's line of credit will be substantially extinguished under Chapter X. It is not inevitable, and I regret that people in the trade may wrongly construe a proceeding in Chapter X to be the harbinger of bankruptcy and liquidation. Hopefully, the proceeding can go forward expeditiously and with minimal expense and if the debtor is not suffering from terminal financial ills, a successful rehabilitation will occur.

MATTER OF BOYDSTON

520 F.2d 1098 (U.S. Fifth Circuit, 1975)

Coleman, Circuit Judge

This appeal arises from the bankruptcy of Mr. and Mrs. Arland D. Boydston. The referee granted the husband's discharge over the objections of two of his creditors, Sears, Roebuck & Co. and Neiman Marcus. On review, the District Court affirmed. Appellants contend that the discharge should have been denied under S. 17(a)(2) of the Bankruptcy Act . . . because the bankrupts were engaged in a scheme to obtain property on credit with the secret intention of not paying for it. Although Boydston's actions appear so highly questionable that if we were hearing this case in the first instance, we would be inclined to deny discharge, we are unable to say as an appellate tribunal that the referee's findings are clearly erroneous. Therefore, we affirm the Judgment of the District Court.

In November of 1969 Arland Boydston, a 40-year-old Army Lt. Colonel, married Carolyn Conner. Their financial downfall began in March 1970 when they borrowed $3,000 to start a wig business, in the Chateau De Monique Wig Salon, in Mineral Wells, Texas. By September, the shop's business had sharply deteriorated because of the projected closing of nearby Fort Wolters. At this time Boydston retired from the service, cutting his income by more than half, to $708 per month. Aside from his retirement income and the small amount of money the couple was taking in from the salon, the Boydstons had no other income. The bankrupt was also involved in a prospective low-income housing project from which

he hoped to make a windfall by sharing in the net profits. In January 1971, the project fell through when FHA approval was denied, again because of the closing of Fort Wolters.

Despite their strained financial condition, however, the Boydstons went on a spending spree which lasted from the latter part of August 1970 until they filed their petition in bankruptcy on February 15, 1971. During this six-month period they incurred almost $32,000 in new indebtedness, the overwhelming portion of which was for luxury items and nonessential personal expenses rather than for salvaging the wig business. Merchandise purchased included a new Cadillac, a mink coat, a very expensive shotgun, a houseful of new furniture, and $1,300 in personal travel expenses. A $6,000 bank loan ostensibly intended to acquire new inventory for the wig salon was diverted to the purchase of a new home in Dallas, and on several occasions personal financial statements submitted to creditors flagrantly failed to disclose a majority of their indebtedness. The substantial portion of the debts was incurred after the Boydstons were no longer able to meet existing obligations when due and the bankrupt had written at least two creditors requesting extension of payment deadlines.

During this period, $2,923.73 worth of personal merchandise was charged at Sears and $2,540.03 at Neiman Marcus. No payments were ever made on either account. Appellants claim that the factors detailed above clearly indicate a purpose to acquire merchandise on credit with no intention of paying for it. Sears also complains that, in completing a credit application with the store in November, Mrs. Boydston grossly overstated the wig salon's monthly earnings and omitted the family's major financial obligations in order to secure an extension of credit which otherwise would not have been granted. The application, however, contained only three blanks for listing present creditors.

Neiman Marcus thwarted Mrs. Boydston's discharge from any of her debts under S. 14(c)(1) of the Bankruptcy Act by showing that she had altered documents pertaining to her bankruptcy for the purpose of deceiving the Court and had given perjured testimony concerning the exhibits. The referee found that there was no evidence to show that Mr. Boydston participated in or knew of these changes.

In mitigation of the husband's apparent disregard of his financial responsibilities, factors cited by the referee or which appear in the record include Boydston's contemplated business venture, the approach of the Christmas gift season, his lack of business experience, the fact that his wife made many of the purchases, particularly furniture and household goods, to replace items that had been used by his deceased wife, and his testimony that he was unaware of the precarious nature of his financial situation or the possibility of bankruptcy until he spoke with an attorney in February. The bankruptcy judge had the opportunity to see and hear the Boydstons firsthand, to weigh the credibility of all the witnesses, and to thoroughly examine the record. In his words, "The evidence offered impresses me more as reckless, irresponsible naivete on the part of a recently retired military man, who had just remarried, than cold, calculating, sophisticated planning by one bent on financial deception." Based on Sears and Neiman Marcus' failure to demonstrate Boydston's insolvency at the time the debts were incurred or to provide sufficient evidence of his subjective intent not to repay the debts, the discharge was granted.

The referee's findings of fact are binding upon the district judge and this Court unless they are clearly erroneous. . . .

There is sufficient evidence in the record before us to sustain the original findings of fact. Boydston could feasibly have felt his financial slump was only temporary. Although he was unable to meet certain obligations as they came due, he did not try to permanently avoid payments, but merely postpone them. His reluctance to attempt to curb his wife's spending may be explained by his desire to stabilize his marriage rather than a secret desire to bilk creditors. The Sears credit application was not materially false since the store asked for the names of only three creditors, not for all outstanding obligations. The wig salon had just begun its decline when Mrs. Boydston stated its earnings in the application, a statement which may have been more optimistic than intentionally deceptive. The bankrupts' expectancy of a windfall from the housing project, the fact that bankruptcy was not contemplated when they made the purchases, and their lack of business expertise all militate against denying a discharge.

PEREZ v. CAMPBELL

402 U.S. 637 (1971)

Justice White

This case raises an important issue concerning the construction of the Supremacy Clause of the Constitution—whether Ariz.Rev.Stat.Ann. S. 28–1163(B) (1956), which is part of Arizona's Motor Vehicle Safety Responsibility Act, is invalid under that clause as being in conflict with the mandate of S. 17 of the Bankruptcy Act, . . . providing that receipt of a discharge fully discharges all but certain specified judgments. The courts below . . . ruled against the claim of conflict and upheld the Arizona statute.

On July 8, 1965, petitioner Adolfo Perez, driving a car registered in his name, was involved in an automobile accident in Tucson, Arizona. The Perez automobile was not covered by liability insurance at the time of the collision. The driver of the second car was the minor daughter of Leonard Pinkerton, and in September 1966 the Pinkertons sued Mr. and Mrs. Perez in state court for personal injuries and property damage sustained in the accident. On October 31, 1967, the petitioners confessed judgment in this suit, and a judgment order was entered against them on November 8, 1967, for $2,425.98 plus court costs.

Mr. and Mrs. Perez each filed a voluntary petition in bankruptcy in Federal District Court on November 6, 1967. Each of them duly scheduled the judgment debt to the Pinkertons. The District Court entered orders on July 8, 1968, discharging both Mr. and Mrs. Perez from all debts and claims provable against their estates, including the Pinkerton judgment. . . .

During the pendency of the bankruptcy proceedings, the provisions of the Arizona Motor

Vehicle Safety Responsibility Act came into play. . . .

Article 4 of the Arizona Act, which includes the only provision at issue here, deals with suspension of licenses and registrations for nonpayment of judgments. Interestingly, it is only when the judgment debtor in an automobile accident lawsuit—usually an owner-operator like Mr. Perez—fails to respond to a judgment entered against him that he must overcome two hurdles in order to regain his driving privileges. Section 28–1161, the first Section of Art. 4, requires the state court clerk or judge, when a judgment has remained unsatisfied for 60 days after entry, to forward a certified copy of the judgment to the superintendent. This was done in the present case, and on March 13, 1968, Mr. and Mrs. Perez were served with notice that their drivers' licenses and registration were suspended pursuant to S. 28–1162(A). Under other provisions of Art. 4, such suspension is to continue until the judgment is paid, and S. 28–1163(B) specifically provides that "[a] discharge in bankruptcy following the rendering of any such judgment shall not relieve the judgment debtor from any of the requirements of this article." In addition to requiring satisfaction of the debt, S. 28–1163(A) provides that the license and registration "shall remain suspended and shall not be renewed, nor shall any license or registration be thereafter issued in the name of the person, . . . until the person gives proof of financial responsibility" for a future period. . . .

With the construction of both statutes clearly established, we proceed immediately to the con-stitutional question whether a state statute that protects judgment creditors from "financially irresponsible persons" is in conflict with a federal statute that gives discharged debtors a new start "unhampered by the pressure and discouragement of preexisting debt. . . ."

We can no longer adhere to the aberrational doctrine of *Kesler* and *Reitz* that state law may frustrate the operation of federal law as long as the state legislature in passing its law had some purpose in mind other than one of frustration. Apart from the fact that it is at odds with the approach taken in nearly all our Supremacy Clause cases, such a doctrine would enable state legislatures to nullify nearly all unwanted federal legislation by simply publishing a legislative committee report articulating some state interest or policy—other than frustration of the federal objective—that would be tangentially furthered by the proposed state law. In view of the consequences, we certainly would not apply the *Kesler* doctrine in all Supremacy Clause cases. Although it is possible to argue that *Kesler* and *Reitz* are somehow confined to cases involving either bankruptcy or highway safety, analysis discloses no reason why the States should have broader power to nullify federal law in these fields than in others. Thus, we conclude that *Kesler* and *Reitz* can have no authoritative effect to the extent they are inconsistent with the controlling principle that any state legislation which frustrates the full effectiveness of federal law is rendered invalid by the Supremacy Clause. Section 28–1163(B) thus may not stand.

PROBLEMS FOR DISCUSSION

1. Tessie Boble stored several valuable antiques with Louie Looper in the warehouse he operated. When Tessie failed to pay the storage charges as required, Louie sold the items to enforce his warehouse lien. Unfortunately, Louie did not comply with all of the required procedural steps in the lien statute. Tessie sued Louie and received a judgment for $50,000, $10,000 of which was a jury award of punitive damages. Louie filed for bankruptcy, listing Tessie as one of his creditors. She says her claim is not dischargeable in bankruptcy. Is she right? Why or why not?

2. Danny Dunaway signed an agreement to sell his Nevada liquor license and related business assets to Ham Jardine for $30,000. As required by the state liquor law, Ham deposited the full $30,000 in an escrow account, and the Alcohol Beverage

Control Department (ABCD) approved the transfer. The statute then provided that the amount in the escrow account should be distributed to the seller and his creditors and that if the proceeds were insufficient to pay all of the creditors' claims, the creditors would be paid in accordance with a state priority list. Included in this list were creditors with claims for goods sold and delivered to the business and for services performed for the business. Before the $30,000 could be paid to anyone, Danny filed for bankruptcy. Danny's trustee in bankruptcy claims the $30,000 for distribution according to bankruptcy priorities. Danny's business creditors claim (1) that the $30,000 is not an asset subject to the bankruptcy, and (2) that the $30,000 should be distributed according to the state liquor law's priorities. Is either argument valid? Explain.

3. Wooden Workship, Inc., leased certain equipment from Rentall, Inc. Erica Bibbs, the owner and president of Wooden, personally guaranteed the lease payments. Wooden later defaulted on several payments, and Rentall demanded payment from Erica, without results. Rentall filed suit against Wooden and Erica on November 14, 1975. Process was finally served on them on March 20, 1976. Meanwhile, Erica had filed for bankruptcy on February 3, 1976, and the next day the bankruptcy court issued a general "stay order" against all other creditor proceedings against the debtor. Erica did not list Rentall as a creditor on the schedule she filed with the bankruptcy court. On March 24, 1976, the bankruptcy court granted her application for discharge. The next day she filed her answer to Rentall's state court suit, indicating the commencement of the voluntary bankruptcy proceedings and including a copy of the stay order. She did not disclose that her discharge had been granted the day before. On May 1, she filed an amended answer in the state lawsuit, asking that it be dismissed because of her discharge in bankruptcy. She says that Rentall's claim is discharged, even though it wasn't scheduled, because the act so provides where "such creditor had notice or actual knowledge of the proceedings in bankruptcy." Is Rentall's claim discharged under this section?

4. Carlos Camaro was declared bankrupt, on his voluntary petition, on February 8, 1972. On November 15, 1971, Carlos had paid Sniper Construction Company $18,350 for work done on his business building. When Carlos filed his petition in early February he listed assets of $55,432.72 and liabilities of $251,980.21. Carlos' trustee in bankruptcy brings an action to set aside the payment to Sniper as a voidable preference. As part of his case, the trustee must prove that Sniper had reasonable cause to believe that Carlos was insolvent when the payment was made. Carlos testified that he told Sniper in September 1971 that he was insolvent, and that his accountant and attorney had suggested that he file for bankruptcy. He also testified that there had been no substantial change in his asset/liability ratio since then. Sniper offered to introduce letters giving Carlos a good credit rating which a local bank had written to third parties. Should Sniper have to repay this money? Why or why not?

5. Emory Catnip, driving his car on a four-lane interstate highway, hit a second car from the rear, causing the death of its driver, Hiram Dallo. Emory's car traveled 468 feet after the collision, 334 feet on the highway and another 134 feet after it left the pavement. Hiram's car traveled 382 feet after impact, 179 feet on the pavement and 203 feet off it, finally turning over. The police found a bottle of gin in Emory's car. He admitted to having taken a couple of drinks that afternoon. The accident occurred between 8:00 P.M. and 8:30 P.M. The pictures of the cars indicated a terrific impact. Emory claimed that Hiram had pulled in front of him just as he was about to pass. Hiram's widow filed a wrongful death action for $200,000 in which she alleged that Emory had been guilty of driving "carelessly, negligently, recklessly, and

wantonly." After she received her judgment, Emory filed for bankruptcy. Will this judgment be discharged by Emory's bankruptcy? Explain.

6. Abner Lumm was forced into involuntary bankruptcy by his creditors. After a hearing he filed an application for discharge. His creditors objected on the grounds (1) that Abner had failed to keep books of account or records, from which his financial condition and business transactions might be ascertained; and (2) that he was uncooperative and evasive and refused to give direct and factual answers to the interrogatories directed to him. Abner says that his missing business records were destroyed by the new tenants who took over the building when Abner moved the location of his business. The new tenants were very eager to take possession, and they threw out some of Abner's things without giving him a chance to come back and pick them up. Abner never actually refused to answer any question, although he was not, in fact, very helpful. Assuming that these are the only two grounds for objection, should Abner be given his discharge? Discuss.

7. Delbert Dedalus sued in the state courts of Vermont, asking for enforcement of an $18,000 Idaho state court judgment against Ike Icarus for the conversion of Delbert's airplane. The Idaho judgment had been taken by default. Delbert introduced a certified copy of his Idaho judgment. Ike then introduced a certified copy of his discharge in bankruptcy, entered after the Idaho judgment, and asked the Vermont court to dismiss Delbert's case. Delbert says that his claim was not discharged by Ike's bankruptcy. How should the court rule, and why?

8. Elvis Ehrlock sued Sally Shurlee, alleging that Sally had been guilty of "fraud and misrepresentation" in a real estate deal in which the parties were involved. The trial judge, in her instructions to the jury, said that it could find for the plaintiff (Elvis) if the defendant (Sally) made a representation which was "known to be false or recklessly made without knowing whether it was true or false." The jury brought in a verdict for Elvis of $65,000. Sally later filed a voluntary petition in bankruptcy and received a discharge. When she went back into business, Elvis started proceedings to enforce his judgment. Sally says he was listed as a creditor and is bound by her bankruptcy discharge. He says he's not. Who's right, and why?

Part XII
Law of the Future

52 | Technology and the Law

It has often been said that the wheels of justice move slowly. Also, as stated in the first chapter of this text, the law must have predictability and stability and yet must be subject to change. The law of today may not be totally applicable to the society of tomorrow. In the past few decades law and technology have clashed because technology has grown by leaps and bounds whereas the law has not changed as readily. There is a very urgent need for changes in the law to accommodate the changes that are taking place in technology, so that both law and technology may continue to serve the best interests of society.

Among the most obvious areas of concern are the legal problems generated by developments in computer technology, medical technology, and the invasion of space by Man. However, many other areas of technology will also require legal study and changes in the legal system. This chapter will try to briefly introduce some of the problem areas of technology and the law.

COMPUTERS AND THE LAW

While the computer has admittedly been a technological advance which has greatly benefited Mankind, it has also created many new legal problems. The most serious problem is the threat of encroachment upon individual privacy. Today's computers have an almost infinite capacity to store, retrieve, and transmit information. Information entered into a computer can be transmitted to other computers anywhere in the world. Compatible electronic storage units harnessed through telephone networks or other transmission devices have created a potential surveillance system of a magnitude and comprehensiveness heretofore deemed impossible.

Along with this new technological capacity to store, retrieve, and transmit data, we find a seemingly insatiable desire on the part of government and business to gather and store information on everything and everyone. Information which required thousands of square feet of storage space when it was stored in conventional filing systems may now be stored on a few thousand feet of magnetic tape. The computer can then search the storage unit in seconds and provide a visual display of information which can be printed out if desired. As a result of this new technology, financial, commercial, and governmental institutions as well as other organizations are amassing great amounts of personal information about individuals.

It is true that businesses have always kept records about individuals. But record keeping was limited, due to the obvious problems of storage, access, and retrievability. The computer has minimized those problems, and consequently more and more information is kept about the individual, and there is more possibility of error and less access by the individual to the records to determine just what they say about him or her. A major concern has been the gathering, storage, and retrieval of information about individuals by various credit bureaus and local merchants' associations which have computerized their files and have dossiers on nearly every American adult.

In order to curb the abuses of credit bureaus, Congress passed the Fair Credit Reporting Act, which became effective on April 25, 1971. The following is a summary of some of its provisions.

1. Credit reporting agencies are authorized to furnish credit information only in connection with credit, insurance, and employment applications, a government license for which a consumer has applied, or any other business transaction in which a consumer is involved; or by written consent of the consumer concerned; or in compliance with a court order.

2. The reporting of adverse information more than seven years old regarding suits, arrests, and other matters is generally prohibited. However, information on bankruptcies can be made available for 14 years, and if the inquiry concerns an application for a life insurance policy of $50,000 or more or an application for a job with an annual salary of $20,000 or more, then there is no age restriction on records and all information may be furnished. Thus the bureaus have an excuse not to clear out the computers periodically.

3. The reporting of adverse information from investigative reports more than three months old is generally prohibited unless the information is reverified.

4. All reporting agencies are required to "follow reasonable procedures to assure maximum accuracy of the information" contained in reports.

5. The type of information which can be furnished to government agencies without a court order is limited.

6. Upon the request of a consumer, a reporting agency must disclose to the consumer all information about him or her in the agency's files, except for medical information or the sources of the information.

7. A person or business ordering an investigative report must notify the consumer that an investigation is being made.

8. An agency must disclose to a consumer on request the names of persons and businesses that have been furnished credit information about the consumer in the preceding six months (two years for employment purposes).

9. An agency must reinvestigate information disputed by a consumer "within a reasonable period of time" unless "it has reasonable grounds to believe that the dispute by the consumer is frivolous or irrelevant." If the information is found to be inaccurate, then the agency must delete the

information from the record. The consumer also has the right to have the agency put in the file a statement of not more than 100 words explaining that the information is disputed, and the agency, at the consumer's request, must send copies of the statement to the persons and businesses that had been sent the disputed information.

10. A person or business that rejects a consumer for credit, insurance, or employment on the basis of a credit report must advise the consumer of the reason for the rejection and identify the reporting agency.

11. A consumer is granted the right to file a civil action in U.S. district court to recover damages resulting from willful and negligent noncompliance with the law.

12. Obtaining information under false pretenses for credit reporting and willfully giving out such information to unauthorized persons is punishable by a fine of up to $5,000 and imprisonment for up to one year.

As noted above, this law gives the aggrieved individual the right to file an action charging that a credit bureau, its informant, or a user of its report violated the Fair Credit Reporting Act. The violation doesn't have to be intentional, but it must have caused demonstrable financial damage. In a successful action a consumer can collect his or her actual damages, legal costs, and an attorney's fee. If he or she can prove that a credit bureau willfully violated the act, the bureau may also have to pay punitive damages and may be subject to criminal penalties.

In passing the Privacy Act of 1974, Congress recognized the problems of invasion of privacy caused by governmental computer record keeping. The act placed many restrictions on computerized record keeping and the handling of computerized records by the various governmental agencies. This act applies only to the records of national governmental agencies, not to those of state agencies or private businesses. In addition to placing restrictions on governmental record keeping and the handling of governmental records, the act gave individuals access to such records about themselves and the right to copy, correct, and challenge personal information held by the national government. The act also prohibited the nonroutine dissemination of records without notification to the individuals involved, and it placed restrictions upon the expanded use of social security numbers.

Many states have passed privacy laws similar to the 1974 Privacy Act. These laws have placed restrictions on record keeping and the handling of computerized information by the various state agencies. The subject of computers and privacy is certainly a key issue in our society today. To date, the major thrust of the various privacy bills has been to regulate only national and state computerized record keeping, and there are still many unsolved legal problems concerning privacy and the record keeping practices of private business.

One of the current electronic record-keeping practices of concern in the private sector is the use of electronic data storage and transmission facilities for electronic fund transfers, as discussed in Chapter 26. The advantages of electronic funds transfer over the traditional cash or check transfer of funds are many, but there are many social and legal problems which must be resolved, particularly the protection of individual privacy and autonomy. The records kept on an individual in an EFT system are very different from the traditional records. For example, a comprehensive EFT system will necessitate massive storage of data about individuals and their financial transactions. It will be necessary for credit purposes to have information about assets, debts, business activities, possessions and many other sensitive bits of information about the individual. That information must be susceptible to easy, fast retrieval, thus creating the potential for access and misuse by unauthorized persons. Thus we have obvious potential privacy problems for the consumer, as computers are not infallible and there is the possibility of invasion of the privacy of the accounts and records about the consumer.

On November 10, 1978, Congress recognized the problems and passed the Electronic Funds Transfer Act. Congress stated that the purpose of this new law was to provide a basic framework establishing the rights, liabilities, and responsibilities of participants in electronic funds transfer systems. The primary objective of the law was to ensure a basic level of protection for the individual consumer's rights.

The Electronic Funds Transfer Act allows the various states to enact more comprehensive and more protective legislation if they desire to do so. A few states have enacted regulatory legislation in the EFT area, and many others are considering such legislation.

In addition to the legal problems concerning individual privacy that have been caused by computerized record keeping, many unique legal problems have been associated with computer-generated evidence, specifically, computerized business records.

Computers certainly represent a major technological revolution in the area of business records and record keeping. The cumbersome ledgers and account books of the past are slowly disappearing from sight; they are being replaced by computer systems which store the information on magnetic tape drums or discs or other storage devices. The role of the bookkeepers who made the daily entries in those ledgers has also disappeared, and these bookkeepers have been replaced by computers.

The increasing use of the computer for record keeping, even though economically profitable and very efficient, has raised a serious legal question: When are computerized records admissible as evidence in a court of law? Traditionally the laws of evidence have required that business records be legible visibly. Computer stored information, however, is not legible visibly. The original tape drum, disc, ferrite core, plated wire, or other storage device cannot be "read" by the naked eye. It must first be deciphered mechanically; a readable printout must be made. To allow a machine printout to be admitted as evidence instead of the traditional record books certainly requires a substantial change in the law of evidence. The old record-keeping books were in the handwriting of the person who made the entries. That person could testify that he or she made the entries, and handwriting experts could check the authenticity of the entries. Any alteration or erasure made in the record books could be seen; anything crossed out or changed would be noticeable to the naked eye. That is not true with the computer. Changes may be made in a computerized record with no telltale sign. Information may be put in, taken out, or changed, with no trace to identify the culprit.

The rule of evidence most often used to object to the introduction of computer printouts as evidence is the hearsay rule. Hearsay can be defined as a written or oral statement made by a person other than the person testifying at the trial, which statement is offered to prove the truth of some issue involved in the trial. In other words, it is a statement made by someone or something, in this case a computer, which is not present at the trial to be cross-examined to determine its truthfulness. There are however, exceptions to the hearsay rule. The most common exception to the hearsay rule by which businesses seek to introduce their computer-generated evidence is the business records exception. For evidence to come within the terms of that exception, it must be shown that the statement referred to is a business record which was made in the regular course of business at or near the time that the act, condition, or event which it evidences occurred. Next a qualified witness must testify as to the identity and mode of preparation of the record. Finally, the sources of information and the method of preparation of the record must be such that there is no question as to the record's trustworthiness. If any of these elements are missing, the evidence is not admissible in court.

Estate of Buddeke
364 N.E.2d 446 (Illinois, 1977)

FACTS MacNeal Memorial Hospital Association filed a claim against the estate of Mary Buddeke for services rendered from August 4 to November 25, 1972. No bill appeared to have been sent to the executor until notification was received from a collection service that $13 was due to the hospital. The executor sent a check marked paid in full, which was cashed by the hospital. The hospital then made a claim for $10,745.19, more than 2½ years after the alleged services had been furnished. The manager of patient accounts testified as the only witness for the hospital. She did not know anything about how the charges were fed into the computer. She could not explain why one line showed a balance due of $745.19 and the next line said, "Please pay $10,745. 19." The trial court admitted the computer printout but refused to admit into evidence the "in full" check. It then allowed the claim against the estate, and the executor appealed.

ISSUE Were the judge's rulings on the admission of evidence correct?

DECISION No. Judgment reversed.

REASONS Justice Dieringer said that the trial court had made errors both in admitting the computer printout and in refusing to admit the check.

"[I]t was reversible error for the trial judge to admit into evidence a computer print-out without some supporting documentation as to what was used to produce the figures on the print-out. The claimant should bring someone into court who can testify as to the correctness of the figures on the print-out. The estate has the right and the executor has the duty to examine all the charges and credits pertaining to the account of the deceased. The executor has the right to examine all the books and records of the hospital pertaining to these charges.

"In the instant case it was also reversible error for the trial judge not to admit into evidence the check of the executor marked 'payment in full' for the estate."

A second question which arises when a computer printout is submitted as evidence is whether the computer printout is the best evidence as required by the best evidence rule. Generally speaking, the best evidence as to the contents of a document is the document itself. However, the "document" of an automated record-keeping system is a magnetic tape, drum, or disc which if produced in court would be useless without transcription. In arguing for the admissibility of computer records, such records might be compared to a document written in a foreign language. In that case the court would admit the document and allow its translation by an interpreter or translator. One might argue that computer records are in a foreign language and that the computer printing machine is essentially a mechanized translator. Generally speaking, courts have been liberal with regard to admitting computerized records if the original documents are unavailable or have been destroyed. However, many businesses such as banks and credit card companies are taking no chances and are keeping either the original signed document or a microfilm copy, both of which are clearly admissible.

Thus it can be seen that although the new computer technology has benefited Mankind in many ways, much remains to be done to secure uniformity clarity concerning its legal ramifications.

Computer technology has also created legal problems in many other areas of law such as patent and copyright law and criminal law. However, space does not permit a discussion of those areas. However, of the problems created by computer technology, those involving the areas of invasion of privacy and the admissibility of computerized evidence are of most concern to business today.

LEGAL PROBLEMS OF NEW MEDICAL TECHNOLOGY

The past few decades have been marked by many great medical discoveries and many new surgical techniques. Heart, kidney, and liver transplants are now almost commonplace. With newly developed machines and medications, it has become possible to extend the life of seriously ill or injured persons for an unprecedented time.

What, then, are the legal problems? First, let us review the legal problems of organ transplantation. An initial problem is the source of the organ. Organs such as a kidney may be donated by a living donor. If the donor is mentally competent, he or she can give an informed consent to the surgical taking of the organ from his or her body and its transplantation in the body of another person. The law acknowledges that a person has rights of ownership to his or her body. If the donor is living, the legal question is whether the donor really understands the consequences of his or her actions.

With the transplantation of organs such as a heart or liver, donor must be dead and the organ must be taken from the donor within a very short period after death—sometimes within minutes, sometimes within hours. Medical experts state that time is more critical for some tissues of the body than for others. For example, the cornea of the eye may be taken from the donor up to approximately six hours after death, whereas the heart, a kidney, or the liver must be taken from the deceased donor within minutes after death. Medical researchers are constantly improving methods for preserving organs for additional periods of time after their removal and before their transplantation, but obtaining the initial consent for the removal of an organ from a deceased donor remains a problem.

A living donor can give an informed consent to the removal of an organ because he or she owns the rights in his or her body. But who owns the deceased body? Who can give consent? The common law gave rights to the deceased body for purposes of its dignified disposition and a decent burial first to the surviving spouse, if any, then to the children, if any, and then to the next of kin as specified by the inheritance statutes. These rights allowed the person who had them to receive the body in the condition it was in when death occurred, and that person could sue anyone who dissected the body, performed an unauthorized autopsy on it, or removed organs from it.

Scarpaci v. *Milwaukee County*
292 N.W.2d 816 (Wisconsin, 1980)

FACTS   James and Linda Scarpaci sued for the wrongful performance of an autopsy on the body of their deceased child Nicole. The defendants were Milwaukee County, county medical examiner Chesley Erwin, deputy medical examiner Joseph LaMonte, and associate medical examiner Elaine Samuels. The plaintiffs alleged that not only was the autopsy done without their permission but that it was done after they had made it known that they did not want one done. The plaintiffs further alleged that the autopsy was not authorized by state statute. As a result of the defendants' wrongful conduct, the plaintiffs claimed to have suffered damages for "the intrusion and defiling of the body of their deceased child, intrusion of their rights of care and burial of their child, extreme disabling emotional distress, and great outrage upon their sensitivities and emotions." The plaintiffs asked for $125,000 compensatory damages and a further $125,000 punitive damages against the individual defendants only. The County Board of Supervisors denied their claim for compensatory damages. They brought suit, and the defendants moved to dismiss, claiming sovereign immunity. The trial court denied the motion to dismiss, and the defendants appealed.

ISSUE   Does the complaint state a cause of action to which sovereign immunity is not a defense?

DECISION   Yes. Judgment affirmed.

REASONS   Justice Abrahamson engaged in an extended review of the powers of a county medical examiner and of the policy choice to be made between granting public officials absolute immunity and granting them qualified immunity in the performance of their duties. He felt that such a decision was best made on the basis of a trial record.

"The law is clear in this state that the family of the deceased has a legally recognized right to entomb the remains of the deceased family member in their integrity and without mutilation. Thus the next of kin have a claim against one who mutilates or otherwise disturbs the corpse. . . .

" 'We can imagine no clearer or dearer right in the gamut of civil liberty and security than to bury our dead in peace and unobstructed; none more sacred to the individual, nor more important of preservation and protection from the point of view of public welfare and decency.' . . .

"The basis for recovery of damages is found not in a property right in a dead body but in the personal right of the family of the deceased to bury the body. The mutilating or disturbing of the corpse is held to be an interference with this right and an actionable wrong.

"The law is not primarily concerned with the extent of physical injury to the bodily remains but with whether there were any improper actions and whether such actions caused emotional or physical suffering to the living kin. The tort rarely involves pecuniary injury; the generally recognized basis of damages is mental suffering. . . .

"Because the complaint in the instant case asserts that the defendants' interference with the right of the parents to bury the body caused the plaintiffs both great emotional distress and physical injuries, we conclude that the complaint is sufficient to survive the initial test of a motion to dismiss because it alleges the factual elements necessary for a claim of intentional or negligent inteference with the body."

Given the need to remove vital organs minutes after death if they are to be transplanted, the surgeons obviously cannot wait for a probate court to make a decision, nor can they always get a written consent from the proper relative. In view of the societal need for organ transplants and the overall importance of organ transplants to the health of persons in society, the National Conference of Commissioners on Uniform State Laws drafted the Uniform Anatomical Gift Act, previously referred to in Chapter 30. This act allows any living person who is competent to make a will, to make a gift of his or her body or any portion or part of it. A great number of the states have adopted the Uniform Anatomical Gift Act as law. Some states have an anatomical gift clause on the back of the driver's license. If the person desires, he or she can sign the anatomical gift clause before two witnesses. Then, if the person is killed, the body can be taken immediately to a hospital as a donor for organs. If no such gift is executed and signed prior to death, then organs may not be removed from the body without complying with proper legal procedure, which in most cases would take too long for the organs to be of benefit.

Another legal problem that has arisen from the medical advances of recent decades involves the question of when a person is determined to be legally dead. Also involved is the question of when orders can be given to disconnect the so-called lifesaving machines from a patient without incurring possible criminal and civil liability.

The key problem involved here is that there is no clear and uniform law in all states as to when a person is legally dead. Medical science explains that persons die in stages. First, there is clinical death; this occurs when respiration and the heartbeat cease. If respiration and the heartbeat cease for a period of time, then the brain is deprived of oxygen and blood circulation and the brain dies. This is defined as biological death. The life of a clinically dead person can be restored if the heart and respiratory systems can be restarted before the brain dies from lack of oxygen. Many persons today are graduates of the CPR course. This is a coronary pulmonary resuscitation procedure which is used to help a heart attack victim whose heart and respiratory system have stopped momentarily. Used properly, the procedure can bring a person back to life from clinical death. Generally speaking, it can be stated that, from a legal standpoint, a person is not legally dead until the brain is dead.

As a practical matter, there are many cases where the brain is not completely dead although the damage to it is irreversible. However, there is still sufficient capacity to allow the heart and the respiratory system to function with the aid of a life-support system. These are the problem cases which raise the question of whether the patient can be separated from the life-support system.

In Re Quinlan
70 N.J. 10 (New Jersey, 1976)

FACTS On the night of April 15, 1975, "for reasons still unclear," Karen Ann Quinlan, age 21, stopped breathing for at least two 15-minute periods. Her friends attempted mouth-to-mouth resuscitation; she was taken to a hospital in an ambulance. Her condition was comatose, with evidence of decortication, a derangement of the cortex of the brain which probably resulted from the prolonged lack of oxygen in the bloodstream. She required a respirator to assist her breathing since her brain function was minimal. She was in a "chronic persistent vegetative state," totally unaware of anyone or anything around her. Medical experts testified that death would probably soon follow removal of the respirator. Her father, Joseph Quinlan, petitioned to have her declared incompetent and himself declared guardian, with an express authorization to discontinue all extraordinary life-support medical systems. Subsequently joined as defendants were the county prosecutor and the treating physicians and the hospital. The state attorney general also intervened in the lawsuit. The trial court appointed a guardian ad litem for Karen and, after a hearing, denied Joseph's requests. He appealed, and the attorney general cross-appealed.

ISSUE Does an individual, acting through her parent as guardian, have a right to make her own decision on the use of extraordinary medical procedures to sustain life?

DECISION Yes. Judgment reversed. Permission given to withdraw the life-support system with the concurrence of the guardian and family *if* the treating physicians and the hospital ethics committee agree that there is no reasonable possibility of Karen's ever emerging from her present comatose condition.

REASONS Chief Justice Hughes recognized a landmark case when he saw one; he said that the case was "of transcendent importance" since it involved "questions related to the definition and existence of death; the prolongation of life through artificial means developed by medical technology undreamed of in past generations of the practice of the healing arts; the impact of such durationally indeterminate and artificial life prolongation on the rights of the incompetent, her family, and society in general; the bearing of constitutional right and the scope of judicial responsibility." After an extensive review of the medical evidence and the constitutional arguments, he felt that the trial court was correct in not giving Joseph a carte blanche authorization to turn off Karen's respirator but that Joseph should be her guardian and should have a more limited authority.

Chief Justice Hughes dismissed the freedom of religion argument because *conduct* might be regulated by the state, though religious beliefs might not. Likewise the claim of cruel and unusual punishment was dismissed since that provision related only to penal sanctions.

"It is the issue of the constitutional right of privacy that has given us most concern, in the exceptional circumstances of this case. Here a loving parent, *qua* parent and raising the rights of his incompetent and profoundly damaged daughter, probably irreversibly doomed to no more than a biologically vegetative remnant of life, is before the court. . . .

"We have no hesitancy in deciding, in the instant . . . case, that no external compelling interest of the State could compel Karen to endure the unendurable, only to vegetate a few measurable months with no realistic possibility of returning to any semblance of cognitive or sapient life. We perceive no thread of logic distinguishing between such a choice on Karen's part and a similar choice which, under the evidence in this case, could be made by a competent patient terminally ill, riddled by cancer, and suffering great pain; such a patient would not be resuscitated or . . . kept *against his will* on a respirator. . . .

"[P]hysicians distinguish between curing the ill and comforting and easing the dying. . . . [M]any of them have refused to inflict an undesired prolongation of the process of dying on the patient in irreversible condition when it is clear that such 'therapy' offers neither human nor humane benefit. We think these attitudes represent a balanced implementation of a profoundly realistic perspective on the meaning of life and death and that they respect the whole Judeo-Christian tradition of regard for human life."

LEGAL ISSUES OF INVASION OF SPACE

Who owns outer space? What rights, what duties do the various nations have with regard to the invasion or occupancy of outer space? We are already occupying outer space with the telecommunication satellites which are used constantly in business and other transactions all over the world. Within a comparatively short time we will see space stations and space shuttles from these stations to various nations. Thus it is imperative that some type of law be established concerning this new technology.

Section 102(a) of the National Aeronautics and Space Act of 1958 states as follows: "The Congress hereby declares that it is the policy of the United States that the activities in space should be devoted to peaceful purposes for the benefit of all mankind."

The United Nations General Assembly in 1962 made a declaration—Resolution no. 1962 (XVIII)—on legal principles covering the activity of states in the exploration and use of outer space. Its first paragraph states that "the exploration and use of outer space shall be carried out for the benefit and interest of all mankind."

In 1967 the United Nations General Assembly adopted an outer space treaty entitled Treaty on Principles Governing the Activity of States in the Exploration and Use of Outer Space, including the Moon and Other Celestial Bodies.

This treaty was ratified by the member nations of the United Nations and is still in effect. Article I of the treaty states that "the exploration and use of outer space, including the moon and other celestial bodies, shall be carried out for the benefit and in the interest of all countries, irrespective of their degree of economic or scientific development, and shall be the province of all mankind. Outer space, including the moon and other celestial bodies, shall be free for exploration and use by all states without discussion of any kind, on a basis of equality and accordance with international law, and there shall be free access to all areas of celestial bodies." Thus, under the 1967 UN treaty no nation can claim ownership of any specific area of space or any specific celestial body.

Article IV of the 1967 treaty specifies that "States, parties to the treaty, undertake not to place in orbit around the earth any objects carrying nuclear weapons or any other kinds of weapons of mass destruction, install such weapons on celestial bodies, or station such weapons in outer space in any other manner."

The 1967 agreement also covers the treatment of astronauts who may have to land in a country other than their own and the problems which may arise in case of accidental damage caused by emergency, unintended, or crash landing of space vehicles.

There are also an International Agreement on International Liability for Damage Caused by Space Objects and an International Agreement on the Rescue of Astronauts, the Return of Astronauts, and the Return of Objects launched into outer space.

Thus the general area of space exploration is viewed as an international problem which must be governed by international agreements. The obvious problem, of course, is the enforcement of these international agreements. Also, these agreements are between governments and not private sector businesses.

The private business sector as well as government is involved in space exploration. Two of the most well known businesses or organizations are Satellite Business Systems, a partnership made up of COMSAT General Corporation, International Business Machines Corporation, and the Aetna Casualty and Surety Company; and the organization known as MARISAT, a joint venture between the COMSAT General Corporation, RCA Global Communication, Western Union International, and ITT World Communications. These business organizations are at present primarily concerned with international communications systems using space satellites. Private sector business involvements in space are high-risk ventures since the law is not settled as to the ownership of a satellite once it is launched. Control and lease arrangements involving space activities have not yet been legally tested, and there are many other legal issues which do not have clear answers. Despite the high-risk nature of space ventures, it is anticipated that there will be more private sector business involvement in this area. As space stations are launched and space shuttles are established, there will be more and more opportunity for business ventures involving space goods and services. Thus this is another area where the law must catch up with technology.

DATA CASH SYSTEMS, INC. v. JS&A GROUP, INC.

628 F.2d 1038 (U.S. Seventh Circuit, 1980)

Nichols, Associate Judge

This is an appeal from an order of the district court denying plaintiff's motion for a preliminary injunction and granting defendants' motion for summary judgment on Count I of plaintiff's complaint, a claim of copyright infringement. We affirm the result of the district court, but we do so on different grounds. Proceedings on Count II of plaintiff's complaint, a claim of unfair competition, are suspended pending resolution of this appeal. . . .

In 1976, plaintiff contracted with D. B. Goodrich and Associates for the creation of a computer program for a computer chess game. During 1976 and 1977, D. B. Goodrich developed such a program called the "Chess One-Move Calculation" (Program).

The program developed for plaintiff was capable of receiving the player's instructions, determining the computer's possible legal moves, choosing among the permissible moves in accordance with tactical principles, and displaying the computer's move. All of the above could be performed at six different levels of expertise. Needless to say, the development of the "Chess One-Move Calculation" involved considerable human time, effort, and ingenuity.

Typically, a computer program evolves through several stages of development before reaching its final form. Initially, the programmer develops a "flow chart," a schematic representation of the program logic. The next step is to render those instructions into a "source code," a programming language such as FORTRAN or COBOL. The source program is then translated into an assembly language or machine language, a series of "ones" and "zeros." Finally, the program is stored in some mechanical medium such as magnetic tape or disk. In this case the final storage medium was in the form of Read-Only-Memory chips (ROM). The ROM is a silicon chip which has been chemically imprinted with tiny switches, an assembly language "one" becoming a connection and a "zero" becoming the absence of a connection.

General Instruments Corporation manufactured the ROM's for plaintiff, and they were electrically integrated into plaintiff's game. Marketing of plaintiff's game, CompuChess, began in the fall of 1977 and continued successfully into 1978.

In June of 1978, it came to the attention of plaintiff that a Hong Kong company claimed to be licensed to sell CompuChess at a lower price. Plaintiff learned from General Instruments that it was manufacturing a ROM for another chess game. At plaintiff's request, General Instruments tested the new ROM and found it to be identical to plaintiff's. Upon further inquiry, plaintiff learned that the other chess game was using a ROM made by General Instruments and was being manufactured by Novag Industries of Hong Kong for JS&A Industries to be marketed as JS&A Computer Chess.

Plaintiff's attempts followed to prevent the manufacture and marketing of JS&A Computer Chess. These efforts were unsuccessful.

In late 1978, JS&A began marketing its computer chess. Shortly thereafter, plaintiff filed this suit for copyright infringement and unfair competition. Defendants moved for summary judgment on both counts of plaintiff's petition on April 13, 1979.

There seems to be no dispute regarding the facts relevant to the issue of whether the program entered the public domain prior to duplication by defendants. The program, in the form of the ROM, was integrated into the CompuChess game, was distributed, and was sold to the general public without restriction in 1977. Over 2,500 CompuChess games were sold that year. Nowhere on the ROM, the game board, the packaging, or the accompanying instructions was there copyright notice. Plaintiff says it did not know that it was possible to read the program, as defendants did, if one had only the ROM. Defendants point out that a purchaser of the CompuChess who removed the ROM and unloaded its contents so as to see a printout of the program would not see a copyright notice because none was there. Plaintiff does not deny this, stating only that the printed readout copies generated by plaintiff and D. B. Goodrich were imprinted with copyright notice. But these were on internal documents and did not inform the public of plaintiff's claim. It does not seem to be denied that a copyright notice could have been placed in the ROM so that one who read out the game could not miss seeing it, and we understand this is now done. Of course a notice on the game board or the printed instructions would have presented no difficulty. Nonetheless plaintiff contends that the program has not entered the public domain. . . .

While there is some philosophical appeal to plaintiff's contention that the absence of copyright notice is irrelevant until someone doesn't see any notice, a proposition akin to the epistemological query as to whether a falling tree makes a sound when there is no one to hear it, we cannot accept plaintiff's assertion. While the 1909 Act did not define "publication," the "date of publication" was defined by section 26 of that Act as ". . . the earliest date when copies of the first authorized edition were placed on sale, sold, or publicly distributed by the proprietor. . . ." In 1977, plaintiff sold over 2,500 CompuChess units to the public without restriction. We do not know whether anyone unloaded the ROM and viewed the program during that year. The point is that plaintiff so gave up control that anyone who wished to do so could have seen the program in 1977, albeit by a technical process of some complexity. . . .

Plaintiff is not in the position of one the statute in section 21 sought to protect. It did not make an effort to comply and fail, through inadvertence or mistake, to comply completely. It made no effort to comply because it thought it was physically impossible to make a copy. It might, but did not, have provided a notice in case its assumption as to the technical limitations of others proved incorrect. Reliance on a more backward state of the art than the facts would have justified is not a covered case. We cannot award the defendants any

accolades for their ethics, but this is not the statutory standard. The arts of the copyist, and his technical resources, were continually advancing in 1909, and have continued since. If Congress had meant to provide that notice would be unnecessary whenever the copyist's techniques were subjectively deemed inadequate to make a copy, it would have said so. We cannot supply the omission.

In conclusion, for the reasons discussed in this opinion, we affirm the district court's grant of summary judgment for defendants and denial of plaintiff's request for injunctive relief. The case is remanded for proceedings on Count II of the complaint.

GOTTSCHALK v. BENSON AND TABBOT
409 U.S. 63 (1972)

Douglas, Justice

Respondents filed in the Patent Office an application for an invention which was described as being related "to the processing of data by program and more particularly to the programmed conversion of numerical information" in general purpose digital computers. They claimed a method for converting binary-coded-decimal (BCD) numerals into pure binary numerals. The claims were not limited to any particular art or technology, to any particular apparatus or machinery, or to any particular end use. They purported to cover any use of the claimed method in a general purpose digital computer of any type. Claims 8 and 13 were rejected by the Patent Office but sustained by the Court of Customs and Patent Appeals. . . . The case is here on a petition for a writ of certiorari. . . .

The question is whether the method described and claimed is a "process" within the meaning of the Patent Act.

A digital computer, as distinguished from an analogue computer, is that which operates on data expressed in digits, solving a problem by doing arithmetic as a person would do it by head and hand. Some of the digits are stored as components of the computer. Others are introduced

1056

into the computer in a form which it is designed to recognize. The computer operates then upon both new and previously stored data. The general purpose computer is designed to perform operations under many different programs.

The representation of numbers may be in the form of a time-series of electrical pulses, magnetized spots on the surface of tapes, drums, or discs, charged spots on cathode ray tube screens, or the presence or absence of punched holes on paper cards, or other devices. The method or program is a sequence of coded instructions for a digital computer.

The patent sought is on a method of programming a general purpose digital computer to convert signals from binary coded decimal form into pure binary form. A procedure for solving a given type of mathematical problem is known as an "algorithm." The procedures set forth in the present claims are of that kind; that is to say, they are generalized formulation for programs to solve mathematical problems of converting one form of numerical representation to another. From the generic formulation, programs may be developed as specific applications.

The decimal system uses as digits the 10 symbols 0, 1, 2, 3, 4, 5, 6, 7, 8, and 9. The value represented by any digit depends, as it does in any positional system of notation, both on its individual value and on its relative position in the numeral. Decimal numerals are written by placing digits in the appropriate positions or columns of the numerical sequence, i.e., "unit" (10^0), "tens" (10^1), "hundreds" (10^2), thousands (10^3), etc. Accordingly, the numeral 1492 signifies $(1 \times 10^3) + (4 \times 10^2) + (9 \times 10^1) + (2 \times 10^0)$.

The pure binary system of positional notation uses two symbols as digits—0 and 1, placed in a numerical sequence with values based on consecutively ascending powers of 2. In pure binary notation, what would be the tens position is the two position; what would be the hundreds position is the fours position; what would be the thousands position is the eights. Any decimal number from 0 to 10 can be represented in the binary system with four digits or positions. . . .

. . . The method sought to be patented varies the ordinary arithmetic steps a human would use by changing the order of the steps, changing the symbolism for writing the multiplier used in some steps, and by taking subtotals after each successive operation. The mathematical procedures can be carried out in existing computers long in use, no new machinery being necessary. And, as noted, they can also be performed without a computer.

The Court stated in *MacKay Co.* v. *Radio Corp.*, 306 U.S. 86, 94, that "While a scientific truth, or the mathematical expression of it, is not a patentable invention, a novel and useful structure created with the aid of knowledge of scientific truth may be." That statement followed the long-standing rule that "An idea of itself is not patentable." . . . "A principle, in the abstract, is a fundamental truth; an original cause; a motive; and these cannot be patented, as no one can claim in either of them an exclusive right." . . . Phenomena of nature, though just discovered, mental processes, abstract intellectual concepts are not patentable, as they are the basic tools of scientific and technological work. . . . "He who discovers a hitherto unknown phenomenon of nature has no claim to a monopoly of it which the law recognizes. If there is to be invention from such a discovery, it must come from the application of the law of nature to a new and useful end." We dealt there with a "product" claim, while the present case deals only with a "process" claim. But we think the same principle applies.

Here the "process" claim is so abstract and sweeping as to cover both known and unknown uses of the BCD to pure binary conversion. The end use may (1) vary from the operation of a train to verification of drivers' licenses to researching the law books for precedents and (2) be performed through any existing machinery or future-devised machinery or without any apparatus.

In *O'Reilly* v. *Morse*, 15 How 62, Morse was allowed a patent for a process of using electromagnetism to produce distinguishable signs for telegraphy. . . . But the Court denied the eighth claim in which Morse claimed the use of "electromagnetism, however, developed for marking or printing intelligible characters, signs, or letters, at any distance." The Court in disallowing that claim said, "If this claim can be maintained, it matters not by what process or machinery, the result is accomplished. For aught that we now know some future inventor, in the onward march of science, may discover a mode of writing or printing at a distance by means of the electric or galvanic current, without using any part of the process or combination set forth in the plaintiff's specification. His invention may be less complicated—less liable to get out of order—less expensive in construction, and its operation. But yet if it is covered by this patent the inventor could not use it, nor the public have the benefit of it without the permission of this patentee." . . .

* * * * *

Transformation and reduction of an article "to a different state or thing" is the clue to the patentability of a process claim that does not include particular machines. So it is that a patent in the process of "manufacturing fat acids and glycerine from fatty bodies by the action of water at a high temperature and pressure" was sustained in the *Tilghman* v. *Proctor*, 102 U.S. 707, 721. The Court said, "The chemical principle or scientific fact upon which it is founded is that the elements of neutral fat require to be severally united with an atomic equivalent of water in order to separate from each other and become free. This chemical was not discovered by Tilghman. He only claims to have invented a particular mode of bringing about the desired chemical union between the fatty elements and water." . . .

* * * * *

It is argued that a process patent must either be tied to a particular machine or apparatus or must operate to change articles or materials to a "different state or thing." We do not hold that no process patent could ever qualify if it did not meet the requirements of our prior precedents. It is said that the decision precludes a patent for any program servicing a computer. We do not so hold. It is said that we have before us a program for a digital computer but extend our holding to

programs for analog computers. We have, however, made clear from the start that we deal with a program only for digital computers. It is said we freeze process patents to old technologies, leaving no room for the revelations of the new, onrushing technology. Such is not our purpose. What we come down to in a nutshell is the following.

It is conceded that one may not patent an idea. But in practical effect that would be the result if the formula for converting binary code to pure binary were patented in this case. The mathematical formula involved here has no substantial practical application except in connection with a digital computer, which means that if the judgment below is affirmed, the patent would wholly pre-empt the mathematical formula and in practical effect would be a patent on the algorithm itself.

It may be that the patent laws should be extended to cover these programs, a policy matter to which we are not competent to speak. The President's Commission on the Patent System rejected the proposal that these programs be patentable:

Uncertainty now exists as to whether the statute permits a valid patent to be granted on programs. Direct attempts to patent programs have been rejected on the ground of nonstatutory subject matter. Indirect attempts to obtain patents and avoid the rejection, by drafting claims as a process, or a machine or components thereof programmed in a given manner, rather than as a program itself, have confused the issue further and should not be permitted.

The Patent Office now cannot examine applications for programs because of a lack of classification technique and the requisite search files. Even if these were available, reliable searchers would not be feasible or economic because of the tremendous volume of prior art being generated. Without this search, the patenting of programs would be tantamount to mere registration and the presumption of validity would be all but nonexistent.

It is noted that the creation of programs has undergone substantial and satisfactory growth in the absence of patent protection and that copyright protection for programs is presently available.

If these programs are to be patentable, considerable

1058

problems are raised which only committees of Congress can manage, for broad powers of investigation are needed, including hearings which canvass the wide variety of views which those operating in this field entertain. The technological problems tendered in the many briefs before us indicate to us that considered action by the Congress is needed.

Reversed.

PROBLEMS FOR DISCUSSION

1. Norris Nerdlinger was chief auditor for Hytone, Inc., before he was summarily fired for incompetence. In the two weeks he worked after receiving notice that he was being terminated, Norris very methodically erased all his company's financial records from its computer tapes. Some of these records might be recoverable at considerable expense; some were gone for good. In addition to the obvious claims against Norris, what other kinds of legal liability might flow from his actions? Discuss.

2. Ivan Lenin was born with serious sight, hearing, and speech defects because his mother contracted German measles (rubella) during the early months of her pregnancy. Dr. Bernie Botch, the treating physician, failed to diagnose her condition, or if he did, he failed to inform her of it. She says that if she had known of the possibility of such serious birth defects, she might have decided to have an abortion. Ivan says that he has been forced into a life of pain, suffering, and disability by the doctors' negligence. Ivan sues the doctor for damages. Does he have a case? Why or why not? If his parents sue the doctor, do they have a case? Why or why not?

3. Lermont Lyman was involved in a serious car accident. He suffered extensive internal injuries and brain damage. He was rushed to a hospital, where he was kept "alive" in a comatose condition by means of a respirator. Doctors agreed that if the respirator were removed, Lermont would die very quickly. Lermont had a $250,000 life insurance policy with a double indemnity clause for accidental death. The double indemnity feature only applied, however, if death resulted from accidental causes within three months of the accident. With the respirator, Lermont might linger on indefinitely in his vegetative state. What legal issues are raised by a situation like this? Discuss.

4. Millie Magnesium attended a backyard barbecue picnic at the home of Herman Malvale. Herman's apartment had a sliding clear glass door which opened onto his backyard. Millie arrived about 5:15 P.M. and was shown through the apartment and out the open back door. She says that she went in and out "several times" during the course of the next hour or so and that she drank only one or two glasses of white wine. Sometime between 6:30 P.M. and 6:45 P.M., she went into the house again, unaware that the glass door had been closed. She said that it "didn't look any different; I could see inside just like before." She walked right into the door, bruising her face and chipping her two front teeth. She sues Artful Industries, Inc., the manufacturer of the door, for manufacturing an unsafe product. Expert testimony will show that it is possible to make a permanent etching or mark in such glass, so that it would not appear to be clear. Is this an "unsafe" product under the law if it can be made in such a way as to probably avoid the accident which occurred? Discuss.

5. Millie's lawyer had done some more thinking about her case (Problem 4). He now wants to amend the complaint to add Herman and the landlord, Tucker Squire, as defendants. Under what theories of liability could he charge Herman and/or Tucker? Explain.

6. Fritz Ferrett, an investigative reporter for *Persons* magazine, was working on a story concerning bankruptcy fraud. Asserting that he had the right to inspect them under the Freedom of Information Act, he gained access to the computerized court records of a particular U.S. district court. When he analyzed the records he discovered that one bankruptcy judge seemed to be appointing the same persons as referees in bankruptcy again and again. Further investigation revealed that these "repeat" referees were either partners in the law firm with which the judge was associated or his business associates or friends. Fritz was ready with his story, which would disclose the above findings. His editor was fearful of a big judgment against the magazine if the story were printed. Of course, the judge could sue, but does he have a good chance for collecting damages against Fritz and the magazine? Discuss.

7. Francis Cuspid brings a lawsuit as guardian ad litem for his six-year-old niece, Chrissie Cuspid. Chrissie's mother, Lorane, was adjudged "mentally deficient" and was confined to a state hospital for the mentally ill. While so confined, Lorane engaged in sexual relations, resulting in the conception and birth of Chrissie. The identity of the father was unknown, as were the circumstances and the exact time of the occurrence. Chrissie says that the state was negligent in failing to prevent this assault on her mother and that as a result Chrissie had been deprived of a normal childhood and home life, proper parental care and support, and property rights and has been caused to bear the stigma of being illegitimate. Assuming that sovereign immunity from suit does not apply here, does Chrissie have a case on the above facts? Explain.

8. Edgar Earnest was charged with the crime of negligent homicide following an accident in which the car he was driving struck and seriously injured Portia Pirgim. Portia was taken to a hospital immediately, but her family refused to permit blood transfusions to be given to her, because of the family's religious beliefs. Portia died shortly thereafter. Edgar's lawyer argues that the accident did not cause Portia's death. How should this criminal case be decided? Discuss. Suppose Portia's family and her estate sue Edgar and his insurance company in a tort action for wrongful death. What result should the court work out in a civil case? Discuss.

International Law—Yesterday, Today, and Tomorrow **53**

Today most large U.S. corporations and many smaller U.S. businesses are engaged in international trade. Contracts may be executed with foreign companies or governments, foreign subsidiaries may be set up, or sales may be made directly to foreign customers through U.S. sales personnel traveling to the foreign country, through local agents, or by direct shipment from the U.S. to the foreign customer. The huge multinationals, corporations operating in many countries—such as Mobil, Gulf, Shell, Hoover, IBM, and Xerox—have been called the "new world order" and the "successor to the nation-state." Foreign business operations are substantial: each of the companies just listed derives 50 percent or more of its income from foreign operations; for Shell Oil, the figure is nearly 90 percent. Ninety percent of all U.S. corporations with sales of over $1 billion are multinationals. Although international trade (exports plus imports) is a relatively small 17 percent of the gross national product of the United States, for other countries international trade dominates the economy. The comparable figures for 1977 shows 53 percent for Italy and West Germany, 58 percent for Sweden, 61 percent for the United Kingdom, and 96 percent for Belgium. Thus the international stakes are high. International business is becoming more rather than less significant; trade has even commenced with the Communist countries of Eastern Europe and Asia. It is important, therefore, that the student have some basic idea of how law operates at the international level.

History of International Law.   International trade, of course, is nothing new. Neither are international relations and treaties between sovereign states. Almost from earliest recorded times, customs developed for the proper handling of international affairs and the problems which inevitably arose. Much of early international law was concerned with the law of the sea—freedom of passage, rights of ships in foreign ports, salvage and fishing rights, and the like—and with the rules covering foreign diplomatic personnel. City-states and nations which were important commercial centers often published collections of the customs which governed international trade. There is evidence that the Egyptians had such certain international law practices as early as 1400 B.C. Rhodes, the largest of the Dodecanese islands, in the Aegean Sea, had a "code" of international law by 700 B.C. The Greek city-states also adopted certain practices for dealing with diplomatic personnel and with international trade. Roman law developed the *ius gentium*, the law which dealt with relations with or between noncitizens, as opposed to the *ius civile*, which covered legal relations between Roman citizens; the *ius gentium* eventually came to dominate the Roman legal system. Important collections of international legal practices were published by Visby, Sweden, one of the most important members of the Hanseatic League, in the 11th century, and by Louis IX of France (the Code of Oléron) in the mid-13th century. Legal historians generally date modern international law from the adoption of the Treaty of Westphalia in 1648.

Sources of International Law. International law is drawn from the widest variety of sources; custom, treaties, judicial precedents, and textbooks have all played a part in its development. Hugo Grotius, a Dutch lawyer, is usually called "the father of international law" because of his great work *De Jure Bellis ac Pacis*, published in 1625. In it he spoke of international law as being based on natural law, which was common to all nations—the "dictate of right reason." This was in marked contrast to the "positivists," who derived international law from the customs of nations in their dealings with each other. In fact, both of these elements have played a part, along with specific treaties governing the international relations of two or more countries, and decisions of arbitrators and national and international courts. The Covenant of the League of Nations established the World Court in the Hague after World War I. A similar body, the International Court of Justice, functions there today under the United Nations Charter. Not all nations have fully accepted the jurisdiction of the ICJ in all matters, and many very important matters remain to be resolved by specific treaties. One of the major unresolved international law problems relates to the use of the seabed of the world's oceans, and the right to the enormous quantities of mineral nodules that are to be found there. The Communist nations and the "have-nots" generally favor some sort of world ownership, through the UN. The United States and most of the developed countries favor an arrangement which will leave substantial room for free enterprise mining of the ocean floor. The economic and political stakes in this one question are enormous.

U.S. v. *The Schooner La Jeune Eugénie*
2 Mason 409 (U.S. Circuit Court, 1822)

FACTS   An American warship, commanded by one Lieutenant Stockton, seized the schooner *La Jeune Eugénie* off the coast of Africa while it was being employed in the slave trade. The schooner was owned by French citizens who objected to the jurisdiction of the U.S. court in this forfeiture action. They contended that even though the slave trade was prohibited by French law, that was a matter which only French courts can decide. The United States contended that the slave trade also violated the law of nations.

ISSUE   Does the slave trade violate international law?

DECISION   Yes. Schooner confiscated from its owners but "delivered over to the consular agent of the King of France, to be dealt with according to his own sense of duty and right."

REASONS   Justice Story did not think himself bound by the fact that slavery was still in force in the United States and that it had been and was recognized in other countries.

"[T]he first question naturally arising out of the asserted facts is, whether the African slave trade be prohibited by the law of nations; for, if it be so, it will not, I presume, be denied, that confiscation of the property ought to follow, for that is the proper penalty denounced by that law for any violation of its precepts. . . .

"I shall take up no time in the examination of the history of slavery, or of the question, how far it is consistent with the natural rights of mankind. . . . That it has existed in all ages of the world, and has been tolerated by some, encouraged by others, and sanctioned by most, of the enlightened and civilized nations of the earth in former ages, admits of no reasonable question. That it has interwoven itself into the municipal institutions of some countries, and forms the foundation of large masses of property in a portion of our own country, is known to all of us. Sitting, therefore, in an American court of judicature, I am not permitted to deny, that under some circumstances it may have a lawful existence; and that the practice may be justified by the condition, or wants, of society, or may form a part of the domestic policy of a nation. . . .

"But this concession carries us but a very short distance towards the decision of this cause. It is not, as the learned counsel for the government have justly stated, on account of the simple fact that the traffic necessarily involves the enslavement of human beings, that it stands reprehended by the present sense of nations; but that it necessarily carries with it a breach of all the moral duties, of all the maxims of justice, mercy, and humanity, and of the admitted rights, which independent Christian nations now hold sacred. . . .

"Now the law of nations may be deduced, first, from the general principles of right and justice, applied to the concerns of individuals, and thence to the relations and duties of nations; or, secondly, in things indifferent or questionable, from the customary observances and recognitions of civilized nations; or, lastly, from the conventional or positive law, that regulates the intercourse between states. . . .

"[N]o practice . . . can obliterate the fundamental distinction between right and wrong. . . .

"[T]he African slave trade . . . is repugnant to the great principles of Christian duty, the dictates of natural religion, the obligations of good faith and morality, and the eternal maxims of social justice."

The International Court of Justice.   Chapter XIV of the Charter of the United Nations set up the International Court of Justice. The following articles in the Charter of the United Nations set out the purpose and jurisdiction of the court:

Art. 92. The International Court of Justice shall be the principal judicial organ of the United Nations. It shall function in accordance with the annexed Statute, which is based upon the Statute of the Permanent Court of International Justice and forms an integral part of the present Charter.

Art. 93. 1. All Members of the United Nations are ipso facto parties to the Statute of the International Court of Justice.

2. A state which is not a Member of the United Nations may become a party to the Statute of the International Court of Justice on conditions to be determined in each case by the General Assembly upon the recommendation of the Security Council.

Art. 94.1. Each Member of the United Nations undertakes to comply with the decision of the International Court of Justice in any case to which it is a party.

2. If any party to a case fails to perform the obligations incumbent upon it under a judgment rendered by the Court, the other party may have recourse to the Security Council, which may, if it deems necessary, make recommendations or decide upon measures to be taken to give effect to the judgment.

Art. 95. Nothing in the present Charter shall prevent Members of the United Nations from entrusting the solution of their differences to other tribunals by virtue of agreements already in existence or which may be concluded in the future.

Art. 96. 1. The General Assembly or the Security Council may request the International Court of Justice to give an advisory opinion on any legal question.

2. Other organs of the United Nations and specialized agencies, which may at any time be so authorized by the General Assembly, may also request advisory opinions of the Court on legal questions arising within the scope of their activities.

Article 93 of Chapter XIV of the United States Charter referred to the "Statute of the International Court of Justice." This statute is a comprehensive code which governs the organization of the court, the jurisdiction of the court, and the procedure to be followed by the court. Following are some of the pertinent provisions.

The statute provides that the International Court of Justice shall consist of 15 judges and that no more than 2 judges may be from the same country. These judges must be persons of high moral character, and they must have the same qualifications as would be required in their respective countries for appointment to the highest judicial offices in those countries, or they must be "jurisconsults" of recognized competence in international law. The judges are elected by the General Assembly and by the Security Council of the United Nations from a list of nominations submitted by nominating bodies from the various member nations. Their term of office is nine years, with five members of the court being reelected or replaced every three years.

The General Assembly and the Security Council must hold their elections independently of each other. If a person's name appears on the list of successful candidates of both the General Assembly and the Security Council, that person is elected. If there are no successful candidates after the first meeting and ballot, then two more meetings may be held and ballots cast. If there is still no agreement, then there is a deadlock procedure which must be followed. Three members of the Security Council and three members of the General Assembly will then meet and make the final selection of the persons to fill the vacancies.

The International Court of Justice was not set up to hear disputes between private citizens concerning international contract or property disputes. Since only nations may be parties in cases which are brought before the International Court of Justice, that court's decisions are of less significance to international business operations than are the decisions of national courts which apply international law.

International Law in U.S. Courts. International law has generally been recognized in U.S. courts, either as a part of the common law or as a body of practice and doctrine which the common-law courts would have recognized and enforced. Two very important constitutional provisions relate to international law. Article III, Section 2 extends the jurisdiction of the national courts to "all cases affecting ambassadors, other public ministers and consuls" and to "all cases of admiralty and maritime jurisdiction." In addition, a citizen of a foreign nation could have a case tried in a U.S. district court under diversity of citizenship rules. It thus appears that most "international" cases heard in this country will be tried in a U.S. district court.

The second important constitutional provision relating to international law produces more controversial results. Article VI, Section 2 provides: "This Constitution, and the laws of the United States which shall be made in pursuance thereof; and all treaties made or which shall be made, under the authority of the United States, shall be the supreme law of the land; and the judges in every state shall be bound thereby, anything in the constitution or laws of any state to the contrary notwithstanding." On its face, this is a logical and commonsense provision: the laws of the whole prevail over those of the parts. The problem arises because of the words used. To be "supreme," national "laws" (acts of Congress) must be made "in pursuance" of the Constitution, that is, subject to its protections and the powers delegated to Congress. Treaties, however, need only have been made "under the authority of the United States," that is, negotiated by the president and ratified by two-thirds of the Senate. This potential problem is starkly illustrated by the following case.

Missouri v. Holland
252 U.S. 416 (1920)

FACTS   In 1913 Congress passed an act prohibiting the killing of migratory birds, except under strict regulations. Since fish and game preservation was not a power delegated to Congress, two lower U.S. courts held the act to be unconstitutional. In 1916 a treaty was negotiated with Great Britain (representing Canada), by the terms of which both parties agreed to protect migratory birds with appropriate legislation. Pursuant to the treaty, Congress passed such a law in 1918. Missouri brought an equity action against Ray Holland, a U.S. game warden, to enjoin him from enforcing the 1918 statute and the secretary of agriculture's regulations adopted under its provisions. The U.S. district court dismissed the suit, and Missouri appealed.

ISSUE   Does the 1918 statute unconstitutionally infringe on the rights reserved to the states by the 10th Amendment to the U.S. Constitution?

DECISION   No. Judgment affirmed.

REASONS   Justice Holmes decided that the treaty power supported the statute even though other grants of authority to Congress would not, or might not.
"To answer this question it is not enough to refer to the 10th Amendment, reserv-

ing the powers not delegated to the United States, because by Article 2, section 2, the power to make treaties is delegated expressly, and by Article 6, treaties made under the authority of the United States, along with the Constitution and laws of the United States, made in pursuance thereof, are declared the supreme law of the land. If the treaty is valid, there can be no dispute about the validity of the statute under Article I, section 8, as a necessary and proper means to execute the powers of the government. The language of the Constitution as to the supremacy of treaties being general, the question before us is narrowed to an inquiry into the ground upon which the present supposed exception is placed.

"It is said that a treaty cannot be valid if it infringes the Constitution, that there are limits, therefore, to the treaty-making power, and that one such limit is that what an act of Congress could not do unaided, in derogation of the powers reserved to the States, a treaty cannot do. An earlier act of Congress that attempted by itself and not in pursuance of a treaty to regulate the killing of migratory birds within the States had been held bad in the District Court. . . .

"Whether the two cases cited were decided rightly or not, they cannot be accepted as a test of the treaty power. Acts of Congress are the supreme law of the land only when made in pursuance of the Constitution, while treaties are declared to be so when made under the authority of the United States. It is open to question whether the authority of the United States means more than the formal acts prescribed to make the convention. We do not mean to imply that there are no qualifications to the treaty-making power; but they must be ascertained in a different way. It is obvious that there may be matters of the sharpest exigency for the national well-being that an act of Congress should not deal with, but that a treaty followed by such an act could, and it is not lightly to be assumed that, in matters requiring national action, 'a power which must belong to and somewhere reside in every civilized government' is not to be found. . . . [W]e may add that when we are dealing with words that are also a constituent act, like the Constitution of the United States, we must realize that they have called into life a being the development of which could not have been foreseen completely by the most gifted of its begetters. . . . The case before us must be considered in the light of our whole experience, and not merely in that of what was said a hundred years ago. The treaty in question does not contravene any prohibitory words to be found in the Constitution. The only question is whether it is forbidden by some invisible radiation from the general terms of the 10th Amendment."

The majority of the Court then decided that the treaty was not so forbidden.

Since the President, by the terms of Article II, Section 2, must get the "advice and consent" of two thirds of the Senate before a treaty becomes the "supreme law of the land," an important check still remained on arbitrary action by the executive which might violate provisions of the Constitution. Presumably, two thirds of the Senate would not vote to ratify a treaty which was blatantly unconstitutional. That protection was removed by a series of cases in the 1930s and 1940s, which dealt with the internal effect of international agreements that had not been submitted to the Senate for ratification as treaties.

U.S. v. Belmont
301 U.S. 324 (1937)

FACTS
As the Bolsheviks consolidated their power in Russia after the 1917 revolution, they engaged in wholesale nationalization of private business assets. The Petrograd Metal Works was nationalized in 1918, under a decree which purported to reach all its assets, wherever situated. Belmont's bank in New York had some of these assets on deposit. President Roosevelt recognized the Soviet government in 1933, by receiving the Soviet ambassador for the first time. A comprehensive settlement of claims between the two countries was worked out in the so-called Litvinov Assignment, by the terms of which all claims which the Soviet government had against U.S. citizens were assigned to the U.S. government. The United States brought this suit to collect the Petrograd Metal Works assets from Belmont. The U.S. district court dismissed the complaint, and the U.S. court of appeals affirmed.

ISSUE
Is this international agreement, not ratified by the Senate as a treaty, part of the supreme law of the land?

DECISION
Yes. Judgment reversed.

REASONS
Justice Sutherland briefly summarized the facts and then proceeded to analyze the foreign affairs function of the national government.

"We do not pause to inquire whether in fact there was any policy of the state of New York to be infringed, since we are of the opinion that no state policy can prevail against the international compact here involved.

"This court has held . . . that every sovereign state must recognize the independence of every other sovereign state; and that the courts of one will not sit in judgment upon the acts of the government of another, done within its own territory. . . .

"That the negotiations, acceptance of the assignment, and agreements and understandings in respect thereof were within the competence of the President may not be doubted. Governmental power over internal affairs is distributed between the national government and the several states. Governmental power over external affairs is not distributed, but is vested exclusively in the national government. And in respect of what was done here, the Executive had authority to speak as the sole organ of that government. . . .

"[A]n international compact, as this was, is not always a treaty which requires the participation of the Senate. . . .

"Plainly, the external powers of the United States are to be exercised without regard to state laws or policies. The supremacy of a treaty in this respect has been recognized from the beginning. . . . And while this rule in respect of treaties is established by the express language of clause 2, article 6, of the Constitution, the same rule would result in the case of all international compacts and agreements from the very fact that complete power over international affairs is in the national government and is not and cannot be subject to any curtailment or interference on the part of the several states. . . . In respect of all international negotiations and compacts, and in respect of our foreign relations generally, state lines disappear. As to such purposes the state of New York does not exist. Within the field of its powers, whatever the United States rightfully undertakes, it necessarily has warrant to consummate. And when judicial authority is involved in aid of such consummation, State Constitutions, state laws, and state policies are irrelevant to the inquiry and decision. It is inconceivable that any of them can be interposed as an obstacle to the effective operation of a federal constitutional power."

While several later cases have indicated that the executive could not enforce an agreement which violated specific provisions of the Bill of Rights, the basic "supremacy" problem remains. From a business standpoint, the danger is that such political settlements may have drastic consequences for the private ownership of property in the foreign country and for the enforceability of contracts.

International Arbitration. It is very common for international business contracts to contain an arbitration clause whereby the parties agree to submit any controversy relating to the contract to an arbitrator or an arbitration panel, rather than to go to court. In any business contract dispute, arbitration will almost certainly save time and legal expense, and the parties can select an arbitrator with expertise in the substantive area involved. These same advantages hold at the international level, but there are additional procedural reasons for including such a clause in the international contract. With an international dispute, there are always potential questions as to which court in what country would have jurisdiction, how service of process can be effected across international boundaries, and which country's law applies. These problems can be minimized with an arbitration clause that specifies the law to be applied, the method of selecting the arbitrator, the procedures to be followed, and the allocation of expenses between the parties. While it is true that arbitrators' awards are sometimes not paid voluntarily, they will generally be enforced by the courts of most nations if a lawsuit is necessary.

Letters of Credit. The letter of credit is a very common, and very useful, financial arrangement in international trade. Of course, it may also be used for business transactions occurring wholly within one country or even as a means of establishing one's credit for nonbusiness purposes, but its main use is in international business transactions.

The basic idea of a letter of credit is simple enough. As defined in UCC 5–103, a letter of credit means "an engagement by a bank or other person made at the request of a customer . . . that the issuer will honor drafts or other demands for payment upon compliance with the condition specified in the credit." A letter of credit may be either revocable or irrevocable. In many cases the draft or demand for payment must be accompanied by the presentation of certain required documents, such as a bill of lading indicating that goods have beeh shipped. Typically the "customer" referred to in the above definition is a foreign buyer of goods. The letter of credit is being used as the payment mechanism for the goods. The buyer goes to its bank, where it has established credit, and requests that the bank issue a letter of credit in favor of the overseas seller, which is the "beneficiary" of the credit. The credit will indicate the maximum amount of money that the seller is authorized to draw and will specify what documents the seller will have to present to the bank in order to get the money. Quite frequently, the arrangement will provide for the buyer's bank to transmit the letter to a bank in the seller's country, for convenience. When the seller ships goods according to the terms of the sales contract, it presents the shipping documents to the bank and gets the contract price for them.

Within the United States, Article 5 of the Uniform Commercial Code governs letters of credit. In international transactions, the parties should specify which country's law controls. In the absence of such a provision in the parties' contract, the general rules of private international law (choice of law rules) would determine which country's law should be applied to the dispute. As to disputes between the customer and its bank relating to the issuance and validity of the letter of credit, the law of the country of issuance would probably be applied. As to the responsibilities of the correspondent bank in the seller's country for handling the credit and verifying the documents presented, that country's law should be applied. Once again, it's best to anticipate such problems and make provisions in the contract for handling them when and if they arise.

American Bell International, Inc. v. Islamic Republic of Iran
474 F. Supp. 420 (New York, 1979)

FACTS   Bell sued for an injunction to prevent defendant Manufacturers Hanover Trust Company from making any payments under its Letter of Credit No. SC 170027 to defendants Iran or Bank Iranshahr or their successors. Bell, a wholly owned subsidiary of AT&T, made a contract on July 23, 1978, with the Imperial Government of Iran—Ministry of War to provide consulting services and equipment to improve Iran's international communications system. The contract provided a complex mechanism of payment to Bell of some $280 million, including a $38 million down payment. Iran could demand return of the down payment at any time, but the amount so refundable would be reduced by 20 percent of the invoices filed by Bell to which Iran did not object. In other words, as satisfactory performance on both sides occurred, Bell got to retain more of the advance guarantee. About $30 million was still refundable at the time of trial. Iran required a guarantee that it would get the money refunded if it asked for it, so Bell had Bank Iranshahr sign an irrevocable letter of guaranty in favor of the Iranian government. To protect Bank Iranshahr in the event that it was forced to honor the guaranty, Bell obtained a letter of credit from Manufacturers in favor of Bank Iranshahr. If Manufacturers received confirmation from Bank Iranshahr that it had been forced to pay the Iranian government, Manufacturers had to reimburse Bank Iranshahr. Bell in turn promised to reimburse Manufacturers for any such amounts paid out under the letter of credit. After the Iranian revolution Bell was left with substantial unpaid invoices and claims, and it terminated its performance under the contract in January 1979. Bell and AT&T filed a state court action for a similar injunction in February 1979; that suit was dismissed. In July 1979 Manufacturers received a demand from Bank Iranshahr for $30,220,724: this demand was refused on the ground that it did not conform to the terms of the letter of credit. Bell then brought this action. A conforming demand for payment had now been received from Bank Iranshahr.

ISSUE   Should an injunction issue against payment of the letter of credit?

DECISION   No. Motion denied, but a payment delay ordered to permit appeal.

REASONS   Judge MacMahon felt that Bell had failed to make out a case for a preliminary injunction because (1) it had not shown irreparable injury; (2) it had not shown a probability of success on the merits at trial; and (3) it had not shown a balance of hardships in its favor.

"There is credible evidence that the Islamic Republic is xenophobic and anti-American and that it has no regard for consulting service contracts such as the one here. Although Bell has made no effort to invoke the aid of the Iranian courts, we think the current situation in Iran, as shown by the evidence, warrants the conclusion that an attempt by Bell to resort to those courts would be futile. . . . However, Bell has not demonstrated that it is without adequate remedy in this court against the Iranian defendants under the Sovereign Immunity Act which it invokes in this very case. . . .

"In order to succeed on the merits, Bell must prove, by a preponderance of the evidence, that either (1) demand for payment of the Manufacturers Letter of Credit conforming to the terms of the Letter has not yet been made . . . or (2) a demand, even though in conformity, should not be honored because of fraud in the transaction. . . .

"[T]he United States now recognizes the present Government of Iran as the legal successor to the Imperial Government of Iran. That recognition is binding on American courts. . . . Though we may decide for ourselves the consequences of such recognition upon the litigants in this case . . . , we point out that American courts have traditionally viewed contract rights as vesting not in any particular government but in the state of which that government is an agent. . . .

"If conformity is established, as here, the issuer of an irrevocable, unconditional letter of credit, such as Manufacturers, normally has an absolute duty to transfer the requisite funds. This duty is wholly independent of the underlying contractual relationship that gives rise to the letter of credit. . . . [P]ayment is enjoinable where a germane document is forged or fraudulent or there is "fraud in the transaction.' . . .

"Even if we accept the proposition that the evidence does show repudiation, plaintiff is still far from demonstrating the kind of evil intent necessary to support a claim of fraud. . . . Absent any showing that Iran would refuse to pay damages upon a contract action here or in Iran, much less a showing that Bell has even attempted to obtain such a remedy, the evidence is ambivalent as to whether the purported repudiation results from nonfraudulent economic calculation or from fraudulent intent to mulct Bell. . . .

"Plaintiff's argument requires us to presume bad faith on the part of the Iranian government. . . . On the evidence before us, fraud is not more inferable than an economically rational decision by the government to recoup its down payment, as it is entitled to do under the consulting contract, and still dispute its liabilities under that Contract."

While certain additional risks are involved in international business, the potential rewards are also great. As the volume of international commerce increases, it will become more and more important for American business managers to have an appreciation for the rules of international law.

NATIONAL AMERICAN CORP. v. FEDERAL REPUBLIC OF NIGERIA

597 F.2d 314 (U.S. Second Circuit, 1978)

Oakes, Circuit Judge

This contract action founded upon diversity jurisdiction is one of the many law suits resulting from the almost incredible massive cement purchase program that appellee Federal Republic of Nigeria (Nigeria) mounted in the spring of 1975. Under this program, Nigeria contracted with 68 international suppliers, of which appellant, National American Corp. (NAC), is one, for the total purchase of over 20 million metric tons of cement to be unloaded within one year at the port of Lagos, a port capable of unloading only 1 million metric tons per year. To add lime to the mix, the contracts—if the one here is a typical example—involved a built-in bonanza for the suppliers: demurrage claims were payable at per diem per vessel rates with no restriction on the number of suppliers that might use and claim demurrage on a single vessel and with no minimum tonnage required from each vessel. As a result, when the inevitable port congestion delayed unloading, huge demurrage claims began piling up because numerous small ships carrying small tonnages for different suppliers waited in the harbor or outside the port, or, in the case of ships carrying cement sold under CIF (cost, insurance, and freight) contracts, simply rested at their home port somewhere in the world. Faced with a national economic disaster because the growing congestion in its only major port threatened the supply of vital consumer goods, Nigeria in August 1975 placed an embargo on all shipping into Lagos. Nigeria notified its suppliers that it would permit no vessels to enter the port except for those already under sail or those giving two months' advance notice of sailing and obtaining permission for departure. Moreover, Nigeria formed a negotiating committee to renegotiate the cement contracts and accompanying letters of credit. It is specifically NAC's contracts as renegotiated that are here in dispute. The United States District Court for the Southern District of New York . . . held that these renegotiation contracts were valid; that they were not executory accords; that they bound the appellant, NAC; and that under the contracts, appellee had fully paid appellant. . . . Appellant principally argues that the negotiated contracts were ineffective because there was no meeting of the minds, that if effective the renegotiated contracts were not novations but were executory accords, and that in any event NAC is entitled to additional payment because the court below erred in computing its damages. Appellees, in addition to arguing that Judge Goettel's rulings were correct, argue that NAC's original claims arise out of governmental and sovereign acts of Nigeria, which are acts of state, thereby rendering the claims nonjusticiable. We affirm for the reasons set out below.

Facts

Assuming the reader may obtain a certain familiarity with Judge Goettel's opinion below, we review the facts only in sufficient detail to elucidate the legal issues on appeal.

As stated, Nigeria's 1975 cement purchase program involved NAC, an American company with Spanish connections. On April 3, 1975, Nigeria entered into a contract with NAC for the purchase of 240,000 tons of Portland Cement at $60 per metric ton CIF Lagos, for a total purchase price of $14 million. The contract provided for demurrage payable by the consignee Nigeria at a rate not exceeding $3,500 per diem. The contract was to be governed by the laws of "New York City" and involved issuance through the state bank, appellee Central Bank of Nigeria (CBN) of an irrevocable letter of credit with a May 31, 1976, expiration date for $14 million, the full amount of the purchase price of the cement, and subsequently agreed to pay for demurrage expenses in excess of the credit amount. NAC assigned portions of the payments due to it under the contract to various corporations, principally two assignments totaling $11,640,000 to International Trade and Finance Espanola, S.A.

(Intrafinsa), headed by one Agustine Arrau. Subsequently, after the renegotiation contracts, hereinafter called the agreements of discharge, Intrafinsa reassigned its rights in the letter of credit to NAC with NAC agreeing to pay the shipowner's claims for demurrage when NAC recovered damages.

Performance of the cement contract started in late July 1975 with the shipment of 500 tons of cement upon the vessel *Cretan Life* (which also carried 10,500 tons consigned by another one of Nigeria's numerous cement suppliers). Five additional vessels, including the *Naimbana, Rio Doro, Cherryfield, Joboy,* and *Jotina,* carried cement to Lagos for NAC. These were the "first six vessels"; and by September 10, 1975, Nigeria had completed payment of $2,257,800 for their combined cargoes of 37,630 tons. Six other ships, the *Aristotle, Astrid, Ardenal, Sandrina, Euna,* and *Nicholaos H.* (the "second six vessels"), were prepared for loading or were partially loaded when Nigeria imposed its embargo. At the time of the embargo CBN also instructed its correspondent Morgan to dishonor all demurrage claims, even those accruing on vessels that entered the harbor prior to the embargo, unless CBN had certified the documents for payment. Nigeria formalized this policy in a government decree issued December 19, 1975.

Of NAC's first six vessels, four were eventually unloaded in Lagos; but the *Joboy* and the *Jotina* departed without discharging their cargoes. Their owners exercised shipholder's liens and seized the cement. Nigeria would not grant the ships priority berthing, and demurrage was running without payment. As to the second six vessels, although there was deposition testimony from Intrafinsa's Arrau that some of them were half loaded when Nigeria imposed the embargo and that the shipowners sold to Saudi Arabia some of the cement under lien, his records were sufficiently inadequate that the court below found that neither NAC nor Intrafinsa had established any losses. . . .

In early January 1976, the Nigerian cement contracts negotiating committee invited NAC's president, Dr. Ilona Gero, to renegotiate the cement contract and letter of credit. Gero and

Arrau prepared a document dated January 28, 1976, which was introduced in evidence as Exhibit 38, that set Intrafinsa's damages at $3,945,000; the amount allegedly represented the demurrage due on all 12 vessels calculated at $3,500 per day. Also in the document, NAC promised to "cause" Nigeria to accept delivery of an additional 28,370 tons of cement. Calculations supporting the demurrage claim appear as a schedule to the document, but the district court noted that this document mysteriously contains a column listing the "ETA" (estimated time of arrival) Lagos date for the first six vessels which had already arrived and an "ETA" date for the second six vessels which had never sailed. . . . As the district judge pointed out, these schedules had an "Alice in Wonderland" character because it is impossible to calculate demurrage at Lagos on vessels that never sailed from their home ports. . . .

At the New York meeting late in January 1976, Gero and Arrau called in another holder of a Nigerian cement contract, Doris Delia, to act as their agent in the cement committee negotiations. Arrau promptly executed a written power of attorney authorizing Delia to negotiate terms paralleling the claims incorporated in Exhibit 38. Delia returned from Nigeria in the first week of February with two form agreements entitled "agreements of discharge," one with the Federal Ministry of Defense concerning the cement contract and one with CBN concerning the letter of credit. These documents provided for payment for 70,830 tons of cement, represented as "either [having] been delivered . . . or . . . at present awaiting delivery in vessels lying within Nigerian territorial waters." The parties acknowledge in the discharge agreements that the port congestion rendered impossible further deliveries of cement. Finally, each of the parties released the others from all liability on the remaining 169,170 tons of cement and NAC and Intrafinsa agreed to indemnify the Nigerian entities against all third-party claims. Two payment provisos are attached to each of the agreements after the "in witness whereof" clause but preceding the signatures of the parties. One is to the effect that CBN would pay within 30 days of execution of the agreement for "the full value of the cement already delivered as reflected in the bills of lading and commercial invoices already in the possession of the Morgan Guaranty Trust Co. in New York." The other is that Nigeria would make payment for demurrage within 14 days of the presentation of the requisite documentation to the Nigerian Port Authority. Following the execution of these agreements of discharge on February 6, 1976, NAC by letter dated February 16, 1976, requested CBN to instruct Morgan Guaranty to release the funds for the 33,200 tons of cement that the second six vessels were to have carried. . . .

On March 12 Morgan paid appellant $1,992,000 for the cargo of the second six vessels bringing the total that the Nigerians had paid to $4,249,800 for 12 shiploads of cement. Nigeria ultimately obtained the cement cargoes of only four ships, however, and thus paid $2,778,000 for cement never received. . . .

Appellant also objects to the trial court's reformation of the tonnage figure in the discharge agreements, contending that there was no meeting of the minds on the amount as reformed. The discharge agreements do specifically refer to 70,830 metric tons of cement, covering the tonnage shipped on the first six vessels as well as the tonnage to have been shipped on the second six. The district court, however, read as controlling, as we do, the provision in the discharge agreements that referred to the tonnage as either actually "delivered under the said Letter of Credit or . . . at present awaiting delivery in vessels lying within Nigerian territorial waters." Appellant argues that the word "delivered" meant delivered under the terms of the original CIF cement contract, that is, that it referred to the second six vessels which had been in the loading process or were preparing to load when Nigeria imposed the embargo. . . .

The court below correctly reformed the agreements of discharge with regard to the tonnage figure on the grounds of either mutual mistake or fraud. It was the cement in the harbor which the parties intended to be covered. By either mutual mistake or fraud the agreements of discharge erroneously indicated that 12 ships were there,

making the tonnage figure greater than it was in fact. Certainly there was mistake on the part of the negotiating committee, which, because of the confusion in the harbor and Nigeria's total lack of capacity to handle the situation, did not find out until after it executed the agreements of discharge that the second six vessels had never arrived. If the court below believed appellant's witness Gero, NAC's president, in her statement that she also did not learn until May 1976 that the second six vessels had never sailed to Lagos, the court could have found a mutual mistake of fact leading up to the negotiation of the agreements of discharge, warranting reformation under well-established principles of law. . . .

Appellant argues that there could have been no reliance on any representation that 12 ships were in Lagos harbor because even with the port congestion appellees "always had control over their own harbor conditions, always had the ability to monitor the arrivals and departure of ships, and did in fact take a census of the ships which where there." But the testimony before Judge Goettel showed that at the time Nigeria imposed the embargo and through the spring of 1976 Nigeria was not able to confirm the presence or absence of particular vessels in their territorial waters; as the court found, there was "a demonstrated inability to verify which vessels were in their waters and for how long they had been there." . . . It was also clear that the negotiating committee did not have the capacity or the responsibility to confirm the location of vessels; that the negotiating committee dealt with the suppliers and their agents in good faith and accepted their representations as to consignments of cement already delivered or aboard vessels in Nigerian waters; and that in fact, in the case of NAC, Nigeria did not become aware of the missing vessels until after Morgan had made payment for their cargoes. . . .

[T]he amount of demurrage owing to NAC, considering the elimination of the *Joboy* and *Jotina* claims and the reduction of the *Rio Doro* claim, is less than Nigeria's overpayment for the cement; and thus NAC has failed to prove any damages.

The judgment is affirmed.

1073

Van Graafeiland, Circuit Judge (dissenting)

Because my understanding of the law of reformation differs markedly from that of my colleagues, I must dissent. . . .

The majority makes sport of the plight of plaintiff and its associates, overlooking the fact that at least one of them, Intrafinsa, is now in the hands of creditors. It is undisputed that Nigeria, imperiously and by threat of force,[1] breached a valid contract to purchase 240,000 tons of cement from plaintiff. Plaintiff is now being deprived of its right to recover damages for that breach by an "Agreement of Discharge," the terms of which were not agreed upon by the parties but were created in the mind of the district judge. I cannot concur in this inequity.

PFIZER, INC. v. GOVERNMENT OF INDIA
434 U.S. 308 (1978)

Justice Stewart

In this case we are asked to decide whether a foreign nation is entitled to sue in our courts for treble damages under the antitrust laws. The respondents are the Government of India, the Imperial Government of Iran, and the Republic of the Philippines. They brought separate actions in Federal District Courts against the petitioners, six pharmaceutical manufacturing companies. The actions were later consolidated for pretrial purposes in the United States District Court of Minnesota. The complaints alleged that the petitioners had conspired to restrain and monopolize interstate and foreign trade in the manufacture, distribution, and sale of broad spectrum antibiotics, in violation of SS.1 and 2 of the Sherman Act. . . . Among the practices the petitioners allegedly engaged in were price fixing, market division, and fraud upon the United States Patent Office. India and Iran each alleged that it was a "sovereign foreign state with whom the United States of America maintains diplomatic relations";

the Philippines alleged that it was a "sovereign and independent government." Each respondent claimed that as a purchaser of antibiotics it had been damaged in its business or property by the alleged violations and sought treble damages under S.4 of the Clayton Act . . . on its own behalf and on behalf of several classes of foreign purchasers of antibiotics.

The petitioners asserted as an affirmative defense to the complaints that the respondents as foreign nations were not "persons" entitled to sue for treble damages under S.4. In response to pretrial motions the District Court held that the respondents were "persons" and refused to dismiss the actions. . . . The Court of Appeals for the Eighth Circuit affirmed . . . and adhered to its decision upon rehearing en banc. . . . We granted certiorari to resolve an important and novel question in the administration of the antitrust laws. . . .

As the Court of Appeals observed, this case "turns on the interpretation of the statute." . . . [W]hether a foreign nation is entitled to sue for treble damages depends upon whether it is a "person" as that word is used in S.4. There is no statutory provision or legislative history that provides a clear answer; it seems apparent that the question was never considered at the time the Sherman and Clayton Acts were enacted.

The Court has previously noted the broad scope of the remedies provided by the antitrust laws. "The Act is comprehensive in its terms and coverage, protecting all who are made victims of the forbidden practices by whomever they may be perpetrated." . . . And the legislative history of the Sherman Act demonstrates that Congress used the phrase "any person" intending it to have its naturally broad and inclusive meaning. There was no mention in the floor debates of any more restrictive definition. Indeed, during the course of those debates the word "person" was used interchangeably with other terms even broader in connotation. For example, Senator Sherman said that the treble-damages remedy was being given to "any party," and Senator Edmunds, one of the principal draftsmen of the final bill, said that it established "the right of anybody to sue who chooses to sue." . . .

---

[1]Plaintiff was informed by telegram on September 22, 1975, that anyone violating Nigeria's embargo "will be liable to have his vessel denied entrance to Nigerian territorial waters by force if necessary. This is a final warning."

In light of the law's expansive remedial purpose, the Court has not taken a technical or semantic approach in determining who is a "person" entitled to sue for treble damages. . . .

The respondents in this case possess two attributes that could arguably exclude them from the scope of the sweeping phrase "any person." They are foreign, and they are sovereign nations. . . .

Yet it is clear that a foreign *corporation* is entitled to sue for treble damages, since the definition of "person" contained in the Sherman and Clayton Acts explicitly includes "corporations and associations existing under or authorized by . . . the laws of any foreign country." . . . Moreover, the antitrust laws extend to trade "with foreign nations" as well as among the several States of the Union. . . . Clearly, therefore, Congress did not intend to make the treble-damages remedy available only to consumers in our own country. . . .

Moreover, an exclusion of all foreign plaintiffs would lessen the deterrent effect of treble damages. The conspiracy alleged by the respondents in this case operated domestically as well as internationally. If foreign plaintiffs were not permitted to seek a remedy for their antitrust injuries, persons doing business both in this country and abroad might be tempted to enter into anticompetitive conspiracies affecting American consumers in the expectation that the illegal profits they could safely extort abroad would offset any liability to plaintiffs at home. If, on the other hand, potential antitrust violators must take into account the full costs of their conduct, American consumers are benefitted by the maximum deterrent effect of treble damages upon all potential violators. . . .

The second distinguishing characteristic of these respondents is that they are sovereign nations. The petitioners contend that the word *person* was clearly understood by Congress when it passed the Sherman Act to exclude sovereign governments. The word *person*, however, is not a term of art with a fixed meaning wherever it is used, nor was it in 1890 when the Sherman Act was passed. . . . Indeed, the Court has expressly noted that use of the word *person* in the Sherman and Clayton Acts did not create a "hard and fast rule of exclusion" of governmental bodies. . . .

On the two previous occasions that the Court has considered whether a sovereign government is a "person" under the antitrust laws, the mechanical rules urged by the petitioners has been rejected. . . .

It is clear that in *Georgia* v. *Evans* the Court rejected the proposition that the word *person* as used in the antitrust laws excludes all sovereign states. And the reasoning of that case leads to the conclusion that a foreign nation, like a domestic State, is entitled to pursue the remedy of treble damages when it has been injured in its business or property by antitrust violations. When a foreign nation enters our commercial markets as a purchaser of goods or services, it can be victimized by anticompetitive practices just as surely as a private person or a domestic State. The antitrust laws provide no alternative remedies for foreign nations as they do for the United States. . . .

Accordingly, the judgment of the Court of Appeals is affirmed.

PROBLEMS FOR DISCUSSION

1. Wilhemena Tussmann was employed in 1972 by the Cord Motor Company in Illinois. Shortly thereafter, a position opened up in Cord's foreign office in Turin, Italy, and Tussmann applied for and was given the job. Cord had a company policy of trying to equalize the effects of foreign income taxes on its overseas employees, by agreeing to reimburse them for any additional foreign income taxes they paid over and above what would normally have been due had they earned the income in the United States and paid income taxes here in full. Tussmann worked in Turin from 1972 to 1975. She alleges that she has some $7,600 coming to her under the tax

repayment arrangement. She filed suit for the money in Illinois in 1978. Cord moved to dismiss the complaint, since Illinois had a two-year statute of limitations for salary and wage claims. Tussmann says her claim is not barred, since Italy has a six-year statute of limitations for contract debts. Who's right, and why?

2. Egbert Leisman, the Norwegian distributor for Filmright, Inc., sued Filmright for commission allegedly due him on sales made through his office. As part of its defense, Filmright argued that any amount it owed Leisman should be set off against amounts that were due it by Swedish Processing Company. Filmright says that Leisman and Swedish entered into a joint venture, thereby making Leisman liable for all debts of the enterprise. Filmright can prove (1) that Swedish did contribute money to set up a local distribution system and (2) that Leisman contributed certain services. Is Filmright entitled to set off its claim against Swedish, against what it owes Leisman? Why or why not?

3. Armando Brile sold 5,000 tons of sheet steel to a customer in Ghana. The contract provided for payment by letter of credit, drawn against a Paris bank. The customer's bank in Ghana sent a cable to its correspondent bank in Paris, instructing the Paris bank to open a conforming letter of credit in the customer's name. For some unknown reason, the French government refused to permit the proposed transfer of funds from the Paris bank. Armando now sues the Ghana bank on the basis that its telegram was itself a letter of credit and that he is entitled to the funds on proof of proper shipment of the goods. Is he correct? Why or why not?

4. In response to certain U.S. foreign policy actions with which it violently disagreed, the government of Bwana nationalized all assets owned by American nationals within its jurisdiction. At that point, a large freighter loaded with bauxite ore belonging to Metallics, Inc., was preparing to leave Bwana's main port. The ship and its cargo were subjected to the seizure order and were later sold by the Bwana government to Ivan Rushoff. Ivan then brought the ship and cargo to New York, to try to resell them at a profit. Metallics has learned what's happening and has filed an appropriate action in New York, asking for immediate possession of the ship and cargo which were illegally seized by Bwana. How should the court rule in this case? Explain.

5. Fishing is very important to the economy of the small nation of Portos. Traditionally it had claimed exclusive fishing rights, or at least the right to regulate fishing by citizens of other nations, only out to a distance of 12 miles from its coastline. As Russia and Japan modernized their fishing fleets, however, it became apparent that they were having a substantial impact on Portos' fishing industry. The government of Portos then declared that henceforth it would claim exclusive fishing rights, or the right to regulate catches by foreigners, out to a distance of 200 miles. Japan and Russia challenge this claim before the ICJ. How should the court go about resolving this dispute? Discuss.

6. The Department of Public Transportation of the nation of Manzaguay entered into a contract to buy 400 small buses for its public transportation system. In order to bid on the contract, the seller, Major Motors, was forced to include a clause which said that any dispute under the contract would be litigated in the Manzaguayan courts, according to Manzaguayan law. Major manufactured and delivered the 400 buses, but the DPT withheld about 20 percent of the contract price, claiming that the buses had substantial defects. Major does not think this claim can be substantiated in a fair court hearing, but it's afraid it won't get a fair hearing in Manzaguay. Manzaguay has a large bank balance in New York City. What chance would Major have of bringing a successful lawsuit in New York? Explain.

7. Stanley Santino, a citizen of Spain, owned and operated a large hardware and general merchandise store in Olambra, a small African nation. In response to a local guerrilla uprising near the city where Stanley's store was located, troops were sent out from the nation's capital. These troops proceeded to "occupy" Stanley's store; to "appropriate" weapons, other equipment, and money from the store; and to lock Stanley in the local prison. Stanley barely escaped with his life in 1957. In 1980 a new government, friendlier to European interests, came to power in Olambra, and so Stanley filed a claim for his earlier losses. How should a national or international court rule in this case if the new Olambra government refuses to recognize and pay Stanley's claim? Discuss.

8. Paula Piquet was a domestic employee of Count Haslagg, the Gavarian minister assigned as the diplomatic agent of his government in the country of Rumination. Paula purchased about $2,000 worth of merchandise on credit, for her own use, in several stores in Rumination. When she didn't pay, her local creditors filed lawsuits under local procedure to have her arrested, pending the posting of a bond, and the merchandise seized and returned to the sellers. What arguments should Paula's lawyer make in these proceedings? Explain.

Appendixes

Glossary

Table of Cases

Index

Appendix | A

Uniform Commercial Code (1978 Text)*

Title
An Act

To be known as the Uniform Commercial Code, Relating to Certain Commercial Transactions in or regarding Personal Property and Contracts and other Documents concerning them, including Sales, Commercial Paper, Bank Deposits and Collections, Letters of Credit, Bulk Transfers, Warehouse Receipts, Bills of Lading, other Documents of Title, Investment Securities, and Secured Transactions, including certain Sales of Accounts, Chattel Paper, and Contract Rights; Providing for Public Notice to Third Parties in Certain Circumstances; Regulating Procedure, Evidence and Damages in Certain Court Actions Involving such Transactions, Contracts or Documents; to Make Uniform the Law with Respect Thereto; and Repealing Inconsistent Legislation.

ARTICLE I GENERAL PROVISIONS

Part 1 Short Title, Construction, Application and Subject Matter of the Act

Section 1–101. Short Title

This Act shall be known and may be cited as Uniform Commercial Code.

*Copyright 1978 by The American Law Institute and the National Conference of Commissioners on Uniform State Laws. Reprinted with permission of The American Law Institute and the National Conference of Commissioners on Uniform State Laws.

Section 1–102. Purposes; Rules of Construction; Variation by Agreement

(1) This Act shall be liberally construed and applied to promote its underlying purposes and policies.

(2) Underlying purposes and policies of this Act are

    (a) to simplify, clarify and modernize the law governing commercial transactions;

    (b) to permit the continued expansion of commercial practices through custom, usage and agreement of the parties;

    (c) to make uniform the law among the various jurisdictions.

(3) The effect of provisions of this Act may be varied by agreement, except as otherwise provided in this Act and except that the obligations of good faith, diligence, reasonableness and care prescribed by this Act may not be disclaimed by agreement but the parties may by agreement determine the standards by which the performance of such obligations is to be measured if such standards are not manifestly unreasonable.

(4) The presence in certain provisions of this Act of the word "unless otherwise agreed" or words of similar import does not imply that the effect of other provisions may not be varied by agreement under subsection (3).

(5) In this Act unless the context otherwise requires

    (a) words in the singular number include the plural, and in the plural include the singular;

    (b) words of the masculine gender include the

feminine and the neuter, and when the sense so indicates words of the neuter gender may refer to any gender.

Section 1–103. Supplementary General Principles of Law Applicable

Unless displaced by the particular provisions of this Act, the principles of law and equity, including the law merchant and the law relative to capacity to contract, principal and agent, estoppel, fraud, misrepresentation, duress, coercion, mistake, bankruptcy, or other validating or invalidating cause shall supplement its provisions.

Section 1–104. Construction Against Implicit Repeal

This Act being a general act intended as a unified coverage of its subject matter, no part of it shall be deemed to be impliedly repealed by subsequent legislation if such construction can reasonably be avoided.

Section 1–105. Territorial Application of the Act; Parties' Power to Choose Applicable Law

(1) Except as provided hereafter in this section, when a transaction bears a reasonable relation to this state and also to another state or nation the parties may agree that the law either of this state or of such other state or nation shall govern their rights and duties. Failing such agreement this Act applies to transactions bearing an appropriate relation to this state.

(2) Where one of the following provisions of this Act specifies the applicable law, that provision governs and a contrary agreement is effective only to the extent permitted by the law (including the conflict of laws rules) so specified:

Rights of creditors against sold goods. Section 2–402.

Applicability of the Article on Bank Deposits and Collections. Section 4–102.

Bulk transfers subject to the Article on Bulk Transfers. Section 6–102.

Applicability of the Article on Investment Securities. Section 8–106.

Perfection provisions of the Article on Secured Transactions. Section 9–103.

Section 1–106. Remedies to Be Liberally Administered

(1) The remedies provided by this Act shall be liberally administered to the end that the aggrieved party may be put in as good a position as if the other party had fully performed but neither consequential or special nor penal damages may be had except as specifically provided in this Act or by other rule of law.

(2) Any right or obligation declared by this Act is enforceable by action unless the provision declaring it specifies a different and limited effect.

Section 1–107. Waiver or Renunciation of Claim or Right After Breach

Any claim or right arising out of an alleged breach can be discharged in whole or in part without consideration by a written waiver or renunciation signed and delivered by the aggrieved party.

Section 1–108. Severability

If any provision or clause of this Act or application thereof to any person or circumstances is held invalid, such invalidity shall not affect other provisions or applications of the Act which can be given effect without the invalid provision or application, and to this end the provisions of this Act are declared to be severable.

Section 1–109. Section Captions

Section captions are parts of this Act.

Part 2 General Definitions and Principles of Interpretation

Section 1–201. General Definitions

Subject to additional definitions contained in the subsequent Articles of this Act which are applicable to specific Articles or Parts thereof, and unless the context otherwise requires, in this Act:

(1) "Action" in the sense of a judicial proceeding includes recoupment, counterclaim, set-off, suit in equity and any other proceedings in which rights are determined.

(2) "Aggrieved party" means a party entitled to resort to a remedy.

(3) "Agreement" means the bargain of the parties in fact as found in their language or by implication from other circumstances including course of dealing or usage of trade or course of performance as provided in

this Act (Sections 1–205 and 2–208). Whether an agreement has legal consequences is determined by the provisions of this Act, if applicable; otherwise by the law of contracts (Section 1–103). (Compare "Contract".)

(4) "Bank" means any person engaged in the business of banking.

(5) "Bearer" means the person in possession of an instrument, document of title, or certificated security payable to bearer or indorsed in blank.

(6) "Bill of lading" means a document evidencing the receipt of goods for shipment issued by a person engaged in the business of transporting or forwarding goods, and includes an airbill. "Airbill" means a document serving for air transportation as a bill of lading does for marine or rail transportation, and includes an air consignment note or air waybill.

(7) "Branch" includes a separately incorporated foreign branch of a bank.

(8) "Burden of establishing" a fact means the burden of persuading the triers of fact that the existence of the fact is more probable than its non-existence.

(9) "Buyer in ordinary course of business" means a person who in good faith and without knowledge that the sale to him is in violation of the ownership rights or security interest of a third party in the goods buys in ordinary course from a person in the business of selling goods of that kind but does not include a pawnbroker. All persons who sell minerals or the like (including oil and gas) at wellhead or minehead shall be deemed to be persons in the business of selling goods of that kind. "Buying" may be for cash or by exchange of other property or on secured or unsecured credit and includes receiving goods or documents of title under a pre-existing contract for sale but does not include a transfer in bulk or as security for or in total or partial satisfaction of a money debt.

(10) "Conspicuous": A term or clause is conspicuous when it is so written that a reasonable person against whom it is to operate ought to have noticed it. A printed heading in capitals (as: NON-NEGOTIABLE BILL OF LADING) is conspicuous. Language in the body of a form is "conspicuous" if it is in larger or other contrasting type or color. But in a telegram any stated term is "conspicuous." Whether a term or clause is "conspicuous" or not is for decision by the court.

(11) "Contract" means the total legal obligation which results from the parties' agreement as affected by this Act and any other applicable rules of law. (Compare "Agreement.")

(12) "Creditor" includes a general creditor, a secured creditor, a lien creditor and any representative of creditors, including an assignee for the benefit of creditors, a trustee in bankruptcy, a receiver in equity and an executor or administrator of an insolvent debtor's or assignor's estate.

(13) "Defendant" includes a person in the position of defendant in a cross-action or counterclaim.

(14) "Delivery" with respect to instruments, documents of title, chattel paper, or certificated securities means voluntary transfer of possession.

(15) "Document of title" includes bill of lading, dock warrant, dock receipt, warehouse receipt or order for the delivery of goods, and also any other document which in the regular course of business or financing is treated as adequately evidencing that the person in possession of it is entitled to receive, hold and dispose of the document and the goods it covers. To be a document of title a document must purport to be issued by or addressed to a bailee and purport to cover goods in the bailee's possession which are either identified or are fungible portions of an identified mass.

(16) "Fault" means wrongful act, omission or breach.

(17) "Fungible" with respect to goods or securities means goods or securities of which any unit is, by nature or usage of trade, the equivalent of any other like unit. Goods which are not fungible shall be deemed fungible for the purposes of this Act to the extent that under a particular agreement or document unlike units are treated as equivalents.

(18) "Genuine" means free of forgery or counterfeiting.

(19) "Good faith" means honesty in fact in the conduct or transaction concerned.

(20) "Holder" means a person who is in possession of a document of title or an instrument or a certificated investment security drawn, issued, or indorsed to him or his order or to bearer or in blank.

(21) To "honor" is to pay or to accept and pay, or where a credit so engages to purchase or discount a draft complying with the terms of the credit.

(22) "Insolvency proceedings" includes any assignment for the benefit of creditors or other proceedings intended to liquidate or rehabilitate the estate of the person involved.

(23) A person is "insolvent" who either has ceased to pay his debts in the ordinary course of business or can-

not pay his debts as they become due or is insolvent within the meaning of the federal bankruptcy law.

(24) "Money" means a medium of exchange authorized or adopted by a domestic or foreign government as a part of its currency.

(25) A person has "notice" of a fact when

    (a) he has actual knowledge of it; or

    (b) he has received a notice or notification of it; or

    (c) from all the facts and circumstances known to him at the time in question he has reason to know that it exists.

A person "knows" or has "knowledge" of a fact when he has actual knowledge of it. "Discover" or "learn" or a word or phrase of similar import refers to knowledge rather than to reason to know. The time and circumstances under which a notice or notification may cease to be effective are not determined by this Act.

(26) A person "notifies" or "gives" a notice or notification to another by taking such steps as may be reasonably required to inform the other in ordinary course whether or not such other actually comes to know of it. A person "receives" a notice or notification when

    (a) it comes to his attention; or

    (b) it is duly delivered at the place of business through which the contract was made or at any other place held out by him as the place for receipt of such communications.

(27) Notice, knowledge or a notice or notification received by an organization is effective for a particular transaction from the time when it is brought to the attention of the individual conducting that transaction, and in any event from the time when it would have been brought to his attention if the organization had exercised due diligence. An organization exercises due diligence if it maintains reasonable routines for communicating significant information to the person conducting the transaction and there is reasonable compliance with the routines. Due diligence does not require an individual acting for the organization to communicate information unless such communication is part of his regular duties or unless he has reason to know of the transaction and that the transaction would be materially affected by the information.

(28) "Organization" includes a corporation, government or governmental subdivision or agency, business trust, estate, trust, partnership or association, two or more persons having a joint or common interest, or any other legal or commercial entity.

(29) "Party," as distinct from "third party," means a person who has engaged in a transaction or made an agreement within this Act.

(30) "Person" includes an individual or an organization (See Section 1–102).

(31) "Presumption" or "presumed" means that the trier of fact must find the existence of the fact presumed unless and until evidence is introduced which would support a finding of its non-existence.

(32) "Purchase" includes taking by sale, discount, negotiation, mortgage, pledge, lien, issue or re-issue, gift or any other voluntary transaction creating an interest in property.

(33) "Purchaser" means a person who takes by purchase.

(34) "Remedy" means any remedial right to which an aggrieved party is entitled with or without resort to a tribunal.

(35) "Representative" includes an agent, an officer of a corporation or association, and a trustee, executor or administrator of an estate, or any other person empowered to act for another.

(36) "Rights" includes remedies.

(37) "Security interest" means an interest in personal property or fixtures which secures payment or performance of an obligation. The retention or reservation of title by a seller of goods notwithstanding shipment or delivery to the buyer (Section 2–401) is limited in effect to a reservation of a "security interest." The term also includes any interest of a buyer of accounts or chattel paper which is subject to Article 9. The special property interest of a buyer of goods on identification of such goods to a contract for sale under Section 2–401 is not a "security interest," but a buyer may also acquire a "security interest" by complying with Article 9. Unless a lease or consignment is intended as security, reservation of title thereunder is not a "security interest" but a consignment is in any event subject to the provisions on consignment sales (Section 2–326). Whether a lease is intended as security is to be determined by the facts of each case; however, (a) the inclusion of an option to purchase does not of itself make the lease one intended for security, and (b) an agreement that upon compliance with the terms of the lease the lessee shall become or has the option to become the owner of the property for no additional consideration or for a nominal consideration does make the lease one intended for security.

(38) "Send" in connection with any writing or notice means to deposit in the mail or deliver for transmission by any other usual means of communication with postage or cost of transmission provided for and properly addressed and in the case of an instrument to an address specified thereon or otherwise agreed, or if there be none to any address reasonable under the circumstances. The receipt of any writing or notice within the time at which it would have arrived if properly sent has the effect of a proper sending.

(39) "Signed" includes any symbol executed or adopted by a party with present intention to authenticate a writing.

(40) "Surety" includes guarantor.

(41) "Telegram" includes a message transmitted by radio, teletype, cable, any mechanical method of transmission, or the like.

(42) "Term" means that portion of an agreement which relates to a particular matter.

(43) "Unauthorized" signature or indorsement means one made without actual, implied or apparent authority and includes a forgery.

(44) "Value." Except as otherwise provided with respect to negotiable instruments and bank collections (Sections 3–303, 4–208 and 4–209) a person gives "value" for rights if he acquires them

    (a) in return for a binding commitment to extend credit or for the extension of immediately available credit whether or not drawn upon and whether or not a chargeback is provided for in the event of difficulties in collection; or

    (b) as security for or in total or partial satisfaction of a pre-existing claim; or

    (c) by accepting delivery pursuant to a pre-existing contract for purchase; or

    (d) generally, in return for any consideration sufficient to support a simple contract.

(45) "Warehouse receipt" means a receipt issued by a person engaged in the business of storing goods for hire.

(46) "Written" or "writing" includes printing, typewriting or any other intentional reduction to tangible form.

Section 1–202. Prima Facie Evidence by Third Party Documents

A document in due form purporting to be a bill of lading, policy or certificate of insurance, official weigher's or inspector's certificate, consular invoice, or any other document authorized or required by the contract to be issued by a third party shall be prima facie evidence of its own authenticity and genuineness and of the facts stated in the document by the third party.

Section 1–203. Obligation of Good Faith

Every contract or duty within this Act imposes an obligation of good faith in its performance or enforcement.

Section 1–204. Time; Reasonable Time; "Seasonably"

(1) Whenever this Act requires any action to be taken within a reasonable time, any time which is not manifestly unreasonable may be fixed by agreement.

(2) What is a reasonable time for taking any action depends on the nature, purpose and circumstances of such action.

(3) An action is taken "seasonably" when it is taken at or within the time agreed or if no time is agreed at or within a reasonable time.

Section 1–205. Course of Dealing and Usage of Trade

(1) A course of dealing is a sequence of previous conduct between the parties to a particular transaction which is fairly to be regarded as establishing a common basis of understanding for interpreting their expressions and other conduct.

(2) A usage of trade is any practice or method of dealing having such regularity of observance in a place, vocation or trade as to justify an expectation that it will be observed with respect to the transaction in question. The existence and scope of such a usage are to be proved as facts. If it is established that such a usage is embodied in a written trade code or similar writing the interpretation of the writing is for the court.

(3) A course of dealing between parties and any usage of trade in the vocation or trade in which they are engaged or of which they are or should be aware give particular meaning to and supplement or qualify terms of an agreement.

(4) The express terms of an agreement and an applicable course of dealing or usage of trade shall be construed wherever reasonable as consistent with each other; but when such construction is unreasonable express terms control both course of dealing and usage of

trade and course of dealing controls usage of trade.

(5) An applicable usage of trade in the place where any part of performance is to occur shall be used in interpreting the agreement as to that part of the performance.

(6) Evidence of a relevant usage of trade offered by one party is not admissible unless and until he has given the other party such notice as the court finds sufficient to prevent unfair surprise to the latter.

Section 1–206. Statute of Frauds for Kinds of Personal Property Not Otherwise Covered

(1) Except in the cases described in subsection (2) of this section a contract for the sale of personal property is not enforceable by way of action or defense beyond five thousand dollars in amount or value of remedy unless there is some writing which indicates that a contract for sale has been made between the parties at a defined or stated price, reasonably identifies the subject matter, and is signed by the party against whom enforcement is sought or by his authorized agent.

(2) Subsection (1) of this section does not apply to contracts for the sale of goods (Section 2–201) nor of securities (Section 8–319) nor to security agreements (Section 9–203).

Section 1–207. Performance or Acceptance Under Reservation of Rights

A party who with explicit reservation of rights performs or promises performance or assents to performance in a manner demanded or offered by the other party does not thereby prejudice the rights reserved. Such words as 'without prejudice," "under protest" or the like are sufficient.

Section 1–208. Option to Accelerate at Will

A term providing that one party or his successor in interest may accelerate payment or performance or require collateral or additional collateral "at will" or "when he deems himself insecure" or in words of similar import shall be construed to mean that he shall have power to do so only if he in good faith believes that the prospect of payment or performance is impaired. The burden of establishing lack of good faith is on the party against whom the power has been exercised.

Section 1–209. Subordinated Obligations

An obligation may be issued as subordinated to payment of another obligation of the person obligated, or a creditor may subordinate his right to payment of an obligation by agreement with either the person obligated or another creditor of the person obligated. Such a subordination does not create a security interest as against either the common debtor or a subordinated creditor. This section shall be construed as declaring the law as it existed prior to the enactment of this section and not as modifying it.

Note: *The new section is proposed as an optional provision to make it clear that a subordination agreement does not create a security interest unless so intended.*

ARTICLE 2   SALES

Part 1   Short Title, General Construction and Subject Matter

Section 2–101.   Short Title

This Article shall be known and may be cited as Uniform Commercial Code—Sales.

Section 2–102.   Scope; Certain Security and Other Transactions Excluded From This Article

Unless the context otherwise requires, this Article applies to transactions in goods; it does not apply to any transaction which although in the form of an unconditional contract to sell or present sale is intended to operate only as a security transaction nor does this Article impair or repeal any statute regulating sales to consumers, farmers or other specified classes of buyers.

Section 2–103.   Definitions and Index of Definitions

(1) In this Article unless the context otherwise requires

    (a) "Buyer" means a person who buys or contracts to buy goods.

    (b) "Good faith" in the case of a merchant means honesty in fact and the observance of reasonable commercial standards of fair dealing in the trade.

    (c) "Receipt" of goods means taking physical possession of them.

    (d) "Seller" means a person who sells or contracts to sell goods.

(2) Other definitions applying to this Article or to specified Parts thereof, and the sections in which they appear are:

"Acceptance." Section 2–606.

"Banker's credit." Section 2–325.

"Between merchants." Section 2–104.

"Cancellation." Section 2–106(4).

"Commercial unit." Section 2–105.

"Confirmed credit." Section 2–325.

"Conforming to contract." Section 2–106.

"Contract for sale." Section 2–106.

"Cover." Section 2–712.

"Entrusting." Section 2–403.

"Financing agency." Section 2–104.

"Future goods." Section 2–105.

"Goods." Section 2–105.

"Identification." Section 2–501.

"Installment contract." Section 2–612.

"Letter of Credit." Section 2–325.

"Lot." Section 2–105.

"Merchant." Section 2–104.

"Overseas." Section 2–323.

"Person in position of seller." Section 2–707.

"Present sale." Section 2–106.

"Sale." Section 2–106.

"Sale on approval." Section 2–326.

"Sale or return." Section 2–326.

"Termination." Section 2–106.

(3) The following definitions in other Articles apply to this Article:

"Check." Section 3–104.

"Consignee." Section 7–102.

"Consignor." Section 7–102.

"Consumer goods." Section 9–109.

"Dishonor." Section 3–507.

"Draft." Section 3–104.

(4) In addition Article I contains general definitions and principles of construction and interpretation applicable throughout this Article.

Section 2–104. Definitions: "Merchant"; "Between Merchants"; "Financing Agency"

(1) "Merchant" means a person who deals in goods of the kind or otherwise by his occupation holds himself out as having knowledge or skill peculiar to the practices or goods involved in the transaction or to whom such knowledge or skill may be attributed by his employment of an agent or broker or other intermediary who by his occupation holds himself out as having such knowledge or skill.

(2) "Financing agency" means a bank, finance company or other person who in the ordinary course of business makes advances against goods or documents of title or who by arrangement with either the seller or the buyer intervenes in ordinary course to make or collect payment due or claimed under the contract for sale, as by purchasing or paying the seller's draft or making advances against it or by merely taking it for collection whether or not documents of title accompany the draft. "Financing agency" includes also a bank or other person who similarly intervenes between persons who are in the position of seller and buyer in respect to the goods (Section 2–707).

(3) "Between merchants" means in any transaction with respect to which both parties are chargeable with the knowledge or skill of merchants.

Section 2–105. Definitions: Transferability; "Goods"; "Future" Goods; "Lot"; "Commercial Unit"

(1) "Goods" means all things (including specially manufactured goods) which are movable at the time of identification to the contract for sale other than the money in which the price is to be paid, investment securities (Article 8) and things in action. "Goods" also includes the unborn young of animals and growing crops and other identified things attached to realty as described in the section on goods to be severed from realty (Section 2–107).

(2) Goods must be both existing and identified before any interest in them can pass. Goods which are not both existing and identified are "future" goods. A purported present sale of future goods or of any interest therein operates as a contract to sell.

(3) There may be a sale of a part interest in existing identified goods.

(4) An undivided share in an identified bulk of fungible goods is sufficiently identified to be sold although the quantity of the bulk is not determined. Any agreed proportion of such a bulk or any quantity thereof agreed upon by number, weight or other measure may to the extent of the seller's interest in the bulk be sold to the buyer who then becomes an owner in common.

(5) "Lot" means a parcel or a single article which is the subject matter of a separate sale or delivery, whether or not it is sufficient to perform the contract.

(6) "Commercial unit" means such a unit of goods as by commercial usage is a single whole for purposes of sale and division of which materially impairs its character or value on the market or in use. A commercial unit may be a single article (as a machine) or a set of articles (as a suite of furniture or an assortment of sizes) or a

quantity (as a bale, gross, or carload) or any other unit treated in use or in the relevant market as a single whole.

Section 2–106. Definitions: "Contract"; "Agreement"; "Contract for Sale"; "Sale"; "Present Sale"; "Conforming" to Contract; "Termination"; "Cancellation"

(1) In this Article unless the context otherwise requires "contract" and "agreement" are limited to those relating to the present or future sale of goods. "Contract for sale" includes both a present sale of goods and a contract to sell goods at a future time. A "sale" consists in the passing of title from the seller to the buyer for a price (Section 2–401). A "present sale" means a sale which is accomplished by the making of the contract.

(2) Goods or conduct including any part of a performance are "conforming" or conform to the contract when they are in accordance with the obligations under the contract.

(3) "Termination" occurs when either party pursuant to a power created by agreement or law puts an end to the contract otherwise than for its breach. On "termination" all obligations which are still executory on both sides are discharged but any right based on prior breach or performance survives.

(4) "Cancellation" occurs when either party puts an end to the contract for breach by the other and its effect is the same as that of "termination" except that the cancelling party also retains any remedy for breach of the whole contract or any unperformed balance.

Section 2–107. Goods to Be Severed From Realty: Recording

(1) A contract for the sale of minerals or the like (including oil and gas) or a structure or its materials to be removed from realty is a contract for the sale of goods within this Article if they are to be severed by the seller but until severance a purported present sale thereof which is not effective as a transfer of an interest in land is effective only as a contract to sell.

(2) A contract for the sale apart from the land of growing crops or other things attached to realty and capable of severance without material harm thereto but not described in subsection (1) or of timber to be cut is a contract for the sale of goods within this Article whether the subject matter is to be severed by the buyer or by the seller even though it forms part of the realty at the time of contracting, and the parties can by identification effect a present sale before severance.

(3) The provisions of this section are subject to any third party rights provided by the law relating to realty records, and the contract for sale may be executed and recorded as a document transferring an interest in land and shall then constitute notice to third parties of the buyer's rights under the contract for sale.

Part 2 Form, Formation and Readjustment of Contract

Section 2–201. Formal Requirements; Statute of Frauds

(1) Except as otherwise provided in this section a contract for the sale of goods for the price of $500 or more is not enforceable by way of action or defense unless there is some writing sufficient to indicate that a contract for sale has been made between the parties and signed by the party against whom enforcement is sought or by his authorized agent or broker. A writing is not insufficient because it omits or incorrectly states a term agreed upon but the contract is not enforceable under this paragraph beyond the quantity of goods shown in such writing.

(2) Between merchants if within a reasonable time a writing in confirmation of the contract and sufficient against the sender is received and the party receiving it has reason to know its contents, it satisfies the requirements of subsection (1) against such party unless written notice of objection to its contents is given within 10 days after it is received.

(3) A contract which does not satisfy the requirements of subsection (1) but which is valid in other respects is enforceable

    (a) if the goods are to be specially manufactured for the buyer and are not suitable for sale to others in the ordinary course of the seller's business and the seller, before notice of repudiation is received and under circumstances which reasonably indicate that the goods are for the buyer, has made either a substantial beginning of their manufacture or commitments for their procurement; or

    (b) if the party against whom enforcement is sought admits in his pleading, testimony or otherwise in court that a contract for sale was made, but the contract is not enforceable under this provision beyond the quantity of goods admitted; or

(c) with respect to goods for which payment has been made and accepted or which have been received and accepted (Sec. 2–606).

Section 2–202.   Final Written Expression: Parol or Extrinsic Evidence

Terms with respect to which the confirmatory memoranda of the parties agree or which are otherwise set forth in a writing intended by the parties as a final expression of their agreement with respect to such terms as are included therein may not be contradicted by evidence of any prior agreement or of a contemporaneous oral agreement but may be explained or supplemented

(a) by course of dealing or usage of trade (Section 1–205) or by course of performance (Section 2–208); and

(b) by evidence of consistent additional terms unless the court finds the writing to have been intended also as a complete and exclusive statement of the terms of the agreement.

Section 2–203.   Seals Inoperative

The affixing of a seal to a writing evidencing a contract for sale or an offer to buy or sell goods does not constitute the writing a sealed instrument and the law with respect to sealed instruments does not apply to such a contract or offer.

Section 2–204.   Formation in General

(1) A contract for sale of goods may be made in any manner sufficient to show agreement, including conduct by both parties which recognizes the existence of such a contract.

(2) An agreement sufficient to constitute a contract for sale may be found even though the moment of its making is undetermined.

(3) Even though one or more terms are left open a contract for sale does not fail for indefiniteness if the parties have intended to make a contract and there is a reasonably certain basis for giving an appropriate remedy.

Section 2–205.   Firm Offers

An offer by a merchant to buy or sell goods in a signed writing which by its terms give assurance that it will be held open is not revocable, for lack of consideration, during the time stated or if no time is stated for a reasonable time, but in no event may such period of irrevocability exceed three months; but any such term

of assurance on a form supplied by the offeree must be separately signed by the offeror.

Section 2–206.   Offer and Acceptance in Formation of Contract

(1) Unless otherwise unambiguously indicated by the language or circumstances

(a) an offer to make a contract shall be construed as inviting acceptance in any manner and by any medium reasonable in the circumstances;

(b) an order or other offer to buy goods for prompt or current shipment shall be construed as inviting acceptance either by a prompt promise to ship or by the prompt or current shipment of conforming or non-conforming goods, but such a shipment of non-conforming goods does not constitute an acceptance if the seller seasonably notifies the buyer that the shipment is offered only as an accommodation to the buyer.

(2) Where the beginning of a requested performance is a reasonable mode of acceptance an offeror who is not notified of acceptance within a reasonable time may treat the offer as having lapsed before acceptance.

Section 2–207.   Additional Terms in Acceptance or Confirmation

(1) A definite and seasonable expression of acceptance or a written confirmation which is sent within a reasonable time operates as an acceptance even though it states terms additional to or different from those offered or agreed upon, unless acceptance is expressly made conditional on assent to the additional or different terms.

(2) The additional terms are to be construed as proposals for addition to the contract. Between merchants such terms become part of the contract unless:

(a) the offer expressly limits acceptance to the terms of the offer;

(b) they materially alter it; or

(c) notification of objection to them has already been given or is given within a reasonable time after notice of them is received.

(3) Conduct by both parties which recognizes the existence of a contract is sufficient to establish a contract for sale although the writings of the parties do not otherwise establish a contract. In such case the terms of the particular contract consist of those terms on

which the writings of the parties agree, together with any supplementary terms incorporated under any other provisions of this Act.

Section 2–208. Course of Performance or Practical Construction

(1) Where the contract for sale involves repeated occasions for performance by either party with knowledge of the nature of the performance and opportunity for objection to it by the other, any course of performance accepted or acquiesced in without objection shall be relevant to determine the meaning of the agreement.

(2) The express terms of the agreement and any such course of performance, as well as any course of dealing and usage of trade, shall be construed whenever reasonable as consistent with each other; but when such construction is unreasonable, express terms shall control course of performance and course of performance shall control both course of dealing and usage of trade (Section 1–205).

(3) Subject to the provisions of the next section on modification and waiver, such course of performance shall be relevant to show a waiver or modification of any term inconsistent with such course of performance.

Section 2–209. Modification, Rescission and Waiver

(1) An agreement modifying a contract within this Article needs no consideration to be binding.

(2) A signed agreement which excludes modification or rescission except by a signed writing cannot be otherwise modified or rescinded, but except as between merchants such a requirement on a form supplied by the merchant must be separately signed by the other party.

(3) The requirements of the statute of frauds section of this Article (Section 2–201) must be satisfied if the contract as modified is within its provisions.

(4) Although an attempt at modification or rescission does not satisfy the requirements of subsection (2) or (3) it can operate as a waiver.

(5) A party who has made a waiver affecting an executory portion of the contract may retract the waiver by reasonable notification received by the other party that strict performance will be required of any term waived, unless the retraction would be unjust in view of a material change of position in reliance on the waiver.

Section 2–210. Delegation of Performance; Assignment of Rights

(1) A party may perform his duty through a delegate unless otherwise agreed or unless the other party has a substantial interest in having his original promisor perform or control the acts required by the contract. No delegation of performance relieves the party delegating of any duty to perform or any liability for breach.

(2) Unless otherwise agreed all rights of either seller or buyer can be assigned except where the assignment would materially change the duty of the other party, or increase materially the burden or risk imposed on him by his contract, or impair materially his chance of obtaining return performance. A right to damages for breach of the whole contract or a right arising out of the assignor's due performance of his entire obligation can be assigned despite agreement otherwise.

(3) Unless the circumstances indicate the contrary a prohibition of assignment of "the contract" is to be construed as barring only the delegation to the assignee of the assignor's performance.

(4) An assignment of "the contract" or of "all my rights under the contract" or an assignment in similar general terms is an assignment of rights and unless the language or the circumstances (as in an assignment for security) indicate the contrary, it is a delegation of performance of the duties of the assignor and its acceptance by the assignee constitutes a promise by him to perform those duties. This promise is enforceable by either the assignor or the other party to the original contract.

(5) The other party may treat any assignment which delegates performance as creating reasonable grounds for insecurity and may without prejudice to his rights against the assignor demand assurances from the assignee (Section 2–609).

Part 3 General Obligation and Construction of Contract

Section 2–301. General Obligations of Parties

The obligation of the seller is to transfer and deliver and that of the buyer is to accept and pay in accordance with the contract.

Section 2–302. Unconscionable Contract or Clause

(1) If the court as a matter of law finds the contract or any clause of the contract to have been unconscionable at the time it was made the court may refuse to enforce

the contract, or it may enforce the remainder of the contract without the unconscionable clause, or it may so limit the application of any unconscionable clause as to avoid any unconscionable result.

(2) When it is claimed or appears to the court that the contract or any clause thereof may be unconscionable the parties shall be afforded a reasonable opportunity to present evidence as to its commercial setting, purpose and effect to aid the court in making the determination.

Section 2–303. Allocation or Division of Risks

Where this Article allocates a risk or a burden as between the parties "unless otherwise agreed," the agreement may not only shift the allocation but may also divide the risk or burden.

Section 2–304. Price Payable in Money, Goods, Realty, or Otherwise

(1) The price can be made payable in money or otherwise. If it is payable in whole or in part in goods each party is a seller of the goods which he is to transfer.

(2) Even though all or part of the price is payable in an interest in realty the transfer of the goods and the seller's obligations with reference to them are subject to this Article, but not the transfer of the interest in realty or the transferor's obligations in connection therewith.

Section 2–305. Open Price Term

(1) The parties if they so intend can conclude a contract for sale even though the price is not settled. In such a case the price is a reasonable price at the time for delivery if

    (a) nothing is said as to price; or

    (b) the price is left to be agreed by the parties and they fail to agree; or

    (c) the price is to be fixed in terms of some agreed market or other standard as set or recorded by a third person or agency and it is not so set or recorded.

(2) A price to be fixed by the seller or by the buyer means a price for him to fix in good faith.

(3) When a price left to be fixed otherwise than by agreement of the parties fails to be fixed through fault of one party the other may at his option treat the contract as cancelled or himself fix a reasonable price.

(4) Where, however, the parties intend not to be bound unless the price be fixed or agreed and it is not fixed or agreed there is no contract. In such a case the buyer must return any goods already received or if unable so to do must pay their reasonable value at the time of delivery and the seller must return any portion of the price paid on account.

Section 2–306. Output, Requirements and Exclusive Dealings

(1) A term which measures the quantity by the output of the seller or the requirements of the buyer means such actual output or requirements as may occur in good faith, except that no quantity unreasonably disproportionate to any stated estimate or in the absence of a stated estimate to any normal or otherwise comparable prior output or requirements may be tendered or demanded.

(2) A lawful agreement by either the seller or the buyer for exclusive dealing in the kind of goods concerned imposes unless otherwise agreed an obligation by the seller to use best efforts to supply the goods and by the buyer to use best efforts to promote the sale.

Section 2–307. Delivery in Single Lot or Several Lots

Unless otherwise agreed all goods called for by a contract for sale must be tendered in a single delivery and payment is due only on such tender but where the circumstances give either party the right to make or demand delivery in lots the price if it can be apportioned may be demanded for each lot.

Section 2–308. Absence of Specified Place for Delivery

Unless otherwise agreed

    (a) the place for delivery of goods is the seller's place of business or if he has none his residence; but

    (b) in a contract for sale of identified goods which to the knowledge of the parties at the time of contracting are in some other place, that place is the place for their delivery; and

    (c) documents of title may be delivered through customary banking channels.

Section 2–309. Absence of Specific Time Provisions; Notice of Termination

(1) The time for shipment or delivery or any other action under a contract if not provided in this Article or agreed upon shall be a reasonable time.

(2) Where the contract provides for successive performances but is indefinite in duration it is valid for a reasonable time but unless otherwise agreed may be terminated at any time by either party.

(3) Termination of a contract by one party except on the happening of an agreed event requires that reasonable notification be received by the other party and an agreement dispensing with notification is invalid if its operation would be unconscionable.

Section 2–310. Open Time for Payment or Running of Credit; Authority to Ship Under Reservation

Unless otherwise agreed

(a) payment is due at the time and place at which the buyer is to receive the goods even though the place of shipment is the place of delivery; and

(b) if the seller is authorized to send the goods he may ship them under reservation, and may tender the documents of title, but the buyer may inspect the goods after their arrival before payment is due unless such inspection is inconsistent with the terms of the contract (Section 2–513); and

(c) if delivery is authorized and made by way of documents of title otherwise than by subsection (b) then payment is due at the time and place at which the buyer is to receive the documents regardless of where the goods are to be received; and

(d) where the seller is required or authorized to ship the goods on credit the credit period runs from the time of shipment but postdating the invoice or delaying its dispatch will correspondingly delay the starting of the credit period.

Section 2–311. Options and Cooperation Respecting Performance

(1) An agreement for sale which is otherwise sufficiently definite (subsection (3) of Section 2–204) to be a contract is not made invalid by the fact that it leaves particulars of performance to be specified by one of the parties. Any such specification must be made in good faith and within limits set by commercial reasonableness.

(2) Unless otherwise agreed specifications relating to assortment of the goods are at the buyer's option and except as otherwise provided in subsections (1) (c) and

(3) of Section 2–319 specifications or arrangements relating to shipment are at the seller's option.

(3) Where such specification would materially affect the other party's performance but is not seasonably made or where one party's cooperation is necessary to the agreed performance of the other but is not seasonably forthcoming, the other party in addition to all other remedies

(a) is excused for any resulting delay in his own performance; and

(b) may also either proceed to perform in any reasonable manner or after the time for a material part of his own performance treat the failure to specify or to cooperate as a breach by failure to deliver or accept the goods.

Section 2–312. Warranty of Title and Against Infringement; Buyer's Obligation Against Infringement

(1) Subject to subsection (2) there is in a contract for sale a warranty by the seller that

(a) the title conveyed shall be good, and its transfer rightful; and

(b) the goods shall be delivered free from any security interest or other lien or encumbrance of which the buyer at the time of contracting has no knowledge.

(2) A warranty under subsection (1) will be excluded or modified only by specific language or by circumstances which give the buyer reason to know that the person selling does not claim title in himself or that he is purporting to sell only such right or title as he or a third person may have.

(3) Unless otherwise agreed a seller who is a merchant regularly dealing in goods of the kind warrants that the goods shall be delivered free of the rightful claim of any third person by way of infringement or the like but a buyer who furnishes specifications to the seller must hold the seller harmless against any such claim which arises out of compliance with the specifications.

Section 2–313. Express Warranties by Affirmation, Promise, Description, Sample

(1) Express warranties by the seller are created as follows:

(a) Any affirmation of fact or promise made by the seller to the buyer which relates to the goods and becomes part of the basis of the bargain creates an express warranty that the goods shall conform to the affirmation or promise.

(b) Any description of the goods which is made part of the basis of the bargain creates an express warranty that the goods shall conform to the description.

(c) Any sample or model which is made part of the basis of the bargain creates an express warranty that the whole of the goods shall conform to the sample or model.

(2) It is not necessary to the creation of an express warranty that the seller use formal words such as "warrant" or "guarantee" or that he have a specific intention to make a warranty, but an affirmation merely of the value of the goods or a statement purporting to be merely the seller's opinion or commendation of the goods does not create a warranty.

Section 2–314.   Implied Warranty: Merchantability; Usage of Trade

(1)   Unless excluded or modified (Section 2–316), a warranty that the goods shall be merchantable is implied in a contract for their sale if the seller is a merchant with respect to goods of that kind. Under this section the serving for value of food or drink to be consumed either on the premises or elsewhere is a sale.

(2)   Goods to be merchantable must be at least such as

(a) pass without objection in the trade under the contract description; and

(b) in the case of fungible goods, are of fair average quality within the description; and

(c) are fit for the ordinary purposes for which such goods are used; and

(d) run, within the variations permitted by the agreement, of even kind, quality and quantity within each unit and among all units involved; and

(e) are adequately contained, packaged, and labeled as the agreement may require; and

(f) conform to the promises or affirmations of fact made on the container or label if any.

(3)   Unless excluded or modified (Section 2–316) other implied warranties may arise from course of dealing or usage of trade.

Section 2–315.   Implied Warranty: Fitness for Particular Purpose

Where the seller at the time of contracting has reason to know any particular purpose for which the goods are required and that the buyer is relying on the seller's skill or judgment to select or furnish suitable goods, there is unless excluded or modified under the next section an implied warranty that the goods shall be fit for such purpose.

Section 2–316.   Exclusion or Modification of Warranties

(1)   Words or conduct relevant to the creation of an express warranty and words or conduct tending to negate or limit warranty shall be construed wherever reasonable as consistent with each other; but subject to the provisions of this Article on parol or extrinsic evidence (Section 2–202) negation or limitation is inoperative to the extent that such construction is unreasonable.

(2)   Subject to subsection (3), to exclude or modify the implied warranty or merchantability or any part of it the language must mention merchantability and in case of a writing must be conspicuous, and to exclude or modify any implied warranty of fitness the exclusion must be by a writing and conspicuous. Language to exclude all implied warranties of fitness is sufficient if it states, for example, that "There are no warranties which extend beyond the description on the face hereof."

(3)   Notwithstanding subsection (2)

(a) unless the circumstances indicate otherwise, all implied warranties are excluded by expressions like "as is," "with all faults" or other languages which in common understanding calls the buyer's attention to the exclusion of warranties and makes plain that there is no implied warranty; and

(b) when the buyer before entering into the contract has examined the goods or the sample or model as fully as he desired or has refused to examine the goods there is no implied warranty with regard to defects which an examination ought in the circumstances to have revealed to him; and

(c) an implied warranty can also be excluded or modified by course of dealing or course of performance or usage of trade.

(4)   Remedies for breach of warranty can be limited in accordance with the provisions of this Article on liquidation or limitation of damages and on contractual modification of remedy (Sections 2–718 and 2–719).

Section 2–317. Cumulation and Conflict of Warranties Express or Implied

Warranties whether express or implied shall be construed as consistent with each other and as cumulative, but if such construction is unreasonable the intention of the parties shall determine which warranty is dominant. In ascertaining that intention the following rules apply:

    (a) Exact or technical specifications displace an inconsistent sample or model or general language of description.

    (b) A sample from an existing bulk displaces inconsistent general language of description.

    (c) Express warranties displace inconsistent implied warranties other than an implied warranty of fitness for a particular purpose.

Section 2–318. Third Party Beneficiaries of Warranties Express or Implied

Note: *If this Act is introduced in the Congress of the United States this section should be omitted. (States to select one alternative.)*

Alternative A

A seller's warranty whether express or implied extends to any natural person who is in the family or household of his buyer or who is a guest in his home if it is reasonable to expect that such person may use, consume or be affected by the goods and who is injured in person by breach of the warranty. A seller may not exclude or limit the operation of this section.

Alternative B

A seller's warranty whether express or implied extends to any natural person who may reasonably be expected to use, consume or be affected by the goods and who is injured in person by breach of the warranty. A seller may not exclude or limit the operation of this section.

Alternative C

A seller's warranty whether express or implied extends to any person who may reasonably be expected to use, consume or be affected by the goods and who is injured by breach of the warranty. A seller may not exclude or limit the operation of this section with respect to injury to the person of an individual to whom the warranty extends.

Section 2–319. F.O.B. and F.A.S. Terms

(1) Unless otherwise agreed the term F.O.B. (which means "free on board") at a named place, even though used only in connection with the stated price, is a delivery term under which

    (a) when the term is F.O.B. the place of shipment, the seller must at that place ship the goods in the manner provided in this Article (Section 2–504) and bear the expense and risk of putting them into the possession of the carrier; or

    (b) when the term is F.O.B. the place of destination, the seller must at his own expense and risk transport the goods to that place and there tender delivery of them in the manner provided in this Article (Section 2–503);

    (c) when under either (a) or (b) the term is also F.O.B. vessel, car or other vehicle, the seller must in addition at his own expense and risk load the goods on board. If the term is F.O.B. vessel the buyer must name the vessel and in an appropriate case the seller must comply with the provisions of this Article on the form of bill of lading (Section 2–323).

(2) Unless otherwise agreed the term F.A.S. vessel (which means "free alongside") at a named port, even though used only in connection with the stated price, is a delivery term under which the seller must

    (a) at his own expense and risk deliver the goods alongside the vessel in the manner usual in that port or on a dock designated and provided by the buyer; and

    (b) obtain and tender a receipt for the goods in exchange for which the carrier is under a duty to issue a bill of lading.

(3) Unless otherwise agreed in any case falling within subsection (1) (a) or (c) or subsection (2) the buyer must seasonably give any needed instructions for making delivery, including when the term is F.A.S. or F.O.B. the loading berth of the vessel and in an appropriate case its name and sailing date. The seller may treat the failure of needed instructions as a failure of cooperation under this Article (Section 2–311). He may also at his option move the goods in any reasonable manner preparatory to delivery or shipment.

(4) Under the term F.O.B. vessel or F.A.S. unless otherwise agreed the buyer must make payment against tender of the required documents and the

seller may not tender nor the buyer demand delivery of the goods in substitution for the documents.

Section 2–320. C.I.F. and C. & F. Terms

(1) The term C.I.F. means that the price includes in a lump sum the cost of the goods and the insurance and freight to the named destination. The term C. & F. or C.F. means that the price so includes cost and freight to the named destination.

(2) Unless otherwise agreed and even though used only in connection with the stated price and destination, the term C.I.F. destination or its equivalent requires the seller at his own expense and risk to

(a) put the goods into the possession of a carrier at the port for shipment and obtain a negotiable bill or bills of lading covering the entire transportation to the named destination; and

(b) load the goods and obtain a receipt from the carrier (which may be contained in the bill of lading) showing that the freight has been paid or provided for; and

(c) obtain a policy or certificate of insurance, including any war risk insurance, of a kind and on terms then current at the port of shipment in the usual amount, in the currency of the contract, shown to cover the same goods covered by the bill of lading and providing for payment of loss to the order of the buyer or for the account of whom it may concern; but the seller may add to the price the amount of the premium for any such war risk insurance; and

(d) prepare an invoice of the goods and procure any other documents required to effect shipment or to comply with the contract; and

(e) forward and tender with commercial promptness all the documents in due form and with any indorsement necessary to perfect the buyer's rights.

(3) Unless otherwise agreed the term C. & F. or its equivalent has the same effect and imposes upon the seller the same obligations and risks as a C.I.F. term except the obligation as to insurance.

(4) Under the term C.I.F. or C. & F. unless otherwise agreed the buyer must make payment against tender of the required documents and the seller may not tender nor the buyer demand delivery of the goods in substitution for the documents.

Section 2–321. C.I.F. or C. & F.: "Net Landed Weights"; "Payment on Arrival"; Warranty of Condition on Arrival

Under a contract containing a term C.I.F. or C. & F.

(1) Where the price is based on or is to be adjusted according to "net landed weights," "delivered weights," "out turn" quantity or quality or the like, unless otherwise agreed the seller must reasonably estimate the price. The payment due on tender of the documents called for by the contract is the amount so estimated, but after final adjustment of the price a settlement must be made with commercial promptness.

(2) An agreement described in subsection (1) or any warranty of quality or condition of the goods on arrival places upon the seller the risk of ordinary deterioration, shrinkage and the like in transportation but has no effect on the place or time of identification to the contract for sale or delivery or on the passing of the risk of loss.

(3) Unless otherwise agreed where the contract provides for payment on or after arrival of the goods the seller must before payment allow such preliminary inspection as is feasible; but if the goods are lost delivery of the documents and payment are due when the goods should have arrived.

Section 2–322. Delivery "Ex-Ship"

(1) Unless otherwise agreed a term for delivery of goods "ex-ship" (which means from the carrying vessel) or in equivalent language is not restricted to a particular ship and requires delivery from a ship which has reached a place at the named port of destination where goods of the kind are usually discharged.

(2) Under such a term unless otherwise agreed

(a) the seller must discharge all liens arising out of the carriage and furnish the buyer with a direction which puts the carrier under a duty to deliver the goods; and

(b) the risk of loss does not pass to the buyer until the goods leave the ship's tackle or are otherwise properly unloaded.

Section 2–323. Form of Bill of Lading Required in Overseas Shipment; "Overseas"

(1) Where the contract contemplates overseas shipment and contains a term C.I.F. or C. & F. or F.O.B.

vessel, the seller unless otherwise agreed must obtain a negotiable bill of lading stating that the goods have been loaded on board or, in the case of a term C.I.F. or C. & F., received for shipment.

(2) Where in a case within subsection (1) a bill of lading has been issued in a set of parts, unless otherwise agreed if the documents are not to be sent from abroad the buyer may demand tender of the full set; otherwise only one part of the bill of lading need be tendered. Even if the agreement expressly requires a full set

(a) due tender of a single part is acceptable within the provisions of this Article on cure of improper delivery (subsection (1) of Section 2–508); and

(b) even though the full set is demanded, if the documents are sent from abroad the person tendering an incomplete set may nevertheless require payment upon furnishing an indemnity which the buyer in good faith deems adequate.

(3) A shipment by water or by air or a contract contemplating such shipment is "overseas" insofar as by usage of trade or agreement it is subject to the commercial, financing or shipping practices characteristic of international deep water commerce.

Section 2–324. "No Arrival, No Sale" Term

Under a term "no arrival, no sale" or terms of like meaning, unless otherwise agreed,

(a) the seller must properly ship conforming goods and if they arrive by any means he must tender them on arrival but he assumes no obligation that the goods will arrive unless he has caused the non-arrival; and

(b) where without fault of the seller the goods are in part lost or have so deteriorated as no longer to conform to the contract or arrive after the contract time, the buyer may proceed as if there had been casualty to identified goods (Section 2–613).

Section 2–325. "Letter of Credit" Term; "Confirmed Credit"

(1) Failure of the buyer seasonably to furnish an agreed letter of credit is a breach of the contract for sale.

(2) The delivery to seller of a proper letter of credit suspends the buyer's obligation to pay. If the letter of

credit is dishonored, the seller may on seasonable notification to the buyer require payment directly from him.

(3) Unless otherwise agreed the term "letter of credit" or "banker's credit" in a contract for sale means an irrevocable credit issued by a financing agency of good repute and, where the shipment is overseas, of good international repute. The term "confirmed credit" means that the credit must also carry the direct obligation of such an agency which does business in the seller's financial market.

Section 2–326. Sale on Approval and Sale or Return; Consignment Sales and Rights of Creditors

(1) Unless otherwise agreed, if delivered goods may be returned by the buyer even though they conform to the contract, the transaction is

(a) a "sale on approval" if the goods are delivered primarily for use, and

(b) a "sale or return" if the goods are delivered primarily for resale.

(2) Except as provided in subsection (3), goods held on approval are not subject to the claims of the buyer's creditors until acceptance; goods held on sale or return are subject to such claims while in the buyer's possession.

(3) Where goods are delivered to a person for sale and such person maintains a place of business at which he deals in goods of the kind involved, under a name other than the name of the person making delivery, then with respect to claims of creditors of the person conducting the business the goods are deemed to be on sale or return. The provisions of this subsection are applicable even though an agreement purports to reserve title to the person making delivery until payment or resale or uses such words as "on consignment" or "on memorandum." However, this subsection is not applicable if the person making delivery

(a) complies with an applicable law providing for a consignor's interest or the like to be evidenced by a sign, or

(b) establishes that the person conducting the business is generally known by his creditors to be substantially engaged in selling the goods of others, or

(c) complies with the filing provisions of the Article on Secured Transactions (Article 9).

(4) Any "or return" term of a contract for sale is to be treated as a separate contract for sale within the statute of frauds section of this Article (Section 2–201) and as

contradicting the sale aspect of the contract within the provisions of this Article or parol or extrinsic evidence (Section 2–202).

Section 2–327. Special Incidents of Sale on Approval and Sale or Return

(1) Under a sale on approval unless otherwise agreed

    (a) although the goods are identified to the contract the risk of loss and the title do not pass to the buyer until acceptance; and

    (b) use of the goods consistent with the purpose of trial is not acceptance but failure seasonably to notify the seller of election to return the goods is acceptance, and if the goods conform to the contract acceptance of any part is acceptance of the whole; and

    (c) after due notification of election to return, the return is at the seller's risk and expense but a merchant buyer must follow any reasonable instructions.

(2) Under a sale or return unless otherwise agreed

    (a) the option to return extends to the whole or any commercial unit of the goods while in substantially their original condition, but must be exercised seasonably; and

    (b) the return is at the buyer's risk and expense.

Section 2–328. Sale by Auction

(1) In a sale by auction if goods are put up in lots each lot is the subject of a separate sale.

(2) A sale by auction is complete when the auctioneer so announces by the fall of the hammer or in other customary manner. Where a bid is made while the hammer is falling in acceptance of a prior bid the auctioneer may in his discretion reopen the bidding or declare the goods sold under the bid on which the hammer was falling.

(3) Such a sale is with reserve unless the goods are in explicit terms put up without reserve. In an auction with reserve the auctioneer may withdraw the goods at any time until he announces completion of the sale. In an auction without reserve, after the auctioneer calls for bids on an article or lot, that article or lot cannot be withdrawn unless no bid is made within a reasonable time. In either case a bidder may retract his bid until the auctioneer's announcement of completion of sale, but a bidder's retraction does not revive any previous bid.

(4) If the auctioneer knowingly receives a bid on the seller's behalf or the seller makes or procures such a bid, and notice has not been given that liberty for such bidding is reserved, the buyer may at his option avoid the sale or take the goods at the price of the last good faith bid prior to the completion of the sale. This subsection shall not apply to any bid at a forced sale.

Part 4 Title, Creditors and Good Faith Purchasers

Section 2–401. Passing of Title; Reservation for Security; Limited Application of This Section

Each provision of this Article with regard to the rights, obligations and remedies of the seller, the buyer, purchasers or other third parties applies irrespective of title to the goods except where the provision refers to such title. Insofar as situations are not covered by the other provisions of this Article and matters concerning title become material the following rules apply:

(1) Title to goods cannot pass under a contract for sale prior to their identification to the contract (Section 2–501), and unless otherwise explicitly agreed the buyer acquires by their identification a special property as limited by this Act. Any retention or reservation by the seller of the title (property) in goods shipped or delivered to the buyer is limited in effect to a reservation of a security interest. Subject to these provisions and to the provisions of the Article on Secured Transactions (Article 9), title to goods passes from the seller to the buyer in any manner and on any conditions explicitly agreed on by the parties.

(2) Unless otherwise explicitly agreed title passes to the buyer at the time and place at which the seller completes his performance with reference to the physical delivery of the goods, despite any reservation of a security interest and even though a document of title is to be delivered at a different time or place; and in particular and despite any reservation of a security interest by the bill of lading

    (a) if the contract requires or authorizes the seller to send the goods to the buyer but does not require him to deliver them at destination, title passes to the buyer at the time and place of shipment; but

    (b) if the contract requires delivery at destination, title passes on tender there.

(3) Unless otherwise explicitly agreed where delivery is to be made without moving the goods,

    (a) if the seller is to deliver a document of title,

title passes at the time when and the place where he delivers such documents; or

(b) if the goods are at the time of contracting already identified and no documents are to be delivered, title passes at the time and place of contracting.

(4) A rejection or other refusal by the buyer to receive or retain the goods, whether or not justified, or a justified revocation of acceptance revests title to the goods in the seller. Such revesting occurs by operation of law and is not a "sale."

Section 2–402. Rights of Seller's Creditors Against Sold Goods

(1) Except as provided in subsections (2) and (3), rights of unsecured creditors of the seller with respect to goods which have been identified to a contract for sale are subject to the buyer's rights to recover the goods under this Article (Sections 2–502 and 2–716).

(2) A creditor of the seller may treat a sale or an identification of goods to a contract for sale as void if as against him a retention of possession by the seller is fraudulent under any rule of law of the state where the goods are situated, except that retention of possession in good faith and current course of trade by a merchant-seller for a commercially reasonable time after a sale or identification is not fraudulent.

(3) Nothing in this Article shall be deemed to impair the rights of creditors of the seller

(a) under the provisions of the Article on Secured Transactions (Article 9); or

(b) where identification to the contract or delivery is made not in current course of trade but in satisfaction of or as security for a pre-existing claim for money, security or the like and is made under circumstances which under any rule of law of the state where the goods are situated would apart from this Article constitute the transaction a fraudulent transfer or voidable preference.

Section 2–403. Power to Transfer; Good Faith Purchase of Goods; "Entrusting"

(1) A purchaser of goods acquires all title which his transferor had or had power to transfer except that a purchaser of a limited interest acquires rights only to the extent of the interest purchased. A person with voidable title has power to transfer a good title to a

good faith purchaser for value. When goods have been delivered under a transaction of purchase the purchaser has such power even though

(a) the transferor was deceived as to the identity of the purchaser, or

(b) the delivery was in exchange for a check which is later dishonored, or

(c) it was agreed that the transaction was to be a "cash sale," or

(d) the delivery was procured through fraud punishable as larcenous under the criminal law.

(2) Any entrusting of possession of goods to a merchant who deals in goods of that kind gives him power to transfer all rights of the entruster to a buyer in ordinary course of business.

(3) "Entrusting" includes any delivery and any acquiescence in retention of possession regardless of any condition expressed between the parties to the delivery or acquiescence and regardless of whether the procurement of the entrusting or the possessor's disposition of the goods have been such as to be larcenous under the criminal law.

(4) The rights of other purchasers of goods and of lien creditors are governed by the Articles on Secured Transactions (Article 9), Bulk Transfers (Article 6) and Documents of Title (Article 7).

Part 5 Performance

Section 2–501. Insurable Interest in Goods; Manner of Identification of Goods

(1) The buyer obtains a special property and an insurable interest in goods by identification of existing goods as goods to which the contract refers even though the goods so identified are nonconforming and he has an option to return or reject them. Such identification can be made at any time and in any manner explicitly agreed to by the parties. In the absence of explicit agreement identification occurs.

(a) when the contract is made if it is for the sale of goods already existing and identified;

(b) if the contract is for the sale of future goods other than those described in paragraph (c), when goods are shipped, marked or otherwise designated by the seller as goods to which the contract refers;

(c) when the crops are planted or otherwise become growing crops or the young are conceived if the contract is for the sale of unborn young to be born within twelve months after contracting or for the sale of crops to be harvested within twelve months or the next normal harvest season after contracting whichever is longer.

(2) The seller retains an insurable interest in goods so long as title to or any security interest in the goods remains in him and where the identification is by the seller alone he may until default or insolvency or notification to the buyer that the identification is final substitute other goods for those identified.

(3) Nothing in this section impairs any insurable interest recognized under any other statute or rule of law.

Section 2–502. Buyer's Right to Goods on Seller's Insolvency

(1) Subject to subsection (2) and even though the goods have not been shipped a buyer who has paid a part or all of the price of goods in which he has a special property under the provisions of the immediately preceding section may on making and keeping good a tender of any unpaid portion of their price recover them from the seller if the seller becomes insolvent within ten days after receipt of the first installment on their price.

(2) If the identification creating his special property has been made by the buyer he acquires the right to recover the goods only if they conform to the contract for sale.

Section 2–503. Manner of Seller's Tender of Delivery

(1) Tender of delivery requires that the seller put and hold conforming goods at the buyer's disposition and give the buyer any notification reasonably necessary to enable him to take delivery. The manner, time and place for tender are determined by the agreement and this Article, and in particular

    (a) tender must be at a reasonable hour, and if it is of goods they must be kept available for the period reasonably necessary to enable the buyer to take possession; but

    (b) unless otherwise agreed the buyer must furnish facilities reasonably suited to the receipt of the goods.

(2) Where the case is within the next section respecting shipment tender requires that the seller comply with its provisions.

(3) Where the seller is required to deliver at a particular destination tender requires that he comply with subsection (1) and also in any appropriate case tender documents as described in subsections (4) and (5) of this section.

(4) Where goods are in the possession of a bailee and are to be delivered without being moved

    (a) tender requires that the seller either tender a negotiable document of title covering such goods or procure acknowledgment by the bailee of the buyer's right to possession of the goods; but

    (b) tender to the buyer of a non-negotiable document of title or of a written direction to the bailee to deliver is sufficient tender unless the buyer seasonably objects, and receipt by the bailee of notification of the buyer's rights fixes those rights as against the bailee and all third persons; but risk of loss of the goods and of any failure by the bailee to honor the non-negotiable document of title or to obey the direction remains on the seller until the buyer has had a reasonable time to present the document or direction, and a refusal by the bailee to honor the document or to obey the direction defeats the tender.

(5) Where the contract requires the seller to deliver documents

    (a) he must tender all such documents in correct form, except as provided in this Article with respect to bills of lading in a set (subsection (2) of Section 2–323); and

    (b) tender through customary banking channels is sufficient and dishonor of a draft accompanying the documents constitutes non-acceptance or rejection.

Section 2–504. Shipment by Seller

Where the seller is required or authorized to send the goods to the buyer and the contract does not require him to deliver them at a particular destination, then unless otherwise agreed he must

    (a) put the goods in the possession of such a carrier and make such a contract for their transportation as may be reasonable having regard to the nature of the goods and other circumstances of the case; and

    (b) obtain and promptly deliver or tender in due

form any document necessary to enable the buyer to obtain possession of the goods or otherwise required by the agreement or by usage of trade; and

(c)   promptly notify the buyer of the shipment.

Failure to notify the buyer under paragraph (c) or to make a proper contract under paragraph (a) is a ground for rejection only if material delay or loss ensues.

Section 2–505.   Seller's Shipment Under Reservation

(1)   Where the seller has identified goods to the contract by or before shipment:

(a)   his procurement of a negotiable bill of lading to his own order or otherwise reserves in him a security interest in the goods. His procurement of the bill to the order of a financing agency or of the buyer indicates in addition only the seller's expectation of transferring that interest to the person named.

(b)   a non-negotiable bill of lading to himself or his nominee reserves possession of the goods as security but except in a case of conditional delivery (subsection (2) of Section 2–507) a non-negotiable bill of lading naming the buyer as consignee reserves no security interest even though the seller retains possession of the bill of lading.

(2)   When shipment by the seller with reservation of a security interest is in violation of the contract for sale it constitutes an improper contract for transportation within the preceding section but impairs neither the rights given to the buyer by shipment and identification of the goods to the contract nor the seller's powers as a holder of a negotiable document.

Section 2–506.   Rights of Financing Agency

(1)   A financing agency by paying or purchasing for value a draft which relates to a shipment of goods acquires to the extent of the payment or purchase and in addition to its own rights under the draft and any document of title securing it any rights of the shipper in the goods including the right to stop delivery and the shipper's right to have the draft honored by the buyer.

(2)   The right to reimbursement of a financing agency which has in good faith honored or purchased the draft under commitment to or authority from the buyer is

not impaired by subsequent discovery of defects with reference to any relevant document which was apparently regular on its face.

Section 2–507.   Effect of Seller's Tender; Delivery on Condition

(1)   Tender of delivery is a condition to the buyer's duty to accept the goods and, unless otherwise agreed, to his duty to pay for them. Tender entitles the seller to acceptance of the goods and to payment according to the contract.

(2)   Where payment is due and demanded on the delivery to the buyer of goods or documents of title, his right as against the seller to retain or dispose of them is conditional upon his making the payment due.

Section 2–508.   Cure by Seller of Improper Tender or Delivery; Replacement

(1)   Where any tender or delivery by the seller is rejected because non-conforming and the time for performance has not yet expired, the seller may seasonably notify the buyer of his intention to cure and may then within the contract time make a conforming delivery.

(2)   Where the buyer rejects a non-conforming tender which the seller had reasonable grounds to believe would be acceptable with or without money allowance the seller may if he seasonably notifies the buyer have a further reasonable time to substitute a conforming tender.

Section 2–509.   Risk of Loss in the Absence of Breach

(1)   Where the contract requires or authorizes the seller to ship the goods by carrier

(a)   if it does not require him to deliver them at a particular destination, the risk of loss passes to the buyer when the goods are duly delivered to the carrier even though the shipment is under reservation (Section 2–505); but

(b)   if it does require him to deliver them at a particular destination and the goods are there duly tendered while in the possession of the carrier, the risk of loss passes to the buyer when the goods are there duly so tendered as to enable the buyer to take delivery.

(2)   Where the goods are held by a bailee to be delivered without being moved, the risk of loss passes to the buyer

(a) on his receipt of a negotiable document of title covering the goods; or

(b) on acknowledgment by the bailee of the buyer's right to possession of the goods; or

(c) after his receipt of a non-negotiable document of title or other written direction to deliver, as provided in subsection (4) (b) of Section 2–503.

(3) In any case not within subsection (1) or (2), the risk of loss passes to the buyer on his receipt of the goods if the seller is a merchant; otherwise the risk passes to the buyer on tender of delivery.

(4) The provisions of this section are subject to contrary agreement of the parties and to the provisions of this Article on sale on approval (Section 2–327) and on effect of breach on risk of loss (Section 2–510).

Section 2–510. Effect of Breach on Risk of Loss

(1) Where a tender or delivery of goods so fails to conform to the contract as to give a right of rejection the risk of their loss remains on the seller until cure or acceptance.

(2) Where the buyer rightfully revokes acceptance he may to the extent of any deficiency in his effective insurance coverage treat the risk of loss as having rested on the seller from the beginning.

(3) Where the buyer as to conforming goods already identified to the contract for sale repudiates or is otherwise in breach before risk of their loss has passed to him, the seller may to the extent of any deficiency in his effective insurance coverage treat the risk of loss as resting on the buyer for a commercially reasonable time.

Section 2–511. Tender of Payment by Buyer; Payment by Check

(1) Unless otherwise agreed tender of payment is a condition to the seller's duty to tender and complete any delivery.

(2) Tender of payment is sufficient when made by any means or in any manner current in the ordinary course of business unless the seller demands payment in legal tender and gives any extension of time reasonably necessary to procure it.

(3) Subject to the provisions of this Act on the effect of an instrument on an obligation (Section 3–802), payment by check is conditional and is defeated as between the parties by dishonor of the check on due presentment.

Section 2–512. Payment by Buyer Before Inspection

(1) Where the contract requires payment before inspection non-conformity of the goods does not excuse the buyer from so making payment unless

(a) the non-conformity appears without inspection; or

(b) despite tender of the required documents the circumstances would justify injunction against honor under the provisions of this Act (Section 5–114).

(2) Payment pursuant to subsection (1) does not constitute an acceptance of goods or impair the buyer's right to inspect or any of his remedies.

Section 2–513. Buyer's Right to Inspection of Goods

(1) Unless otherwise agreed and subject to subsection (3), where goods are tendered or delivered or identified to the contract for sale, the buyer has a right before payment or acceptance to inspect them at any reasonable place and time and in any reasonable manner. When the seller is required or authorized to send the goods to the buyer, the inspection may be after their arrival.

(2) Expenses of inspection must be borne by the buyer but may be recovered from the seller if the goods do not conform and are rejected.

(3) Unless otherwise agreed and subject to the provisions of this Article on C.I.F. contracts (subsection (3) of Section 2–321), the buyer is not entitled to inspect the goods before payment of the price when the contract provides

(a) for delivery "C.O.D." or on other like terms; or

(b) for payment against documents of title, except where such payment is due only after the goods are to become available for inspection.

(4) A place or method of inspection fixed by the parties is presumed to be exclusive but unless otherwise expressly agreed it does not postpone identification or shift the place for delivery or for passing the risk of loss. If compliance becomes impossible, inspection shall be as provided in this section unless the place or method fixed was clearly intended as an indispensable condition failure of which avoids the contract.

Section 2–514.   When Documents Deliverable on Acceptance; When on Payment

Unless otherwise agreed documents against which a draft is drawn are to be delivered to the drawee on acceptance of the draft if it is payable more than three days after presentment; otherwise, only on payment.

Section 2–515.   Preserving Evidence of Goods in Dispute

In furtherance of the adjustment of any claim or dispute

(a)   either party on reasonable notification to the other and for the purpose of ascertaining the facts and preserving evidence has the right to inspect, test and sample the goods including such of them as may be in the possession or control of the other; and

(b)   the parties may agree to a third party inspection or survey to determine the conformity or condition of the goods and may agree that the findings shall be binding upon them in any subsequent litigation or adjustment.

Part 6   Breach, Repudiation and Excuse

Section 2–601.   Buyer's Rights on Improper Delivery

Subject to the provisions of this Article on breach in installment contracts (Section 2–612) and unless otherwise agreed under the sections on contractual limitations of remedy (Sections 2–718 and 2–719), if the goods or the tender of delivery fail in any respect to conform to the contract, the buyer may

(a)   reject the whole; or

(b)   accept the whole; or

(c)   accept any commercial unit or units and reject the rest.

Section 2–602.   Manner and Effect of Rightful Rejection

(1)   Rejection of goods must be within a reasonable time after their delivery or tender. It is ineffective unless the buyer seasonably notifies the seller.

(2)   Subject to the provisions of the two following sections on rejected goods (Sections 2–603 and 2–604),

(a)   after rejection any exercise of ownership by the buyer with respect to any commercial unit is wrongful as against the seller; and

(b)   if the buyer has before rejection taken physical possession of goods in which he does not have a security interest under the provisions of this Article (subsection (3) of Section 2–711), he is under a duty after rejection to hold them with reasonable care at the seller's disposition for a time sufficient to permit the seller to remove them; but

(c)   the buyer has no further obligations with regard to goods rightfully rejected.

(3)   The seller's rights with respect to goods wrongfully rejected are governed by the provisions of this Article on Seller's remedies in general (Section 2–703).

Section 2–603.   Merchant Buyer's Duties as to Rightfully Rejected Goods

(1)   Subject to any security interest in the buyer (subsection (3) of Section 2–711), when the seller has no agent or place of business at the market of rejection a merchant buyer is under a duty after rejection of goods in his possession or control to follow any reasonable instructions received from the seller with respect to the goods and in the absence of such instructions to make reasonable efforts to sell them for the seller's account if they are perishable or threaten to decline in value speedily. Instructions are not reasonable if on demand indemnity for expenses is not forthcoming.

(2)   When the buyer sells goods under subsection (1), he is entitled to reimbursement from the seller or out of the proceeds for reasonable expenses of caring for and selling them, and if the expenses include no selling commission then to such commission as is usual in the trade or if there is none to a reasonable sum not exceeding ten per cent on the gross proceeds.

(3)   In complying with this section the buyer is held only to good faith and good faith conduct hereunder is neither acceptance nor conversion nor the basis of an action for damages.

Section 2–604.   Buyer's Options as to Salvage of Rightfully Rejected Goods

Subject to the provisions of the immediately preceding section on perishables if the seller gives no instructions within a reasonable time after notification of rejection the buyer may store the rejected goods for the seller's account or reship them to him or resell them for the seller's account with reimbursement as provided in the preceding section. Such action is not acceptance or conversion.

Section 2–605.   Waiver of Buyer's Objections by Failure to Particularize

(1)   The buyer's failure to state in connection with rejection a particular defect which is ascertainable by reasonable inspection precludes him from relying on the unstated defect to justify rejection or to establish breach

  (a)   where the seller could have cured it if stated seasonably; or

  (b)   between merchants when the seller has after rejection made a request in writing for a full and final written statement of all defects on which the buyer proposes to rely.

(2)   Payment against documents made without reservation of rights precludes recovery of the payment for defects apparent on the face of the documents.

Section 2–606.   What Constitutes Acceptance of Goods

(1)   Acceptance of goods occurs when the buyer

  (a)   after a reasonable opportunity to inspect the goods signifies to the seller that the goods are conforming or that he will take or retain them in spite of their non-conformity; or

  (b)   fails to make an effective rejection (subsection (1) of Section 2–602), but such acceptance does not occur until the buyer has had a reasonable opportunity to inspect them; or

  (c)   does any act inconsistent with the seller's ownership; but if such act is wrongful as against the seller it is an acceptance only if ratified by him.

(2)   Acceptance of a part of any commercial unit is acceptance of that entire unit.

Section 2–607.   Effect of Acceptance; Notice of Breach; Burden of Establishing Breach After Acceptance; Notice of Claim or Litigation to Person Answerable Over

(1)   The buyer must pay at the contract rate for any goods accepted.

(2)   Acceptance of goods by the buyer precludes rejection of the goods accepted and if made with knowledge of a non-conformity cannot be revoked because of it unless the acceptance was on the reasonable assumption that the non-conformity would be seasonably cured but acceptance does not of itself impair any other remedy provided by this Article for non-conformity.

(3)   Where a tender has been accepted

  (a)   the buyer must within a reasonable time after he discovers or should have discovered any breach notify the seller of breach or be barred from any remedy; and

  (b)   if the claim is one for infringement or the like (subsection (3) of Section 2–312) and the buyer is sued as a result of such a breach he must so notify the seller within a reasonable time after he receives notice of the litigation or be barred from any remedy over for liability established by the litigation.

(4)   The burden is on the buyer to establish any breach with respect to the goods accepted.

(5)   Where the buyer is sued for breach of a warranty or other obligation for which his seller is answerable over

  (a)   he may give his seller written notice of the litigation. If the notice states that the seller may come in and defend and that if the seller does not do so he will be bound in any action against him by his buyer by any determination of fact common to the two litigations, then unless the seller after seasonable receipt of the notice does come in and defend he is so bound.

  (b)   if the claim is one for infringement or the like (subsection (3) of Section 2–312) the original seller may demand in writing that his buyer turn over to him control of the litigation including settlement or else be barred from any remedy over and if he also agrees to bear all expense and to satisfy any adverse judgment, then unless the buyer after seasonable receipt of the demand does turn over control the buyer is so barred.

(6)   The provisions of subsections (3), (4) and (5) apply to any obligation of a buyer to hold the seller harmless against infringement or the like (subsection (3) of Section 2–312).

Section 2–608.   Revocation of Acceptance in Whole or in Part

(1)   The buyer may revoke his acceptance of a lot or commercial unit whose non-conformity substantially impairs its value to him if he has accepted it

(a) on the reasonable assumption that its non-conformity would be cured and it has not been seasonably cured; or

(b) without discovery of such non-conformity if his acceptance was reasonably induced either by the difficulty of discovery before acceptance or by the seller's assurances.

(2) Revocation of acceptance must occur within a reasonable time after the buyer discovers or should have discovered the ground for it and before any substantial change in conditions of the goods which is not caused by their own defects. It is not effective until the buyer notifies the seller of it

(3) A buyer who so revokes has the same rights and duties with regard to the goods involved as if he had rejected them.

Section 2–609. Right to Adequate Assurance of Performance

(1) A contract for sale imposes an obligation on each party that the other's expectation of receiving due performance will not be impaired. When reasonable grounds for insecurity arise with respect to the performance of either party the other may in writing demand adequate assurance of due performance and until he receives such assurance may if commercially reasonable suspend any peformance of which he has not already received the agreed return.

(2) Between merchants the reasonableness of grounds for insecurity and the adequacy of any assurance offered shall be determined according to commercial standards.

(3) Acceptance of any improper delivery or payment does not prejudice the aggrieved party's right to demand adequate assurance of future performance.

(4) After receipt of a justified demand failure to provide within a reasonable time not exceeding thirty days such assurance of due performance as is adequate under the circumstances of the particular case is a repudiation of the contract.

Section 2–610. Anticipatory Repudiation

When either party repudiates the contract with respect to a performance not yet due the loss of which will substantially impair the value of the contract to the other, the aggrieved party may

(a) for a commercially reasonable time await performance by the repudiating party; or

(b) resort to any remedy for breach (Section 2–703 or Section 2–711), even though he has notified the repudiating party that he would await the latter's performance and has urged retraction; and

(c) in either case suspend his own performance or proceed in accordance with the provisions of this Article on the seller's right to identify goods to the contract notwithstanding breach or to salvage unfinished goods (Section 2–704).

Section 2–611. Retraction of Anticipatory Repudiation

(1) Until the repudiating party's next performance is due he can retract his repudiation unless the aggrieved party has since the repudiation cancelled or materially changed his position or otherwise indicated that he considers the repudiation final.

(2) Retraction may be by any method which clearly indicates to the aggrieved party that the repudiating party intends to perform, but must include any assurance justifiably demanded under the provisions of this Article (Section 2–609)

(3) Retraction reinstates the repudiating party's rights under the contract with due excuse and allowance to the aggrieved party for any delay occasioned by the repudiation.

Section 2–612. "Installment Contract"; Breach

(1) An "installment contract" is one which requires or authorizes the delivery of goods in separate lots to be separately accepted, even though the contract contains a clause "each delivery is a separate contract" or its equivalent.

(2) The buyer may reject any installment which is non-conforming if the non-conformity substantially impairs the value of that installment and cannot be cured or if the non-conformity is a defect in the required documents; but if the non-conformity does not fall within subsection (3) and the seller gives adequate assurance of its cure the buyer must accept that installment.

(3) Whenever non-conformity or default with respect to one or more installments substantially impairs the value of the whole contract there is a breach of the whole. But the aggrieved party reinstates the contract if he accepts a non-conforming installment without seasonably notifying of cancellation or if he brings an action with respect only to past installments or demands performance as to future installments.

Section 2–613. Casualty to Identified Goods

Where the contract requires for its performance goods identified when the contract is made, and the goods suffer casualty without fault of either party before the risk of loss passes to the buyer, or in a proper case under a "no arrival, no sale" term (Section 2–324) then

(a) if the loss is total the contract is avoided; and

(b) if the loss is partial or the goods have so deteriorated as no longer to conform to the contract the buyer may nevertheless demand inspection and at his option either treat the contract as avoided or accept the goods with due allowance from the contract price for the deterioration or the deficiency in quantity but without further right against the seller.

Section 2–614. Substituted Performance

(1) Where without fault of either party the agreed berthing, loading, or unloading facilities fail or an agreed type of carrier becomes unavailable or the agreed manner of delivery otherwise becomes commercially impracticable but a commercially reasonable substitute is available, such substitute performance must be tendered and accepted.

(2) If the agreed means or manner of payment fails because of domestic or foreign governmental regulation, the seller may withhold or stop delivery unless the buyer provides a means or manner of payment which is commercially a substantial equivalent. If delivery has already been taken, payment by the means or in the manner provided by the regulation discharges the buyer's obligation unless the regulation is discriminatory, oppressive or predatory.

Section 2–615. Excuse by Failure of Presupposed Conditions

Except so far as a seller may have assumed a greater obligation and subject to the preceding section on substituted performance:

(a) Delay in delivery or non-delivery in whole or in part by a seller who complies with paragraphs (b) and (c) is not a breach of his duty under a contract for sale if performance as agreed has been made impracticable by the occurrence of a contingency the nonoccurrence of which was a basic assumption on which the contract was made or by compliance in good faith with any applicable foreign or domestic governmental regulation or order whether or not it later proves to be invalid.

(b) Where the causes mentioned in paragraph (a) affect only a part of the seller's capacity to perform, he must allocate production and deliveries among his customers but may at his option include regular customers not then under contract as well as his own requirements for further manufacture. He may so allocate in any manner which is fair and reasonable.

(c) The seller must notify the buyer seasonably that there will be delay or non-delivery and, when allocation is required under paragraph (b), of the estimated quota thus made available for the buyer.

Section 2–216. Procedure on Notice Claiming Excuse

(1) Where the buyer receives notification of a material or indefinite delay or an allocation justified under the preceding section he may by written notification to the seller as to any delivery concerned, and where the prospective deficiency substantially impairs the value of the whole contract under the provisions of this Article relating to breach of installment contracts (Section 2–612), then also as to the whole,

(a) terminate and thereby discharge any unexecuted portion of the contract; or

(b) modify the contract by agreeing to take his available quota in substitution.

(2) If after receipt of such notification from the seller the buyer fails so to modify the contract within a reasonable time not exceeding thirty days the contract lapses with respect to any deliveries affected.

(3) The provisions of this section may not be negated by agreement except in so far as the seller has assumed a greater obligation under the preceding section.

Part 7 Remedies

Section 2–701. Remedies for Breach of Collateral Contracts Not Impaired

Remedies for breach of any obligation or promise collateral or ancillary to a contract for sale are not impaired by the provisions of this Article.

Section 2–702. Seller's Remedies on Discovery of Buyer's Insolvency

(1) Where the seller discovers the buyer to be insolvent he may refuse delivery except for cash including

payment for all goods theretofore delivered under the contract, and stop delivery under this Article (Section 2–705).

(2)   Where the seller discovers that the buyer has received goods on credit while insolvent he may reclaim the goods upon demand made within ten days after the receipt, but if misrepresentation of solvency has been made to the particular seller in writing within three months before delivery the ten day limitation does not apply. Except as provided in this subsection the seller may not base a right to reclaim goods on the buyer's fraudulent or innocent misrepresentation of solvency or of intent to pay.

(3)   The seller's right to reclaim under subsection (2) is subject to the rights of a buyer in ordinary course or other good faith purchaser under this Article (Section 2–403). Successful reclamation of goods excludes all other remedies with respect to them.

Section 2–703.   Seller's Remedies in General

Where the buyer wrongfully rejects or revokes acceptance of goods or fails to make a payment due on or before delivery or repudiates with respect to a part or the whole, then with respect to any goods directly affected and, if the breach is of the whole contract (Section 2–612), then also with respect to the whole undelivered balance, the aggrieved seller may

  (a)   withhold delivery of such goods;

  (b)   stop delivery by any bailee as hereafter provided (Section 2–705);

  (c)   proceed under the next section respecting goods still unidentified to the contract;

  (d)   resell and recover damages as hereafter provided (Section 2–706);

  (e)   recover damages for non-acceptance (Section 2–708) or in a proper case the price (Section 2–709);

  (f)   cancel.

Section 2–704.   Seller's Right to Identify Goods to the Contract Notwithstanding Breach or to Salvage Unfinished Goods

(1)   An aggrieved seller under the preceding section may

  (a)   identify to the contract conforming goods not already identified if at the time he learned of the breach they are in his possession or control;

  (b)   treat as the subject of resale goods which have demonstrably been intended for the particular contract even though those goods are unfinished.

(2)   Where the goods are unfinished an aggrieved seller may in the exercise of reasonable commercial judgment for the purposes of avoiding loss and of effective realization either complete the manufacture and wholly identify the goods to the contract or cease manufacture and resell for scrap or salvage value or proceed in any other reasonable manner.

Section 2–705.   Seller's Stoppage of Delivery in Transit or Otherwise

(1)   The seller may stop delivery of goods in the possession of a carrier or other bailee when he discovers the buyer to be insolvent (Section 2–702) and may stop delivery of carload, truckload, planeload or larger shipments of express or freight when the buyer repudiates or fails to make a payment due before delivery or if for any other reason the seller has a right to withhold or reclaim the goods.

(2)   As against such buyer the seller may stop delivery until

  (a)   receipt of the goods by the buyer; or

  (b)   acknowledgment to the buyer by any bailee of the goods except a carrier that the bailee holds the goods for the buyer; or

  (c)   such acknowledgment to the buyer by a carrier by reshipment or as warehouseman; or

  (d)   negotiation to the buyer of any negotiable document of title covering the goods.

(3)   (a)   To stop delivery the seller must so notify as to enable the bailee by reasonable diligence to prevent delivery of the goods.

  (b)   After such notification the bailee must hold and deliver the goods according to the directions of the seller but the seller is liable to the bailee for any ensuing charges or damages.

  (c)   If a negotiable document of title has been issued for goods the bailee is not obliged to obey a notification to stop until surrender of the document.

  (d)   A carrier who has issued a non-negotiable bill of lading is not obliged to obey a notification to stop received from a person other than the consignor.

Section 2–706. Seller's Resale Including Contract for Resale

(1)   Under the conditions stated in Section 2–703 on seller's remedies, the seller may resell the goods concerned or the undelivered balance thereof. Where the resale is made in good faith and in a commercially reasonable manner the seller may recover the difference between the resale price and the contract price together with any incidental damages allowed under the provisions of this Article (Section 2–710), but less expenses saved in consequence of the buyer's breach.

(2)   Except as otherwise provided in subsection (3) or unless otherwise agreed resale may be at public or private sale including sale by way of one or more contracts to sell or of identification of an existing contract of the seller. Sale may be as a unit or in parcels and at any time and place and on any terms but every aspect of the sale including the method, manner, time, place and terms must be commercially reasonable. The resale must be reasonably identified as referring to the broken contract, but it is not necessary that the goods be in existence or that any or all of them have been identified to the contract before the breach.

(3)   Where the resale is at private sale the seller must give the buyer reasonable notification of his intention to resell.

(4)   Where the resale is at public sale

    (a)   only identified goods can be sold except where there is a recognized market for a public sale of futures in goods of the kind; and

    (b)   it must be made at a usual place or market for public sale if one is reasonably available and except in the case of goods which are perishable or threaten to decline in value speedily the seller must give the buyer reasonable notice of the time and place of the resale; and

    (c)   if the goods are not to be within the view of those attending the sale the notification of sale must state the place where the goods are located and provide for their reasonable inspection by prospective bidders; and

    (d)   the seller may buy.

(5)   A purchaser who buys in good faith at a resale takes the goods free of any rights of the original buyer even though the seller fails to comply with one or more of the requirements of this section.

(6)   The seller is not accountable to the buyer for any profit made on any resale. A person in the position of a seller (Section 2–707) or a buyer who has rightfully rejected or justifiably revoked acceptance must account for any excess over the amount of his security interest, as hereinafter defined (subsection (3) of Section 2–711).

Section 2–707.   "Person in the Position of a Seller"

(1)   A "person in the position of a seller" includes as against a principal an agent who has paid or become responsible for the price of goods on behalf of his principal or anyone who otherwise holds a security interest or other right in goods similar to that of a seller.

(2)   A person in the position of a seller may as provided in this Article withhold or stop delivery (Section 2–705) and resell (Section 2–706) and recover incidental damages (Section 2–710).

Section 2–708.   Seller's Damages for Non-acceptance or Repudiation

(1)   Subject to subsection (2) and to the provisions of this Article with respect to proof of market price (Section 2–723), the measure of damages for non-acceptance or repudiation by the buyer is the difference between the market price at the time and place for tender and the unpaid contract price together with any incidental damages provided in this Article (Section 2–710), but less expenses saved in consequence of the buyer's breach.

(2)   If the measure of damages provided in subsection (1) is inadequate to put the seller in as good a position as performance would have done then the measure of damages is the profit (including reasonable overhead) which the seller would have made from full performance by the buyer, together with any incidental damages provided in this Article (Section 2–710), due allowance for costs reasonably incurred and due credit for payments or proceeds of resale.

Section 2–709.   Action for the Price

(1)   When the buyer fails to pay the price as it becomes due the seller may recover, together with any incidental damages under the next section, the price

    (a)   of goods accepted or of conforming goods lost or damaged within a commercially reasonable time after risk of their loss has passed to the buyer; and

    (b)   of goods identified to the contract if the seller is unable after reasonable effort to resell them at a reasonable price or the circumstances reasonably indicate that such effort will be unavailing.

(2) Where the seller sues for the price he must hold for the buyer any goods which have been identified to the contract and are still in his control except that if resale becomes possible he may resell them at any time prior to the collection of the judgment. The net proceeds of any such resale must be credited to the buyer and payment of the judgment entitles him to any goods not resold.

(3) After the buyer has wrongfully rejected or revoked acceptance of the goods or has failed to make a payment due or has repudiated (Section 2–610), a seller who is held not entitled to the price under this section shall nevertheless be awarded damages for non-acceptance under the preceding section.

Section 2–710. Seller's Incidental Damages

Incidental damages to an aggrieved seller include any commercially reasonable charges, expenses or commissions incurred in stopping delivery, in the transportation, care and custody of goods after the buyer's breach, in connection with return or resale of the goods or otherwise resulting from the breach.

Section 2–711. Buyer's Remedies in General; Buyer's Security Interest in Rejected Goods

(1) Where the seller fails to make delivery or repudiates or the buyer rightfully rejects or justifiably revokes acceptance then with respect to any goods involved, and with respect to the whole if the breach goes to the whole contract (Section 2–612), the buyer may cancel and whether or not he has done so may in addition to recovering so much of the price as has been paid

  (a) "cover" and have damages under the next section as to all the goods affected whether or not they have been identified to the contract; or

  (b) recover damages for non-delivery as provided in this Article (Section 2–713).

(2) Where the seller fails to deliver or repudiates the buyer may also

  (a) if the goods have been identified recover them as provided in this Article (Section 2–502); or

  (b) in a proper case obtain specific performance

or replevy the goods as provided in this Article (Section 2–716).

(3) On rightful rejection or justifiable revocation of acceptance a buyer has a security interest in goods in his possession or control for any payments made on their price and any expenses reasonably incurred in their inspection, receipt, transportation, care and custody and may hold such goods and resell them in like manner as an aggrieved seller (Section 2–706).

Section 2–712. "Cover"; Buyer's Procurement of Substitute Goods

(1) After a breach within the preceding section the buyer may "cover" by making in good faith and without unreasonable delay any reasonable purchase of or contract to purchase goods in substitution for those due from the seller.

(2) The buyer may recover from the seller as damages the difference between the cost of cover and the contract price together with any incidental or consequential damages as hereinafter defined (Section 2–715), but less expenses saved in consequence of the seller's breach.

(3) Failure of the buyer to effect cover within this section does not bar him from any other remedy.

Section 2–713. Buyer's Damages for Non-Delivery or Repudiation

(1) Subject to the provisions of this Article with respect to proof of market price (Section 2–723), the measure of damages for non-delivery or repudiation by the seller is the difference between the market price at the time when the buyer learned of the breach and the contract price together with any incidental and consequential damages provided in this Article (Section 2–715), but less expenses saved in consequence of the seller's breach.

(2) Market price is to be determined as of the place for tender or, in cases of rejection after arrival or revocation of acceptance, as of the place of arrival.

Section 2–714. Buyer's Damages for Breach in Regard to Accepted Goods

(1) Where the buyer has accepted goods and given notification (subsection (3) of Section 2–607) he may recover as damages for any non-conformity of tender the loss resulting in the ordinary course of events from the seller's breach as determined in any manner which is reasonable.

(2) The measure of damages for breach of warranty is the difference at the time and place of acceptance between the value of the goods accepted and the value they would have had if they had been as warranted, unless special circumstances show proximate damages of a different amount.

(3) In a proper case any incidental and consequential damages under the next section may also be recovered.

Section 2–715. Buyer's Incidental and Consequential Damages

(1) Incidental damages resulting from the seller's breach include expenses reasonably incurred in inspection, receipt, transportation and care and custody of goods rightfully rejected, any commercially reasonable charges, expenses or commissions in connection with effecting cover and any other reasonable expense incident to the delay or other breach.

(2) Consequential damages resulting from the seller's breach include

    (a) any loss resulting from general or particular requirements and needs of which the seller at the time of contracting had reason to know and which could not reasonably be prevented by cover or otherwise; and

    (b) injury to person or property proximately resulting from any breach of warranty.

Section 2–716. Buyer's Right to Specific Performance or Replevin

(1) Specific performance may be decreed where the goods are unique or in other proper circumstances.

(2) The decree for specific performance may include such terms and conditions as to payment of the price, damages, or other relief as the court may deem just.

(3) The buyer has a right of replevin for goods identified to the contract if after reasonable effort he is unable to effect cover for such goods or the circumstances reasonably indicate that such effort will be unavailing or if the goods have been shipped under reservation and satisfaction of the security interest in them has been made or tendered.

Section 2–717. Deduction of Damages From the Price

The buyer on notifying the seller of his intention to do so may deduct all or any part of the damages resulting from any breach of the contract from any part of the price still due under the same contract.

Section 2–718. Liquidation or Limitation of Damages; Deposits

(1) Damages for breach by either party may be liquidated in the agreement but only at an amount which is reasonable in the light of the anticipated or actual harm caused by the breach, the difficulties of proof of loss, and the inconvenience or nonfeasibility of otherwise obtaining an adequate remedy. A term fixing unreasonably large liquidated damages is void as a penalty.

(2) Where the seller justifiably withholds delivery of goods because of the buyer's breach, the buyer is entitled to restitution of any amount by which the sum of his payments exceeds

    (a) the amount to which the seller is entitled by virtue of terms liquidating the seller's damages in accordance with subsection (1), or

    (b) in the absence of such terms, twenty per cent of the value of the total performance for which the buyer is obligated under the contract or $500, whichever is smaller.

(3) The buyer's right to restitution under subsection (2) is subject to offset to the extent that the seller establishes

    (a) a right to recover damages under the provisions of this Article other than subsection (1), and

    (b) the amount or value of any benefits received by the buyer directly or indirectly by reason of the contract.

(4) Where a seller has received payment in goods their reasonable value or the proceeds of their resale shall be treated as payments for the purposes of subsection (2); but if the seller has notice of the buyer's breach before reselling goods received in part performance, his resale is subject to the conditions laid down in this Article on resale by an aggrieved seller (Section 2–706).

Section 2–719. Contractual Modification or Limitation of Remedy

(1) Subject to the provisions of subsections (2) and (3) of this section and of the preceding section on liquidation and limitation of damages,

    (a) the agreement may provide for remedies in addition to or in substitution for those provided in this Article and may limit or alter the measure of damages recoverable under this Article, as by limiting the buyer's remedies to return of the goods and repayment of the price or to repair and replacement of non-conforming goods or parts; and

(b) resort to a remedy as provided is optional unless the remedy is expressly agreed to be exclusive, in which case it is the sole remedy.

(2) Where circumstances cause an exclusive or limited remedy to fail of its essential purpose, remedy may be had as provided in this Act.

(3) Consequential damages may be limited or excluded unless the limitation or exclusion is unconscionable. Limitation of consequential damages for injury to the person in the case of consumer goods is prima facie unconscionable but limitation of damages where the loss is commercial is not.

Section 2–720. Effect of "Cancellation" or "Rescission" on Claims for Antecedent Breach

Unless the contrary intention clearly appears, expressions of "cancellation" or "rescission" of the contract or the like shall not be construed as a renunciation or discharge of any claim in damages for an antecedent breach.

Section 2–721. Remedies for Fraud

Remedies for material misrepresentation or fraud include all remedies available under this Article for non-fraudulent breach. Neither rescission or a claim for rescission of the contract for sale nor rejection or return of the goods shall bar or be deemed inconsistent with a claim for damages or other remedy.

Section 2–722. Who Can Sue Third Parties for Injury to Goods

Where a third party so deals with goods which have been identified to a contract for sale as to cause actionable injury to a party to that contract

(a) a right of action against the third party is in either party to the contract for sale who has title to or a security interest or a special property or an insurable interest in the goods; and if the goods have been destroyed or converted a right of action is also in the party who either bore the risk of loss under the contract for sale or has since the injury assumed that risk as against the other;

(b) if at the time of the injury the party plaintiff did not bear the risk of loss as against the

other party to the contract for sale and there is no arrangement between them for disposition of the recovery, his suit or settlement is, subject to his own interest, as a fiduciary for the other party to the contract;

(c) either party may with the consent of the other sue for the benefit of whom it may concern.

Section 2–723. Proof of Market Price: Time and Place

(1) If an action based on anticipatory repudiation comes to trial before the time for performance with respect to some or all of the goods, any damages based on market price (Section 2–708 or Section 2–713) shall be determined according to the price of such goods prevailing at the time when the aggrieved party learned of the repudiation.

(2) If evidence of a price prevailing at the times or places described in this Article is not readily available the price prevailing within any reasonable time before or after the time described or at any other place which in commercial judgment or under usage of trade would serve as a reasonable substitute for the one described may be used, making any proper allowance for the cost of transporting the goods to or from such other place.

(3) Evidence of a relevant price prevailing at a time or place other than the one described in this Article offered by one party is not admissible unless and until he has given the other party such notice as the court finds sufficient to prevent unfair surprise.

Section 2–724. Admissibility of Market Quotations

Whenever the prevailing price or value of any goods regularly bought and sold in any established commodity market is in issue, reports in official publications or trade journals or in newspapers or periodicals of general circulation published as the reports of such market shall be admissible in evidence. The circumstances of the preparation of such a report may be shown to affect its weight but not its admissibility.

Section 2–725. Statute of Limitations in Contracts for Sale

(1) An action for breach of any contract for sale must be commenced within four years after the cause of action has accrued. By the original agreement the parties may reduce the period of limitation to not less than one year but may not extend it.

(2) A cause of action accrues when the breach occurs,

regardless of the aggrieved party's lack of knowledge of the breach. A breach of warranty occurs when tender of delivery is made, except that where a warranty explicitly extends to future performance of the goods and discovery of the breach must await the time of such performance the cause of action accrues when the breach is or should have been discovered.

(3) Where an action commenced within the time limited by subsection (1) is so terminated as to leave available a remedy by another action for the same breach such other action may be commenced after the expiration of the time limited and within six months after the termination of the first action unless the termination resulted from voluntary discontinuance or from dismissal for failure or neglect to prosecute.

(4) This section does not alter the law on tolling of the statute of limitations nor does it apply to causes of action which have accrued before this Act becomes effective.

ARTICLE 3   COMMERCIAL PAPER

Part 1   Short Title, Form and Interpretation

Section 3–101.   Short Title

This Article shall be known and may be cited as Uniform Commercial Code—Commercial Paper.

Section 3–102.   Definitions and Index of Definitions

(1) In this Article unless the context otherwise requires

    (a) "Issue" means the first delivery of an instrument to a holder or a remitter.

    (b) An "order" is a direction to pay and must be more than an authorization or request. It must identify the person to pay with reasonable certainty. It may be addressed to one or more such persons jointly or in the alternative but not in succession.

    (c) A "promise" is an undertaking to pay and must be more than an acknowledgment of an obligation.

    (d) "Secondary party" means a drawer or endorser.

    (e) "Instrument" means a negotiable instrument.

(2) Other definitions applying to this Article and the sections in which they appear are:

    "Acceptance." Section 3–410.

    "Accommodation party." Section 3–415.
    "Alteration." Section 3–407.
    "Certificate of deposit." Section 3–104.
    "Certification." Section 3–411.
    "Check." Section 3–104.
    "Definite time." Section 3–109.
    "Dishonor." Section 3–507.
    "Draft." Section 3–104.
    "Holder in due course." Section 3–302.
    "Negotiation." Section 3–202.
    "Note." Section 3–104.
    "Notice of dishonor." Section 3–508.
    "On demand." Section 3–108.
    "Presentment." Section 3–504.
    "Protest." Section 3–509.
    "Restrictive Indorsement." Section 3–205.
    "Signature." Section 3–401.

(3) The following definitions in other Articles apply to this Article:

    "Account." Section 4–104.
    "Banking Day." Section 4–104.
    "Clearing house." Section 4–104.
    "Collecting bank." Section 4–105.
    "Customer." Section 4–104.
    "Depositary Bank." Section 4–105.
    "Documentary Draft." Section 4–104.
    "Intermediary Bank." Section 4–105.
    "Item." Section 4–104.
    "Midnight deadline." Section 4–104.
    "Payor bank." Section 4–105.

(4) In addition Article 1 contains general definitions and principles of construction and interpretation applicable throughout this Article.

Section 3–103.   Limitations on Scope of Article

(1) This Article does not apply to money, documents of title or investment securities.

(2) The provisions of this Article are subject to the provisions of the Article on Bank Deposits and Collections (Article 4) and Secured Transactions (Article 9).

Section 3–104.   Form of Negotiable Instruments; "Draft"; "Check"; "Certificate of Deposit"; "Note"

(1) Any writing to be a negotiable instrument within this Article must

    (a) be signed by the maker or drawer; and

    (b) contain an unconditional promise or order to pay a sum certain in money and no other promise, order, obligation or power given by the maker or drawer except as authorized by this Article; and

(c) be payable on demand or at a definite time; and

(d) be payable to order or to bearer.

(2) A writing which complies with the requirements of this section is

(a) a "draft" ("bill of exchange") if it is an order;

(b) a "check" if it is a draft drawn on a bank and payable on demand;

(c) a "certificate of deposit" if it is an acknowledgment by a bank of receipt of money with an engagement to repay it;

(d) a "note" if it is a promise other than a certificate of deposit.

(3) As used in other Articles of this Act, and as the context may require, the terms "draft," "check," "certificate of deposit" and "note" may refer to instruments which are not negotiable within this Article as well as to instruments which are so negotiable.

Section 3–105. When Promise or Order Unconditional

(1) A promise or order otherwise unconditional is not made conditional by the fact that the instrument

(a) is subject to implied or constructive conditions; or

(b) states its consideration, whether performed or promised, or the transaction which gave rise to the instrument, or that the promise or order is made or the instrument matures in accordance with or "as per" such transaction; or

(c) refers to or states that it arises out of a separate agreement or refers to a separate agreement for rights as to repayment or acceleration; or

(d) states that it is drawn under a letter of credit; or

(e) states that it is secured, whether by mortgage, reservation of title or otherwise; or

(f) indicates a particular account to be debited or any other fund or source from which reimbursement is expected; or

(g) is limited to payment out of a particular fund or the proceeds of a particular source, if the instrument is issued by a government or governmental agency or unit; or

(h) is limited to payment out of the entire assets of a partnership, unincorporated association, trust or estate by or on behalf of which the instrument is issued.

(2) A promise or order is not unconditional if the instrument

(a) states that it is subject to or governed by any other agreement; or

(b) states that it is to be paid only out of a particular fund or source except as provided in this section. As amended 1962.

Section 3–106. Sum Certain

(1) The sum payable is a sum certain even though it is to be paid

(a) with stated interest or by stated installments; or

(b) with stated different rates of interest before and after default or a specified date; or

(c) with a stated discount or addition if paid before or after the date fixed for payment; or

(d) with exchange or less exchange, whether at a fixed rate or at the current rate; or

(e) with costs of collection or an attorney's fee or both upon default.

(2) Nothing in this section shall validate any term which is otherwise illegal.

Section 3–107. Money

(1) An instrument is payable in money if the medium of exchange in which it is payable is money at the time the instrument is made. An instrument payable in "currency" or "current funds" is payable in money.

(2) A promise or order to pay a sum stated in a foreign currency is for a sum certain in money and, unless a different medium of payment is specified in the instrument, may be satisfied by payment of that number of dollars which the stated foreign currency will purchase at the buying sight rate for that currency on the day on which the instrument is payable or, if payable on demand, on the day of demand. If such an instrument specifies a foreign currency as the medium of payment the instrument is payable in that currency.

Section 3–108. Payable on Demand

Instruments payable on demand include those payable at sight or on presentation and those in which no time for payment is stated.

Section 3–109. Definite Time

(1) An instrument is payable at a definite time if by its terms it is payable

    (a) on or before a stated date or at a fixed period after a stated date; or

    (b) at a fixed period after sight; or

    (c) at a definite time subject to any acceleration; or

    (d) at a definite time subject to extension at the option of the holder, or to extension to a further definite time at the option of the maker or acceptor or automatically upon or after a specified act or event.

(2) An instrument which by its terms is otherwise payable only upon an act or event uncertain as to time of occurrence is not payable at a definite time even though the act or event has occurred.

Section 3–110. Payable to Order

(1) An instrument is payable to order when by its terms it is payable to the order or assigns of any person therein specified with reasonable certainty, or to him or his order, or when it is conspicuously designated on its face as "exchange" or the like and names a payee. It may be payable to the order of

    (a) the maker or drawer; or

    (b) the drawee; or

    (c) a payee who is not maker, drawer or drawee; or

    (d) two or more payees together or in the alternative; or

    (e) an estate, trust or fund, in which case it is payable to the order of the representative of such estate, trust or fund or his successors; or

    (f) an office, or an officer by his title as such in which case it is payable to the principal but the incumbent of the office or his successors may act as if he or they were the holder; or

    (g) a partnership or unincorporated association, in which case it is payable to the partnership or association and may be indorsed or transferred by any person thereto authorized.

(2) An instrument not payable to order is not made so payable by such words as "payable upon return of this instrument properly indorsed."

(3) An instrument made payable both to order and to bearer is payable to order unless the bearer words are handwritten or typewritten.

Section 3–111. Payable to Bearer

An instrument is payable to bearer when by its terms it is payable to

    (a) bearer or the order of bearer; or

    (b) a specified person or bearer; or

    (c) "cash" or the order of "cash" or any other indication which does not purport to designate a specific payee.

Section 3–112. Terms and Omissions Not Affecting Negotiability

(1) The negotiability of an instrument is not affected by

    (a) the omission of a statement of any consideration or of the place where the instrument is drawn or payable; or

    (b) a statement that collateral has been given to secure obligations either on the instrument or otherwise of an obligor on the instrument or that in case of default on those obligations the holder may realize on or dispose of the collateral; or

    (c) a promise or power to maintain or protect collateral or to give additional collateral; or

    (d) a term authorizing a confession of judgment on the instrument if it is not paid when due; or

    (e) a term purporting to waive the benefit of any law intended for the advantage or protection of any obligor; or

    (f) a term in a draft providing that the payee by indorsing or cashing it acknowledges full satisfaction of an obligation of the drawer; or

    (g) a statement in a draft drawn in a set of parts (Section 3–801) to the effect that the order is effective only if no other part has been honored.

(2) Nothing in this section shall validate any term which is otherwise illegal.

Section 3–113. Seal

An instrument otherwise negotiable is within this Article even though it is under a seal.

Section 3–114. Date, Antedating, Postdating

(1) The negotiability of an instrument is not affected by the fact that it is undated, antedated or postdated.

(2) Where an instrument is antedated or postdated the time when it is payable is determined by the stated date if the instrument is payable on demand or at a fixed period after date.

(3) Where the instrument or any signature thereon is dated, the date is presumed to be correct.

Section 3–115. Incomplete Instruments

(1) When a paper whose contents at the time of signing show that it is intended to become an instrument is signed while still incomplete in any necessary respect it cannot be enforced until completed, but when it is completed in accordance with authority given it is effective as completed.

(2) If the completion is unauthorized the rules as to material alteration apply (Section 3–407), even though the paper was not delivered by the maker or drawer; but the burden of establishing that any completion is unauthorized is on the party so asserting.

Section 3–116. Instruments Payable to Two or More Persons

An instrument payable to the order of two or more persons

(a) if in the alternative is payable to any one of them and may be negotiated, discharged or enforced by any of them who has possession of it;

(b) if not in the alternative is payable to all of them and may be negotiated, discharged or enforced only by all of them.

Section 3–117. Instruments Payable With Words of Description

An instrument made payable to a named person with the addition of words describing him

(a) as agent or officer of a specified person is payable to his principal but the agent or officer may act as if he were the holder;

(b) as any other fiduciary for a specified person or purpose is payable to the payee and may be negotiated, discharged or enforced by him;

(c) in any other manner is payable to the payee unconditionally and the additional words are without effect on subsequent parties.

Section 3–118. Ambiguous Terms and Rules of Construction

The following rules apply to every instrument:

(a) Where there is doubt whether the instrument is a draft or a note the holder may treat it as either. A draft drawn on the drawer is effective as a note.

(b) Handwritten terms control typewritten and printed terms, and typewritten control printed.

(c) Words control figures except that if the words are ambiguous figures control.

(d) Unless otherwise specified a provision for interest means interest at the judgment rate at the place of payment from the date of the instrument, or if it is undated from the date of issue.

(e) Unless the instrument otherwise specifies two or more persons who sign as maker, acceptor or drawer or indorser and as a part of the same transaction are jointly and severally liable even though the instrument contains such words as "I promise to pay."

(f) Unless otherwise specified consent to extension authorizes a single extension for not longer than the original period. A consent to extension, expressed in the instrument, is binding on secondary parties and accommodation makers. A holder may not exercise his option to extend an instrument over the objection of a maker or acceptor or other party who in accordance with Section 3–604 tenders full payment when the instrument is due.

Section 3–119. Other Writings Affecting Instrument

(1) As between the obligor and his immediate obligee or any transferee the terms of an instrument may be modified or affected by any other written agreement executed as a part of the same transaction, except that a holder in due course is not affected by any limitation of his rights arising out of the separate written agreement if he had no notice of the limitation when he took the instrument.

(2) A separate agreement does not affect the negotiability of an instrument.

Section 3–120.   Instruments "Payable Through" Bank

An instrument which states that it is "payable through" a bank or the like designates that bank as a collecting bank to make presentment but does not of itself authorize the bank to pay the instrument.

Section 3–121.   Instruments Payable at Bank

Note: *If this Act is introduced in the Congress of the United States this section should be omitted. (States to select either alternative)*

Alternative A

A note or acceptance which states that it is payable at a bank is the equivalent of a draft drawn on the bank payable when it falls due out of any funds of the maker or acceptor in current account or otherwise available for such payment.

Alternative B

A note or acceptance which states that it is payable at a bank is not of itself an order or authorization to the bank to pay it.

Section 3–122.   Accrual of Cause of Action

(1)   A cause of action against a maker or an acceptor accrues

    (a)   in the case of a time instrument on the day after maturity;

    (b)   in the case of a demand instrument upon its date or, if no date is stated, on the date of issue.

(2)   A cause of action against the obligor of a demand or time certificate of deposit accrues upon demand, but demand on a time certificate may not be made until on or after the date of maturity.

(3)   A cause of action against a drawer of a draft or an indorser of any instrument accrues upon demand following dishonor of the instrument. Notice of dishonor is a demand.

(4)   Unless an instrument provides otherwise, interest runs at the rate provided by law for a judgment

    (a)   in the case of a maker, acceptor or other primary obligor of a demand instrument, from the date of demand;

    (b)   in all other cases from the date of accrual of the cause of action.

Part 2   Transfer and Negotiation

Section 3–201.   Transfer: Right to Indorsement

(1)   Transfer of an instrument vests in the transferee such rights as the transferor has therein, except that a transferee who has himself been a party to any fraud or illegality affecting the instrument or who as a prior holder had notice of a defense or claim against it cannot improve his position by taking from a later holder in due course.

(2)   A transfer of a security interest in an instrument vests the foregoing rights in the transferee to the extent of the interest transferred.

(3)   Unless otherwise agreed any transfer for value of an instrument not then payable to bearer gives the transferee the specifically enforceable right to have the unqualified indorsement of the transferor. Negotiation takes effect only when the indorsement is made and until that time there is no presumption that the transferee is the owner.

Section 3–202.   Negotiation

(1)   Negotiation is the transfer of an instrument in such form that the transferee becomes a holder. If the instrument is payable to order it is negotiated by delivery with any necessary indorsement; if payable to bearer it is negotiated by delivery.

(2)   An indorsement must be written by or on behalf of the holder and on the instrument or on a paper so firmly affixed thereto as to become a part thereof.

(3)   An indorsement is effective for negotiation only when it conveys the entire instrument or any unpaid residue. If it purports to be of less it operates only as a partial assignment.

(4)   Words of assignment, condition, waiver, guaranty, limitation or disclaimer of liability and the like accompanying an indorsement do not affect its character as an indorsement.

Section 3–203.   Wrong or Misspelled Name

Where an instrument is made payable to a person under a misspelled name or one other than his own he may indorse in that name or his own or both; but signature in both names may be required by a person paying or giving value for the instrument.

Section 3–204. Special Indorsement; Blank Indorsement

(1) A special indorsement specifies the person to whom or to whose order it makes the instrument payable. Any instrument specially indorsed becomes payable to the order of the special indorsee and may be further negotiated by his indorsement.

(2) An indorsement in blank specifies no particular indorsee and may consist of a mere signature. An instrument payable to order and indorsed in blank becomes payable to bearer and may be negotiated by delivery alone until specially indorsed.

(3) The holder may convert a blank indorsement into a special indorsement by writing over the signature of the indorser in blank any contract consistent with the character of the indorsement.

Section 3–205. Restrictive Indorsements

An indorsement is restrictive which either

  (a) is conditional; or

  (b) purports to prohibit further transfer of the instrument; or

  (c) includes the words "for collection," "for deposit," "pay any bank," or like terms signifying a purpose of deposit or collection; or

  (d) otherwise states that it is for the benefit or use of the indorser or of another person.

Section 3–206. Effect of Restrictive Indorsement

(1) No restrictive indorsement prevents further transfer or negotiation of the instrument.

(2) An intermediary bank, or a payor bank which is not the depositary bank, is neither given notice nor otherwise affected by a restrictive indorsement of any person except the bank's immediate transferor or the person presenting for payment.

(3) Except for an intermediary bank, any transferee under an indorsement which is conditional or includes the words "for collection," "for deposit," "pay any bank," or like terms (subparagraphs (a) and (c) of Section 3–205) must pay or apply any value given by him for or on security of the instrument consistently with the indorsement and to the extent that he does so he becomes a holder for value. In addition such transferee is a holder in due course if he otherwise complies with the requirements of Section 3–302 on what constitutes a holder in due course.

(4) The first taker under an indorsement for the benefit of the indorser or another person (subparagraph (d) of Section 3–205) must pay or apply any value given by him for or on the security of the instrument consistently with the indorsement and to the extent that he does so he becomes a holder for value. In addition such taker is a holder in due course if he otherwise complies with the requirements of Section 3–302 on what constitutes a holder in due course. A later holder for value is neither given notice nor otherwise affected by such restrictive indorsement unless he has knowledge that a fiduciary or other person has negotiated the instrument in any transaction for his own benefit or otherwise in breach of duty (subsection (2) of Section 3–304).

Section 3–207. Negotiation Effective Although It May Be Rescinded

(1) Negotiation is effective to transfer the instrument although the negotiation is

  (a) made by an infant, a corporation exceeding its powers, or any other person without capacity; or

  (b) obtained by fraud, duress or mistake of any kind; or

  (c) part of an illegal transaction; or

  (d) made in breach of duty.

(2) Except as against a subsequent holder in due course such negotiation is in an appropriate case subject to rescission, the declaration of a constructive trust or any other remedy permitted by law.

Section 3–208. Reacquisition

Where an instrument is returned to or reacquired by a prior party he may cancel any indorsement which is not necessary to his title and reissue or further negotiate the instrument, but any intervening party is discharged as against the reacquiring party and subsequent holders not in due course and if his indorsement has been cancelled is discharged as against subsequent holders in due course as well.

Part 3   Rights of a Holder

Section 3–301. Rights of a Holder

The holder of an instrument whether or not he is the owner may transfer or negotiate it and, except as otherwise provided in Section 3–603 on payment or satisfaction, discharge it or enforce payment in his own name.

(1)   A holder in due course is a holder who takes the instrument

    (a)   for value, and

    (b)   in good faith; and

    (c)   without notice that it is overdue or has been dishonored or of any defense against or claim to it on the part of any person.

(2)   A payee may be a holder in due course.

(3)   A holder does not become a holder in due course of an instrument:

    (a)   by purchase of it at judicial sale or by taking it under legal process; or

    (b)   by acquiring it in taking over an estate; or

    (c)   by purchasing it as part of a bulk transaction not in regular course of business of the transferor.

(4)   A purchaser of a limited interest can be a holder in due course only to the extent of the interest purchased.

Section 3–303.   Taking for Value

A holder takes the instrument for value

    (a)   to the extent that the agreed consideration has been performed or that he acquires a security interest in or a lien on the instrument otherwise than by legal process; or

    (b)   when he takes the instrument in payment of or as security for an antecedent claim against any person whether or not the claim is due; or

    (c)   when he gives a negotiable instrument for it or makes an irrevocable commitment to a third person.

Section 3–304.   Notice to Purchaser

(1)   The purchaser has notice of a claim or defense if

    (a)   the instrument is so incomplete, bears such visible evidence of forgery or alteration, or is otherwise so irregular as to call into question its validity, terms or ownership or to create an ambiguity as to the party to pay; or

    (b)   the purchaser has notice that the obligation of any party is voidable in whole or in part, or that all parties have been discharged.

(2)   The purchaser has notice of a claim against the instrument when he has knowledge that a fiduciary has negotiated the instrument in payment of or as security

for his own debt or in any transaction for his own benefit or otherwise in breach of duty.

(3)   The purchaser has notice that an instrument is overdue if he has reason to know

    (a)   that any part of the principal amount is overdue or that there is an uncured default in payment of another instrument of the same series; or

    (b)   that acceleration of the instrument has been made; or

    (c)   that he is taking a demand instrument after demand has been made or more than a reasonable length of time after its issue. A reasonable time for a check drawn and payable within the states and territories of the United States and the District of Columbia is presumed to be thirty days.

(4)   Knowledge of the following facts does not of itself give the purchaser notice of a defense or claim

    (a)   that the instrument is antedated or postdated;

    (b)   that it was issued or negotiated in return for an executory promise or accompanied by a separate agreement, unless the purchaser has notice that a defense or claim has arisen from the terms thereof;

    (c)   that any party has signed for accommodation;

    (d)   that an incomplete instrument has been completed, unless the purchaser has notice of any improper completion;

    (e)   that any person negotiating the instrument is or was a fiduciary;

    (f)   that there has been default in payment of interest on the instrument or in payment of any other instrument, except one of the same series.

(5)   The filing or recording of a document does not of itself constitute notice within the provisions of this Article to a person who would otherwise be a holder in due course.

(6)   To be effective notice must be received at such time and in such manner as to give a reasonable opportunity to act on it.

Section 3–305.   Rights of a Holder in Due Course

To the extent that a holder is a holder in due course he takes the instrument free from

(1)   all claims to it on the part of any person; and

(2)   all defenses of any party to the instrument with whom the holder has not dealt except

- (a)   infancy, to the extent that it is a defense to a simple contract; and

- (b)   such other incapacity, or duress, or illegality of the transaction, as renders the obligation of the party a nullity; and

- (c)   such misrepresentation as has induced the party to sign the instrument with neither knowledge nor reasonable opportunity to obtain knowledge of its character or its essential terms; and

- (d)   discharge in solvency proceedings; and

- (e)   any other discharge of which the holder has notice when he takes the instrument.

Section 3–306.   Rights of One Not Holder in Due Course

Unless he has the rights of a holder in due course any person takes the instrument subject to

- (a)   all valid claims to it on the part of any person; and

- (b)   all defenses of any party which would be available in an action on a simple contract; and

- (c)   the defenses of want or failure of consideration, non-performance of any condition precedent, non-delivery, or delivery for a special purpose (Section 3–408); and

- (d)   the defense that he or a person through whom he holds the instrument acquired it by theft, or that payment or satisfaction to such holder would be inconsistent with the terms of a restrictive indorsement. The claim of any third person to the instrument is not otherwise available as a defense to any party liable thereon unless the third person himself defends the action for such party.

Section 3–307.   Burden of Establishing Signatures, Defenses and Due Course

(1)   Unless specifically denied in the pleadings each signature on an instrument is admitted. When the effectiveness of a signature is put in issue

- (a)   the burden of establishing it is on the party claiming under the signature; but

- (b)   the signature is presumed to be genuine or authorized except where the action is to en-

force the obligation of a purported signer who had died or become incompetent before proof is required.

(2)   When signatures are admitted or established, production of the instrument entitles a holder to recover on it unless the defendant establishes a defense.

(3)   After it is shown that a defense exists a person claiming the rights of a holder in due course has the burden of establishing that he or some person under whom he claims is in all respects a holder in due course.

Part 4   Liability of Parties

Section 3–401.   Signature

(1)   No person is liable on an instrument unless his signature appears thereon.

(2)   A signature is made by use of any name, including any trade or assumed name, upon an instrument, or by any word or mark used in lieu of a written signature.

Section 3–402.   Signature in Ambiguous Capacity

Unless the instrument clearly indicates that a signature is made in some other capacity it is an indorsement.

Section 3–403.   Signature by Authorized Representative

(1)   A signature may be made by an agent or other representative, and his authority to make it may be established as in other cases of representation. No particular form of appointment is necessary to establish such authority.

(2)   An authorized representative who signs his own name to an instrument

- (a)   is personally obligated if the instrument neither names the person represented nor shows that the representatives signed in a representative capacity;

- (b)   except as otherwise established between the immediate parties, is personally obligated if the instrument names the person represented but does not show that the representative signed in a representative capacity, or if the instrument does not name the person represented but does show that the representative signed in a representative capacity.

(3)   Except as otherwise established the name of an organization preceded or followed by the name and office of an authorized individual is a signature made in a representative capacity.

Section 3–404.   Unauthorized Signatures

(1)   Any unauthorized signature is wholly inoperative as that of the person whose name is signed unless he ratifies it or is precluded from denying it; but it operates as the signature of the unauthorized signer in favor of any person who in good faith pays the instrument or takes it for value.

(2)   Any unauthorized signature may be ratified for all purposes of this Article. Such ratification does not of itself affect any rights of the person ratifying against the actual signer.

Section 3–405.   Impostors; Signature in Name of Payee

(1)   An indorsement by any person in the name of a named payee is effective if

(a)   an imposter by use of the mails or otherwise has induced the maker or drawer to issue the instrument to him or his confederate in the name of the payee; or

(b)   a person signing as or on behalf of a maker or drawer intends the payee to have no interest in the instrument; or

(c)   an agent or employee of the maker or drawer has supplied him with the name of the payee intending the latter to have no such interest.

(2)   Nothing in this section shall affect the criminal or civil liability of the person so indorsing.

Section 3–406.   Negligence Contributing to Alteration or Unauthorized Signature

Any person who by his negligence substantially contributes to a material alteration of the instrument or to the making of an unauthorized signature is precluded from asserting the alteration or lack of authority against a holder in due course or against a drawee or other payor who pays the instrument in good faith and in accordance with the reasonable commercial standards of the drawee's or payor's business.

Section 3–407.   Alteration

(1)   Any alteration of an instrument is material which changes the contract of any party thereto in any respect, including any such change in

(a)   the number or relations of the parties; or

(b)   an incomplete instrument, by completing it otherwise than as authorized; or

(c)   the writing as signed, by adding to it or by removing any part of it.

(2)   As against any person other than a subsequent holder in due course.

(a)   alteration by the holder which is both fraudulent and material discharges any party whose contract is thereby changed unless that party assents or is precluded from asserting the defense;

(b)   no other alteration discharges any part and the instrument may be enforced according to its original tenor, or as to incomplete instruments according to the authority given.

(3)   A subsequent holder in due course may in all cases enforce the instrument according to its original tenor, and when an incomplete instrument has been completed, he may enforce it as completed.

Section 3–408.   Consideration

Want or failure of consideration is a defense as against any person not having the rights of a holder in due course (Section 3–305), except that no consideration is necessary for an instrument or obligation thereon given in payment of or as security for an antecedent obligation of any kind. Nothing in this section shall be taken to displace any statute outside this Act under which a promise is enforceable notwithstanding lack or failure of consideration. Partial failure of consideration is a defense pro tanto whether or not the failure is in an ascertained or liquidated amount.

Section 3–409.   Draft Not an Assignment

(1)   A check or other draft does not of itself operate as an assignment of any funds in the hands of the drawee available for its payment, and the drawee is not liable on the instrument until he accepts it.

(2)   Nothing in this section shall affect any liability in contract, tort or otherwise arising from any letter of credit or other obligation or representation which is not an acceptance.

Section 3–410.   Definition and Operation of Acceptance

(1)   Acceptance is the drawee's signed engagement to honor the draft as presented. It must be written on the draft, and may consist of his signature alone. It becomes operative when completed by delivery or notification.

(2)   A draft may be accepted although it has not been signed by the drawer or is otherwise incomplete or is overdue or has been dishonored.

(3) Where the draft is payable at a fixed period after sight and the acceptor fails to date his acceptance the holder may complete it by supplying a date in good faith.

Section 3–411. Certification of a Check

(1) Certification of a check is acceptance. Where a holder procures certification the drawer and all prior indorsers are discharged.

(2) Unless otherwise agreed a bank has no obligation to certify a check.

(3) A bank may certify a check before returning it for lack of proper indorsement. If it does so the drawer is discharged.

Section 3–412. Acceptance Varying Draft

(1) Where the drawee's proffered acceptance in any manner varies the draft as presented the holder may refuse the acceptance and treat the draft as dishonored in which case the drawee is entitled to have his acceptance cancelled.

(2) The terms of the draft are not varied by an acceptance to pay at any particular bank or place in the United States, unless the acceptance states that the draft is to be paid only at such bank or place.

(3) Where the holder assents to an acceptance varying the terms of the draft each drawer and indorser who does not affirmatively assent is discharged.

Section 3–413. Contract of Maker, Drawer and Acceptor

(1) The maker or acceptor engages that he will pay the instrument according to its tenor at the time of his engagement or as completed pursuant to Section 3–115 on incomplete instruments.

(2) The drawer engages that upon dishonor of the draft and any necessary notice of dishonor or protest he will pay the amount of the draft to the holder or to any indorser who takes it up. The drawer may disclaim this liability by drawing without recourse.

(3) By making, drawing or accepting the party admits as against all subsequent parties including the drawee the existence of the payee and his then capacity to indorse.

Section 3–414. Contract of Indorser; Order of Liability

(1) Unless the indorsement otherwise specifies (as by such words as "without recourse") every indorser en-

gages that upon dishonor and any necessary notice of dishonor and protest he will pay the instrument according to its tenor at the time of his indorsement to the holder or to any subsequent indorser who takes it up, even though the indorser who takes it up was not obligated to do so.

(2) Unless they otherwise agree indorsers are liable to one another in the order in which they indorse, which is presumed to be the order in which their signatures appear on the instrument.

Section 3–415. Contract of Accommodation Party

(1) An accommodation party is one who signs the instrument in any capacity for the purpose of lending his name to another party to it.

(2) When the instrument has been taken for value before it is due the accommodation party is liable in the capacity in which he has signed even though the taker knows of the accommodation.

(3) As against a holder in due course and without notice of the accommodation oral proof of the accommodation is not admissible to give the accommodation party the benefit of discharges dependent on his character as such. In other cases the accommodation character may be shown by oral proof.

(4) An indorsement which shows that it is not in the chain of title is notice of its accommodation character.

(5) An accommodation party is not liable to the party accommodated, and if he pays the instrument has a right of recourse on the instrument against such party.

Section 3–416. Contract of Guarantor

(1) "Payment guaranteed" or equivalent words added to a signature mean that the signer engages that if the instrument is not paid when due he will pay it according to its tenor without resort by the holder to any other party.

(2) "Collection guaranteed" or equivalent words added to a signature mean that the signer engages that if the instrument is not paid when due he will pay it according to its tenor, but only after the holder has reduced his claim against the maker or acceptor to judgment and execution has been returned unsatisfied, or after the maker or acceptor has become insolvent or it is otherwise apparent that it is useless to proceed against him.

(3) Words of guaranty which do not otherwise specify guarantee payment.

(4) No words of guaranty added to the signature of a sole maker or acceptor affect his liability on the instrument. Such words added to the signature of one of two

or more makers or acceptors create a presumption that the signature is for the accommodation of the others.

(5) When words of guaranty are used presentment, notice of dishonor and protest are not necessary to charge the user.

(6) Any guaranty written on the instrument is enforcible notwithstanding any statute of frauds.

Section 3–417. Warranties on Presentment and Transfer

Section 3–417. Warranties on Presentment and Transfer

(1) Any person who obtains payment or acceptance and any prior transferor warrants to a person who in good faith pays or accepts that

   (a) he has a good title to the instrument or is authorized to obtain payment or acceptance on behalf of one who has a good title; and

   (b) he has no knowledge that the signature of the maker or drawer is unauthorized, except that this warranty is not given by a holder in due course acting in good faith

      (i) to a maker with respect to the maker's own signature; or

      (ii) to a drawer with respect to the drawer's own signature, whether or not the drawer is also the drawee; or

      (iii) to an acceptor of a draft if the holder in due course took the draft after the acceptance or obtained the acceptance without knowledge that the drawer's signature was unauthorized; and

   (c) the instrument has not been materially altered, except that this warranty is not given by a holder in due course acting in good faith

      (i) to the maker of a note; or

      (ii) to the drawer of a draft whether or not the drawer is also the drawee; or

      (iii) to the acceptor of a draft with respect to an alteration made prior to the acceptance if the holder in due course took the draft after the acceptance, even though the acceptance provided "payable as originally drawn" or equivalent terms; or

      (iv) to the acceptor of a draft with respect to an alteration made after the acceptance.

(2) Any person who transfers an instrument and receives consideration warrants to his transferee and if the transfer is by indorsement to any subsequent holder who takes the instrument in good faith that

   (a) he has a good title to the instrument or is authorized to obtain payment or acceptance on behalf of one who has a good title and the transfer is otherwise rightful; and

   (b) all signatures are genuine or authorized; and

   (c) the instrument has not been materially altered; and

   (d) no defense of any party is good against him; and

   (e) he has no knowledge of any insolvency proceeding instituted with respect to the maker or acceptor or the drawer of an unaccepted instrument.

(3) By transferring "without recourse" the transferor limits the obligation stated in subsection (2) (d) to a warranty that he has no knowledge of such a defense.

(4) A selling agent or broker who does not disclose the fact that he is acting only as such gives the warranties provided in this section, but if he makes such disclosure warrants only his good faith and authority.

Section 3–418. Finality of Payment or Acceptance

Except for recovery of bank payments as provided in the Article on Bank Deposits and Collections (Article 4) and except for liability for breach of warranty on presentment under the preceding section, payment or acceptance of any instrument is final in favor of a holder in due course, or a person who has in good faith changed his position in reliance on the payment.

Section 3–419. Conversion of Instrument; Innocent Representative

(1) An instrument is converted when

   (a) a drawee to whom it is delivered for acceptance refuses to return it on demand; or

   (b) any person to whom it is delivered for payment refuses on demand either to pay or to return it; or

   (c) it is paid on a forged indorsement.

(2) In an action against a drawee under subsection (1) the measure of the drawee's liability is the face amount of the instrument. In any other action under subsection (1) the measure of liability is presumed to be the face amount of the instrument.

(3) Subject to the provisions of this Act concerning restrictive indorsements a representative, including a depositary or collecting bank, who has in good faith and in accordance with the reasonable commercial standards applicable to the business of such representative

Uniform Commercial Code

dealt with an instrument or its proceeds on behalf of one who was not the true owner is not liable in conversion or otherwise to the true owner beyond the amount of any proceeds remaining in his hands.

(4) An intermediary bank or payor bank which is not a depositary bank is not liable in conversion solely by reason of the fact that proceeds of an item indorsed restrictively (Sections 3–205 and 3–206) are not paid or applied consistently with the restrictive indorsement of an indorser other than its immediate transferor.

Part 5   Presentment, Notice of Dishonor and Protest

Section 3–501.   When Presentment, Notice of Dishonor, and Protest Necessary or Permissible

(1) Unless excused (Section 3–511) presentment is necessary to charge secondary parties as follows:

   (a) presentment for acceptance is necessary to charge the drawer and indorsers of a draft where the draft so provides, or is payable elsewhere than at the residence or place of business of the drawee, or its date of payment depends upon such presentment. The holder may at his option present for acceptance any other draft payable at a stated date:

   (b) presentment for payment is necessary to charge any indorser;

   (c) in the case of any drawer, the acceptor of a draft payable at a bank or the maker of a note payable at a bank, presentment for payment is necessary, but failure to make presentment discharges such drawer, acceptor or maker only as stated in Section 3–502(1) (b).

(2) Unless excused (Section 3–511)

   (a) notice of any dishonor is necessary to charge any indorser:

   (b) in the case of any drawer, the acceptor of a draft payable at a bank or the maker of a note payable at a bank, notice of any dishonor is necessary, but failure to give such notice discharges such drawer, acceptor or maker only as stated in Section 3–502(1) (b).

(3) Unless excused (Section 3–511) protest of any dishonor is necessary to charge the drawer and indorsers of any draft which on its face appears to be drawn or payable outside of the states, territories, dependencies and possessions of the United States, the District of

Columbia and the Commonwealth of Puerto Rico. The holder may at his option make protest of any dishonor of any other instrument and in the case of a foreign draft may on insolvency of the acceptor before maturity make protest for better security.

(4) Notwithstanding any provision of this section, neither presentment nor notice of dishonor nor protest is necessary to charge an indorser who has indorsed an instrument after maturity.

Section 3–502.   Unexcused Delay; Discharge

(1) Where without excuse any necessary presentment or notice of dishonor is delayed beyond the time when it is due

   (a) any indorser is discharged; and

   (b) any drawer or the acceptor of a draft payable at a bank or the maker of a note payable at a bank who because the drawee or payor bank becomes insolvent during the delay is deprived of funds maintained with the drawee or payor bank to cover the instrument may discharge his liability by written assignment to the holder of his rights against the drawee or payor bank in respect of such funds, but such drawer, acceptor or maker is not otherwise discharged.

(2) Where without excuse a necessary protest is delayed beyond the time when it is due any drawer or indorser is discharged.

Section 3–503.   Time of Presentment

(1) Unless a different time is expressed in the instrument the time for any presentment is determined as follows:

   (a) where an instrument is payable at or a fixed period after a stated date any presentment for acceptance must be made on or before the date it is payable;

   (b) where an instrument is payable after sight it must either be presented for acceptance or negotiated within a reasonable time after date or issue whichever is later;

   (c) where an instrument shows the date on which it is payable presentment for payment is due on that date;

   (d) where an instrument is accelerated presentment for payment is due within a reasonable time after the acceleration;

   (e) with respect to the liability of any secondary party presentment for acceptance or payment of any other instrument is due within a reasonable time after such party becomes liable thereon.

(2) A reasonable time for presentment is determined by the nature of the instrument, any usage of banking or trade and the facts of the particular case. In the case of an uncertified check which is drawn and payable within the United States and which is not a draft drawn by a bank the following are presumed to be reasonable periods within which to present for payment or to initiate bank collection:

(a) with respect to the liability of the drawer, thirty days after date or issue whichever is later; and

(b) with respect to the liability of an indorser, seven days after his indorsement

(3) Where any presentment is due on a day which is not a full business day for either the person making presentment or the party to pay or accept, presentment is due on the next following day which is a full business day for both parties.

(4) Presentment to be sufficient must be made at a reasonable hour, and if at a bank during its banking day.

Section 3–504. How Presentment Made

(1) Presentment is a demand for acceptance or payment made upon the maker, acceptor, drawee or other payor by or on behalf of the holder.

(2) Presentment may be made

(a) by mail, in which event the time of presentment is determined by the time of receipt of the mail; or

(b) through a clearing house; or

(c) at the place of acceptance or payment specified in the instrument or if there be none at the place of business or residence of the party to accept or pay. If neither the party to accept or pay nor anyone authorized to act for him is present or accessible at such place presentment is excused.

(3) It may be made

(a) to any one of two or more makers, acceptors, drawees or other payors; or

(b) to any person who has authority to make or refuse the acceptance or payment.

(4) A draft accepted or a note made payable at a bank in the United States must be presented at such bank.

(5) In the cases described in Section 4–210 present-

ment may be made in the manner and with the result stated in that section.

Section 3–505. Rights of Party to Whom Presentment Is Made

(1) The party to whom presentment is made may without dishonor require

(a) exhibition of the instrument; and

(b) reasonable identification of the person making presentment and evidence of his authority to make it if made for another; and

(c) that the instrument be produced for acceptance or payment at a place specified in it, or if there be none at any place reasonable in the circumstances; and

(d) a signed receipt on the instrument for any partial or full payment and its surrender upon full payment.

(2) Failure to comply with any such requirement invalidates the presentment but the person presenting has a reasonable time in which to comply and the time for acceptance or payment runs from the time of compliance.

Section 3–506. Time Allowed for Acceptance or Payment

(1) Acceptance may be deferred without dishonor until the close of the next business day following presentment. The holder may also in a good faith effort to obtain acceptance and without either dishonor of the instrument or discharge of secondary parties allow postponement of acceptance for an additional business day.

(2) Except as a longer time is allowed in the case of documentary drafts drawn under a letter of credit, and unless an earlier time is agreed to by the party to pay, payment of an instrument may be deferred without dishonor pending reasonable examination to determine whether it is properly payable, but payment must be made in any event before the close of business on the day of presentment.

Section 3–507. Dishonor; Holder's Right of Recourse; Term Allowing Re-Presentment

(1) An instrument is dishonored when

(a) a necessary or optional presentment is duly made and due acceptance or payment is refused or cannot be obtained within the prescribed time or in case of bank collections the instrument is seasonably returned by the midnight deadline (Section 4–301); or

(b) presentment is excused and the instrument is not duly accepted or paid.

(2) Subject to any necessary notice of dishonor and protest, the holder has upon dishonor an immediate right of recourse against the drawers and indorsers.

(3) Return of an instrument for lack of proper indorsement is not dishonor.

(4) A term in a draft or an indorsement thereof allowing a stated time for re-presentment in the event of any dishonor of the draft by nonacceptance if a time draft or by nonpayment if a sight draft gives the holder as against any secondary party bound by the term an option to waive the dishonor without affecting liability of the secondary party and he may present again up to the end of the stated time.

Section 3–508. Notice of Dishonor

(1) Notice of dishonor may be given to any person who may be liable on the instrument by or on behalf of the holder or any party who has himself received notice, or any other party who can be compelled to pay the instrument. In addition an agent or bank in whose hands the instrument is dishonored may give notice to his principal or customer or to another agent or bank from which the instrument was received.

(2) Any necessary notice must be given by a bank before its midnight deadline and by any other person before midnight of the third business day after dishonor or receipt of notice of dishonor.

(3) Notice may be given in any reasonable manner. It may be oral or written and in any terms which identify the instrument and state that it has been dishonored. A misdescription which does not mislead the party notified does not vitiate the notice. Sending the instrument bearing a stamp, ticket or writing stating that acceptance or payment has been refused or sending a notice of debit with respect to the instrument is sufficient.

(4) Written notice is given when sent although it is not received.

(5) Notice to one partner is notice to each although the firm has been dissolved.

(6) When any part is in insolvency proceedings instituted after the issue of the instrument notice may be given either to the party or to the representative of his estate.

(7) When any party is dead or incompetent notice may be sent to his last known address or given to his personal representative.

(8) Notice operates for the benefit of all parties who have rights on the instrument against the party notified.

Section 3–509. Protest; Noting for Protest

(1) A protest is a certificate of dishonor made under the hand and seal of a United States consul or vice consul or a notary public or other person authorized to certify dishonor by the law of the place where dishonor occurs. It may be made upon information satisfactory to such person.

(2) The protest must identify the instrument and certify either that due presentment has been made or the reason why it is excused and that the instrument has been dishonored by nonacceptance or nonpayment.

(3) The protest may also certify that notice of dishonor has been given to all parties or to specified parties.

(4) Subject to subsection (5) any necessary protest is due by the time that notice of dishonor is due.

(5) If, before protest is due, an instrument has been noted for protest by the officer to make protest, the protest may be made at any time thereafter as of the date of the noting.

Section 3–510. Evidence of Dishonor and Notice of Dishonor

The following are admissible as evidence and create a presumption of dishonor and of any notice of dishonor therein shown:

(a) a document regular in form as provided in the preceding section which purports to be a protest;

(b) the purported stamp or writing of the drawee, payor bank or presenting bank on the instrument of accompanying it stating that acceptance or payment has been refused for reasons consistent with dishonor;

(c) any book or record of the drawee, payor bank, or any collecting bank kept in the usual course of business which shows dishonor, even though there is no evidence of who made the entry.

Section 3–511. Waived or Excused Presentment, Protest or Notice of Dishonor or Delay Therein

(1) Delay in presentment, protest or notice of dishonor is excused when the party is without notice that

it is due or when the delay is caused by circumstances beyond his control and he exercises reasonable diligence after the cause of the delay ceases to operate.

(2) Presentment or notice or protest as the case may be is entirely excused when

    (a) the party to be charged has waived it expressly or by implication either before or after it is due; or

    (b) such party has himself dishonored instrument or has countermanded payment or otherwise has no reason to expect or right to require that the instrument be accepted or paid; or

    (c) by reasonable diligence the presentment or protest cannot be made or the notice given.

(3) Presentment is also entirely excused when

    (a) the maker, acceptor, or drawee of any instrument except a documentary draft is dead or in insolvency proceedings instituted after the issue of the instrument; or

    (b) acceptance or payment is refused but not for want of proper presentment.

(4) Where a draft has been dishonored by nonacceptance a later presentment for payment and any notice of dishonor and protest for nonpayment are excused unless in the meantime the instrument has been accepted.

(5) A waiver of protest is also a waiver of presentment and of notice of dishonor even though protest is not required.

(6) Where a waiver of presentment or notice or protest is embodied in the instrument itself it is binding upon all parties; but where it is written above the signature of an indorser it binds him only.

Part 6   Discharge

Section 3–601.   Discharge of Parties

(1) The extent of the discharge of any party from liability on an instrument is governed by the sections on

    (a) payment or satisfaction (Section 3–603); or

    (b) tender of payment (Section 3–604); or

    (c) cancellation or renunciation (Section 3–605); or

    (d) impairment of right of recourse or of collateral (Section 3–606); or

    (e) reacquisition of the instrument by a prior party (Section 3–208); or

    (f) fraudulent and material alteration (Section 3–407); or

    (g) certification of a check (Section 3–411); or

    (h) acceptance varying a draft (section 3–412); or

    (i) unexcused delay in presentment or notice of dishonor or protest (Section 3–502).

(2) Any party is also discharged from his liability on an instrument to another party by any other act or agreement with such party which would discharge his simple contract for the payment of money.

(3) The liability of all parties is discharged when any party who has himself no right of action or recourse on the instrument

    (a) reacquires the instrument in his own right; or

    (b) is discharged under any provision of this Article, except as otherwise provided with respect to discharge for impairment of recourse or of collateral (Section 3–606).

Section 3–602.   Effect of Discharge Against Holder in Due Course

No discharge of any party provided by this Article is effective against a subsequent holder in due course unless he has notice thereof when he takes the instrument.

Section 3–603.   Payment or Satisfaction

(1) The liability of any party is discharged to the extent of his payment or satisfaction to the holder even though it is made with knowledge of a claim of another person to the instrument unless prior to such payment or satisfaction the person making the claim either supplies indemnity deemed adequate by the party seeking the discharge or enjoins payment or satisfaction by order of a court of competent jurisdiction in an action in which the adverse claimant and the holder are parties. This subsection does not, however, result in the discharge of the liability

    (a) of a party who in bad faith pays or satisfies a holder who acquired the instrument by theft or who (unless having the rights of a holder in due course) holds through one who so acquired it; or

    (b) of a party (other than an intermediary bank or a payor bank which is not a depositary bank) who pays or satisfies the holder of an instrument which has been restrictively indorsed in a manner not consistent with the terms of such restrictive indorsement.

(2) Payment or satisfaction may be made with the consent of the holder by any person including a stran-

ger to the instrument. Surrender of the instrument to such a person gives him the rights of a transferee (Section 3–201).

Section 3–604. Tender of Payment

(1) Any party making tender of full payment to a holder when or after it is due is discharged to the extent of all subsequent liability for interest, costs and attorney's fees.

(2) The holder's refusal of such tender wholly discharges any party who has a right of recourse against the party making the tender.

(3) Where the maker or acceptor of an instrument payable otherwise than on demand is able and ready to pay at every place of payment specified in the instrument when it is due, it is equivalent to tender.

Section 3–605. Cancellation and Renunciation

(1) The holder of an instrument may even without consideration discharge any party

    (a) in any manner apparent on the face of the instrument or the indorsement, as by intentionally cancelling the instrument or the party's signature by destruction or mutilation, or by striking out the party's signature; or

    (b) by renouncing his rights by a writing signed and delivered or by surrender of the instrument to the party to be discharged.

(2) Neither cancellation nor renunciation without surrender of the instrument affects the title thereto.

Section 3–606. Impairment of Recourse or of Collateral

(1) The holder discharges any party to the instrument to the extent that without such party's consent the holder

    (a) without express reservation of rights releases or agrees not to sue any person against whom the party has to the knowledge of the holder a right of recourse or agrees to suspend the right to enforce against such person the instrument or collateral or otherwise discharges such person, except that failure or delay in effecting any required presentment, protest or notice of dishonor with respect to any such person does not discharge any party as to

whom presentment, protest or notice of dishonor is effective or unnecessary; or

    (b) unjustifiably impairs any collateral for the instrument given by or on behalf of the party or any person against whom he has a right of recourse.

(2) By express reservation of rights against a party with a right of recourse the holder preserves

    (a) all his rights against such party as of the time when the instrument was originally due; and

    (b) the right of the party to pay the instrument as of that time; and

    (c) all rights of such party to recourse against others.

Part 7 Advice of International Sight Draft

Section 3–701. Letter of Advice of International Sight Draft

(1) A "letter of advice" is a drawer's communication to the drawee that a described draft has been drawn.

(2) Unless otherwise agreed when a bank receives from another bank a letter of advice of an international sight draft the drawee bank may immediately debit the drawer's account and stop the running of interest pro tanto. Such a debit and any resulting credit to any account covering outstanding drafts leaves in the drawer full power to stop payment or otherwise dispose of the amount and creates no trust or interest in favor of the holder.

(3) Unless otherwise agreed and except where a draft is drawn under a credit issued by the drawee, the drawee of an international sight draft owes the drawer no duty to pay an unadvised draft but if it does so and the draft is genuine, may appropriately debit the drawer's account.

Part 8 Miscellaneous

Section 3–801. Drafts in a Set

(1) Where a draft is drawn in a set of parts, each of which is numbered and expressed to be an order only if no other part has been honored, the whole of the parts constitutes one draft but a taker of any part may become a holder in due course of the draft.

(2) Any person who negotiates, indorses or accepts a single part of a draft drawn in a set thereby becomes liable to any holder in due course of that part as if it

were the whole set, but as between different holders in due course to whom different parts have been negotiated the holder whose title first accrues has all rights to the draft and its proceeds.

(3) As against the drawee the first presented part of a draft drawn in a set is the part entitled to payment, or if a time draft to acceptance and payment. Acceptance of any subsequently presented part renders the drawee liable thereon under subsection (2). With respect both to a holder and to the drawer payment of a subsequently presented part of a draft payable at sight has the same effect as payment of a check notwithstanding an effective stop order (Section 4–407).

(4) Except as otherwise provided in this section, where any part of a draft in a set is discharged by payment or otherwise the whole draft is discharged.

Section 3–802. Effect of Instrument on Obligation for Which It is Given

(1) Unless otherwise agreed where an instrument is taken for an underlying obligation

    (a) the obligation is pro tanto discharged if a bank is drawer, maker or acceptor of the instrument and there is no recourse on the instrument against the underlying obligor; and

    (b) in any other case the obligation is suspended pro tanto until the instrument is due or if it is payable on demand until its presentment. If the instrument is dishonored action may be maintained on either the instrument or the obligation; discharge of the underlying obligor on the instrument also discharges him on the obligation.

(2) The taking in good faith of a check which is not postdated does not of itself so extend the time on the original obligation as to discharge a surety.

Section 3–803. Notice to Third Party

Where a defendant is sued for breach of an obligation for which a third person is answerable over under this Article he may give the third person written notice of the litigation, and the person notified may then give similar notice to any other person who is answerable over to him under this Article. If the notice states that the person notified may come in and defend and that if the person notified does not do so he will in any action against him by the person giving the notice be bound by any determination of fact common to the two litigations, then unless after seasonable receipt of the notice the person notified does come in and defend he is so bound.

Section 3–804. Lost, Destroyed or Stolen Instruments

The owner of an instrument which is lost, whether by destruction, theft or otherwise, may maintain an action in his own name and recover from any party liable thereon upon due proof of his ownership, the facts which prevent his production of the instrument and its terms. The court may require security indemnifying the defendant against loss by reason of further claims on the instrument.

Section 3–805. Instruments Not Payable to Order or to Bearer

This Article applies to any instrument whose terms do not preclude transfer and which is otherwise negotiable within this Article but which is not payable to order or to bearer, except that there can be no holder in due course of such an instrument.

ARTICLE 4 BANK DEPOSITS AND COLLECTIONS

Part 1 General Provisions and Definitions

Section 4–101. Short Title

This Article shall be known and may be cited as Uniform Commercial Code—Bank Deposits and Collections.

Section 4–102. Applicability

(1) To the extent that items within this Article are also within the scope of Articles 3 and 8, they are subject to the provisions of those Articles. In the event of conflict the provisions of this Article govern those of Article 3 but the provisions of Article 8 govern those of this Article.

(2) The liability of a bank for action or non-action with respect to any item handled by it for purposes of presentment, payment or collection is governed by the law of the place where the bank is located. In the case of action or non-action by or at a branch or separate office of a bank, its liability is governed by the law of the place where the branch or separate office is located.

Section 4–103. Variation by Agreement; Measure of Damages; Certain Action Constituting Ordinary Care

(1) The effect of the provisions of this Article may be varied by agreement except that no agreement can disclaim a bank's responsibility for its own lack of good faith or failure to exercise ordinary care or can limit the measure of damages for such lack of failure; but the parties may by agreement determine the standards by which such responsibility is to be measured if such standards are not manifestly unreasonable.

(2) Federal Reserve regulations and operating letters, clearing house rules, and the like, have the effect of agreements under subsection (1), whether or not specifically assented to by all parties interested in items handled.

(3) Action or non-action approved by this Article or pursuant to Federal Reserve regulations or operating letters constitutes the exercise of ordinary care and, in the absence of special instructions, action or non-action consistent with clearing house rules and the like or with a general banking usage not disapproved by this Article, prima facie constitutes the exercise of ordinary care.

(4) The specification or approval of certain procedures by this Article does not constitute disapproval of other procedures which may be reasonable under the circumstances.

(5) The measure of damages for failure to exercise ordinary care in handling an item is the amount of the item reduced by an amount which could not have been realized by the use of ordinary care, and where there is bad faith it includes other damages, if any, suffered by the party as a proximate consequence.

Section 4–104. Definitions and Index of Definitions

(1) In this Article unless the context otherwise requires

  (a) "Account" means any account with a bank and includes a checking, time, interest or savings account;

  (b) "Afternoon" means the period of a day between noon and midnight;

  (c) "Banking day" means that part of any day on which a bank is open to the public for carrying on substantially all of its banking functions;

  (d) "Clearing house" means any association of banks or other payor regularly clearing items;

  (e) "Customer" means any person having an account with a bank or for whom a bank has agreed to collect items and includes a bank carrying an account with another bank;

  (f) "Documentary draft" means any negotiable or non-negotiable draft with accompanying documents, securities or other papers to be delivered against honor of the draft;

  (g) "Item" means any instrument for the payment of money even though it is not negotiable but does not include money;

  (h) "Midnight deadline" with respect to a bank is midnight on its next banking day following the banking day on which it receives the relevant item or notice or from which the time for taking action commences to run, whichever is later;

  (i) "Properly payable" includes the availability of funds for payment at the time of decision to pay or dishonor;

  (j) "Settle" means to pay in cash, by clearing house settlement, in a charge or credit or by remittance, or otherwise as instructed. A settlement may be either provisional or final;

  (k) "Suspends payments" with respect to a bank means that it has been closed by order of the supervisory authorities, that a public officer has been appointed to take it over or that it ceases or refuses to make payments in the ordinary course of business.

(2) Other definitions applying to this Article and the sections in which they appear are:

  "Collecting bank." Section 4–105.
  "Depositary bank." Section 4–105.
  "Intermediary bank." Section 4–105.
  "Payor bank." Section 4–105.
  "Presenting bank." Section 4–105.
  "Remitting bank." Section 4–105.

(3) The following definitions in other Articles apply to this Article:

  "Acceptance." Section 3–410.
  "Certificate of deposit." Section 3–104.
  "Certification." Section 3–411.
  "Check." Section 3–104.
  "Draft." Section 3–104.
  "Holder in due course." Section 3–302.
  "Notice of dishonor." Section 3–508.
  "Presentment." Section 3–504.

"Secondary party." Section 3–102.

(4)   In addition Article 1 contains general definitions and principles of construction and interpretation applicable throughout this Article.

Section 4–105.   "Depositary Bank"; "Intermediary Bank"; "Collecting Bank"; "Payor Bank"; "Presenting Bank"; "Remitting Bank"

In this Article unless the context otherwise requires:

(a)   "Depositary bank" means the first bank to which an item is transferred for collection even though it is also the payor bank;

(b)   "Payor bank" means a bank by which an item is payable as drawn or accepted;

(c)   "Intermediary bank" means any bank to which an item is transferred in course of collection except the depositary or payor bank;

(d)   "Collecting bank" means any bank handling the item for collection except the payor bank;

(e)   "Presenting bank" means any bank presenting an item except a payor bank;

(f)   "Remitting bank" means any payor or intermediary bank remitting for an item.

Section 4–106.   Separate Office of a Bank

A branch or separate office of a bank [maintaining its own deposit ledgers] is a separate bank for the purpose of computing the time within which and determining the place at or to which action may be taken or notices or orders shall be given under this Article and under Article 3.

Note: *The brackets are to make it optional with the several states whether to require a branch to maintain its own deposit ledgers in order to be considered to be a separate bank for certain purposes under Article 4. In some states "maintaining its own deposit ledgers" is a satisfactory test. In others branch banking practices are such that this test would not be suitable.*

Section 4–107.   Time of Receipt of Items

(1)   For the purpose of allowing time to process items, prove balances and make the necessary entries on its books to determine its position for the day, a bank may fix an afternoon hour of 2 P.M. or later as a cut-off hour for the handling of money and items and the making of entries on its books.

(2)   Any item or deposit of money received on any day after a cut-off hour so fixed or after the close of the banking day may be treated as being received at the opening of the next banking day.

Section 4–108.   Delays

(1)   Unless otherwise instructed, a collecting bank in a good faith effort to secure payment may, in the case of specific items and with or without the approval of any person involved, waive, modify or extend time limits imposed or permitted by this Act for a period not in excess of an additional banking day without discharge of secondary parties and without liability to its transferor or any prior party.

(2)   Delay by a collecting bank or payor bank beyond time limits prescribed or permitted by this Act or by instructions is excused if caused by interruption of communication facilities, suspension of payments by another bank, war, emergency conditions or other circumstances beyond the control of the bank provided it exercises such diligence as the circumstances require.

Section 4–109.   Process of Posting

The "process of posting" means the usual procedure followed by a payor bank in determining to pay an item and in recording the payment including one or more of the following or other steps as determined by the bank:

(a)   verification of any signature;

(b)   ascertaining that sufficient funds are available;

(c)   affixing a "paid" or other stamp;

(d)   entering a charge or entry to a customer's account;

(e)   correcting or reversing an entry or erroneous action with respect to the item.

Part 2   Collection of Items: Depositary and Collecting Banks

Section 4–201.   Presumption and Duration of Agency Status of Collecting Banks and Provisional Status of Credits; Applicability of Article; Item Indorsed "Pay Any Bank"

(1)   Unless a contrary intent clearly appears and prior to the time that a settlement given by a collecting bank for an item is or becomes final (subsection (3) of Section 4–211 and Sections 4–212 and 4–213) the bank is an agent or sub-agent of the owner of the item and any settlement given for the item is provisional. This provi-

sion applies regardless of the form of indorsement or lack of indorsement and even though credit given for the item is subject to immediate withdrawal as of right or is in fact withdrawn; but the continuance of ownership of an item by its owner and any rights of the owner to proceeds of the item are subject to rights of a collecting bank such as those resulting from outstanding advances on the item and valid rights of set-off. When an item is handled by banks for purposes of presentment, payment and collection, the relevant provisions of this Article apply even though action of parties clearly establishes that a particular bank has purchased the item and is the owner of it.

(2)   After an item has been indorsed with the words "pay any bank" or the like, only a bank may acquire the rights of a holder

(a)   until the item has been returned to the customer initiating collection; or

(b)   until the item has been specially indorsed by a bank to a person who is not a bank.

Section 4–202.   Responsibility for Collection; When Action Seasonable

(1)   A collecting bank must use ordinary care in

(a)   presenting an item or sending it for presentment; and

(b)   sending notice of dishonor or non-payment or returning an item other than a documentary draft to the bank's transferor [or directly to the depositary bank under subsection (2) of Secton 4–212] (*See note to Section 4–212*) after learning that the item has not been paid or accepted, as the case may be; and

(c)   settling for an item when the bank receives final settlement; and

(d)   making or providing for any necessary protest; and

(e)   notifying its transferor of any loss or delay in transit within a reasonable time after discovery thereof.

(2)   A collecting bank taking proper action before its midnight deadline following receipt of an item, notice or payment acts seasonably; taking proper action within a reasonably longer time may be seasonable but the bank has the burden of so establishing.

(3)   Subject to subsection (1) (a), a bank is not liable for the insolvency, neglect, misconduct, mistake or default of another bank or person or for loss or destruction of an item in transit or in the possession of others.

Section 4–203.   Effect of Instructions

Subject to the provisions of Article 3 concerning conversion of instruments (Section 3–419) and the provisions of both Article 3 and this Article concerning restrictive indorsements only a collecting bank's transferor can give instructions which affect the bank or constitute notice to it and a collecting bank is not liable to prior parties for any action taken pursuant to such instructions or in accordance with any agreement with its transferor.

Section 4–204.   Methods of Sending and Presenting; Sending Direct to Payor Bank

(1)   A collecting bank must send items by reasonably prompt method taking into consideration any relevant instructions, the nature of the item, the number of such items on hand, and the cost of collection involved and the method generally used by it or others to present such items.

(2)   A collecting bank may send

(a)   any item direct to the payor bank;

(b)   any item to any non-bank payor if authorized by its transferor; and

(c)   any item other than documentary drafts to any non-bank payor, if authorized by Federal Reserve regulation or operating letter, clearing house rule or the like.

(3)   Presentment may be made by a presenting bank at a place where the payor bank has requested that presentment be made.

Section 4–205.   Supplying Missing Indorsement; No Notice from Prior Indorsement

(1)   A depositary bank which has taken an item for collection may supply any indorsement of the customer which is necessary to title unless the item contains the words "payee's indorsement required" or the like. In the absence of such a requirement a statement placed on the item by the depositary bank to the effect that the item was deposited by a customer or credited to his account is effective as the customer's indorsement.

(2)   An intermediary bank, or payor bank which is not a depositary bank, is neither given notice nor otherwise affected by a restrictive indorsement of any person except the bank's immediate transferor.

Section 4–206.   Transfer Between Banks

Any agreed method which identifies the transferor bank is sufficient for the item's further transfer to another bank.

Section 4–207. Warranties of Customer and Collecting Bank on Transfer or Presentment of Items; Time for Claims

(1) Each customer or collecting bank who obtains payment or acceptance of an item and each prior customer and collecting bank warrants to the payor bank or other payor who in good faith pays or accepts the item that

    (a) he has a good title to the item or is authorized to obtain payment or acceptance on behalf of one who has a good title; and

    (b) he had no knowledge that the signature of the maker or drawer is unauthorized, except that this warranty is not given by any customer or collecting bank that is a holder in due course and acts in good faith

        (i) to a maker with respect to the maker's own signature; or

        (ii) to a drawer with respect to the drawer's own signature, whether or not the drawer is also the drawee; or

        (iii) to an acceptor of an item if the holder in due course took the item after the acceptance or obtained the acceptance without knowledge that the drawer's signature was unauthorized; and

    (c) the item has not been materially altered, except that this warranty is not given by any customer or collecting bank that is a holder in due course and acts in good faith

        (i) to the maker of a note; or

        (ii) to the drawer of a draft whether or not the drawer is also the drawee; or

        (iii) to the acceptor of an item with respect to an alteration made prior to the acceptance if the holder in due course took the item after the acceptance, even though the acceptance provided "payable as originally drawn" or equivalent terms; or

        (iv) to the acceptor of an item with respect to an alteration made after the acceptance.

(2) Each customer and collecting bank who transfers an item and receives a settlement or other consideration for it warrants to his transferee and to any subsequent collecting bank who takes the item in good faith that

    (a) he has a good title to the item or is authorized to obtain payment or acceptance on behalf of one who has a good title and the transfer is otherwise rightful; and

    (b) all signatures are genuine or authorized; and

    (c) the item has not been materially altered; and

    (d) no defense of any party is good against him; and

    (e) he has no knowledge of any insolvency proceeding instituted with respect to the maker or acceptor or the drawer of an unaccepted item.

In addition each customer and collecting bank so transferring an item and receiving a settlement or other consideration engages that upon dishonor and any necessary notice of dishonor and protest he will take up the item.

(3) The warranties and the engagement to honor set forth in the two preceding subsections arise notwithstanding the absence of indorsement or words of guaranty or warranty in the transfer or presentment and a collecting bank remains liable for their breach despite remittance to its transferor. Damages for breach of such warranties or engagement to honor shall not exceed the consideration received by the customer or collecting bank responsible plus finance charges and expenses related to the item, if any.

(4) Unless a claim for breach of warranty under this section is made within a reasonable time after the person claiming learns of the breach, the person liable is discharged to the extent of any loss caused by the delay in making claim.

Section 4–208. Security Interest of Collecting Bank in Items, Accompanying Documents and Proceeds

(1) A bank has a security interest in an item and any accompanying documents or the proceeds of either

    (a) in case of an item deposited in an account to the extent to which credit given for the item has been withdrawn or applied;

    (b) in case of an item for which it has given credit available for withdrawal as of right, to the extent of the credit given whether or not the credit is drawn upon and whether or not there is a right of charge-back; or

    (c) if it makes an advance on or against the item.

(2) When credit which has been given for several items received at one time or pursuant to a single agreement is withdrawn or applied in part the security interest remains upon all the items, any accompanying

53

documents or the proceeds of either. For the purpose of this section, credits first given are first withdrawn.

(3)   Receipt by a collecting bank of a final settlement for an item is a realization on its security interest in the item, accompanying documents and proceeds. To the extent and so long as the bank does not receive final settlement for the item or give up possession of the item or accompanying documents for purposes other than collection, the security interest continues and is subject to the provisions of Article 9 except that

(a)   no security agreement is necessary to make the security interest enforceable (subsection (1) (a) of Section 9–203); and

(b)   no filing is required to perfect the security interest; and

(c)   the security interest has priority over conflicting perfected security interests in the item, accompanying documents or proceeds.

Section 4–209.   When Bank Gives Value for Purposes of Holder in Due Course

For purposes of determining its status as a holder in due course, the bank has given value to the extent that it has a security interest in an item provided that the bank otherwise complies with the requirements of Section 3–302 on what constitutes a holder in due course.

Section 4–210.   Presentment by Notice of Item Not Payable by, Through or at a Bank; Liability of Secondary Parties

(1)   Unless otherwise instructed, a collecting bank may present an item not payable by, through or at a bank by sending to the party to accept or pay a written notice that the bank holds the item for acceptance or payment. The notice must be sent in time to be received on or before the day when presentment is due and the bank must meet any requirement of the party to accept or pay under Section 3–505 by the close of the bank's next banking day after it knows of the requirement.

(2)   Where presentment is made by notice and neither honor nor request for compliance with a requirement under Section 3–505 is received by the close of business on the day after maturity or in the case of demand items by the close of business on the third banking day after notice was sent, the presenting bank may treat the item as dishonored and charge any secondary party by sending him notice of the facts.

54

Section 4–211.   Media of Remittance; Provisional and Final Settlement in Remittance Cases

(1)   A collecting bank may take in settlement of an item

(a)   a check of the remitting bank or of another bank on any bank except the remitting bank; or

(b)   a cashier's check or similar primary obligation of a remitting bank which is a member of or clears through a member of the same clearing house or group as the collecting bank; or

(c)   appropriate authority to charge an account of the remitting bank or of another bank with the collecting bank; or

(d)   if the item is drawn upon or payable by a person other than a bank, a cashier's check, certified check or other bank check or obligation.

(2)   If before its midnight deadline the collecting bank properly dishonors a remittance check or authorization to charge on itself or presents or forwards for collection a remittance instrument of or on another bank which is of a kind approved by subsection (1) or has not been authorized by it, the collecting bank is not liable to prior parties in the event of the dishonor of such check, instrument or authorization.

(3)   A settlement for an item by means of a remittance instrument or authorization to charge is or becomes a final settlement as to both the person making and the person receiving the settlement

(a)   if the remittance instrument or authorization to charge is of a kind approved by subsection (1) or has not been authorized by the person receiving the settlement and in either case the person receiving the settlement acts seasonably before its midnight deadline in presenting, forwarding for collection or paying the instrument or authorization,—at the time the remittance instrument or authorization is finally paid by the payor by which it is payable;

(b)   if the person receiving the settlement has authorized remittance by a non-bank check or obligation or by a cashier's check or similar primary obligation of or a check upon the payor or other remitting bank which is not of a kind approved by subsection (1) (b),—at the time of the receipt of such remittance check or obligation; or

(c)   if in a case not covered by sub-paragraphs (a)

or (b) the person receiving the settlement fails to seasonably present, forward for collection, pay or return a remittance instrument or authorization to it to charge before its midnight deadline,—at such midnight deadline.

Section 4–212. Right of Charge-Back or Refund

(1) If a collecting bank has made provisional settlement with its customer for an item and itself fails by reason of dishonor, suspension of payments by a bank or otherwise to receive a settlement for the item which is or becomes final, the bank may revoke the settlement given by it, charge back the amount of any credit given for the item to its customers' account or obtain refund from its customer whether or not it is able to return the items if by its midnight deadline or within a longer reasonable time after it learns the facts it returns the item or sends notification of the facts. These rights to revoke, charge-back and obtain refund terminate if and when a settlement for the item received by the bank is or becomes final (subsection (3) of Section 4–211 and subsections (2) and (3) of Section 4–213).

[(2) Within the time and manner prescribed by this section and Section 4–301, and intermediary or payor bank, as the case may be, may return an unpaid item directly to the depositary bank and may send for collection a draft on the depositary bank and obtain reimbursement. In such case, if the depositary bank has received provisional settlement for the item, it must reimburse the bank drawing the draft and any provisional credits for the item between banks shall become and remain final.]

Note: *Direct returns is recognized as an innovation that is not yet established bank practice, and therefore. Paragraph 2 has been bracketed. Some lawyers have doubts whether it should be included in legislation or left to development by agreement.*

(3) A depositary bank which is also the payor may charge-back the amount of an item to its customer's account or obtain refund in accordance with the section governing return of an item received by a payor bank for credit on its books (Section 4–301).

(4) The right to charge-back is not affected by

    (a) prior use of the credit given for the item; or

    (b) failure by any bank to exercise ordinary care with respect to the item but any bank so failing remains liable.

(5) A failure to charge-back or claim refund does not affect other rights of the bank against the customer or any other party.

(6) If credit is given in dollars as the equivalent of the value of an item payable in a foreign currency the dollar amount of any charge-back or refund shall be calculated on the basis of the buying sight rate for the foreign currency prevailing on the day when the person entitled to the charge-back or refund learns that it will not receive payment in ordinary course.

Section 4–213. Final Payment of Item by Payor Bank; When Provisional Debits and Credits Become Final; When Certain Credits Become Available for Withdrawal

(1) An item is finally paid by a payor bank when the bank has done any of the following, whichever happens first:

    (a) paid the item in cash; or

    (b) settled for the item without reserving a right to revoke the settlement and without having such right under statute, clearing house rule or agreement; or

    (c) completed the process of posting the item to the indicated account of the drawer, maker or other person to be charged therewith; or

    (d) made a provisional settlement for the item and failed to revoke the settlement in the time and manner permitted by statute, clearing house rule or agreement.

Upon a final payment under subparagraphs (b), (c) or (d) the payor bank shall be accountable for the amount of the item.

(2) If provisional settlement for an item between the presenting and payor banks is made through a clearing house or by debits or credits in an account between them, then to the extent that provisional debits or credits for the item are entered in accounts between the presenting and payor banks or between the presenting and successive prior collecting banks seriatim, they become final upon final payment of the item by the payor bank.

(3) If a collecting bank receives a settlement for an item which is or becomes final (subsection (3) of Section 4–211, subsection (2) of Section 4–213) the bank is accountable to its customer for the amount of the item and any provisional credit given for the item in an account with its customer becomes final.

(4) Subject to any right of the bank to apply the credit to an obligation of the customer, credit given by a bank for an item in an account with its customer becomes available for withdrawal as of right

(a) in any case where the bank has received a provisional settlement for the item,—when such settlement becomes final and the bank has had a reasonable time to learn that the settlement is final;

(b) in any case where the bank is both a depositary bank and a payor bank and the item is finally paid,—at the opening of the bank's second banking day following receipt of the item.

(5) A deposit of money in a bank is final when made but, subject to any right of the bank to apply the deposit to an obligation of the customer, the deposit becomes available for withdrawal as of right at the opening of the bank's next banking day following receipt of the deposit.

Section 4–214. Insolvency and Preference

(1) Any item in or coming into the possession of a payor or collecting bank which suspends payment and which item is not finally paid shall be returned by the receiver, trustee or agent in charge of the closed bank to the presenting bank or the closed bank's customer.

(2) If a payor bank finally pays an item and suspends payments without making a settlement for the item with its customer or the presenting bank which settlement is or becomes final, the owner of the item has a preferred claim against the payor bank.

(3) If a payor bank gives or a collecting bank gives or receives a provisional settlement for an item and thereafter suspends payments, the suspension does not prevent or interfere with the settlement becoming final if such finality occurs automatically upon the lapse of certain time or the happening of certain events (subsection (3) of Section 4–211, subsections (1) (d), (2) and (3) of Section 4–213).

(4) If a collecting bank receives from subsequent parties settlement for an item which settlement is or becomes final and suspends payments without making a settlement for the item with its customer which is or becomes final, the owner of the item has a preferred claim against such collecting bank.

Part 3 Collection of Items; Payor Banks

Section 4–301. Deferred Posting; Recovery of Payment by Return of Items; Time of Dishonor

(1) Where an authorized settlement for a demand item (other than a documentary draft) received by a payor bank otherwise than for immediate payment over the counter has been made before midnight of the banking day of receipt the payor bank may revoke the settlement and recover any payment if before it has made final payment (subsection (1) of Section 4–213) and before its midnight deadline it

(a) returns the item; or

(b) sends written notice of dishonor or nonpayment if the item is held for protest or is otherwise unavailable for return.

(2) If a demand item is received by a payor bank for credit on its books it may return such item or send notice of dishonor and may revoke any credit given or recover the amount thereof withdrawn by its customer, if it acts within the time limit and in the manner specified in the preceding subsection.

(3) Unless previous notice of dishonor has been sent an item is dishonored at the time when for purposes of dishonor it is returned or notice sent in accordance with this section.

(4) An item is returned:

(a) as to an item received through a clearing house, when it is delivered to the presenting or last collecting bank or to the clearing house or is sent or delivered in accordance with its rules; or

(b) in all other cases, when it is sent or delivered to the bank's customer or transferor or pursuant to his instructions.

Section 4–302. Payor Banks' Responsibility for Late Return of Item

In the absence of a valid defense such as breach of a presentment warranty (subsection (1) of Section 4–207), settlement effected or the like, if an item is presented on and received by a payor bank the bank is accountable for the amount of

(a) a demand item other than a documentary draft whether properly payable or not if the bank, in any case where it is not also the depositary bank, retains the item beyond midnight of the banking day of receipt without settling for it or, regardless of whether it is also the depositary bank, does not pay or return the item or send notice of dishonor until after its midnight deadline, or

(b) any other properly payable item unless within the time allowed for acceptance or payment of that item the bank either accepts or pays the item or returns it and accompanying documents.

Section 4–303. When Items Subject to Notice, Stop-Order, Legal Process or Setoff; Order in Which Items May Be Charged or Certified

(1) Any knowledge, notice or stop-order received by, legal process served upon or setoff exercised by a payor bank, whether or not effective under other rules of law to terminate, suspend or modify the bank's right or duty to pay an item or to charge its customer's account for the item, comes too late to so terminate, suspend or modify such right or duty if the knowledge, notice, stop-order or legal process is received or served and a reasonable time for the bank to act thereon expires or the setoff is exercised after the bank has done any of the following:

(a) accepted or certified the item;

(b) paid the item in cash;

(c) settled for the item without reserving a right to revoke the settlement and without having such right under statute, clearing house rule or agreement;

(d) completed the process of posting the item to the indicated account of the drawer, maker or other person to be charged therewith or otherwise has evidenced by examination of such indicated account and by action its decision to pay the item; or

(e) become accountable for the amount of the item under subsection (1) (d) of Section 4–213 and Section 4–302 dealing with the payor bank's responsibility for late return of items.

(2) Subject to the provisions of subsection (1) items may be accepted, paid, certified or charged to the indicated account of its customer in any order convenient to the bank.

Part 4 Relationship Between Payor Bank and Its Customer

Section 4–401. When Bank May Charge Customer's Account

(1) As against its customer, a bank may charge against his account any item which is otherwise properly payable from that account even though the charge creates an overdraft.

(2) A bank which in good faith makes payment to a holder may charge the indicated account of its customer according to

(a) the original tenor of his altered item; or

(b) the tenor of his completed item, even though the bank knows the item has been completed unless the bank has notice that the completion was improper.

Section 4–402. Bank's Liability to Customer for Wrongful Dishonor

A payor bank is liable to its customer for damages proximately caused by the wrongful dishonor of an item. When the dishonor occurs through mistake liability is limited to actual damages proved. If so proximately caused and proved damages may include damages for an arrest or prosecution of the customer or other consequential damages. Whether any consequential damages are proximately caused by the wrongful dishonor is a question of fact to be determined in each case.

Section 4–403. Customer's Right to Stop Payment; Burden of Proof of Loss

(1) A customer may by order to his bank stop payment of any item payable for his account but the order must be received at such time and in such manner as to afford the bank a reasonable opportunity to act on it prior to any action by the bank with respect to the item described in Section 4–303.

(2) An oral order is binding upon the bank only for fourteen calendar days unless confirmed in writing within that period. A written order is effective for only six months unless renewed in writing.

(3) The burden of establishing the fact and amount of loss resulting from the payment of an item contrary to a binding stop payment order is on the customer.

Section 4–404. Bank Not Obligated to Pay Check More Than Six Months Old

A bank is under no obligation to a customer having a checking account to pay a check, other than a certified check, which is presented more than six months after its date, but it may charge its customer's account for a payment made thereafter in good faith.

Section 4–405. Death or Incompetence of Customer

(1) A payor or collecting bank's authority to accept, pay or collect an item or to account for proceeds of its collection if otherwise effective is not rendered ineffective by incompetence of a customer of either bank existing at the time the item is issued or its collection is undertaken if the bank does not know of an adjudication of incompetence. Neither death nor incompetence

of a customer revokes such authority to accept, pay, collect or account until the bank knows of the fact of death or of an adjudication of incompetence and has reasonable opportunity to act on it.

(2)   Even with knowledge a bank may for 10 days after the date of death pay or certify checks drawn on or prior to that date unless ordered to stop payment by a person claiming an interest in the account.

Section 4–406.   Customer's Duty to Discover and Report Unauthorized Signature or Alteration

(1)   When a bank sends to its customer a statement of account accompanied by items paid in good faith in support of the debit entries or holds the statement and items pursuant to a request or instructions of its customer or otherwise in a reasonable manner makes the statement and items available to the customer, the customer must exercise reasonable care and promptness to examine the statement and items to discover his unauthorized signature or any alteration on an item and must notify the bank promptly after discovery thereof.

(2)   If the bank establishes that the customer failed with respect to an item to comply with the duties imposed on the customer by subsection (1) the customer is precluded from asserting against the bank

(a)   his unauthorized signature or any alteration on the item if the bank also establishes that it suffered a loss by reason of such failure; and

(b)   an unauthorized signature or alteration by the same wrongdoer or any other item paid in good faith by the bank after the first item and statement was available to the customer for a reasonable period not exceeding fourteen calendar days and before the bank receives notification from the customer of any such unauthorized signature or alteration.

(3)   The preclusion under subsection (2) does not apply if the customer establishes lack of ordinary care on the part of the bank in paying the item(s).

(4)   Without regard to care or lack of care of either the customer or the bank a customer who does not within one year from the time the statement and items are made available to the customer (subsection (1)) discover and report his unauthorized signature or any alteration on the face or back of the item or does not within 3 years from that time discover and report any unauthorized indorsement is precluded from asserting

against the bank such unauthorized signature or indorsement or such alteration.

(5)   If under this section a payor bank has a valid defense against a claim of a customer upon or resulting from payment of an item and waives or fails upon request to assert the defense the bank may not assert against any collecting bank or other prior party presenting or transferring the item a claim based upon the unauthorized signature or alteration giving rise to the customer's claim.

Section 4–407.   Payor Bank's Right to Subrogation on Improper Payment

If a payor bank has paid an item over the stop payment order of the drawer or maker or otherwise under circumstances giving a basis for objection by the drawer or maker, to prevent unjust enrichment and only to the extent necessary to prevent loss to the bank by reason of its payment of the item, the payor bank shall be subrogated to the rights

(a)   of any holder in due course on the item against the drawer or maker; and

(b)   of the payee or any other holder of the item against the drawer or maker either on the item or under the transaction out of whch the item arose; and

(c)   of the drawer or maker against the payee or any other holder of the item with respect to the transaction out of which the item arose.

Part 5   Collection of Documentary Drafts

Section 4–501.   Handling of Documentary Drafts; Duty to Send for Presentment and to Notify Customer of Dishonor

A bank which takes a documentary draft for collection must present or send the draft and accompanying documents for presentment and upon learning that the draft has not been paid or accepted in due course must seasonably notify its customer of such fact even though it may have discounted or bought the draft or extended credit available for withdrawal as of right.

Section 4–502.   Presentment of "On Arrival" Drafts

When a draft or the relevant instructions require presentment "on arrival," "when goods arrive" or the like, the collecting bank need not present until in its judgment a reasonable time for arrival of the goods has expired. Refusal to pay or accept because the goods have not arrived is not dishonor; the bank must notify its transferor of such refusal but need not present the draft again until it is instructed to do so or learns of the arrival of the goods.

Section 4–503. Responsibility of Presenting Bank for Documents and Goods; Report of Reasons for Dishonor; Referee in Case of Need

Unless otherwise instructed and except as provided in Article 5 a bank presenting a documentary draft

(a) must deliver the documents to the drawee on acceptance of the draft if it is payable more than three days after presentment; otherwise, only on payment; and

(b) upon dishonor, either in the case of presentment for acceptance or presentment for payment, may seek and follow instructions from any referee in case of need designated in the draft or if the presenting bank does not choose to utilize his services it must use diligence and good faith to ascertain the reason for dishonor, must notify its transferor of the dishonor and of the results of its effort to ascertain the reasons therefor and must request instructions.

But the presenting bank is under no obligation with respect to goods represented by the documents except to follow any reasonable instructions seasonably received; it has a right to reimbursement for any expense incurred in following instructions and to prepayment of or indemnity for such expenses.

Section 4–504. Privilege of Presenting Bank to Deal With Goods; Security Interest for Expenses

(1) A presenting bank which, following the dishonor of a documentary draft, has seasonably requested instructions but does not receive them within a reasonable time may store, sell, or otherwise deal with the goods in any reasonable manner.

(2) For its reasonable expenses incurred by action under subsection (1) the presenting bank has a lien upon the goods or their proceeds, which may be foreclosed in the same manner as an unpaid seller's lien.

ARTICLE 5   LETTERS OF CREDIT

Section 5–101.   Short Title

This Article shall be known and may be cited as Uniform Commercial Code—Letters of Credit.

Section 5–102.   Scope

(1) This Article applies

(a) to a credit issued by a bank if the credit requires a documentary draft or a documentary demand for payment; and

(b) to a credit issued by a person other than a bank if the credit requires that the draft or demand for payment be accompanied by a document of title; and

(c) to a credit issued by a bank or other person if the credit is not within subparagraphs (a) or (b) but conspicuously states that it is a letter of credit or is conspicuously so entitled.

(2) Unless the engagement meets the requirements of subsection (1), this Article does not apply to engagements to make advanced or to honor drafts or demands for payment, to authorities to pay or purchase, to guarantees or to general agreements.

(3) This Article deals with some but not all of the rules and concepts of letters of credit as such rules or concepts have developed prior to this act or may hereafter develop. The fact that this Article states a rule does not by itself require, imply or negate application of the same or a converse rule to a situation not provided for or to a person not specified by this Article.

Section 5–103.   Definitions

(1) In this Article unless the context otherwise requires

(a) "Credit" or "letter of credit" means an engagement by a bank or other person made at the request of a customer and of a kind within the scope of this Article (Section 5–102) that the issuer will honor drafts or other demands for payment upon compliance with the conditions specified in the credit. A credit may be either revocable or irrevocable. The engagement may be either an agreement to honor or a statement that the bank or other person is authorized to honor.

(b) A "documentary draft" or a "documentary demand for payment" is one honor of which is conditioned upon the presentation of a document or documents. "Document" means any paper including document of title, security, invoice, certificate, notice of default and the like.

59

(c) An "issuer" is a bank or other person issuing a credit.

(d) A "beneficiary" of a credit is a person who is entitled under its terms to draw or demand payment.

(e) An "advising bank" is a bank which gives notification of the issuance of a credit by another bank.

(f) A "confirming bank" is a bank which engages either that it will itself honor a credit already issued by another bank or that such a credit will be honored by the issuer or a third bank.

(g) A "customer" is a buyer or other person who causes an issuer to issue a credit. The term also includes a bank which procures issuance or confirmation on behalf of that bank's customer.

(2) Other definitions applying to this Article and the sections in which they appear are:

"Notation of Credit." Section 5–108.
"Presenter." Section 5–112(3).

(3) Definitions in other Articles applying to this Article and the sections in which they appear are:

"Accept" or "Acceptance." Section 3–410.
"Contract for sale." Section 2–106.
"Draft." Section 3–104.
"Holder in due course." Section 3–302.
"Midnight deadline." Section 4–104.
"Security." Section 8–102.

(4) In addition, Article 1 contains general definitions and principles of construction and interpretation applicable throughout this Article.

Section 5–104. Formal Requirements; Signing

(1) Except as otherwise required in subsection (1) (c) of Section 5–102 on scope, no particular form of phrasing is required for a credit. A credit must be in writing and signed by the issuer and a confirmation must be in writing and signed by the confirming bank. A modification of the terms of a credit or confirmation must be signed by the issuer or confirming bank.

(2) A telegram may be a sufficient signed writing if it identifies its sender by an authorized authentication. The authentication may be in code and the authorized naming of the issuer in an advice of credit is a sufficient signing.

Section 5–105. Consideration

No consideration is necessary to establish a credit or to enlarge or otherwise modify its terms.

Section 5–106. Time and Effect of Establishment of Credit

(1) Unless otherwise agreed a credit is established

(a) as regards the customer as soon as a letter of credit is sent to him or the letter of credit or an authorized written advice of its issuance is sent to the beneficiary; and

(b) as regards the beneficiary when he receives a letter of credit or an authorized written advice of its issuance.

(2) Unless otherwise agreed once an irrevocable credit is established as regards the customer it can be modified or revoked only with the consent of the customer and once it is established as regards the beneficiary it can be modified or revoked only with his consent.

(3) Unless otherwise agreed after a revocable credit is established it may be modified or revoked by the issuer without notice to or consent from the customer or beneficiary.

(4) Notwithstanding any modification or revocation of a revocable credit any person authorized to honor or negotiate under the terms of the original credit is entitled to reimbursement for or honor of any draft or demand for payment duly honored or negotiated before receipt of notice of the modification or revocation and the issuer in turn is entitled to reimbursement from its customer.

Section 5–107. Advice of Credit; Confirmation; Error in Statement of Terms

(1) Unless otherwise specified an advising bank by advising a credit issued by another bank does not assume any obligation to honor drafts drawn or demands for payment made under the credit but it does assume obligation for the accuracy of its own statement.

(2) A confirming bank by confirming a credit becomes directly obligated on the credit to the extent of its confirmation as though it were its issuer and acquires the rights of an issuer.

(3) Even though an advising bank incorrectly advises the terms of a credit it has been authorized to advise the credit is established as against the issuer to the extent of its original terms.

(4) Unless otherwise specified the customer bears as against the issuer all risks of transmission and reasona-

ble translation or interpretation of any message relating to a credit.

Section 5–108. "Notation Credit"; Exhaustion of Credit

(1) A credit which specifies that any person purchasing or paying drafts drawn or demands for payment made under it must note the amount of the draft or demand on the letter or advice of credit is a "notation credit."

(2) Under a notation credit

    (a) a person paying the beneficiary or purchasing a draft or demand for payment from him acquires a right to honor only if the appropriate notation is made and by transferring or forwarding for honor the documents under the credit such a person warrants to the issuer that the notation has been made; and

    (b) unless the credit or a signed statement that an appropriate notation has been made accompanies the draft or demand for payment the issuer may delay honor until evidence of notation has been procured which is satisfactory to it but its obligation and that of its customer continue for a reasonable time not exceeding thirty days to obtain such evidence.

(3) If the credit is not a notation credit

    (a) the issuer may honor complying drafts or demands for payment presented to it in the order in which they are presented and is discharged pro tanto by honor of any such draft or demand;

    (b) as between competing good faith purchasers of complying drafts or demands the person first purchasing has priority over a subsequent purchaser even though the later purchased draft or demand has been first honored.

Section 5–109. Issuer's Obligation to Its Customer

(1) An issuer's obligation to its customer includes good faith and observance of any general banking usage but unless otherwise agreed does not include liability or responsibility

    (a) for performance of the underlying contract for sale or other transaction between the customer and the beneficiary; or

    (b) for any act or omission of any person other than itself or its own branch or for loss or de-

struction of a draft, demand or document in transit or in the possession of others; or

    (c) based on knowledge or lack of knowledge of any usage of any particular trade.

(2) An issuer must examine documents with care so as to ascertain that on their face they appear to comply with the terms of the credit but unless otherwise agreed assumes no liability of responsibility for the genuineness, falsification or effect of any document which appears on such examination to be regular on its face.

(3) A non-bank issuer is not bound by any banking usage of which it has no knowledge.

Section 5–110. Availability of Credit in Portions; Presenter's Reservation of Lien or Claim

(1) Unless otherwise specified a credit may be used in portions in the discretion of the beneficiary.

(2) Unless otherwise specified a person by presenting a documentary draft or demand for payment under a credit relinquishes upon its honor all claims to the documents and a person by transferring such draft or demand or causing such presentment authorizes such relinquishment. An explicit reservation of claim makes the draft or demand non-complying.

Section 5–111. Warranties on Transfer and Presentment

(1) Unless otherwise agreed the beneficiary by transferring or presenting a documentary draft or demand for payment warrants to all interested parties that the necessary conditions of the credit have been complied with. This is in addition to any warranties arising under Articles 3, 4, 7 and 8.

(2) Unless otherwise agreed a negotiating, advising, confirming, collecting or issuing bank presenting or transferring a draft or demand for payment under a credit warrants only the matters warranted by a collecting bank under Article 4 and any such bank transferring a document warrants only the matters warranted by an intermediary under Articles 7 and 8.

Section 5–112. Time Allowed for Honor or Rejection; Withholding Honor or Rejection by Consent; "Presenter"

(1) A bank to which a documentary draft or demand for payment is presented under a credit may without dishonor of the draft, demand or credit

(a) defer honor until the close of the third banking day following receipt of the documents; and

(b) further defer honor if the presenter has expressly or impliedly consented thereto.

Failure to honor within the time here specified constitutes dishonor of the draft or demand and of the credit [except as otherwise provided in subsection (4) of Section 5–114 on conditional payment].

Note: *The bracketed language in the last sentence of subsection (1) should be included only if the optional provisions of Section 5–114(4) and (5) are included.*

(2) Upon dishonor the bank may unless otherwise instructed fulfill its duty to return the draft or demand and the documents by holding them at the disposal of the presenter and sending him an advice to that effect.

(3) "Presenter" means any person presenting a draft or demand for payment for honor under a credit even though that person is a confirming bank or other correspondent which is acting under an issuer's authorization.

Section 5–113.   Indemnities

(1) A bank seeking to obtain (whether for itself or another) honor, negotiation or reimbursement under a credit may give an indemnity to induce such honor, negotiation or reimbursement.

(2) An indemnity agreement inducing honor, negotiation or reimbursement

(a) unless otherwise explicitly agreed applies to defects in the documents but not in the goods; and

(b) unless a longer time is explicitly agreed expires at the end of ten business days following receipt of the documents by the ultimate customer unless notice of objection is sent before such expiration date. The ultimate customer may send notice of objection to the person from whom he received the documents and any bank receiving such notice is under a duty to send notice to its transferor before its midnight deadline.

Section 5–114.   Issuer's Duty and Privilege to Honor; Right to Reimbursement

(1) An issuer must honor a draft or demand for payment which complies with the terms of the relevant credit regardless of whether the goods or documents conform to the underlying contract for sale or other contract between the customer and the beneficiary. The issuer is not excused from honor of such a draft or demand by reason of an additional general term that all documents must be satisfactory to the issuer, but an issuer may require that specified documents must be satisfactory to it.

(2) Unless otherwise agreed when documents appear on their face to comply with the terms of a credit but a required document does not in fact conform to the warranties made on negotiation or transfer of a document of title (Section 7–507) or of a certificated security (Section 8–306) or is forged or fraudulent or there is fraud in the transaction:

(a) the issuer must honor the draft or demand for payment if honor is demanded by a negotiating bank or other holder of the draft or demand which has taken the draft or demand under the credit and under circumstances which would make it a holder in due course (Section 3–302) and in an appropriate case would make it a person to whom a document of title has been duly negotiated (Section 7–502) or a bona fide purchaser of a certificated security (Section 8–302); and

(b) in all other cases as against its customer, an issuer acting in good faith may honor the draft or demand for payment despite notification from the customer of fraud, forgery or other defect not apparent on the face of the documents but a court of appropriate jurisdiction may enjoin such honor.

(3) Unless otherwise agreed an issuer which has duly honored a draft or demand for payment is entitled to immediate reimbursement of any payment made under the credit and to be put in effectively available funds not later than the day before maturity of any acceptance made under the credit.

[(4) When a credit provides for payment by the issuer on receipt of notice that the required documents are in the possession of a correspondent or other agent of the issuer

(a) any payment made on receipt of such notice is conditional; and

(b) the issuer may reject documents which do not comply with the credit if it does so within three banking days following its receipt of the documents; and

(c) in the event of such rejection, the issuer is entitled by charge back or otherwise to return of the payment made.]

[(5) In the case covered by subsection (4) failure to reject documents within the time specified in sub-paragraph (b) constitutes acceptance of the documents and makes the payment final in favor of the beneficiary.]

Note: *Subsections (4) and (5) are bracketed as optional. If they are included the bracketed language in the last sentence of Section 5–112(1) should also be included.*

Section 5–115. Remedy for Improper Dishonor or Anticipatory Repudiation

(1) When an issuer wrongfully dishonors a draft or demand for payment presented under a credit the person entitled to honor has with respect to any documents the rights of a person in the position of a seller (Section 2–707) and may recover from the issuer the face amount of the draft or demand together with incidental damages under Section 2–710 on seller's incidental damages and interest but less any amount realized by resale or other use or disposition of the subject matter of the transaction. In the event no resale or other utilization is made the documents, goods or other subject matter involved in the transaction must be turned over to the issuer on payment of judgment.

(2) When an issuer wrongfully cancels or otherwise repudiates a credit before presentment of a draft or demand for payment drawn under it the beneficiary has the rights of a seller after anticipatory repudiation by the buyer under Section 2–610 if he learns of the repudiation in time reasonably to avoid procurement of the required documents. Otherwise the beneficiary has an immediate right of action for wrongful dishonor.

Section 5–116. Transfer and Assignment

(1) The right to draw under a credit can be transferred or assigned only when the credit is expressly designated as transferable or assignable.

(2) Even though the credit specifically states that it is nontransferable or nonassignable the beneficiary may before performance of the conditions of the credit assign his right to proceeds. Such an assignment is an assignment of an account under Article 9 on Secured Transactions and is governed by that Article except that

    (a) the assignment is ineffective until the letter of credit or advice of credit is delivered to the assignee which delivery constitutes perfection of the security interest under Article 9; and

    (b) the issuer may honor drafts or demands for payment drawn under the credit until it receives a notification of the assignment signed by the beneficiary which reasonably identifies the credit involved in the assignment and contains a request to pay the assignee; and

    (c) after what reasonably appears to be such a notification has been received the issuer may without dishonor refuse to accept or pay even to a person otherwise entitled to honor until the letter of credit or advice of credit is exhibited to the issuer.

(3) Except where the beneficiary has effectively assigned his right to draw or his right to proceeds, nothing in this section limits his right to transfer or negotiate drafts or demands drawn under the credit.

Section 5–117. Insolvency of Bank Holding Funds for Documentary Credit

(1) Where an issuer or an advising or confirming bank or a bank which has for a customer procured issuance of a credit by another bank becomes insolvent before final payment under the credit and the credit is one to which this Article is made applicable by paragraphs (a) or (b) of Section 5–102(1) on scope, the receipt or allocation of funds or collateral to secure or meet obligations under the credit shall have the following results:

    (a) to the extent of any funds or collateral turned over after or before the insolvency as indemnity against or specifically for the purpose of payment of drafts or demands for payment drawn under the designated credit, the drafts or demands are entitled to payment in preference over depositors or other general creditors of the issuer or bank; and

    (b) on expiration of the credit or surrender of the beneficiary's rights under it unused any person who has given such funds or collateral is similarly entitled to return thereof; and

    (c) a charge to a general or current account with a bank if specifically consented to for the purpose of indemnity against or payment of drafts or demands for payment drawn under the designated credit falls under the same rules as if the funds had been drawn out in cash and then turned over with specific instructions.

(2) After honor or reimbursement under this section the customer or other person for whose account the insolvent bank has acted is entitled to receive the documents involved.

ARTICLE 6   BULK TRANSFERS

Section 6–101.   Short Title

This Article shall be known and may be cited as Uniform Commercial Code–Bulk Transfers.

Section 6–102.   "Bulk Transfers"; Transfers of Equipment; Enterprises Subject to This Article; Bulk Transfers Subject to This Article

(1)   A "bulk transfer" is any transfer in bulk and not in the ordinary course of the transferor's business of a major part of the materials, supplies, merchandise or other inventory (Section 9–109) of an enterprise subject to this Article.

(2)   A transfer of a substantial part of the equipment (Section 9–109) of such an enterprise is a bulk transfer if it is made in connection with a bulk transfer of inventory, but not otherwise.

(3)   The enterprises subject to this Article are all those whose principal business is the sale of merchandise from stock, including those who manufacture what they sell.

(4)   Except as limited by the following section all bulk transfers of goods located within this state are subject to this Article.

Section 6–103.   Transfers Excepted From This Article

The following transfers are not subject to this Article:

(1)   Those made to give security for the performance of an obligation;

(2)   General assignments for the benefit of all the creditors of the transferor, and subsequent transfers by the assignee thereunder;

(3)   Transfers in settlement or realization of a lien or other security interests;

(4)   Sales by executors, administrators, receivers, trustees in bankruptcy, or any public officer under judicial process;

(5)   Sales made in the course of judicial or administrative proceedings for the dissolution or reorganization of a corporation and of which notice is sent to the creditors of the corporation pursuant to order of the court or administrative agency;

(6)   Transfers to a person maintaining a known place of business in this State who becomes bound to pay the debts of the transferor in full and gives public notice of that fact, and who is solvent after becoming so bound;

(7)   A transfer to a new business enterprise organized to take over and continue the business, if public notice of the transaction is given and the new enterprise assumes the debts of the transferor and he receives nothing from the transaction except an interest in the new enterprise junior to the claims of creditors;

(8)   Transfers of property which is exempt from execution.

Public notice under subsection (6) or subsection (7) may be given by publishing once a week for two consecutive weeks in a newspaper of general circulation where the transferor had its principal place of business in this state an advertisement including the names and addresses of the transferor and transferee and the effective date of the transfer.

Section 6–104.   Schedule of Property, List of Creditors

(1)   Except as provided with respect to auction sales (Section 6–108), a bulk transfer subject to this Article is ineffective against any creditor of the transferor unless:

   (a)   The transferee requires the transferor to furnish a list of his existing creditors prepared as stated in this section; and

   (b)   The parties prepare a schedule of the property transferred sufficient to identify it; and

   (c)   The transferee preserves the list and schedule for six months next following the transfer and permits inspection of either or both and copying therefrom at all reasonable hours by any creditor of the transferor, or files the list and schedule in (a public office to be here identified).

(2)   The list of creditors must be signed and sworn to or affirmed by the transferor or his agent. It must contain the names and business addresses of all creditors of the transferor, with the amounts when known, and also the names of all persons who are known to the transferor to assert claims against him even though such claims are disputed. If the transferor is the obligor of an outstanding issue of bonds, debentures or the like as to which there is an indenture trustee, the list of creditors need include only the name and address of the indenture trustee and the aggregate outstanding principal amount of the issue.

(3)   Responsibility for the completeness and accuracy of the list of creditors rests on the transferor, and the transfer is not rendered ineffective by errors or omissions therein unless the transferee is shown to have had knowledge.

Section 6–105.   Notice to Creditors

In addition to the requirements of the preceding section, any bulk transfer subject to this Article except one made by auction sale (Section 6–108) is ineffective against any creditor of the transferor unless at least ten days before he takes possession of the goods or pays for them, whichever happens first, the transferee gives notice of the transfer in the manner and to the persons hereafter provided (Section 6–107).

[Section 6–106.   Application of the Proceeds

In addition to the requirements of the two preceding sections:

(1)   Upon every bulk transfer subject to this Article for which new consideration becomes payable except those made by sale at auction it is the duty of the transferee to assure that such consideration is applied so far as necessary to pay those debts of the transferor which are either shown on the list furnished by the transferor (Section 6–104) or filed in writing in the place stated in the notice (Section 6–107) within thirty days after the mailing of such notice. This duty of the transferee runs to all the holders of such debts, and may be enforced by any of them for the benefit of all.

(2)   If any of said debts are in dispute the necessary sum may be withheld from distribution until the dispute is settled or adjudicated.

(3)   If the consideration payable is not enough to pay all of the said debts in full distribution shall be made pro rata.]

Note: *This section is bracketed to indicate division of opinion as to whether or not it is a wise provision, and to suggest that this is a point on which State enactments may differ without serious damage to the principle of uniformity.*

In any State where this section is omitted, the following parts of sections, also bracketed in the text, should also be omitted, namely:
> *Section 6–107(2) (e).*
> *6–108(3) (c).*
> *6–109(2).*

In any State where this section is enacted, these other provisions should be also.

Optional Subsection (4)

[(4)   The transferee may within ten days after he takes possession of the goods pay the consideration into the (specify court) in the county where the transferor had its principal place of business in this state and thereafter may discharge his duty under this section by giving notice by registered or certified mail to all the persons to whom the duty runs that the consideration has been paid into that court and that they should file their claims there. On motion of any interested party, the court may order the distribution of the consideration to the persons entitled to it.]

Note: *Optional subsection (4) is recommended for those states which do not have a general statute providing for payment of money into court.*

Section 6–107.   The Notice

(1)   The notice to creditors (Section 6–105) shall state:

   (a)   that a bulk transfer is about to be made; and

   (b)   the names and business addresses of the transferor and transferee, and all other business names and addresses used by the transferor within three years last past so far as known to the transferee, and

   (c)   whether or not all the debts of the transferor are to be paid in full as they fall due as a result of the transaction, and if so, the address to which creditors should send their bills.

(2)   If the debts of the transferor are not to be paid in full as they fall due or if the transferee is in doubt on that point then the notice shall state further:

   (a)   the location and general description of the property to be transferred and the estimated total of the transferor's debts;

   (b)   the address where the schedule of property and list of creditors (Section 6–104) may be inspected;

   (c)   whether the transfer is to pay existing debts and if so the amount of such debts and to whom owing;

   (d)   whether the transfer is for new consideration and if so the amount of such consideration and the time and place of payment; [and]

   [(e)   if for new consideration the time and place where creditors of the transferor are to file their claims.]

(3)   The notice in any case shall be delivered personally or sent by registered or certified mail to all the persons shown on the list of creditors furnished by the transferor (Section 6–104) and to all other persons who are known to the transferee to hold or assert claims against the transferor.

Note: *The words in brackets are optional. See Note under Section 6–106.*

Section 6–108.   Auction Sales; "Auctioneer"

(1)   A bulk transfer is subject to this Article even though it is by sale at auction, but only in the manner and with the results stated in this section.

(2)   The transferor shall furnish a list of his creditors and assist in the preparation of a schedule of the property to be sold, both prepared as before stated (Section 6–104).

(3)   The person or persons other than the transferor who direct, control or are responsible for the auction are collectively called the "auctioneer." The auctioneer shall:

> (a)   receive and retain the list of creditors and prepare and retain the schedule of property for the period stated in this Article (Section 6–104);
>
> (b)   give notice of the auction personally or by registered or certified mail at least ten days before it occurs to all persons shown on the list of creditors and to all other persons who are known to him to hold or assert claims against the transferor; [and]
>
> [(c)   assure that the net proceeds of the auction are applied as provided in this Article (Section 6–106).]

(4)   Failure of the auctioneer to perform any of these duties does not affect the validity of the sale or the title of the purchasers, but if the auctioneer knows that the auction constitutes a bulk transfer such failure renders the auctioneer liable to the creditors of the transferor as a class for the sums owing to them from the transferor up to but not exceeding the net proceeds of the auction. If the auctioneer consists of several persons their liability is joint and several.

Note: *The words in brackets are optional. See Note under Section 6–106.*

Section 6–109.   What Creditors Protected; [Credit for Payment to Particular Creditors]

(1)   The creditors of the transferor mentioned in this Article are those holding claims based on transactions or events occurring before the bulk transfer, but creditors who become such after notice to creditors is given (Sections 6–105 and 6–107) are not entitled to notice.

[(2)   Against the aggregate obligation imposed by the provisions of this Article concerning the application of the proceeds (Section 6–106 and subsection (3) (c) of 6–108) the transferee or auctioneer is entitled to credit for sums paid to particular creditors of the transferor,

not exceeding the sums believed in good faith at the time of the payment to be properly payable to such creditors.]

Note: *The words in brackets are optional. See Note under Section 6–106.*

Section 6–110.   Subsequent Transfers

When the title of a transferee to property is subject to a defect by reason of his non-compliance with the requirements of this Article, then:

(1)   A purchaser of any of such property from such transferee who pays no value or who takes with notice of such non-compliance takes subject to such defect, but

(2)   A purchaser for value in good faith and without such notice takes free of such defect.

Section 6–111.   Limitation of Actions and Levies

No action under this Article shall be brought nor levy made more than six months after the date on which the transferee took possession of the goods unless the transfer has been concealed. If the transfer has been concealed, actions may be brought or levies made within six months after its discovery.

Note: *In any State where Section 6–106 is not enacted, the following parts of sections, also bracketed in the text, should also be omitted, namely:*
> *Sec. 6–107(2) (e).*
> *6–108(3) (c).*
> *6–109(2).*
>
> *In any State where Section 6–106 is enacted, these other provisions should be also.*

ARTICLE 7   WAREHOUSE RECEIPTS, BILLS OF LADING AND OTHER DOCUMENTS OF TITLE

Part 1   General

Section 7–101.   Short Title

This Article shall be known and may be cited as Uniform Commercial Code—Documents of Title.

Section 7–102.   Definitions and Index of Definitions

(1)   In this Article, unless the context otherwise requires:

> (a)   "Bailee" means the person who by a warehouse receipt, bill of lading or other document of title acknowledges possession of goods and contracts to deliver them.

(b) "Consignee" means the person named in a bill to whom or to whose order the bill promises delivery.

(c) "Consignor" means the person named in a bill as the person from whom the goods have been received for shipment.

(d) "Delivery order" means a written order to deliver goods directed to a warehouseman, carrier or other person who in the ordinary course of business issues warehouse receipts or bills of lading.

(e) "Document" means document of title as defined in the general definitions in Article 1 (Section 1–201).

(f) "Goods" means all things which are treated as movable for the purposes of a contract of storage or transportation.

(g) "Issuer" means a bailee who issues a document except that in relation to an unaccepted delivery order it means the person who orders the possessor of goods to deliver. Issuer includes any person for whom an agent or employee purports to act in issuing a document if the agent or employee has real or apparent authority to issue documents, notwithstanding that the issuer received no goods or that the goods were misdescribed or that in any other respect the agent or employee violated his instructions.

(h) "Warehouseman" is a person engaged in the business of storing goods for hire.

(2) Other definitions applying to this Article or to specified Parts thereof, and the sections in which they appear are:

"Duly negotiate." Section 7–501.

"Person entitled under the document." Section 7–403(4).

(3) Definitions in other Articles applying to this Article and the sections in which they appear are:

"Contract for sale." Section 2–106.

"Overseas." Section 2–323.

"Receipt" of goods. Section 2–103.

(4) In addition Article 1 contains general definitions and principles of construction and interpretation applicable throughout this Article.

Section 7–103. Relation of Article to Treaty, Statute, Tariff, Classification or Regulation

To the extent that any treaty or statute of the United States, regulatory statute of this State or tariff, classification or regulation filed or issued pursuant thereto is applicable, the provisions of this Article are subject thereto.

Section 7–104. Negotiable and Non-Negotiable Warehouse Receipt, Bill of Lading or Other Document of Title

(1) A warehouse receipt, bill of lading or other document of title is negotiable

(a) if by its terms the goods are to be delivered to bearer or to the order of a named person; or

(b) where recognized in overseas trade, if it runs to a named person or assigns.

(2) Any other document is non-negotiable. A bill of lading in which it is stated that the goods are consigned to a named person is not made negotiable by a provision that the goods are to be delivered only against a written order signed by the same or another named person.

Section 7–105. Construction Against Negative Implication

The omission from either Part 2 or Part 3 of this Article of a provision corresponding to a provision made in the other Part does not imply that a corresponding rule of law is not applicable.

Part 2 Warehouse Receipts: Special Provisions

Section 7–201. Who May Issue a Warehouse Receipt; Storage Under Government Bond

(1) A warehouse receipt may be issued by any warehouseman.

(2) Where goods including distilled spirits and agricultural commodities are stored under a statute requiring a bond against withdrawal or a license for the issuance of receipts in the nature of warehouse receipts, a receipt issued for the goods has like effect as a warehouse receipt even though issued by a person who is the owner of the goods and is not a warehouseman.

Section 7–202. Form of Warehouse Receipt; Essential Terms; Optional Terms

(1) A warehouse receipt need not be in any particular form.

(2) Unless a warehouse receipt embodies within its written or printed terms each of the following, the

warehouseman is liable for damages caused by the omission to a person injured thereby:

(a) the location of the warehouse where the goods are stored;

(b) the date of issue of the receipt;

(c) the consecutive number of the receipt;

(d) a statement whether the goods received will be delivered to the bearer, to a specified person, or to a specified person or his order;

(e) the rate of storage and handling charges, except that where goods are stored under a field warehousing arrangement a statement of that fact is sufficient on a non-negotiable receipt;

(f) a description of the goods or of the packages containing them;

(g) the signature of the warehouseman, which may be made by his authorized agent;

(h) if the receipt is issued for goods of which the warehouseman is owner, either solely or jointly or in common with others, the fact of such ownership; and

(i) a statement of the amount of advances made and of liabilities incurred for which the warehouseman claims a lien or security interest (Section 7–209). If the precise amount of such advances made or of such liabilities incurred is, at the time of the issue of the receipt, unknown to the warehouseman or to his agent who issues it, a statement of the fact that advances have been made or liabilities incurred and the purpose thereof is sufficient.

(3) A warehouseman may insert in his receipt any other terms which are not contrary to the provisions of this Act and do not impair his obligation of delivery (Section 7–403) or his duty of care (Section 7–204). Any contrary provisions shall be ineffective.

Section 7–203. Liability for Non-Receipt or Misdescription

A party to or purchaser for value in good faith of a document of title other than a bill of lading relying in either case upon the description therein of the goods may recover from the issuer damages caused by the non-receipt or misdescription of the goods, except to the extent that the document conspicuously indicates that the issuer does not know whether any part or all of the goods in fact were received or conform to the description, as where the description is in terms of marks or labels or kind, quantity or condition, or the receipt or description is qualified by "contents, condition and quality unknown," "said to contain" or the like, if such indication be true, or the party or purchaser otherwise has notice.

Section 7–204. Duty of Care; Contractual Limitation of Warehouseman's Liability

(1) A warehouseman is liable for damages for loss of or injury to the goods caused by his failure to exercise such care in regard to them as a reasonably careful man would exercise under like circumstances but unless otherwise agreed he is not liable for damages which could not have been avoided by the exercise of such care.

(2) Damages may be limited by a term in the warehouse receipt or storage agreement limiting the amount of liability in case of loss or damage, and setting forth a specific liability per article or item, or value per unit of weight, beyond which the warehouseman shall not be liable; provided, however, that such liability may on written request of the bailor at the time of signing such storage agreement or within a reasonable time after receipt of the warehouse receipt be increased on part or all of the goods thereunder, in which event increased rates may be charged based on such increased valuation, but that no such increase shall be permitted contrary to a lawful limitation of liability contained in the warehouseman's tariff, if any. No such limitation is effective with respect to the warehouseman's liability for conversion to his own use.

(3) Reasonable provisions as to the time and manner of presenting claims and instituting actions based on the bailment may be included in the warehouse receipt or tariff.

(4) This section does not impair or repeal . . .

Note: *Insert in subsection (4) a reference to any statue which imposes a higher responsibility upon the warehouseman or invalidates contractual limitations which would be permissible under this Article.*

Section 7–205. Title Under Warehouse Receipt Defeated in Certain Cases

A buyer in the ordinary course of business of fungible goods sold and delivered by a warehouseman who is also in the business of buying and selling such goods takes free of any claim under a warehouse receipt even though it has been duly negotiated.

Section 7–206. Termination of Storage at Warehouseman's Option

(1) A warehouseman may on notifying the person on whose account the goods are held and any other person known to claim an interest in the goods require payment of any charges and removal of the goods from the warehouse at the termination of the period of storage fixed by the document, or, if no period is fixed, within a stated period not less than thirty days after the notification. If the goods are not removed before the date specified in the notification, the warehouseman may sell them in accordance with the provisions of the section on enforcement of a warehouseman's lien (Section 7–210).

(2) If a warehouseman in good faith believes that the goods are about to deteriorate or decline in value to less than the amount of his lien within the time prescribed in subsection (1) for notification, advertisement and sale, the warehouseman may specify in the notification any reasonable shorter time for removal of the goods and in case the goods are not removed, may sell them at public sale held not less than one week after a single advertisement or posting.

(3) If as a result of a quality or condition of the goods of which the warehouseman had no notice at the time of deposit the goods are a hazard to other property or to the warehouse or to persons, the warehouseman may sell the goods at public or private sale without advertisement on reasonable notification to all persons known to claim an interest in the goods. If the warehouseman after a reasonable effort is unable to sell the goods he may dispose of them in any lawful manner and shall incur no liability by reason of such disposition.

(4) The warehouseman must deliver the goods to any person entitled to them under this Article upon due demand made at any time prior to sale or other disposition under this section.

(5) The warehouseman may satisfy his lien from the proceeds of any sale or disposition under this section but must hold the balance for delivery on the demand of any person to whom he would have been bound to deliver the goods.

Section 7–207. Goods Must Be Kept Separate; Fungible Goods

(1) Unless the warehouse receipt otherwise provides, a warehouseman must keep separate the goods covered by each receipt so as to permit at all times identification and delivery of those goods except that different lots of fungible goods may be commingled.

(2) Fungible goods so commingled are owned in common by the persons entitled thereto and the warehouseman is severally liable to each owner for that owner's share. Where because of overissue a mass of fungible goods is insufficient to meet all the receipts which the warehouseman has issued against it, the persons entitled include all holders to whom overissued receipts have been duly negotiated.

Section 7–208. Altered Warehouse Receipts

Where a blank in a negotiable warehouse receipt has been filled in without authority, a purchaser for value and without notice of the want of authority may treat the insertion as authorized. Any other unauthorized alteration leaves any receipt enforceable against the issuer according to its original tenor.

Section 7–209. Lien of Warehouseman

(1) A warehouseman has a lien against the bailor on the goods covered by a warehouse receipt or on the proceeds thereof in his possession for charges for storage or transportation (including demurrage and terminal charges), insurance, labor, or charges present or future in relation to the goods, and for expenses necessary for preservation of the goods or reasonably incurred in their sale pursuant to law. If the person on whose account the goods are held is liable for like charges or expenses in relation to other goods whenever deposited and it is stated in the receipt that a lien is claimed for charges and expenses in relation to other goods, the warehouseman also has a lien against him for such charges and expenses whether or not the other goods have been delivered by the warehouseman. But against a person to whom a negotiable warehouse receipt is duly negotiated a warehouseman's lien is limited to charges in an amount or at a rate specified on the receipt or if no charges are so specified then to a reasonable charge for storage of the goods covered by the receipt subsequent to the date of the receipt.

(2) The warehouseman may also reserve a security interest against the bailor for a maximum amount specified on the receipt for charges other than those specified in subsection (1), such as for money advanced and interest. Such a security interest is governed by the Article on Secured Transactions (Article 9).

(3) (a) A warehouseman's lien for charges and expenses under subsection (1) or a security interest under subsection (2) is also effective against any person who so entrusted the

bailor with possession of the goods that a pledge of them by him to a good faith purchaser for value would have been valid but is not effective against a person as to whom the document confers no right in the goods covered by it under Section 7–503.

(b) A warehouseman's lien on household goods for charges and expenses in relation to the goods under subsection (1) is also effective against all persons if the depositor was the legal possessor of the goods at the time of deposit. "Household goods" means furniture, furnishings, and personal effects used by the depositor in a dwelling.

(4) A warehouseman loses his lien on any goods which he voluntarily delivers or which he unjustifiably refuses to deliver.

Section 7–210. Enforcement of Warehouseman's Lien

(1) Except as provided in subsection (2), a warehouseman's lien may be enforced by public or private sale of the goods in block or in parcels, at any time or place and on any terms which are commercially reasonable, after notifying all persons known to claim an interest in the goods. Such notification must include a statement of the amount due, the nature of the proposed sale and the time and place of any public sale. The fact that a better price could have been obtained by a sale at a different time or in a different method from that selected by the warehouseman is not of itself sufficient to establish that the sale was not made in a commercially reasonable manner. If the warehouseman either sells the goods in the usual manner in any recognized market therefor, or if he sells at the price current in such market at the time of his sale, or if he has otherwise sold in conformity with commercially reasonable practices among dealers in the type of goods sold, he has sold in a commercially reasonable manner. A sale of more goods than apparently necessary to be offered to insure satisfaction of the obligation is not commercially reasonable except in cases covered by the preceding sentence.

(2) A warehouseman's lien on goods other than goods stored by a merchant in the course of his business may be enforced only as follows:

(a) All persons known to claim an interest in the goods must be notified.

(b) The notification must be delivered in person or sent by registered or certified letter to the last known address of any person to be notified.

(c) The notification must include an itemized statement of the claim, a description of the goods subject to the lien, a demand for payment within a specified time not less than ten days after receipt of the notification, and a conspicuous statement that unless the claim is paid within that time the goods will be advertised for sale and sold by auction at a specified time and place.

(d) The sale must conform to the terms of the notification.

(e) The sale must be held at the nearest suitable place to that where the goods are held or stored.

(f) After the expiration of the time given in the notification, an advertisement of the sale must be published once a week for two weeks consecutively in a newspaper of general circulation where the sale is to be held. The advertisement must include a description of the goods, the name of the person on whose account they are being held, and the time and place of the sale. The sale must take place at least fifteen days after the first publication. If there is no newspaper of general circulation where the sale is to be held, the advertisement must be posted at least ten days before the sale in not less than six conspicuous places in the neighborhood of the proposed sale.

(3) Before any sale pursuant to this section any person claiming a right in the goods may pay the amount necessary to satisfy the lien and the reasonable expenses incurred under this section. In that event the goods must not be sold, but must be retained by the warehouseman subject to the terms of the receipt and this Article.

(4) The warehouseman may buy at any public sale pursuant to this section.

(5) A purchaser in good faith of goods sold to enforce a warehouseman's lien takes the goods free of any rights of persons against whom the lien was valid, despite noncompliance by the warehouseman with the requirements of this section.

(6) The warehouseman may satisfy his lien from the proceeds of any sale pursuant to this section but must hold the balance, if any, for delivery on demand to any

person to whom he would have been bound to deliver the goods.

(7) The rights provided by this section shall be in addition to all other rights allowed by law to a creditor against his debtor.

(8) Where a lien is on goods stored by a merchant in the course of his business the lien may be enforced in accordance with either subsection (1) or (2).

(9) The warehouseman is liable for damages caused by failure to comply with the requirements for sale under this section and in case of willful violation is liable for conversion.

Part 3   Bills of Lading: Special Provisions

Section 7–301.   Liability for Non-Receipt or Misdescription; "Said to Contain"; "Shipper's Load and Count"; Improper Handling

(1) A consignee of a non-negotiable bill who has given value in good faith or a holder to whom a negotiable bill has been duly negotiated relying in either case upon the description therein of the goods, or upon the date therein shown, may recover from the issuer damages caused by the misdating of the bill or the non-receipt or misdescription of the goods, except to the extent that the document indicates that the issuer does not know whether any part or all of the goods in fact were received or conform to the description, as where the description is in terms of marks or labels or kind, quantity, or condition or the receipt or description is qualified by "contents or condition of contents of packages unknown," "said to contain," "shipper's weight, load and count" or the like, if such indication be true.

(2) When goods are loaded by an issuer who is a common carrier, the issuer must count the packages of goods if package freight and ascertain the kind and quantity if bulk freight. In such cases "shipper's weight, load and count" or other words indicating that the description was made by the shipper are ineffective except as to freight concealed by packages.

(3) When bulk freight is loaded by a shipper who makes available to the issuer adequate facilities for weighing such freight, an issuer who is a common carrier must ascertain the kind and quantity within a reasonable time after receiving the written request of the shipper to do so. In such cases "shipper's weight" or other words of like purport are ineffective.

(4) The issuer may be inserting in the bill the words "shipper's weight, load and count" or other words of like purport indicate that the goods were loaded by the shipper; and if such statement be true the issuer shall not be liable for damages caused by the improper loading. But their omission does not imply liability for such damages.

(5) The shipper shall be deemed to have guaranteed to the issuer the accuracy at the time of shipment of the description, marks, labels, number, kind, quantity, condition and weight, as furnished by him; and the shipper shall indemnify the issuer against damage caused by inaccuracies in such particulars. The right of the issuer to such indemnity shall in no way limit his responsibility and liability under the contract of carriage to any person other than the shipper.

Section 7–302.   Through Bills of Lading and Similar Documents

(1) The issuer of a through bill of lading or other document embodying an undertaking to be performed in part by persons acting as its agents or by connecting carriers is liable to anyone entitled to recover on the document for any breach by such other persons or by a connecting carrier of its obligation under the document but to the extent that the bill covers an undertaking to be performed overseas or in territory not contiguous to the continental United States or an undertaking including matters other than transportation this liability may be varied by agreement of the parties.

(2) Where goods covered by a through bill of lading or other document embodying an undertaking to be performed in part by persons other than the issuer are received by any such person, he is subject with respect to his own performance while the goods are in his possession to the obligation of the issuer. His obligation is discharged by delivery of the goods to another such person pursuant to the document, and does not include liability for breach by any other such persons or by the issuer.

(3) The issuer of such through bill of lading or other document shall be entitled to recover from the connecting carrier or such other person in possession of the goods when the breach of the obligation under the document occurred, the amount it may be required to pay to anyone entitled to recover on the document therefor, as may be evidenced by any receipt, judgment, or transcript thereof, and the amount of any expense reasonably incurred by it in defending any action brought by anyone entitled to recover on the document therefor.

Section 7–303. Diversion; Reconsignment; Change of Instructions

(1)   Unless the bill of lading otherwise provides, the carrier may deliver the goods to a person or destination other than that stated in the bill or may otherwise dispose of the goods on instructions from

(a)   the holder of a negotiable bill; or

(b)   the consignor on a non-negotiable bill notwithstanding contrary instructions from the consignee; or

(c)   the consignee on a non-negotiable bill in the absence of contrary instructions from the consignor, if the goods have arrived at the billed destination or if the consignee is in possession of the bill; or

(d)   the consignee on a non-negotiable bill if he is entitled as against the consignor to dispose of them.

(2)   Unless such instructions are noted on a negotiable bill of lading, a person to whom the bill is duly negotiated can hold the bailee according to the original terms.

Section 7–304. Bills of Lading in a Set

(1)   Except where customary in overseas transportation, a bill of lading must not be issued in a set of parts. The issuer is liable for damages caused by violation of this subsection.

(2)   Where a bill of lading is lawfully drawn in a set of parts, each of which is numbered and expressed to be valid only if the goods have not been delivered against any other part, the whole of the parts constitute one bill.

(3)   Where a bill of lading is lawfully issued in a set of parts and different parts are negotiated to different persons, the title of the holder to whom the first due negotiation is made prevails as to both the document and the goods even though any later holder may have received the goods from the carrier in good faith and discharged the carrier's obligation by surrender of his part.

(4)   Any person who negotiates or transfers a single part of a bill of lading drawn in a set is liable to holders of that part as if it were the whole set.

(5)   The bailee is obliged to deliver in accordance with Part 4 of this Article against the first presented part of a bill of lading lawfully drawn in a set. Such delivery discharges the bailee's obligation on the whole bill.

Section 7–305. Destination Bills

(1)   Instead of issuing a bill of lading to the consignor at the place of shipment a carrier may at the request of the consignor procure the bill to be issued at destination or at any other place designated in the request.

(2)   Upon request of anyone entitled as against the carrier to control the goods while in transit and on surrender of any outstanding bill of lading or other receipt covering such goods, the issuer may procure a substitute bill to be issued at any place designated in the request.

Section 7–306. Altered Bills of Lading

An unauthorized alteration or filling in of a blank in a bill of lading leaves the bill enforceable according to its original tenor.

Section 7–307. Lien of Carrier

(1)   A carrier has a lien on the goods covered by a bill of lading for charges subsequent to the date of its receipt of the goods for storage or transportation (including demurrage and terminal charges) and for expenses necessary for preservation of the goods incident to their transportation or reasonably incurred in their sale pursuant to law. But against a purchaser for value of a negotiable bill of lading a carrier's lien is limited to charges stated in the bill or the applicable tariffs, or if no charges are stated then to a reasonable charge.

(2)   A lien for charges and expenses under subsection (1) on goods which the carrier was required by law to receive for transportation is effective against the consignor or any person entitled to the goods unless the carrier had notice that the consignor lacked authority to subject the goods to such charges and expenses. Any other lien under subsection (1) is effective against the consignor and any person who permitted the bailor to have control or possession of the goods unless the carrier had notice that the bailor lacked such authority.

(3)   A carrier loses his lien on any goods which he voluntarily delivers or which he unjustifiably refuses to deliver.

Section 7–308. Enforcement of Carrier's Lien

(1)   A carrier's lien may be enforced by public or private sale of the goods, in block or in parcels, at any time or place and on any terms which are commercially reasonable, after notifying all persons known to claim an interest in the goods. Such notification must include a statement of the amount due, the nature of the proposed sale and the time and place of any public sale.

The fact that a better price could have been obtained by a sale at a different time or in a different method from that selected by the carrier is not of itself sufficient to establish that the sale was not made in a commercially reasonable manner. If the carrier either sells the goods in the usual manner in any recognized market therefor or if he sells at the price current in such market at the time of his sale or if he has otherwise sold in conformity with commercially reasonable practices among dealers in the type of goods sold he has sold in a commercially reasonable manner. A sale of more goods than apparently necessary to be offered to ensure satisfaction of the obligation is not commercially reasonable except in cases covered by the preceding sentence.

(2) Before any sale pursuant to this section any person claiming a right in the goods may pay the amount necessary to satisfy the lien and the reasonable expenses incurred under this section. In that event the goods must not be sold, but must be retained by the carrier subject to the terms of the bill and this Article.

(3) The carrier may buy at any public sale pursuant to this section.

(4) A purchaser in good faith of goods sold to enforce a carrier's lien takes the goods free of any rights of persons against whom the lien was valid, despite noncompliance by the carrier with the requirements of this section.

(5) The carrier may satisfy his lien from the proceeds of any sale pursuant to this section but must hold the balance, if any, for delivery on demand to any person to whom he would have been bound to deliver the goods.

(6) The rights provided by this section shall be in addition to all other rights allowed by law to a creditor against his debtor.

(7) A carrier's lien may be enforced in accordance with either subsection (1) or the procedure set forth in subsection (2) of Section 7–210.

(8) The carrier is liable for damages caused by failure to comply with the requirements for sale under this section and in case of willful violation is liable for conversion.

Section 7–309. Duty of Care; Contractual Limitation of Carrier's Liability

(1) A carrier who issues a bill of lading whether negotiable or non-negotiable must exercise the degree of care in relation to the goods which a reasonably careful man would exercise under like circumstances. This subsection does not repeal or change any law or rule of law which imposes liability upon a common carrier for damages not caused by its negligence.

(2) Damages may be limited by a provision that the carrier's liability shall not exceed a value stated in the document if the carrier's rates are dependent upon value and the consignor by the carrier's tariff is afforded an opportunity to declare a higher value or a value as lawfully provided in the tariff, or where no tariff is filed he is otherwise advised of such opportunity; but no such limitation is effective with respect to the carrier's liability for conversion to its own use.

(3) Reasonable provisions as to the time and manner of presenting claims and instituting actions based on the shipment may be included in a bill of lading or tariff.

Part 4 Warehouse Receipts and Bills of Lading: General Obligations

Section 7–401. Irregularities in Issue of Receipt or Bill or Conduct of Issuer

The obligations imposed by this Article on an issuer apply to a document of title regardless of the fact that

    (a) the document may not comply with the requirements of this Article or of any other law or regulation regarding its issue, form or content; or

    (b) the issuer may have violated laws regulating the conduct of his business; or

    (c) the goods covered by the document were owned by the bailee at the time the document was issued; or

    (d) the person issuing the document does not come within the definition of warehouseman if it purports to be a warehouse receipt.

Section 7–402. Duplicate Receipt or Bill; Overissue

Neither a duplicate nor any other document of title purporting to cover goods already represented by an outstanding document of the same issuer confers any right in the goods, except as provided in the case of bills in a set, overissue of documents for fungible goods and substitutes for lost, stolen or destroyed documents. But the issuer is liable for damages caused by his overissue or failure to identify a duplicate document as such by conspicuous notation on its face.

Section 7–403.   Obligation of Warehouseman or Carrier to Deliver; Excuse

(1)   The bailee must deliver the goods to a person entitled under the document who complies with subsections (2) and (3), unless and to the extent that the bailee establishes any of the following:

    (a)   delivery of the goods to a person whose receipt was rightful as against the claimant;

    (b)   damage to or delay, loss or destruction of the goods for which the bailee is not liable [, but the burden of establishing negligence in such cases is on the person entitled under the document];

Note: *The brackets in (1) (b) indicate that State enactments may differ on this point without serious damage to the principle of uniformity.*

    (c)   previous sale or other disposition of the goods in lawful enforcement of a lien or on warehouseman's lawful termination of storage;

    (d)   the exercise by a seller of his right to stop delivery pursuant to the provisions of the Article on Sales (Section 2–705);

    (e)   a diversion, reconsignment or other disposition pursuant to the provisions of this Article (Section 7–303) or tariff regulating such right;

    (f)   release, satisfaction or any other fact affording a personal defense against the claimant;

    (g)   any other lawful excuse.

(2)   A person claiming goods covered by a document of title must satisfy the bailee's lien where the bailee so requests or where the bailee is prohibited by law from delivering the goods until the charges are paid.

(3)   Unless the person claiming is one against whom the document confers no right under Sec. 7–503(1), he must surrender for cancellation or notation of partial deliveries any outstanding negotiable document covering the goods, and the bailee must cancel the document or conspicuously note the partial delivery thereon or be liable to any person to whom the document is duly negotiated.

(4)   "Person entitled under the document" means holder in the case of a negotiable document, or the person to whom delivery is to be made by the terms of or pursuant to written instructions under a non-negotiable document.

Section 7–404.   No Liability for Good Faith Delivery Pursuant to Receipt or Bill

A bailee who in good faith including observance of reasonable commercial standards has received goods and delivered or otherwise disposed of them according to the terms of the document of title or pursuant to this Article is not liable therefor. This rule applies even though the person from whom he received the goods had no authority to procure the document or to dispose of the goods and even though the person to whom he delivered the goods had no authority to receive them.

Part 5   Warehouse Receipts and Bills of Lading: Negotiation and Transfer

Section 7–501.   Form of Negotiation and Requirements of "Due Negotiation"

(1)   A negotiable document of title running to the order of a named person is negotiated by his indorsement and delivery. After his indorsement in blank or to bearer any person can negotiate it by delivery alone.

(2) (a)   A negotiable document of title is also negotiated by delivery alone when by its original terms it runs to bearer.

     (b)   When a document running to the order of a named person is delivered to him the effect is the same as if the document had been negotiated.

(3)   Negotiation of a negotiable document of title after it has been indorsed to a specified person requires indorsement by the special indorsee as well as delivery.

(4)   A negotiable document of title is "duly negotiated" when it is negotiated in the manner stated in this section to a holder who purchases it in good faith without notice of any defense against or claim to it on the part of any person and for value, unless it is established that the negotiation is not in the regular course of business or financing or involves receiving the document in settlement or payment of a money obligation.

(5)   Indorsement of a non-negotiable document neither makes it negotiable nor adds to the transferee's rights.

(6)   The naming in a negotiable bill of a person to be notified of the arrival of the goods does not limit the negotiability of the bill nor constitute notice to a purchaser thereof of any interest of such person in the goods.

Section 7–502. Rights Acquired by Due Negotiation

(1) Subject to the following section and to the provisions of Section 7–205 on fungible goods, a holder to whom a negotiable document of title has been duly negotiated acquires thereby:

(a) title to the document;

(b) title to the goods;

(c) all rights accruing under the law of agency or estoppel, including rights to goods delivered to the bailee after the document was issued; and

(d) the direct obligation of the issuer to hold or deliver the goods according to the terms of the document free of any defense or claim by him except those arising under the terms of the document or under this Article. In the case of a delivery order the bailee's obligation accrues only upon acceptance and the obligation acquired by the holder is that the issuer and any indorser will procure the acceptance of the bailee.

(2) Subject to the following section, title and rights so acquired are not defeated by any stoppage of the goods represented by the document or by surrender of such goods by the bailee, and are not impaired even though the negotiation or any prior negotiation constituted a breach of duty or even though any person has been deprived of possession of the document by misrepresentation, fraud, accident, mistake, duress, loss, theft or conversion, or even though a previous sale or other transfer of the goods or document has been made to a third person.

Section 7–503. Document of Title to Goods Defeated in Certain Cases

(1) A document of title confers no right in goods against a person who before issuance of the document had a legal interest or a perfected security interest in them and who neither

(a) delivered or entrusted them or any document of title covering them to the bailor or his nominee with actual or apparent authority to ship, store or sell or with power to obtain delivery under this Article (Section 7–403) or with power of disposition under this Act (Sections 2–403 and 9–307) or other statute or rule of law; nor

(b) acquiesced in the procurement by the bailor or his nominee of any document of title.

(2) Title to goods based upon an unaccepted delivery order is subject to the rights of anyone to whom a negotiable warehouse receipt or bill of lading covering the goods has been duly negotiated. Such a title may be defeated under the next section to the same extent as the rights of the issuer or a transferee from the issuer.

(3) Title to goods based upon a bill of lading issued to a freight forwarder is subject to the rights of anyone to whom a bill issued by the freight forwarder is duly negotiated; but delivery by the carrier in accordance with Part 4 of this Article pursuant to its own bill of lading discharges the carrier's obligation to deliver.

Section 7–504. Rights Acquired in the Absence of Due Negotiation; Effect of Diversion; Seller's Stoppage of Delivery

(1) A transferee of a document, whether negotiable or non-negotiable, to whom the document has been delivered but not duly negotiated, acquires the title and rights which his transferor had or had actual authority to convey.

(2) In the case of a non-negotiable document, until but not after the bailee receives notification of the transfer, the rights of the transferee may be defeated

(a) by those creditors of the transferor who could treat the sale as void under Section 2–402; or

(b) by a buyer from the transferor in ordinary course of business if the bailee has delivered the goods to the buyer or received notification of his rights; or

(c) as against the bailee by good faith dealings of the bailee with the transferor.

(3) A diversion or other change of shipping instructions by the consignor in a non-negotiable bill of lading which causes the bailee not to deliver to the consignee defeats the consignee's title to the goods if they have been delivered to a buyer in ordinary course of business and in any event defeats the consignee's rights against the bailee.

(4) Delivery pursuant to a non-negotiable document may be stopped by a seller under Section 2–705, and subject to the requirement of due notification there provided. A bailee honoring the seller's instructions is entitled to be indemnified by the seller against any resulting loss or expense.

Section 7–505. Indorser Not a Guarantor for Other Parties

The indorsement of a document of title issued by a bailee does not make the indorser liable for any default by the bailee or by previous indorsers.

Section 7–506. Delivery Without Indorsement: Right to Compel Indorsement

The transferee of a negotiable document of title has a specifically enforceable right to have his transferor supply any necessary indorsement but the transfer becomes a negotiation only as of the time the indorsement is supplied.

Section 7–507. Warranties on Negotiation or Transfer of Receipt or Bill

Where a person negotiates or transfers a document of title for value otherwise than as a mere intermediary under the next following section, then unless otherwise agreed he warrants to his immediate purchaser only in addition to any warranty made in selling the goods

- (a) that the document is genuine; and
- (b) that he has no knowledge of any fact which would impair its validity or worth; and
- (c) that his negotiation or transfer is rightful and fully effective with respect to the title to the document and the goods it represents.

Section 7–508. Warranties of Collecting Bank as to Documents

A collecting bank or other intermediary known to be entrusted with documents on behalf of another or with collection of a draft or other claim against delivery of documents warrants by such delivery of the documents only its own good faith and authority. This rule applies even though the intermediary has purchased or made advances against the claim or draft to be collected.

Part 6 Warehouse Receipts and Bills of Lading: Miscellaneous Provisions

Section 7–601. Lost and Missing Documents

(1) If a document has been lost, stolen or destroyed, a court may order delivery of the goods or issuance of a substitute document and the bailee may without liability to any person comply with such order. If the document was negotiable the claimant must post security approved by the court to indemnify any person who may suffer loss as a result of non-surrender of the document. If the document was not negotiable, such security may be required at the discretion of the court. The court may also in its discretion order payment of the bailee's reasonable costs and counsel fees.

(2) A bailee who without court order delivers goods to a person claiming under a missing negotiable document is liable to any person injured thereby, and if the delivery is not in good faith becomes liable for conversion. Delivery in good faith is not conversion if made in accordance with a filed classification or tariff or, where no classification or tariff is filed, if the claimant posts security with the bailee in an amount at least double the value of the goods at the time of posting to indemnify any person injured by the delivery who files a notice of claim within one year after the delivery.

Section 7–602. Attachment of Goods Covered by a Negotiable Document

Except where the document was originally issued upon delivery of the goods by a person who had no power to dispose of them, no lien attaches by virtue of any judicial process to goods in the possession of a bailee for which a negotiable document of title is outstanding unless the document be first surrendered to the bailee or its negotiation enjoined, and the bailee shall not be compelled to deliver the goods pursuant to process until the document is surrendered to him or impounded by the court. One who purchases the document for value without notice of the process or injunction takes free of the lien imposed by judicial process.

Section 7–603. Conflicting Claims; Interpleader

If more than one person claims title or possession of the goods, the bailee is excused from delivery until he has had a reasonable time to ascertain the validity of the adverse claims or to bring an action to compel all claimants to interplead and may compel such interpleader, either in defending an action for non-delivery of the goods, or by original action, whichever is appropriate.

ARTICLE 8 INVESTMENT SECURITIES

Part 1 Short Title and General Matters

Section 8–101. Short Title

This Article shall be known and may be cited as Uniform Commercial Code—Investment Securities.

(1)   In this Article, unless the context otherwise requires:

(a)   A "certificated security" is a share, participation, or other interest in property of or an enterprise of the issuer or an obligation of the issuer which is

(i)   represented by an instrument issued in bearer or registered form;

(ii)   of a type commonly dealt in on securities exchanges or markets or commonly recognized in any area in which it is issued or dealt in as a medium for investment; and

(iii)   either one of a class or series or by its terms divisible into a class or series of shares, participations, interests, or obligations.

(b)   An "uncertificated security" is a share, participation, or other interest in property or an enterprise of the issuer or an obligation of the issuer which is

(i)   not represented by an instrument and the transfer of which is registered upon books maintained for that purpose by or on behalf of the issuer;

(ii)   of a type commonly dealt in on securities exchanges or markets; and

(iii)   either one of a class or series or by its terms divisible into a class or series of shares, participations, interests, or obligations.

(c)   A "security" is either a certificated or an uncertificated security. If a security is certificated, the terms "security" and "certificated security" may mean either the intangible interest, the instrument representing that interest, or both, as the context requires. A writing that is a certificated security is governed by this Article and not by Article 3, even though it also meets the requirements of that Article. This Article does not apply to money. If a certificated security has been retained by or surrendered to the issuer or its transfer agent for reasons other than registration of transfer, other temporary purpose, payment, exchange, or acquisition by the issuer, that security shall be treated as an uncertificated security for purposes of this Article.

(d)   A certificated security is in "registered form" if

(i)   it specifies a person entitled to the security or the rights it represents; and

(ii)   its transfer may be registered upon books maintained for that purpose by or on behalf of the issuer, or the security so states.

(e)   A certificated security is in "bearer form" if it runs to bearer according to its terms and not by reason of any indorsement.

(2)   A "subsequent purchaser" is a person who takes other than by original issue.

(3)   A "clearing corporation" is a corporation registered as a "clearing agency" under the federal securities laws or a corporation:

(a)   at least 90 percent of whose capital stock is held by or for one or more organizations, none of which, other than a national securities exchange or association, holds in excess of 20 percent of the capital stock of the corporation, and each of which is

(i)   subject to supervision or regulation pursuant to the provisions of federal or state banking laws or state insurance laws,

(ii)   a broker or dealer or investment company registered under the federal securities laws, or

(iii)   a national securities exchange or association registered under the federal securities laws; and

(b)   any remaining capital stock of which is held by individuals who have purchased it at or prior to the time of their taking office as directors of the corporation and who have purchased only so much of the capital stock as is necessary to permit them to qualify as directors.

(4)   A "custodian bank" is a bank or trust company that is supervised and examined by state or federal authority having supervision over banks and is acting as custodian for a clearing corporation.

(5)   Other definitions applying to this Article or to specified Parts thereof and the sections in which they appear are:

"Adverse claim." Section 8–302.

"Bona fide purchaser." Section 8–302.

"Broker." Section 8–303.

"Debtor." Section 9–105.

"Financial intermediary." Section 8–313.

"Guarantee of the signature." Section 8–402.

"Initial transaction statement." Section 8–408.

"Instruction." Section 8–308.

"Intermediary bank." Section 4–105.

"Issuer." Section 8–201.

"Overissue." Section 8–104.

"Secured Party." Section 9–105.

"Security Agreement." Section 9–105.

(6)   In addition, Article 1 contains general definitions and principles of construction and interpretation applicable throughout this Article.

Section 8–103.   Issuer's Lien

A lien upon a security in favor of an issuer thereof is valid against a purchaser only if:

(a)   the security is certificated and the right of the issuer to the lien is noted conspicuously thereon; or

(b)   the security is uncertificated and a notation of the right of the issuer to the lien is contained in the initial transaction statement sent to the purchaser or, if his interest is transferred to him other than by registration of transfer, pledge, or release, the initial transaction statement sent to the registered owner or the registered pledgee.

Section 8–104.   Effect of Overissue; "Overissue"

(1)   The provisions of this Article which validate a security or compel its issue or reissue do not apply to the extent that validation, issue, or reissue would result in overissue; but if:

(a)   an identical security which does not constitute an overissue is reasonably available for purchase, the person entitled to issue or validation may compel the issuer to purchase the security for him and either to deliver a certificated security or to register the transfer of an uncertificated security to him, against surrender of any certificated security he hold; or

(b)   a security is not so available for purchase, the person entitled to issue or validation may recover from the issuer the price he or the last purchaser for value paid for it with interest from the date of his demand.

(2)   "Overissue" means the issue of securities in excess of the amount the issuer has corporate power to issue.

Section 8–105.   Certificated Securities Negotiable; Statements and Instructions Not Negotiable; Presumptions

(1)   Certificated securities governed by this Article are negotiable instruments.

(2)   Statements (Section 8–408), notices, or the like, sent by the issuer of uncertificated securities and instructions (Section 8–308) are neither negotiable instruments nor certificated securities.

(3)   In any action on a security:

(a)   unless specifically denied in the pleadings, each signature on a certificated security, in a necessary indorsement, on an initial transaction statement, or on an instruction, is admitted;

(b)   if the effectiveness of a signature is put in issue, the burden of establishing it is on the party claiming under the signature, but the signature is presumed to be genuine or authorized;

(c)   if signatures on a certificated security are admitted or established, production of the security entitles a holder to recover on it unless the defendant establishes a defense or a defect going to the validity of the security;

(d)   if signatures on an initial transaction statement are admitted or established, the facts stated in the statement are presumed to be true as of the time of its issuance; and

(e)   after it is shown that a defense or defect exists, the plaintiff has the burden of establishing that he or some person under whom he claims is a person against whom the defense or defect is ineffective (Section 8–202).

Section 8–106.   Applicability

The law (including the conflict of laws rules) of the jurisdiction of organization of the issuer governs the validity of a security, the effectiveness of registration by the issuer, and the rights and duties of the issuer with respect to:

(a)   registration of transfer of a certificated security;

(b)   registration of transfer, pledge, or release of an uncertificated security; and

(c)   sending of statements of uncertificated securities.

Section 8–107. Securities Transferable; Action for Price

(1)   Unless otherwise agreed and subject to any applicable law or regulation respecting short sales, a person obligated to transfer securities may transfer any certificated security of the specified issue in bearer form or registered in the name of the transferee, or indorsed to him or in blank, or he may transfer an equivalent uncertificated security to the transferee or a person designated by the transferee.

(2)   If the buyer fails to pay the price as it comes due under a contract of sale, the seller may recover the price of:

(a)   certificated securities accepted by the buyer;

(b)   uncertificated securities that have been transferred to the buyer or a person designated by the buyer; and

(c)   other securities if efforts at their resale would be unduly burdensome or if there is no readily available market for their resale.

Section 8–108. Registration of Pledge and Release of Uncertificated Securities

A security interest in an uncertificated security may be evidenced by the registration of pledge to the secured party or a person designated by him. There can be no more than one registered pledge of an uncertificated security at any time. The registered owner of an uncertificated security is the person in whose name the security is registered, even if the security is subject to a registered pledge. The rights of a registered pledgee of an uncertificated security under this Article are terminated by the registration of release.

Part 2   Issue–Issuer

Section 8–201.   "Issuer"

(1)   With respect to obligations on or defenses to a security, "issuer" includes a person who:

(a)   places or authorizes the placing of his name on a certificated security (otherwise than as authenticating trustee, registrar, transfer agent, or the like) to evidence that it represents a share, participation, or other interest in his property or in an enterprise, or to evidence his duty to perform an obligation represented by the certificated security;

(b)   creates shares, participations, or other interests in his property or in an enterprise or

undertakes obligations, which shares, participations, interests, or obligations are uncertificated securities;

(c)   directly or indirectly creates fractional interests in his rights or property, which fractional interests are represented by certificated securities; or

(d)   becomes responsible for or in place of any other person described as an issuer in this section.

(2)   With respect to obligations on or defenses to a security, a guarantor is an issuer to the extent of his guaranty, whether or not his obligation is noted on a certificated security or on statements of uncertificated securities sent pursuant to Section 8–408.

(3)   With respect to registration of transfer, pledge, or release (Part 4 of this Article), "issuer" means a person on whose behalf transfer books are maintained.

Section 8–202.   Issuer's Responsibility and Defenses; Notice of Defect or Defense

(1)   Even against a purchaser for value and without notice, the terms of a security include:

(a)   if the security is certificated, those stated on the security;

(b)   if the security is uncertificated, those contained in the initial transaction statement sent to such purchaser, or, if his interest is transferred to him other than by registration of transfer, pledge, or release, the initial transaction statement sent to the registered owner or registered pledgee; and

(c)   those made part of the security by reference, on the certificated security or in the initial transaction statement, to another instrument, indenture, or document or to a constitution, statute, ordinance, rule, regulation, order or the like, to the extent that the terms referred to do not conflict with the terms stated on the certificated security or contained in the statement. A reference under this paragraph does not of itself charge a purchaser for value with notice of a defect going to the validity of the security, even though the certificated security or statement expressly states that a person accepting it admits notice.

(2)   A certificated security in the hands of a purchaser for value or an uncertificated security as to which an

initial transaction statement has been sent to a purchaser for value, other than a security issued by a government or governmental agency or unit, even though issued with a defect going to its validity, is valid with respect to the purchaser if he is without notice of the particular defect unless the defect involves a violation of constitutional provisions, in which case the security is valid with respect to a subsequent purchaser for value and without notice of the defect. This subsection applies to an issuer that is a government or governmental agency or unit only if either there has been substantial compliance with the legal requirements governing the issue or the issuer has received a substantial consideration for the issue as a whole or for the particular security and a stated purpose of the issue is one for which the issuer has power to borrow money or issue the security.

(3) Except as provided in the case of certain unauthorized signatures (Section 8–205), lack of genuiness of a certificated security or an initial transaction statement is a complete defense, even against a purchaser for value and without notice.

(4) All other defenses of the issuer of a certificated or uncertificated security, including nondelivery and conditional delivery of a certificated security, are ineffective against a purchaser for value who has taken without notice of the particular defense.

(5) Nothing in this section shall be construed to affect the right of a party to a "when, as and if issued" or a "when distributed" contract to cancel the contract in the event of a material change in the character of the security that is the subject of the contract or in the plan or arrangement pursuant to which the security is to be issued or distributed.

Section 8–203. Staleness as Notice of Defects or Defenses

(1) After an act or event creating a right to immediate performance of the principal obligation represented by a certificated security or that sets a date on or after which the security is to be presented or surrendered for redemption or exchange, a purchaser is charged with notice of any defect in its issue or defense of the issuer if:

    (a) the act or event is one requiring the payment of money, the delivery of certificated securities, the registration of transfer of uncertificated securities, or any of these on presentation or surrender of the certificated security,

the funds or securities are available on the date set for payment or exchange, and he takes the security more than one year after that date; and

    (b) the act or event is not covered by paragraph (a) and he takes the security more than 2 years after the date set for surrender or presentation or the date on which performance became due.

(2) A call that has been revoked is not within subsection (1).

Section 8–204. Effect of Issuer's Restrictions on Transfer

A restriction on transfer of a security imposed by the issuer, even if otherwise lawful, is ineffective against any person without actual knowledge of it unless:

    (a) the security is certificated and the restriction is noted conspicuously thereon; or

    (b) the security is uncertificated and a notation of the restriction is contained in the initial transaction statement sent to the person or, if his interest is transferred to him other than by registration of transfer, pledge, or release, the initial transaction statement sent to the registered owner or the registered pledgee.

Section 8–205. Effect of Unauthorized Signature on Certificated Security or Initial Transaction Statement

An unauthorized signature placed on a certificated security prior to or in the course of issue or placed on an initial transaction statement is ineffective, but the signature is effective in favor of a purchaser for value of the certificated security or a purchaser for value of an uncertificated security to whom the initial transaction statement has been sent, if the purchaser is without notice of the lack of authority and the signing has been done by:

    (a) an authenticating trustee, registrar, transfer agent, or other person entrusted by the issuer with the signing of the security, of similar securities, or of initial transaction statements or the immediate preparation for signing of any of them; or

    (b) an employee of the issuer, or of any of the foregoing, entrusted with responsible handling of the security or initial transaction statement.

Section 8–206.   Completion or Alteration of Certificated Security or Initial Transaction Statement

(1)   If a certificated security contains the signatures necessary to its issue or transfer but is incomplete in any other respect:

    (a)   any person may complete it by filling in the blanks as authorized; and

    (b)   even though the blanks are incorrectly filled in, the security as completed is enforceable by a purchaser who took it for value and without notice of the incorrectness.

(2)   A complete certificated security that has been improperly altered, even though fraudulently, remains enforceable, but only according to its original terms.

(3)   If an initial transaction statement contains the signatures necessary to its validity, but is incomplete in any other respect:

    (a)   any person may complete it by filling in the blanks as authorized; and

    (b)   even though the blanks are incorrectly filled in, the statement as completed is effective in favor of the person to whom it is sent if he purchased the security referred to therein for value and without notice of the incorrectness.

(4)   A complete initial transaction statement that has been improperly altered, even though fraudulently, is effective in favor of a purchaser to whom it has been sent, but only according to its original terms.

Section 8–207.   Rights and Duties of Issuer With Respect to Registered Owners and Registered Pledgees

(1)   Prior to due presentment for registration of transfer of a certificated security in registered form, the issuer or indenture trustee may treat the registered owner as the person exclusively entitled to vote, to receive notifications, and otherwise to exercise all rights and powers of an owner.

(2)   Subject to the provisions of subsections (3), (4), and (6), the issuer or indenture trustee may treat the registered owner of an uncertificated security as the person exclusively entitled to vote, to receive notifications, and otherwise to exercise all the rights and powers of an owner.

(3)   The registered owner of an uncertificated security that is subject to a registered pledge is not entitled to registration of transfer prior to the due presentment to the issuer of a release instruction. The exercise of conversion rights with respect to a convertible uncertifi-

cated security is a transfer within the meaning of this section.

(4)   Upon due presentment of a transfer instruction from the registered pledgee of an uncertificated security, the issuer shall:

    (a)   register the transfer of the security to the new owner free of pledge, if the instruction specifies a new owner (who may be the registered pledgee) and does not specify a pledgee;

    (b)   register the transfer of the security to the new owner subject to the interest of the existing pledgee, if the instruction specifies a new owner and the existing pledgee; or

    (c)   register the release of the security from the existing pledge and register the pledge of the security to the other pledgee, if the instruction specifies the existing owner and another pledgee.

(5)   Continuity of perfection of a security interest is not broken by registration of transfer under subsection (4)(b) or by registration of release and pledge under subsection (4)(c), if the security interest is assigned.

(6)   If an uncertificated security is subject to a registered pledge:

    (a)   any uncertificated securities issued in exchange for or distributed with respect to the pledged security shall be registered subject to the pledge;

    (b)   any certificated securities issued in exchange for or distributed with respect to the pledged security shall be delivered to the registered pledgee; and

    (c)   any money paid in exchange for or in redemption of part or all of the security shall be paid to the registered pledgee.

(7)   Nothing in this Article shall be construed to affect the liability of the registered owner of a security for calls, assessments, or the like.

Section 8–208.   Effect of Signature of Authenticating Trustee, Registrar, or Transfer Agent

(1)   A person placing his signature upon a certificated security or an initial transaction statement as authenticating trustee, registrar, transfer agent, or the like, warrants to a purchaser for value of the certificated security or a purchaser for value of an uncertificated security to whom the initial transaction statement has

been sent, if the purchaser is without notice of the particular defect, that:

(a) the certificated security or initial transaction statement is genuine;

(b) his own participation in the issue or registration of the transfer, pledge, or release of the security is within his capacity and within the scope of the authority received by him from the issuer; and

(c) he has reasonable grounds to believe the security is in the form and within the amount the issuer is authorized to issue.

(2) Unless otherwise agreed, a person by so placing his signature does not assume responsibility for the validity of the security in other respects.

Part 3 Transfer

Section 8–301. Rights Acquired by Purchaser

(1) Upon transfer of a security to a purchaser (Section 8–313), the purchaser acquires the rights in the security which his transferor had or had actual authority to convey unless the purchaser's rights are limited by Section 8–302(4).

(2) A transferee of a limited interest acquires rights only to the extent of the interest transferred. The creation or release of a security interest in a security is the transfer of a limited interest in that security.

Section 8–302. "Bona Fide Purchaser"; "Adverse Claim"; Title Acquired by Bona Fide Purchaser

(1) A "bona fide purchaser" is a purchaser for value in good faith and without notice of any adverse claim:

(a) who takes delivery of a certificated security in bearer form or in registered form, issued or indorsed to him or in blank;

(b) to whom the transfer, pledge, or release of an uncertificated security is registered on the books of the issuer; or

(c) to whom a security is transferred under the provisions of paragraph (c), (d)(i), or (g) of Section 8–313(1).

(2) "Adverse claim" includes a claim that a transfer was or would be wrongful or that a particular adverse person is the owner of or has an interest in the security.

(3) A bona fide purchaser in addition to acquiring the rights of a purchaser (Section 8–301) also acquires his interest in the security free of any adverse claim.

(4) Notwithstanding Section 8–301(1), the transferee of a particular certificated security who has been a party to any fraud or illegality affecting the security, or who as a prior holder of that certificated security had notice of an adverse claim, cannot improve his position by taking from a bona fide purchaser.

Section 8–303. "Broker"

"Broker" means a person engaged for all or part of his time in the business of buying and selling securities, who in the transaction concerned acts for, buys a security from, or sells a security to, a customer. Nothing in this Article determines the capacity in which a person acts for purposes of any other statute or rule to which the person is subject.

Section 8–304. Notice to Purchaser of Adverse Claims

(1) A purchaser (including a broker for the seller or buyer, but excluding an intermediary bank) of a certificated security is charged with notice of adverse claims if:

(a) the security, whether in bearer or registered form, has been indorsed "for collection" or "for surrender" or for some other purpose not involving transfer; or

(b) the security is in bearer form and has on it an unambiguous statement that it is the property of a person other than the transferor. The mere writing of a name on a security is not such a statement.

(2) A purchaser (including a broker for the seller or buyer, but excluding an intermediary bank) to whom the transfer, pledge, or release of an uncertificated security is registered is charged with notice of adverse claims as to which the issuer has a duty under Section 8–403(4) at the time of registration and which are noted in the initial transaction statement sent to the purchaser or, if his interest is transferred to him other than by registration of transfer, pledge, or release, the initial transaction statement sent to the registered owner or the registered pledgee.

(3) The fact that the purchaser (including a broker for the seller or buyer) of a certificated or uncertificated security has notice that the security is held for a third person or is registered in the name of or indorsed by a fiduciary does not create a duty of inquiry into the rightfulness of the transfer or constitute constructive notice of adverse claims. However, if the purchaser (excluding an intermediary bank) has knowledge that the proceeds are being used or that the transaction is

for the individual benefit of the fiduciary or otherwise in breach of duty, the purchaser is charged with notice of adverse claims.

Section 8–305. Staleness as Notice of Adverse Claims

An act or event that creates a right to immediate performance of the principal obligation represented by a certificated security or sets a date on or after which a certificated security is to be presented or surrendered for redemption or exchange does not itself constitute any notice of adverse claims except in the case of a transfer:

    (a) after one year from any date set for presentment or surrender for redemption or exchange; or

    (b) after 6 months from any date set for payment of money against presentation or surrender of the security if funds are available for payment on that date.

Section 8–306. Warranties on Presentment and Transfer of Certificated Securities; Warranties of Originators of Instructions

(1) A person who presents a certificated security for registration of transfer or for payment or exchange warrants to the issuer that he is entitled to the registration, payment, or exchange. But, a purchaser for value and without notice of adverse claims who receives a new, reissued, or re-registered certificated security on registration of transfer or receives an initial transaction statement confirming the registration of transfer of an equivalent uncertificated security to him warrants only that he has no knowledge of any unauthorized signature (Section 8–311) in a necessary indorsement.

(2) A person by transferring a certificated security to a purchaser for value warrants only that:

    (a) his transfer is effective and rightful;

    (b) the security is genuine and has not been materially altered; and

    (c) he knows of no fact which might impair the validity of the security.

(3) If a certificated security is delivered by an intermediary known to be entrusted with delivery of the security on behalf of another or with collection of a draft or other claim against delivery, the intermediary by delivery warrants only his own good faith and authority, even though he has purchased or made advances against the claim to be collected against the delivery.

(4) A pledgee or other holder for security who redelivers a certificated security received, or after payment and on order of the debtor delivers that security to a third person, makes only the warranties of an intermediary under subsection (3).

(5) A person who originates an instruction warrants to the issuer that:

    (a) he is an appropriate person to originate the instruction; and

    (b) at the time the instruction is presented to the issuer he will be entitled to the registration of transfer, pledge, or release.

(6) A person who originates an instruction warrants to any person specially guaranteeing his signature (subsection 8–312(3)) that:

    (a) he is an appropriate person to originate the instruction; and

    (b) at the time the instruction is presented to the issuer

        (i) he will be entitled to the registration of transfer, pledge, or release; and

        (ii) the transfer, pledge, or release requested in the instruction will be registered by the issuer free from all liens, security interests, restrictions, and claims other than those specified in the instruction.

(7) A person who originates an instruction warrants to a purchaser for value and to any person guaranteeing the instruction (Section 8–312(6)) that:

    (a) he is an appropriate person to originate the instruction;

    (b) the uncertificated security referred to therein is valid; and

    (c) at the time the instruction is presented to the issuer

        (i) the transferor will be entitled to the registration of transfer, pledge, or release;

        (ii) the transfer, pledge, or release requested in the instruction will be registered by the issuer free from all liens, security interests, restrictions, and claims other than those specified in the instruction; and

        (iii) the requested transfer, pledge, or release will be rightful.

(8) If a secured party is the registered pledgee or the registered owner of an uncertificated security, a person who originates an instruction of release or transfer to the debtor or, after payment and on order of the debtor, a transfer instruction to a third person, warrants to the debtor or the third person only that he is an appropriate person to originate the instruction and, at the time the instruction is presented to the issuer, the transferor will be entitled to the registration of release or transfer. If a transfer instruction to a third person who is a purchaser for value is originated on order of the debtor, the debtor makes to the purchaser the warranties of paragraphs (b), (c)(ii) and (c)(iii) of subsection (7).

(9) A person who transfers an uncertificated security to a purchaser for value and does not originate an instruction in connection with the transfer warrants only that:

(a) his transfer is effective and rightful; and

(b) the uncertificated security is valid.

(10) A broker gives to his customer and to the issuer and a purchaser the applicable warranties provided in this section and has the rights and privileges of a purchaser under this section. The warranties of and in favor of the broker, acting as an agent are in addition to applicable warranties given by and in favor of his customer.

Section 8–307. Effect of Delivery Without Indorsement; Right to Compel Indorsement

If a certificated security in registered form has been delivered to a purchaser without a necessary indorsement he may become a bona fide purchaser only as of the time the indorsement is supplied; but against the transferor, the transfer is complete upon delivery and the purchaser has a specifically enforceable right to have any necessary indorsement supplied.

Section 8–308. Indorsements; Instructions

(1) An indorsement of a certificated security in registered form is made when an appropriate person signs on it or on a separate document an assignment or transfer of the security or a power to assign or transfer it or his signature is written without more upon the back of the security.

(2) An indorsement may be in blank or special. An indorsement in blank includes an indorsement to bearer. A special indorsement specifies to whom the security is to be transferred, or who has power to transfer it. A holder may convert a blank indorsement into a special indorsement.

(3) An indorsement purporting to be only of part of a certificated security representing units intended by the issuer to be separately transferable is effective to the extent of the indorsement.

(4) An "instruction" is an order to the issuer of an uncertificated security requesting that the transfer, pledge, or release from pledge of the uncertificated security specified therein be registered.

(5) An instruction originated by an appropriate person is:

(a) a writing signed by an appropriate person; or

(b) a communication to the issuer in any form agreed upon in a writing signed by the issuer and an appropriate person.

If an instruction has been originated by an appropriate person but is incomplete in any other respect, any person may complete it as authorized and the issuer may rely on it as completed even though it has been completed incorrectly.

(6) "An appropriate person" in subsection (1) means the person specified by the certificated security or by special indorsement to be entitled to the security.

(7) "An appropriate person" in subsection (5) means:

(a) for an instruction to transfer or pledge an uncertificated security which is then not subject to a registered pledge, the registered owner; or

(b) for an instruction to transfer or release an uncertificated security which is then subject to a registered pledge, the registered pledgee.

(8) In addition to the persons designated in subsections (6) and (7), "an appropriate person" in subsections (1) and (5) includes:

(a) if the person designated is described as a fiduciary but is no longer serving in the described capacity, either that person or his successor;

(b) if the persons designated are described as more than one person as fiduciaries and one or more are no longer serving in the described capacity, the remaining fiduciary or fiduciaries, whether or not a successor has been appointed or qualified;

(c) if the person designated is an individual and is without capacity to act by virtue of death, incompetence, infancy, or otherwise, his executor, administrator, guardian, or like fiduciary;

(d) if the persons designated are described as more than one person as tenants by the entirety or with right of survivorship and by reason of death all cannot sign, the survivor or survivors;

(e) a person having power to sign under applicable law or controlling instrument; and

(f) to the extent that the person designated or any of the foregoing persons may act through an agent, his authorized agent.

(9) Unless otherwise agreed, the indorser of a certificated security by his indorsement or the originator of an instruction by his origination assumes no obligation that the security will be honored by the issuer but only the obligations provided in Section 8–306.

(10) Whether the person signing is appropriate is determined as of the date of signing and an indorsement made by or an instruction originated by him does not become unauthorized for the purposes of this Article by virtue of any subsequent change of circumstances.

(11) Failure of a fiduciary to comply with a controlling instrument or with the law of the state having jurisdiction of the fiduciary relationship, including any law requiring the fiduciary to obtain court approval of the transfer, pledge, or release, does not render his indorsement or an instruction originated by him unauthorized for the purposes of this Article.

Section 8–309. Effect of Indorsement Without Delivery

An indorsement of a certificated security, whether special or in blank, does not constitute a transfer until delivery of the certificated security on which it appears or, if the indorsement is on a separate document, until delivery of both the document and the certificated security.

Section 8–310. Indorsement of Certificated Security in Bearer Form

An indorsement of a certificated security in bearer form may give notice of adverse claims (Section 8–304) but does not otherwise affect any right to registration the holder possesses.

Section 8–311. Effect of Unauthorized Indorsement or Instruction

Unless the owner or pledgee has ratified an unauthorized indorsement or instruction or is otherwise precluded from asserting its ineffectiveness:

(a) he may assert its ineffectiveness against the issuer or any purchaser, other than a purchaser for value and without notice of adverse claims, who has in good faith received a new, reissued, or re-registered certificated security on registration of transfer or received an initial transaction statement confirming the registration of transfer, pledge, or release of an equivalent uncertificated security to him; and

(b) an issuer who registers the transfer of a certificated security upon the unauthorized indorsement or who registers the transfer, pledge, or release of an uncertificated security upon the unauthorized instruction is subject to liability for improper registration (Section 3–404).

Section 8–312. Effect of Guaranteeing Signature, Indorsement or Instruction

(1) Any person guaranteeing a signature of an indorser of a certificated security warrants that at the time of signing:

(a) the signature was genuine;

(b) the signer was an appropriate person to indorse (Section 8–308); and

(c) the signer had legal capacity to sign.

(2) Any person guaranteeing a signature of the originator of an instruction warrants that at the time of signing:

(a) the signature was genuine;

(b) the signer was an appropriate person to originate the instruction (Section 8–308) if the person specified in the instruction as the registered owner or registered pledgee of the uncertificated security was, in fact, the registered owner or registered pledgee of the security, as to which fact the signature guarantor makes no warranty;

(c) the signer had legal capacity to sign; and

(d) the taxpayer identification number, if any, appearing on the instruction as that of the registered owner or registered pledgee was the taxpayer identification number of the signer or of the owner or pledgee for whom the signer was acting.

(3) Any person specially guaranteeing the signature of the originator of an instruction makes not only the warranties of a signature guarantor (subsection (2)) but also warrants that at the time the instruction is presented to the issuer:

(a) the person specified in the instruction as the registered owner or registered pledgee of the uncertificated security will be the registered owner or registered pledgee; and

(b) the transfer, pledge, or release of the uncertificated security requested in the instruction will be registered by the issuer free from all liens, security interests, restrictions, and claims other than those specified in the instruction.

(4) The guarantor under subsections (1) and (2) or the special guarantor under subsection (3) does not otherwise warrant the rightfulness of the particular transfer, pledge, or release.

(5) Any person guaranteeing an indorsement of a certificated security makes not only the warranties of a signature guarantor under subsection (1) but also warrants the rightfulness of the particular transfer in all respects.

(6) Any person guaranteeing an instruction requesting the transfer, pledge, or release of an uncertificated security makes not only the warranties of a special signature guarantor under subsection (3) but also warrants the rightfulness of the particular transfer, pledge, or release in all respects.

(7) No issuer may require a special guarantee of signature (subsection (3)), a guarantee of indorsement (subsection (5)), or a guarantee of instruction (subsection (6)) as a condition to registration of transfer, pledge, or release.

(8) The foregoing warranties are made to any person taking or dealing with the security in reliance on the guarantee, and the guarantor is liable to the person for any loss resulting from breach of the warranties.

Section 8–313. When Transfer to Purchaser Occurs; Financial Intermediary as Bona Fide Purchaser; "Financial Intermediary"

(1) Transfer of a security or a limited interest (including a security interest) therein to a purchaser occurs only:

(a) at the time he or a person designated by him acquires possession of a certificated security;

(b) at the time the transfer, pledge, or release of an uncertificated security is registered to him or a person designated by him;

(c) at the time his financial intermediary acquires possession of a certificated security

specially indorsed to or issued in the name of the purchaser;

(d) at the time a financial intermediary, not a clearing corporation, sends him confirmation of the purchase and also by book entry or otherwise identifies as belonging to the purchaser

(i) a specific certificated security in the financial intermediary's possession;

(ii) as quantity of securities that constitute or are part of a fungible bulk of certificated securities in the financial intermediary's possession or of uncertificated securities registered in the name of the financial intermediary; or

(iii) a quantity of securities that constitute or are part of a fungible bulk of securities shown on the account of the financial intermediary on the books of another financial intermediary;

(e) with respect to an identified certificated security to be delivered while still in the possession of a third person, not a financial intermediary, at the time that person acknowledges that he holds for the purchaser;

(f) with respect to a specific uncertificated security the pledge or transfer of which has been registered to a third person, not a financial intermediary, at the time that person acknowledges that he holds for the purchaser;

(g) at the time appropriate entries to the account of the purchaser or a person designated by him on the books of a clearing corporation are made under Section 8–320;

(h) with respect to the transfer of a security interest where the debtor has signed a security agreement containing a description of the security, at the time a written notification, which, in the case of the creation of the security interest, is signed by the debtor (which may be a copy of the security agreement) or which, in the case of the release or assignment of the security interest created pursuant to this paragraph, is signed by the secured party, is received by

(i) a financial intermediary on whose books the interest of the transferor in the security appears;

(ii) a third person, not a financial intermediary, in possession of the security, if it is certificated;

(iii) a third person, not a financial intermediary, who is the registered owner of the security, if it is uncertificated and not subject to a registered pledge; or

(iv) a third person, not a financial intermediary, who is the registered pledgee of the security, if it is uncertificated and subject to a registered pledge;

(i) with respect to the transfer of a security interest where the transferor has signed a security agreement containing a description of the security, at the time new value if given by the secured party; or

(j) with respect to the transfer of a security interest where the secured party is a financial intermediary and the security has already been transferred to the financial intermediary under paragraphs (a), (b), (c), (d), or (g), at the time the transferor has signed a security agreement containing a description of the security and value is given by the secured party.

(2) The purchaser is the owner of a security held for him by a financial intermediary, but cannot be a bona fide purchaser of a security so held except in the circumstances specified in paragraphs (c), (d) (i), and (g) of subsection (1). If a security so held is part of a fungible bulk, as in the circumstances specified in paragraphs (d) (ii) and (d) (iii) of subsection (1), the purchaser is the owner of a proportionate property interest in the fungible bulk.

(3) Notice of an adverse claim received by the financial intermediary or by the purchaser after the financial intermediary takes delivery of a certificated security as a holder for value or after the transfer, pledge, or release of an uncertificated security has been registered free of the claim to a financial intermediary who has given value is not effective either as to the financial intermediary or as to the purchaser. However, as between the financial intermediary and the purchaser the purchaser may demand transfer of an equivalent security as to which no notice of adverse claim has been received.

(4) A "financial intermediary" is a bank, broker, clearing corporation, or other person (or the nominee of any of them) which in the ordinary course of its business maintains security accounts for its customers and is acting in that capacity. A financial intermediary may have a security interest in securities held in account for its customer.

Section 8–314. Duty to Transfer, When Completed

(1) Unless otherwise agreed, if a sale of a security is made on an exchange or otherwise through brokers:

(a) the selling customer fulfills his duty to transfer at the time he:

(i) places a certificated security in the possession of the selling broker or a person designated by the broker;

(ii) causes an uncertificated security to be registered in the name of the selling broker or a person designated by the broker;

(iii) if requested, causes an acknowledgment to be made to the selling broker that a certificated or uncertificated security is held for the broker; or

(iv) places in the possession of the selling broker or of a person designated by the broker a transfer instruction for an uncertificated security, providing the issuer does not refuse to register the requested transfer if the instruction is presented to the issuer for registration within 30 days thereafter; and

(b) the selling broker, including a correspondent broker acting for a selling customer, fulfills his duty to transfer at the time he:

(i) places a certificated security in the possession of the buying broker or a person designated by the buying broker;

(ii) causes an uncertificated security to be registered in the name of the buying broker or a person designated by the buying broker;

(iii) places in the possession of the buying broker or of a person designated by the buying broker a transfer instruction for an uncertificated security, providing the issuer does not refuse to register the requested transfer if the instruction is presented to the issuer for registration within 30 days thereafter; or

87

(iv) effects clearance of the sale in accordance with the rules of the exchange on which the transaction took place.

(2) Except as provided in this section or unless otherwise agreed, a transferor's duty to transfer a security under a contract of purchase is not fulfilled until he:

(a) places a certificated security in form to be negotiated by the purhaser in the possession of the purchaser or of a person designated by the purchaser;

(b) causes an uncertificated security to be registered in the name of the purchaser or a person designated by the purchaser; or

(c) if the purchaser requests, causes an acknowledgment to be made to the purchaser that a certificated or uncertificated security is held for the purchaser.

(3) Unless made on an exchange, a sale to a broker purchasing for his own account is within subsection (2) and not within subsection (1).

Section 8–315. Action Against Transferee Based Upon Wrongful Transfer

(1) Any person against whom the transfer of a security is wrongful for any reason, including his incapacity, as against anyone except a bona fide purchaser, may:

(a) reclaim possession of the certificated security wrongfully transferred;

(b) obtain possession of any new certificated security representing all or part of the same rights;

(c) compel the origination of an instruction to transfer to him or a person designated by him an uncertificated security constituting all or part of the same rights; or

(d) have damages.

(2) If the transfer is wrongful because of an unauthorized indorsement of a certificated security, the owner may also reclaim or obtain possession of the security or a new certificated security, even from a bona fide purchaser, if the ineffectiveness of the purported indorsement can be asserted against him under the provisions of this Article on unauthorized indorsements (Section 8–311).

(3) The right to obtain or reclaim possession of a certificated security or to compel the origination of a transfer instruction may be specifically enforced and the transfer of a certificated or uncertificated security

enjoined and a certificated security impounded pending the litigation.

Section 8–316. Purchaser's Right to Requisites for Registration of Transfer, Pledge, or Release on Books

Unless otherwise agreed, the transferor of a certificated security or the transferor, pledgor, or pledgee of an uncertificated security on due demand must supply his purchaser with any proof of his authority to transfer, pledge, or release or with any other requisite necessary to obtain registration of the transfer, pledge, or release of the security; but if the transfer, pledge, or release is not for value, a transferor, pledgor, or pledgee need not do so unless the purchaser furnishes the necessary expenses. Failure within a reasonable time to comply with a demand made gives the purchaser the right to reject or rescind the transfer, pledge, or release.

Section 8–317. Creditors' Rights

(1) Subject to the exceptions in subsections (3) and (4), no attachment or levy upon a certificated security or any share or other interest represented thereby which is outstanding is valid until the security is actually seized by the officer making the attachment or levy, but a certificated security which has been surrendered to the issuer may be reached by a creditor by legal process at the issuer's chief executive office in the United States.

(2) An uncertificated security registered in the name of the debtor may not be reached by a creditor except by legal process at the issuer's chief executive office in the United States.

(3) The interest of a debtor in a certificated security that is in the possession of a secured party not a financial intermediary or in an uncertificated security registered in the name of a secured party not a financial intermediary (or in the name of a nominee of the secured party) may be reached by a creditor by legal process upon the secured party.

(4) The interest of a debtor in a certificated security that is in the possession of or registered in the name of a financial intermediary or in an uncertificated security registered in the name of a financial intermediary may be reached by a creditor by legal process upon the financial intermediary on whose books the interest of the debtor appears.

(5) Unless otherwise provided by law, a creditor's lien upon the interest of a debtor in a security obtained pursuant to subsection (3) or (4) is not a restraint on the transfer of the security, free of the lien, to a third party

for new value; but in the event of a transfer, the lien applies to the proceeds of the transfer in the hands of the secured party or financial intermediary, subject to any claims having priority.

(6) A creditor whose debtor is the owner of a security is entitled to aid from courts of appropriate jurisdiction, by injunction or otherwise, in reaching the security or in satisfying the claim by means allowed at law or in equity in regard to property that cannot readily be reached by ordinary legal process.

Section 8–318. No Conversion by Good Faith Conduct

An agent or bailee who in good faith (including observance of reasonable commercial standards if he is in the business of buying, selling, or otherwise dealing with securities) has received certificated securities and sold, pledged, or delivered them or has sold or caused the transfer or pledge of uncertificated securities over which he had control according to the instructions of his principal, is not liable for conversion or for participation in breach of fiduciary duty although the principal had no right so to deal with the securities.

Section 8–319. Statute of Frauds

A contract for the sale of securities is not enforceable by way of action or defense unless:

(a) there is some writing signed by the party against whom enforcement is sought or by his authorized agent or broker, sufficient to indicate that a contract has been made for sale of a stated quantity of described securities at a defined or stated price;

(b) delivery of a certificated security or transfer instruction has been accepted, or transfer of an uncertificated security has been registered and the transferee has failed to send written objection to the issuer within 10 days after receipt of the initial transaction statement confirming the registration, or payment has been made, but the contract is enforceable under this provision only to the extent of the delivery, registration, or payment;

(c) within a reasonable time a writing in confirmation of the sale or purchase and sufficient against the sender under paragraph (a) has been received by the party against whom enforcement is sought and he has failed to send written objection to its contents within 10 days after its receipt; or

(d) the party against whom enforcement is sought admits in his pleading, testimony, or otherwise in court that a contract was made for the sale of a stated quantity of described securities at a defined or stated price.

Section 8–320. Transfer or Pledge Within Central Depository System

(1) In addition to other methods, a transfer, pledge, or release of a security or any interest therein may be effectd by the making of appropriate entries on the books of a clearing corporation reducing the account of the transferor, pledgor, or pledgee and increasing the account of the transferee, pledgee, or pledgor by the amount of the obligation or the number of shares or rights transferred, pledged, or released, if the security is shown on the account of a transferor, pledgor, or pledgee on the books of the clearing corporation; is subject to the control of the clearing corporation; and

(a) if certificated,

(i) is in the custody of the clearing corporation, another clearing corporation, a custodian bank, or a nominee of any of them; and

(ii) is in bearer form or indorsed in blank by an appropriate person or registered in the name of the clearing corporation, a custodian bank, or a nominee of any of them; or

(b) if uncertificated, is registered in the name of the clearing corporation, another clearing corporation, a custodian bank, or a nominee of any of them.

(2) Under this section entries may be made with respect to like securities or interests therein as a part of a fungible bulk and may refer merely to a quantity of a particular security without reference to the name of the registered owner, certificate or bond number, or the like, and, in appropriate cases, may be on a net basis taking into account other transfers, pledges, or releases of the same security.

(3) A transfer under this section is effective (Section 8–313) and the purchaser acquires the rights of the transferor (Section 8–301). A pledge or release under this section is the transfer of a limited interest. If a pledge or the creation of a security interest is intended, the security interest is perfected at the time when both value is given by the pledgee and the appropriate entries are made (Section 8–321). A transferee or

pledgee under this section may be a bona fide purchaser (Section 8–302).

(4) A transfer or pledge under this section is not a registration of transfer under Part 4.

(5) That entries made on the books of the clearing corporation as provided in subsection (1) are not appropriate does not affect the validity or effect of the entires or the liabilities or obligations of the clearing corporation to any person adversely affected thereby.

Section 8–321. Enforceability, Attachment, Perfection and Termination of Security Interests

(1) A security interest in a security is enforceable and can attach only if it is transferred to the secured party or a person designated by him pursuant to a provision of Section 8–313(1).

(2) A security interest so transferred pursuant to agreement by a transferor who has rights in the security to a transferee who has given value is a perfected security interest, but a security interest that has been transferred solely under paragraph (i) of Section 8–313(1) becomes unperfected after 21 days unless, within that time, the requirements for transfer under any other provision of Section 8–313(1) are satisfied.

(3) A security interest in a security is subject to the provisions of Article 9, but:

  (a) no filing is required to perfect the security interest; and

  (b) no written security agreement signed by the debtor is necessary to make the security interest enforceable, except as provided in paragraph (h), (i), or (j) of Section 8–313(1). The secured party has the rights and duties provided under Section 9–207, to the extent they are applicable, whether or not the security is certificated, and, if certificated, whether or not it is in his possession.

(4) Unless otherwise agreed, a security interest in a security is terminated by transfer to the debtor or a person designated by him pursuant to a provision of Section 8–313(1). If a security is thus transferred, the security interest, if not terminated, becomes unperfected unless the security is certificated and is delivered to the debtor for the purpose of ultimate sale or exchange or presentation, collection, renewal, or registration of transfer. In that case, the security interest becomes unperfected after 21 days unless, within that time, the security (or securities for which it has been

exchanged) is transferred to the secured party or a person designated by him pursuant to a provision of Section 8–313(1).

Part 4 Registration

Section 8–401. Duty of Issuer to Register Transfer, Pledge, or Release

(1) If a certificated security in registered form is presented to the issuer with a request to register transfer or an instruction is presented to the issuer with a request to register transfer, pledge, or release, the issuer shall register the transfer, pledge, or release as requested if:

  (a) the security is indorsed or the instruction was originated by the appropriate person or persons (Section 8–308);

  (b) reasonable assurance is given that those indorsements or instructions are genuine and effective (Section 8–402);

  (c) the issuer has no duty as to adverse claims or has discharged the duty (Section 8–403);

  (d) any applicable law relating to the collection of taxes has been complied with; and

  (e) the transfer, pledge, or release is in fact rightful or is to a bona fide purchaser.

(2) If an issuer is under a duty to register a transfer, pledge, or release of a security, the issuer is also liable to the person presenting a certificated security or an instruction for registration or his principal for loss resulting from any unreasonable delay in registration or from failure or refusal to register the transfer, pledge, or release.

Section 8–402. Assurance that Indorsements and Instructions Are Effective

(1) The issuer may require the following assurance that each necessary indorsement of a certificated security or each instruction (Section 8–308) is genuine and effective:

  (a) in all cases, a guarantee of the signature (Section 8–312(1) or (2)) of the person indorsing a certificated security or originating an instruction including, in the case of an instruction, a warranty of the taxpayer identification number or, in the absence thereof, other reasonable assurance of identity;

  (b) if the indorsement is made or the instruction is originated by an agent, appropriate assurance of authority to sign;

(c) if the indorsement is made or the instruction is originated by a fiduciary, appropriate evidence of appointment or incumbency;

(d) if there is more than one fiduciary, reasonable assurance that all who are required to sign have done so; and

(e) if the indorsement is made or the instruction is originated by a person not covered by any of the foregoing, assurance appropriate to the case corresponding as nearly as may be to the foregoing.

(2) A "guarantee of the signature" in subsection (1) means a guarantee signed by or on behalf of a person reasonably believed by the issuer to be responsible. The issuer may adopt standards with respect to responsibility if they are not manifestly unreasonable.

(3) "Appropriate evidence of appointment or incumbency" in subsection (1) means:

(a) in the case of a fiduciary appointed or qualified by a court, a certificate issued by or under the direction or supervision of that court or an officer thereof and dated within 60 days before the date of presentation for transfer, pledge, or release; or

(b) in any other case, a copy of a document showing the appointment or a certificate issued by or on behalf of a person reasonably believed by the issuer to be responsible or, in the absence of that document or certificate, other evidence reasonably deemed by the issuer to be appropriate. The issuer may adopt standards with respect to the evidence if they are not manifestly unreasonable. The issuer is not charged with notice of the contents of any document obtained pursuant to this paragraph (b) except to the extent that the contents relate directly to the appointment or incumbency.

(4) The issuer may elect to require reasonable assurance beyond that specified in this section, but if it does so and, for a purpose other than that specified in subsection (3)(b), both requires and obtains a copy of a will, trust, indenture, articles of co-partnership, by-laws, or other controlling instrument, it is charged with notice of all matters contained therein affecting the transfer, pledge, or release.

Section 8–403. Issuer's Duty as to Adverse Claims

(1) An issuer to whom a certificated security is presented for registration shall inquire into adverse claims if:

(a) a written notification of an adverse claim is received at a time and in a manner affording the issuer a reasonable opportunity to act on it prior to the issuance of a new, reissued, or re-registered certificated security, and the notification identifies the claimant, the registered owner, and the issue of which the security is a part, and provides an address for communications directed to the claimant; or

(b) the issuer is charged with notice of an adverse claim from a controlling instrument it has elected to require under Section 8–402(4).

(2) The issuer may discharge any duty of inquiry by any reasonable means, including notifying an adverse claimant by registered or certified mail at the address furnished by him or, if there be no such address, at his residence or regular place of business that the certificated security has been presented for registration of transfer by a named person, and that the transfer will be registered unless within 30 days from the date of mailing the notification, either:

(a) an appropriate restraining order, injunction, or other process issues from a court of competent jurisdiction; or

(b) there is filed with the issuer an indemnity bond, sufficient in the issuer's judgment to protect the issuer and any transfer agent, registrar, or other agent of the issuer involved from any loss it or they may suffer by complying with the adverse claim.

(3) Unless an issuer is charged with notice of an adverse claim from a controlling instrument which it has elected to require under Section 8–402(4) or receives notification of an adverse claim under subsection (1), if a certificated security presented for registration is indorsed by the appropriate person or persons the issuer is under no duty to inquire into adverse claims. In particular:

(a) an issuer registering a certificated security in the name of a person who is a fiduciary or who is described as a fiduciary is not bound to inquire into the existence, extent, or correct description of the fiduciary relationship; and thereafter the issuer may assume without inquiry that the newly registered owner continues to be the fiduciary until the issuer receives written notice that the fiduciary is no longer acting as such with respect to the particular security;

(b) an issuer registering transfer on an indorsement by a fiduciary is not bound to inquire whether the transfer is made in compliance with a controlling instrument or with the law of the state having jurisdiction of the fiduciary relationship, including any law requiring the fiduciary to obtain court approval of the transfer; and

(c) the issuer is not charged with notice of the contents of any court record or file or other recorded or unrecorded document even though the document is in its possession and even though the transfer is made on the indorsement of a fiduciary to the fiduciary himself or to his nominee.

(4) An issuer is under no duty as to adverse claims with respect to an uncertificated security except:

(a) claims embodied in a restraining order, injunction, or other legal process served upon the issuer if the process was served at a time and in a manner affording the issuer a reasonable opportunity to act on it in accordance with the requirements of subsection (5);

(b) claims of which the issuer has received a written notification from the registered owner or the registered pledgee if the notification was received at a time and in a manner affording the issuer a reasonable opportunity to act on it in accordance with the requirements of subsection (5);

(c) claims (including restrictions on transfer not imposed by the issuer) to which the registration of transfer to the present registered owner was subject and were so noted in the initial transaction statement sent to him; and

(d) claims as to which an issuer is charged with notice from a controlling instrument it has elected to require under Section 8–402(4).

(5) If the issuer of an uncertificated security is under a duty to an adverse claim, he discharges that duty by:

(a) including a notation of the claim in any statements sent with respect to the security under Sections 8–408 (3), (6), and (7); and

(b) refusing to register the transfer or pledge of the security unless the nature of the claim does not preclude transfer or pledge subject thereto.

(6) If the transfer or pledge of the security is registered subject to an adverse claim, a notation of the claim must be included in the initial transaction statement and all subsequent statements sent to the transferee and pledgee under Section 8–408.

(7) Notwithstanding subsections (4) and (5), if an uncertificated security was subject to a registered pledge at the time the issuer first came under a duty as to a particular adverse claim, the issuer has no duty as to that claim if transfer of the security is requested by the registered pledgee or an appropriate person acting for the registered pledgee unless:

(a) the claim was embodied in legal process which expressly provides otherwise;

(b) the claim was asserted in a written notification from the registered pledgee;

(c) the claim was one as to which the issuer was charged with notice from a controlling instrument it required under Section 8–402(4) in connection with the pledgee's request for transfer; or

(d) the transfer requested is to the registered owner.

Section 8–404. Liability and Non-Liability for Registration

(1) Except as provided in any law relating to the collection of taxes, the issuer in not liable to the owner, pledgee, or any other person suffering loss as a result of the registration of a transfer, pledge, or release of a security if:

(a) there were on or with a certificated security the necessary indorsements or the issuer had received an instruction originated by an appropriate person (Section 8–308); and

(b) the issuer had no duty as to adverse claims or has discharged the duty (Section 8–403).

(2) If an issuer had registered a transfer of a certificated security to a person not entitled to it, the issuer on demand shall deliver a like security to the true owner unless:

(a) the registration was pursuant to subsection (1);

(b) the owner is precluded from asserting any claim for registering the transfer under Section 8–405(1); or

(c) the delivery would result in overissue, in which case the issuer's liability is governed by Section 8–104.

(3) If an issuer has improperly registered a transfer,

pledge, or release of an uncertificated security, the issuer on demand from the injured party shall restore the records as to the injured party to the condition that would have obtained if the improper registration had not been made unless:

(a) the registration was pursuant to subsection (1); or

(b) the registration would result in overissue, in which case the issuer's liability is governed by Section 8–104.

Section 8–405. Lost, Destroyed, and Stolen Certificated Securities

(1) If a certificated security has been lost, apparently destroyed, or wrongfully taken, and the owner fails to notify the issuer of that fact within a reasonable time after he has notice of it and the issuer registers a transfer of the security before receiving notification, the owner is precluded from asserting against the issuer any claim for registering the transfer under Section 8–404 or any claim to a new security under this section.

(2) If the owner of a certificated security claims that the security has been lost, destroyed, or wrongfully taken, the issuer shall issue a new certificated security or, at the option of the issuer, an equivalent uncertificated security in place of the original security if the owner:

(a) so requests before the issuer has notice that the security has been acquired by a bona fide purchaser;

(b) files with the issuer a sufficient indemnity bond; and

(c) satisfies any other reasonable requirements imposed by the issuer.

(3) If, after the issue of a new certificated or uncertificated security, a bona fide purchaser of the original certificated security presents it for registration of transfer, the issuer shall register the transfer unless registration would result in overissue, in which event the issuer's liability is governed by Section 8–104. In addition to any rights on the indemnity bond, the issuer may recover the new certificated security from the person to whom it was issued or any person taking under him except a bona fide purchaser or may cancel the uncertificated security unless a bona fide purchaser or any person taking under a bona fide purchaser is then the registered owner or registered pledgee thereof.

Section 8–406. Duty of Authenticating Trustee, Transfer Agent, or Registrar

(1) If a person acts as authenticating trustee, transfer agent, registrar, or other agent for an issuer in the registration of transfers of its certificated securities or in the registration of transfers, pledges, and releases of its uncertificated securities, in the issue of new securities, or in the cancellation of surrendered securities:

(a) he is under a duty to the issuer to exercise good faith and due diligence in performing his functions; and

(b) with regard to the particular functions he performs, he has the same obligation to the holder or owner of a certificated security or to the owner or pledgee of an uncertificated security and has the same rights and privileges as the issuer has in regard to those functions.

(2) Notice to an authenticating trustee, transfer agent, registrar or other agent is notice to the issuer with respect to the functions performed by the agent.

Section 8–407. Exchangeability of Securities

(1) No issuer is subject to the requirements of this section unless it regularly maintains a system for issuing the class of securities involved under which both certificated and uncertificated securities are regularly issued to the category of owners, which includes the person in whose name the new security is to be registered.

(2) Upon surrender of a certificated security with all necessary indorsements and presentation of a written request by the person surrendering the security, the issuer, if he has no duty as to adverse claims or has discharged the duty (Section 8–403), shall issue to the person or a person designated by him an equivalent uncertificated security subject to all liens, restrictions, and claims that were noted on the certificated security.

(3) Upon receipt of a transfer instruction originated by an appropriate person who so requests, the issuer of an uncertificated security shall cancel the uncertificated security and issue an equivalent certificated security on which must be noted conspicuously any liens and restrictions of the issuer and any adverse claims (as to which the issuer has a duty under Section 8–403(4)) to which the uncertificated security was subject. The certificated security shall be registered in the name of and delivered to:

(a) the registered owner, if the uncertificated security was not subject to a registered pledge; or

(b) the registered pledgee, if the uncertificated security was subject to a registered pledge.

Section 8–408. Statements of Uncertificated Securities

(1) Within 2 business days after the transfer of an uncertificated security has been registered, the issuer shall send to the new registered owner and, if the security has been transferred subject to a registered pledge, to the registered pledgee a written statement containing:

(a) a description of the issue of which the uncertificated security is a part;

(b) the number of shares or units transferred;

(c) the name and address and any taxpayer identification number of the new registered owner and, if the security has been transferred subject to a registered pledge, the name and address and any taxpayer identification number of the registered pledgee;

(d) a notation of any liens and restrictions of the issuer and any adverse claims (as to which the issuer has a duty under Section 8–403(4)) to which the uncertificated security is or may be subject at the time of registration or a statement that there are none of those liens, restrictions, or adverse claims; and

(e) the date the transfer was registered.

(2) Within 2 business days after the pledge of an uncertificated security has been registered, the issuer shall send to the registered owner and the registered pledgee a written statement containing:

(a) a description of the issue of which the uncertificated security is a part;

(b) the number of shares or units pledged;

(c) the name and address and any taxpayer identification number of the registered owner and the registered pledgee;

(d) a notation of any liens and restrictions of the issuer and any adverse claims (as to which the issuer has a duty under Section 8–403(4)) to which the uncertificated security is or may be subject at the time of registration or a statement that there are none of those liens, restrictions, or adverse claims; and

(e) the date the pledge was registered.

(3) Within 2 business days after the release from pledge of an uncertificated security has been registered, the issuer shall send to the registered owner and the pledgee whose interest was released a written statement containing:

(a) a description of the issue of which the uncertificated security is a part;

(b) the number of shares or units released from pledge;

(c) the name and address and any taxpayer identification number of the registered owner and the pledgee whose interest was released;

(d) a notation of any liens and restrictions of the issuer and any adverse claims (as to which the issuer has a duty under Section 8–403(4)) to which the uncertificated security is or may be subject at the time of registration or a statement that there are none of those liens, restrictions, or adverse claims; and

(e) the date the release was registered.

(4) An "initial transaction statement" is the statement sent to:

(a) the new registered owner and, if applicable, to the registered pledgee pursuant to subsection (1);

(b) the registered pledgee pursuant to subsection (2); or

(c) the registered owner pursuant to subsection (3).

Each initial transaction statement shall be signed by or on behalf of the issuer and must be identified as "Initial Transaction Statement."

(5) Within 2 business days after the transfer of an uncertificated security has been registered, the issuer shall send to the former registered owner and the former registered pledgee, if any, a written statement containing:

(a) a description of the issue of which the uncertificated security is a part;

(b) the number of shares or units transferred;

(c) the name and address and any taxpayer identification number of the former registered owner and of any former registered pledgee; and

(d) the date the transfer was registered.

(6) At periodic intervals no less frequent than annually and at any time upon the reasonable written request of the registered owner, the issuer shall send to

the registered owner of each uncertificated security a dated written statement containing:

- (a) a description of the issue of which the uncertificated security is a part;
- (b) the name and address and any taxpayer identification number of the registered owner;
- (c) the number of shares or units of the uncertificated security registered in the name of the registered owner on the date of the statement;
- (d) the name and address and any taxpayer identification number of any registered pledgee and the number of shares of units subject to the pledge; and
- (e) a notation of any liens and restrictions of the issuer and any adverse claims (as to which the issuer has a duty under Section 8–403(4)) to which the uncertificated security is or may be subject or a statement that there are none of those liens, restrictions, or adverse claims.

(7) At periodic intervals no less frequent than annually and at any time upon the reasonable written request of the registered pledgee, the issuer shall send to the registered pledgee of each uncertificated security a dated written statement containing:

- (a) a description of the issue of which the uncertificated security is a part;
- (b) the name and address and any taxpayer identification number of the registered owner;
- (c) the name and address and any taxpayer identification number of the registered pledgee;
- (d) the number of shares or units subject to the pledge; and
- (e) a notation of any liens and restrictions of the issuer and any adverse claims (as to which the issuer has a duty under Section 8–403(4)) to which the uncertificated security is or may be subject or a statement that there are none of those liens, restrictions, or adverse claims.

(8) If the issuer sends the statements described in subsections (6) and (7) at periodic intervals no less frequent than quarterly, the issuer is not obliged to send additional statements upon request unless the owner or pledgee requesting them pays to the issuer the reasonable cost of furnishing them.

(9) Each statement sent pursuant to this section must bear a conspicuous legend reading substantially as follows:"This statement is merely a record of the rights of the addressee as of the time of its issuance. Delivery of this statement, of itself, confers no rights on the re-

cipient. This statement is neither a negotiable instrument nor a security."

ARTICLE 9 SECURED TRANSACTIONS; SALES OF ACCOUNTS AND CHATTEL PAPER

Part 1 Short Title, Applicability and Definitions

Section 9–101. Short Title

This Article shall be known and may be cited as Uniform Commercial Code–Secured Transactions.

Section 9–102. Policy and Subject Matter of Article

(1) Except as otherwise provided in Section 9–104 on excluded transactions, this Article applies

- (a) to any transaction (regardless of its form) which is intended to create a security interest in personal property or fixtures including goods, documents, instruments, general intangibles, chattel paper or accounts; and also
- (b) to any sale of accounts or chattel papter.

(2) This Article applies to security interests created by contract including pledge, assignment, chattel mortgage, chattel trust, trust deed, factor's lien, equipment trust, conditional sale, trust receipt, other lien or title retention contract and lease or consignment intended as security. This Article does not apply to statutory liens except as provided in Section 9–310.

(3) The application of this Article to a security interest in a secured obligation is not affected by the fact that the obligation is itself secured by a transaction or interest to which this Article does not apply.

Note: *The adoption of this Article should be accompanied by the repeal of existing statutes dealing with conditional sales, trust receipts, factor's liens where the factor is given a non-possessory lien, chattel mortgages, crop mortgages, mortgages on railroad equipment, assignment of accounts and generally statutes regulating security interests in personal property.*

Where the state has a retail installment selling act or small loan act, that legislation should be carefully examined to determine what changes in those acts are needed to conform them to this Article. This Article primarily sets out rules defining rights of a secured party against persons dealing with the debtor; it does not prescribe regulations and controls which may be necessary to curb abuses arising in the small loan business or in the financing of consumer purchases on credit. Accordingly there is no intention to repeal existing regulatory acts in those fields by enactment or re-enactment of Article 9. See Section 9–203(4) and the Note thereto.

Section 9–103. Perfection of Security Interest in Multiple State Transactions

(1) Documents, instruments and ordinary goods.

    (a) This subsection applies to documents and instruments and to goods other than those covered by a certificate of title described in subsection (2), mobile goods described in subsection (3), and minerals described in subsection (5).

    (b) Except as otherwise provided in this subsection, perfection and the effect of perfection or non-perfection of a security interest in collateral are governed by the law of the jurisdiction where the collateral is when the last event occurs on which is based the assertion that the security interest is perfected or unperfected.

    (c) If the parties to a transaction creating a purchase money security interest in goods in one jurisdiction understand at the time that the security interest attaches that the goods will be kept in another jurisdiction, then the law of the other jurisdiction governs the perfection and the effect of perfection or non-perfection of the security interest from the time it attaches until thirty days after the debtor receives possession of the goods and thereafter if the goods are taken to the other jurisdiction before the end of the thirty-day period.

    (d) When collateral is brought into and kept in this state while subject to a security interest perfected under the law of the jurisdiction from which the collateral was removed, the security interest remains perfected, but if action is required by Part 3 of this Article to perfect the security interest,

        (i) if the action is not taken before the expiration of the period of perfection in the other jurisdiction or the end of four months after the collateral is brought into this state, whichever period first expires, the security interest becomes unperfected at the end of that period and is thereafter deemed to have been unperfected as against a person who became a purchaser after removal;

        (ii) if the action is taken before the expiration of the period specified in subparagraph (i), the security interest continues perfected thereafter;

        (iii) for the purpose of priority over a buyer of consumer goods (subsection (2) of Section 9–307), the period of the effectiveness of a filing in the jurisdiction from which the collateral is removed is governed by the rules with respect to perfection in subparagraphs (i) and (ii).

(2) Certificate of title.

    (a) This subsection applies to goods covered by a certificate of title issued under a statute of this state or of another jurisdiction under the law of which indication of a security interest on the certificate is required as a condition of perfection.

    (b) Except as otherwise provided in this subsection, perfection and the effect of perfection or non-perfection of the security interest are governed by the law (including the conflict of laws rules) of the jurisdiction issuing the certificate until four months after the goods are removed from that jurisdiction and thereafter until the goods are registered in another jurisdiction, but in any event not beyond surrender of the certificate. After the expiration of that period, the goods are not covered by the certificate of title within the meaning of this section.

    (c) Except with respect to the rights of a buyer described in the next paragraph, a security interest, perfected in another jurisdiction otherwise than by notation on a certificate of title, in goods brought into this state and thereafter covered by a certificate of title issued by this state is subject to the rules stated in paragraph (d) of subsection (1).

    (d) If goods are brought into this state while a security interest therein is perfected in any manner under the law of the jurisdiction from which the goods are removed and a certificate of title is issued by this state and the certificate does not show that the goods are subject to the security interest or that they may be subject to security interests not shown on the certificate, the security interest is subordinate to the rights of a buyer of the goods who is not in the business of selling goods of that kind to the extent that he gives value and receives delivery of the goods after issuance of the certificate and without knowledge of the security interest.

(3) Accounts, general intangibles and mobile goods.

(a) This subsection applies to accounts (other than an acount described in subsection (5) on minerals) and general intangibles (other than uncertificated securities) and to goods which are mobile and which are of a type normally used in more than one jurisdiction, such as motor vehicles, trailers, rolling stock, airplanes, shipping containers, road building and construction machinery and commercial harvesting machinery and the like, if the goods are equipment or are inventory leased or held for lease by the debtor to others, and are not covered by a certificate of title described in subsection (2).

(b) The law (including the conflict of laws rules) of the jurisdiction in which the debtor is located governs the perfection and the effect of perfection or non-perfection of the security interest.

(c) If, however, the debtor is located in a jurisdiction which is not a part of the United States, and which does not provide for perfection of the security interest by filing or recording in that jurisdiction, the law of the jurisdiction in the United States in which the debtor has its major executive office governs the perfection and the effect of perfection or non-perfection of the security interest through filing. In the alternative, if the debtor is located in a jurisdiction which is not a part of the United States or Canada and the collateral is accounts or general intangibles for money due or to become due, the security interest may be perfected by notification to the account debtor. As used in this paragraph, "United States" includes its territories and possessions and the Commonwealth of Puerto Rico.

(d) A debtor shall be deemed located at his place of business if he has one, at his chief executive office if he has more than one place of business, otherwise at his residence. If, however, the debtor is a foreign air carrier under the Federal Aviation Act of 1958, as amended, it shall be deemed located at the designated office of the agent upon whom service of process may be made on behalf of the foreign air carrier.

(e) A security interest perfected under the law of the jurisdiction of the location of the debtor is perfected until the expiration of four months after a change of the debtor's location to another jurisdiction, or until perfection would have ceased by the law of the first jurisdiction, whichever period first expires. Unless perfected in the new jurisdiction before the end of that period, it becomes unperfected thereafter and is deemed to have been unperfected as against a person who became a purchaser after the change.

(4) Chattel paper. The rules stated for goods in subsection (1) apply to a possessory security interest in chattel paper. The rules stated for accounts in subsection (3) apply to a non-possessory security interest in chattel paper, but the security interest may not be perfected by notification to the account debtor.

(5) Minerals. Perfection and the effect of perfection or non-perfection of a security interest which is created by a debtor who has an interest in minerals or the like (including oil and gas) before extraction and which attaches thereto as extracted, or which attaches to an account resulting from the sale thereof at the wellhead or minehead are governed by the law (including the conflict of laws rules) of the jurisdiction wherein the wellhead or minehead is located.

(6) Uncertificated securities. The law (including the conflict of laws rules) of the jurisdiction of organization of the issuer governs the perfection and the effect of perfection or non-perfection of a security interest in uncertificated securities.

Section 9–104. Transactions Excluded From Article

This Article does not apply

(a) to a security interest subject to any statute of the United States, to the extent that such statute governs the rights of parties to and third parties affected by transactions in particular types of property; or

(b) to a landlord's lien; or

(c) to a lien given by statute or other rule of law for services or materials except as provided in Section 9–310 on priority of such liens; or

(d) to a transfer of a claim for wages, salary or other compensation of an employee; or

(e) to a transfer by a government or governmental subdivision or agency; or

(f) to a sale of accounts or chattel paper as part of a sale of the business out of which they arose, or an assignment of accounts or chattel paper which is for the purpose of collection only, or a transfer of a right to payment under a contract to an assignee who is also to do the performance under the contract or a transfer of a single account to an assignee in whole or partial satisfaction of a preexisting indebtedness; or

(g) to a transfer of an interest in or claim in or under any policy of insurance, except as provided with respect to proceeds (Section 9–306) and priorities in proceeds (Section 9–312); or

(h) to a right represented by a judgment (other than a judgment taken on a right to payment which was collateral); or

(i) to any right of set-off; or

(j) except to the extent that provision is made for fixtures in Section 9–313, to the creation or transfer of an interest in or lien on real estate, including a lease or rents thereunder; or

(k) to a transfer in whole or in part of any claim arising out of tort; or

(l) to a transfer of an interest in any deposit account (subsection (1) of Section 9–105), except as provided with respect to proceeds (Section 9–306) and priorities in proceeds (Section 9–312).

Section 9–105. Definitions and Index of Definitions

(1) In this Article unless the context otherwise requires:

(a) "Account debtor" means the person who is obligated on an account, chattel paper or general intangible;

(b) "Chattel paper" means a writing or writings which evidence both a monetary obligation and a security interest in or a lease of specific goods, but a charter or other contract involving the use or hire of a vessel is not chattel paper. When a transaction is evidenced both by such a security agreement or a lease and by an instrument or a series of instruments, the group of writings taken together constitutes chattel paper;

(c) "Collateral" means the property subject to a security interest, and includes accounts and chattel paper which have been sold;

(d) "Debtor" means the person who owes payment or other performance of the obligation secured, whether or not he owns or has rights in the collateral, and includes the seller of accounts or chattel paper. Where the debtor and the owner of the collateral are not the same person, the term "debtor" means the owner of the collateral in any provision of the Article dealing with the collateral, the obligor in any provision dealing with the obligation, and may include both where the context so requires;

(e) "Deposit account" means a demand, time, savings, passbook or like account maintained with a bank, savings and loan association, credit union or like organization, other than an account evidenced by a certificate of deposit;

(f) "Document" means document of title as defined in the general definitions of Article 1 (Section 1–201), and a receipt of the kind described in subsection (2) of Section 7–201;

(g) "Encumbrance" includes real estate mortgages and other liens on real estate and all other rights in real estate that are not ownership interests;

(h) "Goods" includes all things which are movable at the time the security interest attaches or which are fixtures (Section 9–313), but does not include money, documents, insruments, accounts, chattel paper, general intangibles, or minerals or the like (including oil and gas) before extraction. "Goods" also includes standing timber which is to be cut and removed under a conveyance or contract for sale, the unborn young of animals, and growing crops;

(i) "Instrument" means a negotiable instrument (defined in Section 3–104), or a certificated security (defined in Section 8–102) or any other writing which evidences a right to the payment of money and is not itself a security agreement or lease and is of a type which is in ordinary course of business transferred by delivery with any necessary indorsement or assigment;

(j) "Mortgage" means a consensual interest created by a real estate mortgage, a trust deed on real estate, or the like;

(k) An advance is made "pursuant to commitment" if the secured party has bound himself to make it, whether or not a subsequent event of default or other event not within his control has relieved or may relieve him from his obligation;

(l) "Security agreement" means an agreement which creates or provides for a security interest;

(m) "Secured party" means a lender, seller or other person in whose favor there is a security interest, including a person to whom accounts or chattel paper have been sold. When the holders of obligations issued under an indenture of trust, equipment trust agreement or the like are represented by a trustee or other person, the representative is the secured party;

(n) "Transmitting utility" means any person primarily engaged in the railroad, street railway or trolley bus business, the electric or electronics communications transmission business, the transmission of goods by pipeline, or the transmission or the production and transmission of electricity, steam, gas or water, or the provision of sewer service.

(2) Other definitions applying to this Article and the sections in which they appear are:

"Account." Section 9–106.
"Attach." Section 9–203.
"Construction mortgage." Section 9–313 (1).
"Consumer goods." Section 9–109 (1).
"Equipment." Section 9–109 (2).
"Farm products." Section 9–109 (3).
"Fixture." Section 9–313 (1).
"Fixture filing." Section 9–313 (1).
"General intangibles." Section 9–106.
"Inventory." Section 9–109 (4).
"Lien creditor." Section 9–301 (3).
"Proceeds." Section 9–306 (1).
"Purchase money security interest." Section 9–107.
"United States." Section 9–103.

(3) The following definitions in other Articles apply to this Article:

"Check." Section 3–104.
"Contract for sale." Section 2–106.
"Holder in due course." Section 3–302.
"Note." Section 3–104.
"Sale." Section 2–106.

(4) In addition Article 1 contains general definitions and principles of construction and interpretation applicable throughout this Article.

Section 9–106.   Definitions: "Account"; "General Intangibles"

"Account" means any right to payment for goods sold or leased or for services rendered which is not evidenced by an instrument or chattel paper, whether or not it has been earned by performance. "General intangibles" means any personal property (including things in action) other than goods, accounts, chattel paper, documents, instruments, and money. All rights to payment earned or unearned under a charter or other contract involving the use or hire of a vessel and all rights incident to the chart or contract are accounts.

Section 9–107.   Definitions: "Purchase Money Security Interest"

A security interest is a "purchase money security interest" to the extent that it is

(a) taken or retained by the seller of the collateral to secure all or part of its price; or

(b) taken by a person who by making advances or incurring an obligation gives value to enable the debtor to acquire rights in or the use of collateral if such value is in fact so used.

Section 9–108.   When After-Acquired Collateral Not Security for Antecedent Debt

Where a secured party makes an advance, incurs an obligation, releases a perfected security interest, or otherwise gives new value which is to be secured in whole or in part by after-acquired collateral shall be deemed to be taken for new value and not as security for an antecedent debt if the debtor acquires his rights in such collateral either in the ordinary course of his business or under a contract of purchase made pursuant to the security agreement within a reasonable time after new value is given.

Section 9–109.   Classification of Goods; "Consumer Goods"; "Equipment"; "Farm Products"; "Inventory"

Goods are

(1) "consumer goods" if they are used or bought for use primarily for personal, family or household purposes;

(2) "equipment" if they are used or bought for use primarily in business (including farming or a profession) or by a debtor who is a non-profit organization or a governmental subdivision or agency or if the goods are not included in the definitions of inventory, farm products or consumer goods;

(3) "farm products" if they are crops or livestock or supplies used or produced in farming operations or if they are products of crops or livestock in their unmanufactured states (such as ginned cotton, wool-clip, maple syrup, milk and eggs), and if they are in the possession of a debtor engaged in raising, fattening, grazing or other farming operations. If goods are farm products they are neither equipment nor inventory;

(4) "inventory if they are held by a person who holds them for sale or lease or to be furnished under contracts of service or if he has so furnished them, or if they are raw materials, work in process or materials used or consumed in a business. Inventory of a person is not to be classified as his equipment.

Section 9–110.   Sufficiency of Description

For the purposes of this Article any description of personal property or real estate is sufficient whether or not it is specific if it reasonably identifies what is described.

Section 9–111.   Applicability of Bulk Transfer Laws

The creation of a security interest is not a bulk transfer under Article 6 (see Section 6–103).

Section 9–112.   Where Collateral Is Not Owned by Debtor

Unless otherwise agreed, when a secured party knows that collateral is owned by a person who is not the debtor, the owner of the collateral is entitled to receive from the secured party any surplus under Section 9–502(2) or under Section 9–504(1), and is not liable for the debt or for any deficiency after resale, and he has the same right as the debtor

(a) to receive statements under Section 9–208;

(b) to receive notice of and to object to a secured party's proposal to retain the collateral in satisfaction of the indebtedness under Section 9–505;

(c) to redeem the collateral under Section 9–506;

(d) to obtain injunctive or other relief under Section 9–507(1); and

(e) to recover losses caused to him under Section 9–208(2).

Section 9–113.   Security Interests Arising Under Article on Sales

A security interest arising soley under the Article on Sales (Article 2) is subject to the provisions of this Article except that to the extent that and so long as the debtor does not have or does not lawfully obtain possession of the goods

(a) no security agreement is necessary to make the security interest enforceable; and

(b) no filing is required to perfect the security interest; and

(c) the rights of the secured party on default by the debtor are governed by the Article on Sales (Article 2).

Section 9–114.   Consignment

(1)   A person who delivers goods under a consignment which is not a security interest and who would be required to file under this Article by paragraph (3) (c) of Section 2–326 has priority over a secured party who is or becomes a creditor of the consignee and who would have a perfected security interest in the goods if they were the property of the consignee, and also has priority with respect to identifiable cash proceeds received on or before delivery of the goods to a buyer, if

(a) the consignor complies with the filing provision of the Article on Sales with respect to consignments (paragraph (3) (c) of Section 2–326) before the consignee receives possession of the goods; and

(b) the consignor gives notification in writing to the holder of the security interest if the holder has filed a financing statement covering the same types of goods before the date of the filing made by the consignor; and

(c) the holder of the security interest receives the notification within five years before the consignee receives possession of the goods; and

(d) the notification states that the consignor expects to deliver goods on consignment to the consignee, describing the goods by item or type.

(2)   In the case of a consignment which is not a security interest and in which the requirements of the pre-

ceding subsection have not been met, a person who delivers goods to another is subordinate to a person who would have a perfected security interest in the goods if they were the property of the debtor.

Part 2   Validity of Security Agreement and Rights of Parties Thereto

Section 9–201.   General Validity of Security Agreement

Except as otherwise provided by this Act a security agreement is effective according to its terms between the parties, against purchasers of the collateral and against creditors. Nothing in this Article validates any charge or practice illegal under any statute or regulation thereunder governing usury, small loans, retail installment sales, or the like, or extends the application of any such statute or regulation to any transaction not otherwise subject thereto.

Section 9–202.   Title to Collateral Immaterial

Each provision of this Article with regard to rights, obligations and remedies applies whether title to collateral is in the secured party or in the debtor.

Section 9–203.   Attachment and Enforceability of Security Interest; Proceeds; Formal Requisites

(1)   Subject to the provisions of Section 4–208 on the security interest of a collecting bank, Section 8–321 on security interests in securities and Section 9–113 on a security interest arising under the Article on Sales, a security interest is not enforceable against the debtor or third parties with respect to the collateral and does not attach unless:

    (a)   the collateral is in the possession of the secured party pursuant to agreement, or the debtor has signed a security agreement which contains a description of the collateral and in addition, when the security interest covers crops growing or to be grown or timber to be cut, a description of the land concerned;

    (b)   value has been given; and

    (c)   the debtor has rights in the collateral.

(2)   A security interest attaches when it becomes enforceable against the debtor with respect to the collateral. Attachment occurs as soon as all of the events specified in subsection (1) have taken place unless explicit agreement postpones the time of attaching.

(3)   Unless otherwise agreed a security agreement

gives the secured party the rights to proceeds provided by Section 9–306.

(4)   A transaction, although subject to this Article, is also subject to . . . .*, and in the case of conflict between the provisions of this Article and any such statute, the provisions of such statute control. Failure to comply with any applicable statute has only the effect which is specified therein.

Note: *At * in subsection (4) insert reference to any local statute regulating small loans, retail installment sales and the like.*

The foregoing subsection (4) is designed to make it clear that certain transactions, although subject to this Article, must also comply with other applicable legislation.

    This Article is designed to regulate all the "security" aspects of transactions within its scope. There is, however, much regulatory legislation, particularly in the consumer field, which supplements this Article and should not be repealed by its enactment. Examples are small loan acts, retail installment selling acts and the like. Such acts may provide for licensing and rate regulation and may prescribe particular forms of contract. Such provisions should remain in force despite the enactment of this Article. On the other hand if a retail installment selling act contains provisions on filing, rights on default, etc., such provisions should be repealed as inconsistent with this Article except that inconsistent provisions as to deficiencies, penalties, etc., in the Uniform Consumer Credit Code and other recent related legislation should remain because those statutes were drafted after the substantial enactment of the Article and with the intention of modifying certain provisions of this Article as to consumer credit.

Section 9–204.   After-Acquired Property; Future Advances

(1)   Except as provided in subsection (2), a security agreement may provide that any or all obligations covered by the security agreement are to be secured by after-acquired collateral.

(2)   No security interest attaches under an after-acquired property clause to consumer goods other than accessions (Section 9–314) when given as additional security unless the debtor acquires rights in them within ten days after the secured party gives value.

(3)   Obligations covered by a security agreement may include future advances or other value whether or not the advances or value are given pursuant to commitment (subsection (1) of Section 9–105).

Section 9–205.   Use or Disposition of Collateral Without Accounting Permissible

A security interest is not invalid or fraudulent against creditors by reason of liberty in the debtor to use, commingle or dispose of all or part of the collateral (including returned or repossessed goods) or to collect or compromise accounts or chattel paper, or to accept the return of goods or make repossessions, or to use, commingle or dispose of proceeds, or by reason of the failure of the secured party to require the debtor to account for proceeds or replace collateral. This section does not relax the requirements of possession where perfection of a security interest depends upon possession of the collateral by the secured party or by a bailee.

Section 9–206.   Agreement Not to Assert Defenses Against Assignee; Modification of Sales Warranties Where Security Agreement Exists

(1)   Subject to any statute or decision which establishes a different rule for buyers or lessees of consumer goods, an agreement by a buyer or lessee that he will not assert against an assignee any claim or defense which he may have against the seller or lessor is enforceable by an assignee who takes his assignment for value, in good faith and without notice of a claim or defense, except as to defenses of a type which may be asserted against a holder in due course of a negotiable instrument under the Article on Commercial Paper (Article 3). A buyer who as part of one transaction signs both a negotiable instrument and a security agreement makes such an agreement.

(2)   When a seller retains a purchase money security interest in goods the Article on Sales (Article 2) governs the sale and any disclaimer, limitation or modification of the seller's warranties.

Section 9–207.   Rights and Duties When Collateral is in Secured Party's Possession.

(1)   A secured party must use reasonable care in the custody and preservation of collateral in his possession. In the case of an instrument or chattel paper reasonable care includes taking necessary steps to preserve rights against prior parties unless otherwise agreed.

(2)   Unless otherwise agreed, when collateral is in the secured party's possession

(a)   reasonable expenses (including the cost of any insurance and payment of taxes or other charges) incurred in the custody, preservation, use or operation of the collateral are chargeable to the debtor and are secured by the collateral;

(b)   the risk of accidental loss or damage is on the debtor to the extent of any deficiency in any effective insurance coverage;

(c)   the secured party may hold as additional security any increase or profits (except money) received from the collateral, but money so received, unless remitted to the debtor, shall be applied in reduction of the secured obligation;

(d)   the secured party must keep the collateral identifiable but fungible collateral may be commingled;

(e)   the secured party may repledge the collateral upon terms which do not impair the debtor's right to redeem it.

(3)   A secured party is liable for any loss caused by his failure to meet any obligation imposed by the preceding subsections but does not lose his security interest.

(4)   A secured party may use or operate the collateral for the purpose of preserving the collateral or its value or pursuant to the order of a court of appropriate jurisdiction or, except in the case of consumer goods, in the manner and to the extent provided in the security agreement.

Section 9–208.   Request for Statement of Account or List of Collateral

(1)   A debtor may sign a statement indicating what he believes to be the aggregate amount of unpaid indebtedness as of a specified date and may send it to the secured party with a request that the statement be approved or corrected and returned to the debtor. When the security agreement or any other record kept by the secured party identifies the collateral a debtor may similarly request the secured party to approve or correct a list of the collateral.

(2)   The secured party must comply with such a request within two weeks after receipt by sending a written correction or approval. If the secured party claims a security interest in all of a particular type of collateral owned by the debtor he may indicate that fact in his reply and need not approve or correct an itemized list of such collateral. If the secured party without reasonable excuse fails to comply he is liable for any loss caused to the debtor thereby; and if the debtor has properly included in his request a good faith statement of the obligation or a list of the collateral or both the secured party may claim a security interest only as shown in the statement against persons misled by his failure to comply. If he no longer has an interest in the obligation or collateral at the time the request is received he must disclose the name and address of any successor in interest known to him and he is liable for any loss caused to the debtor as a result of failure to

disclose. A successor in interest is not subject to this section until a request is received by him.

(3)   A debtor is entitled to such a statement once every six months without charge. The secured party may require payment of a charge not exceeding $10 for each additonal statement furnished.

Part 3   Rights of Third Parties; Perfected and Unperfected Security Interests; Rules of Priority

Section 9–301.   Persons Who Take Priority Over Unperfected Security Interests; Rights of "Lien Creditor"

(1)   Except as otherwise provided in subsection (2), an unperfected security interest is subordinate to the rights of

(a)   persons entitled to priority under Section 9–312;

(b)   a person who becomes a lien creditor before the security interest is perfected;

(c)   in the case of goods, instruments, documents, and chattel paper, a person who is not a secured party and who is a transferee in bulk or other buyer not in ordinary course of business or is a buyer of farm products in ordinary course of business, to the extent that he gives value and receives delivery of the collateral without knowledge of the security interest and before it is perfected;

(d)   in the case of accounts and general intangibles, a person who is not a secured party and who is a transferee to the extent that he gives value without knowledge of the security interest and before it is perfected.

(2)   If the secured party files with respect to a purchase money security interest before or within ten days after the debtor receives possession of the collateral, he takes priority over the rights of a transferee in bulk or of a lien creditor which arise between the time the security interest attaches and the time of filing.

(3)   A "lien creditor" means a creditor who has acquired a lien on the property involved by attachment, levy or the like and includes an assignee for benefit of creditors from the time of assignment, and a trustee in bankruptcy from the date of the filing of the petition or a receiver in equity from the time of appointment.

(4)   A person who becomes a lien creditor while a security interest is perfected takes subject to the security interest only to the extent that it secures advances made before he becomes a lien creditor or within 45 days thereafter or made without knowledge of the lien or pursuant to a commitment entered into without knowledge of the lien.

Section 9–302.   When Filing Is Required to Perfect Security Interest; Security Interests to Which Filing Provisions of This Article Do Not Apply

(1)   A financing statement must be filed to perfect all security interests except the following:

(a)   a security interest in collateral in possession of the secured party under Section 9–305;

(b)   a security interest temporarily perfected in instruments or documents without delivery under Section 9–304 or in proceeds for a 10 day period under Section 9–306;

(c)   a security interest created by an assignment of a beneficial interest in a trust or a decedent's estate;

(d)   a purchase money security interest in consumer goods; but filing is required for a motor vehicle required to be registered; and fixture filing is required for priority over conflicting interests in fixtures to the extent provided in Section 9–313;

(e)   an assignment of accounts which does not alone or in conjunction with other assignments to the same assignee transfer a significant part of the outstanding accounts of the assignor;

(f)   a security interest of a collecting bank (Section 4–208) or in securities (Section 8–321) or arising under the Article on Sales (see Section 9–113) or covered in subsection (3) of this section;

(g)   an assignment for the benefit of all the creditors of the transferor, and subsequent transfers by the assignee thereunder.

(2)   If a secured party assigns a perfected security interest, no filing under this Article is required in order to continue the perfected status of the security interest against creditors of the transferees from the original debtor.

(3)   The filing of a financing statement otherwise required by this Article is not necessary or effective to perfect a security interest in property subject to

(a)   a statute or treaty of the United States which provides for a national or international registration or a national or international certificate of title or which specifies a place of filing different from that specified in this Article for filing of the security interest; or

(b) the following statutes of this state; [list any certificate of title statute covering automobiles, trailers, mobile homes, boats, farm tractors, or the like, and any central filing statute*.]; but during any period in which collateral is inventory held for sale by a person who is in the business of selling goods of that kind, the filing provisions of this Article (Part 4) apply to a security interest in that collateral created by him as debtor; or

(c) a certificate of title statute of another jurisdiction under the law of which indication of a security interest on the certificate is required as a condition of perfection (subsection (2) of Section 9–103).

(4) Compliance with a statute or treaty described in subsection (3) is equivalent to the filing of a financing statement under this Article, and a security interest in property subject to the statute or treaty can be perfected only by compliance therewith except as provided in Section 9–103 on multiple state transactions. Duration and renewal of perfection of a security interest perfected by compliance with the statute or treaty are governed by the provisions of the statute or treaty; in other respects the security interest is subject to this Article.

Note: *It is recommended that the provisions of certificate of title acts for perfection of security interests by notation on the certificates should be amended to exclude coverage of inventory held for sale.*

Section 9–303. When Security Interest Is Perfected; Continuity of Perfection

(1) A security interest is perfected when it has attached and when all of the applicable steps required for perfection have been taken. Such steps are specified in Sections 9–302, 9–304, 9–305 and 9–306. If such steps are taken before the security interest attaches, it is perfected at the time when it attaches.

(2) If a security interest is originally perfected in any way permitted under this Article and is subsequently perfected in some other way under this Article, without an intermediate period when it was unperfected, the security interest shall be deemed to be perfected continuously for the purposes of this Article.

Section 9–304. Perfection of Security Interest in Instruments, Documents, and Goods Covered by Documents; Perfection by Permissive Filing; Temporary Perfection Without Filing or Transfer of Possession

(1) A security interest in chattel paper or negotiable documents may be perfected by filing. A security interest in money or instruments (other than certificated securities or instruments which constitute part of chattel paper) can be perfected only by the secured party's taking possession, except as provided in subsections (4) and (5) of this section and subsections (2) and (3) of Section 9–306 on proceeds.

(2) During the period that goods are in the possession of the issuer of a negotiable document therefor, a security interest in the goods is perfected by perfecting a security interest in the document, and any security interest in the goods otherwise perfected during such period is subject thereto.

(3) A security interest in goods in the possession of a bailee other than one who has issued a negotiable document therefor is perfected by issuance of a document in the name of the secured party or by the bailee's receipt of notification of the secured party's interest or by filing as to the goods.

(4) A security interest in instruments (other than certificated securities) or negotiable documents is perfected without filing or the taking of possession for a period of 21 days from the time it attaches to the extent that it arises for new value given under a written security agreement.

(5) A security interest remains perfected for a period of 21 days without filing where a secured party having a perfected security interest in an instrument (other than a certificated security), a negotiable document or goods in possession of a bailee other than one who has issued a negotiable document therefor

(a) makes available to the debtor the goods or documents representing the goods for the purpose of ultimate sale or exchange or for the purpose of loading, unloading, storing, shipping, transshipping, manufacturing, processing or otherwise dealing with them in a manner preliminary to their sale or exchange, but priority between conflicting security interests in the goods is subject to subsection (3) of Section 9–312; or

(b) delivers the instrument to the debtor for the purpose of ultimate sale or exchange or of presentation, collection, renewal or registration of transfer.

(6) After the 21 day period in subsections (4) and (5) perfection depends upon compliance with applicable provisions of this Article.

Section 9–305. When Possession by Secured Party Perfects Security Interest Without Filing

A security interest in letters of credit and advices of credit (subsection (2) (a) of Section 5–116), goods, instruments (other than certificated securities), money, negotiable documents, or chattel paper may be perfected by the secured party's taking possession of the collateral. If such collateral other than goods covered by a negotiable document is held by a bailee, the secured party is deemed to have possession from the time the bailee receives notification of the secured party's interest. A security interest is perfected by possession from the time possession is taken without a relation back and continues only so long as possession is retained, unless otherwise specified in this Article. The security interest may be otherwise perfected as provided in this Article before or after the period of possession by the secured party.

Section 9–306. "Proceeds"; Secured Party's Rights on Disposition of Collateral

(1) "Proceeds" includes whatever is received upon the sale, exchange, collection or other disposition of collateral or proceeds. Insurance payable by reason of loss or damage to the collateral is proceeds, except to the extent that it is payable to a person other than a party to the security agreement. Money, checks, deposit accounts, and the like are "cash proceeds." All other proceeds are "non-cash proceeds."

(2) Except where this Article otherwise provides, a security interest continues in collateral notwithstanding sale, exchange or other disposition thereof unless the disposition was authorized by the secured party in the security agreement or otherwise, and also continues in any identifiable proceeds including collections received by the debtor.

(3) The security interest in proceeds is a continuously perfected security interest if the interest in the original collateral was perfected but it ceases to be a perfected security interest and becomes unperfected ten days after receipt of the proceeds by the debtor unless

    (a) a filed financing statement covers the original collateral and the proceeds are collateral in which a security interest may be perfected by filing in the office or offices where the financing statement has been filed and, if the proceeds are acquired with cash proceeds, the description of collateral in the financing statement indicates the types of property constituting the proceeds; or

    (b) a filed financing statement covers the original collateral and the proceeds are identifiable cash proceeds; or

    (c) the security interest in the proceeds is perfected before the expiration of the ten day period.

Except as provided in this section, a security interest in proceeds can be perfected only by the methods or under the circumstances permitted in this Article for original collateral of the same type.

(4) In the event of insolvency proceedings instituted by or against a debtor, a secured party with a perfected security interest in proceeds has a perfected security interest only in the following proceeds:

    (a) in identifiable non-cash proceeds and in separate deposit accounts containing only proceeds;

    (b) in identifiable cash proceeds in the form of money which is neither commingled with other money nor deposited in a deposit account prior to the insolvency proceedings;

    (c) in identifiable cash proceeds in the form of checks and the like which are not deposited in a deposit account prior to the insolvency proceedings; and

    (d) in all cash and deposit accounts of the debtor in which proceeds have been commingled with other funds, but the perfected security interest under this paragraph (d) is

        (i) subject to any right to setoff; and

        (ii) limited to an amount not greater than the amount of any cash proceeds received by the debtor within ten days before the institution of the insolvency proceedings less the sum of (I) the payments to the secured party on account of cash proceeds received by the debtor during such period and (II) the cash proceeds received by the debtor during such period to which the secured party is entitled under paragraphs (a) through (c) of this subsection (4).

(5) If a sale of goods results in an account or chattel paper which is transferred by the seller to a secured party, and if the goods are returned to or are repos-

sessed by the seller or the secured party, the following rules determine priorities:

(a) If the goods were collateral at the time of sale, for an indebtedness of the seller which is still unpaid, the original security interest attaches again to the goods and continues as a perfected security interest if it was perfected at the time when the goods were sold. If the security interest was originally perfected by a filing which is still effective, nothing further is required to continue the perfected status; in any other case, the secured party must take possession of the returned or repossessed goods or must file.

(b) An unpaid transferee of the chattel paper has a security interest in the goods against the transferor. Such security interest is prior to a security interest asserted under paragraph (a) to the extent that the transferee of the chattel paper was entitled to priority under Section 9–308.

(c) An unpaid transferee of the account has a security interest in the goods against the transferor. Such security interest is subordinate to a security interest asserted under paragraph (a).

(d) A security interest of an unpaid transferee asserted under paragraph (b) or (c) must be perfected for protection against creditors of the transferor and purchasers of the returned or repossessed goods.

Section 9–307.   Protection of Buyers of Goods

(1)   A buyer in ordinary course of business (subsection (9) of Section 1–201) other than a person buying farm products from a person engaged in farming operations takes free of a security interest created by his seller even though the security interest is perfected and even though the buyer knows of its existence.

(2)   In the case of consumer goods, a buyer takes free of a security interest even though perfected if he buys without knowledge of the security interest, for value and for his own personal, family or household purposes unless prior to the purchase the secured party has filed a financing statement covering such goods.

(3)   A buyer other than a buyer in ordinary course of business (subsection (1) of this section) takes free of a security interest to the extent that it secures future advances made after the secured party acquires knowl-

edge of the purchase, or more than 45 days after the purchase, whichever first occurs, unless made pursuant to a commitment entered into without knowledge of the purchase and before the expiration of the 45 day period.

Section 9–308.   Purchase of Chattel Paper and Instruments

A purchaser of chattel paper or an instrument who gives new value and takes possession of it in the ordinary course of his business has priority over a security interest in the chattel paper or instrument

(a) which is perfected under Section 9–304 (permissive filing and temporary perfection) or under Section 9–306 (perfection as to proceeds) if he acts without knowledge that the specific paper or instrument is subject to a security interest; or

(b) which is claimed merely as proceeds of inventory subject to a security interest (Section 9–306) even though he knows that the specific paper or instrument is subject to the security interest.

Section 9–309.   Protection of Purchasers of Instruments, Documents and Securities

Nothing in this Article limits the rights of a holder in due course of a negotiable instrument (Section 3–302) or a holder to whom a negotiable document of title has been duly negotiated (Section 7–501) or a bona fide purchaser of a security (Section 8–302) and the holders or purchasers take priority over an earlier security interest even though perfected. Filing under this Article does not constitute notice of the security interest to such holders or purchasers.

Section 9–310.   Priority of Certain Liens Arising by Operation of Law

When a person in the ordinary course of his business furnishes services or materials with respect to goods subject to a security interest, a lien upon goods in the possession of such person given by statute or rule of law for such materials or services takes priority over a perfected security interest unless the lien is statutory and the statute expressly provides otherwise.

Section 9–311.   Alienability of Debtor's Rights: Judicial Process

The debtor's rights in collateral may be voluntarily or involuntarily transferred (by way of sale, creation of a security interest, attachment, levy, garnishment or other judicial process) notwithstanding a provision in the security agreement prohibiting any transfer or making the transfer constitute a default.

Section 9–312. Priorities Among Conflicting Security Interests in the Same Collateral

(1) The rules of priority stated in other sections of this Part and in the following sections shall govern when applicable: Section 4–208 with respect to the security interests of collecting banks in items being collected, accompanying documents and proceeds; Section 9–103 on security interests related to other jurisdictions; Section 9–114 on consignments.

(2) A perfected security interest in crops for new value given to enable the debtor to produce the crops during the production season and given not more than three months before the crops become growing crops by planting or otherwise takes priority over an earlier perfected security interest to the extent that such earlier interest secures obligations due more than six months before the crops become growing crops by planting or otherwise, even though the person giving new value had knowledge of the earlier security interest.

(3) A perfected purchase money security interest in inventory has priority over a conflicting security interest in the same inventory and also has priority in identifiable cash proceeds received on or before the delivery of the inventory to a buyer if

   (a) the purchase money security interest is perfected at the time the debtor receives possession of the inventory; and

   (b) the purchase money secured party gives notification in writing to the holder of the conflicting security interest if the holder had filed a financing statement covering the same types of inventory (i) before the date of the filing made by the purchase money secured party, or (ii) before the beginning of the 21 day period where the purchase money security interest is temporarily perfected without filing or possession (subsection (5) of Section 9–304); and

   (c) the holder of the conflicting security interest receives the notification within five years before the debtor receives possession of the inventory; and

   (d) the notification states that the person giving the notice has or expects to acquire a purchase money security interest in inventory of

the debtor, describing such inventory by item or type.

(4) A purchase money security interest in collateral other than inventory has priority over a conflicting security interest in the same collateral or its proceeds if the purchase money security interest is perfected at the time the debtor receives possession of the collateral or within ten days thereafter.

(5) In all cases not governed by other rules stated in this section (including cases of purchase money security interests which do not qualify for the special priorities set forth in subsections (3) and (4) of this section), priority between conflicting security interests in the same collateral shall be determined according to the following rules:

   (a) Conflicting security interests rank according to priority in time of filing or perfection. Priority dates from the time a filing is first made covering the collateral or the time the security interest is first perfected, whichever is earlier, provided that there is no period thereafter when there is neither filing nor perfection.

   (b) So long as conflicting security interests are unperfected, the first to attach has priority.

(6) For the purposes of subsection (5) a date of filing or perfection as to collateral is also a date of filing or perfection as to proceeds.

(7) If future advances are made while a security interest is perfected by filing, the taking of possession, or under Section 8–321 on securities, the security interest has the same priority for the purposes of subsection (5) with respect to the future advances as it does with respect to the first advance. If a commitment is made before or while the security interest is so perfected, the security interest has the same priority with respect to advances made pursuant thereto. In other cases a perfected security interest has priority from the date the advance is made.

Section 9–313. Priority of Security Interests in Fixtures

(1) In this section and in the provisions of Part 4 of this Article referring to fixture filing, unless the context otherwise requires

   (a) goods are "fixtures" when they become so related to particular real estate that an interest in them arises under real estate law

(b) a "fixture filing" is the filing in the office where a mortgage on the real estate would be filed or recorded of a financing statement covering goods which are or are to become fixtures and conforming to the requirements of subsection (5) of Section 9–402

(c) a mortgage is a "construction mortgage" to the extent that it secures an obligation incurred for the construction of an improvement on land including the acquisition cost of the land, if the recorded writing so indicates.

(2) A security interest under this Article may be created in goods which are fixtures or may continue in goods which become fixtures, but no security interest exists under this Article in ordinary building materials incorporated into an improvement on land.

(3) This Article does not prevent creation of an encumbrance upon fixtures pursuant to real estate law.

(4) A perfected security interest in fixtures has priority over the conflicting interest of an encumbrancer or owner of the real estate where

(a) the security interest is a purchase money security interest, the interest of the encumbrancer or owner arises before the goods become fixtures, the security interest is perfected by a fixture filing before the goods become fixtures or within ten days thereafter, and the debtor has an interest of record in the real estate or is in possession of the real estate; or

(b) the security interest is perfected by a fixture filing before the interest of the encumbrancer or owner is of record, the security interest has priority over any conflicting interest of a predecessor in title of the encumbrancer or owner, and the debtor has an interest of record in the real estate or is in possession of the real estate; or

(c) the fixtures are readily removable factory or office machines or readily removable replacements of domestic appliances which are consumer goods, and before the goods become fixtures the security interest is perfected by any method permitted by this Article; or

(d) the conflicting interest is a lien on the real estate obtained by legal or equitable proceedings after the security interest was perfected by any method permitted by this Article.

(5) A security interest in fixtures, whether or not perfected, has priority over the conflicting interest of an encumbrancer or owner of the real estate where

(a) the encumbrancer or owner has consented in writing to the security interest or has disclaimed an interest in the goods as fixtures; or

(b) the debtor has a right to remove the goods as against the encumbrancer or owner. If the debtor's right terminates, the priority of the security interest continues for a reasonable time.

(6) Notwithstanding paragraph (a) of subsection (4) but otherwise subject to subsections (4) and (5), a security interest in fixtures is subordinate to a construction mortgage recorded before the goods become fixtures if the goods become fixtures before the completion of the construction. To the extent that it is given to refinance a construction mortgage, a mortgage has this priority to the same extent as the construction mortgage.

(7) In cases not within the preceding subsections, a security interest in fixtures is subordinate to the conflicting interest of an encumbrancer or owner of the related real estate who is not the debtor.

(8) When the secured party has priority over all owners and encumbrancers of the real estate, he may, on default, subject to the provisions of Part 5, remove his collateral from the real estate but he must reimburse any encumbrancer or owner of the real estate who is not the debtor and who has not otherwise agreed for the cost of repair of any physical injury, but not for any diminution in value of the real estate caused by the absence of the goods removed or by any necessity of replacing them. A person entitled to reimbursement may refuse permission to remove until the secured party gives adequate security for the performance of this obligation.

Section 9–314. Accessions

(1) A security interest in goods which attaches before they are installed in or affixed to other goods takes priority as to the goods installed or affixed (called in this section "accessions") over the claims of all persons to the whole except as stated in subsection (3) and subject to Section 9–315(1).

(2) A security interest which attaches to goods after they become part of a whole is valid against all persons subsequently acquiring interests in the whole except as stated in subsection (3) but is invalid against any person with an interest in the whole at the time the security interest attaches to the goods who has not in writing consented to the security interest or disclaimed an interest in the goods as part of the whole.

(3) The security interests described in subsections (1) and (2) do not take priority over

(a) a subsequent purchaser for value of any interest in the whole; or

(b) a creditor with a lien on the whole subsequently obtained by judicial proceedings; or

(c) a creditor with a prior perfected security interest in the whole to the extent that he makes subsequent advances

if the subsequent purchase is made, the lien by judicial proceedings obtained or the subsequent advance under the prior perfected security interest is made or contracted for without knowledge of the security interest and before it is perfected. A purchaser of the whole at a foreclosure sale other than the holder of a perfected security interest purchasing at his own foreclosure sale is a subsequent purchaser within this section.

(4) When under subsections (1) or (2) and (3) a secured party has an interest in accessions which has priority over the claims of all persons who have interests in the whole, he may on default subject to the provisions of Part 5 remove his collateral from the whole but he must reimburse any encumbrancer or owner of the whole who is not the debtor and who has not otherwise agreed for the cost of repair of any physical injury but not for any diminution in value of the whole caused by the absence of the goods removed or by any necessity for replacing them. A person entitled to reimbursement may refuse permission to remove until the secured party gives adequate security for the performance of this obligation.

Section 9–315. Priority When Goods Are Commingled or Processed

(1) If a security interest in goods was perfected and subsequently the goods or a part thereof have become part of a product or mass, the security interest continues in the product or mass if

(a) the goods are so manufactured, processed, assembled or commingled that their identity is lost in the product or mass; or

(b) a financing statement covering the original goods also covers the product into which the goods have been manufactured, processed or assembled.

In a case to which paragraph (b) applies, no separate security interest in that part of the original goods which have been manufactured, processed or assembled into the product may be claimed under Section 9–314.

(2) When under subsection (1) more than one security interest attaches to the product or mass, they rank equally according to the ratio that the cost of the goods to which each interest originally attached bears to the cost of the total product or mass.

Section 9–316. Priority Subject to Subordination

Nothing in this Article prevents subordination by agreement by any person entitled to priority.

Section 9–317. Secured Party Not Obligated on Contract of Debtor

The mere existence of a security interest or authority given to the debtor to dispose of or use collateral does not impose contract or tort liability upon the secured party for the debtor's acts or omissions.

Section 9–318. Defenses Against Assignee; Modification of Contract After Notification of Assignment; Term Prohibiting Assignment Ineffective; Identification and Proof of Assignment

(1) Unless an account debtor has made an enforceable agreement not to assert defenses or claims arising out of a sale as provided in Section 9–206 the rights of an assignee are subject to

(a) all the terms of the contract between the account debtor and assignor and any defense or claim arising therefrom; and

(b) any other defense or claim of the account debtor against the assignor which accrues before the account debtor receives notification of the assignment.

(2) So far as the right to payment or a part thereof under an assigned contract has not been fully earned by performance, and notwithstanding notification of the assignment, any modification of or substitution for the contract made in good faith and in accordance with reasonable commercial standards is effective against an assignee unless the account debtor has otherwise agreed but the assignee acquires corresponding rights under the modified or substituted contract. The assignment may provide that such modification or substitution is a breach by the assignor.

(3) The account debtor is authorized to pay the assignor until the account debtor receives notification that the amount due or to become due has been assigned and that payment is to be made to the assignee. A notification which does not reasonably identify the rights assigned is ineffective. If requested by the account debtor, the assignee must seasonably furnish reasonable proof that the assignment has been made and unless he does so the account debtor may pay the assignor.

(4) A term in any contract between an account debtor and an assignor is ineffective if it prohibits assignment

of an account or prohibits creation of a security interest in a general intangible for money due or to become due or requires the account debtor's consent to such assignment or security interest.

Part 4   Filing

Section 9–401.   Place of Filing; Erroneous Filing; Removal of Collateral

First Alternative Subsection (1)

(1)   The proper place to file in order to perfect a security interest is as follows:

(a)   when the collateral is timber to be cut or is minerals or the like (including oil and gas) or accounts subject to subsection (5) of Section 9–103, or when the financing statement is filed as a fixture filing (Section 9–313) and the collateral is goods which are or are to become fixtures, then in the office where a mortgage on the real estate would be filed or recorded;

(b)   in all other cases, in the office of the [Secretary of State].

Second Alternative Subsection (1)

(1)   The proper place to file in order to perfect a security interest is as follows:

(a)   when the collateral is equipment used in farming operations, or farm products, or accounts or general intangibles arising from or relating to the sale of farm products by a farmer, or consumer goods, then in the office of the . . . . in the county of the debtor's residence or if the debtor is not a resident of this state then in the office of the . . . . in the county of the debtor's residence or if the debtor is not a resident of this state then in the office of the . . . . in the county where the goods are kept, and in addition when the collateral is crops growing or to be grown in the office of the . . . . in the county where the land is located;

(b)   when the collateral is timber to be cut or is minerals or the like (including oil and gas) or accounts subject to subsection (5) of Section 9–103, or when the financing statement is filed as a fixture filing (Section 9–313) and the collateral is goods which are or are to become

fixtures, then in the office where a mortgage on the real estate would be filed or recorded;

(c)   in all other cases, in the office of the [Secretary of State].

Third Alternative Subsection (1)

(1)   The proper place to file in order to perfect a security interest is as follows:

(a)   when the collateral is equipment used in farming operations, or farm products, or accounts or general intangibles arising from or relating to the sale of farm products by a farmer, or consumer goods, then in the office of the . . . . . . in the county of the debtor's residence or if the debtor is not a resident of this state then in the office of the . . . . in the county where the goods are kept, and in addition when the collateral is crops growing or to be grown in the office of the . . . . . . in the county where the land is located;

(b)   when the collateral is timber to be cut or is minerals or the like (including oil and gas) or accounts subject to subsection (5) of Section 9–103, or when the financing statement is filed as a fixture filing (Section 9–313) and the collateral is goods which are or are to become fixtures, then in the office where a mortgage on the real estate would be filed or recorded;

(c)   in all other cases, in the office of the [Secretary of State] and in addition, if the debtor has a place of business in only one county of this state, also in the office of . . . . . . of such county, or, if the debtor has no place of business in this state, but resides in the state, also in the office of . . . . . . of the county in which he resides.

Note: *One of the three alternatives should be selected as subsection (1).*

(2)   A filing which is made in good faith in an improper place or not in all of the places required by this section is nevertheless effective with regard to any collateral as to which the filing complied with the requirements of this Article and is also effective with regard to collateral covered by the financing statement against any person who has knowledge of the contents of such financing statement.

(3)   A filing which is made in the proper place in this state continues effective even though the debtor's residence or place of business or the location of the collateral or its use, whichever controlled the original filing, is thereafter changed.

signed by the secured party of record and complying with subsection (2) of Section 9–405, including payment of the required fee. Upon timely filing of the continuation statement, the effectiveness of the original statement is continued for five years after the last date to which the filing was effective whereupon it lapses in the same manner as provided in subsection (2) unless another continuation statement is filed prior to such lapse. Succeeding continuation statements may be filed in the same manner to continue the effectiveness of the original statement. Unless a statute on disposition of public records provides otherwise, the filing officer may remove a lapsed statement from the files and destroy it immediately if he has retained a microfilm or other photographic record, or in other cases after one year after the lapse. The filing officer shall so arrange matters by physical annexation of financing statements to continuation statements or other related filings, or by other means, that if he physically destroys the financing statements of a period more than five years past, those which have been continued by a continuation statement or which are still effective under subsection (6) shall be retained.

(4) Except as provided in subsection (7) a filing officer shall mark each statement with a file number and with the date and hour of filing and shall hold the statement or a microfilm or other photographic copy thereof for public inspection. In addition the filing officer shall index the statement according to the name of the debtor and shall note in the index the file number and the address of the debtor given in the statement.

(5) The uniform fee for filing and indexing and for stamping a copy furnished by the secured party to show the date and place of filing for an original financing statement or for a continuation statement shall be $. . . . . if the statement is in the standard form prescribed by the [Secretary of State] and otherwise shall be $. . . . .,plus in each case, if the financing statement is subject to subsection (5) of Section 9–402, $. . . . . . . The uniform fee for each name more than one required to be indexed shall be $. . . . . The secured party may at his option show a trade name for any person and an extra uniform indexing fee of $. . . . . shall be paid with respect thereto.

(6) If the debtor is a transmitting utility (subsection (5) of Section 9–401) and a filed financing statement so states, it is effective until a termination statement is filed. A real estate mortgage which is effective as a fixture filing under subsection (6) of Section 9–402 remains effective as a fixture filing until the mortgage is released or satisfied of record or its effectiveness otherwise terminates as to the real estate.

(7) When a financing statement covers timber to be cut or covers minerals or the like (including oil and gas) or accounts subject to subsection (5) of Section 9–103, or is filed as a fixture filing, [it shall be filed for record and] the filing officer shall index it under the names of the debtor and any owner of record shown on the financing statement in the same fashion as if they were the mortgagors in a mortgage of the real estate described, and, to the extent that the law of this state provides for indexing of mortgages under the name of the mortgagee, under the name of the secured party as if he were the mortgagee thereunder, or where indexing is by description in the same fashion as if the financing statement were a mortgage of the real estate described.

Note: *In states in which writings will not appear in the real estate records and indices unless actually recorded the bracketed language in subsection (7) should be used.*

Section 9–404. Termination Statement

(1) If a financing statement covering consumer goods is filed on or after . . . ., then within one month or within ten days following written demand by the debtor after there is no outstanding secured obligation and no commitment to make advances, incur obligations or otherwise give value, the secured party must file with each filing officer with whom the financing statement was filed, a termination statement to the effect that he no longer claims a security interest under the financing statement, which shall be identified by file number. In other cases whenever there is no outstanding secured obligation and no commitment to make advances, incur obligations or otherwise give value, the secured party must on written demand by the debtor send the debtor, for each filing officer with whom the financing statement was filed, a termination statement to the effect that he no longer claims a security interest under the financing statement, which shall be identified by file number. A termination statement signed by a person other than the secured party of record must be accompanied by a separate written statement of assignment signed by the secured party of record complying with subsection (2) of Section 9–405, including payment of the required fee. If the affected secured party fails to file such a termination statement as required by this subsection, or to send such a termination statement within ten days after proper demand therefor, he shall be liable to the debtor for one hundred dollars, and in addition for any loss caused to the debtor by such failure.

(2) On presentation to the filing officer of such a termination statement he must note it in the index. If he has received the termination statement in duplicate, he shall return one copy of the termination statement to the secured party stamped to show the time of receipt thereof. If the filing officer has a microfilm or other photographic record of the financing statement, and of any related continuation statement, statement of assignment and statement of release, he may remove the originals from the files at any time after receipt of the termination statement, or if he has no such record, he may remove them from the files at any time after one year after receipt of the termination statement.

(3) If the termination statement is in the standard form prescribed by the [Secretary of State], the uniform fee for filing and indexing the termination statement shall be $. . . . . ., and otherwise shall be $. . . . . ., plus in each case an additional fee of $. . . . . for each name more than one against which the termination statement is required to be indexed.

Note: *The date to be inserted should be the effective date of the revised Article 9.*

Section 9–405. Assignment of Security Interest; Duties of Filing Officer; Fees

(1) A financing statement may disclose an assignment of a security interest in the collateral described in the financing statement by indication in the financing statement of the name and address of the assignee or by an assignment itself or a copy thereof on the face or back of the statement. On presentation to the filing officer of such a financing statement the filing officer shall mark the same as provided in Section 9–403(4). The uniform fee for filing, indexing and furnishing filing data for a financing statement so indicating an assignment shall be $. . . . . if the statement is in the standard form prescribed by the [Secretary of State] and otherwise shall be $. . . . . ., plus in each case an additional fee of $. . . . . for each name more than one against which the financing statement is required to be indexed.

(2) A secured party may assign of record all or part of his rights under a financing statement by the filing in the place where the original financing statement was filed of a separate written statement of assignment signed by the secured party of record and setting forth the name of the secured party of record and the debtor, the file number and the date of filing of the financing statement and the name and address of the assignee and containing a description of the collateral assigned. A copy of the assignment is sufficient as a separate statement if it complies with the preceding sentence. On presentation to the filing officer of such a separate statement, the filing officer shall mark such separate statement with the date and hour of the filing. He shall note the assignment on the index of the financing statement, or in the case of a fixture filing, or a filing covering timber to be cut, or covering minerals or the like (including oil and gas) or accounts subject to subsection (5) of Section 9–103, he shall index the assignment under the name of the assignor as grantor and, to the extent that the law of this state provides for indexing the assignment of a mortgage under the name of the assignee, he shall index the assignment of the financing statement under the name of the assignee. The uniform fee for filing, indexing and furnishing filing data about such a separate statement of assignment shall be $. . . . . if the statement is in the standard form prescribed by the [Secretary of State] and otherwise shall be $. . . . . ., plus in each case an additional fee of $. . . . . for each name more than one against which the statement of assignment is required to be indexed. Notwithstanding the provisions of this subsection, an assignment of record of a security interest in a fixture contained in a mortgage effective as a fixture filing (subsection (6) of Section 9–402) may be made only by an assignment of the mortgage in the manner provided by the law of this state other than this Act.

(3) After the disclosure or filing of an assignment under this section, the assignee is the secured party of record.

Section 9–406. Release of Collateral; Duties of Filing Officer; Fees

A secured party of record may by his signed statement release all or a part of any collateral described in a filed financing statement. The statement of release is sufficient if it contains a description of the collateral being released, the name and address of the debtor, the name and address of the secured party, and the file number of the financing statement. A statement of release signed by a person other than the secured party of record must be accompanied by a separate written statement of assignment signed by the secured party of record and complying with subsection (2) of Section 9–405, including payment of the required fee. Upon presentation of such a statement of release to the filing officer he shall mark the statement with the hour and date of filing and shall note the same upon the margin of the index of the filing of the financing statement. The uniform fee for filing and noting such a statement of release shall be $. . . . . . if the statement is in the standard form prescribed by the [Secretary of State] and otherwise shall be $. . . . . ., plus in each case an additional fee of $. . . . . for each name more than one against which the statement of release is required to be indexed.

[Section 9–407. Information From Filing Officer]

[(1)   If the person filing any financing statement, termination statement, statement of assignment, or statement of release, furnishes the filing officer a copy thereof, the filing officer shall upon request note upon the copy the file number and date and hour of the filing of the original and deliver or send the copy to such person.]

[(2)   Upon request of any person, the filing officer shall issue his certificate showing whether there is on file on the date and hour stated therein, any presently effective financing statement naming a particular debtor and any statement of assignment thereof and if there is, giving the date and hour of filing of each such statement and the names and addresses of each secured party therein. The uniform fee for such a certificate shall be $. . . . . if the request for the certificate is in the standard form prescribed by the [Secretary of State] and otherwise shall be $. . . . . Upon request the filing officer shall furnish a copy of any filed financing statement or statement of assignment for a uniform fee of $. . . . . per page.]

Note: *This section is proposed as an optional provision to require filing officers to furnish certificates. Local law and practices should be consulted with regard to the advisability of adoption.*

Section 9–408.   Financing Statements Covering Consigned or Leased Goods

A consignor or lessor of goods may file a financing statement using the terms "consignor," "consignee," "lessor," "lessee" or the like instead of the terms specified in Section 9–402. The provisions of this Part shall apply as appropriate to such a financing statement but its filing shall not of itself be a factor in determining whether or not the consignment or lease is intended as security (Section 1–201(37)). However, if it is determined for other reasons that the consignment or lease is so intended, a security interest of the consignor or lessor which attaches to the consigned or leased goods is perfected by such filing.

Part 5   Default

Section 9–501.   Default; Procedure When Security Agreement Covers Both Real and Personal Property

(1)   When a debtor is in default under a security agreement, a secured party has the rights and remedies provided in this Part and except as limited by subsection (3) those provided in the security agreement. He may reduce his claim to judgment, foreclose or otherwise enforce the security interest by any available judicial procedure. If the collateral is documents the secured party may proceed either as to the documents or as to the goods covered thereby. A secured party in possession has the rights, remedies and duties provided in Section 9–207. The rights and remedies referred to in this subsection are cumulative.

(2)   After default, the debtor has the rights and remedies provided in this Part, those provided in the security agreement and those provided in Section 9–207.

(3)   To the extent that they give rights to the debtor and impose duties on the secured party, the rules stated in the subsections referred to below may not be waived or varied except as provided with respect to compulsory disposition of collateral (subsection (3) of Section 9–504 and Section 9–505) and with respect to redemption of collateral (Section 9–506) but the parties may be agreement determine the standards by which the fulfillment of these rights and duties is to be measured if such standards are not manifestly unreasonable:

(a)   subsection (2) of Section 9–502 and subsection (2) of Section 9–504 insofar as they require accounting for surplus proceeds of collateral;

(b)   subsection (3) of Section 9–504 and subsection (1) of Section 9–505 which deal with disposition of collateral;

(c)   subsection (2) of Section 9–505 which deals with acceptance of collateral as discharge of obligation;

(d)   Section 9–506 which deals with redemption of collateral; and

(e)   subsection (1) of Section 9–507 which deals with the secured party's liability for failure to comply with this Part.

(4)   If the security agreement covers both real and personal property, the secured party may proceed under this Part as to the personal property or he may

proceed as to both the real and the personal property in accordance with his rights and remedies in respect of the real property in which case the provisions of this Part do not apply.

(5) When a secured party has reduced his claim to judgment the lien of any levy which may be made upon his collateral by virtue of any execution based upon the judgment shall relate back to the date of the perfection of the security interest in such collateral. A judicial sale, pursuant to such execution, is a foreclosure of the security interest by judicial procedure within the meaning of this section, and the secured party may purchase at the sale and thereafter hold the collateral free of any other requirements of this Article.

Section 9–502. Collection Rights of Secured Party

(1) When so agreed and in any event on default the secured party is entitled to notify an account debtor or the obligor on an instrument to make payment to him whether or not the assignor was theretofore making collections on the collateral, and also to take control of any proceeds to which he is entitled under Section 9–306.

(2) A secured party who by agreement is entitled to charge back uncollected collateral or otherwise to full or limited recourse against the debtor and who undertakes to collect from the account debtors or obligors must proceed in a commercially reasonable manner and may deduct his reasonable expenses of realization from the collections. If the security agreement secures an indebtedness, the secured party must account to the debtor for any surplus, and unless otherwise agreed, the debtor is liable for any deficiency. But, if the underlying transaction was a sale of accounts or chattel paper, the debtor is entitled to any surplus or is liable for any deficiency only if the security agreement so provides.

Section 9–503. Secured Party's Right to Take Possession After Default

Unless otherwise agreed a secured party has on default the right to take possession of the collateral. In taking possession a secured party may proceed without judicial process if this can be done without breach of the peace or may proceed by action. If the security agreement so provides the secured party may require the debtor to assemble the collateral and make it available to the secured party at a place to be designated by the secured party which is reasonably convenient to both

parties. Without removal a secured party may render equipment unusable, and may dispose of collateral on the debtor's premises under Section 9–504.

Section 9–504. Secured Party's Right to Dispose of Collateral After Default; Effect of Disposition

(1) A secured party after default may sell, or lease otherwise dispose of any or all of the collateral in its then condition or following any commercially reasonable preparation or processing. Any sale of goods is subject to the Article on Sales (Article 2). The proceeds of disposition shall be applied in the order following to

(a) the reasonable expenses of retaking, holding, preparing for sale or lease, selling, leasing and the like and, to the extent provided for in the agreement and not prohibited by law, the reasonable attorneys' fees and legal expenses incurred by the secured party;

(b) the satisfaction of indebtedness secured by the security interest under which the disposition is made;

(c) the satisfaction of indebtedness secured by any subordinate security interest in the collateral if written notification of demand therefor is received before distribution of the proceeds is completed. If requested by the secured party, the holder of a subordinate security interest must seasonably furnish reasonable proof of his interest, and unless he does so, the secured party need not comply with his demand.

(2) If the security interest secures an indebtedness, the secured party must account to the debtor for any surplus, and, unless otherwise agreed, the debtor is liable for any deficiency. But if the underlying transaction was a sale of accounts or chattel paper, the debtor is entitled to any surplus or is liable for any deficiency only if the security agreement so provides.

(3) Disposition of the collateral may be by public or private proceedings and may be made by way of one or more contracts. Sale or other disposition may be as a unit or in parcels and at any time and place and on any terms but every aspect of the dispositioin including the method, manner, time, place and terms must be commercially reasonable. Unless collateral is perishable or threatens to decline speedily in value or is of a type customarily sold on a recognized market, reasonable notification of the time and place of any public sale or reasonable notification of the time after which any private sale or other intended disposition is to be made shall be sent by the secured party to the debtor, if he

has not signed after default a statement renouncing or modifying his right to notification of sale. In the case of consumer goods no other notification need be sent. In other cases notification shall be sent to any other secured party from whom the secured party has received (before sending his notification to the debtor or before the debtor's renunciation of his rights) written notice of a claim of an interest in the collateral. The secured party may buy at any public sale and if the collateral is of a type customarily sold in a recognized market or is of a type which is the subject of widely distributed standard price quotations he may buy at private sale.

(4) When collateral is disposed of by a secured party after default, the disposition transfers to a purchaser for value all of the debtor's rights therein, discharges the security interest under which it is made and any security interest or lien subordinate thereto. The purchaser takes free of all such rights and interests even though the secured party fails to comply with the requirements of this Part or of any judicial proceedings

    (a) in the case of a public sale, if the purchaser has no knowledge of any defects in the sale and if he does not buy in collusion with the secured party, other bidders or the person conducting the sale; or

    (b) in any other case, if the purchaser acts in good faith.

(5) A person who is liable to a secured party under a guaranty, indorsement, repurchase agreement or the like and who receives a transfer of collateral from the secured party or is subrogated to his rights has thereafter the rights and duties of the secured party. Such a transfer of collateral is not a sale or disposition of the collateral under this Article.

Section 9–505. Compulsory Disposition of Collateral; Acceptance of the Collateral as Discharge of Obligation

(1) If the debtor has paid sixty per cent of the cash price in the case of a purchase money security interest in consumer goods or sixty per cent of the loan in the case of another security interest in consumer goods, and has not signed after default a statement renouncing or modifying his rights under this Part a secured party who has taken possession of collateral must dispose of it under Section 9–504 and if he fails to do so within ninety days after he takes possession the debtor at his option may recover in conversion or under Section 9–507(1) on secured party's liability.

(2) In any other case involving consumer goods or any other collateral a secured party in possession may, after default, propose to retain the collateral in satisfaction of the obligation. Written notice of such proposal shall be sent to the debtor if he has not signed after default a statement renouncing or modifying his rights under this subsection. In the case of consumer goods no other notice need be given. In other cases notice shall be sent to any other secured party from whom the secured party has received (before sending his notice to the debtor or before the debtor's renunciation of his rights) written notice of a claim of an interest in the collateral. If the secured party receives objection in writing from a person entitled to receive notification within twenty-one days after the notice was sent, the secured party must dispose of the collateral under Section 9–504. In the absence of such written objection the secured party may retain the collateral in satisfaction of the debtor's obligation.

Section 9–506. Debtor's Right to Redeem Collateral

At any time before the secured party has disposed of collateral or entered into a contract for its disposition under Section 9–504 or before the obligation has been discharged under Section 9–505(2) the debtor or any other secured party may unless otherwise agreed in writing after default redeem the collateral by tendering fulfillment of all obligations secured by the collateral as well as the expenses reasonably incurred by the secured party in retaking, holding and preparing the collateral for disposition, in arranging for the sale, and to the extent provided in the agreement and not prohibited by law, his reasonable attorneys' fees and legal expenses.

Section 9–507. Secured Party's Liability for Failure to Comply With This Part

(1) If it is established that the secured party is not proceeding in accordance with the provisions of this Part disposition may be ordered or restrained on appropriate terms and conditions. If the disposition has occurred the debtor or any person entitled to notification or whose security interest has been made known to the secured party prior to the disposition has a right to recover from the secured party any loss caused by a failure to comply with the provisions of this Part. If the collateral is consumer goods, the debtor has a right to recover in any event an amount not less than the credit service charge plus ten per cent of the principal

amount of the debt or the time price differential plus 10 per cent of the cash price.

(2) The fact that a better price could have been obtained by a sale at a different time or in a different method from that selected by the secured party is not of itself sufficient to establish that the sale was not made in a commercially reasonable manner. If the secured party either sells the collateral in the usual manner in any recognized market therefor or if he sells at the price current in such market at the time of his sale or if he has otherwise sold in conformity with reasonable commercial practices among dealers in the type of property sold he has sold in a commercially reasonable manner. The principles stated in the two preceding sentences with respect to sales also apply as may be appropriate to other types of disposition. A disposition which has been approved in any judicial proceeding or by any bona fide creditors' committee or representative of creditors shall conclusively be deemed to be commercially reasonable, but this sentence does not indicate that any such approval must be obtained in any case nor does it indicate that any disposition not so approved is not commercially reasonable.

Authors' note: *Articles 10 and 11 have been omitted as unnecessary for the purposes of this text.*

Appendix | B
Uniform Partnership Act (1914)*

Part I Preliminary Provisions

Section 1. Name of Act

This act may be cited as Uniform Partnership Act.

Section 2. Definition of Terms

In this act, "Court" includes every court and judge having jurisdiction in the case.

"Business" includes every trade, occupation, or profession.

"Person" includes individuals, partnerships, corporations, and other associations.

"Bankrupt" includes bankrupt under the Federal Bankruptcy Act or insolvent under any state insolvent act.

"Conveyance" includes every assignment, lease, mortgage, or encumbrance.

"Real property" includes land and any interest or estate in land.

Section 3. Interpretation of Knowledge and Notice

(1) A person has "knowledge" of a fact within the meaning of this act not only when he has actual knowledge thereof, but also when he has knowledge of such other facts as in the circumstances shows bad faith.

(2) A person has "notice" of a fact within the meaning of this act when the person who claims the benefit of the notice:

    (a) States the fact to such person, or

    (b) Delivers through the mail, or by other means of communication, a written statement of the fact to such person or to a proper person at his place of business or residence.

Section 4. Rules of Construction

(1) The rule that statutes in derogation of the common law are to be strictly construed shall have no application to this act.

(2) The law of estoppel shall apply under this act.

(3) The law of agency shall apply under this act.

(4) This act shall be so interpreted and construed as to effect its general purpose to make uniform the law of those states which enact it.

(5) This act shall not be construed so as to impair the obligations of any contract existing when the act goes into effect, nor to affect any action or proceedings begun or right accrued before this act takes effect.

Section 5. Rules for Cases Not Provided for in This Act

In any case not provided for in this act the rules of law and equity, including the law merchant, shall govern.

*Source: National Conference of Commissioners of Uniform State Laws. Reprinted with permission.

Part II   Nature of Partnership

Section 6.   Partnership Defined

(1)   A partnership is an association of two or more persons to carry on as co-owners a business for profit.

(2)   But any association formed under any other statute of this state, or any statute adopted by authority, other than the authority of this state, is not a partnership under this act, unless such association would have been a partnership in this state prior to the adoption of this act; but this act shall apply to limited partnerships except in so far as the statutes relating to such partnerships are inconsistent herewith.

Section 7.   Rules for Determining the Existence of a Partnership

In determining whether a partnership exists, these rules shall apply:

(1)   Except as provided by section 16 persons who are not partners as to each other are not partners as to third persons.

(2)   Joint tenancy, tenancy in common, tenancy by the entireties, joint property, common property, or part ownership does not of itself establish a partnership, whether such co-owners do or do not share any profits made by the use of the property.

(3)   The sharing of gross returns does not of itself establish a partnership, whether or not the persons sharing them have a joint or common right or interest in any property from which the returns are derived.

(4)   The receipt by a person of a share of the profits of a business is prima facie evidence that he is a partner in the business, but no such inference shall be drawn if such profits were received in payment:

    (a)   As a debt by installments or otherwise,

    (b)   As wages of an employee or rent to a landlord,

    (c)   As an annuity to a widow or representative of a deceased partner,

    (d)   As interest on a loan, though the amount of payment vary with the profits of the business,

    (e)   As the consideration for the sale of a goodwill of a business or other property by installments or otherwise.

Section 8.   Partnership Property

(1)   All property originally brought into the partnership stock or subsequently acquired by purchase or otherwise, on account of the partnership, is partnership property.

(2)   Unless the contrary intention appears, property acquired with partnership funds is partnership property.

(3)   Any estate in real property may be acquired in the partnership name. Title so acquired can be conveyed only in the partnership name.

(4)   A conveyance to a partnership in the partnership name, though without words of inheritance, passes the entire estate of the grantor unless a contrary intent appears.

Part III   Relations of Partners to Persons Dealing with the Partnership

Section 9.   Partner Agent of Partnership as to Partnership Business

(1)   Every partner is an agent of the partnership for the purpose of its business, and the act of every partner, including the execution in the partnership name of any instrument, for apparently carrying on in the usual way the business of the partnership of which he is a member binds the partnership, unless the partner so acting has in fact no authority to act for the partnership in the particular matter, and the person with whom he is dealing has knowledge of the fact that he has no such authority.

(2)   An act of a partner which is not apparently for the carrying on of the business of the partnership in the usual way does not bind the partnership unless authorized by the other partners.

(3)   Unless authorized by the other partners or unless they have abandoned the business, one or more but less than all the partners have no authority to:

    (a)   Assign the partnership property in trust for creditors or on the assignee's promise to pay the debts of the partnership,

    (b)   Dispose of the good-will of the business,

    (c)   Do any other act which would make it impossible to carry on the ordinary business of a partnership,

    (d)   Confess a judgment,

    (e)   Submit a partnership claim or liability to arbitration or reference.

(4)   No act of a partner in contravention of a restriction on authority shall bind the partnership to persons having knowledge of the restriction.

Section 10. Conveyance of Real Property of the Partnership

(1) Where title to real property is in the partnership name, any partner may convey title to such property by a conveyance executed in the partnership name; but the partnership may recover such property unless the partner's act binds the partnership under the provisions of paragraph (1) of section 9, or unless such property has been conveyed by the grantee or a person claiming through such grantee to a holder for value without knowledge that the partner, in making the conveyance, has exceeded his authority.

(2) Where title to real property is in the name of the partnership, a conveyance executed by a partner, in his own name, passes the equitable interest of the partnership, provided the act is one within the authority of the partner under the provisions of paragraph (1) of section 9.

(3) Where title to real property is in the name of one or more but not all the partners, and the record does not disclose the right of the partnership, the partners in whose name the title stands may convey title to such property, but the partnership may recover such property if the partners' act does not bind the partnership under the provisions of paragraph (1) of section 9, unless the purchaser or his assignee, is a holder for value, without knowledge.

(4) Where the title to real property is in the name of one or more or all the partners, or in a third person in trust for the partnership, a conveyance executed by a partner in the partnership name, or in his own name, passes the equitable interest of the partnership, provided the act is one within the authority of the partner under the provisions of paragraph (1) of section 9.

(5) Where the title to real property is in the names of all the partners a conveyance executed by all the partners passes all their rights in such property.

Section 11. Partnership Bound by Admission of Partner

An admission or representation made by any partner concerning partnership affairs within the scope of his authority as conferred by this act is evidence against the partnership.

Section 12. Partnership Charged with Knowledge of or Notice to Partner

Notice to any partner of any matter relating to partnership affairs, and the knowledge of the partner acting in the particular matter, acquired while a partner or then present to his mind, and the knowledge of any other partner who reasonably could and should have communicated it to the acting partner, operate as notice to or knowledge of the partnership, except in the case of a fraud on the partnership committed by or with the consent of that partner.

Section 13. Partnership Bound by Partner's Wrongful Act

Where, by any wrongful act or omission of any partner acting in the ordinary course of the business of the partnership or with the authority of his co-partners, loss or injury is caused to any person, not being a partner in the partnership, or any penalty is incurred, the partnership is liable therefor to the same extent as the partner so acting or omitting to act.

Section 14. Partnership Bound by Partner's Breach of Trust

The partnership is bound to make good the loss:

(a) Where one partner acting within the scope of his apparent authority receives money or property of a third person and misapplies it; and

(b) Where the partnership in the course of its business receives money or property of a third person and the money or property so received is misapplied by any partner while it is in the custody of the partnership.

Section 15. Nature of Partner's Liability

All partners are liable

(a) Jointly and severally for everything chargeable to the partnership under sections 13 and 14.

(b) Jointly for all other debts and obligations of the partnership; but any partner may enter into a separate obligation to perform a partnership contract.

Section 16. Partner by Estoppel

(1) When a person, by words spoken or written or by conduct, represents himself, or consents to another representing him to any one, as a partner in an existing partnership or with one or more persons not actual partners, he is liable to any such person to whom such representation has been made, who has, on the faith of such representation, given credit to the actual or ap-

parent partnership, and if he has made such representation or consented to its being made in a public manner he is liable to such person, whether the representation has or has not been made or communicated to such person so giving credit by or with the knowledge of the apparent partner making the representation or consenting to its being made.

    (a) When a partnership liability results, he is liable as though he were an actual member of the partnership.

    (b) When no partnership liability results, he is liable jointly with the other persons, if any, so consenting to the contract or representation as to incur liability, otherwise separately.

(2) When a person has been thus represented to be a partner in an existing partnership, or with one or more persons not actual partners, he is an agent of the persons consenting to such representation to bind them to the same extent and in the same manner as though he were a partner in fact, with respect to persons who rely upon the representation. Where all the members of the existing partnership consent to the representation, a partnership act or obligation results; but in all other cases it is the joint act or obligation of the person acting and the persons consenting to the representation.

Section 17. Liability of Incoming Partner

A person admitted as a partner into an existing partnership is liable for all the obligations of the partnership arising before his admission as though he had been a partner when such obligations were incurred, except that this liability shall be satisfied only out of partnership property.

Part IV   Relations of Partners to One Another

Section 18. Rules Determining Rights and Duties of Partners

The rights and duties of the partners in relation to the partnership shall be determined, subject to any agreement between them, by the following rules:

    (a) Each partner shall be repaid his contributions, whether by way of capital or advances to the partnership property and share equally in the profits and surplus remaining after all liabilities, including those to partners, are satisfied; and must contribute towards the losses, whether of capital or otherwise, sustained by the partnership according to his share in the profits.

    (b) The partnership must indemnify every partner in respect of payments made and personal liabilities reasonably incurred by him in the ordinary and proper conduct of its business, or for the preservation of its business or property.

    (c) A partner, who in aid of the partnership makes any payment or advance beyond the amount of capital which he agreed to contribute, shall be paid interest from the date of the payment or advance.

    (d) A partner shall receive interest on the capital contributed by him only from the date when repayment should be made.

    (e) All partners have equal rights in the management and conduct of the partnership business.

    (f) No partner is entitled to remuneration for acting in the partnership business, except that a surviving partner is entitled to reasonable compensation for his services in winding up the partnership affairs.

    (g) No person can become a member of a partnership without the consent of all the partners.

    (h) Any difference arising as to ordinary matters connected with the partnership business may be decided by a majority of the partners; but no act in contravention of any agreement between the partners may be done rightfully without the consent of all the partners.

Section 19. Partnership Books

The partnership books shall be kept, subject to any agreement between the partners, at the principal place of business of the partnership, and every partner shall at all times have access to and may inspect and copy any of them.

Section 20. Duty of Partners to Render Information

Partners shall render on demand true and full information of all things affecting the partnership to any partner or the legal representative of any deceased partner or partner under legal disability.

Section 21. Partner Accountable as a Fiduciary

(1) Every partner must account to the partnership for any benefit, and hold as trustee for it any profits de-

rived by him without the consent of the other partners from any transaction connected with the formation, conduct, or liquidation of the partnership or from any use by him of its property.

(2) This section applies also to the representatives of a deceased partner engaged in the liquidation of the affairs of the partnership as the personal representatives of the last surviving partner.

Section 22.   Right to an Account

Any partner shall have the right to a formal account as to partnership affairs:

   (a) If he is wrongfully excluded from the partnership business or possession of its property by his co-partners,

   (b) If the right exists under the terms of any agreement,

   (c) As provided by section 21,

   (d) Whenever other circumstances render it just and reasonable.

Section 23.   Continuation of Partnership Beyond Fixed Term

(1) When a partnership for a fixed term or particular undertaking is continued after the termination of such term or particular undertaking without any express agreement, the rights and duties of the partners remain the same as they were at such termination, so far as is consistent with a partnership at will.

(2) A continuation of the business by the partners or such of them as habitually acted therein during the term, without any settlement or liquidation of the partnership affairs, is prima facie evidence of a continuation of the partnership.

Part V   Property Rights of a Partner

Section 24.   Extent of Property Rights of a Partner

The property rights of a partner are (1) his rights in specific partnership property, (2) his interest in the partnership, and (3) his right to participate in the management.

Section 25.   Nature of a Partner's Right in Specific Partnership Property

(1) A partner is co-owner with his partners of specific partnership property holding as a tenant in partnership.

(2) The incidents of this tenancy are such that:

   (a) A partner, subject to the provisions of this act and to any agreement between the partners, has an equal right with his partners to possess specific partnership property for partnership purposes; but he has no right to possess such property for any other purpose without the consent of his partners.

   (b) A partner's right in specific partnership property is not assignable except in connection with the assignment of rights of all the partners in the same property.

   (c) A partner's right in specific partnership property is not subject to attachment or execution, except on a claim against the partnership. When partnership property is attached for a partnership debt the partners, or any of them, or the representatives of a deceased partner, cannot claim any right under the homestead or exemption laws.

   (d) On the death of a partner his right in specific partnership property vests in the surviving partner or partners, except where the deceased was the last surviving partner, when his right in such property vests in his legal representative. Such surviving partner or partners, or the legal representative of the last surviving partner, has no right to possess the partnership property for any but a partnership purpose.

   (e) A partner's right in specific partnership property is not subject to dower, curtesy, or allowances to widows, heirs, or next of kin.

Section 26.   Nature of Partner's Interest in the Partnership

A partner's interest in the partnership is his share of the profits and surplus, and the same is personal property.

Section 27.   Assignment of Partner's Interest

(1) A conveyance by a partner of his interest in the partnership does not of itself dissolve the partnership, nor, as against the other partners in the absence of agreement, entitle the asignee, during the continuance of the partnership, to interfere in the management or administration of the partnership business or affairs, or to require any information or account of partnership transactions, or to inspect the partnership books; but it merely entitles the assignee to receive in accordance

with his contract the profits to which the assigning partner would otherwise be entitled.

(2) In case of a dissolution of the partnership, the assignee is entitled to receive his assignor's interest and may require an account from the date only of the last account agreed to by all the partners.

Section 28.   Partner's Interest Subject to Charging Order

(1) On due application to a competent court by any judgment creditor of a partner, the court which entered the judgment, order, or decree, or any other court, may charge the interest of the debtor partner with payment of the unsatisfied amount of such judgment debt with interest thereon; and may then or later appoint a receiver of his share of the profits, and of any other money due or to fall due to him in respect of the partnership, and make all other orders, directions, accounts and inquiries which the debtor partner might have made, or which the circumstances of the case may require.

(2) The interest charged may be redeemed at any time before foreclosure, or in case of a sale being directed by the court may be purchased without thereby causing a dissolution:

(a) With separate property, by any one or more of the partners, or

(b) With partnership property, by any one or more of the partners with the consent of all the partners whose interests are not so charged or sold.

(3) Nothing in this act shall be held to deprive a partner of his right, if any, under the exemption laws, as regards his interest in the partnership.

Part VI   Dissolution and Winding Up

Section 29.   Dissolution Defined

The dissolution of a partnership is the change in the relation of the partners caused by any partner ceasing to be associated in the carrying on as distinguished from the winding up of the business.

Section 30.   Partnership not Terminated by Dissolution

On dissolution the partnership is not terminated, but continues until the winding up of partnership affairs is completed.

Section 31.   Causes of Dissolution

Dissolution is caused:

(1) Without violation of the agreement between the partners,

(a) By the termination of the definite term or particular undertaking specified in the agreement,

(b) By the express will of any partner when no definite term or particular undertaking is specified,

(c) By the express will of all the partners who have not assigned their interests or suffered them to be charged for their separate debts, either before or after the termination of any specified term or particular undertaking,

(d) By the expulsion of any partner from the business bona fide in accordance with such a power conferred by the agreement between the partners;

(2) In contravention of the agreement between the partners, where the circumstances do not permit a dissolution under any other provision of this section, by the express will of any partner at any time;

(3) By any event which makes it unlawful for the business of the partnership to be carried on or for the members to carry it on in partnership;

(4) By the death of any partner;

(5) By the bankruptcy of any partner or the partnership;

(6) By decree of court under section 32.

Section 32.   Dissolution by Decree of Court

(1) On application by or for a partner the court shall decree a dissolution whenever:

(a) A partner has been declared a lunatic in any judicial proceeding or is shown to be of unsound mind,

(b) A partner becomes in any other way incapable of performing his part of the partnership contract,

(c) A partner has been guilty of such conduct as tends to affect prejudicially the carrying on of the business,

(d) A partner wilfully or persistently commits a breach of the partnership agreement, or otherwise so conducts himself in matters relating to the partnership business that it is not reasonably practicable to carry on the business in partnership with him,

(e) The business of the partnership can only be carried on at a loss,

(f) Other circumstances render a dissolution equitable.

(2) On the application of the purchaser of a partner's interest under sections 28 or 29:

(a) After the termination of the specified term or particular undertaking,

(b) At any time if the partnership was a partnership at will when the interest was assigned or when the charging order was issued.

Section 33. General Effect of Dissolution on Authority of Partner

Except so far as may be necessary to wind up partnership affairs or to complete transactions begun but not then finished, dissolution terminates all authority of any partner to act for the partnership,

(1) With respect to the partners,

(a) When the dissolution is not by the act, bankruptcy or death of a partner; or

(b) When the dissolution is by such act, bankruptcy or death of a partner, in cases where section 34 so requires.

(2) With respect to persons not partners, as declared in section 35.

Section 34. Right of Partner to Contribution from Co-partners after Dissolution

Where the dissolution is caused by the act, death or bankruptcy of a partner, each partner is liable to his co-partners for his share of any liability created by any partner acting for the partnership as if the partnership had not been dissolved unless

(a) The dissolution being by act of any partner, the partner acting for the partnership had knowledge of the dissolution, or

(b) The dissolution being by the death or bankruptcy of a partner, the partner acting for the partnership had knowledge or notice of the death or bankruptcy.

Section 35. Power of Partner to Bind Partnership to Third Persons after Dissolution

(1) After dissolution a partner can bind the partnership except as provided in Paragraph (3).

(a) By any act appropriate for winding up partnership affairs or completing transactions unfinished at dissolution;

(b) By any transaction which would bind the partnership if dissolution had not taken place, provided the other party to the transaction

(i) Had extended credit to the partnership prior to dissolution and had no knowledge or notice of the dissolution; or

(ii) Though he had not so extended credit, had nevertheless known of the partnership prior to dissolution, and, having no knowledge or notice of dissolution, the fact of dissolution had not been advertised in a newspaper of general circulation in the place (or in each place if more than one) at which the partnership business was regularly carried on.

(2) The liability of a partner under Paragraph (1b) shall be satisfied out of partnership assets alone when such partner had been prior to dissolution

(a) Unknown as a partner to the person with whom the contract is made; and

(b) So far unknown and inactive in partnership affairs that the business reputation of the partnership could not be said to have been in any degree due to his connection with it.

(3) The partnership is in no case bound by any act of a partner after dissolution

(a) Where the partnership is dissolved because it is unlawful to carry on the business, unless the act is appropriate for winding up partnership affairs; or

(b) Where the partner has become bankrupt; or

(c) Where the partner has no authority to wind up partnership affairs; except by a transaction with one who

(i) Had extended credit to the partnership prior to dissolution and had no knowledge or notice of his want of authority; or

(ii) Had not extended credit to the partnership prior to dissolution, and, having no knowledge or notice of his want of authority, the fact of his want of authority has not been advertised in the manner provided for advertising the fact of dissolution in Paragraph (1b ii).

(4) Nothing in this section shall affect the liability under Section 16 of any person who after dissolution represents himself or consents to another representing

him as a partner in a partnership engaged in carrying on business.

Section 36. Effect of Dissolution on Partner's Existing Liability

(1)   The dissolution of the partnership does not of itself discharge the existing liability of any partner.

(2)   A partner is discharged from any existing liability upon dissolution of the partnership by an agreement to that effect between himself, the partnership creditor and the person or partnership continuing the business; and such agreement may be inferred from the course of dealing between the creditor having knowledge of the dissolution and the person or partnership continuing the business.

(3)   Where a person agrees to assume the existing obligations of a dissolved partnership, the partners whose obligations have been assumed shall be discharged from any liability to any creditor of the partnership who, knowing of the agreement, consents to a material alteration in the nature or time of payment of such obligations.

(4)   The individual property of a deceased partner shall be liable for all obligations of the partnership incurred while he was a partner but subject to the prior payment of his separate debts.

Section 37. Right to Wind Up

Unless otherwise agreed the partners who have not wrongfully dissolved the partnership or the legal representative of the last surviving partner, not bankrupt, has the right to wind up the partnership affairs; provided, however, that any partner, his legal representative or his assignee, upon cause shown, may obtain winding up by the court.

Section 38. Rights of Partners to Application of Partnership Property

(1)   When dissolution is caused in any way, except in contravention of the partnership agreement, each partner, as against his co-partners and all persons claiming through them in respect of their interests in the partnership, unless otherwise agreed, may have the partnership property applied to discharge its liabilities, and the surplus applied to pay in cash the net amount owing to the respective partners. But if dissolution is caused by expulsion of a partner, bona fide under the partnership agreement and if the expelled partner is discharged from all partnership liabilities, either by payment or agreement under section 36(2), he shall receive in cash only the net amount due him from the partnership.

(2)   When dissolution is caused in contravention of the partnership agreement the rights of the partners shall be as follows:

(a)   Each partner who has not caused dissolution wrongfully shall have,

(i)   All the rights specified in paragraph (1) of this section, and

(ii)   The right, as against each partner who has caused the dissolution wrongfully, to damages for breach of the agreement.

(b)   The partners who have not caused the dissolution wrongfully, if they all desire to continue the business in the same name, either by themselves or jointly with others, may do so, during the agreed term for the partnership and for that purpose may possess the partnership property, provided they secure the payment by bond approved by the court, or pay to any partner who has caused the dissolution wrongfully, the value of his interest in the partnership at the dissolution, less any damages recoverable under clause (2a ii) of this section, and in like manner indemnify him against all present or future partnership liabilities.

(c)   A partner who has caused the dissolution wrongfully shall have:

(i)   If the business is not continued under the provisions of paragraph (2b) all the rights of a partner under paragraph (1), subject to clause (2a ii), of this section,

(ii)   If the business is continued under paragraph (2b) of this section the right as against his co-partners and all claiming through them in respect of their interests in the partnership, to have the value of his interest in the partnership, less any damages caused to his co-partners by the dissolution, ascertained and paid to him in cash, or the payment secured by bond approved by the court, and to be released from all existing liabilities of the partnership; but in ascertaining the value of the partner's interest the value of the good-will of the business shall not be considered.

Section 39. Rights Where Partnership is Dissolved for Fraud or Misrepresentation

Where a partnership contract is rescinded on the ground of the fraud or misrepresentation of one of the parties thereto, the party entitled to rescind is, without prejudice to any other right, entitled,

(a) To a lien on, or a right of retention of, the surplus of the partnership property after satisfying the partnership liabilities to third persons for any sum of money paid by him for the purchase of an interest in the partnership and for any capital or advances contributed by him; and

(b) To stand, after all liabilities to third persons have been satisfied, in the place of the creditors of the partnership for any payments made by him in respect of the partnership liabilities; and

(c) To be indemnified by the person guilty of the fraud or making the representation against all debts and liabilities of the partnership.

Section 40. Rules for Distribution

In settling accounts between the partners after dissolution, the following rules shall be observed, subject to any agreement to the contrary:

(a) The assets of the partnership are:

   (i) The partnership property,

   (ii) The contributions of the partners necessary for the payment of all the liabilities specified in clause (b) of this paragraph.

(b) The liabilities of the partnership shall rank in order of payment, as follows:

   (i) Those owing to creditors other than partners,

   (ii) Those owing to partners other than for capital and profits,

   (iii) Those owing to partners in respect of capital,

   (iv) Those owing to partners in respect of profits.

(c) The assets shall be applied in the order of their declaration in clause (a) of this paragraph to the satisfaction of the liabilities.

(d) The partners shall contribute, as provided by section 18 (a) the amount necessary to satisfy the liabilities; but if any, but not all, of the partners are insolvent, or, not being subject to process, refuse to contribute, the other partners shall contribute their share of the liabilities, and, in the relative proportions in which they share the profits, the additional amount necessary to pay the liabilities.

(e) An assignee for the benefit of creditors or any person appointed by the court shall have the right to enforce the contributions specified in clause (d) of this paragraph.

(f) Any partner or his legal representative shall have the right to enforce the contributions specified in clause (d) of this paragraph, to the extent of the amount which he has paid in excess of his share of the liability.

(g) The individual property of a deceased partner shall be liable for the contributions specified in clause (d) of this paragraph.

(h) When partnership property and the individual properties of the partners are in possession of a court for distribution, partnership creditors shall have priority on partnership property and separate creditors on individual property, saving the rights of lien or secured creditors as heretofore.

(i) Where a partner has become bankrupt or his estate is insolvent the claims against his separate property shall rank in the following order:

   (i) Those owing to separate creditors,

   (ii) Those owing to partnership creditors,

   (iii) Those owing to partners by way of contribution.

Section 41. Liability of Persons Continuing the Business in Certain Cases

(1) When any new partner is admitted into an existing partnership, or when any partner retires and assigns (or the representative of the deceased partner assigns) his rights in partnership property to two or more of the partners, or to one or more of the partners and one or more third persons, if the business is continued without liquidation of the partnership affairs, creditors of the first or dissolved partnership are also creditors of the partnership so continuing the business.

(2) When all but one partner retire and assign (or the representative of a deceased partner assigns) their rights in partnership property to the remaining partner, who continues the business without liquidation of partnership affairs, either alone or with others, credi-

tors of the dissolved partnership are also creditors of the person or partnership so continuing the business.

(3) When any partner retires or dies and the business of the dissolved partnership is continued as set forth in paragraphs (1) and (2) of this section, with the consent of the retired partners or the representative of the deceased partner, but without any assignment of his right in partnership property, rights of creditors of the dissolved partnership and of the creditors of the person or partnership continuing the business shall be as if such assignment has been made.

(4) When all the partners or their representatives assign their rights in partnership property to one or more third persons who promise to pay the debts and who continue the business of the dissolved partnership, creditors of the dissolved partnership are also creditors of the person or partnership continuing the business.

(5) When any partner wrongfully causes a dissolution and the remaining partners continue the business under the provisions of section 38(2b), either alone or with others, and without liquidation of the partnership affairs, creditors of the dissolved partnership are also creditors of the person or partnership continuing the business.

(6) When a partner is expelled and the remaining partners continue the business either alone or with others, without liquidation of the partnership affairs, creditors of the dissolved partnership are also creditors of the person or partnership continuing the business.

(7) The liability of a third person becoming a partner in the partnership continuing the business, under this section, to the creditors of the dissolved partnership shall be satisfied out of partnership property only.

(8) When the business of a partnership after dissolution is continued under any conditions set forth in this section the creditors of the dissolved partnership, as against the separate creditors of the retiring or deceased partner or the representative of the deceased partner, have a prior right to any claim of the retired partner or the representative of the deceased partner against the person or partnership continuing the business, on account of the retired or deceased partner's interest in the dissolved partnership or on account of any consideration promised for such interest or for his right in partnership property.

(9) Nothing in this section shall be held to modify any right of creditors to set aside any assignment on the ground of fraud.

(10) The use by the person or partnership continuing the business of the partnership name, or the name of a deceased partner as part thereof, shall not of itself make the individual property of the deceased partner liable for any debts contracted by such person or partnership.

Section 42. Rights of Retiring or Estate of Deceased Partner When the Business Is Continued

When any partner retires or dies, and the business is continued under any of the conditions set forth in section 41(1, 2, 3, 5, 6), or section 38(2b) without any settlement of accounts as between him or his estate and the person or partnership continuing the business, unless otherwise agreed, he or his legal representative as against such persons or partnership may have the value of his interest at the date of dissolution ascertained, and shall receive as an ordinary creditor an amount equal to the value of his interest in the dissolved partnership with interest, or, at his option or at the option of his legal representative, in lieu of interest, the profits attributable to the use of his right in the property of the dissolved partnership; provided that the creditors of the dissolved partnership as against the separate creditors, or the representative of the retired or deceased partner, shall have priority on any claim arising under this section, as provided by section 41(8) of this act.

Section 43. Accrual of Actions

The right to an account of his interest shall accrue to any partner, or his legal representative, as against the winding up partners or the surviving partners or the person or partnership continuing the business, at the date of dissolution, in the absence of any agreement to the contrary.

Part VII Miscellaneous Provisions

Section 44. When Act Takes Effect

This act shall take effect on the . . . . day of . . . . one thousand nine hundred and . . . .

Section 45. Legislation Repealed

All acts or parts of acts inconsistent with this act are hereby repealed.

Uniform Limited Partnership Act*

Section 1. Limited Partnership Defined

A limited partnership is a partnership formed by two or more persons under the provisions of Section 2, having as members one or more general partners and one or more limited partners. The limited partners as such shall not be bound by the obligations of the partnership.

Section 2. Formation

(1) Two or more persons desiring to form a limited partnership shall

  (a) Sign and swear to a certificate, which shall state

    (i) The name of the partnership,

    (ii) The character of the business,

    (iii) The location of the principal place of business,

    (iv) The name and place of residence of each member; general and limited partners being respectively designated,

    (v) The term for which the partnership is to exist,

    (vi) The amount of cash and a description of and the agreed value of the other property contributed by each limited partner,

    (vii) The additional contributions, if any, agreed to be made by each limited partner and the times at which or events on the happening of which they shall be made,

    (viii) The time, if agreed upon, when the contribution of each limited partner is to be returned,

    (ix) The share of the profits or the other compensation by way of income which each limited partner shall receive by reason of his contribution,

    (x) The right, if given, of a limited partner to substitute an assignee as contributor in his place, and the terms and conditions of the substitution,

    (xi) The right, if given, of the partners to admit additional limited partners,

    (xii) The right, if given, of one or more of the limited partners to priority over other limited partners, as to contributions or as to compensation by way of income, and the nature of such priority,

    (xiii) The right, if given, of the remaining general partner or partners to continue the business on the death, re-

---

Authors' note: A revised Uniform Limited Partnership Act was approved by the Commissioners on Uniform State Laws in 1976. This revised Act has been adopted by only a few states to date. The pertinent revisions have been referred to and discussed in Chapter 42 of this text.

*Source: National Conference of Commissioners of Uniform State Laws. Reprinted with permission.

tirement or insanity of a general partner, and

(xiv) The right, if given, of a limited partner to demand and receive property other than cash in return for his contribution.

(b) File for record the certificate in the office of [here designate the proper office].

(2) A limited partnership is formed if there has been substantial compliance in good faith with the requirements of paragraph (1).

Section 3. Business Which May Be Carried On

A limited partnership may carry on any business which a partnership without limited partners may carry on, except [here designate the business to be prohibited].

Section 4. Character of Limited Partner's Contribution

The contributions of a limited partner may be cash or other property, but not services.

Section 5. A Name Not to Contain Surname of Limited Partner; Exceptions

(1) The surname of a limited partner shall not appear in the partnership name, unless

(a) It is also the surname of a general partner, or

(b) Prior to the time when the limited partner became such the business had been carried on under a name in which his surname appeared.

(2) A limited partner whose name appears in a partnership name contrary to the provisions of paragraph (1) is liable as a general partner to partnership creditors who extend credit to the partnership without actual knowledge that he is not a general partner.

Section 6. Liability for False Statements in Certificate

If the certificate contains a false statement, one who suffers loss by reliance on such statement may hold liable any party to the certificate who knew the statement to be false.

(a) At the time he signed the certificate, or

(b) Subsequently, but within a sufficient time before the statement was relied upon to enable him to cancel or amend the certificate, or to file a petition for its cancellation or amendment as provided in Section 25(3).

Section 7. Limited Partner Not Liable to Creditors

A limited partner shall not become liable as a general partner unless, in addition to the exercise of his rights and powers as a limited partner, he takes part in the control of the business.

Section 8. Admission of Additional Limited Partners

After the formation of a limited partnership, additional limited partners may be admitted upon filing an amendment to the original certificate in accordance with the requirements of Section 25.

Section 9. Rights, Powers and Liabilities of a General Partner

(1) A general partner shall have all the rights and powers and be subject to all the restrictions and liabilities of a partner in a partnership without limited partners, except that without the written consent or ratification of the specific act by all the limited partners, a general partner or all of the general partners have no authority to

(a) Do any act in contravention of the certificate,

(b) Do any act which would make it impossible to carry on the ordinary business of the partnership,

(c) Confess a judgment against the partnership,

(d) Possess partnership property, or assign their rights in specific partnership property, for other than a partnership purpose,

(e) Admit a person as a general partner,

(f) Admit a person as a limited partner, unless the right so to do is given in the certificate,

(g) Continue the business with partnership property on the death, retirement or insanity of a general partner, unless the right so to do is given in the certificate.

Section 10. Rights of a Limited Partner

(1) A limited partner shall have the same rights as a general partner to

(a) Have the partnership books kept at the principal place of business of the partnership, and at all times to inspect and copy any of them,

(b) Have on demand true and full information of all things affecting the partnership, and a formal account of partnership affairs, whenever circumstances render it just and reasonable, and

(c) Have dissolution and winding up by decree of court.

(2) A limited partner shall have the right to receive a share of the profits or other compensation by way of income, and to the return of his contribution as provided in Sections 15 and 16.

Section 11. Status of Person Erroneously Believing Himself a Limited Partner

A person who has contributed to the capital of a business conducted by a person or partnership erroneously believing that he has become a limited partner in a limited partnership, is not, by reason of his exercise of the rights of a limited partner, a general partner with the person or in the partnership carrying on the business, or bound by the obligations of such person or partnership; provided that on ascertaining the mistake he promptly renounces his interest in the profits of the business, or other compensation by way of income.

Section 12. One Person Both General and Limited Partner

(1) A person may be a general partner and a limited partner in the same partnership at the same time.

(2) A person who is a general, and also at the same time a limited partner, shall have all the rights and powers and be subject to all the restrictions of a general partner; except that, in respect to his contribution, he shall have the rights against the other members which he would have had if he were not also a general partner.

Section 13. Loans and Other Business Transactions with Limited Partner

(1) A limited partner also may loan money to and transact other business with the partnership, and, unless he is also a general partner, receive on account of resulting claims against the partnership, with general creditors, a pro rata share of the assets. No limited partner shall in respect to any such claim.

(a) Receive or hold as collateral security any partnership property, or

(b) Receive from a general partner or the partnership any payment, conveyance, or release from liability, if at the time the assets of the partnership are not sufficient to discharge partnership liabilities to persons not claiming as general or limited partners.

(2) The receiving of collateral security, or a payment, conveyance, or release in violation of the provisions of paragraph (1) is a fraud on the creditors of the partnership.

Section 14. Relation of Limited Partners Inter Se

Where there are several limited partners the members may agree that one or more of the limited partners shall have a priority over other limited partners as to the return of their contributions, as to their compensation by way of income, or as to any other matter. If such an agreement is made it shall be stated in the certificate, and in the absence of such a statement all the limited partners shall stand upon equal footing.

Section 15. Compensation of Limited Partner

A limited partner may receive from the partnership the share of the profits or the compensation by way of income stipulated for in the certificate; provided, that after such payment is made, whether from the property of the partnership or that of a general partner, the partnership assets are in excess of all liabilities of the partnership except liabilities to limited partners on account of their contribution and to general partners.

Section 16. Withdrawal or Reduction of Limited Partner's Contribution

(1) A limited partner shall not receive from a general partner or out of partnership property any part of his contribution until

(a) All liabilities of the partnership, except liabilities to general partners and to limited partners on account of their contributions, have been paid or there remains property of the partnership sufficient to pay them,

(b) The consent of all members is had, unless the return of the contribution may be rightfully demanded under the provisions of paragraph (2), and

(c) The certificate is cancelled or so amended as to set forth the withdrawal or reduction.

(2)   Subject to the provisions of paragraph (1) a limited partner may rightfully demand the return of his contribution

   (a)   On the dissolution of a partnership, or

   (b)   When the date specified in the certificate for its return has arrived, or

   (c)   After he has given six months' notice in writing to all other members, if no time is specified in the certificate either for the return of the contribution or for the dissolution of the partnership.

(3)   In the absence of any statement in the certificate to the contrary or the consent of all members, a limited partner, irrespective of the nature of his contribution, has only the right to demand and receive cash in return for his contribution.

(4)   A limited partner may have the partnership dissolved and its affairs wound up when

   (a)   He rightfully but unsuccessfully demands the return of his contribution, or

   (b)   The other liabilities of the partnership have not been paid, or the partnership property is insufficient for their payment as required by paragraph (1a) and the limited partner would otherwise be entitled to the return of his contribution.

Section 17.   Liability of Limited Partner to Partnership

(1)   A limited partner is liable to the partnership

   (a)   For the difference between his contribution as actually made and that stated in the certificate as having been made, and

   (b)   For any unpaid contribution which he agreed in the certificate to make in the future at the time and on the conditions stated in the certificate.

(2)   A limited partner holds as trustee for the partnership

   (a)   Specific property stated in the certificate as contributed by him, but which was not contributed or which has been wrongfully returned, and

   (b)   Money or other property wrongfully paid or conveyed to him on account of his contribution.

(3)   The liabilities of a limited partner as set forth in this section can be waived or compromised only by the consent of all members; but a waiver or compromise shall not affect the right of a creditor of a partnership, who extended credit or whose claim arose after the filing and before a cancellation or amendment of the certificate, to enforce such liabilities.

(4)   When a contributor has rightfully received the return in whole or in part of the capital of his contribution, he is nevertheless liabile to the partnership for any sum, not in excess of such return with interest, necessary to discharge its liabilities to all creditors who extended credit or whose claims arose before such return.

Section 18.   Nature of Limited Partner's Interest in Partnership

A limited partner's interest in lthe partnership is personal property.

Section 19.   Assignment of Limited Partner's Interest

(1)   A limited partner's interest is assignable.

(2)   A substituted limited partner is a person admitted to all the rights of a limited partner who has died or has assigned his interest in a partnership.

(3)   An assignee, who does not become a substituted limited partner, has no right to require any information or account of the partnership transactions or to inspect the partnership books; he is only entitled to receive the share of the profits or other compensation by way of income, or the return of his contribution, to which his assignor would otherwise be entitled.

(4)   An assignee shall have the right to become a substituted limited partner if all the members (except the assignor) consent thereto or if the assignor, being thereunto empowered by the certificate, gives the assignee that right.

(5)   An assignee becomes a substituted limited partner when the certificate is appropriately amended in accordance with Section 25.

(6)   The substituted limited partner has all the rights and powers, and is subject to all the restrictions and liabilities of his assignor, except those liabilities of which he was ignorant at the time he became a limited partner and which could not be ascertained from the certificate.

(7)   The substitution of the assignee as a limited part-

ner does not release the assignor from liability to the partnership under Sections 6 and 17.

Section 20. Effect of Retirement, Death, or Insanity of a General Partner

The retirement, death or insanity of a general partner dissolves the partnership, unless the business is continued by the remaining general partners

(a) Under a right so to do stated in the certificate, or

(b) With the consent of all members.

Section 21. Death of Limited Partner

(1) On the death of a limited partner his executor or administrator shall have all the rights of a limited partner for the purpose of settling his estate, and such power as the deceased had to constitute his assignee a substituted limited partner.

(2) The estate of a deceased limited partner shall be liable for his liabilities as a limited partner.

Section 22. Rights of Creditors of Limited Partner

(1) On due application to a court of competent jurisdiction by any judgment creditor of a limited partner, the court may charge the interest of the indebted limited partner with payment of the unsatisfied amount of the judgment debt; and may appoint a receiver, and make all other orders, directions, and inquiries which the circumstances of the case may require.

[In those states where a creditor on beginning an action can attach debts due the defendant before he has obtained a judgment against the defendant it is recommended that paragraph (1) of this section read as follows:

On due application to a court of competent jurisdiction by any creditor of a limited partner, the court may charge the interest of the indebted limited partner with payment of the unsatisfied amount of such claim; and may appoint a receiver, and make all other orders, directions, and inquiries which the circumstances of the case may require.]

(2) The interest may be redeemed with the separate property of any general partner, but may not be redeemed with partnership property.

(3) The remedies conferred by paragraph (1) shall not be deemed exclusive of others which may exist.

(4) Nothing in this act shall be held to deprive a limited partner of his statutory exemption.

Section 23. Distribution of Assets

(1) In settling accounts after dissolution the liabilities of the partnership shall be entitled to payment in the following order:

(a) Those to creditors, in the order of priority as provided by law, except those to limited partners on account of their contributions, and to general partners,

(b) Those to limited partners in respect to their share of the profits and other compensation by way of income on their contributions,

(c) Those to limited partners in respect to the capital of their contributions,

(d) Those to general partners other than for capital and profits,

(e) Those to general partners in respect to profits,

(f) Those to general partners in respect to capital.

(2) Subject to any statement in the certificate or to subsequent agreement, limited partners share in the partnership assets in respect to their claims for capital, and in respect to their claims for profits or for compensation by way of income on their contributions respectively, in proportion to the respective amounts of such claims.

Section 24. When Certificate Shall Be Cancelled or Amended

(1) The certificate shall be cancelled when the partnership is dissolved or all limited partners cease to be such.

(2) A certificate shall be amended when

(a) There is a change in the name of the partnership or in the amount or character of the contribution of any limited partner,

(b) A person is substituted as a limited partner,

(c) An additional limited partner is admitted,

(d) A person is admitted as a general partner,

(e) A general partner retires, dies or becomes insane, and the business is continued under section 20,

(f) There is a change in the character of the business of the partnership,

(g) There is a false or erroneous statement in the certificate,

(h) There is a change in the time as stated in the certificate for the dissolution of the partnership or for the return of a contribution,

(i) A time is fixed for the dissolution of the partnership, or the return of a contribution, no time having been specified in the certificate, or

(j) The members desire to make a change in any other statement in the certificate in order that it shall accurately represent the agreement between them.

Section 25. Requirements for Amendment and for Cancellation of Certificate

(1) The writing to amend a certificate shall

(a) Conform to the requirements of Section 2(1a) as far as necessary to set forth clearly the change in the certificate which it is desired to make, and

(b) Be signed and sworn to by all members, and an amendment substituting a limited partner or adding a limited or general partner shall be signed also by the member to be substituted or added, and when a limited partner is to be substituted, the amendment shall also be signed by the assigning limited partner.

(2) The writing to cancel a certificate shall be signed by all members.

(3) A person desiring the cancellation or amendment of a certificate, if any person designated in paragraphs (1) and (2) as a person who must execute the writing refuses to do so, may petition the [here designate the proper court] to direct a cancellation or amendment thereof.

(4) If the court finds that the petitioner has a right to have the writing executed by a person who refuses to do so, it shall order the [here designate the responsible official in the office designated in Section 2] in the office where the certificate is recorded to record the cancellation or amendment of the certificate; and where the certificate is to be amended, the court shall also cause to be filed for record in said office a certified copy of its decree setting forth the amendment.

(5) A certificate is amended or cancelled when there is filed for record in the office [here designate the office designated in Section 2] where the certificate is recorded

(a) A writing in accordance with the provisions of paragraph (1), or (2) or

(b) A certified copy of the order of court in accordance with the provisions of paragraph (4).

(6) After the certificate is duly amended in accordance with this section, the amended certificate shall thereafter be for all purposes the certificate provided for by this act.

Section 26. Parties to Actions

A contributor, unless he is a general partner, is not a proper party to proceedings by or against a partnership, except where the object is to enforce a limited partner's right against or liability to the partnership.

Section 27. Name of Act

This act may be cited as The Uniform Limited Partnership Act.

Section 28. Rules of Construction

(1) The rule that statutes in derogation of the common law are to be strictly construed shall have no application to this act.

(2) This act shall be so interpreted and construed as to effect its general purpose to make uniform the law of those states which enact it.

(3) This act shall not be so construed as to impair the obligations of any contract existing when the act goes into effect, nor to affect any action on proceedings begun or right accrued before this act takes affect.

Section 29. Rules for Cases Not Provided for in This Act

In any case not provided for in this act the rules of law and equity, including the law merchant, shall govern.

Section 30.* Provisions for Existing Limited Partnerships

(1) A limited partnership formed under any statute of this state prior to the adoption of this act, may become a limited partnership under this act by complying with the provisions of Section 2; provided the certificate sets forth

(a) The amount of the original contribution of each limited partner, and the time when the contribution was made, and

---

*Sections 30, 31, will be omitted in any state which has not a limited partnership act.

(b) That the property of the partnership exceeds the amount sufficient to discharge its liabilities to persons not claiming as general or limited partners by an amount greater than the sum of the contributions of its limited partners.

(2) A limited partnership formed under any statute of this state prior to the adoption of this act, until or unless it becomes a limited partnership under this act, shall continue to be governed by the provisions of [here insert proper reference to the existing limited partnership act or acts], except that such partnership shall not be renewed unless so provided in the original agreement.

Section 31.* [Acts] Repealed

Except as affecting existing limited partnerships to the extent set forth in Section 30, the act (acts) of [here designate the existing limited partnership act or acts] is (are) hereby repealed.

Model Business Corporation Act (with revisions)*

Section 1.   Short Title.

This Act shall be known and may be cited as the "[supply name of state] . . . Business Corporation Act."

Section 2.   Definitions.

As used in this Act, unless the context otherwise requires, the term:

(a)   "Corporation" or "domestic corporation" means a corporation for profit subject to the provisions of this Act, except a foreign corporation.

(b)   "Foreign corporation" means a corporation for profit organized under laws other than the laws of this State for a purpose or purposes for which a corporation may be organized under this Act.

(c)   "Articles of incorporation" means the original or restated articles of incorporation or articles of consolidation and all amendments thereto including articles of merger.

(d)   "Shares" means the units into which the proprietary interests in a corporation are divided.

(e)   "Subscriber" means one who subscribes for shares in a corporation, whether before or after incorporation.

(f)   "Shareholder" means one who is a holder of record of shares in a corporation. If the articles of incorporation or the by-laws so provide, the board of directors may adopt by resolution a procedure whereby a shareholder of the corporation may certify in writing to the corporation that all or a portion of the shares registered in the name of such shareholder are held for the account of a specified person or persons. The resolution shall set forth (1) the classification of shareholder who may certify, (2) the purpose or purposes for which the certification may be made, (3) the form of certification and information to be contained therein, (4) if the certification is with respect to a record date or closing of the stock transfer books within which the certification must be received by the corporation and (5) such other provisions with respect to the procedure as are deemed necessary or desirable. Upon receipt by the corporation of a certification complying with the procedure, the persons specified in the certification shall be deemed, for the purpose or purposes set forth in the certification, to be the holders of record of the number of shares specified in place of the shareholder making the certification.

(g)   "Authorized shares" means the shares of all classes which the corporation is authorized to issue.

(h)   "Treasury shares" means shares of a corporation which have been issued, have been subsequently acquired by and belong to the corporation, and have not, either by reason of the acquisition or thereafter, been

*Reprinted with the permission of the American Law Institute—American Bar Association Committee on Continuing Professional Education.

cancelled or restored to the status of authorized by unissued shares. Treasury shares shall be deemed to be "issued" shares, but not "outstanding" shares.

(i) "Net assets" means the amount by which the total assets of a corporation exceed the total debts of the corporation.

(j) "Stated capital" means, at any particular time, the sum of (1) the par value of all shares of the corporation having a par value that have been issued, (2) the amount of consideration received by the corporation for all shares of the corporation without par value that have been issued, except such part of the consideration therefor as may have been allocated to capital surplus in a manner permitted by law, and (3) such amounts not included in clauses (1) and (2) of this paragraph as have been transferred to stated capital of the corporation, whether upon the issue of shares as a share dividend or otherwise, minus all reductions from such sum as have been effected in a manner permitted by law. Irrespective of the manner of designation thereof by the laws under which a foreign corporation is organized, the stated capital of a foreign corporation shall be determined on the same basis and in the same manner as the stated capital of a domestic corporation, for the purpose of computing fees, franchise taxes and other charges imposed by this Act.

(k) "Surplus" means the excess of the net assets of a corporation over its stated capital.

(l) "Earned surplus" means the portion of the surplus of a corporation equal to the balance of its net profits, income, gains and losses from the date of incorporation, or from the latest date when a deficit was eliminated by an application of its capital surplus or stated capital or otherwise, after deducting subsequent distributions to shareholders and transfers to stated capital and capital surplus to the extent such distributions and transfers are made out of earned surplus. Earned surplus shall include also any portion of surplus allocated to earned surplus in mergers, consolidations or acquisitions of all or substantially all of the outstanding shares or of the property and assets of another corporation, domestic or foreign.

(m) "Capital surplus" means the entire surplus of a corporation other than its earned surplus.

(n) "Insolvent" means inability of a corporation to pay its debts as they become due in the usual course of its business.

(o) "Employee" includes officers but not directors. A director may accept duties which make him also an employee.

Section 3. Purposes.

Corporations may be organized under this Act for any lawful purpose or purposes, except for the purpose of banking or insurance.

Section 4. General Powers.

Each corporation shall have power:

(a) To have perpetual succession by its corporate name unless a limited period of duration is stated in its articles of incorporation.

(b) To sue and be sued, complain and defend, in its corporate name.

(c) To have a corporate seal which may be altered at pleasure, and to use the same by causing it, or a facsimile thereof, to be impressed or affixed or in any other manner reproduced.

(d) To purchase, take, receive, lease, or otherwise acquire, own, hold, improve, use and otherwise deal in and with, real or personal property, or any interest therein, wherever situated.

(e) To sell, convey, mortgage, pledge, lease, exchange, transfer and otherwise dispose of all or any part of its property and assets.

(f) To lend money and use its credit to assist its employees.

(g) To purchase, take, receive, subscribe for, or otherwise acquire, own, hold, vote, use, employ, sell, mortgage, lend, pledge, or otherwise dispose of, and otherwise use and deal in and with, shares or other interests in, or obligations of, other domestic or foreign corporations, associations, partnerships or individuals, or direct or indirect obligations of the United States or of any other government, state, territory, governmental district or municipality or of any instrumentality thereof.

(h) To make contracts and guarantees and incur liabilities, borrow money at such rates of interest as the corporation may determine, issue its notes, bonds, and other obligations, and secure any of its obligations by mortgage or pledge of all or any of its property, franchises and income.

(i) To lend money for its corporate purposes, invest and reinvest its funds, and take and hold real and personal property as security for the payment of funds so loaned or invested.

(j) To conduct its business, carry on its operations and have offices and exercise the powers granted by this Act, within or without this State.

(k)   To elect or appoint officers and agents of the corporation, and define their duties and fix their compensation.

(l)   To make and alter by-laws, not inconsistent with its articles of incorporation or with the laws of this State, for the administration and regulation of the affairs of the corporation.

(m)   To make donations for the public welfare or for charitable, scientific or educational purposes.

(n)   To transact any lawful business which the board of directors shall find will be in aid of governmental policy.

(o)   To pay pensions and establish pension plans, pension trusts, profit sharing plans, stock bonus plans, stock option plans and other incentive plans for any or all of its directors, officers and employees.

(p)   To be a promoter, partner, member, associate, or manager of any partnership, joint venture, trust or other enterprise.

(q)   To have and exercise all powers necessary or convenient to effect its purposes.

Section 5.   Indemnification of Officers, Directors, Employees and Agents.

(a)   A corporation shall have power to indemnify any person who was or is a party or is threatened to be made a party to any threatened, pending or completed action, suit or proceeding, whether civil, criminal, administrative or investigative (other than an action by or in the right of the corporation) by reason of the fact that he is or was a director, officer, employee or agent of the corporation, or is or was serving at the request of the corporation as a director, officer, employee or agent of another corporation, partnership, joint venture, trust or other enterprise, against expenses (including attorneys' fees), judgments, fines and amounts paid in settlement actually and reasonably incurred by him in connection with such action, suit or proceeding if he acted in good faith and in a manner he reasonably believed to be in or not opposed to the best interests of the corporation, and, with respect to any criminal action or proceeding, had no reasonable cause to believe his conduct was unlawful. The termination of any action, suit or proceeding by judgment, order, settlement, conviction, or upon a plea of nolo contendere or its equivalent, shall not, of itself, create a presumption that the person did not act in good faith and in a manner which he reasonably believed to be in or not opposed to the best interests of the corporation, and,

with respect to any criminal action or proceeding, had reasonable cause to believe that his conduct was unlawful.

(b)   A corporation shall have power to indemnify any person who was or is a party or is threatened to be made a party to any threatened, pending or completed action or suit by or in the right of the corporation to procure a judgment in its favor by reason of the fact that he is or was a director, officer, employee or agent of the corporation, or is or was serving at the request of the corporation as a director, officer, employee or agent of another corporation, partnership, joint venture, trust or other enterprise against expenses (including attorneys' fees) actually and reasonably incurred by him in connection with the defense or settlement of such action or suit if he acted in good faith and in a manner he reasonably believed to be in or not opposed to the best interests of the corporation and except that no indemnification shall be made in respect of any claim, issue or matter as to which such person shall have been adjudged to be liable for negligence or misconduct in the performance of his duty to the corporation unless and only to the extent that the court in which such action or suit was brought shall determine upon application that, despite the adjudication of liability but in view of all circumstances of the case, such person is fairly and reasonably entitled to indemnity for such expenses which such court shall deem proper.

(c)   To the extent that a director, officer, employee or agent of a corporation has been successful on the merits or otherwise in defense of any action, suit or proceeding referred to in subsections (a) or (b), or in defense of any claim, issue or matter therein, he shall be indemnified against expenses (including attorneys' fees) actually and reasonably incurred by him in connection therewith.

(d)   Any indemnification under subsections (a) or (b) (unless ordered by a court) shall be made by the corporation only as authorized in the specific case upon a determination that indemnification of the director, officer, employee or agent is proper in the circumstances because he has met the applicable standard of conduct set forth in subsections (a) or (b). Such determination shall be made (1) by the board of directors by a majority vote of a quorum consisting of directors who were not parties to such action, suit or proceeding, or (2) if such a quorum is not obtainable, or, even if obtainable a quorum of disinterested directors so directs, by independent legal counsel in a written opinion, or (3) by the shareholders.

(e)   Expenses (including attorneys' fees) incurred in defending a civil or criminal action, suit or proceeding may be paid by the corporation in advance of the final disposition of such action, suit or proceeding as authorized in the manner provided in subsection (d) upon receipt of an undertaking by or on behalf of the director, officer, employee or agent to repay such amount unless it shall ultimately be determined that he is entitled to be indemnified by the corporation as authorized in this section.

(f) The indemnification provided by this section shall not be deemed exclusive of any other rights to which those indemnified may be entitled under any by-law, agreement, vote of shareholders or disinterested directors or otherwise, both as to action in his official capacity and as to action in another capacity while holding such office, and shall continue as to a person who has ceased to be a director, officer, employee or agent and shall inure to the benefit of the heirs, executors and administrators of such a person.

(g) A corporation shall have power to purchase and maintain insurance on behalf of any person who is or was a director, officer, employee or agent of the corporation, or is or was serving at the request of the corporation as a director, officer, employee or agent of another corporation, partnership, joint venture, trust or other enterprise against any liability asserted against him and incurred by him in any such capacity or arising out of his status as such, whether or not the corporation would have the power to indemnify him against such liability under the provisions of this section.

Section 6. Right of Corporation to Acquire and Dispose of Its Own Shares.

A corporation shall have the right to purchase, take, receive or otherwise acquire, hold, own, pledge, transfer or otherwise dispose of its own shares, but purchases of its own shares, whether direct or indirect, shall be made only to the extent of unreserved and unrestricted earned surplus available therefor, and, if the articles of incorporation so permit or with the affirmative vote of the holders of a majority of all shares entitled to vote thereon, to the extent of unreserved and unrestricted capital surplus available therefor.

To the extent that earned surplus or capital surplus is used as the measure of the corporation's right to purchase its own shares, such surplus shall be restricted so long as such shares are held as treasury shares, and upon the disposition or cancellation of any such shares the restriction shall be removed pro tanto.

Notwithstanding the foregoing limitation, a corporation may purchase or otherwise acquire its own shares for the purpose of:

(a) Eliminating fractional shares.

(b) Collecting or compromising indebtedness to the corporation.

(c) Paying dissenting shareholders entitled to payment for their shares under the provisions of this Act.

(d) Effecting, subject to the other provisions of this Act, the retirement of its redeemable shares by redemption or by purchase at not to exceed the redemption price.

No purchase of or payment for its own shares shall be made at a time when the corporation is insolvent or when such purchase or payment would make it insolvent.

Section 7. Defense of Ultra Vires.

No act of a corporation and no conveyance or transfer of real or personal property to or by a corporation shall be invalid by reason of the fact that the corporation was without capacity or power to do such act or to make or receive such conveyance or transfer, but such lack of capacity or power may be asserted:

(a) In a proceeding by a shareholder against the corporation to enjoin the doing of any act or the transfer of real or personal property by or to the corporation. If the unauthorized act or transfer sought to be enjoined is being, or is to be, performed or made pursuant to a contract to which the corporation is a party, the court may, if all of the parties to the contract are parties to the proceeding and if it deems the same to be equitable, set aside and enjoin the performance of such contract, and in so doing may allow to the corporation or to the other parties to the contract, as the case may be, compensation for the loss or damage sustained by either of them which may result from the action of the court in setting aside and enjoining the performance of such contract, but anticipated profits to be derived from the performance of the contract shall not be awarded by the court as a loss or damage sustained.

(b) In a proceeding by the corporation, whether acting directly or through a receiver, trustee, or other legal representative, or through shareholders in a representative unit, against the incumbent or former officers or directors of the corporation.

(c) In a proceeding by the Attorney General, as provided in this Act, to dissolve the corporation, or in a proceeding by the Attorney General to enjoin the corporation from the transaction of unauthorized business.

Section 8.   Corporate Name.

The corporate name:

(a)   Shall contain the word "corporation," "company," "incorporated" or "limited," or shall contain an abbreviation of one of such words.

(b)   Shall not contain any word or phrase which indicates or implies that it is organized for any purpose other than one or more of the purposes contained in its articles of incorporation.

(c)   Shall not be the same as, or deceptively similar to, the name of any domestic corporation existing under the laws of this State or any foreign corporation authorized to transact business in this State, or a name the exclusive right to which is, at the time, reserved in the manner provided in this Act, or the name of a corporation which has in effect a registration of its corporate name as provided in this Act, except that this provision shall not apply if the applicant files with the Secretary of State either of the following: (1) the written consent of such other corporation or holder of a reserved or registered name to use the same or deceptively similar name and one or more words are added to make such name distinguishable from such other name, or (2) a certified copy of a final decree of a court of competent jurisdiction establishing the prior right of the applicant to the use of such name in this State.

A corporation with which another corporation, domestic or foreign, is merged, or which is formed by the reorganization or consolidation of one or more domestic or foreign corporations or upon a sale, lease or other disposition to or exchange with, a domestic corporation of all or substantially all the assets of another corporation, domestic or foreign, including its name, may have the same name as that used in this State by any of such corporations if such other corporation was organized under the laws of, or is authorized to transact business in, this State.

Section 9.   Reserved Name.

The exclusive right to the use of a corporate name may be reserved by:

(a)   Any person intending to organize a corporation under this Act.

(b)   Any domestic corporation intending to change its name.

(c)   Any foreign corporation intending to make application for a certificate of authority to transact business in this State.

(d)   Any foreign corporation authorized to transact business in this State and intending to change its name.

(e)   Any person intending to organize a foreign corporation and intending to have such corporation make application for a certificate of authority to transact business in this State.

The reservation shall be made by filing with the Secretary of State an application to reserve a specified corporate name, executed by the applicant. If the Secretary of State finds that the name is available for corporate use, he shall reserve the same for the exclusive use of the applicant for a period of one hundred and twenty days.

The right to the exclusive use of a specified corporate name so reserved may be transferred to any other person or corporation by filing in the office of the Secretary of State a notice of such transfer, executed by the applicant for whom the name was reserved, and specifying the name and address of the transferee.

Section 10.   Registered Name.

Any corporation organized and existing under the laws of any state or territory of the United States may register its corporate name under this Act, provided its corporate name is not the same as, or deceptively similar to, the name of any domestic corporation existing under the laws of this State, or the name of any foreign corporation authorized to transact business in this State, or any corporate name reserved or registered under this Act.

Such registration shall be made by:

(a)   Filing with the Secretary of State (1) an application for registration executed by the corporation by an officer thereof, setting forth the name of the corporation, the state or territory under the laws of which it is incorporated, the date of its incorporation, a statement that it is carrying on or doing business, and a brief statement of the business in which it is engaged, and (2) a certificate setting forth that such corporation is in good standing under the laws of the state or territory wherein it is organized, executed by the Secretary of State of such state or territory or by such other official as may have custody of the records pertaining to corporations, and

(b)   Paying to the Secretary of State a registration fee in the amount of . . . for each month, or fraction thereof, between the date of filing such application and December 31st of the calendar year in which such application is filed.

Such registration shall be effective until the close of the

calendar year in which the application for registration is filed.

Section 11. Renewal of Registered Name [*Text omitted*].

Section 12. Registered Office and Registered Agent.

Each corporation shall have and continuously maintain in this State:

(a) A registered office which may be, but need not be, the same as its place of business.

(b) A registered agent, which agent may be either an individual resident in this State whose business office is identical with such registered office, or a domestic corporation, or a foreign corporation authorized to transact business in this State, having a business office identical with such registered office.

Section 13. Change of Registered Office or Registered Agent.

A corporation may change its registered office or change its registered agent, or both, upon filing in the office of the Secretary of State a statement setting forth:

(a) The name of the corporation.

(b) The address of its then registered office.

(c) If the address of its registered office is to be changed, the address to which the registered office is to be changed.

(d) The name of its then registered agent.

(e) If its registered agent is to be changed, the name of its successor registered agent.

(f) That the address of its registered office and the address of the business office of its registered agent, as changed, will be identical.

(g) That such change was authorized by resolution duly adopted by its board of directors.

Such statement shall be executed by the corporation by its president, or a vice president, and verified by him and delivered to the Secretary of State. If the Secretary of State finds that such statement conforms to the provisions of this Act, he shall file such statement in his office and upon such filing the change of address of the registered office, or the appointment of a new registered agent, or both, as the case may be, shall become effective.

Any registered agent of a corporation may resign as

such agent upon filing a written notice thereof, executed in duplicate, with the Secretary of State, who shall forthwith mail a copy thereof to the corporation at its registered office. The appointment of such agent shall terminate upon the expiration of thirty days after receipt of such notice by the Secretary of State.

If a registered agent changes his or its business address to another place within the same . . . . *, he or it may change such address and the address of the registered office of any corporation of which he or it is registered agent by filing a statement as required above except that it need be signed only by the registered agent and need not be responsive to (e) or (g) and must recite that a copy of the statement has been mailed to the corporation.

Section 14. Service of Process on Corporation.

The registered agent so appointed by a corporation shall be an agent of such corporation upon whom any process, notice or demand required or permitted by law to be served upon the corporation may be served.

Whenever a corporation shall fail to appoint or maintain a registered agent in this State, or whenever its registered agent cannot with reasonable diligence be found at the registered office, then the Secretary of State shall be an agent of such corporation upon whom any such process, notice or demand may be served. Service on the Secretary of State of any such process, notice, or demand shall be made by delivering to and leaving with him, or with any clerk having charge of the corporation department of his office, duplicate copies of such process, notice or demand. In the event any such process, notice or demand is served on the Secretary of State, he shall immediately cause one of the copies thereof to be forwarded by registered mail, addressed to the corporation at its registered office. Any service so had on the Secretary of State shall be returnable in not less than thirty days.

The Secretary of State shall keep a record of all processes, notices and demands served upon him under this section, and shall record therein the time of such service and his action with reference thereto.

Nothing herein contained shall limit or affect the right to serve any process, notice or demand required or permitted by law to be served upon a corporation in any other manner now or hereafter permitted by law.

---

*Supply designation of jurisdiction, such as county, etc., in accordance with local practice.

Section 15. Authorized Shares.

Each corporation shall have power to create and issue the number of shares stated in its articles of incorporation. Such shares may be divided into one or more classes, any or all of which classes may consist of shares with par value or shares without par value, with such designations, preferences, limitations, and relative rights as shall be stated in the articles of incorporation. The articles of incorporation may limit or deny the voting rights of or provide special voting rights for the shares of any class to the extent not inconsistent with the provisions of this Act.

Without limiting the authority herein contained, a corporation, when so provided in its articles of incorporation, may issue shares of preferred or special classes:

(a) Subject to the right of the corporation to redeem any of such shares at the price fixed by the articles of incorporation for the redemption thereof.

(b) Entitling the holders thereof to cumulative, non-cumulative or partially cumulative dividends.

(c) Having preference over any other class or classes of shares as to the payment of dividends.

(d) Having preference in the assets of the corporation over any other class or classes of shares upon the voluntary or involuntary liquidation of the corporation.

(e) Convertible into shares of any other class or into shares of any series of the same or any other class, except a class having prior or superior rights and preferences as to dividends or distribution of assets upon liquidation, but shares without par value shall not be converted into shares with par value unless that part of the stated capital of the corporation represented by such shares without par value is, at the time of conversion, at least equal to the aggregate par value of the shares into which the shares without par value are to be converted or the amount of any such deficiency is transferred from surplus to stated capital.

Section 16. Issuance of Shares of Preferred or Special Classes in Series.

If the articles of incorporation so provide, the shares of any preferred or special class may be divided into and issued in series. If the shares of any such class are to be issued in series, then each series shall be so designated as to distinguish the shares thereof from the shares of all other series and classes. Any or all of the series of any such class and the variations in the relative rights and preferences as between different series may be fixed and determined by the articles of incorporation, but all shares of the same class shall be identical except as to the following relative rights and preferences, as to which there may be variations between different series:

(a) The rate of dividend.

(b) Whether shares may be redeemed and, if so, the redemption price and the terms and conditions of redemption.

(c) The amount payable upon shares in event of voluntary and involuntary liquidation.

(d) Sinking fund provisions, if any, for the redemption or purchase of shares.

(e) The terms and conditions, if any, on which shares may be converted.

(f) Voting rights, if any.

If the articles of incorporation shall expressly vest authority in the board of directors, then, to the extent that the articles of incorporation shall not have established series and fixed and determined the variations in the relative rights and preferences as between series, the board of directors shall have authority to divide any or all of such classes into series and, within the limitations set forth in this section and in the articles of incorporation, fix and determine the relative rights and preferences of the shares of any series so established.

In order for the board of directors to establish a series, where authority so to do is contained in the articles of incorporation, the board of directors shall adopt a resolution setting forth the designation of the series and fixing and determining the relative rights and preferences thereof, or so much thereof as shall not be fixed and determined by the articles of incorporation.

Prior to the issue of any shares of a series established by resolution adopted by the board of directors, the corporation shall file in the office of the Secretary of State a statement setting forth:

(a) The name of the corporation.

(b) A copy of the resolution establishing and designating the series, and fixing and determining the relative rights and preferences thereof.

(c) The date of adoption of such resolution.

(d) That such resolution was duly adopted by the board of directors.

Such statement shall be executed in duplicate by the corporation by its president or a vice president and by its secretary or an assistant secretary, and verified by one of the officers signing such statement, and shall be delivered to the Secretary of State. If the Secretary of State finds that such statement conforms to law, he shall, when all franchise taxes and fees have been paid as in this Act prescribed:

(1) Endorse on each of such duplicate originals the word "Filed," and the month, day, and year of the filing thereof.

(2) File one of such duplicate originals in his office.

(3) Return the other duplicate original to the corporation or its representative.

Upon the filing of such statement by the Secretary of State, the resolution establishing and designating the series and fixing and determining the relative rights and preferences thereof shall become effective and shall constitute an amendment of the articles of incorporation.

Section 17. Subscriptions for Shares.

A subscription for shares of a corporation to be organized shall be irrevocable for a period of six months, unless otherwise provided by the terms of the subscription agreement or unless all of the subscribers consent to the revocation of such subscription.

Unless otherwise provided in the subscription agreement, subscriptions for shares, whether made before or after the organization of a corporation, shall be paid in full at such time, or in such installments and at such times, as shall be determined by the board of directors. Any call made by the board of directors for payment on subscriptions shall be uniform as to all shares of the same class or as to all shares of the same series, as the case may be. In case of default in the payment of any installment or call when such payment is due, the corporation may proceed to collect the amount due in the same manner as any debt due the corporation. The by-laws may prescribe other penalties for failure to pay installments or calls that may become due, but no penalty working a forfeiture of a subscription, or of the amounts paid thereon, shall be declared as against any subscriber unless the amount due thereon shall remain unpaid for a period of twenty days after written demand has been made therefor. If mailed, such written demand shall be deemed to be made when deposited in the United States mail in a sealed envelope addressed to the subscriber at his last post-office address known to the corporation, with postage thereon prepaid. In the event of the sale of any shares by reason of any forfeiture, the excess of proceeds realized over the amount due and unpaid on such shares shall be paid to the delinquent subscriber or to his legal representative.

Section 18. Consideration for Shares.

Shares having a par value may be issued for such consideration expressed in dollars, not less than the par value thereof, as shall be fixed from time to time by the board of directors.

Shares without par value may be issued for such consideration expressed in dollars as may be fixed from time to time by the board of directors unless the articles of incorporation reserve to the shareholders the right to fix the consideration. In the event that such right be reserved as to any shares, the shareholders shall, prior to the issuance of such shares, fix the consideration to be received for such shares, by a vote of the holders of a majority of all shares entitled to vote thereon.

Treasury shares may be disposed of by the corporation for such consideration expressed in dollars as may be fixed from time to time by the board of directors.

That part of the surplus of a corporation which is transferred to stated capital upon the issuance of shares as a share dividend shall be deemed to be the consideration for the issuance of such shares.

In the event of the issuance of shares upon the conversion or exchange of indebtedness or shares, the consideration for the shares so issued shall be (1) the principal sum of, and accrued interest on, the indebtedness so exchanged or converted, or the stated capital then represented by the shares so exchanged or converted, and (2) that part of surplus, if any, transferred to stated capital upon the issuance of shares for the shares so exchanged or converted, and (3) any additional consideration paid to the corporation upon the issuance of shares for the indebtedness or shares so exchanged or converted.

Section 19. Payment for Shares.

The consideration for the issuance of shares may be paid, in whole or in part, in cash, in other property, tangible or intangible, or in labor or services actually performed for the corporation. When payment of the consideration for which shares are to be issued shall have been received by the corporation, such shares shall be deemed to be fully paid and nonassessable.

Neither promissory notes nor future services shall constitute payment or part payment for the issuance of shares of a corporation.

In the absence of fraud in the transaction, the judgment of the board of directors or the shareholders, as the case may be, as to the value of the consideration received for shares shall be conclusive.

Section 20. Stock Rights and Options.

Subject to any provisions in respect thereof set forth in its articles of incorporation, a corporation may create and issue, whether or not in connection with the issuance and sale of any of its shares or other securities, rights or options entitling the holders thereof to purchase from the corporation shares of any class or classes. Such rights or options shall be evidenced in such manner as the board of directors shall approve and, subject to the provisions of the articles of incorporation, shall set forth the terms upon which, the time or times within which and the price or prices at which such shares may be purchased from the corporation upon the exercise of any such right or option. If such rights or options are to be issued to directors, officers or employees as such of the corporation or of any subsidiary thereof, and not to the shareholders generally, their issuance shall be approved by the affirmative vote of the holders of a majority of the shares entitled to vote thereon or shall be authorized by and consistent with a plan approved or ratified by such a vote of shareholders. In the absence of fraud in the transaction, the judgment of the board of directors as to the adequacy of the consideration received for such rights or options shall be conclusive. The price or prices to be received for any shares having a par value, other than treasury shares to be issued upon the exercise of such rights or options, shall not be less than the par value thereof.

Section 21. Determination of Amount of Stated Capital.

In case of the issuance by a corporation of shares having a par value, the consideration received therefor shall constitute stated capital to the extent of the par value of such shares, and the excess, if any, of such consideration shall constitute capital surplus.

In case of the issuance by a corporation of shares without par value, the entire consideration received therefor shall constitute stated capital unless the corporation shall determine as provided in this section that only a part thereof shall be stated capital. Within a period of sixty days after the issuance of any shares without par value, the board of directors may allocate to capital surplus any portion of the consideration received for the issuance of such shares. No such allocation shall be made of any portion of the consideration received for shares without par value having a preference in the assets of the corporation in the event of involuntary liquidation except the amount, if any, of such consideration in excess of such preference.

If shares have been or shall be issued by a corporation in merger or consolidation or in acquisition of all or substantially all of the outstanding shares or of the property and assets of another corporation, whether domestic or foreign, any amount that would otherwise constitute capital surplus under the foregoing provisions of this section may instead by allocated to earned surplus by the board of directors of the issuing corporation except that its aggregate earned surplus shall not exceed the sum of the earned surpluses as defined in this Act of the issuing corporation and of all other corporations, domestic or foreign, that were merged or consolidated or of which the shares or assets were acquired.

The stated capital of a corporation may be increased from time to time by resolution of the board of directors directing that all or a part of the surplus of the corporation be transferred to stated capital. The board of directors may direct that the amount of the surplus so transferred shall be deemed to be stated capital in respect of any designated class of shares.

Section 22. Expenses of Organization. Reorganization and Financing.

The reasonable charges and expenses of organization or reorganization of a corporation, and the reasonable expenses of and compensation for the sale or underwriting of its shares, may be paid or allowed by such corporation out of the consideration received by it in payment for its shares without thereby rendering such shares not fully paid or assessable.

Section 23. Shares Represented by Certificates and Uncertificated Shares.

The shares of a corporation shall be represented by certificates or shall be uncertificated shares. Certificates shall be signed by the chairman or vice-chairman of the board of directors or the president or a vice president and by the treasurer or an assistant treasurer or the secretary or an assistant secretary of the corporation, and may be sealed with the seal of the corporation or a facsimile thereof. Any of or all the signatures upon a certificate may be a facsimile. In case any officer, transfer agent or registrar who has signed or whose facsimile signature has been placed upon such certificate shall have ceased to be such officer, transfer agent or registrar before such certificate is issued, it may be issued by the corporation with the same effect as if he were such officer, transfer agent or registrar at the date of its issue.

Every certificate representing shares issued by a corporation which is authorized to issue shares of more than one class shall set forth upon the face or back of the certificate, or shall state that the corporation will furnish to any shareholder upon request and without charge, a full statement of the designations, preferences, limitations, and relative rights of the shares of each class authorized to be issued, and if the corporation is authorized to issue any preferred or special class in series, the variations in the relative rights and preferences between the shares of each such series so far as the same have been fixed and determined and the authority of the board of directors to fix and determine the relative rights and preferences of subsequent series.

Each certificate representing shares shall state upon the face thereof:

(a)   That the corporation is organized under the laws of this State.

(b)   The name of the person to whom issued.

(c)   The number and class of shares, and the designation of the series, if any, which such certificate represents.

(d)   The par value of each share represented by such certificate, or a statement that the shares are without par value.

No certificate shall be issued for any share until such share is fully paid.

Unless otherwise provided by the articles of incorporation or by-laws, the board of directors of a corporation may provide by resolution that some or all of any or all classes and series of its shares shall be uncertificated shares, provided that such resolution shall not apply to shares represented by a certificate until such certificate is surrendered to the corporation. Within a reasonable time after the issuance or transfer of uncertificated shares, the corporation shall send to the registered owner thereof a written notice containing the information required to be set forth or stated on certificates pursuant to the second and third paragraphs of this section. Except as otherwise expressly provided by law, the rights and obligations of the holders of uncertificated shares and the rights and obligations of the holders of certificates representing shares of the same class and series shall be identical.

Section 24.   Fractional Shares.

A corporation may (1) issue fractions of a share, either represented by a certificate or uncertificated, (2) arrange for the disposition of fractional interests by those entitled thereto, (3) pay in cash the fair value of fractions of a share as of a time when those entitled to receive such fractions are determined, or (4) issue scrip in registered or bearer form which shall entitle the holder to receive a certificate for a full share or an uncertificated full share upon the surrender of such scrip aggregating a full share. A certificate for a fractional share or an uncertificated fractional share shall, but scrip shall not unless otherwise provided therein, entitle the holder to exercise voting rights, to receive dividends thereon, and to participate in any of the assets of the corporation in the event of liquidation. The board of directors may cause scrip to be issued subject to the condition that it shall become void if not exchanged for certificates representing full shares or uncertificated full shares before a specified date, or subject to the condition that the shares for which scrip is exchangeable may be sold by the corporation and the proceeds thereof distributed to the holders of scrip, or subject to any other conditions which the board of directors may deem advisable.

Section 25.   Liability of Subscribers and Shareholders.

A holder of or subscriber to shares of a corporation shall be under no obligation to the corporation or its creditors with respect to such shares other than the obligation to pay to the corporation the full consideration for which such shares were issued or to be issued.

Any person becoming an assignee or transferee of shares or of a subscription for shares in good faith and without knowledge or notice that the full consideration therefor has not been paid shall not be personally liable to the corporation or its creditors for any unpaid portion of such consideration.

An executor, administrator, conservator, guardian, trustee, assignee for the benefit of creditors, or receiver shall not be personally liable to the corporation as a holder of or subscriber to shares of a corporation but the estate and funds in his hands shall be so liable.

No pledgee or other holder of shares as collateral security shall be personally liable as a shareholder.

Section 26.   Shareholders' Preemptive Rights.

The shareholders of a corporation shall have no preemptive right to acquire unissued or treasury shares of the corporation, or securities of the corporation convertible into or carrying a right to subscribe to or acquire shares, except to the extent, if any, that such right is provided in the articles of incorporation.

Section 26A. Shareholders' Preemptive Rights [Alternative].

Except to the extent limited or denied by this section or by the articles of incorporation, shareholders shall have a preemptive right to acquire unissued or treasury shares or securities convertible into such shares or carrying a right to subscribe to or acquire shares.

Unless otherwise provided in the articles of incorporation,

(a) No preemptive right shall exist

    (1) to acquire any shares issued to directors, officers or employees pursuant to approval by the affirmative vote of the holders of a majority of the shares entitled to vote thereon or when authorized by and consistent with a plan theretofore approved by such a vote of shareholders; or

    (2) to acquire any shares sold otherwise than for cash.

(b) Holders of shares of any class that is preferred or limited as to dividends or assets shall not be entitled to any preemptive right.

(c) Holders of shares of common stock shall not be entitled to any preemptive right to shares of any class that is preferred or limited as to dividends or assets or to any obligations, unless convertible into shares of common stock or carrying a right to subscribe to or acquire shares of common stock.

(d) Holders of common stock without voting power shall have no preemptive right to shares of common stock with voting power.

(e) The preemptive right shall be only an opportunity to acquire shares or other securities under such terms and conditions as the board of directors may fix for the purpose of providing a fair and reasonable opportunity for the exercise of such right.

Section 27. By-laws.

The initial by-laws of a corporation shall be adopted by its board of directors. The power to alter, amend or repeal the by-laws or adopt new by-laws, subject to repeal or change by action of the shareholders, shall be vested in the board of directors unless reserved to the shareholders by the articles of incorporation. The by-laws may contain any provisions for the regulation and management of the affairs of the corporation not inconsistent with law or the articles of incorporation.

Section 27A. By-laws and Other Powers in Emergency [Optional].

The board of directors of any corporation may adopt emergency by-laws, subject to repeal or change by action of the shareholders, which shall, notwithstanding any different provision elsewhere in this Act or in the articles of incorporation or by-laws, be operative during any emergency in the conduct of the business of the corporation resulting from an attack on the United States or any nuclear or atomic disaster. The emergency by-laws may make any provision that may be practical and necessary for the circumstances of the emergency, including provisions that:

(a) A meeting of the board of directors may be called by any officer or director in such manner and under such conditions as shall be prescribed in the emergency by-laws;

(b) The director or directors in attendance at the meeting, or any greater number fixed by the emergency by-laws, shall constitute a quorum; and

(c) The officers or other persons designated on a list approved by the board of directors before the emergency, all in such order of priority and subject to such conditions, and for such period of time (not longer than reasonably necessary after the termination of the emergency) as may be provided in the emergency by-laws or in the resolution approving the list shall, to the extent required to provide a quorum at any meeting of the board of directors, be deemed directors for such meeting.

The board of directors, either before or during any such emergency, may provide, and from time to time modify, lines of succession in the event that during such an emergency any or all officers or agents of the corporation shall for any reason be rendered incapable of discharging their duties.

The board of directors, either before or during any such emergency, may, effective in the emergency, change the head office or designate several alternative head offices or regional offices, or authorize the officers so to do.

To the extent not inconsistent with any emergency by-laws so adopted, the by-laws of the corporation shall remain in effect during any such emergency and upon its termination the emergency by-laws shall cease to be operative.

Unless otherwise provided in emergency by-laws, notice of any meeting of the board of directors during any such emergency may be given only to such of the directors as it may be feasible to reach at the time and by such means as may be feasible at the time, including publication or radio.

To the extent required to constitute a quorum at any meeting of the board of directors during any such emergency, the officers of the corporation who are present shall, unless otherwise provided in emergency by-laws, be deemed, in order of rank and within the same rank in order of seniority, directors for such meeting.

No officer, director or employee acting in accordance with any emergency by-laws shall be liable except for willful misconduct. No officer, director or employee shall be liable for any action taken by him in good faith in such an emergency in furtherance of the ordinary business affairs of the corporation even though not authorized by the by-laws then in effect.

Section 28.   Meetings of Shareholders.

Meetings of shareholders may be held at such place within or without this State as may be stated in or fixed in accordance with the by-laws. If no other place is stated or so fixed, meetings shall be held at the registered office of the corporation.

An annual meeting of the shareholders shall be held at such time as may be stated in or fixed in accordance with the by-laws. If the annual meeting is not held within any thirteen-month period the Court of . . . . may, on the application of any shareholder, summarily order a meeting to be held.

Special meetings of the shareholders may be called by the board of directors, the holders of not less than one-tenth of all the shares entitled to vote at the meeting, or such other persons as may be authorized in the articles of incorporation or the by-laws.

Section 29.   Notice of Shareholders' Meetings.

Written notice stating the place, day and hour of the meeting and, in case of a special meeting, the purpose or purposes for which the meeting is called, shall be delivered not less than ten nor more than fifty days before the date of the meeting, either personally or by mail, by or at the direction of the president, the secretary, or the officer or persons calling the meeting, to each shareholder of record entitled to vote at such meeting. If mailed, such notice shall be deemed to be delivered when deposited in the United States mail addressed to the shareholder at his address as it appears on the stock transfer books of the corporation, with postage thereon prepaid.

Section 30.   Closing of Transfer Books and Fixing Record Date.

For the purpose of determining shareholders entitled to notice of or to vote at any meeting of shareholders or any adjournment thereof, or entitled to receive payment of any dividend, or in order to make a determination of shareholders for any other proper purpose, the board of directors of a corporation may provide that the stock transfer books shall be closed for a stated period but not to exceed, in any case, fifty days. If the stock transfer books shall be closed for the purpose of determining shareholders entitled to notice of or to vote at a meeting of shareholders, such books shall be closed for at least ten days immediately preceding such meeting. In lieu of closing the stock transfer books, the by-laws, or in the absence of an applicable by-law the board of directors, may fix in advance a date as the record date for any such determination of shareholders, such date in any case to be not more than fifty days and, in case of a meeting of shareholders, not less than ten days prior to the date on which the particular action, requiring such determination of shareholders, is to be taken. If the stock transfer books are not closed and no record date is fixed for the determination of shareholders entitled to notice of or to vote at a meeting of shareholders, or shareholders entitled to receive payment of a dividend, the date on which notice of the meeting is mailed or the date on which the resolution of the board of directors declaring such dividend is adopted, as the case may be, shall be the record date for such determination of shareholders. When a determination of shareholders entitled to vote at any meeting of shareholders has been made as provided in this section, such determination shall apply to any adjournment thereof.

Section 31.   Voting Record.

The officer or agent having charge of the stock transfer books for shares of a corporation shall make a complete record of the shareholders entitled to vote at such meeting or any adjournment thereof, arranged in alphabetical order, with the address of and the number of shares held by each. Such record shall be produced and kept open at the time and place of the meeting and shall be subject to the inspection of any shareholder during the whole time of the meeting for the purposes thereof.

Failure to comply with the requirements of this section shall not affect the validity of any action taken at such meeting.

An officer or agent having charge of the stock transfer books who shall fail to prepare the record of shareholders, or produce and keep it open for inspection at the meeting, as provided in this section, shall be liable to any shareholder suffering damage on account of such failure, to the extent of such damage.

Section 32.   Quorum of Shareholders.

Unless otherwise provided in the articles of incorporation, a majority of the shares entitled to vote, represented in person or by proxy, shall constitute a quorum at a meeting of shareholders, but in no event shall a quorum consist of less than one-third of the shares entitled to vote at the meeting. If a quorum is present, the affirmative vote of the majority of the shares represented at the meeting and entitled to vote on the subject matter shall be the act of the shareholders, unless the vote of a greater number or voting by classes is required by this Act or the articles of incorporation or by-laws.

Section 33.   Voting of Shares.

Each outstanding share, regardless of class, shall be entitled to one vote on each matter submitted to a vote at a meeting of shareholders, except as may be otherwise provided in the articles of incorporation. If the articles of incorporation provide for more or less than one vote for any share, on any matter, every reference in this Act to a majority or other proportion of shares shall refer to such a majority or other proportion of votes entitled to be cast.

Neither treasury shares, nor shares held by another corporation if a majority of the shares entitled to vote for the election of directors of such other corporation is held by the corporation, shall be voted at any meeting or counted in determining the total number of outstanding shares at any given time.

A shareholder may vote either in person or by proxy executed in writing by the shareholder or by his duly authorized attorney-in-fact. No proxy shall be valid after eleven months from the date of its execution, unless otherwise provided in the proxy.

[Either of the following prefatory phrases may be inserted here: "The articles of incorporation may provide that" or "Unless the articles of incorporation otherwise provide"] . . . at each election for directors every shareholder entitled to vote at such election shall have the right to vote, in person or by proxy, the number of shares owned by him for as many persons as there are

directors to be elected and for whose election he has a right to vote, or to cumulate his votes by giving one candidate as many votes as the number of such directors multiplied by the number of his shares shall equal, or by distributing such votes on the same principle among any number of such candidates.

Shares standing in the name of another corporation, domestic or foreign, may be voted by such officer, agent or proxy as the by-laws of such other corporation may prescribe, or, in the absence of such provision, as the board of directors of such other corporation may determine.

Shares held by an administrator, executor, guardian or conservator may be voted by him, either in person or by proxy, without a transfer of such shares into his name. Shares standing in the name of a trustee may be voted by him, either in person or by proxy, but no trustee shall be entitled to vote shares held by him without a transfer of such shares into his name.

Shares standing in the name of a receiver may be voted by such receiver, and shares held by or under the control of a receiver may be voted by such receiver without the transfer thereof into his name if authority so to do be contained in an appropriate order of the court by which such receiver was appointed.

A shareholder whose shares are pledged shall be entitled to vote such shares until the shares have been transferred into the name of the pledgee, and thereafter the pledgee shall be entitled to vote the shares so transferred.

On and after the date on which written notice of redemption of redeemable shares has been mailed to the holders thereof and a sum sufficient to redeem such shares has been deposited with a bank or trust company with irrevocable instruction and authority to pay the redemption price to the holders thereof upon surrender of certificates therefor, such shares shall not be entitled to vote on any matter and shall not be deemed to be outstanding shares.

Section 34.   Voting Trusts and Agreements among Shareholders.

Any number of shareholders of a corporation may create a voting trust for the purpose of conferring upon a trustee or trustees the right to vote or otherwise represent their shares, for a period of not to exceed ten years, by entering into a written voting trust agreement specifying the terms and conditions of the voting trust, by depositing a counterpart of the agreement with the corporation at its registered office, and by transferring their shares to such trustee or trustees for the purposes of the agreement. Such trustee or trustees shall keep a record of the holders of voting trust certificates evidencing a beneficial interest in the voting trust, giving the names and addresses of all such holders and the number and class of the shares in respect of which the voting trust certificates held by each are issued, and shall deposit a copy of such record with the corporation at its registered office. The counterpart of the voting trust agreement and the copy of such record so deposited with the corporation shall be subject to the same right of examination by a shareholder of the corporation, in person or by agent or attorney, as are the books and records of the corporation, and such counterpart and such copy of such record shall be subject to examination by any holder of record of voting trust certificates, either in person or by agent or attorney, at any reasonable time for any proper purpose.

Agreements among shareholders regarding the voting of their shares shall be valid and enforceable in accordance with their terms. Such agreements shall not be subject to the provisions of this section regarding voting trusts.

Section 35.   Board of Directors.

All corporate powers shall be exercised by or under authority of, and the business and affairs of a corporation shall be managed under the direction of, a board of directors except as may be otherwise provided in this Act or the articles of incorporation. If any such provision is made in the articles of incorporation, the powers and duties conferred or imposed upon the board of directors by this Act shall be exercised or performed to such extent and by such person or persons as shall be provided in the articles of incorporation. Directors need not be residents of this State or shareholders of the corporation unless the articles of incorporation or by-laws so require. The articles of incorporation or by-laws may prescribe other qualifications for directors. The board of directors shall have authority to fix the compensation of directors unless otherwise provided in the articles of incorporation.

A director shall perform his duties as a director, including his duties as a member of any committee of the board upon which he may serve, in good faith, in a manner he reasonably believes to be in the best interests of the corporation, and with such care as an ordinarily prudent person in a like position would use under similar circumstances. In performing his duties, a director shall be entitled to rely on information, opinions, reports or statements, including financial statements and other financial data, in each case prepared or presented by:

(a)   one or more officers or employees of the corporation whom the director reasonably believes to be reliable and competent in the matters presented,

(b)   counsel, public accountants or other persons as to matters which the director reasonably believes to be within such person's professional or expert competence, or

(c)   a committee of the board upon which he does not serve, duly designated in accordance with a provision of the articles of incorporation or the by-laws, as to matters within its designated authority, which committee the director reasonably believes to merit confidence, but he shall not be considered to be acting in good faith if he has knowledge concerning the matter in question that would cause such reliance to be unwarranted. A person who so performs his duties shall have no liability by reason of being or having been a director of the corporation.

A director of a corporation who is present at a meeting of its board of directors at which action on any corporate matter is taken shall be presumed to have assented to the action taken unless his dissent shall be entered in the minutes of the meeting or unless he shall file his written dissent to such action with the secretary of the meeting before the adjournment thereof or shall forward such dissent by registered mail to the secretary of the corporation immediately after the adjournment of the meeting. Such right to dissent shall not apply to a director who voted in favor of such action.

Section 36.   Number and Election of Directors.

The board of directors of a corporation shall consist of one or more members. The number of directors shall be fixed by, or in the manner provided in, the articles of incorporation or the by-laws, except as to the number constituting the initial board of directors, which number shall be fixed by the articles of incorporation. The number of directors may be increased or decreased from time to time by amendment to, or in the manner provided in, the articles of incorporation or the bylaws, but no decrease shall have the effect of shortening the term of any incumbent director. In the absence of a by-law providing for the number of directors, the number shall be the same as that provided for in the articles of incorporation. The names and addresses of the members of the first board of directors shall be stated in the articles of incorporation. Such persons shall hold office until the first annual meeting of shareholders, and until their successors shall have been elected and qualified. At the first annual meeting of shareholders and at each annual meeting thereafter the shareholders shall elect directors to hold office until the next succeeding annual meeting, except in case of the classification of directors as permitted by this Act. Each director shall hold office for the term for which he is elected and until his successor shall have been elected and qualified.

Section 37.   Classification of Directors.

When the board of directors shall consist of nine or more members, in lieu of electing the whole number of directors annually, the articles of incorporation may provide that the directors be divided into either two or three classes, each class to be as nearly equal in number as possible, the term of office of directors of the first class to expire at the first annual meeting of shareholders after their election, that of the second class to expire at the second annual meeting after their election, and that of the third class, if any, to expire at the third annual meeting after their election. At each annual meeting after such classification the number of directors equal to the number of the class whose term expires at the time of such meeting shall be elected to hold office until the second succeeding annual meeting, if there be two classes, or until the third succeeding annual meeting, if there be three classes. No classification of directors shall be effective prior to the first annual meeting of shareholders.

Section 38.   Vacancies.

Any vacancy occurring in the board of directors may be filled by the affirmative vote of a majority of the remaining directors though less than a quorum of the board of directors. A director elected to fill a vacancy shall be elected for the unexpired term of his predecessor in office. Any directorship to be filled by reason of an increase in the number of directors may be filled by the board of directors for a term of office continuing only until the next election of directors by the shareholders.

Section 39.   Removal of Directors.

At a meeting of shareholders called expressly for that purpose, directors may be removed in the manner provided in this section. Any director or the entire board of directors may be removed, with or without cause, by a vote of the holders of a majority of the shares then entitled to vote at an election of directors.

In the case of a corporation having cumulative voting, if less than the entire board is to be removed, no one of the directors may be removed if the votes cast against his removal would be sufficient to elect him if then cumulatively voted at an election of the entire board of directors, or, if there be classes of directors, at an election of the class of directors of which he is part.

Whenever the holders of the shares of any class are entitled to elect one or more directors by the provisions of the articles of incorporation, the provisions of this section shall apply, in respect to the removal of a director or directors so elected, to the vote of the holders of the outstanding shares of that class and not to the vote of the outstanding shares as a whole.

Section 40.   Quorum of Directors.

A majority of the number of directors fixed by or in the manner provided in the by-laws or in the absence of a by-law fixing or providing for the number of directors, then of the number stated in the articles of incorporation, shall constitute a quorum for the transaction of business unless a greater number is required by the articles of incorporation or the by-laws. The act of the majority of the directors present at a meeting at which a quorum is present shall be the act of the board of directors, unless the act of a greater number is required by the articles of incorporation or the by-laws.

Section 41.   Director Conflicts of Interest.

No contract or other transaction between a corporation and one or more of its directors or any other corporation, firm, association or entity in which one or more of its directors are directors or officers or are financially interested, shall be either void or voidable because of such relationship or interest or because such director or directors are present at the meeting of the board of directors or a committee thereof which authorizes, approves or ratifies such contract or transaction or because his or their votes are counted for such purpose, if:

(a)   the fact of such relationship or interest is disclosed or known to the board of directors or committee which authorizes, approves or ratifies the contract or transaction by a vote or consent sufficient for the purpose without counting the votes or consents of such interested directors; or

(b)   the fact of such relationship or interest is disclosed or known to the shareholders entitled to vote and they authorize, approve or ratify such contract or transaction by vote or written consent; or

(c) the contract or transaction is fair and reasonable to the corporation.

Common or interested directors may be counted in determining the presence of a quorum at a meeting of the board of directors or a committee thereof which authorizes, approves or ratifies such a contract or transaction.

Section 42. Executive and Other Committees.

If the articles of incorporation or the by-laws so provide, the board of directors, by resolution adopted by a majority of the full board of directors, may designate from among its members an executive committee and one or more other committees each of which, to the extent provided in such resolution or in the articles of incorporation or the by-laws of the corporation, shall have and may exercise all the authority of the board of directors, except that no such committee shall have authority to (i) declare dividends or distributions, (ii) approve or recommend to shareholders actions or proposals required by this Act to be approved by shareholders, (iii) designate candidates for the office of director, for purposes of proxy solicitation or otherwise, or fill vacancies on the board of directors or any committee thereof, (iv) amend the by-laws, (v) approve a plan of merger not requiring shareholder approval, (vi) reduce earned or capital surplus, (vii) authorize or approve the reacquisition of shares unless pursuant to a general formula or method specified by the board of directors, or (viii) authorize or approve the issuance or sale of, or any contract to issue or sell, shares or designate the terms of a series of a class of shares, provided that the board of directors, having acted regarding general authorization for the issuance or sale of shares, or any contract therefor, and, in the case of a series, the designation thereof, may, pursuant to a general formula or method specified by the board by resolution or by adoption of a stock option or other plan, authorize a committee to fix the terms upon which such shares may be issued or sold, including, without limitation, the price, the dividend rate, provisions for redemption, sinking fund, conversion, voting or preferential rights, and provisions for other features of a class of shares, or a series of a class of shares, with full power in such committee to adopt any final resolution setting forth all terms thereof and to authorize the statement of the terms of a series for filling with the Secretary of State under this Act.

Neither the designation of any such committee, the delegation thereto of authority, nor action by such committee pursuant to such authority shall alone constitute compliance by any member of the board of directors, not a member of the committee in question, with his responsibility to act in good faith, in a manner he reasonably believes to be in the best interests of the corporation, and with such care as an ordinarily prudent person in a like position would use under similar circumstances.

Section 43. Place and Notice of Directors' Meetings; Committee Meetings.

Meetings of the board of directors, regular or special, may be held either within or without this State.

Regular meetings of the board of directors or any committee designated thereby may be held with or without notice as prescribed in the by-laws. Special meetings of the board of directors or any committee designated thereby shall be held upon such notice as is prescribed in the by-laws. Attendance of a director at a meeting shall constitute a waiver of notice of such meeting, except where a director attends a meeting for the express purpose of objecting to the transaction of any business because the meeting is not lawfully called or convened. Neither the business to be transacted at, nor the purpose of, any regular or special meeting of the board of directors or any committee designated thereby need be specified in the notice or waiver of notice of such meeting unless required by the by-laws.

Except as may be otherwise restricted by the articles of incorporation or by-laws, members of the board of directors or any committee designated thereby may participate in a meeting of such board or committee by means of a conference telephone or similar communications equipment by means of which all persons participating in the meeting can hear each other at the same time and participation by such means shall constitute presence in person at a meeting.

Section 44. Action by Directors without a Meeting.

Unless otherwise provided by the articles of incorporation or by-laws, any action required by this Act to be taken at a meeting of the directors of a corporation, or any action which may be taken at a meeting of the directors or of a committee, may be taken without a meeting if a consent in writing, setting forth the action so taken, shall be signed by all of the directors, or all of the members of the committee, as the case may be. Such consent shall have the same effect as a unanimous vote.

Section 45. Dividends.

The board of directors of a corporation may, from time to time, declare and the corporation may pay dividends in cash, property, or its own shares, except when the corporation is insolvent or when the payment thereof would render the corporation insolvent or when the declaration or payment thereof would be contrary to any restriction contained in the articles of incorporation, subject to the following provisions:

(a)   Dividends may be declared and paid in cash or property only out of the unreserved and unrestricted earned surplus of the corporation, except as otherwise provided in this section.

[Alternative] (a) Dividends may be declared and paid in cash or property only out of the unreserved and unrestricted earned surplus of the corporation, or out of the unreserved and unrestricted net earnings of the current fiscal year and the next preceding fiscal year taken as a single period, except as otherwise provided in this section.

(b)   If the articles of incorporation of a corporation engaged in the business of exploiting natural resources so provide, dividends may be declared and paid in cash out of the depletion reserves, but each such dividend shall be identified as a distribution of such reserves and the amount per share paid from such reserves shall be disclosed to the shareholders receiving the same concurrently with the distribution thereof.

(c)   Dividends may be declared and paid in its own treasury shares.

(d)   Dividends may be declared and paid in its own authorized but unissued shares out of any unreserved and unrestricted surplus of the corporation upon the following conditions:

(1)   If a dividend is payable in its own shares having a par value, such shares shall be issued at not less than the par value thereof and there shall be transferred to stated capital at the time such dividend is paid an amount of surplus equal to the aggregate par value of the shares to be issued as a dividend.

(2)   If a dividend is payable in its own shares without par value, such shares shall be issued at such stated value as shall be fixed by the board of directors by resolution adopted at the time such dividend is declared, and there shall be transferred to stated capital at the time such dividend is paid an amount of sur-plus equal to the aggregate stated value so fixed in respect of such shares; and the amount per share so transferred to stated capital shall be disclosed to the shareholders receiving such dividend concurrently with the payment thereof.

(e)   No dividend payable in shares of any class shall be paid to the holders of shares of any other class unless the articles of incorporation so provide or such payment is authorized by the affirmative vote or the written consent of the holders of at least a majority of the outstanding shares of the class in which the payment is to be made.

A split-up or division of the issued shares of any class into a greater number of shares of the same class without increasing the stated capital of the corporation shall not be construed to be a share dividend within the meaning of this section.

Section 46. Distributions from Capital Surplus.

The board of directors of a corporation may, from time to time, distribute to its shareholders out of capital surplus of the corporation a portion of its assets, in cash or property, subject to the following provisions:

(a)   No such distribution shall be made at a time when the corporation is insolvent or when such distribution would render the corporation insolvent.

(b)   No such distribution shall be made unless the articles of incorporation so provide or such distribution is authorized by the affirmative vote of the holders of a majority of the outstanding shares of each class whether or not entitled to vote thereon by the provisions of the articles of incorporation of the corporation.

(c)   No such distribution shall be made to the holders of any class of shares unless all cumulative dividends accrued on all preferred or special classes of shares entitled to preferential dividends shall have been fully paid.

(d)   No such distribution shall be made to the holders of any class of shares which would reduce the remaining net assets of the corporation below the aggregate preferential amount payable in event of involuntary liquidation to the holders of shares having preferential rights to the assets of the corporation in the event of liquidation.

(e)   Each such distribution, when made, shall be identified as a distribution from capital surplus and the amount per share disclosed to the shareholders receiving the same concurrently with the distribution thereof.

The board of directors of a corporation may also, from time to time, distribute to the holders of its outstanding shares having a cumulative preferential right to receive dividends, in discharge of their cumulative dividend rights, dividends payable in cash out of the capital surplus of the corporation, if at the time the corporation has no earned surplus and is not insolvent and would not thereby be rendered insolvent. Each such distribution when made, shall be identified as a payment of cumulative dividends out of capital surplus.

Section 47.   Loans to Employees and Directors.

A corporation shall not lend money to or use its credit to assist its directors without authorization in the particular case by its shareholders, but may lend money to and use its credit to assist any employee of the corporation or of a subsidiary, including any such employee who is a director of the corporation, if the board of directors decides that such loan or assistance may benefit the corporation.

Section 48.   Liabilities of Directors in Certain Cases.

In addition to any other liabilities, a director shall be liable in the following circumstances unless he complies with the standard provided in this Act for the performance of the duties of directors:

(a)   A director who votes for or assents to the declaration of any dividend or other distribution of the assets of a corporation to its shareholders contrary to the provisions of this Act or contrary to any restrictions contained in the articles of incorporation, shall be liable to the corporation, jointly and severally with all other directors so voting or assenting, for the amount of such dividend which is paid or the value of such assets which are distributed in excess of the amount of such dividend or distribution which could have been paid or distributed without a violation of the provisions of this Act or the restrictions in the articles of incorporation.

(b)   A director who votes for or assents to the purchase of the corporation's own shares contrary to the provisions of this Act shall be liable to the corporation, jointly and severally with all other directors so voting or assenting, for the amount of consideration paid for such shares which is in excess of the maximum amount which could have been paid therefor without a violation of the provisions of this Act.

(c)   A director who votes for or assents to any distribution of assets of a corporation to its shareholders during the liquidation of the corporation without the payment and discharge of, or making adequate provision for, all known debts, obligations, and liabilities of the corporation shall be liable to the corporation, jointly and severally with all other directors so voting or assenting, for the value of such assets which are distributed, to the extent that such debts, obligations and liabilities of the corporation are not thereafter paid and discharged.

Any director against whom a claim shall be asserted under or pursuant to this section for the payment of a dividend or other distribution of assets of a corporation and who shall be held liable thereon, shall be entitled to contribution from the shareholders who accepted or received any such dividend or assets knowing such dividend or distribution to have been made in violation of this Act, in proportion to the amounts received by them.

Any director against whom a claim shall be asserted under or pursuant to this section shall be entitled to contribution from the other directors who voted for or assented to the action upon which the claim is asserted.

Section 49.   Provisions Relating to Actions by Shareholders.

No action shall be brought in this State by a shareholder in the right of a domestic or foreign corporation unless the plaintiff was a holder of record of shares or of voting trust certificates therefor at the time of the transaction of which he complains, or his shares or voting trust certificates thereafter devolved upon him by operation of law from a person who was a holder of record at such time.

In any action hereafter instituted in the right of any domestic or foreign corporation by the holder or holders of record of shares of such corporation or of voting trust certificates therefor, the court having jurisdiction, upon final judgment and a finding that the action was brought without reasonable cause, may require the plaintiff or plaintiffs to pay to the parties named as defendant the reasonable expenses, including fees of attorneys, incurred by them in the defense of such action.

In any action now pending or hereafter instituted or maintained in the right of any domestic or foreign corporation by the holder or holders of record of less than five per cent of the outstanding shares of any class of such corporation or of voting trust certificates therefor, unless the shares or voting trust certificates so held have a market value in excess of twenty-five thousand dollars, the corporation in whose right such action is brought shall be entitled at any time before final judgment to require the plaintiff or plaintiffs to give security for the reasonable expenses, including fees of attorneys, that may be incurred by it in connection with such action or may be incurred by other parties named as defendant for which it may become legally liable. Market value shall be determined as of the date that the plaintiff institutes the action or, in the case of an intervenor, as of the date that he becomes a party to the action. The amount of such security may from time to time be increased or decreased, in the discretion of the court, upon showing that the security provided has or may become inadequate or is excessive. The corporation shall have recourse to such security in such amount as the court having jurisdiction shall determine upon the termination of such action, whether or not the court finds the action was brought without reasonable cause.

Section 50.   Officers.

The officers of a corporation shall consist of a president, one or more vice presidents as may be prescribed by the by-laws, a secretary, and a treasurer, each of whom shall be elected by the board of directors at such time and in such manner as may be prescribed by the by-laws. Such other officers and assistant officers and agents as may be deemed necessary may be elected or appointed by the board of directors or chosen in such other manner as may be prescribed by the by-laws.

Any two or more offices may be held by the same person, except the offices of president and secretary.

All officers and agents of the corporation, as between themselves and the corporation, shall have such authority and perform such duties in the management of the corporation as may be provided in the by-laws, or as may be determined by resolution of the board of directors not inconsistent with the by-laws.

Section 51.   Removal of Officers.

Any officer or agent may be removed by the board of directors whenever in its judgment the best interests of the corporation will be served thereby, but such removal shall be without prejudice to the contract rights, if any, of the person so removed. Election or appointment of an officer or agent shall not of itself create contract rights.

Section 52.   Books and Records: Financial Reports to Shareholders; Examination of Records.

Each corporation shall keep correct and complete books and records of account and shall keep minutes of the proceedings of its shareholders and board of directors and shall keep at its registered office or principal place of business, or at the office of its transfer agent or registrar, a record of its shareholders, giving the names and addresses of all shareholders and the number and class of the shares held by each. Any books, records and minutes may be in written form or in any other form capable of being converted into written form with a reasonable time.

Any person who shall have been a holder of record of shares or of voting trust certificates therefor at least six months immediately preceding his demand or shall be the holder of record of, or the holder of record of voting trust certificates for, at least five per cent of all the outstanding shares of the corporation, upon written demand stating the purpose thereof, shall have the right to examine, in person, or by agent or attorney, at any reasonable time or times, for any proper purpose its relevant books and records of accounts, minutes, and record of shareholders and to make extracts therefrom.

Any officer or agent who, or a corporation which, shall refuse to allow any such shareholder or holder of voting trust certificates, or his agent or attorney, so to examine and make extracts from its books and records of account, minutes, and record of shareholders, for any proper purpose, shall be liable to such shareholder or holder of voting trust certificates in a penalty of ten per cent of the value of the shares owned by such shareholder, or in respect of which such voting trust certificates are issued, in addition to any other damages or remedy afforded him by law. It shall be a defense to any action for penalties under this section that the person suing therefor has within two years sold or offered for sale any list of shareholders or of holders of voting trust certificates for shares of such corporation or any other corporation or has aided or abetted any person in procuring any list of shareholders or of holders of voting trust certificates for any such purpose, or has improperly used any information secured through any prior examination of the books and records of account, or minutes, or record of shareholders or of holders of voting trust certificates for shares of such corporation or any other corporation, or was not acting in good faith or for a proper purpose in making his demand.

Nothing herein contained shall impair the power of any court of competent jurisdiction, upon proof by a shareholder or holder of voting trust certificates of proper purpose, irrespective of the period of time during which such shareholder or holder of voting trust certificates shall have been a shareholder of record or a holder of record of voting trust certificates, and irrespective of the number of shares held by him or represented by voting trust certificates held by him, to compel the production for examination by such shareholder or holder of voting trust certificates of the books and records of account, minutes and record of shareholders of a corporation.

Each corporation shall furnish to its shareholders annual financial statements, including at least a balance sheet as of the end of each fiscal year and a statement of income for such fiscal year, which shall be prepared on the basis of generally accepted accounting principles, if the corporation prepares financial statements for such fiscal year on that basis for any purpose, and may be consolidated statements of the corporation and one or more of its subsidiaries. The financial statements shall be mailed by the corporation to each of its shareholders within 120 days after the close of each fiscal year and, after such mailing and upon written request, shall be mailed by the corporation to any shareholder (or holder of a voting trust certificate for its shares) to whom a copy of the most recent annual financial statements has not previously been mailed. In the case of statements audited by a public accountant, each copy shall be accompanied by a report setting forth his opinion thereon; in other cases, each copy shall be accompanied by a statement of the president or the person in charge of the corporation's financial accounting records (1) stating his reasonable belief as to whether or not the financial statements were prepared in accordance with generally accepted accounting principles and, if not, describing the basis of presentation, and (2) describing any respects in which the financial statements were not prepared on a basis consistent with those prepared for the previous year.

Section 53. Incorporators.

One or more persons, or a domestic or foreign corporation, may act as incorporator or incorporators of a corporation by signing and delivering in duplicate to the Secretary of State articles of incorporation for such corporation.

Section 54. Articles of Incorporation.

The articles of incorporation shall set forth:

(a) The name of the corporation.

(b) The period of duration, which may be perpetual.

(c) The purpose or purposes for which the corporation is organized which may be stated to be, or to include, the transaction of any or all lawful business for which corporations may be incorporated under this Act.

(d) The aggregate number of shares which the corporation shall have authority to issue; if such shares are to be

consist of one class only, the par value of each of such shares, or a statement that all of such shares are without par value; or, if such shares are to be divided into classes, the number of shares of each class, and a statement of the par value of the shares of each such class or that such shares are to be without par value.

(e) If the shares are to be divided into classes, the designation of each class and a statement of the preferences, limitations and relative rights in respect of the shares of each class.

(f) If the corporation is to issue the shares of any preferred or special class in series, then the designation of each series and a statement of the variations in the relative rights and preferences as between series insofar as the same are to be fixed in the articles of incorporation, and a statement of any authority to be vested in the board of directors to establish series and fix and determine the variations in the relative rights and preferences as between series.

(g) If any preemptive right is to be granted to shareholders, the provisions therefor.

(h) Any provision, not inconsistent with law, which the incorporators elect to set forth in the articles of incorporation for the regulation of the internal affairs of the corporation, including any provisions restricting the transfer of shares and any provision which under this Act is required or permitted to be set forth in the by-laws.

(i) The address of its initial registered office, and the name of its initial registered agent at such address.

(j) The number of directors constituting the initial board of directors and the names and addresses of the persons who are to serve as directors until the first annual meeting of shareholders or until their successors be elected and qualify.

(k) The name and address of each incorporator.

It shall not be necessary to set forth in the articles of incorporation any of the corporate powers enumerated in this Act.

Section 55. Filing of Articles of Incorporation.

Duplicate originals of the articles of incorporation shall be delivered to the Secretary of State. If the Secretary of State finds that the articles of incorporation conform to law, he shall, when all fees have been paid as in this Act prescribed:

(a) Endorse on each of such duplicate originals the word "Filed," and the month, day and year of the filing thereof.

(b) File one of such duplicate originals in his office.

(c) Issue a certificate of incorporation to which he shall affix the other duplicate original.

The certificate of incorporation, together with the duplicate original of the articles of incorporation affixed thereto by the Secretary of State, shall be returned to the incorporators or their representative.

Section 56. Effect of Issuance of Certificate of Incorporation.

Upon the issuance of the certificate of incorporation, the corporate existence shall begin, and such certificate of incorporation shall be conclusive evidence that all conditions precedent required to be performed by the incorporators have been complied with and that the corporation has been incorporated under this Act, except as against this State in a proceeding to cancel or revoke the certificate of incorporation or for involuntary dissolution of the corporation.

Section 57. Organization Meeting of Directors.

After the issuance of the certificate of incorporation an organization meeting of the board of directors named in the articles of incorporation shall be held, either within or without this State, at the call of a majority of the directors named in the articles of incorporation, for the purpose of adopting by-laws, electing officers and transacting such other business as may come before the meeting. The directors calling the meeting shall give at least three days' notice thereof by mail to each director so named, stating the time and place of the meeting.

Section 58. Right to Amend Articles of Incorporation.

A corporation may amend its articles of incorporation, from time to time, in any and as many respects as may be desired, so long as its articles of incorporation as amended contain only such provisions as might be lawfully contained in original articles of incorporation at the time of making such amendment, and, if a change in shares or the rights of shareholders, or an exchange, reclassification or cancellation of shares or rights of shareholders is to be made, such provisions as may be necessary to effect such change, exchange, reclassification or cancellation.

In particular, and without limitation upon such general power of amendment, a corporation may amend its articles of incorporation, from time to time, so as:

(a) To change its corporate name.

(b) To change its period of duration.

(c) To change, enlarge or diminish its corporate purposes.

(d) To increase or decrease the aggregate number of shares, or shares of any class, which the corporation has authority to issue.

(e) To increase or decrease the par value of the authorized shares of any class having a par value, whether issued or unissued.

(f) To exchange, classify, reclassify or cancel all or any part of its shares, whether issued or unissued.

(g) To change the designation of all or any part of its shares, whether issued or unissued, and to change the preferences, limitations, and the relative rights in respect of all or any part of its shares, whether issued or unissued.

(h) To change shares having a par value, whether issued or unissued, into the same or a different number of shares without par value, and to change shares without par value, whether issued or unissued, into the same or a different number of shares having a par value.

(i) To change the shares of any class, whether issued or unissued, and whether with or without par value, into a different number of shares of the same class or into the same or a different number of shares, either with or without par value, of other classes.

(j) To create new classes of shares having rights and preferences either prior and superior or subordinate and inferior to the shares of any class then authorized, whether issued or unissued.

(k) To cancel or otherwise affect the right of the holders of the shares of any class to receive dividends which have accrued but have not been declared.

(l) To divide any preferred or special class of shares, whether issued or unissued, into series and fix and determine the designations of such series and the variations in the relative rights and preferences as between the shares of such series.

(m) To authorize the board of directors to establish, out of authorized but unissued shares, series of any preferred or special class of shares and fix and determine the relative rights and preferences of the shares of any series so established.

(n) To authorize the board of directors to fix and determine the relative rights and preferences of the authorized but unissued shares of series theretofore established in respect of which either the relative rights and preferences have not been fixed and determined or the relative rights and preferences theretofore fixed and determined are to be changed.

(o) To revoke, diminish, or enlarge the authority of the board of directors to establish series out of authorized but unissued shares of any preferred or special class and fix and determine the relative rights and preferences of the shares of any series so established.

(p) To limit, deny or grant to shareholders of any class the preemptive right to acquire additional or treasury shares of the corporation, whether then or thereafter authorized.

Section 59. Procedure to Amend Articles of Incorporation.

Amendments to the articles of incorporation shall be made in the following manner:

(a) The board of directors shall adopt a resolution setting forth the proposed amendment and, if shares have been issued, directing that it be submitted to a vote at a meeting of shareholders, which may be either the annual or a special meeting. If no shares have been issued, the amendment shall be adopted by resolution of the board of directors and the provisions for adoption by shareholders shall not apply. The resolution may incorporate the proposed amendment in restated articles of incorporation which contain a statement that except for the designated amendment the restated articles of incorporation correctly set forth without change the corresponding provisions of the articles of incororation as theretofore amended, and that the restated articles of incorporation together with the designated amendement supersede the original articles of incorporation and all amendments thereto.

(b) Written notice setting forth the proposed amendment or a summary of the changes to be affected thereby shall be given to each shareholder of record entitled to vote thereon within the time and in the manner provided in this Act for the giving of notice of meetings of shareholders. If the meeting be an annual meeting, the proposed amendment of such summary may be included in the notice of such annual meeting.

(c) At such meeting a vote of the shareholders entitled to vote thereon shall be taken on the proposed amendment. The proposed amendment shall be adopted upon receiving the affirmative vote of the holders of a majority of the shares entitled to vote thereon, unless any class of shares is entitled vote thereon shall be taken on the proposed amendment. The proposed amendment shall be adopted upon receiving vote of the holders of a majority of the shares of each class of shares entitled to vote thereon as a class

and of the total shares entitled to vote thereon.

Any number of amendments may be submitted to the shareholders, and voted upon by them, at one meeting.

Section 60. Class Voting on Amendments.

The holders of the outstanding shares of a class shall be entitled to vote as a class upon a proposed amendment, whether or not entitled to vote thereon by the provisions of the articles of incorporation, if the amendment would:

(a) Increase or decrease the aggregate number of authorized shares of such class.

(b) Increase or decrease the par value of the shares of such class.

(c) Effect an exchange, reclassification or cancellation of all or part of the shares of such class.

(d) Effect an exchange, or create a right of exchange, of all or any part of the shares of another class into the shares of such class.

(e) Change the designations, preferences, limitations or relative rights of the shares of such class.

(f) Change the shares of such class, whether with or without par value, into the same or a different number of shares, either with or without par value, of the same class or another class or classes.

(g) Create a new class of shares having rights and preferences prior and superior to the shares of such class, or increase the rights and preferences or the number of authorized shares, of any class having rights and preferences prior or superior to the shares of such class.

(h) In the case of a preferred or special class of shares, divide the shares of such class into series and fix and determine the designation of such series and the variations in the relative rights and preferences between the shares of such series, or authorize the board of directors to do so.

(i) Limit or deny any existing preemptive rights of the shares of such class.

(j) Cancel or otherwise affect dividends on the shares of such class which have accrued but have not been declared.

Section 61. Articles of Amendment.

The articles of amendment shall be executed in duplicate by the corporation by its president or a vice president and by its secretary or an assistant secretary, and verified by one of the officers signing such articles, and shall set forth:

(a) The name of the corporation.

(b) The amendments so adopted.

(c) The date of the adoption of the amendment by the shareholders, or by the board of directors where no shares have been issued.

(d) The number of shares outstanding, and the number of shares entitled to vote thereon, and if the shares of any class are entitled to vote thereon as a class, the designation and number of outstanding shares entitled to vote thereon of each such class.

(e) The number of shares voted for and against such amendment, respectively, and, if the shares of any class are entitled to vote thereon as a class, the number of shares of each such class voted for and against such amendment, respectively, or if no shares have been issued, a statement to that effect.

(f) If such amendment provides for an exchange, reclassification or cancellation of issued shares, and if the manner in which the same shall be effected is not set forth in the amendment, then a statement of the manner in which the same shall be effected.

(g) If such amendment effects a change in the amount of stated capital, then a statement of the manner in which the same is effected and a statement, expressed in dollars, of the amount of stated capital as changed by such amendment.

Section 62. Filing of Articles of Amendment.

Duplicate originals of the articles of amendment shall be delivered to the Secretary of State. If the Secretary of State finds that the articles of amendment conform to law, he shall, when all fees and franchise taxes have been paid as in this Act prescribed:

(a) Endorse on each of such duplicate originals the word "Filed," and the month, day and year of the filing thereof.

(b) File one of such duplicate originals in his office.

(c) Issue a certificate of amendment to which he shall affix the other duplicate original.

The certificate of amendment, together with the duplicate original of the articles of amendment affixed thereto by the Secretary of State, shall be returned to the corporation or its representative.

Section 63. Effect of Certificate of Amendment.

The amendment shall become effective upon the issuance of the certificate of amendment by the Secretary of State, or on such later date, not more than thirty days subsequent to the filing thereof with the Secretary of State, as shall be provided for in the articles of amendment.

No amendment shall affect any existing cause of action in favor of or against such corporation, or any pending suit to which such corporation shall be a party, or the existing rights of persons other than shareholders; and, in the event the corporate name shall be changed by amendment, no suit brought by or against such corporation under its former name shall abate for that reason.

Section 64. Restated Articles of Incorporation.

A domestic corporation may at any time restate its articles of incorporation as theretofore amended, by a resolution adopted by the board of directors.

Upon the adoption of such resolution, restated articles of incorporation shall be executed in duplicate by the corporation by its president or a vice president and by its secretary or assistant secretary and verified by one of the officers signing such articles and shall set forth all of the operative provisions of the articles of incorporation as theretofore amended together with a statement that the restated articles of incorporation correctly set forth without change the corresponding provisions of the articles of incorporation as theretofore amended and that the restated articles of incorporation supersede the original articles of incorporation and all amendments thereto.

Duplicate originals of the restated articles of incorporation shall be delivered to the Secretary of State. If the Secretary of State finds that such restated articles of incorporation conform to law, he shall, when all fees and franchise taxes have been paid as in this Act prescribed:

(1) Endorse on each of such duplicate originals the word "Filed," and the month, day and year of the filing thereof.

(2) File one of such duplicate originals in his office.

(3) Issue a restated certificate of incorporation, to which he shall affix the other duplicate original.

The restated certificate of incorporation, together with the duplicate original of the restated articles of incorporation affixed thereto by the Secretary of State, shall be returned to the corporation or its representative.

Upon the issuance of the restated certificate of incorporation by the Secretary of State, the restated articles of incorporation shall become effective and shall supersede the original articles of incorporation and all amendments thereto.

Section 65. Amendment of Articles of Incorporation in Reorganization Proceedings.

Whenever a plan of reorganization of a corporation has been confirmed by decree or order of a court of competent jurisdiction in proceedings for the reorganization of such corporation, pursuant to the provisions of any applicable statute of the United States relating to reorganizations of corporations, the articles of incorporation of the corporation may be amended, in the manner provided in this section, in as many respects as may be necessary to carry out the plan and put it into effect, so long as the articles of incorporation as amended contain only such provisions as might be lawfully contained in original articles of incorporation at the time of making such amendment.

In particular and without limitation upon such general power of amendment, the articles of incorporation may be amended for such purpose so as to:

(a)   Change the corporate name, period of duration or corporate purposes of the corporation;

(b)   Repeal, alter or amend the by-laws of the corporation;

(c)   Change the aggregate number of shares or shares of any class, which the corporation has authority to issue;

(d)   Change the preferences, limitations and relative rights in respect of all or any part of the shares of the corporation, and classify, reclassify or cancel all or any part thereof, whether issued or unissued;

(e)   Authorize the issuance of bonds, debentures or other obligations of the corporation, whether or not convertible into shares of any class or bearing warrants or other evidences of optional rights to purchase or subscribe for shares of any class, and fix the terms and conditions thereof; and

(f)   Constitute or reconstitute and classify or reclassify the board of directors of the corporation, and appoint directors and officers in place of or in addition to all or any of the directors or officers then in office.

Amendments to the articles of incorporation pursuant to this section shall be made in the following manner:

(a)   Articles of amendment approved by decree or order of such court shall be executed and verified in duplicate by such person or persons as the court shall designate or appoint for the purpose, and shall set forth the name of the corporation, the amendments of the articles of incorporation approved by the court, the date of the decree or order approving the articles of amendment, the title of the proceedings in which the decree or order was entered, and a statement that such decree or order was entered by a court having jurisdiction of the proceedings for the reorganization of the corporation pursuant to the provisions of an applicable statute of the United States.

(b)   Duplicate originals of the articles of amendment shall be delivered to the Secretary of State. If the Secretary of State finds that the articles of amendment conform to law, he shall, when all fees and franchise taxes have been paid as in his Act prescribed:

> (1)   Endorse on each of such duplicate originals the word "Filed," and the month, day and year of the filing thereof.
>
> (2)   File one of such duplicate originals in his office.
>
> (3)   Issue a certificate of amendment to which he shall affix the other duplicate original.

The certificate of amendment, together with the duplicate original of the articles of amendment affixed thereto by the Secretary of State, shall be returned to the corporation or its representative.

The amendment shall become effective upon the issuance of the certificate of amendment by the Secretary of State, or on such later date, not more than thirty days subsequent to the filing thereof with the Secretary of State, as shall be provided for in the articles of amendment without any action thereon by the directors or shareholders of the corporation and with the same effect as if the amendments had been adopted by unanimous action of the directors and shareholders of the corporation.

Section 66.   Restriction on Redemption or Purchases of Redeemable Shares.

No redemption or purchase of redeemable shares shall be made by a corporation when it is insolvent or when such redemption or purchase would render it insolvent, or which would reduce the net assets below the aggregate amount payable to the holders of shares having prior or equal rights to the assets of the corporation upon involuntary dissolution.

Section 67.   Cancellation of Redeemable Shares by Redemption or Purchase.

When redeemable shares of a corporation are redeemed or purchased by the corporation, the redemption or purchase shall effect a cancellation of such shares, and a statement of cancellation shall be filed as provided in this section. Thereupon such shares shall be restored to the status of authorized but unissued shares, unless the articles of incorporation provide that such shares when redeemed or purchased shall not be reissued, in which case the filing of the statement of cancellation shall constitute an amendment to the articles of incorporation and shall reduce the number of shares of the class so cancelled which the corporation is authorized to issue by the number of shares so cancelled.

The statement of cancellation shall be executed in duplicate by the corporation by its president or a vice president and by its secretary or an assistant secretary, and verified by one of the officers signing such statement, and shall set forth:

(a)   The name of the corporation.

(b)   The number of redeemable shares cancelled through redemption or purchase, itemized by classes and series.

(c)   The aggregate number of issued shares, itemized by classes and series, after giving effect to such cancellation.

(d)   The amount, expressed in dollars, of the stated capital of the corporation after giving effect to such cancellation.

(e)   If the articles of incorporation provide that the cancelled shares shall not be reissued, the number of shares which the corporation will have authority to issue itemized by classes and series, after giving effect to such cancellation.

Duplicate originals of such statement shall be delivered to the Secretary of State. If the Secretary of State finds that such statement conforms to law, he shall, when all fees and franchise taxes have been paid as in this Act prescribed:

(1)   Endorse on each of such duplicate originals the word "Filed," and the month, day and year of the filing thereof.

(2)   File one of such duplicate originals in his office.

(3)   Return the other duplicate original to the corporation or its representative.

Upon the filing of such statement of cancellation, the stated capital of the corporation shall be deemed to be reduced by that part of the stated capital which was, at the time of such cancellation, represented by the shares so cancelled.

Nothing contained in this section shall be construed to forbid a cancellation of shares or a reduction of stated capital in any other manner permitted by this Act.

Section 68.   Cancellation of Other Reacquired Shares.

A corporation may at any time, by resolution of its board of directors, cancel all or any part of the shares of the corporation of any class reacquired by it, other than redeemable shares redeemed or purchased, and in such event a statement of cancellation shall be filed as provided in this section.

The statement of cancellation shall be executed in duplicate by the corporation by its president or a vice president and by its secretary or an assistant secretary, and verified by one of the officers signing such statement, and shall set forth:

(a)   The name of the corporation.

(b)   The number of reacquired shares cancelled by resolution duly adopted by the board of directors, itemized by classes and series, and the date of its adoption.

(c)   The aggregate number of issued shares, itemized by classes and series, after giving effect to such cancellation.

(d)   The amount, expressed in dollars, of the stated capital of the corporation after giving effect to such cancellation.

Duplicate originals of such statement shall be delivered to the Secretary of State. If the Secretary of State finds that such statement conforms to law, he shall, when all fees and franchise taxes have been paid as in this Act prescribed:

(1)   Endorse on each of such duplicate originals the word "Filed," and the month, day and year of the filing thereof.

(2)   File one of such duplicate originals in his office.

(3)   Return the other duplicate original to the corporation or its representative.

Upon the filing of such statement of cancellation, the stated capital of the corporation shall be deemed to be reduced by that part of the stated capital which was, at the time of such cancellation, represented by the shares so cancelled, and the shares so cancelled shall be restored to the status of authorized but unissued shares.

Nothing contained in this section shall be construed to forbid a cancellation of shares or a reduction of stated capital in any other manner permitted by this Act.

Section 69. Reduction of Stated Capital in Certain Cases.

A reduction of the stated capital of a corporation, where such reduction is not accompanied by any action requiring an amendment of the articles of incorporation and not accompanied by a cancellation of shares, may be made in the following manner:

(a) The board of directors shall adopt a resolution setting forth the amount of the proposed reduction and the manner in which the reduction shall be effected, and directing that the question of such reduction be submitted to a vote at a meeting of shareholders, which may be either an annual or a special meeting.

(b) Written notice, stating that the purpose or one of the purposes of such meeting is to consider the question of reducing the stated capital of the corporation in the amount and manner proposed by the board of directors, shall be given to each shareholder of record entitled to vote thereon within the time and in the manner provided in this Act for the giving of notice of meetings of shareholders.

(c) At such meeting a vote of the shareholders entitled to vote thereon shall be taken on the question of approving the proposed reduction of stated capital, which shall require for its adoption the affirmative vote of the holders of a majority of the shares entitled to vote thereon.

When a reduction of the stated capital of a corporation has been approved as provided in this section, a statement shall be executed in duplicate by the corporation by its president or a vice president and by its secretary or an assistant secretary, and verified by one of the officers signing such statement, and shall set forth:

(a) The name of the corporation.

(b) A copy of the resolution of the shareholders approving such reduction, and the date of its adoption.

(c) The number of shares outstanding, and the number of shares entitled to vote thereon.

(d) The number of shares voted for and against such reduction, respectively.

(e) A statement of the manner in which such reduction is effected, and a statement, expressed in dollars, of the amount of stated capital of the corporation after giving effect to such reduction.

Duplicate originals of such statement shall be delivered to the Secretary of State. If the Secretary of State finds that such statement conforms to law, he shall, when all fees and franchise taxes have been paid as in this Act prescribed:

(1) Endorse on each of such duplicate originals the word "Filed," and the month, day and year of the filing thereof.

(2) File one of such duplicate originals in his office.

(3) Return the other duplicate original to the corporation or its representative.

Upon the filing of such statement, the stated capital of the corporation shall be reduced as therein set forth.

No reduction of stated capital shall be made under the provisions of this section which would reduce the amount of the aggregate stated capital of the corporation to an amount equal to or less than the aggregate preferential amounts payable upon all issued shares having a preferential right in the assets of the corporation in the event of involuntary liquidation, plus the aggregate par value of all issued shares having a par value but no preferential right in the assets of the corporation in the event of involuntary liquidation.

Section 70. Special Provisions Relating to Surplus and Reserves.

The surplus, if any, created by or arising out of a reduction of the stated capital of a corporation shall be capital surplus.

The capital surplus of a corporation may be increased from time to time by resolution of the board of directors directing that all or a part of the earned surplus of the corporation be transferred to capital surplus.

A corporation may, by resolution of its board of directors, apply any part or all of its capital surplus to the reduction or elimination of any deficit arising from losses, however incurred, but only after first eliminating the earned surplus, if any, of the corporation by applying such losses against earned surplus and only to the extent that such losses exceed the earned surplus, if any. Each such application of capital surplus shall, to the extent thereof, effect a reduction of capital surplus.

A corporation may, by resolution of its board of directors, create a reserve or reserves out of its earned surplus for any proper purpose or purposes, and may abolish any such reserve in the same manner. Earned surplus of the corporation to the extent so reserved shall not be available for the payment of dividends or other distributions by the corporation except as expressly permitted by this Act.

Section 71.   Procedure for Merger.

Any two or more domestic corporations may merge into one of such corporations pursuant to a plan of merger approved in the manner provided in this Act.

The board of directors of each corporation shall, by resolution adopted by each such board, approve a plan of merger setting forth:

(a)   The names of the corporations proposing to merge, and the name of the corporation into which they propose to merge, which is hereinafter designated as the surviving corporation.

(b)   The terms and conditions of the proposed merger.

(c)   The manner and basis of converting the shares of each corporation into shares, obligations or other securities of the surviving corporation or of any other corporation or, in whole or in part, into cash or other property.

(d)   A statement of any changes in the articles of incorporation of the surviving corporation to be effected by such merger.

(e)   Such other provisions with respect to the proposed merger as are deemed necessary or desirable.

Section 72.   Procedure for Consolidation.

Any two or more domestic corporations may consolidate into a new corporation pursuant to a plan of consolidation approved in the manner provided in this Act.

The board of directors of each corporation shall, by a resolution adopted by each such board, approve a plan of consolidation setting forth:

(a)   The names of the corporations proposing to consolidate, which is hereinafter designated as the new corporation.

(b)   The terms and conditions of the proposed consolidation.

(c)   The manner and basis of converting the shares of each corporation into shares, obligations or other securities of the new corporation or of any other corporation or, in whole or in part, into cash or other property.

(d)   With respect to the new corporation, all of the statements required to be set forth in articles of incorporation for corporations organized under this Act.

(e)   Such other provisions with respect to the proposed consolidation as are deemed necessary or desirable.

Section 72–A.   Procedure for Share Exchange.

All the issued or all the outstanding shares of one or more classes of any domestic corporation may be acquired through the exchange of all such shares of such class or classes by another domestic or foreign corporation pursuant to a plan of exchange approved in the manner provided in this Act.

The board of directors of each corporation shall, by resolution adopted by each such board, approve a plan of exchange setting forth:

(a)   The name of the corporation the shares of which are proposed to be acquired by exchange and the name of the corporation to acquire the shares of such corporation in the exchange, which is hereinafter designated as the acquiring corporation.

(b)   The terms and conditions of the proposed exchange.

(c)   The manner and basis of exchanging the shares to be acquired for shares, obligations or other securities of the acquiring corporation or any other corporation, or, in whole or in part, for cash or other property.

(d)   Such other provisions with respect to the proposed exchange as are deemed necessary or desirable.

The procedure authorized by this section shall not be deemed to limit the power of a corporation to acquire all or part of the shares of any class or classes of a corporation through a voluntary exchange or otherwise by agreement with the shareholders.

Section 73.   Approval by Shareholders

(a)   The board of directors of each corporation in the case of a merger or consolidation, and the board of directors of the corporation the shares of which are to be acquired in the case of an exchange, upon approving such plan of merger, consolidation or exchange, shall, by resolution, direct that the plan be submitted to a vote at a meeting of its shareholders, which may be either an annual or a special meeting. Written notice shall be given to each shareholder of record, whether or not entitled to vote at such meeting, not less than twenty days before such meeting, in the manner provided in this Act for the giving of notice of meetings of shareholders, and, whether the meeting be an annual or a special meeting, shall state that the purpose or one of the purposes is to consider the proposed plan of merger, consolidation or exchange. A copy or a summary of the plan of merger, consolidation or exchange, as the case may be, shall be included in or enclosed with such notice.

(b) At each such meeting, a vote of the shareholders shall be taken on the proposed plan. The plan shall be approved upon receiving the affirmative vote of the holders of a majority of the shares entitled to vote thereon of each such corporation, unless any class of shares of any such corporation is entitled to vote thereon as a class, in which event, as to such corporation, the plan shall be approved upon receiving the affirmative vote of the holders of a majority of the shares of each class of shares entitled to vote thereon as a class and of the total shares entitled to vote thereon. Any class of shares of any such corporation shall be entitled to vote as a class if any such plan contains any provision which, if contained in a proposed amendment to articles of incorporation, would entitle such class of shares to vote as a class and, in the case of an exchange, if the class is included in the exchange.

(c) After such approval by a vote of the shareholders of each such corporation, and at any time prior to the filing of the articles of merger, consolidation or exchange, the merger, consolidation or exchange may be abandoned pursuant to provisions therefore, if any, set forth in the plan.

(d) (1) Notwithstanding the provisions of subsections (a) and (b), submission of a plan of merger to a vote at a meeting of shareholders of a surviving corporation shall not be required if:

(i) the articles of incorporation of the surviving corporation do not differ except in name from those of the corporation before the merger.

(ii) each holder of shares of the surviving corporation which were outstanding immediately before the effective date of the merger is to hold the same number of shares with identical rights immediately after.

(iii) the number of voting shares outstanding immediately after the merger, plus the number of voting shares issuable on conversion of other securities issued by virtue of the terms of the merger and on exercise of rights and warrants so issued, will not exceed by more than 20 per cent the number of voting shares outstanding immediately before the merger, and

(iv) the number of participating shares outstanding immediately after the merger, plus the number of participating shares issuable on conversion of other securities issued by virtue of the terms of the merger and on exercise of rights and warrants so issued, will not exceed by more than 20 per cent the number of participating shares outstanding immediately before the merger.

(2) As used in this subsection:

(i) "voting shares" means shares which entitle their holders to vote unconditionally in elections of directors;

(ii) "participating shares" means shares which entitle their holders to participate without limitation in distribution of earnings or surplus.

Section 74. Articles of Merger, Consolidation or Exchange.

(a) Upon receiving the approvals required by Sections 71, 72 and 73, articles of merger or articles of consolidation shall be executed in duplicate by each corporation by its president or a vice president and by its secretary or an assistant secretary, and verified by one of the officers of each corporation signing such articles, and shall set forth:

(1) The plan of merger or the plan of consolidation;

(2) As to each corporation, either (i) the number of shares outstanding, and, if the shares of any class are entitled to vote as a class, the designation and number of outstanding shares of each such class, or (ii) a statement that the vote of shareholders is not required by virtue of subsection 73(d);

(3) As to each corporation the approval of whose shareholders is required, the number of shares voted for and against such plan, respectively, and, if the shares of any class are entitled to vote as a class, the number of shares of each such class voted for and against such plan, respectively.

(b) Duplicate originals of the articles of merger, consolidation or exchange shall be delivered to the Secretary of State. If the Secretary of State finds that such articles conform to law, he shall, when all fees and franchise taxes have been paid as in this Act prescribed:

(1) Endorse on each of such duplicate originals the word "Filed," and the month, day and year of the filing thereof.

(2) File one of such duplicate originals in his office.

(3) Issue a certificate of merger, consolidation or exchange to which he shall affix the other duplicate original.

(c) The certificate of merger, consolidation or exchange together with the duplicate original of the articles affixed thereto by the Secretary of State, shall be returned to the surviving, new or acquiring corporation, as the case may be, or its representative.

Section 75.   Merger of Subsidiary Corporation.

Any corporation owning at least ninety per cent of the outstanding shares of each class of another corporation may merge such other corporation into itself without approval by a vote of the shareholders of either corporation. Its board of directors shall, by resolution, approve a plan of merger setting forth:

(a) The name of the subsidiary corporation and the name of the corporation owning at least ninety per cent of its shares, which is hereinafter designated as the surviving corporation.

(b) The manner and basis of converting the shares of the subsidiary corporation into shares, obligations or other securities of the surviving corporation or of any other corporation or, in whole or in part, into cash or other property.

A copy of such plan of merger shall be mailed to each shareholder of record of the subsidiary corporation.

Articles of merger shall be executed in duplicate by the surviving corporation by its president or a vice president and by its secretary or an assistant secretary, and verified by one of its officers signing such articles, and shall set forth:

(a) The plan of merger;

(b) The number of outstanding shares of each class of the subsidiary corporation and the number of such shares of each class owned by the surviving corporation; and

(c) The date of the mailing to shareholders of the subsidiary corporation of a copy of the plan of merger.

On and after the thirtieth day after the mailing of a copy of the plan of merger to shareholders of the subsidiary corporation or upon the waiver thereof by the holders of all outstanding shares duplicate originals of

the articles of merger shall be delivered to the Secretary of State. If the Secretary of State finds that such articles conform to law, he shall, when all fees and franchise taxes have been paid as in this Act prescribed:

(1) Endorse on each of such duplicate originals the word "Filed," and the month, day and year of the filing thereof,

(2) File one of such duplicate originals in his office, and

(3) Issue a certificate of merger to which he shall affix the other duplicate original.

The certificate of merger, together with the duplicate original of the articles of merger affixed thereto by the Secretary of State, shall be returned to the surviving corporation or its representative.

Section 76.   Effect of Merger, Consolidation or Exchange

A merger, consolidation or exchange shall become effective upon the issuance of a certificate of merger, consolidation or exchange by the Secretary of State, or on such later date, not more than thirty days subsequent to the filing thereof with the Secretary of State, as shall be provided for in the plan.

When a merger of consolidation has become effective:

(a) The several corporations parties to the plan of merger or consolidation shall be a single corporation, which, in the case of a merger, shall be that corporation designated in the plan of merger as the surviving corporation, and, in the case of a consolidation, shall be the new corporation provided for in the plan of consolidation.

(b) The separate existence of all corporations parties to the plan of merger or consolidation, except the surviving or new corporation, shall cease.

(c) Such surviving or new corporation shall have all the rights, privileges, immunities and powers and shall be subject to all the duties and liabilities of a corporation organized under this Act.

(d) Such surviving or new corporation shall thereupon and thereafter possess all the rights, privileges, immunities, and franchises, of a public as well as of a private nature, of each of the merging or consolidating corporations; and all property, real, personal, and mixed, and all debts due on whatever account, including subscriptions to shares, and all other choses in action, and all and every other interest of or belonging to or due to each of the corporations so merged or consolidated, shall be taken and deemed to be transferred to and vested in such single corporation without further act or deed; and the title to any real estate, or any interest therein, vested in any of such corporations shall not revert or be in any way impaired by reason of such merger or consolidation.

(e) Such surviving or new corporation shall thenceforth be responsible and liable for all the liabilities and obligations of each of the corporations so merged or consolidated; and any claim existing or action or proceeding pending by or against any of such corporations may be prosecuted as if such merger or consolidation had not taken place, or such surviving or new corporation may be substituted in its place. Neither the rights of creditors nor any liens upon the property of any such corporation shall be impaired by such merger or consolidation.

(f) In the case of a merger, the articles of incorporation of the surviving corporation shall be deemed to be amended to the extent, if any, that changes in its articles of incorporation are stated in the plan of merger; and, in the case of a consolidation, the statements set forth in the articles of consolidation and which are required or permitted to be set forth in the articles of incorporation of corporations organized under this Act shall be deemed to be the original articles of incorporation of the new corporation.

When a merger, consolidation or exchange has become effective, the shares of the corporation or corporations party to the plan that are, under the terms of the plan, to be converted or exchanged, shall cease to exist, in the case of a merger or consolidation, or be deemed to be exchanged in the case of an exchange, and the holders of such shares shall thereafter be entitled only to the shares, obligations, other securities, cash or other property into which they shall have been converted or for which they shall have been exchanged, in accordance with the plan, subject to any rights under Section 80 of this Act.

Section 77. Merger, Consolidation or Exchange of Shares between Domestic and Foreign Corporations.

One or more foreign corporations and one or more domestic corporations may be merged or consolidated, or participate in an exchange, in the following manner, if such merger, consolidation or exchange is permitted by the laws of the state under which each such foreign corporation is organized:

(a) Each domestic corporation shall comply with the provisions of this Act with respect to the merger, consolidation or exchange, as the case may be, of domestic corporations and each foreign corporation shall comply with the applicable provisions of the laws of the state under which it is organized.

(b) If the surviving or new corporation in a merger or consolidation is to be governed by the laws of any state other than this State, it shall comply with the provisions of this Act with respect to foreign corporations if it is to transact business in this State, and in every case it shall file with the Secretary of State of this State:

(1) An agreement that it may be served with process in this State in any proceeding for the enforcement of any obligation of any domestic corporation which is a party to such merger or consolidation and in any proceeding for the enforcement of the rights of a dissenting shareholder of any such domestic corporation against the surviving or new corporation.

(2) An irrevocable appointment of the Secretary of State of this State as its agent to accept service of process in any such proceeding; and

(3) An agreement that it will promptly pay to the dissenting shareholders of any such domestic corporation, the amount, if any, to which they shall be entitled under provisions of this Act with respect to the rights of dissenting shareholders.

Section 78. Sale of Assets in Regular Course of Business and Mortgage or Pledge of Assets.

The sale, lease, exchange, or other disposition of all, or substantially all, the property and assets of a corporation in the usual and regular course of its business and the mortgage or pledge of any or all property and assets of a corporation whether or not in the usual and regular course of business may be made upon such terms and conditions and for such consideration, which may consist in whole or in part of cash or other property, including shares, obligations or other securities of any other corporation, domestic or foreign, as shall be authorized by its board of directors; and in any such case no authorization or consent of the shareholders shall be required.

Section 79. Sale of Assets Other Than in Regular Course of Business.

A sale, lease, exchange, or other disposition of all, or substantially all, the property and assets, with or without the good will, of a corporation, if not in the usual and regular course of its business, may be made upon such terms and conditions and for such consideration, which may consist in whole or in part of cash or other property, including shares, obligations or other securities of any other corporation, domestic or foreign, as may be authorized in the following manner:

(a) The board of directors shall adopt a resolution recommending such sale, lease, exchange, or other disposition and directing the submission thereof to a vote at a meeting of shareholders, which may be either an annual or a special meeting.

(b) Written notice shall be given to each shareholder of record, whether or not entitled to vote at such meeting, not less than twenty days before such meeting, in the manner provided in this Act for the giving of notice of meetings of shareholders, and, whether the meeting be an annual or a special meeting, shall state that the purpose, or one of the purposes is to consider the proposed sale, lease, exchange, or other disposition.

(c) At such meeting the shareholders may authorize such sale, lease, exchange, or other disposition and may fix, or may authorize the board of directors to fix, any or all of the terms and conditions thereof and the consideration to be received by the corporation therefor. Such authorization shall require the affirmative vote of the holders of a majority of the shares of the corporation entitled to vote thereon, unless any class of shares is entitled to vote thereon as a class, in which event such authorization shall require the affirmative vote of the holders of a majority of the shares of each class of shares entitled to vote as a class thereon and of the total shares entitled to vote thereon.

(d) After such authorization by a vote of shareholders, the board of directors nevertheless, in its discretion, may abandon such sale, lease, exchange, or other disposition of assets, subject to the rights of third parties under any contracts relating thereto, without further action or approval by shareholders.

Section 80. Right of Shareholders to Dissent and Obtain Payment for Shares.

(a) Any shareholder of a corporation shall have the right to dissent from, and to obtain payment for his shares in the event of, any of the following corporate actions.

(1) Any plan of merger or consolidation to which the corporation is a party, except as provided in subsection (c);

(2) Any sale or exchange of all or substantially all of the property and assets of the corporation not made in the usual or regular course of its business, including a sale in dissolution, but not including a sale pursuant to an order of a court having jurisdiction in the premises or a sale for cash on terms requiring that all or substantially all of the net proceeds of sale be distributed to the shareholders in accordance with their respective interests within one year after the date of sale;

(3) Any plan of exchange to which the corporation is a party as the corporation the shares of which are to be acquired;

(4) Any amendment of the articles of incorporation which materially and adversely affects the rights appurtenant to the share of the dissenting shareholders in that it:

(i) alters or abolishes a preferential right of such shares;

(ii) creates, alters or abolishes a right in respect of the redemption of such shares, including a provision respecting a sinking fund for the redemption or repurchase of such shares;

(iii) alters or abolishes a preemptive right of the holder of such shares to acquire shares or other securities;

(iv) excludes or limits the right of the holder of such shares to vote on any matter, or to cumulate his votes, except as such right may be limited by dilution through the issuance of shares or other securities with similar voting rights; or

(5) Any other corporate action taken pursuant to a shareholder vote with respect to which the articles of incorporation, the bylaws, or a resolution of the board of directors directs that dissenting shareholders shall have a right to obtain payment for their shares.

(b) (1) A record holder of shares may assert dissenters' rights as to less than all of the shares registered in his name only if he dissents with respect to all the shares beneficially owned by any one person, and discloses the name and address of the person or persons on whose behalf he dissents. In that event, his rights shall be determined as if the shares as to which he has dissented and his other shares were registered in the names of different shareholders.

(2) A beneficial owner of shares who is not the record holder may assert dissenters' rights with respect to shares held on his behalf, and

shall be treated as a dissenting shareholder under the terms of this section and Section 31 if he submits to the corporation at the time of or before the assertion of these rights a written consent of the record holder.

(c) The right to obtain payment under this section shall not apply to the shareholders of the surviving corporation in a merger if a vote of the shareholders of such corporation is not necessary to authorize such merger.

(d) A shareholder of a corporation who has a right under this section to obtain payment for his shares shall have no right at law or in equity to attack the validity of the corporate action that gives rise to his right to obtain payment, nor to have the action set aside or rescinded, except when the corporate action is unlawful or fraudulent with regard to the complaining shareholder or to the corporation.

Section 81. Procedures for Protection of Dissenters' Rights.

(a) As used in this section:

  (1) "Dissenter" means a shareholder or beneficial owner who is entitled to and does assert dissenters' rights under Section 80, and who has performed every act required up to the time involved for the assertion of such rights.

  (2) "Corporation" means the issuer of the shares held by the dissenter before the corporate action, or the successor by merger or consolidation of that issuer.

  (3) "Fair value" of shares means their value immediately before the effectuation of the corporate action to which the dissenter objects, excluding any appreciation or depreciation in anticipation of such corporate action unless such exclusion would be inequitable.

  (4) "Interest" means interest from the effective date of the corporate action until the date of payment, at the average rate currently paid by the corporation on its principal bank loans, or, if none, at such rate as is fair and equitable under all the circumstances.

(b) If a proposed corporate action which would give rise to dissenters' rights under Section 80(a) is submitted to a vote at a meeting of shareholders, the notice of meeting shall notify all shareholders that they have or may have a right to dissent and obtain payment for their shares by complying with the terms of this section, and shall be accompanied by a copy of Sections 80 and 81 of this Act.

(c) If the proposed corporate action is submitted to a vote at a meeting of shareholders, any shareholder who wishes to dissent and obtain payment for his shares must file with the corporation, prior to the vote, a written notice of intention to demand that he be paid fair compensation for his shares if the proposed action is effectuated, and shall refrain from voting his shares in approval of such action. A shareholder who fails in either respect shall acquire no right to payment for his shares under this section or Section 80.

(d) If the proposed corporate action is approved by the required vote at a meeting of shareholders, the corporation shall mail a further notice to all shareholders who gave due notice of intention to demand payment and who refrained from voting in favor of the proposed action. If the proposed corporate action is to be taken without a vote of shareholders, the corporation shall send to all shareholders who are entitled to dissent and demand payment for their shares a notice of the adoption of the plan of corporate action. The notice shall (1) state where and when a demand for payment must be sent and certificates of certificated shares must be deposited in order to obtain payment, (2) inform holders of uncertificated shares to what extent transfer of shares will be restricted from the time that demand for payment is received, (3) supply a form for demanding payment which includes a request for certification of the date on which the shareholder, or the person on whose behalf the shareholder dissents, acquired beneficial ownership of the shares, and (4) be accompanied by a copy of Sections 80 and 81 of this Act. The time set for the demand and deposit shall be not less than 30 days from the mailing of the notice.

(e) A shareholder who fails to demand payment, or fails (in the case of certified shares) to deposit certificates, as required by a notice pursuant to subsection (d) shall have no right under this section or Section 80 to receive payment for his shares. If the shares are not represented by certificates, the corporation may restrict their transfer from the time of receipt of demand for payment until effectuation of the proposed corporate action, or the release of restrictions under the terms of subsection (f). The dissenter shall retain all other rights of a shareholder until these rights are modified by effectuation of the proposed corporate action.

(f) (1) Within 60 days after the date set for demanding payment and depositing certificates, if the corporation has not effectuated the proposed corporate action and remitted payment for shares pursuant to paragraph (3), it shall return any certificates that have been deposited, and release uncertificated shares from any transfer restrictions imposed by reason of the demand for payment.

(2) When uncertificated shares have been released from transfer restrictions, and deposited certificates have been returned, the corporation may at any later time send a new notice conforming to the requirements of subsection (d), with like effect.

(3) Immediately upon effectuation of the proposed corporate action, or upon receipt of demand for payment if the corporate action has already been effectuated, the corporation shall remit to dissenters who have made demand and (if their shares are certificated) have deposited their certificates the amount which the corporation estimates to be the fair value of the shares, with interest if any has accrued. The remittance shall be accompanied by:

(i) the corporation's closing balance sheet and statement of income for a fiscal year ending not more than 16 months before the date of remittance, together with the latest available interim financial statements;

(ii) a statement of the corporation's estimate of fair value of the shares; and

(iii) a notice of the dissenter's right to demand supplemental payment, accompanied by a copy of Sections 80 and 81 of this Act.

(g) (1) If the corporation fails to remit as required by subsection (f), or if the dissenter believes that the amount remitted is less than the fair value of his shares, or that the interest is not correctly determined, he may send the corporation his own estimate of the value of the shares or of the interest, and demand payment of the deficiency.

(2) If the dissenter does not file such an estimate within 30 days after the corporation's mailing of its remittance, he shall be entitled to no more than the amount remitted.

(h) (1) Within 60 days after receiving a demand for payment pursuant to subsection (g), if any such demands for payment remain unsettled, the corporation shall file in an appropriate court a petition requesting that the fair value of the shares and interest thereon be determined by the court.

(2) An appropriate court shall be a court of competent jurisdiction in the county of this state where the registered office of the corporation is located. If, in the case of a merger or consolidation or exchange of shares, the corporation is a foreign corporation without a registered office in this state, the petition shall be filed in the county where the registered office of the domestic corporation was last located.

(3) All dissenters, wherever residing, whose demands have not been settled shall be made parties to the proceeding as in an action against their shares. A copy of the petition shall be served on each such dissenter; if a dissenter is a nonresident, the copy may be served on him by registered or certified mail or by publication as provided by law.

(4) The jurisdiction of the court shall be plenary and exclusive. The court may appoint one or more persons as appraisers to receive evidence and recommend a decision on the question of fair value. The appraisers shall have such power and authority as shall be specified in the order of their appointment or in any amendment thereof. The dissenters shall be entitled to discovery in the same manner as parties in other civil suits.

(5) All dissenters who are made parties shall be entitled to judgment for the amount by which the fair value of their shares is found to exceed the amount previously remitted, with interest.

(6) If the corporation fails to file a petition as provided in paragraph (1) of this subsection, each dissenter who made a demand and who has not already settled his claim against the corporation shall be paid by the corporation the amount demanded by him, with interest, and may sue therefor in an appropriate court.

(i) (1) The costs and expenses of any proceeding under subsection (h), including the reasonable compensation and expenses of appraisers appointed by the court, shall be determined by the court and assessed against the corporation, except that any part of the costs and expenses may be apportioned and assessed as the court may deem equitable against all or some of the dissenters who are parties and whose action in demanding supplemental payment the court finds to be arbitrary, vexatious, or not in good faith.

(2) Fees and expenses of counsel and of experts for the respective parties may be assessed as the court may deem equitable against the corporation and in favor of any or all dissenters if the corporation failed to comply substantially with the requirements of this section, and may be assessed against either the corporation or a dissenter, in favor of any other party, if the court finds that the party against whom the fees and expenses are assessed acted arbitrarily, vexatiously, or not in good faith in respect to the rights provided by this section and Section 80.

(3) If the court finds that the services of counsel for any dissenter were of substantial benefit to other dissenters similarly situated, and should not be assessed against the corporation, it may award to these counsel reasonable fees to be paid out of the amounts awarded to the dissenters who were benefitted.

(j) (1) Notwithstanding the foregoing provisions of this section, the corporation may elect to withhold the remittance required by subsection (f) from any dissenter with respect to shares of which the dissenter (or the person on whose behalf the dissenter acts) was not the beneficial owner on the date of the first announcement to news media or to shareholders of the terms of the proposed corporate action. With respect to such shares, the corporation shall, upon effectuating the corporate action, state to each dissenter its estimate of the fair value of the shares, state the rate of interest to be used (explaining the basis thereof) and offer to pay the resulting amounts on receiving the dissenter's agreement to accept them in full satisfaction.

(2) If the dissenter believes that the amount offered is less than the fair value of the shares and interest determined according to this section, he may within 30 days after the date of mailing of the corporation's offer, mail the corporation his own estimate of fair value and interest, and demand their payment. If the dissenter fails to do so, he shall be entitled to no more than the corporation's offer.

(3) If the dissenter makes a demand as provided in paragraph (2), the provisions of subsections (h) and (i) shall apply to further proceedings on the dissenter's demand.

Section 82. Voluntary Dissolution by Incorporators.

A corporation which has not commenced business and which has not issued any shares, may be voluntarily dissolved by its incorporators at any time in the following manner:

(a) Articles of dissolution shall be executed in duplicate by a majority of the incorporators, and verified by them, and shall set forth:

(1) The name of the corporation.

(2) The date of issuance of its certificate of incorporation.

(3) That none of its shares has been issued.

(4) That the corporation has not commenced business.

(5) That the amount, if any, actually paid in on subscriptions for its shares, less any part thereof disbursed for necessary expenses, has been returned to those entitled thereto.

(6) That no debts of the corporation remain unpaid.

(7) That a majority of the incorporators elect that the corporation be dissolved.

(b) Duplicate originals of the articles of dissolution shall be delivered to the Secretary of State. If the Secretary of State finds that the articles of dissolution conform to law, he shall, when all fees and franchise taxes have been paid as in this Act prescribed:

(1) Endorse on each of such duplicate originals the word "Filed," and the month, day and year of the filing thereof.

(2) File one of such duplicate originals in his office.

(3) Issue a certificate of dissolution to which he shall affix the other duplicate original.

The certificate of dissolution, together with the duplicate original of the articles of dissolution affixed thereto by the Secretary of State, shall be returned to the incorporators or their representative. Upon the issuance of such certificate of dissolution by the Secretary of State, the existence of the corporation shall cease.

Appendix D

Section 83. Voluntary Dissolution by Consent of Shareholders.

A corporation may be voluntarily disolved by the written consent of all of its shareholders.

Upon the execution of such written consent, a statement of intent to dissolve shall be executed in duplicate by the corporation by its president or a vice president and by its secretary or an assistant secretary, and verified by one of the officers signing such statement, which statement shall set forth:

(a) The name of the corporation.

(b) The names and respective addresses of its officers.

(c) The names and respective addresses of its directors.

(d) A copy of the written consent signed by all shareholders of the corporation.

(e) A statement that such written consent has been signed by all shareholders of the corporation or signed in their names by their attorneys thereunto duly authorized.

Section 84. Voluntary Dissolution by Act of Corporation.

A corporation may be dissolved by the act of the corporation, when authorized in the following manner:

(a) The board of directors shall adopt a resolution recommending that the corporation be dissolved, and directing that the question of such dissolution be submitted to a vote at a meeting of shareholders, which may be either an annual or a special meeting.

(b) Written notice shall be given to each shareholder of record entitled to vote at such meeting within the time and in the manner provided in this Act for the giving of notice of meetings of shareholders, and, whether the meeting be an annual or special meeting, shall state that the purpose, or one of the purposes, of such meeting is to consider the advisability of dissolving the corporation.

(c) At such meeting a vote of shareholders entitled to vote thereat shall be taken on a resolution to dissolve the corporation. Such resolution shall be adopted upon receiving the affirmative vote of the holders of a majority of the shares of the corporation entitled to vote thereon, unless any class of shares is entitled to vote thereon as a class, in which event the resolution shall be adopted upon receiving the affirmative vote of the holders of a majority of the shares of each class of shares entitled to vote thereon as a class and of the total shares entitled to vote thereon.

170

(d) Upon the adoption of such resolution, a statement of intent to dissolve shall be executed in duplicate by the corporation by its president or a vice president and by its secretary or an assistant secretary, and verified by one of the officers signing such statement, which statement shall set forth:

(1) The name of the corporation.

(2) The names and respective addresses of its officers.

(3) The names and respective addresses of its directors.

(4) A copy of the resolution adopted by the shareholders authorizing the dissolution of the corporation.

(5) The number of shares outstanding, and, if the shares of any class are entitled to vote as a class, the designation and number of outstanding shares of each such class.

(6) The number of shares voted for and against the resolution, respectively, and, if the shares of any class are entitled to vote as a class, the number of shares of each such class voted for and against the resolution, respectively.

Section 85. Filing of Statement of Intent to Dissolve.

Duplicate originals of the statement of intent to dissolve, whether by consent of shareholders or by act of the corporation, shall be delivered to the Secretary of State. If the Secretary of State finds that such statement conforms to law, he shall, when all fees and franchise taxes have been paid as in this Act prescribed:

(a) Endorse on each of such duplicate originals the word "Filed," and the month, day and year of the filing thereof.

(b) File one of such duplicate originals in his office.

(c) Return the other duplicate original to the corporation or its representative.

Section 86. Effect of Statement of Intent to Dissolve.

Upon the filing by the Secretary of State of a statement of intent to dissolve, whether by consent of shareholders or by act of the corporation, the corporation shall cease to carry on its business, except insofar as may be necessary for the winding up thereof, but its corporate existence shall continue until a certificate of dissolution has been issued by the Secretary of State or until a decree dissolving the corporation has been entered by a court of competent jurisdiction as in this Act provided.

Section 87. Procedure after Filing of Statement of Intent to Dissolve.

After the filing by the Secretary of State of a statement of intent to dissolve:

(a) The corporation shall immediately cause notice thereof to be mailed to each known creditor of the corporation.

(b) The corporation shall proceed to collect its assets, convey and dispose of such of its properties as are not to be distributed in kind to its shareholders, pay, satisfy and discharge its liabilities and obligations and do all other acts required to liquidate its business and affairs, and, after paying or adequately providing for the payment of all its obligations, distribute the remainder of its assets, either in cash or in kind, among its shareholders according to their respective rights and interests.

(c) The corporation, at any time during the liquidation of its business and affairs, may make application to a court of competent jurisdiction within the state and judicial subdivision in which the registered office or principal place of business of the corporation is situated, to have the liquidation continued under the supervision of the courts as provided in this Act.

Section 88. Revocation of Voluntary Dissolution Proceedings by Consent of Shareholders. *(Text omitted).*

Section 89. Revocation of Voluntary Dissolution Proceedings by Act of Corporation. *(Text omitted).*

Section 90. Filing of Statement of Revocation of Voluntary Dissolution Proceedings. *(Text omitted).*

Section 91. Effect of Statement of Revocation of Voluntary Dissolution Proceedings.

Upon the filing by the Secretary of State of a statement of revocation of voluntary dissolution proceedings, whether by consent of shareholders or by act of the corporation, the revocation of the voluntary dissolution proceedings shall become effective and the corporation may again carry on its business.

Section 92. Articles of Dissolution.

If voluntary dissolution proceedings have not been revoked, then when all debts, liabilities and obligations of the corporation have been paid and discharged, or adequate provision has been made therefor, and all of the remaining property and assets of the corporation have been distributed to its shareholders, articles of dissolution shall be executed in duplicate by the corpo-

ration by its president or a vice president and by its secretary or an assistant secretary, and verified by one of the officers signing such statement, which statement shall set forth:

(a) The name of the corporation.

(b) That the Secretary of State has theretofore filed a statement of intent to dissolve the corporation, and the date on which such statement was filed.

(c) That all debts, obligations and liabilities of the corporation have been paid and discharged or that adequate provision has been made therefore.

(d) That all the remaining property and assets of the corporation have been distributed among its shareholders in accordance with their respective rights and interests.

(e) That there are no suits pending against the corporation in any court, or that adequate provision has been made for the satisfaction of any judgment, order or decree which may be entered against it in any pending suit.

Section 93. Filing of Articles of Dissolution.

Duplicate originals of such articles of dissolution shall be delivered to the Secretary of State. If the Secretary of State finds that such articles of dissolution conform to law, he shall, when all fees and franchise taxes have been paid as in this Act prescribed:

(a) Endorse on each of such duplicate originals the word "Filed," and the month, day and year of the filing thereof.

(b) File one of such duplicate originals in his office.

(c) Issue a certificate of dissolution to which he shall affix the other duplicate original.

The certificate of dissolution, together with the duplicate original of the articles of dissolution affixed thereto by the Secretary of State, shall be returned to the representative of the dissolved corporation. Upon the issuance of such certificate of dissolution the existence of the corporation shall cease, except for the purpose of suits, other proceedings and appropriate corporate action by shareholders, directors and officers as provided in this Act.

Section 94. Involuntary Dissolution.

A corporation may be dissolved involuntarily by a decree of the . . . . court in an action filed by the Attorney General when it is established that:

(a) The corporation has failed to file its annual report within the time required by this Act, or has failed to pay its franchise tax on or before the first day of August of the year in which such franchise tax becomes due and payable; or

(b) The corporation procured its articles of incorporation through fraud; or

(c) The corporation has continued to exceed or abuse the authority conferred upon it by law; or

(d) The corporation has failed for thirty days to appoint and maintain a registered agent in this State; or

(e) The corporation has failed for thirty days after change of its registered office or registered agent to file in the office of the Secretary of State a statement of such change.

Section 95. Notification to Attorney General.

The Secretary of State, on or before the last day of December of each year, shall certify to the Attorney General the names of all corporations which have failed to file their annual reports or to pay franchise taxes in accordance with the provisions of this Act, together with the facts pertinent thereto. He shall also certify, from time to time, the names of all corporations which have given other cause for dissolution as provided in this Act, together with the facts pertinent thereto. Whenever the Secretary of State shall certify the name of a corporation to the Attorney General as having given any cause for dissolution, the Secretary of State shall concurrently mail to the corporation at its registered office a notice that such certification has been made. Upon the receipt of such certification, the Attorney General shall file an action in the name of the State against such corporation for its dissolution. Every such certificate from the Secretary of State to the Attorney General pertaining to the failure of a corporation to file an annual report or pay a franchise tax shall be taken and received in all courts as prima facie evidence of the facts therein stated. If, before action is filed, the corporation shall file its annual report or pay its franchise tax, together with all penalties thereon, or shall appoint or maintain a registered agent as provided in this Act, or shall file with the Secretary of State the required statement of change of registered office or registered agent, such fact shall be forthwith certified by the Secretary of State to the Attorney General and he shall not file an action against such corporation for such cause. If, after action is filed, the corporation shall file its annual report or pay its franchise tax, together with all penalties thereon, or shall appoint or maintain a registered agent as provided in this Act, or shall file with the Secretary

of State the required statement of change of registered office or registered agent, and shall pay the costs of such action, the action for such cause shall abate.

Section 96. Venue and Process.

Every action for the involuntary dissolution of a corporation shall be commenced by the Attorney General either in the . . . . court of the county in which the registered office of the corporation is situated, or in the . . . . . . court of . . . . county. Summons shall issue and be served as in other civil actions. If process is returned not found, the Attorney General shall cause publication to be made as in other civil cases in some newspaper published in the county where the registered office of the corporation is situated, containing a notice of the pendency of such action, the title of the court, the title of the action, and the date on or after which default may be entered. The Attorney General may include in one notice the names of any number of corporations against which actions are then pending in the same court. The Attorney General shall cause a copy of such notice to be mailed to the corporation at its registered office within ten days after the first publication thereof. The certificate of the Attorney General of the mailing of such notice shall be prima facie evidence thereof. Such notice shall be published at least once each week for two successive weeks, and the first publication thereof may begin at any time after the summons has been returned. Unless a corporation shall have been served with summons, no default shall be taken against it earlier than thirty days after the first publication of such notice.

Section 97. Jurisdiction of Court to Liquidate Assets and Business of Corporation.

The . . . . courts shall have full power to liquidate the assets and business of a corporation:

(a) In an action by a shareholder when it is established:

   (1) That the directors are deadlocked in the management of the corporate affairs and the shareholders are unable to break the deadlock, and that irreparable injury to the corporation is being suffered or is threatened by reason thereof; or

   (2) That the acts of the directors or those in control of the corporation are illegal, oppressive or fraudulent; or

   (3) That the shareholders are deadlocked in voting power, and have failed, for a period which

includes at least two consecutive annual meeting dates, to elect successors to directors whose terms have expired or would have expired upon the election of their successors; or

(4) That the corporate assets are being misapplied or wasted.

(b) In an action by a creditor:

(1) When the claim of the creditor has been reduced to judgment and an execution thereon returned unsatisfied and it is established that the corporation is insolvent; or

(2) When the corporation has admitted in writing that the claim of the creditor is due and owing and it is established that the corporation is insolvent.

(c) Upon application by a corporation which has filed a statement of intent to dissolve, as provided in this Act, to have its liquidation continued under the supervision of the court.

(d) When an action has been filed by the Attorney General to dissolve a corporation and it is established that liquidation of its business and affairs should precede the entry of a decree of dissolution.

Proceedings under clause (a), (b) or (c) of this section shall be brought in the county in which the registered office or the principal office of the corporation is situated.

It shall not be necessary to make shareholders parties to any such action or proceeding unless relief is sought against them personally.

Section 98. Procedure in Liquidation of Corporation by Court.

In proceedings to liquidate the assets and business of a corporation the court shall have power to issue injunctions, to appoint a receiver or receivers pendente lite, with such powers and duties as the court, from time to time, may direct, and to take such other proceedings as may be requisite to preserve the corporate assets wherever situated, and carry on the business of the corporation until a full hearing can be had.

After a hearing had upon such notice as the court may direct to be given to all parties to the proceedings and to any other parties in interest designated by the court, the court may appoint a liquidating receiver or receivers with authority to collect the assets of the corporation, including all amounts owing to the corporation by subscribers on account of any unpaid portion of the consideration for the issuance of shares. Such liquidating receiver or receivers shall have authority, subject to the order of the court, to sell, convey and dispose of all or any part of the assets of the corporation wherever situated, either at public or private sale. The assets of the corporation or the proceeds resulting from a sale, conveyance or other disposition thereof shall be applied to the expenses of such liquidation and to the payment of the liabilities and obligations of the corporation, and any remaining assets or proceeds shall be distributed among its shareholders according to their respective rights and interests. The order appointing such liquidating receiver or receivers shall state their powers and duties. Such powers and duties may be increased or diminished at any time during the proceedings.

The court shall have power to allow from time to time as expenses of the liquidation compensation to the receiver or receivers and to attorneys in the proceeding, and to direct the payment thereof out of the assets of the corporation or the proceeds of any sale or disposition of such assets.

A receiver of a corporation appointed under the provisions of this section shall have authority to sue and defend in all courts in his own name as receiver of such corporation. The court appointing such receiver shall have exclusive jurisdiction of the corporation and its property, wherever situated.

Section 99. Qualifications of Receivers.

A receiver shall in all cases be a natural person or a corporation authorized to act as receiver, which corporation may be a domestic corporation or a foreign corporation authorized to transact business in this State, and shall in all cases give such bond as the court may direct with such sureties as the court may require.

Section 100. Filing of Claims in Liquidation Proceedings.

In proceedings to liquidate the assets and business of a corporation the court may require all creditors of the corporation to file with the clerk of the court or with the receiver, in such form as the court may prescribe, proofs under oath of their respective claims. If the court requires the filing of claims it shall fix a date, which shall be not less than four months from the date of the order, as the last day for the filing of claims, and shall prescribe the notice that shall be given to creditors and claimants of the date so fixed. Prior to the date so fixed the court may extend the time for the filing of claims. Creditors and claimants failing to file proofs of claim on or before the date so fixed may be barred, by order of court, from participating in the distribution of the assets of the corporation.

Section 101. Discontinuance of Liquidation Proceedings.

The liquidation of the assets and business of a corporation may be discontinued at any time during the liquidation proceedings when it is established that cause for liquidation no longer exists. In such event the court shall dismiss the proceedings and direct the receiver to redeliver to the corporation all its remaining property and assets.

Section 102. Decree of Involuntary Dissolution.

In proceedings to liquidate the assets and business of a corporation, when the costs and expenses of such proceedings and all debts, obligations and liabilities of the corporation shall have been paid and discharged and all of its remaining property and assets distributed to its shareholders, or in case its property and assets are not sufficient to satisfy and discharge such costs, expenses, debts and obligations, all the property and assets have been applied so far as they will go to their payment, the court shall enter a decree dissolving the corporation, whereupon the existence of the corporation shall cease.

Section 103. Filing of Decree of Dissolution.

In case the court shall enter a decree dissolving a corporation, it shall be the duty of the clerk of such court to cause a certified copy of the decree to be filed with the Secretary of State. No fee shall be charged by the Secretary of State for the filing thereof.

Section 104. Deposit with State Treasurer of Amount Due Certain Shareholders.

Upon the voluntary or involuntary dissolution of a corporation, the portion of the assets distributable to a creditor or shareholder who is unknown or cannot be found, or who is under disability and there is no person legally competent to receive such distributive portion, shall be reduced to cash and deposited with the State Treasurer and shall be paid over to such creditor or shareholder or to his legal representative upon proof satisfactory to the State Treasurer of his right thereto.

Section 105. Survival of Remedy After Dissolution.

The dissolution of a corporation either (1) by the issuance of a certificate of dissolution by the Secretary of

State, or (2) by a decree of court when the court has not liquidated the assets and business of the corporation as provided in this Act, or (3) by expiration of its period of duration, shall not take away or impair any remedy available to or against such corporation, its directors, officers, or shareholders, for any right or claim existing, or any liability incurred, prior to such dissolution if action or other proceeding thereon is commenced within two years after the date of such dissolution. Any such action or proceeding by or against the corporation may be prosecuted or defended by the corporation in its corporate name. The shareholders, directors and officers shall have power to take such corporate or other action as shall be appropriate to protect such remedy, right or claim. If such corporation was dissolved by the expiration of its period of duration, such corporation may amend its articles of incorporation at any time during such period of two years so as to extend its period of duration.

Section 106. Admission of Foreign Corporation.

No foreign corporation shall have the right to transact business in this State until it shall have procured a certificate of authority so to do from the Secretary of State. No foreign corporation shall be entitled to procure a certificate of authority under this Act to transact in this State any business which a corporation organized under this Act is not permitted to transact. A foreign corporation shall not be denied a certificate of authority by reason of the fact that the laws of the state or country under which such corporation is organized governing its organization and internal affairs differ from the laws of this State, and nothing in this Act contained shall be construed to authorize this State to regulate the organization or the internal affairs of such corporation.

Without excluding other activities which may not constitute transacting business in this State, a foreign corporation shall not be considered to be transacting business in this State, for the purposes of this Act, by reason of carrying on in this State any one or more of the following activities:

(a) Maintaining or defending any action or suit or any administrative or arbitration proceeding, or effecting the settlement thereof or the settlement of claims or disputes.

(b) Holding meetings of its directors or shareholders or carrying on other activities concerning its internal affairs.

(c) Maintaining bank accounts.

(d) Maintaining offices or agencies for the transfer, exchange and registration of its securities, or appointing and maintaining trustees or depositaries with relation to its securities.

(e)   Effecting sales through independent contractors.

(f)   Soliciting or procuring orders, whether by mail or through employees or agents or otherwise, where such orders require acceptance without this State before becoming binding contracts.

(g)   Creating as borrower or lender, or acquiring, indebtedness or mortgages or other security interests in real or personal property.

(h)   Securing or collecting debts or enforcing any rights in property securing the same.

(i)   Transacting any business in interstate commerce.

(j)   Conducting an isolated transaction completed within a period of thirty days and not in the course of a number of repeated transactions of like nature.

Section 107.   Powers of Foreign Corporation.

A foreign corporation which shall have received a certificate of authority under this Act shall, until a certificate of revocation or of withdrawal shall have been issued as provided in this Act, enjoy the same, but no greater, rights and privileges as a domestic corporation organized for the purposes set forth in the application pursuant to which such certificate of authority is issued; and, except as in this Act otherwise provided, shall be subject to the same duties, restrictions, penalties and liabilities now or hereafter imposed upon a domestic corporation of like character.

Section 108.   Corporate Name of Foreign Corporation.

No certificate of authority shall be issued to a foreign corporation unless the corporate name of such corporation:

(a)   Shall contain the word "corporation," "company," "incorporated," or "limited," or shall contain an abbreviation of one of such words, or such corporation shall, for use in this State, add at the end of its name one of such words or an abbreviation thereof.

(b)   Shall not contain any word or phrase which indicates or implies that it is organized for any purpose other than one or more of the purposes contained in its articles of incorporation or that it is authorized or empowered to conduct the business of banking or insurance.

(c)   Shall not be the same as, or deceptively similar to, the name of any domestic corporation existing under the laws of this State or any foreign corporation authorized to transact business in this State, or a name the

exclusive right to which is, at the time, reserved in the manner provided in this Act, or the name of a corporation which has in effect a registration of its name as provided in this Act except that this provision shall not apply if the foreign corporation applying for a certificate of authority files with the Secretary of State any one of the following:

(1)   a resolution of its board of directors adopting a fictitious name for use in transacting business in this State which fictitious name is not deceptively similar to the name of any domestic corporation or of any foreign corporation authorized to transact business in this State or to any name reserved or registered as provided in this Act, or

(2)   the written consent of such other corporation or holder of a reserved or registered name to use the same or deceptively similar name and one or more words are added to make such name distinguishable from such other name, or

(3)   a certified copy of a final decree of a court of competent jurisdiction establishing the prior right of such foreign corporation to the use of such name in this State.

Section 109.   Change of Name by Foreign Corporation.

Whenever a foreign corporation which is authorized to transact business in this State shall change its name to one under which a certificate of authority would not be granted to it on application therefor, the certificate of authority of such corporation shall be suspended and it shall not thereafter transact any business in this State until it has changed its name to a name which is available to it under the laws of this State or has otherwise complied with the provisions of this Act.

Section 110.   Application for Certificate of Authority.

A foreign corporation, in order to procure a certificate of authority to transact business in this State, shall make application therefor to the Secretary of State, which application shall set forth:

(a)   The name of the corporation and the state or country under the laws of which it is incorporated.

(b)   If the name of the corporation does not contain the word "corporation," "company," "incorporated," or "limited," or does not contain an abbreviation of one of such words, then the name of the corporation with the word or abbreviation which it elects to add thereto for use in this State.

(c)   The date of incorporation and the period of duration of the corporation.

(d)   The address of the principal office of the corporation in the state or country under the laws of which it is incorporated.

(e)   The address of the proposed registered office of the corporation in this State, and the name of its proposed registered agent in this State at such address.

(f)   The purpose or purposes of the corporation which it proposes to pursue in the transaction of business in this State.

(g)   The names and respective addresses of the directors and officers of the corporation.

(h)   A statement of the aggregate number of shares which the corporation has authority to issue, itemized by classes, par value of shares, shares without par value, and series, if any, within a class.

(i)   A statement of the aggregate number of issued shares itemized by classes, par value of shares, shares without par value, and series, if any, within a class.

(j)   A statement, expressed in dollar, of the amount of stated capital of the corporation, as defined in this Act.

(k)   An estimate, expressed in dollars, of the value of all property to be owned by the corporation for the following year, wherever located, and an estimate of the value of the property of the corporation to be located within this State during such year, and an estimate, expressed in dollars, of the gross amount of business which will be transacted by the corporation during such year, and an estimate of the gross amount thereof which will be transacted by the corporation at or from places of business in this State during such year.

(1)   Such additional information as may be necessary or appropriate in order to enable the Secretary of State to determine whether such corporation is entitled to a certificate of authority to transact business in this State and to determine and assess the fees and franchise taxes payable as in this Act prescribed.

Such application shall be made on forms prescribed and furnished by the Secretary of State and shall be executed in duplicate by the corporation by its president or a vice president and by its secretary or an assistant secretary, and verified by one of the officers signing such application.

Section 111.   Filing of Application for Certificate of Authority.

Duplicate originals of the application of the corporation for a certificate of authority shall be delivered to the Secretary of State, together with a copy of its articles of incorporation and all amendments thereto, duly authenticated by the proper officer of the state or country under the laws of which it is incorporated.

If the Secretary of State finds that such application conforms to law, he shall, when all fees and franchise taxes have been paid as in this Act prescribed:

(a)   Endorse on each of such documents the word "Filed," and the month, day and year of the filing thereof.

(b)   File in his office one of such duplicate originals of the application and the copy of the articles of incorporation and amendments thereto.

(c)   Issue a certificate of authority to transact business in this State to which he shall affix the other duplicate original application.

The certificate of authority, together with the duplicate original of the application affixed thereto by the Secretary of State, shall be returned to the corporation or its representative.

Section 112.   Effect of Certificate of Authority.

Upon the issuance of a certificate of authority by the Secretary of State, the corporation shall be authorized to transact business in this State for those purposes set forth in its application, subject, however, to the right of this State to suspend or to revoke such authority as provided in this Act.

Section 113.   Registered Office and Registered Agent of Foreign Corporation.

Each foreign corporation authorized to transact business in this State shall have and continuously maintain in this State:

(a)   A registered office which may be, but need not be, the same as its place of business in this State.

(b)   A registered agent, which agent may be either an individual resident in this State whose business office is identical with such registered office, or a domestic corporation, or a foreign corporation authorized to transact business in this State, having a business office identical with such registered office.

Section 114.   Change of Registered Office or Registered Agent of Foreign Corporation.

A foreign corporation authorized to transact business in this State may change its registered office or change its registered agent, or both, upon filing in the office of the Secretary of State a statement setting forth:

(a) The name of the corporation.

(b) The address of its then registered office.

(c) If the address of its registered office be changed, the address to which the registered office is to be changed.

(d) The name of its then registered agent.

(e) If its registered agent be changed, the name of its successor registered agent.

(f) That the address of its registered office and the address of the business office of its registered agent, as changed, will be identical.

(g) That such change was authorized by resolution duly adopted by its board of directors.

Such statement shall be executed by the corporation by its president or a vice president, and verified by him, and delivered to the Secretary of State. If the Secretary of State finds that such statement conforms to the provisions of this Act, he shall file such statement in his office, and upon such filing the change of address of the registered office, or the appointment of a new registered agent, or both, as the case may be, shall become effective.

Any registered agent of a foreign corporation may resign as such agent upon filing a written notice thereof, executed in duplicate, with the Secretary of State, who shall forthwith mail a copy thereof to the corporation at its principal office in the state or country under the laws of which it is incorporated. The appointment of such agent shall terminate upon the expiration of thirty days after receipt of such notice by the Secretary of State.

If a registered agent changes his or its business address to another place within the same . . . .*, he or it may change such address and the address of the registered office of any corporation of which he or it is registered agent by filing a statement as required above except that it need be signed only by the registered agent and need not be responsive to (e) or (g) and must recite that a copy of the statement has been mailed to the corporation.

Section 115. Service of Process on Foreign Corporation.

The registered agent so appointed by a foreign corporation authorized to transact business in this State shall be an agent of such corporation upon whom any proc-

ess, notice or demand required or permitted by law to be served upon the corporation may be served.

Whenever a foreign corporation authorized to transact business in this State shall fail to appoint or maintain a registered agent in this State, or whenever any such registered agent cannot with reasonable diligence be found at the registered office, or whenever the certificate of authority of a foreign corporation shall be suspended or revoked, then the Secretary of State shall be an agent of such corporation upon whom any such process, notice, or demand may be served. Service on the Secretary of State of any such process, notice or demand shall be made by delivering to and leaving with him, or with any clerk having charge of the corporation department of his office, duplicate copies of such process, notice or demand. In the event any such process, notice or demand is served on the Secretary of State, he shall immediately cause one of such copies thereof to be forwarded by registered mail, addressed to the corporation at its principal office in the state or country under the laws of which it is incorporated. Any service so had on the Secretary of State shall be returnable in not less than thirty days.

The Secretary of State shall keep a record of all processes, notices and demands served upon him under this section, and shall record therein the time of such service and his action with reference thereto.

Nothing herein contained shall limit or affect the right to serve any process, notice or demand, required or permitted by law to be served upon a foreign corporation in any other manner now or hereafter permitted by law.

Section 116. Amendment to Articles of Incorporation of Foreign Corporation (Text omitted).

Section 117. Merger of Foreign Corporation Authorized to Transact Business in This State (Text omitted).

Section 118. Amended Certificate of Authority (Text omitted).

Section 119. Withdrawal of Foreign Corporation (Text omitted).

Section 120. Filing of Application for Withdrawal (Text omitted).

---

*Supply designation of jurisdiction, such as county, etc., in accordance with local practice.

Section 121. Revocation of Certificate of Authority *(Text omitted).*

Section 122. Issuance of Certificate of Revocation *(Text omitted).*

Section 123. Application to Corporations Heretofore Authorized to Transact Business in This State *(Text omitted).*

Section 124. Transacting Business without Certificate of Authority.

No foreign corporation transacting business in this State without a certificate of authority shall be permitted to maintain any action, suit or proceeding in any court of this State, until such corporation shall have obtained a certificate of authority. Nor shall any action, suit or proceeding be maintained in any court of this State by any successor or assignee of such corporation on any right, claim or demand arising out of the transaction of business by such corporation in this State, until a certificate of authority shall have been obtained by such corporation or by a corporation which has acquired all or substantially all of its assets.

The failure of a foreign corporation to obtain a certificate of authority to transact business in this State shall not impair the validity of any contract or act of such corporation, and shall not prevent such corporation from defending any action, suit or proceeding in any court of this State.

A foreign corporation which transacts business in this State without a certificate of authority shall be liable to this State, for the years or parts thereof during which it transacted business in this State without a certificate of authority, in an amount equal to all fees and franchise taxes which would have been imposed by this Act upon such corporation had it duly applied for and received a certificate of authority to transact business in this State as required by this Act and thereafter failed all reports required by this Act, plus all penalties imposed by this Act for failure to pay such fees and franchise taxes. The Attorney General shall bring proceedings to recover all amounts due this State under the provisions of this Section.

Section 125. Annual Report of Domestic and Foreign Corporations.

Each domestic corporation, and each foreign corporation authorized to transact business in this State, shall file, within the time prescribed by this Act, an annual report setting forth:

(a) The name of the corporation and the state or country under the laws of which it is incorporated.

(b) The address of the registered office of the corporation in this State, and the name of its registered agent in this State at such address, and, in case of a foreign corporation, the address of its principal office in the state or country under the laws of which it is incorporated.

(c) A brief statement of the character of the business in which the corporation is actually engaged in this State.

(d) The names and respective addresses of the directors and officers of the corporation.

(e) A statement of the aggregate number of shares which the corporation has authority to issue, itemized by classes, par value of shares, shares without par value, and series, if any, within a class.

(f) A statement of the aggregate number of issued shares, itemized by classes, par value of shares, shares without par value, and series, if any, within a class.

(g) A statement, expressed in dollars, of the amount of stated capital of the corporation, as defined in this Act.

(h) A statement, expressed in dollars, of the value of all the property owned by the corporation, wherever located, and the value of the property of the corporation located within this State, and a statement, expressed in dollars, of the gross amount of business transacted by the corporation for the twelve months ended on the thirty-first day of December preceding the date herein provided for the filing of such report and the gross amount thereof transacted by the corporation at or from places of business in this State. If, on the thirty-first day of December preceding the time herein provided for the filing of such report, the corporation had not been in existence for a period of twelve months, or in the case of a foreign corporation had not been authorized to transact business in this State for a period of twelve months, the statement with respect to business transacted shall be furnished for the period between the date of incorporation or the date of its authorization to transact business in this State, as the case may be, and such thirty-first day of December. If all the property of the corporation is located in this State and all of its business is transacted at or from places of business in this State, or if the corporation elects to pay the annual franchise tax on the basis of its entire stated capital, then the information required by this subparagraph need not be set forth in such report.

(i) Such additional information as may be necessary or appropriate in order to enable the Secretary of State to determine and assess the proper amount of franchise taxes payable by such corporation.

Such annual report shall be made on forms prescribed and furnished by the Secretary of State, and the information therein contained shall be given as of the date of the execution of the report, except as to the information required by subparagraphs (g), (h) and (i) which shall be given as of the close of business on the thirty-first day of December next preceding the date herein provided for the filing of such report. It shall be executed by the corporation by its president, a vice president, secretary, an assistant secretary, or treasurer, and verified by the officer executing the report, or, if the corporation is in the hands of a receiver or trustee, it shall be executed on behalf of the corporation and verified by such receiver or trustee.

Section 126.   Filing of Annual Report of Domestic and Foreign Corporations *(Text omitted).*

Section 127.   Fees, Franchise Taxes and Charges to be Collected by Secretary of State *(Text omitted).*

Section 128.   Fees for Filing Documents and Issuing Certificates *(Text omitted).*

Section 129.   Miscellaneous Charges *(Text omitted).*

Section 130.   License Fees Payable by Domestic Corporations *(Text omitted).*

Section 131.   License Fees Payable by Foreign Corporations *(Text omitted).*

Section 132.   Franchise Taxes Payable by Domestic Corporations *(Text omitted).*

Section 133.   Franchise Taxes Payable by Foreign Corporations *(Text omitted).*

Section 134.   Assessment and Collection of Annual Franchise Taxes *(Text omitted).*

Section 135.   Penalties Imposed upon Corporations *(Text omitted).*

Section 136.   Penalties Imposed upon Officers and Directors.

Each officer and director of a corporation, domestic or foreign, who fails or refuses within the time prescribed by this Act to answer truthfully and fully interrogatories propounded to him by the Secretary of State in accordance with the provisions of this Act, or who signs any articles, statement, report, application or other document filed with the Secretary of State which is known to such officer or director to be false in any material respect, shall be deemed to be guilty of a misdemeanor, and upon conviction thereof may be fined in any amount not exceeding . . . . dollars.

Section 137.   Interrogatories by Secretary of State.

Secretary of State may propound to any corporation, domestic or foreign, subject to the provisions of this Act, and to any officer or director thereof, such interrogatories as may be reasonably necessary and proper to enable him to ascertain whether such corporation has complied with all the provisions of this Act applicable to such corporation. Such interrogatories shall be answered within thirty days after the mailing thereof, or within such additional time as shall be fixed by the Secretary of State, and the answers thereto shall be full and complete and shall be made in writing and under oath. If such interrogatories be directed to an individual they shall be answered by him, and if directed to a corporation they shall be answered by the president, vice president, secretary or assistant secretary thereof. The Secretary of State need not file any document to which such interrogatories relate until such interrogatories be answered as herein provided, and not then if the answers thereto disclose that such document is not in conformity with the provisions of this Act. The Secretary of State shall certify to the Attorney General, for such action as the Attorney General may deem appropriate, all interrogatories and answers thereto which disclose a violation of any of the provisions of this Act.

Section 138.   Information Disclosed by Interrogatories.

Interrogatories propounded by the Secretary of State and the answers thereto shall not be open to public inspection nor shall the Secretary of State disclose any facts or information obtained therefrom except insofar as his official duty may require the same to be made public or in the event such interrogatories or the answers thereto are required for evidence in any criminal proceedings or in any other action by this State.

Section 139.   Power of Secretary of State.

The Secretary of State shall have the power and authority reasonably necessary to enable him to administer this Act efficiently and to perform the duties therein imposed upon him.

Section 140. Appeal from Secretary of State *(Text omitted).*

Section 141. Certificates and Certified Copies to Be Received in Evidence *(Text omitted).*

Section 142. Forms to Be Furnished by Secretary of State *(Text omitted).*

Section 143. Greater Voting Requirements.

Whenever, with respect to any action to be taken by the shareholders of a corporation, the articles of incorporation require the vote or concurrence of the holders of a greater proportion of the shares, or of any class or series thereof, than required by this Act with respect to such action, the provisions of the articles in incorporation shall control.

Section 144. Waiver of Notice.

Whenever any notice is required to be given to any shareholder or director of a corporation under the provisions of this Act or under the provisions of the articles of incorporation or by-laws of the corporation, a waiver thereof in writing signed by the person or persons entitled to such notice, whether before or after the time stated therein, shall be equivalent to the giving of such notice.

Section 145. Action by Shareholders without a Meeting.

Any action required by this Act to be taken at a meeting of the shareholders of a corporation, or any action which may be taken at a meeting of the shareholders, may be taken without a meeting if a consent in writing, setting forth the action so taken, shall be signed by all of the shareholders entitled to vote with respect to the subject matter thereof.

Such consent shall have the same effect as a unanimous vote of shareholders, and may be stated as such in any articles or document filed with the Secretary of State under this Act.

Section 146. Unauthorized Assumption of Corporate Powers.

All persons who assume to act as a corporation without authority so to do shall be jointly and severally liable for all debts and liabilities incurred or arising as a result thereof.

Section 147. Application to Existing Corporations *(Text omitted).*

Section 148. Application to Foreign and Interstate Commerce *(Text omitted).*

Section 149. Reservation of Power.

The . . . . . .* shall at all times have power to prescribe such regulations, provisions and limitations as it may deem advisable, which regulations, provisions and limitations shall be binding upon any and all corporations subject to the provisions of this Act, and the . . . . . .* shall have power to amend, repeal or modify this Act at pleasure.

Section 150. Effect of Repeal of Prior Acts *(Text omitted).*

Section 151. Effect of Invalidity of Part of This Act *(Text omitted).*

Section 152. Repeal of Prior Acts *(Text omitted).*

---

*Insert name of legislative body.

Appendix | E

Public Law 95-213—
"Foreign Corrupt Practices
Act of 1977"—Title I

TITLE I—FOREIGN CORRUPT PRACTICES

Short Title

Sec. 101. This title may be cited as the "Foreign Corrupt Practices Act of 1977".

Accounting Standards

Sec. 102. Section 13(b) of the Securities Exchange Act of 1934 (15 U.S.C. 78q(b)) is amended by inserting "(1)" after "(b)" and by adding at the end thereof the following:

"(2) Every issuer which has a class of securities registered pursuant to section 12 of this title and every issuer which is required to file reports pursuant to section 15(d) of this title shall—

"(A) make and keep books, records, and accounts, which, in reasonable detail, accurately and fairly reflect the transactions and dispositions of the assets of the issuer; and

"(B) devise and maintain a system of internal accounting controls sufficient to provide reasonable assurances that—

"(i) transactions are executed in accordance with management's general or specific authorization;

"(ii) transactions are recorded as necessary (I) to permit preparation of financial statements in conformity with generally accepted accounting principles or any other criteria applicable to such statements, and (II) to maintain accountability for assets;

"(iii) access to assets is permitted only in accordance with management's general or specific authorization; and

"(iv) the recorded accountability for assets is compared with the existing assets at reasonable intervals and appropriate action is taken with respect to any differences.

"(3)(A) With respect to matters concerning the national security of the United States, no duty or liability under paragraph (2) of this subsection shall be imposed upon any person acting in cooperation with the head of any Federal department or agency responsible for such matters if such act in cooperation with such head of a department or agency was done upon the specific, written directive of the head of such department or agency pursuant to Presidential authority to issue such directives. Each directive issued under this paragraph shall set forth the specific facts and circumstances with respect to which the provisions of this paragraph are to be invoked. Each such directive shall, unless renewed in writing, expire one year after the date of issuance.

"(B) Each head of a Federal department or agency of

the United States who issues a directive pursuant to this paragraph shall maintain a complete file of all such directives and shall, on October 1 of each year, transmit a summary of matters covered by such directives in force at any time during the previous year to the Permanent Select Committee on Intelligence of the House of Representatives and the Select Committee on Intelligence of the Senate."

Foreign Corrupt Practices
By Issuers

Sec. 103. (a) The Securities Exchange Act of 1934 is amended by inserting after section 30 the following new section:

"Foreign Corrupt Practices
By Issuers

"Sec. 30A. (a) It shall be unlawful for any issuer which has a class of securities registered pursuant to section 12 of this title or which is required to file reports under section 15(d) of this title, or for any officer, director, employee, or agent of such issuer or any stockholder thereof acting on behalf of such issuer, to make use of the mails or any means or instrumentality of interstate commerce corruptly in furtherance of an offer, payment, promise to pay, or authorization of the payment of any money, or offer, gift, promise to give, or authorization of the giving of anything of value to—

"(1) any foreign official for purposes of—

"(A) influencing any act or decision of such foreign official in his official capacity, including a decision to fail to perform his official functions; or

"(B) inducing such foreign official to use his influences with a foreign government or instrumentality thereof to affect or influence any act or decision of such government or instrumentality,

in order to assist such issuer in obtaining or retaining business for or with, or directing business to, any person;

"(2) any foreign political party or official thereof or any candidate for foreign political office for purposes of—

"(A) influencing any act or decision of such party, official, or candidate in its or his official capacity, including a decision to fail to perform its or his official functions; or

"(B) inducing such party, official, or candidate to use

his or its influence with a foreign government or instrumentality thereof to affect or influence any act or decision of such government or instrumentality,

in order to assist such issuer in obtaining or retaining business for or with, or directing business to, any person; or

"(3) any person, while knowing or having reason to know that all or a portion of such money or thing of value will be offered, given, or promised, directly or indirectly, to any foreign official, to any foreign political party or official thereof, or to any candidate for foreign political office, for purposes of—

"(A) influencing any act or decision of such foreign official, political party, party official, or candidate in his or its official capacity, including a decision to fail to perform his or its official functions; or

"(B) inducing such foreign official, political party, party official, or candidate to use his or its influence with a foreign government or instrumentality thereof to affect or influence any act or decision of such government or instrumentality,

in order to assist such issuer in obtaining or retaining business for or with, or directing business to, any person;

"(b) As used in this section, the term 'foreign official' means any officer or employee of a foreign government or any department, agency, or instrumentality thereof, or any person acting in an official capacity for or on behalf of such government or department, agency, or instrumentality. Such term does not include any employee of a foreign government or any department, agency, or instrumentality thereof whose duties are essentially ministerial or clerical."

(b)(1) Section 32(a) of the Securities Exchange Act of 1934 (15 U.S.C. 78ff(a) is amended by inserting "(other than section 30A)" immediately after "title" the first place it appears.

(2) Section 32 of the Securities Exchange Act of 1934 (15 U.S.C. 78ff) is amended by adding at the end thereof the following new subsection:

"(c)(1) Any issuer which violates section 30A(a) of this title shall, upon conviction, be fined not more than $1,000,000.

"(2) Any officer or director of an issuer, or any stockholder acting on behalf of such issuer, who willfully violates section 30A(a) of this title shall, upon conviction, be fined not more than $10,000, or imprisoned not more than five years, or both.

"(3) Whenever an issuer is found to have violated section 30A(a) of this title, any employee or agent of such issuer who is a United States citizen, national, or resident or is otherwise subject to the jurisdiction of the United States (other than an officer, director, or stockholder of such issuer), and who willfully carried out the act or practice constituting such violation shall, upon conviction, be fined not more than $10,000, or imprisoned not more than five years, or both.

"(4) Whenever a fine is imposed under paragraph (2) or (3) of this subsection upon any officer, director, stockholder, employee, or agent of an issuer, such fine shall not be paid, directly or indirectly, by such issuer."

Foreign Corrupt Practices By Domestic Concerns

Sec. 104. (a) It shall be unlawful for any domestic concern, other than an issuer which is subject to section 30A of the Securities Exchange Act of 1934, or any officer, director, employee, or agent of such domestic concern or any stockholder thereof acting on behalf of such domestic concern, to make use of the mails or any means or instrumentality of interstate commerce corruptly in furtherance of an offer, payment, promise to pay, or authorization of the payment of any money, or offer, gift, promise to give, or authorization of the giving of anything of value to—

(1) any foreign official for purposes of—

(A) influencing any act or decision of such foreign official in his official capacity, including a decision to fail to perform his official functions; or

(B) inducing such foreign official to use his influence with a foreign government or instrumentality thereof to affect or influence any act or decision of such government or instrumentality,

in order to assist such domestic concern in obtaining or retaining business for or with, or directing business to, any person;

(2) any foreign political party or official thereof or any candidate for foreign political office for purposes of—

(A) influencing any act or decision of such party, official, or candidate in its or his official capacity, including a decision to fail to perform its or his official functions; or

(B) inducing such party, official, or candidate to use its or his influence with a foreign government or instrumentality thereof to affect or influence any act or decision of such government or instrumentality,

in order to assist such domestic concern in obtaining or retaining business for or with, or directing business to, any person; or

(3) any person, while knowing or having reason to know that all or a portion of such money or thing of value will be offered, given, or promised, directly or indirectly, to any foreign official, to any foreign political party or official thereof, or to any candidate for foreign political office, for purposes of—

(A) influencing any act or decision of such foreign official, political party, party official, or candidate in his or its official capacity, including a decision to fail to perform his or its official functions; or

(B) inducing such foreign official, political party, party official, or candidate to use his or its influence with a foreign government or instrumentality thereof to affect or influence any act or decision of such government or instrumentality,

in order to assist such domestic concern in obtaining or retaining business for or with, or directing business to, any person.

(b)(1)(A) Except as provided in subparagraph (B), any domestic concern which violates subsection (a) shall, upon conviction, be fined not more than $1,000,000.

(B) Any individual who is a domestic concern and who willfully violates subsection (a) shall, upon conviction, be fined not more than $10,000, or imprisoned not more than five years, or both.

(2) Any officer or director of a domestic concern, or stockholder acting on behalf of such domestic concern, who willfully violates subsection (a) shall, upon conviction, be fined not more than $10,000, or imprisoned not more than five years, or both.

(3) Whenever a domestic concern is found to have violated subsection (a) of this section, any employee or agent of such domestic concern who is a United States citizen, national, or resident or is otherwise subject to the jurisdiction of the United States (other than an officer, director, or stockholder acting on behalf of such domestic concern), and who willfully crried out the act or practice constituting such violation shall, upon conviction, be fined not more than $10,000, or imprisoned not more than five years, or both.

(4) Whenever a fine is imposed under paragraph (2) or (3) of this subsection upon any officer, director, stockholder, employee, or agent of a domestic concern, such fine shall not be paid, directly or indirectly, by such domestic concern.

(c) Whenever it appears to the Attorney General that any domestic concern, or officer, director, employee, agent, or stockholder thereof, is engaged, or is about to engage, in any act or practice constituting a violation of subsection (a) of this section, the Attorney General may, in his discretion, bring a civil action in an appropriate district court of the United States to enjoin such act or practice, and upon a proper showing a permanent or temporary injunction or a temporary restraining order shall be granted without bond.

(d) As used in this section:

(1) The term "domestic concern" means (A) any individual who is a citizen, national, or resident of the United States; or (B) any corporation, partnership, association, joint-stock company, business trust, unincorporated organization, or sole proprietorship which has its principal place of business in the United States, or which is organized under the laws of a State of the United States or a territory, possession, or commonwealth of the United States.

(2) The term "foreign official" means any officer or employee of a foreign government or any department, agency, or instrumentality thereof, or any person acting in an official capacity for or on behalf of any such government or department, agency, or instrumentality. Such term does not include any employee of a foreign government or any department, agency, or instrumentality thereof whose duties are essentially ministerial or clerical.

(3) The term "interstate commerce" means trade, commerce, transportation, or communication among the several States, or between any foreign country and any State or between any State and any place or ship outside thereof. Such term includes the intrastate use of (A) a telephone or other interstate means of communication, or (B) any other interstate instrumentality.

Glossary

Abandonment. An owner's voluntary relinquishment of the possession of an item of personal property, with the owner exercising no further interest or control.

Abstract of title. A historical record of the title to a parcel of land, including all changes in the chain of title and all liens and encumbrances recorded against the parcel.

Acceptance. An offeree's manifestation of assent to the terms of an offer made to him or her by an offeror. The acceptance is the act, the oral or written assent, or in certain instances the silence that creates contractual liabilities for both the offeror and the offeree.

Accession. The acquisition of title to something because it has been added to the property one owns. For example, a tenant plants shrubs and trees on the owner's land, and the owner thus acquires title by accession.

Accommodation party. A cosigner to a credit transaction who signs without receiving any payment or value therefor, merely to help a person get credit.

Accord. A new contract which replaces another contract.

Accord and satisfaction. Two persons agree that one of them has a right of action against the other, but they accept a substitute or different act or value as performance.

Account. Any right to payment for goods sold, leased, or delivered or for services performed. Also referred to as an account receivable.

Accretion. Adding to the boundaries of property naturally by gradual deposits of silt, sand, or other solid material. For example, a river deposits sand and silt and builds up the land on its sides.

Acknowledgment. A formally signed statement (usually before a notary public) denoting the execution of a particular legal document.

Act of God. In civil law, an unforeseen accident or casualty caused strictly by the forces of nature, such as flood, drought, and hurricane.

Action. Something that is done; conduct; behavior; In legal terms, a court proceeding for the enforcement of rights.

Adjudication. The pronouncement of a judgment or a decree; a final court determination. (In bankruptcy cases, the proclaiming that a debtor is a bankrupt.)

Administrator, administratrix. In probate law, a person appointed by the court to distribute the property and belongings of the deceased where there was no will. (Administrator refers to a man; administratrix refers to a woman.)

Affiant. A person who subscribes to or makes an affidavit.

Affidavit. A printed or written statement or declaration made under oath before an authorized public official, usually a notary public.

Agency. A contractual relationship whereby the principal contracts with another to act for and on behalf of the principal as an agent and to bind the principal in contract.

Air rights, airspace. Ascertainment of the ownership of the airspace (sky) above one's land.

Alien. Born in one country and residing in another country without being admitted to citizenship in that country.

Alimony. An allowance granted from the husband or wife to his or her spouse, who is living separately or legally divorced. (Laws regarding alimony differ among the states.)

Allegation. The statement or declaration made in a pleading in which a party points out the facts that the party intends to prove.

Amicus curiae. A Latin phrase which means "a friend of the court." An amicus curiae would be a person with a strong interest in the case and the legal principles involved who requests permission to file a legal brief giving his or her views to the court.

Amnesty. In international law, the act of absolution for past offensive acts ("burying the hatchet").

Annuity. In insurance policies, an amount paid periodically to the insured for a specified period or until the death of the insured.

Answer. The defendant's response to the plaintiff's petition or complaint.

Anticipatory breach. Before the performance time on a contract is due, one party announces that he or she will not perform his or her part of the contract, thus giving the nonbreaching party an opportunity to seek a remedy in the courts.

Apparent authority. The assumed authority or permission, not actually granted, which a principal knowingly permits an agent to possess when dealing with a third person.

Appellant. The party appealing to a higher court to overrule a decision made by a lower court.

Appellee. The party against whom an appeal is made; the respondent.

Arbitration. To settle a dispute, an appointed arbitrator (third person) comes in to help the parties make an out-of-court decision. This saves the time and expense of litigation.

Arbitrator. A third person in a dispute who acts as the arbiter (umpire).

Articles of incorporation. A legal document submitted to a designated officer of the state for permission to commence business as a corporation. The articles of incorporation or the corporate charter state the purpose, rights, and duties of the corporation and must comply with state corporation laws.

Articles of partnership. An agreement drawn up to govern a business to be operated by a partnership. The agreement need not be filed with any state official.

Artisan's lien. A possessory claim levied on goods owned by another because of improvements made or work done thereon by the artisan. An artisan is a skilled tradesperson, such as a carpenter or a plumber.

Assignee. The person to whom an assignment is made.

Assignment. A transfer of rights (usually contract rights) from an assignor to an assignee.

Assignor. The person who makes an assignment.

Attachment. The seizure through legal process by proper legal authority, usually the sheriff, of nonexempt property of the defendant, pending a lawsuit for the collection of a debt owed by the defendant to a creditor.

Attestation. The act of witnessing the signing of a legal document.

Attractive nuisance. Any dangerous object or condition on real property which is inviting to children of tender years and tempts them to trespass.

Auction with reserve. A sale whereby the goods sold may be withdrawn before the actual bid is accepted by the owner.

Auction without reserve. An auction sale wherein goods are sold to the highest bidder with no chance of withdrawal by the owner when the goods have been placed on the auction block.

Bailee. A person who receives personal property under contract of bailment.

Bailment. The temporary transfer of possession of personal property without a change of ownership for a specific purpose and with the intent that possession will revert to the owner at a later date. Example: Owner gives his or her car to a mechanic for repairs; owner will get the car back when it has been repaired.

Bailor. A person who entrusts or bails personal property to another under a contract of bailment.

Bankrupt. An insolvent person, one who has been declared by the court to have more debts than assets.

Bankruptcy. When a person is bankrupt, the court proceeds to have that person's nonexempt assets distributed to his or her creditors and releases him or her from further payment of past debts.

Bearer. A person in possession of a security instrument or a document of title payable to the bearer or indorsed in blank.

Beneficiary. A person receiving proceeds from a will,

insurance policy, trust, or third-party beneficiary contract.

Bilateral contract. A contract formed by the mutual exchange of promises between an offeror and an offeree.

Bilateral mistake. Both parties to a contract are in error as to the terms of the contract or the performance expected.

Bill of lading. A formal document issued by a carrier of goods to a shipper of goods. This document identifies the goods and states the terms of the shipping agreement.

Binder. A guarantee of temporary insurance coverage while the policy is being issued.

Blue-sky laws. State regulatory and supervisory laws governing investment companies to avoid fraudulent sales to investors in get-rich-quick schemes.

Board of directors. A specific number of persons elected by a corporation's stockholders to manage and govern the corporation on their behalf.

Bona fide. With good faith or in good faith.

Bond. With regard to corporate financing, a legal instrument which is evidence of a corporation's debt to the bondholder. The instrument obligates the corporation to pay the bondholder a fixed rate of interest on the principal amount and to pay the principal to the bondholder at a fixed maturity date.

Broker. In real property law, a person who acts as an agent and representative of others to negotiate the purchase and sale of real estate.

Bulk transfer. A sale or transfer of all or the major portion of the total inventory of materials, supplies, or merchandise or other inventory not in the ordinary course of the transferor's business.

C&F. Cost plus freight.

Cause of action. The legal grounds needed to successfully pursue a lawsuit in court.

Caveat emptor. A Latin phrase which means "let the buyer beware."

Certiorari. A Latin term which means "to be informed of." It is a writ or certification by which an appellate court orders a review of a case from a lower court. The lower court must then send a certified record of the case to the appellate court.

Chancery court. A court of equity.

Charter. A grant or certification from a state to a corporation granting the corporation the right to operate its business. In maritime law, the leasing or hiring of a vessel.

Chattel. A term used to describe tangible and movable personal property.

Chattel mortgage. A mortgage showing that another person besides the title holder has an interest (lien) on the personal property.

Chattel paper. A writing which shows that there is both a monetary obligation and a security interest in specific goods.

CIF. Cost, insurance, and freight.

COD. Cash on delivery.

Collateral. Something of value, either real or personal property, which a creditor can convert into cash to pay off a debt if the debtor fails to pay the debt. For example, you borrow money from a bank and the bank has you pledge your household furniture as collateral.

Common carrier. A carrier which holds itself out as being for hire to the general public for the transportation of goods and passengers for compensation.

Common law. Written or unwritten laws which have evolved through custom and usage (from English common law) without written legislation.

Common stock. A class of corporate stock which is usually the voting stock in a corporation. Common stockholders have a right to dividends and assets upon dissolution second only to that of preferred stockholders, if any.

Composition agreement. An agreement whereby an insolvent debtor pays each of the creditors a portion of what he or she owes them in return for a release from them for the whole debt.

Condition. A qualifying or limiting provision or clause in a contract which must be taken into consideration by all of the parties involved.

Conditional sales contract. A contract which covers the sale of goods or real estate wherein the seller retains title until the buyer makes the payment in full; however, the buyer has possession and use while he or she makes the payments.

Consignment. The transfer of personal property from one person to another for the purpose of transportation or sale. The owner retains ownership of the property.

Consumer goods. Products primarily purchased for home or private and family use.

Consumer Product Safety Act. This act established the Consumer Product Safety Commission, which oversees the safety of consumer-oriented products.

Contract carrier. A private carrier which transports goods for an individual but not for the general public.

Conveyance. A written instrument which transfers an interest in real property, ordinarily by the execution and delivery of a deed. Personal property can also be conveyed, and this is ordinarily done by a bill of sale.

Corporate express powers. Powers specifically set out in the corporation's articles of incorporation and in statutes.

Corporate implied powers. Those powers reasonable and necessary to carry out the corporation's express powers.

Corporation. A legal entity created by authority of statutory law upon application to a proper state authority. This legal entity is an artificial person with the right to sue or be sued in its own name and to purchase, own, and sell property, real and personal, tangible and intangible.

Counterclaim. In a civil suit, the claim which the defendant makes in opposition to the plaintiff's claim.

Counteroffer. A counterproposal different from an offer which an offeree makes in response to the offer. In making a counteroffer, the offeree rejects the previous offer.

Course of dealing. When two parties have previously been involved in a contract matter, their past performance may be used as a basis for interpreting ambiguities, if any, in the present contract.

Covenant. A contractual promise contained in a deed, mortgage, lease, or contract.

Creditor. A person to whom money or performance is owed.

D/b/a. Doing business as.

Damages. Monetary harm or monetary loss caused by wrongdoing that the injured person may recover in court.

De facto. A Latin phrase which means "in fact." A de facto corporation has not "in fact" complied with the laws of a state, and therefore its existence can be challenged by the state.

De jure corporation. A de jure corporation is one which has been rightfully formed in full compliance with the laws of a state.

De novo. (Latin) Starting anew.

Debtor. One who owes payment or performance.

Deceit. Fraudulent misrepresentation of facts intended to mislead or trick another, which in turn causes financial loss or harm.

Deed. A legal instrument which evidences property ownership.

Defamation. The act of intentionally injuring the character or reputation of another person.

Default. The failure to perform a legal obligation or duty.

Defendant. The person who is being sued in a legal action.

Deficiency judgment. A personal judgment against a debtor in default, where the value of the secured property was not equal to the amount of the indebtedness.

Demurrer. This is a pleading which disputes the legal sufficiency of the other party's pleading. It is also referred to as a motion to dismiss for the failure to state a legal cause of action.

Deposition. Testimony which is taken under oath and subject to cross-examination in order to discover what the witness is going to say and to ensure the preservation of the witness's testimony should the witness die or disappear or forget before the trial.

Derivative suit. An action filed by one or more stockholders of a corporation under the corporation name to enforce a corporate cause of action.

Devise. To give a gift of property by will.

Directed verdict. A verdict that the jury returns as directed by the judge.

Discharge. The termination of a contractual obligation regarding the payment of money or the performance of an act.

Disclaimer. A repudiation or denial of a claim or obligation.

Dissolution. The process by which a corporation or partnership terminates its existence.

Dividend. The portion of corporate profits which is distributed periodically to stockholders.

Document of title. A warehouse receipt, a bill of lading, or any other paper which is evidence of the holder's right to have the goods it covers.

Domestic corporation. A corporation doing business in the state where its incorporation took place.

Donee. A person who receives a gift.

Donor. A person who gives a gift.

Draft. A legal instrument wherein one person orders another person to pay a third party a sum of money.

Duress. Coercion, threat, or force which causes a

person to do something he or she would not have done otherwise.

Earnest money. Money advanced on a contract by a buyer to bind a seller to his or her obligation. This money is given as an indication of good faith by the buyer and usually will be forfeited if the buyer does not perform.

Easement. The right to use the land of another for a special purpose (such as an easement to lay power lines.)

Emancipation. Setting free; release. This term is used with reference to the release of a child from the care and custody of his or her parents before the child reaches the age of majority.

Eminent domain. The government's right to take over private property for public use with just compensation.

Estoppel. This is a rule of law which bars, prevents, and precludes a party from alleging or denying certain facts because of a previous allegation or denial or because of his or her previous conduct or admission.

Eviction. The legal process of removing a tenant from a landlord's property.

Ex contractu. A Latin phrase which means a right arising out of a contract.

Ex delicto. A Latin phrase which refers to a right arising out of a tort.

Ex post facto law. A law passed to punish wrongdoers, which is alleged to apply to acts committed before its passage. Such laws are unconstitutional. Criminal laws may only apply to acts committed after their passage.

Executor, executrix. The person named in a last will and testament to administer the estate of the deceased. *Executor* is the term used if the person is a male, and *executrix* is the term used if the person is a female.

Express authority. The authority which a principal gives to an agent either in writing or orally.

Factor. A person or a legal entity that is employed as an agent to sell goods for a principal. Usually the factor is given possession of the goods for sale and sells them in his or her own name. The factor then receives a commission on the sale.

Fair market value. The price that a willing buyer is willing to pay and that a willing seller will accept for real or personal property.

FAS. An abbreviation of the phrase "free alongside steamer."

Fee simple. Absolute ownership of a specific tract of real estate. This gives the owner the unconditional power to dispose of the property during his or her lifetime and to pass the absolute ownership on to his or her heirs at death.

Felony. A statutory criminal offense which is more serious than a misdemeanor. Felonies are punishable by fine or imprisonment or both, and in some situations, by death.

Fiduciary. A person who handles another person's money or property in a capacity that involves a confidence or trust. Examples of fiduciaries are executors or guardians of the estates of minors or deceased persons.

Fixture. An article of personal property which has been affixed to real property with the intent that it become a permanent part of the real property.

FOB. An abbreviation of the phrase "free on board." This phrase means that the seller or consignor of goods will place them on board a carrier such as a train or truck at a designated place with instructions to ship them through to a designated destination. The expenses of the shipping and insurance for the trip are to be paid by the buyer or consignee, and thus the shipping and insurance free to the seller or consignor.

Foreclosure. The legal process used to enforce the payment of a debt secured by a mortgage whereby the secured property is sold to satisfy the debt.

Foreign corporation. A corporation doing business in a state other than the state in which it was incorporated. *Foreign* does not mean from outside the country, only from outside the particular state.

Forensic medicine. Medical jurisprudence; the science of applying medical knowledge to the law.

Forgery. Falsely making or materially altering with criminal intent a legal document such as a check, power of attorney, or deed.

Franchise. In the public sector, a franchise is a right to operate a certain essential business which a city, county, state, or national authority grants to a private entity. For example, a city grants a bus company a franchise to be the sole bus company that can operate within the city, or it grants an electric company a franchise to be the exclusive supplier of electricity to the city. In the private sector, a franchise is a means by which one person can grant another person the right to use his or her name and use his or her business expertise on a contract basis. Examples include the various fast-food franchises.

Fraud. An intentional concealment or misrepresentation of a material fact with the intent to deceive another person, which concealment or misrepresentation causes damage to the deceived person. Such deceived persons may then sue for their damages, provided they can show that they justifiably relied upon such misrepresentation or concealment and that such reliance caused the damage.

Fungible goods. Goods that if mixed cannot be individually identified, one unit of which is equivalent to any other unit. For example, the milk from five dairy farms is pumped into a storage tank. Each farmer owns the number of gallons taken from him or her but cannot identify the specific milk that he or she contributed once it is mixed with the rest.

Future advances clause. A clause found in security agreements which permits the collateral of the debtor, if sufficiently valuable, to be used to secure future loans.

Garnishment. A legal proceeding whereby a creditor can secure the payment of a judgment against a debtor by securing a court order which requires an employer or other person having funds belonging to the debtor to pay such funds directly to the creditor.

Gift causa mortis. (Latin) A gift which is given in contemplation of death, usually with the understanding that the gift will be returned if the donor survives.

Gift inter vivos. (Latin) An irrevocable gift which is given during the donor's lifetime.

Grantee. The person to whom a conveyance of real property is made.

Grantor. The person by whom a conveyance of real property is made.

Guarantee. A promise by one person to pay some or all of the debts of another person or to answer for the performance of some act or acts by another person.

Heirs. The persons designated by the intestate law of a state to inherit the estate of a deceased where the deceased left no will.

Illusory. Like an illusion, something that seems to be so but really isn't so. An illusory promise appears to be a binding promise but actually promises nothing, as the choice of performance or nonperformance is really left up to the promisor.

Indemnity contract. A contract whereby one party contracts to compensate another party in case of a loss. A fire insurance contract is an indemnity contract.

Indorsement. The signing of one's name on a negotiable instrument such as a check or draft for the purpose of passing title to the instrument to another person. Usually the indorsement is on the back of the instrument.

Infant. A person who has not reached the legal age of majority.

Injunction. An order of a court of equity that tells a person to do or to refrain from doing some act or acts.

In re. A Latin phrase which means "in the matter of." The phrase precedes the name of the party involved in estate and guardian's matters and other non-adversary judicial proceedings. For example: In re Estate of John Jones, Deceased.

In rem. A Latin phrase which means "against the thing."

Inter alia. A Latin phrase which means "among other things."

Intestate. A term which refers to a deceased person who died without leaving a will. If a person dies and had a will, he or she died testate; if the person had no will, he or she died intestate.

Ipso facto. A Latin phrase which means "by the fact itself."

Judgment. The final determination of a court in an action or proceeding instituted in that court.

Jurisdiction. The power of a specific court to hear and decide certain cases.

Lease. A contract whereby an owner of real property, the landlord, agrees to give possession to the tenant, the person requesting possession, for a specific period of time in return for the payment of money or service.

Legal entity. Also referred to as an artificial person. Legal entities include corporations, which exist by legal creation and have the right to contract and the right to own and dispose of property as well as other rights and duties of natural persons.

Lien. A claim against property. A lien can be agreed upon under contract, or it can be imposed by law. A carpenter who works on your home will have a right to a lien on your home if you do not pay the reasonable cost of his or her services.

Liquidated damages. The amount of money which, according to the contract, is to be forfeited or paid as a remedy for breach of the contract.

Long arm statute. A state enactment allowing service of process on out-of-state residents who own property in the state, had an automobile accident in the state, or do business in the state.

Mandamus. A Latin term which means "we command." A mandamus is an order commanding that some specific act be done which a court can issue to an inferior court, a person, or a corporation.

Minor. A person who has not yet reached the age of majority. The common-law age of majority was 21. Most states now set the age of majority for contracts at 18 but still make 21 the age of majority with regard to the drinking of intoxicating beverages.

Misdemeanors. Minor criminal offenses that usually encompass all crimes not classified as felonies or treason.

Necessaries. This term refers to the needs of minors, such as food, reasonable clothing, reasonable lodging, and medical attention. The reasonability of such items as food, clothing, and lodging depends on the minor's earning level and the mode of living of the minor's parents.

Non obstante veredicto. A Latin phrase which means "notwithstanding the verdict." It is used to indicate that the court has entered a judgment contrary to the verdict of the jury. In essence, the judge has vetoed the jury's verdict.

Notary public. An appointed public officer who has the authority to administer oaths; to attest to and certify certain legal documents; and to take and certify acknowledgments of deeds, mortgages, and other such legal documents. A notary public is limited in jurisdiction to the state where he or she is appointed and in some instances to the county where he or she resides.

No-par stock. Corporate stock to which "no par" value is assigned. Before stock is issued, the directors fix a price per share, but that price is not stated on the stock certificate.

Novation. The substitution of a new obligation for a previous one with the understanding that the previous obligation has been discharged and terminated.

Obligee. A person to whom an obligor owes an obligation.

Obligor. A person who owes an obligation to an obligee.

Offer. A proposal to make a contract. It is made orally, in writing, or by other conduct, and it must contain the terms legally necessary to create a contract. Acceptance of the proposal creates the contract.

Offeree. A person to whom an offer is made.

Offeror. A person who makes an offer.

Ordinances. The term used to identify the legislative enactments of a city or municipality.

Par stock. Shares of corporate stock that have been assigned a fixed "par value" by the articles of incorporation. The par value of one share is printed on each stock certificate.

Pari delicto. A Latin term which means "the parties are equally at fault."

Penal damages. A monetary penalty agreed upon in a contractual clause not as compensation for actual losses but as punishment for possible nonperformance or late performance. If in fact the agreed damage amount is a penalty and not a reasonable compensation for loss, the court will not enforce the clause.

Per curiam. A Latin term which means "by the court." The entire court wrote the opinion, not just one justice.

Per se. A Latin term which means "in itself; taken alone; unconnected with other matters."

Plaintiff. A person who files a lawsuit in court.

Pledge. Pawning or giving up the possession of an item of personal property as security for a loan. You borrow $100 from the pawnshop and leave your gold pocket watch as security.

Power of attorney. A writing whereby one person appoints and authorizes another person to act on his or her behalf. This power can be limited or unlimited and can be for a specified time or for life.

Preferred stock. A class of corporate stock, usually nonvoting stock, that has rights to dividends superior to those of common stock and in case of dissolution also has rights to the assets of the corporation superior to those of common stock.

Prima facie. A Latin phrase which means "on the face of it." For example, a valid driver's license in your possession is prima facie evidence that you have a valid right to drive; however, this evidence could be disproved by evidence that there was a court judgment to pick up and suspend your license which had not yet been served upon you.

Principal. A person who has given an agent authority to do some act or acts for him or her.

Pro rata. A Latin phrase which means "proportionately." In other words, to share equally.

Pro tem. A Latin phrase which means "temporarily." For example, a judge pro tem might be a judge who is sitting in temporarily for the regular judge while the regular judge is on vacation.

Probate. The term describing the legal procedure followed in the administration of the estates of deceased persons and persons under guardianship.

Promisee. A person to whom a contractual promise is made.

Promisor. A person who makes a contractual promise.

Promissory estoppel. A rule of law which is often called justifiable reliance. When the promisor makes a promise and the promisee justifiably relies on that promise to his or her detriment, the promisor is estopped from denying liability on the promise.

Proxy. A document which authorizes another to vote for you. Stockholders who will be absent from stockholders' meetings often give their proxy to persons who will attend the meetings.

Punitive damages. Damages awarded against a person to punish him or her. These damages are in addition to compensatory damages, which pay the plaintiff for his or her actual losses. Punitive damages are often also referred to as exemplary damages because they are awarded not only to punish but to set an example for similar wrongdoers.

Quasi contract. The word *quasi* means resembling or somewhat like; thus a quasi contract is not a true contract. It resembles a contract but does not possess all the elements of a legally binding contract. The law does not allow unjust enrichment from quasi contracts, and it provides a restitutory remedy that allows the person with a claim for damages to recover the reasonable value of the goods or services which he or she provided to the other party. Quasi contract is often referred to as a contract implied in law.

Quitclaim deed. A deed which is intended to pass any title or interest which the grantor has in a certain tract of real estate, but does not warrant, profess, or guarantee that the grantor had any title or interest in the real estate or that his or her title was free and clear of liens.

Quo warranto. A Latin phrase which means "by what authority." It is a legal action which a government may commence to remove a person from a public office or to dissolve a corporation.

Quorum. Both incorporated and unincorporated organizations have a governing body, and a quorum is the minimum number of persons in the governing body that have to be present at a meeting to lawfully conduct the business of an organization. The usual requirement for a quorum is a majority of the persons who are eligible to vote, but a lesser number may be agreed upon in the organization charter or bylaws.

Ratification. The present confirmation of a previous promise or act. In the case of a former minor, ratification is the confirmation by that person once he or she has reached the age of majority of the intention to be bound by a contract which he or she had entered into as a minor. In agency law, ratification is the confirmation by a principal of a promise or act made by his or her agent which was unauthorized at the time it was made. The ratification legalizes the previously unauthorized promise or act and creates a binding contract.

Receiver. A person or a bank or other fiduciary institution appointed by the court to receive and preserve property or funds in litigation. The receiver must have no interest in the litigation and will simply hold and manage the property or funds until directed to hand them over to whomever the court awards them.

Redemption. The repurchasing or buying back of property legally taken from a person and sold. In a mortgage foreclosure, a person's land is taken and sold by the sheriff to secure money to pay the person's debt. After the sale the owner has a limited time during which he or she can redeem the property.

Referee. In bankruptcy, this is the person who is in charge of the administration of the bankrupt's estate until the bankrupt has been discharged and the estate has been distributed among the bankrupt's creditors.

Reformation. The rewriting of a contract by the court to correct ambiguities and errors so that the contract reflects the agreement of the parties.

Release. The voluntary giving up of a claim for money or property from another person, usually for consideration.

Replevin. A legal action whereby the owner of goods can legally recover them from someone who is holding them unlawfully.

Res. A Latin word which means "the thing."

Res ipsa loquitur. A Latin phrase which means "the

thing speaks for itself." For example, an airplane may explode in midair. In tort law, the heirs of the deceased passengers would normally have the burden of proving negligence on the defendant. However, it is obvious that planes do not explode unless there was negligence on someone's part. Thus the plaintiff sues and pleads res ipsa loquitur and the defendants must prove that they were not negligent.

Res judicata. A Latin phrase which means "the thing is settled"; that is, the case is finished.

Respondeat superior. A Latin phrase which means "let the master answer." In other words, let the employer be liable for the acts of his or her employees for damages that the employees have caused to others.

Rider. A provision added to an insurance policy to restrict or enlarge its coverage.

Riparian. A term which refers to the bank of a river. A riparian owner is a person who owns land on the bank of a river.

Scienter. The knowledge of a person making a representation that the representation he or she is making is false. In a tort action for deceit, scienter must be proved.

Security agreement. An agreement which gives a security interest in certain property to a creditor. Such an agreement must be in writing to be enforced.

Security interest. An interest in a specific item of personal property, such as possession of the item or its title, which a creditor retains to secure the payment of a debt.

Setoff. A claim which a defendant has against a plaintiff; similar to a counterclaim. For example, if the plaintiff sued the defendant for $100 but owed the defendant $50 the plaintiff's $50 debt to the defendant would be a setoff and the balance owed by the defendant would owe the plaintiff only $50.

Settlor. The term used to describe the donor in a trust document.

Shareholder. A person who owns a portion of the capital stock of a corporation. The shareholder's interest in the corporation is evidenced by a stock certificate.

Shop right. The employer's right to use, without paying royalties, any invention which an employee developed while using the employer's facilities or any invention which the employee conceived in the course of the employee's employment with the employer. An employee who is hired to do research and development agrees by contract that the employer will own the employee's inventions and discoveries

as that is what such an employee would be getting paid for.

Situs. The location of a thing. All tangible property has a situs.

Slander. Defamatory statements orally made by one person which injure the reputation of another person.

Specific performance. A remedy by which a court of equity orders a person to perform in accordance with the terms of his or her contract.

Spendthrift trust. A trust set up to care for an immature, incompetent, or inexperienced beneficiary. Such a trust is also intended to keep money away from a beneficiary who might use it unwisely or foolishly.

Stare decisis. A Latin phrase which means "to abide by." This phrase is also defined as "let the decision stand." Once a case has set a precedent, courts will follow that precedent wherever it is feasible to do so. However, law must change as technology and mores change; thus no precedent is cast in concrete.

Status quo. A Latin phrase which means "the state of things at any given time."

Statute of limitations. A statute which sets limits to the time in which a lawsuit may be filed in certain causes of action. For example, a tort lawsuit must be filed within two years from the day the wrongful act was committed, and if it is not filed by that time, the action is forever barred.

Subpoena. A legal process from a court ordering a witness to appear and testify or ordering a witness to produce certain documents for the court's inspection.

Subrogation. The act of substituting one person for another to prosecute a lawful claim. In insurance, the insurance company pays the collision loss to your automobile and you give the company subrogation rights to sue and collect from the person who negligently damaged your automobile.

Substantive law. The law that is concerned with the rights and duties of the parties, as contrasted with procedural law, which is concerned with the procedure to be followed in the litigation.

Surety. A person who binds himself or herself with another person, called the principal, for the payment of money or the performance of some obligation. However, the principal is already bound to that payment or obligation and the surety serves as a backup person who is available in case the principal does not pay or perform properly.

Tangible property. Property which can be touched—a tract of land, a chair, a table, etc. Intangible property, on the other hand, is property which cannot be touched, such as the ownership of a patent right or of corporate stock and other such ownerships of rights, not things.

Tender. An offer to settle or perform an obligation in contract. If a party offers to perform his or her obligation under a contract, such an offer is called a tender. If the other party unjustifiably refuses to accept the performance offered, that party would be guilty of breach of contract.

Testate. A deceased person who died leaving a will, died testate; a deceased person who died without leaving a will, died intestate.

Testator. A deceased person who left a will.

Third-party beneficiary. A person who was not a party to a contract but was a party to whom the contracting parties intended benefits to be given.

Torrens system. A system of land registration which was developed by Sir Robert Torrens in Australia, in 1858. This system has been adopted in some jurisdictions in the United States.

Tort. A civil wrong for which civil damages may be awarded, as contrasted with a criminal wrong for which punishment may be given. A wrongful act may be both a tort and a crime.

Trade name. A name under which a particular business operates.

Trademark. A distinctive mark or emblem which a manufacturer prints on or affixes to goods so that consumers can identify the manufacturer's goods in the marketplace.

Trespass. Although most commonly used to refer to a person's unauthorized entry onto another person's real property, in its broadest sense this term refers to any intentional injury or damage caused by force to either the person or the property of another.

Ultra vires. A Latin phrase which means "beyond the powers of," or beyond the scope of authority. An ultra vires act is an act which is not within the powers of the person who does it.

Unconscionability. Conduct by a party to a contract which cannot be shown to be fraud and is not duress but is unjust and unfair and because of which the court will not enforce performance of the contract.

Undue influence. A condition which results from the use of unfair persuasion by one person in order to overcome the free will of another person and to influence that person to act in the manner in which he or she is directed to act.

Usury. The charging of an unlawful rate of interest.

Vest. To take effect. To vest a right is to give a right to a present or future benefit. The term *vest* is used in pension law. One's rights in a pension plan will be vested after certain minimum requirements have been met.

Void. No legal effect; not binding. If an agreement is void, it is legally unenforceable.

Voidable. A term which means that a contract is not void but can be avoided by one or both of the parties at their will. A contract between a minor and an adult is voidable by the minor only; a contract between two minors can be avoided by either minor.

Waiver. The voluntary relinquishment by a person of a right which he or she has.

Warehouse receipt. A written acknowledgment of the receipt of goods by a person engaged in the business of storing goods for hire.

Warranty. In the sale of goods, a promise or guarantee by the seller that goods have certain qualities or that the seller has title to the goods. A warranty may be offered by the seller as a contractual term, or a warranty not stated in the contract may be imposed by law. The warranties imposed by law are the warranty of merchantability and the warranty of fitness for purpose. The warranty of merchantability warrants that the goods are of at least fair or average quality. The warranty of fitness for purpose warrants that the goods are fit for the particular purpose of the buyer.

Will. A person's declaration of how his or her property is to be distributed after his or her death.

Writ. A written document issued by a court, directed to a sheriff or some other officer of the law, and ordering that person to carry out a command of the court. For example, a writ of attachment orders a sheriff to attach certain property and hold it for disposition by the court.

Zoning. The process of separating the areas of a city or county by confining them to particular uses, such as residential use, industrial use, or business use.

Table of Cases*

*Cases in capital letters are discussion cases at the ends of chapters; the other cases are located within the chapters.

Index

Index

Index

*This book has been set VIP in 10 and 9 point Cale-
donia, leaded 2 points. Part numbers, part titles,
and chapter numbers are 27 point Caledonia
Bold, and chapter titles are 24 point Caledonia
Bold. The size of the type page is 37 by 48 picas.*